The Holy Bible

NEW CENTURY VERSION

Authentic

KIDSBIBLE.COM™

Copyright © 2001, Thomas Nelson, Inc. All rights reserved.
This anglicised edition copyright © 2005, Authentic Media. All rights reserved.

The Holy Bible, New Century Version. Copyright © 1987, 1988, 1991, Thomas Nelson, Inc. All rights reserved. Anglicised text copyright © 1993, Authentic Media.

The Publisher is pleased hereby to grant permission for the *New Century Version* to be quoted or reprinted without written permission with the following qualifications: up to and including one thousand (1,000) verses may be quoted, except: (a) the verses being quoted may not comprise as much as 50 per cent of the work in which they are quoted, and/or (b) the verses quoted may not comprise an entire book of the Bible when quoted.

Quotations from this Bible may be identified in written form with the abbreviation (NCV) in less formal documents, such as bulletins, newsletters, curriculum, media pieces, posters, transparencies, and where space is limited.

A proper copyright credit line must appear on the title or copyright page of any work quoting from the *New Century Version*, as follows:

"Scriptures quoted from *The Holy Bible, New Century Version* (anglicised edition), copyright © 1993 by Authentic Media. Used by permission."

Quotations of more than 1,000 verses, or other permission requests, must be approved by Authentic Media in writing in advance of use.

All non-Scripture text copyright © 2001 Thomas Nelson, Inc. All excerpts used by permission.

The preliminary research and development of the *New Century Version* was done by the World Bible Translation Center, Inc., Fort Worth, TX 76182.

Hardback   ISBN: 1-86024-482-3
Paperback   ISBN: 1-86024-483-1

Published by Authentic Media, 9 Holdom Avenue, Bletchley, Milton Keynes, Bucks, MK1 1QR, UK.
All Rights Reserved.

Originating producer: Bookprint Creative Services.
Print management by Adare Carwin.
Printed and bound in Great Britain by William Clowes Ltd, Beccles, Suffolk

CONTENTS

Contributors v
KidsBible.com Homepage vi
The FACTs in KidsBible.com (computer glossary) xiii
Get the Info Index xvii
Email from God In-Box List xix
NCV Preface xxv

Old Testament

Genesis	2	Ecclesiastes	871
Exodus	74	Song of Solomon	886
Leviticus	132	Isaiah	894
Numbers	175	Jeremiah	986
Deuteronomy	225	Lamentations	1072
Joshua	274	Ezekiel	1084
Judges	309	Daniel	1148
Ruth	343	Hosea	1171
1 Samuel	352	Joel	1186
2 Samuel	398	Amos	1193
1 Kings	432	Obadiah	1207
2 Kings	474	Jonah	1211
1 Chronicles	517	Micah	1218
2 Chronicles	560	Nahum	1230
Ezra	608	Habakkuk	1235
Nehemiah	623	Zephaniah	1241
Esther	646	Haggai	1247
Job	659	Zechariah	1251
Psalms	708	Malachi	1266
Proverbs	823		

New Testament

Matthew	1272	1 Timothy	1642
Mark	1328	2 Timothy	1650
Luke	1363	Titus	1658
John	1420	Philemon	1662
Acts	1461	Hebrews	1665
Romans	1516	James	1686
1 Corinthians	1543	1 Peter	1697
2 Corinthians	1568	2 Peter	1708
Galatians	1584	1 John	1712
Ephesians	1596	2 John	1721
Philippians	1607	3 John	1723
Colossians	1618	Jude	1725
1 Thessalonians	1628	Revelation	1729
2 Thessalonians	1637		

Search Engine 1756
Top 50 Bible Sites 1785
How to Read Your *KidsBible.com* 1788

CONTRIBUTORS

Our prayer is that KidsBible.com will launch your child on a life-long journey with God's Word.

General Editor
Betsy Todt Schmitt

Design & Editorial Team
Bruce B. Barton, Christopher D. Hudson,
Katie E. Gieser, David R. Veerman

Creative Development
Vicki Wiley

Contributors

Tim Baker, Reverend Eric Titus	New Testament introductions
Jeanette Dall	Livin' It pages
Katie E. Gieser	Email from God
Carol Ochs	Editing
Margaret Reneker, Reverend Eric Titus	Old Testament introductions
Carol Smith	Get the Info features
Randy Southern	Faith Challenges and Connect 2-You features
Ashley Taylor	Editorial assistance
Linda Washington	Faithlinks, FAQs homepages, editorial assistance
Joan Woodhead	Editorial assistance

Anglicising and Proofing of Bible Text and Textual Notes
Louise Stenhouse & Liz Williams

Cover & Colour Page Design
fourninezero design.

▶ KidsBible.com™ Homepage

Welcome!

Hey, newbie, welcome to *KidsBible.com*, the Bible you can surf! You are going to have a totally amazing time downloading all sorts of cool information that you can find in the Bible. So let's boot up and start surfing!

But – hold on a minute – it's all going a bit too fast! First, before you begin, there are a few things to explain about *KidsBible.com*. And let's stop with all the computer lingo for a bit and clear up a few things. Let's try starting this again.

Welcome to *KidsBible.com*. The Bible is an exciting book, and an important feature of *KidsBible.com* is it is the one Bible you can surf. That means you can skip from page to page in *KidsBible.com* by following links, or connections, of related Bible verses, topics, or information. You can read as much or as little as you want about any topic just by connecting to the various links. There are all sorts of sites in *KidsBible.com* that you can surf to help you connect to God's Word. Read on.

Surfing KidsBible.com   vii

This is so cool! You can surf KidsBible.com just as though it is a website. You can surf from link to link simply by opening your Bible to any site, or Bible feature, in KidsBible.com. There are a number of ways for you to start surfing. Here are a few suggestions:

- The easiest place to begin is with the <u>Table of Contents</u> on page iii. You'll find a listing of every book in the Bible. Connect to any book of the Bible and you'll discover the <u>Bible book splash page</u>. Read on!

- Log on to any <u>Bible book splash page</u>. That's the introduction to each book of the Bible. On the splash pages, you'll find a listing of all the different connections in each book, like cool stories to download and read, and other information sites to check out. There's also a summary of the book (what it's about) and a Jesus Watch. (That explains how God's promise for a Saviour – his Son, Jesus – is mentioned in each book of the Bible.)

- Connect to a <u>Livin' it page</u>. These 50 sites are scattered throughout the Bible. Each one talks about a different topic that is important to you – like how to get along in your family, making new friends, or how to handle your money. By logging on to these sites, you can find out what the Bible has to say about each topic. There are more hyperlinks (related connections) called <u>Faithlinks</u> to help you learn more about this topic. You'll find the <u>Livin' it pages</u> listed according to topics in the <u>Search Engine</u>. (Keep going!)

- Or start with the <u>Search Engine</u>. You'll find the Search Engine in the back of the Bible. It has a complete listing of every site you can connect to in *KidsBible.com* according to topics. Maybe you want to learn more about following God. Check out the listings under the heading *Following God* and connect to the links that sound most interesting to you. Or maybe a friend has done something to hurt you and you want to know how to forgive them. Check out the listings under *Forgiving Others* for some straight advice right from God's Word.

Other Connections   viii

But that's not all *KidsBible.com* has to offer. Check out these other "hotspots" that you can connect to and download all sorts of information:

Faithlinks

- There are 500 <u>Faithlinks</u> in *KidsBible.com*. These links discuss important faith issues, such as obeying God and your parents, learning how to be patient, how to deal with the tough times, and how to use your abilities to help others. Each <u>Faithlink</u> has five or six additional links listed so you can surf to as many related links as you want. Check out each <u>Bible book splash page</u> or the <u>Search Engine</u> for a listing of <u>Faithlinks</u>.

Get the Info

- This is the *KidsBible.com* Info BBS – or bulletin board system. There are 75 different info bulletin boards where you can download facts about people in the Bible, like Moses or David; or places in the Bible, like Jerusalem or Bethlehem; or fascinating "did you know" stuff, like about King Hezekiah's amazing water tunnel or why the Israelites cast lots to make decisions. You'll find a complete listing in the <u>Get the Info Index</u> on page xvii.

Faith Challenges

- How are you growing in your faith? Connect to any of these 50 challenges from the Bible and put your faith to the test! There's even a place for you to write down what you learned – but more about writing in your Bible a bit later! You'll find the <u>Faith Challenges</u> listed in the <u>Search Engine</u>.

Other Connections   ix

Email from God

- Everyone loves to get mail, right? And there are a lot of important messages that God has for you in the Bible. Just look for the little envelope icon to check out what God has to say about certain topics, like Angels, Leadership or Music. You can find an entire listing of the 500 Email from God entries in the In-Box List on page xix. Every time you "receive" an email, you can tick it off in the In-Box List.

Connect 2-You

- Got a question about whether it's OK to tell a little white lie, or what to do when you're feeling lonely? Then link up with the Connect 2-You online friends as they talk about these kinds of issues. You'll hear about what other kids your age are struggling with and get some suggestions for other sites to connect to for more help. Look up the Connect 2-You sites in the Search Engine.

The FAQ Homepages

- Throughout *KidsBible.com*, you'll find 16 colourful pages called FAQ home pages, which feature Faith Action Questions about eight men and women of the Bible: Abraham, Moses, Deborah, David, Esther, Mary, Jesus and Paul. Each of these people faced a specific faith challenge. Maybe it was being obedient to God (Abraham), or learning to handle temptations (Jesus). Connect to these sites and download how you can learn from their experiences to deal with your own faith challenges.

> You know, with all these cool connections, you can have a completely different "surfing" experience every time you open *KidsBible.com*.

> You don't have to surf the same places over and over again. But just in case you want to remember some of the cool sites to visit, we've got a place to "bookmark" those sites. Turn the page!

Favourite Places

KidsBible.com

Here it is! Your very own homepage! This is your chance to make *KidsBible.com* uniquely you! Take some time now to fill out some information. Then come back to your homepage whenever you want to write down your thoughts, discoveries and whatever is important to you as you read the Bible.

My Personal Stuff

When I got *KidsBible.com* _____

Why I got this Bible _____

Who gave it to me _____

Questions I have about God, the Bible, faith, etc.

1.

2.

3.

4.

5.

6.

@_____'s dot.com!
(your name)

```
KidsBible.com
```

My Favourite Faithlinks
1.
2.
3.

My Favourite Livin' It Sites
1.
2.
3.

My Favourite Bible Books
1.
2.
3.

My Favourite Bible Heroes
1.
2.
3.

My Favourite Bible Verses
1.
2.
3.

Other Stuff to Think About...
1.
2.
3.

More Cool Stuff! xii

Wow, you can find all that great stuff in one Bible?! Now I'm sure you're even more excited about getting into *KidsBible.com* and doing some major surfing. You might even say you're a little "hyper" -linked! Get it? Just a little computer joke for you newbies!

There are more things you may need to know about *KidsBible.com*. And one is all that computer speak. You may not know exactly what a hyperlink is or what is meant by a newbie. (By the way, a newbie is someone new to a website.)

Not to worry; all of this has already been taken care of. All you have to do is surf over to p. xiii to take a look at The FACTs in *KidsBible.com*. It's a glossary for all the computer terms a person may find in this Bible. And there's one more cool thing for any newbie to *KidsBible.com*.

You may have noticed that *KidsBible.com* has lots of places for you to jot down your favourite Bible verses, Faithlinks, Livin' it sites, and other stuff you want to remember – right in your very own Bible. In fact, on the two pages just before this one, there is a place for you to make up your very own homepage. (That's the main starting point for your *KidsBible.com* journey.) Here are a few do's and don'ts for writing in your Bible:

- Don't use a felt-tip pen or any other kind of marker. Those kinds of pens will "bleed" through the pages and make a real mess!
- Do use a ball-point pen or pencil for jotting down links or sites you want to remember.
- Don't stuff your Bible with extra papers, like Sunday school worksheets or other stuff. Your Bible will last longer if you don't use it as a "collect-all".
- Do use your Bible! It's not just to put on your bookshelf to look good! It's God's rule book for living, and it's meant to be used!

THE FACTs IN
KIDSBIBLE ◯ COM

WHAT'S A <u>FACT</u> ANYWAY?

As you surf through KidsBible.com, you may come across a word or term that may not be so familiar to you. Don't go into panic mode – you're not going to be sent wandering out into cyberspace without a clue as to what's going on – connect here to find out what it means!

FACTs - Frequently Asked Computer Terms - defines the most commonly asked questions about computer terms. Read on!

BBS – Bulletin Board System. In the real computer world, this is a computer system that you can connect to using a modem. At the BBS, you can dial in and leave messages, or play computer games, or send email. In *KidsBible.com*, our BBS is the **Get the Info** feature that gives you interesting data about people, places and things you'll find in *KidsBible.com*.

Boot up – To start up a computer. To start up in *KidsBible.com*, try the **Table of Contents**, which tells you where to find all the great stuff!

Browser – The program, such as the Internet, that allows you to download and display sites and documents on the Web.

Chat room – A place on the Internet where you can "talk" with other online users by typing in messages.

Crash – When a computer doesn't respond to what you ask it to do. Don't worry, *KidsBible.com* will never crash!

Cyberspace – The virtual world created where computers, the Internet and other electronic ways of communication meet.

Data – The computer term for information. All the Bible stories, verses and other information you will read in *KidsBible.com* is data.

▶ FACTs xiv

Database – How data is stored and organised on a computer. The **Table of Contents** and the **Search Engine** are the two main databases for *KidsBible.com*.

Document – Any work that is created on a computer and stored as a file. In *KidsBible.com*, any feature, such as **Get the Info** or a **Faithlink**, is a form of a document.

Download – To get a file from a computer or Internet. In *KidsBible.com*, you can download information every time you read a **Faithlink**, **Livin' It** page, or any other Bible feature.

Email – Electronic mail that is sent over the Internet. In *KidsBible.com*, you can read 500 emails from God's Word that cover a wide variety of topics. Check out the **Email from God** by visiting the inbox list on page xix. When you're reading *KidsBible.com*, you'll always get mail!

Email address – This is your private address on the Internet to which your email is sent. Remember, never give out your private email address without your parent(s)' permission.

FAQs – This is short for Frequently Asked Questions. It is a report that answers the most commonly asked questions on a particular subject. In *KidsBible.com*, you'll find a different kind of **FAQs**, or **Faith Action Questions**. These **FAQs** focus on five different questions involving a Bible character's particular faith challenge. (For example, David's faith challenge was being respectful to people who wanted to do him harm.)

File – Anything stored on a computer. In *KidsBible.com*, this could be **Get the Info**, **Faithlink**, **Connect 2-You**, or other features found in the Bible.

Flash – The facts, as in "What's the flash on this story?"

Header – The top line of an information source, such as an email, which lists the sender's details and the time sent. In *KidsBible.com*, the header will let you know, among other things, the type of information packet it is (for example, a **Faithlink**, **Get the Info**, or **Livin' It** page), a title, and in some cases, where you can find more information about the topic in the Bible. Also, each page of the Bible has its own header that tells you the Bible book with chapter and verse numbers that begins or ends a page. Use these headers to locate a particular Bible story, verse, or feature in *KidsBible.com*.

Homepage – The first page loaded by a browser when you connect to that site. In *KidsBible.com*, you can create your own homepage by recording your favourite places in the Bible to read. See page x.

Hypertext links – On the Web, these are the places where you can "click" that will connect you to other pages on the Web. In *KidsBible.com*, the hypertext links appear as underlined headings. To "connect" to the other pages, you'll have to do the work and turn the pages!

Internet – This is the global collection of computer networks that share a common address so you can connect to a wide variety of websites through one source.

FACTs xv

Link – On a web page, a link is a reference to another document. When you click on a link, that document will be displayed, or played, or downloaded, depending on what kind of document it is. In *KidsBible.com*, links will take you to other Bible references that have a similar topic or theme. You can follow the links by turning to the page number and Bible verse listed for each reference.

Log on – To connect to a computer network. In *KidsBible.com*, you can log on to other Bible references by following the links listed.

MIDI – Stands for Musical Instrument Digital Interface. MIDI files contain synthesized music that can be played when the files are opened. In *KidsBible.com*, you won't find any MIDI files that will actually play music, but only ones that suggest music might be played. (For example, you may find MIDI files mentioned in the Psalms.)

The Net – Shortened form of the Internet.

Newbie – A newcomer to the Internet or to a new website. Anyone who first opens *KidsBible.com* is an official newbie!

Online – To be connected to the Internet or Web. When you read *KidsBible.com*, you are online but with your Bible!

Packet – A unit of data, or information, that is sent over the Internet.

Plug-in – A program that fits into another. In *KidsBible.com*, plug-ins are other Bible features that you will find in each book of the Bible. For example, one plug-in to the Book of Genesis is **The Boat That Saved the World, Genesis 7**.

Post – To send a message on the Internet or a website. In *KidsBible.com*, you can post your favourite places to visit on your homepage or on each Bible book **Splash page**.

○ S

Search Engine – This is where you can look to see if there is information about a particular subject contained in the database for a specific web page. *KidsBible.com* has its own unique **Search Engine** where you can look up topics and see what links are available on that topic.

Splash page – The introductory page to a website that has a listing of everything you'll find on that website. Each book of the Bible in *KidsBible.com* has its own **Splash page** where you will be able to see all the different **Faithlinks**, **Get the Info** and other information available. For a complete listing of the books of the Bible, check out the **Table of Contents**.

Surf – To skip from page to page by following links. In *KidsBible.com*, there are many ways you can surf. Check it out by reading **Surfing *KidsBible.com***, page vii.

Surfwatch – A summary of links that may be found at a particular website.

FACTs xvi

You'll find **Surfwatches** on some of the Bible book **Splash pages**.

The Web – Shortened form of the World Wide Web or WWW. The Web contains all the documents and graphics that are published on the Internet and which are connected through hypertext links.

Web page – A single document.

Website – A collection of related documents.

Get the INFO INDEX

- Garden of Delight
  Genesis 2:8–10, p. 5
- The Boat That Saved the World
  Genesis 7, p. 12
- Tower of Pride
  Genesis 11:3–9, p. 16
- A New Home for Abraham
  Genesis 16, p. 21
- From Deceiver to Wrestler
  Genesis 28:1–19, p. 39
- Ten Curses
  Exodus 9, p. 87
- Church on the Road
  Exodus 27:9–19, p. 111
- God's Presence with the Israelites
  Leviticus 16:1–15, p. 155
- Time for Breakfast
  Numbers 11:4–9, p. 191
- One Potato, Two Potato . . .
  Numbers 26:55–56, p. 212
- Let's Visit the Dead Sea
  Numbers 34:12, p. 222
- A Feast for Remembering
  Deuteronomy 16:1–8, p. 249
- The Deliverer
  Deuteronomy 34, p. 272
- Let's Visit Jericho
  Joshua 5, p. 282
- Claiming the Promised Land
  Joshua 11, p. 291
- Dividing the Land
  Joshua 21, p. 302
- The Judges
  Judges 9, p. 324
- Let's Visit Shiloh
  Judges 18:31, p. 337
- Women Who Made a Difference
  Ruth 4, p. 350
- Samuel, the Prophet
  1 Samuel 4, p. 359
- King Saul, the Soldier
  1 Samuel 14, p. 371
- God to the Rescue!
  1 Samuel 23, p. 386
- Some Bad Guys
  1 Samuel 31:1–4, p. 396
- Elijah, the Prophet
  1 Kings 18:35, p. 465
- Let's Visit the Jordan River
  2 Kings 2:13–15, p. 477
- Elisha's Ministry
  2 Kings 4, p. 482
- A Man After God's Own Heart
  1 Chronicles 17, p. 542
- A Special Angel
  1 Chronicles 21:6–22, p. 547
- Israel's Glory Years
  2 Chronicles 9, p. 572
- Disease or Curse?
  2 Chronicles 26:20–23, p. 593
- A Secret Water Supply
  2 Chronicles 32, p. 599
- The Homecoming
  Nehemiah 8:1–12, p. 635
- A Foreign Queen
  Esther 6, p. 654
- Let's Visit Jerusalem
  Psalm 68:29, p. 758
- God's Glory
  Psalm 115, p. 797
- The Temple in Jerusalem
  Psalm 122, p. 807
- Wise Books
  Ecclesiastes 7, p. 880
- Who Are the Egyptians?
  Isaiah 30:2–5, p. 932

continued on next page

Get the Info INDEX

- True or False Gods?
  Jeremiah 48:7, 13, p. 1057
- Ancient War and Weapons
  Ezekiel 23:24, p. 1112
- Let's Visit Damascus
  Ezekiel 27:18, p. 1117
- The Kings of Egypt
  Ezekiel 29:1–16, p. 1121
- Let's Visit Babylon
  Daniel 2; 7, p. 1152
- Who Are the Greeks?
  Daniel 11:3–35, p. 1167
- Let's Visit Samaria
  Amos 3:11–15, p. 1198
- Let's Visit Nineveh
  Jonah 1—4, p. 1214
- Let's Visit Bethlehem
  Micah 5:2, p. 1225
- Where Is God's Kingdom?
  Zechariah 9:9–10, p. 1260
- Jesus' Sermon Notes
  Matthew 5—7, p. 1282
- The Chosen Dozen
  Matthew 10:1–29, p. 1291
- A Place to Worship
  Mark 6:2, p. 1339
- Saints, Sinners, or Religious Leaders?
  Mark 7:1–13, p. 1341
- Jesus – God with Us
  Mark 16, p. 1361
- A Model Prayer
  Luke 11:1, p. 1390
- Jesus' Last Week
  Luke 22, p. 1412
- Let's Visit Nazareth
  Luke 24:19, p. 1418
- Let's Visit Capernaum
  John 4:46–54, p. 1430
- The Names of Jesus
  John 6:35, p. 1433
- Biographies from Every View
  John 19, p. 1456
- Let's Visit Lake Galilee
  John 21, p. 1460
- Angels Watching Over Us
  Acts 8, p. 1477
- Let's Visit Antioch
  Acts 13:1–3, p. 1486
- Let's Visit Athens
  Acts 17:15—18:1, p. 1496
- Let's Visit Philippi
  Acts 20, p. 1501
- A Man of Two Countries
  Acts 22, p. 1504
- The Life of Paul
  Acts 28, p. 1513
- Let's Visit Rome
  Romans 1:15, p. 1519
- Let's Visit Corinth
  2 Corinthians 6, p. 1575
- Let's Visit Ephesus
  Ephesians 3, p. 1601
- Let's Visit Thessalonica
  1 Thessalonians 3, p. 1632
- Powerful Women of Faith
  2 Timothy 4, p. 1656
- Death on a Cross
  Hebrews 6:6, p. 1672
- A Fisher of People
  1 Peter 1, p. 1699
- The Follower Jesus Loved
  Revelation 1, p. 1731
- What Do You Call the Devil?
  Revelation 12:9, p. 1743

IN-BOX LIST

Tick box when received ☑

✉ Advice
Joshua 3:9 ❑
Psalm 5:12 ❑
Psalm 24:3–6 ❑
James 1:25 ❑

✉ Angels
Genesis 32:1 ❑
2 Samuel 24:16–17 ❑
Psalm 89:6 ❑
Psalm 103:20 ❑
Psalm 148:1–2 ❑
Isaiah 6:2 ❑
Daniel 10:5–6 ❑
Matthew 22:30 ❑
Luke 20:36 ❑
1 Corinthians 6:3 ❑
2 Peter 2:4 ❑

✉ Anger
Proverbs 15:1 ❑
Isaiah 14:5-6 ❑
John 2:13–17 ❑
Ephesians 4:26–27 ❑

✉ Belief
Deuteronomy 27:10 ❑
1 Samuel 15:26 ❑
Ezekiel 36:36 ❑
1 Thessalonians 2:13 ❑

✉ Bible
Joshua 23:6–7 ❑
2 Chronicles 34:31 ❑
Nehemiah 9:14 ❑
Psalm 119:99–100 ❑
Acts 17:11–12 ❑
Acts 18:28 ❑
2 Timothy 3:16 ❑

✉ Blessings
Leviticus 26:3–5 ❑
Nehemiah 13:31 ❑

✉ Caring
Exodus 23:9 ❑
Deuteronomy 7:9 ❑
Psalm 68:5 ❑
Zechariah 7:9 ❑
Luke 6:27 ❑
Luke 14:13–14 ❑

✉ Character
1 Samuel 16:7 ❑
Jeremiah 7:5–7 ❑
Daniel 6:4–5 ❑
Amos 5:24 ❑

✉ Comfort
2 Samuel 19:7 ❑
John 16:33 ❑
2 Corinthians 1:3–11 ❑

✉ Correction
Job 5:17 ❑
Proverbs 4:13 ❑
Proverbs 6:20–23 ❑
Proverbs 15:10 ❑
Hebrews 12:7–11 ❑

✉ Courage
Joshua 1:9 ❑
Isaiah 12:2 ❑
Isaiah 30:15 ❑
1 Corinthians 16:13 ❑
Hebrews 4:16 ❑
James 5:16 ❑

✉ Death
Psalm 49:13–15 ❑

Psalm 116:1–15 ❑
John 14:19 ❑
2 Corinthians 5:6–7 ❑

✉ Decisions
Numbers 14:1–4 ❑
1 Chronicles 13:2 ❑
Psalm 1:1–2 ❑
Psalm 119:105 ❑
Ezekiel 11:12 ❑
Matthew 7:3–5 ❑

✉ Demons
Luke 10:17 ❑
Acts 16:16–18 ❑
Acts 19:13–16 ❑

✉ Encouragement
Nehemiah 5:7–11 ❑
Job 4:4 ❑
Habakkuk 3:17–19 ❑
Zechariah 2:10 ❑
Acts 9:31 ❑

✉ Enemies
Joshua 10:25 ❑
Proverbs 17:9 ❑
Proverbs 24:17–18 ❑
Proverbs 25:21–22 ❑
1 Peter 3:9 ❑

✉ Eternal Life
Matthew 7:21 ❑
John 3:15–16 ❑
John 5:28–29 ❑
John 11:25 ❑
Titus 3:7 ❑

✉ Faith
Luke 17:5–6 ❑

▶ In-Box List xx

Tick box when received ☑

2 Corinthians 3:18 ❏
Philippians 3:12–14 ❏
Hebrews 11:1 ❏

✉ Family
Genesis 47:11–12 ❏
1 Kings 5:13–14 ❏
1 Chronicles 28:8 ❏
Esther 2:11 ❏
Ezekiel 18:19–20 ❏
Luke 12:51–53 ❏

✉ Fears
Deuteronomy 20:1 ❏
Deuteronomy 31:8 ❏
Psalm 23:4 ❏
Psalm 25:15 ❏
Psalm 91:5 ❏
Psalm 112:7 ❏
Isaiah 43:1–2 ❏
Isaiah 51:12–13 ❏
Jeremiah 46:27 ❏
Micah 4:4 ❏
1 John 4:18 ❏

✉ Feelings
Nehemiah 9:27 ❏
Psalm 34:18 ❏

✉ Following God
Leviticus 18:3–5 ❏
Judges 5:31 ❏
1 Samuel 3:10 ❏
2 Chronicles 15:15 ❏
Psalm 27:14 ❏
Proverbs 10:24–25 ❏
Isaiah 35:10 ❏
Ezekiel 11:19 ❏
Ezekiel 36:20–21 ❏
Malachi 3:14–18 ❏
Matthew 16:24 ❏
John 8:12 ❏
John 10:25–27 ❏
John 12:26 ❏
Romans 1:20 ❏
1 Corinthians 11:17–22 ❏
1 Timothy 1:18–19 ❏

1 Timothy 6:11–12 ❏

✉ Forgiveness
Psalm 86:5 ❏
Ezekiel 37:23 ❏
Matthew 18:21–35 ❏
Acts 13:38–39 ❏

✉ Friendship
Samuel 18:1 ❏
1 Samuel 19:1–7 ❏
1 Samuel 20:42 ❏
2 Samuel 9:1 ❏
2 Samuel 19:33 ❏
2 Chronicles 10:1–14 ❏
Job 2:11 ❏
Psalm 55:12–14 ❏
Proverbs 17:17 ❏
Jeremiah 26:24 ❏
John 15:13–15 ❏

✉ Future
Deuteronomy 5:29 ❏
Esther 4:14 ❏
Isaiah 65:17–25 ❏
Jeremiah 18:11 ❏
Jeremiah 31:6 ❏

✉ Giving
Exodus 35:22 ❏
2 Kings 12:4–5 ❏
2 Chronicles 31:4 ❏
Proverbs 11:24–25 ❏
Mark 9:41 ❏
Mark 14:6–9 ❏
Acts 28:10–11 ❏
2 Corinthians 9:6–8 ❏
1 Timothy 6:18 ❏

✉ God
Genesis 8:1 ❏
Exodus 6:7 ❏
Leviticus 11:44 ❏
Joshua 4:24 ❏
1 Samuel 2:6–7 ❏

1 Samuel 6:20 ❏
2 Samuel 7:22 ❏
2 Samuel 23:5 ❏
1 Kings 8:27 ❏
2 Kings 5:15 ❏
2 Kings 20:6 ❏
Job 11:11 ❏
Job 21:22 ❏
Job 40:2 ❏
Psalm 27:1 ❏
Psalm 33:13–18 ❏
Isaiah 41:4 ❏
Ezekiel 38:23 ❏
Hosea 11:1 ❏
Romans 12:2 ❏

✉ God's Family
Deuteronomy 8:5 ❏
Deuteronomy 26:18 ❏
Matthew 12:50 ❏

✉ God's Promises
Psalm 37:23–24 ❏
Jeremiah 32:40–41 ❏
John 5:24 ❏
2 Timothy 1:12 ❏

✉ God's Will
Psalm 16:7 ❏
Psalm 48:14 ❏
Acts 16:6–7 ❏

✉ Good News
Luke 24:46–47 ❏
1 Thessalonians 1:4–5 ❏

✉ Gossip
Proverbs 4:24 ❏
Proverbs 16:28 ❏
Proverbs 26:20 ❏

✉ Greed
Isaiah 5:8 ❏
Jeremiah 8:10 ❏

In-Box List xxi

Tick box when received ☑

✉ Guilt
- Psalm 19:12–13 ☐
- Psalm 32:5 ☐
- Zechariah 13:1 ☐
- Romans 3:9–12 ☐

✉ Hate
- Ezekiel 35:11–12 ☐
- Romans 12:9 ☐

✉ Heaven
- Isaiah 25:8 ☐
- Philippians 1:23 ☐
- Revelation 4:8 ☐
- Revelation 7:17 ☐
- Revelation 21:4 ☐
- Revelation 22:8–9 ☐

✉ Hell
- Psalm 86:13 ☐
- Matthew 8:12 ☐
- Jude 6 ☐

✉ Help
- Genesis 49:25 ☐
- Judges 3:9 ☐
- Psalm 121 ☐
- Hebrews 1:14 ☐

✉ Honesty
- Exodus 20:16 ☐
- Exodus 23:2 ☐
- Isaiah 33:15–16 ☐
- Ezekiel 45:9–11 ☐
- Matthew 15:18 ☐

✉ Honouring God
- Isaiah 29:13 ☐
- Isaiah 58:5–7 ☐

✉ Hope
- Ezra 10:2 ☐
- Psalm 9:18 ☐
- Psalm 42:5–6 ☐
- Psalm 130:5–6 ☐
- Ecclesiastes 5:18–20 ☐
- Jeremiah 23:16 ☐
- Lamentations 3:21–22 ☐

✉ Humbleness
- Job 25:6 ☐
- Proverbs 22:4 ☐
- Isaiah 57:15 ☐
- Zephaniah 2:3 ☐
- Philippians 2:3 ☐

✉ Idols
- Deuteronomy 4:23 ☐
- 1 Kings 14:21–23 ☐

✉ Jealousy
- Acts 7:9 ☐
- Galatians 2:6 ☐

✉ Jesus
- Mark 14:61–62 ☐
- Luke 1:35 ☐
- Luke 19:10 ☐
- John 1:1–5 ☐
- John 4:21–26 ☐
- Acts 3:15 ☐
- Colossians 1:15–16 ☐
- 1 Timothy 1:2 ☐
- 1 Timothy 3:16 ☐
- Hebrews 8:6 ☐

✉ Joy
- Nehemiah 12:43 ☐
- Isaiah 55:12 ☐
- Isaiah 61:10 ☐

✉ Judgement
- Psalm 9:7–8 ☐
- Jeremiah 20:12 ☐
- Ezekiel 7:3–4 ☐
- Ezekiel 12:17–25 ☐
- Obadiah 15 ☐
- Malachi 3:5 ☐
- Matthew 12:36 ☐
- John 7:24 ☐

✉ Kindness
- Joshua 2:12 ☐
- 1 Kings 2:7 ☐
- Proverbs 3:3–4 ☐
- Proverbs 14:31 ☐
- Isaiah 63:7 ☐
- Romans 2:4 ☐
- Romans 15:14 ☐

✉ Laziness
- Proverbs 19:15 ☐
- 1 Thessalonians 5:12–14 ☐

✉ Leadership
- Exodus 18:21 ☐
- Numbers 27:16–17 ☐
- 1 Samuel 24:1–6 ☐
- 2 Kings 15:3–5 ☐
- 2 Kings 23:3 ☐
- 2 Chronicles 19:5–7 ☐
- Esther 10:3 ☐
- Psalm 78:72 ☐
- Matthew 20:25–28 ☐

✉ Learning
- Proverbs 18:2 ☐
- Ephesians 4:13–14 ☐

✉ Life
- Joshua 14:10–11 ☐
- 2 Samuel 4:9–11 ☐
- Luke 9:24 ☐
- John 10:10 ☐
- Philippians 4:8–9 ☐
- Colossians 3:8–9 ☐
- 1 Thessalonians 4:11 ☐
- 3 John 11 ☐

✉ Love
- Ezra 3:11 ☐

▶ In-Box List xxii

Tick box when received ☑

Matthew 5:43–44 ☐
Mark 12:29–30 ☐
John 13:34–35 ☐
1 Corinthians 13:4–8 ☐
Ephesians 4:2 ☐
2 John 5 ☐

✉ Money
1 Chronicles 26:27 ☐
Isaiah 17:10 ☐
Isaiah 31:6–7 ☐
Matthew 6:19–20 ☐
Matthew 19:21–22 ☐
Matthew 22:21 ☐
Mark 8:34–36 ☐
Luke 16:13 ☐
Acts 2:42–45 ☐
Revelation 3:17–18 ☐

✉ Music
Exodus 15:1 ☐
Psalm 81:1–5 ☐
Colossians 3:16 ☐

✉ Obedience
Deuteronomy 12:28 ☐
Deuteronomy 13:17–18 ☐
Deuteronomy 28:1 ☐
1 Samuel 12:14 ☐
1 Samuel 15:22 ☐
1 Kings 6:12–13 ☐
1 Chronicles 6:49 ☐
2 Chronicles 26:4 ☐
Proverbs 5:1 ☐
Jeremiah 11:7–8 ☐
Jeremiah 42:6 ☐
Luke 11:28 ☐
John 14:15–23 ☐
Acts 5:29 ☐
Acts 11:2–18 ☐
Romans 13:1 ☐
Romans 16:19 ☐
Ephesians 6:1–3 ☐
1 Peter 1:2 ☐
1 John 2:3 ☐
1 John 5:1–3 ☐

✉ Pain
Psalm 12:5 ☐
1 Thessalonians 4:18 ☐

✉ Peace
Numbers 6:24–26 ☐
Romans 14:19 ☐
Ephesians 2:14 ☐

✉ Perseverance
Job 17:9 ☐
Matthew 10:22 ☐
Romans 5:3 ☐
1 Corinthians 1:8 ☐
Ephesians 6:13 ☐
Colossians 2:7 ☐
James 5:7–8 ☐
2 Peter 1:5–8 ☐

✉ Prayer
1 Samuel 1:17 ☐
2 Chronicles 1:9–10 ☐
Nehemiah 2:4 ☐
Psalm 17:1–2 ☐
Psalm 40:13 ☐
Isaiah 38:1–6 ☐
Jeremiah 29:7 ☐
Jonah 2:1 ☐
John 16:23–24 ☐
Colossians 4:2 ☐
1 John 5:13–15 ☐
Jude 20 ☐

✉ Pride
Deuteronomy 17:18–20 ☐
2 Kings 19:27–28 ☐
Psalm 131:1 ☐
Proverbs 16:18 ☐
Proverbs 29:23 ☐
Isaiah 10:15–16 ☐
Luke 22:27 ☐
1 Corinthians 1:28 ☐
2 Corinthians 10:12–13 ☐

✉ Protection
Genesis 15:1 ☐

Numbers 18:20 ☐
Psalm 73:24–26 ☐
Psalm 82:3–4 ☐

✉ Purity
Psalm 101:3–8 ☐
Psalm 119:1–20 ☐
Matthew 23:27–28 ☐

✉ Repentance
Luke 3:7–8 ☐
Luke 13:3–5 ☐
Luke 15:7 ☐

✉ Reputation
Deuteronomy 4:6–9 ☐
Malachi 1:11 ☐
2 Corinthians 12:6 ☐

✉ Respect
Exodus 3:5 ☐
Leviticus 19:3 ☐
Job 31:13–14 ☐
Proverbs 31:30 ☐
Acts 10:28 ☐
Galatians 3:28–29 ☐
1 Peter 2:15 ☐

✉ Responsibility
Deuteronomy 11:1 ☐
Joshua 22:5 ☐
Psalm 31:23 ☐
Proverbs 23:26 ☐
Ezekiel 33:1–6 ☐
Matthew 4:10 ☐
Matthew 25:14–30 ☐
Acts 4:19–20 ☐

✉ Resurrection
John 6:38–40 ☐
1 Corinthians 15:12–21 ☐

✉ Revenge
1 Peter 2:21–23 ☐

In-Box List xxiii

Tick box when received ☑

✉ Salvation
- 2 Samuel 22:2 ☐
- 2 Samuel 22:47–48 ☐
- Joel 2:32 ☐
- Luke 15:32 ☐
- John 17:23 ☐
- Acts 2:37–38 ☐
- Romans 10:8–10 ☐
- Hebrews 9:27–28 ☐
- 1 Peter 1:18–19 ☐

✉ Satan
- John 8:44 ☐
- 2 Corinthians 11:14 ☐
- 1 Timothy 4:1 ☐
- 1 Peter 5:8 ☐
- 1 John 3:7–8 ☐

✉ Sickness
- Psalm 41 ☐
- Matthew 25:34–40 ☐

✉ Sin
- Exodus 32:34 ☐
- 2 Chronicles 6:24–25 ☐
- Ezra 9:6 ☐
- Proverbs 21:23 ☐
- Isaiah 53:6 ☐
- Isaiah 59:12–13 ☐
- Isaiah 64:6 ☐
- Jeremiah 16:17 ☐
- Daniel 9:4–8 ☐
- Hosea 7:13 ☐
- Romans 3:23 ☐

✉ Success
- Joshua 6:27 ☐
- 1 Chronicles 11:14 ☐
- 2 Chronicles 7:14 ☐
- 2 Chronicles 12:1 ☐
- Psalm 18:32–50 ☐

✉ Talents
- Ezekiel 28:5 ☐
- Daniel 1:17 ☐

✉ Temptation
- 2 Kings 21:8–9 ☐
- Proverbs 2:10–14 ☐
- 2 Timothy 2:22 ☐
- 1 John 2:16 ☐

✉ Thankfulness
- 1 Chronicles 16:4–36 ☐
- Psalm 100 ☐
- Psalm 107:1–3 ☐
- Psalm 138 ☐
- Isaiah 62:5 ☐
- Acts 27:35 ☐
- Ephesians 1:15–16 ☐
- Ephesians 5:20 ☐
- Hebrews 13:15 ☐

✉ Troubles
- Joshua 8:1 ☐
- 1 Samuel 17:37 ☐
- Job 14:1 ☐
- Psalm 22:19–24 ☐
- Psalm 46:1–2 ☐
- Psalm 142 ☐
- Isaiah 37:20 ☐
- Lamentations 5:16 ☐
- Matthew 11:30 ☐
- Romans 8:17–18 ☐
- 1 Peter 4:12–19 ☐

✉ Trust
- 1 Chronicles 14:10 ☐
- 1 Chronicles 17:26–27 ☐
- Psalm 11:1 ☐
- Psalm 20:7 ☐
- Psalm 52:5–9 ☐
- Psalm 56:11 ☐
- Psalm 62:8 ☐
- Psalm 146:3 ☐
- Proverbs 16:3 ☐
- Proverbs 28:25–26 ☐
- Isaiah 26:4 ☐
- Isaiah 40:25–28 ☐
- Isaiah 50:10 ☐
- Romans 4:5 ☐

✉ Truth
- 1 Samuel 7:3 ☐
- 1 Samuel 12:24 ☐
- Psalm 51:6 ☐
- Jeremiah 9:3 ☐
- Jeremiah 22:3–5 ☐
- John 17:17 ☐
- Hebrews 6:18 ☐

✉ Wisdom
- Genesis 41:16 ☐
- Psalm 90:12 ☐
- Proverbs 1:7 ☐
- Proverbs 8:12–14 ☐
- Proverbs 24:3–4 ☐
- Proverbs 24:13–14 ☐
- Ecclesiastes 9:13–18 ☐
- 1 Corinthians 2:6–8 ☐
- 1 Corinthians 8:1–3 ☐

✉ Witnessing
- Matthew 13:23 ☐
- Matthew 28:19–20 ☐
- John 4:34–38 ☐
- Acts 1:8 ☐
- Acts 18:9 ☐
- Romans 10:14–15 ☐
- 1 Corinthians 3:5–9 ☐
- 2 Corinthians 5:18–21 ☐
- Colossians 4:6 ☐
- 2 Timothy 4:1–2 ☐

✉ Worry
- 1 Chronicles 29:12 ☐
- Psalm 69 ☐
- Proverbs 12:25 ☐
- 2 Corinthians 4:8–12 ☐

✉ Worship
- Exodus 34:14 ☐
- Judges 5:3 ☐
- 2 Samuel 6:21 ☐
- Nehemiah 8:6 ☐
- Psalm 29:1–2 ☐
- Psalm 107:31–32 ☐
- Psalm 150 ☐
- Isaiah 66:2 ☐
- James 4:8 ☐
- Revelation 15:3–4 ☐

Preface to the *New Century Version*

God never intended for the Bible to be too difficult for his people to understand. To make sure God's message was clear, the authors of the Bible wrote it down in everyday language. These books brought a message that the original readers could understand. These first readers knew that God spoke through these books. Down through the centuries, many people wanted a Bible so badly that they copied different Bible books by hand!

Today, now that the Bible is so easy to get, many Christians do not read it every day. Many people feel that it is too hard to understand or doesn't have any answers for their life.

The *New Century Version* translation speaks in clear and simple language that even young readers can understand. The NCV presents God's Word in a clear and dynamic way.

A team of scholars from the World Bible Translation Center worked together with fifty other experienced Bible scholars to translate the verses from the best available Hebrew and Greek texts. You can trust that this Bible accurately presents God's Word as it came to us in the original languages.

Translators kept sentences short and simple. They tried to stay away from difficult words and worked hard to make the verses easier to read. They used more modern words for places and measurements. They put figures of speech and expressions in language that even children could understand. Also included within the text are small ns that refer you to a footnote found at the bottom of the Bible page.

It is with great humility and prayerfulness that this Bible is presented to God's children. We acknowledge the infallibility of God's Word and our own human frailty. We pray that God will use this Bible to help you understand his rich truth for your life. We magnify God's holy name, and for his glory this Bible is given.

THE PUBLISHER

THE OLD TESTAMENT

HOW DID IT ALL BEGIN?

Hi, there! My name is Moses. Does my name sound familiar? I'm the one God chose to lead his people out of Egypt, but you'll have to surf on over to the Book of Exodus for that story. The events in this book, Genesis, happened hundreds of years before I was born, so God told me what to write. Some of the coolest stories in the Bible are in this book. Be sure to check them out.

I wrote this book to tell everyone about the beginning of all things. I described how God created the sky and the earth, the plants and the animals, and finally, the best part of his creation, human beings. I told about the beginning of sin: how Adam and Eve did not obey God and had to leave the Garden of Eden. People have been sinning ever since! Most important, I wrote about the beginning of the special friendship God has with his people, starting with Abraham, and of his plan to save his people.

JESUS WATCH

Many people in Genesis remind us of Jesus. Abel, Adam's son, brought the best parts of his firstborn animals as a sacrifice to God. This sacrifice points to Jesus, the firstborn Son of God, who offered himself as a sacrifice for our sins. Melchizedek, the king of Salem and a priest of God Most High, brought out bread and wine when he blessed Abraham. This reminds us of the Last Supper when Jesus, our high priest, took bread and wine to bless the disciples the night before he died on the cross. In many ways Joseph's life points to the life of Jesus. Both were beloved sons of their fathers, but were hated by many. His own brothers sold Joseph into slavery, and Jesus was betrayed for money by one of his disciples. Both were accused of crimes they did not commit and both were raised to high positions. Joseph was in prison many years before he was freed and made a ruler of Egypt. Jesus died on the cross to take the punishment for our sins. He rose from the dead and later was brought up to heaven to be with God.

my FAVOURITE links

OTHER CONNECTIONS

Livin' it — Ever been hurt badly by a friend? What was your first reaction – to get mad and then get even, or to forgive that friend? Connect to You Want Me to Do What? Genesis 50:15–21, to find out how God wants you to react. You can follow the Faithlinks for more on this topic.

Stop at any of these bulletin boards to find out cool facts about people, places and things mentioned in the Book of Genesis. Here are just a few of the places you can visit:

- The Garden of Delight, Genesis 2:8–10, the first home of Adam and Eve before they were kicked out for disobeying God. No one knows exactly where Eden was located, but check here to find out how many rivers flowed out of the garden.
- Find out what happened when the first rain fell on earth when you visit The Boat That Saved the World, Genesis 7. You'll quickly discover that this was no ordinary boat, but more like a floating zoo!
- Take a trip back in time, tracing the path that Abraham travelled thousands of years ago when you connect to A New Home for Abraham, Genesis 16. Then stop by From Deceiver to Wrestler, Genesis 28:1, to read about Abraham's grandson Jacob and see where his adventures took him.

What's the flash on Noah's boat?

He thought it was going to rain – a lot! Surf on over to Genesis 6 and check it out.

SOME OTHER COOL STORIES TO PLUG INTO. . .

The Tower of Babel, Genesis 11:1–9
God's agreement with Abraham, Genesis 15
Pillar of salt, Genesis 19:23–29
Esau's bowl of soup, Genesis 25:27–34
Jacob's wrestling match with God, Genesis 32:22–32
Joseph's special robe, Genesis 37:1–11

FAITHlinks

- Out of Control?
  Genesis 4
- The Trouble with Sin,
  Genesis 6—8
- Just Kidding?
  Genesis 21:8–10
- Family Feud,
  Genesis 27
- The Best Policy,
  Genesis 29:16–29
- When You're Afraid,
  Genesis 32:9–12
- The Trouble with Jealousy,
  Genesis 37
- Alone and Forgotten?
  Genesis 40:23
- Good Plans,
  Genesis 45:7–8
- More Powerful Than Revenge,
  Genesis 50:14–21

> Genesis 1:1 4

The Beginning of the World

1 In the beginning God created the sky and the earth. 2 The earth was empty and had no form. Darkness covered the ocean, and God's Spirit was moving over the water.

3 Then God said, "Let there be light," and there was light. 4 God saw that the light was good, so he divided the light from the darkness. 5 God named the light "day" and the darkness "night". Evening passed, and morning came. This was the first day.

6 Then God said, "Let there be something to divide the water in two." 7 So God made the air and placed some of the water above the air and some below it. 8 God named the air "sky". Evening passed, and morning came. This was the second day.

9 Then God said, "Let the water under the sky be gathered together so the dry land will appear." And it happened. 10 God named the dry land "earth" and the water that was gathered together "seas". God saw that this was good.

11 Then God said, "Let the earth produce plants—some to make grain for seeds and others to make fruits with seeds in them. Every seed will produce more of its own kind of plant." And it happened. 12 The earth produced plants with grain for seeds, and trees that made fruits with seeds in them. Each seed grew its own kind of plant. God saw that all this was good. 13 Evening passed, and morning came. This was the third day.

14 Then God said, "Let there be lights in the sky to separate day from night. These lights will be used for signs, seasons, days and years. 15 They will be in the sky to give light to the earth." And it happened.

16 So God made the two large lights. He made the brighter light to rule the day and the smaller light to rule the night. He also made the stars. 17 God put all these in the sky to shine on the earth, 18 to rule over the day and over the night, and to separate the light from the darkness. God saw that all these things were good. 19 Evening passed, and morning came. This was the fourth day.

20 Then God said, "Let the water be filled with living things, and let birds fly in the air above the earth."

21 So God created the large sea animals and every living thing that moves in the sea. The sea is filled with these

---

FAITH links

MADE IN HIS IMAGE
GENESIS 1:26-27

Ever have a woe-is-me day, a day when you've wondered, *What's so great about being me?* Here's what's so great: you are one of God's greatest creations. After creating the world and all of the animals and plants, God created people in his own image. News flash: we didn't evolve from apes! Being made in God's image means you have some of his characteristics. Does this mean you have God's nose or chin? No. God doesn't have a body. Instead it means you can love, be forgiving and creative – just like God.

Hey, want to know more about God and how to love like him? Connect to these:

Count on His Mercy, Judges 2:16–17; 3, p. 313

A Model of Forgiveness, Ezekiel 16:59–63, p. 1103

A Blueprint for Living, Amos 5:14–15, p. 1200

Go! No! Jonah 1, p. 1213

Love for Free, Romans 5:8, p. 1524

The Best Choice, 1 Corinthians 13, p. 1560

GARDEN OF DELIGHT
Genesis 2:8–10

We don't know exactly where God created the Garden of Eden. We think it was near the place that we call Arabia today. We do know that four rivers flowed out of the garden. One was called the Tigris and another was called the Euphrates. We may not know exactly where the garden was, but we do know what it was for – it was the home God created for Adam and Eve, the first people on earth. (Check out Genesis 2:4—3:24.) It was a wonderful place to live. *Eden* means "delight" and the Garden of Eden was a place of delightful things. When Adam and Eve had to leave such a wonderful place because of their sin, it was a sad day for all of us.

---

living things, with each one producing more of its own kind. He also made every bird that flies, and each bird produced more of its own kind. God saw that this was good. 22 God blessed them and said, "Have many young ones so that you may grow in number. Fill the water of the seas, and let the birds grow in number on the earth." 23 Evening passed, and morning came. This was the fifth day.

24 Then God said, "Let the earth be filled with animals, each producing more of its own kind. Let there be tame animals and small crawling animals and wild animals, and let each produce more of its kind." And it happened.

25 So God made the wild animals, the tame animals, and all the small crawling animals to produce more of their own kind. God saw that this was good.

26 Then God said, "Let us make human beings in our image and likeness. And let them rule over the fish in the sea and the birds in the sky, over the tame animals, over all the earth, and over all the small crawling animals on the earth."

27 So God created human beings in his image. In the image of God he created them. He created them male and female. 28 God blessed them and said, "Have many children and grow in number. Fill the earth and be its master. Rule over the fish in the sea and over the birds in the sky and over every living thing that moves on the earth."

29 God said, "Look, I have given you all the plants that have grain for seeds and all the trees whose fruits have seeds in them. They will be food for you. 30 I have given all the green plants as food for every wild animal, every bird of the air, and every small crawling animal." And it happened. 31 God looked at everything he had made, and it was very good. Evening passed, and morning came. This was the sixth day.

The Seventh Day—Rest

2 So the sky, the earth, and all that filled them were finished. 2 By the seventh day God finished the work he had been doing, so he rested from all his work. 3 God blessed the seventh day and made it a holy day, because on that day he rested from all the work he had done in creating the world.

The First People

4 This is the story of the creation of the sky and the earth. When the LORD God first made the earth and the sky,

Genesis 2:5 6

5 there were still no plants on the earth. Nothing was growing in the fields because the LORD God had not yet made it rain on the land. And there was no person to care for the ground, 6 but a mist would rise up from the earth and water all the ground.

7 Then the LORD God took dust from the ground and formed a man from it. He breathed the breath of life into the man's nose, and the man became a living person. 8 Then the LORD God planted a garden in the east, in a place called Eden, and put the man he had formed into it. 9 The LORD God caused every beautiful tree and every tree that was good for food to grow out of the ground. In the middle of the garden, God put the tree that gives life and also the tree that gives the knowledge of good and evil.

10 A river flowed through Eden and watered the garden. From there the river branched out to become four rivers. 11 The first river, named Pishon, flows around the whole land of Havilah, where there is gold. 12 The gold of that land is excellent. Bdellium and onyx[n] are also found there. 13 The second river, named Gihon, flows around the whole land of Cush. 14 The third river, named Tigris, flows out of Assyria towards the east. The fourth river is the Euphrates.

15 The LORD God put the man in the garden of Eden to care for it and work it. 16 The LORD God commanded him, "You may eat the fruit from any tree in the garden, 17 but you must not eat the fruit from the tree which gives the knowledge of good and evil. If you ever eat fruit from that tree, you will die!"

The First Woman

18 Then the LORD God said, "It is not good for the man to be alone. I will make a helper who is right for him."

19 From the ground God formed every wild animal and every bird in the sky, and he brought them to the man so the man could name them. Whatever the man called each living thing, that became its name. 20 The man gave names to all the tame animals, to the birds in the sky, and to all the wild animals. But Adam[n] did not find a helper that was right for him. 21 So the LORD God caused the man to sleep very deeply, and while he was asleep, God removed one of the man's ribs. Then God closed up the man's skin at the place where he took the rib. 22 The LORD God used the rib from the man to make a woman, and then he brought the woman to the man.

23 And the man said,
"Now, this is someone whose bones
 came from my bones,
 whose body came from my body.
I will call her 'woman',
 because she was taken out of
  man."

24 So a man will leave his father and mother and be united with his wife, and the two will become one body.

25 The man and his wife were naked, but they were not ashamed.

The Beginning of Sin

3 Now the snake was the most clever of all the wild animals the LORD God had made. One day the snake said to the woman, "Did God really say that you must not eat fruit from any tree in the garden?"

2 The woman answered the snake, "We may eat fruit from the trees in the garden. 3 But God told us, 'You must not eat fruit from the tree that is in the middle of the garden. You must not even touch it, or you will die.'"

4 But the snake said to the woman, "You will not die. 5 God knows that if you eat the fruit from that tree, you will learn about good and evil and you will be like God!"

6 The woman saw that the tree was beautiful, that its fruit was good to eat, and that it would make her wise. So she took some of its fruit and ate it. She also gave some of the fruit to her husband, and he ate it.

7 Then, it was as if their eyes were

2:12 bdellium and onyx Bdellium is an expensive, sweet-smelling resin like myrrh, and onyx is a gem.

2:20 Adam This is the name of the first man. It also means "humans", including men and women.

FAITH links

CAN'T LIVE WITHOUT IT?
GENESIS 3

Is there anything you want that you would do *anything* to get, even something wrong? The snake tempted Eve to eat fruit from the tree in the middle of the garden that God told Adam and Eve not to eat from. (See Genesis 2:16–17.) The snake made the fruit sound wonderful. So Adam and Eve reached for the one thing they felt they didn't have and couldn't live without.

Sometimes we're tempted by the things we think we can't live without. At those times, we also might doubt that God knows what's best for our lives. When that happens, don't give in to temptation and doubt. Instead, ask God for help.

Complaints, Complaints! Exodus 16:1–3, p. 97

A Hidden Sin, Joshua 7, p. 285

Learning to Trust, Psalm 25:4–5, p. 727

Obeying God or Man? Daniel 3:8–30, p. 1154

The Temptation Fighter, Matthew 4:1–11, p. 1278

Faith God Notices, Luke 18:35–43, p. 1406

---

opened. They realised they were naked, so they sewed fig leaves together and made something to cover themselves.

8 Then they heard the LORD God walking in the garden during the cool part of the day, and the man and his wife hid from the LORD God among the trees in the garden. 9 But the LORD God called to the man and said, "Where are you?"

10 The man answered, "I heard you walking in the garden, and I was afraid because I was naked, so I hid."

11 God asked, "Who told you that you were naked? Did you eat fruit from the tree from which I commanded you not to eat?"

12 The man said, "You gave this woman to me and she gave me fruit from the tree, so I ate it."

13 Then the LORD God said to the woman, "How could you have done such a thing?"

She answered, "The snake tricked me, so I ate the fruit."

14 The LORD God said to the snake, "Because you did this,
 a curse will be put on you.
You will be cursed as no other
 animal, tame or wild, will ever be.
You will crawl on your stomach,
 and you will eat dust all the days of your life.
15 I will make you and the woman
 enemies of each other.
Your descendants and her
 descendants
 will be enemies.
One of her descendants will crush
 your head,
 and you will bite his heel."

16 Then God said to the woman,
"I will cause you to have much
 trouble
 when you are pregnant,
and when you give birth to children,
 you will have great pain.
You will greatly desire your
 husband,
 but he will rule over you."

17 Then God said to the man, "You listened to what your wife said, and you ate fruit from the tree from which I commanded you not to eat.

"So I will put a curse on the ground,
 and you will have to work very
 hard for your food.

Genesis 3:18

In pain you will eat its food
all the days of your life.
18 The ground will produce thorns and
weeds for you,
and you will eat the plants of the
field.
19 You will sweat and work hard
for your food.
Later you will return to the ground,
because you were taken from it.
You are dust,
and when you die, you will return
to the dust."

20 The man named his wife Eve,[n] because she is the mother of everyone who has ever lived.

21 The LORD God made clothes from animal skins for the man and his wife and dressed them. 22 Then the LORD God said, "The man has become like one of us; he knows good and evil. We must keep him from eating some of the fruit from the tree of life, or he will live for ever." 23 So the LORD God forced the man out of the garden of Eden to work the ground from which he was taken. 24 After God forced the man out of the garden, he placed angels and a sword of fire that flashed around in every direction on its eastern border. This kept people from getting to the tree of life.

The First Family

4 Adam had sexual relations with his wife Eve, and she became pregnant and gave birth to Cain.[n] Eve said, "With the LORD's help, I have given birth to a man." 2 After that, Eve gave birth to Cain's brother, Abel. Abel took care of flocks, and Cain became a farmer.

3 Later, Cain brought some food from the ground as a gift to God. 4 Abel brought the best parts from some of the firstborn of his flock. The LORD accepted Abel and his gift, 5 but he did not accept Cain and his gift. So Cain became very angry and felt rejected.

3:20 Eve This name sounds like the Hebrew word for "alive".

4:1 Cain This name sounds like the Hebrew word for "I have given birth".

OUT OF CONTROL?
GENESIS 4

Ever been so mad at someone that you were ready to explode? When God did not accept Cain's sacrifice, Cain became angry – angry enough to kill his own brother. Earlier, God had warned Cain to "rule over" his anger. By this, God meant that Cain needed to control his anger. But Cain wouldn't listen.

Feeling angry? Anger itself is not sinful. Sin happens when anger gets out of control. God has tools you can use to master anger before it masters you. One of those tools is a fruit of the Spirit: self-control. (Read about it in Galatians 5:22–23, p. 1593.) Another tool is prayer. Use them when needed!

Need to cool off some more? Surf over to these Faithlinks!

What God "Hates", Proverbs 6:16–19, p. 835

Justice Served, Isaiah 35:3–4, p. 940

The "Ruler" of Our Lives, Amos 7:7–9, p. 1202

Don't Get Mad; Get Even? Matthew 26:57–63; 27:11–14, p.1323

Fear-Fighters, 2 Timothy 1:7, p. 1652

The "Quality" of Life, 2 Peter 1:5–8, p. 1708

6 The LORD asked Cain, "Why are you angry? Why do you look so unhappy? 7 If you do things well, I will accept you, but if you do not do them well, sin is ready to attack you. Sin wants you, but you must rule over it."

8 Cain said to his brother Abel, "Let's go out into the field." While they were out in the field, Cain attacked his brother Abel and killed him.

9 Later, the LORD said to Cain, "Where is your brother Abel?"

Cain answered, "I don't know. Is it my job to take care of my brother?"

10 Then the LORD said, "What have you done? Your brother's blood is crying out to me from the ground. 11 And now you will be cursed in your work with the ground, the same ground where your brother's blood fell and where your hands killed him. 12 You will work the ground, but it will not grow good crops for you any more, and you will wander around on the earth."

13 Then Cain said to the LORD, "This punishment is more than I can stand! 14 Today you have forced me to stop working the ground, and now I must hide from you. I must wander around on the earth, and anyone who meets me can kill me."

15 The LORD said to Cain, "No! If anyone kills you, I will punish that person seven times more." Then the LORD put a mark on Cain warning anyone who met him not to kill him.

Cain's Family

16 So Cain went away from the LORD and lived in the land of Nod,[n] east of Eden. 17 He had sexual relations with his wife, and she became pregnant and gave birth to Enoch. At that time Cain was building a city, which he named after his son Enoch. 18 Enoch had a son named Irad, Irad had a son named Mehujael, Mehujael had a son named Methushael and Methushael had a son named Lamech.

19 Lamech married two women, Adah and Zillah. 20 Adah gave birth to Jabal, who became the first person to live in tents and raise cattle. 21 Jabal's brother was Jubal, the first person to play the harp and flute. 22 Zillah gave birth to Tubal-Cain, who made tools out of bronze and iron. The sister of Tubal-Cain was Naamah.

23 Lamech said to his wives:
"Adah and Zillah, hear my voice!
    You wives of Lamech, listen to
        what I say.
I killed a man for wounding me,
    a young man for hitting me.
24 If Cain's killer is punished seven times,
    then Lamech's killer will be
        punished 77 times."

Adam and Eve Have a New Son

25 Adam had sexual relations with his wife Eve again, and she gave birth to a son. She named him Seth[n] and said, "God has given me another child. He will take the place of Abel, who was killed by Cain." 26 Seth also had a son, and they named him Enosh. At that time people began to pray to the LORD.

Adam's Family History

5 This is the family history of Adam. When God created human beings, he made them in his own likeness. 2 He created them male and female, and on that day he blessed them and named them human beings.

3 When Adam was 130 years old, he became the father of another son in his likeness and image, and Adam named him Seth. 4 After Seth was born, Adam lived 800 years and had other sons and daughters. 5 So Adam lived a total of 930 years, and then he died.

> He created them male and female, and on that day he blessed them and named them human beings.
> – Genesis 5:2

4:16 Nod This name sounds like the Hebrew word for "wander."
4:25 Seth This name sounds like the Hebrew word for "to give."

Genesis 5:6 10

6 When Seth was 105 years old, he had a son named Enosh. 7 After Enosh was born, Seth lived 807 years and had other sons and daughters. 8 So Seth lived a total of 912 years, and then he died.

9 When Enosh was 90 years old, he had a son named Kenan. 10 After Kenan was born, Enosh lived 815 years and had other sons and daughters. 11 So Enosh lived a total of 905 years, and then he died.

12 When Kenan was 70 years old, he had a son named Mahalalel. 13 After Mahalalel was born, Kenan lived 840 years and had other sons and daughters. 14 So Kenan lived a total of 910 years, and then he died.

15 When Mahalalel was 65 years old, he had a son named Jared. 16 After Jared was born, Mahalalel lived 830 years and had other sons and daughters. 17 So Mahalalel lived a total of 895 years, and then he died.

18 When Jared was 162 years old, he had a son named Enoch. 19 After Enoch was born, Jared lived 800 years and had other sons and daughters. 20 So Jared lived a total of 962 years, and then he died.

21 When Enoch was 65 years old, he had a son named Methuselah. 22 After Methuselah was born, Enoch walked with God 300 years more and had other sons and daughters. 23 So Enoch lived a total of 365 years. 24 Enoch walked with God; one day Enoch could not be found, because God took him.

25 When Methuselah was 187 years old, he had a son named Lamech. 26 After Lamech was born, Methuselah lived 782 years and had other sons and daughters. 27 So Methuselah lived a total of 969 years, and then he died.

28 When Lamech was 182, he had a son. 29 Lamech named his son Noah" and said, "He will comfort us in our work, which comes from the ground the LORD has cursed." 30 After Noah was born, Lamech lived 595 years and had other sons and daughters. 31 So Lamech lived a total of 777 years, and then he died.

32 After Noah was 500 years old, he became the father of Shem, Ham and Japheth.

The Human Race Becomes Evil

6 The number of people on earth began to grow, and daughters were born to them. 2 When the sons of God saw that these girls were beautiful, they married any of them they chose. 3 The LORD said, "My Spirit will not remain in human beings for ever, because they are flesh. They will live only 120 years."

4 The Nephilim were on the earth in those days and also later. That was when the sons of God had sexual relations with the daughters of human beings. These women gave birth to children, who became famous and were the mighty warriors of long ago.

5 The LORD saw that the human beings on the earth were very wicked and that everything they thought about was evil. 6 He was sorry he had made human beings on the earth, and his heart was filled with pain. 7 So the LORD said, "I will destroy all human beings that I made on the earth. And I will destroy every animal and everything that crawls on the earth and the birds of the air, because I am sorry I have made them." 8 But Noah pleased the LORD.

Noah and the Great Flood

9 This is the family history of Noah. Noah was a good man, the most innocent man of his time, and he walked with God. 10 He had three sons: Shem, Ham and Japheth.

11 People on earth did what God said was evil, and violence was everywhere. 12 When God saw that everyone on the earth did only evil, 13 he said to Noah, "Because people have made the earth full of violence, I will destroy all of them from the earth. 14 Build a boat of cypress wood for yourself. Make rooms in it and cover it inside and outside with tar. 15 This is how big I want you to build the boat: 150 metres long, 25 metres wide and 15 metres high. 16 Make an opening around the top of the boat that is 50 centimetres high from the edge of the roof down. Put a door in the side

---

5:29 Noah This name sounds like the Hebrew word for "rest."

Genesis 7:11

of the boat. Make an upper, middle and lower deck in it. 17 I will bring a flood of water on the earth to destroy all living things that live under the sky, including everything that has the breath of life. Everything on the earth will die. 18 But I will make an agreement with you— you, your sons, your wife and your sons' wives will all go into the boat. 19 Also, you must bring into the boat two of every living thing, male and female. Keep them alive with you. 20 Two of every kind of bird, animal and crawling thing will come to you to be kept alive. 21 Also, gather some of every kind of food and store it on the boat as food for you and the animals."

22 Noah did everything that God commanded him.

The Flood Begins

7 Then the LORD said to Noah, "I have seen that you are the best person among the people of this time, so you and your family can go into the boat. 2 Take with you seven pairs, each male with its female, of every kind of clean animal; and take one pair, each male with its female, of every kind of unclean animal. 3 Take seven pairs of all the birds of the sky, each male with its female. This will allow all these animals to continue living on the earth after the flood. 4 Seven days from now I will send rain on the earth. It will rain 40 days and 40 nights, and I will wipe from the earth every living thing that I have made."

5 Noah did everything the LORD commanded him.

6 Noah was 600 years old when the flood came. 7 He and his wife and his sons and their wives went into the boat to escape the waters of the flood. 8 The clean animals, the unclean animals, the birds and everything that crawls on the ground 9 came to Noah. They went into the boat in groups of two, male and female, just as God had commanded Noah. 10 Seven days later the flood started.

11 When Noah was 600 years old, the flood started. On the seventeenth day of the second month of that year the underground springs split open, and the

---

FAITH links

THE TROUBLE WITH SIN
GENESIS 6—8

Have you ever heard your mum or dad say, "I've had it up to here"? That usually means, "I'm fed up!" It also means, "You're in trouble." God had "had it up to here" with just about everyone on earth. No one thought about obeying him – no one except Noah. So God decided to destroy almost all human and animal life on earth. Because of Noah's obedience, his whole family was saved from the flood.

Sin has consequences. Those consequences may not involve a flood in your life. But they can mean trouble. That's why God gives us ways to obey. He's given us the Bible, which tells us how to please him.

Connect to these Faithlinks to find out what else God has to say about sin.

The Perfect Sacrifice, Leviticus 1—7, p. 135

Real Repentance, Jeremiah 4:1–4, p. 993

A Fake Apology, Hosea 6:1–7, p. 1177

Hope That Doesn't Fail, Acts 26:4–7, p. 1510

The Sin Habit, Romans 7:15–20, p. 1527

The Finished Product, Philippians 1:6, p. 1609

Genesis 7:12   **12**

THE BOAT THAT SAVED THE WORLD   Genesis 7

Noah built the boat to save himself, his family and animals from a flood that covered the whole earth. (Read about it in Genesis 6:14—9:19.) The boat was about 150 metres long, 25 metres wide and 15 metres high, with three decks. Experts say the boat could hold more than 43,000 tons.

Noah and his family lived in the boat for almost a year as it floated on the floodwaters. The boat finally landed on Mount Ararat in what is now Turkey. No one has ever found the boat if it is still there.

The story of Noah's boat teaches us about God's judgement and his mercy. In the New Testament, Jesus compared the days before the flood to the days before he comes back to earth. (See Matthew 24:37–38, p. 1316; Luke 17:26–27, p. 1404.) Other references to the flood include Hebrews 11:7; 1 Peter 3:20; and 2 Peter 2:5.

---

clouds in the sky poured out rain. **12** The rain fell on the earth for 40 days and 40 nights.

13 On that same day Noah and his wife, his sons Shem, Ham and Japheth, and their wives went into the boat. **14** They had every kind of wild and tame animal, every kind of animal that crawls on the earth and every kind of bird. **15** Every creature that had the breath of life came to Noah in the boat in groups of two. **16** One male and one female of every living thing came, just as God had commanded Noah. Then the LORD closed the door behind them.

17 Water flooded the earth for 40 days, and as it rose it lifted the boat off the ground. **18** The water continued to rise, and the boat floated on it above the earth. **19** The water rose so much that even the highest mountains under the sky were covered by it. **20** It continued to rise until it was more than 7 metres above the mountains.

21 All living things that moved on the earth died. This included all the birds, tame animals, wild animals and creatures that swarm on the earth, as well as all human beings. **22** So everything on dry land that had the breath of life in it died. **23** God destroyed from the earth every living thing that was on the land—every man, animal, crawling thing and bird of the sky. All that was left was Noah and what was there with him in the boat. **24** And the waters continued to cover the earth for 150 days.

The Flood Ends

8 But God remembered Noah and all the wild and tame animals with him in the boat. He made a wind blow over the earth, and the water went down. **2** The underground springs stopped flowing, and the clouds in the sky stopped pouring down rain. **3-4** The water that covered the earth began to go down. After 150 days it had gone down so much that the boat touched land again. It came to rest on one of the mountains of Ararat*[n]*

8:1 God Check out how much God cares for his creation.

8:3-4 Ararat The ancient land of Urartu, an area in eastern Turkey.

on the seventeenth day of the seventh month. 5 The water continued to go down so that by the first day of the tenth month the tops of the mountains could be seen.

6 Forty days later Noah opened the window he had made in the boat, and 7 he sent out a raven. It flew here and there until the water had dried up from the earth. 8 Then Noah sent out a dove to find out if the water had dried up from the ground. 9 The dove could not find a place to land because water still covered the earth, so it came back to the boat. Noah reached out his hand and took the bird and brought it back into the boat.

10 After seven days Noah again sent out the dove from the boat, 11 and that evening it came back to him with a fresh olive leaf in its mouth. Then Noah knew that the ground was almost dry. 12 Seven days later he sent the dove out again, but this time it did not come back.

13 When Noah was 601 years old, in the first day of the first month of that year, the water was dried up from the land. Noah removed the covering of the boat and saw that the land was dry. 14 By the twenty-seventh day of the second month the land was completely dry.

15 Then God said to Noah, 16 "You and your wife, your sons and their wives should go out of the boat. 17 Bring every animal out of the boat with you—the birds, animals and everything that crawls on the earth. Let them have many young ones so that they might grow in number."

18 So Noah went out with his sons, his wife and his sons' wives. 19 Every animal, everything that crawls on the earth and every bird went out of the boat by families.

20 Then Noah built an altar to the LORD. He took some of all the clean birds and animals, and he burned them on the altar as offerings to God. 21 The LORD was pleased with these sacrifices and said to himself, "I will never again curse the ground because of human beings. Their thoughts are evil even when they are young, but I will never again destroy every living thing on the earth as I did this time.

22 "As long as the earth continues,
    planting and harvest,
    cold and hot,
    summer and winter,
    day and night
    will not stop."

The New Beginning

9 Then God blessed Noah and his sons and said to them, "Have many children; grow in number and fill the earth. 2 Every animal on earth, every bird in the sky, every animal that crawls on the ground and every fish in the sea will respect and fear you. I have given them to you.

3 "Everything that moves, everything that is alive, is yours for food. Earlier I gave you the green plants, but now I give you everything for food. 4 But you must not eat meat that still has blood in it, because blood gives life. 5 I will demand blood for life. I will demand the life of any animal that kills a person, and I will demand the life of anyone who takes another person's life.

6 "Whoever kills a human being
    will be killed by a human being,
    because God made humans
    in his own image.

7 "As for you, Noah, I want you and your family to have many children, to grow in number on the earth, and to become many."

8 Then God said to Noah and his sons, 9 "Now I am making my agreement with you and your people who will live after you, 10 and with every living thing that is with you—the birds, the tame and the wild animals, and with everything that came out of the boat with you— with every living thing on earth. 11 I make this agreement with you: I will never again destroy all living things by a flood. A flood will never again destroy the earth."

12 And God said, "This is the sign of the agreement between me and you and every living creature that is with you. 13 I am putting my rainbow in the clouds as the sign of the agreement between me and the earth. 14 When I bring clouds

over the earth and a rainbow appears in them, 15 I will remember my agreement between me and you and every living thing. Floods will never again destroy all life on the earth. 16 When the rainbow appears in the clouds, I will see it and I will remember the agreement that continues for ever between me and every living thing on the earth."

17 So God said to Noah, "The rainbow is a sign of the agreement that I made with all living things on earth."

Noah and His Sons

18 The sons of Noah who came out of the boat with him were Shem, Ham and Japheth. (Ham was the father of Canaan.) 19 These three men were Noah's sons, and all the people on earth came from these three sons.

20 Noah became a farmer and planted a vineyard. 21 When he drank wine made from his grapes, he became drunk and lay naked in his tent. 22 Ham, the father of Canaan, looked at his naked father and told his brothers outside. 23 Then Shem and Japheth got a coat and, carrying it on both their shoulders, they walked backwards into the tent and covered their father. They turned their faces away so that they did not see their father's nakedness.

24 Noah was sleeping because of the wine. When he woke up and learned what his youngest son, Ham, had done to him, 25 he said,

"May there be a curse on Canaan!
    May he be the lowest slave to his
        brothers."

26 Noah also said,

"May the LORD, the God of Shem, be
        praised!
May Canaan be Shem's slave.
27 May God give more land to
        Japheth.
May Japheth live in Shem's
        tents,
and may Canaan be their slave."

28 After the flood Noah lived 350 years. 29 He lived a total of 950 years, and then he died.

Nations Grow and Spread

10 This is the family history of Shem, Ham and Japheth, the sons of Noah. After the flood these three men had sons.

FAITH links

THE RAINBOW PROMISE
GENESIS 9:1-17

Think about the last time you saw a rainbow fill the sky. Some of us may take rainbows for granted. Sure they're nice and colourful. After all, they're the result of the bending and reflecting of sunlight through the moisture in the air. But that rainbow, as routine as it may seem after a spring rain, is the sign of an ancient promise. God promised that he would never again destroy all living creatures by a flood. The rainbow is a sign of his faithfulness. Next time you see a rainbow, let it remind you that God keeps his promises.

Check out God's great love for you by linking up here:

Your Heavenly Parent, Exodus 2:1–10, p. 77

The God of Big Things, Joshua 10, p. 289

How Big Is God? Job 38—41, p. 703

Hope That Doesn't Fail, Acts 26:4–7, p. 1510

But I Want It? Philippians 4:19, p. 1615

His Best Qualities, 2 Peter 3:9, p. 1711

Japheth's Sons

2 The sons of Japheth were Gomer, Magog, Madai, Javan, Tubal, Meshech and Tiras.

3 The sons of Gomer were Ashkenaz, Riphath and Togarmah.

4 The sons of Javan were Elishah, Tarshish, Kittim[n] and Rodanim. 5 Those who lived in the lands around the Mediterranean Sea came from these sons of Japheth. All the families grew and became different nations, each nation with its own land and its own language.

Ham's Sons

6 The sons of Ham were Cush, Mizraim,[n] Put and Canaan.

7 The sons of Cush were Seba, Havilah, Sabtah, Raamah and Sabteca.

The sons of Raamah were Sheba and Dedan.

8 Cush also had a descendant named Nimrod, who became a very powerful man on earth. 9 He was a great hunter before the LORD, which is why people say someone is "like Nimrod, a great hunter before the LORD." 10 At first Nimrod's kingdom covered Babylon, Erech, Akkad and Calneh in the land of Babylonia. 11 From there he went to Assyria, where he built the cities of Nineveh, Rehoboth Ir and Calah. 12 He also built Resen, the great city between Nineveh and Calah.

13 Mizraim was the father of the Ludites, Anamites, Lehabites, Naphtuhites, 14 Pathrusites, Casluhites and the people of Crete. (The Philistines came from the Casluhites.)

15 Canaan was the father of Sidon, his first son, and of Heth. 16 He was also the father of the Jebusites, Amorites, Girgashites, 17 Hivites, Arkites, Sinites, 18 Arvadites, Zemarites and Hamathites. The families of the Canaanites scattered. 19 Their land reached from Sidon to Gerar as far as Gaza and then to Sodom, Gomorrah, Admah and Zeboiim, as far as Lasha.

20 All these people were the sons of Ham and all these families had their own languages, their own lands, and their own nations.

Shem's Sons

21 Shem, Japheth's older brother, also had sons. One of his descendants was the father of all the sons of Eber.

22 The sons of Shem were Elam, Asshur, Arphaxad, Lud and Aram.

23 The sons of Aram were Uz, Hul, Gether and Meshech.

24 Arphaxad was the father of Shelah, who was the father of Eber. 25 Eber was the father of two sons—one named Peleg,[n] because the earth was divided during his life, and the other was named Joktan.

26 Joktan was the father of Almodad, Sheleph, Hazarmaveth, Jerah, 27 Hadoram, Uzal, Diklah, 28 Obal, Abimael, Sheba, 29 Ophir, Havilah and Jobab. All these people were the sons of Joktan. 30 They lived in the area between Mesha and Sephar in the hill country in the east.

31 These are the people from the family of Shem, arranged by families, languages, countries and nations.

32 This is the list of the families from the sons of Noah, arranged according to their nations. From these families came all the nations who spread across the earth after the flood.

> This is the list of the families from the sons of Noah, arranged according to their nations. From these families came all the nations who spread across the earth after the flood.
> – Genesis 10:32

10:4 Kittim His descendants were the people of Cyprus.
10:6 Mizraim This is another name for Egypt.
10:25 Peleg This name sounds like the Hebrew word for "divided."

Genesis 11:1 16

TOWER OF PRIDE — Genesis 11:3–9

The tower of Babel was built like a pyramid. The tower was made of bricks and mortar instead of stone. It was built after the great flood. (Remember Noah and his boat?)

The problem with the tower was that the people built it out of their own pride. They weren't humbly reaching out to God. They were trying to build their own tower to heaven. God did something that got the people's attention as they were building the tower. He confused their languages. That means that all of a sudden different people were talking different languages. Can you imagine talking to your friend, who suddenly starts speaking in Spanish or French? It would be pretty hard to get anything done. That's what happened to the builders of the tower. They got frustrated because they couldn't communicate and finally stopped building altogether. (Look at Genesis 11:3–9.)

The Languages Confused

11 At this time the whole world spoke one language, and everyone used the same words. 2 As people moved from the east, they found a plain in the land of Babylonia and settled there.

3 They said to each other, "Let's make bricks and bake them to make them hard." So they used bricks instead of stones, and tar instead of mortar. 4 Then they said to each other, "Let's build a city and a tower for ourselves, whose top will reach high into the sky. We will become famous. Then we will not be scattered over all the earth."

5 The LORD came down to see the city and the tower that the people had built. 6 The LORD said, "Now, these people are united, all speaking the same language. This is only the beginning of what they will do. They will be able to do anything they want. 7 Come, let us go down and confuse their language so they will not be able to understand each other."

8 So the LORD scattered them from there over all the earth, and they stopped building the city. 9 The place is called Babel[n] since that is where the LORD confused the language of the whole world. So the LORD caused them to spread out from there over the whole world.

The Story of Shem's Family

10 This is the family history of Shem. Two years after the flood, when Shem was 100 years old, his son Arphaxad was born. 11 After that, Shem lived 500 years and had other sons and daughters.

12 When Arphaxad was 35 years old, his son Shelah was born. 13 After that, Arphaxad lived 403 years and had other sons and daughters.

14 When Shelah was 30 years old, his son Eber was born. 15 After that, Shelah lived 403 years and had other sons and daughters.

16 When Eber was 34 years old, his son Peleg was born. 17 After that, Eber lived 430 years and had other sons and daughters.

18 When Peleg was 30 years old, his

11:9 Babel This name sounds like the Hebrew word for "confused."

son Reu was born. **19** After that, Peleg lived 209 years and had other sons and daughters.

20 When Reu was 32 years old, his son Serug was born. **21** After that, Reu lived 207 years and had other sons and daughters.

22 When Serug was 30 years old, his son Nahor was born. **23** After that, Serug lived 200 years and had other sons and daughters.

24 When Nahor was 29 years old, his son Terah was born. **25** After that, Nahor lived 119 years and had other sons and daughters.

26 After Terah was 70 years old, his sons Abram, Nahor and Haran were born.

The Story of Terah's Family

27 This is the family history of Terah. Terah was the father of Abram, Nahor and Haran. Haran was the father of Lot. **28** While his father, Terah, was still alive, Haran died in Ur in Babylonia, where he was born. **29** Abram and Nahor both married. Abram's wife was named Sarai, and Nahor's wife was named Milcah. She was the daughter of Haran, who was the father of both Milcah and Iscah. **30** Sarai was not able to have children.

31 Terah took his son Abram, his grandson Lot (Haran's son), and his daughter-in-law Sarai (Abram's wife) and moved out of Ur of Babylonia. They had planned to go to the land of Canaan, but when they reached the city of Haran, they settled there.

32 Terah lived to be 205 years old, and then he died in Haran.

God Calls Abram

12 The LORD said to Abram,*n* "Leave your country, your relatives and your father's family, and go to the land I will show you.
2 I will make you a great nation,
   and I will bless you.
I will make you famous,
   and you will be a blessing to others.
3 I will bless those who bless you,

12:1 **Abram** This name means "honoured father".

> ## FAITH links
>
> ### LIGHTS, CAMERA,...ACTIONS!
> ### GENESIS 12:1-3
>
> Imagine being asked to pack your things and move to a foreign country – one you know nothing about. Would you go? You would if you were Abraham (called Abram in these verses). Abraham was told to leave his home and relatives in Ur and go to a new land. Abraham showed faith in God by his actions.
>
> Faith in God involves action, not just words. One action is obedience. Many people say that they trust God. Yet their actions tell a different story. What do your actions reveal?
>
> Moses' Champion, Numbers 12, p. 192
>
> Trailblazers of Faith, 2 Kings 22:1–2, p. 510
>
> In the Lions' Den, Daniel 6, p. 1160
>
> Ask, Search, Knock, Matthew 7:7–10, p. 1286
>
> Prove It! Matthew 16:1–4, p. 1302
>
> Our Gift to God, Romans 12:1–2, p. 1536

and I will place a curse on those
   who harm you.
And all the people on earth
   will be blessed through you."

4 So Abram left Haran as the LORD had told him, and Lot went with him. At this time Abram was 75 years old. **5** He took his wife Sarai, his nephew Lot, and everything they owned, as well as all the servants they had gained in Haran. They set out from Haran, planning to go to the land of Canaan, and in time they arrived there.

6 Abram travelled through that land as far as the great tree of Moreh at Shechem. The Canaanites were living in the land at that time. 7 The LORD appeared to Abram and said, "I will give this land to your descendants." So Abram built an altar there to the LORD, who had appeared to him. 8 Then he travelled from Shechem to the mountain east of Bethel and set up his tent there. Bethel was to the west, and Ai was to the east. There Abram built another altar to the LORD and worshipped him. 9 After this, he travelled on towards southern Canaan.

Abram Goes to Egypt

10 At this time there was not much food in the land, so Abram went down to Egypt to live because there was so little food. 11 Just before they arrived in Egypt, he said to his wife Sarai,*n* "I know you are a very beautiful woman. 12 When the Egyptians see you, they will say, 'This woman is his wife.' Then they will kill me but let you live. 13 Tell them you are my sister so that things will go well with me and I may be allowed to live because of you."

14 When Abram came to Egypt, the Egyptians saw that Sarai was very beautiful. 15 The Egyptian officers saw her and told the king of Egypt how beautiful she was. They took her to the king's palace, and 16 the king was kind to Abram because he thought Abram was her brother. He gave Abram sheep, cattle, male and female donkeys, male and female servants and camels.

17 But the LORD sent terrible diseases on the king and all the people in his house because of Abram's wife Sarai. 18 So the king sent for Abram and said, "What have you done to me? Why didn't you tell me Sarai was your wife? 19 Why did you say, 'She is my sister' so that I made her my wife? Now, here is your wife. Take her and leave!" 20 Then the king commanded his men to make Abram leave Egypt; so Abram and his wife left with everything they owned.

Abram and Lot Separate

13 So Abram, his wife and Lot left Egypt, taking everything they owned, and travelled to southern Canaan. 2 Abram was very rich in cattle, silver and gold.

3 He left southern Canaan and went back to Bethel where he had camped before, between Bethel and Ai, 4 and where he had built an altar. So he worshipped the LORD there.

5 During this time Lot was travelling with Abram, and Lot also had flocks, herds and tents. 6 Abram and Lot had so many animals that the land could not support both of them together, 7 so Abram's herdsmen and Lot's herdsmen began to argue. The Canaanites and the Perizzites were living in the land at this time.

8 Abram said to Lot, "There should be no arguing between you and me, or between your herdsmen and mine, because we are brothers. 9 We should separate. The whole land is there in front of you. If you go to the left, I will go to the right. If you go to the right, I will go to the left."

10 Lot looked all around and saw the whole Jordan Valley and that there was much water there. It was like the LORD's garden, like the land of Egypt in the direction of Zoar. (This was before the LORD destroyed Sodom and Gomorrah.) 11 So Lot chose to move east and live in the Jordan Valley. In this way Abram and Lot separated. 12 Abram lived in the land of Canaan, but Lot lived among the cities in the Jordan Valley, very near to Sodom. 13 Now the people of Sodom were very evil and were always sinning against the LORD.

14 After Lot left, the LORD said to Abram, "Look all around you—to the north and south and east and west. 15 All this land that you see I will give to you and your descendants for ever. 16 I will make your descendants as many as the dust of the earth. If anyone could count the dust on the earth, he could count your people. 17 Get up! Walk through all

---

12:11 **Sarai** An Aramaic name meaning "princess".

this land because I am now giving it to you."

18 So Abram moved his tents and went to live near the great trees of Mamre at the city of Hebron. There he built an altar to the LORD.

Lot is Captured

14 Now Amraphel was king of Babylonia, Arioch was king of Ellasar, Kedorlaomer was king of Elam and Tidal was king of Goiim. 2 All these kings went to war against several other kings: Bera, king of Sodom, Birsha, king of Gomorrah, Shinab, king of Admah, Shemeber, king of Zeboiim and the king of Bela. (Bela is also called Zoar.)

3 These kings who were attacked united their armies in the Valley of Siddim (now the Dead Sea). 4 They had served Kedorlaomer for twelve years, but in the thirteenth year, they all turned against him. 5 Then in the fourteenth year, Kedorlaomer and the kings with him came and defeated the Rephaites in Ashteroth Karnaim, the Zuzites in Ham and the Emites in Shaveh Kiriathaim. 6 They also defeated the Horites in the mountains of Edom to El Paran (near the desert). 7 Then they turned back and went to En Mishpat (that is, Kadesh). They defeated all the Amalekites, as well as the Amorites who lived in Hazazon Tamar.

8 At that time the kings of Sodom, Gomorrah, Admah, Zeboiim and Bela went out to fight in the Valley of Siddim. (Bela is called Zoar.) 9 They fought against Kedorlaomer, king of Elam, Tidal, king of Goiim, Amraphel, king of Babylonia and Arioch, king of Ellasar—four kings fighting against five. 10 There were many tar pits in the Valley of Siddim. When the kings of Sodom and Gomorrah and their armies ran away, some of the soldiers fell into the tar pits, but the others ran away to the mountains.

11 Now Kedorlaomer and his armies took everything the people of Sodom and Gomorrah owned, including their food. 12 They took Lot, Abram's nephew, who was living in Sodom, and everything he owned. Then they left. 13 One of the men who was not captured went to Abram, the Hebrew, and told him what had happened. At that time Abram was camped near the great trees of Mamre the Amorite. Mamre was a brother of Eshcol and Aner, and they had all made an agreement to help Abram.

Abram Rescues Lot

14 When Abram learned that Lot had been captured, he called out his 318 trained men who had been born in his camp. He led the men and chased the enemy all the way to the town of Dan. 15 That night he divided his men into groups, and they made a surprise attack against the enemy. They chased them all the way to Hobah, north of Damascus. 16 Then Abram brought back everything the enemy had stolen, the women and the other people and Lot and everything Lot owned.

17 After defeating Kedorlaomer and the kings who were with him, Abram went home. As he was returning, the king of Sodom came out to meet him in the Valley of Shaveh (now called King's Valley).

18 Melchizedek, king of Salem, brought out bread and wine. He was a priest for God Most High 19 and blessed Abram, saying,

"Abram, may you be blessed by God
    Most High,
the God who made heaven and
    earth.
20 And we praise God Most High,
    who has helped you to defeat your
    enemies."

Then Abram gave Melchizedek a tenth of everything he had brought back from the battle.

21 The king of Sodom said to Abram, "You may keep all these things for yourself. Just give me my people who were captured."

Get up! Walk through all this land because I am now giving it to you.
– Genesis 13:17

> **Genesis 14:22   20**

22 But Abram said to the king of Sodom, "I make a promise to the LORD, the God Most High, who made heaven and earth. 23 I promise that I will not keep anything that is yours. I will not keep even a thread or a sandal strap so that you cannot say, 'I made Abram rich.' 24 I will keep nothing but the food my young men have eaten. But give Aner, Eshcol and Mamre their share of what we won, because they went with me into battle."

God's Agreement with Abram

15 After these things happened, the LORD spoke his word to Abram in a vision: "Abram, don't be afraid. I will defend you, and I will give you a great reward."

EMAIL FROM GOD
15:1
Protection
Who will protect you? Check it out here!

2 But Abram said, "Lord GOD, what can you give me? I have no son, so my slave Eliezer from Damascus will get everything I own after I die." 3 Abram said, "Look, you have given me no son, so a slave born in my house will inherit everything I have."

4 Then the LORD spoke his word to Abram: "He will not be the one to inherit what you have. You will have a son of your own who will inherit what you have."

5 Then God led Abram outside and said, "Look at the sky. There are so many stars you cannot count them. Your descendants also will be too many to count."

6 Abram believed the LORD. And the LORD accepted Abram's faith, and that faith made him acceptable to God.

7 God said to Abram, "I am the LORD who led you out of Ur of Babylonia so that I could give you this land to own."

8 But Abram said, "Lord GOD, how can I be sure that I will own this land?"

9 The LORD said to Abram, "Bring me a three-year-old cow, a three-year-old goat, a three-year-old ram, a dove and a young pigeon."

10 Abram brought them all to God. Then Abram killed the animals and cut each of them into two pieces, laying each half opposite the other half. But he did not cut the birds in half. 11 Later, large birds flew down to eat the animals, but Abram chased them away.

FAITH LINKS

A MAJOR PROBLEM
GENESIS 15:6

What is the most impossible problem you've ever faced? Abraham had a major one: his wife Sarah could not have children. Both Abraham and Sarah (called Abram and Sarai in Genesis 15 and 16) were old enough to be grandparents, not parents. But God told Abraham that he would have a son one day. Abraham believed God, even though his situation seemed impossible.

A major problem calls for major faith in God – faith that he can do the impossible. Got a major problem? Talk to God about it. He's always there to help, and all things are possible with God. (Read Luke 18:27, p. 1405.)

The Green Light, 2 Samuel 2:1, p. 401

A Given, 1 Chronicles 5:18–20, p. 526

God's Sure Protection, Psalm 18, p. 721

Rock Solid, Habakkuk 1:12, p. 1236

Perfectly Pleasing? Matthew 5:1–12, p. 1280

Prayer Anywhere, Mark 1:35, p. 1331

GET THE INFO

A NEW HOME FOR ABRAHAM
Genesis 16

1. God called Abram to leave his father's family in Haran and go to a land that God promised to his people. So at the age of 75, Abram left with his wife Sarai and his nephew Lot and moved to Canaan. (Read Genesis 12:4–5.)

2. Abram and his family went to live in Egypt because there wasn't enough food in Canaan. (Look at Genesis 12:10.)

3. Abram returned to Canaan and settled near Hebron. It was here that the Lord promised Abram that he would be the father of a great nation, changing his name to Abraham, which means "honoured father". God also promised Abraham a son, even though he and Sarai (whose name God changed to Sarah) were very old. (See Genesis 17.)

4. God tested Abraham at Mount Moriah in northern Canaan, when he asked Abraham to sacrifice his only son, Isaac. At the last moment, God provided a ram. Because of his obedience, God promised to bless Abraham with descendants – "as many as the stars in the sky and the sand on the seashore". (Look up Genesis 22:1–18.)

---

12 As the sun was going down, Abram fell into a deep sleep. While he was asleep, a very terrible darkness came. 13 Then the LORD said to Abram, "You can be sure that your descendants will be strangers and travel in a land they don't own. The people there will make them slaves and be cruel to them for 400 years. 14 But I will punish the nation where they are slaves. Then your descendants will leave that land, taking great wealth with them. 15 And you, Abram, will die in peace and will be buried at an old age. 16 After your great-great-grandchildren are born, your people will come to this land again. It will take that long, because I am not yet going to punish the Amorites for their evil behaviour."

17 After the sun went down, it was very dark. Suddenly a smoking firepot and a blazing torch passed between the halves of the dead animals." 18 So on that day the LORD made an agreement with Abram and said, "I will give to your descendants the land between the river of Egypt and the great river Euphrates. 19 This is the land of the Kenites, Kenizzites, Kadmonites, 20 Hittites, Perizzites, Rephaites, 21 Amorites, Canaanites, Girgashites and Jebusites."

Ishmael is Born

16 Sarai, Abram's wife, had no children, but she had a slave girl from Egypt named Hagar. 2 Sarai said to Abram, "Look, the LORD has not allowed me to have children, so have sexual relations with my slave girl. If she has a child, may be I can have my own family through her."

Abram did what Sarai said. 3 It was after he had lived ten years in Canaan that Sarai gave Hagar to her husband Abram. (Hagar was her slave girl from Egypt.)

4 Abram had sexual relations with Hagar, and she became pregnant. When

---

15:17 **passed ... animals** This showed that God sealed the agreement between himself and Abram.

Hagar learned she was pregnant, she began to treat her mistress Sarai badly. 5 Then Sarai said to Abram, "This is your fault. I gave my slave girl to you, and when she became pregnant, she began to treat me badly. Let the LORD decide who is right—you or me."

6 But Abram said to Sarai, "You are Hagar's mistress. Do anything you want to her." Then Sarai ill-treated Hagar, and Hagar ran away.

7 The angel of the LORD found Hagar beside a spring of water in the desert, by the road to Shur. 8 The angel said, "Hagar, Sarai's slave girl, where have you come from? Where are you going?"

Hagar answered, "I am running away from my mistress Sarai."

9 The angel of the LORD said to her, "Go home to your mistress and obey her." 10 The angel also said, "I will give you so many descendants they will be too many to count."

11 The angel added,
"You are now
    pregnant,
    and you will have a
    son.
You will name him
    Ishmael,*
    because the LORD
    has heard your
    cries.
12 Ishmael will be like a
    wild donkey.
He will be against
    everyone,
    and everyone will be against him.
He will attack all his brothers."

13 The slave girl gave a name to the LORD who spoke to her: "You are 'God who sees me,'" because she said to herself, "Have I really seen God who sees me?" 14 So the well there, between Kadesh and Bered, was called Beer Lahai Roi.*

15 Hagar gave birth to a son for Abram, and Abram named him Ishmael. 16 Abram was 86 years old when Hagar gave birth to Ishmael.

Proof of the Agreement

17 When Abram was 99 years old, the LORD appeared to him and said, "I am God Almighty. Obey me and do what is right. 2 I will make an agreement between us, and I will make you the ancestor of many people."

3 Then Abram bowed face down on the ground. God said to him, 4 "I am making my agreement with you: I will make you the father of many nations. 5 I am changing your name from Abram* to Abraham* because I am making you a father of many nations. 6 I will give you many descendants. New nations will be born from you, and kings will come from you. 7 And I will make an agreement between me and you and all your descendants from now on: I will be your God and the God of all your descendants. 8 You live in the land of Canaan now as a stranger, but I will give you and your descendants all this land for ever. And I will be the God of your descendants."

9 Then God said to Abraham, "You and your descendants must keep this agreement from now on. 10 This is my agreement with you and all your descendants, which you must obey: every male among you must be circumcised. 11 Cut away your foreskin to show that you are prepared to follow the agreement between me and you. 12 From now on when a baby boy is eight days old, you will circumcise him. This includes any boy born among your people or any who is your slave, who is not one of your descendants. 13 Circumcise every baby boy whether he is born in your family or bought as a slave. Your bodies will be marked to show that you are part of my agreement that lasts for ever. 14 Any male who is not circumcised will be cut off

> I am changing your name from Abram to Abraham because I am making you a father of many nations.
> – Genesis 17:5

16:11 Ishmael The Hebrew words for "Ishmael" and "has heard" sound similar.
16:14 Beer Lahai Roi This means "the well of the Living One who sees me".
17:5 Abram This name means "honoured father".
17:5 Abraham The end of the Hebrew word for "Abraham" sounds like the beginning of the Hebrew word for "many".

Isaac—the Promised Son

15 God said to Abraham, "I will change the name of Sarai,[n] your wife, to Sarah.[n] 16 I will bless her and give her a son, and you will be the father. She will be the mother of many nations. Kings of nations will come from her."

17 Abraham bowed face down on the ground and laughed. He said to himself, "Can a man have a child when he is 100 years old? Can Sarah give birth to a child when she is 90?" 18 Then Abraham said to God, "Please let Ishmael be the son you promised."

19 God said, "No, Sarah your wife will have a son, and you will name him Isaac.[n] I will make my agreement with him to be an agreement that continues for ever with all his descendants.

20 "As for Ishmael, I have heard you. I will bless him and give him many descendants. And I will cause their numbers to grow greatly. He will be the father of twelve great leaders, and I will make him into a great nation. 21 But I will make my agreement with Isaac, the son whom Sarah will have at this same time next year." 22 After God finished talking with Abraham, God rose and left him.

23 Then Abraham gathered Ishmael, all the males born in his camp, and the slaves he had bought. So that day Abraham circumcised every man and boy in his camp as God had told him to do. 24 Abraham was 99 years old when he was circumcised. 25 And Ishmael, his son, was thirteen years old when he was circumcised. 26 Abraham and his son were circumcised on the same day. 27 Also on that day all the men in Abraham's camp were circumcised, including all those born in his camp and all the slaves he had bought from other nations.

The Three Visitors

18 Later, the LORD again appeared to Abraham near the great trees of Mamre. Abraham was sitting at the entrance of his tent during the hottest part of the day. 2 He looked up and saw three men standing near him. When Abraham saw them, he ran from his tent to meet them. He bowed face down on the ground before them 3 and said, "Sir, if you think well of me, please stay awhile with me, your servant. 4 I will bring some water so all of you can wash your feet. You may rest under the tree, 5 and I will get some bread for you so you can regain your strength. Then you may continue your journey."

The three men said, "That is fine. Do as you said."

6 Abraham hurried to the tent where Sarah was and said to her, "Hurry, prepare 22 litres of fine flour, and make it into loaves of bread." 7 Then Abraham ran to his herd and took one of his best calves. He gave it to a servant, who hurried to kill it and to prepare it for food. 8 Abraham gave the three men the calf that had been cooked, milk curds and milk. While they ate, he stood under the tree near them.

9 The men asked Abraham, "Where is your wife, Sarah?"

"There, in the tent," said Abraham.

10 Then the LORD said, "I will certainly return to you about this time a year from now. At that time your wife Sarah will have a son."

Sarah was listening at the entrance of the tent which was behind him. 11 Abraham and Sarah were very old. Since Sarah was past the age when women normally have children, 12 she laughed to herself, "My husband and I are too old to have a baby."

13 Then the LORD said to Abraham, "Why did Sarah laugh? Why did she say, 'I am too old to have a baby'? 14 Is anything too hard for the LORD? No! I will return to you at the right time a year from now, and Sarah will have a son."

15 Sarah was afraid, so she lied and said, "I didn't laugh."

17:15 Sarai An Aramaic name meaning "princess".
17:15 Sarah A Hebrew name meaning "princess".
17:19 Isaac The Hebrew words for "he laughed" (vs. 17) and "Isaac" sound the same.

Genesis 18:16–24

FAITH links

ROLL OUT THE WELCOME WAGON
GENESIS 18:2-8

If three strangers showed up at your door, would you invite them in for a meal? In these days of "Stranger Danger", we're sometimes afraid to be hospitable, even to people we know. When three strangers came to visit, Abraham did everything possible to make his guests feel welcome. These weren't just ordinary visitors. One of them happened to be the Lord himself. The other two were angels.

You can make people feel welcome, just as Abraham did – anywhere, anytime. How? Give a smile, a kind word, or an offer to share your stuff. When you welcome others, you welcome God, too.

Connect to these Faithlinks to find out how else you can care for others like God does.

Care for the Lost, Deuteronomy 22:1–3, p. 255

Help for the Outsiders, Nehemiah 5:9–10, p. 630

Helpful Advice, Job 12:4–5, p. 673

Welcome! Matthew 19:13–15, p. 1307

Kindness Counts, Acts 14:3, p. 1489

Come On In! 1 Peter 4:9–10, p. 1705

But the LORD said, "No. You did laugh."

16 Then the men got up to leave and started out towards Sodom. Abraham walked along with them for a short time to send them on their way.

Abraham's Bargain with God

17 The LORD said, "Should I tell Abraham what I am going to do now? 18 Abraham's children will certainly become a great and powerful nation, and all nations on earth will be blessed through him. 19 I have chosen him so he would command his children and his descendants to live the way the LORD wants them to, to live right and be fair. Then I, the LORD, will give Abraham what I promised him."

20 Then the LORD said, "I have heard many complaints against the people of Sodom and Gomorrah. They are very evil. 21 I will go down and see if they are as bad as I have heard. If not, I will know."

22 So the men turned and went towards Sodom, but Abraham stood there before the LORD. 23 Then Abraham approached him and asked, "Do you plan to destroy the good people along with the evil ones? 24 What if there are 50 good people in that city? Will you still destroy it? Surely you will save the city for the 50 good people living there. 25 Surely you will not destroy the good people along with the evil ones; then they would be treated the same. You are the judge of all the earth. Won't you do what is right?"

26 The LORD said, "If I find 50 good people in the city of Sodom, I will save the whole city because of them."

27 Then Abraham said, "Though I am only dust and ashes, I have been brave to speak to the Lord. 28 What if there are only 45 good people in the city? Will you destroy the whole city for the lack of five good people?"

The LORD said, "If I find 45 there, I will not destroy the city."

29 Again Abraham said to him, "If you find only 40 good people there, will you destroy the city?"

The LORD said, "If I find 40, I will not destroy it."

30 Then Abraham said, "Lord, please don't be angry with me, but let me ask you this. If you find only 30 good people in the city, will you destroy it?"

He said, "If I find 30 good people there, I will not destroy the city."

31 Then Abraham said, "I have been brave to speak to the Lord. But what if there are 20 good people in the city?"

He answered, "If I find 20 there, I will not destroy the city."

32 Then Abraham said, "Lord, please don't be angry with me, but let me bother you this one last time. What if you find ten there?"

He said, "If I find ten there, I will not destroy it."

33 When the LORD finished speaking to Abraham, he left, and Abraham returned home.

Lot Leaves Sodom

19 The two angels came to Sodom in the evening as Lot was sitting near the city gate. When he saw them, he got up and went to them and bowed face down on the ground. 2 Lot said, "Sirs, please come to my house and spend the night. There you can wash your feet, and then tomorrow you may continue your journey."

The angels answered, "No, we will spend the night in the city's public square."

3 But Lot begged them to come, so they agreed and went to his house. Then Lot prepared a meal for them. He baked bread without yeast, and they ate it.

4 Before bedtime, men both young and old and from every part of Sodom surrounded Lot's house. 5 They called to Lot, "Where are the two men who came to you tonight? Bring them out to us so we can have sexual relations with them."

6 Lot went outside to them, closing the door behind him. 7 He said, "No, my brothers! Do not do this evil thing. 8 Look! I have two daughters who have never slept with a man. I will give them to you, and you may do anything you want with them. But please don't do anything to these men. They have come to my house, and I must protect them."

9 The men around the house answered, "Move out of the way!" Then they said to each other, "This man Lot came to our city as a stranger, and now he wants to tell us what to do!" They said to Lot, "We will do worse things to you than to them." They started pushing him back and were ready to break down the door.

10 But the two men staying with Lot opened the door, pulled him back inside the house, and then closed the door. 11 They struck those outside the door with blindness, so the men, both young and old, could not find the door.

12 The two men said to Lot, "Do you have any other relatives in this city? Do you have any sons-in-law, sons, daughters or any other relatives? If you do, tell them to leave now, 13 because we are about to destroy this city. The LORD has heard of all the evil that is here, so he has sent us to destroy it."

14 So Lot went out and said to his future sons-in-law who were pledged to marry his daughters, "Hurry and leave this city! The LORD is about to destroy it!" But they thought Lot was joking.

15 At dawn the next morning, the angels begged Lot to hurry. They said, "Go! Take your wife and your two daughters with you so you will not be destroyed when the city is punished."

16 But Lot delayed. So the two men took the hands of Lot, his wife and his two daughters and led them safely out of the city. So the LORD was merciful to Lot and his family. 17 After they brought them out of the city, one of the men said, "Run for your lives! Don't look back or stop anywhere in the valley. Run to the mountains, or you will be destroyed."

18 But Lot said to one of them, "Sir, please don't force me to go so far! 19 You have been merciful and kind to me and have saved my life. But I can't run to the mountains. The disaster will catch me, and I will die. 20 Look, that little town over there is not too far away. Let me run there. It's really just a little town, and I'll be safe there."

21 The angel said to Lot, "Very well, I will allow you to do this also. I will not destroy that town. 22 But run there fast,

Genesis 19:23–26

because I cannot destroy Sodom until you are safely in that town." (That town is named Zoar,[n] because it is little.)

Sodom and Gomorrah are Destroyed

23 The sun had already come up when Lot entered Zoar. 24 The LORD sent a rain of burning sulphur down from the sky on Sodom and Gomorrah 25 and destroyed those cities. He also destroyed the whole Jordan Valley, everyone living in the cities, and even all the plants.

26 At that point Lot's wife looked back. When she did, she became a pillar of salt.

27 Early the next morning, Abraham got up and went to the place where he had stood before the LORD. 28 He looked down towards Sodom and Gomorrah and all the Jordan Valley and saw smoke rising from the land, like smoke from a furnace.

29 God destroyed the cities in the valley, but he remembered what Abraham had asked. So God saved Lot's life, but he destroyed the city where Lot had lived.

Lot and His Daughters

30 Lot was afraid to continue living in Zoar, so he and his two daughters went to live in the mountains in a cave. 31 One day the older daughter said to the younger, "Our father is old. Everywhere on the earth women and men marry, but there are no men around here for us to marry. 32 Let's get our father drunk and have sexual relations with him. We can use him to have children and continue our family."

33 That night the two girls got their father drunk, and the older daughter went and had sexual relations with him. But Lot did not know when she lay down or when she got up.

34 The next day the older daughter said to the younger, "Last night I had sexual relations with my father. Let's get him drunk again tonight so you can go and have sexual relations with him, too. In this way we can use our father to have children to continue our family." 35 So that night they got their father drunk again, and the younger daughter went and had sexual relations with him. Again, Lot did not know when she lay down or when she got up.

36 So both of Lot's daughters became pregnant by their father. 37 The older daughter gave birth to a son and named him Moab. He is the ancestor of all the Moabite people who are still living today. 38 The younger daughter also gave birth to a son and named him Ben-Ammi. He is the father of all the Ammonite people who are still living today.

Abraham Tricks Abimelech

20 Abraham left Hebron and travelled to southern Canaan where he stayed awhile between Kadesh and Shur. When he moved to Gerar, 2 he told people that his wife Sarah was his sister. Abimelech, king of Gerar, heard this, so he sent some servants to take her. 3 But one night God spoke to Abimelech in a dream and said, "You will die. The woman you took is married."

4 But Abimelech had not gone near Sarah, so he said, "Lord, would you destroy an innocent nation? 5 Abraham himself told me, 'This woman is my sister,' and she also said, 'He is my brother.' I am innocent. I did not know I was doing anything wrong."

6 Then God said to Abimelech in the dream, "Yes, I know you did not realise what you were doing. So I did not allow you to sin against me and touch her. 7 Give Abraham his wife back. He is a prophet. He will pray for you, and you

> God destroyed the cities in the valley, but he remembered what Abraham had asked. So God saved Lot's life, but he destroyed the city where Lot had lived.
> – Genesis 19:29

19:22 **Zoar** This name sounds like the Hebrew word for "little".

will not die. But if you do not give Sarah back, you and all your family will surely die."

8 So early the next morning, Abimelech called all his officers and told them everything that had happened in the dream. They were very afraid. 9 Then Abimelech called Abraham to him and said, "What have you done to us? What wrong did I do against you? Why did you bring this trouble to my kingdom? You should not have done these things to me. 10 What were you thinking that caused you to do this?"

11 Then Abraham answered, "I thought no one in this place respected God and that someone would kill me to get Sarah. 12 And it is true that she is my sister. She is the daughter of my father, but she is not the daughter of my mother. 13 When God told me to leave my father's house and wander in many different places, I told Sarah, 'You must do a special favour for me. Everywhere we go, tell people I am your brother.'"

14 Then Abimelech gave Abraham some sheep, cattle and male and female slaves. He also gave Sarah, Abraham's wife, back to him 15 and said, "Look around you at my land. You may live anywhere you want."

16 Abimelech said to Sarah, "I gave your brother Abraham 1,000 pieces of silver to make up for any wrong that people may think about you. I want everyone to know that you are innocent."

17 Then Abraham prayed to God, and God healed Abimelech, his wife and his servant girls so they could have children. 18 The LORD had kept all the women in Abimelech's house from having children as a punishment to Abimelech for taking Abraham's wife, Sarah.

A Baby for Sarah

21 The LORD cared for Sarah as he had said, and did for her what he had promised. 2 Sarah became pregnant and gave birth to a son for Abraham in his old age. Everything happened at the time God had said it would. 3 Abraham named his son Isaac, the son Sarah gave birth to. 4 He circumcised Isaac when he was eight days old as God had commanded.

5 Abraham was 100 years old when his son Isaac was born. 6 And Sarah said, "God has made me laugh."* Everyone who hears about this will laugh with me. 7 No one thought that I would be able to have Abraham's child, but even though Abraham is old I have given him a son."

Hagar and Ishmael Leave

8 Isaac grew, and when he became old enough to eat food, Abraham gave a great feast. 9 But Sarah saw Ishmael making fun of Isaac. (Ishmael was the son of Abraham by Hagar, Sarah's Egyptian slave.) 10 So Sarah said to Abraham, "Throw out this slave woman and her son. Her son should not inherit anything; my son Isaac should receive it all."

11 This troubled Abraham very much because Ishmael was also his son. 12 But God said to Abraham, "Don't be troubled about the boy and the slave woman. Do whatever Sarah tells you. The descendants I promised you will be from Isaac. 13 I will also make the descendants of Ishmael into a great nation because he is your son, too."

14 Early the next morning Abraham took some food and a leather bag full of water. He gave them to Hagar and sent her away. Carrying these things and her son, Hagar went and wandered in the desert of Beersheba.

15 Later, when all the water was gone from the bag, Hagar put her son under a bush. 16 Then she went away a short distance and sat down. She thought, "My son will

> Then Abraham prayed to God, and God healed Abimelech, his wife and his servant girls so they could have children.
> – Genesis 20:17

21:6 laugh The Hebrew words for "he laughed" and "Isaac" sound the same.

Genesis 21:17 28

FAITH links

JUST KIDDING?
GENESIS 21:8-10

Has anyone ever said something hurtful to you, then added, "I'm just kidding"? "Just kidding" around can lead to trouble sometimes. Take Ishmael for instance. After hearing Ishmael making fun of Isaac, Sarah had Ishmael and his mother Hagar sent away. Although there were other circumstances involved in the decision, Ishmael's behaviour didn't make things better.

There is nothing wrong with a little teasing, if it is done in love. When teasing turns into a put-down, that means trouble. Telling a person "I'm just playing!" does little to heal the pain of a careless remark. Treat others the way you want to be treated.

Just a Little Respect, 1 Chronicles 11:10–19, p. 534

The Problem with Gossip, Proverbs 11:12–13, p. 840

What's Wrong About Rumours, Jeremiah 29:24–32, p. 1032

Say What?! Ephesians 4:22–29, p. 1603

Trouble with the Tongue, James 3:3–12, p. 1692

Who's on First? 3 John 9–10, p. 1723

die, and I cannot watch this happen." She sat there and began to cry.

17 God heard the boy crying, and God's angel called to Hagar from heaven. He said, "What is wrong, Hagar? Don't be afraid! God has heard the boy crying there. **18** Help him up and take him by the hand. I will make his descendants into a great nation."

19 Then God showed Hagar a well of water. So she went to the well and filled her bag with water and gave the boy a drink.

20 God was with the boy as he grew up. Ishmael lived in the desert and became an archer. **21** He lived in the Desert of Paran, and his mother found a wife for him in Egypt.

Abraham's Bargain with Abimelech

22 Then Abimelech came with Phicol, the commander of his army, and said to Abraham, "God is with you in everything you do. **23** So make a promise to me here before God that you will be fair with me and my children and my descendants. Be kind to me and to this land where you have lived as a stranger—as kind as I have been to you."

24 And Abraham said, "I promise." **25** Then Abraham complained to Abimelech about Abimelech's servants who had seized a well of water.

26 But Abimelech said, "I don't know who did this. You never told me about this before today."

27 Then Abraham gave Abimelech some sheep and cattle, and they made an agreement. **28** Abraham also put seven female lambs in front of Abimelech.

29 Abimelech asked Abraham, "Why did you put these seven female lambs by themselves?"

30 Abraham answered, "Accept these lambs from me to prove that you believe I dug this well."

31 So that place was called Beersheba[n] because they made a promise to each other there.

32 After Abraham and Abimelech made the agreement at Beersheba, Abimelech and Phicol, the commander of his

---

21:31 Beersheba This name means "well of the promise" or "well of seven".

army, went back to the land of the Philistines.

33 Abraham planted a tamarisk tree at Beersheba and prayed to the LORD, the God who lives for ever. 34 And Abraham lived as a stranger in the land of the Philistines for a long time.

God Tests Abraham

22 After these things God tested Abraham's faith. God said to him, "Abraham!"

And he answered, "Here I am."

2 Then God said, "Take your only son, Isaac, the son you love, and go to the land of Moriah. Kill him there and offer him as a whole burnt offering on one of the mountains I will tell you about."

3 Abraham got up early in the morning and saddled his donkey. He took Isaac and two servants with him. After he cut the wood for the sacrifice, they went to the place to which God had told them to go. 4 On the third day Abraham looked up and saw the place in the distance. 5 He said to his servants, "Stay here with the donkey. My son and I will go over there and worship, and then we will come back to you."

6 Abraham took the wood for the sacrifice and gave it to his son to carry, but he himself took the knife and the fire. So he and his son went on together.

7 Isaac said to his father Abraham, "Father!"

Abraham answered, "Yes, my son."

Isaac said, "We have the fire and the wood, but where is the lamb we will burn as a sacrifice?"

8 Abraham answered, "God will give us the lamb for the sacrifice, my son."

So Abraham and his son went on together 9 and came to the place God had told him about. Abraham built an altar there. He laid the wood on it and then tied up his son Isaac and laid him on the wood on the altar. 10 Then Abraham took his knife and was about to kill his son.

11 But the angel of the LORD called to him from heaven and said, "Abraham! Abraham!"

Abraham answered, "Yes."

12 The angel said, "Don't kill your son or hurt him in any way. Now I can see that you trust God and that you have not kept your son, your only son, from me."

13 Then Abraham looked up and saw a ram caught in a bush by its horns.

Genesis 22:13 29

FAITH links

THE SACRIFICE
GENESIS 22

If God told you to give up the thing you love most, would you do it? Abraham was obedient to God, no matter what the cost. He was willing to sacrifice his son, the one he had waited *decades* for. God was pleased by his obedience and provided a ram for Abraham to use as a sacrifice.

God may not call you to sacrifice your most-loved possession. But he does call you to obedience. He wants you to put him above anyone or anything else. What are you willing to sacrifice to be obedient to God?

Link here to find out more about how God wants us to obey him.

What You Value, Genesis 25:21–34, p. 34

Remembering What He Said, Deuteronomy 6:4–9, p. 236

I Insist! 1 Samuel 8; 9, p. 363

When God Says No, 2 Samuel 7, p. 407

A Reminder to Do What Is Right and True, Zechariah 7:8–10, p. 1257

Believe It or Not, Luke 1:20, 38, p. 1366

So Abraham went and took the ram and killed it. He offered it as a whole burnt offering to God, and his son was saved. 14 So Abraham named that place The LORD Provides. Even today people say, "On the mountain of the LORD it will be provided."

15 The angel of the LORD called to Abraham from heaven a second time 16 and said, "The LORD says, 'Because you did not keep back your son, your only son, from me, I make you this promise by my own name: 17 I will surely bless you and give you many descendants. They will be as many as the stars in the sky and the sand on the seashore, and they will capture the cities of their enemies. 18 Through your descendants all the nations on the earth will be blessed, because you obeyed me.'"

19 Then Abraham returned to his servants. They all travelled back to Beersheba and Abraham stayed there.

20 After these things happened, someone told Abraham: "Your brother Nahor and his wife Milcah have children now. 21 The first son is Uz, and the second is Buz. The third son is Kemuel (the father of Aram). 22 Then there are Kesed, Hazo, Pildash, Jidlaph and Bethuel." 23 Bethuel became the father of Rebekah. Milcah was the mother of these eight sons, and Nahor, Abraham's brother, was the father. 24 Also Nahor had four other sons by his slave woman, Reumah. Their names were Tebah, Gaham, Tahash and Maacah.

Sarah Dies

23 Sarah lived to be 127 years old. 2 She died in Kiriath Arba (that is, Hebron) in the land of Canaan. Abraham was very sad and cried because of her. 3 After a while he got up from the side of his wife's body and went to talk to the Hittites. He said, 4 "I am only a stranger and a foreigner here. Sell me some of your land so that I can bury my dead wife."

5 The Hittites answered Abraham, 6 "Sir, you are a great leader among us. You may have the best place we have to bury your dead. You may have any of our burying places that you want, and none of us will stop you from burying your dead wife."

7 Abraham rose and bowed to the people of the land, the Hittites. 8 He said to them, "If you truly want to help me bury my dead wife here, speak to Ephron, the son of Zohar, for me. 9 Ask him to sell me the cave of Machpelah at the edge of his field. I will pay him the full price. You can be the witnesses that I am buying it as a burial place."

10 Ephron was sitting among the Hittites at the city gate. He answered Abraham, 11 "No, sir. I will give you the land and the cave that is in it, with these people as witnesses. Bury your dead wife."

12 Then Abraham bowed down before the Hittites. 13 He said to Ephron before all the people, "Please let me pay you the full price for the field. Accept my money, and I will bury my dead there."

14 Ephron answered Abraham, 15 "Sir, the land is worth 400 pieces of silver, but I won't argue with you over the price. Take the land, and bury your dead wife."

16 Abraham agreed and paid Ephron in front of the Hittite witnesses. He weighed out the full price, 400 pieces of silver, and they counted the weight as the traders normally did.

17-18 So Ephron's field in Machpelah, east of Mamre, was sold. Abraham became the owner of the field, the cave in it, and all the trees that were in the field. The sale was made at the city gate, with the Hittites as witnesses. 19 After this, Abraham buried his wife Sarah in the cave in the field of Machpelah, near Mamre. (Mamre was later called Hebron in the land of Canaan.) 20 So Abraham bought

> The Hittites answered Abraham, "Sir, you are a great leader among us. You may have the best place we have to bury your dead."
> – Genesis 23:5–6

the field and the cave in it from the Hittites to use as a burying place.

A Wife for Isaac

24 Abraham was now very old, and the LORD had blessed him in every way. 2 Abraham said to his oldest servant, who was in charge of everything he owned, "Put your hand under my leg.*ⁿ* 3 Make a promise to me before the LORD, the God of heaven and earth. Don't get a wife for my son from the Canaanite girls who live around here. 4 Instead, go back to my country, to the land of my relatives, and get a wife for my son Isaac."

5 The servant said to him, "What if this woman does not want to return with me to this land? Then, should I take your son with me back to your homeland?"

6 Abraham said to him, "No! Don't take my son back there. 7 The LORD, the God of heaven, brought me from the home of my father and the land of my relatives. And he promised me, 'I will give this land to your descendants.' The LORD will send his angel before you to help you get a wife for my son there. 8 If the girl won't come back with you, you will be free from this promise. But you must not take my son back there." 9 So the servant put his hand under his master's leg and made a promise to Abraham about this.

10 The servant took ten of Abraham's camels and left, carrying with him many different kinds of beautiful gifts. He went to North West Mesopotamia, to Nahor's city. 11 In the evening, when the women come out to get water, he made the camels kneel down at the well outside the city.

12 The servant said, "LORD, God of my master Abraham, allow me to find a wife for his son today. Please show this kindness to my master Abraham. 13 Here I am, standing by the spring, and the girls from the city are coming out to get water. 14 I will say to one of them, 'Please put your jar down so I can drink.' Then let her say, 'Drink, and I will also give water to your camels.' If that happens, I will know she is the right one for your servant Isaac and that you have shown kindness to my master."

15 Before the servant had finished praying, Rebekah, the daughter of Bethuel, came out of the city. (Bethuel was the son of Milcah and Nahor, Abraham's brother.) Rebekah was carrying her water jar on her shoulder. 16 She was very pretty, a virgin; she had never had sexual relations with a man. She went down to the spring and filled her jar, then came back up. 17 The servant ran to her and said, "Please give me a little water from your jar."

24:2 **Put . . . leg** This showed that a person would keep a promise.

FAITH CHALLENGE

Here's one for you. Read 24:17-19 to see how one woman responded to a simple request from a servant. How do you usually respond when someone asks you for a favour?

TeSTiNG iT

Genesis 24:17–19
The servant ran to her and said, "Please give me a little water from your jar." Rebekah said, "Drink, sir." She quickly lowered the jar from her shoulder and gave him a drink. After he finished drinking, Rebekah said, "I will also pour some water for your camels."

Genesis 24:18 32

18 Rebekah said, "Drink, sir." She quickly lowered the jar from her shoulder and gave him a drink. **19** After he finished drinking, Rebekah said, "I will also pour some water for your camels." **20** So she quickly poured all the water from her jar into the drinking trough for the camels. Then she kept running to the well until she had given all the camels enough to drink.

21 The servant quietly watched her. He wanted to be sure the LORD had made his trip successful. **22** After the camels had finished drinking, he gave Rebekah a gold ring weighing 5 grammes and two gold arm bracelets weighing about 110 grammes each. **23** He asked, "Who is your father? Is there a place in his house for me and my men to spend the night?"

24 Rebekah answered, "My father is Bethuel, the son of Milcah and Nahor." **25** Then she said, "And, yes, we have straw for your camels and a place for you to spend the night."

26 The servant bowed and worshipped the LORD **27** and said, "Blessed is the LORD, the God of my master Abraham. The LORD has been kind and truthful to him and has led me to my master's relatives."

28 Then Rebekah ran and told her mother's family about all these things. **29** She had a brother named Laban, who ran out to Abraham's servant, who was still at the spring. **30** Laban had heard what she had said and had seen the ring and the bracelets on his sister's arms. So he ran out to the well, and there was the man standing by the camels at the spring. **31** Laban said, "Sir, you are welcome to come in; you don't have to stand outside. I have prepared the house for you and also a place for your camels."

32 So Abraham's servant went into the house. After Laban unloaded the camels and gave them straw and food, he gave water to Abraham's servant so he and the men with him could wash their feet. **33** Then Laban gave the servant food, but the servant said, "I will not eat until I have told you why I came."

So Laban said, "Then tell us."

34 He said, "I am Abraham's servant. **35** The LORD has greatly blessed my master in everything, and he has become a rich man. The LORD has given him many flocks of sheep, herds of cattle, silver and gold, male and female servants, camels and horses. **36** Sarah, my master's wife, gave birth to a son when she was old, and my master has given everything he owns to that son. **37** My master had me make a promise to him and said, 'Don't get a wife for my son from the Canaanite girls who live around here. **38** Instead, you must go to my father's people and to my family. There you must get a wife for my son.' **39** I said to my master, 'What if the woman will not come back with me?' **40** But he said, 'I serve the LORD, who will send his angel with you and will help you. You will get a wife for my son from my family and my father's people. **41** Then you will be free from the promise. But if they will not give you a wife for my son, you will be free from this promise.'

42 "Today I came to this spring. I said, 'LORD, God of my master Abraham, please make my trip successful. **43** I am standing by this spring. I will wait for a young woman to come out to get water, and I will say, "Please give me water from your jar to drink." **44** Then let her say, "Drink this water, and I will also get water for your camels." By this I will know the LORD has chosen her for my master's son.'

45 "Before I finished my silent prayer, Rebekah came out of the city with her water jar on her shoulder. She went down to the spring and got water. I said to her, 'Please give me a drink.' **46** She quickly lowered the jar from her shoulder and said, 'Drink this. I will also get water for your camels.' So I drank, and she gave water to my camels too. **47** When I asked her, 'Who is your father?' she answered, 'My father is Bethuel son of Milcah and Nahor.' Then I put the ring in her nose and the bracelets on her arms, **48** and I bowed my head and thanked the LORD. I praised the LORD, the God of my master Abraham, because he led me on the right road to get the granddaughter of my master's brother for his son. **49** Now, tell me, will you be kind and truthful to my master? And if not, tell me so. Then I will know what I should do."

50 Laban and Bethuel answered, "This is clearly from the LORD, and we cannot change what must happen. 51 Rebekah is yours. Take her and go. Let her marry your master's son as the LORD has commanded."

52 When Abraham's servant heard these words, he bowed face down on the ground before the LORD. 53 Then he gave Rebekah gold and silver jewellery and clothes. He also gave expensive gifts to her brother and mother. 54 The servant and the men with him ate and drank and spent the night there. When they got up the next morning, the servant said, "Now let me go back to my master."

55 Rebekah's mother and her brother said, "Let Rebekah stay with us at least ten days. After that she may go."

56 But the servant said to them, "Do not make me wait, because the LORD has made my trip successful. Now let me go back to my master."

57 Rebekah's brother and mother said, "We will call Rebekah and ask her what she wants to do." 58 They called her and asked her, "Do you want to go with this man now?"

She said, "Yes, I do."

59 So they allowed Rebekah and her nurse to go with Abraham's servant and his men. 60 They blessed Rebekah and said,

"Our sister, may you be the mother
of thousands of people,
and may your descendants capture
the cities of their enemies."

61 Then Rebekah and her servant girls got on the camels and followed the servant and his men. So the servant took Rebekah and left.

62 At this time Isaac had left Beer Lahai Roi and was living in southern Canaan. 63 One evening when he went out to the field to think, he looked up and saw camels coming. 64 Rebekah also looked and saw Isaac. Then she jumped down from the camel 65 and asked the servant, "Who is that man walking in the field to meet us?"

The servant answered, "That is my master." So Rebekah covered her face with her veil.

66 The servant told Isaac everything that had happened. 67 Then Isaac brought Rebekah into the tent of Sarah, his mother, and she became his wife. Isaac loved her very much, and so he was comforted after his mother's death.

Abraham's Family

25 Abraham married again, and his new wife was Keturah. 2 She gave birth to Zimran, Jokshan, Medan, Midian, Ishbak and Shuah. 3 Jokshan was the father of Sheba and Dedan. Dedan's descendants were the people of Assyria, Letush and Leum. 4 The sons of Midian were Ephah, Epher, Hanoch, Abida and Eldaah. All these were descendants of Keturah. 5 Abraham left everything he owned to Isaac. 6 But before Abraham died, he did give gifts to the sons of his other wives, then sent them to the east to be away from Isaac.

7 Abraham lived to be 175 years old. 8 He breathed his last breath and died at an old age, after a long and satisfying life. 9 His sons Isaac and Ishmael buried him in the cave of Machpelah in the field of Ephron east of Mamre. (Ephron was the son of Zohar the Hittite.) 10 So Abraham was buried with his wife Sarah in the same field that he had bought from the Hittites. 11 After Abraham died, God blessed his son Isaac. Isaac was now living at Beer Lahai Roi.

12 This is the family history of Ishmael, Abraham's son. (Hagar, Sarah's Egyptian servant, was Ishmael's mother.) 13 These are the names of Ishmael's sons in the order they were born: Nebaioth, the first son, then Kedar, Adbeel, Mibsam, 14 Mishma, Dumah, Massa, 15 Hadad, Tema, Jetur, Naphish and Kedemah. 16 These were Ishmael's sons, and these are the names of the tribal leaders listed according to their settlements and camps. 17 Ishmael lived for 137 years and then breathed his last breath and died. 18 His descendants lived from Havilah to Shur, which is east of Egypt stretching towards

▶ **Genesis 25:19–34**

Assyria. They often attacked the descendants of his brothers.

Isaac's Family

19 This is the family history of Isaac. 20 When Abraham's son, Isaac, was 40 years old, he married Rebekah, who came from North West Mesopotamia. She was Bethuel's daughter and the sister of Laban the Aramean. 21 Isaac's wife could not have children, so Isaac prayed to the LORD for her. The LORD heard Isaac's prayer, and Rebekah became pregnant.

22 While she was pregnant, the babies struggled inside her. She asked, "Why is this happening to me?" Then she went to get an answer from the LORD.

23 The LORD said to her,
"Two nations are in your body,
   and two groups of people will be taken from you.
One group will be stronger than the other,
   and the older will serve the younger."

24 When the time came, Rebekah gave birth to twins. 25 The first baby was born red. Since his skin was like a hairy robe, he was named Esau.[n] 26 When the second baby was born, he was holding on to Esau's heel, so that baby was named Jacob.[n] Isaac was 60 years old when they were born.

27 When the boys grew up, Esau became a skilled hunter. He loved to be out in the fields. But Jacob was a quiet man and stayed among the tents. 28 Isaac loved Esau because he hunted the wild animals that Isaac enjoyed eating. But Rebekah loved Jacob.

29 One day Jacob was boiling a pot of vegetable soup. Esau came in from hunting in the fields, weak from hunger. 30 So Esau said to Jacob, "Let me eat some of that red soup, because I am weak with hunger." (That is why people call him Edom.[n])

31 But Jacob said, "You must sell me your rights as the firstborn son."[n]

25:25 **Esau** This name may mean "hairy".
25:26 **Jacob** This name sounds like the Hebrew word for "heel". "Holding on to someone's heel" is a Hebrew saying for tricking someone.
25:30 **Edom** This name sounds like the Hebrew word for "red".
25:31 **rights . . . son** Usually the firstborn son had a high rank in the family. The firstborn son usually became the new head of the family.

WHAT YOU VALUE
GENESIS 25:21-34

What's the most valuable thing you have? How much is it worth to you? Esau traded away his rights as the firstborn son for a bowl of soup. Although Esau and his brother Jacob were twins, Esau was still the firstborn. That meant he had more privileges than Jacob did. Unfortunately, Esau didn't value what he had. He also didn't consider what would happen in the long run.

A good reputation is one of the most valuable treasures that anyone can have. If you're a Christian, your relationship with Jesus is also beyond price. In the long run, they're worth hanging on to.

Fatherly Advice, Exodus 18, p. 99

Sitting on the Fence, 1 Kings 18, p. 464

Mind Guard, Proverbs 4:23, p. 831

A Useless Thing, Isaiah 44:9, 18–20, p. 954

Put God First, Acts 5:27-32, p. 1472

That's False! 2 John 7–11, p. 1722

32 Esau said, "I am almost dead from hunger. If I die, all of my father's wealth will not help me." 33 But Jacob said, "First, promise me that you will give it to me." So Esau made a promise to Jacob and sold his part of their father's wealth to Jacob. 34 Then Jacob gave Esau bread and vegetable soup, and he ate and drank, and then left. So Esau showed how little he cared about his rights as the firstborn son.

Isaac Lies to Abimelech

26 Now there was a time of hunger in the land, besides the time of hunger that happened during Abraham's life. So Isaac went to the town of Gerar to see Abimelech king of the Philistines. 2 The LORD appeared to Isaac and said, "Don't go down to Egypt, but live in the land where I tell you to live. 3 Stay in this land, and I will be with you and bless you. I will give you and your descendants all these lands, and I will keep the oath I made to Abraham your father. 4 I will give you many descendants, as hard to count as the stars in the sky, and I will give them all these lands. Through your descendants all the nations on the earth will be blessed. 5 I will do this because your father Abraham obeyed me. He did what I said and obeyed my commands, my teachings and my rules."

6 So Isaac stayed in Gerar. 7 His wife Rebekah was very beautiful, and the men of that place asked Isaac about her. Isaac said, "She is my sister," because he was afraid to tell them she was his wife. He thought they might kill him so they could have her.

8 Isaac lived there a long time. One day as Abimelech king of the Philistines looked out of his window, he saw Isaac holding his wife Rebekah tenderly. 9 Abimelech called for Isaac and said, "This woman is your wife. Why did you say she was your sister?"

Isaac said to him, "I was afraid you would kill me so you could have her."

10 Abimelech said, "What have you done to us? One of our men might have had sexual relations with your wife. Then we would have been guilty of a great sin." 11 So Abimelech warned everyone, "Anyone who touches this man or his wife will be put to death."

Isaac Becomes Rich

12 Isaac planted seed in that land, and that year he gathered a great harvest. The LORD blessed him very much, 13 and he became rich. He gathered more wealth until he became a very rich man. 14 He had so many slaves and flocks and herds that the Philistines envied him. 15 So they stopped up all the wells the servants of Isaac's father Abraham had dug. (They had dug them when Abraham was alive.) The Philistines filled those wells with earth. 16 And Abimelech said to Isaac, "Leave our country because you have become much more powerful than we are."

17 So Isaac left that place and camped in the Valley of Gerar and lived there. 18 Long before this time Abraham had dug many wells, but after he died, the Philistines filled them with earth. So Isaac dug those wells again and gave them the same names his father had given them. 19 Isaac's servants dug a well in the valley, from which a spring of water flowed. 20 But the herdsmen of Gerar argued with them and said, "This water is ours." So Isaac named that well Argue because they argued with him. 21 Then his servants dug another well. When the people also argued about it, Isaac named that well Fight. 22 He moved from there and dug another well. No one argued about this one, so he named it Room Enough. Isaac said, "Now the LORD has made room for us, and we will be successful in this land."

23 From there Isaac went to Beersheba. 24 The LORD appeared to him that night and said, "I am the God of your father Abraham. Don't be afraid, because I am with you. I will bless you and give you many descendants because of my servant Abraham." 25 So Isaac built an altar and worshipped the LORD there. He also made a camp there, and his servants dug a well.

26 Abimelech came from Gerar to see Isaac. He brought with him Ahuzzath, who advised him, and Phicol, the

commander of his army. **27** Isaac asked them, "Why have you come to see me? You were my enemy and forced me to leave your country."

28 They answered, "Now we know that the LORD is with you. Let us swear an oath to each other. Let us make an agreement with you **29** that since we did not hurt you, you will not hurt us. We were good to you and sent you away in peace. Now the LORD has blessed you."

30 So Isaac prepared food for them, and they all ate and drank. **31** Early the next morning the men swore an oath to each other. Then Isaac sent them away, and they left in peace.

32 That day Isaac's servants came and told him about the well they had dug, saying, "We found water in that well." **33** So Isaac named it Shibah[n] and that city is called Beersheba even now.

34 When Esau was 40 years old, he married two Hittite women—Judith daughter of Beeri and Basemath daughter of Elon. **35** These women brought much sorrow to Isaac and Rebekah.

Jacob Tricks Isaac

27 When Isaac was old, his eyes were poor, so he could not see clearly. One day he called his older son Esau to him and said, "Son."

Esau answered, "Here I am."

2 Isaac said, "I am old and don't know when I might die. **3** So take your bow and arrows and go hunting in the field for an animal for me to eat. **4** When you prepare the tasty food that I love, bring it to me, and I will eat. Then I will bless you before I die." **5** So Esau went out in the field to hunt.

Rebekah was listening as Isaac said this to his son Esau. **6** She said to her son Jacob, "Listen, I heard your father saying to your brother Esau, **7** 'Kill an animal and prepare some tasty food for me to eat. Then I will bless you in the presence of the LORD before I die.' **8** So obey me, my son, and do what I tell you. **9** Go out to our goats and bring me two of the best young ones. I will prepare them just the way your father likes them. **10** Then you will take the food to your father, and he will bless you before he dies."

11 But Jacob said to his mother Rebekah, "My brother Esau is a hairy man, and I am smooth! **12** If my father touches me, he will know I am not Esau. Then he will not bless me but will place a curse on me because I tried to trick him."

13 So Rebekah said to him, "If your father puts a curse on you, I will accept the blame. Just do what I said and go, get the goats for me."

14 So Jacob went out and got two goats and brought them to his mother, and she cooked them in the special way Isaac enjoyed. **15** She took the best clothes of her older son Esau that were in the house and put them on the younger son Jacob. **16** She also took the skins of the goats and put them on Jacob's hands and neck. **17** Then she gave Jacob the tasty food and the bread she had made.

18 Jacob went in to his father and said, "Father."

And his father said, "Yes, my son. Who are you?"

19 Jacob said to him, "I am Esau, your first son. I have done what you told me. Now sit up and eat some meat of the animal I hunted for you. Then bless me."

20 But Isaac asked his son, "How did you find and kill the animal so quickly?"

Jacob answered, "Because the LORD your God helped me to find it."

21 Then Isaac said to Jacob, "Come

> The LORD appeared to him that night and said, "I am the God of your father Abraham. Don't be afraid, because I am with you. I will bless you and give you many descendants because of my servant Abraham."
> – Genesis 26:24

26:33 Shibah This name sounds like the Hebrew words for "seven" and "promise."

Genesis 27:34 37

FAITH links

FAMILY FEUD
GENESIS 27

Most of us have moments when someone in our family bugs us. You do, too, right? But have you ever deliberately set out to make someone in your family angry? Jacob did, when he tricked his father into giving him the blessing Esau would have received. A blessing was very important. A blessing was the official "giving" of the firstborn's privileges and rights. After the blessing, these rights could not be taken away. As a result of stealing his brother's blessing, Jacob had to run for his life.

What causes a family feud? Selfish thinking usually does. How can a feud be avoided? Instead of thinking *Me first*, consider *You first*. That means putting someone else's needs ahead of your own.

Need more help in learning to live with your family? Surf over to these links!

Peace in the Family, Psalm 133, p. 811

Some Friendly Advice, Proverbs 17:9, 14, 17, p. 851

The Gentle Way, Titus 3:1–5, p. 1661

Family Time, Hebrews 10:25, p. 1678

---

near so I can touch you, my son. Then I will know if you are really my son Esau."

22 So Jacob came near to Isaac his father. Isaac touched him and said, "Your voice sounds like Jacob's voice, but your hands are hairy like the hands of Esau." 23 Isaac did not know it was Jacob, because his hands were hairy like Esau's hands, so Isaac blessed him. 24 Isaac asked, "Are you really my son Esau?"

Jacob answered, "Yes, I am."

25 Then Isaac said, "Bring me the food, and I will eat it and bless you." So Jacob gave him the food, and he ate. Jacob gave him wine, and he drank. 26 Then Isaac said to him, "My son, come near and kiss me." 27 So Jacob went to his father and kissed him. When Isaac smelled Esau's clothes, he blessed him and said,

"The smell of my son
　is like the smell of the field
　that the LORD has blessed.
28 May God give you plenty of rain
　and good soil
　so that you will have plenty of grain
　and new wine.
29 May nations serve you
　and peoples bow down to you.
May you be master over your
　brothers,
　and may your mother's sons bow
　down to you.
May everyone who curses you be
　cursed,
　and may everyone who blesses you
　be blessed."

30 Isaac finished blessing Jacob. Then, just as Jacob left his father Isaac, Esau came in from hunting. 31 He also prepared some tasty food and brought it to his father. He said, "Father, rise and eat the food that your son killed for you and then bless me."

32 Isaac asked, "Who are you?"

He answered, "I am your son—your firstborn son—Esau."

33 Then Isaac trembled greatly and said, "Then who was it that hunted the animals and brought me food before you came? I ate it, and I blessed him, and it is too late now to take back my blessing."

34 When Esau heard the words of his

father, he let out a loud and bitter cry. He said to his father, "Bless me—me, too, my father!"

35 But Isaac said, "Your brother came and tricked me. He has taken your blessing."

36 Esau said, "Jacob*n* is the right name for him. He has tricked me these two times. He took away my share of everything you own, and now he has taken away my blessing." Then Esau asked, "Haven't you saved a blessing for me?"

37 Isaac answered, "I gave Jacob the power to be master over you, and all his brothers will be his servants. And I kept him strong with grain and new wine. There is nothing left to give you, my son."

38 But Esau continued, "Do you have only one blessing, Father? Bless me, too, Father!" Then Esau began to cry out loud.

39 Isaac said to him,
"You will live far away from the best land,
    far from the rain.
40 You will live by using your sword,
    and you will be a slave to your brother.
But when you struggle,
    you will break free from him."

41 After that Esau hated Jacob because of the blessing from Isaac. He thought to himself, "My father will soon die, and I will be sad for him. Then I will kill Jacob."

42 Rebekah heard about Esau's plan to kill Jacob. So she sent for Jacob and said to him, "Listen, your brother Esau is comforting himself by planning to kill you. 43 So, my son, do what I say. My brother Laban is living in Haran. Go to him at once! 44 Stay with him for a while, until your brother is not so angry. 45 In time, your brother will not be angry, and he will forget what you did to him. Then I will send a servant to bring you back. I don't want to lose both of my sons on the same day."

46 Then Rebekah said to Isaac, "I am tired of Hittite women. If Jacob marries one of these Hittite women here in this land, I want to die."

Jacob Searches for a Wife

28 Isaac called Jacob and blessed him and commanded him, "You must not marry a Canaanite woman. 2 Go to the house of Bethuel, your mother's father, in North West Mesopotamia. Laban, your mother's brother, lives there. Marry one of his daughters. 3 May God Almighty bless you and give you many children, and may you become a group of many peoples. 4 May he give you and your descendants the blessing of Abraham so that you may own the land where you are now living as a stranger, the land God gave to Abraham." 5 So Isaac sent Jacob to North West Mesopotamia, to Laban the brother of Rebekah. Bethuel the Aramean was the father of Laban and Rebekah, and Rebekah was the mother of Jacob and Esau.

6 Esau learned that Isaac had blessed Jacob and sent him to North West Mesopotamia to find a wife there. He also learned that Isaac had commanded Jacob not to marry a Canaanite woman 7 and that Jacob had obeyed his father and mother and had gone to North West Mesopotamia. 8 So Esau saw that his father Isaac did not want his sons to marry Canaanite women. 9 Now Esau already had wives, but he went to Ishmael son of Abraham and he married Mahalath, Ishmael's daughter. Mahalath was the sister of Nebaioth.

Jacob's Dream at Bethel

10 Jacob left Beersheba and set out for Haran. 11 When he came to a place, he spent the night there because the sun had set. He found a stone and laid his head on it to go to sleep. 12 Jacob dreamed that there was a ladder resting on the earth and reaching up into heaven, and he saw angels of God going up and coming down the ladder. 13 Then Jacob saw the LORD standing above the ladder, and he said, "I am the LORD, the God of Abraham your grandfather, and the God of Isaac. I will give you and your descendants the land

---

27:36 Jacob This name sounds like the Hebrew word for "heel". "Holding on to someone's heel" is a Hebrew saying for tricking someone.

Genesis 28:21 39

FROM DECEIVER TO WRESTLER — Genesis 28:1–19

1. Jacob was one of the twin boys born to Rebekah and Isaac in the town of Beersheba. As a young man, Jacob convinced his older twin, Esau, to trade his rights as the firstborn son (which meant a bigger portion of the family wealth) for some vegetable soup! Jacob later tricked his dad into giving him the family blessing instead of giving it to Esau. (See Genesis 25:24–34.)

2. Jacob left home after he tricked his brother and his dad. He travelled to a place where his ancestors came from called Haran to live with his Uncle Laban and find a wife. On his way, he spent the night and dreamed about a ladder with angels coming up and down from heaven. It was at Bethel where God promised Jacob that his descendants would fill the land. (Read Genesis 28:1–19.)

3. Jacob worked for his Uncle Laban for 14 years. He married two of Laban's daughters, first Leah, then her younger sister Rachel. Having two wives is a big enough problem. On top of that, Jacob loved Rachel much more than Leah. This caused even more problems in his family. (Check out Genesis 29:15–28.)

4. Jacob returned home to face his brother Esau. On his way home, Jacob had an amazing wrestling match with God. After this, God changed Jacob's name to Israel. (Look at Genesis 32:22–32.) Jacob's sons and their families formed the 12 tribes of Israel.

5. Jacob moved to Egypt with his sons and their families because there was no food in Canaan where he lived. Jacob died in Egypt, but was buried back in Canaan. (See Genesis 49:1–33; 50:13–14.)

---

on which you are now sleeping. **14** Your descendants will be as many as the dust of the earth. They will spread west and east, north and south, and all the families of the earth will be blessed through you and your descendants. **15** I am with you and will protect you everywhere you go and will bring you back to this land. I will not leave you until I have done what I have promised you."

16 Then Jacob woke from his sleep and said, "Surely the LORD is in this place, but I did not know it." **17** He was afraid and said, "This place frightens me! It is surely the house of God and the gate of heaven."

18 Jacob rose early in the morning and took the stone he had slept on and set it up on its end. Then he poured olive oil on the top of it. **19** At first, the name of that city was Luz, but Jacob named it Bethel."

20 Then Jacob made a promise. He said, "I want God to be with me and to protect me on this journey. I want him to give me food to eat and clothes to wear **21** so I will be able to return in peace to my father's house. If the LORD does

---

28:19 Bethel This name means "house of God".

these things, he will be my God. 22 This stone which I have set up on its end will be the house of God. And I will give God one-tenth of all he gives me."

Jacob Arrives in North West Mesopotamia

29 Then Jacob continued his journey and came to the land of the people of the East. 2 He looked and saw a well in the field and three flocks of sheep lying nearby, because they drank water from this well. A large stone covered the mouth of the well. 3 When all the flocks gathered there, the shepherds would roll the stone away from the well and water the sheep. Then they would put the stone back in its place.

4 Jacob said to the shepherds there, "My brothers, where are you from?"

They answered, "We are from Haran."

5 Then Jacob asked, "Do you know Laban, grandson of Nahor?"

They answered, "We know him."

6 Then Jacob asked, "How is he?"

They answered, "He is well. Look, his daughter Rachel is coming now with his sheep."

7 Jacob said, "But look, it is still the middle of the day. It is not time for the sheep to be gathered for the night, so give them water and let them go back into the pasture."

8 But they said, "We cannot do that until all the flocks are gathered. Then we will roll away the stone from the mouth of the well and water the sheep."

9 While Jacob was talking with the shepherds, Rachel came with her father's sheep, because it was her job to care for the sheep. 10 When Jacob saw Laban's daughter Rachel and Laban's sheep, he went to the well and rolled the stone from its mouth and watered Laban's sheep. Now Laban was the brother of Rebekah, Jacob's mother. 11 Then Jacob kissed Rachel and cried. 12 He told her that he was from her father's family and that he was the son of Rebekah. So Rachel ran home and told her father.

13 When Laban heard the news about his sister's son Jacob, he ran to meet him. Laban hugged him and kissed him and brought him to his house, where Jacob told Laban everything that had happened.

14 Then Laban said, "You are my own flesh and blood."

Jacob is Tricked

Jacob stayed there a month. 15 Then Laban said to Jacob, "You are my relative, but it is not right for you to work for me without pay. What would you like me to pay you?"

16 Now Laban had two daughters. The older was Leah, and the younger was Rachel. 17 Leah had weak eyes, but Rachel was very beautiful. 18 Jacob loved Rachel, so he said to Laban, "Let me marry your younger daughter Rachel. If you will, I will work seven years for you."

19 Laban said, "It would be better for her to marry you than someone else, so stay here with me." 20 So Jacob worked for Laban seven years so he could marry Rachel. But they seemed like just a few days to him because he loved Rachel very much.

21 After seven years Jacob said to Laban, "Give me Rachel so that I may marry her. The time I promised to work for you is over."

22 So Laban gave a feast for all the people there. 23 That evening he brought his daughter Leah to Jacob, and they had sexual relations. 24 (Laban gave his slave girl Zilpah to his daughter to be her servant.) 25 In the morning when Jacob saw that he had had sexual relations with Leah, he said to Laban, "What have you done to me? I worked hard for you so that I could marry Rachel! Why did you trick me?"

26 Laban said, "In our country we do not allow the younger daughter to marry before the older daughter. 27 But complete the full week of the marriage ceremony with Leah, and I will give you Rachel to marry also. But you must serve me another seven years."

28 So Jacob did this, and when he had completed the week with Leah, Laban gave him his daughter Rachel as a wife. 29 (Laban gave his slave girl Bilhah to his daughter Rachel to be her servant.) 30 So Jacob had sexual relations with Rachel

FAITH links

THE BEST POLICY
GENESIS 29:16-29

Know what Jacob's name means? It is a word that means to trick someone. Boy, did he ever. He conned his father into giving him the blessing meant for Esau. Yet the trickster found himself tricked by his uncle – Laban. Jacob had worked several years for Laban in order to marry Laban's daughter Rachel. But Laban tricked him by giving Rachel's sister Leah to Jacob instead.

Think deceiving others is cool? Think again. When you try to deceive others, you might find yourself deceived one day. That's why God instructs us to be honest. As the old saying goes, honesty is always the best policy. Honest!

Surf on to find out what else God has to say about honesty!

A Special Promise, Numbers 30:1–2, p. 217

An Honest Reputation, Nehemiah 13:13, p. 644

Who Do You Prefer? Proverbs 3:32, p. 830

Down on the Ant Farm, Proverbs 6:6–11, p. 833

The Whole Truth, John 8:31–32, 45, p. 1438

The Deadliest Lie, Acts 5:1–11, p. 1471

---

also, and Jacob loved Rachel more than Leah. Jacob worked for Laban for another seven years.

Jacob's Family Grows

31 When the LORD saw that Jacob loved Rachel more than Leah, he made it possible for Leah to have children, but not Rachel. 32 Leah became pregnant and gave birth to a son. She named him Reuben,[n] because she said, "The LORD has seen my troubles. Surely now my husband will love me."

33 Leah became pregnant again and gave birth to another son. She named him Simeon[n] and said, "The LORD has heard that I am not loved, so he has given me this son."

34 Leah became pregnant again and gave birth to another son. She named him Levi[n] and said, "Now, surely my husband will be close to me, because I have given him three sons."

35 Then Leah gave birth to another son. She named him Judah,[n] because she said, "Now I will praise the LORD." Then Leah stopped having children.

30 When Rachel saw that she was not having children for Jacob, she envied her sister Leah. She said to Jacob, "Give me children, or I'll die!" 2 Jacob became angry with her and said, "Can I do what only God can do? He is the one who has kept you from having children."

3 Then Rachel said, "Here is my slave girl Bilhah. Have sexual relations with her so she can give birth to a child for me. Then I can have my own family through her."

4 So Rachel gave Bilhah, her slave girl, to Jacob as a wife, and he had sexual relations with her. 5 She became pregnant and gave Jacob a son. 6 Rachel said, "God has judged me innocent. He has listened

---

29:32 Reuben This name sounds like the Hebrew word for "he has seen my troubles".
29:33 Simeon This name sounds like the Hebrew word for "has heard".
29:34 Levi This name sounds like the Hebrew word for "be close to".
29:35 Judah This name sounds like the Hebrew word for "praise".

to my prayer and has given me a son," so she named him Dan.*

7 Bilhah became pregnant again and gave Jacob a second son. 8 Rachel said, "I have struggled hard with my sister, and I have won." So she named that son Naphtali.*

9 Leah saw that she had stopped having children, so she gave her slave girl Zilpah to Jacob as a wife. 10 When Zilpah had a son, 11 Leah said, "I am lucky," so she named him Gad.* 12 Zilpah gave birth to another son, 13 and Leah said, "I am very happy! Now women will call me happy," so she named him Asher.*

14 During the wheat harvest Reuben went into the field and found some mandrake* plants and brought them to his mother Leah. But Rachel said to Leah, "Please give me some of your son's mandrakes."

15 Leah answered, "You have already taken away my husband, and now you are trying to take away my son's mandrakes."

But Rachel answered, "If you will give me your son's mandrakes, you may sleep with Jacob tonight."

16 When Jacob came in from the field that night, Leah went out to meet him. She said, "You will have sexual relations with me tonight because I have paid for you with my son's mandrakes." So Jacob slept with her that night.

17 Then God answered Leah's prayer, and she became pregnant again. She gave birth to a fifth son 18 and said, "God has given me what I paid for, because I gave my slave girl to my husband." So Leah named her son Issachar.*

19 Leah became pregnant again and gave birth to a sixth son. 20 She said, "God has given me a fine gift. Now surely Jacob will honour me, because I have given him six sons," so she named him Zebulun.*

21 Later Leah gave birth to a daughter and named her Dinah.

22 Then God remembered Rachel and answered her prayer, making it possible for her to have children. 23 When she became pregnant and gave birth to a son, she said, "God has taken away my shame," 24 and she named him Joseph." Rachel said, "I wish the LORD would give me another son."

Jacob Tricks Laban

25 After the birth of Joseph, Jacob said to Laban, "Now let me go to my own home and country. 26 Give me my wives and my children and let me go. I have earned them by working for you, and you know that I have served you well."

27 Laban said to him, "If I have pleased you, please stay. I know the LORD has blessed me because of you. 28 Tell me what I should pay you, and I will give it to you."

29 Jacob answered, "You know that I have worked hard for you, and your flocks have grown while I cared for them. 30 When I came, you had little, but now you have much. Every time I did something for you, the LORD blessed you. But when will I be able to do something for my own family?"

31 Laban asked, "Then what should I give you?"

Jacob answered, "I don't want you to give me anything. Just do this one thing, and I will come back and take care of your flocks. 32 Today let me go through all your flocks. I will take every speckled or spotted sheep, every black lamb and

> Then God remembered Rachel and answered her prayer, making it possible for her to have children.
> – Genesis 30:22

30:6 **Dan** This name means "he has judged".
30:8 **Naphtali** This name sounds like the Hebrew word for "my struggle".
30:11 **Gad** This name may mean "lucky".
30:13 **Asher** This name may mean "happy".
30:14 **mandrake** A plant which was believed to cause a woman to become pregnant.
30:18 **Issachar** This name sounds like the Hebrew word for "paid for".
30:20 **Zebulun** This name sounds like the Hebrew word for "honour".
30:24 **Joseph** This name sounds like the Hebrew word for "he adds".

every spotted or speckled goat. That will be my pay. 33 In the future you can easily see if I am honest. When you come to look at my flocks, if I have any goat that isn't speckled or spotted or any lamb that isn't black, you will know I stole it."

34 Laban answered, "Agreed! We will do what you ask." 35 But that day Laban took away all the male goats that had streaks or spots, all the speckled and spotted female goats (all those that had white on them), and all the black sheep. He told his sons to watch over them. 36 Then he took these animals to a place that was three days' journey away from Jacob. Jacob took care of all the flocks that were left.

37 So Jacob cut green branches from poplar, almond and plane trees, and peeled off some of the bark so that the branches had white stripes on them. 38 He put the branches in front of the flocks at the watering places. When the animals came to drink, they also mated there, 39 so the flocks mated in front of the branches. Then the young that were born were streaked, speckled or spotted. 40 Jacob separated the young animals from the others, and he made them face the streaked and dark animals in Laban's flock. Jacob kept his animals separate from Laban's. 41 When the stronger animals in the flock were mating, Jacob put the branches before their eyes so they would mate near the branches. 42 But when the weaker animals mated, Jacob did not put the branches there. So the animals born from the weaker animals were Laban's, and those born from the stronger animals were Jacob's. 43 In this way Jacob became very rich. He had large flocks, many male and female servants, camels and donkeys.

Jacob Runs Away

31 One day Jacob heard Laban's sons talking. They said, "Jacob has taken everything our father owned, and in this way he has become rich." 2 Then Jacob noticed that Laban was not as friendly as he had been before. 3 The LORD said to Jacob, "Go back to the land where your ancestors lived, and I will be with you."

4 So Jacob told Rachel and Leah to meet him in the field where he kept his flocks. 5 He said to them, "I have seen that your father is not as friendly with me as he used to be, but the God of my father has been with me. 6 You both know that I have worked as hard as I could for your father, 7 but he cheated me and changed my pay ten times. But God has not allowed your father to harm me. 8 When Laban said, 'You can have all the speckled animals as your pay,' all the animals gave birth to speckled young ones. But when he said, 'You can have all the streaked animals as your pay,' all the flocks gave birth to streaked babies. 9 So God has taken the animals away from your father and has given them to me.

10 "I had a dream during the season when the flocks were mating. I saw that the only male goats who were mating were streaked, speckled or spotted. 11 The angel of God spoke to me in that dream and said, 'Jacob!' I answered, 'Yes!' 12 The angel said, 'Look! Only the streaked, speckled or spotted male goats are mating. I have seen all the wrong things Laban has been doing to you. 13 I am the God who appeared to you at Bethel, where you poured olive oil on the stone you set up on end and where you made a promise to me. Now I want you to leave here and go back to the land where you were born.'"

14 Rachel and Leah answered Jacob, "Our father has nothing to give us when he dies. 15 He has treated us like strangers. He sold us to you, and then he spent all of the money you paid for us. 16 God took all this wealth from our father, and now it belongs to us and our children. So do whatever God has told you to do."

17 So Jacob put his children and his wives on camels, 18 and they began their journey back to Isaac, his father, in the land of Canaan. All the flocks of animals that Jacob owned walked ahead of them. He carried everything with him that he had gained while he lived in North West Mesopotamia.

19 While Laban was gone to cut the

wool from his sheep, Rachel stole the idols that belonged to him. 20 And Jacob tricked Laban the Aramean by not telling him he was leaving. 21 Jacob and his family left quickly, crossed the Euphrates River, and travelled towards the mountains of Gilead.

22 Three days later Laban learned that Jacob had run away, 23 so he gathered his relatives and began to chase him. After seven days Laban found him in the mountains of Gilead. 24 That night God came to Laban the Aramean in a dream and said, "Be careful! Do not say anything to Jacob, good or bad."

The Search for the Stolen Idols

25 So Laban caught up with Jacob. Now Jacob had made his camp in the mountains, so Laban and his relatives set up their camp in the mountains of Gilead. 26 Laban said to Jacob, "What have you done? You cheated me and took my daughters as if you had captured them in a war. 27 Why did you run away secretly and trick me? Why didn't you tell me? Then I could have sent you away with joy and singing and with the music of tambourines and harps. 28 You did not even let me kiss my grandchildren and my daughters goodbye. You were very foolish to do this! 29 I have the power to harm you, but last night the God of your father spoke to me and warned me not to say anything to you, good or bad. 30 I know you want to go back to your home, but why did you steal my idols?"

31 Jacob answered Laban, "I left without telling you because I was afraid you would take your daughters away from me. 32 If you find anyone here who has taken your idols, that person will be killed! Your relatives will be my witnesses. You may look for anything that belongs to you and take anything that is yours." (Now Jacob did not know that Rachel had stolen Laban's idols.)

33 So Laban looked in Jacob's tent, in Leah's tent, and in the tent where the two slave women stayed, but he did not find his idols. When he left Leah's tent, he went into Rachel's tent. 34 Rachel had hidden the idols inside her camel's saddle and was sitting on them. Although Laban looked through the whole tent, he did not find them.

35 Rachel said to her father, "Father, don't be angry with me. I am not able to stand up before you because I am having my monthly period." So Laban looked through the camp, but he did not find his idols.

36 Then Jacob became very angry and said, "What wrong have I done? What law have I broken to cause you to chase me? 37 You have looked through everything I own, but you have found nothing that belongs to you. If you have found anything, show it to everyone. Put it in front of your relatives and my relatives, and let them decide which one of us is right. 38 I have worked for you now for 20 years. During all that time none of the lambs and kids died during birth, and I have not eaten any of the rams from your flocks. 39 Any time an animal was killed by wild beasts, I did not bring it to you, but made up for the loss myself. You made me pay for any animal that was stolen during the day or night. 40 In the daytime the sun took away my strength, and at night I was cold and could not sleep. 41 I worked like a slave for you for 20 years—the first fourteen to get your two daughters and the last six to earn your flocks. During that time you changed my pay ten times. 42 But the God of my father, the God of Abraham and the God of Isaac, was with me. Otherwise, you would have sent me away with nothing. But he saw the trouble I had and the hard work I did, and last night he corrected you."

Jacob and Laban's Agreement

43 Laban said to Jacob, "These girls are my daughters. Their children belong to me, and these flocks are mine. Everything you see here belongs to me, but I can do nothing to keep my daughters and their children. 44 Let us make an agreement, and let us set up a pile of stones to remind us of it."

45 So Jacob took a large rock and set it up on its end. 46 He told his relatives to gather rocks, so they took the rocks and

piled them up; then they ate beside the pile. 47 Laban named that place in his language A Pile to Remind Us, and Jacob gave the place the same name in Hebrew. 48 Laban said to Jacob, "This pile of rocks will remind us of the agreement between us." That is why the place was called A Pile to Remind Us. 49 It was also called Mizpah,ⁿ because Laban said, "Let the LORD watch over us while we are separated from each other. 50 Remember that God is our witness even if no one else is around us. He will know if you harm my daughters or marry other women. 51 Here is the pile of rocks that I have put between us and here is the rock I set up on end. 52 This pile of rocks and this rock set on end will remind us of our agreement. I will never go past this pile to hurt you, and you must never come to my side of them to hurt me. 53 Let the God of Abraham, who is the God of Nahor and the God of their fathers, punish either of us if we break this agreement."

So Jacob made a promise in the name of the God whom his father Isaac worshipped. 54 Then Jacob killed an animal and offered it as a sacrifice on the mountain, and he invited his relatives to share in the meal. After they finished eating, they spent the night on the mountain. 55 Early the next morning Laban kissed his grandchildren and his daughters and blessed them, and then he left to return home.

Jacob Meets Esau

32 When Jacob also went his way, the angels of God met him. 2 When he saw them, he said, "This is the camp of God!" So he named that place Mahanaim.ⁿ

32:1 Angels Do angels work among people?

3 Jacob's brother Esau was living in the area called Seir in the country of Edom. Jacob sent messengers to Esau, 4 telling them, "Give this message to my master Esau: 'This is what Jacob, your servant, says: I have lived with Laban and have remained there until now. 5 I have cattle, donkeys, flocks and male and female servants. I send this message to you and ask you to accept us.'"

FAITH links

WHEN YOU'RE AFRAID
GENESIS 32:9-12

Think of a time when you were really afraid. Jacob knew that kind of knock-kneed fear as he thought about returning to his homeland. He had not seen his brother Esau for many years. He was afraid that Esau still had a grudge against him and would cause him harm. But Jacob didn't waste time worrying. Instead, he asked God for help.

When you're afraid, think about handling your fear the way that Jacob did. Give it to God. He'll gladly trade some of his courage for your fear.

Here's some more advice on dealing with things that go bump in the night.

Real Faith or Really Scared?
Judges 4, p. 315

A Message of Courage and Hope, 2 Kings 19:4–10, p. 505

In Deep Water, Psalm 69, p. 760

Future Hope, Joel 3:17–21, p. 1191

A Safe Place, Nahum 1:7, p. 1231

An Energy Boost, Acts 4:31, p. 1469

31:49 Mizpah This name sounds like the Hebrew word for "watch".
32:2 Mahanaim This name means "two camps".

6 The messengers returned to Jacob and said, "We went to your brother Esau. He is coming to meet you and has 400 men with him."

7 Then Jacob was very afraid and worried. He divided the people who were with him and all the flocks, herds and camels into two camps. 8 Jacob thought, "Esau might come and destroy one camp, but the other camp can run away and be saved."

9 Then Jacob said, "God of my father Abraham! God of my father Isaac! LORD, you told me to return to my country and my family. You said that you would treat me well. 10 I am not worthy of the kindness and continual goodness you have shown me. The first time I travelled across the Jordan River, I had only my walking stick, but now I own enough to have two camps. 11 Please save me from my brother Esau. I am afraid he will come and kill all of us, even the mothers with the children. 12 You said to me, 'I will treat you well and will make your children as many as the sand of the seashore. There will be too many to count.'"

13 Jacob stayed there for the night and prepared a gift for Esau from what he had with him: 14 200 female goats and 20 male goats, 200 female sheep and 20 rams, 15 30 female camels and their young, 40 cows and 10 bulls, 20 female donkeys and 10 male donkeys. 16 Jacob gave each separate flock of animals to one of his servants and said to them, "Go ahead of me and keep some space between each herd." 17 Jacob gave them their orders. To the servant with the first group of animals he said, "My brother Esau will come to you and ask, 'Whose servant are you? Where are you going and whose animals are these?' 18 Then you will answer, 'They belong to your servant Jacob. He sent them as a gift to you, my master Esau, and he also is coming behind us.'"

19 Jacob ordered the second servant, the third servant, and all the other servants to do the same thing. He said, "Say the same thing to Esau when you meet him. 20 Say, 'Your servant Jacob is coming behind us.'" Jacob thought, "If I send these gifts ahead of me, maybe Esau will forgive me. Then when I see him, perhaps he will accept me." 21 So Jacob sent the gifts to Esau, but he himself stayed that night in the camp.

Jacob Wrestles with God

22 During the night Jacob rose and crossed the Jabbok River at the crossing, taking with him his two wives, his two slave girls and his eleven sons. 23 He sent his family and everything he had across the river. 24 So Jacob was alone, and a man came and wrestled with him until the sun came up. 25 When the man saw he could not defeat Jacob, he struck Jacob's hip and put it out of joint. 26 Then he said to Jacob, "Let me go. The sun is coming up."

But Jacob said, "I will let you go if you will bless me."

27 The man said to him, "What is your name?"

And he answered, "Jacob."

28 Then the man said, "Your name will no longer be Jacob. Your name will now be Israel," because you have wrestled with God and with people, and you have won."

29 Then Jacob asked him, "Please tell me your name."

But the man said, "Why do you ask my name?" Then he blessed Jacob there.

30 So Jacob named that place Peniel," saying, "I have seen God face to face, but my life was saved." 31 Then the sun rose as he was leaving that place, and Jacob was limping because of his leg. 32 So even today the people of Israel do not eat the muscle that is on the hip joint of animals, because Jacob was touched there.

Jacob Shows His Bravery

33 Jacob looked up and saw Esau coming, and with him were 400 men. So Jacob divided his children among Leah, Rachel and the two slave girls.

32:28 Israel This name means "he wrestles with God."
32:30 Peniel This name means "the face of God."

FAITH links

FORGIVE INSTEAD
GENESIS 33

What's the worst thing anyone has ever done to you? Maybe someone told a lie about you or made fun of you in some way. Jacob tricked Esau out of an important blessing from their father Isaac. Esau was really mad at the time. Several years later, however, Esau's focus changed. Missing out on the blessing didn't seem as important to him anymore. Esau was glad to have his brother back. He gladly forgave Jacob.

Instead of holding a grudge, think about forgiving those who hurt you. Forgiveness doesn't mean that what the person did wasn't wrong. It just means you're willing to do what God did for us: forgive.

Here's some more help on how to handle those hard-to-forgive people in your life.

Mercy for an Enemy, Jonah 4, p. 1216

The Peril of Poisonous Plans, Micah 2:1–3, p. 1221

Quick to Forgive? Mark 11:25, p. 1349

Forgive and Forget, Ephesians 4:32, p. 1604

A Peacemaker or a Peacebreaker? James 3:18, p. 1693

The Way to Get Along, 1 Peter 3:8–9, p. 1703

---

2 Jacob put the slave girls with their children first, then Leah and her children behind them, and Rachel and Joseph last. 3 Jacob himself went out in front of them and bowed down flat on the ground seven times as he was walking towards his brother.

4 But Esau ran to meet Jacob and put his arms around him and hugged him. Then Esau kissed him, and they both cried. 5 When Esau looked up and saw the women and children, he asked, "Who are these people with you?"

Jacob answered, "These are the children God has given me. God has been good to me, your servant."

6 Then the two slave girls and their children came up to Esau and bowed down flat on the earth before him. 7 Leah and her children also came up to Esau and also bowed down flat on the earth. Last of all, Joseph and Rachel came up to Esau, and they, too, bowed down flat before him.

8 Esau said, "I saw many herds as I was coming here. Why did you bring them?"

Jacob answered, "They were to please you, my master."

9 But Esau said, "I already have enough, my brother. Keep what you have."

10 Jacob said, "No! Please! If I have pleased you, then accept the gift I give you. I am very happy to see your face again. It is like seeing the face of God, because you have accepted me. 11 So I beg you to accept the gift I give you. God has been very good to me, and I have more than I need." And because Jacob begged, Esau accepted the gift.

12 Then Esau said, "Let us be going. I will travel with you."

13 But Jacob said to him, "My master, you know that the children are weak. And I must be careful with my flocks and their young ones. If I force them to go too far in one day, all the animals will die. 14 So, my master, you go on ahead of me, your servant. I will follow you slowly and let the animals and the children set the speed at which we travel. I will meet you, my master, in Edom."

15 So Esau said, "Then let me leave some of my people with you."

"No, thank you," said Jacob. "I only want to please you, my master." **16** So that day Esau started back to Edom. **17** But Jacob went to Succoth, where he built a house for himself and shelters for his animals. That is why the place was named Succoth.*

18 Jacob left North West Mesopotamia and arrived safely at the city of Shechem in the land of Canaan. There he camped east of the city. **19** He bought a part of the field where he had camped from the sons of Hamor, father of Shechem, for 100 pieces of silver. **20** He built an altar there and named it after God, the God of Israel.

Dinah is Attacked

34 At this time Dinah, the daughter of Leah and Jacob, went out to visit the women of the land. **2** When Shechem, son of Hamor the Hivite, the ruler of the land, saw her, he took her and forced her to have sexual relations with him. **3** Shechem fell in love with Dinah, and he spoke kindly to her. **4** He told his father, Hamor, "Please get this girl for me so I can marry her."

5 Jacob learned how Shechem had disgraced his daughter, but since his sons were out in the field with the cattle, Jacob said nothing until they came home. **6** While he waited, Hamor, father of Shechem, went to talk with Jacob.

7 When Jacob's sons heard what had happened, they came in from the field. They were very angry that Shechem had done such a wicked thing to Israel. It was wrong for him to have sexual relations with Jacob's daughter; a thing like this should not be done.

8 But Hamor talked to Dinah's brothers and said, "My son Shechem is deeply in love with Dinah. Please let him marry her. **9** Marry our people. Give your women to our men as wives and take our women for your men as wives. **10** You can live in the same land with us. You will be free to own land and to trade here."

11 Shechem also talked to Jacob and to Dinah's brothers and said, "Please accept my offer. I will give anything you ask. **12** Ask as much as you want for the payment for the bride, and I will give it to you. Just let me marry Dinah."

13 Jacob's sons answered Shechem and his father with lies, because Shechem had disgraced their sister Dinah. **14** The brothers said to them, "We cannot allow you to marry our sister, because you are not circumcised. That would be a disgrace to us. **15** But we will allow you to marry her if you do this one thing: every man in your town must be circumcised like us. **16** Then your men can marry our women, and our men can marry your women, and we will live in your land and become one people. **17** If you refuse to be circumcised, we will take Dinah and leave."

18 What they asked seemed fair to Hamor and Shechem. **19** So Shechem quickly went to be circumcised because he loved Jacob's daughter.

Now Shechem was the most respected man in his family. **20** So Hamor and Shechem went to the gate of their city and spoke to the men of their city, saying, **21** "These people want to be friends with us. So let them live in our land and trade here. There is enough land for all of us. Let us marry their women, and we can let them marry our women. **22** But we must agree to one thing: all our men must be circumcised as they are. Then they will agree to live in our land, and we will be one people. **23** If we do this, their cattle and their animals will belong to us. Let us do what they say, and they will stay in our land." **24** All the people who had come to the city gate heard this. They agreed with Hamor and Shechem and every man was circumcised.

25 Three days later the men who were circumcised were still in pain. Two of Jacob's sons, Simeon and Levi (Dinah's brothers), took their swords and made a surprise attack on the city, killing all the men there. **26** They killed Hamor and his son Shechem and then took Dinah out of Shechem's house and left. **27** Jacob's sons came upon the dead bodies and stole

---

33:17 Succoth This name means "shelters."

FAITH links

MY WORSHIP PLACE
GENESIS 35:1-14

Where do you worship God? Jacob built two altars at Bethel to worship God. He wanted to show how thankful he was for God's presence and his help. Each altar was set up in a special place where God had shown himself to Jacob.

Think about where you meet with God or sense his presence. You can worship God in the shower, on the playground – anywhere. You don't need a rock to mark the place. All you need is a heart full of praise. That's where worship really begins.

Serious About the Sabbath, Exodus 31:15, p. 117

A Song of Thanks, 1 Samuel 2, p. 356

Gratitude Attitude, Ezra 3, p. 611

Your Heavenly Dad, Psalm 103:13, p. 786

The Gift of Worship, Matthew 2:10–12, p. 1275

Our Good Shepherd, John 10:11–15, p. 1441

---

everything that was in the city, to pay them back for what Shechem had done to their sister. 28 So the brothers took the flocks, herds and donkeys, and everything in the city and in the fields. 29 They took every valuable thing the people owned, even their wives and children and everything in the houses. 30 Then Jacob said to Simeon and Levi, "You have caused me a lot of trouble. Now the Canaanites and the Perizzites who live in the land will hate me. Since there are only a few of us, if they join together to attack us, my people and I will be destroyed."

31 But the brothers said, "We will not allow our sister to be treated like a prostitute."

Jacob in Bethel

35 God said to Jacob, "Go to the city of Bethel and live there. Make an altar to the God who appeared to you there when you were running away from your brother Esau."

2 So Jacob said to his family and to all who were with him, "Put away the foreign gods you have, and make yourselves clean, and change your clothes. 3 We will leave here and go to Bethel. There I will build an altar to God, who has helped me during my time of trouble. He has been with me everywhere I have gone." 4 So they gave Jacob all the foreign gods they had, and the earrings they were wearing, and he hid them under the great tree near the town of Shechem. 5 Then Jacob and his sons left there. But God caused the people in the nearby cities to be afraid, so they did not follow them. 6 And Jacob and all the people who were with him went to Luz, which is now called Bethel, in the land of Canaan. 7 There Jacob built an altar and named the place Bethel, after God, because God had appeared to him there when he was running from his brother.

8 Deborah, Rebekah's nurse, died and was buried under the oak tree at Bethel, so they named that place Oak of Crying.

Jacob's New Name

9 When Jacob came back from North West Mesopotamia, God appeared to him again and blessed him. 10 God said to him, "Your name is Jacob, but you will not be called Jacob any longer. Your new name will be Israel." So he called him Israel. 11 God said to him, "I am God Almighty. Have many children and grow in number as a nation. You will be the ancestor of

many nations and kings. 12 The same land I gave to Abraham and Isaac I will give to you and your descendants." 13 Then God left him. 14 Jacob set up a stone on edge in that place where God had talked to him, and he poured a drink offering and olive oil on it to make it special for God. 15 And Jacob named the place Bethel.

Rachel Dies Giving Birth

16 Jacob and his group left Bethel. Before they came to Ephrath, Rachel began giving birth to her baby, 17 but she was having much trouble. When Rachel's nurse saw this, she said, "Don't be afraid, Rachel. You are giving birth to another son." 18 Rachel gave birth to the son, but she herself died. As she lay dying, she named the boy Son of My Suffering, but Jacob called him Benjamin.[n]

19 Rachel was buried on the road to Ephrath, a district of Bethlehem, 20 and Jacob set up a rock on her grave to honour her. That rock is still there. 21 Then Israel[n] continued his journey and camped just south of Migdal Eder.

22 While Israel was there, Reuben had sexual relations with Israel's slave woman Bilhah and Israel heard about it.

The Family of Israel

Jacob had twelve sons. 23 He had six sons by his wife Leah: Reuben, his first son, then Simeon, Levi, Judah, Issachar and Zebulun.

24 He had two sons by his wife Rachel: Joseph and Benjamin.

25 He had two sons by Rachel's slave girl Bilhah: Dan and Naphtali.

26 And he had two sons by Leah's slave girl Zilpah: Gad and Asher.

These are Jacob's sons who were born in North West Mesopotamia.

27 Jacob went to his father Isaac at Mamre near Hebron, where Abraham and Isaac had lived. 28 Isaac lived for 180 years. 29 So Isaac breathed his last breath and died when he was very old, and his sons Esau and Jacob buried him.

Esau's Family

36 This is the family history of Esau (also called Edom).

2 Esau married women from the land of Canaan: Adah daughter of Elon the Hittite; and Oholibamah daughter of Anah, the son of Zibeon the Hivite; 3 and Basemath, Ishmael's daughter, the sister of Nebaioth.

4 Adah gave birth to Eliphaz for Esau. Basemath gave him Reuel, 5 and Oholibamah gave him Jeush, Jalam and Korah. These were Esau's sons who were born in the land of Canaan.

6 Esau took his wives, his sons, his daughters and all the people who lived with him, his herds and other animals and all the belongings he had gained in Canaan, and he went to a land away from his brother Jacob.

7 Esau's and Jacob's belongings were becoming too many for them to live in the same land. The land where they had lived could not support both of them, because they had too many herds. 8 So Esau lived in the mountains of Edom. (Esau is also named Edom.)

9 This is the family history of Esau. He is the ancestor of the Edomites, who live in the mountains of Edom.

10 Esau's sons were Eliphaz, son of

> Esau's and Jacob's belongings were becoming too many for them to live in the same land. The land where they had lived could not support both of them, because they had too many herds. So Esau lived in the mountains of Edom. (Esau is also named Edom.)
> – Genesis 36:7–8

35:18 Benjamin This name means "right-hand son" or "favourite son".
35:21 Israel Also called Jacob.

Adah and Esau, and Reuel, son of Basemath and Esau. 11 Eliphaz had five sons: Teman, Omar, Zepho, Gatam and Kenaz. 12 Eliphaz also had a slave woman named Timna, and Timna and Eliphaz gave birth to Amalek. These were Esau's grandsons by his wife Adah.

13 Reuel had four sons: Nahath, Zerah, Shammah and Mizzah. These were Esau's grandsons by his wife Basemath.

14 Esau's third wife was Oholibamah the daughter of Anah. (Anah was the son of Zibeon.) Esau and Oholibamah gave birth to Jeush, Jalam and Korah.

15 These were the leaders that came from Esau: Esau's first son was Eliphaz. From him came these leaders: Teman, Omar, Zepho, Kenaz, 16 Korah, Gatam and Amalek. These were the leaders that came from Eliphaz in the land of Edom. They were the grandsons of Adah.

17 Esau's son Reuel was the father of these leaders: Nahath, Zerah, Shammah and Mizzah. These were the leaders that came from Reuel in the land of Edom. They were the grandsons of Esau's wife Basemath.

18 Esau's wife Oholibamah gave birth to these leaders: Jeush, Jalam and Korah. These are the leaders that came from Esau's wife Oholibamah the daughter of Anah. 19 These were the sons of Esau (also called Edom), and these were their leaders.

20 These were the sons of Seir the Horite, who were living in the land: Lotan, Shobal, Zibeon, Anah, 21 Dishon, Ezer and Dishan. These sons of Seir were the leaders of the Horites in Edom.

22 The sons of Lotan were Hori and Homam. (Timna was Lotan's sister.)

23 The sons of Shobal were Alvan, Manahath, Ebal, Shepho and Onam.

24 The sons of Zibeon were Aiah and Anah. Anah is the man who found the hot springs in the desert while he was caring for his father's donkeys.

25 The children of Anah were Dishon and Oholibamah, daughter of Anah.

26 The sons of Dishon were Hemdan, Eshban, Ithran and Keran.

27 The sons of Ezer were Bilhan, Zaavan and Akan.

28 The sons of Dishan were Uz and Aran.

29 These were the names of the Horite leaders: Lotan, Shobal, Zibeon, Anah, 30 Dishon, Ezer and Dishan.

These men were the leaders of the Horite families who lived in the land of Edom.

31 These are the kings who ruled in the land of Edom before the Israelites ever had a king:

32 Bela son of Beor was the king of Edom. He came from the city of Dinhabah.

33 When Bela died, Jobab son of Zerah became king. Jobab was from Bozrah.

34 When Jobab died, Husham became king. He was from the land of the Temanites.

35 When Husham died, Hadad son of Bedad, who had defeated Midian in the country of Moab, became king. Hadad was from the city of Avith.

36 When Hadad died, Samlah became king. He was from Masrekah.

37 When Samlah died, Shaul became king. He was from Rehoboth on the Euphrates River.

38 When Shaul died, Baal-Hanan son of Acbor became king.

39 When Baal-Hanan son of Acbor died, Hadad became king. He was from the city of Pau. His wife's name was Mehetabel, daughter of Matred, who was the daughter of Me-Zahab.

40 These Edomite leaders, listed by their families and regions, came from Esau. Their names were Timna, Alvah, Jetheth, 41 Oholibamah, Elah, Pinon, 42 Kenaz, Teman, Mibzar, 43 Magdiel and Iram. They were the leaders of Edom. (Esau was the father of the Edomites.) The area where each of these families lived was named after that family.

Joseph the Dreamer

37 Jacob lived in the land of Canaan, where his father had lived. 2 This is the family history of Jacob:

Joseph was a young man, seventeen years old. He and his brothers, the sons of Bilhah and Zilpah, his father's wives, cared for the flocks. Joseph gave his father bad reports about his brothers. 3 Since Joseph was born when his father Israel[n] was old, Israel loved him more than his other sons. He made Joseph a special robe with long sleeves. 4 When Joseph's brothers saw that their father loved him more than he loved them, they hated their brother and could not speak to him politely.

5 One time Joseph had a dream, and when he told his brothers about it, they hated him even more. 6 Joseph said, "Listen to the dream I had. 7 We were in the field tying bundles of wheat together. My bundle stood up, and your bundles of wheat gathered around it and bowed down to it."

8 His brothers said, "Do you really think you will be king over us? Do you truly think you will rule over us?" His brothers hated him even more because of his dreams and what he had said.

9 Then Joseph had another dream, and he told his brothers about it also. He said, "Listen, I had another dream. I saw the sun, moon and eleven stars bowing down to me."

10 Joseph also told his father about this dream, but his father scolded him, saying, "What kind of dream is this? Do you really believe that your mother, your brothers and I will bow down to you?" 11 Joseph's brothers were jealous of him, but his father thought about what all these things could mean.

12 One day Joseph's brothers went to Shechem to herd their father's flocks. 13 Israel said to Joseph, "Go to Shechem where your brothers are herding the flocks."

Joseph answered, "I will go."

14 His father said, "Go and see if your brothers and the flocks are all right. Then come back and tell me." So Joseph's father sent him from the Valley of Hebron.

When Joseph came to Shechem, 15 a man found him wandering in the field and asked him, "What are you looking for?"

16 Joseph answered, "I am looking for my brothers. Can you tell me where they are grazing the flocks?"

17 The man said, "They have already gone. I heard them say they were going to Dothan." So Joseph went to look for his brothers and found them in Dothan.

Joseph Sold into Slavery

18 Joseph's brothers saw him coming from far away. Before he reached them, they made a plan to kill him. 19 They said to each other, "Here comes that dreamer. 20 Let's kill him and throw his body into one of the wells. We can tell our father that a wild animal killed him. Then we will see what will become of his dreams."

21 But Reuben heard their plan and saved Joseph, saying, "Let's not kill him. 22 Don't spill any blood. Throw him into this well here in the desert, but don't hurt him!" Reuben planned to save Joseph later and send him back to his father. 23 So when Joseph came to his brothers, they pulled off his robe with long sleeves 24 and threw him into the well. It was empty, and there was no water in it.

25 While Joseph was in the well, the brothers sat down to eat. When they looked up, they saw a group of Ishmaelites travelling from Gilead to Egypt. Their camels were carrying spices, balm and myrrh.

26 Then Judah said to his brothers, "What will we gain if we kill our brother and hide his death? 27 Let's sell him to these Ishmaelites. Then we will not be guilty of killing our own brother. After all, he is our brother, our own flesh and blood." And the other brothers agreed. 28 So when the Midianite traders came by, the brothers took Joseph out of the well and sold him to the Ishmaelites for 20 pieces of silver. And the Ishmaelites took him to Egypt.

29 When Reuben came back to the well and Joseph was not there, he tore his clothes to show he was sad. 30 Then he went back to his brothers and said, "The boy is not there! What shall I do?" 31 The brothers killed a goat and dipped Joseph's robe in its blood. 32 Then they brought the long-sleeved robe to their father and

---

37:3 **Israel** Also called Jacob.

FAITH links

THE TROUBLE WITH JEALOUSY
GENESIS 37

Did you ever argue with a brother or sister over who the favourite one is in your family? Joseph's brothers were jealous of him because he was the favourite. In fact, Joseph's brothers hated him. Joseph didn't help matters when he bragged about seeing his brothers bowing down to him in his dreams. The fancy coat that Jacob gave to Joseph added more fuel to the fire. The brothers became so jealous that they sold Joseph into slavery.

Jealousy and envy can lead to trouble if you allow them to control you. When you're tempted to be jealous or envious of what someone else has, run – don't walk – to God for help!

Need more advice on dealing with jealousy? Connect to these Faithlinks:

Forgive Instead, Genesis 33, p. 47

Facing the Consequences, Deuteronomy 3:21–29, p. 232

A Right to Get Even? 1 Samuel 24, p. 388

I'll Be the Judge! 1 Corinthians 4:4–5, p. 1549

Winning a Friend, 2 Timothy 2:23–24, p. 1654

The Sin "Braker", Jude 24–25, p. 1727

---

said, "We found this robe. Look it over carefully and see if it is your son's robe." 33 Jacob looked it over and said, "It is my son's robe! Some savage animal has eaten him. My son Joseph has been torn to pieces!" 34 Then Jacob tore his clothes and put on rough cloth to show that he was sad, and he continued to be sad about his son for a long time. 35 All of his sons and daughters tried to comfort him, but he could not be comforted. He said, "I will be sad about my son until the day I die." So Jacob cried for his son Joseph.

36 Meanwhile the Midianites who had bought Joseph had taken him to Egypt. There they sold him to Potiphar, an officer to the king of Egypt, and captain of the palace guard.

Judah and Tamar

38 About that time, Judah left his brothers and went to stay with a man named Hirah in the town of Adullam. 2 There Judah met a Canaanite girl, the daughter of a man named Shua and married her. Judah had sexual relations with her, 3 and she became pregnant and gave birth to a son, whom Judah named Er. 4 Later she gave birth to another son and named him Onan. 5 Still later she had another son and named him Shelah. She was at Kezib when this third son was born.

6 Judah chose a girl named Tamar to be the wife of his first son Er. 7 But Er, Judah's oldest son, did what the LORD said was evil, so the LORD killed him. 8 Then Judah said to Er's brother Onan, "Go and have sexual relations with your dead brother's wife." It is your duty to provide children for your brother in this way."

9 But Onan knew that the children would not belong to him, so when he was supposed to have sexual relations with Tamar he did not complete the sex act. This made it impossible for Tamar to become pregnant and for Er to have

---

38:8 Go . . . wife It was a custom in Israel that if a man died without children, one of his brothers would marry the widow. If a child was born, it would be considered the dead man's child.

descendants. 10 The LORD was displeased by this wicked thing Onan had done, so the LORD killed Onan also. 11 Then Judah said to his daughter-in-law Tamar, "Go back to live in your father's house, and don't marry until my young son Shelah grows up." Judah was afraid that Shelah also would die like his brothers. So Tamar returned to her father's home.

12 After a long time Judah's wife, the daughter of Shua, died. After Judah had got over his sorrow, he went to Timnah to his men who were cutting the wool from his sheep. His friend Hirah from Adullam went with him. 13 Tamar learned that Judah, her father-in-law, was going to Timnah to cut the wool from his sheep. 14 So she took off the clothes that showed she was a widow and covered her face with a veil to hide who she was. Then she sat down by the gate of Enaim on the road to Timnah. She did this because Judah's younger son Shelah had grown up, but Judah had not made plans for her to marry him.

15 When Judah saw her, he thought she was a prostitute, because she had covered her face with a veil. 16 So Judah went to her and said, "Let me have sexual relations with you." He did not know that she was Tamar, his daughter-in-law.

CONNECT 2-YOU

THE TRUTH HURTS

Stop and have a think about honesty. Is it always the best thing to be completely honest with each other?
Charli, aged 9, has something to say about this. Let's welcome Charli to Connect 2-You.

Charli

Well, yesterday I got in trouble for being honest with someone. A load of us were walking home from school together. One of the kids in the group was this boy who always smells bad. Everyone notices it. So I told him he needs to use deodorant. Some of the other kids started laughing, and he got really embarrassed, but he didn't say anything. Anyway, my mum found out about it and grounded me for two days. Can you believe it? Just for telling the truth?

It is easy to see why Charli is confused. She may have thought she was doing her friend a favour by telling him the truth. But Jesus wants us to be compassionate and kind to others. Take a look at the Livin' It page on gentleness, Colossians 3:1-14, p. 1624, to see how you can be honest and kind at the same time.

Here's another idea that might help. Try putting yourself in other people's shoes before you say something to them. Think about whether you would be offended or upset if someone said the same thing to you. If you think you would be, try coming up with a different way of saying it! I think you'll find some very different results.

She asked, "What will you give me if I let you have sexual relations with me?"

17 Judah answered, "I will send you a young goat from my flock."

She answered, "First give me something to keep as a deposit until you send the goat."

18 Judah asked, "What do you want me to give you as a deposit?"

Tamar answered, "Give me your seal and its cord,[n] and give me your walking stick." So Judah gave these things to her. Then Judah and Tamar had sexual relations, and Tamar became pregnant. 19 When Tamar went home, she took off the veil that covered her face and put on the clothes that showed she was a widow.

20 Judah sent his friend Hirah with the young goat to find the woman and get back his seal and the walking stick he had given her, but Hirah could not find her. 21 He asked some of the people at the town of Enaim, "Where is the prostitute who was here by the road?"

They answered, "There has never been a prostitute here."

22 So he went back to Judah and said, "I could not find the woman, and the people who lived there said, 'There has never been a prostitute here.'"

23 Judah said, "Let her keep the things. I don't want people to laugh at us. I sent her the goat as I promised, but you could not find her."

24 About three months later someone told Judah, "Tamar, your daughter-in-law, is guilty of acting like a prostitute, and now she is pregnant."

Then Judah said, "Bring her out and let her be burned to death."

25 When the people went to bring Tamar out, she sent a message to her father-in-law that said, "The man who owns these things has made me pregnant. Look at this seal and its cord and this walking stick, and tell me whose they are."

26 Judah recognised them and said, "She is more in the right than I. She did this because I did not give her to my son Shelah as I promised." And Judah did not have sexual relations with her again.

27 When the time came for Tamar to give birth, there were twins in her body. 28 While she was giving birth, one baby put his hand out. The nurse tied a red string on his hand and said, "This baby came out first." 29 But he pulled his hand back in, so the other baby was born first. The nurse said, "So you are able to break out first," and they named him Perez.[n] 30 After this, the baby with the red string on his hand was born, and they named him Zerah.

Joseph is Sold to Potiphar

39 Now Joseph had been taken down to Egypt. An Egyptian named Potiphar was an officer to the king of Egypt and the captain of the palace guard. He bought Joseph from the Ishmaelites who had brought him down there. 2 The LORD was with Joseph, and he became a successful man. He lived in the house of his master, Potiphar the Egyptian.

3 Potiphar saw that the LORD was with Joseph and that the LORD made Joseph successful in everything he did. 4 So Potiphar was very happy with Joseph and allowed him to be his personal servant. He put Joseph in charge of the house, trusting him with everything he owned.

5 When Joseph was put in charge of the house and everything Potiphar owned, the LORD blessed the people in Potiphar's house because of Joseph. And the LORD blessed everything that belonged to Potiphar, both in the house and in the field.

> The LORD was with Joseph, and he became a successful man. He lived in the house of his master, Potiphar the Egyptian.
> – Genesis 39:2

38:18 seal . . . cord A seal was used like a rubber stamp, and people ran a string through it to tie around the neck. They wrote a contract, folded it, put wax or clay on the contract and pressed the seal onto it as a signature.

38:29 Perez This name means "breaking out".

6 So Potiphar left Joseph in charge of everything he owned and was not concerned about anything except the food he ate.

Joseph is Put into Prison

Now Joseph was well built and handsome. 7 After some time the wife of Joseph's master began to desire Joseph, and one day she said to him, "Have sexual relations with me."

8 But Joseph refused and said to her, "My master trusts me with everything in his house. He has put me in charge of everything he owns. 9 There is no one in his house greater than I. He has not kept anything from me except you, because you are his wife. How can I do such an evil thing? It is a sin against God."

10 The woman talked to Joseph every day, but he refused to have sexual relations with her or even spend time with her.

11 One day Joseph went into the house to do his work as usual and was the only man in the house at that time. 12 His master's wife grabbed his coat and said to him, "Come and have sexual relations with me." But Joseph left his coat in her hand and ran out of the house.

13 When she saw that Joseph had left his coat in her hands and had run outside, 14 she called to the servants in her house and said, "Look! This Hebrew slave was brought here to shame us. He came in and tried to have sex with me, but I screamed. 15 My scream scared him and he ran away, but he left his coat with me." 16 She kept his coat until her husband came home, 17 and she told him the same story. She said, "This Hebrew slave you brought here came in to shame me! 18 When he came near me, I screamed. He ran away, but he left his coat."

19 When Joseph's master heard what his wife said Joseph had done, he became very angry. 20 So Potiphar arrested Joseph and put him into the prison where the king's prisoners were put. And Joseph stayed there in the prison.

21 But the LORD was with Joseph and showed him kindness and caused the prison warden to like Joseph. 22 The prison warden chose Joseph to take care of all the prisoners, and he was responsible for whatever was done in the prison. 23 The warden paid no attention to anything that was in Joseph's care because the LORD was with Joseph and made him successful in everything he did.

Joseph Interprets Two Dreams

40 After these things happened, two of the king's officers displeased the king—the man who served wine to the king, and the king's baker. 2 The king became angry with his officer who served him wine and his baker, 3 so he put them in the prison of the captain of the guard, the same prison where Joseph was kept. 4 The captain of the guard put the two prisoners in Joseph's care, and they stayed in prison for some time.

5 One night both the king's officer who served him wine and the baker had a dream. Each had his own dream with its own meaning. 6 When Joseph came to them the next morning, he saw they were worried. 7 He asked the king's officers who were with him, "Why do you look so unhappy today?"

8 The two men answered, "We both had dreams last night, but no one can explain their meaning to us."

Joseph said to them, "God is the only one who can explain the meaning of dreams. Tell me your dreams."

9 So the man who served wine to the king told Joseph his dream. He said, "I dreamed I saw a vine, and 10 on the vine were three branches. I watched the branches bud and blossom, and then the grapes ripened. 11 I was holding the king's cup, so I took the grapes and squeezed the juice into the cup. Then I gave it to the king."

12 Then Joseph said, "I will explain the dream to you. The three branches stand for three days. 13 Before the end of three days the king will free you, and he will allow you to return to your work. You will serve the king his wine just as you did before. 14 But when you are free, remember me. Be kind to me, and tell the king about me so I can get out of this

ALONE AND FORGOTTEN?
GENESIS 40:23

Ever feel as if everyone in the whole world has forgotten you? Maybe someone forgot your birthday or disappointed you in some way. Joseph could relate to those feelings. While in prison, he did a favour for the chief officer who served the king his wine, and he asked for one in return. But the officer forgot about Joseph for two whole years. God never forgot about him though.

During times of waiting or disappointment, you can trust that God will never forget you. He promises never to leave you or forget about you. (See Hebrews 13:5–6, p. 1684.)

Here are some more Faithlinks on trusting God:

Good Times and Bad, 1 Kings 17, p. 462

Depend on Him! 2 Chronicles 16:1–9, p. 579

Like a Tree, Jeremiah 17:5–8, p. 1016

Flex Your Faith, Acts 3:1–16, p. 1467

It's Under Control, Romans 8:28, p. 1529

Hard Times, 2 Corinthians 1:8–10, p. 1570

prison. 15 I was taken by force from the land of the Hebrews, and I have done nothing here to deserve being put in prison."

16 The baker saw that Joseph's explanation of the dream was good, so he said to him, "I also had a dream. I dreamed there were three bread baskets on my head. 17 In the top basket were all kinds of baked food for the king, but the birds were eating this food out of the basket on my head."

18 Joseph answered, "I will tell you what the dream means. The three baskets stand for three days. 19 Before the end of three days, the king will cut off your head! He will hang your body on a pole, and the birds will eat your flesh."

20 Three days later, on his birthday, the king gave a feast for all his officers. In front of his officers, he released from prison the chief officer who served his wine and the chief baker. 21 The king gave his chief officer who served wine his old position, and once again he put the king's cup of wine into the king's hand. 22 But the king hanged the baker on a pole. Everything happened just as Joseph had said it would, 23 but the officer who served wine did not remember Joseph. He forgot all about him.

The King's Dreams

41 Two years later the king dreamed he was standing on the bank of the Nile River. 2 He saw seven fat and beautiful cows come up out of the river, and they stood there, eating the grass. 3 Then seven more cows came up out of the river, but they were thin and ugly. They stood beside the seven beautiful cows on the bank of the Nile. 4 The seven thin and ugly cows ate the seven beautiful fat cows. Then the king woke up. 5 The king slept again and dreamed a second time. In his dream he saw seven full and good heads of grain growing on one stalk. 6 After that, seven more heads of grain sprang up, but they were thin and burned by the hot east wind. 7 The thin heads of grain ate the seven full and good heads. Then the king woke up again, and he realised it was only a dream. 8 The next morning the king was troubled about these dreams, so he sent for all the magicians and wise men of Egypt. The king told them his dreams,

but no one could explain their meaning to him.

9 Then the chief officer who served wine to the king said to him, "Now I remember something I promised to do, but I forgot about it. 10 There was a time when you were angry with the baker and me, and you put us in prison in the house of the captain of the guard. 11 In prison we each had a dream on the same night, and each dream had a different meaning. 12 A young Hebrew man, a servant of the captain of the guard, was in the prison with us. When we told him our dreams, he explained their meanings to us. He told each man the meaning of his dream, and 13 things happened exactly as he said they would: I was given back my old position, and the baker was hanged."

14 So the king called for Joseph. The guards quickly brought him out of the prison, and he shaved, put on clean clothes and went before the king.

15 The king said to Joseph, "I have had a dream, but no one can explain its meaning to me. I have heard that you can explain a dream when someone tells it to you."

16 Joseph answered the king, "I am not able to explain the meaning of dreams, but God will do this for the king."

41:16 Wisdom
Where can you find wisdom?

17 Then the king said to Joseph, "In my dream I was standing on the bank of the Nile River. 18 I saw seven fat and beautiful cows that came up out of the river and ate the grass. 19 Then I saw seven more cows come out of the river that were thin and lean and ugly—the worst looking cows I have seen in all the land of Egypt. 20 And these thin and ugly cows ate the first seven fat cows, 21 but after they had eaten the seven cows, no one could tell they had eaten them. They looked just as thin and ugly as they did in the beginning. Then I woke up.

22 "I had another dream. I saw seven full and good heads of grain growing on one stalk. 23 Then seven more heads of grain sprang up after them, but these heads were thin and ugly and were burned by the hot east wind. 24 Then the thin heads ate the seven good heads. I told this dream to the magicians, but no one could explain its meaning to me."

Joseph Tells the Dreams' Meaning

25 Then Joseph said to the king, "Both of these dreams mean the same thing. God is telling you what he is about to do. 26 The seven good cows stand for seven years, and the seven good heads of grain stand for seven years. Both dreams mean the same thing. 27 The seven thin and ugly cows stand for seven years, and the seven thin heads of grain burned by the hot east wind stand for seven years of hunger. 28 This will happen as I told you. God is showing the king what he is about to do. 29 You will have seven years of good crops and plenty to eat in all the land of Egypt. 30 But after those seven years, there will come seven years of hunger, and all the food that grew in the land of Egypt will be forgotten. The time of hunger will eat up the land. 31 People will forget what it was like to have plenty of food, because the hunger that follows will be so great. 32 You had two dreams which mean the same thing. This shows that God has firmly decided that this will happen, and he will make it happen soon.

33 "So let the king choose a man who is very wise and understanding and set him over the land of Egypt. 34 And let the king also appoint officers over the land, who should take one-fifth of all the food that is grown during the seven good years. 35 They should gather all the food that is produced during the good years that are coming, and under the king's authority they should store the grain in the cities and guard it. 36 That food should be saved to use during the seven years of hunger that will come on the land of Egypt. Then the people in Egypt will not die during the seven years of hunger."

Joseph is Made Ruler over Egypt

37 This seemed like a very good idea to the king, and all his officers agreed. 38 And the king asked them, "Can we find

FAITH links

A USE FOR YOUR ABILITIES
GENESIS 41

Joseph was a man of many talents. He had the ability to organise and lead others. This was proved during his time as a slave in Potiphar's house and while in prison. He was also wise. But his ability to explain the meaning of dreams was the one that got him noticed by the king of Egypt. Joseph used all of his abilities to bring honour to God.

Everyone has an ability to do something. Some of us have more than one. With these abilities comes a choice: to use them only to win fame and honour for ourselves or to bring honour to God. Which will you choose?

A Serious Promise, Deuteronomy 23:21–23, p. 257

Too Young to Serve, Jeremiah 1:4–9, p. 988

Empty Words, Ezekiel 33:30–33, p. 1127

Just Say Yes! Matthew 9:9–13, p. 1289

One of the Faithful, Acts 10:1–34, p. 1482

Your Faith Example, 1 Timothy 4:12, p. 1646

---

a better man than Joseph to take this job? God's Spirit is truly in him!"

39 So the king said to Joseph, "God has shown you all this. There is no one as wise and understanding as you are, so 40 I will put you in charge of my palace. All the people will obey your orders, and only I will be greater than you."

41 Then the king said to Joseph, "Look! I have put you in charge of all the land of Egypt." 42 Then the king took off from his own finger his ring with the royal seal on it, and he put it on Joseph's finger. He gave Joseph fine linen clothes to wear, and he put a gold chain around Joseph's neck. 43 The king had Joseph ride in the second royal chariot, and people walked ahead of his chariot calling, "Bow down!" By doing these things, the king put Joseph in charge of all of Egypt.

44 The king said to him, "I am the king, and I say that no one in all the land of Egypt may lift a hand or a foot without your permission." 45 The king gave Joseph the name Zaphenath-Paneah. He also gave Joseph a wife named Asenath, who was the daughter of Potiphera, priest of On. So Joseph travelled through all the land of Egypt.

46 Joseph was 30 years old when he began serving the king of Egypt. And he left the king's court and travelled through all the land of Egypt. 47 During the seven good years, the crops in the land grew well. 48 And Joseph gathered all the food which was produced in Egypt during those seven years of good crops and stored the food in the cities. In every city he stored grain that had been grown in the fields around that city. 49 Joseph stored much grain, as much as the sand of the seashore—so much that he could not measure it.

50 Joseph's wife was Asenath, daughter of Potiphera, the priest of On. Before the years of hunger came, Joseph and Asenath had two sons. 51 Joseph named the first son Manasseh[n] and said, "God has made me forget all the troubles I have had and all my father's family." 52 Joseph named the second son Ephraim[n] and said,

---

41:51 Manasseh This name sounds like the Hebrew word for "made me forget".
41:52 Ephraim This name sounds like the Hebrew word for "given me children".

"God has given me children in the land of my troubles."

53 The seven years of good crops came to an end in the land of Egypt. 54 Then the seven years of hunger began, just as Joseph had said. In all the lands people had nothing to eat, but in Egypt there was food. 55 The time of hunger became terrible in all of Egypt, and the people cried to the king for food. He said to all the Egyptians, "Go to Joseph and do whatever he tells you."

56 The hunger was everywhere in that part of the world. And Joseph opened the storehouses and sold grain to the people of Egypt, because the time of hunger became terrible in Egypt. 57 And all the people in that part of the world came to Joseph in Egypt to buy grain because the hunger was terrible everywhere in that part of the world.

The Dreams Come True

42 Jacob learned that there was grain in Egypt, so he said to his sons, "Why are you just sitting here looking at one another? 2 I have heard that there is grain in Egypt. Go down there and buy grain for us to eat, so that we will live and not die."

3 So ten of Joseph's brothers went down to buy grain from Egypt. 4 But Jacob did not send Benjamin, Joseph's brother, with them, because he was afraid that something terrible might happen to him. 5 Along with many other people, the sons of Israel[n] went to Egypt to buy grain, because the people in the land of Canaan were also hungry.

6 Now Joseph was governor over Egypt. He was the one who sold the grain to people who came to buy it. So Joseph's brothers came to him and bowed face down on the ground before him. 7 When Joseph saw his brothers, he knew who they were, but he acted as if he didn't know them. He asked unkindly, "Where do you come from?"

They answered, "We have come from the land of Canaan to buy food."

8 Joseph knew they were his brothers, but they did not know who he was. 9 And Joseph remembered his dreams about his brothers bowing to him. He said to them, "You are spies! You came to learn where the nation is weak!"

10 But his brothers said to him, "No, my master. We come as your servants just to buy food. 11 We are all sons of the same father. We are honest men, not spies."

12 Then Joseph said to them, "No! You have come to learn where this nation is weak!"

13 And they said, "We are ten of twelve brothers, sons of the same father, and we live in the land of Canaan. Our youngest brother is there with our father right now, and our other brother is gone."

14 But Joseph said to them, "I can see I was right! You are spies! 15 But I will give you a way to prove you are telling the truth. As surely as the king lives, you will not leave this place until your youngest brother comes here. 16 One of you must go and get your brother. The rest of you will stay here in prison. We will see if you are telling the truth. If not, as surely as the king lives, you are spies." 17 Then Joseph put them all in prison for three days.

18 On the third day Joseph said to them, "I am a God-fearing man. Do this and I will let you live: 19 if you are honest men, let one of your brothers stay here in prison while the rest of you go and carry grain back to feed your hungry families. 20 Then bring your youngest brother

> They said to each other, "We are being punished for what we did to our brother. We saw his trouble, and he begged us to save him, but we refused to listen. That is why we are in this trouble now."
> – Genesis 42:21

42:5 **Israel** Also called Jacob.

back here to me. If you do this, I will know you are telling the truth, and you will not die."

The brothers agreed to this. 21 They said to each other, "We are being punished for what we did to our brother. We saw his trouble, and he begged us to save him, but we refused to listen. That is why we are in this trouble now."

22 Then Reuben said to them, "I told you not to harm the boy, but you refused to listen to me. So now we are being punished for what we did to him."

23 When Joseph talked to his brothers, he used an interpreter, so they did not know that Joseph understood what they were saying. 24 Then Joseph left them and cried. After a short time he went back and spoke to them. He took Simeon and tied him up while the other brothers watched. 25 Joseph told his servants to fill his brothers' bags with grain and to put the money the brothers had paid for the grain back in their bags. The servants were also to give them what they would need for their trip back home. And the servants did this.

26 So the brothers put the grain on their donkeys and left. 27 When they stopped for the night, one of the brothers opened his sack to get food for his donkey. Then he saw his money in the top of the sack. 28 He said to the other brothers, "The money I paid for the grain has been put back. Here it is in my sack!"

The brothers were very frightened. They said to each other, "What has God done to us?"

The Brothers Return to Jacob

29 The brothers went to their father Jacob in the land of Canaan and told him everything that had happened. 30 They said, "The master of that land spoke unkindly to us. He accused us of spying on his country, 31 but we told him that we were honest men, not spies. 32 We told him that we were ten of twelve brothers—sons of one father. We said that one of our brothers was gone and that our youngest brother was with our father in Canaan.

33 "Then the master of the land said to us, 'Here is a way I can know you are honest men: leave one of your brothers with me, and take grain to feed your hungry families, and go. 34 And bring your youngest brother to me so I will know you are not spies but honest men. Then I will give you back your brother whom you leave with me, and you can move about freely in our land.'"

35 As the brothers emptied their sacks, each of them found his money in his sack. When they and their father saw it, they were afraid.

36 Their father Jacob said to them, "You are robbing me of all my children. Joseph is gone, Simeon is gone, and now you want to take Benjamin away, too. Everything is against me."

37 Then Reuben said to his father, "You may put my two sons to death if I don't bring Benjamin back to you. Trust him to my care, and I will bring him back to you."

38 But Jacob said, "I will not allow Benjamin to go with you. His brother is dead, and he is the only son left from my wife Rachel. I am afraid something terrible might happen to him during the trip to Egypt. Then I would be sad until the day I die."

The Brothers Go Back to Egypt

43 Still no food grew in the land of Canaan. 2 When Jacob's family had eaten all the grain they had brought from Egypt, Jacob said to them, "Go to Egypt again and buy a little more grain for us to eat."

3 But Judah said to Jacob, "The governor of that country strongly warned us, 'If you don't bring your brother back with you, you will not be allowed to see me.' 4 If you will send Benjamin with us, we will go down and buy food for you. 5 But if you refuse to send Benjamin, we will not go. The governor of that country warned us that we would not see him if we didn't bring Benjamin with us."

6 Israel[n] said, "Why did you tell the man you had another brother? You have caused me a lot of trouble."

43:6 **Israel** Also called Jacob.

7 The brothers answered, "He questioned us carefully about ourselves and our family. He asked us, 'Is your father still alive? Do you have another brother?' We just answered his questions. How could we know he would ask us to bring our other brother to him?"

8 Then Judah said to his father Jacob, "Send Benjamin with me, and we will go at once so that we, you, and our children may live and not die. **9** I will guarantee you that he will be safe, and I will be personally responsible for him. If I don't bring him back to you, you can blame me all my life. **10** If we had not wasted all this time, we could have already made two trips."

11 Then their father Jacob said to them, "If it has to be that way, then do this: take some of the best foods in our land in your packs. Give them to the man as a gift: some balm, some honey, spices, myrrh, pistachio nuts and almonds. **12** Take twice as much money with you this time, and take back the money that was returned to you in your sacks last time. Maybe it was a mistake. **13** And take Benjamin with you. Now leave and go to the man. **14** I pray that God Almighty will cause the governor to be merciful to you and that he will allow Simeon and Benjamin to come back with you. If I am robbed of my children, then I am robbed of them!"

15 So the brothers took the gifts. They also took twice as much money as they had taken the first time, and they took Benjamin. They hurried down to Egypt and stood before Joseph.

16 When Joseph saw Benjamin with them, he said to the servant in charge of his house, "Bring those men into my house. Kill an animal and prepare a meal. Those men will eat with me today at noon."

17 The servant did as Joseph told him and brought the men to Joseph's house.

18 The brothers were afraid when they were brought to Joseph's house and thought, "We were brought here because of the money that was put in our sacks on the first trip. He wants to attack us, make us slaves, and take our donkeys." **19** So the brothers went to the servant in charge of Joseph's house and spoke to him at the door of the house. **20** They said, "Master, we came here once before to buy food. **21** While we were going home, we stopped for the night and when we opened our sacks each of us found all his money in his sack. We brought that money with us to give it back to you. **22** And we have brought more money to pay for the food we want to buy this time. We don't know who put that money in our sacks."

23 But the servant answered, "It's all right. Don't be afraid. Your God, the God of your father, must have put the money in your sacks. I got the money you paid me for the grain last time." Then the servant brought Simeon out to them.

24 The servant led the men into Joseph's house and gave them water, and they washed their feet. Then he gave their donkeys food to eat. **25** The men prepared their gift to give to Joseph when he arrived at noon, because they had heard they were going to eat with him there.

26 When Joseph came home, the brothers gave him the gift they had brought into the house and bowed down to the ground in front of him. **27** Joseph asked them how they were. He said, "How is your aged father you told me about? Is he still alive?"

28 The brothers answered, "Your servant, our father, is well. He is still alive." And they bowed low before Joseph to show him respect.

29 When Joseph saw his brother Benjamin, who had the same mother as he, Joseph asked, "Is this your

> Then Joseph hurried off because he had to hold back the tears when he saw his brother Benjamin. So Joseph went into his room and cried there.
> – Genesis 43:30

youngest brother you told me about?" Then he said to Benjamin, "God be good to you, my son!" 30 Then Joseph hurried off because he had to hold back the tears when he saw his brother Benjamin. So Joseph went into his room and cried there. 31 Then he washed his face and came out. He controlled himself and said, "Serve the meal."

32 So they served Joseph at one table, his brothers at another table, and the Egyptians who ate with him at another table. This was because Egyptians did not like Hebrews and never ate with them. 33 Joseph's brothers were seated in front of him in order of their ages, from oldest to youngest. They looked at each other because they were so amazed. 34 Food from Joseph's table was taken to them, but Benjamin was given five times more food than the others. Joseph's brothers ate and drank freely with him.

Joseph Sets a Trap

44 Then Joseph gave a command to the servant in charge of his house. He said, "Fill the men's sacks with as much grain as they can carry, and put each man's money into his sack with the grain. 2 Put my silver cup in the sack of the youngest brother, along with his money for the grain." The servant did what Joseph told him.

3 At dawn the brothers were sent away with their donkeys. 4 They were not far from the city when Joseph said to the servant in charge of his house, "Go after the men. When you catch up with them, say, 'Why have you paid back evil for good? 5 The cup you have stolen is the one my master uses for drinking and for explaining dreams. You have done a very wicked thing!'"

6 So the servant caught up with the brothers and said to them what Joseph had told him to say.

7 But the brothers said to the servant, "Why do you say these things? We would not do anything like that! 8 We brought back to you from the land of Canaan the money we found in our sacks. So surely we would not steal silver or gold from your master's house. 9 If you find that silver cup in the sack of one of us, then let him die, and we will be your slaves."

10 The servant said, "We will do as you say, but only the man who has taken the cup will become my slave. The rest of you may go free."

11 Then every brother quickly lowered his sack to the ground and opened it. 12 The servant searched the sacks, going from the oldest brother to the youngest, and found the cup in Benjamin's sack. 13 The brothers tore their clothes to show they were afraid. Then they put their sacks back on the donkeys and returned to the city.

14 When Judah and his brothers went back to Joseph's house, Joseph was still there, so the brothers bowed face down on the ground before him. 15 Joseph said to them, "What have you done? Didn't you know that a man like me can learn things by signs and dreams?"

16 Judah said, "Master, what can we say? And how can we show we are not guilty? God has uncovered our guilt, so all of us will be your slaves, not just Benjamin."

17 But Joseph said, "I will not make you all slaves! Only the man who stole the cup will be my slave. The rest of you may go back safely to your father."

18 Then Judah went to Joseph and said, "Master, please let me speak plainly to you, and please don't be angry with me. I know that you are as powerful as the king of Egypt himself. 19 When we were here before, you asked us, 'Do you have a father or a brother?' 20 And we answered you, 'We have an old father. And we have

Judah said, "Master, what can we say? And how can we show we are not guilty? God has uncovered our guilt, so all of us will be your slaves, not just Benjamin."
– Genesis 44:16

a younger brother, who was born when our father was old. This youngest son's brother is dead, so he is the only one of his mother's children left alive, and our father loves him very much.' 21 Then you said to us, 'Bring that brother to me. I want to see him.' 22 And we said to you, 'That young boy cannot leave his father, because if he leaves him, his father would die.' 23 But you said to us, 'If you don't bring your youngest brother, you will not be allowed to see me again.' 24 So we went back to our father and told him what you had said.

25 "Later, our father said, 'Go again and buy us a little more food.' 26 We said to our father, 'We cannot go without our youngest brother. Without our youngest brother, we will not be allowed to see the governor.' 27 Then my father said to us, 'You know that my wife Rachel gave me two sons. 28 When one son left me, I thought, "Surely he has been torn apart by a wild animal," and I haven't seen him since. 29 Now you want to take this son away from me also. But something terrible might happen to him, and I would be miserable until the day I die.' 30 Now what will happen if we go home to our father without our youngest brother? He is so important in our father's life that 31 when our father sees the young boy is not with us, he will die. And it will be our fault. We will cause the great sorrow that kills our father.

32 "I gave my father a guarantee that the young boy would be safe. I said to my father, 'If I don't bring him back to you, you can blame me all my life.' 33 So now, please allow me to stay here and be your slave, and let the young boy go back home with his brothers. 34 I cannot go back to my father if the boy is not with me. I couldn't stand to see my father that sad."

Joseph Reveals Who He Is

45 Joseph could not control himself in front of his servants any longer, so he cried out, "Have everyone leave me." When only the brothers were left with Joseph, he told them who he was. 2 Joseph cried so loudly that the Egyptians heard him, and the people in the

---

FAITH links

GOOD PLANS
GENESIS 45:7-8

Think about how you'd feel if your brother or sister sold you into slavery in a foreign country. Could you honestly see the good in such an action? Most of us would say no. Yet after that happened to Joseph, he realised that God had a greater plan beyond his brothers' evil one. God's plan was to save their lives during the great famine that later occurred.

God has good plans for his people – including you! When something bad happens and you're tempted to doubt God's love, think about what Joseph learned. Some people make evil plans. But God's plans are always good.

Thinking about your future? Surf on to see what plans God has in store for you!

The Sign of His Presence, Exodus 40:34–38, p. 130

Full Circle, Job 42, p. 706

Love That Will Last, Psalm 136, p. 813

When the Going Gets Tough, Lamentations 3:22–27, p. 1079

A Soldier's Story, 2 Timothy 2:3, p. 1653

Never Alone, Hebrews 13:5–6, p. 1684

king's palace heard about it. **3** He said to his brothers, "I am Joseph. Is my father still alive?" But the brothers could not answer him, because they were very afraid of him.

4 So Joseph said to them, "Come close to me." When the brothers came close to him, he said to them, "I am your brother Joseph, whom you sold as a slave to go to Egypt. **5** Now don't be worried or angry with yourselves because you sold me here. God sent me here ahead of you to save people's lives. **6** No food has grown on the land for two years now, and there will be five more years without planting or harvest. **7** So God sent me here ahead of you to make sure you have some descendants left on earth and to keep you alive in an amazing way. **8** So it was not you who sent me here, but God. God has made me the highest officer of the king of Egypt. I am in charge of his palace, and I am the master of all the land of Egypt.

9 "So leave quickly and go to my father. Tell him, 'Your son Joseph says: God has made me master over all Egypt. Come down to me quickly. **10** Live in the land of Goshen where you will be near me. Your children, your grandchildren, your flocks and herds, and all that you have will also be near me. **11** I will care for you during the next five years of hunger so that you and your family and all that you have will not starve.'

12 "Now you can see for yourselves, and so can my brother Benjamin, that the one speaking to you is really Joseph. **13** So tell my father about how powerful I have become in Egypt. Tell him about everything you have seen. Now hurry and bring him back to me." **14** Then Joseph hugged his brother Benjamin and cried, and Benjamin cried also. **15** And Joseph kissed all his brothers and cried as he hugged them. After this, his brothers talked with him.

16 When the king of Egypt and his officers learned that Joseph's brothers had come, they were very happy. **17** So the king said to Joseph, "Tell your brothers to load their animals and go back to the land of Canaan **18** and bring their father and their families back here to me. I will give them the best land in Egypt, and they will eat the best food we have here. **19** Tell them to take some wagons from Egypt for their children and their wives and to bring their father back also. **20** Tell them not to worry about bringing any of their things with them, because we will give them the best of what we have in Egypt."

21 So the sons of Israel did this. Joseph gave them wagons as the king had ordered and food for their trip. **22** He gave each brother a change of clothes, but he gave Benjamin five changes of clothes and about 300 pieces of silver. **23** Joseph also sent his father ten donkeys loaded with the best things from Egypt and ten female donkeys loaded with grain, bread and other food for his father on his trip back. **24** Then Joseph told his brothers to go. As they were leaving, he said to them, "Don't quarrel on the way home."

25 So the brothers left Egypt and went to their father Jacob in the land of Canaan. **26** They told him, "Joseph is still alive and is the ruler over all the land of Egypt." Their father was shocked and did not believe them. **27** But when the brothers told him everything Joseph had said, and when Jacob saw the wagons Joseph had sent to carry him back to Egypt, he felt better. **28** Israel[n] said, "Now I believe you. My son Joseph is still alive, and I will go and see him before I die."

Jacob Goes to Egypt

46 So Israel[n] took all he had and started his trip. He went to Beersheba, where he offered sacrifices to the God of his father Isaac. **2** During the night God spoke to Israel in a vision and said, "Jacob, Jacob."

And Jacob answered, "Here I am."

3 Then God said, "I am God, the God of your father. Don't be afraid to go to Egypt, because I will make your descendants a great nation there. **4** I will go to Egypt with you, and I will bring you out of Egypt again. Joseph's own hands will close your eyes when you die."

45:28; 46:1 **Israel** Also called Jacob.

5 Then Jacob left Beersheba. The sons of Israel loaded their father, their children and their wives in the wagons the king of Egypt had sent. 6 They also took their farm animals and everything they had gained in Canaan. So Jacob went to Egypt with all his descendants— 7 his sons and grandsons, his daughters and granddaughters. He took all his family to Egypt with him.

> Then God said, "I am God, the God of your father. Don't be afraid to go to Egypt, because I will make your descendants a great nation there."
> – Genesis 46:3

Jacob's Family

8 Now these are the names of the children of Israel who went into Egypt (Jacob and his descendants).

Reuben was Jacob's first son. 9 Reuben's sons were Hanoch, Pallu, Hezron and Carmi.

10 Simeon's sons were Jemuel, Jamin, Ohad, Jakin, Zohar and Shaul (Simeon's son by a Canaanite woman).

11 Levi's sons were Gershon, Kohath and Merari.

12 Judah's sons were Er, Onan, Shelah, Perez and Zerah (but Er and Onan had died in the land of Canaan). Perez's sons were Hezron and Hamul.

13 Issachar's sons were Tola, Puah, Jashub and Shimron.

14 Zebulun's sons were Sered, Elon and Jahleel.

15 These are the sons of Leah and Jacob born in North West Mesopotamia, in addition to his daughter Dinah. There were 33 persons in this part of Jacob's family.

16 Gad's sons were Zephon, Haggi, Shuni, Ezbon, Eri, Arodi and Areli.

17 Asher's sons were Imnah, Ishvah, Ishvi and Beriah, and their sister was Serah. Beriah's sons were Heber and Malkiel.

18 These are Jacob's sons by Zilpah, the slave girl whom Laban gave to his daughter Leah. There were sixteen persons in this part of Jacob's family.

19 The sons of Jacob's wife Rachel were Joseph and Benjamin. 20 In Egypt, Joseph became the father of Manasseh and Ephraim by his wife Asenath, the daughter of Potiphera, priest of On.

21 Benjamin's sons were Bela, Beker, Ashbel, Gera, Naaman, Ehi, Rosh, Muppim, Huppim and Ard.

22 These are the sons of Jacob by his wife Rachel. There were fourteen persons in this part of Jacob's family.

23 Dan's son was Hushim.

24 Naphtali's sons were Jahziel, Guni, Jezer and Shillem.

25 These are Jacob's sons by Bilhah, the slave girl whom Laban gave to his daughter Rachel. There were seven persons in this part of Jacob's family.

26 So the total number of Jacob's direct descendants who went to Egypt was 66, not counting the wives of Jacob's sons. 27 Joseph had two sons born in Egypt, so the total number in the family of Jacob in Egypt was 70.

Jacob Arrives in Egypt

28 Jacob sent Judah ahead of him to see Joseph in Goshen. When Jacob and his people came into the land of Goshen, 29 Joseph prepared his chariot and went to meet his father Israel in Goshen. As soon as Joseph saw his father, he hugged him, and cried there for a long time.

30 Then Israel said to Joseph, "Now I am ready to die, because I have seen your face and I know you are still alive."

31 Joseph said to his brothers and his father's family, "I will go and tell the king you are here. I will say, 'My brothers and my father's family have left the land of Canaan and have come here to me. 32 They are shepherds and take care of farm animals, and they have brought their flocks and their herds and everything they own with them.' 33 When the king calls you, he will ask, 'What work do you do?' 34 This is what you should tell him: 'We, your servants, have

taken care of farm animals all our lives. Our ancestors did the same thing.' Then the king will allow you to settle in the land of Goshen, away from the Egyptians, because they don't like to be near shepherds."

Jacob Settles in Goshen

47 Joseph went in to the king and said, "My father and my brothers have arrived from Canaan with their flocks and herds and everything they own. They are now in the land of Goshen." 2 Joseph chose five of his brothers to introduce to the king.

3 The king said to the brothers, "What work do you do?"

And they said to him, "We, your servants, are shepherds, just as our ancestors were." 4 They said to the king, "We have come to live in this land, because there is no grass in the land of Canaan for our animals to eat, and the hunger is terrible there. So please allow us to live in the land of Goshen."

5 Then the king said to Joseph, "Your father and your brothers have come to you, 6 and you may choose any place in Egypt for them to live. Give your father and your brothers the best land; let them live in the land of Goshen. And if any of them are skilled shepherds, put them in charge of my sheep and cattle."

7 Then Joseph brought in his father Jacob and introduced him to the king, and Jacob blessed the king.

8 Then the king said to Jacob, "How old are you?"

9 Jacob said to him, "My life has been spent wandering from place to place. It has been short and filled with trouble—only 130 years. My ancestors lived much longer than I." 10 Then Jacob blessed the king and left.

11 Joseph obeyed the king and gave his father and brothers the best land in Egypt, near the city of Rameses. 12 And Joseph gave his father, his brothers and everyone who lived with them the food they needed.

47:11–12 Family
Check out this example of caring for family.

Joseph Buys Land for the King

13 The hunger became worse, and since there was no food anywhere in the land, Egypt and Canaan became very poor. 14 Joseph collected all the money that was to be found in Egypt and Canaan. People paid for the grain they were buying, and he brought that money to the king's palace. 15 After some time, when the people in Egypt and Canaan had no money left, they went to Joseph and said, "Please give us food. Our money is gone, and if we don't eat, we will die here in front of you."

16 Joseph answered, "Since you have no money, give me your farm animals, and I will give you food in return." 17 So people brought their farm animals to Joseph, and he gave them food in exchange for their horses, sheep, goats, cattle and donkeys. And he kept them alive by trading food for their farm animals that year.

18 The next year the people came to Joseph and said, "You know we have no money left, and all our animals belong to you. We have nothing left except our bodies and our land. 19 Surely both we and our land will die here in front of you. Buy us and our land in exchange for food, and we will be slaves to the king, together with our land. Give us seed to plant so that we will live and not die, and the land will not become a desert."

20 So Joseph bought all the land in Egypt for the king. Every Egyptian sold Joseph his field, because the hunger was very great. So the land became the king's, 21 and Joseph made the people slaves from one end of Egypt to the other. 22 The only land he did not buy was the land the priests owned. They did not need to sell their land because the king paid them for their work. So they had money to buy food.

23 Joseph said to the people, "Now I have bought you and your land for the king, so I will give you seed and you can plant your fields. 24 At harvest time you must give one-fifth to the king. You may keep four-fifths for yourselves to use as seed for the field and as food for yourselves, your families and your children."

25 The people said, "You have saved

our lives. If you like, we will become slaves of the king."

26 So Joseph made a law in Egypt, which continues today: one-fifth of everything from the land belongs to the king. The only land the king did not get was the priests' land.

"Don't Bury Me in Egypt"

27 The Israelites continued to live in the land of Goshen in Egypt. There they gained possessions and had many children and grew in number.

28 Jacob* lived in Egypt seventeen years, so he lived to be 147 years old. 29 When Israel knew he soon would die, he called his son Joseph to him and said to him, "If you love me, put your hand under my leg.* Promise me you will not bury me in Egypt. 30 When I die, carry me out of Egypt, and bury me where my ancestors are buried."

Joseph answered, "I will do as you say."

31 Then Jacob said, "Promise me." And Joseph promised him that he would do this. Then Israel worshipped as he leaned on the top of his walking stick.

Blessings for Manasseh and Ephraim

48 Some time later Joseph learned that his father was very sick, so he took his two sons Manasseh and Ephraim and went to his father. 2 When Joseph arrived, someone told Jacob,* "Your son Joseph has come to see you." Jacob was weak, so he used all his strength and sat up on his bed.

3 Then Jacob said to Joseph, "God Almighty appeared to me at Luz in the land of Canaan and blessed me there. 4 He said to me, 'I will give you many children. I will make you the father of many peoples, and I will give your descendants this land for ever.' 5 Your two sons, who were born here in Egypt before I came, will be counted as my own sons. Ephraim and Manasseh will be my sons just as Reuben and Simeon are my sons. 6 But if you have other children, they will be your own, and their land will be part of the land given to Ephraim and Manasseh. 7 When I came from North West Mesopotamia, Rachel died in the land of Canaan, as we were travelling towards Ephrath. This made me very sad, and I buried her there beside the road to Ephrath." (Today Ephrath is Bethlehem.)

8 Then Israel saw Joseph's sons and said, "Who are these boys?"

9 Joseph said to his father, "They are

47:28; 48:2 Jacob Also called Israel.
47:29 put . . . leg This showed that a person would keep a promise.

FAITH CHALLENGE

Read 48:1 to see what one famous Bible character did when he heard that his father was very ill. What would you do if you found out that someone you loved was too sick to get out of bed?

TeSTiNG iT

Genesis 48:1
Some time later Joseph learned that his father was very sick, so he took his two sons Manasseh and Ephraim and went to his father.

my sons that God has given me here in Egypt."

Israel said, "Bring your sons to me so I may bless them."

10 At this time Israel's eyesight was bad because he was old. So Joseph brought the boys close to him, and Israel kissed the boys and put his arms around them. 11 He said to Joseph, "I thought I would never see you alive again, and now God has let me see you and also your children." 12 Then Joseph moved his sons off Israel's lap and bowed face down to the ground. 13 He put Ephraim on his right side and Manasseh on his left. (So Ephraim was near Israel's left hand, and Manasseh was near Israel's right hand.) Joseph brought the boys close to Israel. 14 But Israel crossed his arms and put his right hand on the head of Ephraim, who was younger. He put his left hand on the head of Manasseh, the firstborn son. 15 And Israel blessed Joseph and said,

"My ancestors Abraham and Isaac
　served our God,
and like a shepherd God has led
　me all my life.
16 He was the Angel who saved me from
　all my troubles.
Now I pray that he will bless these
　boys.
May my name be known through
　these boys,
and may the names of my
　ancestors Abraham and Isaac be
　known through them.
May they have many descendants
　on the earth."

17 When Joseph saw that his father put his right hand on Ephraim's head, he didn't like it. So he took hold of his father's hand, wanting to move it from Ephraim's head to Manasseh's head. 18 Joseph said to his father, "You are doing it wrong, Father. Manasseh is the firstborn son. Put your right hand on his head."

19 But his father refused and said, "I know, my son, I know. Manasseh will be great and have many descendants. But his younger brother will be greater, and his descendants will be enough to make a nation."

20 So Israel blessed them that day and said,

"When a blessing is given in Israel,
　they will say:
'May God make you like Ephraim
　and Manasseh.'"

In this way he made Ephraim greater than Manasseh.

21 Then Israel said to Joseph, "Look at me; I am about to die. But God will be with you and will take you back to the land of your fathers. 22 I have given you something that I did not give your brothers—the land of Shechem that I took from the Amorite people with my sword and my bow."

Jacob Blesses His Sons

49 Then Jacob called his sons to him. He said, "Come here to me, and I will tell you what will happen to you in the future.

2 "Come together and listen, sons of
　Jacob.
Listen to Israel, your father.

3 "Reuben, my first son, you are my
　strength.
Your birth showed I could be a
　father.
You have the highest position among
　my sons,
　and you are the most powerful.
4 But you are uncontrolled like water,
　so you will no longer lead your
　brothers.
This is because you got into your
　father's bed
　and shamed me by having sexual
　relations with my slave girl.

5 "Simeon and Levi are brothers
　who used their swords to do
　violence.
6 I will not join their secret talks,
　and I will not meet with them to
　plan evil.
They killed men because they were
　angry,
　and they crippled oxen just for fun.
7 May their anger be cursed, because it
　is too violent.

> Genesis 49:8

May their violence be cursed,
  because it is too cruel.
I will divide them up among the
  tribes of Jacob
  and scatter them through all the
  tribes of Israel."

8 "Judah, your brothers will praise you.
  You will grab your enemies by the
    neck,
  and your brothers will bow down to
    you.
9 Judah is like a young lion.
  You have returned from killing, my
    son.
  Like a lion, he stretches out and lies
    down to rest,
  and no one is brave enough to
    wake him.
10 Kings will come from Judah's family;
  someone from Judah will always be
    on the throne.
  Judah will rule until Shiloh comes,
  and the nations will obey him.
11 He ties his donkey to a grapevine,
  his young donkey to the best
    branch.
  He can afford to use wine to wash his
    clothes
  and the best wine to wash his
    robes.
12 His eyes are dark like the colour of
    wine,
  and his teeth are as white as the
    colour of milk.

13 "Zebulun will live near the sea.
  His shore will be a safe place for
    ships,
  and his land will reach as far as
    Sidon.

14 "Issachar is like a strong donkey
  who lies down while carrying his
    load.
15 When he sees his resting place is
    good
  and how pleasant his land is,
  he will put his back to the load
  and become a slave.

16 "Dan will rule his own people
  like the other tribes in Israel.
17 Dan will be like a snake by the side of
    the road,
  a dangerous snake lying near the
    path.
  That snake bites a horse's leg,
  and the rider is thrown off
    backwards.

18 "LORD, I wait for your salvation.

19 "Robbers will attack Gad,
  but he will defeat them and drive
    them away.

20 "Asher's land will grow much good
    food;
  he will grow food fit for a king.

21 "Naphtali is like a female deer that
    runs free,
  that has beautiful fawns.

22 "Joseph is like a grapevine that
    produces much fruit,
  a healthy vine watered by a spring,
  whose branches grow over the
    wall.
23 Archers attack him violently
  and shoot at him angrily,
24 but he aims his bow well.
  His arms are made strong.
  He gets his power from the Mighty
    God of Jacob
  and his strength from the
    Shepherd, the Rock of Israel.
25 Your father's God helps you.
  God Almighty
    blesses you.
  He blesses you
    with rain
    from above,
    with water
    from
    springs below,
  with many babies born to your wives,
  and many young ones born to your
    animals.
26 The blessings of your father are
    greater
  than the blessings of the oldest
    mountains,
  greater than the good things of the
    long-lasting hills.

**49:25
Help**
Where can you find
dependable help?

Genesis 50:8 71

May these blessings rest on the head of Joseph,
on the forehead of the one who was separated from his brothers.

27 "Benjamin is like a hungry wolf.
In the morning he eats what he has caught,
and in the evening he divides what he has taken."

28 These are the twelve tribes of Israel, and this is what their father said to them. He gave each son the blessing that was right for him. 29 Then Israel gave them a command and said, "I am about to die. Bury me with my ancestors in the cave in the field of Ephron the Hittite. 30 That cave is in the field of Machpelah, east of Mamre, in the land of Canaan. Abraham bought the field and cave from Ephron the Hittite for a burying place. 31 Abraham and Sarah his wife are buried there. Isaac and Rebekah his wife are buried there, and I buried my wife Leah there. 32 The field and the cave in it were bought from the Hittite people." 33 After Jacob finished talking to his sons, he lay down. He put his feet back on the bed, took his last breath and died.

Jacob's Burial

50 When Jacob died, Joseph hugged his father and cried over him and kissed him. 2 He commanded the doctors who served him to prepare his father's body, so the doctors prepared Jacob's body to be buried. 3 It took the doctors 40 days to prepare his body (the usual time it took). And the Egyptians had a time of sorrow for Jacob that lasted 70 days.

4 When this time of sorrow had ended, Joseph spoke to the king's officers and said, "If you think well of me, please tell this to the king: 5 'When my father was near death, I made a promise to him that I would bury him in a cave in the land of Canaan, in a burial place that he cut out for himself. So please let me go and bury my father, and then I will return.'"

6 The king answered, "Keep your promise. Go and bury your father."

7 So Joseph went to bury his father. All the king's officers, the elders and all the leading men of Egypt went with Joseph. 8 Everyone who lived with Joseph and his brothers went with him, as well as everyone who lived with his father. They

---

FAITH links

MORE POWERFUL THAN REVENGE

GENESIS 50:14-21

Imagine being in a position where you could get even with someone who treated you badly. Joseph's brothers had treated him very badly. As the second in command of Egypt, Joseph had the power to do anything he wanted to his brothers. He could have had them thrown into prison or even killed. Instead, when they came to him for forgiveness, he gladly gave it to them. Not only that, he promised to take care of them.

Forgiving others can be hard sometimes. But God wants you to forgive, rather than think about getting even. Forgiveness is more powerful than revenge!

Give Revenge a Rest, Leviticus 19:18, p. 160

Kind or Fair? 1 Samuel 30, p. 395

Putting an Enemy in Check, 2 Kings 6:8–23, p. 486

Wronged for What's Right, Ezra 4:4–5, p. 612

The Best Protection Plan, Matthew 2:13–18, p. 1276

A Friend in Need, Acts 9:27, p. 1480

Genesis 50

FORGIVENESS
Genesis 50:15–21

Livin' it

You Want Me to Do What? What would you do if your friend told a lie about you? Some kids would think of ways to get even. Or they might even stop being friends. But what if your friend is sorry for what he did and asks you to forgive him?

Joseph had ten older brothers who treated him very badly. Joseph had the power to do anything he wanted to his brothers. But when they said they were sorry, Joseph gladly forgave them. (Check out Genesis 50:14–21.)

Sometimes it's hard to forgive others – we would rather get even. But God is always willing to forgive us when we sin against him. God models forgiveness for us so we can forgive others. (See Ezekiel 16:59–63, p. 1102.) How will you react to someone who has hurt you – get even or follow God's example of forgiveness?

MORE FAITH links

Forgive Instead, p. 47

More Powerful Than Revenge, p. 71

A Model of Forgiveness, p. 1103

A Family Celebration, p. 1558

Forgive and Forget, p. 1604

> You know, God really wants us to be able to forgive each other.

Surf these links for more help in how to do this.

A Change of Heart Matthew 3:1–12, p. 1277
- When you do something wrong, are you quick to say, "I'm sorry," but slow to really mean it?
- John told the people to *repent*. To repent means to be sorry for what you did wrong and then to stop doing it. When you want to change, ask God. He's always glad to help!

Quick to Forgive? Mark 11:25, p. 1349
- How quick are you to forgive someone who has hurt you? Are you cheetah-quick or tortoise-slow? God wants you to forgive no matter what – not just when you feel like it. Are you in a cheetah-quick mode of forgiveness?

Forgive Again? Luke 17:3–4, p. 1402
- How many times do you think someone should be forgiven for the same thing?
- Could you forgive a friend if they said the same mean thing to you over and over again? How many times does God forgive you for the same thing?

my FAVOURITE links

left only their children, their flocks and their herds in the land of Goshen. 9 They went with Joseph in chariots and on horses. It was a very large group.

10 When they came to the threshing floor of Atad, near the Jordan River, they cried loudly and bitterly for his father. Joseph's time of sorrow continued for seven days. 11 The people that lived in Canaan saw the sadness at the threshing floor of Atad and said, "Those Egyptians are showing great sorrow!" So now that place is named Sorrow of the Egyptians.

12 So Jacob's sons did as their father commanded. 13 They carried his body to the land of Canaan and buried it in the cave in the field of Machpelah near Mamre. Abraham had bought this cave and field from Ephron the Hittite to use as a burial place. 14 After Joseph buried his father, he returned to Egypt, along with his brothers and everyone who had gone with him to bury his father.

The Brothers Fear Joseph

15 After Jacob died, Joseph's brothers said, "What if Joseph is still angry with us? We did many wrong things to him. What if he plans to pay us back?" 16 So they sent a message to Joseph that said, "Your father gave this command before he died. 17 He said to us, 'You have done wrong and have sinned and done evil to Joseph. Tell Joseph to forgive you, his brothers.' So now, Joseph, we beg you to forgive our wrong. We are the servants of the God of your father." When Joseph received the message, he cried.

18 And his brothers went to him and bowed low before him and said, "We are your slaves."

19 Then Joseph said to them, "Don't be afraid. Can I do what only God can do? 20 You meant to hurt me, but God turned your evil into good to save the lives of many people, which is being done. 21 So don't be afraid. I will take care of you and your children." So Joseph comforted his brothers and spoke kind words to them.

22 Joseph continued to live in Egypt with all his father's family. He died when he was 110 years old. 23 During Joseph's lifetime Ephraim had children and grandchildren, and Joseph's son Manasseh had a son named Makir. Joseph accepted Makir's children as his own.

The Death of Joseph

24 Joseph said to his brothers, "I am about to die, but God will take care of you. He will lead you out of this land to the land he promised to Abraham, Isaac and Jacob." 25 Then Joseph had the sons of Israel make a promise. He said, "Promise me that you will carry my bones with you out of Egypt."

26 Joseph died when he was 110 years old. Doctors prepared his body for burial, and then they put him in a coffin in Egypt.

MOSES, GET US OUT OF HERE!

Hi, it's Moses again. You may already know that I was born a slave and raised a prince, but did you also know that I killed a man and had to flee from the law? (Check out Exodus 2:11–15 for the details.) I still can't figure out why God chose me to be the leader of his people. I had just spent the last 40 years being a shepherd, not a diplomat. Still, when God spoke to me from the burning bush, I knew I had to obey. "Go! Bring my people, the Israelites, out of Egypt!" God said (Exodus 3:10). He promised that he would always be with me.

I wrote this book so that everyone would know how God rescued his people from slavery in Egypt. The king wanted to keep us as slaves, so God sent ten plagues to convince him to let us go. (Read about it in Exodus 7—11.) When the Egyptian soldiers came after us, God sent a great wind to part the water of the Red Sea, so we could escape to the other side (Exodus 14:21–31). Be sure to check out all these awesome stories.

JESUS WATCH

The last, most terrible plague of all that God sent to Egypt was the death of the firstborn. All firstborn sons of the land were going to die, from the sons of the slaves to the son of the king. However, God provided a way for the Israelites to escape this plague. All the Israelite households were to sacrifice a lamb and put its blood on the sides and tops of the door-frames of their houses. Those houses protected by the blood of the sacrificed lamb would be spared. Death would "pass over" their houses. Jesus is like the lamb of Passover. He is the perfect sacrifice for our sins. The punishment for our sins is death, but if we believe in Jesus, the blood of his sacrifice on the cross protects us from the punishment we deserve. Death "passes over" us and we have eternal life.

my FAVOURITE links

OTHER CONNECTIONS

Livin' it — Living with your family can sometimes be tough – especially since we all are so different from each other. Find out some good advice on how to live together by visiting <u>Give Me Space! Exodus 20:12</u>. Then follow the Faithlinks for more help.

Exodus is (literally) a moving story about the journey of God's people from captivity as slaves in Egypt to the border of the land that God promised to them. You can learn more by stopping at these sites:

- <u>Church on the Road, Exodus 27:9–19</u>. You've probably heard about mobile phones and mobile homes, but how about a mobile church? Find out how the Israelites carried their church with them as they wandered through the wilderness.
- Or stop by the <u>Ten Curses, Exodus 9</u>, to get the facts on how God convinced the king of Egypt to finally free the Israelites. (The king was a slow learner, but by the tenth curse, he finally got it! Do you remember which curse finally convinced the king?)

Why do you suppose the Israelites made a gold calf?

Sounds crazy? Connect to <u>Exodus 32</u> and check it out.

did YOU know?

SURFWATCH FOR THESE STORIES:

<u>Who's the baby in the basket? Exodus 2:1–10</u>
<u>Pass over that house, Exodus 12:1–30</u>
<u>Manna – what's this stuff? Exodus 16:31</u>
<u>The Ten Commandments, Exodus 20:1–17</u>
<u>The Ark of the Agreement, Exodus 25:10–22</u>
<u>Levites don't wear blue jeans, Exodus 28</u>

FAITH links

○ Obey? No Way!
<u>Exodus 1:15–21</u>

○ Fearful Service?
<u>Exodus 4:1–17</u>

○ When Bad Turns to Worse,
<u>Exodus 5:6–12</u>

○ Your Worst Enemy,
<u>Exodus 7—11</u>

○ Time to Celebrate,
<u>Exodus 15:1–21</u>

○ Complaints, Complaints!
<u>Exodus 16:1–3</u>

○ Serious About the Sabbath,
<u>Exodus 31:15</u>

○ Share What You Have,
<u>Exodus 35:5–18</u>

○ The Sign of His Presence,
<u>Exodus 40:34–38</u>

Jacob's Family Grows Strong

1 When Jacob[n] went to Egypt, he took his sons, and each son took his own family with him. These are the names of the sons of Israel: 2 Reuben, Simeon, Levi, Judah, 3 Issachar, Zebulun, Benjamin, 4 Dan, Naphtali, Gad and Asher. 5 There was a total of 70 people who were descendants of Jacob. Jacob's son Joseph was already in Egypt.

6 Some time later, Joseph and his brothers died, along with all the people who had lived at that same time. 7 But the people of Israel had many children, and their number grew greatly. They became very strong, and the country of Egypt was filled with them.

Trouble for the People of Israel

8 Then a new king began to rule Egypt, who did not know who Joseph was. 9 This king said to his people, "Look! The people of Israel are too many and too strong for us to handle! 10 If we don't make plans against them, the number of their people will grow even more. Then if there is a war, they might join our enemies and fight us and escape from the country!"

11 So the Egyptians made life hard for the Israelites. They put slave masters over them, who forced the Israelites to build the cities Pithom and Rameses as supply centres for the king. 12 But the harder the Egyptians forced the Israelites to work, the more the Israelites grew in number and spread out. So the Egyptians became very afraid of them 13 and demanded even more of them. 14 They made their lives bitter. They forced the Israelites to work hard to make bricks and mortar and to do all kinds of work in the fields. The Egyptians were not merciful to them in all their painful work.

15 Two Hebrew nurses, named Shiphrah and Puah, helped the Israelite women give birth to their babies. The king of Egypt said to the nurses, 16 "When you are helping the Hebrew women give birth to their babies, watch! If the baby is a girl, let her live, but if it is a boy, kill him!"

1:1 **Jacob** Also called Israel.

FAITH links

OBEY? NO WAY!
EXODUS 1:15-21

Suppose you knew that the headmistress of your school disliked a certain group of kids. Now let's say she asked you to think of a way to get these kids expelled. If you don't, *you'll* be expelled. Would you do what you were told?

The king of Egypt didn't like the fact that the Hebrew population had grown. To decrease the population, he told two Hebrew midwives to kill all Hebrew boy babies. (A midwife is a woman who helps women give birth.) Yet Shiprah and Puah chose to obey God by refusing to kill these babies. God rewarded them by giving them children of their own. Although God wants you to obey people in authority, he would not expect you to obey an order that would cause you to sin.

Take Me to Your Leader, Numbers 27:12–23, p. 214

A Choice to Make, Deuteronomy 30:15–20, p. 265

The Right Thing to Do, 1 Samuel 26, p. 391

When I Need Advice, 1 Kings 12:1–17, p. 455

Going My Way? Hosea 8:1–6, p. 1179

Obey or Disobey? Luke 20:20–26, p. 1409

17 But the nurses feared God, so they did not do as the king told them; they let all the boy babies live. 18 Then the king of Egypt sent for the nurses and said, "Why did you do this? Why did you let the boys live?"

19 The nurses said to him, "The Hebrew women are much stronger than the Egyptian women. They give birth to their babies before we can get there." 20 God was good to the nurses. And the Hebrew people continued to grow in number, so they became even stronger. 21 Because the nurses feared God, he gave them families of their own.

22 So the king commanded all his people, "Every time a boy is born to the Hebrews, you must throw him into the Nile River, but let all the girl babies live."

Baby Moses

2 Now a man from the family of Levi married a woman who was also from the family of Levi. 2 She became pregnant and gave birth to a son. When she saw how wonderful the baby was, she hid him for three months. 3 But after three months she was not able to hide the baby any longer, so she got a basket and covered it with tar so that it would float. She put the baby in the basket. Then she put the basket among the tall stalks of grass at the edge of the Nile River. 4 The baby's sister stood a short distance away to see what would happen to him.

5 Then the daughter of the king of Egypt came to the river to take a bath, and her servant girls were walking beside the river. When she saw the basket in the tall grass, she sent her slave girl to get it. 6 The king's daughter opened the basket and saw the baby boy. He was crying, so she felt sorry for him and said, "This is one of the Hebrew babies."

7 Then the baby's sister asked the king's daughter, "Would you like me to go and find a Hebrew woman to nurse the baby for you?"

8 The king's daughter said, "Go!" So the girl went and got the baby's own mother.

9 The king's daughter said to the

FAITH links

YOUR HEAVENLY PARENT

EXODUS 2:1-10

You know your parents would do anything to protect you, right? They love you and wouldn't want anything to happen to you. Moses' mother felt the same way about her child. The king of Egypt made a cruel law. All of the Hebrew boy babies were to be killed. Moses' mother kept her son hidden. But after a while, she could hide him no longer. She placed him in the river, trusting that God would keep little Moses safe.

That's the kind of trust that God wants you to have. He's a heavenly parent who wants to take care of his earthly kid. If your parents are followers of Jesus, they're also trusting that God will take care of you.

Connect to these Faithlinks on how much God cares for you:

A Major Problem, Genesis 15:6, p. 20

Good Plans, Genesis 45:7–8, p. 64

Lower Than Low, Job 19:13–25, p. 680

Who Ya' Gonna Call? Psalm 3:4, p. 711

When Bad Things Happen, Ecclesiastes 3:16–17, p. 876

Facing Your Fears, Matthew 8:23–27, p. 1288

woman, "Take this baby and nurse him for me, and I will pay you." So the woman took her baby and nursed him. 10 When the child grew older, the woman took him to the king's daughter, and she adopted the baby as her own son. The king's daughter named him Moses,[n] because she had pulled him out of the water.

Moses Tries to Help

11 Moses grew and became a man. One day he visited his people and saw that they were forced to work very hard. He saw an Egyptian beating a Hebrew man, one of Moses' own people. 12 Moses looked all around and saw that no one was watching, so he killed the Egyptian and hid his body in the sand.

13 The next day Moses returned and saw two Hebrew men fighting each other. He said to the one that was in the wrong, "Why are you hitting one of your own people?"

14 The man answered, "Who made you our ruler and judge? Are you going to kill me as you killed the Egyptian?"

Moses was afraid and thought, "Now everyone knows what I did."

15 When the king heard what Moses had done, he tried to kill him. But Moses ran away from the king and went to live in the land of Midian. There he sat down near a well.

Moses in Midian

16 There was a priest in Midian who had seven daughters. His daughters went to that well to get water to fill the water troughs for their father's flock. 17 Some shepherds came and chased the girls away, but Moses defended the girls and watered their flock.

18 When they went back to their father Reuel,[n] he asked them, "Why have you come home early today?"

19 The girls answered, "The shepherds chased us away, but an Egyptian defended us. He got water for us and watered our flock."

20 He asked his daughters, "Where is this man? Why did you leave him? Invite him to eat with us."

21 Moses agreed to stay with Jethro,

FAITH links

PUT PRIDE ASIDE
EXODUS 2:11-15

Ever come up with a plan you thought was good, but it failed? Moses tried to help the Hebrew people in his own strength and timing. His plan was a complete disaster. Because of it, he had to run for his life.

Pride causes us to trust in our own ideas and plans. But sometimes our plans can lead us in the wrong direction. God wants us to put pride aside and give our plans to him for his approval.

Struggle with pride sometimes? Here are some thoughts on how to deal with that:

The Sacrifice, Genesis 22, p. 29

The Weak Link, Judges 16, p. 334

Your Full Trust, Jeremiah 22:20-22, p. 1023

Eating Humble Pie, Daniel 4, p. 1156

Brag on Him! 1 Corinthians 3:18-23, p. 1548

The Way to Be Wise, James 1:5, p. 1689

---

and he gave his daughter Zipporah to Moses to be his wife. 22 Zipporah gave birth to a son. Moses named him

---

2:10 Moses The name Moses sounds like the Hebrew word for "to pull out".
2:18 Reuel He was also called Jethro.

Gershom,[n] because Moses was a stranger in a land that was not his own.

23 After a long time, the king of Egypt died. The people of Israel groaned, because they were forced to work very hard. When they cried for help, God heard them. 24 God heard their cries, and he remembered the agreement he had made with Abraham, Isaac and Jacob. 25 He saw the troubles of the people of Israel, and he was concerned about them.

The Burning Bush

3 One day Moses was taking care of Jethro's flock. (Jethro was the priest of Midian and also Moses' father-in-law.) When Moses led the flock to the west side of the desert, he came to Sinai, the mountain of God. 2 There the angel of the LORD appeared to him in flames of fire coming out of a bush. Moses saw that the bush was on fire, but it was not burning up. 3 So he said, "I will go closer to this strange thing. How can a bush continue burning without burning up?"

4 When the LORD saw Moses was coming to look at the bush, God called to him from the bush, "Moses, Moses!"

And Moses said, "Here I am."

5 Then God said, "Do not come any closer. Take off your sandals, because you are standing on holy ground. 6 I am the God of your ancestors—the God of Abraham, the God of Isaac and the God of Jacob." Moses covered his face because he was afraid to look at God.

7 The LORD said, "I have seen the troubles my people have suffered in Egypt, and I have heard their cries when the Egyptian slave masters hurt them. I am concerned about their pain, 8 and I have come down to save them from the Egyptians. I will bring them out of that land and lead them to a good land with lots of room—a fertile land. It is the land of the Canaanites, Hittites, Amorites, Perizzites, Hivites and Jebusites. 9 I have heard the cries of the people of Israel, and I have seen the way the Egyptians have made life hard for them. 10 So now I am sending you to the king of Egypt. Go! Bring my people, the Israelites, out of Egypt!"

11 But Moses said to God, "I am not a great man! How can I go to the king and lead the Israelites out of Egypt?"

12 God said, "I will be with you. This will be the proof that I am sending you: after you lead the people out of Egypt, all of you will worship me on this mountain."

13 Moses said to God, "When I go to the Israelites, I will say to them, 'The God of your fathers sent me to you.' What if the people say, 'What is his name?' What should I tell them?"

14 Then God said to Moses, "I AM WHO I AM.[n] When you go to the people of Israel, tell them, 'I AM sent me to you.'"

15 God also said to Moses, "This is what you should tell the people: 'The LORD is the God of your ancestors—the God of Abraham, the God of Isaac and the God of Jacob. He sent me to you.' This will always be my name, by which people from now on will know me.

16 "Go and gather the elders and tell them this: 'The LORD, the God of your ancestors Abraham, Isaac and Jacob, has appeared to me. He said, I care about you, and I have seen what has happened to you in Egypt. 17 I promised I would take you out of your troubles in Egypt. I will lead you to the land of the Canaanites, Hittites, Amorites, Perizzites, Hivites and Jebusites—a fertile land.'

18 "The elders will listen to you. And then you and the elders of Israel will go to the king of Egypt and tell him, 'The LORD, the God of the Hebrews, appeared to us. Let us travel three days into the desert to offer sacrifices to the LORD our God.'

19 "But I know that the king of Egypt will not let you go. Only a great power

---

2:22 Gershom This name sounds like the Hebrew word for "a stranger there."

3:14 I . . . I AM The Hebrew words are like the name "Yahweh". This Hebrew name for God, usually called "LORD", shows that God always lives and is always with his people.

Email from God

3:5
Respect
Who is worthy of your respect?

will force him to let you go, 20 so I will use my great power against Egypt. I will strike Egypt with all the miracles that will happen in that land. After I do that, he will let you go. 21 I will cause the Egyptians to think well of the Israelites. So when you leave, they will give gifts to your people. 22 Each woman should ask her Egyptian neighbour and any Egyptian woman living in her house for gifts—silver, gold and clothing. You should put those gifts on your children when you leave Egypt. In this way you will take with you the riches of the Egyptians."

Proof for Moses

4 Then Moses answered, "What if the people of Israel do not believe me or listen to me? What if they say, 'The LORD did not appear to you?'"

2 The LORD said to him, "What is that in your hand?"

Moses answered, "It's my walking stick."

3 The LORD said, "Throw it on the ground."

So Moses threw it on the ground, and it became a snake. Moses ran from the snake, 4 but the LORD said to him, "Reach out and grab the snake by its tail." When Moses reached out and took hold of the snake, it again became a stick in his hand. 5 The LORD said, "This is so that the Israelites will believe that the LORD appeared to you. I am the God of their ancestors, the God of Abraham, the God of Isaac and the God of Jacob."

6 Then the LORD said to Moses, "Put your hand inside your coat." So Moses put his hand inside his coat. When he took it out, it was white with a skin disease.

7 Then he said, "Now put your hand inside your coat again." So Moses put his hand inside his coat again. When he took it out, his hand was healthy again, like the rest of his skin.

8 Then the LORD said, "If the people do not believe you or pay attention to the first miracle, they may believe you when you show them this second miracle. 9 After these two miracles, if they still do not believe or listen to you, take some water from the Nile River and pour it on the dry ground. The water will become blood when it touches the ground."

10 But Moses said to the LORD, "Please, Lord, I have never been a skilled speaker. Even now, after talking to you, I cannot speak well. I speak slowly and can't find the best words."

FAITH links

FEARFUL SERVICE?
EXODUS 4:1-17

What's the biggest fear you have about serving God? Many people fear that God will force them to do something they don't want to do. God wanted Moses to return to Egypt and lead the people out of slavery. The very thought of that terrified Moses. He came up with excuse after excuse. For every excuse, God explained how he would help Moses.

When it comes to serving him, God doesn't want his people to fall back on excuses. God will always give you the resources you need when he calls you to a task. Your part is to be obedient.

What God Wants, Deuteronomy 10:12–13, p. 242

From Zero to Hero, Judges 6; 7, p. 319

The Big Risk, Esther 4:11—5:2, p. 652

Be Brave! Haggai 2:4, p. 1249

Our Gift to God, Romans 12:1–2, p. 1536

Blessed Are the Weak? 2 Corinthians 12:7–10, p. 1582

11 Then the LORD said to him, "Who made a person's mouth? And who makes someone deaf or not able to speak? Or who gives a person sight or blindness? It is I, the LORD. 12 Now go! I will help you speak, and I will teach you what to say."
13 But Moses said, "Please, Lord, send someone else."
14 The LORD became angry with Moses and said, "Your brother Aaron, from the family of Levi, is a skilled speaker. He is already coming to meet you, and he will be happy when he sees you. 15 You will speak to Aaron and tell him what to say. I will help both of you to speak and will teach you what to do. 16 Aaron will speak to the people for you. You will tell him what God says, and he will speak for you. 17 Take your walking stick with you, and use it to do the miracles."

Moses Returns to Egypt

18 Moses went back to Jethro, his father-in-law, and said to him, "Let me go back to my people in Egypt. I want to see if they are still alive."

Jethro said to Moses, "Go! I wish you well."

19 While Moses was still in Midian, the LORD said to him, "Go back to Egypt, because the men who wanted to kill you are dead now."

20 So Moses took his wife and his sons, put them on a donkey, and started back to Egypt. He took with him the walking stick of God.

21 The LORD said to Moses, "When you get back to Egypt, do all the miracles I have given you the power to do. Show them to the king of Egypt. But I will make the king very stubborn, and he will not let the people go. 22 Then say to the king, 'This is what the LORD says: Israel is my firstborn son. 23 I told you to let my son go so he may worship me. But you refused to let Israel go, so I will kill your firstborn son.'"

24 As Moses was on his way to Egypt, he stopped at a resting place for the night. The LORD met him there and tried to kill him. 25 But Zipporah took a flint knife and circumcised her son. Taking the skin, she touched Moses' feet with it and said to him, "You are a bridegroom of blood to me." 26 She said, "You are a bridegroom of blood," because she had to circumcise her son. So the LORD let Moses alone.

27 Meanwhile the LORD said to Aaron, "Go out into the desert to meet Moses." When Aaron went, he met Moses at Sinai, the mountain of God, and kissed him. 28 Moses told Aaron everything the LORD had said to him when he sent him to Egypt. He also told him about the miracles which the LORD had commanded him to do.

29 Moses and Aaron gathered all the elders of the Israelites, 30 and Aaron told them everything that the LORD had told Moses. Then Moses did the miracles for all the people to see, 31 and the Israelites believed. When they heard that the LORD was concerned about them and had seen their troubles, they bowed down and worshipped him.

Moses and Aaron Before the King

5 After Moses and Aaron talked to the people, they went to the king of Egypt and said, "This is what the LORD, the God of Israel, says: 'Let my people go so they may hold a feast for me in the desert.'"

2 But the king of Egypt said, "Who is the LORD? Why should I obey him and let Israel go? I do not know the LORD, and I will not let Israel go."

3 Then Aaron and Moses said, "The God of the Hebrews has met with us. Now let us travel three days into the desert to offer sacrifices to the LORD our God. If we don't do this, he may kill us with a disease or in war."

4 But the king said to them, "Moses and Aaron, why are you taking the people away from their work? Go back to your work! 5 There are very many Hebrews, and now you want them to stop working!"

6 That same day the king gave a command to the slave masters and foremen. 7 He said, "Don't give the people straw to make bricks as you used to do. Let them gather their own straw. 8 But they must still make the same number of bricks as they did before. Do not accept fewer. They

have become lazy, and that is why they are asking me, 'Let us go to offer sacrifices to our God.' **9** Make these people work harder and keep them busy; then they will not have time to listen to the lies of Moses."

10 So the slave masters and foremen went to the Israelites and said, "This is what the king says: 'I will no longer give you straw. **11** Go and get your own straw wherever you can find it. But you must make as many bricks as you made before.'" **12** So the people went everywhere in Egypt looking for dry stalks to use for straw. **13** The slave masters kept forcing the people to work harder. They said, "You must make just as many bricks as you did when you were given straw." **14** The king's slave masters had made the Israelite foremen responsible for the work the people did. The Egyptian slave masters beat these men and asked them, "Why aren't you making as many bricks as you made in the past?"

15 Then the Israelite foremen went to the king and complained, "Why are you treating us, your servants, this way? **16** You give us no straw, but we are commanded to make bricks. Our slave masters beat us, but it is your own people's fault."

17 The king answered, "You are lazy! You don't want to work! That is why you ask to leave here and make sacrifices to the LORD. **18** Now, go back to work! We will not give you any straw, but you must make just as many bricks as you did before."

19 The Israelite foremen knew they were in trouble, because the king had told them, "You must make just as many bricks each day as you did before." **20** As they were leaving the meeting with the king, they met Moses and Aaron, who were waiting for them. **21** So they said to Moses and Aaron, "May the LORD punish you. You caused the king and his officers to hate us. You have given them an excuse to kill us."

Moses Complains to God

22 Then Moses returned to the LORD and said, "Lord, why have you brought

WHEN BAD TURNS TO WORSE
EXODUS 5:6-12

Ever have an already bad day that suddenly took a turn for the worse? Moses didn't want to be the chosen leader of the Israelites. Yet he obeyed God by going to Egypt to tell the king to let the Israelites go. After Moses and Aaron gave the king God's message, the king made the people work harder than ever! Who was blamed for this? Moses!

Sometimes things seem to get worse when we follow God. Has that been your experience? Even when that happens, God still wants you to be obedient. He wants you to trust that he'll see you through the hard times.

How do you handle tough times? Surf over to these links for some help:

Alone and Forgotten? Genesis 40:23, p. 57

Your Worst Enemy, Exodus 7—11, p. 85

A Pity Party, Job 10, p. 671

A Promise from the Heart, Jeremiah 31:31–33, p. 1037

Our Good Shepherd, John 10:11–15, p. 1441

As Strong as Superman? Philippians 4:13, p. 1615

this trouble on your people? Is this why you sent me here? 23 I went to the king and said what you told me to say, but ever since that time he has made the people suffer. And you have done nothing to save them."

6 Then the LORD said to Moses, "Now you will see what I will do to the king of Egypt. I will use my great power against him, and he will let my people go. Because of my power, he will force them out of his country."

2 Then God said to Moses, "I am the LORD. 3 I appeared to Abraham, Isaac and Jacob by the name God Almighty, but they did not know me by my name, the LORD. 4 I also made my agreement with them to give them the land of Canaan. They lived in that land, but it was not their own. 5 Now I have heard the cries of the Israelites, whom the Egyptians are treating as slaves, and I remember my agreement. 6 So tell the people of Israel that I say to them, 'I am the LORD. I will save you from the hard work the Egyptians force you to do. I will make you free, so you will not be slaves to the Egyptians. I will free you by my great power, and I will punish the Egyptians terribly. 7 I will make you my own people, and I will be your God. You will know that I am the LORD your God, the One who saves you from the hard work the Egyptians force you to do. 8 I will lead you to the land that I promised to Abraham, Isaac and Jacob, and I will give you that land to own. I am the LORD.'"

6:7 God
Does God promise to take care of you?

9 So Moses told this to the Israelites, but they would not listen to him. They were discouraged, and their slavery was hard.

10 Then the LORD said to Moses, 11 "Go and tell the king of Egypt that he must let the Israelites leave his land."

12 But Moses answered, "The Israelites will not listen to me, so surely the king will not listen to me either. I am not a good speaker."

13 But the LORD spoke to Moses and Aaron and gave them orders about the

Exodus 6:13 83

FAITH links

FROM HOPELESS TO HOPEFUL

EXODUS 6:9

Have you ever felt hopeless? Imagine feeling like that for months or even years. The Israelites felt hopeless. They had been stuck in slavery for many years. When God sent them a leader, the king increased their work duties out of spite. As a result, they could hardly believe the message of hope that Moses gave them.

When things aren't going very well, you may feel discouraged. You may even doubt that God loves you. God still wants to help you, even if you find that hard to believe. The best thing to do is to not give up on prayer. When you pray, ask God to give you hope.

Here are some more Faithlinks on prayer:

Our Thorough God, Leviticus 13, p. 149

Keep On Praying, 1 Samuel 1, p. 354

Your Best Defence, 2 Chronicles 20:1–12, p. 584

Go for the Gold, Job 23:10, p. 685

Uprooted by Change, Amos 9:15, p. 1205

Keep On Keeping On, Revelation 13:10, p. 1744

Israelites and the king of Egypt. He commanded them to lead the Israelites out of Egypt.

Families of Israel

14 These are the leaders of the families of Israel:

Israel's first son, Reuben, had four sons: Hanoch, Pallu, Hezron and Carmi. These are the family groups of Reuben.

15 Simeon's sons were Jemuel, Jamin, Ohad, Jakin, Zohar and Shaul, the son of a Canaanite woman. These are the family groups of Simeon.

16 Levi lived 137 years. These are the names of his sons according to their family history: Gershon, Kohath and Merari.

17 Gershon had two sons, Libni and Shimei, with their families.

18 Kohath lived for 133 years. The sons of Kohath were Amram, Izhar, Hebron and Uzziel.

19 The sons of Merari were Mahli and Mushi.

These are the family groups of Levi, according to their family history.

20 Amram married his father's sister Jochebed, who gave birth to Aaron and Moses. Amram lived for 137 years.

21 Izhar's sons were Korah, Nepheg and Zicri.

22 Uzziel's sons were Mishael, Elzaphan and Sithri.

23 Aaron married Elisheba, the daughter of Amminadab and the sister of Nahshon. Elisheba gave birth to Nadab, Abihu, Eleazar and Ithamar.

24 The sons of Korah were Assir, Elkanah and Abiasaph. These are the family groups of the Korahites.

25 Eleazar, son of Aaron, married a daughter of Putiel and she gave birth to Phinehas.

These are the leaders of the family groups of the Levites.

26 This was the Aaron and Moses to whom the LORD said, "Lead the people of Israel out of Egypt by their divisions." 27 Aaron and Moses are the ones who talked to the king of Egypt and told him to let the Israelites leave Egypt.

God Repeats His Call to Moses

28 The LORD spoke to Moses in the land of Egypt 29 and said, "I am the LORD. Tell the king of Egypt everything I tell you."

30 But Moses answered, "I am not a good speaker. The king will not listen to me."

7 The LORD said to Moses, "I have made you like God to the king of Egypt, and your brother Aaron will be like a prophet for you. 2 Tell Aaron your brother everything that I command you, and let him tell the king of Egypt to let the Israelites leave his country. 3 But I will make the king stubborn. I will do many miracles in Egypt, 4 but he will still refuse to listen. So then I will punish Egypt terribly, and I will lead my divisions, my people the Israelites, out of that land. 5 I will punish Egypt with my power, and I will bring the Israelites out of that land. Then they will know I am the LORD."

6 Moses and Aaron did just as the LORD had commanded them. 7 Moses was 80 years old and Aaron was 83 when they spoke to the king.

Aaron's Walking Stick Becomes a Snake

8 The LORD said to Moses and Aaron, 9 "Moses, when the king asks you to do a miracle, tell Aaron to throw his walking stick down in front of the king, and it will become a snake."

10 So Moses and Aaron went to the king as the LORD had commanded. Aaron threw his walking stick down in front of the king and his officers, and it became a snake.

11 So the king called in his wise men and his magicians, and with their tricks the Egyptian magicians were able to do the same thing. 12 They threw their walking sticks on the ground, and their sticks became snakes. But Aaron's stick swallowed theirs. 13 Still the king was stubborn and refused to listen to Moses and Aaron, just as the LORD had said.

Exodus 8:3 85

YOUR WORST ENEMY
EXODUS 7–11

You've heard the saying, "You're your own worst enemy," haven't you? That means you've done something to cause pain and suffering in your own life. In the king's case, that was certainly true. He thought he had successfully got even with Moses for daring to ask that the Israelites be freed from slavery. The king's stubbornness led to ten awful plagues that ruined Egypt; and in the last one, his firstborn son also died.

Sometimes we *are* our own worst enemy. What's the cure for that? Trusting that God – not we – knows what's best for our lives.

Who Do You Trust? Joshua 9, p. 287

Big Lack Attack, 2 Kings 4:1–7, p. 480

A Direct Path, Proverbs 3:5–6, p. 829

The Love Magnet, James 4:7–8, p. 1694

Ya' Gotta Love It? 1 John 2:15, p. 1715

Love and Obey, 2 John 6, p. 1721

The Water Becomes Blood

14 Then the LORD said to Moses, "The king is being stubborn and refuses to let the people go. 15 In the morning the king will go out to the Nile River. Go and meet him by the edge of the river, and take with you the walking stick that became a snake. 16 Tell him: the LORD, the God of the Hebrews, sent me to you. He said, 'Let my people go and worship me in the desert.' Until now you have not listened. 17 This is what the LORD says: 'This is how you will know that I am the LORD. I will strike the water of the Nile River with this stick in my hand, and the water will change into blood. 18 Then the fish in the Nile will die, and the river will begin to stink. The Egyptians will not be able to drink the water from the Nile.'"

19 The LORD said to Moses, "Tell Aaron: 'Take the walking stick in your hand and stretch your hand over the rivers, canals, ponds and pools in Egypt.' The water will become blood everywhere in Egypt, both in wooden buckets and in stone jars."

20 So Moses and Aaron did just as the LORD had commanded. In front of the king and his officers, Aaron raised his walking stick and struck the water in the Nile River. So all the water in the Nile changed into blood. 21 The fish in the Nile died, and the river began to stink, so the Egyptians could not drink water from it. Blood was everywhere in the land of Egypt.

22 Using their tricks, the magicians of Egypt did the same thing. So the king was stubborn and refused to listen to Moses and Aaron, just as the LORD had said. 23 The king turned and went into his palace and ignored what Moses and Aaron had done. 24 The Egyptians could not drink the water from the Nile, so all of them dug along the bank of the river, looking for water to drink.

The Frogs

25 Seven days passed after the LORD changed the Nile River into blood.

8 Then the LORD told Moses, "Go to the king of Egypt and tell him, 'This is what the LORD says: let my people go to worship me. 2 If you refuse, I will punish Egypt with frogs. 3 The Nile River will be filled with frogs. They will come up into your palace, into your bedroom, on your bed, into the houses of your officers and onto your people. They will come into

your ovens and into your baking pans. 4 The frogs will jump all over you, your people and your officers.'"

5 Then the LORD said to Moses, "Tell Aaron to hold his walking stick in his hand over the rivers, canals and ponds. Make frogs come up out of the water onto the land of Egypt."

6 So Aaron held his hand over all the waters of Egypt, and the frogs came up out of the water and covered the land of Egypt. 7 The magicians used their tricks to do the same thing, so even more frogs came up onto the land of Egypt.

8 The king called for Moses and Aaron and said, "Pray to the LORD to take the frogs away from me and my people. I will let your people go to offer sacrifices to the LORD."

9 Moses said to the king, "Please set the time when I should pray for you, your people and your officers. Then the frogs will leave you and your houses and will remain only in the Nile."

10 The king answered, "Tomorrow."

Moses said, "What you want will happen. By this you will know that there is no one like the LORD our God. 11 The frogs will leave you, your houses, your officers and your people. They will remain only in the Nile."

12 After Moses and Aaron left the king, Moses asked the LORD about the frogs he had sent to the king. 13 And the LORD did as Moses asked. The frogs died in the houses, in the yards and in the fields. 14 The Egyptians put them in piles, and the whole country began to stink. 15 But when the king saw that they were free of the frogs, he became stubborn again. He did not listen to Moses and Aaron, just as the LORD had said.

The Gnats

16 Then the LORD said to Moses, "Tell Aaron to raise his walking stick and strike the dust on the ground. Then everywhere in Egypt the dust will change into gnats."

> Then the LORD told Moses, "Go to the king of Egypt and tell him, 'This is what the LORD says: let my people go to worship me.'"
> – Exodus 8:1

17 They did this, and when Aaron raised the walking stick that was in his hand and struck the dust on the ground, everywhere in Egypt the dust changed into gnats. The gnats got on the people and animals. 18 Using their tricks, the magicians tried to do the same thing, but they could not make the dust change into gnats. The gnats remained on the people and animals. 19 So the magicians told the king that the power of God had done this. But the king was stubborn and refused to listen to them, just as the LORD had said.

The Flies

20 The LORD told Moses, "Get up early in the morning, and meet the king of Egypt as he goes out to the river. Tell him, 'This is what the LORD says: let my people go so they can worship me. 21 If you don't let them go, I will send swarms of flies into your houses. The flies will be on you, your officers and your people. The houses of Egypt will be full of flies, and they will be all over the ground, too. 22 But I will not treat the Israelites the same as the Egyptian people. There will not be any flies in the land of Goshen, where my people live. By this you will know that I, the LORD, am in this land. 23 I will treat my people differently from your people. This miracle will happen tomorrow.'"

24 So the LORD did as he had said, and great swarms of flies came into the king's palace and his officers' houses. All over Egypt flies were ruining the land. 25 The king called for Moses and Aaron and told them, "Offer sacrifices to your God here in this country."

26 But Moses said, "It wouldn't be right to do that, because the Egyptians hate the sacrifices we offer to the LORD our God. If they see us offering sacrifices they hate, they will throw stones at us and kill us. 27 Let us make a three-day journey into the desert. We must offer

TEN CURSES — Exodus 9

The Israelites had been slaves in Egypt for a long time. Moses went to the king of Egypt and asked him to let the Israelites leave and go back to their homeland. The king said a big "No!" So God sent ten plagues to convince the king to let the Israelites leave. Here's what he did:

1. The water of the River Nile turned to blood (Exodus 7:14–25).
2. Frogs overran the country (Exodus 8:1–15).
3. People and animals were infested with gnats (Exodus 8:16–19).
4. Swarms of flies covered the land and got into Egyptian homes (Exodus 8:20–32).
5. Disease killed the farm animals (Exodus 9:1–7).
6. Boils and sores infected the Egyptians and their animals (Exodus 9:8–12).
7. Hail destroyed crops and vegetation (Exodus 9:13–35).
8. Swarms of locusts covered the land (Exodus 10:1–20).
9. Thick darkness covered Egypt for three days (Exodus 10:21–29).
10. The oldest Egyptian child and animal from each household died (Exodus 11:1—12:30).

Finally, after this last plague, the king of Egypt let Moses and the Israelites leave Egypt.

---

sacrifices to the LORD our God there, as the LORD told us to do."

28 The king said, "I will let you go so that you may offer sacrifices to the LORD your God in the desert, but you must not go very far away. Now go and pray for me."

29 Moses said, "I will leave and pray to the LORD, and he will take the flies away from you, your officers and your people tomorrow. But do not try to trick us again. Do not stop the people from going to offer sacrifices to the LORD."

30 So Moses left the king and prayed to the LORD, **31** and the LORD did as he asked. He removed the flies from the king, his officers and his people so that not one fly was left. **32** But the king became stubborn again and did not let the people go.

The Disease on the Farm Animals

9 Then the LORD told Moses, "Go to the king of Egypt and tell him, 'This is what the LORD, the God of the Hebrews, says: let my people go to worship me. **2** If you refuse to let them go and continue to hold them, **3** the LORD will punish you. He will send a terrible disease on your farm animals that are in the fields. He will cause your horses, donkeys, camels, cattle, goats and sheep to become sick. **4** But the LORD will treat Israel's animals differently from the animals of Egypt. None of the animals that belong to the Israelites will die. **5** The LORD has set tomorrow as the time he will do this in the land.'" **6** The next day the LORD did as he promised. All the farm animals in Egypt died, but none of the animals belonging to the Israelites died. **7** The king sent people to see what had happened to the animals of Israel, and they found that not one of them had died. But the king was still stubborn and did not let the people go.

The Boils

8 The LORD said to Moses and Aaron, "Fill your hands with ashes from a furnace. Moses, throw the ashes into the air in front of the king of Egypt. 9 The ashes will spread like dust through all the land of Egypt. They will cause boils to break out and become sores on the skin of people and animals everywhere in the land."

10 So Moses and Aaron took ashes from a furnace and went and stood before the king. Moses threw ashes into the air, which caused boils to break out and become sores on people and animals. 11 The magicians could not stand before Moses, because all the Egyptians had boils, even the magicians. 12 But the LORD made the king stubborn, so he refused to listen to Moses and Aaron, just as the LORD had said.

The Hail

13 Then the LORD said to Moses, "Get up early in the morning and go to the king of Egypt. Tell him, 'This is what the LORD, the God of the Hebrews, says: let my people go to worship me. 14 If you don't, this time I will punish you, your officers and your people, with all my power. Then you will know there is no one in the whole land like me. 15 By now I could have used my power and caused a terrible disease that would have destroyed you and your people from the earth. 16 But I have let you live for this reason: to show you my power so that my name will be talked about in all the earth. 17 You are still against my people and do not want to let them go. 18 So at this time tomorrow, I will send a terrible hailstorm, the worst in Egypt since it became a nation. 19 Now send for your animals and whatever you have in the fields, and bring them into a safe place. The hail will fall on every person or animal that is still in the fields. If they have not been brought in, they will die.'" 20 Some of the king's officers respected the word of the LORD and hurried to bring their slaves and animals inside. 21 But others ignored the LORD's message and left their slaves and animals in the fields.

22 The LORD told Moses, "Raise your hand towards the sky. Then the hail will start falling in all the land of Egypt. It will fall on people, animals and on everything that grows in the fields of Egypt." 23 When Moses raised his walking stick towards the sky, the LORD sent thunder and hail, and lightning flashed down to the earth. So he caused hail to fall upon the land of Egypt. 24 There was hail, and lightning flashed as it hailed—the worst hailstorm in Egypt since it had become a nation. 25 The hail destroyed all the people and animals that were in the fields in all the land of Egypt. It also destroyed everything that grew in the fields and broke all the trees in the fields. 26 The only place it did not hail was in the land of Goshen, where the Israelites lived.

27 The king sent for Moses and Aaron and told them, "This time I have sinned. The LORD is in the right, and I and my people are in the wrong. 28 Pray to the LORD. We have had enough of God's thunder and hail. I will let you go; you do not have to stay here any longer."

29 Moses told the king, "When I leave the city, I will raise my hands to the LORD in prayer, and the thunder and hail will stop. Then you will know that the earth belongs to the LORD. 30 But I know that you and your officers do not yet fear the LORD God."

31 The flax was in bloom, and the barley had ripened, so these crops were destroyed. 32 But both wheat crops ripen later, so they were not destroyed.

33 Moses left the king and went outside the city. He raised his hands to the LORD, and the thunder and hail stopped. The rain also stopped falling to the ground. 34 When the king saw that the rain, hail and thunder had stopped, he sinned again, and he and his officers became stubborn. 35 So the king became stubborn and refused to let the Israelites go, just as the LORD had said through Moses.

The Locusts

10 The LORD said to Moses, "Go to the king of Egypt. I have made him and his officers stubborn so I could show them my powerful miracles. 2 I also did this so you could tell your children and your grandchildren how I was hard on the Egyptians. Tell them about the miracles I did among them so that all of you will know that I am the LORD."

3 So Moses and Aaron went to the king and told him, "This is what the LORD, the God of the Hebrews, says: 'How long will you refuse to be sorry for what you have done? Let my people go to worship me. 4 If you refuse to let my people go, tomorrow I will bring locusts into your country. 5 They will cover the land so that no one will be able to see the ground. They will eat anything that was left from the hailstorm and the leaves from every tree growing in the field. 6 They will fill your palaces and all your officers' houses, as well as the houses of all the Egyptians. There will be more locusts than your fathers or ancestors have ever seen—more than there have been since people began living in Egypt.'" Then Moses turned and walked away from the king.

7 The king's officers asked him, "How long will this man make trouble for us? Let the Israelites go to worship the LORD their God. Don't you know that Egypt is ruined?"

8 So Moses and Aaron were brought back to the king. He said to them, "Go and worship the LORD your God. But tell me, just who is going?"

9 Moses answered, "We will go with our young and old people, our sons and daughters, and our flocks and herds, because we are going to have a feast to honour the LORD."

10 The king said to them, "The LORD will really have to be with you if ever I let you and all of your children leave Egypt. See, you are planning something evil! 11 No! Only the men may go and worship the LORD, which is what you have been asking for." Then the king forced Moses and Aaron out of his palace.

12 The LORD told Moses, "Raise your hand over the land of Egypt, and the locusts will come. They will spread all over the land of Egypt and will eat all the plants the hail did not destroy."

13 So Moses raised his walking stick over the land of Egypt, and the LORD caused a strong wind to blow from the east. It blew across the land all that day and night, and when morning came, the east wind had brought the locusts. 14 Swarms of locusts covered all the land of Egypt and settled everywhere. There were more locusts than ever before or after, 15 and they covered the whole land so that it was black. They ate everything that was left after the hail—every plant in the field and all the fruit on the trees. Nothing green was left on any tree or plant anywhere in Egypt.

16 The king quickly called for Moses and Aaron. He said, "I have sinned against the LORD your God and against you. 17 Now forgive my sin this time. Pray to the LORD your God, and ask him to stop this punishment that kills."

18 Moses left the king and prayed to the LORD. 19 So the LORD changed the wind. He made a very strong wind blow from the west, and it blew the locusts away into the Red Sea. Not one locust was left anywhere in Egypt. 20 But the LORD caused the king to be stubborn again, and he did not let the Israelites go.

The Darkness

21 Then the LORD told Moses, "Raise your hand towards the sky, and darkness will cover the land of Egypt. It will be so dark you will be able to feel it." 22 Moses raised his hand towards the sky, and total darkness was everywhere in Egypt for three days. 23 No one could see anyone else, and no one could go anywhere for three days. But the Israelites had light where they lived.

24 Again the king of Egypt called for Moses. He said, "All of you may go and worship the LORD. You may take your women and children with you, but you must leave your flocks and herds here."

25 Moses said, "You must let us have animals to use as sacrifices and burnt offerings, because we have to offer them

to the LORD our God. 26 So we must take our animals with us; not a hoof will be left behind. We have to use some of the animals to worship the LORD our God. We won't know exactly what we will need to worship the LORD until we get there."

27 But the LORD made the king stubborn again, so he refused to let them go. 28 Then he told Moses, "Get out of here, and don't come again! The next time you see me, you will die."

29 Then Moses told the king, "I'll do what you say. I will not come to see you again."

The Death of the Firstborn

11 Now the LORD had told Moses, "I have one more way to punish the king and the people of Egypt. After this, the king will send all of you away from Egypt. When he does, he will force you to leave completely. 2 Tell the men and women of Israel to ask their neighbours for things made of silver and gold." 3 The LORD had caused the Egyptians to respect the Israelites, and both the king's officers and the Egyptian people considered Moses to be a great man.

4 So Moses said to the king, "This is what the LORD says: 'About midnight tonight I will go through all Egypt. 5 Every firstborn son in the land of Egypt will die—from the firstborn son of the king, who sits on his throne, to the firstborn of the slave girl grinding grain. Also the firstborn farm animals will die. 6 There will be loud crying everywhere in Egypt, worse than at any time before or after this. 7 But not even a dog will bark at the Israelites or their animals.' Then you will know that the LORD treats Israel differently from Egypt. 8 All your officers will come to me. They will bow face down to the ground before me and say, 'Leave and take all your people with you.' After that, I will leave." Then Moses very angrily left the king.

9 The LORD had told Moses, "The king will not listen to you and Aaron so that I may do many miracles in the land of Egypt." 10 Moses and Aaron did all these great miracles in front of the king. But the LORD made him stubborn, and the king would not let the Israelites leave his country.

The First Passover

12 The LORD spoke to Moses and Aaron in the land of Egypt: 2 "This month will be the beginning of months, the first month of the year for you. 3 Tell the whole community of Israel that on the tenth day of this month each man must get one lamb for the people in his house. 4 If there are not enough people in his house to eat a whole lamb, he must share it with his closest neighbour, considering the number of people. There must be enough lamb for everyone to eat. 5 The lamb must be a one-year-old male that has nothing wrong with it. This animal can be either a young sheep or a young goat. 6 Take care of the animals until the fourteenth day of the month. On that day all the people of the community of Israel will kill them in the evening before dark. 7 The people must take some of the blood and put it on the sides and tops of the doorframes of the houses where they eat the lambs. 8 On this night they must roast the lamb over a fire. They must eat it with bitter herbs and bread made without yeast. 9 Do not eat the lamb raw or boiled in water. Roast the whole lamb over a fire—with its head, legs and inner organs. 10 You must not leave any of it until morning, but if any of it is left over until morning, you must burn it with fire.

11 "This is the way you must eat it: you must be fully dressed as if you were going on a trip. You must have your sandals on and your walking stick in your hand. You must eat it in a hurry; this is the LORD's Passover.

12 "That night I will go through the land of Egypt and kill all the firstborn animals and people in the land of Egypt. I will

> Every firstborn son in the land of Egypt will die – from the firstborn son of the king . . . to the firstborn of the slave girl.
> – Exodus 11:5

also punish all the gods of Egypt. I am the LORD. 13 But the blood will be a sign on the houses where you are. When I see the blood, I will pass over you. Nothing terrible will hurt you when I punish the land of Egypt.

14 "You are always to remember this day and celebrate it with a feast to the LORD. Your descendants are to honour the LORD with this feast from now on. 15 For this feast you must eat bread made without yeast for seven days. On the first day, you are to remove all the yeast from your houses. No one should eat any yeast for the full seven days of the feast, or that person will be cut off from Israel. 16 You are to have holy meetings on the first and last days of the feast. You must not do any work on these days; the only work you may do is to prepare your meals. 17 You must celebrate the Feast of Unleavened Bread, because on this very day I brought your divisions of people out of Egypt. So all of your descendants must celebrate this day. This is a law that will last from now on. 18 In the first month of the year you are to eat bread made without yeast, from the evening of the fourteenth day until the evening of the twenty-first day. 19 For seven days there must not be any yeast in your houses. Anybody who eats yeast during this time, either an Israelite or non-Israelite, must be cut off from the community of Israel. 20 During this feast you must not eat anything made with yeast. You must eat only bread made without yeast wherever you live."

21 Then Moses called all the elders of Israel together and told them, "Get the animals for your families and kill the lamb for the Passover. 22 Take a branch of the hyssop plant, dip it into the bowl filled with blood, and then wipe the blood on the sides and tops of the doorframes. No one may leave that house until morning. 23 When the LORD goes through Egypt to kill the Egyptians, he will see the blood on the sides and tops of the doorframes, and he will pass over that house. He will not let the one who brings death come into your houses and kill you.

24 "You must keep this command as a law for you and your descendants from

---

FAITH links

A THANKSGIVING REMINDER
EXODUS 12

When are you most thankful? When you've received a gift? When things are going well in your life? Holidays or celebrations are times that remind us to be thankful. God instructed the Israelites to establish a holiday to remember how he had saved them from slavery in Egypt. This holiday was known as Passover. For centuries, the Israelites have celebrated the Passover as a way of saying thanks to God.

Holidays like Easter and Christmas remind us that we have a lot to be thankful for. God sent his Son, Jesus, to be our deliverer. He deserves our thanks.

Link here for some more ways to tell God thank you:

A Life of Thanksgiving, 1 Kings 1:47–48, p. 435

A Holiday Letter, Esther 9:20–23, p. 657

The One Who Suffered, Isaiah 53, p. 966

How Do I Love You? Malachi 1:1–5, p. 1267

Too Busy to Worship? Luke 2:8–20, p. 1368

One Big, Happy Family, John 1:12, p. 1422

now on. 25 Do this when you go to the land the LORD has promised to give you. 26 When your children ask you, 'Why are we doing these things?' 27 you will say, 'This is the Passover sacrifice to honour the LORD. When we were in Egypt, the LORD passed over the houses of Israel, and when he killed the Egyptians, he saved our homes.'" Then the people bowed down and worshipped the LORD. 28 They did just as the LORD commanded Moses and Aaron.

29 At midnight the LORD killed all the firstborn sons in the land of Egypt—from the firstborn of the king who sat on the throne to the firstborn of the prisoner in jail. Also, all the firstborn farm animals died. 30 The king, his officers and all the Egyptians got up during the night because someone had died in every house. So there was a loud outcry everywhere in Egypt.

Israel Leaves Egypt

31 During the night the king called for Moses and Aaron and said, "Get up and leave my people. You and your people may do as you have asked; go and worship the LORD. 32 Take all of your flocks and herds as you have asked, and go. And also bless me." 33 The Egyptians also asked the Israelites to hurry and leave, saying, "If you don't leave, we will all die!"

34 So the people took their dough before the yeast was added. They wrapped the bowls for making dough in clothing and carried them on their shoulders. 35 The Israelites did what Moses told them to do and asked their Egyptian neighbours for things made of silver and gold and for clothing. 36 The LORD caused the Egyptians to think well of them, and the Egyptians gave the people everything they asked for. So the Israelites took rich gifts from them.

37 The Israelites travelled from Rameses to Succoth. There were about 600,000 men walking, not including the women and children. 38 Many other people who were not Israelites went with them, as well as a large number of sheep, goats and cattle. 39 The Israelites used the dough they had brought out of Egypt to bake loaves of bread without yeast. The dough had no yeast in it, because they had been rushed out of Egypt and had no time to get food ready for their trip.

40 The people of Israel had lived in Egypt for 430 years; 41 on the very day the 430 years ended, the LORD's divisions of people left Egypt. 42 That night the LORD kept watch to bring them out of Egypt, and so on this same night the Israelites are to keep watch to honour the LORD from now on.

43 The LORD told Moses and Aaron, "Here are the rules for Passover: no foreigner is to eat the Passover. 44 If someone buys a slave and circumcises him, the slave may eat the Passover. 45 But neither a person who lives for a short time in your country nor a hired worker may eat it.

46 "The meal must be eaten inside a house; take none of the meat outside the house. Don't break any of the bones. 47 The whole community of Israel must take part in this feast. 48 A foreigner who lives with you may share in the LORD's Passover if all the males in his house become circumcised. Then, since he will be like a citizen of Israel, he may share in the meal. But a man who is not circumcised may not eat the Passover meal. 49 The same rules apply to an Israelite born in the country or to a foreigner living there."

50 So all the Israelites did just as the LORD had commanded Moses and Aaron. 51 On that same day the LORD led the Israelites out of Egypt by their divisions.

The Law of the Firstborn

13 Then the LORD said to Moses, 2 "Give every firstborn male to me. Every firstborn male among the Israelites belongs to me, whether human or animal."

3 Moses said to the people, "Remember this day, the day you left Egypt. You were slaves in that land, but the LORD with his great power brought you out of

it. You must not eat bread made with yeast. 4 Today, in the month of Abib, you are leaving Egypt. 5 The LORD will lead you to the land of the Canaanites, Hittites, Amorites, Hivites and Jebusites. This is the land he promised your ancestors he would give you, a fertile land. There you must celebrate this feast during the first month of every year. 6 For seven days you must eat bread made without yeast, and on the seventh day there will be a feast to honour the LORD. 7 So for seven days you must not eat any bread made with yeast. There must be no bread made with yeast anywhere in your land. 8 On that day you should tell your son: 'We are having this feast because of what the LORD did for me when I came out of Egypt.' 9 This feast will help you remember, like a mark on your hand or a reminder on your forehead. This feast will remind you to speak the LORD's teachings, because the LORD used his great power to bring you out of Egypt. 10 So celebrate this feast every year at the right time.

11 "And when the LORD takes you into the land of the Canaanites, the land he promised to give you and your ancestors, 12 you must give him every firstborn male. Also every firstborn male animal must be given to the LORD. 13 Buy back every firstborn donkey by offering a lamb. But if you don't want to buy the donkey back, then break its neck. You must buy back from the LORD every firstborn of your sons.

14 "From now on when your son asks you, 'What does this mean?' you will answer, 'With his great power, the LORD brought us out from Egypt, the land where we were slaves. 15 The king of Egypt was stubborn and refused to let us leave. But the LORD killed every firstborn male in Egypt, both human and animal. That is why I sacrifice every firstborn male animal to the LORD, and that is why I buy back each of my firstborn sons from the LORD.' 16 This feast is like a mark on your hand and a reminder on your forehead to help you remember that the LORD brought us out of Egypt with his great power."

The Way Out of Egypt

17 When the king sent the people out of Egypt, God did not lead them on the road through the Philistine country, though that was the shortest way. God said, "If they have to fight, they might change their minds and go back to Egypt." 18 So God led them through the desert towards the Red Sea. The Israelites were dressed for fighting when they left the land of Egypt.

19 Moses carried the bones of Joseph with him, because before Joseph died, he had made the Israelites promise to do this. He had said, "When God saves you, remember to carry my bones with you out of Egypt."

20 The Israelites left Succoth and camped at Etham, on the edge of the desert. 21 The LORD showed them the way; during the day he went ahead of them in a pillar of cloud, and during the night he was in a pillar of fire to give them light. In this way they could travel during the day or night. 22 The pillar of cloud was always with them during the day, and the pillar of fire was always with them at night.

14 Then the LORD said to Moses, 2 "Tell the Israelites to turn back to Pi Hahiroth and to camp between Migdol and the Red Sea. Camp across from Baal Zephon, on the shore of the sea. 3 The king will think, 'The Israelites are lost, trapped by the desert.' 4 I will make the king stubborn again so he will chase after them, but I will defeat the king and his army. This will bring honour to me, and the Egyptians will know that I am the LORD." The Israelites did just as they were told.

The King Chases the Israelites

5 When the king of Egypt was told that the Israelites had left, he and his officers changed their minds about them. They said, "What have we done? We have let the Israelites leave. We have lost our slaves!" 6 So the king prepared his war chariot and took his army with him. 7 He took 600 of his best chariots, together with all the other chariots of Egypt, each with an officer in it. 8 The LORD made

Exodus 14:9 94

the king of Egypt stubborn, so he chased the Israelites, who were leaving victoriously. 9 The Egyptians—with all the king's horses, chariot drivers and army—chased the Israelites. They caught up with them while they were camped by the Red Sea, near Pi Hahiroth and Baal Zephon.

10 When the Israelites saw the king and his army coming after them, they were very frightened and cried to the LORD for help. 11 They said to Moses, "What have you done to us? Why did you bring us out of Egypt to die in the desert? There were plenty of graves for us in Egypt. 12 We told you in Egypt, 'Let us alone; we will stay and serve the Egyptians.' Now we will die in the desert."

13 But Moses answered, "Don't be afraid! Stand still and you will see the LORD save you today. You will never see these Egyptians again after today. 14 You only need to remain calm; the LORD will fight for you."

15 Then the LORD said to Moses, "Why are you crying out to me? Command the Israelites to start moving. 16 Raise your walking stick and hold it over the sea so that the sea will split and the people can cross it on dry land. 17 I will make the Egyptians stubborn so they will chase the Israelites, but I will be honoured when I defeat the king and all of his chariot drivers and chariots. 18 When I defeat the king, his chariot drivers and chariots, the Egyptians will know that I am the LORD."

19 Now the angel of God who usually travelled in front of Israel's army moved behind them. Also, the pillar of cloud moved from in front of the people and stood behind them. 20 So the cloud came between the Egyptians and the Israelites. This made it dark for the Egyptians but gave light to the Israelites. So the cloud kept the two armies apart all night.

21 Then Moses held his hand over the sea. All that night the LORD drove back the sea with a strong east wind, making the sea become dry ground. The water was split, 22 and the Israelites went through the sea on dry land, with a wall of water on their right and on their left.

23 Then all the king's horses, chariots and chariot drivers followed them into the sea. 24 When morning came, the LORD looked down from the pillar of cloud and fire at the Egyptian army and made them panic. 25 He kept the wheels of the chariots from turning, making it hard to drive the chariots. The Egyptians shouted, "Let's get away from the Israelites! The LORD is fighting for them and against Egypt."

26 Then the LORD told Moses, "Hold your hand over the sea so that the water will come back over the Egyptians, their chariots and chariot drivers." 27 So Moses raised his hand over the sea, and at dawn the sea returned to its place. The Egyptians tried to run from it, but the LORD swept them away into the sea. 28 The water returned, covering the chariots, chariot drivers and all the king's army that had followed the Israelites into the sea. Not one of them survived.

29 But the Israelites crossed the sea on dry land, with a wall of water on their right and on their left. 30 So that day the LORD saved the Israelites from the Egyptians, and the Israelites saw the Egyptians lying dead on the seashore. 31 When the Israelites saw the great power the LORD had used against the Egyptians, they feared the LORD, and they trusted him and his servant Moses.

> But Moses answered, "Don't be afraid! Stand still and you will see the LORD save you today. You will never see these Egyptians again after today."
> – Exodus 14:13

The Song of Moses

15:1 Music
Check out what you should sing to.

15 Then Moses and the Israelites sang this song to the LORD:
"I will sing to the LORD,

because he is worthy of great
    honour.
He has thrown the horse and its rider
    into the sea.
2 The LORD gives me strength and
    makes me sing;
he has saved me.
He is my God,
    and I will praise him.
He is the God of my fathers,
    and I will honour him.
3 The LORD is a warrior;
    the LORD is his name.
4 The chariots and soldiers of the king
    of Egypt
he has thrown into the sea.
The king's best officers
    are drowned in the Red Sea.
5 The deep waters covered them,
    and they sank to the bottom like a
        rock.
6 Your right hand, LORD,
    is amazingly strong.
LORD, your right hand
    broke the enemy to pieces.
7 In your great victory
    you destroyed those who were
        against you.
Your anger destroyed them,
    like fire burning straw.
8 Just a blast of your breath,
    and the waters piled up.
The moving waters stood like a wall;
    the deep waters became solid in
        the middle of the sea.

9 "The enemy boasted,
    'I'll chase them and catch them.
I'll take all their riches;
    I'll take all I want.
I'll pull out my sword,
    and my hand will destroy them.'
10 But you blew on them with your
        breath
    and covered them with the sea.
They sank like lead
    in the raging water.

11 "Are there any gods like you, LORD?
    There are no gods like you.
You are wonderfully holy,
    amazingly powerful,
    a worker of miracles.
12 You reached out with your right hand,
    and the earth swallowed our
        enemies.
13 You keep your loving promise
    and lead the people you have
        saved.
With your strength you will guide
        them
    to your holy place.

FAITH links

TIME TO CELEBRATE
EXODUS 15:1-21

How do you celebrate a great victory? When a favourite sports team wins, some towns throw parades in honour of the team. When a person leaves school, family members take him or her out to dinner or throw a party. Moses and the Israelites sang of God's deliverance at the Red Sea. This was their way of celebrating the great victory God had brought about. He had saved them from the wrath of the Egyptians after they left Egypt. Think about what God has done for you. How will you celebrate?

Approaching God, Numbers 3:10, p. 180

A Cause for Celebration, 1 Kings 8:62–66, p. 449

No Thanksgiving? 2 Kings 23:21–23, p. 512

A Love Song, Zephaniah 3:17, p. 1246

The Gift, John 3:16–18, p. 1427

Always Do This! 1 Thessalonians 5:16–18, p. 1636

14 "The other nations will hear this and
       tremble with fear;
   terror will take hold of the
       Philistines.
15 The leaders of the tribes of Edom will
       be very frightened;
   the powerful men of Moab will shake
       with fear;
   the people of Canaan will lose all
       their courage.
16 Terror and fear will fall on them.
   When they see your strength,
       they will be as still as a rock.
   They will be still until your people
       pass by, LORD.
   They will be still until the people
       you have taken as your own pass
       by.
17 You will lead your people and place
       them
   on your very own mountain,
   the place that you, LORD, made for
       yourself to live,
   the temple, Lord, that your hands
       have made.
18 The LORD will be king for ever!"

19 The horses, chariot drivers and chariots of the king of Egypt went into the sea, and the LORD covered them with water from the sea. But the Israelites walked through the sea on dry land. 20 Then Aaron's sister, Miriam, a prophetess, took a tambourine in her hand. All the women followed her, playing tambourines and dancing. 21 Miriam told them:

   "Sing to the LORD,
   because he is worthy of great
       honour;
   he has thrown the horse and its rider
       into the sea."

Bitter Water Becomes Good

22 Moses led the Israelites away from the Red Sea into the Desert of Shur. They travelled for three days in the desert but found no water. 23 Then they came to Marah, where there was water, but they could not drink it because it was too bitter. (That is why the place was named Marah.*) 24 The people grumbled to Moses and asked, "What will we drink?"

25 So Moses cried out to the LORD, and the LORD showed him a tree. When Moses threw the tree into the water, the water became good to drink.

There the LORD gave the people a rule and a law to live by, and there he tested their loyalty to him. 26 He said, "You must obey the LORD your God and do what he says is right. If you obey all his commands and keep his rules, I will not bring on you any of the sicknesses I brought on the Egyptians. I am the LORD who heals you."

27 Then the people travelled to Elim, where there were twelve springs of water and 70 palm trees. So the people camped there near the water.

The People Demand Food

16 The whole Israelite community left Elim and came to the Desert of Sin, which was between Elim and Sinai; they arrived there on the fifteenth day of the second month after they had left Egypt. 2 Then the whole Israelite community grumbled to Moses and Aaron in the desert. 3 They said to them, "It would have been better if the LORD had killed us in the land of Egypt. There we had meat to eat and all the food we wanted. But you have brought us into this desert to starve us to death."

4 Then the LORD said to Moses, "I will cause food to fall like rain from the sky for all of you. Every day the people must go out and gather what they need for that day. I want to see if the people will do what I teach them. 5 On the sixth day of each week, they are to gather twice as much as they gather on other days. Then they are to prepare it."

6 So Moses and Aaron said to all the Israelites: "This evening you will know that the LORD is the one who brought you out of Egypt. 7 Tomorrow morning you will see the glory of the LORD, because he has heard you grumble against him. We are nothing, so you are not grumbling against us, but against the LORD." 8 And Moses said, "Each evening the LORD will give you meat to eat, and every morning he

---

15:23 Marah This name means "bitter".

COMPLAINTS, COMPLAINTS!

EXODUS 16:1-3

Suppose you helped someone with a big project. Instead of thanking you, suppose that person complained to you about something that he felt you *didn't* do. How would you feel? God had delivered the Israelites from slavery. He guided them with a cloud by day and fire by night. Instead of being thankful, the people complained. They felt that God had treated them badly by bringing them out of Egypt. Why? Because they were hungry and wanted food *right now!*

When something isn't going your way, are you tempted to complain? Being thankful is one antidote for having a pity party.

Feeling sorry for yourself? Link here for help:

My Worship Place, Genesis 35:1–14, p. 49

Take My Advice, 1 Kings 2:2–4, p. 436

You're Invited! Psalm 100, p. 784

A Need to Change, Ecclesiastes 1:1–11, p. 873

His Valentine, Jeremiah 31:3, p. 1035

The Power of If, Mark 9:14–24, p. 1344

---

will give you all the bread you want, because he has heard you grumble against him. You are not grumbling against Aaron and me, because we are nothing; you are grumbling against the LORD."

9 Then Moses said to Aaron, "Speak to the whole community of the Israelites, and say to them, 'Meet together in the presence of the LORD, because he has heard your grumblings.'"

10 While Aaron was speaking to the whole community of the Israelites, they looked towards the desert. There the glory of the LORD appeared in a cloud.

11 The LORD said to Moses, **12** "I have heard the grumblings of the people of Israel. So tell them, 'At twilight you will eat meat, and every morning you will eat all the bread you want. Then you will know I am the LORD your God.'"

13 That evening quail came and covered the camp, and in the morning dew lay around the camp. **14** When the dew was gone, thin flakes like frost were on the desert ground. **15** When the Israelites saw it, they asked each other, "What is it?" because they did not know what it was.

So Moses told them, "This is the bread the LORD has given you to eat. **16** The LORD has commanded, 'Each one of you must gather what he needs, about 2 litres for every person in your family.'"

17 So the people of Israel did this; some people gathered much, and some gathered little. **18** Then they measured it. The person who gathered more did not have too much, nor did the person who gathered less have too little. Each person gathered just as much as he needed.

19 Moses said to them, "Don't keep any of it to eat the next day." **20** But some of the people did not listen to Moses and kept part of it to eat the next morning. It became full of worms and began to stink, so Moses was angry with those people.

21 Every morning each person gathered as much food as he needed, but when the sun became hot, it melted away.

22 On the sixth day the people gathered twice as much food—4 litres for every person. When all the leaders of the community came and told this to Moses, **23** he said to them, "This is what the

LORD commanded, because tomorrow is the Sabbath, the LORD's holy day of rest. Bake what you want to bake, and boil what you want to boil today. Save the rest of the food until tomorrow morning."

24 So the people saved it until the next morning, as Moses had commanded, and none of it began to stink or have worms in it. 25 Moses told the people, "Eat the food you gathered yesterday. Today is a Sabbath, the LORD's day of rest; you will not find any out in the field today. 26 You should gather the food for six days, but the seventh day is a Sabbath day. On that day there will not be any food on the ground."

27 On the seventh day some of the people went out to gather food, but they couldn't find any. 28 Then the LORD said to Moses, "How long will you people refuse to obey my commands and teachings? 29 Look, the LORD has made the Sabbath a day of rest for you. So on the sixth day he will give you enough food for two days, but on the seventh day each of you must stay where you are. Do not go anywhere." 30 So the people rested on the seventh day.

31 The people of Israel called the food manna. It was like small white seeds and tasted like wafers made with honey.

32 Then Moses said, "The LORD said, 'Save 2 litres of this food for your descendants. Then they can see the food I gave you to eat in the desert when I brought you out of Egypt.'"

33 Moses told Aaron, "Take a jar and fill it with 2 litres of manna. Then place it before the LORD, and save it for your descendants." 34 So Aaron did what the LORD had commanded Moses. He put the jar of manna in front of the Agreement to keep it safe. 35 The Israelites ate manna for 40 years, until they came to the land where they settled—the edge of the land of Canaan. 36 The measure they used for the manna was about 2 litres, or one-tenth of an ephah.[n]

Water from a Rock

17 The whole Israelite community left the Desert of Sin and travelled from place to place, as the LORD commanded.

They camped at Rephidim, but there was no water there for the people to drink. 2 So they quarrelled with Moses and said, "Give us water to drink."

Moses said to them, "Why do you quarrel with me? Why are you testing the LORD?"

3 But the people were very thirsty for water, so they grumbled against Moses. They said, "Why did you bring us out of Egypt? Was it to kill us, our children and our farm animals with thirst?"

4 So Moses cried to the LORD, "What can I do with these people? They are almost ready to stone me to death."

5 The LORD said to Moses, "Go ahead of the people, and take some of the elders of Israel with you. Carry with you the walking stick that you used to strike the Nile River. Now go! 6 I will stand in front of you on a rock at Mount Sinai. Hit that rock with the stick, and water will come out of it so that the people can drink." Moses did these things as the elders of Israel watched. 7 He named that place Massah,[n] because the Israelites tested the LORD when they asked, "Is the LORD with us or not?" He also named it Meribah,[n] because they quarrelled.

The Amalekites Fight Israel

8 At Rephidim the Amalekites came and fought the Israelites. 9 So Moses said to Joshua, "Choose some men and go and fight the Amalekites. Tomorrow I will stand on the top of the hill, holding the walking stick of God in my hands."

10 Joshua obeyed Moses and went to fight the Amalekites, while Moses, Aaron and Hur went to the top of the hill. 11 As long as Moses held his hands up, the Israelites were winning the fight, but when Moses put his hands down, the Amalekites were winning. 12 Later, when Moses' arms became tired, the men put a

---

16:36 **ephah** An ephah was a measure that equalled 22 litres.
17:7 **Massah** This name is the Hebrew word for "testing."
17:7 **Meribah** This name is the Hebrew word for "quarrel."

large rock under him, and he sat on it. Then Aaron and Hur held up Moses' hands—Aaron on one side and Hur on the other. They kept his hands steady until the sun went down. 13 So Joshua defeated the Amalekites in this battle.

14 Then the LORD said to Moses, "Write about this battle in a book so people will remember. And be sure to tell Joshua, because I will completely destroy the Amalekites from the earth."

15 Then Moses built an altar and named it The LORD is my Banner. 16 Moses said, "I lifted my hands towards the LORD's throne. The LORD will fight against the Amalekites for ever."

Jethro Visits Moses

18 Jethro, Moses' father-in-law, was the priest of Midian. He heard about everything that God had done for Moses and his people, the Israelites, and how the LORD had led the Israelites out of Egypt. 2 Now Moses had sent his wife Zipporah to Jethro, his father-in-law, 3 along with his two sons. The first son was named Gershom,ⁿ because when he was born, Moses said, "I am a stranger in a foreign country." 4 The other son was named Eliezer,ⁿ because when he was born, Moses said, "The God of my father is my help. He saved me from the king of Egypt."

5 So Jethro, Moses' father-in-law, took Moses' wife and his two sons and went to Moses. He was camped in the desert near the mountain of God. 6 Jethro had sent a message ahead to Moses that said, "I, Jethro, your father-in-law, am coming to you with your wife and her two sons."

7 So Moses went out to meet his father-in-law and bowed down and kissed him. After the two men asked about each other's health, they went into Moses' tent. 8 Moses told his father-in-law everything the LORD had done to the king and the Egyptians to help Israel. He told about all the problems they had faced along the way and how the LORD had saved them.

9 Jethro was very happy to hear all the good things the LORD had done for Israel when he had saved them from the Egyptians. 10 He said, "Praise the LORD. He has saved you from the Egyptians and their king, and he has saved the people

---

Exodus 18:10 99

FAITH links

FATHERLY ADVICE
EXODUS 18

When you need help, who do you go to for advice? Moses worked too hard making decisions for the people of Israel. His father-in-law, Jethro, came up with a plan to help Moses with his workload. Moses accepted his father-in-law's advice. He appointed leaders from every tribe to help do some of the work.

God puts people in our lives who care about us. Like Moses, we can learn to listen to the advice of caring family members and trusted adults.

Here is some other good advice to follow:

In Your Best Interests, Ruth 3, p. 349

Choosing Sides, 1 Samuel 20, p. 382

A Wise Wish, 1 Kings 3:5–9, p. 439

A Parent's Advice, Proverbs 1:8–9, p. 825

The Way to Be Wise, James 1:5, p. 1689

What Any Parent Wants, 3 John 3–4, p. 1723

18:3 Gershom This name sounds like the Hebrew word for "a stranger there".
18:4 Eliezer This name sounds like the Hebrew words "My God is my help".

from the power of the Egyptians. 11 Now I know the LORD is greater than all gods, because he did this to those who looked down on Israel." 12 Then Jethro, Moses' father-in-law, gave a whole burnt offering and other sacrifices to God. Aaron and all the elders of Israel came to Moses' father-in-law to eat the holy meal together before God.

13 The next day Moses solved disagreements among the people, and the people stood around him from morning until night. 14 When Moses' father-in-law saw all that Moses was doing for the people, he asked, "What is all this you are doing for the people? Why are you the only one to solve disagreements? All the people are standing around you from morning until night!"

15 Then Moses said to his father-in-law, "It is because the people come to me for God's help in solving their disagreements. 16 When people have a disagreement, they come to me, and I decide who is right. I tell them God's laws and teachings."

17 Moses' father-in-law said to him, "You are not doing this right. 18 You and the people who come to you will get too tired. This is too much work for you; you can't do it by yourself. 19 Now listen to me, and I will give you some advice. I want God to be with you. You must speak to God for the people and tell him about their disagreements. 20 Tell them about the laws and teachings, and teach them the right way to live and what they should do. 21 But choose some capable men from among the people—men who respect God, who can be trusted, and who will not change their decisions for money. Make these men officers over the people, to rule over groups of thousands, hundreds, fifties and tens. 22 Let these officers solve the disagreements among the people all the time. They can bring the hard cases to you, but they can decide the simple cases themselves. That will make it easier for you, because they will share the work with you. 23 If you do this as God commands you, then you will be able to do your job, and all the people will go home with their disagreements solved."

24 So Moses listened to his father-in-law and did everything he said. 25 He chose capable men from all the Israelites and made them leaders over the people; they were officers over groups of thousands, hundreds, fifties and tens. 26 These officers solved disagreements among the people all the time. They brought the hard cases to Moses, but they decided the simple cases themselves.

27 So Moses sent his father-in-law on his way, and Jethro went back to his own home.

Israel Camps at Sinai

19 Exactly three months after the Israelites had left Egypt, they reached the Desert of Sinai. 2 When they left Rephidim, they came to the Desert of Sinai and camped in the desert in front of the mountain. 3 Then Moses went up on the mountain to God. The LORD called to him from the mountain and said, "Say this to the family of Jacob, and tell the people of Israel: 4 'Every one of you has seen what I did to the people of Egypt. You saw how I carried you out of Egypt, as if on eagle's wings. And I brought you here to me. 5 So now if you obey me and keep my agreement, you will be my own possession, chosen from all nations. Even though the whole earth is mine, 6 you will be my kingdom of priests and a holy nation.' You must tell the Israelites these words."

7 So Moses went down and called the elders of the people together. He told them all the words the LORD had commanded him to say. 8 All the people

> Every one of you has seen what I did to the people of Egypt. You saw how I carried you out of Egypt, as if on eagle's wings.
> – Exodus 19:4

18:21 Leadership
What makes a good leader?

answered together, "We will do everything he has said." Then Moses took their answer back to the LORD.

9 And the LORD said to Moses, "I will come to you in a thick cloud and speak to you. The people will hear me speaking with you and will always trust you." Then Moses told the LORD what the people had said.

10 The LORD said to Moses, "Go to the people and have them spend today and tomorrow preparing themselves. They must wash their clothes 11 and be ready by the day after tomorrow. On that day I, the LORD, will come down on Mount Sinai, and all the people will see me. 12 But you must set a limit around the mountain that the people are not to cross. Tell them not to go up on the mountain and not to touch the foot of it. Anyone who touches the mountain must be put to death 13 with stones or shot with arrows. No one is allowed to touch him. Whether it is a person or an animal, he will not live. But the trumpet will make a long blast, and only then may the people go up on the mountain."

14 After Moses went down from the mountain to the people, he made them prepare themselves for service to God, and they washed their clothes. 15 Then Moses said to the people, "Be ready in three days. Do not have sexual relations during this time."

16 On the morning of the third day, there was thunder and lightning with a thick cloud on the mountain. There was a very loud blast from a trumpet, and all the people in the camp trembled. 17 Then Moses led the people out of the camp to meet God, and they stood at the foot of the mountain. 18 Mount Sinai was covered with smoke, because the LORD came down on it in fire. The smoke rose from the mountain like smoke from a furnace, and the whole mountain shook wildly. 19 The sound from the trumpet became louder. Then Moses spoke, and the voice of God answered him.

20 When the LORD came down on top of Mount Sinai, he called Moses to come up to the top of the mountain, and Moses went up. 21 The LORD said to Moses, "Go down and warn the people that they must not force their way through to see me. If they do, many of them will die. 22 Even the priests, who may come near me, must first prepare themselves. If they don't, I, the LORD, will punish them."

23 Moses told the LORD, "The people cannot come up on Mount Sinai, because you yourself told us, 'Set a limit around the mountain, and set it apart as holy.'"

24 The LORD said to him, "Go down and bring Aaron up with you, but don't allow the priests or the people to force their way through. They must not come up to the LORD, or I will punish them."

25 So Moses went down to the people and told them these things.

The Ten Commandments

20 Then God spoke all these words: 2 "I am the LORD your God, who brought you out of the land of Egypt where you were slaves.

3 "You must not have any other gods except me.

4 "You must not make for yourselves an idol that looks like anything in the sky above or on the earth below or in the water below the land. 5 You must not worship or serve any idol, because I, the LORD your God, am a jealous God. If you hate me, I will punish your children, and even your grandchildren and great-grandchildren. 6 But I show kindness to thousands who love me and obey my commands.

7 "You must not use the name of the LORD your God thoughtlessly; the LORD will punish anyone who misuses his name.

8 "Remember to keep the Sabbath holy. 9 Work and get everything done during six days each week, 10 but the seventh day is a day of rest to honour the LORD your God. On that day no one may do any work: not you, your son or daughter, your male or female slaves, your animals, or the foreigners living in your cities. 11 The reason is that in six days the LORD made everything—the sky, the earth, the sea and everything in them. On the seventh day he rested. So the LORD blessed the Sabbath day and made it holy.

Exodus 20 102

LIVING WITH MY FAMILY
Exodus 20:12

Give Me Space! Living with other people isn't always easy – especially in families. Even though you are all part of the same family, you aren't alike in everything. Actually, that would be really boring! How do you handle disagreements that come up in your family?

From the time that God created the first people, Adam and Eve, he told them to live together in love and have children. (Read Genesis 1:27–28, p. 5.) God wants families to be committed to each other in love. That means living together peacefully, helping each other and being loyal to each other.

MORE FAITH links

- Family Feud, **p. 37**
- Fatherly Advice, **p. 99**
- Peace in the Family, **p. 811**
- How to Worship God, **p. 972**
- What Any Parent Wants, **p. 1723**

When someone in your family is really getting on your nerves it can be hard to remember just how important families are to God.

Check out these Faithlinks, they might help you.

God's Valuable Gift: You, Psalm 127:3–5, p. 809
- What's the best gift you've been given recently? Why is it so valuable to you? Want to know a great gift that God gave your parents or guardians? Look in the mirror! God considers families with children blessed – like yours.

The Way to Get Along, 1 Peter 3:8–9, p. 1703
- What was the last thing you argued about with your brother or sister? How did you feel afterwards? How do you feel when you get along? Link here to discover God's formula for getting along with each other.

The True Test, 1 John 3:18, p. 1718
- If someone said that he loved you, but acted like he didn't want to be around you, would you believe him? You would want proof that he loved you. This Faithlink tells you what love really involves. Use the suggestion with your family!

FAITH links

TEN WAYS TO OBEY
EXODUS 20

Who makes the rules at home or at school? These rules help you know the behaviour that is expected of you. They also remind you of the consequences of bad behaviour. God came up with the Ten Commandments to help the people of Israel – and us – know how to obey him and get along with each other. These weren't suggestions that the people could take or leave. These were specific rules God expected them to follow. That goes for you, too!

Think rules aren't important? Surf on!

Do What You Want? Judges 21:25, p. 341

A Travelling Bible Study, 2 Chronicles 17:9, p. 580

The Writing's on the Wall, Daniel 5, p. 1159

The Best Advice, Zechariah 10:2, p. 1261

Attention, Please! Luke 8:11–15, p. 1383

Cut to the Quick, Hebrews 4:12, p. 1670

---

12 "Honour your father and your mother so that you will live a long time in the land that the LORD your God is going to give you.

13 "You must not murder anyone.

14 "You must not be guilty of adultery.

15 "You must not steal.

16 "You must not tell lies about your neighbour.

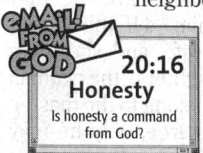

20:16 Honesty
Is honesty a command from God?

17 "You must not want to take your neighbour's house. You must not want his wife or his male or female slaves, or his ox or his donkey, or anything that belongs to your neighbour."

18 When the people heard the thunder and the trumpet, and when they saw the lightning and the smoke rising from the mountain, they shook with fear and stood far away from the mountain. 19 Then they said to Moses, "Speak to us yourself, and we will listen. But don't let God speak to us, or we will die."

20 Then Moses said to the people, "Don't be afraid, because God has come to test you. He wants you to respect him so you will not sin."

21 The people stood far away from the mountain while Moses went near the dark cloud where God was. 22 Then the LORD told Moses to say these things to the Israelites: "You yourselves have seen that I talked with you from heaven. 23 You must not use gold or silver to make idols for yourselves; do not worship these gods in addition to me.

24 "Make an altar of earth for me, and sacrifice on it your whole burnt offerings and fellowship offerings, your sheep and your cattle. Worship me in every place that I choose, and I will come and bless you. 25 If you use stones to make an altar for me, don't use stones that you have shaped with tools. When you use any tools on them, you make them unsuitable for use in worship. 26 And you must not go up to my altar on steps, or people will be able to see under your clothes."

Laws for Living

21 Then God said to Moses, "These are the laws for living that you will give to the Israelites:

2 "If you buy a Hebrew slave, he will serve you for six years. In the seventh year you are to set him free, and he will have to pay nothing. 3 If he is not married when he becomes your slave, he must

leave without a wife. But if he is married when he becomes your slave, he may take his wife with him. 4 If the slave's master gives him a wife, and she gives birth to sons or daughters, the woman and her children will belong to the master. When the slave is set free, only he may leave.

5 "But if the slave says, 'I love my master, my wife and my children, and I don't want to go free,' 6 then the slave's master must take him to God. The master is to take him to a door or doorframe and punch a hole through the slave's ear using a sharp tool. Then the slave will serve that master all his life.

7 "If a man sells his daughter as a slave, the rules for setting her free are different from the rules for setting the male slaves free. 8 If the master wants to marry her but then decides he is not pleased with her, he must let one of her close relatives buy her back. He has no right to sell her to foreigners, because he has treated her unfairly. 9 If the man who bought her promises to let the woman marry his son, he must treat her as a daughter. 10 If the man who bought her marries another woman, he must not keep his first wife from having food or clothing or sexual relations. 11 If he does not give her these three things, she may go free, and she owes him no money.

Laws About Injuries

12 "Anyone who hits a person and kills him must be put to death. 13 But if a person kills someone accidentally, God allowed that to happen, so the person must go to a place I will choose. 14 But if someone plans and murders another person on purpose, put him to death, even if he has run to my altar for safety.

15 "Anyone who hits his father or his mother must be put to death.

16 "Anyone who kidnaps someone and either sells him as a slave or still has him when he is caught must be put to death.

17 "Anyone who says cruel things to his father or mother must be put to death.

18 "If two men argue, and one hits the other with a rock or with his fist, the one who is hurt but not killed might have to stay in bed. 19 Later if he is able to get up and walk around outside with his walking stick, the one who hit him is not to be punished. But he must pay the injured man for the loss of his time, and he must support the injured man until he is completely healed.

20 "If a man beats his male or female slave with a stick, and the slave dies on the spot, the owner must be punished. 21 But if the slave gets well after a day or two, the owner will not be punished since the slave belongs to him.

22 "Suppose two men are fighting and hit a pregnant woman, causing the baby to come out. If there is no further injury, the man who caused the accident must pay money—whatever amount the woman's husband says and the court allows. 23 But if there is further injury, then the punishment that must be paid is life for life, 24 eye for eye, tooth for tooth, hand for hand, foot for foot, 25 burn for burn, wound for wound and bruise for bruise.

26 "If a man hits his male or female slave in the eye, and the eye is blinded, the man is to free the slave to pay for the eye. 27 If a master knocks out a tooth of his male or female slave, the man is to free the slave to pay for the tooth.

28 "If a man's bull kills a man or woman, you must kill that bull by throwing stones at it, and you should not eat the bull. But the owner of the bull is not guilty. 29 However, suppose the bull has hurt people in the past and the owner, though warned, did not keep it in a pen. Then if it kills a man or woman, the bull must be stoned to death, and the owner must also be put to death. 30 But if the family of the dead person accepts money, the one who owned the bull may buy back his life, but he must pay whatever is demanded. 31 Use this same law if the bull kills a person's son or daughter. 32 If the bull kills a male or female slave, the owner must pay the master the price for a new slave, or 30 pieces of silver, and the bull must also be stoned to death.

33 "If a man takes the cover off a pit, or digs a pit and does not cover it, and

another man's ox or donkey comes and falls into it, 34 the owner of the pit must pay the owner of the animal for the loss. The dead animal will belong to the one who pays.

35 "If a man's bull kills another man's bull, they must sell the bull that is alive. Both men will get half of the money and half of the bull that was killed. 36 But if a person's bull has hurt other animals in the past and the owner did not keep it in a pen, that owner must pay bull for bull, and the dead animal is his.

Property Laws

22 "If a man steals a bull or a sheep and kills or sells it, he must pay back five bulls for the one bull he stole and four sheep for the one sheep he stole.

2-4 "The robber who is caught must pay back what he stole. If he owns nothing, he must be sold as a slave to pay for what he stole. If the stolen animal is found alive with the robber, he must give the owner two animals for every animal he stole, whether it was a bull, donkey or sheep.

"If a thief is killed while breaking into a house at night, the one who killed him is not guilty of murder. But if this happens during the day, he is guilty of murder.

5 "If a man lets his farm animal graze in his field or vineyard, and it wanders into another man's field or vineyard, the owner of the animal must pay back the loss from the best of his crop.

6 "Suppose a man starts a fire that spreads through the thorn bushes to his neighbour's field. If the fire burns his neighbour's growing grain or grain that has been stacked, or if it burns his whole field, the person who started the fire must pay for what was burned.

7 "Suppose a man gives his neighbour money or other things to keep for him and those things are stolen from the neighbour's house. If the thief is caught, he must pay back twice as much as he stole. 8 But if the thief is never found, the owner of the house must make a promise before God that he has not stolen his neighbour's things.

9 "Suppose two men disagree about who owns something—whether ox, donkey, sheep, clothing or something else that is lost. If each says, 'This is mine,' each man must bring his case to God. God's judges will decide who is guilty, and that person must pay the other man twice as much as the object is worth.

10 "Suppose a man asks his neighbour to keep his donkey, ox, sheep or some other animal for him, and that animal dies, gets hurt or is taken away, without anyone seeing what happened. 11 That neighbour must promise before the LORD that he did not harm or kill the other man's animal, and the owner of the animal must accept his promise made before God. The neighbour does not have to pay the owner for the animal. 12 But if the animal was stolen from the neighbour, he must pay the owner for it. 13 If wild animals killed it, the neighbour must bring the body as proof, and he will not have to pay for the animal that was killed.

14 "If a man borrows an animal from his neighbour, and it gets hurt or dies while the owner is not there, the one who borrowed it must pay the owner for the animal. 15 But if the owner is with the animal, the one who borrowed it does not have to pay. If the animal was rented, the rental price covers the loss.

Laws and Relationships

16 "Suppose a man finds a woman who is not pledged to be married and has never had sexual relations with a man. If he tricks her into having sexual relations with him, he must give her family the payment to marry her and she will become his wife. 17 But if her father refuses to allow his daughter to marry him, the man must still give the usual payment for a bride who has never had sexual relations.

18 "Put to death any woman who does evil magic.

19 "Put to death anyone who has sexual relations with an animal.

20 "Destroy completely any person who makes a sacrifice to any god except the LORD.

21 "Do not cheat or hurt a foreigner,

because you were foreigners in the land of Egypt.

22 "Do not cheat a widow or an orphan. 23 If you do, and they cry out to me for help, I certainly will hear their cry. 24 And I will be very angry and kill you in war. Then your wives will become widows, and your children will become orphans.

25 "If you lend money to one of my people who is poor, do not treat him as a moneylender would. Charge him nothing for using your money. 26 If your neighbour gives you his coat as a promise for the money he owes you, you must give it back to him by sunset, 27 because it is the only cover to keep his body warm. He has nothing else to sleep in. If he cries out to me for help, I will listen, because I am merciful.

28 "You must not speak against God or curse a leader of your people.

29 "Do not hold back your offering from the first of your harvest and the first wine that you make. Also, you must give me your firstborn sons. 30 You must do the same with your bulls and your sheep. Let the firstborn males stay with their mothers for seven days, and on the eighth day you must give them to me.

31 "You are to be my holy people. You must not eat the meat of any animal that has been killed by wild animals. Instead, give it to the dogs.

Laws About Fairness

23 "You must not tell lies. If you are a witness in court, don't help a wicked person by telling lies.

23:2 Honesty
Don't follow the crowd.

2 "You must not do wrong just because everyone else is doing it. If you are a witness in court, you must not ruin a fair trial. You must not tell lies just because everyone else does. 3 If a poor person is in court, you must not take his side just because he is poor.

4 "If you see your enemy's ox or donkey wandering away, you must return it to him. 5 If you see that your enemy's donkey has fallen because its load is too heavy, do not leave it there. You must help your enemy get the donkey back on its feet.

6 "You must not be unfair to a poor person when he is in court. 7 You must not lie when you accuse someone in court. Never allow an innocent or honest person to be put to death as punishment, because I will not treat guilty people as if they were innocent.

8 "You must not accept money from a person who wants you to lie in court, because such money will not let you see what is right. Such money makes good people tell lies.

FAITH CHALLENGE

Got another challenge for you. Read 22:28 to find out what God says about respecting people in authority. What would you say to someone who was saying bad things about the prime minister?

TesTiNG iT

Exodus 22:28
You must not speak against God or curse a leader of your people.

23:9 Caring
Do you have to be nice to everyone?

9 "You must not mistreat a foreigner. You know how it feels to be a foreigner, because you were foreigners in Egypt.

Laws for the Sabbath

10 "For six years you are to plant and harvest crops on your land. 11 Then during the seventh year, do not plough or plant your land. If any food grows there, allow the poor people to have it, and let the wild animals eat what is left. You should do the same with your vineyards and your orchards of olive trees.

12 "You should work six days a week, but on the seventh day you must rest. This lets your ox and your donkey rest, and it also lets the slave born in your house and the foreigner be refreshed.

13 "Be sure to do all that I have said to you. You must not even say the names of other gods; those names must not come out of your mouth.

Three Yearly Feasts

14 "Three times each year you must hold a feast to honour me. 15 You must celebrate the Feast of Unleavened Bread in the way I commanded you. For seven days you must eat bread that is made without yeast at the set time during the month of Abib, the month when you came out of Egypt. No one is to come to worship me without bringing an offering.

16 "You must celebrate the Feast of Weeks. Offer to God the first things you harvest from the crops you planted in your fields.

"You must celebrate the Feast of Shelters in the autumn, when you gather all the crops from your fields.

17 "So three times during every year all your males must come to worship the LORD God.

18 "You must not offer animal blood along with anything that has yeast in it.

"You must not save any of the fat from the sacrifice for the next day.

19 "You must bring the best of the firstfruits of your land to the Holy Tent[n] of the LORD your God.

"You must not cook a young goat in its mother's milk.

God Will Help Israel

20 "I am sending an angel ahead of you, who will protect you as you travel. He will lead you to the place I have prepared. 21 Pay attention to the angel and obey him. Do not turn against him; he will not forgive such turning against him because my power is in him. 22 If you listen carefully to all he says and do everything that I tell you, I will be an enemy to your enemies. I will fight all who fight against you. 23 My angel will go ahead of you and take you into the land of the Amorites, Hittites, Perizzites, Canaanites, Hivites and Jebusites, and I will destroy them.

24 "You must not bow down to their gods or worship them. You must not live in the way those people live. You must destroy their idols, breaking into pieces the stone pillars they use in worship. 25 If you worship the LORD your God, I will bless your bread and your water. I will take away sickness from you. 26 None of your women will have her baby die before it is born, and all women will have children. I will allow you to live long lives.

27 "I will make your enemies afraid of me. I will confuse any people you fight against, and I will make all your enemies run away from you. 28 I will send terror ahead of you that will force the Hivites, Canaanites and Hittites out of your way. 29 But I will not force all those people out in only one year. If I did, the land would become a desert and the wild animals would become too many for you. 30 Instead, I will force those people out slowly, until there are enough of you to take over the land.

31 "I will give you the land from the Red Sea to the Mediterranean Sea, and from the desert to the Euphrates River. I will give you power over the people who now live in the land, and you will

---

23:19 Holy Tent Literally, "house of the LORD your God." See Exodus 25:9.

force them out ahead of you. 32 You must not make an agreement with those people or with their gods. 33 You must not let them live in your land, or they will make you sin against me. If you worship their gods, you will be caught in a trap."

God and Israel Make Their Agreement

24 The LORD told Moses, "You, Aaron, Nadab, Abihu and 70 of the elders of Israel must come up to me and worship me from a distance. 2 Then Moses alone must come near me; the others must not come near. The rest of the people must not come up the mountain with Moses."

3 Moses told the people all the LORD's words and laws for living. Then all of the people answered out loud together, "We will do all the things the LORD has said." 4 So Moses wrote down all the words of the LORD. And he got up early the next morning and built an altar near the bottom of the mountain. He set up twelve stones, one stone for each of the twelve tribes of Israel. 5 Then Moses sent young Israelite men to offer whole burnt offerings and to sacrifice young bulls as fellowship offerings to the LORD. 6 Moses put half of the blood of these animals in bowls, and he sprinkled the other half of the blood on the altar. 7 Then he took the Book of the Agreement and read it so the people could hear him. And they said, "We will do everything that the LORD has said; we will obey."

8 Then Moses took the blood from the bowls and sprinkled it on the people, saying, "This is the blood that begins the Agreement, the Agreement which the LORD has made with you about all these words."

9 Moses, Aaron, Nadab, Abihu and 70 of the elders of Israel went up the mountain 10 and saw the God of Israel. Under his feet was a surface that looked as if it were paved with blue sapphire stones and it was as clear as the sky! 11 These leaders of the Israelites saw God, but God did not destroy them. Then they ate and drank together.

God Promises Moses the Stone Tablets

12 The LORD said to Moses, "Come up the mountain to me. Wait there, and I will give you two stone tablets. On these are the teachings and the commands I have written to teach the people."

13 So Moses and his helper Joshua set out, and Moses went up to Sinai, the mountain of God. 14 Moses said to the elders, "Wait here for us until we come back to you. Aaron and Hur are with you, and anyone who has a disagreement with others can take it to them."

Moses Meets with God

15 When Moses went up on the mountain, the cloud covered it. 16 The glory of the LORD came down on Mount Sinai, and the cloud covered it for six days. On the seventh day the LORD called to Moses from inside the cloud. 17 To the Israelites the glory of the LORD looked like a fire burning on top of the mountain. 18 Then Moses went into the cloud and went higher up the mountain. He was on the mountain for 40 days and 40 nights.

Gifts for the LORD

25 The LORD said to Moses, 2 "Tell the Israelites to bring me gifts. Receive for me the gifts each person wants to give. 3 These are the gifts that you should receive from them: gold, silver and bronze; 4 blue, purple and red thread; fine linen, goat hair and 5 ram's skins that are dyed red; fine leather; acacia wood; 6 olive oil to burn in the lamps; spices for sweet-smelling incense, and the special olive oil poured on a person's head to make him a priest; and 7 onyx stones and other jewels to be put on the holy robe and the chest covering.

8 "The people must build a holy place for me so that I can live among them.

> The LORD said to Moses, "Come up the mountain to me. Wait there, and I will give you two stone tablets."
> – Exodus 24:12

9 Build this Holy Tent and everything in it by the plan I will show you.

The Ark of the Agreement

10 "Use acacia wood and build an Ark 110 centimetres long, 70 centimetres wide and 70 centimetres high. 11 Cover the Ark inside and out with pure gold, and put a gold strip all around it. 12 Make four gold rings for the Ark and attach them to its four feet, two rings on each side. 13 Then make poles from acacia wood and cover them with gold. 14 Put the poles through the rings on the sides of the Ark, and use these poles to carry it. 15 These poles must always stay in the rings of the Ark. Do not take them out. 16 Then put in the Ark the Agreement which I will make with you.

17 "Then make a lid of pure gold for the Ark; this is the mercy seat. Make it 110 centimetres long and 70 centimetres wide. 18 Then hammer gold to make two creatures with wings, and put one on each end of the lid. 19 Attach one creature on one end of the lid and the other creature on the other end. Make them to be one piece with the lid at the ends. 20 The creatures' wings should be spread upwards, covering the lid, and the creatures are to face each other across the lid. 21 Put this lid on top of the Ark, and put in the Ark the Agreement which I will make with you. 22 I will meet with you there, above the lid between the two winged creatures on the Ark of the Agreement. There I will give you all my commands for the Israelites.

The Table

23 "Make a table out of acacia wood, 90 centimetres long, 50 centimetres wide and 70 centimetres high. 24 Cover it with pure gold, and put a gold strip around it. 25 Make a frame 8 centimetres high that stands up all around the edge, and put a gold strip around it. 26 Then make four gold rings. Attach them to the four corners of the table where the four legs are. 27 Put the rings close to the frame around the top of the table, because they will hold the poles for carrying it. 28 Make the poles out of acacia wood, cover them with gold, and carry the table with these poles. 29 Make the plates and bowls for the table, as well as the jars and cups, out of pure gold. They will be used for pouring out the drink offerings. 30 On this table put the bread that shows you are in my presence so that it is always there in front of me.

The Lampstand

31 "Hammer pure gold to make a lampstand. Its base, stand, flower-like cups, buds and petals must all be joined together in one piece. 32 The lampstand must have six branches going out from its sides—three on one side and three on the other. 33 Each branch must have three cups shaped like almond flowers on it. Each cup must have a bud and a petal. Each of the six branches going out from the lampstand must be the same. 34 And there must be four more cups made like almond flowers on the lampstand itself. These cups must also have buds and petals. 35 Put a bud under each pair of branches that goes out from the lampstand. Each of the six branches going out from the lampstand must be the same. 36 The branches, buds and lampstand must be made of one piece, hammered out of pure gold.

37 "Then make seven small oil lamps and put them on the lampstand so that they give light to the area in front of it. 38 The wick trimmers and trays must be made of pure gold. 39 Use 34 kilogrammes of pure gold to make the lampstand and everything with it. 40 Be very careful to make them by the plan I showed you on the mountain.

> "The people must build a holy place for me so that I can live among them."
> – Exodus 25:8

The Holy Tent

26 "Make for the Holy Tent ten curtains of fine linen and blue, purple and red thread. Have a skilled craftsman sew designs of creatures with wings on the pieces of cloth. 2 Make each curtain the same size—14 metres long and 2 metres wide. 3 Sew five curtains together for one set, and sew the other curtains together for the second set. 4 Make loops of blue cloth on the edge of the end curtain of one set, and do the same for the end curtain of the other set. 5 Make 50 loops on the end curtain of the first set and 50 loops on the end curtain of the second set. These loops must be opposite each other. 6 And make 50 gold hooks to join the two sets of curtains so that the Holy Tent is one piece.

7 "Then make another tent that will cover the Holy Tent, using eleven curtains made from goat hair. 8 All these curtains must be the same size—15 metres long and 2 metres wide. 9 Sew five of the curtains together into one set. Then sew the other six curtains together into the second set. Fold the sixth curtain double over the front of the Tent. 10 Make 50 loops down the edge of the end curtain of one set, and do the same for the end curtain of the other set. 11 Then make 50 bronze hooks and put them in the loops to join the tent together so that the covering is one piece. 12 Let the extra half piece of cloth hang over the back of the Holy Tent. 13 There will be 50 centimetres hanging over the sides of the Holy Tent, to protect it. 14 Make a covering for the Holy Tent from ram's skins coloured red, and over that make a covering from fine leather.

15 "Use acacia wood to make upright frames for the Holy Tent. 16 Each frame must be 5 metres long and 70 centimetres wide, 17 with two pegs side by side. Every frame must be made in this way. 18 Make 20 frames for the south side of the Holy Tent. 19 Each frame must have two silver bases to go under it, a peg fitting into each base. You must make 40 silver bases for the frames. 20 Make 20 more frames for the north side of the Holy Tent 21 and 40 silver bases for them—two bases for each frame. 22 You must make six frames for the rear or west end of the Holy Tent 23 and two frames for each corner at the rear. 24 The two frames are to be doubled at the bottom and joined at the top with a metal ring. Both corner frames must be made in this way. 25 So there will be a total of eight frames at the rear of the Tent, and there will be sixteen silver bases—two bases under each frame.

26 "Make crossbars of acacia wood to connect the upright frames of the Holy Tent. Make five crossbars to hold the frames together on one side 27 and five to hold the frames together on the other side. Also make five crossbars to hold the frames together on the west end, at the rear. 28 The middle crossbar is to be set halfway up the frames, and it is to run along the entire length of each side and rear. 29 Make gold rings on the sides of the frames to hold the crossbars, and cover the frames and the crossbars with gold. 30 Set up the Holy Tent by the plan shown to you on the mountain.

31 "Make a curtain of fine linen and blue, purple and red thread, and have a skilled craftsman sew designs of creatures with wings on it. 32 Hang the curtain by gold hooks on four posts of acacia wood that are covered with gold, and set them in four silver bases. 33 Hang the curtain from the hooks in the roof, and put the Ark of the Agreement containing the two flat stones behind it. This curtain will separate the Holy Place from the Most Holy Place. 34 Put the lid on the Ark of the Agreement in the Most Holy Place.

35 "Outside the curtain, put the table on the north side of the Holy Tent. Put the lampstand on the south side of the Holy Tent across from the table.

> Set up the Holy Tent by the plan shown to you on the mountain.
> – Exodus 26:30

CHURCH ON THE ROAD Exodus 27:9–19

The Meeting Tent was a moveable church tent. The Israelites used the Meeting Tent as their church when they were wandering through the wilderness on their way back home from Egypt. Sometimes it is called the "Holy Tent". Wherever they stopped to camp, they put up the Meeting Tent in the centre of the camp. God himself taught the Israelites how to build the Meeting Tent and how to take care of it.

The Meeting Tent measured 5 by 15 metres and had two main sections: the outer room, known as the Holy Place, and the inner room called the Most Holy Place. (See Exodus 26:33.) The only person who went into the Most Holy Place was the high priest. He only went in there once a year to offer a sacrifice for his sins and the sins of all the people. There was only one thing in this place: the Ark of the Agreement.

The Israelites used the Meeting Tent for their place of worship until Solomon built the Temple in Jerusalem.

The Entrance of the Holy Tent

36 "Then, for the entrance of the Tent, make a curtain with fine linen and blue, purple and red thread. Someone who can sew well is to sew designs on it. 37 Make five posts of acacia wood covered with gold. Make gold hooks for them on which to hang the curtain, and make five bronze bases for them.

The Altar for Burnt Offerings

27 "Make an altar of acacia wood, 1.5 metres high. It should be square—2.5 metres long and 2.5 metres wide. 2 Make each of the four corners of the altar stick out like a horn, in such a way that the corners with their horns are all one piece. Then cover the whole altar with bronze.

3 "Use bronze to make all the tools and dishes that will be used on the altar: the pots to remove the ashes, the shovels, the bowls for sprinkling blood, the meat forks and the pans for carrying the burning wood.

4 "Make a large bronze screen to hold the burning wood, and put a bronze ring at each of the four corners of it. 5 Put the screen inside the altar, under its rim, halfway up from the bottom.

6 "Make poles of acacia wood for the altar, and cover them with bronze. 7 Put the poles through the rings on both sides of the altar to carry it. 8 Make the altar out of boards and leave the inside hollow. Make it as you were shown on the mountain.

The Courtyard of the Holy Tent

9 "Make a wall of curtains to form a courtyard around the Holy Tent. The south side should have a wall of fine linen curtains 50 metres long. 10 Hang the curtains with silver hooks and bands on 20 bronze posts with 20 bronze bases. 11 The north side must also be 50 metres long. Hang its curtains on silver hooks and bands on 20 bronze posts with 20 bronze bases.

12 "The west end of the courtyard

must have a wall of curtains 25 metres long, with ten posts and ten bases on that wall. 13 The east end of the courtyard must also be 25 metres long. 14 On one side of the entry, there is to be a wall of curtains 7.5 metres long, held up by three posts on three bases. 15 On the other side of the entry, there is also to be a wall of curtains 7.5 metres long, held up by three posts on three bases.

16 "The entry to the courtyard is to be a curtain 10 metres wide, made of fine linen with blue, purple and red thread. Someone who can sew well is to sew designs on it. It is to be held up by four posts on four bases. 17 All the posts around the courtyard must have silver bands and hooks and bronze bases. 18 The courtyard must be 50 metres long and 25 metres wide, with a wall of curtains around it 2.5 metres high, made of fine linen. The bases in which the posts are set must be bronze. 19 All the things used in the Holy Tent and all the tent pegs for the Holy Tent and the wall around the courtyard must be made of bronze.

Oil for the Lamp

20 "Command the people of Israel to bring you pure olive oil, made from pressed olives, to keep the lamps on the lampstand burning. 21 Aaron and his sons must keep the lamps burning before the LORD from evening till morning. This will be in the Meeting Tent, outside the curtain which is in front of the Ark. The Israelites and their descendants must obey this rule from now on.

Clothes for the Priests

28 "Tell your brother Aaron to come to you, along with his sons Nadab, Abihu, Eleazar and Ithamar. Separate them from the other Israelites to serve me as priests. 2 Make holy clothes for your brother Aaron to give him honour and beauty. 3 Tell all the skilled craftsmen to whom I have given wisdom to make special clothes for Aaron—clothes to show that he belongs to me so that he may serve me as a priest. 4 These are the clothes they must make: a chest covering, a holy robe, an outer robe, a woven inner robe, a turban and a cloth belt. The craftsmen must make these holy clothes for your brother Aaron and his sons. Then they may serve me as priests. 5 The craftsmen must use gold and blue, purple and red thread, and fine linen.

The Holy Robe

6 "Use gold and blue, purple and red thread, and fine linen to make the holy robe; skilled craftsmen are to make it. 7 At each top corner of this holy robe there will be a pair of shoulder straps tied together over each shoulder.

8 "The craftsmen will very carefully weave a belt on the holy robe that is made with the same materials—gold and blue, purple and red thread, and fine linen.

9 "Take two onyx stones and write the names of the twelve sons of Israel on them, 10 six on one stone and six on the other. Write the names in order, from the oldest son to the youngest. 11 Carve the names of the sons of Israel on these stones in the same way that a person carves words and designs on a seal. Put gold around the stones to hold them on the holy robe. 12 Then put the two stones on the two straps of the holy robe as reminders of the twelve sons of Israel. Aaron is to wear their names on his shoulders in the presence of the LORD as reminders of the sons of Israel. 13 Make two gold pieces to hold the stones 14 and two chains of pure gold, twisted together like a rope. Attach the chains to the two gold pieces that hold the stones.

The Chest Covering

15 "Make a chest covering to help in making decisions. The craftsmen should make it as they made the holy robe, using gold and blue, purple and red thread, and fine linen. 16 The chest covering must be square—23 centimetres long and 23 centimetres wide—and folded double to make a pocket. 17 Put four rows of beautiful gems on the chest covering: the first row must have a ruby, a topaz and a yellow quartz; 18 the second must have turquoise, a sapphire and an emerald;

19 the third must have a jacinth, an agate and an amethyst; 20 the fourth must have a chrysolite, an onyx and a jasper. Put gold around these jewels to attach them to the chest covering. 21 There must be twelve jewels on the chest covering—one jewel for each of the names of the sons of Israel. Carve the name of one of the twelve tribes on each of the stones as you would carve a seal.

22 "Make chains of pure gold, twisted together like rope, for the chest covering. 23 Make two gold rings and put them on the two upper corners of the chest covering. 24 Attach the two gold chains to the two rings at the upper corners of the chest covering. 25 Attach the other ends of the two chains to the two gold pieces on the shoulder straps in the front of the holy robe.

26 "Make two gold rings and put them at the two lower corners of the chest covering, on the inside edge next to the holy robe. 27 Make two more gold rings and attach them to the bottom of the shoulder straps in the front of the holy robe. Put them close to the seam above the woven belt of the holy robe. 28 Join the rings of the chest covering to the rings of the holy robe with blue ribbon, connecting it to the woven belt so the chest covering will not swing out from the holy robe.

29 "When Aaron enters the Holy Place, he will wear the names of the sons of Israel over his heart, on the chest covering that helps in making decisions. This will be a continual reminder before the LORD. 30 And put the Urim and Thummim inside the chest covering so that they will be on Aaron's heart when he goes before the LORD. They will help in making decisions for the Israelites. So Aaron will always carry them with him when he is before the LORD.

31 "Make the outer robe to be worn under the holy robe, using only blue cloth. 32 Make a hole in the centre for Aaron's head, with a woven collar around the hole so it will not tear. 33 Make balls like pomegranates of blue, purple and red thread, and hang them around the bottom of the outer robe with gold bells between them. 34 All around the bottom of the outer robe there should be a gold bell and a pomegranate ball, a gold bell and a pomegranate ball. 35 Aaron must wear this robe when he serves as priest. The ringing of the bells will be heard when he enters and leaves the Holy Place before the LORD so that Aaron will not die.

36 "Make a strip of pure gold and carve these words on it as you would carve a seal: 'Holy to the LORD'. 37 Use blue ribbon to tie it to the turban; put it on the front of the turban. 38 Aaron must wear this on his forehead. In this way, he will be blamed if anything is wrong with the gifts of the Israelites. Aaron must always wear this on his head so the LORD will accept the gifts of the people.

39 "Make the woven inner robe of fine linen, and make the turban of fine linen also. Make the cloth belt with designs sewn on it. 40 Also make woven inner robes, cloth belts and headbands for Aaron's sons, to give them honour and beauty. 41 Put these clothes on your brother Aaron and his sons, and pour olive oil on their heads to appoint them as priests. Make them belong to me so they may serve me as priests.

42 "Make for them linen underclothes to cover them from the waist to the upper parts of the legs. 43 Aaron and his sons must wear these underclothes when they enter the Meeting Tent and whenever they come near the altar to serve as priests in the Holy Place. If they do not wear these clothes, they will be guilty of wrong, and they will die. This will be a law that will last from now on for Aaron and all his descendants.

Appointing the Priests

29 "This is what you must do to appoint Aaron and his sons to

> Make a strip of pure gold and carve these words on it as you would carve a seal: "Holy to the LORD".
> – Exodus 28:36

serve me as priests. Take one young bull and two rams that have nothing wrong with them. 2 Use fine wheat flour without yeast to make bread, cakes mixed with olive oil, and wafers brushed with olive oil. 3 Put these in one basket, and bring them along with the bull and two rams. 4 Bring Aaron and his sons to the entrance of the Meeting Tent and wash them with water. 5 Take the clothes and dress Aaron in the inner robe and the outer robe of the holy robe. Then put on him the holy robe and the chest covering, and tie the holy robe on him with its skilfully woven belt. 6 Put the turban on his head, and put the holy crown on the turban. 7 Take the special olive oil and pour it on his head to make him a priest.

8 "Then bring his sons and put the inner robes on them. 9 Put the headbands on their heads, and tie cloth belts around their waists. Aaron and his descendants will be priests in Israel, according to a rule that will continue from now on. This is how you will appoint Aaron and his sons as priests.

10 "Bring the bull to the front of the Meeting Tent, and Aaron and his sons must put their hands on the bull's head. 11 Then kill the bull before the LORD at the entrance to the Meeting Tent. 12 Use your finger to put some of the bull's blood on the corners of the altar, and then pour the blood that is left at the bottom of the altar. 13 Take all the fat that covers the inner organs, as well as the best part of the liver, both kidneys and the fat around them, and burn them on the altar. 14 Take the bull's meat, skin and intestines, and burn them outside the camp. This is an offering to take away sin.

15 "Take one of the rams, and have Aaron and his sons put their hands on its head. 16 Kill it, and take its blood and sprinkle it on all four sides of the altar. 17 Then cut it into pieces and wash its inner organs and its legs, putting them with its head and its other pieces. 18 Burn the whole ram on the altar; it is a burnt offering made by fire to the LORD. Its smell is pleasing to the LORD.

19 "Take the other ram, and have Aaron and his sons put their hands on its head. 20 Kill it and take some of its blood. Put the blood on the bottom of the right ears of Aaron and his sons and on the thumbs of their right hands and on the big toes of their right feet. Then sprinkle the rest of the blood against all four sides of the altar. 21 Take some of the blood from the altar, and mix it with the special oil used in appointing priests. Sprinkle this on Aaron and his clothes, and on his sons and their clothes. This will show that Aaron and his sons and their clothes are given to my service.

22 "Then take the fat from the rams, the fat tail and the fat that covers the inner organs. In addition, take the best part of the liver, both kidneys, and the fat around them, and the right thigh. (This is the ram to be used in appointing priests.)

23 "Then take the basket of bread that you made without yeast, which you put before the LORD. From it take a loaf of bread, a cake made with olive oil and a wafer. 24 Put all these in the hands of Aaron and his sons, and tell them to present them as an offering to the LORD. 25 Then take them from their hands and burn them on the altar with the whole burnt offering. This is an offering made by fire to the LORD; its smell is pleasing to the LORD. 26 Then take the breast of the ram used to appoint Aaron as priest, and present it before the LORD as an offering. This part of the animal will be your share. 27 Set aside the breast and the thigh of the sheep that were used to appoint Aaron and his sons as priests. These parts belong to them. 28 They are to be the regular share which the Israelites will always give to Aaron and his sons. It is the gift the Israelites must give to the LORD from their fellowship offerings.

29 "The holy clothes made for Aaron will belong to his descendants so that they can wear these clothes when they are appointed as priests. 30 Aaron's son, who will become high priest after Aaron, will come to the Meeting Tent to serve in the Holy Place. He is to wear these clothes for seven days.

31 "Take the ram used to appoint

priests and boil its meat in a place that is holy. 32 Then at the entrance of the Meeting Tent, Aaron and his sons must eat the meat of the ram and the bread that is in the basket. 33 They should eat these offerings that were used to remove their sins and to make them holy when they were made priests. But no one else is to eat them, because they are holy things. 34 If any of the meat from that sheep or any of the bread is left the next morning, it must be burned. It must not be eaten, because it is holy.

35 "Do all these things that I commanded you to do to Aaron and his sons, and spend seven days appointing them. 36 Each day you are to offer a bull to remove the sins of Aaron and his sons so they will be given for service to the LORD. Make the altar ready for service to the LORD, and pour oil on it to make it holy. 37 Spend seven days making the altar ready for service to God and making it holy. Then the altar will become very holy, and anything that touches it must be holy.

The Daily Sacrifices

38 "Every day from now on, offer on the altar two lambs that are one year old. 39 Offer one lamb in the morning and the other in the evening before dark. 40 In the morning, when you offer the first lamb, offer also two litres of fine flour mixed with one litre of oil from pressed olives. Pour out one litre of wine as a drink offering. 41 Offer the second lamb in the evening with the same grain offering and drink offering as you did in the morning. This is an offering made by fire to the LORD, and its smell is pleasing to him.

42 "You must burn these things as an offering to the LORD every day, from now on, at the entrance of the Meeting Tent before the LORD. When you make the offering, I, the LORD, will meet you there and speak to you. 43 I will meet with the people of Israel there, and that place will be holy because of my glory.

44 "So I will make the Meeting Tent and the altar holy; I will also make Aaron and his sons holy so they may serve me as priests. 45 I will live with the people of Israel and be their God. 46 And they will know that I am the LORD their God who led them out of Egypt so that I could live with them. I am the LORD their God.

> I will live with the people of Israel and be their God.
> – Exodus 29:45

The Altar for Burning Incense

30 "Make an altar out of acacia wood for burning incense. 2 Make it square—50 centimetres long and 50 centimetres wide—and make it 90 centimetres high. The corners that stick out like horns must be one piece with the altar. 3 Cover its top, its sides and its corners with pure gold, and put a gold strip all around the altar. 4 Make two gold rings beneath the gold strip on opposite sides of the altar, and slide poles through them to carry the altar. 5 Make the poles from acacia wood and cover them with gold. 6 Put the altar of incense in front of the curtain that is near the Ark of the Agreement, in front of the lid that covers that Ark. There I will meet with you.

7 "Aaron must burn sweet-smelling incense on the altar every morning when he comes to take care of the oil lamps. 8 He must burn incense again in the evening when he lights the lamps, so incense will burn before the LORD every day from now on. 9 Do not use this altar for offering any other incense or burnt offering, or any kind of grain offering or drink offering. 10 Once a year Aaron must make the altar ready for service to God by putting blood on its corners—the blood of the animal offered to remove sins. He is to do this once a year from now on. This altar belongs completely to the LORD's service."

The Tax for the Meeting Tent

11 The LORD said to Moses, 12 "When you count the people of Israel, every

person must buy back his life from the LORD so that no terrible things will happen to the people when you number them. 13 Every person who is counted must pay 6 grammes of silver. (This is set by using a half of the Holy Place measure, which weighs 12 grammes.) This amount is a gift to the LORD. 14 Every person who is counted and is 20 years old or older must give this amount to the LORD. 15 A rich person must not give more than 6 grammes, and a poor person must not give less. You are paying this to the LORD to buy back your lives. 16 Gather from the people of Israel this money paid to buy back their lives, and spend it on things for the service in the Meeting Tent. This payment will remind the LORD that the Israelites' lives have been bought back."

The Bronze Bowl

17 The LORD said to Moses, 18 "Make a bronze bowl, on a bronze stand, for washing. Put the bowl and stand between the Meeting Tent and the altar, and put water in the bowl. 19 Aaron and his sons must wash their hands and feet with the water from this bowl. 20 Each time they enter the Meeting Tent they must wash with water so they will not die. Each time they approach the altar to serve as priests and offer a sacrifice to the LORD by fire, 21 they must wash their hands and their feet so that they will not die. This is a rule which Aaron and his descendants are to keep from now on."

Oil for Appointing

22 Then the LORD said to Moses, 23 "Take the finest spices: 6 kilogrammes of liquid myrrh, half that amount (that is, 3 kilogrammes) of sweet-smelling cinnamon, 3 kilogrammes of sweet-smelling cane 24 and 6 kilogrammes of cassia. Weigh all these by the Holy Place measure. Also take 4 litres of olive oil, 25 and mix all these things like a perfume to make a holy olive oil. This special oil must be put on people and things to make them ready for service to God. 26 Put this oil on the Meeting Tent and the Ark of the Agreement, 27 on the table and all its dishes, on the lampstand and all its tools, and on the incense altar. 28 Also, put the oil on the altar for burnt offerings and on all its tools, as well as on the bowl and the stand under the bowl. 29 You will prepare all these things for service to God, and they will be very holy. Anything that touches these things must be holy.

30 "Put the oil on Aaron and his sons to give them for service to me, that they may serve me as priests. 31 Tell the Israelites, 'This is to be my holy olive oil from now on. It is to be put on people and things to make them ready for service to God. 32 Do not pour it on the bodies of ordinary people, and do not make perfume in the same way that you make this oil. It is holy, and you must treat it as holy. 33 If anyone makes perfume like it or puts it on someone who is not a priest, that person must be cut off from his people.'"

Incense

34 Then the LORD said to Moses, "Take these sweet-smelling spices: resin, onycha, galbanum and pure frankincense. Be sure that you have equal amounts of each. 35 Make incense as a person who makes perfume would do. Add salt to it to keep it pure and holy. 36 Beat some of the incense into a fine powder, and put it in front of the Ark of the Agreement in the Meeting Tent, where I will meet with you. You must use this incense powder only for its very special purpose. 37 Do not make incense for yourselves in the same way that you make this incense. Treat it as holy to the LORD. 38 Whoever makes incense like this to use as perfume must be cut off from his people."

Bezalel and Oholiab Help

31 Then the LORD said to Moses, 2 "See, I have chosen Bezalel, son of Uri, from the tribe of Judah. (Uri was the son of Hur.) 3 I have filled Bezalel with the Spirit of God and have given him the skill, ability and knowledge to do all kinds of work. 4 He is able to design pieces to be made from gold, silver and bronze, 5 to cut jewels and put them in metal, to carve wood, and to do all kinds of work.

FAITH links

SERIOUS ABOUT THE SABBATH
EXODUS 31:15

What's the best day of the week for you? Friday? Saturday? Any day that you don't have to go to school? God has a special day, too – the Sabbath day. God set this as a day for the people to rest and think about him. How serious was God about keeping the Sabbath? Serious enough to slap the death penalty on anyone who broke the Sabbath. That's why keeping the Sabbath is mentioned a number of times in Exodus (16:23; 20:8; 23:12; 35:2) and other places. (Look up Leviticus 19:30, p. 161.)

For Christians, the Sabbath day is Sunday. Most Christians attend a worship service as their way of keeping the Sabbath. How do you show how special this day is for you?

Time to Celebrate, Exodus 15:1–21, p. 95

A Holiday Every Week, Leviticus 23:1–3, p. 166

Plans for a Son, 1 Chronicles 22:5–19, p. 548

The Number One Rule, Mark 12:28–31, p. 1351

A Christian's Responsibility, Acts 11:26, p. 1484

Meeting Together, 1 Corinthians 16:19, p. 1567

Exodus 31:18 117

6 I have also chosen Oholiab, son of Ahisamach, from the tribe of Dan to work with Bezalel. I have given skills to all the craftsmen, and they will be able to make all these things I have commanded you: 7 the Meeting Tent, the Ark of the Agreement, the lid that covers the Ark, and everything in the Tent. 8 This includes the table and everything on it, the pure gold lampstand and everything with it, the altar of incense, 9 the altar for burnt offerings and everything used with it, and the bowl and the stand under it. 10 They will make the woven clothes and the holy clothes for Aaron and the clothes for his sons to wear when they serve as priests. 11 They will also make the special olive oil used in appointing people and things to the service of the LORD, and the sweet-smelling incense for the Holy Place.

"These workers will make all these things just as I have commanded you."

The Day of Rest

12 Then the LORD said to Moses, 13 "Tell the Israelites, 'You must keep the rules about my Sabbaths, because they will be a sign between you and me from now on. In this way you will know that I, the LORD, make you holy.

14 "Make the Sabbath a holy day. If anyone treats the Sabbath like any other day, that person must be put to death; anyone who works on the Sabbath day must be cut off from his people. 15 There are six days for working, but the seventh day is a day of rest, a day holy for the LORD. Anyone who works during the Sabbath day must be put to death. 16 The Israelites must remember the Sabbath day as an agreement between them and me that will continue from now on. 17 The Sabbath day will be a sign between me and the Israelites for ever, because in six days I, the LORD, made the sky and the earth. On the seventh day I did not work: I rested.'"

18 When the LORD finished speaking to Moses on Mount Sinai, he gave him the two stone tablets with the Agreement written on them, written by the finger of God.

The People Make a Gold Calf

32 The people saw that a long time had passed and Moses had not come down from the mountain. So they gathered around Aaron and said, "Moses led us out of Egypt, but we don't know what has happened to him. Make us gods who will lead us."

2 Aaron said to the people, "Take off the gold earrings that your wives, sons and daughters are wearing, and bring them to me." 3 So all the people took their gold earrings and brought them to Aaron. 4 He took the gold from the people and formed it with a tool and made a statue of a calf. Then the people said, "Israel, these are your gods who brought you out of the land of Egypt!"

5 When Aaron saw all this, he built an altar before the calf and announced, "Tomorrow there will be a special feast to honour the LORD." 6 The people got up early the next morning and offered whole burnt offerings and fellowship offerings. They sat down to eat and drink, and then they got up and sinned sexually.

7 Then the LORD said to Moses, "Go down from this mountain, because your people, the people you brought out of the land of Egypt, have ruined themselves. 8 They have quickly turned away from the things I commanded them to do. They have made for themselves a calf covered with gold, and they have worshipped it and offered sacrifices to it. They have said, 'Israel, these are your gods who brought you out of Egypt.'"

9 The LORD said to Moses, "I have seen these people, and I know that they are very stubborn. 10 So now do not stop me. I am so angry with them that I am going to destroy them. Then I will make you and your descendants a great nation."

11 But Moses begged the LORD his God and said, "LORD, don't let your anger destroy your people, whom you brought out of Egypt with your great power and strength. 12 Don't let the people of Egypt say, 'The LORD brought the Israelites out of Egypt for an evil purpose. He planned to kill them in the mountains and destroy them from the earth.' So stop being angry, and don't destroy your people.

13 Remember the men who served you— Abraham, Isaac and Israel. You promised with an oath to them and said, 'I will make your descendants as many as the stars in

---

FAITH links

IDOL TALK

EXODUS 32

What is an idol? It is anyone or anything that takes the place of God in your life. The Israelites sinned by worshipping a gold calf that Aaron made. When God gave the Ten Commandments, he told the people of Israel never to worship anyone or anything besides him. The consequences of disobedience were high for the people of Israel. Many died that day.

Some people "worship" money, other people, or fame. That's all they can think about. Got any idols in your life? Give 'em the heave-ho! God wants first place in your life. He won't share that place with anyone or anything!

What He's Really Like, Deuteronomy 4:15–20, p. 233

No Middle Ground, Joshua 24:14–15, p. 307

What I've Got, 2 Kings 20:12–17, p. 508

The Foundation of Our Hope, Isaiah 31:1–8, p. 934

Faith That Pleases God, Luke 7:1–9, p. 1380

Your Heart's Desire, Luke 16:13–15, p. 1401

the sky. I will give your descendants all this land that I have promised them, and it will be theirs for ever.'" 14 So the LORD changed his mind and did not destroy the people as he had said he might.

15 Then Moses went down the mountain, and in his hands he had the two stone tablets with the Agreement on them. The commands were written on both sides of each stone, front and back. 16 God himself had made the tablets, and God himself had written the commands on the tablets.

17 When Joshua heard the sound of the people shouting, he said to Moses, "It sounds like war down in the camp."

18 Moses answered:
"It is not a shout of victory;
it is not a cry of defeat.
It is the sound of singing that I hear."

19 When Moses came close to the camp, he saw the gold calf and the dancing, and he became very angry. He threw down the stone tablets that he was carrying and broke them at the bottom of the mountain. 20 Then he took the calf that the people had made and melted it in the fire. He ground it into powder. Then he threw the powder into the water and forced the Israelites to drink it.

21 Moses said to Aaron, "What did these people do to you? Why did you cause them to do such a terrible sin?"

22 Aaron answered, "Don't be angry, master. You know that these people are always ready to do wrong. 23 The people said to me, 'Moses led us out of Egypt, but we don't know what has happened to him. Make us gods who will lead us.' 24 So I told the people, 'Take off your gold jewellery.' When they gave me the gold, I threw it into the fire and out came this calf!"

25 Moses saw that the people were acting wildly. Aaron had let them get out of control and become fools in front of their enemies. 26 So Moses stood at the entrance to the camp and said, "Let anyone who wants to follow the LORD come to me." And all the people from the family of Levi gathered around Moses.

27 Then Moses said to them, "The LORD, the God of Israel, says this: 'Every man must put on his sword and go through the camp from one end to the other. Each man must kill his brother, his friend and his neighbour.'" 28 The people from the family of Levi obeyed Moses, and that day about 3,000 of the Israelites died. 29 Then Moses said, "Today you have been given for service to the LORD. You were willing to kill your own sons and brothers, and God has blessed you for this."

30 The next day Moses told the people, "You have done a terrible sin. But now I will go up to the LORD. Maybe I can do something so your sins will be removed." 31 So Moses went back to the LORD and said, "How terribly these people have sinned! They have made for themselves gods from gold. 32 Now, please forgive them this sin. If you will not, then erase my name from the book in which you have written the names of your people."

33 But the LORD told Moses, "I will erase from my book the names of the people who sin against me. 34 So now, go. Lead the people where I have told you, and my angel will lead you. When the time comes to punish, I will punish them for their sin."

EMAIL FROM GOD
32:34
Sin
Is there punishment for your sin?

35 So the LORD caused terrible things to happen to the people because of what they did with the calf Aaron had made.

33 Then the LORD said to Moses, "You and the people you brought out of Egypt must leave this place. Go to the land that I promised with an oath to give to Abraham, Isaac and Jacob when I said, 'I will give that land to your descendants.' 2 I will send an angel to lead you, and I will force these people out of the land: the Canaanites, Amorites, Hittites, Perizzites, Hivites and Jebusites. 3 Go up to a fertile land. But I will not go with you, because I might destroy you on the way, since you are such a stubborn people."

4 When the people heard this bad news, they became very sad, and none of

them put on jewellery. 5 This was because the LORD had said to Moses, "Tell the Israelites, 'You are a stubborn people. If I were to go with you even for a moment, I would destroy you. So take off all your jewellery, and I will decide what to do with you.'" 6 So the people of Israel took off their jewellery at Mount Sinai.

The Meeting Tent

7 Moses used to take a tent and set it up a long way outside the camp; he called it the "Meeting Tent". Anyone who wanted to ask the LORD about something would go to the Meeting Tent outside the camp. 8 Whenever Moses went out to the Tent, all the people would rise and stand at the entrances of their tents, watching him until he entered the Meeting Tent. 9 When Moses went into the Tent, the pillar of cloud would always come down and stay at the entrance of the Tent while the LORD spoke with Moses. 10 Whenever the people saw the pillar of cloud at the entrance of the Tent, they stood and worshipped, each person at the entrance of his own tent.

11 The LORD spoke to Moses face to face as a man speaks with his friend. Then Moses would return to the camp, but Moses' young helper, Joshua son of Nun, did not leave the Tent.

12 Moses said to the LORD, "You have told me to lead these people, but you did not say whom you would send with me. You have said to me, 'I know you very well, and I am pleased with you.' 13 If I have truly pleased you, show me your plans so that I may know you and continue to please you. Remember that this nation is your people."

14 The LORD answered, "I myself will go with you, and I will give you victory."

15 Then Moses said to him, "If you yourself don't go with us, then don't send us away from this place. 16 If you don't go with us, no one will know that you are pleased with me and with your people. These people and I will be no different from any other people on earth."

17 Then the LORD said to Moses, "I will do what you ask, because I know you very well, and I am pleased with you."

FAITH links

THE NAME OF THE LORD
EXODUS 33:19-23; 34:5-8

Ever wish you could see God face-to-face? Although he could hear God speak to him, Moses wanted to "see" God. He wanted to know that God was around. God allowed him to understand the richness of his love in a special way. He passed by Moses calling out his own name. God's character is wrapped up in his name. His name describes what he does.

We can understand the richness of God's love through one name: *Jesus*. His name describes what he did. The name *Jesus* means "salvation". He saved us from sin. When we pray, we go to God in Jesus' name. One day, we will see Jesus face-to-face!

What's in a Name? Isaiah 9:6, p. 908

God's New Temple, Ezekiel 40—44, p. 1135

Concern for All, Daniel 9, p. 1165

Name with a Purpose, Matthew 1:21, p. 1274

Remembering Jesus, Matthew 26:26–29, p. 1321

MVFM? Galatians 3:26–27, p. 1589

Moses Sees God's Glory

18 Then Moses said, "Now, please show me your glory."

19 The LORD answered, "I will cause all my goodness to pass in front of you, and I will announce my name, the LORD, so you can hear it. I will show kindness to anyone to whom I want to show kindness, and I will show mercy to anyone to whom I want to show mercy. 20 But you cannot see my face, because no one can see me and live.

21 "There is a place near me where you may stand on a rock. 22 When my glory passes that place, I will put you in a large crack in the rock and cover you with my hand until I have passed by. 23 Then I will take away my hand, and you will see my back. But my face must not be seen."

Moses Gets New Stone Tablets

34 The LORD said to Moses, "Cut two more stone tablets like the first two, and I will write the same words on them that were on the first two stones which you broke. 2 Be ready tomorrow morning, and then come up on Mount Sinai. Stand before me there on the top of the mountain. 3 No one may come with you or even be seen anywhere on the mountain. Not even the flocks or herds may eat grass near that mountain."

4 So Moses cut two stone tablets like the first ones. Then early the next morning he went up Mount Sinai, just as the LORD had commanded him, carrying the two stone tablets with him. 5 Then the LORD came down in the cloud and stood there with Moses, and the LORD called out his name: the LORD.

6 The LORD passed in front of Moses and said, "I am the LORD. The LORD is a God who shows mercy, who is kind, who doesn't become angry quickly, who has great love and faithfulness 7 and is kind to thousands of people. The LORD forgives people for evil, for sin and for turning against him, but he does not forget to punish guilty people. He will punish not only the guilty people, but also their children, their grandchildren, their great-grandchildren and their great-great-grandchildren."

8 Then Moses quickly bowed to the ground and worshipped. 9 He said, "Lord, if you are pleased with me, please go with us. I know that these are stubborn people, but forgive our evil and our sin. Take us as your own people."

10 Then the LORD said, "I am making this agreement with you. I will do miracles in front of all your people—things that have never before been done for any other nation on earth—and the people with you will see my work. I, the LORD, will do wonderful things for you. 11 Obey the things I command you today, and I will force out the Amorites, Canaanites, Hittites, Perizzites, Hivites and Jebusites ahead of you. 12 Be careful that you don't make an agreement with the people who live in the land where you are going, because it will bring you trouble. 13 Destroy their altars, break their stone pillars and cut down their Asherah idols. 14 Don't worship any other god, because I, the LORD, the Jealous One, am a jealous God.

34:14 Worship
Is worship meant for anyone besides God?

15 "Be careful that you don't make an agreement with the people who live in that land. When they worship their gods, they will invite you to join them. Then you will eat their sacrifices. 16 If you choose some of their daughters as wives for your sons and those daughters worship gods, they will lead your sons to do the same thing.

17 "Do not make gods of melted metal.

18 "Celebrate the Feast of Unleavened Bread. For seven days you must eat bread made without yeast as I commanded you. Do this during the month I have chosen, the month of Abib, because in that month you came out of Egypt.

19 "The firstborn of every mother belongs to me, including every firstborn male animal that is born in your flocks and herds. 20 You may buy back a donkey by paying for it with a lamb, but if you don't want to buy back a donkey, you

must break its neck. You must buy back all your firstborn sons.

"No one is to come before me without a gift.

21 "You must work for six days, but on the seventh day you must rest—even during the planting season and the harvest season.

22 "Celebrate the Feast of Weeks when you gather the first grain of the wheat harvest. And celebrate the Feast of Shelters in the autumn.

23 "Three times each year all your males must come before the Lord GOD, the God of Israel. 24 I will force out nations ahead of you and expand the borders of your land. You will go before the LORD your God three times each year, and at that time no one will try to take your land from you.

25 "Do not offer the blood of a sacrifice to me with anything containing yeast, and do not leave any of the sacrifice of the Feast of Passover until the next morning.

26 "Bring the best first crops that you harvest from your ground to the Tent of the LORD your God.

"You must not cook a young goat in its mother's milk."

27 Then the LORD said to Moses, "Write down these words, because with these words I have made an agreement with you and Israel."

28 Moses stayed there with the LORD 40 days and 40 nights, and during that time he did not eat food or drink water. And Moses wrote the words of the Agreement—the Ten Commandments—on the stone tablets.

The Face of Moses Shines

29 Then Moses came down from Mount Sinai, carrying the two stone tablets of the Agreement in his hands. But he did not know that his face was shining because he had talked with the LORD. 30 When Aaron and all the people of Israel saw that Moses' face was shining, they were afraid to go near him. 31 But Moses called to them, so Aaron and all the leaders of the people returned to Moses, and he talked with them. 32 After that, all the people of Israel came near him, and he gave them all the commands that the LORD had given him on Mount Sinai.

33 When Moses finished speaking to the people, he put a covering over his face. 34 Whenever Moses went before the LORD to speak with him, Moses took off the covering until he came out. Then Moses would come out and tell the Israelites what the LORD had commanded. 35 They would see that Moses' face was shining. So he would cover his face again until the next time he went in to speak with the LORD.

Rules About the Sabbath

35 Moses gathered all the Israelite community together and said to them, "These are the things the LORD has commanded you to do. 2 You are to work for six days, but the seventh day will be a holy day, a Sabbath of rest to honour the LORD. Anyone who works on that day must be put to death. 3 On the Sabbath day you must not light a fire in any of your houses."

4 Moses said to all the Israelites, "This is what the LORD has commanded: 5 From what you have, take an offering for the LORD. Let everyone who is willing bring this offering to the LORD: gold, silver, bronze, 6 blue, purple and red thread, and fine linen, goat hair 7 and rams' skins that are coloured red. They may also bring fine leather, acacia wood, 8 olive oil for the lamps, spices for the special olive oil used for appointing priests and for the sweet-smelling incense, 9 onyx stones and other jewels to be put on the holy robe and chest covering of the priests.

10 "Let all the skilled workers come and make everything the LORD commanded: 11 the Holy Tent, its outer tent and its covering, the hooks, frames, crossbars, posts and bases; 12 the Ark of the Agreement, its poles, lid and the curtain in front of it; 13 the table and its poles, all the things that go with the table, and the bread that shows we are in God's presence; 14 the lampstand for the light and all the things that go with it, the lamps and olive oil for the light; 15 the altar of incense and its poles, the special oil and the sweet-smelling incense, the curtain

FAITH links

SHARE WHAT YOU HAVE
EXODUS 35:5-18

Moses and the Israelites wanted to build a place where God could be worshipped. God told them to build the Meeting Tent. This was to be a portable "house" for God. The Israelites gave generously to help with the building. Moses also asked them to share their skills and talents to build it.

God wants us to share what we have with others. We can share our money, time and talents to do the work of God. When we share what we have, everyone is helped.

Here are some more Faithlinks on sharing:

Help for the Poor, Leviticus 5:7, p. 138

Give What You Can, Numbers 7:1–11, p. 186

A Robbery in Progress, Malachi 3:8–10, p. 1270

Give from the Heart, Luke 21:1–4, p. 1410

Share and Share Alike? Acts 2:43–47, p. 1466

Help for the Body, Romans 12:3–8, p. 1536

---

for the entrance of the Meeting Tent; 16 the altar of burnt offering and its bronze screen, its poles and all its tools, the bronze bowl and its base; 17 the curtains around the courtyard, their posts and bases, and the curtain at the entrance to the courtyard; 18 the pegs of the Holy Tent and of the courtyard and their ropes; 19 the special clothes that the priest will wear in the Holy Place. These are the holy clothes for Aaron the priest and his sons to wear when they serve as priests."

20 Then all the people of Israel went away from Moses. 21 Everyone who wanted to give, came and brought a gift to the LORD for making the Meeting Tent, all the things in the Tent, and the special clothes.

35:22 Giving
Check out this attitude of giving.

22 All the men and women who wanted to give, brought gold jewellery of all kinds—pins, earrings, rings and bracelets. They all presented their gold to the LORD. 23 Everyone who had blue, purple and red thread, and fine linen, and anyone who had goat hair or ram's skins coloured red or fine leather brought them to the LORD. 24 Everyone who could give silver or bronze brought that as a gift to the LORD, and everyone who had acacia wood to be used in the work brought it. 25 Every skilled woman used her hands to make the blue, purple and red thread, and fine linen, and they brought what they had made. 26 All the women who were skilled and wanted to help made thread of the goat hair. 27 The leaders brought onyx stones and other jewels to put on the holy robe and chest covering for the priest. 28 They also brought spices and olive oil for the sweet-smelling incense, the special oil, and the oil to burn in the lamps. 29 All the men and women of Israel who wanted to help brought gifts to the LORD for all the work the LORD had commanded Moses and the people to do.

30 Then Moses said to the Israelites, "Look, the LORD has chosen Bezalel, son of Uri, the son of Hur, from the tribe of Judah. 31 The LORD has filled Bezalel with the Spirit of God and has given him the skill, ability and knowledge to do all kinds of work. 32 He is able to design pieces to be made of gold, silver and bronze, 33 to cut stones and jewels and put them in metal, to carve wood, and to do all kinds of work. 34 Also, the LORD has given Bezalel and Oholiab, the son of Ahisamach from the tribe of Dan, the

ability to teach others. 35 The LORD has given them the skill to do all kinds of work. They are able to cut designs in metal and stone. They can plan and sew designs in the fine linen with the blue, purple and red thread. And they are also able to weave things.

36 So Bezalel, Oholiab and every skilled person will do the work the LORD has commanded, because he gave them the wisdom and understanding to do all the skilled work needed to build the Holy Tent."

2 Then Moses called Bezalel, Oholiab and all the other skilled people to whom the LORD had given skills, and they came because they wanted to help with the work. 3 They received from Moses everything the people of Israel had brought as gifts to build the Holy Tent. The people continued to bring gifts each morning because they wanted to. 4 So all the skilled workers left the work they were doing on the Holy Tent, 5 and they said to Moses, "The people are bringing more than we need to do the work the LORD commanded."

6 Then Moses sent this command throughout the camp: "No man or woman should make anything else as a gift for the Holy Tent." So the people were kept from giving more, 7 because what they had was already more than enough to do all the work.

The Holy Tent

8 Then the skilled workers made the Holy Tent. They made the ten curtains of blue, purple and red cloth, and they sewed designs of creatures with wings on the curtains. 9 Each curtain was the same size—14 metres long and 2 metres wide. 10 Five of the curtains were fastened together to make one set, and the other five were fastened together to make another set. 11 Then they made loops of blue cloth along the edge of the end curtain on the first set of five, and they did the same thing with the other set of five. 12 There were 50 loops on one curtain and 50 loops on the other curtain, with the loops opposite each other. 13 They made 50 gold hooks to join the two curtains together so that the Holy Tent was joined together as one piece.

14 Then the workers made another tent of eleven curtains made of goat hair, to put over the Holy Tent. 15 All eleven curtains were the same size—15 metres long and 2 metres wide. 16 The workers sewed five curtains together into one set and six together into another set. 17 They made 50 loops along the edge of the outside curtain of one set and 50 loops along the edge of the outside curtain of the other set. 18 Then they made 50 bronze rings to join the two sets of cloth together and make the tent one piece. 19 They made two more coverings for the outer tent—one made of ram's skins coloured red and the other made of fine leather.

> So Bezalel, Oholiab and every skilled person will do the work the LORD has commanded.
> – Exodus 36:1

20 Then they made upright frames of acacia wood for the Holy Tent. 21 Each frame was 5 metres tall and 70 centimetres wide, 22 and there were two pegs side by side on each one. Every frame of the Holy Tent was made in this way. 23 They made 20 frames for the south side of the Tent, 24 and they made 40 silver bases that went under the 20 frames. There were two bases for every frame— one for each peg of each frame. 25 They also made 20 frames for the north side of the Holy Tent 26 and 40 silver bases— two to go under each frame. 27 They made six frames for the rear or west end of the Holy Tent 28 and two frames for the corners at the rear of the Holy Tent. 29 These two frames were doubled at the bottom and joined at the top with a metal ring. They did this for each of these corners. 30 So there were eight frames and sixteen silver bases—two bases under each frame.

31 Then they made crossbars of acacia

wood to connect the upright frames of the Holy Tent. Five crossbars held the frames together on one side of the Tent, 32 and five held the frames together on the other side. Also, five crossbars held the frames together on the west end, at the rear of the Tent. 33 They made the middle crossbar run along the entire length of each side and rear of the Tent. It was set halfway up the frames. 34 They made gold rings on the sides of the frames to hold the crossbars, and they covered the frames and the crossbars with gold.

35 Then they made the curtain of blue, purple and red thread, and fine linen. A skilled craftsman sewed designs of creatures with wings on it. 36 They made four posts of acacia wood for it and covered them with gold. Then they made gold hooks for the posts, as well as four silver bases in which to set the posts. 37 For the entrance to the Tent, they made a curtain of blue, purple and red thread, and fine linen. A person who sewed well, sewed designs on it. 38 Then they made five posts and hooks for it. They covered the tops of the posts and their bands with gold, and they made five bronze bases for the posts.

The Ark of the Agreement

37 Bezalel made the Ark of acacia wood; it was 110 centimetres long, 70 centimetres wide and 70 centimetres high. 2 He covered it, both inside and out, with pure gold, and he put a gold strip around it. 3 He made four gold rings for it and attached them to its four feet, with two rings on each side. 4 Then he made poles of acacia wood and covered them with gold. 5 He put the poles through the rings on each side of the Ark to carry it. 6 Then he made a lid of pure gold that was 110 centimetres long and 70 centimetres wide. 7 Then Bezalel hammered gold to make two creatures with wings and attached them to each end of the lid. 8 He made one creature on one end of the lid and the other creature on the other end. He attached them to the lid so that it would be one piece. 9 The creatures' wings were spread upwards, covering the lid, and the creatures faced each other across the lid.

The Table

10 Then he made the table of acacia wood; it was 90 centimetres long, 50 centimetres wide and 70 centimetres high. 11 He covered it with pure gold and put a gold strip around it. 12 He made a frame 8 centimetres high that stood up all around the edge, and he put a gold strip around it. 13 Then he made four gold rings for the table and attached them to the four corners of the table where the four legs were. 14 The rings were put close to the frame around the top of the table, because they held the poles for carrying it. 15 The poles for carrying the table were made of acacia wood and were covered with gold. 16 He made of pure gold all the things that were used on the table: the plates, bowls, cups and jars used for pouring the drink offerings.

The Lampstand

17 Then he made the lampstand of pure gold, hammering out its base and stand. Its flower-like cups, buds and petals were joined together in one piece with the base and stand. 18 Six branches went out from the sides of the lampstand— three on one side and three on the other. 19 Each branch had three cups shaped like almond flowers, and each cup had a bud and a petal. Each of the six branches going out from the lampstand was the same. 20 There were four more cups shaped like almond flowers on the lampstand itself, each with its buds and petals. 21 Three pairs of branches went out from the lampstand. A bud was under the place where each pair was attached to the lampstand. Each of the six branches going out from the lampstand was the same. 22 The buds, branches and lampstand were all one piece of pure, hammered gold. 23 He made seven pure gold lamps for this lampstand, and he made pure gold wick trimmers and trays. 24 He used about 35 kilogrammes of pure gold to make the lampstand and all the things that went with it.

The Altar for Burning Incense

25 Then he made the altar of incense out of acacia wood. It was square—50 centimetres long and 50 centimetres wide—and it was 90 centimetres high. Each corner that stuck out like a horn was joined into one piece with the altar. 26 He covered the top and all the sides and the corners with pure gold, and he put gold trim around the altar. 27 He made two gold rings and put them below the trim on opposite sides of the altar; these rings held the poles for carrying it. 28 He made the poles of acacia wood and covered them with gold.

29 Then he made the holy olive oil for appointing the priests and the pure, sweet-smelling incense. He made them like a person who mixes perfumes.

The Altar for Burnt Offerings

38 Then he built the altar for burnt offerings out of acacia wood. The altar was square—2.5 metres long and 2.5 metres wide—and it was 1.5 metres high. 2 He made each corner stick out like a horn so that the horns and the altar were joined together in one piece. Then he covered the altar with bronze. 3 He made all the tools of bronze to use on the altar: the pots, shovels, bowls for sprinkling blood, meat forks and pans

YOU'RE NOT ALONE

Have a think about what it's like to be lonely. Here is someone who knows the feeling. Let's welcome Lindsay, aged 10, to Connect 2-You.

Well, my best friend moved away a few weeks ago. The two of us used to do everything together. Now that she's gone, I feel like I'm all alone. I have other people that I hang out with sometimes, but it just isn't the same. I feel so lonely. What can I do?

Have you ever felt the way Lindsay's feeling? Losing your best friend can hurt a lot. God created us with a desire to connect with other people. Friendships are some of the best gifts he gives us. Take a look at the Livin' It page on friendship, 1 Samuel 18:1, p. 378, to see what else the Bible says about friends.

It's OK to be sad about losing your friend, but that shouldn't keep you from looking for new ones. You never know where your new best friend is going to come from. The key is to be patient. God promises to give us what we need when we need it – and that includes friends!

for carrying the fire. 4 He made a large bronze screen to hold the burning wood for the altar and put it inside the altar, under its rim, halfway up from the bottom. 5 He made bronze rings to hold the poles for carrying the altar, and he put them at the four corners of the screen. 6 Then he made poles of acacia wood and covered them with bronze. 7 He put the poles through the rings on both sides of the altar, to carry it. He made the altar of boards and left the inside hollow.

The Bronze Bowl

8 He made the bronze bowl for washing, and he built it on a bronze stand. He used the bronze from mirrors that belonged to the women who served at the entrance to the Meeting Tent.

The Courtyard of the Holy Tent

9 Then he made a wall of curtains to form a courtyard around the Holy Tent. On the south side the curtains were 50 metres long and were made of fine linen. 10 The curtains hung on silver hooks and bands, placed on 20 bronze posts with 20 bronze bases. 11 On the north side the wall of curtains was also 50 metres long, and it hung on silver hooks and bands on 20 posts with 20 bronze bases.
12 On the west side of the courtyard, the wall of curtains was 25 metres long. It was held up by silver hooks and bands on ten posts with ten bases. 13 The east side was also 25 metres long. 14 On one side of the entry there was a wall of curtains 7.5 metres long, held up by three posts and three bases. 15 On the other side of the entry there was also a wall of curtains 7.5 metres long, held up by three posts and three bases. 16 All the curtains around the courtyard were made of fine linen. 17 The bases for the posts were made of bronze. The hooks and the bands on the posts were made of silver, and the tops of the posts were covered with silver also. All the posts in the courtyard had silver bands.
18 The curtain for the entrance of the courtyard was made of blue, purple and red thread, and fine linen, sewn by a person who could sew well. The curtain was 10 metres long and 2.5 metres high, the same height as the curtains around the courtyard. 19 It was held up by four posts and four bronze bases. The hooks and bands on the posts were made of silver, and the tops on the posts were covered with silver. 20 All the tent pegs for the Holy Tent and for the curtains around the courtyard were made of bronze.

21 This is a list of the materials used to make the Holy Tent, where the Agreement was kept. Moses ordered the Levites to make this list, and Ithamar, son of Aaron, was in charge of keeping it. 22 Bezalel, son of Uri, the son of Hur, of the tribe of Judah, made everything the LORD commanded Moses. 23 Oholiab, son of Ahisamach, of the tribe of Dan, helped him. He could cut designs into metal and stone; he was a designer and also skilled at sewing the blue, purple and red thread, and fine linen.

24 The total amount of gold used to build the Holy Tent was presented to the LORD. It weighed about a tonne, as set by the Holy Place measure.

25 The silver was given by the members of the community who were counted. It weighed 3.5 tonnes, as set by the Holy Place measure. 26 All the men 20 years old or older were counted. There were 603,550 men, and each man had to pay 6 grammes of silver, as set by the Holy Place measure. 27 Of this silver, 3.5 tonnes were used to make the 100 bases for the Holy Tent and for the curtain— 35 kilogrammes of silver in each base. 28 They used 20 kilogrammes of silver to make the hooks for the posts and to cover the tops of the posts and to make the bands on them.

29 The bronze which was presented to the LORD weighed about 2.5 tonnes. 30 They used the bronze to make the bases at the entrance of the Meeting Tent, to make the altar and the bronze screen, and to make all the tools for the altar. 31 This bronze was also used to make bases for the wall of curtains around

Clothes for the Priests

39 They used blue, purple and red thread to make woven clothes for the priests to wear when they served in the Holy Place. They made the holy clothes for Aaron as the LORD had commanded Moses.

2 They made the holy robe of gold and blue, purple and red thread, and fine linen. 3 They hammered the gold into sheets and then cut it into long, thin strips. They worked the gold into the blue, purple and red thread, and fine linen. This was done by skilled craftsmen. 4 They made the shoulder straps for the holy robe, which were attached to the top corners of the robe and tied together over each shoulder. 5 The skilfully woven belt was made in the same way; it was joined to the holy robe as one piece. It was made of gold and blue, purple and red thread, and fine linen, in the way the LORD commanded Moses.

6 They put gold around the onyx stones and then wrote the names of the sons of Israel on these gems, as a person carves words and designs on a seal. 7 Then they attached the gems on the shoulder straps of the holy robe, as reminders of the twelve sons of Israel. This was done just as the LORD had commanded Moses.

8 The skilled craftsmen made the chest covering like the holy robe; it was made of gold and blue, purple and red thread, and fine linen. 9 The chest covering was square—23 centimetres long and 23 centimetres wide—and it was folded double to make a pocket. 10 Then they put four rows of beautiful jewels on it: in the first row there was a ruby, a topaz and a yellow quartz; 11 in the second there was a turquoise, a sapphire and an emerald; 12 in the third there was a jacinth, an agate and an amethyst; 13 in the fourth there was a chrysolite, an onyx and a jasper. Gold was put around these jewels to attach them to the chest covering, 14 and the names of the sons of Israel were carved on these twelve jewels as a person carves a seal. Each jewel had the name of one of the twelve tribes of Israel.

15 They made chains of pure gold, twisted together like a rope, for the chest covering. 16 The workers made two gold pieces and two gold rings. They put the two gold rings on the two upper corners of the chest covering. 17 Then they put two gold chains in the two rings at the ends of the chest covering, 18 and they fastened the other two ends of the chains to the two gold pieces. They attached these gold pieces to the two shoulder straps in the front of the holy robe. 19 They made two gold rings and put them at the lower corners of the chest covering on the inside edge next to the holy robe. 20 They made two more gold rings on the bottom of the shoulder straps in front of the holy robe, near the seam, just above the woven belt of the holy robe. 21 They used a blue ribbon and tied the rings of the chest covering to the rings of the holy robe, connecting it to the woven belt. So that the chest covering would not swing out from the holy robe. They did all these things in the way the LORD commanded.

22 Then they made the outer robe to be worn under the holy robe. It was woven only of blue cloth. 23 They made a hole in the centre of the outer robe, with a woven collar sewn around it so it would not tear. 24 Then they made balls like pomegranates of blue, purple and red thread, and fine linen, and hung them around the bottom of the outer robe. 25 They also made bells of pure gold and hung these around the bottom of the outer robe between the balls. 26 So around the bottom of the outer robe there was a bell and a pomegranate ball, a bell and a pomegranate ball. The priest wore this outer robe when he served as priest, just as the LORD had commanded Moses.

27 They wove inner robes of fine linen for Aaron and his sons, 28 and they made turbans, headbands and underclothes of fine linen. 29 Then they made the cloth

belt of fine linen, and blue, purple and red thread, and designs were sewn onto it, just as the LORD had commanded Moses. 30 They made a strip of pure gold, which is the holy crown, and carved these words in the gold, as one might carve on a seal: "Holy to the LORD". 31 Then they tied this flat piece to the turban with a blue ribbon, as the LORD had commanded Moses.

32 So all the work on the Meeting Tent was finished. The Israelites did everything just as the LORD had commanded Moses. 33 Then they brought the Holy Tent to Moses: the Tent and all its furniture, hooks, frames, crossbars, posts and bases; 34 the covering made of rams' skins coloured red, the covering made of fine leather and the curtain that covered the entrance to the Most Holy Place; 35 the Ark of the Agreement, its poles and lid; 36 the table, all its containers, and the bread that showed they were in God's presence; 37 the pure gold lampstand with its lamps in a row, all its tools and the olive oil for the light; 38 the gold altar, the special olive oil used for appointing priests, the sweet-smelling incense, and the curtain that covered the entrance to the Tent; 39 the bronze altar and its screen, its poles and all its tools, the bowl and its stand; and 40 the curtains for the courtyard with their posts and bases, the curtain that covered the entrance to the courtyard, the cords, pegs, and all the things in the Meeting Tent. 41 They brought the clothes for the priests to wear when they served in the Holy Tent—the holy clothes for Aaron the priest and the clothes for his sons, which they wore when they served as priests.

42 The Israelites had done all this work just as the LORD had commanded Moses. 43 Moses looked closely at all the work and saw they had done it just as the LORD had commanded. So Moses blessed them.

> The Israelites had done all this work just as the LORD had commanded Moses.
> – Exodus 39:42

Setting Up the Holy Tent

40 Then the LORD said to Moses: 2 "On the first day of the first month, set up the Holy Tent, which is the Meeting Tent. 3 Put the Ark of the Agreement in it and hang the curtain in front of the Ark. 4 Bring in the table and arrange everything on the table that should be there. Then bring in the lampstand and set up its lamps. 5 Put the gold altar for burning incense in front of the Ark of the Agreement, and put the curtain at the entrance to the Holy Tent.

6 "Put the altar of burnt offerings in front of the entrance of the Holy Tent, the Meeting Tent. 7 Put the bowl between the Meeting Tent and the altar, and put water in it. 8 Set up the courtyard around the Holy Tent, and put the curtain at the entrance to the courtyard.

9 "Use the special olive oil and pour it on the Holy Tent and everything in it, in order to give the Tent and all that is in it for service to the LORD. They will be holy. 10 Pour the special oil on the altar for burnt offerings and on all its tools. Give the altar for service to God, and it will be very holy. 11 Then pour the special olive oil on the bowl and the base under it so that they will be given for service to God.

12 "Bring Aaron and his sons to the entrance of the Meeting Tent, and wash them with water. 13 Then put the holy clothes on Aaron. Pour the special oil on him, and give him for service to God so that he may serve me as a priest. 14 Bring Aaron's sons and put the inner robes on them. 15 Pour the special oil on them in the same way that you appointed their father as priest, so that they may also serve me as priests. Pouring oil on them will make them a family of priests, they and their descendants from now on." 16 Moses did everything that the LORD commanded him.

17 So the Holy Tent was set up on the first day of the first month during the second year after they left Egypt. 18 When

Moses set up the Holy Tent, he put the bases in place, and he put the frames on the bases. Next he put the crossbars through the rings of the frames and set up the posts. 19 After that, Moses spread the cloth over the Holy Tent and put the covering over it, just as the LORD commanded.

20 Moses put the stone tablets that had the Agreement written on them into the Ark. He put the poles through the rings of the Ark and put the lid on it. 21 Next he brought the Ark into the Tent and hung the curtain to cover the Ark, just as the LORD commanded him.

22 Moses put the table in the Meeting Tent on the north side of the Holy Tent in front of the curtain. 23 Then he put the bread on the table before the LORD, just as the LORD commanded him. 24 Moses put the lampstand in the Meeting Tent on the south side of the Holy Tent across from the table. 25 Then he put the lamps on the lampstand before the LORD, just as the LORD commanded him.

26 Moses put the gold altar for burning incense in the Meeting Tent in front of the curtain. 27 Then he burned sweet-smelling incense on it, just as the LORD commanded him. 28 Then he hung the curtain at the entrance to the Holy Tent.

29 He put the altar for burnt offerings at the entrance to the Holy Tent, the Meeting Tent, and offered a whole burnt offering and grain offerings on it, just as the LORD commanded him. 30 Moses put the bowl between the Meeting Tent and the altar for burnt offerings, and he put water in it for washing. 31 Moses, Aaron and Aaron's sons used this water to wash their hands and feet. 32 They washed themselves every time they entered the Meeting Tent and every time they went near the altar for burnt offerings, just as the LORD commanded Moses.

33 Then Moses set up the courtyard around the Holy Tent and the altar, and he put up the curtain at the entrance to the courtyard. So Moses finished the work.

The Cloud over the Holy Tent

34 Then the cloud covered the Meeting Tent, and the glory of the LORD filled the Holy Tent. 35 Moses could not enter the Meeting Tent, because the cloud had settled on it, and the glory of the LORD filled the Holy Tent.

36 When the cloud rose from the Holy Tent, the Israelites would begin to travel, 37 but as long as the cloud stayed on the Holy Tent, they did not travel. They

THE SIGN OF HIS PRESENCE

EXODUS 40:34-38

God appeared to the Israelites in the form of a cloud. When the people of Israel saw the cloud hovering over the Meeting Tent, they knew that God was with them. The Holy Spirit is the sign of God's presence today. Before leaving the earth, Jesus promised that the Holy Spirit would come. He came at Pentecost. Jesus promised that the Holy Spirit would come and live within anyone who believes in Jesus. Although we can't see him, we can trust that he's there.

A Priest Without Sin, Leviticus 4:3–7, p. 136

The Cloud Guide, Numbers 9:15–23, p. 188

God's New Home, 2 Chronicles 7:11–22, p. 570

The Dead End of Occult, Ezekiel 13:17–23, p. 1098

Fully God, Fully Human, John 11:35, p. 1444

Just for the Asking, Romans 3:23–28, p. 1522

stayed in that place until the cloud rose. **38** So the cloud of the LORD was over the Holy Tent during the day, and there was a fire in the cloud at night. So all the Israelites could see the cloud while they travelled.

RULES, RULES, RULES

It's me, Moses, the leader of God's people. Perhaps you've read my previous book, Exodus? I wrote the Book of Leviticus shortly after we escaped Egypt and were camped in the desert near Mount Sinai. (For the incredible story of how God appeared on the mountain and spoke to me, be sure to read Exodus 19:16–25, p. 101.) Leviticus is a rulebook for the nation of Israel. You may not like rules, but they are important. God gave us rules so we could be healthy (in Leviticus 11, God even told the people what to eat!) and rules for special holidays, like Passover.

I wrote this book so that the people of Israel would know how to please God. As you probably already figured out from the title, Leviticus has many rules for the Levites, the family God chose to be our priests. Because God is holy, the people could not come into his presence without a sacrifice for their sins. This book tells the priests how to make sacrifices, so sins will be forgiven.

JESUS WATCH

God is holy and wants us to be holy, too. Because of our sins we could never be holy enough to be with God. In Leviticus, God gave rules for offerings so the people could atone or "pay" for their sins with the sacrifice of an animal. The animal was to be young and have nothing wrong with it. When the animal was sacrificed on the altar, it took the place of the person who sinned and deserved punishment. Because people sin more than once, sacrifices had to be offered again and again. All of these sacrifices point to the perfect sacrifice, Jesus, who died one time to take away all our sins. Like the sacrificed animals, he took the punishment we deserve for our sins. When our sins are forgiven, we are made holy by the sacrifice Jesus made for us.

my FAVOURITE links

OTHER CONNECTIONS

Livin' it — How important is it to you to be one of the crowd? Will you do *anything* just to fit in with your friends, or are you willing to stand against those things you think are wrong? It's not easy to go against the crowd. That's why God has a lot to say about it. Check it out by connecting to Totally "Uncool"? Leviticus 18:1–5.

Do you know what was the most important possession the Israelites had? Find out more about this most holy item by checking into:
- God's Presence with the Israelites, Leviticus 16:1–15. The Israelites believed they had God's presence with them at all times because they carried around the Ark of the Agreement. How do you know God is with you?

MORE STUFF . . .

Rules to Eat By   Check out what God said to the Israelites about what they could and could not eat. You can read about it in Leviticus 11.
- The people could eat cows, but not camels, rabbits, or pigs.
- They could not eat eagles, vultures, owls, storks, or bats.
- They could eat locusts, grasshoppers and crickets.

Boy, there really are a lot of rules in Leviticus.

But the rules are there to help God's people live healthy and happy lives. Connect to these sites to find out more.

OTHER SITES TO VISIT:
Bugs you can eat, Leviticus 11:21–25
The goat that removes sin, Leviticus 16:7–10
Don't go to fortune-tellers, Leviticus 20:6
One day to rest, Leviticus 23:3
The year of Jubilee, Leviticus 25:8–22

FAITH links

○ A Priest Without Sin,
Leviticus 4:3–7

○ Help for the Poor,
Leviticus 5:7

○ A Different Kind of People,
Leviticus 11

○ An Example Not to Follow,
Leviticus 18:1–3

○ Show Some Respect,
Leviticus 19:32

○ A Holiday Every Week,
Leviticus 23:1–3

○ Reward for Obedience,
Leviticus 26:3–13

○ Giving Your Part,
Leviticus 27:30

The Burnt Offering

1 The LORD called to Moses and spoke to him from the Meeting Tent, saying, 2 "Tell the people of Israel: 'When you bring an offering to the LORD, bring as your offering an animal from the herd or flock.

3 "'If the offering is a whole burnt offering from the herd, it must be a male that has nothing wrong with it. The person must take the animal to the entrance of the Meeting Tent so that the LORD will accept the offering. 4 He must put his hand on the animal's head, and the LORD will accept it to remove the person's sin so that he will once again belong to God. 5 He must kill the young bull before the LORD, and Aaron's sons, the priests, must bring its blood and sprinkle it on all sides of the altar at the entrance to the Meeting Tent. 6 After that he will skin the animal and cut it into pieces. 7 The priests, when they have put wood and fire on the altar, 8 are to lay the head, the fat and other pieces on the wood that is on the fire of the altar. 9 The animal's inner organs and legs must be washed with water. Then the priest must burn all the animal's parts on the altar. It is a whole burnt offering, an offering made by fire, and its smell is pleasing to the LORD.

10 "'If the burnt offering is a sheep or a goat from the flock, it must be a male that has nothing wrong with it. 11 The person must kill the animal on the north side of the altar before the LORD, and Aaron's sons, the priests, must sprinkle its blood on all sides of the altar. 12 The person must cut the animal into pieces, and the priest must lay them, with the head and fat, on the wood that is on the fire of the altar. 13 The person must wash the animal's inner organs and legs with water, and then the priest must burn all its parts on the altar. It is a whole burnt offering, an offering made by fire, and its smell is pleasing to the LORD.

14 "'If the whole burnt offering for the LORD is a bird, it must be a dove or a young pigeon. 15 The priest will bring it to the altar and pull off its head, which he will burn on the altar; the bird's blood must be drained out on the side of the altar. 16 The priest must remove the bird's crop[n] and its contents and throw them on the east side of the altar, where the ashes are. 17 Then he must tear the bird open by its wings without dividing it into two parts. He must burn the bird on the altar, on the wood which is on the fire. It is a whole burnt offering, an offering made by fire, and its smell is pleasing to the LORD.

The Grain Offering

2 "'When anyone offers a grain offering to the LORD, it must be made from fine flour. The person must pour oil on it, put incense on it, 2 and then take it to Aaron's sons, the priests. The priest must take a handful of the fine flour and oil and all the incense, and burn it on the altar as a memorial portion. It is an offering made by fire, and its smell is pleasing to the LORD. 3 The rest of the grain offering will belong to Aaron and the priests; it is a most holy part of the offerings made by fire to the LORD.

4 "'If you bring a grain offering that was baked in the oven, it must be made from fine flour. It may be loaves made without yeast and mixed with oil, or it may be wafers made without yeast that have oil poured over them. 5 If your grain offering is cooked on a griddle, it must be made, without yeast, of fine flour mixed with oil. 6 Crumble it and pour oil over it; it is a grain offering. 7 If your grain offering is cooked in a pan, it must be made from fine flour and oil. 8 Bring the grain offering made of these things to the LORD. Give it to the priest, and he will take it to the altar. 9 He will take out the memorial portion from the grain offering and burn it on the altar, as an offering made by fire. Its smell is pleasing to the LORD. 10 The rest of the grain offering belongs to Aaron and the priests. It is a most holy part of the offerings made to the LORD by fire.

11 "'Every grain offering you bring to the LORD must be made without yeast,

---

1:16 crop A small bag inside a bird's throat. When a bird eats, its food goes into this part first. There, the food is made soft before it goes into the stomach.

FAITH links

THE PERFECT SACRIFICE
LEVITICUS 1–7

During Old Testament times, the Israelites were required to offer many different kinds of sacrifices. Each sacrifice had very specific instructions. Sacrifices were the only way that sins could be forgiven. An animal or grain sacrifice was offered on the altar at the Meeting Tent. The animal or crops had to be perfect – no flaws.

Today we do not need to offer sacrifices to God. Why? Because Jesus has already been sacrificed for us. He is the only one perfect enough to be offered for the sins of the whole world. No other sacrifice will ever be needed. Anyone who accepts that sacrifice on his or her behalf will be forgiven.

Can't Live Without It? Genesis 3, p. 7

Count on His Mercy, Judges 2:16–17; 3, p. 313

The Cover-up, Psalm 32:1–2, p. 733

The Watchman, Ezekiel 3:16–22, p. 1088

A Change of Heart, Matthew 3:1–12, p. 1277

The Sin Habit, Romans 7:15–20, p. 1527

---

to the Lord as an offering from the first harvest, but they must not be burned on the altar as a pleasing smell. 13 You must also put salt on all your grain offerings. Salt stands for your agreement with God that will last for ever; do not leave it out of your grain offering. You must add salt to all your offerings.

14 "If you bring a grain offering from the first harvest to the Lord, bring crushed heads of new grain roasted in the fire. 15 Put oil and incense on it; it is a grain offering. 16 The priest will burn the memorial portion of the crushed grain and oil, with the incense on it. It is an offering by fire to the Lord.

The Fellowship Offering

3 "If a person's fellowship offering to the Lord is from the herd, it may be a male or female, but it must have nothing wrong with it. 2 The person must put his hand on the animal's head and kill it at the entrance to the Meeting Tent. Then Aaron's sons, the priests, must sprinkle the blood on all sides of the altar. 3 From the fellowship offering he must make a sacrifice by fire to the Lord. He must offer the fat of the animal's inner organs (both the fat that is in them and that covers them), 4 both kidneys with the fat that is on them near the lower back muscle, and the best part of the liver, which he will remove with the kidneys. 5 Then the priests will burn these parts on the altar, on the whole burnt offering that is on the wood of the fire. It is an offering made by fire, and its smell is pleasing to the Lord.

6 "If a person's fellowship offering to the Lord is a lamb or a goat, it may be a male or female, but it must have nothing wrong with it. 7 If he offers a lamb, he must bring it before the Lord 8 and put his hand on its head. Then he must kill the animal in front of the Meeting Tent, and the priests must sprinkle its blood on all sides of the altar. 9 From the fellowship offering the person must make a sacrifice by fire to the Lord. He must bring the fat, the whole fat tail cut off close to the backbone, the fat of the inner organs (both the fat that is in them and that covers them), 10 both kidneys with the fat that is

---

because you must not burn any yeast or honey in an offering made by fire to the Lord. 12 You may bring yeast and honey on them, near the lower back muscle, and the best part of the liver, which he will remove with the kidneys. 11 Then the priest will burn these parts on the altar as food; it will be an offering made by fire to the LORD.

12 "'If a person's offering is a goat, he must offer it before the LORD 13 and put his hand on its head. Then he must kill it in front of the Meeting Tent, and the priests must sprinkle its blood on all sides of the altar. 14 From this offering the person must make a sacrifice by fire to the LORD. He must offer all the fat of the goat's inner organs (both the fat that is in them and that covers them), 15 both kidneys with the fat that is on them near the lower back muscle, and the best part of the liver, which he will remove with the kidneys. 16 The priest will burn these parts on the altar as food. It is an offering made by fire, and its smell is pleasing to the LORD. All the fat belongs to the LORD.

17 "'This law will continue for people from now on, wherever you live: you must not eat any fat or blood.'"

The Sin Offering

4 The LORD said to Moses, 2 "Tell the people of Israel this: 'When a person sins by accident and does some things the LORD has commanded not to be done, that person must do these things:

3 "'If the appointed priest sins so that he brings guilt on the people, then he must offer a young bull to the LORD, one that has nothing wrong with it, as a sin offering for the sin he has done. 4 He will bring the bull to the entrance of the Meeting Tent in front of the LORD, put his hand on its head, and kill it before the LORD. 5 Then the appointed priest must bring some of the bull's blood into the Meeting Tent. 6 The priest is to dip his finger into the blood and sprinkle it seven times before the LORD in front of the curtain of the Most Holy Place. 7 The priest must also put some of the blood on the corners of the altar of incense that stands before the LORD in the Meeting Tent. The rest of the blood he must pour out at the bottom of the altar of burnt offering, which is at the entrance of the Meeting Tent. 8 He must remove all the fat from the bull of the sin offering—the fat on and around the inner organs, 9 both kidneys

---

FAITH links

A PRIEST WITHOUT SIN
LEVITICUS 4:3-7

Even people of God sin. God required a certain sacrifice to be made when the appointed priest (the high priest) sinned. When this priest sinned, however, his sin brought guilt on everyone. After all, he was the one who usually offered the sacrifices. He had to offer a special sacrifice to cleanse all of their sin.

Jesus is called our "great high priest". (Check out Hebrews 4:14, p. 1671.) Jesus is the only sinless high priest. When God looks at your sin, he sees only the sacrifice that Jesus made for you.

Check out these other Faithlinks on how God forgives us:

Own Up to It, 2 Samuel 12:1–3, p. 412

Dirty Inside, Isaiah 6:1–7, p. 904

Believe the Impossible? Ezekiel 37, p. 1131

Inside the Heart of God, Micah 7:18–20, p. 1228

Clean Inside and Out, Luke 11:39–40, p. 1392

That's Much Better! Ephesians 2:4–5, p. 1599

with the fat that is on them near the lower back muscle, and the best part of the liver which he will remove with the kidneys. 10 (He must do this in the same way that the fat is removed from the bull of the fellowship offering.) Then the priest must burn the animal parts on the altar of burnt offering. 11 But the priest must carry off the skin of the bull and all its meat, along with the rest of the bull—its head, legs, intestines and other inner organs. 12 He must take it outside the camp to the special clean place where the ashes are poured out. He must burn it on a wood fire on the pile of ashes.

13 "'If the whole nation of Israel sins accidentally without knowing it and does something the LORD has commanded not to be done, they are guilty. 14 When they learn about the sin they have done, they must offer a young bull as a sin offering and bring it before the Meeting Tent. 15 The elders of the group of people must put their hands on the bull's head before the LORD, and it must be killed before the LORD. 16 Then the appointed priest must bring some of the bull's blood into the Meeting Tent. 17 Dipping his finger in the blood, he must sprinkle it seven times before the LORD in front of the curtain. 18 Then he must put some of the blood on the corners of the altar that is before the LORD in the Meeting Tent. The priest must pour out the rest of the blood at the bottom of the altar of burnt offering, which is at the entrance to the Meeting Tent. 19 He must remove all the fat from the animal and burn it on the altar; 20 he will do the same thing with this bull that he did with the first bull of the sin offering. In this way the priest removes the sins of the people so they will belong to the LORD and be forgiven. 21 Then the priest must carry the bull outside the camp and burn it, just as he did with the first bull. This is the sin offering for the whole community.

22 "'If a ruler sins by accident and does something the LORD his God has commanded must not be done, he is guilty. 23 When he learns about his sin, he must bring a male goat that has nothing wrong with it as his offering. 24 The ruler must put his hand on the goat's head and kill it in the place where they kill the whole burnt offering before the LORD; it is a sin offering. 25 The priest must take some of the blood of the sin offering on his finger and put it on the corners of the altar of burnt offering. He must pour out the rest of the blood at the bottom of the altar of burnt offering. 26 He must burn all the goat's fat on the altar in the same way that he burns the fat of the fellowship offerings. In this way the priest removes the ruler's sin so that he belongs to the LORD, and the LORD will forgive him.

27 "'If any person in the community sins by accident and does something which the LORD has commanded must not be done, he is guilty. 28 When the person learns about his sin, he must bring a female goat that has nothing wrong with it as an offering for his sin. 29 He must put his hand on the animal's head and kill it at the place of the whole burnt offering. 30 Then the priest must take some of the goat's blood on his finger and put it on the corners of the altar of burnt offering. He must pour out the rest of the goat's blood at the bottom of the altar. 31 Then the priest must remove all the goat's fat in the same way the fat is removed from the fellowship offerings. He must burn it on the altar as a smell pleasing to the LORD. In this way the priest will remove that person's sin so he will belong to the LORD, and the LORD will forgive him.

32 "'If this person brings a lamb as his offering for sin, he must bring a female that has nothing wrong with it. 33 He must put his hand on the animal's head and kill it as a sin offering in the place where the whole burnt offering is killed. 34 The priest must take some of the blood from the sin offering on his finger and put it on the corners of the altar of burnt offering. He must pour out the rest of the lamb's blood at the bottom of the altar. 35 Then the priest must remove all the lamb's fat in the same way that the lamb's fat is removed from the fellowship offerings. He must burn the pieces on the altar on top of the offerings made by fire to the LORD. In this way the priest will remove that person's sins so he will

Leviticus 5:1   138

belong to the LORD, and the LORD will forgive him.

Special Types of Accidental Sins

5 "'If a person is ordered to tell in court what he has seen or what he knows and he does not tell the court, he is guilty of sin.

2 "'Or someone might touch something unclean, such as the dead body of an unclean wild animal or an unclean farm animal or an unclean crawling animal. Even if he does not know that he touched it, he will still be unclean and guilty of sin.

3 "'Someone might touch human uncleanness—anything that makes someone unclean—and not know it. But when he learns about it, he will be guilty.

4 "'Or someone might make a promise before the LORD without thinking. It might be a promise to do something bad or something good; it might be about anything. Even if he forgets about it, when he remembers, he will be guilty.

5 "'When anyone is guilty of any of these things, he must tell how he sinned. **6** He must bring an offering to the LORD as a penalty for sin; it must be a female lamb or goat from the flock. The priest will perform the acts to remove that person's sin so that he will once again belong to the LORD.

7 "'But if the person cannot afford a lamb, he must bring two doves or two young pigeons to the LORD as the penalty for his sin. One bird must be for a sin offering, and the other must be for a whole burnt offering. **8** He must bring them to the priest, who will first offer the one for the sin offering. He will pull the bird's head from its neck, but he will not pull it completely off. **9** He must sprinkle the blood from the sin offering on the side of the altar, and then he must pour the rest of the blood at the bottom of the altar; it is a sin offering. **10** Then the priest must offer the second bird as a whole burnt offering, as the law says. In this way the priest will remove the person's sin so he will belong to the LORD, and the LORD will forgive him.

11 "'If the person cannot afford two doves or two pigeons, he must bring about 2 litres of fine flour as an offering for sin. He must not put oil or incense on the flour, because it is a sin offering. **12** He must bring the flour to the priest. The priest will take a handful of the flour

---

FAITH links

HELP FOR THE POOR
LEVITICUS 5:7

Throughout the Old Testament are laws written with the poor in mind. God had great concern for the poor. He even came up with a sin offering that the poor could afford. They could sacrifice two doves or two pigeons. This is the offering Mary brought to the temple when Jesus was presented. (See Luke 2:22–24, p. 1369.)

God still looks out for those who are poor or suffering in some way. Sometimes he shows his kindness through people. How will you show God's kindness to those who are poor or suffering?

Yours, Mine and Ours? 1 Samuel 25, p. 389

Your Best Work, 1 Kings 6, p. 443

You Are What You Do, Proverbs 20:11, p. 854

Love Him? Show It! Amos 2:6–7, p. 1196

The Greatest Commandment, Matthew 22:36–40, p. 1313

The Person Most Likely to Give? Acts 9:36–42, p. 1481

Leviticus 6:13

as a memorial offering and burn it on the altar on top of the offerings made by fire to the LORD; it is a sin offering. 13 In this way the priest will remove the person's sins so that he will belong to the LORD, and the LORD will forgive him. What is left of the sin offering belongs to the priest, like the grain offering.'"

The Penalty Offering

14 The LORD said to Moses, 15 "If a person accidentally sins and does something against the holy things of the LORD, he must bring from the flock a ram that has nothing wrong with it. This will be his penalty offering to the LORD. Its value in silver must be correct as set by the Holy Place measure. It is a penalty offering. 16 That person must pay for the sin he did against the holy thing, adding one-fifth to its value. Then he must give it all to the priest. In this way the priest will remove the person's sin so he will belong to the LORD, by using the ram as the penalty offering. And the LORD will forgive the person.

17 "If a person sins and does something the LORD has commanded not to be done, even if he does not know it, he is still guilty. He is responsible for his sin. 18 He must bring the priest a ram from the flock, one that has nothing wrong with it and that is worth the correct amount. It will be a penalty offering. Though the person sinned without knowing it, with this offering the priest will remove the sin so that the person will belong to the LORD, and the LORD will forgive him. 19 The person is guilty of doing wrong, so he must give the penalty offering to the LORD."

6 The LORD said to Moses, 2 "A person might sin against the LORD by doing one of these sins: he might lie about what happened to something he was taking care of for someone else, or he might lie about a promise he made. He might steal something or cheat someone. 3 He might find something that had been lost and then lie about it. He might make a promise before the LORD about something and not mean it, or he might do some other sin. 4 If he does any of these things, he is guilty of sin. He must bring back whatever he stole or whatever he took by cheating. He must bring back the thing he took care of for someone else. He must bring back what he found and lied about 5 or what he made a false promise about. He must pay the full price plus an extra one-fifth of the value of what he took. He must give the money to the true owner on the day he brings his penalty offering. 6 He must bring his penalty to the priest—a ram from the flock, one that does not have anything wrong with it and that is worth the correct amount. It will be a penalty offering to the LORD. 7 Then the priest will perform the acts to remove that person's sin so that he will belong to the LORD, and the LORD will forgive him for the sins that made him guilty."

> If he does any of these things, he is guilty of sin.
> – Leviticus 6:4

The Whole Burnt Offering

8 The LORD said to Moses, 9 "Give this command to Aaron and the priests: 'These are the teachings about the whole burnt offering: the burnt offering must stay on the altar all night until morning, and the altar's fire must be kept burning. 10 The priest must put on his linen robe and linen underclothes next to his body. Then he will remove the ashes from the burnt offering on the altar and put them beside the altar. 11 Then he must take off those clothes and put on others and carry the ashes outside the camp to a special clean place. 12 But the fire must be kept burning on the altar; it must not be allowed to go out. The priest must put more firewood on the altar every morning, place the whole burnt offering on the fire, and burn the fat of the fellowship offerings. 13 The fire must be kept burning on the altar all the time; it must not go out.

The Grain Offering

14 "These are the teachings about the grain offering: the priests must bring it to the LORD in front of the altar. 15 The priest must take a handful of fine flour, with the oil and all of the incense on it, and burn the grain offering on the altar as a memorial offering to the LORD. Its smell is pleasing to him. 16 Aaron and the priests may eat what is left, but it must be eaten without yeast in a holy place. They must eat it in the courtyard of the Meeting Tent. 17 It must not be cooked with yeast. I have given it as their share of the offerings made to me by fire; it is most holy, like the sin offering and the penalty offering. 18 Any male descendant of Aaron may eat it as his share of the offerings made to the LORD by fire, and this will continue from now on. Whatever touches these offerings shall become holy.'"

19 The LORD said to Moses, 20 "This is the offering Aaron and the priests must bring to the LORD on the day they appoint Aaron as high priest: they must bring 2 litres of fine flour for a continual grain offering, half of it in the morning and half in the evening. 21 The fine flour must be mixed with oil and cooked on a griddle. Bring it when it is well mixed. Present the grain offering that is broken into pieces, and it will be a smell that is pleasing to the LORD. 22 One of the priests appointed to take Aaron's place as high priest must make the grain offering. It is a rule for ever that the grain offering must be completely burned to the LORD. 23 Every grain offering made by a priest must be completely burned; it must not be eaten."

The Sin Offering

24 The LORD said to Moses, 25 "Tell Aaron and the priests: 'These are the teachings about the sin offering: the sin offering must be killed in front of the LORD in the same place that the whole burnt offering is killed; it is most holy. 26 The priest who offers the sin offering must eat it in a holy place, in the courtyard of the Meeting Tent. 27 Whatever touches the meat of the sin offering must be holy, and if the blood is sprinkled on any clothes, you must wash them in a holy place. 28 The clay pot the meat is cooked in must be broken, or if a bronze pot is used, it must be scrubbed and rinsed with water. 29 Any male in a priest's family may eat the offering; it is most holy. 30 But if the blood of the sin offering is taken into the Meeting Tent and used to remove sin in the Holy Place, that sin offering must be burned with fire. It must not be eaten.

The Penalty Offering

7 "These are the teachings about the penalty offering, which is most holy: 2 the penalty offering must be killed where the whole burnt offering is killed. Then the priest must sprinkle its blood on all sides of the altar. 3 He must offer all the fat from the penalty offering—the fat tail, the fat that covers the inner organs, 4 both kidneys with the fat that is on them near the lower back muscle, and the best part of the liver, which is to be removed with the kidneys. 5 The priest must burn all these things on the altar as an offering made by fire to the LORD. It is a penalty offering. 6 Any male in a priest's family may eat it. It is most holy, so it must be eaten in a holy place.

7 "'The penalty offering is like the sin offering in that the teachings are the same for both. The priest who offers the sacrifice to remove sins will get the meat for food. 8 The priest who offers the burnt offering may also have the skin from it. 9 Every grain offering that is baked in an oven, cooked on a griddle or baked in a dish belongs to the priest who offers it. 10 Every grain offering, either dry or mixed with oil, belongs to the priests, and all priests will share alike.

The Fellowship Offering

11 "These are the teachings about the fellowship offering a person may offer to the LORD: 12 if he brings the fellowship offering to show his thanks, he should also bring loaves of bread made without yeast that are mixed with oil, wafers made without yeast that have oil poured over them, and loaves of fine flour that are

mixed with oil. **13** He must also offer loaves of bread made with yeast along with his fellowship offering, which he gives to show thanks. **14** One of each kind of offering will be for the LORD; it will be given to the priest who sprinkles the blood of the fellowship offering. **15** When the fellowship offering is given to thank the LORD, the meat from it must be eaten the same day it is offered; none of it must be left until morning.

16 "If a person brings a fellowship offering just to give a gift to God or because of a special promise to him, the sacrifice should be eaten the same day he offers it. If there is any left, it may be eaten the next day. **17** If any meat from this sacrifice is left on the third day, it must be burned up. **18** Any meat of the fellowship offering eaten on the third day will not be accepted, nor will the sacrifice count for the person who offered it. It will become unclean, and anyone who eats the meat will be guilty of sin.

19 "People must not eat meat that touches anything unclean; they must burn this meat with fire. Anyone who is clean may eat other meat. **20** But if anyone is unclean and eats the meat from the fellowship offering that belongs to the LORD, he must be cut off from his people.

21 "If anyone touches something

CONNECT 2-YOU

CHEEK TO CHEEK

Some people are really hard to get along with. Scott, aged 10, knows someone who fits that exact description!

Scott

It's my older brother. He picks on me all the time. Sometimes he pushes me around, but most of the time he just makes fun of me. It seems like I can't say or do anything without him laughing at me or telling me how stupid I am. Sometimes I get so mad that I try to hit him. Other times I just tell my mum what he's doing. But nothing seems to stop him.

Jesus set the example we should follow when someone hurts us. When people made fun of him, he did nothing. When people lied about him, he said nothing. When people hit him on one cheek, he gave them the other cheek to hit. "Turning the other cheek" is a tough thing to do, but it's the best way to handle people like Scott's brother.

Scott can't control what his brother does, but he can make sure that he does everything possible to keep things peaceful between the two of them. Check out the Livin' It page on being a peacemaker, Romans 14:19, p. 1539. You may find some more tips on dealing with people who are hard to get along with.

unclean—uncleanness that comes from people, from an animal or from some hated thing—touching it will make him unclean. If he then eats meat from the fellowship offering that belongs to the LORD, he must be cut off from his people.'"

22 The LORD said to Moses, 23 "Tell the people of Israel: 'You must not eat any of the fat from cattle, sheep or goats. 24 If an animal is found dead or torn by wild animals, you may use its fat for other things, but you must not eat it. 25 If someone eats fat from an animal offering made by fire to the LORD, he must be cut off from his people. 26 No matter where you live, you must not eat blood from any bird or animal. 27 Anyone who eats blood must be cut off from his people.'"

The Priests' Share

28 The LORD said to Moses, 29 "Tell the people of Israel: 'If someone brings a fellowship offering to the LORD, he must give part of it as his sacrifice to the LORD. 30 He must carry that part of the gift in his own hands as an offering made by fire to the LORD. He must bring the fat and the breast of the animal to the priest, to be presented to the LORD as the priests' share. 31 Then the priest must burn the fat on the altar, but the breast of the animal will belong to Aaron and the priests. 32 You must also give the right thigh from the fellowship offering to the priest as a gift; 33 it will belong to the priest who offers the blood and fat of the fellowship offering. 34 I have taken the breast and the thigh from the fellowship offerings of the Israelites, and I have given these parts to Aaron and the priests as their share for all time from the Israelites.'"

35 This is the portion that belongs to Aaron and his sons from the offerings made by fire to the LORD. They were given this share on the day they were presented to the LORD as priests. 36 On the day the LORD appointed the priests, he commanded Israel to give this share to them, and it is to be given to the priests as their share from now on.

37 These are the teachings about the whole burnt offering, the grain offering, the sin offering, the penalty offering, the offering for the appointment of priests and the fellowship offering. 38 The LORD gave these teachings to Moses on Mount Sinai on the day he commanded the Israelites to bring their offerings to the LORD in the Sinai Desert.

Aaron and His Sons Appointed

8 The LORD said to Moses, 2 "Bring Aaron and his sons and their clothes, the special olive oil used in appointing people and things to the service of the LORD, the bull of the sin offering and the two rams, and the basket of bread made without yeast. 3 Then gather the people together at the entrance to the Meeting Tent." 4 Moses did as the LORD commanded him, and the people met together at the entrance to the Meeting Tent.

5 Then Moses spoke to the people and said, "This is what the LORD has commanded to be done." 6 Bringing Aaron and his sons forwards, Moses washed them with water. 7 He put the inner robe on Aaron and tied the cloth belt around him. Then Moses put the outer robe on him and placed the holy robe on him. He tied the skilfully woven belt around him so that the holy robe was tied to Aaron. 8 Then Moses put the chest covering on him and put the Urim and the Thummim in the chest covering. 9 He also put the turban on Aaron's head. He put the strip of gold, the holy crown, on the front of the turban, as the LORD commanded him to do.

10 Then Moses put the special oil on the Holy Tent and everything in it, making them holy for the LORD. 11 He sprinkled some oil on the altar seven times, sprinkling the altar and all its tools and the large bowl and its base. In this way he made them holy for the LORD. 12 He poured some of the special oil on Aaron's head to make Aaron holy for the LORD. 13 Then Moses brought Aaron's sons forwards. He put the inner robes on them, tied cloth belts around them, and put headbands on them, as the LORD had commanded him.

14 Then Moses brought the bull for the sin offering, and Aaron and his sons

put their hands on its head. 15 Moses killed the bull, took the blood, and with his finger put some of it on all the corners of the altar, to make it pure. Then he poured out the rest of the blood at the bottom of the altar. In this way he made it holy and ready for service to God. 16 Moses took all the fat from the inner organs of the bull, the best part of the liver, and both kidneys with the fat that is on them, and he burned them on the altar. 17 But he took the bull's skin, its meat and its intestines and burned them in a fire outside the camp, as the LORD had commanded him.

18 Next Moses brought the ram of the burnt offering, and Aaron and his sons put their hands on its head. 19 Then Moses killed it and sprinkled the blood on all sides of the altar. 20 He cut the ram into pieces and burned the head, the pieces and the fat. 21 He washed the inner organs and legs with water and burned the whole ram on the altar as a burnt offering made by fire to the LORD; its smell was pleasing to the LORD. Moses did these things as the LORD had commanded him.

22 Then Moses brought the other ram, the one used in appointing Aaron and his sons as priests, and Aaron and his sons put their hands on its head. 23 Then Moses killed the sheep and put some of its blood on the bottom of Aaron's right ear, some on the thumb of Aaron's right hand, and some on the big toe of his right foot. 24 Then Moses brought Aaron's sons close to the altar. He put some of the blood on the bottom of their right ears, some on the thumbs of their right hands, and some on the big toes of their right feet. Then he sprinkled blood on all sides of the altar. 25 He took the fat, the fat tail, all the fat on the inner organs, the best part of the liver, both kidneys with their fat and the right thigh. 26 From the basket of bread made without yeast that is put before the LORD each day, Moses took a loaf of bread, a loaf made with oil and a wafer. He put these pieces of bread on the fat and right thigh of the ram. 27 All these things he put in the hands of Aaron and his sons and presented them as an offering before the LORD. 28 Then Moses took them from their hands and burned them on the altar on top of the burnt offering. So this was the offering for appointing Aaron and his sons as priests. It was an offering made by fire to the LORD, and its smell was pleasing to him. 29 Moses also took the breast and presented it as an offering before the LORD. It was Moses' share of the ram used in appointing the priests, as the LORD had commanded him.

30 Moses took some of the special oil and some of the blood which was on the altar, and he sprinkled them on Aaron and Aaron's clothes, and on Aaron's sons and their clothes. In this way Moses made Aaron, his clothes, his sons and their clothes holy for the LORD.

31 Then Moses said to Aaron and his sons, "I gave you a command, saying, 'Aaron and his sons will eat these things.' So take the meat and basket of bread from the offering for appointing priests. Boil the meat at the door of the Meeting Tent, and eat it there with the bread. 32 If any of the meat or bread is left, burn it. 33 The time of appointing will last seven days; you must not go outside the entrance of the Meeting Tent until that time is up. Stay there until the time of your appointing is finished. 34 The LORD commanded the things that were done today to remove your sins so you will belong to him. 35 You must stay at the entrance of the Meeting Tent day and night for seven days. If you don't obey the LORD's commands, you will die. The LORD has given me these commands."

36 So Aaron and his sons did everything the LORD had commanded through Moses.

> So Aaron and his sons did everything the LORD had commanded through Moses.
> – Leviticus 8:36

Aaron and His Sons Offer Sacrifices

9 On the eighth day after the time of appointing, Moses called for Aaron and his sons and for the elders of Israel. 2 He said to Aaron, "Take a bull calf and a ram that have nothing wrong with them, and offer them to the LORD. The calf will be a sin offering, and the ram will be a whole burnt offering. 3 Tell the people of Israel, 'Take a male goat for a sin offering and a calf and a lamb for a whole burnt offering; each must be one year old, and it must have nothing wrong with it. 4 Also take a bull and a ram for fellowship offerings, along with a grain offering mixed with oil. Offer all these things to the LORD, because the LORD will appear to you today.'"

5 So all the people came to the front of the Meeting Tent, bringing the things Moses had commanded them to bring, and they stood before the LORD. 6 Moses said, "You have done what the LORD commanded, so you will see the LORD's glory."

7 Then Moses told Aaron, "Go to the altar and offer sin offerings and whole burnt offerings. Do this to remove your sins and the people's sins so you will belong to God. Offer the sacrifices for the people and perform the acts to remove their sins for them so they will belong to the LORD, as the LORD has commanded."

8 So Aaron went to the altar and killed the bull calf as a sin offering for himself. 9 Then his sons brought the blood to him, and he dipped his finger in the blood and put it on the corners of the altar. He poured out the rest of the blood at the bottom of the altar. 10 Aaron took the fat, the kidneys and the best part of the liver from the sin offering and burned them on the altar, in the way the LORD had commanded Moses. 11 The meat and skin he burned outside the camp.

12 Then Aaron killed the animal for the whole burnt offering. His sons brought the blood to him, and he sprinkled it on all sides of the altar. 13 As they gave him the pieces and head of the burnt offering, Aaron burned them on the altar. 14 He also washed the inner organs and the legs of the burnt offering and burned them on top of the burnt offering on the altar.

15 Then Aaron brought the offering that was for the people. He took the goat of the people's sin offering and killed it and offered it for the sin offering, just as he had done for the first sin offering.

16 Then Aaron brought the whole burnt offering and offered it in the way that the LORD had commanded. 17 He also brought the grain offering to the altar. He took a handful of the grain and burned it on the altar, in addition to the morning's burnt offering.

18 Aaron also killed the bull and the ram as the fellowship offerings for the people. His sons brought him the blood, and he sprinkled it on all sides of the altar. 19 Aaron's sons also brought to Aaron the fat of the bull and the ram—the fat tail, the fat covering the inner organs, the kidneys and the best part of the liver. 20 Aaron's sons put them on the breasts of the bull and the sheep. Then Aaron burned these fat parts on the altar. 21 He presented the breasts and the right thigh before the LORD as the priests' share of the offering, as Moses had commanded.

22 Then Aaron lifted his hands towards the people and blessed them. When he had finished offering the sin offering, the burnt offering and the fellowship offering, he stepped down from the altar.

23 Moses and Aaron went into the Meeting Tent. Then they came out and blessed the people, and the LORD's glory came to all the people. 24 Fire came out from the LORD and burned up the burnt offering and fat on the altar. When the people saw this, they shouted with joy and bowed face down on the ground.

> Then Aaron lifted his hands toward the people and blessed them.
> – Leviticus 9:22

God Destroys Nadab and Abihu

10 Aaron's sons Nadab and Abihu took their pans for burning incense, put fire in them, and added incense; but they did not use the special fire Moses had commanded them to use in the presence of the LORD. 2 So fire came down from the LORD and destroyed Nadab and Abihu, and they died in front of the LORD. 3 Then Moses said to Aaron, "This is what the LORD was speaking about when he said,

'I must be respected as holy
by those who come near me;
before all the people
I must be given honour.'"

So Aaron did not say anything about the death of his sons.

4 Aaron's uncle Uzziel had two sons named Mishael and Elzaphan. Moses said to them, "Come here and pick up your cousins' bodies. Carry them outside the camp away from the front of the Holy Place." 5 So Mishael and Elzaphan obeyed Moses and carried the bodies of Nadab and Abihu, still clothed in the special priest's inner robes, outside the camp.

6 Then Moses said to Aaron and his other sons, Eleazar and Ithamar, "Don't show sadness by tearing your clothes or leaving your hair uncombed. If you do, you will die, and the LORD will be angry with all the people. All the people of Israel, your relatives, may cry loudly about the LORD burning Nadab and Abihu, 7 but you must not even leave the Meeting Tent. If you go out of the entrance, you will die, because the LORD has appointed you to his service." So Aaron, Eleazar and Ithamar obeyed Moses.

8 Then the LORD said to Aaron, 9 "You and your sons must not drink wine or beer when you go into the Meeting Tent. If you do, you will die. This law will continue from now on. 10 You must keep what is holy separate from what is not holy; you must keep what is clean separate from what is unclean. 11 You must teach the people all the laws that the LORD gave to them through Moses."

12 Moses said to Aaron and his remaining sons, Eleazar and Ithamar, "Eat the part of the grain offering that is left from the sacrifices offered by fire to the LORD, but do not add yeast to it. Eat it near the altar because it is most holy. 13 You must eat it in a holy place, because this part of the offering made by fire to the LORD belongs to you and your sons. I have been commanded to tell you this.

14 "Also, you and your sons and daughters may eat the breast and thigh of the fellowship offering that was presented to the LORD. You must eat them in a clean place; they are your share of the fellowship offerings given by the Israelites. 15 The people must bring the fat from

---

FAITH CHALLENGE

Here's another one for you. Read 10:3 to find out how God wants us to treat him. How do you show respect and honour to God when you are with your friends?

TeSTiNG iT

Leviticus 10:3
This is what the LORD was speaking about when he said, "I must be respected as holy by those who come near me; before all the people I must be given honour."

their animals that was part of the offering made by fire, and they must present it to the LORD along with the thigh and the breast of the fellowship offering. They will be the regular share of the offerings for you and your children, as the LORD has commanded."

16 Moses looked for the goat of the sin offering, but it had already been burned up. So he became very angry with Eleazar and Ithamar, Aaron's remaining sons. He said, 17 "Why didn't you eat that goat in a holy place? It is most holy, and the LORD gave it to you to take away the guilt of the people, to remove their sins so that they will belong to the LORD. 18 You didn't bring the goat's blood inside the Holy Place. You were supposed to eat the goat in a holy place, as I commanded!"

19 But Aaron said to Moses, "Today they brought their sin offering and burnt offering before the LORD, but these terrible things have still happened to me! Do you think the LORD would be any happier if I ate the sin offering today?" 20 When Moses heard this, he was satisfied.

Rules About What May Be Eaten

11 The LORD said to Moses and Aaron, 2 "Tell the Israelites this: 'These are the land animals you may eat: 3 you may eat any animal that has split hoofs completely divided and that chews the cud.

4 "'Some animals only chew the cud or only have split hoofs, and you must not eat them. The camel chews the cud but does not have a split hoof; it is unclean for you. 5 The rock badger chews the cud but does not have a split hoof; it is unclean for you. 6 The rabbit chews the cud but does not have a split hoof; it is unclean for you. 7 Now the pig has a split hoof that is completely divided, but it does not chew the cud; it is unclean for you. 8 You must not eat the meat from these animals or even touch their dead bodies; they are unclean for you.

9 "'Of the animals that live in the sea or in a river, if the animal has fins and scales, you may eat it. 10 But whatever lives in the sea or in a river and does not have fins and scales—including the things

FAITH links

A DIFFERENT KIND OF PEOPLE

LEVITICUS 11

God wanted the Israelites to be different from other nations. That's why he gave them a lot of rules to follow. Some of these rules had to do with food. The Israelites were told which types of animals they could eat and which ones they could not eat. The ones they could eat were known as "clean" animals.

We don't have strict laws about the foods we eat today. But God still expects our behaviour as Christians to be different from that of nonbelievers. Knowing Jesus makes all the difference.

Want to know what else the Bible has to say about following God? Check out these Faithlinks:

Lights, Camera, . . . Actions! Genesis 12:1–3, p. 17

The Wisdom of Obeying God, 1 Kings 11:1–13, p. 453

The Bible: Good for Your Faith, Psalm 119, p. 802

Your Spiritual Roots, Zechariah 1:1–6, p. 1253

When We Agree, Matthew 18:19–20, p. 1306

Faith That Pleases God, Luke 7:1–9, p. 1380

that fill the water and all other things that live in it—you should hate. 11 You must not eat any meat from them or even touch their dead bodies, because you should hate them. 12 You must hate any animal in the water that does not have fins and scales.

13 "'Also, these are the birds you are to hate. They are hateful and should not be eaten. You must not eat eagles, vultures, black vultures, 14 kites, any kind of falcon, 15 any kind of raven, 16 horned owls, screech owls, sea gulls, any kind of hawk, 17 little owls, cormorants, great owls, 18 white owls, desert owls, ospreys, 19 storks, any kind of heron, hoopoes or bats.

20 "'Don't eat insects that have wings and walk on all four feet; they also are to be hated.

21 "'But you may eat certain insects that have wings and walk on four feet. You may eat those that have legs with joints above their feet so that they can jump. 22 These are the insects you may eat: all kinds of locusts, winged locusts, crickets and grasshoppers. 23 But all other insects that have wings and walk on four feet you are to hate. 24 Those insects will make you unclean, and anyone who touches the dead body of one of these insects will become unclean until evening. 25 Anyone who picks up one of these dead insects must wash his clothes and be unclean until evening.

26 "'Some animals have split hoofs, but the hoofs are not completely divided; others do not chew the cud. They are unclean for you, and anyone who touches the dead body of one of these animals will become unclean. 27 Of all the animals that walk on four feet, the animals that walk on their paws are unclean for you. Anyone who touches the dead body of one of these animals will become unclean until evening. 28 Anyone who picks up their dead bodies must wash his clothes and be unclean until evening; these animals are unclean for you.

29 "'These crawling animals are unclean for you: moles, rats, all kinds of great lizards, 30 geckos, crocodiles, lizards, sand reptiles and chameleons. 31 These crawling animals are unclean for you; anyone who touches their dead bodies will be unclean until evening.

32 "'If an unclean animal dies and falls on something, that thing will also become unclean. This includes anything made from wood, cloth, leather or rough cloth, regardless of its use. Whatever the animal falls on must be washed with water and be unclean until evening; then it will become clean again. 33 If the dead, unclean animal falls into a clay bowl, anything in the bowl will become unclean, and you must break the bowl. 34 If water from the unclean clay bowl gets on any food, that food will become unclean. 35 If any dead, unclean animal falls on something, it becomes unclean. If it is a clay oven or a clay baking pan, it must be broken into pieces. These things will be unclean; they are unclean for you.

36 "'A spring or well that collects water will stay clean, but anyone who touches the dead body of any unclean animal will become unclean. 37 If a dead, unclean animal falls on a seed to be planted, that seed is still clean. 38 But if you put water on some seeds and a dead, unclean animal falls on them, they are unclean for you.

39 "'Also, if an animal which you use for food dies, anyone who touches its body will be unclean until evening. 40 Anyone who eats meat from this animal's dead body must wash his clothes and be unclean until evening. Anyone who picks up the animal's dead body must wash his clothes and be unclean until evening.

41 "'Every animal that crawls on the ground is to be hated; it must not be eaten. 42 You must not eat any of the animals that crawl on the ground, including those that crawl on their stomachs, that walk on all four feet, or on many feet. They are to be hated. 43 Do not make yourself unclean by these animals; you must not become unclean by them. 44 I am the LORD your God. Keep yourselves holy for me because I am holy. Don't make yourselves unclean with any

11:44
God
What is a characteristic of God?

of these crawling animals. 45 I am the LORD who brought you out of Egypt to be your God; you must be holy because I am holy.

46 "These are the teachings about all of the cattle, birds and other animals on earth, as well as the animals in the sea and those that crawl on the ground. 47 These teachings help people know the difference between unclean animals and clean animals; they help people know which animals may be eaten and which ones must not be eaten.'"

Rules for New Mothers

12 The LORD said to Moses, 2 "Tell the people of Israel this: 'If a woman gives birth to a son, she will become unclean for seven days, as she is unclean during her monthly period. 3 On the eighth day the boy must be circumcised. 4 Then it will be 33 days before she becomes clean from her loss of blood. She must not touch anything that is holy or enter the Holy Tent until her time of cleansing is finished. 5 But if she gives birth to a daughter, the mother will be unclean for two weeks, as she is unclean during her monthly period. It will be 66 days before she becomes clean from her loss of blood.

6 "After she has a son or daughter and her days of cleansing are over, the new mother must bring certain sacrifices to the Meeting Tent. She must give the priest at the entrance a year-old lamb for a burnt offering and a dove or young pigeon for a sin offering. 7 He will offer them before the LORD to make her clean so she will belong to the LORD again; then she will be clean from her loss of blood. These are the teachings for a woman who gives birth to a boy or girl.

8 "If she cannot afford a lamb, she is to bring two doves or two young pigeons, one for a burnt offering and one for a sin offering. In this way the priest will make her clean so she will belong to the LORD again, and she will be clean.'"

> In this way the priest will make her clean so she will belong to the LORD again, and she will be clean.
> – Leviticus 12:8

Rules About Skin Diseases

13 The LORD said to Moses and Aaron, 2 "Someone might have on his skin a swelling or a sore or a bright spot. If the sore looks like a harmful skin disease, the person must be brought to Aaron, the priest, or to one of Aaron's sons, the priests. 3 The priest must look at the sore on the person's skin. If the hair in the sore has become white, and the sore seems deeper than the person's skin, it is a harmful skin disease. When he has finished looking at the person, the priest must announce that the person is unclean.

4 "If there is a white spot on a person's skin, but the spot does not seem deeper than the skin, and if the hair from the spot has not turned white, the priest must separate that person from other people for seven days. 5 On the seventh day the priest must look at the person again. If he sees that the sore has not changed and it has not spread on the skin, the priest must keep the person seprated for seven more days. 6 On the seventh day the priest must look at the person again. If the sore has faded and has not spread on the skin, the priest must announce that the person is clean. The sore is only a rash. The person must wash his clothes, and he will become clean again.

7 "But if the sore spreads again after the priest has announced him clean, the person must come again to the priest. 8 The priest must look at him, and if the rash has spread on the skin, the priest must announce that the person is unclean; it is a harmful skin disease.

9 "If a person has a harmful skin disease, he must be brought to the priest, 10 and the priest must look at him. If there is a white swelling in the skin, and the hair has become white, and the skin looks raw in the swelling, 11 it is a harmful skin disease. It is one he has had for a long time. The priest must announce that the person is unclean. He will not need to

OUR THOROUGH GOD
LEVITICUS 13

Do you think your local council has a law about fungus? What about a law about mildew? The people of Israel had laws about both, plus several other laws about contagious diseases like harmful skin diseases. (This skin disease was often referred to as leprosy. Today it's also known as Hansen's disease.) Obeying these laws kept infections from spreading.

Reading this chapter reminds us that God cares about every part of our lives. God is pretty thorough! He makes rules for our protection and to protect others. Don't be afraid to take any concern you have to him. He cares about everything you care about.

The Name of the Lord, Exodus 33:19–23; 34:5–8, p. 120

Problem Solved, 2 Kings 20:1–11, p. 507

Our Heavenly Shepherd, Psalm 23, p. 726

Our Awesome God, Ezekiel 1:26–28, p. 1087

Faith God Notices, Luke 18:35–43, p. 1406

You've Got the Power! Acts 1:1–8; 2:1–4, p. 1463

---

12 "If the skin disease spreads all over a person's body, covering his skin from his head to his feet, as far as the priest can see, the priest must look at the person's whole body. 13 If the priest sees that the disease covers the whole body and has turned all of the person's skin white, he must announce that the person is clean.

14 "But when the person has an open sore, he is unclean. 15 When the priest sees the open sore, he must announce that the person is unclean. The open sore is not clean; it is a harmful skin disease. 16 If the open sore becomes white again, the person must come to the priest. 17 The priest must look at him, and if the sores have become white, the priest must announce that the person with the sores is clean. Then he will be clean.

18 "Someone may have a boil on his skin that is healed. 19 If in the place where the boil was, there is a white swelling or a bright red spot, this place on the skin must be shown to the priest. 20 And the priest must look at it. If the spot seems deeper than the skin and the hair on it has become white, the priest must announce that the person is unclean. The spot is a harmful skin disease that has broken out from inside the boil. 21 But if the priest looks at the spot and there are no white hairs in it and the spot is not deeper than the skin and it has faded, the priest must separate the person from other people for seven days. 22 If the spot spreads on the skin, the priest must announce that the person is unclean; it is a disease that will spread. 23 But if the bright spot does not spread or change, it is only the scar from the old boil. Then the priest must announce that the person is clean.

24 "When a person gets a burn on his skin, if the open sore becomes white or red, 25 the priest must look at it. If the white spot seems deeper than the skin and the hair at that spot has become white, it is a harmful skin disease. The disease has broken out in the burn, and the priest must announce that the person is unclean. It is a harmful skin disease. 26 But if the priest looks at the spot and

---

separate that person from other people, because everyone already knows that the person is unclean.

there is no white hair in the bright spot, and the spot is no deeper than the skin and has faded, the priest must separate the person from other people for seven days. 27 On the seventh day the priest must look at him again. If the spot has spread on the skin, the priest must announce that the person is unclean. It is a harmful skin disease. 28 But if the bright spot has not spread on the skin but has faded, it is the swelling from the burn. The priest must announce that the person is clean, because the spot is only a scar from the burn.

29 "When a man or a woman gets a sore on the scalp or on the chin, 30 a priest must look at the sore. If it seems deeper than the skin and the hair around it is thin and yellow, the priest must announce that the person is unclean. It is an itch, a harmful skin disease of the head or chin. 31 But if the priest looks at it and it does not seem deeper than the skin and there is no black hair in it, the priest must separate the person from other people for seven days. 32 On the seventh day the priest must look at the sore. If it has not spread, and there are no yellow hairs growing in it, and the sore does not seem deeper than the skin, 33 the person must shave himself, but he must not shave the sore place. The priest must separate that person from other people for seven more days. 34 On the seventh day the priest must look at the sore. If it has not spread on the skin and it does not seem deeper than the skin, the priest must announce that the person is clean. So the person must wash his clothes and become clean. 35 But if the sore spreads on the skin after the person has become clean, 36 the priest must look at him again. If the sore has spread on the skin, the priest doesn't need to look for the yellowish hair; the person is unclean. 37 But if the priest thinks the sore has stopped spreading, and black hair is growing in it, the sore has healed. The person is clean, and the priest must announce that he is clean.

38 "When a man or a woman has white spots on the skin, 39 a priest must look at them. If the spots on the skin are dull white, the disease is only a harmless rash. That person is clean.

40 "When anyone loses hair from his head and is bald, he is clean. 41 If he loses hair from the front of his head and has a bald forehead, he is clean. 42 But if there is a red-white sore on his bald head or forehead, it is a skin disease breaking out in those places. 43 A priest must look at that person. If the swelling of the sore on his bald head or forehead is red-white, like a skin disease that spreads, 44 that person has a skin disease. He is unclean. The priest must announce that the person is unclean because of the sore on his head.

45 "If a person has a skin disease that spreads, he must warn other people by shouting, 'Unclean, unclean!' His clothes must be torn at the seams, he must let his hair stay uncombed, and he must cover his mouth. 46 That person will remain unclean while he has the disease; he is unclean. He must live alone outside the camp.

Rules About Mildew

47 "Clothing might have mildew on it. It might be clothing made of linen or wool 48 (either woven or knitted), or of leather, or something made from leather. 49 If the mildew in the clothing, leather or woven or knitted material is green or red, it is a spreading mildew. It must be shown to the priest. 50 The priest must look at the mildew, and he must put that piece of clothing in a separate place for seven days. 51 On the seventh day he must look at the mildew again. If the mildew has spread on the cloth (either woven or knitted) or the leather, no matter what the leather was used for, it is a mildew that destroys; it is unclean. 52 The priest must burn the clothing. It does not matter if it is woven or knitted, wool or linen, or made of leather, because the mildew is spreading. It must be burned.

53 "If the priest sees that the mildew has not spread in the cloth (either knitted or woven) or leather, 54 he must order the people to wash that piece of leather or cloth. Then he must separate the clothing for seven more days. 55 After the

piece with the mildew has been washed, the priest must look at it again. If the mildew still looks the same, the piece is unclean, even if the mildew has not spread. You must burn it in fire; it does not matter if the mildew is on one side or the other.

56 "But when the priest looks at that piece of leather or cloth, the mildew might have faded after the piece has been washed. Then the priest must tear the mildew out of the piece of leather or cloth (either woven or knitted). 57 But if the mildew comes back to that piece of leather or cloth (either woven or knitted), the mildew is spreading. And whatever has the mildew must be burned with fire. 58 When the cloth (either woven or knitted) or the leather is washed and the mildew is gone, it must be washed again; then it will be clean.

59 "These are the teachings about mildew on pieces of cloth (either woven or knitted) or leather, to decide if they are clean or unclean."

Rules for Cleansing from Skin Diseases

14 The LORD said to Moses, 2 "These are the teachings for the time at which people who had a harmful skin disease are made clean.

"The person shall be brought to the priest, 3 and the priest must go outside the camp and look at the one who had the skin disease. If the skin disease is healed, 4 the priest will command that two living, clean birds, a piece of cedar wood, a piece of red string and a hyssop plant be brought for cleansing the person with the skin disease.

5 "The priest must order one bird to be killed in a clay bowl containing fresh water. 6 Then he will take the living bird, the piece of cedar wood, the red string and the hyssop; all these he will dip into the blood of the bird that was killed over the fresh water. 7 The priest will sprinkle the blood seven times on the person being cleansed from the skin disease. He must announce that the person is clean and then go to an open field and let the living bird go free.

8 "The person to be cleansed must wash his clothes, shave off all his hair, and bathe in water. Then he will be clean and may go into the camp, though he must stay outside his tent for the first seven days. 9 On the seventh day he must shave off all his hair—the hair from his head, his beard, his eyebrows and the rest of his hair. He must wash his clothes and bathe his body in water, and he will be clean.

10 "On the eighth day the person who had the skin disease must take two male lambs that have nothing wrong with them and a year-old female lamb that has nothing wrong with it. He must also take 7 litres of fine flour mixed with oil for a grain offering and a third of a litre of olive oil. 11 The priest who is to announce that the person is clean must bring him and his sacrifices before the LORD at the entrance of the Meeting Tent. 12 The priest will take one of the male lambs and offer it with the olive oil as a penalty offering; he will present them before the LORD as an offering. 13 Then he will kill the male lamb in the holy place, where the sin offering and the whole burnt offering are killed. The penalty offering is like the sin offering—it belongs to the priest and it is most holy.

14 "The priest will take some of the blood of the penalty offering and put it on the bottom of the right ear of the person to be made clean. He will also put some of it on the thumb of the person's right hand and on the big toe of the person's right foot. 15 Then the priest will take some of the oil and pour it into his own left hand. 16 He will dip a finger of his right hand into the oil that is in his left hand, and with his finger he will sprinkle some of the oil seven times before the LORD. 17 The priest will put some oil from his hand on the bottom of the right ear of the person to be made clean, some on the thumb of the person's right hand, and some on the big toe of the person's right foot. The oil will go on these places on top of the blood for the penalty offering. 18 He will put the rest of the oil that is in his left hand on the head of the person to be made clean. In this way the priest

will make that person clean so he can belong to the LORD again.

19 "Next the priest will offer the sin offering to make that person clean so he can belong to the LORD again. After this the priest will kill the animal for the whole burnt offering, 20 and he will offer the burnt offering and grain offering on the altar. In this way he will make that person clean so he can belong to the LORD again.

21 "But if the person is poor and unable to afford these offerings, he must take one male lamb for a penalty offering. It will be presented to the LORD to make him clean so he can belong to the LORD again. The person must also take 2.2 litres of fine flour mixed with oil for a grain offering. He must also take 0.3 litres of olive oil 22 and two doves or two young pigeons, which he can afford. One bird is for a sin offering and the other for a whole burnt offering. 23 On the eighth day the person will bring them for his cleansing to the priest at the entrance of the Meeting Tent, before the LORD. 24 The priest will take the lamb for the penalty offering and the oil, and he will present them as an offering before the LORD. 25 Then he will kill the lamb of the penalty offering, take some of its blood, and put it on the bottom of the right ear of the person to be made clean. The priest will put some of this blood on the thumb of the person's right hand and some on the big toe of the person's right foot. 26 He will also pour some of the oil into his own left hand. 27 Then with a finger of his right hand, he will sprinkle some of the oil from his left hand seven times before the LORD. 28 The priest will take some of the oil from his hand and put it on the bottom of the right ear of the person to be made clean. He will also put some of it on the thumb of the person's right hand and some on the big toe of the person's right foot. The oil will go on these places on top of the blood from the penalty offering. 29 The priest must put

> The priest must put the rest of the oil that is in his hand on the head of the person to be made clean, to make him clean so he can belong to the LORD again.
> – Leviticus 14:29

the rest of the oil that is in his hand on the head of the person to be made clean, to make him clean so that he can belong to the LORD again. 30 Then the priest will offer one of the doves or young pigeons, which the person can afford. 31 He must offer one of the birds for a sin offering and the other for a whole burnt offering, along with the grain offering. In this way the priest will make the person clean so that he can belong to the LORD again; he will become clean.

32 "These are the teachings for making a person clean after he has had a skin disease, if he cannot afford the regular sacrifices for becoming clean."

Rules for Cleaning Mildew

33 The LORD also said to Moses and Aaron, 34 "I am giving the land of Canaan to your people. When they enter that land, if I cause mildew to grow in someone's house in that land, 35 the owner of that house must come and tell the priest. He should say, 'I have seen something like mildew in my house.' 36 Then the priest must order the people to empty the house before he goes in to look at the mildew. This is so he will not have to say that everything in the house is unclean. After this, the priest will go in to look at it. 37 He will look at the mildew, and if the mildew on the walls of the house is green or red and goes into the walls' surfaces, 38 he must go out and close up the house for seven days. 39 On the seventh day the priest must come back and check the house. If the mildew has spread on the walls of the house, 40 the priest must order the people to tear out the stones with the mildew on them. They should throw them away, at a certain unclean place outside the city. 41 Then the priest must have all the inside of the house scraped. The people must throw away the plaster they scraped off the walls, at a certain unclean place outside the city. 42 Then the owner must put new stones

in the walls, and he must cover the walls with new clay plaster.

43 "Suppose a person has taken away the old stones and plaster and put in new stones and plaster. If mildew again appears in his house, 44 the priest must come back and check the house again. If the mildew has spread in the house, it is a mildew that destroys things; the house is unclean. 45 Then the owner must tear down the house, remove all its stones, plaster and wood, and take them to the unclean place outside the city. 46 Anyone who goes into that house while it is closed up will be unclean until evening. 47 Anyone who eats in that house or lies down there must wash his clothes.

48 "Suppose after new stones and plaster have been put in a house, the priest checks it again and the mildew has not spread. Then the priest will announce that the house is clean, because the mildew is gone.

49 "Then, to make the house clean, the priest must take two birds, a piece of cedar wood, a piece of red string and a hyssop plant. 50 He will kill one bird in a clay bowl containing fresh water. 51 Then he will take the bird that is still alive, the cedar wood, the hyssop and the red string, and he will dip them into the blood of the bird that was killed over the fresh water. The priest will sprinkle the blood on the house seven times. 52 He will use the bird's blood, the fresh water, the live bird, the cedar wood, the hyssop and the red string to make the house clean. 53 He will then go to an open field outside the city and let the living bird go free. This is how the priest makes the house clean and ready for service to the LORD."

54 These are the teachings about any kind of skin disease, 55 mildew on pieces of cloth or in a house, 56 swellings, rashes or bright spots on the skin; 57 they help people decide when things are unclean and when they are clean. These are the teachings about all these kinds of diseases.

Rules About a Person's Body

15 The LORD also said to Moses and Aaron, 2 "Say to the people of Israel: 'When a fluid comes from a person's body, the fluid is unclean. 3 It doesn't matter if the fluid flows freely or if it is blocked from flowing; the fluid will make him unclean. This is the way the fluid makes him unclean:

4 "'If the person who discharges the body fluid lies on a bed, that bed becomes unclean, and everything he sits on becomes unclean. 5 Anyone who touches his bed must wash his clothes and bathe in water, and the person will be unclean until evening. 6 Whoever sits on something that the person who discharges the fluid sat on must wash his clothes and bathe in water; he will be unclean until evening. 7 Anyone who touches the person who discharges the body fluid must wash his clothes and bathe in water; he will be unclean until evening.

8 "'If the person who discharges the body fluid spits on someone who is clean, that person must wash his clothes and bathe in water; he will be unclean until evening. 9 Everything on which the person who is unclean sits when riding will become unclean. 10 Anyone who touches something that was under him will be unclean until evening. And anyone who carries these things must wash his clothes and bathe in water; he will be unclean until evening.

11 "'If the person who discharges a body fluid has not washed his hands in water and touches another person, that person must wash his clothes and bathe in water; he will be unclean until evening.

12 "'If a person who discharges a body fluid touches a clay bowl, that bowl must be broken. If he touches a wooden bowl, that bowl must be washed in water.

13 "'When a person who discharges a body fluid is made clean, he must count seven days for himself for his cleansing. He must wash his clothes and bathe his body in fresh water, and he will be clean. 14 On the eighth day he must take two doves or two young pigeons before the LORD at the entrance of the Meeting Tent. He will give the two birds to the priest. 15 The priest will offer the birds, one for a sin offering and the other for a burnt

offering. And the priest will make that person clean so he can belong to the LORD again.

16 "'If semen[n] goes out from a man, he must bathe in water; he will be unclean until evening. 17 If the fluid gets on any clothing or leather, it must be washed with water; it will be unclean until evening.

18 "'If a man has sexual relations with a woman and semen comes out, both people must bathe in water; they will be unclean until evening.

Rules About a Woman's Body

19 "'When a woman has her monthly period, she is unclean for seven days; anyone who touches her will be unclean until evening. 20 Anything she lies on during this time will be unclean, and everything she sits on during this time will be unclean. 21 Anyone who touches her bed must wash his clothes and bathe in water; that person will be unclean until evening. 22 Anyone who touches something she has sat on must wash his clothes and bathe in water; that person will be unclean until evening. 23 It does not matter if the person touched the woman's bed or something she sat on; he will be unclean until evening.

24 "'If a man has sexual relations with a woman and her monthly period touches him, he will be unclean for seven days; every bed he lies on will be unclean.

25 "'If a woman has a loss of blood for many days and it is not during her regular monthly period, or if she continues to have a loss of blood after her regular period, she will be unclean, as she is during her monthly period. She will be unclean for as long as she continues to bleed. 26 Any bed she lies on during all the time of her bleeding will be like her bed during her regular monthly period. Everything she sits on will be unclean, as during her regular monthly period.

27 "'Whoever touches those things will be unclean and must wash his clothes and bathe in water; he will be unclean until evening. 28 When the woman becomes clean from her bleeding, she must wait seven days, and after this she will be clean. 29 Then on the eighth day she must take two doves or two young pigeons and bring them to the priest at the entrance of the Meeting Tent. 30 The priest must offer one bird for a sin offering and the other for a whole burnt offering. In this way the priest will make her clean so she can belong to the LORD again.

31 "'So you must warn the people of Israel to stay separated from things that make them unclean. If you don't warn the people, they might make my Holy Tent unclean, and then they would have to die!'"

32 These are the teachings for the person who discharges a body fluid and for the man who becomes unclean from semen[n] coming out of his body. 33 These are the teachings for the woman who becomes unclean from her monthly period, for a man or woman who has a discharge, and for a man who becomes unclean by having sexual relations with a woman who is unclean.

The Day of Cleansing

16 Now two of Aaron's sons had died while offering incense to the LORD, and after that time the LORD spoke to Moses. 2 The LORD said to him, "Tell your brother Aaron that there are times when he cannot go behind the curtain into the Most Holy Place where the Ark is. If he goes in when I appear in a cloud over the lid on the Ark, he will die.

3 "This is how Aaron may enter the Most Holy Place: before he enters, he must offer a bull for a sin offering and a ram for a whole burnt offering. 4 He must put on the holy linen inner robe, with the linen underclothes next to his body. His belt will be the cloth belt, and he will wear the linen turban. These are holy clothes, so he must bathe his body in water before he puts them on.

5 "Aaron must take from the people of Israel two male goats for a sin offering and one ram for a burnt offering. 6 Then he will offer the bull for the sin offering

---

15:16, 32 semen A man's body fluid by which he can make a woman pregnant.

GOD'S PRESENCE WITH THE ISRAELITES
Leviticus 16:1–15

The Ark of the Agreement was like a box. It was about 110 centimetres long and about 70 centimetres wide and high. It was made from acacia wood. There were two rings on each side so that poles could be slipped through them. This way men could carry the Ark without touching it. Why would they want to do that? Because this Ark was the most holy thing that the Israelites had. They believed that God's presence was with the Ark. That's why they kept it in a special place in the Meeting Tent. This was a holy place the Israelites had built, so God could live among them. They also carried it to some battles because they wanted God to be with them.

Inside the Ark, the Israelites kept the Ten Commandments (check out Exodus 20, p. 101), a golden jar of manna (the food that God sent them while they were wandering in the desert), and Aaron's miraculous rod – reminders that God provided for them in the wilderness. (Read Hebrews 9:4, p. 1676.)

---

for himself to remove sins from him and his family so that they will belong to the LORD.

7 "Next Aaron will take the two goats and bring them before the LORD at the entrance to the Meeting Tent. 8 He will throw lots for the two goats—one will be for the LORD and the other for the goat that removes sin. 9 Then Aaron will take the goat that was chosen for the LORD by throwing the lot, and he will offer it as a sin offering. 10 The other goat, which was chosen by lot to remove the sin, must be brought alive before the LORD. The priest will use it to perform the acts that remove Israel's sin so that they will belong to the LORD. Then this goat will be sent out into the desert as a goat that removes sin.

11 "Then Aaron will offer the bull as a sin offering for himself, to remove the sins from him and his family so they will belong to the LORD; he will kill the bull for the sin offering for himself. 12 Then he must take a pan full of burning coals from the altar before the LORD and two handfuls of sweet incense that has been ground into powder. He must bring it into the room behind the curtain. 13 He must put the incense on the fire before the LORD so that the cloud of incense will cover the lid on the Ark. Then, when Aaron comes in, he will not die. 14 Also, he must take some of the blood from the bull and sprinkle it with his finger on the front of the lid; with his finger he will sprinkle the blood seven times in front of the lid.

15 "Then Aaron must kill the goat of the sin offering for the people and bring its blood into the room behind the curtain. He must do with the goat's blood as he did with the bull's blood, sprinkling it on the lid and in front of the lid. 16 Because the people of Israel have been unclean, Aaron will perform the acts to make the Most Holy Place ready for service to the LORD. Then it will be clean from the sins and crimes of the Israelites. He must also do this for the Meeting Tent,

because it stays in the middle of unclean people. 17 When Aaron makes the Most Holy Place ready for service to the LORD, no one is allowed in the Meeting Tent until he comes out. So Aaron will perform the acts to remove sins from himself, his family and all the people of Israel, so that they will belong to the LORD. 18 Afterwards he will go out to the altar that is before the LORD and will make it ready for service to the LORD. Aaron will take some of the bull's blood and some of the goat's blood and put it on the corners of the altar on all sides. 19 Then, with his finger, he will sprinkle some of the blood on the altar seven times to make the altar holy for the LORD and clean from all the sins of the Israelites.

20 "When Aaron has finished making the Most Holy Place, the Meeting Tent and the altar ready for service to the LORD, he will offer the living goat. 21 He will put both his hands on the head of the living goat, and he will confess over it all the sins and crimes of Israel. In this way Aaron will put the people's sins on the goat's head. Then he will send the goat away into the desert, and a man who has been appointed will lead the goat away. 22 So the goat will carry on itself all the people's sins to a lonely place in the desert. The man who leads the goat will let it loose there.

23 "Then Aaron will enter the Meeting Tent and take off the linen clothes he had put on before he went into the Most Holy Place; he must leave these clothes there. 24 He will bathe his body in water in a holy place and put on his regular clothes. Then he will come out and offer the whole burnt offering for himself and for the people, to remove sins from himself and the people so they will belong to the LORD. 25 Then he will burn the fat of the sin offering on the altar.

26 "The person who led the goat, the goat to remove sins, into the desert must wash his clothes and bathe his body in water. After that, he may come back into the camp.

27 "The bull and the goat for the sin offerings, whose blood was brought into the Most Holy Place to make it ready for service to the LORD, must be taken outside the camp; the animals' skins, bodies and intestines will be burned in the fire. 28 Then the one who burns them must wash his clothes and bathe his body in water. After that, he may come back into the camp.

29 "This law will always continue for you: on the tenth day of the seventh month, you must not eat and you must not do any work. The travellers or foreigners living with you must not work either. 30 It is on this day that the priests will make you clean so you will belong to the LORD again. All your sins will be removed. 31 This is a very important day of rest for you, and you must not eat. This law will continue for ever.

32 "The priest appointed to take his father's place, on whom the oil was poured, will perform the acts for making things ready for service to the LORD. He must put on the holy linen clothes 33 and make the Most Holy Place, the Meeting Tent and the altar ready for service to the LORD. He must also remove the sins of the priests and all the people of Israel so that they will belong to the LORD. 34 That law for removing the sins of the Israelites so they will belong to the LORD will continue for ever. You will do these things once a year."

So they did the things the LORD had commanded Moses.

Offering Sacrifices

17 The LORD said to Moses, 2 "Speak to Aaron, his sons and all the people of Israel. Tell them: 'This is what the LORD has commanded. 3 If an Israelite kills an ox, a lamb or a goat either inside the camp or outside it, 4 when he should have brought the animal to the entrance of the Meeting Tent as a gift to the LORD in front of the LORD's Holy Tent, he is guilty of killing. He has killed, and he must be cut off from the people. 5 This rule is so people will bring their sacrifices, which they have been sacrificing in the open fields, to the LORD. They must bring those animals to the LORD at the entrance of the Meeting Tent; they must bring them to the priest and offer them as

fellowship offerings. 6 Then the priest will sprinkle the blood from those animals on the Lord's altar near the entrance of the Meeting Tent. And he will burn the fat from those animals on the altar, as a smell pleasing to the Lord. 7 They must not offer any more sacrifices to their goat idols, which they have chased like prostitutes. These rules will continue for people from now on.'

8 "Tell the people this: 'If any citizen of Israel or foreigner living with you offers a burnt offering or sacrifice, 9 that person must take his sacrifice to the entrance of the Meeting Tent to offer it to the Lord. If he does not do this, he must be cut off from the people.

10 "'I will be against any citizen of Israel or foreigner living with you who eats blood. I will cut off that person from the people. 11 This is because the life of the body is in the blood, and I have given you rules for pouring that blood on the altar to remove your sins so that you will belong to the Lord. It is the blood that removes the sins, because it is life. 12 So I tell the people of Israel this: "None of you may eat blood, and no foreigner living among you may eat blood."

13 "'If any citizen of Israel or foreigner living among you catches a wild animal or bird that can be eaten, that person must pour the blood on the ground and cover it with earth. 14 If blood is still in the meat, the animal's life is still in it. So I give this command to the people of Israel: "Don't eat meat that still has blood in it, because the animal's life is in its blood. Anyone who eats blood must be cut off."

15 "'If a person, either a citizen or a foreigner, eats an animal that died by itself or was killed by another animal, he must wash his clothes and bathe in water. He will be unclean until evening; then he will be clean. 16 If he does not wash his clothes and bathe his body, he will be guilty of sin.'"

Rules About Sexual Relations

18 The Lord said to Moses, 2 "Tell the people of Israel: 'I am the Lord your God. 3 In the past you lived in Egypt,

FAITH links

AN EXAMPLE NOT TO FOLLOW
LEVITICUS 18:1-3

Did your mum or dad ever tell you not to act like someone you know? Maybe this person behaves in a way that would cause you to break a rule your parents made. God warned the Israelites not to follow the ways of the people of Canaan. The Canaanites did many things that God did not like. He expected his people to obey his rules.

God doesn't want you to imitate those who do wrong. When someone tries to pressure you to do wrong, think about what God tells you to do in the Bible. Don't follow the crowd if the crowd leads you the wrong way.

Surf on to these Faithlinks for some other good advice:

Good Advice? Leviticus 20:6, p. 162

Following the Crowd, Numbers 13; 14, p. 193

Learning to Listen, 1 Samuel 3, p. 358

Wisdom in Store, Proverbs 2:6–7, p. 828

Get Ready! Mark 13:26–27, p. 1354

How Do You Grow? Titus 1:1, p. 1659

PEER PRESSURE
Leviticus 18:1–5

Totally "Uncool"? Did your mum and dad ever tell you not to act like a certain friend? Do they want you to do totally "uncool" things like being polite and not using bad language? Are you expected to do this even though your friends laugh at you and give you a hard time? Going against the crowd can be tough.

God warns us not to follow the crowd, especially when the crowd is going in the opposite direction of what God wants us to do. Following those who are doing the wrong things goes against what God says. (Check out Leviticus 18:1–3.)

Some people like to follow the crowd and it can get them in big trouble! (Read Numbers 13; 14.) Are you a crowd-follower, or are you willing to take a stand for God?

MORE FAITH links

An Example Not to Follow, p. 157

Following the Crowd, p. 193

Fear God or People? p. 1047

A Real Crowd-pleaser? p. 1222

Have you got some friends who think it's "cool" to make fun of other kids? If you're not too sure that what they're doing is a good idea, stop and think before you follow the crowd. Sometimes that could get you into lots of trouble.

Check out these Faithlinks, too, for some more good advice.

Give In or Take a Stand? 1 Kings 22:13–14, p. 472
- "C'mon and try it. Everybody's doing it." Ever heard words like that before? What do you do when you feel pressured to do something "everybody else" is doing?
- Have you ever been the only one to stand up for what's right? How did you feel? Whenever you stand for what's right, remember God stands with you.

Two Kinds of People, Psalm 1, p. 710
- Link here to find out how to choose between the two different kinds of people you meet.

The Unpopular Choice, Mark 15:42–43, p. 1360
- How important is popularity to you? Would you be willing to admit you believed in something if doing so made you unpopular?
- It often takes courage to follow Jesus. Are you courageous enough to make an unpopular choice and to take the risk of being thought of as "uncool"?

but you must not do what was done in that country. And you must not do as they do in the land of Canaan, where I am bringing you. Do not follow their customs. 4 You must obey my rules and follow them. I am the LORD your God. 5 Obey my laws and rules; a person who obeys them will live because of them. I am the LORD.

> **18:3–5 Following God**
> Should you follow other people?

6 "You must never have sexual relations with your close relatives. I am the LORD.

7 "You must not shame your father by having sexual relations with your mother. She is your mother; do not have sexual relations with her. 8 You must not have sexual relations with your father's wife; that would shame your father.

9 "You must not have sexual relations with your sister, either the daughter of your father or your mother. It doesn't matter if she was born in your house or somewhere else.

10 "You must not have sexual relations with your son's daughter or your daughter's daughter; that would bring shame on you.

11 "If your father and his wife have a daughter, she is your sister. You must not have sexual relations with her.

12 "You must not have sexual relations with your father's sister; she is your father's close relative. 13 You must not have sexual relations with your mother's sister; she is your mother's close relative. 14 You must not have sexual relations with the wife of your father's brother, because this would shame him. She is your aunt.

15 "You must not have sexual relations with your daughter-in-law; she is your son's wife. Do not have sexual relations with her.

16 "You must not have sexual relations with your brother's wife. That would shame your brother.

17 "You must not have sexual relations with both a woman and her daughter. And do not have sexual relations with this woman's granddaughter, either the daughter of her son or her daughter; they are her close relatives. It is evil to do this.

18 "While your wife is still living, you must not take her sister as another wife. Do not have sexual relations with her.

19 "You must not go near a woman to have sexual relations with her during her monthly period, when she is unclean.

20 "You must not have sexual relations with your neighbour's wife and make yourself unclean with her.

21 "You must not give any of your children to be sacrificed to Molech, because this would show that you do not respect your God. I am the LORD.

22 "You must not have sexual relations with a man as you would a woman. That is a hateful sin.

23 "You must not have sexual relations with an animal and make yourself unclean with it. Also a woman must not have sexual relations with an animal; it is not natural.

24 "Don't make yourself unclean by any of these wrong things. I am forcing nations out of their countries because they did these sins, and I am giving their land to you. 25 The land has become unclean, and I punished it for its sins, so the land is throwing out those people who live there.

26 "You must obey my laws and rules, and you must not do any of these hateful sins. These rules are for the citizens of Israel and for the people who live with you. 27 The people who lived in the land before you did all these hateful things and made the land unclean. 28 If you do these things, you will also make the land unclean, and it will throw you out as it threw out the nations before you. 29 Anyone who does these hateful sins must be cut off from the people. 30 Keep my command not to do these hateful sins that were done by the people who lived in the land before you. Don't make yourself unclean by doing them. I am the LORD your God.'"

Other Laws

19 The LORD said to Moses, 2 "Tell all the people of Israel: 'I am the LORD your God. You must be holy because I am holy.

19:3 Respect
Respect your parents.

3 "You must respect your mother and father, and you must keep my Sabbaths. I am the LORD your God.

4 "Do not worship idols or make statues or gods for yourselves. I am the LORD your God.

5 "When you sacrifice a fellowship offering to the LORD, offer it in such a way that it will be accepted. 6 You may eat it on the same day you offer it or on the next day. But if any is left on the third day, you must burn it up. 7 If any of it is eaten on the third day, it is unclean, and it will not be accepted. 8 Anyone who eats it then will be guilty of sin, because he did not respect the holy things that belong to the LORD. He must be cut off from the people.

9 "When you harvest your crops on your land, do not harvest all the way to the corners of your fields. If grain falls onto the ground, don't gather it up. 10 Don't pick all the grapes in your vineyards, and don't pick up the grapes that fall to the ground. You must leave those things for poor people and for people travelling through your country. I am the LORD your God.

11 "You must not steal. You must not cheat people, and you must not lie to each other. 12 You must not make a false promise by my name, or you will show that you don't respect your God. I am the LORD.

13 "You must not cheat your neighbour or rob him. You must not keep a hired worker's salary all night until morning. 14 You must not curse a deaf person or put something in front of a blind person to make him fall. But you must respect your God. I am the LORD.

15 "Be fair in your judging. You must not show special favour to poor people or great people, but be fair when you judge your neighbour. 16 You must not spread false stories against other people, and you must not do anything that would put your neighbour's life in danger. I am the LORD.

17 "You must not hate your fellow

FAITH links

GIVE REVENGE A REST
LEVITICUS 19:18

More than likely, you've heard someone talk about getting even with someone for what that person did. Maybe the person talking *was* you. A special law was given to the people of Israel about getting even with others. That law is also for us today. God told the people to avoid getting even with someone or holding a grudge. Instead, they were to love their neighbours.

Thoughts of revenge are natural for humans. But God doesn't want us to do what comes naturally. When we're angry, we easily sin. That's why God commands us to give revenge a rest. Instead, we're to love our neighbours.

Want to know more about loving your enemies? Check out these links:

More Powerful Than Revenge, Genesis 50:14–21, p. 71

Play Fair or Play Favourites? Deuteronomy 1:16–18, p. 227

Mourning for an Enemy, 2 Samuel 1, p. 399

Anger: Quick or Slow? Psalm 86:15, p. 776

Get Hot or Keep Cool? Proverbs 12:16, p. 842

Forgive Again? Luke 17:3–4, p. 1402

FAITH links

SHOW SOME RESPECT
LEVITICUS 19:32

Ever feel like grown-ups put you down or ignore you because you're a kid? Guess what. Many elderly people feel the same way. They often find themselves forgotten or disrespected by those who are younger.

God commanded the people of Israel to show respect to the elderly. That command is for you as well. Elderly people have a lot of wisdom and experience to offer. If you can, take time to get to know someone older. He or she will be pleased with the respect you offer.

Roll Out the Welcome Wagon, Genesis 18:2–8, p. 24

Obey? No Way! Exodus 1:15–21, p. 76

Play Fair or Play Favourites? Deuteronomy 1:16–18, p. 227

A Blueprint for Living, Amos 5:14–15, p. 1200

The Right Ingredients, Micah 6:8, p. 1227

Full of Faith, 1 Thessalonians 4:1, p. 1633

---

citizen in your heart. If your neighbour does something wrong, tell him about it, or you will be partly to blame. 18 Forget about the wrong things people do to you, and do not try to get even. Love your neighbour as you love yourself. I am the LORD.

19 "'Obey my laws. You must not mate two different kinds of cattle or sow your field with two different kinds of seed. You must not wear clothing made from two different kinds of material mixed together.

20 "'If a man has sexual relations with a slave girl of another man, but this slave girl has not been bought or given her freedom, there must be punishment. But they are not to be put to death, because the woman was not free. 21 The man must bring a ram as his penalty offering to the LORD at the entrance to the Meeting Tent. 22 The priest will offer the ram as a penalty offering before the LORD for the man's sin, to remove the sins of the man so that he will belong to the LORD. Then he will be forgiven for his sin.

23 "'In the future, when you enter your country, you will plant many kinds of trees for food. After planting a tree, wait three years before using its fruit. 24 In the fourth year the fruit from the tree will be the LORD's, a holy offering of praise to him. 25 Then in the fifth year, you may eat the fruit from the tree. The tree will then produce more fruit for you. I am the LORD your God.

26 "'You must not eat anything with the blood in it.

"'You must not try to tell the future by signs or black magic.

27 "'You must not cut the hair on the sides of your heads or cut the edges of your beard. 28 You must not cut your body to show sadness for someone who died or put tattoo marks on yourselves. I am the LORD.

29 "'Do not dishonour your daughter by making her become a prostitute. If you do this, the country will be filled with all kinds of sin.

30 "'Obey the laws about Sabbaths, and respect my Most Holy Place. I am the LORD.

31 "'Do not go to mediums or fortune-tellers for advice, or you will become unclean. I am the LORD your God.

32 "'Show respect to old people; stand up in their presence. Show respect also to your God. I am the LORD.

33 "'Do not mistreat foreigners living in your country, 34 but treat them just as you treat your own citizens. Love foreigners as you love yourselves, because

you were once foreigners in Egypt. I am the LORD your God.

35 "'Do not cheat when you measure the length or weight or amount of something. 36 Your weights and balances should weigh correctly, with your weighing baskets the right size and your jars holding the right amount of liquid. I am the LORD your God. I brought you out of the land of Egypt.

37 "'Remember all my laws and rules, and obey them. I am the LORD.'"

Warnings About Various Sins

20 The LORD said to Moses, 2 "You must also tell the people of Israel these things: 'If a person in your country gives one of his children to Molech, that person must be killed. It doesn't matter if he is a citizen or a foreigner living in Israel; you must throw stones at him and kill him. 3 I will be against him and cut him off from his people, because he gave his children to Molech. He showed that he did not respect my holy name, and he made my Holy Place unclean. 4 The people of the community might ignore that person and not kill the one who gave his children to Molech. 5 But I will be against him and his family, and I will cut him off from his people. I will do this to anyone who follows him in being unfaithful to me by worshipping Molech.

6 "'I will be against anyone who goes to mediums and fortune-tellers for advice, because that person is being unfaithful to me. So I will cut him off from his people.

7 "'Be my holy people. Be holy because I am the LORD your God. 8 Remember and obey my laws. I am the LORD, and I have made you holy.

9 "'Anyone who curses his father or mother must be put to death. He has cursed his father or mother, so he has brought his own death on himself.

Punishments for Sexual Sins

10 "'If a man has sexual relations with his neighbour's wife, both the man and the woman are guilty of adultery and must be put to death. 11 If a man has sexual relations with his father's wife, he has shamed his father, and both the man and his father's wife must be put to death. They have brought it on themselves.

12 "'If a man has sexual relations with his daughter-in-law, both of them must be put to death. What they have done is not

---

FAITH links

GOOD ADVICE?
LEVITICUS 20:6

What do you depend on for answers when you need direction? Some people call up the psychic hotline. Others don't make a move without checking their horoscope in the newspaper or online. Still others think that Magic 8 balls or Ouija boards are fun ways to find out information.

God told the Israelites to avoid asking fortune-tellers or mediums for advice. He knew that these individuals offered "quick-fix" information that did not come from him. God wanted the people to trust him for answers. That's what he wants you to do, too.

An Example Not to Follow, Leviticus 18:1–3, p. 157

The Cloud Guide, Numbers 9:15–23, p. 188

Facts About Following, Joshua 6, p. 283

Help to Understand, 2 Samuel 14, p. 416

What God Thinks, Isaiah 55:8–9, p. 969

One Thing to Do, Romans 4:1–5, p. 1523

natural. They have brought their own deaths on themselves.

13 "'If a man has sexual relations with another man as a man does with a woman, these two men have done a hateful sin. They must be put to death. They have brought it on themselves.

14 "'If a man has sexual relations with both a woman and her mother, this is evil. The people must burn that man and the two women in fire so that your people will not be evil.

15 "'If a man has sexual relations with an animal, he must be put to death. You must also kill the animal. 16 If a woman approaches an animal and has sexual relations with it, you must kill the woman and the animal. They must be put to death. They have brought it on themselves.

17 "'It is shameful for a brother to marry his sister, the daughter of either his father or his mother, and to have sexual relations with her. In front of everyone they must both be cut off from their people. The man has shamed his sister, and he is guilty of sin.

18 "'If a man has sexual relations with a woman during her monthly period, both the woman and the man must be cut off from their people. They have sinned because they have showed the source of her blood.

19 "'Do not have sexual relations with your mother's sister or your father's sister, because that would shame a close relative. Both of you are guilty of this sin.

20 "'If a man has sexual relations with his uncle's wife, he has shamed his uncle. That man and his uncle's wife will die without children; they are guilty of sin.

21 "'It is unclean for a man to marry his brother's wife. That man has shamed his brother, and they will have no children.

22 "'Remember all my laws and rules, and obey them. I am leading you to your own land, and if you obey my laws and rules, that land will not throw you out. 23 I am forcing out ahead of you the people who live there. Because they did all these sins, I have hated them. Do not live the way those people lived.

24 "'I have told you that you will get their land, which I will give to you as your very own; it is a fertile land. I am the LORD your God, and I have set you apart from other people and made you my own. 25 So you must treat clean animals and birds differently from unclean animals and birds. Do not make yourselves unclean by any of these unclean birds or animals or things that crawl on the ground, which I have made unclean for you. 26 So you must be holy to me because I, the LORD, am holy, and I have set you apart from other people to be my own.

27 "'A man or woman who is a medium or a fortune-teller must be put to death. You must stone them to death; they have brought it on themselves.'"

How Priests Must Behave

21 The LORD said to Moses, "Tell these things to Aaron's sons, the priests: 'A priest must not make himself unclean by touching a dead person. 2 But if the dead person was one of his close relatives, he may touch him. The priest may make himself unclean if the dead person is his mother or father, son or daughter, brother or 3 unmarried sister who is close to him because she has no husband. The priest may make himself unclean for her if she dies. 4 But a priest must not make himself unclean if the dead person was only related to him by marriage.

5 "'Priests must not shave their heads, or shave off the edges of their beards, or cut their bodies. 6 They must be holy to their God and show respect for God's name, because they present the offerings made by fire to the LORD, which is the food of their God. So they must be holy.

7 "'A priest must not marry an unclean prostitute or a divorced woman, because he is holy to his God. 8 Treat him as holy, because he offers up the food of your God. Think of him as holy; I am the LORD who makes you holy, and I am holy.

9 "'If a priest's daughter makes herself unclean by becoming a prostitute, she shames her father. She must be burned with fire.

10 "'The high priest, who was chosen

from among his brothers, had the special olive oil poured on his head. He was also appointed to wear the priestly clothes. So he must not show his sadness by letting his hair go uncombed or tearing his clothes. 11 He must not go into a house where there is a dead body. He must not make himself unclean, even if it is for his own father or mother. 12 The high priest must not go out of the Holy Place, because if he does and becomes unclean, he will make God's Holy Place unclean. The special oil used in appointing priests was poured on his head to separate him from the rest of the people. I am the LORD.

13 "The high priest must marry a woman who is a virgin. 14 He must not marry a widow, a divorced woman or a prostitute. He must marry a virgin from his own people 15 so the people will respect his children as his own. I am the LORD. I have set the high priest apart for his special job.'"

16 The LORD said to Moses, 17 "Tell Aaron: 'If any of your descendants have something wrong with them, they must never come near to offer the special food of their God. 18 Anyone who has something wrong with him must not come near: blind men, crippled men, men with damaged faces, deformed men, 19 men with a crippled foot or hand, 20 hunchbacks, dwarfs, men who have something wrong with their eyes, men who have an itching disease or a skin disease or men who have damaged sex glands.

21 "'If one of Aaron's descendants has something wrong with him, he cannot come near to make the offerings made by fire to the LORD. He has something wrong with him; he cannot offer the food of his God. 22 He may eat the most holy food and also the holy food. 23 But he may not go through the curtain into the Most Holy Place, and he may not go near the altar, because he has something wrong with him. He must not make my Holy Place unfit. I am the LORD who makes these places holy.'"

24 So Moses told these things to Aaron, Aaron's sons and all the people of Israel.

22 The LORD said to Moses, 2 "Tell Aaron and his sons: 'The people of Israel will give offerings to me. These offerings are holy, and they are mine, so you must respect them to show that you respect my holy name. I am the LORD. 3 Say to them: if any one of your descendants from now on is unclean and comes near the offerings that the Israelites made holy for me, that person must be cut off from appearing before me. I am the LORD.

4 "'If one of Aaron's descendants has a harmful skin disease, or if he discharges a body fluid, he cannot eat the holy offerings until he becomes clean. He could also become unclean from touching a dead body, from his own semen,* 5 from touching any unclean crawling animal or from touching an unclean person (no matter what made the person unclean). 6 Anyone who touches those things will become unclean until evening. That person must not eat the holy offerings unless he washes with water. 7 He will be clean only after the sun goes down. Then he may eat the holy offerings; the offerings are his food.

8 "'If a priest finds an animal that died by itself or that was killed by some other animal, he must not eat it. If he does, he will become unclean. I am the LORD.

9 "'If the priests keep all the rules I have given, they will not become guilty; if they are careful, they will not die. I am the LORD who has made them holy. 10 Only people in a priest's family may eat the holy offering. A visitor staying with the priest or a hired worker must not eat it. 11 But if the priest buys a slave with his own money, that slave may eat the holy offerings; slaves who were born in his house may

> These offerings are holy, and they are mine, so you must respect them to show that you respect my holy name.
> – Leviticus 22:2

22:4 semen A man's body fluid by which he can make a woman pregnant.

also eat his food. 12 If a priest's daughter marries a person who is not a priest, she must not eat any of the holy offerings. 13 But if the priest's daughter becomes widowed or divorced, with no children to support her, and if she goes back to her father's house where she lived as a child, she may eat some of her father's food. But only people from a priest's family may eat this food.

14 "'If someone eats some of the holy offering by mistake, that person must pay back the priest for that holy food, adding another one-fifth of the price of that food.

15 "'When the Israelites give their holy offerings to the LORD, the priest must not treat these holy things as though they were not holy. 16 The priests must not allow those who are not priests to eat the holy offerings. If they do, they cause the ones who eat the holy offerings to become guilty, and they will have to pay for it. I am the LORD, who makes them holy.'"

17 The LORD said to Moses, 18 "Tell Aaron and his sons and all the people of Israel: 'A citizen of Israel or a foreigner living in Israel might want to bring a whole burnt offering, either for some special promise he has made or for a special gift he wants to give to the LORD. 19 If he does, he must bring a male animal that has nothing wrong with it—a bull, a sheep or a goat—so it might be accepted for him. 20 He must not bring an animal that has something wrong with it, or it will not be accepted for him.

21 "'If someone brings a fellowship offering to the LORD, either as payment for a special promise the person has made or as a special gift the person wants to give the LORD, it might be from the herd or from the flock. But it must be healthy, with nothing wrong with it, so that it will be accepted. 22 You must not offer to the LORD any animal that is blind, that has broken bones or is crippled, that has running sores or any sort of skin disease. You must not offer any animals like these on the altar as an offering by fire to the LORD.

23 "'If an ox or lamb is smaller than normal or is not perfectly formed, you may give it as a special gift to the LORD; it will be accepted. But it will not be accepted as payment for a special promise you have made.

24 "'If an animal has bruised, crushed, torn or cut sex glands, you must not offer it to the LORD. You must not do this in your own land, 25 and you must not take such animals from foreigners as sacrifices to the LORD. Because the animals have been hurt in some way and have something wrong with them, they will not be accepted for you.'"

26 The LORD said to Moses, 27 "When an ox, a sheep or a goat is born, it must stay seven days with its mother. But from the eighth day on, this animal will be accepted as a sacrifice by fire to the LORD. 28 But you must not kill the animal and its mother on the same day, either an ox or a sheep.

29 "If you want to offer some special offering of thanks to the LORD, you must do it in a way that pleases him. 30 You must eat the whole animal that same day and not leave any of the meat for the next morning. I am the LORD.

31 "Remember my commands and obey them; I am the LORD. 32 Show respect for my holy name. You Israelites must remember that I am holy; I am the LORD, who has made you holy. 33 I brought you out of Egypt to be your God. I am the LORD."

Special Holidays

23 The LORD said to Moses, 2 "Tell the people of Israel: 'You will announce the LORD's appointed feasts as holy meetings. These are my special feasts.

The Sabbath

3 "'There are six days for you to work, but the seventh day will be a special day of rest. It is a day for a holy meeting; you must not do any work. It is a Sabbath to the LORD in all your homes.

The Passover and Unleavened Bread

4 "'These are the LORD's appointed feasts, the holy meetings, which you will

FAITH links

A HOLIDAY EVERY WEEK
LEVITICUS 23:1-3

Wouldn't it be great to have a holiday every week? Well, guess what? God took care of that! There *is* a special day each week that is considered a holiday. That day is Sunday. God set aside the Sabbath day for his people to rest and worship him. That makes Sunday a mini-holiday every week.

Many people spend time preparing for holidays in special ways. You can prepare for Sunday, too. How? One way to prepare is to get your heart ready to worship God. You can do this by reminding yourself of what God has done for you. You can also tell him you're sorry for anything you did wrong.

Here are some more Faithlinks about the importance of spending time with God:

A Thanksgiving Reminder, Exodus 12, p. 91

Idol Talk, Exodus 32, p. 118

You're Invited! Psalm 100, p. 784

The One Who Suffered, Isaiah 53, p. 966

First Place, Haggai 1:7–11, p. 1248

From Useless to Useful, Philemon 11, p. 1663

---

announce at the times set for them. 5 The LORD's Passover is on the fourteenth day of the first month, beginning at twilight. 6 The Feast of Unleavened Bread begins on the fifteenth day of the same month. You will eat bread made without yeast for seven days. 7 On the first day of this feast you will have a holy meeting, and you must not do any work. 8 For seven days you will bring an offering made by fire to the LORD. There will be a holy meeting on the seventh day, and on that day you must not do any regular work.'"

The First of the Harvest

9 The LORD said to Moses, 10 "Tell the people of Israel: 'You will enter the land I will give you and gather its harvest. At that time you must bring the first bundle of grain from your harvest to the priest. 11 The priest will present the bundle before the LORD, and it will be accepted for you; he will present the bundle on the day after the Sabbath.

12 "'On the day when you present the bundle of grain, offer a male lamb, one year old, that has nothing wrong with it, as a burnt offering to the LORD. 13 You must also offer a grain offering—4 litres of fine flour mixed with olive oil as an offering made by fire to the LORD; its smell will be pleasing to him. You must also offer a litre of wine as a drink offering. 14 Until the day you bring your offering to your God, do not eat any new grain, roasted grain or bread made from new grain. This law will always continue for people from now on, wherever you live.

The Feast of Weeks

15 "'Count seven full weeks from the morning after the Sabbath. (This is the Sabbath on which you bring the bundle of grain to present as an offering.) 16 On the fiftieth day, the first day after the seventh week, you will bring a new grain offering to the LORD. 17 On that day bring two loaves of bread from your homes to be presented as an offering. Use yeast and 4 litres of flour to make those loaves of bread; they will be your gift to the LORD from the first wheat of your harvest.

18 "'Offer with the bread one young bull, two rams and seven male lambs that are one year old and have nothing wrong with them. Offer them with their grain offerings and drink offerings, as a burnt offering to the LORD. They will be an offering made by fire, and the smell will be pleasing to the LORD. 19 You must also offer one male goat for a sin offering and two male, one-year-old lambs as a fellowship offering.

20 "'The priest will present the two lambs as an offering before the LORD, along with the bread from the first wheat of the harvest. They are holy to the LORD, and they will belong to the priest. 21 On that same day you will call a holy meeting; you must not do any work on that day. This law will continue for you from now on, wherever you live.

22 "'When you harvest your crops on your land, do not harvest all the way to the corners of your field. If grain falls onto the ground, don't gather it up. Leave it for poor people and foreigners in your country. I am the LORD your God.'"

The Feast of Trumpets

23 Again the LORD said to Moses, 24 "Tell the people of Israel: 'On the first day of the seventh month you must have a special day of rest, a holy meeting, when you blow the trumpet for a special time of remembering. 25 Do not do any work, and bring an offering made by fire to the LORD.'"

The Day of Cleansing

26 The LORD said to Moses, 27 "The Day of Cleansing will be on the tenth day of the seventh month. There will be a holy meeting, and you will give up eating and bring an offering made by fire to the LORD. 28 Do not do any work on that day, because it is the Day of Cleansing. On that day the priests will go before the LORD and perform the acts to make you clean so that you will belong to the LORD.

29 "Anyone who refuses to give up food on this day must be cut off from the people. 30 If anyone works on this day, I will destroy that person from among the people. 31 You must not do any work at all; this law will continue for people from now on wherever you live. 32 It will be a special day of rest for you, and you must not eat. You will start this special day of rest on the evening after the ninth day of the month, and it will continue from that evening until the next evening."

The Feast of Shelters

33 Again the LORD said to Moses, 34 "Tell the people of Israel: 'On the fifteenth day of the seventh month is the Feast of Shelters. This feast to the LORD will continue for seven days. 35 There will be a holy meeting on the first day; do not do any work. 36 You will bring an offering made by fire to the LORD each day for seven days. On the eighth day you will have another holy meeting, and you will bring an offering made by fire to the LORD. This will be a holy meeting; do not do any work.

37 ("'These are the LORD's special feasts, when there will be holy meetings and when you bring offerings made by fire to the LORD. You will bring whole burnt offerings, grain offerings, sacrifices and drink offerings—each at the right time. 38 These offerings are in addition to those for the LORD's Sabbath days, in addition to offerings you give as payment for special promises, and in addition to special offerings you want to give to the LORD.)

39 "'So on the fifteenth day of the seventh month, after you have gathered in the crops of the land, celebrate the LORD's festival for seven days. You must rest on the first day and the eighth day. 40 On the first day you will take good fruit from the fruit trees, as well as branches from palm trees, poplars and other leafy trees. You will celebrate before the LORD your God for seven days. 41 Celebrate this festival to the LORD for seven days each year. This law will continue from now on; you will celebrate it in the seventh month. 42 Live in shelters for seven days. All the people born in Israel must live in shelters 43 so that all your descendants will know I made Israel live in shelters during the time I brought them out of Egypt. I am the LORD your God.'"

44 So Moses told the people of Israel about all of the LORD's appointed feast days.

The Lampstand and the Holy Bread

24 The LORD said to Moses, 2 "Command the people of Israel to bring you pure oil from crushed olives. That oil is for the lamps so that these lamps may never go out. 3 Aaron will keep the lamps burning in the Meeting Tent from evening until morning before the LORD; this is in front of the curtain of the Ark of the Agreement. This law will continue from now on. 4 Aaron must always keep the lamps burning on the lampstands of pure gold before the LORD.

5 "Take fine flour and bake twelve loaves of bread with it, using 4 litres of flour for each loaf. 6 Put them in two rows on the golden table before the LORD, six loaves in each row. 7 Put pure incense on each row as the memorial portion to take the place of the bread. It is an offering made by fire to the LORD. 8 Every Sabbath day Aaron will put the bread in order before the LORD, as an agreement with the people of Israel that will continue for ever. 9 That bread will belong to Aaron and his sons. They will eat it in a holy place, because it is a most holy part of the offerings made by fire to the LORD. That bread is their share for ever."

The Man Who Cursed God

10 Now there was a son of an Israelite woman and an Egyptian father who was walking among the Israelites. A fight broke out in the camp between him and an Israelite. 11 The son of the Israelite woman began cursing and speaking against the LORD, so the people took him to Moses. (The mother's name was Shelomith, the daughter of Debri from the family of Dan.) 12 The people held him as a prisoner while they waited for the LORD's command to be made clear to them.

13 Then the LORD said to Moses, 14 "Take the one who spoke against me outside the camp. Then all the people who heard him must put their hands on his head, and all the people must throw stones at him and kill him. 15 Tell the people of Israel this: 'If anyone curses his God, he is guilty of sin. 16 Anyone who speaks against the LORD must be put to death; all the people must kill him by throwing stones at him. Foreigners must be punished just like the people born in Israel; if they speak against the LORD, they must be put to death.

17 "'Whoever kills another person must be put to death. 18 Whoever kills an animal that belongs to another person must give that person another animal to take its place. 19 And whoever causes an injury to a neighbour must receive the same kind of injury in return: 20 broken bone for broken bone, eye for eye, tooth for tooth. Anyone who injures another person must be injured in the same way in return. 21 Whoever kills another person's animal must give that person another animal to take its place. But whoever kills another person must be put to death.

22 "'The law will be the same for the foreigner as for those from your own country. I am the LORD your God.'"

23 Then Moses spoke to the people of Israel, and they took the person who had cursed outside the camp and killed him by throwing stones at him. So the people of Israel did as the LORD had commanded Moses.

> The law will be the same for the foreigner as for those from your own country. I am the LORD your God.
> – Leviticus 24:22

The Time of Rest for the Land

25 The LORD said to Moses at Mount Sinai, 2 "Tell the people of Israel this: 'When you enter the land I will give you, let it have a special time of rest, to honour the LORD. 3 You may plant seed in your field for six years, and you may trim your vineyards for six years and bring in their fruits. 4 But during the seventh year, you must let the land rest. This will be a special time to honour the LORD. You

must not plant seed in your field or trim your vineyards. 5 You must not cut the crops that grow by themselves after harvest, or gather the grapes from your vines that are not trimmed. The land will have a year of rest.

6 "You may eat whatever the land produces during that year of rest. It will be food for your men and women servants, for your hired workers and for the foreigners living in your country. 7 It will also be food for your cattle and the wild animals of your land. Whatever the land produces may be eaten.

The Year of Jubilee

8 "Count off seven groups of seven years, or 49 years. During that time there will be seven years of rest for the land. 9 On the Day of Cleansing, you must blow the horn of a ram; this will be on the tenth day of the seventh month. You must blow the horn through the whole country. 10 Make the fiftieth year a special year, and announce freedom for all the people living in your country. This time will be called Jubilee.ⁿ You will each go back to your own property, each to your own family and family group. 11 The fiftieth year will be a special time for you to celebrate. Don't plant seeds, or harvest the crops that grow by themselves, or gather grapes from the vines that are not trimmed. 12 That year is Jubilee; it will be a holy time for you. You may eat only the crops that come from the field. 13 In the year of Jubilee you each must go back to your own property.

14 "If you sell your land to your neighbour, or if you buy land from your neighbour, don't cheat each other. 15 If you want to buy your neighbour's land, count the number of years since the last Jubilee, and use that number to decide the right price. If your neighbour sells the land to you, count the number of years left for harvesting crops, and use that number to decide the right price. 16 If there are many years, the price will be high. But if there are only a few years, lower the price, because your neighbour is really selling only a few crops to you. 17 You must not cheat each other, but you must respect your God. I am the LORD your God.

18 "Remember my laws and rules, and obey them so that you will live safely in the land. 19 The land will give good crops to you, and you will eat as much as you want and live safely in the land.

20 "But you might ask, "If we don't plant seeds or gather crops, what will we eat during the seventh year?" 21 I will send you such a great blessing during the sixth year that the land will produce enough crops for three years. 22 When you plant in the eighth year, you will still be eating from the old crop; you will eat the old crop until the harvest of the ninth year.

Property Laws

23 "The land really belongs to me, so you can't sell it for all time. You are only foreigners and travellers living for a while on my land. 24 People might sell their land, but it must always be possible for the family to get its land back. 25 If a person in your country becomes very poor and sells some land, then close relatives must come and buy it back. 26 If there is not a close relative to buy the land back, but if the person makes enough money to be able to buy it back, 27 the years must be counted since the land was sold. That number must be used to decide how much the first owner should pay back the one who bought it. Then the land will belong to the first owner again. 28 But if there is not enough money to buy it back, the one who bought it will keep it until the year of Jubilee. During that celebration, the land will go back to the first owner's family.

29 "If someone sells a home in a walled city, for a full year after it is sold the person has the right to buy it back. 30 But if the owner does not buy back the house before a full year has passed, it will belong to the one who bought it and to his future sons. The house will not go back to the first owner at Jubilee. 31 But houses in small towns without walls are like open country; they can be bought back, and

---

25:10 Jubilee This word comes from the Hebrew word for a horn of a ram.

they must be returned to their first owner at Jubilee.

32 "The Levites may always buy back their houses in the cities that belong to them. 33 If someone buys a house from a Levite, that house in the Levites' city will again belong to the Levites in the Jubilee. This is because houses in Levite cities belong to the people of Levi; the Israelites gave these cities to them. 34 Also the fields and pastures around the Levites' cities cannot be sold, because those fields belong to the Levites for ever.

Rules for Slave Owners

35 "If anyone from your country becomes too poor to support himself, help him to live among you as you would a stranger or foreigner. 36 Do not charge him any interest on money you loan to him, but respect your God; let the poor live among you. 37 Don't lend him money for interest, and don't try to make a profit from the food he buys. 38 I am the LORD your God, who brought you out of the land of Egypt to give the land of Canaan to you and to become your God.

39 "If anyone from your country becomes very poor and sells himself as a slave to you, you must not make him work like a slave. 40 He will be like a hired worker and a visitor with you until the year of Jubilee. 41 Then he may leave you, take his children, and go back to his family and the land of his ancestors. 42 This is because the Israelites are my servants, and I brought them out of slavery in Egypt. They must not become slaves again. 43 You must not rule this person cruelly, but you must respect your God.

44 "Your men and women slaves must come from other nations around you; from them you may buy slaves. 45 Also you may buy as slaves children from the families of foreigners living in your land. These child slaves will belong to you, 46 and you may even pass them on to your children after you die; you can make them slaves for ever. But you must not rule cruelly over your own people, the Israelites.

47 "Suppose a foreigner or visitor among you becomes rich. If someone in your country becomes so poor that he has to sell himself as a slave to the foreigner living among you or to a member of the foreigner's family, 48 the poor person has the right to be bought back and become free. One of his relatives may buy him back: 49 His uncle, his uncle's son, or any one of his close relatives may buy him back. Or, if he gets enough money, he may pay the money to free himself.

50 "He and the one who bought him must count the time from when he sold himself up to the next year of Jubilee. Use that number to decide the price, because the person really only hired himself out for a certain number of years. 51 If there are still many years before the year of Jubilee, the person must pay back a large part of the price. 52 If there are only a few years left until Jubilee, the person must pay a small part of the first price. 53 But he will live like a hired person with the foreigner every year; don't let the foreigner rule cruelly over him.

54 "Even if no one buys him back, at the year of Jubilee, he and his children will become free. 55 This is because the people of Israel are servants to me. They are my servants, whom I brought out of Egypt. I am the LORD your God."

Rewards for Obeying God

26 "Don't make idols for yourselves or set up statues or memorials. Don't put stone statues in your land to bow down to, because I am the LORD your God.

2 "Remember my Sabbaths, and respect my Holy Place. I am the LORD.

26:3–5 Blessings
Find out the key to God's blessings.

3 "If you remember my laws and commands and obey them, 4 I will give you rains at the right season; the land will produce crops, and the trees of the field will produce their fruit. 5 Your threshing will continue until the grape harvest, and your grape harvest will continue until it is time to plant. Then you will have plenty to eat and live

Leviticus 26:22 171

defeat them, killing them with your sword. 8 Five of you will chase 100 men; 100 of you will chase 10,000 men. You will defeat your enemies and kill them with your sword.

9 "Then I will show kindness to you and let you have many children; I will keep my agreement with you. 10 You will have enough crops to last for more than a year. When you harvest the new crops, you will have to throw out the old ones to make room for them. 11 Also I will place my Holy Tent among you, and I will not turn away from you. 12 I will walk with you and be your God, and you will be my people. 13 I am the LORD your God, who brought you out of Egypt, where you were slaves. I broke the heavy weights that were on your shoulders and let you walk proudly again.

Punishment for Not Obeying God

14 "But if you do not obey me and keep all my commands, 15 and if you turn away from my rules and hate my laws, refusing to obey all my commands, you have broken our agreement. 16 As a result, I will do this to you: I will cause terrible things to happen to you. I will cause you to have disease and fever that will destroy your eyes and slowly kill you. You will not have success when you plant your seed, and your enemy will eat your crops. 17 I will be against you, and your enemies will defeat you. These people who hate you will rule over you, and you will run away even when no one is chasing you.

18 "If after all this you still do not obey me, I will punish you seven times more for your sins. 19 I will break your great pride, and I will make the sky like iron and the earth like bronze." 20 You will work hard, but it will not help. Your land will not grow any crops, and your trees will not give their fruit.

21 "If you still turn against me and refuse to obey me, I will beat you seven times harder. The more you sin, the more you will be punished. 22 I will send wild

---

FAITH links

REWARD FOR OBEDIENCE
LEVITICUS 26:3-13

Have you ever been rewarded for doing the right thing? God told the people of Israel that he would reward them for obeying him. He would give them children and they would have a good harvest. Best of all, he promised not to turn away from them.

God does not always reward us with material things in this life. But he does promise to supply what we need. He also promises never to leave us. As a Christian, you can look forward to the biggest reward of all – living for ever with Jesus.

A Special Promise, Numbers 30:1–2, p. 217

Your Stats, 1 Kings 15; 16, p. 460

All Talk, No Action, Jeremiah 5:1–2, p. 996

The God of Second Chances, Jonah 3, p. 1215

Perfectly Pleasing? Matthew 5:1–12, p. 1280

The Way to Heaven, John 14:1–6, p. 1448

---

safely in your land. 6 I will give peace to your country; you will lie down in peace, and no one will make you afraid. I will keep harmful animals out of your country, and armies will not pass through it.

7 "You will chase your enemies and

26:19 sky . . . bronze This means the sky will give no rain and the earth will produce no crops.

animals to attack you, and they will take your children away from you and destroy your cattle. They will make you so few in number the roads will be empty.

23 "If you don't learn your lesson after all these things, and if you still turn against me, 24 I will also turn against you. I will punish you seven more times for your sins. 25 You broke my agreement, and I will punish you. I will bring armies against you, and if you go into your cities for safety, I will cause diseases to spread among you so that your enemy will defeat you. 26 There will be very little bread to eat; ten women will be able to cook all your bread in one oven. They will measure each piece of bread, and you will eat, but you will still be hungry.

27 "If you still refuse to listen to me and still turn against me, 28 I will show my great anger; I will punish you seven more times for your sins. 29 You will eat the bodies of your sons and daughters. 30 I will destroy your places where gods are worshipped and cut down your incense altars. I will pile your dead bodies on the lifeless forms of your idols. I will hate you. 31 I will destroy your cities and make your holy places empty, and I will not smell the pleasing smell of your offerings. 32 I will make the land empty so that your enemies who come to live in it will be shocked at it. 33 I will scatter you among the nations, and I will pull out my sword and destroy you. Your land will become empty, your cities a waste. 34 When you are taken to your enemy's country, your land will finally get its rest. It will enjoy its time of rest all the time it lies empty. 35 During the time the land is empty, it will have the rest you should have given it while you lived in it.

36 "Those of you who are left alive will lose their courage in the land of their enemies. They will be frightened by the sound of a leaf being blown by the wind. They will run as if someone were chasing them with a sword, and they will fall even when no one is chasing them. 37 They will fall over each other, as if someone were chasing them with a sword, even though no one is chasing them. You will not be strong enough to stand up against your enemies. 38 You will die among other nations and disappear in your enemies' countries. 39 So those who are left alive will rot away in their enemies' countries because of their sins. They will also rot away because of their ancestors' sins.

There is Always Hope

40 "But perhaps the people will confess their sins and the sins of their ancestors; maybe they will admit they turned against me and sinned against me, 41 which made me turn against them and send them into the land of their enemies. If these disobedient people are sorry for what they did and accept punishment for their sin, 42 I will remember my agreement with Jacob, my agreement with Isaac and my agreement with Abraham, and I will remember the land. 43 The land will be left empty by its people, and it will enjoy its time of rest as it lies bare without them. Then those who are left alive will accept the punishment for their sins. They will learn that they were punished because they hated my laws and refused to obey my rules. 44 But even though this is true, I will not turn away from them when they are in the land of their enemies. I will not hate them so much that I completely destroy them and break my agreement with them, because I am the LORD their God. 45 For their good I will remember the agreement with their ancestors, whom I brought out of the land of Egypt so I could become their God; the other nations saw these things. I am the LORD.'"

46 These are the laws, rules and teachings the LORD made between himself and the Israelites through Moses at Mount Sinai.

Promises are Important

27 The LORD said to Moses, 2 "Speak to the people of Israel and tell them: 'If someone makes a special promise to give a person as a servant to the LORD by paying a price that is the same value as that person, 3 the price for a man 20 to 60 years old is about 50 pieces of silver. (You must use the measure as set

by the Holy Place.) **4** The price for a woman 20 to 60 years old is about 30 pieces of silver. **5** The price for a man five to 20 years old is about 20 pieces of silver; for a woman it is about 10 pieces of silver. **6** The price for a baby boy one month to five years old is about 5 pieces of silver; for a baby girl the price is about 3 pieces of silver. **7** The price for a man 60 years old or older is about 15 pieces of silver; for a woman it is about 10 pieces of silver.

8 "If anyone is too poor to pay the price, bring him to the priest, and the priest will set the price. The priest will decide how much money the person making the vow can afford to pay.

Gifts to the LORD

9 "Some animals may be used as sacrifices to the LORD. If someone promises to bring one of these to the LORD, it will become holy. **10** That person must not try to put another animal in its place or exchange it, a good animal for a bad one, or a bad animal for a good one. If this happens, both animals will become holy.

11 "'Unclean animals cannot be offered as sacrifices to the LORD, and if someone brings one of them to the LORD, that animal must be brought to the priest. **12** The priest will decide a price for the animal, according to whether it is good or bad; as the priest decides, that is the price for the animal. **13** If the person wants to buy back the animal, an additional one-fifth must be added to the price.

Value of a House

14 "'If a person gives a house as holy to the LORD, the priest must decide its value, according to whether the house is good or bad; as the priest decides, that is the price for the house. **15** But if the person who gives the house wants to buy it back, an additional one-fifth must be added to the price. Then the house will belong to that person again.

Value of Land

16 "'If a person gives some family property to the LORD, the value of the fields will depend on how much seed is needed to plant them. It will cost about 50 pieces of silver for each 100 kilogrammes of barley seed needed. **17** If the person gives a field at the year of Jubilee, its value will stay at what the priest has decided. **18** But if the person gives the field after

---

FAITH links

GIVING YOUR PART
LEVITICUS 27:30

Through Moses, God told the Israelites to give one-tenth or 10 per cent of their harvest to him. The offerings given to God were given to the priests and Levites who served at the Meeting Tent. Many Christians today give a tithe or 10 per cent of the money they earn to God. This money goes to support the work of the church.

God wants you to give from the heart, not out of obligation. He wants you to be willing to share what you have with others. How will you do your part to share with others?

Share What You Have, Exodus 35:5–18, p. 123

Gifts from the Heart, 1 Chronicles 29, p. 557

Operation Co-operation, Ezra 1:5, p. 609

Seeing the Needs, Nehemiah 1, p. 625

A Half-hearted Offering, Malachi 1:6–14, p. 1268

One of the Faithful, Acts 10:1–34, p. 1482

the Jubilee, the priest must decide the exact price by counting the number of years to the next year of Jubilee. Then he will subtract that number from its value. 19 If the person who gave the field wants to buy it back, one-fifth must be added to that price, and the field will belong to the first owner again.

20 " 'If the person does not buy back the field, or if it is sold to someone else, the first person cannot ever buy it back. 21 When the land is released at the year of Jubilee, it will become holy to the LORD, like land specially given to him. It will become the property of the priests.

22 " 'If someone gives to the LORD a field he has bought, which is not a part of his family land, 23 the priest must count the years to the next Jubilee. He must decide the price for the land, and the price must be paid on that day. Then that land will be holy to the LORD. 24 At the year of Jubilee, the land will go back to its first owner, to the family who sold the land.

25 " 'You must use the measure as set by the Holy Place in paying these prices; it weighs 11.5 grammes.

Value of Animals

26 " 'If an animal is the first one born to its parent, it already belongs to the LORD, so people may not give it again. If it is a cow or a sheep, it is the LORD's. 27 If the animal is unclean, the person must buy it back for the price set by the priest, and the person must add one-fifth to that price. If it is not bought back, the priest must sell it for the price he had decided.

28 " 'There is a special kind of gift that people set apart to give to the LORD; it may be a person, animal or field from the family property. That gift cannot be bought back or sold. Every special kind of gift is most holy to the LORD.

29 " 'If anyone is given for the purpose of being destroyed, he cannot be bought back; he must be put to death.

30 " 'One-tenth of all crops belongs to the LORD, including the crops from fields and the fruit from trees. That one-tenth is holy to the LORD. 31 If a person wants to get back that tenth, one-fifth must be added to its price.

32 " 'The priest will take every tenth animal from a person's herd or flock, and it will be holy to the LORD. 33 The owner should not pick out the good animals from the bad or exchange one animal for another. If that happens, both animals will become holy; they cannot be bought back.' "

34 These are the commands the LORD gave to Moses at Mount Sinai for the people of Israel.

LET'S COUNT

Hi! Moses here. Remember me from Exodus, leading God's people out of Egypt? In Numbers I tell the next part of the story. You probably think Numbers sounds like a maths book, but the title actually refers to the number of Israelites in our army. With over 600,000 soldiers, we were ready to conquer the land God promised to us, but the people were afraid to go. Some actually thought we should go back to Egypt and be slaves again! Surf on over to the story of the 12 spies in Numbers 13:26–33 to find out why they were so afraid.

I wrote this book to remind people how important it is to obey God. Because Israel disobeyed, we had to wander the desert for nearly 40 more years. Life was hard, and the people complained all the time. You may not think complaining is that big a deal, but God punished us severely. One time God sent poisonous snakes when the people complained about the food. Check out that story in Numbers 21:4–9.

JESUS WATCH

Many things in Numbers make us think of Jesus. Moses made a bronze snake and put it on a pole. When he lifted the pole up, people who looked at the snake were saved from snakebites. This is like the cross, on which Jesus was lifted up to die. The people who believed in him were saved. Many times Moses struck a rock and life-saving water came out for the people. This points to Jesus who gives us living water, the Holy Spirit, so that we will enjoy eternal life with God. (See the story of the woman at the well in John 4:1–26, p. 1428.) God fed the Israelites with manna every day when they were in the desert. This reminds us of Jesus who is the bread that gives life. (Read about Jesus as the bread of life in John 6:25–58, p. 1432.) Just as the manna was the food that kept the Israelites alive in the desert, Jesus is the bread who gives us eternal life with God.

my FAVOURITE links

OTHER CONNECTIONS

GET THE INFO

Check out these amazing facts and places mentioned in the Book of Numbers by connecting to:

- <u>Time for Breakfast, Numbers 11:4–9</u>. Can you imagine being hungry and having bags of crisps falling from the sky? Well, it was almost like that for the Israelites when they were wandering in the wilderness and God provided them with miracle food. Check it out!
- Ever have trouble making a decision? The Israelites had a unique way of finding out what God wanted them to do. Read all about it in <u>One Potato, Two Potato . . . Numbers 26:55–56</u>.
- True or false: The Dead Sea is really a lake. Find out the answer by linking to <u>Let's Visit the Dead Sea, Numbers 34:12</u>. You also will learn how the Dead Sea got its name.

Why did Moses hit the rock twice with a stick?

Not sure? You can download that information by reading <u>Numbers 20:1-13</u>.

FAITH LINKS

- Approaching God, **Numbers 3:10**
- Give What You Can, **Numbers 7:1–11**
- The Cloud Guide, **Numbers 9:15–23**
- Following the Crowd, **Numbers 13; 14**
- The Perfect Leader? **Numbers 20:1–13**
- An Attention-Getter, **Numbers 22**
- Take Me to Your Leader, **Numbers 27:12–23**
- A Special Promise, **Numbers 30:1–2**

OTHER COOL STORIES:
<u>Follow that cloud! Numbers 9:15–23</u>
<u>Knee-deep in quail, Numbers 11:31–35</u>
<u>Are there really giants in the land? Numbers 13</u>
<u>The angel and the talking donkey, Numbers 22</u>

The People of Israel are Counted

1 The LORD spoke to Moses in the Meeting Tent in the Desert of Sinai. This was on the first day of the second month in the second year after the Israelites left Egypt. He said to Moses: 2 "You and Aaron must count all the people of Israel by families and family groups, listing the name of each man. 3 You and Aaron must count every man 20 years old or older who will serve in the army of Israel, and list them by their divisions. 4 One man from each tribe, the leader of his family, will help you. 5 These are the names of the men who will help you:

> from the tribe of Reuben—Elizur son of Shedeur;
> 6 from the tribe of Simeon—Shelumiel son of Zurishaddai;
> 7 from the tribe of Judah—Nahshon son of Amminadab;
> 8 from the tribe of Issachar—Nethanel son of Zuar;
> 9 from the tribe of Zebulun—Eliab son of Helon;
> 10 from the tribe of Ephraim son of Joseph—Elishama son of Ammihud;
> from the tribe of Manasseh son of Joseph—Gamaliel son of Pedahzur;
> 11 from the tribe of Benjamin—Abidan son of Gideoni;
> 12 from the tribe of Dan—Ahiezer son of Ammishaddai;
> 13 from the tribe of Asher—Pagiel son of Ocran;
> 14 from the tribe of Gad—Eliasaph son of Deuel;
> 15 from the tribe of Naphtali—Ahira son of Enan."

16 These were the men chosen from the people to be leaders of their tribes, the heads of Israel's family groups.

17 Moses and Aaron took these men who had been picked 18 and called all the people of Israel together on the first day of the second month. Then the people were listed by their families and family groups, and all the men who were 20 years old or older were listed by name. 19 Moses did exactly what the LORD had commanded and listed the people while they were in the Desert of Sinai.

20 The tribe of Reuben, the first son born to Israel, was counted; all the men 20 years old or older who were able to serve in the army were listed by name with their families and family groups. 21 The tribe of Reuben totalled 46,500 men.

22 The tribe of Simeon was counted; all the men 20 years old or older who were able to serve in the army were listed by name with their families and family groups. 23 The tribe of Simeon totalled 59,300 men.

24 The tribe of Gad was counted; all the men 20 years old or older who were able to serve in the army were listed by name with their families and family groups. 25 The tribe of Gad totalled 45,650 men.

26 The tribe of Judah was counted; all the men 20 years old or older who were able to serve in the army were listed by name with their families and family groups. 27 The tribe of Judah totalled 74,600 men.

28 The tribe of Issachar was counted; all the men 20 years old or older who were able to serve in the army were listed by name with their families and family groups. 29 The tribe of Issachar totalled 54,400 men.

30 The tribe of Zebulun was counted; all the men 20 years old or older who were able to serve in the army were listed by name with their families and family groups. 31 The tribe of Zebulun totalled 57,400 men.

32 The tribe of Ephraim, a son of Joseph, was counted; all the men 20 years old or older who were able to serve in the army were listed by name with their families and family groups. 33 The tribe of Ephraim totalled 40,500 men.

34 The tribe of Manasseh, also a son of Joseph, was counted; all the men 20 years old or older who were able to serve in the army were listed by name with their families and family groups. 35 The tribe of Manasseh totalled 32,200 men.

36 The tribe of Benjamin was counted; all the men 20 years old or older who

were able to serve in the army were listed by name with their families and family groups. 37 The tribe of Benjamin totalled 35,400 men.

38 The tribe of Dan was counted; all the men 20 years old or older who were able to serve in the army were listed by name with their families and family groups. 39 The tribe of Dan totalled 62,700 men.

40 The tribe of Asher was counted; all the men 20 years old or older who were able to serve in the army were listed by name with their families and family groups. 41 The tribe of Asher totalled 41,500 men.

42 The tribe of Naphtali was counted; all the men 20 years old or older who were able to serve in the army were listed by name with their families and family groups. 43 The tribe of Naphtali totalled 53,400 men.

44 Moses, Aaron and the twelve leaders of Israel, one from each of the families, counted these men. 45 Every man of Israel 20 years old or older who was able to serve in the army was counted and listed with his family. 46 The total number of men was 603,550.

47 The families from the tribe of Levi were not listed with the others, because 48 the LORD had told Moses: 49 "Do not count the tribe of Levi or include them with the other Israelites. 50 Instead put the Levites in charge of the Holy Tent of the Agreement and everything that is with it. They must carry the Holy Tent and everything in it, and they must take care of it and make their camp around it. 51 Any time the Holy Tent is moved, the Levites must take it down, and any time it is set up, the Levites must do it. Anyone else who goes near the Holy Tent will be put to death. 52 The Israelites will make their camps in separate divisions, each family near its flag. 53 But the Levites must make their camp around the Holy Tent of the Agreement so that I will not be angry with the Israelites. The Levites will take care of the Holy Tent of the Agreement."

54 So the Israelites did everything just as the LORD commanded Moses.

The Camp Arrangement

2 The LORD said to Moses and Aaron: 2 "The Israelites should make their camps around the Meeting Tent, but they should not camp too close to it. They should camp under their family flag and banners."

3 The camp of Judah will be on the east side, where the sun rises, and they will camp by divisions there under their flag. The leader of the people of Judah is Nahshon son of Amminadab. 4 There are 74,600 men in his division.

5 Next to them the tribe of Issachar will camp. The leader of the people of Issachar is Nethanel son of Zuar. 6 There are 54,400 men in his division.

7 Next is the tribe of Zebulun. The leader of the people of Zebulun is Eliab son of Helon. 8 There are 57,400 men in his division.

9 There are a total of 186,400 men in the camps of Judah and its neighbours, in all their divisions. They will be the first to march out of camp.

10 The divisions of the camp of Reuben will be on the south side, where they will camp under their flag. The leader of the people of Reuben is Elizur son of Shedeur. 11 There are 46,500 men in his division.

12 Next to them the tribe of Simeon will camp. The leader of the people of Simeon is Shelumiel son of Zurishaddai. 13 There are 59,300 men in his division.

14 Next is the tribe of Gad. The leader of the people of Gad is Eliasaph son of Deuel. 15 There are 45,650 men in his division.

16 There are a total of 151,450 men in the camps of Reuben and its neighbours, in all their divisions. They will be the second group to march out of camp.

17 When the Levites march out with the Meeting Tent, they will be in the middle of the other camps. The tribes will march out in the same order as they camp, each in its place under its flag.

18 The divisions of the camp of Ephraim will be on the west side, where they will camp under their flag. The leader of the people of Ephraim is Elishama son

of Ammihud. **19** There are 40,500 men in his division.

20 Next to them the tribe of Manasseh will camp. The leader of the people of Manasseh is Gamaliel son of Pedahzur. **21** There are 32,200 men in his division.

22 Next is the tribe of Benjamin. The leader of the people of Benjamin is Abidan son of Gideoni. **23** There are 35,400 men in his division.

24 There are a total of 108,100 men in the camps of Ephraim and its neighbours, in all their divisions. They will be the third group to march out of camp.

25 The divisions of the camp of Dan will be on the north side, where they will camp under their flag. The leader of the people of Dan is Ahiezer son of Ammishaddai. **26** There are 62,700 men in his division.

27 Next to them the tribe of Asher will camp. The leader of the people of Asher is Pagiel son of Ocran. **28** There are 41,500 men in his division.

29 Next is the tribe of Naphtali. The leader of the people of Naphtali is Ahira son of Enan. **30** There are 53,400 men in his division.

31 There are 157,600 men in the camps of Dan and its neighbours. They will be the last to march out of camp, and they will travel under their own flag.

32 These are the Israelites who were counted by families. The total number of Israelites in the camps, counted by divisions, is 603,550. **33** Moses obeyed the LORD and did not count the Levites among the other people of Israel.

34 So the Israelites obeyed everything the LORD commanded Moses. They camped under their flags and marched out by families and family groups.

Aaron's Family, the Priests

3 This is the family history of Aaron and Moses at the time the LORD talked to Moses on Mount Sinai.

2 Aaron had four sons: Nadab, the oldest, Abihu, Eleazar and Ithamar. **3** These were the names of Aaron's sons, who were appointed to serve as priests. **4** But Nadab and Abihu died in the presence of the LORD when they offered the wrong kind of fire before the LORD in the Desert of Sinai. They had no sons. So Eleazar and Ithamar served as priests during the lifetime of their father Aaron.

5 The LORD said to Moses, **6** "Bring the tribe of Levi and present them to Aaron the priest to help him. **7** They will help him and all the Israelites at the Meeting Tent, doing the work in the Holy Tent. **8** The Levites must take care of everything in the Meeting Tent and serve the people of Israel by doing the work in the Holy Tent. **9** Give the Levites to Aaron and his sons; of all the Israelites, the Levites are given completely to him. **10** Appoint Aaron and his sons to serve as priests, but anyone else who comes near the holy things must be put to death."

11 The LORD also said to Moses, **12** "I am choosing the Levites from all the Israelites to take the place of all the firstborn children of Israel. The Levites will be mine, **13** because the firstborn are mine. When you were in Egypt, I killed all the firstborn children of the Egyptians and took all the firstborn of Israel to be mine, both animals and children. They are mine. I am the LORD."

14 The LORD again said to Moses in the Desert of Sinai, **15** "Count the Levites by families and family groups. Count every male one month old or older." **16** So Moses obeyed the LORD and counted them all.

17 Levi had three sons, whose names were Gershon, Kohath and Merari.

18 The Gershonite family groups were Libni and Shimei.

19 The Kohathite family groups were Amram, Izhar, Hebron and Uzziel.

20 The Merarite family groups were Mahli and Mushi.

These were the family groups of the Levites.

> They camped under their flags and marched out by families and family groups.
> – Numbers 2:34

FAITH links

APPROACHING GOD
NUMBERS 3:10

How would you react if your pastor or vicar one Sunday suddenly announced, "Anyone but me who touches the altar or puts anything on it will instantly be put to death"? In Moses' day, that statement was true. Certain items and areas of the Meeting Tent were considered off-limits to everyone except Aaron and his sons, who served as priests. These items and areas were symbols of God's holiness. Only appointed priests could handle these items and enter these special areas.

Jesus' death makes it possible for anyone to approach him, without the fear of death. You don't have to go through a minister. All you have to do is pray.

Check out these other Faithlinks on prayer:

The Rainbow Promise, Genesis 9:1–17, p. 14

The Name of the Lord, Exodus 33:19–23; 34:5–8, p. 120

A Friend in Deed, Job 2:13, p. 662

The Prayer Habit, Psalm 5:1–3, p. 712

A Hopeful Name, Hosea 1:3–11, p. 1172

Praise Him! Revelation 5:12, p. 1736

---

21 The family groups of Libni and Shimei belonged to Gershon; they were the Gershonite family groups. 22 The number that was counted was 7,500 males one month old or older. 23 The Gershonite family groups camped on the west side, behind the Holy Tent. 24 The leader of the families of Gershon was Eliasaph son of Lael. 25 In the Meeting Tent the Gershonites were in charge of the Holy Tent, its covering, the curtain at the entrance to the Meeting Tent, 26 the curtains in the courtyard, the curtain at the entrance to the courtyard around the Holy Tent and the altar, the ropes and all the work connected with these things.

27 The family groups of Amram, Izhar, Hebron and Uzziel belonged to Kohath; they were the Kohathite family groups. 28 They had 8,600 males one month old or older, and they were responsible for taking care of the Holy Place. 29 The Kohathite family groups camped south of the Holy Tent. 30 The leader of the Kohathite families was Elizaphan son of Uzziel. 31 They were responsible for the Ark, the table, the lampstand, the altars, the tools of the Holy Place which they were to use, the curtain and all the work connected with these things. 32 The main leader of the Levites was Eleazar son of Aaron, the priest, who was in charge of all those responsible for the Holy Place.

33 The family groups of Mahli and Mushi belonged to Merari; they were the Merarite family groups. 34 The number that was counted was 6,200 males one month old or older. 35 The leader of the Merari families was Zuriel son of Abihail, and they were to camp north of the Holy Tent. 36 The Merarites were responsible for the frames of the Holy Tent, the braces, the posts, the bases and all the work connected with these things. 37 They were also responsible for the posts in the courtyard around the Holy Tent and their bases, tent pegs and ropes.

38 Moses, Aaron and his sons camped east of the Holy Tent, towards the sunrise, in front of the Meeting Tent. They were responsible for the Holy Place for the Israelites. Anyone else who came near the Holy Place was to be put to death.

39 Moses and Aaron counted the Levite men by their families, as the LORD commanded, and there were 22,000 males one month old or older.

Levites Take the Place of the Firstborn Sons

40 The LORD said to Moses, "Count all the firstborn sons in Israel one month old or older, and list their names. 41 Take the Levites for me instead of the firstborn sons of Israel; take the animals of the Levites instead of the firstborn animals from the rest of Israel. I am the LORD."

42 So Moses did what the LORD commanded and counted all the firstborn sons of the Israelites. 43 When he listed all the firstborn sons one month old or older, there were 22,273 names.

44 The LORD also said to Moses, 45 "Take the Levites instead of all the firstborn sons of the Israelites, and take the animals of the Levites instead of the animals of the other people. The Levites are mine. I am the LORD. 46 Since there are 273 more firstborn sons than Levites, 47 collect 5 pieces of silver for each of the 273 sons. Use the measure as set by the Holy Place, which is 11.5 grammes. 48 Give the silver to Aaron and his sons as the payment for the 273 Israelites."

49 So Moses collected the money for the people the Levites could not replace. 50 From the firstborn of the Israelites, he collected 1,365 pieces of silver, using the measure set by the Holy Place. 51 Moses obeyed the command of the LORD and gave the silver to Aaron and his sons.

The Jobs of the Kohath Family

4 The LORD said to Moses and Aaron, 2 "Count the Kohathites among the Levites by family groups and families. 3 Count the men from 30 to 50 years old, all who come to serve in the Meeting Tent.

4 "The Kohathites are responsible for the most holy things in the Meeting Tent. 5 When the Israelites are ready to move, Aaron and his sons must go into the Holy Tent, take down the curtain, and cover the Ark of the Agreement with it. 6 Over this they must put a covering made from fine leather, then spread the solid blue cloth over that, and put the poles in place.

7 "Then they must spread a blue cloth over the table for the bread that shows a

---

FAITH links

EVERYONE CAN HELP

NUMBERS 4

Does the minister of your church preach the sermon, collect the offering, teach Sunday school, lead the choir, clean the church and pass out the bulletins each Sunday? No way, right? One person couldn't do all that needs to be done. That's the way it was in Moses' day. Everyone had specific duties within the Meeting Tent. Certain families were responsible for certain jobs.

Everyone has specific duties within the church today. We all work together as a body to worship God. This allows everyone the opportunity to serve. How will you serve?

A Use for Your Abilities, Genesis 41, p. 59

His OK to Obey, Deuteronomy 2:24–36, p. 230

Your Response to Responsibility, Ruth 2:1–7, p. 346

The Way to Serve God, 1 Kings 9:4, p. 450

My Best Serve, Acts 6:1–6, p. 1473

Glad to Help! Romans 15:17–20, p. 1541

person is in God's presence. They must put the plates, pans, bowls and the jars for drink offerings on the table; they must leave the bread that is always there on the table. 8 Then they must put a red cloth over all of these things, cover everything with fine leather, and put the poles in place.

9 "With a blue cloth they must cover the lampstand, its lamps, its wick trimmers, its trays and all the jars for the oil used in the lamps. 10 Then they must wrap everything in fine leather and put all these things on a frame for carrying them.

11 "They must spread a blue cloth over the gold altar, cover it with fine leather and put the poles in place.

12 "They must gather all the things used for serving in the Holy Place and wrap them in a blue cloth. Then they must cover that with fine leather and put these things on a frame for carrying them.

13 "They must clean the ashes off the bronze altar and spread a purple cloth over it. 14 They must gather all the things used for serving at the altar—the pans for carrying the fire, the meat forks, the shovels and the bowls—and put them on the bronze altar. Then they must spread a covering of fine leather over it and put the poles in place.

15 "When the Israelites are ready to move, and when Aaron and his sons have covered the holy furniture and all the holy things, the Kohathites may go in and carry them away. In this way they won't touch the holy things and die. It is the Kohathites' job to carry the things that are in the Meeting Tent.

16 "Eleazar son of Aaron, the priest, will be responsible for the Holy Tent and for everything in it, for all the holy things it has: the oil for the lamp, the sweet-smelling incense, the continual grain offering and the oil used to appoint priests and things to the LORD's service."

17 The LORD said to Moses and Aaron, 18 "Don't let the Kohathites be cut off from the Levites. 19 Do this for the Kohathites so that they may go near the Most Holy Place and not die: Aaron and his sons must go in and show each Kohathite what to do and what to carry. 20 The Kohathites must not enter and look at the holy things, even for a second, or they will die."

The Jobs of the Gershon Family

21 The LORD said to Moses, 22 "Count the Gershonites by families and family groups. 23 Count the men from 30 to 50 years old, all who have a job to do in the Meeting Tent.

24 "This is what the Gershonite family groups must do and what they must carry. 25 They must carry the curtains of the Holy Tent, the Meeting Tent, its covering and its outer covering made from fine leather. They must also carry the curtains for the entrance to the Meeting Tent, 26 the curtains of the courtyard that go around the Holy Tent and the altar, the curtain for the entrance to the courtyard, the ropes and all the things used with the curtains. They must do everything connected with these things. 27 Aaron and his sons are in charge of what the Gershonites do or carry; you tell them what they are responsible for carrying. 28 This is the work of the Gershonite family group at the Meeting Tent. Ithamar son of Aaron, the priest, will direct their work.

The Jobs of the Merari Family

29 "Count the Merarite families and family groups. 30 Count the men from 30 to 50 years old, all who work at the Meeting Tent. 31 It is their job to carry the following as they serve in the Meeting Tent: the frames of the Holy Tent, the crossbars, the posts and bases, 32 in addition to the posts that go around the courtyard, their bases, tent pegs, ropes and everything that is used with the poles around the courtyard. Tell each man exactly what to carry. 33 This is the work the Merarite family group will do for the Meeting Tent. Ithamar son of Aaron, the priest, will direct their work."

The Levite Families

34 Moses, Aaron and the leaders of Israel counted the Kohathites by families and family groups, 35 the men from 30

to 50 years old who were to work at the Meeting Tent. 36 There were 2,750 men in the family groups. 37 This was the total of the Kohath family groups who worked at the Meeting Tent, whom Moses and Aaron counted as the LORD had commanded Moses.

38 Also, the Gershonites were counted by families and family groups, 39 the men from 30 to 50 years old who were given work at the Meeting Tent. 40 The families and family groups had 2,630 men. 41 This was the total of the Gershon family groups who worked at the Meeting Tent, whom Moses and Aaron counted as the LORD had commanded.

42 Also, the men in the families and family groups of the Merari family were counted, 43 the men from 30 to 50 years old who were to work at the Meeting Tent. 44 The family groups had 3,200 men. 45 This was the total of the Merari family groups, whom Moses and Aaron counted as the LORD had commanded Moses.

46 So Moses, Aaron and the leaders of Israel counted all the Levites by families and family groups. 47 They counted the men from 30 to 50 years old who were given work at the Meeting Tent and who carried the Tent. 48 The total number of these men was 8,580. 49 Each man was counted as the LORD had commanded Moses; each man was given his work and told what to carry as the LORD had commanded Moses.

Rules About Cleanliness

5 The LORD said to Moses, 2 "Command the Israelites to send away from camp anyone with a harmful skin disease. Send away anyone who gives off body fluid or who has become unclean by touching a dead body. 3 Send both men and women outside the camp so that they won't spread the disease there, where I am living among you." 4 So Israel obeyed the LORD's command and sent those people outside the camp. They did just as the LORD had told Moses.

Paying for Doing Wrong

5 The LORD said to Moses, 6 "Tell the Israelites: 'When a man or woman does something wrong to another person, that is really sinning against the LORD. That person is guilty 7 and must admit the wrong that has been done. The person must fully pay for the wrong that has been done, adding one-fifth to it, and giving it to the person who was wronged. 8 But if that person is dead and does not have any close relatives to receive the payment, the one who did wrong owes the LORD and must pay the priest. In addition, the priest must sacrifice a ram to remove the wrong so that the person will belong to the LORD. 9 When an Israelite brings a holy gift, it should be given to the priest. 10 No one has to give these holy gifts, but if someone does give them, they belong to the priest.'"

> The person must fully pay for the wrong that has been done, adding one-fifth to it.
> – Numbers 5:7

Suspicious Husbands

11 Then the LORD said to Moses, 12 "Tell the Israelites: 'A man's wife might be unfaithful to him 13 and have sexual relations with another man. Her sin might be kept hidden from her husband so that he does not know about the wrong she did. Perhaps no one saw it, and she wasn't caught. 14 But if her husband has feelings of jealousy and suspects she has sinned—whether she has or not— 15 he should take her to the priest. The husband must also take an offering for her of 2 litres of barley flour. He must not pour oil or incense on it, because this is a grain offering for jealousy, an offering of remembrance. It is to find out if she is guilty.

16 "'The priest will bring in the woman and make her stand before the LORD. 17 He will take some holy water in a clay jar, and he will put some earth from the floor of the Holy Tent into the water.

18 The priest will make the woman stand before the LORD, and he will loosen her hair. He will hand her the offering of remembrance, the grain offering for jealousy; he will hold the bitter water that brings a curse. 19 The priest will make her take an oath and ask her, "Has another man had sexual relations with you? Have you been unfaithful to your husband? If you haven't, this bitter water that brings a curse won't hurt you. 20 But if you have been unfaithful to your husband and have had sexual relations with a man besides him"— 21 the priest will then put on her the curse that the oath will bring—"the LORD will make the people curse and reject you. He will make your stomach get big, and he will make your body unable to give birth to another baby. 22 This water that brings a curse will go inside you and make your body unable to give birth to another baby."

"'The woman must say, "I agree."

23 "'The priest should write these curses on a scroll, wash the words off into the bitter water, 24 and make the woman drink the bitter water that brings a curse. If she is guilty, the water will make her sick. 25 Then the priest will take the grain offering for jealousy from her. He will present it before the LORD and bring it to the altar. 26 He will take a handful of the grain, which is a memorial offering, and burn it on the altar. After that he will make the woman drink the water 27 to see if she is not pure and if she has sinned against her husband. When it goes into her, if her stomach gets big so that she is not able to have another baby, her people will reject her. 28 But if the woman has not sinned, she is pure. She is not guilty, and she will be able to have babies.

29 "'So this is the teaching about jealousy. This is what to do when a woman does wrong and is unfaithful while she is married to her husband. 30 It also should be done if the man gets jealous because he suspects his wife. The priest will have her stand before the LORD, and he will do all these things, just as the teaching commands. 31 In this way the husband can be proven correct, and the woman will suffer if she has done wrong.'"

Rules for the Nazirites

6 The LORD said to Moses, 2 "Tell the Israelites: 'If men or women want to promise to belong to the LORD in a special way, they will be called Nazirites. 3 During this time, they must not drink wine or beer, or vinegar made from wine or beer. They must not even drink grape juice or eat grapes or raisins. 4 While they are Nazirites, they must not eat anything that comes from the grapevine, even the seeds or the skin.

5 "'During the time they have promised to belong to the LORD, they must not cut their hair. They must be holy until this special time is over. They must let their hair grow long. 6 During their special time of belonging to the LORD, Nazirites must not go near a dead body. 7 Even if their own father, mother, brother or sister dies, they must not touch them, or they will become unclean. They must still keep their promise to belong to God in a special way. 8 While they are Nazirites, they belong to the LORD in a special way.

9 "'If they are next to someone who dies suddenly, their hair, which was part of their promise, has been made unclean. So they must shave their head seven days later to be clean. 10 Then on the eighth day, they must bring two doves or two young pigeons to the priest at the entrance to the Meeting Tent. 11 The priest will offer one as a sin offering and the other as a burnt offering. This removes sin so they will belong to the LORD. (They had sinned because they were near a dead body.) That same day they will again promise to let their hair grow 12 and give themselves to the LORD for another special time. They must bring a male lamb a year old as a penalty offering. The days of the special time before don't count, because they became unclean during their first special time.

13 "'This is the teaching for the Nazirites. When the promised time is over, they must go to the entrance of the Meeting Tent 14 and give their offerings to the LORD. They must offer a year-old male lamb that has nothing wrong with it, as a burnt offering, a year-old female lamb

that has nothing wrong with it, as a sin offering, and a ram that has nothing wrong with it, for a fellowship offering. 15 They must also bring the grain offerings and drink offerings that go with them. And they must bring a basket of bread made without yeast, loaves made with fine flour mixed with oil, and wafers made without yeast, spread with oil.

16 "The priest will give these offerings to the LORD and make the sin offering and the burnt offering. 17 Then he will kill the ram as a fellowship offering to the LORD; along with it, he will present the basket of bread made without yeast, the grain offering and the drink offering.

18 "The Nazirites must go to the entrance of the Meeting Tent and shave off their hair that they grew for their promise. The hair will be put in the fire that is under the sacrifice of the fellowship offering.

19 "'After the Nazirites cut off their hair, the priest will give them a boiled shoulder from the ram. From the basket he will also give a loaf and a wafer, both made without yeast. 20 Then the priest will present them to the LORD. They are holy and belong to the priest. Also, he is to present the breast and the thigh from the ram. After that, the Nazirites may drink wine.

21 "This is the teaching for the Nazirites who make a promise. Everyone who makes the Nazirite promise must give all these gifts to the LORD. If they promised to do more, they must keep their promise, according to the teaching of the Nazirites.'"

The Priests' Blessings

22 The LORD said to Moses, 23 "Tell Aaron and his sons, 'This is how you should bless the Israelites. Say to them:
24 "May the LORD bless you
   and keep you.
25 May the LORD
   show you
   his kindness
   and have mercy
   on you.

6:24–26
Peace
What does God give you?

26 May the LORD watch over you
   and give you peace."'

27 "So Aaron and his sons will bless the Israelites with my name, and I will bless them."

The Holy Tent

7 When Moses finished setting up the Holy Tent, he gave it for service to the LORD by pouring olive oil on the Tent and on everything used in it. He also poured oil on the altar and all its tools to prepare them for service to the LORD. 2 Then the leaders of Israel made offerings. These were the heads of the families, the leaders of each tribe who counted the people. 3 They brought to the LORD six covered carts and twelve oxen—each leader giving an ox, and every two leaders giving a cart. They brought these to the Holy Tent.

4 The LORD said to Moses, 5 "Accept these gifts from the leaders and use them in the work of the Meeting Tent. Give them to the Levites as they need them."

6 So Moses accepted the carts and the oxen and gave them to the Levites. 7 He gave two carts and four oxen to the Gershonites, which they needed for their work. 8 Then Moses gave four carts and eight oxen to the Merarites, which they needed for their work. Ithamar son of Aaron, the priest, directed the work of all of them. 9 Moses did not give any oxen or carts to the Kohathites, because their job was to carry the holy things on their shoulders.

10 When the oil was poured on the altar, the leaders brought their offerings to it to give it to the LORD's service; they presented them in front of the altar. 11 The LORD told Moses, "Each day one leader must bring his gift to make the altar ready for service to me."

12-83 Each of the twelve leaders brought these gifts. Each leader brought one silver plate that weighed about 1,500 grammes, and one silver bowl that weighed about 800 grammes. These weights were set by the Holy Place measure. The bowl and the plate were filled with fine flour mixed with oil for a grain offering. Each

Numbers 7:84   186

FAITH links

GIVE WHAT YOU CAN
NUMBERS 7:1-11

If you've ever been a member of a football club, you know that you will have had to pay your subscriptions and you may have been asked to help with fundraising. In order to keep the club going, money needs to be given in support.

When the Meeting Tent was finished, the leaders of the twelve tribes gave gifts to the priests. The offerings were given to support the work. This way everyone shared in supplying the needs of the priests. Our offerings today help to support the activities of the church. We all have the responsibility to give what we can, whether it's money, time, or help.

Giving Your Part, Leviticus 27:30, p. 173

What's the Use? 2 Kings 12:6–12, p. 495

Service with a Smile, 1 Chronicles 6:31–49, p. 527

A Reminder to Be Fair, 2 Chronicles 19:5–11, p. 583

The Way to Greatness, Matthew 20:20–28, p. 1309

The Most Fun, Acts 20:35, p. 1502

In addition, each of the leaders brought one young bull, one ram and one male lamb a year old for a burnt offering; one male goat for a sin offering; and two oxen, five rams, five male goats and five male lambs a year old for a fellowship offering.

On the first day Nahshon son of Amminadab brought his gifts. He was the leader of the tribe of Judah.

On the second day Nethanel son of Zuar brought his gifts. He was the leader of the tribe of Issachar.

On the third day Eliab son of Helon brought his gifts. He was the leader of the tribe of Zebulun.

On the fourth day Elizur son of Shedeur brought his gifts. He was the leader of the tribe of Reuben.

On the fifth day Shelumiel son of Zurishaddai brought his gifts. He was the leader of the tribe of Simeon.

On the sixth day Eliasaph son of Deuel brought his gifts. He was the leader of the tribe of Gad.

On the seventh day Elishama son of Ammihud brought his gifts. He was the leader of the tribe of Ephraim.

On the eighth day Gamaliel son of Pedahzur brought his gifts. He was the leader of the tribe of Manasseh.

On the ninth day Abidan son of Gideoni brought his gifts. He was the leader of the tribe of Benjamin.

On the tenth day Ahiezer son of Ammishaddai brought his gifts. He was the leader of the tribe of Dan.

On the eleventh day Pagiel son of Ocran brought his gifts. He was the leader of the tribe of Asher.

On the twelfth day Ahira son of Enan brought his gifts. He was the leader of the tribe of Naphtali.

84 So these were the gifts from the Israelite leaders when oil was poured on the altar and it was given for service to the LORD: twelve silver plates, twelve silver bowls and twelve gold dishes. 85 Each silver plate weighed about 1,500 grammes, and each bowl weighed about 800 grammes. All the silver plates and silver bowls together weighed about 27 kilogrammes according to a weight set

leader also brought a large gold dish that weighed about 110 grammes and was filled with incense.

by the Holy Place measure. 86 The twelve gold dishes filled with incense weighed 110 grammes each, according to the weight set by the Holy Place measure. Together the gold dishes weighed about 1,400 grammes. 87 The total number of animals for the burnt offering was twelve bulls, twelve rams and twelve male lambs a year old. There was also a grain offering, and there were twelve male goats for a sin offering. 88 The total number of animals for the fellowship offering was 24 bulls, 60 rams, 60 male goats and 60 male lambs a year old. All these offerings were for giving the altar to the service of the LORD after the oil had been poured on it.

89 When Moses went into the Meeting Tent to speak with the LORD, he heard the LORD speaking to him. The voice was coming from between the two gold creatures with wings that were above the lid of the Ark of the Agreement. In this way the LORD spoke with him.

The Lampstand

8 The LORD said to Moses, 2 "Speak to Aaron and tell him, 'Put the seven lamps where they can light the area in front of the lampstand.'"

3 Aaron did this, placing the lamps so that they lighted the area in front of the lampstand; he obeyed the command the LORD gave Moses. 4 The lampstand was made from hammered gold, from its base to the flowers. It was made in exactly the way the LORD had showed Moses.

The Levites are Given to God

5 The LORD said to Moses, 6 "Take the Levites away from the other Israelites and make them clean. 7 This is what you should do to make them clean: sprinkle the cleansing water on them, and make them shave their bodies and wash their clothes so that they are clean. 8 They must take a young bull and the grain offering of flour mixed with oil that goes with it. Then take a second young bull for a sin offering. 9 Bring the Levites to the front of the Meeting Tent, and gather all the Israelites around. 10 When you bring the Levites before the LORD, the Israelites should put their hands on them.[n] 11 Aaron will present the Levites before the LORD as an offering presented from the Israelites. Then the Levites will be ready to do the work of the LORD.

12 "The Levites will put their hands on the bulls' heads—one bull will be a sin offering to the LORD, and the other will be a burnt offering, to remove the sins of the Levites so they will belong to the LORD. 13 Make the Levites stand in front of Aaron and his sons and present the Levites as an offering to the LORD. 14 In this way you must set apart the Levites from the other Israelites; the Levites will be mine.

15 "Make the Levites pure, and present them as an offering so that they may come to work at the Meeting Tent. 16 They will be given completely to me from the Israelites; I have taken them for myself instead of the firstborn of every Israelite woman. 17 All the firstborn in Israel—people or animals—are mine. When I killed all the firstborn in Egypt, I set the firstborn in Israel aside for myself. 18 But I have taken the Levites instead of all the firstborn in Israel. 19 From all the Israelites I have given the Levites to Aaron and his sons so that they may serve the Israelites at the Meeting Tent. They will help remove the Israelites' sins so that they belong to the LORD and so that no disaster strikes the Israelites when they approach the Holy Place."

20 So Moses, Aaron and all the Israelites obeyed and did with the Levites what the LORD commanded Moses. 21 The Levites made themselves clean and washed their clothes. Then Aaron presented them as an offering to the LORD.

> In this way you must set apart the Levites from the other Israelites; the Levites will be mine.
> – Numbers 8:14

8:10 put . . . them This showed that the people had a part in giving the Levites their special work.

He also removed their sins so they would be pure. 22 After that, the Levites came to the Meeting Tent to work, and Aaron and his sons told them what to do. They did with the Levites what the LORD commanded Moses.

23 The LORD said to Moses, 24 "This command is for the Levites. Everyone 25 years old or older must come to the Meeting Tent, because they all have jobs to do there. 25 At the age of 50, they must retire from their jobs and not work again. 26 They may help their fellow Levites with their work at the Meeting Tent, but they must not do the work themselves. This is how you are to give the Levites their jobs."

The Passover is Celebrated

9 The LORD spoke to Moses in the Desert of Sinai in the first month of the second year after the Israelites left Egypt. He said, 2 "Tell the Israelites to celebrate the Passover at the appointed time. 3 That appointed time is the fourteenth day of this month at twilight; they must obey all the rules about it."

4 So Moses told the Israelites to celebrate the Passover, 5 and they did; it was in the Desert of Sinai at twilight on the fourteenth day of the first month. The Israelites did everything just as the LORD commanded Moses.

6 But some of the people could not celebrate the Passover on that day because they were unclean from touching a dead body. So they went to Moses and Aaron that day and 7 said to Moses, "We are unclean because of touching a dead body. But why should we be kept from offering gifts to the LORD at this appointed time? Why can't we join the other Israelites?"

8 Moses said to them, "Wait, and I will find out what the LORD says about you."

9 Then the LORD said to Moses, 10 "Tell the Israelites this: 'If you or your descendants become unclean because of a dead body, or if you are away on a trip during the Passover, you must still celebrate the LORD's Passover. 11 But celebrate it at twilight on the fourteenth day of the second month. Eat the lamb with bitter herbs and bread made without yeast.

FAITH links

THE CLOUD GUIDE
NUMBERS 9:15-23

Certain clouds are a sign of changing weather conditions. Black clouds are the sign of a thunderstorm. For the Israelites, a cloud was the sign of change. God's presence took the form of a cloud over the Meeting Tent. When the cloud moved, the people knew that the time had come to break camp and move out.

Today, God doesn't use a cloud to guide his people. God is present with us through the Holy Spirit. He has also given us the Bible and wise advice from fellow Christians.

Try to Remember, Deuteronomy 11:18–21, p. 243

Learning to Listen, 1 Samuel 3, p. 358

Deciding Wisely, 1 Kings 3:16–28, p. 440

Like Silver, Psalm 12:6–8, p. 717

A Hopeful Future, Jeremiah 29:11, p. 1031

Out of Your Mind? 1 Corinthians 2:16, p. 1547

12 Don't leave any of it until the next morning or break any of its bones. When you celebrate the Passover, follow all the rules. 13 Anyone who is clean and is not away on a trip but does not eat the Passover must be cut off from the people. That person did not give an offering to the LORD at the appointed time and must be punished for the sin.

14 "'Foreigners among you may celebrate the LORD's Passover, but they must follow all the rules. You must have the same rules for foreigners as you have for yourselves.'"

The Cloud Above the Tent

15 On the day the Holy Tent, the Tent of the Agreement, was set up, a cloud covered it. From dusk until dawn the cloud above the Tent looked like fire. 16 The cloud stayed above the Tent, and at night it looked like fire. 17 When the cloud moved from its place over the Tent, the Israelites moved, and wherever the cloud stopped, the Israelites camped. 18 So the Israelites moved at the LORD's command, and they camped at his command. While the cloud stayed over the Tent, they remained camped. 19 Sometimes the cloud stayed over the Tent for a long time, but the Israelites obeyed the LORD and did not move. 20 Sometimes the cloud was over it only a few days. At the LORD's command the people camped, and at his command they moved. 21 Sometimes the cloud stayed only from dusk until dawn; when the cloud lifted the next morning, the people moved. When the cloud lifted, day or night, the people moved. 22 The cloud might stay over the Tent for two days, a month or a year. As long as it stayed, the people camped, but when it lifted, they moved. 23 At the LORD's command the people camped, and at his command they moved. They obeyed the LORD's order that he commanded through Moses.

The Silver Trumpets

10 The LORD said to Moses, 2 "Make two trumpets of hammered silver, and use them to call the people together and to march out of camp. 3 When both trumpets are blown, the people should gather before you at the entrance to the Meeting Tent. 4 If you blow only one trumpet, the leaders, the heads of the family groups of Israel, should meet before you. 5 When you loudly blow the trumpets, the tribes camping on the east should move. 6 When you loudly blow them again, the tribes camping on the south should move; the loud sound will tell them to move. 7 When you want to gather the people, blow the trumpets, but don't blow them as loudly.

8 "Aaron's sons, the priests, should blow the trumpets. This is a law for you and your descendants from now on. 9 When you are fighting an enemy who attacks you in your own land, blow the trumpets loudly. The LORD your God will take notice of you and will save you from your enemies. 10 Also blow your trumpets at happy times and during your feasts and at New Moon festivals. Blow them over your burnt offerings and fellowship offerings, because they will help you remember your God. I am the LORD your God."

The Israelites Move Camp

11 The cloud lifted from the Tent of the Agreement on the twentieth day of the second month of the second year. 12 So the Israelites moved from the Desert of Sinai and continued until the cloud stopped in the Desert of Paran. 13 This was their first time to move, and they did it as the LORD had commanded Moses.

14 The divisions from the camp of Judah moved first under their flag. Nahshon son of Amminadab was the commander. 15 Nethanel son of Zuar was over the division of the tribe of Issachar. 16 Eliab son of Helon was over the division of the tribe of Zebulun. 17 Then the Holy Tent was taken down, and the Gershonites and Merarites, who carried it, moved next.

18 Then came the divisions from the camp of Reuben under their flag, and Elizur son of Shedeur was the commander. 19 Shelumiel son of Zurishaddai was over the division of the tribe of Simeon. 20 Eliasaph son of Deuel was over the division of the tribe of Gad. 21 Then came the Kohathites, who carried the holy things; the Holy Tent was to be set up before they arrived.

22 Next came the divisions from the camp of Ephraim under their flag, and Elishama son of Ammihud was the commander. 23 Gamaliel son of Pedahzur was over the division of the tribe of Manasseh,

24 and Abidan son of Gideoni was over the division of the tribe of Benjamin.

25 The last ones were the rearguard for all the tribes. These were the divisions from the camp of Dan under their flag, and Ahiezer son of Ammishaddai was the commander. 26 Pagiel son of Ocran was over the division of the tribe of Asher; 27 Ahira son of Enan was over the division of the tribe of Naphtali. 28 This was the order the Israelite divisions marched in when they moved.

29 Hobab was the son of Reuel the Midianite,[n] who was Moses' father-in-law. Moses said to Hobab, "We are moving to the land the LORD promised to give us. Come with us and we will be good to you, because the LORD has promised good things to Israel."

30 But Hobab answered, "No, I will not go. I will go back to my own land where I was born."

31 But Moses said, "Please don't leave us. You know where we can camp in the desert, and you can be our guide. 32 Come with us. We will share with you all the good things the LORD gives us." 33 So they left the mountain of the LORD and travelled for three days. The Ark of the LORD's Agreement went in front of the people for those three days, as they looked for a place to camp. 34 The LORD's cloud was over them during the day when they left their camp.

35 When the Ark left the camp, Moses said,
"Rise up, LORD!
Scatter your enemies:
make those who hate you run from you."

36 And when the Ark was set down, Moses said,
"Return, LORD,
to the thousands of people of Israel."

Fire from the LORD

11 Now the people complained to the LORD about their troubles, and when he heard them, he became angry. Then fire from the LORD burned among the people at the edge of the camp. 2 The people cried out to Moses, and when he prayed to the LORD, the fire stopped burning. 3 So that place was called Taberah,[n] because the LORD's fire had burned among them.

Seventy Elders Help Moses

4 Some troublemakers among them wanted better food, and soon all the Israelites began complaining. They said, "We want meat! 5 We remember the fish we ate for free in Egypt. We also had cucumbers, melons, leeks, onions and garlic. 6 But now we have lost our appetite; we never see anything but this manna!"

7 The manna was like small white seeds. 8 The people would go to gather it, and then grind it in handmills, or crush it between stones. After they cooked it in a pot or made cakes with it, it tasted like bread baked with olive oil. 9 When the dew fell on the camp each night, so did the manna.

10 Moses heard every family crying as they stood in the entrances of their tents. Then the LORD became very angry, and Moses got upset. 11 He asked the LORD, "Why have you brought me, your servant, this trouble? What have I done wrong that you made me responsible for all these people? 12 I am not the father of all these people, and I didn't give birth to them. So why do you make me carry them to the land you promised to our ancestors? Must I carry them in my arms as a nurse carries a baby? 13 Where can I get meat for all these people? They keep crying to me, 'We want meat!' 14 I can't take care of all these people alone. It's too much for me. 15 If you are going to continue doing this to me, then kill me now. If you care about me, put me to

> The LORD's cloud was over them during the day when they left their camp.
> – Numbers 10:34

10:29 Reuel the Midianite Also called Jethro.
11:3 Taberah This name means "burning".

TIME FOR BREAKFAST Numbers 11:4–9

Manna was a food. You can't find it anywhere in the world today. It was a miracle food God supplied to the Israelites. During the years that the Israelites wandered through the wilderness, God made "food fall like rain from the sky". (Read Exodus 16:4, p. 96.) Each morning when the people woke up, there was manna on the ground. It looked like thin flakes of frost. (See Exodus 16:14, p. 97.)

The Israelites gathered the manna every day except on the Sabbath. The left-over manna would melt in the sun. No one was supposed to gather more than they needed. If they did, it would become infested with worms. (Look at Exodus 16:16–18, 20–21, p. 97.) When manna appeared on the ground, it was sticky. Later when it dried it became solid and could be ground up like flour and baked into wafers or cakes. It tasted a little like wafers made with honey. (Check out Exodus 16:31, p. 98.)

death, and then I won't have any more troubles."

16 The LORD said to Moses, "Bring me 70 of Israel's elders, men that you know are leaders among the people. Bring them to the Meeting Tent, and have them stand there with you. 17 I will come down and speak with you there. I will take some of the Spirit that is in you, and I will give it to them. They will help you care for the people so that you will not have to care for them alone.

18 "Tell the people this: 'Make yourselves holy for tomorrow, and you will eat meat. You cried to the LORD, "We want meat! We were better off in Egypt!" So now the LORD will give you meat to eat. 19 You will eat it not for just one, two, five, ten or even twenty days, 20 but you will eat that meat for a whole month. You will eat it until it comes out your nose, and you will grow to hate it. This is because you have rejected the LORD, who is with you. You have cried to him, saying, "Why did we ever leave Egypt?"'"

21 Moses said, "LORD, here are 600,000 people standing around me, and you say, 'I will give them enough meat to eat for a month!' 22 If we killed all the flocks and herds, that would not be enough. If we caught all the fish in the sea, that would not be enough."

23 But the LORD said to Moses, "Do you think I'm weak? Now you will see if I can do what I say."

24 So Moses went out to the people and told them what the LORD had said. He gathered 70 of the elders together and had them stand around the Tent. 25 Then the LORD came down in the cloud and spoke to Moses. The LORD took some of the Spirit Moses had, and he gave it to the 70 leaders. With the Spirit in them, they prophesied, but just that one time.

26 Two men named Eldad and Medad were also listed as leaders, but they did not go to the Tent. They stayed in the camp, but the Spirit was also given to them, and they prophesied in the camp. 27 A young man ran to Moses and said, "Eldad and Medad are prophesying in the camp."

28 Joshua son of Nun said, "Moses, my

master, stop them!" (Ever since he was a young boy, Joshua had been Moses' assistant.)

29 But Moses answered, "Are you jealous for me? I wish all the LORD's people could prophesy. I wish the LORD would give his Spirit to all of them!" 30 Then Moses and the leaders of Israel went back to the camp.

The LORD Sends Quail

31 The LORD sent a strong wind from the sea, and it blew quail into the area all around the camp. The quail were about a metre deep on the ground, and there were quail a day's walk in any direction. 32 The people went out and gathered quail all that day, that night and the next day. Everyone gathered at least a tonne, and they spread them around the camp. 33 But the LORD became very angry, and he gave the people a terrible sickness that came while the meat was still in their mouths. 34 So the people named that place Kibroth Hattaavah,[n] because there they buried those who wanted other food.

35 From Kibroth Hattaavah the people went to stay at Hazeroth.

Miriam and Aaron Speak Against Moses

12 Miriam and Aaron began to talk against Moses because of his Cushite wife (he had married a Cushite). 2 They said, "Is Moses the only one the LORD speaks through? Doesn't he also speak through us?" And the LORD heard this.

3 (Now Moses was very humble. He was the least proud person on earth.)

4 So the LORD suddenly spoke to Moses, Aaron and Miriam and said, "All three of you come to the Meeting Tent." So they went. 5 The LORD came down in a pillar of cloud and stood at the entrance to the Tent. He called to Aaron and Miriam, and they both came near. 6 He said, "Listen to my words:
When a prophet is among you,
    I, the LORD, will show myself to him in visions;

11:34 Kibroth Hattaavah This name in Hebrew means "graves of wanting".

FAITH links

MOSES' CHAMPION
NUMBERS 12

If you've ever been picked on by a brother or sister, you can understand how Moses felt. He was criticised by his brother Aaron and his sister Miriam. But Moses did not try to get even with them or criticise them in return for their harsh words. When they put him down, God stuck up for him in a powerful way.

When you're criticised by others, it's easy to think you have to defend yourself or strike back in some way. Consider the Moses way of dealing with criticism. Let God handle it. Although he may not use a skin disease to correct the person who wronged you, he does have a way of protecting his people.

Here's some more advice on forgiving others:

Forgive Instead, Genesis 33, p. 47

An Attention-Getter, Numbers 22, p. 207

What's Out Becomes In, Judges 11, p. 327

A Tight Spot, Jonah 2, p. 1215

Justice Desserts, Habakkuk 2:4–8, p. 1237

Two Birthdays, John 3:1–7, p. 1426

I will speak to him in dreams.
7 But this is not true with my servant Moses.
I trust him to lead all my people.
8 I speak face to face with him—
clearly, not with hidden meanings.
He has even seen the form of the LORD.
You should be afraid
to speak against my servant Moses."

9 The LORD was very angry with them, and he left.

10 When the cloud lifted from the Tent and Aaron turned towards Miriam, she was as white as snow; she had a skin disease. **11** Aaron said to Moses, "Please, my master, forgive us for our foolish sin. **12** Don't let her be like a baby who is born dead. (Sometimes a baby is born with half of its flesh eaten away.)"

13 So Moses cried out to the LORD, "God, please heal her!"

14 The LORD answered Moses, "If her father had spat in her face, she would have been shamed for seven days, so put her outside the camp for seven days. After that, she may come back." **15** So Miriam was put outside the camp for seven days, and the people did not move on until she came back.

16 After that, the people left Hazeroth and camped in the Desert of Paran.

The Spies Explore Canaan

13 The LORD said to Moses, **2** "Send men to explore the land of Canaan, which I will give to the Israelites. Send one leader from each tribe."

3 So Moses obeyed the LORD's command and sent the Israelite leaders out from the Desert of Paran. **4** These are their names: from the tribe of Reuben, Shammua son of Zaccur; **5** from the tribe of Simeon, Shaphat son of Hori; **6** from the tribe of Judah, Caleb son of Jephunneh; **7** from the tribe of Issachar, Igal son of Joseph; **8** from the tribe of Ephraim, Hoshea son of Nun; **9** from the tribe of Benjamin, Palti son of Raphu; **10** from the tribe of Zebulun, Gaddiel son of Sodi; **11** from the tribe of Manasseh (a tribe of Joseph), Gaddi son of Susi; **12** from the

FAITH links

FOLLOWING THE CROWD

NUMBERS 13; 14

Some people like to follow the crowd. Whatever the group thinks is right is fine with them. Is that your belief? The people of Israel would agree. Joshua, Caleb and ten others went to explore the land of Canaan. Ten returned with a fearful story of giants in the land. But Joshua and Caleb believed that God would help them take possession of the land. Because the Israelites chose not to trust God, they were forced to wander in the wilderness for 40 years.

Following the crowd can get you into trouble at times. If the crowd decides to disobey God, are you willing to take a stand for God?

An Example Not to Follow, Leviticus 18:1–3, p. 157

I'll Never Forget What's-His-Name, Deuteronomy 8, p. 239

The Green Light, 2 Samuel 2:1, p. 401

Give In or Take a Stand? 1 Kings 22:13–14, p. 472

Choosing a Friend, Proverbs 28:7, p. 865

Heavenly Treasure, Luke 12:32–34, p. 1394

tribe of Dan, Ammiel son of Gemalli; **13** from the tribe of Asher, Sethur son of Michael; **14** from the tribe of Naphtali,

Nahbi son of Vophsi; 15 from the tribe of Gad, Geuel son of Maki.

16 These are the names of the men Moses sent to explore the land. (Moses gave Hoshea son of Nun the new name Joshua.)

17 Moses sent them to explore Canaan and said, "Go through southern Canaan and then into the mountains. 18 See what the land looks like. Are the people who live there strong or weak? Are there a few or many? 19 What kind of land do they live in? Is it good or bad? What about the towns they live in—are they open like camps, or do they have walls? 20 What about the soil? Is it fertile or poor? Are there trees there? Try to bring back some of the fruit from that land." (It was the season for the first grapes.)

21 So they went up and explored the land, from the Desert of Zin all the way to Rehob by Lebo Hamath. 22 They went through the southern area to Hebron, where Ahiman, Sheshai and Talmai, the descendants of Anak lived. (The city of Hebron had been built seven years before Zoan in Egypt.) 23 In the Valley of Eshcol, they cut off a branch of a grapevine that had one bunch of grapes on it and carried that branch on a pole between two of them. They also got some pomegranates and figs. 24 That place was called the Valley of Eshcol," because the Israelites cut off the bunch of grapes there. 25 After 40 days of exploring the land, the men returned to the camp.

26 They came back to Moses and Aaron and all the Israelites at Kadesh, in the Desert of Paran. The men reported to them and showed everybody the fruit from the land. 27 They told Moses, "We went to the land where you sent us, and it is a fertile land! Here is some of its fruit. 28 But the people who live there are strong. Their cities are walled and very large. We even saw some Anakites there. 29 The Amalekites live in the southern area; the Hittites, Jebusites and Amorites live in the mountains; and the Canaanites live near the sea and along the Jordan River."

30 Then Caleb told the people near Moses to be quiet, and he said, "We should certainly go up and take the land for ourselves. We can certainly do it."

31 But the men who had gone with him said, "We can't attack those people; they are stronger than we are." 32 And those men gave the Israelites a bad report about the land they explored, saying, "The land that we explored is too large to conquer. All the people we saw are very tall. 33 We saw the Nephilim people there. (The Anakites come from the Nephilim people.) We felt like grasshoppers, and we looked like grasshoppers to them."

The People Complain Again

14 That night all the people in the camp began crying loudly. 2 All the Israelites complained against Moses and Aaron, and all the people said to them, "We wish we had died in Egypt or in this desert. 3 Why is the LORD bringing us to this land to be killed with swords? Our wives and children will be taken away. We would be better off going back to Egypt." 4 They said to each other, "Let's choose a leader and go back to Egypt."

14:1–4 Decisions Find out what poor decisions the Israelites want to make.

5 Then Moses and Aaron bowed face down in front of all the Israelites gathered there. 6 Joshua son of Nun and Caleb son of Jephunneh, who had explored the land, tore their clothes. 7 They said to all of the Israelites, "The land we explored is very good. 8 If the LORD is pleased with us, he will lead us into that land and give us that fertile land. 9 Don't turn against the LORD! Don't be afraid of the people in that land! We will chew them up. They have no protection, but the LORD is with us. So don't be afraid of them."

10 Then all the people talked about killing them with stones. But the glory of the LORD appeared at the Meeting Tent to all the Israelites. 11 The LORD said to Moses, "How long will these people

---

13:24 Eshcol This name in Hebrew means "bunch".

ignore me? How long will they not believe me in spite of the miracles I have done among them? 12 I will give them a terrible sickness and get rid of them. But I will make you into a great nation that will be stronger than they are."

13 Then Moses said to the LORD, "The Egyptians will hear about it! You brought these people from there by your great power, 14 and the Egyptians will tell this to those who live in this land. They have already heard about you, LORD. They know that you are with your people and that you were seen face to face. They know that your cloud stays over your people and that you lead your people with that cloud during the day and with fire at night. 15 If you put these people to death all at once, the nations who have heard about your power will say, 16 'The LORD was not able to bring them into the land he promised them. So he killed them in the desert.'

17 "So show your strength now, Lord. Do what you said: 18 'The LORD doesn't become angry quickly, but he has great love. He forgives sin and law breaking. But the LORD never forgets to punish guilty people. When parents sin, he will also punish their children, their grandchildren, their great-grandchildren and their great-great-grandchildren.' 19 By your great love, forgive these people's sin, just as you have forgiven them from the time they left Egypt until now."

20 The LORD answered, "I have forgiven them as you asked. 21 But, as surely as I live and as surely as my glory fills the whole earth, I make this promise: 22 all these men saw my glory and the miracles I did in Egypt and in the desert, but they disobeyed me and tested me ten times. 23 So not one of them will see the land I promised to their ancestors. No one who rejected me will see that land. 24 But my servant Caleb thinks differently and follows me completely. So I will bring him into the land he has already seen, and his children will own that land. 25 Since the Amalekites and the Canaanites are living in the valleys, leave tomorrow and follow the desert road towards the Red Sea."

The LORD Punishes the People

26 The LORD said to Moses and Aaron, 27 "How long will these evil people complain about me? I have heard the grumbling and complaining of these Israelites. 28 So tell them, 'This is what the LORD says. I heard what you said, and as surely as I live, I will do those very things to you: 29 you will die in this desert. Every one of you who is 20 years old or older and who was counted with the people—all of you who complained against me—will die. 30 Not one of you will enter the land where I promised you would live; only Caleb son of Jephunneh and Joshua son of Nun will go in. 31 You said that your children would be taken away, but I will bring them into the land to enjoy what you refused. 32 As for you, you will die in this desert. 33 Your children will be shepherds here for 40 years. Because you were not loyal, they will suffer until you lie dead in the desert. 34 For 40 years you will suffer for your sins—a year for each of the 40 days you explored the land. You will know me as your enemy.' 35 I, the LORD, have spoken, and I will certainly do these things to all these evil people who have come together against me. So they will all die here in this desert."

36 The men Moses had sent to explore the land had returned and spread complaints among all the people. They had given a bad report about the land. 37 The men who gave a very bad report died; the LORD killed them with a terrible sickness. 38 Only two of the men who explored the land did not die—Joshua son of Nun and Caleb son of Jephunneh.

39 When Moses told these things to all the Israelites, they were very sad. 40 Early the next morning they started to go towards the top of the mountains, saying, "We have sinned. We will go where the LORD told us."

41 But Moses said, "Why are you disobeying the LORD's command? You will not win! 42 Don't go, because the LORD is not with you and you will be beaten by your enemies. 43 You will run into the Amalekites and Canaanites, who will kill you with swords. You have turned away

from the LORD, so the LORD will not be with you."

44 But they were proud. They went towards the top of the mountains, but Moses and the Ark of the Agreement with the LORD did not leave the camp. 45 The Amalekites and the Canaanites who lived in those mountains came down and attacked the Israelites and beat them back all the way to Hormah.

Rules About Sacrifices

15 The LORD said to Moses, 2 "Speak to the Israelites and say to them, 'When you enter the land that I am giving you as a home, 3 give the LORD offerings made by fire. These may be from your herds or flocks, as a smell pleasing to the LORD. These may be burnt offerings or sacrifices for special promises, or as gifts to him, or as festival offerings. 4 The one who brings the offering shall also give the LORD a grain offering. It should be 2 litres of fine flour mixed with 1 litre of olive oil. 5 Each time you offer a lamb as a burnt offering or sacrifice, also prepare 1 litre of wine as a drink offering.

6 "'If you are giving a ram, also prepare a grain offering of 4 litres of fine flour mixed with one and a half litres of olive oil. 7 Also prepare one and a half litres of wine as a drink offering. Its smell will be pleasing to the LORD.

8 "'If you prepare a young bull as a burnt offering or sacrifice, whether it is for a special promise or a fellowship offering to the LORD, 9 bring a grain offering with the bull. It should be 7 litres of fine flour mixed with 2 litres of olive oil. 10 Also bring 2 litres of wine as a drink offering. This offering is made by fire, and its smell will be pleasing to the LORD. 11 Prepare each bull or ram, lamb or young goat in this way. 12 Do this for every one of the animals you bring.

13 "'All citizens must do these things in this way, and the smell of their offerings by fire will be pleasing to the LORD. 14 From now on if foreigners who live among you want to make offerings by fire so the smell will be pleasing to the LORD, they must offer them in the same way that you do. 15 The law is the same for you and for foreigners, and it will be from now on; you and the foreigners are alike before the LORD. 16 The teachings and rules are the same for you and for the foreigners among you.'"

17 The LORD said to Moses, 18 "Tell the Israelites: 'You are going to another land, where I am taking you. 19 When you eat the food there, offer part of it to the LORD. 20 Offer a loaf of bread from the first of your grain, which will be your offering from the threshing floor. 21 From now on offer to the LORD the first part of your grain.

22 "'Now what if you forget to obey any of these commands the LORD gave Moses? 23 These are the LORD's commands given to you through Moses, which began the day the LORD gave them to you and will continue from now on. 24 If the people forget to obey one of these commands, all the people must offer a young bull as a burnt offering, a smell pleasing to the LORD. By law you must also give the grain offering and the drink offering with it, and you must bring a male goat as a sin offering.

25 "'The priest will remove that sin for all the Israelites so they will belong to the LORD. They are forgiven, because they didn't know they were sinning. For the wrong they did they brought offerings to the LORD, an offering by fire and a sin offering. 26 So all of the people of Israel and the foreigners living among them will be forgiven. No one meant to do wrong.

27 "'If just one person sins without meaning to, a year-old female goat must be brought for a sin offering. 28 The priest will remove the sin of the person who sinned accidentally. He will remove it before the LORD, and the person will be forgiven. 29 The same teaching is for everyone who sins accidentally—for those born Israelites and for foreigners living among you.

30 "'But anyone who sins on purpose is against the LORD and must be cut off from the people, whether it is someone born among you or a foreigner. 31 That

person has turned against the LORD's word and has not obeyed his commands. Such a person must surely be cut off from the others. He is guilty.'"

A Man Worked on the Sabbath

32 When the Israelites were still in the desert, they found a man gathering wood on the Sabbath day. 33 Those who found him gathering wood brought him to Moses and Aaron and all the people. 34 They held the man under guard, because they did not know what to do with him. 35 Then the LORD said to Moses, "The man must surely die. All the people must kill him by throwing stones at him outside the camp." 36 So all the people took him outside the camp and stoned him to death, as the LORD commanded Moses.

The Tassels

37 The LORD said to Moses, 38 "Speak to the Israelites and tell them this: 'Tie several pieces of thread together and attach them to the corners of your clothes. Put a blue thread in each one of these tassels. Wear them from now on. 39 You will have these tassels to look at to remind you of all the LORD's commands. Then you will obey them and not be disloyal by following what your bodies and eyes want. 40 Then you will remember to obey all my commands, and you will be God's holy people. 41 I am the LORD your God, who brought you out of Egypt to be your God. I am the LORD your God.'"

Korah, Dathan, Abiram and On

16 Korah, Dathan, Abiram and On turned against Moses. (Korah was the son of Izhar, the son of Kohath, the son of Levi; Dathan and Abiram were brothers, the sons of Eliab; and On was the son of Peleth; Dathan, Abiram and On were from the tribe of Reuben.) 2 These men gathered 250 other Israelite men, well-known leaders chosen by the community, and challenged Moses. 3 They came as a group to speak to Moses and Aaron and said, "You have gone too far. All the people are holy, every one of them, and the LORD is among them. So why do you put yourselves above all the people of the LORD?"

4 When Moses heard this, he bowed face down. 5 Then he said to Korah and all his followers: "Tomorrow morning the LORD will show who belongs to him. He will bring the one who is holy near to him; he will bring to himself the person he chooses. 6 So Korah, you and all your followers do this: get some pans for burning incense. 7 Tomorrow put fire and incense in them and take them before the LORD. He will choose the man who is holy. You Levites have gone too far."

8 Moses also said to Korah, "Listen, you Levites. 9 The God of Israel has separated you from the rest of the Israelites. He brought you near to himself to do the work in the LORD's Holy Tent and to stand before all the Israelites and serve them. Isn't that enough? 10 He has brought you and all your fellow Levites near to himself, yet now you want to be priests. 11 You and your followers have joined together against the LORD. Your complaint is not against Aaron."

12 Then Moses called Dathan and Abiram, the sons of Eliab, but they said, "We will not come! 13 You have brought us out of a fertile land to this desert to kill us, and now you want to order us around. 14 You haven't brought us into a fertile land; you haven't given us any land with fields and vineyards. Will you put out the eyes of these men? No! We will not come!"

15 Then Moses became very angry and said to the LORD, "Don't accept their gifts. I have not taken anything from them, not even a donkey, and I have not done wrong to any of them."

16 Then Moses said to Korah, "You and all your followers must stand before the LORD tomorrow. And Aaron will stand

> The God of Israel has separated you from the rest of the Israelites.
> – Numbers 16:9

there with you and them. 17 Each of you must take your pan and put incense in it; present these 250 pans before the LORD. You and Aaron must also present your pans." 18 So each man got his pan and put burning incense in it and stood with Moses and Aaron at the entrance to the Meeting Tent. 19 Korah gathered all his followers who were against Moses and Aaron, and they stood at the entrance to the Meeting Tent. Then the glory of the LORD appeared to everyone.

20 The LORD said to Moses and Aaron, 21 "Move away from these men so I can destroy them quickly."

22 But Moses and Aaron bowed face down and cried out, "God, you are the God over the spirits of all people. Please don't be angry with this whole group. Only one man has really sinned."

23 Then the LORD said to Moses, 24 "Tell everyone to move away from the tents of Korah, Dathan and Abiram."

25 Moses stood and went to Dathan and Abiram; the elders of Israel followed him. 26 Moses warned the people, "Move away from the tents of these evil men! Don't touch anything of theirs, or you will be destroyed because of their sins." 27 So they moved away from the tents of Korah, Dathan and Abiram. Dathan and Abiram were standing outside their tents with their wives, children and little babies.

28 Then Moses said, "Now you will know that the LORD has sent me to do all these things; it was not my idea. 29 If these men die a normal death—the way men usually die—then the LORD did not really send me. 30 But if the LORD does something new, you will know they have insulted the LORD. The ground will open and swallow them. They will be buried alive and will go to the place of the dead, and everything that belongs to them will go with them."

31 When Moses finished saying these things, the ground under the men split open. 32 The earth opened and swallowed them and all their families. All Korah's men and everything they owned went down. 33 They were buried alive, going to the place of the dead, and everything they owned went with them. Then the earth covered them. They died and were gone from the community. 34 The people of Israel around them heard their screams and ran away, saying, "The earth will swallow us, too!"

35 Then a fire came down from the LORD and destroyed the 250 men who had presented the incense.

36 The LORD said to Moses, 37 "Tell Eleazar son of Aaron, the priest, to take all the incense pans out of the fire. Have him scatter the coals a long distance away. But the incense pans are still holy. 38 Take the pans of these men who sinned and lost their lives, and hammer them into flat sheets that will be used to cover the altar. They are holy, because they were presented to the LORD, and they will be a sign to the Israelites."

39 So Eleazar the priest gathered all the bronze pans that had been brought by the men who were burned up. He had the pans hammered into flat sheets to put on the altar, 40 as the LORD had commanded him through Moses. These sheets were to remind the Israelites that only descendants of Aaron should burn incense before the LORD. Anyone else would die like Korah and his followers.

Aaron Saves the People

41 The next day all the Israelites complained against Moses and Aaron and said, "You have killed the LORD's people."

42 When the people gathered to complain against Moses and Aaron, they turned towards the Meeting Tent, and the cloud covered it. The glory of the LORD appeared. 43 Then Moses and Aaron went in front of the Meeting Tent.

44 The LORD said to Moses, 45 "Move away from these people so I can destroy them quickly." So Moses and Aaron bowed face down.

46 Then Moses said to Aaron, "Get your pan, and put fire from the altar and incense in it. Hurry to the people and remove their sin. The LORD is angry with them; the sickness has already started." 47 So Aaron did as Moses said. He ran to the middle of the people, where the sickness had already started among them.

Numbers 17:8 199

So Aaron offered the incense to remove their sin. 48 He stood between the dead and the living, and the sickness stopped there. 49 But 14,700 people died from that sickness, in addition to those who died because of Korah. 50 Then Aaron went back to Moses at the entrance to the Meeting Tent. The terrible sickness had been stopped.

Aaron's Walking Stick Buds

17 The LORD said to Moses, 2 "Speak to the people of Israel and get twelve walking sticks from them—one from the leader of each tribe. Write the name of each man on his stick, and 3 on the stick from Levi, write Aaron's name. There must be one stick for the head of each tribe. 4 Put them in the Meeting Tent in front of the Ark of the Agreement, where I meet with you. 5 I will choose one man whose walking stick will begin to grow leaves; in this way I will stop the Israelites from always complaining against you."

6 So Moses spoke to the Israelites. Each of the twelve leaders gave him a walking stick—one from each tribe—and Aaron's walking stick was among them. 7 Moses put them before the LORD in the Tent of the Agreement.

8 The next day, when Moses entered

SHARING WITH A FRIEND

Do you have a problem telling your friends about Jesus? Welcome Kelly, aged 12, to Connect 2-You. She's going to tell us about the problem she has.

Kelly

Well, my best friend knows I go to church, but we've never really talked about spiritual things. I'm pretty sure she's not a Christian, but I don't know what to do. I really want to tell her about Jesus, but I'm afraid she'll think I'm weird or something. I want her to know about Jesus, but I don't want her to feel uncomfortable around me.

Know the feeling? It takes a lot of courage to share your faith with a friend. But the Bible tells us that before someone can become a Christian, they have to hear about Jesus. If your best friend doesn't hear about Jesus from you, can you be sure that they'll hear about him from someone else? Check out the Livin' It page on sharing your faith, Romans 10:14-17, p. 1532, for some tips on how to talk to your friends about Jesus.

You may be surprised. Your best friend may be more interested in talking about spiritual things than you think. Ask them what they think happens to us after we die, or how they think the world began. After they give you their answer, they may ask what you think. Then you'll have a chance to tell them why you believe what you do.

the Tent, he saw that Aaron's stick (which stood for the family of Levi) had grown leaves. It had even budded, blossomed and produced almonds. 9 So Moses brought out to the Israelites all the walking sticks from the LORD's presence. They all looked, and each man took back his stick.

10 Then the LORD said to Moses, "Put Aaron's walking stick back in front of the Ark of the Agreement. It will remind these people who are always turning against me to stop their complaining against me so they won't die." 11 So Moses obeyed what the LORD commanded him.

12 The people of Israel said to Moses, "We are going to die! We are destroyed. We are all destroyed! 13 Anyone who even comes near the Holy Tent of the LORD will die. Will we all die?"

The Work of the Priests and Levites

18 The LORD said to Aaron, "You, your sons and your family are now responsible for any wrongs done against the Holy Place; you and your sons are responsible for any wrongs done against the priests. 2 Bring with you your fellow Levites from your tribe, and they will help you and your sons serve in the Tent of the Agreement. 3 They are under your control, to do all the work that needs to be done in the Tent. But they must not go near the things in the Holy Place or near the altar. If they do, both you and they will die. 4 They will join you in taking care of the Meeting Tent. They must do the work at the Tent, and no one else may come near you.

5 "You must take care of the Holy Place and the altar so that I won't become angry with the Israelites again. 6 I myself chose your fellow Levites from among the Israelites as a gift given for you to the LORD, to work at the Meeting Tent. 7 But only you and your sons may serve as priests. Only you may serve at the altar or go behind the curtain. I am giving you this gift of serving as a priest, and anyone else who comes near the Holy Place will be put to death."

8 Then the LORD said to Aaron, "I myself make you responsible for the offerings given to me. All the holy offerings that the Israelites give to me, I give to you and your sons as your share, your continual portion. 9 Your share of the holy offerings is that part which is not burned. When the people bring me gifts as most holy offerings, whether they are grain or sin or penalty offerings, they will be set apart for you and your sons. 10 You must eat the offering in a most holy place. Any male may eat it, but you must respect it as holy.

11 "I also give you the offerings the Israelites present to me. I give these to you and your sons and daughters as your continual share. Anyone in your family who is clean may eat it.

12 "And I give you all the best olive oil and all the best new wine and grain. This is what the Israelites give to me, the LORD, from the first crops they harvest. 13 When they bring to the LORD all the first things they harvest, they will be yours. Anyone in your family who is clean may eat these things.

14 "Everything in Israel that is given to the LORD is yours. 15 The first one born to any family, whether people or animals, will be offered to the LORD. And that will be yours. But you must make a payment for every firstborn child and every firstborn animal that is unclean. 16 When they are one month old, you must make a payment for them of 5 pieces of silver, as set by the Holy Place measure.

17 "But you must not make a payment for the firstborn ox or sheep or goat. Those animals are holy. Sprinkle their blood on the altar and burn their fat as an offering made by fire. The smell is pleasing to the LORD. 18 But the meat will be yours, just as the breast that is presented and the right thigh will be yours. 19 Anything the Israelites present as holy gifts I, the LORD, give to you, your sons and daughters as your continual portion. This is a lasting agreement of salt[n] before the

---

18:19 agreement of salt The meaning is not clear, but Leviticus 2:13 says, "Salt stands for your agreement with God that will last for ever."

LORD for you and your children for ever."

18:20
Protection
Who provides for you?

20 The LORD also said to Aaron, "You will not inherit any of the land, and you will not own any land among the other people. I will be yours. Out of all the Israelites, only you will inherit me.

21 "When the people of Israel give me a tenth of what they make, I will give that tenth to the Levites. This is their payment for the work they do serving at the Meeting Tent. 22 But the other Israelites must never go near the Meeting Tent, or they will die for their sin. 23 Only the Levites should work in the Meeting Tent and be responsible for any sins against it. This is a rule from now on. The Levites will not inherit any land among the other Israelites, 24 but when the Israelites give a tenth of everything they make to me, I will give that tenth to the Levites as a reward. That is why I said about the Levites: 'They will not inherit any land among the Israelites.'"

25 The LORD said to Moses, 26 "Speak to the Levites and tell them: 'You will receive a tenth of everything the Israelites make, which I will give to you. But you must give a tenth of that back to the LORD. 27 I will accept your offering just as much as I accept the offerings from others, who give new grain or new wine. 28 In this way you will present an offering to the LORD as the other Israelites do. When you receive a tenth from the Israelites, you will give a tenth of that to Aaron, the priest, as the LORD's share. 29 Choose the best and holiest part from what you are given as the portion you must give to the LORD.'

30 "Say to the Levites: 'When you present the best, it will be accepted as much as the grain and wine from the other people. 31 You and your families may eat all that is left anywhere, because it is your pay for your work in the Meeting Tent. 32 And if you always give the best part to the LORD, you will never be guilty. If you do not sin against the holy offerings of the Israelites, you will not die.'"

FAITH CHALLENGE

Try this one. Read 18:25-26 to find out what God says we should do with everything we own. How can you give one-tenth of everything you have back to the Lord?

TeSTiNG iT

Numbers 18:25-26
The LORD said to Moses, "Speak to the Levites and tell them: 'You will receive a tenth of everything the Israelites make, which I will give to you. But you must give a tenth of that back to the LORD.'"

The Offering for Cleansing

19 The LORD said to Moses and Aaron, 2 "These are the teachings that the LORD commanded. Tell the Israelites to get a young red cow that does not have anything wrong with it and that has never been worked. 3 Give the cow to Eleazar the priest; he will take it outside the camp and kill it. 4 Then Eleazar the priest must put some of its blood on his finger and sprinkle it seven times towards the front of the Meeting Tent. 5 The whole cow must be burned while he watches; the skin, the meat, the blood and the intestines must all be burned. 6 Then the priest

must take a cedar stick, a hyssop branch and a red string and throw them onto the burning cow. 7 After the priest has washed himself and his clothes with water, he may come back into the camp, but he will be unclean until evening. 8 The man who burns the cow must wash himself and his clothes in water; he will be unclean until evening.

9 "Then someone who is clean will collect the ashes from the cow and put them in a clean place outside the camp. The Israelites will keep these ashes to use in the cleansing water, in a special ceremony to cleanse away sin. 10 The man who collected the cow's ashes must wash his clothes and be unclean until evening. This is a lasting rule for the Israelites and for the foreigners among them.

11 "Those who touch a dead person's body will be unclean for seven days. 12 They must wash themselves with the cleansing water on the third day and on the seventh day; then they will be clean. But if they do not wash themselves on the third day and the seventh day, they cannot be clean. 13 If those who touch a dead person's body stay unclean and go to the LORD's Holy Tent, it becomes unclean; they must be cut off from Israel. If the cleansing water is not sprinkled on them, they are unclean and will stay unclean.

14 "This is the teaching about someone who dies in a tent: anyone in the tent or anyone who enters it will be unclean for seven days. 15 And every open jar or pot without a cover becomes unclean. 16 If anyone is outside and touches someone who was killed by a sword or who died a natural death, or if anyone touches a human bone or a grave, that person will be unclean for seven days.

17 "So you must use the ashes from the burnt offering to make that person clean again. Pour fresh water over the ashes into a jar. 18 A clean person must take a hyssop branch and dip it into the water, and then he must sprinkle it over the Tent and all its objects. He must also sprinkle the people who were there, as well as anyone who touched a bone, or the body of someone who was killed, or a dead person, or a grave. 19 The person who is clean must sprinkle this water on the unclean people on the third day and on the seventh day. On the seventh day they will become clean. They must wash their clothes and take a bath, and they will be clean that evening. 20 If any who are unclean do not become clean, they must be cut off from the community. Since they were not sprinkled with the cleansing water, they stay unclean, and they could make the LORD's Holy Tent unclean. 21 This is a lasting rule. Those who sprinkle the cleansing water must also wash their clothes, and anyone who touches the water will be unclean until evening. 22 Anything an unclean person touches becomes unclean, and whoever touches it will be unclean until evening."

> Tell the Israelites to get a young red cow that does not have anything wrong with it and that has never been worked.
> – Numbers 19:2

Moses Disobeys God

20 In the first month all the people of Israel arrived at the Desert of Zin, and they stayed at Kadesh. There Miriam died and was buried. 2 There was no water for the people, so they came together against Moses and Aaron. 3 They argued with Moses and said, "We should have died in front of the LORD as our brothers did. 4 Why did you bring the LORD's people into this desert? Are we and our animals to die here? 5 Why did you bring us from Egypt to this terrible place? It has no grain, figs, grapevines or pomegranates, and there's no water to drink!"

6 So Moses and Aaron left the people and went to the entrance of the Meeting Tent. There they bowed face down, and the glory of the LORD appeared to them. 7 The LORD said to Moses, 8 "Take your walking stick, and you and your brother Aaron should gather the people. Speak to that rock in front of them so that its water

FAITH links

THE PERFECT LEADER?
NUMBERS 20:1-13

Quick! Think of someone you know right now who has never sinned. (Someone besides Jesus.) Can't think of anyone? What about someone in history, someone like . . . Moses? There was a time when Moses blew his cool. The people of Israel made him angry. Moses reacted in sin. Because of his disobedience, God told him that he would not enter the Promised Land.

As humans, we sometimes "worship" our leaders. We think they can do no wrong. But sometimes they disappoint us by being all too human. None of us is without sin. That's why all of us – including leaders – need Jesus.

Surf over to these Faithlinks for more on sin.

The Trouble with Sin, Genesis 6—8, p. 11

The Weak Link, Judges 16, p. 334

Plan for Success, 1 Chronicles 14:8-17, p. 538

Dirty Inside, Isaiah 6:1-7, p. 904

A Model of Forgiveness, Ezekiel 16:59-63, p. 1103

It's Free! Ephesians 2:8-9, p. 1600

---

will flow from it. When you bring the water out from that rock, give it to the people and their animals."

9 So Moses took the stick from in front of the LORD, as he had said. 10 Moses and Aaron gathered the people in front of the rock, and Moses said, "Now listen to me, you who turn against God! Do you want us to bring water out of this rock?" 11 Then Moses lifted his hand and hit the rock twice with his stick. Water began pouring out, and the people and their animals drank it.

12 But the LORD said to Moses and Aaron, "Because you did not believe me, and because you did not honour me as holy before the people, you will not lead them into the land I will give them."

13 These are the waters of Meribah,[n] where the Israelites argued with the LORD and where he showed them he was holy.

Edom will Not Let Israel Pass

14 From Kadesh, Moses sent messengers to the king of Edom. He said, "Your brothers, the Israelites, say to you: you know about all the troubles we have had, 15 how our ancestors went down into Egypt and we lived there for many years. The people of Egypt were cruel to us and our ancestors, 16 but when we cried out to the LORD, he heard us and sent us an angel to bring us out of Egypt.

"Now we are here at Kadesh, a town on the edge of your land. 17 Please let us pass through your country. We will not touch any fields of grain or vineyards, and will not drink water from the wells. We will travel only along the king's road, not turning right or left until we have passed through your country."

18 But the king of Edom answered: "You may not pass through here. If you try, I will come and meet you with swords."

19 The Israelites answered: "We will go along the main road, and if we or our animals drink any of your water, we will

---

20:13 *Meribah* This name in Hebrew means "argument".

pay for it. We only want to walk through. That's all."

20 But he answered: "You may not pass through here."

Then the Edomites went out to meet the Israelites with a large and powerful army. 21 The Edomites refused to let them pass through their country, so the Israelites turned back.

Aaron Dies

22 All the Israelites moved from Kadesh to Mount Hor, 23 near the border of Edom. There the LORD said to Moses and Aaron, 24 "Aaron will die. He will not enter the land that I'm giving to the Israelites, because you both acted against my command at the waters of Meribah. 25 Take Aaron and his son Eleazar up on Mount Hor, 26 and take off Aaron's special clothes and put them on his son Eleazar. Aaron will die there; he will join his ancestors."

27 Moses obeyed the LORD's command. They climbed up Mount Hor, and all the people saw them go. 28 Moses took off Aaron's clothes and put them on Aaron's son Eleazar. Then Aaron died there on top of the mountain. Moses and Eleazar came back down the mountain, 29 and when all the people learned that Aaron was dead, everyone in Israel cried for him for 30 days.

War with the Canaanites

21 The Canaanite king of Arad lived in the southern area. When he heard that the Israelites were coming on the road to Atharim, he attacked them and captured some of them. 2 Then the Israelites made this promise to the LORD: "If you will help us defeat these people, we will completely destroy their cities." 3 The LORD listened to the Israelites, and he let them defeat the Canaanites. The Israelites completely destroyed the Canaanites and their cities, so the place was named Hormah.*n*

The Bronze Snake

4 The Israelites left Mount Hor and went on the road towards the Red Sea, in order to go around the country of Edom. But the people became impatient on the way 5 and grumbled at God and Moses. They said, "Why did you bring us out of Egypt to die in this desert? There is no bread and no water, and we hate this terrible food!"

6 So the LORD sent them poisonous snakes; they bit the people, and many of the Israelites died. 7 The people came to Moses and said, "We sinned when we grumbled at you and the LORD. Pray that the LORD will take away these snakes." So Moses prayed for the people.

8 The LORD said to Moses, "Make a bronze snake, and put it on a pole. When anyone who is bitten looks at it, that person will live." 9 So Moses made a bronze snake and put it on a pole. Then when a snake bit anyone, that person looked at the bronze snake and lived.

The Journey to Moab

10 The Israelites went and camped at Oboth. 11 They went from Oboth to Iye Abarim, in the desert east of Moab. 12 From there they went and camped in the Zered Valley. 13 From there they went and camped across the Arnon, in the desert just inside the Amorite country. The Arnon is the border between the Moabites and the Amorites. 14 That is why the Book of the Wars of the LORD says:

"... and Waheb in Suphah, and the ravines,
the Arnon, 15 and the slopes of the ravines
that lead to the settlement of Ar.
These places are at the border of Moab."

16 The Israelites went from there to Beer; a well is there where the LORD said to Moses, "Gather the people and I will give them water."

17 Then the Israelites sang this song:
"Pour out water, well!
Sing about it.
18 Princes dug this well.
Important men made it.
With their sceptres and poles, they dug it."

21:3 Hormah This name in Hebrew means "completely destroyed".

The people went from the desert to Mattanah. 19 From Mattanah they went to Nahaliel and on to Bamoth. 20 From Bamoth they went to the valley of Moab where the top of Mount Pisgah looks over the desert.

Israel Kills Sihon and Og

21 The Israelites sent messengers to Sihon, king of the Amorites, saying, 22 "Let us pass through your country. We will not go through any fields of grain or vineyards, or drink water from the wells. We will travel only along the king's road until we have passed through your country." 23 But King Sihon would not let the Israelites pass through his country. He gathered his whole army together, and they marched out to meet Israel in the desert. At Jahaz they fought the Israelites. 24 Israel killed the king and captured his land from the Arnon River to the Jabbok River. They took the land as far as the Ammonite border, which was strongly defended. 25 Israel catured all the Amorite cities and lived in them, taking Heshbon and all the towns around it. 26 Heshbon was the city where Sihon, the Amorite king, lived. In the past he had fought with the king of Moab and had taken all the land as far as the Arnon.

27 That is why the poets say:
"Come to Heshbon
    and rebuild it;
    rebuild Sihon's city.
28 A fire began in Heshbon;
    flames came from Sihon's city.
It destroyed Ar in Moab,
    and it burned the Arnon highlands.
29 How terrible for you, Moab!
The people of Chemosh are
        ruined.
His sons ran away
    and his daughters were captured
    by Sihon, king of the Amorites.
30 But we defeated those Amorites.
    We ruined their towns from
        Heshbon to Dibon,
    and we destroyed them as far as
        Nophah, near Medeba."

31 So Israel lived in the land of the Amorites.

32 After Moses sent spies to the town of Jazer, they captured the towns around it, forcing out the Amorites who lived there.

33 Then the Israelites went up the road towards Bashan. Og king of Bashan and his whole army marched out to meet the Israelites, and they fought at Edrei.

34 The LORD said to Moses, "Don't be afraid of him. I will hand him, his whole army and his land over to you. Do to him what you did to Sihon, the Amorite king who lived in Heshbon."

35 So the Israelites killed Og and his sons and all his army; no one was left alive. And they took his land.

Balak Sends for Balaam

22 Then the people of Israel went to the plains of Moab, and they camped near the Jordan River across from Jericho.

2 Balak son of Zippor saw everything the Israelites had done to the Amorites. 3 And Moab was scared of so many Israelites; truly, Moab was terrified by them.

4 The Moabites said to the elders of Midian, "These people will take everything around us like an ox eating grass."

Balak son of Zippor was the king of Moab at this time. 5 He sent messengers to Balaam son of Beor at Pethor, near the Euphrates River in his native land. Balak said, "A nation has come out of Egypt that covers the land. They have camped next to me, 6 and they are too powerful for me. So come and put a curse on them. Maybe then I can defeat them and make them leave the area. I know that if you bless someone, the blessings happen, and if you put a curse on someone, it happens."

7 The elders of Moab and Midian went with payment in their hands. When they

> The LORD said to Moses, "Don't be afraid of him. I will hand him, his whole army, and his land over to you."
> – Numbers 21:34

found Balaam, they told him what Balak had said.

8 Balaam said to them, "Stay here for the night, and I will tell you what the LORD tells me." So the Moabite leaders stayed with him.

9 God came to Balaam and asked, "Who are these men with you?"

10 Balaam said to God, "The king of Moab, Balak son of Zippor, sent them to me with this message: 11 'A nation has come out of Egypt that covers the land. So come and put a curse on them, and maybe I can fight them and force them out of my land.'"

12 But God said to Balaam, "Do not go with them. Don't put a curse on those people, because I have blessed them."

13 The next morning Balaam awoke and said to Balak's leaders, "Go back to your own country; the LORD has refused to let me go with you."

14 So the Moabite leaders went back to Balak and said, "Balaam refused to come with us."

15 So Balak sent other leaders—this time there were more of them, and they were more important. 16 They went to Balaam and said, "Balak son of Zippor says this: Please don't let anything stop you from coming to me. 17 I will pay you very well, and I will do what you say. Come and put a curse on these people for me."

18 But Balaam answered Balak's servants, "King Balak could give me his palace full of silver and gold, but I cannot disobey the LORD my God in anything, great or small. 19 You stay here tonight as the other men did, and I will find out what more the LORD tells me."

20 That night God came to Balaam and said, "These men have come to ask you to go with them. Go, but only do what I tell you."

Balaam's Donkey Speaks

21 Balaam got up the next morning and put a saddle on his donkey. Then he went with the Moabite leaders. 22 But God became angry because Balaam went, so the angel of the LORD stood in the road to stop Balaam. Balaam was riding his donkey, and he had two servants with him. 23 When the donkey saw the angel of the LORD standing in the road with a sword in his hand, the donkey left the road and went into the field. Balaam hit the donkey to force her back on the road.

24 Later, the angel of the LORD stood on a narrow path between two vineyards, with walls on both sides. 25 Again the donkey saw the angel of the LORD, and she walked close to one wall, crushing Balaam's foot against it. So he hit her again.

26 The angel of the LORD went ahead again and stood at a narrow place, too narrow to turn left or right. 27 When the donkey saw the angel of the LORD, she lay down under Balaam. This made him so angry that he hit her with his stick. 28 Then the LORD made the donkey talk, and she said to Balaam, "What have I done to make you hit me three times?"

29 Balaam answered the donkey, "You have made me look foolish! I wish I had a sword in my hand! I would kill you right now!"

30 But the donkey said to Balaam, "I am your very own donkey, which you have ridden for years. Have I ever done this to you before?"

"No," Balaam said.

31 Then the LORD let Balaam see the angel of the LORD, who was standing in the road with his sword drawn. Then Balaam bowed face down on the ground.

32 The angel of the LORD asked Balaam, "Why have you hit your donkey three times? I have stood here to stop you, because what you are doing is wrong. 33 The donkey saw me and turned away from me three times. If she had not turned away, I would have killed you by now, but I would have let her live."

34 Then Balaam said to the angel of the LORD, "I have sinned; I did not know you were standing in the road to stop me. If I am wrong, I will go back."

35 The angel of the LORD said to Balaam, "Go with these men, but say only what I tell you." So Balaam went with Balak's leaders.

36 When Balak heard that Balaam was coming, he went out to meet him at Ar in Moab, which was beside the Arnon, at

FAITH links

AN ATTENTION-GETTER
NUMBERS 22

Do you have a pet? What would you do if your pet suddenly talked to you one morning, instead of barking or meowing? That would certainly get your attention, wouldn't it? Balaam was a prophet who was determined to curse the people of Israel, all because a king told him to do so. But God told him not to do it. Since Balaam resisted God, God used a talking donkey to get his attention.

God will do whatever it takes to protect his people from harm and to keep people from harming others. He knows how to get someone's attention. Does he have yours?

Ten Ways to Obey, Exodus 20, p. 103

Our Thorough God, Leviticus 13, p. 149

Reward for Obedience, Leviticus 26:3–13, p. 171

A Shortcut, 1 Samuel 13:1–14, p. 369

Listen Up! 1 Kings 19:11–13, p. 467

The Doubt Remover, Romans 10:8–10, p. 1533

---

to you now, but I can't say just anything. I can only say what God tells me to say."
39 Then Balaam went with Balak to Kiriath Huzoth. 40 Balak offered cattle and sheep as a sacrifice and gave some meat to Balaam and the leaders with him.
41 The next morning Balak took Balaam to Bamoth Baal; from there he could see the edge of the Israelite camp.

Balaam's First Message

23 Balaam said to Balak, "Build me seven altars here, and prepare seven bulls and seven rams for me." 2 Balak did what Balaam asked, and they offered a bull and a ram on each of the altars.

3 Then Balaam said to Balak, "Stay here beside your burnt offering and I will go. If the LORD comes to me, I will tell you whatever he shows me." Then Balaam went to a higher place.

4 God came to Balaam there, and Balaam said to him, "I have prepared seven altars, and I have offered a bull and a ram on each altar."

5 The LORD told Balaam what he should say. Then the LORD said, "Go back to Balak and give him this message."

6 So Balaam went back to Balak. Balak and all the leaders of Moab were still standing beside his burnt offering 7 when Balaam gave them this message:

"Balak brought me here from Aram;
  the king of Moab brought me from
    the eastern mountains.
Balak said, 'Come, put a curse on the
    people of Jacob for me.
Come, call down evil on the people
    of Israel.'
8 But God has not cursed them,
  so I cannot curse them.
The LORD has not called down evil
    on them,
  so I cannot call down evil on them.
9 I see them from the top of the
    mountains;
  I see them from the hills.
I see a people who live alone,
  who think they are different from
    other nations.
10 No one can number the many people
    of Jacob,

---

the edge of his country. 37 Balak said to Balaam, "I had asked you before to come quickly. Why didn't you come to me? I am able to reward you well."
38 But Balaam answered, "I have come

and no one can count a fourth of
  Israel.
Let me die like good men,
  and let me end up like them!"

11 Balak said to Balaam, "What have you done to me? I brought you here to curse my enemies, but you have only blessed them!"

12 But Balaam answered, "I must say what the LORD tells me to say."

Balaam's Second Message

13 Then Balak said to him, "Come with me to another place, where you can also see the people. But you can only see part of them, not all of them. Curse them for me from there." 14 So Balak took Balaam to the field of Zophim, on top of Mount Pisgah. There Balak built seven altars and offered a bull and a ram on each altar.

15 So Balaam said to Balak, "Stay here by your burnt offering, and I will meet with God over there."

16 So the LORD came to Balaam and told him what to say. Then he said, "Go back to Balak and say such and such."

17 So Balaam went to Balak, where he and the leaders of Moab were standing beside his burnt offering. Balak asked him, "What did the LORD say?"

18 Then Balaam gave this message:
"Stand up, Balak, and listen.
  Hear me, son of Zippor.
19 God is not a human being, and he will
    not lie.
  He is not a human, and he does not
    change his mind.
  What he says he will do, he does.
    What he promises, he makes come
    true.
20 He told me to bless them,
  so I cannot change the blessing.
21 He has found no wrong in the people
    of Jacob;
  he saw no fault in Israel.
  The LORD their God is with them,
    and they praise their King.
22 God brought them out of Egypt;
  they are as strong as a wild ox.
23 No tricks will work on the people of
    Jacob,

and no magic will work against
  Israel.
People now say about them,
  'Look what God has done for
    Israel!'
24 The people rise up like a lioness;
  they get up like a lion.
Lions don't rest until they have
  eaten,

FAITH links

ALWAYS TRUTHFUL
NUMBERS 23:19

Is there anyone you know who has never lied? Some people think that George Washington never told a lie because of a popular story about a cherry tree. That story may or may not be true. One thing is true, though: God never lies. He always does what he says he will do. He won't suddenly change his mind or say, "Whoops! I made a mistake!" When he makes a promise, you can be sure that he will keep it.

Find out what else God has to say about keeping your word.

A Long Wait, Joshua 14:6–15, p. 294

An Unsung Hero, Ruth 2:12, 15–16, p. 347

A Given, 1 Chronicles 5:18–20, p. 526

All Talk, No Action, Jeremiah 5:1–2, p. 996

The Whole Truth, John 8:31–32, 45, p. 1438

The Finished Product, Philippians 1:6, p. 1609

until they have drunk their
  enemies' blood."
25 Then Balak said to Balaam, "You haven't cursed these people, so at least, don't bless them!"
26 Balaam answered Balak, "I told you before that I can only do what the LORD tells me."

Balaam's Third Message

27 Then Balak said to Balaam, "Come, I will take you to another place. Maybe God will be pleased to let you curse them from there." 28 So Balak took Balaam to the top of Peor, the mountain that looks over the desert.
29 Balaam told Balak, "Build me seven altars here and prepare for me seven bulls and seven rams." 30 Balak did what Balaam asked, and he offered a bull and a ram on each altar.

24 Balaam saw that the LORD wanted to bless Israel, so he did not try to use any magic but looked towards the desert. 2 When Balaam saw the Israelites camped in their tribes, the Spirit of God took control of him, 3 and he gave this message:

"This is the message of Balaam son
    of Beor,
  the message of a man who sees
    clearly;
4 this is the message of a man who
  hears the words of God.
I see a vision from the Almighty,
  and my eyes are open as I fall
    before him.
5 Your tents are beautiful, people of
    Jacob!
  So are your homes, Israel!
6 Your tents spread out like valleys,
  like gardens beside a river.
They are like spices planted by the
    LORD,
  like cedar trees growing by the
    water.
7 Israel's water buckets will always be
    full,
  and their crops will have plenty of
    water.
Their king will be greater than Agag;
  their kingdom will be very great.
8 God brought them out of Egypt;
  they are as strong as a wild ox.
They will defeat their enemies
  and break their enemies' bones;
  they will shoot them with arrows.
9 Like a lion, they lie waiting to
    attack;
  like a lioness, no one would be
    brave enough to wake them.
Anyone who blesses you will be
    blessed,
  and anyone who curses you will be
    cursed."

10 Then Balak was angry with Balaam, and he pounded his fist. He said to Balaam, "I called you here to curse my enemies, but you have continued to bless them three times. 11 Now go home! I said I would pay you well, but the LORD has made you lose your reward."

12 Balaam said to Balak, "When you sent messengers to me, I told them, 13 'Balak could give me his palace filled with silver and gold, but I still cannot go against the LORD's commands. I could not do anything, good or bad, on my own, but I must say what the LORD says.' 14 Now I am going back to my own people, but I will tell you what these people will do to your people in the future."

Balaam's Final Message

15 Then Balaam gave this message:
"This is the message of Balaam son
    of Beor,
  the message of a man who sees
    clearly;
16 this is the message of a man who
  hears the words of God.
I know well the Most High God.
I see a vision from the Almighty,
  and my eyes are open as I fall
    before him.
17 I see someone who will come some
    day,
  someone who will come, but not
    soon.
A star will come from Jacob;
  a ruler will rise from Israel.
He will crush the heads of the
    Moabites
  and smash the skulls of the sons of
    Sheth.
18 Edom will be conquered;

his enemy Edom will be
    conquered,
but Israel will grow wealthy.
19 A ruler will come from the
    descendants of Jacob
and will destroy those left in the
    city."

20 Then Balaam saw Amalek and gave this message:
"Amalek was the most important
    nation,
but Amalek will be destroyed at
    last."

21 Then Balaam saw the Kenites and gave this message:
"Your home is safe,
    like a nest on a
    cliff.
22 But you Kenites will
    be burned up;
Assyria will keep
    you captive."

23 Then Balaam gave this message:
"No one can live when God does this.
24 Ships will sail from the shores of
    Cyprus
and defeat Assyria and Eber,
    but they will also be destroyed."

25 Then Balaam got up and returned home, and Balak also went on his way.

Israel Worships Baal at Peor

25 While the people of Israel were still camped at Acacia, the men began sinning sexually with Moabite women. 2 The women invited them to their sacrifices to their gods, and the Israelites ate food there and worshipped these gods. 3 So the Israelites began to worship Baal of Peor, and the LORD was very angry with them.

4 The LORD said to Moses, "Get all the leaders of the people and kill them in open daylight in the presence of the LORD. Then the LORD will not be angry with the people of Israel."

5 So Moses said to Israel's judges, "Each of you must put to death your people who have become worshippers of Baal of Peor."

6 Moses and the Israelites were gathered at the entrance to the Meeting Tent, crying there. Then an Israelite man brought a Midianite woman to his brothers in plain sight of Moses and all the people. 7 Phinehas son of Eleazar, the son of Aaron, the priest, saw this, so he left the meeting and got his spear. 8 He followed the Israelite into his tent and drove his spear through both the Israelite man and the Midianite woman. Then the terrible sickness among the Israelites stopped.

9 This sickness had killed 24,000 people.

10 The LORD said to Moses, 11 "Phinehas son of Eleazar, the son of Aaron, the priest, has saved the Israelites from my anger. He hates sin as much as I do. Since he tried to save my honour among them, I will not kill them. 12 So tell Phinehas that I am making my peace agreement with him. 13 He and his descendants will always be priests, because he had great concern for the honour of his God. He removed the sins of the Israelites so that they would belong to God."

14 The Israelite man who was killed with the Midianite woman was named Zimri son of Salu. He was the leader of a family in the tribe of Simeon. 15 And the name of the Midianite woman who was put to death was Cozbi daughter of Zur, who was the chief of a Midianite family.

16 The LORD said to Moses, 17 "The Midianites are your enemies, and you should kill them. 18 They have already made you their enemies, because they tricked you at Peor and because of their sister Cozbi, the daughter of a Midianite leader. She was the woman who was killed when the sickness came because the people sinned at Peor."

The People are Counted

26 After the great sickness, the LORD said to Moses and Eleazar son of

> So the Israelites began to worship Baal of Peor, and the LORD was very angry with them.
> – Numbers 25:3

Aaron, the priest, 2 "Count all the people of Israel by families. Count all the men who are 20 years old or older who will serve in the army of Israel." 3 Moses and Eleazar the priest spoke to the people on the plains of Moab near the Jordan River, across from Jericho. They said, 4 "Count the men 20 years old or older, as the LORD commanded Moses."

Here are the Israelites who came out of Egypt:

5 The tribe of Reuben, the first son born to Israel, was counted. From Hanoch came the Hanochite family group; from Pallu came the Palluite family group; 6 from Hezron came the Hezronite family group; from Carmi came the Carmite family group. 7 These were the family groups of Reuben, and the total number of men was 43,730.

8 The son of Pallu was Eliab, 9 and Eliab's sons were Nemuel, Dathan and Abiram. Dathan and Abiram were the leaders who turned against Moses and Aaron and followed Korah when he turned against the LORD. 10 The earth opened up and swallowed them and Korah; they died at the same time the fire burned up the 250 men. This was a warning, 11 but the children of Korah did not die.

12 These were the family groups in the tribe of Simeon: from Nemuel came the Nemuelite family group; from Jamin came the Jaminite family group; from Jakin came the Jakinite family group; 13 from Zerah came the Zerahite family group; from Shaul came the Shaulite family group. 14 These were the family groups of Simeon, and the total number of men was 22,200.

15 These were the family groups in the tribe of Gad: from Zephon came the Zephonite family group; from Haggi came the Haggite family group; from Shuni came the Shunite family group; 16 from Ozni came the Oznite family group; from Eri came the Erite family group; 17 from Arodi came the Arodite family group; from Areli came the Arelite family group. 18 These were the family groups of Gad, and the total number of men was 40,500.

19 Two of Judah's sons, Er and Onan, died in Canaan.

20 These were the family groups in the tribe of Judah: from Shelah came the Shelanite family group; from Perez came the Perezite family group; from Zerah came the Zerahite family group. 21 These were the family groups from Perez: from Hezron came the Hezronite family group; from Hamul came the Hamulite family group. 22 These were the family groups of Judah, and the total number of men was 76,500.

23 These were the family groups in the tribe of Issachar: from Tola came the Tolaite family group; from Puah came the Puthite family group; 24 from Jashub came the Jashubite family group; from Shimron came the Shimronite family group. 25 These were the family groups of Issachar, and the total number of men was 64,300.

26 These were the family groups in the tribe of Zebulun: from Sered came the Seredite family group; from Elon came the Elonite family group; from Jahleel came the Jahleelite family group. 27 These were the family groups of Zebulun, and the total number of men was 60,500.

28 These were the family groups of Joseph through Manasseh and Ephraim. 29 These were the family groups of Manasseh: from Makir came the Makirite family group (Makir was the father of Gilead); from Gilead came the Gileadite family group. 30 These were the family groups that came from Gilead: from Iezer came the Iezerite family group; from Helek came the Helekite family group; 31 from Asriel came the Asrielite family group; from Shechem came the Shechemite family group; 32 from Shemida came the Shemidaite family group; from Hepher came the Hepherite family group. 33 (Zelophehad son of Hepher had no sons; he had only daughters, and their names were Mahlah, Noah, Hoglah, Milcah and Tirzah.) 34 These were the family groups of Manasseh, and the total number of men was 52,700.

35 These were the family groups in the tribe of Ephraim: from Shuthelah came the Shuthelahite family group; from Beker came the Bekerite family group;

ONE POTATO, TWO POTATO . . .   Numbers 26:55-56

Have you ever made a decision by counting off, "One-potato, two-potato, three-potato, four"? It's an easy way to get a quick answer to who should be "it". Throwing lots was a little like that. It was kind of like drawing straws (to see who gets the short straw) or flipping a coin (heads or tails). We don't know what the lots were made of or exactly how they were thrown. We just know they were used to make big and important decisions. Throwing lots was the way that people in biblical times gave God some room to help them make their decisions, like:

Choosing the goat to remove sins on the Day of Cleansing.
(Read Leviticus 16:8-10, p. 155.)

Dividing the land after the Israelites moved back into it. (Check out Numbers 26:55-56, p. 213; Joshua 14:2, p. 294.)

Dividing Jesus' garments among the soldiers. (Look at Matthew 27:35, p. 1325.)

Even choosing the new disciple to take the place of Judas.
(Check out Acts 1:24-26, p. 1464.)

from Tahan came the Tahanite family group. 36 This was the family group from Shuthelah: from Eran came the Eranite family group. 37 These were the family groups of Ephraim, and the total number of men was 32,500. These are the family groups that came from Joseph.

38 These were the family groups in the tribe of Benjamin: from Bela came the Belaite family group; from Ashbel came the Ashbelite family group; from Ahiram came the Ahiramite family group; 39 from Shupham came the Shuphamite family group; from Hupham came the Huphamite family group. 40 These were the family groups from Bela through Ard and Naaman: from Ard came the Ardite family group; from Naaman came the Naamite family group. 41 These were the family groups of Benjamin, and the total number of men was 45,600.

42 This was the family group in the tribe of Dan: from Shuham came the Shuhamite family group. That was the family of Dan, 43 and the total number of men in the Shuhamite family group of Dan was 64,400.

44 These were the family groups in the tribe of Asher: from Imnah came the Imnite family group; from Ishvi came the Ishvite family group; from Beriah came the Beriite family group. 45 These were the family groups that came from Beriah: from Heber came the Heberite family group; from Malkiel came the Malkielite family group. 46 (Asher also had a daughter named Serah.) 47 These were the family groups of Asher, and the total number of men was 53,400.

48 These were the family groups in the tribe of Naphtali: from Jahzeel came the Jahzeelite family group; from Guni came the Gunite family group; 49 from Jezer came the Jezerite family group; from Shillem came the Shillemite family group. 50 These were the family groups of Naphtali, and the total number of men was 45,400.

51 So the total number of the men of Israel was 601,730.

52 The LORD said to Moses, 53 "Divide the land among these people by the number of names. 54 A large tribe will get more land, and a small tribe will get less land; the amount of land each tribe gets will depend on the number of its people. 55 Divide the land by drawing lots, and the land each tribe gets will be named after that tribe. 56 Divide the land between large and small groups by drawing lots."

57 The tribe of Levi was also counted. These were the family groups of Levi: from Gershon came the Gershonite family group; from Kohath came the Kohathite family group; from Merari came the Merarite family group. 58 These also were Levite family groups: the Libnite family group, the Hebronite family group, the Mahlite family group, the Mushite family group and the Korahite family group. (Kohath was the ancestor of Amram, 59 whose wife was named Jochebed. She was from the tribe of Levi and she was born in Egypt. She and Amram had two sons, Aaron and Moses, and their sister Miriam. 60 Aaron was the father of Nadab, Abihu, Eleazar and Ithamar. 61 But Nadab and Abihu died because they made an offering before the LORD with the wrong kind of fire.)

62 The total number of male Levites one month old or older was 23,000. But these men were not counted with the other Israelites, because they were not given any of the land among the other Israelites.

63 Moses and Eleazar the priest counted all these people. They counted the Israelites on the plains of Moab across the Jordan River from Jericho. 64 Moses and Aaron the priest had counted the Israelites in the Desert of Sinai, but no one Moses counted on the plains of Moab was in the first counting. 65 The LORD had told the Israelites they would all die in the desert, and the only two left were Caleb son of Jephunneh and Joshua son of Nun.

Zelophehad's Daughters

27 Then the daughters of Zelophehad came near. Zelophehad was the son of Hepher, the son of Gilead, the son of Makir, the son of Manasseh. Zelophehad's daughters belonged to the family groups of Manasseh son of Joseph. The daughters' names were Mahlah, Noah, Hoglah, Milcah and Tirzah. 2 They went to the entrance of the Meeting Tent and stood before Moses, Eleazar the priest, the leaders and all the people. They said, 3 "Our father died in the desert. He was not one of Korah's followers who came together against the LORD, but he died because of his own sin, and he had no sons. 4 Our father's name will die out because he had no sons. Give us property among our father's relatives."

5 So Moses brought their case to the LORD, 6 and the LORD said to him, 7 "The daughters of Zelophehad are right; they should certainly get what their father owned. Give them property among their father's relatives.

8 "Tell the Israelites, 'If a man dies and has no son, then everything he owned should go to his daughter. 9 If he has no daughter, then everything he owned should go to his brothers. 10 If he has no brothers, then everything he owned should go to his father's brothers. 11 And if his father had no brothers, then everything he owned should go to the nearest relative in his family group. This should be a rule among the people of Israel, as the LORD has given this command to Moses.'"

Joshua is the New Leader

12 Then the LORD said to Moses, "Climb this mountain in the Abarim Mountains, and look at the land I have given to the Israelites. 13 After you have seen it, you will die and join your ancestors as your brother Aaron did, 14 because you both acted against my command in the Desert of Zin. You did not honour me as holy before the people at the waters of Meribah." (This was at Meribah in Kadesh in the Desert of Zin.)

27:16–17 Leadership
The leader is a shepherd.

15 Moses said to the LORD, 16 "The LORD is the God of the

Numbers 27:17 214

FAITH links

TAKE ME TO YOUR LEADER
NUMBERS 27:12-23

God told the Israelites that their leader, Moses, would not enter the land God promised to them. God knew that the people would need another leader. So he chose Joshua to lead the Israelites. He told the Israelites to give Joshua the same respect that they had given to Moses.

God gives us leaders in the church, in our communities and in the government. Those in authority over us deserve our respect and obedience. How do you show your respect for your leaders?

Family Feud, Genesis 27, p. 37

Fatherly Advice, Exodus 18, p. 99

Show Some Respect, Leviticus 19:32, p. 161

The Heart of the Matter, 1 Samuel 16, p. 375

Help to Understand, 2 Samuel 14, p. 416

The Verdict Is In? Matthew 7:1-2, p. 1285

---

spirits of all people. May he choose a leader for these people, 17 who will go in and out before them. He must lead them out like sheep and bring them in; the LORD's people must not be like sheep without a shepherd."

18 So the LORD said to Moses, "Take Joshua son of Nun, because my Spirit is in him. Put your hand on him, 19 and have him stand before Eleazar the priest and all the people. Then give him his orders as they watch. 20 Let him share your honour so that all the Israelites will obey him. 21 He must stand before Eleazar the priest, and Eleazar will get advice from the LORD by using the Urim. At his command all the Israelites will go out, and at his command they will all come in."

22 Moses did what the LORD told him. He took Joshua and had him stand before Eleazar the priest and all the people, 23 and he put his hands on him and gave him orders, just as the LORD had told him.

Daily Offerings

28 The LORD said to Moses, 2 "Give this command to the Israelites. Tell them: 'Bring me food offerings made by fire, for a smell that is pleasing to me, and be sure to bring them at the right time.' 3 Say to them, 'These are the offerings you must bring to the LORD: two male lambs, a year old, as a burnt offering each day. They must have nothing wrong with them. 4 Offer one lamb in the morning and the other lamb at twilight. 5 Also bring a grain offering of 2 litres of fine flour, mixed with 1 litre of oil from pressed olives. 6 This is the daily burnt offering which began at Mount Sinai; its smell is pleasing to the LORD. 7 Offer 1 litre of wine with each lamb as a drink offering; pour it out to the LORD at the Holy Place. 8 Offer the second lamb at twilight. As in the morning, also give a grain offering and a drink offering. This offering is made by fire, and its smell is pleasing to the LORD.

Sabbath Offerings

9 "'On the Sabbath day you must give two male lambs, a year old, that have nothing wrong with them. Also give a drink offering and a grain offering; the grain offering must be 4 litres of fine flour mixed with olive oil. 10 This is the burnt offering for every Sabbath, in addition to the daily burnt offering and drink offering.

Monthly Offerings

11 "'On the first day of each month bring a burnt offering to the LORD. This will be two young bulls, one ram and seven male lambs a year old, and they must have nothing wrong with them. **12** Give a grain offering with each bull of 6.6 litres of fine flour mixed with olive oil. Also give a grain offering with the ram. It must be 4 litres of fine flour mixed with olive oil. **13** And give a grain offering with each lamb of 2 litres of fine flour mixed with olive oil. This is a burnt offering, and its smell is pleasing to the LORD. **14** The drink offering with each bull will be 2 litres of wine, with the ram it will be one and a half litres, and with each lamb it will be 1 litre of wine. This is the burnt offering that must be offered each month of the year. **15** Besides the daily burnt offerings and drink offerings, bring a sin offering of one goat to the LORD.

The Passover

16 "'The LORD's Passover will be on the fourteenth day of the first month. **17** The Feast of Unleavened Bread begins on the fifteenth day of that month. For seven days, you may eat only bread made without yeast. **18** Have a holy meeting on the first day of the festival, and don't work that day. **19** Bring to the LORD an offering made by fire, a burnt offering of two young bulls, one ram and seven male lambs a year old. They must have nothing wrong with them. **20** With each bull give a grain offering of 6 litres of fine flour mixed with olive oil. With the ram it must be 4 litres of fine flour mixed with oil. **21** With each of the seven lambs, it must be 2 litres of fine flour mixed with oil. **22** Bring one goat as a sin offering, to remove your sins so you will belong to God. **23** Bring these offerings in addition to the burnt offerings you give every morning. **24** So bring food for the offering made by fire each day for seven days, for a smell that is pleasing to the LORD.

Do it in addition to the daily burnt offering and its drink offering. **25** On the seventh day have a holy meeting, and don't work that day.

The Feast of Weeks

26 "'On the day of firstfruits when you bring new grain to the LORD during the Feast of Weeks, have a holy meeting. Don't work that day. **27** Bring this burnt offering to the LORD: two young bulls, one ram and seven male lambs a year old. This smell is pleasing to the LORD. **28** Also, with each bull give a grain offering of 6 litres of fine flour mixed with oil. With the ram, it must be 4 litres of flour, **29** and with each of the seven lambs offer 2 litres of flour. **30** Offer one male goat to remove your sins so that you will belong to God. **31** Bring these offerings and their drink offerings in addition to the daily burnt offering and its grain offering. The animals must have nothing wrong with them.

The Feast of Trumpets

29 "'Have a holy meeting on the first day of the seventh month, and don't work on that day. That is the day you blow the trumpets. **2** Bring these burnt offerings as a smell pleasing to the LORD: one young bull, one ram and seven male lambs a year old. They must have nothing wrong with them. **3** With the bull give a grain offering of 7 litres of fine flour mixed with oil. With the ram offer 4 litres, **4** and with each of the seven lambs offer 2 litres. **5** Offer one male goat for a sin offering to remove your sins so that you will belong to God. **6** These offerings are in addition to the monthly and daily burnt offerings. Their grain offerings and drink offerings must be done as you have been told. These offerings are made by fire to the LORD, and their smell is pleasing to him.

> The LORD's Passover will be on the fourteenth day of the first month.
> – Numbers 28:16

The Day of Cleansing

7 "'Have a holy meeting on the tenth day of the seventh month. On that day do not eat and do not work. 8 Bring these burnt offerings as a smell pleasing to the LORD: one young bull, one ram and seven male lambs a year old. They must have nothing wrong with them. 9 With the bull give a grain offering of 7 litres of fine flour mixed with oil. With the ram it must be 4 litres, 10 and with each of the seven lambs it must be 2 litres. 11 Offer one male goat as a sin offering. This will be in addition to the sin offering which removes your sins, the daily burnt offering with its grain offering and the drink offerings.

The Feast of Shelters

12 "'Have a holy meeting on the fifteenth day of the seventh month, and do not work on that day. Celebrate a festival to the LORD for seven days. 13 Bring these burnt offerings, made by fire, as a smell pleasing to the LORD: thirteen young bulls, two rams and fourteen male lambs a year old. They must have nothing wrong with them. 14 With each of the thirteen bulls offer a grain offering of 7 litres of fine flour mixed with oil. With each of the two rams it must be 4 litres, 15 and with each of the fourteen lambs it must be 2 litres. 16 Offer one male goat as a sin offering in addition to the daily burnt offering with its grain and drink offerings.

17 "'On the second day of this festival give an offering of twelve bulls, two rams and fourteen male lambs a year old. They must have nothing wrong with them. 18 Bring the grain and drink offerings for the bulls, rams and lambs, according to the number required. 19 Offer one male goat as a sin offering, in addition to the daily burnt offering with its grain and drink offerings.

20 "'On the third day offer eleven bulls, two rams and fourteen male lambs a year old. They must have nothing wrong with them. 21 Bring the grain and drink offerings for the bulls, rams and lambs, according to the number required. 22 Offer one male goat as a sin offering, in addition to the daily burnt offering with its grain and drink offerings.

23 "'On the fourth day offer ten bulls, two rams and fourteen male lambs a year old. They must have nothing wrong with them. 24 Bring the grain and drink offerings for the bulls, rams and lambs, according to the number required. 25 Offer one male goat as a sin offering, in addition to the daily burnt offering with its grain and drink offerings.

26 "'On the fifth day offer nine bulls, two rams and fourteen male lambs a year old. They must have nothing wrong with them. 27 Bring the grain and drink offerings for the bulls, rams and lambs, according to the number required. 28 Offer one male goat as a sin offering, in addition to the daily burnt offering with its grain and drink offerings.

29 "'On the sixth day offer eight bulls, two rams and fourteen male lambs a year old. They must have nothing wrong with them. 30 Bring the grain and drink offerings for the bulls, rams and lambs, according to the number required. 31 Offer one male goat as a sin offering, in addition to the daily burnt offering with its grain and drink offerings.

32 "'On the seventh day offer seven bulls, two rams and fourteen male lambs a year old. They must have nothing wrong with them. 33 Bring the grain and drink offerings for the bulls, rams and lambs, according to the number required. 34 Offer one male goat as a sin offering, in addition to the daily burnt offering with its grain and drink offerings.

35 "'On the eighth day have a closing meeting and do not work on that day. 36 Bring an offering made by fire, a burnt offering, as a smell pleasing to the LORD. Offer one bull, one ram and seven male lambs a year old. They must have nothing wrong with them. 37 Bring the grain and drink offerings for the bull, the rams and the lambs, according to the number required. 38 Offer one male goat as a sin offering, in addition to the daily burnt offering with its grain and drink offerings.

39 "'At your festivals you should bring these to the LORD: your burnt offerings,

grain offerings, drink offerings and fellowship offerings. These are in addition to other promised offerings and special gifts you want to give to the LORD.'"

40 Moses told the Israelites everything the LORD had commanded him.

Rules About Special Promises

30 Moses spoke with the leaders of the Israelite tribes. He told them these commands from the LORD.

2 "If a man makes a promise to the LORD or says he will do something special, he must keep his promise. He must do what he said. 3 If a young woman still living at home makes a promise to the LORD or pledges to do something special, 4 and if her father hears about the promise or pledge and says nothing, she must do what she promised. She must keep her pledge. 5 But if her father hears about the promise or pledge and does not allow it, then the promise or pledge does not have to be kept. Her father would not allow it, so the LORD will free her from her promise.

6 "If a woman makes a pledge or a careless promise and then gets married, 7 and if her husband hears about it and says nothing, she must keep her promise or the pledge she made. 8 But if her husband hears about it and does not allow it, he cancels her pledge or the careless promise she made. The LORD will free her from keeping it.

9 "If a widow or divorced woman makes a promise, she must do whatever she promised.

10 "If a woman makes a promise or pledge while she is married, 11 and if her husband hears about it but says nothing and does not stop her, she must keep her promise or pledge. 12 But if her husband hears about it and cancels it, she does not have to do what she said. Her husband has cancelled it, so the LORD will free her from it. 13 A woman's husband may make her keep or cancel any promise or pledge she has made. 14 If he says nothing to her about it for several days, she must keep her promises. If he hears about them and says nothing, she must keep her promises. 15 But if he cancels them long after he heard about them, he is responsible if she breaks her promise."

16 These are commands that the LORD

Numbers 30:16 217

FAITH links

A SPECIAL PROMISE
NUMBERS 30:1-2

Do you believe in keeping your word? During Bible times, people often made vows to God or to someone else. A vow was a special promise. For example, Hannah made a promise to God that if he gave her a son, she would give her son back to him. (See 1 Samuel 1, p. 354.) Moses told the people of Israel that anyone who made this kind of promise to God had to keep it. That's why Jesus later warned against making rash promises. (Read Matthew 5:33–37, p. 1281.)

God wants you to avoid making promises that you don't intend to keep. When you give your word about something, make sure you keep it.

Just Kidding? Genesis 21:8–10, p. 28

Promises, Promises, Judges 2:1–3, p. 312

Who Do You Prefer? Proverbs 3:32, p. 830

The Problem with Gossip, Proverbs 11:12–13, p. 840

A Gentle Answer, Proverbs 15:1, p. 847

Your Choice of Fruit, Matthew 12:33–35, p. 1295

gave to Moses for husbands and wives, and for fathers with daughters living at home.

Israel Attacks the Midianites

31 The LORD spoke to Moses and said, 2 "Pay back the Midianites for what they did to the Israelites; after that you will die."

3 So Moses said to the people, "Get some men ready for war. The LORD will use them to pay back the Midianites. 4 Send to war 1,000 men from each of the tribes of Israel." 5 So 12,000 men got ready for war, 1,000 men from each tribe. 6 Moses sent those men to war; Phinehas son of Eleazar the priest was with them. He took with him the holy things and the trumpets for giving the alarm. 7 They fought the Midianites as the LORD had commanded Moses, and they killed every Midianite man. 8 Among those they killed were Evi, Rekem, Zur, Hur and Reba, who were the five kings of Midian. They also killed Balaam son of Beor with a sword.

9 The Israelites captured the Midianite women and children, and they took all their flocks, herds and goods. 10 They burned all the Midianite towns where they had settled and all their camps, 11 but they took all the people and animals and goods. 12 Then they brought the captives, the animals and the goods back to Moses and Eleazar the priest and all the Israelites. Their camp was on the plains of Moab near the Jordan River, across from Jericho.

13 Moses, Eleazar the priest, and all the leaders of the people went outside the camp to meet them. 14 Moses was angry with the army officers, the commanders over 1,000 men and those over 100 men, who returned from war.

15 He asked them, "Why did you let the women live? 16 They were the ones who followed Balaam's advice and turned the Israelites from the LORD at Peor. Then a terrible sickness struck the LORD's people. 17 Kill all the Midianite boys, and kill all the Midianite women who have had sexual relations. 18 But save for yourselves the girls who have not had sexual relations with a man.

19 "All you men who killed anyone or touched a dead body must stay outside the camp for seven days. On the third and seventh days you and your captives must make yourselves clean. 20 You must clean all your clothes and anything made of leather, goat hair or wood."

21 Then Eleazar the priest said to the soldiers who had gone to war, "These are the teachings that the LORD gave to Moses. 22 Put any gold, silver, bronze, iron, tin or lead— 23 anything that will not burn—into the fire, and then it will be clean. But also purify those things with the cleansing water. Then they will be clean. If something cannot stand the fire, wash it with the water. 24 On the seventh day wash your clothes, and you will be clean. After that you may come into the camp."

Dividing the Goods

25 The LORD said to Moses, 26 "You, Eleazar the priest, and the leaders of the family groups should take a count of the goods, the men and the animals that were taken. 27 Then divide those possessions between the soldiers who went to war and the rest of the people. 28 From the soldiers who went to war, take a tax for the LORD of one thing out of every 500. This includes people, cattle, donkeys or sheep. 29 Take it from the soldiers' half, and give it to Eleazar the priest as the LORD's share. 30 And from the people's half, take one thing out of every 50. This includes people, cattle, donkeys, sheep or other animals. Give that to the Levites, who take care of the LORD's Holy Tent." 31 So Moses and Eleazar did as the LORD commanded Moses.

32 There remained from what the soldiers had taken 675,000 sheep, 33 72,000 cattle, 34 61,000 donkeys 35 and 32,000 women who had not had sexual relations with a man. 36 The soldiers who went to war got 337,500 sheep 37 and they gave 675 of them to the LORD. 38 They got 36,000 cattle and they gave 72 of them to the LORD. 39 They got 30,500 donkeys and they gave 61 of them to the LORD.

40 They got 16,000 people, and they gave 32 of them to the LORD. 41 Moses gave the LORD's share to Eleazar the priest, as the LORD had commanded him. 42 Moses separated the people's half from the soldiers' half. 43 The people got 337,500 sheep, 44 36,000 cattle, 45 30,500 donkeys 46 and 16,000 people. 47 From the people's half Moses took one thing out of every 50 for the LORD. This included the animals and the people. Then he gave them to the Levites, who took care of the LORD's Holy Tent. This was what the LORD had commanded Moses.

48 Then the officers of the army, the commanders of 1,000 men and commanders of 100 men, came to Moses. 49 They told Moses, "We, your servants, have counted our soldiers under our command, and not one of them is missing. 50 So we have brought the LORD a gift of the gold things that each of us found: arm bands, bracelets, signet rings, earrings and necklaces. These are to remove our sins so we will belong to the LORD."

51 So Moses and Eleazar the priest took the gold from them, which had been made into all kinds of objects. 52 The commanders of 1,000 men and the commanders of 100 men gave the LORD the gold, and all of it together weighed about 190 kilogrammes; 53 each soldier had taken something for himself. 54 Moses and Eleazar the priest took the gold from the commanders of 1,000 men and the commanders of 100 men. Then they put it in the Meeting Tent as a memorial before the LORD for the people of Israel.

> We, your servants, have counted our soldiers under our command, and not one of them is missing.
> – Numbers 31:49

The Tribes East of the Jordan

32 The people of Reuben and Gad had large flocks and herds. When they saw that the lands of Jazer and Gilead were good for the animals, 2 they came to Moses, Eleazar the priest and the leaders of the people. 3-4 They said, "We, your servants, have flocks and herds. The LORD has captured for the Israelites a land that is good for animals—the land around Ataroth, Dibon, Jazer, Nimrah, Heshbon, Elealeh, Sebam, Nebo and Beon. 5 If it pleases you, we would like this land to be given to us. Don't make us cross the Jordan River."

6 Moses told the people of Gad and Reuben, "Shall your brothers go to war while you stay behind? 7 You will discourage the Israelites from going over to the land the LORD has given them. 8 Your ancestors did the same thing. I sent them from Kadesh Barnea to look at the land. 9 They went as far as the Valley of Eshcol, and when they saw the land, they discouraged the Israelites from going into the land the LORD had given them. 10 The LORD became very angry that day and made this promise: 11 'None of the people who came from Egypt and who are 20 years old or older will see the land that I promised to Abraham, Isaac and Jacob. These people have not followed me completely. 12 Only Caleb son of Jephunneh the Kenizzite and Joshua son of Nun followed the LORD completely.'

13 "The LORD was angry with Israel, so he made them wander in the desert for 40 years. Finally all the people who had sinned against the LORD died, 14 and now you are acting just like your ancestors! You sinful people are making the LORD even more angry with Israel. 15 If you stop following him, it will add to their stay in the desert, and you will destroy all these people."

16 Then the Reubenites and Gadites came up to Moses and said, "We will build pens for our animals and cities for our children here. 17 Then our children will be in fortified cities, safe from the people who live in this land. Then we will prepare for war. We will help the other Israelites get their land, 18 and we will not return home until every Israelite has received his land. 19 We won't take any of the land west of the Jordan River; our part of the land is east of the Jordan."

20 So Moses told them, "You must do these things. You must go before the LORD into battle 21 and cross the Jordan River armed, until the LORD forces out the enemy. 22 After the LORD helps us take the land, you may return home. You will have done your duty to the LORD and Israel, and you may have this land as your own.

23 "But if you don't do these things, you will be sinning against the LORD; know for sure that you will be punished for your sin. 24 Build cities for your children and pens for your animals, but then you must do what you promised."

25 The Gadites and Reubenites said to Moses, "We are your servants, and we will do what you, our master, command. 26 Our children, wives and all our cattle will stay in the cities of Gilead, 27 but we, your servants, will prepare for battle. We will go over and fight for the LORD, as you, our master, have said."

28 So Moses gave orders about them to Eleazar the priest, to Joshua son of Nun, and to the leaders of the tribes of Israel. 29 Moses said to them, "If the Gadites and Reubenites prepare for battle and cross the Jordan River with you, to go before the LORD and help you take the land, give them the land of Gilead for their own. 30 But if they do not go over armed, they will not receive it; their land will be in Canaan with you."

31 The Gadites and Reubenites answered, "We are your servants, and we will do as the LORD said. 32 We will cross over into Canaan and go before the LORD ready for battle. But our land will be east of the Jordan River."

33 So Moses gave that land to the tribes of Gad, Reuben and East Manasseh. (Manasseh was Joseph's son.) That land had been the kingdom of Sihon, king of the Amorites, and the kingdom of Og, king of Bashan, as well as all the cities and the land around them.

34 The Gadites rebuilt the cities of Dibon, Ataroth, Aroer, 35 Atroth Shophan, Jazer, Jogbehah, 36 Beth Nimrah and Beth Haran. These were fortified cities. And they built sheep pens.

37 The Reubenites rebuilt Heshbon, Elealeh, Kiriathaim, 38 Nebo, Baal Meon and Sibmah. They renamed Nebo and Baal Meon when they rebuilt them.

39 The descendants of Makir son of Manasseh went and captured Gilead and forced out the Amorites who were there. 40 So Moses gave Gilead to the family of Makir son of Manasseh and they settled there. 41 Jair son of Manasseh went out and captured the small towns there, and he called them the Towns of Jair. 42 Nobah went and captured Kenath and the small towns around it; then he named it Nobah after himself.

Israel's Journey from Egypt

33 These are the places where the Israelites went as Moses and Aaron led them out of Egypt in divisions. 2 At the LORD's command Moses recorded the places where they went, and these are the places they went.

3 On the fifteenth day of the first month, the day after the Passover, the Israelites left Rameses and marched out boldly in front of all the Egyptians. 4 The Egyptians were burying their firstborn sons, whom the LORD had killed; the LORD showed that the gods of Egypt were false.

5 The Israelites left Rameses and camped at Succoth.

6 They left Succoth and camped at Etham, at the edge of the desert.

7 They left Etham and went back to Pi Hahiroth, to the east of Baal Zephon, and camped near Migdol.

8 They left Pi Hahiroth and walked through the sea into the desert. After going three days through the Desert of Etham, they camped at Marah.

9 They left Marah and went to Elim; there were twelve springs of water and 70 palm trees where they camped.

> These are the places the Israelites went as Moses and Aaron led them out of Egypt in divisions.
> – Numbers 33:1

10 They left Elim and camped near the Red Sea.
11 They left the Red Sea and camped in the Desert of Sin.
12 They left the Desert of Sin and camped at Dophkah.
13 They left Dophkah and camped at Alush.
14 They left Alush and camped at Rephidim, where the people had no water to drink.
15 They left Rephidim and camped in the Desert of Sinai.
16 They left the Desert of Sinai and camped at Kibroth Hattaavah.
17 They left Kibroth Hattaavah and camped at Hazeroth.
18 They left Hazeroth and camped at Rithmah.
19 They left Rithmah and camped at Rimmon Perez.
20 They left Rimmon Perez and camped at Libnah.
21 They left Libnah and camped at Rissah.
22 They left Rissah and camped at Kehelathah.
23 They left Kehelathah and camped at Mount Shepher.
24 They left Mount Shepher and camped at Haradah.
25 They left Haradah and camped at Makheloth.
26 They left Makheloth and camped at Tahath.
27 They left Tahath and camped at Terah.
28 They left Terah and camped at Mithcah.
29 They left Mithcah and camped at Hashmonah.
30 They left Hashmonah and camped at Moseroth.
31 They left Moseroth and camped at Bene Berak Jaakan.
32 They left Bene Berak Jaakan and camped at Hor Haggidgad.
33 They left Hor Haggidgad and camped at Jotbathah.
34 They left Jotbathah and camped at Abronah.
35 They left Abronah and camped at Ezion Geber.
36 They left Ezion Geber and camped at Kadesh in the Desert of Zin.
37 They left Kadesh and camped at Mount Hor, on the border of Edom.
38 Aaron the priest obeyed the LORD and went up Mount Hor. There he died on the first day of the fifth month in the fortieth year after the Israelites left Egypt.
39 Aaron was 123 years old when he died on Mount Hor.
40 The Canaanite king of Arad, who lived in the southern area of Canaan, heard that the Israelites were coming.
41 The people left Mount Hor and camped at Zalmonah.
42 They left Zalmonah and camped at Punon.
43 They left Punon and camped at Oboth.
44 They left Oboth and camped at Iye Abarim, on the border of Moab.
45 They left Iye Abarim and camped at Dibon Gad.
46 They left Dibon Gad and camped at Almon Diblathaim.
47 They left Almon Diblathaim and camped in the mountains of Abarim, near Nebo.
48 They left the mountains of Abarim and camped on the plains of Moab near the Jordan River across from Jericho.
49 They camped along the Jordan on the plains of Moab, and their camp went from Beth Jeshimoth to Abel Acacia.
50 On the plains of Moab by the Jordan River across from Jericho, the LORD spoke to Moses. He said, **51** "Speak to the Israelites and tell them, 'When you cross the Jordan River and go into Canaan, **52** force out all the people who live there. Destroy all of their carved statues and metal idols. Wreck all of their places of worship. **53** Take over the land and settle there, because I have given this land to you to own. **54** Throw lots to divide up the land by family groups, giving larger portions to larger family groups and smaller portions to smaller family groups. The land will be given as the lots decide; each tribe will get its own land.
55 "'But if you don't force those people out of the land, they will bring you trouble. They will be like sharp hooks in

Numbers 33:56 222

LET'S VISIT THE DEAD SEA   Numbers 34:12

Check this out: the Dead Sea is really a lake, not a sea. While the Jordan and some other waters run *into* it, nothing runs *out* of it. The water slowly evaporates but the salt and other minerals stay in the lake. The water is so full of these minerals that no water creatures can live in it. That's why it's called the Dead Sea. (It's also sometimes called the Salt Sea.)

Some famous Bible events happened nearby. God used fire to totally destroy Sodom and Gomorrah because they were so evil. (Check out Genesis 19:23–29, p. 26.) David hid from King Saul in some caves. (See 1 Samuel 24:1, p. 387.) More recently, someone found some old, old copies of parts of the Bible. We call these copies the "Dead Sea Scrolls".

---

your eyes and thorns in your sides. They will bring trouble to the land where you live. **56** Then I will punish you as I had planned to punish them.'"

The Borders of Canaan

34 The LORD said to Moses, **2** "Give this command to the people of Israel: 'You will soon enter Canaan and it will be yours. These shall be the borders: **3** On the south you will get part of the Desert of Zin near the border of Edom. On the east side your southern border will start at the south end of the Dead Sea, **4** cross south of Scorpion Pass, and go through the Desert of Zin and south of Kadesh Barnea. Then it will go to Hazar Addar and over to Azmon. **5** From Azmon it will go to the brook of Egypt, and it will end at the Mediterranean Sea.

6 "'Your western border will be the Mediterranean Sea.

7 "'Your northern border will begin at the Mediterranean Sea and go to Mount Hor. **8** From Mount Hor it will go to Lebo Hamath, and on to Zedad. **9** Then the border will go to Ziphron, and it will end at Hazar Enan. This will be your northern border.

10 "'Your eastern border will begin at Hazar Enan and go to Shepham. **11** From Shepham the border will go east of Ain to Riblah and along the hills east of Lake Galilee. **12** Then the border will go down along the Jordan River and end at the Dead Sea.

"'These are the borders around your country.'"

13 So Moses gave this command to the Israelites: "This is the land you will receive. Throw lots to divide it among the nine and a half tribes, because the LORD commanded that it should be theirs. **14** The tribes of Reuben, Gad and East Manasseh have already received their land. **15** These two and a half tribes received land east of the Jordan River, across from Jericho."

16 Then the LORD said to Moses, **17** "These are the men who will divide the land: Eleazar the priest and Joshua son of Nun. **18** Also take one leader from each tribe to help divide the land. **19** These are the names of the leaders: from the tribe of Judah, Caleb son of Jephunneh; **20** from the tribe of Simeon, Shemuel son of Ammihud; **21** from the tribe of Benjamin, Elidad son of Kislon; **22** from the tribe of Dan,

Bukki son of Jogli; 23 from the tribe of Manasseh son of Joseph, Hanniel son of Ephod; 24 from the tribe of Ephraim son of Joseph, Kemuel son of Shiphtan; 25 from the tribe of Zebulun, Elizaphan son of Parnach; 26 from the tribe of Issachar, Paltiel son of Azzan; 27 from the tribe of Asher, Ahihud son of Shelomi; 28 from the tribe of Naphtali, Pedahel son of Ammihud."

29 The LORD commanded these men to divide the land of Canaan among the Israelites.

The Levites' Towns

35 The LORD spoke to Moses on the plains of Moab across from Jericho by the Jordan River. He said, 2 "Command the Israelites to give the Levites cities to live in from the land they receive. Also give the Levites the pastureland around these cities. 3 Then the Levites will have cities where they may live and pastureland for their cattle, flocks and other animals. 4 The pastureland you give the Levites will extend 500 metres from the city wall. 5 Also measure 1,000 metres in each direction outside the city wall—1,000 metres east of the city, 1,000 metres south of the city, 1,000 metres west of the city and 1,000 metres north of the city, with the city in the centre. This will be pastureland for the Levites' cities.

Cities of Safety

6 "Six of the cities you give the Levites will be cities of safety. A person who accidentally kills someone may run to one of those cities for safety. You must also give 42 other cities to the Levites; 7 give the Levites a total of 48 cities and their pastures. 8 The larger tribes of Israel must give more cities, and the smaller tribes must give fewer cities. Each tribe must give some of its cities to the Levites, but the number of cities they give will depend on the size of their land."

9 Then the LORD said to Moses, 10 "Tell the Israelites these things: 'When you cross the Jordan River and go into Canaan, 11 you must choose cities to be cities of safety, so that a person who accidentally kills someone may run to them for safety. 12 There the person will be safe from the dead person's relative who has the duty of punishing the killer. He will not die before he receives a fair trial in court. 13 The six cities you give will be cities of safety. 14 Give three cities east of the Jordan River and three cities in Canaan as cities of safety. 15 These six cities will be places of safety for citizens of Israel, as well as for foreigners and other people living with you. Any of these people who accidentally kills someone may run to one of these cities.

16 "'Anyone who uses an iron weapon to kill someone is a murderer. He must be put to death. 17 Anyone who takes a rock and kills a person with it is a murderer. He must be put to death. 18 Anyone who picks up a piece of wood and kills someone with it is a murderer. He must be put to death. 19 A relative of the dead person must put the murderer to death; when they meet, the relative must kill the murderer. 20 A person might shove someone or throw something at someone and cause death. 21 Or a person might hit someone with his hand and cause death. If it were done from hate, the person is a murderer and must be put to death. A relative of the dead person must kill the murderer when they meet.

22 "'But a person might suddenly push someone, and not from hatred. Or a person might accidentally throw something and hit someone. 23 Or a person might drop a rock on someone he couldn't see and kill that person. There was no plan to hurt anyone and no hatred for the one who was killed. 24 If that happens, the community must judge between the relative of the dead person and the killer, according to these rules. 25 They must

> You must choose... cities of safety, so that a person who accidentally kills someone may run to them for safety.
> – Numbers 35:11

protect the killer from the dead person's relative, sending the killer back to the original city of safety, to stay there until the high priest dies (the high priest had the holy oil poured on him).

26 "Such a person must never go outside the limits of the city of safety. 27 If a relative of the dead person finds the killer outside the city, the relative may kill that person and not be guilty of murder. 28 The killer must stay in the city of safety until the high priest dies. After the high priest dies, the killer may go home.

29 "These laws are for you from now on, wherever you live.

30 "If anyone kills a person, the murderer may be put to death only if there are witnesses. No one may be put to death with only one witness.

31 "Don't take money to spare the life of a murderer who should be put to death. A murderer must be put to death.

32 "If someone has run to a city of safety, don't take money to let the person go back home before the high priest dies.

33 "Don't let murder spoil your land. The only way to remove the sin of killing an innocent person is for the murderer to be put to death. 34 I am the LORD, and I live among the Israelites. I live in that land with you, so do not spoil it with murder.'"

Land for Zelophehad's Daughters

36 The leaders of Gilead's family group went to talk to Moses and the leaders of the families of Israel. (Gilead was the son of Makir, the son of Manasseh, the son of Joseph.) 2 They said, "The LORD commanded you, our master, to give the land to the Israelites by throwing lots, and the LORD commanded you to give the land of Zelophehad, our brother, to his daughters. 3 But if his daughters marry men from other tribes of Israel, then that land will leave our family, and the people of the other tribes will get that land. So we will lose some of our land. 4 When the time of Jubilee comes for the Israelites, their land will go to the tribes of the people they marry; their land will be taken away from us, the land we received from our fathers."

5 Then Moses gave the Israelites this command from the LORD: "These men from the tribe of Joseph are right. 6 This is the LORD's command to Zelophehad's daughters: you may marry anyone you wish, as long as the person is from your own tribe. 7 In this way the Israelites' land will not pass from tribe to tribe, and each Israelite will keep the land in the tribe that belonged to his ancestors. 8 A woman who inherits her father's land may marry, but she must marry someone from her own tribe. In this way every Israelite will keep the land that belonged to his ancestors. 9 The land must not pass from tribe to tribe, and each Israelite tribe will keep the land it received from its ancestors."

10 Zelophehad's daughters obeyed the LORD's command to Moses.

11 So Zelophehad's daughters—Mahlah, Tirzah, Hoglah, Milcah and Noah—married their cousins, their father's relatives. 12 Their husbands were from the tribe of Manasseh son of Joseph, so their land stayed in their father's family group and tribe.

13 These were the laws and commands that the LORD gave to the Israelites through Moses on the plains of Moab by the Jordan River, across from Jericho.

Deuteronomy

TELL US AGAIN, MOSES
Remember me? I'm Moses and this is my last book. By the time I wrote Deuteronomy, I was a very old man, and this book was my farewell speech. I remembered all the awesome things God did for us when he brought us out of Egypt (read about it in Deuteronomy 4:32–38), and I looked forward to the day when Israel would live in the Promised Land. I warned the people that they must not worship the false gods of the land but only the Lord our God.

I wrote this book to remind people to follow God's laws. So that people would understand how important the laws were, I wrote them down a second time. (The word *Deuteronomy* means "second law".) In fact, the laws were so important, I told the people to write them down and tie them to their foreheads! (See Deuteronomy 6:4–9 for other ways to remember God's law.) God promises great blessings for those who obey his laws.

JESUS WATCH

In many ways Moses was very much like Jesus. Just like Jesus, Moses was chosen by God to serve his people as prophet, priest and king. As a prophet, Moses performed miracles so that everyone would know that he spoke for God. He gave the people the Law so that they could honour God and get along with each other. Jesus also performed many miracles that proved he was from God and he explained the laws of God. Moses warned the people not to sin and spoke of their future in the land God promised to them. Today Jesus is our high priest, asking God to forgive our sins and blot them out for ever. Because of him, our future is in heaven. Like a priest, Moses prayed many times that God would forgive the Israelites and that their punishment would not be too harsh. (See Deuteronomy 9:7–29.) Although Moses was not a king, he served as ruler of Israel, just as Jesus is king of all who believe in him.

my FAVOURITE links

OTHER CONNECTIONS

Livin' it

It's easy to become proud when you've accomplished something, or you love something you have, but God warns us over and over again about being proud. Check it out by linking to Struttin' Our Stuff, Deuteronomy 8:11–18, to find out what God has to say about pride.

Making good choices is tough. Something may appear to be a good choice, but later turns out to be a bad choice. How can you know you're making the right decision? Connect to This or That? Deuteronomy 30:15–20, for help on making good choices.

Learn more cool facts about events and places mentioned in the Book of Deuteronomy by connecting here:

- A Feast for Remembering, Deuteronomy 16:1–8. You and your family probably remember special days in different ways – with celebrations, festivals, family traditions. The Israelites had a special feast to help them remember an important event in their history. Check it out by linking here.
- Follow Moses' life by tracking his many journeys – from Egypt to the wilderness and back, when you visit The Deliverer, Deuteronomy 34.

What's the data on a 'safe city'?

Don't know? Try connecting to Deuteronomy 19:1–7, and see if you can find out.

did YOU know?

OTHER STORIES TO BOOKMARK:

The Ten Commandments, Deuteronomy 5:1–22
Burn the idols, Deuteronomy 7:1–6
One-tenth of all we have, Deuteronomy 14:22–29
Follow the new leader: Joshua, Deuteronomy 31:1–8
Moses dies, Deuteronomy 34

FAITH links

Play Fair or Play Favourites?
Deuteronomy 1:16–18

His OK to Obey,
Deuteronomy 2:24–36

Facing the Consequences,
Deuteronomy 3:21–29

I'll Never Forget What's-His-Name,
Deuteronomy 8

What God Wants,
Deuteronomy 10:12–13

Care for the Lost,
Deuteronomy 22:1–3

A Serious Promise,
Deuteronomy 23:21–23

Read My Lips?
Deuteronomy 26:16–19

A Choice to Make,
Deuteronomy 30:15–20

Moses Talks to the Israelites

1 This is the message Moses gave to all the people of Israel in the desert east of the Jordan River. They were in the desert area near Suph, between Paran and the towns of Tophel, Laban, Hazeroth and Dizahab.

2 (The trip from Mount Sinai to Kadesh Barnea on the Mount Seir road takes eleven days.) 3 40 years after the Israelites had left Egypt, on the first day of the eleventh month, Moses told the people of Israel everything the LORD had commanded him to tell them. 4 This was after the LORD had defeated Sihon and Og. Sihon was king of the Amorite people and lived in Heshbon. Og was king of Bashan and lived in Ashteroth and Edrei.

5 Now the Israelites were east of the Jordan River in the land of Moab, and there Moses began to explain what God had commanded. He said:

6 The LORD our God spoke to us at Mount Sinai and said, "You have stayed long enough at this mountain. 7 Get ready, and go to the mountain country of the Amorites, and to all the places around there—the Jordan Valley, the mountains, the western hills, the southern area, the sea coast, the land of Canaan and Lebanon. Go as far as the great river, the Euphrates. 8 See, I have given you this land, so go in and take it for yourselves. The LORD promised it to your ancestors—Abraham, Isaac and Jacob and their descendants."

Moses Appoints Leaders

9 At that time I said, "I am not able to take care of you by myself. 10 The LORD your God has made you grow in number so that there are as many of you as there are stars in the sky. 11 I pray that the LORD, the God of your ancestors, will give you a thousand times more people and do all the wonderful things he promised. 12 But I cannot take care of your problems, your troubles and your arguments by myself. 13 So choose some men from each tribe—wise men who have understanding and experience—and I will make them leaders over you."

14 And you said, "That's a good thing to do."

15 So I took the wise and experienced leaders of your tribes, and I made them your leaders. I appointed commanders

FAITH links

PLAY FAIR OR PLAY FAVOURITES?

DEUTERONOMY 1:16-18

"That's not fair!" Have you said that statement within the last week? Many of us hope to be treated fairly, especially by people in authority. Moses talked to the leaders of the Israelites about being fair. God commanded them to be fair. When these leaders ruled on arguments between two people, they were to decide with fairness. They were not to play favourites.

Often we act with more fairness towards the people we like than we do towards those people we don't like. Is that true for you? God doesn't want us to be fair to some and not to others. He has one rule for all: be fair!

Made in His Image, Genesis 1:26–27, p. 4

Moses' Champion, Numbers 12, p. 192

The Right Thing to Do, 1 Samuel 26, p. 391

Mercy for an Enemy, Jonah 4, p. 1216

The Way to Greatness, Matthew 20:20–28, p. 1309

Who Needs Love? Luke 6:27–36, p. 1379

over 1,000 people, over 100 people, over 50 people and over ten people and made them officers over your tribes. 16 Then I told your leaders, "Listen to the arguments between your people. Judge fairly between two Israelites or between an Israelite and a foreigner. 17 When you judge, be fair to everyone; don't act as if one person is more important than another, and don't be afraid of anyone, because your decision comes from God. Bring the hard cases to me, and I will judge them." 18 At that time I told you everything you must do.

Spies Enter the Land

19 Then, as the LORD our God commanded us, we left Mount Sinai and went towards the mountain country of the Amorite people. We went through that large and terrible desert you saw, and then we came to Kadesh Barnea. 20 I said to you, "You have now come to the mountain country of the Amorites, to the land the LORD our God will give us. 21 Look, here it is! Go up and take it. The LORD, the God of your ancestors, told you to do this, so don't be afraid and don't worry."

22 Then all of you came to me and said, "Let's send men before us to spy out the land. They can come back and tell us about the way we should go and the cities we will find."

23 I thought that was a good idea, so I chose twelve of your men, one for each tribe. 24 They left and went up to the mountains, and when they came to the Valley of Eshcol they explored it. 25 They took some of the fruit from that land and brought it down to us, saying, "It is a good land that the LORD our God is giving us."

Israel Refuses to Enter

26 But you refused to go. You would not obey the command of the LORD your God, 27 but grumbled in your tents, saying, "The LORD hates us. He brought us out of Egypt just to give us to the Amorites, who will destroy us. 28 Where can we go now? The spies we sent have made us afraid, because they said, 'The people there are stronger and taller than we are. The cities are big, with walls up to the sky. And we saw the Anakites there!'"

29 Then I said to you, "Don't be frightened; don't be afraid of those people. 30 The LORD your God will go ahead of you and fight for you as he did in Egypt; you saw him do it. 31 And in the desert you saw how the LORD your God carried you, as one carries a child. And he has brought you safely all the way to this place."

32 But you still did not trust the LORD your God, even though 33 he had always gone before you to find places for you to camp. In a fire at night and in a cloud during the day, he showed you which way to go.

34 When the LORD heard what you said, he was angry and made an oath, saying, 35 "I promised a good land to your ancestors, but none of you evil people will see it. 36 Only Caleb son of Jephunneh will see it. I will give him and his descendants the land he walked on, because he followed the LORD completely."

37 Because of you, the LORD was also angry with me and said, "You won't enter the land either, 38 but your assistant, Joshua son of Nun, will enter it. Encourage him, because he will lead Israel to take the land for their own.

39 "Your little children that you said would be captured, who do not know right from wrong at this time, will go into the land. I will give the land to them, and they will take it for their own. 40 But you must turn round and follow the desert road towards the Red Sea."

41 Then you said to me, "We have sinned against the LORD, but now we will go up and fight, as the LORD our God commanded us." Then all of you put on weapons, thinking it would be easy to go into the mountains.

42 But the LORD said to me, "Tell the people, 'You must not go up there and fight. I will not be with you, and your enemies will defeat you.'"

43 So I told you, but you would not listen. You would not obey the LORD's command. You were proud, so you went on up into the mountains, 44 and the Amorites who lived in those mountains came out and fought you. They chased you like

FAITH links

YOUR TOTAL TRUST
DEUTERONOMY 1:32

During their journey to the land God promised them, God helped the Israelites many times. While they wandered through the wilderness, he kept them safe, gave them food and took care of them. Still, they had a hard time trusting him, as Moses reminded them. Do you trust God all of the time or only when you really need help? God wants your total trust always.

Link here for some more thoughts on trusting God:

Lights, Camera, . . . Actions! Genesis 12:1–3, p. 17

Always Truthful, Numbers 23:19, p. 208

Love for a Lifetime, Song of Solomon 6:8–9, p. 891

A Broken Promise, Jeremiah 2:1–8, p. 989

Exercising Patience, Luke 2:25–28, 36–37, p. 1369

Keeping Clean, 2 Corinthians 7:1, p. 1576

---

bees and defeated you from Edom to Hormah. 45 So you came back and cried before the LORD, but the LORD did not listen to you; he refused to pay attention to you. 46 So you stayed in Kadesh a long time.

Israel Wanders in the Desert

2 Then we turned round, and we travelled on the desert road towards the Red Sea, as the LORD had told me to do. We travelled through the mountains of Edom for many days.

2 Then the LORD said to me, 3 "You have travelled through these mountains long enough. Turn north 4 and give the people this command: 'You will soon go through the land that belongs to your relatives, the descendants of Esau who live in Edom. They will be afraid of you, but be very careful. 5 Do not go to war against them. I will not give you any of their land—not even a foot of it—because I have given the mountains of Edom to Esau as his own. 6 You must pay them in silver for any food you eat or water you drink.'"

7 The LORD your God has blessed everything you have done; he has protected you while you travelled through this great desert. The LORD your God has been with you for the past 40 years, and you have had everything you needed.

8 So we passed by our relatives, the descendants of Esau who lived in Edom. We turned off the Jordan Valley road that comes from the towns of Elath and Ezion Geber and travelled along the desert road to Moab.

The Land of Ar

9 Then the LORD said to me, "Don't bother the people of Moab. Don't go to war against them, because I will not give you any of their land as your own; I have given Ar to the descendants of Lot as their own." 10 (The Emites, who lived in Ar before, were strong people, and there were many of them. They were very tall, like the Anakites. 11 The Emites were thought to be Rephaites, like the Anakites, but the Moabite people called them Emites. 12 The Horites also lived in Edom before, but the descendants of Esau forced them out and destroyed them, taking their place as Israel did in the land the LORD gave them as their own.)

13 And the LORD said to me, "Now get up and cross the Zered Valley." So we crossed the valley. 14 It had been 38 years from the time we left Kadesh Barnea until we crossed the Zered Valley. By then, all the fighting men from that time had died, as the LORD had promised would happen.

15 The LORD continued to work against them to remove them from the camp until they were all dead.

16 When the last of those fighting men had died, 17 the LORD said to me, 18 "Today you will pass by Ar, on the border of Moab. 19 When you come near the people of Ammon, don't bother them or go to war against them, because I will not give you any of their land as your own. I have given it to the descendants of Lot for their own."

20 (That land was also thought to be a land of the Rephaites, because those people used to live there, but the Ammonites called them Zamzummites. 21 They were strong people, and there were many of them; they were very tall, like the Anakites. The LORD destroyed the Zamzummites and the Ammonites forced them out of the land and took their place. 22 The LORD did the same thing for the descendants of Esau, who lived in Edom, when he destroyed the Horites. The Edomites forced them out of the land and took their place, and they live there to this day. 23 The Cretan people came from Crete and destroyed the Avvites, who lived in towns all the way to Gaza; the Cretan people destroyed them and took their place.)

Fighting the Amorites

24 The LORD said, "Get up and cross the Arnon Ravine. See, I am giving you the power to defeat Sihon the Amorite, king of Heshbon, and I am giving you his land. So fight against him and begin taking his land. 25 Today I will begin to make all the people in the world afraid of you. When they hear reports about you, they will shake with fear, and they will be terrified of you."

26 I sent messengers from the desert of Kedemoth to Sihon king of Heshbon. They offered him peace, saying, 27 "If you let us pass through your country, we will stay on the road and not turn right or left. 28 We will pay you in silver for any food we eat or water we drink. We only want to walk through your country. 29 The descendants of Esau in Edom let us go through their land, and so did the Moabites in Ar. We want to cross the Jordan River into the land the LORD our God has given us." 30 But Sihon king of Heshbon would not let us pass, because

---

FAITH links

HIS OK TO OBEY

DEUTERONOMY 2:24-36

Think of the biggest kid at your school. Suppose God told you that he would give you something that kid owns. All you have to do is tell him of God's plans. Would you do it? How do you think that kid would react?

God told the Israelites many times that he would give them land. To begin taking possession of that land, they had to fight an enemy nation. But the Lord kept them safe because they were obedient.

When God wants you to do something, he gives you the resources and the ability to do it. He'll never tell you to do something that you can't do with his help.

Fearful Service? Exodus 4:1–17, p. 80

God's Pep Talk, Joshua 1:5–9, p. 276

Building Together, Nehemiah 3, p. 627

Standing for What's Right, Esther 3:2–4, p. 651

Stand! Jeremiah 19:14—20:6, p. 1019

Your Civic Duty, Matthew 17:24–27, p. 1304

the LORD your God had made him stubborn. The LORD wanted you to defeat Sihon, and now this has happened.

31 The LORD said to me, "See, I have begun to give Sihon and his country to you. Begin taking the land as your own."

32 Then Sihon and all his army came out and fought us at Jahaz, 33 but the LORD our God gave Sihon to us. We defeated him, his sons and all his army. 34 We captured all his cities at that time and completely destroyed them, as well as the men, women and children. We left no one alive. 35 But we kept the cattle and valuable things from the cities for ourselves. 36 We defeated Aroer on the edge of the Arnon Ravine, and we defeated the town in the ravine, and even as far as Gilead. No town was too strong for us; the LORD our God gave us all of them. 37 But you did not go near the land of the Ammonites, on the shores of the Jabbok River, or the towns in the mountains, as the LORD our God had commanded.

The Battle at Bashan

3 When we turned and went up the road towards Bashan, Og king of Bashan and all his army came out to fight us at Edrei. 2 The LORD said to me, "Don't be afraid of Og, because I will hand him, his whole army and his land over to you. Do to him what you did to Sihon king of the Amorites, who ruled in Heshbon."

3 So the LORD our God gave us Og king of Bashan and all his army; we defeated them and left no one alive. 4 Then we captured all of Og's cities, all 60 of them, and took the whole area of Argob, Og's kingdom in Bashan. 5 All these were strong cities, with high walls and gates with bars. And there were also many small towns with no walls. 6 We completely destroyed them, just like the cities of Sihon king of Heshbon. We killed all the men, women and children, 7 but we kept all the cattle and valuable things from the cities for ourselves.

8 So at that time we took the land east of the Jordan River, from the Arnon Ravine to Mount Hermon, from these two Amorite kings. 9 (Hermon is called Sirion by the Sidonian people, but the Amorites call it Senir.) 10 We captured all the cities on the high plain and all of Gilead, and we took all of Bashan as far as Salecah and Edrei, towns in Og's kingdom of Bashan. 11 (Only Og king of Bashan was left of the few Rephaites. His bed was made of iron, and it was more than 4 metres long and 2 metres wide! It is still in the Ammonite city of Rabbah.)

The Land is Divided

12 At that time we took this land to be our own. I gave the people of Reuben and Gad the land from Aroer by the Arnon Ravine, as well as half of the mountain country of Gilead and the cities in it. 13 To the people of East Manasseh I gave the rest of Gilead and all of Bashan, the kingdom of Og. (The area of Argob in Bashan was called the land of the Rephaites. 14 Jair, a descendant of Manasseh, took the whole area of Argob, all the way to the border of the Geshurites and Maacathites. So that land was named for Jair, and even today Bashan is called the Towns of Jair.) 15 I gave Gilead to Makir. 16 I gave the Reubenites and the Gadites the land that begins at Gilead and goes from the Arnon Ravine (the middle of the Arnon is the border) to the Jabbok River, which is the Ammonite border. 17 The border on the west was the Jordan River in the Jordan Valley, and it goes from Lake Galilee to the Dead Sea west of Mount Pisgah.

18 At that time I gave you this command: "The LORD your God has given you this land as your own. Now your fighting men must take their weapons, and you must lead the other Israelites across the river. 19 Your wives, your young children and your cattle may stay here. I know you have many cattle, and they may stay here in the cities I have given you, 20 until the LORD also gives your Israelite relatives a place to rest. They will receive the land the LORD your God has given them on the other side of the Jordan River. After that, you may each return to the land I have given you."

21 Then I gave this command to Joshua: "You have seen for yourself all that the LORD your God has done to these

FACING THE CONSEQUENCES
DEUTERONOMY 3:21-29

Think about the last time that you did something wrong. Did you get into trouble for it? Wrong behaviour has consequences. When Moses sinned, the consequence was that he would not be allowed to enter the land God promised to the Israelites. Even though Moses pleaded with God, God did not change his mind.

Although God forgives us when we sin, we still have to face the consequences of our actions. A consequence is when a parent grounds you for doing something wrong. Before you take a step in the wrong direction, consider this: can you afford to pay the consequences?

Can't Live Without It? Genesis 3, p. 7

A Hidden Sin, Joshua 7, p. 285

Above the Law, 1 Kings 21, p. 470

A Life-Saving Message, Esther 2:19–22, p. 650

Just a Test, Luke 4:1–13, p. 1373

Just Say No! Titus 2:11–12, p. 1660

two kings. The LORD will do the same thing to all the kingdoms where you are going. 22 Don't be afraid of them, because the LORD your God will fight for you."

Moses Cannot Enter the Land

23 Then I begged the LORD: 24 "Lord GOD, you have begun to show me, your servant, how great you are. You have great strength, and no other god in heaven or on earth can do the powerful things you do. There is no other god like you. 25 Please let me cross the Jordan River so that I may see the good land by the Jordan. I want to see the beautiful mountains and Lebanon."

26 But the LORD was angry with me because of you, and he would not listen to me. The LORD said to me, "That's enough. Don't talk to me any more about it. 27 Climb to the top of Mount Pisgah and look west, north, south and east. You can look at the land, but you will not cross the Jordan River. 28 Appoint Joshua and help him be brave and strong. He will lead the people across the river and give them the land that they are to inherit, but you can only look at it." 29 So we stayed in the valley opposite Beth Peor.

Moses Tells Israel to Obey

4 Now, Israel, listen to the laws and commands I will teach you. Obey them so that you will live and so that you will go over and take the land the LORD, the God of your ancestors, is giving to you. 2 Don't add to these commands, and don't leave anything out, but obey the commands of the LORD your God that I give you.

3 You have seen for yourselves what the LORD did at Baal Peor, how the LORD your God destroyed everyone among you who followed Baal in Peor. 4 But all of you who continued following the LORD your God are still alive today.

5 Look, I have taught you the laws and rules the LORD my God commanded me. Now you can obey the laws in the land you are entering, in the land you will take. 6 Obey these laws carefully, in order to show the other nations that you have wisdom and understanding. When they hear about these laws, they will say, "This great nation of Israel is wise and understanding." 7 No other nation is as great as we are. Their gods do not come near them, but the LORD our God comes near

when we pray to him. 8 And no other nation has such good teachings and commands as those I am giving to you today.

9 But be careful! Watch out and don't forget the things you have seen. Don't forget them as long as you live, but teach them to your children and grandchildren. 10 Remember the day you stood before the LORD your God at Mount Sinai. He said to me, "Bring the people together so I can tell them what I have to say. Then they will respect me as long as they live in the land, and they will teach these things to their children." 11 When you came and stood at the bottom of the mountain, it blazed with fire that reached to the sky, and black clouds made it very dark. 12 The LORD spoke to you from the fire. You heard the sound of words, but you did not see him; there was only a voice. 13 The LORD told you about his Agreement, the Ten Commandments. He told you to obey them, and he wrote them on two stone tablets. 14 Then the LORD commanded me to teach you the laws and rules that you must obey in the land you will take when you cross the Jordan River.

4:6–9 Reputation
Check out how to build a good reputation.

Laws About Idols

15 Since the LORD spoke to you from the fire at Mount Sinai, but you did not see him, watch yourselves carefully! 16 Don't sin by making idols of any kind, and don't make statues—of men or women, 17 of animals on earth or birds that fly in the air, 18 of anything that crawls on the ground or of fish in the water below. 19 When you look up at the sky, you see the sun, moon and stars and everything in the sky. But don't bow down and worship them, because the LORD your God has made these things for all people everywhere. 20 But the LORD brought you out of Egypt, which tested you like a furnace for melting iron, and he made you his very own people, as you are now.

21 The LORD was angry with me because of you, and he swore that I would not cross the Jordan River to go into the

FAITH links

WHAT HE'S REALLY LIKE
DEUTERONOMY 4:15-20

Ever wonder what God looks like? Moses reminded the people of Israel that God did not physically appear to them when he talked to them at Mount Sinai. God is spirit. (See John 4:24, p. 1428.) He has no physical shape. God warned the people not to make statues of what they thought he looked like. These statues were called idols. God did not want the people to worship a man-made image. A statue could not represent what God was like.

Although we may not worship statues of God, we can have ideas about him that are just as wrong. We sometimes try to limit God by what we think he's like. If you want to know what he's really like, just ask him, or read his Book!

Want to know more about the danger of having false gods in our lives? Read on!

Idol Talk, Exodus 32, p. 118

A Look for the Book, 2 Chronicles 34:14–18, p. 603

Remember Your Creator, Ecclesiastes 12:1, 13, p. 885

What God Thinks, Isaiah 55:8–9, p. 969

Two Ways to Grow, Luke 2:46–52, p. 1370

Life's Rule Book, 2 Timothy 3:15–17, p. 1655

good land the LORD your God is giving you as your own. 22 I will die here in this land and not cross the Jordan, but you will soon go across and take that good land. 23 Be careful. Don't forget the Agreement of the LORD your God that he made with you, and don't make any idols for yourselves, as the LORD your God has commanded you not to do. 24 The LORD your God is a jealous God, like a fire that burns things up.

email FROM GOD 4:23
Idols
Is it OK to love something more than God?

25 Even after you have lived in the land a long time and have had children and grandchildren, don't do evil things. Don't make any kind of idol, and don't do what the LORD your God says is evil, because that will make him angry. 26 If you do, I ask heaven and earth to speak against you this day that you will quickly be removed from this land that you are crossing the Jordan River to take. You will not live there long after that, but you will be completely destroyed. 27 The LORD will scatter you among the other nations. Only a few of you will be left alive, and those few will be in other nations where the LORD will send you. 28 There you will worship gods made by people, gods made of wood and stone, that cannot see, hear, eat or smell. 29 But even there you can look for the LORD your God, and you will find him if you look for him with your whole being. 30 It will be hard when all these things happen to you. But after that you will come back to the LORD your God and obey him, 31 because the LORD your God is a merciful God. He will not leave you or destroy you. He will not forget the Agreement with your ancestors, which he swore to them.

The LORD is Great

32 Nothing like this has ever happened before! Look at the past, long before you were even born. Go all the way back to when God made man on the earth, and look from one end of heaven to the other. Nothing like this has ever been heard of! 33 No other people have ever heard God speak from a fire and have still lived. But you have. 34 No other god has ever taken for himself one nation out of another. But the LORD your God did this for you in Egypt, right before your own eyes. He did it with tests, signs, miracles, war and great sights, by his great power and strength.

35 He showed you things so you would know that the LORD is God, and there is no other God besides him. 36 He spoke to you from heaven to teach you. He showed you his great fire on earth, and you heard him speak from the fire. 37 Because the LORD loved your ancestors, he chose you, their descendants, and he brought you out of Egypt himself by his great strength. 38 He forced nations out of their land ahead of you, nations that were bigger and stronger than you were. The LORD did this so he could bring you into their land and give it to you as your own, and this land is yours today.

39 Know and believe today that the LORD is God. He is God in heaven above and on the earth below. There is no other god! 40 Obey his laws and commands that I am giving you today so that things will go well for you and your children. Then you will live a long time in the land that the LORD your God is giving to you for ever.

Cities of Safety

41 Moses chose three cities east of the Jordan River, 42 where a person who accidentally killed someone could go. If the person was not killed because of hatred, the murderer's life could be saved by running to one of these cities. 43 These were the cities: Bezer in the desert high plain was for the Reubenites; Ramoth in Gilead was for the Gadites; and Golan in Bashan was for the Manassites.

The Laws Moses Gave

44 These are the teachings Moses gave to the people of Israel. 45 They are the rules, commands and laws he gave them when they came out of Egypt. 46 They were in the valley near Beth Peor, east of the Jordan River, in the land of Sihon. Sihon king of the Amorites ruled in Heshbon and was defeated by Moses

and the Israelites as they came out of Egypt. 47 The Israelites took his land and the land of Og king of Bashan, the two Amorite kings east of the Jordan River. 48 This land went from Aroer, on the edge of the Arnon Ravine, to Mount Hermon. 49 It included all the Jordan Valley east of the Jordan River, and it went as far as the Dead Sea below Mount Pisgah.

The Ten Commandments

5 Moses called all the people of Israel together and said: Listen, Israel, to the commands and laws I am giving you today. Learn them and obey them carefully. 2 The LORD our God made an Agreement with us at Mount Sinai. 3 He did not make this Agreement with our ancestors, but he made it with us, with all of us who are alive here today. 4 The LORD spoke to you face to face from the fire on the mountain. 5 (At that time I stood between you and the LORD in order to tell you what the LORD said; you were afraid of the fire, so you would not go up on the mountain.) The LORD said:

6 "I am the LORD your God; I brought you out of the land of Egypt where you were slaves.

7 "You must not have any other gods except me.

8 "You must not make for yourselves any idols or anything to worship that looks like something in the sky above or on the earth below or in the water below the land. 9 You must not worship or serve any idol, because I, the LORD your God, am a jealous God. If people sin against me and hate me, I will punish their children, even their grandchildren and great-grandchildren. 10 But I will be very kind for 1,000 lifetimes to those who love me and obey my commands.

11 "You must not use the name of the LORD your God thoughtlessly, because the LORD will punish anyone who uses his name in this way.

12 "Keep the Sabbath as a holy day, as the LORD your God has commanded you. 13 You may work and get everything done during six days each week, 14 but the seventh day is a day of rest to honour the LORD your God. On that day no one may do any work: not you, your son or daughter, your male or female slaves, your ox, your donkey or any of your animals, or the foreigners living in your cities. That way your servants may rest as you do. 15 Remember that you were slaves in Egypt and that the LORD your God brought you out of there by his great power and strength. So the LORD your God has commanded you to rest on the Sabbath day.

16 "Honour your father and your mother as the LORD your God has commanded you. Then you will live a long time, and things will go well for you in the land that the LORD your God is going to give you.

17 "You must not murder anyone.

18 "You must not be guilty of adultery.

19 "You must not steal.

20 "You must not tell lies about your neighbour.

21 "You must not want to take your neighbour's wife. You must not want to take your neighbour's house or land, his male or female slaves, his ox or his donkey, or anything that belongs to your neighbour."

22 The LORD spoke these commands to all of you on the mountain in a loud voice out of the fire, the cloud and the deep darkness; he did not say anything else. Then he wrote them on two stone tablets, and he gave them to me.

23 When you heard the voice from the darkness, as the mountain was blazing with fire, all your elders and leaders of your tribes came to me. 24 And you said, "The LORD our God has shown us his glory and majesty, and we have heard his voice from the fire. Today we have seen that a person can live even if God speaks to him. 25 But now, we will die! This great fire will burn us up, and we will die if we hear the LORD our God speak any more. 26 No human being has ever heard the living God speaking from a fire and still lived, but we have. 27 Moses, you go near and listen to everything the LORD our God says. Then you tell us what the LORD our God tells you, and we will listen and obey."

28 The LORD heard what you said to me, and he said to me, "I have heard what

the people said to you. Everything they said was good. 29 I wish their hearts would always respect me and that they would always obey my commands so that things would go well for them and their children for ever!

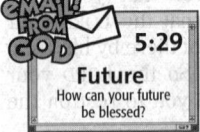

5:29 Future
How can your future be blessed?

30 "Go and tell the people to return to their tents, 31 but you stay here with me so that I may give you all the commands, rules and laws that you must teach the people to obey in the land I am giving them as their own."

32 So be careful to do what the LORD your God has commanded you, and follow the commands exactly. 33 Live the way the LORD your God has commanded you so that you may live and have what is good and have a long life in the land you will take.

The Command to Love God

6 These are the commands, rules and laws that the LORD your God told me to teach you to obey in the land you are crossing the Jordan River to take. 2 You, your children and your grandchildren must respect the LORD your God as long as you live. Obey all his rules and commands I give you so that you will live a long time. 3 Listen, Israel, and carefully obey these laws. Then all will go well for you, and you will become a great nation in a fertile land, just as the LORD, the God of your ancestors, has promised you.

4 Listen, people of Israel! The LORD our God is the only LORD. 5 Love the LORD your God with all your heart, all your soul and all your strength. 6 Always remember these commands I give you today. 7 Teach them to your children, and talk about them when you sit at home and walk along the road, when you lie down and when you get up. 8 Write them down and tie them to your hands as a sign. Tie them on your forehead to remind you, 9 and write them on your doors and gates.

10 The LORD your God will bring you into the land he promised to your ancestors, to Abraham, Isaac and Jacob, and he will give it to you. The land has large,

FAITH links

REMEMBERING WHAT HE SAID

DEUTERONOMY 6:4-9

Think of something your parents have spent a lot of time teaching you. Perhaps they taught you how to read or play a sport. They probably helped you remember what they taught by telling you the same thing over and over again. God wanted the parents of Israel to spend a lot of time teaching their children how to obey God. That was the most important lesson they could teach their children. They weren't to say these things once and never again. They were to tell their children over and over again. How have your parents helped you to learn about God? What will you do to remember what they said?

Good Advice? Leviticus 20:6, p. 162

An Attention-Getter, Numbers 22, p. 207

A Wise Wish, 1 Kings 3:5–9, p. 439

Teaching Others, Ezra 7:8–10, p. 617

God's Instructions, Ezekiel 4:1–15, p. 1089

Want to Know? Ask! Luke 9:45, p. 1386

growing cities you did not build, 11 houses full of good things you did not buy, wells you did not dig and vineyards and olive trees you did not plant. You will eat as much as you want. 12 But be careful! Do not forget the LORD, who brought you out of the land of Egypt where you were slaves.

13 Respect the LORD your God. You must worship him and make your promises only in his name. 14 Do not worship other gods as the people around you do, 15 because the LORD your God is a jealous God. He is present with you, and if you worship other gods, he will become angry with you and destroy you from the earth. 16 Do not test the LORD your God as you did at Massah. 17 Be sure to obey the commands of the LORD your God and the rules and laws he has given you. 18 Do what the LORD says is good and right so that things will go well for you. Then you may go in and take the good land the LORD promised to your ancestors. 19 He will force all your enemies out as you go in, as the LORD has said.

20 In the future when your children ask you, "What is the meaning of the laws, commands and rules the LORD our God gave us?" 21 tell them, "We were slaves to the king of Egypt, but the LORD brought us out of Egypt by his great power. 22 The LORD showed us great and terrible signs and miracles, which he did to Egypt, the king and his whole family. 23 The LORD brought us out of Egypt to lead us here and to give us the land he promised our ancestors. 24 The LORD ordered us to obey all these commands and to respect the LORD our God so that we will always do well and stay alive, as we are today. 25 The right thing for us to do is this: obey all these rules in the presence of the LORD our God, as he has commanded."

You are God's People

7 The LORD your God will bring you into the land that you are entering and that you will have as your own. As you go in, he will force out these nations: the Hittites, Girgashites, Amorites, Canaanites, Perizzites, Hivites and Jebusites—seven nations that are stronger than you. 2 The LORD your God will hand these nations over to you, and when you defeat them, you must destroy them completely. Do not make a peace treaty with them or show them any mercy. 3 Do not marry any of them, or let your daughters marry their sons, or let your sons marry their daughters. 4 If you do, those people will turn your children away from me, to begin serving other gods. Then the LORD will be very angry with you, and he will quickly destroy you. 5 This is what you must do to those people: tear down their altars, smash their holy stone pillars, cut down their Asherah idols and burn their idols in the fire. 6 You are holy people who belong to the LORD your God. He has chosen you from all the people on earth to be his very own.

7 The LORD did not care for you and choose you because there were many of you—you are the smallest nation of all. 8 But the LORD chose you because he loved you, and he kept his promise to your ancestors. So he brought you out of Egypt by his great power and freed you from the land of slavery, from the power of the king of Egypt. 9 So know that the LORD your God is God, the faithful God. He will keep his agreement of love for 1,000 lifetimes for people who love him and obey his commands. 10 But he will pay back those people who hate him. He will destroy them, and he will not be slow to pay back those who hate him. 11 So be careful to obey the commands, rules and laws I give you today.

12 If you pay attention to these laws and obey them carefully, the LORD your God will keep his agreement and show his love to you, as he promised your ancestors. 13 He will love and bless you. He will make the number of your people grow; he will bless you with children. He will bless your fields with good crops and will give you grain, new wine and oil. He will bless your herds with calves and your flocks with lambs in the land he promised your ancestors he would give you. 14 You will be blessed more than any other people. Every husband and wife will

> **MAIL FROM GOD**
> **7:9**
> **Caring**
> Who does God care for?

PRIDE
Deuteronomy 8:11–18

Livin' it

Struttin' Our Stuff How do you feel when a classmate gets an A* for a science project? Or a teammate scores a hat-trick? You're probably OK with those things *unless* they keep bragging about how good they are. Sometimes braggers are said to be "proud as peacocks". Got any peacock feathers on your back?

Pride in what we have or can do makes us trust in our own ideas or plans. But God wants us to put our pride aside and give our plans to him for his OK. (Look at Exodus 2:11–15, p. 78.)

Samson was a real-life superman – but he had a weakness. Samson was proud of his strength and believed it could get him out of anything. This led to total disaster. (Read Judges 16, p. 334.) Want to be a "proud peacock" or the world's most powerful Christian? Faith in God makes the difference!

MORE FAITH links

Put Pride Aside, **p. 78**

Best Seat in the House, **p. 1398**

Glad to Help! **p. 1541**

The "Eyes" Have It? **p. 1559**

Most Wanted? **p. 1580**

Being excited about something you've done, somewhere you've been, or something you've just been given – like the best super-fast computer or the latest video-messaging mobile phone – is one thing. But boasting about it in front of other kids is not exactly going to win you any friends! Connect to these Faithlinks for some advice on pride.

The Problem with Pride, Isaiah 2:11, p. 898
- What do you think when someone "rolls her eyes"? Or raises his eyebrows? Or wrinkles up her nose? What would make you do one of those things? How about a nose-in-the-air look? That usually means someone thinks he or she is better than everyone else is – it's called being proud. Where is your nose pointed?

Eating Humble Pie, Daniel 4, p. 1156
- Link here to discover the best "food" for someone who has an appetite for being proud.

Better Than Some? Luke 18:9–14, p. 1405
- Do you feel you're pretty good – or at least better than some people are? Does your pride make you feel superior? Surf over here to find out how God feels about a proud attitude.

Brag on Him! 1 Corinthians 3:18–23, p. 1548
- Link here to discover something God wants us to brag about.

my FAVOURITE links

have children, and all your cattle will have calves. **15** The LORD will take away all disease from you; you will not have the terrible diseases that were in Egypt, but he will give them to all the people who hate you. **16** You must destroy all the people the LORD your God hands over to you. Do not feel sorry for them, and do not worship their gods, or they will trap you.

17 You might say to yourselves, "Because these nations are stronger than we are, we can't force them out." **18** But don't be afraid of them. Remember what the LORD your God did to all of Egypt and its king. **19** You saw for yourselves the troubles, signs and miracles he did, how the LORD's great power and strength brought you out of Egypt. The LORD your God will do the same thing to all the nations you now fear. **20** The LORD your God will also send terror among them so that even those who are alive and hiding from you will die. **21** Don't be afraid of them, because the LORD your God is with you; he is a great God and people are afraid of him. **22** When the LORD your God forces those nations out of the land, he will do it little by little ahead of you. You won't be able to destroy them all at once; otherwise, the wild animals will grow too many in number. **23** But the LORD your God will hand those nations over to you, confusing them until they are destroyed. **24** The LORD will help you defeat their kings, and the world will forget who they were. No one will be able to stop you; you will destroy them all. **25** Burn up their idols in the fire. Do not wish for the silver and gold they have, and don't take it for yourselves, or you will be trapped by it. The LORD your God hates it. **26** Do not bring one of those hateful things into your house, or you will be completely destroyed along with it. Hate and reject those things; they must be completely destroyed.

Remember the LORD

8 Carefully obey every command I give you today. Then you will live and grow in number, and you will enter and take the land the LORD promised your ancestors. **2** Remember how the LORD your God has led you in the desert for these 40 years, taking away your pride and testing you, because he wanted to know what was in your heart. He wanted to know if you would obey his commands. **3** He took away your pride when he let

---

FAITH links

I'LL NEVER FORGET WHAT'S-HIS-NAME
DEUTERONOMY 8

Did you ever forget someone's name? That's easy to do if you've only met the person once or haven't spent much time with that person. God reminded the people of Israel to make an effort to remember him and his commands. He didn't want them to forget all that he had done for them. That reminder is for you, too. One way to remember God is to spend time with him each day. If you make time with God a priority, you won't easily forget him.

Here's some more advice on taking time to be with God:

Try to Remember, Deuteronomy 11:18–21, p. 243

I Insist! 1 Samuel 8; 9, p. 363

When God Says No, 2 Samuel 7, p. 407

More Precious Than Gold, Psalm 19:7–10, p. 723

My Favourite! Mark 10:17–23, p. 1347

Faith Workout, Acts 16:4–5, p. 1493

you get hungry, and then he fed you with manna, which neither you nor your ancestors had ever seen. This was to teach you that a person does not live by eating only bread, but by everything the LORD says. 4 During these 40 years, your clothes did not wear out, and your feet did not swell. 5 Know in your heart that the LORD your God corrects you as a parent corrects a child.

8:5
God's Family
Find out how God helps his children to grow.

6 Obey the commands of the LORD your God, living as he has commanded you, and respect him. 7 The LORD your God is bringing you into a good land, a land with rivers and pools of water, with springs that flow in the valleys and hills, 8 a land that has wheat and barley, vines, fig trees, pomegranates, olive oil and honey. 9 It is a land where you will have plenty of food, where you will have everything you need, where the rocks are iron, and where you can dig copper out of the hills.

10 When you have all you want to eat, then praise the LORD your God for giving you a good land. 11 Be careful not to forget the LORD your God so that you fail to obey his commands, laws and rules that I am giving to you today. 12 When you eat all you want and build nice houses and live in them, 13 when your herds and flocks grow large and your silver and gold increase, when you have more of everything, 14 then your heart will become proud. You will forget the LORD your God, who brought you out of the land of Egypt, where you were slaves. 15 He led you through the large and terrible desert that was dry and had no water, and that had poisonous snakes and stinging insects. He gave you water from a solid rock 16 and manna to eat in the desert. Manna was something your ancestors had never seen. He did this to take away your pride and to test you, so things would go well for you in the end. 17 You might say to yourself, "I am rich because of my own power and strength." 18 but remember the LORD your God! It is he who gives you the power to become rich, keeping the

agreement he promised to your ancestors, as it is today.

19 If you ever forget the LORD your God and follow other gods and worship them and bow down to them, I warn you today that you will be destroyed. 20 Just as the LORD destroyed the other nations for you, you can be destroyed if you do not obey the LORD your God.

The LORD will be with Israel

9 Listen, Israel. You will soon cross the Jordan River to go in and force out nations that are bigger and stronger than you. They have large cities with walls up to the sky. 2 The people there are Anakites, who are strong and tall. You know about them, and you have heard it said: "No one can stop the Anakites." 3 But today remember that the LORD your God goes in before you to destroy them like a fire that burns things up. He will defeat them ahead of you, and you will force them out and destroy them quickly, just as the LORD has said.

4 After the LORD your God has forced those nations out ahead of you, don't say to yourself, "The LORD brought me here to take this land because I am so good." No! It is because these nations are evil that the LORD will force them out ahead of you. 5 You are going in to take the land, not because you are good and honest, but because these nations are evil. That is why the LORD your God will force them out ahead of you, to keep his promise to your ancestors, to Abraham, Isaac and Jacob. 6 The LORD your God is giving you this good land to take as your own. But know this: it is not because you are good; you are a stubborn people.

Remember the LORD's Anger

7 Remember this and do not forget it: you made the LORD your God angry in the desert. You would not obey the LORD from the day you left Egypt until you arrived here. 8 At Mount Sinai you made the LORD angry—angry enough to destroy you. 9 When I went up on the mountain to receive the stone tablets, the tablets with the Agreement the LORD had made

with you, I stayed on the mountain for 40 days and 40 nights; I did not eat bread or drink water. 10 The Lord gave me two stone tablets, which God had written on with his own finger. On them were all the commands that the Lord gave to you on the mountain out of the fire, on the day you were gathered there.

11 When the 40 days and 40 nights were over, the Lord gave me the two stone tablets, the tablets with the Agreement on them. 12 Then the Lord told me, "Get up and go down quickly from here, because the people you brought out from Egypt are ruining themselves. They have quickly turned away from what I commanded and have made an idol for themselves."

13 The Lord said to me, "I have watched these people, and they are very stubborn! 14 Get away so that I may destroy them and make the whole world forget who they are. Then I will make another nation from you that will be bigger and stronger than they are."

15 So I turned and came down the mountain that was burning with fire and the two stone tablets with the Agreement were in my hands. 16 When I looked, I saw you had sinned against the Lord your God and had made an idol in the shape of a calf. You had quickly turned away from what the Lord had told you to do. 17 So I took the two stone tablets and threw them down, breaking them into pieces right in front of you.

18 Then I again bowed face down on the ground before the Lord for 40 days and 40 nights; I did not eat bread or drink water. You had sinned by doing what the Lord said was evil, and you made him angry. 19 I was afraid of the Lord's anger and rage, because he was angry enough with you to destroy you, but the Lord listened to me again. 20 And the Lord was angry enough with Aaron to destroy him, but then I prayed for Aaron too. 21 I took that sinful calf idol you had made and burned it in the fire. I crushed it into a powder like dust and threw the dust into a stream that flowed down the mountain.

22 You also made the Lord angry at Taberah, Massah and Kibroth Hattaavah.

23 Then the Lord sent you away from Kadesh Barnea and said, "Go up and take the land I have given you." But you rejected the command of the Lord your God. You did not trust him or obey him. 24 You have refused to obey the Lord as long as I have known you.

25 The Lord had said he would destroy you, so I threw myself down in front of him for those 40 days and 40 nights. 26 I prayed to the Lord and said, "Lord God, do not destroy your people, your own people, whom you freed and brought out of Egypt by your great power and strength. 27 Remember your servants Abraham, Isaac and Jacob. Don't look at how stubborn these people are, and don't look at their sin and evil. 28 Otherwise, Egypt will say, 'It was because the Lord was not able to take his people into the land he promised them, and it was because he hated them that he took them into the desert to kill them.' 29 But they are your people, Lord, your own people, whom you brought out of Egypt with your great power and strength."

> But today remember that the Lord your God goes in before you to destroy them like a fire that burns things up.
> – Deuteronomy 9:3

New Stone Tablets

10 At that time the Lord said to me, "Cut two stone tablets like the first ones and come up to me on the mountain. Also make a wooden Ark. 2 I will write on the tablets the same words that were on the first tablets, which you broke, and you will put the new tablets in the Ark."

3 So I made the Ark out of acacia wood, and I cut out two stone tablets like the first ones. Then I went up on the mountain with the two tablets in my hands. 4 The Lord wrote the same things on these tablets he had written before—the Ten Commandments that he had told you on

the mountain from the fire, on the day you were gathered there. And the LORD gave them to me. 5 Then I turned and came down the mountain; I put the tablets in the Ark I had made, as the LORD had commanded, and they are still there.

6 (The people of Israel went from the wells of the Jaakanites to Moserah. Aaron died there and was buried; his son Eleazar became priest in his place. 7 From Moserah they went to Gudgodah, and from Gudgodah they went to Jotbathah, a place with streams of water. 8 At that time the LORD chose the tribe of Levi to carry the Ark of the Agreement with the LORD. They were to serve the LORD and to bless the people in his name, which they still do today. 9 That is why the Levites did not receive any land of their own; instead, they received the LORD himself as their gift, as the LORD your God told them.)

10 I stayed on the mountain 40 days and 40 nights just like the first time, and the LORD listened to me this time also. He did not want to destroy you. 11 The LORD said to me, "Go and lead the people so that they will go in and take the land I promised their ancestors."

What the LORD Wants You to Do

12 Now, Israel, this is what the LORD your God wants you to do: respect the LORD your God, and do what he has told you to do. Love him. Serve the LORD your God with your whole being, 13 and obey the LORD's commands and laws that I am giving you today for your own good.

14 The LORD owns the world and everything in it—the heavens, even the highest heavens, are his. 15 But the LORD cared for and loved your ancestors, and he chose you, their descendants, over all the other nations, just as it is today. 16 Give yourselves completely to serving him, and do not be stubborn any longer. 17 The LORD your God is God of all gods and Lord of all lords. He is the great God, who is strong and wonderful. He does not take sides, and he will not be talked into doing evil. 18 He helps orphans and widows, and he loves foreigners and gives them food and clothes. 19 You also must love foreigners, because you were foreigners in Egypt. 20 Respect the LORD your God and serve him. Be loyal to him and make your promises in his name. 21 He is the one you should praise; he is

---

FAITH links

WHAT GOD WANTS
DEUTERONOMY 10:12-13

Ever wonder what God wants from you? Wonder no more. God wants you to love him and others. He also wants your obedience. That's what he told the people of Israel through Moses. That doesn't sound so hard, does it? Yet, we sometimes allow fear to keep us from giving God what he wants. Many times we worry that God has some horrible task just waiting to assign us. So we spend our lives trying to avoid doing what he wants. God doesn't want fear to keep you from obeying him. That's why he promises to help you respect, love and obey him.

Fearful Service? Exodus 4:1–17, p. 80

Everyone Can Help, Numbers 4, p. 181

The Gift of Friendship, 1 Samuel 18:1–3; 19, p. 381

Sitting on the Fence, 1 Kings 18, p. 464

A Reminder to Do What Is Right and True, Zechariah 7:8–10, p. 1257

The Unpopular Choice, Mark 15:42–43, p. 1360

Deuteronomy 11:14 **243**

your God, who has done great and wonderful things for you, which you have seen with your own eyes. 22 There were only 70 of your ancestors when they went down to Egypt, and now the LORD your God has made you as many as the stars in the sky.

Great Things Israel Saw

11 Love the LORD your God and always obey his orders, rules, laws and commands. 2 Remember today it was not your children who saw and felt the correction of the LORD your God. They did not see his majesty, his power, his strength 3 or his signs and the things he did in Egypt to the king and his whole country. 4 They did not see what he did to the Egyptian army, its horses and chariots, when he drowned them in the Red Sea as they were chasing you. The LORD ruined them for ever. 5 They did not see what he did for you in the desert until you arrived here. 6 They did not see what he did to Dathan and Abiram, the sons of Eliab the Reubenite, when the ground opened up and swallowed them, their families, their tents and everyone who stood with them in Israel. 7 It was you who saw all these great things the LORD has done.

8 So obey all the commands I am giving you today so that you will be strong and can go in and take the land you are going to take as your own. 9 Then you will live a long time in the land that the LORD promised to give to your ancestors and their descendants, a fertile land. 10 The land you are going to take is not like Egypt, where you were. There you had to plant your seed and water it, like a vegetable garden, by using your feet. 11 But the land that you will soon cross the Jordan River to take is a land of hills and valleys, a land that drinks rain from heaven. 12 It is a land the LORD your God cares for. His eyes are on it continually, and he watches it from the beginning of the year to the end.

13 If you carefully obey the commands

11:1 Responsibility
Your responsibilities!

FAITH links

TRY TO REMEMBER
DEUTERONOMY 11:18-21

What do you do to remember what you need to remember? Some people use memory tools like making up a song, tying a string around their finger, or sticking a self-adhesive note on a backpack or a bathroom mirror. God gave Moses different ways that the people of Israel could use to remember his commands. They could write them down and tie them to their hands or foreheads. They were to remember these words wherever they went. God wants you to remember his words, too. What is your favourite way to memorise God's Word?

Surf over here to find out more about learning God's Word:

When I Need Advice, 1 Kings 12:1–17 , p. 455

Comfort from the Word, Job 26:3–4, p. 688

Our Thirst Quencher, Psalm 42:1–3, p. 741

If You Want My Advice . . . Proverbs 13:1, p. 843

Long-lasting Hope, Hosea 14, p. 1184

Our Heavenly Connection, Matthew 6:9–13, p. 1283

I am giving you today and love the LORD your God and serve him with your whole being, 14 then he will send rain on your land at the right time, in the autumn and spring, and you will be able to gather your grain, new wine and oil. 15 He will put grass in the fields for your cattle, and you will have plenty to eat.

16 Be careful, or you will be fooled and will turn away to serve and worship other gods. 17 If you do, the LORD will become angry with you and will shut the heavens so it will not rain. Then the land will not grow crops, and you will soon die in the good land the LORD is giving you. 18 Remember my words with your whole being. Write them down and tie them to your hands as a sign; tie them on your foreheads to remind you. 19 Teach them well to your children, talking about them when you sit at home and walk along the road, when you lie down and when you get up. 20 Write them on your doors and gates 21 so that both you and your children will live a long time in the land the LORD promised your ancestors, as long as the skies are above the earth.

22 If you are careful to obey every command I am giving you to follow, and love the LORD your God, and do what he has told you to do, and are loyal to him, 23 then the LORD will force all those nations out of the land ahead of you, and you will take the land from nations that are bigger and stronger than you. 24 Everywhere you step will be yours. Your land will go from the desert to Lebanon and from the Euphrates River to the Mediterranean Sea. 25 No one will be able to stop you. The LORD your God will do what he promised and will make the people afraid everywhere you go.

26 See, today I am letting you choose a blessing or a curse. 27 You will be blessed if you obey the commands of the LORD your God that I am giving you today. 28 But you will be cursed if you disobey the commands of the LORD your God. So do not disobey the commands I am giving you today, and do not worship other gods you do not know. 29 When the LORD your God brings you into the land you will take as your own, you are to announce the blessings from Mount Gerizim and the curses from Mount Ebal. 30 (These mountains are on the other side of the Jordan River, to the west, towards the sunset. They are near the great trees of Moreh in the land of the Canaanites who live in the Jordan Valley opposite Gilgal.) 31 You will soon cross the Jordan River to enter and take the land the LORD your God is giving you. When you take it over and live there, 32 be careful to obey all the commands and laws I am giving you today.

The Place for Worship

12 These are the commands and laws you must carefully obey in the land the LORD, the God of your ancestors, is giving you. Obey them as long as you live in the land. 2 When you inherit the lands of these nations, you must completely destroy all the places where they serve their gods, on high mountains and hills and under every green tree. 3 Tear down their altars, smash their holy stone pillars and burn their Asherah idols in the fire. Cut down their idols and destroy their names from those places.

4 Don't worship the LORD your God that way, 5 but look for the place the LORD your God will choose—a place among your tribes where he is to be worshipped. Go there, 6 and bring to that place your burnt offerings and sacrifices; bring a tenth of what you gain and your special gifts; bring what you have promised and the special gifts you want to give the LORD, and bring the first animals born to your herds and flocks.

7 There you will be together with the LORD your God. There you and your families will eat, and you will enjoy all the good things for which you have worked, because the LORD your God has blessed you.

8 Do not worship the way we have been doing today, each person doing what he thinks is right. 9 You have not yet come to a resting place, to the land the LORD your God will give you as your own. 10 But soon you will cross the Jordan River to live in the land the LORD your God is giving you as your own, where he will give you rest from all your enemies and you will live in safety. 11 Then the LORD your God will choose a place where

he is to be worshipped. To that place you must bring everything I tell you: your burnt offerings and sacrifices, your offerings of a tenth of what you gain, your special gifts and all your best things you promised to the LORD. 12 There rejoice before the LORD your God. Everyone should rejoice: you, your sons and daughters, your male and female servants and the Levites from your towns who have no land of their own. 13 Be careful that you don't sacrifice your burnt offerings just anywhere you please. 14 Offer them only in the place the LORD will choose. He will choose a place in one of your tribes, and there you must do everything I am commanding you.

15 But you may kill your animals in any of your towns and eat as much of the meat as you want, as if it were a deer or a gazelle; this is the blessing the LORD your God is giving you. Anyone, clean or unclean, may eat this meat, 16 but do not eat the blood. Pour it out on the ground like water. 17 Do not eat in your own towns what belongs to the LORD: one-tenth of your grain, new wine or oil; the first animals born to your herds or flocks; whatever you have promised to give; the special gifts you want to give to the LORD, or any other gifts. 18 Eat these things when you are together with the LORD your God, in the place the LORD your God chooses to be worshipped. Everyone must do this: you, your sons and daughters, your male and female servants and the Levites from your towns. Rejoice in the LORD your God's presence about the things you have worked for. 19 Be careful not to forget the Levites as long as you live in the land.

20 When the LORD your God enlarges your country as he has promised, and you want some meat so you say, "I want some meat," you may eat as much meat as you want. 21 If the LORD your God chooses a place where he is to be worshipped that is too far away from you, you may kill animals from your herds and flocks, which the LORD has given to you. I have commanded that you may do this. You may eat as much of them as you want in your own towns, 22 as you would eat gazelle or deer meat. Both clean and unclean people may eat this meat, 23 but be sure you don't eat the blood, because the life is in the blood. Don't eat the life with the meat. 24 Don't eat the blood, but pour it out on the ground like water. 25 If you don't eat it, things will go well for you and your children, because you will be doing what the LORD says is right.

26 Take your holy things and the things you have promised to give, and go to the place the LORD will choose. 27 Present your burnt offerings on the altar of the LORD your God, both the meat and the blood. The blood of your sacrifices should be poured beside the altar of the LORD your God, but you may eat the meat. 28 Be careful to obey all the rules I am giving you so that things will always go well for you and your children, and you will be doing what the LORD your God says is good and right.

29 You will enter the land and take it away from the nations that the LORD your God will destroy ahead of you. When you force them out and live in their land, 30 they will be destroyed for you, but be careful not to be trapped by asking about their gods. Don't say, "How do these nations worship? I will do the same." 31 Don't worship the LORD your God that way, because the LORD hates the evil ways they worship their gods. They even burn their sons and daughters as sacrifices to their gods!

32 Be sure to do everything I have commanded you. Do not add anything to it, and do not take anything away from it.

False Prophets

13 Prophets or those who tell the future with dreams might come to you and say they will show you a miracle or a sign. 2 The miracle or sign might even happen, and then they might say, "Let's serve other gods" (gods you have not known) "and let's worship them." 3 But you must not listen to those prophets or dreamers. The LORD your God is testing you, to find out if you love him with

> **12:28 Obedience**
> Check out what happens when you obey.

your whole being. 4 Serve only the LORD your God. Respect him, keep his commands and obey him. Serve him and be loyal to him. 5 The prophets or dreamers must be killed, because they said you should turn against the LORD your God, who brought you out of Egypt and saved you from the land where you were slaves. They tried to turn you from doing what the LORD your God commanded you to do. You must get rid of the evil among you.

6 Someone might try to lead you to serve other gods—it might be your brother, your son or daughter, the wife you love or a close friend. The person might say, "Let's go and worship other gods." (These are gods that neither you nor your ancestors have known, 7 gods of the people who live around you, either nearby or far away, from one end of the land to the other.) 8 Do not give in to such people. Do not listen or feel sorry for them, and do not let them go free or protect them. 9 You must put them to death. You must be the first one to start to kill them, and then everyone else must join in. 10 You must throw stones at them until they die, because they tried to turn you away from the LORD your God, who brought you out of the land of Egypt, where you were slaves. 11 Then everyone in Israel will hear about this and be afraid, and no one among you will ever do such an evil thing again.

Cities to Destroy

12 The LORD your God is giving you cities in which to live, and you might hear something about one of them. Someone might say 13 that evil people have moved in among you. And they might lead the people of that city away from God, saying, "Let's go and worship other gods." (These are gods you have not known.) 14 Then you must ask about it, looking into the matter and checking carefully whether it is true. If it is proved that a hateful thing has happened among you, 15 you must kill with a sword everyone who lives in that city. Destroy the city completely and kill everyone in it, as well as the animals, with a sword. 16 Gather up everything those people owned, and put it in the middle of the city square. Then completely burn the city and everything they owned as a burnt offering to the LORD your God. That city should never be rebuilt; let it be ruined for ever. 17 Don't keep for yourselves any of the things found in that city, so the LORD will not be angry any more. He will give you mercy and feel sorry for you, and he will make your nation grow larger, as he promised to your ancestors. 18 You will have obeyed the LORD your God by keeping all his commands that I am giving to you today, and you will be doing what the LORD says is right.

> **EMAIL FROM GOD**
> **13:17–18**
> **Obedience**
> Is it important to listen to God?

God's Special People

14 You are the children of the LORD your God. When someone dies, do not cut yourselves or shave your heads to show your sadness. 2 You are holy people, who belong to the LORD your God. He has chosen you from all the people on earth to be his very own.

3 Do not eat anything the LORD hates. 4 These are the animals you may eat: oxen, sheep, goats, 5 deer, gazelle, roe deer, wild goats, ibex, antelope and mountain sheep. 6 You may eat any animal that has a split hoof and chews the cud, 7 but you may not eat camels, rabbits or rock badgers. These animals chew the cud, but they do not have split hoofs, so they are unclean for you. 8 Pigs are also unclean for you; they have split hoofs, but they do not chew the cud. Do not eat their meat or touch their dead bodies.

9 There are many things that live in the water. You may eat anything that has fins and scales, 10 but do not eat anything that does not have fins and scales. It is unclean for you.

11 You may eat any clean bird. 12 But do not eat these birds: eagles, vultures, black vultures, 13 red kites, falcons, any kind of kite, 14 any kind of raven, 15 horned owls, screech owls, sea gulls, any kind of hawk, 16 little owls, great

FAITH links

A SMALL PERCENT
DEUTERONOMY 14:22-23

Do you receive pocket-money? Suppose God told you, "I want 10 per cent of your pocket-money each month." Would you give it? God commanded the people of Israel to give him one-tenth of their crops. Giving it was a sign of their respect for him. These crops went to provide for the priests who served in the Meeting Tent.

God wants us to be willing givers. He doesn't force us to give. How much are you willing to give to God?

Giving Your Part, Leviticus 27:30, p. 173

Yours, Mine and Ours? 1 Samuel 25, p. 389

Wisdom About Wealth, Ecclesiastes 5:10–12, p. 878

The Gift of Worship, Matthew 2:10–12, p. 1275

Give to Give, 1 Corinthians 16:1–4, p. 1566

More Money? 1 Timothy 6:10, p. 1649

---

owls, white owls, 17 desert owls, ospreys, cormorants, 18 storks, any kind of heron, the hoopoes or bats.

19 All insects with wings are unclean for you; do not eat them. 20 Other things with wings are clean, and you may eat them.

21 Do not eat anything you find that is already dead. You may give it to a foreigner living in your town, and he may eat it, or you may sell it to a foreigner. But you are holy people, who belong to the LORD your God.

Do not cook a baby goat in its mother's milk.

Giving One-Tenth

22 Be sure to save one-tenth of all your crops each year. 23 Take it to the place the LORD your God will choose where he is to be worshipped. There, where you will be together with the LORD, eat the tenth of your grain, new wine and oil, and eat the animals born first to your herds and flocks. Do this so that you will learn to respect the LORD your God always. 24 But if the place the LORD will choose to be worshipped is too far away and he has blessed you so much you cannot carry a tenth, 25 exchange your one-tenth for silver. Then take the silver with you to the place the LORD your God shall choose. 26 Use the silver to buy anything you wish—cattle, sheep, wine, beer or anything you wish. Then you and your family will eat and celebrate there before the LORD your God. 27 Do not forget the Levites in your town, because they have no land of their own among you.

28 At the end of every third year, everyone should bring one-tenth of that year's crop and store it in your towns. 29 This is for the Levites so they may eat and be full. (They have no land of their own among you.) It is also for strangers, orphans and widows who live in your towns so that all of them may eat and be full. Then the LORD your God will bless you and all the work you do.

The Special Seventh Year

15 At the end of every seven years, you must tell those who owe you anything that they do not have to pay you back. 2 This is how you must do it: everyone who has loaned money must cancel the loan and not make a neighbour or relative pay it back. This is the LORD's time for cancelling what people owe. 3 You may make a foreigner pay what is owed to you,

but you must not collect what another Israelite owes you. 4 But there should be no poor people among you, because the LORD your God will richly bless you in the land he is giving you as your own. 5 He will bless you if you obey the LORD your God completely, but you must be careful to obey all the commands I am giving you today. 6 The LORD your God will bless you as he promised, and you will lend to other nations, but you will not need to borrow from them. You will rule over many nations, but none will rule over you.

7 If there are poor among you, in one of the towns of the land the LORD your God is giving you, do not be selfish or greedy towards them. 8 But give freely to them, and freely lend them whatever they need. 9 Beware of evil thoughts. Don't think, "The seventh year is near, the year to cancel what people owe." You might be mean to the needy and not give them anything. Then they will complain to the LORD about you, and he will find you guilty of sin. 10 Give freely to the poor person, and do not wish that you didn't have to give. The LORD your God will bless your work and everything you touch. 11 There will always be poor people in the land, so I command you to give freely to your neighbours and to the poor and needy in your land.

Letting Slaves Go Free

12 If one of your own people sells himself to you as a slave, whether it is a Hebrew man or woman, that person will serve you for six years. But in the seventh year you must let the slave go free. 13 When you let slaves go, don't send them away without anything. 14 Give them some of your flock, your grain and your wine, giving to them as the LORD has given to you. 15 Remember that you were slaves in Egypt, and the LORD your God saved you. That is why I give you this command today.

16 But if your slave says to you, "I don't want to leave you," because he loves you and your family and has a good life with you, 17 stick an awl[n] through his ear into the door; he will be your slave for life. Also do this to a female slave.

18 Do not think of it as a hard thing when you let your slaves go free. After all, they served you six years and did twice the work of a hired person. The LORD your God will bless you in everything you do.

Rules About Firstborn Animals

19 Save all the first male animals born to your herds and flocks. They are for the LORD your God. Do not work the first calf

---

FAITH CHALLENGE

Here's one for you. Read 15:6 to find out what God said about taking care of his people. How do you respond when your brother, sister, or one of your friends asks to borrow something from you?

TESTING IT

Deuteronomy 15:6
The LORD your God will bless you as he promised, and you will lend to other nations, but you will not need to borrow from them.

15:17 **awl** A tool like a big needle with a handle at one end.

A FEAST FOR REMEMBERING   Deuteronomy 16:1–8

God sent ten plagues to convince the king of Egypt to let the Israelites leave his country. The last plague was a plague of death. One night God passed through the city. If a house was not protected by lamb's blood on the door-frame, then the firstborn child and animal of that household died. If there was lamb's blood on the door-frame, then God would "pass over" that house. It was a sad and horrible night. But it was a night the Israelites would never forget. (Check out Exodus 12:1—13:16, p. 90.)

So that they would remember how God protected and delivered them, every year they had a feast to celebrate his "passing over". They called it the Passover Feast. Each year for the feast they would eat the same meal that they ate that sad night. They also kept certain customs to remind them that God had performed a miracle and that he would always take care of them.

born to your oxen, and do not cut off the wool from the first lamb born to your sheep. 20 Each year you and your family are to eat these animals in the presence of the LORD your God, in the place he will choose to be worshipped. 21 If an animal is crippled or blind or has something else wrong, do not sacrifice it to the LORD your God. 22 But you may eat that animal in your own town. Both clean and unclean people may eat it, as they would eat a gazelle or a deer. 23 But don't eat its blood; pour it out on the ground like water.

The Passover

16 Celebrate the Passover of the LORD your God during the month of Abib, because it was during Abib that he brought you out of Egypt at night. 2 As the sacrifice for the Passover to the LORD your God, offer an animal from your flock or herd at the place the LORD will choose to be worshipped. 3 Do not eat it with bread made with yeast. But for seven days eat bread made without yeast, the bread of suffering, because you left Egypt in a hurry. So all your life you will remember the time you left Egypt. 4 There must be no yeast anywhere in your land for seven days. Offer the sacrifice on the evening of the first day, and eat all the meat before morning; do not leave it overnight.

5 Do not offer the Passover sacrifice in just any town the LORD your God gives you, 6 but offer it in the place he will choose to be worshipped. Offer it in the evening as the sun goes down, which is when you left Egypt. 7 Roast the meat and eat it at the place the LORD your God will choose. The next morning go back to your tents. 8 Eat bread made without yeast for six days. On the seventh day have a special meeting for the LORD your God, and do not work that day.

The Feast of Weeks

9 Count seven weeks from the time you begin to harvest the grain, 10 and then celebrate the Feast of Weeks for the LORD your God. Bring an offering as a special gift to him, giving to him just as he has blessed you. 11 Rejoice before the LORD your God at the place he will choose to be worshipped. Everybody should rejoice: you, your sons and daughters, your male and female servants, the Levites in your town, the strangers, orphans and widows

living among you. 12 Remember that you were slaves in Egypt, and carefully obey all these laws.

The Feast of Shelters

13 Celebrate the Feast of Shelters for seven days, after you have gathered your harvest from the threshing floor and winepress. 14 Everybody should rejoice at your Feast: you, your sons and daughters, your male and female servants, the Levites, strangers, orphans and widows who live in your towns. 15 Celebrate the Feast to the LORD your God for seven days at the place he will choose, because the LORD your God will bless all your harvest and all the work you do, and you will be completely happy.

16 All your men must come before the LORD three times a year to the place he will choose. They must come at these times: the Feast of Unleavened Bread, the Feast of Weeks and the Feast of Shelters. No man should come before the LORD without a gift. 17 Each of you must bring a gift that will show how much the LORD your God has blessed you.

Judges for the People

18 Appoint judges and officers for your tribes in every town the LORD your God is giving you; they must judge the people fairly. 19 Do not judge unfairly or take sides. Do not let people pay you to make wrong decisions, because that kind of payment makes wise people seem blind, and it changes the words of good people. 20 Always do what is right so that you will live and always have the land the LORD your God is giving you.

God Hates Idols

21 Do not set up a wooden Asherah idol next to the altar you build for the LORD your God, 22 and do not set up holy stone pillars. The LORD your God hates them.

17 If an ox or sheep has something wrong with it, do not offer it as a sacrifice to the LORD your God. He would hate that.

2 A man or woman in one of the towns the LORD gave you might be found doing something evil and breaking the Agreement. 3 That person may have served other gods and bowed down to them or to the sun or moon or stars of the sky, which I have commanded should not be done. 4 If someone has told you about it, you must look into the matter carefully. If it is true that such a hateful thing has happened in Israel, 5 take the man or woman who has done the evil thing to the city gates and throw stones at that person until he dies. 6 There must be two or three witnesses that it is true before the person is put to death; if there is only one witness, the person should not be put to death. 7 The witnesses must be the first to throw stones at the person, and then everyone else will follow. You must get rid of the evil among you.

Courts of Law

8 Some cases that come before you, such as murder, quarrelling or attack, may be too difficult to judge. Take these cases to the place the LORD your God will choose. 9 Go to the priests who are Levites and to the judge who is on duty at that time. Ask them about the case, and they will decide. 10 You must follow the decision they give you at the place the LORD your God will choose. Be careful to do everything they tell you. 11 Follow the teachings they give you, and do whatever they decide, exactly as they tell you. 12 The person who does not show respect for the judge or priest who is there serving the LORD your God must be put to death. You must get rid of that evil from Israel. 13 Then everyone will hear about this and will be afraid, and they will not show disrespect any more.

> You must follow the decision they give you at the place the LORD your God will choose.
> – Deuteronomy 17:10

Choosing a King

14 When you enter the land the LORD your God is giving you, taking it as your own and living in it, you will say, "Let's appoint a king over us like the nations all around us." 15 Be sure to appoint over you the king the LORD your God chooses. He must be one of your own people. Do not appoint as your king a foreigner who is not a fellow Israelite. 16 The king must not have too many horses for himself, and he must not send people to Egypt to get more horses, because the LORD has told you, "Don't return that way again." 17 The king must not have many wives, or his heart will be led away from God. He must not have too much silver and gold.

18 When he becomes king, he should write a copy of the teachings on a scroll for himself, a copy taken from the priests and Levites. 19 He should keep it with him all the time and read from it every day of his life. Then he will learn to respect the LORD his God, and he will obey all the teachings and commands. 20 He should not think he is better than his fellow Israelites, and he must not stop obeying the law in any way so that he and his descendants may rule the kingdom for a long time.

17:18–20 Pride
Find out how to keep from being proud.

Shares for Priests and Levites

18 The priests are from the tribe of Levi, and that tribe will not receive a share of the land with the Israelites. They will eat the offerings made to the LORD by fire, which is their share. 2 They will not inherit any of the land like their brothers, but they will inherit the LORD himself, as he has promised them.

3 When you offer a bull or sheep as a sacrifice, you must share with the priests, giving them the shoulder, the cheeks and the inner organs. 4 Give them the first of your grain, new wine and oil, as well as the first wool you cut from your sheep. 5 The LORD your God has chosen the priests and their descendants out of all your tribes to stand and serve the LORD always.

6 If a Levite moves from one of your towns anywhere in Israel where he lives and comes to the place the LORD will choose, because he wants to serve the LORD there, 7 he may serve the LORD his God. He will be like his fellow Levites who serve there before the LORD. 8 They all will have an equal share of the food. That is separate from what he has received from the sale of family possessions.

Do Not Follow Other Nations

9 When you enter the land the LORD your God is giving you, don't learn to do the hateful things the other nations do. 10 Don't let anyone among you offer a son or daughter as a sacrifice in the fire. Don't let anyone use magic or witchcraft, or try to explain the meaning of signs. 11 Don't let anyone try to control others with magic, and don't let them be mediums or try to talk with the spirits of dead people. 12 The LORD hates anyone who does these things. Because the other nations do these things, the LORD your God will force them out of the land ahead of you. 13 But you must be innocent in the presence of the LORD your God.

The LORD's Special Prophet

14 The nations you will force out listen to people who use magic and witchcraft, but the LORD your God will not let you do those things. 15 The LORD your God will give you a prophet like me, who is one of your own people. Listen to him. 16 This is what you asked the LORD your God to do when you were gathered at Mount Sinai. You said, "Don't make us listen to the voice of the LORD our God again, and don't make us look at this terrible fire any more, or we will die."

17 So the LORD said to me, "What they have said is good. 18 So I will give them a prophet like you, who is one of their own people. I will tell him what to say, and he will tell them everything I command. 19 This prophet will speak for me; anyone who does not listen when he speaks will answer to me. 20 But if a prophet says

something I did not tell him to say as though he were speaking for me, or if a prophet speaks in the name of other gods, that prophet must be killed."

21 You might be thinking, "How can we know if a message is not from the LORD?" 22 If what a prophet says in the name of the LORD does not happen, it is not the LORD's message. That prophet was speaking his own ideas. Don't be afraid of him.

Cities of Safety

19 When the LORD your God gives you land that belongs to the other nations, nations that he will destroy, you will force them out and live in their cities and houses. 2 Then choose three cities in the middle of the land the LORD your God is giving you as your own. 3 Build roads to these cities, and divide the land the LORD is giving you into three parts so that someone who kills another person may run to these cities.

4 This is the rule for someone who kills another person and runs to one of these cities in order to save his life. But the person must have killed a neighbour without meaning to, not out of hatred. 5 For example, suppose someone goes into the forest with a neighbour to cut wood and swings an axe to cut down a tree. If the axe head flies off the handle, hitting and killing the neighbour, the one who killed him may run to one of these cities to save his life. 6 Otherwise, the dead person's relative who has the duty of punishing a murderer might be angry and chase him. If the city is far away, the relative might catch and kill the person, even though he should not be killed because there was no intent to kill his neighbour. 7 This is why I command you to choose these three cities.

8-9 Carefully obey all these laws I'm giving you today. Love the LORD your God, and always do what he wants you to do. Then the LORD your God will enlarge your land as he promised your ancestors, giving you the whole land he promised to them. After that, choose three more cities of safety 10 so that innocent people will not be killed in your land, the land that the LORD your God is giving you as your own. By doing this you will not be guilty of allowing the death of innocent people.

11 But if a person hates his neighbour and, after hiding and waiting, attacks and kills him and then runs to one of these cities for safety, 12 the elders of his own city should send for the murderer. They should bring the person back from the city of safety and hand him over to the relative who has the duty of punishing the murderer. 13 Show no mercy. You must remove from Israel the guilt of murdering innocent people so that things will go well for you.

14 Do not move the stone that marks the border of your neighbour's land, which people long ago set in place. It marks what you inherit in the land the LORD your God is giving you as your own.

Rules About Witnesses

15 One witness is not enough to accuse a person of a crime or sin. A case must be proved by two or three witnesses.

16 If a witness lies and accuses a person of a crime, 17 the two people who are arguing must stand in the presence of the LORD before the priests and judges who are on duty. 18 The judges must check the matter carefully. The witness who is a liar, lying about a fellow Israelite, 19 must be punished. He must be punished in the same way the other person would have been punished. You must get rid of the evil among you. 20 The rest of the people will hear about this and be afraid, and no one among you will ever do such an evil thing again. 21 Show no mercy. A life must be paid for a life, an eye for an eye, a tooth for a tooth, a hand for a hand, a foot for a foot.

Laws for War

20 When you go to war against your enemies and you see horses and chariots and an army that is bigger than yours, don't be afraid of them. The LORD

20:1
Fears
When is God with you?

your God, who brought you out of Egypt, will be with you. 2 The priest must come and speak to the army before you go into battle. 3 He will say, "Listen, Israel! Today you are going into battle against your enemies. Don't lose your courage or be afraid. Don't panic or be frightened, 4 because the LORD your God goes with you, to fight for you against your enemies and to save you."

5 The officers should say to the army, "Has anyone built a new house but not given it to God? He may go home, because he might die in battle and someone else would get to give his house to God. 6 Has anyone planted a vineyard and not begun to enjoy it? He may go home, because he might die in battle and someone else would enjoy his vineyard. 7 Is any man engaged to a woman and not yet married to her? He may go home, because he might die in battle and someone else would marry her." 8 Then the officers should also say, "Is anyone here afraid? Has anyone lost his courage? He may go home so that he will not cause others to lose their courage too." 9 When the officers finish speaking to the army, they should appoint commanders to lead it.

10 When you march up to attack a city, first make them an offer of peace. 11 If they accept your offer and open their gates to you, all the people of that city will become your slaves and work for you. 12 But if they do not make peace with you and fight you in battle, you should surround that city. 13 The LORD your God will give it to you. Then kill all the men with your swords, 14 and you may take everything else in the city for yourselves. Take the women, children and animals, and you may use these things the LORD your God gives you from your enemies. 15 Do this to all the cities that are far away, that do not belong to the nations nearby.

16 But leave nothing alive in the cities of the land the LORD your God is giving you. 17 Completely destroy these people: the Hittites, Amorites, Canaanites, Perizzites, Hivites and Jebusites, as the LORD your God has commanded. 18 Otherwise, they will teach you what they do for their gods, and if you do these hateful things, you will sin against the LORD your God.

19 If you surround and attack a city for a long time, trying to capture it, do not destroy its trees with an axe. You can eat the fruit from the trees, but do not cut them down. These trees are not the enemy, so don't make war against them. 20 But you may cut down trees that you know are not fruit trees and use them to build devices to attack the city walls, until the city is captured.

A Person Found Murdered

21 Suppose someone is found murdered, lying in a field in the land the LORD your God is giving you as your own, and no one knows who killed the person. 2 Your elders and judges should go to where the body was found, and they should measure how far it is to the nearby cities. 3 The elders of the city nearest the body must take a young cow that has never worked or worn a yoke, 4 and they must lead her down to a valley that has never been ploughed or planted, with a stream flowing through it. There they must break the young cow's neck. 5 The priests, the sons of Levi, should come forward, because they have been chosen by the LORD your God to serve him and to give blessings in the LORD's name. They are the ones who decide cases of quarrelling and attacks. 6 Then all the elders of the city nearest the murdered person should wash their hands over the young cow whose neck was broken in the valley. 7 They should declare: "We did not kill this person, and we did not see it happen. 8 LORD, remove this sin from your people Israel, whom you have saved. Don't blame your people, the Israelites, for the murder of this innocent person." And so the murder will be paid for.

> But if they do not make peace with you and fight you in battle, you should surround that city.
> – Deuteronomy 20:12

9 Then you will have removed from yourselves the guilt of murdering an innocent person, because you will be doing what the LORD says is right.

Captive Women as Wives

10 When you go to war against your enemies, the LORD will help you defeat them so that you will take them captive. 11 If you see a beautiful woman among the captives and are attracted to her, you may take her as your wife. 12 Bring her into your home, where she must shave her head and cut her nails 13 and change the clothes she was wearing when you captured her. After she has lived in your house and cried for her parents for a month, you may marry her. You will be her husband, and she will be your wife. 14 But if you are not pleased with her, you must let her go anywhere she wants. You must not sell her for money or make her a slave, because you have taken away her honour.

The Oldest Son

15 A man might have two wives, one he loves and one he doesn't. Both wives might have sons by him. If the older son belongs to the wife he does not love, 16 when that man wills his property to his sons he must not give the son of the wife he loves what belongs to the older son, the son of the wife he does not love. 17 He must agree to give the older son two shares of everything he owns, even though the older son is from the wife he does not love. That son was the first to prove his father could have children, so he has the rights that belong to the older son.

Sons Who Refuse to Obey

18 If someone has a son who is stubborn, who turns against his father and mother and doesn't obey them or listen when they correct him, 19 his parents must take him to the elders at the city gate. 20 They will say to the leaders, "Our son is stubborn and turns against us. He will not obey us. He eats too much, and he is always drunk." 21 Then all the men in his town must throw stones at him until he dies. Get rid of the evil among you, because then all the people of Israel will hear about this and be afraid.

Other Laws

22 If someone is guilty of a sin worthy of death, he must be put to death and his body displayed on a tree. 23 But don't leave his body hanging on the tree overnight; be sure to bury him that same day, because anyone whose body is displayed on a tree is cursed by God. You must not ruin the land the LORD your God is giving you as your own.

22 If you see your fellow Israelite's ox or sheep wandering away, don't ignore it. Take it back to its owner. 2 If the owner does not live close to you, or if you do not know who the owner is, take the animal home with you. Keep it until the owner comes looking for it; then give it back. 3 Do the same thing if you find a donkey or coat or anything someone lost. Don't just ignore it.

4 If you see your fellow Israelite's donkey or ox fallen on the road, don't ignore it. Help the owner get it up.

5 A woman must not wear men's clothes, and a man must not wear women's clothes. The LORD your God hates anyone who does that.

6 If you find a bird's nest by the road, either in a tree or on the ground, and the mother bird is sitting on the young birds or eggs, do not take the mother bird with the young birds. 7 You may take the young birds, but you must let the mother bird go free. Then things will go well for you, and you will live a long time.

8 When you build a new house, build a low wall around the edge of the roof[n] so you will not be guilty if someone falls off the roof.

9 Don't plant two different kinds of seeds in your vineyard. Otherwise, both crops will be ruined.

10 Don't plough with an ox and a donkey tied together.

22:8 roof In Bible times houses were built with flat roofs. The roof was used for drying things such as flax and fruit. And it was used as an extra room, as a place for worship and as a place to sleep in the summer.

FAITH links

CARE FOR THE LOST
DEUTERONOMY 22:1-3

Have you ever found a lost dog or cat? Even if you wanted to keep it, you knew that finding the owner was the right thing to do. God made a rule for the people of Israel about lost animals. Animals were very important to them. Having livestock was a sign of God's blessing. If a poor person lost a sheep, often he couldn't afford to get another one. That's why God commanded the people to return lost animals.

After God created Adam, he was given the job of caring for and naming the animals. We're still caretakers of the earth. Being a caretaker includes caring for animals.

God really wants us to care for others. Read on!

Help for the Poor, Leviticus 5:7, p. 138

Help for the Hurting, Job 6:29–30, p. 666

You Are What You Do, Proverbs 20:11, p. 854

Let's Make a Deal, Daniel 1:8–21, p. 1150

The Greatest Commandment, Matthew 22:36–40, p. 1313

The Worst Chore, John 13:3–17, p. 1447

---

11 Don't wear clothes made of wool and linen woven together.

12 Tie several pieces of thread together; then put these tassels on the four corners of your coat.

Marriage Laws

13 If a man marries a girl and has sexual relations with her but then decides he does not like her, 14 he might talk badly about her and give her a bad name. He might say, "I married this woman, but when I had sexual relations with her, I did not find that she was a virgin." 15 Then the girl's parents must bring proof that she was a virgin to the elders at the city gate. 16 The girl's father will say to the leaders, "I gave my daughter to this man to be his wife, but now he does not want her. 17 This man has told lies about my daughter. He has said, 'I did not find your daughter to be a virgin,' but here is the proof that my daughter was a virgin." Then her parents are to show the sheet to the city leaders, 18 and the leaders must take the man and punish him. 19 They must make him pay about a kilogramme of silver to the girl's father, because the man has given an Israelite virgin a bad name. The girl will continue to be the man's wife, and he may not divorce her as long as he lives.

20 But if the things the husband said about his wife are true, and there is no proof that she was a virgin, 21 the girl must be brought to the door of her father's house. Then the men of the town must put her to death by throwing stones at her. She has done a disgraceful thing in Israel by having sexual relations before she was married. You must get rid of the evil among you.

22 If a man is found having sexual relations with another man's wife, both the woman and the man who had sexual relations with her must die. Get rid of this evil from Israel.

23 If a man meets a virgin in a city and has sexual relations with her, but she is engaged to another man, 24 you must take both of them to the city gate and put them to death by throwing stones at them. Kill the girl, because she was in a city and

did not scream for help. And kill the man for having sexual relations with another man's wife. You must get rid of the evil among you.

25 But if a man meets an engaged girl out in the country and forces her to have sexual relations with him, only the man who had sexual relations with her must be put to death. 26 Don't do anything to the girl, because she has not done a sin worthy of death. This is like the person who attacks and murders a neighbour; 27 the man found the engaged girl in the country and she screamed, but no one was there to save her.

28 If a man meets a virgin who is not engaged to be married and forces her to have sexual relations with him and people find out about it, 29 the man must pay the girl's father about 50 pieces of silver. He must also marry the girl, because he has dishonoured her, and he may never divorce her for as long as he lives.

30 A man must not marry his father's wife; he must not dishonour his father in this way.

The LORD's People

23 No man who has had part of his sex organ cut off may come into the meeting to worship the LORD.

2 No one born to parents who were forbidden by law to marry may come into the meeting to worship the LORD. The descendants for ten generations may not come in either.

3 No Ammonite or Moabite may come into the meeting to worship the LORD, and none of their descendants for ten generations may come in. 4 This is because the Ammonites and Moabites did not give you bread and water when you came out of Egypt. And they hired Balaam son of Beor, from Pethor in North West Mesopotamia, to put a curse on you. 5 But the LORD your God would not listen to Balaam. He turned the curse into a blessing for you, because the LORD your God loves you. 6 Don't wish for their peace or success as long as you live.

7 Don't hate Edomites; they are your close relatives. Don't hate Egyptians, because you were foreigners in their country. 8 The great-grandchildren of these two peoples may come into the meeting to worship the LORD.

Keeping the Camp Clean

9 When you are camped in time of war, keep away from unclean things. 10 If a man becomes unclean during the night, he must go outside the camp and not come back. 11 But when evening comes, he must wash himself, and at sunset he may come back into the camp.

12 Choose a place outside the camp where people may go to relieve themselves. 13 Carry a tent peg with you, and when you relieve yourself, dig a hole and cover up your dung. 14 The LORD your God moves around through your camp to protect you and to defeat your enemies for you, so the camp must be holy. He must not see anything unclean among you so that he will not leave you.

Other Laws

15 If an escaped slave comes to you, do not hand over the slave to his master. 16 Let the slave live with you anywhere he likes, in any town he chooses. Do not mistreat him.

17 No Israelite man or woman must ever become a temple prostitute. 18 Do not bring a male or female prostitute's pay to the Temple of the LORD your God to pay what you have promised to the LORD, because the LORD your God hates prostitution.

19 If you loan your fellow Israelites money or food or anything else, don't make them pay back more than you loaned them. 20 You may charge foreigners, but not fellow Israelites. Then the LORD your God will bless everything you do in the land you are entering to take as your own.

21 If you make a promise to give something to the LORD your God, do not be slow to pay it, because the LORD your God demands it from you. Do not be guilty of sin. 22 But if you do not make the promise, you will not be guilty. 23 You must do whatever you say you will do,

Deuteronomy 24:15 257

24 A man might marry a woman but later decide she doesn't please him because he has found something bad about her. He writes out divorce papers for her, gives them to her and sends her away from his house. 2 After she leaves his house, she goes and marries another man, 3 but her second husband does not like her either. So he writes out divorce papers for her, gives them to her and sends her away from his house. Or the second husband might die. 4 In either case, her first husband who divorced her must not marry her again, because she has become unclean. The LORD would hate this. Don't bring this sin into the land the LORD your God is giving you as your own.

5 A man who has just married must not be sent to war or be given any other duty. He should be free to stay home for a year to make his new wife happy.

6 If someone owes you something, do not take his two stones for grinding grain—not even the upper one—in place of what he owes, because this is how the person makes a living.

7 If someone kidnaps a fellow Israelite, either to make him a slave or sell him, the kidnapper must be killed. You must get rid of the evil among you.

8 Be careful when someone has a skin disease. Do exactly what the priests, the Levites, teach you, being careful to do what I have commanded them. 9 Remember what the LORD your God did to Miriam on your way out of Egypt.

10 When you make a loan to your neighbours, don't go into their homes to get something in place of it. 11 Stay outside and let them go in and get what they promised you. 12 If a poor person gives you a coat to show he will pay the loan back, don't keep it overnight. 13 Give the coat back at sunset, because your neighbour needs that coat to sleep in, and he will thank you. And the LORD your God will see that you have done a good thing.

14 Don't cheat hired servants who are poor and needy, whether they are fellow Israelites or foreigners living in one of your towns. 15 Pay them each day before

---

FAITH links

A SERIOUS PROMISE
DEUTERONOMY 23:21-23

Has someone ever borrowed money from you and promised to pay it back but didn't? When that person did not keep his or her word, how did that make you feel? God takes promises made to him just as seriously as you do. He told Moses to tell the Israelites to always keep their promises to him. If a person promised to give an offering to the Meeting Tent, God expected him to do it. When you make a promise to God, keep it!

A Different Kind of People, Leviticus 11, p. 146

Loyal to a Friend, 2 Samuel 9, p. 409

"Handle" Your Responsibilities, 2 Kings 6:5–7, p. 485

The Salt Promise, 2 Chronicles 13:5, p. 576

Fear God or People? Jeremiah 38:14–21, p. 1047

A Christian's Responsibility, Acts 11:26, p. 1484

---

because you chose to make the promise to the LORD your God.

24 If you go into your neighbour's vineyard, you may eat as many grapes as you wish, but do not put any grapes into your basket. 25 If you go into your neighbour's grainfield, you may pick grain with your hands, but you must not cut down your neighbour's grain with your sickle.

sunset, because they are poor and need the money. Otherwise, they may complain to the LORD about you, and you will be guilty of sin.

FAIRNESS FOR ALL
DEUTERONOMY 24:17

How would you react if someone passed out biscuits to you and your friends, but gave you less than everyone else had? Everyone likes to be treated fairly. God commanded the Israelites to treat widows, orphans and people from other nations fairly. Why them? They were the people who had the least of all the people in Israel. Sometimes they were treated unfairly. Others tried to ignore them. God did not want the Israelites to treat them unkindly. God wants us to treat everyone fairly, especially those whom we feel do not deserve fairness.

Link here for some more thoughts on fairness:

Just Kidding? Genesis 21:8–10, p. 28

Care to Be Fair? Joshua 18:1–8, p. 299

Fair All the Time? 2 Samuel 8:15, p. 408

Meaningless Words, Job 21:34, p. 684

My Favourite! Mark 10:17–23, p. 1347

I'll Be the Judge! 1 Corinthians 4:4–5, p. 1549

16 Parents must not be put to death if their children do wrong, and children must not be put to death if their parents do wrong. Each person must die for his own sin.

17 Do not be unfair to a foreigner or an orphan. Don't take a widow's coat to make sure she pays you back. 18 Remember that you were slaves in Egypt, and the LORD your God saved you from there. That is why I am commanding you to do this.

19 When you are gathering your harvest in the field and leave behind a bundle of grain, don't go back and get it. Leave it there for foreigners, orphans and widows so that the LORD your God can bless everything you do. 20 When you beat your olive trees to knock the olives off, don't beat the trees a second time. Leave what is left for foreigners, orphans and widows. 21 When you harvest the grapes in your vineyard, don't pick the vines a second time. Leave what is left for foreigners, orphans and widows. 22 Remember that you were slaves in Egypt; that is why I am commanding you to do this.

25 If two people have an argument and go to court, the judges will decide the case. They will declare one person right and the other guilty. 2 If the guilty person has to be punished with a beating, the judge will make that person lie down and be beaten in front of him. The number of lashes should match the crime. 3 But don't hit a person more than 40 times, because more than that would disgrace him before others.

4 When an ox is working in the grain, do not cover its mouth to keep it from eating.

5 If two brothers are living together, and one of them dies without having a son, his widow must not marry someone outside her husband's family. Her husband's brother must marry her, which is his duty to her as a brother-in-law. 6 The first son she has counts as the son of the dead brother so that his name will not be forgotten in Israel.

7 But if a man does not want to marry

his brother's widow, she should go to the elders at the town gate. She should say, "My brother-in-law will not carry on his brother's name in Israel. He refuses to do his duty for me."

8 Then the elders of the town must call for the man and talk to him. But if he is stubborn and says, "I don't want to marry her," 9 the woman must go up to him in front of the elders. She must take off one of his sandals and spit in his face and say, "This is for the man who won't continue his brother's family!" 10 Then that man's family shall be known in Israel as the Family of the Unsandaled.

11 If two men are fighting and one man's wife comes to save her husband from his attacker, grabbing the attacker by his sex organs, 12 you must cut off her hand. Show her no mercy.

13 Don't carry two sets of weights with you, one heavy and one light. 14 Don't have two different sets of measures in your house, one large and one small. 15 You must have true and honest weights and measures so that you will live a long time in the land the LORD your God is giving you. 16 The LORD your God hates anyone who is dishonest and uses dishonest measures.

17 Remember what the Amalekites did to you when you came out of Egypt. 18 When you were tired and worn out, they met you on the road and attacked all those lagging behind. They were not afraid of God. 19 When the LORD your God gives you rest from all the enemies around you in the land he is giving you as your own, you shall destroy any memory of the Amalekites on the earth. Do not forget!

The First Harvest

26 When you go into the land the LORD your God is giving you as your own, to take it over and live in it, 2 you must take some of the first harvest of crops that grow from the land the LORD your God is giving you. Put the food in a basket and go to the place where the LORD your God will choose to be worshipped. 3 Say to the priest on duty at that time, "Today I declare before the LORD your God that I have come into the land the LORD promised our ancestors that he would give us." 4 The priest will take your basket and set it down in front of the altar of the LORD your God. 5 Then you shall announce before the LORD your God: "My father was a wandering Aramean. He went down to Egypt with only a few people, but they became a great, powerful and large nation there. 6 But the Egyptians were cruel to us, making us suffer and work very hard. 7 So we prayed to the LORD, the God of our ancestors, and he heard us. When he saw our trouble, hard work and suffering, 8 the LORD brought us out of Egypt with his great power and strength, using great terrors, signs and miracles. 9 Then he brought us to this place and gave us this fertile land. 10 Now I bring part of the first harvest from this land that you, LORD, have given me." Place the basket before the LORD your God and bow down before him. 11 Then you and the Levites and foreigners among you should rejoice, because the LORD your God has given good things to you and your family.

12 Bring a tenth of all your harvest the third year (the year to give a tenth of your harvest). Give it to the Levites, foreigners, orphans and widows so that they may eat in your towns and be full. 13 Then say to the LORD your God, "I have taken out of my house the part of my harvest that belongs to God, and I have given it to the Levites, foreigners, orphans and widows. I have done everything you commanded me; I have not broken your commands, and I have not forgotten any of them. 14 I have not eaten any of the holy part while I was in sorrow. I have not removed any of it while I was unclean, and I have not offered it for dead people. I have obeyed you, the LORD my God, and

> You must have true and honest weights and measures.
> – Deuteronomy 25:15

have done everything you commanded me. 15 So look down from heaven, your holy home. Bless your people Israel and bless the land you have given us, which you promised to our ancestors—a fertile land."

Obey the LORD's Commands

16 Today the LORD your God commands you to obey all these rules and laws; be careful to obey them with your whole being. 17 Today you have said that the LORD is your God, and you have promised to do what he wants you to do—to keep his rules, commands and laws. You have said you will obey him. 18 And today the LORD has said that you are his very own people, as he has promised you. But you must obey his commands. 19 He will make you greater than all the other nations he made. He will give you praise, fame and honour, and you will be a holy people to the LORD your God, as he has said.

26:18 God's Family
What are God's people supposed to do?

The Law Written on Stones

27 Then Moses, along with the elders of Israel, commanded the people, saying, "Keep all the commands I have given you today. 2 Soon you will cross the Jordan River to go into the land the LORD your God is giving you. On that day set up some large stones and cover them with plaster. 3 When you cross over, write all the words of these teachings on them. Then you may enter the land the LORD your God is giving you, a fertile land, just as the LORD, the God of your ancestors, promised. 4 After you have crossed the Jordan River, set up these stones on Mount Ebal, as I command you today, and cover them with plaster. 5 Build an altar of stones there to the LORD your God, but don't use any iron tool to cut the stones; 6 build the altar of the LORD your God with stones from the field. Offer burnt offerings on it to the LORD your God, 7 and offer fellowship offerings there, and eat them and rejoice before the LORD your God. 8 Then write clearly all the words of these teachings on the stones."

Curses of the Law

9 Then Moses and the Levites who were priests spoke to all Israel and said, "Be quiet, Israel. Listen! Today you have become the people of the LORD

27:10 Belief
What else should go with belief in God?

READ MY LIPS?
DEUTERONOMY 26:16-19

Suppose you told your mother you would take out the rubbish, but didn't do it. Do you think she would believe that you really meant what you said? Nope!

The Israelites told the Lord that they would follow his commands. Through Moses, God called the people to do what they said they would do. God still calls people to action, not lip service. Do you mean what you say? Then act like you mean it by doing it!

Always Truthful, Numbers 23:19, p. 208

A Special Promise, Numbers 30:1–2, p. 217

A Broken Promise, Jeremiah 2:1–8, p. 989

The Verdict Is In? Matthew 7:1–2, p. 1285

Calling Anyone! Acts 23:12–22, p. 1506

Say What?! Ephesians 4:22–29, p. 1603

your God. 10 Obey the LORD your God, and keep his commands and laws that I give you today."

11 That day Moses also gave the people this command:

12 When you cross the Jordan River, these tribes must stand on Mount Gerizim to bless the people: Simeon, Levi, Judah, Issachar, Joseph and Benjamin. 13 And these tribes must stand on Mount Ebal to announce the curses: Reuben, Gad, Asher, Zebulun, Dan and Naphtali. 14 The Levites will say to all the people of Israel in a loud voice:

15 "Anyone will be cursed who makes an idol or statue and secretly sets it up, because the LORD hates the idols people make."

Then all the people will say, "Amen!"

16 "Anyone will be cursed who dishonours his father or mother."

Then all the people will say, "Amen!"

17 "Anyone will be cursed who moves the stone that marks a neighbour's border."

Then all the people will say, "Amen!"

18 "Anyone will be cursed who sends a blind person down the wrong road."

Then all the people will say, "Amen!"

19 "Anyone will be cursed who is unfair to foreigners, orphans or widows."

Then all the people will say, "Amen!"

20 "A man will be cursed who has sexual relations with his father's wife, because it is a dishonour to his father."

Then all the people will say, "Amen!"

21 "Anyone will be cursed who has sexual relations with an animal."

Then all the people will say, "Amen!"

22 "A man will be cursed who has sexual relations with his sister, whether she is his father's daughter or his mother's daughter."

Then all the people will say, "Amen!"

23 "A man will be cursed who has sexual relations with his mother-in-law."

Then all the people will say, "Amen!"

24 "Anyone will be cursed who kills a neighbour secretly."

Then all the people will say, "Amen!"

25 "Anyone will be cursed who takes money to murder an innocent person."

Then all the people will say, "Amen!"

26 "Anyone will be cursed who does not agree with the words of these teachings and does not obey them."

Then all the people will say, "Amen!"

Blessings for Obeying

28 You must completely obey the LORD your God, and you must carefully follow all his commands I am giving you today. Then the LORD your God will make you greater than any other nation on earth. 2 Obey the LORD your God so that all these blessings will come and stay with you:

28:1
Obedience
How does God reward obedience?

3 You will be blessed in the city and blessed in the country.

4 Your children will be blessed, as well as your crops; your herds will be blessed with calves and your flocks with lambs.

5 Your basket and your kitchen will be blessed.

6 You will be blessed when you come in and when you go out.

7 The LORD will help you defeat the enemies that come to fight you. They will attack you from one direction, but they will run from you in seven directions.

8 The LORD your God will bless you with full barns, and he will bless everything you do. He will bless the land he is giving you.

9 The LORD will make you his holy people, as he promised. But you must obey his commands and do what he wants you to do. 10 Then everyone on earth will see that you are the LORD's people, and they will be afraid of you. 11 The LORD will make you rich: you will have many children, your animals will have many young, and your land will give good crops. It is the land that the LORD promised your ancestors he would give to you.

12 The LORD will open up his heavenly storehouse so that the skies send rain on your land at the right time, and he will bless everything you do. You will lend to other nations, but you will not need to borrow from them. 13 The LORD will make you like the head and not like the tail; you will be on top and not on the bottom. But you must obey the commands

of the LORD your God that I am giving you today, being careful to keep them. 14 Do not disobey anything I command you today. Do exactly as I command, and do not follow other gods or serve them.

Curses for Disobeying

15 But if you do not obey the LORD your God and carefully follow all his commands and laws I am giving you today, all these curses will come upon you and stay:
16 You will be cursed in the city and cursed in the country.
17 Your basket and your kitchen will be cursed.
18 Your children will be cursed, as well as your crops; the calves of your herds and the lambs of your flocks will be cursed.
19 You will be cursed when you go in and when you go out.
20 The LORD will send you curses, confusion and punishment in everything you do. You will be destroyed and suddenly ruined because you did wrong when you left him. 21 The LORD will give you terrible diseases and destroy you from the land you are going to take. 22 The LORD will punish you with disease, fever, swelling, heat, lack of rain, plant diseases and mildew, until you die. 23 The sky above will be like bronze, and the ground below will be like iron.*n* 24 The LORD will turn the rain into dust and sand, which will fall from the skies until you are destroyed.
25 The LORD will help your enemies defeat you. You will attack them from one direction, but you will run from them in seven directions. And you will become a thing of horror among all the kingdoms on earth. 26 Your dead bodies will be food for all the birds and wild animals, and there will be no one to scare them away.
27 The LORD will punish you with boils like those the Egyptians had. You will have bad growths, sores and itches that can't be cured. 28 The LORD will give you madness, blindness and a confused mind. 29 You will have to feel around in the daylight like a blind person. You will fail in everything you do. People will hurt you and steal from you every day, and no one will save you.
30 You will be engaged to a woman, but another man will force her to have sexual relations with him. You will build a house, but you will not live in it. You will plant a vineyard, but you will not get its grapes. 31 Your ox will be killed before your eyes, but you will not eat any of it. Your donkey will be taken away from you, and it will not be brought back. Your sheep will be given to your enemies, and no one will save you. 32 Your sons and daughters will be given to another nation, and you will grow tired looking for them every day, but there will be nothing you can do. 33 People you don't know will eat the crops your land and hard work have produced. You will be mistreated and abused all your life. 34 The things you see will cause you to go mad. 35 The LORD will give you sore boils on your knees and legs that cannot be cured, and they will go from the soles of your feet to the tops of your heads.
36 The LORD will send you and your king away to a nation neither you nor your ancestors know, where you will serve other gods made of wood and stone. 37 You will become a hated thing to the nations where the LORD sends you; they will laugh at you and make fun of you.
38 You will plant much seed in your field, but your harvest will be small, because locusts will eat the crop. 39 You will plant vineyards and work hard in them, but you will not pick the grapes or drink the wine, because the worms will eat them. 40 You will have olive trees in all your land, but you will not get any olive oil, because the olives will drop off the trees. 41 You will have sons and

> Obey the LORD your God so that all these blessings will come and stay with you.
> – Deuteronomy 28:2

28:23 **sky . . . iron** This means the sky will give no rain and the earth will produce no crops.

daughters, but you will not be able to keep them, because they will be taken captive. 42 Locusts will destroy all your trees and crops.

43 The foreigners who live among you will get stronger and stronger, and you will get weaker and weaker. 44 Foreigners will lend money to you, but you will not be able to lend to them. They will be like the head, and you will be like the tail.

45 All these curses will come upon you. They will chase you and catch you and destroy you, because you did not obey the LORD your God and keep the commands and laws he gave you. 46 The curses will be signs and miracles to you and your descendants for ever. 47 You had plenty of everything, but you did not serve the LORD your God with joy and a pure heart, 48 so you will serve the enemies the LORD sends against you. You will be hungry, thirsty, naked and poor, and the LORD will put a load on you until he has destroyed you.

The Curse of an Enemy Nation

49 The LORD will bring a nation against you from far away, from the end of the world, and it will swoop down like an eagle. You won't understand their language, 50 and they will look fierce. They will not respect old people or feel sorry for the young. 51 They will eat the calves from your herds and the harvest of your field, and you will be destroyed. They will not leave you any grain, new wine or oil, or any calves from your herds or lambs from your flocks. You will be ruined. 52 That nation will surround and attack all your cities. You trust in your high, strong walls, but they will fall down. That nation will surround all your cities everywhere in the land the LORD your God is giving you.

53 Your enemy will surround you. Those people will make you starve so that you will eat your own babies, the bodies of the sons and daughters the LORD your God gave you. 54 Even the most gentle and kind man among you will become cruel to his brother, his wife whom he loves and his children who are still alive. 55 He will not even give them any of the flesh of his children he is eating, because it will be all he has left. Your enemy will surround you and make you starve in all your cities. 56 The most gentle and kind woman among you, so gentle and kind she would hardly even walk on the ground, will be cruel to her husband whom she loves and to her son and daughter. 57 She will give birth to a baby, but she will plan to eat the baby and what comes after the birth itself. She will eat them secretly while the enemy surrounds the city. Those people will make you starve in all your cities.

58 Be careful to obey everything in these teachings that are written in this book. You must respect the glorious and wonderful name of the LORD your God, 59 or the LORD will give terrible diseases to you and your descendants. You will have long and serious diseases, and long and miserable sicknesses. 60 He will give you all the diseases of Egypt that you dread, and the diseases will stay with you. 61 The LORD will also give you every disease and sickness not written in this Book of the Teachings, until you are destroyed. 62 You people may have outnumbered the stars, but only a few of you will be left, because you did not obey the LORD your God. 63 Just as the LORD was once happy with you and gave you good things and made you grow in number, so then the LORD will be happy to ruin and destroy you, and you will be removed from the land you are entering to take as your own.

64 Then the LORD will scatter you among the nations—from one end of the earth to the other. There you will serve other gods of wood and stone, gods that neither you nor your ancestors have known. 65 You will have no rest among those nations and no place that is yours. The LORD will make your mind worried, your sight weak and your soul sad. 66 You will live with danger and be afraid night and day. You will not be sure that you will live. 67 In the morning you will say, "I wish it were evening," and in the evening you will say, "I wish it were morning." Terror will be in your heart,

and the things you have seen will scare you. 68 The LORD will send you back to Egypt in ships, even though I, Moses, said you would never go back to Egypt. And there you will try to sell yourselves as slaves to your enemies, but no one will buy you.

The Agreement in Moab

29 The LORD commanded Moses to make an agreement with the Israelites in Moab in addition to the agreement he had made with them at Mount Sinai. These are the words of that agreement.

2 Moses called all the Israelites together and said to them: You have seen everything the LORD did before your own eyes to the king of Egypt and to the king's leaders and to the whole country. 3 With your own eyes you saw the great troubles, signs and miracles. 4 But to this day the LORD has not given you a mind that understands; you don't really understand what you see with your eyes or hear with your ears. 5 I led you through the desert for 40 years, and during that time neither your clothes nor sandals wore out. 6 You ate no bread and drank no wine or beer. This was so you would understand that I am the LORD your God.

7 When you came to this place, Sihon king of Heshbon and Og king of Bashan came out to fight us, but we defeated them. 8 We captured their land and gave it to the tribes of Reuben, Gad and East Manasseh to be their own.

9 You must carefully obey everything in this agreement so that you will succeed in everything you do. 10 Today you are all standing here before the LORD your God—your leaders and important men, your elders, officers and all the other men of Israel, 11 your wives and children and the foreigners who live among you, who chop your wood and carry your water. 12 You are all here to enter into an agreement and a promise with the LORD your God, an agreement the LORD your God is making with you today. 13 This will make you today his own people. He will be your God, as he told you and as he promised your ancestors Abraham, Isaac and Jacob. 14 But I am not just making this agreement and its promises with you 15 who are standing here before the LORD your God today, but also with those who are not here today.

16 You know how we lived in Egypt and how we passed through the countries when we came here. 17 You saw their hateful idols made of wood, stone, silver and gold. 18 Make sure no man, woman, family group or tribe among you leaves the LORD our God to go and serve the gods of those nations. They would be to you like a plant that grows bitter, poisonous fruit.

19 These are the kind of people who hear these curses but bless themselves, thinking, "We will be safe even though we continue doing what we want to do." Those people may destroy all of your land, both wet and dry. 20 The LORD will not forgive them. His anger will be like a burning fire against those people, and all the curses written in this book will come on them. The LORD will destroy any memory of them on the earth. 21 He will separate them from all the tribes of Israel for punishment. All the curses of the Agreement that are written in this Book of the Teachings will happen to them.

22 Your children who will come after you, as well as foreigners from faraway lands, will see the disasters that come to this land and the diseases the LORD will send on it. They will say, 23 "The land is nothing but burning cinders and salt. Nothing is planted, nothing grows and nothing blooms. It is like Sodom and Gomorrah, and Admah and Zeboiim, which the LORD destroyed because he was very angry." 24 All the other nations will ask, "Why has the LORD done this to the land? Why is he so angry?"

25 And the answer will be, "It is

> There are some things the LORD our God has kept secret, but there are some things he has let us know.
> – Deuteronomy 29:29

because the people broke the Agreement of the LORD, the God of their ancestors, which he made with them when he brought them out of Egypt. 26 They went and served other gods and bowed down to gods they did not even know. The LORD did not allow that, 27 so he became very angry at the land and brought all the curses on it that are written in this book. 28 Since the LORD became angry and furious with them, he took them out of their land and put them in another land where they are today."

29 There are some things the LORD our God has kept secret, but there are some things he has let us know. These things belong to us and our children forever so that we will do everything in these teachings.

The Israelites will Return

30 When all these blessings and curses I have described happen to you, and the LORD your God has sent you away to other nations, think about these things. 2 Then you and your children will return to the LORD your God, and you will obey him with your whole being in everything I am commanding you today. 3 Then the LORD your God will give you back your freedom. He will feel sorry for you, and he will bring you back again from the nations where he scattered you. 4 He may send you to the ends of the earth, but he will gather you and bring you back from there, 5 back to the land that belonged to your ancestors. It will be yours. He will give you success, and there will be more of you than there were of your ancestors. 6 The LORD your God will prepare you and your descendants to love him with your whole being so that you will live. 7 The LORD your God will put all these curses on your enemies, who hate you and are cruel to you. 8 And you will again obey the LORD, keeping all his commands that I give you today. 9 The LORD your God will make you successful in everything you do. You will have many children, your cattle will have many calves, and your fields will produce good crops, because the LORD will again be happy with you, just as he was with your

FAITH links

A CHOICE TO MAKE
DEUTERONOMY 30:15-20

If someone offered you a choice between eating a nice, juicy apple and eating a poisoned one, which would you choose? That's an easy one, right? Life is full of choices, some of which seem like no-brainers. God offered the people of Israel a choice between doing what was right and what was wrong. That was an easy choice for those who truly wanted to obey God. For those who weren't sure, well . . . the choice was a lot harder.

God gives you the same choice. He can help you make right choices. But you have to *want* his help first.

Connect to these links to find out what else God has to say about making the right choice:

What You Value, Genesis 25:21–34, p. 34

I Want It Now! Judges 14:1–3, p. 332

A Memorial for Two Thieves, 1 Chronicles 7:21, p. 530

Two Kinds of People, Psalm 1, p. 710

Love Him? Show It! Amos 2:6–7, p. 1196

That Thing You Do, Matthew 25:14–30, p. 1319

ancestors. 10 But you must obey the LORD your God by keeping all his commands and rules that are written in this Book of the Teachings. You must return to the LORD your God with your whole being.

Choose Life or Death

11 This command I give you today is not too hard for you; it is not beyond what you can do. 12 It is not up in heaven. You do not have to ask, "Who will go up to heaven and get it for us so we can obey it and keep it?" 13 It is not on the other side of the sea. You do not have to ask, "Who will go across the sea and get it? Who will tell it to us so we can keep it?" 14 No, the word is very near you. It is in your mouth and in your heart so you may obey it.

15 Look, today I offer you life and success, death and destruction. 16 I command you today to love the LORD your God, to do what he wants you to do, and to keep his commands, his rules and his laws. Then you will live and grow in number, and the LORD your God will bless you in the land you are entering to take as your own.

17 But if you turn away from the LORD and do not obey him, if you are led to bow and serve other gods, 18 I tell you today that you will surely be destroyed. And you will not live long in the land you are crossing the Jordan River to enter and take as your own.

19 Today I ask heaven and earth to be witnesses. I am offering you life or death, blessings or curses. Now, choose life! Then you and your children may live. 20 To choose life is to love the LORD your God, obey him and stay close to him. He is your life, and he will let you live many years in the land, the land he promised to give your ancestors Abraham, Isaac and Jacob.

Joshua Takes Moses' Place

31 Then Moses went and spoke these words to all the Israelites: 2 "I am now 120 years old, and I cannot lead you any more. The LORD told me I would not cross the Jordan River; 3 the LORD your God will lead you across himself. He will destroy those nations for you, and you will take over their land. Joshua will also lead you across, as the LORD has said. 4 The LORD will do to those nations what he did to Sihon and Og, the kings of the Amorites, when he destroyed them and their land. 5 The LORD will give those nations to you; do to them everything I told you. 6 Be strong and brave. Don't be afraid of them and don't be frightened, because the LORD your God will go with you. He will not leave you or forget you."

7 Then Moses called Joshua and said to him in front of the people, "Be strong and brave, because you will lead these people into the land the LORD promised to give their ancestors, and help them take it as their own. 8 The LORD himself will go before you. He will be with you; he will not leave you or forget you. Don't be afraid and don't worry."

31:8 Fears
Where is God when you are afraid?

Moses Writes the Teachings

9 So Moses wrote down these teachings and gave them to the priests and all the elders of Israel. (The priests are the sons of Levi, who carry the Ark of the Agreement with the LORD.) 10-11 Then Moses commanded them: "Read these teachings for all Israel to hear at the end of every seven years, which is the year to cancel what people owe. Do it during the Feast of Shelters, when all the Israelites will come to appear before the LORD your God and stand at the place he will choose. 12 Gather all the people: the men, women, children and foreigners living in your towns so that they can listen and learn to respect the LORD your God and carefully obey everything in this law. 13 Since their children do not know this law, they must hear it. They must learn to respect the LORD your God for as long as they live in the land you are crossing the Jordan River to take for your own."

The LORD Calls Moses and Joshua

14 The LORD said to Moses, "Soon you will die. Get Joshua and come to the

Making Good Choices
Deuteronomy 30:15–20

Livin' it

This or That? Which would you rather do, stay at home and do chores or go to an amusement park for the day? No-brainer, right? Some choices are like that – easy to make. Others, though, are tougher. How about doing what you know is right even if your friends make fun of you? Is that a harder choice for you to make? How would you decide what to do?

God offered the people of Israel a choice between doing what was right and what was wrong. That was an easy choice for those who truly wanted to obey God. For some of the others the choice was a lot harder. (Read Deuteronomy 30:15–20.) God gives you the same choice. He can help you make the right choices. How badly do you want his help?

MORE FAITH links

What You Value, **p. 34**

A Choice to Make, **p. 265**

Sitting on the Fence, **p. 464**

Mind Guard, **p. 831**

The Choices of a Choice, **p. 1375**

Have you decided what you want to do when you get older?

It's a pretty important decision to make. Maybe you ought to check out these links for some help in making good choices!

Choosing Sides, 1 Samuel 20, p. 382
- In an argument between two people, do you find yourself taking sides? How do you decide whose side you're on? Link here to learn about being on the side of what's right.

Let's Make a Deal, Daniel 1:8–21, p. 1150
- Suppose your teacher involved your class in an activity that you and your parents agreed was wrong for you. Should you go along with it in order to obey your teacher? Or should you refuse to go along with it in order to obey your parents? What could help you make that choice? This Faithlink explains how Daniel resolved a similar situation.

Keeping Clean, 2 Corinthians 7:1, p. 1576
- Suppose you've just put on some cool new clothes. Would you immediately leap into the nearest muddy puddle? Probably not. You would want to keep them clean and looking good. God wants Christians to be clean on the *inside*. What are some things that can make you have bad or wrong ideas and do wrong things (so that you become *dirty* on the inside)? How can you get clean inside? God can help with the clean-up – just ask!

my FAVOURITE links

Meeting Tent so that I may command him." So Moses and Joshua went to the Meeting Tent.

15 The LORD appeared at the Meeting Tent in a cloud; the cloud stood over the entrance of the Tent. 16 And the LORD said to Moses, "You will soon die. Then these people will not be loyal to me but will worship the foreign gods of the land they are entering. They will leave me, breaking the Agreement I made with them. 17 Then I will become very angry at them, and I will leave them. I will turn away from them, and they will be destroyed. Many terrible things will happen to them. Then they will say, 'It is because God is not with us that these terrible things are happening.' 18 I will surely turn away from them then, because they have done wrong and have turned to other gods.

19 "Now write down this song and teach it to the Israelites. Then have them sing it, because it will be my witness against them. 20 When I bring them into the land I promised to their ancestors, a fertile land, they will eat as much as they want and get fat. Then they will turn to other gods and serve them. They will reject me and break my Agreement. 21 Then when many troubles and terrible things happen to them, this song will testify against them, because the song will not be forgotten by their descendants. I know what they plan to do, even before I take them into the land I promised them." 22 So Moses wrote down the song that day, and he taught it to the Israelites.

23 Then the LORD gave this command to Joshua son of Nun: "Be strong and brave, because you will lead the people of Israel to the land I promised them, and I will be with you."

24 After Moses finished writing all the words of the teachings in a book, 25 he gave a command to the Levites, who carried the Ark of the Agreement with the LORD. 26 He said, "Take this Book of the Teachings and put it beside the Ark of the Agreement with the LORD your God. It must stay there as a witness against you. 27 I know how stubborn and disobedient you are. You have disobeyed the LORD while I am alive and with you, and you will disobey even more after I die! 28 Gather all the elders of your tribes and all your officers to me so that I may say these things for them to hear, and so that I may ask heaven and earth to testify against them. 29 I know that after I die you will become completely evil. You will turn away from the commands I have given you. Terrible things will happen to you in the future when you do what the LORD says is evil, and you will make him angry with the idols you have made."

Moses' Song

30 And Moses spoke this whole song for all the people of Israel to hear:

32 Hear, heavens, and I will speak.
Listen, earth, to what I say.
2 My teaching will drop like rain;
  my words will fall like dew.
They will be like showers on the grass;
  they will pour down like rain on young plants.
3 I will announce the name of the LORD.
  Praise God because he is great!
4 He is like a rock; what he does is perfect,
  and he is always fair.
He is a faithful God who does no wrong,
  who is right and fair.

5 They have done evil against him.
  To their shame they are no longer his children;
  they are an evil and lying people.
6 This is not the way to repay the LORD,
  you foolish and unwise people.
He is your Father and Maker,
  who made you and formed you.

7 Remember the old days.
  Think of the years already passed.
Ask your father and he will tell you;
  ask your elders and they will inform you.
8 God Most High gave the nations their lands,

dividing up the human race.
He set up borders for the people
    and even numbered the Israelites.
9 The LORD took his people as his
        share,
    the people of Jacob as his very
        own.

10 He found them in a desert,
    a windy, empty land.
He surrounded them and brought
        them up,
    guarding them as those he loved
        very much.
11 He was like an eagle building its nest
    that flutters over its young.
It spreads its wings to catch them
    and carries them on its feathers.
12 The LORD alone led them,
    and there was no foreign god
        helping him.

13 The LORD brought them to the
        heights of the land
    and fed them the fruit of the
        fields.
He gave them honey from the rocks,
    bringing oil from the solid rock.
14 There were milk curds from the cows
        and milk from the flock;
    there were fat sheep and goats.
There were rams and goats from
        Bashan
    and the best of the wheat.
You drank the juice of grapes.

15 Israel grew fat and kicked;
    they were fat and full and firm.
They left the God who made them
    and rejected the Rock who saved
        them.
16 They made God jealous with foreign
        gods
    and angry with hateful idols.
17 They made sacrifices to demons, not
        God,
    to gods they had never known,
    new gods from nearby,
    gods your ancestors did not fear.
18 You left God who is the Rock, your
        Father,
    and you forgot the God who gave
        you birth.

19 The LORD saw this and rejected
        them;
    his sons and daughters had made
        him angry.
20 He said, "I will turn away from them
    and see what will happen to them.
They are evil people,
    unfaithful children.
21 They used things that are not gods to
        make me jealous
    and worthless idols to make me
        angry.
So I will use those who are not a
        nation to make them jealous;
    I will use a nation that does not
        understand to make them angry.
22 My anger has started a fire
    that burns down to the place of the
        dead.
It will burn up the ground and its
        crops,
    and it will set fire to the base of the
        mountains.

23 "I will pile troubles upon them
    and shoot my arrows at them.
24 They will be starved and sick,
    destroyed by terrible diseases.
I will send them vicious animals
    and gliding, poisonous snakes.
25 In the streets the sword will kill;
    in their homes there will be
        terror.
Young men and women will die,
    and so will babies and grey-haired
        men.
26 I will scatter them as I said,
    and no one will remember them.
27 But I didn't want their enemy to
        boast;
    their enemy might misunderstand
        and say, 'We have won!
The LORD has done none of this.'"

28 Israel has no sense;
    they do not understand.
29 I wish they were wise and understood
        this;
    I wish they could see what will
        happen to them.
30 One person cannot chase 1,000
        people,
    and two people cannot fight 10,000

unless their Rock has sold them,
>   unless the Lord has given them
>   up.
> 31 The rock of these people is not like
>   our Rock;
>   our enemies agree to that.
> 32 Their vine comes from Sodom,
>   and their fields are like Gomorrah.
>   Their grapes are full of poison;
>   their bunches of grapes are bitter.
> 33 Their wine is like snake poison,
>   like the deadly poison of cobras.

> 34 "I have been saving this,
>   and I have it locked in my
>   storehouses.
> 35 I will punish those who do wrong; I
>   will repay them.
>   Soon their foot will slip,
>   because their day of trouble is near,
>   and their punishment will come
>   quickly."

> 36 The Lord will defend his people
>   and have mercy on his servants.
>   He will see that their strength is
>   gone,
>   that nobody is left, slaves or free.
> 37 Then he will say, "Where are their
>   gods?
>   Where is the rock they trusted?
> 38 Who ate the fat from their sacrifices,
>   and who drank the wine of their
>   drink offerings?
>   Let those gods come to help you!
>   Let them protect you!

> 39 "Now you will see that I am the one
>   God!
>   There is no god but me.
>   I send life and death;
>   I can hurt, and I can heal.
>   No one can escape from me.
> 40 I raise my hand towards heaven and
>   make this promise:
>   As surely as I live for ever,
> 41 I will sharpen my flashing sword,
>   and I will take it in my hand to
>   judge.
>   I will punish my enemies
>   and pay back those who hate me.
> 42 My arrows will be covered with their
>   blood;

>   my sword will eat their flesh.
>   The blood will flow from those who
>   are killed and the captives.
>   The heads of the enemy leaders
>   will be cut off."

> 43 Be happy, nations, with his people,
>   because he will repay you for the
>   blood of his servants.
>   He will punish his enemies,
>   and he will remove the sin of his
>   land and people.

44 Moses came with Joshua son of Nun, and they spoke all the words of this song for the people to hear. 45 When Moses finished speaking these words to all Israel, 46 he said to them: "Pay careful attention to all the words I have said to you today, and command your children to obey carefully everything in these teachings. 47 These should not be unimportant words for you, but rather they mean life for you! By these words you will live a long time in the land you are crossing the Jordan River to take as your own."

Moses Goes Up to Mount Nebo

48 The Lord spoke to Moses again that same day and said, 49 "Go up the Abarim Mountains, to Mount Nebo in the country of Moab, across from Jericho. Look at the land of Canaan that I am giving to the Israelites as their own. 50 On that mountain that you climb, you will die and join your ancestors, just as your brother Aaron died on Mount Hor and joined his ancestors. 51 You both sinned against me at the waters of Meribah Kadesh in the Desert of Zin, and you did not honour me as holy there among the Israelites. 52 So now you will only look at the land from far away. You will not enter the land I am giving the people of Israel."

Moses Blesses the People

33 Moses, the man of God, gave this blessing to the Israelites before he died. 2 He said:

> "The Lord came from Mount Sinai
>   and rose like the sun from
>   Edom;

he showed his greatness from
    Mount Paran.
He came with thousands of angels
    from the southern mountains.
3 The LORD surely loves his people
    and takes care of all those who
    belong to him.
They bow down at his feet,
    and they are taught by him.
4 Moses gave us the teachings
    that belong to the
    people of Jacob.
5 The LORD became
    king of Israel
    when the leaders
    of the people
    gathered,
    when the tribes of
    Israel came
    together.

6 "Let the people of Reuben live and
    not die,
    but let the people be few."

7 Moses said this about the people of
Judah:
    "LORD, listen to Judah's prayer;
    bring them back to their people.
    They defend themselves with their
    hands.
    Help them fight their enemies!"

8 Moses said this about the people of
Levi:
    "LORD, your Thummim and Urim
    belong
    to Levi, whom you love.
    LORD, you tested him at Massah
    and argued with him at the waters
    of Meribah.
9 He said about his father and mother,
    'I don't care about them.'
    He did not treat his brothers as
    favourites
    or give special favours to his
    children,
    but he protected your word
    and guarded your agreement.
10 He teaches your laws to the people of
    Jacob
    and your teachings to the people of
    Israel.

He burns incense before you
    and makes whole burnt offerings
    on your altar.
11 LORD, make them strong;
    be pleased with the work they do.
    Defeat those who attack them,
    and don't let their enemies rise up
    again."

12 Moses said this about the people of
    Benjamin:
    "The LORD's loved
    ones will lie down in
    safety,
    because he protects
    them all day long.
    The ones he loves rest
    with him."

> The LORD's loved ones will lie down in safety, because he protects them all day long.
> – Deuteronomy 33:12

13 Moses said this
    about the people of Joseph:
    "May the LORD bless their land with
    wonderful dew from heaven,
    with water from the springs below,
14 with the best fruits that the sun
    brings,
    and with the best fruits that the
    moon brings.
15 Let the old mountains give the finest
    crops,
    and let the everlasting hills give the
    best fruits.
16 Let the full earth give the best fruits,
    and let the LORD who lived in the
    burning bush be pleased.
    May these blessings rest on the head
    of Joseph,
    on the forehead of the one who
    was blessed among his brothers.
17 Joseph has the majesty of a firstborn
    bull;
    he is as strong as a wild ox.
    He will stab other nations,
    even those nations far away.
    These are the ten thousands of
    Ephraim,
    and these are the thousands of
    Manasseh."

18 Moses said this about the people of
Zebulun:
    "Be happy when you go out,
    Zebulun,

Deuteronomy 33:19   272

THE DELIVERER   Deuteronomy 34

1. Moses was born in Egypt to Israelite slaves. But Moses got to grow up in the king's palace when the king's daughter rescued him from a basket floating down the River Nile. Later, as a young man, he ran away to Midian because he killed an Egyptian guard to protect the Hebrew slaves. (Check out Exodus 2:1–15, p. 77.)

2. Moses worked for 40 years as a shepherd in Midian. He stayed with a man named Jethro and married one of his daughters, Zipporah. While he lived there, God talked to him from a burning bush and instructed Moses to return to Egypt and lead the Israelites out of Egypt. (Read Exodus 2:16—3:22, p. 78.)

3. Moses returned to Egypt. It took a series of 10 plagues – the final one where the firstborn son of every Egyptian died – to convince the king of Egypt to let the Israelites go free. (Look at Exodus 4:18—12:50, p. 81.)

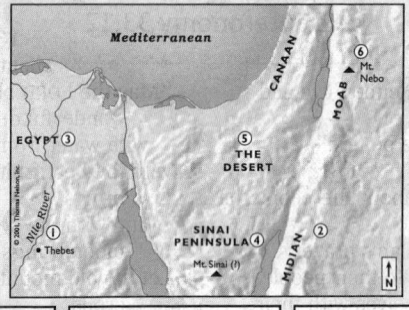

4. Moses and the Israelites travelled through the Sinai Peninsula. At Mount Sinai, God gave the Ten Commandments. (See Exodus 19 and 20, p. 100.)

5. Moses led the Israelites through the desert for 40 years while God prepared them to re-enter their homeland of Canaan. (Look up Numbers 14:20–34, p. 195.)

6. Joshua was appointed the new leader and the one to lead the people into the land God promised them. Moses died near Mount Nebo, overlooking the land of Canaan. (Check out Numbers 27:12–23, p. 213; Deuteronomy 34:1–9, p. 273.)

and be happy in your tents,
   Issachar.
19 They will call the people to the
      mountain,
   and there they will offer the right
      sacrifices.
   They will do well from all that is in
      the sea,
   and they will do well from the
      treasures hidden in the sand on
      the shore."

20 Moses said this about the people of Gad:
   "Praise God who gives Gad more
      land!

Gad lives there like a lion,
   who tears off arms and heads.
21 They chose the best land for
      themselves.
   They received a large share, like
      that given to an officer.
   When the leaders of the people
      gathered,
   the people of Gad did what the
      Lord said was right,
   and they judged Israel fairly."

22 Moses said this about the people of Dan:
   "Dan is like a lion's cub,
      who jumps out of Bashan."

23 Moses said this about the people of Naphtali:

"Naphtali enjoys special kindnesses,
  and they are full of the LORD's
    blessings.
Take as your own the west and
    south."

24 Moses said this about the people of Asher:

"Asher is the most blessed of the
    sons;
  let him be his brothers' favourite.
  Let him bathe his feet in olive oil.
25 Your gates will have locks of iron and
    bronze,
  and you will be strong as long as
    you live.

26 "There is no one like the God of
    Israel,
  who rides through the skies to
    help you,
  who rides on the clouds in his
    majesty.
27 The everlasting God is your place of
    safety,
  and his arms will hold you up for
    ever.
He will force your enemy out ahead
    of you,
  saying, 'Destroy the enemy!'
28 The people of Israel will lie down in
    safety.
Jacob's spring is theirs alone.
Theirs is a land full of grain and new
    wine,
  where the skies drop their dew.
29 Israel, you are blessed!
  No one else is like you,
  because you are a people saved by
    the LORD.
He is your shield and helper,
  your glorious sword.
Your enemies will be afraid of you,
  and you will walk all over their holy
    places."

Moses Dies

34 Then Moses climbed Mount Nebo from the plains of Moab to the top of Mount Pisgah, across from Jericho. From there the LORD showed him all the land from Gilead to Dan, 2 all of Naphtali and the lands of Ephraim and Manasseh, all the land of Judah as far as the Mediterranean Sea, 3 as well as the southern desert and the whole Valley of Jericho up to Zoar. (Jericho is called the city of palm trees.) 4 Then the LORD said to Moses, "This is the land I promised to Abraham, Isaac and Jacob when I said to them, 'I will give this land to your descendants.' I have let you look at it, Moses, but you will not cross over there."

5 Then Moses, the servant of the LORD, died there in Moab, as the LORD had said. 6 He buried Moses in Moab in the valley opposite Beth Peor, but even today no one knows where his grave is. 7 Moses was 120 years old when he died. His eyes were not weak, and he was still strong. 8 The Israelites cried for Moses for 30 days, staying in the plains of Moab until the time of sadness was over.

9 Joshua son of Nun was then filled with wisdom, because Moses had put his hands on him. So the Israelites listened to Joshua, and they did what the LORD had commanded Moses.

10 There has never been another prophet in Israel like Moses. The LORD knew Moses face to face 11 and sent him to do signs and miracles in Egypt—to the king, to all his officers and to the whole land of Egypt. 12 Moses had great power, and he did great and wonderful things for all the Israelites to see.

CONQUER THE LAND!

Hello! My name is Joshua. You may remember me as one of the 12 spies sent out by Moses to check out the land God promised to the Israelites. (Surf on over to Numbers 13, p. 193 for that story.) After Moses died, God made me the leader of his people. In this book, I describe how Israel conquered the land God promised them. Because the people already living in the land worshipped false gods and did many evil things, God wanted us to defeat these people completely. Don't miss any of the exciting stories of our many battles.

I wrote this book so everyone would know that God gave us victory in conquering the land he promised to us. When we followed his commands, he was with us in battle. You have probably already heard of our most famous victory: how we marched around the city of Jericho seven times, blew some trumpets, and the city walls fell down. (See Joshua 6 for the whole story. Also visit the plug-in about the town of Jericho, Let's Visit Jericho, Joshua 5.) When we were unfaithful, God allowed us to be defeated. (See the details of our most stunning defeat, when one man, Achan, sinned against God in Joshua 7.) After most of the country had been defeated, we divided the land among the tribes, or families, of God's people.

JESUS WATCH

Many people believe that the commander of the Lord's army mentioned in Joshua 5 is really Jesus. Notice that Joshua takes off his sandals in respect and calls the commander "master". In many ways, Joshua himself reminds us of Jesus. In fact, in Hebrew their names are the same and mean "the LORD saves". As a young man, Joshua was with Moses when Moses wrote down the laws of God. When he was a boy, Jesus studied these same laws. As a leader, Joshua urged the people to follow God and obey his laws. Jesus taught that the law pointed out our need for a saviour. Joshua led the people into a new land where God had promised to bless them richly. Jesus leads us to heaven where we will live for ever.

my FAVOURITE links

OTHER CONNECTIONS

Livin' it: Has anyone ever called you "brave" or "courageous"? What do you think it takes to be brave? Connect to Captain Courageous? Joshua 1:6–9, for some thoughts from God on being brave. Follow the Faithlinks for more information.

 The Book of Joshua has some incredible stories of adventures, battles and victories as the Israelites entered the land that God promised them. Connect to these sites for more information about:

- The stunning defeat of the town of Jericho at the hands – or should we say sounds – of the Israelites. Check it out and the other historical significance of this old Bible city by linking to Let's Visit Jericho, Joshua 5.

- Joshua's Victories, Joshua 11. Surf here for the highlights of Joshua and the Israelites' battle plan against the kings and people who occupied Canaan.

- After the Israelites had conquered the land, Joshua and the leaders had to fairly divide up the land among the 12 tribes. Find out how they did it by visiting Dividing the Land, Joshua 21.

Here's a puzzle for you. Why did the Gibeonites wear old clothes and carry old sacks?

Clue: it was a trick. Log on to Joshua 9 for the answer.

did you know?

OTHER COOL STORIES:
Spies in Jericho, Joshua 2
Rocks to remind us, Joshua 4:1–7
The commander of the Lord's army, Joshua 5:13–15
The sun stands still, Joshua 10:12–14

FAITH links

○ God's Pep Talk, Joshua 1:5–9

○ What Will You Risk? Joshua 2

○ Facts About Following, Joshua 6

○ Who Do You Trust? Joshua 9

○ The God of Big Things, Joshua 10

○ A Long Wait, Joshua 14:6–15

○ No Middle Ground, Joshua 24:14–15

God's Command to Joshua

1 After Moses, the servant of the LORD, died, the LORD spoke to Joshua son of Nun, Moses' assistant. 2 The LORD said, "My servant Moses is dead. Now you and all these people go across the Jordan River into the land I am giving to the Israelites. 3 I promised Moses I would give you this land, so I will give you every place you go in the land. 4 All the land from the desert in the south to Lebanon in the north will be yours. All the land from the great river, the Euphrates, in the east, to the Mediterranean Sea in the west will be yours too, including the land of the Hittites. 5 No one will be able to defeat you all your life. Just as I was with Moses, so I will be with you. I will not leave you or forget you.

6 "Joshua, be strong and brave! You must lead these people so they can take the land that I promised their fathers I would give them. 7 Be strong and brave. Be sure to obey all the teachings my servant Moses gave you. If you follow them exactly, you will be successful in everything you do. 8 Always remember what is written in the Book of the Teachings. Study it day and night to be sure to obey everything that is written there. If you do this, you will be wise and successful in everything. 9 Remember that I commanded you to be strong and brave. Don't be afraid, because the LORD your God will be with you everywhere you go."

1:9 Courage
How can you be brave?

Joshua's Orders to the People

10 Then Joshua gave orders to the officers of the people: 11 "Go through the camp and tell the people, 'Get your supplies ready. Three days from now you will cross the Jordan River and take the land the LORD your God is giving you.'"

12 Then Joshua said to the people of Reuben, Gad and East Manasseh, 13 "Remember what Moses, the servant of the LORD, told you. He said the LORD your God would give you rest and would give you this land. 14 Now the LORD has given you this land east of the Jordan

---

FAITH links

GOD'S PEP TALK
JOSHUA 1:5-9

How do you usually face the big challenges of your life? Many sports team coaches give their teams a pep talk when they're about to go into the big game. That pep talk helps them to be strong and brave. Joshua and the Israelites were about to face one of the biggest challenges of their lives. They were about to move into the land that God promised them. They would have to fight many battles. That was scary! So God gave Joshua "the pep talk". After all, Joshua was the one who would lead them into battle. God's command to be strong and brave is one to remember when you're afraid.

Check out these other Faithlinks on being brave!

When You're Afraid, Genesis 32:9–12, p. 45

Listen Up! 1 Kings 19:11–13, p. 467

A Life-Saving Message, Esther 2:19–22, p. 650

Who Ya' Gonna Call? Psalm 3:4, p. 711

A Word About Worry, Matthew 6:25–34, p. 1284

Thoughts on Thoughts, Philippians 4:8–9, p. 1614

Joshua 1 277

COURAGE
Joshua 1:6–9

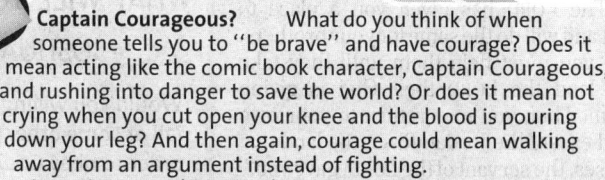

Captain Courageous? What do you think of when someone tells you to "be brave" and have courage? Does it mean acting like the comic book character, Captain Courageous, and rushing into danger to save the world? Or does it mean not crying when you cut open your knee and the blood is pouring down your leg? And then again, courage could mean walking away from an argument instead of fighting.

Sometimes coaches give their teams pep talks to help them be strong and courageous. God gave Joshua a pep talk, too, before Joshua was about to lead the Israelites into enemy territory. (Check Joshua 1:5–9.) How can God's pep talk help you when you are not feeling especially courageous?

The king of Assyria made fun of King Hezekiah because of his faith in God. But God gave Hezekiah a message of courage and hope. (Read 2 Kings 19:4–10, p. 505.)

MORE FAITH links

What Will You Risk? **p. 278**

Give In or Take a Stand? **p. 472**

Standing for What's Right, **p. 651**

Who Ya' Gonna Call? **p. 711**

Stand! **p. 1019**

If you want to be courageous, it doesn't mean you have to go around in a flowing cape and black mask, with your undies on over a pair of your mum's old tights (although that does sound pretty courageous!).

If you want to know more about real courage why don't you connect to these thinks?

The Big Risk, Esther 4:11—5:2, p. 652
- What's the biggest risk you've ever taken? What happened when you took this risk?
- What are some risks you may have to take in life? Where will you find the courage to deal with them? Surf here to find out where Esther got her courage.

Your Feet on High Places, Habakkuk 3:18–19, p. 1239
- Are you like a mountain goat, unafraid and skipping along, no matter what? Link here to discover how to deal with the good and bad times in your life.

Be Brave! Haggai 2:4, p. 1249
- What fears, if any, stop you from serving God? How do you handle fear of failure and discouragement? Find out how to trust God to help you be courageous and do whatever he has called you to do.

As Strong as Superman? Philippians 4:13, p. 1615
- Do you ever worry about what you can't do? Find out how you can "do all things" by linking here.

River. Your wives, children and animals may stay here, but your fighting men must dress for war and cross the Jordan River ahead of your brothers to help them. **15** The LORD has given you a place to rest and will do the same for your brothers. But you must help them until they take the land the LORD their God is giving them. Then you may return to your own land east of the Jordan River, the land that Moses, the servant of the LORD, gave you."

16 Then the people answered Joshua, "Whatever you command us to do, we will do. Wherever you send us, we will go. **17** Just as we fully obeyed Moses, we will obey you. We ask only that the LORD your God be with you just as he was with Moses. **18** Whoever refuses to obey your commands or turns against you will be put to death. Just be strong and brave!"

Spies Sent to Jericho

2 Joshua son of Nun secretly sent out two spies from Acacia and said to them, "Go and look at the land, particularly at the city of Jericho."

So the men went to Jericho and stayed at the house of a prostitute named Rahab. **2** Someone told the king of Jericho, "Some men from Israel have come here tonight to spy out the land." **3** So the king of Jericho sent this message to Rahab: "Bring out the men who came to you and entered your house. They have come to spy out our whole land."

4 But the woman had hidden the two men. She said, "They did come here, but I didn't know where they came from. **5** In the evening, when it was time to close the city gate, they left. I don't know where they went, but if you go quickly, maybe you can catch them." **6** (The woman had taken the men up to the roof[n] and had hidden them there under stalks of flax that she had spread out.) **7** So the king's men went out looking for the spies on the road that leads to the crossings of the Jordan River. The city gate was closed just after the king's men left the city.

8 Before the spies went to sleep for the night, Rahab went up to the roof. **9** She said to them, "I know the LORD has given this land to your people. You frighten us very much. Everyone living in this land is terribly afraid of you **10** because

---

FAITH links

WHAT WILL YOU RISK?
JOSHUA 2

Would you willingly risk going to jail or some other punishment in order to obey God? Rahab chose to hide two spies from Israel. The king of her city found out about the spies and wanted to capture them. But Rahab knew that God was with them. She disobeyed a command of the king in order to save the two men from Israel. Had she been caught, she would have been punished.

Obeying God takes courage. It takes a willingness to face the risks that come your way. What are you willing to risk to serve God?

Give In or Take a Stand? 1 Kings 22:13–14, p. 472

A Message of Courage and Hope, 2 Kings 19:4–10, p. 505

Fear God or People? Jeremiah 38:14–21, p. 1047

A Real Crowd-pleaser? Micah 2:6–11, p. 1222

Be Brave! Haggai 2:4, p. 1249

Facing Your Fears, Matthew 8:23–27, p. 1288

2:6 roof In Bible times houses were built with flat roofs. The roof was used for drying things such as flax and fruit. And it was used as an extra room, as a place for worship and as a place to sleep in the summer.

we have heard how the LORD dried up the Red Sea when you came out of Egypt. We have heard how you destroyed Sihon and Og, two Amorite kings who lived east of the Jordan. 11 When we heard this, we were very frightened. Now our men are afraid to fight you because the LORD your God rules the heavens above and the earth below! 12 So now, promise me before the LORD that you will show kindness to my family just as I showed kindness to you. Give me some proof that you will do this. 13 Allow my father, mother, brothers, sisters and all of their families to live. Save us from death."

2:12 Kindness
Show kindness to others.

14 The men agreed and said, "It will be our lives for your lives if you don't tell anyone what we are doing. When the LORD gives us the land, we will be kind and true to you."

15 The house Rahab lived in was built on the city wall, so she used a rope to let the men down through a window. 16 She said to them, "Go into the hills so the king's men will not find you. Hide there for three days. After the king's men return, you may go on your way."

17 The men said to her, "You must do as we say. If not, we cannot be responsible for keeping this oath you have made us swear. 18 When we return to this land, you must tie this red rope in the window through which you let us down. Bring your father, mother, brothers and all your family into your house. 19 If anyone leaves your house and is killed, it is his own fault. We cannot be responsible for him. If anyone in your house is hurt, we will be responsible. 20 But if you tell anyone about this, we will be free from the oath you made us swear."

21 Rahab answered, "I agree to this." So she sent them away, and they left. Then she tied the red rope in the window.

22 The men left and went into the hills where they stayed for three days. The king's men looked for them all along the road, but after three days, they returned to the city without finding them. 23 Then the two men started back. They left the hills and crossed the river and came to Joshua son of Nun and told him everything that had happened to them. 24 They said, "The LORD surely has given us all of the land. All the people in that land are terribly afraid of us."

Crossing the Jordan

3 Early the next morning Joshua and all the Israelites left Acacia. They travelled to the Jordan River and camped there before crossing it. 2 After three days the officers went through the camp 3 and gave orders to the people: "When you see the priests and Levites carrying the Ark of the Agreement with the LORD your God, leave where you are and follow it. 4 That way you will know which way to go since you have never been here before. But do not follow too closely. Stay about a kilometre behind the Ark."

5 Then Joshua told the people, "Make yourselves holy, because tomorrow the LORD will do amazing things among you."

6 Joshua said to the priests, "Take the Ark of the Agreement and go ahead of the people." So the priests lifted the Ark and carried it ahead of the people.

7 Then the LORD said to Joshua, "Today I will begin to make you great in the opinion of all the Israelites so the people will know I am with you just as I was with Moses. 8 Tell the priests who carry the Ark of the Agreement to go to the edge of the Jordan River and stand in the water."

9 Then Joshua said to the Israelites, "Come here and listen to the words of the LORD your God. 10 Here is proof that the living God is with you and that he will force out the

3:9 Advice
Need advice? Here's the place to start.

Canaanites, Hittites, Hivites, Perizzites, Girgashites, Amorites and Jebusites. 11 The Ark of the Agreement with the Lord of the whole world will go ahead of you into the Jordan River. 12 Now choose twelve men from among you, one from each of the twelve tribes of Israel. 13 The priests will carry the Ark of the LORD, the Master of the whole world, into the

Jordan ahead of you. When they step into the water, it will stop. The river will stop flowing and will stand up in a heap."

14 So the people left the place where they had camped, and they followed the priests who carried the Ark of the Agreement across the Jordan River. 15 During harvest the Jordan overflows its banks. When the priests carrying the Ark came to the edge of the river and stepped into the water, 16 the water a great distance away stopped flowing. It stood up in a heap a great distance away at Adam, a town near Zarethan. The water flowing down to the Sea of Arabah (the Dead Sea) was completely cut off. So the people crossed the river near Jericho. 17 The priests carried the Ark of the Agreement with the LORD to the middle of the river and stood there on dry ground. They waited there while all the people of Israel walked across the Jordan River on dry land.

Rocks to Remind the People

4 After all the people had finished crossing the Jordan, the LORD said to Joshua, 2 "Choose twelve men from among the people, one from each tribe. 3 Tell them to get twelve rocks from the middle of the river, from where the priests stood. Carry the rocks and put them down where you stay tonight."

4 So Joshua chose one man from each tribe. Then he called the twelve men together 5 and said to them, "Go out into the river where the Ark of the LORD your God is. Each of you bring back one rock, one for each tribe of Israel, and carry it on your shoulder. 6 They will be a sign among you. In the future your children will ask you, 'What do these rocks mean?' 7 Tell them the water stopped flowing in the Jordan when the Ark of the Agreement with the LORD crossed the river. These rocks will always remind the Israelites of this."

8 So the Israelites obeyed Joshua and carried twelve rocks from the middle of the Jordan River, one rock for each of the twelve tribes of Israel, just as the LORD had commanded Joshua. They carried the rocks with them and put them down where they made their camp. 9 Joshua also put twelve rocks in the middle of the

---

FAITH links

FAITH OF OUR FATHERS
JOSHUA 4:4-9

Whenever something special happens to a group of people or a country, the story of that event is usually passed on from one generation to another. We know about most wars because the stories of what happened have been passed down. The Israelites were about to cross the River Jordan and enter the land God promised to them. Joshua had them build a memorial out of stones. He knew how important it was to pass on the story of their journey to the children yet to come.

Stories of faith are important to pass on. They remind us of the ways that God helps people. If you think about it, ask your parents to tell you their faith story. They'll be glad that you asked.

Link here for other thoughts on sharing your faith:

Learning from Mistakes, Psalm 51:12–13, p. 748

A Picture of the Past, Psalm 105, p. 789

A Bad Reaction, Jeremiah 36, p. 1043

Pass It On! Joel 1:2–3, p. 1187

Flex Your Faith, Acts 3:1–16, p. 1467

The Doubt Remover, Romans 10:8–10, p. 1533

Jordan River where the priests had stood while carrying the Ark of the Agreement. These rocks are still there today.

10 The priests carrying the Ark continued standing in the middle of the river until everything was done that the LORD had commanded Joshua to tell the people, just as Moses had told Joshua. The people hurried across the river. 11 After they finished crossing the river, the priests carried the Ark of the LORD to the other side as the people watched. 12 The men from the tribes of Reuben, Gad and East Manasseh obeyed what Moses had told them. They were dressed for war, and they crossed the river ahead of the other people. 13 About 40,000 soldiers, prepared for war, passed before the LORD as they marched across the river, going towards the plains of Jericho.

14 That day the LORD made Joshua great in the opinion of all the Israelites. They respected Joshua all his life, just as they had respected Moses.

15 Then the LORD said to Joshua, 16 "Command the priests to bring the Ark of the Agreement out of the river."

17 So Joshua commanded the priests, "Come up out of the Jordan."

18 Then the priests carried the Ark of the Agreement with the LORD out of the river. As soon as their feet touched dry land, the water began flowing again. The river again overflowed its banks, just as it had before they crossed.

19 The people crossed the Jordan on the tenth day of the first month and camped at Gilgal, east of Jericho. 20 They carried with them the twelve rocks taken from the Jordan, and Joshua set them up at Gilgal. 21 Then he spoke to the Israelites: "In the future your children will ask you, 'What do these rocks mean?' 22 Tell them, 'Israel crossed the Jordan River on dry land. 23 The LORD your God caused the water to stop flowing until you finished crossing it, just as the LORD did to the Red Sea. He stopped the water until we crossed it. 24 The LORD did this so all people would know

4:24
God
Is God powerful?

he has great power and so you would always respect the LORD your God.'"

5 All the kings of the Amorites west of the Jordan and the Canaanite kings living by the Mediterranean Sea heard that the LORD dried up the Jordan River until the Israelites had crossed it. After that they were scared and too afraid to face the Israelites.

The Israelites are Circumcised

2 At that time the LORD said to Joshua, "Make knives from flint stones and circumcise the Israelites." 3 So Joshua made knives from flint stones and circumcised the Israelites at Gibeath Haaraloth.

4 This is why Joshua circumcised the men: after the Israelites left Egypt, all the men old enough to serve in the army died in the desert on the way out of Egypt. 5 The men who had come out of Egypt had been circumcised, but none of those who were born in the desert on the trip from Egypt had been circumcised. 6 The Israelites had moved about in the desert for 40 years. During that time all the fighting men who had left Egypt had died because they had not obeyed the LORD. So the LORD swore they would not see the land he had promised their ancestors to give them, a fertile land. 7 Their sons took their places. But none of the sons born on the trip from Egypt had been circumcised, so Joshua circumcised them. 8 After all the Israelites had been circumcised, they stayed in camp until they were healed.

9 Then the LORD said to Joshua, "As slaves in Egypt you were ashamed, but today I have removed that shame." So Joshua named that place Gilgal, which it is still named today.

10 The people of Israel were camped at Gilgal on the plains of Jericho. It was there, on the evening of the fourteenth day of the month, they celebrated the Passover Feast. 11 The day after the Passover, the people ate food grown on that land: bread made without yeast and roasted grain. 12 The day they ate this food, the manna stopped coming. The Israelites no longer got the manna from

Joshua 5:13

LET'S VISIT JERICHO   Joshua 5

The city of Jericho is an old, old city that was built just north of the Dead Sea. In the Old Testament, when the Hebrews entered the Promised Land, Jericho was the first city they captured. They marched around the walls of Jericho for six days. On the seventh day, the walls of the city miraculously fell down when the priests blew their trumpets and the people shouted, and the Israelites took over the city. (Check out Joshua 6.)

In the New Testament, Jesus spent time in Jericho. This is where he told the story of the Good Samaritan. (Check out Luke 10:30–37, p. 1388.) It's also where he met blind Bartimaeus (read Mark 10:46–52, p. 1348) and Zacchaeus (look at Luke 19:1–10, p. 1406).

Today Jericho is called er-Riha. It sits at the bottom of a deep gorge, like a canyon, and is a hot, tropical place.

---

heaven. They ate the food grown in the land of Canaan that year.

13 Joshua was near Jericho when he looked up and saw a man standing in front of him with a sword in his hand. Joshua went to him and asked, "Are you a friend or an enemy?"

14 The man answered, "I am neither. I have come as the commander of the LORD's army."

Then Joshua bowed face down on the ground and asked, "Does my master have a command for me, his servant?"

15 The commander of the LORD's army answered, "Take off your sandals, because the place where you are standing is holy." So Joshua did.

The Fall of Jericho

6 The people of Jericho were afraid because the Israelites were near. They closed the city gates and guarded them. No one went into the city, and no one came out.

2 Then the LORD said to Joshua, "Look, I have given you Jericho, its king, and all its fighting men. 3 March around the city with your army once a day for six days. 4 Have seven priests carry trumpets made from horns of rams and have them march in front of the Ark. On the seventh day march around the city seven times and have the priests blow the trumpets as they march. 5 They will make one long blast on the trumpets. When you hear that sound, have all the people give a loud shout. Then the walls of the city will fall so the people can go straight into the city."

6 So Joshua son of Nun called the priests together and said to them, "Carry the Ark of the Agreement. Tell seven priests to carry trumpets and march in front of it." 7 Then Joshua ordered the people, "Now go! March around the city. The soldiers with weapons should march in front of the Ark of the Agreement with the LORD."

8 When Joshua finished speaking to the people, the seven priests began marching before the LORD. They carried the seven trumpets and blew them as they marched. The priests carrying the Ark of the Agreement with the LORD followed them. 9 Soldiers with weapons marched in front of the priests, and armed men walked behind the Ark. The priests were blowing their trumpets. 10 But Joshua had told the people not to give a war cry. He said, "Don't shout. Don't say a word until the day I tell you. Then shout." 11 So Joshua had the Ark of the LORD carried around the city once. Then they went back to camp for the night.

front of the Ark of the LORD, blowing their trumpets. Soldiers with weapons marched in front of them, and other soldiers walked behind the Ark of the LORD. All this time the priests were blowing their trumpets. 14 So on the second day they marched around the city once and then went back to camp. They did this every day for six days.

15 On the seventh day they got up at dawn and marched around the city, just as they had on the days before. But on that day they marched around the city seven times. 16 The seventh time around the priests blew their trumpets. Then Joshua gave the command: "Now, shout! The LORD has given you this city! 17 The city and everything in it are to be destroyed as an offering to the LORD. Only Rahab the prostitute and everyone in her house should remain alive. They must not be killed, because Rahab hid the two spies we sent out. 18 Don't take any of the things that are to be destroyed as an offering to the LORD. If you take them and bring them into our camp, you yourselves will be destroyed, and you will bring trouble to all of Israel. 19 All the silver and gold and things made from bronze and iron belong to the LORD and must be saved for him."

20 When the priests blew the trumpets, the people shouted. At the sound of the trumpets and the people's shout, the walls fell, and everyone ran straight into the city. So the Israelites defeated that city. 21 They completely destroyed with the sword every living thing in the city—men and women, young and old, cattle, sheep and donkeys.

22 Joshua said to the two men who had spied out the land, "Go into the prostitute's house. Bring her out and bring out those who are with her, because of the promise you made to her." 23 So the two men went into the house and brought out Rahab, her father, mother, brothers and all those with her. They put all of her family in a safe place outside the camp of Israel.

24 Then Israel burned the whole city and everything in it, but they did not burn the things made from silver, gold, bronze

FAITH links

FACTS ABOUT FOLLOWING
JOSHUA 6

What are the weirdest instructions you ever had to follow? More than likely those instructions didn't involve walking around a city once a day for six days and seven times on the seventh day. Yet those were the instructions the people of Israel had to follow for taking over the city of Jericho! They had to listen carefully and do exactly what God told them. Otherwise, nothing would happen. Because of their obedience, the wall around the city of Jericho fell.

God expects you to listen carefully to his instructions. Listening is the first step to obedience.

Help to Understand, 2 Samuel 14, p. 416

A Look for the Book, 2 Chronicles 34:14–18, p. 603

If You Want My Advice... Proverbs 13:1, p. 843

Like a Tree, Jeremiah 17:5–8, p. 1016

Going My Way? Hosea 8:1–6, p. 1179

Two Ways to Grow, Luke 2:46–52, p. 1370

12 Early the next morning Joshua got up, and the priests carried the Ark of the LORD again. 13 The seven priests carried the seven trumpets and marched in

and iron. These were saved for the LORD. 25 Joshua saved Rahab the prostitute, her family and all who were with her, because Rahab had helped the men he had sent to spy out Jericho. Rahab still lives among the Israelites today.

26 Then Joshua made this oath:
"Anyone who tries to rebuild this city
of Jericho
will be cursed by the LORD.
The one who lays the foundation of
this city
will lose his oldest son,
and the one who sets up the gates
will lose his youngest son."

6:27 Success
Who gives you success?

27 So the LORD was with Joshua, and Joshua became famous through all the land.

The Sin of Achan

7 But the Israelites did not obey the LORD. There was a man from the tribe of Judah named Achan. (He was the son of Carmi and grandson of Zabdi, who was the son of Zerah.) Because Achan kept some of the things that were to be given to the LORD, the LORD became very angry at the Israelites.

2 Joshua sent some men from Jericho to Ai, which was near Beth Aven, east of Bethel. He told them, "Go to Ai and spy out the area." So the men went to spy on Ai.

3 Later they came back to Joshua and said, "There are only a few people in Ai, so we will not need all our people to defeat them. Send only 2,000 to 3,000 men to fight. There is no need to send all of our people." 4 So about 3,000 men went up to Ai, but the people of Ai beat them badly. 5 The people of Ai killed about 36 Israelites and then chased the rest from the city gate all the way down to the quarry, killing them as they went down the hill. When the Israelites saw this, they lost their courage.

6 Then Joshua tore his clothes in sorrow. He bowed face down on the ground before the Ark of the LORD and stayed there until evening. The elders of Israel did the same thing. They also threw dust on their heads to show their sorrow. 7 Then Joshua said, "Lord GOD, you brought our people across the Jordan River. Why did you bring us this far and then let the Amorites destroy us? We would have been happy to stay on the other side of the Jordan. 8 Lord, there is nothing I can say now. Israel has been beaten by the enemy. 9 The Canaanites and all the other people in this country will hear about this and will surround and kill us all! Then what will you do for your own great name?"

10 The LORD said to Joshua, "Stand up! Why are you down on your face? 11 The Israelites have sinned; they have broken the agreement I commanded them to obey. They took some of the things I commanded them to destroy. They have stolen and lied and have taken those things for themselves. 12 That is why the Israelites cannot face their enemies. They turn away from the fight and run, because I have commanded that they be destroyed. I will not help you any more unless you destroy everything as I commanded you.

13 "Now go! Make the people holy. Tell them, 'Set yourselves apart to the LORD for tomorrow. The LORD, the God of Israel, says some of you are keeping things he commanded you to destroy. You will never defeat your enemies until you throw away those things.

14 "'Tomorrow morning you must be present with your tribes. The LORD will choose one tribe to stand alone before him. Then the LORD will choose one family group from that tribe to stand before him. Then the LORD will choose one family from that family group to stand before him, person by person. 15 The one who is keeping what should have been destroyed will himself be destroyed by fire. Everything he owns will be destroyed with him. He has broken the agreement with the LORD and has done a disgraceful thing among the people of Israel!'"

16 Early the next morning Joshua led all of Israel to present themselves in their tribes, and the LORD chose the tribe of Judah. 17 So the family groups of Judah

FAITH links

A HIDDEN SIN
JOSHUA 7

Ever hear the expression, "You can run, but you can't hide"? That means you'll be found out, no matter what you do. Many people think they can do something wrong and never be found out. That's what Achan believed. He stole some items from the ruins of the city of Jericho despite strict instructions from God not to take anything. He tried to hide what he did, but God found out anyway.

Sin can never be hidden from God. He sees everything, because he is everywhere. We may fool others, but we can never fool God. Don't be an Achan or you'll be achin' spiritually. You can run, but you can't hide.

Here's some more advice on what to do with your sin.

A Priest Without Sin, Leviticus 4:3–7, p. 136

When the Green-eyed Monster Strikes, 1 Samuel 18:6–9, p. 379

This Hurts Me More? 2 Chronicles 36:17–22, p. 606

A Swarm of Trouble, Joel 2:25–27, p. 1190

The Choices of a Choice, Luke 5:1–11, p. 1375

The Sin "Braker", Jude 24–25, p. 1727

---

presented themselves, and the LORD then chose the family group of Zerah. When all the families of Zerah presented themselves, the family of Zabdi was chosen. 18 And Joshua told all the men in that family to present themselves. The LORD chose Achan son of Carmi. (Carmi was the son of Zabdi, who was the son of Zerah.)

19 Then Joshua said to Achan, "My son, tell the truth. Confess to the LORD, the God of Israel. Tell me what you did, and don't try to hide anything from me."

20 Achan answered, "It is true! I have sinned against the LORD, the God of Israel. This is what I did: 21 among the things I saw was a beautiful coat from Babylonia and about 2 kilogrammes of silver and more than half a kilogramme of gold. I wanted these things very much for myself, so I took them. You will find them buried in the ground under my tent, with the silver underneath."

22 So Joshua sent men who ran to the tent and found the things hidden there, with the silver. 23 The men brought them out of the tent, took them to Joshua and all the Israelites, and spread them out on the ground before the LORD. 24 Then Joshua and all the people led Achan son of Zerah to the Valley of Trouble. They also took the silver, the coat, the gold, Achan's sons, daughters, cattle, donkeys, sheep, tent and everything he owned. 25 Joshua said, "I don't know why you caused so much trouble for us, but now the LORD will bring trouble to you." Then all the people threw stones at Achan and his family until they died. Then the people burned them. 26 They piled rocks over Achan's body, and they are still there today. That is why it is called the Valley of Trouble. After this the LORD was no longer angry.

Ai is Destroyed

8 Then the LORD said to Joshua, "Don't be afraid or give up. Lead all your fighting men to Ai. I will help you defeat the king of Ai, his people, his city and his land. 2 You will do to Ai and its king what you did to Jericho

8:1 Troubles
Who cheers you on to win victories?

and its king. Only this time you may take all the wealth and keep it for yourselves. Now tell some of your soldiers to set up an ambush behind the city."

3 So Joshua led his whole army towards Ai. Then he chose 30,000 of his best fighting men and sent them out at night. 4 Joshua gave them these orders: "Listen carefully. You must set up an ambush behind the city. Don't go far from it, but continue to watch and be ready. 5 I and the men who are with me will march towards the city, and the men in the city will come out to fight us, just as they did before. Then we will turn and run away from them. 6 They will chase us away from the city, thinking we are running away from them as we did before. When we run away, 7 come out from your ambush and take the city. The LORD your God will give you the power to win. 8 After you take the city, burn it. See to it! You have your orders."

9 Then Joshua sent them to wait in ambush between Bethel and Ai, to the west of Ai. But Joshua stayed the night with his people.

10 Early the next morning Joshua gathered his men together. He and the elders of Israel led them up to Ai. 11 All of the soldiers who were with Joshua marched up to Ai and stopped in front of the city and made camp north of it. There was a valley between them and the city. 12 Then Joshua chose about 5,000 men and set them in ambush in the area west of the city between Bethel and Ai. 13 So the people took their positions; the main camp was north of the city, and the other men were hiding to the west. That night Joshua went down into the valley.

14 Now when the king of Ai saw the army of Israel, he and his people got up early the next morning and hurried out to fight them. They went out to a place east of the city, but the king did not know soldiers were waiting in ambush behind the city. 15 Joshua and all the men of Israel let the army of Ai push them back. Then they ran towards the desert. 16 The men in Ai were called to chase Joshua and his men, so they left the city and went after them. 17 All the men of Ai and Bethel chased the army of Israel. The city was left open; not a man stayed to protect it.

18 Then the LORD said to Joshua, "Hold your spear towards Ai, because I will give you that city." So Joshua held his spear towards the city of Ai. 19 When the Israelites who were in ambush saw this, they quickly came out of their hiding place and hurried towards the city. They entered the city, took control of it, and quickly set it on fire.

20 When the men of Ai looked back, they saw smoke rising from their city. At the same time the Israelites stopped running and turned against the men of Ai, who could not escape in any direction. 21 When Joshua and all his men saw that the army had taken control of the city and saw the smoke rising from it, they stopped running and turned to fight the men of Ai. 22 The men who were in ambush also came out of the city to help with the fight. So the men of Ai were caught between the armies of Israel. None of the enemy escaped. The Israelites fought until not one of the men of Ai was left alive, except 23 the king of Ai, and they brought him to Joshua.

A Review of the Fighting

24 During the fighting the army of Israel chased the men of Ai into the fields and desert and killed all of them. Then they went back to Ai and killed everyone there. 25 All the people of Ai died that day, 12,000 men and women. 26 Joshua had held his spear towards Ai, as a sign to destroy the city, and did not draw it back until all the people of Ai were destroyed. 27 The people of Israel kept for themselves the animals and the other things the people of Ai had owned, as the LORD had commanded Joshua to do.

28 Then Joshua burned the city of Ai and made it a pile of ruins. And it is still like that today. 29 Joshua hanged the king of Ai on a tree and left him there until evening. At sunset Joshua told his men to take the king's body down from the tree and to throw it down at the city gate. Then they covered it with a pile of rocks, which is still there today.

30 Joshua built an altar for the LORD, the God of Israel, on Mount Ebal, as 31 Moses, the LORD's servant, had commanded. Joshua built the altar as it was explained in the Book of the Teachings of Moses. It was made from uncut stones; no tool was ever used on them. On that altar the Israelites offered burnt offerings to the LORD and fellowship offerings. 32 There Joshua wrote the teachings of Moses on stones for all the people of Israel to see. 33 The elders, officers, judges and all the Israelites were there; Israelites and non-Israelites were all standing around the Ark of the Agreement with the LORD in front of the priests, the Levites who had carried the Ark. Half of the people stood in front of Mount Ebal, and half stood in front of Mount Gerizim. This was the way the LORD's servant Moses had earlier commanded the people to be blessed.

34 Then Joshua read all the words of the teachings, the blessings and the curses, exactly as they were written in the Book of the Teachings. 35 All the Israelites were gathered together—men, women and children—along with the non-Israelites who lived among them. Joshua read every command that Moses had given.

The Gibeonite Trickery

9 All the kings west of the Jordan River heard about these things: the kings of the Hittites, Amorites, Canaanites, Perizzites, Hivites and Jebusites. They lived in the mountains and on the western hills and along the whole Mediterranean Sea coast. 2 So all these kings gathered to fight Joshua and the Israelites.

3 When the people of Gibeon heard how Joshua had defeated Jericho and Ai, 4 they decided to trick the Israelites. They gathered old sacks and old leather wine bags that were cracked and mended, and they put them on the backs of their donkeys. 5 They put old sandals on their feet and wore old clothes, and they took some dry, mouldy bread. 6 Then they went to Joshua in the camp near Gilgal. The men said to Joshua and the

FAITH links

WHO DO YOU TRUST?
JOSHUA 9

Do you know when someone is trying to trick you? The Israelites would have to answer no to that question. The people of Gibeon tricked them into believing that they lived far away. But they really lived nearby. God had told Israel not to make a treaty with the people in Canaan. But the Israelites made an agreement with the people of Gibeon before they realised that they had been tricked.

We need God's wisdom to know when to trust and when not to. When in doubt about who to trust, here's a simple rule to remember. *Always* trust God. When you do that, you've already begun to be wise.

Surf here for some more thoughts on being a wise guy – or girl!

From Zero to Hero, Judges 6; 7, p. 319

An Admirable Quality, 1 Kings 10:1–13, p. 451

Wisdom in Store, Proverbs 2:6–7, p. 828

Down on Discipline? Proverbs 29:15, p. 867

Small Beginnings, Zechariah 4:10, p. 1255

The Winner's Crown, 1 Corinthians 9:24–27, p. 1555

Israelites, "We have travelled from a faraway country. Make a peace agreement with us."

7 The Israelites said to these Hivites, "Maybe you live near us. How can we make a peace agreement with you?"

8 The Hivites said to Joshua, "We are your servants."

But Joshua asked, "Who are you? Where do you come from?"

9 The men answered, "We are your servants who have come from a far country, because we heard of the fame of the LORD your God. We heard about what he has done and everything he did in Egypt. 10 We heard that he defeated the two kings of the Amorites from the east side of the Jordan River—Sihon king of Heshbon and Og king of Bashan who ruled in Ashtaroth. 11 So our elders and our people said to us, 'Take food for your journey and go and meet the Israelites. Tell them, "We are your servants. Make a peace agreement with us."'

12 "Look at our bread. On the day we left home to come to you it was warm and fresh, but now it is dry and mouldy. 13 Look at our leather wine bags. They were new and filled with wine, but now they are cracked and old. Our clothes and sandals are worn out from the long journey."

14 The men of Israel tasted the bread, but they did not ask the LORD what to do. 15 So Joshua agreed to make peace with the Gibeonites and to let them live. And the leaders of the Israelites swore an oath to keep the agreement.

16 Three days after they had made the agreement, the Israelites learned that the Gibeonites lived nearby. 17 So the Israelites went to where they lived and on the third day came to their cities: Gibeon, Kephirah, Beeroth and Kiriath Jearim. 18 But the Israelites did not attack those cities, because they had made a promise to them before the LORD, the God of Israel.

All the Israelites grumbled against the leaders. 19 But the leaders answered, "We have given our promise before the LORD, the God of Israel, so we cannot attack them now. 20 This is what we must do. We must let them live. Otherwise, God's anger will be against us for breaking the oath we swore to them. 21 So let them live, but they will cut wood and carry water for our people." So the leaders kept their promise to them.

22 Joshua called for the Gibeonites and asked, "Why did you lie to us? Your land was near our camp, but you told us you were from a far country. 23 Now, you will be placed under a curse to be our slaves. You will have to cut wood and carry water for the house of my God."

24 The Gibeonites answered Joshua, "We lied to you because we were afraid you would kill us. We heard that the LORD your God commanded his servant Moses to give you all of this land and to kill all the people who lived in it. That is why we did this. 25 Now you can decide what to do with us, whatever you think is right."

26 So Joshua saved their lives by not allowing the Israelites to kill them, 27 but he made the Gibeonites slaves. They cut wood and carried water for the Israelites, and they did it for the altar of the LORD— wherever he chose it to be. They are still doing this today.

The Sun Stands Still

10 At this time Adoni-Zedek king of Jerusalem heard that Joshua had defeated Ai and completely destroyed it, as he had also done to Jericho and its king. The king also learned that the Gibeonites had made a peace agreement with Israel and that they lived nearby. 2 Adoni-Zedek and his people were very afraid because of this. Gibeon was not a little town like Ai; it was a large city, as big as a city that had a king, and all its men were good fighters. 3 So Adoni-Zedek king of Jerusalem sent a message to Hoham king of Hebron, Piram king of Jarmuth, Japhia king of Lachish and Debir king of Eglon. He begged them, 4 "Come with me and help me attack Gibeon, which has made a peace agreement with Joshua and the Israelites."

5 Then these five Amorite kings—the kings of Jerusalem, Hebron, Jarmuth, Lachish and Eglon—gathered their armies, went to Gibeon, surrounded it and attacked it.

Joshua 10:21   289

his whole army, including his best fighting men. 8 The LORD said to Joshua, "Don't be afraid of those armies, because I will hand them over to you. None of them will be able to stand against you."

9 Joshua and his army marched all night from Gilgal for a surprise attack. 10 The LORD confused those armies when Israel attacked, so Israel defeated them in a great victory at Gibeon. They chased them along the road going up to Beth Horon and killed men all the way to Azekah and Makkedah. 11 As they chased the enemy down the Beth Horon Pass to Azekah, the LORD threw large hailstones on them from the sky and killed them. More people were killed by the hailstones than by the Israelites' swords.

12 On the day that the LORD gave up the Amorites to the Israelites, Joshua stood before all the people of Israel and said to the LORD:

"Sun, stand still over Gibeon.
Moon, stand still over the Valley of Aijalon."
13 So the sun stood still,
and the moon stopped
until the people defeated their enemies.

These words are written in the Book of Jashar.

The sun stopped in the middle of the sky and waited to go down for a full day. 14 That has never happened at any time before that day or since. That was the day the LORD listened to a human being. Truly the LORD was fighting for Israel!

15 After this, Joshua and his army went back to the camp at Gilgal.

16 During the fight the five kings ran away and hid in a cave near Makkedah, 17 but someone found them hiding in the cave at Makkedah and told Joshua. 18 So he said, "Cover the opening of the cave with large rocks. Put some men there to guard it, 19 but don't stay there yourselves. Continue chasing the enemy and attacking them from behind. Don't let them get to their cities, because the LORD your God will hand them over to you."

20 So Joshua and the Israelites killed the enemy, but a few were able to get back to their fortified cities. 21 After

---

FAITH links

THE GOD OF BIG THINGS
JOSHUA 10

Have you ever read a tall story? Tall stories are fictitious tales about real people who did amazing things. The story of King Canute is a tall story. He was a very powerful king whose followers thought he was so great he could control the sea. He couldn't, of course, and got soaking wet! One of the most amazing things that ever happened did not take place in a made-up story. It happened in real life! God made the sun stand still during one of Israel's battles. Only God can control the forces of nature. Since he can do that, we can trust that God can do anything.

From Hopeless to Hopeful, Exodus 6:9, p. 83

How God Speaks, Job 33:14–17, p. 696

In Deep Water, Psalm 69, p. 760

Believe the Impossible? Ezekiel 37, p. 1131

A Safe Place, Nahum 1:7, p. 1231

Go for It! Hebrews 12:1–4, p. 1682

---

6 The Gibeonites sent this message to Joshua in his camp at Gilgal: "Don't let us, your servants, be destroyed. Come quickly and help us! Save us! All the Amorite kings from the mountains have joined their armies and are fighting against us."

7 So Joshua marched out of Gilgal with

the fighting, Joshua's men came back safely to him at Makkedah. No one was brave enough to say a word against the Israelites.

22 Joshua said, "Move the rocks that are covering the opening of the cave and bring those five kings out to me." 23 So Joshua's men brought the five kings out of the cave—the kings of Jerusalem, Hebron, Jarmuth, Lachish and Eglon. 24 When they brought the five kings out to Joshua, he called for all his men. He said to the commanders of his army, "Come here! Put your feet on the necks of these kings." So they came close and put their feet on their necks.

**10:25
Enemies**
Who can defeat your enemies?

25 Joshua said to his men, "Be strong and brave! Don't be afraid, because I will show you what the LORD will do to the enemies you will fight in the future." 26 Then Joshua killed the five kings and hung their bodies on five trees, where he left them until evening.

27 At sunset Joshua told his men to take the bodies down from the trees. Then they threw them into the same cave where they had been hiding and covered the opening of the cave with large rocks, which are still there today.

28 That day Joshua defeated Makkedah. He killed the king and completely destroyed all the people in that city as an offering to the LORD; no one was left alive. He did the same thing to the king of Makkedah that he had done to the king of Jericho.

Defeating Southern Cities

29 Joshua and all the Israelites travelled from Makkedah to Libnah and attacked it. 30 The LORD handed over the city and its king. They killed every person in the city; no one was left alive. And they did the same thing to that king that they had done to the king of Jericho.

31 Then Joshua and all the Israelites left Libnah and went to Lachish, which they surrounded and attacked. 32 The LORD handed over Lachish on the second day. The Israelites killed everyone in that city just as they had done to Libnah. 33 During this same time Horam king of Gezer came to help Lachish, but Joshua also defeated him and his army; no one was left alive.

34 Then Joshua and all the Israelites went from Lachish to Eglon. They surrounded Eglon, attacked it and 35 captured it the same day. They killed all its people and completely destroyed everything in it as an offering to the LORD, just as they had done to Lachish.

36 Then Joshua and the Israelites went from Eglon to Hebron and attacked it, 37 capturing it and all the little towns near it. The Israelites killed everyone in Hebron; no one was left alive there. Just as they had done to Eglon, they completely destroyed the city and all its people as an offering to the LORD.

38 Then Joshua and the Israelites went back to Debir and attacked it. 39 They captured that city, its king and all the little towns near it, completely destroying everyone in Debir as an offering to the LORD; no one was left alive there. Israel did to Debir and its king just as they had done to Libnah and its king, just as they had done to Hebron.

40 So Joshua defeated all the kings of the cities of these areas: the mountains, southern Canaan, the western hills and the slopes. The LORD, the God of Israel, had told Joshua to completely destroy all the people as an offering to the LORD, so he left no one alive in those places. 41 Joshua captured all the cities from Kadesh Barnea to Gaza, and from Goshen to Gibeon. 42 He captured all these cities and their kings on one trip, because the LORD, the God of Israel, was fighting for Israel.

43 Then Joshua and all the Israelites returned to their camp at Gilgal.

Defeating Northern Kings

11 When Jabin king of Hazor heard about all that had happened, he sent messages to Jobab king of Madon, to the king of Shimron and to the king of Achshaph. 2 He sent messages to the kings in the northern mountains and also

GET THE INFO

CLAIMING THE PROMISED LAND — Joshua 11

Under Joshua's leadership, the Israelites were able to enter Canaan and defeat the people living there. It took Joshua and the Israelites about seven years to conquer the many kings and armies in the land. Here are some highlights of those important battles:

1. Under Joshua's military plan, the Israelites set up their main camp in the central part of Canaan at Gilgal. Joshua launched all his battles from there. (Read Joshua 4:19.)

2. In his first victory, Joshua and the Israelites conquered Jericho. The city walls toppled over when the Israelites shouted and blew their trumpets. (Check out Joshua 6.)

3. At Gibeon, the Israelites completed their conquest of the central part of Canaan when they defeated five Canaanite kings. God made the sun stand still until all Israel's enemies were defeated. (Look up Joshua 10:1–14.)

4. Joshua then turned south. He defeated and destroyed the cities of Lachish, Eglon, Hebron and Debir. (Read Joshua 10:29–43.)

5. Next Joshua headed north. He defeated three northern kings and their armies at the waters of Merom. (See Joshua 11:11–9.)

6. Joshua's last battle was an important one. His army destroyed and burned Hazor, a strong Canaanite fort. With that victory, Joshua and his army controlled all the area of Canaan. (Look up Joshua 11:10–16.)

---

to the kings in the Jordan Valley south of Lake Galilee and in the western hills. He sent a message to the king of Naphoth Dor in the west 3 and to the kings of the Canaanites in the east and in the west. He sent messages to the Amorites, Hittites, Perizzites and Jebusites in the mountains. Jabin also sent one to the Hivites, who lived below Mount Hermon in the area of Mizpah. 4 So the armies of all these kings came together with their horses and chariots. There were as many soldiers as grains of sand on the seashore.

5 All of these kings met together at the waters of Merom, joined their armies together into one camp, and made plans to fight against the Israelites.

6 Then the LORD said to Joshua, "Don't be afraid of them, because at this time tomorrow I will give them to you. You will cripple their horses and burn all their chariots."

7 So Joshua and his whole army surprised the enemy by attacking them at the waters of Merom. 8 The LORD handed them over to Israel. They chased them to Greater Sidon, Misrephoth Maim and the Valley of Mizpah in the east. Israel fought until none of the enemy was left alive. 9 Joshua did what the LORD said to do: he crippled their horses and burned their chariots.

10 Then Joshua went back and captured the city of Hazor and killed its king. (Hazor had been the leader of all the kingdoms that fought against Israel.) 11 Israel

killed everyone in Hazor, completely destroying them; no one was left alive. Then they burned Hazor itself.

12 Joshua captured all of these cities, killed all of their kings, and completely destroyed everything in these cities. He did this just as Moses, the servant of the LORD, had commanded. 13 But the Israelites did not burn any cities that were built on their hills, except Hazor; only that city was burned by Joshua. 14 The people of Israel kept for themselves everything they found in the cities, including all the animals. But they killed all the people there; they left no one alive. 15 Long ago the LORD had commanded his servant Moses to do this, and then Moses had commanded Joshua to do it. Joshua did everything the LORD had commanded Moses.

16 So Joshua defeated all the people in the land. He had control of the mountains and the area of southern Canaan, all the areas of Goshen, the western hills and the Jordan Valley. He controlled the mountains of Israel and all the hills near them. 17 Joshua controlled all the land from Mount Halak near Edom to Baal Gad in the Valley of Lebanon, below Mount Hermon. Joshua also captured all the kings in the land and killed them. 18 He fought against them for many years. 19 The people of only one city in all the land had made a peace agreement with Israel—the Hivites living in Gibeon. All the other cities were defeated in war. 20 The LORD made those people stubborn so they would fight against Israel and he could completely destroy them without mercy. This is what the LORD had commanded Moses to do.

21 Now Joshua fought the Anakites who lived in the mountains of Hebron, Debir, Anab, Judah and Israel, and he completely destroyed them and their towns. 22 There were no Anakites left living in the land of the Israelites and only a few were left in Gaza, Gath and Ashdod. 23 Joshua took control of all the land of Israel as the LORD had told Moses to do long ago. He gave the land to Israel, because he had promised it to them. Then Joshua divided the land among the tribes of Israel, and there was peace in the land.

Kings Defeated by Israel

12 The Israelites took control of the land east of the Jordan River from the Arnon Ravine to Mount Hermon and all the land along the eastern side of the Jordan Valley. These lands belonged to the kings whom the Israelites defeated.

2 Sihon king of the Amorites lived in the city of Heshbon and ruled the land from Aroer at the Arnon Ravine to the Jabbok River. His land started in the middle of the ravine, which was their border with the Ammonites. Sihon ruled over half the land of Gilead 3 and over the eastern side of the Jordan Valley from Lake Galilee to the Dead Sea. And he ruled from Beth Jeshimoth south to the slopes of Pisgah.

4 Og king of Bashan was one of the last of the Rephaites. He ruled the land in Ashtaroth and Edrei. 5 He ruled over Mount Hermon, Salecah and all the area of Bashan up to where the people of Geshur and Maacah lived. Og also ruled half the land of Gilead up to the border of Sihon king of Heshbon.

6 The LORD's servant Moses and the Israelites defeated all these kings, and Moses gave that land to the tribes of Reuben and Gad and to East Manasseh as their own.

7 Joshua and the Israelites also defeated kings in the land west of the Jordan River. He gave the people the land and divided it among the twelve tribes to be their own. It was between Baal Gad in the Valley of Lebanon and Mount Halak near Edom. 8 This included the mountains, the western hills, the Jordan Valley, the slopes, the desert and southern Canaan. This was the land where the Hittites, Amorites, Canaanites, Perizzites, Hivites and Jebusites had lived. The Israelites defeated the king of each of the following cities: 9 Jericho, Ai (near Bethel), 10 Jerusalem, Hebron, 11 Jarmuth, Lachish, 12 Eglon, Gezer, 13 Debir, Geder, 14 Hormah, Arad, 15 Libnah, Adullam, 16 Makkedah, Bethel, 17 Tappuah, Hepher, 18 Aphek, Lasharon, 19 Madon,

Hazor, 20 Shimron Meron, Achshaph, 21 Taanach, Megiddo, 22 Kedesh, Jokneam in Carmel, 23 Dor (in Naphoth Dor), Goyim in Gilgal and 24 Tirzah. The total number of kings was 31.

Land Still to be Taken

13 When Joshua was very old, the LORD said to him, "Joshua, you have grown old, but there is still much land for you to take. 2 This is what is left: the regions of Geshur and of the Philistines; 3 the area from the Shihor River at the border of Egypt to Ekron in the north, which belongs to the Canaanites; the five Philistine leaders at Gaza, Ashdod, Ashkelon, Gath and Ekron; the Avvites, 4 who live south of the Canaanite land; 5 the Gebalites, and the area of Lebanon east of Baal Gad below Mount Hermon to Lebo Hamath.

6 "The Sidonians are living in the hill country from Lebanon to Misrephoth Maim, but I will force all of them out ahead of the Israelites. Be sure to remember this land when you divide the land among the Israelites, as I told you.

7 "Now divide the land among the nine tribes and West Manasseh."

Dividing the Land

8 East Manasseh and the tribes of Reuben and Gad had received their land. The LORD's servant Moses had given them the land east of the Jordan River. 9 Their land started at Aroer at the Arnon Ravine and continued to the town in the middle of the ravine, and it included the whole plain from Medeba to Dibon. 10 All the towns ruled by Sihon king of the Amorites, who ruled in the city of Heshbon, were in that land. The land continued to the area where the Ammonites lived. 11 Gilead was also there, as well as the area where the people of Geshur and Maacah lived, and all of Mount Hermon and Bashan as far as Salecah. 12 All the kingdom of Og king of Bashan was in the land. Og was one of the last of the Rephaites, and in the past he had ruled in Ashtaroth and Edrei. Moses had defeated them and had taken their land. 13 Because the Israelites did not force out the people of Geshur and Maacah, they still live among the Israelites today.

14 The tribe of Levi was the only one that did not get any land. Instead, they were given all the burned sacrifices made to the LORD, the God of Israel, as he had promised them.

15 Moses had given each family group from the tribe of Reuben some land: 16 theirs was the land from Aroer near the Arnon Ravine to the town of Medeba, including the whole plain and the town in the middle of the ravine; 17 Heshbon and all the towns on the plain: Dibon, Bamoth Baal and Beth Baal Meon, 18 Jahaz, Kedemoth, Mephaath, 19 Kiriathaim, Sibmah, Zereth Shahar on the hill in the valley, 20 Beth Peor, the hills of Pisgah and Beth Jeshimoth. 21 So that land included all the towns on the plain and all the area that Sihon king of the Amorites had ruled from the town of Heshbon. Moses had defeated him along with the leaders of the Midianites, including Evi, Rekem, Zur, Hur and Reba. All these leaders fought together with Sihon and lived in that country. 22 The Israelites killed many people during the fighting, including Balaam of Beor, who tried to use magic to tell the future. 23 The land given to Reuben stopped at the shore of the Jordan River. So the land given to the family groups of Reuben included all these towns and their villages that were listed.

24 This is the land Moses gave to the tribe of Gad, to all its family groups: 25 the land of Jazar and all the towns of Gilead; half the land of the Ammonites that went as far as Aroer near Rabbah; 26 the area from Heshbon to Ramath Mizpah and Betonim; the area from Mahanaim to the land of Debir; 27 in the valley, Beth Haram, Beth Nimrah, Succoth and

Now divide the land among the nine tribes and West Manasseh.
— Joshua 13:7

Zaphon with the other land that Sihon king of Heshbon had ruled east of the Jordan River and continuing to the end of Lake Galilee. 28 All this land went to the family groups of Gad, including all these towns and their villages.

29 This is the land Moses had given to East Manasseh. Half of all the family groups in the tribe of Manasseh were given this land: 30 the land started at Mahanaim and included all of Bashan and the land ruled by Og king of Bashan; all the towns of Jair in Bashan, 60 cities in all; 31 half of Gilead, Ashtaroth and Edrei, the cities where Og king of Bashan had ruled. All this went to the family of Makir son of Manasseh, and half of all his sons were given this land.

32 Moses had given this land to these tribes on the plains of Moab across the Jordan River east of Jericho. 33 But Moses had given no land to the tribe of Levi because the LORD, the God of Israel, promised that he himself would be the gift for the Levites.

14 Eleazar the priest, Joshua son of Nun, and the leaders of all the tribes of Israel decided what land to give to the people in the land of Canaan. 2 The LORD had commanded Moses long ago how he wanted the people to choose their land. The people of the nine-and-a-half tribes threw lots to decide which land they would receive. 3 Moses had already given the two-and-a-half tribes their land east of the Jordan River. But the tribe of Levi was not given any land like the others. 4 The sons of Joseph had divided into two tribes—Manasseh and Ephraim. The tribe of Levi was not given any land. It was given only some towns in which to live and pastures for its animals. 5 The LORD had told Moses how to give the land to the tribes of Israel, and the Israelites divided the land.

Caleb's Land

6 One day some men from the tribe of Judah went to Joshua at Gilgal. Among them was Caleb son of Jephunneh the Kenizzite. He said to Joshua, "You remember what the LORD said at Kadesh Barnea when he was speaking to the prophet Moses about you and me. 7 Moses, the LORD's servant, sent me to look

---

FAITH links

A LONG WAIT
JOSHUA 14:6-15

Could you imagine having to wait 40 years to get something you were promised? Caleb was one of ten spies whom Moses sent to look over the land. Because of Israel's sin, both Caleb and Joshua had to wait 40 years to receive their inheritance. Caleb was 85 years old when he finally received his land!

God keeps his promises, although his timing might seem long in your understanding. God may not make you wait until you're 85 to give you something you've always wanted. He just wants you to trust his timing.

Don't like to wait? Connect to these Faithlinks to find out what God wants you to do:

I Want It Now! Judges 14:1–3, p. 332

Learning to Trust, Psalm 25:4–5, p. 727

Patience, Please, Psalm 145:8–9, p. 819

Think About Him, Isaiah 26:3, p. 926

Ask, Search, Knock, Matthew 7:7–10, p. 1286

At the Right Time, Galatians 4:4, p. 1590

Abraham: Open to Obedience

How quick are you to obey? When told to do something, would you rather whine or would you rather say "OK"? Being obedient to God takes faith and persistence. Sometimes it means following God even when you don't know where he is taking you! Don't believe it? Read the story of Abram, who God later renamed Abraham. Check out how Abraham responded when God told him to do something by turning the page to

Here's the Scoop

You'll find the number matches the question number on this page. Then decide for yourself: how open are you to obedience?

1. Have you ever moved to another house or to another part of the country? If your family had to move to a place you knew nothing about, how would you feel? What would you do?

2. Suppose your mum or dad promised to give you something you've always wanted, like a dog or your very own computer. The only condition is that you have to be obedient. And you would have to wait – a very long time. Would you be willing to be obedient even if you had to wait years to receive what you wanted?

3. Dependability is part of obedience. Would your friends and others around you consider you a dependable friend? Abram, who was now called Abraham, was considered a good friend. Find out what he did to earn that reputation.

4. If someone told you to change your first name, would you? Would you still do it if that person chose the name? Abram got a new name that changed his life.

5. Would you give up your most valued possession, immediately and willingly, if God told you to do so? Or would you try to "make a deal" with God and give up something of less value to you?

Here's the Scoop

1. God told Abram to leave most of his relatives in Ur and move. Abram didn't even know where he was going! He was 75 years old when he and his wife Sarai (later called Sarah) and nephew Lot set out. But Abram did exactly what God told him to do. God led him to a land called Canaan. Hundreds of years later, this land would be the land promised to Moses and the Israelites after they left Egypt. (See **Genesis 12:1-9**, p. 17.)

2. Imagine being able to have what you've always wanted. Abraham and his wife Sarah were unable to have children. But God had promised that one day they would have a son. During the wait, Abraham wasn't always obedient. But God kept his promise anyway. Finally, the promised son arrived. Abraham obediently named him Isaac, a name that God had given him (**Genesis 17:19**). (Read about it in **Genesis 21:1-3**, p. 27.)

3. Abraham was a friend of God. That's why God didn't keep his plans hidden from Abraham. He knew that Abraham would "command his children and his descendants to live the way the LORD wants them to, to live right and be fair" (**Genesis 18:19**). Obedience is the mark of friendship with God. That's why Jesus later told his disciples, "You are my friends if you do what I command you" (**John 15:14**). Are you a friend of God? (Check it out in **Genesis 18:17-19**, p. 24. See also **2 Chronicles 20:7**, p. 583.)

4. God had a good reason for telling Abram to change his name. His new name, Abraham, was like a promise from God. Abraham would be a "father of nations" and Abraham would have many descendants. But God also told him to "obey me and do what is right" (**Genesis 17:1**). Abraham was to continue following God. His change in name would be a constant reminder of God's special agreement between Abraham and his descendants. (Look up **Genesis 17:1-9**, p. 22.)

5. This was the ultimate test of obedience. Abraham was told to take the one thing he loved the most – his beloved and long-awaited son – and sacrifice him on a mountain. Abraham didn't ask questions. He didn't try to make a deal with God. He didn't whine or complain. He simply obeyed. Would you have made the same choice? God did not really want Abraham to sacrifice his son. But he was pleased that Abraham was obedient. (Read about it in **Genesis 22:1-19**, p. 29.)

Answers Page

Moses: Faith to Grow On

What do you know about Moses? That he was a Hebrew raised in an Egyptian palace? That he took on Pharaoh and won, thanks to God and the ten plagues? That he led the Israelites out of Egypt? Do you think that Moses instantly became mature in the faith or grew into it? Like you, Moses had to grow in faith. It didn't come overnight. God had a lot to teach the man who would become Israel's greatest prophet. Discover more about the lessons Moses had to learn by checking out

Here's the Scoop

on the following page. The numbers match the numbered questions on this page. As you see how Moses' faith developed, ask yourself: how is my faith growing?

1 Have you ever tried, but failed to do something good? When you failed, did you want to give up or try again? Everyone knows about Moses' successes. But did you also know about Moses' failures? Find out how Moses handled his failures and how God was able to take those failures and use them to help Moses grow in his faith.

2 When someone gives you a difficult task, is your first response to make excuses about why you can't do it? Or do you look for the possible ways to tackle the problem?

3 What do you think helps your faith to grow? Is it learning from your parents or Sunday school teacher? Is it reading the Bible or being with other Christians? Or is it seeing how God works in your life and in the lives of others?

4 When you've had a victory, what do you do first? Do you celebrate straight away, or do you say thanks to those people who helped you win? Do you stop to thank God?

5 When you haven't seen someone for a long time, what are they most likely to say to you? It's probably, "My, haven't you grown!" right? What do you think someone would say about your faith? Would they say that you've grown in that, too?

Here's the Scoop

1. Moses was the deliverer God planned to use to lead Israel out of slavery. After all, God had rescued him when other Hebrew baby boys were put to death. But when Moses became a man, he tried to do things his own way. Doing so caused him to have to run for his life. He had not yet learned what God could do. Many years would pass before he saw Egypt again. (Check it out in **Exodus 2:11–15**, p. 78.)

2. Moses spent 40 years as a shepherd in the desert of Midian. Watching sheep and goats was good training for being a leader of people! (Don't believe it? Try it sometime!) But when God called him through a burning bush to return to Egypt, Moses didn't want to go. He gave every excuse in the book to get out of going. Although Moses said, "No," God said, "Go!" (Read about it in **Exodus 3:1—4:17**, p. 79.)

3. Through the ten plagues, Moses and his brother Aaron delivered God's message to Pharaoh. That wasn't always easy! Moses and Aaron had to be persistent. Pharaoh's hard heart and God's strong hand helped Moses learn to rely on God. Finally, Pharaoh agreed to do what God had said all along that he would do. He let the people go. Seeing God at work was a real faith-builder for Moses! (See **Exodus 6—14**, p. 83.)

4. The Israelites had not gone very far when they encountered their first test of faith. With their backs to the Red Sea, they watched the approaching Egyptian army coming to capture them and take them back into slavery. Yet Moses remained confident in his faith that God would deliver them – and God did! Moses and the people responded by showing their gratitude and faith with this song of praise. (Read **Exodus 15:1–18**, p. 94.)

5. The closing sentences in the Book of Deuteronomy are a glowing tribute to a man who learned to be a great leader. Moses didn't do everything perfectly. In fact, one mistake cost him a home in the Promised Land. (For that story, read **Numbers 20:2–13**, p. 202 and **Deuteronomy 3:23–28**, p. 232.) Yet, despite the hardships, the failures and the setbacks, Moses' life is an example of how anyone can grow in faith. All it takes is a willingness to trust God. (Look up **Deuteronomy 34:10–12**, p. 273.)

at the land where we were going. I was 40 years old then. When I came back, I told Moses what I thought about the land. 8 The other men who went with me frightened the people, but I fully believed the LORD would allow us to take the land. 9 So that day Moses promised me, 'The land where you went will become your land, and your children will own it for ever. I will give you that land because you fully believed in the LORD, my God.'

10 "Now then, the LORD has kept his promise. He has kept me alive for 45 years from the time he said this to Moses during the time we all wandered in the desert. Now here I am, 85 years old. 11 I am still as strong today as I was the day Moses sent me out, and I am just as ready to fight now as I was then. 12 So give me the mountain country the LORD promised me that day long ago. Back then you heard that the Anakite people lived there and the cities were large and well protected. But now with the LORD helping me, I will force them out, just as the LORD said."

13 Joshua blessed Caleb son of Jephunneh and gave him the city of Hebron as his own. 14 Hebron still belongs to the family of Caleb son of Jephunneh the Kenizzite because he had faith and obeyed the LORD, the God of Israel. 15 (In the past it was called Kiriath Arba, named after Arba, the greatest man among the Anakites.)

After this there was peace in the land.

**14:10–11
Life**
Where do you get your strength?

Land for Judah

15 The land that was given to the tribe of Judah was divided among all the family groups. It went all the way to the Desert of Zin in the far south, at the border of Edom.

2 The southern border of Judah's land started at the south end of the Dead Sea 3 and went south of Scorpion Pass to Zin. From there it passed to the south of Kadesh Barnea and continued past Hezron to Addar. From Addar it turned and went to Karka. 4 It continued to Azmon, the brook of Egypt, and then to the Mediterranean Sea. This was the southern border.

5 The eastern border was the shore of the Dead Sea, as far as the mouth of the Jordan River.

The northern border started at the shore of the sea at the mouth of the Jordan River. 6 Then it went to Beth Hoglah and continued north of Beth Arabah to the stone of Bohan son of Reuben. 7 Then the northern border went through the Valley of Achor to Debir where it turned towards the north and went to Gilgal. Gilgal is across from the road that goes through Adummim Pass, on the south side of the ravine. The border continued to the waters of En Shemesh and stopped at En Rogel. 8 Then it went through the Valley of Ben Hinnom, next to the southern side of the Jebusite city (which is called Jerusalem). There the border went to the top of the hill on the west side of Hinnom Valley, at the northern end of the Valley of Giants. 9 From there it went to the spring of the waters of Nephtoah and then it went to the cities near Mount Ephron. There it turned and went towards Baalah, which is called Kiriath Jearim. 10 At Baalah the border turned west and went towards Mount Seir. It continued along the north side of Mount Jearim (also called Kesalon) and came to Beth Shemesh. From there it went past Timnah 11 to the hill north of Ekron. Then it turned towards Shikkeron and went past Mount Baalah and continued on to Jabneel, ending at the sea.

12 The Mediterranean Sea was the western border. Inside these borders lived the family groups of Judah.

13 The LORD had commanded Joshua to give Caleb son of Jephunneh part of the land in Judah, so he gave Caleb the town of Kiriath Arba, also called Hebron. (Arba was the father of Anak.) 14 Caleb forced out the three Anakite families living in Hebron: Sheshai, Ahiman and Talmai, the descendants of Anak. 15 Then he left there and went to fight against the people living in Debir. (In the past Debir had been called Kiriath Sepher.) 16 Caleb said, "I will give Achsah, my daughter, as a

wife to the man who attacks and captures the city of Kiriath Sepher." 17 Othniel son of Kenaz, Caleb's brother, captured the city, so Caleb gave his daughter Achsah to Othniel to be his wife. 18 When Achsah came to Othniel, she told him to ask her father for a field.

So Achsah went to her father. When she got down from her donkey, Caleb asked her, "What do you want?"

19 Achsah answered, "Do me a special favour. Since you have given me land in southern Canaan, also give me springs of water." So Caleb gave her the upper and lower springs.

20 The tribe of Judah got the land God had promised them. Each family group got part of the land.

21 The tribe of Judah got all these towns in the southern part of Canaan near the border of Edom: Kabzeel, Eder, Jagur, 22 Kinah, Dimonah, Adadah, 23 Kedesh, Hazor, Ithnan, 24 Ziph, Telem, Bealoth, 25 Hazor Hadattah, Kerioth Hezron (also called Hazor), 26 Amam, Shema, Moladah, 27 Hazar Gaddah, Heshmon, Beth Pelet, 28 Hazar Shual, Beersheba, Biziothiah, 29 Baalah, Iim, Ezem, 30 Eltolad, Kesil, Hormah, 31 Ziklag, Madmannah, Sansannah, 32 Lebaoth, Shilhim, Ain

CONNECT 2-YOU

A CHANCE TO BE POPULAR

Sometimes being seen to be part of the right crowd can feel like the most important thing. Let's welcome Amy, aged 12, to Connect 2-You. She's struggling with a serious popularity problem.

Amy

Well, lately, one of the most popular girls at school and I have been talking to each other. Last week she even asked me to eat lunch with her and her friends. To top it all off, yesterday she invited me to her birthday party. The only problem is, I know what kind of a party it's going to be. All the popular kids will be there – but her parents won't. She told me some of the things she has planned, and my parents would have heart attacks if they knew. But this is my big chance to be part of the popular crowd! What should I do?

It's pretty tempting to go to the party, isn't it? But is popularity worth more than your relationship with Jesus, your bond with your parents, and your reputation? No way. Popularity fades as fast as it comes. Your relationship with Jesus, your bond with your parents, and your reputation are things to hold on to. Check out the Livin' It page on peer pressure, Leviticus 18:1–5, p. 158, for some other ways to handle tempting situations.

Think of it this way. If you have to change who you are to become popular, then it's not really you who's popular.

and Rimmon. There were 29 towns and their villages.

33 The tribe of Judah got these towns in the western hills: Eshtaol, Zorah, Ashnah, 34 Zanoah, En Gannim, Tappuah, Enam, 35 Jarmuth, Adullam, Socoh, Azekah, 36 Shaaraim, Adithaim and Gederah (also called Gederothaim). There were fourteen towns and their villages.

37 Judah was also given these towns in the western hills: Zenan, Hadashah, Migdal Gad, 38 Dilean, Mizpah, Joktheel, 39 Lachish, Bozkath, Eglon, 40 Cabbon, Lahmas, Kitlish, 41 Gederoth, Beth Dagon, Naamah and Makkedah. There were sixteen towns and their villages.

42 Judah was also given these towns in the western hills: Libnah, Ether, Ashan, 43 Iphtah, Ashnah, Nezib, 44 Keilah, Achzib and Mareshah. There were nine towns and their villages.

45 The tribe of Judah was also given these towns: Ekron and all the small towns and villages near it; 46 the area west of Ekron and all the villages and small towns near Ashdod; 47 Ashdod and the small towns and villages around it; the villages and small towns around Gaza as far as the brook of Egypt and along the coast of the Mediterranean Sea.

48 The tribe of Judah was also given these towns in the mountains: Shamir, Jattir, Socoh, 49 Dannah, Kiriath Sannah (also called Debir), 50 Anab, Eshtemoh, Anim, 51 Goshen, Holon and Giloh. There were eleven towns and their villages.

52 They were also given these towns in the mountains: Arab, Dumah, Eshan, 53 Janim, Beth Tappuah, Aphekah, 54 Humtah, Kiriath Arba (also called Hebron) and Zior. There were nine towns and their villages.

55 Judah was also given these towns in the mountains: Maon, Carmel, Ziph, Juttah, 56 Jezreel, Jokdeam, Zanoah, 57 Kain, Gibeah and Timnah. There were ten towns and their villages.

58 They were also given these towns in the mountains: Halhul, Beth Zur, Gedor, 59 Maarath, Beth Anoth and Eltekon. There were six towns and their villages.

60 The people of Judah were also given the two towns of Rabbah and Kiriath Baal (also called Kiriath Jearim) and their villages.

61 Judah was given these towns in the desert: Beth Arabah, Middin, Secacah, 62 Nibshan, the City of Salt and En Gedi. There were six towns and all their villages.

63 The army of Judah was not able to force out the Jebusites living in Jerusalem, so the Jebusites still live among the people of Judah to this day.

Land for Ephraim and Manasseh

16 This is the land the tribe of Joseph received. It started at the Jordan River near Jericho and continued to the waters of Jericho, just east of the city. The border went up from Jericho to the mountains of Bethel. 2 Then it continued from Bethel (also called Luz) to the Arkite border at Ataroth. 3 From there it went west to the border of the Japhletites and continued to the area of the Lower Beth Horon. Then it went to Gezer and ended at the sea.

4 So Manasseh and Ephraim, sons of Joseph, received their land.

5 This is the land that was given to the family groups of Ephraim: their border started at Ataroth Addar in the east, went to Upper Beth Horon, 6 and then to the sea. From Micmethath it turned eastwards towards Taanath Shiloh and continued eastwards to Janoah. 7 Then it went down from Janoah to Ataroth and to Naarah. It continued until it touched Jericho and stopped at the Jordan River. 8 The border went from Tappuah west to Kanah Ravine and ended at the sea. This is all the land that was given to each family group in the tribe of the Ephraimites. 9 Many of the towns were actually within Manasseh's borders, but the people of Ephraim got those towns and their villages. 10 The Ephraimites could not force the Canaanites to leave Gezer, so the Canaanites still live among the Ephraimites today, but they became slaves of the Ephraimites.

17 Then land was given to the tribe of Manasseh, Joseph's first son. Manasseh's first son was Makir, the father of

Gilead. Makir was a great soldier, so the lands of Gilead and Bashan were given to his family. 2 Land was also given to the other family groups of Manasseh—Abiezer, Helek, Asriel, Shechem, Hepher and Shemida. These were all the other sons of Manasseh son of Joseph.

3 Zelophehad was the son of Hepher, who was the son of Gilead, who was the son of Makir, who was the son of Manasseh. Zelophehad had no sons, but he had five daughters, named Mahlah, Noah, Hoglah, Milcah and Tirzah. 4 They went to Eleazar the priest and to Joshua son of Nun and all the leaders. They said, "The LORD told Moses to give us land like the men received." So Eleazar obeyed the LORD and gave the daughters some land, just like the brothers of their father. 5 So the tribe of Manasseh had ten sections of land west of the Jordan River and two more sections, Gilead and Bashan, on the east side of the Jordan River. 6 The daughters of Manasseh received land just as the sons did. Gilead was given to the rest of the families of Manasseh.

7 The lands of Manasseh were in the area between Asher and Micmethath, near Shechem. The border went south to the En Tappuah area, 8 which belonged to Manasseh, except for the town of Tappuah. It was along the border of Manasseh's land and belonged to the sons of Ephraim. 9 The border of Manasseh continued south to Kanah Ravine. The cities in this area of Manasseh belonged to Ephraim. Manasseh's border was on the north side of the ravine and went to the sea. 10 The land to the south belonged to Ephraim, and the land to the north belonged to Manasseh. The Mediterranean Sea was the western border. The border touched Asher's land on the north and Issachar's land on the east.

11 In the areas of Issachar and Asher, the people of Manasseh owned these towns: Beth Shan and its small towns; Ibleam and its small towns; the people who lived in Dor and its small towns; the people in Naphoth Dor and its small towns; the people who lived in Taanach and its small towns; the people in Megiddo and its small towns. 12 Manasseh was not able to defeat those cities, so the Canaanites continued to live there. 13 When the Israelites grew strong, they forced the Canaanites to work for them, although they did not force them to leave the land.

14 The people from the tribes of Joseph said to Joshua, "You gave us only one area of land, but we are many people. Why did you give us only one part of all the land the LORD gave his people?"

15 And Joshua answered them, "If you have too many people, go up to the forest and make a place for yourselves to live there in the land of the Perizzites and the Rephaites. The mountain country of Ephraim is too small for you."

16 The people of Joseph said, "It is true. The mountain country of Ephraim is not enough for us, but the land where the Canaanites live is dangerous. They are skilled fighters. They have powerful weapons in Beth Shan and all the small towns in that area, and they are also in the Valley of Jezreel."

17 Then Joshua said to the people of Joseph—to Ephraim and Manasseh, "There are many of you, and you have great power. You should be given more than one share of land. 18 You also will have the mountain country. It is a forest, but you can cut down the trees and make it a good place to live. You will own all of it because you will force the Canaanites to leave the land even though they have powerful weapons and are strong."

The Rest of the Land Divided

18 All of the Israelites gathered together at Shiloh where they set up the Meeting Tent. The land was now under their control. 2 But there were still seven tribes of Israel that had not yet received their land.

3 So Joshua said to the Israelites:

> So Eleazar obeyed the LORD and gave the daughters some land, just like the brothers of their father.
> – Joshua 17:4

FAITH links

CARE TO BE FAIR?
JOSHUA 18:1-8

When you need to share with someone, what do you do to be fair? The Israelites chose a fair way to divide up the land. They cast lots and let God do the choosing. Using lots was a special way of choosing. When Joshua had been chosen to be the leader, God told him to use lots. (See Numbers 27:21, p. 214.) In this way, no one had to argue over who received what.

God wants his people to care about being fair. We can learn fair ways to share with others. What is one way you've come up with to share what God gives you with others?

Link here to find out some ways to share with others:

A Small Percent, Deuteronomy 14:22–23, p. 247

Kind or Fair? 1 Samuel 30, p. 395

A Reminder to Be Fair, 2 Chronicles 19:5–11, p. 583

The Person Most Likely to Give? Acts 9:36–42, p. 1481

You're Welcomed! Acts 16:14–15, p. 1494

Give Till It Hurts? 2 Corinthians 8:6–9; 9:6–9, p. 1578

"Why do you wait so long to take your land? The LORD, the God of your ancestors, has given this land to you. 4 Choose three men from each tribe, and I will send them out to study the land. They will describe in writing the land their tribe wants as its share, and then they will come back to me. 5 They will divide the land into seven parts. The people of Judah will keep their land in the south, and the people of Joseph will keep their land in the north. 6 You should describe the seven parts of land in writing and bring what you have written to me. Then I will throw lots in the presence of the LORD our God. 7 But the Levites do not get any part of these lands, because they are priests, and their work is to serve the LORD. Gad, Reuben and East Manasseh have received the land promised to them, which is east of the Jordan River. Moses, the servant of the LORD, gave it to them."

8 So the men who were chosen to map the land started out. Joshua told them, "Go and study the land and describe it in writing. Then come back to me, and I will throw lots in the presence of the LORD here in Shiloh." 9 So the men left and went into the land. They described in a scroll each town in the seven parts of the land. Then they came back to Joshua, who was still at the camp at Shiloh. 10 There Joshua threw lots in the presence of the LORD to choose the lands that should be given to each tribe.

Land for Benjamin

11 The first part of the land was given to the tribe of Benjamin. Each family group received some land between the land of Judah and the land of Joseph. This is the land chosen for Benjamin: 12 the northern border started at the Jordan River and went along the northern edge of Jericho, and then it went west into the mountains. That boundary continued until it was just east of Beth Aven. 13 From there it went south to Luz (also called Bethel) and then down to Ataroth Addar, which is on the hill south of Lower Beth Horon.

14 At the hill to the south of Beth Horon, the border turned and went south

near the western side of the hill. It went to Kiriath Baal (also called Kiriath Jearim), a town where people of Judah lived. This was the western border. 15 The southern border started near Kiriath Jearim and went west to the waters of Nephtoah. 16 Then it went down to the bottom of the hill, which was near the Valley of Ben Hinnom, on the north side of the Valley of Rephaim. The border continued down the Hinnom Valley just south of the Jebusite city to En Rogel. 17 There it turned north and went to En Shemesh. It continued to Geliloth near the Adummim Pass. Then it went down to the great Stone of Bohan son of Reuben. 18 The border continued to the northern part of Beth Arabah and went down into the Jordan Valley. 19 From there it went to the northern part of Beth Hoglah and ended at the north shore of the Dead Sea, where the Jordan River flows into the sea. This was the southern border.

20 The Jordan River was the border on the eastern side. So this was the land given to the family groups of Benjamin with the borders on all sides.

21 The family groups of Benjamin received these cities: Jericho, Beth Hoglah, Emek Keziz, 22 Beth Arabah, Zemaraim, Bethel, 23 Avvim, Parah, Ophrah, 24 Kephar Ammoni, Ophni and Geba. There were twelve towns and all their villages. 25 The tribe of Benjamin also received Gibeon, Ramah, Beeroth, 26 Mizpah, Kephirah, Mozah, 27 Rekem, Irpeel, Taralah, 28 Zelah, Haeleph, the Jebusite city (Jerusalem), Gibeah and Kiriath. There were fourteen towns and their villages. All these areas are the lands the family groups of Benjamin were given.

Land for Simeon

19 The second part of the land was given to the tribe of Simeon. Each family group received some of the land inside the area of Judah. 2 They received Beersheba (also called Sheba), Moladah, 3 Hazar Shual, Balah, Ezem, 4 Eltolad, Bethul, Hormah, 5 Ziklag, Beth Marcaboth, Hazar Susah, 6 Beth Lebaoth and Sharuhen. There were thirteen towns and their villages.

7 They received the towns of Ain, Rimmon, Ether and Ashan, four towns and their villages. 8 They also received all the very small areas with people living in them as far as Baalath Beer (this is the same as Ramah in southern Canaan). So these were the lands given to the family groups in the tribe of Simeon. 9 The land of the Simeonites was taken from part of the land of Judah. Since Judah had much more land than they needed, the Simeonites received part of their land.

Land for Zebulun

10 The third part of the land was given to the tribe of Zebulun. Each family group of Zebulun received some of the land. The border of Zebulun went as far as Sarid. 11 Then it went west to Maralah and came near Dabbesheth and then near Jokneam. 12 Then it turned to the east. It went from Sarid to the area of Kisloth Tabor and on to Daberath and to Japhia. 13 It continued eastwards to Gath Hepher and Eth Kazin, ending at Rimmon. There the border turned and went towards Neah. 14 At Neah it turned again and went to the north to Hannathon and continued to the Valley of Iphtah El. 15 Inside this border were the cities of Kattath, Nahalal, Shimron, Idalah and Bethlehem. There were twelve towns and their villages.

16 So these are the towns and the villages that were given to the family groups of Zebulun.

Land for Issachar

17 The fourth part of the land was given to the tribe of Issachar. Each family group of Issachar received some of the land. 18 Their land included Jezreel, Kesulloth, Shunem, 19 Hapharaim, Shion, Anaharath, 20 Rabbith, Kishion, Ebez, 21 Remeth, En Gannim, En Haddah and Beth Pazzez.

22 The border of their land touched the area called Tabor, Shahazumah and Beth Shemesh and stopped at the Jordan River. There were sixteen towns and their villages.

23 These cities and towns were part of the land that was given to the family groups of Issachar.

Land for Asher

24 The fifth part of the land was given to the tribe of Asher. Each family group of Asher received some of the land. 25 Their land included Helkath, Hali, Beten, Achshaph, 26 Allammelech, Amad and Mishal. The western border touched Mount Carmel and Shihor Libnath. 27 Then it turned east and went to Beth Dagon, touching Zebulun and the Valley of Iphtah El. Then it went north of Beth Emek and Neiel and passed north to Cabul. 28 From there it went to Abdon, Rehob, Hammon and Kanah and continued to Greater Sidon. 29 Then the border went back south towards Ramah and continued to the fortified city of Tyre. There it turned and went towards Hosah, ending at the sea. This was in the area of Achzib, 30 Ummah, Aphek and Rehob. There were 22 towns and their villages.

31 These cities and their villages were part of the land that was given to the family groups of Asher.

Land for Naphtali

32 The sixth part of the land was given to the tribe of Naphtali. Each family group of Naphtali received some of the land. 33 The border of their land started at the large tree in Zaanannim, which is near Heleph. Then it went through Adami Nekeb and Jabneel, as far as Lakkum, and ended at the Jordan River. 34 Then it went to the west through Aznoth Tabor and stopped at Hukkok. It went to the area of Zebulun on the south, Asher on the west, and Judah, at the Jordan River, on the east. 35 The fortified cities inside these borders were called Ziddim, Zer, Hammath, Rakkath, Kinnereth, 36 Adamah, Ramah, Hazor, 37 Kedesh, Edrei, En Hazor, 38 Iron, Migdal El, Horem, Beth Anath and Beth Shemesh. There were nineteen towns and all their villages.

39 The towns and the villages around them were in the land that was given to the family groups of Naphtali.

Land for Dan

40 The seventh part of the land was given to the tribe of Dan. Each family group of Dan received some of the land. 41 Their land included Zorah, Eshtaol, Ir Shemesh, 42 Shaalabbin, Aijalon, Ithlah, 43 Elon, Timnah, Ekron, 44 Eltekeh, Gibbethon, Baalath, 45 Jehud, Bene Berak, Gath Rimmon, 46 Me Jarkon, Rakkon and the area near Joppa.

47 (But the Danites had trouble taking their land. They went and fought against Leshem, defeated it, and killed the people who lived there. So the Danites moved into the town of Leshem and changed its name to Dan, because he was the father of their tribe.) 48 All of these towns and villages were given to the family groups of Dan.

Land for Joshua

49 After the leaders finished dividing the land and giving it to the different tribes, the Israelites gave Joshua son of Nun his land also. 50 They gave Joshua the town he asked for, Timnath Serah in the mountains of Ephraim, just as the LORD commanded. He built up the town and lived there.

51 So these lands were given to the different tribes of Israel. Eleazar the priest, Joshua son of Nun and the leaders of each tribe divided up the land by lots at Shiloh. They met in the presence of the LORD at the entrance to the Meeting Tent. Now they had finished dividing the land.

> Eleazar the priest, Joshua son of Nun and the leaders of each tribe divided up the land by lots at Shiloh.
> – Joshua 19:51

Cities of Safety

20 Then the LORD said to Joshua: 2 "Tell the Israelites to choose the special cities of safety," as I had Moses command you to do. 3 If a person kills someone accidentally and without meaning to kill him, that person may go to a city of safety to hide. There the killer will be

---

20:2 **cities of safety** A person who had accidentally killed someone could go to one of the six cities of safety to receive protection and a fair trial.

▶ Joshua 20:4 302

DIVIDING THE LAND   Joshua 21

The land of Israel is called that because the land was divided among the 12 sons of a man named Israel. (He was born with the name Jacob, but God later changed it to Israel.) The land of Israel stretched from the River Jordan on the east to the Mediterranean Sea on the west. From the north to the south it covered the land between the Sinai Peninsula and the boundary of Phoenicia.

Israel's sons were: Reuben, Simeon, Levi, Judah, Zebulun, Issachar, Dan, Gad, Asher, Naphtali, Joseph and Benjamin.

The only son of Israel whose descendants didn't get a tract of land was Levi. (Check out Joshua 13:33.) That's because Levi's descendants (the Levites) were selected to be priests. (Read Numbers 18:20, p. 201.) They would work and live from the Temple, so they didn't need any land. The land that would have gone to the Levites was divided between the two sons of Joseph — Manasseh and Ephraim.

safe from the relative who has the duty of punishing a murderer.

4 "When the killer runs to one of those cities, he must stop at the entrance gate, stand there, and tell the elders of the people what happened. Then that person will be allowed to enter the city and will be given a place to live among them. 5 But if the one who is chasing him follows him to that city, the leaders of the city must not hand over the killer. It was an accident. He did not hate him beforehand or kill him on purpose. 6 The killer must stay in the city until a court comes to a decision and until the high priest dies. Then he may go back home to the town from which he ran away."

7 So the Israelites chose these cities to be cities of safety: Kedesh in Galilee in the mountains of Naphtali; Shechem in the mountains of Ephraim; Kiriath Arba (also called Hebron) in the mountains of Judah; 8 Bezer on the east side of the Jordan River near Jericho in the desert in the land of Reuben; Ramoth in Gilead in the land of Gad; and Golan in Bashan in the land of Manasseh. 9 Any Israelite or anyone living among them who killed someone accidentally was to be allowed to run to one of these cities of safety. There he would not be killed, before he was judged, by the relative who had the duty of punishing a murderer.

Towns for the Levites

21 The heads of the Levite families went to talk to Eleazar the priest, to Joshua son of Nun and to the heads of the families of all the tribes of Israel. 2 At Shiloh in the land of Canaan, the heads of the Levite families said to them, "The LORD commanded Moses that you give us towns where we may live and pastures for our animals." 3 So the Israelites obeyed this command of the LORD and gave the Levite people these towns and pastures for their own land: 4 the Kohath family groups were part of the tribe of Levi. Some of the Levites in the Kohath family groups were from the family of Aaron the priest. To these Levites were given thirteen towns in the areas of Judah, Simeon and Benjamin. 5 The other family groups of

Kohath were given ten towns in the areas of Ephraim, Dan and West Manasseh.

6 The people from the Gershon family groups were given thirteen towns in the land of Issachar, Asher, Naphtali and East Manasseh in Bashan.

7 The family groups of Merari were given twelve towns in the areas of Reuben, Gad and Zebulun.

8 So the Israelites gave the Levites these towns and the pastures around them, just as the LORD had commanded Moses.

9 These are the names of the towns that came from the lands of Judah and Simeon. **10** The first choice of towns was given to the Kohath family groups of the Levites. **11** They gave them Kiriath Arba, also called Hebron, and all its pastures in the mountains of Judah. (Arba was the father of Anak.) **12** But the fields and the villages around Kiriath Arba had been given to Caleb son of Jephunneh.

13 So they gave the city of Hebron to the descendants of Aaron (Hebron was a city of safety*ⁿ*). They also gave them the towns of Libnah, **14** Jattir, Eshtemoa, **15** Holon, Debir, **16** Ain, Juttah and Beth Shemesh, and all the pastures around them. Nine towns were given from these two tribes.

17 They also gave the people of Aaron these cities that belonged to the tribe of Benjamin: Gibeon, Geba, **18** Anathoth and Almon. They gave them these four towns and the pastures around them.

19 So these thirteen towns with their pastures were given to the priests, who were from the family of Aaron.

20 The other Kohathite family groups of the Levites were given these towns from the tribe of Ephraim: **21** Shechem in the mountains of Ephraim (which was a city of safety), Gezer, **22** Kibzaim and Beth Horon. There were four towns and their pastures.

23 The tribe of Dan gave them Eltekeh, Gibbethon, **24** Aijalon and Gath Rimmon. There were four towns and their pastures.

25 West Manasseh gave them Taanach and Gath Rimmon and the pastures around these two towns.

26 So these ten towns and the pastures around them were given to the rest of the Kohathite family groups.

27 The Gershonite family groups of the Levite tribe were given these towns: East Manasseh gave them Golan in Bashan, which was a city of safety, and Be Eshtarah, and the pastures around these two towns.

28 The tribe of Issachar gave them Kishion, Daberath, **29** Jarmuth and En Gannim, and the pastures around these four towns.

30 The tribe of Asher gave them Mishal, Abdon, **31** Helkath and Rehob, and the pastures around these four towns.

32 The tribe of Naphtali gave them Kedesh in Galilee (a city of safety), Hammoth Dor and Kartan, and the pastures around these three towns.

33 So the Gershonite family groups received thirteen towns and the pastures around them.

34 The Merarite family groups (the rest of the Levites) were given these towns: the tribe of Zebulun gave them Jokneam, Kartah, **35** Dimnah and Nahalal, and the pastures around these four towns.

36 The tribe of Reuben gave them Bezer, Jahaz, **37** Kedemoth and Mephaath, along with the pastures around these four towns.

38 The tribe of Gad gave them Ramoth in Gilead (a city of safety), Mahanaim, **39** Heshbon and Jazer, and the pastures around these four towns.

40 So the total number of towns given to the Merarite family groups was twelve.

41 A total of 48 towns with their pastures in the land of Israel were given to the Levites. **42** Each town had pastures around it.

43 So the LORD gave the people all the land he had promised their ancestors. The people took the land and lived there. **44** The LORD gave them peace on all sides, as he had promised their ancestors. None of their enemies defeated them; the LORD

21:13 city of safety A person who had accidentally killed someone could go to one of the six cities of safety to receive protection and a fair trial.

handed all their enemies over to them. 45 He kept every promise he had made to the Israelites; each one came true.

Three Tribes Go Home

22 Then Joshua called a meeting of all the people from the tribes of Reuben, Gad and East Manasseh. 2 He said to them, "You have done everything Moses, the LORD's servant, told you to do. You have also obeyed all my commands. 3 For a long time you have supported the other Israelites. You have been careful to obey the commands the LORD your God gave you. 4 The LORD your God promised to give the Israelites peace, and he has kept his promise. Now you may go back to your homes, to the land that Moses, the LORD's servant, gave you, on the east side of the Jordan River. 5 But be careful to obey the teachings and laws Moses, the LORD's servant, gave you: to love the LORD your God and obey his commands, to continue to follow him and serve him the very best you can."

6 Then Joshua said goodbye to them, and they left and went away to their homes. 7 Moses had given the land of Bashan to East Manasseh. Joshua gave land on the west side of the Jordan River to West Manasseh. And he sent them to their homes and he blessed them. 8 He said, "Go back to your homes and your riches. You have many animals, silver, gold, bronze and iron, and many beautiful clothes. Also, you have taken many things from your enemies that you should divide among yourselves."

9 So the people from the tribes of Reuben, Gad and East Manasseh left the other Israelites at Shiloh in Canaan and went back to Gilead. It was their own land, given to them by Moses as the LORD had commanded.

10 The people of Reuben, Gad and East Manasseh went to Geliloth, near the Jordan River in the land of Canaan. There they built a beautiful altar. 11 The other Israelites still at Shiloh heard about the altar these three tribes built at the border of Canaan at Geliloth, near the Jordan River on Israel's side. 12 All the Israelites became very angry at these three tribes, so they met together and decided to fight them.

13 The Israelites sent Phinehas son of Eleazar the priest to Gilead to talk to the people of Reuben, Gad and East Manasseh. 14 They also sent one leader from each of the ten tribes at Shiloh. Each of them was a leader of his family group of Israelites.

15 These leaders went to Gilead to talk to the people of Reuben, Gad and East Manasseh. They said: 16 "All the Israel-

EMAIL FROM GOD
22:5
Responsibility
Be careful to do this!

FAITH CHALLENGE
Got another challenge for you. Read 22:18 to find out what warning the Israelites received from God. How can you make sure that the Lord does not get angry with you?

TESTING IT

Joshua 22:18
And now are you turning against the LORD and refusing to follow him? If you don't stop what you're doing today, the LORD will be angry with everyone in Israel tomorrow.

ites ask you: 'Why did you turn against the God of Israel by building an altar for yourselves? You know that this is against God's law. 17 Remember what happened at Peor? We still suffer today because of that sin, for which God made many Israelites very sick. 18 And now are you turning against the LORD and refusing to follow him?

"'If you don't stop what you're doing today, the LORD will be angry with everyone in Israel tomorrow. 19 If your land is unclean, come over into our land where the LORD's Tent is. Share it with us. But don't turn against the LORD and us by building another altar for the LORD our God. 20 Remember how Achan son of Zerah refused to obey the command about what must be completely destroyed. That one man broke God's law, but all the Israelites were punished. Achan died because of his sin, but others also died.'"

21 The people from Reuben, Gad and East Manasseh answered, 22 "The LORD is God of gods! The LORD is God of gods! God knows, and we want you to know also. If we have done something wrong, you may kill us. 23 If we broke God's law, we ask the LORD himself to punish us. We did not build this altar to offer burnt offerings or grain and fellowship offerings. 24 "We did not build it for that reason. We feared that some day your people would not accept us as part of your nation. Then they might say, 'You cannot worship the LORD, the God of Israel. 25 The LORD made the Jordan River a border between us and you people of Reuben and Gad. You cannot worship the LORD.' So we feared that your children might make our children stop worshipping the LORD.

26 "That is why we decided to build this altar. But it is not for burnt offerings and sacrifices. 27 This altar is proof to you and us and to all our children who will come after us that we worship the LORD with our whole burnt offerings, grain and fellowship offerings. This was so your children would not say to our children, 'You are not the LORD's.'

28 "In the future if your children say that, our children can say, 'See the altar made by our ancestors. It is exactly like the LORD's altar, but we do not use it for sacrifices. It shows that we are part of Israel.'

29 "Truly, we don't want to be against the LORD or to stop following him by building an altar for burnt offerings, grain offerings or sacrifices. We know the only true altar to the LORD our God is in front of the Holy Tent."

30 When Phinehas the priest and the ten leaders heard the people of Reuben, Gad and East Manasseh, they were pleased. 31 So Phinehas, son of Eleazar the priest, said, "Now we know the LORD is with us and that you didn't turn against him. Now the Israelites will not be punished by the LORD."

32 Then Phinehas and the leaders left the people of Reuben and Gad in Gilead and went back to Canaan where they told the Israelites what had happened. 33 They were pleased and thanked God. So they decided not to fight the people of Reuben and Gad and destroy those lands.

34 And the people of Reuben and Gad named the altar Proof that We Believe the LORD Is God.

The Last Words of Joshua

23 The LORD gave Israel peace from their enemies around them. Many years passed, and Joshua grew very old. 2 He called a meeting of all the elders, heads of families, judges and officers of Israel. He said, "I am now very old. 3 You have seen what the LORD has done to our enemies to help us. The LORD your God fought for you. 4 Remember that your people have been given their land between the Jordan River and the Mediterranean Sea in the west, the land I promised to give you. 5 The LORD your God will force out the people living there. The LORD will push them out ahead of you. And you will own the land, as he has promised you.

23:6–7 Bible
Read this to see what God's teachings tell you to do.

6 "Be strong. You must be careful to obey everything commanded in the Book of the Teachings of Moses. Do exactly as it says. 7 Don't become friends with the people living among us who are not

Israelites. Don't say the names of their gods or make anyone swear by them. Don't serve or worship them. 8 You must continue to follow the LORD your God, as you have done in the past.

9 "The LORD has forced many great and powerful nations to leave ahead of you. No nation has been able to defeat you. 10 With his help, one Israelite could defeat 1,000, because the LORD your God fights for you, as he promised to do. 11 So you must be careful to love the LORD your God.

12 "If you turn away from the way of the LORD and become friends with these people who are not part of Israel and marry them, 13 the LORD your God will not help you defeat your enemies. They will be like traps for you, like whips on your back and thorns in your eyes, and none of you will be left in this good land the LORD your God has given you.

14 "It's almost time for me to die. You know and fully believe that the LORD has done great things for you. You know that he has not failed to keep any of his promises. 15 Every good promise that the LORD your God made has come true, and in the same way, his other promises will come true. He promised that evil will come to you and that he will destroy you from this good land that he gave you. 16 This will happen if you don't keep your agreement with the LORD your God. If you go and serve other gods and worship them, the LORD will become very angry with you. Then none of you will be left in this good land he has given you."

24 Joshua gathered all the tribes of Israel together at Shechem. He called the elders, heads of families, judges and officers of Israel to stand before God.

2 Then Joshua said to all the people, "Here's what the LORD, the God of Israel, says to you: 'A long time ago your ancestors lived on the other side of the Euphrates River. Terah, the father of Abraham and Nahor, worshiped other gods. 3 But I, the LORD, took your ancestor Abraham from the other side of the river and led him through the land of Canaan. And I gave him many children, including his son Isaac. 4 I gave Isaac two sons named Jacob and Esau. I gave the land around the mountains of Edom to Esau, but Jacob and his sons went down to Egypt. 5 Then I sent Moses and Aaron to Egypt, where I brought many disasters on the Egyptians. Afterwards I brought you out. 6 When I brought your ancestors out of Egypt, they came to the Red Sea, and the Egyptians chased them with chariots and men on horses. 7 So the people called out to the LORD. And I brought darkness between you and the Egyptians and created the sea to cover them. You yourselves saw what I did to the army of Egypt. After that, you lived in the desert for a long time.

8 "'Then I brought you to the land of the Amorites, east of the Jordan River. They fought against you, but I handed them over to you. I destroyed them before you, and you took control of that land. 9 But the king of Moab, Balak son of Zippor, prepared to fight against the Israelites. The king sent for Balaam son of Beor to curse you, 10 but I refused to listen to Balaam. So he asked for good things to happen to you! I saved you and brought you out of his power.

11 "'Then you crossed the Jordan River and came to Jericho, where the people of Jericho fought against you. Also, the Amorites, Perizzites, Canaanites, Hittites, Girgashites, Hivites and Jebusites fought against you. But I handed them over to you. 12 I sent terror ahead of you to force out two Amorite kings. You took the land without using swords and bows. 13 I gave you that land where you did not have to work. I gave you cities that you did not have to build. And now you live in that land and in those cities, and you eat from vineyards and olive trees that you did not plant.'"

14 Then Joshua said to the people, "Now respect the LORD and serve him fully and sincerely. Throw away the gods that your ancestors worshiped on the other side of the Euphrates River and in Egypt. Serve the LORD. 15 But if you don't want to serve the LORD, you must choose for yourselves today whom you will serve. You may serve the gods that your ancestors worshiped when they lived on the

NO MIDDLE GROUND
JOSHUA 24:14-15

Some choices we have to make are cut and dried – either this or that. Joshua told the people of Israel to choose either to worship God or to worship idols made by people. There was no choice in between.

God offers you the same choice. An idol is someone or something you value more than God. You can either choose him or choose someone or something else you value more. You decide.

The Wisdom of Obeying God, 1 Kings 11:1–13, p. 453

A Useless Thing, Isaiah 44:9, 18–20, p. 954

How to Worship God, Isaiah 58, p. 972

Obeying God or Man? Daniel 3:8–30, p. 1154

First Place, Haggai 1:7–11, p. 1248

Heavenly Treasure, Luke 12:32–34, p. 1394

---

other side of the Euphrates River, or you may serve the gods of the Amorites who lived in this land. As for me and my family, we will serve the LORD."

16 Then the people answered, "We will never stop following the LORD to serve other gods! 17 It was the LORD our God who brought our ancestors out of Egypt. We were slaves in that land, but the LORD did great things for us there. He brought us out and protected us while we travelled through other lands. 18 Then he forced out all the people living in these lands, even the Amorites. So we will serve the LORD, because he is our God."

19 Then Joshua said, "You are not able to serve the LORD, because he is a holy God and a jealous God. If you turn against him and sin, he will not forgive you. 20 If you leave the LORD and serve other gods, he will send you great trouble. The LORD may have been good to you, but if you turn against him, he will destroy you."

21 But the people said to Joshua, "No! We will serve the LORD."

22 Then Joshua said, "You are your own witnesses that you have chosen to serve the LORD."

The people said, "Yes, we are."

23 Then Joshua said, "Now throw away the gods that you have. Love the LORD, the God of Israel, with all your heart."

24 Then the people said to Joshua, "We will serve the LORD our God, and we will obey him."

25 On that day at Shechem, Joshua made an agreement for the people. He made rules and laws for them to follow. 26 Joshua wrote these things in the Book of the Teachings of God. Then he took a large stone and set it up under the oak tree near the LORD's Holy Tent.

27 Joshua said to all the people, "See this stone! It will remind you of what we did today. It was here the LORD spoke to us today. It will remind you of what happened so you will not turn against your God."

Joshua Dies

28 Then Joshua sent the people back to their land.

29 After that, Joshua son of Nun died at the age of 110. 30 They buried him in his own land at Timnath Serah, in the mountains of Ephraim, north of Mount Gaash.

31 The Israelites served the LORD during the lifetime of Joshua and during the lifetimes of the elders who lived after Joshua who had seen what the LORD had done for Israel.

Joseph Comes Home

32 When the Israelites left Egypt, they carried the bones of Joseph with them. They buried them at Shechem, in the land Jacob had bought for 100 pieces of silver from the sons of Hamor (Hamor was the father of Shechem). This land now belonged to Joseph's children.

33 And Eleazar son of Aaron died and was buried at Gibeah in the mountains of Ephraim, which had been given to Eleazar's son Phinehas.

SAVE US FROM OUR ENEMIES!

Greetings! My name is Samuel, and I was the last judge of Israel. (Although I wrote the Book of Judges, my story is in 1 Samuel. Link with 1 Samuel 1:1–20, p. 354, for the story of my birth.) Seeing a title like Judges, you might think that this would be a boring book about court cases, but Judges has some of the most interesting and strangest stories in the Bible. You'll need to do some surfing through this book!

I wrote the Book of Judges to remind people to be faithful to God. "At that time Israel did not have a king, so everyone did what seemed right" (Judges 17:6). Unfortunately, for most people it did not "seem right" to follow God, so God allowed them to be conquered by their enemies. It was not until the people were sorry for their sins and called out to God that God sent a judge, or leader, to save them.

JESUS WATCH

In the Book of Judges, we see many people who point to Jesus. Each judge was a ruler and a saviour of the nation of Israel as Jesus is the ruler and saviour for those who believe in him. The judges in this book were imperfect, and the effects of their actions were only temporary. Jesus is perfect, and his salvation is for ever. Several judges ruled Israel. Some, like Gideon, were warrior-rulers who defeated Israel's enemies. Jesus defeated Satan and rules his kingdom from heaven. Other judges, like Deborah and Samuel, were prophets who urged the people to follow God's laws. Jesus was the ultimate prophet who showed us God's love. Some judges were priests who prayed and sacrificed for the people. Jesus is our high priest who sacrificed himself for our sins and is always asking God to forgive us.

my FAVOURITE links

OTHER CONNECTIONS

 Surf these connections to find out more about what some consider to be Israel's "dark ages", a time when people strayed from God and began to worship other gods.

- The Judges, Judges 9, will introduce you to some of the main leaders of the young nation of Israel as they began to settle in the land God had promised to them.
- Check out the earliest religious capital for the Israelites when you connect to Let's Visit Shiloh, Judges 18:31. This ancient Canaan city was where the Israelites kept the Holy Tent of God. It's also where a young woman named Hannah prayed for God to give her a son.

FAITH links

○ Promises, Promises, **Judges 2:1–3**

○ Count on His Mercy, **Judges 2:16–17; 3**

○ From Zero to Hero, **Judges 6; 7**

○ What's Out Becomes In, **Judges 11**

○ I Want it *Now*! **Judges 14:1–3**

○ The Weak Link, **Judges 16**

○ Do What You Want? **Judges 21:25**

Do you know what Ehud's secret message for the king of Moab was?

No? If you connect to Judges 3:12–28, you can find out.

CHECK OUT THESE STRANGE STORIES:
A stake through the head? Judges 4:14–24
Gideon's fleece, Judges 6:36–40
Samson eats honey from a dead lion, Judges 14:5–9
Samson's seven braids, Judges 16:15–22

Judah Fights the Canaanites

1 After Joshua died, the Israelites asked the LORD, "Who will be first to go and fight for us against the Canaanites?" 2 The LORD said to them, "The tribe of Judah will go. I have handed the land over to them."

3 The men of Judah said to the men of Simeon, their relatives, "Come and help us fight the Canaanites for our land. If you do, we will go and help you fight for your land." So the men of Simeon went with them.

4 When Judah attacked, the LORD handed over the Canaanites and the Perizzites to them, and they defeated 10,000 men at the city of Bezek. 5 There they found Adoni-Bezek, the ruler of the city, and fought him. The men of Judah defeated the Canaanites and the Perizzites, 6 but Adoni-Bezek ran away. The men of Judah chased him, and when they caught him, they cut off his thumbs and big toes.

7 Adoni-Bezek said, "Seventy kings whose thumbs and big toes had been cut off used to eat scraps that fell from my table. Now God has paid me back for what I did to them." The men of Judah took Adoni-Bezek to Jerusalem, and he died there.

8 Then the men of Judah fought against Jerusalem and captured it. They attacked with their swords and burned the city.

9 Later, they went down to fight the Canaanites who lived in the mountains, in the dry country to the south and in the western hills. 10 The men of Judah went to fight against the Canaanites in the city of Hebron (which used to be called Kiriath Arba). And they defeated Sheshai, Ahiman and Talmai.

Caleb and His Daughter

11 Then they left there and went to fight against the people living in Debir. (In the past Debir had been called Kiriath Sepher.) 12 Before attacking the city, Caleb said, "I will give Achsah, my daughter, as a wife to the man who attacks and captures the city of Kiriath Sepher." 13 Othniel son of Kenaz, Caleb's younger brother, captured the city, so Caleb gave his daughter Achsah to Othniel to be his wife. 14 When Achsah came to Othniel, she told him to ask her father for a field. When she got down from her donkey, Caleb asked her, "What do you want?"

15 Achsah answered him, "Do me a special favour. Since you have given me land in southern Canaan, also give me springs of water." So Caleb gave her the upper and lower springs.

Fights with the Canaanites

16 The Kenite people, who were from the family of Moses' father-in-law, left Jericho, the city of palm trees. They went with the men of Judah to the Desert of Judah to live with them there in southern Judah near the city of Arad.

17 The men of Judah and the men of Simeon, their relatives, defeated the Canaanites who lived in Zephath. They completely destroyed the city, so they called it Hormah.*ⁿ* 18 The men of Judah captured Gaza, Ashkelon, Ekron and the lands around them.

19 The LORD was with the men of Judah. They took the land in the mountains, but they could not force out the people living on the plain, because they had iron chariots. 20 As Moses had promised, Hebron was given to Caleb, and Caleb forced out the three sons of Anak. 21 But the people of Benjamin could not make the Jebusite people leave Jerusalem. Since that time the Jebusites have lived with the people of Benjamin in Jerusalem.

22 The men of Joseph went to fight against the city of Bethel, and the LORD was with them. 23 They sent some spies to Bethel (which used to be called Luz).

> After Joshua died, the Israelites asked the LORD, "Who will be first to go and fight for us against the Canaanites?"
> – Judges 1:1

1:17 Hormah Hormah sounds like the Hebrew word meaning "to destroy completely".

24 The spies saw a man coming out of the city and said to him, "Show us a way into the city, and we will be kind to you." 25 So the man showed them the way into the city. The men of Joseph attacked with swords the people in Bethel, but they let the man and his family go free. 26 He went to the land where the Hittites lived and built a city. He named it Luz, which it is called even today.

27 There were Canaanites living in the cities of Beth Shan, Taanach, Dor, Ibleam, Megiddo and the small towns around them. The people of Manasseh did not force those people out of their towns, because the Canaanites were determined to stay there. 28 Later, the Israelites grew strong and forced the Canaanites to work as slaves, but they did not make all the Canaanites leave their land. 29 The people of Ephraim did not force out all of the Canaanites living in Gezer. So the Canaanites continued to live in Gezer with the people of Ephraim. 30 The people of Zebulun did not force out the Canaanites living in the cities of Kitron and Nahalol. They stayed and lived with the people of Zebulun, but Zebulun made them work as slaves.

31 The people of Asher did not force the Canaanites from the cities of Acco, Sidon, Ahlab, Achzib, Helbah, Aphek and Rehob. 32 Since the people of Asher did not force them out, the Canaanites continued to live with them. 33 The people of Naphtali did not force out the people of the cities of Beth Shemesh and Beth Anath. So they continued to live with the Canaanites in those cities, and the Canaanites worked as slaves. 34 The Amorites forced the Danites back into the mountains and would not let them come down to live in the plain. 35 The Amorites were determined to stay in Mount Heres, Aijalon and Shaalbim. But when the Israelites grew stronger, they made the Amorites work as slaves. 36 The land of the Amorites was from Scorpion Pass to Sela and beyond.

The Angel of the Lord at Bokim

2 The angel of the Lord went up from Gilgal to Bokim*n* and said, "I brought you up from Egypt and led you to the land I promised to give your ancestors. I said, 'I will never break my agreement with you. 2 But you must not make an agreement with the people who live in this land. You

---

FAITH links

PROMISES, PROMISES
JUDGES 2:1-3

Have you ever made a promise that you did not keep? The Israelites broke a promise to God. They promised not to make peace treaties with other nations. They also promised to get rid of the idols in the land. Because the Israelites broke their promise, God said he would not help them to conquer the land.

Sometimes people break promises because they don't want to go through the trouble of keeping them. Being a person of your word means keeping the promises you make, even if you face difficulty in doing so.

A Serious Promise, Deuteronomy 23:21–23, p. 257

A Big Responsibility, 2 Kings 11, p. 494

Said It? Do It! Lamentations 2:17, p. 1077

Your Choice of Fruit, Matthew 12:33–35, p. 1295

Your Civic Duty, Matthew 17:24–27, p. 1304

Another Lazy Day? 2 Thessalonians 3:6–13, p. 1640

2:1 **Bokim** This name means "crying".

FAITH links

COUNT ON HIS MERCY
JUDGES 2:16-17; 3

Time and time again, the Israelites sinned. You'd think that God would be done with them, wouldn't you? Nope. God showed them love and forgiveness by raising-up judges to lead them against their enemies. You've seen the superheroes in comic books or on video games, right? Well, meet the real superheroes. Judges were the leaders God equipped to help his people. They didn't have X-ray vision or cool costumes. But they did have access to God's power and wisdom.

When we blow it, we can count on God's love and forgiveness, just as the people of Israel did. We don't deserve it. But it sure helps when we're in trouble.

Think you've messed up big time? Link here to see what God can do for you!

Own Up to It, 2 Samuel 12:1–13, p. 412

The Cover-up, Psalm 32:1–2, p. 733

Red to White, Isaiah 1:18, p. 896

A Hard Place, Ezekiel 28:25–26, p. 1120

Clean Inside and Out, Luke 11:39–40, p. 1392

A Friendly Welcome, Philemon 18, p. 1664

---

must destroy their altars.' But you did not obey me. How could you do this? 3 Now I tell you, 'I will not force out the people in this land. They will be your enemies, and their gods will be a trap for you.'"

4 After the angel gave Israel this message from the LORD, they cried loudly. 5 So they named the place Bokim. There they offered sacrifices to the LORD.

Joshua Dies

6 Then Joshua sent the people back to their land. 7 The people served the LORD during the lifetime of Joshua and during the lifetimes of the elders who lived after Joshua and who had seen what great things the LORD had done for Israel. 8 Joshua son of Nun, the servant of the LORD, died at the age of 110. 9 They buried him in his own land at Timnath Serah in the mountains of Ephraim, north of Mount Gaash.

The People Disobey

10 After those people had died, their children grew up and did not know the LORD or what he had done for Israel. 11 So they did what the LORD said was wrong, and they worshipped the Baal idols. 12 They stopped following the LORD, the God of their ancestors who had brought them out of Egypt. They began to worship the gods of the people who lived around them, and that made the LORD angry. 13 The Israelites stopped following the LORD and worshipped Baal and Ashtoreth. 14 The LORD was angry with the people of Israel, so he handed them over to robbers who took their possessions. He let their enemies who lived around them defeat them; they could not protect themselves. 15 When the Israelites went out to fight, they always lost, because the LORD was not with them. The LORD had sworn to them this would happen. So the Israelites suffered very much.

God Chooses Judges

16 Then the LORD chose leaders called judges," who saved the Israelites from

---

2:16 judges They were not judges in courts of law, but leaders of the people in times of emergency.

the robbers. 17 But the Israelites did not listen to their judges. They were not faithful to God but worshipped other gods instead. Their ancestors had obeyed the LORD's commands, but they quickly turned away and did not obey. 18 When their enemies hurt them, the Israelites cried for help. So the LORD felt sorry for them and sent judges to save them from their enemies. The LORD was with those judges all their lives. 19 But when the judges died, the Israelites again sinned and worshipped other gods. They became worse than their ancestors. The Israelites were very stubborn and refused to change their evil ways.

20 So the LORD became angry with the Israelites. He said, "These people have broken the agreement I made with their ancestors. They have not listened to me. 21 I will no longer defeat the nations who were left when Joshua died. 22 I will use them to test Israel, to see if Israel will keep the LORD's commands as their ancestors did." 23 In the past the LORD had permitted those nations to stay in the land. He did not quickly force them out or help Joshua's army defeat them.

3 These are the nations the LORD did not force to leave. He wanted to test the Israelites who had not fought in the wars of Canaan. 2 (The only reason the LORD left those nations in the land was to teach the descendants of the Israelites who had not fought in those wars how to fight.) 3 These are the nations: the five rulers of the Philistines, all the Canaanites, the people of Sidon and the Hivites who lived in the Lebanon mountains from Mount Baal Hermon to Lebo Hamath. 4 Those nations were in the land to test the Israelites— to see if they would obey the commands the LORD had given to their ancestors by Moses.

5 The people of Israel lived with the Canaanites, Hittites, Amorites, Perizzites, Hivites and Jebusites. 6 The Israelites began to marry the daughters of those people, and they allowed their daughters to marry the sons of those people. Israel also served their gods.

Othniel, the First Judge

7 The Israelites did what the LORD said was wrong. They forgot about the LORD their God and served the idols of Baal and Asherah. 8 So the LORD was angry with Israel and allowed Cushan-Rishathaim king of North West Mesopotamia to rule over the Israelites for eight years. 9 When Israel cried to the LORD, the LORD sent someone to save them. Othniel son of Kenaz, Caleb's younger brother, saved the Israelites. 10 The Spirit of the LORD entered Othniel, and he became Israel's judge. When he went to war, the LORD handed over to him Cushan-Rishathaim, king of North West Mesopotamia. 11 So the land was at peace for 40 years. Then Othniel son of Kenaz died.

3:9
Help
Who should you call for help?

Ehud, the Judge

12 Again the people of Israel did what the LORD said was wrong. So the LORD gave Eglon king of Moab power to defeat Israel because of the evil Israel did. 13 Eglon got the Ammonites and the Amalekites to join him. Then he attacked Israel and took Jericho, the city of palm trees. 14 So the people of Israel were ruled by Eglon king of Moab for eighteen years.

15 When the people cried to the LORD, he sent someone to save them. He was Ehud, son of Gera from the people of Benjamin, who was left-handed. Israel sent Ehud to give Eglon king of Moab the payment he demanded. 16 Ehud made himself a sword with two edges, about half a metre long, and he tied it to his right hip under his clothes. 17 Ehud gave Eglon king of Moab the payment he demanded. Now Eglon was a very fat man. 18 After he had given Eglon the payment, Ehud sent away the people who had carried it. 19 When he passed the statues near Gilgal, he turned around and said to Eglon, "I have a secret message for you, King Eglon."

The king said, "Be quiet!" Then he sent all of his servants out of the room.

20 Ehud went to King Eglon, as he was sitting alone in the room above his summer palace.

Ehud said, "I have a message from God for you." As the king stood up from his chair, 21 Ehud reached with his left hand and took out the sword that was tied to his right hip. Then he stabbed the sword deep into the king's belly! 22 Even the handle sank in, and the blade came out of his back. The king's fat covered the whole sword, so Ehud left the sword in Eglon. 23 Then he went out of the room and closed and locked the doors behind him.

24 When the servants returned just after Ehud left, they found the doors to the room locked. So they thought the king was relieving himself. 25 They waited for a long time. Finally they became worried because he still had not opened the doors. So they got the key and unlocked them and saw their king lying dead on the floor!

26 While the servants were waiting, Ehud had escaped. He passed by the statues and went to Seirah. 27 When he reached the mountains of Ephraim he blew the trumpet. The people of Israel heard it and went down from the hills with Ehud leading them.

28 He said to them, "Follow me! The LORD has helped you to defeat your enemies, the Moabites." So Israel followed Ehud and captured the crossings of the Jordan River. They did not allow the Moabites to cross the Jordan River. 29 Israel killed about 10,000 strong and able men from Moab; not one escaped. 30 So that day Moab was forced to be under the rule of Israel, and there was peace in the land for 80 years.

Shamgar, the Judge

31 After Ehud, Shamgar son of Anath saved Israel. Shamgar killed 600 Philistines with a sharp stick used to guide oxen.

Deborah, the Woman Judge

4 After Ehud died, the Israelites again did what the LORD said was wrong. 2 So he let Jabin, a king of Canaan who ruled in the city of Hazor, defeat Israel. Sisera, who lived in Harosheth Haggoyim, was the commander of Jabin's army. 3 Because he had 900 iron chariots and was very cruel to the people of Israel for 20 years, they cried to the LORD for help.

FAITH LINKS

REAL FAITH OR REALLY SCARED?

JUDGES 4

When you think about facing something scary, are you a Barak or a Deborah? Deborah told Barak that he had been chosen by God to fight Sisera and his army. Sisera, with his 900 chariots, seemed impossible to beat. Barak said he wouldn't go unless Deborah went with him. Deborah agreed to go with him into battle. As a leader of Israel, Deborah had faith in God. She trusted that God would do the fighting.

God wants you to have faith in him when you're scared. That means focusing on him, rather than on your fear. Trust him to handle what you're afraid of.

Alone and Forgotten? Genesis 40:23, p. 57

How Big Is God? Job 38—41, p. 703

999, Psalm 28:6, p. 730

Long-lasting Hope, Hosea 14, p. 1184

Our Heavenly Connection, Matthew 6:9–13, p. 1283

A Word About Worry, Matthew 6:25–34, p. 1284

4 A prophetess named Deborah, the wife of Lappidoth, was judge of Israel at that time. 5 Deborah would sit under the Palm Tree of Deborah, which was between the cities of Ramah and Bethel, in the mountains of Ephraim. And the people of Israel would come to her to settle their arguments.

6 Deborah sent a message to Barak son of Abinoam. Barak lived in the city of Kedesh, which is in the area of Naphtali. Deborah said to Barak, "The LORD, the God of Israel, commands you: 'Go and gather 10,000 men of Naphtali and Zebulun and lead them to Mount Tabor. 7 I will make Sisera, the commander of Jabin's army, and his chariots, and his army meet you at the Kishon River. I will hand Sisera over to you.'"

8 Then Barak said to Deborah, "I will go if you will go with me, but if you won't go with me, I won't go."

9 "Of course I will go with you," Deborah answered, "but you will not get credit for the victory. The LORD will let a woman defeat Sisera." So Deborah went with Barak to Kedesh. 10 At Kedesh, Barak called the people of Zebulun and Naphtali together. From them, he gathered 10,000 men to follow him, and Deborah went with him also.

11 Now Heber the Kenite had left the other Kenites, the descendants of Hobab, Moses' brother-in-law. Heber had put up his tent by the great tree in Zaanannim, near Kedesh.

12 When Sisera was told that Barak son of Abinoam had gone to Mount Tabor, 13 Sisera gathered his 900 iron chariots and all the men with him, from Harosheth Haggoyim to the Kishon River.

14 Then Deborah said to Barak, "Get up! Today is the day the LORD will hand over Sisera. The LORD has already cleared the way for you." So Barak led 10,000 men down Mount Tabor. 15 As Barak approached, the LORD confused Sisera and his army and chariots. The LORD defeated them with the sword, but Sisera left his chariot and ran away on foot. 16 Barak and his men chased Sisera's chariots and army to Harosheth Haggoyim. With their swords they killed all of Sisera's men; not one of them was left alive.

17 But Sisera himself ran away to the tent where Jael lived. She was the wife of Heber, one of the Kenite family groups. Heber's family was at peace with Jabin king of Hazor. 18 Jael went out to meet Sisera and said to him, "Come into my tent, master! Come in. Don't be afraid." So Sisera went into Jael's tent, and she covered him with a rug.

19 Sisera said to Jael, "I am thirsty. Please give me some water to drink." So she opened a leather bag of milk and gave him a drink. Then she covered him up.

20 He said to her, "Go and stand at the entrance to the tent. If anyone comes and asks you, 'Is anyone here?' say, 'No.'"

21 But Jael, the wife of Heber, took a tent peg and a hammer and quietly went to Sisera. Since he was very tired, he was in a deep sleep. She hammered the tent peg through the side of Sisera's head and into the ground. And so Sisera died.

22 At that very moment Barak came by Jael's tent, chasing Sisera. Jael went out to meet him and said, "Come. I will show you the man you are looking for." So Barak entered her tent, and there Sisera lay dead, with the tent peg in his head.

23 On that day God defeated Jabin king of Canaan in the sight of Israel.

24 Israel became stronger and stronger against Jabin king of Canaan until finally they destroyed him.

The Song of Deborah

5 On that day Deborah and Barak son of Abinoam sang this song:

2 "The leaders led Israel.
    The people
      volunteered
      to go to
      battle.
    Praise the
      LORD!
3 Listen, kings.
    Pay attention,
      rulers!
    I myself will sing to the LORD.

eMAIL FROM GOD 5:3
Worship
Who should you worship?

I will make music to the LORD, the
  God of Israel.

4 "LORD, when you came from Edom,
  when you marched from the land
    of Edom,
  the earth shook,
  the skies rained,
  and the clouds dropped water.
5 The mountains shook before the
    LORD, the God of Mount Sinai,
  before the LORD, the God of Israel!

6 "In the days of Shamgar son of
    Anath,
  in the days of Jael, the main roads
    were empty.
  Travellers went on the back roads.
7 There were no warriors in Israel
  until I, Deborah, arose,
  until I arose to be a mother to
    Israel.
8 At that time they chose to follow new
    gods.
  Because of this, enemies fought us
    at our city gates.
  No one could find a shield or a
    spear
  among the 40,000 people of Israel.
9 My heart is with the commanders of
    Israel.
  They volunteered freely from
    among the people.
  Praise the LORD!

10 "You who ride on white donkeys
  and sit on saddle blankets,
  and you who walk along the road,
    listen!
11 Listen to the sound of the singers
    at the watering holes.
  There they tell about the victories of
    the LORD,
  the victories of the LORD's warriors
    in Israel.
  Then the LORD's people went down
    to the city gates.

12 "Wake up, wake up, Deborah!
  Wake up, wake up, sing a song!
  Get up, Barak!
  Go and capture your enemies, son
    of Abinoam!

13 "Then those who were left came
    down to the important leaders.
  The LORD's people came down to
    me with strong men.
14 They came from Ephraim in the
    mountains of Amalek.
  Benjamin was among the people
    who followed you.
  From the family group of Makir, the
    commanders came down.
  And from Zebulun came those who
    lead.
15 The princes of Issachar were with
    Deborah.
  The people of Issachar were loyal
    to Barak
  and followed him into the valley.
  The Reubenites thought hard
    about what they would do.
16 Why did you stay by the
    sheepfold?
  Was it to hear the music played for
    your sheep?
  The Reubenites thought hard
    about what they would do.
17 The people of Gilead stayed east of
    the Jordan River.
  People of Dan, why did you stay by
    the ships?
  The people of Asher stayed at the
    seashore,
  at their safe harbours.
18 But the people of Zebulun risked
    their lives,
  as did the people of Naphtali on the
    battlefield.

19 "The kings came, and they fought.
  At that time the kings of Canaan
    fought
  at Taanach, by the waters of
    Megiddo.
  But they took away no silver or
    possessions of Israel.
20 The stars fought from heaven;
  from their paths, they fought
    Sisera.
21 The Kishon River swept Sisera's
    men away,
  that old river, the Kishon River.
  March on, my soul, with strength!
22 Then the horses' hoofs beat the
    ground.

Galloping, galloping go Sisera's
  mighty horses.
23 'May the town of Meroz be cursed,'
    said the angel of the LORD.
  'Bitterly curse its people,
  because they did not come to help
    the LORD.
  They did not fight the strong
    enemy.'

24 "May Jael, the wife of Heber the
    Kenite,
  be blessed above all women who
    live in tents.
25 Sisera asked for water,
  but Jael gave him milk.
  In a bowl fit for a ruler,
    she brought him cream.
26 Jael reached out and took the tent
    peg.
  Her right hand reached for the
    workman's hammer.
  She hit Sisera! She smashed his
    head!
  She crushed and pierced the side
    of his head!
27 At Jael's feet he sank.
  He fell, and he lay there.
  At her feet he sank. He fell.
  Where Sisera sank, there he fell,
    dead!

28 "Sisera's mother looked out through
    the window.
  She looked through the curtains
    and cried out,
  'Why is Sisera's chariot so late in
    coming?
  Why are sounds of his chariots'
    horses delayed?'
29 The wisest of her servant ladies
    answer her,
  and Sisera's mother says to
    herself,
30 'Surely they are robbing the people
    they defeated!
  Surely they are dividing those
    things among themselves!
  Each soldier is given a girl or two.
  Maybe Sisera is taking pieces of
    dyed cloth.
  Maybe they are even taking
  pieces of dyed, embroidered cloth
    for the necks of the victors!'

31 "Let all your enemies die this way,
    LORD!
  But let all the
    people who
    love you
    be as strong as
    the rising
    sun!"
Then there was
peace in the land for 40 years.

5:31
Following God
Check to see what God's people are like.

The Midianites Attack Israel

6 Again the Israelites did what the LORD said was wrong. So for seven years the LORD handed them over to Midian. 2 Because the Midianites were very powerful and were cruel to Israel, the Israelites made hiding places in the mountains, in caves and in safe places. 3 Whenever the Israelites planted crops, the Midianites, Amalekites and other peoples from the east would come and attack them. 4 They camped in the land and destroyed the crops that the Israelites had planted as far away as Gaza. They left nothing for Israel to eat, and no sheep, cattle or donkeys. 5 The Midianites came with their tents and their animals like swarms of locusts to ruin the land. There were so many people and camels they could not be counted. 6 Israel became very poor because of the Midianites, so they cried out to the LORD.

7 When the Israelites cried out to the LORD against the Midianites, 8 the LORD sent a prophet to them. He said, "This is what the LORD, the God of Israel, says: I brought you out of Egypt, the land of slavery. 9 I saved you from the Egyptians and from all those who were against you. I forced the Canaanites out of their land and gave it to you. 10 Then I said to you, 'I am the LORD your God. Live in the land of the Amorites, but do not worship their gods.' But you did not obey me."

The Angel of the LORD Visits Gideon

11 The angel of the LORD came and sat down under the oak tree at Ophrah that

FAITH links

FROM ZERO TO HERO
JUDGES 6; 7

Would you get up and conquer an army of people if God said that you could? Or, would you head for the hills? When Gideon learned that he had been chosen to lead the people of Israel against the Midianites, he was ready to head for the hills. He could hardly believe that God had chosen him for the job. After all, he was a nobody! He was the youngest in his family. He was no hero! But God proved him wrong.

Faith in God makes anyone go from being a zero to being a hero. With God on your side, you are a conqueror!

Want to be a real hero? Connect to these Faithlinks:

The Way to Serve God, 1 Kings 9:4, p. 450

Building Together, Nehemiah 3, p. 627

The Foundation of Our Hope, Isaiah 31:1–8, p. 934

Jesus' Mission and Yours, Isaiah 61:1–2, p. 978

Go! No! Jonah 1, p. 1213

Just a Test, Luke 4:1–13, p. 1373

Midianites. 12 The angel of the LORD appeared to Gideon and said, "The LORD is with you, mighty warrior!"

13 Then Gideon said, "Sir, if the LORD is with us, why are we having so much trouble? Where are the miracles our ancestors told us he did when the LORD brought them out of Egypt? But now he has left us and has handed us over to the Midianites."

14 The LORD turned to Gideon and said, "Go with your strength and save Israel from the Midianites. I am the one who is sending you."

15 But Gideon answered, "Lord, how can I save Israel? My family group is the weakest in Manasseh, and I am the least important member of my family."

16 The LORD answered him, "I will be with you. It will seem as if the Midianites you are fighting are only one man."

17 Then Gideon said to the LORD, "If you are pleased with me, give me proof that it is really you talking with me. 18 Please wait here until I come back to you. Let me bring my offering and set it in front of you."

And the LORD said, "I will wait until you return."

19 So Gideon went in and cooked a young goat, and with 10 kilogrammes of flour, made bread without yeast. Then he put the meat into a basket and the broth into a pot. He brought them out and gave them to the angel under the oak tree.

20 The angel of God said to Gideon, "Put the meat and the bread without yeast on that rock over there. Then pour the broth on them." And Gideon did as he was told. 21 The angel of the LORD touched the meat and the bread with the end of the stick that was in his hand. Then fire jumped up from the rock and completely burned up the meat and the bread! And the angel of the LORD disappeared! 22 Then Gideon understood he had been talking to the angel of the LORD. So Gideon cried out, "Lord GOD! I have seen the angel of the LORD face to face!"

23 But the LORD said to Gideon, "Calm down! Don't be afraid! You will not die!"

24 So Gideon built an altar there to worship the LORD and named it The LORD

---

belonged to Joash, one of the Abiezrite people. Gideon, Joash's son, was separating some wheat from the chaff in a winepress to keep the wheat from the

Is Peace. It still stands at Ophrah, where the Abiezrites live.

Gideon Tears Down the Altar of Baal

25 That same night the LORD said to Gideon, "Take the bull that belongs to your father and a second bull seven years old. Pull down your father's altar to Baal, and cut down the Asherah idol beside it. 26 Then build an altar to the LORD your God with its stones in the right order on this high ground. Kill and burn a second bull on this altar, using the wood from the Asherah idol."

27 So Gideon got ten of his servants and did what the LORD had told him to do. But Gideon was afraid that his family and the men of the city might see him, so he did it at night, not in the daytime.

28 When the men of the city got up the next morning, they saw that the altar for Baal had been destroyed and that the Asherah idol beside it had been cut down! They also saw the altar Gideon had built and the second bull that had been sacrificed on it. 29 The men of the city asked each other, "Who did this?"

After they asked many questions, someone told them, "Gideon son of Joash did this."

30 So they said to Joash, "Bring your son out. He has pulled down the altar of Baal and cut down the Asherah idol beside it. He must die!"

31 But Joash said to the angry crowd around him, "Are you going to take Baal's side? Are you going to defend him? Anyone who takes Baal's side will be killed by morning! If Baal is a god, let him fight for himself. It's his altar that has been pulled down." 32 So on that day Gideon got the name Jerub-Baal, which means "let Baal fight against him," because Gideon pulled down Baal's altar.

Gideon Defeats Midian

33 All the Midianites, the Amalekites and other peoples from the east joined together and came across the Jordan River and camped in the Valley of Jezreel. 34 But the Spirit of the LORD entered Gideon, and he blew a trumpet to call the Abiezrites to follow him. 35 He sent messengers to all of Manasseh, calling them to follow him. He also sent messengers to the people of Asher, Zebulun and Naphtali. So they also went up to meet Gideon and his men.

36 Then Gideon said to God, "You said you would help me save Israel. 37 I will put some wool on the threshing floor. If there is dew only on the wool but all of the ground is dry, then I will know that you will use me to save Israel, as you said." 38 And that is just what happened. When Gideon got up early the next morning and squeezed the wool, he got a full bowl of water from it.

39 Then Gideon said to God, "Don't be angry with me if I ask just one more thing. Please let me make one more test. Let only the wool be dry while the ground around it gets wet with dew." 40 That night God did that very thing. Just the wool was dry, but the ground around it was wet with dew.

7 Early in the morning Jerub-Baal (also called Gideon) and all his men set up their camp at the spring of Harod. The Midianites were camped north of them in the valley at the bottom of the hill called Moreh. 2 Then the LORD said to Gideon, "You have too many men to defeat the Midianites. I don't want the Israelites to boast that they saved themselves. 3 So now, announce to the people, 'Anyone who is afraid may leave Mount Gilead and go back home.'" So 22,000 men returned home, but 10,000 remained.

4 Then the LORD said to Gideon, "There are still too many men. Take the men down to the water, and I will test them for you there. If I say, 'This man will go with you,' he will go. But if I say, 'That one will not go with you,' he will not go."

5 So Gideon led the men down to the water. There the LORD said to him, "Separate them into those who drink water by lapping it up like a dog and those who bend down to drink." 6 There were 300 men who used their hands to bring water to their mouths, lapping it as a dog does. All the rest got down on their knees to drink.

7 Then the LORD said to Gideon, "Using the 300 men who lapped the water, I will save you and hand Midian over to you. Let all the others go home." 8 So Gideon sent the rest of Israel to their homes. But he kept the 300 men and took the jars and the trumpets of those who left.

Now the camp of Midian was in the valley below Gideon. 9 That night the LORD said to Gideon, "Get up. Go down and attack the camp of the Midianites, because I will give them to you. 10 But if you are afraid to go down, take your servant Purah with you. 11 When you come to the camp of Midian, you will hear what they are saying. Then you will not be afraid to attack the camp."

Gideon is Encouraged

So Gideon and his servant Purah went down to the edge of the enemy camp. 12 The Midianites, the Amalekites and all the peoples from the east were camped in that valley. There were so many of them they seemed like locusts. Their camels could not be counted because they were as many as the grains of sand on the seashore!

13 When Gideon came to the enemy camp, he heard a man telling his friend about a dream. He was saying, "I dreamed that a loaf of barley bread rolled into the camp of Midian. It hit the tent so hard that the tent turned over and fell flat!"

14 The man's friend said, "Your dream is about the sword of Gideon son of Joash, a man of Israel. God will hand Midian and the whole army over to him!"

15 When Gideon heard about the dream and what it meant, he worshiped God. Then Gideon went back to the camp of Israel and called out to them, "Get up! The LORD has handed the army of Midian over to you!" 16 Gideon divided the 300 men into three groups. He gave each man a trumpet and an empty jar with a burning torch inside.

17 Gideon told the men, "Watch me and do what I do. When I get to the edge of the camp, do what I do. 18 Surround the enemy camp. When I and everyone with me blow our trumpets, you blow your trumpets too. Then shout, 'For the LORD and for Gideon!'"

Midian is Defeated

19 So Gideon and the 100 men with him came to the edge of the enemy camp just after they had changed guards. It was during the middle watch of the night. Then Gideon and his men blew their trumpets and smashed their jars. 20 All three groups of Gideon's men blew their trumpets and smashed their jars. They held the torches in their left hands and the trumpets in their right hands. Then they shouted, "A sword for the LORD and for Gideon!" 21 Each of Gideon's men stayed in his place around the camp, but the Midianites began shouting and running to escape.

22 When Gideon's 300 men blew their trumpets, the LORD made all the Midianites fight each other with their swords! The enemy army ran away to the city of Beth Shittah towards Zererah. They ran as far as the border of Abel Meholah, near the city of Tabbath. 23 Then men of Israel from Naphtali, Asher and all of Manasseh were called out to chase the Midianites. 24 Gideon sent messengers through all the mountains of Ephraim, saying, "Come down and attack the Midianites. Take control of the Jordan River as far as Beth Barah before the Midianites can get to it."

So they called out all the men of Ephraim, who took control of the Jordan River as far as Beth Barah. 25 The men of Ephraim captured two princes of Midian named Oreb and Zeeb. They killed Oreb at the rock of Oreb and Zeeb at the winepress of Zeeb, and they continued chasing the Midianites. They brought the heads of Oreb and Zeeb to Gideon, who was east of the Jordan River.

8 The men of Ephraim asked Gideon, "Why did you treat us this way? Why didn't you call us when you went to fight against Midian?" They argued angrily with Gideon.

2 But he answered them, "I have not done as well as you! The small part you did was better than all that my people of Abiezer did. 3 God let you capture Oreb

and Zeeb, the princes of Midian. How can I compare what I did with what you did?" When the men of Ephraim heard Gideon's answer, they were not as angry any more.

Gideon Captures Two Kings

4 When Gideon and his 300 men came to the Jordan River, they were tired, but they chased the enemy across to the other side. 5 Gideon said to the men of Succoth, "Please give my soldiers some bread because they are very tired. I am chasing Zebah and Zalmunna, the kings of Midian."

6 But the leaders of Succoth said, "Why should we give your soldiers bread? You haven't caught Zebah and Zalmunna yet."

7 Then Gideon said, "The LORD will surrender Zebah and Zalmunna to me. After that, I will whip your skin with thorns and briers from the desert."

8 Gideon left Succoth and went to the city of Peniel and asked them for food. But the people of Peniel gave him the same answer as the people of Succoth. 9 So Gideon said to the men of Peniel, "After I win the victory, I will return and pull down this tower."

10 Zebah and Zalmunna and their army were in the city of Karkor. About 15,000 men were left of the armies of the peoples of the east. Already 120,000 soldiers had been killed. 11 Gideon went up the road of those who live in tents east of Nobah and Jogbehah, and he attacked the enemy army when they did not expect it. 12 Zebah and Zalmunna, the kings of Midian, ran away, but Gideon chased and captured them and frightened away their army.

13 Then Gideon son of Joash returned from the battle by the Pass of Heres. 14 Gideon captured a young man from Succoth and asked him some questions. So the young man wrote down for Gideon the names of 77 officers and elders of Succoth.

Gideon Punishes Succoth

15 When Gideon came to Succoth, he said to the people of that city, "Here are Zebah and Zalmunna. You made fun of me by saying, 'Why should we give bread to your tired men? You have not caught Zebah and Zalmunna yet.'" 16 So Gideon took the elders of the city and punished them with thorns and briers from the desert. 17 He also pulled down the tower of Peniel and killed the people in that city.

18 Gideon asked Zebah and Zalmunna, "What were the men like that you killed on Mount Tabor?"

They answered, "They were like you. Each one of them looked like a prince."

19 Gideon said, "Those were my brothers, my mother's sons. As surely as the LORD lives, I would not kill you if you had spared them." 20 Then Gideon said to Jether, his oldest son, "Kill them." But Jether was only a boy and was afraid, so he did not take out his sword.

21 Then Zebah and Zalmunna said to Gideon, "Come on. Kill us yourself. As the saying goes, 'It takes a man to do a man's job.'" So Gideon got up and killed Zebah and Zalmunna and took the decorations off their camels' necks.

Gideon Makes an Idol

22 The people of Israel said to Gideon, "You saved us from the Midianites. Now, we want you and your son and your grandson to rule over us."

23 But Gideon told them, "The LORD will be your ruler. I will not rule over you, nor will my son rule over you." 24 He said, "I want you to do this one thing for me. I want each of you to give me a gold earring from the things you took in the fighting." (The Ishmaelites[n] wore gold earrings.)

25 They said, "We will gladly give you what you want." So they spread out a coat, and everyone threw down an earring from what he had taken. 26 The gold earrings weighed about 20 kilogrammes. This did not include the decorations, necklaces and purple robes worn by the kings of Midian, nor the chains from the camels' necks. 27 Gideon used the

---

8:24 Ishmaelites Another name for the Midianites. See Genesis 37:25-28.

FAITH CHALLENGE

Here's a challenge for you. Read 8:23 to find out what a famous Israelite leader told his people about their government. What could you do to let your friends know that the Lord is ruler of your life?

Testing It

Judges 8:23
But Gideon told them, "The LORD will be your ruler. I will not rule over you, nor will my son rule over you."

_____
_____
_____
_____
_____

gold to make a holy robe, which he put in his home town of Ophrah. But all the Israelites were unfaithful to God and worshipped it, so it became a trap for Gideon and his family.

The Death of Gideon

28 So Midian was under the rule of Israel; they did not cause trouble any more. And the land had peace for 40 years, as long as Gideon was alive.

29 Gideon[n] son of Joash went to his home to live. 30 He had 70 sons of his own, because he had many wives. 31 He had a slave woman who lived in Shechem, and he had a son by her, whom he named Abimelech. 32 So Gideon son of Joash died at a good old age. He was buried in the tomb of Joash, his father, in Ophrah, where the Abiezrites live.

33 As soon as Gideon died, the people of Israel were again unfaithful to God and followed the Baals. They made Baal-of-the-Agreement their god. 34 The Israelites did not remember the LORD their God, who had saved them from all their enemies living all around them. 35 And they were not kind to the family of Jerub-Baal, also called Gideon, for all the good he had done for Israel.

Abimelech Becomes King

9 Abimelech son of Gideon[n] went to his uncles in the city of Shechem. He said to his uncles and all of his mother's family group, 2 "Ask the leaders of Shechem, 'Is it better for the 70 sons of Gideon to rule over you or for one man to rule?' Remember, I am your relative."

3 Abimelech's uncles spoke to all the leaders of Shechem about this. And they decided to follow Abimelech, because they said, "He is our relative." 4 So the leaders of Shechem gave Abimelech about 70 pieces of silver from the temple of the god Baal-of-the-Agreement. Abimelech used the silver to hire some worthless, reckless men, who followed him wherever he went. 5 He went to Ophrah, the home town of his father, and murdered his 70 brothers, the sons of Gideon. He killed them all on one stone. But Gideon's youngest son, Jotham, hid from Abimelech and escaped. 6 Then all of the leaders of Shechem and Beth Millo gathered beside the great tree standing in Shechem. There they made Abimelech their king.

Jotham's Story

7 When Jotham heard this, he went and stood on the top of Mount Gerizim. He shouted to the people: "Listen to me, you leaders of Shechem, so that God will listen to you! 8 One day the trees decided to appoint a king to rule over

---

8:29, 9:1 **Gideon** Also called Jerub-Baal.

Judges 9:9 324

THE JUDGES
Judges 9

After the death of Joshua, the Israelites were ruled by judges, or leaders, for about 300 years. This was a dark time in Israel's history because "everyone did what seemed right" and did not obey God. The judges tried to steer the people back to God, but many of them were also disobedient. Here are some of the judges from that time:

1. Othniel was the first judge of Israel. He delivered the Israelites from the king of Northwest Mesopotamia. (Check out Judges 3:7–11.)

2. Shamgar was famous for killing 600 men with a sharp stick used to guide oxen. He delivered Israel from the Philistines. (Look up Judges 3:31.)

3. Deborah was the only woman judge of Israel. She and her military commander, Barak, fought against Jabin, king of Canaan, and his commander, Sisera. (See Judges 4:1–24.)

4. Gideon wasn't a judge or a soldier. Still God used him to be a judge of Israel and to lead a small army of 300 men to defeat the much greater forces of Midian. (Look up Judges 6—8.)

5. Samson was a judge in Israel. He ruled for 20 years. His body was strong, but his character was weak. Because of that, the Philistines captured him and made him a slave. Samson died when he destroyed a pagan temple, but he killed many Philistine enemies at the same time. (See Judges 13—16.)

them. They said to the olive tree, 'You be king over us!'

9 "But the olive tree said, 'Men and gods are honoured by my oil. Should I stop making it and go and sway over the other trees?'

10 "Then the trees said to the fig tree, 'Come and be king over us!'

11 "But the fig tree answered, 'Should I stop making my sweet and good fruit and go and sway over the other trees?'

12 "Then the trees said to the vine, 'Come and be king over us!'

13 "But the vine answered, 'My new wine makes men and gods happy. Should I stop making it and go and sway over the trees?'

14 "Then all the trees said to the thornbush, 'Come and be king over us.'

15 "But the thornbush said to the trees, 'If you really want to appoint me king over you, come and find shelter in my shade! But if not, let fire come out of the thornbush and burn up the cedars of Lebanon!'

16 "Now, were you completely honest

and sincere when you made Abimelech king? Have you been fair to Gideon[n] and his family? Have you treated Gideon as you should? 17 Remember, my father fought for you and risked his life to save you from the power of the Midianites. 18 But now you have turned against my father's family and have killed his 70 sons on one stone. You have made Abimelech, the son of my father's slave girl, king over the leaders of Shechem just because he is your relative! 19 So then, if you have been honest and sincere to Gideon and his family today, be happy with Abimelech as your king. And may he be happy with you! 20 But if not, may fire come out of Abimelech and completely burn you leaders of Shechem and Beth Millo! Also may fire come out of the leaders of Shechem and Beth Millo and burn up Abimelech!"

21 Then Jotham ran away and escaped to the city of Beer. He lived there because he was afraid of his brother Abimelech.

Abimelech Fights Against Shechem

22 Abimelech ruled Israel for three years. 23 Then God sent an evil spirit to make trouble between Abimelech and the leaders of Shechem so that the leaders of Shechem turned against him. 24 Abimelech had killed Gideon's[n] 70 sons, his own brothers, and the leaders of Shechem had helped him. So God sent the evil spirit to punish them. 25 The leaders of Shechem were against Abimelech then. They put men on the hilltops in ambush who robbed everyone going by. And Abimelech was told.

26 A man named Gaal son of Ebed and his brothers moved into Shechem, and the leaders of Shechem trusted him. 27 They went out to the vineyards to pick grapes, and they squeezed the grapes. Then they had a feast in the temple of their god, where they ate and drank and cursed Abimelech. 28 Gaal son of Ebed said, "We are the men of Shechem. Who is Abimelech that we should serve him? Isn't he one of Gideon's sons, and isn't Zebul his officer? We should serve the men of Hamor, Shechem's father. Why should we serve Abimelech? 29 If you made me commander of these people, I would get rid of Abimelech. I would say to him, 'Get your army ready and come out to battle.'"

30 Now when Zebul, the ruler of Shechem, heard what Gaal son of Ebed said, he was very angry. 31 He sent secret messengers to Abimelech, saying, "Gaal son of Ebed and Gaal's brothers have come to Shechem, and they are turning the city against you! 32 You and your men should get up during the night and hide in the fields outside the city. 33 As soon as the sun comes up in the morning, attack the city. When Gaal and his men come out to fight you, do what you can to them."

34 So Abimelech and all his soldiers got up during the night and hid near Shechem in four groups. 35 Gaal son of Ebed went out and was standing at the entrance to the city gate. As he was standing there, Abimelech and his soldiers came out of their hiding places.

36 When Gaal saw the soldiers, he said to Zebul, "Look! There are people coming down from the mountains!"

But Zebul said, "You are seeing the shadows of the mountains. The shadows just look like people."

37 But again Gaal said, "Look, there are people coming down from the centre of the land, and there is a group coming from the fortune-tellers' tree!"

38 Zebul said to Gaal, "Where is your boasting now? You said, 'Who is Abimelech that we should serve him?' You made fun of these men. Now go out and fight them."

39 So Gaal led the men of Shechem out to fight Abimelech. 40 Abimelech and his men chased them, and many of Gaal's men were killed before they could get back to the city gate. 41 While Abimelech stayed at Arumah, Zebul forced Gaal and his brothers to leave Shechem.

42 The next day the people of Shechem went out to the fields. When Abimelech was told about it, 43 he separated his men into three groups and hid them in

---

9:16, 24 Gideon Also called Jerub-Baal.

the fields. When he saw the people coming out of the city, he jumped up and attacked them. 44 Abimelech and his group ran to the entrance gate to the city. The other two groups ran out to the people in the fields and struck them down. 45 Abimelech and his men fought the city of Shechem all day until they captured it and killed its people. Then he tore it down and threw salt[n] over the ruins.

The Tower of Shechem Burns

46 When the leaders who were in the Tower of Shechem heard what had happened to Shechem, they gathered in the safest room of the temple of El Berith. 47 Abimelech heard that all the leaders of the Tower of Shechem had gathered there. 48 So he and all his men went up Mount Zalmon, near Shechem. Abimelech took an axe and cut some branches and put them on his shoulders. He said to all those with him, "Hurry! Do what I have done!" 49 So all those men cut branches and followed Abimelech and piled them against the safest room of the temple. Then they set them on fire and burned the people inside. So all the people who were at the Tower of Shechem also died—about 1,000 men and women.

Abimelech's Death

50 Then Abimelech went to the city of Thebez. He surrounded the city, attacked it and captured it. 51 But inside the city was a strong tower, so all the men, women and leaders of that city ran to the tower. When they got inside, they locked the door behind them. Then they climbed up to the roof of the tower. 52 Abimelech came to the tower to attack it. He approached the door of the tower to set it on fire, 53 but as he came near, a woman dropped a grinding stone on his head, crushing his skull.

54 He quickly called to the officer who carried his armour and said, "Take out your sword and kill me. I don't want people to say, 'A woman killed Abimelech.'" So the officer stabbed Abimelech, and he died. 55 When the people of Israel saw Abimelech was dead, they all returned home.

56 In that way God punished Abimelech for all the evil he had done to his father by killing his 70 brothers. 57 God also punished the men of Shechem for the evil they had done. So the curse spoken by Jotham, the youngest son of Gideon,[n] came true.

Tola, the Judge

10 After Abimelech died, another judge came to save Israel. He was Tola son of Puah, the son of Dodo. Tola was from the people of Issachar and lived in the city of Shamir in the mountains of Ephraim. 2 Tola was a judge for Israel for 23 years. Then he died and was buried in Shamir.

Jair, the Judge

3 After Tola died, Jair from the region of Gilead became judge. He was a judge for Israel for 22 years. 4 Jair had 30 sons, who rode 30 donkeys. These 30 sons controlled 30 towns in Gilead, which are called the Towns of Jair to this day. 5 Jair died and was buried in the city of Kamon.

The Ammonites Trouble Israel

6 Again the Israelites did what the LORD said was wrong. They worshipped Baal and Ashtoreth, the gods of Aram, Sidon, Moab and Ammon, and the gods of the Philistines. The Israelites left the LORD and stopped serving him. 7 So the LORD was angry with them and handed them over to the Philistines and the Ammonites. 8 In the same year those people destroyed the Israelites who lived east of the Jordan River in the region of Gilead, where the Amorites lived. So the Israelites suffered for eighteen years. 9 The

> So the LORD was angry with them and handed them over to the Philistines and the Ammonites.
> – Judges 10:7

9:45 salt The salt would stop crops from growing there.
9:57 Gideon Also called Jerub-Baal.

Ammonites then crossed the Jordan River to fight the people of Judah, Benjamin and Ephraim, causing much trouble to the people of Israel. 10 So the Israelites cried out to the LORD, "We have sinned against you. We left our God and worshipped the Baal idols."

11 The LORD answered the Israelites, "When the Egyptians, Amorites, Ammonites, Philistines, 12 Sidonians, Amalekites and Maonites were cruel to you, you cried out to me, and I saved you. 13 But now you have left me again and have worshipped other gods. So I refuse to save you again. 14 You have chosen those gods. So go and call to them for help. Let them save you when you are in trouble."

15 But the people of Israel said to the LORD, "We have sinned. Do to us whatever you want, but please save us today!" 16 Then the Israelites threw away the foreign gods among them, and they worshipped the LORD again. So he felt sorry for them when he saw their suffering.

17 The Ammonites gathered for war and camped in Gilead. The Israelites gathered and camped at Mizpah. 18 The leaders of the people of Gilead said, "Who will lead us to attack the Ammonites? He will become the head of all those who live in Gilead."

Jephthah Is Chosen as Leader

11 Jephthah was a strong soldier from Gilead. His father was named Gilead, and his mother was a prostitute. 2 Gilead's wife had several sons. When they grew up, they forced Jephthah to leave his home, saying to him, "You will not get any of our father's property, because you are the son of another woman." 3 So Jephthah ran away from his brothers and lived in the land of Tob. There some worthless men began to follow him.

4 After a time the Ammonites fought against Israel. 5 When the Ammonites made war against Israel, the elders of Gilead went to Jephthah to bring him back from Tob. 6 They said to him, "Come and lead our army so we can fight the Ammonites."

7 But Jephthah said to them, "Didn't

FAITH links

WHAT'S OUT BECOMES IN

JUDGES 11

If someone called you a loser, then turned around and asked you for help, what would you do? That was the situation Jephthah found himself in. His own family told him they didn't want him around. But when the Ammonites attacked, they begged Jephthah for help. Suddenly, Jephthah the outcast was in. Jephthah didn't let their first opinion of him affect his behaviour. He agreed to help them because he knew that God would help him.

If someone treats you unkindly, you don't have to respond with unkindness. You also don't have to accept someone else's bad opinion as the truth. Instead, trust God to help you see the truth and do what's right.

When Bad Turns to Worse,
Exodus 5:6–12, p. 82

Play Fair or Play Favourites?
Deuteronomy 1:16–18, p. 227

Wronged for What's Right, Ezra 4:4–5, p. 612

Does Crime Pay? Psalm 37:1–7, p. 736

In the Lions' Den, Daniel 6, p. 1160

Who Needs Love? Luke 6:27–36, p. 1379

you hate me? You forced me to leave my father's house. Why are you coming to me now that you are in trouble?"

8 The elders of Gilead said to Jephthah, "It is because of those troubles that we come to you now. Please come with us and fight against the Ammonites. You will be the ruler over everyone who lives in Gilead."

9 Then Jephthah answered, "If you take me back to Gilead to fight the Ammonites and the LORD helps me win, I will be your ruler."

10 The elders of Gilead said to him, "The LORD is listening to everything we are saying. We promise to do all that you tell us to do." 11 So Jephthah went with the elders of Gilead, and the people made him their leader and commander of their army. Jephthah repeated all of his words in front of the LORD at Mizpah.

Jephthah Sends Messengers to the Ammonite King

12 Jephthah sent messengers to the king of the Ammonites, asking, "What have you got against Israel? Why have you come to attack our land?"

13 The king of the Ammonites answered the messengers of Jephthah, "We are fighting Israel because you took our land when you came up from Egypt. You took our land from the Arnon River to the Jabbok River to the Jordan River. Now give our land back to us peacefully."

14 Jephthah sent the messengers to the Ammonite king again. 15 They said:

"This is what Jephthah says: Israel did not take the land of the people of Moab or Ammon. 16 When the Israelites came out of Egypt, they went into the desert to the Red Sea and then to Kadesh. 17 Israel sent messengers to the king of Edom, saying, 'Let the people of Israel go across your land.' But the king of Edom refused. We sent the same message to the king of Moab, but he also refused. So the Israelites stayed at Kadesh.

18 "Then the Israelites went into the desert around the borders of the lands of Edom and Moab. Israel went east of the land of Moab and camped on the other side of the Arnon River, the border of Moab. They did not cross it to go into the land of Moab.

19 "Then Israel sent messengers to Sihon king of the Amorites, king of the city of Heshbon, asking, 'Let the people of Israel pass through your land to go to our land.' 20 But Sihon did not trust the Israelites to cross his land. So he gathered all of his people and camped at Jahaz and fought with Israel.

21 "But the LORD, the God of Israel, handed Sihon and his army over to Israel. All the land of the Amorites became the property of Israel. 22 So Israel took all the land of the Amorites from the Arnon River to the Jabbok River, from the desert to the Jordan River.

23 "It was the LORD, the God of Israel, who forced out the Amorites ahead of the people of Israel. So do you think you can make them leave? 24 Take the land that your god Chemosh has given you. We will live in the land the LORD our God has given us!

25 "Are you any better than Balak son of Zippor, king of Moab? Did he ever quarrel or fight with the people of Israel? 26 For 300 years the Israelites have lived in Heshbon and Aroer and the towns around them and in all the cities along the Arnon River. Why have you not taken these cities back in all that time? 27 I have not sinned against you, but you are sinning against me by making war on me. May the LORD, the Judge, decide whether the Israelites or the Ammonites are right."

28 But the king of the Ammonites ignored this message from Jephthah.

Jephthah's Promise

29 Then the Spirit of the LORD entered Jephthah. Jephthah passed through Gilead and Manasseh and the city of Mizpah in Gilead to the land of the Ammonites. 30 Jephthah made a promise to the LORD, saying, "If you will hand over the Ammonites to me, 31 I will give you as a burnt offering the first thing that comes out of my house to meet me when I return from the victory. It will be the LORD's."

32 Then Jephthah went over to fight the Ammonites, and the LORD handed them over to him. 33 In a great defeat Jephthah struck them down from the city of Aroer to the area of Minnith, and 20 cities as far as the city of Abel Keramim. So the Ammonites were defeated by the Israelites.

34 When Jephthah returned to his home in Mizpah, his daughter was the first one to come out to meet him, playing a tambourine and dancing. She was his only child; he had no other sons or daughters. 35 When Jephthah saw his daughter, he tore his clothes to show his sorrow. He said, "My daughter! You have made me so sad because I made a promise to the LORD, and I cannot break it!"

36 Then his daughter said, "Father, you made a promise to the LORD. So do to me just what you promised, because the LORD helped you defeat your enemies, the Ammonites." 37 She also said, "But let me do one thing. Let me be alone for two months to go to the mountains. Since I will never marry, let me and my friends go and cry together."

38 Jephthah said, "Go." So he sent her away for two months. She and her friends stayed in the mountains and cried for her because she would never marry. 39 After two months she returned to her father, and Jephthah did to her what he had promised. Jephthah's daughter never had a husband.

From this came a custom in Israel that 40 every year the young women of Israel would go out for four days to remember the daughter of Jephthah from Gilead.

Jephthah and Ephraim

12 The men of Ephraim called all their soldiers together and crossed the river to the town of Zaphon. They said to Jephthah, "Why didn't you call us to help you fight the Ammonites? We will burn your house down with you in it."

2 Jephthah answered them, "My people and I fought a great battle against the Ammonites. I called you, but you didn't come to help me. 3 When I saw that you would not help me, I risked my own life and went against the Ammonites. The LORD handed them over to me. So why have you come to fight against me today?"

4 Then Jephthah called the men of Gilead together and fought the men of Ephraim. The men of Gilead struck them down because the Ephraimites had said, "You men of Gilead are nothing but deserters from Ephraim—living between Ephraim and Manasseh." 5 The men of Gilead captured the crossings of the Jordan River that led to the country of Ephraim. A person from Ephraim trying to escape would say, "Let me cross the river." Then the men of Gilead would ask him, "Are you from Ephraim?" If he replied "No," 6 they would say to him, "Say the word 'Shibboleth'." The men of Ephraim could not say that word correctly. So if the person from Ephraim said, "Sibboleth," the men of Gilead would kill him at the crossing. So 42,000 people from Ephraim were killed at that time.

7 Jephthah was a judge for Israel for six years. Then Jephthah, the man from Gilead, died and was buried in a town in Gilead.

Ibzan, the Judge

8 After Jephthah died, Ibzan from Bethlehem was a judge for Israel. 9 He had 30 sons and 30 daughters. He let his daughters marry men who were not in his family group, and he brought 30 women who were not in his tribe to be wives for his sons. Ibzan judged Israel for seven years. 10 Then he died and was buried in Bethlehem.

Elon, the Judge

11 After Ibzan died, Elon from the tribe of Zebulun was a judge for Israel. He judged Israel for ten years. 12 Then Elon, the man of Zebulun, died and was buried in the city of Aijalon in the land of Zebulun.

Abdon, the Judge

13 After Elon died, Abdon son of Hillel from the city of Pirathon was a judge for Israel. 14 He had 40 sons and 30 grandsons, who rode on 70 donkeys. He judged

Judges 12:15 330

Israel for eight years. 15 Then Abdon son of Hillel died and was buried in Pirathon in the land of Ephraim, in the mountains where the Amalekites lived.

The Birth of Samson

13 Again the people of Israel did what the LORD said was wrong. So he handed them over to the Philistines for 40 years.

2 There was a man named Manoah from the tribe of Dan, who lived in the city of Zorah. He had a wife, but she could not have children. 3 The angel of the LORD appeared to Manoah's wife and said, "You have not been able to have children, but you will become pregnant and give birth to a son. 4 Be careful not to drink wine or beer or eat anything that is unclean, 5 because you will become pregnant and have a son. You must never cut his hair, because he will be a Nazirite, given to God from birth. He will begin to save Israel from the power of the Philistines."

6 Then Manoah's wife went to him and told him what had happened. She said, "A man from God came to me. He looked like an angel from God; his appearance was frightening. I didn't ask him where he was from, and he didn't tell me his name. 7 But he said to me, 'You will become

ME AND MY PARENTS

How do you get on with your parents? Do they have rules for you that you think are OK, or do you think they are too strict?

Let's welcome Erik, aged 10, to Connect 2-You. He's having a problem with his parents and he'd like some help.

My problem is that my parents are much stricter than all my friends' parents! My friends can play whatever video games, movies and music they want. But my parents ruin my fun with a billion rules about that stuff. They say it's for my own good, but sometimes I feel like just doing what I want and not listening to what they say.

Do you know how Erik's feeling? It's tough to do what other people tell us to do – but God tells us that obeying your mum and dad is always best. God gives us parents to help "light our path". Their job is to steer us away from danger areas – no matter how badly we may want to explore those areas. It's not an easy job. That's why God wants us to honour our parents. Honouring means more than obeying. It means treating them with respect, love and appreciation.

A funny thing happens when you honour your parents. They start to honour you back. When you show them that you're responsible enough to follow their rules, you may find that your parents give you more freedom and trust. For some tips on how to obey your parents, take a look at the Livin' It page on obeying your mum and dad, <u>Proverbs 6:20-23, p. 834</u>. It may encourage you!

pregnant and will have a son. Don't drink wine or beer or eat anything that is unclean, because the boy will be a Nazirite to God from his birth until the day of his death.'"

8 Then Manoah prayed to the LORD: "Lord, I beg you to let the man of God come to us again. Let him teach us what we should do for the boy who will be born to us."

9 God heard Manoah's prayer, and the angel of God came to Manoah's wife again while she was sitting in the field. But her husband Manoah was not with her. 10 So she ran to tell him, "He is here! The man who appeared to me the other day is here!"

11 Manoah got up and followed his wife. When he came to the man, he said, "Are you the man who spoke to my wife?"

The man said, "I am."

12 So Manoah asked, "When what you say happens, what kind of life should the boy live? What should he do?"

13 The angel of the LORD said, "Your wife must be careful to do everything I told her to do. 14 She must not eat anything that grows on a grapevine, or drink any wine or beer, or eat anything that is unclean. She must do everything I have commanded her."

15 Manoah said to the angel of the LORD, "We would like you to stay awhile so we can cook a young goat for you."

16 The angel of the LORD answered, "Even if I stay awhile, I would not eat your food. But if you want to prepare something, offer a burnt offering to the LORD." (Manoah did not understand that the man was really the angel of the LORD.)

17 Then Manoah asked the angel of the LORD, "What is your name? Then we will honour you when what you have said really happens."

18 The angel of the LORD said, "Why do you ask my name? It is too amazing for you to understand." 19 So Manoah sacrificed a young goat on a rock and offered some grain as a gift to the LORD. Then an amazing thing happened as Manoah and his wife watched. 20 The flames went up to the sky from the altar. As the fire burned, the angel of the LORD went up to heaven in the flame. When Manoah and his wife saw that, they bowed face down on the ground. 21 The angel of the LORD did not appear to them again. Then Manoah understood that the man was really the angel of the LORD. 22 Manoah said, "We have seen God, so we will surely die."

23 But his wife said to him, "If the LORD wanted to kill us, he would not have accepted our burnt offering or grain offering. He would not have shown us all these things or told us all this."

24 So the woman gave birth to a boy and named him Samson. He grew, and the LORD blessed him. 25 The Spirit of the LORD began to work in Samson while he was in the city of Mahaneh Dan, between the cities of Zorah and Eshtaol.

Samson's First Marriage

14 Samson went down to the city of Timnah where he saw a Philistine woman. 2 When he returned home, he said to his father and mother, "I saw a Philistine woman in Timnah. I want you to get her for me so I can marry her."

3 His father and mother answered, "Surely there is a woman from Israel you can marry. Do you have to marry a woman from the Philistines, who are not circumcised?"

But Samson said, "Get that woman for me! She is the one I want!" 4 (Samson's parents did not know that the LORD wanted this to happen because he was looking for a way to challenge the Philistines, who were ruling over Israel at this time.) 5 Samson went down with his father and mother to Timnah, as far as the vineyard near there. Suddenly, a young lion came roaring towards Samson! 6 The Spirit of the LORD entered Samson with great power, and he tore the lion apart with his bare hands. For him it was as easy as tearing apart a young goat. But Samson did not tell his father or mother what he had done. 7 Then he went down to the city and talked to the Philistine woman, and he liked her.

8 Several days later Samson went back to marry her. On his way he went over to

FAITH links

I WANT IT NOW!
JUDGES 14:1-3

Samson wanted what he wanted when he wanted it. He demanded that his parents get him the wife he wanted, even though they knew his choice was not good. His lack of self-control and his failure to make good choices led him into trouble.

Part of self-control means learning to control your need to have everything *right now!* It means learning the value of waiting. Self-control is a fruit of the Spirit. (Read about it in Galatians 5:22–23, p. 1593.) A person with self-control takes the time to make wise choices about his or her wants. One way to make wise choices is to seek wise advice.

Connect here to find out more about self-control:

Obey? No Way! Exodus 1:15–21, p. 76

Choosing Sides, 1 Samuel 20, p. 382

Mind Guard, Proverbs 4:23, p. 831

The Right Ingredients, Micah 6:8, p. 1227

Exercising Patience, Luke 2:25–28, 36–37, p. 1369

Best Seat in the House, Luke 14:7–11, p. 1398

look at the body of the dead lion and found a swarm of bees and honey in it. 9 Samson got some of the honey with his hands and walked along eating it. When he came to his parents, he gave some to them. They ate it, too, but Samson did not tell them he had taken the honey from the body of the dead lion.

10 Samson's father went down to see the Philistine woman. And Samson gave a feast, as was the custom for the bridegroom. 11 When the people saw him, they sent 30 friends to be with him.

Samson's Riddle

12 Samson said to them, "Let me tell you a riddle. Try to find the answer during the seven days of the feast. If you can, I will give you 30 linen shirts and 30 changes of clothes. 13 But if you can't, you must give me 30 linen shirts and 30 changes of clothes."

So they said, "Tell us your riddle so we can hear it."

14 Samson said,

"Out of the eater comes something
   to eat.
Out of the strong comes something
   sweet."

After three days, they had not found the answer.

15 On the fourth[n] day they said to Samson's wife, "Did you invite us here to make us poor? Trick your husband into telling us the answer to the riddle. If you don't, we will burn you and everyone in your father's house."

16 So Samson's wife went to him, crying, and said, "You hate me! You don't really love me! You told my people a riddle, but you won't tell me the answer."

Samson said, "I haven't even told my father or mother. Why should I tell you?"

17 Samson's wife cried for the rest of the seven days of the feast. So he finally gave her the answer on the seventh day, because she kept bothering him. Then she told her people the answer to the riddle.

14:15 *fourth* The Hebrew word is "seventh." Some old translations say "fourth," which fits the order of events better.

18 Before sunset on the seventh day of the feast, the Philistine men had the answer. They came to Samson and said, "What is sweeter than honey?
What is stronger than a lion?"
Then Samson said to them,
"If you had not ploughed with my young cow,
you would not have solved my riddle!"
19 Then the Spirit of the LORD entered Samson and gave him great power. Samson went down to the city of Ashkelon and killed 30 of its men and took all that they had and gave the clothes to the men who had answered his riddle. Then he went to his father's house very angry. 20 And Samson's wife was given to his best man.

Samson Troubles the Philistines

15 At the time of the wheat harvest, Samson went to visit his wife, taking a young goat with him. He said, "I'm going to my wife's room," but her father would not let him go in.

2 He said to Samson, "I thought you really hated your wife, so I gave her to your best man. Her younger sister is more beautiful. Take her instead."

3 But Samson said to them, "This time no one will blame me for hurting you Philistines!" 4 So Samson went out and caught 300 foxes. He took two foxes at a time, tied their tails together and then tied a torch to the tails of each pair of foxes. 5 After he lit the torches, he let the foxes loose in the grain fields of the Philistines so that he burned up their standing grain, the piles of grain, their vineyards and their olive trees.

6 The Philistines asked, "Who did this?"
Someone told them, "Samson, the son-in-law of the man from Timnah, did because his father-in-law gave his wife to his best man."

So the Philistines burned Samson's wife and her father to death. 7 Then Samson said to the Philistines, "Since you did this, I won't stop until I pay you back!" 8 Samson attacked the Philistines and killed many of them. Then he went down and stayed in a cave in the rock of Etam.

9 The Philistines went up and camped in the land of Judah, near a place named Lehi. 10 The men of Judah asked them, "Why have you come here to fight us?"

They answered, "We have come to make Samson our prisoner, to pay him back for what he did to our people."

11 Then 3,000 men of Judah went to the cave in the rock of Etam and said to Samson, "What have you done to us? Don't you know that the Philistines rule over us?"

Samson answered, "I only paid them back for what they did to me."

12 Then they said to him, "We have come to tie you up and to hand you over to the Philistines."

Samson said to them, "Promise me you will not hurt me yourselves."

13 The men from Judah said, "We agree. We will just tie you up and give you to the Philistines. We will not kill you." So they tied Samson with two new ropes and led him up from the cave in the rock. 14 When Samson came to the place named Lehi, the Philistines came to meet him, shouting for joy. Then the Spirit of the LORD entered Samson and gave him great power. The ropes on him weakened like burned strings and fell off his hands! 15 Samson found the jawbone of a dead donkey, took it, and killed 1,000 men with it!

16 Then Samson said,
"With a donkey's jawbone
I made donkeys out of them.
With a donkey's jawbone
I killed 1,000 men!"

17 When he finished speaking, he threw away the jawbone. So that place was named Ramath Lehi."

18 Samson was very thirsty, so he

> Then Samson said, "With a donkey's jawbone... I killed 1,000 men!"
> – Judges 15:16

15:17 Ramath Lehi This name means Jawbone Hill.

cried out to the LORD, "You gave me, your servant, this great victory. Do I have to die of thirst now? Do I have to be captured by people who are not circumcised?" 19 Then God opened up a hole in the ground at Lehi, and water came out. When Samson drank, he felt better; he felt strong again. So he named that spring Caller's Spring, which is still in Lehi.

20 Samson judged Israel for 20 years in the days of the Philistines.

Samson Goes to the City of Gaza

16 One day Samson went to Gaza and saw a prostitute there. He went in to spend the night with her. 2 When the people of Gaza heard, "Samson has come here!" they surrounded the place and waited for him near the city gate all night. They said to each other, "When dawn comes, we will kill Samson!"

3 But Samson only stayed with the prostitute until midnight. Then he got up and took hold of the doors and the two posts of the city gate and tore them loose, along with the bar. He put them on his shoulders and carried them to the top of the hill that faces the city of Hebron.

Samson and Delilah

4 After this, Samson fell in love with a woman named Delilah, who lived in the Valley of Sorek. 5 The Philistine rulers went to Delilah and said, "Find out what makes Samson so strong. Trick him into telling you how we can overpower him, capture him and tie him up. If you do this, each one of us will give you 1,100 pieces of silver."

6 So Delilah said to Samson, "Tell me why you are so strong. How can someone tie you up and capture you?"

7 Samson answered, "Someone would have to tie me up with seven new bowstrings that have not been dried. Then I would be as weak as any other man."

8 The Philistine rulers brought Delilah seven new bowstrings that had not been dried, and she tied Samson with them. 9 Some men were hiding in another room. Delilah said to him, "Samson, the Philistines are here!" But Samson broke the bowstrings like pieces of burned string.

FAITH links

THE WEAK LINK
JUDGES 16

You've heard of Hercules, right? Well, he's just a myth. Samson, however, was the real thing. God gave Samson super strength to use in defeating Israel's enemies, the Philistines. But the world's strongest man had a weakness – he relied on himself and his super strength, rather than on God. He was soon led into a trap that cost him his strength.

God gives each of us the ability to serve him. But he expects us to rely on him – not on our abilities. Want to be the world's most powerful Christian? Then take time to see the God behind your abilities. Faith in God gives you the power to serve him.

Complaints, Complaints! Exodus 16:1–3, p. 97

Weak? Great! 2 Chronicles 14:11, p. 577

Remember Your Creator, Ecclesiastes 12:1, 13, p. 885

Your Feet on High Places, Habakkuk 3:18–19, p. 1239

Small Beginnings, Zechariah 4:10, p. 1255

The Way to Greatness, Matthew 20:20–28, p. 1309

So the Philistines did not find out the secret of Samson's strength.

10 Then Delilah said to Samson, "You

made a fool of me. You lied to me. Now tell me how someone can tie you up."

11 Samson said, "They would have to tie me with new ropes that have not been used before. Then I would become as weak as any other man."

12 So Delilah took new ropes and tied Samson. Some men were hiding in another room. She called out to him, "Samson, the Philistines are here!" But he broke the ropes as easily as if they were threads.

13 Then Delilah said to Samson, "Again you have made a fool of me. You lied to me. Tell me how someone can tie you up."

He said, "Using the loom,[n] weave the seven plaits of my hair into the cloth, and tighten it with a pin. Then I will be as weak as any other man."

While Samson slept, Delilah wove the seven plaits of his hair into the cloth. 14 Then she fastened it with a pin.

Again she said to him, "Samson, the Philistines are here!" Samson woke up and pulled out the pin and the loom with the cloth.

15 Then Delilah said to him, "How can you say, 'I love you,' when you don't even trust me? This is the third time you have made a fool of me. You haven't told me the secret of your great strength." 16 She kept bothering Samson about his secret day after day until he felt he was going to die!

17 So he told her everything. He said, "I have never had my hair cut, because I have been set apart to God as a Nazirite since I was born. If someone shaved my head, I would lose my strength and be as weak as any other man."

18 When Delilah saw that he had told her everything sincerely, she sent a message to the Philistine rulers. She said, "Come back one more time, because he has told me everything." So the Philistine rulers came back to Delilah and brought the silver with them. 19 Delilah got Samson to sleep, lying in her lap. Then she called in a man to shave off the seven plaits of Samson's hair. In this way she began to make him weak, and his strength left him.

20 Then she said, "Samson, the Philistines are here!"

He woke up and thought, "I'll leave as I did before and shake myself free." But he did not know that the Lord had left him.

21 Then the Philistines captured Samson and tore out his eyes. They took him down to Gaza, where they put bronze chains on him and made him grind grain in the prison. 22 But his hair began to grow again.

Samson Dies

23 The Philistine rulers gathered to celebrate and to offer a great sacrifice to their god Dagon. They said, "Our god has handed Samson our enemy over to us." 24 When the people saw him, they praised their god, saying,

"This man destroyed our country.
He killed many of us!
But our god handed over
    our enemy to us."

25 While the people were enjoying the celebration, they said, "Bring Samson out to perform for us." So they brought Samson from the prison, and he performed for them. They made him stand between the pillars. 26 Samson said to the servant holding his hand, "Let me feel the pillars that hold up the temple so I can lean against them." 27 Now the temple was full of men and women. All the Philistine rulers were there, and about 3,000 men and women were on the roof[n] watching Samson perform. 28 Then Samson prayed to the Lord, "Lord God, remember me. God, please give me strength one more time so I can pay these Philistines back for putting out my two eyes!" 29 Then Samson turned to the two centre pillars that supported the whole temple. He braced himself between the two pillars, with his right hand on one and his left hand on the other. 30 Samson said,

---

16:13 loom A machine for making cloth from thread.
16:27 roof In Bible times houses were built with flat roofs. The roof was used for drying things such as flax and fruit. And it was used as an extra room, as a place for worship and as a place to sleep in the summer.

"Let me die with these Philistines!" Then he pushed as hard as he could, causing the temple to fall on the rulers and all the people in it. So Samson killed more of the Philistines when he died than when he was alive.

31 Samson's brothers and his whole family went down to get his body. They brought him back and buried him in the tomb of Manoah, his father, between the cities of Zorah and Eshtaol. Samson was a judge for the people of Israel for 20 years.

Micah's Idols

17 There was a man named Micah who lived in the mountains of Ephraim. 2 He said to his mother, "I heard you speak a curse about the 1,100 pieces of silver that were taken from you. I have the silver with me; I took it."

His mother said, "The LORD bless you, my son!"

3 Micah gave the 1,100 pieces of silver to his mother. Then she said, "I will give this silver to the LORD. I will have my son make an idol and a statue. So I will give the silver back to you."

4 When he gave the silver back to his mother, she took about 200 pieces and gave it to a silversmith. With it he made an idol and a statue, which stood in Micah's house. 5 Micah had a special holy place, and he made a holy robe and some household idols. Then Micah chose one of his sons to be his priest. 6 At that time Israel did not have a king, so everyone did what seemed right.

7 There was a young man who was a Levite" from the city of Bethlehem in Judah who was from the people of Judah. 8 He left Bethlehem to look for another place to live, and on his way he came to Micah's house in the mountains of Ephraim. 9 Micah asked him, "Where are you from?"

He answered, "I'm a Levite from Bethlehem in Judah. I'm looking for a place to live."

10 Micah said to him, "Live with me and be my father and my priest. I will give you 10 pieces of silver each year and clothes and food." So the Levite went in. 11 He agreed to live with Micah and became like one of Micah's own sons. 12 Micah made him a priest, and he lived in Micah's house. 13 Then Micah said, "Now I know the LORD will be good to me, because I have a Levite as my priest."

> At that time Israel did not have a king, so everyone did what seemed right.
> – Judges 17:6

Dan's Family Captures Laish

18 At that time Israel did not have a king. And at that time the tribe of Dan was still looking for a land where they could live, a land of their own. The Danites had not yet been given their own land among the tribes of Israel. 2 So, from their family groups, they chose five soldiers from the cities of Zorah and Eshtaol to spy out and explore the land. They were told, "Go, explore the land."

They came to the mountains of Ephraim, to Micah's house, where they spent the night. 3 When they came near Micah's house, they recognised the voice of the young Levite." So they stopped there and asked him, "Who brought you here? What are you doing here? Why are you here?"

4 He told them what Micah had done for him, saying, "He hired me. I am his priest."

5 They said to him, "Please ask God if our journey will be successful."

6 The priest said to them, "Go in peace. The LORD is pleased with your journey."

7 So the five men left. When they came to the city of Laish, they saw that the people there lived in safety, like the people of

---

17:7; 18:3 Levite The Levites were the only ones God had appointed as priests.

Judges 18:21   337

LET'S VISIT SHILOH Judges 18:31

At one time, Shiloh was the religious capital for the Hebrews. This was because they kept the Holy Tent of God there. (See Judges 18:31.) Shiloh is also where a woman named Hannah prayed to God to give her a son. That little boy, Samuel, grew up at the Lord's house at Shiloh. You might remember that while Samuel lived there, God woke him up and actually talked to him. When Samuel grew up, he became the priest in the Lord's house. (Look at 1 Samuel 1:9, p. 354.)

Later, Solomon built the Temple in Jerusalem, the capital of Israel. When that happened, Shiloh was not as important to the Israelites. For a while it was like a ghost town, but hundreds of years later the Greeks and Romans moved in and rebuilt the city.

Sidon. They thought they were safe and had plenty of everything. They lived a long way from the Sidonians and had no dealings with anyone else.

8 When the five men returned to Zorah and Eshtaol, their relatives asked them, "What did you find?"

9 They answered, "We have seen the land, and it is very good. We should attack them. Aren't you going to do something? Don't wait! Let's go and take that land! 10 When you go, you will see there is plenty of land—plenty of everything! The people are not expecting an attack. Surely God has handed that land over to us!"

11 So 600 Danites left Zorah and Eshtaol ready for war. 12 On their way they set up camp near the city of Kiriath Jearim in Judah. That is why the place west of Kiriath Jearim is named Mahaneh Dan[n] to this day. 13 From there they travelled on to the mountains of Ephraim. Then they came to Micah's house.

14 The five men who had explored the land around Laish said to their relatives, "Do you know, in one of these houses there are a holy robe, household gods, an idol and a statue? You know what to do." 15 So they stopped at the Levite's house, which was also Micah's house, and greeted the Levite. 16 The 600 Danites stood at the entrance gate, wearing their weapons of war. 17 The five spies went into the house and took the idol, the holy robe, the household idols and the statue. The priest and the 600 men armed for war stood by the entrance gate.

18 When the spies went into Micah's house and took the image, the holy robe, the household idols and the statue, the priest asked them, "What are you doing?"

19 They answered, "Be quiet! Don't say a word. Come with us and be our father and priest. Is it better for you to be a priest for one man's house or for a tribe and family group in Israel?" 20 This made the priest happy. So he took the holy robe, the household idols and the idol and went with the Danites. 21 They left Micah's house, putting their little children, their

---

18:12 Mahaneh Dan This name means "the camp of Dan".

animals and everything they owned in front of them.

22 When they had gone a little way from Micah's house, the men who lived near Micah were called out and caught up with them. 23 The men with Micah shouted at the Danites, who turned round and said to Micah, "What's the matter with you? Why have you been called out to fight?"

24 Micah answered, "You took my gods that I made and my priest. What do I have left? How can you ask me, 'What's the matter?'"

25 The Danites answered, "You should not argue with us. Some of our angry men might attack you, killing you and your family." 26 Then the Danites went on their way. Micah knew they were too strong for him, so he turned and went back home.

27 Then the Danites took what Micah had made and his priest and went on to Laish. They attacked those peaceful people and killed them with their swords and then burned the city. 28 There was no one to save the people of Laish. They lived too far from Sidon, and they had no dealings with anyone else. Laish was in a valley near Beth Rehob.

The people of Dan rebuilt the city and lived there. 29 They changed the name of Laish to Dan, naming it after their ancestor Dan, one of the sons of Israel.

30 The people of Dan set up the idols in the city of Dan. Jonathan son of Gershom, Moses' son, and his sons served as priests for the tribe of Dan until the land was captured. 31 The people of Dan set up the idols Micah had made as long as the Holy Tent of God was in Shiloh.

A Levite and His Servant

19 At that time Israel did not have a king.

There was a Levite who lived in the faraway mountains of Ephraim. He had taken a slave woman from the city of Bethlehem in the land of Judah to live with him, 2 but she was unfaithful to him. She left him and went back to her father's house in Bethlehem in Judah and stayed there for four months. 3 Then her husband went to ask her to come back to him, taking with him his servant and two donkeys. When the Levite came to her father's house, she invited him to come in, and her father was happy to see him. 4 The father-in-law, the young woman's father, asked him to stay. So he stayed for three days and ate, drank and slept there.

5 On the fourth day they got up early in the morning. The Levite was getting ready to leave, but the woman's father said to his son-in-law, "Refresh yourself by eating something. Then go." 6 So the two men sat down to eat and drink together. After that, the father said to him, "Please stay tonight. Relax and enjoy yourself." 7 When the man got up to go, his father-in-law asked him to stay. So he stayed again that night. 8 On the fifth day the man got up early in the morning to leave. The woman's father said, "Refresh yourself. Wait until this afternoon." So the two men ate together.

9 When the Levite, his slave woman, and his servant got up to leave, the father-in-law, the young woman's father, said, "It's almost night. The day is almost gone. Spend the night here and enjoy yourself. Tomorrow morning you can get up early and go home." 10 But the Levite did not want to stay another night. So he took his two saddled donkeys and his slave woman and travelled towards the city of Jebus (also called Jerusalem).

11 As the day was almost over, they came near Jebus. So the servant said to his master, "Let's stop at this city of the Jebusites, and spend the night here."

12 But his master said, "No. We won't go inside a foreign city. Those people are not Israelites. We will go on to the city of Gibeah." 13 He said, "Come on. Let's try to make it to Gibeah or Ramah so we can spend the night in one of those cities." 14 So they went on. The sun went down as they came near Gibeah, which belongs to the tribe of Benjamin. 15 They stopped there to spend the night. They came to the public square of the city and sat down, but no one invited them home to spend the night.

16 Late in the evening an old man

came in from his work in the fields. His home was in the mountains of Ephraim, but now he was living in Gibeah. (The people of Gibeah were from the tribe of Benjamin.) 17 He saw the traveller in the public square and asked, "Where are you going? Where did you come from?"

18 The Levite answered, "We are travelling from Bethlehem in Judah to my home in the mountains of Ephraim. I have been to Bethlehem in Judah, but now I am going to the Holy Tent of the LORD. No one has invited me to stay in his house. 19 We already have straw and food for our donkeys and bread and wine for me, the young woman and my servant. We don't need anything."

20 The old man said, "You are welcome to stay at my house. Let me give you anything you need, but don't spend the night in the public square." 21 So the old man took the Levite into his house, and he fed their donkeys. They washed their feet and had something to eat and drink.

22 While they were enjoying themselves, some wicked men of the city surrounded the house and beat on the door. They shouted to the old man who owned the house, "Bring out the man who came to your house. We want to have sexual relations with him."

23 The owner of the house went outside and said to them, "No, my friends. Don't be so evil. This man is a guest in my house. Don't do this terrible thing! 24 Look, here is my daughter, who has never had sexual relations before, and also the man's slave woman. I will bring them out to you now. Do anything you want with them, but don't do such a terrible thing to this man."

25 But the men would not listen to him. So the Levite took his slave woman and sent her outside to them. They forced her to have sexual relations with them, and they abused her all night long. Then, at dawn, they let her go. 26 She came back to the house where her master was staying and fell down at the door and lay there until daylight.

27 In the morning when the Levite got up, he opened the door of the house and went outside to go on his way. But his slave woman was lying at the doorway of the house, with her hands on the doorsill. 28 The Levite said to her, "Get up; let's go." But she did not answer. So he put her on his donkey and went home.

29 When the Levite got home, he took a knife and cut his slave woman into twelve parts, limb by limb. Then he sent a part to each area of Israel. 30 Everyone who saw this said, "Nothing like this has ever happened before, not since the people of Israel came out of Egypt. Think about it. Tell us what to do."

The War Between Israel and Benjamin

20 So all the Israelites from Dan to Beersheba,[n] including the land of Gilead, joined together before the LORD in the city of Mizpah. 2 The leaders of all the tribes of Israel took their places in the meeting of the people of God. There were 400,000 soldiers with swords. 3 (The people of Benjamin heard that the Israelites had gone up to Mizpah.) Then the Israelites said to the Levite, "Tell us how this evil thing happened."

4 So the husband of the murdered woman answered, "My slave woman and I came to Gibeah in Benjamin to spend the night. 5 During the night the men of Gibeah came after me. They surrounded the house and wanted to kill me. They forced my slave woman to have sexual relations and she died. 6 I took her and cut her into parts and sent one part to each area of Israel because the people of Benjamin did this wicked and terrible thing in Israel. 7 Now, all you Israelites, speak up. What is your decision?"

8 Then all the people stood up at the same time, saying, "None of us will go home. Not one of us will go back to his house! 9 Now this is what we will do to Gibeah. We will throw lots. 10 That way we will choose ten men from every 100 men from all the tribes of Israel, and we

---

20:1 Dan to Beersheba Dan was the city farthest north in Israel and Beersheba was the city farthest south. So this means all the people of Israel.

will choose 100 men from every 1,000, and 1,000 men from every 10,000. These will find supplies for the army. Then the army will go to the city of Gibeah of Benjamin to repay them for the terrible thing they have done in Israel." 11 So all the men of Israel were united and gathered against the city.

12 The tribes of Israel sent men throughout the tribe of Benjamin demanding, "What is this evil thing some of your men have done? 13 Hand over the wicked men in Gibeah so that we can put them to death. We must remove this evil from Israel."

But the Benjaminites would not listen to their fellow Israelites. 14 The Benjaminites left their own cities and met at Gibeah to fight the Israelites. 15 In only one day the Benjaminites got 26,000 soldiers together who were trained with swords. They also had 700 chosen men from Gibeah. 16 Seven hundred of these trained soldiers were left-handed, each of whom could sling a stone at a hair and not miss!

17 The Israelites, except for the Benjaminites, gathered 400,000 soldiers with swords.

18 The Israelites went up to the city of Bethel and asked God, "Which tribe shall be first to attack the Benjaminites?"

The LORD answered, "Judah shall go first."

19 The next morning the Israelites got up and made a camp near Gibeah. 20 The men of Israel went out to fight the Benjaminites and took their battle position at Gibeah. 21 Then the Benjaminites came out of Gibeah and killed 22,000 Israelites during the battle that day. 22-23 The Israelites went before the LORD and cried until evening. They asked the LORD, "Shall we go to fight our relatives, the Benjaminites, again?"

The LORD answered, "Go up and fight them." The men of Israel encouraged each other. So they took the same battle positions as they had taken on the first day.

24 The Israelites came to fight the Benjaminites on the second day. 25 The Benjaminites came out of Gibeah to attack the Israelites. This time, the Benjaminites killed 18,000 Israelites, all of whom carried swords.

26 Then the Israelites went up to Bethel. There they sat down and cried to the LORD and went without food all day until evening. They also brought burnt offerings and fellowship offerings to the LORD. 27 The Israelites asked the LORD a question. (In those days the Ark of the Agreement with God was there at Bethel. 28 A priest named Phinehas son of Eleazar, the son of Aaron, served before the Ark of the Agreement.) They asked, "Shall we go to fight our relatives, the Benjaminites, again, or shall we stop fighting?"

The LORD answered, "Go, because tomorrow I will hand them over to you."

29 Then the Israelites set up ambushes all around Gibeah. 30 They went to fight against the Benjaminites at Gibeah on the third day, getting into position for battle as they had done before. 31 When the Benjaminites came out to fight them, the Israelites backed up and led the Benjaminites away from the city. The Benjaminites began to kill some of the Israelites as they had done before. About 30 Israelites were killed—some in the fields and some on the roads leading to Bethel and to Gibeah.

32 The Benjaminites said, "We are winning as before!"

But the Israelites said, "Let's run. Let's trick them into going farther away from their city and onto the roads."

33 All the Israelites moved from their places and got into battle positions at a place named Baal Tamar. Then the Israelites ran out from their hiding places west of Gibeah. 34 Ten thousand of the best trained soldiers from all of Israel attacked Gibeah. The battle was very hard. The Benjaminites did not know disaster was about to come to them. 35 The LORD used the Israelites to defeat the Benjaminites. On that day the Israelites killed 25,100 Benjaminites, all armed with swords. 36 Then the Benjaminites saw that they were defeated.

The Israelites had moved back because they were depending on the surprise attack they had set up near Gibeah. 37 The men in hiding rushed into Gibeah, spread out and killed everyone in the city with their swords. 38 Now the Israelites had set up a signal with the men in hiding. The men in the surprise attack were to send up a cloud of smoke from the city. 39 Then the army of Israel turned round in the battle.

The Benjaminites had killed about 30 Israelites. They were saying, "We are winning, as in the first battle!" 40 But then a cloud of smoke began to rise from the city. The Benjaminites turned round and saw that the whole city was going up in smoke. 41 Then the Israelites turned and began to fight. The Benjaminites were terrified because they knew that disaster was coming to them. 42 So the Benjaminites ran away from the Israelites towards the desert, but they could not escape the battle. And the Israelites who came out of the cities killed them. 43 They surrounded the Benjaminites and chased them and caught them in the area east of Gibeah. 44 So 18,000 brave Benjaminite fighters were killed. 45 The Benjaminites ran towards the desert to the rock of Rimmon, but the Israelites killed 5,000 Benjaminites along the roads. They chased them as far as Gidom and killed 2,000 more Benjaminites there.

46 On that day 25,000 Benjaminites were killed, all of whom had fought bravely with swords. 47 But 600 Benjaminites ran to the rock of Rimmon in the desert, where they stayed for four months. 48 Then the Israelites went back to the land of Benjamin and killed the people in every city and also the animals and everything they could find. And they burned every city they found.

Wives for the Men of Benjamin

21 At Mizpah the men of Israel had sworn, "Not one of us will let his daughter marry a man from the tribe of Benjamin."

2 The people went to the city of Bethel and sat before God until evening, crying loudly. 3 They said, "LORD, God of Israel, why has this terrible thing happened to us so that one tribe of Israel is missing today?"

4 Early the next day the people built an altar and put burnt offerings and fellowship offerings to God on it.

5 Then the Israelites asked, "Did any tribe of Israel not come here to meet with

---

FAITH links

DO WHAT YOU WANT?

JUDGES 21:25

Ever hear the same message over and over again? The same message occurs in the Book of Judges over and over again. You can find it in the last verse of the book. "Everyone did what seemed right." (Check out Judges 17:6.) The Israelites did what *they* thought was right, rather than what God taught them. This is the pattern throughout the Book of Judges. Does that sound familiar to you? It should. People do the same thing today.

God wants us to be obedient to him. He doesn't want us to follow our own opinions of what's right or wrong. Do you want what he wants?

Take My Advice, 1 Kings 2:2–4, p. 436

See the Heart Behind It, Nehemiah 8; 9, p. 636

More Precious Than Gold, Psalm 19:7–10, p. 723

Said It? Do It! Lamentations 2:17, p. 1077

Get Ready! Mark 13:26–27, p. 1354

Hold On! 2 Thessalonians 2:15–17, p. 1639

us in the presence of the LORD?" They asked this question because they had sworn that anyone who did not meet with them at Mizpah would be killed.

6 The Israelites felt sorry for their relatives, the Benjaminites. They said, "Today one tribe has been cut off from Israel. 7 We swore before the LORD that we would not allow our daughters to marry a Benjaminite. How can we make sure that the remaining men of Benjamin will have wives?" 8 Then they asked, "Which one of the tribes of Israel did not come here to Mizpah?" They found that no one from the city of Jabesh Gilead had come. 9 The people of Israel counted everyone, but there was no one from Jabesh Gilead.

10 So the whole group of Israelites sent 12,000 soldiers to Jabesh Gilead to kill the people with their swords, even the women and children.

11 "This is what you must do," they said. "Kill every man in Jabesh Gilead and every married woman." 12 The soldiers found 400 young unmarried women in Jabesh Gilead, so they brought them to the camp at Shiloh in Canaan.

13 Then the whole group of Israelites sent a message to the men of Benjamin, who were at the rock of Rimmon, offering to make peace with them. 14 So the men of Benjamin came back at that time. The Israelites gave them the women from Jabesh Gilead who had not been killed, but there were not enough women.

15 The people of Israel felt sorry for the Benjaminites because the LORD had separated the tribes of Israel. 16 The elders of the Israelites said, "The women of Benjamin have been killed. Where can we get wives for the men of Benjamin who are still alive? 17 These men must have children to continue their families so a tribe in Israel will not die out. 18 But we cannot allow our daughters to marry them, because we swore, 'Anyone who gives a wife to a man of Benjamin is cursed.' 19 We have an idea! There is a yearly festival of the LORD at Shiloh, which is north of the city of Bethel, east of the road that goes from Bethel to Shechem, and south of the city of Lebonah."

20 So the elders told the men of Benjamin, "Go and hide in the vineyards. 21 Watch for the young women from Shiloh to come out to join the dancing. Then run out from the vineyards and take one of the young Shiloh women and return to the land of Benjamin. 22 If their fathers or brothers come to us and complain, we will say: 'Be kind to the men of Benjamin. We did not get wives for Benjamin during the war, and you did not give the women to the men from Benjamin. So you are not guilty.'"

23 So that is what the Benjaminites did. While the young women were dancing, each man caught one of them, took her away and married her. Then they went back to the land God had given them and rebuilt their cities and lived there.

24 Then the Israelites went home to their own tribes and family groups, to their own land that God had given them.

25 In those days Israel did not have a king. Everyone did what seemed right.

ALWAYS FAITHFUL

Hello! My name is Ruth. No one is sure who wrote this book, but I can tell you that it is the true story of my life. You may have heard the famous quote: "Where you go, I will go. Where you live, I will live. Your people will be my people, and your God will be my God" (Ruth 1:16). Did you know that I was speaking to my mother-in-law when I said that? With no husband or sons to care for her, Naomi had decided to go back to Israel to be with other relatives. I could not bear to be separated from my mother-in-law, so I went with her. Most importantly, I decided to follow the true God of Israel.

This book was written to tell about the love and devotion my family had for God and for each other. God rewarded me for my devotion to Naomi by giving me a husband and a son in my new land. I was especially honoured to be the great-grandmother of King David and an ancestor of Jesus. (You can see my name listed in Jesus' family history in Matthew 1:5, p. 1274.)

JESUS WATCH

In Israel a near relative or "kinsman" had the right to buy or "redeem" the property of a poor person to keep the property in the family. Naomi's closest relative chose not to buy her land, so Boaz willingly bought her land and took on the responsibility of her family. In his sacrifice for others, Boaz points to Jesus, who promises to take care of us. Jesus became a man, so he could be our kinsman; and he willingly paid the price for our lives. Because Jesus died on the cross and took the punishment for our sins, we have eternal life.

my FAVOURITE links

OTHER CONNECTIONS

- **Women Who Made a Difference, Ruth 4.** Connect here to learn more about some amazing and faithful women whose stories can be found in the Old Testament – women such as Ruth, Naomi, Hannah and Esther.

MORE STUFF . . .
It's the Custom! There are many Israelite customs found in the Book of Ruth that are important to the story. Here are a couple:
- Gathering the leftover grain in the field (Ruth 2:2) was a practice called gleaning. According to the law, any grain that was dropped during the harvest was to be left for the poor people to pick up and use for food. (See Leviticus 19:9, p. 160.) For Ruth and Naomi, this was the only way for them to get food.
- The "one who should take care of us" (Ruth 2:20) refers to the closest relative, or the kinsman-redeemer. According to social customs, the closest relative was responsible for helping a person if a catastrophe struck, like a death in the family.

FAITH links

- The MLP, **Ruth 1:16–17**
- Your Response to Responsibility, **Ruth 2:1–7**
- An Unsung Hero, **Ruth 2:12, 15–16**
- In Your Best Interests, **Ruth 3**

did YOU know?

What's the flash on Boaz's relative taking off his sandal?

Maybe he had sore feet! Let's connect to Ruth 4:7–8 to find out.

TAKE A LOOK AT THESE:
Ruth follows Naomi, Ruth 1:16–22
Boaz first notices Ruth, Ruth 2:5–13
Ruth uncovers Boaz's feet, Ruth 3:5–14
Naomi's grandson, Ruth 4:13–17

1 ¹⁻² Long ago when the judges[n] ruled Israel, there was a shortage of food in the land. So a man named Elimelech left the town of Bethlehem in Judah to live in the country of Moab with his wife and his two sons. His wife was named Naomi, and his two sons were named Mahlon and Kilion. They were from the Ephrathah district from Bethlehem in Judah. When they came to Moab, they settled there.

³ Then Naomi's husband, Elimelech, died, and she was left with her two sons. ⁴ These sons married women from Moab. One was named Orpah and the other was named Ruth. Naomi and her sons had lived in Moab about ten years ⁵ when Mahlon and Kilion also died. So Naomi was left alone without her husband or her two sons.

⁶ While Naomi was in Moab, she heard that the LORD had come to help his people and had given them food again. So she and her daughters-in-law got ready to leave Moab and return home. ⁷ Naomi and her daughters-in-law left the place where they had lived and started back to the land of Judah. ⁸ But Naomi said to her two daughters-in-law, "Go back home, each of you to your own mother's house. May the LORD be as kind to you as you have been to me and my sons who are now dead. ⁹ May the LORD give you another happy home and a new husband."

When Naomi kissed the women good-bye, they began to cry out loud. ¹⁰ They said to her, "No, we want to go with you to your people."

¹¹ But Naomi said, "My daughters, return to your own homes. Why do you want to go with me? I cannot give birth to more sons to give you new husbands; ¹² go back, my daughters, to your own homes. I am too old to have another husband. Even if I told myself, 'I still have hope' and had another husband tonight, and even if I had more sons, ¹³ should you wait until they were grown into men? Should you live for so many years without husbands? Don't do that, my daughters.

1:1-2 judges They were not judges in courts of law, but leaders of the people in times of emergency.

FAITH links

THE MLP
RUTH 1:16-17

Who is the most loyal person you know? In the Bible, one candidate for the MLP (Most Loyal Person) award is Ruth. Ruth showed loyalty to her mother-in-law, Naomi, by refusing to leave her. Naomi tried to convince Ruth to stay in Moab. But instead of staying put, Ruth chose to stay loyal and leave her homeland to be with Naomi.

Loyalty is more than just admitting you're someone's friend. It involves sticking with that friend even through tough times. It also means offering your friendship without a thought of what you might get out of it. Would someone consider you an MLP? How do you show your loyalty for friends or family?

Want to be a good friend? Connect here:

A Use for Your Abilities, Genesis 41, p. 59

What God Wants, Deuteronomy 10:12–13, p. 242

Loyal to a Friend, 2 Samuel 9, p. 409

A Friend in Deed, Job 2:13, p. 662

Two Are Better, Ecclesiastes 4:9–12, p. 877

Kindness First, Matthew 9:35–36, p. 1290

My life is much too sad for you to share, because the LORD has been against me!"

14 The women cried together out loud again. Then Orpah kissed her mother-in-law Naomi goodbye, but Ruth held on to her tightly.

15 Naomi said to Ruth, "Look, your sister-in-law is going back to her own people and her own gods. Go back with her."

Ruth Stays with Naomi

16 But Ruth said, "Don't beg me to leave you or to stop following you. Where you go, I will go. Where you live, I will live. Your people will be my people, and your God will be my God. 17 And where you die, I will die, and there I will be buried. I ask the LORD to punish me terribly if I do not keep this promise: not even death will separate us."

18 When Naomi saw that Ruth had firmly made up her mind to go with her, she stopped arguing with her. 19 So Naomi and Ruth went on until they came to the town of Bethlehem. When they entered Bethlehem, all the people became very excited. The women of the town said, "Is this really Naomi?"

20 Naomi answered the people, "Don't call me Naomi.ⁿ Call me Mara,ⁿ because the Almighty has made my life very sad. 21 When I left, I had all I wanted, but now, the LORD has brought me home with nothing. Why should you call me Naomi when the LORD has spoken against me and the Almighty has given me so much trouble?"

22 So Naomi and her daughter-in-law Ruth, the Moabite, returned from Moab and arrived at Bethlehem at the beginning of the barley harvest.

Ruth Meets Boaz

2 Now Naomi had a rich relative named Boaz, from Elimelech's family.

2 One day Ruth, the Moabite, said to Naomi, "I am going to the fields. Maybe someone will be kind enough to let me gather the grain he leaves behind."

1:20 **Naomi** This name means "happy" or "pleasant".
1:20 **Mara** This name means "bitter" or "sad".

FAITH links

YOUR RESPONSE TO RESPONSIBILITY

RUTH 2:1-7

Of all the qualities others notice about you, is being *responsible* one of them? Ruth was not only loyal, but she was also responsible. She had a "What can I do to help others?" attitude rather than an attitude of "What can others do for me?" Since Ruth and Naomi were poor when they returned to Bethlehem, Ruth volunteered to gather grain left in the fields by the harvesters. That was hard work! But Ruth's hard work provided food for herself and for Naomi.

Showing responsibility for others means taking an active role to care for others. Part of learning to be responsible is being willing to work hard if necessary. What is your response to responsibility?

Roll Out the Welcome Wagon, Genesis 18:2–8, p. 24

Loyal to a Friend, 2 Samuel 9, p. 409

On the Wrong Foot, 2 Kings 21:1–2, 16, p. 509

You Are What You Do, Proverbs 20:11, p. 854

A Half-hearted Offering, Malachi 1:6–14, p. 1268

The Worst Chore, John 13:3–17, p. 1447

FAITH links

AN UNSUNG HERO
RUTH 2:12, 15-16

Have you ever felt unappreciated in what you do to help others? Or maybe you're convinced that the hard work you do goes totally unnoticed by anyone. Ruth worked hard to support herself and her mother-in-law, Naomi. God caused the servant in charge of the land to notice how faithful and responsible she was. Boaz, the owner of the field, rewarded Ruth for her faithfulness to her mother-in-law.

Feeling unnoticed? Don't forget that God sees everything. He wants you to be faithful in doing what's right even if no one else notices.

Here are some more thoughts on doing the right thing:

Your Total Trust, Deuteronomy 1:32, p. 229

Care for the Lost, Deuteronomy 22:1–3, p. 255

Trailblazers of Faith, 2 Kings 22:1–2, p. 510

Good Enough? Ezekiel 8, p. 1093

Just Say Yes! Matthew 9:9–13, p. 1289

Another Lazy Day? 2 Thessalonians 3:6–13, p. 1640

Naomi said, "Go, my daughter."

3 So Ruth went to the fields and gathered the grain that the workers cutting the grain had left behind. It just so happened that the field belonged to Boaz, from Elimelech's family.

4 Soon Boaz came from Bethlehem and greeted his workers, "The LORD be with you!"

And the workers answered, "May the LORD bless you!"

5 Then Boaz asked his servant in charge of the workers, "Whose girl is that?"

6 The servant answered, "She is the young Moabite woman who came back with Naomi from the country of Moab. 7 She said, 'Please let me follow the workers cutting grain and gather what they leave behind.' She came and has remained here, from morning until just now. She has stopped only a few moments to rest in the shelter."

8 Then Boaz said to Ruth, "Listen, my daughter. Don't go to gather grain for yourself in another field. Don't even leave this field at all, but continue following closely behind my women workers. 9 Watch to see into which fields they go to cut grain and follow them. I have warned the young men not to bother you. When you are thirsty, you may go and drink from the water jugs that the young men have filled."

10 Then Ruth bowed low with her face to the ground and said to him, "I am not an Israelite. Why have you been so kind to notice me?"

11 Boaz answered her, "I know about all the help you have given your mother-in-law after your husband died. You left your father and mother and your own country to come to a nation where you did not know anyone. 12 May the LORD reward you for all you have done. May your wages be paid in full by the LORD, the God of Israel, under whose wings you have come for shelter."

13 Then Ruth said, "I hope I can continue to please you, sir. You have said kind and encouraging words to me, your servant, though I am not one of your servants."

14 At mealtime Boaz told Ruth, "Come here. Eat some of our bread and dip it in our vinegar."

So Ruth sat down beside the workers. Boaz handed her some roasted grain, and she ate until she was full; she even had some food left over. 15 When Ruth rose and went back to work, Boaz commanded his workers, "Let her gather even around the piles of cut grain. Don't tell her to go away. 16 In fact, drop some full heads of grain for her from what you have in your hands, and let her gather them. Don't tell her to stop."

17 So Ruth gathered grain in the field until evening. Then she separated the grain from the chaff, and there was about 10 kilogrammes of barley. 18 Ruth carried the grain into town, and her mother-in-law saw how much she had gathered. Ruth also took out the food that was left over from lunch and gave it to Naomi.

19 Naomi asked her, "Where did you gather all this grain today? Where did you work? Blessed be whoever noticed you!"

Ruth told her mother-in-law whose field she had worked in. She said, "The man I worked with today is named Boaz."

20 Naomi told her daughter-in-law, "The LORD bless him! He continues to be kind to us—both the living and the dead!" Then Naomi told Ruth, "Boaz is one of our close relatives,[n] one who should take care of us."

21 Then Ruth, the Moabite, said, "Boaz also told me, 'Keep close to my workers until they have finished my whole harvest.'"

22 But Naomi said to her daughter-in-law Ruth, "It is better for you to continue working with his women workers. If you work in another field, someone might hurt you." 23 So Ruth continued working closely with the workers of Boaz, gathering grain until the barley harvest and the wheat harvest were finished. And she continued to live with Naomi, her mother-in-law.

Naomi's Plan

3 Then Naomi, Ruth's mother-in-law, said to her, "My daughter, I must find a suitable home for you, one that will be good for you. 2 Now Boaz, whose young women you worked with, is our close relative.[n] Tonight he will be working at the threshing floor. 3 Wash yourself, put on perfume, change your clothes and go down to the threshing floor. But don't let him know you're there until he has finished his dinner. 4 Watch him so you will know where he lies down to sleep. When he lies down, go and lift the cover off his feet[n] and lie down. He will tell you what you should do."

5 Then Ruth answered, "I will do everything you say."

6 So Ruth went down to the threshing floor and did all her mother-in-law told her to do. 7 After his evening meal, Boaz felt good and went to sleep lying beside the pile of grain. Ruth went to him quietly and lifted the cover from his feet and lay down.

8 About midnight Boaz was startled and rolled over. There was a woman lying near his feet! 9 Boaz asked, "Who are you?"

She said, "I am Ruth, your servant girl. Spread your cover over me, because you are a relative who is supposed to take care of me."[n]

10 Then Boaz said, "The LORD bless you, my daughter. This act of kindness is greater than the kindness you showed to Naomi in the beginning. You didn't look for a young man to marry, either rich or poor. 11 Now, my daughter, don't be afraid. I will do everything you ask, because all the people in our town know you are a good woman. 12 It is true that I am a relative who is to take care of you, but you have a closer relative than I. 13 Stay here tonight, and in the morning we will see if he will take care of you. If he decides to take care of you, that is fine. But if he refuses, I will take care of you myself, as surely as the LORD lives. So stay here until morning."

14 So Ruth stayed near his feet until morning but got up while it was still too dark to recognise anyone. Boaz thought, "People in town must not know that the woman came here to the threshing floor."

2:20; 3:2 close relatives In Bible times the closest relative could marry a widow without children so she could have children. He would care for this family, but they and their property would not belong to him. They would belong to the dead husband.

3:4 lift . . . feet This showed Ruth was asking him to be her husband.

3:9 Spread . . . me By this, Ruth was asking Boaz to marry her.

Ruth 4:7 349

IN YOUR BEST INTERESTS
RUTH 3

When your parents offer you advice, how do you usually respond? Choose one of the following or come up with your own (be honest!). (1) The advice goes in one ear and out the other. (2) I usually take their advice. (3) I listen, then offer my advice about their advice. (4) I complain about being given advice. (5) Other. When Ruth's mother-in-law, Naomi, offered Ruth advice, Ruth's response was No. 2. She respected Naomi's wisdom. She also knew that Naomi had her best interests at heart.

Unwanted advice can seem annoying at times. But when you know that a person has your best interests at heart, advice is easier to take.

Take Me to Your Leader, Numbers 27:12–23, p. 214

See the Heart Behind It, Nehemiah 8; 9, p. 636

Peace in the Family, Psalm 133, p. 811

A Parent's Advice, Proverbs 1:8–9, p. 825

Sow It and Reap, Lamentations 1:18, p. 1075

How to Make God Glad, Ephesians 6:1–2, p. 1605

---

15 So Boaz said to Ruth, "Bring me your shawl and hold it open."

So Ruth held her shawl open, and Boaz poured six portions of barley into it. Boaz then put it on her head and went back to the city.

16 When Ruth went back to her mother-in-law, Naomi asked, "How did you do, my daughter?"

Ruth told Naomi everything that Boaz did for her. 17 She said, "Boaz gave me these six portions of barley, saying, 'You must not go home without a gift for your mother-in-law.'"

18 Naomi answered, "Ruth, my daughter, wait here until you see what happens. Boaz will not rest until he has finished doing what he should do today."

Boaz Marries Ruth

4 Boaz went to the city gate and sat there until the close relative he had mentioned passed by. Boaz called to him, "Come here, friend, and sit down." So the man came over and sat down. 2 Boaz gathered ten of the elders of the city and told them, "Sit down here!" So they sat down.

3 Then Boaz said to the close relative, "Naomi, who has come back from the country of Moab, wants to sell the piece of land that belonged to our relative Elimelech. 4 So I decided to tell you about it. If you want to buy back the land, then buy it in front of the people who are sitting here and in front of the elders of my people. But if you don't want to buy it, tell me, because you are the only one who can buy it, and I am next after you."

The close relative answered, "I will buy back the land."

5 Then Boaz explained, "When you buy the land from Naomi, you must also marry Ruth, the Moabite, the dead man's wife. That way, the land will stay in the dead man's name."

6 The close relative answered, "I can't buy back the land. If I did, I might harm what I can pass on to my own sons. I cannot buy the land back, so buy it yourself."

7 Long ago in Israel when people traded or bought back something, one

WOMEN WHO MADE A DIFFERENCE — Ruth 4

One of the outstanding women of the Old Testament was Hannah, who prayed for a son and dedicated him to the Lord even before he was born. Hannah's faithfulness was rewarded. Her son, Samuel, became a great prophet, priest and judge. He led Israel to be a great nation. (Read 1 Samuel 1—7, p. 354.)

Other outstanding women you'll read about in the Old Testament include:

Deborah	Hebrew judge who defeated the Canaanites under Sisera	Judges 4:4, p. 316
Esther	Jewish queen who saved her people from destruction	Esther 7:3–4, p. 655
Eve	First woman	Genesis 3:20, p. 8
Miriam	Aaron's sister; a prophetess	Exodus 15:20, p. 96
Naomi	Ruth's mother-in-law	Ruth 1:2, 4, p. 345
Rachel	Wife of Jacob	Genesis 29:28, p. 40
Rahab	Cared for Israel's spies; ancestor of Jesus	Joshua 2:3–21, p. 278; Matthew 1:5, p. 1274
Ruth	Boaz's wife; ancestor of Jesus	Ruth 4:13–17, p. 351; Matthew 1:5, p. 1274
Sarah (Sarai)	Abraham's wife; Isaac's mum	Genesis 11:29, p. 17; 21:2–3, p. 27
Zipporah	Wife of Moses	Exodus 2:21, p. 78

person took off his sandal and gave it to the other person. This was the proof of purchase in Israel.

8 So the close relative said to Boaz, "Buy the land yourself," and he took off his sandal.

9 Then Boaz said to the elders and to all the people, "You are witnesses today. I am buying from Naomi everything that belonged to Elimelech and Kilion and Mahlon. 10 I am also taking Ruth, the Moabite who was the wife of Mahlon, as my wife. I am doing this so her dead husband's property will stay in his name and his name will not be separated from his family and his home town. You are witnesses today."

11 So all the people and elders who were at the city gate said, "We are witnesses. May the LORD make this woman, who is coming into your home, like Rachel and Leah, who had many children and built

up the people of Israel. May you become powerful in the district of Ephrathah and famous in Bethlehem. 12 As Tamar gave birth to Judah's son Perez,*n* may the LORD give you many children through Ruth. May your family be great like his."

13 So Boaz took Ruth home as his wife and had sexual relations with her. The LORD let her become pregnant, and she gave birth to a son. 14 The women told Naomi, "Praise the LORD who gave you this grandson. May he become famous in Israel. 15 He will give you new life and will take care of you in your old age because of your daughter-in-law who loves you. She is better for you than seven sons, because she has given birth to your grandson."

16 Naomi took the boy, held him in her arms and cared for him. 17 The neighbours gave the boy his name, saying, "This boy was born for Naomi." They named him Obed. Obed was the father of Jesse, and Jesse was the father of David.

18 This is the family history of Perez, the father of Hezron. 19 Hezron was the father of Ram, who was the father of Amminadab. 20 Amminadab was the father of Nahshon, who was the father of Salmon. 21 Salmon was the father of Boaz, who was the father of Obed. 22 Obed was the father of Jesse, and Jesse was the father of David.

4:12 Perez One of Boaz's ancestors.

WAITING TO BE KING

Hi, there! My name is David. You may remember me, the shepherd boy who defeated the terrible giant Goliath? The stories in this book are true, but no one is sure who wrote them. It may have been the prophet Samuel. I was only a boy when God chose me to be the next king of Israel. (For that surprising story, link to 1 Samuel 16:1–13.) For many years I faithfully served Saul, the first king of Israel. His son Jonathan was my best friend. I never could understand why Saul was so angry with me. He even tried to kill me! (See 1 Samuel 19:9–10.)

This book was written to tell the story of how Israel became a nation ruled by kings. Soon after Saul became our first king, he disobeyed God and turned away from him. God rejected Saul and chose me to be the next king. I always respected Saul because he was appointed by God to be king. When Saul and his soldiers tried to kill me, I relied on God to protect me. Check out the MIDI file on Psalm 18, p. 721, for the words to a song I wrote after God saved me from my enemies.

JESUS WATCH

David reminds us of Jesus. David and Jesus were both born in Bethlehem and were from the family of Judah. David spent many years watching sheep in his father's fields, risking his life to defend them from lions and bears. Jesus is our good shepherd. He knows us by name and loves us so much that he laid down his life for us. When David was anointed by Samuel, the Spirit of God came to him and set him apart to be king of Israel. The Spirit of God came to Jesus when he was baptised by John, equipping him to be our saviour and king. David suffered at the hands of his enemies before becoming king. Jesus, too, suffered before God exalted him in heaven.

my FAVOURITE links

OTHER CONNECTIONS

Livin' it — One of the best examples of true friendship can be found between David and his friend Jonathan, the son of King Saul. Despite many obstacles, these two remained loyal to one another. Connect to The Perfect Friend, 1 Samuel 18:1, to learn more about the qualities that make up a good friend.

 Find out more about the transition from Samuel, the last judge of Israel, to when Saul became Israel's first king and other interesting facts found in the first Book of Samuel by linking here:

- Samuel, the Prophet, 1 Samuel 4. Follow the life of Samuel, Israel's last judge before God granted the people's request for a king.
- King Saul, the Soldier, 1 Samuel 14. As long as King Saul obeyed God, he achieved many successes on the battlefield. Check out the highlights of his battles here.
- God to the Rescue! 1 Samuel 23. Link here to learn more about some pretty amazing rescues found throughout the Old Testament that only God could make happen.
- Israel was surrounded by enemies, but the biggest bullies in the neighbourhood were a people called the Philistines. Learn more about Israel's arch-enemies by linking to Some Bad Guys, 1 Samuel 31:1–4.

DOWNLOAD THESE EXCITING STORIES:

Wake up; God is calling, 1 Samuel 3
The idol that bowed down to God, 1 Samuel 5
The shepherd and the giant, 1 Samuel 17
David escapes out a window, 1 Samuel 19:9–17
Best friends, 1 Samuel 20:41–42
The corner of Saul's robe, 1 Samuel 24
Nabal insults David, 1 Samuel 25

FAITH links

- Learning to Listen, **1 Samuel 3**
- I Insist! **1 Samuel 8; 9**
- A Shortcut, **1 Samuel 13:1–14**
- A Giant Problem, **1 Samuel 17:32–51**
- When the Green-eyed Monster Strikes, **1 Samuel 18:6–9**
- The Gift of Friendship, **1 Samuel 18:1–3; 19**
- A Right to Get Even? **1 Samuel 24**
- The Right Thing to Do, **1 Samuel 26**
- Kind or Fair? **1 Samuel 30**

did YOU know?

Samuel's Birth

1 There was a man named Elkanah son of Jeroham from Ramathaim in the mountains of Ephraim. Elkanah was from the family of Zuph. (Jeroham was Elihu's son. Elihu was Tohu's son, and Tohu was the son of Zuph from the family group of Ephraim.) 2 Elkanah had two wives named Hannah and Peninnah. Peninnah had children, but Hannah had none.

3 Every year Elkanah left his town of Ramah and went up to Shiloh to worship the LORD All-powerful and to offer sacrifices to him. Shiloh was where Hophni and Phinehas, the sons of Eli, served as priests of the LORD. 4 When Elkanah offered sacrifices, he always gave a share of the meat to his wife Peninnah and to her sons and daughters. 5 But Elkanah always gave a special share of the meat to Hannah, because he loved Hannah and because the LORD had kept her from having children. 6 Peninnah would tease Hannah and upset her, because the LORD had made her unable to have children. 7 This happened every year when they went up to the house of the LORD at Shiloh. Peninnah would upset Hannah until Hannah would cry and not eat anything. 8 Her husband Elkanah would say to her, "Hannah, why are you crying and why won't you eat? Why are you sad? Don't I mean more to you than ten sons?"

9 Once, after they had eaten their meal in Shiloh, Hannah got up. Now Eli the priest was sitting on a chair near the entrance to the LORD's house. 10 Hannah was so sad that she cried and prayed to the LORD. 11 She made a promise, saying, "LORD All-powerful, see how sad I am. Remember me and don't forget me. If you will give me a son, I will give him back to you all his life, and no one will ever cut his hair with a razor."[n]

12 While Hannah kept praying, Eli watched her mouth. 13 She was praying in her heart so her lips moved, but her voice was not heard. Eli thought she was drunk 14 and said to her, "Stop getting drunk! Throw away your wine!"

15 Hannah answered, "No, sir, I have not drunk any wine or beer. I am a deeply troubled woman, and I was telling the LORD about all my problems. 16 Don't think I am an evil woman. I have been

---

FAITH links

KEEP ON PRAYING
1 SAMUEL 1

When it comes to prayer, how persistent are you? Many times, we might pray about something once. If God doesn't answer right away, we give up. Hannah was persistent in asking God for a son. She desperately wanted one! She didn't just ask once. She kept on asking. God wants you to have this kind of perseverance about prayer. You won't annoy God if you keep on asking him about something. So . . . keep on asking!

Link here for some more encouraging words on prayer:

From Hopeless to Hopeful, Exodus 6:9, p. 83

What He's Really Like, Deuteronomy 4:15–20, p. 233

Two Enemies, Nehemiah 6, p. 631

The Prayer Habit, Psalm 5:1–3, p. 712

Ask, Search, Knock, Matthew 7:7–10, p. 1286

While You Wait, Jude 21, p. 1726

1:11 cut . . . razor People who made special promises not to cut their hair or to drink wine or beer were called Nazirites. These people gave a specific time in their lives, or sometimes their entire lives, to the LORD. See Numbers 6:1–5.

praying because I have many troubles and am very sad."

1:17 Prayer Who answers prayer?

17 Eli answered, "Go! I wish you well. May the God of Israel give you what you asked of him." 18 Hannah said, "May I always please you." When she left and ate something, she was not sad any more.

19 Early the next morning Elkanah's family got up and worshipped the LORD. Then they went back home to Ramah. Elkanah had sexual relations with his wife Hannah, and the LORD remembered her. 20 So Hannah became pregnant, and in time she gave birth to a son. She named him Samuel,ⁿ saying, "His name is Samuel because I asked the LORD for him."

Hannah Gives Samuel to God

21 Every year Elkanah went with his whole family to Shiloh to offer sacrifices and to keep the promise he had made to God. 22 But one year Hannah did not go with him. She told him, "When the boy is old enough to eat solid food, I will take him to Shiloh. Then I will give him to the LORD, and he will always live there."

23 Elkanah, Hannah's husband, said to her, "Do what you think is best. You may stay home until the boy is old enough to eat. May the LORD do what you have said." So Hannah stayed at home to nurse her son until he was old enough to eat.

24 When Samuel was old enough to eat, Hannah took him to the house of the LORD at Shiloh, along with a three-year-old bull, ten kilogrammes of flour, and a leather bag filled with wine. 25 After they had killed the bull for the sacrifice, Hannah brought Samuel to Eli. 26 She said to Eli, "As surely as you live, sir, I am the same woman who stood near you praying to the LORD. 27 I prayed for this child, and the LORD answered my prayer and gave him to me. 28 Now I give him back to the LORD. He will belong to the LORD all his life." And he worshipped the LORD there.

Hannah Gives Thanks

2 Hannah prayed:
"The LORD has filled my heart with joy;
I feel very strong in the LORD.
I can laugh at my enemies;
I am glad because you have helped me!

2 "There is no one holy like the LORD.
There is no God but you;
there is no Rock like our God.

3 "Don't continue boasting,
don't speak proud words.
The LORD is a God who knows everything,
and he judges what people do.

4 "The bows of warriors break,
but weak people become strong.
5 Those who once had plenty of food
now must work for food,
but people who were hungry are hungry no more.
The woman who could not have children now has seven,
but the woman who had many children now is sad.

6 "The LORD sends death,
and he brings to life.
He sends people to the grave,
and he raises them to life again.
7 The LORD makes some people poor,
and others he makes rich.
He makes some people humble,
and others he makes great.
8 The LORD raises the poor up from the dust,
and he lifts the needy from the ashes.
He lets the poor sit with princes
and receive a throne of honour.

2:6–7 God Does God rule over everything?

1:20 Samuel This name sounds like the Hebrew word for "God heard".

"The foundations of the earth belong to the LORD,
and the LORD set the world upon them.
9 He protects those who are loyal to him,
but evil people will be silenced in darkness.
Power is not the key to success.
10 The LORD destroys his enemies;
he will thunder in heaven against them.
The LORD will judge all the earth.
He will give power to his king
and make his appointed king strong."

Eli's Evil Sons

11 Then Elkanah went home to Ramah, but the boy continued to serve the LORD under Eli the priest.

12 Now Eli's sons were evil men; they did not care about the LORD. 13 This is what the priests would normally do to the people: every time someone brought a sacrifice, the meat would be cooked in a pot. The priest's servant would then come carrying a fork that had three prongs. 14 He would plunge the fork into the pot or the kettle. Whatever the fork brought out of the pot belonged to the priest. But this is how they treated all the Israelites who came to Shiloh to offer sacrifices. 15 Even before the fat was burned, the priest's servant would come to the person offering sacrifices and say, "Give the priest some meat to roast. He won't accept boiled meat from you, only raw meat."

16 If the one who offered the sacrifice said, "Let the fat be burned up first as usual, and then take anything you want," the priest's servant would answer, "No, give me the meat now. If you don't, I'll take it by force."

17 The LORD saw that the sin of the servants was very great because they did not show respect for the offerings made to the LORD.

Samuel Grows Up

18 But Samuel obeyed the LORD. As a boy he wore a linen holy robe. 19 Every year Samuel's mother made a little coat for him and took it to him when she went with her husband to Shiloh for the sacrifice. 20 When Eli blessed Elkanah and his

---

A SONG OF THANKS
1 SAMUEL 2

When you're feeling thankful, how do you show it? Hannah was thankful that God answered her prayer. She showed thanks to God with a song. Other people in the Bible also sang songs to thank God: Moses and Miriam (check out Exodus 15, p. 94); Deborah and Barak (read Judges 5, p. 316); David (look up 2 Samuel 22, p. 427; Psalm 18, p. 721, and Psalms 23—25, p. 726, just to name a few); Mary (read Luke 1:46–55, p. 1366); Zechariah (see Luke 1:68–79, p. 1367); and Simeon (check out Luke 2:29–32, p. 1369). What are you thankful to God for? How will you show your thanks?

A Thanksgiving Reminder, Exodus 12, p. 91

No Thanksgiving? 2 Kings 23:21–23, p. 512

Love That Will Last, Psalm 136, p. 813

Bragging Rights, Jeremiah 9:23–24, p. 1005

Your Spiritual Roots, Zechariah 1:1–6, p. 1253

A Family Meal, Mark 14:23–26, p. 1356

wife, he would say, "May the LORD repay you with children through Hannah to take the place of the boy Hannah prayed for and gave back to the LORD." Then Elkanah and Hannah would go home. 21 The LORD was kind to Hannah, so she became the mother of three sons and two daughters. And the boy Samuel grew up serving the LORD.

22 Now Eli was very old. He heard about everything his sons were doing to all the Israelites and how his sons had sexual relations with the women who served at the entrance to the Meeting Tent. 23 Eli said to his sons, "Why do you do these evil things that the people tell me about? 24 No, my sons. The LORD's people are spreading a bad report about you. 25 If you sin against someone, God can help you. But if you sin against the LORD himself, no one can help you!" But Eli's sons would not listen to him, because the LORD had decided to put them to death.

26 The boy Samuel grew physically. He pleased the LORD and the people.

27 A man of God came to Eli and said, "This is what the LORD says: 'I clearly showed myself to the family of your ancestor Aaron when they were slaves to the king of Egypt. 28 I chose them from all the tribes of Israel to be my priests. I wanted them to go up to my altar, to burn incense and to wear the holy robe. I also let the family of your ancestor have part of all the offerings sacrificed by the Israelites. 29 So why don't you respect the sacrifices and gifts? You honour your sons more than me. You grow fat on the best parts of the meat the Israelites bring to me.'

30 "So the LORD, the God of Israel, says: 'I promised that your family and your ancestor's family would serve me always.' But now the LORD says: 'This must stop! I will honour those who honour me, but I will dishonour those who ignore me. 31 The time is coming when I will destroy the descendants of both you and your ancestors. No man will grow old in your family. 32 You will see trouble in my house. No matter what good things happen to Israel, there will never be an old man in your family. 33 I will not totally cut off your family from my altar. But your eyes will cry and your heart be sad, because all your descendants will die.

34 "'I will give you a sign. Both your sons, Hophni and Phinehas, will die on the same day. 35 I will choose a loyal priest for myself who will listen to me and do what I want. I will make his family continue, and he will always serve before my appointed king. 36 Then everyone left in your family will come and bow down before him. They will beg for a little money or a little food and say, "Please give me a job as priest so I can have food to eat."'"

God Calls Samuel

3 The boy Samuel served the LORD under Eli. In those days the LORD did not speak directly to people very often; there were very few visions.

2 Eli's eyes were so weak he was almost blind. One night he was lying in bed. 3 Samuel was also in bed in the LORD's house, where the Ark of the Agreement was. God's lamp was still burning.

4 Then the LORD called Samuel, and Samuel answered, "I am here!" 5 He ran to Eli and said, "I am here. You called me."

But Eli said, "I didn't call you. Go back to bed." So Samuel went back to bed.

6 The LORD called again, "Samuel!"

Samuel again went to Eli and said, "I am here. You called me."

Again Eli said, "I didn't call you. Go back to bed."

7 Samuel did not yet know the LORD, and the LORD had not spoken directly to him yet.

8 The LORD called Samuel for the third time. Samuel got up and went to Eli and said, "I am here. You called me."

Then Eli realised the LORD was calling the boy. 9 So he told Samuel, "Go to bed. If he calls you again, say, 'Speak, LORD. I am your servant and I am listening.'" So Samuel went and lay down in bed.

10 The LORD came and stood there and called as he had before, "Samuel, Samuel!"

> **EMAIL FROM GOD 3:10**
> Following God
> Who should you listen to?

FAITH links

LEARNING TO LISTEN
1 SAMUEL 3

When you were a baby, your parents probably spoke your name to you often. They wanted you to learn your name. They also wanted you to learn to listen to them.

Hundreds of years had passed since the Israelites had heard from God directly. That all changed one night when Samuel heard someone call his name. At first, he didn't know who had called him. He had to learn how to listen and respond to God. God wants you to learn to listen to him, too. There are many ways that God can speak to you. He uses the Bible, prayer and the wise advice of Christians. Are you ready to listen?

The Cloud Guide, Numbers 9:15–23, p. 188

Plan for Success, 1 Chronicles 14:8–17, p. 538

How God Speaks, Job 33:14–17, p. 696

The Bible: Good for Your Faith, Psalm 119, p. 802

A Word to the Wise, Proverbs 10:1, p. 838

That's False! 2 John 7–11, p. 1722

Samuel said, "Speak, LORD. I am your servant and I am listening."

11 The LORD said to Samuel, "Watch, I am going to do something in Israel that will shock those who hear about it. 12 At that time I will do to Eli and his family everything I promised, from beginning to end. 13 I told Eli I would punish his family always, because he knew his sons were evil. They acted without honour, but he did not stop them. 14 So I swore to Eli's family, 'Your guilt will never be removed by sacrifice or offering.'"

15 Samuel lay down until morning. Then he opened the doors of the house of the LORD. He was afraid to tell Eli about the vision, 16 but Eli called to him, "Samuel, my son!"

Samuel answered, "I am here."

17 Eli asked, "What did the LORD say to you? Don't hide it from me. May God punish you terribly if you hide from me anything he said to you." 18 So Samuel told Eli everything and did not hide anything from him. Then Eli said, "He is the LORD. Let him do what he thinks is best."

19 The LORD was with Samuel as he grew up; he did not let any of Samuel's messages fail to come true. 20 Then all Israel, from Dan to Beersheba,ⁿ knew Samuel was a true prophet of the LORD. 21 And the LORD continued to show himself at Shiloh, and he showed himself to Samuel through his word.

4 So, news about Samuel spread through all of Israel.

The Philistines Capture the Ark of the Agreement

At that time the Israelites went out to fight the Philistines. The Israelites camped at Ebenezer and the Philistines at Aphek. 2 The Philistines went to meet the Israelites in battle. And as the battle spread, they defeated the Israelites, killing about 4,000 soldiers on the battlefield. 3 When some Israelite soldiers went back to their camp, the elders of Israel asked, "Why did the LORD let the Philistines defeat us? Let's bring the Ark of the Agreement with the LORD here from Shiloh and take it with us into battle. Then God will save us from our enemies."

3:20 Dan to Beersheba Dan was the city farthest north in Israel, and Beersheba was the city farthest south. So this means all the people of Israel.

Get the Info

SAMUEL, THE PROPHET — 1 Samuel 4

1. Hannah prayed for a son at the Lord's house near Shiloh. She promised if God would give her a son that she would dedicate him to the Lord's service. (Read 1 Samuel 1:10–17.)

2. Samuel was born to Hannah and Elkanah at Ramah. (Look up 1 Samuel 1:19–20.)

3. Hannah brought Samuel to live at the Lord's house at Shiloh when he was "old enough to eat solid food". Samuel became a helper to Eli, a priest at the Lord's house. While Samuel was there, God called him to do a special job. (See 1 Samuel 2:18—3:21.)

4. As a grown-up, Samuel served as a prophet and a judge. In the district of Zuph, Samuel secretly appointed Saul to be the first king of Israel. (Check out 1 Samuel 9:1—10:1.)

5. After Saul failed to obey God, Samuel appointed David, the youngest son of Jesse, to become the second king of Israel. (Read 1 Samuel 16:1–13.)

---

4 So the people sent men to Shiloh. They brought back the Ark of the Agreement with the LORD All-powerful, who sits between the gold creatures with wings. Eli's two sons, Hophni and Phinehas, were there with the Ark.

5 When the Ark of the Agreement with the LORD came into the camp, all the Israelites gave a great shout of joy that made the ground shake. 6 When the Philistines heard Israel's shout, they asked, "What's all this shouting in the Hebrew camp?"

Then the Philistines found out that the Ark of the LORD had come into the Hebrew camp. 7 They were afraid and said, "A god has come into the Hebrew camp! We're in trouble! This has never happened before! 8 How terrible it will be for us! Who can save us from these powerful gods? They are the ones who struck the Egyptians with all kinds of disasters in the desert. 9 Be brave, Philistines! Fight like men! In the past they were our slaves. So fight like men, or we will become their slaves."

10 So the Philistines fought hard and defeated the Israelites, and every Israelite soldier ran away to his own home. It was a

great defeat for Israel, because 30,000 Israelite soldiers were killed. 11 The Ark of God was taken by the Philistines, and Eli's two sons, Hophni and Phinehas, died.

12 That same day a man from the tribe of Benjamin ran from the battle. He tore his clothes and put dust on his head to show his great sadness. 13 When he arrived in Shiloh, Eli was by the side of the road. He was sitting there in a chair, watching, because he was worried about the Ark of God. When the Benjaminite entered Shiloh, he told the bad news. Then all the people in town cried loudly. 14 Eli heard the crying and asked, "What's all this noise?"

The Benjaminite ran to Eli and told him what had happened. 15 Eli was now 98 years old, and he was blind. 16 The Benjaminite told him, "I have come from the battle. I ran all the way here today."

Eli asked, "What happened, my son?"

17 The Benjaminite answered, "Israel ran away from the Philistines, and the Israelite army has lost many soldiers. Your two sons are both dead, and the Philistines have taken the Ark of God."

18 When he mentioned the Ark of God, Eli fell backwards off his chair. He fell beside the gate, broke his neck, and died, because he was old and fat. He had led Israel for 40 years.

The Glory is Gone

19 Eli's daughter-in-law, the wife of Phinehas, was pregnant and was about to give birth. When she heard the news that the Ark of God had been taken and that Eli, her father-in-law, and Phinehas, her husband, were both dead, she began to give birth to her child. The child was born, but the mother had much trouble in giving birth. 20 As she was dying, the women who helped her said, "Don't worry! You've given birth to a son!" But she did not answer or pay attention. 21 She named the baby Ichabod,[n] saying, "Israel's glory is gone." She said this because the Ark of God had been taken and her father-in-law and husband were dead. 22 She said, "Israel's glory is gone, because the Ark of God has been taken away."

Trouble for the Philistines

5 After the Philistines had captured the Ark of God, they took it from Ebenezer to Ashdod. 2 They carried it into Dagon's temple and put it next to Dagon. 3 When the people of Ashdod rose early the next morning, they found that Dagon had fallen on his face on the ground before the Ark of the LORD. So they put Dagon back in his place. 4 The next morning when they rose, they again found Dagon fallen on the ground before the Ark of the LORD. His head and hands had broken off and were lying in the doorway. Only his body was still in one piece. 5 So, even today, Dagon's priests and others who enter his temple at Ashdod refuse to step on the doorsill.

6 The LORD was hard on the people of Ashdod and their neighbours. He caused them to suffer and gave them growths on their skin. 7 When the people of Ashdod saw what was happening, they said, "The Ark of the God of Israel can't stay with us. God is punishing us and Dagon our god." 8 The people of Ashdod called all five Philistine kings together and asked them, "What should we do with the Ark of the God of Israel?"

The rulers answered, "Move the Ark of the God of Israel to Gath." So the Philistines moved it to Gath.

9 But after they moved it to Gath, there was a great panic. The LORD was hard on that city also, and he gave both old and young people in Gath growths on their skin. 10 Then the Philistines sent the Ark of God to Ekron.

But when it came into Ekron, the people of Ekron yelled, "Why are you bringing the Ark of the God of Israel to our city? Do you want to kill us and our people?" 11 So they called all the kings of the Philistines together and said, "Send the Ark of the God of Israel back to its place before it kills us and our people!" All the people in the city were struck with terror because God was so hard on them there.

4:21 **Ichabod** This name means "no glory".

12 The people who did not die were troubled with growths on their skin. So the people of Ekron cried loudly to heaven.

The Ark of God is Sent Home

6 The Philistines kept the Ark of God in their land seven months. 2 Then they called for their priests and magicians and said, "What should we do with the Ark of the LORD? Tell us how to send it back home!"

3 The priests and magicians answered, "If you send back the Ark of the God of Israel, don't send it back empty. You must give a penalty offering. If you are then healed, you will know that it was because of the Ark that you had such trouble."

4 The Philistines asked, "What kind of penalty offering should we send to Israel's God?"

They answered, "Make five gold models of the growths on your skin and five gold models of rats. The number of models must match the number of Philistine kings, because the same sickness has come on you and your kings. 5 Make models of the growths and the rats that are ruining the country, and give honour to Israel's God. Then maybe he will stop being so hard on you, your gods and your land. 6 Don't be stubborn like the king of Egypt and the Egyptians. God punished them terribly until they let the Israelites leave Egypt.

7 "You must build a new cart and get two cows that have just had calves. These must be cows that have never had yokes on their necks. Hitch the cows to the cart, and take the calves home, away from their mothers. 8 Put the Ark of the LORD on the cart and the gold models for the penalty offering in a box beside the Ark. Then send the cart straight on its way. 9 Watch the cart. If it goes towards Beth Shemesh in Israel's own land, the LORD has given us this great sickness. But if it doesn't, we will know that Israel's God has not punished us. Our sickness just happened by chance."

10 The Philistines did what the priests and magicians said. They took two cows that had just had calves and hitched them to the cart, but they kept their calves at home. 11 They put the Ark of the LORD and the box with the gold rats and models of growths on the cart. 12 Then the cows went straight towards Beth Shemesh. They stayed on the road, mooing all the way, and did not turn right or left. The Philistine kings followed the cows as far as the border of Beth Shemesh.

13 Now the people of Beth Shemesh were harvesting their wheat in the valley. When they looked up and saw the Ark of the LORD, they were very happy. 14 The cart came to the field belonging to Joshua of Beth Shemesh and stopped near a large rock. The people of Beth Shemesh chopped up the wood of the cart. Then they sacrificed the cows as burnt offerings to the LORD. 15 The Levites took down the Ark of the LORD and the box that had the gold models, and they put both on the large rock. That day the people of Beth Shemesh offered whole burnt offerings and made sacrifices to the LORD. 16 After the five Philistine kings saw this, they went back to Ekron the same day.

17 The Philistines had sent these gold models of the growths as penalty offerings to the LORD. They sent one model for each Philistine town: Ashdod, Gaza, Ashkelon, Gath and Ekron. 18 And the Philistines also sent gold models of rats. The number of rats matched the number of towns belonging to the Philistine kings, including both fortified cities and country villages. The large rock on which they put the Ark of the LORD is still there in the field of Joshua of Beth Shemesh.

19 But some of the men of Beth Shemesh looked into the Ark of the LORD. So God killed 70 of them. The people of Beth Shemesh cried because the LORD had struck them down. 20 They said, "Who can stand before the LORD, this holy God? Whom will he strike next?"

6:20 God
Who can stand before God?

21 Then they sent messengers to the people of Kiriath Jearim, saying, "The Philistines have brought back the Ark of

the LORD. Come down and take it to your city."

7 The men of Kiriath Jearim came and took the Ark of the LORD to Abinadab's house on a hill. There they made Abinadab's son Eleazar holy for the LORD so he could guard the Ark of the LORD.

The LORD Saves the Israelites

2 The Ark stayed at Kiriath Jearim a long time—20 years in all. And the people of Israel began to follow the LORD again. 3 Samuel spoke to the whole group of Israel, saying, "If you're turning back to the LORD with all your hearts, you must remove your foreign gods and your idols of Ashtoreth. You must give yourselves fully to the LORD and serve only him. Then he will save you from the Philistines."

> **7:3 Truth**
> How does following truth help you?

4 So the Israelites put away their idols of Baal and Ashtoreth, and they served only the LORD.

5 Samuel said, "All Israel must meet at Mizpah, and I will pray to the LORD for you." 6 So the Israelites met together at Mizpah. They drew water from the ground and poured it out before the LORD and did not eat that day. They confessed, "We have sinned against the LORD." And Samuel served as judge of Israel at Mizpah.

7 The Philistines heard the Israelites were meeting at Mizpah, so the Philistine kings came up to attack them. When the Israelites heard they were coming, they were afraid. 8 They said to Samuel, "Don't stop praying to the LORD our God for us! Ask him to save us from the Philistines!" 9 Then Samuel took a baby lamb and offered it to the LORD as a whole burnt offering. He called to the LORD for Israel's sake, and the LORD answered him.

10 While Samuel was burning the offering, the Philistines came near to attack Israel. But the LORD thundered against them with loud thunder. They were so frightened they became confused. So the Israelites defeated the Philistines in battle. 11 The men of Israel ran out of Mizpah and chased the Philistines almost to Beth Car, killing the Philistines along the way.

Peace Comes to Israel

12 After this happened Samuel took a stone and set it up between Mizpah and Shen. He named the stone Ebenezer,* saying, "The LORD has helped us to this point." 13 So the Philistines were defeated and did not enter the Israelites' land again.

The LORD was against the Philistines all Samuel's life. 14 Earlier the Philistines had taken towns from the Israelites, but the Israelites won them back, from Ekron to Gath. They also took back from the Philistines the lands near these towns. There was peace also between Israel and the Amorites.

15 Samuel continued as judge of Israel all his life. 16 Every year he went from Bethel to Gilgal to Mizpah and judged the Israelites in all these towns. 17 But Samuel always went back to Ramah, where his home was. There he judged Israel and built an altar to the LORD.

Israel Asks for a King

8 When Samuel was old, he made his sons judges for Israel. 2 His first son was named Joel, and his second son was named Abijah. Joel and Abijah were judges in Beersheba. 3 But Samuel's sons did not live as he did. They tried to get money dishonestly, and they accepted money secretly to make wrong judgements.

4 So all the elders came together and met Samuel at Ramah. 5 They said to him, "You're old, and your sons don't live as you do. Give us a king to rule over us like all the other nations."

6 When the elders said that, Samuel was not pleased. He prayed to the LORD, 7 and the LORD told Samuel, "Listen to whatever the people say to you. They have not rejected you. They have rejected me from being their king. 8 They are doing as they have always done. When I took them out of Egypt, they left me and served

---

7:12 Ebenezer This name means "stone of help".

FAITH links

I INSIST!
1 SAMUEL 8; 9

Have you ever begged your parents for something that you later regretted having? Maybe this was something your parents insisted was not good for you. The people didn't want Samuel's sons to rule over them. God knew that the people really did not want *him* to rule over them. He also knew they would later regret having a king. He told Samuel to warn the people not to insist on having a king. But they wouldn't listen.

Have you ever insisted on having your own way? If your way is God's way, there's no problem. But if your way involves disobeying God, there is one way to avoid having regrets. Follow his way!

Here are some more Faithlinks on obeying God:

An Attention-Getter, Numbers 22, p. 207

Try to Remember, Deuteronomy 11:18–21, p. 243

Your Stats, 1 Kings 15; 16, p. 460

God's Instructions, Ezekiel 4:1–15, p. 1089

The Writing's on the Wall, Daniel 5, p. 1159

The Choices of a Choice, Luke 5:1–11, p. 1375

---

other gods. They are doing the same to you. 9 Now listen to the people, but warn them what the king who rules over them will do."

10 So Samuel told those who had asked him for a king what the LORD had said. 11 Samuel said, "If you have a king ruling over you, this is what he will do: he will take your sons and make them serve with his chariots and his horses, and they will run in front of the king's chariot. 12 The king will make some of your sons commanders over thousands or over fifties. He will make some of your other sons plough his ground and reap his harvest. He will take others to make weapons of war and equipment for his chariots. 13 He will take your daughters to make perfume and cook and bake for him. 14 He will take your best fields, vineyards and olive groves and give them to his servants. 15 He will take one-tenth of your grain and grapes and give it to his officers and servants. 16 He will take your male and female servants, your best cattle and your donkeys and use them all for his own work. 17 He will take one-tenth of your flocks, and you yourselves will become his slaves. 18 When that time comes, you will cry out because of the king you chose. But the LORD will not answer you then."

19 But the people would not listen to Samuel. They said, "No! We want a king to rule over us. 20 Then we will be the same as all the other nations. Our king will judge for us and go with us and fight our battles."

21 After Samuel heard all that the people said, he repeated their words to the LORD. 22 The LORD answered, "You must listen to them. Give them a king."

Then Samuel told the people of Israel, "Go back to your towns."

Saul Looks for His Father's Donkeys

9 Kish, son of Abiel from the tribe of Benjamin, was an important man. (Abiel was the son of Zeror, who was the son of Becorath, who was the son of Aphiah of Benjamin.) 2 Kish had a son named Saul, who was a fine young man.

There was no Israelite better than he. Saul stood a head taller than any other man in Israel.

3 Now the donkeys of Saul's father, Kish, were lost. So Kish said to Saul, his son, "Take one of the servants, and go and look for the donkeys." 4 Saul went through the mountains of Ephraim and the land of Shalisha, but he and the servant could not find the donkeys. They went into the land of Shaalim, but the donkeys were not there. They went through the land of Benjamin, but they still did not find them. 5 When they arrived in the area of Zuph, Saul said to his servant, "Let's go back or my father will stop thinking about the donkeys and will start worrying about us."

6 But the servant answered, "A man of God is in this town. People respect him because everything he says comes true. Let's go into the town now. Maybe he can tell us something about the journey we have taken."

7 Saul said to his servant, "If we go into the town, what can we give him? The food in our bags is gone. We have no gift to give him. Do we have anything?"

8 Again the servant answered Saul. "Look, I have nearly a piece of silver. Give it to the man of God. Then he will tell us about our journey." 9 (In the past, if someone in Israel wanted to ask something from God, he would say, "Let's go to the seer." We call the person a prophet today, but in the past he was called a seer.)

10 Saul said to his servant, "That's a good idea. Come, let's go." So they went towards the town where the man of God was.

11 As Saul and the servant were going up the hill to the town, they met some young women coming out to get water. Saul and the servant asked them, "Is the seer here?"

12 The young women answered, "Yes, he's here. He's ahead of you. Hurry now. He has just come to our town today, because the people will offer a sacrifice at the place of worship. 13 As soon as you enter the town, you will find him before he goes up to the place of worship to eat. The people will not begin eating until the seer comes, because he must bless the sacrifice. After that, the guests will eat. Go now, and you should find him."

Saul Meets Samuel

14 Saul and the servant went up to the town. Just as they entered it, they saw Samuel coming towards them on his way up to the place of worship.

15 The day before Saul came, the LORD had told Samuel: 16 "About this time tomorrow I will send you a man from the land of Benjamin. Appoint him to lead my people Israel. He will save my people from the Philistines. I have seen the suffering of my people, and I have listened to their cry."

17 When Samuel first saw Saul, the LORD said to Samuel, "This is the man I told you about. He will organise my people."

18 Saul approached Samuel at the gate and said, "Please tell me where the seer's house is."

19 Samuel answered, "I am the seer. Go with me to the place of worship. Today you and your servant are to eat with me. Tomorrow morning I will answer all your questions and send you home. 20 Don't worry about the donkeys you lost three days ago, because they have been found. Soon all the wealth of Israel will belong to you and your family."

21 Saul answered, "But I am from the tribe of Benjamin, the smallest tribe in Israel. And my family group is the smallest in the tribe of Benjamin. Why are you saying such things?"

22 Then Samuel took Saul and his servant into a large room and gave them a choice place at the table. About 30 guests were there. 23 Samuel said to the cook, "Bring the meat I gave you, the portion I told you to set aside."

> When Samuel first saw Saul, the LORD said to Samuel, "This is the man I told you about. He will organise my people."
> – 1 Samuel 9:17

24 So the cook took the thigh and put it on the table in front of Saul. Samuel said, "This is the meat saved for you. Eat it, because it was set aside for you for this special time. As I said, 'I had invited the people.'" So Saul ate with Samuel that day.

25 After they finished eating, they came down from the place of worship and went to the town. Then Samuel talked with Saul on the roof[n] of his house. 26 At dawn they got up, and Samuel called to Saul on the roof. He said, "Get up, and I will send you on your way." So Saul got up and went out of the house with Samuel. 27 As Saul, his servant and Samuel were getting near the edge of the city, Samuel said to Saul, "Tell the servant to go on ahead of us, but you stay, because I have a message from God for you."

Samuel Appoints Saul

10 Samuel took a jar of olive oil and poured it on Saul's head. He kissed Saul and said, "The LORD has appointed you to lead his people. 2 After you leave me today, you will meet two men near Rachel's tomb on the border of Benjamin at Zelzah. They will say to you, 'The donkeys you were looking for have been found. But now your father has stopped thinking about his donkeys and is worrying about you. He is asking, "What will I do about my son?"'

3 "Then you will go on until you reach the big tree at Tabor. Three men on their way to worship God at Bethel will meet you there. One man will be carrying three goats. Another will be carrying three loaves of bread. And the third will have a leather bag full of wine. 4 They will greet you and offer you two loaves of bread, which you must accept. 5 Then you will go to Gibeah of God, where a Philistine camp is. When you approach this town, a group of prophets will come down from the place of worship. They will be playing harps, tambourines, flutes and lyres, and they will be prophesying. 6 Then the Spirit of the LORD will rush upon you with power. You will prophesy with these prophets, and you will be changed into a different man. 7 After these signs happen, do whatever you find to do, because God is with you.

8 "Go ahead of me to Gilgal. I will come down to you to offer whole burnt offerings and fellowship offerings. But you must wait seven days. Then I will come and tell you what to do."

Saul Made King

9 When Saul turned to leave Samuel, God changed Saul's heart. All these signs came true that day. 10 When Saul and his servant arrived at Gibeah, Saul met a group of prophets. The Spirit of God rushed upon him, and he prophesied with the prophets. 11 When people who had known Saul before saw him prophesying with the prophets, they asked each other, "What has happened to Kish's son? Is even Saul one of the prophets?"

12 A man who lived there said, "Who is the father of these prophets?" So this became a famous saying: "Is even Saul one of the prophets?" 13 When Saul finished prophesying, he went to the place of worship.

14 Saul's uncle asked him and his servant, "Where have you been?"

Saul said, "We were looking for the donkeys. When we couldn't find them, we went to talk to Samuel."

15 Saul's uncle asked, "Please tell me. What did Samuel say to you?"

16 Saul answered, "He told us the donkeys had already been found." But Saul did not tell his uncle what Samuel had said about his becoming king.

17 Samuel called all the people of Israel to meet with the LORD at Mizpah. 18 He said, "This is what the LORD, the God of Israel, says: 'I led Israel out of Egypt. I saved you from Egypt's control and from other kingdoms that were troubling you.' 19 But now you have rejected your God. He saves you from all your troubles and problems, but you said, 'No! We want a king to rule over us.' Now come,

---

9:25 roof In Bible times houses were built with flat roofs. The roof was used for drying things such as flax and fruit. And it was used as an extra room, as a place for worship and as a place to sleep in the summer.

stand before the LORD in your tribes and family groups."

20 When Samuel gathered all the tribes of Israel, the tribe of Benjamin was picked. 21 Samuel had them pass by in family groups, and Matri's family was picked. Then he had each man of Matri's family pass by, and Saul son of Kish was picked. But when they looked for Saul, they could not find him. 22 They asked the LORD, "Has Saul come here yet?"

The LORD said, "Yes. He's hiding behind the baggage."

23 So they ran and brought him out. When Saul stood among the people, he was a head taller than anyone else. 24 Then Samuel said to the people, "See the man the LORD has chosen. There is no one like him among all the people."

Then the people shouted, "Long live the king!"

25 Samuel explained the rights and duties of the king and then wrote them in a book and put it before the LORD. Then he told the people to go to their homes.

26 Saul also went to his home in Gibeah. God touched the hearts of certain brave men who went along with him. 27 But some troublemakers said, "How can this man save us?" They disapproved of Saul and refused to bring gifts to him. But Saul kept quiet.

Nahash Troubles Jabesh Gilead

11 About a month later Nahash the Ammonite and his army surrounded the city of Jabesh in Gilead. All the people of Jabesh said to Nahash, "Make a treaty with us, and we will serve you."

2 But he answered, "I will make a treaty with you only if I'm allowed to tear out the right eye of each of you. Then all Israel will be ashamed!"

3 The elders of Jabesh said to Nahash, "Give us seven days to send messengers through all Israel. If no one comes to help us, we will give ourselves up to you."

4 When the messengers came to Gibeah where Saul lived and told the people the news, they cried loudly. 5 Saul was coming home from ploughing the fields with his oxen when he heard the people crying. He asked, "What's wrong with the people that they are crying?" Then they told Saul what the messengers from Jabesh had said. 6 When Saul heard their words, God's Spirit rushed upon him with power, and he became very angry. 7 So he took a pair of oxen and cut them into pieces. Then he gave the pieces of the oxen to messengers and ordered them to carry them through all the land of Israel.

The messengers said, "This is what will happen to the oxen of anyone who does not follow Saul and Samuel." So the people became very afraid of the LORD. They all came together as if they were one person. 8 Saul gathered the people together at Bezek. There were 300,000 men from Israel and 30,000 men from Judah.

> Then Samuel said to the people, "See the man the LORD has chosen. There is no one like him among all the people."
> – 1 Samuel 10:24

9 They said to the messengers who had come, "Tell the people at Jabesh Gilead this: 'Before the day warms up tomorrow, you will be saved.'" So the messengers went and reported this to the people at Jabesh, and they were very happy. 10 The people said to Nahash the Ammonite, "Tomorrow we will come out to meet you. Then you can do anything you want to us."

11 The next morning Saul divided his soldiers into three groups. At dawn they entered the Ammonite camp and defeated them before the heat of the day. The Ammonites who escaped were scattered; no two of them were still together.

12 Then the people said to Samuel, "Who didn't want Saul as king? Bring them here and we will kill them!"

13 But Saul said, "No! No one will be put to death today. Today the LORD has saved Israel!"

14 Then Samuel said to the people, "Come, let's go to Gilgal. There we will

again promise to obey the king." 15 So all the people went to Gilgal, and there, before the LORD, the people made Saul king. They offered fellowship offerings to the LORD, and Saul and all the Israelites had a great celebration.

Samuel's Farewell Speech

12 Samuel said to all Israel, "I have done everything you wanted me to do and have put a king over you. 2 Now you have a king to lead you. I am old and grey, and my sons are here with you. I have been your leader since I was young. 3 Here I am. If I have done anything wrong, you must testify against me before the LORD and his appointed king. Did I steal anyone's ox or donkey? Did I hurt or cheat anyone? Did I ever secretly accept money to pretend not to see something wrong? If I did any of these things, I will make it right."

4 The Israelites answered, "You have not cheated us, or hurt us or taken anything unfairly from anyone."

5 Samuel said to them, "The LORD is a witness to what you have said. His appointed king is also a witness today that you did not find anything wrong in me."

"He is our witness," they said.

6 Then Samuel said to the people, "It is the LORD who chose Moses and Aaron

LOOK AT ME!

What are some things you're proud of? Everyone has something they do well and can be proud of what they do. But sometimes pride can cause problems. Let's listen as Danielle, aged 11, tells us about her problem with pride.

Danielle

My sister says I'm a conceited show-off because I told her friends about all the medals I've won in gymnastics. I say she's just jealous. I've been competing for seven years now, and my coach says I'm one of the best students she's ever had. If I'm that good, what's wrong with telling people about it?

It sounds like Danielle's quite a gymnast. The question she needs to ask herself is why she wants to tell other people how good she is. The Bible tells us that pride makes us forget about God because we're too busy focusing on ourselves. Danielle needs to ask herself this: How good a gymnast would she be if God hadn't given her a healthy body?

Also, she shouldn't forget other people's feelings. Maybe Danielle's sister is jealous. Maybe she wishes she had her talent. The Bible instructs us to build each other up, not make each other feel miserable. Maybe, instead of talking about her own skills, she should think of something her sister is good at and talk about that. For more tips on how to keep pride under control, check out the Livin' It page on pride, Deuteronomy 8:11-18, p. 238.

and brought your ancestors out of Egypt. 7 Now, stand there, and I will remind you of all the good things the LORD did for you and your ancestors.

8 "After Jacob entered Egypt, his descendants cried to the LORD for help. So the LORD sent Moses and Aaron, who took your ancestors out of Egypt and brought them to live in this place.

9 "But they forgot the LORD their God. So he handed them over as slaves to Sisera, the commander of the army of Hazor, and as slaves to the Philistines and the king of Moab. They all fought against your ancestors. 10 Then your ancestors cried to the LORD and said, 'We have sinned. We have left the LORD and served the Baals and the Ashtoreths. But now save us from our enemies, and we will serve you.' 11 So the LORD sent Gideon,[n] Barak, Jephthah and Samuel. He saved you from your enemies around you, and you lived in safety. 12 But when you saw Nahash king of the Ammonites coming against you, you said, 'No! We want a king to rule over us!'—even though the LORD your God was your king. 13 Now here is the king you chose, the one you asked for. The LORD has put him over you. 14 You must honour the LORD and serve him. You must obey his word and not turn against his commands. Both you and the king ruling over you must follow the LORD your God. If you do, it will be well with you. 15 But if you don't obey the LORD, and if you turn against his commands, he will be against you. He will do to you what he did to your ancestors.

16 "Now stand still and see the great thing the LORD will do before your eyes. 17 It is now the time of the wheat harvest.[n] I will pray for the LORD to send thunder and rain. Then you will know what an evil thing you did against the LORD when you asked for a king."

18 Then Samuel prayed to the LORD, and that same day the LORD sent thunder and rain. So the people were very afraid of the LORD and Samuel. 19 They said to Samuel, "Pray to the LORD your God for us, your servants! Don't let us die! We've added to all our sins the evil of asking for a king."

20 Samuel answered, "Don't be afraid. It's true that you did wrong, but don't turn away from the LORD. Serve the LORD with all your heart. 21 Idols are of no use, so don't worship them. They can't help you or save you. They are useless! 22 For his own sake, the LORD won't leave his people. Instead, he was pleased to make you his own people. 23 I will surely not stop praying for you, because that would be sinning against the LORD. I will teach you what is good and right. 24 You must honour the LORD and truly serve him with all your heart. Remember the wonderful things he did for you! 25 But if you are stubborn and do evil, he will sweep you and your king away."

12:14 Obedience How do you follow God?

12:24 Truth Find out how to serve God.

13 Saul was 30 years old when he became king, and he was king over Israel for 42 years.[n] 2 Saul chose 3,000 men from Israel. 2,000 men stayed with him at Michmash in the mountains of Bethel, and 1,000 men stayed with Jonathan at Gibeah in Benjamin. Saul sent the other men in the army back home.

3 Jonathan attacked the Philistine camp in Geba, and the other Philistines heard about it. Saul said, "Let the Hebrews hear what happened." So he told the men to blow trumpets through all the land of Israel. 4 All the Israelites heard the news. The men said, "Saul has defeated the Philistine camp. Now the Philistines will really hate us!" Then the Israelites were called to join Saul at Gilgal.

5 The Philistines gathered to fight Israel with 3,000[n] chariots and 6,000 men

---

12:11 Gideon Also called Jerub-Baal.
12:17 time . . . harvest This was a dry time in the summer when no rains fell.
13:1 Saul . . . years This is how the verse is worded in some early Greek copies. The Hebrew is not clear here.
13:5 3,000 Some Greek copies say 3,000. The Hebrew copies say 30,000.

A SHORTCUT
1 SAMUEL 13:1-14

Ever take a shortcut? They can save you time sometimes. But there are some instances where taking shortcuts can get you into trouble. Obeying God is one of those instances. Instead of doing what Samuel told him to do, Saul couldn't wait. He wanted to take a shortcut instead. His impatience cost him the kingdom.

God wants you to obey him fully, not just when or how you might feel like doing it. After all, when it comes to loving you, God never takes shortcuts. Why should you?

Your Worst Enemy, Exodus 7—11, p. 85

A Long Wait, Joshua 14:6–15, p. 294

Hurry Up and Wait, 2 Samuel 5, p. 405

Fly Like an Eagle, Isaiah 40:28–31, p. 947

A Hopeful Future, Jeremiah 29:11, p. 1031

Faith That Pleases God, Luke 7:1–9, p. 1380

---

to ride in them. Their soldiers were as many as the grains of sand on the seashore. The Philistines went and camped at Michmash, which is east of Beth Aven. 6 When the Israelites saw that they were in trouble, they went to hide in caves and bushes, among the rocks and in pits and wells. 7 Some Hebrews even went across the Jordan River to the land of Gad and Gilead.

But Saul stayed at Gilgal, and all the men in his army were shaking with fear. 8 Saul waited seven days, because Samuel had said he would meet him then. But Samuel did not come to Gilgal, and the soldiers began to leave.

9 So Saul said, "Bring me the whole burnt offering and the fellowship offerings." Then Saul offered the whole burnt offering. 10 Just as he finished, Samuel arrived, and Saul went to greet him.

11 Samuel asked, "What have you done?"

Saul answered, "I saw the soldiers leaving me, and you were not here when you said you would be. The Philistines were gathering at Michmash. 12 Then I thought, 'The Philistines will come against me at Gilgal, and I haven't asked for the LORD's approval.' So I forced myself to offer the whole burnt offering."

13 Samuel said, "You acted foolishly! You haven't obeyed the command of the LORD your God. If you had obeyed him, the LORD would have made your kingdom continue in Israel always, 14 but now your kingdom will not continue. The LORD has looked for the kind of man he wants. He has appointed him to rule his people, because you haven't obeyed his command."

15 Then Samuel left Gilgal and went to Gibeah in Benjamin. Saul counted the men who were still with him, and there were about 600.

Hard Times for Israel

16 Saul and his son Jonathan and the soldiers with him stayed in Gibeah in the land of Benjamin. The Philistines made their camp at Michmash. 17 Three groups went out from the Philistine camp to make attacks. One group went on the Ophrah road in the land of Shual. 18 The second group went on the Beth Horon road. The third group went on the border road that overlooks the Valley of Zeboim towards the desert.

19 The whole land of Israel had no blacksmith because the Philistines had said, "The Hebrews might make swords

and spears." 20 So all the Israelites had to go down to the Philistines to have their ploughs, hoes, axes and sickles sharpened. 21 The Philistine blacksmiths charged about 8 grammes of silver for sharpening ploughs and hoes. And they charged 4 grammes of silver for sharpening picks, axes and the sticks used to guide oxen.

22 So when the battle came, the soldiers with Saul and Jonathan had no swords or spears. Only Saul and his son Jonathan had them.

Israel Defeats the Philistines

23 A group from the Philistine army had gone out to the pass at Michmash.

14 One day Jonathan, Saul's son, said to the officer who carried his armour, "Come, let's go over to the Philistine camp on the other side." But Jonathan did not tell his father.

2 Saul was sitting under a pomegranate tree at the threshing floor near Gibeah. He had about 600 men with him. 3 One man was Ahijah who was wearing the holy robe. (Ahijah was a son of Ichabod's brother Ahitub. Ichabod was the son of Phinehas, the son of Eli, the LORD's priest in Shiloh.) No one knew Jonathan had left.

4 There was a steep slope on each side of the pass that Jonathan planned to go through to reach the Philistine camp. The cliff on one side was named Bozez, and the cliff on the other side was named Seneh. 5 One cliff faced north towards Michmash. The other faced south towards Geba.

6 Jonathan said to his officer who carried his armour, "Come. Let's go to the camp of those men who are not circumcised. Maybe the LORD will help us. The LORD can give us victory if we have many people, or just a few."

7 The officer who carried Jonathan's armour said to him, "Do whatever you think is best. Go ahead. I'm with you."

8 Jonathan said, "Then come. We will cross over to the Philistines and let them see us. 9 If they say to us, 'Stay there until we come to you,' we will stay where we are. We won't go up to them. 10 But if they say, 'Come up to us,' we will climb up, and the LORD will let us defeat them. This will be the sign for us."

11 When both Jonathan and his officer let the Philistines see them, the Philistines said, "Look! The Hebrews are crawling out of the holes they were hiding in!" 12 The Philistines in the camp shouted to Jonathan and his officer, "Come up to us. We'll teach you a lesson!"

Jonathan said to his officer, "Climb up behind me, because the LORD has given the Philistines to Israel!" 13 So Jonathan climbed up, using his hands and feet, and his officer climbed just behind him. Jonathan struck down the Philistines as he went, and his officer killed them as he followed behind him. 14 In that first fight Jonathan and his officer killed about 20 Philistines over a fifth of a hectare of ground.

15 All the Philistine soldiers panicked—those in the camp and those in the raiding party. The ground itself shook! God had caused the panic.

16 Saul's guards were at Gibeah in the land of Benjamin when they saw the Philistine soldiers running in every direction. 17 Saul said to his army, "Check to see who has left our camp." When they checked, they learned that Jonathan and his officer were gone.

18 So Saul said to Ahijah the priest, "Bring the Ark of God." (At that time it was with the Israelites.) 19 While Saul was talking to the priest, the confusion in the Philistine camp was growing. Then Saul said to Ahijah, "Put your hand down!"

20 Then Saul gathered his army and entered the battle. They found the Philistines confused, striking each other with their swords! 21 Earlier, there were Hebrews who had served the Philistines and had stayed in their camp, but now they joined the Israelites with Saul and Jonathan. 22 When all the Israelites hidden in the mountains of Ephraim heard that the Philistine soldiers were running away, they also joined the battle and chased the Philistines. 23 So the LORD saved the Israelites that day, and the battle moved on past Beth Aven.

1 Samuel 14:30   371

KING SAUL, THE SOLDIER   1 Samuel 14

As the first king of a united Israel, Saul's first priority was to conquer his enemies. At first, Saul won many important battles. But as he became more concerned about chasing and capturing David, his armies began to lose. Ultimately, Saul and his sons were killed by the Philistines. Here are some important highlights from Saul's battles:

1. King Saul won his first battle against the Philistines at Geba. (See 1 Samuel 13 and 14.)

2. Saul's army also won battles against the Moabites, Ammonites and Edomites. (Look up 1 Samuel 14:47.)

3. Saul and his armies defeated the Amalekites, but Saul disobeyed God by sparing the life of King Agag and not destroying some of the best Amalekite possessions. (Check out 1 Samuel 15:1–9.)

4. Saul took his own life after being seriously wounded at the end of a losing battle with the Philistines. (Read 1 Samuel 31.)

Saul Makes Another Mistake

24 The men of Israel were miserable that day because Saul had made an oath for all of them. He had said, "No one should eat food before evening and before I finish defeating my enemies. If he does, he will be cursed!" So no Israelite soldier ate food.

25 Now the army went into the woods, where there was some honey on the ground. 26 They came upon some honey, but no one took any because they were afraid of the oath. 27 Jonathan had not heard the oath Saul had put on the army, so he dipped the end of his stick into the honey and lifted some out and ate it. Then he felt better. 28 Then one of the soldiers told Jonathan, "Your father made an oath for all the soldiers. He said any man who eats today will be cursed! That's why they are so weak."

29 Jonathan said, "My father has made trouble for the land! See how much better I feel after just tasting a little of this honey! 30 It would have been much better for the men to eat the food they took from their enemies today. We could have killed many more Philistines!"

31 That day the Israelites defeated the Philistines from Michmash to Aijalon. After that, they were very tired. 32 They had taken sheep, cattle and calves from the Philistines. Now they were so hungry they killed the animals on the ground and ate them, without draining the blood from them! 33 Someone said to Saul, "Look! The men are sinning against the LORD. They're eating meat without draining the blood from it!"

Saul said, "You have sinned! Roll a large stone over here now!" 34 Then he said, "Go to the men and tell them that each person must bring his ox and sheep to me and kill it here and eat it. Don't sin against the LORD by eating meat without draining the blood from it."

That night everyone brought his animals and killed them there. 35 Then Saul built an altar to the LORD. It was the first altar he had built to the LORD.

36 Saul said, "Let's go after the Philistines tonight and rob them. We won't let any of them live!"

The men answered, "Do whatever you think is best."

But the priest said, "Let's ask God."

37 So Saul asked God, "Should I chase the Philistines? Will you let us defeat them?" But God did not answer Saul at that time. 38 Then Saul said to all the leaders of his army, "Come here. Let's find out what sin has been done today. 39 As surely as the LORD lives who has saved Israel, even if my son Jonathan did the sin, he must die." But no one in the army spoke.

40 Then Saul said to all the Israelites, "You stand on this side. I and my son Jonathan will stand on the other side."

The men answered, "Do whatever you think is best."

41 Then Saul prayed to the LORD, the God of Israel, "Give me the right answer."

And Saul and Jonathan were picked; the other men went free. 42 Saul said, "Now let us discover if it is I or Jonathan my son who is guilty." And Jonathan was picked.

43 Saul said to Jonathan, "Tell me what you have done."

So Jonathan told Saul, "I only tasted a little honey from the end of my stick. And must I die now?"

44 Saul said, "Jonathan, if you don't die, may God punish me terribly."

45 But the soldiers said to Saul, "Must Jonathan die? Never! He is responsible for saving Israel today! As surely as the LORD lives, not even a hair of his head will fall to the ground! Today Jonathan fought against the Philistines with God's help!" So the army saved Jonathan, and he did not die.

46 Then Saul stopped chasing the Philistines, and they went back to their own land.

Saul Fights Israel's Enemies

47 When Saul became king over Israel, he fought against Israel's enemies all around. He fought Moab, the Ammonites, Edom, the king of Zobah and the Philistines. Everywhere Saul went he defeated Israel's enemies. 48 He fought bravely and defeated the Amalekites. He saved the Israelites from their enemies who had robbed them.

49 Saul's sons were Jonathan, Ishvi and Malki-Shua. His older daughter was named Merab, and his younger daughter was named Michal. 50 Saul's wife was Ahinoam, daughter of Ahimaaz. The commander of his army was Abner son of Ner, Saul's uncle. 51 Saul's father Kish and Abner's father Ner were sons of Abiel.

52 All Saul's life he fought hard against the Philistines. When he saw strong or brave men, he took them into his army.

Saul Rejected as King

15 Samuel said to Saul, "The LORD sent me to appoint you king over Israel. Now listen to his message. 2 This is what the LORD All-powerful says: 'When the Israelites came out of Egypt, the Amalekites tried to stop them from going to Canaan. So I will punish them. 3 Now go, attack the Amalekites and destroy everything they own as an offering to the LORD. Don't let anything live. Put to death men and women, children and small babies, cattle and sheep, camels and donkeys.'"

1 Samuel 15:29 373

4 So Saul called the army together at Telaim. There were 200,000 foot soldiers and 10,000 men from Judah. 5 Then Saul went to the city of Amalek and set up an ambush in the ravine. 6 He said to the Kenites, "Go away. Leave the Amalekites so that I won't destroy you with them, because you showed kindness to the Israelites when they came out of Egypt." So the Kenites moved away from the Amalekites.

7 Then Saul defeated the Amalekites. He fought them all the way from Havilah to Shur, at the border of Egypt. 8 He took King Agag of the Amalekites alive, but he killed all of Agag's army with the sword. 9 Saul and the army let Agag live, along with the best sheep, fat cattle and lambs. They let every good animal live, because they did not want to destroy them. But when they found an animal that was weak or useless, they killed it.

10 Then the LORD spoke his word to Samuel: 11 "I am sorry I made Saul king, because he has stopped following me and has not obeyed my commands." Samuel was upset, and he cried out to the LORD all night long.

12 Early the next morning Samuel got up and went to meet Saul. But the people told Samuel, "Saul has gone to Carmel, where he has put up a monument in his own honour. Now he has gone down to Gilgal."

13 When Samuel came to Saul, Saul said, "May the LORD bless you! I have obeyed the LORD's commands."

14 But Samuel said, "Then why do I hear cattle mooing and sheep bleating?"

15 Saul answered, "The soldiers took them from the Amalekites. They saved the best sheep and cattle to offer as sacrifices to the LORD your God, but we destroyed all the other animals."

16 Samuel said to Saul, "Stop! Let me tell you what the LORD said to me last night."

Saul answered, "Tell me."

17 Samuel said, "Once you didn't think much of yourself, but now you have become the leader of the tribes of Israel. The LORD appointed you to be king over Israel. 18 And he sent you on a mission. He said, 'Go and destroy those evil people, the Amalekites. Make war on them until all of them are dead.' 19 Why didn't you obey the LORD? Why did you take the best things? Why did you do what the LORD said was wrong?"

20 Saul said, "But I did obey the LORD. I did what the LORD told me to do. I destroyed all the Amalekites, and I brought back Agag their king. 21 The soldiers took the best sheep and cattle to sacrifice to the LORD your God at Gilgal."

22 But Samuel answered,
"What pleases the LORD more:
   burnt offerings and sacrifices
   or obedience to his voice?
It is better to
   obey than
   to sacrifice.
It is better to
   listen to
   God than to
   offer the fat
   of rams.
23 Refusing to obey is as bad as the sin
      of sorcery.
   Pride is as bad as the sin of
      worshipping idols.
   You have rejected the LORD's
      command.
   Now he rejects you as king."

15:22 Obedience
Find out what pleases God the most.

24 Then Saul said to Samuel, "I have sinned. I didn't obey the LORD's commands and your words. I was afraid of the people, and I did what they said. 25 Now, I beg you, forgive my sin. Come back with me so I may worship the LORD."

26 But Samuel said to Saul, "I won't go back with you. You rejected the LORD's command, and now he rejects you as king of Israel."

15:26 Belief
What happens if you reject God?

27 As Samuel turned to leave, Saul caught his robe, and it tore. 28 Samuel said to him, "The LORD has torn the kingdom of Israel from you today and has given it to one of your neighbours who is better than you. 29 The LORD is the Eternal One of Israel. He does not lie or change his mind. He is not a human being, so he does not change his mind.

30 Saul answered, "I have sinned. But please honour me in front of the elders of my people and in front of the Israelites. Come back with me so that I can worship the LORD your God." 31 So Samuel went back with Saul, and Saul worshipped the LORD.

32 Then Samuel said, "Bring me King Agag of the Amalekites."

Agag came to Samuel in chains, but Agag thought, "Surely the threat of death has passed."

33 Samuel said to him, "Your sword made other mothers lose their children. Now your mother will have no children." And Samuel cut Agag to pieces before the LORD at Gilgal.

34 Then Samuel left and went to Ramah, but Saul went up to his home in Gibeah. 35 And Samuel never saw Saul again for the rest of his life, but he was sad for Saul. And the LORD was very sorry he had made Saul king of Israel.

Samuel Goes to Bethlehem

16 The LORD said to Samuel, "How long will you continue to feel sorry for Saul? I have rejected him as king of Israel. Fill your container with olive oil and go. I am sending you to Jesse who lives in Bethlehem, because I have chosen one of his sons to be king."

2 But Samuel said, "If I go, Saul will hear the news and will try to kill me."

The LORD said, "Take a young calf with you. Say, 'I have come to offer a sacrifice to the LORD.' 3 Invite Jesse to the sacrifice. Then I will tell you what to do. You must appoint the one I show you."

4 Samuel did what the LORD told him to do. When he arrived at Bethlehem, the elders of Bethlehem shook with fear. They met him and asked, "Are you coming in peace?"

5 Samuel answered, "Yes, I come in peace. I have come to make a sacrifice to the LORD. Set yourselves apart to the LORD and come to the sacrifice with me." Then he set Jesse and his sons apart to the LORD, and he invited them to come to the sacrifice.

6 When they arrived, Samuel saw Eliab, and he thought, "Surely the LORD has appointed this person standing here before him."

7 But the LORD said to Samuel, "Don't look at how handsome Eliab is or how tall he is, because I have not chosen him. God does not see the same way people see. People look at the outside of a person, but the LORD looks at the heart."

16:7
Character
God cares most about what's on the inside.

8 Then Jesse called Abinadab and told him to pass by Samuel. But Samuel said, "The LORD has not chosen this man either." 9 Then Jesse had Shammah pass by. But Samuel said, "No, the LORD has not chosen this one." 10 Jesse had seven of his sons pass by Samuel. But Samuel said to him, "The LORD has not chosen any of these."

11 Then he asked Jesse, "Are these all the sons you have?"

Jesse answered, "I still have the youngest son. He is out taking care of the sheep."

Samuel said, "Send for him. We will not sit down to eat until he arrives."

12 So Jesse sent and had his youngest son brought in. He was a fine boy, tanned and handsome.

The LORD said to Samuel, "Go, appoint him, because he is the one."

13 So Samuel took the container of olive oil and poured it on Jesse's youngest son to appoint him in front of his brothers. From that day on, the LORD's Spirit worked in David. Samuel then went back to Ramah.

David Serves Saul

14 But the LORD's Spirit had left Saul, and an evil spirit from the LORD troubled him.

15 Saul's servants said to him, "See, an evil spirit from God is troubling you. 16 Give us the command to look for someone who can play the harp. When the evil spirit from God troubles you, he will play, and you will feel better."

17 So Saul said to his servants, "Find someone who can play well and bring him to me."

FAITH links

THE HEART OF THE MATTER

1 SAMUEL 16

How do you choose someone to hang around with? Many of us make choices based on how a person looks or acts. God has a different way of choosing people to serve him. When God was ready to anoint a king to take Saul's place, Samuel assumed that God wanted the biggest and best looking of Jesse's sons. Instead, God chose David, the youngest in his family, to be king. God didn't consider how David looked on the outside. How David was on the inside was more important.

When you meet someone new, remember to look not just at the outside of a person's appearance, but look at the inside. That's what counts!

Want to fit in with God? Link here:

Following the Crowd, Numbers 13; 14, p. 193

Facts About Following, Joshua 6, p. 283

Choosing a Friend, Proverbs 28:7, p. 865

Going My Way? Hosea 8:1–6, p. 1179

That Thing You Do, Matthew 25:14–30, p. 1319

Help for a Friend, Mark 2:1–5, p. 1332

---

18 One of the servants said, "I have seen a son of Jesse of Bethlehem play the harp. He is brave and courageous. He is a good speaker and handsome, and the LORD is with him."

19 Then Saul sent messengers to Jesse, saying, "Send me your son David, who is with the sheep." 20 So Jesse loaded a donkey with bread, a leather bag full of wine and a young goat, and he sent them with his son David to Saul.

21 When David came to Saul, he began to serve him. Saul liked David and made him the officer who carried his armour. 22 Saul sent a message to Jesse, saying, "Let David stay and serve me because I like him."

23 When the evil spirit from God troubled Saul, David would take his harp and play. Then the evil spirit would leave him, and Saul would feel better.

David and Goliath

17 The Philistines gathered their armies for war. They met at Socoh in Judah and camped at Ephes Dammim between Socoh and Azekah. 2 Saul and the Israelites gathered in the Valley of Elah and camped there and took their positions to fight the Philistines. 3 The Philistines controlled one hill while the Israelites controlled another. The valley was between them.

4 The Philistines had a champion fighter from Gath named Goliath. He was about 3 metres tall. He came out of the Philistine camp 5 with a bronze helmet on his head and a coat of bronze armour that weighed about 60 kilogrammes. 6 He wore bronze protectors on his legs, and he had a bronze spear on his back. 7 The wooden part of his larger spear was like a weaver's rod, and its blade weighed about 7 kilogrammes. The officer who carried his shield walked in front of him.

8 Goliath stood and shouted to the Israelite soldiers, "Why have you taken positions for battle? I am a Philistine, and you are Saul's servants! Choose a man and send him to fight me. 9 If he can fight and kill me, we will be your servants. But if I can kill him, you will be our servants."

10 Then he said, "Today I stand and challenge the army of Israel! Send one of your men to fight me!" 11 When Saul and the Israelites heard the Philistine's words, they were very scared.

12 Now David was the son of Jesse, an Ephrathite from Bethlehem in Judah. Jesse had eight sons. In Saul's time Jesse was an old man. 13 His three oldest sons followed Saul to the war. The first son was Eliab, the second was Abinadab, and the third was Shammah. 14 David was the youngest. Jesse's three oldest sons followed Saul, 15 but David went back and forth from Saul to Bethlehem, where he took care of his father's sheep.

16 For 40 days the Philistine came out every morning and evening and stood before the Israelite army.

17 Jesse said to his son David, "Take this 10 kilogrammes of cooked grain and ten loaves of bread to your brothers in the camp. 18 Also take ten pieces of cheese to the commander and to your brothers. See how your brothers are and bring back some proof to show me that they are all right. 19 Your brothers are with Saul and the army in the Valley of Elah, fighting against the Philistines."

20 Early in the morning David left the sheep with another shepherd. He took the food and left as Jesse had told him. When David arrived at the camp, the army was going out to their battle positions, shouting their war cry. 21 The Israelites and Philistines were lining up their men to face each other in battle.

22 David left the food with the man who kept the supplies and ran to the battle line to talk to his brothers. 23 While he was talking with them, Goliath, the Philistine champion from Gath, came out. He shouted things against Israel as usual, and David heard him. 24 When the Israelites saw Goliath, they were very much afraid and ran away.

25 They said, "Look at this man! He keeps coming out to challenge Israel. The king will give much money to whoever kills him. He will also let whoever kills him marry his daughter. And his father's family will not have to pay taxes in Israel."

26 David asked the men who stood near him, "What will be done to reward the man who kills this Philistine and takes away the shame from Israel? Who does this uncircumcised Philistine think he is? Does he think he can speak against the armies of the living God?"

27 The Israelites told David what would be done for the man who would kill Goliath.

28 When David's oldest brother Eliab heard David talking with the soldiers, he was angry with David. He asked David, "Why did you come here? Who's taking care of those few sheep of yours in the desert? I know you are proud and wicked at heart. You came down here just to watch the battle."

29 David asked, "Now what have I done wrong? Can't I even talk?" 30 When he turned to other people and asked the same questions, they gave him the same answer as before. 31 Yet what David said was told to Saul, and he sent for David.

32 David said to Saul, "Don't let anyone be discouraged. I, your servant, will go and fight this Philistine!"

33 Saul answered, "You can't go out against this Philistine and fight him. You're only a boy. Goliath has been a warrior since he was a young man."

34 But David said to Saul, "I, your servant, have been keeping my father's sheep. When a lion or bear came and took a sheep from the flock, 35 then I would chase it. I would attack it and save the sheep from its mouth. When it attacked me, I caught it by its fur and hit it and killed it. 36 I, your servant, have killed both a lion and a bear! This uncircumcised Philistine will be like them, because he has spoken against the armies of the living God. 37 The LORD who saved me from a lion and a bear will save me from this Philistine."

17:37
Troubles
Where can you find strength?

Saul said to David, "Go, and may the LORD be with you." 38 Saul put his own clothes on David. He put a bronze helmet on his head and dressed him in armour. 39 David put on Saul's sword and tried to

FAITH links

A GIANT PROBLEM
1 SAMUEL 17:32-51

If you've ever seen a sumo wrestler, you know how huge they can be. Now compare your size to that of a sumo wrestler. Feeling puny? Imagine how David felt when he saw Goliath. But David had something that Goliath didn't have: faith in God. His faith led to Goliath's downfall. He succeeded where stronger and older men had failed.

Some problems in life can seem as big as Goliath. But faith in God makes you the giant. Got a giant problem? Talk to God about it. He'll soon cut that problem down to size.

A Major Problem, Genesis 15:6, p. 20

God's Pep Talk, Joshua 1:5–9, p. 276

Good Times and Bad, 1 Kings 17, p. 462

A Home Town Hurt, Jeremiah 11:8—12:6, p. 1008

Prayer Anywhere, Mark 1:35, p. 1331

Mission Impossible? Mark 5:21–24, 35–43, p. 1337

---

walk around, but he was not used to all the armour Saul had put on him.

He said to Saul, "I can't go in this, because I'm not used to it." Then David took it all off. 40 He took his stick in his hand and chose five smooth stones from a stream. He put them in his shepherd's bag. With his sling in his hand, he went to meet the Philistine.

41 At the same time, the Philistine was coming closer to David. The man who held his shield walked in front of him. 42 When Goliath looked at David and saw that he was only a boy, tanned and handsome, he looked down on David with disgust. 43 He said, "Do you think I am a dog, that you come at me with a stick?" He used his gods' names to curse David. 44 He said to David, "Come here. I'll feed your body to the birds of the air and the wild animals!"

45 But David said to him, "You come to me using a sword and two spears. But I come to you in the name of the Lord All-powerful, the God of the armies of Israel! You have spoken against him. 46 Today the Lord will hand you over to me, and I'll kill you and cut off your head. Today I'll feed the bodies of the Philistine soldiers to the birds of the air and the wild animals. Then all the world will know there is a God in Israel! 47 Everyone gathered here will know the Lord does not need swords or spears to save people. The battle belongs to him, and he will hand you over to us."

48 As Goliath came near to attack him, David ran quickly to meet him. 49 He took a stone from his bag, put it into his sling, and slung it. The stone hit the Philistine and went deep into his forehead, and Goliath fell face down on the ground.

50 So David defeated the Philistine with only a sling and a stone. He hit him and killed him. He did not even have a sword in his hand. 51 Then David ran and stood beside him. He took Goliath's sword out of its holder and killed him by cutting off his head.

When the Philistines saw that their champion was dead, they turned and ran. 52 The men of Israel and Judah shouted and chased the Philistines all the way to the entrance of the city of Gath and to the gates of Ekron.

The Philistines' bodies lay on the Shaaraim road as far as Gath and Ekron. 53 The Israelites returned after chasing the Philistines and robbed their camp.

1 Samuel 17 378

FRIENDSHIP
1 Samuel 18:1

The Perfect Friend If you advertised for a friend in the newspaper or on the Internet, what would you look for? What kind of person would be the perfect friend for you? Would you ask for a brilliant footballer, or a rich kid, or maybe someone who is a genius? What if you could find all of these things in one person – would they be the perfect friend?

If God advertised for a special friend, he wouldn't choose someone by how he looks or what he can do. God looks at the inside – what's in a person's heart. (Look at <u>1 Samuel 16</u>.)

One of the best things in the world is having a friend you can count on. But being a good friend takes a lot of work. One person can't do it alone – friendship means sharing. (Check out <u>1 Samuel 18:1–3; 20</u>.) How do you show your friend that he or she is special to you?

MORE FAITH links

The Heart of the Matter, **p. 375**

The Gift of Friendship, **p. 381**

Choosing a Friend, **p. 865**

A Fair-weather Friend, **p. 1209**

An Encouraging Word, **p. 1545**

> What do you think makes up a good friend?

> Surf on to find out what the Bible has to say about being a good friend.

The MLP (Most Loyal Person), <u>Ruth 1:16–17, p. 345</u>
- Who is the most loyal person you know? How does he or she show loyalty to you?
- Would someone consider you an MLP? How do you show loyalty for friends or family?

Two Are Better, <u>Ecclesiastes 4:9–12, p. 877</u>
- God made us to need each other. What are the things you do to help your family or friends?
- To earn a friend, you have to be a friend. What can you do to be the best friend possible?

Help for a Friend, <u>Mark 2:1–5, p. 1332</u>
- Would you go out of your way to help a friend? Link up here to find out about some people who became "house wreckers" to help a friend!

Thanks for a Friend, <u>1 Thessalonians 1:1–3, p. 1630</u>
- Do you ever say thanks to your friend for being a friend? Stop and do it right now!

my FAVOURITE links

54 David took Goliath's head to Jerusalem and put Goliath's weapons in his own tent.

55 When Saul saw David go out to meet Goliath, Saul asked Abner, commander of the army, "Abner, who is that young man's father?"

Abner answered, "As surely as you live, my king, I don't know."

56 The king said, "Find out whose son he is."

57 When David came back from killing Goliath, Abner brought him to Saul. David was still holding Goliath's head.

58 Saul asked him, "Young man, who is your father?"

David answered, "I am the son of your servant Jesse of Bethlehem."

Saul Fears David

18 When David finished talking with Saul, Jonathan felt very close to David. He loved David as much as he loved himself. 2 Saul kept David with him from that day on and did not let him go home to his father's house.

18:1 Friendship
Check out this great friend.

3 Jonathan made an agreement with David, because he loved David as much as himself. 4 He took off his coat and gave it to David, along with his armour, including his sword, bow and belt.

5 Saul sent David to fight in different battles, and David was very successful. Then Saul put David over the soldiers, which pleased Saul's officers and all the other people.

6 After David had killed the Philistine, he and the men returned home. Women came out from all the towns of Israel to meet King Saul. They sang songs of joy, danced, and played tambourines and stringed instruments. 7 As they played, they sang,

"Saul has killed thousands of his enemies,
but David has killed tens of thousands."

8 The women's song upset Saul, and he became very angry. He thought, "The

---

FAITH links

WHEN THE GREEN-EYED MONSTER STRIKES
1 SAMUEL 18:6-9

Has someone ever compared you with someone else? If we're thought to be better than others are, that can be easier to take. When we're compared unfavourably with someone, trouble can be the result. Saul grew jealous of David when the Israelite women cheered louder for David than for him. Saul wanted the people to praise only him. So, he tried to get rid of David.

We call jealousy the "green-eyed monster". That's because it can lead us to act like one. When jealousy strikes, you don't have to give in to it. Instead, talk to God about how you feel.

Here are some more hints on battling that green-eyed monster:

The Trouble with Jealousy, Genesis 37, p. 53

Complaints, Complaints! Exodus 16:1–3, p. 97

A Life of Thanksgiving, 1 Kings 1:47–48, p. 435

Weak? Great! 2 Chronicles 14:11, p. 577

A Need to Change, Ecclesiastes 1:1–11, p. 873

Eating Humble Pie, Daniel 4, p. 1156

women say David has killed tens of thousands, but they say I have killed only thousands. The only thing left for him to have is the kingdom!" 9 So Saul watched David closely from then on, because he was jealous.

10 The next day an evil spirit from God rushed upon Saul, and he prophesied in his house. David was playing the harp as he usually did, but Saul had a spear in his hand. 11 He threw the spear, thinking, "I'll pin David to the wall." But David escaped from him twice.

12 The LORD was with David but had left Saul. So Saul was afraid of David. 13 He sent David away and made him commander of 1,000 soldiers. So David led them in battle. 14 He had great success in everything he did because the LORD was with him. 15 When Saul saw that David was very successful, he feared David even more. 16 But all the people of Israel and Judah loved David because he led them well in battle.

Saul's Daughter Marries David

17 Saul said to David, "Here is my older daughter Merab. I will let you marry her. All I ask is that you remain brave and fight the LORD's battles." Saul thought, "I won't have to kill David. The Philistines will do that."

18 But David answered Saul, saying, "Who am I? My family is not important enough for me to become the king's son-in-law." 19 So, when the time came for Saul's daughter Merab to marry David, Saul gave her instead to Adriel of Meholah.

20 Now Saul's other daughter, Michal, loved David. When they told Saul, he was pleased. 21 He thought, "I will let her marry David. Then she will be a trap for him, and the Philistines will defeat him." So Saul said to David a second time, "You may become my son-in-law."

22 And Saul ordered his servants to talk with David in private and say, "Look, the king likes you. His servants love you. You should be his son-in-law."

23 Saul's servants said these words to David, but David answered, "Do you think it is easy to become the king's son-in-law? I am poor and unimportant."

24 When Saul's servants told him what David had said, 25 Saul said, "Tell David, 'The king doesn't want money for the bride. All he wants is 100 Philistine foreskins to get even with his enemies.'" Saul planned to let the Philistines kill David.

26 When Saul's servants told this to David, he was pleased to become the king's son-in-law. 27 So he and his men went out and killed 200 Philistines. David brought all their foreskins to Saul so he could be the king's son-in-law. Then Saul gave him his daughter Michal for his wife. 28 Saul saw that the LORD was with David and that his daughter Michal loved David. 29 So he grew even more afraid of David, and he was David's enemy all his life.

30 The Philistine commanders continued to go out to fight the Israelites, but every time, David was more skilful than Saul's officers. So he became famous.

Saul Tries to Kill David

19 Saul told his son Jonathan and all his servants to kill David, but Jonathan liked David very much. 2 So he warned David, "My father Saul is looking for a chance to kill you. Watch out in the morning. Hide in a secret place. 3 I will go out and stand with my father in the field where you are hiding, and I'll talk to him about you. Then I'll let you know what I find out."

4 When Jonathan talked to Saul his father, he said good things about David. Jonathan said, "The king should do no wrong to your servant David since he has done nothing wrong to you. What he has done has helped you greatly. 5 David risked his life when he killed Goliath the Philistine, and the LORD won a great victory for all Israel. You saw it and were happy. Why would you do wrong against David? He's innocent. There's no reason to kill him!"

> **MAIL FROM GOD**
> **19:1–7**
> **Friendship**
> How can you be a good friend?

FAITH links

THE GIFT OF FRIENDSHIP
1 SAMUEL 18:1-3; 19

Do you have a best friend? One of life's blessings is having a friend you can count on. David and Jonathan were best friends. Jonathan showed his friendship by sharing what he had with David. David and Jonathan promised to be loyal to each other.

Friendship is a gift that's meant to be shared. Being a friend takes effort. One person can't do it alone. How do you show your friend that he or she is special to you?

Link here to find out how to be a good friend:

Family Feud, Genesis 27, p. 37

Show Some Respect, Leviticus 19:32, p. 161

The MLP, Ruth 1:16–17, p. 345

The Salt Promise, 2 Chronicles 13:5, p. 576

A Fair-weather Friend, Obadiah 7, p. 1209

Help for a Friend, Mark 2:1–5, p. 1332

---

6 Saul listened to Jonathan and then made this promise: "As surely as the LORD lives, David won't be put to death."

7 So Jonathan called to David and told him everything that had been said. He brought David to Saul, and David was with Saul as before.

8 When war broke out again, David went out to fight the Philistines. He defeated them, and they ran away from him.

9 But once again an evil spirit from the LORD rushed upon Saul as he was sitting in his house with his spear in his hand. David was playing the harp. 10 Saul tried to pin David to the wall with his spear, but David jumped out of the way. So Saul's spear went into the wall, and David ran away that night.

11 Saul sent messengers to David's house to watch him and to kill him in the morning. But Michal, David's wife, warned him, saying, "Tonight you must run for your life. If you don't, you will be dead in the morning." 12 So she let David down out of a window, and he ran away and escaped. 13 Then Michal took an idol, laid it on the bed, covered it with clothes and put goats' hair on its head.

14 Saul sent messengers to take David prisoner, but Michal said, "He is sick."

15 Saul sent them back to see David, saying, "Bring him to me on his bed so I can kill him."

16 When the messengers entered David's house, they found just an idol on the bed with goats' hair on its head.

17 Saul said to Michal, "Why did you trick me this way? You let my enemy go so he could run away!"

Michal answered Saul, "David told me if I did not help him escape, he would kill me."

18 After David had escaped from Saul, he went to Samuel at Ramah and told him everything Saul had done to him. Then David and Samuel went to Naioth and stayed there. 19 Saul heard that David was in Naioth at Ramah. 20 So he sent messengers to capture him. But they met a group of prophets prophesying, with Samuel standing there leading them. So the Spirit of God entered Saul's men, and they also prophesied.

21 When Saul heard the news, he sent more messengers, but they also prophesied. Then he sent messengers a third time, but they also prophesied. 22 Finally, Saul himself went to Ramah, to the well at Secu. He asked, "Where are Samuel and David?"

The people answered, "In Naioth at Ramah."

23 When Saul went to Naioth at Ramah, the Spirit of God also rushed upon him. And he walked on, prophesying until he came to Naioth at Ramah. 24 He took off his robes and prophesied in front of Samuel. He lay that way all day and all night. That is why people ask, "Is even Saul one of the prophets?"

Jonathan Helps David

20 Then David ran away from Naioth in Ramah. He went to Jonathan and asked, "What have I done? What is my crime? How did I sin against your father? Why is he trying to kill me?"

2 Jonathan answered, "No! You won't die! See, my father doesn't do anything great or small without first telling me. Why would he keep this from me? It's not true!"

3 But David took an oath, saying, "Your father knows very well that you like me. He says to himself, 'Jonathan must not know about it, or he will tell David.' As surely as the LORD lives and as you live, I am only a step away from death!"

4 Jonathan said to David, "I'll do anything you want me to do."

5 So David said, "Look, tomorrow is the New Moon festival. I am supposed to eat with the king, but let me hide in the field until the third evening. 6 If your father notices I am gone, tell him, 'David begged me to let him go to his home town of Bethlehem. Every year at this time his family group offers a sacrifice.' 7 If your father says, 'Fine,' I am safe. But if he becomes angry, you will know that he wants to hurt me. 8 Jonathan, be loyal to me, your servant. You have made an agreement with me before the LORD. If I am guilty, you may kill me yourself! Why hand me over to your father?"

9 Jonathan answered, "No, never! If I learn that my father plans to hurt you, I will warn you!"

10 David asked, "Who will let me know if your father answers you unkindly?"

11 Then Jonathan said, "Come, let's go out into the field." So the two of them went out into the field.

12 Jonathan said to David, "I promise this before the LORD, the God of Israel: at this same time the day after tomorrow,

---

FAITH links

CHOOSING SIDES
1 SAMUEL 20

In an argument between two people, do you ever find yourself taking sides? How do you decide whose side you're on? Jonathan was caught in the middle when his father, King Saul, declared David to be his enemy. When Jonathan chose to do what was right, his father became angry with him. He could not stop being loyal to David, even though his father demanded that he do so.

God wants you to do the right thing, even if choosing to do so makes someone angry with you. The side of right is always the best side to choose to be on.

An Example Not to Follow, Leviticus 18:1–3, p. 157

Remembering What He Said, Deuteronomy 6:4–9, p. 236

Sow It and Reap, Lamentations 1:18, p. 1075

A Blueprint for Living, Amos 5:14–15, p. 1200

The "Eyes" Have It? 1 Corinthians 12, p. 1559

Keeping Clean, 2 Corinthians 7:1, p. 1576

I will find out how my father feels. If he feels good towards you, I will send word to you and let you know. 13 But if my father plans to hurt you, I will let you know and send you away safely. May the LORD punish me terribly if I don't do this. And may the LORD be with you as he has been with my father. 14 But show me the kindness of the LORD as long as I live so that I may not die. 15 You must never stop showing your kindness to my family, even when the LORD has destroyed all your enemies from the earth."

16 So Jonathan made an agreement with David. He said, "May the LORD hold David's enemies responsible." 17 And Jonathan asked David to repeat his promise of love for him, because he loved David as much as he loved himself.

18 Jonathan said to David, "Tomorrow is the New Moon festival. Your seat will be empty, so my father will miss you. 19 On the third day go to the place where you hid when this trouble began. Wait by the rock Ezel. 20 On the third day I will shoot three arrows to the side of the rock as if I am shooting at a target. 21 Then I will send a boy to find the arrows. If I say to him, 'The arrows are near you; bring them here,' you may come out of hiding. You are safe. As the LORD lives, there is no danger. 22 But if I say to the boy, 'Look, the arrows are beyond you,' you must go, because the LORD is sending you away. 23 Remember what we talked about. The LORD is a witness between you and me for ever."

24 So David hid in the field. When the New Moon festival came, the king sat down to eat. 25 He sat where he always sat, near the wall. Jonathan sat across from him, and Abner sat next to Saul, but David's place was empty. 26 That day Saul said nothing. He thought, "Maybe something has happened to David so that he is unclean." 27 But the next day was the second day of the month, and David's place was still empty. So Saul said to Jonathan, "Why hasn't the son of Jesse come to the feast yesterday or today?"

28 Jonathan answered, "David begged me to let him go to Bethlehem. 29 He said, 'Let me go, because our family has a sacrifice in the town, and my brother has ordered me to be there. Now if I am your friend, please let me go to see my brothers.' That is why he has not come to the king's table."

30 Then Saul became very angry with Jonathan. He said, "You son of a wicked, worthless woman! I know you are on the side of David son of Jesse! You bring shame on yourself and on your mother who gave birth to you. 31 As long as Jesse's son lives, you will never be king or have a kingdom. Now send for David and bring him to me. He must die!"

32 Jonathan asked his father, "Why should David be killed? What wrong has he done?" 33 Then Saul threw his spear at Jonathan, trying to kill him. So Jonathan knew that his father really wanted to kill David. 34 Jonathan was very angry and left the table. That second day of the month he refused to eat. He was ashamed of his father and upset over David.

35 The next morning Jonathan went out to the field to meet David as they had agreed. He had a young boy with him. 36 Jonathan said to the boy, "Run and find the arrows I shoot." When he ran, Jonathan shot an arrow beyond him. 37 The boy ran to the place where Jonathan's arrow fell, but Jonathan called, "The arrow is beyond you!" 38 Then he shouted, "Hurry! Go quickly! Don't stop!" The boy picked up the arrow and brought it back to his master. 39 (The boy knew nothing about what this meant; only Jonathan and David knew.) 40 Then Jonathan gave his weapons to the boy and told him, "Go back to town."

41 When the boy left, David came out from the south side of the rock. He bowed face down on the ground before Jonathan three times. Then David and Jonathan kissed each other and cried together, but David cried the most.

20:42 Friendship
See what bonds friends together.

42 Jonathan said to David, "Go in peace. We have promised by the LORD that we will be friends. We said, 'The LORD will be a witness between you and me, and between our descendants always.'" Then

David left, and Jonathan went back to town.

David Goes to See Ahimelech

21 David went to Nob to see Ahimelech the priest. Ahimelech shook with fear when he saw David, and he asked, "Why are you alone? Why is no one with you?"

2 David answered him, "The king gave me a special order. He told me, 'No one must know what I am sending you to do or what I told you to do.' I told my men where to meet me. 3 Now, what food do you have with you? Give me five loaves of bread or anything you find."

4 The priest said to David, "I don't have any plain bread here, but I do have some holy bread.ⁿ You may eat it if your men have kept themselves from women."

5 David answered, "No women have been near us for days. My men always keep themselves holy, even when we do ordinary work. And this is especially true when the work is holy."

6 So the priest gave David the holy bread from the presence of God because there was no other. Each day the holy bread was replaced with hot bread.

7 One of Saul's servants happened to be there that day. He had been held there before the LORD. He was Doeg the Edomite, the chief of Saul's shepherds.

8 David asked Ahimelech, "Do you have a spear or sword here? The king's business was very important, so I left without my sword or any other weapon."

9 The priest answered, "The sword of Goliath the Philistine, the one you killed in the Valley of Elah, is here. It is wrapped in a cloth behind the holy robe. If you want it, you may take it. There's no other sword here but that one."

David said, "There is no other sword like it. Give it to me."

David Goes to Gath

10 That day David ran away from Saul and went to Achish king of Gath. 11 But the servants of Achish said to him, "This is David, the king of the Israelites. He's the man they dance and sing about, saying:

'Saul has killed thousands of his
    enemies,
but David has killed tens of
    thousands.'"

12 David paid attention to these words and was very much afraid of Achish king of Gath. 13 So he pretended to be insane in front of Achish and his servants. While he was with them, he acted like a madman and made marks on the doors of the gate and let spit run down his beard.

14 Achish said to his servants, "Look at the man! He's insane! Why do you bring him to me? 15 I have enough madmen. I don't need you to bring him here to act like this in front of me! Don't let him in my house!"

David at Adullam and Mizpah

22 David left Gath and escaped to the cave of Adullam. When his brothers and other relatives heard that he was there, they went to see him. 2 Everyone who was in trouble, or who owed money, or who was unsatisfied gathered around David, and he became their leader. About 400 men were with him.

3 From there David went to Mizpah in Moab and spoke to the king of Moab. He said, "Please let my father and mother come and stay with you until I learn what God is going to do for me." 4 So he left them with the king of Moab, and they stayed with him as long as David was hiding in the stronghold.

5 But the prophet Gad said to David, "Don't stay in the stronghold. Go to the land of Judah." So David left and went to the forest of Hereth.

> Saul has killed thousands of his enemies, but David has killed tens of thousands.
> – 1 Samuel 21:11

21:4 holy bread This was the bread that showed the people were in the presence of God. Normally only the priests ate this bread.

Saul Destroys Ahimelech's Family

6 Saul heard that David and his men had been seen. Saul was sitting under the tamarisk tree on the hill at Gibeah, and all his officers were standing around him. He had a spear in his hand. 7 Saul said to them, "Listen, men of Benjamin! Do you think the son of Jesse will give all of you fields and vineyards? Will David make you commanders over thousands of men or hundreds of men? 8 You have all made plans against me! No one tells me when my son makes an agreement with the son of Jesse! No one cares about me! No one tells me when my son has encouraged my servant to ambush me this very day!"

9 Doeg the Edomite, who was standing there with Saul's officers, said, "I saw the son of Jesse. He came to see Ahimelech son of Ahitub at Nob. 10 Ahimelech prayed to the LORD for David and gave him food and gave him the sword of Goliath the Philistine."

11 Then the king sent for the priest Ahimelech son of Ahitub and for all of Ahimelech's relatives who were priests at Nob. And they all came to the king. 12 Saul said to Ahimelech, "Listen now, son of Ahitub."

Ahimelech answered, "Yes, master."

13 Saul said, "Why are you and Jesse's son against me? You gave him bread and a sword! You prayed to God for him. David has turned against me and is waiting to attack me even now!"

14 Ahimelech answered, "You have no other servant who is as loyal as David, your own son-in-law and captain of your bodyguards. Everyone in your house respects him. 15 That was not the first time I prayed to God for David. Don't blame me or any of my relatives. I, your servant, know nothing about what is going on."

16 But the king said, "Ahimelech, you and all your relatives must die!" 17 Then he told the guards at his side, "Go and kill the priests of the LORD, because they are on David's side. They knew he was running away, but they didn't tell me."

But the king's officers refused to kill the priests of the LORD.

18 Then the king ordered Doeg, "Go and kill the priests." So Doeg the Edomite went and killed the priests. That day he killed 85 men who wore the linen holy robe. 19 He also killed the people of Nob, the city of the priests. With the sword he killed men, women, children, babies, cattle, donkeys and sheep.

20 But Abiathar, a son of Ahimelech, who was the son of Ahitub, escaped. He ran away and joined David. 21 He told David that Saul had killed the LORD's priests. 22 Then David told him, "Doeg the Edomite was there at Nob that day. I knew he would surely tell Saul. So I am responsible for the death of all your father's family. 23 Stay with me. Don't be afraid. The man who wants to kill you also wants to kill me. You will be safe with me."

> Everyone who was in trouble, or who owed money, or who was unsatisfied gathered around David, and he became their leader.
> – 1 Samuel 22:2

David Saves the People of Keilah

23 Someone told David, "Look, the Philistines are fighting against Keilah and stealing grain from the threshing floors."

2 David asked the LORD, "Should I go and fight these Philistines?"

The LORD answered him, "Go. Attack them, and save Keilah."

3 But David's men said to him, "We're afraid here in Judah. We will be more afraid if we go to Keilah where the Philistine army is."

4 David again asked the LORD, and the LORD answered, "Go down to Keilah. I will help you defeat the Philistines." 5 So David and his men went to Keilah and fought the Philistines and took their cattle. David killed many Philistines and saved the people of Keilah. 6 (Now Abiathar son of Ahimelech had brought the holy robe with him when he came to David at Keilah.)

GOD TO THE RESCUE!   1 Samuel 23

In the Old Testament, God helped his people over and over again. Sometimes he helped them through the miracles he sent. Once, the angel of the Lord went through an enemy camp outside of Jerusalem and killed nearly *two hundred thousand* soldiers. In the morning, the Israelites woke up to discover that God had already saved them from their enemies. (Look at 2 Kings 19:35, p. 507.)

God delivered these people too:

Noah and his family were delivered from the flood.	Genesis 6—8, p. 10
Lot and his family were saved from Sodom and Gomorrah.	Genesis 19:29, p. 26
The Israelites were delivered from slavery and cared for on their journey.	Exodus 12:1—17:7, p. 90
David and his army were saved from Saul's army more than once.	1 Samuel 23:7–29, p. 386
Birds fed Elijah when he was in the wilderness.	1 Kings 17:2–6, p. 462
Daniel's friends were delivered from a fiery furnace.	Daniel 3:19–30, p. 1155
Daniel was saved from a den of hungry lions.	Daniel 6:1–24, p. 1160

Saul Chases David

7 Someone told Saul that David was now at Keilah. Saul said, "God has handed David over to me! He has trapped himself, because he has entered a town with gates and bars." 8 Saul called all his army together for battle, and they prepared to go down to Keilah to attack David and his men.

9 David learned Saul was making evil plans against him. So he said to Abiathar the priest, "Bring the holy robe." 10 David prayed, "LORD, God of Israel, I have heard that Saul plans to come to Keilah to destroy the town because of me. 11 Will the leaders of Keilah hand me over to Saul? Will Saul come down to Keilah, as I heard? LORD, God of Israel, tell me, your servant!"

The LORD answered, "Saul will come down."

12 Again David asked, "Will the leaders of Keilah hand me and my men over to Saul?"

The LORD answered, "They will."

13 So David and his 600 men left Keilah and kept moving from place to place. When Saul found out that David

had escaped from Keilah, he did not go there.

14 David stayed in the desert hideouts and in the hills of the Desert of Ziph. Every day Saul looked for David, but the LORD did not surrender David to him.

15 While David was at Horesh in the Desert of Ziph, he learned that Saul was coming to kill him. 16 But Saul's son Jonathan went to David at Horesh and strengthened his faith in God. 17 Jonathan told him, "Don't be afraid, because my father won't touch you. You will be king of Israel, and I will be second to you. Even my father Saul knows this." 18 The two of them made an agreement before the LORD. Then Jonathan went home, but David stayed at Horesh.

19 The people from Ziph went to Saul at Gibeah and told him, "David is hiding in our land. He's at the protected places of Horesh, on the hill of Hakilah, south of Jeshimon. 20 Now, our king, come down any time you want. It's our duty to hand David over to you."

21 Saul answered, "The LORD bless you for helping me. 22 Go and learn more about him. Find out where he is staying and who has seen him there. I have heard that he is clever. 23 Find all the hiding places he uses, and come back and tell me everything. Then I'll go with you. If David is in the area, I will track him down among all the families in Judah."

24 So they went back to Ziph ahead of Saul. Now David and his men were in the Desert of Maon* in the desert area south of Jeshimon. 25 Saul and his men went to look for David, but David heard about it and went down to a rock and stayed in the Desert of Maon. When Saul heard that, he followed David into the Desert of Maon.

26 Saul was going along one side of the mountain, and David and his men were on the other side. They were hurrying to get away from Saul, because Saul and his men were closing in on them. 27 But a messenger came to Saul, saying, "Come quickly! The Philistines are attacking our land!" 28 So Saul stopped chasing David and went to challenge the Philistines. That is why people call this place Rock of Parting. 29 David also left the Desert of Maon and stayed in the protected places of En Gedi.

David Shames Saul

24 After Saul returned from chasing the Philistines, he was told, "David is in the Desert of En Gedi." 2 So he took 3,000 chosen men from all Israel and began looking for David and his men near the Rocks of the Wild Goats.

> **EMAIL FROM GOD**
> **24:1–6**
> **Leadership**
> Why should you respect your leaders?

3 Saul came to the sheep pens beside the road. A cave was there, and he went in to relieve himself. Now David and his men were hiding far back in the cave. 4 The men said to David, "Today is the day the LORD spoke of when he said, 'I will give your enemy over to you. Do anything you want with him.'"

Then David crept up to Saul and quietly cut off a corner of Saul's robe. 5 Later David felt guilty because he had cut off a corner of Saul's robe. 6 He said to his men, "May the LORD keep me from doing such a thing to my master! Saul is the LORD's appointed king. I should not do anything against him, because he is the LORD's appointed king!" 7 David used these words to stop his men; he did not let them attack Saul. Then Saul left the cave and went on his way.

8 When David came out of the cave, he shouted to Saul, "My master and king!" Saul looked back, and David bowed face down on the ground. 9 He said to Saul, "Why do you listen when people say, 'David wants to harm you'? 10 You have seen something with your own eyes today. The LORD put you in my power in the cave. They said I should kill you, but I was merciful. I said, 'I won't harm my master, because he is the LORD's appointed king.' 11 My father, look at this piece of your robe in my hand! I cut off the corner of your robe, but I didn't kill you. Now understand and know I am not

---

23:24 Maon Some early Greek copies say "Maon". The Hebrew copies say "Paran".

FAITH links

A RIGHT TO GET EVEN?
1 SAMUEL 24

If you've ever felt like getting even with someone, consider David's story. David had an opportunity to kill Saul and stop Saul from trying to kill him. Instead, David showed respect for Saul and for God by not harming Saul. David knew that God had placed Saul in his position. He knew that he did not have the right to judge Saul, even though Saul had treated him disrespectfully.

A person's disrespectful actions do not give you the right to respond to him or her in the same way. Not getting even with someone shows your respect for that person and for God.

It's not easy to turn away from an "enemy". Here's some more advice on how to do just that:

The Trouble with Jealousy, Genesis 37, p. 53

Mourning for an Enemy, 2 Samuel 1, p. 399

God's Sure Protection, Psalm 18, p. 721

Justice Served, Isaiah 35:3–4, p. 940

Don't Get Mad; Get Even? Matthew 26:57–63; 27:11–14, p. 1323

Full of Faith, 1 Thessalonians 4:1, p. 1633

---

planning any evil against you. I did nothing wrong to you, but you are hunting me to kill me. 12 May the LORD judge between us, and may he punish you for the wrong you have done to me! But I am not against you. 13 There is an old saying: 'Evil things come from evil people.' But I am not against you. 14 Whom is the king of Israel coming out against? Whom are you chasing? It's as if you are chasing a dead dog or a flea. 15 May the LORD be our judge and decide between you and me. May he support me and show that I am right. May he save me from you!"

16 When David finished saying these words, Saul asked, "Is that your voice, David my son?" And he cried loudly. 17 He said, "You are a better man than I am. You have been good to me, but I have done wrong to you. 18 You told me what good things you did. The LORD handed me over to you, but you did not kill me. 19 If a person finds his enemy, he doesn't just send him on his way, does he? May the LORD reward you because you were good to me today. 20 I know you will surely be king, and you will rule the kingdom of Israel. 21 Now swear to me by the LORD that you will not kill my descendants and that you won't wipe out my name from my father's family."

22 So David made the promise to Saul. Then Saul went back home, and David and his men went up to their protected place.

Nabal Insults David

25 Now Samuel died, and all the Israelites met and had a time of sadness for him. Then they buried him at his home in Ramah.

David moved to the Desert of Maon." 2 A man in Maon who had land at Carmel was very rich. He had 3,000 sheep and 1,000 goats. He was cutting the wool off his sheep at Carmel. 3 His name was Nabal, and he was a descendant of Caleb. His wife was named Abigail. She was wise and beautiful, but Nabal was cruel and mean.

4 While David was in the desert, he

25:1 **Maon** Some early Greek copies say "Maon". The Hebrew copies say "Paran".

1 Samuel 25:22

FAITH links

YOURS, MINE AND OURS?

1 SAMUEL 25

Has someone ever refused to share something with you? Nabal didn't want to share when David asked him for food for himself and his men. David's men had protected Nabal's flocks. But Nabal wanted to keep all that he had for himself.

God wants his people to be generous towards others. Since he graciously gives us all that we have and need, he wants us to share that grace with others.

A Small Percent, Deuteronomy 14:22–23, p. 247

Fairness for All, Deuteronomy 24:17, p. 258

Two Are Better, Ecclesiastes 4:9–12, p. 877

The Right Ingredients, Micah 6:8, p. 1227

Give from the Heart, Luke 21:1–4, p. 1410

The Most Fun, Acts 20:35, p. 1502

---

heard that Nabal was cutting the wool from his sheep. 5 So he sent ten young men and told them, "Go to Nabal at Carmel, and greet him for me. 6 Say to Nabal, 'May you and your family and all who belong to you have good health! 7 I have heard that you are cutting the wool from your sheep. When your shepherds were with us, we did not harm them. All the time your shepherds were at Carmel, we stole nothing from them. 8 Ask your servants, and they will tell you. We come at a happy time, so be kind to my young men. Please give anything you can find for them and for your son David.'"

9 When David's men arrived, they gave the message to Nabal, but Nabal insulted them. 10 He answered them, "Who is David? Who is this son of Jesse? Many slaves are running away from their masters today! 11 I have bread and water, and I have meat that I killed for my servants who cut the wool. But I won't give it to men I don't know."

12 David's men went back and told him all Nabal had said. 13 Then David said to them, "Put on your swords!" So they put on their swords, and David put on his also. About 400 men went with David, but 200 men stayed with the supplies.

14 One of Nabal's servants said to Abigail, Nabal's wife, "David sent messengers from the desert to greet our master, but Nabal insulted them. 15 These men were very good to us. They did not harm us. They stole nothing from us during all the time we were out in the field with them. 16 Night and day they protected us. They were like a wall around us while we were with them caring for the sheep. 17 Now think about it, and decide what you can do. Terrible trouble is coming to our master and all his family. Nabal is such a wicked man that no one can even talk to him."

18 Abigail hurried. She took 200 loaves of bread, two leather bags full of wine, five cooked sheep, 15 kilogrammes of cooked grain, 100 cakes of raisins and 200 cakes of pressed figs and put all these on donkeys. 19 Then she told her servants, "Go on. I'll follow you." But she did not tell her husband.

20 Abigail rode her donkey and came down towards the mountain ravine. There she met David and his men coming down towards her.

21 David had just said, "It's been useless! I watched over Nabal's property in the desert. I made sure none of his sheep was missing. I did good to him, but he has paid me back with evil. 22 May God

punish my enemies even more. I will not leave one of Nabal's men alive until morning."

23 When Abigail saw David, she quickly got off her donkey and bowed face down on the ground before him. 24 She fell at David's feet and said, "My master, let the blame be on me! Please let me talk to you. Listen to what I say. 25 My master, don't pay attention to this worthless man Nabal. He is like his name. His name means 'fool', and he is truly a fool. But I, your servant, didn't see the men you sent. 26 The LORD has kept you from killing and punishing anyone. As surely as the LORD lives and as surely as you live, may your enemies become like Nabal! 27 I have brought a gift to you for the men who follow you. 28 Please forgive my wrong. The LORD will certainly let your family have many kings, because you fight his battles. As long as you live, may you do nothing bad. 29 Someone might chase you to kill you, but the LORD your God will keep you alive. He will throw away your enemies' lives as he would throw a stone from a sling. 30 The LORD will keep all his promises of good things for you. He will make you leader over Israel. 31 Then you won't feel guilty or troubled because you killed innocent people and punished them. Please remember me when the LORD brings you success."

32 David answered Abigail, "Praise the LORD, the God of Israel, who sent you to meet me. 33 May you be blessed for your wisdom. You have kept me from killing or punishing people today. 34 As surely as the LORD, the God of Israel, lives, he has kept me from hurting you. If you hadn't come quickly to meet me, not one of Nabal's men would have lived until morning."

35 Then David accepted Abigail's gifts. He told her, "Go home in peace. I have heard your words, and I will do what you have asked."

Nabal's Death

36 When Abigail went back to Nabal, he was in the house, eating like a king. He was very drunk and in a good mood. So she told him nothing until the next morning. 37 In the morning when he was not drunk, his wife told him everything. His heart stopped, and he became like stone. 38 About ten days later the LORD struck Nabal and he died.

39 When David heard that Nabal was dead, he said, "Praise the LORD! Nabal insulted me, but the LORD has supported me! He has kept me from doing wrong. The LORD has punished Nabal for his wrong."

Then David sent a message to Abigail, asking her to be his wife. 40 His servants went to Carmel and said to Abigail, "David sent us to take you so you can become his wife."

41 Abigail bowed face down on the ground and said, "I am your servant. I'm ready to serve you and to wash the feet of my master's servants." 42 Abigail quickly got on a donkey and went with David's messengers, with her five maids following her. And she became David's wife.

43 David also had married Ahinoam of Jezreel. So they were both David's wives. 44 Saul's daughter Michal was also David's wife, but Saul had given her to Paltiel son of Laish, who was from Gallim.

David Shames Saul Again

26 The people of Ziph went to Saul at Gibeah and said to him, "David is hiding on the hill of Hakilah opposite Jeshimon."

2 So Saul went down to the Desert of Ziph with 3,000 chosen men of Israel to look for David there. 3 Saul made his camp beside the road on the hill of Hakilah opposite Jeshimon, but David stayed in the desert. When he heard Saul had followed him, 4 he sent out spies and learned for certain that Saul had come to Hakilah.

5 Then David went to the place where Saul had camped. He saw where Saul and Abner son of Ner, the commander of Saul's army, were sleeping. Saul was sleeping in the middle of the camp with all the army around him.

6 David asked Ahimelech the Hittite and Abishai son of Zeruiah, Joab's brother, "Who will go down into Saul's camp with me?"

FAITH links

THE RIGHT THING TO DO
1 SAMUEL 26

What if a friend tried to convince you to do something by telling you God wanted you to do it? What would you do? One of David's men, Abishai, tried to get David to kill Saul. He told David that God had created the opportunity for him to do so. But David chose not to harm Saul, even though Saul had wronged him. David knew that God would not allow him to get even with Saul.

God will never tell you to do something wrong. If you're not sure about what God wants you to do, you can always ask him to help you know what to do. He'll be glad to do it!

Here are some more Faithlinks on doing the right thing:

What's Out Becomes In, Judges 11, p. 327

Fair All the Time? 2 Samuel 8:15, p. 408

On the Wrong Foot, 2 Kings 21:1–2, 16, p. 509

Just a Little Respect, 1 Chronicles 11:10–19, p. 534

Forgive and Forget, Ephesians 4:32, p. 1604

The Leaders in Your Life, 1 Timothy 2:1–4, p. 1645

Abishai answered, "I'll go with you."

7 So that night David and Abishai went into Saul's camp. Saul was asleep in the middle of the camp with his spear stuck in the ground near his head. Abner and the army were sleeping around Saul. 8 Abishai said to David, "Today God has handed your enemy over to you. Let me pin Saul to the ground with my spear. I'll only have to do it once. I won't need to hit him twice."

9 But David said to Abishai, "Don't kill Saul! No one can harm the LORD's appointed king and still be innocent! 10 As surely as the LORD lives, the LORD himself will punish Saul. Maybe Saul will die naturally, or maybe he will go into battle and be killed. 11 But may the LORD keep me from harming his appointed king! Take the spear and water jug that are near Saul's head. Then let's go."

12 So David took the spear and water jug that were near Saul's head, and they left. No one saw them or knew about it or woke up, because the LORD had put them into a deep sleep.

13 David crossed over to the other side of the hill and stood on top of the mountain far from Saul's camp. They were a long way away from each other. 14 David shouted to the army and to Abner son of Ner, "Won't you answer me, Abner?"

Abner answered, "Who is calling for the king? Who are you?"

15 David said, "You're the greatest man in Israel. Isn't that true? Why didn't you guard your master the king? Someone came into your camp to kill your master the king! 16 You have not done well. As surely as the LORD lives, you and your men should die. You haven't guarded your master, the LORD's appointed king. Look! Where are the king's spear and water jug that were near his head?"

17 Saul knew David's voice. He said, "Is that your voice, David my son?"

David answered, "Yes, it is, my master and king." 18 David also said, "Why are you chasing me, my master? What wrong have I done? What evil am I guilty of? 19 My master and king, listen to me. If the LORD made you angry with me, let him accept an offering. But if people did it, may the LORD curse them! They have made me leave the land the LORD gave me. They have told me, 'Go and serve other gods.' 20 Now don't let me die far away from the LORD's presence. The king of Israel has come out looking for a flea! You're just hunting a bird in the mountains!"

21 Then Saul said, "I have sinned. Come back, David my son. Today you respected my life, so I will not try to hurt you. I have been very stupid and foolish."

22 David answered, "Here is your spear. Let one of your young men come here and get it. 23 The LORD rewards us for the things we do right and for our loyalty to him. The LORD handed you over to me today, but I wouldn't harm the LORD's appointed king. 24 As I respected your life today, may the LORD also respect my life and save me from all trouble."

25 Then Saul said to David, "You are blessed, my son David. You will do great things and succeed."

So David went on his way, and Saul went back home.

David Lives with the Philistines

27 But David thought to himself, "Saul will catch me some day. The best thing I can do is escape to the land of the Philistines. Then he will give up looking for me in Israel, and I can get away from him."

2 So David and his 600 men left Israel and went to Achish son of Maoch, king of Gath. 3 David, his men and their families made their home in Gath with Achish. David had his two wives with him—Ahinoam of Jezreel and Abigail of Carmel, the widow of Nabal. 4 When Saul heard that David had run away to Gath, he stopped looking for him.

5 Then David said to Achish, "If you are pleased with me, give me a place in one of the country towns where I can live. I don't need to live in the royal city with you."

6 That day Achish gave David the town of Ziklag, and Ziklag has belonged to the kings of Judah ever since. 7 David lived in the Philistine land a year and four months.

8 David and his men went to raid the people of Geshur, Girzi and Amalek. (These people had lived for a long time in the land that reached to Shur and Egypt.) 9 When David fought them, he killed all the men and women and took their sheep, cattle, donkeys, camels and clothes. Then he returned to Achish.

10 Achish would ask David, "Where did you go raiding today?" And David would tell him that he had gone to the southern part of Judah, or Jerahmeel, or to the land of the Kenites. 11 David never brought a man or woman alive to Gath. He thought, "If we bring people alive, they may tell Achish, 'This is what David really did.'" David did this all the time he lived in the Philistine land. 12 So Achish trusted David and said to himself, "David's own people, the Israelites, now hate him very much. He will serve me for ever."

Saul and the Witch of Endor

28 Later, the Philistines gathered their armies to fight against Israel. Achish said to David, "You understand that you and your men must join my army."

2 David answered, "You will see for yourself what I, your servant, can do!"

Achish said, "Fine, I'll make you my bodyguard for life."

3 Now Samuel was dead, and all the Israelites had shown their sadness for him. They had buried Samuel in his home town of Ramah.

And Saul had forced out the mediums and fortune-tellers from the land.

4 The Philistines came together and made camp at Shunem. Saul gathered all the Israelites and made camp at Gilboa. 5 When he saw the Philistine army, he was afraid, and his heart pounded with fear. 6 He prayed to the LORD, but the LORD did not answer him through dreams, Urim or prophets. 7 Then Saul said to his servants, "Find me a woman who is a medium so I may go and ask her what will happen."

His servants answered, "There is a medium in Endor."

8 Then Saul put on other clothes to

disguise himself, and at night he and two of his men went to see the woman. Saul said to her, "Talk to a spirit for me. Bring up the person I name."

9 But the woman said to him, "Surely you know what Saul has done. He has forced the mediums and fortune-tellers from the land. You are trying to trap me and get me killed."

10 Saul made a promise to the woman in the name of the LORD. He said, "As surely as the LORD lives, you won't be punished for this."

11 The woman asked, "Whom do you want me to bring up?"

FAITH CHALLENGE

Here's another challenge for you. Read 28:7 to discover the terrible mistake King Saul made when he tried to learn about his future. What would you say to a friend who reads and depends on horoscopes for advice?

Testing it

1 Samuel 28:7
Then Saul said to his servants, "Find me a woman who is a medium so I may go and ask her what will happen."

He answered, "Bring up Samuel."

12 When the woman saw Samuel, she screamed. She said, "Why have you tricked me? You are Saul!"

13 The king said to the woman, "Don't be afraid! What do you see?"

The woman said, "I see a spirit coming up out of the ground."

14 Saul asked, "What does he look like?"

The woman answered, "An old man wearing a coat is coming up."

Then Saul knew it was Samuel, and he bowed face down on the ground.

15 Samuel asked Saul, "Why have you disturbed me by bringing me up?"

Saul said, "I am greatly troubled. The Philistines are fighting against me, and God has left me. He won't answer me any more, either by prophets or in dreams. That's why I called for you. Tell me what to do."

16 Samuel said, "The LORD has left you and has become your enemy. So why do you call on me? 17 He has done what he said he would do—the things he said through me. He has torn the kingdom out of your hands and given it to one of your neighbours, David. 18 You did not obey the LORD; you did not show the Amalekites how angry he was with them. That's why he has done this to you today. 19 The LORD will hand over both Israel and you to the Philistines. Tomorrow you and your sons will be with me. The LORD will hand over the army of Israel to the Philistines."

20 Saul quickly fell flat on the ground and was afraid of what Samuel had said. He was also very weak because he had eaten nothing all that day and night.

21 Then the woman came to Saul and saw that he was really frightened. She said, "Look, I, your servant, have obeyed you. I have risked my life and done what you told me to do. 22 Now please listen to me. Let me give you some food so you may eat and have enough strength to go on your way."

23 But Saul refused, saying, "I won't eat."

His servants joined the woman in asking him to eat, and he listened to them.

So he got up from the ground and sat on the bed.

24 At the house the woman had a fat calf, which she quickly killed. She took some flour and mixed dough with her hands. Then she baked some bread without yeast. 25 She put the food before them, and they ate. That same night they got up and left.

David Goes Back to Ziklag

29 The Philistines gathered all their soldiers at Aphek. Israel camped by the spring at Jezreel. 2 The Philistine kings were marching with their groups of 100 and 1,000 men. David and his men were marching behind Achish. 3 The Philistine commanders asked, "What are these Hebrews doing here?"

Achish told them, "This is David. He served Saul king of Israel, but he has been with me for over a year now. I have found nothing wrong in David since the time he left Saul."

4 But the Philistine commanders were angry with Achish and said, "Send David back to the city you gave him. He cannot go with us into battle. If he does, we'll have an enemy in our own camp. He could please his king by killing our own men. 5 David is the one the Israelites dance and sing about, saying:

'Saul has killed thousands of his
    enemies,
but David has killed tens of
    thousands.'"

6 So Achish called David and said to him, "As surely as the LORD lives, you are loyal. I would be pleased to have you serve in my army. Since the day you came to me, I have found no wrong in you. But the other kings don't trust you. 7 Go back in peace. Don't do anything to displease the Philistine kings."

8 David asked, "What wrong have I done? What evil have you found in me from the day I came to you until now? Why can't I go and fight your enemies, my lord and king?"

9 Achish answered, "I know you are as good as an angel from God. But the Philistine commanders have said, 'David must not go with us into battle.' 10 Early in the morning you and your master's servants should leave. Get up as soon as it is light and go."

11 So David and his men got up early in the morning and went back to the country of the Philistines. And the Philistines went up to Jezreel.

David's War with the Amalekites

30 On the third day, when David and his men arrived at Ziklag, he found that the Amalekites had raided southern Judah and Ziklag, attacking Ziklag and burning it. 2 They captured the women and everyone, young and old, but they had not killed anyone. They had only taken them away.

3 When David and his men came to Ziklag, they found the town had been burned and their wives, sons and daughters had been taken as prisoners. 4 Then David and his army cried loudly until they were too weak to cry any more. 5 David's two wives had also been taken—Ahinoam of Jezreel and Abigail the widow of Nabal from Carmel. 6 The men in the army were threatening to kill David with stones, which greatly upset David. Each man was sad and angry because his sons and daughters had been captured, but David found strength in the LORD his God. 7 David said to Abiathar the priest, "Bring me the holy robe."

8 Then David asked the LORD, "Should I chase the people who took our families? Will I catch them?"

The LORD answered, "Chase them. You will catch them, and you will succeed in saving your families."

9 David and the 600 men with him came to the Besor Ravine, where some of the men stayed. 10 David and 400 men

> As surely as the LORD lives, you are loyal. I would be pleased to have you serve in my army.
> — 1 Samuel 29:6

FAITH links

KIND OR FAIR?
1 SAMUEL 30

Suppose you and a friend did a project together to win a prize, but a third friend chose not to help you. Would it be fair to let the third friend share in the prize? When a group of enemy soldiers burned down their village and stole their possessions, David and 400 of his men went after them. But 200 of David's 600 men were too tired to go. Some of the men who fought the enemy didn't want to share with the men who didn't go. They felt that sharing with them wasn't fair. But David agreed to share and share alike. Sometimes, you might have to choose between kindness and your idea of fairness. Which will you choose?

Forgive Instead, Genesis 33, p. 47

Share What You Have, Exodus 35:5–18, p. 123

Play Fair or Play Favourites? Deuteronomy 1:16–18, p. 227

Fairness for All, Deuteronomy 24:17, p. 258

Wronged for What's Right, Ezra 4:4–5, p. 612

The Way to Get Along, 1 Peter 3:8–9, p. 1703

---

11 They found an Egyptian in a field and brought him to David. They gave the Egyptian some water to drink and some food to eat. 12 And they gave him a piece of a fig cake and two clusters of raisins. Then he felt better, because he had not eaten any food or drunk any water for three days and nights.

13 David asked him, "Who is your master? Where do you come from?"

He answered, "I'm an Egyptian, the slave of an Amalekite. Three days ago my master left me, because I was sick. 14 We had attacked the southern area of the Kerethites, the land of Judah and the southern area of Caleb. We burned Ziklag, as well.

15 David asked him, "Can you lead me to the people who took our families?"

He answered, "Yes, if you promise me before God that you won't kill me or give me back to my master. Then I will take you to them."

16 So the Egyptian led David to the Amalekites. They were lying around on the ground, eating and drinking and celebrating with the things they had taken from the land of the Philistines and from Judah. 17 David fought them from sunset until the evening of the next day. None of them escaped, except 400 young men who rode off on their camels. 18 David got his two wives back and everything the Amalekites had taken. 19 Nothing was missing. David brought back everyone, young and old, sons and daughters. He recovered the valuable things and everything the Amalekites had taken. 20 David took all the sheep and cattle, and his men made these animals go in front, saying, "They are David's prize."

21 Then David came to the 200 men who had been too tired to follow him, who had stayed at the Besor Ravine. They came out to meet David and the people with him. When he came near, David greeted the men at the ravine.

22 But the evil men and troublemakers among those who followed David said, "Since these 200 men didn't go with us, we shouldn't give them any of the things we recovered. Just let each man take his wife and children and go."

---

kept up the chase. The other 200 men stayed behind because they were too tired to cross the ravine.

1 Samuel 30:23 396

SOME BAD GUYS 1 Samuel 31:1–4

The Philistines were a fierce tribe of people. They were called the "sea people" because they probably came from an island in the Mediterranean Sea. (See Genesis 10:14, p. 15, and Amos 9:7, p. 1204.) The land that they lived in was called Philistia. Maybe the most famous Philistine was Goliath, the giant that David killed with a slingshot and five stones.

The Philistines are mostly mentioned in the Bible at two different times. First, they were mentioned in the stories about Abraham. These Philistines were peaceful and were ruled by King Abimelech. Later on, the Philistines were mentioned when the Israelites were just about to get their first two kings: Saul and David. These Philistines were made up of a confederation of five different Philistine states ruled by five different leaders. They were dangerous, and the Israelites were afraid of them. In fact, one of the main reasons that the Israelites wanted a king was for protection against the Philistines. King David was the king who finally broke the power of the great Philistines.

23 David answered, "No, my brothers. Don't do that after what the LORD has given us. He has protected us and given us the enemy who attacked us. 24 Who will listen to what you say? The share will be the same for the one who stayed with the supplies as for the one who went into battle. All will share alike." 25 David made this an order and rule for Israel, which continues even today.

26 When David arrived in Ziklag, he sent some of the things he had taken from the Amalekites to his friends, the elders of Judah. He said, "Here is a present for you from the things we took from the LORD's enemies."

27 David also sent some things to the leaders in Bethel, Ramoth in the southern part of Judah, Jattir, 28 Aroer, Siphmoth, Eshtemoa, 29 Racal, the cities of the Jerahmeelites and the Kenites, 30 Hormah, Bor Ashan, Athach, 31 Hebron and to the people in all the other places where he and his men had been.

The Death of Saul

31 The Philistines fought against Israel, and the Israelites ran away from them. Many Israelites were killed on Mount Gilboa. 2 The Philistines fought hard against Saul and his sons, killing his sons Jonathan, Abinadab and Malki-Shua. 3 The fighting was heavy around Saul. The archers shot him, and he was badly wounded. 4 He said to the officer who carried his armour, "Pull out your sword and kill me. Then those uncircumcised men won't make fun of me and kill me." But Saul's officer refused, because he was afraid. So Saul took his own sword and threw himself on it. 5 When the officer saw that Saul was dead, he threw himself on his own sword, and he died with Saul. 6 So Saul, his three sons and the officer who carried his armour died together that day.

7 When the Israelites who lived across the Jezreel Valley and those who lived across the Jordan River saw how the

Israelite army had run away, and that Saul and his sons were dead, they left their cities and ran away. Then the Philistines came and lived there.

8 The next day when the Philistines came to take all the valuable things from the dead soldiers, they found Saul and his three sons dead on Mount Gilboa. 9 They cut off Saul's head and took off his armour. Then they sent messengers through all the land of the Philistines to tell the news in the temple of their idols and to their people. 10 They put Saul's armour in the temple of the Ashtoreths and hung his body on the wall of Beth Shan.

11 When the people living in Jabesh Gilead heard what the Philistines had done to Saul, 12 the brave men of Jabesh marched all night and came to Beth Shan. They removed the bodies of Saul and his sons from the wall of Beth Shan and brought them to Jabesh. There they burned the bodies. 13 They took their bones and buried them under the tamarisk tree in Jabesh. Then the people of Jabesh gave up eating for seven days.

KING AT LAST

Greetings! I am King David. You may remember me, the shepherd boy who played the harp for King Saul? This book tells how I was made king over all of Israel. No one is sure who wrote these stories, but I know they are true. These were exciting days for God's people. We defeated our enemies, and Israel became a great nation. I danced for joy when we brought the Ark of God to Jerusalem. Check out 2 Samuel 6 for the big celebration.

This book was written to tell the story of my rule. God was good to me and gave me many victories. Sadly, I did not always obey God, and I had times of trouble, too. When the prophet Nathan pointed out my sin, I asked God to forgive me. Check out the MIDI in Psalm 51, p. 748, for the words of the song I wrote telling God I was sorry.

JESUS WATCH

David had a close relationship with God and a desire to bring him glory, just as Jesus did. Even though David sinned, he remained close to God because he was willing to ask God for forgiveness. David wrote many psalms praising God and made worship the most important part of his kingdom. His rule was known for justice and compassion. God made a special promise to David that his family would rule for ever. Israel and the prophets looked forward to the Son of David, the Messiah, who would bring people to God and make Israel a great nation again. The angel Gabriel told Mary that Jesus would reign on the throne of King David and that his kingdom would never end. People were looking for a military hero who would defeat Israel's enemies, but Jesus rules for ever from heaven. When we believe in Jesus, he becomes our king. His justice and mercy never end.

FAITH links

Do you know why King David's son, Absalom, was hanging by his hair in a tree? Sounds like trouble, doesn't it? Surf over to 2 Samuel 18 to find out more.

- The Green Light, 2 Samuel 2:1
- When God Says No, 2 Samuel 7
- Loyal to a Friend, 2 Samuel 9
- Help to Understand, 2 Samuel 14

David Learns About Saul's Death

1 Now Saul was dead. After David had defeated the Amalekites, he returned to Ziklag and stayed there for two days. 2 On the third day a young man from Saul's camp came to Ziklag. To show his sadness, his clothes were torn and he had dust on his head. He came and bowed face down on the ground before David.

3 David asked him, "Where did you come from?"

The man answered, "I escaped from the Israelite camp."

4 David asked him, "What happened? Please tell me!"

The man answered, "The people have run away from the battle, and many of them have fallen and are dead. Saul and his son Jonathan are dead also."

5 David asked him, "How do you know Saul and his son Jonathan are dead?"

6 The young man answered, "I happened to be on Mount Gilboa. There I saw Saul leaning on his spear. The Philistine chariots and the men riding in them were coming closer to Saul. 7 When he looked back and saw me, he called to me. I answered him, 'Here I am!'

8 "Then Saul asked me, 'Who are you?'

"I told him, 'I am an Amalekite.'

9 "Then Saul said to me, 'Please come here and kill me. I am badly hurt and am almost dead already.'

10 "So I went over and killed him. He had been hurt so badly I knew he couldn't live. Then I took the crown from his head and the bracelet from his arm, and I have brought them here to you, my master."

11 Then David tore his clothes to show his sorrow, and all the men with him did also. 12 They were very sad and cried and did not eat until evening. They cried for Saul and his son Jonathan and for all the people of the LORD and for all the Israelites who had died in the battle.

David Orders the Amalekite Killed

13 David asked the young man who brought the report, "Where are you from?"

The young man answered, "I am the son of a foreigner, an Amalekite."

14 David asked him, "Why were you not afraid to kill the LORD's appointed king?"

15 Then David called one of his men

FAITH links

MOURNING FOR AN ENEMY

2 SAMUEL 1

If you had an enemy, would you feel glad if that enemy got into trouble? Even though Saul had been his enemy for several years, David remained respectful to Saul. He did not celebrate when his enemy was killed. Instead he mourned the loss of Saul. He even sang a song in honour of his fallen enemy.

Are you tempted to laugh when your enemy gets hit with trouble? Taking pleasure in your enemy's misfortune, or causing it, doesn't make you a hero. Showing respect for an enemy does. When you're respectful even to an enemy, God is pleased.

Give Revenge a Rest, Leviticus 19:18, p. 160

A Right to Get Even? 1 Samuel 24, p. 388

The Problem with Pride, Isaiah 2:11, p. 898

A Home Town Hurt, Jeremiah 11:8—12:6, p. 1008

Quick to Forgive? Mark 11:25, p. 1349

Better Than Some? Luke 18:9–14, p. 1405

and told him, "Go! Kill the Amalekite!" So the Israelite killed him. 16 David had said to the Amalekite, "You are responsible for your own death. You confessed by saying, 'I have killed the LORD's appointed king.'"

David's Song About Saul and Jonathan

17 David sang a funeral song about Saul and his son Jonathan, 18 and he ordered that the people of Judah be taught this song. It is called "The Bow", and it is written in the Book of Jashar:

19 "Israel, your leaders have been killed
on the hills.
How the mighty have fallen in
battle!
20 Don't tell it in Gath.
Don't announce it in the streets of
Ashkelon.
If you do, the Philistine women will
be happy.
The daughters of the Philistines
will rejoice.
21 "May there be no dew or rain on the
mountains of Gilboa,
and may their fields produce no
grain,
because there the mighty warrior's
shield was dishonoured.
Saul's shield will no longer be
rubbed with oil.
22 Jonathan's bow did not fail
to kill many soldiers.
Saul's sword did not fail
to wound many strong men.

23 "We loved Saul and Jonathan
and enjoyed them while they
lived.
They are together even in death.
They were faster than eagles.
They were stronger than lions.

24 "You daughters of Israel, cry for Saul.
Saul clothed you with red dresses
and put gold decorations on them.

25 "How the mighty have fallen in
battle!
Jonathan is dead on Gilboa's hills.

26 I cry for you, my brother Jonathan.
I enjoyed your friendship so much.
Your love to me was wonderful,
better than the love of women.

27 "How the mighty have fallen!
The weapons of war are gone."

David is Made King of Judah

2 Later, David prayed to the LORD, saying, "Should I go up to any of the cities of Judah?"

The LORD said to David, "Go."
David asked, "Where should I go?"
The LORD answered, "To Hebron."

2 So David went up to Hebron with his two wives: Ahinoam from Jezreel and Abigail, the widow of Nabal from Carmel. 3 David also brought his men and their families, and they all made their homes in the cities of Hebron. 4 Then the men of Judah came to Hebron and appointed David king over Judah.

They told David that the men of Jabesh Gilead had buried Saul. 5 So David sent messengers to the men of Jabesh Gilead and said to them, "The LORD bless you. You have shown loyalty to your master Saul by burying him. 6 May the LORD now be loyal and true to you. I will also treat you well because you have done this. 7 Now be strong and brave. Saul your master is dead, and the people of Judah have appointed me their king."

War Between Judah and Israel

8 Abner son of Ner was the commander of Saul's army. Abner took Saul's son Ish-Bosheth to Mahanaim 9 and made him king of Gilead, Ashuri, Jezreel, Ephraim, Benjamin and all Israel. 10 Saul's son Ish-Bosheth was 40 years old when he became king over Israel, and he ruled two years. But the people of Judah followed David. 11 David was king in Hebron for seven years and six months.

12 Abner son of Ner and the servants of Ish-Bosheth son of Saul left Mahanaim and went to Gibeon. 13 Joab son of Zeruiah and David's men also went there and met Abner and Ish-Bosheth's men at the pool of Gibeon. Abner's group sat on one side of the pool; Joab's group sat on the other.

FAITH links

THE GREEN LIGHT
2 SAMUEL 2:1

When a producer in Hollywood is given permission to make a film, the project is said to be "green-lighted". That means he or she can go ahead with it. God gave David "the green light" to move to Hebron. David didn't make a move before checking with God. He trusted God's timing.

When you're about to make plans, do you ever think about checking with God for his approval? Although you may not want to stop and ask God about things like whether you should wear orange socks or red, consider talking over the major decisions of your life. God cares about you. Commit your plans to God. Wait for him to give you the green light.

Here are some more Faithlinks on making good plans:

A Giant Problem, 1 Samuel 17:32–51, p. 377

When God Says No, 2 Samuel 7, p. 407

A Need to Change, Ecclesiastes 1:1–11, p. 873

First Place, Haggai 1:7–11, p. 1248

The Best Advice, Zechariah 10:2, p. 1261

Prayer Priority, Luke 5:15–16, p. 1376

---

14 Abner said to Joab, "Let the young men have a contest here."

Joab said, "Yes, let them have a contest."

15 Then the men got up and were counted—twelve from the people of Benjamin for Ish-Bosheth son of Saul, and twelve from David's men. 16 Each man grabbed the one opposite him by the head and stabbed him in the side with a knife. So the men fell down together. For that reason, that place in Gibeon is called the Field of Knives. 17 That day there was a terrible battle, and David's men defeated Abner and the Israelites.

Abner Kills Asahel

18 Zeruiah's three sons, Joab, Abishai and Asahel, were there. Now Asahel was a fast runner, as fast as a deer in the field. 19 Asahel chased Abner, going straight towards him. 20 Abner looked back and asked, "Is that you, Asahel?"

Asahel said, "Yes, it is."

21 Then Abner said to Asahel, "Turn to your right or left and catch one of the young men and take his armour." But Asahel refused to stop chasing him.

22 Abner again said to Asahel, "Stop chasing me! If you don't stop, I'll have to kill you! Then I won't be able to face your brother Joab again!"

23 But Asahel refused to stop chasing Abner. So using the back end of his spear, Abner stabbed Asahel in the stomach, and the spear came out of his back. Asahel died right there, and everyone stopped when they came to the place where Asahel's body lay.

24 But Joab and Abishai continued chasing Abner. As the sun was going down, they arrived at the hill of Ammah, near Giah on the way to the desert near Gibeon. 25 The men of Benjamin came to Abner, and all stood together at the top of the hill.

26 Abner shouted to Joab, "Must the sword kill for ever? Surely you must know this will only end in sadness! Tell the people to stop chasing their own brothers!"

27 Then Joab said, "As surely as God lives, if you had not said anything, the

people would have chased their brothers until morning." 28 Then Joab blew a trumpet, and his people stopped chasing the Israelites. They did not fight them any more.

29 Abner and his men marched all night through the Jordan Valley. They crossed the Jordan River, and after marching all day, arrived at Mahanaim.

30 After he had stopped chasing Abner, Joab came back and gathered the people together. Asahel and nineteen of David's men were missing. 31 But David's men had killed 360 Benjaminites who had followed Abner. 32 David's men took Asahel and buried him in the tomb of his father at Bethlehem. Then Joab and his men marched all night. The sun came up as they reached Hebron.

3 There was a long war between the people who supported Saul's family and those who supported David's family. The supporters of David's family became stronger and stronger, but the supporters of Saul's family became weaker and weaker.

David's Sons

2 Sons were born to David at Hebron. The first was Amnon, whose mother was Ahinoam from Jezreel. 3 The second son was Kileab, whose mother was Abigail, the widow of Nabal from Carmel. The third son was Absalom, whose mother was Maacah daughter of Talmai, the king of Geshur. 4 The fourth son was Adonijah, whose mother was Haggith. The fifth son was Shephatiah, whose mother was Abital. 5 The sixth son was Ithream, whose mother was Eglah, David's wife. These sons were born to David at Hebron.

Abner Joins David

6 During the war between the supporters of Saul's family and the supporters of David's family, Abner made himself a main leader among the supporters of Saul.

7 Saul once had a slave woman named Rizpah, who was the daughter of Aiah. Ish-Bosheth said to Abner, "Why did you have sexual relations with my father's slave woman?"

8 Abner was very angry because of what Ish-Bosheth said, and he replied, "I have been loyal to Saul and his family and friends! I didn't hand you over to David. I am not a traitor working for Judah! But now you are saying I did something wrong with this woman! 9 May God help me if I don't join David! I will make sure that what the LORD promised does happen! 10 I will take the kingdom from the family of Saul and make David king of Israel and Judah, from Dan to Beersheba!"[n]

11 Ish-Bosheth couldn't say anything to Abner, because he was afraid of him.

12 Then Abner sent messengers to ask David, "Who is going to rule the land? Make an agreement with me, and I will help you unite all Israel."

13 David answered, "Good! I will make an agreement with you, but I ask you one thing. I will not meet with you unless you bring Saul's daughter Michal to me."

14 Then David sent messengers to Saul's son Ish-Bosheth, saying, "Give me my wife Michal. She was promised to me, and I killed 100 Philistines to get her."

15 So Ish-Bosheth sent men to take Michal from her husband Paltiel son of Laish. 16 Michal's husband went with her, crying as he followed her to Bahurim. But Abner said to Paltiel, "Go back home." So he went home.

17 Abner sent this message to the elders of Israel: "You have been wanting to make David your king. 18 Now do it! The LORD said of David, 'Through my servant David, I will save my people Israel from the Philistines and all their enemies.'"

19 Abner also said these things to the people of Benjamin. He then went to Hebron to tell David what the Benjaminites and Israel wanted to do. 20 Abner came with 20 men to David at Hebron. There David prepared a feast for them. 21 Abner said to David, "My master and

---

3:10 Dan to Beersheba Dan was the city farthest north in Israel, and Beersheba was the city farthest south. So this means all the people of Israel.

king, I will go and bring all the Israelites to you. Then they will make an agreement with you so you will rule over all Israel as you wanted." So David let Abner go, and he left in peace.

Abner's Death

22 Just then Joab and David's men came from a battle, bringing many valuable things they had taken from the enemy. David had let Abner leave in peace, so he was not with David at Hebron. 23 When Joab and all his army arrived at Hebron, the army said to Joab, "Abner son of Ner came to King David, and David let him leave in peace."

24 Joab came to the king and said, "What have you done? Abner came to you. Why did you let him go? Now he's gone. 25 You know Abner son of Ner! He came to trick you! He came to learn about everything you are doing!"

26 After Joab left David, he sent messengers after Abner, and they brought him back from the well of Sirah. But David did not know this. 27 When Abner arrived at Hebron, Joab took him aside into the gateway. He acted as though he wanted to talk with Abner in private, but Joab stabbed him in the stomach, and Abner died. Abner had killed Joab's brother Asahel, so Joab killed Abner to pay him back.

28 Later when David heard the news, he said, "My kingdom and I are innocent for ever of the death of Abner son of Ner. The LORD knows this. 29 Joab and his family are responsible for this. May his family always have someone with sores or with a skin disease. May they always have someone who must lean on a crutch. May some of his family be killed in war. May they always have someone without food to eat."

30 (Joab and his brother Abishai killed Abner, because he had killed their brother Asahel in the battle at Gibeon.)

31 Then David said to Joab and to all the people with Joab, "Tear your clothes and put on rough cloth to show how sad you are. Cry for Abner." King David himself followed the body of Abner. 32 They buried Abner in Hebron, and David and all the people cried at Abner's grave.

33 King David sang this funeral song for Abner.

"Did Abner die like a fool?
34 His hands were not tied.
    His feet were not in chains.
He fell at the hands of evil men."

Then all the people cried again for Abner. 35 They came to encourage David to eat while it was still day. But he made a promise, saying, "May God punish me terribly if I eat bread or anything else before the sun sets!"

36 All the people saw what happened, and they agreed with what the king was doing, just as they agreed with everything he did. 37 That day all the people of Judah and Israel understood that David did not order the killing of Abner son of Ner.

38 David said to his officers, "You know that a great man died today in Israel. 39 Even though I am the appointed king, I feel empty. These sons of Zeruiah are too much for me. May the LORD give them the punishment they should have."

Ish-Bosheth's Death

4 When Ish-Bosheth son of Saul heard that Abner had died at Hebron, he was shocked and all Israel became frightened. 2 Two men who were captains in Saul's army came to Ish-Bosheth. One was named Baanah, and the other was named Recab. They were the sons of Rimmon of Beeroth, who was a Benjaminite. (The town Beeroth belonged to the tribe of Benjamin. 3 The people of Beeroth ran away to Gittaim, and they still live there as foreigners today.)

4 (Saul's son Jonathan had a son named Mephibosheth, who was crippled in both feet. He was five years old when the news came from Jezreel that Saul and Jonathan were dead. Mephibosheth's

> Tear your clothes and put on rough cloth to show how sad you are. Cry for Abner.
> – 2 Samuel 3:31

nurse had picked him up and run away. But as she hurried to leave, she dropped him, and now he was lame.)

5 Recab and Baanah, sons of Rimmon from Beeroth, went to Ish-Bosheth's house in the afternoon while he was having his midday rest. 6-7 They went into the middle of the house as if to get some wheat. Ish-Bosheth was lying on his bed in his bedroom. Then Recab and Baanah stabbed him in the stomach, killed him, cut off his head and took it with them. They escaped and travelled all night through the Jordan Valley. 8 When they arrived at Hebron, they gave his head to David and said to the king, "Here is the head of Ish-Bosheth son of Saul, your enemy. He tried to kill you! Today the LORD has paid back Saul and his family for what they did to you!"

9 David answered Recab and his brother Baanah, the sons of Rimmon of Beeroth, "As surely as the LORD lives, he has saved me from all trouble! 10 Once a man thought he was bringing me good news. When he told me, 'Saul is dead!' I seized him and killed him at Ziklag. That was the reward I gave him for his news! 11 So even more I must put you evil men to death because you have killed an innocent man on his own bed in his own house!"

4:9–11
Life
Is life sacred?

12 So David commanded his men to kill Recab and Baanah. They cut off the hands and feet of Recab and Baanah and hung them over the pool of Hebron. Then they took Ish-Bosheth's head and buried it in Abner's tomb at Hebron.

David is Made King of Israel

5 Then all the tribes of Israel came to David at Hebron and said to him, "Look, we are your own family. 2 Even when Saul was king, you were the one who led Israel in battle. The LORD said to you, 'You will be a shepherd for my people Israel. You will be their leader.'"

3 So all the elders of Israel came to King David at Hebron, and he made an agreement with them in Hebron in the presence of the LORD. Then they poured oil on David to make him king over Israel.

4 David was 30 years old when he became king, and he ruled 40 years. 5 He was king over Judah in Hebron for seven years and six months, and he was king over all Israel and Judah in Jerusalem for 33 years.

6 When the king and his men went to Jerusalem to attack the Jebusites who lived there, the Jebusites said to David, "You can't get inside our city. Even the blind and the crippled can stop you." They thought David could not enter their city. 7 But David did take the city of Jerusalem with its strong walls, and it became the City of David.

8 That day David said to his men, "To defeat the Jebusites you must go through the water tunnel. Then you can reach those 'crippled' and 'blind' enemies. This is why people say, 'The blind and the crippled may not enter the palace.'"

9 So David lived in the fortified city and called it the City of David. David built more buildings around it, beginning where the land was filled in. He also built more buildings inside the city. 10 He became stronger and stronger, because the LORD God All-powerful was with him.

11 Hiram king of the city of Tyre sent messengers to David, along with cedar logs, carpenters and stonecutters. They built a palace for David. 12 Then David knew that the LORD really had made him king of Israel and that the LORD had made his kingdom great because the LORD loved his people Israel.

13 After he came from Hebron, David took for himself more slave women and wives in Jerusalem. More sons and daughters were born to David. 14 These are the names of the sons born to David in Jerusalem: Shammua, Shobab, Nathan, Solomon, 15 Ibhar, Elishua, Nepheg, Japhia, 16 Elishama, Eliada and Eliphelet.

David Defeats the Philistines

17 When the Philistines heard that David had been made king over Israel, all

FAITH links

HURRY UP AND WAIT
2 SAMUEL 5

When it comes to waiting for something, how would you rate yourself on a scale of 1 to 10 (1 = not at all patient; 10 = very patient)? Several years passed between David's anointing as king and his taking the throne. He had several opportunities to force his way onto the throne. But he chose to be patient and wait for God to bring him to the throne.

Patience doesn't come overnight. One step to take on the path to patience is to let go of your expectations about when something should take place. Another step is to trust in God's timing.

Want to know how to trust God? Link here:

A Long Wait, Joshua 14:6–15, p. 294

A Shortcut, 1 Samuel 13:1–14, p. 369

Does Crime Pay? Psalm 37:1–7, p. 736

Think About Him, Isaiah 26:3, p. 926

Faith God Notices, Luke 18:35–43, p. 1406

A Different Kind of Fruit, Galatians 5:22–23, p. 1592

---

the Philistines went to look for him. But when David heard the news, he went down to the stronghold. 18 The Philistines came and camped in the Valley of Rephaim. 19 David asked the LORD, "Should I attack the Philistines? Will you hand them over to me?"

The LORD said to David, "Go! I will certainly hand them over to you."

20 So David went to Baal Perazim and defeated the Philistines there. David said, "Like a flood of water, the LORD has broken through my enemies in front of me." So David named the place Baal Perazim.ⁿ 21 The Philistines left their idols behind at Baal Perazim, so David and his men carried them away.

22 Once again the Philistines came and camped in the Valley of Rephaim. 23 When David prayed to the LORD, he answered, "Don't attack the Philistines from the front. Instead, go around and attack them in front of the balsam trees. 24 When you hear the sound of marching in the tops of the balsam trees, act quickly. I, the LORD, will have gone ahead of you to defeat the Philistine army." 25 So David did what the LORD commanded. He defeated the Philistines and chased them all the way from Gibeon to Gezer.

The Ark is Brought to Jerusalem

6 David again gathered all the chosen men of Israel—30,000 of them. 2 Then he and all his people went to Baalah in Judahⁿ to bring back the Ark of God. The Ark is called by the Name, the name of the LORD All-powerful, whose throne is between the gold creatures with wings. 3 They put the Ark of God on a new cart and brought it out of Abinadab's house on the hill. Uzzah and Ahio, sons of Abinadab, led the new cart 4 which had the Ark of God on it. Ahio was walking in front of it. 5 David and all the Israelites were celebrating in the presence of the LORD. They were playing wooden instruments: lyres, harps, tambourines, rattles and cymbals.

6 When David's men came to the threshing floor of Nacon, the oxen stumbled. So Uzzah reached out to steady the Ark of God. 7 The LORD was angry with

---

5:20 Baal Perazim This name means "the LORD breaks through".
6:2 Baalah in Judah Another name for Kiriath Jearim.

Uzzah and killed him because of what he did. So Uzzah died there beside the Ark of God. 8 David was angry because the LORD had killed Uzzah. Now that place is called the Punishment of Uzzah.

9 David was afraid of the LORD that day, and he said, "How can the Ark of the LORD come to me now?" 10 So David would not move the Ark of the LORD to be with him in Jerusalem. Instead, he took it to the house of Obed-Edom, a man from Gath. 11 The Ark of the LORD stayed in Obed-Edom's house for three months, and the LORD blessed Obed-Edom and all his family.

12 The people told David, "The LORD has blessed the family of Obed-Edom and all that belongs to him, because the Ark of God is there." So David went and brought it up from Obed-Edom's house to Jerusalem with joy. 13 When the men carrying the Ark of the LORD had walked six steps, David sacrificed a bull and a fat calf. 14 Then David danced with all his might before the LORD. He had on a holy linen robe. 15 David and all the Israelites shouted with joy and blew the trumpets as they brought the Ark of the LORD to the city.

16 As the Ark of the LORD came into the city, Saul's daughter Michal looked out of the window. When she saw David jumping and dancing in the presence of the LORD, she hated him.

17 David put up a tent for the Ark of the LORD, and then the Israelites put it in its place inside the tent. David offered whole burnt offerings and fellowship offerings before the LORD. 18 When David finished offering the whole burnt offerings and the fellowship offerings, he blessed the people in the name of the LORD All-powerful. 19 David gave a loaf of bread, a cake of dates and a cake of raisins to every Israelite, both men and women. Then all the people went home.

20 David went back to bless the people in his home, but Saul's daughter Michal came out to meet him. She said, "With what honour the king of Israel acted today! You took off your clothes in front of the servant girls of your officers like one who takes off his clothes without shame!"

21 Then David said to Michal, "I did it in the presence of the LORD. The LORD chose me, not your father or anyone from Saul's family. The LORD appointed me to be over Israel. So I will celebrate in the presence of the LORD. 22 Maybe I will lose even more honour, and maybe I will be brought down in my own opinion, but the girls you talk about will honour me!"

23 And Saul's daughter Michal had no children to the day she died.

6:21 Worship
How should you worship God?

David Wants to Build a Temple

7 King David was living in his palace, and the LORD had given him peace from all his enemies around him. 2 Then David said to Nathan the prophet, "Look, I am living in a palace made of cedar wood, but the Ark of God is in a tent!"

3 Nathan said to the king, "Go and do what you really want to do, because the LORD is with you."

4 But that night the LORD spoke his word to Nathan, 5 "Go and tell my servant David, 'This is what the LORD says: will you build a house for me to live in? 6 From the time I brought the Israelites out of Egypt until now I have not lived in a house. I have been moving around all this time with a tent as my home. 7 As I have moved with the Israelites, I have never said to the tribes, whom I commanded to take care of my people Israel, "Why haven't you built me a house of cedar?"'

8 "You must tell my servant David, 'This is what the LORD All-powerful says: I took you from the pasture and from tending the sheep and made you leader of my people Israel. 9 I have been with you everywhere you have gone and have defeated your enemies for you. I will make you as famous as any of the great people on the earth. 10 Also I will choose a place for my people Israel, and I will plant them so they can live in their own homes. They will not be bothered any more. Wicked people will no longer bother them as they have in the past 11 when I chose judges for my people Israel. But I will give you

2 Samuel 7:26

FAITH links

WHEN GOD SAYS NO
2 SAMUEL 7

Whatever plans you might make to go out with your friends, your parents have the right to veto those plans. That's a fancy way of saying that your mum and dad have the power to say no to something. David wanted to build a temple for God, but God said no to his plan. Even though David's desire to build was good, God knew that he wasn't the right man for the job. (Connect to this same story by reading 1 Chronicles 17, p. 541.)

If we say that God is our heavenly Father, that gives him veto power. He has the right to say no to our plans. Are you willing to trust that he knows what's best?

The Sacrifice, Genesis 22, p. 29

I'll Never Forget What's-His-Name, Deuteronomy 8, p. 239

Sitting on the Fence, 1 Kings 18, p. 464

The Foundation of Our Hope, Isaiah 31:1–8, p. 934

Prayer Priority, Luke 5:15–16, p. 1376

The "Quality" of Life, 2 Peter 1:5–8, p. 1708

---

peace from all your enemies. I also tell you that I will make your descendants kings of Israel after you.

12 "When you die and join your ancestors, I will make one of your sons the next king, and I will set up his kingdom. 13 He will build a house for me, and I will let his kingdom rule always. 14 I will be his father, and he will be my son. When he sins, I will use other people to punish him. They will be my whips. 15 I took away my love from Saul, whom I removed before you, but I will never stop loving your son. 16 But your family and your kingdom will continue always before me. Your throne will last for ever.'"

17 Nathan told David everything God had said in this vision.

David Prays to God

18 Then King David went in and sat in front of the LORD. David said, "Lord GOD, who am I? What is my family? Why did you bring me to this point? 19 But even this is not enough for you, Lord GOD. You have also made promises about my future family. This is not normal, Lord GOD.

20 "What more can I say to you, Lord GOD, since you know me, your servant, so well! 21 You have done this great thing because you said you would and because you wanted to, and you have let me know about it. 22 This is why you are great, Lord GOD! There is no one like you. There is no God except you. We have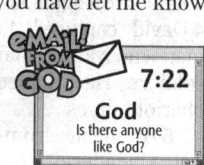

7:22 God Is there anyone like God?

heard all this ourselves! 23 There is no nation like your people Israel. They are the only people on earth that God chose to be his own. You made your name well known. You did great and wonderful miracles for them. You went ahead of them and forced other nations and their gods out of the land. You freed your people from slavery in Egypt. 24 You made the people of Israel your very own people for ever, and, LORD, you are their God.

25 "Now, LORD God, keep the promise for ever that you made about my family and me, your servant. Do what you have said. 26 Then you will be honoured always, and people will say, 'The LORD All-powerful is God over Israel!' And the family of your servant David will continue before you.

27 "LORD All-powerful, the God of Israel, you have said to me, 'I will make your family great.' So I, your servant, am brave enough to pray to you. 28 Lord GOD, you are God, and your words are true. And you have promised these good things to me, your servant. 29 Please, bless my family. Let it continue before you always. Lord GOD, you have said so. With your blessing let my family always be blessed."

David Wins Many Wars

8 Later, David defeated the Philistines, conquered them, and took the city of Metheg Ammah.

2 He also defeated the people of Moab. He made them lie on the ground, and then he used a rope to measure them. Those who were measured within two rope lengths were killed, but those who were within the next rope length were allowed to live. So the people of Moab became servants of David and gave him the payment he demanded.

3 David also defeated Hadadezer son of Rehob, king of Zobah, as he went to take control again at the Euphrates River. 4 David captured 1,000 chariots, 7,000 men who rode in chariots, and 20,000 foot soldiers. He crippled all but 100 of the chariot horses.

5 Arameans from Damascus came to help Hadadezer king of Zobah, but David killed 22,000 of them. 6 Then David put groups of soldiers in Damascus in Aram. The Arameans became David's servants and gave him the payment he demanded. The LORD gave David victory everywhere he went.

7 David took the shields of gold that had belonged to Hadadezer's officers and brought them to Jerusalem. 8 David also took many things made of bronze from Tebah and Berothai, which had been cities under Hadadezer's control.

9 Toi king of Hamath heard that David had defeated all the army of Hadadezer. 10 So Toi sent his son Joram to greet and congratulate King David for defeating Hadadezer. (Hadadezer had been at war with Toi.) Joram brought things made of silver, gold and bronze. 11 King David gave them to the LORD, along with the silver and gold he had taken from the other nations he had defeated. 12 These nations were Edom, Moab, Ammon, Philistia and Amalek. David also gave the LORD what he had taken from Hadadezer son of Rehob, king of Zobah.

13 David was famous after he returned from defeating 18,000 Arameans in the Valley of Salt. 14 He put groups of soldiers all over Edom, and all the Edomites became his servants. The LORD gave David victory everywhere he went.

FAITH links

FAIR ALL THE TIME?
2 SAMUEL 8:15

Do you treat everyone the same way? As a king, David was known to be fair to everyone. That meant he made good laws and was merciful towards those who were punished. He was able to do this because he trusted God to help him. Respecting God and others helps you to be fair not some of the time, but all of the time.

Show Some Respect, Leviticus 19:32, p. 161

Fairness for All, Deuteronomy 24:17, p. 258

Kind or Fair? 1 Samuel 30, p. 395

Service with a Smile, 1 Chronicles 6:31–49, p. 527

Seeing the Needs, Nehemiah 1, p. 625

I'll Be the Judge! 1 Corinthians 4:4–5, p. 1549

15 David was king over all Israel, and he did what was fair and right for all his people. 16 Joab son of Zeruiah was commander over the army. Jehoshaphat son of Ahilud was the recorder. 17 Zadok son of Ahitub and Abiathar son of Ahimelech were priests. Seraiah was the royal secretary. 18 Benaiah son of Jehoiada was over the Kerethites and Pelethites." And David's sons were priests.

David Helps Saul's Family

9 David asked, "Is anyone still left in Saul's family? I want to show kindness to that person for Jonathan's sake!"

9:1 Friendship Check out a friendship that outlasted death.

2 Now there was a servant named Ziba from Saul's family. So David's servants called Ziba to him. King David said to him, "Are you Ziba?"

He answered, "Yes, I am your servant."

3 The king asked, "Is anyone left in Saul's family? I want to show God's kindness to that person."

Ziba answered the king, "Jonathan has a son still living who is crippled in both feet."

4 The king asked Ziba, "Where is this son?"

Ziba answered, "He is at the house of Makir son of Ammiel in Lo Debar."

5 Then King David had servants bring Jonathan's son from the house of Makir son of Ammiel in Lo Debar. 6 Mephibosheth, Jonathan's son, came before David and bowed face down on the floor.

David said, "Mephibosheth!"

Mephibosheth said, "I am your servant."

7 David said to him, "Don't be afraid. I will be kind to you for your father Jonathan's sake. I will give you back all the land of your grandfather Saul, and you will always eat at my table."

8 Mephibosheth bowed to David again

8:18 Kerethites and Pelethites These were probably special units of the army that were responsible for the king's safety, a kind of palace guard.

FAITH links

LOYAL TO A FRIEND
2 SAMUEL 9

How long should you be loyal to a friend? Does loyalty end when a friend dies? David's best friend, Jonathan, had died. But David was kind to Jonathan's son, Mephibosheth, because of his loyalty to Jonathan. Long before, David and Jonathan made a promise of loyalty to each other and to each other's family. David faithfully kept that promise.

Loyalty is like a promise two people make to each other. You both promise to be faithful to each other and to care for one another. Loyalty doesn't have a time limit. Aren't you glad that it doesn't?

Are you good at keeping promises? Connect here for some hints:

A Special Promise, Numbers 30:1–2, p. 217

Read My Lips? Deuteronomy 26:16–19, p. 260

The Gift of Friendship, 1 Samuel 18:1–3; 19, p. 381

A Fair-weather Friend, Obadiah 7, p. 1209

The Right Ingredients, Micah 6:8, p. 1227

The Number One Rule, Mark 12:28–31, p. 1351

and said, "You are being very kind to me, your servant! And I am no better than a dead dog!"

9 Then King David called Saul's servant Ziba. David said to him, "I have given your master's grandson everything that belonged to Saul and his family. 10 You, your sons and your servants will farm the land and harvest the crops. Then your family will have food to eat. But Mephibosheth, your master's grandson, will always eat at my table."

(Now Ziba had fifteen sons and 20 servants.) 11 Ziba said to King David, "I, your servant, will do everything my master, the king, commands me."

So Mephibosheth ate at David's table as if he were one of the king's sons. 12 Mephibosheth had a young son named Mica. Everyone in Ziba's family became Mephibosheth's servants. 13 Mephibosheth lived in Jerusalem, because he always ate at the king's table. And he was crippled in both feet.

War with the Ammonites and Arameans

10 When Nahash king of the Ammonites died, his son Hanun became king after him. 2 David said, "Nahash was loyal to me, so I will be loyal to his son Hanun." So David sent his messengers to comfort Hanun about his father's death.

David's officers went to the land of the Ammonites. 3 But the Ammonite leaders said to Hanun, their master, "Do you think David wants to honour your father by sending men to comfort you? No! David sent them to study the city and spy it out and capture it!" 4 So Hanun arrested David's officers. To shame them he shaved off half their beards and cut off their clothes at the hips. Then he sent them away.

5 When the people told David, he sent messengers to meet his officers because they were very ashamed. King David said, "Stay in Jericho until your beards have grown back. Then come home."

6 The Ammonites knew that they had insulted David. So they hired 20,000 Aramean foot soldiers from Beth Rehob and Zobah. They also hired the king of Maacah with 1,000 men and 12,000 men from Tob.

7 When David heard about this, he sent Joab with the whole army. 8 The Ammonites came out and prepared for battle at the city gate. The Arameans from Zobah and Rehob and the men from Tob and Maacah were out in the field by themselves.

9 Joab saw that there were enemies both in front of him and behind him. So he chose some of the best soldiers of Israel and sent them out to fight the Arameans. 10 Joab put the rest of the army under the command of Abishai, his brother. Then he sent them out to fight the Ammonites. 11 Joab said to Abishai, "If the Arameans are too strong for me, you must help me. Or, if the Ammonites are too strong for you, I will help you. 12 Be strong. We must fight bravely for our people and the cities of our God. The LORD will do what he thinks is right."

13 Then Joab and the army with him went to attack the Arameans, and the Arameans ran away. 14 When the Ammonites saw that the Arameans were running away, they also ran away from Abishai and went back to their city. So Joab returned from the battle with the Ammonites and came to Jerusalem.

15 When the Arameans saw that Israel had defeated them, they came together into one big army. 16 Hadadezer sent messengers to bring the Arameans from east of the Euphrates River, and they went to Helam. Their leader was Shobach, the commander of Hadadezer's army.

17 When David heard about this, he gathered all the Israelites together. They crossed over the Jordan River and went to Helam. There the Arameans prepared for battle and attacked him. 18 But the Arameans ran away from the Israelites. David killed

> David said, "Nahash was loyal to me, so I will be loyal to his son Hanun."
> – 2 Samuel 10:2

700 Aramean chariot drivers and 40,000 Aramean horsemen. He also killed Shobach, the commander of the Aramean army.

19 When the kings who served Hadadezer saw that the Israelites had defeated them, they made peace with the Israelites and served them. And the Arameans were afraid to help the Ammonites again.

David Sins with Bathsheba

11 In the spring, when the kings normally went out to war, David sent out Joab, his servants and all the Israelites. They destroyed the Ammonites and attacked the city of Rabbah. But David stayed in Jerusalem. 2 One evening David got up from his bed and walked around on the roof[n] of his palace. While he was on the roof, he saw a woman bathing. She was very beautiful. 3 So David sent his servants to find out who she was. A servant answered, "That woman is Bathsheba daughter of Eliam. She is the wife of Uriah the Hittite." 4 So David sent messengers to bring Bathsheba to him. When she came to him, he had sexual relations with her. (Now Bathsheba had purified herself from her monthly period.) Then she went back to her house. 5 But Bathsheba became pregnant and sent word to David, saying, "I am pregnant."

6 So David sent a message to Joab: "Send Uriah the Hittite to me." And Joab sent Uriah to David. 7 When Uriah came to him, David asked him how Joab was, how the soldiers were and how the war was going. 8 Then David said to Uriah, "Go home and rest."

So Uriah left the palace, and the king sent a gift to him. 9 But Uriah did not go home. Instead, he slept outside the door of the palace as all the king's officers did.

10 The officers told David, "Uriah did not go home."

Then David said to Uriah, "You came from a long trip. Why didn't you go home?"

11 Uriah said to him, "The Ark and the soldiers of Israel and Judah are staying in tents. My master Joab and his officers are camping out in the fields. It isn't right for me to go home to eat and drink and have sexual relations with my wife!"

12 David said to Uriah, "Stay here today. Tomorrow I'll send you back to the battle." So Uriah stayed in Jerusalem that day and the next. 13 Then David called Uriah to come to see him, so Uriah ate and drank with David. David made Uriah drunk, but he still did not go home. That evening Uriah again slept with the king's officers.

14 The next morning David wrote a letter to Joab and sent it by Uriah. 15 In the letter David wrote, "Put Uriah on the front lines where the fighting is worst and leave him there alone. Let him be killed in battle."

16 Joab watched the city and saw where its strongest defenders were and put Uriah there. 17 When the men of the city came out to fight against Joab, some of David's men were killed. And Uriah the Hittite was one of them.

18 Then Joab sent David a complete account of the war. 19 Joab told the messenger, "Tell King David what happened in the war. 20 After you finish, the king may be angry and ask, 'Why did you go so near the city to fight? Didn't you know they would shoot arrows from the city wall? 21 Do you remember who killed Abimelech son of Jerub-Besheth?[n] It was a woman on the city wall. She threw a large stone for grinding grain on Abimelech and killed him there in Thebez. Why did you go so near the wall?' If King David asks that, tell him, 'Your servant Uriah the Hittite also died.'"

22 The messenger left and went to David and told him everything Joab had told him to say. 23 The messenger told David, "The men of Ammon were winning. They came out and attacked us in the field, but we fought them back to the city gate. 24 The archers on the city wall shot at your servants, and some of your

---

11:2 roof In Bible times houses were built with flat roofs. The roof was used for drying things such as flax and fruit. And it was used as an extra room, as a place for worship, and as a cool place to sleep in the summer.
11:21 Jerub-Besheth Another name for Gideon.

men were killed. Your servant Uriah the Hittite also died."

25 David said to the messenger, "Say this to Joab: 'Don't be upset about this. The sword kills everyone the same. Make a stronger attack against the city and capture it.' Encourage Joab with these words."

26 When Bathsheba heard that her husband was dead, she cried for him. 27 After she finished her time of sadness, David sent servants to bring her to his house. She became David's wife and gave birth to his son, but the LORD did not like what David had done.

David's Son Dies

12 The LORD sent Nathan to David. When he came to David, he said, "There were two men in a city. One was rich, but the other was poor. 2 The rich man had many sheep and cattle. 3 But the poor man had nothing except one little female lamb he had bought. The poor man fed the lamb, and it grew up with him and his children. It shared his food and drank from his cup and slept in his arms. The lamb was like a daughter to him.

4 "Then a traveller stopped to visit the rich man. The rich man wanted to feed the traveller, but he didn't want to take one of his own sheep or cattle. Instead, he took the lamb from the poor man and cooked it for his visitor."

5 David became very angry at the rich man. He said to Nathan, "As surely as the LORD lives, the man who did this should die! 6 He must pay for the lamb four times for doing such a thing. He had no mercy!"

7 Then Nathan said to David, "You are the man! This is what the LORD, the God of Israel, says: 'I appointed you king of Israel and saved you from Saul. 8 I gave you his kingdom and his wives. And I made you king of Israel and Judah. And if that had not been enough, I would have given you even more. 9 So why did you ignore the LORD's command? Why did you do what he says is wrong? You killed Uriah the Hittite with the sword of the Ammonites and took his wife to be your wife! 10 Now there will always be people in your family who will die by a sword, because you did not respect me; you took the wife of Uriah the Hittite for yourself!'

11 "This is what the LORD says: 'I am bringing trouble to you from your own family. While you watch, I will take your wives from you and give them to someone

---

FAITH links

OWN UP TO IT
2 SAMUEL 12:1-13

When someone tells you about something you've done wrong, do you usually own up to it? Or do you make excuses or try to find someone else to take the blame? That's called "playing the blame game". When David did wrong, he didn't play the blame game or excuse his way out of it. Instead, he owned up to it. God forgave him for his disobedience.

When God confronts us about something we've done wrong, he doesn't want excuses. He just wants us to admit that we were wrong. No matter what you do, God will forgive you. Just ask him.

A Priest Without Sin, Leviticus 4:3–7, p. 136

You're Out! 2 Kings 17:5–7, p. 501

Red to White, Isaiah 1:18, p. 896

Real Repentance, Jeremiah 4:1–4, p. 993

Just for the Asking, Romans 3:23–28, p. 1522

It's Guaranteed! 1 John 1:9–10, p. 1714

who is very close to you. He will have sexual relations with your wives, and everyone will know it. 12 You had sexual relations with Bathsheba in secret, but I will do this so all the people of Israel can see it.'"

13 Then David said to Nathan, "I have sinned against the LORD."

Nathan answered, "The LORD has taken away your sin. You will not die. 14 But what you did caused the LORD's enemies to lose all respect for him. For this reason the son who was born to you will die."

15 Then Nathan went home. And the LORD caused the son of David and Bathsheba, Uriah's widow, to be very sick. 16 David prayed to God for the baby. David refused to eat or drink. He went into his house and stayed there, lying on the ground all night. 17 The elders of David's family came to him and tried to pull him up from the ground, but he refused to get up or to eat food with them.

18 On the seventh day the baby died. David's servants were afraid to tell him that the baby was dead. They said, "Look, we tried to talk to David while the baby was alive, but he refused to listen to us. If we tell him the baby is dead, he may do something awful."

19 When David saw his servants whispering, he knew that the baby was dead. So he asked them, "Is the baby dead?"

They answered, "Yes, he is dead."

20 Then David got up from the floor, washed himself, put lotions on and changed his clothes. Then he went into the LORD's house to worship. After that, he went home and asked for something to eat. His servants gave him some food, and he ate.

21 David's servants said to him, "Why are you doing this? When the baby was still alive, you refused to eat and you cried. Now that the baby is dead, you get up and eat food."

22 David said, "While the baby was still alive, I refused to eat, and I cried. I thought, 'Who knows? Maybe the LORD will feel sorry for me and let the baby live.' 23 But now that the baby is dead, why should I go without food? I can't bring him back to life. Some day I will go to him, but he cannot come back to me."

24 Then David comforted Bathsheba his wife. He slept with her and had sexual relations with her. She became pregnant again and had another son, whom David named Solomon. The LORD loved Solomon. 25 The LORD sent word through Nathan the prophet to name the baby Jedidiah,*n* because the LORD loved the child.

David Captures Rabbah

26 Joab fought against Rabbah, a royal city of the Ammonites, and he was about to capture it. 27 Joab sent messengers to David and said, "I have fought against Rabbah and have captured its water supply. 28 Now bring the other soldiers together and attack this city. Capture it before I capture it myself and call it by my name!"

29 So David gathered all the army and went to Rabbah and fought against it and captured it. 30 David took the crown off their king's head and had it placed on his own head. That gold crown weighed about 35 kilogrammes, and it had valuable gems in it. And David took many valuable things from the city. 31 He also brought out the people of the city and forced them to work with saws, iron picks and axes. He also made them build with bricks. David did this to all the Ammonite cities. Then David and all his army returned to Jerusalem.

Amnon and Tamar

13 David had a son named Absalom and a son named Amnon. Absalom had a beautiful sister named Tamar, and Amnon loved her. 2 Tamar was a virgin. Amnon made himself sick just thinking about her, because he could not find any chance to be alone with her.

3 Amnon had a friend named Jonadab son of Shimeah, David's brother. Jonadab was a very clever man. 4 He asked Amnon, "Son of the king, why do you look so sad day after day? Tell me what's wrong!"

12:25 Jedidiah This name means "loved by the LORD."

Amnon told him, "I love Tamar, the sister of my half-brother Absalom."

5 Jonadab said to Amnon, "Go to bed and act as if you are sick. Then your father will come to see you. Tell him, 'Please let my sister Tamar come in and give me food to eat. Let her make the food in front of me so I can watch and eat it from her hand.'"

6 So Amnon went to bed and acted sick. When King David came in to see him, Amnon said to him, "Please let my sister Tamar come in. Let her make two of her special cakes for me while I watch. Then I will eat them from her hands."

7 David sent for Tamar in the palace, saying, "Go to your brother Amnon's house and make some food for him." 8 So Tamar went to her brother Amnon's house, and he was in bed. Tamar took some dough and pressed it together with her hands. She made some special cakes while Amnon watched. Then she baked them. 9 Next she took the pan and served him, but he refused to eat.

He said to his servants, "All of you, leave me alone!" So they all left him alone. 10 Amnon said to Tamar, "Bring the food into the bedroom so I may eat from your hand."

Tamar took the cakes she had made and brought them to her brother Amnon in the bedroom. 11 She went to him so he could eat from her hands, but Amnon grabbed her. He said, "Sister, come to bed with me."

12 Tamar said to him, "No, brother! Don't force me! This should never be done in Israel! Don't do this shameful thing! 13 I could never get rid of my shame! And you will be like the shameful fools in Israel! Please talk with the king, and he will let you marry me."

14 But Amnon refused to listen to her. He was stronger than she was, so he forced her to have sexual relations with him. 15 After that, Amnon hated Tamar. He hated her more than he had loved her before. Amnon said to her, "Get up and leave!"

16 Tamar said to him, "No! Sending me away would be worse than what you've already done!"

But he refused to listen to her. 17 He called his young servant back in and said, "Get this woman out of here and away from me! Lock the door after her." 18 So his servant led her out of the room and bolted the door after her.

Tamar was wearing a special robe with long sleeves, because the king's virgin daughters wore this kind of robe. 19 To show how upset she was, Tamar put ashes on her head and tore her special robe and put her hand on her head. Then she went away, crying loudly.

20 Absalom, Tamar's brother, said to her, "Has Amnon, your brother, forced you to have sexual relations with him? For now, sister, be quiet. He is your half-brother. Don't let this upset you so much!" So Tamar lived in her brother Absalom's house and was sad and lonely.

21 When King David heard the news, he was very angry. 22 Absalom did not say a word, good or bad, to Amnon. But he hated Amnon for disgracing his sister Tamar.

Absalom's Revenge

23 Two years later Absalom had some men come to Baal Hazor, near Ephraim, to cut the wool from his sheep. Absalom invited all the king's sons to come also. 24 Absalom went to the king and said, "I have men coming to cut the wool. Please come with your officers and join me."

25 King David said to Absalom, "No, my son. We won't all go, because it would be too much trouble for you." Although Absalom begged David, he would not go, but he did give his blessing.

26 Absalom said, "If you don't want to come, then please let my brother Amnon come with us."

King David asked, "Why should he go with you?"

27 Absalom kept begging David until he let Amnon and all the king's sons go with Absalom.

28 Then Absalom commanded his servants, "Watch Amnon. When he is drunk, I will tell you, 'Kill Amnon.' Right then, kill him! Don't be afraid, because I have commanded you! Be strong and brave!" 29 So Absalom's young men killed Amnon as

Absalom commanded, but all of David's other sons got on their mules and escaped.

30 While the king's sons were on their way, the news came to David, "Absalom has killed all of the king's sons! Not one of them is left alive!" 31 King David tore his clothes and lay on the ground to show his sadness. All his servants standing nearby tore their clothes also.

32 Jonadab son of Shimeah, David's brother, said to David, "Don't think all the young men, your sons, are killed. No, only Amnon is dead! Absalom has planned this ever since Amnon forced his sister Tamar to have sexual relations with him. 33 My master and king, don't think that all of the king's sons are dead. Only Amnon is dead!"

34 In the meantime Absalom had run away.

A guard standing on the city wall saw many people coming from the other side of the hill. 35 So Jonadab said to King David, "Look, I was right! The king's sons are coming!"

36 As soon as Jonadab had said this, the king's sons arrived, crying loudly. David and all his servants began crying also. 37 David cried for his son every day.

But Absalom ran away to Talmai*n* son of Ammihud, the king of Geshur. 38 After Absalom ran away to Geshur, he stayed there for three years. 39 When King David got over Amnon's death, he missed Absalom greatly.

Joab Sends a Wise Woman to David

14 Joab son of Zeruiah knew that King David missed Absalom very much. 2 So Joab sent messengers to Tekoa to bring a wise woman from there. He said to her, "Pretend to be very sad. Put on funeral clothes and don't put lotion on yourself. Act like a woman who has been crying many days for someone who died. 3 Then go to the king and say these words." Then Joab told her what to say.

4 So the woman from Tekoa spoke to the king. She bowed face down on the ground to show respect and said, "My king, help me!"

5 King David asked her, "What is the matter?"

The woman said, "I am a widow; my husband is dead. 6 I had two sons. They were out in the field fighting, and no one was there to stop them. So one son killed the other son. 7 Now all the family group is against me. They said to me, 'Bring the son who killed his brother so we may kill him for killing his brother. That way we will also get rid of the one who would receive what belonged to his father.' My son is like the last spark of a fire. He is all I have left. If they kill him, my husband's name and property will be gone from the earth."

8 Then the king said to the woman, "Go home. I will take care of this for you."

9 The woman of Tekoa said to him, "Let the blame be on me and my father's family. My master and king, you and your throne are innocent."

10 King David said, "Bring me anyone who says anything bad to you. Then he won't bother you again."

11 The woman said, "Please promise in the name of the LORD your God. Then my relative who has the duty of punishing a murderer won't add to the destruction by killing my son."

David said, "As surely as the LORD lives, no one will hurt your son. Not one hair from his head will fall to the ground."

12 The woman said, "Let me say something to you, my master and king." The king said, "Speak."

13 Then the woman said, "Why have you decided this way against the people of God? When you judge this way, you show that you are guilty for not bringing back your son who was forced to leave

David cried for his son every day.
— 2 Samuel 13:37

13:37 Talmai He was Absalom's grandfather.

FAITH links

HELP TO UNDERSTAND
2 SAMUEL 14

Have you ever heard the phrase "You can't see the wood for the trees"? That means you're so close to something you can't see it for what it is. Sometimes we can't see the wood for the trees about situations in life. King David couldn't understand the problems within his own family. A wise woman went to David with helpful advice.

Part of learning to listen to God is learning to listen to people who provide wise advice. God brings these people into your life to help you understand his truths. As you pay attention to what you hear, your faith will grow.

Surf these links to see how your faith can grow:

The Cloud Guide, Numbers 9:15–23, p. 188

Facts About Following, Joshua 6, p. 283

The Right Thing to Do, 1 Samuel 26, p. 391

Plan for Success, 1 Chronicles 14:8–17, p. 538

Like Silver, Psalm 12:6–8, p. 717

Just Like a Tree, Colossians 1:23, p. 1621

---

home. 14 We will all die some day. We're like water spilled on the ground; no one can gather it back. But God doesn't take away life. Instead, he plans ways that those who have been sent away will not have to stay away from him! 15 My master and king, I came to say this to you because the people have made me afraid! I thought, 'Let me talk to the king. Maybe he will do what I ask. 16 Maybe he will listen. Perhaps he will save me from those who want to keep both me and my son from getting what God gave us.'

17 "Now I say, 'May the words of my master the king give me rest. Like an angel of God, you know what is good and what is bad. May the LORD your God be with you!'"

18 Then King David said, "Do not hide the truth. Answer me one question."

The woman said, "My master the king, please ask your question."

19 The king said, "Did Joab tell you to say all these things?"

The woman answered, "As you live, my master the king, no one could avoid that question. You are right. Your servant Joab did tell me to say these things. 20 Joab did it so you would see things differently. My master, you are wise like an angel of God who knows everything that happens on earth."

Absalom Returns to Jerusalem

21 The king said to Joab, "Look, I will do what I promised. Bring back the young man Absalom."

22 Joab bowed face down on the ground and blessed the king. Then he said, "Today I know you are pleased with me, because you have done what I asked."

23 Then Joab got up and went to Geshur and brought Absalom back to Jerusalem. 24 But King David said, "Absalom must go to his own house. He may not come to see me." So Absalom went to his own house and did not go to see the king.

25 Absalom was greatly praised for his handsome appearance. No man in Israel was as handsome as he. No blemish was on him from his head to his foot. 26 At the end of every year, Absalom would cut his hair, because it became too heavy. When

he weighed it, it would weigh about 2 kilogrammes by the royal measure.

27 Absalom had three sons and one daughter. His daughter's name was also Tamar, and she was a beautiful woman. 28 Absalom lived in Jerusalem for two full years without seeing King David. 29 Then Absalom sent for Joab so he could send him to the king, but Joab would not come. Absalom sent a message a second time, but Joab still refused to come. 30 Then Absalom said to his servants, "Look, Joab's field is next to mine, and he has barley growing there. Go and burn it." So Absalom's servants set fire to Joab's field.

31 Then Joab went to Absalom's house and said to him, "Why did your servants burn my field?"

32 Absalom said to Joab, "I sent a message to you, asking you to come here. I wanted to send you to the king to ask him why he brought me home from Geshur. It would have been better for me to stay there! Now let me see the king. If I have sinned, he can put me to death!"

33 So Joab went to the king and told him Absalom's words. Then the king called for Absalom. Absalom came and bowed face down on the ground before the king, and the king kissed him.

Absalom Plans to Take David's Kingdom

15 After this, Absalom got a chariot and horses for himself and 50 men to run before him. 2 Absalom would get up early and stand near the city gate.ⁿ Anyone who had a problem for the king to settle would come here. When someone came, Absalom would call out and say, "What city are you from?"

The person would answer, "I'm from one of the tribes of Israel."

3 Then Absalom would say, "Look, your claims are right, but the king has no one to listen to you." 4 Absalom would also say, "I wish someone would make me judge in this land! Then people with problems could come to me, and I could help them get justice."

5 People would come near Absalom to bow to him. When they did, Absalom would reach out his hand and take hold of them and kiss them. 6 Absalom did that to all the Israelites who came to King David for decisions. In this way, Absalom stole the hearts of all Israel.

7 After four years Absalom said to King David, "Please let me go to Hebron. I want to carry out my promise that I made to the LORD 8 while I was living in Geshur in Aram. I said, 'If the LORD takes me back to Jerusalem, I will worship him in Hebron.'"

9 The king said, "Go in peace."

So Absalom went to Hebron. 10 But he sent secret messengers through all the tribes of Israel. They told the people, "When you hear the trumpets, say this: 'Absalom is the king at Hebron!'"

11 Absalom had invited 200 men to go with him. So they went from Jerusalem with him, but they didn't know what he was planning. 12 While Absalom was offering sacrifices, he sent for Ahithophel, one of the people who advised David, to come from his home town of Giloh. So Absalom's plans were working very well. More and more people began to support him.

13 A messenger came to David, saying, "The Israelites are giving their loyalty to Absalom."

14 Then David said to all his officers who were with him in Jerusalem, "We must leave quickly! If we don't, we won't be able to get away from Absalom. We must hurry before he catches us and destroys us and kills the people of Jerusalem."

15 The king's officers said to him, "We will do anything you say."

16 The king set out with everyone in his house, but he left ten slave women to take care of the palace. 17 The king left with all his people following him, and they stopped at a house far away. 18 All the king's servants passed by him—the Kerethites and Pelethites,ⁿ all those from

---

15:2 city gate People came here to conduct business. Public meetings and court cases were also held here.

15:18 Kerethites and Pelethites These were probably special units of the army that were responsible for the king's safety, a kind of palace guard.

Gath, and the 600 men who had followed him.

19 The king said to Ittai, a man from Gath, "Why are you also going with us? Turn back and stay with King Absalom because you are a foreigner. This is not your homeland. 20 You joined me only a short time ago. Should I make you wander with us when I don't even know where I'm going? Turn back and take your brothers with you. May kindness and loyalty be shown to you."

21 But Ittai said to the king, "As surely as the LORD lives and as you live, I will stay with you, whether it means life or death."

22 David said to Ittai, "Go, march on." So Ittai from Gath and all his people with their children marched on. 23 All the people cried loudly as everyone passed by. King David crossed the Kidron Valley, and then all the people went on to the desert. 24 Zadok and all the Levites with him carried the Ark of the Agreement with God. They set it down, and Abiathar offered sacrifices until all the people had left the city.

25 The king said to Zadok, "Take the Ark of God back into the city. If the LORD is pleased with me, he will bring me back and will let me see both it and Jerusalem again. 26 But if the LORD says he is not pleased with me, I am ready. He can do what he wants with me."

27 The king also said to Zadok the priest, "Aren't you a seer? Go back to the city in peace and take your son Ahimaaz and Abiathar's son Jonathan with you. 28 I will wait near the crossings into the desert until I hear from you." 29 So Zadok and Abiathar took the Ark of God back to Jerusalem and stayed there.

30 David went up the Mount of Olives, crying as he went. He covered his head and went barefoot. All the people with David covered their heads also and cried as they went. 31 Someone told David, "Ahithophel is one of the people with Absalom who made secret plans against you."

So David prayed, "LORD, please make Ahithophel's advice foolish."

32 When David reached the top of the mountain where people used to worship God, Hushai the Arkite came to meet him. Hushai's coat was torn, and there was dust on his head to show how sad he was. 33 David said to Hushai, "If you go with me, you will be just one more person for me to take care of. 34 But if you return to the city, you can make Ahithophel's advice useless. Tell Absalom, 'I am your servant, my king. In the past I served your father, but now I will serve you.' 35 The priests Zadok and Abiathar will be with you. Tell them everything you hear in the royal palace. 36 Zadok's son Ahimaaz and Abiathar's son Jonathan are with them. Send them to tell me everything you hear." 37 So David's friend Hushai entered Jerusalem just as Absalom arrived.

Ziba Meets David

16 When David had passed a short way over the top of the Mount of Olives, Ziba, Mephibosheth's servant, met him. Ziba had a row of donkeys loaded with 200 loaves of bread, 100 cakes of raisins, 100 cakes of figs and leather bags full of wine. 2 The king asked Ziba, "What are these things for?"

Ziba answered, "The donkeys are for your family to ride. The bread and cakes of figs are for the servants to eat. And the wine is for anyone to drink who might become weak in the desert."

3 The king asked, "Where is Mephibosheth?"

Ziba answered him, "Mephibosheth is staying in Jerusalem because he thinks, 'Today the Israelites will give my father's kingdom back to me!'"

4 Then the king said to Ziba, "All right. Everything that belonged to Mephibosheth, I now give to you!"

Ziba said, "I bow to you. I hope I will always be able to please you."

Shimei Curses David

5 As King David came to Bahurim, a man came out and cursed him. He was from Saul's family group, and his name was Shimei son of Gera. 6 He threw stones at David and his officers, but the people and soldiers gathered all around

David. 7 Shimei cursed David, saying, "Get out, get out, you murderer, you troublemaker. 8 The LORD is punishing you for the people in Saul's family you killed! You took Saul's place as king, but now the LORD has given the kingdom to your son Absalom! Now you are ruined because you are a murderer!"

9 Abishai son of Zeruiah said to the king, "Why should this dead dog curse you, the king? Let me go over and cut off his head!"

10 But the king answered, "This does not concern you, sons of Zeruiah! If he is cursing me because the LORD told him to, who can question him?"

11 David also said to Abishai and all his officers, "My own son is trying to kill me! This man is a Benjaminite and has more right to kill me! Leave him alone, and let him curse me because the LORD told him to do this. 12 Maybe the LORD will see my misery and repay me with something good for Shimei's curses today!"

13 So David and his men went on down the road, but Shimei followed on the nearby hillside. He kept cursing David and throwing stones and earth at him. 14 When the king and all his people arrived at the Jordan, they were very tired, so they rested there.

15 Meanwhile, Absalom, Ahithophel and all the Israelites arrived at Jerusalem. 16 David's friend Hushai the Arkite came to Absalom and said to him, "Long live the king! Long live the king!"

17 Absalom asked, "Why are you not loyal to your friend David? Why didn't you leave Jerusalem with your friend?"

18 Hushai said, "I belong to the one chosen by the LORD and by these people and everyone in Israel. I will stay with you. 19 In the past I served your father. So whom should I serve now? David's son! I will serve you as I served him."

Ahithophel's Advice

20 Absalom said to Ahithophel, "Tell us what we should do."

> If he is cursing me because the LORD told him to, who can question him?
> – 2 Samuel 16:10

21 Ahithophel said, "Your father left behind some of his slave women to take care of the palace. Have sexual relations with them. Then all Israel will hear that your father is your enemy, and all your people will be encouraged to give you more support." 22 So they put up a tent for Absalom on the roof[n] of the palace where everyone in Israel could see it. And Absalom had sexual relations with his father's slave women.

23 At that time people thought Ahithophel's advice was as reliable as God's own word. Both David and Absalom thought it was that reliable.

17 Ahithophel said to Absalom, "Let me choose 12,000 men and chase David tonight. 2 I'll catch him while he is tired and weak, and I'll frighten him so all his people will run away. But I'll kill only King David. 3 Then I'll bring everyone back to you. If the man you are looking for is dead, everyone else will return safely." 4 This plan seemed good to Absalom and to all the leaders of Israel.

5 But Absalom said, "Now call Hushai the Arkite, so I can hear what he says." 6 When Hushai came to Absalom, Absalom said to him, "This is the plan Ahithophel gave. Should we follow it? If not, tell us."

7 Hushai said to Absalom, "Ahithophel's advice is not good this time." 8 Hushai added, "You know your father and his men are strong. They are as angry as a bear that is robbed of its cubs. Your father is a skilled fighter. He won't stay all night with the army. 9 He is probably already hiding in a cave or some other place. If the first attack fails, people will hear the news and think, 'Absalom's followers are losing!' 10 Then even the men who are as brave as lions will be frightened, because all the Israelites know

---

16:22 roof In Bible times houses were built with flat roofs. The roof was used for drying things such as flax and fruit. And it was used as an extra room, as a place for worship and as a place to sleep in the summer.

your father is a fighter. They know his men are brave!

11 "This is what I suggest: gather all the Israelites from Dan to Beersheba." There will be as many people as grains of sand by the sea. Then you yourself must go into the battle. **12** We will go to David wherever he is hiding. We will fall on him as dew falls on the ground. We will kill him and all of his men so that no one will be left alive. **13** If David escapes into a city, all the Israelites will bring ropes to that city and pull it into the valley. Not a stone will be left!"

14 Absalom and all the Israelites said, "The advice of Hushai the Arkite is better than that of Ahithophel." (The LORD had planned to destroy the good advice of Ahithophel so the LORD could bring disaster on Absalom.)

15 Hushai told Zadok and Abiathar, the priests, what Ahithophel had suggested to Absalom and the elders of Israel. He also reported to them what he himself had suggested. Hushai said, **16** "Quickly! Send a message to David. Tell him not to stay tonight at the crossings into the

---

17:11 Dan to Beersheba Dan was the city farthest north in Israel, and Beersheba was the city farthest south. So this means all the people of Israel.

I CAN'T DO IT!

Do you avoid trying something new because you're afraid it will be too hard? Devon, aged 9, is having a problem just like that. Devon is struggling to develop a new skill, and it's not going very well. Let him tell you about it.

Devon

Piano lessons. I've been taking them for over a year now. My mum thinks I'm going to be a great musician someday, but I'm not. I'm terrible. Every other note I play is wrong. The piano is just too hard. I want to quit, but I don't know what to tell my mum. I guess I'll just tell her that I'll never be any good.

Sounds like Devon's having a tough time. It would be nice to be able to say that his lessons will get easier, but that's not necessarily so. What is true is that Devon's reward for sticking with them will be worth the work. Check out what Proverbs 13:4, p. 843, says about those who continue to work hard. Then take a look at the tips in the Livin' It page on the need to keep going when the going gets tough! (Check out Job 17:9, p. 679.)

Sticking with something is called perseverance. God likes it when we persevere. As a result, he makes all kinds of good things happen if we refuse to give up when things get tough.

desert but to cross over the Jordan River at once. If he crosses the river, he and all his people won't be destroyed."

17 Jonathan and Ahimaaz were waiting at En Rogel. They did not want to be seen going into the city, so a servant girl would go out to them and give them messages. Then Jonathan and Ahimaaz would go and tell King David.

18 But a boy saw Jonathan and Ahimaaz and told Absalom. So Jonathan and Ahimaaz left quickly and went to a man's house in Bahurim. He had a well in his courtyard, and they climbed down into it. 19 The man's wife spread a sheet over the opening of the well and covered it with grain. No one could tell that anyone was hiding there.

20 Absalom's servants came to the woman at the house and asked, "Where are Ahimaaz and Jonathan?"

She said to them, "They have already crossed the brook."

Absalom's servants then went to look for Jonathan and Ahimaaz, but they could not find them. So they went back to Jerusalem.

21 After Absalom's servants left, Jonathan and Ahimaaz climbed out of the well and went to tell King David. They said, "Hurry, cross over the river! Ahithophel has said these things against you!" 22 So David and all his people crossed the Jordan River. By dawn, everyone had crossed the Jordan.

23 When Ahithophel saw that the Israelites did not accept his advice, he saddled his donkey and went to his home town. He left orders for his family and property, and then he hanged himself. He died and was buried in his father' tomb.

War Between David and Absalom

24 David arrived at Mahanaim. And Absalom and all his Israelites crossed over the Jordan River. 25 Absalom had made Amasa captain of the army instead of Joab. Amasa was the son of a man named Jether the Ishmaelite. Amasa's mother was Abigail daughter of Nahash and sister of Zeruiah, Joab's mother. 26 Absalom and the Israelites camped in the land of Gilead.

27 Shobi, Makir and Barzillai were at Mahanaim when David arrived. Shobi son of Nahash was from the Ammonite town of Rabbah. Makir son of Ammiel was from Lo Debar, and Barzillai was from Rogelim in Gilead. 28 They brought beds, bowls, clay pots, wheat, barley, flour, roasted grain, beans, small peas, 29 honey, milk curds, sheep and cheese made from cows' milk for David and his people. They said, "The people are hungry and tired and thirsty in the desert."

18 David counted his men and placed over them commanders of thousands and commanders of hundreds. 2 He sent the troops out in three groups. Joab commanded one-third of the men. Joab's brother Abishai son of Zeruiah commanded another third. And Ittai from Gath commanded the last third. King David said to them, "I will also go with you."

3 But the men said, "You must not go with us! If we run away in the battle, Absalom's men won't care. Even if half of us are killed, Absalom's men won't care. But you're worth 10,000 of us! You can help us most by staying in the city."

4 The king said to his people, "I will do what you think is best." So the king stood at the side of the gate as the army went out in groups of 100 and 1,000.

5 The king commanded Joab, Abishai and Ittai, "Be gentle with young Absalom for my sake." Everyone heard the king's orders to the commanders about Absalom.

6 David's army went out into the field against Absalom's Israelites, and they fought in the forest of Ephraim. 7 There David's army defeated the Israelites. Many died that day—20,000 men. 8 The battle spread through all the country, but that day more men died in the forest than in the fighting.

Absalom Dies

9 Then Absalom happened to meet David's troops. As Absalom was riding his mule, it went under the thick branches of a large oak tree. Absalom's head got caught in the tree, and his mule ran out

from under him. So Absalom was left hanging above the ground.

10 When one of the men saw it happen, he told Joab, "I saw Absalom hanging in an oak tree!"

11 Joab said to him, "You saw him? Why didn't you kill him and let him fall to the ground? I would have given you a belt and ten pieces of silver!"

12 The man answered, "I wouldn't touch the king's son even if you gave me 1,000 pieces of silver. We heard the king command you, Abishai and Ittai, 'Be careful not to hurt young Absalom.' 13 If I had killed him, the king would have found out, and you would not have protected me!"

14 Joab said, "I won't waste time here with you!" Absalom was still alive in the oak tree, so Joab took three spears and stabbed him in the heart. 15 Ten young men who carried Joab's armour also gathered around Absalom and struck him and killed him.

16 Then Joab blew the trumpet, so the troops stopped chasing the Israelites. 17 Then Joab's men took Absalom's body and threw it into a large pit in the forest and filled the pit with many stones. All the Israelites ran away to their homes.

18 When Absalom was alive, he had set up a pillar for himself in the King's Valley. He said, "I have no son to keep my name alive." So he named the pillar after himself, and it is called Absalom's Monument even today.

19 Ahimaaz son of Zadok said to Joab, "Let me run and take the news to King David. I'll tell him the LORD has saved him from his enemies."

20 Joab answered Ahimaaz, "No, you are not the one to take the news today. You may do it another time, but do not take it today, because the king's son is dead."

21 Then Joab said to a man from Cush, "Go, tell the king what you have seen." The Cushite bowed to Joab and ran to tell David.

22 But Ahimaaz son of Zadok begged Joab again, "No matter what happens, please let me go along with the Cushite!"

Joab said, "Son, why do you want to carry the news? You won't get any reward."

23 Ahimaaz answered, "No matter what happens, I will run."

So Joab said to Ahimaaz, "Run!" Then Ahimaaz ran by way of the Jordan Valley and passed the Cushite.

24 David was sitting between the inner and outer gates of the city. The watchman went up to the roof of the gate by the walls, and as he looked up, he saw a man running alone. 25 He shouted the news to the king.

The king said, "If he is alone, he is bringing good news!"

The man came nearer and nearer to the city. 26 Then the watchman saw another man running, and he called to the gatekeeper, "Look! Another man is running alone!"

The king said, "He is also bringing good news!"

27 The watchman said, "I think the first man runs like Ahimaaz son of Zadok."

The king said, "Ahimaaz is a good man. He must be bringing good news!"

28 Then Ahimaaz called a greeting to the king. He bowed face down on the ground before the king and said, "Praise the LORD your God! The LORD has defeated those who were against you, my king."

29 The king asked, "Is young Absalom all right?"

Ahimaaz answered, "When Joab sent me, I saw some great excitement, but I don't know what it was."

30 The king said, "Step over here and wait." So Ahimaaz stepped aside and stood there.

31 Then the Cushite arrived. He said, "Master and king, hear the good news! Today the LORD has punished those who were against you!"

32 The king asked the Cushite, "Is young Absalom all right?"

The Cushite answered, "May your enemies and all who come to hurt you be like that young man!"

33 Then the king was very upset, and he went to the room over the city gate and cried. As he went, he cried out, "My son Absalom, my son Absalom! I wish I had

died and not you. Absalom, my son, my son!"

Joab Scolds David

19 People told Joab, "Look, the king is sad and crying because of Absalom." 2 David's army had won the battle that day. But it became a very sad day for all the people, because they heard that the king was very sad for his son. 3 The people came into the city quietly that day. They were like an army that had been defeated in battle and had run away. 4 The king covered his face and cried loudly, "My son Absalom! Absalom, my son, my son!"

5 Joab went into the king's house and said, "Today you have shamed all your men. They saved your life and the lives of your sons, daughters, wives and slave women. 6 You have shamed them because you love those who hate you, and you hate those who love you. Today you have made it clear that your commanders and men mean nothing to you. What if Absalom had lived and all of us were dead? I can see you would be pleased. 7 Now go out and encourage your servants. I swear by the LORD that if you don't go out, no man will be left with you by tonight! That will be worse than all the troubles you have had from your youth until today."

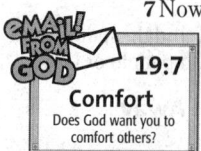

19:7 Comfort Does God want you to comfort others?

8 So the king went to the city gate.[n] When the news spread that the king was at the gate, everyone came to see him.

David Goes Back to Jerusalem

All the Israelites who had followed Absalom had run away to their homes. 9 People in all the tribes of Israel began to argue, saying, "The king saved us from the Philistines and our other enemies, but he left the country because of Absalom. 10 We appointed Absalom to rule us, but now he has died in battle. We should make David the king again."

11 King David sent a message to Zadok and Abiathar, the priests, that said, "Speak to the elders of Judah. Say, 'Even in my house I have heard what all the Israelites are saying. So why are you the last tribe to bring the king back to his palace? 12 You are my brothers, my own family. Why are you the last tribe to bring back the king?' 13 And say to Amasa, 'You are part of my own family. May God punish me terribly if I don't make you commander of the army in Joab's place!'"

14 David touched the hearts of all the people of Judah at once. They sent a message to the king that said, "Return with all your men." 15 Then the king returned as far as the Jordan River. The men of Judah came to Gilgal to meet him and to bring him across the Jordan.

16 Shimei son of Gera, a Benjaminite who lived in Bahurim, hurried down with the men of Judah to meet King David. 17 With Shimei came 1,000 Benjaminites. Ziba, the servant from Saul's family, also came, bringing his fifteen sons and 20 servants with him. They all hurried to the Jordan River to meet the king. 18 The people went across the Jordan to help bring the king's family back to Judah and to do whatever the king wanted. As the king was crossing the river, Shimei son of Gera came to him and bowed face down on the ground in front of the king. 19 He said to the king, "My master, don't hold me guilty. Don't remember the wrong I did when you left Jerusalem! Don't hold it against me. 20 I know I have sinned. That is why I am the first person from Joseph's family to come down and meet you today, my master and king!"

21 But Abishai son of Zeruiah said, "Shimei should die because he cursed you, the LORD's appointed king!"

22 David said, "This does not concern you, sons of Zeruiah! Today you're against me! No one will be put to death in Israel today. Today I know I am king over Israel!" 23 Then the king promised Shimei, "You won't die."

24 Mephibosheth, Saul's grandson, also went down to meet King David. Mephibosheth had not cared for his feet, cut

---

19:8 city gate People came here to conduct business. Public meetings and court cases were also held here.

his beard or washed his clothes from the time the king had left Jerusalem until he returned safely. 25 When Mephibosheth came from Jerusalem to meet the king, the king asked him, "Mephibosheth, why didn't you go with me?"

26 He answered, "My master, my servant Ziba tricked me! I said to Ziba, 'I am crippled, so saddle a donkey. Then I will ride it so I can go with the king.' 27 But he lied about me to you. You, my master and king, are like an angel from God. Do what you think is good. 28 You could have killed all my grandfather's family. Instead, you put me with those people who eat at your own table. So I don't have a right to ask anything more from the king!"

29 The king said to him, "Don't say anything more. I have decided that you and Ziba will divide the land."

30 Mephibosheth said to the king, "Let Ziba take all the land now that my master the king has arrived safely home."

31 Barzillai of Gilead came down from Rogelim to cross the Jordan River with the king. 32 Barzillai was a very old man, 80 years old. He had taken care of the king when David was staying at Mahanaim, because Barzillai was a very rich man. 33 David said to Barzillai, "Cross the river with me. Come with me to Jerusalem, and I will take care of you."

19:33 Friendship
How should you care for your friends?

34 But Barzillai answered the king, "Do you know how old I am? Do you think I can go with you to Jerusalem? 35 I am 80 years old! I am too old to taste what I eat or drink. I am too old to hear the voices of men and women singers. Why should you be bothered with me? 36 I am not worthy of a reward from you, but I will cross the Jordan River with you. 37 Then let me go back so I may die in my own city near the grave of my father and mother. But here is Kimham, your servant. Let him go with you, my master and king. Do with him whatever you want."

38 The king answered, "Kimham will go with me. I will do for him anything you wish, and I will do anything for you that you wish." 39 The king kissed Barzillai and blessed him. Then Barzillai returned home, and the king and all the people crossed the Jordan.

40 When the king crossed over to Gilgal, Kimham went with him. All the troops of Judah and half the troops of Israel led David across the river.

41 Soon all the Israelites came to the king and said to him, "Why did our relatives, the people of Judah, steal you away? Why did they bring you and your family across the Jordan River with your men?"

42 All the people of Judah answered the Israelites, "We did this because the king is our close relative. Why are you angry about it? We have not eaten food at the king's expense or taken anything for ourselves!"

43 The Israelites answered the people of Judah, "We have ten tribes in the kingdom, so we have more right to David than you do! But you ignored us! We were the first ones to talk about bringing our king back!"

But the people of Judah spoke even more unkindly than the people of Israel.

Sheba Leads Israel Away from David

20 It happened that a troublemaker named Sheba son of Bicri from the tribe of Benjamin was there. He blew the trumpet and said:

"We have no share in David!
We have no part in the son of Jesse!
People of Israel, let's go home!"

2 So all the Israelites left David and followed Sheba son of Bicri. But the people of Judah stayed with their king all the way from the Jordan River to Jerusalem.

3 David came back to his palace in Jerusalem. He had left ten of his slave women there to take care of the palace. Now he put them in a locked house. He gave them food, but he did not have sexual relations with them. So they lived like widows until they died.

4 The king said to Amasa, "Tell the

men of Judah to meet with me in three days, and you must also be here." 5 So Amasa went to call the men of Judah together, but he took more time than the king had said.

6 David said to Abishai, "Sheba son of Bicri is more dangerous to us than Absalom was. Take my men and chase him before he finds walled cities and escapes from us." 7 So Joab's men, the Kerethites and the Pelethites,[n] and all the soldiers went with Abishai. They went out from Jerusalem to chase Sheba son of Bicri.

8 When Joab and the army came to the great rock at Gibeon, Amasa came out to meet them. Joab was wearing his uniform, and at his waist he wore a belt that held his sword in its case. As Joab stepped forwards, his sword fell out of its case. 9 Joab asked Amasa, "Brother, is everything all right with you?" Then with his right hand he took Amasa by the beard to kiss him. 10 Amasa was not watching the sword in Joab's hand. So Joab pushed the sword into Amasa's stomach, causing Amasa's insides to spill onto the ground. Joab did not have to stab Amasa again; he was already dead. Then Joab and his brother Abishai continued to chase Sheba son of Bicri.

11 One of Joab's young men stood by Amasa's body and said, "Everyone who is for Joab and David should follow Joab!" 12 Amasa lay in the middle of the road, covered with his own blood. When the young man saw that everyone was stopping to look at the body, he dragged it from the road, laid it in a field and put a cloth over it. 13 After Amasa's body was taken off the road, all the men followed Joab to chase Sheba son of Bicri.

14 Sheba went through all the tribes of Israel to Abel Beth Maacah. All the Berites also came together and followed him. 15 So Joab and his men came to Abel Beth Maacah and surrounded it. They piled earth up against the city wall, and they began digging under the walls to bring them down.

16 But a wise woman shouted out from the city, "Listen! Listen! Tell Joab to come here. I want to talk to him!"

17 So Joab came near her. She asked him, "Are you Joab?"

He answered, "Yes, I am."

Then she said, "Listen to what I say."

Joab said, "I'm listening."

18 Then the woman said, "In the past people would say, 'Ask for advice at Abel,' and the problem would be solved. 19 I am one of the peaceful, loyal people of Israel. You are trying to destroy an important city of Israel. Why must you destroy what belongs to the LORD?"

20 Joab answered, "I would prefer not to destroy or ruin anything! 21 That is not what I want. But there is a man here from the mountains of Ephraim, who is named Sheba son of Bicri. He has turned against King David. If you bring him to me, I will leave the city alone."

The woman said to Joab, "His head will be thrown over the wall to you."

22 Then the woman spoke very wisely to all the people of the city. They cut off the head of Sheba son of Bicri and threw it over the wall to Joab. So he blew the trumpet, and the army left the city. Every man returned home, and Joab went back to the king in Jerusalem.

23 Joab was commander of all the army of Israel. Benaiah son of Jehoiada led the Kerethites and Pelethites. 24 Adoniram was in charge of the men who were forced to do hard work. Jehoshaphat son of Ahilud was the recorder. 25 Sheba was the royal secretary. Zadok and Abiathar were the priests, 26 and Ira the Jairite was David's priest.

The Gibeonites Punish Saul's Family

21 During the time David was king, there was a shortage of food that lasted for three years. So David prayed to the LORD.

The LORD answered, "Saul and his family of murderers are the reason for this shortage, because he killed the Gibeonites." 2 (Now the Gibeonites were not Israelites; they were a group of Amorites who were left alive. The Israelites had

---

20:7 **Kerethites and Pelethites** These were probably special units of the army that were responsible for the king's safety, a kind of palace guard.

promised not to hurt the Gibeonites, but Saul had tried to kill them, because he was eager to help the people of Israel and Judah.)

King David called the Gibeonites together and spoke to them. 3 He asked, "What can I do for you? How can I make up for the harm done so you can bless the LORD's people?"

4 The Gibeonites said to David, "We cannot demand silver or gold from Saul or his family. And we don't have the right to kill anyone in Israel."

Then David asked, "What do you want me to do for you?"

5 The Gibeonites said, "Saul made plans against us and tried to destroy all our people who are left in the land of Israel. 6 So bring seven of his sons to us. Then we will kill them and hang them on stakes in the presence of the LORD at Gibeah, the home town of Saul, the LORD's chosen king."

The king said, "I will give them to you." 7 But the king protected Mephibosheth, the son of Jonathan, the son of Saul, because of the promise he had made to Jonathan in the LORD's name. 8 The king did take Armoni and Mephibosheth,[n] sons of Rizpah and Saul. (Rizpah was the daughter of Aiah.) And the king took the five sons of Saul's daughter Merab. (Adriel son of Barzillai the Meholathite was the father of Merab's five sons.) 9 David gave these seven sons to the Gibeonites. Then the Gibeonites killed them and hung them on stakes on a hill in the presence of the LORD. All seven sons died together. They were put to death during the first days of the harvest season at the beginning of barley harvest.

10 Aiah's daughter Rizpah took the rough cloth that was worn to show sadness and put it on a rock for herself. She stayed there from the beginning of the harvest until the rain fell on her sons' bodies. During the day she did not let the birds of the sky touch her sons' bodies, and during the night she did not let the wild animals touch them.

11 People told David what Aiah's daughter Rizpah, Saul's slave woman, was doing. 12 Then David took the bones of Saul and Jonathan from the men of Jabesh Gilead. (The Philistines had hung the bodies of Saul and Jonathan in the public square of Beth Shan after they had killed Saul at Gilboa. Later the men of Jabesh Gilead had secretly taken them from there.) 13 David brought the bones of Saul and his son Jonathan from Gilead. Then the people gathered the bodies of Saul's seven sons who were hanged on stakes. 14 The people buried the bones of Saul and his son Jonathan at Zela in Benjamin in

FAITH CHALLENGE

Try this one. Read 21:7 to find out how David kept a promise to his friend. How far would you be willing to go to keep a promise to one of your friends?

TeSTiNG iT

2 Samuel 21:7
But the king protected Mephibosheth, the son of Jonathan, the son of Saul, because of the promise he had made to Jonathan in the LORD's name.

21:8 Mephibosheth This is not Jonathan's son but another man with the same name.

the tomb of Saul's father Kish. The people did everything the king commanded. Then God answered the prayers for the land.

Wars with the Philistines

15 Again there was war between the Philistines and Israel. David and his men went out to fight the Philistines, but David became tired. 16 Ishbi-Benob, one of the sons of Rapha, had a bronze spearhead weighing about 3.5 kilogrammes and a new sword. He planned to kill David, 17 but Abishai son of Zeruiah killed the Philistine and saved David's life.

Then David's men made a promise to him, saying, "Never again will you go out with us to battle. If you were killed, Israel would lose its greatest leader."

18 Later, at Gob, there was another battle with the Philistines. Sibbecai the Hushathite killed Saph, another one of the sons of Rapha.

19 Later, there was another battle at Gob with the Philistines. Elhanan son of Jaare-Oregim from Bethlehem killed Goliath[n] from Gath. His spear was as large as a weaver's rod.

20 At Gath another battle took place. A very large man was there; he had six fingers on each hand and six toes on each foot—24 fingers and toes in all. This man also was one of the sons of Rapha. 21 When he challenged Israel, Jonathan son of Shimeah, David's brother, killed him.

22 These four sons of Rapha from Gath were killed by David and his men.

David's Song of Praise

22 David sang this song to the LORD when the LORD saved him from Saul and all his other enemies. 2 He said:

"The LORD is my
  rock, my
  protection,
  my Saviour.
3 My God is
  my rock.
I can run to
  him for safety.

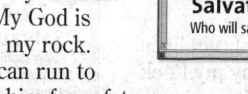

22:2 Salvation
Who will save you?

He is my shield and my saving
  strength,
my defender and my place of
  safety.
The LORD saves me from those
  who want to harm me.
4 I will call to the LORD, who is worthy
  of praise,
and I will be saved from my
  enemies.

5 "The waves of death came around me;
  the deadly rivers overwhelmed me.
6 The ropes of death wrapped around
  me.
The traps of death were before me.
7 In my trouble I called to the LORD;
  I cried out to my God.
From his temple he heard my voice;
  my call for help reached his ears.

8 "The earth trembled and shook.
  The foundations of heaven began
    to shake.
  They trembled because the LORD
    was angry.
9 Smoke came out of his nose,
  and burning fire came out of his
    mouth.
  Burning coals went before him.
10 He tore open the sky and came down
  with dark clouds under his feet.
11 He rode a creature with wings and
  flew.
He raced on the wings of the wind.
12 He made darkness his shelter,
  surrounded by fog and clouds.
13 Out of the brightness of his presence
  came flashes of lightning.
14 The LORD thundered from heaven;
  the Most High raised his voice.
15 He shot his arrows and scattered his
  enemies.
His bolts of lightning confused
  them with fear.
16 The LORD spoke strongly.
  The wind blew from his nose.
Then the valleys of the sea appeared,
  and the foundations of the earth
    were seen.

21:19 **Goliath** In 1 Chronicles 20:5 he is called Lahmi brother of Goliath.

17 "The LORD reached down from above and took me;
  he pulled me from the deep water.
18 He saved me from my powerful enemies,
  from those who hated me, because they were too strong for me.
19 They attacked me at my time of trouble,
  but the LORD supported me.
20 He took me to a safe place.
  Because he delights in me, he saved me.
21 "The LORD spared me because I did what was right.
  Because I have not done evil, he has rewarded me.
22 I have followed the ways of the LORD;
  I have not done evil by turning from my God.
23 I remember all his laws
  and have not broken his rules.
24 I am innocent before him;
  I have kept myself from doing evil.
25 The LORD rewarded me because I did what was right,
  because I did what the LORD said was right.
26 "LORD, you are loyal to those who are loyal,
  and you are good to those who are good.
27 You are pure to those who are pure,
  but you are against those who are evil.
28 You save the humble,
  but you bring down those who are proud.
29 LORD, you give light to my lamp.
  The LORD brightens the darkness around me.
30 With your help I can attack an army.
  With God's help I can jump over a wall.
31 "The ways of God are without fault;
  the LORD's words are pure.
He is a shield to those who trust him.
32 Who is God? Only the LORD.
  Who is the Rock? Only our God.
33 God is my protection.
  He makes my way free from fault.
34 He makes me like a deer that does not stumble;
  he helps me stand on the steep mountains.
35 He trains my hands for battle
  so my arms can bend a bronze bow.
36 You protect me with your saving shield.
  You have stooped to make me great.
37 You give me a better way to live,
  so I live as you want me to.
38 I chased my enemies and destroyed them.
  I did not stop till they were destroyed.
39 I destroyed and crushed them
  so they couldn't rise up again.
  They fell beneath my feet.
40 You gave me strength in battle.
  You made my enemies bow before me.
41 You made my enemies turn back,
  and I destroyed those who hated me.
42 They called for help,
  but no one came to save them.
  They called to the LORD,
  but he did not answer them.
43 I beat my enemies into pieces,
  like dust on the ground.
  I poured them out and walked on them
  like mud in the streets.
44 "You saved me when my people attacked me.
  You kept me as the leader of nations.
  People I never knew serve me.
45 Foreigners obey me.
  As soon as they hear me, they obey me.
46 They all become afraid
  and tremble in their hiding places.
47 "The LORD lives!
  May my Rock be praised!

22:47–48
Salvation
Why should you praise God?

Praise God, the Rock, who saves
    me!
48 God gives me victory over my
    enemies
   and brings people under my rule.
49 He frees me from my enemies.

"You set me over those who hate me.
   You saved me from cruel men.
50 So I will praise you, LORD, among the
    nations.
   I will sing praises to your name.
51 The LORD gives great victories to his
    king.
   He is loyal to his appointed king,
   to David and his descendants for
    ever."

David's Last Words

23 These are the last words of David.

This is the message of David son of
    Jesse.
   The man made
    great by the Most
    High God speaks.
   He is the appointed
    king of the God
    of Jacob;
   he is the sweet
    singer of Israel.

2 "The LORD's Spirit
    spoke through
    me,
   and his word was on my tongue.
3 The God of Israel spoke;
   the Rock of Israel said to me:
   'Whoever rules fairly over people,
    who rules with respect for God,
4 is like the morning light at dawn,
    like a morning without clouds.
   He is like sunshine after a rain
    that makes the grass grow from
     the ground.'

5 "This is how
    God has
    cared for
    my family.
   God made a
    lasting agreement with me,

   right and sure in every way.
   He will accomplish my salvation
    and satisfy all my desires.

6 "But all evil people will be thrown
    away like thorns
    that cannot be held in a hand.
7 No one can touch them
    except with a tool of iron or wood.
   They will be thrown in the fire and
    burned where they lie."

David's Army

8 These are the names of David's warriors:

Josheb-Basshebeth, the Tahkemonite, was head of the Three.*n* He killed 800 men at one time.

9 Next was Eleazar son of Dodai the Ahohite. Eleazar was one of the three soldiers who were with David when they challenged the Philistines. The Philistines were gathered for battle, and the Israelites drew back. 10 But Eleazar stayed where he was and fought the Philistines until he was so tired his hand stuck to his sword. The LORD gave a great victory for the Israelites that day. The troops came back after Eleazar had won the battle, but only to take weapons and armour from the enemy.

11 Next there was Shammah son of Agee the Hararite. The Philistines came together to fight in a vegetable field. Israel's troops ran away from the Philistines, 12 but Shammah stood in the middle of the field and fought for it and killed the Philistines. And the LORD gave a great victory.

13 Once, three of the Thirty, David's chief soldiers, came down to him at the cave of Adullam during harvest. The Philistine army had camped in the Valley of Rephaim. 14 At that time David was in the stronghold, and some of the Philistines were in Bethlehem.

23:8 Three, or maybe "Thirty" These were David's most powerful soldiers. See 1 Chronicles 11:11.

> Whoever rules fairly over people, who rules with respect for God, is like the morning light at dawn.
> – 2 Samuel 23:3–4

23:5 God Does God keep his promises?

15 David had a strong desire for some water. He said, "Oh, I wish someone would get me water from the well near the city gate of Bethlehem!" 16 So the three warriors broke through the Philistine army and took water from the well near the city gate of Bethlehem. Then they brought it to David, but he refused to drink it. He poured it out before the LORD, 17 saying, "May the LORD keep me from drinking this water! It would be like drinking the blood of the men who risked their lives!" So David refused to drink it. These were the brave things that the three warriors did.

18 Abishai, brother of Joab son of Zeruiah, was captain of the Three. Abishai fought 300 soldiers with his spear and killed them. He became as famous as the Three 19 and was more honoured than the Three. He became their commander even though he was not one of them.

20 Benaiah son of Jehoiada was a brave fighter from Kabzeel who did mighty things. He killed two of the best warriors from Moab. He also went down into a pit and killed a lion on a snowy day. 21 Benaiah killed a large Egyptian who had a spear in his hand. Benaiah had a club, but he grabbed the spear from the Egyptian's hand and killed him with his own spear. 22 These were the things Benaiah son of Jehoiada did. He was as famous as the Three. 23 He received more honour than the Thirty, but he did not become a member of the Three. David made him leader of his bodyguards.

The Thirty Chief Soldiers

24 The following men were among the Thirty:

> Asahel brother of Joab;
> Elhanan son of Dodo from
>   Bethlehem;
> 25 Shammah the Harodite;
>   Elika the Harodite;
> 26 Helez the Paltite;
>   Ira son of Ikkesh from Tekoa;
> 27 Abiezer the Anathothite;
>   Mebunnai the Hushathite;
> 28 Zalmon the Ahohite;
>   Maharai the Netophathite;
> 29 Heled son of Baanah the
>   Netophathite;
>   Ithai son of Ribai from Gibeah
>   in Benjamin;
> 30 Benaiah the Pirathonite;
>   Hiddai from the ravines of
>   Gaash;
> 31 Abi-Albon the Arbathite;
>   Azmaveth the Barhumite;
> 32 Eliahba the Shaalbonite;
>   the sons of Jashen;
>   Jonathan 33 son of Shammah
>   the Hararite;
>   Ahiam son of Sharar the Hararite;
> 34 Eliphelet son of Ahasbai the
>   Maacathite;
>   Eliam son of Ahithophel the
>   Gilonite;
> 35 Hezro the Carmelite;
>   Paarai the Arbite;
> 36 Igal son of Nathan of Zobah;
>   the son of Hagri;
> 37 Zelek the Ammonite;
>   Naharai the Beerothite, who
>   carried the armour of Joab
>   son of Zeruiah;
> 38 Ira the Ithrite;
>   Gareb the Ithrite,
> 39 and Uriah the Hittite.

There were 37 in all.

David Counts His Army

24 The LORD was angry with Israel again, and he caused David to turn against the Israelites. He said, "Go, count the people of Israel and Judah."

2 So King David said to Joab, the commander of the army, "Go through all the tribes of Israel, from Dan to Beersheba," and count the people. Then I will know how many there are."

3 But Joab said to the king, "May the LORD your God give you 100 times more people, and may my master the king live to see this happen. Why do you want to do this?"

24:2 Dan to Beersheba Dan was the city farthest north in Israel, and Beersheba was the city farthest south. So this means all the people of Israel.

4 But the king commanded Joab and the commanders of the army, so they left the king to count the Israelites.

5 After crossing the Jordan River, they camped near Aroer on the south side of the city in the ravine. They went through Gad and on to Jazer. 6 Then they went to Gilead and the land of Tahtim Hodshi and to Dan Janai and around to Sidon. 7 They went to the fortified city of Tyre and to all the cities of the Hivites and Canaanites. Finally, they went to southern Judah, to Beersheba. 8 After nine months and 20 days, they had gone through all the land. Then they came back to Jerusalem.

9 Joab gave the list of the people to the king. There were 800,000 men in Israel who could use the sword and 500,000 men in Judah.

10 David felt ashamed after he had counted the people. He said to the LORD, "I have sinned greatly by what I have done. LORD, I beg you to forgive me, your servant, because I have been very foolish."

11 When David got up in the morning, the LORD spoke his word to Gad, who was a prophet and David's seer. 12 The LORD told Gad, "Go and tell David, 'This is what the LORD says: I offer you three choices. Choose one of them and I will do it to you.'"

13 So Gad went to David and said to him, "Should three years of hunger come to you and your land? Or should your enemies chase you for three months? Or should there be three days of disease in your land? Think about it. Then decide which of these things I should tell the LORD who sent me."

14 David said to Gad, "I am in great trouble. Let the LORD punish us, because the LORD is very merciful. Don't let my punishment come from human beings!"

15 So the LORD sent a terrible disease on Israel. It began in the morning and continued until the chosen time to stop. From Dan to Beersheba 70,000 people died. 16 When the angel raised his arm towards Jerusalem to destroy it, the LORD felt very sorry about the terrible things that had happened. He said to the angel who was destroying the people, "That is enough! Put down your arm!" The angel of the LORD was then by the threshing floor of Araunah the Jebusite.

> **24:16–17 Angels**
> This angel has a terrible job.

17 When David saw the angel that killed the people, he said to the LORD, "I am the one who sinned and did wrong. These people only followed me like sheep. They did nothing wrong. Please punish me and my family."

18 That day Gad came to David and said, "Go and build an altar to the LORD on the threshing floor of Araunah the Jebusite." 19 So David did what Gad told him to do, just as the LORD commanded.

20 Araunah looked and saw the king and his servants coming to him. So he went out and bowed face down on the ground before the king. 21 He said, "Why has my master the king come to me?"

David answered, "To buy the threshing floor from you so I can build an altar to the LORD. Then the terrible disease will stop."

22 Araunah said to David, "My master and king, you may take anything you want for a sacrifice. Here are some oxen for the whole burnt offering and the threshing boards and the yokes for the wood. 23 My king, I give everything to you." Araunah also said to the king, "May the LORD your God be pleased with you."

24 But the king answered Araunah, "No, I will pay you for the land. I won't offer to the LORD my God burnt offerings that cost me nothing."

So David bought the threshing floor and the oxen for 50 pieces of silver. 25 He built an altar to the LORD there and offered whole burnt offerings and fellowship offerings. Then the LORD answered his prayer for the country, and the disease in Israel stopped.

GIVE ME WISDOM

Hello. My name is Jeremiah and I am a prophet of God. Have you ever heard of King Solomon, the one who asked God for wisdom? God was so pleased with his request that he made Solomon wiser than anyone else on earth and gave him fabulous riches as well. In gratitude, Solomon built the Temple of the Lord, which was the centre of worship for the whole nation of Israel. Check out the details of the Temple in 1 Kings 6. Even the floors were covered with gold!

I wrote this book to tell the history of King Solomon and the kings who came after him. When Solomon died, his kingdom was split into two nations: Israel and Judah. The kings of both nations led the people into worshipping false gods, so God sent prophets to tell people about the true God. Don't miss the story of the famous contest on Mount Carmel between Elijah, the prophet of God, and 450 prophets of Baal. Log onto 1 Kings 18 for the amazing way God answered Elijah's prayer.

JESUS WATCH

In many ways Solomon reminds us of Jesus. Solomon was well known for his wisdom. People came from all over to hear him speak. Jesus, too, was known for wisdom. People followed Jesus all over the country, listening to him talk about God. Solomon, however, was not always wise. He married many foreign women and, towards the end of his life, he started to follow their false gods. Jesus is always wise, pointing the way to the true God. Solomon's reign was a time of peace because Israel was strong and Solomon was skillful in diplomacy. When Solomon died, the peaceful time ended and the kingdom split into two countries. Because Jesus took our punishment for the sin that separates us from God, our peace with God will never end. The magnificence of the Temple is a picture of the splendour of heaven where we will worship God for ever.

my FAVOURITE links

OTHER CONNECTIONS

 Find out more about the many adventures and struggles Elijah encountered during his ministry in the Northern Kingdom of Israel by connecting to Elijah, the Prophet, 1 Kings 18.

MORE STUFF . . .
What a miracle! The story of Elijah, one of the most famous prophets in the Old Testament, is filled with miracles. Here are just a few you can read about:
- Elijah predicted there would be a drought in the land (1 Kings 17:1).
- Elijah helped a widow and her son survive the drought by providing, through God's power, a never-ending supply of flour and oil (1 Kings 17:10–16).
- Elijah was used by God to bring the widow's son back to life after he had died from an illness (1 Kings 17:17–24).
- Elijah was God's representative in a battle between him and the prophets of the idols Baal and Asherah (1 Kings 18:18–40).

Here's one for you. Why did Solomon tell his servants to cut the baby in two?

Yikes! That doesn't sound very wise. Better surf over to 1 Kings 3:16–28 to find out.

DON'T MISS THESE HOT SITES:
Give me wisdom! 1 Kings 3:4–15
The queen of Sheba, 1 Kings 10:1–13
Air-express food, 1 Kings 17:1–6
The boy who came back to life, 1 Kings 17:17–24
Running on God's power, 1 Kings 18:41–46
God's whisper, 1 Kings 19:9–13

FAITH links

○ Take My Advice, **1 Kings 2:2–4**

○ A Wise Wish, **1 Kings 3:5–9**

○ Your Best Work, **1 Kings 6**

○ The Way to Serve God, **1 Kings 9:4**

○ An Admirable Quality, **1 Kings 10:1–13**

○ Your Stats, **1 Kings 15; 16**

○ Good Times and Bad, **1 Kings 17**

○ Sitting on the Fence, **1 Kings 18**

○ Listen Up! **1 Kings 19: 11–13**

○ Give In or Take a Stand? **1 Kings 22:13–14**

Adonijah Tries to Become King

1 At this time King David was very old, and although his servants covered him with blankets, he could not keep warm. 2 They said to him, "We will look for a young woman to care for you. She will lie close to you and keep you warm." 3 After searching everywhere in Israel for a beautiful young woman, they found a girl named Abishag from Shunam and brought her to the king. 4 The girl was very beautiful, and she cared for the king and served him. But the king did not have sexual relations with her.

5 Adonijah was the son of King David and Haggith, and he was very proud. "I will be the king," he said. So he got chariots and horses for himself and 50 men for his personal bodyguard. 6 Now David had never interfered with Adonijah by questioning what he did. Born next after Absalom, Adonijah was a very handsome man.

7 Adonijah spoke with Joab son of Zeruiah and Abiathar the priest, and they agreed to help him. 8 But Zadok the priest, Benaiah son of Jehoiada, Nathan the prophet, Shimei, Rei and King David's special guard did not join Adonijah.

9 Then Adonijah killed some sheep, cows and fat calves for sacrifices at the Stone of Zoheleth near the spring of Rogel. He invited all his brothers, the other sons of King David, to come, as well as all the men of Judah. 10 But Adonijah did not invite Nathan the prophet, Benaiah, his father's special guard or his brother Solomon.

11 When Nathan heard about this, he went to Bathsheba, Solomon's mother. "Have you heard that Adonijah, Haggith's son, has made himself king?" Nathan asked. "Our real king, David, does not know it. 12 Let me tell you how you can save yourself and your sons. 13 Go to King David and tell him, 'My master and king, you promised that my son Solomon would be king and would rule on your throne after you. Why then has Adonijah become king?' 14 While you are still talking to the king, I will come in and tell him that what you have said about Adonijah is true."

15 So Bathsheba went in to see the aged king in his bedroom, where Abishag, the girl from Shunam, was caring for him. 16 Bathsheba bowed and knelt before the king. He asked, "What do you want?"

17 She answered, "My master, you made a promise to me in the name of the LORD your God. You said, 'Your son Solomon will become king after me, and he will rule on my throne.' 18 But now, unknown to you, Adonijah has become king. 19 He has killed many cows, fat calves and sheep for sacrifices. And he has invited all your sons, as well as Abiathar the priest and Joab the commander of the army, but he did not invite Solomon, who serves you. 20 My master and king, all the Israelites are watching you, waiting for you to decide who will be king after you. 21 As soon as you die, Solomon and I will be treated as criminals."

22 While Bathsheba was still talking with the king, Nathan the prophet arrived. 23 The servants told the king, "Nathan the prophet is here." So Nathan went to the king and bowed face down on the ground before him.

24 Nathan said, "My master and king, have you said that Adonijah will be the king after you and that he will rule on your throne? 25 Today he has sacrificed many cows, fat calves and sheep, and he has invited all your other sons, the commanders of the army, and Abiathar the priest. Right now they are eating and drinking with him. They are saying, 'Long live King Adonijah!' 26 But he did not invite me, your own servant, or Zadok the priest, or Benaiah son of Jehoiada or your son Solomon. 27 Did you do this? Since we are your servants, why didn't you tell us who should be king after you?"

David Makes Solomon King

28 Then the king said, "Tell Bathsheba to come in!" So she came in and stood before the king.

29 Then the king made this promise, "The LORD has saved me from all trouble. As surely as he lives, 30 I will do today what I have promised you in the name of the LORD, the God of Israel. I promised

that your son Solomon would be king after me and rule on my throne in my place."

31 Then Bathsheba bowed face down on the ground and knelt before the king and said, "Long live my master King David!"

32 Then King David said, "Tell Zadok the priest, Nathan the prophet and Benaiah son of Jehoiada to come in." When they came before the king, 33 he said to them, "Take my servants with you and put my son Solomon on my own mule. Take him down to the spring called Gihon. 34 There Zadok the priest and Nathan the prophet should pour olive oil on him and make him king over Israel. Blow the trumpet and shout, 'Long live King Solomon!' 35 Then come back up here with him. He will sit on my throne and rule in my place, because he is the one I have chosen to be the ruler over Israel and Judah."

36 Benaiah son of Jehoiada answered the king, "Amen! This is what the LORD, the God of my master, has declared! 37 The LORD has always helped you, our king. May he also help Solomon and make King Solomon's throne an even greater throne than yours."

38 So Zadok the priest, Nathan the prophet, and Benaiah son of Jehoiada left with the Kerethites and Pelethites.[n] They put Solomon on King David's mule and took him to the spring called Gihon. 39 Zadok the priest took the container of olive oil from the Holy Tent and poured the oil on Solomon's head to show he was the king. Then they blew the trumpet, and all the people shouted, "Long live King Solomon!" 40 All the people followed Solomon into the city. Playing flutes and shouting for joy, they made so much noise the ground shook.

41 At this time Adonijah and all the guests with him were finishing their meal. When he heard the sound from the trumpet, Joab asked, "What does all that noise from the city mean?"

1:38 Kerethites and Pelethites These were probably special units of the army that were responsible for the king's safety, a kind of palace guard.

FAITH links

A LIFE OF THANKSGIVING
1 KINGS 1:47-48

Your parents may tell you to make the most of your life. That means they want you to have a full life. Think about the activities you do the most. What would you say your life is full of right now? Fun? Boring activities? Complaints? David's life was full of thankfulness to God. Just before he died, David thanked God for making his son, Solomon, king.

Want to have a life full of thankfulness? Instead of always asking God for things, every once in a while you can say "thanks" to God for who he is and for what he does. When you do that, you're building a life of thanksgiving like David's.

Check out these links on being thankful:

Serious About the Sabbath, Exodus 31:15, p. 117

The Name of the Lord, Exodus 33:19–23; 34:5–8, p. 120

When the Green-eyed Monster Strikes, 1 Samuel 18:6–9, p. 379

Gratitude Attitude, Ezra 3, p. 611

Happiness or Joy? Job 29:18–19, p. 691

Thanks for a Friend, 1 Thessalonians 1:1–3, p. 1630

42 While Joab was speaking, Jonathan son of Abiathar the priest arrived. Adonijah said, "Come in! You are an important man, so you must be bringing good news."

43 But Jonathan answered, "No! Our master King David has made Solomon the new king. 44 King David sent Zadok the priest, Nathan the prophet, Benaiah son of Jehoiada, and all the king's bodyguards with him, and they have put Solomon on the king's own mule. 45 Then Zadok the priest and Nathan the prophet poured olive oil on Solomon at Gihon to make him king. After that they went into the city, shouting with joy. Now the whole city is excited, and that is the noise you hear. 46 Solomon has now become the king. 47 All the king's officers have come to tell King David that he has done a good thing. They are saying, 'May your God make Solomon even more famous than you and an even greater king than you.'" Jonathan continued, "And King David bowed down on his bed to worship God, 48 saying, 'Bless the LORD, the God of Israel. Today he has made one of my sons the king and allowed me to see it.'"

49 Then all of Adonijah's guests were afraid, and they left quickly and scattered. 50 Adonijah was also afraid of Solomon, so he went and took hold of the corners of the altar." 51 Then someone told Solomon, "Adonijah is afraid of you, so he is at the altar, holding on to its corners. He says, 'Tell King Solomon to promise me today that he will not kill me.'"

52 So Solomon answered, "Adonijah must show that he is a man of honour. If he does that, I promise he will not lose even a single hair from his head. But if he does anything wrong, he will die." 53 Then King Solomon sent some men to get Adonijah. When he was brought from the altar, he came before King Solomon and bowed down. Solomon told him, "Go home."

The Death of David

2 Since it was almost time for David to die, he gave his son Solomon his last commands. 2 David said, "My time to die is near. Be a good and strong leader.

FAITH links

TAKE MY ADVICE
1 KINGS 2:2-4

What is the most important advice your parents have passed on to you? Think about that for a moment as you consider this. King David was about to die. He had one last chance to talk to his son Solomon. David did not teach him how to fight a battle or how to make the people of Israel happy. He told Solomon that the most important thing he could do in life was to obey the Lord. Is that your goal, too? How do your actions show that you've taken this advice to heart?

A Use for Your Abilities, Genesis 41, p. 59

Prayer + Action = Success, Nehemiah 2:4–9, p. 626

Our Thirst Quencher, Psalm 42:1–3, p. 741

Think About Him, Isaiah 26:3, p. 926

Empty Words, Ezekiel 33:30–33, p. 1127

That Thing You Do, Matthew 25:14–30, p. 1319

3 Obey the LORD your God. Follow him by obeying his demands, his commands, his laws and his rules that are written in

---

1:50 corners of the altar If a person were innocent of a crime, he could run into the Holy Place where the altar was. If he held on to the corners of the altar, which looked like horns, he would be safe.

the teachings of Moses. If you do these things, you will be successful in all you do and wherever you go. 4 And if you obey the LORD, he will keep the promise he made to me. He said: 'If your descendants live as I tell them and have complete faith in me, a man from your family will always be king over the people of Israel.'

5 "Also, you remember what Joab son of Zeruiah did to me. He killed the two commanders of Israel's armies: Abner son of Ner and Amasa son of Jether. He did this as if he and they were at war, although it was a time of peace. He put their blood on the belt around his waist and on his sandals on his feet. 6 Punish him in the way you think is wisest, but do not let him die peacefully of old age.

7 "Be kind to the children of Barzillai of Gilead, and allow them to eat at your table. They welcomed me when I ran away from your brother Absalom.

2:7
Kindness
How should you treat those who have been kind to you?

8 "And remember, Shimei son of Gera, the Benjaminite, is here with you. He cursed me the day I went to Mahanaim. But when he came down to meet me at the Jordan River, I promised him before the LORD, 'Shimei, I will not kill you.' 9 But you should not leave him unpunished. You are a wise man, and you will know what to do to him, but you must be sure he is killed."

10 Then David died and was buried with his ancestors in Jerusalem. 11 He had ruled over Israel 40 years—seven years in Hebron and 33 years in Jerusalem.

Solomon Takes Control as King

12 Solomon became king after David, his father, and he was in firm control of his kingdom.

13 At this time Adonijah son of Haggith went to Bathsheba, Solomon's mother. "Do you come in peace?" Bathsheba asked.

"Yes. This is a peaceful visit," Adonijah answered. 14 "I have something to say to you."

"You may speak," she said.

15 "You remember that at one time the kingdom was mine," Adonijah said. "All the people of Israel recognised me as their king, but things have changed. Now my brother is the king, because the LORD chose him. 16 Now I have one thing to ask you; please do not refuse me."

Bathsheba answered, "What do you want?"

17 "I know King Solomon will do anything you ask him," Adonijah continued. "Please ask him to give me Abishag the Shunammite to be my wife."

18 "Very well," she answered. "I will speak to the king for you."

19 So Bathsheba went to King Solomon to speak to him for Adonijah. When Solomon saw her, he stood up to meet her, then bowed down and sat on the throne. He told some servants to bring another throne for his mother. Then she sat down at his right side.

20 Bathsheba said, "I have one small thing to ask you. Please do not refuse me."

"Ask, mother," the king answered. "I will not refuse you."

21 So she said, "Allow Abishag the Shunammite to marry your brother Adonijah."

22 King Solomon answered his mother, "Why do you ask me to give him Abishag? Why don't you also ask for him to become the king since he is my older brother? Abiathar the priest and Joab son of Zeruiah would support him!"

23 Then King Solomon swore by the name of the LORD, saying, "May God punish me terribly if this doesn't cost Adonijah his life! 24 By the LORD who has given me the throne that belonged to my father David and who has kept his promise and given the kingdom to me and my people, Adonijah will die today!" 25 Then King Solomon gave orders to Benaiah son of Jehoiada, and he went and killed Adonijah.

26 King Solomon said to Abiathar the priest, "I should kill you too, but I will allow you to go back to your fields in Anathoth. I will not kill you at this time, because you helped carry the Ark of the Lord GOD while marching with my

father David. And I know you shared in all the hard times with him." 27 Then Solomon removed Abiathar from being the Lord's priest. This happened as the Lord had said it would, when he was speaking in Shiloh about the priest Eli and his descendants.

28 When Joab heard about what had happened, he was afraid. He had supported Adonijah but not Absalom. So Joab ran to the Tent of the Lord and took hold of the corners of the altar.ⁿ 29 Someone told King Solomon that Joab had run to the Tent of the Lord and was beside the altar. Then Solomon ordered Benaiah to go and kill him.

30 Benaiah went into the Tent of the Lord and said to Joab, "The king says, 'Come out!'"

But Joab answered, "No, I will die here."

So Benaiah went back to the king and told him what Joab had said. 31 Then the king ordered Benaiah, "Do as he says! Kill him there and bury him. Then my family and I will be free of the guilt of Joab, who has killed innocent people. 32 Without my father knowing it, he killed two men who were much better than he was—Abner son of Ner, the commander of Israel's army, and Amasa son of Jether, the commander of Judah's army. So the Lord will pay him back for those deaths. 33 Joab and his family will be for ever guilty of their deaths, but there will be peace from the Lord for David, his descendants, his family and his throne for ever."

34 So Benaiah son of Jehoiada killed Joab, and he was buried near his home in the desert. 35 The king then made Benaiah son of Jehoiada commander of the army in Joab's place. He also made Zadok the new high priest in Abiathar's place.

36 Next the king sent for Shimei. Solomon said to him, "Build a house for yourself in Jerusalem and live there. Don't leave the city. 37 The very day you leave and cross the Kidron Valley, someone will kill you, and it will be your own fault."

38 So Shimei answered the king, "I agree with what you say. I will do what you say, my master and king." So Shimei lived in Jerusalem for a long time.

39 But three years later two of Shimei's slaves ran away to Achish king of Gath, who was the son of Maacah. Shimei heard that his slaves were in Gath, 40 so he put his saddle on his donkey and went to Achish at Gath to find them. Then he brought them back from Gath.

41 Someone told Solomon that Shimei had gone from Jerusalem to Gath and had returned. 42 So Solomon sent for Shimei and said, "I made you promise in the name of the Lord not to leave Jerusalem. I warned you if you went out anywhere you would die, and you agreed to what I said. 43 Why did you break your promise to the Lord and disobey my command?" 44 The king also said, "You know the many wrong things you did to my father David, so now the Lord will punish you for those wrongs. 45 But the Lord will bless me and make the rule of David safe before the Lord for ever."

46 Then the king ordered Benaiah to kill Shimei, and he did. Now Solomon was in full control of his kingdom.

Solomon Asks for Wisdom

3 Solomon made an agreement with the king of Egypt by marrying his daughter and bringing her to Jerusalem. At this time Solomon was still building his palace and the Temple of the Lord, as well as a wall around Jerusalem. 2 The Temple for the worship of the Lord had not yet been finished, so people were still sacrificing at altars in many places of worship. 3 Solomon showed he loved the Lord by following the commands his father David had given him, except many other places of worship were still used to offer sacrifices and to burn incense.

4 King Solomon went to Gibeon to offer a sacrifice, because it was the most important place of worship. He offered a

---

2:28 corners of the altar If a person were innocent of a crime, he could run into the Holy Place where the altar was. If he held on to the corners of the altar, which looked like horns, he would be safe.

thousand burnt offerings on that altar. 5 While he was at Gibeon, the LORD appeared to him in a dream during the night. God said, "Ask for whatever you want me to give you."

6 Solomon answered, "You were very kind to your servant, my father David. He obeyed you, and he was honest and lived right. You showed great kindness to him when you allowed his son to be king after him. 7 LORD my God, now you have made me, your servant, king in my father's place. But I am like a little child; I don't know how to do what must be done. 8 I, your servant, am here among your chosen people, and there are too many of them to count. 9 I ask that you give me an obedient heart so I can rule the people in the right way and will know the difference between right and wrong. Otherwise, it is impossible to rule this great people of yours."

10 The Lord was pleased that Solomon had asked this. 11 So God said to him, "You did not ask for a long life, or riches for yourself or the death of your enemies. Since you asked for wisdom to make the right decisions, 12 I will do what you asked. I will give you wisdom and understanding that is greater than anyone has had in the past or will have in the future. 13 I will also give you what you did not ask for: riches and honour. During your life no other king will be as great as you. 14 If you follow me and obey my laws and commands as your father David did, I will also give you a long life."

15 After Solomon woke up from the dream, he went to Jerusalem. He stood before the Ark of the Agreement with the Lord, where he made burnt offerings and fellowship offerings. After that, he gave a feast for all his leaders and officers.

Solomon Makes a Wise Decision

16 One day two women who were prostitutes came to Solomon. As they stood before him, 17 one of the women said, "My master, this woman and I live in the same house. I gave birth to a baby while she was there with me. 18 Three days later this woman also gave birth to a baby. No one else was in the house with us; it was just the two of us. 19 One night this woman rolled over on her baby, and he died. 20 So she took my son from my bed during the night while I was asleep, and she carried him to her bed. Then she put the dead baby in my bed. 21 The next morning when I got up to feed my baby, I

FAITH links

A WISE WISH
1 KINGS 3:5-9

If you could have one wish, what would you ask for? That is what happened to Solomon. God told him that he would give him whatever he asked for. Solomon did not ask for money or a huge palace. Solomon took a step of faith and asked for wisdom. He became wiser than anyone who ever lived. (Link to 2 Chronicles 1:7–13, p. 563, for another version of this story.)

Want to be like Solomon? When you pray, ask God for wisdom. He will give it to you. (Download James 1:5, p. 1688, for more on getting God's wisdom.)

Remembering What He Said, Deuteronomy 6:4–9, p. 236

The Green Light, 2 Samuel 2:1, p. 401

Learning to Trust, Psalm 25:4–5, p. 727

A Need to Change, Ecclesiastes 1:1–11, p. 873

A Hopeful Future, Jeremiah 29:11, p. 1031

The Power of Prayer, Acts 12:5, p. 1485

FAITH links

DECIDING WISELY
1 KINGS 3:16-28

Ever have a tough decision to make? What helped you make the decision? Solomon made a good decision by asking God for wisdom. That wisdom was put to the test when he was asked to decide a very difficult case. But Solomon was able to make a fair decision because he had great wisdom from God. Everyone respected Solomon for his wisdom.

When you have a hard decision to make, you can use God's wisdom, too. The wise person knows when to ask for help to make a decision. God has given us the Bible, which is full of wise advice. God also gives us godly people who can help us make good choices.

Wise up by linking on to these notes:

Learning to Listen, 1 Samuel 3, p. 358

A Travelling Bible Study, 2 Chronicles 17:9, p. 580

Let's Make a Deal, Daniel 1:8–21, p. 1150

Want to Know? Ask! Luke 9:45, p. 1386

Faith Workout, Acts 16:4–5, p. 1493

How Do You Grow? Titus 1:1, p. 1659

---

saw that he was dead! When I looked at him more closely, I realised he was not my son."

22 "No!" the other woman cried. "The living baby is my son, and the dead baby is yours!"

But the first woman said, "No! The dead baby is yours, and the living one is mine!" So the two women argued before the king.

23 Then King Solomon said, "One of you says, 'My son is alive and your son is dead.' Then the other one says, 'No! Your son is dead and my son is alive.'"

24 The king sent his servants to get a sword. When they brought it to him, 25 he said, "Cut the living baby into two pieces, and give each woman half."

26 The real mother of the living child was full of love for her son. So she said to the king, "Please, my master, don't kill him! Give the baby to her!"

But the other woman said, "Neither of us will have him. Cut him into two pieces!"

27 Then King Solomon said, "Don't kill him. Give the baby to the first woman, because she is the real mother."

28 When the people of Israel heard about King Solomon's decision, they respected him very much. They saw he had wisdom from God to make the right decisions.

Solomon's Officers

4 King Solomon ruled over all Israel. 2 These are the names of his leading officers:

Azariah son of Zadok was the priest;

3 Elihoreph and Ahijah, sons of Shisha, recorded what happened in the courts;

Jehoshaphat son of Ahilud recorded the history of the people;

4 Benaiah son of Jehoiada was commander of the army;

Zadok and Abiathar were priests;

5 Azariah son of Nathan was in charge of the district governors;

Zabud son of Nathan was a priest and adviser to the king;

6 Ahishar was responsible for everything in the palace;

Adoniram son of Abda was in charge of the slaves.

7 Solomon placed twelve governors over the districts of Israel, who gathered food from their districts for the king and his family. Each governor was responsible for bringing food to the king for one month of each year. 8 These are the names of the twelve governors:

Ben-Hur was governor of the mountain country of Ephraim;

9 Ben-Deker was governor of Makaz, Shaalbim, Beth Shemesh and Elon Bethhanan;

10 Ben-Hesed was governor of Arubboth, Socoh and all the land of Hepher;

11 Ben-Abinadab was governor of Naphoth Dor (he was married to Taphath, Solomon's daughter);

12 Baana son of Ahilud was governor of Taanach, Megiddo and all of Beth Shan next to Zarethan, this was below Jezreel from Beth Shan to Abel Meholah across from Jokmeam;

13 Ben-Geber was governor of Ramoth in Gilead (he was governor of all the towns of Jair in Gilead—Jair was the son of Manasseh; Ben-Geber was also over the district of Argob in Bashan, which had 60 large, walled cities with bronze bars on their gates);

14 Ahinadab son of Iddo was governor of Mahanaim;

15 Ahimaaz was governor of Naphtali (he was married to Basemath, Solomon's daughter);

16 Baana son of Hushai was governor of Asher and Aloth;

17 Jehoshaphat son of Paruah was governor of Issachar;

18 Shimei son of Ela was governor of Benjamin;

19 Geber son of Uri was governor of Gilead. Gilead had been the country of Sihon king of the Amorites and Og king of Bashan. But Geber was the only governor over this district.

Solomon's Kingdom

20 There were as many people in Judah and Israel as grains of sand on the seashore. The people ate, drank and were happy. 21 Solomon ruled over all the kingdoms from the Euphrates River to the land of the Philistines, as far as the border of Egypt. These countries brought Solomon the payments he demanded, and they were under his control all his life.

22 Solomon needed much food each day to feed himself and all the people who ate at his table: 6,000 litres of fine flour, 12,000 litres of grain, 23 ten cows that were fed on good grain, 20 cows that were raised in the fields, 100 sheep, three kinds of deer, and fattened birds.

24 Solomon controlled all the countries west of the Euphrates River—the land from Tiphsah to Gaza. And he had peace on all sides of his kingdom. 25 During Solomon's life Judah and Israel, from Dan to Beersheba,[n] also lived in peace; all of his people were able to sit under their own fig trees and grapevines.

26 Solomon had 4,000 stalls for his chariot horses and 12,000 horses. 27 Each month one of the district governors gave King Solomon all the food he needed—enough for every person who ate at the king's table. The governors made sure he had everything he needed. 28 They also brought enough barley and straw for Solomon's chariot and work horses; each person brought this grain to the right place.

Solomon's Wisdom

29 God gave Solomon great wisdom so he could understand many things. His wisdom was as hard to measure as the grains of sand on the seashore. 30 His wisdom was greater than any wisdom of the East, or any wisdom in Egypt. 31 He was wiser than anyone on earth. He was even wiser than Ethan the Ezrahite, as well as Heman, Calcol and Darda—the three sons of Mahol. King Solomon became famous in all the surrounding countries. 32 During his life he spoke 3,000 wise sayings and also wrote 1,005 songs. 33 He taught about many kinds of plants—everything from the great

---

4:25 Dan to Beersheba Dan was the city farthest north in Israel, and Beersheba was the city farthest south. So this means all the people of Israel.

cedar trees of Lebanon to the weeds that grow out of the walls. He also taught about animals, birds, crawling things and fish. 34 People from all nations came to listen to King Solomon's wisdom. The kings of all nations sent them to him, because they had heard of Solomon's wisdom.

Preparing to Build the Temple

5 Hiram, the king of Tyre, had always been David's friend. When Hiram heard that Solomon had been made king in David's place, he sent his messengers to Solomon. 2 Solomon sent this message back to King Hiram: 3 "You remember my father David had to fight many wars with the countries around him, so he was never able to build a temple for worshipping the LORD his God. David was waiting until the LORD allowed him to defeat all his enemies. 4 But now the LORD my God has given me peace on all sides of my country. I have no enemies now, and no danger threatens my people.

5 "The LORD promised my father David, 'I will make your son king after you, and he will build a temple for worshipping me.' Now, I plan to build that temple for worshipping the LORD my God. 6 So send your men to cut down cedar trees for me from Lebanon. My servants will work with yours, and I will pay them whatever wages you decide. We don't have anyone who can cut down trees as well as the people of Sidon."

7 When Hiram heard what Solomon asked, he was very happy. He said, "Praise the LORD today! He has given David a wise son to rule over this great nation!" 8 Then Hiram sent back this message to Solomon: "I received the message you sent, and I will give you all the cedar and pine trees you want. 9 My servants will bring them down from Lebanon to the sea. There I will tie them together and float them along the shore to the place you choose. Then I will separate the logs there, and you can take them away. In return it is my wish that you give food to all those who live with me." 10 So Hiram gave Solomon as much cedar and pine as he wanted. 11 And Solomon gave Hiram about 2,000 tonnes of wheat each year to feed the people who lived with him. Solomon also gave him about 4,000 litres of pure olive oil every year.

12 The LORD gave Solomon wisdom as he had promised. And there was peace between Hiram and Solomon; these two kings made a treaty between themselves.

**5:13–14
Family**
What's more important: family or work?

13 King Solomon forced 30,000 men of Israel to help in this work. 14 He sent a group of 10,000 men each month to Lebanon. Each group worked in Lebanon for a month, then went home for two months. A man named Adoniram was in charge. 15 Solomon forced 80,000 men to work in the hill country, cutting stone, and he had 70,000 men to carry the stones. 16 There were also 3,300 men who directed the workers.

17 King Solomon commanded them to cut large blocks of fine stone to be used for the foundation of the Temple. 18 Solomon's and Hiram's builders and the men from Byblos carved the stones and prepared the stones and the logs for building the Temple.

> Praise the LORD today! He has given David a wise son to rule over this great nation!
> – 1 Kings 5:7

Solomon Builds the Temple

6 Solomon began to build the Temple 480 years after the people of Israel had left Egypt. This was during the fourth year of King Solomon's rule over Israel. It was the second month, the month of Ziv.

2 The Temple was 30 metres long, 10 metres wide and 15 metres high. 3 The porch in front of the main room of the Temple was 5 metres deep and 10 metres

wide. This room ran along the front of the Temple itself. Its width was equal to that of the Temple. 4 The Temple also had windows that opened and closed. 5 Solomon also built some side rooms against the walls of the main room and the inner room of the Temple. He built rooms all around. 6 The rooms on the bottom floor were 2.5 metres wide. Those on the middle floor were 3 metres wide, and the rooms above them were 3.5 metres wide. The Temple wall that formed the side of each room was thinner than the wall in the room below. These rooms were pushed against the Temple wall, but they did not have their main beams built into this wall.

7 The stones were prepared at the same place where they were cut from the ground. Since these stones were the only ones used to build the Temple, there was no noise of hammers, axes or any other iron tools at the Temple.

8 The entrance to the ground floor beside the Temple was on the south side. From there, stairs went up to the first floor. And from there, stairs went on to the second-floor rooms. 9 Solomon put a roof made from beams and cedar boards on the Temple. So he finished building the Temple 10 as well as the ground floor that was beside the Temple. This ground floor was 2.5 metres high and was attached to the Temple by cedar beams.

11 The LORD said to Solomon: 12 "If you obey all my laws and commands, I will do for you what I promised your father David. 13 I will live among the Israelites in this Temple, and I will never leave my people Israel."

14 So Solomon finished building the Temple. 15 The inside walls were covered from floor to ceiling with cedar boards. The floor was made from pine boards. 16 A room 10 metres long was built in the back part of the Temple. This room, called the Most Holy Place, was separated from the rest of the Temple by cedar boards which reached from floor to ceiling. 17 The main room, the one in front of the Most Holy Place, was 20 metres long. 18 Everything inside the Temple was covered with

6:12–13 Obedience
Read this to see God's promises.

FAITH links

YOUR BEST WORK
1 KINGS 6

What activities do you put the most effort into? Only the things you like to do? Everything you do? You know what doing your best is like. Solomon used the best labourers and the best material to work on God's Temple. He knew that God's house deserved the very best materials he could find. The people he hired worked very hard to complete the Temple.

Part of learning to do your best means putting effort into whatever you do. When you do your best, your efforts show.

Check out these links on giving it your all:

Everyone Can Help, Numbers 4, p. 181

An Unsung Hero, Ruth 2:12, 15–16, p. 347

Operation Co-operation, Ezra 1:5, p. 609

Said It? Do It! Lamentations 2:17, p. 1077

A Half-hearted Offering, Malachi 1:6–14, p. 1268

With All Your Heart, Colossians 3:23, p. 1626

cedar, which was carved with pictures of flowers and plants. A person could not see the stones of the wall, only the cedar.

19 Solomon prepared the inner room at the back of the Temple to keep the Ark of the Agreement with the LORD. 20 This inner room was 10 metres long, 10 metres wide and 10 metres high. He covered this room with pure gold, and he also covered the altar of cedar. 21 He covered the inside of the Temple with pure gold, placing gold chains across the front of the inner room, which was also covered with gold. 22 So all the inside of the Temple, as well as the altar of the Most Holy Place, was covered with gold.

23 Solomon made two creatures from olive wood and placed them in the Most Holy Place. Each creature was 5 metres tall 24 and had two wings. Each wing was 2.5 metres long, so it was 5 metres from the end of one wing to the end of the other. 25 The creatures were the same size and shape; 26 each was 5 metres tall. 27 These creatures were put beside each other in the Most Holy Place with their wings spread out. One creature's wing touched one wall, and the other creature's wing touched the other wall with their wings touching each other in the middle of the room. 28 These two creatures were covered with gold.

29 All the walls around the Temple were carved with pictures of creatures with wings, as well as palm trees and flowers. This was true for both the main room and the inner room. 30 The floors of both rooms were covered with gold.

31 Doors made from olive wood were placed at the entrance to the Most Holy Place. These doors had frames with five sides. 32 Creatures with wings, as well as palm trees and flowers, were also carved on the two olive wood doors that were covered with gold. The creatures and the palm trees on the doors were covered with gold as well. 33 At the entrance to the main room there was a square door frame made of olive wood. 34 Two doors were made from pine. Each door had two parts so the doors folded. 35 The doors were covered with pictures of creatures with wings, as well as palm trees and flowers. All of the carvings were covered with gold, which was evenly spread over them.

36 The inner courtyard was enclosed by walls, which were made of three rows of cut stones and one row of cedar boards.

37 Work began on the Temple in Ziv, the second month, during the fourth year Solomon was king over Israel. 38 The Temple was finished during the eleventh year he was king, in the eighth month, the month of Bul. It was built exactly as it was planned. Solomon had spent seven years building it.

Solomon's Palace

7 King Solomon also built a palace for himself; it took him thirteen years to finish it. 2 Built of cedars from the Forest of Lebanon, it was 50 metres long, 25 metres wide and 15 metres high. It had four rows of cedar columns which supported the cedar beams. 3 There were 45 beams on the roof, with 15 beams in each row, and the ceiling was covered with cedar above the beams. 4 Windows were placed in three rows facing each other. 5 All the doors were square, and the three doors at each end faced each other.

6 Solomon also built the porch that had pillars. This porch was 25 metres long and 15 metres wide. Along the front of the porch was a roof supported by pillars.

7 Solomon also built a throne room where he judged people, called the Hall of Justice. This room was covered with cedar from the floor to the ceiling. 8 The palace where Solomon lived was built like the Hall of Justice, and it was behind this hall. Solomon also built the same kind of palace for his wife, who was the daughter of the king of Egypt.

9 All these buildings were made with blocks of fine stone. First they were carefully cut. Then they were trimmed with a saw in the front and back. These fine stones went from the foundations of the buildings to the top of the walls. Even the courtyard was made with blocks of

stone. 10 The foundations were made with large blocks of fine stone, some as long as 5 metres. Others were 4 metres long. 11 On top of these foundation stones were other blocks of fine stone and cedar beams. 12 The palace courtyard, the courtyard inside the Temple and the porch of the Temple were surrounded by walls. All of these walls had three rows of stone blocks and one row of cedar beams.

The Temple is Completed Inside

13 King Solomon sent to Tyre and had Huram brought to him. 14 Huram's mother was a widow from the tribe of Naphtali. His father was from Tyre and had been skilled in making things from bronze. Huram was also very skilled and experienced in bronze work. So he came to King Solomon and did all the bronze work.

15 He made two bronze pillars, each one 9 metres tall and 6 metres around. 16 He also made two bronze capitals that were 2.5 metres tall, and he put them on top of the pillars. 17 Then he made a net of seven chains for each capital, which covered the capitals on top of the two pillars. 18 He made two rows of bronze pomegranates to go on the nets. These covered the capitals at the top of the pillars. 19 The capitals on top of the pillars in the porch were shaped like lilies, and they were 2 metres tall. 20 The capitals were on top of both pillars, above the bowl-shaped section and next to the nets. At that place there were 200 pomegranates in rows all around the capitals. 21 Huram put these two bronze pillars at the porch of the Temple. He named the south pillar He Establishes and the north pillar In Him Is Strength. 22 The capitals on top of the pillars were shaped like lilies. So the work on the pillars was finished.

23 Then Huram made from bronze a large round bowl, which was called the Sea. It was 15 metres around, 5 metres across and 2.5 metres deep. 24 Around the outer edge of the bowl was a rim. Under this rim were two rows of bronze plants which surrounded the bowl. There were ten plants every 50 centimetres, and these plants were made in one piece with the bowl. 25 The bowl rested on the backs of twelve bronze bulls that faced outwards from the centre of the bowl. Three bulls faced north, three faced west, three faced south and three faced east. 26 The sides of the bowl were 10 centimetres thick, and it held about 40,000 litres. The rim of the bowl was like the rim of a cup or like a lily blossom.

27 Then Huram made ten bronze stands, each one 2 metres long, 2 metres wide and 1.5 metres high. 28 The stands were made from square sides, which were put on frames. 29 On the sides were bronze lions, bulls and creatures with wings. On the frames above and below the lions and bulls were designs of flowers hammered into the bronze. 30 Each stand had four bronze wheels with bronze axles. At the corners there were bronze supports for a large bowl, and the supports had designs of flowers. 31 There was a frame on top of the bowls, 50 centimetres high above the bowls. The opening of the bowl was round, 75 centimetres deep. Designs were carved into the bronze on the frame, which was square, not round. 32 The four wheels, placed under the frame, were 75 centimetres high. The axles between the wheels were made as one piece with the stand. 33 The wheels were like a chariot's wheels. Everything on the wheels—the axles, rims, spokes and hubs—was made of bronze.

34 The four supports were on the four corners of each stand. They were made as one piece with the stand. 35 A strip of bronze around the top of each stand was 25 centimetres deep. It was also made as one piece with the stand. 36 The sides of the stand and the frames were covered with carvings of creatures with wings, as well as lions, palm trees and flowers. 37 This is the way Huram made the ten stands. The bronze for each stand was melted and poured into a mould, so all the stands were the same size and shape.

38 Huram also made ten bronze bowls,

one bowl for each of the ten stands. Each bowl was 2 metres across and could hold about 800 litres. 39 Huram put five stands on the south side of the Temple and five on the north side. He put the large bowl in the south-east corner of the Temple. 40 Huram also made bowls, shovels and small bowls.

So Huram finished all his work for King Solomon on the Temple of the LORD:
41 two pillars;
two large bowls for the capitals on top of the pillars;
two nets to cover the two large bowls for the capitals on top of the pillars;
42 400 pomegranates for the two nets (there were two rows of pomegranates for each net covering the bowls for the capitals on top of the pillars);
43 ten stands with a bowl on each stand;
44 the large bowl with twelve bulls under it;
45 the pots, shovels, small bowls and all the dishes for the Temple of the LORD.

Huram made everything King Solomon wanted from polished bronze. 46 The king had these things poured into clay moulds that were made in the plain of the Jordan River between Succoth and Zarethan. 47 Solomon never weighed the bronze used to make these things, because there was too much to weigh. So the total weight of all the bronze was never known.

48 Solomon also made all the things for the Temple of the LORD:
the golden altar;
the golden table which held the bread that shows God's people are in his presence;
49 the lampstands of pure gold (five on the right side and five on the left side in front of the Most Holy Place);
the flowers, lamps and tongs of gold;
50 the pure gold bowls, wick trimmers, small bowls, pans and dishes used to carry coals;
the gold hinges for the doors of the Most Holy Place and the main room of the Temple.

51 Finally the work King Solomon did for the Temple of the LORD was finished. Solomon brought in everything his father David had set apart for the Temple—silver, gold and other articles. He put everything in the treasuries of the Temple of the LORD.

> Finally the work King Solomon did for the Temple of the LORD was finished.
> —1 Kings 7:51

The Ark is Brought into the Temple

8 King Solomon called for the elders of Israel, the heads of the tribes and the leaders of the families to come to him in Jerusalem. He wanted them to bring the Ark of the Agreement with the LORD from the older part of the city 2 So all the Israelites came together with King Solomon during the festival in the month of Ethanim, the seventh month.

3 When all the elders of Israel arrived, the priests lifted up the Ark. 4 They carried the Ark of the LORD, the Meeting Tent and the holy things; the priests and the Levites brought them up. 5 King Solomon and all the Israelites gathered before the Ark and sacrificed so many sheep and cattle no one could count them all. 6 Then the priests put the Ark of the Agreement with the LORD in its place inside the Most Holy Place in the Temple, under the wings of the golden creatures. 7 The wings of these creatures were spread out over the place for the Ark, covering it and its carrying poles. 8 The carrying poles were so long that anyone standing in the Holy Place in front of the Most Holy Place could see the ends of the poles, but no one could see them

from outside the Holy Place. The poles are still there today. 9 The only things inside the Ark were two stone tablets*ⁿ* that Moses had put in the Ark at Mount Sinai. That was where the LORD made his agreement with the Israelites after they came out of Egypt.

10 When the priests left the Holy Place, a cloud filled the Temple of the LORD. 11 The priests could not continue their work, because the Temple was filled with the glory of the LORD.

Solomon Speaks to the People

12 Then Solomon said, "The LORD said he would live in a dark cloud. 13 LORD, I have truly built a wonderful Temple for you—a place for you to live for ever."

14 While all the Israelites were standing there, King Solomon turned to them and blessed them.

15 Then he said, "Praise the LORD, the God of Israel. He has done what he promised to my father David. The LORD said, 16 'Since the time I brought my people Israel out of Egypt, I have not chosen a city in any tribe of Israel where a temple will be built for me. But I have chosen David to lead my people Israel.'

17 "My father David wanted to build a temple for the LORD, the God of Israel. 18 But the LORD said to my father David, 'It was good that you wanted to build a temple for me. 19 But you are not the one to build it. Your son, who comes from your own body, is the one who will build my temple.'

20 "Now the LORD has kept his promise. I am the king now in place of David my father. Now I rule Israel as the LORD promised, and I have built the Temple for the LORD, the God of Israel. 21 I have made a place there for the Ark, in which is the Agreement the LORD made with our ancestors when he brought them out of Egypt."

Solomon's Prayer

22 Then Solomon stood facing the LORD's altar, and all the Israelites were standing behind him. He spread out his hands towards the sky 23 and said:

"LORD, God of Israel, there is no god like you in heaven above or on earth below. You keep your agreement of love with your servants who truly follow you. 24 You have kept the promise you made to your servant David, my father. You spoke it with your own mouth and finished it with your hands today. 25 Now LORD, God of Israel, keep the promise you made to your servant David, my father. You said, 'If your sons are careful to obey me as you have obeyed me, there will always be someone from your family ruling Israel.' 26 Now, God of Israel, please continue to keep that promise you made to your servant David, my father.

27 "But, God, can you really live here on the earth? The sky and the highest place in heaven cannot contain you. Surely this house which I have built cannot contain you. 28 But please listen to my prayer and my request, because I am your servant. LORD my God, hear this prayer your servant prays to you today. 29 Night and day please watch over this Temple where you have said, 'I will be worshipped there.' Hear the prayer I pray facing this Temple. 30 Hear my prayers and the prayers of your people Israel when we pray facing this place. Hear from your home in heaven, and when you hear, forgive us.

31 "If someone wrongs another person, he will be brought to the altar in this Temple. If he swears an oath that he is not guilty, 32 then hear in heaven. Judge the case, punish the guilty, but declare that the innocent person is not guilty.

33 "When your people, the Israelites, sin against you, their enemies will defeat them. But if they come back to you and praise you and pray to you in this Temple, 34 then hear them in heaven. Forgive the sins of your people Israel, and bring them back to the land you gave to their ancestors.

35 "When they sin against you, you will stop the rain from falling on their land.

8:27
God
Where does God live?

8:9 stone tablets They were the two tablets on which God wrote the Ten Commandments.

Then they will pray, facing this place and praising you; they will stop sinning when you make them suffer. 36 When this happens, please hear their prayer in heaven, and forgive the sins of your servants, the Israelites. Teach them to do what is right. Then please send rain to this land you have given particularly to them.

37 "At times the land will become so dry that no food will grow, or a great sickness will spread among the people. Sometimes all the crops will be destroyed by locusts or grasshoppers. Your people will be attacked in their cities by their enemy or will become sick. 38 When any of these things happen, the people will become truly sorry. If your people spread their hands in prayer towards this Temple, 39 then hear their prayers from your home in heaven. Forgive and treat each person as he should be treated because you know what is in a person's heart. Only you know what is in everyone's heart. 40 Then your people will respect you as long as they live in this land you gave to our ancestors.

41-42 "People who are not Israelites, foreigners from other lands, will hear about your greatness and power. They will come from far away to pray at this Temple. 43 Then hear from your home in heaven, and do whatever they ask you. Then people everywhere will know you and respect you, just as your people in Israel do. Then everyone will know I built this Temple as a place to worship you.

44 "When your people go out to fight their enemies along some road on which you send them, your people will pray to you, facing the city which you have chosen and the Temple I have built for you. 45 Then hear in heaven their prayers, and do what is right.

46 "Everyone sins, so your people will also sin against you. You will become angry with them and hand them over to their enemies. Their enemies will capture them and take them away to their countries far or near. 47 Your people will be sorry for their sins when they are held as prisoners in another country. They will be sorry and pray to you in the land where they are held as prisoners, saying, 'We have sinned. We have done wrong and acted wickedly.' 48 They will truly turn back to you in the land of their enemies. They will pray to you, facing this land you gave their ancestors, this city you have chosen and the Temple I have built for you. 49 Then hear their prayers from your home in heaven, and do what is right. 50 Forgive your people for all their sins and for turning against you. Make those who have captured them show them mercy. 51 Remember, they are your special people. You brought them out of Egypt, as if you were pulling them out of a blazing furnace.

52 "Give your attention to my prayers and the prayers of your people Israel. Listen to them whenever they ask you for help. 53 You chose them from all the nations on earth to be your very own people. This is what you promised through Moses your servant when you brought our ancestors out of Egypt, Lord GOD."

54 Solomon prayed this prayer to the LORD, kneeling in front of the altar with his arms raised towards heaven. When he finished praying, he got up. 55 Then, in a loud voice, he stood and blessed all the people of Israel, saying: 56 "Praise the LORD! He promised he would give rest to his people Israel, and he has given us rest. The LORD has kept all the good promises he gave through his servant Moses. 57 May the LORD our God be with us as he was with our ancestors. May he never leave us, 58 and may he turn us to himself so we will follow him. Let us obey all the laws and commands he gave our ancestors. 59 May the LORD our God remember this prayer day and night and do what is right for his servant and his people Israel day by day. 60 Then all the people of the world will know the LORD is the only true God. 61 You must fully obey the LORD our God and follow all his laws and commands. Continue to obey in the future as you do now."

Sacrifices are Offered

62 Then King Solomon and all Israel with him offered sacrifices to the LORD. 63 Solomon killed 22,000 cattle and

FAITH links

A CAUSE FOR CELEBRATION
1 KINGS 8:62-66

What are some occasions you like to celebrate? Birthdays? Anniversaries? Many churches hold a celebration when the church anniversary comes around. Church anniversaries are a reminder of how a church has grown together as a family. They're also a way to thank God for what he has done. The people of Israel celebrated after the completion of the Temple. A lot of hard work went into building the Temple. The people showed their thankfulness to God for blessing them.

You don't have to wait for a church anniversary to express your thanks to God. You can do it right now. In fact, why not make a habit of it? That's how holiday celebrations get their start.

My Worship Place, Genesis 35:1-14, p. 49

A Holiday Every Week, Leviticus 23:1-3, p. 166

A Song of Thanks, 1 Samuel 2, p. 356

The Gift of Worship, Matthew 2:10-12, p. 1275

Ten Things I Like About You, 2 Thessalonians 1:3-4, p. 1638

Touched by an Angel? Hebrews 1:3-4, p. 1667

120,000 sheep as fellowship offerings. So the king and all the people gave the Temple to the LORD.

64 On that day King Solomon made holy the middle part of the courtyard which is in front of the Temple of the LORD. There he offered whole burnt offerings, grain offerings and the fat of the fellowship offerings. He offered them in the courtyard, because the bronze altar before the LORD was too small to hold all the burnt offerings, the grain offerings and the fat of the fellowship offerings.

65 Solomon and all the Israelites celebrated the other festival that came at that time. People came from as far away as Lebo Hamath and the brook of Egypt. A great many people celebrated before the LORD for seven days, then seven more days, for a total of fourteen days. 66 On the following day Solomon sent the people home. They blessed the king as they went, happy because of all the good things the LORD had done for his servant David and his people Israel.

The LORD Appears to Solomon Again

9 Solomon finished building the Temple of the LORD and his royal palace and everything he wanted to build. 2 Then the LORD appeared to him again just as he had done before, in Gibeon. 3 The LORD said to him: "I have heard your prayer and what you have asked me to do. You built this Temple, and I have made it a holy place. I will be worshipped there for ever and will watch over it and protect it always.

4 "But you must serve me as your father David did; he was fair and sincere. You must obey all I have commanded and keep my laws and rules. 5 If you do, I will make your kingdom strong. This is the promise I made to your father David—that someone from his family would always rule Israel.

6 "But you and your children must follow me and obey the laws and commands I have given you. You must not serve or worship other gods. 7 If you do, I will force Israel to leave the land I have

FAITH links

THE WAY TO SERVE GOD
1 KINGS 9:4

If God were to describe your character to someone else, what do you think he would say? What would you want him to say? When God talked to Solomon about his father David, he described David as "fair and sincere". God wanted Solomon to be like that when he served God. God has that in mind for you as well. Are you like that?

What words come to mind to describe how you serve God? Connect here to see how God wants us to serve:

Share What You Have, Exodus 35:5–18, p. 123

Your Response to Responsibility, Ruth 2:1–7, p. 346

A Reminder to Be Fair, 2 Chronicles 19:5–11, p. 583

Let's Make a Deal, Daniel 1:8–21, p. 1150

Perfectly Pleasing? Matthew 5:1–12, p. 1280

Our Gift to God, Romans 12:1–2, p. 1536

---

given them, and I will leave this Temple that I have made holy. All the nations will make fun of Israel and speak evil about them. 8 If the Temple is destroyed, everyone who passes by will be shocked. They will make fun of you and ask, 'Why did the LORD do this terrible thing to this land and this Temple?' 9 People will answer, 'This happened because they left the LORD their God. This was the God who brought their ancestors out of Egypt, but they decided to follow other gods. They worshipped and served those gods, so the LORD brought all this disaster on them.'"

Solomon's Other Achievements

10 By the end of 20 years, King Solomon had built two buildings—the Temple of the LORD and the royal palace. 11 At that time King Solomon gave 20 towns in Galilee to Hiram king of Tyre, because Hiram had helped with the buildings. Hiram had given Solomon all the cedar, pine and gold he wanted. 12 So Hiram travelled from Tyre to see the towns Solomon had given him, but when he saw them, he was not pleased. 13 He asked, "What good are these towns you have given me, my brother?" So he named them the Land of Cabul,[n] and they are still called that today. 14 Hiram had sent Solomon about 4 tonnes of gold.

15 This is the account of the forced labour Solomon used to build the Temple and the palace. He had them fill in the land and build the wall around Jerusalem. He also had them rebuild the cities of Hazor, Megiddo and Gezer. 16 (In the past the king of Egypt had attacked and captured Gezer. After burning it, he killed the Canaanites who lived there. Then he gave it as a wedding present to his daughter, who married Solomon. 17 So Solomon rebuilt it.) He also built the cities of Lower Beth Horon 18 and Baalath, as well as Tadmor, which is in the desert. 19 King Solomon also built cities for storing grain and supplies and cities for his chariots and horses. He built whatever he wanted in Jerusalem, Lebanon and everywhere he ruled.

20 There were other people in the land who were not Israelites—Amorites, Hittites, Perizzites, Hivites and Jebusites. 21 They were descendants of people that the Israelites had not destroyed. Solomon forced them to work for him as slaves, as is still true today. 22 But Solomon did not make slaves of the Israelites. They were his soldiers, government leaders,

---

9:13 Cabul This name sounds like the Hebrew word for "worthless".

officers, captains, chariot commanders and drivers. 23 These were his most important officers over the work. There were 550 supervisors over the people who did the work on Solomon's projects.

24 The daughter of the king of Egypt moved from the old part of Jerusalem to the palace that Solomon had built for her. Then Solomon filled in the surrounding land.

25 Three times each year Solomon offered whole burnt offerings and fellowship offerings on the altar he had built for the LORD. He also burned incense before the LORD. So he finished the work on the Temple.

26 King Solomon also built ships at Ezion Geber, a town near Elath on the shore of the Red Sea, in the land of Edom. 27 Hiram had skilled sailors, so he sent them to serve in these ships with Solomon's men. 28 The ships sailed to Ophir and brought back about 14 tonnes of gold to King Solomon.

The Queen of Sheba Visits Solomon

10 When the queen of Sheba heard about Solomon, she came to test him with hard questions. 2 She travelled to Jerusalem with a large group of servants and camels carrying spices, jewels and much gold. When she came to Solomon, she talked with him about all she had in mind, 3 and Solomon answered all her questions. Nothing was too hard for him to explain to her. 4 The queen of Sheba learned that Solomon was very wise. She saw the palace he had built, 5 the food on his table, his many officers, the palace servants and their good clothes. She saw the servants who served him at feasts and the whole burnt offerings he made in the Temple of the LORD. All these things amazed her.

6 So she said to King Solomon, "What I heard in my own country about your achievements and wisdom is true. 7 I could not believe it then, but now I have come and seen it with my own eyes. I was not told even half of it! Your wisdom and wealth are much greater than I had heard. 8 Your men and officers are very happy, because in always serving you, they are able to hear your wisdom. 9 Praise the LORD your God, who was pleased to make you king of Israel. The LORD has

---

FAITH links

AN ADMIRABLE QUALITY
1 KINGS 10:1-13

Who is the person you most admire? What qualities make this person worth admiring? The queen of Sheba admired Solomon's wisdom. Even though there were no newspapers or TV, people all over the world had heard about Solomon's wisdom. The queen travelled a long way to ask Solomon questions and bring him gifts.

In today's society wisdom isn't prized as much as wealth or power. Still, God wants you to value having wisdom. Why? Because it comes from him. (Check out 2 Chronicles 9, p. 571, which also tells this story.)

A Different Kind of People, Leviticus 11, p. 146

Who Do You Trust? Joshua 9, p. 287

Our Thirst Quencher, Psalm 42:1–3, p. 741

The Best Advice, Zechariah 10:2, p. 1261

Put God First, Acts 5:27–32, p. 1472

Out of Your Mind? 1 Corinthians 2:16, p. 1547

constant love for Israel, so he made you king to keep justice and to rule fairly."

10 Then she gave the king about 4 tonnes of gold and many spices and jewels. No one since that time has brought more spices than the queen of Sheba gave to King Solomon.

11 (Hiram's ships brought gold from Ophir, as well as much juniper wood and jewels. 12 Solomon used the juniper wood to build supports for the Temple of the LORD and the palace, and to make harps and lyres for the musicians. Such fine juniper wood has not been brought in or been seen since that time.)

13 King Solomon gave the queen of Sheba everything she wanted and asked for, in addition to what he had already given her of his wealth. Then she and her servants returned to her own country.

Solomon's Wealth

14 Every year King Solomon received about 23 tonnes of gold. 15 Besides that, he also received gold from the traders and merchants, as well as from the kings of Arabia and governors of the land.

16 King Solomon made 200 large shields of hammered gold, each of which contained about 7 kilogrammes of gold. 17 He also made 300 smaller shields of hammered gold, each of which contained about 2 kilogrammes of gold. The king put them in the Palace of the Forest of Lebanon.

18 The king built a large throne of ivory and covered it with fine gold. 19 The throne had six steps on it, and its back was round at the top. There were armrests on both sides of the chair, and each armrest had a lion beside it. 20 Twelve lions stood on the six steps, one lion at each end of each step. Nothing like this had ever been made for any other kingdom. 21 All of Solomon's drinking cups, as well as the dishes in the Palace of the Forest of Lebanon, were made of pure gold. Nothing was made from silver, because silver was not so valuable in Solomon's time.

22 King Solomon also had many trading ships at sea, along with Hiram's ships. Every three years the ships returned, bringing back gold, silver, ivory, apes and baboons.

23 So Solomon had more riches and wisdom than all the other kings on earth. 24 People everywhere wanted to see King Solomon and listen to the wisdom God had given him. 25 Every year those who came brought gifts of silver and gold, clothes, weapons, spices, horses and mules.

26 Solomon had 1,400 chariots and 12,000 horses. He kept some in special cities for the chariots, and others he kept with him in Jerusalem. 27 In Jerusalem Solomon made silver as common as stones and cedar trees as common as the fig trees on the western hills. 28 He brought in horses from Egypt and Kue. His traders bought them in Kue. 29 A chariot from Egypt cost about 600 pieces of silver, and a horse cost nearly 150 pieces of silver. Solomon's traders also sold horses and chariots to all the kings of the Hittites and the Arameans.

Solomon's Many Wives

11 King Solomon loved many women who were not from Israel. He loved the daughter of the king of Egypt, as well as women of the Moabites, Ammonites, Edomites, Sidonians and Hittites. 2 The LORD had told the Israelites, "You must not marry people of other nations. If you do, they will cause you to follow their gods." But Solomon fell in love with these women. 3 He had 700 wives who were from royal families and 300 slave women who gave birth to his children. His wives caused him to turn away from God. 4 As Solomon grew old, his wives caused him to follow other gods. He did not follow the LORD completely as his father David had done. 5 Solomon worshipped Ashtoreth, the goddess of the people of Sidon, and Molech, the hated god of the Ammonites. 6 So Solomon did what the LORD said was wrong and did not follow the LORD completely as his father David had done.

7 On a hill east of Jerusalem, Solomon built two places for worship. One was a

place to worship Chemosh, the hated god of the Moabites, and the other was a place to worship Molech, the hated god of the Ammonites. 8 Solomon did the same thing for all his foreign wives so they could burn incense and offer sacrifices to their gods.

9 The LORD had appeared to Solomon twice, but the king turned away from following the LORD, the God of Israel. The LORD was angry with Solomon, 10 because he had commanded Solomon not to follow other gods. But Solomon did not obey the LORD's command. 11 So the LORD said to Solomon, "Because you have chosen to break your agreement with me and have not obeyed my commands, I will tear your kingdom away from you and give it to one of your officers. 12 But I will not take it away while you are alive because of my love for your father David. I will tear it away from your son when he becomes king. 13 I will not tear away all the kingdom from him, but I will leave him one tribe to rule. I will do this because of David, my servant, and because of Jerusalem, the city I have chosen."

Solomon's Enemies

14 The LORD caused Hadad the Edomite, a member of the family of the king of Edom, to become Solomon's enemy. 15 Earlier, David had defeated Edom. When Joab, the commander of David's army, went into Edom to bury the dead, he killed all the males. 16 Joab and all the Israelites stayed in Edom for six months and killed every male in Edom. 17 At that time Hadad was only a young boy, so he ran away to Egypt with some of his father's officers. 18 They left Midian and went to Paran, where they were joined by other men. Then they all went to Egypt to see the king, who gave Hadad a house, some food and some land.

19 The king liked Hadad so much he gave Hadad a wife—the sister of Tahpenes, the king's wife. 20 They had a son named Genubath. Queen Tahpenes brought him up in the royal palace with the king's own children.

21 While he was in Egypt, Hadad heard that David had died and that Joab, the commander of the army, was dead also. So Hadad said to the king, "Let me go; I will return to my own country."

22 "Why do you want to go back to your own country?" the king asked. "What haven't I given you here?"

"Nothing," Hadad answered, "but please, let me go."

THE WISDOM OF OBEYING GOD
1 KINGS 11:1-13

On his deathbed, David told his son Solomon to always obey God. Solomon obeyed God for a while. But later he disobeyed God's law by marrying foreign women and by worshipping other gods. Solomon had forgotten his father's wise advice.

Want to be wise? Don't forget the wise advice you've been given. If you have trouble remembering anything else, remember David's advice to Solomon: always obey God.

The Best Policy, Genesis 29:16–29, p. 41

Ten Ways to Obey, Exodus 20, p. 103

A Word to the Wise, Proverbs 10:1, p. 838

A Useless Thing, Isaiah 44:9, 18–20, p. 954

A Home Town Hurt, Jeremiah 11:8—12:6, p. 1008

Faith God Notices, Luke 18:35–43, p. 1406

23 God also caused another man to be Solomon's enemy—Rezon son of Eliada. Rezon had run away from his master, Hadadezer king of Zobah. 24 After David defeated the army of Zobah, Rezon gathered some men and became the leader of a small army. They went to Damascus and settled there, and Rezon became king of Damascus. 25 Rezon ruled Aram, and he hated Israel. So he was an enemy of Israel all the time Solomon was alive. Both Rezon and Hadad made trouble for Israel.

26 Jeroboam son of Nebat was one of Solomon's officers. He was an Ephraimite from the town of Zeredah, and he was the son of a widow named Zeruah. Jeroboam turned against the king.

27 This is the story of how Jeroboam turned against the king. Solomon was filling in the land and repairing the wall of Jerusalem, the city of David, his father. 28 Jeroboam was a capable man, and Solomon saw that this young man was a good worker. So Solomon put him over all the workers from the tribes of Ephraim and Manasseh.

29 One day as Jeroboam was leaving Jerusalem, Ahijah, the prophet from Shiloh, who was wearing a new coat, met him on the road. The two men were alone out in the country. 30 Ahijah took his new coat and tore it into twelve pieces. 31 Then he said to Jeroboam, "Take ten pieces of this coat for yourself. The LORD, the God of Israel, says: 'I will tear the kingdom away from Solomon and give you ten tribes. 32 But I will allow him to control one tribe. I will do this for the sake of my servant David and for Jerusalem, the city I have chosen from all the tribes of Israel. 33 I will do this because Solomon has stopped following me and has worshiped the Sidonian god Ashtoreth, the Moabite god Chemosh, and the Ammonite god Molech. Solomon has not obeyed me by doing what I said is right and obeying my laws and commands, as his father David did.

34 "'But I will not take all the kingdom away from Solomon. I will let him rule all his life because of my servant David, whom I chose, who obeyed all my commands and laws. 35 But I will take the kingdom away from his son, and I will allow you to rule over the ten tribes. 36 I will allow Solomon's son to continue to rule over one tribe so that there will always be a descendant of David, my servant, in Jerusalem, the city where I chose to be worshiped. 37 But I will make you rule over everything you want. You will rule over all of Israel, 38 and I will always be with you if you do what I say is right. You must obey all my commands. If you obey my laws and commands as David did, I will be with you. I will make your family a lasting family of kings, as I did for David, and give Israel to you. 39 I will punish David's children because of this, but I will not punish them for ever.'"

Solomon's Death

40 Solomon tried to kill Jeroboam, but he ran away to Egypt, to Shishak king of Egypt, where he stayed until Solomon died.

41 Everything else King Solomon did, and the wisdom he showed, is written in the book of the history of Solomon. 42 Solomon ruled in Jerusalem over all Israel for 40 years. 43 Then he died and was buried in Jerusalem, the city of David, his father. And his son Rehoboam became king in his place.

Israel Turns Against Rehoboam

12 Rehoboam went to Shechem, where all the Israelites had gone to make him king. 2 Jeroboam son of Nebat was still in Egypt, where he had gone to escape from Solomon. When Jeroboam heard about Rehoboam being made king, he was living in Egypt. 3 After the people sent for him, he and the people went to Rehoboam and said to him, 4 "Your father forced us to work very hard. Now, make it easier for us, and don't make us work as hard as he did. Then we will serve you."

5 Rehoboam answered, "Go away for three days, and then come back to me." So the people left.

6 King Rehoboam asked the elders who had advised Solomon during his lifetime, "How do you think I should answer these people?"

FAITH links

WHEN I NEED ADVICE
1 KINGS 12:1-17

What is your favourite source of advice: your friends or adults? After Solomon died, his son Rehoboam became king of Israel. Two groups of people came to him with advice on running the kingdom: a group of older leaders and a group of his friends. The older leaders told him to be kind to the people. The friends told him to be hard on the people. Rehoboam took his friends' advice. When he did, most of the kingdom rebelled against him.

There's nothing wrong with asking your friends for advice. But take time to consider the advice of godly adults as well. Their wisdom and experience might be just what you need.

Who do you ask for advice? Connect here to find out some good sources:

Good Advice? Leviticus 20:6, p. 162

I Want It Now! Judges 14:1–3, p. 332

Teaching Others, Ezra 7:8–10, p. 617

The Dead End of the Occult, Ezekiel 13:17–23, p. 1098

Going My Way? Hosea 8:1–6, p. 1179

Two Ways to Grow, Luke 2:46–52, p. 1370

---

7 They said, "You should be like a servant to them today. If you serve them and give them a kind answer, they will serve you always."

8 But Rehoboam rejected this advice. Instead, he asked the young men who had grown up with him and who served as his advisers. 9 Rehoboam asked them, "What is your advice? How should we answer these people who said, 'Don't make us work as hard as your father did'?"

10 The young men who had grown up with him answered, "Those people said to you, 'Your father forced us to work very hard. Now make our work easier.' You should tell them, 'My little finger is bigger than my father's legs. 11 He forced you to work hard, but I will make you work even harder. My father beat you with whips, but I will beat you with whips that have sharp points.'"

12 Rehoboam had told the people, "Come back to me in three days." So after three days Jeroboam and all the people returned to Rehoboam. 13 King Rehoboam spoke cruel words to them, because he had rejected the advice the elders had given him. 14 He followed the advice of the young men and said to the people, "My father forced you to work hard, but I will make you work even harder. My father beat you with whips, but I will beat you with whips that have sharp points." 15 So the king did not listen to the people. The LORD caused this to happen to keep the promise he had made to Jeroboam son of Nebat through Ahijah, a prophet from Shiloh.

16 When all the Israelites saw that the new king refused to listen to them, they said to the king,

"We have no share in David!
 We have no part in the son of Jesse!
People of Israel, let's go to our own homes!
 Let David's son rule his own people!"

So the Israelites went home. 17 But Rehoboam still ruled over the Israelites who lived in the towns of Judah.

18 Adoniram was in charge of the people who were forced to work. When

Rehoboam sent him to the people of Israel, they threw stones at him until he died. But King Rehoboam ran to his chariot and escaped to Jerusalem. 19 Since then, Israel has been against the family of David.

20 When all the Israelites heard that Jeroboam had returned, they called him to a meeting and made him king over all Israel. Only the tribe of Judah continued to follow the family of David.

21 When Rehoboam arrived in Jerusalem, he gathered 180,000 of the best soldiers from the tribes of Judah and Benjamin. As son of Solomon, Rehoboam wanted to fight the people of Israel to take back his kingdom.

22 But God spoke his word to Shemaiah, a man of God, saying, 23 "Speak to Solomon's son Rehoboam, the king of Judah, and to all the people of Judah and Benjamin and the rest of the people. Say to them, 24 'The LORD says you must not go to war against your brothers, the Israelites. Every one of you should go home, because I made all these things happen.'" So they obeyed the LORD's command and went home as the LORD had commanded.

25 Then Jeroboam made Shechem in the mountains of Ephraim a very strong city, and he lived there. He also went to the city of Peniel and made it stronger.

Jeroboam Builds Golden Calves

26 Jeroboam said to himself, "The kingdom will probably go back to David's family. 27 If the people continue going to the Temple of the LORD in Jerusalem to offer sacrifices, they will want to be ruled again by Rehoboam. Then they will kill me and follow Rehoboam king of Judah."

28 King Jeroboam asked for advice. Then he made two golden calves. "It is too long a journey for you to go to Jerusalem to worship," he said to the people. "Israel, here are your gods who brought you out of Egypt." 29 Jeroboam put one golden calf in the city of Bethel and the other in the city of Dan. 30 This became a very great sin, because the people travelled as far as Dan to worship the calf there.

31 Jeroboam built temples on the places of worship. He also chose priests from all the people, not just from the tribe of Levi. 32 And he started a new festival on the fifteenth day of the eighth month, just like the festival in Judah. During that time the king offered sacrifices on the altar, along with sacrifices to the calves in Bethel he had made. He also chose priests in Bethel to serve at the places of worship he had made. 33 So Jeroboam chose his own time for a festival for the Israelites—the fifteenth day of the eighth month. During that time he offered sacrifices on the altar he had built in Bethel. He set up a festival for the Israelites and offered sacrifices on the altar.

The Man of God Speaks Against Bethel

13 The LORD commanded a man of God from Judah to go to Bethel. When he arrived, Jeroboam was standing by the altar to offer a sacrifice. 2 The LORD had commanded the man of God to speak against the altar. The man said, "Altar, altar, the LORD says to you: 'David's family will have a son named Josiah. The priests for the places of worship now make their sacrifices on you, but Josiah will sacrifice those priests on you. Human bones will be burned on you.'" 3 That same day the man of God gave proof that these things would happen. "This is the LORD's sign that this will happen," he said. "This altar will break apart, and the ashes on it will fall to the ground."

4 When King Jeroboam heard what the man of God said about the altar in Bethel, the king raised his hand from the altar and pointed at the man. "Take him!" he said. But when the king said this, his arm was paralysed, and he could not move it. 5 The altar also broke into pieces, and its ashes fell to the ground. This was the sign the LORD had told the man of God to give.

6 Then the king said to the man of God, "Please pray to the LORD your God for me, and ask him to heal my arm."

So the man of God prayed to the LORD, and the king's arm was healed, becoming as it was before.

7 Then the king said to the man of God, "Please come home and eat with me, and I will give you a gift." 8 But the man of God answered the king, "Even if you gave me half of your kingdom, I would not go with you. I will not eat or drink anything in this place. 9 The LORD commanded me not to eat or drink anything nor to return on the same road by which I came." 10 So he took a different road and did not return on the same road by which he had come to Bethel.

11 Now an old prophet was living in Bethel. His sons came and told him what the man of God had done there that day. They also told their father what he had said to King Jeroboam. 12 The father asked, "Which road did he use when he left?" So his sons showed him the road the man of God from Judah had taken. 13 Then the prophet told his sons to put a saddle on his donkey. So they saddled the donkey, and he left.

14 He went after the man of God and found him sitting under an oak tree. The prophet asked, "Are you the man of God who came from Judah?"

The man answered, "Yes, I am."

15 The prophet said, "Please come home and eat with me."

16 "I can't go home with you," the man of God answered. "I can't eat or drink with you in this place. 17 The LORD said to me, 'Don't eat or drink anything there or return on the same road by which you came.'"

18 Then the old prophet said, "But I also am a prophet like you." Then he told a lie. He said, "An angel from the LORD came to me and told me to bring you to my home. He said you should eat and drink with me." 19 So the man of God went to the old prophet's house, and he ate and drank with him there.

20 While they were sitting at the table, the LORD spoke his word to the old prophet. 21 The old prophet cried out to the man of God from Judah, "The LORD said you did not obey him! He said you did not do what the LORD your God commanded you. 22 The LORD commanded you not to eat or drink anything in this place, but you came back and ate and drank. So your body will not be buried in your family grave."

23 After the man of God finished eating and drinking, the prophet put a saddle on his donkey for him, and the man left. 24 As he was travelling home, a lion attacked and killed him. His body lay on the road, with the donkey and the lion standing nearby. 25 Some men who were travelling on that road saw the body and the lion standing nearby. So they went to the city where the old prophet lived and told what they had seen.

26 The old prophet who had brought back the man of God heard what had happened. "It is the man of God who did not obey the LORD's command," he said. "So the LORD sent a lion to kill him, just as he said he would."

27 Then the prophet said to his sons, "Put a saddle on my donkey," which they did. 28 The old prophet went out and found the body lying on the road, with the donkey and the lion still standing nearby. The lion had not eaten the body or hurt the donkey. 29 The prophet put the body on his donkey and carried it back to the city to have a time of sadness for him and to bury him. 30 The prophet buried the body in his own family grave, and they were sad for the man of God and said, "Oh, my brother."

31 After the prophet buried the body, he said to his sons, "When I die, bury me in this same grave. Put my bones next to his. 32 Through him the LORD spoke against the altar at Bethel and against the places of worship in the towns of Samaria. What the LORD spoke through him will certainly come true."

33 After this incident King Jeroboam did not stop doing evil. He continued to choose priests for the places of worship from among all the people. Anyone who wanted to be a priest for the places of worship was allowed to be one. 34 In this way the family of Jeroboam sinned, and this sin caused its ruin and destruction from the earth.

Jeroboam's Son Dies

14 At that time Jeroboam's son Abijah became very sick. 2 So Jeroboam

said to his wife, "Go to Shiloh to see the prophet Ahijah. He is the one who said I would become king of Israel. But dress yourself so people won't know you are my wife. 3 Take the prophet ten loaves of bread, some cakes and a jar of honey. Then ask him what will happen to our son, and he will tell you." 4 So the king's wife did as he said and went to Ahijah's home in Shiloh.

Now Ahijah was very old and blind. 5 The LORD said to him, "Jeroboam's son is sick, and Jeroboam's wife is coming to ask you about him. When she arrives, she will pretend to be someone else." Then the LORD told Ahijah what to say.

6 When Ahijah heard her walking to the door, he said, "Come in, wife of Jeroboam. Why are you pretending to be someone else? I have bad news for you. 7 Go back and tell Jeroboam that this is what the LORD, the God of Israel, says: 'Jeroboam, I chose you from among all the people and made you the leader of my people Israel. 8 I tore the kingdom away from David's family, and I gave it to you. But you are not like my servant David, who always obeyed my commands and followed me with all my heart. He did only what I said was right. 9 But you have done more evil than anyone who ruled before you. You have stopped following me and have made other gods and idols of metal. This has made me very angry, 10 so I will soon bring disaster to your family. I will kill all the men in your family, both slaves and free men. I will destroy your family as completely as fire burns up manure. 11 Anyone from your family who dies in the city will be eaten by dogs, and those who die in the fields will be eaten by the birds. The LORD has spoken.'"

12 Then Ahijah said to Jeroboam's wife, "Go home now. As soon as you enter your city, your son will die, 13 and all Israel will be sad for him and bury him. He is the only one of Jeroboam's family who will be buried, because he is the only one in the king's family who pleased the LORD, the God of Israel.

14 "The LORD will put a new king over Israel, who will destroy Jeroboam's family, and this will happen soon. 15 Then the LORD will punish Israel, which will be like grass moving in the water. The LORD will pull up Israel from this good land, the land he gave their ancestors. He will scatter Israel beyond the Euphrates River, because he is angry with the people. They made the LORD angry when they set up idols to worship Asherah. 16 Jeroboam sinned, and then he made the people of Israel sin. So the LORD will let the people of Israel be defeated."

17 Then Jeroboam's wife left and returned to Tirzah. As soon as she entered her home, the boy died. 18 After they buried him, all Israel had a time of sadness for him, just as the LORD had said through his servant, the prophet Ahijah.

19 Everything else Jeroboam did is written in the book of the history of the kings of Israel. He fought wars and continued to rule the people, 20 serving as king for 22 years. Then he died, and his son Nadab became king in his place.

The Death of Rehoboam

21 Solomon's son Rehoboam was 41 years old when he became king of Judah. His mother was Naamah from Ammon. Rehoboam ruled in Jerusalem for seventeen years. (The LORD had chosen that city from all the land of Israel as the place where he would be worshipped.)

22 The people of Judah did what the LORD said was wrong. Their sins made the LORD very angry, even more angry than he had been at their ancestors. 23 The people built stone pillars and places to worship gods and Asherah idols on every high hill and under every green tree.

> But you are not like my servant David, who always obeyed my commands and followed me with all his heart.
> – 1 Kings 14:8

14:21–23 Idols
What does God think of worshipping other things?

24 There were even male prostitutes in the land. They acted like the people who had lived in the land before the Israelites. They had done many evil things, and God had taken the land away from them.

25 During the fifth year Rehoboam was king, Shishak king of Egypt attacked Jerusalem. 26 He took the treasures from the Temple of the LORD and the king's palace. He took everything, even the gold shields Solomon had made. 27 So King Rehoboam made bronze shields to put in their place and gave them to the commanders of the guards for the palace gates. 28 Whenever the king went to the Temple of the LORD, the guards carried the shields. Later, they would put them back in the guardroom.

29 Everything else King Rehoboam did is written in the book of the history of the kings of Judah. 30 There was hostility between Rehoboam and Jeroboam continually. 31 Rehoboam, son of Naamah from Ammon, died and was buried with his ancestors in Jerusalem, and his son Abijah became king in his place.

Abijah King of Judah

15 Abijah became king of Judah during the eighteenth year Jeroboam son of Nebat was king of Israel. 2 Abijah ruled in Jerusalem for three years. His mother was Maacah daughter of Abishalom. 3 He did all the same sins his father before him had done. Abijah was not faithful to the LORD his God as David, his great-grandfather, had been. 4 Because the LORD loved David, the LORD gave him a kingdom in Jerusalem and allowed him to have a son to be king after him. The LORD also kept Jerusalem safe. 5 David always did what the LORD said was right and obeyed his commands all his life, except the one time when David sinned against Uriah the Hittite.

6 There was war between Abijah and Jeroboam during Abijah's lifetime. 7 Everything else Abijah did is written in the book of the history of the kings of Judah. During the time Abijah ruled, there was war between Abijah and Jeroboam. 8 Abijah died and was buried in Jerusalem, and his son Asa became king in his place.

Asa King of Judah

9 During the twentieth year Jeroboam was king of Israel, Asa became king of Judah. 10 His grandmother's name was Maacah, the daughter of Abishalom. Asa ruled in Jerusalem for 41 years.

11 Asa did what the LORD said was right, as his ancestor David had done. 12 He forced the male prostitutes at the worship places to leave the country. He also took away the idols that his ancestors had made. 13 His grandmother Maacah had made a terrible Asherah idol, so Asa removed her from being queen mother. He cut down that idol and burned it in the Kidron Valley. 14 The places of worship to gods were not removed. Even so, Asa was faithful to the LORD all his life. 15 Asa brought into the Temple of the LORD the gifts he and his father had given: gold, silver and utensils.

16 There was war between Asa and Baasha king of Israel all the time they were kings. 17 Baasha attacked Judah, and he made the town of Ramah strong so he could keep people from leaving or entering Judah, Asa's country.

18 Asa took the rest of the silver and gold from the treasuries of the Temple of the LORD and his own palace and gave it to his officers. Then he sent them to Ben-Hadad son of Tabrimmon, who was the son of Hezion. Ben-Hadad was the king of Aram and ruled in the city of Damascus. Asa said, 19 "Let there be a treaty between you and me as there was between my father and your father. I am sending you a gift of silver and gold. Break your treaty with Baasha king of Israel so he will leave my land."

20 Ben-Hadad agreed with King Asa, so he sent the commanders of his armies to attack the towns of Israel. They defeated the towns of Ijon, Dan and Abel Beth Maacah, as well as all Galilee and the area of Naphtali. 21 When Baasha heard about these attacks, he stopped building up Ramah and returned to Tirzah. 22 Then King Asa gave an order to all the people of Judah; everyone had to help. They carried away all the stones and wood Baasha had been using in Ramah, and they used them to build

1 Kings 15:23   460

FAITH links

YOUR STATS
1 KINGS 15; 16

You can look at any sports player's stats to know whether or not they are good at what they do. Any football card, poster or match programme will tell you players' statistics. The listings or "stats" of the kings of Israel in 1 Kings reveal only one important item: whether or not they were obedient to God.

Your life is one big scorecard. Although you're at the beginning of your game right now, people can still tell by your life whether or not obeying God is important to you. Is it?

Obey? No Way! Exodus 1:15–21, p. 76

Remembering What He Said, Deuteronomy 6:4–9, p. 236

Bragging Rights, Jeremiah 9:23–24, p. 1005

Obeying God or Man? Daniel 3:8–30, p. 1154

Perfectly Pleasing? Matthew 5:1–12, p. 1280

Out with the Old! Colossians 3:1–14, p. 1625

up Geba and Mizpah in the land of Benjamin.

23 Everything else Asa did—his victories and the cities he built—is written in the book of the history of the kings of Judah. When he became old, he got a disease in his feet. 24 After Asa died, he was buried with his ancestors in Jerusalem, the city of David, his ancestor. Then Jehoshaphat, Asa's son, became king in his place.

Nadab King of Israel

25 Nadab son of Jeroboam became king of Israel during the second year Asa was king of Judah. Nadab was king of Israel for two years, 26 and he did what the LORD said was wrong. Jeroboam had led the people of Israel to sin, and Nadab sinned in the same way as his father Jeroboam.

27 Baasha son of Ahijah, from the tribe of Issachar, made plans to kill Nadab. Nadab and all Israel were attacking the Philistine town of Gibbethon, so Baasha killed Nadab there. 28 This happened during Asa's third year as king of Judah, and Baasha became the next king of Israel.

Baasha King of Israel

29 As soon as Baasha became king, he killed all of Jeroboam's family, leaving no one in Jeroboam's family alive. He destroyed them all as the LORD had said would happen through his servant Ahijah from Shiloh. 30 King Jeroboam had sinned very much and had led the people of Israel to sin, so he made the LORD, the God of Israel, very angry.

31 Everything else Nadab did is written in the book of the history of the kings of Israel. 32 There was war between Asa king of Judah and Baasha king of Israel all the time they ruled.

33 Baasha son of Ahijah became king of Israel during Asa's third year as king of Judah. Baasha ruled in Tirzah for 24 years, 34 and he did what the LORD said was wrong. Jeroboam had led the people of Israel to sin, and Baasha sinned in the same way as Jeroboam.

16 Jehu son of Hanani spoke the word of the LORD against King Baasha. 2 The LORD said, "You were nothing, but I took you and made you a leader over my people Israel. But you have followed the ways of Jeroboam and have led my people Israel to sin. Their sins have made me angry, 3 so, Baasha, I will soon destroy you and your family. I will do to you what I did to the family of Jeroboam son of Nebat. 4 Anyone from your family who

dies in the city will be eaten by dogs, and anyone from your family who dies in the fields will be eaten by birds."

5 Everything else Baasha did and all his victories are written down in the book of the history of the kings of Israel. 6 So Baasha died and was buried in Tirzah, and his son Elah became king in his place.

7 The LORD spoke his word against Baasha and his family through the prophet Jehu son of Hanani. Baasha had done many things the LORD said were wrong, which made the LORD very angry. He did the same evil deeds that Jeroboam's family had done before him. The LORD also spoke against Baasha because he killed all of Jeroboam's family.

Elah King of Israel

8 Elah son of Baasha became king of Israel during Asa's twenty-sixth year as king of Judah, and Elah ruled in Tirzah for two years.

9 Zimri, one of Elah's officers, commanded half of Elah's chariots. Zimri made plans against Elah while the king was in Tirzah, getting drunk at Arza's home. (Arza was in charge of the palace at Tirzah.) 10 Zimri went into Arza's house and killed Elah during Asa's twenty-seventh year as king of Judah. Then Zimri became king of Israel in Elah's place.

Zimri King of Israel

11 As soon as Zimri became king, he killed all of Baasha's family, not allowing any of Baasha's family or friends to live. 12 So Zimri destroyed all of Baasha's family just as the LORD had said it would happen through the prophet Jehu. 13 Baasha and his son Elah sinned and led the people of Israel to sin, and they made the LORD, the God of Israel, angry because of their worthless idols.

14 Everything else Elah did is written in the book of the history of the kings of Israel.

15 So during Asa's twenty-seventh year as king of Judah, Zimri became king of Israel and ruled in Tirzah seven days.

The army of Israel was camped near Gibbethon, a Philistine town. 16 The men in the camp heard that Zimri had made secret plans against King Elah and had killed him. So that day in the camp they made Omri, the commander of the army, king over Israel. 17 So Omri and all the Israelite army left Gibbethon and attacked Tirzah. 18 When Zimri saw that the city had been captured, he went into the palace and set it on fire, burning the palace and himself with it. 19 So Zimri died because he had sinned by doing what the LORD said was wrong. Jeroboam had led the people of Israel to sin, and Zimri sinned in the same way as Jeroboam.

20 Everything else Zimri did and the story of how he turned against King Elah are written down in the book of the history of the kings of Israel.

Omri King of Israel

21 The people of Israel were divided into two groups. Half of the people wanted Tibni son of Ginath to be king, while the other half wanted Omri. 22 Omri's followers were stronger than the followers of Tibni son of Ginath, so Tibni died and Omri became king.

23 Omri became king of Israel during the thirty-first year Asa was king of Judah. Omri ruled Israel for twelve years, six of those years in the city of Tirzah. 24 He bought the hill of Samaria from Shemer for about 6,000 pieces of silver. Omri built a city on that hill and called it Samaria after the name of its earlier owner, Shemer.

25 But Omri did what the LORD said was wrong; he did more evil than all the kings who came before him. 26 Jeroboam son of Nebat had led the people of Israel to sin, and Omri sinned in the same way as Jeroboam. The Israelites made the LORD, the God of Israel, very angry because they worshiped worthless idols.

27 Everything else Omri did and all his successes are written in the book of the history of the kings of Israel. 28 So Omri died and was buried in Samaria, and his son Ahab became king in his place.

Ahab King of Israel

29 Ahab son of Omri became king of Israel during Asa's thirty-eighth year as

king of Judah, and Ahab ruled Israel in the city of Samaria for 22 years. 30 More than any king before him, Ahab son of Omri did many things the LORD said were wrong. 31 He sinned in the same ways as Jeroboam son of Nebat, but he did even worse things. He married Jezebel daughter of Ethbaal, the king of Sidon. Then Ahab began to serve Baal and worship him. 32 He built a temple in Samaria for worshipping Baal and put an altar there for Baal. 33 Ahab also made an idol for worshipping Asherah. He did more things to make the LORD, the God of Israel, angry than all the other kings before him.

34 During the time of Ahab, Hiel from Bethel rebuilt the city of Jericho. It cost Hiel the life of Abiram, his oldest son, to begin work on the city, and it cost the life of Segub, his youngest son, to build the city gates. This happened just as the LORD, speaking through Joshua son of Nun, said it would happen."

Elijah Stops the Rain

17 Now Elijah the Tishbite was a prophet from the settlers in Gilead. "I serve the LORD, the God of Israel," Elijah said to Ahab. "As surely as the LORD lives, no rain or dew will fall during the next few years unless I command it."

2 Then the LORD spoke his word to Elijah: 3 "Leave this place and go east and hide near Kerith Ravine east of the Jordan River. 4 You may drink from the stream, and I have commanded ravens to bring you food there." 5 So Elijah did what the LORD said; he went to Kerith Ravine, east of the Jordan, and lived there. 6 The birds brought Elijah bread and meat every morning and evening, and he drank water from the stream.

7 After a while the stream dried up because there was no rain. 8 Then the LORD spoke his word to Elijah, 9 "Go to Zarephath in Sidon and live there. I have commanded a widow there to take care of you."

10 So Elijah went to Zarephath. When he reached the town gate, he saw a widow gathering wood for a fire. Elijah asked

FAITH links

GOOD TIMES AND BAD
1 KINGS 17

Did you ever think that serving God means you'd never have problems? During the prophet Elijah's time, there was no rain for three years. Without rain, food became scarce. But God took care of Elijah and a poor widow during the drought.

Jesus once said that God causes the rain to fall on "those who do right and . . . those who do wrong" (Matthew 5:45). Good times and hard times fall in the lives of Christians as well as people who don't believe in Jesus. God wants his people to have faith that he'll take care of them and bring them through the hard times.

Find out how your faith can get you through the tough times:

Good Plans, Genesis 45:7–8, p. 64

Your Best Defence, 2 Chronicles 20:1–12, p. 584

A Really Bad Day, Job 1:20–22; 2:10, p. 661

Facing Your Fears, Matthew 8:23–27, p. 1288

Hard Times, 2 Corinthians 1:8–10, p. 1570

A Good Habit, Ephesians 6:18, p. 1606

16:34 the LORD . . . happen When Joshua destroyed Jericho, he said whoever rebuilt the city would lose his oldest and youngest sons. See Joshua 6:26.

her, "Would you bring me a little water in a cup so I may have a drink." 11 As she was going to get his water, Elijah said, "Please bring me a piece of bread, too."

12 The woman answered, "As surely as the LORD your God lives, I have no bread. I have only a handful of flour in a jar and only a little olive oil in a jug. I came here to gather some wood so I could go home and cook our last meal. My son and I will eat it and then die from hunger."

13 "Don't worry," Elijah said to her. "Go home and cook your food as you have said. But first make a small loaf of bread from the flour you have, and bring it to me. Then cook something for yourself and your son. 14 The LORD, the God of Israel, says, 'That jar of flour will never be empty, and the jug will always have oil in it, until the day the LORD sends rain to the land.'"

15 So the woman went home and did what Elijah told her to do. And the woman and her son and Elijah had enough food every day. 16 The jar of flour and the jug of oil were never empty, just as the LORD, through Elijah, had promised.

Elijah Brings a Boy Back to Life

17 Some time later the son of the woman who owned the house became sick. He grew worse and worse and finally stopped breathing. 18 The woman said to Elijah, "Man of God, what have you done to me? Did you come here to remind me of my sin and to kill my son?"

19 Elijah said to her, "Give me your son." Elijah took the boy from her, carried him upstairs and laid him on the bed in the room where he was staying. 20 Then he prayed to the LORD: "LORD my God, this widow is letting me stay in her house. Why have you done this terrible thing to her and caused her son to die?" 21 Then Elijah lay on top of the boy three times. He prayed to the LORD, "LORD my God, let this boy live again!"

22 The LORD answered Elijah's prayer; the boy began breathing again and was alive. 23 Elijah carried the boy downstairs and gave him to his mother and said, "See! Your son is alive!"

24 "Now I know you really are a man from God," the woman said to Elijah. "I know that the LORD truly speaks through you!"

Elijah Kills the Prophets of Baal

18 During the third year without rain, the LORD spoke his word to Elijah: "Go and meet King Ahab, and I will soon send rain." 2 So Elijah went to meet Ahab.

By this time there was no food in Samaria. 3 King Ahab sent for Obadiah, who was in charge of the king's palace. (Obadiah was a true follower of the LORD. 4 When Jezebel was killing all the LORD's prophets, Obadiah hid 100 of them in two caves, 50 in one cave and 50 in another. He also brought them food and water.) 5 Ahab said to Obadiah, "Let's check every spring and valley in the land. Maybe we can find enough grass to keep our horses and mules alive and not have to kill our animals." 6 So each one chose a part of the country to search; Ahab went in one direction and Obadiah in another.

7 While Obadiah was on his way, Elijah met him. Obadiah recognised Elijah, so he bowed down to the ground and said, "Elijah? Is it really you, master?"

8 "Yes," Elijah answered. "Go and tell your master that I am here."

9 Then Obadiah said, "What wrong have I done for you to hand me over to Ahab like this? He will put me to death. 10 As surely as the LORD your God lives, the king has sent people to every country to search for you. If the ruler said you were not there, Ahab forced the ruler to swear you could not be found in his country. 11 Now you want me to go to my master and tell him, 'Elijah is here'? 12 The Spirit of the LORD may carry you to some other place after I leave. If I go and tell King Ahab you are here, and he comes and doesn't find you, he will kill me! I have followed the LORD since I was a boy. 13 Haven't you been told what I did? When Jezebel was killing the LORD's prophets, I hid 100 of them, 50 in one cave and 50 in another. I brought them food and water. 14 Now you want me to go and tell my master you are here? He will kill me!"

FAITH links

SITTING ON THE FENCE
1 KINGS 18

Ever hear someone say, "You're sitting on the fence"? That means, "You're not on one side or the other." Elijah knew that the Israelites sat on the fence about God. Sometimes they wanted to serve God. Other times, they wanted to worship Baal, a false god the people of Canaan worshipped. Elijah told the people to get off the fence and choose between God and Baal once and for all. Once they saw how amazing God was, they chose God.

Are you sitting on the fence about God? Maybe you're not sure about being a Christian. Or, maybe you're not sure how much of your life you want God to have. Want to come off the fence? It's up to you to choose a side.

The Perfect Leader? Numbers 20:1–13, p. 203

Remember Your Creator, Ecclesiastes 12:1, 13, p. 885

How to Worship God, Isaiah 58, p. 972

A Fake Apology, Hosea 6:1–7, p. 1177

Prove It! Matthew 16:1–4, p. 1302

Keeping Clean, 2 Corinthians 7:1, p. 1576

15 Elijah answered, "As surely as the LORD All-powerful lives, whom I serve, I will be seen by Ahab today."

16 So Obadiah went to Ahab and told him where Elijah was. Then Ahab went to meet Elijah.

17 When he saw Elijah, he asked, "Is it you—the biggest troublemaker in Israel?"

18 Elijah answered, "I have not made trouble in Israel. You and your father's family have made all this trouble by not obeying the LORD's commands. You have gone after the Baals. 19 Now tell all Israel to meet me at Mount Carmel. Also bring the 450 prophets of Baal and the 400 prophets of Asherah, who eat at Jezebel's table."

20 So Ahab called all the Israelites and those prophets to Mount Carmel. 21 Elijah approached the people and said, "How long will you not decide between two choices? If the LORD is the true God, follow him, but if Baal is the true God, follow him!" But the people said nothing.

22 Elijah said, "I am the only prophet of the LORD here, but there are 450 prophets of Baal. 23 Bring two bulls. Let the prophets of Baal choose one bull and kill it and cut it into pieces. Then let them put the meat on the wood, but they are not to set fire to it. I will prepare the other bull, putting the meat on the wood but not setting fire to it. 24 You prophets of Baal, pray to your god, and I will pray to the LORD. The god who answers by setting fire to his wood is the true God."

All the people agreed that this was a good idea.

25 Then Elijah said to the prophets of Baal, "There are many of you, so you go first. Choose a bull and prepare it. Pray to your god, but don't start the fire."

26 So they took the bull that was given to them and prepared it. They prayed to Baal from morning until noon, shouting, "Baal, answer us!" But there was no sound, and no one answered. They danced around the altar they had built.

27 At noon Elijah began to make fun of them. "Pray louder!" he said. "If Baal really is a god, maybe he is thinking, or

Get the Info

ELIJAH, THE PROPHET — 1 Kings 18

1. Elijah was known as a Tishbite, which probably means he was from a town called Tishbe. (Read 1 Kings 17:1.)

2. As God's prophet, Elijah predicted a drought (a water shortage) as a punishment against the wicked kings of Samaria, Ahab and Ahaziah.

3. During the drought, Elijah hid by a brook near the Kerith Ravine. He drank the water there and was miraculously fed by ravens. (Look at 1 Kings 17:1–7.)

4. Elijah helped a widow and her son in a town called Zarephath. Through a miracle, her oil and flour never ran out until the drought was over. (See 1 Kings 17:8–24.)

5. Elijah had a big showdown with 450 prophets of Baal on Mount Carmel. God sent fire from heaven to burn the altar and proved his power. (Look up 1 Kings 18:20–40.)

6. Elijah was taken up into heaven in a chariot of fire. (Look at 2 Kings 2:1–12, p. 476.)

---

busy, or travelling! Maybe he is sleeping so you will have to wake him!" 28 The prophets prayed louder, cutting themselves with swords and spears until their blood flowed, which was the way they worshipped. 29 The afternoon passed, and the prophets continued to act like this until it was time for the evening sacrifice. But no voice was heard; Baal did not answer, and no one paid attention.

30 Then Elijah said to all the people, "Now come to me." So they gathered around him, and Elijah rebuilt the altar of the LORD, which had been torn down. 31 He took twelve stones, one stone for each of the twelve tribes, the number of Jacob's sons. (The LORD changed Jacob's name to Israel.) 32 Elijah used these stones to rebuild the altar in honour of the LORD. Then he dug a ditch around the altar that was big enough to hold about 14 litres of seed. 33 Elijah put the wood on the altar, cut the bull into pieces and laid the pieces on the wood. 34 Then he said, "Fill four jars with water, and pour it on the meat and on the wood." Then Elijah said, "Do it again," and they did it again. Then he said, "Do it a third time," and they did it the third time. 35 So the water ran off the altar and filled the ditch.

36 At the time for the evening sacrifice, the prophet Elijah went near the altar. "LORD, you are the God of Abraham, Isaac and Israel," he prayed. "Prove that you are the God of Israel and that I am your servant. Show these people that you commanded me to do all these things. 37 LORD, answer my prayer so these people will know that you, LORD, are God and that you will change their minds."

38 Then fire from the LORD came down and burned the sacrifice, the wood, the stones and the ground around the altar. It also dried up the water in the ditch. 39 When all the people saw this, they fell down to the ground, crying, "The LORD is God! The LORD is God!"

40 Then Elijah said, "Capture the prophets of Baal! Don't let any of them run away!" The people captured all the prophets. Then Elijah led them down to the Kishon Valley, where he killed them.

The Rain Comes Again

41 Then Elijah said to Ahab, "Now, go, eat and drink, because a heavy rain is coming." 42 So King Ahab went to eat and drink. At the same time Elijah climbed to the top of Mount Carmel, where he bent down to the ground with his head between his knees.

43 Then Elijah said to his servant, "Go and look towards the sea."

The servant went and looked. "I see nothing," he said.

Elijah told him to go and look again. This happened seven times. 44 The seventh time, the servant said, "I see a small cloud, the size of a human fist, coming from the sea."

Elijah told the servant, "Go to Ahab and tell him to get his chariot ready and go home now. Otherwise, the rain will stop him."

45 After a short time the sky was covered with dark clouds. The wind began to blow, and soon a heavy rain began to fall. Ahab got in his chariot and started back to Jezreel. 46 The LORD gave his power to Elijah, who tightened his clothes around him and ran ahead of King Ahab all the way to Jezreel.

Elijah Runs Away

19 King Ahab told Jezebel everything Elijah had done and how Elijah had killed all the prophets with a sword. 2 So Jezebel sent a messenger to Elijah, saying, "May the gods punish me terribly if by this time tomorrow I don't kill you just as you killed those prophets."

3 When Elijah heard this, he was afraid and ran for his life, taking his servant with him. When they came to Beersheba in Judah, Elijah left his servant there. 4 Then Elijah walked for a whole day into the desert. He sat down under a bush and asked to die. "I have had enough, LORD," he prayed. "Let me die. I am no better than my ancestors." 5 Then he lay down under the tree and slept.

Suddenly an angel came to him and touched him. "Get up and eat," the angel said. 6 Elijah saw near his head a loaf baked over coals and a jar of water, so he ate and drank. Then he went back to sleep.

7 Later the LORD's angel came to him a second time. The angel touched him and said, "Get up and eat. If you don't, the journey will be too hard for you." 8 So Elijah got up and ate and drank. The food made him strong enough to walk for 40 days and nights to Mount Sinai, the mountain of God. 9 There Elijah went into a cave and stayed all night.

Then the LORD spoke his word to him: "Elijah! Why are you here?"

10 He answered, "LORD God All-powerful, I have always served you as well as I could. But the people of Israel have broken their agreement with you, destroyed your altars and killed your prophets with swords. I am the only prophet left, and now they are trying to kill me, too."

11 The LORD said to Elijah, "Go, stand in front of me on the mountain, and I will pass by you." Then a very strong wind blew until it caused the mountains to fall apart and large rocks to break in front of the LORD. But the LORD was not in the wind. After the wind, there was an earthquake, but the LORD was not in the earthquake. 12 After the earthquake, there was a fire, but the LORD was not in the fire. After the fire, there was a quiet, gentle

FAITH links

LISTEN UP!
1 KINGS 19:11-13

When you're feeling discouraged, what cheers you up? Elijah needed some encouragement. Queen Jezebel, the wife of Ahab, wanted to give him a new address – six feet under. So he ran for his life. During that time, God taught him how to listen for his voice. God's voice was a "quiet, gentle sound". Elijah had not expected God to come to him in that way!

In what ways do you expect God to speak to you? Some might want God to speak in a noticeable way (like dropping a note to earth from heaven). But God wants you to be ready to listen in whatever way he speaks. Are you ready?

Here are some other Faithlinks on listening to God's word:

Comfort from the Word, Job 26:3-4, p. 688

Our Heavenly Shepherd, Psalm 23, p. 726

Learning from Mistakes, Psalm 51:12-13, p. 748

How Do I Love You? Malachi 1:1-5, p. 1267

Flex Your Faith, Acts 3:1-16, p. 1467

One Thing to Do, Romans 4:1-5, p. 1523

---

sound. 13 When Elijah heard it, he covered his face with his coat and went out and stood at the entrance to the cave.

Then a voice said to him, "Elijah! Why are you here?"

14 He answered, "LORD God All-powerful, I have always served you as well as I could. But the people of Israel have broken their agreement with you, destroyed your altars and killed your prophets with swords. I am the only prophet left, and now they are trying to kill me, too."

15 The LORD said to him, "Go back on the road that leads to the desert around Damascus. Enter that city, and pour olive oil on Hazael to make him king over Aram. 16 Then pour oil on Jehu son of Nimshi to make him king over Israel. Next, pour oil on Elisha son of Shaphat from Abel Meholah to make him a prophet in your place. 17 Jehu will kill anyone who escapes from Hazael's sword, and Elisha will kill anyone who escapes from Jehu's sword. 18 I have 7,000 people left in Israel who have never bowed down before Baal and whose mouths have never kissed his idol."

Elisha Becomes a Prophet

19 So Elijah left that place and found Elisha son of Shaphat ploughing a field with a team of oxen. He owned twelve teams of oxen and was ploughing with the twelfth team. Elijah came up to Elisha, took off his coat and put it on Elisha. 20 Then Elisha left his oxen and ran to follow Elijah. "Let me kiss my father and my mother goodbye," Elisha said. "Then I will go with you."

Elijah answered, "Go back. It does not matter to me."

21 So Elisha went back and took his pair of oxen and killed them. He used their wooden yoke for a fire. Then he cooked the meat and gave it to the people. After they ate it, Elisha left and followed Elijah and became his helper.

Ben-Hadad and Ahab Go to War

20 Ben-Hadad king of Aram gathered together all his army. There were 32 kings with their horses and chariots who went with him and surrounded

Samaria and attacked it. 2 The king sent messengers into the city to Ahab king of Israel.

This was his message: "Ben-Hadad says, 3 'Your silver and gold belong to me, as well as the best of your wives and children.'"

4 Ahab king of Israel answered, "My master and king, I agree to what you say. I and everything I have belong to you."

5 Then the messengers came to Ahab again. They said, "Ben-Hadad says, 'I told you before that you must give me your silver and gold, your wives and your children. 6 About this time tomorrow I will send my men, who will search everywhere in your palace and in the homes of your officers. Whatever they want they will take and carry off.'"

7 Then Ahab called a meeting of all the elders of his country. He said, "Ben-Hadad is looking for trouble. First he said I had to give him my wives, my children, my silver and my gold, and I have not refused him."

8 The elders and all the people said, "Don't listen to him or agree to this."

9 So Ahab said to Ben-Hadad's messengers, "Tell my master the king: 'I will do what you said at first, but I cannot allow this second command.'" And King Ben-Hadad's men carried the message back to him.

10 Then Ben-Hadad sent another message to Ahab: "May the gods punish me terribly if I don't completely destroy Samaria. There won't be enough left for each of my men to get a handful of dust!"

11 Ahab answered, "Tell Ben-Hadad, 'The man who puts on his armour should not boast. It's the man who lives to take it off who has the right to boast.'"

12 Ben-Hadad was drinking in his tent with the other rulers when the message came from Ahab. Ben-Hadad commanded his men to prepare to attack the city, and they moved into place for battle.

13 At the same time a prophet came to Ahab king of Israel. The prophet said, "Ahab, the LORD says to you, 'Do you see that big army? I will hand it over to you today so you will know I am the LORD.'"

14 Ahab asked, "Who will you use to defeat them?"

The prophet answered, "The LORD says, 'The young officers of the district governors will defeat them.'"

Then the king asked, "Who will command the main army?"

The prophet answered, "You will."

15 So Ahab gathered the young officers of the district governors, 232 of them. Then he called together the army of Israel, about 7,000 people in all.

16 They marched out at noon, while Ben-Hadad and the 32 rulers helping him were getting drunk in their tents. 17 The young officers of the district governors attacked first. Ben-Hadad sent out scouts who told him that soldiers were coming from Samaria. 18 Ben-Hadad said, "They may be coming to fight, or they may be coming to ask for peace. In either case capture them alive."

19 The young officers of the district governors led the attack, followed by the army of Israel. 20 Each officer of Israel killed the man who came against him. The men from Aram ran away as Israel chased them, but Ben-Hadad king of Aram escaped on a horse with some of his horsemen. 21 Ahab king of Israel led the army and destroyed the Arameans' horses and chariots. King Ahab thoroughly defeated the Aramean army.

22 Then the prophet went to Ahab king of Israel and said, "The king of Aram will attack you again next spring. So go home now and strengthen your army and see what you need to do."

23 Meanwhile the officers of Ben-Hadad king of Aram said to him, "The gods of Israel are mountain gods. Since we fought in a mountain area, Israel won. Let's fight them on the flat land, and then we will win. 24 This is what you should do. Don't allow the 32 rulers to command the armies, but put other commanders in their places. 25 Gather an army like the one that was destroyed and as many horses and chariots as before. We will fight the Israelites on flat land, and then we will win." Ben-Hadad agreed with their advice and did what they said.

26 The next spring Ben-Hadad gathered the army of Aram and went up to Aphek to fight against Israel. 27 The Israelites also had prepared for war. They marched out to meet the Arameans and camped opposite them. The Israelites looked like two small flocks of goats, but the Arameans covered the area.

28 A man of God came to the king of Israel with this message: "The LORD says, 'The people of Aram say that I, the LORD, am a god of the mountains, not a god of the valleys. So I will allow you to defeat this big army, and then you will know I am the LORD.'"

29 The armies were camped across from each other for seven days. On the seventh day the battle began. The Israelites killed 100,000 Aramean soldiers in one day. 30 The rest of them ran away to the city of Aphek, where a city wall fell on 27,000 of them. Ben-Hadad also ran away to the city and hid in a room.

31 His officers said to him, "We have heard that the kings of Israel are trustworthy. Let's dress in rough cloth to show our sadness, and wear ropes on our heads. Then we will go to the king of Israel, and perhaps he will let you live."

32 So they dressed in rough cloth and wore ropes on their heads and went to the king of Israel. They said, "Your servant Ben-Hadad says, 'Please let me live.'"

Ahab answered, "Is he still alive? He is my brother."

33 Ben-Hadad's men had wanted a sign from Ahab. So when Ahab called Ben-Hadad his brother, they quickly said, "Yes! Ben-Hadad is your brother."

Ahab said, "Bring him to me." When Ben-Hadad came, Ahab asked him to join him in the chariot.

34 Ben-Hadad said to him, "Ahab, I will give you back the cities my father took from your father. And you may put shops in Damascus, as my father did in Samaria."

Ahab said, "If you agree to this, I will allow you to go free." So the two kings made a peace agreement. Then Ahab let Ben-Hadad go free.

A Prophet Speaks Against Ahab

35 One prophet from one of the groups of prophets told another, "Hit me!" He said this because the LORD had commanded it, but the other man refused. 36 The prophet said, "You did not obey the LORD's command, so a lion will kill you as soon as you leave me." When the man left, a lion found him and killed him.

37 The prophet went to another man and said, "Hit me, please!" So the man hit him and hurt him. 38 The prophet wrapped his face in a cloth so no one could tell who he was. Then he went and waited by the road for the king. 39 As Ahab king of Israel passed by, the prophet called out to him. "I went to fight in the battle," the prophet said. "One of our men brought an enemy soldier to me. Our man said, 'Guard this man. If he runs away, you will have to give your life in his place. Or, you will have to pay a fine of 3,000 pieces of silver.' 40 But I was busy doing other things, so the man ran away."

The king of Israel answered, "You have already said what the punishment is. You must do what the man said."

41 Then the prophet quickly took the cloth from his face. When the king of Israel saw him, he knew he was one of the prophets. 42 The prophet said to the king, "This is what the LORD says: 'You freed the man I said should die, so your life will be taken instead of his. The lives of your people will also be taken instead of the lives of his people.'"

43 Then King Ahab went back to his palace in Samaria, angry and upset.

Ahab Takes Naboth's Vineyard

21 After these things had happened, this is what followed. A man named Naboth owned a vineyard in Jezreel, near the palace of Ahab king of Israel. 2 One day Ahab said to Naboth, "Give me your vineyard. It is near my palace, and I want to make it into a vegetable garden. I will give you a better vineyard in its place, or, if you prefer, I will pay you what it is worth."

3 Naboth answered, "May the LORD

keep me from ever giving my land to you. It belongs to my family."

4 Ahab went home angry and upset, because he did not like what Naboth from Jezreel had said. (Naboth had said, "I will not give you my family's land.") Ahab lay down on his bed, turned his face to the wall and refused to eat.

5 His wife, Jezebel, came in and asked him, "Why are you so upset that you refuse to eat?"

6 Ahab answered, "I talked to Naboth, the man from Jezreel. I said, 'Sell me your vineyard, or, if you prefer, I will give you another vineyard for it.' But Naboth refused."

7 Jezebel answered, "Is this how you rule as king over Israel? Get up, eat something, and cheer up. I will get Naboth's vineyard for you."

8 So Jezebel wrote some letters, signed Ahab's name to them, and used his own seal to seal them. Then she sent them to the elders and important men who lived in Naboth's town. 9 The letter she wrote said: "Declare a day during which the people are to give up eating. Call the people together, and give Naboth a place of honour among them. 10 Seat two troublemakers across from him, and have them say they heard Naboth speak against God and the king. Then take Naboth out of the city and kill him with stones."

11 The elders and important men of Jezreel obeyed Jezebel's command, just as she wrote in the letters. 12 They declared a special day on which the people were to give up eating. And they put Naboth in a place of honour before the people. 13 Two troublemakers sat across from Naboth and said in front of everybody that they had heard him speak against God and the king. So the people carried Naboth out of the city and killed him with stones. 14 Then the leaders sent a message to Jezebel, saying, "Naboth has been killed."

15 When Jezebel heard that Naboth had been killed, she told Ahab, "Naboth of Jezreel is dead. Now you may go and take for yourself the vineyard he would not sell to you." 16 When Ahab heard that Naboth of Jezreel was dead, he got up and went to the vineyard to take it for his own.

17 At this time the LORD spoke his

FAITH links

ABOVE THE LAW
1 KINGS 21

Ahab, the king of the northern kingdom of Israel, was considered one of the worst kings ever. With his wife Jezebel, he did whatever he had to do to get what he wanted. When he disobeyed God's laws (don't steal; don't kill) by taking a vineyard that didn't belong to him, he thought he was above the law. After all, he *was* the king. But God had one law about sin for all people.

When it comes to sin, a person's name, rank and serial number don't matter to God. Fame or influence won't get you out of the consequences of sin. What can make a difference in your life is who you know: Jesus.

The Trouble with Sin, Genesis 6—8, p. 11

Facing the Consequences, Deuteronomy 3:21–29, p. 232

What God "Hates", Proverbs 6:16–19, p. 835

Believe the Impossible? Ezekiel 37, p. 1131

A High Price, Romans 6:23, p. 1526

The Winner's Crown, 1 Corinthians 9:24–27, p. 1555

word to the prophet Elijah the Tishbite. The LORD said, 18 "Go to Ahab king of Israel in Samaria. He is at Naboth's vineyard, where he has gone to take it as his own. 19 Tell Ahab that I, the LORD, say to him, 'You have murdered Naboth and taken his land. So I tell you this: in the same place the dogs licked up Naboth's blood, they will also lick up your blood!'"

20 When Ahab saw Elijah, he said, "So you have found me, my enemy!"

Elijah answered, "Yes, I have found you. You have always chosen to do what the LORD says is wrong. 21 So the LORD says to you, 'I will soon destroy you. I will kill you and every male in your family, both slave and free. 22 Your family will be like the family of King Jeroboam son of Nebat and like the family of King Baasha son of Ahijah. I will destroy you, because you have made me angry and have led the people of Israel to sin.'

23 "And the LORD also says, 'Dogs will eat the body of Jezebel in the city of Jezreel.'

24 "Anyone in your family who dies in the city will be eaten by dogs, and anyone who dies in the fields will be eaten by birds.'"

25 There was no one like Ahab who had chosen so often to do what the LORD said was wrong, because his wife Jezebel influenced him to do evil. 26 Ahab sinned terribly by worshipping idols, just as the Amorite people did. And the LORD had taken away their land and given it to the people of Israel.

27 After Elijah finished speaking, Ahab tore his clothes. He put on rough cloth, refused to eat and even slept in the rough cloth to show how sad and upset he was.

28 The LORD spoke his word to Elijah the Tishbite: 29 "I see that Ahab is now sorry for what he has done. So I will not cause the trouble to come to him during his life, but I will wait until his son is king. Then I will bring this trouble to Ahab's family."

The Death of Ahab

22 For three years there was peace between Israel and Aram. 2 During the third year Jehoshaphat king of Judah went to visit Ahab king of Israel.

3 At that time Ahab asked his officers, "Do you remember that the king of Aram took Ramoth in Gilead from us? Why have we done nothing to get it back?" 4 So Ahab asked King Jehoshaphat, "Will you go with me to fight at Ramoth in Gilead?"

"I will go with you," Jehoshaphat answered. "My soldiers are yours, and my horses are yours." 5 Jehoshaphat also said to Ahab, "But first we should ask if this is the LORD's will."

6 Ahab called about 400 prophets together and asked them, "Should I go to war against Ramoth in Gilead or not?"

They answered, "Go, because the Lord will hand them over to you."

7 But Jehoshaphat asked, "Isn't there a prophet of the LORD here? Let's ask him what we should do."

8 Then King Ahab said to Jehoshaphat, "There is one other prophet. We could ask the LORD through him, but I hate him. He never prophesies anything good about me, but something bad. He is Micaiah son of Imlah."

Jehoshaphat said, "King Ahab, you shouldn't say that!"

9 So Ahab king of Israel told one of his officers to bring Micaiah to him at once.

10 Ahab king of Israel and Jehoshaphat king of Judah had on their royal robes and were sitting on their thrones at the threshing floor, near the entrance to the gate of Samaria. All the prophets were standing before them, speaking their messages. 11 Zedekiah son of Kenaanah had made some iron horns. He said to Ahab, "This is what the LORD says, 'You will use these horns to fight the Arameans until they are destroyed.'"

12 All the other prophets said the same thing. "Attack Ramoth in Gilead and win, because the LORD will hand the Arameans over to you."

13 The messenger who had gone to get Micaiah said to him, "All the other prophets are saying King Ahab will succeed. You should agree with them and give the king a good answer."

FAITH links

GIVE IN OR TAKE A STAND?
1 KINGS 22:13-14

"C'mon and try it. Everybody's doing it." Have you heard words like that before? You feel pressured to do something that "everyone else" is doing. Even Old Testament prophets know what being pressured is like. King Ahab tried to pressure Micaiah into siding with him about going to war. Four hundred other prophets told the king what he wanted to hear. Micaiah was the only one who spoke for the Lord. (Surf over to 2 Chronicles 18, p. 581, for another version of this story.)

There may be times when you'll have to stand alone in order to do what's right. That can seem pretty scary. But whenever you stand for what's right, God stands with you.

Who do you stand for? Connect here for some links on that:

His OK to Obey, Deuteronomy 2:24–36, p. 230

No Middle Ground, Joshua 24:14–15, p. 307

The Big Risk, Esther 4:11—5:2, p. 652

When Bad Things Happen, Ecclesiastes 3:16–17, p. 876

Stand! Jeremiah 19:14—20:6, p. 1019

The Unpopular Choice, Mark 15:42–43, p. 1360

---

14 But Micaiah answered, "As surely as the LORD lives, I can tell him only what the LORD tells me."

15 When Micaiah came to Ahab, the king asked him, "Micaiah, should we attack Ramoth in Gilead or not?"

Micaiah answered, "Attack and win! The LORD will hand them over to you."

16 But Ahab said to Micaiah, "How many times do I have to tell you to speak only the truth to me in the name of the LORD?"

17 So Micaiah answered, "I saw the army of Israel scattered over the hills like sheep without a shepherd. The LORD said, 'They have no leaders. They should go home and not fight.'"

18 Then Ahab king of Israel said to Jehoshaphat, "I told you! He never prophesies anything good about me, but only bad."

19 But Micaiah said, "Hear the message from the LORD: I saw the LORD sitting on his throne with his heavenly army standing near him on his right and on his left. 20 The LORD said, 'Who will trick Ahab into attacking Ramoth in Gilead where he will be killed?'

"Some said one thing; some said another. 21 Then one spirit came and stood before the LORD and said, 'I will trick him.'

22 "The LORD asked, 'How will you do it?'

"The spirit answered, 'I will go to Ahab's prophets and make them tell lies.'

"So the LORD said, 'You will succeed in tricking him. Go and do it.'"

23 Micaiah said, "Ahab, the LORD has made your prophets lie to you, and the LORD has decided that disaster should come to you."

24 Then Zedekiah son of Kenaanah went up to Micaiah and slapped him in the face. Zedekiah said, "Has the LORD's spirit left me to speak through you?"

25 Micaiah answered, "You will find out on the day you go to hide in an inside room."

26 Then Ahab king of Israel ordered, "Take Micaiah and send him to Amon, the governor of the city, and to Joash, the king's son. 27 Tell them I said to put this

man in prison and give him only bread and water until I return safely from the battle."

28 Micaiah said, "Ahab, if you come back safely from battle, the LORD has not spoken through me. Remember my words, all you people!"

29 So Ahab king of Israel and Jehoshaphat king of Judah went to Ramoth in Gilead. 30 King Ahab said to Jehoshaphat, "I will go into battle, but I will wear other clothes so no one will recognise me. But you wear your royal clothes." So Ahab wore other clothes and went into battle.

31 The king of Aram had ordered his 32 chariot commanders, "Don't fight with anyone—important or unimportant—except the king of Israel." 32 When these commanders saw Jehoshaphat, they thought he was certainly the king of Israel, so they turned to attack him. But Jehoshaphat began shouting. 33 When they saw he was not King Ahab, they stopped chasing him.

34 By chance, a soldier shot an arrow, but he hit Ahab king of Israel between the pieces of his armour. King Ahab said to his chariot driver, "Turn round and get me out of the battle, because I am hurt!" 35 The battle continued all day. King Ahab was held up in his chariot and faced the Arameans. His blood flowed down to the bottom of the chariot. That evening he died. 36 Near sunset a cry went out through the army of Israel: "Each man go back to his own city and land."

37 In that way King Ahab died. His body was carried to Samaria and buried there. 38 The men cleaned Ahab's chariot at a pool in Samaria where prostitutes bathed, and the dogs licked his blood from the chariot. These things happened as the LORD had said they would.

39 Everything else Ahab did is written in the book of the history of the kings of Israel. It tells about the palace Ahab built and decorated with ivory and the cities he built. 40 So Ahab died, and his son Ahaziah became king in his place.

Jehoshaphat King of Judah

41 Jehoshaphat son of Asa became king of Judah during Ahab's fourth year as king of Israel. 42 Jehoshaphat was 35 years old when he became king, and he ruled in Jerusalem for 25 years. His mother's name was Azubah daughter of Shilhi. 43 Jehoshaphat was good, like his father Asa, and he did what the LORD said was right. But Jehoshaphat did not destroy the places where gods were worshipped, so the people continued offering sacrifices and burning incense there. 44 Jehoshaphat was at peace with the king of Israel. 45 Jehoshaphat fought many wars, and these wars and his successes are written in the book of the history of the kings of Judah. 46 There were male prostitutes still in the places of worship from the days of his father, Asa. So Jehoshaphat forced them to leave.

47 During this time the land of Edom had no king; it was ruled by a governor.

48 King Jehoshaphat built trading ships to sail to Ophir for gold. But the ships were destroyed at Ezion Geber, so they never set sail. 49 Ahaziah son of Ahab went to help Jehoshaphat, offering to give Jehoshaphat some men to sail with his men, but Jehoshaphat refused.

50 Jehoshaphat died and was buried with his ancestors in Jerusalem, the city of David, his ancestor. Then his son Jehoram became king in his place.

Ahaziah King of Israel

51 Ahaziah son of Ahab became king of Israel in Samaria during Jehoshaphat's seventeenth year as king over Judah. Ahaziah ruled Israel for two years, 52 and he did what the LORD said was wrong. He did the same evil his father Ahab, his mother Jezebel and Jeroboam son of Nebat had done. All these rulers led the people of Israel into more sin. 53 Ahaziah worshipped and served the god Baal, and this made the LORD, the God of Israel, very angry. In these ways Ahaziah did what his father had done.

A SAD STORY

Welcome! Jeremiah, the prophet, here. Have you ever tried to go up the stairs when *everyone* else is coming down? That's what it was like to be a prophet during the time I wrote about in this book. The prophets were sent by God to tell the people to obey his commands, but few people listened. Because of their unwillingness to worship God and obey him, God allowed his people to be conquered by their enemies and driven away from the land he had given them. The saddest day of all was the day Jerusalem was destroyed. You can find out more about that terrible day by surfing over to 2 Kings 25:8–21.

I wrote this book to remind people to be faithful to the true God and to worship only him. By the time Josiah was king (did you know that Josiah was only eight years old when he became king?), people were worshipping all sorts of false idols and had forgotten about God. Imagine Josiah's surprise when the book of God's laws (called the Book of the Teachings) was found! Check out 2 Kings 23 to see how Josiah obeyed God.

JESUS WATCH

The many miracles Elisha performed show God's concern for the people and point to the miracles of Jesus. Elisha cared for the family of a poor widow by multiplying her supply of oil so that she could pay off debts and save her sons from being sold into slavery. This reminds us of how Jesus showed his concern for family friends at the wedding in Cana. (Surf over to John 2:1–11, p. 1424, for the story.) Elisha healed the Aramean army's commander of leprosy to show that he was God's prophet. Jesus showed his power and love by healing people of leprosy, blindness and other physical problems. A family in Shunem showed their love for Elisha by preparing a room for him to use whenever he needed it. When their son died, Elisha prayed to the Lord and the boy came back to life. This reminds us of the special compassion Jesus had for his friends Mary and Martha when he raised their brother Lazarus from the dead. (Check out that miracle in John 11:37–44, p. 1443.)

my FAVOURITE links

OTHER CONNECTIONS

 Stop at these information bulletin boards to find out more about some of the key people and places found in the second Book of Kings:

- Let's Visit the Jordan River, 2 Kings 2:13–15. The Jordan is frequently mentioned in both Old and New Testament stories. It's where the Israelites had to cross in order to enter the land God promised them, and it's where Jesus was baptised. For more about this famous body of water, connect here!

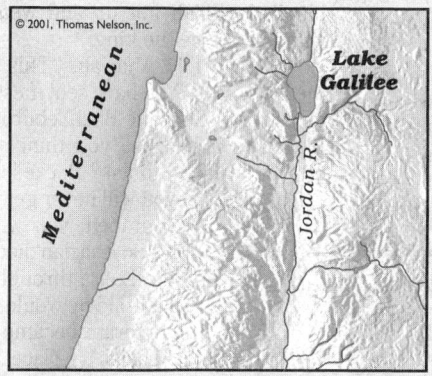

- Link to Elisha's Ministry, 2 Kings 4, to find out more about this hand-picked successor to Elijah.

Here's an FAQ for you – who went to heaven in a chariot of fire?

Don't know? If you link to 2 Kings 2:7-12, you should find the answer.

CHECK OUT THESE STORIES:
A dip in the Jordan, 2 Kings 5:1–15
The floating axe-head, 2 Kings 6:1–7
Elisha and the army of angels, 2 Kings 6:8–23
Joash repairs the Temple, 2 Kings 12:4–16

FAITH links

- Big Lack Attack, **2 Kings 4:1–7**
- Advice from a Kid, **2 Kings 5**
- Putting an Enemy in Check, **2 Kings 6:8–23**
- A Big Responsibility, **2 Kings 11**
- You're Out! **2 Kings 17:5–7**
- A Message of Courage and Hope, **2 Kings 19:4–10**
- Problem Solved, **2 Kings 20:1–11**
- On the Wrong Foot, **2 Kings 21:1–2, 16**
- Trailblazers of Faith, **2 Kings 22:1–2**
- No Thanksgiving? **2 Kings 23:21–23**

Elijah and King Ahaziah

1 After Ahab died, Moab broke away from Israel's rule. 2 Ahaziah fell down through the wooden bars in his upstairs room in Samaria and was badly hurt. He sent messengers and told them, "Go, ask Baal-Zebub, god of Ekron, if I will recover from my injuries."

3 But the LORD's angel said to Elijah the Tishbite, "Go up and meet the messengers sent by the king of Samaria. Ask them, 'Why are you going to ask questions of Baal-Zebub, god of Ekron? Is it because you think there is no God in Israel?' 4 This is what the LORD says: 'You will never get up from the bed you are lying on; you will die.'" Then Elijah left.

5 When the messengers returned to Ahaziah, he asked them, "Why have you returned?"

6 They said, "A man came to meet us. He said, 'Go back to the king who sent you and tell him what the LORD says: "Why do you send messengers to ask questions of Baal-Zebub, god of Ekron? Is it because you think there is no God in Israel? You will never get up from the bed you are lying on; you will die."'"

7 Ahaziah asked them, "What did the man look like who met you and told you this?"

8 They answered, "He was a hairy man and wore a leather belt around his waist."

Ahaziah said, "It was Elijah the Tishbite."

9 Then he sent a captain with his 50 men to Elijah. The captain went to Elijah, who was sitting on top of the hill, and said to him, "Man of God, the king says, 'Come down!'"

10 Elijah answered the captain, "If I am a man of God, let fire come down from heaven and burn up you and your 50 men." Then fire came down from heaven and burned up the captain and his 50 men.

11 Ahaziah sent another captain and 50 men to Elijah. The captain said to him, "Man of God, this is what the king says: 'Come down quickly!'"

12 Elijah answered, "If I am a man of God, let fire come down from heaven and burn up you and your 50 men!" Then fire came down from heaven and burned up the captain and his 50 men.

13 Ahaziah then sent a third captain with his 50 men. The third captain came and fell down on his knees before Elijah and begged, "Man of God, please respect my life and the lives of your 50 servants. 14 See, fire came down from heaven and burned up the first two captains of 50 with all their men. But now, respect my life."

15 The LORD's angel said to Elijah, "Go down with him and don't be afraid of him." So Elijah got up and went down with him to see the king.

16 Elijah told Ahaziah, "This is what the LORD says: 'You have sent messengers to ask questions of Baal-Zebub, god of Ekron. Is it because you think there is no God in Israel to ask? Because of this, you will never get up from your bed; you will die.'"

17 So Ahaziah died, just as the LORD, through Elijah, had said he would.

Joram became king in Ahaziah's place during the second year Jehoram son of Jehoshaphat was king of Judah. Joram ruled because Ahaziah had no son to take his place. 18 The other things Ahaziah did are written in the book of the history of the kings of Israel.

> Elijah answered the captain, "If I am a man of God, let fire come down from heaven and burn up you and your 50 men."
> – 2 Kings 1:10

Elijah is Taken to Heaven

2 It was almost time for the LORD to take Elijah by a whirlwind up into heaven. While Elijah and Elisha were leaving Gilgal, 2 Elijah said to Elisha, "Please stay here. The LORD has told me to go to Bethel."

But Elisha said, "As the LORD lives, and as you live, I won't leave you." So they went down to Bethel. 3 The groups of prophets at Bethel came out to Elisha and said to him, "Do you know the LORD

2 Kings 2:14 **477**

LET'S VISIT THE JORDAN RIVER   2 Kings 2:13–15

The Jordan River is a famous river that starts near Mount Hermon, passes through the Sea of Galilee, and empties out into the Dead Sea. That means it starts at the top of a mountain and ends at the lowest point on earth. Its name is thought to mean "the river that rushes down".

In the Old Testament, Abraham let Lot choose his own land, and he chose land by the Jordan. (See Genesis 13:10–11, p. 18.) The Jordan was also the place where the Israelites crossed into the land of Canaan with Joshua. (Look at Deuteronomy 3:20, 25, 27, p. 231.) A man named Naaman once washed in the river to be healed of leprosy. (Look up 2 Kings 5:10–12.) In the New Testament, John the Baptist baptised Jesus in the Jordan. Because of that, a lot of people who visit Israel ask to be baptised in these waters. (Read Matthew 3:13, p. 1278.)

will take your master away from you today?"

Elisha said, "Yes, I know, but don't talk about it."

4 Elijah said to him, "Stay here, Elisha, because the LORD has sent me to Jericho."

But Elisha said, "As the LORD lives, and as you live, I won't leave you."

So they went to Jericho. 5 The groups of prophets at Jericho came to Elisha and said, "Do you know that the LORD will take your master away from you today?"

Elisha answered, "Yes, I know, but don't talk about it."

6 Elijah said to Elisha, "Stay here. The LORD has sent me to the Jordan River."

Elisha answered, "As the LORD lives, and as you live, I won't leave you."

So the two of them went on. 7 Fifty men of the groups of prophets came and stood at a distance from where Elijah and Elisha were by the Jordan. 8 Elijah took off his coat, rolled it up, and hit the water. The water divided to the right and to the left, and Elijah and Elisha crossed over on dry ground.

9 After they had crossed over, Elijah said to Elisha, "What can I do for you before I am taken from you?"

Elisha said, "Leave me a double share of your spirit."[n]

10 Elijah said, "You have asked a hard thing. But if you see me when I am taken from you, it will be yours. If you don't, it won't happen."

11 As they were walking and talking, a chariot and horses of fire appeared and separated Elijah from Elisha. Then Elijah went up to heaven in a whirlwind. 12 Elisha saw it and shouted, "My father! My father! The chariots of Israel and their horsemen!" And Elisha did not see him any more. Then Elisha grabbed his own clothes and tore them to show how sad he was.

13 He picked up Elijah's coat that had fallen from him. Then he returned and stood on the bank of the Jordan. 14 Elisha hit the water with Elijah's coat and said,

---

2:9 Leave . . . spirit By law, the first son in a family would inherit a double share of his father's possessions. Elisha is asking to inherit a share of his master's power as his follower. He is not asking for twice as much power as Elijah had.

"Where is the LORD, the God of Elijah?" When he hit the water, it divided to the right and to the left, and Elisha crossed over.

15 The groups of prophets at Jericho were watching and said, "Elisha now has the spirit Elijah had." And they came to meet him, bowing down to the ground before him. 16 They said to him, "There are 50 strong men with us. Please let them go and look for your master. Maybe the Spirit of the LORD has taken Elijah up and set him down on some mountain or in some valley."

But Elisha answered, "No, don't send them."

17 When the groups of prophets had begged Elisha until he couldn't refuse them any more, he said, "Send them." So they sent 50 men who looked for three days, but they could not find him. 18 Then they came back to Elisha at Jericho where he was staying. He said to them, "I told you not to go, didn't I?"

Elisha Makes the Water Pure

19 The people of the city said to Elisha, "Look, master, this city is a nice place to live as you can see. But the water is so bad the land cannot grow crops."

20 Elisha said, "Bring me a new bowl and put salt in it." So they brought it to him.

21 Then he went out to the spring and threw the salt in it. He said, "This is what the LORD says: 'I have healed this water. From now on it won't cause death, and it won't keep the land from growing crops.'" 22 So the water has been healed to this day just as Elisha had said.

Boys Make Fun of Elisha

23 From there Elisha went up to Bethel. On the way some boys came out of the city and made fun of him. They said to him, "Go up too, you baldhead! Go up too, you baldhead!" 24 Elisha turned around, looked at them and put a curse on them in the name of the LORD. Then two mother bears came out of the woods and tore 42 of the boys to pieces. 25 Elisha went to Mount Carmel and from there he returned to Samaria.

War Between Israel and Moab

3 Joram son of Ahab became king over Israel at Samaria in Jehoshaphat's eighteenth year as king of Judah. And Joram ruled twelve years. 2 He did what the LORD said was wrong, but he was not like his father and mother; he removed the stone pillars his father had made for Baal. 3 But he continued to sin like Jeroboam son of Nebat who had led Israel to sin. Joram did not stop doing these same sins.

4 Mesha king of Moab raised sheep. He paid the king of Israel 100,000 lambs and the wool of 100,000 sheep. 5 But when Ahab died, the king of Moab turned against the king of Israel. 6 So King Joram went out from Samaria and gathered Israel's army. 7 He also sent messengers to Jehoshaphat king of Judah. "The king of Moab has turned against me," he said. "Will you go with me to fight Moab?"

Jehoshaphat replied, "I will go with you. My soldiers and my horses are yours."

8 Jehoshaphat asked, "Which way should we attack?"

Joram answered, "Through the Desert of Edom."

9 So the king of Israel went with the king of Judah and the king of Edom. After they had marched seven days, there was no more water for the army or for their animals that were with them. 10 The king of Israel said, "This is terrible! The LORD has called us three kings together to hand us over to the Moabites!"

11 But Jehoshaphat asked, "Is there a prophet of the LORD here? We can ask the LORD through him."

An officer of the king of Israel answered, "Elisha son of Shaphat is here. He was Elijah's servant."

12 Jehoshaphat said, "He speaks the LORD's truth." So the king of Israel and Jehoshaphat and the king of Edom went down to see Elisha.

13 Elisha said to the king of Israel, "I have nothing to do with you. Go to the prophets of your father and to the prophets of your mother!"

The king of Israel said to Elisha, "No, the LORD has called us three kings together to hand us over to the Moabites." 14 Elisha said, "As surely as the LORD All-powerful lives, whom I serve, I tell you the truth. I wouldn't even look at you or notice you if Jehoshaphat king of Judah were not here. I respect him. 15 Now bring me someone who plays the harp."

While the harp was being played, the LORD gave Elisha power. 16 Then Elisha said, "The LORD says to dig holes in the valley. 17 The LORD says you won't see wind or rain, but the valley will be filled with water. Then you, your cattle and your other animals can drink. 18 This is easy for the LORD to do; he will also hand Moab over to you. 19 You will destroy every fortified city and every important town. You will cut down every good tree and stop up all springs. You will ruin every good field with rocks."

20 The next morning, about the time the sacrifice was offered, water came from the direction of Edom and filled the valley.

21 All the Moabites heard that the kings had come up to fight against them. So they gathered everyone old enough to put on armour and waited at the border. 22 But when the Moabites got up early in the morning, the sun was shining on the water. They saw the water across from them, and it looked as red as blood. 23 Then they said, "This is blood! The kings must have fought and killed each other! Come, Moabites, let's take the valuable things from the dead bodies!"

24 When the Moabites came to the camp of Israel, the Israelites came out and fought them until they ran away. Then the Israelites went on into the land, killing the Moabites. 25 They tore down the cities and threw rocks all over every good field. They stopped up all the springs and cut down all the good trees. Kir Hareseth was the only city with its stones still in place, but the men with slings surrounded it and conquered it too.

26 When the king of Moab saw that the battle was too much for him, he took 700 men with swords to try to break through to the king of Edom. But they could not break through. 27 Then the king of Moab took his oldest son, who would have been king after him, and offered him as a burnt offering on the wall. So there was great anger against the Israelites, who left and went back to their own land.

A Widow Asks Elisha for Help

4 The wife of a man from the groups of prophets said to Elisha, "Your servant, my husband, is dead. You know he honoured the LORD. But now the man he owes money to is coming to take my two boys as his slaves!"

2 Elisha answered, "How can I help you? Tell me, what do you have in your house?"

The woman said, "I don't have anything there except a pot of oil."

3 Then Elisha said, "Go and get empty jars from all your neighbours. Don't ask for just a few. 4 Then go into your house and shut the door behind you and your sons. Pour oil into all the jars, and set the full ones aside."

5 So she left Elisha and shut the door behind her and her sons. As they brought the jars to her, she poured out the oil. 6 When the jars were all full, she said to her son, "Bring me another jar."

But he said, "There are no more jars." Then the oil stopped flowing.

7 She went and told Elisha. And the prophet said to her, "Go, sell the oil and pay what you owe. You and your sons can live on what is left."

The Shunammite Woman

8 One day Elisha went to Shunem, where an important woman lived. She begged Elisha to stay and eat. So every time Elisha passed by, he stopped there to eat. 9 The woman said to her husband, "I know that this is a holy man of God who passes by our house all the time. 10 Let's

> While the harp was being played, the LORD gave Elisha power.
> – 2 Kings 3:15

make a small room on the roof[n] and put a bed in the room for him. We can put a table, a chair and a lampstand there. Then when he comes by, he can stay there."

11 One day Elisha came to the woman's house. After he went to his room and rested, **12** he said to his servant Gehazi, "Call the Shunammite woman."

When the servant had called her, she stood in front of him. **13** Elisha had told his servant, "Now say to her, 'You have gone to all this trouble for us. What can I do for you? Do you want me to speak to the king or the commander of the army for you?'"

She answered, "I live among my own people."

14 Elisha said to Gehazi, "But what can we do for her?"

He answered, "She has no son, and her husband is old."

15 Then Elisha said to Gehazi, "Call her." When he called her, she stood in the doorway. **16** Then Elisha said, "About this time next year, you will hold a son in your arms."

The woman said, "No, master, man of God, don't lie to me, your servant!"

17 But the woman became pregnant and gave birth to a son at that time the next year, just as Elisha had told her.

18 The boy grew up and one day went out to his father, who was with the men harvesting grain. **19** The boy said to his father, "My head! My head!"

The father said to his servant, "Take him to his mother!" **20** The servant took him to his mother, and he lay on his mother's lap until noon. Then he died. **21** So she took him up and laid him on Elisha's bed. Then she shut the door and left.

22 She called to her husband, "Send me one of the servants and one of the donkeys. Then I can go quickly to the man of God and return."

23 The husband said, "Why do you want to go to him today? It isn't the New Moon or the Sabbath day."

She said, "It will be all right."

24 Then she saddled the donkey and said to her servant, "Lead on. Don't slow down for me unless I tell you." **25** So she went to Elisha, the man of God, at Mount Carmel.

FAITH links

BIG LACK ATTACK
2 KINGS 4:1-7

Ever worry that you'll run out of what you need? An Old Testament widow faced that problem. Because she lacked money, her sons would be sold as slaves to pay her debts. She asked Elisha for help. God miraculously provided for her by multiplying the oil that she had. During New Testament times, Jesus did something similar with loaves and fish. (Download Matthew 14:13–21, p. 1299, for that story.) Both stories show how God took care of his people. He can do the same for you.

The Rainbow Promise, Genesis 9:1–17, p. 14

From Hopeless to Hopeful, Exodus 6:9, p. 83

His Valentine, Jeremiah 31:3, p. 1035

Rock Solid, Habakkuk 1:12, p. 1236

When We Agree, Matthew 18:19–20, p. 1306

Two Birthdays, John 3:1–7, p. 1426

4:10 roof In Bible times houses were built with flat roofs. The roof was used for drying things such as flax and fruit. And it was used as an extra room, as a place for worship and as a place to sleep in the summer.

2 Kings 4:38 481

27 Then she came to Elisha at the hill and grabbed his feet. Gehazi came near to pull her away, but Elisha said to him, "Leave her alone. She's very upset, and the LORD has not told me about it. He has hidden it from me."

28 She said, "Master, did I ask you for a son? Didn't I tell you not to lie to me?"

29 Then Elisha said to Gehazi, "Get ready. Take my walking stick in your hand and go quickly. If you meet anyone, don't say hello. If anyone greets you, don't answer. Lay my walking stick on the boy's face."

30 The boy's mother said, "As surely as the LORD lives and as you live, I won't leave you!" So Elisha got up and followed her.

31 Gehazi went on ahead and laid the walking stick on the boy's face, but the boy did not talk or move. Then Gehazi went back to meet Elisha. "The boy has not awakened," he said.

32 When Elisha came into the house, the boy was lying dead on his bed. 33 Elisha entered the room and shut the door, so only he and the boy were in the room. Then he prayed to the LORD. 34 He went to the bed and lay on the boy, putting his mouth on the boy's mouth, his eyes on the boy's eyes, and his hands on the boy's hands. He stretched himself out on top of the boy. Soon the boy's skin became warm. 35 Elisha turned away and walked around the room. Then he went back and put himself on the boy again. The boy sneezed seven times and opened his eyes.

36 Elisha called Gehazi and said, "Call the Shunammite!" So he did. When she came, Elisha said, "Pick up your son." 37 She came in and fell at Elisha's feet, bowing face down to the floor. Then she picked up her son and went out.

Elisha and the Stew

38 When Elisha returned to Gilgal, there was a shortage of food in the land. While the groups of prophets were sitting in front of him, he said to his servant, "Put the large pot on the fire, and boil some stew for these men."

SHOW YOU CARE
2 KINGS 4:10

How do you show others that you care? Some people show their love by opening their homes to others. An important woman in Shunem went out of her way to welcome Elisha. What are some ways you can show you care for others? Make someone feel welcome in your home, give someone a hug, or make a card. You don't have to do anything major. Sometimes a warm smile can say "I care" better than anything else.

Check out these Faithlinks to see how you can show others you care:

Give What You Can, Numbers 7:1–11, p. 186

Care to Be Fair? Joshua 18:1–8, p. 299

Help for the Hurting, Job 6:29–30, p. 666

Mercy for an Enemy, Jonah 4, p. 1216

Kindness First, Matthew 9:35–36, p. 1290

Come On In! 1 Peter 4:9–10, p. 1705

When he saw her coming from far away, he said to his servant Gehazi, "Look, there's the Shunammite woman! 26 Run to meet her and ask, 'Are you all right? Is your husband all right? Is the boy all right?'"

She answered, "Everything is all right."

2 Kings 4:39 482

Get the Info

ELISHA'S MINISTRY

2 Kings 4

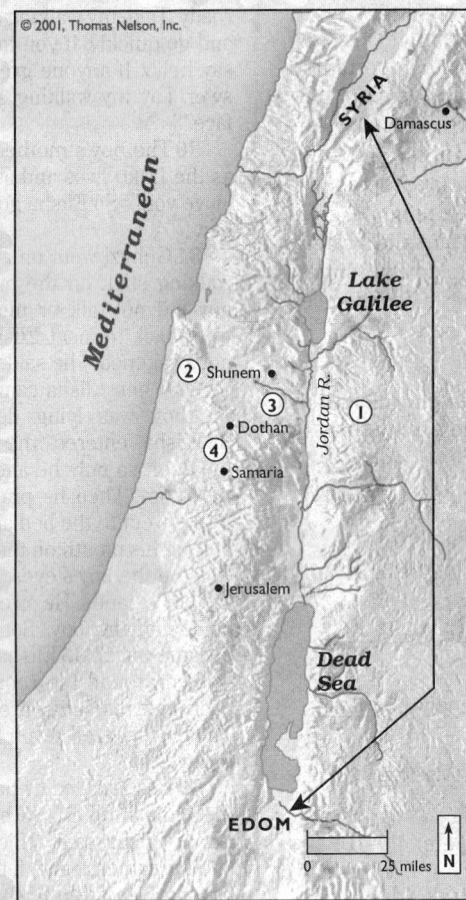

1. Elijah chose Elisha to carry on his ministry in the northern kingdom of Israel. (See 1 Kings 19:16–21, p. 467.)

2. At Shunem, an important woman offered Elisha a place to stay. Elisha repaid the woman's hospitality by promising her a son. (Read about what happens later by looking up 2 Kings 4:8–37.)

3. Elisha healed Naaman, commander of the army of Aram, of a terrible skin disease by ordering him to wash himself seven times in the River Jordan. (Check out this amazing story in 2 Kings 5:1–15.)

4. Elisha helped defeat the Aramean army at Dothan by blinding them and leading them into the city of Samaria. (To learn more about Elisha's battle plan, read 2 Kings 6:8–23.)

39 One of them went out into the field to gather plants. Finding a wild vine, he picked fruit from the vine and filled his robe with it. Then he came and cut up the fruit into the pot. But they didn't know what kind of fruit it was. 40 They poured out the stew for the others to eat. When they began to eat it, they shouted, "Man of God, there's death in the pot!" And they could not eat it.

41 Elisha told them to bring some flour. He threw it into the pot and said, "Pour it out for the people to eat." This time there was nothing harmful in the pot.

Elisha Feeds the People

42 A man from Baal Shalishah came to Elisha, bringing him 20 loaves of barley bread from the first harvest. He also brought fresh grain in his sack. Elisha said, "Give it to the people to eat."

43 Elisha's servant asked, "How can I feed 100 people with so little?"

"Give the bread to the people to eat," Elisha said. "This is what the LORD says: 'They will eat and will have food left over.'"

44 After he gave it to them, the people ate and had food left over, as the LORD had said.

Naaman is Healed

5 Naaman was commander of the army of the king of Aram. He was honoured by his master, and he had much respect because the LORD used him to give victory to Aram. He was a mighty and brave man, but he had a skin disease.

2 The Arameans had gone out to steal from the Israelites and had taken a little girl as a captive. This little girl served Naaman's wife. 3 She said to her mistress, "I wish my master would meet the prophet who lives in Samaria. He would cure him of his disease."

4 Naaman went to the king and told him what the girl from Israel had said. 5 The king of Aram said, "Go ahead, and I will send a letter to the king of Israel." So Naaman left and took with him about 30,000 pieces of silver, as well as 6,000 pieces of gold and ten changes of clothes. 6 He brought the letter to the king of Israel, which read, "I am sending my servant Naaman to you so you can heal him of his skin disease."

7 When the king of Israel read the letter, he tore his clothes to show how upset he was. He said, "I'm not God! I can't kill and make alive again! Why does this man send someone with a skin disease for me to heal? You can see that the king of Aram is trying to start trouble with me."

8 When Elisha, the man of God, heard that the king of Israel had torn his clothes, he sent the king this message: "Why have you torn your clothes? Let Naaman come to me. Then he will know there is a prophet in Israel." 9 So Naaman went with his horses and chariots to Elisha's house and stood outside the door.

10 Elisha sent Naaman a messenger who said, "Go and wash in the Jordan River seven times. Then your skin will be healed, and you will be clean."

11 Naaman became angry and left. He said, "I thought Elisha would surely come out and stand before me and call on the name of the LORD his God. I thought he would wave his hand over the place and heal the disease. 12 The Abana and the Pharpar, the rivers of Damascus, are better than all the waters of Israel. Why can't I wash in them and become clean?" So Naaman went away very angry.

13 Naaman's servants came near and said to him, "My father, if the prophet had told you to do some great thing, wouldn't you have done it? Doesn't it make more sense just to do it? After all, he only told you, 'Wash, and you will be clean.'" 14 So Naaman went down and dipped in the Jordan seven times, just as Elisha had said. Then his skin became new again, like the skin of a child. And he was clean.

15 Naaman and all his group returned to Elisha. He stood before Elisha and said, "Look, I now know there is no God in all the earth except in Israel. Now please accept a gift from me."

> **5:15 God**
> Read to see how to honour God.

16 But Elisha said, "As surely as the LORD lives whom I serve, I won't accept anything." Naaman urged him to take the gift, but he refused.

17 Then Naaman said, "If you won't take the gift, then please give me some soil—as much as two of my mules can carry. From now on I'll not offer any burnt offering or sacrifice to any other gods but the LORD. 18 But let the LORD pardon me for this: When my master goes into the temple of Rimmon[n] to worship, he leans on my arm. Then I must bow in that temple. May the LORD pardon me when I do that."

5:18 temple of Rimmon The place where the Aramean people worshipped the god Rimmon.

FAITH links

ADVICE FROM A KID
2 KINGS 5

Do you think you have to be older before you can do anything for God? Think again. Naaman was a great army commander with a terrible skin disease. He never would have been cured if he had not listened to the advice of a servant girl. She told Naaman's wife about a prophet who could cure him. Naaman's wife then told him about this prophet. Elisha was that prophet. That little piece of advice changed Naaman's life for ever.

You never know what great things you can do for God. Yes, you! You'll never know unless you make yourself available.

Think you're too young to serve God? Surf on to these links:

The Heart of the Matter, 1 Samuel 16, p. 375

The Way to Serve God, 1 Kings 9:4, p. 450

Too Young to Serve, Jeremiah 1:4–9, p. 988

Love Him? Show It! Amos 2:6–7, p. 1196

A Friend of Jesus, John 15:9–17, p. 1450

Helpful Hints, 3 John 11, p. 1724

---

19 Elisha said to him, "Go in peace."

Naaman left Elisha and went a short way. 20 Gehazi, the servant of Elisha the man of God, thought, "My master has not accepted what Naaman the Aramean brought. As surely as the LORD lives, I'll run after him and get something from him." 21 So Gehazi went after Naaman.

When Naaman saw someone running after him, he got off the chariot to meet Gehazi. He asked, "Is everything all right?"

22 Gehazi said, "Everything is all right. My master has sent me. He said, 'Two young men from the groups of prophets in the mountains of Ephraim just came to me. Please give them 3,000 pieces of silver and two changes of clothes.'"

23 Naaman said, "Please take 6,000 pieces," and he urged Gehazi to take it. He tied 68 kilogrammes of silver in two bags with two changes of clothes. Then he gave them to two of his servants to carry for Gehazi. 24 When they came to the hill, Gehazi took these things from Naaman's servants and put them in the house. Then he let Naaman's servants go, and they left.

25 When he came in and stood before his master, Elisha said to him, "Where have you been, Gehazi?"

"I didn't go anywhere," he answered.

26 But Elisha said to him, "My spirit was with you. I knew when the man turned from his chariot to meet you. This isn't a time to take money, clothes, olives, grapes, sheep, oxen, male servants or female servants. 27 So Naaman's skin disease will come on you and your children for ever." When Gehazi left Elisha, he had the disease and was as white as snow.

An Axehead Floats

6 The groups of prophets said to Elisha, "The place where we meet with you is too small for us. 2 Let's go to the Jordan River. There everyone can get a log, and let's build a place there to live."

Elisha said, "Go."

3 One of them said, "Please go with us."

FAITH links

"HANDLE" YOUR RESPONSIBILITIES
2 KINGS 6:5-7

Have you ever borrowed something from one of your friends but then lost it? It isn't a good feeling, is it? An unnamed Old Testament man could relate! He had borrowed an axe, and the axe-head fell into the water. There he was, left with the handle! That axe-head was too expensive to lose. Yet, he showed responsibility by going to the one person he felt could do something about it – Elisha. The prophet made the heavy iron axe-head float so the man could grab it!

The things we have are meant to be taken care of. The things we borrow should receive the same care.

The Sacrifice, Genesis 22, p. 29

A Serious Promise, Deuteronomy 23:21–23, p. 257

Promises, Promises, Judges 2:1–3, p. 312

Wisdom About Wealth, Ecclesiastes 5:10–12, p. 878

Obeying God or Man? Daniel 3:8–30, p. 1154

That Thing You Do, Matthew 25:14–30, p. 1319

---

head of his axe fell into the water. He yelled, "Oh, my master! I borrowed that axe!"

6 Elisha asked, "Where did it fall?" The man showed him the place. Then Elisha cut down a stick and threw it into the water, and it made the iron head float. 7 Elisha said, "Pick up the axehead." Then the man reached out and took it.

Elisha and the Blinded Arameans

8 The king of Aram was at war with Israel. He had a council meeting with his officers and said, "I will set up my camp in this place."

9 Elisha, the man of God, sent a message to the king of Israel, saying, "Be careful! Don't pass that place, because the Arameans are going down there!"

10 The king of Israel checked the place about which Elisha had warned him. Elisha warned him several times, so the king protected himself there.

11 The king of Aram was angry about this. He called his officers together and demanded, "Tell me who of us is working for the king of Israel."

12 One of the officers said, "None, my master and king. It's Elisha, the prophet from Israel. He can tell you what you speak in your bedroom."

13 The king said, "Go and find him so I can send men and catch him."

The servants came back and reported, "He is in Dothan."

14 Then the king sent horses, chariots and many troops to Dothan. They arrived at night and surrounded the city.

15 Elisha's servant got up early, and when he went out, he saw an army with horses and chariots all around the city. The servant said to Elisha, "Oh, my master, what can we do?"

16 Elisha said, "Don't be afraid. The army that fights for us is larger than the one against us."

17 Then Elisha prayed, "Lord, open my servant's eyes, and let him see."

The Lord opened the eyes of the young man, and he saw that the mountain was full of horses and chariots of fire all around Elisha.

18 As the enemy came down towards

Elisha answered, "I will go," 4 so he went with them. When they arrived at the Jordan, they cut down some trees. 5 As one man was cutting down a tree, the

PUTTING AN ENEMY IN CHECK
2 KINGS 6:8-23

In the game of chess the object is to capture your opponent's king. You do this by putting the king in "check". That means making sure the king cannot be moved without being captured. During Elisha's day, an enemy king tried to put Elisha in "check" by sending his army after him. They surrounded the city where Elisha stayed. But God put *them* in "check" by having them captured instead. But this game had a surprise ending. Instead of calling "checkmate" and destroying the enemy, Elisha showed mercy.

Mercy for an enemy won't win you any chess games. But it makes you a winner in God's eyes.

Connect here to find out how you can be a winner!

Forgive Instead, <u>Genesis 33, p. 47</u>

The Right Thing to Do, <u>1 Samuel 26, p. 391</u>

Anger: Quick or Slow? <u>Psalm 86:15, p. 776</u>

Mercy for an Enemy, <u>Jonah 4, p. 1216</u>

Forgive Again? <u>Luke 17:3-4, p. 1402</u>

Forgive and Forget, <u>Ephesians 4:32, p. 1604</u>

Elisha, he prayed to the LORD, "Make these people blind." So he made the Aramean army blind, as Elisha had asked.

19 Elisha said to them, "This is not the right road or the right city. Follow me and I'll take you to the man you are looking for." Then Elisha led them to Samaria.

20 After they entered Samaria, Elisha said, "LORD, open these men's eyes so they can see." So the LORD opened their eyes, and the Aramean army saw that they were inside the city of Samaria!

21 When the king of Israel saw the Aramean army, he said to Elisha, "My father, should I kill them? Should I kill them?"

22 Elisha answered, "Don't kill them. You wouldn't kill people whom you captured with your sword and bow. Give them food and water, and let them eat and drink and then go home to their master." 23 So he prepared a great feast for the Aramean army. After they ate and drank, the king sent them away, and they went home to their master. The soldiers of Aram did not come any more into the land of Israel.

A Shortage of Food

24 Later, Ben-Hadad king of Aram gathered his whole army and surrounded and attacked Samaria. 25 There was a shortage of food in Samaria. It was so bad that a donkey's head sold for about 80 pieces of silver, and 8 litres of dove's dung sold for about 5 pieces of silver.

26 As the king of Israel was passing by on the wall, a woman yelled out to him, "Help me, my master and king!"

27 The king said, "If the LORD doesn't help you, how can I? Can I get help from the threshing floor or from the winepress?" 28 Then the king said to her, "What is your trouble?"

She answered, "This woman said to me, 'Give up your son so we can eat him today. Then we will eat my son tomorrow.' 29 So we boiled my son and ate him. Then the next day I said to her, 'Give up your son so we can eat him.' But she had hidden him."

30 When the king heard the woman's words, he tore his clothes in sadness. As he walked along the wall, the people looked and saw he had on rough cloth under his clothes to show his sadness. 31 He said, "May God punish me terribly if the head of Elisha son of Shaphat isn't cut off from his body today!" 32 The king sent a messenger to Elisha, who was sitting in his house with the elders. But before the messenger arrived, Elisha said to them, "See, this murderer is sending men to cut off my head. When the messenger arrives, shut the door and hold it; don't let him in. The sound of his master's feet is behind him."

33 Elisha was still talking to the leaders when the messenger arrived. The king said, "This trouble has come from the LORD. Why should I wait for the LORD any longer?"

7 Elisha said, "Listen to the LORD's word. This is what the LORD says: 'About this time tomorrow 8 litres of fine flour will be sold for a piece of silver, and 6 kilogrammes of barley will be sold for a piece of silver. This will happen at the gate of Samaria.'"

2 Then the officer who was close to the king answered Elisha, "Even if the LORD opened windows in the sky, that couldn't happen."

Elisha said, "You will see it with your eyes, but you will not eat any of it."

3 There were four men with a skin disease at the entrance to the city gate. They said to each other, "Why should we sit here until we die? 4 There is no food in the city. So if we go into the city, we will die there. If we stay here, we will die. So let's go to the Aramean camp. If they let us live, we will live. If they kill us, we die."

5 So they got up at twilight and went to the Aramean camp, but when they arrived, no one was there. 6 The Lord had caused the Aramean army to hear the sound of chariots, horses and a large army. They had said to each other, "The king of Israel has hired the Hittite and Egyptian kings to attack us!" 7 So they got up and ran away in the twilight, leaving their tents, horses and donkeys. They left the camp standing and ran for their lives.

8 When the men with the skin disease came to the edge of the camp, they went into one of the tents and ate and drank. They carried silver, gold and clothes out of the camp and hid them. Then they came back and entered another tent. They carried things from this tent and hid them, as well. 9 Then they said to each other, "We're doing wrong. Today we have good news, but we are silent. If we wait until the sun comes up, we'll be discovered. Let's go right now and tell the people in the king's palace."

10 So they went and called to the gatekeepers of the city. They said, "We went to the Aramean camp, but no one is there; we didn't hear anyone. The horses and donkeys were still tied up, and the tents were still standing." 11 Then the gatekeepers shouted out and told the people in the palace.

12 The king got up in the night and said to his officers, "I'll tell you what the Arameans are doing to us. They know we are starving. They have gone out of the camp to hide in the field. They're saying, 'When the Israelites come out of the city, we'll capture them alive. Then we'll enter the city.'"

13 One of his officers answered, "Let some men take five of the horses that are still left in the city. These men are like all the Israelites who are left; they are also about to die. Let's send them to see what has happened."

14 So the men took two chariots with horses. The king sent them after the Aramean army, saying, "Go and see what has happened." 15 The men followed the Aramean army as far as the Jordan River. The road was full of clothes and equipment that the Arameans had thrown away as they had hurriedly left. So the messengers returned and told the king. 16 Then the people went out and took valuable things from the Aramean camp. So 8 litres of fine flour were sold for a piece of silver, and 6 kilogrammes of barley were sold for a piece of silver, just as the LORD had said.

17 The king chose the officer who was close to him to guard the gate, but the people trampled the officer to death. This happened just as Elisha had told the king when the king came to his house. 18 He had said, "6 kilogrammes of barley and 8 litres of fine flour will each sell for a piece of silver about this time tomorrow at the gate of Samaria."

19 But the officer had answered, "Even if the LORD opened windows in the sky, that couldn't happen." And Elisha had told him, "You will see it with your eyes, but you won't eat any of it." 20 It happened to the officer just that way. The people trampled him in the gateway, and he died.

The Shunammite Regains Her Land

8 Elisha spoke to the woman whose son he had brought back to life. He said, "Get up and go with your family. Stay wherever you can, because the LORD has called for a time without food that will last seven years." 2 So the woman got up and did as the man of God had said. She left with her family, and they stayed in the land of the Philistines for seven years. 3 After seven years she returned from the land of the Philistines and went to beg the king for her house and land. 4 The king was talking with Gehazi, the servant of the man of God. The king had said, "Please tell me all the great things Elisha has done." 5 Gehazi was telling the king how Elisha had brought a dead boy back to life. Just then the woman whose son Elisha had brought back to life came and begged the king for her house and land.

Gehazi said, "My master and king, this is the woman, and this is the son Elisha brought back to life."

6 The king asked the woman, and she told him about it. Then the king chose an officer to help her. "Give the woman everything that is hers," the king said. "Give her all the money made from her land from the day she left until now."

Ben-Hadad is Killed

7 Then Elisha went to Damascus, where Ben-Hadad king of Aram was sick. Someone told him, "The man of God has arrived."

8 The king said to Hazael, "Take a gift in your hand and go and meet him. Ask the LORD through him if I will recover from my sickness."

9 So Hazael went to meet Elisha, taking with him a gift of 40 camels loaded with every good thing in Damascus. He came and stood before Elisha and said, "Your son Ben-Hadad king of Aram sent me to you. He asks if he will recover from his sickness."

10 Elisha said to Hazael, "Go and tell Ben-Hadad, 'You will surely recover,' but the LORD has told me he will really die." 11 Hazael stared at Elisha until he felt ashamed. Then Elisha cried.

12 Hazael asked, "Why are you crying, master?"

Elisha answered, "Because I know what evil you will do to the Israelites. You will burn their fortified cities with fire and kill their young men with swords. You will throw their babies to the ground and split open their pregnant women."

13 Hazael said, "Am I a dog? How could I do such things?"

Elisha answered, "The LORD has shown me that you will be king over Aram."

14 Then Hazael left Elisha and came to his master. Ben-Hadad said to him, "What did Elisha say to you?"

Hazael answered, "He told me that you will surely recover." 15 But the next day Hazael took a blanket and dipped it in water. Then he put it over Ben-Hadad's face, and he died. So Hazael became king in Ben-Hadad's place.

Jehoram King of Judah

16 While Jehoshaphat was king in Judah, Jehoram son of Jehoshaphat became king of Judah. This was during the fifth year Joram son of Ahab was king of Israel. 17 Jehoram was 32 years old when he began to rule, and he ruled eight years in Jerusalem. 18 He followed the ways of the kings of Israel, just as the family of Ahab had done, because he married Ahab's daughter. Jehoram did what the LORD said was wrong. 19 But the LORD

would not destroy Judah because of his servant David. The LORD had promised that one of David's descendants would always rule.

20 In Jehoram's time Edom broke away from Judah's rule and chose their own king. 21 So Jehoram and all his chariots went to Zair. The Edomites surrounded him and his chariot commanders. Jehoram got up and attacked the Edomites at night, but his army ran away to their tents. 22 From then until now the country of Edom has fought against the rule of Judah. At the same time Libnah also broke away from Judah's rule.

23 The other acts of Jehoram and all the things he did are written in the book of the history of the kings of Judah. 24 Jehoram died and was buried with his ancestors in Jerusalem, and Jehoram's son Ahaziah ruled in his place.

25 Ahaziah son of Jehoram became king of Judah during the twelfth year Joram son of Ahab was king of Israel. 26 Ahaziah was 22 years old when he became king, and he ruled one year in Jerusalem. His mother's name was Athaliah, a granddaughter of Omri king of Israel. 27 Ahaziah followed the ways of Ahab's family. He did what the LORD said was wrong, as Ahab's family had done, because he was a son-in-law to Ahab.

28 Ahaziah went with Joram son of Ahab to Ramoth in Gilead, where they fought against Hazael king of Aram. The Arameans wounded Joram. 29 So King Joram returned to Jezreel to heal from the wound he had received from the Arameans at Ramoth when he fought Hazael king of Aram. Ahaziah son of Jehoram king of Judah went down to visit Joram son of Ahab at Jezreel, because he had been wounded.

Jehu is Chosen King

9 At the same time, Elisha the prophet called a man from the groups of prophets. Elisha said, "Get ready, and take this small bottle of olive oil in your hand. Go to Ramoth in Gilead. 2 When you arrive, find Jehu son of Jehoshaphat, the son of Nimshi. Go in and make Jehu get up from among his brothers, and take him to an inner room. 3 Then take the bottle and pour the oil on Jehu's head and say, 'This is what the LORD says: I have appointed you king over Israel.' Then open the door and run away. Don't wait!"

4 So the young man, the prophet, went to Ramoth in Gilead. 5 When he arrived, he saw the officers of the army sitting together. He said, "Commander, I have a message for you."

Jehu asked, "For which one of us?"

The young man said, "For you, commander."

6 Jehu got up and went into the house. Then the young prophet poured the olive oil on Jehu's head and said to him, "This is what the LORD, the God of Israel says: 'I have appointed you king over the LORD's people Israel. 7 You must destroy the family of Ahab your master. I will punish Jezebel for the deaths of my servants the prophets and for all the LORD's servants who were murdered. 8 All of Ahab's family must die. I will not let any male child in Ahab's family live in Israel, whether slave or free. 9 I will make Ahab's family like the family of Jeroboam son of Nebat and like the family of Baasha son of Ahijah. 10 The dogs will eat Jezebel at Jezreel, and no one will bury her.'"

Then the young prophet opened the door and ran away.

11 When Jehu went back to his master's officers, one of them said to Jehu, "Is everything all right? Why did this madman come to you?"

Jehu answered, "You know the man and how he talks."

12 They answered, "That's not true. Tell us."

Jehu said, "He said to me, 'This is what the LORD says: I have appointed you to be king over Israel.'"

> The LORD had promised that one of David's descendants would always rule.
> – 2 Kings 8:19

13 Then the officers hurried, and each man took off his own coat and put it on the stairs for Jehu. They blew the trumpet and shouted, "Jehu is king!"

Joram and Ahaziah are Killed

14 So Jehu son of Jehoshaphat, the son of Nimshi, made plans against Joram. Now Joram and all Israel had been defending Ramoth in Gilead from Hazael king of Aram. **15** But King Joram had to return to Jezreel to heal from the injuries the Arameans had given him when he fought against Hazael king of Aram.

Jehu said, "If you agree with this, don't let anyone leave the city. They might tell the news in Jezreel." **16** Then he got into his chariot and set out for Jezreel, where Joram was resting. Ahaziah king of Judah had gone down to see him.

17 The look-out was standing on the watchtower in Jezreel when he saw Jehu's troops coming. He said, "I see some soldiers!"

Joram said, "Take a horseman and send him to meet them. Tell him to ask, 'Is all in order?'"

18 The horseman rode out to meet Jehu, and he said, "This is what the king says: 'Is all in order?'"

Jehu said, "Why bother yourself with order? Come along behind me."

CONNECT 2-YOU

TV OR NOT TV: THAT IS THE QUESTION

Do you have favourite ways of spending your time? Let's welcome Justin, aged 11, to Connect 2-You and hear what he likes to do with his spare time.

Justin

I love TV. I'd have it on 24 hours a day if I could. Of course, there's no way my mum would ever let that happen. She says I spend far too much time in front of the telly as it is. She says that TV is too much of a "priority" to me, and that it's interfering with what's really important in life. I don't know what she's talking about. What's wrong with TV?

It's a good question. Let's go back to what Justin's mum said about it being a priority in his life. God warns us not to have any other gods except him. A "god" could be anything that is more important to you than your relationship with Jesus. That includes TV. Maybe you've never bowed down and worshipped your television, but if watching TV is a higher priority in your life than things like praying or reading the Bible, you may have a new god in your life.

Think of it this way. Someday we'll all stand before God, and he'll ask us to explain how we spent our time on earth – and why. How pleased do you think he'll be if you tell him you spent most of it in front of a TV? For tips on how to spend your time wisely, take a look at the Livin' It page on making good choices, <u>Deuteronomy 30:15–20, p. 267</u>.

The look-out reported, "The messenger reached them, but he is not coming back."

19 Then Joram sent out a second horseman. This rider came to Jehu's group and said, "This is what the king says: 'Is all in order?'"

Jehu answered, "Why bother yourself with order? Come along behind me."

20 The look-out reported, "The second man reached them, but he is not coming back. The man in the chariot is driving like Jehu son of Nimshi. He drives as if he were mad!"

21 Joram said, "Get my chariot ready." Then the servant got Joram's chariot ready. Joram king of Israel and Ahaziah king of Judah went out, each in his own chariot, to meet Jehu at the property of Naboth the Jezreelite.

22 When Joram saw Jehu, he said, "Is all in order, Jehu?"

Jehu answered, "There will never be any order as long as your mother Jezebel worships idols and uses witchcraft."

23 Joram turned the horses to run away and yelled to Ahaziah, "It's a trick, Ahaziah!"

24 Then Jehu drew his bow and shot Joram between his shoulders. The arrow went through Joram's heart, and he fell down in his chariot.

25 Jehu ordered Bidkar, his chariot officer, "Pick up Joram's body, and throw it into the field of Naboth the Jezreelite. Remember when you and I rode together with Joram's father Ahab. The LORD made this prophecy against him: 26 'Yesterday I saw the blood of Naboth and his sons, says the LORD, so I will punish Ahab in his field, says the LORD.' Take Joram's body and throw it into the field, as the LORD has said."

27 When Ahaziah king of Judah saw this, he ran away towards Beth Haggan. Jehu chased him, saying, "Shoot Ahaziah, too!" Ahaziah was wounded in his chariot on the way up to Gur near Ibleam. He got as far as Megiddo but died there. 28 Ahaziah's servants carried his body in a chariot to Jerusalem and buried him with his ancestors in his tomb in Jerusalem. 29 (Ahaziah had become king over Judah in the eleventh year Joram son of Ahab was king.)

Death of Jezebel

30 When Jehu came to Jezreel, Jezebel heard about it. She put on her eye paint and fixed her hair. Then she looked out of the window. 31 When Jehu entered the city gate, Jezebel said, "Have you come in peace, you Zimri," you who killed your master?"

32 Jehu looked up at the window and said, "Who is on my side? Who?" Two or three servants looked out the window at Jehu. 33 He said to them, "Throw her down." So they threw Jezebel down, and the horses ran over her. Some of her blood splashed on the wall and on the horses.

34 Jehu went into the house and ate and drank. Then he said, "Now see about this cursed woman. Bury her, because she is a king's daughter."

35 The men went to bury Jezebel, but they could not find her. They found only her skull, feet and the palms of her hands. 36 When they came back and told Jehu, he said, "The LORD said this through his servant Elijah the Tishbite: 'The dogs will eat Jezebel at Jezreel. 37 Her body will be like manure on the field in the land at Jezreel. No one will be able to say that this is Jezebel.'"

Families of Ahab and Ahaziah Killed

10 Ahab had 70 sons in Samaria. Jehu wrote letters and sent them to Samaria to the officers and elders of Jezreel and to the guardians of the sons of Ahab. Jehu said, 2 "You have your master's sons with you, and you have chariots, horses, a city with strong walls and weapons. When you get this letter, 3 choose the best and most worthy person among your master's sons, and make him king. Then fight for your master's family."

4 But the officers and leaders of Jezreel were frightened. They said, "Two

---

9:31 Zimri He was the man who killed Elah and the family of Baasha. Read 1 Kings 16:8-12.

kings could not stand up to Jehu, so how can we?"

5 The palace manager, the city governor, the elders and the guardians sent a message to Jehu. "We are your servants," they said. "We will do everything you tell us to do. We won't make any man king, so do whatever you think is best."

6 Then Jehu wrote a second letter, saying, "If you are on my side and will obey me, cut off the heads of your master's sons and come to me at Jezreel tomorrow about this time."

Now the 70 sons of the king's family were with the leading men of the city who were their guardians. 7 When the leaders received the letter, they took the king's sons and killed all 70 of them. They put their heads in baskets and sent them to Jehu at Jezreel. 8 The messenger came to Jehu and told him, "They have brought the heads of the king's sons."

Then Jehu said, "Lay the heads in two piles at the city gate" until morning."

9 In the morning, Jehu went out and stood before the people and said to them, "You are innocent. Look, I made plans against my master and killed him. But who killed all these? 10 You should know that everything the LORD said about Ahab's family will come true. The LORD has spoken through his servant Elijah, and the LORD has done what he said." 11 So Jehu killed every one of Ahab's family in Jezreel who was still alive. He also killed all Ahab's leading men, close friends and priests. No one who had helped Ahab was left alive.

12 Then Jehu left and went to Samaria by way of the road to Beth Eked of the Shepherds. 13 There Jehu met some relatives of Ahaziah king of Judah. Jehu asked, "Who are you?"

They answered, "We are relatives of Ahaziah. We have come down to get revenge for the families of the king and the king's mother."

14 Then Jehu said, "Take them alive!" So they captured Ahaziah's relatives alive and killed them at the well near Beth Eked—42 of them. Jehu did not leave anyone alive.

15 After Jehu left there, he met Jehonadab son of Recab, who was also on his way to meet Jehu. Jehu greeted him and said, "Are you as good a friend to me as I am to you?"

Jehonadab answered, "Yes, I am."

Jehu said, "If you are, then give me your hand." So Jehonadab gave him his hand, and Jehu pulled him into the chariot. 16 "Come with me," Jehu said. "You can see how strong my feelings are for the LORD." So Jehu had Jehonadab ride in his chariot.

17 When Jehu came to Samaria, he killed all of Ahab's family in Samaria. He destroyed all those who were left, just as the LORD had told Elijah it would happen.

Baal Worshippers Killed

18 Then Jehu gathered all the people together and said to them, "Ahab served Baal a little, but Jehu will serve Baal much. 19 Now call for me all Baal's prophets and priests and all the people who worship Baal. Don't let anyone miss this meeting, because I have a great sacrifice for Baal. Anyone who is not there will not live." But Jehu was tricking them so he could destroy the worshippers of Baal. 20 He said, "Prepare a holy meeting for Baal." So they announced the meeting. 21 Then Jehu sent word through all Israel, and all the worshippers of Baal came; not one stayed at home. They came into the temple of Baal, and the temple was filled from one side to the other.

22 Jehu said to the man who kept the robes, "Bring out robes for all the worshippers of Baal." After he brought out robes for them, 23 Jehu and Jehonadab son of Recab went into the temple of Baal.

> You should know that everything the LORD said about Ahab's family will come true.
> — 2 Kings 10:10

10:8 city gate People came here to conduct business. Public meetings and court cases were also held here.

Jehu said to the worshippers of Baal, "Look around, and make sure there are no servants of the LORD with you. Be sure there are only worshippers of Baal." 24 Then the worshippers of Baal went in to offer sacrifices and burnt offerings.

Jehu had 80 men waiting outside. He had told them, "Don't let anyone escape. If you do, you must pay with your own life."

25 As soon as Jehu finished offering the burnt offering, he ordered the guards and the captains, "Go in and kill the worshippers of Baal. Don't let anyone come out." So the guards and captains killed the worshippers of Baal with the sword and threw their bodies out. Then they went to the inner rooms of the temple 26 and brought out the pillars of the temple of Baal and burned them. 27 They tore down the stone pillar of Baal, as well as the temple of Baal. And they made it into a sewage pit, as it is today.

28 So Jehu destroyed Baal worship in Israel, 29 but he did not stop doing the sins Jeroboam son of Nebat had done. Jeroboam had led Israel to sin by worshipping the golden calves in Bethel and Dan.

30 The LORD said to Jehu, "You have done well in obeying what I said was right. You have done to the family of Ahab as I wanted. Because of this, your descendants as far as your great-great-grandchildren will be kings of Israel." 31 But Jehu was not careful to follow the teachings of the LORD, the God of Israel, with all his heart. He did not stop doing the same sins Jeroboam had done, by which he had led Israel to sin.

32 At that time the LORD began to make Israel smaller. Hazael defeated the Israelites in all the land of Israel, 33 taking all the land of the Jordan known as the land of Gilead. (It was the region of Gad, Reuben and Manasseh.) He took land from Aroer by the Arnon Ravine through Gilead to Bashan.

34 The other things Jehu did—everything he did and all his victories—are recorded in the book of the history of the kings of Israel. 35 Jehu died and was buried in Samaria, and his son Jehoahaz became king in his place. 36 Jehu was king over Israel in Samaria for 28 years.

Athaliah and Joash

11 When Ahaziah's mother, Athaliah, saw that her son was dead, she killed all the royal family. 2 But Jehosheba, King Jehoram's daughter and Ahaziah's sister, took Joash, Ahaziah's son. She stole him from among the other sons of the king who were about to be murdered. She put Joash and his nurse in a bedroom to hide him from Athaliah, so he was not killed. 3 He hid with her in the Temple of the LORD for six years. During that time Athaliah ruled the land.

4 In the seventh year Jehoiada sent for the commanders of groups of 100 men, as well as the Carites." He brought them together in the Temple of the LORD and made an agreement with them. There, in the Temple of the LORD, he made them promise loyalty, and then he showed them the king's son. 5 He commanded them, "This is what you must do. A third of you who go on duty on the Sabbath will guard the king's palace. 6 A third of you will be at the Sur Gate, and another third will be at the gate behind the guard. This way you will guard the Temple. 7 The two groups who go off duty on the Sabbath must protect the Temple of the LORD for the king. 8 All of you must stand around the king, each man with his weapons in his hand. If anyone comes near, kill him. Stay close to the king when he goes out and when he comes in."

9 The commanders of groups of 100 men obeyed everything Jehoiada the priest had commanded. Each one took his men who came on duty on the Sabbath and those who went off duty on the Sabbath, and they came to Jehoiada the priest. 10 He gave the commanders the spears and shields that had belonged to King David and that were kept in the Temple of the LORD.

Joash Becomes King

11 Then each guard took his place with his weapons in his hand. There were

---

11:4 Carites This was probably a special unit of the army that was responsible for the king's safety, a kind of palace guard similar to the Kerethites and the Pelethites.

FAITH links

A BIG RESPONSIBILITY
2 KINGS 11

Think back to the time when you were seven (all the way back then!). Imagine being told that you were the new Prime Minister. How would you react? Joash was only seven when he became king of Judah. Although he had people to help him run the country, he still had to learn how to be responsible. (You can also read this story in 2 Chronicles 24, p. 588.)

You may not have a country to run, but you can still learn to be responsible. One of the first steps is to take your responsibilities seriously whatever they may be – chores, homework, going to school. That means doing what's expected of you.

A Use for Your Abilities, Genesis 41, p. 59

Read My Lips? Deuteronomy 26:16–19, p. 260

Your Best Work, 1 Kings 6, p. 443

Down on the Ant Farm, Proverbs 6:6–11, p. 833

Calling Anyone! Acts 23:12–22, p. 1506

Help for the Body, Romans 12:3–8, p. 1536

---

guards from the south side of the Temple to the north side. They stood by the altar and the Temple and around the king. 12 Jehoiada brought out the king's son and put the crown on him and gave him a copy of the agreement. They appointed him king and poured olive oil on him. Then they clapped their hands and said, "Long live the king!"

13 When Athaliah heard the noise of the guards and the people, she went to them at the Temple of the LORD. 14 She looked, and there was the king, standing by the pillar, as the custom was. The officers and trumpeters were standing beside him, and all the people of the land were very happy and were blowing trumpets. Then Athaliah tore her clothes and screamed, "Traitors! Traitors!"

15 Jehoiada the priest gave orders to the commanders of the groups of 100 men, who led the army. He said, "Surround her with soldiers and kill with a sword anyone who follows her." He commanded this because he had said, "Don't put Athaliah to death in the Temple of the LORD." 16 So they caught her when she came to the horses' entrance near the palace. There she was put to death.

17 Then Jehoiada made an agreement between the LORD and the king and the people that they would be the LORD's special people. He also made an agreement between the king and the people. 18 All the people of the land went to the temple of Baal and tore it down, smashing the altars and idols. They also killed Mattan, the priest of Baal, in front of the altars.

Then Jehoiada the priest placed guards at the Temple of the LORD. 19 He took with him the commanders of 100 men and the Carites, the royal bodyguards, as well as the guards and all the people of the land. Together they took the king out of the Temple of the LORD and went into the palace through the gate of the guards. Then the king sat on the royal throne. 20 So all the people of the land were very happy, and Jerusalem had peace, because Athaliah had been put to death with the sword at the palace.

21 Joash was seven years old when he became king.

12 Joash became king of Judah in Jehu's seventh year as king of Israel, and he ruled for 40 years in Jeru-

salem. His mother's name was Zibiah, and she was from Beersheba. 2 Joash did what the LORD said was right as long as Jehoiada the priest taught him. 3 But the places where gods were worshipped were not removed; the people still made sacrifices and burned incense there.

Joash Repairs the Temple

4 Joash said to the priests, "Take all the money brought as offerings to the Temple of the LORD. This includes the money each person owes in taxes and the money each person promises or brings freely to the LORD. 5 Each priest will take the money from the people he serves. Then the priests must repair any damage they find in the Temple."

**12:4–5
Giving**
How much should you give to God?

6 But by the twenty-third year Joash was king, the priests still had not repaired the Temple. 7 So King Joash called for Jehoiada the priest and the other priests and said to them, "Why aren't you repairing the damage of the Temple? Don't take any more money from the people you serve, but hand over the money for the repair of the Temple." 8 The priests agreed not to take any more money from the people and not to repair the Temple themselves.

9 Jehoiada the priest took a box and made a hole in the top of it. Then he put it by the altar, on the right side as the people came into the Temple of the LORD. The priests guarding the doorway put all the money brought to the Temple of the LORD into the box.

10 Each time the priests saw that the box was full of money, the king's royal secretary and the high priest came. They counted the money that had been brought to the Temple of the LORD, and they put it into bags. 11 Next they weighed the money and gave it to the people in charge of the work on the Temple. With it they paid the carpenters and the builders who worked on the Temple of the LORD, 12 as well as the bricklayers and stonecutters. They also used the money to buy

FAITH links

WHAT'S THE USE?
2 KINGS 12:6-12

What's your first thought when you see the offering plate go by? Do you think *I have to give* or *I want to give*? Many people grumble about giving because they're not sure what their money is used for. During Old Testament times, the Temple was in need of repair. Instead of demanding money from the people to repair the Temple, King Joash had a wooden box placed at the entrance to the Temple. All of the money in the box was used to repair the Temple. When the people saw how the money was used, they gave more.

If you're not sure what your offerings are used for, ask your pastor or church treasurer. Knowing where your money goes can help you be more generous.

Connect here for more on being generous:

A Small Percent, Deuteronomy 14:22–23, p. 247

Gifts from the Heart, 1 Chronicles 29, p. 557

Wisdom About Wealth, Ecclesiastes 5:10–12, p. 878

Set for Life? Obadiah 2–4, p. 1208

One of the Faithful, Acts 10:1–34, p. 1482

Give to Give, 1 Corinthians 16:1–4, p. 1566

timber and cut stone to repair the damage of the Temple of the LORD. It paid for everything.

13 The money brought into the Temple of the LORD was not used to make silver cups, wick trimmers, bowls, trumpets, or gold or silver vessels. 14 They paid the money to the workers, who used it to repair the Temple of the LORD. 15 They did not demand to know how the money was spent, because the workers were honest. 16 The money from the penalty offerings and sin offerings was not brought into the Temple of the LORD, because it belonged to the priests.

Joash Saves Jerusalem

17 About this time Hazael king of Aram attacked Gath and captured it. Then he went to attack Jerusalem. 18 Joash king of Judah took all the holy things given by his ancestors, the kings of Judah—Jehoshaphat, Jehoram and Ahaziah. He also took his own holy things as well as the gold that was found in the treasuries of the Temple of the LORD and the gold from the palace. Joash sent all this treasure to Hazael king of Aram, who turned away from Jerusalem.

19 Everything else Joash did is written in the book of the history of the kings of Judah. 20 His officers made plans against him and killed him at Beth Millo on the road down to Silla. 21 The officers who killed him were Jozabad son of Shimeath and Jehozabad son of Shomer. Joash was buried with his ancestors in Jerusalem, and Amaziah, his son, became king in his place.

Jehoahaz King of Israel

13 Jehoahaz son of Jehu became king over Israel in Samaria during the twenty-third year Joash son of Ahaziah was king of Judah. Jehoahaz ruled for seventeen years, 2 and he did what the LORD said was wrong. Jehoahaz did the same sins Jeroboam son of Nebat had done. Jeroboam had led Israel to sin, and Jehoahaz did not stop doing these same sins. 3 So the LORD was angry with Israel and handed them over to Hazael king of Aram and his son Ben-Hadad for a long time.

4 Then Jehoahaz begged the LORD, and the LORD listened to him. The LORD had seen the troubles of Israel; he saw how terribly the king of Aram was treating them. 5 He gave Israel a man to save them, and they escaped from the Arameans. The Israelites then lived in their own homes as they had before, 6 but they still did not stop doing the same sins that the family of Jeroboam had done. He had led Israel to sin, and they continued doing those sins. The Asherah idol also was left standing in Samaria.

7 Nothing was left of Jehoahaz's army except 50 horsemen, ten chariots and 10,000 foot soldiers. The king of Aram had destroyed them and made them like chaff.

8 Everything else Jehoahaz did and all his victories are written in the book of the history of the kings of Israel. 9 Jehoahaz died and was buried in Samaria, and his son Jehoash became king in his place.

Jehoash King of Israel

10 Jehoash son of Jehoahaz became king of Israel in Samaria during Joash's thirty-seventh year as king of Judah. Jehoash ruled for sixteen years, 11 and he did what the LORD said was wrong. He did not stop doing the same sins Jeroboam son of Nebat had done. Jeroboam had led Israel to sin, and Jehoash continued to do the same thing. 12 Everything else he did and all his victories, including his war against Amaziah king of Judah, are written in the book of the history of the kings of Israel. 13 Jehoash died, and Jeroboam took his place on the throne. Jehoash was buried in Samaria with the kings of Israel.

The Death of Elisha

14 At this time Elisha became sick. Before he died, Jehoash king of Israel went to Elisha and cried for him. Jehoash said, "My father, my father! The chariots of Israel and their horsemen!"

15 Elisha said to Jehoash, "Take a bow and arrows." So he took a bow and arrows. 16 Then Elisha said to him, "Put your hand on the bow." So Jehoash put his hand on the bow. Then Elisha put his hands on the king's hands. 17 Elisha said,

"Open the east window." So Jehoash opened the window. Then Elisha said, "Shoot," and Jehoash shot. Elisha said, "The LORD's arrow of victory over Aram! You will defeat the Arameans at Aphek until you destroy them." 18 Elisha said, "Take the arrows." So Jehoash took them. Then Elisha said to him, "Strike the ground." So Jehoash struck the ground three times and stopped. 19 The man of God was angry with him. "You should have struck five or six times!" Elisha said. "Then you would have struck Aram until you had completely destroyed it. But now you will defeat it only three times."

20 Then Elisha died and was buried.

At that time groups of Moabites would rob the land in the springtime. 21 Once as some Israelites were burying a man, suddenly they saw a group of Moabites coming. The Israelites threw the dead man into Elisha's grave. When the man touched Elisha's bones, the man came back to life and stood on his feet.

War with Aram

22 During all the days Jehoahaz was king, Hazael king of Aram troubled Israel. 23 But the LORD was kind to the Israelites; he had mercy on them and helped them because of his agreement with Abraham, Isaac and Jacob. To this day he has never wanted to destroy them or reject them.

24 When Hazael king of Aram died, his son Ben-Hadad became king in his place. 25 During a war Hazael had taken some cities from Jehoahaz, Jehoash's father. Now Jehoash took back those cities from Hazael's son Ben-Hadad. He defeated Ben-Hadad three times and took back the cities of Israel.

Amaziah King of Judah

14 Amaziah son of Joash became king of Judah during the second year Jehoash son of Jehoahaz was king of Israel. 2 Amaziah was 25 years old when he became king, and he ruled for 29 years in Jerusalem. His mother was named Jehoaddin, and she was from Jerusalem. 3 Amaziah did what the LORD said was right. He did everything his father Joash had done, but he did not do as his ancestor David had done. 4 The places where gods were worshipped were not removed, so the people still sacrificed and burned incense there.

5 As soon as Amaziah took control of the kingdom, he put to death the officers who had murdered his father the king. 6 But he did not put to death the children of the murderers because of the rule written in the Book of the Teachings of Moses. The LORD had commanded: "Parents must not be put to death when their children do wrong, and children must not be put to death when their parents do wrong. Each must die for his own sins."[n]

7 In battle Amaziah killed 10,000 Edomites in the Valley of Salt. He also took the city of Sela. He called it Joktheel, as it is still called today.

8 Amaziah sent messengers to Jehoash son of Jehoahaz, the son of Jehu, king of Israel. They said, "Come, let's meet face to face."

9 Then Jehoash king of Israel answered Amaziah king of Judah, "A thornbush in Lebanon sent a message to a cedar tree in Lebanon. It said, 'Let your daughter marry my son.' But then a wild animal from Lebanon came by, walking on and crushing the thornbush. 10 You have defeated Edom, but you have become proud. Stay at home and boast. Don't ask for trouble, or you and Judah will be defeated."

11 But Amaziah would not listen, so Jehoash king of Israel went to attack. He and Amaziah king of Judah faced each other in battle at Beth Shemesh in Judah. 12 Israel defeated Judah, and every man of Judah ran away to his home. 13 At Beth Shemesh Jehoash king of Israel captured Amaziah king of Judah. (Amaziah was the son of Joash, who was the son of Ahaziah.) Jehoash went up to Jerusalem and broke down the wall of Jerusalem from the Gate of Ephraim to the Corner Gate, which was about 200 metres. 14 He took all the gold

---

14:6 "Parents . . . sin." See Deuteronomy 24:16.

and silver and everything in the Temple of the LORD, and he took the treasuries of the palace and some hostages. Then he returned to Samaria.

15 The other acts of Jehoash and his victories, including his war against Amaziah king of Judah, are written in the book of the history of the kings of Israel. 16 Jehoash died and was buried in Samaria with the kings of Israel, and his son Jeroboam became king in his place.

17 Amaziah son of Joash, the king of Judah, lived fifteen years after the death of Jehoash son of Jehoahaz, the king of Israel. 18 The other things Amaziah did are written in the book of the history of the kings of Judah. 19 The people in Jerusalem made plans against him. So he ran away to the town of Lachish, but they sent men after him to Lachish and killed him. 20 They brought his body back on horses, and he was buried with his ancestors in Jerusalem, in the city of David. 21 Then all the people of Judah made Uzziah[n] king in place of his father Amaziah. Uzziah was sixteen years old. 22 He rebuilt the town of Elath and made it part of Judah again after Amaziah died.

Jeroboam King of Israel

23 Jeroboam son of Jehoash became king of Israel in Samaria during the fifteenth year Amaziah was king of Judah. (Amaziah was the son of Joash.) Jeroboam ruled for 41 years, 24 and he did what the LORD said was wrong. Jeroboam son of Nebat had led Israel to sin, and Jeroboam son of Jehoash did not stop doing the same sins. 25 Jeroboam won back Israel's border from Lebo Hamath to the Dead Sea. This happened as the LORD, the God of Israel, had said through his servant Jonah son of Amittai, the prophet from Gath Hepher. 26 The LORD had seen how the Israelites, both slave and free, were suffering terribly. No one was left who could help Israel. 27 The LORD had not said he would completely destroy Israel from the world, so he saved the Israelites through Jeroboam son of Jehoash.

28 Everything else Jeroboam did is written down—all his victories and how he won back from Judah the towns of Damascus and Hamath for Israel. All this is written in the book of the history of the kings of Israel. 29 Jeroboam died and was buried with his ancestors, the kings of Israel. Jeroboam's son Zechariah became king in his place.

Uzziah King of Judah

15 Uzziah[n] son of Amaziah became king of Judah during Jeroboam's twenty-seventh year as king of Israel. 2 Uzziah was sixteen years old when he became king, and he ruled for 52 years in Jerusalem. His mother was named Jecoliah, and she was from Jerusalem. 3 He did what the LORD said was right, just as his father Amaziah had done. 4 But the places where gods were worshipped were not removed, so the people still made sacrifices and burned incense there.

> **EMAIL FROM GOD**
> **15:3–5**
> **Leadership**
> Does God hold leaders accountable for how they lead?

5 The LORD struck Uzziah with a skin disease, which he had until the day he died. So he had to live in a separate house. Jotham, the king's son, was in charge of the palace, and he governed the people of the land.

6 All the other things Uzziah did are written in the book of the history of the kings of Judah. 7 Uzziah died and was buried near his ancestors in Jerusalem, and his son Jotham became king in his place.

Zechariah King of Israel

8 Zechariah son of Jeroboam was king over Israel in Samaria. He ruled for six months during Uzziah's[n] thirty-eighth

> The LORD had seen how the Israelites, both slave and free, were suffering terribly.
> – 2 Kings 14:26

14:21, 15:1, 15:8 Uzziah Also called Azariah.

year as king of Judah. 9 Zechariah did what the LORD said was wrong, just as his ancestors had done. Jeroboam son of Nebat had led the people of Israel to sin, and Zechariah did not stop doing the same sins.

10 Shallum son of Jabesh made plans against Zechariah and killed him in front of the people. Then Shallum became king in his place. 11 The other acts of Zechariah are written in the book of the history of the kings of Israel. 12 The LORD had told Jehu: "Your sons down to your great-great-grandchildren will be kings of Israel," and the LORD's word came true.

Shallum King of Israel

13 Shallum son of Jabesh became king during Uzziah's[n] thirty-ninth year as king of Judah. Shallum ruled for a month in Samaria. 14 Then Menahem son of Gadi came up from Tirzah to Samaria and attacked Shallum son of Jabesh in Samaria. He killed him and became king in Shallum's place.

15 The other acts of Shallum and his secret plans are written in the book of the history of the kings of Israel.

Menahem King of Israel

16 Menahem started out from Tirzah and attacked Tiphsah, destroying the city and the area nearby. This was because the people had refused to open the city gate for him. He defeated them and ripped open all their pregnant women.

17 Menahem son of Gadi became king over Israel during Uzziah's thirty-ninth year as king of Judah. Menahem ruled for ten years in Samaria, 18 and he did what the LORD said was wrong. Jeroboam son of Nebat had led Israel to sin, and all the time Menahem was king, he did not stop doing the same sins.

19 Pul king of Assyria came to attack the land. Menahem gave him about 35 tonnes of silver so Pul would support him and make his hold on the kingdom stronger. 20 Menahem taxed Israel to pay about 50 pieces of silver to each soldier of the king of Assyria. So the king left and did not stay in the land.

21 Everything else Menahem did is written in the book of the history of the kings of Israel. 22 Then Menahem died, and his son Pekahiah became king in his place.

Pekahiah King of Israel

23 Pekahiah son of Menahem became king over Israel in Samaria during Uzziah's[n] fiftieth year as king of Judah. Pekahiah ruled for two years, 24 and he did what the LORD said was wrong. Jeroboam son of Nebat had led Israel to sin, and Pekahiah did not stop doing the same sins.

25 Pekah son of Remaliah was one of Pekahiah's captains, and he made plans against Pekahiah. He took 50 men of Gilead with him and killed Pekahiah, as well as Argob and Arieh, in the palace at Samaria. Then Pekah became king in Pekahiah's place.

26 Everything else Pekahiah did is written in the book of the history of the kings of Israel.

Pekah King of Israel

27 Pekah son of Remaliah became king over Israel in Samaria during Uzziah's[n] fifty-second year as king of Judah. Pekah ruled for 20 years, 28 and he did what the LORD said was wrong. Jeroboam son of Nebat had led Israel to sin, and Pekah did not stop doing the same sins.

29 Tiglath-Pileser[n] was king of Assyria. He attacked while Pekah was king of Israel, capturing the cities of Ijon, Abel Beth Maacah, Janoah, Kedesh and Hazor. He also captured Gilead and Galilee and all the land of Naphtali and carried the people away to Assyria. 30 Then Hoshea son of Elah made plans against Pekah son of Remaliah and attacked and killed him. Then Hoshea became king in Pekah's place during the twentieth year Jotham son of Uzziah was king.

31 Everything else Pekah did is written in the book of the history of the kings of Israel.

15:13, 15:23, 15:27 Uzziah Also called Azariah.
15:29 Tiglath-Pileser Also called Pul.

Jotham King of Judah

32 Jotham son of Uzziah became king of Judah during the second year Pekah son of Remaliah was king of Israel. 33 Jotham was 25 years old when he became king, and he ruled for sixteen years in Jerusalem. His mother's name was Jerusha, daughter of Zadok. 34 Jotham did what the LORD said was right, just as his father Uzziah had done. 35 But the places where gods were worshipped were not removed, and the people still made sacrifices and burned incense there. Jotham rebuilt the Upper Gate of the Temple of the LORD.

36 The other things Jotham did while he was king are written in the book of the history of the kings of Judah. 37 At that time the LORD began to send Rezin king of Aram and Pekah son of Remaliah against Judah. 38 Jotham died and was buried with his ancestors in Jerusalem, the city of David, his ancestor. Then Jotham's son Ahaz became king in his place.

Ahaz King of Judah

16 Ahaz was the son of Jotham king of Judah. Ahaz became king of Judah in the seventeenth year Pekah son of Remaliah was king of Israel. 2 Ahaz was 20 years old when he became king, and he ruled for sixteen years in Jerusalem. Unlike his ancestor David, he did not do what the LORD his God said was right. 3 Ahaz did the same things the kings of Israel had done. He even made his son pass through fire. He did the same hateful sins as the nations had done whom the LORD had forced out of the land ahead of the Israelites. 4 Ahaz offered sacrifices and burned incense at the places where gods were worshipped, on the hills and under every green tree.

5 Rezin king of Aram and Pekah son of Remaliah, the king of Israel, came up to attack Jerusalem. They surrounded Ahaz but could not defeat him. 6 At that time Rezin king of Aram took back the city of Elath for Aram, and he forced out all the people of Judah. Then Edomites moved into Elath, and they still live there today. 7 Ahaz sent messengers to Tiglath-Pileser[n] king of Assyria, saying, "I am your servant and your friend. Come and save me from the king of Aram and the king of Israel, who are attacking me." 8 Ahaz took the silver and gold that was in the Temple of the LORD and in the treasuries of the palace, and he sent these as a gift to the king of Assyria. 9 So the king of Assyria listened to Ahaz. He attacked Damascus and captured it and sent all its people away to Kir. And he killed Rezin.

10 Then King Ahaz went to Damascus to meet Tiglath-Pileser king of Assyria. Ahaz saw an altar at Damascus, and he sent plans and a pattern of this altar to Uriah the priest. 11 So Uriah the priest built an altar, following the plans King Ahaz had sent him from Damascus. Uriah finished the altar before King Ahaz came back from Damascus. 12 When the king arrived from Damascus, he saw the altar and went near and offered sacrifices on it. 13 He burned his burnt offerings and grain offerings and poured out his drink offering. He also sprinkled the blood of his fellowship offerings on the altar.

14 Ahaz moved the bronze altar that was before the LORD at the front of the Temple. It was between Ahaz's altar and the Temple of the LORD, but he put it on the north side of his altar. 15 King Ahaz commanded Uriah the priest, "On the large altar burn the morning burnt offering, the evening grain offering, the king's burnt offering and grain offering, and the whole burnt offering, the grain offering and the drink offering for all the people of the land. Sprinkle on the altar all the blood of the burnt offering and of the sacrifice. But I will use the bronze altar to ask questions of God." 16 So Uriah the priest did everything as King Ahaz commanded him.

17 Then King Ahaz took off the side panels from the bases and removed the washing bowls from the top of the bases. He also took the large bowl, which was called the Sea, off the bronze bulls that held it up, and he put it on a stone base. 18 Ahaz took away the platform for the royal throne, which had been built at the

---

16:7 **Tiglath-Pileser** Also called Pul.

Temple of the LORD. He also took away the outside entrance for the king. He did these things because of the king of Assyria.

19 The other things Ahaz did as king are written in the book of the history of the kings of Judah. 20 Ahaz died and was buried with his ancestors in Jerusalem, and Ahaz's son Hezekiah became king in his place.

Hoshea, Last King of Israel

17 Hoshea son of Elah became king over Israel during Ahaz's twelfth year as king of Judah. Hoshea ruled in Samaria for nine years. 2 He did what the LORD said was wrong, but he was not as bad as the kings of Israel who had ruled before him.

3 Shalmaneser king of Assyria came to attack Hoshea. Hoshea had been Shalmaneser's servant and had made the payments to Shalmaneser that he had demanded. 4 But the king of Assyria found out that Hoshea had made plans against him by sending messengers to So, the king of Egypt. Hoshea had also stopped giving Shalmaneser the payments, which he had paid every year in the past. For that, the king put Hoshea in prison. 5 Then the king of Assyria came and attacked all the land of Israel. He surrounded Samaria and attacked it for three years. 6 He defeated Samaria in the ninth year Hoshea was king, and he took the Israelites away to Assyria. He settled them in Halah, in Gozan on the Habor River and in the cities of the Medes.

Israelites Punished for Sin

7 All these things happened because the Israelites had sinned against the LORD their God. He had brought them out of Egypt and had rescued them from the power of the king of Egypt, but the Israelites had honoured other gods. 8 They lived like the nations the LORD had forced out of the land ahead of them. They lived as their evil kings had shown them, 9 secretly sinning against the LORD their God. They built places to worship gods in all their cities, from the watchtower to the fortified city. 10 They put up stone pillars to gods and Asherah idols on every high hill and

FAITH links

YOU'RE OUT!
2 KINGS 17:5-7

The old saying "three strikes and you're out" applies to the Israelites. Time and time again they had sinned. God allowed an enemy nation – the Assyrians – to invade the land three times. This was a warning for the Israelites to stop worshipping false gods and to worship him instead. But they kept on doing what they wanted to do. So the third time, God didn't rescue them. The king of Assyria sent his army to carry them away to another land.

Sin puts you "out" with God. When you sin, God wants you to confess it and ask for his forgiveness.

Are you "out" with God? Link here to find out how to get back "in".

Count on His Mercy, Judges 2:16–17; 3, p. 313

Dirty Inside, Isaiah 6:1–7, p. 904

World News, Isaiah 13—19, p. 913

The Watchman, Ezekiel 3:16–22, p. 1088

Just for the Asking, Romans 3:23–28, p. 1522

Lost Love? Revelation 2:4, p. 1733

under every green tree. 11 The Israelites burned incense everywhere gods were worshipped, just as the nations who lived there before them had done, whom the LORD had forced out of the land. The Israelites did wicked things that made the LORD angry. 12 They served idols when the LORD had said, "You must not do this." 13 The LORD used every prophet and seer to warn Israel and Judah. He said, "Stop your evil ways and obey my commands and laws. Follow all the teachings that I commanded your ancestors, the teachings that I gave you through my servants the prophets."

14 But the people would not listen. They were stubborn, just as their ancestors had been who did not believe in the LORD their God. 15 They rejected the LORD's laws and the agreement he had made with their ancestors. And they refused to listen to his warnings. They worshipped useless idols and became useless themselves. They did what the nations around them did, which the LORD had warned them not to do.

16 The people rejected all the commands of the LORD their God. They moulded statues of two calves, and they made an Asherah idol. They worshipped all the stars of the sky and served Baal. 17 They made their sons and daughters pass through fire and tried to find out the future by magic and witchcraft. They always chose to do what the LORD said was wrong, which made him angry. 18 Because he was very angry with the people of Israel, he removed them from his presence. Only the tribe of Judah was left.

Judah is Also Guilty

19 But even Judah did not obey the commands of the LORD their God. They did what the Israelites had done, 20 so the LORD rejected all the people of Israel. He punished them and let others destroy them; he threw them out of his presence. 21 When the LORD separated them from the family of David, the Israelites made Jeroboam son of Nebat their king. Jeroboam led the Israelites away from the LORD and led them to sin greatly. 22 So they continued to do all the sins Jeroboam did. They did not stop doing these sins 23 until the LORD removed the Israelites from his presence, just as he had said through all his servants the prophets. So the Israelites were taken out of their land to Assyria, and they have been there to this day.

The Beginning of the Samaritan People

24 The king of Assyria brought people from Babylon, Cuthah, Avva, Hamath and Sepharvaim and put them in the cities of Samaria to replace the Israelites. These people took over Samaria and lived in the cities. 25 At first they did not worship the LORD, so he sent lions among them which killed some of them. 26 The king of Assyria was told, "You sent foreigners into the cities of Samaria who do not know the law of the god of the land. This is why he has sent lions among them. The lions are killing them because they don't know what the god wants."

27 Then the king of Assyria commanded, "Send back one of the priests you took away. Let him live there and teach the people what the god wants." 28 So one of the priests who had been carried away from Samaria returned to live in Bethel. And he taught the people how to honour the LORD.

29 But each nation made gods of its own and put them in the cities where they lived and in the temples where gods were worshipped. These temples had been built by the Samaritans. 30 The people from Babylon made Succoth Benoth their god. The people from Cuthah worshipped Nergal. The people of Hamath worshipped Ashima. 31 The Avvites worshipped Nibhaz and Tartak. The Sepharvites burned their children in the fire, sacrificing them to Adrammelech and Anammelech, the gods of Sepharvaim. 32 They also honoured the LORD, but they chose priests for the places where gods were worshipped. The priests were chosen from among themselves, and they made sacrifices for the people. 33 The people honoured the LORD but also served their own gods, just as the nations did from which they had been brought. 34 Even today

they do as they did in the past. They do not worship the LORD nor obey his rules and commands. They do not obey the teachings or the commands of the LORD, which he gave to the children of Jacob, whom he had named Israel. 35 The LORD had made an agreement with them and had commanded them, "Do not honour other gods. Do not bow down to them or worship them or offer sacrifices to them. 36 Worship the LORD who brought you up out of the land of Egypt with great power and strength. Bow down to him and offer sacrifices to him. 37 Always obey the rules, orders, teachings and commands he wrote for you. Do not honour other gods. 38 Do not forget the agreement I made with you, and do not honour other gods. 39 Instead worship the LORD your God, who will save you from all your enemies."

40 But the Israelites did not listen. They kept on doing the same things they had done before. 41 So these nations honoured the LORD but also worshipped their idols, and their children and grandchildren still do as their ancestors did.

Hezekiah King of Judah

18 Hezekiah son of Ahaz king of Judah became king during the third year Hoshea son of Elah was king of Israel. 2 Hezekiah was 25 years old when he became king, and he ruled for 29 years in Jerusalem. His mother's name was Abijah daughter of Zechariah. 3 Hezekiah did what the LORD said was right, just as his ancestor David had done. 4 He removed the places where gods were worshipped. He smashed the stone pillars and cut down the Asherah idols. Also the Israelites had been burning incense to Nehushtan, the bronze snake Moses had made. But Hezekiah broke it into pieces.

5 Hezekiah trusted in the LORD, the God of Israel. There was no one like him among all the kings of Judah, either before him or after him. 6 Hezekiah was loyal to the LORD and did not stop following him; he obeyed the commands the LORD had given Moses. 7 And the LORD was with Hezekiah, so he had success in everything he did. He turned against the king of Assyria and stopped serving him. 8 Hezekiah defeated the Philistines all the way to Gaza and its borders, including the watchtowers and the fortified cities.

The Assyrians Capture Samaria

9 Shalmaneser king of Assyria surrounded Samaria and attacked it in the fourth year Hezekiah was king. This was the seventh year Hoshea son of Elah was king of Israel. 10 After three years the Assyrians captured Samaria. This was in the sixth year Hezekiah was king, which was Hoshea's ninth year as king of Israel. 11 The king of Assyria took the Israelites away to Assyria and settled them in Halah, in Gozan on the Habor River and in the cities of the Medes. 12 This happened because they did not obey the LORD their God. They broke his agreement and did not obey all that Moses, the LORD's servant, had commanded. They would not listen to the commands or do them.

Assyria Attacks Judah

13 During Hezekiah's fourteenth year as king, Sennacherib king of Assyria attacked all the fortified cities of Judah and captured them. 14 Then Hezekiah king of Judah sent a message to the king of Assyria at Lachish. He said, "I have done wrong. Leave me alone, and I will pay anything you ask." So the king of Assyria made Hezekiah pay about 10 tonnes of silver and 1 tonne of gold. 15 Hezekiah gave him all the silver that was in the Temple of the LORD and in the palace treasuries. 16 Hezekiah stripped all the gold that covered the doors and doorposts of the Temple of the LORD. Hezekiah had put gold on these

> Hezekiah did what the LORD said was right, just as his ancestor David had done.
> – 2 Kings 18:3

doors himself, but he gave it all to the king of Assyria.

17 The king of Assyria sent out his supreme commander, his chief officer and his field commander. They went with a large army from Lachish to King Hezekiah in Jerusalem. When they came near the waterway from the upper pool on the road where people do their laundry, they stopped. 18 They called for the king, so the king sent Eliakim, Shebna and Joah out to meet them. Eliakim son of Hilkiah was the palace manager, Shebna was the royal secretary and Joah son of Asaph was the recorder.

19 The field commander said to them, "Tell Hezekiah this:

"'The great king, the king of Assyria, says: What can you trust in now? 20 You say you have battle plans and power for war, but your words mean nothing. Whom are you trusting for help so that you turn against me? 21 Look, you are depending on Egypt to help you, but Egypt is like a splintered walking stick. If you lean on it for help, it will stab your hand and hurt you. The king of Egypt will hurt all those who depend on him. 22 You might say, "We are depending on the LORD our God," but Hezekiah destroyed the LORD's altars and the places of worship. Hezekiah told Judah and Jerusalem, "You must worship only at this one altar in Jerusalem."

23 "'Now make an agreement with my master, the king of Assyria: I will give you 2,000 horses if you can find enough men to ride them. 24 You cannot defeat one of my master's least important officers, so why do you depend on Egypt to give you chariots and horsemen? 25 I have not come to attack and destroy this place without an order from the LORD. The LORD himself told me to come to this country and destroy it.'"

26 Then Eliakim son of Hilkiah, Shebna and Joah said to the field commander, "Please speak to us in the Aramaic language. We understand it. Don't speak to us in Hebrew, because the people on the city wall can hear you."

27 "No," the commander said, "my master did not send me to tell these things only to you and your king. He sent me to speak also to those people sitting on the wall who will have to eat their own dung and drink their own urine like you."

28 Then the commander stood and shouted loudly in the Hebrew language, "Listen to what the great king, the king of Assyria, says! 29 The king says you should not let Hezekiah fool you, because he can't save you from my power. 30 Don't let Hezekiah talk you into trusting the LORD by saying, 'The LORD will surely save us. This city won't be handed over to the king of Assyria.'

31 "Don't listen to Hezekiah. The king of Assyria says, 'Make peace with me, and come out of the city to me. Then everyone will be free to eat the fruit from his own grapevine and fig tree and to drink water from his own well. 32 After that I will come and take you to a land like your own—a land with grain and new wine, bread and vineyards, olives and honey. Choose to live and not to die!'

"Don't listen to Hezekiah. He is fooling you when he says, 'The LORD will save us.' 33 Has a god of any other nation saved his people from the power of the king of Assyria? 34 Where are the gods of Hamath and Arpad? Where are the gods of Sepharvaim, Hena and Ivvah? They did not save Samaria from my power. 35 Not one of all the gods of these countries has saved his people from me. Neither can the LORD save Jerusalem from my power."

36 The people were silent. They didn't answer the commander at all, because King Hezekiah had ordered, "Don't answer him."

37 Then Eliakim, Shebna and Joah tore their clothes to show how upset they were. (Eliakim son of Hilkiah was the palace manager, Shebna was the royal secretary and Joah son of Asaph was the recorder.) The three men went to Hezekiah and told him what the field commander had said.

Jerusalem will Be Saved

19 When King Hezekiah heard the message, he tore his clothes and put on rough cloth to show how sad he was. Then he went into the Temple of the

LORD. 2 Hezekiah sent Eliakim, the palace manager and Shebna, the royal secretary, and the elders of the priests to Isaiah. They were all wearing rough cloth when they came to Isaiah the prophet, the son of Amoz. 3 They told Isaiah, "This is what Hezekiah says: 'Today is a day of sorrow and punishment and disgrace, as when a child should be born, but the mother is not strong enough to give birth to it. 4 The king of Assyria sent his field commander to make fun of the living God. Maybe the LORD your God will hear what the commander said and will punish him for it. So pray for the few of us who are left alive.'"

5 When Hezekiah's officers came to Isaiah, 6 he said to them, "Tell your master this: the LORD says, 'Don't be afraid of what you have heard. Don't be frightened by the words the servants of the king of Assyria have spoken against me. 7 Listen! I am going to put a spirit in the king of Assyria. He will hear a report that will make him return to his own country, and I will cause him to die by the sword there.'"

8 The field commander heard that the king of Assyria had left Lachish. When he went back, he found the king fighting against the city of Libnah.

9 The king received a report that Tirhakah, the Cushite king of Egypt, was coming to attack him. When the king of Assyria heard this, he sent messengers to Hezekiah, saying, 10 "Tell Hezekiah king of Judah: 'Don't be fooled by the god you trust. Don't believe him when he says Jerusalem will not be handed over to the king of Assyria. 11 You have heard what the kings of Assyria have done. They have completely defeated every country, so do not think you will be saved. 12 Did the gods of those people save them? My ancestors destroyed them, defeating the cities of Gozan, Haran and Rezeph, and the people of Eden living in Tel Assar. 13 Where are the kings of Hamath and Arpad? Where are the kings of Sepharvaim, Hena and Ivvah?'"

Hezekiah Prays to the LORD

14 When Hezekiah received the letter from the messengers and read it, he went up to the Temple of the LORD. He spread the letter out before the LORD 15 and prayed to the LORD: "LORD, God of Israel, whose throne is between the gold creatures with wings, only you are God of all the kingdoms of the earth. You made the heavens and the earth. 16 Hear,

---

FAITH links

A MESSAGE OF COURAGE AND HOPE
2 KINGS 19:4-10

Has anyone ever made fun of you because of your faith? The king of Assyria made fun of King Hezekiah because of his faith in God. But God gave Hezekiah a message of hope. He told Hezekiah not to be afraid. He would help Hezekiah and his people.

People who don't believe in God may call you names or think you're weird for believing in a God you can't see. When that happens, the same message of hope that God gave to Hezekiah is there for you, too.

When You're Afraid, Genesis 32:9–12, p. 45

Moses' Champion, Numbers 12, p. 192

God's Sure Protection, Psalm 18, p. 721

Uprooted by Change, Amos 9:15, p. 1205

A Real Crowd-pleaser? Micah 2:6–11, p. 1222

Hope That Doesn't Fail, Acts 26:4–7, p. 1510

LORD, and listen. Open your eyes, LORD, and see. Listen to the words Sennacherib has said to insult the living God. **17** It is true, LORD, that the kings of Assyria have destroyed these countries and their lands. **18** They have thrown the gods of these nations into the fire, but they were only wood and rock statues that people made. So the kings have destroyed them. **19** Now, LORD our God, save us from the king's power so that all the kingdoms of the earth will know that you, LORD, are the only God."

God Answers Hezekiah

20 Then Isaiah son of Amoz sent a message to Hezekiah that said, "This is what the LORD, the God of Israel, says: 'I have heard your prayer to me about Sennacherib king of Assyria.' **21** This is what the LORD has said against Sennacherib:

'The people of Jerusalem
  hate you and make fun of you.
The people of Jerusalem
  laugh at you as you run away.
22 You have insulted me and spoken
    against me;
  you have raised your voice against
    me.
  You have a proud look on your face,
    which is against me, the Holy One
      of Israel.
23 You have sent your messengers to
    insult the Lord.
  You have said, "With my many
    chariots
  I have gone to the tops of the
    mountains,
  to the highest mountains of
    Lebanon.
  I have cut down its tallest cedars
    and its best pine trees.
  I have gone to its farthest places
    and to its best forests.
24 I have dug wells in foreign
    countries
  and drunk water there.
  By the soles of my feet,
    I have dried up all the rivers of
      Egypt."
25 "'King of Assyria, surely you have
    heard.
Long ago I, the LORD, planned
  these things.
Long ago I designed them,
  and now I have made them happen.
I allowed you to turn those fortified
  cities
  into piles of rocks.
26 The people in those cities were weak;
  they were frightened and put to
    shame.
They were like grass in the field,
  like tender, young grass,
  like grass on the housetop
  that is burned by the wind before it
    can grow.

27 "'I know when you rest,
  when you come and go,
  and how you rage against me.
28 Because you rage against me,
  and because I have heard your
    proud words,
I will put my hook in your nose
  and my bit in
    your mouth.
Then I will force
  you to leave
  my country
  the same way
  you came.'

**19:27–28
Pride**
Read to see how God
views pride.

29 "Then the LORD said, 'Hezekiah, I will give you this sign:

This year you will eat the grain that
  grows wild,
and the second year you will eat
  what grows wild from that.
But in the third year, plant grain and
  harvest it.
Plant vineyards and eat their
  fruit.
30 Some of the people in the family of
    Judah
  will escape.
Like plants that take root,
  they will grow strong and have
    many children.
31 A few people will come out of
    Jerusalem alive;
  a few from Mount Zion will live.
The strong love of the LORD
  All-powerful
  will make this happen.'

2 Kings 20:7 **507**

32 "So this is what the LORD says about the king of Assyria:
'He will not enter this city
or even shoot an arrow here.
He will not fight against it with shields
or build a ramp to attack the city walls.
33 He will return to his country the same way he came,
and he will not enter this city,' says the LORD.
34 'I will defend and save this city for my sake and for the sake of David, my servant.'"

35 That night the angel of the LORD went out and killed 185,000 men in the Assyrian camp. When the people got up early the next morning, they saw all the dead bodies. 36 So Sennacherib king of Assyria left and went back to Nineveh and stayed there.

37 One day as Sennacherib was worshipping in the temple of his god Nisroch, his sons Adrammelech and Sharezer killed him with a sword. Then they escaped to the land of Ararat. So Sennacherib's son Esarhaddon became king of Assyria.

Hezekiah's Illness

20 At that time Hezekiah became so sick he almost died. The prophet Isaiah son of Amoz went to see him and told him, "This is what the LORD says: 'Make arrangements because you are not going to live, but die.'"

2 Hezekiah turned towards the wall and prayed to the LORD, 3 "LORD, please remember that I have always obeyed you. I have given myself completely to you and have done what you said was right." Then Hezekiah cried loudly.

4 Before Isaiah had left the middle courtyard, the LORD spoke his word to Isaiah: 5 "Go back and tell Hezekiah, the leader of my people: 'This is what the LORD, the God of your ancestor David, says: I have heard your prayer and seen your tears, so I will heal you. Three days from now you will go up to the Temple of the LORD. 6 I will add fifteen years to your life. I will save you and this city from the king of Assyria; I will protect the city for my sake and for the sake of my servant David.'"

7 Then Isaiah said, "Make a paste

FAITH links

PROBLEM SOLVED
2 KINGS 20:1-11

Who do you turn to when you're worried about a problem? Some problems can only be solved by God. Hezekiah was dying of an illness. No one could help him. He prayed to God. God heard his prayer and let him live 15 more years. When the king asked for proof of God's answer, God made the sun go backwards!

When you're worried, pray. God may not always answer yes or make the sun go backwards, but he will answer.

Got a problem? Link here for help:

When You're Afraid, Genesis 32:9–12, p. 45

God's Pep Talk, Joshua 1:5–9, p. 276

A Really Bad Day, Job 1:20–22; 2:10, p. 661

Who Ya' Gonna Call? Psalm 3:4, p. 711

The Best Protection Plan, Matthew 2:13–18, p. 1276

You've Got the Power! Acts 1:1–8; 2:1–4, p. 1463

20:6
God
How does God fight for his people?

from figs." So they made it and put it on Hezekiah's boil, and he got well.

8 Hezekiah had asked Isaiah, "What will be the sign that the LORD will heal me and that I will go up to the Temple of the LORD on the third day?"

9 Isaiah said, "The LORD will do what he says. This is the sign from the LORD to show you: do you want the shadow to go forwards ten steps or back ten steps?"

10 Hezekiah answered, "It's easy for the shadow to go forwards ten steps. Instead, let it go back ten steps."

11 Then Isaiah the prophet called to the LORD, and the LORD brought the shadow ten steps back up the stairway of Ahaz that it had gone down.

Messengers from Babylon

12 At that time Merodach-Baladan son of Baladan was king of Babylon. He sent letters and a gift to Hezekiah, because he had heard that Hezekiah was sick. 13 Hezekiah listened to the messengers, so he showed them what was in his storehouses: the silver, gold, spices, expensive perfumes, his swords and shields, and all his wealth. He showed them everything in his palace and his kingdom.

14 Then Isaiah the prophet went to King Hezekiah and asked him, "What did these men say? Where did they come from?"

Hezekiah said, "They came from a faraway country—from Babylon."

15 So Isaiah asked him, "What did they see in your palace?"

Hezekiah said, "They saw everything in my palace. I showed them all my wealth."

16 Then Isaiah said to Hezekiah, "Listen to the words of the LORD: 17 'In the future everything in your palace and everything your ancestors have stored up until this day will be taken away to Babylon. Nothing will be left,' says the LORD. 18 'Some of your own children, those who will be born to you, will be taken away. And they will become servants in the palace of the king of Babylon.'"

19 Hezekiah told Isaiah, "These words from the LORD are good." He said this because he thought, "There will be peace and security in my lifetime."

20 Everything else Hezekiah did—all his victories, his work on the pool, his work on the tunnel to bring water into the

---

FAITH links

WHAT I'VE GOT
2 KINGS 20:12-17

Are you ever tempted to brag about all the stuff you have? Maybe you think that what you have makes you cool. What would you do if one day you no longer had those things? King Hezekiah showed some messengers from Babylon all of his treasures. The prophet Isaiah warned him that these valuable things would one day be taken away.

There is nothing wrong with having nice things. But your possessions are not what make you special. If you want to boast, boast about someone who made it possible for you to have what you have: God.

Put Pride Aside, Exodus 2:11–15, p. 78

Uniquely You, Psalm 139:13–14, p. 815

The Problem with Pride, Isaiah 2:11, p. 898

Bragging Rights, Jeremiah 9:23–24, p. 1005

Set for Life? Obadiah 2–4, p. 1208

Better Than Some? Luke 18:9–14, p. 1405

city—is written in the book of the history of the kings of Judah. 21 Then Hezekiah died, and his son Manasseh became king in his place.

Manasseh King of Judah

21 Manasseh was twelve years old when he became king, and he was king for 55 years in Jerusalem. His mother's name was Hephzibah. 2 He did what the LORD said was wrong. He did the hateful things the other nations had done—the nations that the LORD had forced out of the land ahead of the Israelites. 3 Manasseh's father, Hezekiah had destroyed the places where gods were worshipped, but Manasseh rebuilt them. He built altars for Baal, and he made an Asherah idol as Ahab king of Israel had done. Manasseh also worshipped all the stars of the sky and served them. 4 The LORD had said about the Temple, "I will be worshipped in Jerusalem," but Manasseh built altars in the Temple of the LORD. 5 He built altars to worship the stars in the two courtyards of the Temple of the LORD. 6 He made his own son pass through fire. He practised magic and told the future by explaining signs and dreams, and he got advice from mediums and fortune-tellers. He did many things the LORD said were wrong, which made the LORD angry.

7 Manasseh carved an Asherah idol and put it in the Temple. The LORD had said to David and his son Solomon about the Temple, "I will be worshipped for ever in this Temple and in Jerusalem, which I have chosen from all the tribes of Israel. 8 I will never again make the Israelites wander out of the land I gave their ancestors. But they must obey everything I have commanded them and all the teachings my servant Moses gave them." 9 But the people did not listen. Manasseh led them to do more evil than the nations the LORD had destroyed ahead of the Israelites.

10 The LORD said through his servants the prophets, 11 "Manasseh king of Judah has done these hateful things. He has done more evil than the Amorites before him. He has also led Judah to sin with his idols. 12 So this is what the LORD, the God of Israel, says: 'I will bring so much trouble on Jerusalem and Judah that anyone who

21:8–9 Temptation
What can you do to avoid temptation?

FAITH links

ON THE WRONG FOOT
2 KINGS 21:1-2, 16

Ever have your parents warn you about someone's bad influence? Israel had a number of kings who were a bad influence. One was Manasseh, who became king at the age of 12. Unlike Joash, Manasseh started off on the wrong foot. He did things and influenced others to do things that God considered evil.

Believe it or not, you can influence people for good or evil. Being a Christian starts you off on the right foot for influencing people for good.

Connect here to see how you can be a good influence on others:

A Choice to Make,
Deuteronomy 30:15–20, p. 265

The Right Thing to Do,
1 Samuel 26, p. 391

A Useless Thing, Isaiah 44:9, 18–20, p. 954

The Dead End of the Occult,
Ezekiel 13:17–23, p. 1098

Kindness Counts, Acts 14:3, p. 1489

Love for Free, Romans 5:8, p. 1524

hears about it will be shocked. 13 I will stretch the measuring line of Samaria over Jerusalem, and the plumb line used against Ahab's family will be used on Jerusalem. I will wipe out Jerusalem as a person wipes a dish and turns it upside down. 14 I will throw away the rest of my people who are left. I will give them to their enemies, and they will be robbed by all their enemies, 15 because my people did what I said was wrong. They have made me angry from the day their ancestors left Egypt until now.'"

16 Manasseh also killed many innocent people, filling Jerusalem from one end to the other with their blood. This was besides the sin he led Judah to do; he led Judah to do what the LORD said was wrong.

17 The other things Manasseh did as king, even the sin he did, are written in the book of the history of the kings of Judah. 18 Manasseh died and was buried in the garden of his own palace, the garden of Uzza. Then Manasseh's son Amon became king in his place.

Amon King of Judah

19 Amon was 22 years old when he became king, and he was king for two years in Jerusalem. His mother's name was Meshullemeth daughter of Haruz, who was from Jotbah. 20 Amon did what the LORD said was wrong, as his father Manasseh had done. 21 He lived in the same way his father had lived: he worshipped the idols his father had worshipped, and he bowed down before them. 22 Amon rejected the LORD, the God of his ancestors, and did not follow the ways of the LORD.

23 Amon's officers made plans against him and killed him in his palace. 24 Then the people of the land killed all those who had made plans to kill King Amon, and they made his son Josiah king in his place.

25 Everything else Amon did is written in the book of the history of the kings of Judah. 26 He was buried in his grave in the garden of Uzza, and his son Josiah became king in his place.

Josiah King of Judah

22 Josiah was eight years old when he became king, and he ruled for 31 years in Jerusalem. His mother's name was Jedidah daughter of Adaiah, who was from Bozkath. 2 Josiah did what the LORD

TRAILBLAZERS OF FAITH
2 KINGS 22:1-2

Did you ever walk in someone else's footprints in sand or snow? If you were lost, following someone else's steps could lead you in the right direction. Josiah was only eight years old when he became king of Judah. He followed in David's footsteps. That means he did the right things that David did.

If you have parents or grandparents who are Christians, they've blazed a path of faith for you to follow. Although they've shown you the way to go, you need to have your own relationship with God in order to follow in those faith-steps.

Lights, Camera, . . . Actions! Genesis 12:1–3, p. 17

An Unsung Hero, Ruth 2:12, 15–16, p. 347

A Memorial for Two Thieves, 1 Chronicles 7:21, p. 530

Jesus' Mission and Yours, Isaiah 61:1–2, p. 978

Pass It On! Joel 1:2–3, p. 1187

Our Good Shepherd, John 10: 11–15, p. 1441

said was right. He lived as his ancestor David had lived, and he did not stop doing what was right.

3 In Josiah's eighteenth year as king, he sent Shaphan to the Temple of the LORD. Shaphan son of Azaliah, the son of Meshullam, was the royal secretary. Josiah said, 4 "Go up to Hilkiah the high priest, and have him empty out the money the gatekeepers have gathered from the people. This is the money they have brought into the Temple of the LORD. 5 Have him give the money to the supervisors of the work on the Temple of the LORD. They must pay the workers who repair the Temple of the LORD— 6 the carpenters, builders and bricklayers. Also use the money to buy timber and cut stone to repair the Temple. 7 They do not need to report how they use the money given to them, because they are working honestly."

The Book of the Teachings is Found

8 Hilkiah the high priest said to Shaphan the royal secretary, "I've found the Book of the Teachings in the Temple of the LORD." He gave it to Shaphan, who read it.

9 Then Shaphan the royal secretary went to the king and reported to Josiah, "Your officers have paid out the money that was in the Temple of the LORD. They have given it to the workers and supervisors at the Temple." 10 Then Shaphan the royal secretary told the king, "Hilkiah the priest has given me a book." And Shaphan read from the book to the king.

11 When the king heard the words of the Book of the Teachings, he tore his clothes to show how upset he was. 12 He gave orders to Hilkiah the priest, Ahikam son of Shaphan, Acbor son of Micaiah, Shaphan the royal secretary and Asaiah the king's servant. These were the orders: 13 "Go and ask the LORD about the words in the book that was found. Ask for me, for all the people and for all Judah. The LORD's anger is burning against us, because our ancestors did not obey the words of this book; they did not do all the things written for us to do."

14 So Hilkiah the priest, Ahikam, Acbor, Shaphan and Asaiah went to talk to Huldah the prophetess. She was the wife of Shallum son of Tikvah, the son of Harhas, who took care of the king's clothes. Huldah lived in Jerusalem, in the new area of the city.

15 She said to them, "This is what the LORD, the God of Israel, says: 'Tell the man who sent you to me, 16 "This is what the LORD says: 'I will bring trouble to this place and to the people living here, as it is written in the book which the king of Judah has read. 17 The people of Judah have left me and have burned incense to other gods. They have made me angry by all that they have done. My anger burns against this place like a fire, and it will not be put out.'" 18 Tell the king of Judah, who sent you to ask the LORD, "This is what the LORD, the God of Israel, says about the words you heard: 19 When you heard my words against this place and its people, you became sorry for what you had done and upset yourself before me. I said they would be cursed and would be destroyed. You tore your clothes to show how upset you were, and you cried in my presence. This is why I have heard you, says the LORD. 20 So I will let you die, and you will be buried in peace. You won't see all the trouble I will bring to this place."'"

So they took her message back to the king.

The People Hear the Agreement

23 Then the king gathered all the elders of Judah and Jerusalem together. 2 He went up to the Temple of the LORD, and all the people from Judah and Jerusalem went with him. The priests, prophets and all the people—from the least important to the most important—went with him. He read to them all the words of the Book of the Agreement that was found in the Temple of the LORD. 3 The king stood by the pillar and made an agreement in the presence of the LORD to follow the LORD

23:3
Leadership
Read about a good leader.

and obey his commands, rules and laws with his whole being, and to obey the words of the agreement written in this book. Then all the people promised to obey the agreement.

Josiah Destroys the Places for Idol Worship

4 The king commanded Hilkiah the high priest and the priests of the next rank and the gatekeepers to bring out of the Temple of the LORD everything made for Baal, Asherah and all the stars of the sky. Then Josiah burnt them outside Jerusalem in the open country of the Kidron Valley and carried their ashes to Bethel. 5 The kings of Judah had chosen priests for these gods. These priests burnt incense in the places where gods were worshipped in the cities of Judah and the towns around Jerusalem. They burnt incense to Baal, the sun, the moon, the planets and all the stars of the sky. But Josiah took those priests away. 6 He removed the Asherah idol from the Temple of the LORD and took it outside Jerusalem to the Kidron Valley, where he burnt it and beat it into dust. Then he threw the ashes on the graves of the common people. 7 He also tore down the houses of the male prostitutes who were in the Temple of the LORD, where the women did weaving for Asherah.

8 King Josiah brought all the false priests from the cities of Judah. He ruined the places where gods were worshipped, where the priests had burnt incense, from Geba to Beersheba. He destroyed the places of worship at the entrance to the Gate of Joshua, the ruler of the city, on the left side of the city gate. 9 The priests at the places where gods were worshipped were not allowed to serve at the LORD's altar in Jerusalem. But they could eat bread made without yeast with their brothers.

10 Josiah ruined Topheth, in the Valley of Ben Hinnom, so no one could sacrifice his son or daughter to Molech. 11 Judah's kings had placed horses at the front door of the Temple of the LORD in the courtyard near the room of Nathan-Melech, an officer. These horses were for the worship of the sun. So Josiah removed them

---

FAITH links

NO THANKSGIVING?
2 KINGS 23:21-23

Can you imagine what it would be like if your mum and dad waited until the end of the year to say thank you to you for doing your weekly chores? Strange, huh? For the Israelites, Passover was a time of thanksgiving. When they celebrated Passover they remembered how thankful they were to God. He had rescued them from slavery in Egypt and had taken care of them. Yet, for many years, the Israelites did not celebrate Passover. King Josiah wanted them to start celebrating once more.

We don't have to wait for a special time of year to be thankful. Each time we go to church, take communion, talk with someone about God, or read the Bible we are reminded about what God has done for us.

Want to say thank you to God? Click here:

Time to Celebrate, Exodus 15:1-21, p. 95

A Cause for Celebration, 1 Kings 8:62-66, p. 449

Like Silver, Psalm 12:6-8, p. 717

Uniquely You, Psalm 139:13-14, p. 815

Too Busy to Worship? Luke 2:8-20, p. 1368

Always Do This! 1 Thessalonians 5:16-18, p. 1636

and burnt the chariots that were for sun worship also. **12** The kings of Judah had built altars on the roof[n] of the upstairs room of Ahaz. Josiah broke down these altars and the altars Manasseh had made in the two courtyards of the Temple of the LORD. Josiah smashed them to pieces and threw their dust into the Kidron Valley. **13** King Josiah ruined the places where gods were worshipped east of Jerusalem, south of the Mount of Olives.[n] Solomon king of Israel had built these places. One was for Ashtoreth, the hated goddess of the Sidonians. One was for Chemosh, the hated god of Moab. And one was for Molech, the hated god of the Ammonites. **14** Josiah smashed to pieces the stone pillars they worshipped, and he cut down the Asherah idols. Then he covered the places with human bones.

15 Josiah also broke down the altar at Bethel—the place of worship made by Jeroboam son of Nebat, who had led Israel to sin. Josiah burnt that place, broke the stones of the altar into pieces, then beat them into dust. He also burnt the Asherah idol. **16** When he turned round, he saw the graves on the mountain. He had the bones taken from the graves, and he burnt them on the altar to ruin it. This happened as the LORD had said it would through the man of God.

17 Josiah asked, "What is that monument I see?"

The people of the city answered, "It's the grave of the man of God who came from Judah. This prophet announced the things you have done against the altar of Bethel."

18 Josiah said, "Leave the grave alone. No one may move this man's bones." So they left his bones and the bones of the prophet who had come from Samaria.

19 The kings of Israel had built temples for worshipping gods in the cities of Samaria, which had caused the LORD to be angry. Josiah removed all those temples and did the same things as he had done at Bethel. **20** He killed all the priests of those places of worship; he killed them on the altars and burnt human bones on the altars. Then he went back to Jerusalem.

Josiah Celebrates the Passover

21 The king commanded all the people, "Celebrate the Passover to the LORD your God as it is written in this Book of the Agreement." **22** The Passover had not been celebrated like this since the judges led Israel. Nor had one like it happened while there were kings of Israel and kings of Judah. **23** This Passover was celebrated to the LORD in Jerusalem in the eighteenth year of King Josiah's rule.

24 Josiah destroyed the mediums, fortune-tellers, house gods and idols. He also destroyed all the hated gods seen in the land of Judah and Jerusalem. This was to obey the words of the teachings written in the book Hilkiah the priest had found in the Temple of the LORD.

25 There was no king like Josiah before or after him. He obeyed the LORD with all his heart, soul and strength, following all the Teachings of Moses.

26 Even so, the LORD did not stop his strong and terrible anger. His anger burned against Judah because of all Manasseh had done to make him angry. **27** The LORD said, "I will send Judah out of my sight, as I have sent Israel away. I will reject Jerusalem, which I chose. And I will take away the Temple about which I said, 'I will be worshipped there.'"

28 Everything else Josiah did is written in the book of the history of the kings of Judah.

29 While Josiah was king, Neco king of Egypt went to help the king of Assyria at the Euphrates River. King Josiah marched out to fight against Neco, but at Megiddo, Neco faced him and killed him. **30** Josiah's servants carried his body in a chariot from Megiddo to Jerusalem and buried him in his own grave. Then the people of Judah chose Josiah's son Jehoahaz and poured olive oil on him to make him king in his father's place.

23:12 roof In Bible times houses were built with flat roofs. The roof was used for drying things such as flax and fruit. And it was used as an extra room, as a place for worship and as a place to sleep in the summer.

23:13 Mount of Olives Literally, "The Mountain of Ruin".

Jehoahaz King of Judah

31 Jehoahaz was 23 years old when he became king, and he was king in Jerusalem for three months. His mother's name was Hamutal, who was the daughter of Jeremiah from Libnah. 32 Jehoahaz did what the LORD said was wrong, just as his ancestors had done.

33 King Neco took Jehoahaz prisoner at Riblah in the land of Hamath so that Jehoahaz could not rule in Jerusalem. Neco made the people of Judah pay about 3.5 tonnes of silver and about 35 kilogrammes of gold.

34 King Neco made Josiah's son Eliakim the king in place of Josiah his father. Then Neco changed Eliakim's name to Jehoiakim. But Neco took Jehoahaz to Egypt, where he died. 35 Jehoiakim gave King Neco the silver and gold he demanded. Jehoiakim taxed the land and took silver and gold from the people of the land to give to King Neco. Each person had to pay his share.

Jehoiakim King of Judah

36 Jehoiakim was 25 years old when he became king, and he was king in Jerusalem for eleven years. His mother's name was Zebidah daughter of Pedaiah, who was from Rumah. 37 Jehoiakim did what the LORD said was wrong, just as his ancestors had done.

24 While Jehoiakim was king, Nebuchadnezzar king of Babylon attacked the land of Judah. So Jehoiakim became Nebuchadnezzar's servant for three years. Then he turned against Nebuchadnezzar and broke away from his rule. 2 The LORD sent raiding men from Babylon, Aram, Moab and Ammon against Jehoiakim to destroy Judah. This happened as the LORD had said it would through his servants the prophets.

3 The LORD commanded this to happen to the people of Judah, to remove them from his presence, because of all the sins of Manasseh. 4 He had killed many innocent people and had filled Jerusalem with their blood. And the LORD would not forgive these sins.

5 The other things that happened while Jehoiakim was king and all he did are written in the book of the history of the kings of Judah. 6 Jehoiakim died, and his son Jehoiachin became king in his place.

7 The king of Egypt did not leave his land again, because the king of Babylon had captured all that belonged to the king of Egypt, from the brook of Egypt to the Euphrates River.

Jehoiachin King of Judah

8 Jehoiachin was eighteen years old when he became king, and he was king for three months in Jerusalem. His mother's name was Nehushta daughter of Elnathan from Jerusalem. 9 Jehoiachin did what the LORD said was wrong, just as his father had done.

10 At that time the officers of Nebuchadnezzar king of Babylon came up to Jerusalem. When they reached the city, they attacked it. 11 Nebuchadnezzar himself came to the city while his officers were attacking it. 12 Jehoiachin king of Judah surrendered to the king of Babylon, along with Jehoiachin's mother, servants, elders and officers. So Nebuchadnezzar made Jehoiachin a prisoner in the eighth year he was king of Babylon. 13 Nebuchadnezzar took all the treasures from the Temple of the LORD and from the palace. He cut up all the gold objects Solomon king of Israel had made for the Temple of the LORD. This happened as the LORD had said it would. 14 Nebuchadnezzar took away all the people of Jerusalem, including all the leaders, all the wealthy people, and all the craftsmen and metal workers. There were 10,000 prisoners in all. Only the poorest people in the land were left. 15 Nebuchadnezzar carried away Jehoiachin to Babylon, as well as the king's mother and his wives, the

> Nebuchadnezzar took all the treasures from the Temple of the LORD and from the palace.
> – 2 Kings 24:13

officers and the leading men of the land. They were taken captive from Jerusalem to Babylon. 16 The king of Babylon also took all 7,000 soldiers, who were strong and able to fight in war, and about 1,000 craftsmen and metal workers. Nebuchadnezzar took them as prisoners to Babylon. 17 Then he made Mattaniah, Jehoiachin's uncle, king in Jehoiachin's place. He also changed Mattaniah's name to Zedekiah.

Zedekiah King of Judah

18 Zedekiah was 21 years old when he became king, and he was king in Jerusalem for eleven years. His mother's name was Hamutal daughter of Jeremiah[n] from Libnah. 19 Zedekiah did what the LORD said was wrong, just as Jehoiakim had done. 20 All this happened in Jerusalem and Judah because the LORD was angry with them. Finally, he threw them out of his presence.

The Fall of Jerusalem

Zedekiah turned against the king of Babylon.

25 Nebuchadnezzar king of Babylon marched against Jerusalem with his whole army during Zedekiah's ninth year as king, on the tenth day of the tenth month. He made a camp around the city and piled earth against the city walls to attack it. 2 The city was under attack until Zedekiah's eleventh year as king. 3 By the ninth day of the fourth month, the hunger was terrible in the city. There was no food for the people to eat. 4 Then the city was broken into, and the whole army ran away at night through the gate between the two walls by the king's garden. While the Babylonians were still surrounding the city, Zedekiah and his men ran away towards the Jordan Valley. 5 But the Babylonian army chased King Zedekiah and caught up with him in the plains of Jericho. All of his army was scattered from him, 6 so they captured Zedekiah and took him to the king of Babylon at Riblah. There he passed sentence on Zedekiah. 7 They killed Zedekiah's sons as he watched. Then they put out his eyes and put bronze chains on him and took him to Babylon.

8 Nebuzaradan was the commander of the king's special guards. This officer of the king of Babylon came to Jerusalem on the seventh day of the fifth month, in Nebuchadnezzar's nineteenth year as king of Babylon. 9 Nebuzaradan set fire to the Temple of the LORD and the palace and all the houses of Jerusalem. Every important building was burned. 10 The whole Babylonian army, led by the commander of the king's special guards, broke down the walls around Jerusalem. 11 Nebuzaradan, the commander of the guards, captured the people left in Jerusalem, those who had surrendered to the king of Babylon and the rest of the people. 12 But the commander left behind some of the poorest people of the land to take care of the vineyards and fields.

13 The Babylonians broke up the bronze pillars, the bronze stands and the large bronze bowl, which was called the Sea, in the Temple of the LORD. Then they carried the bronze to Babylon. 14 They also took the pots, shovels, wick trimmers, dishes and all the bronze objects used to serve in the Temple. 15 The commander of the king's special guards took away the pans for carrying hot coals, the bowls and everything made of pure gold or silver. 16 There were two pillars and the large bronze bowl and the movable stands which Solomon had made for the Temple of the LORD. There was so much bronze that it could not be weighed. 17 Each pillar was about 9 metres high. The bronze capital on top of the pillar was about 1.5 metres high. It was decorated with a net design and bronze pomegranates all around it. The

---

24:18 Jeremiah This is not the prophet Jeremiah, but another man with the same name.

Judah is Taken Prisoner

18 The commander of the guards took some prisoners—Seraiah the chief priest, Zephaniah the priest next in rank, and the three doorkeepers. 19 Of the people who were still in the city, he took the officer in charge of the fighting men, as well as five people who advised the king. He took the royal secretary who selected people for the army and 60 other men who were in the city. 20 Nebuzaradan, the commander, took all these people and brought them to the king of Babylon at Riblah. 21 There at Riblah, in the land of Hamath, the king had them killed. So the people of Judah were led away from their country as captives.

Gedaliah Becomes Governor

22 Nebuchadnezzar king of Babylon left some people in the land of Judah. He appointed Gedaliah son of Ahikam, the son of Shaphan, as governor.

23 The army captains and their men heard that the king of Babylon had made Gedaliah governor, so they came to Gedaliah at Mizpah. They were Ishmael son of Nethaniah, Johanan son of Kareah, Seraiah son of Tanhumeth the Netophathite, Jaazaniah son of the Maacathite, and their men. 24 Then Gedaliah promised these army captains and their men, "Don't be afraid of the Babylonian officers. Live in the land and serve the king of Babylon, and everything will go well for you."

25 In the seventh month Ishmael son of Nethaniah, son of Elishama from the king's family, came with ten men and killed Gedaliah. They also killed the men of Judah and Babylon who were with Gedaliah at Mizpah. 26 Then all the people, from the least important to the most important, along with the army leaders, ran away to Egypt, because they were afraid of the Babylonians.

Jehoiachin is Set Free

27 Jehoiachin king of Judah was held in Babylon for 37 years. In the thirty-seventh year Evil-Merodach became king of Babylon, and he let Jehoiachin out of prison on the twenty-seventh day of the twelfth month. 28 Evil-Merodach spoke kindly to Jehoiachin and gave him a seat of honour above the seats of the other kings who were with him in Babylon. 29 So Jehoiachin put away his prison clothes. For the rest of his life, he ate at the king's table. 30 Every day, for as long as Jehoiachin lived, the king gave him an allowance.

1 Chronicles

GOD MAKES A LIST

Hello. My name is Ezra, and I am a teacher and priest. Have you ever asked your parents and grandparents about the history of your family? First Chronicles is a history book of God's family, starting with the first man, Adam, and ending with our great King David. Israel became a strong nation under David's rule because David loved God and obeyed his commands. Download 1 Chronicles 17 to read about God's promise to David that his family would rule for ever.

I wrote this book so that people would know that God is faithful through all generations. The people of God were returning to Israel from exile in a foreign land and needed to be reminded of God's blessing for those who love and obey him. Don't miss the MIDI file on David's song of praise celebrating God's love for the people of Israel at 1 Chronicles 16:8–36.

JESUS WATCH

At first glance, 1 Chronicles seems packed with boring lists, but take a second look. All the people on the lists were important to God and to his plan for salvation. Jesus often called himself the Son of Man; and his family history can be traced all the way back to Adam, the first man. Jesus was also called the Son of David. Notice the special emphasis placed on the genealogy of the tribe of Judah, David's family. God promised David that his son would rule for ever. David's descendants did rule as kings until Judah was conquered and the people were exiled to Babylon. The list of family generations continues in Matthew 1 and ends with Jesus, the promised Son of David. Jesus is our king, but his rule lasts for ever!

my FAVOURITE links

OTHER CONNECTIONS

Connect to these info bulletin boards for more fascinating facts about David and God's special messengers, angels:

- **A Man After God's Own Heart, 1 Chronicles 17.** David – shepherd boy, warrior, musician, poet, king – answered to all these descriptions, but he is perhaps best known for being called "a man after God's own heart". Discover more about this man by following key events in his life.
- **A Special Angel, 1 Chronicles 21:6–22.** Learn about the angel of the Lord, who appeared to numerous people throughout the Old Testament, performing special jobs for God. Consider what you would do if you had a visit from God's special messenger.

MORE STUFF...

David's Mighty Men David had a strong and loyal following of soldiers. Read about them and their adventures in 1 Chronicles 11; 12. Here are a few facts about them:
- Joab defeated the Jebusites living in Jerusalem and became commander of David's army.
- Jashobeam was commander of the Three, David's most powerful soldiers. He once used his spear to fight 300 men, and he killed all of them.
- Benaiah killed an Egyptian who was about 2.5 metres tall.

FAITH links

- A Given, **1 Chronicles 5:18–20**
- Service with a Smile, **1 Chronicles 6:31–49**
- A Memorial for Two Thieves, **1 Chronicles 7:21**
- Just a Little Respect, **1 Chronicles 11:10–19**
- Plan for Success, **1 Chronicles 14:8–17**
- Plans for a Son, **1 Chronicles 22:5–19**
- Gifts from the Heart, **1 Chronicles 29**

---

did YOU know?

Do you know who was the commander of David's army?

No clue? How about downloading 1 Chronicles 11:4–9 to find out?

SOME OTHER PLACES TO SURF IN 1 CHRONICLES:

David's mighty warriors, 1 Chronicles 11:15–25
Don't touch – or else! 1 Chronicles 13
The "how-to" on carrying the Ark, 1 Chronicles 15
David tells Solomon to build the Temple, 1 Chronicles 28

From Adam to Abraham

1 Adam was the father of Seth. Seth was the father of Enosh. Enosh was the father of Kenan. 2 Kenan was the father of Mahalalel. Mahalalel was the father of Jared. Jared was the father of Enoch. 3 Enoch was the father of Methuselah. Methuselah was the father of Lamech and Lamech was the father of Noah.

4 The sons of Noah were Shem, Ham and Japheth.

5 Japheth's sons were Gomer, Magog, Madai, Javan, Tubal, Meshech and Tiras.

6 Gomer's sons were Ashkenaz, Riphath and Togarmah.

7 Javan's sons were Elishah, Tarshish, Kittim[n] and Rodanim.

8 Ham's sons were Cush, Mizraim,[n] Put and Canaan.

9 Cush's sons were Seba, Havilah, Sabta, Raamah and Sabteca.

Raamah's sons were Sheba and Dedan.

10 Cush was the father of Nimrod, who grew up to become a mighty warrior on the earth.

11 Mizraim was the father of the Ludites, Anamites, Lehabites and Naphtuhim,

12 Pathrusites, Casluhites and Caphtorites. (The Philistines came from the Casluhites.)

13 Canaan's first child was Sidon. He was also the father of the Hittites, 14 Jebusites, Amorites, Girgashites, 15 Hivites, Arkites, Sinites, 16 Arvadites, Zemarites and Hamathites.

17 Shem's sons were Elam, Asshur, Arphaxad, Lud and Aram.

Aram's sons were Uz, Hul, Gether and Meshech.

18 Arphaxad was the father of Shelah, who was the father of Eber.

19 Eber had two sons. One son was named Peleg,[n] because the people on the earth were divided into different languages during his life. Peleg's brother was named Joktan.

20 Joktan was the father of Almodad, Sheleph, Hazarmaveth, Jerah, 21 Hadoram, Uzal, Diklah, 22 Obal, Abimael, Sheba, 23 Ophir, Havilah and Jobab. All these were Joktan's sons. 24 The family line included Shem, Arphaxad, Shelah, 25 Eber, Peleg, Reu, 26 Serug, Nahor, Terah 27 and Abram, who was called Abraham.

Abraham's Family

28 Abraham's sons were Isaac and Ishmael.

29 These were the sons of Isaac and Ishmael. Ishmael's first son was Nebaioth. His other sons were Kedar, Adbeel, Mibsam, 30 Mishma, Dumah, Massa, Hadad, Tema, 31 Jetur, Naphish and Kedemah. These were Ishmael's sons. 32 Keturah, Abraham's slave woman, gave birth to Zimran, Jokshan, Medan, Midian, Ishbak and Shuah.

Jokshan's sons were Sheba and Dedan.

33 Midian's sons were Ephah, Epher, Hanoch, Abida and Eldaah. All these were descendants of Keturah.

34 Abraham was the father of Isaac and Isaac's sons were Esau and Israel.

35 Esau's sons were Eliphaz, Reuel, Jeush, Jalam and Korah.

36 Eliphaz's sons were Teman, Omar, Zepho, Gatam, Kenaz, Timna and Amalek.

37 Reuel's sons were Nahath, Zerah, Shammah and Mizzah.

The Edomites from Seir

38 Seir's sons were Lotan, Shobal, Zibeon, Anah, Dishon, Ezer and Dishan.

39 Lotan's sons were Hori, Homam and his sister was Timna.

40 Shobal's sons were Alvan, Manahath, Ebal, Shepho and Onam.

1:7 Kittim His descendants were the people of Cyprus.
1:8 Mizraim This is another name for Egypt.
1:19 Peleg This name sounds like the Hebrew word for "divided."

> Cush was the father of Nimrod, who grew up to become a mighty warrior on the earth.
> – 1 Chronicles 1:10

Zibeon's sons were Aiah and Anah. 41 Anah's son was Dishon. Dishon's sons were Hemdan, Eshban, Ithran and Keran. 42 Ezer's sons were Bilhan, Zaavan and Akan. Dishan's sons were Uz and Aran.

The Kings of Edom

43 These kings ruled in Edom before there were kings in Israel. Bela son of Beor was king of Edom, and his city was named Dinhabah. 44 When Bela died, Jobab son of Zerah became king. He was from Bozrah. 45 When Jobab died, Husham became king. He was from the land of the Temanites. 46 When Husham died, Hadad son of Bedad became king, and his city was named Avith. Hadad defeated Midian in the country of Moab. 47 When Hadad died, Samlah became king. He was from Masrekah. 48 When Samlah died, Shaul became king. He was from Rehoboth by the river. 49 When Shaul died, Baal-Hanan son of Acbor became king. 50 When Baal-Hanan died, Hadad became king, and his city was named Pau. Hadad's wife was named Mehetabel, and she was the daughter of Matred, who was the daughter of Me-Zahab. 51 Then Hadad died.

The leaders of the family groups of Edom were Timna, Alvah, Jetheth, 52 Oholibamah, Elah, Pinon, 53 Kenaz, Teman, Mibzar, 54 Magdiel and Iram. These were the leaders of Edom.

Israel's Family

2 The sons of Israel[n] were Reuben, Simeon, Levi, Judah, Issachar, Zebulun, 2 Dan, Joseph, Benjamin, Naphtali, Gad and Asher.

Judah's Family

3 Judah's sons were Er, Onan and Shelah. A Canaanite woman, the daughter of Shua, was their mother. Judah's first son, Er, did what the LORD said was wicked, so the LORD put him to death. 4 Judah's daughter-in-law Tamar gave birth to Perez and Zerah. Judah was the father, so Judah had five sons. 5 Perez's sons were Hezron and Hamul. 6 Zerah had five sons: Zimri, Ethan, Heman, Calcol and Darda. 7 Carmi's son was Achan, who caused trouble for Israel because he took things that had been given to the LORD to be destroyed. 8 Ethan's son was Azariah.

9 Hezron's sons were Jerahmeel, Ram and Caleb. 10 Ram was Amminadab's father, and Amminadab was Nahshon's father. Nahshon was the leader of the people of Judah. 11 Nahshon was the father of Salmon, who was the father of Boaz. 12 Boaz was the father of Obed, and Obed was the father of Jesse.

13 Jesse's first son was Eliab. His second son was Abinadab, his third was Shimea, 14 his fourth was Nethanel, his fifth was Raddai, 15 his sixth was Ozem and his seventh son was David. 16 Their sisters were Zeruiah and Abigail. Zeruiah's three sons were Abishai, Joab and Asahel. 17 Abigail was the mother of Amasa and his father was Jether, an Ishmaelite.

Caleb's Family

18 Caleb son of Hezron had children by his wife Azubah and by Jerioth. Caleb and Azubah's sons were Jesher, Shobab and Ardon. 19 When Azubah died, Caleb married Ephrath. They had a son named Hur, 20 who was the father of Uri, who was the father of Bezalel.

21 Later, when Hezron was 60 years old, he married the daughter of Makir, Gilead's father. Hezron had sexual rela-

> Carmi's son was Achan, who . . . took things that had been given to the LORD to be destroyed.
> – 1 Chronicles 2:7

2:1 **Israel** Another name for Jacob.

tions with Makir's daughter, and she had a son named Segub. 22 Segub was the father of Jair. Jair controlled 23 cities in the country of Gilead. 23 (But Geshur and Aram captured the towns of Jair, as well as Kenath and the small towns around it—60 towns in all.) All these were descendants of Makir, the father of Gilead.

24 After Hezron died in Caleb Ephrathah, his wife Abijah had his son, named Ashhur. Ashhur became the father of Tekoa.

Jerahmeel's Family

25 Hezron's first son was Jerahmeel. Jerahmeel's sons were Ram, Bunah, Oren, Ozem and Ahijah. Ram was Jerahmeel's first son. 26 Jerahmeel had another wife, named Atarah. She was the mother of Onam.

27 Jerahmeel's first son, Ram, had sons. They were Maaz, Jamin and Eker.

28 Onam's sons were Shammai and Jada.

Shammai's sons were Nadab and Abishur.

29 Abishur's wife was named Abihail, and their sons were Ahban and Molid.

30 Nadab's sons were Seled and Appaim. Seled died without having children.

31 Appaim's son was Ishi, who became the father of Sheshan.

Sheshan was the father of Ahlai.

32 Jada was Shammai's brother, and Jada's sons were Jether and Jonathan. Jether died without having children.

33 Jonathan's sons were Peleth and Zaza.

These were Jerahmeel's descendants.

34 Sheshan did not have any sons, only daughters. He had a servant from Egypt named Jarha. 35 Sheshan let his daughter marry his servant Jarha, and she had a son named Attai.

36 Attai was the father of Nathan. Nathan was the father of Zabad. 37 Zabad was the father of Ephlal. Ephlal was the father of Obed. 38 Obed was the father of Jehu. Jehu was the father of Azariah. 39 Azariah was the father of Helez. Helez was the father of Eleasah. 40 Eleasah was the father of Sismai. Sismai was the father of Shallum. 41 Shallum was the father of Jekamiah, and Jekamiah was the father of Elishama.

The Clans of Caleb

42 Caleb was Jerahmeel's brother. Caleb's first son was Mesha. Mesha was the father of Ziph, and his son Mareshah was the father of Hebron.

43 Hebron's sons were Korah, Tappuah, Rekem and Shema. 44 Shema was the father of Raham, who was the father of Jorkeam. Rekem was the father of Shammai. 45 Shammai was the father of Maon, and Maon was the father of Beth Zur.

46 Caleb's slave woman was named Ephah and she was the mother of Haran, Moza and Gazez. Haran was the father of Gazez.

47 Jahdai's sons were Regem, Jotham, Geshan, Pelet, Ephah and Shaaph.

48 Caleb had another slave woman named Maacah. She was the mother of Sheber, Tirhanah, 49 Shaaph and Sheva. Shaaph was the father of Madmannah. Sheva was the father of Macbenah and Gibea. Caleb's daughter was Achsah.

50-51 These were Caleb's descendants: Caleb's son Hur was the first son of his mother Ephrathah. Hur's sons were Shobal, Salma and Hareph. Shobal was the father of Kiriath Jearim. Salma was the father of Bethlehem. And Hareph was the father of Beth Gader.

52 Shobal was the father of Kiriath Jearim. Shobal's descendants were Haroeh, half the Manahathites, 53 and the family groups of Kiriath Jearim: the Ithrites, Puthites, Shumathites and Mishraites. The Zorathites and the Eshtaolites came from the Mishraite people.

54 Salma's descendants were Bethlehem, the Netophathites, Atroth Beth Joab, half the Manahathites and the Zorites. 55 His descendants included the families who lived at Jabez, who wrote and copied important papers. They were called the Tirathites, Shimeathites and Sucathites and were from the Kenite family group who came from Hammath. He was the father of the people living in Recab.

1 Chronicles 3:1 522

David's Family

3 These are David's sons who were born in Hebron. The first was Amnon, whose mother was Ahinoam from Jezreel. The second son was Daniel, whose mother was Abigail from Carmel. 2 The third son was Absalom, whose mother was Maacah daughter of Talmai, the king of Geshur. The fourth son was Adonijah, whose mother was Haggith. 3 The fifth son was Shephatiah, whose mother was Abital. The sixth son was Ithream, whose mother was Eglah. 4 These six sons of David were born to him in Hebron, where David ruled for seven and a half years.

David ruled in Jerusalem for 33 years. 5 These were his children who were born in Jerusalem: Shammua, Shobab, Nathan and Solomon—the four children of David and Bathsheba, Ammiel's daughter. 6-8 David's other nine children were Ibhar, Elishua, Eliphelet, Nogah, Nepheg, Japhia, Elishama, Eliada and Eliphelet. 9 These were all of David's sons, except for those born to his slave women. David also had a daughter named Tamar.

The Kings of Judah

10 Solomon's son was Rehoboam. Rehoboam's son was Abijah. Abijah's son

FOR BETTER OR WORSHIP

Do you ever stop and think about what it means to worship God. Please welcome Maria, aged 10, to Connect 2-You. She has something to say about worship.

Maria

I want to know why we have to go to Sunday school and church. Everything is so boring – especially at my church. We never talk about anything interesting in Sunday school, the hymns in church are old and slow, and I can't understand a word of the sermon. Church is for grown-ups. I think kids should be allowed to stay at home.

Do you know how Maria's feeling? Many church services and many Sunday school classes aren't very "kid-friendly". But the reason we go to church is not to have a good time or to be entertained, but to give worship to God. It gives us a chance to let God know how we feel about him – through the things we talk about, the things we think about, the songs we sing and the way we act. Think of it as "paying him back" once a week for everything he does for you.

If there are things that would make your Sunday school class or church service better for you, tell your teacher or pastor. They will probably be glad to hear your ideas. For some tips on how to make worship meaningful to you, check out the Livin' It page on worshipping God, <u>Nehemiah 8:6, p. 634</u>.

was Asa. Asa's son was Jehoshaphat. **11** Jehoshaphat's son was Jehoram. Jehoram's son was Ahaziah. Ahaziah's son was Joash. **12** Joash's son was Amaziah. Amaziah's son was Azariah. Azariah's son was Jotham. **13** Jotham's son was Ahaz. Ahaz's son was Hezekiah. Hezekiah's son was Manasseh. **14** Manasseh's son was Amon, and Amon's son was Josiah.

15 These were Josiah's sons: his first son was Johanan, his second was Jehoiakim, his third was Zedekiah and his fourth was Shallum.

16 Jehoiakim was followed by Jehoiachin, and he was followed by Zedekiah.

David's Descendants After the Babylonian Captivity

17 Jehoiachin was taken as a prisoner. His sons were Shealtiel, **18** Malkiram, Pedaiah, Shenazzar, Jekamiah, Hoshama and Nedabiah.

19 Pedaiah's sons were Zerubbabel and Shimei.

Zerubbabel's sons were Meshullam and Hananiah, and their sister was Shelomith. **20** Zerubbabel also had five other sons: Hashubah, Ohel, Berekiah, Hasadiah and Jushab-Hesed.

21 Hananiah's descendants were Pelatiah and Jeshaiah, and the sons of Rephaiah, Arnan, Obadiah and Shecaniah.

22 Shecaniah's son was Shemaiah. Shemaiah's sons were Hattush, Igal, Bariah, Neariah and Shaphat. There were six in all.

23 Neariah had three sons: Elioenai, Hizkiah and Azrikam.

24 Elioenai had seven sons: Hodaviah, Eliashib, Pelaiah, Akkub, Johanan, Delaiah and Anani.

Other Family Groups of Judah

4 Judah's descendants were Perez, Hezron, Carmi, Hur and Shobal.

2 Reaiah was Shobal's son. Reaiah was the father of Jahath, and Jahath was the father of Ahumai and Lahad. They were the family groups of the Zorathite people.

3-4 Hur was the oldest son of Caleb and his wife Ephrathah. Hur was the leader of Bethlehem. His three sons were Etam, Penuel and Ezer. Etam's sons were Jezreel, Ishma and Idbash. They had a sister named Hazzelelponi. Penuel was the father of Gedor and Ezer was the father of Hushah.

5 Tekoa's father was Ashhur. Ashhur had two wives named Helah and Naarah.

6 The sons of Ashhur and Naarah were Ahuzzam, Hepher, Temeni and Haahashtari. These were the descendants of Naarah.

7 Helah's sons were Zereth, Zohar, Ethnan **8** and Koz. Koz was the father of Anub, Hazzobebah and the Aharhel family group. Aharhel was the son of Harum.

9 There was a man named Jabez, who was respected more than his brothers. His mother named him Jabez[n] because she said, "I was in much pain when I gave birth to him." **10** Jabez prayed to the God of Israel, "Please do good things for me and give me more land. Stay with me, and don't let anyone hurt me. Then I won't have any pain." And God did what Jabez had asked.

> Please do good things for me and give me more land. Stay with me, and don't let anyone hurt me.
> – 1 Chronicles 4:10

11 Kelub, Shuhah's brother, was the father of Mehir. Mehir was the father of Eshton. **12** Eshton was the father of Beth Rapha, Paseah and Tehinnah. Tehinnah was the father of the people from the town of Nahash. These people were from Recah.

13 The sons of Kenaz were Othniel and Seraiah.

Othniel's sons were Hathath and Meonothai. **14** Meonothai was the father of Ophrah.

Seraiah was the father of Joab. Joab was the ancestor of the people from Craftsmen's Valley, named that because the people living there were craftsmen.

15 Caleb was Jephunneh's son. Caleb's

4:9 Jabez This name in Hebrew sounds like the word for "pain."

sons were Iru, Elah and Naam. Elah's son was Kenaz.

16 Jehallelel's sons were Ziph, Ziphah, Tiria and Asarel.

17-18 Ezrah's sons were Jether, Mered, Epher and Jalon. Mered married Bithiah, the daughter of the king of Egypt. The children of Mered and Bithiah were Miriam, Shammai and Ishbah. Ishbah was the father of Eshtemoa. Mered also had a wife from Judah, who gave birth to Jered, Heber and Jekuthiel. Jered became the father of Gedor. Heber became the father of Soco. And Jekuthiel became the father of Zanoah.

19 Hodiah's wife was Naham's sister. The sons of Hodiah's wife were Eshtemoa and the father of Keilah. Keilah was from the Garmite people, and Eshtemoa was from the Maacathite people.

20 Shimon's sons were Amnon, Rinnah, Ben-Hanan and Tilon.

Ishi's sons were Zoheth and Ben-Zoheth.

21-22 Shelah was Judah's son. Shelah's sons were Er, Laadah, Jokim, the men from Cozeba, Joash and Saraph. Er was the father of Lecah. Laadah was the father of Mareshah and the family groups of linen workers at Beth Ashbea. Joash and Saraph ruled in Moab and Jashubi Lehem. The writings about this family are very old. 23 These sons of Shelah were potters. They lived in Netaim and Gederah and worked for the king.

Simeon's Children

24 Simeon's sons were Nemuel, Jamin, Jarib, Zerah and Shaul. 25 Shaul's son was Shallum. Shallum's son was Mibsam. Mibsam's son was Mishma.

26 Mishma's son was Hammuel. Hammuel's son was Zaccur. Zaccur's son was Shimei. 27 Shimei had sixteen sons and six daughters, but his brothers did not have many children, so there were not as many people in their family group as there were in Judah.

28 Shimei's children lived in Beersheba, Moladah, Hazar Shual, 29 Bilhah, Ezem, Tolad, 30 Bethuel, Hormah, Ziklag, 31 Beth Marcaboth, Hazar Susim, Beth Biri and Shaaraim. They lived in these cities until David became king. 32 The five villages near these cities were Etam, Ain, Rimmon, Token and Ashan. 33 There were also other villages as far away as Baalath. This is where they lived. And they wrote the history of their family.

34-38 The men in this list were leaders of their family groups: Meshobab, Jamlech, Joshah son of Amaziah, Joel, Jehu son of Joshibiah (Joshibiah was the son of Seraiah, who was the son of Asiel), Elioenai, Jaakobah, Jeshohaiah, Asaiah, Adiel, Jesimiel, Benaiah and Ziza. (Ziza was the son of Shiphi, who was the son of Allon. Allon was the son of Jedaiah, who was the son of Shimri. And Shimri was the son of Shemaiah.)

These families grew very large. 39 They went outside the city of Gedor to the east side of the valley to look for pasture for their flocks. 40 They found good pastures with plenty of grass, and the land was open country and peaceful and quiet. Ham's descendants had lived there in the past.

41 These men who were listed came to Gedor while Hezekiah was king of Judah. They fought against the Hamite people, destroying their tents, and also against the Meunites who lived there, and completely destroyed them. So there are no Meunites there even today. Then these men began to live there, because there was pasture for their flocks. 42 Ishi's sons, Pelatiah, Neariah, Rephaiah and Uzziel, led 500 of the Simeonites and attacked the people living in the mountains of Edom. 43 They killed the few Amalekites who were still alive. From that time until now these Simeonites have lived in Edom.

Reuben's Children

5 Reuben was Israel's first son. Reuben should have received the special privileges of the oldest son, but he had sexual relations with his father's slave woman. So those special privileges were given to Joseph's sons. (Joseph was a son of Israel.) In the family history Reuben's name is not listed as the first

son. 2 Judah became stronger than his brothers, and a leader came from his family. But Joseph's family received the privileges that belonged to the oldest son. 3 Reuben was Israel's first son. Reuben's sons were Hanoch, Pallu, Hezron and Carmi.

4 These were the children of Joel: Shemaiah was Joel's son. Gog was Shemaiah's son. Shimei was Gog's son. 5 Micah was Shimei's son. Reaiah was Micah's son. Baal was Reaiah's son. 6 Beerah was Baal's son. Beerah was a leader of the tribe of Reuben. Tiglath-Pileser king of Assyria captured him and took him away.

7 Joel's brothers and all his family groups are listed just as they are written in their family histories: Jeiel was the first, then Zechariah 8 and Bela. (Bela was the son of Azaz. Azaz was the son of Shema, and Shema was the son of Joel.) They lived in the area of Aroer all the way to Nebo and Baal Meon. 9 Bela's people lived to the east—as far as the edge of the desert, which is beside the Euphrates River—because they had too many cattle for the land of Gilead.

10 When Saul was king, Bela's people fought a war against the Hagrite people and defeated them. Then Bela's people lived in the tents that had belonged to the Hagrites in all the area east of Gilead.

Gad's Children

11 The people from the tribe of Gad lived near the Reubenites. The Gadites lived in the area of Bashan all the way to Salecah. 12 Joel was the main leader, Shapham was second, and then Janai and Shaphat were leaders in Bashan.

13 The seven relatives in their families were Michael, Meshullam, Sheba, Jorai, Jacan, Zia and Eber. 14 They were the descendants of Abihail. Abihail was Huri's son. Huri was Jaroah's son. Jaroah was Gilead's son. Gilead was Michael's son. Michael was Jeshishai's son. Jeshishai was Jahdo's son, and Jahdo was the son of Buz. 15 Ahi was Abdiel's son, and Abdiel was Guni's son. Ahi was the leader of their family.

16 The Gadites lived in Gilead, Bashan and the small towns around it, and on all the pasturelands in the Plain of Sharon all the way to the borders.

17 All these names were written in the family history of Gad during the time Jotham was king of Judah and Jeroboam was king of Israel.

Soldiers Skilled in War

18 There were 44,760 soldiers from the tribes of Reuben and Gad and East Manasseh who carried shields and swords and bows. They were skilled in war. 19 They started a war against the Hagrites and the people of Jetur, Naphish and Nodab. 20 The men from the tribes of Manasseh, Reuben and Gad prayed to God during the war, asking him to help them. So he helped them because they trusted him. He handed over to them the Hagrites and all those who were with them. 21 They took the animals that belonged to the Hagrites: 50,000 camels, 250,000 sheep and 2,000 donkeys. They also captured 100,000 people. 22 Many Hagrites were killed because God helped the people of Reuben, Gad and Manasseh. Then they lived there until Babylon captured them and took them away.

East Manasseh

23 There were many people in East Manasseh, and they lived in the area of Bashan all the way to Baal Hermon, Senir and Mount Hermon.

24 These were the family leaders: Epher, Ishi, Eliel, Azriel, Jeremiah, Hodaviah and Jahdiel. They were all strong, brave and famous men, and leaders in their families. 25 But they sinned against the God that their ancestors had worshipped. They began worshiping the gods of the people in that land, and those were the people God was destroying. 26 So the God of Israel made Pul king of Assyria want to go to war. (Pul was also called Tiglath-Pileser.) He captured the people of Reuben, Gad and East Manasseh, and he took them away to Halah, Habor, Hara and near the Gozan River. They have lived there from that time until this day.

1 Chronicles 6:1 526

FAITH links

A GIVEN
1 CHRONICLES 5:18-20

Certain things in life are givens. That means you can count on them to happen. You expect the sun to come up. Even if it rains, you know the sun is still there somewhere. Certain things about faith are givens, too. In 1 Chronicles 5:20, eight little words explain one of the "givens". Some men of Israel prayed to God for help. "So he [God] helped them because they trusted him" (5:20). Read those eight words again. That means he'll help you if you trust him. The key word is *trust*. Do you trust him?

Here are some more Faithlinks on trust:

From Hopeless to Hopeful, Exodus 6:9, p. 83

God's New Home, 2 Chronicles 7:11–22, p. 570

A Mother's Love, Isaiah 49:13–16, p. 961

A Safe Place, Nahum 1:7, p. 1231

Jesus' Prayer, John 17, p. 1453

The Finished Product, Philippians 1:6, p. 1609

Levi's Children

6 Levi's sons were Gershon, Kohath and Merari.

2 Kohath's sons were Amram, Izhar, Hebron and Uzziel.

3 Amram's children were Aaron, Moses and Miriam.

Aaron's sons were Nadab, Abihu, Eleazar and Ithamar. **4** Eleazar was the father of Phinehas. Phinehas was the father of Abishua. **5** Abishua was the father of Bukki. Bukki was the father of Uzzi. **6** Uzzi was the father of Zerahiah. Zerahiah was the father of Meraioth. **7** Meraioth was the father of Amariah. Amariah was the father of Ahitub. **8** Ahitub was the father of Zadok. Zadok was the father of Ahimaaz. **9** Ahimaaz was the father of Azariah. Azariah was the father of Johanan. **10** Johanan was the father of Azariah. (Azariah was a priest in the Temple Solomon built in Jerusalem.) **11** Azariah was the father of Amariah. Amariah was the father of Ahitub. **12** Ahitub was the father of Zadok. Zadok was the father of Shallum. **13** Shallum was the father of Hilkiah. Hilkiah was the father of Azariah. **14** Azariah was the father of Seraiah, and Seraiah was the father of Jehozadak.

15 Jehozadak was forced to leave his home when the LORD sent Judah and Jerusalem into captivity under the control of Nebuchadnezzar.

16 Levi's sons were Gershon, Kohath and Merari.

17 The names of Gershon's sons were Libni and Shimei.

18 Kohath's sons were Amram, Izhar, Hebron and Uzziel.

19 Merari's sons were Mahli and Mushi.

This is a list of the family groups of Levi, listed by the name of the father of each group.

20 Gershon's son was Libni. Libni's son was Jehath. Jehath's son was Zimmah. **21** Zimmah's son was Joah. Joah's son was Iddo. Iddo's son was Zerah. And Zerah's son was Jeatherai.

22 Kohath's son was Amminadab. Amminadab's son was Korah. Korah's son was Assir. **23** Assir's son was Elkanah. Elkanah's son was Ebiasaph. Ebiasaph's son was Assir. **24** Assir's son was Tahath. Tahath's son was Uriel. Uriel's son was Uzziah, and Uzziah's son was Shaul.

25 Elkanah's sons were Amasai and Ahimoth. **26** Ahimoth's son was Elkanah.

Elkanah's son was Zophai. Zophai's son was Nahath. 27 Nahath's son was Eliab. Eliab's son was Jeroham. Jeroham's son was Elkanah, and Elkanah's son was Samuel.

28 Samuel's sons were Joel, the first son, and Abijah, the second son.

29 Merari's son was Mahli. Mahli's son was Libni. Libni's son was Shimei. Shimei's son was Uzzah. 30 Uzzah's son was Shimea. Shimea's son was Haggiah, and Haggiah's son was Asaiah.

The Temple Musicians

31 David chose some people to be in charge of the music in the house of the LORD. They began their work after the Ark of the Agreement was put there. 32 They served by making music at the Holy Tent (also called the Meeting Tent), and they served until Solomon built the Temple of the LORD in Jerusalem. They followed the rules for their work.

33 These are the musicians and their sons:

From Kohath's family there was Heman the singer. Heman was Joel's son. Joel was Samuel's son. 34 Samuel was Elkanah's son. Elkanah was Jeroham's son. Jeroham was Eliel's son. Eliel was Toah's son. 35 Toah was Zuph's son. Zuph was Elkanah's son. Elkanah was Mahath's son. Mahath was Amasai's son. 36 Amasai was Elkanah's son. Elkanah was Joel's son. Joel was Azariah's son. Azariah was Zephaniah's son. 37 Zephaniah was Tahath's son. Tahath was Assir's son. Assir was Ebiasaph's son. Ebiasaph was Korah's son. 38 Korah was Izhar's son. Izhar was Kohath's son. Kohath was Levi's son. Levi was Israel's son.

39 There was Heman's helper Asaph, whose group stood by Heman's right side. Asaph was Berekiah's son. Berekiah was Shimea's son. 40 Shimea was Michael's son. Michael was Baaseiah's son. Baaseiah was Malkijah's son. 41 Malkijah was Ethni's son. Ethni was Zerah's son. Zerah was Adaiah's son. 42 Adaiah was Ethan's son. Ethan was Zimmah's son. Zimmah was Shimei's son. 43 Shimei was Jahath's son. Jahath was Gershon's son, and Gershon was Levi's son.

FAITH links

SERVICE WITH A SMILE
1 CHRONICLES 6:31-49

Think about something you do well that brings a smile to your face when you do it. Maybe you like to paint or sing. Music brought a smile to David's face. He used his musical ability to serve God. He played the harp and wrote many of the psalms. David wanted others to please God with their talents, too. As king, David chose certain people who were good musicians to be in charge of the music in the Temple. Other groups had different roles.

You can serve God with what you enjoy doing, too. God is pleased when you serve him with a smile.

How do you serve? Connect to these links for thoughts on serving:

Share What You Have, Exodus 35:5–18, p. 123

Help for the Poor, Leviticus 5:7, p. 138

What God Wants, Deuteronomy 10:12–13, p. 242

Advice from a Kid, 2 Kings 5, p. 484

The Way to Greatness, Matthew 20:20–28, p. 1309

My Best Serve, Acts 6:1–6, p. 1473

44 Merari's family were the helpers of Heman and Asaph, and they stood by Heman's left side. In this group was Ethan son of Kishi. Kishi was Abdi's son. Abdi was Malluch's son. 45 Malluch was Hashabiah's son. Hashabiah was Amaziah's son. Amaziah was Hilkiah's son. 46 Hilkiah was Amzi's son. Amzi was Bani's son. Bani was Shemer's son. 47 Shemer was Mahli's son. Mahli was Mushi's son. Mushi was Merari's son, and Merari was Levi's son.

48 The other Levites served by doing their own special work in the Holy Tent, the house of God. 49 Aaron and his descendants offered the sacrifices on the altar of burnt offering and burned the incense on the altar of incense. They offered the sacrifices that removed the Israelites' sins so they could belong to God. They did all the work in the Most Holy Place and followed all the laws that Moses, God's servant, had commanded.

6:49 Obedience How did the Israelites obey God?

50 These were Aaron's sons: Eleazar was Aaron's son. Phinehas was Eleazar's son. Abishua was Phinehas' son. 51 Bukki was Abishua's son. Uzzi was Bukki's son. Zerahiah was Uzzi's son. 52 Meraioth was Zerahiah's son. Amariah was Meraioth's son. Ahitub was Amariah's son. 53 Zadok was Ahitub's son and Ahimaaz was Zadok's son.

Land for the Levites

54 These are the places where Aaron's descendants lived. His descendants from the Kohath family group received the first share of the land.

55 They were given the city of Hebron in Judah and the pastures around it, 56 but the fields farther from the city and the villages near Hebron were given to Caleb son of Jephunneh. 57 So the descendants of Aaron were given Hebron, one of the cities of safety.[n] They also received the towns and pastures of Libnah, Jattir, Eshtemoa, 58 Hilen, Debir, 59 Ashan, Juttah and Beth Shemesh. 60 They also received these towns and pastures from the tribe of Benjamin: Gibeon, Geba, Alemeth and Anathoth.

The Kohath family groups received a total of thirteen towns.

61 The rest of the Kohath family group was given ten towns from the family groups of West Manasseh. The towns were chosen by throwing lots.

62 The Gershon family group received thirteen towns from the tribes of Issachar, Asher, Naphtali and the part of Manasseh living in Bashan.

63 The Merari family group received twelve towns from the tribes of Reuben, Gad and Zebulun. Those towns were chosen by throwing lots.

64 So the Israelites gave these towns and their pastures to the Levites. 65 The towns from the tribes of Judah, Simeon and Benjamin, which were named, were chosen by throwing lots.

66 Some of the Kohath family groups received towns and pastures from the tribe of Ephraim. 67 They received Shechem, one of the cities of safety, with its pastures in the mountains of Ephraim. They also received the towns and pastures of Gezer, 68 Jokmeam, Beth Horon, 69 Aijalon and Gath Rimmon.

70 The rest of the people in the Kohath family group received the towns of Aner and Bileam and their pastures from West Manasseh.

71 From East Manasseh, the Gershon family received the towns and pastures of Golan in Bashan and Ashtaroth.

72-73 From the tribe of Issachar, the Gershon family received the towns and pastures of Kedesh, Daberath, Ramoth and Anem.

74-75 From the tribe of Asher, the Gershon family received the towns and pastures of Mashal, Abdon, Hukok and Rehob.

76 From the tribe of Naphtali, the Gershon family received the towns and pastures of Kedesh in Galilee, Hammon and Kiriathaim.

6:57 cities of safety A person who had accidentally killed someone could go to one of the six cities of safety to receive protection and a fair trial.

77 The rest of the Levites, the people from the Merari family, received from the tribe of Zebulun the towns and pastures of Jokneam, Kartah, Rimmono and Tabor.

78-79 From the tribe of Reuben, the Merari family received the towns and pastures of Bezer in the desert, Jahzah, Kedemoth and Mephaath. (The tribe of Reuben lived east of the Jordan River, across from Jericho.)

80-81 From the tribe of Gad, the Merari family received the towns and pastures of Ramoth in Gilead, Mahanaim, Heshbon and Jazer.

Issachar's Children

7 Issachar had four sons: Tola, Puah, Jashub and Shimron.

2 Tola's sons were Uzzi, Rephaiah, Jeriel, Jahmai, Ibsam and Samuel, and they were leaders of their families. In the family history of Tola's descendants, 22,600 men were listed as fighting men during the time David was king.

3 Uzzi's son was Izrahiah.

Izrahiah's sons were Michael, Obadiah, Joel and Isshiah. All five of them were leaders. 4 Their family history shows they had 36,000 men ready to serve in the army, because they had many wives and children.

5 The records of the family groups of Issachar show there were 87,000 fighting men.

Benjamin's Children

6 Benjamin had three sons: Bela, Beker and Jediael.

7 Bela had five sons: Ezbon, Uzzi, Uzziel, Jerimoth and Iri, and they were leaders of their families. Their family history shows they had 22,034 fighting men.

8 Beker's sons were Zemirah, Joash, Eliezer, Elioenai, Omri, Jeremoth, Abijah, Anathoth and Alemeth. They all were Beker's sons. 9 Their family history listed the family leaders and 20,200 fighting men.

10 Jediael's son was Bilhan.

Bilhan's sons were Jeush, Benjamin, Ehud, Kenaanah, Zethan, Tarshish and Ahishahar. 11 All these sons of Jediael were leaders of their families. They had 17,200 fighting men ready to serve in the army.

12 The Shuppites and Huppites were descendants of Ir and the Hushites were descendants of Aher.

Naphtali's Children

13 Naphtali's sons were Jahziel, Guni, Jezer and Shillem. They were Bilhah's grandsons.

Manasseh's Children

14 These are Manasseh's descendants. Manasseh had an Aramean slave woman, who was the mother of Asriel and Makir. Makir was Gilead's father. 15 Makir took a wife from the Huppites and Shuppites. His sister was named Maacah. His second son was named Zelophehad, and he had only daughters. 16 Makir's wife Maacah had a son whom she named Peresh. Peresh's brother was named Sheresh. Sheresh's sons were Ulam and Rakem.

17 Ulam's son was Bedan.

These were the sons of Gilead, who was the son of Makir. Makir was Manasseh's son. 18 Makir's sister Hammoleketh gave birth to Ishhod, Abiezer and Mahlah.

19 The sons of Shemida were Ahian, Shechem, Likhi and Aniam.

Ephraim's Children

20 These are the names of Ephraim's descendants. Ephraim's son was Shuthelah. Shuthelah's son was Bered. Bered's son was Tahath. Tahath's son was Eleadah. Eleadah's son was Tahath. 21 Tahath's son was Zabad. Zabad's son was Shuthelah.

Ezer and Elead went to Gath to steal cows and sheep and were killed by some men who grew up in that city. 22 Their father Ephraim cried for them many days, and his family came to comfort him. 23 Then he had sexual relations with his wife again. She became pregnant and gave birth to a son whom Ephraim named

FAITH links

A MEMORIAL FOR TWO THIEVES
1 CHRONICLES 7:21

Genealogies, or family histories, are records of people's lives. You'll find many of them in the Bible. They tell what people did, both good and bad. Two men, Ezer and Elead, had only one deed listed: they stole some cows and sheep! Would you want to be remembered for that?

If someone wrote about your life, what would your actions say about you? Each day, you're adding to the record of your life. Following Jesus can guarantee you a better memorial than the one for two thieves.

Show Some Respect, Leviticus 19:32, p. 161

I'll Never Forget What's-His-Name, Deuteronomy 8, p. 239

What's Out Becomes In, Judges 11, p. 327

Trailblazers of Faith, 2 Kings 22:1–2, p. 510

Good Enough? Ezekiel 8, p. 1093

The Worst Chore, John 13:3–17, p. 1447

Beriah[n] because of the trouble that had happened to his family. 24 Ephraim's daughter was Sheerah. She built Lower Beth Horon, Upper Beth Horon and Uzzen Sheerah.

25 Rephah was Ephraim's son. Resheph was Rephah's son. Telah was Resheph's son. Tahan was Telah's son. 26 Ladan was Tahan's son. Ammihud was Ladan's son. Elishama was Ammihud's son. 27 Nun was Elishama's son, and Joshua was the son of Nun.

28 Ephraim's descendants lived in these lands and towns: Bethel and the villages near it, Naaran on the east, Gezer and the villages near it on the west, and Shechem and the villages near it. These villages went all the way to Ayyah and its villages. 29 Along the borders of Manasseh's land were the towns of Beth Shan, Taanach, Megiddo, Dor and the villages near them. The descendants of Joseph son of Israel lived in these towns.

Asher's Children

30 Asher's sons were Imnah, Ishvah, Ishvi and Beriah. Their sister was Serah.

31 Beriah's sons were Heber and Malkiel. Malkiel was Birzaith's father.

32 Heber was the father of Japhlet, Shomer, Hotham and their sister Shua.

33 Japhlet's sons were Pasach, Bimhal and Ashvath. They were Japhlet's children.

34 Japhlet's brother was Shomer. Shomer's sons were Rohgah, Hubbah and Aram.

35 Shomer's brother was Hotham. Hotham's sons were Zophah, Imna, Shelesh and Amal.

36 Zophah's sons were Suah, Harnepher, Shual, Beri, Imrah, 37 Bezer, Hod, Shamma, Shilshah, Ithran and Beera.

38 Jether's sons were Jephunneh, Pispah and Ara.

39 Ulla's sons were Arah, Hanniel and Rizia.

40 All these men were descendants of Asher and leaders of their families. They were powerful warriors and outstanding leaders. Their family history lists that they had 26,000 soldiers ready to serve in the army.

The Family History of King Saul

8 Benjamin was the father of Bela, his first son. Ashbel was his second son,

---

7:23 **Beriah** This name sounds like the Hebrew word for "trouble."

Aharah was his third, 2 Nohah was his fourth and Rapha was his fifth son.

3 Bela's sons were Addar, Gera, Abihud, 4 Abishua, Naaman, Ahoah, 5 Gera, Shephuphan and Huram.

6 These were the descendants of Ehud and leaders of their families in Geba. They were forced to move to Manahath. 7 Ehud's descendants were Naaman, Ahijah and Gera. Gera forced them to leave. He was the father of Uzza and Ahihud.

8-11 Shaharaim and his wife Hushim had sons named Abitub and Elpaal. In Moab, Shaharaim divorced his wives Hushim and Baara. Shaharaim and his wife Hodesh had these sons: Jobab, Zibia, Mesha, Malcam, Jeuz, Sakia and Mirmah. They were leaders of their families.

12-13 Elpaal's sons were Eber, Misham, Shemed, Beriah and Shema. Shemed built the towns of Ono and Lod and the villages around them. Beriah and Shema were leaders of the families living in Aijalon, and they forced out the people who lived in Gath.

14 Beriah's sons were Ahio, Shashak, Jeremoth, 15 Zebadiah, Arad, Eder, 16 Michael, Ishpah and Joha.

17 Elpaal's sons were Zebadiah, Meshullam, Hizki, Heber, 18 Ishmerai, Izliah and Jobab.

19 Shimei's sons were Jakim, Zicri, Zabdi, 20 Elienai, Zillethai, Eliel, 21 Adaiah, Beraiah and Shimrath.

22 Shashak's sons were Ishpan, Eber, Eliel, 23 Abdon, Zicri, Hanan, 24 Hananiah, Elam, Anthothijah, 25 Iphdeiah and Penuel.

26 Jeroham's sons were Shamsherai, Shehariah, Athaliah, 27 Jaareshiah, Elijah and Zicri.

28 The family histories show that all these men were leaders of their families and lived in Jerusalem.

29 Jeiel lived in the town of Gibeon, where he was the leader. His wife was named Maacah. 30 Jeiel's first son was Abdon. His other sons were Zur, Kish, Baal, Ner, Nadab, 31 Gedor, Ahio, Zeker 32 and Mikloth. Mikloth was the father of Shimeah. These sons also lived near their relatives in Jerusalem.

33 Ner was the father of Kish. Kish was the father of Saul, and Saul was the father of Jonathan, Malki-Shua, Abinadab and Esh-Baal.

34 Jonathan's son was Merib-Baal, who was the father of Micah.

35 Micah's sons were Pithon, Melech, Tarea and Ahaz. 36 Ahaz was the father of Jehoaddah. Jehoaddah was the father of Alemeth, Azmaveth and Zimri. Zimri was the father of Moza. 37 Moza was the father of Binea. Raphah was Binea's son. Eleasah was Raphah's son and Azel was Eleasah's son.

38 Azel had six sons: Azrikam, Bokeru, Ishmael, Sheariah, Obadiah and Hanan. All these were Azel's sons.

39 Azel's brother was Eshek. Eshek's first son was Ulam, his second was Jeush and Eliphelet was his third. 40 Ulam's sons were mighty warriors and good archers. They had many sons and grandsons—150 of them in all.

All these men were Benjamin's descendants.

9 The names of all the people of Israel were listed in their family histories, and those family histories were put in the book of the kings of Israel.

The People in Jerusalem

The people of Judah were captured and forced to go to Babylon, because they were not faithful to God. 2 The first people to come back and live in their own lands and towns were some Israelites, priests, Levites and Temple servants.

3 People from the tribes of Judah, Benjamin, Ephraim and Manasseh lived in Jerusalem. This is a list of those people.

4 There was Uthai son of Ammihud. (Ammihud was Omri's son. Omri was Imri's son. Imri was Bani's son. Bani was

> The names of all the people of Israel were listed in their family histories.
> – 1 Chronicles 9:1

a descendant of Perez, and Perez was Judah's son.)

5 Of the Shilonite people there were Asaiah and his sons. Asaiah was the oldest son in his family.

6 Of the Zerahite people there were Jeuel and other relatives of Zerah. There were 690 of them in all.

7 From the tribe of Benjamin there was Sallu son of Meshullam. (Meshullam was Hodaviah's son, and Hodaviah was Hassenuah's son.) 8 There was also Ibneiah son of Jeroham and Elah son of Uzzi. (Uzzi was Micri's son.) And there was Meshullam son of Shephatiah. (Shephatiah was Reuel's son, and Reuel was Ibnijah's son.) 9 The family history of Benjamin lists 956 people living in Jerusalem, and all these were leaders of their families.

10 Of the priests there were Jedaiah, Jehoiarib, Jakin and 11 Azariah son of Hilkiah. (Hilkiah was Meshullam's son. Meshullam was Zadok's son. Zadok was Meraioth's son. Meraioth was Ahitub's son. Ahitub was the officer responsible for the Temple of God.) 12 Also there was Adaiah son of Jeroham. (Jeroham was Pashhur's son, and Pashhur was Malkijah's son.) And there was Maasai son of Adiel. (Adiel was Jahzerah's son. Jahzerah was Meshullam's son. Meshullam was Meshillemith's son, and Meshillemith was Immer's son.) 13 There were 1,760 priests. They were leaders of their families, and they were responsible for serving in the Temple of God.

14 Of the Levites there was Semaiah son of Hasshub. (Hasshub was Azrikam's son, and Azrikam was Hashabiah's son. Hashabiah was from the family of Merari.) 15 There were also Bakbakkar, Heresh, Galal and Mattaniah son of Mica. (Mica was Zicri's son, and Zicri was Asaph's son.) 16 There was also Obadiah son of Shemaiah. (Shemaiah was Galal's son and Galal was Jeduthun's son.) And there was Berekiah son of Asa. (Asa was the son of Elkanah, who lived in the villages of the Netophathites.)

17 Of the gatekeepers there were Shallum, Akkub, Talmon, Ahiman and their relatives. Shallum was their leader. 18 These gatekeepers from the tribe of Levi still stand next to the King's Gate on the east side of the city. 19 Shallum was Kore's son. Kore was Ebiasaph's son, and Ebiasaph was Korah's son. Shallum and his relatives from the family of Korah were gatekeepers and were responsible for guarding the gates of the Temple. Their ancestors had also been responsible for guarding the entrance to the Temple of the LORD. 20 In the past Phinehas, Eleazar's son, was in charge of the gatekeepers, and the LORD was with Phinehas. 21 Zechariah son of Meshelemiah was the gatekeeper at the entrance to the Temple.

22 In all, 212 men were chosen to guard the gates, and their names were written in their family histories in their villages. David and Samuel the seer chose these men because they were dependable. 23 The gatekeepers and their descendants had to guard the gates of the Temple of the LORD. (The Temple took the place of the Holy Tent.) 24 There were gatekeepers on all four sides of the Temple: east, west, north and south. 25 The gatekeepers' relatives who lived in the villages had to come and help them at times. Each time they came they helped the gatekeepers for seven days. 26 Because they were dependable, four gatekeepers were made the leaders of all the gatekeepers. They were Levites, and they were responsible for the rooms and treasures in the Temple of God. 27 They stayed up all night guarding the Temple of God, and they opened it every morning.

28 Some of the gatekeepers were responsible for the dishes used in the Temple services. They counted these utensils when people took them out and when they brought them back. 29 Other gatekeepers were chosen to take care of the furniture and utensils in the Holy Place. They also took care of the flour, wine, oil, incense and spices, 30 but some of the priests took care of mixing the spices. 31 There was a Levite named Mattithiah who was dependable and had the job of baking the bread used for the offerings. He was the first son of Shallum, who

was from the family of Korah. 32 Some of the gatekeepers from the Kohath family had the job of preparing the special bread that was put on the table every Sabbath day.

33 Some of the Levites were musicians in the Temple. The leaders of these families stayed in the rooms of the Temple. Since they were on duty day and night, they did not do other work in the Temple.

34 These are the leaders of the Levite families. Their names were listed in their family histories, and they lived in Jerusalem.

The Genealogy of King Saul

35 Jeiel lived in the town of Gibeon, where he was the leader. His wife was named Maacah. 36 Jeiel's first son was Abdon. His other sons were Zur, Kish, Baal, Ner, Nadab, 37 Gedor, Ahio, Zechariah and Mikloth. 38 Mikloth was Shimeam's father. Jeiel's family lived near their relatives in Jerusalem.

39 Ner was Kish's father. Kish was Saul's father. Saul was the father of Jonathan, Malki-Shua, Abinadab and Esh-Baal.

40 Jonathan's son was Merib-Baal, who was the father of Micah.

41 Micah's sons were Pithon, Melech, Tahrea and Ahaz. 42 Ahaz was Jadah's father. Jadah was the father of Alemeth, Azmaveth and Zimri. Zimri was Moza's father. 43 Moza was Binea's father. Rephaiah was Binea's son. Eleasah was Rephaiah's son, and Azel was Eleasah's son.

44 Azel had six sons: Azrikam, Bokeru, Ishmael, Sheariah, Obadiah and Hanan. They were Azel's sons.

The Death of King Saul

10 The Philistines fought against Israel, and the Israelites ran away from them. Many Israelites were killed on Mount Gilboa. 2 The Philistines fought hard against Saul and his sons, killing his sons Jonathan, Abinadab and Malki-Shua. 3 The fighting was heavy around Saul, and the archers shot him with their arrows and wounded him.

4 Then Saul said to the officer who carried his armour, "Pull out your sword and stab me. If you don't, these Philistines who are not circumcised will come and hurt me." But Saul's officer refused, because he was afraid. So Saul took his own sword and threw himself on it. 5 When the officer saw that Saul was dead, he threw himself on his own sword and died. 6 So Saul and three of his sons died; all his family died together.

7 When the Israelites living in the valley saw that their army had run away and that Saul and his sons were dead, they left their towns and ran away. Then the Philistines came and settled in them.

8 The next day when the Philistines came to strip the dead soldiers, they found Saul and his sons dead on Mount Gilboa. 9 The Philistines stripped Saul's body and took his head and his armour. Then they sent messengers through all their country to tell the news to their idols and to their people. 10 The Philistines put Saul's armour in the temple of their idols and hung his head in the temple of Dagon.

11 All the people in Jabesh Gilead heard what the Philistines had done to Saul. 12 So the brave men of Jabesh went and got the bodies of Saul and his sons and brought them to Jabesh. They buried their bones under the large tree in Jabesh. Then the people of Jabesh gave up eating for seven days.

13 Saul died because he was not faithful to the LORD and did not obey the LORD. He even went to a medium and asked her for advice 14 instead of asking the LORD. This is why the LORD put Saul to death and gave the kingdom to Jesse's son David.

> Saul died because he was not faithful to the LORD and did not obey the LORD.
> – 1 Chronicles 10:13

David Becomes King

11 Then the people of Israel came to David at the town of Hebron and said, "Look, we are your own family. ² Even when Saul was king, you were the one who led Israel in battle. The LORD your God said to you, 'You will be the shepherd for my people Israel. You will be their leader.'"

³ So all the elders of Israel came to King David at Hebron. He made an agreement with them in Hebron in the presence of the LORD. Then they poured oil on David to make him king over Israel. The LORD had promised through Samuel that this would happen.

David Captures Jerusalem

⁴ David and all the Israelites went to the city of Jerusalem. At that time Jerusalem was called Jebus, and the people living there were named Jebusites. ⁵ They said to David, "You can't get inside our city." But David did take the city of Jerusalem with its strong walls, and it became the City of David.

⁶ David had said, "The person who leads the attack against the Jebusites will become the commander over all my army." Joab son of Zeruiah led the attack, so he became the commander of the army.

⁷ Then David made his home in the fortified city, which is why it was named the City of David. ⁸ David rebuilt the city, beginning where the land was filled in and going to the wall that was around the city. Joab repaired the other parts of the city. ⁹ David became stronger and stronger, and the LORD All-powerful was with him.

David's Mighty Warriors

¹⁰ This is a list of the leaders over David's warriors who helped make David's kingdom strong. All the people of Israel also supported David's kingdom. These heroes and all the people of Israel made David king, just as the LORD had promised.

¹¹ This is a list of David's warriors:

Jashobeam was from the Hacmonite people. He was the head of the Three,*n*

FAITH links

JUST A LITTLE RESPECT
1 CHRONICLES 11:10-19

Think about the leaders in your life: teachers, Sunday school leaders, pastors and so on. What would you do to show your respect for them? David's men once risked their lives to cross enemy lines just to bring him some water. Their actions showed his value as a leader. David was touched by their act. Instead of drinking the water, he offered it to God.

You can offer the leaders in your life a gift. You don't have to cross enemy lines to get it, either. You can offer them your respect and encouragement. You can also offer to pray for them. That's the best gift you can give.

Link here for more tips on helping the leaders in your life:

Play Fair or Play Favourites?
Deuteronomy 1:16–18, p. 227

The MLP, Ruth 1:16–17, p. 345

Seeing the Needs, Nehemiah 1, p. 625

Help for a Friend, Mark 2:1–5, p. 1332

Best Seat in the House, Luke 14:7–11, p. 1398

The True Test, 1 John 3:18, p. 1718

11:11 Three Or maybe "Thirty". These were David's most powerful soldiers. See 2 Samuel 23:8.

David's most powerful soldiers. He used his spear to fight 300 men at one time, and he killed them all.

12 Next was Eleazar, one of the Three. Eleazar was Dodai's son from the Ahohite people. 13 Eleazar was with David at Pas-Dammim when the Philistines came there to fight. There was a field of barley at that place. The Israelites ran away from the Philistines, 14 but they stopped in the middle of that field and fought for it and killed the Philistines. The LORD gave them a great victory.

11:14 Success
Can you trust God for your success?

15 Once, three of the Thirty, David's chief soldiers, came down to him at the rock by the cave near Adullam. At the same time the Philistine army had camped in the Valley of Rephaim.

16 At that time David was in a stronghold, and some of the Philistines were in Bethlehem. 17 David had a strong desire for some water. He said, "Oh, I wish someone would get me water from the well near the city gate*n* of Bethlehem!" 18 So the Three broke through the Philistine army and took water from the well near the city gate in Bethlehem. Then they brought it to David, but he refused to drink it. He poured it out before the LORD, 19 saying, "May God keep me from drinking this water! It would be like drinking the blood of the men who risked their lives to bring it to me!" So David refused to drink it.

These were the brave things that the three warriors did.

20 Abishai brother of Joab was the captain of the Three. Abishai fought 300 soldiers with his spear and killed them. He became as famous as the Three 21 and was more honoured than the Three. He became their commander even though he was not one of them.

22 Benaiah son of Jehoiada was a brave fighter from Kabzeel who did mighty things. He killed two of the best warriors from Moab. He also went down into a pit and killed a lion on a snowy day. 23 Benaiah killed an Egyptian who was about 2.5 metres tall and had a spear as large as a weaver's rod. Benaiah had a club, but he grabbed the spear from the Egyptian's hand and killed him with his own spear. 24 These were the things Benaiah son of Jehoiada did. He was as famous as the Three. 25 He received more honour than the Thirty, but he did not become a member of the Three. David made him leader of his bodyguards.

The Thirty Chief Soldiers

26 These were also mighty warriors:
Asahel brother of Joab;
Elhanan son of Dodo from Bethlehem;
27 Shammoth the Harorite; Helez the Pelonite;
28 Ira son of Ikkesh from Tekoa; Abiezer the Anathothite;
29 Sibbecai the Hushathite; Ilai the Ahohite;
30 Maharai the Netophathite; Heled son of Baanah the Netophathite;
31 Ithai son of Ribai from Gibeah in Benjamin; Benaiah the Pirathonite;
32 Hurai from the ravines of Gaash; Abiel the Arbathite;
33 Azmaveth the Baharumite; Eliahba the Shaalbonite;
34 the sons of Hashem the Gizonite; Jonathan son of Shagee the Hararite;
35 Ahiam son of Sacar the Hararite; Eliphal son of Ur;
36 Hepher the Mekerathite; Ahijah the Pelonite;
37 Hezro the Carmelite; Naarai son of Ezbai;
38 Joel brother of Nathan; Mibhar son of Hagri;
39 Zelek the Ammonite; Naharai the Berothite, the officer who carried the armour for Joab son of Zeruiah;
40 Ira the Ithrite; Gareb the Ithrite;

11:17 city gate People came here to conduct business. Public meetings and court cases were also held here.

41 Uriah the Hittite;
Zabad son of Ahlai;
42 Adina son of Shiza the Reubenite, who was the leader of the Reubenites, and his 30 soldiers;
43 Hanan son of Maacah; Joshaphat the Mithnite;
44 Uzzia the Ashterathite; Shama and Jeiel sons of Hotham the Aroerite;
45 Jediael son of Shimri; Joha, Jediael's brother, the Tizite;
46 Eliel the Mahavite; Jeribai and Joshaviah, Elnaam's sons; Ithmah the Moabite;
47 Eliel, Obed and Jaasiel the Mezobaites.

Warriors Join David

12 These were the men who came to David at Ziklag when David was hiding from Saul son of Kish. They were among the warriors who helped David in battle. 2 They came with bows for weapons and could use either their right or left hands to shoot arrows or to sling rocks. They were Saul's relatives from the tribe of Benjamin. 3 Ahiezer was their leader, and there was Joash. (Ahiezer and Joash were sons of Shemaah, who was from the town of Gibeah.) There were also Jeziel and Pelet, the sons of Azmaveth. There were Beracah and Jehu from the town of Anathoth. 4 And there was Ishmaiah from the town of Gibeon; he was one of the Thirty. In fact, he was the leader of the Thirty. There were Jeremiah, Jahaziel, Johanan and Jozabad from Gederah. 5 There were Eluzai, Jerimoth, Bealiah and Shemariah. There was Shephatiah from Haruph. 6 There were Elkanah, Isshiah, Azarel, Joezer and Jashobeam from the family group of Korah. 7 And there were Joelah and Zebadiah, the sons of Jeroham, from the town of Gedor.

8 Part of the people of Gad joined David at his stronghold in the desert. They were brave warriors trained for war and skilled with shields and spears. They were as fierce as lions and as fast as gazelles over the hills.

9 Ezer was the leader of Gad's army, and Obadiah was second in command. Eliab was third, 10 Mishmannah was fourth, Jeremiah was fifth, 11 Attai was sixth, Eliel was seventh, 12 Johanan was eighth, Elzabad was ninth, 13 Jeremiah was tenth and Macbannai was eleventh in command.

14 They were the commanders of the army from Gad. The least of these leaders was in charge of 100 soldiers, and the greatest was in charge of 1,000. 15 They crossed the Jordan River and chased away the people living in the valleys, to the east and to the west. This happened in the first month of the year when the Jordan floods the valley.

16 Other people from the tribes of Benjamin and Judah also came to David at his stronghold. 17 David went out to meet them and said to them, "If you have come peacefully to help me, I welcome you. Join me. But if you have come to turn me over to my enemies, even though I have done nothing wrong, the God of our fathers will see this and punish you."

18 Then the Spirit entered Amasai, the leader of the Thirty, and he said:

"We belong to you, David.
We are with you, son of Jesse.
Success, success to you.
Success to those who help you,
because your God helps you."

So David welcomed these men and made them leaders of his army.

19 Some of the men from Manasseh also joined David when he went with the Philistines to fight Saul. But David and his men did not really help the Philistines. After talking about it, the Philistine leaders decided to send David away. They said, "If David goes back to his master Saul, we will be killed." 20 These are the men from Manasseh who joined David when he went to Ziklag: Adnah, Jozabad, Jediael, Michael, Jozabad, Elihu and Zillethai. Each of them was a leader of 1,000 men from Manasseh. 21 All these men of Manasseh were brave soldiers, and they helped David fight against groups of men who went around the country robbing people. These soldiers became commanders in David's army.

22 Every day more men joined David, and his army became large, like the army of God.

Others Join David at Hebron

23 These are the numbers of the soldiers ready for battle who joined David at Hebron. They came to help turn the kingdom of Saul over to David, just as the LORD had said.

24 There were 6,800 men with their weapons from Judah. They carried shields and spears.

25 There were 7,100 men from Simeon. They were warriors ready for war.

26 There were 4,600 men from Levi. 27 Jehoiada, a leader from Aaron's family, was in that group. There were 3,700 with him. 28 Zadok was also in that group. He was a strong young warrior, and with him came 22 leaders from his family.

29 There were 3,000 men from Benjamin, who were Saul's relatives. Most of them had remained loyal to Saul's family until then.

30 There were 20,800 men from Ephraim. They were brave warriors and were famous men in their own family groups.

31 There were 18,000 men from West Manasseh. Each one was especially chosen to make David king.

32 There were 200 leaders from Issachar. They knew what Israel should do, and they knew the right time to do it. Their relatives were with them and under their command.

33 There were 50,000 men from Zebulun. They were trained soldiers and knew how to use every kind of weapon of war. They followed David completely.

34 There were 1,000 officers from Naphtali. They had 37,000 soldiers with them who carried shields and spears.

35 There were 28,600 men from Dan, who were ready for war.

36 There were 40,000 trained soldiers from Asher, who were ready for war.

37 There were 120,000 soldiers from the east side of the Jordan River from the people of Reuben, Gad and East Manasseh. They had every kind of weapon.

38 All these fighting men were ready to go to war. They came to Hebron fully agreed to make David king of all Israel. All the other Israelites also agreed to make David king. 39 They spent three days there with David, eating and drinking, because their relatives had prepared food for them. 40 Also, their neighbours came from as far away as Issachar, Zebulun and Naphtali, bringing food on donkeys, camels, mules and oxen. They brought much flour, fig cakes, raisins, wine, oil, cows and sheep, because the people of Israel were very happy.

Bringing Back the Ark

13 David talked with all the officers of his army, the commanders of 100 men and the commanders of 1,000 men. 2 Then David called the people of Israel together and said, "If you think it is a good idea, and if it is what the LORD our God wants, let's send a message. Let's tell our fellow Israelites in all the areas of Israel and the priests and Levites living with them in their towns and pastures to come and join us. 3 Let's bring the Ark of our God back to us. We did not use it to ask God for help while Saul was king." 4 All the people agreed with David, because they all thought it was the right thing to do.

13:2 Decisions Check out what goes into making a decision.

5 So David gathered all the Israelites, from the Shihor River in Egypt to Lebo Hamath, to bring the Ark of God back from the town of Kiriath Jearim. 6 David and all the Israelites with him went to Baalah of Judah, which is Kiriath Jearim, to get the Ark of God the LORD. God's throne is between the golden, winged creatures on the Ark, and the Ark is called by his name.

7 The people carried the Ark of God from Abinadab's house on a new cart, and Uzzah and Ahio guided it. 8 David and all the Israelites were celebrating in the presence of God. With all their strength they were singing and playing

lyres, harps, tambourines, cymbals and trumpets.

9 When David's men came to the threshing floor of Kidon, the oxen stumbled, and Uzzah reached out his hand to steady the Ark. 10 The LORD was angry with Uzzah and killed him, because he had touched the Ark. So Uzzah died there in the presence of God.

11 David was angry because the LORD had punished Uzzah in his anger. Now that place is called The Punishment of Uzzah.

12 David was afraid of God that day and asked, "How can I bring the Ark of God home to me?" 13 So David did not take the Ark with him to Jerusalem. Instead, he took it to the house of Obed-Edom who was from Gath. 14 The Ark of God stayed with Obed-Edom's family in his house for three months, and the LORD blessed Obed-Edom's family and everything he owned.

David's Kingdom Grows

14 Hiram king of the city of Tyre sent messengers to David. He also sent cedar logs, bricklayers and carpenters to build a palace for David. 2 Then David knew that the LORD really had made him king of Israel and that he had made his kingdom great. The LORD did this because he loved his people Israel.

3 David married more women in Jerusalem and had more sons and daughters. 4 These are the names of David's children born in Jerusalem: Shammua, Shobab, Nathan, Solomon, 5 Ibhar, Elishua, Elpelet, 6 Nogah, Nepheg, Japhia, 7 Elishama, Beeliada and Eliphelet.

David Defeats the Philistines

8 When the Philistines heard that David had been made king of all Israel, they went to look for him. But David heard about it and went out to fight them. 9 The Philistines had attacked and robbed the people in the Valley of Rephaim. 10 David asked God, "Should

14:10 Trust
You can trust God to lead you.

FAITH links

PLAN FOR SUCCESS
1 CHRONICLES 14:8-17

Many successful business people write books or make videos about their success strategies. People buy these books to copy the success of these individuals. David, the king who defeated the Philistines, had a strategy for success. He didn't write a book about it, but you can still know his strategy. Here it is: seek God's wisdom; then do what he says. In other words, have faith in God. That's a strategy you can follow, too.

Choosing Sides, 1 Samuel 20, p. 382

A Wise Wish, 1 Kings 3:5–9, p. 439

The Wisdom of Obeying God, 1 Kings 11:1–13, p. 453

999, Psalm 28:6, p. 730

What God Thinks, Isaiah 55:8–9, p. 969

When We Agree, Matthew 18:19–20, p. 1306

I go and attack the Philistines? Will you hand them over to me?"

The LORD answered him, "Go, I will hand them over to you."

11 So David and his men went up to the town of Baal Perazim and defeated the Philistines. David said, "Like a flood of water, God has broken through my enemies by using me." So that place was

named Baal Perazim.[n] 12 The Philistines had left their idols there, so David ordered his men to burn them.

13 Soon the Philistines attacked the people in the valley again. 14 David prayed to God again, and God answered him, saying, "Don't attack the Philistines from the front. Instead, go around them and attack them in front of the balsam trees. 15 When you hear the sound of marching in the tops of the balsam trees, then attack. I, God, will have gone out before you to defeat the Philistine army." 16 David did as God commanded, and he and his men defeated the Philistine army all the way from Gibeon to Gezer.

17 So David became famous in all the countries, and the LORD made all nations afraid of him.

The Ark is Brought to Jerusalem

15 David built houses for himself in Jerusalem. Then he prepared a place for the Ark of God, and he set up a tent for it. 2 David said, "Only the Levites may carry the Ark of God. The LORD chose them to carry the Ark of the LORD and to serve him for ever."

3 David called all the people of Israel to come to Jerusalem. He wanted to bring the Ark of the LORD to the place he had made for it. 4 David called together the descendants of Aaron and the Levites. 5 There were 120 people from Kohath's family group, with Uriel as their leader. 6 There were 220 people from Merari's family group, with Asaiah as their leader. 7 There were 130 people from Gershon's family group, with Joel as their leader. 8 There were 200 people from Elizaphan's family group, with Shemaiah as their leader. 9 There were 80 people from Hebron's family group, with Eliel as their leader. 10 And there were 112 people from Uzziel's family group, with Amminadab as their leader.

11 Then David asked the priests Zadok and Abiathar and these Levites to come to him: Uriel, Asaiah, Joel, Shem-aiah, Eliel and Amminadab. 12 David said to them, "You are the leaders of the families of Levi. You and the other Levites must give yourselves for service to the LORD. Bring up the Ark of the LORD, the God of Israel, to the place I have made for it. 13 The last time we did not ask the LORD how to carry it. You Levites didn't carry it, so the LORD our God punished us."

14 Then the priests and Levites prepared themselves for service to the LORD so they could carry the Ark of the LORD, the God of Israel. 15 The Levites used special poles to carry the Ark of God on their shoulders, as Moses had commanded, just as the LORD had said they should.

16 David told the leaders of the Levites to appoint their brothers as singers to play their lyres, harps and cymbals and to sing happy songs.

17 So the Levites appointed Heman and his relatives Asaph and Ethan. Heman was Joel's son. Asaph was Berekiah's son. And Ethan, from the Merari family group, was Kushaiah's son. 18 There was also a second group of Levites: Zechariah, Jaaziel, Shemiramoth, Jehiel, Unni, Eliab, Benaiah, Maaseiah, Mattithiah, Eliphelehu, Mikneiah, Obed-Edom and Jeiel. They were the Levite guards.

19 The singers Heman, Asaph and Ethan played bronze cymbals. 20 Zechariah, Jaaziel, Shemiramoth, Jehiel, Unni, Eliab, Maaseiah and Benaiah played the lyres. 21 Mattithiah, Eliphelehu, Mikneiah, Obed-Edom, Jeiel and Azaziah played the harps. 22 The Levite leader Kenaniah was in charge of the singing, because he was very good at it.

23 Berekiah and Elkanah were two of the guards for the Ark of the Agreement. 24 The priests Shebaniah, Joshaphat,

> David said, "Only the Levites may carry the Ark of God. The LORD chose them to carry the Ark of the LORD and to serve him for ever."
> – 1 Chronicles 15:2

14:11 Baal Perazim This name means "the LORD breaks through".

Nethanel, Amasai, Zechariah, Benaiah and Eliezer had the job of blowing trumpets in front of the Ark of God. Obed-Edom and Jehiah were also guards for the Ark.

25 David, the elders of Israel, and the commanders of 1,000 soldiers went to get the Ark of the Agreement with the LORD. They all went to bring the Ark from Obed-Edom's house with great joy. 26 Because God helped the Levites who carried the Ark of the Agreement with the LORD, they sacrificed seven bulls and seven rams. 27 All the Levites who carried the Ark, and Kenaniah, the man in charge of the singing, and all the singers wore robes of fine linen. David also wore a robe of fine linen and a holy robe of fine linen. 28 So all the people of Israel brought up the Ark of the Agreement with the LORD. They shouted, blew horns and trumpets and played cymbals, lyres and harps.

29 As the Ark of the Agreement with the LORD entered Jerusalem, Saul's daughter Michal watched from a window. When she saw King David dancing and celebrating, she hated him.

16 They brought the Ark of God and put it inside the tent that David had set up for it. Then they offered burnt offerings and fellowship offerings to God. 2 When David had finished giving the burnt offerings and fellowship offerings, he blessed the people in the name of the LORD. 3 He gave a loaf of bread, some dates and raisins to every Israelite man and woman.

16:4–36
Thankfulness
A song of thanks!

4 Then David appointed some of the Levites to serve before the Ark of the LORD. They had the job of leading the worship and giving thanks and praising the LORD, the God of Israel. 5 Asaph, who played the cymbals, was the leader. Zechariah was second to him. The other Levites were Jaaziel, Shemiramoth, Jehiel, Mattithiah, Eliab, Benaiah, Obed-Edom and Jeiel. They played the lyres and harps. 6 Benaiah and Jahaziel were priests who blew the trumpets regularly before the Ark of the Agreement with God. 7 That day David first gave Asaph and his relatives the job of singing praises to the LORD.

David's Song of Thanks

8 Give thanks to the LORD and pray to
    him.
Tell the nations what he has done.
9 Sing to him; sing praises to him.
Tell about all his miracles.
10 Be glad that you are his;
    let those who seek the LORD be
    happy.
11 Depend on the LORD and his
    strength;
always go to him for help.
12 Remember the miracles he has
    done,
his wonders, and his decisions.
13 You are the descendants of his
    servant, Israel;
you are the children of Jacob, his
    chosen people.

14 He is the LORD our God.
His laws are for all the world.
15 He will keep his agreement for ever;
he will keep his promises always.
16 He will keep the agreement he made
    with Abraham
and the promise he made to Isaac.
17 He made it a law for the people of
    Jacob;
he made it an agreement with
    Israel to last for ever.
18 He said, "I will give the land of
    Canaan to you,
to belong to you."

19 Then God's people were few in
    number,
and they were strangers in the
    land.
20 They went from one nation to
    another,
from one kingdom to another.
21 But he did not let anyone hurt them;
he warned kings not to harm
    them.
22 He said, "Don't touch my chosen
    people,
and don't harm my prophets."

23 Sing to the LORD, all the earth.
Every day tell how he saves us.
24 Tell the nations about his glory;
tell all peoples the miracles he does.
25 The LORD is great; he should be praised.
He should be respected more than all the gods.
26 All the gods of the nations are only idols,
but the LORD made the skies.
27 He has glory and majesty;
he has power and joy in his Temple.

28 Praise the LORD, all nations on earth.
Praise the LORD's glory and power;
29 praise the glory of the LORD's name.
Bring an offering and come to him.
Worship the LORD because he is holy.
30 Tremble before him, everyone on earth.
The earth is set, and it cannot be moved.
31 Let the skies rejoice and the earth be glad.
Let people everywhere say, "The LORD is king!"
32 Let the sea and everything in it shout;
let the fields and everything in them rejoice.
33 Then the trees of the forest will sing for joy before the LORD.
They will sing because he is coming to judge the world.

34 Thank the LORD because he is good.
His love continues for ever.
35 Say to him, "Save us, God our Saviour,
and bring us back and save us from other nations.
Then we will thank you
and will gladly praise you."
36 Praise the LORD, the God of Israel.
He always was and always will be.
All the people said "Amen" and praised the LORD.

37 Then David left Asaph and the other Levites there in front of the Ark of the Agreement with the LORD. They were to serve there every day. 38 David also left Obed-Edom and 68 other Levites to serve with them. Hosah and Obed-Edom son of Jeduthun were guards.

39 David left Zadok the priest and the other priests who served with him in front of the Tent of the LORD at the place of worship in Gibeon. 40 Every morning and evening they offered burnt offerings on the altar of burnt offerings, following the rules written in the Teachings of the LORD, which he had given Israel. 41 With them were Heman and Jeduthun and other Levites. They were chosen by name to sing praises to the LORD because his love continues for ever. 42 Heman and Jeduthun also had the job of playing the trumpets and cymbals and other musical instruments when songs were sung to God. Jeduthun's sons guarded the gates.

43 Then all the people left. Each person went home, and David also went home to bless the people in his home.

God's Promise to David

17 When David moved into his palace, he said to Nathan the prophet, "Look, I am living in a palace made of cedar, but the Ark of the Agreement with the LORD sits in a tent."

2 Nathan said to David, "Do what you want to do, because God is with you."

3 But that night God spoke his word to Nathan, saying, 4 "Go and tell David my servant, 'This is what the LORD says: You are not the person to build a house for me to live in. 5 From the time I brought Israel out of Egypt until now I have not lived in a house. I have moved from one tent site to another and from one place to another. 6 As I have moved with the Israelites to different places, I have never said to the leaders, whom I commanded to take care of my people, "Why haven't you built me a house of cedar?"'

7 "Now, tell my servant David: 'This is what the LORD All-powerful says: I took you from the pasture and from tending the sheep and made you king of my people Israel. 8 I have been with you everywhere you have gone. I have defeated

Get the Info

A MAN AFTER GOD'S OWN HEART — 1 Chronicles 17

1. David was born in Bethlehem, the youngest of Jesse's eight sons. David was given the job of caring for the family sheep. (Look at 1 Samuel 17:12–15, p. 376.)

2. As a boy, David helped the army of Israel defeat the Philistines when he killed the giant Goliath with a slingshot in the Valley of Elah. (Get all the details of this familiar story in 1 Samuel 17:19–50, p. 376.)

3. David became a popular and successful warrior for King Saul. Saul, though, was jealous of David's success and began a campaign to have David killed. David was forced to run and hide in the hill country from his enemy, Saul. (Follow David's chase in 1 Samuel 19:1—23:29, p. 380.)

4. After Saul's death, David became the king of Judah. He made his first capital at Hebron. (Read 2 Samuel 2:1–4, p. 400.)

5. After defeating his enemies, David united the tribes of Israel and Judah and made Jerusalem his capital. (See 2 Samuel 5:1–5, p. 404.)

---

your enemies for you. I will make you as famous as any of the great people on the earth. 9 I will choose a place for my people Israel, and I will plant them so they can live in their own homes. They will not be bothered any more. Wicked people will no longer hurt them as they have in the past 10 when I chose judges for my people Israel. I will defeat all your enemies.

"'I tell you that the LORD will make your descendants kings of Israel after you. 11 When you die and join your ancestors, I will make one of your sons the new king, and I will set up his kingdom. 12 He will build a house for me, and I will let his kingdom rule always. 13 I will be his father, and he will be my son. I took away my love from Saul, who ruled before you, but I will never stop loving your son. 14 I will put him in charge of my house and kingdom for ever. His family will rule for ever.'"

15 Nathan told David everything God had said in this vision.

David Prays to God

16 Then King David went in and sat in front of the LORD. David said, "LORD God, who am I? What is my family? Why did you bring me to this point? 17 But that was not enough for you, God. You have

also made promises about my future family. LORD God, you have treated me like a very important person.

18 "What more can I say to you for honouring me, your servant? You know me so well. 19 LORD, you have done this wonderful thing for my sake and because you wanted to. You have made known all these great things.

20 "There is no one like you, LORD. There is no God except you. We have heard all this ourselves! 21 There is no nation like your people Israel. They are the only people on earth that God chose to be his own. You made your name well known by the great and wonderful things you did for them. You went ahead of them and forced other nations out of the land. You freed your people from slavery in Egypt. 22 You made the people of Israel your very own people for ever, and, LORD, you are their God.

23 "LORD, keep the promise for ever that you made about my family and me, your servant. Do what you have said. 24 Then you will be honoured always, and people will say, 'The LORD All-powerful, the God over Israel, is Israel's God!' And the family of your servant David will continue before you.

25 "My God, you have told me that you would make my family great. So I, your servant, am brave enough to pray to you. 26 LORD, you are God, and you have promised these good things to me, your servant. 27 You have chosen to bless my family. Let it continue before you always. LORD, you have blessed my family, so it will always be blessed."

17:26–27
Trust
You can count on this!

David Defeats Nations

18 Later, David defeated the Philistines, conquered them, and took the city of Gath and the small towns around it.

2 He also defeated the people of Moab. So the people of Moab became servants of David and gave him the payment he demanded.

3 David also defeated Hadadezer king of Zobah all the way to the town of Hamath as he tried to spread his kingdom to the Euphrates River. 4 David captured 1,000 of his chariots, 7,000 men who rode in chariots and 20,000 foot soldiers. He crippled all but 100 of the chariot horses.

5 Arameans from Damascus came to help Hadadezer king of Zobah, but David killed 22,000 of them. 6 Then David put groups of soldiers in Damascus in Aram. The Arameans became David's servants and gave him the payments he demanded. So the LORD gave David victory everywhere he went.

7 David took the shields of gold that had belonged to Hadadezer's officers and brought them to Jerusalem. 8 David also took many things made of bronze from Tebah and Cun, which had been cities under Hadadezer's control. Later, Solomon used this bronze to make things for the Temple: the large bronze bowl, which was called the Sea, the pillars and other bronze utensils.

9 Toi king of Hamath heard that David had defeated all the army of Hadadezer king of Zobah. 10 So Toi sent his son Hadoram to greet and congratulate King David for defeating Hadadezer. (Hadadezer had been at war with Toi.) Hadoram brought things made of gold, silver and bronze. 11 King David gave them to the LORD, along with the silver and gold he had taken from these nations: Edom, Moab, the Ammonites, the Philistines and Amalek.

12 Abishai son of Zeruiah killed 18,000 Edomites in the Valley of Salt. 13 David put groups of soldiers in Edom, and all the Edomites became his servants. The LORD gave David victory everywhere he went.

David's Important Officers

14 David was king over all of Israel, and he did what was fair and right for all his people. 15 Joab son of Zeruiah was commander over the army. Jehoshaphat son of Ahilud was the recorder. 16 Zadok son of Ahitub and Abiathar son of Ahimelech were priests. Shavsha was the royal

secretary. **17** Benaiah son of Jehoiada was over the Kerethites and Pelethites.*ⁿ* And David's sons were important officers who served at his side.

War with the Ammonites and Arameans

19 When Nahash king of the Ammonites died, his son became king after him. **2** David said, "Nahash was loyal to me, so I will be loyal to his son Hanun." So David sent messengers to comfort Hanun about his father's death.

David's officers went to the land of the Ammonites to comfort Hanun. **3** But the Ammonite leaders said to Hanun, "Do you think David wants to honour your father by sending men to comfort you? No! David sent them to study the land and capture it and spy it out."

4 So Hanun arrested David's officers. To shame them he shaved their beards and cut off their clothes at the hips. Then he sent them away.

5 When the people told David what had happened to his officers, he sent messengers to meet them, because they were very ashamed. King David said, "Stay in Jericho until your beards have grown back. Then come home."

6 The Ammonites knew that they had insulted David. So Hanun and the Ammonites sent about 35 tonnes of silver to hire chariots and chariot drivers from North West Mesopotamia, Aram Maacah and Zobah. **7** The Ammonites hired 32,000 chariots and the king of Maacah and his army. So they came and set up camp near the town of Medeba. The Ammonites themselves came out of their towns and got ready for battle.

8 When David heard about this, he sent Joab with the whole army. **9** The Ammonites came out and prepared for battle at the city gate.*ⁿ* The kings who had come to help were out in the field by themselves.

10 Joab saw that there were enemies both in front of him and behind him. So he chose some of the best soldiers of Israel and sent them out to fight the Arameans. **11** Joab put the rest of the army under the command of Abishai, his brother. Then they went out to fight the Ammonites. **12** Joab said to Abishai, "If the Arameans are too strong for me, you must help me. Or, if the Ammonites are too strong for you, I will help you. **13** Be strong. We must fight bravely for our people and the cities of our God. The LORD will do what he thinks is right."

14 Then Joab and the army with him went to attack the Arameans, and the Arameans ran away. **15** When the Ammonites saw that the Arameans were running away, they also ran away from Joab's brother Abishai and went back to their city. So Joab went back to Jerusalem.

16 When the Arameans saw that Israel had defeated them, they sent messengers to bring other Arameans from east of the Euphrates River. Their leader was Shophach, the commander of Hadadezer's army.

17 When David heard about this, he gathered all the Israelites, and they crossed over the Jordan River. He prepared them for battle, facing the Arameans. The Arameans fought with him, **18** but they ran away from the Israelites. David killed 7,000 Aramean chariot drivers and 40,000 Aramean foot soldiers. He also killed Shophach, the commander of the Aramean army.

19 When those who served Hadadezer saw that the Israelites had defeated them, they made peace with David and served him. So the Arameans refused to help the Ammonites again.

> Be strong. We must fight bravely for our people and the cities of our God. The LORD will do what he thinks is right.
> – 1 Chronicles 19:13

18:17 Kerethites and Pelethites These were probably special units of the army that were responsible for the king's safety, a kind of palace guard.
19:9 city gate People came here to conduct business. Public meetings and court cases were also held here.

Joab Destroys the Ammonites

20 In the spring, the time of year when kings normally went out to battle, Joab led out the army of Israel. But David stayed in Jerusalem. The army of Israel destroyed the land of Ammon and went to the city of Rabbah and attacked it. 2 David took the crown off the head of their king,[n] and had it placed on his own head. That gold crown weighed about 35 kilogrammes, and it had valuable gems in it. And David took many valuable things from the city. 3 He also brought out the people of the city and forced them to work with saws, iron picks and axes. David did this to all the Ammonite cities. Then David and all his army returned to Jerusalem.

Philistine Giants are Killed

4 Later, at Gezer, war broke out with the Philistines. Sibbecai the Hushathite killed Sippai, who was one of the descendants of the Rephaites. So those Philistines were defeated.

5 Later, there was another battle with the Philistines. Elhanan son of Jair killed Lahmi, the brother of Goliath, who was from the town of Gath. His spear was as large as a weaver's rod.

6 At Gath another battle took place. A very large man was there; he had six fingers on each hand and six toes on each foot—24 fingers and toes in all. This man also was one of the sons of Rapha. 7 When he spoke against Israel, Jonathan son of Shimea, David's brother, killed him.

8 These descendants of Rapha from Gath were killed by David and his men.

David Counts the Israelites

21 Satan was against Israel, and he caused David to count the people of Israel. 2 So David said to Joab and the commanders of the troops, "Go and count all the Israelites from Beersheba to Dan.[n] Then tell me so I will know how many there are."

3 But Joab said, "May the LORD give the nation a hundred times more people. My master the king, all the Israelites are your servants. Why do you want to do this, my master? You will make Israel guilty of sin."

4 But the king commanded Joab, so Joab left and went through all Israel. Then he returned to Jerusalem. 5 Joab gave the list of the people to David. There were 1,100,000 men in all of Israel who could use the sword, and there were

---

> ### FAITH CHALLENGE
> Read 21:8 to find out what King David did after he disobeyed God. What do you do after you know you've done something wrong – either to your brother or sister, your parents, or God?
>
> ### TeSTiNG iT
>
> **1 Chronicles 21:8**
> Then David said to God, "I have sinned greatly by what I have done! Now, I beg you to forgive me, your servant, because I have been very foolish."

20:2 *their king* Or, "Milcom," the god of the Ammonite people.
21:2 *Beersheba to Dan* Beersheba was the city farthest south in Israel, and Dan was the city farthest north. So this means all the people of Israel.

470,000 men in Judah who could use the sword. 6 But Joab did not count the tribes of Levi and Benjamin, because he disliked King David's order. 7 David had done something God had said was wrong, so God punished Israel.

8 Then David said to God, "I have sinned greatly by what I have done! Now, I beg you to forgive me, your servant, because I have been very foolish."

9 The LORD said to Gad, who was David's seer, 10 "Go and tell David, 'This is what the LORD says: I offer you three choices. Choose one of them and I will do it.'"

11 So Gad went to David and said to him, "This is what the LORD says: 'Choose for yourself 12 three years of hunger. Or choose three months of running from your enemies as they chase you with their swords. Or choose three days of punishment from the LORD, in which a terrible disease will spread through the country. The angel of the LORD will go through Israel destroying the people.' Now, David, decide which of these things I should tell the LORD who sent me."

13 David said to Gad, "I am in great trouble. Let the LORD punish me, because the LORD is very merciful. Don't let my punishment come from human beings."

14 So the LORD sent a terrible disease on Israel, and 70,000 people died. 15 God sent an angel to destroy Jerusalem, but when the angel started to destroy it, the LORD saw and felt very sorry about the terrible things that had happened. So he said to the angel who was destroying, "That is enough! Put down your arm!" The angel of the LORD was then standing at the threshing floor of Araunah the Jebusite.

16 David looked up and saw the angel of the LORD in the sky, holding his sword drawn and pointed at Jerusalem. Then David and the elders bowed face down on the ground. They were wearing rough cloth to show their grief. 17 David said to God, "I am the one who sinned and did wrong. I gave the order for the people to be counted. These people only followed me like sheep. They did nothing wrong. LORD my God, please punish me and my family, but stop the terrible disease that is killing your people."

18 Then the angel of the LORD told Gad to tell David that he should build an altar to the LORD on the threshing floor of Araunah the Jebusite. 19 So David did what Gad told him to do, in the name of the LORD.

20 Araunah was separating the wheat from the straw. When he turned round, he saw the angel. Araunah's four sons who were with him hid. 21 David came to Araunah, and when Araunah saw him, he left the threshing floor and bowed face down on the ground before David.

22 David said to him, "Sell me your threshing floor so I can build an altar to the LORD here. Then the terrible disease will stop. Sell it to me for the full price."

23 Araunah said to David, "Take this threshing floor. My master the king, do anything you want. Look, I will also give you oxen for the whole burnt offerings, the threshing boards for the wood, and wheat for the grain offering. I give everything to you."

24 But King David answered Araunah, "No, I will pay the full price for the land. I won't take anything that is yours and give it to the LORD. I won't offer a burnt offering that costs me nothing."

25 So David paid Araunah about 7 kilogrammes of gold for the place. 26 David built an altar to the LORD there and offered whole burnt offerings and fellowship offerings. David prayed to the LORD, and he answered him by sending down fire from heaven on the altar of burnt offering. 27 Then the LORD commanded the angel to put his sword back into its holder.

28 When David saw that the LORD had answered him on the threshing floor of Araunah, he offered sacrifices there. 29 The Holy Tent that Moses made while the Israelites were in the desert and the altar of burnt offerings were in Gibeon at the place of worship. 30 But David could not go to the Holy Tent to speak with God, because he was afraid of the angel of the LORD and his sword.

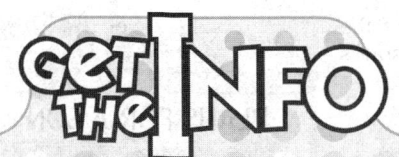

A SPECIAL ANGEL — 1 CHRONICLES 21:6–22

In the Old Testament, the angel of the Lord is a mysterious messenger of God. God used this angel to appear to human beings who would not be able to see him and live. The angel of the Lord accomplished God's work. Sometimes that work was revelation (giving a message), or deliverance, or even judgement. The angel of the Lord was a special angel, like the other angels, but responsible for more.

In the Old Testament, the angel of the Lord appeared to many people. Check out the chart below for some special sightings of how the angel of the Lord helped different people in the Bible:

Abraham	Prevented Abraham from sacrificing his son Isaac	Genesis 22:11–13, p. 29
Jacob	Wrestled with Jacob through the night and blessed him at daybreak	Genesis 32:24–30, p. 46
Moses	Spoke to Moses from the burning bush, promising to deliver the Israelites from enslavement	Exodus 3:1–8, p. 79
Israelites	Protected them from the pursuing Egyptian army	Exodus 14:19–20, p. 94
Balaam	Blocked Balaam's path, then sent him to deliver a message to Balak	Numbers 22:22–35, p. 206
Joshua	Reassured Joshua in his role as commander of the Lord's people	Joshua 5:13—6:5, p. 282
Gideon	Commissioned Gideon to fight against the Midianites	Judges 6:11–24, p. 318
Elijah	Provided food for Elijah in the wilderness	1 Kings 19:4–8, p. 466
David	Appeared to David at the threshing floor of Araunah, where David built an altar	1 Chronicles 21:16–27, p. 546
Three Hebrew Men	Protected them in Nebuchadnezzar's fiery furnace	Daniel 3:25, p. 1155

22 David said, "The Temple of the LORD God and the altar for Israel's burnt offerings will be built here."

David Makes Plans for the Temple

2 So David ordered all foreigners living in Israel to gather together. From that group David chose stonecutters to cut stones to be used in building the Temple of God. 3 David supplied a large amount of iron to be used for making nails and hinges for the gate doors. He also supplied more bronze than could be weighed, 4 and he supplied more cedar logs than could be counted. Much of the cedar had been brought to David by the people from Sidon and Tyre.

5 David said, "We should build a great Temple for the LORD, which will be famous everywhere for its greatness and beauty. But my son Solomon is young. He hasn't yet learned what he needs to know, so I will prepare for the building of it." So David got many of the materials ready before he died.

6 Then David called for his son Solomon and told him to build the Temple for the LORD, the God of Israel. 7 David said to him, "My son, I wanted to build a temple for worshipping the LORD my God. 8 But the LORD spoke his word to me, 'David, you have killed many people. You have fought many wars. You cannot build a temple for worship to me, because you have killed many people. 9 But, you will have a son, a man of peace and rest. I will give him rest from all his enemies around him. His name will be Solomon,*n* and I will give Israel peace and quiet while he is king. 10 Solomon will build a temple for worship to me. He will be my son, and I will be his father. I will make his kingdom strong; someone from his family will rule Israel for ever.'"

11 David said, "Now, my son, may the LORD be with you. May you build a temple for the LORD your God, as he said you would. 12 He will make you the king of Israel. May the LORD give you wisdom and understanding so you will be able to obey the teachings of the LORD your God. 13 Be careful to obey the rules and laws

FAITH links

PLANS FOR A SON
1 CHRONICLES 22:5-19

David wanted to help his son honour God by building a Temple. He gathered the materials necessary and told the Israelite leaders to be ready to help Solomon.

Have you noticed lately what your mum and dad do to help you follow God? Maybe he yanks the covers off your bed on Sundays to encourage you to get ready for church. Maybe she drops you off at the youth meeting on Friday evening. They do things like this to make sure you live a life that honours God. That makes your mum and dad pretty special, don't you think?

Check out these other Faithlinks on obeying your parents:

Reward for Obedience, Leviticus 26:3–13, p. 171

A Look for the Book, 2 Chronicles 34:14–18, p. 603

All Talk, No Action, Jeremiah 5:1–2, p. 996

Just Say Yes! Matthew 9:9–13, p. 1289

The Number One Rule, Mark 12:28–31, p. 1351

Glad to Help! Romans 15:17–20, p. 1541

22:9 **Solomon** This name sounds like the Hebrew word for "peace".

the LORD gave Moses for Israel. If you obey them, you will have success. Be strong and brave. Don't be afraid or discouraged.

14 "Solomon, I have worked hard getting many of the materials for building the Temple of the LORD. I have supplied about 3,550 tonnes of gold, about 35,000 tonnes of silver, so much bronze and iron it cannot be weighed, and wood and stone. You may add to them. 15 You have many workmen—stonecutters, bricklayers, carpenters and people skilled in every kind of work. 16 They are skilled in working with gold, silver, bronze and iron. You have more craftsmen than can be counted. Now begin the work, and may the LORD be with you."

17 Then David ordered all the leaders of Israel to help his son Solomon. 18 David said to them, "The LORD your God is with you. He has given you rest from our enemies. He has handed over to me the people living around us. The LORD and his people are in control of this land. 19 Now give yourselves completely to obeying the LORD your God. Build the holy place of the LORD God; build the Temple for worship to the LORD. Then bring the Ark of the Agreement with the LORD and the holy things that belong to God into the Temple."

The Levites

23 After David had lived long and was old, he made his son Solomon the new king of Israel. 2 David gathered all the leaders of Israel, along with the priests and Levites. 3 He counted the Levites who were 30 years old and older. In all, there were 38,000 Levites. 4 David said, "Of these, 24,000 Levites will direct the work of the Temple of the LORD, 6,000 Levites will be officers and judges, 5 4,000 Levites will be gatekeepers and 4,000 Levites will praise the LORD with musical instruments I made for giving praise."

6 David separated the Levites into three groups that were led by Levi's three sons: Gershon, Kohath and Merari.

The People of Gershon

7 From the people of Gershon, there were Ladan and Shimei.

8 Ladan had three sons. His first son was Jehiel, and his other sons were Zetham and Joel.

9 Shimei's sons were Shelomoth, Haziel and Haran. These three sons were leaders of Ladan's families. 10 Shimei had four sons: Jahath, Ziza, Jeush and Beriah. 11 Jahath was the first son, and Ziza was the second son. But Jeush and Beriah did not have many children, so they were counted as if they were one family.

The People of Kohath

12 Kohath had four sons: Amram, Izhar, Hebron and Uzziel.

13 Amram's sons were Aaron and Moses. Aaron and his descendants were chosen to be special for ever. They were chosen to prepare the holy things for the LORD's service, to offer sacrifices before the LORD, and to serve him as priests. They were to give blessings in his name for ever.

14 Moses was the man of God, and his sons were counted as part of the tribe of Levi. 15 Moses' sons were Gershom and Eliezer. 16 Gershom's first son was Shubael. 17 Eliezer's first son was Rehabiah. Eliezer had no other sons, but Rehabiah had many sons.

18 Izhar's first son was Shelomith.

19 Hebron's first son was Jeriah, his second was Amariah, his third was Jahaziel, and his fourth was Jekameam.

20 Uzziel's first son was Micah and his second was Isshiah.

The People of Merari

21 Merari's sons were Mahli and Mushi. Mahli's sons were Eleazar and Kish. 22 Eleazar died without sons; he

> After David had lived long and was old, he made his son Solomon the new king of Israel.
> – 1 Chronicles 23:1

had only daughters. Eleazar's daughters married their cousins, the sons of Kish. 23 Mushi's three sons were Mahli, Eder and Jerimoth.

The Levites' Work

24 These were Levi's descendants listed by their families. They were the leaders of families. Each person who was 20 years old or older was listed. They served in the LORD's Temple.

25 David had said, "The LORD, the God of Israel, has given rest to his people. He has come to live in Jerusalem for ever. 26 So the Levites don't need to carry the Holy Tent or any of the things used in its services any more." 27 David's last instructions were to count the Levites who were 20 years old and older.

28 The Levites had the job of helping Aaron's descendants in the service of the Temple of the LORD. They cared for the Temple courtyard and side rooms, and they made all the holy things pure. Their job was to serve in the Temple of God. 29 They were responsible for putting the holy bread on the table, for the flour in the grain offerings, for the bread made without yeast, for the baking and mixing, and for the measuring. 30 The Levites also stood every morning and gave thanks and praise to the LORD. They also

LIFE AFTER LIFE

Here is someone who has a question that at one time or another we've all probably wondered about. Please welcome Joe, aged 9, to Connect 2-You.

Joe: My grandmother died last month, and I miss her a lot. She was the first person who ever told me about Jesus. She was also the nicest person in the world. I don't understand why God let her die. Can you tell me?

It's natural to have questions like this. Joe's grandmother sounds like a very special person. We can't tell why God let her die, but we do know that Joe won't be separated from her for ever. Death is just the beginning for people who believe in Christ. We will be resurrected (raised up) to live for ever with God. That doesn't mean Joe won't miss his grandmother here on earth. It's natural to feel grief. But if he knows that he will see her again someday, the grief isn't quite as bad. If you'd like to learn more about dealing with the death of a loved one, check out the Livin' It page on death, <u>1 Corinthians 15:50-57, p. 1564</u>.

did this every evening. 31 The Levites offered all the burnt offerings to the LORD on the special days of rest, at the New Moon festivals and at all appointed feasts. They served before the LORD every day. They were to follow the rules for how many Levites should serve each time. 32 So the Levites took care of the Meeting Tent and the Holy Place. And they helped their relatives, Aaron's descendants, with the services at the Temple of the LORD.

The Groups of the Priests

24 These were the groups of Aaron's sons:

Aaron's sons were Nadab, Abihu, Eleazar and Ithamar. 2 But Nadab and Abihu died before their father did, and they had no sons. So Eleazar and Ithamar served as the priests. 3 David, with the help of Zadok, a descendant of Eleazar, and Ahimelech, a descendant of Ithamar, separated their family groups into two different groups. Each group had certain duties. 4 There were more leaders from Eleazar's family than from Ithamar's— sixteen leaders from Eleazar's family and eight leaders from Ithamar's family. 5 Men were chosen from Eleazar's and Ithamar's families by throwing lots. Some men from each family were chosen to be in charge of the Holy Place, and some were chosen to serve as priests.

6 Shemaiah son of Nethanel, from the tribe of Levi, was the secretary. He recorded the names of those descendants in front of King David, the officers, Zadok the priest, Ahimelech son of Abiathar, and the leaders of the families of the priests and Levites. The work was divided by lots among the families of Eleazar and Ithamar. The following men with their groups were chosen.

7 The first one chosen was Jehoiarib. The second was Jedaiah. 8 The third was Harim. The fourth was Seorim. 9 The fifth was Malkijah. The sixth was Mijamin. 10 The seventh was Hakkoz. The eighth was Abijah. 11 The ninth was Jeshua. The tenth was Shecaniah. 12 The eleventh was Eliashib. The twelfth was Jakim. 13 The thirteenth was Huppah. The fourteenth was Jeshebeab. 14 The fifteenth was Bilgah.

The sixteenth was Immer. 15 The seventeenth was Hezir. The eighteenth was Happizzez. 16 The nineteenth was Pethahiah. The twentieth was Jehezkel. 17 The twenty-first was Jakin. The twenty-second was Gamul. 18 The twenty-third was Delaiah. The twenty-fourth was Maaziah.

19 These were the groups chosen to serve in the Temple of the LORD. They obeyed the rules given them by Aaron, just as the LORD, the God of Israel, had commanded him.

The Other Levites

20 These are the names of the rest of Levi's descendants:

Shubael was a descendant of Amram, and Jehdeiah was a descendant of Shubael.

21 Isshiah was the first son of Rehabiah.

22 From the Izhar family group, there was Shelomoth, and Jahath was a descendant of Shelomoth.

23 Hebron's first son was Jeriah, Amariah was his second, Jahaziel was his third and Jekameam was his fourth.

24 Uzziel's son was Micah. Micah's son was Shamir. 25 Micah's brother was Isshiah and Isshiah's son was Zechariah.

26 Merari's descendants were Mahli and Mushi. Merari's son was Jaaziah. 27 Jaaziah son of Merari had sons named Shoham, Zaccur and Ibri. 28 Mahli's son was Eleazar, but Eleazar did not have any sons.

29 Kish's son was Jerahmeel.

30 Mushi's sons were Mahli, Eder and Jerimoth.

These are the Levites, listed by their families. 31 They were chosen for special jobs by throwing lots in front of King David, Zadok, Ahimelech, the leaders of the families of the priests and of the Levites. They did this just as their relatives, the priests, Aaron's descendants, had done. The families of the oldest brother and the youngest brother were treated the same.

The Music Groups

25 David and the commanders of the army chose some of the sons of

Asaph, Heman and Jeduthun to preach and play harps, lyres and cymbals. Here is a list of the men who served in this way:

2 Asaph's sons who served were Zaccur, Joseph, Nethaniah and Asarelah. King David chose Asaph to preach, and Asaph directed his sons.

3 Jeduthun's sons who served were Gedaliah, Zeri, Jeshaiah, Shimei, Hashabiah and Mattithiah. There were six of them, and Jeduthun directed them. He preached and used a harp to give thanks and praise to the LORD.

4 Heman's sons who served were Bukkiah, Mattaniah, Uzziel, Shubael, Jerimoth, Hananiah, Hanani, Eliathah, Giddalti, Romamti-Ezer, Joshbekashah, Mallothi, Hothir and Mahazioth. 5 All these were sons of Heman, David's seer. God promised to make Heman strong, so Heman had many sons. God gave him fourteen sons and three daughters. 6 Heman directed all his sons in making music for the Temple of the LORD with cymbals, lyres and harps; that was their way of serving in the Temple of God. King David was in charge of Asaph, Jeduthun and Heman. 7 These men and their relatives were trained and skilled in making music for the LORD. There were 288 of them. 8 Everyone threw lots to choose the time his family was to serve at the Temple. The young and the old, the teacher and the student, had to throw lots.

9 First, the lot fell to Joseph, from the family of Asaph.

Second, twelve men were chosen from Gedaliah, his sons and relatives.

10 Third, twelve men were chosen from Zaccur, his sons and relatives.

11 Fourth, twelve men were chosen from Izri, his sons and relatives.

12 Fifth, twelve men were chosen from Nethaniah, his sons and relatives.

13 Sixth, twelve men were chosen from Bukkiah, his sons and relatives.

14 Seventh, twelve men were chosen from Jesarelah, his sons and relatives.

15 Eighth, twelve men were chosen from Jeshaiah, his sons and relatives.

16 Ninth, twelve men were chosen from Mattaniah, his sons and relatives.

17 Tenth, twelve men were chosen from Shimei, his sons and relatives.

18 Eleventh, twelve men were chosen from Azarel, his sons and relatives.

19 Twelfth, twelve men were chosen from Hashabiah, his sons and relatives.

20 Thirteenth, twelve men were chosen from Shubael, his sons and relatives.

21 Fourteenth, twelve men were chosen from Mattithiah, his sons and relatives.

22 Fifteenth, twelve men were chosen from Jerimoth, his sons and relatives.

23 Sixteenth, twelve men were chosen from Hananiah, his sons and relatives.

24 Seventeenth, twelve men were chosen from Joshbekashah, his sons and relatives.

25 Eighteenth, twelve men were chosen from Hanani, his sons and relatives.

26 Nineteenth, twelve men were chosen from Mallothi, his sons and relatives.

27 Twentieth, twelve men were chosen from Eliathah, his sons and relatives.

28 Twenty-first, twelve men were chosen from Hothir, his sons and relatives.

29 Twenty-second, twelve men were chosen from Giddalti, his sons and relatives.

30 Twenty-third, twelve men were chosen from Mahazioth, his sons and relatives.

31 Twenty-fourth, twelve men were chosen from Romamti-Ezer, his sons and relatives.

The Gatekeepers

26 These are the groups of the gatekeepers.

From the family of Korah, there was Meshelemiah son of Kore, who was from Asaph's family. 2 Meshelemiah had sons. Zechariah was his first son,

> These men and their relatives were trained and skilled in making music for the LORD.
> – 1 Chronicles 25:7

Jediael was second, Zebadiah was third, Jathniel was fourth, 3 Elam was fifth, Jehohanan was sixth and Eliehoenai was seventh. 4 Obed-Edom had sons. Shemaiah was his first son, Jehozabad was second, Joah was third, Sacar was fourth, Nethanel was fifth, 5 Ammiel was sixth, Issachar was seventh and Peullethai was eighth. God blessed Obed-Edom with children. 6 Obed-Edom's son Shemaiah also had sons. They were leaders in their father's family because they were capable men. 7 Shemaiah's sons were Othni, Rephael, Obed, Elzabad, Elihu and Semakiah. Elihu and Semakiah were skilled workers. 8 All these were Obed-Edom's descendants. They and their sons and relatives were capable men and strong workers. Obed-Edom had 62 descendants in all.

9 Meshelemiah had sons and relatives who were skilled workers. In all, there were eighteen.

10 From the Merari family, Hosah had sons. Shimri was chosen to be in charge. Although he was not the oldest son, his father chose him to be in charge. 11 Hilkiah was his second son, Tabaliah was third and Zechariah was fourth. In all, Hosah had thirteen sons and relatives.

12 These were the leaders of the groups of gatekeepers, and they served in the Temple of the LORD. Their relatives also worked in the Temple. 13 By throwing lots, each family chose a gate to guard. Young and old threw lots.

14 Meshelemiah was chosen by lot to guard the East Gate. Then lots were thrown for Meshelemiah's son Zechariah. He was a wise counsellor and was chosen for the North Gate. 15 Obed-Edom was chosen for the South Gate, and Obed-Edom's sons were chosen to guard the storehouse. 16 Shuppim and Hosah were chosen for the West Gate and the Shalleketh Gate on the upper road.

> Other Levites were responsible for guarding the treasuries of the Temple of God.
> – 1 Chronicles 26:20

Guards stood side by side with guards. 17 Six Levites stood guard every day at the East Gate; four Levites stood guard every day at the North Gate; four Levites stood guard every day at the South Gate; and two Levites at a time guarded the storehouse. 18 There were two guards at the western court and four guards on the road to the court.

19 These were the groups of the gatekeepers from the families of Korah and Merari.

Other Leaders

20 Other Levites were responsible for guarding the treasuries of the Temple of God and for the places where the holy things were kept.

21 Ladan was Gershon's son and the ancestor of several family groups. Jehiel was a leader of one of the family groups. 22 His sons were Zetham and Joel his brother, and they were responsible for the treasuries of the Temple of the LORD.

23 Other leaders were chosen from the family groups of Amram, Izhar, Hebron and Uzziel. 24 Shubael, the descendant of Gershom, who was Moses' son, was the leader responsible for the treasuries. 25 These were Shubael's relatives from Eliezer: Eliezer's son Rehabiah, Rehabiah's son Jeshaiah, Jeshaiah's son Joram, Joram's son Zicri and Zicri's son Shelomith. 26 Shelomith and his relatives were responsible for everything that had been collected for the Temple by King David, by the heads of families, by the commanders of 1,000 men and of 100 men, and by other army commanders. 27 They also gave some of the things they had taken in wars to be used in repairing the Temple of the LORD. 28 Shelomith and his relatives took care of all the holy things. Some had been given by Samuel the seer, Saul son of Kish, Abner son of Ner and Joab son of Zeruiah.

26:27 Money
What's a good way to spend some of the money you earn?

29 Kenaniah was from the Izhar family. He and his sons worked outside the Temple as officers and judges in different places in Israel.

30 Hashabiah was from the Hebron family. He and his relatives were responsible for the LORD's work and the king's business in Israel west of the Jordan River. There were 1,700 skilled men in Hashabiah's group. 31 The history of the Hebron family shows that Jeriah was their leader. In David's fortieth year as king, the records were searched, and some capable men of the Hebron family were found living at Jazer in Gilead. 32 Jeriah had 2,700 relatives who were skilled men and leaders of families. King David gave them the responsibility of directing the tribes of Reuben, Gad and East Manasseh in God's work and the king's business.

Army Divisions

27 This is the list of the Israelites who served the king in the army. Each division was on duty one month each year. There were leaders of families, commanders of 100 men, commanders of 1,000 men, and other officers. Each division had 24,000 men.

2 Jashobeam son of Zabdiel was in charge of the first division for the first month. There were 24,000 men in his division. 3 Jashobeam, one of the descendants of Perez, was leader of all the army officers for the first month.

4 Dodai, from the Ahohites, was in charge of the division for the second month. Mikloth was a leader in the division. There were 24,000 men in Dodai's division.

5 The third commander, for the third month, was Benaiah son of Jehoiada the priest. There were 24,000 men in his division. 6 He was the Benaiah who was one of the Thirty[n] soldiers. Benaiah was a brave warrior who led those men. Benaiah's son Ammizabad was in charge of Benaiah's division.

7 The fourth commander, for the fourth month, was Asahel, the brother of Joab. Later, Asahel's son Zebadiah took his place as commander. There were 24,000 men in his division.

8 The fifth commander, for the fifth month, was Shamhuth, from Izrah's family. There were 24,000 men in his division.

9 The sixth commander, for the sixth month, was Ira son of Ikkesh from the town of Tekoa. There were 24,000 men in his division.

10 The seventh commander, for the seventh month, was Helez. He was from the Pelonites and a descendant of Ephraim. There were 24,000 men in his division.

11 The eighth commander, for the eighth month, was Sibbecai. He was from Hushah and was from Zerah's family. There were 24,000 men in his division.

12 The ninth commander, for the ninth month, was Abiezer. He was from Anathoth in Benjamin. There were 24,000 men in his division.

13 The tenth commander, for the tenth month, was Maharai. He was from Netophah and was from Zerah's family. There were 24,000 men in his division.

14 The eleventh commander, for the eleventh month, was Benaiah. He was from Pirathon in Ephraim. There were 24,000 men in his division.

15 The twelfth commander, for the twelfth month, was Heldai. He was from Netophah and was from Othniel's family. There were 24,000 men in his division.

Leaders of the Tribes

16 These were the leaders of the tribes of Israel. Eliezer son of Zicri was over the tribe of Reuben. Shephatiah son of Maacah was over the tribe of Simeon. 17 Hashabiah son of Kemuel was over the tribe of Levi. Zadok was over the people of Aaron. 18 Elihu, one of David's brothers, was over the tribe of Judah. Omri son of Michael was over the tribe of Issachar. 19 Ishmaiah son of Obadiah was over the

---

27:6 Thirty These were David's most powerful soldiers. See 2 Samuel 23:20-39.

tribe of Zebulun. Jerimoth son of Azriel was over the tribe of Naphtali. 20 Hoshea son of Azaziah was over the tribe of Ephraim. Joel son of Pedaiah was over West Manasseh. 21 Iddo son of Zechariah was over East Manasseh. Jaasiel son of Abner was over the tribe of Benjamin. 22 Azarel son of Jeroham was over the tribe of Dan.

These were the leaders of the tribes of Israel.

23 The LORD had promised to make the Israelites as many as the stars in the sky. So David only counted the men who were 20 years old and older. 24 Joab son of Zeruiah began to count the people, but he did not finish. God became angry with Israel for counting the people, so the number of the people was not put in the history book about King David's rule.

The King's Directors

25 Azmaveth son of Adiel was in charge of the royal storehouses.

Jonathan son of Uzziah was in charge of the storehouses in the country, towns, villages and towers.

26 Ezri son of Kelub was in charge of the field workers who farmed the land.

27 Shimei, from the town of Ramah, was in charge of the vineyards.

Zabdi, from Shapham, was in charge of storing the wine that came from the vineyards.

28 Baal-Hanan, from Geder, was in charge of the olive trees and sycamore trees in the western hills.

Joash was in charge of storing the olive oil.

29 Shitrai, from Sharon, was in charge of the herds that fed in the Plain of Sharon.

Shaphat son of Adlai was in charge of the herds in the valleys.

30 Obil, an Ishmaelite, was in charge of the camels.

Jehdeiah, from Meronoth, was in charge of the donkeys.

31 Jaziz, from the Hagrites, was in charge of the flocks.

All these men were the officers who took care of King David's property.

32 Jonathan was David's uncle, and he advised David. Jonathan was a wise man and a teacher of the law. Jehiel son of Hacmoni took care of the king's sons. 33 Ahithophel advised the king. Hushai, from the Arkite people, was the king's friend. 34 Jehoiada and Abiathar later took Ahithophel's place in advising the king. Jehoiada was Benaiah's son. Joab was the commander of the king's army.

David's Plans for the Temple

28 David commanded all the leaders of Israel to come to Jerusalem. There were the leaders of the tribes, commanders of the divisions serving the king, commanders of 1,000 men and of 100 men, leaders who took care of the property and animals that belonged to the king and his sons, men over the palace, the powerful men and all the brave warriors.

The LORD had promised to make the Israelites as many as the stars in the sky.
– 1 Chronicles 27:23

2 King David stood up and said, "Listen to me, my relatives and my people. I wanted to build a place to keep the Ark of the Agreement with the LORD. I wanted it to be God's footstool. So I made plans to build a temple. 3 But God said to me, 'You must not build a temple for worshipping me, because you are a soldier and have killed many people.'

4 "But the LORD, the God of Israel, chose me from my whole family to be king of Israel for ever. He chose the tribe of Judah to lead, and from the people of Judah, he chose my father's family. From that family God was pleased to make me king of Israel. 5 The LORD has given me many sons, and from those sons he has chosen Solomon to be the new king of Israel. Israel is the LORD's kingdom. 6 The LORD said to me, 'Your son Solomon will build my Temple and its courtyards. I have chosen Solomon to be my son, and

FAITH CHALLENGE

Here's one for you. Read 28:6-7 to find out what God said to King David about David's son. What do you think God would say to your parents about you?

TeSTiNG iT

1 Chronicles 28:6-7
I have chosen Solomon to be my son, and I will be his father. He is obeying my laws and commands now. If he continues to obey them, I will make his kingdom strong for ever.

I will be his father. **7** He is obeying my laws and commands now. If he continues to obey them, I will make his kingdom strong for ever.'"

8 David said, "Now, in front of all Israel, the assembly of the LORD, and in the hearing of God, I tell you these things: be careful to obey all the commands of the LORD your God. Then you will keep this good land and pass it on to your descendants for ever.

28:8 Family
Check out David's advice to his children.

9 "And you, my son Solomon, accept the God of your father. Serve him completely and willingly, because the LORD knows what is in everyone's mind. He understands everything you think. If you go to him for help, you will get an answer. But if you turn away from him, he will leave you for ever. **10** Solomon, you must understand this. The LORD has chosen you to build the Temple as his holy place. Be strong and finish the job."

11 Then David gave his son Solomon the plans for building the Temple and the courtyard around the Temple. They included its buildings, its storerooms, its upper rooms, its inside rooms and the place where the people's sins were cancelled. **12** David gave him plans for everything he had in mind: the courtyards around the LORD's Temple and all the rooms around it, the Temple treasuries and the treasuries of the holy things used in the Temple. **13** David gave Solomon directions for the groups of the priests and Levites. David told him about all the work of serving in the Temple of the LORD and about the things to be used in the Temple service **14** that were made of gold or silver. David told Solomon how much gold or silver should be used to make each thing. **15** David told him how much gold to use for each gold lampstand and its lamps and how much silver to use for each silver lampstand and its lamps. The different lampstands were to be used where needed. **16** David told him how much gold should be used for each table that held the holy bread and how much silver should be used for the silver tables. **17** He told how much pure gold should be used to make the forks, bowls and pitchers and how much gold should be used to make each gold dish. He told how much silver should be used to make each silver dish **18** and how much pure gold should be used for the altar of incense. He also gave Solomon the plans for the chariot of the golden creatures that spread their wings over the Ark of the Agreement with the LORD.

19 David said, "All these plans were written with the LORD guiding me. He helped me understand everything in the plans."

20 David also said to his son Solomon, "Be strong and brave, and do the work. Don't be afraid or discouraged, because the LORD God, my God, is with you. He will not fail you or leave you until all the work for the Temple of the LORD is finished. 21 The groups of the priests and Levites are ready for all the work on the Temple of God. Every skilled worker is ready to help you with all the work. The leaders and all the people will obey every command you give."

Gifts for Building the Temple

29 King David said to all the Israelites who were gathered, "God chose my son Solomon, who is young and hasn't yet learned what he needs to know, but the work is important. This palace is not for people; it is for the LORD God. 2 I have done my best to prepare for building the Temple of God. I have given gold for the things made of gold and silver for the things made of silver. I have given bronze for the things made of bronze and iron for the things made of iron. I have given wood for the things made of wood and onyx for the settings. I have given turquoise gems of many different colours, valuable stones and white marble. I have given much of all these things. 3 I have already given this for the Temple, but now I am also giving my own treasures of gold and silver, because I really want the Temple of my God to be built. 4 I have given about 100 tonnes of pure gold from Ophir and about 236 tonnes of pure silver. They will be used to cover the walls of the buildings 5 and for all the gold and silver work. Skilled men may use the gold and silver to make things for the Temple. Now, who is ready to give himself to the service of the LORD today?"

6 The family leaders and the leaders of the tribes of Israel, the commanders of 1,000 men and of 100 men, and the leaders responsible for the king's work gave their valuable things. 7 They gave about 170 tonnes of gold, about 350 tonnes of silver, about 600 tonnes of bronze and about 3,500 tonnes of iron to the Temple of God. 8 People who had valuable gems gave them to the treasury of the Temple of the LORD, and Jehiel, from the Gershon family, took care of the valuable gems. 9 The leaders gave willingly and completely to the LORD. The people rejoiced to see their leaders give so gladly, and King David was also very happy.

FAITH links

GIFTS FROM THE HEART
1 CHRONICLES 29

Have you ever participated in a fund-raising event? Meeting your goal can be pretty exciting! King David asked the Israelites to give to the building fund for the Temple. They gave generously and cheerfully. They celebrated because so much was given!

Giving that takes place from the heart is always exciting. Whatever is given – whether money, time or a smile – it's all good! Search your heart. What would you like to give?

Giving Your Part, Leviticus 27:30, p. 173

Wisdom About Wealth, Ecclesiastes 5:10–12, p. 878

The Foundation of Our Hope, Isaiah 31:1–8, p. 934

Your Feet on High Places, Habakkuk 3:18–19, p. 1239

Your Heart's Desire, Luke 16:13–15, p. 1401

More Money? 1 Timothy 6:10, p. 1649

David's Prayer

10 David praised the LORD in front of all the people who were gathered. He said:
"We praise you, LORD,
   God of our father Israel.
We praise you for ever and ever.
11 LORD, you are great and powerful.
   You have glory, victory and honour.
   Everything in heaven and on earth belongs to you.
   The kingdom belongs to you, LORD;
   you are the ruler over everything.
12 Riches and honour come from you.
   You rule everything.
   You have the power and strength
   to make anyone great and strong.
13 Now, our God, we thank you
   and praise your glorious name.

14 "These things did not really come from me and my people.
   Everything comes from you;
   we have given you back what you gave us.
15 We are like foreigners and strangers, as our ancestors were.
   Our time on earth is like a shadow.
   There is no hope.
16 LORD our God, we have gathered all this
   to build your Temple for worship of you.
   But everything has come from you; everything belongs to you.
17 I know, my God, that you test people's hearts.
   You are happy when people do what is right.
   I was happy to give all these things,
   and I gave with an honest heart.
   Your people gathered here are happy to give to you,
   and I rejoice to see their giving.
18 LORD, you are the God of our ancestors,
   the God of Abraham, Isaac and Jacob.
   Make your people want to serve you always,
   and make them want to obey you.
19 Give my son Solomon a desire to serve you.
   Help him always obey your commands, laws and rules.
   Help him build the Temple for which I have prepared."

20 Then David said to all the people who were gathered, "Praise the LORD your God." So they all praised the LORD, the God of their ancestors, and they bowed to the ground to give honour to the LORD and the king.

Solomon Becomes King

21 The next day the people sacrificed to the LORD. They offered burnt offerings to him of 1,000 bulls, 1,000 rams and 1,000 male lambs. They also brought drink offerings. Many sacrifices were made for all the people of Israel. 22 That day the people ate and drank with much joy, and the LORD was with them.

And they made David's son Solomon king for the second time. They poured olive oil on Solomon to appoint him king in the presence of the LORD. And they poured oil on Zadok to appoint him as priest. 23 Then Solomon sat on the LORD's throne as king and took his father David's place. Solomon was very successful, and all the people of Israel obeyed him. 24 All the leaders and soldiers and King David's sons accepted Solomon as king and promised to obey him. 25 The LORD made Solomon great before all the Israelites and gave Solomon much honour. No king of Israel before Solomon had such honour.

David's Death

26 David son of Jesse was king over all Israel. 27 He had ruled over Israel 40 years—seven years in Hebron and 33 years in Jerusalem. 28 David died when he was old. He had lived a good, long life and had received many riches and honours. His son Solomon became king after him.

29:12 Worry
Where do you find confidence?

29 Everything David did as king, from beginning to end, is recorded in the records of Samuel the seer, the records of Nathan the prophet and the records of Gad the seer. 30 Those writings tell what David did as king of Israel. They tell about his power and what happened to him and to Israel and to all the kingdoms around them.

2 Chronicles

THE GLORIOUS TEMPLE

Hello, there! I'm Ezra – teacher and historian. Step back in time with me to the day Solomon dedicated the Temple to the Lord. Imagine as you walk up the hill, the Temple of stone glitters in the sun. In the courtyard stands the huge bronze altar where the priests make sacrifices to the Lord. To the side is an enormous basin of water resting on 12 bronze bulls. Walk up the steps and through the doors. Every surface is coated with gold and is encrusted with jewels. Admire the golden lampstands, tables and bowls. What a day! God was pleased with the Temple that Solomon built. Link to 2 Chronicles 7:1–3 to read about the awesome way his presence filled the Temple. (You can also connect to The Temple in Jerusalem, p. 564.)

I wrote this book to remind people to be faithful to God and to worship only him. After Solomon died, many people turned away from God and started to worship idols. They did not take care of the Temple and even gave away some of its treasures. King Hezekiah remembered God and restored the Temple. He united the whole nation to worship the true God. Be sure to check out how God saved Jerusalem from the Assyrians in 2 Chronicles 32:1–23.

JESUS WATCH

The Temple had two rooms that were divided by a thick curtain: the Holy Place and the Most Holy Place. Bread offerings from the 12 tribes were placed on gold tables in the Holy Place. Behind the curtain, shielded from sight, the Ark of God was placed in the Most Holy Place. This was God's throne room in Israel. Only the high priest was allowed access. Once a year, on the Day of Cleansing, the high priest entered into the Most Holy Place with the sacrifice for the people's sins. In a similar, but more permanent way, Jesus is our high priest. When he died on the cross, Jesus became our perfect sacrifice, giving up his life for our sins. Unlike the high priests in the Old Testament, though, Jesus does not need to make this sacrifice every year; his one sacrifice is enough for all our sins. When Jesus died, the curtain shielding the Most Holy Place was torn. (Check out Matthew 27:45–51, p. 1325, for that story.)

my FAVOURITE links

OTHER CONNECTIONS

Livin' it

Want to know a secret for success? Surf over to Eyes on the Prize, 2 Chronicles 1:7–12, to learn the importance of setting goals for yourself and of learning the goals God has set for you. Your life will never be the same!

Visit these information bulletin boards for some interesting facts that you will read about in 2 Chronicles:

- Israel's Glory Years, 2 Chronicles 9. Stop here for some cool facts about one of Israel's most famous builders, Solomon. Under King Solomon, Israel stretched its empire to its limits and built the Temple and a breathtaking palace.
- Skin diseases are mentioned frequently in the Bible. Check out the facts behind these skin diseases by connecting to Disease or Curse? 2 Chronicles 26:20–23.
- King Hezekiah had a secret weapon to defend Jerusalem when their enemies surrounded the city and attempted to stop food and water supplies from coming in. Find out what his secret was by linking to A Secret Water Supply, 2 Chronicles 32.

FAITH links

God's New Home, **2 Chronicles 7:11–22**

The Salt Promise, **2 Chronicles 13:5**

Weak? Great! **2 Chronicles 14:11**

Depend on Him! **2 Chronicles 16:1–9**

A Travelling Bible Study, **2 Chronicles 17:9**

A Reminder to Be Fair, **2 Chronicles 19:5–11**

Your Best Defence, **2 Chronicles 20:1–12**

A Look for the Book, **2 Chronicles 34:14–18**

This Hurts Me More? **2 Chronicles 36:17–22**

Did you know?

What's the flash on Josiah? The story is that he was only a kid when he became king.

Link to 2 Chronicles 34:1–2 to find out.

CHECK OUT THESE COOL STORIES:

Solomon builds the Temple, 2 Chronicles 3
Joash restores the Temple, 2 Chronicles 24
Hezekiah's water supply, 2 Chronicles 32:1–5, 30
God's Temple on fire, 2 Chronicles 36:15–21

SETTING GOALS
2 Chronicles 1:7–12

Eyes on the Prize Have you ever played in a championship football or hockey tournament? How did you feel when you saw the trophy that would be awarded to the winning team? Did it make you play your very best – setting your goal on helping your team win that trophy? What are some of the things you set goals for in your life? Sometimes it's difficult to reach the goals we set for ourselves. Bad things happen and we face hard times. But just like Paul, we can trust God to help us no matter what. (Read 2 Corinthians 1:8–10, p. 1570.) Set your goals and then trust God to help you reach them.

MORE FAITHlinks

- I'll Never Forget What's-His-Name, **p. 239**
- A Need to Change, **p. 873**
- My Favourite! **p. 1347**
- Heavenly Treasure, **p. 1394**
- Put God First, **p. 1472**

Do you have any goals for the future?

You do? Are they that you want to grow up so you can stay up as late as you want and eat all the junk food you want?

Although those are interesting ideas, maybe you ought to log on to these Faithlinks for more info on setting goals!

A Hopeful Future, Jeremiah 29:11, p. 1031
- What are some of the plans you and your parents have made concerning your future? What will you need to do to carry out those plans and reach your goals? Why were the plans made? Link here to learn about God's plans for your future.

First Place, Haggai 1:7–11, p. 1248
- Suppose your parents' goal was to redecorate every room in the house – except yours. How would that make you feel? What would you think of the goal they had set?
- How many goals have you set concerning God and serving him? God wants his work to be important to us. How important is it to you?

The Choices of a Choice, Luke 5:1–11, p. 1375
- You have plans and goals for your life, right? Now, suppose you met someone who could do amazing things. Would you give up your life plans to work with that person? Link here to discover some people who made life-changing choices.

my FAVOURITE links

Solomon Asks for Wisdom

1 Solomon, David's son, became a powerful king, because the LORD his God was with him and made him very great.

2 Solomon spoke to all the people of Israel—the commanders of 100 men and of 1,000 men, the judges, every leader in all Israel and the leaders of the families. 3 Then Solomon and all the people with him went to the place of worship at the town of Gibeon. God's Meeting Tent, which Moses the LORD's servant had made in the desert, was there. 4 David had brought the Ark of God from Kiriath Jearim to Jerusalem, where he had made a place for it and had set up a tent for it. 5 The bronze altar that Bezalel son of Uri, who was the son of Hur, had made was in Gibeon in front of the Holy Tent. So Solomon and the people worshipped there. 6 Solomon went up to the bronze altar in the presence of the LORD at the Meeting Tent and offered 1,000 burnt offerings on it.

7 That night God appeared to Solomon and said to him, "Ask for whatever you want me to give you."

8 Solomon answered, "You have been very kind to my father David, and you have made me king in his place. 9 Now, LORD God, may your promise to my father David come true. You have made me king of a people who are as many as the dust of the earth. 10 Now give me wisdom and knowledge so that I can lead these people in the right way, because no one can rule them without your help."

11 God said to Solomon, "You have not asked for wealth or riches or honour, or for the death of your enemies, or for a long life. But since you have asked for wisdom and knowledge to lead my people, over whom I have made you king, 12 I will give you wisdom and knowledge. I will also give you more wealth, riches and honour than any king who has lived before you or any who will live after you."

13 Then Solomon left the place of worship, the Meeting Tent, at Gibeon and went back to Jerusalem. There King Solomon ruled over Israel.

Solomon's Wealth

14 Solomon had 1,400 chariots and 12,000 horses. He kept some in special cities for the chariots, and others he kept with him in Jerusalem. 15 In Jerusalem Solomon made silver and gold as plentiful as stones and cedar trees as plentiful as the fig trees on the western hills. 16 He imported horses from Egypt and Kue; his traders bought them in Kue. 17 They imported chariots from Egypt for about 600 pieces of silver each, and horses cost nearly 150 pieces of silver apiece. Then they sold the horses and chariots to all the kings of the Hittites and the Arameans.

Solomon Prepares for the Temple

2 Solomon decided to build a temple as a place to worship the LORD and also a palace for himself. 2 He chose 70,000 men to carry loads, 80,000 men to cut stone in the hill country and 3,600 men to direct the workers.

3 Solomon sent this message to Hiram king of the city of Tyre: "Help me as you helped my father David by sending him cedar logs so he could build himself a palace to live in. 4 I will build a temple for worshipping the LORD my God, and I will give this temple to him. There we will burn sweet-smelling spices in his presence. We will continually set out the holy bread in God's presence. And we will burn sacrifices every morning and evening, on Sabbath days and New Moons, and on the other feast days commanded by the LORD our God. This is a rule for Israel to obey for ever.

**1:9–10
Prayer**
What can you pray for?

> Solomon decided to build a temple as a place to worship the LORD and also a palace for himself.
> – 2 Chronicles 2:1

5 "The temple I build will be great, because our God is greater than all gods. 6 But no one can really build a house for our God. Not even the highest of heavens can hold him. How then can I build a temple for him except as a place to burn sacrifices to him?

7 "Now send me a man skilled in working with gold, silver, bronze and iron, and with purple, red and blue thread. He must also know how to make engravings. He will work with my skilled craftsmen in Judah and Jerusalem, whom my father David chose.

8 "Also send me cedar, pine and juniper logs from Lebanon. I know your servants are experienced at cutting down the trees in Lebanon, and my servants will help them. 9 Send me a lot of wood, because the temple I am going to build will be large and wonderful. 10 I will give your servants who cut the wood 2,000 tonnes of wheat, 2,000 tonnes of barley, 400 kilolitres of wine and 400 kilolitres of oil."

11 Then Hiram king of Tyre answered Solomon with this letter: "Solomon, because the LORD loves his people, he chose you to be their king." 12 Hiram also said: "Praise the LORD, the God of Israel, who made heaven and earth! He has given King David a wise son, one with wisdom and understanding, who will build a temple for the LORD and a palace for himself.

13 "I will send you a skilled and wise man named Huram-Abi. 14 His mother was from the people of Dan, and his father was from Tyre. Huram-Abi is skilled in working with gold, silver, bronze, iron, stone and wood, and with purple, blue and red thread, and expensive linen. He is skilled in making engravings and can make any design you show him. He will help your craftsmen and the craftsmen of your father David.

15 "Now send my servants the wheat, barley, oil and wine you promised. 16 We will cut as much wood from Lebanon as you need and will bring it on rafts by sea to Joppa. Then you may carry it to Jerusalem."

17 Solomon counted all the foreigners living in Israel. (This was after the time his father David had counted the people.) There were 153,600 foreigners in the country. 18 Solomon chose 70,000 of them to carry loads, 80,000 of them to cut stone in the mountains and 3,600 of them to direct the workers and to keep the people working.

Solomon Builds the Temple

3 Then Solomon began to build the Temple of the LORD in Jerusalem on Mount Moriah. This was where the LORD had appeared to David, Solomon's father. Solomon built the Temple on the place David had prepared on the threshing floor of Araunah the Jebusite. 2 Solomon began building in the second month of the fourth year he ruled Israel.

3 Solomon used these measurements for building the Temple of God. It was 30 metres long and 10 metres wide, using the old measurement. 4 The porch in front of the main room of the Temple was 10 metres long and 10 metres high.

He covered the inside of the porch with pure gold. 5 He put panels of pine on the walls of the main room and covered them with pure gold. Then he put designs of palm trees and chains in the gold. 6 He decorated the Temple with gems and gold from Parvaim." 7 He put gold on the Temple's ceiling beams, doorposts, walls and doors, and he carved creatures with wings on the walls.

8 Then he made the Most Holy Place. It was 10 metres long and 10 metres wide, as wide as the Temple. He covered

> Solomon built the Temple on the place David had prepared on the threshing floor of Araunah the Jebusite.
> – 2 Chronicles 3:1

3:6 Parvaim There was a lot of gold there. It may have been in the country of Ophir.

its walls with over 20 tonnes of pure gold. 9 The gold nails weighed over 500 grammes. He also covered the upper rooms with gold.

10 He made two creatures with wings for the Most Holy Place and covered them with gold. 11 The wings of the gold creatures were 10 metres across. One wing of one creature was 2.5 metres long and touched the Temple wall. The creature's other wing was also 2.5 metres long, and it touched a wing of the second creature. 12 One wing of the second creature touched the other side of the room and was also 2.5 metres long. The second creature's other wing touched the first creature's wing, and it was also 2.5 metres long. 13 Together, the creatures' wings were 10 metres across. The creatures stood on their feet, facing the main room.

14 He made the curtain of blue, purple and red thread, and expensive linen, and he put designs of creatures with wings in it.

15 He made two pillars to stand in front of the Temple. They were about 16 metres tall, and the capital of each pillar was over 2 metres tall. 16 He made a net of chains and put them on the tops of the pillars. He made 100 pomegranates and put them on the chains. 17 Then he put the pillars up in front of the Temple. One pillar stood on the south side, the other on the north. He named the south pillar He Establishes and the north pillar In Him Is Strength.

Things for the Temple

4 He made a bronze altar 10 metres long, 10 metres wide and 5 metres tall. 2 Then he made from bronze a large round bowl, which was called the Sea. It was 15 metres around, 5 metres across and 2.5 metres deep. 3 There were carvings of bulls under the rim of the bowl— ten bulls every 50 centimetres. They were in two rows and were made in one piece with the bowl.

4 The bowl rested on the backs of twelve bronze bulls that faced outwards from the centre of the bowl. Three bulls faced north, three faced west, three faced south and three faced east. 5 The sides of the bowl were 8 centimetres thick, and it held about 60,000 litres. The rim of the bowl was like the rim of a cup or like a lily blossom.

6 He made ten smaller bowls and put five on the south side and five on the north. They were for washing the animals for the burnt offerings, but the large bowl was for the priests to wash in.

7 He made ten lampstands of gold, following the plans. He put them in the Temple, five on the south side and five on the north.

8 He made ten tables and put them in the Temple, five on the south side and five on the north. And he used gold to make 100 other bowls.

9 He also made the priests' courtyard and the large courtyard. He made the doors that opened to the courtyard and covered them with bronze. 10 Then he put the large bowl in the south-east corner of the Temple.

11 Huram-Abi also made bowls, shovels and small bowls. So he finished his work for King Solomon on the Temple of God:

12 two pillars;
  two large bowls for the capitals on top of the pillars;
  two nets to cover the two large bowls for the capitals on top of the pillars;
13 400 pomegranates for the two nets (there were two rows of pomegranates for each net covering the bowls for the capitals on top of the pillars);
14 the stands with a bowl on each stand;
15 the large bowl with twelve bulls under it;
16 the pots, shovels, forks and all the objects to go with them.

All the things that Huram-Abi made for King Solomon for the Temple of the LORD were made of polished bronze. 17 The king had these things poured into clay moulds that were made in the plain of the Jordan River between Succoth and Zarethan. 18 Solomon had so many things made that the total weight of all the bronze was never known.

19 Solomon also made all the things for God's Temple: the golden altar; tables which held the bread that shows God's people are in his presence; 20 the lampstands and their lamps of pure gold, to burn in front of the Most Holy Place as planned; 21 the flowers, lamps and tongs of pure gold; 22 the pure gold wick trimmers, small bowls, pans and dishes used to carry coals; the gold doors for the Temple; and the inside doors of the Most Holy Place and of the main room.

5 Finally all the work Solomon did for the Temple of the LORD was finished. He brought in everything his father David had set apart for the Temple—all the silver and gold and everything. And he put everything in the treasuries of God's Temple.

The Ark is Brought into the Temple

2 Solomon called for the elders of Israel, the heads of the tribes and the leaders of the families to come to him in Jerusalem. He wanted them to bring the Ark of the Agreement with the LORD from the older part of the city. 3 So all the

THE HAVES AND HAVE NOTS

Ever wish you had all the money in the world to buy whatever you wanted? Let's welcome Geoff, aged 11, to Connect 2-You. Geoff has something to share about what it's like to have a rich friend.

Geoff

I have this friend who has everything. And if there's ever anything he doesn't have, his parents will go and buy it for him. Whenever I hang around with him, I feel like a total loser. My parents want me to invite him round, but there's no way. I'd freak if he ever saw how old and run down our house is. I always wonder what it would be like if I could swap places with him.

Do you sometimes feel the same way as Geoff? Don't forget, though, God's Word makes it clear that money does not equal happiness. If Geoff could trade places with his friend, he might find that he got the worst part of the deal.

Geoff should think about everything God has given him – not just money or possessions, but loving relationships, health, unique talents and everything else that makes life valuable.

There are probably people who are jealous of everything Geoff has. They see what he has and wish that they could swap places with him. The key to happiness is to learn to be content with what God has given us. If you're interested in learning how to do that, check out the tips in the Livin' It page on being content, Philippians 4:10-13, p. 1616.

Israelites came together with the king during the festival in the seventh month. 4 When all the elders of Israel arrived, the Levites lifted up the Ark. 5 They carried the Ark of the Agreement, the Meeting Tent and the holy utensils in it; the priests and the Levites brought them up. 6 King Solomon and all the Israelites gathered before the Ark of the Agreement and sacrificed so many sheep and bulls no one could count them.

7 Then the priests put the Ark of the Agreement with the LORD in its place inside the Most Holy Place in the Temple, under the wings of the golden creatures. 8 The wings of these creatures were spread out over the place for the Ark, covering it and its carrying poles. 9 The carrying poles were so long that anyone standing in the Holy Place in front of the Most Holy Place could see the ends of the poles. But no one could see them from outside the Holy Place. The poles are still there today. 10 The only things inside the Ark were two stone tablets[n] that Moses had put in the Ark at Mount Sinai. That was where the LORD made his agreement with the Israelites after they came out of Egypt.

11 Then all the priests left the Holy Place. (All the priests from each group had made themselves ready to serve the LORD.) 12 All the Levite musicians—Asaph, Heman, Jeduthun and all their sons and relatives—stood on the east side of the altar. They were dressed in white linen and played cymbals, harps and lyres. With them were 120 priests who blew trumpets. 13 Those who blew the trumpets and those who sang together sounded like one person as they praised and thanked the LORD. They sang as others played their trumpets, cymbals and other instruments. They praised the LORD with this song:

"He is good;
his love continues for ever."

Then the Temple of the LORD was filled with a cloud. 14 The priests could not continue their work because of the cloud, because the LORD's glory filled the Temple of God.

Solomon Speaks to the People

6 Then Solomon said, "The LORD said he would live in the dark cloud. 2 LORD, I have built a wonderful Temple for you—a place for you to live for ever."

3 While all the Israelites were standing there, King Solomon turned to them and blessed them. 4 Then he said, "Praise the LORD, the God of Israel. He has done what he promised to my father David. The LORD said, 5 'Since the time I brought my people out of Egypt, I have not chosen a city in any tribe of Israel where a temple will be built for me. I did not choose a man to lead my people Israel. 6 But now I have chosen Jerusalem as the place I am to be worshipped, and I have chosen David to lead my people Israel.'

7 "My father David wanted to build a temple for the LORD, the God of Israel. 8 But the LORD said to my father David, 'It was good that you wanted to build a temple for me. 9 But you are not the one to build it. Your son, who comes from your own body, is the one who will build my temple.'

10 "Now the LORD has kept his promise. I am the king now in place of David my father. Now I rule Israel as the LORD promised, and I have built the Temple for the LORD, the God of Israel. 11 There I have put the Ark, in which is the Agreement the LORD made with the Israelites."

Solomon's Prayer

12 Then Solomon stood facing the LORD's altar, and all the Israelites were standing behind him. He spread out his hands. 13 He had made a bronze platform 2.5

> They praised the LORD with this song:
> "He is good; his love continues for ever."
> – 2 Chronicles 5:13

5:10 *stone tablets* They were the two stone tablets on which God wrote the Ten Commandments.

metres long, 2.5 metres wide and 1.5 metres high, and he had placed it in the middle of the outer courtyard. Solomon stood on the platform. Then he kneeled in front of all the people of Israel gathered there, and he spread out his hands towards the sky. 14 He said, "LORD, God of Israel, there is no god like you in heaven or on earth. You keep your agreement of love with your servants who truly follow you. 15 You have kept the promise you made to your servant David, my father. You spoke it with your own mouth and finished it with your hands today.

16 "Now, LORD, God of Israel, keep the promise you made to your servant David, my father. You said, 'If your sons are careful to obey my teachings as you have obeyed, there will always be someone from your family ruling Israel.' 17 Now, LORD, God of Israel, please continue to keep that promise you made to your servant.

18 "But, God, can you really live here on the earth with people? The sky and the highest place in heaven cannot contain you. Surely this house which I have built cannot contain you. 19 But please listen to my prayer and my request, because I am your servant. LORD my God, hear this prayer your servant prays to you. 20 Day and night please watch over this Temple where you have said you would be worshipped. Hear the prayer I pray facing this Temple. 21 Hear my prayers and the prayers of your people Israel when we pray facing this place. Hear from your home in heaven, and when you hear, forgive us.

22 "If someone wrongs another person, he will be brought to the altar in this Temple. If he swears an oath that he is not guilty, 23 then hear in heaven. Judge the case, punish the guilty, but declare that the innocent person is not guilty.

24 "When your people, the Israelites, sin against you, their enemies will defeat them. But if they come back to you and praise you and pray to you in this Temple, 25 then listen from heaven. Forgive the sin of your people Israel, and bring them back to the land you gave to them and their ancestors.

26 "When they sin against you, you will stop the rain from falling on their land. Then they will pray, facing this place and praising you; they will stop sinning when you make them suffer. 27 When this happens, hear their prayer in heaven, and forgive the sins of your servants, the Israelites. Teach them to do what is right. Then please send rain to this land you have given particularly to them.

28 "At times the land will get so dry that no food will grow, or a great sickness will spread among the people. Sometimes the crops will be destroyed by locusts or grasshoppers. Your people will be attacked in their cities by their enemies, or will become sick. 29 When any of these things happens, the people will become truly sorry. If your people spread their hands in prayer towards this Temple, 30 then hear their prayers from your home in heaven. Forgive and treat each person as he should be treated because you know what is in a person's heart. Only you know what is in people's hearts. 31 Then the people will respect and obey you as long as they live in this land you gave our ancestors.

32 "People who are not Israelites, foreigners from other lands, will hear about your greatness and power. They will come from far away to pray at this Temple. 33 Then hear from your home in heaven, and do whatever they ask you. Then people everywhere will know you and respect you, just as your people Israel do. Then everyone will know that I built this Temple as a place to worship you.

34 "When your people go out to fight their enemies along some road on which you send them, your people will pray to you, facing this city which you have chosen and the Temple I have built for you. 35 Then hear in heaven their prayers and do what is right.

36 "Everyone sins, so your people will also sin against you. You will become

---

**6:24–25
Sin**
Do you need to confess your sins?

angry with them and will hand them over to their enemies. Their enemies will capture them and take them away to a country far or near. 37 Your people will be sorry for their sins when they are held as prisoners in another country. They will be sorry and pray to you in the land where they are held as prisoners, saying, 'We have sinned. We have done wrong and acted wickedly.' 38 They will truly turn back to you in the land where they are captives. They will pray, facing this land you gave their ancestors, this city you have chosen and the Temple I have built for you. 39 Then hear their prayers from your home in heaven and do what is right. Forgive your people who have sinned against you.

40 "Now, my God, look at us. Listen to the prayers we pray in this place.
41 Now, rise, LORD God, and come to your resting place.
Come with the Ark of the Agreement that shows your strength.
Let your priests receive your salvation, LORD God, and may your holy people be happy because of your goodness.
42 LORD God, do not reject your appointed one.
Remember your love for your servant David."

The Temple is Given to the LORD

7 When Solomon finished praying, fire came down from the sky and burned up the burnt offering and the sacrifices. The LORD's glory filled the Temple. 2 The priests could not enter the Temple of the LORD, because the LORD's glory filled it. 3 When all the people of Israel saw the fire come down from heaven and the LORD's glory on the Temple, they bowed down on the pavement with their faces to the ground. They worshipped and thanked the LORD, saying,
"He is good;
his love continues for ever."
4 Then King Solomon and all the people offered sacrifices to the LORD. 5 King Solomon offered a sacrifice of 22,000 cattle and 120,000 sheep. So the king and all the people gave the Temple to God. 6 The priests stood ready to do their work. The Levites also stood with the instruments of the LORD's music that King David had made for praising the LORD. The priests and Levites were saying, "His love continues for ever." The priests, who stood across from the Levites, blew their trumpets, and all the Israelites were standing.

7 Solomon made holy the middle part of the courtyard, which is in front of the Temple of the LORD. There he offered whole burnt offerings and the fat of the fellowship offerings. He offered them in the courtyard, because the bronze altar he had made could not hold the burnt offerings, grain offerings and fat.

8 Solomon and all the Israelites celebrated the festival for seven days. There were many people, and they came from as far away as Lebo Hamath and the brook of Egypt. 9 For seven days they celebrated giving the altar for the worship of God. Then they celebrated the festival for seven days. On the eighth day they had a meeting. 10 On the twenty-third day of the seventh month Solomon sent the people home, full of joy. They were happy because the LORD had been so good to David, Solomon and his people Israel.

The LORD Appears to Solomon

11 Solomon finished the Temple of the LORD and his royal palace. He had success in doing everything he planned in the Temple of the LORD and his own palace. 12 Then the LORD appeared to Solomon at night and said to him, "I have heard your prayer and have chosen this place for myself to be a Temple for sacrifices.

13 "I may stop the sky from sending rain. I may command the locusts to destroy the land. I may send sicknesses to my people. 14 Then if my people, who are called by my name, are sorry for what they have done, if they pray and obey me and stop their

7:14
Success
Check out what will bring success.

2 Chronicles 7:15

FAITH links

GOD'S NEW HOME
2 CHRONICLES 7:11-22

Have you ever moved to a new house? New homeowners like to inspect the house they've bought before moving in. Once everything looks OK, they feel comfortable enough to move in. After Solomon had the Temple built, God appeared to him to give him advice. He also wanted Solomon to know how pleased he was with his new house. God told him that he would always love it. These days, however, God has a different sort of house on earth. If you're a Christian, he's made his home in you. He will always love this new house, too!

Ever think of yourself as a temple? God does! Surf on:

Good Plans, Genesis 45:7–8, p. 64

The God of Big Things, Joshua 10, p. 289

Your Heavenly Dad, Psalm 103:13, p. 786

God's New Temple, Ezekiel 40—44, p. 1135

One Big, Happy Family, John 1:12, p. 1422

Life After Death? 1 Corinthians 15:12–13, p. 1563

evil ways, I will hear them from heaven. I will forgive their sin, and I will heal their land. 15 Now I will see them, and I will listen to the prayers prayed in this place. 16 I have chosen this Temple and made it holy. So I will be worshipped there for ever. Yes, I will always watch over it and love it.

17 "But you must serve me as your father David did. You must obey all I have commanded and keep my laws and rules. 18 If you do, I will make your kingdom strong. This is the agreement I made with your father David, saying, 'Someone from your family will always rule in Israel.'

19 "But you must follow me and obey the laws and commands I have given you. You must not serve or worship other gods. 20 If you do, I will take the Israelites out of my land, the land I have given them, and I will leave this Temple that I have made holy. All the nations will make fun of it and speak evil about it. 21 This Temple is honoured now, but then, everyone who passes by will be shocked. They will ask, 'Why did the LORD do this terrible thing to this land and this Temple?' 22 People will answer, 'This happened because they left the LORD, the God of their ancestors, the God who brought them out of Egypt. They decided to follow other gods and worshipped and served them, so he brought all this disaster on them.'"

Solomon's Other Achievements

8 By the end of 20 years, Solomon had built the Temple of the LORD and the royal palace. 2 Solomon rebuilt the towns that Hiram had given him, and Solomon sent Israelites to live in them. 3 Then he went to Hamath Zobah and captured it. 4 Solomon also built the town of Tadmor in the desert, and he built all the towns in Hamath as towns for storing grain and supplies. 5 He rebuilt the towns of Upper Beth Horon and Lower Beth Horon, protecting them with strong walls, gates and bars in the gates. 6 He also rebuilt the town of Baalath. And he built all the other towns for storage and all the cities for his chariots and horses. He built all he wanted in Jerusalem, Lebanon and everywhere he ruled.

7 There were other people in the land who were not Israelites—the Hittites, Amorites, Perizzites, Hivites and Jebusites. 8 They were descendants of the

people that the Israelites had not destroyed. Solomon forced them to be slave workers, as is still true today. 9 But Solomon did not make slaves of the Israelites. They were his soldiers, chief captains, commanders of his chariots and his chariot drivers. 10 These were his most important officers. There were 250 of them to direct the people.

11 Solomon brought the daughter of the king of Egypt from the older part of Jerusalem to the palace he had built for her. Solomon said, "My wife must not live in King David's palace, because the places where the Ark of the Agreement has been are holy."

12 Then Solomon offered burnt offerings to the LORD on the altar he had built for the LORD in front of the Temple porch. 13 He offered sacrifices every day as Moses had commanded. They were offered on the Sabbath days, New Moons and the three yearly feasts—the Feast of Unleavened Bread, the Feast of Weeks and the Feast of Shelters. 14 Solomon followed his father David's instructions and chose the groups of priests for their service and the Levites to lead the praise and to help the priests do their daily work. And he chose the gatekeepers by their groups to serve at each gate, as David, the man of God, had commanded. 15 They obeyed all of Solomon's commands to the priests and Levites, as well as his commands about the treasuries.

16 All Solomon's work was done as he had said from the day the foundation of the Temple of the LORD was begun, until it was finished. So the Temple was finished.

17 Then Solomon went to the towns of Ezion Geber and Elath near the Red Sea in the land of Edom. 18 Hiram sent ships to Solomon that were commanded by his own men, who were skilled sailors. Hiram's men went with Solomon's men to Ophir and brought back about 15 tonnes of gold to King Solomon.

> But Solomon did not make slaves of the Israelites.
> – 2 Chronicles 8:9

The Queen of Sheba Visits

9 When the queen of Sheba heard about Solomon's fame, she came to Jerusalem to test him with hard questions. She had a large group of servants with her and camels carrying spices, jewels and much gold. When she came to Solomon, she talked with him about all she had in mind, 2 and Solomon answered all her questions. Nothing was too hard for him to explain to her. 3 The queen of Sheba saw that Solomon was very wise. She saw the palace he had built, 4 the food on his table, his many officers, the palace servants and their good clothes, the servants who served Solomon his wine and their good clothes. She saw the whole burnt offerings he made in the Temple of the LORD. All these things amazed her.

5 So she said to King Solomon, "What I heard in my own country about your achievements and wisdom is true. 6 I did not believe it then, but now I have come and seen it with my own eyes. I was not told even half of your great wisdom! You are much greater than I had heard. 7 Your men and officers are very happy, because in always serving you, they are able to hear your wisdom. 8 Praise the LORD your God who was pleased to make you king. He has put you on his throne to rule for the LORD your God, because your God loves the people of Israel and supports them for ever. He has made you king over them to keep justice and to rule fairly."

9 Then she gave the king about 4 tonnes of gold and many spices and jewels. No one had ever given such spices as the queen of Sheba gave to King Solomon.

10 Hiram's men and Solomon's men brought gold from Ophir, juniper wood and jewels. 11 King Solomon used the juniper wood to build steps for the Temple of the LORD and the palace and to make lyres and harps for the musicians. No one in Judah had ever seen such beautiful things as these.

2 Chronicles 9:12   572

Get the Info

ISRAEL'S GLORY YEARS

2 Chronicles 9

1. It took thousands of men 7 years to build the Temple at Jerusalem and another 13 years to finish King Solomon's royal palace. (Find out about it in 1 Kings 5—7, p. 442.)

2. The Euphrates River marked the possible northern limits of King Solomon's empire. It was said all Israel and Judah lived at peace "from Dan to Beersheba". (Read about it in 1 Kings 4:24-25, p. 441.)

3. The area around Gaza was probably the southern border of King Solomon's kingdom. (Look up 1 Kings 4:21, p. 441.)

4. Solomon built a tremendous shipping fleet at Ezion Geber, a town near Elath on the shore of the Red Sea. (Read 1 Kings 9:26-28, p. 451.)

5. Solomon also rebuilt the cities of Hazor, Megiddo, Gezer and others as important outposts to defend his empire. (Check it out in 1 Kings 9:15-19, p. 450.)

12 King Solomon gave the queen of Sheba everything she wanted and asked for, even more than she had brought to him. Then she and her servants returned to her own country.

Solomon's Wealth

13 Every year King Solomon received about 23 tonnes of gold. 14 Besides that, he also received gold from traders and merchants. All the kings of Arabia and the governors of the land also brought gold and silver.

15 King Solomon made 200 large shields of hammered gold, each of which contained about 7 kilogrammes of hammered gold. 16 He also made 300 smaller shields of hammered gold, each of which contained about 3 kilogrammes of gold.

The king put them in the Palace of the Forest of Lebanon.

17 The king built a large throne of ivory and covered it with pure gold. 18 The throne had six steps on it and a gold footstool. There were armrests on both sides of the chair, and each armrest had a lion beside it. 19 Twelve lions stood on the six steps, one lion at each end of each step. Nothing like this had ever been made for any other kingdom. 20 All of Solomon's drinking cups, as well as the dishes in the Palace of the Forest of Lebanon, were made of pure gold. In Solomon's time people did not think silver was valuable.

21 King Solomon had many ships that he sent out to trade, with Hiram's men as the crews. Every three years the ships returned, bringing back gold, silver, ivory, apes and baboons.

22 King Solomon had more riches and wisdom than all the other kings on earth. 23 All the kings of the earth wanted to see Solomon and listen to the wisdom God had given him. 24 Year after year everyone who came brought gifts of silver and gold, clothes, weapons, spices, horses and mules.

25 Solomon had 4,000 stalls for horses and chariots, and he had 12,000 horses. He kept some in special cities for the chariots, and others he kept with him in Jerusalem. 26 Solomon ruled over all the kingdoms from the Euphrates River to the land of the Philistines, as far as the border of Egypt. 27 In Jerusalem the king made silver as common as stones and cedar trees as plentiful as the fig trees on the western hills. 28 Solomon imported horses from Egypt and all other countries.

Solomon's Death

29 Everything else Solomon did, from the beginning to the end, is written in the records of Nathan the prophet, and in the prophecy of Ahijah the Shilonite and in the visions of Iddo the seer, who wrote about Jeroboam, Nebat's son. 30 Solomon ruled in Jerusalem over all Israel for 40 years. 31 Then Solomon died and was buried in Jerusalem, the city of David, his father. And Solomon's son Rehoboam became king in his place.

Israel Turns Against Rehoboam

10 Rehoboam went to Shechem, where all the Israelites had gone to make him king. 2 Jeroboam son of Nebat was in Egypt, where he had gone to escape from King Solomon. When Jeroboam heard about Rehoboam being made king, he returned from Egypt. 3 After the people sent for him, he and the people went to Rehoboam and said to him, 4 "Your father forced us to work very hard. Now, make it easier for us, and don't make us work as he did. Then we will serve you."

10:1–14 Friendship
How can friends pull you down?

5 Rehoboam answered, "Come back to me in three days." So the people left.

6 King Rehoboam asked the elders who had advised Solomon during his lifetime, "How do you think I should answer these people?"

7 They answered, "Be kind to these people. If you please them and give them a kind answer, they will serve you always."

8 But Rehoboam rejected this advice. Instead, he asked the young men who had grown up with him and who served as his advisers. 9 Rehoboam asked them, "What is your advice? How should we answer these people who said, 'Don't make us work as hard as your father did'?"

10 The young men who had grown up with him answered, "The people said to you, 'Your father forced us to work very hard. Now make our work easier.' You should tell them, 'My little finger is bigger than my father's legs. 11 He forced you to work hard, but I will make you work even harder. My father beat you with whips, but I will beat you with whips that have sharp points.'"

12 Rehoboam had told the people, "Come back to me in three days." So after three days Jeroboam and all the people returned to Rehoboam. 13 King Rehoboam spoke cruel words to them, because

he had rejected the advice of the older leaders. 14 He followed the advice of the young men and said, "My father forced you to work hard, but I will make you work even harder. My father beat you with whips, but I will beat you with whips that have sharp points." 15 So the king did not listen to the people. God caused this to happen so that the LORD could keep the promise he had made to Jeroboam son of Nebat through Ahijah, a prophet from Shiloh.

16 When all the Israelites saw that the king refused to listen to them, they said to the king,
"We have no share in David!
We have no part in the son of Jesse!
People of Israel, let's go to our own homes!
Let David's son rule his own people."
So all the Israelites went home. 17 But Rehoboam still ruled over the Israelites who lived in the towns of Judah.

18 Adoniram was in charge of the people who were forced to work. When Rehoboam sent him to the people, they threw stones at him until he died. But King Rehoboam ran to his chariot and escaped to Jerusalem. 19 Since then, Israel has been against the family of David.

11 When Rehoboam arrived in Jerusalem, he gathered 180,000 of the best soldiers from Judah and Benjamin. He wanted to fight Israel to take back his kingdom. 2 But the LORD spoke his word to Shemaiah, a man of God, saying, 3 "Speak to Solomon's son Rehoboam, the king of Judah, and to all the Israelites living in Judah and Benjamin. Say to them, 4 'The LORD says you must not go to war against your brothers. Every one of you should go home, because I made all these things happen.'" So they obeyed the LORD's command and turned back and did not attack Jeroboam.

Rehoboam Makes Judah Strong

5 Rehoboam lived in Jerusalem and built strong cities in Judah to defend it. 6 He built up the cities of Bethlehem, Etam, Tekoa, 7 Beth Zur, Soco, Adullam, 8 Gath, Mareshah, Ziph, 9 Adoraim, Lachish, Azekah, 10 Zorah, Aijalon and Hebron. These were fortified cities in Judah and Benjamin. 11 When Rehoboam made those cities strong, he put commanders and supplies of food, oil and wine in them. 12 Also, Rehoboam put shields and spears in all the cities and made them very strong. Rehoboam kept the people of Judah and Benjamin under his control.

13 The priests and the Levites from all over Israel joined Rehoboam. 14 The Levites even left their pasturelands and property and came to Judah and Jerusalem, because Jeroboam and his sons refused to let them serve as priests to the LORD. 15 Jeroboam chose his own priests for the places of worship and for the goat and calf idols he had made. 16 There were people from all the tribes of Israel who wanted to obey the LORD, the God of Israel. So they went to Jerusalem with the Levites to sacrifice to the LORD, the God of their fathers. 17 These people made the kingdom of Judah strong, and they supported Solomon's son Rehoboam for three years. During this time they lived the way David and Solomon had lived.

Rehoboam's Family

18 Rehoboam married Mahalath, the daughter of Jerimoth and Abihail. Jerimoth was David's son, and Abihail was the daughter of Eliab, Jesse's son. 19 Mahalath gave Rehoboam these sons: Jeush, Shemariah and Zaham. 20 Then Rehoboam married Absalom's daughter Maacah, and she gave Rehoboam these children: Abijah, Attai, Ziza and Shelomith. 21 Rehoboam loved Maacah more than his other wives and slave women. Rehoboam had eighteen wives and 60 slave women

> These people made the kingdom of Judah strong, and they supported Solomon's son Rehoboam for three years.
> – 2 Chronicles 11:17

and was the father of 28 sons and 60 daughters.

22 Rehoboam chose Abijah son of Maacah to be the leader of his own brothers, because he planned to make Abijah king. 23 Rehoboam acted wisely. He spread his sons through all the areas of Judah and Benjamin, sending them to every fortified city. He gave plenty of supplies to his sons, and he also found wives for them.

Shishak Attacks Jerusalem

12 After Rehoboam's kingdom was set up and he became strong, he and the people of Judah stopped obeying the teachings of the LORD. 2 During the fifth year Rehoboam was king, Shishak king of Egypt attacked Jerusalem, because Rehoboam and the people were unfaithful to the LORD. 3 Shishak had 1,200 chariots and 60,000 horsemen. He brought troops of Libyans, Sukkites and Cushites from Egypt with him, so many they couldn't be counted. 4 Shishak captured the fortified cities of Judah and came as far as Jerusalem.

5 Then Shemaiah the prophet came to Rehoboam and the leaders of Judah who had gathered in Jerusalem because they were afraid of Shishak. Shemaiah said to them, "This is what the LORD says: 'You have left me, so now I will leave you to face Shishak alone.'"

6 Then the leaders of Judah and King Rehoboam were sorry for what they had done. They said, "The LORD does what is right."

7 When the LORD saw they were sorry for what they had done, the LORD spoke his word to Shemaiah, saying, "The king and the leaders are sorry. So I will not destroy them but will save them soon. I will not use Shishak to punish Jerusalem in my anger. 8 But the people of Jerusalem will become Shishak's servants so they may learn that serving me is different from serving the kings of other nations."

12:1
Success
Find out when success is bad.

9 Shishak king of Egypt attacked Jerusalem and took the treasures from the Temple of the LORD and the king's palace. He took everything, even the gold shields Solomon had made. 10 So King Rehoboam made bronze shields to take their place and gave them to the commanders of the guards for the palace gates. 11 Whenever the king went to the Temple of the LORD, the guards went with him, carrying the shields. Later, they would put them back in the guardroom.

12 When Rehoboam was sorry for what he had done, the LORD held his anger back and did not fully destroy Rehoboam. There was some good in Judah.

13 King Rehoboam made himself a strong king in Jerusalem. He was 41 years old when he became king, and he was king in Jerusalem for seventeen years. Jerusalem is the city that the LORD chose from all the tribes of Israel in which he was to be worshipped. Rehoboam's mother was Naamah from the country of Ammon. 14 Rehoboam did evil because he did not want to obey the LORD.

15 The things Rehoboam did as king, from the beginning to the end, are written in the records of Shemaiah the prophet and Iddo the seer, in the family histories. There were wars between Rehoboam and Jeroboam all the time they ruled. 16 Rehoboam died and was buried in Jerusalem, and his son Abijah became king in his place.

Abijah King of Judah

13 Abijah became the king of Judah during the eighteenth year Jeroboam was king of Israel. 2 Abijah ruled in Jerusalem for three years. His mother was Maacah daughter of Uriel from the town of Gibeah.

And there was war between Abijah and Jeroboam. 3 Abijah led an army of 400,000 capable soldiers into battle, and Jeroboam prepared to fight him with 800,000 capable soldiers.

4 Abijah stood on Mount Zemaraim in the mountains of Ephraim and said, "Jeroboam and all Israel, listen to me! 5 You should know that the LORD, the God of Israel, gave David and his sons

> ## FAITH links
>
> ### THE SALT PROMISE
> ### 2 CHRONICLES 13:5
>
> Salt has many uses, but did you ever think of it as a symbol of loyalty? King Abijah of Judah recalled God's promise to David that his family would rule over Israel for ever. Salt was the sign that God would keep this promise.
>
> Loyalty is a gift we give to each other. It is a promise of faithfulness. What do you do to show *your* loyalty? How do your friends show their loyalty to you?
>
> A Special Promise, Numbers 30:1–2, p. 217
>
> Promises, Promises, Judges 2:1–3, p. 312
>
> The Heart of the Matter, 1 Samuel 16, p. 375
>
> A Big Responsibility, 2 Kings 11, p. 494
>
> A Promise from the Heart, Jeremiah 31:31–33, p. 1037
>
> A Friend of Jesus, John 15:9–17, p. 1450

the right to rule Israel for ever by an agreement of salt." 6 But Jeroboam son of Nebat, one of the officers of Solomon, David's son, turned against his master. 7 Then worthless, evil men joined Jeroboam against Rehoboam, Solomon's son. He was young and didn't know what to do, so he could not stop them.

8 "Now you people are making plans against the LORD's kingdom, which belongs to David's sons. There are many of you, and you have the gold calves Jeroboam made for you as gods. 9 You have thrown out the Levites and the LORD's priests, Aaron's sons. You have chosen your own priests as people in other countries do. Anyone who comes with a young bull and seven rams can become a priest of idols that are not gods.

10 "But as for us, the LORD is our God; we have not left him. The priests who serve the LORD are Aaron's sons, and the Levites help them. 11 They offer burnt offerings and sweet-smelling incense to the LORD every morning and evening. They put the bread on the special table in the Temple. And they light the lamps on the gold lampstand every evening. We obey the command of the LORD our God, but you have left him. 12 God himself is with us as our ruler. His priests blow the trumpet to call us to war against you. Men of Israel, don't fight against the LORD, the God of your ancestors, because you won't succeed."

13 But Jeroboam had sent some troops to sneak behind Judah's army. So while Jeroboam was in front of Judah's army, Jeroboam's soldiers were behind them. 14 When the soldiers of Judah turned around, they saw Jeroboam's army attacking both in front and at the back. So they cried out to the LORD, and the priests blew the trumpets. 15 Then the men of Judah gave a battle cry. When they shouted, God caused Jeroboam and the army of Israel to run away from Abijah and the army of Judah. 16 When the army of Israel ran away from the men of Judah, God handed them over to Judah. 17 Abijah's army struck Israel so that 500,000 of Israel's best men were killed. 18 So at that time the people of Israel were defeated. And the people of Judah won, because they depended on the LORD, the God of their ancestors.

19 Abijah's army chased Jeroboam's army and captured from him the towns of Bethel, Jeshanah and Ephron, and the small villages near them. 20 Jeroboam never became strong again while Abijah

---

13:5 **an agreement of salt** An unbreakable agreement.

was alive. The LORD struck Jeroboam, and he died.

21 But Abijah became strong. He married fourteen women and was the father of 22 sons and sixteen daughters. 22 Everything else Abijah did—what he said and what he did—is recorded in the writings of the prophet Iddo.

14 Abijah died and was buried in Jerusalem. His son Asa became king in his place, and there was peace in the country for ten years during Asa's time.

Asa King of Judah

2 Asa did what the LORD his God said was good and right. 3 He removed the foreign altars and the places where gods were worshipped. He smashed the stone pillars that honoured other gods, and he tore down the Asherah idols. 4 Asa commanded the people of Judah to follow the LORD, the God of their ancestors, and to obey his teachings and commandments. 5 He also removed the places where gods were worshipped and the incense altars from every town in Judah. So the kingdom had peace while Asa was king. 6 Asa built fortified cities in Judah during the time of peace. He had no war in these years, because the LORD gave him peace.

7 Asa said to the people of Judah, "Let's build up these towns and put walls around them. Let's make towers, gates and bars in the gates. This country is ours, because we have obeyed the LORD our God. We have followed him, and he has given us peace all around." So they built and had success.

8 Asa had an army of 300,000 men from Judah and 280,000 men from Benjamin. The men from Judah carried large shields and spears. The men from Benjamin carried small shields and bows and arrows. All of them were brave fighting men.

9 Then Zerah from Cush came out to fight them with an enormous army and 300 chariots. They came as far as the town of Mareshah. 10 So Asa went out to fight Zerah and prepared for battle in the Valley of Zephathah at Mareshah.

11 Asa called out to the LORD his God, saying, "LORD, only you can help weak

---

FAITH links

WEAK? GREAT!
2 CHRONICLES 14:11

What's so great about being weak? If you asked five or six of your friends that question, how would they respond? Most of us, if we're honest, would not have an answer. In our society, weakness is not considered a good thing.

When an enemy nation threatened Judah, King Asa asked God for help. He admitted how weak his people were. The enemy nation was much stronger. God, however, was much stronger still. He had the power to defeat the enemy.

When we're weak, God is strong. What's so great about being weak? We can rely on God's strength to help us.

Check out these Faithlinks on being strong – in God:

Out of Control? Genesis 4, p. 8

Put Pride Aside, Exodus 2:11–15, p. 78

The Perfect Leader? Numbers 20:1–13, p. 203

When the Green-eyed Monster Strikes, 1 Samuel 18:6–9, p. 379

An Energy Boost, Acts 4:31, p. 1469

Thoughts on Thoughts, Philippians 4:8–9, p. 1614

people against the strong. Help us, LORD our God, because we depend on you. We fight against this enormous army in your name. LORD, you are our God. Don't let anyone win against you."

12 So the LORD defeated the Cushites when Asa's army from Judah attacked them, and the Cushites ran away. 13 Asa's army chased them as far as the town of Gerar. So many Cushites were killed that the army could not fight again; they were crushed by the LORD and his army. Asa and his army carried many valuable things away from the enemy. 14 They destroyed all the towns near Gerar, because the people living in these towns were afraid of the LORD. Since these towns had many valuable things, Asa's army took them away. 15 Asa's army also attacked the camps where the shepherds lived and took many sheep and camels. Then they returned to Jerusalem.

Asa's Changes

15 The Spirit of God entered Azariah son of Oded. 2 Azariah went to meet Asa and said, "Listen to me, Asa and all you people of Judah and Benjamin. The LORD is with you when you are with him. If you obey him, you will find him, but if you leave him, he will leave you. 3 For a long time Israel was without the true God and without a priest to teach them and without the teachings. 4 But when they were in trouble, they turned to the LORD, the God of Israel. They looked for him and found him. 5 In those days no one could travel safely. There was much trouble in all the nations. 6 One nation would destroy another nation, and one city would destroy another city, because God troubled them with all kinds of distress. 7 But you should be strong. Don't give up, because you will get a reward for your good work."

8 Asa felt brave when he heard these words and the message from Azariah son of Oded the prophet. So he removed the hateful idols from all of Judah and Benjamin and from the towns he had captured in the hills of Ephraim. He repaired the LORD's altar that was in front of the porch of the Temple of the LORD.

9 Then Asa gathered all the people from Judah and Benjamin and from the tribes of Ephraim, Manasseh and Simeon who were living in Judah. Many people came to Asa even from Israel, because they saw that the LORD, Asa's God, was with him.

10 Asa and these people gathered in Jerusalem in the third month of the fifteenth year of Asa's rule. 11 At that time they sacrificed to the LORD 700 bulls and 7,000 sheep and goats from the valuable things Asa's army had taken from their enemies. 12 Then they made an agreement to obey the LORD, the God of their ancestors, with their whole being. 13 Anyone who refused to obey the LORD, the God of Israel, was to be killed. It did not matter if that person was important or unimportant, a man or woman. 14 Then Asa and the people made a promise before the LORD, shouting with a loud voice and blowing trumpets and sheep's horns. 15 All the people of Judah were happy about the promise, because they had promised with all their heart. They looked for God and found him. So the LORD gave them peace in all the country.

15:15 Following God How should you follow God?

16 King Asa also removed Maacah, his grandmother, from being queen mother, because she had made a terrible Asherah idol. Asa cut down that idol, smashed it into pieces and burned it in the Kidron Valley. 17 But the places of worship to gods were not removed from Judah. Even so, Asa was faithful all his life.

18 Asa brought into the Temple of God the gifts he and his father had given: silver, gold and utensils.

19 There was no more war until the thirty-fifth year of Asa's rule.

Asa's Last Years

16 In the thirty-sixth year of Asa's rule, Baasha king of Israel attacked Judah. He made the town of Ramah strong so he could keep people from leaving or entering Judah, Asa's country.

2 Asa took silver and gold from the

FAITH links

DEPEND ON HIM!
2 CHRONICLES 16:1-9

When you fall into trouble, who do you depend on for help? King Asa of Judah needed help. Instead of asking God for help, he depended on the help of the king of Aram and his army. A prophet predicted disaster for King Asa.

God wants us to ask him for help. But, many times, he's the last one we go to. Whenever you have a problem, even if you think you can find a solution by yourself, ask God to help you. Getting help from a parent is fine, too. God wants you to depend on trusted adults. He also wants you to learn to depend on him.

Need someone to depend on? Link here:

Two Enemies, Nehemiah 6, p. 631

A Pity Party, Job 10, p. 671

Uprooted by Change, Amos 9:15, p. 1205

Our Heavenly Connection, Matthew 6:9–13, p. 1283

At the Right Time, Galatians 4:4, p. 1590

Keep Going! James 1:2–3, p. 1688

---

treasuries of the Temple of the LORD and out of his own palace. Then he sent it with messengers to Ben-Hadad king of Aram, who lived in Damascus. Asa said, 3 "Let there be a treaty between you and me as there was between my father and your father. I am sending you silver and gold. Break your treaty with Baasha king of Israel so he will leave my land."

4 Ben-Hadad agreed with King Asa and sent the commanders of his armies to attack the towns of Israel. They defeated the towns of Ijon, Dan and Abel Beth Maacah, and all the towns in Naphtali where treasures were stored. 5 When Baasha heard about this, he stopped building up Ramah and left his work. 6 Then King Asa brought all the people of Judah to Ramah, and they carried away the rocks and wood that Baasha had used. And they used them to build up Geba and Mizpah.

7 At that time Hanani the seer came to Asa king of Judah and said to him, "You depended on the king of Aram to help you and not on the LORD your God. So the king of Aram's army escaped from you. 8 The Cushites and Libyans had a large and powerful army and many chariots and horsemen. But you depended on the LORD to help you, so he handed them over to you. 9 The LORD searches all the earth for people who have given themselves completely to him. He wants to make them strong. Asa, you did a foolish thing, so from now on you will have wars."

10 Asa was angry with Hanani the seer because of what he had said; he was so angry that he put Hanani in prison. And Asa was cruel to some of the people at the same time.

11 Everything Asa did as king, from the beginning to the end, is written in the book of the kings of Judah and Israel. 12 In the thirty-ninth year of his rule, Asa got a disease in his feet. Though his disease was very bad, he did not ask for help from the LORD, but only from the doctors. 13 Then Asa died in the forty-first year of his rule. 14 The people buried Asa in the tomb he had made for himself in Jerusalem. They laid him on a bed filled with spices and different kinds of mixed perfumes, and they made a large fire to honour him.

Jehoshaphat King of Judah

17 Jehoshaphat, Asa's son, became king of Judah in his place.

Jehoshaphat made Judah strong so they could fight against Israel. 2 He put troops in all the fortified cities of Judah, in the land of Judah and in the towns of Ephraim that his father Asa had captured.

3 The LORD was with Jehoshaphat, because he lived as his ancestor David had lived when he first became king. Jehoshaphat did not ask for help from the Baal idols, 4 but from the God of his father. He obeyed God's commands and did not live as the people of Israel lived. 5 The LORD made Jehoshaphat a strong king over Judah. All the people of Judah brought gifts to Jehoshaphat, so he had much wealth and honour. 6 He wanted very much to obey the LORD. He also removed the places for worshipping gods and the Asherah idols from Judah.

7 During the third year of his rule, Jehoshaphat sent his officers to teach in the towns of Judah. These officers were Ben-Hail, Obadiah, Zechariah, Nethanel and Micaiah. 8 Jehoshaphat sent with them these Levites: Shemaiah, Nethaniah, Zebadiah, Asahel, Shemiramoth, Jehonathan, Adonijah, Tobijah and Tob-Adonijah. He also sent the priests Elishama and Jehoram. 9 These leaders, Levites and priests taught the people in Judah. They took the Book of the Teachings of the LORD and went through all the towns of Judah and taught the people.

10 The nations near Judah were afraid of the LORD, so they did not start a war against Jehoshaphat. 11 Some of the Philistines brought gifts and silver to Jehoshaphat as he demanded. Some Arabs brought him flocks: 7,700 rams and 7,700 goats.

12 Jehoshaphat grew more and more powerful. He built strong, walled cities and towns for storing supplies in Judah. 13 He kept many supplies in the towns of Judah, and he kept trained soldiers in Jerusalem. 14 These soldiers were listed by families. From the families of Judah, these were the commanders of groups of 1,000 men: Adnah was the commander of 300,000 soldiers; 15 Jehohanan was the commander of 280,000 soldiers;

FAITH links

A TRAVELLING BIBLE STUDY
2 CHRONICLES 17:9

King Jehoshaphat of Judah knew the importance of obeying God. One of the ways to obey God was to study God's law. He had two priests carry God's law, called the Book of the Teachings of the Lord, throughout Judah and teach the people about God. At that time, the people did not have the whole Bible. They only had the Book of the Teachings.

You don't have to wait for a teacher to travel to your town to teach you about God. God has provided teachers in your church to teach you about the Bible. You also have the Bible itself to read and study. And Bible reference books like a concordance, a dictionary and Bible study guides can help you understand what you read.

Check out these links on reading the Bible:

The Cloud Guide, Numbers 9:15–23, p. 188

Facts About Following, Joshua 6, p. 283

Do What You Want? Judges 21:25, p. 341

The "Ruler" of Our Lives, Amos 7:7–9, p. 1202

The Power of If, Mark 9:14–24, p. 1344

Just Like a Tree, Colossians 1:23, p. 1621

16 Amasiah was the commander of 200,000 soldiers. Amasiah son of Zicri had volunteered to serve the LORD. 17 These were the commanders from the families of Benjamin: Eliada, a brave soldier, had 200,000 soldiers who used bows and shields. 18 And Jehozabad had 180,000 men armed for war. 19 All these soldiers served King Jehoshaphat. The king also put other men in the fortified cities through all of Judah.

Micaiah Warns King Ahab

18 Jehoshaphat had much wealth and honour, and he made an agreement with King Ahab through marriage.ⁿ 2 A few years later Jehoshaphat went to visit Ahab in Samaria. Ahab sacrificed many sheep and cattle at a great feast to honour Jehoshaphat and the people with him. He encouraged Jehoshaphat to attack Ramoth in Gilead. 3 Ahab king of Israel asked Jehoshaphat king of Judah, "Will you go with me to attack Ramoth in Gilead?"

Jehoshaphat answered, "I will go with you, and my soldiers are yours. We will join you in the battle." 4 Jehoshaphat also said to Ahab, "But first we should ask if this is the LORD's will."

5 So King Ahab called 400 prophets together and asked them, "Should we go to war against Ramoth in Gilead or not?"

They answered, "Go, because God will hand them over to you."

6 But Jehoshaphat asked, "Isn't there a prophet of the LORD here? Let's ask him what we should do."

7 Then King Ahab said to Jehoshaphat, "There is one other prophet. We could ask the LORD through him, but I hate him. He never prophesies anything good about me, but always something bad. He is Micaiah son of Imlah."

Jehoshaphat said, "King Ahab, you shouldn't say that!"

8 So Ahab king of Israel told one of his officers to bring Micaiah to him at once.

9 Ahab king of Israel and Jehoshaphat king of Judah had on their royal robes and were sitting on their thrones at the threshing floor, near the entrance to the gate of Samaria. All the prophets were standing before them speaking their messages. 10 Zedekiah son of Kenaanah had made some iron horns. He said to Ahab, "This is what the LORD says: 'You will use these horns to fight the Arameans until they are destroyed.'"

11 All the other prophets said the same thing, "Attack Ramoth in Gilead and win, because the LORD will hand the Arameans over to you."

12 The messenger who had gone to get Micaiah said to him, "All the other prophets are saying King Ahab will win. You should agree with them and give the king a good answer."

13 But Micaiah answered, "As surely as the LORD lives, I can tell him only what my God says."

14 When Micaiah came to Ahab, the king asked him, "Micaiah, should we attack Ramoth in Gilead or not?"

Micaiah answered, "Attack and win! They will be handed over to you."

15 But Ahab said to Micaiah, "How many times do I have to tell you to speak only the truth to me in the name of the LORD?"

16 So Micaiah answered, "I saw the army of Israel scattered over the hills like sheep without a shepherd. The LORD said, 'They have no leaders. They should go home and not fight.'"

17 Then Ahab king of Israel said to Jehoshaphat, "I told you! He never prophesies anything good about me, but only bad."

18 But Micaiah said, "Hear the

> He never prophesies anything good about me, but always something bad.
> – 2 Chronicles 18:7

18:1 **agreement . . . through marriage** Jehoshaphat's son Jehoram married Athaliah, Ahab's daughter. See 2 Chronicles 21:6.

message from the LORD: I saw the LORD sitting on his throne with his heavenly army standing on his right and on his left. 19 The LORD said, 'Who will trick King Ahab of Israel into attacking Ramoth in Gilead where he will be killed?'

"Some said one thing; some said another. 20 Then one spirit came and stood before the LORD and said, 'I will trick him.'

"The LORD asked, 'How will you do it?'

21 "The spirit answered, 'I will go to Ahab's prophets and make them tell lies.'

"So the LORD said, 'You will succeed in tricking him. Go and do it.'"

22 Micaiah said, "Ahab, the LORD has made your prophets lie to you, and the LORD has decided that disaster should come to you."

23 Then Zedekiah son of Kenaanah went up to Micaiah and slapped him in the face. Zedekiah said, "Has the LORD's Spirit left me to speak through you?"

24 Micaiah answered, "You will find out on the day you go to hide in an inside room."

25 Then Ahab king of Israel ordered, "Take Micaiah and send him to Amon, the governor of the city, and to Joash, the king's son. 26 Tell them I said to put this man in prison and give him only bread and water until I return safely from the battle."

27 Micaiah said, "Ahab, if you come back safely from the battle, the LORD has not spoken through me. Remember my words, all you people!"

Ahab is Killed

28 So Ahab king of Israel and Jehoshaphat king of Judah went to Ramoth in Gilead. 29 King Ahab said to Jehoshaphat, "I will go into battle, but I will wear other clothes so no one will recognise me. But you wear your royal clothes." So Ahab wore other clothes and they went into battle.

30 The king of Aram ordered his chariot commanders, "Don't fight with anyone—important or unimportant— except the king of Israel." 31 When these commanders saw Jehoshaphat, they thought he was the king of Israel, so they turned to attack him. But Jehoshaphat began shouting and the LORD helped him. God made the chariot commanders turn away from Jehoshaphat. 32 When they saw he was not King Ahab, they stopped chasing him.

33 By chance, a soldier shot an arrow which hit Ahab king of Israel between the pieces of his armour. King Ahab said to his chariot driver, "Turn around and get me out of the battle, because I am hurt!" 34 The battle continued all day. King Ahab held himself up in his chariot and faced the Arameans until evening. Then he died at sunset.

19 Jehoshaphat king of Judah came back safely to his palace in Jerusalem. 2 Jehu son of Hanani, a seer, went out to meet him and said to the king, "Why did you help evil people? Why do you love those who hate the LORD? That is the reason the LORD is angry with you. 3 But there is some good in you. You took the Asherah idols out of this country, and you have tried to obey God."

Jehoshaphat Chooses Judges

4 Jehoshaphat lived in Jerusalem. He went out again to be with the people, from Beersheba to the mountains of Ephraim, and he turned them back to the LORD, the God of their ancestors. 5 Jehoshaphat appointed judges in all the land, in each of the strong, walled cities of Judah. 6 Jehoshaphat said to them, "Watch what you do, because you are not judging for people but for the LORD. He will be with you when you make a decision. 7 Now let each of you fear the LORD. Watch what you do, because the LORD our God wants people to be fair. He wants all people to be treated the same, and he doesn't want decisions influenced by money."

8 And in Jerusalem Jehoshaphat appointed some of the Levites, priests and leaders of Israelite families to be judges. They were to decide cases about the law of the LORD and settle problems between the people who lived in Jerusalem.

19:5–7 Leadership Check out how to make good decisions.

9 Jehoshaphat commanded them, "You must always serve the LORD completely, and you must fear him. 10 Your people living in the cities will bring you cases about killing, about the teachings, commands, rules or some other law. In all these cases you must warn the people not to sin against the LORD. If you don't, he will be angry with you and your people. But if you warn them, you won't be guilty.

11 "Amariah, the leading priest, will be over you in all cases about the LORD. Zebadiah son of Ishmael, a leader in the tribe of Judah, will be over you in all cases about the king. Also, the Levites will serve as officers for you. Have courage. May the LORD be with those who do what is right."

Jehoshaphat Faces War

20 Later the Moabites, Ammonites and some Meunites came to start a war with Jehoshaphat. 2 Messengers came and told Jehoshaphat, "A large army is coming against you from Edom, from the other side of the Dead Sea. They are already in Hazazon Tamar!" (Hazazon Tamar is also called En Gedi.) 3 Jehoshaphat was afraid, so he decided to ask the LORD what to do. He announced that no one in Judah should eat during this special time of prayer to God. 4 The people of Judah came together to ask the LORD for help; they came from every town in Judah.

5 The people of Judah and Jerusalem met in front of the new courtyard in the Temple of the LORD. Then Jehoshaphat stood up, 6 and he said, "LORD, God of our ancestors, you are the God in heaven. You rule over all the kingdoms of the nations. You have power and strength, so no one can stand against you. 7 Our God, you forced out the people who lived in this land as your people Israel moved in. And you gave this land for ever to the descendants of your friend Abraham. 8 They lived in this land and built a Temple for you. They said, 9 'If trouble comes upon us, or war, punishment, sickness or hunger, we will stand before you and before this Temple where you have chosen to be worshipped. We will cry out to you when we are in trouble. Then you will hear and save us.'

10 "But now here are men from Ammon, Moab and Edom. You wouldn't let the Israelites enter their lands when

---

FAITH links

A REMINDER TO BE FAIR
2 CHRONICLES 19:5-11

Have you ever had to be reminded to be fair? King Jehoshaphat of Judah wanted to rule his people wisely. But he couldn't be everywhere at the same time. So, he assigned judges to make fair decisions over the people they governed. He also reminded them to be obedient to the Lord while they did their jobs. Obedience to God would help them be fair.

Remembering to do what God says can help you be fair to others, too. One of God's rules that can help you be fair is called the Golden Rule: "Do to others what you would want them to do to you" (Luke 6:31).

Fairness for All, Deuteronomy 24:17, p. 258

Fair All the Time? 2 Samuel 8:15, p. 408

Help for the Outsiders, Nehemiah 5:9–10, p. 630

A Bad Reaction, Jeremiah 36, p. 1043

One of the Faithful, Acts 10:1–34, p. 1482

The Sacrifice of Service, Philippians 2:17, 25–30, p. 1612

FAITH links

YOUR BEST DEFENCE
2 CHRONICLES 20:1-12

In video or computer games, you're often faced with an overwhelming problem. The game gives you several defence resources you can use to overcome the problem. If you run out of resources, you can shut the game off. Ta-da! You're no longer facing that problem. In life, though, when you're facing an overwhelming problem, you can't push a button to turn it off. King Jehoshaphat of Judah felt overwhelmed when an enemy army marched to attack his people. He faced certain defeat until he used the best resource a person can have when trouble comes: prayer. When an overwhelming problem comes your way, remember: God is your best defence.

Need a good defence against problems? Check out these links:

Your Heavenly Parent, Exodus 2:1–10, p. 77

Keep On Praying, 1 Samuel 1, p. 354

No Doubt About It, Job 36:5, p. 699

A Tight Spot, Jonah 2, p. 1215

Our Heavenly Connection, Matthew 6:9–13, p. 1283

Hold On! 2 Thessalonians 2:15–17, p. 1639

---

the Israelites came from Egypt. So the Israelites turned away and did not destroy them. 11 But see how they repay us for not destroying them! They have come to force us out of your land, which you gave us as our own. 12 Our God, punish those people. We have no power against this large army that is attacking us. We don't know what to do, so we look to you for help."

13 All the men of Judah stood before the LORD with their babies, wives and children. 14 Then the Spirit of the LORD entered Jahaziel. (Jahaziel was Zechariah's son. Zechariah was Benaiah's son. Benaiah was Jeiel's son and Jeiel was Mattaniah's son.) Jahaziel, a Levite and a descendant of Asaph, stood up in the meeting. 15 He said, "Listen to me, King Jehoshaphat and all you people living in Judah and Jerusalem. The LORD says this to you: 'Don't be afraid or discouraged because of this large army. The battle is not your battle, it is God's. 16 Tomorrow go down there and fight those people. They will come up through the Pass of Ziz. You will find them at the end of the ravine that leads to the Desert of Jeruel. 17 You won't need to fight in this battle. Just stand strong in your places and you will see the LORD save you. Judah and Jerusalem, don't be afraid or discouraged because the LORD is with you. So go out against those people tomorrow.'"

18 Jehoshaphat bowed face down on the ground. All the people of Judah and Jerusalem bowed down before the LORD and worshipped him. 19 Then some Levites from the Kohathite and Korahite people stood up and praised the LORD, the God of Israel, with very loud voices.

20 Jehoshaphat's army went out into the Desert of Tekoa early in the morning. As they were starting out, Jehoshaphat stood and said, "Listen to me, people of Judah and Jerusalem. Have faith in the LORD your God, and you will stand strong. Have faith in his prophets, and you will succeed." 21 Jehoshaphat listened to the people's advice. Then he chose men to be singers to the LORD, to praise him because he is holy and wonderful. As they marched in front of the army, they said,

"Thank the LORD,
because his love continues for ever."

22 As they began to sing and praise God, the LORD set ambushes for the people of Ammon, Moab and Edom who had come to attack Judah. And they were defeated. 23 The Ammonites and Moabites attacked the Edomites, destroying them completely. After they had killed the Edomites, they killed each other. 24 When the men from Judah came to a place where they could see the desert, they looked at the enemy's large army. But they only saw dead bodies lying on the ground; no one had escaped. 25 When Jehoshaphat and his army came to take their valuables, they found many supplies, much clothing and other valuable things. There was more than they could carry away; there was so much it took three days to gather it all. 26 On the fourth day Jehoshaphat and his army met in the Valley of Beracah and praised the LORD. That is why that place has been called the Valley of Beracah[n] to this day. 27 Then Jehoshaphat led all the men from Judah and Jerusalem back to Jerusalem. The LORD had made them happy because their enemies were defeated. 28 They entered Jerusalem with harps, lyres and trumpets and went to the Temple of the LORD. 29 When all the kingdoms of the lands around them heard how the LORD had fought Israel's enemies, they feared God. 30 So Jehoshaphat's kingdom was not at war. His God gave him peace from all the countries around him.

Jehoshaphat's Rule Ends

31 Jehoshaphat ruled over the country of Judah. He was 35 years old when he became king, and he ruled in Jerusalem for 25 years. His mother's name was Azubah daughter of Shilhi. 32 Jehoshaphat was good like his father Asa, and he did what the LORD said was right. 33 But the places where gods were worshiped were not removed, and the people did not really want to follow the God of their ancestors.

34 The other things Jehoshaphat did as king, from the beginning to the end, are written in the records of Jehu son of Hanani, which are in the book of the kings of Israel.

35 Later, Jehoshaphat king of Judah made a treaty with Ahaziah king of Israel, which was a wrong thing to do. 36 Jehoshaphat agreed with Ahaziah to build trading ships, which they built in the town of Ezion Geber. 37 Then Eliezer son of Dodavahu from the town of Mareshah spoke against Jehoshaphat. He said, "Jehoshaphat, because you joined with Ahaziah, the LORD will destroy what you have made." The ships were wrecked so they could not sail out to trade.

21 Jehoshaphat died and was buried with his ancestors in Jerusalem, the city of David. Then his son Jehoram became king in his place. 2 Jehoram's brothers were Azariah, Jehiel, Zechariah, Azariahu, Michael and Shephatiah. They were the sons of Jehoshaphat king of Judah. 3 Jehoshaphat gave his sons many gifts of silver, gold and valuable things, and he gave them fortified cities in Judah. But Jehoshaphat gave the kingdom to Jehoram, because he was the first son.

Jehoram King of Judah

4 When Jehoram took control of his father's kingdom, he killed all his brothers with a sword and also killed some of the leaders of Judah. 5 He was 32 years old when he began to rule, and he ruled eight years in Jerusalem. 6 He followed in the ways of the kings of Israel, just as the family of Ahab had done, because he married Ahab's daughter. Jehoram did what the LORD said was wrong. 7 But the LORD would not destroy David's family because of the agreement he had made with David. He had promised that one of David's descendants would always rule.

8 In Jehoram's time, Edom broke away from Judah's rule and chose their own king. 9 So Jehoram went to Edom

---

20:26 Beracah This name means "blessing" or "praise".

with all his commanders and chariots. The Edomites surrounded him and his chariot commanders, but Jehoram got up and attacked the Edomites at night. 10 From then until now the country of Edom has fought against the rule of Judah. At the same time the people of Libnah also broke away from Jehoram because Jehoram left the LORD, the God of his ancestors.

11 Jehoram also built places to worship gods on the hills in Judah. He led the people of Jerusalem to sin, and he led the people of Judah away from the LORD. 12 Then Jehoram received this letter from Elijah the prophet:

This is what the LORD, the God of your ancestor David, says, "Jehoram, you have not lived as your father Jehoshaphat lived and as Asa king of Judah lived. 13 But you have lived as the kings of Israel lived, leading the people of Judah and Jerusalem to sin against God, as Ahab and his family did. You have killed your brothers and they were better than you. 14 So now the LORD is about to punish your people, your children, wives and everything you own. 15 You will have a terrible disease in your intestines that will become worse every day. Finally it will cause your intestines to come out."

16 The LORD caused the Philistines and the Arabs who lived near the Cushites to be angry with Jehoram. 17 So the Philistines and Arabs attacked Judah and carried away all the wealth of Jehoram's palace, as well as his sons and wives. Only Jehoram's youngest son, Ahaziah, was left.

18 After these things happened, the LORD gave Jehoram a disease in his intestines that could not be cured. 19 After he was sick for two years, Jehoram's intestines came out because of the disease, and he died in terrible pain. The people did not make a fire to honour Jehoram as they had done for his ancestors.

20 Jehoram was 32 years old when he became king, and he ruled for eight years in Jerusalem. No one was sad when he died. He was buried in Jerusalem, but not in the graves for the kings.

Ahaziah King of Judah

22 The people of Jerusalem chose Ahaziah, Jehoram's youngest son, to be king in his place. The robbers who had come with the Arabs to attack Jehoram's camp had killed all of Jehoram's older sons. So Ahaziah began to rule Judah. 2 Ahaziah was 22 years old when he became king, and he ruled for a year in Jerusalem. His mother's name was Athaliah, a granddaughter of Omri. 3 Ahaziah followed the ways of Ahab's family, because his mother encouraged him to do wrong. 4 Ahaziah did what the LORD said was wrong, as Ahab's family had done. They gave advice to Ahaziah after his father died, and their bad advice led to his death. 5 Following their advice, Ahaziah went with Joram son of Ahab to Ramoth in Gilead, where they fought against Hazael king of Aram. The Arameans wounded Joram. 6 So Joram returned to Jezreel to heal from the wounds he received at Ramoth when he fought Hazael king of Aram.

Ahaziah son of Jehoram and king of Judah went down to visit Joram son of Ahab at Jezreel because he had been wounded.

7 God caused Ahaziah's death when he went to visit Joram. Ahaziah arrived and went out with Joram to meet Jehu son of Nimshi, whom the LORD had appointed to destroy Ahab's family. 8 While Jehu was punishing Ahab's family, he found the leaders of Judah and the sons of Ahaziah's relatives who served Ahaziah, and Jehu killed them all. 9 Then Jehu looked for Ahaziah. Jehu's men caught him hiding in Samaria, so they brought

> Ahaziah followed the ways of Ahab's family, because his mother encouraged him to do wrong.
> – 2 Chronicles 22:3

him to Jehu. Then they killed and buried him. They said, "Ahaziah is a descendant of Jehoshaphat, and Jehoshaphat obeyed the LORD with all his heart." No one in Ahaziah's family had the power to take control of the kingdom of Judah.

Athaliah and Joash

10 When Ahaziah's mother, Athaliah, saw that her son was dead, she killed all the royal family in Judah. 11 But Jehosheba, King Jehoram's daughter, took Joash, Ahaziah's son. She stole him from among the other sons of the king who were going to be murdered and put him and his nurse in a bedroom. So Jehosheba, who was King Jehoram's daughter and Ahaziah's sister and the wife of Jehoiada the priest, hid Joash so Athaliah could not kill him. 12 He hid with them in the Temple of God for six years. During that time Athaliah ruled the land.

23 In the seventh year Jehoiada decided to do something. He made an agreement with the commanders of the groups of 100 men: Azariah son of Jeroham, Ishmael son of Jehohanan, Azariah son of Obed, Maaseiah son of Adaiah and Elishaphat son of Zicri. 2 They went around in Judah and gathered the Levites from all the towns, and they gathered the leaders of the families of Judah. Then

MY FAULT

Have you ever made any really embarrassing mistakes? Here's someone who's still trying to recover from one of his mistakes. Let's welcome Tom, aged 10, to Connect 2-You.

Tom

The problem is, I did something really stupid at church camp last summer. I don't really want to go into all the details about it, so I'll just say it was bad enough to get me sent home from camp and grounded by my parents for a month. I've never done anything like it before, and I don't even know why I did it. What do you think is wrong with me?

Well, we're all human and we all make mistakes – some just seem worse than others. The good news is that no matter how bad our mistakes are, God will forgive us for them – if we sincerely ask him to. The Bible tells us that nothing, not even the worst mistake in the world, can separate us from God. You can read about that in Romans 8:38-39, p. 1530. For more tips on how to deal with mistakes, check out the Livin' It page on failures and weaknesses, Luke 22:54-62, p. 1414.

Also, look at the men Jesus chose for his disciples. They were always making mistakes – especially Peter, one of Jesus' closest friends. But Peter didn't let his mistakes ruin his life. He learned from them and became a stronger person in the process. With God's help, you can, too!

they went to Jerusalem. 3 All the people together made an agreement with the king in the Temple of God.

Jehoiada said to them, "The king's son will rule, as the LORD promised about David's descendants. 4 Now this is what you must do: you priests and Levites go on duty on the Sabbath. A third of you will guard the doors. 5 A third of you will be at the king's palace, and a third of you will be at the Foundation Gate. All the other people will stay in the courtyards of the Temple of the LORD. 6 Don't let anyone come into the Temple of the LORD except the priests and Levites who serve. They may come because they have been made ready to serve the LORD, but all the others must do the job the LORD has given them. 7 The Levites must stay near the king, each man with his weapon in his hand. If anyone tries to enter the Temple, kill him. Stay close to the king when he goes in and when he goes out."

Joash Becomes King

8 The Levites and all the people of Judah obeyed everything Jehoiada the priest had commanded. He did not excuse anyone from the groups of the priests. So each commander took his men who came on duty on the Sabbath with those who went off duty on the Sabbath. 9 Jehoiada gave the commanders of 100 men the spears and the large and small shields that had belonged to King David and that were kept in the Temple of God. 10 Then Jehoiada told the men where to stand, each man with his weapon in his hand. There were guards from the south side of the Temple to the north side. They stood by the altar and the Temple and around the king.

11 Jehoiada and his sons brought out the king's son and put the crown on him and gave him a copy of the agreement. Then they appointed him king and poured olive oil on him and shouted, "Long live the king!"

12 When Athaliah heard the noise of the people running and praising the king, she went to them at the Temple of the LORD. 13 She looked, and there was the king standing by his pillar at the entrance. The officers and the trumpeters were standing beside him, and all the people of the land were happy and blowing trumpets. The singers were playing musical instruments and leading praises. Then Athaliah tore her clothes and screamed, "Traitors! Traitors!"

14 Jehoiada the priest sent out the commanders of 100 men, who led the army. He said, "Surround her with soldiers and take her out of the Temple area. Kill with a sword anyone who follows her." He had said, "Don't put Athaliah to death in the Temple of the LORD." 15 So they caught her when she came to the entrance of the Horse Gate near the palace. There they put her to death.

16 Then Jehoiada made an agreement with the people and the king that they would be the LORD's special people. 17 All the people went to the temple of Baal and tore it down, smashing the altars and idols. They killed Mattan, the priest of Baal, in front of the altars.

18 Then Jehoiada chose the priests, who were Levites, to be responsible for the Temple of the LORD. David had given them duties in the Temple of the LORD. They were to offer the burnt offerings to the LORD as the Teachings of Moses commanded, and they were to offer them with much joy and singing as David had commanded. 19 Jehoiada put guards at the gates of the Temple of the LORD so that anyone who was unclean in any way could not enter.

20 Jehoiada took with him the commanders of 100 men, the important men, the rulers of the people, and all the people of the land to take the king out of the Temple of the LORD. They went through the Upper Gate into the palace, and then they seated the king on the throne. 21 So all the people of the land were very happy, and Jerusalem had peace, because Athaliah had been put to death with the sword.

Joash Repairs the Temple

24 Joash was seven years old when he became king, and he ruled for 40 years in Jerusalem. His mother's name was Zibiah, and she was from Beersheba.

2 Joash did what the LORD said was right as long as Jehoiada the priest was alive. 3 Jehoiada chose two wives for Joash, and Joash had sons and daughters.

4 Later, Joash decided to repair the Temple of the LORD. 5 He called the priests and the Levites together and said to them, "Go to the towns of Judah and gather the money all the Israelites have to pay every year. Use it to repair the Temple of your God. Do this now." But the Levites did not hurry.

6 So King Joash called for Jehoiada the leading priest and said to him, "Why haven't you made the Levites bring in from Judah and Jerusalem the tax money that Moses, the LORD's servant, and the people of Israel used for the Holy Tent?"

7 In the past the sons of wicked Athaliah had broken into the Temple of God and used its holy things for worshipping the Baal idols.

8 King Joash commanded that a box for contributions be made. They put it outside, at the gate of the Temple of the LORD. 9 Then the Levites made an announcement in Judah and Jerusalem, telling people to bring to the LORD the tax money Moses, the servant of God, had made the Israelites give while they were in the desert. 10 All the officers and people were happy to bring their money, and they put it in the box until the box was full. 11 When the Levites would take the box to the king's officers, they would see that it was full of money. Then the king's royal secretary and the leading priest's officer would come and take out the money and return the box to its place. They did this often and gathered much money. 12 King Joash and Jehoiada gave the money to the people who worked on the Temple of the LORD. And they hired stoneworkers and carpenters to repair the Temple of the LORD. They also hired people to work with iron and bronze to repair the Temple.

13 The people worked hard, and the work to repair the Temple went well. They rebuilt the Temple of God to be as it was before, but even stronger. 14 When the workers finished, they brought the money that was left to King Joash and Jehoiada. They used that money to make utensils for the Temple of the LORD, utensils for the service in the Temple and for the burnt offerings, and bowls and other utensils from gold and silver. Burnt offerings were given every day in the Temple of the LORD while Jehoiada was alive.

15 Jehoiada grew old and lived many years. Then he died when he was 130 years old. 16 Jehoiada was buried in Jerusalem with the kings, because he had done much good in Judah for God and his Temple.

> Joash was seven years old when he became king, and he ruled for 40 years in Jerusalem.
> – 2 Chronicles 24:1

Joash Does Evil

17 After Jehoiada died, the officers of Judah came and bowed down to King Joash, and he listened to them. 18 The king and these leaders stopped worshipping in the Temple of the LORD, the God of their ancestors. Instead, they began to worship the Asherah idols and other idols. Because they did wrong, God was angry with the people of Judah and Jerusalem. 19 Even though the LORD sent prophets to the people to turn them back to him and even though the prophets warned them, they refused to listen.

20 Then the Spirit of God entered Zechariah son of Jehoiada the priest. Zechariah stood before the people and said, "This is what God says: 'Why do you disobey the LORD's commands? You will not be successful. Because you have left the LORD, he has also left you.'"

21 But the king and his officers made plans against Zechariah. At the king's command they threw stones at him in the courtyard of the Temple of the LORD until he died. 22 King Joash did not remember Jehoiada's kindness to him, so Joash killed Zechariah, Jehoiada's son. Before Zechariah died, he said, "May the LORD see what you are doing and punish you."

23 At the end of the year, the Aramean army came against Joash. They attacked Judah and Jerusalem, killed all the leaders of the people, and sent all the valuable things to their king in Damascus. 24 The Aramean army came with only a small group of men, but the LORD handed over to them a very large army from Judah, because the people of Judah had left the LORD, the God of their ancestors. So Joash was punished. 25 When the Arameans left, Joash was badly wounded. His own officers made plans against him because he had killed Zechariah son of Jehoiada the priest. So they killed Joash in his own bed. He died and was buried in Jerusalem but not in the graves of the kings.

26 The officers who made plans against Joash were Jozabad and Jehozabad. Jozabad was the son of Shimeath, a woman from Ammon. And Jehozabad was the son of Shimrith, a woman from Moab. 27 The story of Joash's sons, the great prophecies against him, and how he repaired the Temple of God are written in the book of the kings. Joash's son Amaziah became king in his place.

Amaziah King of Judah

25 Amaziah was 25 years old when he became king, and he ruled for 29 years in Jerusalem. His mother's name was Jehoaddin, and she was from Jerusalem. 2 Amaziah did what the LORD said was right, but he did not really want to obey him. 3 As soon as Amaziah took strong control of the kingdom, he put to death the officers who had murdered his father the king. 4 But Amaziah did not put to death their children. He obeyed what was written in the Book of Moses, where the LORD commanded, "Parents must not be put to death when their children do wrong, and children must not be put to death when their parents do wrong. Each must die for his own sins."[n]

5 Amaziah gathered the people of Judah together. He grouped all the people of Judah and Benjamin by families, and he put commanders over groups of 1,000 and over groups of 100. He counted the men who were 20 years old and older. In all there were 300,000 soldiers ready to fight and skilled with spears and shields. 6 Amaziah also hired 100,000 soldiers from Israel for about 3.5 tonnes of silver. 7 But a man of God came to Amaziah and said, "My king, don't let the army of Israel go with you. The LORD is not with Israel or the people from the tribe of Ephraim. 8 You can make

---

25:4 "Parents . . . sin." See Deuteronomy 24:16.

FAITH CHALLENGE

Here's another for you! Read 25:2 to see how one king responded to God's rules. How do you respond when you're faced with something you really don't want to do – like playing with your baby brother while your mum goes to the shops, or doing your homework before going out with your friends?

TeSTiNG iT

2 Chronicles 25:2
Amaziah did what the LORD said was right, but he did not really want to obey him.

yourself strong for war, but God will defeat you. He has the power to help you or to defeat you."

9 Amaziah said to the man of God, "But what about the 3.5 tonnes of silver I paid to the Israelite army?"

The man of God answered, "The LORD can give you much more than that."

10 So Amaziah sent the Israelite army back home to Ephraim. They were very angry with the people of Judah and went home angry.

11 Then Amaziah became very brave and led his army to the Valley of Salt in the country of Edom. There Amaziah's army killed 10,000 Edomites. 12 The army of Judah also captured 10,000 and took them to the top of a cliff and threw them off so that they split open.

13 At the same time the Israelite troops that Amaziah had not allowed to fight in the war were robbing towns in Judah. From Samaria to Beth Horon they killed 3,000 people and took many valuable things.

14 When Amaziah came home after defeating the Edomites, he brought back the idols they worshipped and started to worship them himself. He bowed down to them and offered sacrifices to them.

15 The LORD was very angry with Amaziah, so he sent a prophet to him who said, "Why have you asked their gods for help? They could not even save their own people from you!"

16 As the prophet spoke, Amaziah said to him, "We never gave you the job of advising the king. Stop, or you will be killed."

The prophet stopped speaking except to say, "I know that God has decided to destroy you because you have done this. You did not listen to my advice."

17 Amaziah king of Judah talked with those who advised him. Then he sent a message to Jehoash son of Jehoahaz, who was the son of Jehu king of Israel. Amaziah said to Jehoash, "Come, let's meet face to face."

18 Then Jehoash king of Israel answered Amaziah king of Judah, "A thornbush in Lebanon sent a message to a cedar tree in Lebanon. It said, 'Let your daughter marry my son.' But then a wild animal from Lebanon came by, walking on and crushing the thornbush. 19 You say to yourself that you have defeated Edom, but you have become proud and you boast. But stay at home! Don't ask for trouble, or you and Judah will be defeated."

20 But Amaziah would not listen. God caused this to happen so that Jehoash would defeat Judah, because Judah asked for help from the gods of Edom. 21 So Jehoash king of Israel went to attack. He and Amaziah king of Judah faced each other in battle at Beth Shemesh in Judah. 22 Israel defeated Judah, and every man of Judah ran away to his home. 23 At Beth Shemesh, Jehoash king of Israel captured Amaziah king of Judah. (Amaziah was the son of Joash, who was the son of Ahaziah.) Then Jehoash brought him to Jerusalem. Jehoash broke down the wall of Jerusalem, from the Gate of Ephraim to the Corner Gate, about 200 metres. 24 He took all the gold and silver and all the utensils from the Temple of God that Obed-Edom had taken care of. He also took the treasures from the palace and some hostages. Then he returned to Samaria.

25 Amaziah son of Joash, the king of Judah, lived fifteen years after the death of Jehoash son of Jehoahaz, the king of Israel. 26 The other things Amaziah did as king, from the beginning to the end, are written in the book of the kings of Judah and Israel. 27 When Amaziah stopped obeying the LORD, the people in Jerusalem made plans against him. So he ran away to the town of Lachish, but they sent men after him to Lachish and killed him. 28 They brought his body back on horses, and he was buried with his ancestors in Jerusalem, the city of David.

Uzziah King of Judah

26 Then all the people of Judah made Uzziah[n] king in place of his father Amaziah. Uzziah was sixteen years old. 2 He rebuilt the town of Elath and made

---

26:1 **Uzziah** Also called Azariah.

it part of Judah again after Amaziah died.

3 Uzziah was sixteen years old when he became king, and he ruled for 52 years in Jerusalem. His mother's name was Jecoliah, and she was from Jerusalem. 4 He did what the LORD said was right, just as his father Amaziah had done. 5 Uzziah obeyed God while Zechariah was alive, because he taught Uzziah how to respect and obey God. And as long as Uzziah obeyed the LORD, God gave him success.

26:4 Obedience What's an example of obedience?

6 Uzziah fought a war against the Philistines. He tore down the walls around their towns of Gath, Jabneh and Ashdod and built new towns near Ashdod and in other places among the Philistines. 7 God helped Uzziah fight the Philistines, the Arabs living in Gur Baal and the Meunites. 8 Also, the Ammonites made the payments Uzziah demanded. He was very powerful, so his name became famous all the way to the border of Egypt.

9 Uzziah built towers in Jerusalem at the Corner Gate, the Valley Gate and where the wall turned, and he made them strong. 10 He also built towers in the desert and dug many wells, because he had many cattle on the western hills and in the plains. He had people who worked his fields and vineyards in the hills and in the fertile lands, because he loved the land.

11 Uzziah had an army of trained soldiers. They were counted and put in groups by Jeiel the royal secretary and Maaseiah the officer. Hananiah, one of the king's commanders, was their leader. 12 There were 2,600 leaders over the soldiers. 13 They were in charge of an army of 307,500 men who fought with great power to help the king against the enemy. 14 Uzziah gave his army shields, spears, helmets, armour, bows and stones for their slings. 15 In Jerusalem Uzziah made devices that were invented by clever men. These devices on the towers and corners of the city walls were used to shoot arrows and large rocks. So Uzziah became famous in faraway places, because he had much help until he became powerful.

16 But when Uzziah became powerful, his pride led to his ruin. He was unfaithful to the LORD his God; he went into the Temple of the LORD to burn incense on the altar for incense. 17 Azariah and 80 other brave priests who served the LORD followed Uzziah into the Temple. 18 They told him he was wrong and said to him, "You don't have the right to burn incense to the LORD. Only the priests, Aaron's descendants, should burn the incense, because they have been made holy. Leave this holy place. You have been unfaithful, and the LORD God will not honour you for this."

19 Uzziah was standing beside the altar for incense in the Temple of the LORD, and in his hand was a pan for burning incense. He was very angry with the priests. As he was standing in front of the priests, a skin disease broke out on his forehead. 20 Azariah, the leading priest, and all the other priests looked at him and saw the skin disease on his forehead. So they hurried him out of the Temple. Uzziah also rushed out, because the LORD was punishing him. 21 So King Uzziah had the skin disease until the day he died. He had to live in a separate house and could not enter the Temple of the LORD. His son Jotham was in charge of the palace, and he governed the people of the land.

22 The other things Uzziah did as king, from beginning to end, were written down by the prophet Isaiah son of Amoz. 23 Uzziah died and was buried near his ancestors in a graveyard that belonged to the kings. This was because people said, "He had a skin disease." And his son Jotham became king in his place.

Jotham King of Judah

27 Jotham was 25 years old when he became king, and he ruled for sixteen years in Jerusalem. His mother's name was Jerusha daughter of Zadok. 2 Jotham did what the LORD said was right, just as his father Uzziah[n] had done. (But Jotham did not enter the Temple of

---

27:2 **Uzziah** Also called Azariah.

DISEASE OR CURSE? 2 Chronicles 26:20-23

Skin diseases are mentioned in many places in the Bible. In Bible times, there was no cure for these skin diseases, so when a person got the disease they had to move away from their home and family. It was like a curse. It was such a big deal that one book of the Bible, Leviticus, gave detailed instructions about how to spot skin diseases and how to keep from getting them. One of the symptoms of a particular skin disease, sometimes called leprosy, was shiny white spots under the skin. (See Leviticus 13:3-4, p. 148.)

The Bible tells about several times when skin diseases were cured miraculously. Both Moses (Exodus 4:6-7, p. 80) and Miriam (Numbers 12:10-15, p. 193) were cured of skin diseases. God used the prophet Elisha to heal Naaman, a Syrian military officer, of his skin disease. (Read 2 Kings 5:1-14, p. 483.) Once, Jesus even healed ten people suffering from skin diseases at the same time. (See Luke 17:11-19, p. 1402.) After a person was cured from skin disease, they had to show themselves to the priests to prove they were healed. (Look at Luke 17:14, p. 1402.)

Today, we know there are many different kinds of skin diseases, and we know what to do to take care of most of them. The skin disease leprosy often described in the Bible is sometimes called Hansen's disease today.

---

the LORD to burn incense as his father had.) But the people continued doing wrong. 3 Jotham rebuilt the Upper Gate of the Temple of the LORD and he added greatly to the wall at Ophel. 4 He also built towns in the hill country of Judah, as well as walled cities and towers in the forests.

5 Jotham also fought the king of the Ammonites and defeated them. So each year for three years they gave Jotham about 3.5 tonnes of silver, about 1,000 tonnes of wheat and about 1,000 tonnes of barley. 6 Jotham became powerful, because he always obeyed the LORD his God.

7 The other things Jotham did while he was king and all his wars are written in the book of the kings of Israel and Judah. 8 Jotham was 25 years old when he became king, and he ruled for sixteen years in Jerusalem. 9 Jotham died and was buried in Jerusalem, the city of David. Then Jotham's son Ahaz became king in his place.

Ahaz King of Judah

28 Ahaz was 20 years old when he became king, and he ruled for sixteen years in Jerusalem. Unlike his ancestor David, he did not do what the LORD said was right. 2 Ahaz did the same things the kings of Israel had done. He made metal idols to worship Baal. 3 He burnt incense in the Valley of Ben Hinnom and made his children pass*n* through the fire. He did the same hateful sins as the nations had done whom the LORD had forced out of the land ahead of the Israelites. 4 Ahaz offered sacrifices and burnt incense at the places where gods were worshipped, and on the hills and under every green tree.

28:3 pass This means that Ahaz sacrificed his children in the fire.

5 So the LORD his God handed over Ahaz to the king of Aram. The Arameans defeated Ahaz and took many people of Judah as prisoners to Damascus.

He also handed over Ahaz to Pekah king of Israel, and Pekah's army killed many soldiers of Ahaz. 6 The army of Pekah son of Remaliah killed 120,000 brave soldiers from Judah in one day. Pekah defeated them because they had left the LORD, the God of their ancestors. 7 Zicri, a warrior from Ephraim, killed King Ahaz's son Maaseiah. He also killed Azrikam, the officer in charge of the palace and Elkanah, who was second in command to the king. 8 The Israelite army captured 200,000 of their own relatives. They took women, sons and daughters and many valuable things from Judah and carried them back to Samaria. 9 But a prophet of the LORD named Oded was there. He met the Israelite army when it returned to Samaria and said to them, "The LORD, the God of your ancestors, handed Judah over to you, because he was angry with those people. But God has seen the cruel way you killed them. 10 Now you plan to make the people of Judah and Jerusalem your slaves, but you also have sinned against the LORD your God. 11 Now listen to me. Send back your brothers and sisters whom you captured, because the LORD is very angry with you."

12 Then some of the leaders in Ephraim—Azariah son of Jehohanan, Berekiah son of Meshillemoth, Jehizkiah son of Shallum and Amasa son of Hadlai—met the Israelite soldiers coming home from war. 13 They warned the soldiers, "Don't bring the prisoners from Judah here. If you do, we will be guilty of sin against the LORD, and that will make our sin and guilt even worse. Our guilt is already so great that he is angry with Israel."

14 So the soldiers left the prisoners and valuable things in front of the officers and people there. 15 The leaders who were named took the prisoners and gave those who were naked the clothes that the Israelite army had taken. They gave the prisoners clothes, sandals, food, drink and medicine. They put the weak prisoners on donkeys and took them back to their families in Jericho, the city of palm trees. Then they returned home to Samaria.

16-17 At that time the Edomites came again and attacked Judah and carried away prisoners. So King Ahaz sent to the king of Assyria for help. 18 The Philistines also robbed the towns in the western hills and in southern Judah. They captured the towns of Beth Shemesh, Aijalon, Gederoth, Soco, Timnah and Gimzo, and the villages around them. Then the Philistines lived in those towns. 19 The LORD brought trouble on Judah because Ahaz their king led the people of Judah to sin, and he was unfaithful to the LORD. 20 Tiglath-Pileser king of Assyria came to Ahaz, but he gave Ahaz trouble instead of help. 21 Ahaz took some valuable things from the Temple of the LORD, from the palace and from the princes, and he gave them to the king of Assyria, but it did not help.

22 During Ahaz's troubles he was even more unfaithful to the LORD. 23 He offered sacrifices to the gods of the people of Damascus, who had defeated him. He thought, "The gods of the kings of Aram helped them. If I offer sacrifices to them, they will help me also." But this brought ruin to Ahaz and all Israel.

24 Ahaz gathered the things from the Temple of God and broke them into pieces. Then he closed the doors of the Temple of the LORD. He made altars and put them on every street corner in Jerusalem. 25 In every town in Judah, Ahaz made places for burning sacrifices to worship other gods. So he made the LORD, the God of his ancestors, very angry.

26 The other things Ahaz did as king, from beginning to end, are written in the book of the kings of Judah and Israel. 27 Ahaz died and was buried in the city of Jerusalem, but not in the graves of the kings of Israel. Ahaz's son Hezekiah became king in his place.

Hezekiah Purifies the Temple

29 Hezekiah was 25 years old when he became king, and he ruled for

29 years in Jerusalem. His mother's name was Abijah daughter of Zechariah. 2 Hezekiah did what the LORD said was right, just as his ancestor David had done.

3 Hezekiah opened the doors of the Temple of the LORD and repaired them in the first month of the first year he was king. 4 Hezekiah brought in the priests and Levites and gathered them in the courtyard on the east side of the Temple. 5 Hezekiah said, "Listen to me, Levites. Make yourselves ready for the LORD's service, and make holy the Temple of the LORD, the God of your ancestors. Remove from the Temple everything that makes it impure. 6 Our ancestors were unfaithful to God and did what the LORD said was wrong. They left the LORD and stopped worshipping at the Temple where he lives. They rejected him. 7 They shut the doors of the porch of the Temple, and they let the fire go out in the lamps. They stopped burning incense and offering burnt offerings in the holy place to the God of Israel. 8 So the LORD became very angry with the people of Judah and Jerusalem, and he punished them. Other people are frightened and shocked by what he did to them. So they insult the people of Judah. You know these things are true. 9 That is why our ancestors were killed in battle and our sons, daughters and wives were taken captive. 10 Now I, Hezekiah, have decided to make an agreement with the LORD, the God of Israel, so he will not be angry with us any more. 11 My sons, don't waste any more time. The LORD chose you to stand before him, to serve him, to be his servants and to burn incense to him."

12 These are the Levites who started to work. From the Kohathite family there were Mahath son of Amasai and Joel son of Azariah. From the Merarite family there were Kish son of Abdi and Azariah son of Jehallelel. From the Gershonite family there were Joah son of Zimmah and Eden son of Joah. 13 From Elizaphan's family there were Shimri and Jeiel. From Asaph's family there were Zechariah and Mattaniah. 14 From Heman's family there were Jehiel and Shimei. From Jeduthun's family there were Shemaiah and Uzziel.

15 These Levites gathered their brothers together and made themselves holy for service in the Temple. Then they went into the Temple of the LORD to purify it. They obeyed the king's command that had come from the LORD. 16 When the priests went into the Temple of the LORD to purify it, they took out all the unclean things they found in the Temple of the LORD and put them in the Temple courtyard. Then the Levites took these things out to the Kidron Valley. 17 Beginning on the first day of the first month, they made the Temple holy for the LORD's service. On the eighth day of the month, they came to the porch of the Temple, and for eight more days they made the Temple of the LORD holy. So they finished on the sixteenth day of the first month.

18 Then they went to King Hezekiah and said, "We have purified the entire Temple of the LORD, the altar for burnt offerings and its utensils, and the table for the holy bread and all its utensils. 19 When Ahaz was king, he was unfaithful to God and removed some things from the Temple. But we have put them back and made them holy for the LORD. They are now in front of the LORD's altar."

20 Early the next morning King Hezekiah gathered the leaders of the city and went up to the Temple of the LORD. 21 They brought seven bulls, seven rams, seven lambs and seven male goats. These animals were an offering to remove the sin of the people and the kingdom of Judah and to make the Temple ready for service to God. King Hezekiah commanded the priests, the descendants of Aaron, to offer these animals on the LORD's altar. 22 So the priests killed the bulls and sprinkled their blood on the

> Now I, Hezekiah, have decided to make an agreement with the LORD.
> – 2 Chronicles 29:10

altar. They killed the rams and sprinkled their blood on the altar. Then they killed the lambs and sprinkled their blood on the altar. 23 Then the priests brought the male goats for the sin offering before the king and the people there. After the king and the people put their hands on the goats, 24 the priests killed them. With the goats' blood they made an offering on the altar to remove the sins of the Israelites so they would belong to God. The king had said that the burnt offering and sin offering should be made for all Israel.

25 King Hezekiah put the Levites in the Temple of the LORD with cymbals, harps and lyres, as David, Gad and Nathan had commanded. (Gad was the king's seer and Nathan was a prophet.) This command came from the LORD through his prophets. 26 So the Levites stood ready with David's instruments of music, and the priests stood ready with their trumpets.

27 Then Hezekiah gave the order to sacrifice the burnt offering on the altar. When the burnt offering began, the singing to the LORD also began. The trumpets were blown and the musical instruments of David king of Israel were played. 28 All the people worshiped, the singers sang and the trumpeters blew their trumpets until the burnt offering was finished.

29 When the sacrifices were completed, King Hezekiah and everyone with him bowed down and worshiped. 30 King Hezekiah and his officers ordered the Levites to praise the LORD, using the words David and Asaph the seer had used. So they praised God with joy and bowed down and worshiped.

31 Then Hezekiah said, "Now that you people of Judah have given yourselves to the LORD, come near to the Temple of the LORD. Bring sacrifices and offerings to show thanks to him." So the people brought sacrifices and thank offerings, and anyone who was willing also brought burnt offerings. 32 For burnt offerings they brought a total of 70 bulls, 100 rams and 200 lambs; all these animals were sacrificed as burnt offerings to the LORD. 33 The holy offerings totalled 600 bulls and 3,000 sheep and goats. 34 There were not enough priests to skin all the animals for the burnt offerings. So their relatives the Levites helped them until the work was finished and other priests could be made holy. The Levites had been more careful to make themselves holy for the LORD's service than the priests. 35 There were many burnt offerings along with the fat of fellowship offerings and drink offerings. So the service in the Temple of the LORD began again. 36 And Hezekiah and the people were very happy that God had made it happen so quickly for his people.

The Passover Celebration

30 King Hezekiah sent messages to all the people of Israel and Judah, and he wrote letters to the people of Ephraim and Manasseh. Hezekiah invited all these people to come to the Temple of the LORD in Jerusalem to celebrate the Passover for the LORD, the God of Israel. 2 King Hezekiah, his officers and all the people in Jerusalem agreed to celebrate the Passover in the second month. 3 They could not celebrate it at the normal time, because not enough priests had made themselves ready to serve the LORD, and the people had not yet gathered in Jerusalem. 4 This plan satisfied King Hezekiah and all the people. 5 So they made an announcement everywhere in Israel, from Beersheba to Dan,[n] telling the people to come to Jerusalem to celebrate the Passover for the LORD, the God of Israel. For a long time most of the people had not celebrated the Passover as the law commanded. 6 At the king's command, the messengers took letters from him and his officers all through Israel and Judah. This is what the letters said:

People of Israel, return to the LORD, the God of Abraham, Isaac

---

30:5 **Beersheba to Dan** Dan was the city farthest north in Israel, and Beersheba was the city farthest south. So this means all the people of Israel.

and Israel. Then God will return to you who are still alive, who have escaped from the kings of Assyria. 7 Don't be like your ancestors or your relatives. They turned against the LORD, the God of their ancestors, so he caused other people to be disgusted with them. You know this is true. 8 Don't be stubborn as your ancestors were, but obey the LORD willingly. Come to the Temple, which he has made holy for ever. Serve the LORD your God so he will not be angry with you. 9 Come back to the LORD. Then the people who captured your relatives and children will be kind to them and will let them return to this land. The LORD your God is kind and merciful. He will not turn away from you if you return to him.

10 The messengers went to every town in Ephraim and Manasseh, and all the way to Zebulun, but the people laughed at them and made fun of them. 11 But some men from Asher, Manasseh and Zebulun were sorry for what they had done and went to Jerusalem. 12 And God united all the people of Judah in obeying King Hezekiah and his officers, because their command had come from the LORD.

13 In the second month a large crowd came together in Jerusalem to celebrate the Feast of Unleavened Bread. 14 The people removed the altars and incense altars to gods in Jerusalem and threw them into the Kidron Valley.

15 They killed the Passover lamb on the fourteenth day of the second month. The priests and the Levites were ashamed, so they made themselves holy and brought burnt offerings into the Temple of the LORD. 16 They took their regular places in the Temple as the Teachings of Moses, the man of God, commanded. The Levites gave the blood of the sacrifices to the priests, who sprinkled it on the altar. 17 Since many people in the crowd had not made themselves holy, the Levites killed the Passover lambs for everyone who was not clean. The Levites made each lamb holy for the LORD. 18-19 Although many people from Ephraim, Manasseh, Issachar and Zebulun had not purified themselves for the feast, they ate the Passover even though it was against the law. So Hezekiah prayed for them, saying, "LORD, you are good. You are the LORD, the God of our ancestors. Please forgive all those who try to obey you even if they did not make themselves clean as the rules of the Temple command." 20 The LORD listened to Hezekiah's prayer, and he healed the people. 21 The Israelites in Jerusalem celebrated the Feast of Unleavened Bread for seven days with great joy to the LORD. The Levites and priests praised the LORD every day with loud music. 22 Hezekiah encouraged all the Levites who showed they understood well how to do their service for the LORD. The people ate the feast for seven days, offered fellowship offerings and praised the LORD, the God of their ancestors.

23 Then all the people agreed to stay seven more days, so they celebrated with joy for seven more days. 24 Hezekiah king of Judah gave 1,000 bulls and 7,000 sheep to the people. The officers gave 1,000 bulls and 10,000 sheep to the people. Many priests made themselves holy. 25 All the people of Judah, the priests, the Levites, those who came from Israel, the foreigners from Israel and the foreigners living in Judah were very happy. 26 There was much joy in Jerusalem, because there had not been a celebration like this since the time of Solomon son of David and king of Israel. 27 The priests and Levites stood up and blessed the people, and God heard them because their prayer reached heaven, his holy home.

> Don't be stubborn as your ancestors were, but obey the LORD willingly.
> – 2 Chronicles 30:8

The Collection for the Priests

31 When the Passover celebration was finished, all the Israelites in Jerusalem went out to the towns of Judah. There they smashed the stone pillars used to worship gods. They cut down the Asherah idols and destroyed the altars and places for worshipping gods in all of Judah, Benjamin, Ephraim and Manasseh. After they had destroyed all of them, the Israelites returned to their own towns and homes.

2 King Hezekiah appointed groups of priests and Levites for their special duties. They were to offer burnt offerings and fellowship offerings, to worship and to give thanks and praise at the gates of the LORD's house. 3 Hezekiah gave some of his own animals for the burnt offerings, which were given every morning and evening on Sabbath days, during New Moons and at other feasts commanded in the LORD's Teachings.

4 Hezekiah commanded the people living in Jerusalem to give the priests and Levites the portion that belonged to them. Then the priests and Levites could give all their time to the LORD's Teachings. 5 As soon as the king's command went out to the Israelites, they gave freely of the first portion of their grain, new wine, oil, honey and everything they grew in their fields. They brought a large amount, one-tenth of everything. 6 The people of Israel and Judah who lived in Judah also brought one-tenth of their cattle and sheep and one-tenth of the holy things that were given to the LORD their God, and they put all of them in piles. 7 The people began the piles in the third month and finished in the seventh month. 8 When Hezekiah and his officers came and saw the piles, they praised the LORD and his people, the people of Israel. 9 Hezekiah asked the priests and Levites about the piles. 10 Azariah, the leading priest from Zadok's family, answered Hezekiah, "Since the people began to bring their offerings to the Temple of the LORD, we have had plenty to eat and plenty left over, because the LORD has blessed his people. So we have all this left over."

11 Then Hezekiah commanded the priests to prepare the storerooms in the Temple of the LORD. So this was done. 12 Then the priests brought in the offerings and the things given to the LORD and a tenth of everything the people had given. Conaniah the Levite was in charge of these things, and his brother Shimei was second to him. 13 Conaniah and his brother Shimei were over these supervisors: Jehiel, Azaziah, Nahath, Asahel, Jerimoth, Jozabad, Eliel, Ismachiah, Mahath and Benaiah. King Hezekiah and Azariah the officer in charge of the Temple of God had chosen them.

14 Kore, son of Imnah the Levite, was in charge of the special gifts the people wanted to give to God. He was responsible for giving out the contributions made to the LORD and the holy gifts. Kore was the guard at the East Gate. 15 Eden, Miniamin, Jeshua, Shemaiah, Amariah and Shecaniah helped Kore in the towns where the priests lived. They gave from what was collected to the other groups of priests, both young and old.

16 From what was collected, these men also gave to the males three years old and older who had their names in the Levite family histories. They were to enter the Temple of the LORD for their daily service, each group having its own responsibilities. 17 The priests were given their part of the collection, by families, as listed in the family histories. The Levites 20 years old and older were given their part of the collection, based on their responsibilities and their groups. 18 The Levites' babies, wives, sons and daughters also got part of the collection. This was done for all the Levites who were listed in the family histories, because they always kept themselves ready to serve the LORD.

19 Some of Aaron's descendants, the priests, lived on the farmlands near the towns or in the towns. Men were chosen by name to give part of the collection to these priests. All the males and those named in the family histories of the

31:4 Giving
How can you help your church?

A SECRET WATER SUPPLY — 2 Chronicles 32

A tunnel built by King Hezekiah runs under the city wall of Jerusalem. One crew of men started digging at the Gihon Spring, outside the city walls. Another crew started digging at the Pool of Siloam, inside the city walls. They dug and dug until they met in the middle of the tunnel. This was a difficult job because the tunnel had to be dug through solid rock.

Can you figure out why King Hezekiah built the tunnel? When an enemy attacked a city like Jerusalem, the army surrounded the city. That meant that no one from inside the city could go outside of the wall without being captured or killed. Once a city started running out of food and water, they *had* to try and sneak out to find some. (Check out 2 Kings 6:25–29, p. 486.) But with King Hezekiah's tunnel, Jerusalem never ran out of water no matter how long an enemy camped around them.

King Hezekiah's tunnel was 530 metres long. At some places it was 20 metres below ground. Today water doesn't run through the tunnel. In fact, these days, tourists can walk through what is left of the tunnel when they visit Jerusalem.

Levites received part of the collection. 20 This is what King Hezekiah did in Judah. He did what was good and right and obedient before the LORD his God. 21 Hezekiah tried to obey God in his service of the Temple of God, and he tried to obey God's teachings and commands. He gave himself fully to his work for God. So he had success.

Assyria Attacks Judah

32 After Hezekiah did all these things to serve the LORD, Sennacherib king of Assyria came and attacked Judah. He and his army surrounded and attacked the fortified cities, hoping to take them for himself. 2 Hezekiah knew that Sennacherib had come to Jerusalem to attack it. 3 So Hezekiah and his officers and army commanders decided to cut off the water from the springs outside the city. So the officers and commanders helped Hezekiah. 4 Many people came and cut off all the springs and the stream that flowed through the land. They said, "The king of Assyria will not find much water when he comes here." 5 Then Hezekiah made Jerusalem stronger. He rebuilt all the broken parts of the wall and put towers on it. He also built another wall outside the first one and strengthened the area that was filled in on the east side of the old part of Jerusalem. He also made many weapons and shields.

6 Hezekiah put army commanders over the people and met with them at the open place near the city gate. Hezekiah encouraged them, saying, 7 "Be strong and brave. Don't be afraid or worried because of the king of Assyria or his large army. There is a greater power with us than with him. 8 He only has men, but we have the LORD our God to help us and to fight our battles." The people were encouraged by the words of Hezekiah king of Judah.

9 After this King Sennacherib of Assyria and all his army surrounded and attacked Lachish. Then he sent his officers to Jerusalem with this message for

King Hezekiah of Judah and all the people of Judah in Jerusalem:

10 Sennacherib king of Assyria says this: "You have nothing to trust in to help you. It is no use for you to stay in Jerusalem under attack. 11 Hezekiah says to you, 'The LORD our God will save us from the king of Assyria,' but he is fooling you. If you stay in Jerusalem, you will die from hunger and thirst. 12 Hezekiah himself removed your LORD's places of worship and altars. He told you people of Judah and Jerusalem that you must worship and burn incense on only one altar.

13 "You know what my ancestors and I have done to all the people in other nations. The gods of those nations could not save their people from my power. 14 My ancestors destroyed those nations; none of their gods could save them from me. So your god cannot save you from my power. 15 Do not let Hezekiah fool you or trick you, and do not believe him. No god of any nation or kingdom has been able to save his people from me or my ancestors. Your god is even less able to save you from me."

16 Sennacherib's officers said worse things against the LORD God and his servant Hezekiah. 17 King Sennacherib also wrote letters insulting the LORD, the God of Israel. They spoke against him, saying, "The gods of the other nations could not save their people from me. In the same way Hezekiah's God won't be able to save his people from me." 18 Then the king's officers shouted in Hebrew, calling out to the people of Jerusalem who were on the city wall. The officers wanted to scare the people away so they could capture Jerusalem. 19 They spoke about the God of Jerusalem as though he were like the gods the people of the world worshipped, which are made by human hands.

20 King Hezekiah and the prophet Isaiah son of Amoz prayed to heaven about this. 21 Then the LORD sent an angel who killed all the soldiers, leaders and officers in the camp of the king of Assyria. So the king went back to his own country in disgrace. When he went into the temple of his god, some of his own sons killed him with a sword.

22 So the LORD saved Hezekiah and the people in Jerusalem from Sennacherib king of Assyria and from all other people. He took care of them on every side. 23 Many people brought gifts for the LORD to Jerusalem, and they also brought valuable gifts to King Hezekiah of Judah. From then on all the nations respected Hezekiah.

Hezekiah Dies

24 At that time Hezekiah became so sick he almost died. When he prayed to the LORD, the LORD spoke to him and gave him a sign." 25 But Hezekiah did not thank God for his kindness, because he was so proud. So the LORD was angry with him and the people of Judah and Jerusalem. 26 But later Hezekiah and the people of Jerusalem were sorry and stopped being proud, so the LORD did not punish them while Hezekiah was alive.

27 Hezekiah had many riches and much honour. He made treasuries for his silver, gold, gems, spices, shields and other valuable things. 28 He built storage buildings for grain, new wine and oil, stalls for all the cattle and pens for the sheep. 29 He also built many towns. He had many flocks and herds, because God had given Hezekiah much wealth.

30 It was Hezekiah who cut off the upper pool of the Gihon spring and made those waters flow straight down to the west side of the older part of Jerusalem. And Hezekiah was successful in everything he did. 31 But once the leaders of Babylon sent messengers to Hezekiah, asking him about a strange sign" that had happened in the land. When they came, God left Hezekiah alone to test

---

32:24, 31 sign See Isaiah 38:1-8. It tells the story about the sign and how the Lord gave Hezekiah fifteen more years to live.

him so he could know everything that was in Hezekiah's heart.ⁿ

32 Hezekiah's love for God and the other things he did as king are written in the vision of the prophet Isaiah son of Amoz. This is in the book of the kings of Judah and Israel. 33 Hezekiah died and was buried on a hill, where the graves of David's ancestors are. All the people of Judah and Jerusalem honoured Hezekiah when he died, and his son Manasseh became king in his place.

Manasseh King of Judah

33 Manasseh was twelve years old when he became king, and he was king for 55 years in Jerusalem. 2 He did what the LORD said was wrong. He did the hateful things the nations had done— the nations that the LORD had forced out of the land ahead of the Israelites. 3 Manasseh's father, Hezekiah, had torn down the places where gods were worshipped, but Manasseh rebuilt them. He also built altars for the Baal gods, and he made Asherah idols and worshipped all the stars of the sky and served them. 4 The LORD had said about the Temple, "I will be worshipped in Jerusalem for ever," but Manasseh built altars in the Temple of the LORD. 5 He built altars to worship the stars in the two courtyards of the Temple of the LORD. 6 He made his children pass through fire in the Valley of Ben Hinnom. He practised magic and witchcraft and told the future by explaining signs and dreams. He got advice from mediums and fortune-tellers. He did many things the LORD said were wrong, which made the LORD angry.

7 Manasseh carved an idol and put it in the Temple of God. God had said to David and his son Solomon about the Temple, "I will be worshipped for ever in this Temple and in Jerusalem, which I have chosen from all the tribes of Israel. 8 I will never again make the Israelites leave the land I gave to their ancestors.

But they must obey everything I have commanded them in all the teachings, rules and commands I gave them through Moses." 9 But Manasseh led the people of Judah and Jerusalem to do wrong. They did more evil than the nations the LORD had destroyed ahead of the Israelites.

10 The LORD spoke to Manasseh and his people, but they did not listen. 11 So the LORD brought the king of Assyria's army commanders to attack Judah. They captured Manasseh, put hooks in him, placed bronze chains on his hands and took him to Babylon. 12 As Manasseh suffered, he begged the LORD his God for help and humbled himself before the God of his ancestors. 13 When Manasseh prayed, the LORD heard him and had pity on him. So the LORD let him return to Jerusalem and to his kingdom. Then Manasseh knew that the LORD is the true God.

14 After that happened, Manasseh rebuilt the outer wall of Jerusalem and made it higher. It was in the valley on the west side of the Gihon spring and went to the entrance of the Fish Gate and around the hill of Ophel. Then he put commanders in all the fortified cities in Judah.

15 Manasseh removed the idols of other nations, including the idol in the Temple of the LORD. He removed all the altars he had built on the Temple hill and in Jerusalem and threw them out of the city. 16 Then he set up the LORD's altar and sacrificed on it fellowship offerings and offerings to show thanks to God. Manasseh commanded all the people of Judah to serve the LORD, the God of Israel. 17 The people continued to offer sacrifices at the places of worship, but their sacrifices were only to the LORD their God. 18 The other things Manasseh did as king, his prayer to his God, and what the seers said to him in the name of the LORD, the God of Israel—all are

> As Manasseh suffered, he begged the LORD his God for help and humbled himself before the God of his ancestors.
> – 2 Chronicles 33:12

32:31 God ... heart See 2 Kings 20:12-19.

recorded in the book of the history of the kings of Israel. 19 Manasseh's prayer and God's pity for him, his sins, his unfaithfulness, the places he built for worshipping gods and the Asherah idols before he humbled himself—all are written in the book of the seers. 20 Manasseh died and was buried in his palace. Then Manasseh's son Amon became king in his place.

Amon King of Judah

21 Amon was 22 years old when he became king, and he was king for two years in Jerusalem. 22 He did what the LORD said was wrong, as his father Manasseh had done. Amon worshipped and offered sacrifices to all the carved idols Manasseh had made. 23 Amon did not humble himself before the LORD as his father Manasseh had done. Instead, Amon sinned even more.

24 King Amon's officers made plans against him and killed him in his palace. 25 Then the people of the land killed all those who had made plans to kill King Amon, and they made his son Josiah king in his place.

Josiah King of Judah

34 Josiah was eight years old when he became king, and he ruled for 31 years in Jerusalem. 2 He did what the LORD said was right. He lived as his ancestor David had lived, and he did not stop doing what was right.

3 In his eighth year as king while he was still young, Josiah began to obey the God of his ancestor David. In his twelfth year as king, Josiah began to remove from Judah and Jerusalem the gods, the places for worshipping gods, the Asherah idols, and the wooden and metal idols. 4 The people tore down the altars for the Baal gods as Josiah directed. Then Josiah cut down the incense altars that were above them. He broke up the Asherah idols and the wooden and metal idols and beat them into powder. Then he sprinkled the powder on the graves of the people who had offered sacrifices to these gods. 5 He burned the bones of their priests on their own altars. So Josiah removed idol worship from Judah and Jerusalem, 6 and from the towns in the areas of Manasseh, Ephraim and Simeon all the way to Naphtali, and in the ruins near these towns. 7 Josiah broke down the altars and Asherah idols and beat the idols into powder. He cut down all the incense altars in all of Israel. Then he went back to Jerusalem.

8 In Josiah's eighteenth year as king, he made Judah and the Temple pure again. He sent Shaphan son of Azaliah, Maaseiah the city leader and Joah son of Joahaz the recorder to repair the Temple of the LORD, the God of Josiah. 9 These men went to Hilkiah the high priest and gave him the money the Levite gatekeepers had gathered from the people of Manasseh, Ephraim and all the Israelites who were left alive, and also from all the people of Judah, Benjamin and Jerusalem. This is the money they had brought into the Temple of God. 10 Then the Levites gave it to the supervisors of the work on the Temple of the LORD, and they paid the workers who rebuilt and repaired the Temple. 11 They gave money to carpenters and builders to buy cut stone and wood. The wood was used to rebuild the buildings and to make beams for them, because the kings of Judah had let the buildings fall into ruin. 12 The men did their work well. Their supervisors were Jahath and Obadiah, who were Levites from the family of Merari, and Zechariah and Meshullam, who were from the family of Kohath. These Levites were all skilled musicians. 13 They were also in charge of the workers who carried loads and all the other workers. Some Levites worked as secretaries, officers and gatekeepers.

The Book of the Teachings is Found

14 The Levites brought out the money that was in the Temple of the LORD. As they were doing this, Hilkiah the priest found the Book of the LORD's Teachings that had been given through Moses. 15 Hilkiah said to Shaphan the royal secretary, "I've found the Book

2 Chronicles 34:28

FAITH links

A LOOK FOR THE BOOK
2 CHRONICLES 34:14-18

Imagine living in a world where there was only one copy of the Bible – and only part of one at that. Now imagine what would happen if that copy became lost. In King Josiah's day, the book of the law was lost. A priest, Hilkiah, discovered it buried in the Temple. When King Josiah heard that the book had been found, he wanted to read it to find out what God wanted his people to do.

Making a habit of reading the Bible can help you remember what God wants you to do. So don't bury your Bible somewhere under your bed. Be a discoverer of the hidden treasures inside it.

Learning to Listen, 1 Samuel 3, p. 358

Your Stats, 1 Kings 15; 16, p. 460

The Best Advice, Zechariah 10:2, p. 1261

Believe It or Not, Luke 1:20, 38, p. 1366

Pay Attention! Hebrews 2:1, p. 1668

You're a Fake! 2 Peter 2:1, p. 1709

---

of the Teachings in the Temple of the LORD!" Then he gave it to Shaphan.

16 Shaphan took the book to the king and reported to Josiah, "Your officers are doing everything you told them to do. 17 They have paid out the money that was in the Temple of the LORD and have given it to the supervisors and the workers." 18 Then Shaphan the royal secretary told the king, "Hilkiah the priest has given me a book." And Shaphan read from the book to the king.

19 When the king heard the words of the Teachings, he tore his clothes to show how upset he was. 20 He gave orders to Hilkiah, Ahikam son of Shaphan, Acbor son of Micaiah, Shaphan the royal secretary and Asaiah, the king's servant. These were the orders: 21 "Go and ask the LORD about the words in the book that was found. Ask for me and for the people who are left alive in Israel and Judah. The LORD is very angry with us, because our ancestors did not obey the LORD's word; they did not do everything this book says to do."

22 So Hilkiah and those the king sent with him went to talk to Huldah the prophetess. She was the wife of Shallum son of Tikvah, the son of Harhas, who took care of the king's clothes. Huldah lived in Jerusalem, in the new area of the city.

23 She said to them, "This is what the LORD, the God of Israel, says: Tell the man who sent you to me, 24 'This is what the LORD says: I will bring trouble to this place and to the people living here. I will bring all the curses that are written in the book that was read to the king of Judah. 25 The people of Judah have left me and have burned incense to other gods. They have made me angry by all the evil things they have made. So I will punish them in my anger, which will not be put out.' 26 Tell the king of Judah, who sent you to ask the LORD, 'This is what the LORD, the God of Israel, says about the words you heard: 27 When you heard my words against this place and its people, you became sorry for what you had done and you upset yourself before me. You tore your clothes to show how upset you were, and you cried in my presence. This is why I have heard you, says the LORD. 28 So I will let you die and be buried in peace. You won't see all the trouble I will bring to this place and the people living here.'"

So they took her message back to the king.

29 Then the king gathered all the elders of Judah and Jerusalem together. 30 He went up to the Temple of the LORD, and all the people from Judah and from Jerusalem went with him. The priests, the Levites and all the people—from the most important to the least important—went with him. He read to them all the words in the Book of the Agreement that was found in the Temple of the LORD. 31 The king stood by his pillar and made an agreement in the presence of the LORD to follow the LORD and obey his commands, rules and laws with his whole being and to obey the words of the agreement written in this book. 32 Then Josiah made all the people in Jerusalem and Benjamin promise to accept the agreement. So the people of Jerusalem obeyed the agreement of God, the God of their ancestors.

33 And Josiah threw out the hateful idols from all the land that belonged to the Israelites. He led everyone in Israel to serve the LORD their God. While Josiah lived, the people obeyed the LORD, the God of their ancestors.

email FROM GOD
34:31 Bible
How hard should you try to obey the Bible?

Josiah Celebrates the Passover

35 King Josiah celebrated the Passover to the LORD in Jerusalem. The Passover lamb was killed on the fourteenth day of the first month. 2 Josiah chose the priests to do their duties, and he encouraged them as they served in the Temple of the LORD. 3 The Levites taught the Israelites and were made holy for service to the LORD. Josiah said to them, "Put the Holy Ark in the Temple that David's son Solomon, the king of Israel, built. Do not carry it from place to place on your shoulders any more. Now serve the LORD your God and his people Israel. 4 Prepare yourselves by your family groups for service, and do the jobs that King David and his son Solomon gave you to do.

5 "Stand in the holy place with a group of the Levites for each family group of the people. 6 Kill the Passover lambs, and make yourselves holy to the LORD. Prepare the lambs for your relatives, the people of Israel, as the LORD through Moses commanded us to do."

7 Josiah gave the Israelites 30,000 sheep and goats to kill for the Passover sacrifices, and he gave them 3,000 cattle. They were all his own animals.

8 Josiah's officers also gave willingly to the people, the priests and the Levites. Hilkiah, Zechariah and Jehiel, the officers in charge of the Temple, gave the priests 2,600 lambs and goats and 300 cattle for Passover sacrifices. 9 Conaniah, his brothers Shemaiah and Nethanel, and Hashabiah, Jeiel and Jozabad gave the Levites 5,000 sheep and goats and 500 cattle for Passover sacrifices. These men were leaders of the Levites.

10 When everything was ready for the Passover service, the priests and Levites went to their places, as the king had commanded. 11 The Passover lambs were killed. Then the Levites skinned the animals and gave the blood to the priests, who sprinkled it on the altar. 12 Then they gave the animals for the burnt offerings to the different family groups so the burnt offerings could be offered to the LORD as was written in the book of Moses. They also did this with the cattle. 13 The Levites roasted the Passover sacrifices over the fire as they were commanded, and they boiled the holy offerings in pots, kettles and pans. Then they quickly gave the meat to the people. 14 After this was finished, the Levites prepared meat for themselves and for the priests, the descendants of Aaron. The priests worked until night, offering the burnt offerings and burning the fat of the sacrifices.

15 The Levite singers from Asaph's family stood in the places chosen for them by King David, Asaph, Heman and Jeduthun, the king's seer. The gatekeepers at each gate did not have to leave their places, because their fellow Levites had prepared everything for them for the Passover.

16 So everything was done that day for the worship of the LORD, as King

Josiah commanded. The Passover was celebrated, and the burnt offerings were offered on the LORD's altar. 17 The Israelites who were there celebrated the Passover and the Feast of Unleavened Bread for seven days. 18 The Passover had not been celebrated like this in Israel since the prophet Samuel was alive. None of the kings of Israel had ever celebrated a Passover as did King Josiah, the priests, the Levites, the people of Judah and Israel who were there, and the people of Jerusalem. 19 This Passover was celebrated in the eighteenth year Josiah was king.

The Death of Josiah

20 After Josiah did all this for the Temple, Neco king of Egypt led an army to attack Carchemish, a town on the Euphrates River. And Josiah marched out to fight against Neco. 21 But Neco sent messengers to Josiah, saying, "King Josiah, there should not be war between us. I did not come to fight you, but my enemies. God told me to hurry and he is on my side. So don't fight God, or he will destroy you."

22 But Josiah did not go away. He wore different clothes so no one would know who he was. Refusing to listen to what Neco said at God's command, Josiah went to fight on the plain of Megiddo. 23 In the battle King Josiah was shot by archers. He told his servants, "Take me away because I am badly wounded." 24 So they took him out of his chariot and put him in another chariot and carried him to Jerusalem. There he died and was buried in the graves where his ancestors were buried. All the people of Judah and Jerusalem were very sad because he was dead.

25 Jeremiah wrote some sad songs about Josiah. Even to this day all the men and women singers remember and honour Josiah with these songs. It became a custom in Israel to sing these songs that are written in the collection of sad songs.

> The Passover had not been celebrated like this in Israel since the prophet Samuel was alive.
> – 2 Chronicles 35:18

26-27 The other things Josiah did as king, from beginning to end, are written in the book of the kings of Israel and Judah. It tells how he loved what was written in the LORD's teachings.

Jehoahaz King of Judah

36 The people of Judah chose Josiah's son Jehoahaz and made him king in Jerusalem in his father's place.

2 Jehoahaz was 23 years old when he became king, and he was king in Jerusalem for three months. 3 Then King Neco of Egypt removed Jehoahaz from being king in Jerusalem. Neco made the people of Judah pay about 3.5 tonnes of silver and about 35 kilogrammes of gold. 4 The king of Egypt made Jehoahaz's brother Eliakim the king of Judah and Jerusalem and changed his name to Jehoiakim. But Neco took his brother Jehoahaz to Egypt.

Jehoiakim King of Judah

5 Jehoiakim was 25 years old when he became king, and he was king in Jerusalem for eleven years. He did what the LORD his God said was wrong. 6 King Nebuchadnezzar of Babylon attacked Judah, captured Jehoiakim, put bronze chains on him and took him to Babylon. 7 Nebuchadnezzar removed some of the things from the Temple of the LORD, took them to Babylon and put them in his own palace.

8 The other things Jehoiakim did as king, the hateful things he did and everything he was guilty of doing, are written in the book of the kings of Israel and Judah. And Jehoiakim's son Jehoiachin became king in his place.

Jehoiachin King of Judah

9 Jehoiachin was eighteen years old when he became king of Judah, and he was king in Jerusalem for three months and ten days. He did what the LORD said was wrong. 10 In the spring King

Nebuchadnezzar sent for Jehoiachin and brought him and some valuable treasures from the Temple of the LORD to Babylon. Then Nebuchadnezzar made Jehoiachin's uncle Zedekiah the king of Judah and Jerusalem.

Zedekiah King of Judah

11 Zedekiah was 21 years old when he became king of Judah, and he was king in Jerusalem for eleven years. 12 Zedekiah did what the LORD his God said was wrong. The prophet Jeremiah spoke messages from the LORD, but Zedekiah did not obey. 13 Zedekiah turned against King Nebuchadnezzar, who had forced him to swear in God's name to be loyal to him. But Zedekiah became stubborn and refused to obey the LORD, the God of Israel. 14 Also, all the leaders of the priests and the people of Judah became more wicked, following the evil example of the other nations. The LORD had made the Temple in Jerusalem holy, but the leaders made it unholy.

The Fall of Jerusalem

15 The LORD, the God of their ancestors, sent prophets again and again to warn his people, because he had pity on them and on his Temple. 16 But they made fun of God's prophets and hated God's messages. They refused to listen to the prophets until, finally, the LORD became so angry with his people that he could not be stopped. 17 So God brought the king of Babylon to attack them. The king killed the young men even when they were in the Temple. He had no mercy on the young men or women, the old men or those who were sick. God handed all of them over to Nebuchadnezzar. 18 Nebuchadnezzar carried away to Babylon all the things from the Temple of God, both large and small, and all the treasures from the Temple of the LORD and from the king and his officers. 19 Nebuchadnezzar and his army set fire to God's Temple and broke down Jerusalem's wall and burned all the palaces. They took or destroyed every valuable thing in Jerusalem.

20 Nebuchadnezzar took captive to Babylon the people who were left alive,

---

FAITH links

THIS HURTS ME MORE?
2 CHRONICLES 36:17-22

"This hurts me more than it hurts you." Ever hear your mum or dad say that after punishing you for breaking a rule? When a rule is broken, a punishment typically follows. God had warned his people of the consequences for their disobedience. The Israelites were not obedient to him, so God allowed an enemy army to destroy the Temple and take the Israelites to another land.

God established his rules to show his people that he knew what was best for them. He never enjoyed seeing his people suffer the consequences of their behaviour. Your parents don't like to see you suffer either. So, why make them, God, or yourself miserable? You know what you have to do. Do it!

Fatherly Advice, Exodus 18, p. 99

Above the Law, 1 Kings 21, p. 470

If You Want My Advice . . . Proverbs 13:1, p. 843

Sow It and Reap, Lamentations 1:18, p. 1075

A Reminder to Do What Is Right and True, Zechariah 7:8–10, p. 1257

A Change of Heart, Matthew 3:1–12, p. 1277

and he forced them to be slaves for him and his descendants. They remained there as slaves until the Persian kingdom defeated Babylon. 21 And so what the LORD had told Israel through the prophet Jeremiah happened: the country was an empty wasteland for 70 years to make up for the years of Sabbath rest[n] that the people had not kept.

22 In the first year Cyrus was king of Persia, the LORD had Cyrus send an announcement to his whole kingdom. This happened so the LORD's message spoken by Jeremiah would come true. He wrote:

23 This is what Cyrus king of Persia says:

The LORD, the God of heaven, has given me all the kingdoms of the earth, and he has appointed me to build a Temple for him at Jerusalem in Judah. Now may the LORD your God be with all of you who are his people. You are free to go to Jerusalem.

36:21 Sabbath rest The Law said that every seventh year the land was not to be farmed. See Leviticus 25:1-7.

Ezra

GOING HOME

Hi! My name is Ezra and I am a teacher of God's law. Imagine returning "home" to a place you have never been. Think about leaving your house, your friends, your school and starting again in the land where your grandparents once lived. Many years ago God's people were conquered by their enemies and forced to live in foreign lands as punishment for their disobedience. As I wrote this book, the long time of exile was over, and the people were allowed to return to Israel. Download Ezra 1:5–11 to find out what treasure they brought with them.

I wrote this book to remind people of God's faithfulness to them. The people were discouraged when their enemies prevented them from rebuilding the Temple of the Lord. To our surprise, the new king of Persia ordered the Temple to be rebuilt at government expense. He even asked us to pray for his family. When the Temple was finished, I urged the people to confess their sins and ask God to forgive them.

JESUS WATCH

When Judah was conquered by Babylon, all of God's people were forced to leave the land that God had given them. The Temple was destroyed and the people had no central place of worship. While they were held captive in Babylon, God sent prophets to assure the people that he loved them and that he would bring them back to their homeland. In Ezra we see the first people return to rebuild their nation. God promised that a Messiah, a Son of David, would come to save his people and rule for ever. The ancestors of Jesus came back to the land God had promised them, so Jesus would be born in the land where David ruled, not in Babylon. Zerubbabel, one of the men who rebuilt the Temple, was an ancestor of Jesus. (Surf over to Matthew 1, p. 1274, to see Zerubbabel's name listed in Jesus' family history.)

DON'T MISS THESE EXCITING STORIES:
Cyrus sends the captives home, Ezra 1
Letters from enemies, Ezra 4
The Temple is completed, Ezra 6:13–18
Why Ezra pulled his hair out, Ezra 9

FAITH links
- Operation Co-operation, Ezra 1:5
- Gratitude Attitude, Ezra 3
- Wronged for What's Right, Ezra 4:4–5
- Building Tools, Ezra 6:15
- Teaching Others, Ezra 7:8–10

Cyrus Helps the Captives Return

1 In the first year Cyrus was king of Persia, the LORD caused Cyrus to send an announcement to his whole kingdom and to put it in writing. This happened so the LORD's message spoken by Jeremiah would come true. He wrote:

2 This is what Cyrus king of Persia says:

The LORD, the God of heaven, has given all the kingdoms of the earth to me, and he has appointed me to build a Temple for him at Jerusalem in Judah. 3 May God be with all of you who are his people. You are free to go to Jerusalem in Judah and build the Temple of the LORD, the God of Israel, who is in Jerusalem. 4 Those who stay behind, wherever they live, should support those who want to go. Give them silver and gold, supplies and cattle, and special gifts for the Temple of God in Jerusalem.

5 Then the family leaders of Judah and Benjamin and the priests and Levites got ready to go to Jerusalem—everyone God had caused to want to go to Jerusalem to build the Temple of the LORD. 6 All their neighbours helped them, giving them things made of silver and gold, along with supplies, cattle, valuable gifts and special gifts for the Temple. 7 Also, King Cyrus brought out the bowls and pans that belonged in the Temple of the LORD, which Nebuchadnezzar had taken from Jerusalem and put in the temple of his own god. 8 Cyrus king of Persia had Mithredath the treasurer bring them and count them out for Sheshbazzar, the prince of Judah.

9 He listed 30 gold dishes, 1,000 silver dishes, 29 pans, 10 30 gold bowls, 410 matching silver bowls and 1,000 other pieces.

11 There was a total of 5,400 pieces of gold and silver. Sheshbazzar brought all these things along when the captives went from Babylon to Jerusalem.

OPERATION CO-OPERATION
EZRA 1:5

When you have a big project to do, isn't it great to have help? In Ezra's day, the Israelites had lived in Babylon for a long while. They wanted to return to their own land to rebuild the Temple. The plan was to work together to get things done. Some would do the actual work of rebuilding. Others gave valuable items to pay for the work.

Learning to co-operate with others is one way to serve God. No one can do everything by themselves. We all need to work together.

Connect here for tips on working with others:

A Use for Your Abilities, Genesis 41, p. 59

Building Together, Nehemiah 3, p. 627

A Half-hearted Offering, Malachi 1:6–14, p. 1268

With All Your Heart, Colossians 3:23, p. 1626

From Useless to Useful, Philemon 11, p. 1663

Come On In! 1 Peter 4:9–10, p. 1705

The Captives who Returned

2 These are the people of the area who returned from captivity, whom Nebuchadnezzar king of Babylon had taken

away to Babylon. They returned to Jerusalem and Judah, each going back to his own town. **2** These people returned with Zerubbabel, Jeshua, Nehemiah, Seraiah, Reelaiah, Mordecai, Bilshan, Mispar, Bigvai, Rehum and Baanah.

These are the people from Israel: **3** the descendants of Parosh—2,172; **4** the descendants of Shephatiah—372; **5** the descendants of Arah—775; **6** the descendants of Pahath-Moab (through the family of Jeshua and Joab)—2,812; **7** the descendants of Elam—1,254; **8** the descendants of Zattu—945; **9** the descendants of Zaccai—760; **10** the descendants of Bani—642; **11** the descendants of Bebai—623; **12** the descendants of Azgad—1,222; **13** the descendants of Adonikam—666; **14** the descendants of Bigvai—2,056; **15** the descendants of Adin—454; **16** the descendants of Ater (through the family of Hezekiah)—98; **17** the descendants of Bezai—323; **18** the descendants of Jorah—112; **19** the descendants of Hashum—223; **20** the descendants of Gibbar—95.

21 These are the people from the towns: of Bethlehem—123; **22** of Netophah—56; **23** of Anathoth—128; **24** of Azmaveth—42; **25** of Kiriath Jearim, Kephirah and Beeroth—743; **26** of Ramah and Geba—621; **27** of Michmash—122; **28** of Bethel and Ai—223; **29** of Nebo—52; **30** of Magbish—156; **31** of the other town of Elam—1,254; **32** of Harim—320; **33** of Lod, Hadid and Ono—725; **34** of Jericho—345; **35** of Senaah—3,630.

36 These are the priests: the descendants of Jedaiah (through the family of Jeshua)—973; **37** the descendants of Immer—1,052; **38** the descendants of Pashhur—1,247; **39** the descendants of Harim—1,017.

40 These are the Levites: the descendants of Jeshua and Kadmiel (through the family of Hodaviah)—74.

41 These are the singers: the descendants of Asaph—128.

42 These are the gatekeepers of the Temple: the descendants of Shallum, Ater, Talmon, Akkub, Hatita and Shobai—139.

43 These are the Temple servants: the descendants of Ziha, Hasupha, Tabbaoth, **44** Keros, Siaha, Padon, **45** Lebanah, Hagabah, Akkub, **46** Hagab, Shalmai, Hanan, **47** Giddel, Gahar, Reaiah, **48** Rezin, Nekoda, Gazzam, **49** Uzza, Paseah, Besai, **50** Asnah, Meunim, Nephussim, **51** Bakbuk, Hakupha, Harhur, **52** Bazluth, Mehida, Harsha, **53** Barkos, Sisera, Temah, **54** Neziah and Hatipha.

55 These are the descendants of the servants of Solomon: the descendants of Sotai, Hassophereth, Peruda, **56** Jaala, Darkon, Giddel, **57** Shephatiah, Hattil, Pokereth-Hazzebaim and Ami.

58 The Temple servants and the descendants of the servants of Solomon numbered 392.

59 Some people came to Jerusalem from the towns of Tel Melah, Tel Harsha, Kerub, Addon and Immer, but they could not prove that their ancestors came from Israel. **60** They were the descendants of Delaiah, Tobiah and Nekoda—652.

61 Also these priests: the descendants of Hobaiah, Hakkoz and Barzillai, who had married a daughter of Barzillai from Gilead and was called by her family name. **62** These people searched for their family records but could not find them. So they could not be priests, because they were thought to be unclean. **63** The governor ordered them not to eat any of the food offered to God until a priest had settled this matter by using the Urim and Thummim.

64 The total number of those who returned was 42,360. **65** This is not counting their 7,337 male and female servants and the 200 male and female singers they had with them. **66** They had 736 horses, 245 mules, **67** 435 camels and 6,720 donkeys.

68 When they arrived at the Temple of the LORD in Jerusalem, some of the leaders of families gave offerings to rebuild the Temple of God on the same site as

> Some of the leaders of families gave offerings to rebuild the Temple of God on the same site as before.
> — Ezra 2:68

before. 69 They gave as much as they could to the treasury to rebuild the Temple—about 500 kilogrammes of gold, about 2,800 kilogrammes of silver and 100 pieces of clothing for the priests. 70 All the Israelites settled in their home towns. The priests, Levites, singers, gatekeepers and Temple servants, along with some of the other people, settled in their own towns as well.

Rebuilding the Altar

3 In the seventh month, after the Israelites were settled in their home towns, they met together in Jerusalem. 2 Then Jeshua son of Jozadak and his fellow priests joined Zerubbabel son of Shealtiel and began to build the altar of the God of Israel where they could offer burnt offerings, just as it is written in the Teachings of Moses, the man of God. 3 Even though they were afraid of the people living around them, they built the altar where it had been before. And they offered burnt offerings on it to the LORD morning and evening. 4 Then, to obey what was written, they celebrated the Feast of Shelters. They offered the right number of sacrifices for each day of the festival. 5 After the Feast of Shelters, they had regular sacrifices every day, as well as sacrifices for the New Moon and all the festivals commanded by the LORD. Also there were special offerings brought as gifts to the LORD. 6 On the first day of the seventh month they began to bring burnt offerings to the LORD, but the foundation of the LORD's Temple had not yet been laid.

Rebuilding the Temple

7 Then they gave money to the bricklayers and carpenters. They also gave food, wine and oil to the cities of Sidon and Tyre so they would float cedar logs from Lebanon to the seacoast town of Joppa. Cyrus king of Persia had given permission for this.

8 In the second month of the second year after their arrival at the Temple of God in Jerusalem, Zerubbabel son of Shealtiel, Jeshua son of Jozadak, their fellow priests and Levites, and all who

---

FAITH links

GRATITUDE ATTITUDE
EZRA 3

What is the most exciting project you've ever worked on? This could be something you've wanted to do for a long time. The Israelites were happy about rebuilding the Temple. For years they had lived in a foreign land. Now that they were back home, they could repair the damage done to God's house. They gave thanks to God at every step of the building process to show how happy they were to work.

Next time you're working on an exciting project, think about giving God thanks each step of the way. It helps to build an attitude of gratitude that will make the work even more fun!

How's your gratitude attitude? Link here to find out:

My Worship Place, Genesis 35:1–14, p. 49

The Name of the Lord, Exodus 33:19–23; 34:5–8, p. 120

Everyone Can Help, Numbers 4, p. 181

You're Invited! Psalm 100, p. 784

Small Beginnings, Zechariah 4:10, p. 1255

Glad to Help! Romans 15:17–20, p. 1541

had returned from captivity to Jerusalem began to work. They chose Levites 20 years old and older to be in charge of the building of the Temple of the LORD. 9 These men were in charge of the work of building the Temple of God: Jeshua and his sons and brothers; Kadmiel and his sons who were the descendants of Hodaviah; and the sons of Henadad and their sons and brothers. They were all Levites.

10 The builders finished laying the foundation of the Temple of the LORD. Then the priests, dressed in their robes, stood with their trumpets, and the Levites, the sons of Asaph, stood with their cymbals. They all took their places and praised the LORD just as David king of Israel had said to do. 11 With praise and thanksgiving, they sang to the LORD:

"He is good;
his love for Israel continues
for ever."

And then all the people shouted loudly, "Praise the LORD! The foundation of his Temple has been laid." 12 But many of the older priests, Levites and family leaders who had seen the first Temple cried when they saw the foundation of this Temple. Most of the other people were shouting with joy. 13 The people made so much noise it could be heard far away, and no one could tell the difference between the joyful shouting and the sad crying.

3:11
Love
The Lord's love continues for ever.

Enemies of the Rebuilding

4 When the enemies of the people of Judah and Benjamin heard that the returned captives were building a Temple for the LORD, the God of Israel, 2 they came to Zerubbabel and the leaders of the families. The enemies said, "Let us help you build, because we are like you and want to worship your God. We have been offering sacrifices to him since the time of Esarhaddon king of Assyria, who brought us here."

3 But Zerubbabel, Jeshua and the leaders of Israel answered, "You will not help us build a Temple to our God. We will build it ourselves for the LORD, the God of Israel, as King Cyrus, the king of Persia, commanded us to do."

FAITH LINKS

WRONGED FOR WHAT'S RIGHT
EZRA 4:4-5

Ever have someone try to stop you from doing something you knew was right? The Israelites faced trouble for rebuilding the Temple. A group of people who lived in the area tried to stop the Israelites from working. As a Christian, you can expect trouble whenever you do anything for the Lord. Jesus told his followers that trouble would find them. Why? Christians have an enemy – Satan. He doesn't want to see the good results God's work brings about. But Jesus said, "Be brave! I have defeated the world" (John 16:33). That means your enemy has already lost. So be brave!

Family Feud, Genesis 27, p. 37

What Will You Risk? Joshua 2, p. 278

A Right to Get Even? 1 Samuel 24, p. 388

Quick to Forgive? Mark 11:25, p. 1349

A Peacemaker or a Peacebreaker? James 3:18, p. 1693

Who's on First? 3 John 9–10, p. 1723

4 Then the people around them tried to discourage the people of Judah by making them afraid to build. 5 Their enemies hired others to delay the building plans during the time Cyrus was king of Persia. And it continued to the time Darius was king of Persia.

More Problems for the Builders

6 When Xerxes first became king, those enemies wrote a letter against the people of Judah and Jerusalem.

7 When Artaxerxes became king of Persia, Bishlam, Mithredath, Tabeel and those with them wrote a letter to Artaxerxes. It was written in the Aramaic language and translated.

8 Rehum the governor and Shimshai the governor's secretary wrote a letter against Jerusalem to Artaxerxes the king. It said:

9 This letter is from Rehum the governor, Shimshai the secretary and their fellow workers—the judges and important officers over the men who came from Tripolis, Persia, Erech and Babylon, the Elamite people of Susa, 10 and those whom the great and honourable Ashurbanipal forced out of their countries and settled in the city of Samaria and in other places of the west of the Euphrates River.

11 (This is a copy of the letter they sent to Artaxerxes.)

To King Artaxerxes.

From your servants who live west of the Euphrates River.

12 King Artaxerxes, you should know that the Jewish people who came to us from you have gone to Jerusalem to rebuild that evil city that refuses to obey. They are fixing the walls and repairing the foundations of the buildings.

13 Now, King Artaxerxes, you should know that if Jerusalem is built and its walls are fixed, Jerusalem will not pay taxes of any kind. Then the amount of money your government collects will be less. 14 Since we must be loyal to the government, we don't want to see the king dishonoured. So we are writing to let the king know. 15 We suggest you search the records of the kings who ruled before you. You will find out that the city of Jerusalem refuses to obey and makes trouble for kings and areas controlled by Persia. Since long ago it has been a place where disobedience has started. That is why it was destroyed. 16 We want you to know, King Artaxerxes, that if this city is rebuilt and its walls fixed, you will be left with nothing west of the Euphrates River.

17 King Artaxerxes sent this answer:

To Rehum the governor and Shimshai the secretary, to all their fellow workers living in Samaria, and to those in other places west of the Euphrates River.

Greetings.

18 The letter you sent to us has been translated and read to me. 19 I ordered the records to be searched, and it was done. We found that Jerusalem has a history of disobedience to kings and has been a place of problems and trouble. 20 Jerusalem has had powerful kings who have ruled over the whole area west of the Euphrates River, and taxes of all kinds have been paid to them. 21 Now, give an order for those men to stop work. The city of Jerusalem will not be rebuilt until I say so. 22 Make sure you do this, because if they continue, it will hurt the government.

23 A copy of the letter that King Artaxerxes sent was read to Rehum and Shimshai the secretary and the others. Then they quickly went to the Jewish people in Jerusalem and forced them to stop building.

24 So the work on the Temple of God in Jerusalem stopped until the second year Darius was king of Persia.

Tattenai's Letter to Darius

5 The prophets Haggai and Zechariah, a descendant of Iddo, prophesied to the Jewish people in Judah and Jerusalem in the name of the God of Israel, who was over them. 2 Then Zerubbabel son of Shealtiel and Jeshua son of Jozadak started working again to rebuild the Temple of God in Jerusalem. And the prophets of God were there, helping them.

3 At that time Tattenai, who was the governor west of the Euphrates River, and Shethar-Bozenai and their fellow workers went to the Jewish people and asked, "Who gave you permission to rebuild this Temple and fix these walls?" 4 They also asked, "What are the names of the men working on this building?" 5 But their God was watching over the elders of the Jewish people. The builders were not stopped until a report could go to King Darius and his written answer could be received.

6 This is a copy of the letter that was sent to King Darius by Tattenai, who was the governor of west of the Euphrates River, Shethar-Bozenai and the other important officers of west of the Euphrates River. 7 This is what was said in the report they sent to him:

To King Darius.

Greetings. May you have peace.

8 King Darius, you should know that we went to the district of Judah where the Temple of the great God is. The people are building that Temple with large stones and they are putting timbers in the walls. They are working very hard and are building very fast.

9 We asked their elders, "Who gave you permission to rebuild this Temple and these walls?" 10 We also asked for their names, and we wrote down the names of their leaders so you would know who they are.

11 This is the answer they gave to us: "We are the servants of the God of heaven and earth. We are rebuilding the Temple that a great king of Israel built and finished many years ago. 12 But our ancestors made the God of heaven angry, so he handed them over to Nebuchadnezzar king of Babylon, who destroyed this Temple and took the people to Babylon as captives.

13 "Later, in the first year Cyrus was king of Babylon, he gave a special order for this Temple to be rebuilt. 14 Cyrus brought out from the temple in Babylon the gold and silver bowls and pans that came from the Temple of God. Nebuchadnezzar had taken them from the Temple in Jerusalem and had put them in the temple in Babylon.

"Then King Cyrus gave them to Sheshbazzar, his appointed governor. 15 Cyrus said to him, 'Take these gold and silver bowls and pans, and put them back in the Temple in Jerusalem and rebuild the Temple of God where it was.' 16 So Sheshbazzar came and laid the foundations of the Temple of God in Jerusalem. From that day until now the work has been going on, but it is not yet finished."

17 Now, if the king wishes, let a search be made in the royal records of Babylon. See if King Cyrus gave an order to rebuild this Temple in Jerusalem. Then let the king write to us and tell us what he has decided.

The Order of Darius

6 So King Darius gave an order to search the records kept in the treasury in Babylon. 2 A scroll was found in

> We are rebuilding the Temple that a great king of Israel built and finished many years ago.
> – Ezra 5:11

Ecbatana, the capital city of Media. This is what was written on it:

Note:

3 King Cyrus gave an order about the Temple of God in Jerusalem in the first year he was king. This was the order: "Let the Temple be rebuilt as a place to present sacrifices. Let its foundations be laid; it should be 30 metres high and 30 metres wide. 4 It must have three layers of large stones and then one layer of timbers. The costs should be paid from the king's treasury. 5 The gold and silver utensils from the Temple of God should be put back in their places. Nebuchadnezzar took them from the Temple in Jerusalem and brought them to Babylon, but they are to be put back in the Temple of God in Jerusalem."

6 Now then, Tattenai, governor of west of the Euphrates River, Shethar-Bozenai and all the officers of that area, stay away from there. 7 Do not bother the work on that Temple of God. Let the governor of the Jewish people and the Jewish elders rebuild this Temple where it was before.

8 Also, I order you to do this for those elders of the Jewish people who are building this Temple: the cost of the building is to be fully paid from the royal treasury, from taxes collected from west of the Euphrates River. Do this so the work will not stop. 9 Give those people anything they need—young bulls, rams or lambs for burnt offerings to the God of heaven, or wheat, salt, wine or olive oil. Give the priests in Jerusalem anything they ask for every day without fail. 10 Then they may offer sacrifices pleasing to the God of heaven, and they may pray for the life of the king and his sons.

11 Also, I give this order: if anyone changes this order, a wooden beam is to be pulled from his house and driven through his body. Because of his crime, make his house

FAITH links

BUILDING TOOLS
EZRA 6:15

What gets you through a project that takes a long time to finish? Plenty of bags of crisps or bars of chocolate? The promise of a reward? How about hard work and perseverance (another way to say not quitting)? Both helped the Israelites to rebuild the Temple. Without these "tools", they would not have completed such a long, hard project.

Hard work and perseverance may not seem as appetising or fun as chocolate. But they can help you do all sorts of things that a bar of chocolate can't.

Stuck on something? Connect to these links for help in getting back on track:

Keep On Praying, 1 Samuel 1, p. 354

The Green Light, 2 Samuel 2:1, p. 401

Plan for Success, 1 Chronicles 14:8–17, p. 538

Two Enemies, Nehemiah 6, p. 631

Fly Like an Eagle, Isaiah 40:28–31, p. 947

Exercising Patience, Luke 2:25–28, 36–37, p. 1369

a pile of ruins. 12 God has chosen Jerusalem as the place he is to be worshipped. May he punish any king or person who tries to change this order and destroy this Temple.

I, Darius, have given this order. Let it be obeyed quickly and carefully.

Completion of the Temple

13 So, Tattenai, the governor west of the Euphrates River, Shethar-Bozenai and their fellow workers carried out King Darius' order quickly and carefully. 14 The Jewish elders continued to build and were successful because of the preaching of Haggai the prophet and Zechariah, a descendant of Iddo. They finished building the Temple as the God of Israel had commanded and as kings Cyrus, Darius and Artaxerxes of Persia had ordered. 15 The Temple was finished on the third day of the month of Adar in the sixth year Darius was king.

16 Then the people of Israel celebrated and gave the Temple to God to honour him. Everybody was happy: the priests, the Levites and the rest of the Jewish people who had returned from captivity. 17 They gave the Temple to God by offering 100 bulls, 200 rams and 400 lambs as sacrifices. And as an offering to forgive the sins of all Israel, they offered twelve male goats, one goat for each tribe in Israel. 18 Then they put the priests and the Levites into their separate groups. Each group had a certain time to serve God in the Temple at Jerusalem as it is written in the Book of Moses.

The Passover is Celebrated

19 The Jewish people who returned from captivity celebrated the Passover on the fourteenth day of the first month. 20 The priests and Levites had made themselves clean. Then the Levites killed the Passover lambs for all the people who had returned from captivity, for their relatives the priests and for themselves. 21 So all the people of Israel who returned from captivity ate the Passover lamb. So did the people who had given up the unclean ways of their non-Jewish neighbours in order to worship the LORD, the God of Israel. 22 For seven days they celebrated the Feast of Unleavened Bread in a very joyful way. The LORD had made them happy by changing the mind of the king of Assyria so that he helped them in the work on the Temple of the God of Israel.

Ezra Comes to Jerusalem

7 After these things[n] during the rule of Artaxerxes king of Persia, Ezra came up from Babylon. Ezra was the son of Seraiah, the son of Azariah, the son of Hilkiah, 2 the son of Shallum, the son of Zadok, the son of Ahitub, 3 the son of Amariah, the son of Azariah, the son of Meraioth, 4 the son of Zerahiah, the son of Uzzi, the son of Bukki, 5 the son of Abishua, the son of Phinehas, the son of Eleazar, the son of Aaron the high priest. 6 This Ezra came to Jerusalem from Babylon. He was a teacher and knew well the Teachings of Moses that had been given by the LORD, the God of Israel. Ezra received everything he asked for from the king, because the LORD his God was helping him. 7 In the seventh year of King Artaxerxes more Israelites came to Jerusalem. Among them were priests, Levites, singers, gatekeepers and Temple servants.

8 Ezra arrived in Jerusalem in the fifth month of Artaxerxes' seventh year as king. 9 Ezra had left Babylon on the first day of the first month, and he arrived in Jerusalem on the first day of the fifth month, because God was helping him. 10 Ezra had worked hard to know and obey the Teachings of the LORD and to teach his rules and commands to the Israelites.

Artaxerxes' Letter to Ezra

11 King Artaxerxes had given a letter to Ezra, a priest and teacher who taught about the commands and laws the LORD gave Israel. This is a copy of the letter:

7:1 **After these things** There is a time period of about 60 years between chapters six and seven.

FAITH links

TEACHING OTHERS
EZRA 7:8-10

Have you ever taught someone how to play a game or helped someone with their homework? If so, you know how important it is for you to know the game or subject well before teaching someone else. Ezra worked hard to know the Teachings of the Lord in order to teach others about God's laws.

Your Sunday school teacher, youth leader or youth pastor also worked hard to learn what they know in order to teach you about God. They do it to encourage you to study the Bible for yourself. Who knows? Maybe *you'll* teach someone about the Bible someday!

An Example Not to Follow, Leviticus 18:1-3, p. 157

The Prayer Habit, Psalm 5:1-3, p. 712

Your Full Trust, Jeremiah 22:20-22, p. 1023

God's Instructions, Ezekiel 4:1-15, p. 1089

Attention, Please! Luke 8:11-15, p. 1383

How to Make God Glad, Ephesians 6:1-2, p. 1605

---

12 From Artaxerxes, king of kings, to Ezra the priest, a teacher of the Law of the God of heaven.

Greetings.

13 Now I give this order: Any Israelite in my kingdom who wishes may go with you to Jerusalem, including priests and Levites. 14 Ezra, you are sent by the king and the seven people who advise him to ask how Judah and Jerusalem are obeying the Law of your God, which you are carrying with you. 15 Also take with you the silver and gold that the king and those who advise him have given freely to the God of Israel, whose Temple is in Jerusalem. 16 Also take the silver and gold you receive from the area of Babylon. Take the offerings the Israelites and their priests have given as gifts for the Temple of your God in Jerusalem. 17 With this money buy bulls, rams and lambs, and the grain offerings and drink offerings that go with those sacrifices. Then sacrifice them on the altar in the Temple of your God in Jerusalem.

18 You and your fellow Jews may spend the silver and gold left over as you want and as God wishes. 19 Take to the God of Jerusalem all the utensils for worship in the Temple of your God, 20 which we have given you. Use the royal treasury to pay for anything else you need for the Temple of your God.

21 Now I, King Artaxerxes, give this order to all the men in charge of the treasury of west of the Euphrates River: Give Ezra, a priest and a teacher of the Law of the God of heaven, whatever he asks for. 22 Give him up to 3.5 tonnes of silver, 10 tonnes of wheat, 2,000 litres of wine and 2,000 litres of olive oil. And give him as much salt as he wants. 23 Carefully give him whatever the God of heaven wants for the Temple of the God of heaven. We do not want God to be angry with the king and his sons. 24 Remember, you must not make these people pay taxes of any kind: priests, Levites, singers, gatekeepers, Temple servants and

other workers in this Temple of God.

25 And you, Ezra, use the wisdom you have from your God to choose judges and lawmakers to rule the Jewish people, west of the Euphrates River. They know the laws of your God, and you may teach anyone who does not know them. 26 Whoever does not obey the law of your God or of the king must be punished. He will be killed, or sent away, or have his property taken away, or be put in jail.

27 Praise the LORD, the God of our ancestors. He caused the king to want to honour the Temple of the LORD in Jerusalem. 28 The LORD has shown me, Ezra, his love in the presence of the king, those who advise the king and the royal officers. Because the LORD my God was helping me, I had courage, and I gathered the leaders of Israel to return with me.

Leaders Who Returned with Ezra

8 These are the leaders of the family groups and those who were listed with them who came back with me from Babylon during the rule of King Artaxerxes.

2 From the descendants of Phinehas: Gershom.

From the descendants of Ithamar: Daniel.

From the descendants of David: Hattush 3 of the descendants of Shecaniah.

From the descendants of Parosh: Zechariah, with 150 men.

4 From the descendants of Pahath-Moab: Eliehoenai son of Zerahiah, with 200 men.

5 From the descendants of Zattu: Shecaniah son of Jahaziel, with 300 men.

6 From the descendants of Adin: Ebed son of Jonathan, with 50 men.

7 From the descendants of Elam: Jeshaiah son of Athaliah, with 70 men.

8 From the descendants of Shephatiah: Zebadiah son of Michael, with 80 men.

9 From the descendants of Joab: Obadiah son of Jehiel, with 218 men.

10 From the descendants of Bani: Shelomith son of Josiphiah, with 160 men.

11 From the descendants of Bebai: Zechariah son of Bebai, with 28 men.

12 From the descendants of Azgad: Johanan son of Hakkatan, with 110 men.

13 From the descendants of Adonikam, these were the last ones: Eliphelet, Jeuel and Shemaiah, with 60 men.

14 From the descendants of Bigvai: Uthai and Zaccur, with 70 men.

The Return to Jerusalem

15 I called all those people together at the canal that flows towards Ahava, where we camped for three days. I checked all the people and the priests, but I did not find any Levites. 16 So I called these leaders: Eliezer, Ariel, Shemaiah, Elnathan, Jarib, Elnathan, Nathan, Zechariah and Meshullam. And I called Joiarib and Elnathan, who were teachers. 17 I sent these men to Iddo, the leader at Casiphia, and told them what to say to Iddo and his relatives, who are the Temple servants in Casiphia. I sent them to bring servants to us for the Temple of our God. 18 Our God was helping us, so Iddo's relatives gave us Sherebiah, a wise man from the descendants of Mahli son of Levi, who was the son of Israel. And they brought Sherebiah's sons and brothers, for a total of eighteen men. 19 And they brought to us Hashabiah and Jeshaiah from the descendants of Merari, and his brothers and nephews. In all there were 20 men. 20 They also brought 220 of the Temple servants, a group David and the officers had set up to help the Levites. All of those men were listed by name.

21 There by the Ahava Canal, I announced we would all give up eating and humble ourselves before our God. We would ask God for a safe trip for ourselves, our children and all our possessions. 22 I was ashamed to ask the king for soldiers and horsemen to protect us from enemies on the road. We had said to the king, "Our God helps

everyone who obeys him, but he is very angry with all who reject him." 23 So we gave up eating and prayed to our God about our trip, and he answered our prayers.

24 Then I chose twelve of the priests who were leaders, Sherebiah, Hashabiah and ten of their relatives. 25 I weighed the offering of silver and gold and the utensils given for the Temple of our God, and I gave them to the twelve priests I had chosen. The king, the people who advised him, his officers and all the Israelites there with us had given these things for the Temple. 26 I weighed out and gave them about 22 tonnes of silver, about 14 tonnes of silver objects and about 14 tonnes of gold. 27 I gave them 20 gold bowls that weighed about 8.5 kilogrammes and two fine pieces of polished bronze that were as valuable as gold.

28 Then I said to the priests, "You and these utensils belong to the LORD for his service. The silver and gold are gifts to the LORD, the God of your ancestors. 29 Guard these things carefully. In Jerusalem, weigh them in front of the leading priests, Levites and the leaders of the family groups of Israel in the rooms of the Temple of the LORD." 30 So the priests and Levites accepted the silver, the gold and the utensils that had been weighed to take them to the Temple of our God in Jerusalem.

31 On the twelfth day of the first month we left the Ahava Canal and started towards Jerusalem. Our God helped us and protected us from enemies and robbers along the way. 32 Finally we arrived in Jerusalem where we rested three days.

33 On the fourth day we weighed out the silver, the gold and the utensils in the Temple of our God. We handed them to the priest Meremoth son of Uriah. Eleazar son of Phinehas was with him, as were the Levites Jozabad son of Jeshua and Noadiah son of Binnui. 34 We checked everything by number and by weight, and the total weight was written down.

35 Then the captives who returned made burnt offerings to the God of Israel. They sacrificed twelve bulls for all Israel, 96 rams and 77 lambs. For a sin offering there were twelve male goats. All this was a burnt offering to the LORD. 36 They took King Artaxerxes' orders to the royal officers and to the governors, west of the Euphrates River. Then these men gave help to the people and the Temple of God.

Ezra's Prayer

9 After these things had been done, the leaders came to me and said, "Ezra,

FAITH CHALLENGE

Here's a challenge for you. Read 8:36 to discover how the leaders of Babylon helped the Israelites who were rebuilding their temple. How could you and your friends help the people who work at your church?

TeSTiNG iT

Ezra 8:36
They took King Artaxerxes' orders to the royal officers and to the governors west of the Euphrates River. Then these men gave help to the people and the Temple of God.

the Israelites, including the priests and Levites, have not kept themselves separate from the people around us. Those neighbours do evil things, as the Canaanites, Hittites, Perizzites, Jebusites, Ammonites, Moabites, Egyptians and Amorites did. 2 The Israelite men and their sons have married these women. They have mixed the people who belong to God with the people around them. The leaders and officers of Israel have led the rest of the Israelites to do this unfaithful thing."

3 When I heard this, I angrily tore my robe and coat, pulled hair from my head and beard, and sat down in shock. 4 Everyone who trembled in fear at the word of the God of Israel gathered around me because of the unfaithfulness of the captives who had returned. I sat there in shock until the evening sacrifice.

9:6
Sin
How to deal with your sins.

5 At the evening sacrifice I got up from where I had shown my shame. My robe and coat were torn, and I fell on my knees with my hands spread out to the LORD my God. 6 I prayed, "My God, I am too ashamed and embarrassed to lift up my face to you, my God, because our sins are so many. They are higher than our heads. Our guilt even reaches up to the sky. 7 From the days of our ancestors until now, our guilt has been great. Because of our sins, we, our kings and our priests have been punished by the sword and captivity. Foreign kings have taken away our things and shamed us, even as it is today.

8 "But now, for a short time, the LORD our God has been kind to us. He has let some of us come back from captivity and has let us live in safety in his holy place. And so our God gives us hope and a little relief from our slavery. 9 Even though we are slaves, our God has not left us. He caused the kings of Persia to be kind to us and has given us new life. We can rebuild the Temple and repair its ruins. And he has given us a wall to protect us in Judah and Jerusalem.

10 "But now, our God, what can we say after you have done all this? We have disobeyed your commands 11 that you gave through your servants the prophets. You said, 'The land you are entering to own is ruined; the people living there have spoiled it by the evil they do. Their evil filled the land with uncleanness from one end to the other. 12 So do not let your daughters marry their sons, and do not let their daughters marry your sons. Do not wish for their peace or success. Then you will be strong and eat the good things of the land. Then you can leave this land to your descendants for ever.'

13 "What has happened to us is our own fault. We have done evil things, and our guilt is great. But you, our God, have punished us less than we deserve; you have left a few of us alive. 14 We should not again break your commands by allowing marriages with these wicked people. If we did, you would get angry enough to destroy us, and none of us would be left alive. 15 LORD, God of Israel, by your goodness a few of us are left alive today. We admit that we are guilty and none of us should be allowed to stand before you."

The People Confess Sin

10 As Ezra was praying and confessing and crying and throwing himself down in front of the Temple, a large group of Israelite men, women and children gathered around him who were also crying loudly. 2 Then Shecaniah son of Jehiel the Elamite said to Ezra, "We have been unfaithful to our God by marrying women from the peoples around us. But even so, there is still hope for Israel. 3 Now let us make an agreement before our God. We will send away all these women and their children as you and those who respect the commands of our God advise. Let it be done to obey God's Teachings. 4 Get up, Ezra. You are in charge, and we will support you. Have courage and do it."

10:2
Hope
Will God still love you even if you sin?

5 So Ezra got up and made the priests,

Levites and all the people of Israel promise to do what was suggested; and they promised. 6 Then Ezra left the Temple and went to the room of Jehohanan son of Eliashib. While Ezra was there, he did not eat or drink, because he was still sad about the unfaithfulness of the captives who had returned.

7 They sent out an order in Judah and Jerusalem for all the captives who had returned to meet together in Jerusalem. 8 Whoever did not come to Jerusalem within three days would lose his property and would no longer be a member of the community of the returned captives. That was the decision of the officers and elders.

9 So within three days all the people of Judah and Benjamin gathered in Jerusalem. It was the twentieth day of the ninth month. All the people were sitting in the open place in front of the Temple and were upset because of the meeting and because it was raining. 10 Ezra the priest stood up and said to them, "You have been unfaithful and have married non-Jewish women. You have made Israel more guilty. 11 Now, confess it to the LORD, the God of your ancestors. Do his will and separate yourselves from the people living around you and from your non-Jewish wives."

12 Then the whole group answered Ezra with a loud voice, "Ezra, you're right! We must do what you say. 13 But there are many people here, and it's the rainy season. We can't stand outside, and this problem can't be solved in a day or two, because we have sinned badly. 14 Let our officers make a decision for the whole group. Then let everyone in our towns who has married a non-Jewish woman meet with the elders and judges of each town at a planned time, until the hot anger of our God turns away from us." 15 Only Jonathan son of Asahel, Jahzeiah son of Tikvah, Meshullam and Shabbethai the Levite were against the plan.

16 So the returned captives did what was suggested. Ezra the priest chose men who were leaders of the family groups and named one from each family division. On the first day of the tenth month they sat down to study each case. 17 By the first day of the first month, they dealt with all the men who had married non-Jewish women.

Those Guilty of Marrying Non-Jewish Women

18 These are the descendants of the priests who had married foreign women:

From the descendants of Jeshua son of Jozadak and Jeshua's brothers: Maaseiah, Eliezer, Jarib and Gedaliah. 19 (They all promised to divorce their wives, and each one brought a ram from the flock as a penalty offering.)

20 From the descendants of Immer: Hanani and Zebadiah.

21 From the descendants of Harim: Maaseiah, Elijah, Shemaiah, Jehiel and Uzziah.

22 From the descendants of Pashhur: Elioenai, Maaseiah, Ishmael, Nethanel, Jozabad and Elasah.

23 Among the Levites: Jozabad, Shimei, Kelaiah (also called Kelita), Pethahiah, Judah and Eliezer.

24 Among the singers: Eliashib.

Among the gatekeepers: Shallum, Telem and Uri.

25 And among the other Israelites, these married non-Jewish women:

From the descendants of Parosh: Ramiah, Izziah, Malkijah, Mijamin, Eleazar, Malkijah and Benaiah.

26 From the descendants of Elam: Mattaniah, Zechariah, Jehiel, Abdi, Jeremoth and Elijah.

27 From the descendants of Zattu: Elioenai, Eliashib, Mattaniah, Jeremoth, Zabad and Aziza.

28 From the descendants of Bebai: Jehohanan, Hananiah, Zabbai and Athlai.

29 From the descendants of Bani: Meshullam, Malluch, Adaiah, Jashub, Sheal and Jeremoth.

30 From the descendants of Pahath-Moab: Adna, Kelal, Benaiah, Maaseiah, Mattaniah, Bezalel, Binnui and Manasseh.

31 From the descendants of Harim: Eliezer, Ishijah, Malkijah, Shemaiah, Shimeon, 32 Benjamin, Malluch and Shemariah.

33 From the descendants of Hashum: Mattenai, Mattattah, Zabad, Eliphelet, Jeremai, Manasseh and Shimei.

34 From the descendants of Bani: Maadai, Amram, Uel, **35** Benaiah, Bedeiah, Keluhi, **36** Vaniah, Meremoth, Eliashib, **37** Mattaniah, Mattenai and Jaasu.

38 From the descendants of Binnui: Shimei, **39** Shelemiah, Nathan, Adaiah, **40** Macnadebai, Shashai, Sharai, **41** Azarel, Shelemiah, Shemariah, **42** Shallum, Amariah and Joseph.

43 From the descendants of Nebo: Jeiel, Mattithiah, Zabad, Zebina, Jaddai, Joel and Benaiah.

44 All these men had married non-Jewish women, and some of them had children by these wives.

BUILD THE WALL

Hi! My name is Nehemiah. I was the one who served wine to the king of Persia. When I heard about the poor conditions in Israel, the land of my parents and grandparents, I was very sad. The city of Jerusalem had no wall and the people were not following God's laws. The king noticed how sad I was; and when he asked me why, I told him about my homeland. He gave me permission to go to Jerusalem and rebuild the walls.

Have you ever run an obstacle course? Rebuilding the wall of Jerusalem was like running an obstacle course, but in this case the obstacles were people! Foreigners living in our land tried to stop our work and even threatened to kill us. Half of our workers had to stand guard while the other half built the wall. Link to Nehemiah 4:7–23 to see how we prepared for attack.

I wrote this book to tell people to be faithful to God. When the wall was finished, Ezra, the teacher, read God's laws to the people. The people cried when they understood what God's law said and how disobedient they were. But I told them, "Today is a holy day to the Lord. Don't be sad, because the joy of the LORD will make you strong" (Nehemiah 8:10). We offered the wall of Jerusalem as a gift to God. Check out Nehemiah 12:27–43 for the big party we had after the work was done.

JESUS WATCH

Nehemiah had the privilege of selecting and serving the finest wine to the king, as well as the responsibility of tasting it to make sure it was not poisoned. He earned the respect of the king and was a trusted advisor. Nehemiah gave up his high-ranking job so that he could help his people in Jerusalem. This reminds us of Jesus, the Son of God, who left his place in heaven so that he could become our saviour.

Like Jesus, Nehemiah showed great compassion for the poor. As governor of Jerusalem, Nehemiah did not demand all that was owed to him, because he knew the people were already working very hard. Nehemiah also spent a lot of time in prayer. He asked God to make him strong. Jesus often went to a quiet place to pray to his Father in heaven.

OTHER CONNECTIONS

Livin' it
What are some ways that you worship God? Can God only be worshipped at church on Sundays, or when you are with other Christians? Find out more about worshipping God by connecting to An Awesome God, Nehemiah 8:6.

It was a sad day for Israel when the city of Jerusalem finally was captured and destroyed and its people taken as captives to a foreign land. But, just as God had promised, the day came when the people were allowed to return to their homeland. Read about it at The Homecoming, Nehemiah 8:1–12.

my FAVOURITE links
_____
_____
_____

FAITH links

○ Seeing the Needs, **Nehemiah 1**

○ Prayer + Action = Success, **Nehemiah 2:4–9**

○ Building Together, **Nehemiah 3**

○ Help for the Outsiders, **Nehemiah 5:9–10**

○ Two Enemies, **Nehemiah 6**

○ See the Heart Behind It, **Nehemiah 8; 9**

○ An Honest Reputation, **Nehemiah 13:13**

Do you know how the people decided who should live in Jerusalem?

Not sure? If you link to Nehemiah 11:1-2, you can find out.

THE NEHEMIAH SURFWATCH:
Nehemiah's sad face, Nehemiah 2:1–10
Nehemiah shakes his robe, Nehemiah 5:1–13
The people build shelters, Nehemiah 8:13–18
Let's celebrate, Nehemiah 12:27–43

Nehemiah's Prayer

1 These are the words of Nehemiah son of Hacaliah.

In the month of Kislev in the twentieth year,[n] I, Nehemiah, was in the capital city of Susa. 2 One of my brothers named Hanani came with some other men from Judah. I asked them about Jerusalem and the Jewish people who lived through the captivity.

3 They answered me, "Those who are left from the captivity are back in Judah, but they are in much trouble and are full of shame. The wall around Jerusalem is broken down, and its gates have been burnt."

4 When I heard these things, I sat down and cried for several days. I was sad and ate nothing. I prayed to the God of heaven, 5 "LORD, God of heaven, you are the great God who is to be respected. You are loyal, and you keep your agreement with those who love you and obey your commands. 6 Look and listen carefully. Hear the prayer that I, your servant, am praying to you day and night for your servants, the Israelites. I confess the sins we Israelites have done against you. My father's family and I have sinned against you. 7 We have been wicked towards you and have not obeyed the commands, rules and laws you gave your servant Moses.

8 "Remember what you taught your servant Moses, saying, 'If you are unfaithful, I will scatter you among the nations. 9 But if you return to me and obey my commands, I will gather your people from the far ends of the earth. And I will bring them from captivity to where I have chosen to be worshipped.'

10 "They are your servants and your people, whom you have saved with your great strength and power. 11 Lord, listen carefully to the prayer of your servant and the prayers of your servants who love to honour you. Give me, your servant, success today; allow this king to show kindness to me."

I was the one who served wine to the king.

Nehemiah is Sent to Jerusalem

2 It was the month of Nisan in the twentieth year Artaxerxes was king. He wanted some wine, so I took some and gave it to the king. I had not been sad in his presence before. 2 So the king said,

---

SEEING THE NEEDS
NEHEMIAH 1

What's the first thing you need to do in order to help someone? If your answer is pray, you're half right. You first need to know what kind of help is needed. Nehemiah saw a need and wanted to do something about it. He heard how the Israelites had returned to their land. The wall around Jerusalem had been destroyed. So the people were defenceless. Nehemiah then talked to God about that need.

God wants us to notice the needs of the people around us. Seeing the needs of others reminds us to care for them.

Your Response to Responsibility, Ruth 2:1–7, p. 346

Just a Little Respect, 1 Chronicles 11:10–19, p. 534

Meaningless Words, Job 21:34, p. 684

You Are What You Do, Proverbs 20:11, p. 854

Your Choice of Fruit, Matthew 12:33–35, p. 1295

An Encouraging Word, 1 Corinthians 1:3–5, p. 1545

1:1 *twentieth year* This is probably referring to the twentieth year King Artaxerxes I ruled Persia.

"Why does your face look sad even though you are not sick? Your heart must be sad."

Then I was very afraid. 3 I said to the king, "May the king live for ever! My face is sad because the city where my ancestors are buried lies in ruins, and its gates have been destroyed by fire."

2:4 Prayer
Do you need to kneel to pray?

4 Then the king said to me, "What do you want?"

First I prayed to the God of heaven. 5 Then I answered the king, "If you are willing and if I have pleased you, send me to the city in Judah where my ancestors are buried so I can rebuild it."

6 The queen was sitting next to the king. He asked me, "How long will your trip take, and when will you get back?" It pleased the king to send me, so I set a time.

7 I also said to him, "If you are willing, give me letters for the governors west of the Euphrates River. Tell them to let me pass safely through their lands on my way to Judah. 8 And may I have a letter for Asaph, the keeper of the king's forest, telling him to give me timber? I will need it to make boards for the gates of the palace, which is by the Temple, and for the city wall and for the house in which I will live." So the king gave me the letters, because God was showing kindness to me. 9 Then I went to the governors west of the Euphrates River and gave them the king's letters. The king had also sent army officers and soldiers on horses with me.

10 When Sanballat the Horonite and Tobiah the Ammonite officer heard about this, they were upset that someone had come to help the Israelites.

Nehemiah Inspects Jerusalem

11 I went to Jerusalem and stayed there three days. 12 Then at night I started out with a few men. I had not told anyone what God had caused me to do for Jerusalem. There were no animals with me except the one I was riding.

13 I went out at night through the Valley Gate. I rode towards the Dragon

---

FAITH links

PRAYER + ACTION = SUCCESS

NEHEMIAH 2:4-9

Suppose you had a big homework project to do. Would just thinking about it get the project done? Nope. You've also got to do it. Nehemiah knew that the wall around Jerusalem needed to be repaired. But just thinking about it wouldn't move a brick. First, he prayed about the problem. Second, he acted. God gave Nehemiah the wisdom to know what to do next. Nehemiah didn't expect God to do all the work. But he knew that God would help *him* do the work.

Prayer and action make a winning combination. It's one you can use often to get things done.

Link here to find out more about that winning combination:

The Right Thing to Do, 1 Samuel 26, p. 391

A Wise Wish, 1 Kings 3:5–9, p. 439

Mind Guard, Proverbs 4:23, p. 831

Your Civic Duty, Matthew 17:24–27, p. 1304

You've Got the Power! Acts 1:1–8; 2:1–4, p. 1463

Keep Up the Good Work! Galatians 6:9–10, p. 1593

Well and the Rubbish Gate, inspecting the walls of Jerusalem that had been broken down and the gates that had been destroyed by fire. 14 Then I rode on towards the Fountain Gate and the King's Pool, but there was not enough room for the animal I was riding to pass through. 15 So I went up the valley at night, inspecting the wall. Finally, I turned and went back in through the Valley Gate. 16 The guards did not know where I had gone or what I was doing. I had not yet said anything to the Jewish people, the priests, the important men, the officers or any of the others who would do the work.

17 Then I said to them, "You can see the trouble we have here. Jerusalem is a pile of ruins, and its gates have been burned. Come, let's rebuild the wall of Jerusalem so we won't be full of shame any longer." 18 I also told them how God had been kind to me and what the king had said to me.

Then they answered, "Let's start rebuilding." So they began to work hard.

19 But when Sanballat the Horonite, Tobiah the Ammonite officer and Geshem the Arab heard about it, they made fun of us and laughed at us. They said, "What are you doing? Are you turning against the king?"

20 But I answered them, "The God of heaven will give us success. We, his servants, will start rebuilding, but you have no share, claim or memorial in Jerusalem."

Builders of the Wall

3 Eliashib the high priest and his fellow priests went to work and rebuilt the Sheep Gate. They gave it to the Lord's service and set its doors in place. They worked as far as the Tower of the Hundred and gave it to the Lord's service. Then they went on to the Tower of Hananel. 2 Next to them, the men of Jericho built part of the wall, and Zaccur son of Imri built next to them.

3 The sons of Hassenaah rebuilt the Fish Gate, laying its boards and setting its doors, bolts and bars in place. 4 Meremoth son of Uriah, the son of Hakkoz, made repairs next to them. Meshullam son of Berekiah, the son of Meshezabel, made repairs next to Meremoth. And Zadok son of Baana made repairs next to Meshullam. 5 The men from Tekoa made

FAITH links

BUILDING TOGETHER
NEHEMIAH 3

Do you ever read the credits at the end of a film? They remind us that the actors weren't the only ones involved in making the film. Many people with different skills work together to make a film. In Nehemiah's day, many people with different skills helped to rebuild the wall around Jerusalem.

God gave you the skills you have. You can use those skills to serve God. When God's people work together using the skills God provided each person with, much is accomplished.

Connect here to discover how God wants you to use your skills:

Kind or Fair? 1 Samuel 30, p. 395

Your Best Work, 1 Kings 6, p. 443

A Big Responsibility, 2 Kings 11, p. 494

Operation Co-operation, Ezra 1:5, p. 609

Get Ready! Mark 13:26–27, p. 1354

The Worst Chore, John 13:3–17, p. 1447

repairs next to them, but the leading men of Tekoa would not work under their supervisors.

6 Joiada son of Paseah and Meshullam son of Besodeiah repaired the Old Gate. They laid its boards and set its doors, bolts and bars in place. 7 Next to them, Melatiah from Gibeon, other men from Gibeon and Mizpah, and Jadon from Meronoth made repairs. These places were ruled by the governor west of the Euphrates River. 8 Next to them, Uzziel son of Harhaiah, a goldsmith, made repairs. And next to him, Hananiah, a perfume maker, made repairs. These men rebuilt Jerusalem as far as the Broad Wall. 9 The next part of the wall was repaired by Rephaiah son of Hur, the ruler of half of the district of Jerusalem. 10 Next to him, Jedaiah son of Harumaph made repairs opposite his own house. And next to him, Hattush son of Hashabneiah made repairs. 11 Malkijah son of Harim and Hasshub son of Pahath-Moab repaired another part of the wall and the Tower of the Ovens. 12 Next to them Shallum son of Hallohesh, the ruler of half of the district of Jerusalem, and his daughters made repairs.

13 Hanun and the people of Zanoah repaired the Valley Gate, rebuilding it and setting its doors, bolts and bars in place. They also repaired the 500 metres of the wall to the Rubbish Gate.

14 Malkijah son of Recab, the ruler of the district of Beth Hakkerem, repaired the Rubbish Gate. He rebuilt that gate and set its doors, bolts and bars in place.

15 Shallun son of Col-Hozeh, the ruler of the district of Mizpah, repaired the Fountain Gate. He rebuilt it, put a roof over it and set its doors, bolts and bars in place. He also repaired the wall of the Pool of Siloam next to the King's Garden all the way to the steps that went down from the older part of the city. 16 Next to Shallun was Nehemiah[n] son of Azbuk, the ruler of half of the district of Beth Zur. He made repairs opposite the tombs of David and as far as the man-made pool and the House of the Heroes.

17 Next to him, the Levites made repairs, working under Rehum son of Bani. Next to him, Hashabiah, the ruler of half of the district of Keilah, for his district. 18 Next to him, Binnui son of Henadad and his Levites made repairs. Binnui was the ruler of the other half of the district of Keilah. 19 Next to them, Ezer son of Jeshua, the ruler of Mizpah, repaired another part of the wall. He worked across from the way up to the storehouse for weapons, as far as the bend. 20 Next to him, Baruch son of Zabbai worked hard on the wall that went from the bend to the entrance to the house of Eliashib, the high priest. 21 Next to him, Meremoth son of Uriah, the son of Hakkoz, repaired the wall that went from the entrance to Eliashib's house to the far end of it.

22 Next to him worked the priests from the surrounding area. 23 Next to them, Benjamin and Hasshub made repairs in front of their own house. Next to them, Azariah son of Maaseiah, the son of Ananiah, made repairs beside his own house. 24 Next to him, Binnui son of Henadad repaired the wall that went from Azariah's house to the bend and on to the corner. 25 Palal son of Uzai worked across from the bend and by the tower on the upper palace, which is near the courtyard of the king's guard. Next to Palal, Pedaiah son of Parosh made repairs. 26 The Temple servants who lived on the hill of Ophel made repairs as far as a point opposite the Water Gate. They worked towards the east and the tower that extends from the palace. 27 Next to them, the people of Tekoa repaired the wall from the great tower that extends from the palace to the wall of Ophel.

28 The priests made repairs above the Horse Gate, each working in front of his own house. 29 Next to them, Zadok son of Immer made repairs across from his own house. Next to him, Shemaiah son of Shecaniah, the guard of the East Gate, made repairs. 30 Next to him, Hananiah son of Shelemiah, and Hanun, the sixth son of Zalaph, made repairs on another part of the wall. Next to them, Meshullam son of Berekiah made repairs across from where he lived. 31 Next

---

3:16 Nehemiah This is a different Nehemiah from the one who wrote this book.

to him, Malkijah, one of the goldsmiths, made repairs. He worked as far as the house of the Temple servants and the traders, which is across from the Inspection Gate, and as far as the room above the corner of the wall. 32 The goldsmiths and the traders made repairs between the room above the corner of the wall and the Sheep Gate.

Those Against the Rebuilding

4 When Sanballat heard we were rebuilding the wall, he was very angry, even furious. He made fun of the Jewish people. 2 He said to his friends and those with power in Samaria, "What are these weak Jews doing? Will they rebuild the wall? Will they offer sacrifices? Can they finish it in one day? Can they bring stones back to life from piles of rubbish and ashes?"

3 Tobiah the Ammonite, who was next to Sanballat, said, "If a fox climbed up on the stone wall they are building, it would break it down."

4 I prayed, "Hear us, our God. We are hated. Turn the insults of Sanballat and Tobiah back on their own heads. Let them be captured and stolen like valuables. 5 Do not hide their guilt or take away their sins so that you can't see them, because they have insulted the builders."

6 So we rebuilt the wall to half its height, because the people were willing to work.

7 But Sanballat, Tobiah, the Arabs, the Ammonites and the people from Ashdod were very angry when they heard that the repairs to Jerusalem's walls were continuing and that the holes in the wall were being closed. 8 So they all made plans to come to Jerusalem and fight and stir up trouble. 9 But we prayed to our God and appointed guards to watch for them day and night.

10 The people of Judah said, "The workers are getting tired. There is so much rubbish we cannot rebuild the wall."

11 And our enemies said, "The Jews won't know or see anything until we come among them and kill them and stop the work."

12 Then the Jewish people who lived near our enemies came and told us ten times, "Everywhere you turn, the enemy will attack us." 13 So I put people behind the lowest places along the wall—the open places—and I put families together with their swords, spears and bows. 14 Then I looked around and stood up and said to the important men, the leaders and the rest of the people: "Don't be afraid of them. Remember the Lord, who is great and powerful. Fight for your brothers, your sons and daughters, your wives and your homes."

15 Then our enemies heard that we knew about their plans and that God had ruined their plans. So we all went back to the wall, each to his own work.

16 From that day on, half my people worked on the wall. The other half was ready with spears, shields, bows and armour. The officers stood behind the people of Judah 17 who were building the wall. Those who carried materials did their work with one hand and carried a weapon with the other. 18 Each builder wore his sword at his side as he worked. The man who blew the trumpet to warn the people stayed next to me.

19 Then I said to the important men, the leaders and the rest of the people, "This is a very big job. We are spreading out along the wall so that we are far apart. 20 Wherever you hear the sound of the trumpet, assemble there. Our God will fight for us."

21 So we continued to work with half the men holding spears from sunrise till the stars came out. 22 At that time I also said to the people, "Let every man and his helper stay inside Jerusalem at night. They can be our guards at night and workmen during the day." 23 Neither I, my brothers, my workers nor the guards with me ever took off our clothes. Each person carried his weapon even when he went for water.

> Don't be afraid of them. Remember the Lord, who is great and powerful.
> – Nehemiah 4:14

Nehemiah Helps Poor People

5 The men and their wives complained loudly against their fellow Jews. 2 Some of them were saying, "We have many sons and daughters in our families. To eat and stay alive, we need grain."

3 Others were saying, "We are borrowing money against our fields, vineyards and homes to get grain because there is not much food."

4 And still others were saying, "We are borrowing money to pay the king's tax on our fields and vineyards. 5 We are just like our fellow Jews, and our sons are like their sons. But we have to sell our sons and daughters as slaves. Some of our daughters have already been sold. But there is nothing we can do, because our fields and vineyards already belong to other people."

6 When I heard their complaints about these things, I was very angry. 7 After I thought about it, I accused the important people and the leaders, "You are charging your own brothers too much interest." So I called a large meeting to deal with them. 8 I said to them, "As much as possible, we have bought freedom for our fellow Jews who had been sold to foreigners. Now you are selling your fellow Jews to us!" The leaders were quiet and had nothing to say.

9 Then I said, "What you are doing is not right. Don't you fear God? Don't let our foreign enemies shame us. 10 I, my brothers and my men are also lending money and grain to the people. But stop charging them so much for this. 11 Give back their fields, vineyards, olive trees and houses right now. Also give back the extra amount you charged—the hundredth part of the money, grain, new wine and oil."

12 They said, "We will give it back and not demand anything more from them. We will do as you say."

Then I called for the priests, and I made the important men and leaders take an oath to do what they had said. 13 Also I shook out the folds of my robe and said,

5:7-11
Encouragement
How should you stand up for those who need help?

FAITH links

HELP FOR THE OUTSIDERS
NEHEMIAH 5:9-10

Think of somebody in your school or in your neighbourhood who is made fun of or ignored by everyone else. In Nehemiah's day, the poor were like that person in your neighbourhood. Nehemiah wanted to do something to help them. When he saw how people who had more treated the poor, he put a stop to it.

It is easy to forget how important it is to treat all people kindly. God wants you to be kind to other people. What could you do to help those whom others ignore or treat badly?

How do you treat those on the "outside" at school? Link here for some good advice:

Help for the Poor, Leviticus 5:7, p. 138

Fairness for All, Deuteronomy 24:17, p. 258

I Want It Now! Judges 14:1–3, p. 332

A Friend in Deed, Job 2:13, p. 662

Two Are Better, Ecclesiastes 4:9–12, p. 877

You're Correct! Hebrews 12:5–7, p. 1683

"In this way may God shake out everyone who does not keep his promise. May God shake him out of his house and out of the things that are his. Let that person be shaken out and emptied!"

Then the whole group said, "Amen," and they praised the LORD. So the people did what they had promised.

14 I was appointed governor in the land of Judah in the twentieth year of King Artaxerxes' rule. I was governor of Judah for twelve years, until his thirty-second year. During that time neither my brothers nor I ate the food that was allowed for a governor. 15 But the governors before me had placed a heavy load on the people. They took about 40 pieces of silver from each person, along with food and wine. The governors' helpers before me also controlled the people, but I did not do that, because I feared God. 16 I worked on the wall, as did all my men who were gathered there. We did not buy any fields.

17 Also, I fed 150 Jewish people and officers at my table, as well as those who came from the nations around us. 18 This is what was prepared every day: one ox, six good sheep, and birds. And every ten days there were all kinds of wine. But I never demanded the food that was allowed a governor, because the people were already working very hard.

19 Remember to be kind to me, my God, for all the good I have done for these people.

More Problems for Nehemiah

6 Then Sanballat, Tobiah, Geshem the Arab and our other enemies heard that I had rebuilt the wall and that there was not one gap in it. But I had not yet set the doors in the gates. 2 So Sanballat and Geshem sent me this message: "Come, Nehemiah, let's meet together in Kephirim on the plain of Ono."

But they were planning to harm me. 3 So I sent messengers to them with this answer: "I am doing a great work and I can't come down. I don't want the work to stop while I leave to meet you." 4 Sanballat and Geshem sent the same message to me four times, and each time I sent back the same answer.

5 The fifth time Sanballat sent his helper to me with the message, and in his hand was an unsealed letter. 6 This is what was written:

Nehemiah 6:6 631

FAITH links

TWO ENEMIES
NEHEMIAH 6

When you're faced with a long project, are you ever tempted to put off doing the work? Enemies led by two men, Sanballat and Tobiah, tried to get Nehemiah and the Israelites to put off working on the wall.

There are two other enemies that can keep you from doing your work: procrastination and worry. *Procrastination* is a long word that means to keep putting off doing something. It can become a habit after a while. Worried thoughts like *I'll never get this done* can also sap your energy. One way to fight both can be found in one word: *perseverance*. Don't give up! Ask God to give you the desire to get to work and keep on doing it.

When Bad Turns to Worse, Exodus 5:6–12, p. 82

Building Tools, Ezra 6:15, p. 615

When the Going Gets Tough, Lamentations 3:22–27, p. 1079

Small Beginnings, Zechariah 4:10, p. 1255

Faith God Notices, Luke 18:35–43, p. 1406

Just Like a Tree, Colossians 1:23, p. 1621

A report is going around to all the nations, and Geshem says it is true, that you and the Jewish people are planning to turn against the king and that you are rebuilding the wall. They say you are going to be their king 7 and that you have appointed prophets to announce in Jerusalem: "There is a king of Judah!" The king will hear about this. So come, let's discuss this together.

8 So I sent him back this answer: "Nothing you are saying is really happening. You are just making it up in your own mind."

9 Our enemies were trying to scare us, thinking, "They will get too weak to work. Then the wall will not be finished."

But I prayed, "God, make me strong."

10 One day I went to the house of Shemaiah son of Delaiah, the son of Mehetabel. Shemaiah had to stay at home. He said, "Nehemiah, let's meet in the Temple of God. Let's go inside the Temple and close the doors, because men are coming at night to kill you."

11 But I said, "Should a man like me run away? Should I run for my life into the Temple? I will not go." 12 I knew that God had not sent him but that Tobiah and Sanballat had paid him to prophesy against me. 13 They paid him to frighten me so I would do this and sin. Then they could give me a bad name to shame me.

14 I prayed, "My God, remember Tobiah and Sanballat and what they have done. Also remember the prophetess Noadiah and the other prophets who have been trying to frighten me."

The Wall is Finished

15 The wall of Jerusalem was completed on the twenty-fifth day of the month of Elul. It took 52 days to rebuild. 16 When all our enemies heard about it and all the nations around us saw it, they were shamed. They then understood that the work had been done with the help of our God.

17 Also in those days the important men of Judah sent many letters to Tobiah, and he answered them. 18 Many Jewish people had promised to be faithful to Tobiah, because he was the son-in-law of Shecaniah son of Arah. And Tobiah's son Jehohanan had married the daughter of Meshullam son of Berekiah. 19 These important men kept telling me about the good things Tobiah was doing, and then they would tell Tobiah what I said about him. So Tobiah sent letters to frighten me.

7 After the wall had been rebuilt and I had set the doors in place, the gatekeepers, singers and Levites were chosen. 2 I put my brother Hanani, along with Hananiah, the commander of the palace, in charge of Jerusalem. Hananiah was honest and feared God more than most people. 3 I said to them, "The gates of Jerusalem should not be opened until the sun is hot. While the gatekeepers are still on duty, have them shut and bolt the doors. Appoint people who live in Jerusalem as guards, and put some at guard posts and some near their own houses."

The Captives Who Returned

4 The city was large and roomy, but there were few people in it, and the houses had not yet been rebuilt. 5 Then my God caused me to gather the important men, the leaders and the common people so I could register them by families. I found the family history of those who had returned first. This is what I found written there:

6 These are the people of the area who returned from captivity, whom Nebuchadnezzar king of Babylon had taken away. They returned to Jerusalem and Judah, each going back to his own town. 7 These people returned with Zerubbabel, Jeshua, Nehemiah, Azariah, Raamiah, Nahamani, Mordecai, Bilshan, Mispereth, Bigvai, Nehum and Baanah.

These are the people from Israel: 8 the descendants of Parosh—2,172; 9 the descendants of Shephatiah—372; 10 the

> Then my God caused me to gather the important men, the leaders and the common people so I could register them.
> – Nehemiah 7:5

descendants of Arah—652; **11** the descendants of Pahath-Moab (through the family of Jeshua and Joab)—2,818; **12** the descendants of Elam—1,254; **13** the descendants of Zattu—845; **14** the descendants of Zaccai—760; **15** the descendants of Binnui—648; **16** the descendants of Bebai—628; **17** the descendants of Azgad—2,322; **18** the descendants of Adonikam—667; **19** the descendants of Bigvai—2,067; **20** the descendants of Adin—655; **21** the descendants of Ater (through Hezekiah)—98; **22** the descendants of Hashum—328; **23** the descendants of Bezai—324; **24** the descendants of Hariph—112; **25** the descendants of Gibeon—95.

26 These are the people from the towns of Bethlehem and Netophah—188; **27** of Anathoth—128; **28** of Beth Azmaveth—42; **29** of Kiriath Jearim, Kephirah and Beeroth—743; **30** of Ramah and Geba—621; **31** of Michmash—122; **32** of Bethel and Ai—123; **33** of the other Nebo—52; **34** of the other Elam—1,254; **35** of Harim—320; **36** of Jericho—345; **37** of Lod, Hadid and Ono—721; **38** of Senaah—3,930.

39 These are the priests: the descendants of Jedaiah (through the family of Jeshua)—973; **40** the descendants of Immer—1,052; **41** the descendants of Pashhur—1,247; **42** the descendants of Harim—1,017.

43 These are the Levites: the descendants of Jeshua (through Kadmiel through the family of Hodaviah)—74.

44 These are the singers: the descendants of Asaph—148.

45 These are the gatekeepers: the descendants of Shallum, Ater, Talmon, Akkub, Hatita and Shobai—138.

46 These are the Temple servants: the descendants of Ziha, Hasupha, Tabbaoth, **47** Keros, Sia, Padon, **48** Lebana, Hagaba, Shalmai, **49** Hanan, Giddel, Gahar, **50** Reaiah, Rezin, Nekoda, **51** Gazzam, Uzza, Paseah, **52** Besai, Meunim, Nephussim, **53** Bakbuk, Hakupha, Harhur, **54** Bazluth, Mehida, Harsha, **55** Barkos, Sisera, Temah, **56** Neziah and Hatipha.

57 These are the descendants of the servants of Solomon: the descendants of Sotai, Sophereth, Perida, **58** Jaala, Darkon, Giddel, **59** Shephatiah, Hattil, Pokereth-Hazzebaim and Amon.

60 The Temple servants and the descendants of the servants of Solomon totalled 392 people.

61 Some people came to Jerusalem from the towns of Tel Melah, Tel Harsha, Kerub, Addon and Immer, but they could not prove that their ancestors came from Israel. Here are their names and their number: **62** the descendants of Delaiah, Tobiah and Nekoda—642.

63 And these priests could not prove that their ancestors came from Israel: the descendants of Hobaiah, Hakkoz and Barzillai. (He had married a daughter of Barzillai from Gilead and was called by her family name.)

64 These people searched for their family records, but they could not find them. So they could not be priests, because they were thought to be unclean. **65** The governor ordered them not to eat any of the holy food until a priest settled this matter by using the Urim and Thummim.

66 The total number of those who returned was 42,360. **67** This is not counting their 7,337 male and female servants and the 245 male and female singers with them. **68** They had 736 horses, 245 mules, **69** 435 camels and 6,720 donkeys.

70 Some of the family leaders gave to the work. The governor gave to the treasury about 8 kilogrammes of gold, 50 bowls and 530 pieces of clothing for the priests. **71** Some of the family leaders gave about 170 kilogrammes of gold and about 1.3 tonnes of silver to the treasury for the work. **72** The total of what the other people gave was about 170 kilogrammes of gold, about a tonne of silver and 67 pieces of clothing for the priests. **73** So these people all settled in their own towns: the priests, the Levites, the gatekeepers, the singers, the Temple servants and all the other people of Israel.

Ezra Reads the Teachings

By the seventh month the Israelites were settled in their own towns.

8 All the people of Israel gathered together in the square by the Water Gate.

Nehemiah 8 634

WORSHIPPING GOD
Nehemiah 8:6

Livin' it

An Awesome God How would you explain the word *worship* to someone? Would you talk about going to church? Or maybe singing? Maybe you'd mention prayers. Good answers, but they're only the beginning. You can worship God anytime, anywhere and in many ways.

When God answered Job's prayer for understanding, God told Job how big he was. God is big, yet loving. God is in control of everything. When we begin to understand how awesome God is, we can't help but worship him in our everyday life. (Check out Job 38—41, p. 701.) How do you worship God when you're alone? When you're with others?

More Faith Links

My Worship Place, **p. 49**
Time to Celebrate, **p. 95**
How to Worship God, **p. 972**
The Gift of Worship, **p. 1275**
Meeting Together, **p. 1567**
Praise Him! **p. 1736**

You know, some people love to sing in a really loud voice when they worship.

But did you know that worship can be very quiet, too? Read on to find out what the Bible has to say about worship.

You're Invited! Psalm 100, p. 784
- When someone invites you to a special event, how do you feel? Excited? Glad to be invited? You would probably go and have a good time. Link here for a special invitation. Feel free to invite a friend to join in!

God's New Temple, Ezekiel 40—44, p. 1135
- Where do you meet with other believers to worship God? In a church? A school? A house? Or maybe outdoors? Does it matter where you worship? Why or why not?
- If you're a Christian, you provide a temple for God within your own body. That's where the Holy Spirit lives. How do you worship God in your "body" temple?

Too Busy to Worship? Luke 2:8–20, p. 1368
- Too busy to worship God? Take time to make worship an important part of your life. Link here to meet some very busy people who dropped everything to worship.

My Favourite Links

THE HOMECOMING — Nehemiah 8:1–12

Because the Israelites didn't stay obedient to God, they became a weak nation. Eventually, the city of Jerusalem (the capital city) was destroyed by the Babylonians, and many Israelites were carried away to Babylon to live. Later, Babylon was taken over by the Persians, and the Israelites finally were allowed to return home.

Not all of the Israelites wanted to go back home. They had lived in Babylon a long time. It felt like home. The ones who did make the trip went back in three groups. Each of these groups had a specific job to do.

1. The first group, led by Zerubbabel, returned home to rebuild the Temple. (See Ezra 6:3–22, p. 615.)

2. Ezra's group helped the people relearn how to follow God's laws. (Read Nehemiah 8:1–12.)

3. The last group, led by Nehemiah, rebuilt the wall around Jerusalem in just 52 days. (See Nehemiah 6:15.)

There were three prophets God sent to encourage and teach the people as they returned – Haggai, Zechariah and Malachi.

They asked Ezra the teacher to bring out the Book of the Teachings of Moses, which the LORD had given to Israel.

2 So on the first day of the seventh month, Ezra the priest brought out the Teachings for the crowd. Men, women and all who could listen and understand had gathered. 3 At the square by the Water Gate Ezra read the Teachings out loud from early morning until noon to the men, women and everyone who could listen and understand. All the people listened carefully to the Book of the Teachings.

4 Ezra the teacher stood on a high wooden platform that had been built just for this time. On his right were Mattithiah, Shema, Anaiah, Uriah, Hilkiah and Maaseiah. And on his left were Pedaiah, Mishael, Malkijah, Hashum, Hashbaddanah, Zechariah and Meshullam.

5 Ezra opened the book in full view of everyone, because he was above them. As he opened it, all the people stood up. 6 Ezra praised the LORD, the great God, and all the people held up their hands and said, "Amen! Amen!" Then they bowed down and worshipped the LORD with their faces to the ground.

7 These Levites explained the Teachings to the people as they stood there: Jeshua, Bani, Sherebiah, Jamin, Akkub, Shabbethai, Hodiah, Maaseiah, Kelita, Azariah, Jozabad, Hanan and Pelaiah. 8 They read from the Book of the Teachings of God and explained what it meant so the people understood what was being read.

9 Then Nehemiah the governor, Ezra the priest and teacher, and the Levites who were teaching said to all the people, "This is a holy day to the LORD your God. Don't be sad or cry." All the people had been crying as they listened to the words of the Teachings.

> **8:6 Worship** — What should your attitude be towards God?

FAITH links

SEE THE HEART BEHIND IT
NEHEMIAH 8; 9

Picture your mum or dad in full lecture mode. They are telling you about the kind of behaviour they expect from you. Picture your own expression as you're listening to this. What does it show? Boredom? Restlessness? When the Temple was completed, Ezra read the Book of the Teachings to the people. Everyone stood there for hours listening. In response, they confessed their sins. What made them do it? They could see the heart behind the words. They understood how much God loved them.

Your parents and God want you to have the best life possible. When your mum or dad goes into lecture mode, look for the heart behind it.

Check out these other Faithlinks on listening:

Faith of Our Fathers, Joshua 4:4–9, p. 280

In Your Best Interests, Ruth 3, p. 349

Deciding Wisely, 1 Kings 3:16–28, p. 440

A Word to the Wise, Proverbs 10:1, p. 838

Cut to the Quick, Hebrews 4:12, p. 1670

The Way to Be Wise, James 1:5, p. 1689

---

10 Nehemiah said, "Go and enjoy good food and sweet drinks. Send some to people who have none, because today is a holy day to the Lord. Don't be sad, because the joy of the LORD will make you strong."

11 The Levites helped calm the people, saying, "Be quiet, because this is a holy day. Don't be sad."

12 Then all the people went away to eat and drink, to send some of their food to others and to celebrate with great joy. They finally understood what they had been taught.

13 On the second day of the month, the leaders of all the families, the priests and the Levites met with Ezra the teacher. They gathered to study the words of the Teachings. 14 This is what they found written in the Teachings: the LORD commanded through Moses that the people of Israel were to live in shelters during the feast of the seventh month. 15 The people were supposed to preach this message and spread it through all their towns and in Jerusalem: "Go out into the mountains, and bring back branches from olive and wild olive trees, myrtle trees, palms and shade trees. Make shelters with them, as it is written."

16 So the people went out and got tree branches. They built shelters on their roofs,[n] in their courtyards, in the courtyards of the Temple, in the square by the Water Gate and in the square next to the Gate of Ephraim. 17 The whole group that had come back from captivity built shelters and lived in them. The Israelites had not done this since the time of Joshua son of Nun. And they were very happy.

18 Ezra read to them every day from the Book of the Teachings, from the first day to the last. The people of Israel celebrated the feast for seven days, and then on the eighth day the people gathered as the law said.

8:16 roofs In Bible times houses were built with flat roofs. The roof was used for drying things such as flax and fruit. And it was used as an extra room, as a place for worship and as a place to sleep in the summer.

Israel Confesses Sins

9 On the twenty-fourth day of that same month, the people of Israel gathered. They did not eat, and they wore rough cloth and put dust on their heads to show their sadness. 2 Those people whose ancestors were from Israel had separated themselves from all foreigners. They stood and confessed their sins and their ancestors' sins. 3 For a quarter of the day they stood where they were and read from the Book of the Teachings of the LORD their God. For another quarter of the day they confessed their sins and worshipped the LORD their God. 4 These Levites were standing on the stairs: Jeshua, Bani, Kadmiel, Shebaniah, Bunni, Sherebiah, Bani and Kanani. They called out to the LORD their God with loud voices. 5 Then these Levites spoke: Jeshua, Kadmiel, Bani, Hashabneiah, Sherebiah, Hodiah, Shebaniah and Pethahiah. They said, "Stand up and praise the LORD your God, who lives for ever and ever."

The People's Prayer

"Blessed be your wonderful name.
It is more wonderful than all
blessing and praise.
6 You are the only LORD.
You made the heavens, even the
highest heavens,
with all the stars.
You made the earth and everything
on it,
the seas and everything in them;
you give life to everything.
The heavenly army worships you.

7 "You are the LORD,
the God who chose Abram
and brought him out of Ur in
Babylonia
and named him Abraham.
8 You found him faithful to you,
so you made an agreement with
him
to give his descendants the land of
the Canaanites,
Hittites, Amorites,
Perizzites, Jebusites and
Girgashites.
You have kept your promise,
because you do what is right.

9 "You saw our ancestors suffering in
Egypt
and heard them cry out at the Red
Sea.
10 You did signs and miracles against
the king of Egypt,
and against all his officers and all
his people,
because you knew how proud they
were.
You became as famous as you are
today.
11 You divided the sea in front of our
ancestors;
they walked through on dry
ground.
But you threw the people chasing
them into the deep water,
like a stone thrown into mighty
waters.
12 You led our ancestors with a pillar of
cloud by day
and with a pillar of fire at night.
It lit the way
they were supposed to go.
13 You came down to Mount Sinai
and spoke from heaven to our
ancestors.
You gave them fair rules and true
teachings,
good orders and commands.
14 You told them
about your
holy Sabbath
and gave them
commands,
orders and
teachings
through your servant Moses.
15 When they were hungry, you gave
them bread from heaven.
When they were thirsty, you
brought them water from the
rock.
You told them to enter and take over
the land you had promised to give
them.

16 "But our ancestors were proud and
stubborn

9:14
Bible
Where did the Bible come from?

and did not obey your commands.
17 They refused to listen;
   they forgot the miracles you did for them.
   So they became stubborn and turned against you,
   choosing a leader to take them back to slavery.
   But you are a forgiving God.
   You are kind and full of mercy.
   You do not become angry quickly and you have great love.
   So you did not leave them.
18 Our ancestors even made an idol of a calf for themselves.
   They said, 'This is your god, Israel,
   who brought you up out of Egypt.'
   They spoke against you.
19 "You have great mercy,
   so you did not leave them in the desert.
   The pillar of cloud guided them by day,
   and the pillar of fire led them at night,
   lighting the way they were to go.
20 You gave your good Spirit to teach them.
   You gave them manna to eat
   and water when they were thirsty.
21 You took care of them for 40 years in the desert;
   they needed nothing.
   Their clothes did not wear out,
   and their feet did not swell.
22 "You gave them kingdoms and nations;
   you gave them more land.
   They took over the country of Sihon king of Heshbon
   and the country of Og king of Bashan.
23 You made their children as many as the stars in the sky,
   and you brought them into the land
   that you told their fathers to enter and take over.
24 So their children went into the land and took over.
   The Canaanites lived there, but you defeated them for our ancestors.
   You handed over to them the Canaanites, their kings and the people of the land.
   Our ancestors could do what they wanted with them.
25 They captured strong, walled cities and fertile land.
   They took over houses full of good things,
   wells that were already dug,
   vineyards, olive trees and many fruit trees.
   They ate until they were full and grew fat;
   they enjoyed your great goodness.
26 "But they were disobedient and turned against you
   and ignored your teachings.
   Your prophets warned them to come back to you,
   but they killed those prophets and spoke against you.
27 So you handed them over to their enemies,
   and their enemies treated them badly.
   But in this time of trouble our ancestors cried out to you,
   and you heard from heaven.
   You had great mercy
   and gave them saviours who saved them from the power of their enemies.
28 But as soon as they had rest,
   they again did what was evil.
   So you left them to their enemies who ruled over them.
   When they cried out to you again,
   you heard from heaven.
   Because of your mercy, you saved them again and again.
29 You warned them to return to your teachings,
   but they were proud and did not obey your commands.

eMAIL FROM GOD 9:27
Feelings
Does God care when you hurt?

If someone obeys your laws, he will live,
but they sinned against your laws.
They were stubborn, unwilling and disobedient.
30 You were patient with them for many years
and warned them by your Spirit through the prophets,
but they did not pay attention.
So you handed them over to other countries.
31 But because your mercy is great, you did not kill them all or leave them.
You are a kind and merciful God.

32 "And so, our God, you are the great and mighty and wonderful God.
You keep your agreement of love.
Do not let all our trouble seem unimportant to you.
This trouble has come to us, to our kings and our leaders,
to our priests and prophets,
to our ancestors and all your people
from the days of the kings of Assyria until today.
33 You have been fair in everything that has happened to us;
you have been loyal, but we have been wicked.
34 Our kings, leaders, priests and ancestors did not obey your teachings;
they did not pay attention to the commands and warnings you gave them.
35 Even when our ancestors were living in their kingdom,
enjoying all the good things you had given them,
enjoying the land that was fertile and full of room,
they did not stop their evil ways.

36 "Look, we are slaves today in the land you gave our ancestors.
They were to enjoy its fruit and its good things,
but look, we are slaves here.
37 The land's great harvest belongs to the kings you have put over us because of our sins.
Those kings rule over us and our cattle as they please,
so we are in much trouble.

The People's Agreement

38 "Because of all this, we are making an agreement in writing, and our leaders, Levites and priests are putting their seals on it."

10 These are the men who sealed the agreement:
Nehemiah the governor, son of Hacaliah.

2 Zedekiah, Seraiah, Azariah, Jeremiah, 3 Pashhur, Amariah, Malkijah, 4 Hattush, Shebaniah, Malluch, 5 Harim, Meremoth, Obadiah, 6 Daniel, Ginnethon, Baruch, 7 Meshullam, Abijah, Mijamin, 8 Maaziah, Bilgai and Shemaiah. These are the priests.

9 These are the Levites who sealed it: Jeshua son of Azaniah, Binnui of the sons of Henadad, Kadmiel 10 and their fellow Levites: Shebaniah, Hodiah, Kelita, Pelaiah, Hanan, 11 Mica, Rehob, Hashabiah, 12 Zaccur, Sherebiah, Shebaniah, 13 Hodiah, Bani and Beninu.

14 These are the leaders of the people who sealed the agreement: Parosh, Pahath-Moab, Elam, Zattu, Bani, 15 Bunni, Azgad, Bebai, 16 Adonijah, Bigvai, Adin, 17 Ater, Hezekiah, Azzur, 18 Hodiah, Hashum, Bezai, 19 Hariph, Anathoth, Nebai, 20 Magpiash, Meshullam, Hezir, 21 Meshezabel, Zadok, Jaddua, 22 Pelatiah, Hanan, Anaiah, 23 Hoshea, Hananiah, Hasshub, 24 Hallohesh, Pilha, Shobek, 25 Rehum, Hashabnah, Maaseiah, 26 Ahiah, Hanan, Anan, 27 Malluch, Harim and Baanah.

28 The rest of the people took an oath. They were the priests, Levites, gatekeepers, singers, Temple servants, all those who separated themselves from foreigners to keep the Teachings of God and also their wives and their sons and daughters who could understand. 29 They joined their fellow Israelites and their leading men in taking an oath, which was tied to a curse in case they broke the oath.

They promised to follow the Teachings of God, which they had been given through Moses the servant of God, and to obey all the commands, rules and laws of the LORD our God.

30 They said:

We promise not to let our daughters marry foreigners nor to let our sons marry their daughters. 31 Foreigners may bring goods or grain to sell on the Sabbath, but we will not buy on the Sabbath or any holy day. Every seventh year we will not plant, and that year we will forget all that people owe us.

32 We will be responsible for the commands to pay for the service of the Temple of our God. We will give 4 grammes of silver each year. 33 It is for the bread that is set out on the table; the regular grain offerings and burnt offerings; the offerings on the Sabbaths, New Moon festivals and special feasts; the holy offerings; the offerings to remove the sins of the Israelites so they will belong to God; and for the work of the Temple of our God.

34 We, the priests, the Levites and the people, have thrown lots to decide at what time of year each family must bring wood to the Temple. The wood is for burning on the altar of the LORD our God, and we will do this as it is written in the Teachings.

35 We also will bring the first fruits from our crops and the first fruits of every tree to the Temple each year.

36 We will bring to the Temple our firstborn sons and cattle and the firstborn of our herds and flocks, as it is written in the Teachings. We will bring them to the priests who are serving in the Temple.

37 We will bring to the priests at the storerooms of the Temple the first of our ground meal, our offerings, the fruit from all our trees and our new wine and oil. And we will bring a tenth of our crops to the Levites, who will collect these things in all the towns where we work. 38 A priest of Aaron's family must be with the Levites when they receive the tenth of the people's crops. The Levites must bring a tenth of all they receive to the Temple of our God to put in the storerooms of the treasury. 39 The people of Israel and the Levites are to bring to the storerooms the gifts of grain, new wine and oil. That is where the utensils for the Temple are kept and where the priests who are serving, the gatekeepers and singers stay.

We will not ignore the Temple of our God.

New People Move into Jerusalem

11 The leaders of Israel lived in Jerusalem. But the rest of the people threw lots to choose one person out of every ten to come and live in Jerusalem, the holy city. The other nine could stay in their own cities. 2 The people blessed those who volunteered to live in Jerusalem.

3 These are the area leaders who lived in Jerusalem. (Some people lived on their own land in the cities of Judah. These included Israelites, priests, Levites, Temple servants and descendants of Solomon's servants. 4 Others from the families of Judah and Benjamin lived in Jerusalem.)

These are the descendants of Judah who moved into Jerusalem. There was Athaiah son of Uzziah. (Uzziah was the son of Zechariah, the son of Amariah. Amariah was the son of Shephatiah, the son of Mahalalel. Mahalalel was a descendant of Perez.) 5 There was also Masseiah son of Baruch. (Baruch was the son of

---

> We also will bring the first fruits from our crops and the first fruits of every tree to the Temple each year.
> – Nehemiah 10:35

Col-Hozeh, the son of Hazaiah. Hazaiah was the son of Adaiah, the son of Joiarib. Joiarib was the son of Zechariah, a descendant of Shelah.) **6** All the descendants of Perez who lived in Jerusalem totalled 468 men. They were soldiers.

7 These are descendants of Benjamin who moved into Jerusalem. There was Sallu son of Meshullam. (Meshullam was the son of Joed, the son of Pedaiah. Pedaiah was the son of Kolaiah, the son of Maaseiah. Maaseiah was the son of Ithiel, the son of Jeshaiah.) **8** Following him were Gabbai and Sallai, for a total of 928 men. **9** Joel son of Zicri was appointed over them, and Judah son of Hassenuah was second in charge of the new area of the city.

10 These are the priests who moved into Jerusalem. There was Jedaiah son of Joiarib, Jakin **11** and Seraiah son of Hilkiah, the supervisor in the Temple. (Hilkiah was the son of Meshullam, the son of Zadok. Zadok was the son of Meraioth, the son of Ahitub.) **12** And there were others with them who did the work for the Temple. Altogether there were 822 men. Also there was Adaiah son of Jeroham. (Jeroham was the son of Pelaliah, the son of Amzi. Amzi was the son of Zechariah, the son of Pashhur. Pashhur was the son of Malkijah.) **13** And there were family heads with him. Altogether there were 242 men. Also there was Amashsai son of Azarel. (Azarel was the son of Ahzai, the son of Meshillemoth. Meshillemoth was the son of Immer.) **14** And there were brave men with Amashsai. Altogether there were 128 men. Zabdiel son of Haggedolim was appointed over them.

15 These are the Levites who moved into Jerusalem. There was Shemaiah son of Hasshub. (Hasshub was the son of Azrikam, the son of Hashabiah. Hashabiah was the son of Bunni.) **16** And there were Shabbethai and Jozabad, two of the leaders of the Levites who were in charge of the work outside the Temple. **17** There was Mattaniah son of Mica. (Mica was the son of Zabdi, the son of Asaph.) Mattaniah was the director who led the people in thanksgiving and prayer. There was Bakbukiah, who was second in charge over his fellow Levites. And there was Abda son of Shammua. (Shammua was the son of Galal, the son of Jeduthun.) **18** Altogether 284 Levites lived in the holy city of Jerusalem.

19 The gatekeepers who moved into Jerusalem were Akkub, Talmon and others with them. There was a total of 172 men who guarded the city gates.

20 The other Israelites, priests and Levites lived on their own land in all the cities of Judah.

21 The Temple servants lived on the hill of Ophel, and Ziha and Gishpa were in charge of them.

22 Uzzi son of Bani was appointed over the Levites in Jerusalem. (Bani was the son of Hashabiah, the son of Mattaniah. Mattaniah was the son of Mica.) Uzzi was one of Asaph's descendants, who were the singers responsible for the service of the Temple. **23** The singers were under the king's orders, which regulated them day by day.

24 Pethahiah son of Meshezabel was the king's spokesman. (Meshezabel was a descendant of Zerah, the son of Judah.)

25 Some of the people of Judah lived in villages with their surrounding fields. They lived in Kiriath Arba and its surroundings, in Dibon and its surroundings, in Jekabzeel and its surroundings, **26** in Jeshua, Moladah, Beth Pelet, **27** Hazar Shual, Beersheba and its surroundings, **28** in Ziklag and Meconah and its surroundings, **29** in En Rimmon, Zorah, Jarmuth, **30** Zanoah, Adullam and their villages, in Lachish and the fields around it, and in Azekah and its surroundings. So they settled from Beersheba all the way to the Valley of Hinnom.

31 The descendants of the Benjaminites from Geba lived in Michmash, Aija,

> The people blessed those who volunteered to live in Jerusalem.
> – Nehemiah 11:2

Bethel and its surroundings, 32 in Anathoth, Nob, Ananiah, 33 Hazor, Ramah, Gittaim, 34 Hadid, Zeboim, Neballat, 35 Lod, Ono and in the Valley of the Craftsmen.

36 Some groups of the Levites from Judah settled in the land of Benjamin.

Priests and Levites

12 These are the priests and Levites who returned with Zerubbabel son of Shealtiel and with Jeshua. There were Seraiah, Jeremiah, Ezra, 2 Amariah, Malluch, Hattush, 3 Shecaniah, Rehum, Meremoth, 4 Iddo, Ginnethon, Abijah, 5 Mijamin, Moadiah, Bilgah, 6 Shemaiah, Joiarib, Jedaiah, 7 Sallu, Amok, Hilkiah and Jedaiah. They were the leaders of the priests and their relatives in the days of Jeshua.

8 The Levites were Jeshua, Binnui, Kadmiel, Sherebiah, Judah and Mattaniah. Mattaniah and his relatives were in charge of the songs of thanksgiving. 9 Bakbukiah and Unni, their relatives, stood across from them in the services.

10 Jeshua was the father of Joiakim. Joiakim was the father of Eliashib. Eliashib was the father of Joiada. 11 Joiada was the father of Jonathan and Jonathan was the father of Jaddua.

12 In the days of Joiakim, these priests were the leaders of the families of priests: Meraiah, from Seraiah's family; Hananiah, from Jeremiah's family; 13 Meshullam, from Ezra's family; Jehohanan, from Amariah's family; 14 Jonathan, from Malluch's family; Joseph, from Shecaniah's family; 15 Adna, from Harim's family; Helkai, from Meremoth's family; 16 Zechariah, from Iddo's family; Meshullam, from Ginnethon's family; 17 Zicri, from Abijah's family; Piltai, from Miniamin's and Moadiah's families; 18 Shammua, from Bilgah's family; Jehonathan, from Shemaiah's family; 19 Mattenai, from Joiarib's family; Uzzi, from Jedaiah's family; 20 Kallai, from Sallu's family; Eber, from Amok's family; 21 Hashabiah, from Hilkiah's family; and Nethanel, from Jedaiah's family.

22 The leaders of the families of the Levites and the priests were written down in the days of Eliashib, Joiada, Johanan and Jaddua, while Darius the Persian was king. 23 The family leaders among the Levites were written down in the history book, but only up to the time of Johanan son of Eliashib. 24 The leaders of the Levites were Hashabiah, Sherebiah, Jeshua son of Kadmiel and their relatives. Their relatives stood across from them and gave praise and thanksgiving to God. One group answered the other group, as David, the man of God, had commanded.

25 These were the gatekeepers who guarded the storerooms next to the gates:

FAITH CHALLENGE

Here's one for you. Read 12:27 to discover how the people of Israel gave thanks to God for everything he had done for them. What are your favourite and least favourite ways to worship God?

TeSTiNG iT

Nehemiah 12:27
When the wall of Jerusalem was offered as a gift to God, they asked the Levites to come from wherever they lived to Jerusalem to celebrate with joy the gift of the wall. They were to celebrate with songs of thanksgiving and with the music of cymbals, harps and lyres.

Mattaniah, Bakbukiah, Obadiah, Meshullam, Talmon and Akkub. 26 They served in the days of Joiakim son of Jeshua, the son of Jozadak. They also served in the days of Nehemiah the governor and Ezra the priest and teacher.

The Wall of Jerusalem

27 When the wall of Jerusalem was offered as a gift to God, they asked the Levites to come from wherever they lived to Jerusalem to celebrate with joy the gift of the wall. They were to celebrate with songs of thanksgiving and with the music of cymbals, harps and lyres. 28 They also brought together singers from all around Jerusalem, from the Netophathite villages, 29 from Beth Gilgal and from the areas of Geba and Azmaveth. The singers had built villages for themselves around Jerusalem. 30 The priests and Levites made themselves pure, and they also made the people, the gates and the wall of Jerusalem pure.

31 I had the leaders of Judah go up on top of the wall, and I appointed two large choruses to give thanks. One chorus went to the right on top of the wall, towards the Rubbish Gate. 32 Behind them went Hoshaiah and half the leaders of Judah. 33 Azariah, Ezra, Meshullam, 34 Judah, Benjamin, Shemaiah and Jeremiah also went. 35 Some priests with trumpets also went, along with Zechariah son of Jonathan. (Jonathan was the son of Shemaiah, the son of Mattaniah. Mattaniah was the son of Micaiah, the son of Zaccur. Zaccur was the son of Asaph.) 36 Zechariah's relatives also went. They were Shemaiah, Azarel, Milalai, Gilalai, Maai, Nethanel, Judah and Hanani. These men played the musical instruments of David, the man of God, and Ezra the teacher walked in front of them. 37 They went from the Fountain Gate straight up the steps to the highest part of the wall by the older part of the city. They went on above the house of David to the Water Gate on the east.

38 The second chorus went to the left, while I followed them on top of the wall with half the people. We went from the Tower of the Ovens to the Broad Wall, 39 over the Gate of Ephraim to the Old Gate and the Fish Gate, to the Tower of Hananel and the Tower of the Hundred. We went as far as the Sheep Gate and stopped at the Gate of the Guard.

40 The two choruses took their places at the Temple. Half of the leaders and I did also. 41 These priests were there with their trumpets: Eliakim, Maaseiah, Miniamin, Micaiah, Elioenai, Zechariah and Hananiah. 42 These people were also there: Maaseiah, Shemaiah, Eleazar, Uzzi, Jehohanan, Malkijah, Elam and Ezer. The choruses sang, led by Jezrahiah. 43 The people offered many sacrifices that day and were happy because God had given them great joy. The women and children were happy. The sound of happiness in Jerusalem could be heard far away.

12:43
Joy
Who gives you joy?

44 At that time the leaders appointed men to be in charge of the storerooms. These rooms were for the gifts, the first fruits and the tenth that the people brought. The Teachings said they should bring a share for the priests and Levites from the fields around the towns. The people of Judah were happy to do this for the priests and Levites who served. 45 They performed the service of their God in making things pure. The singers and gatekeepers also did their jobs, as David had commanded his son Solomon. 46 Earlier, in the time of David and Asaph, there was a leader of the singers and of the songs of praise and thanksgiving to God. 47 So it was in the days of Zerubbabel and Nehemiah. All the people of Israel gave something to the singers and gatekeepers, and they also set aside part for the Levites. Then the Levites set aside part for the descendants of Aaron.

Foreign People are Sent Away

13 On that day they read the Book of Moses to the people, and they found that it said no Ammonite or Moabite should ever be allowed in the meeting to worship. 2 The Ammonites and Moabites had not welcomed the Israelites with

food and water. Instead, they had hired Balaam to put a curse on Israel. (But our God turned the curse into a blessing.) 3 When the people heard this teaching, they separated all foreigners from Israel.

Nehemiah Returns to Jerusalem

4 Before that happened, Eliashib the priest, who was in charge of the Temple storerooms, was friendly with Tobiah. 5 Eliashib let Tobiah use one of the large storerooms. Earlier it had been used for grain offerings, incense, the utensils and the tenth offerings of grain, new wine and olive oil that belonged to the Levites, singers and gatekeepers. It had also been used for gifts for the priests.

6 I was not in Jerusalem when this happened. I had gone back to Artaxerxes king of Babylon in the thirty-second year he was king. Finally I asked the king to let me leave. 7 When I returned to Jerusalem, I found out the evil Eliashib had done by letting Tobiah have a room in the Temple courtyard. 8 I was very upset at this, so I threw all of Tobiah's goods out of the room. 9 I ordered the rooms to be purified, and I brought back the utensils for God's Temple, the grain offerings and the incense.

10 Then I found out the people were not giving the Levites their shares. So the Levites and singers who served had gone back to their own farms. 11 I argued with the officers, saying, "Why haven't you taken care of the Temple?" Then I gathered the Levites and singers and put them back at their places.

12 All the people of Judah then brought to the storerooms a tenth of their crops, new wine and olive oil. 13 I put these men in charge of the storerooms: Shelemiah the priest, Zadok the teacher and Pedaiah a Levite. I made Hanan son of Zaccur, the son of Mattaniah, their helper. Everyone knew they were honest men. They gave out the portions that went to their relatives.

14 Remember me, my God, for this. Do not ignore my love for the Temple and its service.

15 In those days I saw people in Judah working in the winepresses on the Sabbath day. They were bringing in grain and loading it on donkeys. And they were bringing loads of wine, grapes and figs into Jerusalem on the Sabbath day. So I warned them about selling food on that

FAITH links

AN HONEST REPUTATION

NEHEMIAH 13:13

If you needed someone to watch your wallet for a while, would you hand it to someone who has the reputation for being a thief? Not likely! When Nehemiah looked for people to put in charge of the Temple storerooms, he looked for people he could count on. It was a position of great responsibility! So he found three men who had a reputation for honesty.

What's your reputation at home? At school? You're known by how you act. Are you known for honesty? Dependability? If you want a good reputation, you've got to earn it by consistent behaviour.

The Best Policy, Genesis 29:16–29, p. 41

Always Truthful, Numbers 23:19, p. 208

Down on the Ant Farm, Proverbs 6:6–11, p. 833

A Broken Promise, Jeremiah 2:1–8, p. 989

The Deadliest Lie, Acts 5:1–11, p. 1471

Say What?! Ephesians 4:22–29, p. 1603

day. 16 People from the city of Tyre who were living in Jerusalem brought in fish and other things and sold them there on the Sabbath day to the people of Judah. 17 I argued with the important men of Judah and said to them, "What is this evil thing you are doing? You are ruining the Sabbath day. 18 This is just what your ancestors did. So our God did terrible things to us and this city. Now you are making him even more angry at Israel by ruining the Sabbath day."

19 So I ordered that the doors be shut at sunset before the Sabbath and not be opened until the Sabbath was over. I put my servants at the gates so no load could come in on the Sabbath. 20 Once or twice traders and sellers of all kinds of goods spent the night outside Jerusalem. 21 So I warned them, "Why are you spending the night by the wall? If you do it again, I will force you away." After that, they did not come back on the Sabbath. 22 Then I ordered the Levites to purify themselves and to guard the city gates to make sure the Sabbath remained holy.

Remember me, my God, for this. Have mercy on me because of your great love.

23 In those days I saw men of Judah who had married women from Ashdod, Ammon and Moab. 24 Half their children were speaking the language of Ashdod or some other place, and they couldn't speak the language of Judah. 25 I argued with those people, put curses on them, hit some of them and pulled out their hair. I forced them to make a promise to God, saying, "Do not let your daughters marry the sons of foreigners, and do not take the daughters of foreigners as wives for your sons or yourselves. 26 Foreign women made King Solomon of Israel sin. There was never a king like him in any of the nations. God loved Solomon and made him king over all Israel, but foreign women made him sin. 27 And now you are not obedient when you do this evil thing. You are unfaithful to our God when you marry foreign wives."

28 Joiada was the son of Eliashib the high priest. One of Joiada's sons married a daughter of Sanballat the Horonite, so I sent him away from me.

29 Remember them, my God, because they made the priesthood unclean and the agreement of the priests and Levites unclean.

30 So I purified them of everything that was foreign. I appointed duties for the priests and Levites, giving each man his own job. 31 I also made sure wood was brought for the altar at regular times and that the first fruits were brought.

Remember me, my God; be kind to me.

13:31 Blessings
See what Nehemiah asks for from God.

IN THE RIGHT PLACE
Greetings! I am Esther, queen of Persia. I did not write this book, but the author was probably a fellow Jew living in Persia. Have you ever heard the expression "being in the right place at the right time"? I was very young when I was brought to the royal palace; but after a year of beauty treatments and training, I was ready to meet the king. Imagine my surprise when the king chose me to be his queen! Little did I know that my position was part of God's plan to save his people. Haman, one of the king's trusted servants, plotted to have all the Jews in the kingdom put to death. My cousin Mordecai urged me to beg the king for mercy: "Who knows, you may have been chosen queen for just such a time as this" (Esther 4:14).

This book was written to show how God takes care of his people. Sometimes he uses ordinary people like you and me as part of his plan. God placed me in a high position so I would be able to influence the king. Has God placed you in a position to serve him in a special way?

JESUS WATCH

Esther may have been queen, but she risked her life by attempting to see the king when he had not sent for her. She prepared for her meeting by fasting and praying for three days and asking other people to do the same. She was willing to give up her own life in the hope of saving God's people. Jesus was not only willing, but he did give up his life to save God's people. Jesus became a man, knowing that he would die as punishment for our wrongdoings. Jesus was willing to die on the cross so that we can be saved from a life of sin.

my FAVOURITE links

OTHER CONNECTIONS

 Imagine – somebody who isn't British becoming king or queen.

Not possible? God made something similar to that happen when Esther, an Israelite woman, became queen of Persia! Read more about it by linking to A Foreign Queen, Esther 6.

MORE STUFF...
Behind the Scenes   God's name is never mentioned in the Book of Esther. Yet, he makes himself known in many different ways throughout the book.

Consider one way in which God is at work in Esther. Esther was part of the Jewish community that had been taken captive from Jerusalem by Nebuchadnezzar to Babylon and that worshipped God. She was taken to the royal palace and later made queen (Esther 2:5–18). (See also Mordecai's comment in Esther 4:13–14.)

What happened to the plan Haman had for the king to honour him?

Well, the king used Haman's ideas, but not exactly in the way Haman had planned! Connect to Esther 6:6-12 to see what happened!

DON'T MISS THESE OTHER COOL STORIES:
Esther's beauty plan, Esther 2:8–18
Haman's evil plan, Esther 3
A robe and a horse for Mordecai, Esther 6
Haman begs for his life, Esther 7

FAITH links

○ A Life-Saving Message, **Esther 2:19–22**

○ Standing for What's Right, **Esther 3:2–4**

○ The Big Risk, **Esther 4:11—5:2**

○ A Holiday Letter, **Esther 9:20–23**

Queen Vashti Disobeys the King

1 This is what happened during the time of King Xerxes, the king who ruled the 127 areas from India to Cush. 2 In those days King Xerxes ruled from his capital city of Susa. 3 In the third year of his rule, he gave a banquet for all his important men and royal officers. The army leaders from the countries of Persia and Media and the important men from all Xerxes' empire were there.

4 The banquet lasted 180 days. All during that time King Xerxes was showing off the great wealth of his kingdom and his own great riches and glory. 5 When the 180 days were over, the king gave another banquet. It was held in the courtyard of the palace garden for seven days, and it was for everybody in the palace at Susa, from the greatest to the least. 6 The courtyard had fine white curtains and purple linen that were tied to silver rings on marble pillars by white and purple cords. And there were gold and silver couches on a floor set with tiles of white marble, shells and gems. 7 Wine was served in gold cups of various kinds. And there was plenty of the king's wine, because he was very generous. 8 The king commanded that the guests be permitted to drink as much as they wished. He told the wine servers to serve each person what he wanted.

9 Queen Vashti also gave a banquet for the women in the royal palace of King Xerxes.

10 On the seventh day of the banquet, King Xerxes was very happy, because he had been drinking much wine. He gave a command to the seven eunuchs who served him—Mehuman, Biztha, Harbona, Bigtha, Abagtha, Zethar and Carcas. 11 He commanded them to bring him Queen Vashti, wearing her royal crown. She was to come to show her beauty to the people and important men, because she was very beautiful. 12 The eunuchs told Queen Vashti about the king's command, but she refused to come. Then the king became very angry; his anger was like a burning fire.

13 It was a custom for the king to ask advice from experts about law and order. So King Xerxes spoke with the wise men who would know the right thing to do. 14 The wise men the king usually talked to were Carshena, Shethar, Admatha, Tarshish, Meres, Marsena and Memucan, seven of the important men of Persia and Media. These seven had special privileges to see the king and had the highest rank in the kingdom. 15 The king asked them, "What does the law say must be done to Queen Vashti? She has not obeyed the command of King Xerxes, which the eunuchs took to her."

16 Then Memucan said to the king and the other important men, "Queen Vashti has not done wrong to the king alone. She has also done wrong to all the important men and all the people in all the empire of King Xerxes. 17 All the wives of the important men of Persia and Media will hear about the queen's actions. Then they will no longer honour their husbands. They will say, 'King Xerxes commanded Queen Vashti to be brought to him, but she refused to come.' 18 Today the wives of the important men of Persia and Media have heard about the queen's actions. So they will speak in the same way to their husbands, and there will be no end to disrespect and anger.

19 "So, our king, if it pleases you, give a royal order, and let it be written in the laws of Persia and Media, which cannot be changed. The law should say Vashti is never again to enter the presence of King Xerxes. Also let the king give her place as queen to someone who is better than she is. 20 And let the king's order be announced everywhere in his great kingdom. Then all the women will respect their husbands, from the greatest to the least."

> Also let the king give her place as queen to someone who is better than she is.
> – Esther 1:19

21 The king and his important men were happy with this advice, so King Xerxes did as Memucan suggested. 22 He sent letters to all the areas of the kingdom in the writing of each area and in the language of each group of people. These letters announced that each man was to be the ruler of his own family.

Esther is Made Queen

2 Later, when King Xerxes was not so angry, he remembered Vashti and what she had done and his order about her. 2 Then the king's personal servants suggested, "Let a search be made for beautiful young girls for the king. 3 Let the king choose supervisors in every area of his kingdom to bring every beautiful young girl to the palace at Susa. They should be taken to the women's quarters and put under the care of Hegai, the king's eunuch in charge of the women. And let beauty treatments be given to them. 4 Then let the girl who most pleases the king become queen in place of Vashti." The king liked this idea, so he did as they said.

5 Now there was a Jewish man in the palace of Susa whose name was Mordecai son of Jair. Jair was the son of Shimei, the son of Kish. Mordecai was from the tribe of Benjamin, 6 which had been taken captive from Jerusalem by Nebuchadnezzar king of Babylon. They were part of the group taken into captivity with Jehoiachin king of Judah. 7 Mordecai had a cousin named Hadassah, who had no father or mother, so Mordecai took care of her. Hadassah was also called Esther, and she had a very pretty figure and face. Mordecai had adopted her as his own daughter when her father and mother died.

8 When the king's command and order had been heard, many girls had been brought to the palace in Susa and put under the care of Hegai. Esther was also taken to the king's palace and put under the care of Hegai, who was in charge of the women. 9 Esther pleased Hegai, and he liked her. So Hegai quickly began giving Esther her beauty treatments and special food. He gave her seven servant girls chosen from the king's palace. Then he moved her and her seven servant girls to the best part of the women's quarters.

10 Esther did not tell anyone about her family or who her people were, because Mordecai had told her not to. 11 Every day Mordecai walked back and forth near the courtyard where the king's women lived to find out how Esther was and what was happening to her.

> **EMAIL FROM GOD**
> **2:11**
> **Family**
> Here's a good example of love for family.

12 Before a girl could take her turn with King Xerxes, she had to complete twelve months of beauty treatments that were ordered for the women. For six months she was treated with oil and myrrh and for six months with perfumes and cosmetics. 13 Then she was ready to go to the king. Anything she asked for was given to her to take with her from the women's quarters to the king's palace. 14 In the evening she would go to the king's palace, and in the morning she would return to another part of the women's quarters. There she would be placed under the care of Shaashgaz, the king's eunuch in charge of the slave women. The girl would not go back to the king again unless he was pleased with her and asked for her by name.

15 The time came for Esther daughter of Abihail, Mordecai's uncle, who had been adopted by Mordecai, to go to the king. She asked for only what Hegai suggested she should take. (Hegai was the king's eunuch who was in charge of the women.) Everyone who saw Esther liked her. 16 So Esther was taken to King Xerxes in the royal palace in the tenth month, the month of Tebeth, during Xerxes' seventh year as king.

17 And the king was pleased with Esther more than with any of the other girls. He liked her more than any of the other girls, so he put a royal crown on her head and made her queen in place of Vashti. 18 Then the king gave a great banquet for Esther and invited all his important men and royal officers. He announced a holiday for all the empire and had the government give away gifts.

Esther 2:19 650

FAITH links

A LIFE-SAVING MESSAGE
ESTHER 2:19-22

Some things in life take courage, even if they're the right things to do. Mordecai had the courage to tell the king of an assassination attempt on his life. By doing what was right, Mordecai risked his own safety and risked looking foolish had the king not chosen to believe him.

Even though you may not hear about an assassination attempt against someone, you do have important news to share. The gospel message reminds us that because of sin, we're all under a penalty of death. But Jesus saved our lives by dying for us. Do you have the courage to share that news with someone?

His OK to Obey, Deuteronomy 2:24-36, p. 230

Faith of Our Fathers, Joshua 4:4-9, p. 280

The One Who Suffered, Isaiah 53, p. 966

A Friend in Need, Acts 9:27, p. 1480

Blessed Are the Weak? 2 Corinthians 12:7-10, p. 1582

Keep Up the Good Work! Galatians 6:9-10, p. 1593

Mordecai Discovers an Evil Plan

19 Now Mordecai was sitting at the king's gate when the girls were gathered the second time. 20 Esther still had not told anyone about her family or who her people were, just as Mordecai had commanded her. She obeyed Mordecai just as she had done when she was under his care.

21 Now Bigthana and Teresh were two of the king's officers who guarded the doorway. While Mordecai was sitting at the king's gate, they became angry and began to make plans to kill King Xerxes. 22 But Mordecai found out about their plans and told Queen Esther. Then Esther told the king how Mordecai had discovered the evil plan. 23 When the report was investigated, it was found to be true, and the two officers who had planned to kill the king were hanged. All this was written down in the daily court record in the king's presence.

Haman Plans to Destroy the Jewish People

3 After these things happened, King Xerxes honoured Haman son of Hammedatha the Agagite. He gave him a new rank that was higher than all the important men. 2 All the royal officers at the king's gate would bow down and kneel before Haman, as the king had ordered. But Mordecai would not bow down or show him honour.

3 Then the royal officers at the king's gate asked Mordecai, "Why don't you obey the king's command?" 4 And they said this to him every day. When he did not listen to them, they told Haman about it. They wanted to see if Haman would accept Mordecai's behaviour because Mordecai had told them he was Jewish.

5 When Haman saw that Mordecai would not bow down to him or honour him, he became very angry. 6 He thought of himself as too important to try to kill only Mordecai. He had been told who the people of Mordecai were, so he looked for a way to destroy all of Mordecai's people, the Jews, in all of Xerxes' kingdom.

7 It was in the first month of the twelfth year of King Xerxes' rule—the month of Nisan. Pur (that is, the lot) was thrown before Haman to choose a day and a month. So the twelfth month, the month of Adar, was chosen.

8 Then Haman said to King Xerxes,

FAITH links

STANDING FOR WHAT'S RIGHT
ESTHER 3:2-4

Suppose the headmaster or headmistress of your school told you to stand up whenever they entered your classroom. No problem, right? They deserve respect because of their position as the head of your school. Now suppose they told you to do something you know is against God's laws. Suddenly there's a problem, right? Mordecai refused to bow down to Haman, a Persian official. Bowing to Haman was a law the king made. Mordecai felt that bowing to Haman was not what God wanted him to do. Even though Haman tried to get even with Mordecai, Mordecai stood firm. Are you willing to stand for what's right, even if no one else does?

Check out these Faithlinks on standing up for what you believe:

A Choice to Make, Deuteronomy 30:15–20, p. 265

Learning to Listen, 1 Samuel 3, p. 358

Give In or Take a Stand? 1 Kings 22:13–14, p. 472

Wronged for What's Right, Ezra 4:4–5, p. 612

Facing Your Fears, Matthew 8:23–27, p. 1288

Don't Play Favourites, James 2:1–7, p. 1691

"There is a certain group of people scattered among the other people in all the areas of your kingdom. Their customs are different from those of all the other people, and they do not obey the king's laws. It is not right for you to allow them to continue living in your kingdom. 9 If it pleases the king, let an order be given to destroy those people. Then I will pay 350 tonnes of silver to those who do the king's business, and they will put it into the royal treasury."

10 So the king took his signet ring off and gave it to Haman son of Hammedatha, the Agagite, the enemy of the Jewish people. 11 Then the king said to Haman, "The money and the people are yours. Do with them as you please."

12 On the thirteenth day of the first month, the royal secretaries were called, and they wrote out all of Haman's orders. They wrote to the king's governors and to the captains of the soldiers in each area and to the important men of each group of people. The orders were written in the writing of each area and in the language of each people. They were written in the name of King Xerxes and sealed with his signet ring. 13 Letters were sent by messengers to all the king's empire ordering them to destroy, kill and completely wipe out all the Jewish people. That meant young and old, women and little children too. It was to happen on a single day—the thirteenth day of the twelfth month, which was Adar. And they could take everything the Jewish people owned. 14 A copy of the order was given out as a law in every area so all the people would be ready for that day.

15 The messengers set out, hurried by the king's command, as soon as the order was given in the palace at Susa. The king and Haman sat down to drink, but the city of Susa was in confusion.

Mordecai Asks Esther to Help

4 When Mordecai heard about all that had been done, he tore his clothes, put on rough cloth and ashes, and went out into the city crying loudly and painfully. 2 But Mordecai went only as far as

the king's gate, because no one was allowed to enter that gate dressed in rough cloth. 3 As the king's order reached every area, there was great sadness and loud crying among the Jewish people. They gave up eating and cried out loudly, and many of them lay down on rough cloth and ashes to show how sad they were.

4 When Esther's servant girls and eunuchs came to her and told her about Mordecai, she was very upset and afraid. She sent clothes for Mordecai to put on instead of the rough cloth, but he would not wear them. 5 Then Esther called for Hathach, one of the king's eunuchs chosen by the king to serve her. Esther ordered him to find out what was bothering Mordecai and why.

6 So Hathach went to Mordecai, who was in the city square in front of the king's gate. 7 Mordecai told Hathach everything that had happened to him, and he told Hathach about the amount of money Haman had promised to pay into the king's treasury for the killing of the Jewish people. 8 Mordecai also gave him a copy of the order to kill the Jewish people, which had been given in Susa. He wanted Hathach to show it to Esther and to tell her about it. And Mordecai told him to order Esther to go into the king's presence to beg for mercy and to plead with him for her people.

9 Hathach went back and reported to Esther everything Mordecai had said. 10 Then Esther told Hathach to tell Mordecai, 11 "All the royal officers and people of the royal areas know that no man or woman may go to the king in the inner courtyard without being called. There is only one law about this: anyone who enters must be put to death unless the king holds out his gold sceptre. Then that person may live. And I have not been called to go to the king for 30 days."

12 Esther's message was given to Mordecai. 13 Then Mordecai sent back word to Esther: "Just because you live in the king's palace, don't think that out of all the Jewish people you alone will escape. 14 If you keep quiet at this time, someone else will help and save the Jewish people, but you and your father's family will all die. And who knows, you may have been chosen queen for just such a time as this."

4:14 Future
Does God put you in situations to make a difference?

FAITH links

THE BIG RISK
ESTHER 4:11—5:2

Think about the biggest risk you've ever taken. What made you decide to do it? Taking a risk can be very scary. Esther faced a big risk when Mordecai told her about Haman's plot to have the Jewish people killed. He knew that she needed to tell the king. But to go to the king without his permission meant death! Esther had to take that risk in order to save lives – including her own.

There are certain risks you'll have to take in life. God will give you the courage to take any risk you face on his behalf.

How brave are you? Link here to find out:

Fearful Service? Exodus 4:1–17, p. 80

Everyone Can Help, Numbers 4, p. 181

When Bad Things Happen, Ecclesiastes 3:16–17, p. 876

A Bad Reaction, Jeremiah 36, p. 1043

The Unpopular Choice, Mark 15:42–43, p. 1360

Obey or Disobey? Luke 20:20–26, p. 1409

15 Then Esther sent this answer to Mordecai: 16 "Go and get all the Jewish people in Susa together. For my sake, give up eating; do not eat or drink for three days, night and day. I and my servant girls will also give up eating. Then I will go to the king, even though it is against the law, and if I die, I die."

17 So Mordecai went away and did everything Esther had told him to do.

Esther Speaks to the King

5 On the third day Esther put on her royal robes and stood in the inner courtyard of the king's palace, facing the king's hall. The king was sitting on his royal throne in the hall, facing the doorway. 2 When the king saw Queen Esther standing in the courtyard, he was pleased. He held out to her the gold sceptre that was in his hand, so Esther went forwards and touched the end of it.

3 The king asked, "What is it, Queen Esther? What do you want to ask me? I will give you as much as half of my kingdom."

4 Esther answered, "My king, if it pleases you, come today with Haman to a banquet that I have prepared for him."

5 Then the king said, "Bring Haman quickly so we may do what Esther asks."

So the king and Haman went to the banquet Esther had prepared for them. 6 As they were drinking wine, the king said to Esther, "Now, what are you asking for? I will give it to you. What is it you want? I will give you as much as half of my kingdom."

7 Esther answered, "This is what I want and what I ask for. 8 My king, if you are pleased with me and if it pleases you, give me what I ask for and do what I want. Come with Haman tomorrow to the banquet I will prepare for you. Then I will answer your question about what I want."

Haman's Plans Against Mordecai

9 Haman left the king's palace that day happy and content. But when he saw Mordecai at the king's gate and saw that Mordecai did not stand up or tremble with fear before him, Haman became very angry with Mordecai. 10 But he controlled his anger and went home.

Then Haman called together his friends and his wife, Zeresh. 11 He told them how wealthy he was and how many sons he had. He also told them all the ways the king had honoured him and how the king had placed him higher than his important men and his royal officers. 12 He also said, "I'm the only person Queen Esther invited to come with the king to the banquet she gave. And tomorrow also the queen has asked me to be her guest with the king. 13 But all this does not really make me happy when I see that Jew Mordecai sitting at the king's gate."

14 Then Haman's wife, Zeresh, and all his friends said, "Have a 25-metre-high platform built, and in the morning ask the king to have Mordecai hanged on it. Then go to the banquet with the king and be happy." Haman liked this suggestion, so he ordered the platform to be built.

> The king asked, "What is it, Queen Esther? What do you want to ask me? I will give you as much as half of my kingdom."
> – Esther 5:3

Mordecai is Honoured

6 That same night the king could not sleep. So he gave an order for the daily court record to be brought in and read to him. 2 It was found recorded that Mordecai had warned the king about Bigthana and Teresh, two of the king's officers who guarded the doorway and who had planned to kill the king.

3 The king asked, "What honour and reward have been given to Mordecai for this?"

The king's personal servants answered, "Nothing has been done for Mordecai."

4 The king said, "Who is in the courtyard?" Now Haman had just entered the outer court of the king's palace. He had come to ask the king about hanging Mordecai on the platform he had prepared.

A FOREIGN QUEEN   Esther 6

Esther was an Israelite woman who became a queen of Persia. That was an amazing thing! Esther's people were captives in Persia, and yet she became queen. While she was the queen, Esther helped save the life of her uncle and the lives of all her people. She also gave us some insight into how the Persians lived.

Royal Persian feasts were fancy, fancy, fancy. The guests ate while lying back on a bed or couch, sort of like when you lie back on a sun-lounger. All the cups were made of gold and each was different from the others. (Check out Esther 1:7.)

Special laws protected the Persian king. There were only seven important men who could meet with the king. (Read Esther 1:14.) Nobody else could come to see the king unless he called them in. (See Esther 4:11.) That's why Esther took such a risk when she went to the king to ask for his help.

5 The king's personal servants said, "Haman is standing in the courtyard."

The king said, "Bring him in."

6 So Haman came in. And the king asked him, "What should be done for a man whom the king wants very much to honour?"

And Haman thought to himself, "Whom would the king want to honour more than me?" 7 So he answered the king, "This is what you could do for the man you want very much to honour. 8 Have the servants bring a royal robe that the king himself has worn. And also bring a horse with a royal crown on its head, a horse that the king himself has ridden. 9 Let the robe and the horse be given to one of the king's most important men. Let the servants put the robe on the man the king wants to honour, and let them lead him on the horse through the city streets. As they are leading him, let them announce: 'This is what is done for the man whom the king wants to honour!'"

10 The king commanded Haman, "Go quickly. Take the robe and the horse just as you have said, and do all this for Mordecai the Jew who sits at the king's gate. Do not leave out anything you have suggested."

11 So Haman took the robe and the horse, and he put the robe on Mordecai. Then he led him on horseback through the city streets, announcing before Mordecai: "This is what is done for the man whom the king wants to honour!"

12 Then Mordecai returned to the king's gate, but Haman hurried home with his head covered, because he was embarrassed and ashamed. 13 He told his wife, Zeresh, and all his friends everything that had happened to him.

Haman's wife and the men who gave him advice said, "You are starting to lose power to Mordecai. Since he is a Jew, you cannot win against him. You will surely be ruined." 14 While they were still talking, the king's eunuchs came to Haman's house and made him hurry to the banquet Esther had prepared.

Haman is Hanged

7 So the king and Haman went in to eat with Queen Esther. 2 As they were drinking wine on the second day, the king asked Esther again, "What are you asking

for? I will give it to you. What is it you want? I will give you as much as half of my kingdom."

3 Then Queen Esther answered, "My king, if you are pleased with me, and if it pleases you, let me live. This is what I ask. And let my people live, too. This is what I want. 4 My people and I have been sold to be destroyed, to be killed and completely wiped out. If we had been sold as male and female slaves, I would have kept quiet, because that would not be enough of a problem to bother the king."

5 Then King Xerxes asked Queen Esther, "Who is he, and where is he? Who has done such a thing?"

6 Esther said, "Our enemy and foe is this wicked Haman!"

Then Haman was filled with terror before the king and queen. 7 The king was very angry, so he got up, left his wine and went out into the palace garden. But Haman stayed inside to beg Queen Esther to save his life. He could see that the king had already decided to kill him.

8 When the king returned from the palace garden to the banquet hall, he saw Haman falling on the couch where Esther was lying. The king said, "Will he even attack the queen while I am in the house?"

As soon as the king said that, servants came in and covered Haman's face. 9 Harbona, one of the eunuchs there serving the king, said, "Look, a 25-metre-high platform stands near Haman's house. This is the one Haman had prepared for Mordecai, who gave the warning that saved the king."

The king said, "Hang Haman on it!" 10 So they hanged Haman on the platform he had prepared for Mordecai. Then the king was not so angry any more.

The King Helps the Jewish People

8 That same day King Xerxes gave Queen Esther everything Haman, the enemy of the Jewish people, had left when he died. And Mordecai came in to see the king, because Esther had told the king how he was related to her. 2 Then the king took off his signet ring that he had taken back from Haman, and he gave it to Mordecai. Esther put Mordecai in charge of everything Haman left when he died.

3 Once again Esther spoke to the king. She fell at the king's feet and cried and begged him to stop the evil plan that Haman the Agagite had planned against the Jews. 4 The king held out the gold sceptre to Esther. So Esther got up and stood in front of him.

5 She said, "My king, if you are pleased with me, and if it pleases you to do this, if you think it is the right thing to do, and if you are happy with me, let an order be written to cancel the letters Haman wrote. Haman the Agagite sent messages to destroy all the Jewish people in all of your kingdom. 6 I could not stand to see that terrible thing happen to my people. I could not stand to see my family killed."

7 King Xerxes answered Queen Esther and Mordecai the Jew, "Because Haman was against the Jewish people, I have given his things to Esther and my soldiers have hanged him. 8 Now, in the king's name, write another order to the Jewish people as it seems best to you. Then seal the order with the king's signet ring, because no letter written in the king's name and sealed with his signet ring can be cancelled."

9 At that time the king's secretaries were called. This was the twenty-third day of the third month, which is Sivan. The secretaries wrote out all of Mordecai's orders to the Jews, to the governors, to the captains of the soldiers in each area and to the important men of the 127 areas that reached from India to Cush. They wrote in the writing of each area and in the language of each people. They also wrote to the Jewish

---

> Esther said, "Our enemy and foe is this wicked Haman!" Then Haman was filled with terror before the king and queen.
>
> – Esther 7:6

people in their own writing and language. 10 Mordecai wrote orders in the name of King Xerxes and sealed the letters with the king's signet ring. Then he sent the king's orders by messengers on fast horses, horses that were raised just for the king.

11 These were the king's orders: the Jewish people in every city have the right to gather together to protect themselves. They may destroy, kill and completely wipe out the army of any area or people who attack them. And they are to do the same to the women and children of that army. They may also take by force the property of their enemies. 12 The one day set for the Jewish people to do this in all the empire of King Xerxes was the thirteenth day of the twelfth month, the month of Adar. 13 A copy of the king's order was to be sent out as a law in every area. It was to be made known to the people of every nation living in the kingdom so the Jewish people would be ready on that set day to strike back at their enemies.

14 The messengers hurried out, riding on the royal horses, because the king commanded those messengers to hurry. And the order was also given in the palace at Susa.

15 Mordecai left the king's presence wearing royal clothes of blue and white and a large gold crown. He also had a purple robe made of the best linen. And the people of Susa shouted for joy. 16 It was a time of happiness, joy, gladness and honour for the Jewish people. 17 As the king's order went to every area and city, there was joy and gladness among the Jewish people. In every area and city to which the king's order went, they were having feasts and celebrating. And many people through all the empire became Jews, because they were afraid of the Jewish people.

Victory for the Jewish People

9 The order the king had commanded was to be done on the thirteenth day of the twelfth month, the month of Adar. That was the day the enemies of the Jewish people had hoped to defeat them, but that was changed. So the Jewish people themselves defeated those who hated them. 2 The Jews met in their cities in all the empire of King Xerxes in order to attack those who wanted to harm them. No one was strong enough to fight against them, because all the other people living in the empire were afraid of them. 3 All the important men of the areas, the governors, captains of the soldiers, and the king's officers helped the Jewish people, because they were afraid of Mordecai. 4 Mordecai was very important in the king's palace. He was famous in all the empire, because he was becoming a leader of more and more people.

5 And, with their swords, the Jewish people defeated all their enemies, killing and destroying them. And they did what they wanted with those people who hated them. 6 In the palace at Susa, they killed and destroyed 500 men. 7 They also killed: Parshandatha, Dalphon, Aspatha, 8 Poratha, Adalia, Aridatha, 9 Parmashta, Arisai, Aridai and Vaizatha, 10 the ten sons of Haman, son of Hammedatha, the enemy of the Jewish people. But the Jewish people did not take their belongings.

> She fell at the king's feet and cried and begged him to stop the evil plan that Haman ... had planned against the Jews.
> — Esther 8:3

11 On that day the number killed in the palace at Susa was reported to the king. 12 The king said to Queen Esther, "The Jewish people have killed and destroyed 500 people in the palace at Susa, and they have also killed Haman's ten sons. What have they done in the rest of the king's empire! Now what else are you asking? I will do it! What else do you want? It will be done!"

13 Esther answered, "If it pleases the king, give the Jewish people who are in Susa permission to do again tomorrow what the king ordered for today. And let the bodies of Haman's ten sons be hanged on the platform."

14 So the king ordered that it be done.

FAITH links

A HOLIDAY LETTER
ESTHER 9:20-23

Many people write letters at Christmas. They tell friends and relatives about the events that happened to them during the year. Quite often, they mention their thankfulness to God. Esther and Mordecai started a holiday called Purim to remember how God protected the Jewish people. Mordecai wrote letters to remind people to celebrate this festival. He recorded the main reason to celebrate: God had saved their lives.

We celebrate Christmas and Easter for the same reason. Both holidays remind us of God's love and grace. Jesus came to earth to save us from the penalty of death. Because of Jesus, we have eternal life.

Here are some more links on celebrating our great God:

Approaching God, Numbers 3:10, p. 180

Love That Will Last, Psalm 136, p. 813

A Need to Change, Ecclesiastes 1:1–11, p. 873

Inside the Heart of God, Micah 7:18–20, p. 1228

A Love Song, Zephaniah 3:17, p. 1246

Life After Death? 1 Corinthians 15:12–13, p. 1563

A law was given in Susa, and the bodies of the ten sons of Haman were hanged. 15 The Jewish people in Susa came together on the fourteenth day of the month of Adar. They killed 300 people in Susa, but they did not take their belongings.

16 At that same time, all the Jewish people in the king's empire also met to protect themselves and get rid of their enemies. They killed 75,000 of those who hated them, but they did not take their belongings. 17 This happened on the thirteenth day of the month of Adar. On the fourteenth day they rested and made it a day of joyful feasting.

The Feast of Purim

18 But the Jewish people in Susa met on the thirteenth and fourteenth days of the month of Adar. Then they rested on the fifteenth day and made it a day of joyful feasting.

19 This is why the Jewish people who live in the country and small villages celebrate on the fourteenth day of the month of Adar. It is a day of joyful feasting and a day for exchanging gifts.

20 Mordecai wrote down everything that had happened. Then he sent letters to all the Jewish people in all the empire of King Xerxes, far and near. 21 He told them to celebrate every year on the fourteenth and fifteenth days of the month of Adar, 22 because that was when the Jewish people got rid of their enemies. They were also to celebrate it as the month their sadness was turned to joy and their crying for the dead was turned into celebration. He told them to celebrate those days as days of joyful feasting and as a time for giving food to each other and presents to the poor.

23 So the Jewish people agreed to do what Mordecai had written to them, and they agreed to hold the celebration every year. 24 Haman son of Hammedatha, the Agagite, was the enemy of all the Jewish people. He had made an evil plan against the Jewish people to destroy them, and he had thrown the Pur (that is, the lot) to choose a day to ruin and destroy them. 25 But when the king learned of the evil plan, he sent out written orders that the

evil plans Haman had made against the Jewish people would be used against him. And those orders said that Haman and his sons should be hanged on the platform. 26 So these days were called Purim, which comes from the word "Pur" (the lot). Because of everything written in this letter and what they had seen and what happened to them, 27 the Jewish people set up this custom. They and their descendants and all those who join them are always to celebrate these two days every year. They should do it in the right way and at the time Mordecai had ordered them in the letter. 28 These two days should be remembered and celebrated from now on in every family, in every area and in every city. These days of Purim should always be celebrated by the Jewish people, and their descendants should always remember to celebrate them too.

29 So Queen Esther daughter of Abihail, along with Mordecai the Jew, wrote this second letter about Purim. Using the power they had, they wrote to prove the first letter was true. 30 And Mordecai sent letters to all the Jewish people in the 127 areas of the kingdom of Xerxes, writing them a message of peace and truth. 31 He wrote to set up these days of Purim at the chosen times. Mordecai the Jew and Queen Esther had sent out the order for the Jewish people, just as they had set up things for themselves and their descendants: On these two days the people should give up eating and cry loudly. 32 Esther's letter set up the rules for Purim and they were written down in the records.

The Greatness of Mordecai

10 King Xerxes demanded taxes everywhere, even from the cities on the seacoast. 2 And all the great things Xerxes did by his power and strength are written in the record books of the kings of Media and Persia. Also written in those record books are all the things done by Mordecai, whom the king made great. 3 Mordecai the Jew was second in importance to King Xerxes, and he was the most important man among the Jewish people. His fellow Jews respected him very much, because he worked for the good of his people and spoke up for the safety of all the Jewish people.

> **EMAIL FROM GOD 10:3**
> **Leadership**
> What's a good way to get your followers to like you?

WHY ME, GOD?

Hi, there! My name is Job and I lived a very long time ago. Today no one remembers who wrote this book, but I can tell you that it is the true story of my life. Do you think you have bad days? I hope you never have a day like *this*: one day enemies stole all of my oxen, donkeys and camels; lightning struck and killed all my servants and all my sheep; and then a great wind collapsed the house my sons and daughters were in and killed them all. The next day I was covered from head to toe with painful sores. My wife thought I should curse God and die, but I said, "Should we take only good things from God and not trouble?" (Job 2:10). You'll have to read my book to see how things turned out for me.

This book was written to tell people to be faithful to God even when life is difficult. My friends thought I was being punished for a great sin, but I knew that this was not true. I didn't understand why God allowed me to suffer, but can anyone understand God? He is *always* worthy of our worship, no matter what he chooses to do. You won't want to miss the amazing way God spoke to me from a storm in Job 38—41.

JESUS WATCH

At the beginning of the story, we learn that Job was an honest and innocent man. He honoured God and stayed away from evil. Yet, God allowed Satan to destroy Job's health, his possessions and all of his children. Job suffered greatly, but not because he had sinned against God. Job is a picture of innocent suffering that reminds us of Jesus. Jesus had no sin. He lived a perfect life and did not deserve to suffer in any way. Jesus chose to become a man so that he could take the punishment we deserve for our sins. The punishment for sin is death, and Jesus willingly died in our place. Because Jesus suffered for us, we can have eternal life with him in heaven.

My FAVOURITE links

OTHER CONNECTIONS

 Sometimes the hardest part of getting a difficult task done is to keep going. It's tempting to throw in the towel when things get difficult. Check out a few thoughts on the value of getting the job done by visiting Hang in There! Job 17:9. How do you show respect to others? Is that important to you? Is it important that other people respect you? Find out what God has to say about this topic by surfing over to Just a Little Respect, Job 31:13–14.

MORE STUFF . . .

Take the Challenge! Job went through a lot. He lost his children, his home, his possessions and his wealth. Throughout it all, what Job really wanted was a chance to tell God that he was innocent and not deserving of these terrible things. Instead of answering his questions, God had a few questions of his own for Job. Take a look and see how you would answer:

- "Where were you when I made the earth's foundation? Tell me, if you understand?" Job 38:4
- "Have you ever ordered the morning to begin, or shown the dawn where its place was?" Job 38:12
- "Job, are you the one who gives the horse its strength or puts a flowing mane on its neck?" Job 39:19
- "Are you as strong as God? Can your voice thunder like his?" Job 40:9

Who made the behemoth?

Are you thinking – what's a behemoth? Better connect to Job 40:15-24 to find out.

MORE THINGS TO LOOK FOR IN JOB:
Satan makes trouble, Job 1:6–11
More trouble for Job, Job 2
Job cries out to God, Job 10
Job confesses; God blesses, Job 42

FAITH links

○ A Really Bad Day,
  Job 1:20–22; 2:10

○ A Friend in Deed,
  Job 2:13

○ A Pity Party,
  Job 10

○ Helpful Advice,
  Job 12:4–5

○ Meaningless Words,
  Job 21:34

○ Go for the Gold,
  Job 23:10

○ Happiness or Joy?
  Job 29:18–19

○ No Doubt About It,
  Job 36:5

○ How Big Is God?
  Job 38—41

○ Full Circle,
  Job 42

Job, the Good Man

1 A man named Job lived in the land of Uz. He was an honest and innocent man; he honoured God and stayed away from evil. **2** Job had seven sons and three daughters. **3** He owned 7,000 sheep, 3,000 camels, 500 teams of oxen and 500 female donkeys. He also had a large number of servants. He was the greatest man among all the people of the East.

4 Job's sons took turns holding feasts in their homes and invited their sisters to eat and drink with them. **5** After a feast was over, Job would send and have them made clean. Early in the morning Job would offer a burnt offering for each of them, because he thought, "My children may have sinned and cursed God in their hearts." Job did this every time.

Satan Appears Before the Lord

6 One day the angels came to show themselves before the Lord, and Satan was with them. **7** The Lord said to Satan, "Where have you come from?"

Satan answered the Lord, "I have been wandering around the earth, going back and forth in it."

8 Then the Lord said to Satan, "Have you noticed my servant Job? No one else on earth is like him. He is an honest and innocent man, honouring God and staying away from evil."

9 But Satan answered the Lord, "Job honours God for a good reason. **10** You have put a wall around him, his family and everything he owns. You have blessed the things he has done. His flocks and herds are so large they almost cover the land. **11** But reach out your hand and destroy everything he has, and he will curse you to your face."

12 The Lord said to Satan, "All right, then. Everything Job has is in your power, but you must not touch Job himself." Then Satan left the Lord's presence.

13 One day Job's sons and daughters were eating and drinking wine together at the oldest brother's house. **14** A messenger came to Job and said, "The oxen were ploughing and the donkeys were eating grass nearby, **15** when the Sabeans attacked and carried them away. They killed the servants with swords, and I am the only one who escaped to tell you!"

16 The messenger was still speaking

FAITH links

A REALLY BAD DAY
JOB 1:20-22; 2:10

There are good days and there are bad days. But some days are worse than anything you can imagine. One day, Job had everything going for him. The next day, his family and wealth were wiped out. How would you respond to a disaster like that? Job didn't blame or yell at God. He gave a faithful response, even in the worst times imaginable.

Hard times are hard – that's how they get their name! Like Job, you can seek God's help when life gets rough. Don't let hard times turn you away from God. Instead, turn towards God.

What do you do when you have a bad day? Check out these links:

A Major Problem, Genesis 15:6, p. 20

From Hopeless to Hopeful, Exodus 6:9, p. 83

Our Heavenly Shepherd, Psalm 23, p. 726

A Swarm of Trouble, Joel 2:25–27, p. 1190

A Word About Worry, Matthew 6:25–34, p. 1284

Our Interpreter, Romans 8:26, p. 1528

when another messenger arrived and said, "Lightning from God fell from the sky. It burned up the sheep and the servants, and I am the only one who escaped to tell you!"

17 The second messenger was still speaking when another messenger arrived and said, "The Babylonians sent three groups of attackers that swept down and stole your camels and killed the servants. I am the only one who escaped to tell you!"

18 The third messenger was still speaking when another messenger arrived and said, "Your sons and daughters were eating and drinking wine together at the oldest brother's house. 19 Suddenly a great wind came from the desert, hitting all four corners of the house at once. The house fell in on the young people, and they are all dead. I am the only one who escaped to tell you!"

20 When Job heard this, he got up and tore his robe and shaved his head to show how sad he was. Then he bowed down to the ground to worship God. 21 He said:

"I was naked when I was born,
and I will be naked when I die.
The LORD gave these things to me,
and he has taken them away.
Praise the name of the LORD."

22 In all this Job did not sin or blame God.

Satan Appears Before the Lord Again

2 On another day the angels came to show themselves before the LORD, and Satan was with them again. 2 The LORD said to Satan, "Where have you come from?"

Satan answered the LORD, "I have been wandering around the earth, going back and forth in it."

3 Then the LORD said to Satan, "Have you noticed my servant Job? No one else on earth is like him. He is an honest and innocent man, honouring God and staying away from evil. You caused me to ruin him for no good reason, but he continues to be without blame."

4 "One skin for another!" Satan answered. "A man will give all he has to save

A FRIEND IN DEED
JOB 2:13

The test of friendship is when you go through hard times. A friend who sticks with you through hard times is a true friend. Three of Job's friends stayed with him during the first week of his terrible loss. They mourned with him.

When you have a friend who is going through a hard time, don't be afraid to be around him, even if you don't know what to say. Just be available, ready to listen. You don't have to say a word. If you're going through hard times, what friend can you count on? If you can't think of one, here is a name to call: Jesus. He can "be more loyal than a brother" (Proverbs 18:24).

Connect here to find out how to help a friend:

God's Pep Talk, Joshua 1:5–9, p. 276

Loyal to a Friend, 2 Samuel 9, p. 409

A Direct Path, Proverbs 3:5–6, p. 829

The Right Ingredients, Micah 6:8, p. 1227

A Friend in Need, Acts 9:27, p. 1480

Toss Those Troubles! 1 Peter 5:7, p. 1706

his own life. 5 But reach out your hand and destroy his flesh and bones, and he will curse you to your face."

6 The LORD said to Satan, "All right, then. Job is in your power, but you may not take his life."

7 So Satan left the LORD's presence. He put painful sores on Job's body, from the top of his head to the soles of his feet. 8 Job took a piece of broken pottery to scrape himself, and he sat in ashes in misery.

9 Job's wife said to him, "Why are you trying to stay innocent? Curse God and die!"

10 Job answered, "You are talking like a foolish woman. Should we take only good things from God and not trouble?" In spite of all this Job did not sin in what he said.

Job's Three Friends Come to Help

11 Now Job had three friends: Eliphaz the Temanite, Bildad the Shuhite and Zophar the Naamathite. When these friends heard about Job's troubles, they agreed to meet and visit him. They wanted to show their concern and to comfort him. 12 They saw Job from far away, but he looked so different they almost didn't recognise him. They began to cry loudly and tore their robes and put earth on their heads to show how sad they were. 13 Then they sat on the ground with Job for seven days and seven nights. No one said a word to him because they saw how much he was suffering.

2:11 Friendship
How can you help hurting friends?

Job Curses His Birth

3 After seven days Job cried out and cursed the day he had been born, 2 saying:

3 "Let the day I was born be destroyed,
and the night it was said, 'A boy is born!'
4 Let that day turn to darkness.
Don't let God care about it.
Don't let light shine on it.
5 Let darkness and gloom have that day.
Let a cloud hide it.
Let thick darkness cover its light.
6 Let thick darkness capture that night.
Don't count it among the days of the year
or put it in any of the months.
7 Let that night be empty,
with no shout of joy to be heard.
8 Let those who curse days curse that day.
Let them prepare to wake up the sea monster Leviathan.
9 Let that day's morning stars never appear;
let it wait for daylight that never comes.
Don't let it see the first light of dawn,
10 because it allowed me to be born
and did not hide trouble from my eyes.

11 "Why didn't I die as soon as I was born?
Why didn't I die when I came out of the womb?
12 Why did my mother's lap receive me,
and my mother's breasts feed me?
13 If they had not been there,
I would be lying dead in peace;
I would be asleep and at rest
14 with kings and wise men of the earth
who built places for themselves that are now ruined.
15 I would be asleep with rulers
who filled their houses with gold and silver.
16 Why was I not buried like a child born dead,
like a baby who never saw the light of day?
17 In the grave the wicked stop making trouble,
and the tired workers are at rest.
18 In the grave there is rest for the captives
who no longer hear the shout of the slave driver.

19 People great and small are in the grave,
and the slave is freed from his master.
20 "Why is light given to those in misery?
Why is life given to those who are so unhappy?
21 They want to die, but death does not come.
They search for death more than for hidden treasure.
22 They are very happy when they get to the grave.
23 They cannot see where they are going.
God has hidden the road ahead.
24 I make sad sounds as I eat;
my groans pour out like water.
25 Everything I feared and dreaded has happened to me.
26 I have no peace or quietness.
I have no rest, only trouble."

Eliphaz Speaks

4 Then Eliphaz the Temanite answered:
2 "If someone tried to speak with you, would you be upset?
I cannot keep from speaking.
3 Think about the many people you have taught
and the weak hands you have made strong.
4 Your words have comforted those who fell,
and you have strengthened those who could not stand.

4:4 Encouragement
How can you encourage others?

5 But now trouble comes to you, and you are discouraged;
trouble hits you, and you are terrified.
6 You should have confidence because you respect God;
you should have hope because you are innocent.

7 "Remember that the innocent will not die;

honest people will never be destroyed.
8 I have noticed that people who plough evil
and plant trouble, harvest it.
9 God's breath destroys them,
and a blast of his anger kills them.
10 Lions may roar and growl,
but when the teeth of a strong lion are broken,
11 that lion dies of hunger.
The cubs of the mother lion are scattered.

12 "A word was brought to me in secret,
and my ears heard a whisper of it.
13 It was during a troublesome dream when people are in deep sleep.
14 I was trembling with fear;
all my bones were shaking.
15 A spirit glided past my face,
and the hair on my body stood on end.
16 The spirit stopped,
but I could not see what it was.
A shape stood before my eyes,
and I heard a quiet voice.
17 It said, 'Can a human be more right than God?
Can a person be pure before his maker?
18 God does not trust his angels;
he blames them for mistakes.
19 So he puts even more blame on people who live in clay houses,"
whose foundations are made of dust,
who can be crushed like a moth.
20 Between dawn and sunset many people are broken to pieces;
without being noticed, they die and are gone for ever.
21 The ropes of their tents are pulled up,
and they die without wisdom.'

5 "Call if you want to, Job, but no one will answer you.
You can't turn to any of the holy ones.

4:19 clay houses This is probably talking about people's bodies.

2 Anger kills the fool,
and jealousy kills the stupid.
3 I have seen a fool succeed,
but I cursed his home immediately.
4 His children are far from safety
and are crushed in court with no
defence.
5 The hungry eat his harvest,
even taking what grew among the
thorns,
and thirsty people want his wealth.
6 Hard times do not come up from the
ground,
and trouble does not grow from the
earth.
7 People produce trouble
as surely as sparks fly upwards.

8 "But if I were you, I would call on
God
and bring my problem before him.
9 God does wonders that cannot be
understood;
he does so many miracles they
cannot be counted.
10 He gives rain to the earth
and sends water on the fields.
11 He makes the humble person
important
and lifts the sad to places of safety.
12 He ruins the plans of those who trick
others
so they have no success.
13 He catches the wise in their own
clever traps
and sweeps away the plans of those
who try to trick others.
14 Darkness covers them up in the
daytime;
even at noon they feel around in
the dark.
15 God saves the needy from their lies
and from the harm done by
powerful people.
16 So the poor have hope,
while those
who are
unfair are
silenced.
17 "The one whom
God corrects
is happy,

**5:17
Correction**
Is God's correction good?

so do not hate being corrected by
the Almighty.
18 God hurts, but he also bandages up;
he injures, but his hands also heal.
19 He will save you from six troubles;
even seven troubles will not harm
you.
20 God will buy you back from death in
times of hunger,
and in battle he will save you from
the sword.
21 You will be protected from the tongue
that strikes like a whip,
and you will not be afraid when
destruction comes.
22 You will laugh at destruction and
hunger,
and you will not fear the wild
animals,
23 because you will have an agreement
with the stones in the field,
and the wild animals will be at
peace with you.
24 You will know that your tent is safe,
because you will check the things
you own and find nothing
missing.
25 You will know that you will have
many children,
and your descendants will be like
the grass on the earth.
26 You will come to the grave with all
your strength,
like bundles of grain gathered at
the right time.
27 "We have checked this, and it is true,
so hear it and decide what it means
to you."

Job Answers Eliphaz

6 Then Job answered:

2 "I wish my suffering could be
weighed
and my misery put on scales.
3 My sadness would be heavier than
the sand of the seas.
No wonder my words seem
careless.
4 The arrows of the Almighty are in
me;
my spirit drinks in their poison;

God's terrors are gathered against me.
5 A wild donkey does not bray when it has grass to eat,
and an ox is quiet when it has food.
6 Tasteless food is not eaten without salt,
and there is no flavour in the white of an egg.
7 I refuse to touch it;
such food makes me sick.

8 "How I wish that I might have what I ask for
and that God would give me what I hope for.
9 How I wish God would crush me
and reach out his hand to destroy me.
10 Then I would have this comfort
and be glad even in this unending pain,
because I would know I did not reject the words of the Holy One.

11 "I do not have the strength to wait.
There is nothing to hope for,
so why should I be patient?
12 I do not have the strength of stone;
my flesh is not bronze.
13 I have no power to help myself,
because success has been taken away from me.

14 "They say, 'A man's friends should be kind to him when he is in trouble,
even if he stops fearing the Almighty.'
15 But my brothers cannot be counted on.
They are like streams that do not always flow,
streams that sometimes run over.
16 They are made dark by melting ice
and rise with melting snow.
17 But they stop flowing in the dry season;
they disappear when it is hot.
18 Travellers turn away from their paths
and go into the desert and die.
19 The groups of travellers from Tema look for water,
and the traders of Sheba look hopefully.
20 They are upset because they had been sure;

FAITH links

HELP FOR THE HURTING
JOB 6:29-30

Have you ever been tempted to judge someone by the way they reacted to a problem? Maybe you thought a friend overreacted when you made a comment that seemed to hurt them. Or maybe you wondered why a friend didn't just snap out of a bad mood. We tend to judge people by how we would react. Job's friends didn't know how to help Job. Their judgements about his behaviour made him feel worse.

God warns us not to judge others, especially not those who are going through hard times. Since we really don't know how others *should* feel, the best thing to do for a person who's hurting is to pray for them.

Care for the Lost, Deuteronomy 22:1–3, p. 255

Show You Care, 2 Kings 4:10, p. 481

Depend on Him! 2 Chronicles 16:1–9, p. 579

A Gentle Answer, Proverbs 15:1, p. 847

Concern for All, Daniel 9, p. 1165

An Encouraging Word, 1 Corinthians 1:3–5, p. 1545

when they arrive, they are
   disappointed.
21 You also have been of no help.
   You see something terrible, and
     you are afraid.
22 I have never said, 'Give me a gift.
   Use your wealth to pay my debt.
23 Save me from the enemy's power.
   Buy me back from the clutches of
     cruel people.'
24 "Teach me, and I will be quiet.
   Show me where I have been
     wrong.
25 Honest words are painful,
   but your arguments prove
     nothing.
26 Do you mean to correct what I say?
   Will you treat the words of a
     troubled man as if they were
     only wind?
27 You would even gamble for orphans
   and would trade away your friend.

28 "But now please look at me.
   I would not lie to your face.
29 Change your mind; do not be unfair;
   think again, because my innocence
     is being questioned.
30 What I am saying is not wicked;
   I can tell the difference between
     right and wrong.

7 "People have a hard task on earth,
   and their days are like those of a hired
     man.
2 They are like a slave wishing for the
     evening shadows,
   like a labourer waiting to be paid.
3 But I am given months
     that are empty,
   and nights of
     misery have
     been given to
     me.
4 When I lie down, I
     think, 'How long
     until I get up?'
   The night is long,
     and I toss until
     dawn.
5 My body is covered with worms and
     scabs,

and my skin is broken and full of
     sores.

6 "My days go by faster than a
     weaver's tool,
   and they come to an end without
     hope.
7 Remember, God, that my life is only a
     breath.
   My eyes will never see happy times
     again.
8 Those who see me now will see me
     no more;
   you will look for me, but I will be
     gone.
9 As a cloud disappears and is gone,
   people go to the grave and never
     return.
10 They will never come back to their
     houses again,
   and their places will not know them
     any more.

11 "So I will not stay quiet;
   I will speak out in the suffering of
     my spirit.
   I will complain because I am so
     unhappy.
12 I am not the sea or the sea monster.
   So why have you set a guard over
     me?
13 Sometimes I think my bed will
     comfort me
   or that my couch will stop my
     complaint.
14 Then you frighten me with dreams
   and terrify me with visions.
15 My throat prefers to be choked;
   my bones welcome
     death.
16 I hate my life; I don't
     want to live for
     ever.
   Leave me alone,
     because my days
     have no meaning.
17 "Why do you make
     people so
     important
   and give them so
     much attention?
18 You examine them every morning

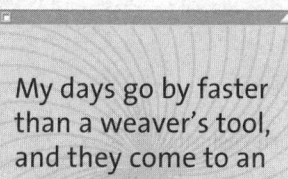

My days go by faster
than a weaver's tool,
and they come to an
end without hope.
   – Job 7:6

and test them every moment.
19 Will you never look away from me
or leave me alone even long
enough to swallow?
20 If I have sinned, what have I done to
you,
you watcher of men?
Why have you made me your target?
Have I become a heavy load for
you?
21 Why don't you pardon my wrongs
and forgive my sins?
I will soon lie down in the dust of
death.
Then you will search for me, but I
will be no more."

Bildad Speaks to Job

8 Then Bildad the Shuhite answered:

2 "How long will you say such things?
Your words are no more than
wind.
3 God does not twist justice;
the Almighty does not make wrong
what is right.
4 Your children sinned against God,
and he punished them for their
sins.
5 But you should ask God for help
and pray to the Almighty for
mercy.
6 If you are good and honest,
he will stand up for you
and bring you back where you
belong.
7 Where you began will seem
unimportant,
because your future will be so
successful.

8 "Ask old people;
find out what their ancestors
learned,
9 because we were only born yesterday
and know nothing.
Our days on earth are only a
shadow.
10 Those people will teach you and tell
you
and speak about what they know.
11 Papyrus plants cannot grow where
there is no swamp,
and reeds cannot grow tall without
water.
12 While they are still growing and not
yet cut,
they will dry up quicker than grass.
13 That is what will happen to those who
forget God;
the hope of the wicked will be gone.
14 What they hope in is easily broken;
what they trust is like a spider's
web.
15 They lean on the spider's web, but it
breaks.
They hold on to it, but it does not
hold up.

FAITH CHALLENGE

Here's one for you. Read 8:20 to find out what God does to make sure that evil does not overcome good in this world. How can you tell the difference between an innocent person and an evil person?

TeSTiNG iT

Job 8:20
Surely God does not reject the innocent or give strength to those who do evil.

16 They are like well-watered plants in the sunshine
that spread their roots all through the garden.
17 They wrap their roots around a pile of rocks
and look for a place among the stones.
18 But if a plant is torn from its place,
then that place rejects it and says, 'I never saw you.'
19 Now joy has gone away;
other plants grow up from the same earth.

20 "Surely God does not reject the innocent
or give strength to those who do evil.
21 God will yet fill your mouth with laughter
and your lips with shouts of joy.
22 Your enemies will be covered with shame,
and the tents of the wicked will be gone."

Job Answers Bildad

9 Then Job answered:

2 "Yes, I know that this is true,
but how can anyone be right in the presence of God?
3 Someone might want to argue with God,
but no one could answer God, not even one out of a thousand.
4 God's wisdom is deep, and his power is great;
no one can fight him without getting hurt.
5 God moves mountains without anyone knowing it
and turns them over when he is angry.
6 He shakes the earth out of its place
and makes its foundations tremble.
7 He commands the sun not to shine
and shuts off the light of the stars.
8 He alone stretches out the skies
and walks on the waves of the sea.
9 It is God who made the Bear, Orion and the Pleiades[n]
and the groups of stars in the southern sky.
10 He does wonders that cannot be understood;
he does so many miracles they cannot be counted.
11 When he passes me, I cannot see him;
when he goes by me, I do not recognise him.
12 If he snatches something away, no one can stop him
or say to him, 'What are you doing?'
13 God will not hold back his anger.
Even the helpers of the monster Rahab lie at his feet in fear.
14 So how can I argue with God,
or even find words to argue with him?
15 Even if I were right, I could not answer him;
I could only beg God, my Judge, for mercy.
16 If I called to him and he answered,
I still don't believe he would listen to me.
17 He would crush me with a storm
and multiply my wounds for no reason.
18 He would not let me catch my breath
but would overwhelm me with misery.
19 When it comes to strength, God is stronger than I;
when it comes to justice, no one can accuse him.
20 Even if I were right,
my own mouth would say I was wrong;
if I were innocent, my mouth would say I was guilty.

> God's wisdom is deep, and his power is great; no one can fight him without getting hurt.
> – Job 9:4

9:9 Bear . . . Pleiades Names of well-known groups of stars.

21 "I am innocent,
but I don't care about myself.
I hate my own life.
22 It is all the same. That is why I say,
'God destroys both the innocent
and the guilty.'
23 If the whip brings sudden death,
God will laugh at the suffering of
the innocent.
24 When the land falls into the hands of
evil people,
he covers the judges' faces so they
can't see it.
If it is not God who does this, then
who is it?
25 "My days go by faster than a runner;
they fly away without my seeing
any joy.
26 They glide past like paper boats.
They attack like eagles swooping
down to feed.
27 Even though I say, 'I will forget my
complaint;
I will change the look on my face
and smile,'
28 I still dread all my suffering.
I know you will hold me guilty.
29 I have already been found guilty,
so why should I struggle for no
reason?
30 I might wash myself with soap
and scrub my hands with strong
soap,
31 but you would push me into a dirty
pit,
and even my clothes would hate
me.
32 "God is not a man like me, so I
cannot answer him.
We cannot meet each other in
court.
33 I wish there were someone to make
peace between us,
someone to decide our case.
34 Maybe he could remove God's
punishment
so his terror would no longer
frighten me.
35 Then I could speak without being
afraid,
but I am not able to do that.

10 "I hate my life,
so I will complain without holding
back;
I will speak because I am so
unhappy.
2 I will say to God: Do not hold me
guilty,
but tell me what you have against
me.
3 Does it make you happy to trouble
me?
Don't you care about me, the work
of your hands?
Are you happy with the plans of
evil people?
4 Do you have human eyes
that see as we see?
5 Are your days like the days of man,
and your years like our years?
6 You look for the evil I have done
and search for my sin.
7 You know I am not guilty,
but no one can save me from your
power.
8 "Your hands shaped and made me.
Do you now turn around and
destroy me?
9 Remember that you moulded me like
a piece of clay.
Will you now turn me back into
dust?
10 You formed me inside my mother
like cheese formed from milk.
11 You dressed me with skin and
flesh;
you sewed me together with bones
and muscles.
12 You gave me life and showed me
kindness,
and in your care you watched over
my life.
13 "But in your heart you hid other
plans.
I know this was in your mind.
14 If I sinned, you would watch me
and would not let my sin go
unpunished.
15 How terrible it will be for me if I am
guilty!
Even if I am right, I cannot lift my
head.

> ## FAITH links
>
> ### A PITY PARTY
> ### JOB 10
>
> Ever feel sorry for yourself? Usually that feeling comes when hard times hit. During times like those, many people question God. Job had a hard time understanding why God allowed such trouble in his life. He began to feel sorry for himself. When things were going well, Job could easily sense God's love for him. Now when things were not going well, he had a hard time sensing God's concern.
>
> It's natural to feel sorry for yourself when you're having a hard time. That's what's known as a "pity party". But that feeling only makes matters worse, not better. Remembering God's love for you, even when things seem rotten, can help.
>
> Feeling sorry for yourself? Surf on to these links:
>
> A Giant Problem, 1 Samuel 17:32–51, p. 377
>
> A Home Town Hurt, Jeremiah 11:8—12:6, p. 1008
>
> A Hard Place, Ezekiel 28:25–26, p. 1120
>
> Your Feet on High Places, Habakkuk 3:18–19, p. 1239
>
> Sad Times, Matthew 14:13–14, p. 1299
>
> Hard Times, 2 Corinthians 1:8–10, p. 1570

I am full of shame
and experience only pain.
16 If I hold up my head, you hunt me
like a lion
and again show your terrible power
against me.
17 You bring new witnesses against me
and increase your anger against
me.
Your armies come against me.

18 "So why did you allow me to be
born?
I wish I had died before anyone
saw me.
19 I wish I had never lived,
but had been carried straight from
birth to the grave.
20 The few days of my life are almost
over.
Leave me alone so I can have a
moment of joy.
21 Soon I will leave; I will not return
from the land of darkness and
gloom,
22 the land of darkest night,
from the land of gloom and
confusion,
where even the light is darkness."

Zophar Speaks to Job

11 Then Zophar the Naamathite answered:

2 "Should these words go
unanswered?
Is this talker in the right?
3 Your lies do not make people quiet;
people should correct you when
you make fun of God.
4 You say, 'My teachings are right,
and I am clean in God's sight.'
5 I wish God would speak
and open his lips against you
6 and tell you the secrets of wisdom,
because wisdom has two sides.
Know this: God has even forgotten
some of your sin.

7 "Can you understand the secrets of
God?
Can you search the limits of the
Almighty?

8 His limits are higher than the heavens;
you cannot reach them!
They are deeper than the grave;
you cannot understand them!
9 His limits are longer than the earth
and wider than the sea.
10 "If God comes along and puts you in prison
or calls you into court, no one can stop him.
11 God knows who is evil,
and when he sees evil,
he takes note of it.
12 A fool cannot become wise
any more than a wild donkey
can be born tame.
13 "You must give your whole heart to him
and hold out your hands to him for help.
14 Put away the sin that is in your hand;
let no evil remain in your tent.
15 Then you can lift up your face without shame,
and you can stand strong without fear.
16 You will forget your trouble
and remember it only as water gone by.
17 Your life will be as bright as the noonday sun,
and darkness will seem like morning.
18 You will feel safe because there is hope;
you will look around and rest in safety.
19 You will lie down and no one will scare you.
Many people will want favours from you.
20 But the wicked will not be able to see,
so they will not escape.
Their only hope will be to die."

eMAIL FROM GOD

11:11 God
Does God know when you do wrong?

Job Answers Zophar

12 Then Job answered:

2 "You really think you are the only wise people
and that when you die, wisdom will die with you!
3 But my mind is as good as yours;
you are not better than I am.
Everyone knows all these things.
4 My friends all laugh at me
when I call on God and expect him to answer me;
they laugh at me even though I am right and innocent!
5 Those who are comfortable don't care that others have trouble;
they think it right that those people should have troubles.
6 The tents of robbers are not bothered,
and those who make God angry are safe.
They have their god in their pocket.
7 "But ask the animals, and they will teach you,
or ask the birds of the air, and they will tell you.
8 Speak to the earth, and it will teach you,
or let the fish of the sea tell you.
9 Every one of these knows
that the hand of the LORD has done this.
10 The life of every creature
and the breath of all people are in God's hand.
11 The ear tests words
as the tongue tastes food.
12 Older people are wise,
and long life brings understanding.

13 "But only God has wisdom and power,
good advice and understanding.
14 What he tears down cannot be rebuilt;
anyone he puts in prison cannot be let out.
15 If God holds back the waters, there is no rain;

Job 13:9

FAITH links

HELPFUL ADVICE
JOB 12:4-5

When life is going well for you, it's easy to forget about those who don't have it as good. We might pass someone who is homeless and think *Why doesn't he just get a job?* Or we might see someone who isn't wearing the latest clothes and think *Why doesn't she dress better?*

Job was angry with his friends for the way they judged him. He felt that others made fun of him for the trouble in his life. Like Job's friends did, it's far easier to judge someone than to offer a helping hand. Next time you're tempted to offer an opinion about someone in need, offer your help instead.

The MLP, Ruth 1:16–17, p. 345

Some Friendly Advice, Proverbs 17:9, 14, 17, p. 851

Love for a Lifetime, Song of Solomon 6:8–9, p. 891

A Safe Place, Nahum 1:7, p. 1231

Welcome! Matthew 19:13–15, p. 1307

Most Wanted? 2 Corinthians 10:1, p. 1580

---

if he lets the waters go, they flood the land.
16 He is strong and victorious;
both the one who fools others and the one who is fooled belong to him.
17 God leads the wise away as captives and turns judges into fools.
18 He takes off chains that kings put on and puts a cloth on their bodies.
19 He leads priests away naked and destroys the powerful.
20 He makes trusted people be silent and takes away the wisdom of older leaders.
21 He brings disgrace on important people
and takes away the weapons of the strong.
22 He uncovers the deep things of darkness
and brings dark shadows into the light.
23 He makes nations great and then destroys them;
he makes nations large and then scatters them.
24 He takes understanding away from the leaders of the earth
and makes them wander through a desert without paths.
25 They feel around in darkness with no light;
he makes them stumble like drunkards.

13 "Now my eyes have seen all this; my ears have heard and understood it.
2 What you know, I also know.
You are not better than I am.
3 But I want to speak to the Almighty and to argue my case with God.
4 But you smear me with lies.
You are worthless doctors, all of you!
5 I wish you would just stop talking; then you would really be wise!
6 Listen to my argument,
and hear the pleading of my lips.
7 You should not speak evil in the name of God;
you cannot speak God's truth by telling lies.
8 You should not unfairly choose his side against mine;
you should not argue the case for God.
9 You will not do well if he examines you;

you cannot fool God as you might
 fool humans.
10 God would surely scold you
 if you unfairly took one person's
 side.
11 His bright glory would scare you,
 and you would be very much afraid
 of him.
12 Your wise sayings are worth no more
 than ashes,
 and your arguments are as weak as
 clay.
13 "Be quiet and let me speak.
 Let things happen to me as they
 will.
14 Why should I put myself in danger
 and take my life in my own hands?
15 Even if God kills me, I have hope in
 him;
 I will still defend my ways to his
 face.
16 This is my salvation.
 The wicked cannot come before
 him.
17 Listen carefully to my words;
 let your ears hear what I say.
18 See, I have prepared my case,
 and I know I will be proved right.
19 No one can accuse me of doing
 wrong.
 If someone can, I will be quiet and
 die.
20 "God, please just give me these two
 things,
 and then I will not hide from you:
21 Take your punishment away from
 me,
 and stop frightening me with your
 terrors.
22 Then call me, and I will answer,
 or let me speak, and you answer.
23 How many evil things and sins have I
 done?
 Show me my wrong and my sin.
24 Don't hide your face from me;
 don't think of me as your enemy.
25 Don't punish a leaf that is blown by
 the wind;
 don't chase after straw.
26 You write down cruel things against
 me

and make me suffer for my
 boyhood sins.
27 You put my feet in chains
 and keep close watch wherever I
 go.
 You even mark the soles of my
 feet.

28 "Everyone wears out like something
 rotten,
 like clothing eaten by moths.

14
"All of us born to women
 live only a few days and
 have lots of
 trouble.
2 We grow up like
 flowers and
 then dry up
 and die.

We are like a
 passing shadow that does not
 last.
3 Lord, do you need to watch me like
 this?
 Must you bring me before you to
 be judged?
4 No one can bring something clean
 from something dirty.
5 Our time is limited.
 You have given us only so many
 months to live
 and have set limits we cannot go
 beyond.
6 So look away from us and leave us
 alone
 until we put in our time like a
 labourer.

7 "If a tree is cut down,
 there is hope that it will grow
 again
 and will send out new branches.
8 Even if its roots grow old in the
 ground,
 and its stump dies in the earth,
9 at the smell of water it will bud
 and put out new shoots like a plant.
10 But we die, and our bodies are laid in
 the ground;
 we take our last breath and are
 gone.
11 Water disappears from a lake,

and a river loses its water and
dries up.
12 In the same way, we lie down and do
not rise again;
we will not get up or be awakened
until the heavens disappear.
13 "I wish you would hide me in the
grave;
hide me until your anger is gone.
I wish you would set a time
and then remember me!
14 If a person dies, will he live again?
All my days are a struggle;
I will wait until things change for me.
15 You will call, and I will answer you;
you will desire the creature your
hands have made.
16 Then you will count my steps,
but you will not keep track of my
sin.
17 My wrongs will be closed up in a bag,
and you will cover up my sin.
18 "A mountain washes away and
crumbles;
and a rock can be moved from its
place.
19 Water washes over stones and wears
them down,
and rushing waters wash away the
earth.
In the same way, you destroy my
hope.
20 You defeat a person for ever, and he
is gone;
you change his appearance and
send him away.
21 His sons are honoured, but he does
not know it;
his sons are disgraced, but he does
not see it.
22 He only feels the pain of his body
and feels sorry for himself."

Eliphaz Answers Job

15 Then Eliphaz the Temanite answered:

2 "A wise person would not answer
with empty words
or fill his stomach with the hot
east wind.
3 He would not argue with useless
words
or make speeches that have no
value.
4 But you even destroy respect for God
and limit the worship of him.
5 Your sin teaches your mouth what to
say;
you use words to trick others.
6 It is your own mouth, not mine, that
shows you are wicked;
your own lips testify against you.

7 "You are not the first man ever born;
you are not older than the hills.
8 You did not listen in on God's secret
advice.
But you limit wisdom to yourself.
9 You don't know any more than we
know.
You don't understand any more
than we understand.
10 Old people with grey hair are on our
side;
they are even older than your
father.
11 Is the comfort God gives you not
enough for you,
even when words are spoken
gently to you?
12 Has your heart carried you away
from God?
Why do your eyes flash with
anger?
13 Why do you speak out your anger
against God?
Why do these words pour out of
your mouth?

14 "How can anyone be pure?
How can someone born to a
woman be good?
15 God places no trust in his holy ones,
and even the heavens are not pure
in his eyes.
16 How much less pure is one who is
terrible and rotten
and drinks up evil as if it were
water!

17 "Listen to me, and I will tell you
about it;
I will tell you what I have seen.

Job 15:18

18 These are things wise men have told;
   their fathers told them, and they
      have hidden nothing.
19 (The land was given to their fathers
      only,
   and no foreigner lived among
      them.)
20 The wicked suffer pain all their lives;
   the cruel suffer during all the years
      saved up for them.
21 Terrible sounds fill their ears,
   and when things seem to be going
      well, robbers attack them.
22 Evil people give up trying to escape
      from the darkness;
   it has been decided that they will
      die by the sword.
23 They wander around and will become
      food for vultures.
   They know darkness will soon
      come.
24 Worry and suffering terrify them;
   they overwhelm them, like a king
      ready to attack,
25 because they shake their fists at
      God
   and try to get their own way
      against the Almighty.
26 They stubbornly charge at God
   with thick, strong shields.

NO FEAR

Are there some things that make you really nervous, like speaking in front of a large group, or maybe listening to a thunderstorm? Please welcome Millie, aged 10, to Connect 2-You. She's facing a nervous time at the moment.

Millie

Well, my family moved to a new city this summer. That means I'm starting the school year in a new building, with new teachers and nobody around that I know. I'm really scared. What if I don't make any new friends? Who will I eat lunch with? Who's going to make sure that I get to where I need to be?

It's normal to be nervous. Being the new kid is never easy. But Millie shouldn't let her fears get the better of her. The Bible tells us that God is with us no matter where we go. He will not abandon us. Trust him – he will take care of everything you need. If you look at the Livin' It page on fear, Isaiah 43:1-2, p. 951, you'll find some tips on what the Bible has to say about overcoming your fears.

When Millie walks into school on her first day, she should remind herself that she is not walking alone. God is right beside her. And he'll stay there every minute of the day.

27 "Although the faces of the wicked are
         heavy with fat,
     and their waists are fat with flesh,
28 they will live in towns that are
         ruined,
     in houses where no one lives,
         which are crumbling into ruins.
29 The wicked will no longer get rich,
     and the riches they have will not
         last;
     the things they own will no longer
         spread over the land.
30 They will not escape the darkness.
     A flame will dry up their branches;
     God's breath will carry the wicked
         away.
31 The wicked should not fool
         themselves by
         trusting what is
         useless.
     If they do, they
         will get nothing
         in return.
32 Their branches will
         dry up before
         they finish
         growing
     and will never turn
         green.
33 They will be like a vine whose grapes
         are pulled off before they are
         ripe,
     like an olive tree that loses its
         blossoms.
34 People without God can produce
         nothing.
     Fire will destroy the tents of those
         who take money to do evil,
35 who plan trouble and give birth to
         evil,
     whose hearts plan ways to trick
         others."

Job Answers Eliphaz

16 Then Job answered:

2 "I have heard many things like these.
     You are all painful comforters!
3 Will your long speeches
         never end?
     What makes you keep on arguing?
4 I also could speak as you do
     if you were in my place.

I could make great speeches against
         you
     and shake my head at you.
5 But, instead, I would encourage you,
     and my words would bring you
         relief.

6 "Even if I speak, my pain is not less,
     and if I don't speak, it still does not
         go away.
7 God, you have surely taken away my
         strength
     and destroyed my whole family.
8 You have made me thin and weak,
     and this shows I have done wrong.
9 God attacks me and tears me with
         anger;
     he grinds his teeth
         at me;
     my enemy stares at
         me with his
         angry eyes.
10 People open their
         mouths to make
         fun of me
     and slap my cheeks
         to insult me.
     They unite against
         me.
11 God has turned me over to evil
         people
     and has handed me over to the
         wicked.
12 Everything was fine with me,
     but God broke me into pieces;
     he held me by the neck and
         crushed me.
     He has made me his target;
13   his archers surround me.
     He stabs my kidneys without
         mercy;
     he spills my blood on the
         ground.
14 Again and again God attacks me;
     he runs at me like a soldier.

15 "I have sewed rough cloth over my
         skin to show my sadness
     and have buried my face in the
         dust.
16 My face is red from crying;
     I have dark circles around my
         eyes.

> I have heard many
> things like these.
> You are all painful
> comforters!
>   – Job 16:2

17 Yet my hands have never done
anything cruel,
and my prayer is pure.

18 "Earth, please do not cover up my
blood.
Don't let my cry ever stop being
heard!
19 Even now I have one who speaks for
me in heaven;
the one who is on my side is high
above.
20 The one who speaks for me is my
friend.
My eyes pour out tears to God.
21 He begs God on behalf of a human
as a person begs for his friend.

22 "Only a few years will pass
before I go on the journey of no
return.

17 My spirit is broken;
the days of my life are almost
gone.
The grave is waiting for me.
2 Those who laugh at me surround me;
I watch them insult me.

3 "God, make me a promise.
No one will make a pledge for me.
4 You have closed their minds to
understanding.
Do not let them win over me.
5 A person might speak against his
friends for money,
but if he does, the eyes of his
children go blind.

6 "God has made my name a curse
word;
people spit in my face.
7 My sight has grown weak because of
my sadness,
and my body is as thin as a
shadow.
8 Honest people are upset about this;
innocent people are upset with
those who
do wrong.
9 But those who
do right will
continue to
do right,

and those whose hands are not
dirty with sin will grow stronger.
10 "But, all of you, come and try again!
I do not find a wise person among
you.
11 My days are gone, and my plans have
been destroyed,
along with the desires of my heart.
12 These men think night is day;
when it is dark, they say, 'Light is
near.'
13 If the only home I hope for is the
grave,
if I spread out my bed in darkness,
14 if I say to the grave, 'You are my
father,'
and to the worm, 'You are my
mother' or 'You are my sister,'
15 where, then, is my hope?
Who can see any hope for me?
16 Will hope go down to the gates of
death?
Will we go down together into the
dust?"

Bildad Answers Job

18 Then Bildad the Shuhite answered:
2 "When will you stop these speeches?
Be sensible, and then we can
talk.
3 You think of us as cattle,
as if we are stupid.
4 You tear yourself to pieces in your
anger.
Should the earth be vacant just for
you?
Should the rocks move from their
places?

5 "The lamp of the wicked will be put
out,
and the flame in their lamps will
stop burning.
6 The light in their tents will grow
dark,
and the lamps by their sides will go
out.
7 Their strong steps will grow weak;
they will fall into their own evil
traps.
8 Their feet will be caught in a net

17:9
Perseverance
Why should you keep
doing right?

Deborah
Ready for Responsibility

When it comes to being responsible in word or deed, how would you rate on a scale of 1 to 10 (1 being not responsible at all)? Don't worry if you're not a perfect 10. For most people being responsible is challenging. As a judge in Israel, Deborah was faced with this challenge. Deborah's responsibilities included giving the people wise counsel and settling their arguments, providing rest and stability for the people and providing leadership in times of war and turmoil. How did she rate? You can "judge" by checking out

Here's the Scoop

on the following page. The numbers match the numbered questions on this page.

1 Are you always careful about what you say? Or do you think your words don't matter. Words mattered a lot to Deborah because of her job. She had to set a good example through her words for the people.

2 Ever have good news and bad news to tell someone? Maybe the good news is that you found your missing library book, but the bad news is that you now have an enormous fine! If you had bad news to give, would you be tempted to avoid delivering the message? Deborah had both good and bad news to give to someone else.

3 What does it take to be a good leader? Do you think a good leader tells everyone else what to do? Or do you think a good leader shows everyone what to do? Part of Deborah's responsibilities included providing leadership for the Israelites.

4 Are you quick to take all of the credit or look for congratulations when you accomplish something? Deborah was part of a great victory. Did she take all of the credit?

5 If a friend needed help to face a bully at school or in the neighbourhood, would you take on the responsibility? Would you have to consider the situation first? Would it depend on whether you thought you could win? Deborah had to make this decision.

Here's the Scoop

1. As a prophet of God, Deborah had to always watch what she said. Why? Because she told God's words to the people of Israel. She was also the only woman called to be a judge in Israel. A judge was a leader who ruled on legal cases. Deborah helped people to decide what was right. This was a position of great responsibility. But Deborah was responsible and wise. (Check out **Judges 4:4–5**, p. 316.)

2. Imagine having to tell someone to go to war against an army that is impossible to beat! That was the news Deborah had for Barak. He was called to lead an army against Sisera, the general of the powerful army of Canaan. But Deborah also had good news: God would help Barak and Israel to defeat their enemy. Deborah didn't worry about how Barak might respond to the news. She just did what God told her to do. (Read about it in **Judges 4:6–7**, p. 316.)

3. Deborah was the kind of leader people wanted to follow. Deborah didn't just tell the people what to do; she showed them. She took the responsibility of being a good leader very seriously. When Deborah gave the order to Barak to fight Sisera, she didn't sit safely behind the battle-lines. She went with Barak to rally the troops and then she marched with the army into battle. Deborah demonstrated that her confidence was in God, not herself, and that inspired others to follow her. (Read **Judges 4:6–10**, p. 316.)

4. Part of being responsible means giving credit where credit is due. Deborah could have claimed the victory for defeating the Canaanites. After all, she was the leader of the Israelites; she gave the order to attack Sisera; and she agreed to accompany Barak to the battlefield or else he would not have gone. Yet, Deborah didn't take the credit for winning the battle. She knew who was really behind the Israelites' victory – God! Look at her praise song to God following the battle in **Judges 5**, p. 316.

5. When Barak heard that God wanted him to fight the fierce Canaanite army, he did what he thought was the only sensible thing – he refused to go without Deborah! Deborah risked being responsible and agreed to go with him. Because Barak passed the buck, a woman would claim the victory later on! (Read about that in **Judges 4:9, 15–22**, p. 316.) Deborah showed that being a responsible leader means standing up for what's right, even when doing so is risky. (Look up **Judges 4:8–10**, p. 316.)

David Willing to Respect

Would you say that respecting others comes easily for you? Why or why not? Sometimes the behaviour of others can make respecting them a challenge! David, who was considered a man after God's own heart, understood that truth. As David discovered, respect for others often requires an act of will and the help of God. Check out the challenges David faced, then turn the page to

Here's the Scoop

to discover how David earned that reputation of being a godly man. The numbers match the question numbers on this page.

1 Quick – is it easier to respect someone who treats you well or to respect someone who is not so nice to you? Do you think respecting someone depends on how that person treats you? Think about a classmate who won't let you join the game of footie at lunchtime. How do you show that person respect? David had to show respect to a very difficult person in his life, and it wasn't always easy.

2 In what ways do you show respect for friends or members of your family? Do you go out of your way to show kindness to a brother or sister? Are you willing to help your friends?

3 Ever hear the phrase *Kick a man when he's down*? That means to cause further injury to someone who has already been defeated. How do you react when an "enemy" is defeated? Do you think it is OK to talk badly about an enemy?

4 When someone does something to hurt you, how do you respond? What if you were given a chance to get even with that person? David was given that opportunity.

5 Would you go out of your way to help someone whose family has been mean to you? Imagine that the family next door is not nice to you. Then one day you are walking past when the youngest child of that family is hurt in a bike accident. What would you do?

Here's the Scoop

1. King Saul was jealous of David. Saul even tried to kill David. But David still showed respect for Saul. He knew that God had made Saul king of Israel. By respecting Saul, David also showed respect for God. He knew that he could please God by respecting others. (Check out **1 Samuel 18:18; 19:1, 9–11**, p. 380.)

2. David showed respect and love for Jonathan, Saul's son. Because they were friends, they made a promise to be loyal to each other. Part of that loyalty involved being kind to the members of each other's families. David remembered this promise throughout his life. (Read about it in **1 Samuel 18:1–4; 19:1–2; 20:14–17, 42**, p. 379.)

3. It was the perfect opportunity for David to take revenge on Saul. King Saul fell asleep in the very cave where David and his men were hiding. David's own men begged him to kill Saul. After all, Saul tried several times to kill David. But David showed respect for Saul by refusing to harm him when he had the chance. David said no to revenge and yes to respect. Would you have made the same choice? (Look up **1 Samuel 24**, p. 387.)

4. David had a second chance to harm his enemy, Saul. David and one of his soldiers sneaked into Saul's camp while the king was sleeping. David's soldier volunteered to kill Saul right then and there. But David refused. David knew that he was going to be the next king of Israel. (See **1 Samuel 16:1–13**, p. 374.) But David did not want to push himself onto a throne that Saul still occupied. He wanted to wait for God's timing. (Read **1 Samuel 26**, p. 390.)

5. In Bible times, it was a common practice for the new king to kill off the surviving members of rival families. They wanted to make sure that no one tried to take the throne away from them. But as the new king of Israel, David showed respect and love for his friend Jonathan by choosing to be kind to Jonathan's son Mephibosheth. He made sure that Mephibosheth ate at his table and was given the land that belonged to his grandfather Saul. (See **2 Samuel 9**, p. 409.)

Job 18 679

PERSEVERANCE
Job 17:9

Livin' it

Hang in There! What keeps you going on a project that seems to last for ever? Promise of a trip to the pictures? Some money? How about hard work and perseverance (another way to say not quitting)?

Hard work and perseverance don't seem as much fun as seeing a film but they can help you do all sorts of things a movie could never do! Both helped the Israelites rebuild the Temple. Without perseverance they wouldn't have completed such a hard, long project. (Read Ezra 6:15, p. 616.)

Two things can keep you from persevering – putting off doing something and worry. Nehemiah and the Israelites faced these things as they were rebuilding the wall, but they didn't give up. (Check Nehemiah 6, p. 631.) What project needs your perseverance? Pray for God's help, and hang in there to the end!

MORE FAITH links

Two Enemies, **p. 631**

Fly Like an Eagle, **p. 947**

Small Beginnings, **p. 1255**

Keep Going! **p. 1688**

Sometimes you can work hard all day and still not finish a project. Wouldn't it be easy to say, "I quit!"

But before you do quit, why don't you download some of these Faithlinks about not giving up, no matter what! They may help you get the work done.

A Soldier's Story, 2 Timothy 2:3, p. 1653
- Think a soldier's life is easy? No way! A soldier's life is one of long marches and difficulties. It's a job that requires a lot of perseverance. Sometimes Christians are called soldiers of the Lord. In what ways do you think Christians are like soldiers? How can you persevere at the Christian life?

Go for It! Hebrews 12:1–4, p. 1682
- Do you have what it takes to be a marathon runner? Could you go the distance and do all 26 miles? Link here to see how the Christian life can be compared to a race.

While You Wait, Jude 21, p. 1726
- What events do you find the hardest to wait for? Your birthday? Christmas? Holidays? Many believers have a hard time waiting for Jesus' return to earth. How can you persevere and stick with God while you are waiting?

Keep On Keeping On, Revelation 13:10, p. 1744
- Everyone has hard times in life. Hard times help develop perseverance. Find out about the most wonderful reward for hanging in there by linking here.

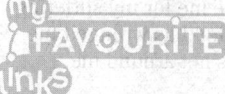
my FAVOURITE links

when they walk into its web.
9 A trap will catch them by the heel
  and hold them tight.
10 A trap for them is hidden on the
   ground,
   right in their path.
11 Terrible things startle them from
   every side
   and chase them at every step.
12 Hunger takes away their strength,
   and disaster is at their side.
13 Disease eats away parts of their skin;
   death eats away at their arms and
   legs.
14 They are torn from the safety of their
   tents
   and dragged off to Death, the King
   of Terrors.
15 Their tents are set on fire,
   and sulphur is scattered over their
   homes.
16 Their roots dry up below ground,
   and their branches die above
   ground.
17 People on earth will not remember
   them;
   their names will be forgotten in the
   land.
18 They will be driven from light into
   darkness
   and chased out of the world.
19 They have no children or
   descendants among their people,
   and no one will be left alive where
   they once lived.
20 People of the west will be shocked at
   what has happened to them,
   and people of the east will be very
   frightened.
21 Surely this is what will happen to the
   wicked;
   such is the place of one who does
   not know God."

Job Answers Bildad

19 Then Job answered:

2 "How long will you hurt me
  and crush me with your words?
3 You have insulted me ten times now
  and attacked me without shame.
4 Even if I have sinned,
  it is my worry alone.

5 If you want to make yourselves look
  better than I,
  you can blame me for my suffering.
6 But know that God has wronged me
  and pulled his net around me.

7 "I shout, 'I have been wronged!'
  But I get no answer.

FAITH links

LOWER THAN LOW

JOB 19:13-25

Some problems in life don't have easy answers. Job's problems made him feel miserable. All of his children had died. His livestock had been taken. Everyone made fun of him. Now his health was bad. Job was lower than low. Yet, even through the lowest times a person could face, Job still had hope in God.

We call the place where Job was "rock bottom". That means life can't get any worse than this. When you're at rock bottom, do what Job did. Look up. Remember that Jesus still cares about you.

Listen Up! 1 Kings 19:11–13, p. 467

A Message of Courage and Hope, 2 Kings 19:4–10, p. 505

999, Psalm 28:6, p. 730

Your Full Trust, Jeremiah 22:20–22, p. 1023

Our Heavenly Connection, Matthew 6:9–13, p. 1283

Toss Those Troubles! 1 Peter 5:7, p. 1706

I scream for help
  but I get no justice.
8 God has blocked my way so I cannot pass;
  he has covered my paths with darkness.
9 He has taken away my honour
  and removed the crown from my head.
10 He beats me down on every side until I am gone;
  he destroys my hope like a fallen tree.
11 His anger burns against me,
  and he treats me like an enemy.
12 His armies gather;
  they prepare to attack me.
  They camp around my tent.
13 "God has made my brothers my enemies,
  and my friends have become strangers.
14 My relatives have gone away,
  and my friends have forgotten me.
15 My guests and my female servants treat me like a stranger;
  they look at me as if I were a foreigner.
16 I call for my servant, but he does not answer,
  even when I beg him with my own mouth.
17 My wife can't stand my breath,
  and my own family dislikes me.
18 Even the little boys hate me
  and talk about me when I leave.
19 All my close friends hate me;
  even those I love have turned against me.
20 I am nothing but skin and bones;
  I have escaped by the skin of my teeth.
21 Pity me, my friends, pity me,
  because the hand of God has hit me.
22 Why do you chase me as God does?
  Haven't you hurt me enough?
23 "How I wish my words were written down,
  written on a scroll.
24 I wish they were carved with an iron pen into lead,
  or carved into stone for ever.
25 I know that my Defender lives,
  and in the end he will stand upon the earth.
26 Even after my skin has been destroyed,
  in my flesh I will see God.
27 I will see him myself;
  I will see him with my very own eyes.
  How my heart wants that to happen!
28 "If you say, 'We will continue to trouble Job,
  because the problem lies with him,'
29 you should be afraid of the sword yourselves.
  God's anger will bring punishment by the sword.
  Then you will know there is judgement."

Zophar Answers

20 Then Zophar the Naamathite answered:

2 "My troubled thoughts cause me to answer,
  because I am very upset.
3 You correct me and I am insulted,
  but I understand how to answer you.

4 "You know how it has been for a long time,
  ever since people were first put on the earth.
5 The happiness of evil people is brief,
  and the joy of the wicked lasts only a moment.
6 Their pride may be as high as the heavens,

> The happiness of evil people is brief, and the joy of the wicked lasts only a moment.
> – Job 20:5

and their heads may touch the clouds,
7 but they will be gone for ever, like their own dung.
People who knew them will say, 'Where are they?'
8 They will fly away like a dream and not be found again;
they will be chased away like a vision in the night.
9 Those who saw them will not see them again;
the places where they lived will see them no more.
10 Their children will have to pay back the poor,
and they will have to give up their wealth.
11 They had the strength of their youth in their bones,
but it will lie with them in the dust of death.
12 "Evil may taste sweet in their mouths,
and they may hide it under their tongues.
13 They cannot stand to let go of it; they keep it in their mouths.
14 But their food will turn sour in their stomachs,
like the poison of a snake inside them.
15 They have swallowed riches, but they will spit them out;
God will make them vomit their riches up.
16 They will suck the poison of snakes,
and the snake's fangs will kill them.
17 They will not admire the sparkling streams
or the rivers flowing with honey and cream.
18 They must give back what they worked for without eating it;
they will not enjoy the money they made from their trading,
19 because they troubled the poor and left them with nothing.
They have taken houses they did not build.
20 "Evil people never lack an appetite, and nothing escapes their selfishness.
21 But nothing will be left for them to eat;
their riches will not continue.
22 When they still have plenty, trouble will catch up with them,
and great misery will come down on them.
23 When the wicked fill their stomachs, God will send his burning anger against them,
and blows of punishment will fall on them like rain.
24 The wicked may run away from an iron weapon,
but a bronze arrow will stab them.
25 They will pull the arrows out of their backs
and pull the points out of their livers.
Terrors will come over them;
26 total darkness waits for their treasure.
A fire not fanned by people will destroy them
and burn up what is left of their tents.
27 The heavens will show their guilt, and the earth will rise up against them.
28 A flood will carry their houses away, swept away on the day of God's anger.
29 This is what God plans for evil people;
this is what he has decided they will receive."

Job Answers Zophar

21 Then Job answered:

2 "Listen carefully to my words, and let this be the way you comfort me.
3 Be patient while I speak.
After I have finished, you may continue to make fun of me.

4 "My complaint is not just against people;
I have reason to be impatient.

5 Look at me and be shocked;
    put your hand over your mouth in
        shock.
6 When I think about this, I am terribly
        afraid
    and my body shakes.
7 Why do evil people live a long time?
    They grow old and become more
        powerful.
8 They see their children around them;
    they watch them grow up.
9 Their homes are safe and without
        fear;
    God does not punish them.
10 Their bulls never fail to mate;
    their cows have healthy calves.
11 They send out their children like a
        flock;
    their little ones dance about.
12 They sing to the music of
        tambourines and harps,
    and the sound of the flute makes
        them happy.
13 Evil people enjoy successful lives
    and then go peacefully to the
        grave.
14 They say to God, 'Leave us alone!
    We don't want to know your ways.
15 Who is the Almighty that we should
        serve him?
    What would we gain by praying to
        him?'
16 The success of the wicked is not their
        own doing.
    Their way of thinking is different
        from mine.
17 Yet how often are the lamps of evil
        people turned off?
    How often does trouble come to
        them?
    How often do they suffer God's
        angry punishment?
18 How often are they like straw in the
        wind
    or like chaff that is blown away by
        a storm?
19 It is said, 'God saves up a person's
        punishment for his children.'
    But God should punish the
        wicked themselves so they will
        know it.
20 Their eyes should see their own
        destruction,

and they should suffer the anger of
    the Almighty.
21 They do not care about the families
        they leave behind
    when their lives have come to an
        end.
22 "No one can
        teach
        knowledge
        to God;

> **21:22 God** Is God above all others?

    he is the one who judges even the
        most important people.
23 One person dies while he still has all
        his strength,
    feeling completely safe and
        comfortable.
24 His body was well fed,
    and his bones were strong and
        healthy.
25 But another person dies with an
        unhappy heart,
    never enjoying any happiness.
26 They are buried next to each other,
    and worms cover them both.
27 "I know very well your thoughts
    and your plans to wrong me.
28 You ask about me, 'Where is this
        great man's house?
    Where are the tents where the
        wicked live?'
29 Have you never asked those who
        travel?
    Have you never listened to their
        stories?
30 On the day of God's anger and
        punishment,
    it is the wicked who are spared.
31 Who will accuse them to their faces?
    Who will pay them back for the evil
        they have done?
32 They are carried to their graves,
    and someone keeps watch over
        their tombs.
33 The earth in the valley seems sweet
        to them.
    Everybody follows after them,
    and many people go before them.
34 "So how can you comfort me with
        this nonsense?
    Your answers are only lies!"

FAITH links

MEANINGLESS WORDS
JOB 21:34

Have you ever listened to someone talking in a foreign language? If you don't know the language, the words spoken have little meaning to you. Sometimes when we try to comfort someone who is hurting, our words may seem as meaningless as if we were speaking in a foreign language. That's the way Job felt when his friends tried to comfort him. He could find no comfort in their words.

One of the best ways to help someone who is suffering is to listen. A true listening ear is often more valuable than words.

Know how to be a good listener? Link here to find out:

Problem Solved, 2 Kings 20:1–11, p. 507

A Gentle Answer, Proverbs 15:1, p. 847

How to Worship God, Isaiah 58, p. 972

Love Him? Show It! Amos 2:6–7, p. 1196

Help for a Friend, Mark 2:1–5, p. 1332

Kindness Counts, Acts 14:3, p. 1489

Eliphaz Answers

22 Then Eliphaz the Temanite answered:

2 "Can anyone be of real use to God?
    Can even a wise person do him good?
3 Does it help the Almighty for you to be good?
    Does he gain anything if you are innocent?
4 Does God punish you for respecting him?
    Does he bring you into court for this?
5 No! It is because your evil is without limits
    and your sins have no end.
6 You took your brothers' things for a debt they didn't owe;
    you took clothes from people and left them naked.
7 You did not give water to tired people,
    and you kept food from the hungry.
8 You were a powerful man who owned land;
    you were honoured and lived in the land.
9 But you sent widows away empty-handed,
    and you mistreated orphans.
10 That is why traps are all around you
    and sudden danger frightens you.
11 That is why it is so dark you cannot see
    and a flood of water covers you.
12 "God is in the highest part of heaven.
    See how high the highest stars are!
13 But you ask, 'What does God know?
    Can he judge us through the dark clouds?
14 Thick clouds cover him so he cannot see us
    as he walks around high up in the sky.'
15 Are you going to stay on the old path
    where evil people walk?
16 They were carried away before their time was up,
    and their foundations were washed away by a flood.
17 They said to God, 'Leave us alone!
    The Almighty can do nothing to us.'

18 But it was God who filled their
    houses with good things.
    Their way of thinking is different
    from mine.

19 "Good people can watch and be glad;
    the innocent can laugh at them and
    say,
20 'Surely our enemies are destroyed,
    and fire burns up their wealth.'

21 "Obey God and be at peace with him;
    this is the way to happiness.
22 Accept teaching from his mouth,
    and keep his words in your heart.
23 If you return to the Almighty, you will
    be blessed again.
    So remove evil from your house.
24 Throw your gold nuggets into the
    dust
    and your fine gold among the
    rocks in the ravines.
25 Then the Almighty will be your gold
    and the best silver for you.
26 You will find pleasure in the Almighty,
    and you will look up to him.
27 You will pray to him, and he will hear
    you,
    and you will keep your promises to
    him.
28 Anything you decide will be done,
    and light will shine on your ways.
29 When people are made humble and
    you say, 'Have courage,'
    then the humble will be saved.
30 Even a guilty person will escape
    and be saved because your hands
    are clean."

Job Answers

23 Then Job answered:

2 "My complaint is still bitter today.
    I am groaning because God's heavy
    hand is on me.
3 I wish I knew where to find God
    so I could go to where he lives.
4 I would present my case before him
    and fill my mouth with arguments.
5 I would learn how he would answer
    me
    and would think about what he
    would say.

FAITH links

GO FOR THE GOLD
JOB 23:10

Job was confident that once God had finished testing him, he would "come out like gold". Do you know what happens to gold when it is refined? To refine something means to purify it. The impurities have to be removed from gold to make it useful. Nowadays, two of the methods used to refine gold are electrolysis or acid.

You're like gold to God. Throughout your life he works on you to remove the things that aren't pure in your life. Sometimes, you'll go through hard times as part of the refining process. Although this is not always easy, God promises to be with you all the way.

Check out how valuable you are to God:

Alone and Forgotten? Genesis 40:23, p. 57

Moses' Champion, Numbers 12, p. 192

In Deep Water, Psalm 69, p. 760

Believe the Impossible? Ezekiel 37, p. 1131

Prayer Anywhere, Mark 1:35, p. 1331

Thoughts on Thoughts, Philippians 4:8–9, p. 1614

---

6 Would he not argue strongly against
    me?
    No, he would really listen to me.

7 Then an honest person could present his case to God,
and I would be saved for ever by my judge.

8 "If I go to the east, God is not there; if I go to the west, I do not see him.
9 When he is at work in the north, I catch no sight of him;
when he turns to the south, I cannot see him.
10 But God knows the way that I take, and when he has tested me, I will come out like gold.
11 My feet have closely followed his steps;
I have stayed in his way;
I did not turn aside.
12 I have never left the commands he has spoken;
I have treasured his words more than my own.

13 "But he is the only God. Who can come against him?
He does anything he wants.
14 He will do to me what he said he would do,
and he has many plans like this.
15 That is why I am frightened of him; when I think of this, I am afraid of him.
16 God has made me afraid;
the Almighty terrifies me.
17 But I am not hidden by the darkness,
by the thick darkness that covers my face.

24 "I wish the Almighty would set a time for judging.
Those who know God do not see such a day.
2 Wicked people take other people's land;
they steal flocks and take them to new pastures.

3 They chase away the orphan's donkey
and take the widow's ox when she has no money.
4 They push needy people off the path; all the poor of the land hide from them.
5 The poor become like wild donkeys in the desert
who go about their job of finding food.
The desert gives them food for their children.
6 They gather hay and straw in the fields
and pick up leftover grapes from the vineyard of the wicked.
7 They spend the night naked, because they have no clothes,
nothing to cover themselves in the cold.
8 They are soaked from mountain rains
and stay near the large rocks because they have no shelter.
9 The fatherless child is grabbed from its mother's breast;
they take a poor mother's baby to pay for what she owes.
10 So the poor go around naked without any clothes;
they carry bundles of grain but still go hungry;
11 they crush olives to get oil and grapes to get wine, but they still go thirsty.
12 Dying people groan in the city,
and the injured cry out for help,
but God accuses no one of doing wrong.

13 "Those who fight against the light
do not know God's ways
or stay in his paths.
14 When the day is over, the murderers get up
to kill the poor and needy.
At night they go about like thieves.

> Those who fight against the light do not know God's ways or stay in his paths.
> – Job 24:13

15 Those who are guilty of adultery
    watch for the night,
  thinking, 'No one will see us,'
  and they keep their faces
    covered.
16 In the dark, evil people break into
    houses.
  In the daytime they shut
    themselves up in their own
    houses,
  because they want nothing to do
    with the light.
17 Darkness is like morning to all these
    evil people
  who make friends with the terrors
    of darkness.

18 "They are like foam floating on the
    water.
  Their part of the land is cursed;
  no one uses the road that goes by
    their vineyards.
19 As heat and dryness quickly melt the
    snow,
  so the grave quickly takes away the
    sinners.
20 Their mothers forget them,
  and worms will eat their bodies.
  They will not be remembered,
  so wickedness is broken in pieces
    like a stick.
21 These evil people abuse women who
    cannot have children
  and show no kindness to
    widows.
22 But God drags away the strong by his
    power.
  Even though they seem strong,
    they do not know how long they
    will live.
23 God may let these evil people feel
    safe,
  but he is watching their ways.
24 For a little while they are important,
    and then they die;
  they are laid low and buried like
    everyone else;
  they are cut off like the heads of
    grain.
25 If this is not true, who can prove I am
    wrong?
  Who can show that my words are
    worth nothing?"

Bildad Answers

25 Then Bildad the Shuhite answered:

2 "God rules and he must be
    honoured;
  he set up order in his high heaven.
3 No one can count God's armies.
  His light shines on all people.
4 So no one can be good in the
    presence of God,
  and no one born to a woman can
    be pure.
5 Even the moon is not bright
  and the stars
    are not
    pure in his
    eyes.
6 People are much
    less! They are
    like insects.
  They are only worms!"

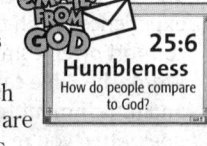

25:6 Humbleness How do people compare to God?

Job Answers Bildad

26 Then Job answered:

2 "You are no help to the helpless!
  You have not given help to the weak!
3 Your advice lacks wisdom!
  You have shown little
    understanding!
4 Who has helped you say these words?
  And where did you get these
    words?

5 "The spirits of the dead tremble,
    those who are beneath and in the
    waters.
6 Death is naked before God;
  destruction is uncovered before
    him.
7 God stretches the northern sky out
    over empty space
  and hangs the earth on nothing.
8 He wraps up the waters in his thick
    clouds,
  but the clouds do not break under
    their weight.
9 He covers the face of the moon,
  spreading his clouds over it.
10 He draws the horizon like a circle on
    the water

FAITH links

COMFORT FROM THE WORD
JOB 26:3-4

Have you experienced someone trying but failing to cheer you up during a tough time? Job could relate to that. His friends offered him words of advice that really didn't hit the spot. When we experience tough times, true comfort often comes from God's Word. The Bible can offer comfort and refreshment to you like water does when you're thirsty. It's the ultimate thirst quencher!

The God of Big Things, Joshua 10, p. 289

God's Sure Protection, Psalm 18, p. 721

Learning to Trust, Psalm 25:4–5, p. 727

Like a Tree, Jeremiah 17:5–8, p. 1016

The Best Advice, Zechariah 10:2, p. 1261

Flex Your Faith, Acts 3:1–16, p. 1467

---

at the place where light and darkness meet.
11 Heaven's foundations shake
when he thunders at them.
12 With his power he controls the sea;
by his wisdom he destroys Rahab, the sea monster.
13 He breathes, and the sky clears.
His hand stabs the fleeing snake.
14 And these are only a small part of God's works.
We only hear a small whisper of him.
Who could understand God's thundering power?"

27

And Job continued speaking:
2 "As surely as God lives, who has taken away my rights,
the Almighty, who has made me unhappy,
3 as long as I am alive
and God's breath of life is in my nose,
4 my lips will not speak evil,
and my tongue will not tell a lie.
5 I will never agree you are right;
until I die, I will never stop saying I am innocent.
6 I will insist that I am right; I will not back down.
My sense of right and wrong will never bother me.

7 "Let my enemies be like evil people, my foes like those who are wrong.
8 What hope do the wicked have when they die,
when God takes their life away?
9 God will not listen to their cries
when trouble comes to them.
10 They will not find joy in the Almighty,
even though they call out to God all the time.

11 "I will teach you about the power of God
and will not hide the ways of the Almighty.
12 You have all seen this yourselves.
So why are we having all this talk that means nothing?

13 "Here is what God has planned for evil people,
and what the Almighty will give to cruel people:
14 They may have many children, but the sword will kill them.
Their children who are left will never have enough to eat.

15 Then they will die of disease and be
buried,
and the widows will not even cry
for them.
16 The wicked may heap up silver like
piles of earth
and have so many clothes they are
like piles of clay.
17 But good people will wear what evil
people have gathered,
and the innocent will divide up
their silver.
18 The houses the wicked build are like
a spider's web,
like a hut that a guard builds.
19 The wicked are rich when they go to
bed,
but they are rich for the last time;
when they open their eyes,
everything is gone.
20 Fears come over them like a flood,
and a storm snatches them away in
the night.
21 The east wind will carry them away,
and then they are gone,
because it sweeps them out of their
place.
22 The wind will hit them without
mercy
as they try to run away from its
power.
23 It will be as if the wind is clapping its
hands;
it will whistle at them as they run
from their place.

28
"There are mines where people
dig silver
and places where gold is made
pure.
2 Iron is taken from the ground,
and copper is melted out of rocks.
3 Miners bring lights
and search deep into the mines
for metal in thick darkness.
4 Miners dig a tunnel far from where
people live,
where no one has ever walked;
they work far from people,
swinging and swaying from
ropes.
5 Food grows on top of the earth,
but below ground things are
changed as if by fire.
6 Sapphires are found in rocks,
and gold dust is also found there.
7 No hawk knows that path;
the falcon has not seen it.
8 Proud animals have not walked
there,
and no lions cross over it.
9 Miners hit the rocks of flint
and dig away at the bottom of the
mountains.
10 They cut tunnels through the rock
and see all the treasures there.
11 They search for places where rivers
begin
and bring things hidden out into
the light.

12 "But where can wisdom be found,
and where does understanding
live?
13 People do not understand the value of
wisdom;
it cannot be found among those
who are alive.
14 The deep ocean says, 'It's not in me;'
the sea says, 'It's not in me.'
15 Wisdom cannot be bought with gold,
and its cost cannot be weighed in
silver.
16 Wisdom cannot be bought with fine
gold
or with valuable onyx or sapphire
gems.
17 Gold and crystal are not as valuable
as wisdom,
and you cannot buy it with jewels
of gold.
18 Coral and jasper are not worth talking
about,
and the price of wisdom is much
greater than rubies.
19 The topaz from Cush cannot compare
with wisdom;
it cannot be bought with the purest
gold.

20 "So where does wisdom come from,
and where does understanding
live?
21 It is hidden from the eyes of every
living thing,
even from the birds of the air.

22 The places of destruction and death say,
   'We have heard reports about it.'
23 Only God understands the way to wisdom,
   and he alone knows where it lives,
24 because he looks to the farthest parts of the earth
   and sees everything under the sky.
25 When God gave power to the wind
   and measured the water,
26 when he made rules for the rain
   and set a path for a thunderstorm to follow,
27 then he looked at wisdom and decided its worth;
   he set wisdom up and tested it.
28 Then he said to humans,
   'The fear of the Lord is wisdom;
   to stay away from evil is understanding.'"

Job Continues

29 Job continued to speak:
2 "How I wish for the months that have passed
   and the days when God watched over me.
3 God's lamp shone on my head,
   and I walked through darkness by his light.
4 I wish for the days when I was strong,
   when God's close friendship blessed my house.
5 The Almighty was still with me,
   and my children were all around me.
6 It was as if my path were covered with cream
   and the rocks poured out olive oil for me.
7 I would go to the city gate
   and sit in the public square.
8 When the young men saw me, they would step aside,
   and the old men would stand up in respect.
9 The leading men stopped speaking
   and covered their mouths with their hands.
10 The voices of the important men were quiet,
   as if their tongues stuck to the roof of their mouths.
11 Anyone who heard me spoke well of me,
   and those who saw me praised me,
12 because I saved the poor who called out
   and the orphan who had no one to help.
13 The dying person blessed me,
   and I made the widow's heart sing.
14 I put on right living as if it were clothing;
   I wore fairness like a robe and a turban.
15 I was eyes for the blind
   and feet for the lame.
16 I was like a father to needy people,
   and I took the side of strangers who were in trouble.
17 I broke the fangs of evil people
   and snatched the captives from their teeth.
18 "I thought, 'I will live for as many days as there are grains of sand,
   and I will die in my own house.
19 My roots will reach down to the water.
   The dew will lie on the branches all night.
20 New honours will come to me continually,
   and I will always have great strength.'
21 "People listened to me carefully
   and waited quietly for my advice.
22 After I finished speaking, they spoke no more.
   My words fell very gently on their ears.

> Then he said to humans, "The fear of the Lord is wisdom; to stay away from evil is understanding."
> – Job 28:28

FAITH links

HAPPINESS OR JOY?
JOB 29:18-19

Have you ever wished that everything in life would just freeze during a happy moment? That's how Job felt. Before trouble came, he had everything that he wanted. Job wished that he still felt that happiness.

Do you know the difference between happiness and joy? Happiness depends on circumstances. If everything is going great, you feel happy. But happiness doesn't last for ever. Joy, on the other hand, doesn't depend on what you have. Joy comes from God. You can be joyful even when things aren't going great. Joy is more long lasting than happiness. Which would you prefer: joy or happiness?

Are you happy? Or do you have joy? Check it out at these links:

A Life of Thanksgiving, 1 Kings 1:47–48, p. 435

When Bad Things Happen, Ecclesiastes 3:16–17, p. 876

The Foundation of Our Hope, Isaiah 31:1–8, p. 934

Mission Impossible? Mark 5:21–24, 35–43, p. 1337

Always Do This! 1 Thessalonians 5:16–18, p. 1636

The "Quality" of Life, 2 Peter 1:5–8, p. 1708

---

23 They waited for me as they would for rain
and drank in my words like spring rain.
24 I smiled at them when they doubted,
and my approval was important to them.
25 I chose the way for them and was their leader.
I lived like a king among his army,
like a person who comforts sad people.

30 "But now men who are younger than I make fun of me.
I would not even have let their fathers sit with my sheep dogs.
2 What use did I have for their strength
since they had lost their strength to work?
3 They were thin from hunger
and wandered the dry and ruined land at night.
4 They gathered desert plants among the brush
and ate the root of the broom tree.
5 They were forced to live away from people;
people shouted at them as if they were thieves.
6 They lived in dried up stream beds,
in caves and among the rocks.
7 They howled like animals among the bushes
and huddled together in the brush.
8 They are worthless people without names
and were forced to leave the land.

9 "Now they make fun of me with songs;
my name is a joke among them.
10 They hate me and stay far away from me,
but they do not mind spitting in my face.
11 God has taken away my strength and made me suffer,
so they attack me with all their anger.

12 On my right side they rise up like a mob.
They lay traps for my feet
and prepare to attack me.
13 They break up my road
and work to destroy me,
and no one helps me.
14 They come at me as if through a hole in the wall,
and they roll in among the ruins.
15 Great fears overwhelm me.
They blow my honour away as if by a great wind,
and my safety disappears like a cloud.
16 "Now my life is almost over;
my days are full of suffering.
17 At night my bones ache;
gnawing pains never stop.
18 In his great power God grabs hold of my clothing
and chokes me with the collar of my coat.
19 He throws me into the mud,
and I become like earth and ashes.
20 "I cry out to you, God, but you do not answer;
I stand up, but you just look at me.
21 You have turned on me without mercy;
with your powerful hand you attacked me.
22 You snatched me up and threw me into the wind
and tossed me about in the storm.
23 I know you will bring me down to death,
to the place where all living people must go.
24 "Surely no one would hurt a ruined man
when he cries for help in his time of trouble.
25 I cried for those who were in trouble;
I have been very sad for poor people.
26 But when I hoped for good, only evil came to me;
when I looked for light, darkness came.
27 I never stop being upset;
days of suffering are ahead of me.
28 I have turned black, but not by the sun.
I stand up in public and cry for help.
29 I have become a brother to wild dogs
and a friend to ostriches.
30 My skin has become black and peels off,
as my body burns with fever.
31 My harp is tuned to sing a sad song,
and my flute is tuned to moaning.

> I cried for those who were in trouble; I have been very sad for poor people.
> – Job 30:25

31

"But I made an agreement with my eyes
not to look with desire at a girl.
2 What has God above promised for people?
What has the Almighty planned from on high?
3 It is ruin for evil people
and disaster for those who do wrong.
4 God sees my ways
and counts every step I take.
5 "If I have been dishonest
or lied to others,
6 then let God weigh me on honest scales.
Then he will know I have done nothing wrong.
7 If I have turned away from doing what is right,
or my heart has been led by my eyes to do wrong,
or my hands have been made unclean,
8 then let other people eat what I have planted,
and let my crops be ploughed up.

9 "If I have desired another woman
    or have waited at my neighbour's
        door for his wife,
10 then let my wife grind another man's
        grain,
    and let other men have sexual
        relations with her.
11 That would be shameful,
    a sin to be punished.
12 It is like a fire that burns and destroys;
    all I have done would be ploughed
        up.

13 "If I have been unfair to my male and
        female slaves
    when they had a complaint against
        me,
14 how could I tell God what I did?
    What will I answer when he asks me to explain what I've done?
15 God made me in my mother's womb,
        and he also made them;
    the same God formed both of us in
        our mothers' wombs.

16 "I have never refused the appeals of
        the poor
    or let widows give up hope while
        looking for help.
17 I have not kept my food to myself
    but have given it to the orphans.
18 Since I was young, I have been like a
        father to the orphans.
    From my birth I guided the
        widows.
19 I have not let anyone die for lack of
        clothes
    or let a needy person go without a
        coat.
20 That person's heart blessed me,
    because I warmed him with the
        wool of my sheep.
21 I have never hurt an orphan
    even when I knew I could win in
        court.
22 If I have, then let my arm fall off my
        shoulder
    and be broken at the joint.
23 I fear destruction from God,
    and I fear his majesty, so I could
        not do such things.

24 "I have not put my trust in gold
    or said to pure gold, 'You are my
        security.'
25 I have not celebrated my great
        wealth
    or the riches my hands had gained.
26 I have not thought about worshipping
        the sun in its brightness
    nor admired the moon moving in
        glory
27 so that my heart was pulled away
        from God.
    My hand has never offered the sun
        and moon a kiss of worship.
28 If I had, these also would have been
        sins to be punished,
    because I would have been
        unfaithful to God.

29 "I have not been happy when my
        enemy fell
    or laughed when he had trouble.
30 I have not let my mouth sin
    by cursing my enemy's life.
31 The men of my house have always
        said,
    'Everyone has eaten all he wants of
        Job's food.'
32 No stranger ever had to spend the
        night in the street,
    because I always let travellers stay
        in my home.
33 I have not hidden my sin as others
        do,
    secretly keeping my guilt to
        myself.
34 I was not so afraid of the crowd
    that I kept quiet and stayed inside
    because I feared being hated by
        other families.

35 ("How I wish a court would hear my
        case!
    Here I sign my name to show I
        have told the truth.
    Now let the Almighty answer me;
    let the one who accuses me write it
        down.
36 I would wear the writing on my
        shoulder;

---

eMAIL FROM GOD

31:13–14
Respect

Treat others with respect.

RESPECTING OTHERS
Job 31:13–14

Just a Little Respect Do you bow or give a salute when you meet members of your family or friends? Probably not. But if you were in the army, you would do a lot of saluting. And if you were presented to the Queen, you would bow or curtsy. These are special ways of showing respect. But there are other ways of showing respect to people. How do you show respect to your family or to older people?

God wants us to respect him and the people he places in our life. David's soldiers risked their lives out of respect for him. (Read 1 Chronicles 11:10–19, p. 534.) You may never have to risk your life for someone to show them respect, but think of the leaders in your life: parents, teachers, youth leaders, pastors and so on. Do you listen to them when they speak? Do you answer them politely? What would you do to show respect for them?

MORE FAITH links

- Show Some Respect, **p. 161**
- Take Me to Your Leader, **p. 214**
- In Your Best Interests, **p. 349**
- Just a Little Respect, **p. 534**
- Who's on First? **p. 1723**

Sometimes, people are greeted by others bowing or curtsying in front of them, or by a fanfare of trumpets. These are all ways to show people respect.

Why don't you log on to these Faithlinks to find some other ways of showing respect?

Fairness for All, Deuteronomy 24:17, p. 258
- What if someone passed out sweets to you and your friends, but gave you the least? Would you feel that person had respect for you? Treating people fairly is one way to show respect for others. Link here to find out more.

Fair All the Time? 2 Samuel 8:15, p. 408
- Do you show the same respect to everyone and treat everyone the same way? Check out this link to find out about King David's treatment of others.

The Verdict Is In? Matthew 7:1–2, p. 1285
- Do you make judgements about others? Are you always right in your opinion? This Faithlink tells you what Jesus taught about judging others.

Best Seat in the House, Luke 14:7–11, p. 1398
- Suppose you and a friend were invited to a party for a famous person. There is only one seat next to this person. Would you sit there or let your friend have the seat? Jesus teaches us to be humble – not try to make ourselves important. How does being humble show respect for others?

my FAVOURITE links

I would put it on like a crown.
37 I would explain to God every step I
took,
and I would come near to him like
a prince.)

38 "If my land cries out against me
and its ploughed rows are not wet
with tears,
39 if I have taken the land's harvest
without paying
or have broken the spirit of those
who worked the land,
40 then let thorns come up instead of
wheat,
and let weeds come up instead of
barley."

The words of Job are finished.

Elihu Speaks

32 These three men stopped trying to answer Job, because he was so sure he was right. 2 But Elihu son of Barakel the Buzite, from the family of Ram, became very angry with Job, because Job claimed he was right instead of God. 3 Elihu was also angry with Job's three friends who had no answer to show that Job was wrong, yet continued to blame him. 4 Elihu had waited before speaking to Job, because the three friends were older than he was. 5 But when Elihu saw that the three men had nothing more to say, he became very angry.

6 So Elihu son of Barakel the Buzite said this:

"I am young,
and you are old.
That is why I was afraid
to tell you what I know.
7 I thought, 'Older people should
speak,
and those who have lived many
years should teach wisdom.'
8 But it is the spirit in a person,
the breath of the Almighty, that
gives understanding.

> But it is the spirit in a person, the breath of the Almighty, that gives understanding.
> – Job 32:8

9 It is not just older people who are
wise;
they are not the only ones who
understand what is right.
10 So I say, listen to me.
I too will tell you what I know.
11 I waited while you three spoke,
and listened to your explanations.
While you looked for words to use,
12 I paid close attention to you.
But not one of you has proved Job
wrong;
none of you has answered his
arguments.
13 Don't say, 'We have found wisdom;
only God will show Job to be
wrong, not people.'
14 Job has not spoken his words against
me,
so I will not use your arguments to
answer Job.

15 "These three friends are defeated and
have no more to say;
words have failed them.
16 Now they are standing there with no
answers for Job.
Now that they are quiet, must I
wait to speak?
17 No, I too will speak
and tell what I
know.
18 I am full of words,
and the spirit in me
causes me to
speak.
19 I am like wine that
has been bottled
up;
I am ready to burst
like a new
leather wine bag.
20 I must speak so I will feel relief;
I must open my mouth and answer.
21 I will be fair to everyone
and not flatter anyone.
22 I don't know how to flatter,
and if I did, my Maker would
quickly take me away.

33 "Now, Job, listen to my words.
Pay attention to everything I say.
2 I open my mouth

and am ready to speak.
3 My words come from an honest heart,
and I am sincere in saying what I know.
4 The Spirit of God created me,
and the breath of the Almighty gave me life.
5 Answer me if you can;
get yourself ready and stand before me.
6 I am just like you before God;
I too am made out of clay.

7 Don't be afraid of me;
I will not be hard on you.

8 "But I heard what you have said;
I heard every word.
9 You said, 'I am pure and without sin;
I am innocent and free from guilt.'
10 But God has found fault with me;
he considers me his enemy.
11 He locks my feet in chains
and closely watches everywhere I go.'

12 "But I tell you, you are not right in saying this,
because God is greater than we are.
13 Why do you accuse God
of not answering anyone?
14 God does speak—sometimes one way and sometimes another—
even though people may not understand it.
15 He speaks in a dream or a vision of the night
when people are in a deep sleep, lying on their beds.
16 He speaks in their ears
and frightens them with warnings
17 to turn them away from doing wrong
and to keep them from being proud.
18 God does this to save a person from death,
to keep him from dying.
19 A person may be corrected while in bed in great pain;
he may have continual pain in his very bones.
20 He may be in such pain that he even hates food,
even the very best meal.
21 His body becomes so thin there is almost nothing left of it,
and his bones that were hidden now stick out.
22 He is near death,
and his life is almost over.

23 "But there may be an angel to speak for him,
one out of a thousand, who will tell him what to do.

HOW GOD SPEAKS
JOB 33:14-17

Ever wonder how God speaks to a person? Elihu, one of Job's friends, told Job about the different ways God used to speak to people. God still speaks to people today, although we don't always recognise his voice. He speaks to you through the Bible, through the Holy Spirit and through the people he puts in your life. You have to learn to listen for his voice.

Help to Understand, 2 Samuel 14, p. 416

Deciding Wisely, 1 Kings 3:16–28, p. 440

Teaching Others, Ezra 7:8–10, p. 617

The Bible: Good for Your Faith, Psalm 119, p. 802

Heavenly Treasure, Luke 12:32–34, p. 1394

Pay Attention! Hebrews 2:1, p. 1668

24 The angel will beg for mercy and say:
'Save him from death.
I have found a way to pay for his life.'
25 Then his body is made new like a child's.
It will return to the way it was when he was young.
26 That person will pray to God, and God will listen to him.
He will see God's face and will shout with happiness.
And God will set things right for him again.
27 Then he will say to others,
'I sinned and twisted what was right,
but I did not receive the punishment I should have received.
28 God bought my life back from death, and I will continue to enjoy life.'
29 "God does all these things to a person
two or even three times
30 so he won't die as punishment for his sins
and so he may still enjoy life.
31 "Job, pay attention and listen to me; be quiet, and I will speak.
32 If you have anything to say, answer me;
speak up, because I want to prove you right.
33 But if you have nothing to say, then listen to me;
be quiet, and I will teach you wisdom."

34

Then Elihu said:
2 "Hear my words, you wise men; listen to me, you who know a lot.
3 The ear tests words
as the tongue tastes food.
4 Let's decide for ourselves what is right,
and let's learn together what is good.
5 "Job says, 'I am not guilty,
and God has refused me a fair trial.
6 Instead of getting a fair trial,
I am called a liar.
I have been seriously hurt,
even though I have not sinned.'
7 There is no other man like Job;
he takes insults as if he were drinking water.
8 He keeps company with those who do evil
and spends time with wicked men,
9 because he says, 'It is no use trying to please God.'
10 "So listen to me, you who can understand.
God can never do wrong!
It is impossible for the Almighty to do evil.
11 God pays a person back for what he has done
and gives him what his actions deserve.
12 Truly God will never do wrong;
the Almighty will never twist what is right.
13 No one chose God to rule over the earth
or put him in charge of the whole world.
14 If God should decide
to take away life and breath,
15 then everyone would die together
and turn back into dust.
16 "If you can understand, hear this; listen to what I have to say.
17 Can anyone govern who hates what is right?
How can you blame God who is both fair and powerful?
18 God is the one who says to kings, 'You are worthless,'
or to important people, 'You are evil.'
19 He is not nicer to princes than other people,
nor kinder to rich people than poor people,
because he made them all with his own hands.
20 They can die in a moment, in the middle of the night.

They are struck down, and then
    they pass away;
powerful people die without help.
21 "God watches where people go;
    he sees every step
        they take.
22 There is no dark place
    or deep shadow
        where those who do
        evil can hide from
        him.
23 He does not set a time
    for people to come
        before him for
        judging.
24 Without asking
    questions, God breaks powerful
        people into pieces
    and puts others in their place.
25 Because God knows what people do,
    he defeats them in the night, and
        they are crushed.
26 He punishes them for the evil they
        do
    so that everyone else can watch,
27 because they stopped following
        God
    and did not care about any of his
        ways.
28 The cry of the poor comes to God;
    he hears the cry of the needy.
29 But if God keeps quiet, who can
        blame him?
    If he hides his face, who can see
        him?
    God still rules over both nations and
        persons alike.
30   He keeps the wicked from ruling
    and from trapping others.

31 "But suppose someone says to
        God,
    'I am guilty, but I will not sin
        any more.
32 Teach me what I cannot see.
    If I have done wrong, I will not do
        it again.'
33 So, Job, should God reward you as
        you want
    when you refuse to change?
    You must decide, not I,
        so tell me what you know.

> God watches where people go; he sees every step they take.
> — Job 34:21

34 "Those who understand speak,
    and the wise who hear me say,
35 'Job speaks without knowing what is
        true;
    his words show he does not
        understand.'
36 I wish Job would be
        tested completely,
        because he
        answered like an
        evil man!
37 Job now adds to his sin
        by turning
        against God.
    He claps his hands
        in protest,
        speaking more and
        more against
        God."

35
Then Elihu said:
2 "Do you think this is fair?
    You say, 'God will show that I am
        right,'
3 but you also ask, 'What's the use?
    I don't gain anything by not sinning.'

4 "I will answer you
    and your friends who are with you.
5 Look up at the sky
    and see the clouds so high above
        you.
6 If you sin, it does nothing to God;
    even if your sins are many, they do
        nothing to him.
7 If you are good, you give nothing to
        God;
    he receives nothing from your hand.
8 Your evil ways only hurt a man like
        yourself,
    and the good you do only helps
        other human beings.

9 "People cry out when they are in
        trouble;
    they beg for relief from powerful
        people.
10 But no one asks, 'Where is God, my
        Maker,
    who gives us songs in the night,
11 who teaches more to us than the
        animals of the earth

and wiser than the birds of the
air?'
12 God does not answer evil people
when they cry out,
because the wicked are proud.
13 God does not listen to their useless
begging;
the Almighty pays no attention to
them.
14 He will listen to you even less
when you say that you do not see
him,
that your case is before him,
that you must wait for him,
15 that his anger never punishes,
and that he doesn't notice evil.
16 So Job is only speaking nonsense,
saying many words without
knowing what is true."

Elihu's Speech Continues

36 Elihu continued:

2 "Listen to me a little longer, and I will
show you
that there is more to be said for
God.
3 What I know comes from far away.
I will show that my Maker is
right.
4 You can be sure that my words are
not false;
one who really knows is with you.

5 "God is powerful, but he does not
hate people;
he is powerful and sure of what he
wants to do.
6 He will not keep evil people alive,
but he gives the poor their rights.
7 He always watches over those who do
right;
he sets them on thrones with
kings
and they are honoured for ever.
8 If people are bound in chains,
or if trouble, like ropes, ties them
up,
9 God tells them what they have done,
that they have sinned in their
pride.
10 God makes them listen to his
warning
and commands them to change
from doing evil.
11 If they obey and serve him,

FAITH links

NO DOUBT ABOUT IT
JOB 36:5

Think about the things you're certain that you know – no doubts cross your mind at all. You're certain about what your name is and where you live. (You *are* sure of that, right?) You're sure that your parents love you. You can be sure of something else: God cares. One of Job's friends talked to Job about God. He told Job that God was all-powerful, but still cared about everyone. No matter what happens in your life, you can be sure that God cares about you. Since he's all-powerful, he can help you through the toughest problems you will ever face. No doubt about it.

Here are some more Faithlinks on God's care for you:

Good Plans, Genesis 45:7–8, p. 64

What God Thinks, Isaiah 55:8–9, p. 969

A Tight Spot, Jonah 2, p. 1215

Your Feet on High Places, Habakkuk 3:18–19, p. 1239

But I Want It? Philippians 4:19, p. 1615

A Happy Ending, Revelation 22:16–21, p. 1754

the rest of their lives will be successful,
and the rest of their years will be happy.
12 But if they do not listen,
they will die by the sword,
and they will die without knowing why.

13 "Those who have wicked hearts hold on to anger.
Even when God punishes them, they do not cry for help.
14 They die while they are still young,
and their lives end in disgrace.
15 But God saves those who suffer through their suffering;
he gets them to listen through their pain.

16 "God is gently calling you from the jaws of trouble
to an open place of freedom
where he has set your table full of the best food.
17 But now you are being punished like the wicked;
you are getting justice.
18 Be careful! Don't be led away from God by riches;
don't let much money turn you away.
19 Neither your wealth nor all your great strength
will keep you out of trouble.
20 Don't wish for the night
when people are taken from their homes.
21 Be careful not to turn to evil,
which you seem to want more than suffering.

22 "God is great and powerful;
no other teacher is like him.
23 No one has planned his ways for him;
no one can say to God, 'You have done wrong.'
24 Remember to praise his work,
about which people have sung.
25 Everybody has seen it;
people look at it from far off.
26 God is so great, greater than we can understand!
No one knows how old he is.
27 "He takes up the drops of water from the earth
and turns them into rain.
28 The rain then pours down from the clouds,
and showers fall on people.
29 No one understands how God spreads out the clouds
or how he sends thunder from where he lives.
30 Watch how God scatters his lightning around him,
lighting up the deepest parts of the sea.
31 This is the way God governs the nations;
this is how he gives us enough food.
32 God fills his hands with lightning
and commands it to strike its target.
33 His thunder announces the coming storm,
and even the cattle know it is near.

37 "At the sound of his thunder, my heart pounds
as if it will jump out of my chest.
2 Listen! Listen to the thunder of God's voice
and to the rumbling that comes from his mouth.
3 He turns his lightning loose under the whole sky
and sends it to the farthest parts of the earth.
4 After that you can hear the roar
when he thunders with a great sound.
He does not hold back the flashing
when his voice is heard.
5 God's voice thunders in wonderful ways;
he does great things we cannot understand.
6 He says to the snow, 'Fall on the earth,'
and to the shower, 'Be a heavy rain.'
7 With it, he stops everyone from working
so everyone knows it is the work of God.

8 The animals take cover from the rain
    and stay in their dens.
9 The storm comes from where it was
      stored;
    the cold comes with the strong
      winds.
10 The breath of God makes ice,
    and the wide waters become
      frozen.
11 He fills the clouds with water
    and scatters his lightning through
      them.
12 At his command they swirl around
      over the whole earth,
    doing whatever he commands.

FAITH CHALLENGE

Got another challenge for you. Read 37:14 to discover the good advice Job got from one of his friends. What's the most amazing thing you've ever seen God do in your life or in the life of someone you know?

TeSTiNG iT

Job 37:14
Job, listen to this: Stop and notice God's miracles.

13 He uses the clouds to punish people
    or to water his earth and show his
      love.
14 "Job, listen to this:
    Stop and notice God's miracles.
15 Do you know how God controls the
      clouds
    and makes his lightning flash?
16 Do you know how the clouds hang in
      the sky?
    Do you know the miracles of God,
      who knows everything?
17 You suffer in your clothes
    when the land is silenced by the
      hot, south wind.
18 You cannot stretch out the sky like God
    and make it look as hard as
      polished bronze.
19 Tell us what we should say to him;
    we cannot get our arguments ready
      because we do not have enough
      understanding.
20 Should God be told that I want to
      speak?
    Would a person ask to be
      swallowed up?
21 No one can look at the sun
    when it is bright in the sky
      after the wind has blown all the
      clouds away.
22 God comes out of the north in golden
      light,
    in overwhelming greatness.
23 The Almighty is too high for us to
      reach.
    He has great strength;
    he is always right and never
      punishes unfairly.
24 That is why people honour him;
    he does not respect those who say
      they are wise."

The Lord Questions Job

38 Then the LORD answered Job from the storm. He said:

2 "Who is this that makes my purpose
      unclear
    by saying things that are not true?
3 Be strong like a man!
    I will ask you questions,
    and you must answer me.

4 Where were you when I made the earth's foundation?
Tell me, if you understand.
5 Who marked off how big it should be?
Surely you know!
Who stretched a ruler across it?
6 What were the earth's foundations set on,
or who put its cornerstone in place
7 while the morning stars sang together
and all the angels shouted with joy?

8 "Who shut the doors to keep the sea in
when it broke through and was born,
9 when I made the clouds like a coat for the sea
and wrapped it in dark clouds,
10 when I put limits on the sea
and put its doors and bars in place,
11 when I said to the sea, 'You may come this far, but no farther;
this is where your proud waves must stop'?

12 "Have you ever ordered the morning to begin,
or shown the dawn where its place was
13 in order to take hold of the earth by its edges
and shake evil people out of it?
14 At dawn the earth changes like clay being pressed by a seal;
the hills and valleys stand out like folds in a coat.
15 Light is not given to evil people;
their arm is raised to do harm, but it is broken.

16 "Have you ever gone to where the sea begins
or walked in the valleys under the sea?
17 Have the gates of death been opened to you?
Have you seen the gates of the deep darkness?
18 Do you understand how wide the earth is?
Tell me, if you know all these things.

19 "What is the path to the source of light,
and where does darkness live?
20 Can you take them to their places?
Do you know the way to their homes?
21 Surely you know, if you were already born when all this happened!
Have you lived that many years?

22 "Have you ever gone into the storehouse of the snow
or seen the storehouses for hail,
23 which I save for times of trouble,
for days of war and battle?
24 Where is the place from which light comes?
Where is the place from which the east winds blow over the earth?
25 Who cuts a waterway for the heavy rains
and sets a path for the thunderstorm?
26 Who waters the land where no one lives,
the desert that has no one in it?
27 Who sends rain to satisfy the empty land
so the grass begins to grow?
28 Does the rain have a father?
Who is father to the drops of dew?
29 Who is the mother of the ice?
Who gives birth to the frost from the sky
30 when the water becomes hard as stone,
and even the surface of the ocean is frozen?

31 "Can you tie up the stars of the Pleiades
or loosen the ropes of the stars in Orion?
32 Can you bring out the stars on time
or lead out the stars of the Bear with its cubs?
33 Do you know the laws of the sky
and understand their rule over the earth?

FAITH links

HOW BIG IS GOD?
JOB 38—41

Want to know how big God is? When God answered Job's prayer for understanding about his situation, God told him how big he was. God was big enough to create the world and everything in it and big enough to order the stars in the sky. That information made Job feel small.

God is in control of everything. He's big, yet loving. When we begin to understand how much we don't know about God, we begin to understand how awesome he is.

Think God can't handle your problems? Check it out again at these links:

Your Heavenly Dad, Psalm 103:13, p. 786

Our Awesome God, Ezekiel 1:26–28, p. 1087

A Love Song, Zephaniah 3:17, p. 1246

The Best Protection Plan, Matthew 2:13–18, p. 1276

Who Needs Love? Luke 6:27–36, p. 1379

Hope That Doesn't Fail, Acts 26:4–7, p. 1510

---

34 "Can you shout an order to the clouds
  and cover yourself with a flood of water?
35 Can you send lightning bolts on their way?
  Do they come to you and say, 'Here we are'?
36 Who put wisdom inside the mind
  or understanding in the heart?
37 Who has the wisdom to count the clouds?
  Who can pour water from the jars of the sky
38 when the dust becomes hard
  and the clumps of earth stick together?
39 "Do you hunt food for the female lion
  to satisfy the hunger of the young lions
40 while they lie in their dens
  or hide in the bushes waiting to attack?
41 Who gives food to the birds
  when their young cry out to God
  and wander about without food?

39 "Do you know when the mountain goats give birth?
  Do you watch when the deer gives birth to her fawn?
2 Do you count the months until they give birth
  and know the right time for them to give birth?
3 They lie down, their young are born,
  and then the pain of giving birth is over.
4 Their young ones grow big and strong in the wild country.
  Then they leave their homes and do not return.

5 "Who let the wild donkey go free?
  Who untied its ropes?
6 I am the one who gave the donkey the desert as its home;
  I gave it the desert lands as a place to live.
7 The wild donkey laughs at the confusion in the city,
  and it does not hear the drivers shout.
8 It roams the hills looking for pasture,
  looking for anything green to eat.

9 "Will the wild ox agree to serve you
and stay by your feeding box at
night?
10 Can you hold it to the ploughed row
with a harness
so it will plough the valleys for
you?
11 Will you depend on the wild ox for its
great strength
and leave your heavy work for it to
do?
12 Can you trust the ox to bring in your
grain
and gather it to your threshing
floor?

13 "The wings of the ostrich flap
happily,
but they are not like the feathers of
the stork.
14 The ostrich lays its eggs on the
ground
and lets them warm in the sand.
15 It does not stop to think that a foot
might step on them and crush
them;
it does not care that some animal might walk on them.
16 The ostrich is cruel to its young, as if
they were not even its own.
It does not care that its work is for
nothing,
17 because God did not give the ostrich
wisdom;
God did not give it a share of good
sense.
18 But when the ostrich gets up to run,
it is so fast
that it laughs at the horse and its
rider.

19 "Job, are you the one who gives the
horse its strength
or puts a flowing mane on its neck?
20 Do you make the horse jump like a
locust?
It scares people with its proud
snorting.

21 It paws wildly, enjoying its strength,
and charges into battle.
22 It laughs at fear and is afraid of
nothing;
it does not run away from the
sword.
23 The bag of arrows rattles against the
horse's side,
along with the flashing spears and
swords.
24 With great excitement, the horse
races over the ground;
and it cannot stand still when it
hears the trumpet.
25 When the trumpet blows, the horse
snorts, 'Aha!'
It smells the battle from far away;
it hears the shouts of commanders
and the battle cry.

> Is it through your wisdom that the hawk flies and spreads its wings towards the south?
> – Job 39:26

26 "Is it through your wisdom that the
hawk flies
and spreads its wings towards
the south?
27 Are you the one that commands the
eagle to fly
and build its nest so high?
28 It lives on a high cliff and stays there
at night;
the rocky peak is its protected
place.
29 From there it looks for its food;
its eyes can see it from far away.
30 Its young eat blood,
and where there is something
dead, the eagle is there."

40 The LORD said to Job:
2 "Will the person who argues
with the Almighty correct him?
Let the person who accuses
God answer him."

40:2 God Can you correct God?

3 Then Job answered the LORD:
4 "I am not worthy; I cannot answer
you anything,

so I will put my hand over my
    mouth.
5 I spoke once, but I will not answer
    again;
  I even spoke twice, but I will say
    nothing more."

6 Then the LORD spoke to Job from the storm:
7 "Be strong, like a man!
  I will ask you questions,
    and you must answer me.
8 Would you say that I am unfair?
  Would you blame me to make
    yourself look right?
9 Are you as strong as God?
  Can your voice thunder like his?
10 If so, then decorate yourself with
    glory and beauty;
  dress in honour and greatness as if
    they were clothing.
11 Let your great anger punish;
  look at the proud and bring them
    down.
12 Look at the proud and make them
    humble.
  Crush the wicked wherever they
    are.
13 Bury them all in the earth together;
  cover their faces in the grave.
14 If you can do that,
    then I myself will praise you,
  because you are strong enough to
    save yourself.

15 "Look at the behemoth,"
    which I made just as I made you.
  It eats grass like an ox.
16 Look at the strength it has in its
    body;
  the muscles of its stomach are
    powerful.
17 Its tail moves like a cedar tree;
  the muscles of its thighs are woven
    together.
18 Its bones are like tubes of bronze;
  its legs are like bars of iron.
19 It is one of the first of God's works,
    but its Maker can destroy it.
20 The hills, where the wild animals
    play,
  provide food for it.
21 It lies under the lotus plants,
  hidden by the tall grass in the
    swamp.
22 The lotus plants hide it in their
    shadow;
  the poplar trees by the streams
    surround it.
23 If the river floods, it will not be afraid;
  it is safe even if the Jordan River
    rushes to its mouth.
24 Can anyone blind its eyes and capture
    it?
  Can anyone put hooks in its nose?

41 "Can you catch the leviathan" on a
    fish-hook
  or tie its tongue down with a rope?
2 Can you put a cord through its nose
  or a hook in its jaw?
3 Will it keep begging you for mercy
  and speak to you with gentle
    words?
4 Will it make an agreement with you
  and let you take it as your slave for
    life?
5 Can you make a pet of the leviathan as
  you would a bird
  or put it on a leash for your girls?
6 Will traders try to bargain with you
    for it?
  Will they divide it up among the
    merchants?
7 Can you stick darts all over its skin
  or fill its head with fishing spears?
8 If you put one hand on it,
  you will never forget the battle,
    and you will never do it again!
9 There is no hope of defeating it;

> Can you catch the leviathan on a fish-hook or tie its tongue down with a rope?
> – Job 41:1

40:15 behemoth A large land animal. It could refer to the hippopotamus, the elephant, or a monster.
41:1 leviathan Possibly a crocodile or a sea monster.

just seeing it overwhelms people.
10 No one is brave enough to make it angry,
so who would be able to stand up against me?
11 No one has ever given me anything that I must pay back,
because everything under the sky belongs to me.

12 "I will speak about Leviathan's arms and legs,
its great strength and well-formed body.
13 No one can tear off its outer hide
or poke through its double armour.
14 No one can force open its great jaws;
they are filled with frightening teeth.
15 It has rows of shields on its back
that are tightly sealed together.
16 Each shield is so close to the next one
that no air can go between them.
17 They are joined strongly to one another;
they hold on to each other and cannot be separated.
18 When it snorts, flashes of light are thrown out,
and its eyes look like the light at dawn.
19 Flames blaze from its mouth;
sparks of fire shoot out.
20 Smoke pours out of its nose,
as if coming from a large pot over a hot fire.
21 Its breath sets coals on fire,
and flames come out of its mouth.
22 There is great strength in its neck.
People are afraid and run away.
23 The folds of its skin are tightly joined;
they are set and cannot be moved.
24 Its chest is as hard as a rock,
even as hard as a grinding stone.
25 The powerful fear its terrible looks
and draw back in fear as it moves.
26 The sword that hits it does not hurt it,
nor the arrows, darts and spears.
27 It treats iron as if it were straw

FAITH links

FULL CIRCLE
JOB 42

Picture in your mind a skater gracefully spinning in a circle. When someone is said to "do a 360", that means they have turned around in a complete circle. They're right back where they started. That's also known as "coming full circle". Job did a 360 after having a talk with God. He realised that since God knew everything, he could put his whole trust in God. After that, God gave him a new family and restored his wealth. Job had come full circle.

If you're having a hard time right now, you might wonder when you'll ever "come full circle". God waits for you to put your full trust in him, just as Job did.

Our Thorough God, Leviticus 13, p. 149

A Long Wait, Joshua 14:6–15, p. 294

Fly Like an Eagle, Isaiah 40:28–31, p. 947

Future Hope, Joel 3:17–21, p. 1191

It's Under Control, Romans 8:28, p. 1529

Keep On Keeping On, Revelation 13:10, p. 1744

and bronze metal as if it were rotten wood.
28 It does not run away from arrows;

stones from slings are like chaff to it.
29 Clubs feel like pieces of straw to it, and it laughs when they shake a spear at it.
30 The underside of its body is like broken pieces of pottery.
It leaves a trail in the mud like a threshing board.
31 It makes the deep sea bubble like a boiling pot;
it stirs up the sea like a pot of oil.
32 When it swims, it leaves a shining path in the water
that makes the sea look as if it had white hair.
33 Nothing else on earth is equal to it; it is a creature without fear.
34 It looks down on all those who are too proud;
it is king over all proud creatures."

Job Answers the Lord

42 Then Job answered the LORD: 2 "I know that you can do all things and that no plan of yours can be ruined.
3 You asked, 'Who is this that made my purpose unclear by saying things that are not true?'
Surely I spoke of things I did not understand;
I talked of things too wonderful for me to know.

4 "You said, 'Listen now, and I will speak.
I will ask you questions, and you must answer me.'
5 My ears had heard of you before, but now my eyes have seen you.
6 So now I hate myself;
I will change my heart and life.
I will sit in the dust and ashes."

End of the Story

7 After the LORD had said these things to Job, he said to Eliphaz the Temanite, "I am angry with you and your two friends, because you have not said what is right about me, as my servant Job did. 8 Now take seven bulls and seven rams, and go to my servant Job, and offer a burnt offering for yourselves. My servant Job will pray for you, and I will listen to his prayer. Then I will not punish you for being foolish. You have not said what is right about me, as my servant Job did." 9 So Eliphaz the Temanite, Bildad the Shuhite and Zophar the Naamathite did as the LORD said, and the LORD listened to Job's prayer.

10 After Job had prayed for his friends, the LORD gave him success again. The LORD gave Job twice as much as he had owned before. 11 Job's brothers and sisters came to his house, along with everyone who had known him before, and they all ate with him there. They comforted him and made him feel better about the trouble the LORD had brought on him, and each one gave Job a piece of silver and a gold ring.

12 The LORD blessed the last part of Job's life even more than the first part. Job had 14,000 sheep, 6,000 camels, 1,000 teams of oxen and 1,000 female donkeys. 13 Job also had seven sons and three daughters. 14 He named the first daughter Jemimah, the second daughter Keziah and the third daughter Keren-Happuch. 15 There were no other women in all the land as beautiful as Job's daughters. And their father Job gave them land to own along with their brothers.

16 After this, Job lived 140 years. He lived to see his children, grandchildren, great-grandchildren and great-great-grandchildren. 17 Then Job died; he was old and had lived many years.

SONGS OF PRAISE

Hello! Do you remember me, David, the shepherd boy who became the king of the great nation of Israel? My days of watching sheep inspired me to write my most famous song –The Lord is My Shepherd, Psalm 23. Maybe you've heard of it? Over the years I wrote many songs. Check out the MIDI on Psalm 19 for my song praising God for his wonderful creation and his perfect law. Do you want to worship God in a special way? Try writing your own song of praise!

The Book of Psalms is a book of songs written to praise God. I was not the only author of Psalms. Asaph and the sons of Korah, our chief musicians, also wrote many psalms to use in the Temple. Check out Psalm 136. The leader praises God in the first part of each verse; and the people sing, "His love continues for ever." Try reading this psalm out loud with your family or friends. You can be the leader!

JESUS WATCH

We can see Jesus, the promised Messiah, in many of the psalms. In some psalms the words are true for the writer, but are truer of the life of Jesus. David wrote Psalm 22 when he was hiding from his enemies. The words that describe David's trouble also give us a picture of Jesus' death on the cross. Evil people made fun of David and took his clothes. Like dogs, they trapped him and bit his arms and legs. Compare this psalm to Matthew 27, p. 1324. The soldiers who arrested Jesus made fun of him and gambled for his clothes. They nailed his hands and feet to the cross and put him in a public place so people could stare at him. Jesus knew that this psalm was written about him. He quoted the first verse just before he died: "My God, my God, why have you rejected me?" (Psalm 22:1). Other psalms, like Psalms 96—99, describe Jesus as our king who will rule for ever in heaven. Worship him because he is holy! Sing praise to him for he rules in glory and majesty! Turn to these psalms for other reasons to praise Jesus.

my FAVOURITE links

OTHER CONNECTIONS

Livin' it — Think it's OK to tell a little fib now and then? Find out what God has to say about being honest by connecting to Friends with God, Psalm 15.

Who is it in your life that you totally trust with your deepest secrets? Your parents? Maybe your best friend? Discover who you can entrust everything to by checking out Trustometer, Psalm 56.

What's the first thing you do when you're feeling down, or you've got an exam to take, or your mum is ill in hospital? Does prayer come to mind? Learn more about this important lifeline to God by checking out No Answering Machine, Psalm 86:1–7.

Quick! What's the most precious thing you own? While you're thinking, surf over to A Burning Lamp, Psalm 119:12–18, to discover what the psalmist has to say about it.

Check out these information bulletin boards:

- Jerusalem was the centre of Israel's worship life and its government. It was an important centre for Jesus' ministry and today is a holy city for three different religions. Find out more by linking to Let's Visit Jerusalem, Psalm 68:29.
- God's Glory, Psalm 115. What does the Bible mean when it refers to "the glory of the Lord"? Is it something people actually saw? Check it out here.
- The Temple in Jerusalem, Psalm 122. Nothing was more important to the Israelite people in terms of worship than the Temple. Find out more about it here.

Whose voice makes the lightning flash?

Sounds pretty electrifying, doesn't it! Check out Psalm 29 to find out.

did YOU know?

THE PSALMS SURFWATCH:
Lower than angels, Psalm 8
A thirsty deer, Psalm 42
Why do the bad guys get rich? Psalm 73
Before I was born, Psalm 139
A musical tribute, Psalm 150

FAITH links

○ Who Ya' Gonna Call?
Psalm 3:4

○ Like Silver,
Psalm 12:6–8

○ Our Heavenly Shepherd,
Psalm 23

○ 999,
Psalm 28:6

○ Does Crime Pay?
Psalm 37:1–7

○ Learning from Mistakes,
Psalm 51:12–13

○ In Deep Water,
Psalm 69

○ A Picture of the Past,
Psalm 105

○ God's Valuable Gift: You,
Psalm 127:3–5

○ Love That Will Last,
Psalm 136

Book 1

Two Ways to Live

1 Happy are those who don't listen to the wicked,
who don't go where sinners go,
who don't do what evil people do.
2 They love the LORD's teachings,
and they think about those teachings day and night.
3 They are strong, like a tree planted by a river.
The tree produces fruit in season,
and its leaves don't die.
Everything they do will succeed.

4 But wicked people are not like that.
They are like chaff that the wind blows away.
5 So the wicked will not escape God's punishment.
Sinners will not worship with God's people.

6 This is because the LORD takes care of his people,
but the wicked will be destroyed.

The Lord's Chosen King

2 Why are the nations so angry?
Why are the people making useless plans?
2 The kings of the earth prepare to fight,
and their leaders make plans together
against the LORD
and his appointed one.
3 They say, "Let's break the chains that hold us back
and throw off the ropes that tie us down."

4 But the one who sits in heaven laughs;
the Lord makes fun of them.
5 Then the LORD warns them
and frightens them with his anger.
6 He says, "I have appointed my own king
to rule in Jerusalem on my holy mountain, Zion."

7 Now I will tell you what the LORD has declared:
he said to me, "You are my son.

1:1–2 Decisions
What's the best way to spend your time? Check it out!

TWO KINDS OF PEOPLE
PSALM 1

You've been at your school long enough to observe the different groups of kids there are: the popular kids, the smart kids, the athletic kids. Every school has similar groups. Some kids try to fit into one group or another, depending on what's important to them. This psalm describes two kinds of people. One group of people follows those who do evil things. The other group follows those who do good things. Those who do good things are happier than those who do evil things.

The people you hang around with can influence you to do good or to do evil. Which will you choose?

What You Value, Genesis 25:21–34, p. 34

An Example Not to Follow, Leviticus 18:1–3, p. 157

The Gift of Friendship, 1 Samuel 18:1–3; 19, p. 381

Deciding Wisely, 1 Kings 3:16–28, p. 440

The Verdict Is In? Matthew 7:1–2, p. 1285

Don't Play Favourites, James 2:1–7, p. 1691

Today I have become your father.
8 If you ask me,
   I will give you the nations;
   all the people on earth will be
      yours.
9 You will rule over them with an iron
      rod.
   You will break them into pieces
      like pottery."

10 So, kings, be wise;
   rulers, learn this lesson.
11 Obey the LORD with great fear.
   Be happy, but tremble.
12 Show that you are loyal to his son,
      or you will be destroyed by his
         anger,
   because he can quickly become
      angry.
   But happy are those who trust him
      for protection.

A Morning Prayer

David sang this when he ran away from his son Absalom.

3 LORD, I have many enemies!
   Many people have turned against
      me.
2 Many are saying about me,
   "God won't rescue him."   *Selah*

3 But, LORD, you are my shield,
   my wonderful God who gives me
      courage.
4 I will pray to the LORD,
   and he will answer me from his
      holy mountain.   *Selah*

5 I can lie down and go to sleep,
   and I will wake up again,
   because the LORD gives me
      strength.
6 Thousands of troops may surround
      me,
   but I am not afraid.

7 LORD, rise up!
   My God, come and save me!
   You have struck my enemies on the
      cheek;
   you have broken the teeth of the
      wicked.

8 The LORD can save his people.
   LORD, bless your people.   *Selah*

An Evening Prayer

For the director of music. With stringed instruments. A psalm of David.

4 Answer me when I pray to you,
   my God who does what is right.
   Make things easier for me when I am
      in trouble.

FAITH links

WHO YA' GONNA CALL?

PSALM 3:4

What is the most scared you've ever been? At one point, King David's son Absalom was his enemy. He was on the run from Absalom's army when he wrote this psalm. He told God that he was afraid and needed help. Even while he was afraid, he knew that God would answer his prayer.

David's psalm provides good advice to use when you're scared. For those heart-pounding times, call on God.

Need help? Call God!

A Major Problem, Genesis 15:6, p. 20

A Given, 1 Chronicles 5:18–20, p. 526

A Really Bad Day, Job 1:20–22; 2:10, p. 661

When the Going Gets Tough, Lamentations 3:22–27, p. 1079

The Best Protection Plan, Matthew 2:13–18, p. 1276

Prayer for a Friend, Colossians 1:9–12, p. 1620

Have mercy on me and hear my prayer.

2 People, how long will you turn my honour into shame?
How long will you love what is false and look for new lies? *Selah*
3 You know that the LORD has chosen for himself those who are loyal to him.
The LORD listens when I pray to him.

4 When you are angry, do not sin.
Think about these things quietly as you go to bed. *Selah*

5 Do what is right as a sacrifice to the LORD
and trust the LORD.

6 Many people ask,
"Who will give us anything good?"
LORD, be kind to us.
7 But you have made me very happy,
happier than they are,
even with all their grain and new wine.
8 I go to bed and sleep in peace,
because, LORD, only you keep me safe.

A Morning Prayer for Protection

For the director of music. For flutes. A psalm of David.

5 LORD, listen to my words.
Understand my sadness.
2 Listen to my cry for help, my King and my God,
because I pray to you.
3 LORD, every morning you hear my voice.
Every morning, I tell you what I need,
and I wait for your answer.

4 You are not a God who is pleased with the wicked;
you do not live with those who do evil.
5 Those people who make fun of you cannot stand before you.
You hate all those who do evil.
6 You destroy liars;
the LORD hates those who kill and trick others.

7 Because of your great love,
I can come into your Temple.
Because I fear and respect you,
I can worship in your holy Temple.
8 LORD, since I have many enemies,
show me the right thing to do.
Show me clearly how you want me to live.

FAITH links

THE PRAYER HABIT
PSALM 5:1-3

There are certain things you can do regularly to make your life better in the long run. Eating fruit and veg, studying and spending time with friends are important habits to get into. Prayer is another habit to develop. David, the writer of this psalm, prayed every morning.

Do you have a special time to pray? Whenever or wherever you pray, God will hear you. Make prayer a part of your daily routine.

Approaching God, Numbers 3:10, p. 180

Good Times and Bad, 1 Kings 17, p. 462

Your Best Defence, 2 Chronicles 20:1–12, p. 584

Wisdom in Store, Proverbs 2:6–7, p. 828

Prayer Priority, Luke 5:15–16, p. 1376

Go for It! Hebrews 12:1–4, p. 1682

9 My enemies' mouths do not tell the
      truth;
   in their hearts they want to destroy
      others.
   Their throats are like open graves;
      they use their tongues for telling
         lies.
10 God, declare them guilty!
    Let them fall into their own traps.
    Send them away because their sins
       are many;
       they have turned against you.

11 But let everyone who trusts you be
      happy;
    let them sing glad songs for ever.
    Protect those who love you
       and who are
          happy
          because of
          you.
12 LORD, you bless
    those who do
    what is right;
    you protect them like a soldier's
       shield.

A Prayer for Mercy in Troubled Times

For the director of music. With stringed instruments. Upon the sheminith. A psalm of David.

6 LORD, don't punish
     me when you are
     angry;
   don't punish me
     when you are
     very angry.
2 LORD, have mercy on
     me because I am
     weak.
   Heal me, LORD,
     because my
     bones ache.
3 I am very upset.
   LORD, how long will it be?

4 LORD, return and save me;
   save me because of your love.
5 Dead people don't remember you;
   those in the grave don't praise
     you.

6 I am tired of crying to you.
   Every night my bed is wet with
      tears;
   my bed is soaked from my crying.
7 My eyes are weak from so much
      crying;
   they are weak from crying about
      my enemies.

8 Get away from me, all you who do
      evil,
   because the LORD has heard my
      crying.
9 The LORD has heard my cry for help;
   the LORD will answer my prayer.
10 All my enemies will be ashamed and
      troubled.
    They will turn and suddenly leave
      in shame.

A Prayer for Fairness

A shiggaion of David which he sang to the LORD about Cush, from the tribe of Benjamin.

7 LORD my God, I trust in you for
     protection.
   Save me and rescue me
     from those who are chasing me.
2 Otherwise, like a lion they will tear
     me apart.
   They will rip me to pieces, and no
     one can save me.

3 LORD my God, what
     have I done?
   Have my hands done
     something wrong?
4 Have I done wrong to
     my friend
   or stolen without
     reason from my
     enemy?
5 If I have, let my enemy
     chase me and
     capture me.
   Let him trample me into the dust
     and bury me in the ground.   Selah

6 LORD, rise up in your anger;
   stand up against my enemies'
     anger.
   Get up and demand fairness.

5:12 Blessings
What kind of people does God bless?

LORD, have mercy on me because I am weak.
– Psalm 6:2

Psalm 7:7

FAITH CHALLENGE

Here's one for you. Read the first part of 7:4 to learn how David, the writer of the psalm, felt about his friends. How can you make sure that you don't do wrong to any of your friends?

TeSTiNG iT

**Psalm 7:4
Have I done wrong to my friend?**

---

7 Gather the nations around you
 and rule them from above.
8 LORD, judge the people.
  LORD, defend me because I am right,
   because I have done no wrong, God Most High.
9 God, you do what is right.
  You know our thoughts and feelings.
  Stop those wicked actions done by evil people,
  and help those who do what is right.
10 God protects me like a shield;
   he saves those whose hearts are right.
11 God judges by what is right,
   and God is always ready to punish the wicked.
12 If they do not change their lives,
   God will sharpen his sword;
   he will string his bow and take aim.
13 He has prepared his deadly weapons;
   he has made his flaming arrows.

14 There are people who think up evil
   and plan trouble and tell lies.
15 They dig a hole to trap others,
   but they will fall into it themselves.
16 They will get themselves into trouble;
   the violence they cause will hurt only themselves.

17 I praise the LORD because he does what is right.
   I sing praises to the LORD Most High.

The Lord's Greatness

For the director of music. On the gittith. A psalm of David.

8 LORD our Lord,
 your name is the most wonderful name in all the earth!

  It brings you praise in heaven above.
2 You have taught children and babies
  to sing praises to you
  because of your enemies.
  And so you silence your enemies
  and destroy those who try to take revenge.

3 I look at your heavens,
  which you made with your fingers.
  I see the moon and stars,
  which you created.
4 But why are people important to you?
  Why do you take care of human beings?
5 You made them a little lower than the angels

and crowned them with glory and
  honour.
6 You put them in charge of everything
  you made.
  You put all things under their
    control:
7 all the sheep, the cattle
  and the wild animals,
8 the birds in the sky,
  the fish in the sea
  and everything that
    lives underwater.

9 LORD our Lord,
  your name is the
    most wonderful
    name in all the
    earth!

Thanksgiving for Victory

For the director of music. To the tune of "The Death of the Son". A psalm of David.

9 I will praise you, LORD, with all my
    heart.
  I will tell of all the miracles you
    have done.
2 I will be happy because of you;
  God Most High, I will sing praises
    to your name.

3 My enemies turn back;
  they are overwhelmed and die
    because of you.
4 You have heard my complaint;
  you sat on your throne and judged
    by what was right.
5 You spoke strongly against the
    foreign nations
  and destroyed the wicked;
  you wiped out their names for ever
    and ever.
6 The enemy is gone for ever.
  You destroyed their cities;
  no one even
    remembers
    them.
7 But the LORD
  rules for
    ever.

> LORD our Lord, your
> name is the most
> wonderful name in
> all the earth!
> – Psalm 8:9

He sits on his throne to judge,
8 and he will judge the world in
    fairness;
  he will decide what is fair for the
    nations.
9 The LORD defends those who suffer;
  he defends them in times of
    trouble.
10 Those who know the
    LORD trust him,
    because he will not
    leave those who
    come to him.
11 Sing praises to the
    LORD who is king
    on Mount Zion.
  Tell the nations what
    he has done.
12 He remembers who
    the murderers are;
  he will not forget the cries of those
    who suffer.

13 LORD, have mercy on me.
  See how my enemies hurt me.
  Do not let me go through the gates
    of death.
14 Then, at the gates of Jerusalem, I will
    praise you;
  I will rejoice because you saved me.

15 The nations have fallen into the pit
    they dug.
  Their feet are caught in the nets
    they laid.
16 The LORD has made himself known
    by his fair decisions;
  the wicked get trapped by what
    they do.   *Higgaion. Selah*

17 Wicked people will go to the grave,
    and so will all those who forget God.
18 But those who have troubles will not
    be forgotten.
  The hopes of
    the poor will
    never die.

19 LORD, rise up
    and judge the
    nations.
  Don't let people think they are
    strong.

**9:7–8
Judgement**
Who is the ultimate authority?

**9:18
Hope**
Who does God give hope to?

20 Teach them to fear you, LORD.
The nations must learn that they
are only human. *Selah*

A Complaint About Evil People

10 LORD, why are you so far away?
Why do you hide when there is
trouble?

2 Proudly the wicked chase down those
who suffer.
Let them be caught
in their own
traps.
3 They boast about the
things they want.
They bless the
greedy but hate
the LORD.
4 The wicked people
are too proud.
They do not look
for God;
there is no room for God in their
thoughts.
5 They always succeed.
They are far from keeping your
laws;
they make fun of their enemies.
6 They say to themselves, "Nothing
bad will ever happen to me;
I will never be ruined."
7 Their mouths are full of curses, lies
and threats;
they use their tongues for sin and
evil.
8 They hide near the villages.
They look for innocent people to
kill;
they watch in secret for the
helpless.
9 They wait in hiding like a lion.
They wait to catch poor people;
they catch the poor in nets.
10 The poor are thrown down and
crushed;
they are defeated because the
others are stronger.
11 The wicked think, "God has forgotten
us.
He doesn't see what is happening."

12 LORD, rise up and punish the wicked.
Don't forget those who need help.
13 Why do wicked people hate God?
They say to themselves, "God
won't punish us."
14 LORD, surely you see these cruel and
evil things;
look at them and do something.
People in trouble look to you for
help.
You are the one who helps the
orphans.
15 Break the power of
wicked people.
Punish them for the
evil they have
done.

16 The LORD is King for
ever and ever.
Destroy from your
land those nations
that do not
worship you.
17 LORD, you have heard what the poor
people want.
Do what they ask, and listen to
them.
18 Protect the orphans and put an end to
suffering
so they will no longer be afraid of
evil people.

Trust in the Lord

For the director of music. Of David.

11 I trust in the LORD for protection.
So why do you say to me,
"Fly like a bird to your mountain.
2 Like hunters,
the wicked
string their
bows;
they set their
arrows on
the bowstrings.
They shoot from dark places
at those who are honest.
3 When all that is good falls apart,
what can good people do?"
4 The LORD is in his holy temple;
the LORD sits on his throne in
heaven.

> LORD, you have heard
> what the poor
> people want. Do
> what they ask, and
> listen to them.
> – Psalm 10:17

11:1 Trust
Where is your trust?

He sees what people do;
  he keeps his eye on them.
5 The LORD tests those who do right,
  but he hates the wicked and those
    who love to hurt others.
6 He will send hot coals and burning
    sulphur on the wicked.
  A whirlwind is what they will get.

7 The LORD does what is right, and he
    loves justice,
  so honest people will see his face.

A Prayer Against Liars

For the director of music. Upon the sheminith. A psalm of David.

12 Save me, LORD, because the good people are all gone;
  no true believers are left on earth.
2 Everyone lies to his neighbours;
  they say one thing and mean
    another.

3 The LORD will stop those flattering
    lips
  and cut off those boasting tongues.
4 They say, "Our tongues will help us
    win.
  We can say what we wish; no one is
    our master."

5 But the LORD says,
  "I will now rise up,
    because the poor are being hurt.
  Because of the moans of the helpless,
    I will give
    them the
    help they
    want."
6 The LORD's
  words are
  pure,
  like silver purified by fire,
  like silver purified seven times
    over.

7 LORD, you will keep us safe;
  you will always protect us from
    such people.
8 But the wicked are all around us;
  everyone loves what is wrong.

12:5 Pain — Who does God watch over?

FAITH links

LIKE SILVER
PSALM 12:6-8

Do you own anything silver? Silver is valuable to many people. That's why David compared God's Word (the Bible) to silver. Like gold, the impurities in silver have to be removed in order for the silver to be useful. When silver is heated in a furnace, it becomes more pure. When you test the truth of the Bible against some of what you hear at school or read in the newspaper or on the Internet, it will seem more pure to you. The more you read it, the more valuable it will become.

What do you value? Is one of those items the Bible? Connect here to find out what God values:

Lights, Camera, . . . Actions!
Genesis 12:1–3, p. 17

Comfort from the Word, Job 26:3–4, p. 688

The Foundation of Our Hope, Isaiah 31:1–8, p. 934

Your Full Trust, Jeremiah 22:20–22, p. 1023

Faith Workout, Acts 16:4–5, p. 1493

Pay Attention! Hebrews 2:1, p. 1668

A Prayer for God to be Near

For the director of music.
A psalm of David.

13 How long will you forget me,
    LORD? For ever?
  How long will you
    hide from me?
2 How long must I
    worry
  and feel sad in my
    heart all day?
  How long will my
    enemy win over
    me?

3 LORD, look at me.
  Answer me, my
    God;
  tell me, or I will die.
4 Otherwise my enemy will say, "I have
    won!"
  Those against me will rejoice that
    I've been defeated.

5 I trust in your love.
  My heart is happy because you
    saved me.
6 I sing to the LORD
  because he has taken care of me.

The Unbelieving Fool

For the director of music. Of David.

14 Fools say to themselves,
    "There is no God."
  Fools are evil and do terrible
    things;
  there is no one who does anything
    good.

2 The LORD looked down from heaven
    on all people
  to see if anyone understood,
  if anyone was looking to God for
    help.
3 But all have turned away.
  Together, everyone has become
    evil.
  There is no one who does anything
    good,
    not even one.

4 Don't the wicked understand?
  They destroy my people as if they
    were eating bread.
  They do not ask the LORD for help.
5 But the wicked are filled with terror,
  because God is with those who do
    what is right.
6 The wicked upset the
    plans of the poor,
  but the LORD will
    protect them.

7 I pray that victory will
    come to Israel
    from Mount Zion!
  May the LORD bring
    them back.
  Then the people of
    Jacob will rejoice,
  and the people of Israel will be
    glad.

What the Lord Demands

A psalm of David.

15 LORD, who may enter your Holy
    Tent?
  Who may live on your holy
    mountain?

2 Only those who are innocent
  and who do what is right.
  Such people speak the truth from
    their hearts
3   and do not tell lies about others.
  They do no wrong to their
    neighbours
  and do not gossip.
4 They do not respect hateful
    people
  but honour those who honour the
    LORD.
  They keep their promises to their
    neighbours,
    even when it hurts.
5 They do not charge interest on money
    they lend
  and do not take money to hurt
    innocent people.

Whoever does all these things will
    never be destroyed.

> I trust in your love.
> My heart is happy
> because you saved
> me.
> — Psalm 13:5

HONESTY
Psalm 15

Friends with God Who do you like to hang around with? The cool kids or the kids who are into football? Kids who are smart? Or maybe the kids that you hang about with like to get into trouble. There's an old saying that goes "birds of a feather flock together". What kind of "birds" are you flying with?

Nehemiah needed people to look after the Temple storerooms, which was a big responsibility. What kind of people did he look for? (Check out Nehemiah 13:13, p. 644, to see.)

God tells us he is a friend of those who are honest. (Look at Proverbs 3:32, p. 829.) That means God values honesty. A person usually hangs around with others who have the same interests and values that he or she has. Is being honest important to you? If you want to be friends with God, your answer had better be yes.

Do you sometimes tell little fibs – not big lies but just not quite the truth? Do you think that's OK?

Link up with what God has to say about telling the truth. Check it out below!

MORE FAITH links

- Always Truthful, **p. 208**
- An Honest Reputation, **p. 644**
- Who Do You Prefer? **p. 830**
- All Talk, No Action, **p. 996**
- What's Wrong About Rumours, **p. 1032**

The Best Policy, Genesis 29:16–29, p. 41
- Do you think tricking someone is cool? Think again! When you try to trick others, be prepared – you may be on the receiving end someday. How cool would that be?

A Serious Promise, Deuteronomy 23:21–23, p. 257
- Has someone ever borrowed money from you and promised to pay it back, but didn't? How did that make you feel?
- God expects us to keep our promises to him and to others. How well do you keep the promises you make?

The Whole Truth, John 8:31–32, 45, p. 1438
- It's hard to believe someone who has lied to you in the past, isn't it? Find out what Jesus said about the truth by linking here.

The Deadliest Lie, Acts 5:1–11, p. 1471
- Link here to read a very scary story about lying!

The Lord Takes Care of His People

A miktam of David.

16 ¹ Protect me, God,
because I trust in you.

² I said to the LORD, "You are my Lord.
Every good thing I have comes
from you."

³ As for the godly people in the world,
they are the wonderful ones I
enjoy.

⁴ But those who turn to idols
will have much pain.
I will not offer blood to those idols
or even speak their names.

⁵ No, the LORD is all I need.
He takes care of me.
⁶ My share in life has been pleasant;
my part has been beautiful.

⁷ I praise the LORD because he advises
me.
Even at night,
I feel his
leading.
⁸ I keep the LORD
before me
always.
Because he is close by my side,
I will not be hurt.

16:7 God's Will
Who can you trust in decisions?

⁹ So I rejoice and am glad.
Even my body has hope,
¹⁰ because you will not leave me in the
grave.
You will not let your holy one rot.
¹¹ You will teach me how to live a holy life.
Being with you will fill me with joy;
at your right hand I will find
pleasure for ever.

A Prayer for Protection

A prayer of David.

17 LORD, hear
me begging
for fairness;
listen to my
cry for help.
Pay attention to my
prayer,

17:1–2 Prayer
Does God hear your prayers?

because I speak the truth.
² You will judge that I am right;
your eyes can see what is true.

³ You have examined my heart;
you have tested me all night.
You questioned me without finding
anything wrong;
I have not sinned with my mouth.
⁴ I have obeyed your commands,
so I have not done what evil people
do.
⁵ I have done what you told me;
I have not failed.

⁶ I call to you, God,
and you answer me.
Listen to me now,
and hear what I say.
⁷ Your love is wonderful.
By your power you save those who
trust you
from their enemies.

⁸ Protect me as you would protect your
own eye.
Hide me under the shadow of your
wings.
⁹ Keep me from the wicked who attack
me,
from my enemies who surround me.

¹⁰ They are selfish
and boast about themselves.
¹¹ They have chased me until they have
surrounded me.
They plan to throw me to the
ground.
¹² They are like lions ready to kill;
like lions, they sit in hiding.

¹³ LORD, rise up, face the enemy and
throw them down.
Save me from the wicked with your
sword.
¹⁴ LORD, save me by your power
from those whose reward is in this
life.

They have plenty of food.
They have many sons
and leave much money to their
children.

¹⁵ Because I have lived right, I will see
your face.

When I wake up, I will see your
likeness and be satisfied.

A Song of Victory

For the director of music. By the LORD's
servant, David. David sang this song to the
LORD when the LORD had saved him from
Saul and all his other enemies.

18 I love you, LORD. You are my
strength.

2 The LORD is my rock, my protection,
my Saviour.
My God is my rock.
I can run to him for safety.
He is my shield and my saving
strength, my defender.
3 I will call to the LORD, who is worthy
of praise,
and I will be saved from my
enemies.

4 The ropes of death came around
me;
the deadly rivers overwhelmed me.
5 The ropes of death wrapped around
me.
The traps of death were before me.
6 In my trouble I called to the LORD.
I cried out to my God for help.
From his temple he heard my voice;
my call for help reached his ears.

7 The earth trembled and shook.
The foundations of the mountains
began to shake.
They trembled because the LORD
was angry.
8 Smoke came out of his nose,
and burning fire came out of his
mouth.
Burning coals went before him.
9 He tore open the sky and came down
with dark clouds under his feet.
10 He rode a creature with wings and
flew.
He raced on the wings of the wind.
11 He made darkness his covering, his
shelter around him,
surrounded by fog and clouds.
12 Out of the brightness of his presence
came clouds
with hail and lightning.
13 The LORD thundered from heaven;
the Most High raised his voice,
and there was hail and lightning.
14 He shot his arrows and scattered his
enemies.
His many bolts of lightning
confused them with fear.
15 LORD, you spoke strongly.

FAITH links

GOD'S SURE PROTECTION
PSALM 18

What is the largest rock or stone you have ever seen? If you live in an area with mountains, you're face-to-face with the biggest rocks of all! A large rock is tough to move. A mountain is impossible to move. That's why David, the writer of this psalm, called God his "rock". David was constantly on the run from his enemies. He often needed God's protection. Like David, we can count on God's protection. It's a sure thing!

When You're Afraid, Genesis 32:9–12, p. 45

Real Faith or Really Scared? Judges 4, p. 315

Fly Like an Eagle, Isaiah 40:28–31, p. 947

The Best Protection Plan, Matthew 2:13–18, p. 1276

Prayer Anywhere, Mark 1:35, p. 1331

Fully God, Fully Human, John 11:35, p. 1444

The wind blew from your nose.
Then the valleys of the sea appeared,
and the foundations of the earth
were seen.

16 The LORD reached down from above
and took me;
he pulled me from the deep water.
17 He saved me from my powerful
enemies,
from those who hated me, because
they were too strong for me.
18 They attacked me at my time of
trouble,
but the LORD supported me.
19 He took me to a safe place.
Because he delights in me, he
saved me.

20 The LORD spared me because I did
what was right.
Because I have not done evil, he
has rewarded me.
21 I have followed the ways of the
LORD;
I have not done evil by turning
away from my God.
22 I remember all his laws
and have not broken his rules.
23 I am innocent before him;
I have kept myself from doing
evil.
24 The LORD rewarded me because I did
what was right,
because I did what the LORD said
was right.

25 LORD, you are loyal to those who are
loyal,
and you are good to those who are
good.
26 You are pure to those who are pure,
but you are against those who are
bad.
27 You save the humble,
but you bring down those who are
proud.
28 LORD, you give light to my lamp.
My God brightens the darkness
around me.
29 With your help I can attack an army.
With God's help I can jump over a
wall.

30 The ways of God are without fault.
The LORD's words are pure.
He is a shield to those who trust him.
31 Who is God? Only the LORD.
Who is the Rock? Only our God.
32 God is my
protection.
He makes my
way free
from fault.
33 He makes me
like a deer
that does not stumble;
he helps me stand on the steep
mountains.
34 He trains my hands for battle
so my arms can bend a bronze bow.
35 You protect me with your saving
shield.
You support me with your right
hand.
You have stooped to make me great.
36 You give me a better way to live,
so I live as you want me to.
37 I chased my enemies and caught
them.
I did not stop until they were
destroyed.
38 I crushed them so they couldn't rise
up again.
They fell beneath my feet.
39 You gave me strength in battle.
You made my enemies bow before
me.
40 You made my enemies turn back,
and I destroyed those who hated
me.
41 They called for help,
but no one came to save them.
They called to the LORD,
but he did not answer them.
42 I beat my enemies into pieces, like
dust in the wind.
I poured them out like mud in the
streets.

43 You saved me when the people
attacked me.
You made me the leader of nations.
People I never knew serve me.
44 As soon as they hear me, they obey
me.

> **E-MAIL FROM GOD**
> **18:32–50 Success**
> Where do you turn for success?

Foreigners obey me.
45 They all become afraid
and tremble in their hiding
places.

46 The LORD lives!
May my Rock be praised.
Praise the God who saves me!
47 God gives me victory over my
enemies
and brings people under my rule.
48 He saves me from my enemies.

You set me over those who hate me.
You saved me from cruel men.
49 So I will praise you, LORD, among the
nations.
I will sing praises to your name.
50 The LORD gives great victories to his
king.
He is loyal to his appointed king,
to David and his descendants for
ever.

God's Works and Word

*For the director of music.
A psalm of David.*

19 The heavens tell the glory of
God,
and the skies announce what his
hands have made.
2 Day after day they tell the story;
night after night they tell it again.
3 They have no speech or words;
they have no voice to be heard.
4 But their message goes out through
all the world;
their words go everywhere on
earth.

The sky is like a home for the sun.
5 The sun comes out like a bridegroom
from his bedroom.
It rejoices like an athlete eager to
run a race.
6 The sun rises at one end of the sky
and follows its path to the other
end.
Nothing hides from its heat.
7 The teachings of the LORD are
perfect;
they give new strength.
The LORD's rules can be
trusted;
they make plain people wise.
8 The orders of the LORD are right;
they make people happy.
The commands of the LORD are pure;
they light up the way.
9 Respect for the LORD is good;
it will last for ever.

FAITH links

MORE PRECIOUS THAN GOLD

PSALM 19:7-10

Name something you own that's worth more than anything else you have. Maybe it's your CD collection or your favourite sweatshirt. The psalm writer described God's commands and promises as "worth more than gold". That's pretty valuable! They're not only priceless; they're perfect. Many people value gold more than they value what God said. Yet gold is here today and gone tomorrow. Only God's Word will last for ever.

Ten Ways to Obey, Exodus 20, p. 103

When I Need Advice, 1 Kings 12:1–17, p. 455

Plan for Success, 1 Chronicles 14:8–17, p. 538

Said It? Do It! Lamentations 2:17, p. 1077

Want to Know? Ask! Luke 9:45, p. 1386

Life's Rule Book, 2 Timothy 3:15–17, p. 1655

The judgements of the LORD are true;
   they are completely right.
10 They are worth more than gold,
      even the purest gold.
   They are sweeter than honey,
      even the finest honey.
11 By them your servant is warned.
      Keeping them brings great reward.

12 People cannot see their own mistakes.
   Forgive me for my secret sins.
13 Keep me from the sins of pride;
      don't let them rule me.
   Then I can be pure
      and innocent of the greatest of sins.

14 I hope my words and thoughts please you.
   LORD, you are my Rock, the one who saves me.

19:12–13 Guilt
Can you hide sins from God?

A Prayer for the King

*For the director of music.
A psalm of David.*

20 May the LORD answer you in times of trouble.
   May the God of Jacob protect you.
2 May he send you help from his Temple
   and support you from Mount Zion.
3 May he remember all your offerings
   and accept all your sacrifices. *Selah*

4 May he give you what you want
   and make all your plans succeed,
5 and we will shout for joy when you succeed,
   and we will raise a flag in the name of our God.
   May the LORD give you all that you ask for.

6 Now I know the LORD helps his appointed king.
   He answers him from his holy heaven
      and saves him with his strong right hand.
7 Some trust in chariots,
      others in horses,
   but we trust the LORD our God.
8 They are overwhelmed and defeated,
   but we march forwards and win.

9 LORD, save the king!
   Answer us when we call for help.

20:7 Trust
What do some people trust in?

Thanksgiving for the King

*For the director of music.
A psalm of David.*

21 LORD, the king rejoices because of your strength;
   he is so happy when you save him!
2 You gave the king what he wanted
   and did not refuse what he asked for. *Selah*
3 You put good things before him
   and placed a gold crown on his head.
4 He asked you for life,
   and you gave it to him,
      so his years go on and on.
5 He has great glory because you gave him victories;
   you gave him honour and praise.
6 You always gave him blessings;
   you made him glad because you were with him.
7 The king truly trusts the LORD.
   Because God Most High always loves him,
      he will not be overwhelmed.

8 Your hand is against all your enemies;
   those who hate you will feel your power.
9 When you appear,
      you will burn them as in a furnace.
   In your anger you will swallow them up,
      and fire will burn them up.
10 You will destroy their families from the earth;
   their children will not live.
11 They made evil plans against you,

but their traps won't work.
12 You will make them
turn their backs
when you aim your
arrows at them.

13 Be supreme, LORD, in
your power.
We sing and praise
your greatness.

The Prayer of a Suffering Man

For the director of music. To the tune of "The Doe of Dawn". A psalm of David.

22 My God, my God, why have you rejected me?
You seem far from saving me,
far from the words of my moans.
2 My God, I call to you during the day,
but you do not answer.
I call at night;
I am not silent.

3 You sit as the Holy One.
The praises of Israel are your throne.
4 Our ancestors trusted you;
they trusted, and you saved them.
5 They called to you for help
and were rescued.
They trusted you
and were not disappointed.

6 But I am like a worm instead of a man.
People make fun of me and hate me.
7 Those who look at me laugh.
They stick out their tongues and
shake their heads.
8 They say, "Turn to the LORD for help.
Maybe he will save you.
If he likes you,
maybe he will rescue you."

9 You had my mother give birth to me.
You made me trust you
while I was just a baby.
10 I have leaned on you since the day I was born;
you have been my God since my
mother gave birth to me.

11 So don't be far away from me.
Now trouble is near,
and there is no one to help.

12 People have
surrounded me
like angry bulls.
Like the strong bulls
of Bashan, they
are on every side.
13 Like hungry, roaring lions
they open their mouths at me.
14 My strength is gone,
like water poured out onto the ground,
and my bones are out of joint.
My heart is like wax;
it has melted inside me.
15 My strength has dried up like a clay pot,
and my tongue sticks to the top of my mouth.
You laid me in the dust of death.
16 Evil people have surrounded me;
like dogs they have trapped me.
They have bitten my arms and legs.
17 I can count all my bones;
people look and stare at me.
18 They divided my clothes among them,
and they threw lots for my clothing.

19 But, LORD, don't be far away.
You are my strength; hurry to help me.
20 Save me from the sword;
save my life from the dogs.
21 Rescue me from
the lion's mouth;
save me from
the horns
of the bulls.
22 Then I will tell
my fellow Israelites about you;
I will praise you in the public meeting.

> Be supreme, LORD, in your power. We sing and praise your greatness.
> – Psalm 21:13

MAIL FROM GOD
**22:19–24
Troubles**
Does God care if you have problems?

23 Praise the LORD, all you who respect him.
All you descendants of Jacob, honour him;
fear him, all you Israelites.
24 He does not ignore those in trouble.
He doesn't hide from them
but listens when they call out to him.
25 LORD, I praise you in the great meeting of your people;
these worshippers will see me do what I promised.
26 Poor people will eat until they are full;
those who look to the LORD will praise him.
May your hearts live for ever!
27 People everywhere will remember and will turn to the LORD.
All the families of the nations will worship him
28 because the LORD is King,
and he rules the nations.
29 All the powerful people on earth will eat and worship.
Everyone will bow down to him, all who will one day die.
30 The people in the future will serve him;
they will always be told about the Lord.
31 They will tell that he does what is right.
People who are not yet born will hear what God has done.

The Lord the Shepherd

A psalm of David.

23 The LORD is my shepherd;
I have everything I need.
2 He lets me rest in green pastures.
He leads me to calm water.
3 He gives me new strength.
He leads me on paths that are right for the good of his name.
4 Even if I walk through a very dark valley,
I will not be afraid, because you are with me.
Your rod and your staff[n] comfort me.

23:4 Fears
Who is your comforter?

FAITH links

OUR HEAVENLY SHEPHERD
PSALM 23

One of the most well-known psalms in the Bible is Psalm 23. This psalm may be familiar, but its message never gets old. God watches over us as a shepherd watches over sheep. David wrote this psalm based on his own experiences as a shepherd. He knew the kind of care sheep needed. The best shepherds took good care of their sheep. That's the kind of care God provides for you.

Here are some more Faithlinks on how much God cares for you:

A Thanksgiving Reminder, Exodus 12, p. 91

See the Heart Behind It, Nehemiah 8; 9, p. 636

How Big Is God? Job 38—41, p. 703

Your Heavenly Dad, Psalm 103:13, p. 786

Justice Desserts, Habakkuk 2:4–8, p. 1237

Two Birthdays, John 3:1–7, p. 1426

23:4 staff The stick a shepherd uses to guide and protect his sheep.

5 You prepare a meal for me
   in front of my enemies.
  You pour oil on my head;[n]
   you fill my cup to overflowing.
6 Surely your goodness and love will
   be with me
  all my life,
  and I will live in the house of the
   LORD for ever.

A Welcome for God into the Temple

A psalm of David.

24 The earth belongs to the LORD,
    and everything in it—
  the world and all its people.
2 He built it on the waters
  and set it on the rivers.

3 Who may go up on the mountain of
   the LORD?
  Who may stand in his holy
   Temple?
4 Only those with
   clean hands
   and pure
   hearts,
  who have not
   worshipped
   idols,
  who have not made promises in the
   name of a false god.
5 They will receive a blessing from the
   LORD;
  the God who saves them will
   declare them right.
6 They try to follow God;
   they look to the God of Jacob for
   help. *Selah*

7 Gates, open all the way.
  Open wide, aged doors
  so the glorious King will come in.
8 Who is this glorious King?
  The LORD, strong and mighty.
  The LORD, the powerful warrior.
9 Gates, open all the way.
  Open wide, aged doors
  so the glorious King will come in.
10 Who is this glorious King?
  The LORD All-powerful—
  he is the glorious King. *Selah*

A Prayer for God to Guide

Of David.

25 LORD, I give myself to you;
2 my God, I trust you.
  Do not let me be disgraced;

23:5 pour oil ... head This can mean that God gave him great wealth and blessed him.

FAITH links

LEARNING TO TRUST
PSALM 25:4-5

When you were little, you had to be taught everything. All you knew how to do was dribble. As you grew older, you learned more and more new things. (Hopefully, you stopped dribbling.) If you're a Christian, there are also new things to learn. Trusting God is one of them.

David wrote this psalm as a prayer for help to learn how to live a life that honoured God. He wanted God to teach him his ways. Is this your prayer, too? You can learn God's ways by reading the Bible and getting involved in your church.

The Name of the Lord, Exodus 33:19-23; 34:5-8, p. 120

What He's Really Like, Deuteronomy 4:15-20, p. 233

Listen Up! 1 Kings 19:11-13, p. 467

The Writing's on the Wall, Daniel 5, p. 1159

Ask, Search, Knock, Matthew 7:7-10, p. 1286

Faith God Notices, Luke 18:35-43, p. 1406

MAIL FROM GOD

24:3-6 Blessings
Who can get a blessing from God?

do not let my enemies laugh at me.
3 No one who trusts you will be
    disgraced,
  but those who sin without excuse
    will be disgraced.

4 LORD, tell me your ways.
  Show me how to live.
5 Guide me in your truth,
  and teach me, my God, my Saviour.
  I trust you all day long.
6 LORD, remember your mercy and
    love
  that you have shown since long
    ago.
7 Do not remember the sins
  and wrong things I did when I was
    young.
  But remember to love me always
    because you are good, LORD.

8 The LORD is good and right;
  he points sinners to the right way.
9 He shows those who are humble how
    to do right,
  and he teaches them his ways.
10 All the LORD's ways
    are loving and
    true
    for those who
    follow the
    demands of his
    agreement.
11 For the sake of your
    name, LORD,
    forgive my many
    sins.
12 Are there those who
    respect the LORD?
  He will point them to the best way.
13 They will enjoy a good life,
  and their children will inherit the
    land.
14 The LORD tells his secrets to those
    who respect him;
  he tells them
    about his
    agreement.
15 My eyes are
    always
    looking to
    the LORD
    for help.

He will keep me from any traps.

16 Turn to me and have mercy on me,
    because I am lonely and hurting.
17 My troubles have grown larger;
    free me from my problems.
18 Look at my suffering and troubles,
    and take away all my sins.
19 Look at how many enemies I have!
    See how much they hate me!
20 Protect me and save me.
    I trust you, so do not let me be
      disgraced.
21 My hope is in you,
    so may goodness and honesty
      guard me.
22 God, save Israel from all their troubles!

The Prayer of an Innocent Believer

Of David.

26 LORD, defend me because I have
    lived an innocent life.
  I have trusted the LORD and never
    doubted.

2 LORD, try me and test
    me;
  look closely into my
    heart and mind.
3 I see your love,
    and I live by your
    truth.
4 I do not spend time
    with liars,
  nor do I make friends
    with those who hide
    their sin.

> LORD, try me and test me; look closely into my heart and mind.
> – Psalm 26:2

5 I hate the company of evil people,
    and I won't sit with the wicked.
6 I wash my hands to show I am
    innocent,
  and I come to your altar, LORD.
7 I raise my voice in praise
    and tell of all the miracles you have
      done.
8 LORD, I love the Temple where you live,
    where your glory is.

9 Do not kill me with those sinners
    or take my life with those
      murderers.
10 Evil is in their hands,

25:15 Fears
Who should you look to for help?

and they do wrong for money.
11 But I have lived an innocent life,
so save me and have mercy on me.
12 I stand in a safe place.
LORD, I praise you in the great meeting.

A Song of Trust in God

Of David.

27 The LORD is my light and the one who saves me.
I fear no one.
The LORD protects my life;
I am afraid of no one.
2 Evil people may try to destroy my body.
My enemies and those who hate me attack me,
but they are overwhelmed and defeated.
3 If an army surrounds me,
I will not be afraid.
If war breaks out,
I will trust the LORD.
4 I ask only one thing from the LORD.
This is what I want:
let me live in the LORD's house all my life.
Let me see the LORD's beauty
and look with my own eyes at his Temple.
5 During danger he will keep me safe in his shelter.
He will hide me in his Holy Tent,
or he will keep me safe on a high mountain.
6 My head is higher than my enemies around me.
I will offer joyful sacrifices in his Holy Tent.
I will sing and praise the LORD.
7 LORD, hear me when I call;
have mercy and answer me.
8 My heart said of you, "Go, worship him."
So I come to worship you, LORD.
9 Do not turn away from me.
Do not turn your servant away in anger;
you have helped me.
Do not push me away or leave me alone,
God, my Saviour.
10 If my father and mother leave me,
the LORD will take me in.
11 LORD, teach me your ways,
and guide me to do what is right
because I have enemies.
12 Do not hand me over to my enemies,
because they tell lies about me
and say they will hurt me.
13 I truly believe
I will live to see the LORD's goodness.
14 Wait for the LORD's help.
Be strong and brave,
and wait for the LORD's help.

> **27:1 God** Check out who is your light.

> **27:14 Following God** What will come from waiting on the Lord?

A Prayer in Troubled Times

Of David.

28 LORD, my Rock, I call out to you for help.
Do not be deaf to me.
If you are silent,
I will be like those in the grave.
2 Hear the sound of my prayer,
when I cry out to you for help.
I raise my hands
towards your Most Holy Place.
3 Don't drag me away with the wicked,
with those who do evil.
They say "Peace" to their neighbours,
but evil is in their hearts.
4 Pay them back for what they have done,
for their evil deeds.
Pay them back for what they have done;
give them their reward.
5 They don't understand what the LORD has done
or what he has made.
So he will knock them down
and not lift them up.

FAITH links

999
PSALM 28:6

Whenever someone dials 999, they expect a quick answer. After all, the situation is usually a life-or-death emergency! For many years, David was surrounded by trouble. He often prayed for relief from life-threatening situations. He begged God not to ignore him.

Do you ever wish that God would respond as quickly as the 999 operators do? He doesn't always answer quickly. When you pray, just know that God *will* answer you, even if you have to wait a while for the answer.

Got an emergency? Link here for quick help:

Problem Solved, 2 Kings 20:1–11, p. 507

Full Circle, Job 42, p. 706

When the Going Gets Tough, Lamentations 3:22–27, p. 1079

Long-lasting Hope, Hosea 14, p. 1184

Prayer Anywhere, Mark 1:35, p. 1331

Hold On! 2 Thessalonians 2:15–17, p. 1639

---

6 Praise the LORD,
   because he heard my prayer for help.
7 The LORD is my strength and shield.
   I trust him, and he helps me.
   I am very happy,
   and I praise him with my song.
8 The LORD is powerful;
   he gives victory to his chosen one.
9 Save your people
   and bless those who are your own.
   Be their shepherd and carry them for ever.

God in the Thunderstorm

A psalm of David.

29 Praise the LORD, you angels;
   praise the LORD's glory and power.
2 Praise the LORD for the glory of his name;
   worship the LORD
   because he is holy.

> **eMAIL FROM GOD**
> **29:1–2**
> **Worship**
> What should you give to the Lord during worship?

3 The LORD's voice
   is heard over the sea.
   The glorious God thunders;
   the LORD thunders over the ocean.
4 The LORD's voice is powerful;
   the LORD's voice is majestic.
5 The LORD's voice breaks the trees;
   the LORD breaks the cedars of Lebanon.
6 He makes the land of Lebanon dance like a calf
   and Mount Hermon jump like a baby bull.
7 The LORD's voice makes the lightning flash.
8 The LORD's voice shakes the desert;
   the LORD shakes the Desert of Kadesh.
9 The LORD's voice shakes the oaks
   and strips the leaves off the trees.
   In his Temple everyone says, "Glory to God!"

10 The LORD controls the flood.
   The LORD will be King for ever.
11 The LORD gives strength to his people;
   the LORD blesses his people with peace.

Thanksgiving for Escaping Death

A psalm of David. A song for giving the Temple to the LORD.

30 I will praise you, LORD,
because you rescued me.
You did not let my enemies laugh at me.
2 LORD, my God, I prayed to you,
and you healed me.
3 You lifted me out of the grave;
you spared me from going down to the place of the dead.

4 Sing praises to the LORD, you who belong to him;
praise his holy name.
5 His anger lasts only a moment,
but his kindness lasts for a lifetime.
Crying may last for a night,
but joy comes in the morning.

6 When I felt safe, I said,
"I will never fear."
7 LORD, in your kindness you made my mountain safe.
But when you turned away, I was frightened.

8 I called to you, LORD,
and asked you to have mercy on me.
9 I said, "What good will it do if I die or if I go down to the grave?
Dust cannot praise you;
it cannot speak about your truth.
10 LORD, hear me and have mercy on me.
LORD, help me."

11 You changed my sorrow into dancing.
You took away my clothes of sadness,
and clothed me in happiness.
12 I will sing to you and not be silent.
LORD, my God, I will praise you forever.

A Prayer of Faith in Troubled Times

For the director of music. A psalm of David.

31 LORD, I trust in you;
let me never be disgraced.
Save me because you do what is right.
2 Listen to me
and save me quickly.
Be my rock of protection,
a strong city to save me.
3 You are my rock and my protection.
For the good of your name, lead me and guide me.
4 Set me free from the trap they set for me,
because you are my protection.
5 I give you my life.
Save me, LORD, God of truth.

6 I hate those who worship false gods.
I trust only in the LORD.
7 I will be glad and rejoice in your love,
because you saw my suffering;
you knew my troubles.
8 You have not handed me over to my enemies
but have set me in a safe place.

9 LORD, have mercy, because I am in misery.
My eyes are weak from so much crying,
and my whole being is tired from grief.
10 My life is ending in sadness,
and my years are spent in crying.
My troubles are using up my strength,
and my bones are getting weaker.
11 Because of all my troubles, my enemies hate me,

> His anger lasts only a moment, but his kindness lasts for a lifetime.
> — Psalm 30:5

and even my neighbours look
  down on me.
When my friends see me,
  they are afraid and run.
12 I am like a piece of a broken pot.
  I am forgotten as if I were dead.
13 I have heard many insults.
  Terror is all around me.
  They make plans against me
  and want to kill me.

14 LORD, I trust you.
  I have said, "You are my God."
15 My life is in your hands.
  Save me from my enemies
  and from those who are chasing
    me.
16 Show your kindness to me, your
    servant.
  Save me because of your love.
17 LORD, I called to you,
  so do not let me be disgraced.
  Let the wicked be disgraced
  and lie silent in the grave.
18 With pride and hatred
  they speak against those who do
    right.
  So silence their lying lips.

19 How great is your goodness
  that you have stored up for those
    who fear you,
  that you have given to those who
    trust you.
  You do this for all to see.
20 You protect them by your presence
  from what people plan against them.
  You shelter them from evil words.
21 Praise the LORD.
  His love to me was wonderful
  when my city was attacked.
22 In my distress, I said,
  "God cannot see me!"
  But you heard my prayer
  when I cried out to you for help.

23 Love the LORD, all
  you who
  belong to him.
  The LORD
  protects
  those who
  truly believe,

31:23
Responsibility
God is responsible for you.

but he punishes the proud as much
  as they have sinned.
24 All you who put your hope in the
  LORD
  be strong and brave.

It is Better to Confess Sin

A maskil of David.

32 Happy is the person
  whose sins are forgiven,
  whose wrongs are pardoned.
2 Happy is the person
  whom the LORD does not consider
    guilty
  and in whom there is nothing false.

3 When I kept things to myself,
  I felt weak deep inside me.
  I moaned all day long.
4 Day and night you punished me.
  My strength was gone as in the
    summer heat.   *Selah*
5 Then I confessed my sins to you
  and didn't hide my guilt.
  I said, "I will
    confess my
    sins to the
    LORD",
    and you
    forgave my
    guilt.   *Selah*

32:5
Guilt
Check out how to get rid of guilt.

6 For this reason, all who obey you
  should pray to you while they still
    can.
  When troubles rise like a flood,
  they will not reach them.
7 You are my hiding place.
  You protect me from my troubles
  and fill me with songs of salvation.
                                Selah

8 The LORD says, "I will make you wise
  and show you where to go.
  I will guide you and watch over
    you.
9 So don't be like a horse or donkey
  that doesn't understand.
  They must be led with bits and reins,
  or they will not come near you."

10 Wicked people have many troubles,

FAITH links

THE COVER-UP
PSALM 32:1-2

How long do you think you could hide a bag of smelly rubbish – old food, that sort of thing – in your room? Not very long, right? The smell would give it away. Sin is like that bag of rubbish. When we try to cover it up, God sniffs it out. Confessing it is the only way to really "cover up" sin. God's forgiveness completely covers it and takes it away. David knew great joy because of this. You can, too!

Made in His Image, Genesis 1:26–27, p. 4

Think About Him, Isaiah 26:3, p. 926

A Hard Place, Ezekiel 28:25–26, p. 1120

A Swarm of Trouble, Joel 2:25–27, p. 1190

Inside the Heart of God, Micah 7:18–20, p. 1228

Just for the Asking, Romans 3:23–28, p. 1522

---

but the LORD's love surrounds
   those who trust him.
11 Good people, rejoice and be happy in
   the LORD.
   Sing all you whose hearts are
      right.

Praise God Who Creates and Saves

33 Sing to the LORD, you who do
      what is right;

Psalm 33:18 733

honest people should praise him.
2 Praise the LORD on the harp;
   make music for him on a
      ten-stringed lyre.
3 Sing a new song to him;
   play well and joyfully.

4 God's word is true,
   and everything he does is right.
5 He loves what is right and fair;
   the LORD's love fills the earth.

6 The sky was made at the LORD's
      command.
   By the breath from his mouth, he
      made all the stars.
7 He gathered the water of the sea into
      a heap.
   He made the great ocean stay in its
      place.
8 All the earth should worship the
      LORD;
   the whole world should fear him.
9 He spoke, and it happened.
   He commanded, and it appeared.
10 The LORD upsets the plans of nations;
   he ruins all their plans.
11 But the LORD's plans will stand for
      ever;
   his ideas will last from now on.

12 Happy is the nation whose God is the
      LORD,
   the people he chose for his very
      own.
13 The LORD looks down from heaven
   and sees every person.
14 From his throne he watches
   all who live on earth.
15 He made their hearts
   and understands everything they
      do.
16 No king is saved by his great army.
   No warrior escapes by his great
      strength.
17 Horses can't bring victory;
   they can't save
      by their
      strength.
18 But the LORD
   looks after
   those who
   fear him,

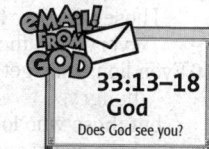
33:13–18
God
Does God see you?

those who put their hope in his
love.
19 He saves them from death
and spares their lives in times of
hunger.

20 So our hope is in the LORD.
He is our help, our shield to
protect us.
21 We rejoice in him,
because we trust his holy name.
22 LORD, show your love to us
as we put our hope in you.

Praise God Who Judges and Saves

*David's song from the time he pretended
to be insane so that Abimelech
would send him away.*

34 I will praise the LORD at all times;
his praise is always on my lips.
2 My whole being praises the LORD.
The poor will hear and be glad.
3 Praise the LORD with me,
and let us praise his name
together.

4 I asked the LORD for help, and he
answered me.
He saved me from all that I feared.
5 Those who go to him for help are
happy,
and they are never disgraced.
6 This poor man called, and the LORD
heard him
and saved him from all his
troubles.
7 The angel of the LORD camps around
those who fear God,
and he saves them.

8 Examine and see how good the LORD
is.
Happy is the person who trusts
him.
9 You who belong to the LORD, fear
him!
Those who fear him will have
everything they need.
10 Even lions may get weak and
hungry,
but those who look to the LORD will
have every good thing.

11 Children, come and listen to me.
I will teach you to worship the LORD.
12 You must do these things
to enjoy life and have many happy
days.
13 You must not say evil things,
and you must not tell lies.
14 Stop doing evil and do good.
Look for peace and work for it.

15 The LORD sees the good people
and listens to their prayers.
16 But the LORD is against those who do
evil;
he makes the world forget them.

17 The LORD hears good people when
they cry out to him,
and he saves them from all their
troubles.
18 The LORD is close to the
broken-hearted,
and he saves
those whose
spirits have
been
crushed.

34:18 Feelings
Who heals a broken heart?

19 People who do
what is right may have many
problems,
but the LORD will solve them all.
20 He will protect their very bones;
not one of them will be broken.

21 Evil will kill the wicked;
those who hate good people will be
judged guilty.
22 But the LORD saves his servants' lives;
no one who trusts him will be
judged guilty.

A Prayer for Help

Of David.

35 LORD, battle against those who
battle with me.
Fight against those who fight
against me.
2 Pick up the shield and armour.
Rise up and help me.
3 Lift up your spears, both large and
small,

against those who chase me.
Tell me, "I will save you."

4 Make those who want to kill me
   be ashamed and disgraced.
  Make those who plan to harm me
   turn back and run away.
5 Make them like chaff blown by the
   wind
   as the angel of the LORD forces
   them away.
6 Let their road be dark and slippery
   as the angel of the LORD chases
   them.
7 For no reason they spread out their
   net to trap me;
  for no reason they dug a pit for me.
8 So let ruin strike them suddenly.
  Let them be caught in their own
   nets;
  let them fall into the pit and die.
9 Then I will rejoice in the LORD;
  I will be happy when he saves me.
10 Even my bones will say,
   "LORD, who is like you?
   You save the weak from the strong,
   the weak and poor from robbers."

11 Men without mercy stand up to
   testify.
  They ask me things I do not know.
12 They repay me with evil for the good
    I have done,
   and they make me
    very sad.
13 Yet when they were
    sick, I put on
    clothes of
    sadness
   and showed my
    sorrow by going
    without food.
   But my prayers were
    not answered.
14   I acted as if they
    were my friends
    or brothers.
   I bowed in sadness as if I were crying
    for my mother.
15 But when I was in trouble, they
    gathered and laughed;
   they gathered to attack before I
    knew it.

They insulted me without
   stopping.
16 They made fun of me and were cruel
    to me
   and ground their teeth at me in
    anger.
17 Lord, how long will you watch this
    happen?
   Save my life from their attacks;
   save me from these people who are
    like lions.
18 I will praise you in the great meeting.
   I will praise you among crowds of
    people.

19 Do not let my enemies laugh at me;
    they hate me for no reason.
   Do not let them make fun of me;
    they have no cause to hate me.
20 Their words are not friendly
   but are lies about peace-loving
    people.
21 They speak against me
   and say, "Aha! We saw what you
    did!"

22 LORD, you have been watching. Do
    not keep quiet.
   Lord, do not leave me alone.
23 Wake up! Come and defend me!
   My God and Lord, fight for me!
24 LORD my God, defend me with your
    justice.
   Don't let them laugh
    at me.
25 Don't let them think,
    "Aha! We got
    what we
    wanted!"
   Don't let them say,
    "We destroyed
    him."

26 Let them be ashamed
    and embarrassed,
   because they were
    happy when I
    hurt.
   Cover them with shame and disgrace,
    because they thought they were
    better than I was.
27 May my friends sing and shout for
    joy.

> LORD, you have been watching. Do not keep quiet. Lord, do not leave me alone.
> – Psalm 35:22

May they always say, "Praise the
greatness of the LORD,
who loves to see his servants do
well."
28 I will tell of your goodness
and will praise you every day.

Wicked People and a Good God

For the director of music. Of David,
the servant of the LORD.

36 Sin speaks to the wicked in their
hearts.
They have no fear of God.
2 They think too much of themselves
so they don't see their sin and hate
it.
3 Their words are wicked lies;
they are no longer wise or good.
4 At night they make evil plans;
what they do leads to nothing
good.
They don't refuse things that are
evil.

5 LORD, your love reaches to the
heavens,
your loyalty to the skies.
6 Your goodness is as high as the
mountains.
Your justice is as deep as the great
ocean.
LORD, you protect both people and
animals.
7 God, your love is so precious!
You protect people in the shadow
of your wings.
8 They eat the rich food in your house,
and you let them drink from your
river of pleasure.
9 You are the giver of life.
Your light lets us enjoy life.

10 Continue to love those who know you
and to do good to those who are
good.
11 Don't let proud people attack me
and the wicked force me away.
12 Those who do evil have been
defeated.
They are overwhelmed;
they cannot do evil any longer.

God will Reward Fairly

Of David.

37 Don't be upset because of evil
people.
Don't be jealous of those who do
wrong,
2 because, like the grass, they will soon
dry up.
Like green plants, they will soon
die away.

FAITH links

DOES CRIME PAY?

PSALM 37:1-7

Did you ever wonder whether people who do evil things are punished? Maybe you know of someone who bullies others at school and never gets into trouble. If so, David offers this advice to you from his psalm: don't worry when those who do evil seem to get away with it. Instead, trust God. Wait for him to even things out.

Connect here to find out how to get God – not get even:

More Powerful Than Revenge, Genesis 50:14–21, p. 71

Learning from Mistakes, Psalm 51:12–13, p. 748

A Change of Heart, Matthew 3:1–12, p. 1277

Forgive Again? Luke 17:3–4, p. 1402

A Friend in Need, Acts 9:27, p. 1480

His Best Qualities, 2 Peter 3:9, p. 1711

3 Trust the LORD and do good.
   Live in the land and feed on truth.
4 Enjoy serving the LORD,
   and he will give you what you want.
5 Depend on the LORD;
   trust him, and he will take care of you.
6 Then your goodness will shine like the sun,
   and your fairness like the noonday sun.
7 Wait and trust the LORD.
   Don't be upset when others get rich
   or when someone else's plans succeed.
8 Don't get angry.
   Don't be upset; it only leads to trouble.
9 Evil people will be sent away,
   but those who trust the LORD will inherit the land.
10 In a little while the wicked will be no more.
   You may look for them, but they will be gone.
11 People who are not proud will inherit the land
   and will enjoy complete peace.
12 The wicked make evil plans against good people.
   They grind their teeth at them in anger.
13 But the Lord laughs at the wicked,
   because he sees that their day is coming.
14 The wicked draw their swords
   and bend their bows
   to kill the poor and helpless,
   to kill those who are honest.
15 But their swords will stab their own hearts,
   and their bows will break.
16 It is better to have little and be right
   than to have much and be wrong.
17 The power of the wicked will be broken,
   but the LORD supports those who do right.
18 The LORD watches over the lives of the innocent,
   and their reward will last for ever.
19 They will not be ashamed when trouble comes.
   They will be full in times of hunger.
20 But the wicked will die.
   The LORD's enemies will be like the flowers of the fields;
   they will disappear like smoke.
21 The wicked borrow and don't pay back,
   but those who do right give freely to others.
22 Those whom the LORD blesses will inherit the land,
   but those he curses will be sent away.
23 When a person's steps follow the LORD,
   God is pleased with his ways.
24 If he stumbles, he will not fall,
   because the LORD holds his hand.
25 I was young, and now I am old,
   but I have never seen good people left helpless
   or their children begging for food.
26 Good people always lend freely to others,
   and their children are a blessing.
27 Stop doing evil and do good,
   so you will live for ever.
28 The LORD loves justice
   and will not leave those who worship him.
   He will always protect them,
   but the children of the wicked will die.
29 Good people will inherit the land
   and will live in it for ever.
30 A good person speaks with wisdom,
   and he says what is fair.
31 The teachings of his God are in his heart,
   so he does not fail to keep them.

37:23–24 God's Promises
Find out how God cares for his children.

32 The wicked watch for good people
  so that they may kill them.
33 But the LORD will not take away his
    protection
  or let good people be judged guilty.

34 Wait for the LORD's help
    and follow him.
  He will honour you and give you the
    land,
    and you will see the wicked sent
    away.

35 I saw a wicked and cruel man
    who looked strong like a healthy
    tree in good soil.
36 But he died and was gone;
    I looked for him,
    but he couldn't be found.

37 Think of the innocent person,
    and watch the honest one.
  The man who has peace
    will have children to live after him.
38 But sinners will be destroyed;
    in the end the wicked will die.

39 The LORD saves good people;
    he is their strength in times of
    trouble.
40 The LORD helps them and saves
    them;
    he saves them from the wicked,
    because they trust in him for
    protection.

A Prayer in Time of Sickness

A psalm of David to remember.

38 LORD, don't punish me when you
    are angry.
  Don't punish me when you are
    furious.
2 Your arrows have wounded me,
    and your hand has come down on
    me.
3 My body is sick from your
    punishment.
  Even my bones are not healthy
    because of my sin.
4 My guilt has overwhelmed me;
    like a load it weighs me down.

5 My sores stink and become infected
    because I was foolish.
6 I am bent over and bowed down;
    I am sad all day long.
7 I am burning with fever,
    and my whole body is sore.
8 I am weak and faint.
    I moan from the pain I feel.

9 Lord, you know everything I want;
    my cries are not hidden from you.
10 My heart pounds, and
    my strength is gone.
    I am losing my sight.
11 Because of my wounds, my
    friends and neighbours avoid
    me,
    and my relatives stay far away.
12 Some people set traps to kill me.
    Those who want to hurt me plan
    trouble;
    all day long they think up lies.

13 I am like a deaf man; I cannot hear.
    Like a mute, I cannot speak.
14 I am like a person who does not
    hear,
    who has no answer to give.
15 I trust you, LORD.
    You will answer, my Lord and
    God.
16 I said, "Don't let them laugh at me
    or boast when I am defeated."

17 I am about to die,
    and I cannot forget my pain.
18 I confess my guilt;
    I am troubled by my sin.
19 My enemies are strong and healthy,
    and many hate me for no reason.
20 They repay me with evil for the good
    I did.
    They lie about me because I try to
    do good.

> Lord, you know everything I want; my cries are not hidden from you.
> – Psalm 38:9

21 LORD, don't leave me;
   my God, don't go away.
22 Quickly come and help me,
   my Lord and Saviour.

Life is Short

*For the director of music. For Jeduthun.
A psalm of David.*

39 I said, "I will be careful how I act
   and will not sin by what I say.
I will be careful what I say
   around wicked people."
2 So I kept very quiet.
   I didn't even say anything good,
   but I became even more upset.
3 I became very angry inside,
   and as I thought about it, my anger burned.
   So I spoke:

4 "LORD, tell me when the end will come
   and how long I will live.
   Let me know how long I have.
5 You have given me only a short life;
   my lifetime is like nothing to you.
   Everyone's life is only a breath.
                                    Selah
6 People are like shadows moving about.
   All their work is for nothing;
   they collect things
      but don't know
      who will get them.

7 "So, Lord, what hope do I have?
   You are my hope.
8 Save me from all my sins.
   Don't let wicked fools make fun of me.
9 I am quiet; I do not open my mouth,
   because you are the one who has done this.
10 Stop punishing me;
   your beating is about to kill me.
11 You correct and punish people for their sins;
   like a moth, you destroy what they love.
Everyone's life is only a breath.
                                    Selah

12 "LORD, hear my prayer,
   and listen to my cry.
   Do not ignore my tears.
   I am like a visitor with you.
   Like my ancestors, I'm only here
      for a short time.
13 Leave me alone so I can be happy
   before I leave and am no more."

Praise and Prayer for Help

*For the director of music.
A psalm of David.*

40 I waited patiently for the LORD.
   He turned to me and heard my cry.
2 He lifted me out of the pit of destruction,
   out of the sticky mud.
   He stood me on a rock
   and made my feet steady.
3 He put a new song in my mouth,
   a song of praise to our God.
   Many people will see this and worship him.
   Then they will trust the LORD.

4 Happy is the person
      who trusts the LORD,
      who doesn't turn to those who are proud
      or to those who worship false gods.
5 LORD my God, you have done many miracles.
   Your plans for us are many.
   If I tried to tell them all,
      there would be too many to count.

6 You do not want sacrifices and offerings.
   But you have made a hole in my ear
   to show that my body and life are yours.

> Save me from all my sins. Don't let wicked fools make fun of me.
> – Psalm 39:8

You do not ask for burnt offerings
   and sacrifices to take away sins.
7 Then I said, "Look, I have come.
   It is written about me in the book.
8 My God, I want to do what you want.
   Your teachings are in my heart."

9 I will tell about your goodness in the
      great meeting of your people.
   LORD, you know my lips are not
      silent.
10 I do not hide your goodness in my
      heart;
   I speak about your loyalty and
      salvation.
   I do not hide your love and truth
      from the people in the great
      meeting.

11 LORD, do not hold back your mercy
      from me;
   let your love and truth always
      protect me.
12 Troubles have surrounded me;
      there are too many to count.
   My sins have caught me
      so that I cannot see a way to
      escape.
   I have more sins than hairs on my
      head,
      and I have lost my courage.

13 Please, LORD,
      save me.
   Hurry, LORD,
      to help me.
14 People are trying
      to kill me.
   Shame them and disgrace them.
   People want to hurt me.
      Let them run away in disgrace.
15 People are making fun of me.
   Let them be shamed into silence.
16 But let those who follow you
      be happy and glad.
   They love you for saving them.
   May they always say, "Praise the
      LORD!"

17 Lord, because I am poor and helpless,
      please remember me.
   You are my helper and saviour.
   My God, do not wait.

40:13 Prayer
Who should you go to for help?

A Prayer in Time of Sickness

For the director of music.
A psalm of David.

41 Happy is the person who thinks
      about the poor.
   When trouble comes, the LORD will
      save him.
2 The LORD will protect him and spare
      his life
   and will bless
      him in the
      land.
   He will not let
      his enemies
      take him.
3 The LORD will
      give him
      strength when he is sick,
   and he will make him well again.

41 Sickness
Check out how God cares for the sick.

4 I said, "LORD, have mercy on me.
   Heal me, because I have sinned
      against you."
5 My enemies are saying evil things
      about me.
   They say, "When will he die and be
      forgotten?"
6 Some people come to see me,
      but they lie.
   They just come to get bad news.
      Then they go and gossip.

7 All my enemies whisper about me
   and think the worst about me.
8 They say, "He has a terrible disease.
   He will never get out of bed again."
9 My best and truest friend, who ate at
      my table,
   has even turned against me.

10 LORD, have mercy on me.
   Give me strength so I can pay
      them back.
11 Because my enemies do not defeat
      me,
   I know you are pleased with me.
12 Because I am innocent, you support
      me
   and will let me be with you for ever.

13 Praise the LORD, the God of Israel.
   He has always been,

and he will always be.
    Amen and amen.

Book 2

Wishing to be Near God

For the director of music.
A maskil of the sons of Korah.

42 As a deer thirsts for streams of water,
    so I thirst for you, God.
2 I thirst for the living God.
    When can I go to meet with him?
3 Day and night, my tears have been my food.
    People are always saying,
        "Where is your God?"
4 When I remember these things,
    I speak with a broken heart.
    I used to walk with the crowd
        and lead them to God's Temple
            with songs of praise.

5 Why am I so sad?
    Why am I so upset?
    I should put my hope in God
        and keep praising him,
    my Saviour and 6 my God.

I am very sad.
    So I remember you where the Jordan River begins,
        near the peaks of Hermon and Mount Mizar.
7 Troubles have come again and again,
        sounding like waterfalls.
    Your waves are crashing all around me.

8 The LORD shows his true love every day.
    At night I have a song,
    and I pray to my living God.

9 I say to God, my Rock,
    "Why have you forgotten me?
    Why am I sad
        and troubled by my enemies?"
10 My enemies' insults make me feel as if my bones were broken.
    They are always saying,
        "Where is your God?"

11 Why am I so sad?
    Why am I so upset?

FAITH links

OUR THIRST QUENCHER
PSALM 42:1-3

Think of a time when you were really thirsty. If someone had handed you a juice drink or a glass of milk, would that have quenched your thirst? Only partially, right? Water is the only liquid that can fully quench someone's thirst. Both animals and humans need water to live. That's why David compared our need for God to a deer's need for water. Our hearts "thirst" for God. Only God can satisfy the need we have. The more you get to know about God, the more you will "thirst" for him.

I'll Never Forget What's-His-Name, Deuteronomy 8, p. 239

Help to Understand, 2 Samuel 14, p. 416

Choosing a Friend, Proverbs 28:7, p. 865

A Need to Change, Ecclesiastes 1:1–11, p. 873

Two Ways to Grow, Luke 2:46–52, p. 1370

That's False! 2 John 7–11, p. 1722

42:5–6
Hope
How can you chase away the blues?

I should put my hope in God
and keep praising him,
my Saviour and my God.

A Prayer for Protection

43 God, defend me.
Argue my case against those who
don't follow you.
Save me from liars and those who
do evil.
2 God, you are my strength.
Why have you rejected me?
Why am I sad
and troubled by my enemies?
3 Send me your light and truth
to guide me.
Let them lead me to your holy
mountain,
to where you live.
4 Then I will go to the altar of God,
to God who is my joy and
happiness.
I will praise you with a harp,
God, my God.

5 Why am I so sad?
Why am I so upset?
I should put my hope in God
and keep praising him,
my Saviour and my God.

CONNECT 2-YOU

TEMPER, TEMPER

Have you ever got so angry you could hardly see straight? Here's someone who has a problem with his temper. Let's welcome David, aged 11, to Connect 2-You.

David: My mum says I have a "short fuse" and I have to admit she's right. When something makes me mad, I just explode. I get so angry with my brother sometimes that I feel like hitting him – or worse. Does that make me a bad person?

We all get mad sometimes, don't we? There's nothing wrong with feeling angry. But the way we handle our anger says a lot about us, whether we like it or not. God wants us to turn anger over to him, admit what we're feeling, and let him deal with it. If you'd like to find out more about this process, check out the Livin' It page on anger, James 1:19-21, p. 1690.

One of the best ways to keep your temper under control is to pray before you do anything out of anger. Praying gives you the chance to ask God for help and it gives you time to cool down. Why not give it a try the next time you feel your temperature rising?

A Prayer for Help

For the director of music.
A maskil of the sons of Korah.

44 God, we have heard about you.
Our ancestors told us
what you did in their days,
in days long ago.
2 With your power you forced the
nations out of the land
and placed our ancestors here.
You destroyed those other nations,
but you made our ancestors grow
strong.
3 It wasn't their swords that took the
land.
It wasn't their power that gave
them victory.
But it was your great power and
strength.
You were with them because you
loved them.

4 My God, you are my King.
Your commands led Jacob's people
to victory.
5 With your help we pushed back our
enemies.
In your name we trampled those
who came against us.
6 I don't trust my bow to
help me,
and my sword can't
save me.
7 You saved us from our
foes,
and you made our
enemies
ashamed.
8 We will praise God
every day;
we will praise your
name for ever.

Selah

9 But you have rejected us and shamed
us.
You don't march with our armies
any more.
10 You let our enemies push us back,
and those who hate us have taken
our wealth.
11 You gave us away like sheep to be
eaten

and have scattered us among the
nations.
12 You sold your people for nothing
and made no profit on the sale.

13 You made us a joke to our neighbours;
those around us laugh and make
fun of us.
14 You made us a joke to the other
nations;
people shake their heads.
15 I am always in disgrace,
and I am covered with shame.
16 My enemy is getting even
with insults and curses.

17 All these things have happened to us,
but we have not forgotten you
or failed to keep our agreement
with you.
18 Our hearts haven't turned away from
you,
and we haven't stopped following
you.
19 But you crushed us in this place
where wild dogs live,
and you covered us with deep
darkness.

20 If we had forgotten our God
or lifted our hands in
prayer to foreign
gods,
21 God would have
known,
because he knows
what is in our
hearts.
22 But for you we are in
danger of death all
the time.
People think we are
worth no more
than sheep to
be killed.

23 Wake up, Lord! Why are you
sleeping?
Get up! Don't reject us for
ever.
24 Why do you hide from us?
Have you forgotten our pain and
troubles?

> I don't trust my bow
> to help me, and my
> sword can't save me.
> – Psalm 44:6

25 We have been pushed down into the ground;
 we are flat on the ground.
26 Get up and help us.
 Because of your love, save us.

A Song for the King's Wedding

For the director of music. To the tune of "Lilies". A maskil. A love song of the sons of Korah.

45 Beautiful words fill my mind.
 I am speaking of royal things.
 My tongue is like the pen of a skilled writer.

2 You are more handsome than anyone,
 and you are an excellent speaker,
 so God has blessed you for ever.
3 Put on your sword, powerful warrior.
 Show your glory and majesty.
4 In your majesty win the victory
 for what is true and right.
 Your power will do amazing things.
5 Your sharp arrows will enter
 the hearts of the king's enemies.
 Nations will be defeated before you.
6 God, your throne will last for ever and ever.
 You will rule your kingdom with fairness.
7 You love right and hate evil,
 so God has chosen you from among your friends;
 he has set you apart with much joy.
8 Your clothes smell like myrrh, aloes and cassia.
 From palaces of ivory music comes to make you happy.
9 Kings' daughters are among your honoured women.
 Your bride stands at your right side wearing gold from Ophir.

10 Listen to me, daughter; look and pay attention.
 Forget your people and your father's family.
11 The king loves your beauty.
 Because he is your master, you should obey him.
12 People from the city of Tyre have brought a gift.
 Wealthy people will want to meet you.

13 The princess is very beautiful.
 Her gown is woven with gold.
14 In her beautiful clothes she is brought to the king.
 Her bridesmaids follow behind her,
 and they are also brought to him.
15 They come with happiness and joy;
 they enter the king's palace.

16 You will have sons to replace your fathers.
 You will make them rulers through all the land.
17 I will make your name famous from now on,
 so people will praise you for ever and ever.

> God, your throne will last for ever and ever. You will rule your kingdom with fairness.
> – Psalm 45:6

God Protects His People

For the director of music. By alamoth. A psalm of the sons of Korah.

46 God is our protection and our strength.
 He always helps in times of trouble.
2 So we will not be afraid even
 if the earth shakes,
 or the mountains fall into the sea,
3 even if the oceans roar and foam,
 or the mountains shake at the raging sea. *Selah*

46:1–2 Troubles
Who is your help in bad times?

4 There is a river that brings joy to the
      city of God,
   the holy place where God Most
      High lives.
5 God is in that city, and so it will not be
      shaken.
   God will help her at dawn.
6 Nations tremble and kingdoms shake.
   God shouts and the earth
      crumbles.

7 The LORD All-powerful is with us;
   the God of Jacob is our defender.
                                          Selah

8 Come and see what the LORD has
      done,
   the amazing things he has done on
      the earth.
9 He stops wars everywhere on the
      earth.
   He breaks all bows and spears
   and burns up the chariots with fire.
10 God says, "Be quiet and know that I
      am God.
   I will be supreme over all the
      nations;
   I will be supreme in the earth."

11 The LORD All-powerful is with us;
   the God of Jacob is our defender.
                                          Selah

God, the King of the World

*For the director of music.
A psalm of the sons of Korah.*

47 Clap your hands, all you people.
   Shout to God with joy.
2 The LORD Most High
      is wonderful.
   He is the great
      King over all the
         earth!
3 He defeated nations
      for us
   and put them under
      our control.
4 He chose the land we
      would inherit.
   We are the children
      of Jacob, whom he loved.   *Selah*

5 God has risen with a shout of joy;
   the LORD has risen as the trumpets
      sounded.
6 Sing praises to God. Sing praises.
   Sing praises to our King. Sing
      praises.

7 God is King of all the earth,
   so sing a song of praise to him.
8 God is King over the nations.
   God sits on his holy throne.
9 The leaders of the nations meet
      with the people of the God of
         Abraham,
   because the leaders of the earth
      belong to God.
   He is supreme.

Jerusalem, the City of God

A psalm of the sons of Korah.

48 The LORD is great; he should be
      praised
   in the city of our God, on his holy
      mountain.
2 It is high and beautiful
   and brings joy to the whole world.
   Mount Zion is like the high
      mountains of the north;
   it is the city of the Great King.
3 God is within its palaces;
   he is known as its defender.

4 Kings joined together
   and came to attack the city.
5 But when they saw it, they were
      amazed.
   They ran away in fear.
6 Fear took hold of them;
   they hurt like a woman having a baby.
7 You destroyed the large trading ships
   with an east wind.

8 First we heard
   and now we have
      seen
   that God will always
      keep his city
         safe.
   It is the city of
      the LORD
         All-powerful,
   the city of our God.
                                          Selah

> Clap your hands, all
> you people. Shout to
> God with joy.
>   – Psalm 47:1

9 God, we come into your Temple
   to think about your love.
10 God, your name is known
      everywhere;
   all over the earth people praise
      you.
   Your right hand is full of goodness.
11 Mount Zion is happy
   and all the towns of Judah rejoice,
   because your decisions are fair.

12 Walk around Jerusalem
   and count its towers.
13 Notice how strong they are.
   Look at the palaces.

   Then you can tell your children
      about them.
14 This God is our God for ever
   and ever.
   He will guide us from now on.

eMail FROM GOD
48:14
God's Will
Why can you be hopeful about the future?

Trusting Money is Foolish

For the director of music.
A psalm of the sons of Korah.

49 Listen to this, all you nations;
   listen, all you who live on earth.
2 Listen, both great and small,
   rich and poor together.
3 What I say is wise,
   and my heart speaks with
      understanding.
4 I will pay attention to a wise saying;
   I will explain my riddle on the harp.

5 Why should I be afraid of bad days?
   Why should I fear when evil men
      surround me?
6 They trust in their money
   and boast about their riches.
7 No one can buy back the life of
      another.
   No one can pay God for his own
      life,
8 because the price of a life is high.
   No payment is ever enough.
9 Do people live for ever?
   Don't they all face death?

10 See, even wise people die.
   Fools and stupid people also die
   and leave their wealth to others.
11 Their graves will always be their
      homes.
   They will live there from now on,
   even though they named places
      after themselves.

12 Even rich people do not live for ever;
   like the animals, people die.

13 This is what will happen to those who
      trust in themselves
   and to their followers who believe
      them.   *Selah*

FAITH CHALLENGE

Here's another one for you. Read 48:9 to discover what the writer of the psalm thought about when he worshipped God. What can you do to make sure that you think about the right things when you're in church?

TeSTiNG iT

Psalm 48:9
God, we come into your Temple to think about your love.

14 Like sheep, they must die,
    and death will be their shepherd.
  Honest people will rule over them in
      the morning,
    and their bodies will
      rot in a
      grave far
      from home.
15 But God will save
      my life
    and will take me from the grave.
                                    Selah

49:13–15
Death
Who will God save from death?

16 Don't be afraid of rich people
    because their houses are more
      beautiful.
17 They don't take anything to the grave;
    their wealth won't go down with
      them.
18 Even though they were praised when
      they were alive—
    and people may praise you when
      you succeed—
19 they will go to where their ancestors
      are.
    They will never see light again.

20 Rich people with no understanding
    are just like animals that die.

God Wants True Worship

A psalm of Asaph.

50 The God of gods, the LORD,
      speaks.
    He calls the earth from the rising
      to the setting sun.
 2 God shines from Jerusalem,
    whose beauty is perfect.
 3 Our God comes, and he will not be
      silent.
    A fire burns in front of him,
    and a powerful storm surrounds
      him.
 4 He calls to the sky above and to the
      earth
    that he might judge his people.
 5 He says, "Gather around, you who
      worship me,
    who have made an agreement with
      me, using a sacrifice."
 6 God is the judge,
    and even the skies say he is right.
                                    Selah

 7 God says, "My people, listen to me;
    Israel, I will testify against you.
    I am God, your God.
 8 I do not scold you for your sacrifices.
    You always bring me your burnt
      offerings.
 9 But I do not need bulls from your stalls
    or goats from your pens,
10 because every animal of the forest is
      already mine.
    The cattle on a thousand hills are
      mine.
11 I know every bird on the mountains,
    and every living thing in the fields
      is mine.
12 If I were hungry, I would not tell you,
    because the earth and everything
      in it are mine.
13 I don't eat the meat of bulls
    or drink the blood of goats.
14 Give an offering to show thanks to
      God.
    Give God Most High what you
      have promised.
15 Call to me in times of trouble.
    I will save you, and you will honour
      me."

16 But God says to the wicked:
    "Why do you talk about my laws?
    Why do you mention my
      agreement?
17 You hate my teachings
    and turn your back on what I say.
18 When you see a thief, you join him.
    You take part in adultery.
19 You don't stop your mouth from
      speaking evil,
    and your tongue makes up lies.
20 You speak against your brother
    and lie about your mother's son.
21 I have kept quiet while you did these
      things,
    so you thought I was just like you.
    But I will scold you
    and accuse you to your face.

22 "Think about this, you who forget
      God.

Psalm 50:23 748

Otherwise, I will tear you apart,
and no one will save you.
23 Those people honour me
who bring me offerings to show
thanks.
And I, God, will save those who do
that."

A Prayer for Forgiveness

*For the director of music. A psalm
of David when the prophet Nathan
came to David after David's
sin with Bathsheba.*

51 God, be merciful to me
because you are loving.
Because you are always ready to be
merciful,
wipe out all my wrongs.
2 Wash away all my guilt
and make me clean again.

3 I know about my wrongs,
and I can't forget my sin.
4 You are the only one I have sinned
against;
I have done what you say is wrong.
You are right when you speak
and fair when you judge.
5 I was brought into this world in sin.
In sin my mother gave birth to me.

6 You want me
to be
completely
truthful,
so teach me
wisdom.

51:6 Truth
How does God want
you to live?

7 Take away my sin, and I will be clean.
Wash me, and I will be whiter than
snow.
8 Make me hear sounds of joy and
gladness;
let the bones you crushed be
happy again.
9 Turn your face from my sins
and wipe out all my guilt.
10 Create in me a pure heart, God,
and make my spirit right again.
11 Do not send me away from you
or take your Holy Spirit away from
me.

FAITH links

LEARNING FROM MISTAKES

PSALM 51:12-13

Suppose you were punished for something you did wrong. If you saw a friend about to do the same thing that got you into trouble, you would try to stop him, wouldn't you? That's what is known as learning from your mistakes.

David wrote this psalm after God sent a prophet to tell David about a sin that David tried to cover up. Once God forgave him, David wanted to encourage others to ask God for forgiveness. Telling others about God – and even about the mistakes for which you've received forgiveness – helps you and others grow in faith.

How can you help others learn from your mistakes? Link here to find out:

An Attention-Getter, Numbers 22, p. 207

On the Wrong Foot, 2 Kings 21:1–2, 16, p. 509

A Useless Thing, Isaiah 44:9, 18–20, p. 954

Real Repentance, Jeremiah 4:1–4, p. 993

Prayer for a Friend, Colossians 1:9–12, p. 1620

You're a Fake! 2 Peter 2:1, p. 1709

12 Give me back the joy of your
      salvation.
    Keep me strong by giving me a
      willing spirit.

13 Then I will teach your ways to those
      who do wrong,
    and sinners will turn back to you.
14 God, save me from the guilt of
      murder,
    God of my salvation,
    and I will sing about your
      goodness.
15 Lord, let me speak
    so I may praise you.
16 You are not pleased by sacrifices, or I
      would give them.
    You don't want burnt offerings.
17 The sacrifice God wants is a broken
      spirit.
    God, you will not reject a heart that
      is broken and sorry for sin.

18 Do whatever good you wish for
      Jerusalem.
    Rebuild the walls of Jerusalem.
19 Then you will be pleased with right
      sacrifices and whole burnt
      offerings,
    and bulls will be offered on your
      altar.

God will Punish the Proud

*For the director of music. A maskil of
David. When Doeg the Edomite came
to Saul and said to him, "David is
in Ahimelech's house."*

52 Mighty warrior, why do you boast
      about the evil you do?
    God's love will continue for ever.
2 You think up evil plans.
    Your tongue is like a sharp razor,
      making up lies.
3 You love wrong more than right
    and lies more than truth.   *Selah*
4 You love words that bite
    and tongues that lie.

5 But God will ruin you for ever.
    He will seize you and throw you
      out of your tent;
    he will tear you away from the land
      of the living.   *Selah*
6 Those who do right will see this and
      fear God.
    They will laugh at you and say,
7 "Look what happened to the man
      who did not depend on God
    but depended on his money.
    He grew strong by his evil plans."
8 But I am like an
      olive tree
      growing in
      God's
      Temple.
    I trust God's love
      for ever and
      ever.
9 God, I will thank you for ever for what
      you have done.
    With those who worship you, I will
      trust you because you are good.

52:5–9 Trust
Trusting in God makes a difference.

The Unbelieving Fool

*For the director of music. By mahalath.
A maskil of David.*

53 Fools say to themselves,
      "There is no God."
    Fools are evil and do terrible things;
      none of them does anything good.

2 God looked down from heaven on all
      people
    to see if anyone was wise,
    if anyone was looking to God for
      help.
3 But all have turned away.
    Together, everyone has become
      evil;
    none of them does anything good.
    Not a single person.

4 Don't the wicked understand?
    They destroy my people as if they
      were eating bread.
    They do not ask God for help.
5 The wicked are filled with terror
    where there had been nothing to
      fear.
    God will scatter the bones of your
      enemies.
    You will defeat them,
    because God has rejected them.

6 I pray that victory will come to Israel
    from Mount Zion!
  May God bring them back.
  Then the people of Jacob will
    rejoice,
  and the people of Israel will be glad.

A Prayer for Help

For the director of music. With stringed instruments. A maskil of David when the Ziphites went to Saul and said, "We think David is hiding among our people."

54 God, save me because of who you
    are.
  By your strength show that I am
    innocent.
2 Hear my prayer, God;
  listen to what I say.
3 Strangers turn against me,
  and cruel men want to kill me.
  They do not care about God. *Selah*
4 See, God will help me;
  the Lord will support me.
5 Let my enemies be punished with
    their own evil.
  Destroy them because you are
    loyal to me.
6 I will offer a sacrifice as a special gift
    to you.
  I will thank you, LORD, because you
    are good.
7 You have saved me from all my
    troubles,
  and I have seen my enemies
    defeated.

A Prayer About a False Friend

For the director of music. With stringed instruments. A maskil of David.

55 God, listen to my prayer
  and do not ignore my cry for help.
2 Pay attention to me and answer me.
  I am troubled and upset
3 by what the enemy says
    and how the wicked look at me.
  They bring troubles down on me,
    and in anger they attack me.

4 I am frightened inside;
  the terror of death has attacked
    me.
5 I am scared and shaking,
  and terror grips me.
6 I said, "I wish I had wings like a
    dove.
  Then I would fly away and rest.
7 I would wander far away
  and stay in the desert. *Selah*
8 I would hurry to my place of escape,
  far away from the wind and storm."
9 Lord, destroy and confuse their
    words,
  because I see violence and fighting
    in the city.
10 Day and night they are all around its
    walls,
  and evil and trouble are
    everywhere inside.
11 Destruction is everywhere in the
    city;
  trouble and lying never leave its
    streets.

55:12–14
Friendship
Can friends cause
you pain?

12 It was not an enemy insulting me.
  I could stand that.
  It was not someone who hated me.
  I could hide from him.
13 But it is you, a person like me,
  my companion and good friend.
14 We had a good friendship
  and walked together to God's
    Temple.
15 Let death take away my enemies.
  Let them die while they are still
    young
  because evil lives with them.
16 But I will call to God for help,
  and the LORD will save me.
17 Morning, noon and night I am
    troubled and upset,
  but he will listen to me.
18 Many are against me,
  but he keeps me safe in battle.
19 God who lives for ever
  will hear me and punish them. *Selah*

But they will not change;
    they do not fear God.

20 The one who was my friend attacks his friends
    and breaks his promises.
21 His words are slippery like butter,
    but war is in his heart.
    His words are smoother than oil,
    but they cut like knives.

22 Give your worries to the LORD,
    and he will take care of you.
    He will never let good people down.
23 But, God, you will bring down the wicked to the grave.
    Murderers and liars will live only half a lifetime.

But I will trust in you.

Trusting God for Help

For the director of music. To the tune of "The Dove in the Distant Oak". A miktam of David when the Philistines captured him in Gath.

56 God, be merciful to me because people are chasing me;
    the battle has pressed me all day long.
2 My enemies have chased me all day;
    there are many proud people fighting me.

3 When I am afraid,
    I will trust you.
4 I praise God for his word.
    I trust God, so I am not afraid.
    What can human beings do to me?

5 All day long they twist my words;
    all their evil plans are against me.
6 They wait. They hide.
    They watch my steps,
    hoping to kill me.

7 God, do not let them escape;
    punish the foreign nations in your anger.
8 You have recorded my troubles.
    You have kept a list of my tears.
    Aren't they in your records?

9 On the day I call for help, my enemies will be defeated.
    I know that God is on my side.
10 I praise God for his word to me;
    I praise the LORD for his word.
11 I trust in God. I will not be afraid.
    What can people do to me?

56:11 Trust Why you should not fear.

12 God, I must keep my promises to you.
    I will give you my offerings to thank you,
13 because you have saved me from death.
    You have kept me from being defeated.
    So I will walk with God
    in the light among the living.

A Prayer in Troubled Times

For the director of music. To the tune of "Do Not Destroy". A miktam of David when he escaped from Saul in the cave.

57 Be merciful to me, God; be merciful to me
    because I come to you for protection.
    Let me hide under the shadow of your wings
    until the trouble has passed.

2 I cry out to God Most High,
    to the God who does everything for me.
3 He sends help from heaven and saves me.
    He punishes those who chase me.
        Selah
    God sends me his love and truth.

4 Enemies, like lions, are all around me;
    I must lie down among them.
    Their teeth are like spears and arrows,
    their tongues as sharp as swords.

5 God is supreme over the skies;
    his majesty covers the earth.

6 They set a trap for me.
    I am very worried.

TRUSTING IN GOD
Psalm 56

Trustometer Who can you count on to always stick with you – someone you can trust completely? Imagine having a "trustometer" marked off from 1 to 10. Who would send the pointer up to 10? Is there anyone who wouldn't even move the pointer to 1?

Sometimes it's hard to know who you can trust. And sometimes people we trust let us down. But we can always trust God in everything, no matter what comes up. (Check it out in Psalm 18.)

You can count on certain things to happen. You know everyone will get older, the sun is always in the sky, and God will help those who trust him. (Read 1 Chronicles 5:18–20, p. 525.) God always rates a 10+ on the trustometer!

MORE FAITH links

- Your Total Trust, **p. 229**
- Learning to Trust, **p. 727**
- A Direct Path, **p. 829**
- When Bad Things Happen, **p. 876**
- The Power of *If*, **p. 1344**
- Toss Those Troubles! **p. 1706**

Where would you rate on the trustometer?

Not sure? Some days, we may all do quite well, but other days we probably rate pretty low. We can be sure, though, that God's not like that! Download some of these Faithlinks about trusting God.

From Zero to Hero, Judges 6; 7, p. 319
- Would you stand up to all the toughest kids in school if God said you could, or would you hide in your room for a month?
- Gideon faced a tough situation – and he was scared. But faith in God made him go from zero to hero. Where do you fit in – zero or hero – or somewhere in between?

The Foundation of Our Hope, Isaiah 31:1–8, p. 934
- Some people trust money or power. But those things can disappear overnight. What should your hope be based on? This Faithlink will give you the answer.

Our Good Shepherd, John 10:11–15, p. 1441
- Sheep are pretty helpless by themselves. They trust the shepherd for everything. How are you like a sheep? What do you trust Jesus, the good shepherd, to do for you?

My FAVOURITE links

They dug a pit in my path,
but they fell into it themselves.
Selah

7 My heart is steady, God; my heart is steady.
I will sing and praise you.
8 Wake up, my soul.
Wake up, harp and lyre!
I will wake up the dawn.
9 Lord, I will praise you among the nations;
I will sing songs of praise about you to all the nations.
10 Your great love reaches to the skies,
your truth to the clouds.
11 God, you are supreme above the skies.
Let your glory be over all the earth.

Unfair Judges

For the director of music. To the tune of "Do Not Destroy". A miktam of David.

58 Do you rulers really say what is right?
Do you judge people fairly?
2 No, in your heart you plan evil;
you think up violent crimes in the land.
3 From birth, evil people turn away from God;
they wander off and tell lies as soon as they are born.
4 They are like poisonous snakes,
like deaf cobras that stop up their ears
5 so they cannot hear the music of the snake charmer
no matter how well he plays.

6 God, break the teeth in their mouths!
Tear out the fangs of those lions, Lord!
7 Let them disappear like water that flows away.
Let them be cut short like a broken arrow.
8 Let them be like snails that melt as they move.
Let them be like a child born dead who never saw the sun.
9 His anger will blow them away alive
faster than burning thorns can heat a pot.
10 Good people will be glad when they see him take revenge.
They will wash their feet in the blood of the wicked.
11 Then people will say,
"There really are rewards for doing what is right.
There really is a God who judges the world."

A Prayer for Protection

For the director of music. To the tune of "Do Not Destroy". A miktam of David when Saul sent men to watch David's house to kill him.

59 God, save me from my enemies.
Protect me from those who come against me.
2 Save me from those who do evil
and from murderers.
3 Look, men are waiting to ambush me.
Cruel men attack me,
but I have not sinned or done wrong, Lord.
4 I have done nothing wrong, but they are ready to attack me.
Wake up to help me, and look.
5 You are the Lord God All-powerful, the God of Israel.
Arise and punish those people.
Do not give those traitors any mercy.
Selah
6 They come back at night.
Like dogs they growl and roam round the city.
7 Notice what comes from their mouths.

> From birth, evil people turn away from God; they wander off and tell lies as soon as they are born.
> – Psalm 58:3

Insults come from their lips,
because they say, "Who's listening?"
8 But, LORD, you laugh at them;
you make fun of all of them.
9 God, my strength, I am looking to you,
because God is my defender.
10 My God loves me,
and he goes in front of me.

He will help me defeat my
enemies.
11 Lord, our protector, do not kill them,
or my people will forget.
With your power scatter them and
defeat them.
12 They sin by what they say;
they sin with their words.
They curse and tell lies,
so let their pride trap them.
13 Destroy them in your anger;
destroy them completely!
Then they will know
that God rules over Israel
and to the ends of the earth. *Selah*

14 They come back at night.
Like dogs they growl
and roam round the city.
15 They wander about looking for food,
and they howl if they do not find
enough.
16 But I will sing about your strength.
In the morning I will sing about
your love.
You are my defender,
my place of safety in times of trouble.

17 God, my strength, I will sing praises
to you.
God, my defender, you are the God
who loves me.

A Prayer After a Defeat

For the director of music. To the tune of
"Lily of the Agreement". A miktam
of David. For teaching. When David
fought the Arameans of North West
Mesopotamia and Zobah, and when Joab
returned and defeated 12,000
Edomites at the Valley of Salt.

60 God, you have rejected us and
scattered us.
You have been angry, but please
come back to us.
2 You made the earth shake and crack.
Heal its breaks because it is
shaking.
3 You have given your people trouble.
You made us unable to walk
straight, like people drunk with
wine.

4 You have raised a banner to gather
those who fear you.
Now they can stand up against the
enemy. *Selah*

5 Answer us and save us by your power
so the people you love will be
rescued.
6 God has said from his Temple,
"When I win, I will divide Shechem
and measure off the Valley of
Succoth.
7 Gilead and Manasseh are mine.
Ephraim is like my helmet.
Judah holds my royal sceptre.
8 Moab is like my washbowl.
I throw my sandals at Edom.
I shout at Philistia."

9 Who will bring me to the fortified
city?
Who will lead me to Edom?
10 God, surely you have rejected us;
you do not go out with our armies.
11 Help us fight the enemy.
Human help is useless,
12 but we can win with God's help.
He will defeat our enemies.

A Prayer for Protection

For the director of music. With stringed
instruments. Of David.

61 God, hear my cry;
listen to my prayer.

2 I call to you from the ends of the
earth
when I am afraid.
Carry me away to a high mountain.
3 You have been my protection,
like a strong tower against my
enemies.

4 Let me live in your Holy Tent for ever.
　Let me find safety in the shelter of
　　your wings.　　　　　　　Selah

5 God, you have heard my promises.
　You have given me what belongs to
　　those who fear you.

6 Give the king a long life;
　let him live many years.
7 Let him rule in the
　　presence of God
　　for ever.
　Protect him with
　　your love and
　　truth.

8 Then I will praise
　　your name for
　　ever,
　and every day I will
　　keep my promises.

Trust Only in God

*For the director of music. For Jeduthun.
A psalm of David.*

62 I find rest in God;
　　only he can save me.
2 He is my rock and my salvation.
　He is my defender;
　I will not be defeated.

3 How long will you attack someone?
　Will all of you kill that person?
　Who is like a leaning wall, like a
　　fence ready to fall?
4 They are planning to make that
　　person fall.
　They enjoy telling lies.
　With their mouths they bless,
　　but in their hearts they curse.
　　　　　　　　　　　　Selah

5 I find rest in God alone;
　only he gives me hope.
6 He is my rock and my salvation.
　He is my defender;
　I will not be defeated.
7 My honour and salvation come from
　　God.
　He is my mighty rock and my
　　protection.

8 People, trust God
　　all the time.
　Tell him all
　　your
　　problems,
　　because God
　　is our
　　protection.　　　Selah

62:8 Trust
Who do you trust with your problems?

*You have been my protection.
　– Psalm 61:3*

9 The least of people are only a breath,
　　and even the
　　　greatest are just a
　　　lie.
　On the scales, they
　　weigh nothing;
　　together they are
　　only a breath.
10 Do not trust in force.
　Stealing is of no
　　use.
　Even if you gain more
　　riches,
　don't put your trust in them.

11 God has said this,
　　and I have heard it over and over:
　God is strong.
12 The Lord is loving.
　You reward people for what they
　　have done.

Wishing to be Near God

*A psalm of David when he was
in the Desert of Judah.*

63 God, you are my God.
　　I search for you.
　I thirst for you
　　like someone in a dry, empty land
　　where there is no water.

2 I have seen you in the Temple
　and have seen your strength and
　　glory.
3 Because your love is better than life,
　I will praise you.
4 I will praise you as long as I live.
　I will lift up my hands in prayer to
　　your name.
5 I will be content as if I had eaten the
　　best foods.
　My lips will sing, and my mouth
　　will praise you.

6 I remember you while I'm lying in my bed;
  I think about you through the night.
7 You are my help.
  Because of your protection, I sing.
8 I stay close to you;
  you support me with your right hand.

9 Some people are trying to kill me,
  but they will go down to the grave.
10 They will be killed with swords
  and eaten by wild dogs.
11 But the king will rejoice in his God.
  All who make promises in his name will praise him,
  but the mouths of liars will be shut.

> I remember you while I'm lying in my bed; I think about you through the night.
> – Psalm 63:6

A Prayer Against Enemies

For the director of music.
A psalm of David.

64 God, listen to my complaint.
  I am afraid of my enemies;
  protect my life from them.
2 Hide me from those who plan wicked things,
  from that mob who does evil.
3 They sharpen their tongues like swords
  and shoot bitter words like arrows.
4 From their hiding places they shoot at innocent people;
  they shoot suddenly and are not afraid.
5 They encourage each other to do wrong.
  They talk about setting traps,
  thinking no one will see them.
6 They plan wicked things and say,
  "We have a perfect plan."
  The mind of human beings is hard to understand.

7 But God will shoot them with arrows;
  they will suddenly be struck down.
8 Their own words will be used against them.
  All who see them will shake their heads.
9 Then everyone will fear God.
  They will tell what God has done,
  and they will learn from what he has done.
10 Good people will be happy in the LORD
  and will find protection in him.
  Let everyone who is honest praise the LORD.

A Hymn of Thanksgiving

For the director of music.
A psalm of David. A song.

65 God, you will be praised in Jerusalem.
  We will keep our promises to you.
2 You hear our prayers.
  All people will come to you.
3 Our guilt overwhelms us,
  but you forgive our sins.
4 Happy are the people you choose
  and invite to stay in your court.
  We are filled with good things in your house,
  your holy Temple.

5 You answer us in amazing ways,
  God our Saviour.
  People everywhere on the earth
  and beyond the sea trust you.
6 You made the mountains by your strength;
  you are dressed in power.
7 You stopped the roaring seas,
  the roaring waves,
  and the uproar of the nations.
8 Even those people at the ends of the earth fear your miracles.
  You are praised from where the sun rises to where it sets.
9 You take care of the land and water it;

    you make it very fertile.
  The rivers of God are full of water.
  Grain grows because you make it
      grow.
10 You send rain to the ploughed fields;
  you fill the rows with water.
  You soften the ground with rain,
    and then you bless it with crops.
11 You give the year a good harvest,
    and you load the wagons with
      many crops.
12 The desert is covered with grass
    and the hills with happiness.
13 The pastures are full of flocks,
    and the valleys are covered with
      grain.
    Everything shouts and sings for
      joy.

Praise God for What He Has Done

  *For the director of music.
  A song. A psalm.*

66 Everything on earth, shout with joy to God!
2 Sing about his glory!
  Make his praise glorious!
3 Say to God, "Your
    works are
    amazing!
  Because your
    power is great,
    your enemies fall
    before you.
4 All the earth worships
    you
    and sings praises
      to you.
    They sing praises
      to your name."   *Selah*

5 Come and see what God has done,
    the amazing things he has done for
      people.
6 He turned the sea into dry land.
  The people crossed the river on
    foot.
  So let us rejoice because of what
    he has done.
7 He rules for ever with his power.
  He keeps his eye on the nations,
    so people should not turn against
      him.   *Selah*

8 You people, praise our God;
  loudly sing his praise.
9 He protects our lives
  and does not let us be defeated.
10 God, you have tested us;
  you have purified us like silver.
11 You let us be trapped
  and put a heavy load on us.
12 You let our enemies walk on our
    heads.
  We went through fire and flood,
    but you brought us to a place with
      good things.
13 I will come to your Temple with burnt
    offerings.
  I will give you what I promised,
14   objects I promised to you when
      I was in trouble.
15 I will bring you offerings of fat
    animals,
    and I will offer rams, bulls and
      goats.   *Selah*

16 All of you who fear God, come and
    listen,
    and I will tell you what he has
      done for me.
17 I cried out to him with
    my mouth
    and praised him
    with my
    tongue.
18 If I had known of any
    sin in my heart,
    the Lord would not
    have listened to
    me.
19 But God has listened;
  he has heard my prayer.
20 Praise God,
  who did not ignore my prayer
    or hold back his love from me.

Everyone Should Praise God

  *For the director of music. With stringed
  instruments. A psalm. A song.*

67 God, have mercy on us and bless us
  and show us your kindness   *Selah*

2 so the world will learn your ways,

> And all nations will
> learn that you can
> save.
> – Psalm 67:2

Psalm 67:3 758

LET'S VISIT JERUSALEM   Psalm 68:29

The city of Jerusalem was on top of a hill. That was a great thing for a city in those days because the city guards could see any enemies that might come to attack them. When David was king, one of the first things he did was make Jerusalem the capital of Israel. (Check out 2 Samuel 5:6–10, p. 404; 1 Chronicles 11:4–9, p. 534.) This made Jerusalem the most important city for the people of Israel. It was important to their religion and their politics. When Solomon (David's son) became king, he built an amazing Temple in Jerusalem. (Read 1 Kings 6; 7, p. 442; 2 Chronicles 3; 4, p. 564.) Jerusalem became the most beautiful city in the country.

Later, Jerusalem played an important role in Jesus' life and ministry. Jesus went to Temple in Jerusalem. It was also in Jerusalem that Jesus was crucified and buried, and it was there that God brought him back to life.

Today, Jerusalem is a holy city for three world religions: Christianity, Judaism and Islam.

and all nations will learn that you
  can save.

3 God, the people should praise you;
  all people should praise you.
4 The nations should be glad and sing
  because you judge people fairly.
  You guide all the nations on earth.
                                    Selah

5 God, the people should praise you;
  all people should praise you.

6 The land has given its crops.
  God, our God, blesses us.
7 God blesses us
  so people all over the earth will
    fear him.

Praise God Who Saved the Nation

For the director of music. A psalm
  of David. A song.

68 Let God rise up and scatter his
      enemies;
  let those who hate him run away
    from him.
2 Blow them away as smoke
    is driven away by the wind.
  As wax melts before a fire,
    let the wicked be destroyed before
      God.
3 But those who do right should be
    glad
  and should rejoice before God;
    they should be happy and glad.

4 Sing to God; sing praises to his
    name.
  Prepare the way for him
    who rides
      through the
        desert,
  whose name is
    the LORD.
  Rejoice before
    him.
5 God is in his holy Temple.
  He is a father to orphans,
  and he defends the widows.

68:5
Caring
Check out if God cares for needy people.

6 God gives the lonely a home.
 He leads prisoners out with joy,
 but those who turn against God
  will live in a dry land.
7 God, you led your people out
  when you marched through the
  desert. *Selah*
8 The ground shook
  and the sky poured down rain
  before God, the God of Mount Sinai,
  before God, the God of Israel.
9 God, you sent much rain;
  you refreshed your tired land.
10 Your people settled there.
  God, in your goodness
  you took care of the poor.

11 The Lord gave the command,
  and a great army told the news:
12 "Kings and their armies run away.
  In camp they divide the wealth
  taken in war.
13 Those who stayed by the campfires
  will share the riches taken in
  battle."
14 The Almighty scattered kings
  like snow on Mount Zalmon.

15 The mountains of Bashan are high;
  the mountains of Bashan have
  many peaks.
16 Why do you mountains with many
  peaks look with envy
  on the mountain that God chose for
  his home?
  The LORD will live there for ever.
17 God comes with millions of chariots;
  the Lord comes from Mount Sinai
  to his holy place.
18 When you went up to the heights,
  you led a parade of captives.
  You received gifts from the
  people,
  even from those who turned against
  you.
  And the LORD God will live there.

19 Praise the Lord, God our Saviour,
  who helps us every day. *Selah*
20 Our God is a God who saves us;
  the LORD God saves us from
  death.

21 God will crush his enemies' heads,
  the hairy skulls of those who
  continue to sin.
22 The Lord said, "I will bring the
  enemy back from Bashan;
  I will bring them back from the
  depths of the sea.
23 Then you can stick your feet in their
  blood,
  and your dogs can lick their
  share."

24 God, people have seen your victory
  march;
  God my King marched into the
  holy place.
25 The singers are in front and the
  instruments are behind.
  In the middle are the girls with the
  tambourines.
26 Praise God in the meeting place;
  praise the LORD in the gathering of
  Israel.
27 There is the smallest tribe, Benjamin,
  leading them.
  And there are the leaders of Judah
  with their group.
  There also are the leaders of
  Zebulun and of Naphtali.

28 God, order up your power;
  show the mighty power you have
  used for us before.
29 Kings will bring their wealth to you,
  to your Temple in Jerusalem.
30 Punish Egypt, the beast in the tall
  grass along the river.
  Punish the leaders of nations,
  those bulls among the cows.
  Defeated, they will bring you their
  silver.
  Scatter those nations that love war.
31 Messengers will come from Egypt;
  the people of Cush will pray to
  God.

32 Kingdoms of the earth, sing to God;
  sing praises to the Lord. *Selah*
33 Sing to the one who rides through
  the skies, which are from long
  ago.
  He speaks with a thundering voice.
34 Announce that God is powerful.

He rules over Israel,
and his power is in the skies.
35 God, you are wonderful in your
Temple.
The God of Israel gives his people
strength and power.

Praise God!

A Cry for Help

For the director of music. To the tune of "Lilies". A psalm of David.

69 God, save me,
because the water has risen to my neck.
2 I'm sinking down into the mud,
and there is nothing to stand on.
I am in deep water,
and the flood covers me.
3 I am tired from calling for help;
my throat is sore.
My eyes are tired from waiting
for God to help me.
4 There are more people who hate me
for no reason than hairs on my head;
powerful enemies want to destroy
me for no reason.
They make me pay back
what I did not steal.

5 God, you know what I have done wrong;
I cannot hide my guilt from you.
6 Lord GOD All-powerful,
do not let those who hope in you
be ashamed because of me.
God of Israel,
do not let your worshippers be
disgraced because of me.
7 For you, I carry this shame,
and my face is covered with disgrace.
8 I am like a stranger to my closest relatives
and a foreigner to my mother's children.
9 My strong love for your Temple
completely controls me.
When people insult you, it hurts me.
10 When I cry and go without food,
they make fun of me.
11 When I wear clothes of sadness,
they joke about me.
12 They make fun of me in public places,
and the drunkards make up songs about me.

FAITH links

IN DEEP WATER
PSALM 69

If you've ever been in an ocean or in the deep end of a swimming pool, you know what water up to the neck feels like. Conflicts in life can make you feel like you're in deep water, or even mud. David wrote psalms like this one to express his feelings of distress. These psalms were prayers to God for help to handle the conflicts in his life.

You can't go through life without having some conflict. But you can follow David's example and rely on God. He offers wisdom and other tools to help you handle the conflicts in life.

More Powerful Than Revenge, Genesis 50:14–21, p. 71

Approaching God, Numbers 3:10, p. 180

Real Faith or Really Scared? Judges 4, p. 315

Learning to Trust, Psalm 25:4–5, p. 727

Sad Times, Matthew 14:13–14, p. 1299

How Do You Grow? Titus 1:1, p. 1659

13 But I pray to you, LORD, for favour.
   God, because of your great love,
      answer me.
   You are truly able to save.
14 Pull me from the mud,
      and do not let me sink.
   Save me from those who hate me
      and from the deep water.
15 Do not let the flood drown me
      or the deep water swallow me
      or the grave close its mouth over
         me.
16 LORD, answer me because your love
      is so good.
   Because of your great kindness,
      turn to me.
17 Do not hide from me, your servant.
   I am in trouble. Hurry to help me!
18 Come near and save me;
      rescue me from my enemies.
19 You see my shame and disgrace.
   You know all
      my enemies
      and what
      they have
      said.
20 Insults have
      broken my
      heart
   and left me weak.
   I looked for sympathy, but there was
      none;
   I found no one to comfort me.
21 They put poison in my food
      and gave me vinegar to drink.

22 Let their own feasts cause their ruin;
   let their feasts trap them and pay
      them back.
23 Let their eyes be closed so they
      cannot see
   and their backs be for ever weak
      from troubles.
24 Pour your anger out on them;
      let your anger catch up with them.
25 May their place be empty;
      leave no one to live in their tents.
26 They chase after those you have
      hurt,
   and they talk about the pain of
      those you have wounded.
27 Charge them with crime after crime,
   and do not let them have anything
      good.
28 Wipe their names from the book of
      life,
   and do not list them with those
      who do what is right.
29 I am sad and hurting.
   God, save me and protect me.
30 I will praise God in a song
   and will honour him by giving
      thanks.
31 That will please the LORD more than
      offering him cattle,
   more than sacrificing a bull with
      horns and hoofs.
32 Poor people will see this and be glad.
   Be encouraged, you who worship
      God.
33 The LORD listens to those in need
   and does not look down on
      captives.
34 Heaven and earth should praise him,
      the seas and everything in them.
35 God will save Jerusalem
      and rebuild the cities of Judah.
   Then people will live there and own
      the land.
36 The descendants of his servants will
      inherit that land,
   and those who love him will live
      there.

A Cry for God to Help Quickly

*For the director of music.
A psalm of David. To help
people remember.*

70 God, come quickly and save me.
   LORD, hurry to help me.
2 Let those who are trying to kill me
      be ashamed and disgraced.
   Let those who want to hurt me
      run away in disgrace.
3 Let those who make fun of me
      stop because of their shame.
4 But let all those who worship you
      rejoice and be glad.
   Let those who love your salvation
      always say, "Praise the greatness
      of God."

5 I am poor and helpless;
  God, hurry to me.
  You help me and save me.
  LORD, do not wait.

An Old Person's Prayer

71 In you, LORD, is my protection.
  Never let me be ashamed.
2 Because you do what is right, save and rescue me;
  listen to me and save me.
3 Be my place of safety
  where I can always come.
  Give the command to save me,
  because you are my rock and my fortified city.
4 My God, save me from the power of the wicked
  and from the hold of evil and cruel people.

5 LORD, you are my hope.
  LORD, I have trusted you since I was young.
6 I have depended on you since I was born;
  you helped me even on the day of my birth.
  I will always praise you.

7 I am an example to many people,
  because you are my strong protection.
8 I am always praising you;
  all day long I honour you.

9 Do not reject me when I am old;
  do not leave me when my strength is gone.
10 My enemies make plans against me,
  and they meet together to kill me.
11 They say, "God has left him.
  Go after him and take him,
  because no one will save him."
12 God, don't be far off.
  My God, hurry to help me.
13 Let those who accuse me
  be ashamed and destroyed.
  Let those who are trying to hurt me
  be covered with shame and disgrace.

14 But I will always have hope
  and will praise you more and more.
15 I will tell how you do what is right.
  I will tell about your salvation all day long,
  even though it is more than I can tell.
16 I will come and tell about your powerful works, Lord GOD.
  I will remind people that only you do what is right.
17 God, you have taught me since I was young.
  To this day I tell about the miracles you do.
18 Even though I am old and grey,
  do not leave me, God.
  I will tell the children about your power;
  I will tell those who live after me about your might.

19 God, your justice reaches to the skies.
  You have done great things;
  God, there is no one like you.
20 You have given me many troubles and bad times,
  but you will give me life again.
  When I am almost dead,
  you will keep me alive.
21 You will make me greater than ever,
  and you will comfort me again.

22 I will praise you with the harp.
  I trust you, my God.
  I will sing to you with the lyre,
  Holy One of Israel.
23 I will shout for joy when I sing praises to you.
  You have saved me.
24 I will tell about your justice all day long.
  And those who want to hurt me
  will be ashamed and disgraced.

> God, your justice reaches to the skies. You have done great things; God, there is no one like you.
> — Psalm 71:19

A Prayer for the King

Of Solomon.

72 God, give the king your good judgement
and the king's son your goodness.
2 Help him judge your people fairly
and decide what is right for the poor.
3 Let there be peace on the mountains
and goodness on the hills for the people.
4 Help him be fair to the poor
and save the needy
and punish those who hurt them.

5 May they respect you as long as the sun shines
and as long as the moon glows.
6 Let him be like rain on the grass,
like showers that water the earth.
7 Let goodness be plentiful while he lives.
Let peace continue as long as there is a moon.

8 Let his kingdom go from sea to sea,
and from the Euphrates River to the ends of the earth.
9 Let the people of the desert bow down to him,
and make his enemies lick the dust.
10 Let the kings of Tarshish and the faraway lands
bring him gifts.
Let the kings of Sheba and Seba
bring their presents to him.
11 Let all kings bow down to him
and all nations serve him.

12 He will help the poor when they cry out
and will save the needy when no one else will help.
13 He will be kind to the weak and poor,
and he will save their lives.
14 He will save them from cruel people
who try to hurt them,
because their lives are precious to him.

15 Long live the king!
Let him receive gold from Sheba.
Let people always pray for him
and bless him all day long.
16 Let the fields grow plenty of grain
and the hills be covered with crops.
Let the land be as fertile as Lebanon,
and let the cities grow like the grass in a field.
17 Let the king be famous for ever;
let him be remembered as long as the sun shines.

Let the nations be blessed because of him,
and may they all bless him.

18 Praise the LORD God, the God of Israel,
who alone does such miracles.
19 Praise his glorious name for ever.
Let his glory fill the whole world.
Amen and amen.
20 This ends the prayers of David son of Jesse.

Book 3

Should the Wicked Be Rich?

A psalm of Asaph.

73 God is truly good to Israel,
to those who have pure hearts.

2 But I had almost stopped believing;
I had almost lost my faith
3 because I was jealous of proud people.
I saw wicked people doing well.

4 They are not suffering;
they are healthy and strong.
5 They don't have troubles like the rest of us;
they don't have problems like other people.
6 They wear pride like a necklace
and put on violence as their clothing.
7 They are looking for profits
and do not control their selfish desires.
8 They make fun of others and speak evil;

proudly they speak of hurting
    others.
9 They boast to the sky.
    They say that they own the earth.
10 So their people turn to them
    and give them whatever they want.
11 They say, "How can God know?
    What does God Most High know?"

12 These people are wicked,
    always at ease and getting richer.
13 So why have I kept my heart pure?
    Why have I kept my hands from
    doing wrong?
14 I have suffered all day long;
    I have been punished every
    morning.

15 God, if I had decided to talk like this,
    I would have let your people down.
16 I tried to understand all this,
    but it was too hard for me to see
17 until I went to the Temple of God.
    Then I understood what will
    happen to them.

18 You have put them in danger;
    you cause them to be destroyed.
19 They are destroyed in a moment;
    they are swept away by terrors.
20 It will be like waking from a dream.
    Lord, when you rise up, they will
    disappear.

21 When my heart was sad
    and I was angry,
22 I was senseless and stupid.
    I acted like an animal towards you.

23 But I am always with you;
    you have held my hand.
24 You guide me with your advice,
    and later you will receive me in honour.
25 I have no one in heaven but you;
    I want nothing on earth besides you.
26 My body and my mind may become
    weak,
    but God is my strength.
    He is mine for ever.

73:24–26 Protection
Who is your strength?

27 Those who are far from God will die;
    you destroy those who are
    unfaithful.
28 But I am close to God, and that is good.
    The Lord GOD is my protection.
    I will tell all that you have done.

A Nation in Trouble Prays

A maskil of Asaph.

74 God, why have you rejected us for
    so long?
    Why are you angry with us, the
    sheep of your pasture?
2 Remember the people you bought
    long ago.
    You saved us, and we are your very
    own.
    After all, you live on Mount Zion.
3 Make your way through these old
    ruins;
    the enemy wrecked everything in
    the Temple.

4 Those who were against you shouted
    in your meeting place
    and raised their flags there.
5 They came with axes raised
    as if to cut down a forest of trees.
6 They smashed the carved panels
    with their axes and hatchets.
7 They burned your Temple to the
    ground;
    they have made the place where
    you live unclean.
8 They thought, "We will completely
    crush them!"
    They burned every place where
    God was worshipped in the land.
9 We do not see any signs.
    There are no more prophets,
    and no one knows how long this
    will last.

10 God, how much longer will the
    enemy make fun of you?
    Will they insult you for ever?
11 Why do you hold back your power?
    Bring your power out in the open
    and destroy them!

12 God, you have been our king for a
    long time.
    You bring salvation to the earth.

13 You split open the sea by your power
 and broke the heads of the sea
 monster.
14 You smashed the heads of the
 monster Leviathan
 and gave him to the desert
 creatures as food.
15 You opened up the springs and
 streams
 and made the flowing rivers run
 dry.
16 Both the day and the night are yours;
 you made the sun and the moon.
17 You set all the limits on the earth;
 you created summer and winter.

18 LORD, remember how
 the enemy
 insulted you.
 Remember how
 those foolish
 people made fun
 of you.
19 Do not give us, your
 doves, to those
 wild animals.
 Never forget your
 poor people.
20 Remember the agreement you made
 with us,
 because violence fills every dark
 corner of this land.
21 Do not let your suffering people be
 disgraced.
 Let the poor and helpless praise you.

22 God, arise and defend yourself.
 Remember the insults that come
 from those foolish people all day
 long.
23 Don't forget what your enemies said;
 don't forget their roar as they rise
 against you always.

God the Judge

For the director of music. To the tune
of "Do Not Destroy". A psalm
of Asaph. A song.

75 God, we thank you;
 we thank you because you are
 near.
 We tell about the miracles you do.

2 You say, "I set the time for trial,
 and I will judge fairly.
3 The earth with all its people may
 shake,
 but I am the one who holds it
 steady. *Selah*
4 I say to those who are proud, 'Don't
 boast,'
 and to the wicked, 'Don't show
 your power.
5 Don't try to use your power against
 heaven.
 Don't be stubborn.'"

6 No one from the east or the west
 or the desert can
 judge you.
7 God is the judge;
 he judges one
 person as guilty
 and another as
 innocent.
8 The LORD holds a cup
 of anger in his
 hand;
 it is full of wine
 mixed with
 spices.
 He pours it out even to the last drop,
 and the wicked drink it all.

9 I will tell about this for ever;
 I will sing praise to the God of
 Jacob.
10 He will take all power away from the
 wicked,
 but the power of the good people
 will grow.

The God Who Always Wins

For the director of music.
With stringed instruments.
A psalm of Asaph. A song.

76 People in Judah know God;
 his fame is great in Israel.
2 His Tent is in Jerusalem;
 his home is on Mount Zion.
3 There God broke the flaming arrows,
 the shields, the swords and the
 weapons of war. *Selah*

4 God, how wonderful you are!

> You set all the limits
> on the earth; you
> created summer and
> winter.
> – Psalm 74:17

You are more wonderful than the
   hills full of animals.
5 The brave soldiers were stripped
      as they lay asleep in death.
   Not one warrior
      had the strength to stop it.
6 God of Jacob, when you spoke
      strongly,
   horses and riders fell dead.
7 You are feared;
   no one can stand
      against you when
      you are angry.
8 From heaven you gave
      the decision,
   and the earth was
      afraid and silent.
9 God, you stood up to
      judge
   and to save the
      needy people of
      the earth. *Selah*
10 People praise you for your anger
      against evil.
   Those who live through your anger
      are stopped from doing more
      evil.
11 Make and keep your promises to the
      LORD your God.
   From all around, gifts should come
      to the God we worship.
12 God breaks the spirits of great
      leaders;
   the kings on earth fear him.

Remembering God's Help

*For the director of music. For Jeduthun.
A psalm of Asaph.*

77 I cry out to God;
      I call to God, and he will hear me.
2 I look for the Lord on the day of
      trouble.
   All night long I reach out my hands,
      but I cannot be comforted.

3 When I remember you God, I become
      upset;
   when I think, I become afraid. *Selah*

4 You keep my eyes from closing.
   I am too upset to say anything.

5 I keep thinking about the old days,
   the years of long ago.
6 At night I remember my songs.
   I think and I ask myself:

7 "Will the Lord reject us for ever?
   Will he never be kind to us again?
8 Is his love gone for ever?
   Has he stopped speaking for all
      time?
9 Has God forgotten
      mercy?
   Is he too angry to
      pity us?" *Selah*

10 Then I say, "This is
      what makes me
      sad:
   for years the power
      of God Most High
      was with us."

11 I remember what the LORD did;
   I remember the miracles you did
      long ago.
12 I think about all the things you did
   and consider your deeds.

13 God, your ways are holy.
   No god is as great as our God.
14 You are the God who does miracles;
   you have shown people your power.
15 By your great power you have saved
      your people,
   the descendants of Jacob and
      Joseph. *Selah*

16 God, the waters saw you;
      they saw you and became afraid;
   the deep waters shook with fear.
17 The clouds poured down their rain.
   The sky thundered.
   Your lightning flashed back and
      forth like arrows.
18 Your thunder could be heard in the
      whirlwind.
   Lightning lit up the world.
   The earth trembled and shook.
19 You made a way through the sea
      and paths through the deep waters,
   but your footprints were not seen.
20 You led your people like a flock
   by using Moses and Aaron.

> Make and keep your promises to the LORD your God.
> – Psalm 76:11

God Saved Israel from Egypt

A maskil of Asaph.

78 My people, listen to my teaching;
listen to what I say.
2 I will speak using stories;
I will tell secret things from long ago.
3 We have heard them and known them
by what our ancestors have told us.
4 We will not keep them from our children;
we will tell those who come later
about the praises of the LORD.
We will tell about his power
and the miracles he has done.
5 The LORD made an agreement with Jacob
and gave the Teachings to Israel,
which he commanded our ancestors
to teach to their children.
6 Then their children would know them,
even their children not yet born.
And they would tell their children.
7 So they would all trust God
and would not forget what he had done

ASK AND YOU SHALL RECEIVE

Do you ever think about why prayer is such a cool thing? Here's someone who has some questions about prayer. Let's welcome Michael, aged 9, to Connect 2-You.

Michael

I don't understand prayer. I always hear people in church talk about how God answered their prayers. But when I ask God for the things that I want, I never get them. Does that mean he's not listening to me – or that he doesn't like me?

It sounds as though Michael's getting prayer mixed up with his Christmas list! It's much, much more than that. Prayer gives us the chance to talk personally with the Creator of the universe. We can thank God for the things he does for us every day. We can ask him to forgive us for the bad things we've done. We can ask him to guide our lives. He will listen to everything we say and then answer us. He may say "Yes", he may say "No", or he may say, "Not yet" – but he hears and will answer every prayer. For tips on talking to God, check out the Livin' It page on prayer, Psalm 86:1-7, p. 775.

Remember, prayer is a two-way conversation. You talk to God and then let him talk to you. He may speak through a Bible verse or through some events in your life, but he will speak. And if you keep your eyes and ears open, you'll know when he does.

but would obey his commands.
8 They would not be like their ancestors
who were stubborn and disobedient.
Their hearts were not loyal to God,
and they were not true to him.

9 The men of Ephraim had bows for weapons,
but they ran away on the day of battle.
10 They didn't keep their agreement with God
and refused to live by his teachings.
11 They forgot what he had done
and the miracles he had shown them.
12 He did miracles while their ancestors watched,
in the fields of Zoan in Egypt.
13 He divided the Red Sea and led them through.
He made the water stand up like a wall.
14 He led them with a cloud by day
and by the light of a fire by night.
15 He split the rocks in the desert
and gave them more than enough water, as if from the deep ocean.
16 He brought streams out of the rock
and caused water to flow down like rivers.

17 But the people continued to sin against him;
in the desert they turned against God Most High.
18 They decided to test God
by asking for the food they wanted.
19 Then they spoke against God,
saying, "Can God prepare food in the desert?
20 When he hit the rock, water poured out
and rivers flowed down.
But can he give us bread also?
Will he provide his people with meat?"
21 When the Lord heard them, he was very angry.
His anger was like fire to the people of Jacob;
his anger grew against the people of Israel.
22 They had not believed God
and had not trusted him to save them.
23 But he gave a command to the clouds above
and opened the doors of heaven.
24 He rained manna down on them to eat;
he gave them grain from heaven.
25 So they ate the bread of angels.
He sent them all the food they could eat.
26 He sent the east wind from heaven
and led the south wind by his power.
27 He rained meat on them like dust.
The birds were as many as the sand of the sea.
28 He made the birds fall inside the camp,
all around the tents.
29 So the people ate and became very full.
God had given them what they wanted.
30 While they were still eating,
and while the food was still in their mouths,
31 God became angry with them.
He killed some of the healthiest of them;
he struck down the best young men of Israel.

32 But they kept on sinning;
they did not believe even with the miracles.
33 So he ended their days without meaning
and their years in terror.
34 Any time he killed them, they would look to him for help;
they would come back to God and follow him.
35 They would remember that God was their Rock,
that God Most High had saved them.
36 But their words were false,

and their tongues lied to him.
37 Their hearts were not really loyal to God;
they did not keep his agreement.
38 Still God was merciful.
He forgave their sins
and did not destroy them.
Many times he held back his anger
and did not stir up all his anger.
39 He remembered that they were only human,
like a wind that blows and does not come back.

40 They turned against God so often in the desert
and made him very sad there.
41 Again and again they tested God
and brought pain to the Holy One of Israel.
42 They did not remember his power
or the time he saved them from the enemy.
43 They forgot the signs he did in Egypt
and his wonders in the fields of Zoan.
44 He turned their rivers to blood
so no one could drink the water.
45 He sent flies that bit the people.
He sent frogs that destroyed them.
46 He gave their crops to grasshoppers
and what they worked for to locusts.
47 He destroyed their vines with hail
and their sycamore trees with sleet.
48 He killed their animals with hail
and their cattle with lightning.
49 He showed them his hot anger.
He sent his strong anger against them,
his destroying angels.
50 He found a way to show his anger.
He did not keep them from dying
but let them die by a terrible disease.
51 God killed all the firstborn sons in Egypt,
the oldest son of each family of Ham."
52 But God led his people out like sheep
and he guided them like a flock through the desert.

53 He led them to safety so they had nothing to fear,
but their enemies drowned in the sea.
54 So God brought them to his holy land,
to the mountain country he took with his own power.
55 He forced out the other nations,
and he had his people inherit the land.
He let the tribes of Israel settle there in tents.

56 But they tested God
and turned against God Most High;
they did not keep his rules.
57 They turned away and were disloyal just like their ancestors.
They were like a crooked bow that does not shoot straight.
58 They made God angry by building places to worship gods;
they made him jealous with their idols.
59 When God heard them, he became very angry
and rejected the people of Israel completely.
60 He left his dwelling at Shiloh,
the Tent where he lived among the people.
61 He let the Ark, his power, be captured;
he let the Ark, his glory, be taken by enemies.
62 He let his people be killed;
he was very angry with his children.
63 The young men died by fire,
and the young women had no one to marry.
64 Their priests fell by the sword,
but their widows were not allowed to cry.
65 Then the Lord got up as if he had been asleep;

78:51 Ham The people in Egypt were descendants of Ham, one of Noah's sons. See Genesis 10:6.

he awoke like a man who had been drunk with wine.
66 He struck down his enemies
and disgraced them for ever.
67 But God rejected the family of Joseph;
he did not choose the tribe of Ephraim.
68 Instead, he chose the tribe of Judah
and Mount Zion, which he loves.
69 And he built his Temple high like the mountains.
Like the earth, he built it to last for ever.
70 He chose David to be his servant
and took him from the sheep pens.
71 He brought him from tending the sheep
so he could lead the flock, the people of Jacob,
his own people, the people of Israel.
72 And David led them with an innocent heart
and guided them with skilful hands.

78:72 Leaderships
Is it important for leaders to have integrity?

The Nation Cries for Jerusalem

A psalm of Asaph.

79 God, nations have come against your chosen people.
They have ruined your holy Temple.
They have turned Jerusalem into ruins.
2 They have given the bodies of your servants as food to the wild birds.
They have given the bodies of those who worship you to the wild animals.
3 They have spilled blood like water all around Jerusalem.
No one was left to bury the dead.
4 We are a joke to the other nations;
they laugh and make fun of us.
5 LORD, how long will this last?
Will you be angry for ever?
How long will your jealousy burn like a fire?
6 Be angry with the nations that do not know you
and with the kingdoms that do not honour you.
7 They have destroyed the people of Jacob
and destroyed their land.
8 Don't punish us for our past sins.
Show your mercy to us soon,
because we are helpless!
9 God our Saviour, help us
so people will praise you.
Save us and forgive our sins
so people will honour you.
10 Why should the nations say,
"Where is their God?"
Tell the other nations in our presence
that you punish those who kill your servants.
11 Hear the moans of the prisoners.
Use your great power
to save those sentenced to die.
12 Repay those around us seven times over
for their insults to you, Lord.
13 We are your people, the sheep of your flock.
We will thank you always;
for ever and ever we will praise you.

A Prayer to Bring Israel Back

*For the director of music. To the tune of "Lilies of the Agreement".
A psalm of Asaph.*

80 Shepherd of Israel, listen to us.
You lead the people of Joseph like a flock.
You sit on your throne between the gold creatures with wings.
Show your greatness 2 to the people of Ephraim, Benjamin and Manasseh.
Use your strength,
and come to save us.

3 God, take us back.
Show us your kindness so we can be saved.

4 LORD God All-powerful,
    how long will you be angry
    at the prayers of your people?
5 You have fed your people with tears;
    you have made them drink many
        tears.
6 You made those around us fight over
        us,
    and our enemies make fun of us.

7 God All-powerful, take us back.
    Show us your kindness so we can
        be saved.

8 You brought us out of Egypt as if we
        were a vine.
    You forced out other nations and
        planted us in the land.
9 You cleared the ground for us.
    Like a vine, we took root and filled
        the land.
10 We covered the mountains with our
        shade.
    We had limbs like the mighty cedar
        tree.
11 Our branches reached the
        Mediterranean Sea,
    and our shoots went to the
        Euphrates River.

12 So why did you pull down our walls?
    Now everyone who passes by
        steals from us.
13 Like wild pigs they walk over us;
    like wild animals they feed on us.

14 God All-powerful, come back.
    Look down from heaven and see.
    Take care of us, your vine.
15   You planted this shoot with your
        own hands
    and strengthened this child.

16 Now it is cut down and burned with
        fire;
    you destroyed us by your angry
        looks.
17 With your hand,
    strengthen the one you have
        chosen for yourself.
18 Then we will not turn away from you.
    Give us life again, and we will call
        to you for help.

19 LORD God All-powerful, take us back.
    Show us your kindness so we can
        be saved.

A Song for a Holiday

*For the director of music. By the gittith.
A psalm of Asaph.*

81 Sing for joy to God, our strength;
    shout out loud to the God of
        Jacob.
2 Begin the music. Play the
        tambourines.
    Play pleasant
        music on
        the harps
        and lyres.
3 Blow the trumpet
    at the time of the New Moon,
    when the moon is full, when our
        feast begins.
4 This is the law for Israel;
    it is the command of the God of
        Jacob.
5 He gave this rule to the people of
        Joseph
    when they went out of the land of
        Egypt.

81:1–5
Music
How is music useful?

I heard a language I did not know,
        saying:
6 "I took the load off their shoulders;
    I let them put down their baskets.
7 When you were in trouble, you called,
        and I saved you.
    I answered you with thunder.
    I tested you at the waters of
        Meribah.   *Selah*
8 My people, listen. I am warning you.
    Israel, please listen to me!
9 You must not have foreign gods;
    you must not worship any false
        god.
10 I, the LORD, am your God,
    who brought you out of Egypt.
    Open your mouth and I will feed
        you.

11 "But my people did not listen to me;
    Israel did not want me.
12 So I let them go their stubborn way
    and follow their own advice.

> Psalm 81:13

FAITH CHALLENGE

Read 81:8-9 to find out the serious warning the writer had for his fellow Israelites. Let's say a false god is anything that has a higher priority in your life than God. How can you keep false gods out of your life?

TESTING IT

Psalm 81:8-9
My people, listen. I am warning you. Israel, please listen to me! You must not have foreign gods; you must not worship any false god.

13 "I wish my people would listen to me;
   I wish Israel would live my way.
14 Then I would quickly defeat their enemies
   and turn my hand against their foes.
15 Those who hate the LORD would bow before him.
   Their punishment would continue for ever.
16 But I would give you the finest wheat
   and fill you with honey from the rocks."

A Cry for Justice

A psalm of Asaph.

82 God is in charge of the great meeting;
   he judges among the "gods".
2 He says, "How long will you defend evil people?
   How long will you show greater kindness to the wicked?" *Selah*
3 Defend the weak and the orphans;
   defend the rights of the poor and suffering.
4 Save the weak and helpless;
   free them from the power of the wicked.

EMAIL FROM GOD
82:3-4
Protection
Protect the helpless!

5 "You know nothing. You don't understand.
   You walk in the dark,
   while the world is falling apart.

6 "I said, 'You are "gods".
   You are all sons of God Most High.'
7 But you will die like any other person;
   you will fall like all the leaders."

8 God, come and judge the earth,
   because you own all the nations.

A Prayer Against the Enemies

A song. A psalm of Asaph.

83 God, do not keep quiet;
   God, do not be silent or still.
2 Your enemies are making noises;
   those who hate you are getting ready to attack.
3 They are making secret plans against your people;
   they plot against those you love.
4 They say, "Come, let's destroy them as a nation.
   Then no one will ever remember the name 'Israel'."

5 They are united in their plan.
   These have made an agreement against you:

6 the families of Edom and the
    Ishmaelites,
  Moab and the Hagrites,
7 the people of Byblos, Ammon, Amalek,
    Philistia and Tyre.
8 Even Assyria has joined them
    to help Ammon and Moab, the
    descendants of Lot.   *Selah*

9 God, do to them what you did to
    Midian,
  what you did to Sisera and Jabin at
    the Kishon River.
10 They died at Endor,
  and their bodies rotted on the
    ground.
11 Do to their important leaders what
    you did to Oreb and Zeeb.
  Do to their princes
    what you did to
    Zebah and
    Zalmunna.
12 They said, "Let's take
    for ourselves
    the pasturelands that
    belong to God."

13 My God, make them
    like tumbleweed,
    like chaff blown
    away by the wind.
14 Be like a fire that burns a forest
  or like flames that blaze through
    the hills.
15 Chase them with your storm,
  and frighten them with your wind.
16 Cover them with shame.
  Then people will look for you, LORD.

17 Make them afraid and ashamed for
    ever.
  Disgrace them and destroy them.
18 Then they will know that you are the
    LORD,
  that only you are God Most High
    over all the earth.

Wishing to Be in the Temple

For the director of music. On the gittith.
A psalm of the sons of Korah.

84 LORD All-powerful,
   how lovely is your Temple!

2 I want more than anything
    to be in the courtyards of the
    LORD's Temple.
  My whole being wants
    to be with the living God.

3 The sparrows have found a home,
    and the swallows have nests.
  They raise their young near your
    altars,
    LORD All-powerful, my King and
    my God.
4 Happy are the people who live at your
    Temple;
  they are always praising you.   *Selah*

5 Happy are those whose strength
    comes from you,
  who want to travel to
    Jerusalem.
6 As they pass through
    the Valley of
    Baca,
  they make it like a
    spring.
  The autumn rains
    fill it with pools
    of water.
7 The people get
    stronger as they
    go,
  and everyone meets with God in
    Jerusalem.

8 LORD God All-powerful, hear my
    prayer;
  God of Jacob, listen to me.   *Selah*
9 God, look at our shield;
  be kind to your appointed king.

10 One day in the courtyards of your
    Temple is better
  than a thousand days anywhere else.
  I would rather be a doorkeeper in the
    Temple of my God
  than live in the homes of the
    wicked.
11 The LORD God is like a sun and shield;
    the LORD gives us kindness and
    honour.
  He does not hold back anything good
    from those whose lives are
    innocent.

> One day in the courtyards of your Temple is better than a thousand days anywhere else.
> – Psalm 84:10

Psalm 84:12

12 LORD All-powerful,
   happy are the people who trust
      you!

A Prayer for the Nation

For the director of music.
A psalm of the sons of Korah.

85 LORD, you have been kind to your
      land;
   you brought back the people of
      Jacob.
2 You forgave the guilt of the people
   and covered all their sins. *Selah*
3 You stopped all your anger;
   you turned back from your strong
      anger.

4 God our Saviour, bring us back again.
   Stop being angry
      with us.
5 Will you be angry with
      us for ever?
   Will you stay angry
      from now on?
6 Won't you give us life
      again?
   Your people would
      rejoice in you.
7 LORD, show us your
      love,
   and save us.

8 I will listen to God the LORD.
   He has ordered peace for those
      who worship him.
   Don't let them go back to
      foolishness.
9 God will soon save those who respect
      him,
   and his glory will be seen in our
      land.

10 Love and truth belong to God's
      people;
   goodness and peace will be theirs.
11 On earth people will be loyal to God,
   and God's goodness will shine
      down from heaven.
12 The LORD will give his goodness,
   and the land will give its crops.
13 Goodness will go before God
   and prepare the way for him.

A Cry for Help

A prayer of David.

86 LORD, listen to me and answer
      me.
   I am poor and helpless.
2 Protect me, because I worship you.
   My God, save me, your servant
      who trusts in you.
3 Lord, have mercy on me,
   because I have called to you all day.
4 Give happiness to
      me, your
      servant,
   because I give
      my life to
      you, Lord.

5 Lord, you are kind and forgiving
   and have great love
      for those who call
         to you.
6 LORD, hear my prayer,
   and listen when I ask
      for mercy.
7 I call to you in times
      of trouble,
   because you will
      answer me.

8 Lord, there is no god
      like you
   and no works like yours.
9 Lord, all the nations you have made
   will come and worship you.
   They will honour you.
10 You are great and you do miracles.
   Only you are God.

11 LORD, teach me what you want me to do,
   and I will live by your truth.
   Teach me to respect you completely.
12 Lord, my God, I will praise you with
      all my heart,
   and I will honour your name for
      ever.
13 You have great
      love for me.
   You have
      saved me
      from death.
14 God, proud men
   are attacking me;

> Goodness will go before God and prepare the way for him.
> — Psalm 85:13

Psalm 86 775

PRAYER
Psalm 86:1–7

No Answering Machine How do you feel when you really want to talk to someone or ask him or her a question and all you get is an answering machine, or an engaged tone, or someone telling you to "call back later"? It's *really* annoying, isn't it?

God always hears our prayers – no answering machines and no engaged tones. God doesn't always answer prayers immediately, but he *will* answer. (Read Psalm 28:6, p. 730.) How do you wait for God's answer?

Don't give up if God doesn't answer right away. Just keep on praying! (Check out 1 Samuel 1, p. 354.) You won't annoy God if you keep on asking him about something. So . . . keep on asking!

How do you think prayer works? Do you think, "If I pray every day at the same time, God will save that time slot for me so my prayers will get heard"?

God hears all our prayers – no matter what time we pray or how often we pray. Maybe these Faithlinks will help you understand more about prayer.

MORE FAITHlinks

- Your Best Defence, **p. 584**
- Prayer + Action = Success, **p. 626**
- Our Heavenly Connection, **p. 1283**
- Prayer Anywhere, **p. 1331**
- Prayer Priority, **p. 1376**
- The Power of Prayer, **p. 1485**

The Prayer Habit, Psalm 5:1–3, p. 712
- When you do the same thing every day, you develop a habit. What are some good habits you've developed? How do these habits help you? Do you have a special time to pray? What can you do to make prayer a daily habit?

Concern for All, Daniel 9, p. 1165
- How would you show concern for a large group of people? If you could, would you buy everyone an ice cream? Link here to discover a great way to show concern for others.

Ask, Search, Knock, Matthew 7:7–10, p. 1286
- Have you ever wanted to ask for something, but weren't sure what to ask? Jesus said to just keep asking for what you need.
- Do you think this means that God will automatically give you what you ask for if you keep asking him? God knows what we need and the final decision is up to him.

Our Interpreter, Romans 8:26, p. 1528
- An interpreter translates for two people who can't understand each other. Did you know you have an interpreter? Link here to find out about him.

FAITHlinks

ANGER: QUICK OR SLOW?
PSALM 86:15

Which do you do the quickest: become angry or show mercy and forgiveness? When someone does something to annoy you, getting angry is usually the easiest, right? Now, which do you think God does the quickest: become angry or show mercy and forgiveness? Many people believe that God is angry all the time, but that's not true. God is slow to anger, but quick on the draw as far as mercy and forgiveness are concerned. He wants you to be the same way.

Here are some more Faithlinks on anger:

Out of Control? Genesis 4, p. 8

Get Hot or Keep Cool? Proverbs 12:16, p. 842

Justice Served, Isaiah 35:3–4, p. 940

The Peril of Poisonous Plans, Micah 2:1–3, p. 1221

Don't Get Mad; Get Even? Matthew 26:57–63; 27:11–14, p. 1323

The Best Choice, 1 Corinthians 13, p. 1560

---

a gang of cruel men is trying to kill me.
They do not respect you.
15 But Lord, you are a God who shows mercy and is kind.
You don't become angry quickly.
You have great love and faithfulness.
16 Turn to me and have mercy.
Give me, your servant, strength.
Save me, the son of your female servant.
17 Show me a sign of your goodness.
When my enemies look, they will be ashamed.
You, LORD, have helped me and comforted me.

God Loves Jerusalem

A song. A psalm of the sons of Korah.

87 The LORD built Jerusalem on the holy mountain.
2 He loves its gates more than any other place in Israel.
3 City of God,
wonderful things are said about you.   *Selah*
4 God says, "I will put Egypt and Babylonia
on the list of nations that know me.
People from Philistia, Tyre and Cush will be born there."

5 They will say about Jerusalem,
"This one and that one were born there.
God Most High will strengthen her."
6 The LORD will keep a list of the nations.
He will note, "This person was born there."   *Selah*

7 They will dance and sing,
"All good things come from Jerusalem."

A Sad Complaint

A song. A psalm of the sons of Korah. For the director of music. By the mahalath leannoth. A maskil of Heman the Ezrahite.

88 LORD, you are the God who saves me.
I cry out to you day and night.

2 Receive my prayer,
and listen to my cry.

3 My life is full of troubles,
and I am nearly dead.
4 They think I am on the way to my
grave.
I am like a man with no strength.
5 I have been left as dead,
like a body lying in a grave
whom you don't remember any more,
cut off from your care.

6 You have brought me close to death;
I am almost in the dark place of the
dead.
7 You have been very angry with me;
all your waves crush me. *Selah*
8 You have taken my friends away from
me
and have made them hate me.
I am trapped and cannot escape.

9 My eyes are weak from crying.
LORD, I have prayed to you every day;
I have lifted my hands in prayer to
you.

10 Do you show your miracles for the
dead?
Do their spirits rise up and praise
you? *Selah*
11 Will your love be told in the grave?
Will your loyalty be told in the
place of death?
12 Will your miracles be known in the
dark grave?
Will your goodness be known in
the land of forgetfulness?

13 But, LORD, I have called out to you for
help;
every morning I pray to you.
14 LORD, why do you reject me?
Why do you hide from me?

15 I have been weak and dying since I
was young.
I suffer from your terrors, and I am
helpless.
16 You have been angry with me,
and your terrors have destroyed me.
17 They surround me daily like a flood;
they are all around me.
18 You have taken away my loved ones
and friends.
Darkness is my only friend.

A Song About God's Loyalty

A maskil of Ethan the Ezrahite.

89 I will always sing about the LORD's
love;
I will tell of his loyalty from now on.
2 I will say, "Your love continues for
ever;
your loyalty goes on and on like
the sky."

3 You said, "I made an agreement with
the man of my choice;
I made a promise to my servant
David.
4 I told him, 'I will make your family
continue for ever.
Your kingdom will go on and on.'"
Selah

5 LORD, the heavens praise you for your
miracles
and for your loyalty in the meeting
of your holy ones.
6 Who in heaven is equal to the LORD?
None of the
angels is like
the LORD.
7 When the holy
ones meet,
it is God
they fear.
He is more frightening than all
who surround him.
8 Lord GOD All-powerful, who is like you?
LORD, you are powerful and
completely trustworthy.

89:6 Angels
Are angels equal to God?

9 You rule the mighty sea
and calm the stormy waves.
10 You crushed the sea monster Rahab;
by your power you scattered your
enemies.

11 The skies and the earth belong to
you.
You made the world and
everything in it.

12 You created the north and the south.
   Mount Tabor and Mount Hermon
     sing for joy at your name.
13 Your arm has great power.
   Your hand is strong; your right
     hand is lifted up.
14 Your kingdom is built on what is right
     and fair.
   Love and truth are in all you do.
15 Happy are the people who know how
     to praise you.
   LORD, let them live in the light of
     your presence.
16 In your name they rejoice
   and continually praise your
     goodness.
17 You are their glorious strength,
   and in your kindness you honour
     our king.
18 Our king, our shield, belongs to the
     LORD,
   to the Holy One of Israel.
19 Once, in a vision, you spoke
     to those who worship you.
   You said, "I have given strength to a
     warrior;
   I have raised up a young man from
     my people.
20 I have found my servant David;
   I appointed him by pouring holy oil
     on him.
21 I will steady him with my hand
   and strengthen him with my arm.
22 No enemy will make him give forced
     payments,
   and wicked people will not defeat
     him.
23 I will crush his enemies in front of him;
   I will defeat those who hate him.
24 My loyalty and love will be with him.
   Through me he will be strong.
25 I will give him power over the sea
   and control over the rivers.
26 He will say to me, 'You are my father,
   my God, the Rock, my Saviour.'
27 I will make him my firstborn son,
   the greatest king on earth.
28 My love will watch over him for ever,
   and my agreement with him will
     never end.

29 I will make his family continue,
   and his kingdom will last as long as
     the skies.
30 "If his descendants reject my
     teachings
   and do not follow my laws,
31 if they ignore my demands
   and disobey my commands,
32 then I will punish their sins with a
     rod
   and their wrongs with a whip.
33 But I will not hold back my love from
     David,
   nor will I stop being loyal.
34 I will not break my agreement
   nor change what I have said.
35 I have promised by my holiness,
   I will not lie to David.
36 His family will go on for ever.
   His kingdom will last before me
     like the sun.
37 It will continue for ever, like the
     moon,
   like a dependable witness in the
     sky."   *Selah*

38 But now you have refused and
     rejected your appointed king.
   You have been angry with him.
39 You have abandoned the agreement
     with your servant
   and thrown his crown to the
     ground.
40 You have torn down all his city walls;
   you have turned his strong cities
     into ruins.
41 Everyone who passes by steals from
     him.
   His neighbours insult him.
42 You have given strength to his
     enemies
   and have made them all happy.
43 You have made his sword useless;
   you did not help him stand in
     battle.
44 You have kept him from winning
   and have thrown his throne to the
     ground.
45 You have cut his life short
   and covered him with shame. *Selah*

46 LORD, how long will this go on?

Will you ignore us for ever?
How long will your anger burn like a fire?
47 Remember how short my life is.
Why did you create us? For nothing?
48 What person alive will not die?
Who can escape the grave? *Selah*
49 Lord, where is your love from times past,
which in your loyalty you promised to David?
50 Lord, remember how they insulted your servant;
remember how I have suffered the insults of the nations.
51 LORD, remember how your enemies insulted you
and how they insulted your appointed king wherever he went.

52 Praise the LORD for ever!
Amen and amen.

Book 4

God is Eternal, and We are Not

A prayer of Moses, the man of God.

90 Lord, you have been our home since the beginning.
2 Before the mountains were born
and before you created the earth and the world,
you are God.
You have always been, and you will always be.
3 You turn people back into dust.
You say, "Go back into dust, human beings."
4 To you, a thousand years
is like the passing of a day,
or like a few hours in the night.
5 While people sleep, you take their lives.
They are like grass that grows up in the morning.
6 In the morning they are fresh and new,
but by evening they dry up and die.

7 We are destroyed by your anger;
we are terrified by your hot anger.
8 You have put the evil we have done right in front of you;
you clearly see our secret sins.
9 All our days pass while you are angry.
Our years end with a moan.
10 Our lifetime is 70 years
or, if we are strong, 80 years.
But the years are full of hard work and pain.
They pass quickly, and then we are gone.
11 Who knows the full power of your anger?
Your anger is as great as our fear of you should be.
12 Teach us how short our lives really are
so that we may be wise.

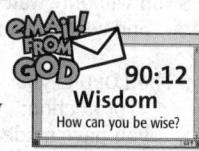
90:12
Wisdom
How can you be wise?

13 LORD, how long before you return
and show kindness to your servants?
14 Fill us with your love every morning.
Then we will sing and rejoice all our lives.
15 We have seen years of trouble.
Now give us as much joy as you gave us sorrow.
16 Show your servants the wonderful things you do;
show your greatness to their children.
17 Lord our God, treat us well.
Give us success in what we do;
yes, give us success in what we do.

Safe in the Lord

91 Those who go to God Most High for safety
will be protected by the Almighty.
2 I will say to the LORD, "You are my place of safety and protection.
You are my God and I trust you."

3 God will save you from hidden traps

and from deadly diseases.
4 He will cover you with his feathers,
and under his wings you can hide.
His truth will be your shield and
protection.
5 You will not fear
any danger
by night
or an arrow
during the
day.

**91:5
Fears**
Don't fear these things!

6 You will not be afraid of diseases that
come in the dark
or sickness that strikes at noon.
7 At your side a thousand people may
die,
or even ten thousand right beside
you,
but you will not be hurt.
8 You will only watch
and see the wicked punished.

9 The LORD is your
protection;
you have made God
Most High your
place of safety.
10 Nothing bad will
happen to you;
no disaster will
come to your
home.
11 He has put his angels
in charge of you
to watch over you wherever you
go.
12 They will catch you in their hands
so that you will not hit your foot on
a rock.
13 You will walk on lions and cobras;
you will step on strong lions and
snakes.
14 The LORD says, "Whoever loves me, I
will save.
I will protect those who know me.
15 They will call to me, and I will answer
them.
I will be with them in trouble;
I will rescue them and honour
them.
16 I will give them a long, full life,
and they will see how I can save."

Thanksgiving for God's Goodness

A psalm. A song for the Sabbath day.

92 It is good to praise you, LORD,
to sing praises to God Most High.
2 It is good to tell of your love in the
morning
and of your loyalty at night.
3 It is good to praise you with the
ten-stringed lyre
and with the soft-sounding harp.

4 LORD, you have made me happy by
what you have done;
I will sing for joy about what your
hands have done.
5 LORD, you have done such great
things!
How deep are your thoughts!
6 Stupid people don't know these things,
and fools don't understand.
7 Wicked people grow
like the grass.
Evil people seem to
do well,
but they will be
destroyed for ever.
8 But, LORD, you will be
honoured for ever.

9 LORD, surely your
enemies,
surely your enemies will be
destroyed,
and all who do evil will be
scattered.
10 But you have made me as strong as
an ox.
You have poured fine oils on me.
11 When I looked, I saw my enemies;
I heard the cries of those who are
against me.

12 But good people will grow like palm
trees;
they will be tall like the cedars of
Lebanon.
13 Like trees planted in the Temple of
the LORD,
they will grow strong in the
courtyards of our God.

> It is good to tell of
> your love in the
> morning and of your
> loyalty at night.
> — Psalm 92:2

14 When they are old, they will still produce fruit;
   they will be healthy and fresh.
15 They will say that the LORD is good.
   He is my Rock, and there is no wrong in him.

The Majesty of the Lord

93 The LORD is king. He is clothed in majesty.
   The LORD is clothed in majesty and armed with strength.
   The world is set, and it cannot be moved.
2 LORD, your kingdom was set up long ago;
   you are everlasting.

3 LORD, the seas raise, the seas raise their voice.
   The seas raise up their pounding waves.
4 The sound of the water is loud;
   the ocean waves are powerful,
   but the LORD above is much greater.
5 LORD, your laws will stand for ever.
   Your Temple will be holy for ever.

God will Pay Back His Enemies

94 The LORD is a God who punishes.
   God, show your greatness and punish!
2 Rise up, Judge of the earth,
   and give the proud what they deserve.
3 How long will the wicked be happy? How long, LORD?
4 They are full of proud words;
   those who do evil boast about what they have done.
5 LORD, they crush your people
   and make your children suffer.
6 They kill widows and foreigners
   and murder orphans.
7 They say, "The LORD doesn't see;
   the God of Jacob doesn't notice."
8 You stupid ones among the people, pay attention.
   You fools, when will you understand?
9 Can't the creator of ears hear?
   Can't the maker of eyes see?
10 Won't the one who corrects nations punish you?
   Doesn't the teacher of people know everything?
11 The LORD knows what people think.
   He knows their thoughts are just a puff of wind.

12 LORD, those you correct are happy;
   you teach them from your law.
13 You give them rest from times of trouble
   until a pit is dug for the wicked.
14 The LORD won't leave his people
   nor give up his children.
15 Judgement will again be fair,
   and all who are honest will follow it.

> LORD, those you correct are happy;
> you teach them from your law.
> — Psalm 94:12

16 Who will help me fight against the wicked?
   Who will stand with me against those who do evil?
17 If the LORD had not helped me,
   I would have died in a minute.
18 I said, "I am about to fall,"
   but, LORD, your love kept me safe.
19 I was very worried,
   but you comforted me and made me happy.

20 Crooked leaders cannot be friends with you.
   They use the law to cause suffering.
21 They join forces against people who do right
   and sentence to death the innocent.

22 But the LORD is my defender;
      my God is the rock of my
         protection.
23 God will pay them back for their sins
      and will destroy them for their
         evil.
      The LORD our God will destroy
         them.

A Call to Praise and Obedience

95 Come, let's sing for joy to the
      LORD.
   Let's shout praises to the Rock who
      saves us.
2 Let's come to him with thanksgiving.
   Let's sing songs to him,

3 because the LORD is the great God,
      the great King over all gods.
4 The deepest places on earth are his,
      and the highest mountains
         belong to him.
5 The sea is his because he made it,
      and he created the land with his
         own hands.

6 Come, let's worship him and bow
      down.
   Let's kneel before the LORD who
      made us,
7 because he is our God
      and we are the people he takes
         care of
      and the sheep that he tends.

   Today listen to what he says:
8 "Do not be stubborn, as your
      ancestors were at Meribah,
   as they were that day at Massah in
      the desert.
9 There your ancestors tested me
      and tried me even though they saw
         what I did.
10 I was angry with those people for
      forty years.
   I said, 'They are not loyal to me
      and have not understood my
         ways.'
11 I was angry and made a promise,
      'They will never enter my rest.'"

Praise for the Lord's Glory

96 Sing to the LORD a new song;
      sing to the LORD, all the earth.
2 Sing to the LORD and praise his
      name;
   every day tell how he saves us.
3 Tell the nations of his glory;
      tell all peoples the miracles he
         does,

4 because the LORD is great; he should
      be praised at all times.
   He should be honoured more than
      all the gods,
5 because all the gods of the nations are
      only idols,
   but the LORD made the heavens.
6 The LORD has glory and majesty;
      he has power and beauty in his
         Temple.

7 Praise the LORD, all nations on earth;
      praise the LORD's glory and
         power.
8 Praise the glory of the LORD's name.
   Bring an offering and come into his
      Temple courtyards.
9 Worship the LORD because he is holy.
   Tremble before him, everyone on
      earth.

10 Tell the nations, "The LORD is king."
   The earth is set, and it cannot be
      moved.
   He will judge the people fairly.
11 Let the skies rejoice and the earth be
      glad;
   let the sea and everything in it shout.
12 Let the fields and everything in
      them rejoice.
   Then all the trees of the forest will
      sing for joy
13 before the LORD, because he is
      coming.
   He is coming to judge the world;

> Come, let's worship him and bow down. Let's kneel before the LORD who made us.
> – Psalm 95:6

he will judge the world with fairness
and the peoples with truth.

A Hymn About the Lord's Power

97 The LORD is king. Let the earth rejoice;
faraway lands should be glad.

2 Thick, dark clouds surround him.
His kingdom is built on what is right and fair.
3 A fire goes before him
and burns up his enemies all around.
4 His lightning lights up the world;
when the people see it, they tremble.
5 The mountains melt like wax before the LORD,
before the Lord of all the earth.
6 The heavens tell about his goodness,
and all the people see his glory.

7 Those who worship idols should be ashamed;
they boast about their gods.
All the gods should worship the LORD.

8 When Jerusalem hears this, she is glad,
and the towns of Judah rejoice.
They are happy because of your judgements, LORD.
9 You are the LORD Most High over all the earth;
you are supreme over all gods.

10 People who love the LORD hate evil.
The LORD watches over those who follow him
and frees them from the power of the wicked.
11 Light shines on those who do right;
joy belongs to those who are honest.
12 Rejoice in the LORD, you who do right.
Praise his holy name.

The Lord of Power and Justice

A psalm.

98 Sing to the LORD a new song,
because he has done miracles.
By his right hand and holy arm
he has won the victory.
2 The LORD has made known his power to save;
he has shown the other nations his victory for his people.
3 He has remembered his love
and his loyalty to the people of Israel.
All the ends of the earth have seen God's power to save.

4 Shout with joy to the LORD, all the earth;
burst into songs and make music.
5 Make music to the LORD with harps,
with harps and the sound of singing.
6 Blow the trumpets and the sheep's horns;
shout for joy to the LORD the King.

He will judge the world fairly; he will judge the peoples with fairness.
— Psalm 98:9

7 Let the sea and everything in it shout;
let the world and everyone in it sing.
8 Let the rivers clap their hands;
let the mountains sing together for joy.
9 Let them sing before the LORD,
because he is coming to judge the world.
He will judge the world fairly;
he will judge the peoples with fairness.

The Lord, the Fair and Holy King

99 The LORD is king.
Let the peoples shake with fear.
He sits between the gold creatures with wings.
Let the earth shake.
2 The LORD in Jerusalem is great;
he is supreme over all the peoples.

3 Let them praise your name;
    it is great, holy and to be feared.

4 The King is powerful and loves
      justice.
  LORD, you made things fair;
    you have done what is fair and right
      for the people of Jacob.
5 Praise the LORD our God,
    and worship at the Temple, his
      footstool.
    He is holy.

6 Moses and Aaron were among his
      priests,
    and Samuel was among his
      worshippers.
  They called to the LORD,
    and he answered them.
7 He spoke to them from the pillar of
      cloud.
    They kept the rules and laws he
      gave them.

8 LORD our God, you answered them.
    You showed them that you are a
      forgiving God,
    but you punished them for their
      wrongs.
9 Praise the LORD our God,
    and worship at his holy mountain,
      because the LORD our God is holy.

A Call to Praise the Lord

A psalm of thanks.

100 Shout to the LORD, all the earth.
2   Serve the LORD with joy;
      come before him with singing.
3   Know that the LORD is God.
      He made us,
        and we belong to him;
      we are his people, the sheep he tends.
4   Come into his city with songs of thanksgiving
      and into his courtyards with songs of praise.
    Thank him and praise his name.
5 The LORD is good. His love is for ever,
    and his loyalty goes on and on.

A Promise to Rule Well

A psalm of David.

101 I will sing of your love and fairness;

FAITH links

YOU'RE INVITED!
PSALM 100

When someone hands you a special invitation to a party or some other gathering, how do you feel? Excited? Glad to be invited? More than likely you wouldn't grumble about it. You would go and have a good time. This psalm is a special invitation to praise God. You're invited to come and tell him how amazing he is. You're also encouraged to thank him for all that he does. Feel free to invite a friend to join in!

A Holiday Every Week, Leviticus 23:1–3, p. 166

Gratitude Attitude, Ezra 3, p. 611

Uniquely You, Psalm 139:13–14, p. 815

Jesus' Mission and Yours, Isaiah 61:1–2, p. 978

A Family Meal, Mark 14:23–26, p. 1356

Your Faith Story, 2 Timothy 1:5, p. 1650

---

100 Thankfulness
How can you express thankfulness?

LORD, I will sing praises to you.
2 I will be careful to live an innocent life.
   When will you come to me?
   I will live an innocent life in my house.
3 I will not look at anything wicked.
   I hate those who turn against you;
   they will not be found near me.
4 Let those who want to do wrong stay away from me;
   I will have nothing to do with evil.
5 If anyone secretly says things against his neighbour,
   I will stop him.
   I will not allow people
   to be proud and look down on others.
6 I will look for trustworthy people
   so I can live with them in the land.
   Only those who live innocent lives
   will be my servants.
7 No one who is dishonest will live in my house;
   no liars will stay around me.
8 Every morning I will destroy the wicked in the land.
   I will rid the LORD's city of people who do evil.

> **eMAIL FROM GOD**
> **101:3–8 Being pure**
> Find out why we should stay away from evil.

A Cry for Help

A prayer of a person who is suffering when he is discouraged and tells the LORD his complaints.

102 LORD, listen to my prayer;
   let my cry for help come to you.
2 Do not hide from me
   in my time of trouble.
   Pay attention to me.
   When I cry for help, answer me quickly.
3 My life is passing away like smoke,
   and my bones are burned up with fire.
4 My heart is like grass that has been cut and dried.
   I forget to eat.
5 Because of my grief,
   my skin hangs on my bones.
6 I am like a desert owl,
   like an owl living among the ruins.
7 I lie awake.
   I am like a lonely bird on a housetop.
8 All day long enemies insult me;
   those who make fun of me use my name as a curse.
9 I eat ashes for food,
   and my tears fall into my drink.
10 Because of your great anger,
   you have picked me up and thrown me away.
11 My days are like a passing shadow;
   I am like dried grass.
12 But, LORD, you rule for ever,
   and your fame goes on and on.
13 You will come and have mercy on Jerusalem,
   because the time has now come to be kind to her;
   the right time has come.
14 Your servants love even her stones;
   they even care about her dust.
15 Nations will fear the name of the LORD,
   and all the kings on earth will honour you.
16 The LORD will rebuild Jerusalem;
   there his glory will be seen.
17 He will answer the prayers of the needy;
   he will not reject their prayers.
18 Write these things for the future
   so that people who are not yet born
   will praise the LORD.
19 The LORD looked down from his holy place above;
   from heaven he looked down at the earth.
20 He heard the moans of the prisoners,
   and he freed those sentenced to die.
21 The name of the LORD will be heard in Jerusalem;
   his praise will be heard there.

22 People will come together,
  and kingdoms will serve the LORD.

23 God has made me tired of living;
  he has cut short my life.
24 So I said, "My God, do not take me in
    the middle of my life.
  Your years go on and on.
25 In the beginning you made the earth,
  and your hands made the skies.
26 They will be destroyed, but you will
    remain.
  They will all wear out like clothes.
  And, like clothes, you will change
    them
  and throw them away.
27 But you never change,
  and your life will never end.
28 Our children will live in your
    presence,
  and their children will remain with
    you."

Praise to the Lord of Love

Of David.

103 My whole being, praise the
    LORD;
  all my being, praise his holy name.
2 My whole being, praise the LORD
  and do not forget all his kindnesses.
3 He forgives all my sins
  and heals all my diseases.
4 He saves my life from the grave
  and loads me with love and mercy.
5 He satisfies me with good things
  and makes me young again, like
    the eagle.

6 The LORD does what is right and fair
  for all who are wronged by others.

7 He showed his ways to Moses
  and his deeds to the people of Israel.
8 The LORD shows mercy and is kind.
  He does not become angry quickly,
  and he has great love.
9 He will not always accuse us,
  and he will not be angry for ever.
10 He has not punished us as our sins
    should be punished;
  he has not repaid us for the evil we
    have done.

11 As high as the sky is above the earth,
  so great is his love for those who
    respect him.
12 He has taken our sins away from us
  as far as the east is from the west.
13 The LORD has mercy on those who
    respect him,
  as a father has mercy on his
    children.
14 He knows how we were made;
  he remembers that we are dust.

FAITH links

YOUR HEAVENLY DAD
PSALM 103:13

Stop a minute to think about your dad or someone who is like a father to you. Think about what he does to show his love for you. Would you hesitate to talk to him or ask him for anything, knowing how much he cares about you? God cares for us, just as a father cares for his children. That means you can talk to him like you talk to your dad.

Need to talk to God?
He's available any time!
Read on:

My Worship Place, Genesis 35:1–14, p. 49

Your Heavenly Parent, Exodus 2:1–10, p. 77

A Holiday Letter, Esther 9:20–23, p. 657

How God Speaks, Job 33:14–17, p. 696

What's in a Name? Isaiah 9:6, p. 908

Jesus' Prayer, John 17, p. 1453

15 Human life is like grass;
  we grow like a flower in the field.
16 After the wind blows, the flower is gone,
  and there is no sign of where it was.
17 But the LORD's love for those who respect him
  continues for ever and ever,
  and his goodness continues to their grandchildren
18 and to those who keep his agreement
  and who remember to obey his orders.

19 The LORD has set his throne in heaven,
  and his kingdom rules over everything.
20 You who are his angels,
  praise the LORD.
  You are the mighty warriors who do what he says
  and who obey his voice.
21 You, his armies, praise the LORD;
  you are his servants who do what he wants.
22 Everything the LORD has made
  should praise him in all the places he rules.

My whole being, praise the LORD.

103:20 Angels
Find out who are God's mighty warriors.

Praise to God Who Made the World

104 My whole being, praise the LORD.
  LORD my God, you are very great.
  You are clothed with glory and majesty;
2   you wear light like a robe.
  You stretch out the skies like a tent.
3   You build your room above the clouds.
  You make the clouds your chariot,
  and you ride on the wings of the wind.
4 You make the winds your messengers,
  and flames of fire are your servants.
5 You built the earth on its foundations
  so it can never be moved.
6 You covered the earth with oceans;
  the water was above the mountains.
7 But at your command, the water rushed away.
  When you thundered your orders, it hurried away.
8 The mountains rose; the valleys sank.
  The water went to the places you made for it.
9 You set borders for the seas that they cannot cross,
  so water will never cover the earth again.

10 You make springs pour into the ravines;
  they flow between the mountains.
11 They water all the wild animals;
  the wild donkeys come there to drink.
12 Wild birds make nests by the water;
  they sing among the tree branches.
13 You water the mountains from above.
  The earth is full of the things you made.
14 You make the grass for cattle
  and vegetables for the people.
  You make food grow from the earth.
15 You give us wine that makes happy hearts
  and olive oil that makes our faces shine.
  You give us bread that gives us strength.
16 The LORD's trees have plenty of water;
  they are the cedars of Lebanon, which he planted.
17 The birds make their nests there;
  the stork's home is in the fir trees.
18 The high mountains belong to the wild goats.
  The rocks are hiding places for the badgers.

19 You made the moon to mark the seasons,

and the sun always knows when to set.
20 You make it dark, and it becomes night.
Then all the wild animals creep around.
21 The lions roar as they attack.
They look to God for food.
22 When the sun rises, they leave and go back to their dens to lie down.
23 Then people go to work and work until evening.

24 LORD, you have made many things; with your wisdom you made them all.
The earth is full of your riches.
25 Look at the sea, so big and wide, with creatures large and small that cannot be counted.
26 Ships travel over the ocean, and there is the sea monster Leviathan, which you made to play there.
27 All these things depend on you to give them their food at the right time.
28 When you give it to them, they gather it up.
When you open your hand, they are filled with good food.
29 When you turn away from them, they become frightened.
When you take away their breath, they die and turn to dust.
30 When you breathe on them, they are created, and you make the land new again.

31 May the glory of the LORD be for ever.
May the LORD enjoy what he has made.
32 He just looks at the earth, and it shakes.
He touches the mountains, and they smoke.

33 I will sing to the LORD all my life;
I will sing praises to my God as long as I live.
34 May my thoughts please him;
I am happy in the LORD.
35 Let sinners be destroyed from the earth,
and let the wicked live no longer.

My whole being, praise the LORD.

Praise the LORD.

God's Love for Israel

105 Give thanks to the LORD and pray to him.
Tell the nations what he has done.
2 Sing to him; sing praises to him.
Tell about all his miracles.
3 Be glad that you are his;
let those who seek the LORD be happy.
4 Depend on the LORD and his strength;
always go to him for help.
5 Remember the miracles he has done;
remember his wonders and his decisions.
6 You are descendants of his servant Abraham,
the children of Jacob, his chosen people.
7 He is the LORD our God.
His laws are for all the world.

8 He will keep his agreement for ever;
he will keep his promises always.
9 He will keep the agreement he made with Abraham
and the promise he made to Isaac.
10 He made it a law for the people of Jacob;
he made it an agreement with Israel to last for ever.
11 The LORD said, "I will give you the land of Canaan,
and it will belong to you."

> May my thoughts please him; I am happy in the LORD.
> – Psalm 104:34

FAITH links

A PICTURE OF THE PAST
PSALM 105

Your family photo album or videos tell the story of the past. When you look at old pictures, you can see the events of your family's life. Reading this psalm is like looking at a photo album of Israel's history. How many of these stories do you remember? Throughout Israel's history, leaders like Joseph and Moses reminded people to pass on the stories of what God did for their people.

Maybe your family never crossed the Red Sea or followed a cloud through a wilderness. But the message of this psalm is still for you: remember what God has done for you, and pass it on!

Here's some more advice on telling others about God:

Care for the Lost, Deuteronomy 22:1–3, p. 255

Faith of Our Fathers, Joshua 4:4–9, p. 280

Remember Your Creator, Ecclesiastes 12:1, 13, p. 885

A Bad Reaction, Jeremiah 36, p. 1043

Pass It On! Joel 1:2–3, p. 1187

Tell All About Him! Matthew 28:19, p. 1326

Psalm 105:28 789

12 Then God's people were few in number.
They were strangers in the land.
13 They went from one nation to another,
from one kingdom to another.
14 But the LORD did not let anyone hurt them;
he warned kings not to harm them.
15 He said, "Don't touch my chosen people,
and don't harm my prophets."
16 God ordered a time of hunger in the land,
and he destroyed all the food.
17 Then he sent a man ahead of them—
Joseph, who was sold as a slave.
18 They put chains around his feet
and an iron ring around his neck.
19 Then the time he had spoken of came,
and the LORD's words proved that Joseph was right.
20 The king of Egypt sent for Joseph and freed him;
the ruler of the people set him free.
21 He made him the master of his house;
Joseph was in charge of his riches.
22 He could order the princes as he wished.
He taught the older men to be wise.
23 Then his father Israel came to Egypt;
Jacob[n] lived in Egypt.[n]
24 The LORD made his people grow in number,
and he made them stronger than their enemies.
25 He caused the Egyptians to hate his people
and to make plans against his servants.
26 Then he sent his servant Moses,
and Aaron, whom he had chosen.
27 They did many signs among the Egyptians
and worked wonders in Egypt.
28 The LORD sent darkness and made the land dark,

105:23 Jacob Also called Israel.
105:23 Egypt Literally, "the land of Ham". Also in verse 27. The people in Egypt were descendants of Ham, one of Noah's sons. See Genesis 10:6.

but the Egyptians turned against
what he said.
29 So he changed their water into blood
and made their fish die.
30 Then their country was filled with
frogs,
even in the bedrooms of their
rulers.
31 The LORD spoke and flies came,
and gnats were everywhere in the
country.
32 He made hail fall like rain
and sent lightning through their
land.
33 He struck down their grapevines and
fig trees,
and he destroyed every tree in the
country.
34 He spoke and grasshoppers came;
the locusts were too many to count.
35 They ate all the plants in the land
and everything the earth
produced.
36 The LORD also killed all the firstborn
sons in the land,
the oldest son of each family.
37 Then he brought his people out,
and they carried with them silver
and gold.
Not one of his people stumbled.
38 The Egyptians were glad when they
left,
because the Egyptians were afraid
of them.
39 The LORD covered them with a cloud
and lit up the night with fire.
40 When they asked, he brought them
quail
and filled them with bread from
heaven.
41 God split the rock, and water flowed
out;
it ran like a river through the
desert.
42 He remembered his holy promise
to his servant Abraham.
43 So God brought his people out with
joy,
his chosen ones with singing.
44 He gave them the lands of other
nations,
so they received what others had
worked for.
45 This was so they would keep his
orders
and obey his teachings.

Praise the LORD!

Israel's Failure to Trust God

106 Praise the LORD!

Thank the LORD because he is good.
His love continues for ever.
2 No one can tell all the mighty things
the LORD has done;
no one can speak all his praise.

FAITH CHALLENGE

Here's another one for you. Read 106:3 to find out what kind of people are most likely to be happy. How do you respond when you see people cheating or not doing what they're supposed to do?

TESTING IT

Psalm 106:3
Happy are those who do right,
who do what is fair at all times.

3 Happy are those who do right,
   who do what is fair at all times.

4 LORD, remember me when you are
   kind to your people;
   help me when you save them.
5 Let me see the good things you do for
   your chosen people.
   Let me be happy along with your
   happy nation;
   let me join your own people in
   praising you.

6 We have sinned just as our ancestors
   did.
   We have done wrong; we have
   done evil.
7 Our ancestors in Egypt
   did not learn from your
   miracles.
   They did not remember all your
   kindnesses,
   so they turned against you at the
   Red Sea.
8 But the LORD saved them for his own
   sake,
   to show his great power.
9 He commanded the Red Sea, and it
   dried up.
   He led them through the deep sea
   as if it were a desert.
10 He saved them from those who hated
   them.
   He saved them from their
   enemies,
11 and the water covered their foes.
   Not one of them escaped.
12 Then the people believed what the
   LORD said,
   and they sang praises to him.

13 But they quickly forgot what he had
   done;
   they did not wait for his advice.
14 They became greedy for food in the
   desert,
   and they tested God there.
15 So he gave them what they wanted,
   but he also sent a terrible disease
   among them.

16 The people in the camp were jealous
   of Moses

and of Aaron, the holy priest of the
   LORD.
17 Then the ground opened up and
   swallowed Dathan
   and closed over Abiram's group.
18 A fire burned among their followers,
   and flames burned up the wicked.

19 The people made a gold calf at Mount
   Sinai
   and worshipped a metal statue.
20 They exchanged their glorious God
   for a statue of a bull that eats
   grass.
21 They forgot the God who saved
   them,
   who had done great things in
   Egypt,"
22 who had done miracles in Egypt
   and amazing things by the Red
   Sea.
23 So God said he would destroy them.
   But Moses, his chosen one, stood
   before him
   and stopped God's anger from
   destroying them.

24 Then they refused to go into the
   beautiful land of Canaan;
   they did not believe what God
   promised.
25 They grumbled in their tents
   and did not obey the LORD.
26 So he swore to them
   that they would die in the desert.
27 He said their children would be killed
   by other nations
   and that they would be scattered
   among other countries.

28 They joined in worshipping Baal at
   Peor
   and ate meat that had been
   sacrificed to lifeless statues.
29 They made the LORD angry by what
   they did,
   so many people became sick with a
   terrible disease.
30 But Phinehas prayed to the LORD,

106:21 Egypt Literally, "the land of Ham". The people in Egypt were descendants of Ham, one of Noah's sons. See Genesis 10:6.

and the disease stopped.
31 Phinehas did what was right,
and it will be remembered from now on.

32 The people also made the LORD angry at Meribah,
and Moses was in trouble because of them.
33 The people turned against the Spirit of God,
so Moses spoke without stopping to think.

34 The people did not destroy the other nations
as the LORD had told them to do.
35 Instead, they mixed with the other nations
and learned their customs.
36 They worshipped other nations' idols
and were trapped by them.
37 They even killed their sons and daughters
as sacrifices to demons.
38 They killed innocent people,
their own sons and daughters,
as sacrifices to the idols of Canaan.
So the land was made unholy by their blood.
39 The people became unholy by their sins;
they were unfaithful to God in what they did.

40 So the LORD became angry with his people
and hated his own children.
41 He handed them over to other nations
and let their enemies rule over them.
42 Their enemies were cruel to them
and kept them under their power.
43 The LORD saved his people many times,
but they continued to turn against him.
So they became even more wicked.

44 But God saw their misery
when he heard their cry.
45 He remembered his agreement with them,
and he felt sorry for them because of his great love.
46 He caused them to be pitied
by those who held them captive.

47 LORD our God, save us
and bring us back from other nations.
Then we will thank you
and will gladly praise you.

48 Praise the LORD, the God of Israel.
He always was and always will be.
Let all the people say, "Amen!"

Praise the LORD!

Book 5

God Saves from Many Dangers

107 Thank the Lord because he is good.
His love continues for ever.
2 That is what those whom the LORD has saved should say.
He has saved them from the enemy
3 and has gathered them from other lands,
from east and west, north and south.

107:1–3
Thankfulness
Why should you thank the Lord?

4 Some people had wandered in the desert lands.
They found no city in which to live.
5 They were hungry and thirsty,
and they were discouraged.
6 In their misery they cried out to the LORD,
and he saved them from their troubles.
7 He led them on a straight road
to a city where they could live.
8 Let them give thanks to the LORD for his love
and for the miracles he does for people.
9 He satisfies the thirsty
and fills up the hungry.

10 Some sat in gloom and darkness;
    they were prisoners suffering in
        chains.
11 They had turned against the words of
        God
    and had refused the advice of God
        Most High.
12 So he broke their pride by hard work.
    They stumbled, and no one helped.
13 In their misery they cried out to the
        LORD,
    and he saved them from their
        troubles.
14 He brought them out of their gloom
        and darkness
    and broke their chains.
15 Let them give thanks to the LORD for
        his love
    and for the miracles he does for
        people.
16 He breaks down bronze gates
    and cuts apart iron bars.
17 Some fools turned against God
    and suffered for the evil they did.
18 They refused to eat anything,
    so they almost died.
19 In their misery they cried out to the
        LORD,
    and he saved them from their
        troubles.
20 God gave the command and healed
        them,
    so they were saved from dying.
21 Let them give thanks to the LORD for
        his love
    and for the miracles he does for
        people.
22 Let them offer sacrifices to thank
        him.
    With joy they should tell what he
        has done.
23 Others went out to sea in ships
    and did business on the great
        oceans.
24 They saw what the LORD could do,
    the miracles he did in the deep
        oceans.
25 He spoke, and a storm came up,
    which blew up high waves.
26 The ships were tossed as high as the
        sky and fell low to the depths.

Psalm 107:40   793

The storm was so bad that they
        lost their courage.
27 They stumbled and fell like people
        who were drunk.
    They did not know what to do.
28 In their misery they cried out to the
        LORD,
    and he saved them from their
        troubles.
29 He stilled the storm
    and calmed the waves.
30 They were happy that it was quiet,
    and God guided them to the port
        they wanted.
31 Let them give thanks to the LORD for
        his love
    and for the
        miracles he
        does for
        people.
32 Let them praise
        his greatness
        in the
        meeting of
        the people;
    let them praise him in the meeting
        of the elders.

**107:31–32
Worship**
A call to worship.

33 He changed rivers into a desert
    and springs of water into dry
        ground.
34 He made fertile land salty,
    because the people there did evil.
35 He changed the desert into pools of
        water
    and dry ground into springs of
        water.
36 He had the hungry settle there
    so they could build a city in which
        to live.
37 They planted seeds in the fields and
        vineyards,
    and they had a good harvest.
38 God blessed them, and they grew in
        number.
    Their cattle did not become fewer.
39 Because of disaster, troubles and
        sadness,
    their families grew smaller and
        weaker.
40 He showed he was displeased with
        their leaders

and made them wander in a pathless desert.

41 But he lifted the poor out of their suffering
and made their families grow like flocks of sheep.

42 Good people see this and are happy, but the wicked say nothing.

43 Whoever is wise will remember these things
and will think about the love of the LORD.

A Prayer for Victory

A song. A psalm of David.

108 God, my heart is steady.
I will sing and praise you with all my being.

2 Wake up, harp and lyre!
I will wake up the dawn.

3 LORD, I will praise you among the nations;
I will sing songs of praise about you to all the nations.

4 Your great love reaches to the skies, your truth to the heavens.

5 God, you are supreme above the skies.
Let your glory be over all the earth.

6 Answer us and save us by your power
so the people you love will be rescued.

7 God has said from his Temple,
"When I win, I will divide Shechem and measure off the Valley of Succoth.

8 Gilead and Manasseh are mine.
Ephraim is like my helmet.
Judah holds my royal sceptre.

9 Moab is like my washbowl.
I throw my sandals at Edom.
I shout at Philistia."

10 Who will bring me to the fortified city?
Who will lead me to Edom?

11 God, surely you have rejected us;
you do not go out with our armies.

12 Help us fight the enemy.
Human help is useless,

13 but we can win with God's help.
He will defeat our enemies.

A Prayer Against an Enemy

For the director of music. A psalm of David.

109 God, I praise you.
Do not be silent.

2 Wicked people and liars have spoken against me;
they have told lies about me.

3 They have said hateful things about me
and attack me for no reason.

4 They attacked me, even though I loved them
and prayed for them.

5 I was good to them, but they repay me with evil.
I loved them, but they hated me in return.

6 They say about me, "Have an evil person work against him,
and let an accuser stand against him.

7 When he is judged, let him be found guilty,
and let even his prayers show his guilt.

8 Let his life be cut short,
and let another man replace him as leader.

9 Let his children become orphans and his wife a widow.

10 Make his children wander around, begging for food.
Let them be forced out of the ruins in which they live.

11 Let the people to whom he owes money take everything he owns,
and let strangers steal everything he has worked for.

12 Let no one show him love
or have mercy on his orphaned children.

13 Let all his descendants die
and be forgotten by those who live after him.

14 Lord, remember how wicked his
    ancestors were,
    and don't let the sins of his mother
        be wiped out.
15 Lord, always remember their sins.
    Then make people forget about
        them completely.

16 "He did not remember to be loving.
    He hurt the poor, the needy and
        those who were sad
    until they were
        nearly dead.
17 He loved to put
        curses on others,
    so let those same
        curses fall on
        him.
    He did not like to
        bless others,
    so do not let good
        things happen to
        him.
18 He cursed others as often as he wore
        clothes.
    Cursing others filled his body and
        his life,
    like drinking water and using olive
        oil.
19 So let curses cover him like clothes
    and wrap round him like a belt."
20 May the Lord do these things to
        those who accuse me,
    to those who speak evil against
        me.
21 But you, Lord God,
    be kind to me so others will know
        you are good.
    Because your love is good, save
        me.
22 I am poor and helpless
    and very sad.
23 I am dying like an evening shadow;
    I am shaken off like a locust.
24 My knees are weak from hunger,
    and I have grown thin.
25 My enemies insult me;
    they look at me and shake their
        heads.

26 Lord my God, help me;
    because you are loving, save me.

27 Then they will know that your power
        has done this;
    they will know that you have done
        it, Lord.
28 They may curse me, but you bless
        me.
    They may attack me, but they will
        be disgraced.
    Then I, your servant, will be glad.
29 Let those who accuse me be
        disgraced
        and covered with
        shame like a coat.

30 I will thank the Lord
        very much;
    I will praise him in
        front of many
        people.
31 He defends the
        helpless
    and saves them from
        those who accuse
        them.

> I will thank the Lord very much; I will praise him in front of many people.
> – Psalm 109:30

The Lord Appoints a King

A psalm of David.

110 The Lord said to my Lord,
    "Sit by me at my right side
    until I put your enemies under
        your control."

2 The Lord will enlarge your kingdom
        beyond Jerusalem,
    and you will rule over your
        enemies.
3 Your people will join you on your day
        of battle.
    You have been dressed in holiness
        from birth;
    you have the freshness of a child.

4 The Lord has made a promise
    and will not change his mind.
    He said, "You are a priest for ever,
        a priest like Melchizedek."

5 The Lord is beside you to help you.
    When he becomes angry, he will
        crush kings.
6 He will judge those nations, filling
        them with dead bodies;

he will defeat rulers all over the
world.
7 The king will drink from the brook on
the way.
Then he will be strengthened.

Praise the Lord's Goodness

111 Praise the LORD!
I will thank the LORD with all my
heart
in the meeting of his good people.

2 The LORD does great things;
those who enjoy them seek them.
3 What he does is glorious and
splendid,
and his goodness continues for ever.
4 His miracles are unforgettable.
The LORD is kind and merciful.
5 He gives food to those who fear him.
He remembers his agreement for
ever.
6 He has shown his people his power
when he gave them the lands of
other nations.

7 Everything he does is good and fair;
all his orders can be trusted.
8 They will continue for ever.
They were made true and right.
9 He sets his people free.
He made his agreement
everlasting.
He is holy and wonderful.

10 Wisdom begins with respect for the
LORD;
those who obey his orders have
good understanding.
He should be praised for ever.

Honest People are Blessed

112 Praise the LORD!
Happy are those who respect the
LORD,
who want what he commands.

2 Their descendants will be powerful in
the land;
the children of honest people will
be blessed.

3 Their houses will be full of wealth and
riches,
and their goodness will continue
for ever.
4 A light shines in the dark for honest
people,
for those who are merciful and
kind and good.
5 It is good to be merciful and
generous.
Those who are fair in their
business
6 will never be defeated.
Good people will always be
remembered.
7 They won't be
afraid of bad
news;
their hearts
are steady
because
they trust
the LORD.

112:7
Fears
Should we fear
bad news?

8 They are confident and will not be
afraid;
they will look down on their
enemies.
9 They give freely to the poor.
The things they do are right and
will continue for ever.
They will be given great honour.

10 The wicked will see this and become
angry;
they will grind their teeth in anger
and then disappear.
The wishes of the wicked will come
to nothing.

Praise for the Lord's Kindness

113 Praise the LORD!
Praise him, you servants of the LORD;
praise the name of the LORD.
2 The LORD's name should be praised
now and for ever.
3 The LORD's name should be praised
from where the sun rises to where
it sets.

4 The LORD is supreme over all the
nations;
his glory reaches to the skies.

GOD'S GLORY — Psalm 115

The "glory of the Lord" is the appearance of God's presence. God doesn't have a body with a face, like you do. He is a spirit. When people catch a glimpse of him, they see his "glory". Moses saw God's glory in a bush that was on fire but never burned up. (Look at Exodus 3:1–6, p. 79.) Moses also saw God's glory in a cloud on Mount Sinai. (Check out Exodus 24:9–17, p. 108.) Aaron and all the Israelites saw God's glory when Aaron made his first sacrifice in the wilderness as a priest. (Read Leviticus 9:23, p. 144.) God showed his glory the most through his Son, Jesus Christ. (See John 1:14, p. 1422.)

God has shown himself to people in some amazing ways. He has spoken through dreams. (Look at Genesis 37:5–10, p. 52, and Matthew 1:20–21, p. 1275.) He has also shown himself through nature. (Check out Romans 1:20, p. 1519.) He has shown himself through his Son and then through giving us the Holy Spirit to lead us. (Read John 3:16, p. 1426; 14:16–17, p. 1449.)

God shows himself to us so that we can know him and worship him for who he really is.

---

5 No one is like the LORD our God,
   who rules from heaven,
6 who bends down to look
   at the skies and the earth.

7 The LORD lifts the poor from the ground
   and takes the helpless from the ashes.
8 He seats them with princes,
   the princes of his people.
9 He gives children to the woman who has none
   and makes her a happy mother.

   Praise the LORD!

God Brought Israel from Egypt

114 When the Israelites went out of Egypt,
   the people of Jacob left that foreign country.
2 Then Judah became God's holy place;
   Israel became the land he ruled.

3 The Red Sea looked and ran away;
   the Jordan River turned back.
4 The mountains danced like rams
   and the hills like little lambs.

5 Sea, why did you run away?
   Jordan, why did you turn back?
6 Mountains, why did you dance like rams?
   Hills, why did you dance like little lambs?

7 Earth, shake with fear before the Lord,
   before the God of Jacob.
8 He turned a rock into a pool of water,
   a hard rock into a spring of water.

The One True God

115 It does not belong to us, LORD.
   The glory belongs to you
   because of your love and loyalty.
2 Why do the nations ask,
   "Where is their God?"

3 Our God is in heaven.
   He does what he pleases.
4 Their idols are made of silver and
      gold,
   the work of human hands.
5 They have mouths, but they cannot
      speak.
   They have eyes, but they cannot
      see.
6 They have ears, but they cannot
      hear.
   They have noses, but they cannot
      smell.
7 They have hands, but they cannot
      feel.
   They have feet, but they cannot
      walk.
   No sounds come from their
      throats.
8 People who make idols will be like
      them,
   and so will those who trust them.

9 Family of Israel, trust the LORD;
   he is your helper and your
      protection.
10 Family of Aaron, trust the LORD;
    he is your helper and your
       protection.
11 You who respect the LORD should
       trust him;
    he is your helper and your
       protection.

12 The LORD remembers us and will
       bless us.
    He will bless the family of Israel;
    he will bless the family of Aaron.
13 The LORD will bless those who
       respect him,
    from the smallest to the greatest.

14 May the LORD give you success,
    and may he give you and your
       children success.
15 May you be blessed by the LORD,
    who made heaven and earth.

16 Heaven belongs to the LORD,
    but he gave the earth to people.
17 Dead people do not praise the
       LORD;
    those in the grave are silent.
18 But we will praise the LORD
    now and for ever.

Praise the LORD!

Thanksgiving for Escaping Death

116 I love the LORD,
       because he listens to my
          prayers for help.
2 He paid attention to me,
   so I will call to him for help as long
      as I live.
3 The ropes of death bound me,
   and the fear of the grave took hold
      of me.
   I was troubled
      and sad.
4 Then I called out
      the name of
      the LORD.
   I said, "Please,
      LORD, save me!"

EMAIL FROM GOD
116:1–15
Death
Should Christians be
afraid of death?

5 The LORD is kind and does what is
      right;
   our God is merciful.
6 The LORD watches over the foolish;
   when I was helpless, he saved me.

7 I said to myself, "Relax,
   because the LORD takes care of you."

8 LORD, you saved me from death.
   You stopped my eyes from crying;
   you kept me from being defeated.
9 So I will walk with the LORD
   in the land of the living.
10 I believed, so I said,
    "I am completely ruined."
11 In my distress I said,
    "All people are liars."

12 What can I give the LORD
    for all the good things he has given
       to me?
13 I will lift up the cup of salvation,
    and I will pray to the LORD.
14 I will give the LORD what I promised
    in front of all his people.

15 The death of one that belongs to the
       LORD
    is precious in his sight.
16 LORD, I am your servant;

I am your servant and the son of
   your female servant.
You have freed me from my chains.

17 I will give you an offering to show
     thanks to you,
   and I will pray to the LORD.
18 I will give the LORD what I promised
     in front of all his people,
19 in the Temple courtyards
     in Jerusalem.

Praise the LORD!

A Hymn of Praise

117 All you nations, praise the
       LORD.
   All you people, praise him
2 because the LORD loves us very
     much,
   and his truth is everlasting.

Praise the LORD!

Thanksgiving for Victory

118 Thank the LORD because he is
       good.
   His love continues for ever.

2 Let the people of Israel say,
   "His love continues for ever."
3 Let the family of Aaron say,
   "His love continues for ever."
4 Let those who respect the LORD say,
   "His love continues for ever."
5 I was in trouble, so I called to the LORD.
   The LORD answered me and set me
     free.
6 I will not be afraid, because the LORD
     is with me.
   People can't do anything to me.
7 The LORD is with me to help me,
   so I will see my enemies defeated.

8 It is better to trust the LORD
     than to trust people.
9 It is better to trust the LORD
     than to trust princes.

10 All the nations surrounded me,
     but I defeated them in the name of
       the LORD.
11 They surrounded me on every side,
     but with the LORD's power I
       defeated them.
12 They surrounded me like a swarm of
     bees,
   but they died as quickly as thorns
     burn.
   By the LORD's power, I defeated
     them.

13 They chased me until I was almost
     defeated,
   but the LORD helped me.
14 The LORD gives me strength and a
     song.
   He has saved me.

FAITH CHALLENGE

Got another challenge for you. Read 118:18 to discover the bright side of learning hard lessons. What's the hardest lesson you've ever had to learn? What made it so hard?

TESTING IT

Psalm 118:18
The LORD has taught me a hard lesson, but he did not let me die.

15 Shouts of joy and victory
  come from the tents of those who do right:
  "The LORD has done powerful things."
16 The power of the LORD has won the victory;
  with his power the LORD has done mighty things.
17 I will not die, but live,
  and I will tell what the LORD has done.
18 The LORD has taught me a hard lesson,
  but he did not let me die.
19 Open for me the Temple gates.
  Then I will come in and thank the LORD.
20 This is the LORD's gate;
  only those who are good may enter through it.
21 LORD, I thank you for answering me.
  You have saved me.
22 The stone that the builders rejected
  became the cornerstone.
23 The LORD did this,
  and it is wonderful to us.
24 This is the day that the LORD has made.
  Let us rejoice and be glad today!
25 Please, LORD, save us;
  please, LORD, give us success.
26 God bless the one who comes in the name of the LORD.
  We bless all of you from the Temple of the LORD.
27 The LORD is God,
  and he has shown kindness to us.
  With branches in your hands, join the feast.
  Come to the corners of the altar.
28 You are my God, and I will thank you;
  you are my God, and I will praise your greatness.
29 Thank the LORD because he is good.
  His love continues for ever.

The Word of God

119 Happy are those who live pure lives,
  who follow the LORD's teachings.
2 Happy are those who keep his rules,
  who try to obey him with their whole heart.
3 They don't do what is wrong;
  they follow his ways.
4 LORD, you gave your orders
  to be obeyed completely.
5 I wish I were more loyal
  in obeying your demands.
6 Then I would not be ashamed
  when I study your commands.
7 When I learned that your laws are fair,
  I praised you with an honest heart.
8 I will obey your demands,
  so please don't ever leave me.
9 How can a young person live a pure life?
  By obeying your word.
10 With all my heart I try to obey you.
  Don't let me break your commands.
11 I have taken your words to heart
  so I would not sin against you.
12 LORD, you should be praised.
  Teach me your demands.
13 My lips will tell about
  all the laws you have spoken.
14 I enjoy living by your rules
  as people enjoy great riches.
15 I think about your orders
  and study your ways.
16 I enjoy obeying your demands,
  and I will not forget your word.
17 Do good to me, your servant, so I can live,
  so I can obey your word.
18 Open my eyes to see
  the miracles in your teachings.
19 I am a stranger on earth.
  Do not hide your commands from me.
20 I wear myself out with desire

EMAIL FROM GOD
119:1–20
Being Pure
How can you live a pure life?

GOD'S WORD
Psalm 119:12–18

Livin' it

A Burning Lamp What's one thing you would need and want if you were camping overnight in the woods? A computer? A TV? Crisps? Probably more than anything else you would need a good torch – or something to light the way. Computers and TVs won't help you find your way in the dark, and they certainly won't scare off any animals that may be lurking about! A trusty light can show you where to go and keep you from tripping.

God's Word is like a strong light showing you how to live. God's Word tells you how much he loves you and how to please him. (Check out Psalm 119:105.) Do you have God's burning lamp to use in the dark world?

MORE FAITH links

More Precious Than Gold, **p. 723**

The Bible: Good for Your Faith, **p. 802**

Said It? Do It! **p. 1077**

The "Ruler" of Our Lives, **p. 1202**

Cut to the Quick, **p. 1670**

OK. So you think you're ready for anything. You've got your map, your compass, your torch, your first-aid kit, six bottles of water and a dozen bars of chocolate!

Although you look the part, are you really prepared? Do you know what is the best thing to have to prepare you for life in the real world? Take a look at these Faithlinks to find out!

A Look for the Book, 2 Chronicles 34:14–18, p. 603
- How many Bibles are in your house or in your church? Imagine that there was only one copy of the Bible in the world – and only part of one at that. And then it was lost! King Josiah was eager to read God's teachings when the Book of the Teachings was found. Do you read the Bible to learn about God? Discover hidden treasures inside it!

Life's Rule Book, 2 Timothy 3:15–17, p. 1655
- Have you ever tried to learn a new sport? What did you do to learn the rules? Link here to learn about the "rule book" for life.

Pay Attention! Hebrews 2:1, p. 1668
- What are the things that grab your attention? A favourite TV programme or DVD? A computer game? We usually pay attention to things that interest us. The writer of Hebrews wanted to remind Christians to pay attention to God's Word. Link here to find out why that's so important.

my FAVOURITE links

Psalm 119:21 802

FAITH links

THE BIBLE: GOOD FOR YOUR FAITH
PSALM 119

When a subject is important enough for the public to know about, you'll find the information splashed across billboards and ads. You've seen ads about drinking milk, not smoking, and eating healthily. Although the subject discussed in Psalm 119 can't be found on a billboard, it's also important. That subject is God's Word. Through God's Word you can learn how much God loves you and how you can please him. What you learn about God helps your faith in him to grow. Reading the Bible won't give you a milk moustache, but it will keep you spiritually healthy.

Want to grow spiritually? Link here to find out how:

Try to Remember, Deuteronomy 11:18–21, p. 243

Learning to Listen, 1 Samuel 3, p. 358

A Travelling Bible Study, 2 Chronicles 17:9, p. 580

Future Hope, Joel 3:17–21, p. 1191

Heavenly Treasure, Luke 12:32–34, p. 1394

Life's Rule Book, 2 Timothy 3:15–17, p. 1655

---

for your laws all the time.
21 You scold proud people;
   those who ignore your commands are cursed.
22 Don't let me be insulted and hated because I keep your rules.
23 Even if princes speak against me, I, your servant, will think about your demands.
24 Your rules give me pleasure; they give me good advice.

25 I am about to die.
   Give me life, as you have promised.
26 I told you about my life, and you answered me.
   Teach me your demands.
27 Help me understand your orders.
   Then I will think about your miracles.
28 I am sad and tired.
   Make me strong again as you have promised.
29 Don't let me be dishonest;
   have mercy on me by helping me obey your teachings.
30 I have chosen the way of truth;
   I have obeyed your laws.
31 I hold on to your rules.
   LORD, do not let me be disgraced.
32 I will quickly obey your commands, because you have made me happy.

33 LORD, teach me your demands, and I will keep them until the end.
34 Help me understand, so I can keep your teachings,
   obeying them with all my heart.
35 Lead me in the path of your commands,
   because that makes me happy.
36 Make me want to keep your rules instead of wishing for riches.
37 Keep me from looking at worthless things.
   Let me live by your word.
38 Keep your promise to me, your servant,
   so you will be respected.
39 Take away the shame I fear, because your laws are good.
40 How I want to follow your orders.

Give me life because of your
    goodness.

41 LORD, show me your love,
    and save me as you have promised.
42 I have an answer for people who
        insult me,
    because I trust what you say.
43 Never keep me from speaking your
        truth,
    because I depend on your fair laws.
44 I will obey your teachings
    for ever and ever.
45 So I will live in freedom,
    because I want to follow your
        orders.
46 I will discuss your rules with kings
    and will not be ashamed.
47 I enjoy obeying your commands,
    which I love.
48 I praise your commands, which I
        love,
    and I think about your demands.

49 Remember your promise to me,
        your servant;
    it gives me hope.
50 When I suffer, this comforts me:
    your promise gives me life.
51 Proud people always make fun of me,
    but I do not reject your teachings.
52 I remember your laws from long ago,
    and they comfort me, LORD.
53 I become angry with wicked people
    who do not keep your teachings.
54 I sing about your demands
    wherever I live.
55 LORD, I remember you at night,
    and I will obey your teachings.
56 This is what I do:
    I follow your orders.

57 LORD, you are my share in life;
    I have promised to obey your
        words.
58 I prayed to you with all my heart.
    Have mercy on me as you have
        promised.
59 I thought about my life,
    and I decided to follow your rules.
60 I hurried and did not wait
    to obey your commands.
61 Wicked people have tied me up,
    but I have not forgotten your
        teachings.
62 In the middle of the night, I get up
        to thank you
    because your laws are right.
63 I am a friend to everyone who fears
        you,
    to anyone who obeys your orders.
64 LORD, your love fills the earth.
    Teach me your demands.

65 You have done good things for your
        servant,
    as you have promised, LORD.
66 Teach me wisdom and knowledge
    because I trust your commands.
67 Before I suffered, I did wrong,
    but now I obey your word.
68 You are good, and you do what is
        good.
    Teach me your demands.
69 Proud people have made up lies
        about me,
    but I will follow your orders with
        all my heart.
70 Those people have no feelings,
    but I love your teachings.
71 It was good for me to suffer
    so I would learn your demands.
72 Your teachings are worth more to me
    than thousands of pieces of gold
        and silver.

73 You made me and formed me with
        your hands.
    Give me understanding so I can
        learn your commands.
74 Let those who respect you rejoice
        when they see me,
    because I put my hope in your
        word.
75 LORD, I know that your laws are right
    and that it was right for you to
        punish me.
76 Comfort me with your love,
    as you promised me, your servant.
77 Have mercy on me so that I may live.
    I love your teachings.
78 Make proud people ashamed
    because they lied about me.
    But I will think about your orders.
79 Let those who respect you return to
        me,

those who know your rules.
80 Let me obey your demands perfectly
    so I will not be ashamed.

81 I am weak from waiting for you to
    save me,
    but I hope in your word.
82 My eyes are tired from looking for
    your promise.
    When will you comfort me?
83 Even though I am like a wine bag
    going up in smoke,
    I do not forget your demands.
84 How long will I live?
    When will you judge those who are
    hurting me?
85 Proud people have dug pits to trap
    me.
    They have nothing to do with your
    teachings.
86 All of your commands can be trusted.
    Liars are hurting me. Help me!
87 They have almost put me in the
    grave,
    but I have not rejected your
    orders.
88 Give me life by your love
    so I can obey your rules.
89 LORD, your word is everlasting;
    it continues for ever in heaven.
90 Your loyalty will go on and on;
    you made the earth, and it still
    stands.
91 All things continue to this day
    because of your laws,
    because all things serve you.
92 If I had not loved your teachings,
    I would have died from my
    sufferings.
93 I will never forget your orders,
    because you have given me life by
    them.
94 I am yours. Save me.
    I want to obey your orders.
95 Wicked people are waiting to
    destroy me,
    but I will think about your rules.
96 Everything I see has its limits,
    but your commands have none.
97 How I love your teachings!
    I think about them all day long.

98 Your commands make me wiser
    than my enemies,
    because they are mine for ever.
99 I am wiser than all my teachers,
    because I
    think about
    your rules.
100 I have more
    understanding
    than the older
    leaders,
    because I follow
    your orders.

**119:99–100
Bible**
What does the Bible give you?

101 I have avoided every evil way
    so I could obey your word.
102 I haven't walked away from your
    laws,
    because you yourself are my
    teacher.
103 Your promises are sweet to me,
    sweeter than honey in my mouth!
104 Your orders give me understanding,
    so I hate lying ways.

105 Your word is
    like a lamp
    for my feet
    and a light for
    my path.

**119:105
Decisions**
What helps you make decisions?

106 I will do what I
    have promised
    and obey your fair laws.
107 I have suffered for a long time.
    LORD, give me life by your word.
108 LORD, accept my willing praise
    and teach me your laws.
109 My life is always in danger,
    but I haven't forgotten your
    teachings.
110 Wicked people have set a trap for me,
    but I haven't strayed from your
    orders.
111 I will follow your rules for ever,
    because they make me happy.
112 I will try to do what you demand
    for ever, until the end.

113 I hate disloyal people,
    but I love your teachings.
114 You are my hiding place and my
    shield;
    I hope in your word.
115 Get away from me, you who do evil,

so I can keep my God's commands.
116 Support me as you promised so I
    can live.
    Don't let me be embarrassed
    because of my hopes.
117 Help me, and I will be saved.
    I will always respect your
    demands.
118 You reject those who ignore your
    demands,
    because their lies mislead them.
119 You throw away the wicked of the
    world like rubbish.
    So I will love your rules.
120 I shake in fear of you;
    I respect your laws.

121 I have done what is fair and right.
    Don't leave me to those who wrong
    me.
122 Promise that you will help me, your
    servant.
    Don't let proud people wrong me.
123 My eyes are tired from looking for
    your salvation
    and for your good promise.
124 Show your love to me, your servant,
    and teach me your demands.
125 I am your servant. Give me wisdom
    so I can understand your rules.
126 LORD, it is time for you to do
    something,
    because people have disobeyed
    your teachings.
127 I love your commands
    more than the purest gold.
128 I respect all your orders,
    so I hate lying ways.

129 Your rules are wonderful.
    That is why I keep them.
130 Learning your words gives wisdom
    and understanding for the
    foolish.
131 I am nearly out of breath.
    I really want to learn your
    commands.
132 Look at me and have mercy on me
    as you do for those who love you.
133 Guide my steps as you promised;
    don't let any sin control me.
134 Save me from harmful people
    so I can obey your orders.

135 Show your kindness to me, your
    servant.
    Teach me your demands.
136 Tears stream from my eyes,
    because people do not obey your
    teachings.

137 LORD, you do what is right,
    and your laws are fair.
138 The rules you commanded are right
    and completely trustworthy.
139 I am so upset I am worn out,
    because my enemies have
    forgotten your words.
140 Your promises are proven,
    so I, your servant, love them.
141 I am unimportant and hated,
    but I have not forgotten your
    orders.
142 Your goodness continues for ever,
    and your teachings are true.
143 I have had troubles and misery,
    but I love your commands.
144 Your rules are always good.
    Help me understand so I can live.

145 LORD, I call to you with all my heart.
    Answer me, and I will keep your
    demands.
146 I call to you.
    Save me so I can obey your rules.
147 I wake up early in the morning and
    cry out.
    I hope in your word.
148 I stay awake all night
    so I can think about your
    promises.
149 Listen to me because of your love;
    LORD, give me life by your laws.
150 Those who love evil are near,
    but they are far from your
    teachings.
151 But, LORD, you are also near,
    and all your commands are true.
152 Long ago I learned from your rules
    that you made them to continue for
    ever.

153 See my suffering and rescue me,
    because I have not forgotten your
    teachings.
154 Argue my case and save me.
    Let me live by your promises.

155 Wicked people are far from being saved,
because they do not want your demands.
156 LORD, you are very kind;
give me life by your laws.
157 Many enemies are chasing me,
but I have not rejected your rules.
158 I see those traitors, and I hate them,
because they do not obey what you say.
159 See how I love your orders.
LORD, give me life by your love.
160 Your words are true from the start,
and all your laws will be fair for ever.

161 Leaders attack me for no reason,
but I fear your law in my heart.
162 I am as happy over your promises
as if I had found a great treasure.
163 I hate and despise lies,
but I love your teachings.
164 Seven times a day I praise you
for your fair laws.
165 Those who love your teachings will find true peace,
and nothing will defeat them.
166 I am waiting for you to save me, LORD.
I will obey your commands.
167 I obey your rules,
and I love them very much.
168 I obey your orders and rules,
because you know everything I do.

169 Hear my cry to you, LORD.
Let your word help me understand.
170 Listen to my prayer;
save me as you promised.
171 Let me speak your praise,
because you have taught me your demands.
172 Let me sing about your promises,
because all your commands are fair.
173 Give me your helping hand,
because I have chosen your commands.
174 I want you to save me, LORD.
I love your teachings.
175 Let me live so I can praise you,
and let your laws help me.
176 I have wandered like a lost sheep.
Look for your servant, because I have not forgotten your commands.

A Prayer of Someone Far from Home

A psalm for going up to worship.

120 When I was in trouble, I called to the LORD,
and he answered me.
2 LORD, save me from liars
and from those who plan evil.

3 You who plan evil, what will God do to you?
How will he punish you?
4 He will punish you with the sharp arrows of a warrior
and with burning coals of wood.

5 How terrible it is for me to live in the land of Meshech,
to live among the people of Kedar.
6 I have lived too long
with people who hate peace.
7 When I talk peace,
they want war.

The Lord Guards His People

A song for going up to worship.

121 I look up to the hills,
but where does my help come from?
2 My help comes from the LORD,
who made heaven and earth.

3 He will not let you be defeated.
He who guards you never sleeps.
4 He who guards Israel
never rests or sleeps.
5 The LORD guards you.

The LORD is the shade that protects you from the sun.
6 The sun cannot hurt you during the day,

email from GOD
121
Help
Where does your help come from?

GET THE INFO

THE TEMPLE IN JERUSALEM — Psalm 122

The Temple in Jerusalem was a very important place for the Israelite people. Through Temple services, the Israelite people pledged their lives to follow the laws and teachings of their Creator. They worshipped God there, and they offered sacrifices for their sins.

Three different Temples were actually built in Jerusalem. All three were built on the same site on a hill called Mount Moriah. (See 2 Chronicles 3:1, p. 564.)

The first Temple, built by King Solomon, stood on a platform about three metres high. Thousands of labourers and craftsmen built this Temple. (Read 1 Kings 6 and 7, p. 442; 2 Chronicles 3 and 4, p. 564.) This building was destroyed by the Babylonians when they captured Jerusalem. Then Cyrus, king of Persia, had the Temple rebuilt on the same site when he allowed the Israelite people to return to Jerusalem. (Check out Ezra 1, p. 609.) This Temple was known as Zerubbabel's Temple. (Look at Ezra 6:13–15, p. 616.) Several centuries later, Herod the Great (Roman ruler of Palestine) ordered construction of the third Temple – a cream-coloured building of stone and gold. The Romans destroyed this Temple about 40 years after Jesus' resurrection and ascension.

---

and the moon cannot hurt you at
    night.

7 The LORD will protect you from all
    dangers;
  he will guard your life.
8 The LORD will guard you as you come
    and go,
  both now and for ever.

Happy People in Jerusalem

*A song for going up to worship.
Of David.*

122 I was happy when they said to
    me,
"Let's go to the Temple of the LORD."
2 Jerusalem, we are standing
    at your gates.
3 Jerusalem is built as a city
    with the buildings close together.
4 The tribes go up there,
    the tribes who belong to the
    LORD.
  It is the rule in Israel
    to praise the LORD at Jerusalem.
5 There the descendants of David
    set their thrones to judge the
    people.
6 Pray for peace in Jerusalem:
    "May those who love her be safe.
7 May there be peace within her
    walls
    and safety within her strong
    towers."
8 To help my relatives and friends,
    I say, "Let Jerusalem have
    peace."
9 For the sake of the Temple of the
    LORD our God,
    I wish good for her.

A Prayer for Mercy

A song for going up to worship.

123 LORD, I look upwards to you,
you who live in heaven.
2 Slaves depend on their masters,
and a female servant depends on her mistress.
In the same way, we depend on the LORD our God;
we wait for him to show us mercy.

3 Have mercy on us, LORD. Have mercy on us,
because we have been insulted.
4 We have suffered many insults from lazy people
and much cruelty from the proud.

The Lord Saves His People

*A song for going up to worship.
Of David.*

124 What if the LORD had not been on our side?
(Let Israel repeat this.)
2 What if the LORD had not been on our side
when we were attacked?
3 When they were angry with us,
they would have swallowed us alive.
4 They would have been like a flood drowning us;
they would have poured over us like a river.
5 They would have swept us away like a mighty stream.

6 Praise the LORD,
who did not let them chew us up.
7 We escaped like a bird
from the hunter's trap.
The trap broke,
and we escaped.
8 Our help comes from the LORD,
who made heaven and earth.

God Protects Those Who Trust Him

A song for going up to worship.

125 Those who trust the LORD are like Mount Zion,
which sits unmoved for ever.
2 As the mountains surround Jerusalem,
the LORD surrounds his people
now and for ever.

3 The wicked will not rule
over those who do right.
If they did, the people who do right
might use their power to do evil.

4 LORD, be good to those who are good,
whose hearts are honest.

FAITH CHALLENGE

Here's a challenge for you. Read 123:3-4 to find out why it's sometimes tough to follow the Lord. What do you do when someone insults you or calls you a name?

TESTING IT

Psalm 123:3-4
Have mercy on us, LORD. Have mercy on us, because we have been insulted. We have suffered many insults from lazy people and much cruelty from the proud.

5 But, LORD, when you remove those
          who do evil,
    also remove those who stop
          following you.

    Let there be peace in Israel.

Lord, Bring Your People Back

A song for going up to worship.

126 When the LORD brought the
          prisoners back to
          Jerusalem,
    it seemed as if we were dreaming.
2 Then we were filled with laughter,
    and we sang happy songs.
    Then the other nations said,
    "The LORD has done great things
          for them."
3 The LORD has done great things for us,
    and we are very glad.

4 LORD, return our prisoners again,
    as you bring streams to the desert.
5 Those who cry as they plant crops
    will sing at harvest time.
6 Those who cry
          as they carry out the seeds
    will return singing
          and carrying bundles of grain.

All Good Things Come from God

*A song for going up to worship.
Of Solomon.*

127 If the LORD doesn't build the
          house,
    the builders are working for
          nothing.
    If the LORD doesn't guard the city,
          the guards are watching for
          nothing.
2 It is no use for you to get up early
          and stay up late,
    working for a living.
    The LORD gives sleep to those he
          loves.

3 Children are a gift from the LORD;
    babies are a reward.
4 Children who are born to a young man
    are like arrows in the hand of a
          warrior.

Psalm 128:1 809

FAITH links

GOD'S VALUABLE GIFT: YOU
PSALM 127:3-5

What's the best gift you've been given recently? What makes that gift so valuable to you? Want to know a great gift that God gave your parents or guardians? Take a look in the mirror. One of the main points of this psalm by Solomon is how much God values children. Families with children – like yours – are considered blessed.

Check out these Faithlinks to see how God loves his creations:

Made in His Image, Genesis 1:26–27, p. 4

The MLP, Ruth 1:16–17, p. 345

Love for a Lifetime, Song of Solomon 6:8–9, p. 891

Rock Solid, Habakkuk 1:12, p. 1236

One Big, Happy Family, John 1:12, p. 1422

A Family Celebration, 1 Corinthians 11:23–29, p. 1558

---

5 Happy is the man
    who has his bag full of arrows.
    They will not be defeated
          when they fight their enemies at
          the city gate.

The Happy Home

A song for going up to worship.

128 Happy are those who respect
          the LORD and obey him.

2 You will enjoy what you work for,
   and you will be blessed with good
       things.
3 Your wife will give you many
       children,
   like a vine that produces much
       fruit.
   Your children will bring you much
       good,
   like olive branches that produce
       many olives.
4 This is how the man who respects the
       LORD
   will be blessed.

5 May the LORD bless you from Mount
       Zion;
   may you enjoy the good things of
       Jerusalem all your life.
6 May you see your grandchildren.

   Let there be peace in Israel.

A Prayer Against the Enemies

   A song for going up to worship.

129 They have treated me badly all
       my life.
   (Let Israel repeat this.)
2 They have treated me badly all my
       life,
   but they have not defeated me.
3 Like farmers ploughing, they
       ploughed over my back,
   making long wounds.
4 But the LORD does what is right;
   he has set me free from those
       wicked people.

5 Let those who hate Jerusalem
   be turned back in shame.
6 Let them be like the grass on the
       roof
   that dries up before it has grown.
7 There is not enough of it to fill a
       hand
   or to make into a bundle to fill
       one's arms.
8 Let those who pass by them not
       say,
   "May the LORD bless you.
   We bless you by the power of the
       LORD."

A Prayer for Mercy

   A song for going up to worship.

130 Lord, I am in great trouble,
   so I call out to you.
2 Lord, hear my voice;
   listen to my prayer for help.
3 LORD, if you punished people for all
       their sins,
   no one would be left, Lord.
4 But you forgive us,
   so we respect you.

5 I wait for the LORD to help me,
   and I trust his
       word.
6 I wait for the
   Lord to help
   me
   more than
   night-watchmen wait for the
       dawn,
   more than night-watchmen wait for
       the dawn.

130:5–6
Hope
Wait for the Lord.

7 People of Israel, put your hope in the
       LORD
   because he is loving
   and able to save.
8 He will save Israel
   from all their sins.

Childlike Trust in the Lord

   A song for going up to worship.
   Of David.

131 LORD, my heart is not proud;
   I don't look down on others.
   I don't do great
       things,
   and I can't do
       miracles.
2 But I am calm
   and quiet,
   like a baby with
       its mother.
   I am at peace, like a baby with its
       mother.

3 People of Israel, put your hope in the
       LORD
   now and for ever.

131:1
Pride
What should your
attitude be like?

In Praise of the Temple

A song for going up to worship.

132 LORD, remember David and all his suffering.
2 He made an oath to the LORD,
 a promise to the Mighty God of Jacob.
3 He said, "I will not go home to my house,
 or lie down on my bed,
4 or close my eyes,
 or let myself sleep
5 until I find a place for the LORD.
 I want to provide a home for the Mighty God of Jacob."

6 We heard about the Ark in Bethlehem.
 We found it at Kiriath Jearim.
7 Let's go to the LORD's house.
 Let's worship at his footstool.
8 Rise, LORD, and come to your resting place;
 come with the Ark that shows your strength.
9 May your priests do what is right.
 May your people sing for joy.

10 For the sake of your servant David,
 do not reject your appointed king.
11 The LORD made a promise to David,
 a sure promise that he will not take back.
 He promised, "I will make one of your descendants
 rule as king after you.
12 If your sons keep my agreement
 and the rules that I teach them,
 then their sons after them will rule on your throne for ever and ever."

13 The LORD has chosen Jerusalem;
 he wants it for his home.
14 He says, "This is my resting place for ever.
 Here is where I want to stay.
15 I will bless her with plenty;
 I will fill her poor with food.
16 I will cover her priests with salvation,
 and those who worship me will really sing for joy.

17 "I will make a king come from the family of David.
 I will provide my appointed one descendants to rule after him.
18 I will cover his enemies with shame,
 but his crown will shine."

FAITH links

PEACE IN THE FAMILY
PSALM 133

"He started it!" "No she did!" Sounds familiar? Maybe you've said something similar in an argument with a sister or brother. Ever wish you and your siblings could get along all the time? Maybe you also wish that for your brothers and sisters in Christ. That is the hope expressed in this psalm. Getting along with siblings is not an impossible dream. God's love makes it possible for people to "live together in peace". Even siblings.

Link here to find out how to live with your brothers and sisters:

Family Feud, Genesis 27, p. 37

Fair All the Time? 2 Samuel 8:15, p. 408

In Deep Water, Psalm 69, p. 760

Better Than Some? Luke 18:9–14, p. 1405

The Gentle Way, Titus 3:1–5, p. 1661

Who's on First? 3 John 9–10, p. 1723

The Love of God's People

*A song for going up to worship.
Of David.*

133 It is good and pleasant
when God's people live
together in peace!
2 It is like perfumed oil poured on the
priest's head
and running down his beard.
It ran down Aaron's beard
and on to the collar of his robes.
3 It is like the dew of Mount Hermon
falling on the hills of Jerusalem.
There the LORD gives his blessing
of life for ever.

Temple Guards, Praise the Lord

A song for going up to worship.

134 Praise the LORD, all you
servants of the LORD,
you who serve at night in the
Temple of the LORD.
2 Raise your hands in the Temple
and praise the LORD.

3 May the LORD bless you from Mount
Zion,
he who made heaven and earth.

The Lord Saves, Idols do Not

135 Praise the LORD!

Praise the name of the LORD;
praise him, you servants of the
LORD,
2 you who stand in the
LORD's Temple
and in the Temple
courtyards.

3 Praise the LORD,
because he is
good;
sing praises to him,
because it is
pleasant.
4 The LORD has chosen
the people of Jacob for himself;
he has chosen the people of Israel
for his very own.

5 I know that the LORD is great.
Our Lord is greater than all the
gods.
6 The LORD does what he pleases,
in heaven and on earth,
in the seas and the deep oceans.
7 He brings the clouds from the ends of
the earth.
He sends the lightning with the
rain.
He brings out the wind from his
storehouses.

8 He destroyed the firstborn sons in
Egypt
the firstborn of both people and
animals.
9 He did many signs and miracles in
Egypt
against the king and his servants.
10 He defeated many nations
and killed powerful kings:
11 Sihon king of the Amorites,
Og king of Bashan,
and all the kings of Canaan.
12 Then he gave their land as a gift,
a gift to his people, the Israelites.

13 LORD, your name is everlasting;
LORD, you will be remembered for
ever.
14 The LORD defends his people
and has mercy on his servants.

15 The idols of other nations are made
of silver and gold,
the work of human hands.
16 They have mouths, but they cannot
speak.
They have eyes,
but they cannot
see.
17 They have ears, but
they cannot hear.
They have no
breath in their
mouths.
18 People who make
idols will be like
them,
and so will those who trust them.

19 Family of Israel, praise the LORD.

Our Lord is greater
than all the gods.
– Psalm 135:5

Family of Aaron, praise the LORD.
20 Family of Levi, praise the LORD.
You who respect the LORD should praise him.
21 You people of Jerusalem, praise the LORD on Mount Zion.

Praise the LORD!

God's Love Continues For Ever

136 Give thanks to the LORD because he is good.
His love continues for ever.
2 Give thanks to the God of gods.
His love continues for ever.
3 Give thanks to the Lord of lords.
His love continues for ever.
4 Only he can do great miracles.
His love continues for ever.
5 With his wisdom he made the skies.
His love continues for ever.
6 He spread out the earth on the seas.
His love continues for ever.
7 He made the sun and the moon.
His love continues for ever.
8 He made the sun to rule the day.
His love continues for ever.
9 He made the moon and stars to rule the night.
His love continues for ever.

10 He killed the firstborn sons of the Egyptians.
His love continues for ever.
11 He brought the people of Israel out of Egypt.
His love continues for ever.
12 He did it with his great power and strength.
His love continues for ever.

13 He parted the water of the Red Sea.
His love continues for ever.
14 He brought the Israelites through the middle of it.
His love continues for ever.
15 But the king of Egypt and his army drowned in the Red Sea.
His love continues for ever.

16 He led his people through the desert.
His love continues for ever.
17 He defeated great kings.
His love continues for ever.
18 He killed powerful kings.
His love continues for ever.
19 He defeated Sihon king of the Amorites.
His love continues for ever.
20 He defeated Og king of Bashan.

FAITH links

LOVE THAT WILL LAST
PSALM 136

Is there anything you know of that lasts for ever? Some things like spots, or your gran's fish pie may seem to last for ever, but eventually they disappear. Even some friendships don't seem to last. Maybe you had a friend you thought you'd have for ever. Throughout this psalm of praise, one statement stands out: "His love continues for ever." God's love will never end. Even though others may disappoint you, you can count on God.

Surf over to these Faithlinks to find out about the One who will never disappoint you:

Your Worst Enemy, Exodus 7—11, p. 85

God's New Home, 2 Chronicles 7:11–22, p. 570

Lower Than Low, Job 19:13–25, p. 680

The One Who Suffered, Isaiah 53, p. 966

His Valentine, Jeremiah 31:3, p. 1035

A Heavenly Sight, Revelation 21:1–4, p. 1753

His love continues for ever.
21 He gave their land as a gift.
His love continues for ever.
22 It was a gift to his servants, the Israelites.
His love continues for ever.

23 He remembered us when we were in trouble.
His love continues for ever.
24 He freed us from our enemies.
His love continues for ever.
25 He gives food to every living creature.
His love continues for ever.

26 Give thanks to the God of heaven.
His love continues for ever.

Israelites in Captivity

137 By the rivers in Babylon we sat and cried
when we remembered Jerusalem.
2 On the poplar trees nearby
we hung our harps.
3 Those who captured us asked us to sing;
our enemies wanted happy songs.
They said, "Sing us a song about Jerusalem!"

4 But we cannot sing songs about the LORD
while we are in this foreign country!
5 Jerusalem, if I forget you,
let my right hand lose its skill.
6 Let my tongue stick to the roof of my mouth
if I do not remember you,
if I do not think about Jerusalem
as my greatest joy.

7 LORD, remember what the Edomites did
on the day Jerusalem fell.
They said, "Tear it down!
Tear it down to its foundations!"

8 People of Babylon, you will be destroyed.
The people who pay you back for what you did to us will be happy.
9 They will grab your babies
and throw them against the rocks.

A Hymn of Thanksgiving

A psalm of David.

138 LORD, I will thank you with all my heart;
I will sing to you before the gods.
2 I will bow down facing your holy Temple,
and I will thank you for your love and loyalty.
You have made your name and your word
greater than anything.
3 On the day I called to you, you answered me.
You made me strong and brave.

4 LORD, let all the kings of the earth praise you
when they hear the words you speak.
5 They will sing about what the LORD has done,
because the LORD's glory is great.

138
Thankfulness
What should you be thankful for?

6 Though the LORD is supreme,
he takes care of those who are humble,
but he stays away from the proud.
7 LORD, even when I have trouble all around me,
you will keep me alive.
When my enemies are angry,
you will reach down and save me by your power.
8 LORD, you do everything for me.
LORD, your love continues for ever.
Do not leave us, whom you made.

God Knows Everything

For the director of music. A psalm of David.

139 LORD, you have examined me
and know all about me.

2 You know when I sit down and when I get up.
You know my thoughts before I think them.
3 You know where I go and where I lie down.
You know thoroughly everything I do.
4 LORD, even before I say a word, you already know it.
5 You are all around me—in front and at the back—
and have put your hand on me.
6 Your knowledge is amazing to me; it is more than I can understand.
7 Where can I go to get away from your Spirit?
Where can I run from you?
8 If I go up to the heavens, you are there.
If I lie down in the grave, you are there.
9 If I rise with the sun in the east and settle in the west beyond the sea,
10 even there you would guide me.
With your right hand you would hold me.
11 I could say, "The darkness will hide me.
Let the light around me turn into night."
12 But even the darkness is not dark to you.
The night is as light as the day; darkness and light are the same to you.

13 You made my whole being; you formed me in my mother's body.
14 I praise you because you made me in an amazing and wonderful way.
What you have done is wonderful.
I know this very well.
15 You saw my bones being formed as I took shape in my mother's body.
When I was put together there,
16 you saw my body as it was formed.
All the days planned for me were written in your book before I was one day old.
17 God, your thoughts are precious to me.
They are so many!
18 If I could count them, they would be more than all the grains of sand.
When I wake up, I am still with you.

FAITH LINKS

UNIQUELY YOU
PSALM 139:13-14

Take a good look at yourself in the mirror. You've probably heard relatives tell you how much you look like various members of your family. Maybe you have your mother's eyebrows or your grandfather's left ear. Maybe there are some features you like and some you wish you could change. But guess what? God made you exactly the way he wanted you to be. You are unique. That means there is only one of you. And that makes you pretty cool.

Complaints, Complaints! Exodus 16:1–3, p. 97

The Perfect Sacrifice, Leviticus 1—7, p. 135

How to Worship God, Isaiah 58, p. 972

The Way to Heaven, John 14:1–6, p. 1448

The "Eyes" Have It?
1 Corinthians 12, p. 1559

It's Free! Ephesians 2:8–9, p. 1600

19 God, I wish you would kill the wicked!
  Get away from me, you murderers!
20 They say evil things about you.
  Your enemies use your name thoughtlessly.
21 LORD, I hate those who hate you;
  I hate those who rise up against you.
22 I feel only hate for them;
  they are my enemies.

23 God, examine me and know my heart;
  test me and know my nervous thoughts.
24 See if there is any bad thing in me.
  Lead me on the road to everlasting life.

A Prayer for Protection

For the director of music. A psalm of David.

140 LORD, rescue me from evil people;
  protect me from cruel people
2 who make evil plans,
  who always start fights.
3 They make their tongues sharp as a snake's;
  their words are like snake poison. *Selah*

4 LORD, guard me from the power of wicked people;
  protect me from cruel people
  who plan to trip me up.
5 The proud hid a trap for me.
  They spread out a net beside the road;
  they set traps for me. *Selah*

6 I said to the LORD, "You are my God."
  LORD, listen to my prayer for help.
7 LORD God, my mighty Saviour,
  you protect me in battle.

8 LORD, do not give the wicked what they want.
  Don't let their plans succeed,
  or they will become proud. *Selah*

9 Those around me have planned trouble.
  Now let it come to them.
10 Let burning coals fall on them.
  Throw them into the fire
  or into pits from which they cannot escape.
11 Don't let liars settle in the land.
  Let evil quickly hunt down cruel people.

12 I know the LORD will get justice for the poor
  and will defend the needy in court.
13 Good people will praise his name;
  honest people will live in his presence.

A Prayer Not to Sin

A psalm of David.

141 LORD, I call to you. Come quickly.
  Listen to me when I call to you.
2 Let my prayer be like incense placed before you,
  and my praise like the evening sacrifice.

3 LORD, help me control my tongue;
  help me be careful about what I say.
4 Take away my desire to do evil
  or to join others in doing wrong.
  Don't let me eat tasty food
  with those who do evil.

5 If a good person punished me, that would be kind.
  If he corrected me, that would be like perfumed oil on my head.
  I shouldn't refuse it.
  But I pray against those who do evil.

> LORD, help me control my tongue; help me be careful about what I say.
> – Psalm 141:3

6 Let their leaders be thrown down the cliffs.
Then people will know that I have spoken correctly:
7 "The ground is ploughed and broken up.
In the same way, our bones have been scattered at the grave."
8 GOD, I look to you for help.
I trust in you, LORD. Don't let me die.
9 Protect me from the traps they set for me
and from the net that evil people have spread.
10 Let the wicked fall into their own nets, but let me pass by safely.

A Prayer for Safety

A maskil of David when he was in the cave. A prayer.

142 I cry out to the Lord;
I pray to the Lord for mercy.
2 I pour out my problems to him;
I tell him my troubles.

3 When I am afraid,
you, LORD, know the way out.
In the path where I walk,
a trap is hidden for me.
4 Look around me and see.
No one cares about me.
I have no place of safety;
no one cares if I live.

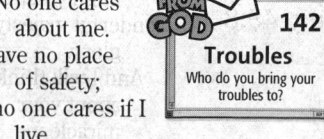

142 Troubles
Who do you bring your troubles to?

5 LORD, I cry out to you.
I say, "You are my protection.
You are all I want in this life."
6 Listen to my cry,
because I am helpless.
Save me from those who are chasing me,
because they are too strong for me.
7 Free me from my prison,
and then I will praise your name.
Then good people will surround me,
because you have taken care of me.

A Prayer Not to be Killed

A psalm of David.

143 LORD, hear my prayer;
listen to my cry for mercy.
Answer me
because you are loyal and good.
2 Don't judge me, your servant,
because no one alive is right before you.

3 My enemies are chasing me;
they crushed me to the ground.
They made me live in darkness
like those long dead.
4 I am afraid;
my courage is gone.

5 I remember what happened long ago;
I consider everything you have done.
I think about all you have made.
6 I lift my hands to you in prayer.
As a dry land needs rain, I thirst for you.   *Selah*

7 LORD, answer me quickly,
because I am getting weak.
Don't turn away from me,
or I will be like those who are dead.
8 Tell me in the morning about your love,
because I trust you.
Show me what I should do,
because my prayers go up to you.
9 LORD, save me from my enemies;
I hide in you.
10 Teach me to do what you want,
because you are my God.
Let your good Spirit
lead me on level ground.

11 LORD, let me live
so people will praise you.
In your goodness
save me from my troubles.
12 In your love defeat my enemies.
Destroy all those who trouble me,
because I am your servant.

A Prayer for Victory

Of David.

144 ¹ Praise the LORD, my Rock,
who trains me for war,
who trains me for battle.
² He protects me like a fortified city,
and he loves me.
He is my defender and my Saviour,
my shield and my protection.
He helps me keep my people under
control.

³ LORD, why are people important to
you?
Why do you even think about
human beings?
⁴ People are like a breath;
their lives are like passing
shadows.

⁵ LORD, tear open the sky and come
down.
Touch the mountains so they will
smoke.
⁶ Send the lightning and scatter my
enemies.
Shoot your arrows
and force them
away.
⁷ Reach down from
above.
Save me and
rescue me out of
this sea of
enemies,
from these
foreigners.
⁸ They are liars;
they are dishonest.

⁹ God, I will sing a new song to you;
I will play to you on the ten-
stringed harp.
¹⁰ You give victory to kings.
You save your servant David from
cruel swords.

¹¹ Save me, rescue me from these
foreigners.
They are liars; they are dishonest.
¹² Let our sons in their youth
grow like plants.
Let our daughters be
like the decorated stones in the
Temple.
¹³ Let our barns be filled
with crops of all kinds.
Let our sheep in the fields have
thousands and tens of thousands of
lambs.
¹⁴ Let our cattle be strong.
Let no one break in.
Let there be no war,
no screams in our streets.

¹⁵ Happy are those who are like this;
happy are the people whose God is
the LORD.

Praise to God the King

A psalm of praise. Of David.

145 ¹ I praise your greatness, my
God the King;
I will praise you for ever and ever.
² I will praise you every day;
I will praise you for ever and ever.
³ The LORD is great and worthy of our
praise;
no one can
understand how
great he is.

⁴ Parents will tell their
children what you
have done.
They will retell your
mighty acts,
⁵ wonderful majesty and
glory.
And I will think
about your
miracles.
⁶ They will tell about the amazing
things you do,
and I will tell how great you are.
⁷ They will remember your great
goodness
and will sing about your fairness.

⁸ The LORD is kind and shows mercy.
He does not become angry quickly
but is full of love.
⁹ The LORD is good to everyone;
he is merciful to all he has made.

> The LORD is kind and
> shows mercy. He
> does not become
> angry quickly but is
> full of love.
> – Psalm 145:8

FAITH links

PATIENCE, PLEASE
PSALM 145:8-9

Who among your family has the most patience? Have you ever noticed how this person acts towards others? Maybe he doesn't seem to mind when others go ahead of him. Or maybe she takes time to answer your questions or explain things. A patient person never seems to do things in a hurry.

That's a description of God. This psalm mentions one thing that God doesn't do in a hurry: become angry. That means he's always patient with us. He never demands that we "hurry up" and do something. He wants his people to be just as patient with each other as he is with us.

Here are some more Faithlinks on patience:

Just Kidding? Genesis 21:8–10, p. 28

Give Revenge a Rest, Leviticus 19:18, p. 160

Putting an Enemy in Check, 2 Kings 6:8–23, p. 486

Helpful Advice, Job 12:4–5, p. 673

Ask, Search, Knock, Matthew 7:7–10, p. 1286

Your Civic Duty, Matthew 17:24–27, p. 1304

---

10 LORD, everything you have made will praise you;
   those who belong to you will bless you.
11 They will tell about the glory of your kingdom
   and will speak about your power.
12 Then everyone will know the mighty things you do
   and the glory and majesty of your kingdom.
13 Your kingdom will go on and on,
   and you will rule for ever.

The LORD will keep all his promises;
   he is loyal to all he has made.
14 The LORD helps those who have been defeated
   and takes care of those who are in trouble.
15 All living things look to you for food,
   and you give it to them at the right time.
16 You open your hand,
   and you satisfy all living things.

17 Everything the LORD does is right.
   He is loyal to all he has made.
18 The LORD is close to everyone who prays to him,
   to all who truly pray to him.
19 He gives those who respect him what they want.
   He listens when they cry, and he saves them.
20 The LORD protects everyone who loves him,
   but he will destroy the wicked.

21 I will praise the LORD.
   Let everyone praise his holy name for ever.

Praise God Who Helps the Weak

146 Praise the LORD!

My whole being, praise the LORD.
2 I will praise the LORD all my life;
   I will sing praises to my God as long as I live.

3 Do not put your trust in princes

Psalm 146:4 820

or other people, who cannot save you.
4 When people die, they are buried.
Then all of their plans come to an end.

5 Happy are those who are helped by the God of Jacob.
Their hope is in the LORD their God.
6 He made heaven and earth,
the sea and everything in it.
He remains loyal for ever.
7 He does what is fair for those who have been wronged.

146:3 Trust
Don't put your trust here.

FAITH CHALLENGE

Try this one. Read 146:8 to find out how God helps people who have special needs. When you find yourself in trouble, what's the first thing you usually do?

Testing it

Psalm 146:8
The LORD gives sight to the blind. The LORD lifts up people who are in trouble. The LORD loves those who do right.

He gives food to the hungry.
The LORD sets the prisoners free.
8 The LORD gives sight to the blind.
The LORD lifts up people who are in trouble.
The LORD loves those who do right.
9 The LORD protects the foreigners.
He defends the orphans and widows,
but he blocks the way of the wicked.

10 The LORD will be King for ever.
Jerusalem, your God is everlasting.

Praise the LORD!

Praise God Who Helps His People

147 Praise the LORD!
It is good to sing praises to our God;
it is good and pleasant to praise him.

2 The LORD rebuilds Jerusalem;
he brings back the captured Israelites.
3 He heals the broken-hearted
and bandages their wounds.

4 He counts the stars
and names each one.
5 Our Lord is great and very powerful.
There is no limit to what he knows.
6 The LORD defends the humble,
but he throws the wicked to the ground.

7 Sing praises to the LORD;
praise our God with harps.
8 He fills the sky with clouds
and sends rain to the earth
and makes grass grow on the hills.
9 He gives food to cattle
and to the little birds that call.

10 He does not enjoy the strength of a horse
or the strength of a man.

11 The LORD is pleased with those who
respect him,
with those who trust his love.

12 Jerusalem, praise the LORD;
Jerusalem, praise
your God.
13 He makes your city
gates strong
and blesses your
children inside.
14 He brings peace to
your country
and fills you with
the finest grain.

15 He gives a command
to the earth,
and it quickly obeys him.
16 He spreads the snow like wool
and scatters the frost like ashes.
17 He throws down hail like rocks.
No one can stand the cold he
sends.
18 Then he gives a command, and it
melts.
He sends the breezes, and the
waters flow.
19 He gave his word to Jacob,
his laws and demands to Israel.
20 He didn't do this for any other nation.
They don't know his laws.

Praise the LORD!

The World Should Praise the Lord

148 Praise the LORD!

Praise the LORD from the skies.
Praise him high above the earth.
2 Praise him, all
you angels.
Praise him, all
you armies
of heaven.
3 Praise him, sun
and moon.
Praise him, all
you shining stars.
4 Praise him, highest heavens
and you waters above the sky.
5 Let them praise the LORD,

> He counts the stars
> and names each
> one.
> – Psalm 147:4

148:1–2
Angels
Who do angels praise?

because they were created by his
command.
6 He put them in place for ever and
ever;
he made a law that will never
change.

7 Praise the LORD from
the earth,
you large sea
animals and all the
oceans,
8 lightning and hail,
snow and mist
and stormy winds
that obey him,
9 mountains and all hills,
fruit trees and all cedars,
10 wild animals and all cattle,
crawling animals and birds,
11 kings of the earth and all nations,
princes and all rulers of the earth,
12 young men and women,
old people and children.

13 Praise the LORD,
because he alone is great.
He is more wonderful than heaven
and earth.
14 God has given his people a king.
He should be praised by all who
belong to him;
he should be praised by the
Israelites, the people closest to
his heart.

Praise the LORD!

Praise the God of Israel

149 Praise the LORD!

Sing a new song to the LORD;
sing his praise in the meeting of
his people.

2 Let the Israelites be happy because of
God, their Maker.
Let the people of Jerusalem rejoice
because of their King.
3 They should praise him with dancing.
They should sing praises to him
with tambourines and harps.
4 The LORD is pleased with his people;

he saves the humble.
5 Let those who worship him rejoice in his glory.
 Let them sing for joy even in bed!

6 Let them shout his praise
 with their two-edged swords in their hands.
7 They will punish the nations
 and defeat the people.
8 They will put those kings in chains
 and those important men in iron bands.
9 They will punish them as God has written.
 God is honoured by all who worship him.

Praise the LORD!

Praise the Lord with Music

150 Praise the LORD!

Praise God in his Temple;
 praise him in his mighty heaven.
2 Praise him for his strength;
 praise him for his greatness.
3 Praise him with trumpet blasts;
 praise him with harps and lyres.
4 Praise him with tambourines and dancing;
 praise him with stringed instruments and flutes.
5 Praise him with loud cymbals;
 praise him with crashing cymbals.

6 Let everything that breathes praise the LORD.

Praise the LORD!

150
Worship
Check out ways to worship God.

BE WISE!

Greetings! I am Solomon, the king of Israel and the builder of the Lord's Temple. One night, shortly after I became king, God appeared to me in a dream and said he would give me whatever I wanted. Whatever I wanted! Can you imagine? What would you ask for? Toys? Money? Popularity? I could have asked for a long life or money or victory over my enemies, but I asked for wisdom so that I could rule my kingdom well. God granted my request and I became famous for my wisdom. People said that I was the wisest man who had ever lived!

I wrote Proverbs to share God's wisdom. This book is a collection of proverbs (or wise sayings) that help us make good decisions in daily life. Many proverbs show a choice between two paths: the way of the wise and the way of the fool. Here's an example: "Wise people are careful and stay out of trouble, but fools are careless and quick to act" (Proverbs 14:16). Do you want to be wise? Read some proverbs today!

JESUS WATCH

Solomon describes wisdom as a woman who has set up her house on the highest hill. She calls out for all to come and learn the ways of God. Her teachings are more precious than gold and silver and rubies. Those who follow her teachings will make good decisions and will be richly rewarded. Those who find wisdom will find life with God. Those who hate wisdom will find death. In 1 Corinthians 1:30, Paul says that Jesus has become wisdom for us. Jesus invites everyone to believe in him and obey his teachings. It is wise to follow Jesus because the reward is more precious than gold. It is eternal life with God.

my FAVOURITE links

OTHER CONNECTIONS

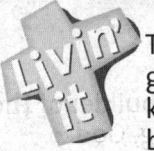 The Book of Proverbs is all about gaining wisdom – not just the kind that comes from reading books and studying hard, but wisdom that comes from God. Find out what the difference is by linking to Wise or Wise Guy? Proverbs 2.

- It may not be the easiest thing to do, but listening to and obeying your parents is the wisest thing you can do! Surf over to How to Be a Real Wise Guy! Proverbs 6:20–23, and find out all about what it takes to have true wisdom. Really!

- It may be one of the hardest things to do – to walk away from a fight or a kid who has just insulted you – but that's what the Bible tells you to do. Check it out by downloading Now You're Asking for It! Proverbs 25:21–22.

FAITH links

- A Parent's Advice, Proverbs 1:8–9
- A Direct Path, Proverbs 3:5–6
- Down on the Ant Farm, Proverbs 6:6–11
- What God "Hates", Proverbs 6:16–19
- The Problem with Gossip, Proverbs 11:12–13
- If You Want My Advice . . . Proverbs 13:1
- A Gentle Answer, Proverbs 15:1
- Choosing a Friend, Proverbs 28:7
- Down on Discipline? Proverbs 29:15

did you know?

Can you name seven things the Lord can't stand?

That's a tough one, isn't it? Surf over to Proverbs 6:16–19 to find out.

SOME MORE COOL STUFF FROM PROVERBS:

Who do you trust? Proverbs 3:5–6
Be like an ant? Proverbs 6:6–8
Like a gold ring in a pig's snout, Proverbs 11:22
Reward this woman! Proverbs 31:10–31

The Importance of Proverbs

1 These are the wise words of Solomon son of David, king of Israel.

2 They teach wisdom and self-control;
    they will help you understand wise
      words.
3 They will teach you how to be wise
      and self-controlled
    and will teach you to do what is
      honest and fair and right.
4 They make the uneducated clever
    and give knowledge and sense to
      the young.
5 Wise people can also listen and learn;
    even clever people can find good
      advice in these words.
6 Then anyone can understand wise
      words and stories,
    the words of the wise and their
      riddles.

7 Knowledge begins with respect for the LORD,
    but fools hate wisdom and self-control.

1:7 Wisdom
Where does wisdom begin?

Warnings Against Evil

8 My child, listen to your father's
      teaching
    and do not forget your mother's
      advice.
9 Their teaching will be like flowers in
      your hair
    or a necklace around your neck.

10 My child, if sinners try to lead you
      into sin,
    do not follow them.
11 They will say, "Come with us.
      Let's ambush and kill someone;
      let's attack some innocent people
        just for fun.
12 Let's swallow them alive, as death
      does;
    let's swallow them whole, as the
      grave does.
13 We will take all kinds of valuable
      things
    and fill our houses with stolen goods.
14 Come and join us,
    and we will share with you stolen
      goods."
15 My child, do not go along with them;
    do not do what they do.
16 They are eager to do evil
    and are quick to kill.
17 It is useless to spread out a net
    right where the birds can see it.
18 But sinners will fall into their own
      traps;
    they will only catch themselves!
19 All greedy people end up this way;
    greed kills selfish people.

FAITH links

A PARENT'S ADVICE
PROVERBS 1:8-9

You can find advice all over the place: the newspaper, the Internet, magazines, the radio and your friends. But there is only one source of advice that this proverb tells you to listen to: your parents. Listening to them is one way to show your respect for them. If you really want to be wise, lend your parents your ear.

His OK to Obey, Deuteronomy 2:24–36, p. 230

In Your Best Interests, Ruth 3, p. 349

God's Valuable Gift: You, Psalm 127:3–5, p. 809

Sow It and Reap, Lamentations 1:18, p. 1075

Obey or Disobey? Luke 20:20–26, p. 1409

The Best Choice, 1 Corinthians 13, p. 1560

Wisdom Speaks

20 Wisdom is like a woman shouting in the street;
  she raises her voice in the city squares.
21 She cries out in the noisy street
  and shouts at the city gates:*
22 "You fools, how long will you be foolish?
  How long will you make fun of wisdom
  and hate knowledge?
23 If only you had listened when I corrected you,
  I would have told you what's in my heart;
  I would have told you what I am thinking.
24 I called, but you refused to listen;
  I held out my hand, but you paid no attention.
25 You did not follow my advice
  and did not listen when I corrected you.
26 So I will laugh when you are in trouble.
  I will make fun when disaster strikes you,
27 when disaster comes over you like a storm,
  when trouble strikes you like a whirlwind,
  when pain and trouble overwhelm you.

28 "Then you will call to me,
  but I will not answer.
  You will look for me,
  but you will not find me.
29 It is because you rejected knowledge
  and did not choose to respect the LORD.
30 You did not accept my advice,
  and you rejected my correction.
31 So you will get what you deserve;
  you will get what you planned for others.
32 Fools will die because they refuse to listen;
  they will be destroyed because they do not care.
33 But those who listen to me will live in safety
  and be at peace, without fear of injury."

Rewards of Wisdom

2 My child, listen to what I say
  and remember what I command you.
2 Listen carefully to wisdom;
  set your mind on understanding.
3 Cry out for wisdom,
  and beg for understanding.
4 Search for it like silver,
  and hunt for it like hidden treasure.
5 Then you will understand respect for the LORD,
  and you will find that you know God.
6 Only the LORD gives wisdom;
  he gives knowledge and understanding.
7 He stores up wisdom for those who are honest.
  Like a shield he protects the innocent.
8 He makes sure that justice is done,
  and he protects those who are loyal to him.

9 Then you will understand what is honest and fair
  and what is the good and right thing to do.
10 Wisdom will come into your mind,
  and knowledge will be pleasing to you.
11 Good sense will protect you;
  understanding will guard you.
12 It will keep you from the wicked,
  from those whose words are bad,
13 who don't do what is right
  but what is evil.
14 They enjoy doing wrong
  and are happy to do what is crooked and evil.
15 What they do is wrong,
  and their ways are dishonest.

EMAIL FROM GOD
2:10–14 Temptation
Check out how to guard against temptation.

1:21 city gates People came here to conduct business. Public meetings and court cases were also held here.

GROWING IN WISDOM
Proverbs 2

Livin' it

Wise or Wise Guy? Which of these titles fits you? You probably wouldn't want to be called a wise guy – someone who thinks he knows everything about everything. But being called *wise* is a compliment. It means you really think about things and make good decisions. What is the difference between being smart and being wise? How can someone be smart and not wise?

Where does true wisdom come from? The Bible tells us it comes from God because he is the source of all wisdom. (Check out Proverbs 2:6–7.) God has plenty of wisdom for everyone. When you need it, be wise – just ask.

MORE FAITH links

Deciding Wisely, **p. 440**
Plan for Success, **p. 538**
Like Silver, **p. 717**
Wisdom in Store, **p. 828**
Want to Know? Ask! **p. 1386**

Are you a wise guy?

You may know a lot about lots of things – but that doesn't make you wise. Better read up on it!

Fatherly Advice, Exodus 18, p. 99
- When you need help, who do you go to for advice? Why do you go to them? Do you accept their advice and follow through on what they suggest? God puts people in your life who care about you and can give you good advice. Be wise – learn to listen to them.

Take My Advice, 1 Kings 2:2–4, p. 436
- What is the most important advice your parents have passed on to you? Link here to find out the advice King David gave his son, Solomon.

The Way to Be Wise, James 1:5, p. 1689
- What do you think is the secret to being wise? What does having wisdom mean to you? Where do you get this wisdom?
- When you are looking for some wisdom, remember God is the source of all wisdom. The best thing about having wisdom is this: God helps you to use it.

my FAVOURITE links

16 It will save you from the unfaithful wife
 who tries to lead you into adultery
 with pleasing words.
17 She leaves the husband she married
 when she was young.
 She ignores the promise she made
 before God.
18 Her house is on the way to death;
 those who took that path are now
 all dead.
19 No one who goes to her comes back
 or walks the path of life again.
20 But wisdom will help you be good
 and do what is right.
21 Those who are honest will live in the
 land,
 and those who are innocent will
 remain in it.
22 But the wicked will be removed from
 the land,
 and the unfaithful will be thrown
 out of it.

Advice to Children

3 My child, do not forget my teaching,
 but keep my commands in mind.
2 Then you will live a long time,
 and your life will be successful.

3 Don't ever forget kindness and truth.
 Wear them like a necklace.
 Write them on your heart as if on a
 tablet.
4 Then you will be respected
 and will please both God and people.

3:3–4
Kindness
Remember kindness and truth.

5 Trust the LORD
 with all your heart,
 and don't depend on your own
 understanding.
6 Remember the LORD in all you do,
 and he will give you success.
7 Don't depend on your own wisdom.
 Respect the LORD and refuse to do
 wrong.
8 Then your body will be healthy,
 and your bones will be strong.
9 Honour the LORD with your wealth
 and the first fruits from all your
 crops.
10 Then your barns will be full,
 and your wine barrels will overflow
 with new wine.

11 My child, do not reject the LORD's
 discipline,
 and don't get angry when he
 corrects you.
12 The LORD corrects those he loves,
 just as parents correct the child
 they delight in.

FAITH links

WISDOM IN STORE

PROVERBS 2:6-7

Do you have a savings account? If you do, you know that you collect interest, maybe every month or perhaps once a year. The more you store in the bank, the more interest you receive. God is a "storehouse" of wisdom. That means he is the source of wisdom. It also means he has plenty in reserve for those who might need it. When you need it, just ask. (See James 1:5, p. 1688.)

Looking for some good advice? Check out these Faithlinks:

Good Advice? Leviticus 20:6, p. 162

Who Do You Trust? Joshua 9, p. 287

A Promise from the Heart, Jeremiah 31:31–33, p. 1037

How Do You Grow? Titus 1:1, p. 1659

The Way to Be Wise, James 1:5, p. 1689

That's False! 2 John 7–11, p. 1722

13 Happy is the person who finds wisdom,
    the one who gets understanding.
14 Wisdom is worth more than silver;
    it brings more profit than gold.
15 Wisdom is more precious than rubies;
    nothing you could want is equal to it.
16 With her right hand wisdom offers you a long life,
    and with her left hand she gives you riches and honour.
17 Wisdom will make your life pleasant
    and will bring you peace.
18 As a tree produces fruit, wisdom gives life to those who use it,
    and everyone who uses it will be happy.
19 The LORD made the earth, using his wisdom.
    He set the sky in place, using his understanding.
20 With his knowledge, he made springs flow into rivers
    and the clouds drop rain on the earth.
21 My child, hold on to wisdom and good sense.
    Don't let them out of your sight.
22 They will give you life
    and beauty like a necklace around your neck.
23 Then you will go your way in safety,
    and you will not get hurt.
24 When you lie down, you won't be afraid;
    when you lie down, you will sleep in peace.
25 You won't be afraid of sudden trouble;
    you won't fear the ruin that comes to the wicked,
26 because the LORD will keep you safe.
    He will keep you from being trapped.
27 Whenever you are able,
    do good to people who need help.
28 If you have what your neighbour asks for,
    don't say, "Come back later. I will give it to you tomorrow."
29 Don't make plans to hurt your neighbour
    who lives nearby and trusts you.
30 Don't accuse a person for no good reason;
    don't accuse someone who has not harmed you.
31 Don't be jealous of those who use violence,
    and don't choose to be like them.
32 The LORD hates those who do wrong,
    but he is a friend to those who are honest.

FAITH links

A DIRECT PATH
PROVERBS 3:5-6

If you were a tourist in a city, would you depend on your own instincts or ideas about how to get around? You wouldn't, would you? You would ask someone knowledgeable to give you directions. You would also look at a map. Trusting God is like looking at a map. He promises to direct your steps and "give you success" (3:6).

The Wisdom of Obeying God, 1 Kings 11:1–13, p. 453

A Picture of the Past, Psalm 105, p. 789

What God Thinks, Isaiah 55:8–9, p. 969

Obeying God or Man? Daniel 3:8–30, p. 1154

The Writing's on the Wall, Daniel 5, p. 1159

Perfectly Pleasing? Matthew 5:1–12, p. 1280

FAITH links

WHO DO YOU PREFER?
PROVERBS 3:32

Who do you like to hang around with the most? The popular kids? Cool kids? Kids who know a lot about computers? Kids who get into trouble? A person usually hangs around with those who value the same things he or she values. This proverb describes God as a friend to those who are honest. That means he values honesty. Is being honest important to you? If you want to be friends with God, that means yes, right?

Here are some more Faithlinks on being honest:

The Best Policy, Genesis 29:16–29, p. 41

Read My Lips? Deuteronomy 26:16–19, p. 260

The Salt Promise, 2 Chronicles 13:5, p. 576

The Problem with Gossip, Proverbs 11:12–13, p. 840

What's Wrong About Rumours, Jeremiah 29:24–32, p. 1032

The Verdict Is In? Matthew 7:1–2, p. 1285

33 The LORD will curse the evil person's house,
   but he will bless the home of those who do right.
34 The LORD laughs at those who laugh at him,
   but he gives grace to those who are not proud.
35 Wise people will receive honour,
   but fools will be disgraced.

Wisdom is Important

4 My children, listen to your father's teaching;
   pay attention so you will understand.
2 What I am telling you is good,
   so do not forget what I teach you.
3 When I was a young boy in my father's house
   and like an only child to my mother,
4 my father taught me and said,
   "Hold on to my words with all your heart.
   Keep my commands and you will live.
5 Get wisdom and understanding.
   Don't forget or ignore my words.
6 Hold on to wisdom, and it will take care of you.
   Love it, and it will keep you safe.
7 Wisdom is the most important thing;
   so get wisdom.
   If it costs everything you have, get understanding.
8 Treasure wisdom, and it will make you great;
   hold on to it, and it will bring you honour.
9 It will be like flowers in your hair
   and like a beautiful crown on your head."

10 My child, listen and accept what I say.
   Then you will have a long life.
11 I am guiding you in the way of wisdom,
   and I am leading you on the right path.
12 Nothing will hold you back;
   you will not be overwhelmed.
13 Always remember what you have been taught,
   and don't let go of it.
   Keep all that you have learned;
   it is the most important thing in life.
14 Don't follow the ways of the wicked;
   don't do what evil people do.

4:13
Correction
What is important to remember?

Proverbs 5:3   831

15 Avoid their ways, and don't follow them.
   Stay away from them and keep on going,
16 because they cannot sleep until they do evil.
   They cannot rest until they harm someone.
17 They feast on wickedness and cruelty
   as if they were eating bread and drinking wine.
18 The way of the good person is like the light of dawn,
   growing brighter and brighter until full daylight.
19 But the wicked walk around in the dark;
   they can't even see what makes them stumble.

20 My child, pay attention to my words;
   listen closely to what I say.
21 Don't ever forget my words;
   keep them always in mind.
22 They are the key to life for those who find them;
   they bring health to the whole body.
23 Be careful what you think,
   because your thoughts run your life.
24 Don't use your mouth to tell lies;
   don't ever say things that are not true.

4:24 Gossip
Should you repeat gossip?

25 Keep your eyes focused on what is right,
   and look straight ahead to what is good.
26 Be careful what you do,
   and always do what is right.
27 Don't turn off the road of goodness;
   keep away from evil paths.

Warning About Adultery

5:1 Obedience
Should you listen to your parents?

5 My son, pay attention to my wisdom;
   listen to my words of understanding.
2 Be careful to use good sense,
   and watch what you say.
3 The words of another man's wife may seem sweet as honey;

FAITH links

MIND GUARD
PROVERBS 4:23

What are you thinking of right now? Did you ever see or hear something that you had a problem getting off your mind? Some images and songs stay with you a long time. That's why this proverb advises you to be careful about what you think. Thoughts are what lead a person to do good or evil. The more you think about something, the more it influences your actions. Memorising Bible verses can help you guard your thoughts. Think about it.

Here are some more thoughts on thinking!

An Example Not to Follow, Leviticus 18:1–3, p. 157

The Right Thing to Do, 1 Samuel 26, p. 391

Take My Advice, 1 Kings 2:2–4, p. 436

A Reminder to Do What Is Right and True, Zechariah 7:8–10, p. 1257

Just Say No! Titus 2:11–12, p. 1660

The "Quality" of Life, 2 Peter 1:5–8, p. 1708

they may be as smooth as olive oil.
4 But in the end she will bring you sorrow,
causing you pain like a two-edged sword.
5 She is on the way to death;
her steps are headed straight to the grave.
6 She gives little thought to life.
She doesn't even know that her ways are wrong.

7 Now, my sons, listen to me,
and don't ignore what I say.
8 Stay away from such a woman.
Don't even go near the door of her house,
9 or you will give your riches to others,
and the best years of your life will be given to someone cruel.
10 Strangers will enjoy your wealth,
and what you worked so hard for will go to someone else.
11 You will groan at the end of your life when your health is gone.
12 Then you will say, "I hated being told what to do!
I would not listen to correction!
13 I would not listen to my teachers or pay attention to my instructors.
14 I came close to being completely ruined
in front of a whole group of people."

15 Be faithful to your own wife,
just as you drink water from your own well.
16 Don't pour your water in the streets;
don't give your love to just any woman.
17 These things are yours alone
and shouldn't be shared with strangers.
18 Be happy with the wife you married when you were young.
She gives you joy, as your fountain gives you water.
19 She is as lovely and graceful as a deer.
Let her love always make you happy;
let her love always hold you captive.

20 My son, don't be held captive by a woman who takes part in adultery.
Don't hold another man's wife.
21 The LORD sees everything you do,
and he watches where you go.
22 An evil man will be caught in his wicked ways;
the ropes of his sins will tie him up.
23 He will die because he does not control himself,
and he will be held captive by his foolishness.

Dangers of Being Foolish

6 My child, be careful about giving a guarantee for somebody else's loan,
about promising to pay what someone else owes.
2 You might get trapped by what you say;
you might be caught by your own words.
3 My child, if you have done this and are under your neighbour's control,
here is how to get free.
Don't be proud. Go to your neighbour and beg to be free from your promise.
4 Don't go to sleep
or even rest your eyes,
5 but free yourself like a deer running from a hunter,
like a bird flying away from a trapper.

6 Go and watch the ants, you lazy person.
Watch what they do and be wise.
7 Ants have no commander,
no leader or ruler,
8 but they store up food in the summer and gather their supplies at harvest.
9 How long will you lie there, you lazy person?
When will you get up from sleeping?
10 You sleep a little; you take a nap.
You fold your hands and lie down to rest.

Proverbs 6:24 833

FAITH links

DOWN ON THE ANT FARM
PROVERBS 6:6-11

Have you ever watched ants working away on an anthill or in an ant farm? Ants work very hard to store up food before they need it. No one has to tell them to do it. The wise person follows the ants' example by working hard and getting things done ahead of time. The unwise person prefers every day to be a lazy, sleep-in sort of day.

Sleeping-in can be fun sometimes. However, you can't get much done if you do it all the time. Think about the things you have to do right now. If you're a do-it-at-the-last-minute kind of person, take a lesson from the ants.

Your Response to Responsibility, Ruth 2:1–7, p. 346

Listen Up! 1 Kings 19:11–13, p. 467

Operation Co-operation, Ezra 1:5, p. 609

Our Thirst Quencher, Psalm 42:1–3, p. 741

A Gentle Answer, Proverbs 15:1, p. 847

That Thing You Do, Matthew 25:14–30, p. 1319

11 So you will be as poor as if you had been robbed;
  you will have as little as if you had been held up.

12 Some people are wicked and no good.
  They go around telling lies,
13 winking with their eyes, signalling with their feet
  and making signs with their fingers.
14 They make evil plans in their hearts
  and are always starting arguments.
15 So trouble will strike them in an instant;
  suddenly they will be so hurt no one can help them.

16 There are six things the LORD hates.
  There are seven things he cannot stand:
17   a proud look,
    a lying tongue,
    hands that kill innocent people,
18   a mind that thinks up evil plans,
    feet that are quick to do evil,
19   a witness who lies,
    and someone who starts arguments among families.

Warning About Adultery

20 My son, keep your father's commands,
  and don't forget your mother's teaching.
21 Keep their words in mind for ever
  as though you had them tied around your neck.

6:20–23
Correction
What are the benefits of listening to instructions?

22 They will guide you when you walk.
  They will guard you when you sleep.
  They will speak to you when you are awake.
23 These commands are like a lamp;
  this teaching is like a light.
  And the correction that comes from them
  will help you have life.
24 They will keep you from sinful women
  and from the pleasing words of another man's unfaithful wife.

HONOURING MUM AND DAD
Proverbs 6:20–23

Livin' it

How to Be a Real Wise Guy! Got a big problem? Where do you go to find help? There are lots of places to go for advice: your friends, magazines, newspapers, the Internet, TV. But the best place to go is to your parents. You may not always like what they say, but listening to them is a way of showing them respect. (Check out Proverbs 1:8–9.)

Being a wise son or daughter or a foolish one has to do with how willingly you obey your parents. A foolish child makes her parents sad, but a wise one makes his parents happy. (Read about it in Proverbs 10:1.) How can you be a wise kid and make your parents happy?

MORE FAITH links

- A Parent's Advice, p. 825
- A Word to the Wise, p. 838
- If You Want My Advice… p. 843
- Down on Discipline? p. 867
- Sow It and Reap, p. 1075
- What Any Parent Wants, p. 1723

Sometimes you probably don't feel like obeying your parents. Especially when you've got something better to do – like playing on the computer!

But you'd better wise up! God doesn't say obey your parents when you want to – he says always obey your parents. Read on to see how you can really be wise!

Plans for a Son, 1 Chronicles 22:5–19, p. 548
- Have you noticed what your mum or dad does to help you follow and obey God? Why do you think they do these things? How do you react to the things they do?

See the Heart Behind It, Nehemiah 8; 9, p. 636
- What expression is usually on your face when your mum or dad tells you exactly what kind of behaviour they expect from you? Do you look bored? Or do you stare blankly off into space somewhere?
- Your parents and God want the best life possible for you. How can you change your response to their advice?

How to Make God Glad, Ephesians 6:1–2, p. 1605
- Link here to find out how to really please God – and your parents.

my FAVOURITE links

Proverbs 7:5 835

FAITH links

WHAT GOD "HATES"
PROVERBS 6:16-19

So much is said about God's love. But did you know there are things that God hates? They all have to do with sin: pride; lying; murder; evil thoughts; feet that hurry to commit crimes; lying about others; causing others to fight among themselves. This kind of hatred isn't like the hatred people sometimes feel for each other. After all, God cannot sin. He doesn't hate the people who do wrong. He hates sin. He wants you to hate it even more than he does. But don't just talk about hating it. Do something about it.

Take a look at some other sins that God hates:

Out of Control? Genesis 4, p. 8

Patience, Please, Psalm 145:8-9, p. 819

God's Instructions, Ezekiel 4:1-15, p. 1089

Good Enough? Ezekiel 8, p. 1093

Want to Know? Ask! Luke 9:45, p. 1386

The Deadliest Lie, Acts 5:1-11, p. 1471

25 Don't desire her because she is beautiful.
   Don't let her capture you by the way she looks at you.

26 A prostitute will treat you like a loaf of bread,
   and a woman who takes part in adultery may cost you your life.
27 You cannot carry hot coals against your chest
   without burning your clothes,
28 and you cannot walk on hot coals
   without burning your feet.
29 The same is true if you have sexual relations with another man's wife.
   Anyone who does so will be punished.

30 People don't hate a thief
   when he steals because he is hungry.
31 But if he is caught, he must pay back seven times what he stole,
   and it may cost him everything he owns.
32 A man who takes part in adultery has no sense;
   he will destroy himself.
33 He will be beaten up and disgraced,
   and his shame will never go away.
34 Jealousy makes a husband very angry,
   and he will have no pity when he gets revenge.
35 He will accept no payment for the wrong;
   he will take no amount of money.

The Woman of Adultery

7 My son, remember what I say,
   and treasure my commands.
2 Obey my commands, and you will live.
   Guard my teachings as you would your own eyes.
3 Remind yourself of them;
   write them on your heart as if on a tablet.
4 Treat wisdom as a sister,
   and make understanding your closest friend.
5 Wisdom and understanding will keep you away from adultery,
   away from the unfaithful wife and her pleasing words.

6 Once while I was at the window of my house
I looked out through the shutters
7 and saw some foolish young men.
I noticed one of them had no wisdom.
8 He was walking down the street near the corner
on the road leading to her house.
9 It was the twilight of the evening;
the darkness of the night was just beginning.
10 Then the woman approached him,
dressed like a prostitute
and planning to trick him.
11 She was loud and stubborn
and never stayed at home.
12 She was always out in the streets or in the city squares,
waiting around on the corners of the streets.
13 She took hold of him and kissed him.
Without shame she said to him,
14 "I made my fellowship offering and took some of the meat home.
Today I have kept my special promises.
15 So I have come out to meet you;
I have been looking for you and have found you.
16 I have covered my bed
with coloured sheets from Egypt.
17 I have made my bed smell sweet
with myrrh, aloes and cinnamon.
18 Come, let's make love until morning.
Let's enjoy each other's love.
19 My husband is not home;
he has gone on a long trip.
20 He took a lot of money with him
and won't be home for weeks."
21 By her clever words she made him give in;
by her pleasing words she led him into doing wrong.
22 All at once he followed her,
like an ox led to the butcher,
like a deer caught in a trap
23 and shot through the liver with an arrow.
Like a bird caught in a trap,
he didn't know what he did would kill him.

24 Now, my sons, listen to me;
pay attention to what I say.
25 Don't let yourself be tricked by such a woman;
don't go where she leads you.
26 She has ruined many good men,
and many have died because of her.
27 Her house is on the road to death,
the road that leads down to the grave.

Listen to Wisdom

8 Wisdom calls to you like someone shouting;
understanding raises her voice.
2 On the hilltops along the road
and at the crossroads, she stands calling.
3 Beside the city gates,"
at the entrances into the city, she calls out:
4 "Listen, everyone, I'm calling out to you;
I am shouting to all people.
5 You who are uneducated, be cleverer.
You who are foolish, get understanding.
6 Listen, because I have important things to say,
and what I tell you is right.
7 What I say is true,
I refuse to speak evil.
8 Everything I say is honest;
nothing I say is crooked or false.
9 People with good sense know what I say is true;
and those with knowledge know my words are right.
10 Choose my teachings instead of silver,
and knowledge rather than the finest gold.
11 Wisdom is more precious than rubies.
Nothing you could want is equal to it.
12 "I am wisdom,
and I am clever.
I also have knowledge and good sense.

8:12–14 Wisdom
What comes with wisdom?

8:3 city gates People came here to conduct business. Public meetings and court cases were also held here.

13 If you respect the LORD, you will also hate evil.
I hate pride and boasting, evil ways and lies.
14 I have good sense and advice, and I have understanding and power.
15 I help kings to govern and rulers to make fair laws.
16 Princes use me to lead, and so do all important people who judge fairly.
17 I love those who love me, and those who seek me find me.
18 Riches and honour are mine to give. So are wealth and lasting success.
19 What I give is better than the finest gold, better than the purest silver.
20 I do what is right and follow the path of justice.
21 I give wealth to those who love me, filling their houses with treasures.

22 "I, wisdom, was with the LORD when he began his work, long before he made anything else.
23 I was created in the very beginning, even before the world began.
24 I was born before there were oceans, or springs overflowing with water,
25 before the hills were there, before the mountains were put in place.
26 God had not made the earth or fields, not even the first dust of the earth.
27 I was there when God put the skies in place, when he stretched the horizon over the oceans,
28 when he made the clouds above and put the deep underground springs in place.
29 I was there when he ordered the sea not to go beyond the borders he had set.
I was there when he laid the earth's foundation.

30 I was like a child by his side.
I was delighted every day, enjoying his presence all the time,
31 enjoying the whole world, and delighted with all its people.

32 "Now, my children, listen to me, because those who follow my ways are happy.
33 Listen to my teaching, and you will be wise; do not ignore it.
34 Happy are those who listen to me, watching at my door every day, waiting at my open doorway.
35 Those who find me find life, and the LORD will be pleased with them.
36 Those who do not find me hurt themselves.
Those who hate me love death."

Being Wise or Foolish

9 Wisdom has built her house; she has made its seven columns.
2 She has prepared her food and wine; she has set her table.
3 She has sent out her servant girls, and she calls out from the highest place in the city.
4 She says to those who are uneducated, "Come in here, you foolish people!
5 Come and eat my food and drink the wine I have prepared.
6 Stop your foolish ways, and you will live; take the road of understanding.

7 "If you correct someone who makes fun of wisdom, you will be insulted.
If you correct an evil person, you will get hurt.
8 Do not correct those who make fun of wisdom, or they will hate you.
But correct the wise, and they will love you.

> Stop your foolish ways, and you will live; take the road of understanding.
> – Proverbs 9:6

9 Teach the wise, and they will become
     even wiser;
   teach good people, and they will
     learn even more.

10 "Wisdom begins with respect for the
     LORD,
   and understanding begins with
     knowing the Holy One.
11 If you live wisely, you will live a long
     time;
   wisdom will add years to your life.
12 The wise person is rewarded by
     wisdom,
   but whoever makes fun of wisdom
     will suffer for it."

13 Foolishness is like a loud woman;
   she does not have wisdom or
     knowledge.
14 She sits at the door of her house
   at the highest place in the city.
15 She calls out to those who are
     passing by,
   who are going along, minding their
     own business.
16 She says to those who are
     uneducated,
   "Come in here, you foolish people!
17 Stolen water is sweeter,
   and food eaten in secret tastes
     better."
18 But these people don't know that
     everyone who goes there dies,
   that her guests end up deep in the
     grave.

The Wise Words of Solomon

10 These are the wise words of Solomon:
   A wise son makes his father happy,
   but a foolish son makes his mother
     sad.

2 Riches gained by doing wrong have
     no value,
   but right living will save you from
     death.

3 The LORD does not let good people go
     hungry,
   but he keeps evil people from
     getting what they want.

4 A lazy person will end up poor,
   but a hard worker will become
     rich.

5 Those who gather crops on time are
     wise,
   but those who sleep through the
     harvest are a disgrace.

FAITH links

A WORD TO THE WISE
PROVERBS 10:1

Want to know how you can make your parents joyful? Be a wise kid. Being a wise son or daughter or a foolish one has to do with how much you listen to your parents. Solomon mentioned that a foolish child makes his parents sad. A wise child makes her parents happy. So, how can you be wise? Do what your parents tell you to do. It's as simple as that!

Fatherly Advice, Exodus 18, p. 99

What God Wants, Deuteronomy 10:12–13, p. 242

Advice from a Kid, 2 Kings 5, p. 484

A Reminder to Do What Is Right and True, Zechariah 7:8–10, p. 1257

How to Make God Glad, Ephesians 6:1–2, p. 1605

Full of Faith, 1 Thessalonians 4:1, p. 1633

6 Good people will have rich blessings,
but the wicked will be overwhelmed by violence.

7 Good people will be remembered as a blessing,
but evil people will soon be forgotten.

8 The wise do what they are told,
but a talkative fool will be ruined.

9 The honest person will live in safety,
but the dishonest will be caught.

10 A wink may get you into trouble,
and foolish talk will lead to your ruin.

11 The words of a good person give life,
like a fountain of water,
but the words of the wicked contain nothing but violence.

12 Hatred stirs up trouble,
but love forgives all wrongs.

13 Clever people speak wisely,
but people without wisdom should be punished.

14 The wise don't tell everything they know,
but the foolish talk too much and are ruined.

15 Having lots of money protects the rich,
but having no money destroys the poor.

16 Good people are rewarded with life,
but evil people are paid with punishment.

17 Whoever accepts correction is on the way to life,
but whoever ignores correction will lead others away from life.

18 Whoever hides hate is a liar.
Whoever tells lies is a fool.

19 If you talk a lot, you are sure to sin;
if you are wise, you will keep quiet.

20 The words of a good person are like pure silver,
but an evil person's thoughts are worth very little.

21 Good people's words will help many others,
but fools will die because they don't have wisdom.

22 The LORD's blessing brings wealth,
and no sorrow comes with it.

23 A foolish person enjoys doing wrong,
but a person with understanding enjoys doing what is wise.

24 Evil people will get what they fear most,
but good people will get what they want most.

25 A storm will blow the evil person away,
but a good person will always be safe.

**10:24–25
Following God**
What's the hope of a person who does good?

26 A lazy person bothers the one he works for
like vinegar on the teeth or smoke in the eyes.

27 Whoever respects the LORD will have a long life,
but the life of an evil person will be cut short.

28 A good person can look forward to happiness,
but an evil person can expect nothing.

29 The LORD will protect good people
but will ruin those who do evil.

30 Good people will always be safe,
but evil people will not remain in the land.

31 A good person says wise things,
    but a liar's tongue will be stopped.

32 Good people know the right thing to say,
    but evil people only tell lies.

11

The LORD hates dishonest scales,
    but he is pleased with honest weights.

2 Pride leads only to shame;
    it is wise to be humble.

3 Good people will be guided by honesty;
    dishonesty will destroy those who are not trustworthy.

4 Riches will not help when it's time to die,
    but right living will save you from death.

5 The goodness of the innocent makes life easier,
    but the wicked will be destroyed by their wickedness.

6 Doing right brings freedom to honest people,
    but those who are not trustworthy will be caught by their own desires.

7 When the wicked die, hope dies with them;
    their hope in riches will come to nothing.

8 The good person is saved from trouble;
    it comes to the wicked instead.

9 With words an evil person can destroy a neighbour,
    but a good person will escape by being clever.

10 When good people succeed, the city is happy.
    When evil people die, there are shouts of joy.

FAITH links

THE PROBLEM WITH GOSSIP

PROVERBS 11:12-13

Let's say a friend told you a secret and made you promise not to tell. Now suppose you came upon another friend of yours. Let's say that person asked you about your other friend. Would you tell the secret anyway?

Gossip doesn't always mean passing on a rumour about someone. It can also mean repeating to someone else something told in confidence to you. Know what else gossip is? Trouble. Gossip and rumours have never been known to strengthen friendships. However, trustworthiness and faithfulness do. Want to be a trustworthy friend? Learn to keep a secret.

How do you rate in the friendship department? Link here to find out:

The MLP, Ruth 1:16–17, p. 345

Loyal to a Friend, 2 Samuel 9, p. 409

An Honest Reputation, Nehemiah 13:13, p. 644

Fear God or People? Jeremiah 38:14–21, p. 1047

Your Civic Duty, Matthew 17:24–27, p. 1304

The Whole Truth, John 8:31–32, 45, p. 1438

11 Good people bless and build up their city,
   but the wicked can destroy it with their words.

12 People without good sense find fault with their neighbours,
   but those with understanding keep quiet.

13 Gossips can't keep secrets,
   but a trustworthy person can.

14 Without leadership a nation falls,
   but lots of good advice will save it.

15 Whoever guarantees to pay somebody else's loan will suffer.
   It is safer to avoid such promises.

16 A kind woman gets respect,
   but cruel men get only wealth.

17 Kind people do themselves a favour,
   but cruel people bring trouble on themselves.

18 An evil person really earns nothing,
   but a good person will surely be rewarded.

19 Those who are truly good will live,
   but those who chase after evil will die.

20 The LORD hates those with evil hearts
   but is pleased with those who are innocent.

21 Evil people will certainly be punished,
   but those who do right will be set free.

22 A beautiful woman without good sense
   is like a gold ring in a pig's snout.

23 Those who do right only wish for good,
   but the wicked can expect to be defeated by God's anger.

24 Some people give much but get back even more.
   Others don't give what they should and end up poor.

25 Whoever gives to others will get richer;
   those who help others will themselves be helped.

11:24–25 Giving
What's the bonus in giving?

26 People curse those who keep all the grain,
   but they bless the one who is willing to sell it.

27 Whoever looks for good will find kindness,
   but whoever looks for evil will find trouble.

28 Those who trust in riches will be ruined,
   but a good person will be healthy like a green leaf.

29 Whoever brings trouble to his family will be left with nothing but the wind.
   A fool will be a servant to the wise.

30 A good person gives life to others;
   the wise person teaches others how to live.

31 Good people will be rewarded on earth,
   and the wicked and the sinners will be punished.

12

Anyone who loves learning accepts correction,
but a person who hates being corrected is stupid.

2 The LORD is pleased with a good person,
   but he will punish anyone who plans evil.

3 Doing evil brings no safety at all,
   but a good person has safety and security.

4 A good wife is like a crown for her husband,
   but a disgraceful wife is like a disease in his bones.

5 The plans that good people make are fair,
   but the advice of the wicked will trick you.

6 The wicked talk about killing people,
   but the words of good people will save them.

7 Wicked people die and they are no more,
   but a good person's family continues.

8 The wisdom of the wise wins praise,
   but there is no respect for the stupid.

9 A person who is not important but has a servant is better off
   than someone who acts important but has no food.

10 Good people take care of their animals,
    but even the kindest acts of the wicked are cruel.

11 Those who work their land will have plenty of food,
    but the one who chases empty dreams is not wise.

12 The wicked want what other evil people have stolen,
    but good people want to give what they have to others.

13 Evil people are trapped by their evil talk,
    but good people stay out of trouble.

14 People will be rewarded for what they say,
    and they will also be rewarded for what they do.

15 Fools think they are doing right,
    but the wise listen to advice.

16 Fools quickly show that they are upset,
    but the wise ignore insults.

17 An honest witness tells the truth,
    but a dishonest witness tells lies.

18 Careless words stab like a sword,
    but wise words bring healing.

FAITH links

GET HOT OR KEEP COOL?
PROVERBS 12:16

If someone called you a name, what would you do? Get mad and call that person a worse name? Sulk about it? Keep your cool and ignore it? Some people might tell you that ignoring an insult makes you a wimp. But God's way is to be self-controlled. When someone insults you, remember Jesus' example. When he was insulted, he didn't try to get even. Thanks to him, we have the power to do likewise.

I Want It *Now!* Judges 14:1–3, p. 332

Anger: Quick or Slow? Psalm 86:15, p. 776

Peace in the Family, Psalm 133, p. 811

Kindness First, Matthew 9:35–36, p. 1290

Don't Get Mad; Get Even? Matthew 26:57–63; 27:11–14, p. 1323

Out with the Old! Colossians 3:1–14, p. 1625

19 Truth will continue for ever,
  but lies are only for a moment.

20 Those who plan evil are full of lies,
  but those who plan peace are happy.

21 No harm comes to a good person,
  but an evil person's life is full of trouble.

22 The LORD hates those who tell lies
  but is pleased with those who keep their promises.

23 Wise people keep what they know to themselves,
  but fools can't keep from showing how foolish they are.

24 Hard workers will become leaders,
  but those who are lazy will be slaves.

25 Worry is a heavy load,
  but a kind word cheers you up.

**12:25
Worry**
What's the cure for worry?

26 Good people take advice from their friends,
  but an evil person is easily led to do wrong.

27 The lazy catch no food to cook,
  but a hard worker will have great wealth.

28 Doing what is right is the way to life,
  but there is another way that leads to death.

13 Wise children take their parents' advice;
  but whoever makes fun of wisdom won't listen to correction.

2 People will be rewarded for what they say,
  but those who can't be trusted want only violence.

3 Those who are careful about what they say protect their lives,
  but whoever speaks without thinking will be ruined.

4 The lazy will not get what they want,
  but those who work hard will.

5 Good people hate what is false,
  but the wicked do shameful and disgraceful things.

Proverbs 13:5 843

FAITH links

IF YOU WANT MY ADVICE . . .

PROVERBS 13:1

When your parents give you advice or discipline you, do you get angry or do you accept what they say? Solomon, the writer of this proverb, mentioned that wise children accept their parents' advice. But don't think of it as yet one more adult telling you what to do. Think of it as God showing you the way to be wise.

Check out these Faithlinks on learning to be wise:

Your Stats, 1 Kings 15; 16, p. 460

This Hurts Me More? 2 Chronicles 36:17–22, p. 606

Help for the Outsiders, Nehemiah 5:9–10, p. 630

The Problem with Pride, Isaiah 2:11, p. 898

A Friend of Jesus, John 15:9–17, p. 1450

You're a Fake! 2 Peter 2:1, p. 1709

6 Doing what is right protects the honest person,
but doing evil ruins the sinner.

7 Some people pretend to be rich but really have nothing.
Others pretend to be poor but really are wealthy.

8 The rich may have to pay a ransom for their lives,
but the poor will face no such danger.

9 Good people can look forward to a bright future,
but the future of the wicked is like a flame going out.

10 Pride only leads to arguments,
but those who take advice are wise.

11 Money that comes easily disappears quickly,
but money that is gathered little by little will grow.

12 It is sad not to get what you hoped for.
But wishes that come true are like eating fruit from the tree of life.

13 Those who reject what they are taught will pay for it,
but those who obey what they are told will be rewarded.

14 The teaching of a wise person gives life.
It is like a fountain that can save people from death.

15 People with good understanding will be well liked,
but the lives of those who are not trustworthy are hard.

16 Every wise person acts with good sense,
but fools show how foolish they are.

17 A wicked messenger brings nothing but trouble,
but a trustworthy one makes everything right.

18 A person who refuses correction will end up poor and disgraced,
but the one who accepts correction will be honoured.

19 It is so good when wishes come true,
but fools hate to stop doing evil.

20 Spend time with the wise and you will become wise,
but the friends of fools will suffer.

21 Trouble always comes to sinners,
but good people enjoy success.

22 Good people leave their wealth to their grandchildren,
but a sinner's wealth is stored up for good people.

23 A poor person's field might produce plenty of food,
but others often steal it away.

24 If you do not punish your children, you don't love them,
but if you love your children, you will correct them.

25 Good people have enough to eat,
but the wicked will go hungry.

14

A wise woman strengthens her family,
but a foolish woman destroys hers by what she does.

2 People who live good lives respect the LORD,
but those who live evil lives don't.

3 Fools will be punished for their proud words,
but the words of the wise will protect them.

4 When there are no oxen, there is no
    food in the barn.
    But with a strong ox, much grain
        can be grown.

5 A truthful witness does not lie,
    but a false witness tells nothing but
        lies.

6 Those who make fun of wisdom look
        for it and do not find it,
    but knowledge comes easily to
        those with understanding.

7 Stay away from fools,
    because they can't teach you
        anything.

8 A wise person will understand what to
        do,
    but a foolish person is dishonest.

9 Fools don't care if they sin,
    but honest people work at being
        right.

10 No one else can know your sadness,
    and strangers cannot share your joy.

11 The wicked person's house will be
        destroyed,
    but a good person's tent will still be
        standing.

12 Some people think they are doing
        right,
    but in the end it leads to death.

13 Someone who is laughing may be sad
        inside,
    and joy may end in sadness.

14 Evil people will be paid back for their
        evil ways,
    and good people will be rewarded
        for their good ones.

15 Fools will believe anything,
    but the wise think about what they
        do.

16 Wise people are careful and stay out
        of trouble,
    but fools are careless and quick to
        act.

17 Someone with a quick temper does
        foolish things,
    but someone with understanding
        remains calm.

18 Fools are rewarded with nothing but
        more foolishness,
    but the wise are rewarded with
        knowledge.

19 Evil people will bow down to those
        who are good;
    the wicked will bow down at the
        door of those who do right.

20 The poor are rejected, even by their
        neighbours,
    but the rich have many friends.

21 It is a sin to hate your neighbour,
    but being kind to the needy brings
        happiness.

22 Those who make evil plans will be
        ruined,
    but those who plan to do good will
        be loved and trusted.

23 Those who work hard make a profit,
    but those who only talk will be
        poor.

24 Wise people are rewarded with
        wealth,
    but fools only get more foolishness.

25 A truthful witness saves lives,
    but a false witness is a traitor.

26 Those who respect the LORD will
        have security,
    and their children will be
        protected.

27 Respect for the LORD gives life.
    It is like a fountain that can save
        people from death.

28 A king is honoured when he has
        many people to rule,

FAITH CHALLENGE

Here's a challenge! Read 14:21 to discover what God says about helping people in need. What can you and your friends do to help needy people in your community?

TESTING IT

Proverbs 14:21
It is a sin to hate your neighbour, but being kind to the needy brings happiness.

but a prince is ruined if he has none.

29 Patient people have great understanding,
   but people with quick tempers show their foolishness.

30 Peace of mind means a healthy body,
   but jealousy will rot your bones.

31 Whoever mistreats the poor insults their Maker,

14:31 Kindness
Be kind to the poor.

but whoever is kind to the needy honours God.

32 The wicked are ruined by their own evil,
   but those who do right are protected even in death.

33 Wisdom lives in those with understanding,
   and even fools recognise it.

34 Doing what is right makes a nation great,
   but sin will bring disgrace to any people.

35 A king is pleased with a wise servant,
   but he will become angry with one who causes him shame.

15

1 A gentle answer will calm a person's anger,
   but an unkind answer will cause more anger.

15:1 Anger
Check out a cure for anger.

2 Wise people use knowledge when they speak,
   but fools pour out foolishness.

3 The LORD's eyes see everything;
   he watches both evil and good people.

4 As a tree gives fruit, healing words give life,
   but dishonest words crush the spirit.

5 Fools reject their parents' correction,
   but anyone who accepts correction is wise.

6 Much wealth is in the houses of good people,
   but evil people get nothing but trouble.

FAITH links

A GENTLE ANSWER
PROVERBS 15:1

Have you ever noticed that when someone makes you mad and you say something mean back to that person, you both feel angrier? That's why Solomon advised giving a gentle answer to a person, even someone who has made you angry. A gentle answer has a calming effect. A mean or sarcastic answer just fans the flames of anger. Giving a gentle answer isn't always easy. It takes self-control – a gift from the Holy Spirit. (Surf over to Galatians 5:22–23, p. 1593, to read more about this special gift.)

Just Kidding? Genesis 21:8–10, p. 28

A Friend in Deed, Job 2:13, p. 662

Patience, Please, Psalm 145:8–9, p. 819

World News, Isaiah 13—19, p. 913

Kindness Counts, Acts 14:3, p. 1489

A Different Kind of Fruit, Galatians 5:22–23, p. 1592

---

7 Wise people use their words to spread knowledge,
  but there is no knowledge in the thoughts of fools.

8 The LORD hates the sacrifice that the wicked offer,
  but he likes the prayers of honest people.

9 The LORD hates what evil people do,
  but he loves those who do what is right.

10 The person who stops doing what is right will be punished,
  and the one who hates to be corrected will die.

15:10 Correction
What happens if you hate correction?

11 The LORD knows what is happening in the world of the dead,
  so he surely knows the thoughts of the living.

12 Those who make fun of wisdom don't like to be corrected;
  they will not ask the wise for advice.

13 Happiness makes a person smile,
  but sadness can break a person's spirit.

14 People with understanding want more knowledge,
  but fools just want more foolishness.

15 Every day is hard for those who suffer,
  but a happy heart is like a continual feast.

16 It is better to be poor and respect the LORD
  than to be wealthy and have much trouble.

17 It is better to eat vegetables with those who love you
  than to eat meat with those who hate you.

18 People with quick tempers cause trouble,
  but those who control their tempers stop a quarrel.

19 A lazy person's life is like a patch of thorns,
   but an honest person's life is like a smooth highway.

20 A wise son makes his father happy,
   but a foolish son hates his mother.

21 A person without wisdom enjoys being foolish,
   but someone with understanding does what is right.

22 Plans fail without good advice,
   but they succeed with the advice of many others.

23 People enjoy giving good advice.
   Saying the right word at the right time is so pleasing.

24 Wise people's lives get better and better.
   They avoid whatever would cause their death.

25 The LORD will tear down the proud person's house,
   but he will protect the widow's property.

26 The LORD hates evil thoughts
   but is pleased with kind words.

27 Greedy people bring trouble to their families,
   but the person who can't be paid to do wrong will live.

28 Good people think before they answer,
   but the wicked simply pour out evil.

29 The LORD does not listen to the wicked,
   but he hears the prayers of those who do right.

30 Good news makes you feel better.
   Your happiness will show in your eyes.

31 If you listen to correction to improve your life,
   you will live among the wise.

32 Those who refuse correction hate themselves,
   but those who accept correction gain understanding.

33 Respect for the LORD will teach you wisdom.
   If you want to be honoured, you must be humble.

16

People may make plans in their minds,
   but only the LORD can make them come true.

2 You may believe you are doing right,
   but the LORD will judge your reasons.

3 Depend on the LORD in whatever you do,
   and your plans will succeed.

16:3 Trust — The key to success.

4 The LORD makes everything go as he pleases.
   He has even prepared a day of disaster for evil people.

5 The LORD hates those who are proud.
   They will surely be punished.

6 Love and truth bring forgiveness of sin.
   By respecting the LORD you will avoid evil.

7 When people live so that they please the LORD,
   even their enemies will make peace with them.

8 It is better to be poor and right
   than to be wealthy and dishonest.

9 People may make plans in their minds,

but the LORD decides what they
   will do.

10 The words of a king are like a
      message from God,
   so his decisions should be fair.

11 The LORD wants honest balances and
      scales;
   all the weights are his work.

12 Kings hate those who do wrong,
   because governments only
      continue if they are fair.

13 Kings like honest people;
   they value someone who speaks
      the truth.

14 An angry king can put someone to
      death,
   so a wise person will try to make
      him happy.

15 A smiling king can give people life;
   his kindness is like a spring shower.

16 It is better to get wisdom than gold,
   and to choose understanding
      rather than silver!

17 Good people stay away from evil.
   By watching what they do, they
      protect their lives.

18 Pride will destroy
      a person;
   a proud attitude
      leads to ruin.

16:18
Pride
What can pride do?

19 It is better to be
      humble and be with those who
      suffer
   than to share stolen property with
      the proud.

20 Whoever listens to what is taught will
      succeed,
   and whoever trusts the LORD will
      be happy.

21 The wise are known for their
      understanding.
   Their pleasant words make them
      better teachers.

22 Understanding is like a fountain
      which gives life to those who
      use it,
   but foolishness brings punishment
      to fools.

23 Wise people's minds tell them what to
      say,
   and that helps them be better
      teachers.

24 Pleasant words are like a honeycomb,
   making people happy and healthy.

25 Some people think they are doing
      right,
   but in the end it leads to death.

26 The workers' hunger helps them,
   because their desire to eat makes
      them work.

27 Useless people make evil plans,
   and their words are like a burning
      fire.

28 A useless person
      causes
      trouble,
   and a gossip
      ruins
      friendships.

16:28
Gossip
Check out the bad results
of gossip.

29 Cruel people trick their neighbours
   and lead them to do wrong.

30 Someone who winks is planning evil,
   and the one who grins is planning
      something wrong.

31 Grey hair is like a crown of honour;
   it is earned by living a good life.

32 Patience is better than strength.
   Controlling your temper is better
      than capturing a city.

33 People throw lots to make a decision,
   but the answer comes from the
      LORD.

Proverbs 17:1

17 It is better to eat a dry crust of bread in peace
than to have a feast where there is quarrelling.

2 A wise servant will rule over the master's disgraceful child
and will even inherit a share of what the master leaves his children.

3 A hot furnace tests silver and gold,
but the LORD tests hearts.

4 Evil people listen to evil words.
Liars pay attention to cruel words.

5 Whoever mistreats the poor insults their Maker;
whoever enjoys someone's trouble will be punished.

6 Old people are proud of their grandchildren,
and children are proud of their parents.

7 Fools should not be proud,
and rulers should not be liars.

8 Some people think they can pay others to do anything they ask.
They think it will work every time.

9 Whoever forgives someone's sin makes a friend,
but telling about the sin breaks up friendships.

17:9 Enemies
How can you avoid making enemies?

10 A wise person will learn more from a warning
than a fool will learn from a hundred lashings.

11 Disobedient people look only for trouble,
so a cruel messenger will be sent against them.

12 It is better to meet a bear robbed of her cubs
than to meet a fool doing foolish things.

13 Whoever gives evil in return for good
will always have trouble at home.

14 Starting a quarrel is like a leak in a dam,
so stop it before a fight breaks out.

15 The LORD hates both of these things:
freeing the guilty and punishing the innocent.

16 It won't do a fool any good to try to buy wisdom,
because he doesn't have the ability to be wise.

17 A friend loves you all the time,
and a brother helps in time of trouble.

17:17 Friendship
Why are friends special?

18 It is not wise to promise
to pay what your neighbour owes.

19 Whoever loves to argue loves to sin.
Whoever is proud a lot is asking for trouble.

20 A person with an evil heart will find no success,
and the person whose words are evil will get into trouble.

21 It is sad to have a foolish child;
there is no joy in being the parent of a fool.

22 A happy heart is like good medicine,
but a broken spirit drains your strength.

23 When the wicked accept money to do wrong
there can be no justice.

FAITH links

SOME FRIENDLY ADVICE
PROVERBS 17:9, 14, 17

What can two people share that one person can't own and that also lasts a lifetime? Give up? Friendship. Solomon offers some friendly advice about friendship. Everyone wants to have friends. Being a friend takes effort. It takes forgiveness and love. It also takes a willingness to stop quarrels before they start. Both people in a friendship need to be willing to do whatever is necessary to be a good friend. How willing are you to be a good friend?

Want to be a good friend? Check out these Faithlinks:

Yours, Mine and Ours?
1 Samuel 25, p. 389

Peace in the Family, Psalm 133, p. 811

Two Are Better, Ecclesiastes 4:9–12, p. 877

Concern for All, Daniel 9, p. 1165

The Right Ingredients, Micah 6:8, p. 1227

I'll Be the Judge!
1 Corinthians 4:4–5, p. 1549

24 The person with understanding is always looking for wisdom, but the mind of a fool wanders everywhere.

25 A foolish son makes his father sad and causes his mother great sorrow.

26 It is not good to punish the innocent or to beat leaders for being honest.

27 The clever person says very little, and one with understanding stays calm.

28 Even fools seem to be wise if they keep quiet; if they don't speak, they appear to understand.

18 Unfriendly people are selfish and hate all good sense.

2 Fools do not want to understand anything. They only want to tell others what they think.

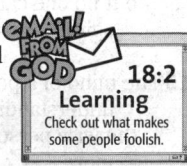
18:2 Learning
Check out what makes some people foolish.

3 Do something evil, and people won't like you.
Do something shameful, and they will make fun of you.

4 Spoken words can be like deep water, but wisdom is like a flowing stream.

5 It is not good to honour the wicked or to be unfair to the innocent.

6 The words of fools start quarrels. They make people want to beat them.

7 The words of fools will ruin them; their own words will trap them.

8 The words of a gossip are like tasty bits of food.
People like to take them all up.

9 A person who doesn't work hard is just like someone who destroys things.

10 The LORD is like a strong tower; those who do right can run to him for safety.

11 Rich people trust their wealth to
  protect them.
 They think it is like the high walls
  of a city.

12 Proud people will be ruined,
 but the humble will be honoured.

13 Anyone who answers without
  listening
 is foolish and confused.

14 The will to live can get you through
  sickness,
 but no one can live with a broken
  spirit.

15 The mind of a person with
  understanding gets knowledge;
 the wise person listens to learn
  more.

16 Taking a gift to an important man
  will help get you in to see him.

17 The person who tells one side of a
  story seems right,
 until someone else comes and asks
  questions.

18 Throwing lots can settle arguments
 and keep the two sides from
  fighting.

19 A brother who has been insulted is
  harder to win back than a walled
  city,
 and arguments separate people like
  the barred gates of a palace.

20 People will be rewarded for what they
  say;
 they will be rewarded by how they
  speak.

21 What you say can mean life or death.
 Those who speak with care will be
  rewarded.

22 When a man finds a wife, he finds
  something good.
 It shows that the LORD is pleased
  with him.

23 The poor beg for mercy,
 but the rich give rude answers.

24 Some friends may ruin you,
 but a real friend will be more loyal
  than a brother.

19 It is better to be poor and honest
  than to be foolish and tell lies.

2 Enthusiasm without knowledge is not
  good.
 If you act too quickly, you might
  make a mistake.

3 People's own foolishness ruins their
  lives,
 but in their minds they blame the
  LORD.

4 Wealthy people are always finding
  more friends,
 but the poor lose all theirs.

5 A witness who lies will not go free;
 liars will never escape.

6 Many people want to please a leader,
 and everyone is friends with those
  who give gifts.

7 Poor people's relatives avoid them;
 even their friends stay far away.
 They run after them, begging,
  but they are gone.

8 Those who get wisdom do themselves
  a favour,
 and those who love learning will
  succeed.

9 A witness who lies will not go free;
 liars will die.

10 A fool should not live in luxury.
 A slave should not rule over
  princes.

11 Clever people are patient;
 they will be honoured if they
  ignore insults.

12 An angry king is like a roaring lion,

but his kindness is like the dew on the grass.

13 A foolish son will ruin his father, and a quarrelling wife is like dripping water.

14 Houses and wealth are inherited from parents, but a wise wife is a gift from the LORD.

15 Lazy people sleep a lot, and idle people will go hungry.

19:15
Laziness
What the lazy can expect.

16 Those who obey the commands protect themselves, but those who are careless will die.

17 Being kind to the poor is like lending to the LORD; he will reward you for what you have done.

18 Correct your children while there is still hope; do not let them destroy themselves.

19 People with quick tempers will have to pay for it. If you help them out once, you will have to do it again.

20 Listen to advice and accept correction, and in the end you will be wise.

21 People can make all kinds of plans, but only the LORD's plan will happen.

22 People want others to be loyal, so it is better to be poor than to be a liar.

23 Those who respect the LORD will live and be satisfied, unbothered by trouble.

24 Though the lazy person puts his hand in the dish, he won't lift the food to his mouth.

25 Whip those who make fun of wisdom, and perhaps foolish people will gain some wisdom. Correct those with understanding, and they will gain knowledge.

26 A son who robs his father and sends away his mother brings shame and disgrace on himself.

27 Don't stop listening to correction, my child, or you will forget what you have already learned.

28 An evil witness makes fun of fairness, and wicked people love what is evil.

29 People who make fun of wisdom will be punished, and the backs of foolish people will be beaten.

20 Wine and beer make people loud and uncontrolled; it is not wise to get drunk on them.

2 An angry king is like a roaring lion. Making him angry may cost you your life.

3 Foolish people are always fighting, but avoiding quarrels will bring you honour.

4 Lazy farmers don't plough when they should; they expect a harvest, but there is none.

5 People's thoughts can be like a deep well, but someone with understanding can find the wisdom there.

6 Many people claim to be loyal,

but it is hard to find a trustworthy person.

7 The good people who live honest lives
will be a blessing to their children.

8 When a king sits on his throne to judge,
he knows evil when he sees it.

9 No one can say, "I am innocent;
I have never done anything wrong."

10 The LORD hates both these things:
dishonest weights and dishonest measures.

11 Even children are known by their behaviour;
their actions show if they are innocent and good.

12 The LORD has made both these things:
ears to hear and eyes to see.

13 If you love to sleep, you will be poor.
If you stay awake, you will have plenty of food.

14 Buyers say, "This is bad. It's no good."
Then they go away and boast about what they bought.

15 There is gold and plenty of rubies,
but only a few people speak with knowledge.

16 Take the coat of someone who promises to pay a stranger's debts,
and keep it until he pays what the stranger owes.

17 Stolen food may taste sweet at first,
but later it will feel like a mouth full of gravel.

18 Get advice if you want your plans to work.
If you go to war, get the advice of others.

19 Gossips can't keep secrets,
so avoid people who talk too much.

FAITH links

YOU ARE WHAT YOU DO
PROVERBS 20:11

Have you heard the old saying "You are what you eat"? That means the foods you eat make you healthy or unhealthy. Now what about the expression "Actions speak louder than words"? You've heard that before, right? This proverb suggests that your character is shown by your actions. In other words, you are what you do. What do your actions show? If you claim to love others, your actions should be loving. You are known by what you do. Let Jesus be the model for the things you do and say.

Looking for a good role model? Connect here:

A Different Kind of People, Leviticus 11, p. 146

Your Response to Responsibility, Ruth 2:1–7, p. 346

Choosing Sides, 1 Samuel 20, p. 382

"Handle" Your Responsibilities, 2 Kings 6:5–7, p. 485

Calling Anyone! Acts 23:12–22, p. 1506

An Unselfish Example, Philippians 2:5–8, p. 1611

Proverbs 21:13 855

20 Those who curse their father or mother
will be like a light going out in darkness.

21 Wealth inherited quickly in the beginning
will do you no good in the end.

22 Don't say, "I'll pay you back for the wrong you did."
Wait for the LORD, and he will make things right.

23 The LORD hates dishonest weights,
and dishonest scales do not please him.

24 The LORD decides what a person will do;
no one understands what his life is all about.

25 It's dangerous to promise something to God too quickly.
After you've thought about it, it may be too late.

26 A wise king separates out the evil people,
and he drives the threshing wheel over them as they deserve.

27 The LORD looks deep inside people
and searches through their thoughts.

28 Loyalty and truth keep a king in power;
he continues to rule if he is loyal.

29 Young men glory in their strength,
and old men are honoured for their grey hair.

30 Hard punishment will get rid of evil,
and whippings can change an evil heart.

21 The LORD can control a king's mind as he controls a river;
he can direct it as he pleases.

2 You may believe you are doing right,
but the LORD judges your reasons.

3 Doing what is right and fair
is more important to the LORD than sacrifices.

4 Proud looks, proud thoughts
and evil actions are sin.

5 The plans of people who work hard earn a profit,
but those who act too quickly become poor.

6 Wealth that comes from telling lies
vanishes like a mist and leads to death.

7 The violence of the wicked will destroy them,
because they refuse to do what is right.

8 Guilty people live dishonest lives,
but honest people do right.

9 It is better to live in a corner on the roof[n]
than inside the house with a quarrelling wife.

10 Evil people only want to harm others.
Their neighbours get no mercy from them.

11 If you punish those who make fun of wisdom, a foolish person may gain some wisdom.
But if you teach the wise, they will get knowledge.

12 God, who is always right, watches the house of the wicked
and brings ruin on every evil person.

13 Whoever ignores the poor when they cry for help
will also cry for help and not be answered.

21:9 roof In Bible times houses were built with flat roofs. The roof was used for drying things such as flax and fruit. And it was used as an extra room, as a place for worship and as a place to sleep in the summer.

Proverbs 21:14 856

14 A secret gift will calm an angry person;
a present given in secrecy will still great anger.

15 When justice is done, good people are happy,
but evil people are ruined.

16 Whoever does not use good sense will end up among the dead.

17 Whoever loves pleasure will become poor;
whoever loves wine and perfume will never be rich.

18 Wicked people will suffer instead of good people,
and those who cannot be trusted will suffer instead of those who do right.

19 It is better to live alone in the desert than with a quarrelling and complaining wife.

20 Wise people's houses are full of the best foods and olive oil,
but fools waste everything they have.

21 Whoever tries to live right and be loyal
finds life, success and honour.

22 A wise person can defeat a city full of warriors
and tear down the defences they trust in.

23 Those who are careful about what they say keep themselves out of trouble.

21:23 Sin — Why is it important to watch what you say?

24 People who act with stubborn pride are called "proud", "boaster" and "mocker".

25 Lazy people's desire for sleep will kill them,
because they refuse to work.

26 All day long they wish for more,
but good people give without holding back.

27 The LORD hates sacrifices brought by evil people,
particularly when they offer them for the wrong reasons.

28 A lying witness will be forgotten,
but a truthful witness will speak on.

29 Wicked people are stubborn,
but good people think carefully about what they do.

30 There is no wisdom, understanding or advice
that can succeed against the LORD.

31 You can get the horses ready for battle,
but it is the LORD who gives the victory.

22 Being respected is more important than having great riches.
To be well thought of is better than silver or gold.

2 The rich and the poor are alike in that the LORD made them all.

3 The wise see danger ahead and avoid it,
but fools keep going and get into trouble.

4 Respecting the LORD and not being proud
will bring you wealth, honour and life.

22:4 Humbleness — Don't be proud.

5 Evil people's lives are like paths covered with thorns and traps.

> **FAITH CHALLENGE**
>
> Here's one for you. Read 22:6 to find out what happens to children with good parents. What is the most important thing your parents have taught you – the one thing you will remember for the rest of your life?
>
> ## TeSTiNG iT
>
> **Proverbs 22:6**
> Train children how to live right, and when they are old, they will not change.

People who guard themselves don't have such problems.

6 Train children how to live right,
  and when they are old, they will not change.

7 The rich rule over the poor,
  and borrowers are servants to those who lend.

8 Those who plan evil will receive trouble.
  Their cruel anger will come to an end.

9 Generous people will be blessed,
  because they share their food with the poor.

10 Get rid of the one who makes fun of wisdom.
   Then fighting, quarrels and insults will stop.

11 Whoever loves pure thoughts and kind words
   will have even the king as a friend.

12 The LORD guards knowledge,
   but he destroys false words.

13 The lazy person says, "There's a lion outside!
   I might get killed out in the street!"

14 The words of an unfaithful wife are like a deep trap.
   Those who make the LORD angry will get caught by them.

15 Every child is full of foolishness,
   but punishment can get rid of it.

16 Whoever gets rich by mistreating the poor,
   and gives presents to the wealthy, will become poor.

Other Wise Sayings

17 Listen carefully to what wise people say;
   pay attention to what I am teaching you.

18 It will be good to keep these things in mind
   so that you are ready to repeat them.

19 I am teaching them to you now
   so that you will put your trust in the LORD.

20 I have written thirty sayings for you,
   which give knowledge and good advice.

21 I am teaching you true and reliable words
   so that you can give true answers to anyone who asks.

22 Do not abuse poor people because
    they are poor,
    and do not take away the rights of
    the needy in court.
23 The LORD will defend them in court
    and will take the life of those who
    take away their rights.

24 Don't make friends with bad-
    tempered people
    or spend time with those who have
    bad tempers.
25 If you do, you will be like them.
    Then you will be in real danger.

26 Don't promise to pay what someone
    else owes,
    and don't guarantee anyone's loan.
27 If you cannot pay the loan,
    your own bed may be taken right
    out from under you.

28 Don't move an old stone that marks a
    border,
    because those stones were set up
    by your ancestors.

29 Do you see people skilled in their
    work?
    They will work for kings, not for
    ordinary people.

23

If you sit down to eat with a ruler,
    notice the food that is in front of
    you.
2 Control yourself
    if you have a big appetite.
3 Don't be greedy for his fine foods,
    because that food might be a trick.

4 Don't wear yourself out trying to get
    rich;
    be wise enough to control yourself.
5 Wealth can vanish in the wink of an
    eye.
    It can seem to grow wings
    and fly away like an eagle.

6 Don't eat the food of selfish people;
    don't be greedy for their fine foods.
7 Selfish people are always worrying
    about how much the food costs.
    They tell you, "Eat and drink,"
    but they don't really mean it.
8 You will throw up the little you have
    eaten,
    and you will have wasted your kind
    words.

9 Don't speak to fools;
    they will only ignore your wise
    words.

10 Don't move an old stone that marks a
    border,
    and don't take fields that belong to
    orphans.
11 God, their defender, is strong;
    he will take their side against you.

12 Remember what you are taught,
    and listen carefully to words of
    knowledge.

13 Don't fail to punish children.
    If you spank them, they won't die.
14 If you spank them,
    you will save them from death.

15 My child, if you are wise,
    then I will be happy.
16 I will be so pleased
    if you speak what is right.

17 Don't envy sinners,
    but always respect the LORD.
18 Then you will have hope for the
    future,
    and your wishes will come true.

19 Listen, my child, and be wise.
    Keep your mind on what is right.
20 Don't drink too much wine
    or eat too much food.
21 Those who drink and eat too much
    become poor.
    They sleep too much and end up
    wearing rags.

22 Listen to your father, who gave you
    life,
    and do not forget your mother
    when she is old.
23 Learn the truth and never reject it.
    Get wisdom, self-control and
    understanding.

24 The father of a good child is very happy;
parents who have wise children are glad because of them.
25 Make your father and mother happy;
give your mother a reason to be glad.
26 My son, pay attention to me,
and watch closely what I do.

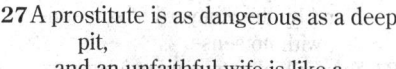
23:26 Responsibility
How can you learn to be responsible?

27 A prostitute is as dangerous as a deep pit,
and an unfaithful wife is like a narrow well.
28 They ambush you like robbers
and cause many men to be unfaithful to their wives.
29 Who has trouble? Who has pain?
Who fights? Who complains?
Who has unnecessary bruises?
Who has bloodshot eyes?
30 It is people who drink too much wine,
who try out all different kinds of strong drinks.
31 Don't stare at the wine when it is red,
when it sparkles in the cup,
when it goes down smoothly.
32 Later it bites like a snake
with poison in its fangs.
33 Your eyes will see strange sights,
and your mind will be confused.
34 You will feel dizzy as if you're in a storm on the ocean,
as if you're on top of a ship's sails.
35 You will think, "They hit me, but I'm not hurt.
They beat me up, but I don't remember it.
I wish I could wake up.
Then I would get another drink."

24 Don't envy evil people
or try to be friends with them.
2 Their minds are always planning violence,
and they always talk about making trouble.
3 It takes wisdom to have a good family,
and it takes understanding to make it strong.

24:3–4 Wisdom
Why is wisdom important?

4 It takes knowledge to fill a home
with rare and beautiful treasures.
5 Wise people have great power,
and those with knowledge have great strength.
6 So you need advice when you go to war.
If you have lots of good advice, you will win.
7 Foolish people cannot understand wisdom.
They have nothing to say in a discussion.
8 Whoever makes evil plans
will be known as a troublemaker.
9 Making foolish plans is sinful,
and making fun of wisdom is hateful.
10 If you give up when trouble comes,
it shows that you are weak.
11 Save those who are being led to their death;
rescue those who are about to be killed.
12 If you say, "We don't know anything about this,"
God, who knows what's in your mind, will notice.
He is watching you, and he will know.
He will reward each person for what he has done.
13 My child, eat honey because it is good.
Honey from the honeycomb tastes sweet.
14 In the same way, wisdom is pleasing to you.

24:13–14 Wisdom
Check out what wisdom is like.

If you find it, you have hope for the future,
and your wishes will come true.

15 Don't be wicked and attack a good family's house;
don't rob the place where they live.
16 Even though good people may be bothered by trouble seven times, they are never defeated,
but the wicked are overwhelmed by trouble.
17 Don't be happy when your enemy is defeated;
don't be glad when he is overwhelmed.
18 The LORD will notice and be displeased.
He may not be angry with them any more.
19 Don't envy evil people,
and don't be jealous of the wicked.
20 An evil person has nothing to hope for;
the wicked will die like a flame that is put out.

21 My child, respect the LORD and the king.
Don't join those people who refuse to obey them.
22 The LORD and the king will quickly destroy such people.
Those two can cause great disaster!

More Words of Wisdom

23 These are also sayings of the wise:
It is not good to take sides when you are the judge.
24 Don't tell the wicked that they are innocent;
people will curse you, and nations will hate you.
25 But things will go well if you punish the guilty,
and you will receive rich blessings.

24:17–18
Enemies
Should you be glad when your enemy gets hurt?

26 An honest answer is as pleasing as a kiss on the lips.
27 First, finish your outside work and prepare your fields.
After that, you can build your house.
28 Don't testify against your neighbour for no good reason.
Don't say things that are false.
29 Don't say, "I'll get even;
I'll do to him what he did to me."

30 I passed by a lazy person's field
and by the vineyard of someone with no sense.
31 Thorns had grown up everywhere.
The ground was covered with weeds,
and the stone walls had fallen down.
32 I thought about what I had seen;
I learned this lesson from what I saw.
33 You sleep a little; you take a nap.
You fold your hands and lie down to rest.
34 Soon you will be as poor as if you had been robbed;
you will have as little as if you had been held up.

More Wise Sayings of Solomon

25 These are more wise sayings of Solomon, copied by the men of Hezekiah king of Judah.

2 God is honoured for what he keeps secret.
Kings are honoured for what they can discover.

3 No one can measure the height of the skies or the depth of the earth.
So also no one can understand the mind of a king.

4 Remove the scum from the silver,
so the silver can be used by the silversmith.
5 Remove wicked people from the king's presence;
then his government will be honest and last a long time.

6 Don't boast to the king
and act as if you are great.
7 It is better for him to give you a
higher position
than to bring you down in front of
the prince.

Because of something you have seen,
8 do not quickly take someone to
court.
What will you do later
when your neighbour proves you
wrong?

9 If you have an argument with your
neighbour,
don't tell other people what was
said.
10 Whoever hears it might shame you,
and you might not ever be
respected again.

11 The right word spoken at the right
time
is as beautiful as golden apples in a
silver bowl.

12 A wise warning to someone who will
listen
is as valuable as gold earrings or
fine gold jewellery.

13 Trustworthy messengers refresh
those who send them,
like the coolness of snow in the
summer-time.

14 People who boast about gifts they
never give
are like clouds and wind that give
no rain.

15 With patience you can convince a
ruler,
and a gentle word can get through
to the hard-headed.

16 If you find honey, don't eat too
much,
or it will make you vomit.
17 Don't go to your neighbour's house
too often;
too much of you will make him
hate you.

18 When you lie about your neighbours,
it hurts them as much as a club, a
sword or a sharp arrow.

19 Trusting unfaithful people when you
are in trouble
is like eating with a broken tooth
or walking with a crippled foot.

20 Singing songs to someone who is sad
is like taking away his coat on a
cold day
or pouring vinegar on soda.

21 If your enemy is
hungry, feed
him.
If he is thirsty,
give him a
drink.
22 Doing this will be
like pouring burning coals on his
head,
and the LORD will reward you.

**25:21-22
Enemies**
How should you treat
your enemies?

23 As the north wind brings rain,
telling gossip brings angry looks.

24 It is better to live in a corner on the
roof*n*
than inside the house with a
quarrelling wife.

25 Good news from a faraway place
is like a cool drink when you are
tired.

26 A good person who gives in to evil
is like a muddy spring or a dirty
well.

27 It is not good to eat too much honey,
nor does it bring you honour to
boast about yourself.

25:24 roof In Bible times houses were built with flat roofs. The roof was used for drying things such as flax and fruit. And it was used as an extra room, as a place for worship and as a place to sleep in the summer.

HANDLING MY ENEMIES
Proverbs 25:21–22

Now You're Asking for It! In TV programmes and films, we feel like cheering when the "bad guy" gets what he deserves. What do you do when someone makes you angry or does something rotten to you? Do you feel like getting even? Or do you forgive and forget?

God has a different idea about justice. He claims revenge as part of his territory. (Look at Isaiah 35:3–4, p. 940.) When someone acts like an enemy, tell God about it. Let him take care of it. In Israel, a special law was given to the people about getting even with others. (Check out Leviticus 19:18, p. 161.) When we are angry, we easily sin. What are some things you can do instead of getting even?

MORE FAITH links

- Give Revenge a Rest, **p. 160**
- What's Out Becomes In, **p. 327**
- Putting an Enemy in Check, **p. 486**
- Mercy for an Enemy, **p. 1216**
- Who Needs Love? **p. 1379**

If someone plays a mean trick on you or makes fun of you, do you bide your time – with a water bomb at the ready – waiting to get your own back?

There are better ways than revenge to deal with your enemies. Why don't you forget about the water bomb and log on to these Faithlinks for some ideas?

A Right to Get Even? 1 Samuel 24, p. 388
- If you've ever felt like getting even with someone, think of David's story. King Saul was David's enemy, determined to kill David. Link here to discover how David reacted when he had a chance to get even.

Justice Desserts, Habakkuk 2:4–8, p. 1237
- Have you ever heard someone say, "There's no justice in the world!"? Have *you* ever said that? How do you feel when you see people get away with doing wrong things? What would you like to see happen to them? This Faithlink points out God's faithfulness in serving justice.

Don't Get Mad; Get Even? Matthew 26:57–63; 27:11–14, p. 1323
- When someone treats you terribly, what do you do? Do you get mad or think about getting even? When we are mistreated, many of us are tempted to get even. Would that solve the problem? How could getting even make things worse? Next time you feel like getting even, ask yourself, "What would Jesus do?" and try to follow his example.

my FAVOURITE links

28 Those who do not control themselves
are like a city whose walls are
broken down.

26

It shouldn't snow in summer or
rain at harvest.
Neither should a foolish person
ever be honoured.

2 Curses will not harm someone who is
innocent;
they are like sparrows or swallows
that fly around and never land.

3 Whips are for horses, and harnesses
are for donkeys,
so paddles are good for fools.

4 Don't give fools a foolish answer,
or you will be just like them.

5 But answer fools as they should be
answered,
or they will think they are really
wise.

6 Sending a message by a foolish
person
is like cutting off your feet or
drinking poison.

7 A wise saying spoken by a fool
is as useless as the legs of a
crippled person.

8 Giving honour to a foolish person
is like tying a stone in a catapult.

9 A wise saying spoken by a fool
is like a thorn stuck in the hand of
a drunkard.

10 Employing a foolish person or anyone
just passing by
is like an archer shooting at just
anything.

11 A fool who repeats his foolishness
is like a dog that goes back to what
it has vomited.

12 There is more hope for a foolish
person
than for those who think they are
wise.

13 The lazy person says, "There's a lion
in the road!
There's a lion in the streets!"

14 Like a door turning back and forth on
its hinges,
the lazy person turns over and over
in bed.

15 Lazy people may put their hands in
the dish,
but they are too tired to lift the
food to their mouths.

16 The lazy person thinks he is wiser
than seven people who give
sensible answers.

17 Interfering in someone else's quarrel
as you pass by
is like grabbing a dog by the ears.

18 Like a madman shooting
deadly, burning arrows
19 is the one who tricks a neighbour
and then says, "I was just joking."

20 Without wood,
a fire will
go out,
and without
gossip,
quarrelling
will stop.

**26:20
Gossip**
What happens when
gossip is stopped?

21 Just as charcoal and wood keep a fire
going,
a quarrelsome person keeps an
argument going.

22 The words of a gossip are like tasty
bits of food;
people like to take them all up.

23 Kind words from a wicked mind
are like a shiny coating on a clay
pot.

24 Those who hate you may try to fool
you with their words,

but in their minds they are
  planning evil.
25 People's words may be kind, but don't
    believe them,
  because their minds are full of evil
    thoughts.
26 Lies can hide hate,
  but the evil will be plain to
    everyone.
27 Whoever digs a pit for others will fall
    into it.
  Whoever tries to roll a boulder
    down on others will be crushed
    by it.
28 Liars hate the people they hurt,
  and false praise can ruin others.

27

Don't boast about tomorrow;
  you don't know what may
    happen then.
2 Don't praise yourself.
  Let someone
    else do it.
  Let the praise come
    from a stranger
    and not from
    your own mouth.
3 Stone is heavy, and
    sand is weighty,
  but a complaining fool is worse
    than either.
4 Anger is cruel and destroys like a
    flood,
  but no one can put up with
    jealousy!
5 It is better to correct someone
    openly
  than to have love and not show it.
6 The slap of a friend can be trusted to
    help you,
  but the kisses of an enemy are
    nothing but lies.
7 When you are full, not even honey
    tastes good,
  but when you are hungry, even
    something bitter tastes sweet.
8 A person who leaves his home
  is like a bird that leaves its nest.
9 The sweet smell of perfume and oils
    is pleasant,
  and so is good advice from a friend.
10 Don't forget your friend or your
    parent's friend.
  Don't always go to your family for
    help when trouble comes.
  A neighbour close by is better than
    a family far away.
11 Be wise, my child, and make me
    happy.
  Then I can respond to any insult.
12 The wise see danger
    ahead and avoid
    it,
  but fools keep
    going and get
    into trouble.
13 Take the coat of
    someone who
    promises to pay
    a stranger's loan,
    and keep it until he
    pays what the
    stranger owes.
14 If you loudly greet your neighbour
    early in the morning,
  he will think of it as a curse.
15 A quarrelling wife is as bothersome
    as a continual dripping on a rainy
    day.
16 Stopping her is like stopping the wind
    or trying to hold oil in your hand.
17 As iron sharpens iron,
    so people can improve each other.
18 Whoever tends a fig tree gets to eat
    its fruit,
  and whoever takes care of his
    master will receive honour.

> The wise see danger
> ahead and avoid it.
> — Proverbs 27:12

19 As water reflects your face,
    so your mind shows what kind of
    person you are.
20 People will never stop dying and
    being destroyed,
    and they will never stop wanting
    more than they have.
21 A hot furnace tests silver and gold,
    and people are tested by the praise
    they receive.
22 Even if you ground up a foolish
    person like grain in a bowl,
    you couldn't remove the
    foolishness.
23 Be sure you know how your sheep
    are doing,
    and pay attention to the condition
    of your cattle.
24 Riches will not go on for ever,
    nor do governments go on for ever.
25 Bring in the hay, and let the new
    grass appear.
    Gather the grass from the hills.
26 Make clothes from the lambs' wool,
    and sell some goats to buy a field.
27 There will be plenty of goat's milk
    to feed you and your family
    and to make your servant girls
    healthy.

28

Evil people run even though no
    one is chasing them,
    but good people are as brave as a
    lion.
2 When a country is disobedient, it has
    one ruler after another;
    but when it is led by a man with
    understanding and knowledge, it
    continues strong.
3 Rulers who mistreat the poor
    are like a hard rain that destroys
    the crops.
4 Those who disobey what they have
    been taught praise the wicked,
    but those who obey what they have
    been taught are against them.

5 Evil people do not understand justice,
    but those who follow the LORD
    understand it completely.
6 It is better to be poor and innocent
    than to be rich and wicked.
7 Children who obey what they have
    been taught are clever,
    but friends of troublemakers
    disgrace their parents.

FAITH links

CHOOSING A FRIEND

PROVERBS 28:7

Have you ever done a magazine quiz on choosing a friend? Those same magazines usually offer advice on making friends. The friends you choose are not only important to you; they're important to your parents as well. As this proverb mentions, those who have troublemakers for friends wind up embarrassing their parents. If that's not your goal, choose your friends wisely.

An Admirable Quality, 1 Kings 10:1–13, p. 451

Two Kinds of People, Psalm 1, p. 710

A Hopeful Future, Jeremiah 29:11, p. 1031

A Blueprint for Living, Amos 5:14–15, p. 1200

A Real Crowd-pleaser? Micah 2:6–11, p. 1222

My Favourite! Mark 10:17–23, p. 1347

Proverbs 28:8

8 Some people get rich by overcharging others,
  but their wealth will be given to those who are kind to the poor.

9 If you refuse to obey what you have been taught,
  your prayers will not be heard.

10 Those who lead good people to do wrong
  will be ruined by their own evil,
  but the innocent will be rewarded with good things.

11 Rich people may think they are wise,
  but the poor with understanding will prove them wrong.

12 When good people triumph, there is great happiness,
  but when the wicked get control, everybody hides.

13 If you hide your sins, you will not succeed.
  If you confess and reject them, you will receive mercy.

14 Those who are always respectful will be happy,
  but those who are stubborn will get into trouble.

15 A wicked ruler is as dangerous to poor people
  as a roaring lion or a charging bear.

16 A ruler without wisdom will be cruel,
  but the one who refuses to take dishonest money will rule a long time.

17 Don't help those who are guilty of murder;
  let them run until they die.

18 Innocent people will be kept safe,
  but those who are dishonest will suddenly be ruined.

19 Those who work their land will have plenty of food,
  but the ones who chase empty dreams instead will end up poor.

20 A truthful person will have many blessings,
  but those eager to get rich will be punished.

21 It is not good for a judge to take sides,
  but some will sin for only a piece of bread.

22 Selfish people are in a hurry to get rich
  and do not realise they soon will be poor.

23 Those who correct others will later be liked
  more than those who give false praise.

24 Whoever robs his father or mother and says, "It's not wrong,"
  is just like someone who destroys things.

25 A greedy person causes trouble,
  but the one who trusts the LORD will succeed.

26 Those who trust in themselves are foolish,
  but those who live wisely will be kept safe.

28:25–26 Trust How successful will you be?

27 Whoever gives to the poor will have everything he needs,
  but the one who ignores the poor will receive many curses.

28 When the wicked get control, everybody hides,
  but when they die, good people do well.

29 Whoever is stubborn after being corrected many times
  will suddenly be hurt beyond cure.

2 When good people do well, everyone is happy,

but when evil people rule,
everyone groans.

3 Those who love wisdom make their
parents happy,
but friends of prostitutes waste
their money.

4 If a king is fair, he makes his country
strong,
but if he takes gifts dishonestly, he
tears his country down.

5 Those who give false praise to their
neighbours
are setting a trap for them.

6 Evil people are trapped by their own
sin,
but good people can sing and be
happy.

7 Good people care about justice for the
poor,
but the wicked are not concerned.

8 People who make fun of wisdom
cause trouble in a city,
but wise people calm anger down.

9 When a wise person takes a foolish
person to court,
the fool only shouts or laughs, and
there is no peace.

10 Murderers hate an honest person
and try to kill those who do right.

11 Foolish people lose their tempers,
but wise people control theirs.

12 If a ruler pays attention to lies,
all his officers will become
wicked.

13 The poor person and the cruel person
are alike
in that the LORD gave eyes to both
of them.

14 If a king judges poor people fairly,
his government will continue for
ever.

15 Correction and punishment make
children wise,
but those left alone will disgrace
their mother.

FAITH links

DOWN ON DISCIPLINE?
PROVERBS 29:15

If you wish your parents would never nag about something you've done wrong, raise your hand. Is your hand up? Thought so. Now, if you would like to be wise, raise your hand. Is your hand up? If so, consider this: a parent's discipline provides wisdom for each child. You've probably seen or heard enough news stories about kids who were "left alone" as this proverb states. The result is usually trouble. So... want to change your answer to the first question?

No one likes to be disciplined, but connect here to see why it's important:

In Your Best Interests, Ruth 3, p. 349

This Hurts Me More? 2 Chronicles 36:17–22, p. 606

See the Heart Behind It, Nehemiah 8; 9, p. 636

A Word to the Wise, Proverbs 10:1, p. 838

Remember Your Creator, Ecclesiastes 12:1, 13, p. 885

Just Say No! Titus 2:11–12, p. 1660

Proverbs 29:16

16 When there are many wicked people,
   there is much sin,
   but those who do right will see
   them destroyed.

17 Correct your children, and you will
   be proud;
   they will give you satisfaction.

18 Where there is no word from God,
   people are uncontrolled,
   but those who obey what they have
   been taught are happy.

19 Words alone cannot correct a
   servant,
   because even if he understands, he
   won't respond.

20 Do you see people who speak too
   quickly?
   There is more hope for a foolish
   person than for them.

21 If you spoil your servants when
   they are young,
   they will bring you grief later on.

22 An angry person causes trouble;
   a person with a quick temper sins
   a lot.

23 Pride will ruin people,
   but those who are humble will be
   honoured.

29:23 Pride
Check out who will be honoured.

24 Partners of thieves are their own
   worst enemies.
   If they have to testify in court, they
   are afraid to say anything.

25 Being afraid of people can get you
   into trouble,
   but if you trust the LORD, you will
   be safe.

26 Many people want to speak to a ruler,
   but justice comes only from the
   LORD.

27 Good people hate those who are
   dishonest,
   and the wicked hate those who are
   honest.

Wise Words from Agur

30 These are the words of Agur son
   of Jakeh.
   This is his message to Ithiel and
   Ucal:

2 "I am the most stupid person there
   is,
   and I have no understanding.
3 I have not learned to be wise,
   and I don't know much about God,
   the Holy One.
4 Who has gone up to heaven and come
   back down?
   Who can hold the wind in his hand?
   Who can gather up the waters in his
   coat?
   Who has set in place the ends of
   the earth?
   What is his name or his son's
   name?
   Tell me, if you know!

> Every word of God is true.
> – Proverbs 30:5

5 "Every word of God is true.
   He guards those who come to him
   for safety.
6 Do not add to his words,
   or he will correct you and prove
   you are a liar.

7 "I ask two things from you, LORD.
   Don't refuse me before I die.
8 Keep me from lying and being
   dishonest.
   And don't make me either rich or
   poor;
   just give me enough food for each
   day.

9 If I have too much, I might reject you
and say, 'I don't know the LORD.'
If I am poor, I might steal
and disgrace the name of my God.

10 "Do not say bad things about
servants to their masters,
or they will curse you, and you will
suffer for it.

11 "Some people curse their fathers
and do not bless their mothers.
12 Some people think they are pure,
but they are not really free from
evil.
13 Some people have such a proud
look!
They look down on others.
14 Some people have teeth like swords;
their jaws seem full of knives.
They want to remove the poor from
the earth
and the needy from the land.

15 "Greed has two daughters
named 'Give' and 'Give'.
There are three things that are never
satisfied,
really four that never say, 'I've had
enough!':
16 the cemetery, the childless mother,
the land that never gets enough
rain
and fire that never says, 'I've had
enough!'

17 "If you make fun of your father
and refuse to obey your mother,
the birds of the valley will peck out
your eyes,
and the vultures will eat them.

18 "There are three things that are too
hard for me,
really four I don't understand:
19 the way an eagle flies in the sky,
the way a snake slides over a rock,
the way a ship sails on the sea
and the way a man and a woman
fall in love.

20 "This is the way of a woman who
takes part in adultery:
she acts as if she had eaten and
washed her face;
she says, 'I haven't done anything
wrong.'

21 "There are three things that make
the earth tremble,
really four it cannot stand:
22 a servant who becomes a king,
a foolish person who has plenty to
eat,
23 a hated woman who gets married
and a maid who replaces her
mistress.

24 "There are four things on earth that
are small,
but they are very wise:
25 Ants are not very strong,
but they store up food in the
summer.
26 Rock badgers are not very powerful,
but they can live among the rocks.
27 Locusts have no king,
but they all go forwards in
formation.
28 Lizards can be caught in the hand,
but they are found even in kings'
palaces.

29 "There are three things that strut
proudly,
really four that walk as if they were
important:
30 a lion, the proudest animal,
which is strong and runs from
nothing,
31 a rooster, a male goat
and a king when his army is
around him.

32 "If you have been foolish and proud,
or if you have planned evil, shut
your mouth.
33 Just as stirring milk makes butter,
and twisting noses makes them
bleed,
so stirring up anger causes trouble."

Wise Words of King Lemuel

31 These are the words of King
Lemuel, the message his mother
taught him:

2 "My son, I gave birth to you.
  You are the son I prayed for.
3 Don't waste your strength on women
  or your time on those who ruin
  kings.

4 "Kings should not drink wine,
  Lemuel,
  and rulers should not desire beer.
5 If they drink, they might forget the
  law
  and keep the needy from getting
  their rights.
6 Give beer to people who are dying
  and wine to those who are sad.
7 Let them drink and forget their need
  and remember their misery no
  more.

8 "Speak up for those who cannot
  speak for themselves;
  defend the rights of all those who
  have nothing.
9 Speak up and judge fairly,
  and defend the rights of the poor
  and needy."

The Good Wife

10 It is hard to find a good wife,
   because she is worth far more than
   rubies.
11 Her husband trusts her completely.
   With her, he has everything he
   needs.
12 She does him good and not harm
   for as long as she lives.
13 She looks for wool and flax
   and likes to work with her hands.
14 She is like a trader's ship,
   bringing food from far away.
15 She gets up while it is still dark
   and prepares food for her family
   and feeds her servant girls.
16 She inspects a field and buys it.
   With money she earned, she plants
   a vineyard.
17 She does her work with energy,
   and her arms are strong.
18 She knows that what she makes is
   good.
   Her lamp burns late into the night.
19 She makes thread with her hands
   and weaves her own cloth.
20 She welcomes the poor
   and helps the needy.
21 She does not worry about her family
   when it snows,
   because they all have fine clothes
   to keep them warm.
22 She makes coverings for herself;
   her clothes are made of linen and
   other expensive material.
23 Her husband is known at the city
   meetings,
   where he makes decisions as one
   of the elders of the land.
24 She makes linen clothes and sells
   them
   and provides belts for the
   merchants.
25 She is strong and is respected by the
   people.
   She looks forward to the future
   with joy.
26 She speaks wise words
   and teaches others to be kind.
27 She watches over her family
   and never wastes her time.
28 Her children speak well of her.
   Her husband also praises her,
29 saying, "There are many fine women,
   but you are
   better than
   all of them."
30 Charm can fool
   you, and
   beauty can
   trick you,
   but a woman
   who respects the LORD should
   be praised.
31 Give her the reward she has earned;
   she should be praised in public for
   what she has done.

31:30 Respect
Check out how to gain respect.

USELESS! USELESS!

Hi! Solomon, here. You've probably heard of me, the king who asked God for wisdom. (I also wrote Proverbs.) Not only did God grant my request for wisdom, but he also blessed me with fabulous riches and power. I did great things with my wealth. I built houses and vineyards, bought large herds of animals, and gathered gold and silver treasure for myself. Anything I wanted, I got. But something was missing. Have you ever put together a puzzle and discovered that a piece in the middle was missing? The missing piece of my life was God.

I wrote this book to tell others that life without God is useless. Don't think you can find meaning in your life by collecting treasure or gaining a high position. It's like chasing the wind. The best advice I can give is to obey God and enjoy the life he gives you.

JESUS WATCH

How empty is life without God! The pleasures of this life will never satisfy us. We always want more. The need for Jesus is clearly seen in this book. When we believe in Jesus, our lives are full of his love and care for us. The work we do is not useless, but is pleasing to God. Jesus takes care of us like a good shepherd. He knows each one of us by name, and he protects us from our enemies. Jesus is not only our shepherd; he is also our friend. How rich and full our lives are when Jesus is our friend! Without Jesus, our life, like Solomon said, is useless.

my FAVOURITE links

OTHER CONNECTIONS

 Want to find out what real wisdom is all about? Connect to Wise Books, Ecclesiastes 7 and you can learn more about what books in the Bible are considered the "Wisdom Literature" and in what forms you will discover wisdom in the Bible.

MORE STUFF...

Some Good Advice King Solomon had a lot of questions in the Book of Ecclesiastes. But he also had some good advice to share. Take a look at some advice that Solomon had to offer:
- Two people are better than one because they can help each other, can get more done and can protect one another (Ecclesiastes 4:9–12).
- Think before you speak and be careful about what you promise God (Ecclesiastes 5:1–7).
- Enjoy the things that God has given you to do (Ecclesiastes 5:18–20).
- Don't get angry quickly (Ecclesiastes 7:9).
- Don't make fun of others because your words may get back to them (Ecclesiastes 10:20).
- Honour and obey all God's commands (Ecclesiastes 12:13–14).

FAITH links

○ A Need to Change, **Ecclesiastes 1:1–11**

○ When Bad Things Happen, **Ecclesiastes 3:16–17**

○ Two Are Better, **Ecclesiastes 4:9–12**

○ Wisdom About Wealth, **Ecclesiastes 5:10–12**

○ Remember Your Creator, **Ecclesiastes 12:1, 13**

What is Solomon's final advice?

Let's be wise and look it up in Ecclesiastes 12:13-14.

IT'S NOT USELESS TO LOOK THESE UP:

A time for everything, Ecclesiastes 3:1–8
Two are better than one, Ecclesiastes 4:9–12
Never enough, Ecclesiastes 5:10–12
Enjoy every day, Ecclesiastes 11:7–10

1 These are the words of the Teacher, a son of David, king in Jerusalem. 2 The Teacher says,
"Useless! Useless!
Completely useless!
Everything is useless."

3 What do people really gain
   from all the hard work they do
   here on earth?

Things Never Change

4 People live, and people die,
   but the earth continues for ever.
5 The sun rises, the sun sets,
   and then it hurries back to where it rises again.
6 The wind blows to the south;
   it blows to the north.
   It blows from one direction and then another.
   Then it turns round and repeats the same pattern, going nowhere.
7 All the rivers flow to the sea,
   but the sea never becomes full.
8 Everything is boring,
   so boring that you don't even want to talk about it.
   Words come again and again to our ears,
   but we never hear enough,
   nor can we ever really see all we want to see.
9 All things continue the way they have been since the beginning.
   What has happened will happen again;
   there is nothing new here on earth.
10 Someone might say,
   "Look, this is new,"
   but really it has always been here.
   It was here before we were.
11 People don't remember what happened long ago,
   and in the future people will not remember what happens now.
   Even later, other people will not remember what was done before them.

FAITH links

A NEED TO CHANGE
ECCLESIASTES 1:1-11

Booooorrrring! Have you uttered that word lately? Solomon was very wise and rich, but he was not satisfied with his life. Nothing seemed new or exciting to him. Solomon could already have anything he wanted. Yet he felt that he needed something else.

Boredom is sometimes a sign of a lack of contentment or a need to change. When you're stuck in the "everything is boring" (v. 8) mode, think about what you could do to change your situation.

Bored? Connect here:

Complaints, Complaints! Exodus 16:1–3, p. 97

A Life of Thanksgiving, 1 Kings 1:47–48, p. 435

Our Thirst Quencher, Psalm 42:1–3, p. 741

First Place, Haggai 1:7–11, p. 1248

My Favourite! Mark 10:17–23, p. 1347

A Different Kind of Fruit, Galatians 5:22–23, p. 1592

Does Wisdom Bring Happiness?

12 I, the Teacher, was king over Israel in Jerusalem. 13 I decided to use my wisdom to learn about everything that happens on earth. I learned that God has given us terrible things to face. 14 I looked at everything done on earth and

saw that it is all useless, like chasing the wind.

15 If something is crooked,
you can't make it straight.
If something is missing,
you can't say it is there.

16 I said to myself, "I have become very wise and am now wiser than anyone who ruled Jerusalem before me. I know what wisdom and knowledge really are." 17 So I decided to find out about wisdom and knowledge and also about foolish thinking, but this turned out to be like chasing the wind.

18 With much wisdom comes much
disappointment;
the person who gains more
knowledge also gains more
sorrow.

Does "Having Fun" Bring Happiness?

2 I said to myself, "I will try having fun. I will enjoy myself." But I found that this is also useless. 2 It is foolish to laugh all the time, and having fun doesn't accomplish anything. 3 I decided to cheer myself up with wine while my mind was still thinking wisely. I wanted to find a way to enjoy myself and see what was good for people to do during their few days of life.

Does Hard Work Bring Happiness?

4 Then I did great things: I built houses and planted vineyards for myself. 5 I made gardens and parks and I planted all kinds of fruit trees in them. 6 I made pools of water for myself and used them to water my growing trees. 7 I bought male and female slaves, and slaves were also born in my house. I had large herds and flocks, more than anyone in Jerusalem had ever had before. 8 I also gathered silver and gold for myself, treasures from kings and other areas. I had male and female singers and all the women a man could ever want. 9 I became very famous, even greater than anyone who had lived in Jerusalem before me. My wisdom helped me in all this.

10 Anything I saw and wanted, I got for
myself;
I did not miss any pleasure I
desired.
I was pleased with everything I did,
and this pleasure was the reward
for all my hard work.

11 But then I looked at what I had done,
and I thought about all the hard
work.
Suddenly I realised it was useless,
like chasing the wind.
There is nothing to gain from
anything we do here on earth.

Maybe Wisdom is the Answer

12 Then I began to think again about
being wise,
and also about being foolish and
doing mad things.
But after all, what more can anyone
do?
He can't do more than what the
other king has already done.
13 I saw that being wise is certainly
better than being foolish,
just as light is better than
darkness.
14 Wise people see where they are
going,
but fools walk around in the dark.
Yet I saw that
both wise and foolish people end
the same way.

15 I thought to myself,
"What happens to a fool will happen
to me too,
so what is the reward for being
wise?"
I said to myself,
"Being wise is also useless."
16 The wise person and the fool
will both die,
and no one will remember either one
for long.
In the future, both will be
forgotten.

Is There Real Happiness in Life?

17 So I hated life. It made me sad to think that everything here on earth is useless, like chasing the wind. 18 I hated all

the things I had worked for here on earth, because I must leave them to someone who will live after me. 19 Someone else will control everything for which I worked so hard here on earth, and I don't know if he will be wise or foolish. This is also useless. 20 So I became sad about all the hard work I had done here on earth. 21 People can work hard using all their wisdom, knowledge and skill, but they will die, and other people will get the things for which they worked. They did not do the work, but they will get everything. This is also unfair and useless. 22 What do people get for all their work and struggling here on earth? 23 All of their lives their work is full of pain and sorrow, and even at night their minds don't rest. This is also useless.

24 The best that people can do is eat, drink and enjoy their work. I saw that even this comes from God, 25 because no one can eat or enjoy life without him. 26 If people please God, God will give them wisdom, knowledge and joy. But sinners will get only the work of gathering and storing wealth that they will have to give to the ones who please God. So all their work is useless, like chasing the wind.

There is a Time for Everything

3 There is a time for everything,
and everything on earth has its special season.
2 There is a time to be born
and a time to die.
There is a time to plant
and a time to pull up plants.
3 There is a time to kill
and a time to heal.
There is a time to destroy
and a time to build.
4 There is a time to cry
and a time to laugh.
There is a time to be sad
and a time to dance.
5 There is a time to throw away stones
and a time to gather them.
There is a time to embrace
and a time to refrain.
6 There is a time to look for something
and a time to stop looking for it.
There is a time to keep things
and a time to throw things away.
7 There is a time to tear apart
and a time to sew together.
There is a time to be silent
and a time to speak.
8 There is a time to love
and a time to hate.
There is a time for war
and a time for peace.

God Controls His World

9 Do people really gain anything from their work? 10 I saw the hard work God has given people to do. 11 God has given them a desire to know the future. He does everything just right and on time, but people can never completely understand what he is doing. 12 So I realise that the best thing for them is to be happy and enjoy themselves as long as they live. 13 God wants all people to eat and drink and be happy in their work, which are gifts from God. 14 I know that everything God does will continue for ever. People cannot add anything to what God has done, and they cannot take anything away from it. God does it this way to make people respect him.

15 What happens now has happened in
the past,
and what will happen in the future
has happened before.
God makes the same things
happen again and again.

Unfairness on Earth

16 I also saw this here on earth:
where there should have been justice,
there was evil;
where there should have been
right, there was wrong.
17 I said to myself,

> The best that people can do is eat, drink and enjoy their work.
> – Ecclesiastes 2:24

FAITH links

WHEN BAD THINGS HAPPEN
ECCLESIASTES 3:16-17

You can't go through life without hearing about something bad happening to someone. Sometimes bad things happen even to people who trust God. When that happens, we call it an injustice. Often people use the evil in the world as an excuse not to believe in God. "Why would a good God allow evil?" they might ask.

God wants you to trust him, even when bad things happen. He wants you to trust that he's still in control of everything.

When You're Afraid, Genesis 32:9–12, p. 45

A Giant Problem, 1 Samuel 17:32–51, p. 377

Fly Like an Eagle, Isaiah 40:28–31, p. 947

Small Beginnings, Zechariah 4:10, p. 1255

An Energy Boost, Acts 4:31, p. 1469

It's Under Control, Romans 8:28, p. 1529

God has planned a time for
　　everything and every action,
so he will judge both good people
　　and bad.
18 I decided that God leaves it the way it is to test people and to show them they are just like animals. 19 The same thing happens to animals and to people; they both have the same breath, so they both die. People are no better off than the animals, because everything is useless. 20 Both end up the same way; both came from dust and both will go back to dust. 21 Who can be sure that the human spirit goes up to God and that the spirit of an animal goes down into the ground? 22 So I saw that the best thing people can do is to enjoy their work, because that is all they have. No one can help another person see what will happen in the future.

Is It Better to be Dead?

4 Again I saw all the people who were mistreated here on earth.
　I saw their tears
　　and that they had no one to
　　　comfort them.
　Cruel people had all the power,
　　and there was no one to comfort
　　　those they hurt.
2 I decided that the dead
　　are better off than the living.
3 But those who have never been
　　born
　are better off still;
　they have not seen the evil
　　that is done here on earth.

Why Work So Hard?

4 I realised the reason people work hard and try to succeed: they are jealous of each other. This, too, is useless, like chasing the wind.

5 Some say it is foolish to fold your
　　hands and do nothing,
　because you will starve to death.
6 Maybe so, but I say it is better to be
　　content
　with what little you have.
　Otherwise, you will always be
　　struggling for more,
　and that is like chasing the wind.

7 Again I saw something here on earth
　　that was useless:
8 I saw a man who had no family,
　　no son or brother.
　He always worked hard
　　but was never satisfied with what
　　　he had.

He never asked himself, "For whom am I working so hard? Why don't I let myself enjoy life?" This also is very sad and useless.

Friends and Family Give Strength

9 Two people are better than one,
  because they get more done by working together.
10 If one falls down,
  the other can help him up.
  But it is bad for the person who is alone and falls,
  because no one is there to help.
11 If two lie down together, they will be warm,
  but a person alone will not be warm.
12 An enemy might defeat one person,
  but two people together can defend themselves;
  a rope that is woven of three strings is hard to break.

Fame and Power are Useless

13 A poor but wise boy is better than a foolish but old king who doesn't listen to advice. 14 A boy became king. He had been born poor in the kingdom and had even gone to prison before becoming king. 15 I watched all the people who live on earth follow him and make him their king. 16 Many followed him at first, but later, they did not like him, either. So fame and power are useless, like chasing the wind.

Be Careful About Making Promises

5 Be careful when you go to worship at the Temple. It is better to listen than to offer foolish sacrifices without even knowing you are doing wrong.

2 Think before you speak,
  and be careful about what you say to God.
  God is in heaven,
  and you are on the earth,
  so say only a few words to God.
3 The saying is true: bad dreams come from too much worrying,
  and too many words come from foolish people.

4 If you make a promise to God, don't be slow to keep it. God is not happy with fools, so give God what you promised. 5 It is better not to promise anything than to promise something and not do it. 6 Don't let your words cause you to sin, and don't say to the priest at the Temple, "I didn't mean what I promised." If you do, God will become angry with your words and

---

FAITH links

TWO ARE BETTER
ECCLESIASTES 4:9-12

What are the things you do to help your family or friends? God made us to need each other. Friends and family support each other by being there for each other. If your friends and family love God like you do, they can encourage you in your faith.

To earn a friend, you have to be a friend. You can do that by sharing with someone, helping that person, and offering words of encouragement.

Want a recipe for being a good friend? Link here:

Help for the Poor, Leviticus 5:7, p. 138

An Unsung Hero, Ruth 2:12, 15–16, p. 347

Show You Care, 2 Kings 4:10, p. 481

Some Friendly Advice, Proverbs 17:9, 14, 17, p. 851

How to Worship God, Isaiah 58, p. 972

An Encouraging Word, 1 Corinthians 1:3–5, p. 1545

will destroy everything you have worked for. 7 Many useless promises are like so many dreams; they mean nothing. You should respect God.

Officers Cheat Each Other

8 In some places you will see poor people mistreated. Don't be surprised when they are not treated fairly or given their rights. One officer is cheated by a higher officer who in turn is cheated by even higher officers. 9 The wealth of the country is divided up among them all. Even the king makes sure he gets his share of the profits.

Wealth Cannot Buy Happiness

10 Whoever loves money
    will never have enough money;
  Whoever loves wealth
    will not be satisfied with it.
  This is also useless.
11 The more wealth people have,
    the more friends they have to help spend it.
  So what do people really gain?
    They gain nothing except to look at their riches.
12 Those who work hard sleep in peace;
    it is not important if they eat little or much.
  But rich people worry about their wealth
    and cannot sleep.

13 I have seen real misery here on earth:
  money saved is a curse to its owners.
14   They lose it all in a bad deal
    and have nothing to give to their children.
15 People come into this world with nothing,
    and when they die they leave with nothing.
  In spite of all their hard work,
    they leave just as they came.
16 This, too, is real misery:
    they leave just as they came.
    So what do they gain from chasing the wind?
17 All they get are days full of sadness and sorrow,

FAITH links

WISDOM ABOUT WEALTH

ECCLESIASTES 5:10-12

Did you ever believe that all of your problems would be solved if your family just had a little more money? Maybe you believe that right now. Solomon was the wisest man in the world. He was also the richest at one time. Even though he had money, it didn't satisfy him.

The more money a person has, the more he or she wants. Want to be wise about money? Don't make it the centre of your life.

Here are some more Faithlinks on handling your money:

Idol Talk, Exodus 32, p. 118

What I've Got, 2 Kings 20:12–17, p. 508

Gifts from the Heart, 1 Chronicles 29, p. 557

A Robbery in Progress, Malachi 3:8–10, p. 1270

Your Heart's Desire, Luke 16:13–15, p. 1401

More Money? 1 Timothy 6:10, p. 1649

and they end up sick, defeated and angry.

Enjoy Your Life's Work

18 I have seen what is best for people here on earth. They should eat and drink and enjoy their work, because the life

God has given them on earth is short. 19 God gives some people the ability to enjoy the wealth and property he gives them, as well as the ability to accept their area in life and enjoy their work. 20 They do not worry about how short life is, because God keeps them busy with what they love to do.

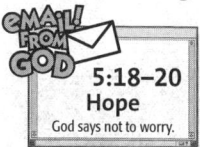

5:18–20
Hope
God says not to worry.

6 I have seen something else wrong here on earth that causes serious problems for people. 2 God gives great wealth, riches and honour to some people; they have everything they want. But God does not let them enjoy such things; a stranger enjoys them instead. This is useless and very wrong. 3 A man might have 100 children and live a long time, but what good is it if he can't enjoy the good God gives him or have a proper burial? I say a baby born dead is better off than he is. 4 A baby born dead is useless. It returns to darkness without even a name. 5 That baby never saw the sun and never knew anything, but it finds more rest than that man. 6 Even if he lives 2,000 years, he doesn't enjoy the good God gives him. Everyone is going to the same place.

7 People work just to feed themselves,
but they never seem to get enough
to eat.
8 In this way a wise person
is no better off than a fool.
Then, too, it does a poor person little
good
to know how to get along in life.
9 It is better to see what you have
than to want more.
Wanting more is useless—
like chasing the wind.

Who Can Understand God's Plan?

10 Whatever happens was planned long
ago.
Everyone knows what people are
like.
No one can argue with God,
who is stronger than anyone.
11 The more you say,
the more useless it is.
What good does it do?

12 People have only a few useless days of life on the earth; their short life passes like a shadow. Who knows what is best for them while they live? Who can tell them what the future will bring?

Some Benefits of Serious Thinking

7 It is better to have respect than good
perfume.
The day of death is better than the
day of birth.
2 It is better to go to a funeral
than to a party.
We all must die,
and everyone living should think
about this.
3 Sorrow is better than laughter,
and sadness has a good influence
on you.
4 A wise person thinks about death,
but a fool thinks only about having
a good time.
5 It is better to be criticised by a wise
person
than to be praised by a fool.
6 The laughter of fools
is like the burning of thorns in a
cooking fire.
Both are useless.

7 Even wise people are fools
if they let money change their
thinking.

8 It is better to finish something
than to start it.
It is better to be patient
than to be proud.
9 Don't become angry quickly,
because getting angry is foolish.

10 Don't ask, "Why was life better in the
'good old days?'"
It is not wise to ask such
questions.

11 Wisdom is better when it comes with
money.
They both help those who are
alive.

WISE BOOKS   Ecclesiastes 7

The Israelite word for "wisdom" means "skill for living". There are a few books in the Bible that are all about wisdom: Job, Proverbs, Ecclesiastes and some of the Psalms. In these books, we will find helpful advice on how to live our lives. We call these books the Wisdom Literature. The wisdom you'll find in these books is in three different forms:

1. proverbs or short, little nuggets of truth;
2. riddles or stories with a spiritual meaning; and
3. discussions about the problems of life.

The Book of Proverbs is a book filled with nuggets of truth about attitudes and behaviours. Ecclesiastes is a discussion about how empty life is without God. (Check out Ecclesiastes 1:2, 14.) Job is a story about evil and suffering. (Read Job 28:20–28, p. 689.) Many of the Psalms talk about how to face the problems of life. (See Psalm 37:9, p. 737.)

12 Wisdom is like money:
    they both help.
But wisdom is better,
    because it can save whoever has it.
13 Look at what God has done:
    no one can straighten what he has made crooked.
14 When life is good, enjoy it.
    But when life is hard, remember:
    God gives good times and hard times,
    and no one knows what tomorrow will bring.

It is Impossible to be Truly Good

15 In my useless life I have seen both of these:
    I have seen good people die in spite of their goodness
    and evil people live a long time in spite of their evil.
16 Don't be too right,
    and don't be too wise.
    Why destroy yourself?
17 Don't be too wicked,
    and don't be foolish.
    Why die before your time?
18 It is good to grasp the one and not let go of the other;
    those who honour God will hold them both.
19 Wisdom makes a person stronger than ten leaders in a city.
20 Surely there is not a good person on earth
    who always does good and never sins.
21 Don't listen to everything people say,
    or you might hear your servant insulting you.
22 You know that many times
    you have insulted others.
23 I used wisdom to test all these things.
    I wanted to be wise,
    but it was too hard for me.
24 I cannot understand why things are as they are.

It is too hard for anyone to understand.
25 I studied and tried very hard to find wisdom,
to find some meaning for everything.
I learned that it is foolish to be evil, and it is mad to act like a fool.

26 I found that some women are worse than death
and are as dangerous as traps.
Their love is like a net,
and their arms hold men like chains.
A man who pleases God will be saved from them,
but a sinner will be caught by them.

27 The Teacher says, "This is what I learned:
I added all these things together
to find some meaning for everything.
28 While I was searching but not finding
I found one man among the thousands.
But not one woman among all these.
29 One thing I have learned:
God made people good,
but they have found all kinds of ways to be bad."

Obey the King

8 No one is like the wise person
who can understand what things mean.
Wisdom brings happiness;
it makes sad faces happy.

2 Obey the king's command, because you made a promise to God. 3 Don't be too quick to leave the king. Don't support something that is wrong, because the king does whatever he pleases. 4 What the king says is law; no one tells him what to do.

5 Whoever obeys the king's command will be safe.
A wise person does the right thing at the right time.
6 There is a right time and a right way for everything,
yet people often have many troubles.
7 They do not know what the future holds,
and no one can tell them what will happen.
8 No one can control the wind or stop his own death.
No soldier is released in times of war,
and evil does not set free those who do evil.

Justice, Rewards and Punishment

9 I saw all of this as I considered all that is done here on earth. Sometimes men harm those they control. 10 I saw the funerals of evil people who used to go in and out of the holy place. They were honoured in the same towns where they had done evil. This is useless too.

11 When evil people are not punished right away, it makes others want to do evil too. 12 Though a sinner might do 100 evil things and might live a long time, I know it will be better for those who honour God. 13 I also know it will not go well for evil people, because they do not honour God. Like a shadow, they will not last.

14 Sometimes something useless happens on earth. Bad things happen to good people, and good things happen to bad people. I say that this is also useless. 15 So I decided it was more important to enjoy life. The best that people can do here on earth is to eat, drink and enjoy life, because these joys will help them do the hard work God gives them here on earth.

Wisdom brings happiness; it makes sad faces happy.
– Ecclesiastes 8:1

We Cannot Understand All God Does

16 I tried to understand all that happens on earth. I saw how busy people are, working day and night and hardly ever sleeping. 17 I also saw all that God has done. Nobody can understand what God does here on earth. No matter how hard people try to understand it, they cannot. Even if wise people say they understand, they cannot; no one can really understand it.

Is Death Fair?

9 I thought about all this and tried to understand it. I saw that God controls good people and wise people and what they do, but no one knows if they will experience love or hate.

2 Good and bad people end up the same—
> those who are right and those who are wrong,
> those who are good and those who are evil,
> those who are clean and those who are unclean,
> those who sacrifice and those who do not.
> The same things happen to a good person
>   as happen to a sinner,
> to a person who makes promises to God
>   and to one who does not.

3 This is something wrong that happens here on earth: what happens to one happens to all. So people's minds are full of evil and foolish thoughts while they live. After that, they join the dead. 4 But anyone still alive has hope; even a live dog is better off than a dead lion!

5 The living know they will die,
>   but the dead know nothing.
> Dead people have no more reward,
>   and people forget them.
6 After people are dead,
>   they can no longer love or hate or envy.
> They will never again share
>   in what happens here on earth.

Enjoy Life While You Can

7 So go and eat your food and enjoy it;
>   drink your wine and be happy,
> because that is what God wants you to do.
8 Put on nice clothes
>   and make yourself look good.
9 Enjoy life with the wife you love. Enjoy all the useless days of this useless life God has given you here on earth, because it is all you have. So enjoy the work you do here on earth. 10 Whatever work you do, do your best, because you are going to the grave, where there is no working, no planning, no knowledge and no wisdom.

Time and Chance

11 I also saw something else here on earth:
>   the fastest runner does not always win the race,
>   the strongest soldier does not always win the battle,
>   the wisest does not always have food,
>   the cleverest man does not always become wealthy
>   and the talented one does not always receive praise.
> Time and chance happen to everyone.
12 No one knows what will happen next.
> Like a fish caught in a net,
>   or a bird caught in a trap,
> people are trapped by evil
>   when it suddenly falls on them.

Wisdom Does Not Always Win

13 I also saw something wise here on earth that was very impressive to me. 14 There was a small town with only a few people in it. A great king fought against it and put his armies all around it. 15 Now there was a poor but wise man in the town who used his wisdom to save his town. But later on, everyone forgot about him. 16 I still think wisdom is better than strength. But those people forgot about the poor man's wisdom and stopped listening to what he said.

> **E-MAIL FROM GOD**
> **9:13–18 Wisdom**
> What do you think is better than wisdom?

17 The quiet words of a wise person are better
    than the shouts of a foolish ruler.
18 Wisdom is better than weapons of war,
    but one sinner can destroy much good.

10 Dead flies can make even perfume stink.
    In the same way, a little foolishness can spoil wisdom.
2 The heart of the wise leads to right,
    but the heart of a fool leads to wrong.
3 Even in the way fools walk along the road,
    they show they are not wise;
    they show everyone how stupid they are.
4 Don't leave your job
    just because your ruler is angry with you.
    Remaining calm solves great problems.
5 There is something else wrong that happens here on earth.
    It is the kind of mistake rulers make:
6 fools are given important positions
    while rich people are given lower ones;
7 I have seen servants ride horses
    while princes walk like servants on foot.
8 Anyone who digs a pit might fall into it;
    anyone who knocks down a wall might be bitten by a snake;
9 anyone who moves boulders might be hurt by them;
    and anyone who cuts logs might be harmed by them.
10 A dull axe means harder work.
    Being wise will make it easier.
11 If a snake bites the tamer before it is tamed,
    what good is the tamer?
12 The words of the wise bring them praise,
    but the words of a fool will destroy them.

13 A fool begins by saying foolish things
    and ends by saying insane and wicked things.
14 A fool talks too much.
    No one knows the future,
    and no one can tell what will happen after death.
15 Work wears fools out;
    they don't even know how to get home.

The Value of Work

16 How terrible it is for a country whose king is a child

FAITH CHALLENGE

Here's a good one! Read 10:20 to see what can happen when people talk about others behind their backs. What would you do if you heard that someone was making fun of you behind your back? Why is it important to watch your words?

TESTING IT

Ecclesiastes 10:20
Don't make fun of the king, and don't make fun of rich people, even in your bedroom. A little bird might carry your words; a bird might fly and tell what you said.

and whose leaders eat all morning.
17 How happy a country is whose king
 comes from a good family,
 whose leaders eat only at
 mealtimes
 and for strength, not to get drunk.

18 If someone is lazy, the
 roof will begin to
 fall.
 If he doesn't fix it,
 the house will
 leak.

19 A party makes you
 feel good,
 wine makes you feel
 happy
 and money buys
 anything.

20 Don't make fun of the king,
 and don't make fun of rich people,
 even in your bedroom.
 A little bird might carry your words;
 a bird might fly and tell what you
 said.

Boldly Face the Future

11 Invest what you have,
 because after a while you will get
 a return.
2 Invest what you have in several
 different businesses,
 because you don't know what
 disasters might happen.

3 If clouds are full of rain,
 they will shower on the earth.
 A tree can fall to the north or south,
 but it will stay where it falls.
4 Those who wait for perfect weather
 will never plant seeds;
 those who look at every cloud
 will never harvest crops.

5 You don't know where the wind will
 blow,
 and you don't know how a baby
 grows inside the mother.
 In the same way, you don't know
 what God is doing,
 or how he created everything.

6 Plant early in the morning,
 and work until evening,
 because you don't know if this or that
 will succeed.
 They might both do well.

Serve God While You are Young

7 Sunshine is sweet;
 it is good to see the
 light of day.
8 People ought to enjoy
 every day of
 their lives,
 no matter how long
 they live.
 But they should also
 remember this:
 you will be dead a
 long time.
 Everything that
 happens then is
 useless.
9 Young people, enjoy yourselves while
 you are young;
 be happy while you are young.
 Do whatever your heart desires,
 whatever you want to do.
 But remember that God will judge
 you
 for everything you do.
10 Don't worry,
 and forget the troubles of your body,
 because youth and childhood are
 useless.

The Problems of Old Age

12 Remember your Creator
 while you are young,
 before the days of trouble come
 and the years when you say,
 "I find no pleasure in them."
2 When you get old,
 the light from the sun, moon and
 stars will grow dark;
 the rain clouds will never seem to
 go away.
3 At that time your arms will shake
 and your legs will become weak.
 Your teeth will fall out so you cannot
 chew,
 and your eyes will not see clearly.
4 Your ears will be deaf to the noise in
 the streets,

> Sunshine is sweet;
> it is good to see the
> light of day.
> – Ecclesiastes 11:7

FAITH links

REMEMBER YOUR CREATOR
ECCLESIASTES 12:1, 13

If you learn a musical instrument or a foreign language when you're young, you'll have a better chance of being good at it and remembering it later. Why? Your brain is like a sponge. It soaks information up quickly. As you get older, learning new things gets harder. That's why Solomon advises you to remember your Creator while you are young. If you get to know God now, your faith will grow with you.

Listen Up! 1 Kings 19:11–13, p. 467

More Precious Than Gold, Psalm 19:7–10, p. 723

Jesus' Mission and Yours, Isaiah 61:1–2, p. 978

The Writing's on the Wall, Daniel 5, p. 1159

The Best Advice, Zechariah 10:2, p. 1261

Prove It! Matthew 16:1–4, p. 1302

---

5 You will fear high places
and will be afraid to go for a walk.
Your hair will become white like the
flowers on an almond tree.
You will limp along like a
grasshopper when you walk.
Your appetite will be gone.
Then you will go to your everlasting
home,
and people will go to your funeral.

6 Soon your life will snap like a silver
chain
or break like a golden bowl.
You will be like a broken pitcher at a
spring,
or a broken wheel at a well.
7 You will turn back into the dust of the
earth again,
but your spirit will return to God
who gave it.

8 Everything is useless!
The Teacher says that everything
is useless.

Conclusion: Honour God

9 The Teacher was very wise and taught the people what he knew. He very carefully thought about, studied and set in order many wise teachings. 10 The Teacher looked for just the right words to write what is dependable and true.

11 Words from wise people are like sharp sticks used to guide animals. They are like nails that have been driven in firmly. Altogether they are wise teachings that come from one Shepherd. 12 So be careful, my son, about other teachings. People are always writing books, and too much study will make you tired.

13 Now, everything has been heard,
so I give my final advice:
honour God and obey his
commands,
because this is all people must do.
14 God will judge everything,
even what is done in secret,
the good and the evil.

---

and you will barely hear the
millstone grinding grain.
You will wake up when a bird starts
singing,
but you will barely hear the faint
singing.

Song of Solomon

A SONG OF LOVE

Hi! I'm Solomon, king of the great nation of Israel. You probably already know that I asked God for wisdom and that he not only made me wise but fantastically wealthy as well. You may also know that I built the Temple of the Lord, a splendid building that was the centre of worship for all of Israel. I was a powerful king, but I also had a private life. One day, as I was travelling in the northern part of my kingdom, I met a beautiful young woman who was tending her vineyard. I loved her so much that I made her my bride. This book is a song describing the love we had for each other.

I wrote this book to let people know that marriage is a wonderful gift from God. God wants husbands and wives to share the joys – and the sorrows – of life together. They are to be faithful in their love for each other for the rest of their lives. Maybe one day you will be married and enjoy life with a special person.

JESUS WATCH

The Song of Solomon tells about the love that Solomon had for his bride, which is also a picture of the love that Jesus has for his church. In Ephesians 5, the church is described as the bride of Christ. Jesus is the head of the church and the saviour of all who believe. Jesus loved the church so much that he gave up his life to make it holy and pure, like a bride. The church is to be faithful to Jesus and love only him. Someday all the members of the church will live for ever with Jesus in heaven.

Where did the bride work?

Not sure? Let's connect to **Song of Solomon 1:5-7** to find out.

FAITH links

- Love for a Lifetime, **Song of Solomon 6:8–9**

OTHER STUFF TO LOOK UP:
Apple (tree) of my eye, Song of Solomon 2:3–6
Springtime! Song of Solomon 2:8–13
Moonstruck, Song of Solomon 6:10

1

Solomon's Greatest Song.

The Woman Speaks to the Man She Loves

2 Kiss me with the kisses of your mouth,
   because your love is better than wine.
3 The smell of your perfume is pleasant,
   and your name is pleasant like expensive perfume.
   That's why the young women love you.
4 Take me with you; let's run together.
   The king takes me into his rooms.

Friends Speak to the Man

We will rejoice and be happy with you;
   we praise your love more than wine.
With good reason, the young women love you.

The Woman Speaks

5 I'm dark but lovely,
   women of Jerusalem,
   dark like the tents of Kedar,
   like the curtains of Solomon.
6 Don't look at how dark I am,
   at how dark the sun has made me.
   My brothers were angry with me
   and made me tend the vineyards,
   so I haven't tended my own vineyard!
7 Tell me, you whom I love,
   where do you feed your sheep?
   Where do you let them rest at noon?
   Why should I look for you near your friend's sheep,
   like a woman who wears a veil?[n]

The Man Speaks to the Woman

8 You are the most beautiful of women.
   Surely you know to follow the sheep
   and feed your young goats
   near the shepherds' tents.
9 My darling, you are like a mare among the king's stallions.
10 Your cheeks are beautiful with ornaments,
   and your neck with jewels.
11 We will make for you gold earrings with silver hooks.

The Woman Speaks

12 The smell of my perfume spreads out
   to the king on his couch.
13 My lover is like a bag of myrrh
   that lies all night between my breasts.
14 My lover is like a bunch of flowers
   from the vineyards at En Gedi.

The Man Speaks

15 My darling, you are beautiful!
   Oh, you are beautiful,
   and your eyes are like doves.

The Woman Answers the Man

16 You are so handsome, my lover,
   and so pleasant!
   Our bed is the grass.
17 Cedar trees form our roof;
   our ceiling is made of juniper wood.

The Woman Speaks Again

2

I am a rose in the Plain of Sharon,
   a lily in the valleys.

The Man Speaks Again

2 Among the young women, my darling
   is like a lily among thorns!

The Woman Answers

3 Among the young men, my lover
   is like an apple tree in the woods!
   I enjoy sitting in his shadow;
   his fruit is sweet to my taste.
4 He brought me to the banquet room,
   and his banner over me is love.
5 Strengthen me with raisins,
   and refresh me with apples,
   because I am weak with love.
6 My lover's left hand is under my head,
   and his right arm holds me tight.

1:7 veil This was the way a prostitute usually dressed.

The Woman Speaks to the Friends

7 Women of Jerusalem, promise me
   by the gazelles and the deer
not to awaken
   or excite my feelings of love
      until it is ready.

The Woman Speaks Again

8 I hear my lover's voice.
   Here he comes jumping across the mountains,
      skipping over the hills.
9 My lover is like a gazelle or a young deer.
   Look, he stands behind our wall
      looking through the windows,
      looking through the blinds.
10 My lover spoke and said to me,
   "Get up, my darling;
      let's go away, my beautiful one.
11 Look, the winter is past;
      the rains are over and gone.
12 Blossoms appear through all the land.
   The time has come to sing;
      the cooing of doves is heard in our land.
13 There are young figs on the fig trees,
      and the blossoms on the vines smell sweet.
   Get up, my darling;
      let's go away, my beautiful one."

The Man Speaks

14 My beloved is like a dove hiding in the cracks of the rock,
      in the secret places of the cliff.
   Show me your face,
      and let me hear your voice.
   Your voice is sweet,
      and your face is lovely.
15 Catch the foxes for us—
   the little foxes that ruin the vineyards
      while they are in blossom.

The Woman Speaks

16 My lover is mine, and I am his.
   He feeds among the lilies
17 until the day dawns
   and the shadows disappear.
   Turn, my lover.
   Be like a gazelle or a young deer
      on the mountain valleys.

The Woman Dreams

3 At night on my bed,
   I looked for the one I love;
   I looked for him, but I could not find him.
2 I got up and went around the city,
      in the streets and squares,
      looking for the one I love.
   I looked for him, but I could not find him.
3 The watchmen found me as they patrolled the city,
      so I asked, "Have you seen the one I love?"
4 As soon as I had left them,
   I found the one I love.
   I held him and would not let him go
      until I brought him to my mother's house,
      to the room where I was born.

The Woman Speaks to the Friends

5 Women of Jerusalem, promise me
   by the gazelles and the deer
not to awaken
   or excite my feelings of love
      until it is ready.
6 Who is this coming out of the desert
   like a cloud of smoke?
   Who is this that smells like myrrh, incense
      and other spices?
7 Look, it's Solomon's couch[n]
   with 60 soldiers around it,
      the finest soldiers of Israel.

> Blossoms appear through all the land. The time has come to sing.
> – Song of Solomon 2:12

3:7 *couch* Something like a bed carried by slaves on which the king lay or sat while travelling.

8 These soldiers all carry swords
    and have been trained in war.
  Every man wears a sword at his side
    and is ready for the dangers of the
      night.
9 King Solomon had a couch made for
    himself
  of wood from Lebanon.
10 He made its posts of silver
    and its braces of gold.
  The seat was covered with purple
      cloth
    that the women of Jerusalem wove
      with love.
11 Women of Jerusalem, go out and see
    King Solomon.
  He is wearing the crown his
    mother put on his head
  on his wedding day,
    when his heart was happy!

The Man Speaks to the Woman

4 How beautiful you are, my darling!
    Oh, you are beautiful!
  Your eyes behind your veil are like
      doves.
    Your hair is like a flock of goats
      streaming down Mount Gilead.
2 Your teeth are white like newly
      sheared sheep
    just coming from their bath.
  Each one has a twin,
    and none of them is missing.
3 Your lips are like red silk thread,
    and your mouth is lovely.
  Your cheeks behind your veil
    are like slices of a pomegranate.
4 Your neck is like David's tower,
    built with rows of stones.
  A thousand shields hang on its walls;
    each shield belongs to a strong
      soldier.
5 Your breasts are like two fawns,
    like twins of a gazelle,
    feeding among the lilies.
6 Until the day dawns
    and the shadows disappear,
  I will go to that mountain of myrrh
    and to that hill of incense.
7 My darling, everything about you is
      beautiful,
    and there is nothing at all wrong
      with you.

8 Come with me from Lebanon, my
    bride.
  Come with me from Lebanon,
    from the top of Mount Amana,
    from the tops of Mount Senir and
      Mount Hermon.
  Come from the lions' dens
    and from the leopards' hills.
9 My sister, my bride,
    you have thrilled my heart;
  you have thrilled my heart
    with a glance of your eyes,
    with one sparkle from your
      necklace.
10 Your love is so sweet, my sister, my
      bride.
  Your love is better than wine,
    and your perfume smells better
      than any spice.
11 My bride, your lips drip honey;
    honey and milk are under your
      tongue.
  Your clothes smell like the cedars
    of Lebanon.
12 My sister, my bride, you are like a
      garden locked up,
    like a walled-in spring, a closed
      fountain.
13 Your limbs are like an orchard
    of pomegranates with all the best
      fruit,
  filled with flowers and nard,
14 nard and saffron, calamus and
      cinnamon,
    with trees of incense, myrrh and
      aloes—
  all the best spices.
15 You are like a garden fountain—
    a well of fresh water
  flowing down from the mountains
    of Lebanon.

The Woman Speaks

16 Awake, north wind.
    Come, south wind.
  Blow on my garden,
    and let its sweet smells flow out.
  Let my lover enter the garden
    and eat its best fruits.

The Man Speaks

5 I have entered my garden, my sister,
    my bride.

I have gathered my myrrh with my
    spice.
I have eaten my honeycomb and my
    honey.
I have drunk my wine and my milk.

The Friends Speak

Eat, friends, and drink;
    yes, drink deeply, lovers.

The Woman Dreams

2 I sleep, but my heart is awake.
    I hear my lover knocking.
"Open to me, my sister, my darling,
    my dove, my perfect one.
My head is wet with dew,
    and my hair with the dampness of
        the night."
3 I have taken off my garment
    and don't want to put it on again.
I have washed my feet
    and don't want to get them dirty
        again.
4 My lover put his hand through the
        opening,
    and I felt excited inside.
5 I got up to open the door for my lover.
    Myrrh was dripping from my
        hands
    and flowing from my fingers,
        onto the handles of the lock.
6 I opened the door for my lover,
    but my lover had left and was
        gone.
    When he spoke, he took my breath
        away.
    I looked for him, but I could not find
        him;
    I called for him, but he did not
        answer.
7 The watchmen found me
    as they patrolled the city.
    They hit me and hurt me;
        the guards on the wall took away
            my veil.
8 Promise me, women of Jerusalem,
    if you find my lover,
    tell him I am weak with love.

The Friends Answer the Woman

9 How is your lover better than other
        lovers,
    most beautiful of women?
How is your lover better than other
    lovers?
Why do you want us to promise
    this?

The Woman Answers the Friends

10 My lover is healthy and tanned,
    the best of ten thousand men.
11 His head is like the finest gold;
    his hair is wavy and black like a
        raven.
12 His eyes are like doves
    by springs of water.
    They seem to be bathed in cream
        and are set like jewels.
13 His cheeks are like beds of spices;
    they smell like mounds of
        perfume.
His lips are like lilies
    flowing with myrrh.
14 His hands are like gold hinges,
    filled with jewels.
His body is like shiny ivory
    covered with sapphires.
15 His legs are like large marble posts,
    standing on bases of fine gold.
He is like a cedar of Lebanon,
    like the finest of the trees.
16 His mouth is sweet to kiss,
    and I desire him very much.
Yes, daughters of Jerusalem,
    this is my lover
    and my friend.

The Friends Speak to the Woman

6 Where has your lover gone,
    most beautiful of women?
Which way did your lover turn?
    We will look for him with you.

The Woman Answers the Friends

2 My lover has gone down to his
        garden,
    to the beds of spices,
    to feed in the gardens
        and to gather lilies.
3 I belong to my lover,
    and my lover belongs to me.
He feeds among the lilies.

The Man Speaks to the Woman

4 My darling, you are as beautiful as
        the city of Tirzah,

FAITH links

LOVE FOR A LIFETIME
SONG OF SOLOMON 6:8-9

Who in your family has been married the longest? Part of loving someone involves making a commitment to that person. When two people decide to marry, they agree to be faithful to each other. The vows they say at their wedding are a public sign of their commitment to each other.

God helps a person to make a commitment and stick to it, even through hard times. Maybe you can't imagine being married right now. But you've certainly seen the results of a committed marriage. You can begin learning to make commitments to others by the way you treat your friends and family.

Connect to these Faithlinks for more thoughts on being a part of a family:

Fatherly Advice, Exodus 18, p. 99

Yours, Mine and Ours? 1 Samuel 25, p. 389

A Parent's Advice, Proverbs 1:8–9, p. 825

A Broken Promise, Jeremiah 2:1–8, p. 989

A Friend of Jesus, John 15:9–17, p. 1450

MVFM? Galatians 3:26–27, p. 1589

---

as lovely as the city of Jerusalem,
   like an army flying flags.
5 Turn your eyes from me,
   because they excite me too much.
Your hair is like a flock of goats
   streaming down Mount Gilead.
6 Your teeth are white like sheep
   just coming from their bath;
each one has a twin,
   and none of them is missing.
7 Your cheeks behind your veil
   are like slices of a pomegranate.
8 There may be sixty queens and eighty slave women
and so many girls you cannot count them,
9 but there is only one like my dove,
   my perfect one.
She is her mother's only daughter,
   the brightest of the one who gave her birth.
The young women saw her and called her happy;
   the queens and the slave women also praised her.

The Young Women Praise the Woman

10 Who is that young woman
   that shines out like the dawn?
She is as pretty as the moon,
   as bright as the sun,
   as wonderful as an army flying flags.

The Man Speaks

11 I went down into the orchard of nut trees
   to see the blossoms of the valley,
to look for buds on the vines,
   to see if the pomegranate trees had bloomed.
12 Before I realised it, my desire for you made me feel
   like a prince in a chariot.

The Friends Call to the Woman

13 Come back, come back, woman of Shulam.
Come back, come back,
   so we may look at you!

The Woman Answers the Friends

Why do you want to look at the
  woman of Shulam
  as you would at the dance of two
    armies?

The Man Speaks to the Woman

7 Your feet are beautiful in sandals,
  you daughter of a prince.
  Your round thighs are like jewels
    shaped by an artist.
2 Your navel is like a round drinking
    cup
  always filled with wine.
  Your stomach is like a pile of wheat
    surrounded with lilies.
3 Your breasts are like two fawns,
    like twins of a gazelle.
4 Your neck is like an ivory tower.
  Your eyes are like the pools in
    Heshbon
    near the gate of Bath Rabbim.
  Your nose is like the mountain of
    Lebanon
    that looks down on Damascus.
5 Your head is like Mount Carmel,
  and your hair is like purple cloth;
    the king is captured in its folds.
6 You are beautiful and pleasant;
    my love, you are full of delights.
7 You are tall like a palm tree,
  and your breasts are like its
    bunches of fruit.
8 I said, "I will climb up the palm tree
    and take hold of its fruit."
  Let your breasts be like bunches of
    grapes,
    the smell of your breath like apples,
9   and your mouth like the best wine.

The Woman Speaks to the Man

  Let this wine go down sweetly for my
    lover;
    may it flow gently past the lips and
      teeth.
10 I belong to my lover,
    and he desires only me.
11 Come, my lover,
    let's go out into the country
    and spend the night in the fields.
12 Let's go early to the vineyards
    and see if the buds are on the
      vines.
  Let's see if the blossoms have already
    opened
    and if the pomegranates have
      bloomed.
  There I will give you my love.
13 The mandrake flowers give their
    sweet smell,
  and all the best fruits are at our
    gates.
  I have saved them for you, my
    lover,
    the old delights and the new.

8 I wish you were like my brother
  who fed at my mother's breasts.
  If I found you outside,
    I would kiss you,
    and no one would look down on
      me.
2 I would lead you and bring you
    to my mother's house;
    she is the one who taught me.
  I would give you a drink of spiced
    wine
    from my pomegranates.

The Woman Speaks to the Friends

3 My lover's left hand is under my
    head,
    and his right arm holds me tight.
4 Women of Jerusalem,
    promise not to awaken
    or excite my feelings of love
    until it is ready.

The Friends Speak

5 Who is this coming out of the desert,
    leaning on her lover?

The Man Speaks to the Woman

  I woke you under the apple tree
    where you were born;
    there your mother gave birth to
      you.
6 Put me like a seal on your heart,
    like a seal on your arm.
  Love is as strong as death;
    jealousy is as strong as the grave.
  Love bursts into flames
    and burns like a hot fire.
7 Even much water cannot put out the
    flame of love;
    floods cannot drown love.

If a man offered everything in his
    house for love,
    people would totally reject it.

The Woman's Brothers Speak

8 We have a little sister,
    and her breasts are not yet grown.
    What should we do for our sister
    on the day she becomes engaged?
9 If she is a wall,
    we will put silver
    towers on her.
  If she is a door,
    we will protect her
    with cedar boards.

The Woman Speaks

10 I am a wall,
    and my breasts are
    like towers.
  So I was to him,
    as one who brings happiness.
11 Solomon had a vineyard at Baal
    Hamon.
  He rented the vineyards for others
    to tend,
  and everyone who rented had to pay
    a thousand silver pieces for the
    fruit.
12 But my own vineyard is mine to
    give.
  Solomon, the thousand silver
    pieces are for you,
  and two hundred pieces are for
    those who tend the fruit.

The Man Speaks to the Woman

13 You who live in the
    gardens,
    my friends are
    listening for your
    voice;
    let me hear it.

The Woman Speaks to the Man

14 Hurry, my lover,
    be like a gazelle
    or a young deer
    on the mountains where spices
    grow.

> Put me like a seal on your heart, like a seal on your arm.
> – Song of Solomon 8:6

BURNING COALS ON THE LIPS

Hello! I'm Isaiah, prophet of God. Would you like to see a picture of heaven? God gave me this picture of heaven when he called me to be his messenger. I saw the Lord sitting on a very high throne with heavenly creatures of fire all around him. The creatures had six wings and they called, "Holy, holy, holy." One of the creatures touched my mouth with a hot coal. Why? You'd better surf on over to Isaiah 6 to find out.

I wrote this book to tell people to stop worshipping idols and turn back to God. I urged them to trust in the power of God, not in friendships with other nations. The people of Israel did not follow God's laws, so God allowed the king of Assyria to conquer them. The southern kingdom of Judah would have been conquered, too, but good King Hezekiah wisely asked God for help. Check out Isaiah 37:14–20 for this important prayer.

JESUS WATCH

Even though he lived 700 years before Jesus was born, Isaiah told us many things about Jesus, the promised Messiah. In Isaiah 9, we learn the Messiah will be born into the family of David and that he will rule as king on David's throne. His kingdom will be strong for he will rule with justice and goodness. The Messiah will be a great leader and will have the following names: Wonderful Counsellor, Powerful God, Father Who Lives For Ever, Prince of Peace. Jesus is not only our king; but he is also our saviour. In Isaiah 53 we find a picture of Jesus as the sacrifice for our sins. He was willing to die so that we can have eternal life in heaven. Jesus knew that much of the Book of Isaiah was about him. During his ministry, Jesus quoted passages from Isaiah to announce that he was the long-awaited Messiah.

my FAVOURITE links

OTHER CONNECTIONS

Livin' it

Try it, you'll like it! Sounds pretty harmless, but temptation often starts with something small and then grows into something big. Check out how to handle those trying times by linking to Go Ahead; Try It, Isaiah 33:15–16.

What frightens you? You can find some practical advice on what to do when your fears try to get the better of you by connecting to Scared to Death! Isaiah 43:1–2.

Do you think your sin problem is not so bad? It only takes a little sin to separate us from God. But God has the best sin-cleaner in the world. Discover what it is by logging onto Covered with Mud! Isaiah 59:12–13.

FAITH links

○ The Problem with Pride, **Isaiah 2:11**

○ Dirty Inside, **Isaiah 6:1–7**

○ What's in a Name? **Isaiah 9:6**

○ World News, **Isaiah 13—19**

○ The Foundation of Our Hope, **Isaiah 31:1–8**

○ Fly Like an Eagle, **Isaiah 40:28–31**

○ A Useless Thing, **Isaiah 44:9, 18–20**

○ The One Who Suffered, **Isaiah 53**

○ What God Thinks, **Isaiah 55:8–9**

○ Jesus' Mission and Yours, **Isaiah 61:1–2**

Get the Info

The Egyptians play an important role in Bible history. Check out some cool facts about these amazing ancient people by connecting to Who Are the Egyptians? Isaiah 30:2–5.

Did you know?

Here's one for you. What good are false gods?

Well, they seem pretty useless, don't they, but let's plug into Isaiah 44:9–20 to find out what God had to say about them.

HAVE YOU HEARD ABOUT. . .

Whispering fortune-tellers, Isaiah 8:19–20
God's greatest gift, Isaiah 9:6–7
Party time! Isaiah 25:6–12
A happy desert, Isaiah 35
Get ready! Isaiah 40

Isaiah 1:1

1 This is the vision Isaiah son of Amoz saw about what would happen to Judah and Jerusalem. Isaiah saw these things while Uzziah,[n] Jotham, Ahaz and Hezekiah were kings of Judah.

God's Case Against His Children

2 Heaven and earth, listen,
  because the LORD is speaking:
"I raised my children and helped
    them grow up,
  but they have turned against me.
3 An ox knows its master,
  and a donkey knows where its
    owner feeds it,
  but the people of Israel do not know
    me;
  my people do not understand."

4 How terrible! Israel is a nation of sin,
  a people loaded down with guilt,
  a group of children doing evil,
    children who are full of evil.
They have left the LORD;
  they hate God, the Holy One of
    Israel,
  and have turned away from him as
    if he were a stranger.

5 Why should you continue to be
    punished?
  Why do you continue to turn
    against him?
Your whole head is hurt,
  and your whole heart is sick.
6 There is no healthy spot
  from the bottom of your foot to the
    top of your head;
  you are covered with wounds,
    hurts and open sores
  that are not cleaned and covered,
    and no medicine takes away the pain.

7 Your land is ruined;
  your cities have been burnt with fire.
While you watch,
  your enemies are stealing
    everything from your land;
  it is ruined like a country
    destroyed by enemies.
8 Jerusalem is left alone

1:1 **Uzziah** Also called Azariah.

FAITH links

RED TO WHITE
ISAIAH 1:18

Think about the colour red. If you've ever spilled red paint or tomato sauce on your clothes, you know that the stain it leaves is difficult to wash out. Now picture a blanket of newly fallen snow. We may not get to see snow all that often but, when it comes, you know that it will cover everything. It can turn a brown and green world into a soft, cottony white one. When you do something wrong, your sin is like the tomato sauce stain – very noticeable. God's forgiveness can make it the colour of newly fallen snow. In other words, he can make it disappear. All you have to do is ask for his forgiveness.

Link here for other thoughts on our sin problem:

A Priest Without Sin, Leviticus 4:3–7, p. 136

The Cover-up, Psalm 32:1–2, p. 733

Our Awesome God, Ezekiel 1:26–28, p. 1087

The God of Second Chances, Jonah 3, p. 1215

A High Price, Romans 6:23, p. 1526

The Sin "Braker", Jude 24–25, p. 1727

like an empty shelter in a vineyard,
like a hut left in a field of melons,
like a city surrounded by enemies.
9 The LORD All-powerful
allowed a few of our people to live.
Otherwise we would have been
completely destroyed
like the cities of Sodom and
Gomorrah.

10 Jerusalem, your rulers are like those
of Sodom,
and your people are like those of
Gomorrah.
Hear the word of the LORD;
listen to the teaching of our God!
11 The LORD says,
"I do not want all these sacrifices.
I have had enough of your burnt
sacrifices
of rams and fat from fine animals.
I am not pleased
by the blood of bulls, lambs and
goats.
12 You come to meet with me,
but who asked you to do
all this running in and out of my
Temple's rooms?
13 Don't continue bringing me worthless
sacrifices!
I hate the incense you burn.
I can't stand your New Moons,
Sabbaths and other feast days;
I can't stand the evil you do in your
holy meetings.
14 I hate your New Moon feasts
and your other yearly feasts.
They have become a heavy weight on
me,
and I am tired of carrying it.
15 When you raise your arms to me in
prayer,
I will refuse to look at you.
Even if you say many prayers,
I will not listen to you,
because your hands are full of
blood.
16 Wash yourselves and make
yourselves clean.
Stop doing the evil things I see you
do.
Stop doing wrong.
17 Learn to do good.
Seek justice.
Punish those who hurt others.
Help the orphans.
Stand up for the rights of widows."

18 The LORD says,
"Come, let us talk about these
things.
Though your sins are bright red,
they can be as white as snow.
Though your sins are deep red,
they can be white like wool.
19 If you become willing and obey me,
you will eat good crops from the
land.
20 But if you refuse to obey and if you
turn against me,
you will be destroyed by your
enemies' swords."
The LORD himself said these things.

Jerusalem is Not Loyal to God
21 The city of Jerusalem once followed
the LORD,
but she is no longer loyal to him.
She used to be filled with fairness;
people there lived the way God
wanted.
But now, murderers live there.
22 Jerusalem, you have become like the
scum left when silver is purified;
you are like wine mixed with water.
23 Your rulers are rebels
and friends of thieves.
They all accept money for doing
wrong,
and they are paid to cheat people.
They don't seek justice for the
orphans
or listen to the widows' needs.
24 So the Lord GOD All-powerful,
the Mighty One of Israel, says:
"You, my enemies, will not cause me
any more trouble.
I will pay you back for what you
did.
25 I will turn against you
and clean away all your wrongs as
if with soap;
I will take all the worthless things
out of you.
26 I will bring back judges as you had
long ago;

your counsellors will be like those
you had in the beginning.
Then you will be called the City That
Is Right with God,
the Loyal City."

27 By doing what is fair,
Jerusalem will be free again.
By doing what is right,
her people who come back to the
Lord will have freedom.
28 But sinners and those who turn
against him will be destroyed;
those who have left the Lord will
die.
29 "You will be ashamed,
because you have worshipped gods
under the oak trees.
You will be disgraced,
because you have worshipped idols
in your gardens.
30 You will be like an oak whose leaves
are dying
or like a garden without water.
31 Powerful people will be like small,
dry pieces of wood,
and their works will be like sparks.
They will burn together,
and no one will be able to put out
that fire."

The Message About Jerusalem

2 Isaiah son of Amoz saw this message
about Judah and Jerusalem:
2   In the last days
the mountain on which the Lord's
Temple stands
will become the most important of
all mountains.
It will be raised above the hills,
and people from all nations will
come streaming to it.
3 Many nations will come and say,
"Come, let us go up to the
mountain of the Lord,
to the Temple of the God of Jacob.
Then God will teach us his ways,
and we will obey his teachings."
His teachings will go out from
Jerusalem;
the message of the Lord will go
out from Jerusalem.
4 He will settle arguments among the
nations
and will make decisions for many
nations.
Then they will make their swords
into ploughs

FAITH links

THE PROBLEM WITH PRIDE

ISAIAH 2:11

A look can mean a lot. When someone rolls their eyes, that can mean, "Get real." You may have even flashed one of your parents a look that inspired them to say, "Don't give me that look." There's a certain look that the prophet Isaiah wrote about: a proud look. A proud look isn't always a kind of nose-in-the-air look. A person could have no expression at all and still be proud. Pride starts in the heart. It's when you feel that no one is better than you. The opposite of pride is humility. God plans to humble those who are proud.

The Weak Link, Judges 16, p. 334

Mourning for an Enemy, 2 Samuel 1, p. 399

Help for the Outsiders, Nehemiah 5:9–10, p. 630

Fear God or People? Jeremiah 38:14–21, p. 1047

The "Eyes" Have It? 1 Corinthians 12, p. 1559

The Sacrifice of Service, Philippians 2:17, 25–30, p. 1612

and their spears into hooks for
      trimming trees.
Nations will no longer fight other
      nations,
   nor will they train for war any
      more.
5 Come, family of Jacob,
   and let us follow the way of the
      LORD.

A Terrible Day is Coming

6 LORD, you have left your people,
      the family of Jacob,
   because they have become filled with
      wrong ideas from people in the
      East.
   They try to tell the future like the
      Philistines,
   and they have completely accepted
      those foreign ideas.
7 Their land has been filled with silver
      and gold;
   there are a great many treasures
      there.
   Their land has been filled with
      horses;
   there are many chariots there.
8 Their land is full of idols.
   The people worship these idols
      they made with their own hands
      and shaped with their own fingers.
9 People will not be proud any longer
      but will bow low with shame.
   God, do not forgive them.

10 Go into the caves of the cliffs;
      dig holes and hide in the ground
   from the anger of the LORD
      and from his great power!
11 Proud people will be made humble,
      and they will bow low with shame.
   At that time only the LORD will still be
      praised.
12 The LORD All-powerful has a certain
      day planned
   when he will punish the proud and
      those who boast,
   and they will no longer be
      important.
13 He will bring down the tall cedar
      trees from Lebanon

   and the great oak trees of Bashan,
14 all the tall mountains
      and the high hills,
15 every tall tower
      and every high, strong wall,
16 all the trading ships
      and the beautiful ships.
17 At that time proud people will be
      made humble,
   and they will bow low with shame.
   At that time only the LORD will be
      praised,
18   but all the idols will be gone.

19 People will run to caves in the rocky
      cliffs
   and will dig holes and hide in the
      ground
   from the anger of the LORD
      and his great power,
   when he stands to shake the earth.
20 At that time people will throw away
      their gold and silver idols,
   which they made for themselves to
      worship;
   they will throw them away to the
      bats and moles.
21 Then the people will hide in caves
      and cracks in the rocks
   from the anger of the LORD
      and his great power,
   when he stands to shake the earth.
22 You should stop trusting in people to
      save you,
   because people are only human;
      they aren't able to help you.

God Will Punish Judah and Jerusalem

3 Understand this:
   the Lord GOD All-powerful
   will take away everything Judah and
      Jerusalem need—
      all the food and water,
2 the heroes and great soldiers,
      the judges and prophets,
   people who do magic and older
      leaders,
3 the military leaders and government
      leaders,
   the counsellors, the skilled

craftsmen and those who try to tell the future.

4 The LORD says, "I will cause young boys to be your leaders,
and foolish children will rule over you.
5 People will be against each other; everyone will be against his neighbour.
Young people will not respect older people,
and common people will not respect important people."
6 At that time a man will seize one of his brothers
from his own family and say,
"You have a coat, so you will be our leader.
These ruins will be under your control."
7 But that brother will stand up and say,
"I cannot help you,
because I do not have food or clothes in my house.
You will not make me your leader."
8 This will happen because Jerusalem has stumbled,
and Judah has fallen.
The things they say and do are against the LORD; they turn against him.
9 The look on their faces shows they are guilty;
like the people of Sodom, they are proud of their sin.
They don't care who sees it.
How terrible it will be for them, because they have brought much trouble on themselves.

10 Tell those who do what is right that things will go well for them,
because they will receive a reward for what they do.
11 But how terrible it will be for the wicked!
They will be punished for all the wrong they have done.
12 Children treat my people cruelly, and women rule over them.
My people, your guides lead you in the wrong way
and turn you away from what is right.
13 The LORD takes his place in court and stands to judge the people.
14 The LORD presents his case
against the older leaders and other leaders of his people:
"You have burned the vineyard.
Your houses are full of what you took from the poor.
15 What gives you the right to crush my people
and grind the faces of the poor into the ground?"
The Lord GOD All-powerful says this.

A Warning to Women of Jerusalem

16 The LORD says,
"The women of Jerusalem are proud.
They walk around with their heads held high,
and they flirt with their eyes.
They take quick, short steps,
making noise with their ankle bracelets."
17 So the Lord will put sores on the heads of those women in Jerusalem,
and he will make them lose their hair.

18 At that time the Lord will take away everything that makes them proud: their beautiful ankle bracelets, their headbands, their necklaces shaped like the moon, 19 their ear-rings, bracelets and veils, 20 their scarves, ankle chains, the cloth

Tell those who do what is right that things will go well for them.
– Isaiah 3:10

belts worn around their waists, their bottles of perfume and charms, 21 their signet rings, nose rings, 22 their fine robes, capes, shawls and purses, 23 their mirrors, linen dresses, turbans and long shawls.
24 Instead of wearing sweet-smelling
  perfume, they will stink.
 Instead of fine cloth belts, they will
  wear the ropes of captives.
 Instead of having their hair fixed in
  fancy ways, they will be bald.
 Instead of fine clothes, they will
  wear clothes of sadness.
 Instead of being beautiful, they will
  wear the brand of a captive.

25 At that time your men will be killed
  with swords,
 and your heroes will die in war.
26 There will be crying and sadness
  near the city gates.
 Jerusalem will be like a woman
  who has lost everything and sits
  on the ground.

4 At that time seven women will seize one man
 and say, "We will eat our own bread
  and make our own clothes,
 but please marry us!
  Please, take away our shame."

THE B-I-B-L-E

Do you have some favourite verses from God's Word? Let's welcome Harry, aged 11, to Connect 2-You. Harry has something different to say about the Bible.

Harry

Well, I'm sort of embarrassed to admit it, but I really don't understand the Bible. It's OK when someone tells a story from it, but when I read it on my own, nothing really makes sense. I don't think the Bible is written for kids.

Some Bibles are – like this one you're holding in your hands. That's why it's important to find a version of the Bible that you can understand. It's also important to pray before you read the Bible and ask God to help you understand what you're reading. For some other tips on understanding the Bible, check out the Livin' It page on studying God's Word, Psalm 119:12–18, p. 801.

Nothing brings us closer to God than reading and understanding his Word. If you try to read a version of the Bible that you can't understand, you don't know what you're missing.

The Branch of the LORD

2 At that time the LORD's branch will be very beautiful and great. The people still living in Israel will be proud of what the land grows. 3 Those who are still living in Jerusalem will be called holy; their names are recorded among the living in Jerusalem. 4 The Lord will wash away the filth from the women of Jerusalem. He will wash the bloodstains out of Jerusalem and clean the city with the spirit of fairness and the spirit of fire. 5 Then the LORD will cover Mount Zion and the people who meet there with a cloud of smoke during the day and with a bright, flaming fire at night. There will be a covering over every person. 6 This covering will protect the people from the heat of the sun and will provide a safe place to hide from the storm and rain.

Israel, the LORD's Vineyard

5 Now I will sing for my friend a song about his vineyard.
  My friend had a vineyard
    on a hill with very rich soil.
2 He dug and cleared the field of stones
    and planted the best grapevines there.
  He built a tower in the middle of it
    and cut out a winepress as well.
  He hoped good grapes would grow there,
    but only bad ones grew.

3 My friend says, "You people living in Jerusalem,
    and you people of Judah,
  judge between me and my vineyard.
4 What more could I have done for my vineyard
    than I have already done?
  Although I expected good grapes to grow,
    why were there only bad ones?
5 Now I will tell you
    what I will do to my vineyard:
  I will remove the hedge,
    and it will be burnt.
  I will break down the stone wall,
    and it will be walked on.
6 I will ruin my field.
  It will not be trimmed or hoed,
    and weeds and thorns will grow there.
  I will command the clouds
    not to rain on it."

7 The vineyard belonging to the LORD All-powerful
    is the nation of Israel;
  the garden that he loves
    is the people of Judah.
  He looked for justice, but there was only killing.
  He hoped for right living, but there were only cries of pain.

8 How terrible it will be for you who
    add more houses to your houses
    and more fields to your fields
  until there is no room left for other people.
  Then you are left alone in the land.

9 The LORD All-powerful said this to me:
  "The fine houses will be destroyed;
    the large and beautiful houses will be left empty.
10 At that time a 25-hectare vineyard will
    make only 20 litres of wine,
    and 200 litres of seed will grow
    only 20 litres of grain."

11 How terrible it will be for people who
    rise early in the morning
    to look for strong drink,
  who stay awake late at night,
    becoming drunk with wine.
12 At their parties they have lyres, harps,
    tambourines, flutes and wine.
  They don't see what the LORD has done
    or notice the work of his hands.
13 So my people will be captured and taken away,
    because they don't really know me.

5:8 Greed
What's wrong with greed?

All the great people will die of hunger,
and the common people will die of
thirst.
14 So the place of the dead wants more
and more people,
and it opens wide its mouth.
Jerusalem's important people and
common people will go down
into it,
with their happy and noisy ones.
15 So the common people and the great
people will be brought down;
those who are proud will be
humbled.
16 The LORD All-powerful will receive
glory by judging fairly;
the holy God will show himself
holy by doing what is right.
17 Then the sheep will go anywhere
they want,
and lambs will feed on the land that
rich people once owned.

18 How terrible it will be for those
people!
They pull their guilt and sins
behind them
as people pull wagons with ropes.
19 They say, "Let God hurry;
let him do his work soon
so we may see it.
Let the plan of the Holy One of Israel
happen soon
so that we will know what it is."

20 How terrible it will be for people who
call good things bad
and bad things good,
who think darkness is light
and light is darkness,
who think sour is sweet
and sweet is sour.

21 How terrible it will be for people who
think they are wise
and believe they are clever.

22 How terrible it will be for people who
are famous for drinking wine
and are champions at mixing
drinks.
23 They take money to set the guilty
free
and don't allow good people to be
judged fairly.
24 They will be destroyed
just as fire burns straw or dry grass.
They will be destroyed
like a plant whose roots rot
and whose flower dies and blows
away like dust.
They have refused to obey the
teachings of the LORD All-
powerful
and have hated the message from
the Holy God of Israel.
25 So the LORD has become very angry
with his people,
and he has raised his hand to
punish them.
Even the mountains are frightened.
Dead bodies lie in the streets like
rubbish.
But the LORD is still angry;
his hand is still raised to strike
down the people.

26 He raises a banner for the nations far
away.
He whistles to call those people
from the ends of the earth.
Look! The enemy comes quickly!
27 Not one of them becomes tired or
falls down.
Not one of them gets sleepy and
falls asleep.
Their weapons are close at hand,
and their sandal straps are not
broken.
28 Their arrows are sharp,
and all of their bows are ready to
shoot.
The horses' hoofs are as hard as
rocks,
and their chariot wheels move like
a whirlwind.
29 Their shout is like the roar of a lion;
it is loud like a young lion.
They growl as they capture their
captives.
There is no one to stop them from
taking their captives away.
30 On that day they will roar
like the waves of the sea.
And when people look at the land,

they will see only darkness and
    pain;
all light will become dark in this
    thick cloud.

Isaiah Becomes a Prophet

6 In the year that King Uzziah died, I saw the Lord sitting on a very high throne. His long robe filled the Temple. 2 Heavenly creatures of fire stood above him. Each creature had six wings: it used two wings to cover its face, two wings to cover its feet and two wings for flying. 3 Each creature was calling to the others:

6:2 Angels Check out what some angels look like.

"Holy, holy, holy is the LORD All-
    powerful.
His glory fills the whole earth."

4 Their calling caused the frame around the door to shake, as the Temple filled with smoke.

5 I said, "Oh, no! I will be destroyed. I am not pure, and I live among people who are not pure, but I have seen the King, the LORD All-powerful."

6 One of the heavenly creatures used a pair of tongs to take a hot coal from the altar. Then he flew to me with the hot coal in his hand. 7 The creature touched my mouth with the hot coal and said, "Look, your guilt is taken away, because this hot coal has touched your lips. Your sin is taken away."

8 Then I heard the Lord's voice, saying, "Whom can I send? Who will go for us?"

So I said, "Here I am. Send me!"

9 Then the Lord said, "Go and tell this to the people:

'You will listen and listen, but you will
    not understand.
You will look and look, but you will
    not learn.'

10 Make the minds of these people dumb.
Shut their ears. Cover their eyes.
Otherwise, they might really
    understand
what they see with their eyes
    and hear with their ears.
They might really understand in their
    minds

FAITH links

DIRTY INSIDE
ISAIAH 6:1-7

If Jesus were to suddenly walk into your room right now, what would you think? How would you act? The prophet Isaiah saw a vision of God in the Temple. Angels surrounded God's throne. In such a holy place, Isaiah couldn't help but realise his own sin. Instead of trying to sweep it under the carpet, he cried out his need to be made clean.

When you sin, it's as if you went outside and rolled around in the mud. Instead of being dirty on the outside, sin makes you dirty inside. Only God can remove the dirt and make you clean once more.

Need a sin "cleaning"? Check out these Faithlinks:

Facing the Consequences, Deuteronomy 3:21–29, p. 232

Real Repentance, Jeremiah 4:1–4, p. 993

The Watchman, Ezekiel 3:16–22, p. 1088

A Model of Forgiveness, Ezekiel 16:59–63, p. 1103

Clean Inside and Out, Luke 11:39–40, p. 1392

The Gift, John 3:16–18, p. 1427

and come back to me and be
    healed."

11 Then I asked, "Lord, how long
    should I do this?"

He answered,
"Until the cities are destroyed
  and the people are gone,
until there are no people left in the
  houses,
until the land is destroyed and left
  empty.
12 The LORD will send the people far
  away,
  and the land will be left empty.
13 One-tenth of the people will be left in
  the land,
  but it will be destroyed again.
These people will be like an oak
  tree
  whose stump is left when the tree
  is chopped down.
The people who remain will be
  like a stump that will sprout
  again."

Trouble with Aram

7 Now Ahaz was the son of Jotham, who was the son of Uzziah.*ⁿ* When Ahaz was king of Judah, Rezin king of Aram and Pekah son of Remaliah, the king of Israel, went up to Jerusalem to fight against it. But they were not able to defeat the city.

2 Ahaz king of Judah received a message saying, "The armies of Aram and Israel*ⁿ* have joined together."

When Ahaz heard this, he and the people were frightened. They shook with fear like trees of the forest blown by the wind.

3 Then the LORD told Isaiah, "You and your son Shear-Jashub*ⁿ* should go and meet Ahaz at the place where the water flows into the upper pool, on the road where people do their laundry. 4 Tell Ahaz, 'Be careful. Be calm and don't worry. Don't let those two men, Rezin and Pekah son of Remaliah, scare you. Don't be afraid of their anger or Aram's anger, because they are like two barely burning sticks that are ready to go out. 5 They have made plans against you, saying, 6 "Let's fight against Judah and tear it apart. We will divide the land for ourselves and make the son of Tabeel the new king of Judah." 7 But I, the Lord GOD, say,
  "'Their plan will not succeed;
    it will not happen,
  8 because Aram is led by the city of
    Damascus,
    and Damascus is led by its weak
      king, Rezin.
  Within 65 years Israel will no longer
    be a nation.
  9 Israel is led by the city of Samaria,
    and Samaria is led by its weak
      king, the son of Remaliah.
  If your faith is not strong,
    you will not have strength enough
    to last.'"

Immanuel—God is With Us

10 Then the LORD spoke to Ahaz again, saying, 11 "Ask for a sign from the LORD your God to prove to yourself that these things are true. It may be a sign from as deep as the place of the dead or as high as the heavens."

12 But Ahaz said, "I will not ask for a sign or test the LORD."

13 Then Isaiah said, "Ahaz, descendant of David, listen carefully! Isn't it bad enough that you wear out the patience of people? Do you also have to wear out the patience of my God? 14 The Lord himself will give you a sign: the virgin*ⁿ* will be pregnant. She will have a son, and she will name him Immanuel.*ⁿ* 15 He will be eating milk curds and honey when he learns to reject what is evil and to choose what is good. 16 You are afraid of the kings of Israel and Aram now. But before the child

> The Lord himself will give you a sign: the virgin will be pregnant. She will have a son, and she will name him Immanuel.
> – Isaiah 7:14

7:1 Uzziah Also called Azariah.
7:2 Israel Literally, "Ephraim". Isaiah often uses "Ephraim" to mean all of Israel.
7:3 Shear-Jashub This name means "a part of the people will come back".
7:14 virgin The Hebrew word means "a young woman". Often this meant a girl who was not married and had not yet had sexual relations with anyone.
7:14 Immanuel This name means "God is with us".

learns to choose good and reject evil, the lands of Israel and Aram will be empty. 17 The LORD will bring troubled times to you, your people and to the people of your father's family. They will be worse than anything that has happened since Israel separated from Judah. The LORD will bring the king of Assyria to fight against you.

18 "At that time the LORD will whistle for the Egyptians, and they will come like flies from Egypt's faraway streams. He will call for the Assyrians, and they will come like bees. 19 These enemies will camp in the deep ravines and in the cliffs, by the thorn-bushes and watering holes. 20 The Lord will hire Assyria and use it like a razor to punish Judah. It will be as if the Lord is shaving the hair from Judah's head and legs and removing Judah's beard.

21 "At that time a person will be able to keep only one young cow and two sheep alive. 22 There will be only enough milk for that person to eat milk curds. All who remain in the land will go back to eating just milk curds and honey. 23 In this land there are now vineyards that have 1,000 grapevines, which are worth about 1,000 pieces of silver. But these fields will become full of weeds and thorns. 24 The land will become wild and useful only as a hunting ground. 25 People once worked and grew food on these hills, but at that time people will not go there, because the land will be filled with weeds and thorns. Only sheep and cattle will go to those places."

Assyria will Come Soon

8 The LORD told me, "Take a large scroll and write on it with an ordinary pen: 'Maher-Shalal-Hash-Baz'. 2 I will gather some men to be reliable witnesses: Uriah the priest and Zechariah son of Jeberekiah."

3 Then I went to the prophetess, and she became pregnant and had a son. The LORD told me, "Name the boy Maher-Shalal-Hash-Baz,[n] 4 because the king of Assyria will take away all the wealth and possessions of Damascus and Samaria before the boy learns to say 'my father' or 'my mother'."

5 Again the LORD spoke to me, saying,
6 "These people refuse to accept
    the slow-moving waters of the pool
        of Shiloah
    and are terrified of Rezin
        and Pekah son of Remaliah.
7 So I, the Lord, will bring
    the king of Assyria and all his
        power against them,
    like a powerful flood of water from
        the Euphrates River.
The Assyrians will be like water
    rising over the banks of the
        river,
    flowing over the land.
8 That water will flow into Judah and
        pass through it,
    rising to Judah's throat.
Immanuel, this army will spread its
        wings like a bird
    until it covers your whole country."

9 Be broken, all you nations,
    and be smashed to pieces.
Listen, all you faraway countries.
    Prepare for battle and be smashed
        to pieces!
    Prepare for battle and be smashed
        to pieces!
10 Make your plans for the fight,
    but they will be defeated.
Give orders to your armies,
    but they will be useless,
because God is with us.

Warnings to Isaiah

11 The LORD spoke to me with his great power and warned me not to follow the lead of the rest of the people. He said, 12 "People are saying that others make
        plans against them,
    but you should not believe them.
Don't be afraid of what they fear;
    do not dread those things.
13 But remember that the LORD All-
        powerful is holy.
He is the one you should fear;
    he is the one you should dread.
14 Then he will be a place of safety for
        you.

8:3 **Maher-Shalal-Hash-Baz** This name means "there will soon be looting and stealing".

But for the two families of Israel,
he will be like a stone that causes
people to stumble,
like a rock that makes them fall.
He will be like a trap for the people of
Jerusalem,
and he will catch them in his trap.
15 Many people will fall over this rock.
They will fall and be broken;
they will be trapped and caught."

16 Make an agreement.
Seal up the teaching while my
followers are watching.
17 I will wait for the LORD to help us,
the LORD who is ashamed of the
family of Israel.
I will wait for him.

18 I am here, and with me are the children the LORD has given me. We are signs and proofs for the people of Israel from the LORD All-powerful, who lives on Mount Zion.

19 Some people say, "Ask the mediums and fortune-tellers, who whisper and mutter, what to do." But I tell you that people should ask their God for help. Why should people who are still alive ask something from the dead? 20 You should follow the teachings and the agreement with the LORD. The mediums and fortune-tellers do not speak the word of the LORD, so their words are worth nothing.

21 People will wander through the land troubled and hungry. When they become hungry, they will become angry and will look up and curse their king and their God. 22 They will look around them at their land and see only trouble, darkness and awful gloom. And they will be forced into the darkness.

A New Day is Coming

9 But suddenly there will be no more gloom for the land that suffered. In the past God made the lands of Zebulun and Naphtali hang their heads in shame, but in the future those lands will be made great. They will stretch from the road along the Mediterranean Sea to the land beyond the Jordan River and north to Galilee, the land of people who are not Israelites.

2 Before those people lived in darkness,
but now they have seen a great
light.
They lived in a dark land,
but a light has shone on them.
3 God, you have caused the nation to
grow
and made the people happy.
And they have shown their happiness
to you,
like the joy during harvest time,
like the joy of people
taking what they have won in war.
4 Like the time you defeated Midian,
you have taken away their heavy
load
and the heavy pole from their backs
and the rod the enemy used to
punish them.
5 Every boot that marched in battle
and every uniform stained with
blood
has been thrown into the fire.
6 A child has been born to us;
God has given a son to us.
He will be responsible for leading
the people.
His name will be Wonderful
Counsellor, Powerful God,
Father Who Lives For Ever, Prince
of Peace.
7 Power and peace will be in his
kingdom
and will continue to grow for ever.
He will rule as king on David's throne
and over David's kingdom.
He will make it strong
by ruling with justice and
goodness
from now on and for ever.
The LORD All-powerful will do this
because of his strong love for his
people.

God Will Punish Israel

8 The Lord sent a message against the
people of Jacob;
it says that God will judge Israel.
9 Then everyone in Israel, even the
leaders in Samaria,

FAITH links

WHAT'S IN A NAME?
ISAIAH 9:6

How many names do you have? If you have a middle name, you have three names – a first, a middle and a last name. A nickname adds a fourth to your list. Speaking of names, have you ever heard Handel's *Messiah*, or at least part of it? It describes the names of the Messiah, which are included in this verse. In Isaiah's time, the people looked forward to the coming of the Messiah. Who was that Messiah? Jesus. These names are a way to describe his character. After reading these names, wouldn't you like to add another one to the list? How about *My Saviour*?

Surf on to these Faithlinks about the importance of names:

The Name of the Lord, Exodus 33:19–23; 34:5–8, p. 120

A Hopeful Name, Hosea 1:3–11, p. 1172

Uprooted by Change, Amos 9:15, p. 1205

Name with a Purpose, Matthew 1:21, p. 1274

A Family Meal, Mark 14:23–26, p. 1356

Our Gift to God, Romans 12:1–2, p. 1536

---

will know that God has sent it.
Those people are proud and boast by saying,
10 "These bricks have fallen,
but we will build again with cut stones.
These small trees have been chopped down,
but we will put great cedars there."
11 But the LORD has brought the enemies of Rezin against them;
he has stirred up their enemies against them.
12 The Arameans came from the east and the Philistines from the west,
and they ate up Israel with their armies.

But the LORD was still angry;
his hand was still raised to punish the people.

13 But the people did not return to the one who had struck them;
they did not follow the LORD All-powerful.
14 So the LORD cut off Israel's head and tail,
taking away both the branch and stalk in one day.
15 The older leaders and important men were the head,
and the prophets who speak lies were the tail.
16 Those who led the people led them in the wrong direction,
and those who followed them were destroyed.
17 So the Lord is not happy with the young people,
nor will he show mercy to the orphans and widows.
All the people are separated from God and are very evil;
they all speak lies.

But the LORD is still angry;
his hand is still raised to strike down the people.

18 Evil is like a small fire.
First, it burns weeds and thorns.

Next, it burns the larger bushes in
 the forest,
 and they all go up in a column of
  smoke.
19 The LORD All-powerful is angry,
 so the land will be burnt.
The people are like fuel for the fire;
 no one will try to save his brother
  or sister.
20 People will grab something on the
  right,
 but they will still be hungry.
They will eat something on the left,
 but they will not be filled.
Then they will each turn and eat their
 own children.
21 The people of Manasseh will fight
  against the people of Ephraim,
 and Ephraim will fight against
  Manasseh.
Then both of them will turn against
 Judah.

But the LORD is still angry;
 his hand is still raised to strike
  down the people.

10 How terrible it will be for those
 who make unfair laws,
 and those who write laws that
  make life hard for people.
2 They are not fair to the poor,
 and they rob my people of their
  rights.
They allow people to steal from
 widows
 and to take from orphans what
  really belongs to them.
3 How will you explain the things you
  have done?
 What will you do when your
  destruction comes from far
   away?
Where will you run for help?
 Where will you hide your riches
  then?
4 You will have to bow down among the
  captives
 or fall down among the dead
  bodies.
But the LORD is still angry;
 his hand is still raised to strike
  down the people.

God Will Punish Assyria

5 God says, "How terrible it will be for
  the king of Assyria.
 I use him like a rod to show my
  anger;
 in anger I use Assyria like a club.
6 I send it to fight against a nation that
  is separated from God.
 I am angry with those people,
 so I command Assyria to fight
  against them,
 to take their wealth from them,
 to trample them down like mud in
  the streets.
7 But Assyria's king doesn't understand
  that I am using him;
 he doesn't know he is a tool for me.
 He only wants to destroy other
  people
 and to defeat many nations.
8 The king of Assyria says to himself,
 'All of my commanders are like
  kings.
9 The city Calno is like the city
  Carchemish.
 The city Hamath is like the city
  Arpad.
 The city Samaria is like the city
  Damascus.
10 I defeated those kingdoms that
  worship idols,
 and those idols were more than the
  idols of Jerusalem and Samaria.
11 As I defeated Samaria and her idols,
 I will also defeat Jerusalem and her
  idols.'"

12 When the Lord finishes doing what he planned to Mount Zion and Jerusalem, he will punish Assyria. The king of Assyria is very proud, and his pride has made him do these evil things, so God will punish him. 13 The king of Assyria says this:

"By my own power I have done these
  things;
 by my wisdom I have defeated
  many nations.
I have taken their wealth,
 and, like a mighty one, I have
  taken their people.
14 I have taken the riches of all these
  people,

like a person reaching into a bird's
    nest.
I have taken these nations,
    like a person taking eggs.
Not one raised a hand
    or opened its mouth to stop me."

15 An axe is not better than the person
        who swings it.
    A saw is not
        better than
        the one
        who uses it.
    A stick cannot
        control the
        person who
        picks it up.
    A club cannot pick up the person!
16 So the Lord GOD All-powerful
        will send a terrible disease upon
        Assyria's soldiers.
    The strength of Assyria will be
        burned up
    like a fire burning until everything
        is gone.
17 God, the Light of Israel, will be like a
        fire;
    the Holy One will be like a flame.
    He will be like a fire
        that suddenly burns the weeds and
        thorns.
18 The fire burns away the great trees
        and rich farmlands,
    destroying everything.
    It will be like a sick person who
        wastes away.
19 The trees left standing will be so
        few
        that even a child could count
        them.

20 At that time some people will be left
        alive in Israel
        from the family of Jacob.
    They will not continue to depend
        on the person who defeated them.
    They will learn truly to depend on
        the LORD,
        the Holy One of Israel.
21 Those who are left alive in Jacob's
        family
        will again follow the powerful God.
22 Israel, your people are many,

like the grains of sand by the sea.
    But only a few of them will be left
        alive to return to the LORD.
God has announced that he will
        destroy the land
        completely and fairly.
23 The Lord GOD All-powerful will
        certainly destroy this land
        as he has announced.
24 This is what the Lord GOD All-
        powerful says:
    "My people living in Jerusalem,
        don't be afraid of the Assyrians,
    who beat you with a rod
        and raise a stick against you, as
        Egypt did.
25 After a short time my anger against
        you will stop,
    and then I will turn my anger to
        destroying them."

26 Then the LORD All-powerful will beat
        the Assyrians with a whip
    as he defeated Midian at the rock
        of Oreb.
    He will raise his stick over the
        waters
    as he did in Egypt.
27 Then the troubles that Assyria puts
        on you
        will be removed,
    and the load they make you carry
        will be taken away.

Assyria Invades Israel

28 The army of Assyria will enter near
        Aiath.
    Its soldiers will walk through
        Migron.
    They will store their food in
        Michmash.
29 The army will go over the pass.
    The soldiers will sleep at Geba.
    The people of Ramah will be afraid,
    and the people of Saul at Gibeah
        will run away.
30 Cry out, Bath Gallim!
    Laishah, listen!
    Poor Anathoth!
31 The people of Madmenah are
        running away;
    the people of Gebim are hiding.
32 This day the army will stop at Nob.

> **10:15–16
> Pride**
> Why should you not
> boast?

They will shake their fist at Mount
Zion,
at the hill of Jerusalem.

33 Watch! The Lord GOD All-powerful
with his great power will chop
them down like a great tree.
Those who are great will be cut
down;
those who are important will fall to
the ground.
34 He will cut them down
as a forest is cut down with an axe.
And the great trees of Lebanon
will fall by the power of the Mighty
One.

The King of Peace is Coming

11 A new branch will grow
from a stump of a tree;
so a new king will come
from the family of Jesse.[n]
2 The Spirit of the LORD will rest upon
that king.
The Spirit will give
him wisdom and
understanding,
guidance and
power.
The Spirit will
teach him to
know and
respect the
LORD.
3 This king will be glad
to obey the LORD.
He will not judge by the way things
look
or decide by what he hears.
4 But he will judge the poor
honestly;
he will be fair in his decisions for
the poor people of the land.
At his command evil people will be
punished,
and by his words the wicked will
be put to death.
5 Goodness and fairness will give him
strength,
like a belt around his waist.

6 Then wolves will live in peace with
lambs,
and leopards will lie down to rest
with goats.
Calves, lions and young bulls will eat
together,
and a little child will lead them.
7 Cows and bears will eat together in
peace.
Their young will lie down to rest
together.
Lions will eat hay as oxen do.
8 A baby will be able to play near a
cobra's hole,
and a child will be able to put his
hand into the nest of a poisonous
snake.
9 They will not hurt or destroy each other
on all my holy mountain,
because the earth will be full of the
knowledge of the LORD,
as the sea is full of water.

10 At that time the new king from
the family of Jesse[n] will stand as a banner
for all peoples. The nations
will come together around
him, and the place where
he lives will be filled with
glory. 11 At that time the
Lord will again reach out
and take his people who
are left alive in Assyria,
North Egypt, South Egypt,
Cush, Elam, Babylonia,
Hamath and all the islands
of the sea.

12 God will raise a banner as a sign for
all nations,
and he will gather the people of
Israel who were forced from
their country.
He will gather the scattered people of
Judah
from all parts of the earth.
13 At that time Israel will not be jealous
any more,
and Judah will have no more
enemies.
Israel will not be jealous of Judah,
and Judah will not hate Israel.

> The Spirit will give
> him wisdom and
> understanding,
> guidance and power.
> – Isaiah 11:2

11:1,10 Jesse King David's father.

14 But Israel and Judah will attack the Philistines on the west.
Together they will take the riches from the people of the east.
They will conquer Edom and Moab, and the people of Ammon will be under their control.
15 The LORD will dry up the Red Sea of Egypt.
He will wave his arm over the Euphrates River
and dry it up with a scorching wind.
He will divide it into seven small rivers
so that people can walk across them with their sandals on.
16 So God's people who are left alive will have a way to leave Assyria,
just like the time the Israelites came out of Egypt.

A Song of Praise to God

12 At that time you will say:
"I praise you, LORD!
You were angry with me,
but you are not angry with me now!
You have comforted me.
2 God is the one who saves me;
I will trust him and not be afraid.
The LORD, the LORD gives me strength and makes me sing.
He has saved me."
3 You will receive your salvation with joy
as you would draw water from a well.
4 At that time you will say,
"Praise the LORD and worship him.
Tell everyone what he has done and how great he is.
5 Sing praise to the LORD, because he has done great things.
Let all the world know what he has done.
6 Shout and sing for joy, you people of Jerusalem,
because the Holy One of Israel does great things before your eyes."

12:2 Courage Where can you get courage?

God's Message to Babylon

13 God showed Isaiah son of Amoz this message about Babylon:
2 Raise a flag on the bare mountain.
Call out to the men.
Raise your hand to signal them to enter through the gates for important people.
3 I myself have commanded those people whom I have separated as mine.
I have called those warriors to carry out my anger.
They rejoice and are glad to do my will.

4 Listen to the loud noise in the mountains,
the sound of many people.
Listen to the noise among the kingdoms,
the sound of nations gathering together.
The LORD All-powerful is calling his army together for battle.
5 This army is coming from a faraway land,
from the edge of the horizon.
In anger the LORD is using this army like a weapon
to destroy the whole country.
6 Cry, because the LORD's day of judging is near;
the Almighty is sending destruction.
7 People will be weak with fear,
and their courage will melt away.
8 Everyone will be afraid.
Pain and hurt will grab them;
they will hurt like a woman giving birth to a baby.
They will look at each other in fear, with their faces red like fire.

God's Judgement Against Babylon

9 Look, the LORD's day of judging is coming—
a terrible day, a day of God's anger.
He will destroy the land and the sinners who live in it.
10 The stars will not show their light;
the skies will be dark.

The sun will grow dark as it rises,
and the moon will not give its
light.
11 The LORD says, "I will punish the
world for its evil
and wicked people for their sins.
I will cause proud people to lose their
pride,
and I will destroy the pride of those
who are cruel to others.
12 People will be harder to find than
pure gold;
there will be fewer people than
there is fine gold in Ophir.
13 I will make the sky shake,
and the earth will be moved from
its place
by the anger of the LORD
All-powerful
at the time of his burning anger.

14 "Then the people from Babylon will
run away like hunted deer
or like sheep who have no
shepherd.
Everyone will turn back to his own
people;
each will run back to his own land.
15 Everyone who is captured will be
killed;
everyone who is caught will be
killed with a sword.
16 Their little children will be beaten to
death in front of them.
Their houses will be robbed
and their wives raped.

17 "Look, I will cause the armies of
Media to attack Babylon.
They do not care about silver
or delight in gold.
18 Their soldiers will shoot the young
men with arrows;
they will show no mercy on
children,
nor will they feel sorry for little
ones.
19 Babylon is the most beautiful of all
kingdoms,
and the Babylonians are very
proud of it.
But God will destroy it

like Sodom and Gomorrah.
20 No one will ever live there
or settle there again.
No Arab will put a tent there;
no shepherd will bring sheep
there.
21 Only desert animals will live there,

FAITH links

WORLD NEWS
ISAIAH 13—19

If you've ever watched the news on TV, you know that a section of the news focuses on what's going on in the world. Isaiah's prophecies included a "world news" segment. Many important nations around the world did not obey God. God planned to punish them.

Many people view God as always angry, always ready to punish someone. Is that your view of God? God would prefer not to punish people. Instead, he offers mercy when we repent of our sin.

Out of Control? Genesis 4, p. 8

Facing the Consequences, Deuteronomy 3:21–29, p. 232

Count on His Mercy, Judges 2:16–17; 3, p. 313

Don't Get Mad; Get Even? Matthew 26:57–63; 27:11–14, p. 1323

That's Much Better! Ephesians 2:4–5, p. 1599

It's Guaranteed! 1 John 1:9–10, p. 1714

and their houses will be full of wild
    dogs.
Owls will live there,
    and wild goats will leap about in
        the houses.
22 Wolves will howl within the strong
        walls,
    and wild dogs will bark in the
        beautiful buildings.
The end of Babylon is near;
    its time is almost over."

Israel will Return Home

14 The LORD will show mercy to the people of Jacob, and he will again choose the people of Israel. He will settle them in their own land. Then non-Israelite people will join the Israelites and will become a part of the family of Jacob. 2 Nations will take the Israelites back to their land. Then those men and women from the other nations will become slaves to Israel in the LORD's land. In the past the Israelites were their slaves, but now the Israelites will defeat those nations and rule over them.

The King of Babylon will Fall

3 The LORD will take away the Israelites' hard work and will comfort them. They will no longer have to work hard as slaves. 4 On that day Israel will sing this song about the king of Babylon:
    The cruel king who ruled us is finished;
        his angry rule is finished!
5 The LORD has broken the sceptre of
        evil rulers
    and taken away their power.
6 The king of Babylon struck people in
        anger
    again and
        again.
    He ruled nations
        in anger
    and continued to
        hurt them.

**14:5–6
Anger**
Find out if God will punish anger.

7 But now, the whole world rests and is
        quiet.
    Now the people begin to sing.
8 Even the pine trees are happy,
    and the cedar trees of Lebanon
        rejoice.
They say, "The king has fallen,
    so no one will ever cut us down
        again."
9 The place of the dead is excited
    to meet you when you come.
It wakes the spirits of the dead,
    the leaders of the world.
It makes kings of all nations
    stand up from their thrones to
        greet you.
10 All these leaders will make fun of you
        and will say,
"Now you are weak, as we are.
    Now you are just like us."
11 Your pride has been sent down to the
        place of the dead.
    The music from your harps goes
        with it.
    Flies are spread out like your bed
        beneath you,
    and worms cover your body like a
        blanket.
12 King of Babylon, morning star, you
        have fallen from heaven,
    even though you were as bright as
        the rising sun!
In the past all the nations on earth
        bowed down before you,
    but now you have been cut down.
13 You told yourself,
    "I will go up to heaven.
    I will put my throne
        above God's stars.
    I will sit on the mountain of the gods,
        on the slopes of the sacred
            mountain.
14 I will go up above the tops of the
        clouds.
    I will be like God Most High."
15 But you were brought down to the
        grave,
    to the deep places where the dead
        are.
16 Those who see you stare at you.
    They think about what has
        happened to you
    and say, "Is this the same man who
        caused great fear on earth,
    who shook the kingdoms,
17 who turned the world into a desert,
    who destroyed its cities,

who captured people in war
and would not let them go home?"

18 Every king of the earth has been
buried with honour,
each in his own grave.
19 But you are thrown out of your grave,
like an unwanted branch.
You are covered by bodies
that died in battle,
by bodies to be buried in a rocky pit.
You are like a dead body other
soldiers walk on.
20 You will not be buried with those
bodies,
because you ruined your own country
and killed your own people.
The children of evil people
will never be mentioned again.

21 Prepare to kill his children,
because their father is guilty.
They will never again take control of
the earth;
they will never again fill the world
with their cities.

22 The LORD All-powerful says this:
"I will fight against those people;
I will destroy Babylon and its people,
its children and their descendants,"
says the LORD.
23 "I will make Babylon fit only for owls
and for swamps.
I will sweep Babylon as with a broom
of destruction,"
says the LORD All-powerful.

God will Punish Assyria

24 The LORD All-powerful has made
this promise:
"These things will happen exactly as
I planned them;
they will happen exactly as I set
them up.
25 I will destroy the king of Assyria in
my country;
I will trample him on my mountains.
He placed a heavy load on my people,
but that weight will be removed.

26 "This is what I plan to do for all the
earth.
And this is the hand that I have
raised over all nations."
27 When the LORD All-powerful makes a
plan,
no one can stop it.
When the LORD raises his hand to
punish people,
no one can stop it.

God's Message to Philistia

28 This message was given in the year
that King Ahaz died:
29 Country of Philistia, don't be happy
that the king who struck you is
now dead.
He is like a snake that will give birth
to another dangerous snake.
The new king will be like a quick,
dangerous snake to bite you.
30 Even the poorest of my people will be
able to eat safely,
and people in need will be able to
lie down in safety.
But I will kill your family with hunger,
and all your people who are left will
die.

31 People near the city gates,ⁿ cry out!
Philistines, be frightened,
because a cloud of dust comes from
the north.
It is an army, full of men ready to
fight.
32 What shall we tell the messengers
from Philistia?
Say that the LORD has made
Jerusalem strong
and that his poor people will go
there for safety.

God's Message to Moab

15 This is a message about Moab:
In one night armies took the
wealth from Ar in Moab,
and it was destroyed.
In one night armies took the wealth
from Kir in Moab,
and it was destroyed.
2 The people of Dibon go to the places

14:31 **city gates** People came here to conduct business. Public meetings and court cases were also held there.

of worship to cry.
The people of Moab cry for the
  cities of Nebo and Medeba.
Every head and beard has been
  shaved to show how sad Moab is.
3 In the streets they wear rough cloth
  to show their sadness.
On the roofs* and in the public
  squares,
they are crying loudly.
4 People in the cities Heshbon and
  Elealeh cry out loud.
You can hear their voices far away
  in the city Jahaz.
Even the soldiers are frightened;
  they are shaking with fear.

5 My heart cries with sorrow for Moab.
Its people run away to Zoar for
  safety;
they run to Eglath Shelishiyah.
People are going up the mountain
  road to Luhith,
crying as they go.
People are going on the road to
  Horonaim,
crying over their
  destruction.
6 But the water of
  Nimrim has
  dried up.
The grass has
  dried up,
and all the plants are
  dead;
nothing green is
  left.
7 So the people gather
  up what they have saved
and carry it across the Ravine of
  the Poplars.
8 Crying is heard everywhere in Moab.
Their crying is heard as far away
  as the city Eglaim;
it is heard as far away as Beer
  Elim.
9 The water of the city Dibon is full of
  blood,
and I, the LORD, will bring even
  more troubles to Dibon.
A few people living in Moab have
  escaped the enemy,
but I will send lions to kill them.

16 Send the king of the land
   the payment he demands.
Send a lamb from Sela through the
  desert
to the mountain of Jerusalem.
2 The women of Moab
  try to cross the river Arnon
like little birds
  that have fallen from their nest.

3 They say: "Help us.
  Tell us what to do.
Protect us from our enemies
  as shade protects us from the noon
  sun.
Hide us, because we are running for
  safety!
Don't give us to our enemies.
4 Let those of us who were forced out
  of Moab live in your land.
Hide us from our enemies."

The robbing of Moab will stop.
The enemy will be defeated;
those who hurt others will
  disappear from the land.
5 Then a new loyal king
  will come;
this faithful king
  will be from the
  family of David.
He will judge fairly
  and do what is
  right.

6 We have heard that the
  people of Moab
  are proud and
  very conceited.
They are very proud and angry,
  but their boasting means nothing.
7 So the people of Moab will cry;
  they will all be sad.
They will moan and groan
  for the raisin cakes they had in Kir
  Hareseth.
8 But the fields of Heshbon and the vines

> This faithful king will be from the family of David. He will judge fairly and do what is right.
> — Isaiah 16:5

15:3 roofs In Bible times houses were built with flat roofs. The roof was used for drying things such as flax and fruit. And it was used as an extra room, as a place for worship and as a place to sleep in the summer.

of Sibmah cannot grow grapes;
foreign rulers have destroyed the
grapevines.
The grapevines once spread as far as
the city of Jazer and into the
desert;
they had spread as far as the sea.
9 I cry with the people of Jazer
for the grapevines of Sibmah.
I will cry with the people of Heshbon
and Elealeh.
There will be no shouts of joy,
because there will be no harvest or
ripe fruit.
10 There will be no joy and happiness in
the orchards
and no songs or shouts of joy in
the vineyards.
No one makes wine in the winepresses,
because I have put an end to
shouts of joy.
11 My heart cries for Moab like a harp
playing a funeral song;
I am very sad for Kir Hareseth.
12 The people of Moab will go to their
places of worship
and will try to pray.
But when they go to their temple to
pray,
they will not be able.

13 Earlier the LORD said these things about Moab. 14 Now the LORD says, "In three years all those people and what they take pride in will be hated. (This is three years as a hired helper would count time.) There will be a few people left, but they will be weak."

God's Message to Aram

17 This is a message about Damascus:
"The city of Damascus will be
destroyed;
only ruins will remain.
2 People will leave the cities of Aroer.
Flocks will wander freely in those
empty towns,
and there will be no one to bother
them.
3 The fortified cities of Israel will be
destroyed.
The government in Damascus will
end.
Those left alive of Aram will be
like the glory of Israel," says the
LORD All-powerful.
4 "At that time Israel's wealth will all be
gone.
Israel will be like someone who has
lost much weight from sickness.
5 That time will be like the grain
harvest in the Valley of Rephaim.
The workers cut the wheat.
Then they cut the heads of grain
from the plants
and collect the grain.
6 That time will also be like the olive
harvest,
when a few olives are left.
Two or three olives are left in the top
branches.
Four or five olives are left on full
branches," says the LORD, the
God of Israel.

7 At that time people will look to God,
their Maker;
their eyes will see the Holy One of
Israel.
8 They will not trust the altars they
have made,
nor will they trust what their hands
have made,
not even the Asherah idols
and altars.

9 In that day all their strong cities will be empty. They will be like the cities the Hivites and the Amorites left when the Israelites came to take the land. Everything will be ruined.

10 You have forgotten the God who
saves you;
you have not remembered that
God is your
place of
safety.
You plant the
finest
grapevines
and grapevines
from faraway places.

17:10 Money
What can all your stuff distract you from?

11 You plant your grapevines one day
and try to make them grow,
and the next day you make them
blossom.
But at harvest time everything will be
dead;
a sickness will kill all the plants.

12 Listen to the many people!
Their crying is like the noise from
the sea.
Listen to the nations!
Their crying is like the crashing of
great waves.
13 The people roar like the waves,
but when God speaks harshly to
them, they will
run away.
They will be like
chaff on the hills
being blown by
the wind,
or like
tumbleweeds
blown away by a
storm.
14 At night the people
will be very
frightened.
Before morning, no one will be
left.
So our enemies will come to our
land,
but they will become nothing.

God's Message to Cush

18 How terrible it will be for the land
beyond the rivers of Cush.
It is filled with the sound of
wings.
2 That land sends messengers across
the sea;
they go on the water in boats made
of reeds.

Go, quick messengers,
to a people who are tall and
smooth-skinned,
who are feared everywhere.
They are a powerful nation that
defeats other nations.
Their land is divided by rivers.

3 All you people of the world, look!
Everyone who lives in the world,
look!
You will see a banner raised on a
mountain.
You will hear a trumpet sound.
4 The LORD said to me,
"I will quietly watch from where I
live,
like heat in the sunshine,
like the dew in the heat of harvest
time."
5 The time will come, after the flowers
have bloomed and before the
harvest,
when new grapes will be budding
and growing.
The enemy will cut
the plants with
knives;
he will cut down
the vines and
take them away.
6 They will be left for
the birds of the
mountains
and for the wild
animals.
Birds will feed on
them all
summer,
and wild animals will eat them that
winter."

7 At that time a gift will be brought to
the LORD All-powerful
from the people who are tall and
smooth-skinned,
who are feared everywhere.
They are a powerful nation that
defeats other nations.
Their land is divided by rivers.
These gifts will be brought to the
place of the LORD All-powerful,
to Mount Zion.

God's Message to Egypt

19 This is a message about Egypt:
Look, the LORD is coming on a fast
cloud
to enter Egypt.
The idols of Egypt will tremble before
him,

> The idols of Egypt will tremble before him, and Egypt's courage will melt away.
> — Isaiah 19:1

and Egypt's courage will melt away.

2 The LORD says, "I will cause the Egyptians to fight against themselves.
People will fight with their relatives;
neighbours will fight neighbours;
cities will fight cities;
kingdoms will fight kingdoms.
3 The Egyptians will be afraid, and I will ruin their plans.
They will ask advice from their idols and spirits of the dead,
from their mediums and fortune-tellers."
4 The Lord GOD All-powerful says, "I will hand Egypt over to a hard master,
and a powerful king will rule over them."

5 The sea will become dry, and the water will disappear from the Nile River.
6 The canals will stink;
the streams of Egypt will decrease and dry up.
All the water plants will rot;
7 all the plants along the banks of the Nile will die.
Even the planted fields by the Nile will dry up, blow away and disappear.
8 The fishermen, all those who catch fish from the Nile,
will groan and cry;
those who fish in the Nile will be sad.
9 All the people who make cloth from flax will be sad,
and those who weave linen will lose hope.
10 Those who weave cloth will be broken.
All those who work for money will be sad.

11 The officers of the city of Zoan are fools;
the wise men who advise the king of Egypt give wrong advice.
How can you say to him, 'I am wise'?
How can you say, 'I am from the old family of the kings'?
12 Egypt, where are your wise men?
Let them show you
what the LORD All-powerful has planned for Egypt.
13 The officers of Zoan have been fooled;
the leaders of Memphis have believed false things.
So the leaders of Egypt
lead that nation the wrong way.
14 The LORD has made the leaders confused.
They have led Egypt to wander in the wrong ways,
like drunk people stumbling in their own vomit.
15 There is nothing Egypt can do; no one there can help.

16 In that day the Egyptians will be like women. They will be afraid of the LORD All-powerful, because he will raise his hand to strike them down. 17 The land of Judah will bring fear to Egypt. Anyone there who hears the name Judah will be afraid, because the LORD All-powerful has planned terrible things for them. 18 At that time five cities in Egypt will speak Hebrew, the language of Canaan, and they will promise to be loyal to the LORD All-powerful. One of these cities will be named the City of Destruction. 19 At that time there will be an altar for the LORD in the middle of Egypt and a monument to the LORD at the border of Egypt. 20 This will be a sign and a witness to the LORD All-powerful in the land of Egypt. When the people cry to the LORD for help, he will send someone to save and defend them. He will rescue them from those who hurt them.

21 So the LORD will show himself to the Egyptians, and then they will know he is the LORD. They will worship God and offer many sacrifices. They will make promises to the LORD and will keep them. 22 The LORD will punish the Egyptians, but then he will heal them. They will come back to the LORD, and he will listen to their prayers and heal them.

23 At that time there will be a highway

from Egypt to Assyria, and the Assyrians will go to Egypt, and the Egyptians will go to Assyria. The Egyptians and Assyrians will worship God together. 24 At that time Israel, Assyria and Egypt will join together, which will be a blessing for the earth. 25 The LORD All-powerful will bless them, saying, "Egypt, you are my people. Assyria, I made you. Israel, I own you. You are all blessed!"

Assyria will Defeat Egypt and Cush

20 Sargon king of Assyria sent a military commander to Ashdod to attack that city. So the commander attacked and captured it. 2 Then the LORD spoke through Isaiah son of Amoz, saying, "Take the rough cloth off your body, and take your sandals off your feet." So Isaiah obeyed and walked around naked and barefoot.

3 Then the LORD said, "Isaiah my servant has walked around naked and barefoot for three years as a sign against Egypt and Cush. 4 The king of Assyria will carry away prisoners from Egypt and Cush. Old people and young people will be led away naked and barefoot, with their buttocks bare. So the Egyptians will be shamed. 5 People who looked to Cush for help will be afraid, and those who were amazed by Egypt's glory will be shamed. 6 People who live near the sea will say, 'Look at those countries. We trusted them to help us. We ran to them so they would save us from the king of Assyria. So how will we be able to escape?'"

God's Message to Babylon

21 This is a message about the Desert by the Sea:"
Disaster is coming from the desert
    like wind blowing in the south.
It is coming from a terrible
    country.
2 I have seen a terrible vision.

I see traitors turning against you
    and people taking your wealth.

Elam, attack the people!
Media, surround the city and
    attack it!
I will bring an end to the pain the
    city causes.

3 I saw those terrible things, and now I
    am in pain;
my pains are like the pains of
    giving birth.
What I hear makes me very afraid;
    what I see causes me to shake with
    fear.
4 I am worried,
    and I am shaking with fear.
My pleasant evening
    has become a night of fear.

5 They set the table;
    they spread the rugs;
    they eat and drink.
Leaders, stand up.
Prepare the shields for battle!

6 The Lord said to me,
    "Go, place a lookout
        for the city
    and have him report
        what he sees.
7 If he sees chariots
        and teams of
        horses, donkeys
        or camels,
    he should pay very
        close attention."

8 Then the lookout
        called out,
"My master, each day I stand in the
    watchtower watching;
every night I have been on guard.
9 Look, I see a man coming in a chariot
    with a team of horses."
The man gives back the answer,
    "Babylon has fallen. It has fallen!
All the statues of her gods
    lie broken on the ground."

> Disaster is coming from the desert like wind blowing in the south.
> – Isaiah 21:1

21:1 **Desert by the Sea** Probably Babylon.

10 My people are crushed like grain on
    the threshing floor.
  My people, I tell you what I have
    heard
  from the Lord All-powerful,
    from the God of Israel.

God's Message to Edom

11 This is a message about Dumah:[n]
  Someone calls to me from Edom,
  "Watchman, how much of the
    night is left?
  Watchman, how much longer will it
    be night?"
12 The watchman answers,
  "Morning is coming, but then
    night will come again.
  If you have something to ask,
    then come back and ask."

God's Message to Arabia

13 This is a message about Arabia:
  A group of traders from Dedan
  spent the night near some trees in
    Arabia.
14   They gave water to thirsty
    travellers;
  the people of Tema gave food
    to those who were escaping.
15 They were running from swords,
    from swords ready to kill,
  from bows ready to shoot,
    from a hard battle.

16 This is what the Lord said to me:
"In one year all the glory of the country of
Kedar will be gone. (This is a year as a
hired helper counts time.) 17 At that time
only a few of the archers, the soldiers of
Kedar, will be left alive." The Lord, the
God of Israel, has spoken.

God's Message to Jerusalem

22 This is a message about the Valley
  of Vision:[n]
  What is wrong with you people?
    Why are you on your roofs?[n]
2 This city was a very busy city,
    full of noise and wild parties.
  Now your people have been killed,
    but not with swords,
    nor did they die in battle.
3 All your leaders ran away together,
    but they have been captured
    without using a bow.
  All you who were captured
    tried to run away before the enemy
    came.
4 So I say, "Don't look at me.
    Let me cry loudly.
  Don't hurry to comfort me
    about the destruction of
    Jerusalem."
5 The Lord God All-powerful has
    chosen a special day
    of riots and confusion.
  People will trample each other in
    the Valley of Vision.
  The city walls will be knocked down,
    and the people will cry out to the
    mountain.
6 The soldiers from Elam will gather
    their arrows
  and their chariots and men on
    horses.
  Kir will prepare their shields.
7 Your nicest valleys will be filled with
    chariots.
  Horsemen will be ordered to guard
    the gates of the city.
8 The walls protecting Judah will fall.

  At that time the people of Jerusalem
    depended on
  the weapons kept at the Palace of
    the Forest.
9 You saw that the walls of Jerusalem
    had many cracks that needed
    repairing.
  You stored up water in the lower
    pool.
10 You counted the houses of Jerusalem,
    and you tore down houses to repair
    the walls with their stones.
11 You made a pool between the two walls
    to save water from the old pool,
  but you did not trust the God who
    made these things;

21:11 Dumah Another name for Edom.
22:1 Valley of Vision This probably means a valley near Jerusalem.
22:1 roofs In Bible times houses were built with flat roofs. The roof was used for drying things such as flax and fruit. And it was used as an extra room, as a place for worship and as a place to sleep in the summer.

you did not respect the One who
   planned them long ago.

12 The Lord GOD All-powerful told the
      people
   to cry and be sad,
   to shave their heads and wear
      rough cloth.
13 But look, the people are happy
      and are having
      wild parties.
   They kill the cattle
      and the sheep;
   they eat the food
      and drink the
      wine.
   They say, "Let us eat
      and drink,
      because tomorrow
      we will die."
14 The LORD All-powerful said to me: "You people will die before this guilt is forgiven." The Lord GOD All-powerful said this.

God's Message to Shebna

15 This is what the Lord GOD All-powerful says:
   "Go to this servant Shebna,
      the manager of the palace.
16 Say to him, 'What are you doing
      here?
   Who said you could cut out a tomb
      for yourself here?
   Why are you preparing your tomb in
      a high place?
   Why are you carving out a tomb
      from the rock?
17 Look, mighty one! The LORD will
      throw you away.
   He will take firm hold of you
18 and roll you tightly into a ball
      and throw you into another
      country.
   There you will die,
      and there your fine chariots will
      remain.
   You are a disgrace to your master's
      house.
19 I will force you out of your important
      job,
      and you will be thrown down from
      your important place.'

20 "At that time I will call for my servant Eliakim son of Hilkiah. 21 I will take your robe and put it on him and give him your belt. I will hand over to him the important job you have, and he will be like a father to the people of Jerusalem and the family of Judah. 22 I will put the key to the house of David around his neck. If he opens a door, no one will be able to close it; if he closes a door, no one will be able to open it. 23 He will be like an honoured chair in his father's house. I will make him strong like a peg that is hammered into a strong board. 24 All the honoured and important things of his family will depend on him; all the adults and little children will depend on him. They will be like bowls and jars hanging on him.

25 "At that time," says the LORD All-powerful, "the peg hammered into the strong board will weaken. It will break and fall, and everything hanging on it will be destroyed." The LORD says this.

God's Message to Lebanon

23 This is a message about Tyre:
   You trading ships, cry!
   The houses and harbour of Tyre
      are destroyed.
   This news came to the ships
      from the land of Cyprus.
2 Be silent, you who live on the island
      of Tyre;
   you merchants of Sidon, be silent.
   Sailors have made you rich.
3 They travelled the sea to bring grain
      from Egypt;
   the sailors of Tyre brought grain
      from the Nile Valley
   and sold it to other nations.

4 Sidon, be ashamed.
   Strong city of the sea, be ashamed,
      because the sea says:
   "I have not felt the pain of giving
      birth;
   I have not reared young men or
      women."

> They say, "Let us eat and drink, because tomorrow we will die."
> – Isaiah 22:13

5 Egypt will hear the news about Tyre,
    and it will make Egypt hurt with
    sorrow.

6 You ships should return to
    Tarshish.
  You people living near the sea
    should be sad.
7 Look at your once happy city!
  Look at your old, old city!
  People from that city have travelled
    far away to live.
8 Who planned Tyre's destruction?
  Tyre made others rich.
  Its merchants were treated like
    princes,
  and its traders were greatly
    respected.
9 It was the LORD All-powerful who
    planned this.
  He decided to make these proud
    people unimportant;
  he decided to disgrace those who
    were greatly respected.
10 Go through your land, people of
    Tarshish,
  like the Nile goes through Egypt.
  There is no harbour for you now!
11 The LORD has stretched his hand
    over the sea
  and made its kingdoms tremble.
  He commands that Canaan's

A GOOD KIND OF SUFFERING

How do you go about letting people know that you're a Christian? Here's somebody who can share her own experience in this area. Let's welcome Sue, aged 12, to Connect 2-You.

Sue

Well, in my biology lesson we were talking about how everything was created. The teacher explained evolution; then he asked if any of us believed anything different. I raised my hand and told him that I believe God created the world like the Bible says. Now some kids are calling me names like Bible Girl and Jesus Freak. What should I do?

Sue should take it as a compliment. You may think that's a joke, but it's not. The Bible says that when people insult you for following Jesus, you are blessed. That means God likes what he sees in you. You might want to check out the tips on the Livin' It page on handling bad times, 1 Peter 4:12-19, p. 1704.

Sue may not enjoy being teased, but just think! Kids who may have never considered where life comes from may start wondering about the possibility of a Creator. Other Christian kids who were too insecure to share their faith might learn from her example. It's worth taking the risk.

fortified cities be destroyed.
12 He said, "Sidon, you will not rejoice
any longer,
because you are destroyed.
Even if you cross the sea to Cyprus,
you will not find a place to rest."
13 Look at the land of the Babylonians;
it is not a country now.
Assyria has made it a place for wild
animals.
Assyria built towers to attack it;
the soldiers took all the treasures
from its cities,
and they turned it into ruins.
14 So be sad, you trading ships,
because your strong city is
destroyed.
15 At that time people will forget about Tyre for 70 years, which is the length of a king's life. After 70 years, Tyre will be like the prostitute in this song:

16 "Oh woman, you are forgotten.
Take your harp and walk through
the city.
Play your harp well. Sing your song
often.
Then people will remember
you."

17 After 70 years the LORD will deal with Tyre, and it will again have trade. It will be like a prostitute for all the nations of the earth. 18 The profits will be saved for the LORD. Tyre will not keep the money she earns but will give them to the people who serve the LORD, so they will have plenty of food and nice clothes.

The LORD will Punish the World

24 Look! The LORD will destroy the
earth and leave it empty;
he will ruin the surface of the land
and scatter its people.
2 At that time the same thing will
happen to everyone:
to common people and priests,
to slaves and masters,
to women slaves and their women
masters,
to buyers and sellers,
to those who borrow and those
who lend,
to bankers and those who owe the
bank.
3 The earth will be completely empty.
The wealth will all be taken,
because the LORD has commanded
it.
4 The earth will dry up and die;
the world will grow weak and
die;
the great leaders in this land will
become weak.
5 The people of the earth have ruined
it,
because they do not follow God's
teachings
or obey God's laws
or keep their agreement with God
that was to last for ever.
6 So a curse will destroy the earth.
The people of the world are
guilty,
so they will be burned up;
only a few will be left.
7 The new wine will be bad, and the
grapevines will die.
People who were happy will be sad.
8 The happy music of the tambourines
will end.
The happy sounds
of wild parties
will stop.
The joyful music
from the harps
will end.
9 People will no longer
sing while they
drink their wine.
The beer will taste bitter
to those who drink it.
10 The ruined city will be empty,
and people will hide behind closed
doors.
11 People in the streets will ask for
wine,
but joy will have turned to
sadness;
all the happiness will have left.
12 The city will be left in ruins,

Look! The LORD will
destroy the earth
and leave it empty.
– Isaiah 24:1

and its gates will be smashed to
  pieces.
13 This is what will happen all over the
    earth
  and to all the nations.
  The earth will be like an olive tree
    after the harvest
  or like the few grapes left on a vine
    after harvest.

14 The people shout for joy.
  From the west they praise the
    greatness of the LORD.
15 People in the east, praise the LORD.
  People in the islands of the sea,
    praise the name of the LORD, the
    God of Israel.
16 We hear songs from every part of the
    earth
  praising God, the Righteous One.

  But I said, "I am dying! I am dying!
    How terrible it will be for me!
  Traitors turn against people;
    with their dishonesty, they turn
    against people."
17 There are terrors, holes and traps
    for the people of the earth.
18 Anyone who tries to escape from the
    sound of terror
  will fall into a hole.
  Anyone who climbs out of the hole
    will be caught in a trap.
  The clouds in the sky will pour out
    rain,
  and the foundations of the earth
    will shake.
19 The earth will be broken up;
  the earth will split open;
  the earth will shake violently.
20 The earth will stumble around like
    someone who is drunk;
  it will shake like a hut in a storm.
  Its sin is like a heavy weight on its
    back;
  it will fall and never rise again.

21 At that time the LORD will punish
  the powers in the sky above
  and the rulers on earth below.
22 They will be gathered together
  like prisoners thrown into
    a pit;
  they will be shut up in prison.
  After much time they will be
    punished.
23 The moon will be embarrassed,
  and the sun will be ashamed,
  because the LORD All-powerful will
    rule as king
  on Mount Zion in Jerusalem.
  Jerusalem's leaders will see his
    greatness.

A Song of Praise to God

25 LORD, you are my God.
  I honour you and praise you,
  because you have done amazing
    things.
  You have always done what you
    said you would do;
  you have done what you planned
    long ago.
2 You have made the city a pile of
    rocks
  and have destroyed her walls.
  The city our enemies built with
    strong walls is gone;
  it will never be built again.
3 People from powerful nations will
    honour you;
  cruel people from strong cities will
    fear you.
4 You protect the poor;
  you protect the helpless when they
    are in danger.
  You are like a shelter from storms,
  like shade that protects them from
    the heat.
  The cruel people attack
  like a rainstorm beating against the
    wall,
5 like the heat in the desert.
  But you, God, stop their violent
    attack.
  As a cloud cools a hot day,
  you silence the songs of those who
    have no mercy.

God's Banquet for His Servants

6 The LORD All-powerful will prepare a
    feast
  on this mountain for all people.
  It will be a feast with all the best food
    and wine,
  the finest meat and wine.

7 On this mountain God will destroy
    the veil that covers all nations,
    the veil that stretches over all
        peoples;
8 he will destroy
    death for
    ever.
  The Lord GOD
    will wipe
    away every
    tear from
    every face.
  He will take away the shame of his
    people from the earth.
  The LORD has spoken.
9 At that time people will say,
    "Our God is doing this!
  We have waited for him, and he has
        come to save us.
  This is the LORD. We waited for
        him,
  so we will rejoice and be happy when
        he saves us."
10 The LORD will protect Jerusalem,
    but he will crush our enemy Moab
  like straw that is trampled down in
        the manure.
11 They will spread their arms in it
    like a person who is swimming.
  But God will bring down their pride,
    and all the clever things they have
        made will mean nothing.
12 Moab's high walls protect them,
    but God will destroy these walls.
  He will throw them down to the
        ground,
    even to the dust.

A Song of Praise to God

26 At that time people will sing this
   song in Judah:
  We have a strong city.
    God protects us with its strong
        walls and defences.
2 Open the gates,
    and the good people will enter,
    those who follow God.
3 You, LORD, give true peace
    to those who depend on you,
    because they trust you.
4 So, trust the LORD always,
    because he is our Rock for ever.
5 He will destroy the proud city,
    and he will punish the people living
        there.
  He will bring
    that high
    city down to
    the ground
    and throw it
    down into
    the dust.

25:8 Heaven
What will be missing in heaven?

FAITH links

THINK ABOUT HIM
ISAIAH 26:3

Quick! Don't think of elephants, starting . . . now. Can't stop thinking of elephants, huh? Whenever you're told to stop thinking about something, your mind instantly focuses on that something. That's why Isaiah said that those who depend on God will be given true peace. By this he meant that those whose thoughts are often on God will experience his peace. God is the only source of true peace.

Feel like things are out of control? Check out these Faithlinks for help:

A Life of Thanksgiving, 1 Kings 1:47–48, p. 435

A Need to Change, Ecclesiastes 1:1–11, p. 873

Like a Tree, Jeremiah 17:5–8, p. 1016

Faith God Notices, Luke 18:35–43, p. 1406

A Different Kind of Fruit, Galatians 5:22–23, p. 1592

The "Quality" of Life, 2 Peter 1:5–8, p. 1708

26:4 Trust
Who is your Rock?

6 Then those who were hurt by the city
    will walk on its ruins;
  those who were made poor by the
    city will trample it under their
    feet.
7 The path of life is level for those who
    are right with God;
  LORD, you make the way of life
    smooth for those people.
8 But, LORD, we are waiting
    for your way of justice.
  Our souls want to remember
    you and your name.
9 My soul wants to be with you at night,
  and my spirit wants to be with you
    at the dawn of every day.
  When your way of justice comes to
    the land,
  people of the world will learn the
    right way of living.
10 Evil people will not learn to do good
    even if you show them kindness.
  They will continue doing evil, even if
    they live in a good world;
  they never see the LORD's
    greatness.
11 LORD, you are ready to punish those
    people,
  but they do not see that.
  Show them your strong love for your
    people.
  Then those who are evil will be
    ashamed.
  Burn them in the fire
    you have prepared for your
    enemies.
12 LORD, all our success is because of
    what you have done,
  so give us peace.
13 LORD, our God, other masters besides
    you have ruled us,
  but we honour only you.
14 Those masters are now dead;
    their ghosts will not rise from
    death.
  You punished and destroyed them
    and destroyed any memory of
    them.
15 LORD, you multiplied the number of
    your people;
  you multiplied them and brought
    honour to yourself.
  You made the borders of the land
    wide.
16 LORD, people remember you when
    they are in trouble;
  they say quiet prayers to you when
    you punish them.
17 LORD, when we are with you,
  we are like a woman giving birth to
    a baby;
  she cries and has pain from the
    birth.
18 In the same way, we had pain.
  We gave birth, but only to wind.
  We don't bring salvation to the land
    or make new people for the world.
19 Your people have died, but they will
    live again;
  their bodies will rise from death.
  You who lie in the ground,
    wake up and be happy!
  The dew covering you is like the dew
    of a new day;
  the ground will give birth to the
    dead.

Judgement: Reward or Punishment

20 My people, go into your rooms
    and shut your doors behind you.
  Hide in your rooms for a short time
    until God's anger is finished.
21 The LORD will leave his place
    to punish the people of the world
    for their sins.
  The earth will show the blood of the
    people who have been killed;
  it will not cover the dead any
    longer.

27 At that time the LORD will punish
    Leviathan, the gliding snake.
  He will punish Leviathan, the
    coiled snake,
  with his great and hard and
    powerful sword.
  He will kill the monster in the sea.

2 At that time
  people will sing about the pleasant
    vineyard.
3 "I, the LORD, will care for that
    vineyard;
  I will water it at the right time.
  No one will hurt it,

because I will guard it day and
        night.
4 I am not angry.
    If anyone builds a wall of
            thorn-bushes in war,
        I will march to it
            and burn it.
5 But if anyone comes
            to me for safety
        and wants to make
            peace with me,
        he should come
            and make peace
            with me."
6 In the days to come,
        the people of
        Jacob will be like
        a plant with good roots;
    Israel will grow like a plant
        beginning to bloom.
    Then the world will be filled with
        their children.

The Lord will Send Israel Away

7 The LORD has not hurt his people as
        he hurt their enemies;
    his people have not been killed like
        those who tried to kill them.
8 He will settle his argument with Israel
        by sending it far away.
    Like a hot desert wind, he will
        drive it away.
9 This is how Israel's guilt will be
        forgiven;
    this is how its sins will be taken
        away:
    Israel will crush the rocks of the altar
        to dust,
    and no statues or altars will be left
        standing for the Asherah
        idols.
10 At that time the fortified city will be
        empty
    like a desert.
    Calves will eat grass there.
    They will lie down there
        and eat leaves from the branches.
11 The limbs will become dry and break
        off,
    so women will use them for
        firewood.
    The people refuse to understand,
        so God will not comfort them;

their Maker will not be kind to
        them.
12 At that time the LORD will begin
    gathering his people one by one from the
    Euphrates River to the brook of Egypt. He
    will separate them from
    others as grain is separated from chaff. 13 Many
    of my people are now lost
    in Assyria. Some have run
    away to Egypt. But at that
    time a great trumpet will
    be blown, and all those
    people will come and worship the LORD on that holy
    mountain in Jerusalem.

> But if anyone comes
> to me for safety and
> wants to make peace
> with me, he should
> come and make
> peace with me.
> – Isaiah 27:5

Warnings to Israel

28 How terrible it will be for Samaria,
        the pride of Israel's drunken
        people!
    That beautiful crown of flowers is
        just a dying plant
    set on a hill above a rich valley where
        drunkards live.
2 Look, the Lord has someone who is
        strong and powerful.
    Like a storm of hail and strong
        wind,
    like a sudden flood of water pouring
        over the country,
    he will throw Samaria down to the
        ground.
3 That city, the pride of Israel's
        drunken people,
    will be trampled underfoot.
4 That beautiful crown of flowers is just
        a dying plant
    set on a hill above a rich valley.
    That city will be like the first fig of
        summer.
    Anyone who sees it
        quickly picks it and eats it.

5 At that time the LORD All-powerful
    will be like a beautiful crown,
    like a wonderful crown of flowers
        for his people who are left alive.
6 Then he will give wisdom to the
        judges who must decide cases
    and strength to those who battle at
        the city gate.

7 But now those leaders are drunk with wine;
    they stumble from drinking too much beer.
  The priests and prophets are drunk with beer
    and are filled with wine.
  They stumble from too much beer.
  The prophets are drunk when they see their visions;
    the judges stumble when they make their decisions.
8 Every table is covered with vomit,
    so there is not a clean place anywhere.

9 The LORD is trying to teach the people a lesson;
    he is trying to make them understand his teachings.
  But the people are like babies too old for breast milk,
    like those who no longer nurse at their mother's breast.
10 So they make fun of the LORD's prophet and say:
  "A command here, a command there.
    A rule here, a rule there.
    A little lesson here, a little lesson there."
11 So the LORD will use strange words and foreign languages
    to speak to these people.
12 God said to them,
  "Here is a place of rest;
    let the tired people come and rest.
  This is the place of peace."
    But the people would not listen.
13 So the words of the LORD will be,
  "A command here, a command there.
    A rule here, a rule there.
    A little lesson here, a little lesson there."
  They will fall back and be defeated;
    they will be trapped and captured.

14 So listen to the LORD's message, you who boast,
    you leaders in Jerusalem.
15 You say, "We have made an agreement with death;
    we have a contract with death.
  When terrible punishment passes by, it won't hurt us.
  Our lies will keep us safe,
    and our tricks will hide us."

16 Because of these things, this is what the Lord GOD says:
  "I will put a stone in the ground in Jerusalem,
    a tested stone.
  Everything will be built on this important and precious rock.
  Anyone who trusts in it will never be disappointed.
17 I will use justice as a measuring line
    and goodness as the standard.
  The lies you hide behind will be destroyed as if by hail.
  They will be washed away as if in a flood.
18 Your agreement with death will be erased;
    your contract with death will not help you.
  When terrible punishment comes, you will be crushed by it.
19 Whenever punishment comes, it will take you away.
  It will come morning after morning;
    it will defeat you by day and by night.
  Those who understand this punishment will be terrified."
20 You will be like the person who tried to sleep
    on a bed that was too short
  and with a blanket that was too narrow
    to wrap around himself.
21 The LORD will fight as he did at Mount Perazim.

> The LORD is trying to teach the people a lesson; he is trying to make them understand his teachings.
> – Isaiah 28:9

He will be angry as he was in the
Valley of Gibeon.
He will do his work, his strange work.
He will finish his job, his strange
job.
22 Now, you must not make fun of these
things,
or the ropes around you will
become tighter.
The Lord GOD All-powerful has told
me
how the whole earth will be
destroyed.

The LORD Punishes Fairly

23 Listen closely to what I tell you;
listen carefully to what I say.
24 A farmer does not plough his field all
the time;
he does not go on working the soil.
25 He makes the ground flat and
smooth.
Then he plants the dill and scatters
the cumin.
He plants the wheat in rows,
the barley in its special place
and other wheat as a border
around the field.
26 His God teaches him
and shows him the right way.
27 A farmer doesn't use heavy boards to
crush dill;
he doesn't use a wagon wheel to
crush cumin.
He uses a small stick to break open
the dill,
and with a stick he opens the
cumin.
28 The grain is ground to make bread.
People do not ruin it by crushing it
for ever.
The farmer separates the wheat from
the chaff with his cart,
but he does not let his horses grind
it.
29 This lesson also comes from the
LORD All-powerful,
who gives wonderful advice, who is
very wise.

Warnings to Jerusalem

29 How terrible it will be for you,
Jerusalem,
the city where David camped.
Your festivals have continued
year after year.
2 I will attack Jerusalem,
and that city will be filled with
sadness and crying.
It will be like an altar to me.
3 I will put armies all around you,
Jerusalem;
I will surround you with towers
and with devices to attack you.
4 You will be pulled down and will
speak from the ground;
I will hear your voice rising from
the ground.
It will sound like the voice of a ghost;
your words will come like a
whisper from the dust.
5 Your many enemies will become like
fine dust;
the many cruel people will be like
chaff that is blown away.
Everything will happen very quickly.
6 The LORD All-powerful will come
with thunder, earthquakes and great
noises,
with storms, strong winds and a
fire that destroys.
7 Then all the nations that fight against
Jerusalem
will be like a dream;
all the nations that attack her
will be like a vision in the night.
8 They will be like a hungry man who
dreams he is eating,
but when he awakens, he is still
hungry.
They will be like a thirsty man who
dreams he is drinking,
but when he awakens, he is still
weak and thirsty.
It will be the same way with all the
nations
who fight against Mount Zion.

9 Be surprised and amazed.
Blind yourselves so that you cannot
see.
Become drunk, but not from wine.
Trip and fall, but not from beer.
10 The LORD has made you go into a
deep sleep.

He has closed your eyes. (The
  prophets are your eyes.)
He has covered your heads. (The
  seers are your heads.)

11 This vision is like the words of a book that is closed and sealed. You may give the book to someone who can read and tell that person to read it. But he will say, "I can't read the book, because it is sealed." 12 Or you may give the book to someone who cannot read and tell him to read it. But he will say, "I don't know how to read."

13 The Lord says:
"These people
  say they
  love me;
they show
  honour to
  me with
  words,
but their hearts
  are far from me.
The honour they show me
  is nothing but human rules.
14 So I will continue to amaze these
    people
  by doing more and more
    miracles.
Their wise men will lose their
    wisdom;
  their wise men will not be able to
    understand."

29:13
Honouring
God
What is hypocrisy?

Warnings About Other Nations

15 How terrible it will be for those who
    try
  to hide things from the LORD
  and who do their work in darkness.
  They think no one will see them or
    know what they do.
16 You are confused.
  You think the clay is equal to the
    potter.
  You think that an object can tell the
    one who made it,
    "You didn't make me."
  This is like a pot telling its maker,
    "You don't know anything."

A Better Time is Coming

17 In a very short time, Lebanon will
    become rich farmland,
  and the rich farmland will seem
    like a forest.
18 At that time the deaf will hear the
    words in a book.
  Instead of having darkness and
    gloom, the blind will see.
19 The LORD will make the poor people
    happy;
  they will rejoice in the Holy One of
    Israel.
20 Then the people without mercy will
    come to an end;
  those who do not respect God will
    disappear.
  Those who enjoy doing evil will be
    gone:
21 those who lie about others in court,
  those who trap people in court,
  those who lie and take justice from
    innocent people in court.

22 This is what the LORD who set Abraham free says to the family of Jacob:
"Now the people of Jacob will not be
    ashamed
  or disgraced any longer.
23 When they see all their children,
    the children I made with my hands,
  they will say my name is holy.
  They will agree that the Holy One
    of Jacob is holy,
  and they will respect the God of
    Israel.
24 People who do wrong will now
    understand.
  Those who complain will accept
    being taught."

Warnings to the Stubborn Nation

30 The LORD said,
  "How terrible it will be for these stubborn children.
  They make plans, but they don't ask
    me to help them.
  They make agreements with other
    nations, without asking my Spirit.
  They are adding more and more
    sins to themselves.
2 They go down to Egypt for help
    without asking me about it first.
  They hope they will be saved by the
    king of Egypt;

Isaiah 30:3 932

WHO ARE THE EGYPTIANS?   Isaiah 30:2–5

The Egyptians were from the country founded by Mizraim, one of Noah's grandsons. Egyptians worshipped different parts of nature, like the sun, as if those parts were gods. They even worshipped the River Nile, which ran through their country.

It was in Egypt that the Israelites grew to be a nation. One man, Israel, and his sons moved to Egypt because there was no food in their land. After about 400 years, Israel's descendants had become a whole nation within Egypt, but they were a nation of slaves. (Look at Exodus 12:40, p. 92.) When they decided they wanted to leave, the king of Egypt wouldn't let them. He didn't want to lose all those hard workers. Finally, using a man named Moses, God convinced the king to let them go. Their leaving was called the "Exodus". After the Exodus, Egypt became a much weaker nation.

they want Egypt to protect them.
3 But hiding in Egypt will bring you
    only shame;
Egypt's protection will only
    disappoint you.
4 Your officers have gone to Zoan,
    and your messengers have gone to
    Hanes,
5 but they will be put to shame,
    because Egypt is useless to them.
It will give no help and will be of no
    use;
it will cause them only shame and
    embarrassment."

God's Message to Judah

6 This is a message about the animals
    in southern Judah:
Southern Judah is a dangerous place
    full of lions and lionesses,
    poisonous snakes and darting
    snakes.
The messengers travel through there
    with their wealth on the backs of
    donkeys
and their treasure on the backs of
    camels.
They carry them to a nation that
    cannot help them,

7 to Egypt whose help is useless.
    So I call that country Rahab the Do-
    Nothing.

8 Now write this on a sign for the
    people,
    write this on a scroll,
so that for the days to come
    this will be a witness for ever.
9 These people are like children who lie
    and refuse to obey;
    they refuse to listen to the LORD's
    teachings.
10 They tell the seers,
    "Don't see any more visions!"
They say to the prophets,
    "Don't tell us the truth!
Say things that will make us feel
    good;
    see only good things for us.
11 Stop blocking our path.
    Get out of our way.
Stop telling us
    about God, the Holy One of Israel."

12 So this is what the Holy One of Israel says:
    "You people have refused to accept
    this message

and have depended on cruelty and
    lies to help you.
13 You are guilty of these things.
    So you will be like a high wall with
        cracks in it
    that falls suddenly and breaks into
        small pieces.
14 You will be like a clay jar that breaks,
    smashed into many pieces.
    Those pieces will be too small
    to take coals from the fire
    or to get water from a well."

15 This is what
the Lord GOD, the
Holy One of Israel,
says:
    "If you come back
        to me and
    trust me, you will be saved.
    If you will be calm and trust me,
        you will be strong."
    But you don't want to do that.
16 You say, "No, we need horses to run
        away on."
    So you will run away on horses.
    You say, "We will ride away on fast
        horses."
    So those who chase you will be
        fast.
17 One enemy will make threats,
    and 1,000 of your men will run
        away.
    Five enemies will make threats,
    and all of you will run from them.
    You will be left alone like a flagpole
        on a hilltop,
    like a banner on a hill.
18 The LORD wants to show his mercy to
        you.
    He wants to rise and comfort you.
    The LORD is a fair God,
    and everyone who waits for his
        help will be happy.

The LORD will Help His People

19 You people who live on Mount Zion in Jerusalem will not cry any more. The LORD will hear your crying, and he will comfort you. When he hears you, he will help you. 20 The Lord has given you sorrow and hurt like the bread and water you ate every day. He is your teacher; he will not continue to hide from you, but you will see your teacher with your own eyes. 21 If you go the wrong way—to the right or to the left—you will hear a voice behind you saying, "This is the right way. You should go this way." 22 You have statues covered with silver and gold, but you will ruin them for further use. You will throw them away like filthy rags and say, "Go away!"

23 At that time the LORD will send rain for the seeds you plant in the ground, and the ground will grow food for you. The harvest will be rich and great, and you will have plenty of food in the fields for your animals. 24 Your oxen and donkeys that work the soil will have all the food they need. You will have to use shovels and pitchforks to spread all their food. 25 Every mountain and hill will have streams filled with water. These things will happen after many people are killed and the towers are pulled down. 26 At that time the light from the moon will be bright like the sun, and the light from the sun will be seven times brighter than now, like the light of seven days. These things will happen when the LORD bandages his broken people and heals the hurts he gave them.

27 Look! The LORD comes from far
        away.
    His anger is like a fire with thick
        clouds of smoke.
    His mouth is filled with anger,
    and his tongue is like a burning
        fire.
28 His breath is like a rushing river,
    which rises to the throat.
    He will judge the nations as if he is
        sifting them through the strainer
        of destruction.
    He will place in their mouths a bit
        that will lead them the wrong
        way.
29 You will sing happy songs
    as on the nights you begin a
        festival.
    You will be happy like people
        listening to flutes
    as they come to the mountain of
        the LORD,

---

eMAIL FROM GOD

30:15 Courage

Check out where to go to find courage.

to the Rock of Israel.
30 The LORD will cause all people to
hear his great voice
and to see his powerful arm come
down with anger,
like a great fire that burns
everything,
like a great storm with much rain
and hail.
31 Assyria will be afraid when it hears
the voice of the LORD,
because he will strike Assyria with
a rod.
32 When the LORD punishes Assyria
with a rod,
he will beat them to the music of
tambourines and harps;
he will fight against them with his
mighty weapons.
33 Topheth*n* has been made ready for a
long time;
it is ready for the king.
It was made deep and wide
with much wood and fire.
And the LORD's breath will come
like a stream of burning sulphur
and set it on fire.

Warnings About Relying on Egypt

31 How terrible it will be for those
people who go down to Egypt
for help.
They think horses will save
them.
They think their many chariots
and strong horsemen will save
them.
But they don't trust God, the Holy
One of Israel,
or ask the LORD for help.
2 But he is wise and can bring them
disaster.
He does not change his warnings.
He will rise up and fight against the
evil people
and against those who try to help
evil people.
3 The Egyptians are only people and
are not God.
Their horses are only animals and
are not spirit.
The LORD will stretch out his arm,

FAITH links

THE FOUNDATION OF OUR HOPE
ISAIAH 31:1-8

Did you ever strongly believe something was true that turned out not to be true? When a person's belief crumbles, we usually say that his belief had no foundation. It's like trying to build a house without including a foundation. Sooner or later, the house will fall apart, because it has nothing to stand on.

Isaiah warned the Israelites against trusting the Egyptians for help. He knew that their hope in Egypt would soon crumble. Trusting God to defend them was the only hope with a solid foundation. What is your hope based on? Some people trust in money or power. Neither will last for ever. Only God is all-powerful and everlasting.

Following the Crowd, Numbers 13; 14, p. 193

Down on Discipline? Proverbs 29:15, p. 867

Long-lasting Hope, Hosea 14, p. 1184

Set for Life? Obadiah 2–4, p. 1208

Put God First, Acts 5:27–32, p. 1472

More Money? 1 Timothy 6:10, p. 1649

30:33 Topheth Gehenna; the Valley of Hinnom. Here people burned the bodies of criminals and animals, along with rubbish.

and the one who helps will
   stumble,
and the people who wanted help
   will fall.
All of them will be destroyed
   together.
4 The LORD says this to me:
"When a lion or a lion's cub kills an
   animal to eat,
it stands over the dead animal and
   roars.
A band of shepherds
   may be assembled against it,
but the lion will not be afraid of their
   yelling
or upset by their noise.
So the LORD All-powerful will come
   down
to fight on Mount Zion and on its
   hill.
5 The LORD All-powerful will defend
   Jerusalem
like birds flying over their nests.
He will defend and save it;
he will 'pass over' and save
   Jerusalem."
6 You children of Israel, come back to
   the God you fought
   against. 7 The time
   is coming when
   each of you will stop
   worshipping idols of
   gold and silver,
   which you sinned
   by making.

31:6–7
Money
What is more lasting than your things?

8 "Assyria will be defeated by a
   sword, but not the sword of a
   person;
Assyria will be destroyed, but not
   by a person's sword.
Assyria will run away from the sword
   of God,
but its young men will be caught
   and made slaves.
9 They will panic, and their protection
   will be destroyed.
Their commanders will be terrified
   when they see God's battle flag,"
says the LORD,
   whose fire is in Jerusalem
   and whose furnace is in
      Jerusalem.

A Good Kingdom is Coming

32 A king will rule in a way that
      brings justice,
and leaders will make fair
   decisions.
2 Then each ruler will be like a shelter
   from the wind,
like a safe place in a storm,
like streams of water in a dry land,
like a cool shadow from a large
   rock in a hot land.

3 People will look to the king for help,
   and they will truly listen to what he
      says.
4 People who are now worried will be
   able to understand.
Those who cannot speak clearly
   now will then be able to speak
   clearly and quickly.
5 Fools will not be called great,
   and people will not respect the
      wicked.
6 A fool says foolish things,
   and in his mind he plans evil.
A fool does things that are wicked,
   and he says wrong things about
      the LORD.
A fool does not feed the hungry
   or let thirsty people drink water.
7 The wicked person uses evil like a
   tool.
He plans ways to take everything
   from the poor.
He destroys the poor with lies,
   even when the poor person is in
      the right.
8 But a good leader plans to do good,
   and those good things make him a
      good leader.

Hard Times are Coming

9 You women who are calm now,
   stand up and listen to me.
You women who feel safe now,
   hear what I say.
10 You women feel safe now,
   but after one year you will be
      afraid.
There will be no grape harvest
   and no summer fruit to gather.
11 Women, you are calm now, but you
   should shake with fear.

Women, you feel safe now, but you
should tremble.
Take off your nice clothes
and put rough cloth around your
waist to show your sadness.
12 Beat your breasts in grief, because
the fields that were pleasant are
now empty.
Cry, because the vines that once
had fruit now have no more
grapes.
13 Cry for the land of my people,
in which only thorns and weeds
now grow.
Cry for the city that once was happy
and for all the houses that once
were filled with joy.
14 The palace will be empty;
people will leave the noisy city.
Strong cities and towers will be
empty.
Wild donkeys will love to live
there, and sheep will go there to
eat.

Things will Get Better

15 This will continue until God pours his
Spirit from above upon us.
Then the desert will be like a
fertile field
and the fertile field like a forest.
16 Justice will be found
even in the
desert,
and fairness will be
found in the
fertile fields.
17 That fairness will
bring peace,
and it will bring
calm and safety
for ever.
18 My people will live in
peaceful places
and in safe homes
and in calm places of rest.
19 Hail will destroy the forest,
and the city will be completely
destroyed.
20 But you will be happy as you plant
seeds near every stream
and as you let your cattle and
donkeys wander freely.

Warnings to Assyria and Promises to God's People

33 How terrible it will be for you who
destroy others
but have not been destroyed yet.
How terrible it will be for you, traitor,
whom no one has turned against
yet.
When you stop destroying,
others will destroy you.
When you stop turning against
others,
they will turn against you.

2 LORD, be kind to us.
We have waited for your help.
Give us strength every morning.
Save us when we are in trouble.
3 Your powerful voice makes people
run away in fear;
your greatness causes the nations
to run away.
4 Like locusts, your enemies will take
away the things you stole in
war.
Like locusts rushing about, they
will take your wealth.
5 The LORD is very great, and he lives
in a high place.
He fills Jerusalem with fairness
and justice.
6 He will be your safety.
He is full of
salvation,
wisdom and
knowledge.
Respect for the
LORD is the
greatest treasure.
7 See, brave men are
crying out in the
streets;
those who tried to bring peace are
crying loudly.
8 There is no one on the roads,
no one walking in the paths.
People have broken the agreements
they made.
They refuse to believe the proof
from witnesses.
No one respects other people.
9 The land is sick and dying;

> Justice will be found
> even in the desert,
> and fairness will be
> found in the fertile
> fields.
> — Isaiah 32:16

TEMPTATiONS
Isaiah 33:15–16

Livin' it

Go Ahead; Try It Is there something that you would like to do, even though you know it's wrong? What tempts you? Maybe it's playing a computer game at your friend's house – one that your parents consider too violent. Or maybe it's copying test answers from the kid in front of you. How do you keep from giving in to these temptations – or do you?

Are you sometimes tempted to do something wrong because everyone else is doing it and you don't want to look like a nerd? God wants us to follow his laws even though it may be the unpopular thing to do. (Read Esther 3:2–4, p. 650.) Are you willing to stand for what's right, even when no one else does?

MORE FAITH links

Facing the Consequences, **p. 232**

A Hidden Sin, **p. 285**

Just a Test, **p. 1373**

Just Say No! **p. 1660**

The Sin "Braker", **p. 1727**

Are you ever tempted to do something that you know is wrong? It could be something as simple as taking a chocolate biscuit that was meant for somebody else.

A good way to avoid temptation is by making yourself busy. How about connecting to these Faithlinks instead?

Can't Live Without It? Genesis 3, p. 7
- Is there anything you want that you would do *anything* to get? Link here to discover the disastrous results of giving in to temptation.

A Real Crowd-pleaser? Micah 2:6–11, p. 1222
- Have you ever been tempted to tell someone something you thought that person wanted to hear? Why? Did you want him to like you? Did it work?
- Are you a people-pleaser or a God-pleaser? Being a God-pleaser takes courage. God gives you the courage to go against the crowd if necessary.

The Temptation Fighter, Matthew 4:1–11, p. 1278
- How do you handle the temptation to do something wrong? Do you walk away? Blame your parents for not letting you do it? Or get busy doing something else? This Faithlink tells you what Jesus did when he was tempted by the devil. Following his example is the best defence against temptation.

my FAVOURITE links

Lebanon is ashamed and dying.
The Plain of Sharon is dry like the desert,
and the trees of Bashan and Carmel are dying.

10 The LORD says, "Now, I will stand up and show my greatness.
Now, I will become important to the people.
11 You people do useless things that are like hay and straw.
A destructive wind will burn you like fire.
12 People will be burned until their bones become like lime;
they will burn quickly like dry thorn-bushes."

13 You people in faraway lands, hear what I have done.
You people who are near me, learn about my power.
14 The sinners in Jerusalem are afraid; those who are separated from God shake with fear.
They say, "Can any of us live through this fire that destroys?
Who can live near this fire that burns on and on?"
15 A person who does what is right and speaks what is right,
who refuses to take money unfairly,
who refuses to take money to hurt others,
who does not listen to plans of murder,
who refuses to think about evil—
16 this is the kind of person who will be safe.
He will be protected as he would be in a high, walled city.
He will always have bread,
and he will not run out of water.
17 Your eyes will see the king in his beauty.
You will see the land that stretches far away.
18 You will think about the terror of the past:

33:15–16 Honesty Read how you should act.

"Where is that officer?
Where is the one who collected the taxes?
Where is the officer in charge of our defence towers?"
19 No longer will you see those proud people from other countries,
whose strange language you couldn't understand.

God will Protect Jerusalem

20 Look at Jerusalem, the city of our festivals.
Look at Jerusalem, that beautiful place of rest.
It is like a tent that will never be moved;
the pegs that hold her in place will never be pulled up,
and her ropes will never be broken.
21 There the LORD will be our Mighty One.
That land is a place with streams and wide rivers,
but there will be no enemy boats on those rivers;
no powerful ship will sail on them.
22 This is because the LORD is our judge.
The LORD makes our laws.
The LORD is our king.
He will save us.
23 You sailors from other lands, hear:
The ropes on your boats hang loose.
The mast is not held firm.
The sails are not spread open.
Then your great wealth will be divided.
There will be so much wealth that even the crippled people will carry off a share.
24 No one living in Jerusalem will say, "I am sick."
The people who live there will have their sins forgiven.

God will Punish His Enemies

34 All you nations, come near and listen.
Pay attention, you peoples!

The earth and all the people in it
should listen,
the world and everything in it.
2 The LORD is angry with all the
nations;
he is angry with their armies.
He will destroy them and kill them
all.
3 Their bodies will be thrown outside.
The stink will rise from the bodies,
and the blood will flow down the
mountains.
4 The sun, moon and stars will dissolve,
and the sky will be rolled up like a
scroll.
The stars will fall
like dead leaves from a vine
or dried-up figs from a fig tree.
5 The LORD's sword in the sky is
covered with blood.
It will cut through Edom
and destroy those people as an
offering to the LORD.
6 The LORD's sword will be covered
with blood;
it will be covered with fat,
with the blood from lambs and goats,
with the fat from the kidneys of
rams.
This is because the LORD decided
there will be a sacrifice in
Bozrah
and much killing in Edom.
7 The oxen will be
killed,
and the cattle and
the strong bulls.
The land will be filled
with their blood,
and the earth will
be covered with
their fat.
8 The LORD has chosen
a time for
punishment.
He has chosen a
year when people must pay for
the wrongs they did to
Jerusalem.
9 Edom's rivers will be like hot tar.
Its earth will be like burning
sulphur.
Its land will be like burning tar.

10 The fires will burn night and day;
the smoke will rise from Edom for
ever.
Year after year that land will be
empty;
no one will ever travel through that
land again.
11 Birds and small animals will own that
land,
and owls and ravens will live there.
God will make it an empty wasteland;
it will have nothing left in it.
12 The important people will have no
one left to rule them;
the leaders will all be gone.
13 Thorns will take over the strong
towers,
and wild bushes will grow in the
walled cities.
It will be a home for wild dogs
and a place for owls to live.
14 Desert animals will live with the
hyenas,
and wild goats will call to their
friends.
Night animals will live there
and find a place of rest.
15 Owls will nest there and lay eggs.
When the eggs open, the owls will
gather their young under their
wings.
Hawks will gather
with their own kind.

16 Look at the LORD's
scroll and read
what is written
there:
None of these will be
missing;
none will be
without its mate.
God has given the
command,
so his Spirit will
gather them
together.
17 God has divided the land among
them,
and he has given them each their
portion.
So they will own that land for ever
and will live there year after year.

> The LORD has chosen a time for punishment.
> – Isaiah 34:8

Isaiah 35:1

God will Comfort His People

35 The desert and dry land will become happy;
  the desert will be glad and will produce flowers.
Like a flower, **2** it will have many blooms.
  It will show its happiness, as if it were shouting with joy.
It will be beautiful like the forest of Lebanon,
  as beautiful as the hill of Carmel and the Plain of Sharon.
Everyone will see the glory of the LORD
  and the splendour of our God.

3 Make the weak hands strong
  and the weak knees steady.
4 Say to people who are frightened,
  "Be strong. Don't be afraid.
Look, your God will come,
  and he will punish your enemies.
He will make them pay for the wrongs they did,
  but he will save you."

5 Then the blind people will see again,
  and the deaf will hear.
6 Crippled people will jump like deer,
  and those who can't talk now will shout with joy.
Water will flow in the desert,
  and streams will flow in the dry land.
7 The burning desert will have pools of water,
  and the dry ground will have springs.
Where wild dogs once lived,
  grass and water plants will grow.
8 A road will be there;
  this highway will be called "The Road to Being Holy".
Evil people will not be allowed to walk on that road;
  only good people will walk on it. No fools will go on it.
9 No lions will be there,
  nor will dangerous animals be on that road.
They will not be found there.
That road will be for the people God saves;

FAITH links

JUSTICE SERVED
ISAIAH 35:3-4

In television programmes and films, one of the most satisfying things is to see a villain brought to justice. Isaiah wrote of a future time, when God would return. Finally the enemies of his people would be brought to justice. Isaiah did not say that God's people would be the ones to get even with their enemies. God would do the punishing.

Has someone made you angry recently? Feel like getting even? God claims revenge as part of his territory. That means only he can do it. When someone treats you unkindly, tell God all about it. Let him handle it.

Want to know how to handle that kid who always teases you? Check out these Faithlinks:

Can't Live Without It?
Genesis 3, p. 7

The Cover-up, Psalm 32:1-2, p. 733

Anger: Quick or Slow?
Psalm 86:15, p. 776

Quick to Forgive? Mark 11:25, p. 1349

Say What?! Ephesians 4:22-29, p. 1603

As Strong as Superman?
Philippians 4:13, p. 1615

10 the people the LORD has freed will return there. They will enter Jerusalem with joy, and their happiness will last for ever. Their gladness and joy will fill them completely, and sorrow and sadness will go far away.

35:10 Following God
Where will following God lead you?

The Assyrians Invade Judah

36 During Hezekiah's fourteenth year as king, Sennacherib king of Assyria attacked all the fortified cities of Judah and captured them. 2 The king of Assyria sent out his field commander with a large army from Lachish to King Hezekiah in Jerusalem. When the commander came near the waterway from the upper pool on the road where people do their laundry, he stopped. 3 Eliakim, Shebna and Joah went out to meet him. Eliakim son of Hilkiah was the palace manager, Shebna was the royal secretary and Joah son of Asaph was the recorder.

4 The field commander said to them, "Tell Hezekiah this:

"'The great king, the king of Assyria, says: What can you trust in now? 5 You say you have battle plans and power for war, but your words mean nothing. Whom are you trusting for help so that you turn against me? 6 Look, you are depending on Egypt to help you, but Egypt is like a splintered walking stick. If you lean on it for help, it will stab your hand and hurt you. The king of Egypt will hurt all those who depend on him. 7 You might say, "We are depending on the LORD our God," but Hezekiah destroyed the LORD's altars and the places of worship. Hezekiah told Judah and Jerusalem, "You must worship only at this one altar."

8 "'Now make an agreement with my master, the king of Assyria: I will give you 2,000 horses if you can find enough men to ride them. 9 You cannot defeat one of my master's least important officers, so why do you depend on Egypt to give you chariots and horsemen? 10 I have not come to attack and destroy this country without an order from the LORD. The LORD himself told me to come to this country and destroy it.'"

11 Then Eliakim, Shebna and Joah said to the field commander, "Please speak to us in the Aramaic language. We understand it. Don't speak to us in Hebrew, because the people on the city wall can hear you."

12 But the commander said, "My master did not send me to tell these things only to you and your king. He sent me to speak also to those people sitting on the wall who will have to eat their own dung and drink their own urine like you."

13 Then the commander stood and shouted loudly in the Hebrew language, "Listen to what the great king, the king of Assyria says. 14 The king says you should not let Hezekiah fool you, because he can't save you. 15 Don't let Hezekiah talk you into trusting the LORD by saying, 'The LORD will surely save us. This city won't be handed over to the king of Assyria.'

16 "Don't listen to Hezekiah. The king of Assyria says, 'Make peace with me, and come out of the city to me. Then everyone will be free to eat the fruit from his own grapevine and fig tree and to drink water from his own well. 17 After that I will come and take you to a land like your own—a land with grain and new wine, bread and vineyards.'

18 "Don't let Hezekiah fool you, saying, 'The LORD will save us.' Has a god of any other nation saved his people from the power of the king of Assyria? 19 Where are the gods of Hamath and Arpad? Where are the gods of Sepharvaim? They did not save Samaria from my power. 20 Not one of all the gods of these countries has saved his people from me. Neither can the LORD save Jerusalem from my power."

21 The people were silent. They didn't answer the commander at all, because King Hezekiah had ordered, "Don't answer him."

22 Then Eliakim, Shebna and Joah tore their clothes to show how upset they

were. (Eliakim son of Hilkiah was the palace manager, Shebna was the royal secretary and Joah son of Asaph was the recorder.) The three men went to Hezekiah and told him what the field commander had said.

Hezekiah Asks God to Help

37 When King Hezekiah heard the message, he tore his clothes and put on rough cloth to show how sad he was. Then he went into the Temple of the LORD. 2 Hezekiah sent Eliakim, the palace manager, and Shebna, the royal secretary, and the older priests to Isaiah. They were all wearing rough cloth when they came to Isaiah the prophet, the son of Amoz. 3 They told Isaiah, "This is what Hezekiah says: Today is a day of sorrow and punishment and disgrace, as when a child should be born, but the mother is not strong enough to give birth to it. 4 The king of Assyria sent his field commander to make fun of the living God. Maybe the LORD your God will hear what the commander said and will punish him for it. So pray for the few of us who are left alive."

5 When Hezekiah's officers came to Isaiah, 6 he said to them, "Tell your master this: The LORD says, 'Don't be afraid of what you have heard. Don't be frightened by the words the servants of the king of Assyria have spoken against me. 7 Listen! I am going to put a spirit in the king of Assyria. He will hear a report that will make him return to his own country, and I will cause him to die by the sword there.'"

8 The field commander heard that the king of Assyria had left Lachish. When he went back, he found the king fighting against the city of Libnah.

9 The king received a report that Tirhakah, the Cushite king of Egypt, was coming to attack him. When the king of Assyria heard this, he sent messengers to Hezekiah, saying, 10 "Tell Hezekiah king of Judah: don't be fooled by the god you trust. Don't believe him when he says Jerusalem will not be handed over to the king of Assyria. 11 You have heard what the kings of Assyria have done. They have completely defeated every country, so do not think you will be saved. 12 Did the gods of those people save them? My ancestors destroyed them, defeating the cities of Gozan, Haran and Rezeph, and the people of Eden living in Tel Assar. 13 Where are the kings of Hamath and Arpad? Where are the kings of Sepharvaim, Hena and Ivvah?"

Hezekiah Prays to the LORD

14 When Hezekiah received the letter from the messengers and read it, he went up to the Temple of the LORD. He spread the letter out before the LORD 15 and prayed to the LORD: 16 "LORD All-powerful, you are the God of Israel, whose throne is between the gold creatures with wings, only you are God of all the kingdoms of the earth. You made the heavens and the earth. 17 Hear, LORD, and listen. Open your eyes, LORD, and see. Listen to all the words Sennacherib has said to insult the living God.

18 "It is true, LORD, that the kings of Assyria have destroyed all these countries and their lands. 19 They have thrown the gods of these nations into the fire, but they were only wood and rock statues that people made. So the kings have destroyed them. 20 Now, LORD our God, save us from the king's power so that all the kingdoms of the earth will know that you, LORD, are the only God."

37:20 Troubles
Who will help you overcome problems?

The LORD Answers Hezekiah

21 Then Isaiah son of Amoz sent a message to Hezekiah that said, "This is what the LORD, the God of Israel, says: 'You prayed to me about Sennacherib king of Assyria. 22 So this is what the LORD has said against Sennacherib:
The people of Jerusalem
　hate you and make fun of you;
the people of Jerusalem
　laugh at you as you run away.
23 You have insulted me and spoken
　against me;
you have raised your voice
　against me.

You have a proud look on your face,
  which is against me, the Holy One
  of Israel!
24 You have sent your messengers to
  insult the Lord.
  You have said, "With my many
  chariots
  I have gone to the tops of the
  mountains,
  to the highest mountains of
  Lebanon.
  I have cut down its tallest cedars
  and its best pine trees.
  I have gone to its greatest heights
  and its best forests.
25 I have dug wells in foreign countries
  and drunk water there.
  By the soles of my feet,
  I have dried up all the rivers of
  Egypt."

26 "'King of Assyria, surely you have
  heard.
  Long ago I, the LORD, planned
  these things.
  Long ago I designed them,
  and now I have made them happen.
  I allowed you to turn those fortified
  cities
  into piles of rocks.
27 The people in those cities were weak;
  they were frightened and put to
  shame.
  They were like grass in the field,
  like tender, young grass,
  like grass on the housetop
  that is burned by the wind before it
  can grow.

28 "'I know when you rest,
  when you come and go,
  and how you rage against me.
29 Because you rage against me,
  and because I have heard your
  proud words,
  I will put my hook in your nose
  and my bit in your mouth.
  Then I will force you to leave my
  country
  the same way you came.'

30 "Then the LORD said, 'Hezekiah, I
will give you this sign:

This year you will eat the grain that
  grows wild,
  and the second year you will eat
  what grows wild from that.
  But in the third year, plant grain and
  harvest it.
  Plant vineyards and eat their fruit.
31 Some of the people in the family of
  Judah
  will escape.
  Like plants that take root,
  they will grow strong and have
  many children.
32 A few people will come out of
  Jerusalem alive;
  a few from Mount Zion will live.
  The strong love of the LORD All-
  powerful
  will make this happen.'

33 "So this is what the LORD says
about the king of Assyria:
  'He will not enter this city
  or even shoot an arrow here.
  He will not fight against it with
  shields
  or build a ramp to attack the city
  walls.
34 He will return to his country the
  same way he came,
  and he will not enter this city,'
  says the LORD.
35 'I will defend and save this city
  for my sake and for David, my
  servant.'"

36 Then the angel of the LORD went out and killed 185,000 men in the Assyrian camp. When the people got up early the next morning, they saw all the dead bodies. 37 So Sennacherib king of Assyria left and went back to Nineveh and stayed there.

38 One day as Sennacherib was worshipping in the temple of his god Nisroch, his sons Adrammelech and Sharezer killed him with a sword. Then they escaped to the land of Ararat. So Sennacherib's son Esarhaddon became king of Assyria.

Hezekiah's Illness

38 At that time Hezekiah became very sick; he was almost dead. The

prophet Isaiah son of Amoz went to see him and told him, "This is what the LORD says: Make arrangements, because you are not going to live, but die."

2 Hezekiah turned towards the wall and prayed to the LORD, 3 "LORD, please remember that I have always obeyed you. I have given myself completely to you and have done what you said was right." Then Hezekiah cried loudly.

4 Then the LORD spoke his word to Isaiah: 5 "Go to Hezekiah and tell him: 'This is what the LORD, the God of your ancestor David, says: I have heard your prayer and seen your tears. So I will add fifteen years to your life. 6 I will save you and this city from the king of Assyria; I will defend this city.

7 "'The LORD will do what he says. This is the sign from the LORD to show you: 8 the sun has made a shadow go down the stairway of Ahaz, but I will make it go back ten steps.'" So the shadow made by the sun went back up the ten steps it had gone down.

9 After Hezekiah king of Judah got well, he wrote this song:

10 I said, "I am in the middle of my life.
Do I have to go through the gates of death?
Will I have the rest of my life taken away from me?"
11 I said, "I will not see the LORD in the land of the living again.
I will not again see the people who live on the earth.
12 Like a shepherd's tent,
my home has been pulled down and taken from me.
I am finished
like the cloth a weaver rolls up and cuts from the loom."
In one day you brought me to this end.
13 All night I cried loudly.
Like a lion, he crushed all my bones.
In one day you brought me to this end.

14 I cried like a bird
and moaned like a dove.
My eyes became tired as I looked to the heavens.
Lord, I have troubles. Please help me."

15 What can I say?
The Lord told me what would happen and then made it happen.
I have had these troubles in my soul, so now I will be humble all my life.
16 Lord, because of you, people live.
Because of you, my spirit also lives; you made me well and let me live.
17 It was for my own good
that I had such troubles.
Because you love me very much, you did not let me die
but threw my sins
far away.
18 People in the place of the dead cannot praise you;
those who have died cannot sing praises to you;
those who die don't trust you to help them.
19 The people who are alive are the ones who praise you.
They praise you as I praise you today.
A father should tell his children that you provide help.

20 The LORD saved me,
so we will play songs on stringed instruments
in the Temple of the LORD
all the days of our lives.

21 Then Isaiah said, "Make a paste from figs and put it on Hezekiah's boil. Then he will get well." 22 Hezekiah then asked Isaiah, "What will be the sign? What will show that I will go up to the Temple of the LORD?"

Messengers from Babylon

39 At that time Merodach-Baladan son of Baladan was king of Bab-

---

38:12 loom A machine for making cloth from thread.

> **MAIL FROM GOD**
> **38:1–6**
> **Prayer**
> Check out this example of answered prayer.

ylon. He sent letters and a gift to Hezekiah, because he had heard that Hezekiah had been sick and was now well. 2 Hezekiah was pleased and showed the messengers what was in his storehouses: the silver, gold, spices, expensive perfumes, his swords and shields, and all his wealth. He showed them everything in his palace and in his kingdom.

3 Then Isaiah the prophet went to King Hezekiah and asked him, "What did these men say? Where did they come from?"

Hezekiah said, "They came from a faraway country—from Babylon."

4 So Isaiah asked him, "What did they see in your palace?"

Hezekiah said, "They saw everything in my palace. I showed them all my wealth."

5 Then Isaiah said to Hezekiah: "Listen to the words of the LORD All-powerful: 6 'In the future everything in your palace and everything your ancestors have stored up until this day will be taken away to Babylon. Nothing will be left,' says the LORD. 7 Some of your own children, those who will be born to you, will be taken away, and they will become servants in the palace of the king of Babylon."

8 Hezekiah told Isaiah, "These words from the LORD are good." He said this because he thought, "There will be peace and security in my lifetime."

Israel's Punishment will End

40 Your God says, "Comfort, comfort my people.
2 Speak kindly to the people of
    Jerusalem
    and tell them
  that their time of service is finished,
    that they have paid for their sins,
    that the LORD has punished
      Jerusalem
    twice for every sin they did."

3 This is the voice of one who calls out:
  "Prepare in the desert
    the way for the LORD.
  Make a straight road in the dry
      lands
    for our God.
4 Every valley should be raised up,
    and every mountain and hill should
      be made flat.
  The rough ground should be made
      level,
    and the rugged ground should be
      made smooth.
5 Then the glory of the LORD will be
      shown,
    and all people together will see it.
  The LORD himself said these things."

6 A voice says, "Cry out!"
  Then I said, "What shall I cry out?"

  "Say all people are like the grass,
    and all their glory is like the
      flowers of the field.
7 The grass dies and the flowers fall
    when the breath of the LORD blows
      on them.
  Surely the people
      are like grass.
8 The grass dies and
    the flowers fall,
    but the word of our
      God will live for
      ever."

> The grass dies and the flowers fall, but the word of our God will live for ever.
> – Isaiah 40:8

9 Jerusalem, you have
      good news to tell.
  Go up on a high
      mountain.
  Jerusalem, you have good news to
      tell.
  Shout out loud the good news.
  Shout it out and don't be afraid.
  Say to the towns of Judah,
    "Here is your God."
10 Look, the Lord GOD is coming with
      power
    to rule all the people.
  Look, he will bring reward for his
      people;
    he will have their payment with
      him.
11 He takes care of his people like a
      shepherd.
  He gathers them like lambs in his
      arms

and carries them close to him.
He gently leads the mothers of the
  lambs.

God is Supreme

12 Who has measured the oceans in the
  palm of his hand?
  Who has used his hand to measure
    the sky?
  Who has used a bowl to measure all
    the dust of the earth
  and scales to weigh the mountains
    and hills?
13 Who has known the mind of the
  LORD
  or been able to give him advice?
14 Whom did he ask for help?
  Who taught him the right way?
  Who taught him knowledge
  and showed him the way to
    understanding?

15 The nations are like one small drop in
    a bucket;
  they are no more than the dust on
    his measuring scales.
  To him the islands are no more
    than fine dust on his scales.
16 All the trees in Lebanon are not
    enough for the altar fires,
  and all the animals in Lebanon are
    not enough for burnt offerings.
17 Compared to the LORD all the nations
    are worth nothing;
  to him they are less than nothing.

18 Can you compare God to anything?
  Can you compare him to an image
    of anything?
19 An idol is formed by a craftsman,
  and a goldsmith covers it with gold
  and makes silver chains for it.
20 A poor person cannot buy those
    expensive statues,
  so he finds a tree that will not rot.
  Then he finds a skilled craftsman
  to make it into an idol that will not
    fall over.

21 Surely you know. Surely you have
    heard.
  Surely from the beginning
    someone told you.

Surely you understand how the
    earth was created.
22 God sits on his throne above the
    circle of the earth,
  and compared to him, people are
    like grasshoppers.
  He stretches out the skies like a
    piece of cloth
  and spreads them out like a tent to
    sit under.
23 He makes rulers unimportant
  and the judges of this world worth
    nothing.
24 They are like plants that are placed in
    the ground,
  like seeds that are planted.
  As soon as they begin to grow
    strong,
  he blows on them and they die,
  and the wind blows them away like
    chaff.

25 God, the Holy
  One, says,
  "Can you
  compare
  me to anyone?
  Is anyone equal
  to me?"
26 Look up to the skies.
  Who created all these stars?
  He leads out the army of heaven one
    by one
  and calls all the stars by name.
  Because he is strong and powerful,
  not one of them is missing.

27 People of Jacob, why do you
    complain?
  People of Israel, why do you say,
  "The LORD does not see what
    happens to me;
  he does not care if I am treated
    fairly"?
28 Surely you know.
  Surely you have heard.
  The LORD is the God who lives for
    ever,
  who created all the world.
  He does not become tired or need to
    rest.
  No one can understand how great
    his wisdom is.

eMAIL FROM GOD
40:25–28
Trust
Why can you trust God?

Isaiah 41:7 947

FAITH links

FLY LIKE AN EAGLE
ISAIAH 40:28-31

Could you run two miles and not get tired? If you're not sure, try it and see. If you were an eagle, you could easily go two miles – above the ground that is. An eagle glides along on currents of warm air. Gliding keeps it from having to constantly flap its wings and grow tired. That's why Isaiah mentioned eagles when he shared God's message of comfort. Whenever we try to work for God in our own strength, we grow tired. But trusting in God allows us to build up strength. His strength is like a current of warm air that causes us to soar.

Here are some more links to keep you going:

God's Pep Talk, Joshua 1:5–9, p. 276

Keep On Praying, 1 Samuel 1, p. 354

Standing for What's Right, Esther 3:2–4, p. 651

When the Going Gets Tough, Lamentations 3:22–27, p. 1079

Small Beginnings, Zechariah 4:10, p. 1255

Facing Your Fears, Matthew 8:23–27, p. 1288

---

30 Even children become tired and need to rest,
and young people trip and fall.
31 But the people who trust the LORD will become strong again.
They will rise up as an eagle in the sky;
they will run and not need rest;
they will walk and not become tired.

The LORD will Help Israel

41 The LORD says, "Faraway countries, listen to me.
Let the nations become strong.
Come to me and speak;
we will meet together to decide who is right.

2 "Who caused the one to come from the east?
Who gives him victories everywhere he goes?
The one who brought him gives nations over to him
and defeats kings.
He uses his sword, and kings become like dust.
He uses his bow, and they are blown away like chaff.
3 He chases them and is never hurt, going places he has never been before.
4 Who caused this to happen?
Who has controlled history since the beginning?
I, the LORD, am the one. I was here at the beginning,
and I will be here when all things are finished."
5 All you faraway places, look and be afraid;
all you places far away on the earth, shake with fear.
Come close and listen to me.
6 The workers help each other
and say to each other, "Be strong!"
7 The craftsman encourages the goldsmith,

EMAIL FROM GOD 41:4
God
How long has God been around?

---

29 He gives strength to those who are tired
and more power to those who are weak.

and the workman who smooths the
  metal with a hammer
encourages the one who shapes
  the metal.
He says, "This metal work is good."
He nails the statue to a base so it
  can't fall over.

Only the LORD Can Save Us

8 The LORD says, "People of Israel, you
    are my servants.
  People of Jacob, I chose you.
  You are from the family of my
    friend Abraham.
9 I took you from places far away on the
    earth
  and called you from a faraway
    country.
  I said, 'You are my servants.'
  I have chosen you and have not
    turned against you.
10 So don't worry, because I am with
    you.
  Don't be afraid, because I am your
    God.
  I will make you strong and will help
    you;
  I will support you with my right
    hand that saves you.

11 "All those people who are angry with
    you
    will be ashamed and disgraced.
  Those who are against you
    will disappear and be lost.
12 You will look for your enemies,
    but you will not find them.
  Those who fought against you
    will vanish completely.
13 I am the LORD your God,
    who holds your right hand,
  and I tell you, 'Don't be afraid.
    I will help you.'
14 You few people of Israel who are left,
    do not be afraid even though you
    are weak as a worm.
  I myself will help you," says the
    LORD.
  "The one who saves you is the
    Holy One of Israel.
15 Look, I have made you like a new
    threshing board
    with many sharp teeth.
So you will walk on mountains and
    crush them;
  you will make the hills like chaff.
16 You will throw them into the air, and
    the wind will carry them away;
  a windstorm will scatter them.
Then you will be happy in the LORD;
  you will be proud of the Holy One
    of Israel.

17 "The poor and needy people look for
    water,
    but they can't find any.
  Their tongues are dry with thirst.
But I, the LORD, will answer their
    prayers;
  I, the God of Israel, will not leave
    them to die.
18 I will make rivers flow on the dry
    hills
  and springs flow through the
    valleys.
  I will change the desert into a lake of
    water
  and the dry land into fountains of
    water.
19 I will make trees grow in the desert—
    cedars, acacia, myrtle and olive
    trees.
  I will put pine, fir and cypress trees
    growing together in the desert.
20 People will see these things and
    understand;
  they will think carefully about
    these things and learn
  that the LORD's power did this,
    that the Holy One of Israel made
    these things."

The Lord Challenges False Gods

21 The LORD says, "Present your case."
  The King of Jacob says, "Tell me
    your arguments.
22 Bring in your idols to tell us
    what is going to happen.
  Have them tell us what happened in
    the beginning.
  Then we will think about these
    things,
  and we will know how they will
    turn out.
  Or tell us what will happen in the
    future.

23 Tell us what is coming next
so we will believe that you are
gods.
Do something, whether it is good or
bad,
and make us afraid.
24 You gods are less than nothing;
you can't do anything.
Those who worship you should be
hated.

25 "I have brought someone to come out
of the north.*
I have called by name a man from
the east, and he knows me.
He walks on kings as if they were
mud,
just as a potter walks on the clay.
26 Who told us about this before it
happened?
Who told us ahead of time so we
could say, 'He was right'?
None of you told us anything;
none of you told us before it
happened;
no one heard you tell about it.
27 I, the LORD, was the first one to tell
Jerusalem that the people were
coming home.
I sent a messenger to Jerusalem
with the good news.
28 I look at the idols, but there is not
one that can answer.
None of them can give advice;
none of them can answer my
questions.
29 Look, all these idols are false.
They cannot do anything;
they are worth nothing.

The Lord's Special Servant

42 "Here is my servant, the one I
support.
He is the one I chose, and I am
pleased with him.
I have put my Spirit upon him,
and he will bring justice to all
nations.
2 He will not cry out or yell
or speak loudly in the streets.
3 He will not break a crushed blade of
grass
or put out even a weak flame.

He will truly bring justice;
4 he will not lose hope or give up
until he brings justice to the world.
And people far away will trust his
teachings."

5 God, the LORD, said these things.
He created the skies and stretched
them out.
He spread out the earth and
everything on it.
He gives life to all people on earth,
to everyone who walks on the
earth.
6 The LORD says, "I, the LORD, called
you to do right,
and I will hold your hand
and protect you.
You will be the sign of my
agreement with the people,
a light to shine for all people.
7 You will help the blind to see.
You will free those who are in
prison,
and you will lead those who live in
darkness out of their prison.

8 "I am the LORD. That is my name.
I will not give my glory to
another;
I will not let idols take the praise
that should be mine.
9 The things I said would happen have
happened,
and now I tell you about new
things.
Before those things happen,
I tell you about them."

A Song of Praise to the LORD

10 Sing a new song to the LORD;
sing his praise everywhere on the
earth.
Praise him, you people who sail on
the seas and you animals who
live in them.
Praise him, you people living in
faraway places.
11 The deserts and their cities should
praise him.

41:25 someone . . . north This probably means
Cyrus, a king of Persia.

The settlements of Kedar should
  praise him.
The people living in Sela should sing
  for joy;
    they should shout from the
      mountain tops.
12 They should give glory to the LORD.
  People in faraway lands should
    praise him.
13 The LORD will march out like a strong
    soldier;
  he will be excited like a man ready
    to fight a war.
He will shout out the battle cry
  and defeat his enemies.

14 The LORD says, "For a long time I
    have said nothing;
  I have been quiet and held myself
    back.
But now I will cry out
  and strain like a woman giving
    birth to a child.
15 I will destroy the hills and
    mountains
  and dry up all their plants.
I will make the rivers become dry
    land
  and dry up the pools of water.
16 Then I will lead the blind along a way
    they never knew;
  I will guide them along paths they
    have not known.
I will make the darkness become
    light for them,
  and the rough ground smooth.
These are the things I will do;
  I will not leave my people.
17 But those who trust in idols,
  who say to their statues,
'You are our gods'
  will be rejected in disgrace.

Israel Refused to Listen to the LORD

18 "You who are deaf, hear me.
  You who are blind, look and see.
19 No one is more blind than my servant
    Israel
  or more deaf than the messenger I
    send.
No one is more blind than the person
  I own

or more blind than the servant of
  the LORD.
20 Israel, you have seen much, but you
    have not obeyed.
  You hear, but you refuse to listen."
21 The LORD made his teachings
    wonderful,
  because he is good.
22 These people have been defeated and
    robbed.
  They are trapped in pits
    or locked up in prison.
Like robbers, enemies have taken
    them away,
  and there is no one to save them.
Enemies carried them off,
  and no one said, "Bring them
    back."

23 Will any of you listen to this?
  Will you listen carefully in the
    future?
24 Who let the people of Jacob be
    carried off?
  Who let robbers take Israel away?
The LORD allowed this to happen,
  because we sinned against him.
We did not live the way he wanted us
    to live
  and did not obey his teaching.
25 So he became very angry with us
  and brought terrible wars against
    us.
It was as if the people of Israel had
    fire all around them,
  but they didn't know what was
    happening.
It was as if they were burning,
  but they didn't pay any attention.

God is Always with His People

43 Now this is what the LORD says.
He created you, people of Jacob;
  he formed you, people of Israel.
He says, "Don't
  be afraid,
  because I
    have saved
    you.
I have called you
    by name, and
    you are mine.

43:1-2
Fears
Check to see if God is always with you.

FEARS
Isaiah 43:1–2

Scared to Death! What makes you break out in a cold sweat or want to run away and hide? Creepy, crawly things? The biggest bully in school? Or giving a speech in front of your class? What do you do when you're so afraid your stomach is turning cartwheels? Do you try to stop thinking about it? That's pretty hard to do, isn't it?

Isaiah had a better solution to overcoming fears. He said to focus on God and what he does for you. Then you will experience true peace. (Check out Isaiah 26:3.) How can you trust God to chase out the fear monsters?

Deborah, a leader of Israel, trusted God to handle a very scary situation. However, the commander of her army, Barak, didn't. Find out what happened by linking to Judges 4, p. 315. When you face something scary, are you a Barak or a Deborah?

MORE FAITH links

God's Pep Talk, **p. 276**

Real Faith or Really Scared? **p. 315**

Uprooted by Change, **p. 1205**

A Safe Place, **p. 1231**

Fear-Fighters, **p. 1652**

> Boy, there's a lot of stuff about that can be scary – thunderstorms, scary films, spiders, big dogs. Who do you think can help chase those fear monsters away?
>
> Read on to find out how God can help you fight your fears!

Big Lack Attack, 2 Kings 4:1–7, p. 480
- Link here to discover why you don't need to worry about running out of what you need.

Who Ya' Gonna Call? Psalm 3:4, p. 711
- What's the most scared you've ever been? What did you do? Did you call someone?
- David's life was in danger and he was really scared. Link here to find out how his solution can help you when you're scared.

A Word About Worry, Matthew 6:25–34, p. 1284
- Fears and worry usually go together. What do you worry about? How much does worrying help you? Link here to discover what Jesus has to say about worries.

Facing Your Fears, Matthew 8:23–27, p. 1288
- Imagine you are in a small boat in the middle of a large lake. Suddenly a fierce storm threatens to sink the boat – and you can't swim! How would you feel? Tell Jesus about your fears. He can handle any "storms" that come into your life.

my FAVOURITE links

2 When you pass through the waters, I
    will be with you.
  When you cross rivers, you will not
    drown.
  When you walk through fire, you will
    not be burnt,
  nor will the flames hurt you.
3 This is because I, the LORD, am your
    God,
  the Holy One of Israel, your
    Saviour.
  I gave Egypt to pay for you,
    and I gave Cush and Seba to make
    you mine.
4 Because you are precious to me,
  because I give you honour and love
    you,
  I will give other people in your place;
  I will give other nations to save
    your life.
5 Don't be afraid, because I am with
    you.
  I will bring your children from the
    east
  and gather you from the west.
6 I will tell the north: give my people to
    me.
  I will tell the south: don't keep my
    people in prison.
  Bring my sons from far away
  and my daughters from faraway
    places.
7 Bring to me all the people who are
    mine,
  whom I made for my glory,
  whom I formed and made."

Judah is God's Witness

8 Bring out the people who have eyes
    but don't see
  and those who have ears but don't
    hear.
9 All the nations gather together,
  and all the people come together.
  Which of their gods said this would
    happen?
  Which of their gods can tell what
    happened in the beginning?
  Let them bring their witnesses to
    prove they were right.
  Then others will say, "It is true."
10 The LORD says, "You are my
    witnesses
  and the servant I chose.
  I chose you so you would know and
    believe me,
  so you would understand that I am
    the true God.
  There was no God before me,
  and there will be no God after me.
11 I myself am the LORD;
  I am the only Saviour.
12 I myself have spoken to you, saved
    you and told you these things.
  It was not some foreign god among
    you.
  You are my witnesses, and I am
    God,"
  says the LORD.
13 "I have always been God.
  No one can save people from my
    power;
  when I do something, no one can
    change it."
14 This is what the LORD, who saves
    you,
  the Holy One of Israel, says:
  "I will send armies to Babylon for
    you,
  and I will knock down all its locked
    gates.
  The Babylonians will shout their cries
    of sorrow.
15 I am the LORD, your Holy One,
  the Creator of Israel, your King."

God will Save His People Again

16 This is what the LORD says.
  He is the one who made a road
    through the sea
  and a path through rough waters.
17 He is the one who defeated the
    chariots and horses
  and the mighty armies.
  They fell together and will never rise
    again.
  They were destroyed as a flame is
    put out.
18 The LORD says, "Forget what
    happened before,
  and do not think about the past.
19 Look at the new thing I am going to
    do.
  It is already happening. Don't you
    see it?

I will make a road in the desert
    and rivers in the dry land.
20 Even the wild animals will be thankful
    to me—
    the wild dogs and owls.
They will honour me when I put
    water in the desert
    and rivers in the dry land
to give water to my people, the ones I
    chose.
21 The people I made
    will sing songs to praise me.

22 "People of Jacob, you have not called
    to me;
    people of Israel, you have become
    tired of me.
23 You have not brought me your
    sacrifices of sheep
    nor honoured me with your
    sacrifices.
I did not weigh you down with
    sacrifices to offer
    or make you tired with incense to
    burn.
24 So you did not buy incense for me;
    you did not freely bring me fat
    from your sacrifices.
Instead you have weighed me down
    with your many sins;
    you have made me tired of your
    many wrongs.

25 "I, I am the One who forgives all your
    sins, for my sake;
    I will not remember your sins.
26 But you should remind me.
    Let's meet and decide what is right.
    Tell what you have done and show
    you are right.
27 Your first father sinned,
    and your leaders have turned
    against me.
28 So I will make your holy rulers
    unholy.
I will bring destruction on the
    people of Jacob,
    and I will let Israel be insulted."

The Lord is the Only God

44 The LORD says, "People of Jacob, you are my servants. Listen to me!
People of Israel, I chose you."
2 This is what the LORD says, who
    made you,
    who formed you in your mother's
    body,
    who will help you:
"People of Jacob, my servants, don't
    be afraid.
Israel, I chose you.
3 I will pour out water for the thirsty
    land
    and make streams flow on dry land.
I will pour out my Spirit into your
    children
    and my blessing on your
    descendants.
4 Your children will grow like a tree in
    the grass,
    like poplar trees growing beside
    streams of water.
5 One person will say, 'I belong to the
    LORD,'
    and another will use the name
    Jacob.
Another will sign his name 'I am the
    LORD's,'
    and another will use the name
    Israel."

6 The LORD, the king of Israel,
    is the LORD All-powerful, who
    saves Israel.
This is what he says: "I am the
    beginning and the end.
I am the only God.
7 Who is a god like me?
    That god should come and prove it.
Let him tell and explain all that has
    happened since I set up my
    ancient people.
He should also tell what will
    happen in the future.
8 Don't be afraid! Don't worry!
    I have always told you what will
    happen.
You are my witnesses.
    There is no other God but me.
    I know of no other Rock; I am the
    only One."

Idols are Useless

9 Some people make idols, but they are
    worth nothing.

FAITH links

A USELESS THING
ISAIAH 44:9, 18-20

Would you expect a telegraph pole to offer you comfort when you're feeling sad? A telegraph pole is only useful for holding up phone lines. Yet the Israelites worshipped man-made wooden objects. Isaiah warned them against worshipping false gods. The false gods had replaced God in their hearts.

Worshipping a block of wood may seem silly. However, there are things in *our* lives that can seem more important to us than God. For example, we might think of money, popularity and possessions more than we think about God. To God, these things are just as useless as a block of wood. God wants us to worship only him.

What You Value, Genesis 25:21–34, p. 34

Idol Talk, Exodus 32, p. 118

Sitting on the Fence, 1 Kings 18, p. 464

How Big Is God? Job 38—41, p. 703

Bragging Rights, Jeremiah 9:23–24, p. 1005

That's False! 2 John 7–11, p. 1722

People treasure them, but they are useless.
Those people are witnesses for the statues, but those people cannot see.
They know nothing, so they will be ashamed.
10 Who made these gods?
Who made these useless idols?
11 The workmen who made them will be ashamed,
because they are only human.
If they all would come together,
they would all be ashamed and afraid.

12 One workman uses tools to heat iron,
and he works over hot coals.
With his hammer he beats the metal
and makes a statue,
using his powerful arms.
But when he becomes hungry, he loses his power.
If he does not drink water, he becomes tired.

13 Another workman uses a line and a compass
to draw on the wood.
Then he uses his chisels to cut a statue
and his calipers to measure the statue.
In this way, the workman makes the wood look exactly like a person,
and this statue of a person sits in the house.
14 He cuts down cedars
or cypress or oak trees.
Those trees grew by their own power in the forest.
Or he plants a pine tree, and the rain makes it grow.
15 Then he burns the tree.
He uses some of the wood for a fire
to keep himself warm.
He also starts a fire to bake his bread.
But he uses part of the wood to make a god, and then he worships it!
He makes the idol and bows down to it.
16 The man burns half of the wood in the fire.
He uses the fire to cook his meat,
and he eats the meat until he is full.

He also burns the wood to keep
    himself warm. He says,
    "Good! Now I am warm. I can see
    because of the fire's light."
17 But he makes a statue from the wood
    that is left and calls it his god.
    He bows down to it and worships
    it.
    He prays to it and says,
    "You are my god. Save me!"
18 Those people don't know what they
    are doing. They don't
    understand!
    It is as if their eyes are covered so
    they can't see.
    Their minds don't understand.
19 They have not thought about these
    things;
    they don't understand.
    They have never thought to
    themselves,
    "I burnt half of the wood in the
    fire
    and used the hot coals to bake my
    bread.
    I cooked and ate my meat.
    And I used the wood that was left to
    make this hateful thing.
    I am worshiping a block of wood!"
20 He doesn't know what he is doing;
    his confused mind leads him the
    wrong way.
    He cannot save himself
    or say, "This statue I am holding is
    a false god."

The Lord is the True God

21 "People of Jacob, remember these
    things!
    People of Israel, remember you are
    my servants.
    I made you, and you are my servants.
    So Israel, I will not forget you.
22 I have swept away your sins like a big
    cloud;
    I have removed your sins like a
    cloud that disappears into the
    air.
    Come back to me because I saved
    you."
23 Skies, sing for joy because the Lord
    did great things!

Earth, shout for joy, even in your
    deepest parts!
Sing, you mountains, with thanks to
    God.
Sing, too, you trees in the forest!
The Lord saved the people of Jacob!
    He showed his glory when he
    saved Israel.
24 This is what the Lord says, who
    saved you,
    who formed you in your mother's
    body:
    "I, the Lord, made everything,
    stretching out the skies by myself
    and spreading out the earth all
    alone.
25 I show that the lying prophets' signs
    are false;
    I make fools of those who do
    magic.
    I confuse even wise men;
    they think they know much, but I
    make them look foolish.
26 I make the messages of my servants
    come true;
    I make the advice of my
    messengers come true.
    I say to Jerusalem,
    'People will live in you again!'
    I say to the towns of Judah,
    'You will be built again!'
    I say to Jerusalem's ruins,
    'I will repair you.'
27 I tell the deep waters, 'Become dry!
    I will make your streams become
    dry!'
28 I say of Cyrus,ⁿ 'He is my shepherd
    and will do all that I want him to
    do.
    He will say to Jerusalem, "You will
    be built again!"
    He will tell the Temple, "Your
    foundations will be rebuilt."'"

God Chooses Cyrus to Free Israel

45 This is what the Lord says to
    Cyrus, his appointed king:
    "I hold your right hand
    and will help you defeat nations
    and take away other kings' power.

44:28 **Cyrus** A king of Persia who ruled from about 550 to 530 B.C.

I will open doors for you
    so city gates will not stop you.
2 I will go before you
    and make the mountains flat.
  I will break down the bronze gates of
      the cities
    and cut through their iron bars.
3 I will give you the wealth that is
      stored away
    and the hidden riches
  so you will know I am the LORD,
    the God of Israel, who calls you by
      name.
4 I do these things for my servants, the
      people of Jacob,
    and for my chosen people, the
      Israelites.
  Cyrus, I call you by name,
    and I give you a title of honour
    even though you don't know me.
5 I am the LORD. There
      is no other God;
    I am the only God.
  I will make you
      strong,
    even though you
      don't know me,
6 so that everyone will
      know
    there is no other
      God.
  From the east to the
      west they will know
    I alone am the LORD.
7 I made the light and the darkness.
  I bring peace, and I cause troubles.
    I, the LORD, do all these things.

8 "Sky above, make victory fall like
      rain;
    clouds, pour down victory.
  Let the earth receive it,
    and let salvation grow,
    and let victory grow with it.
  I, the LORD, have created it.

9 "How terrible it will be for those who
      argue with the God who made
      them.
  They are like a piece of broken
      pottery among many pieces.
  The clay does not ask the potter,
    'What are you doing?'

The thing that is made doesn't say to
      its maker,
    'You have no hands.'
10 How terrible it will be for the child
      who says to his father,
    'Why are you giving me life?'
  How terrible it will be for the child
      who says to his mother,
    'Why are you giving birth to me?'"

11 This is what the LORD,
    the Holy One of Israel, and its
      Maker, says:
  "You ask me about what will happen.
  You question me about my
      children.
  You give me orders about what I
      have made.
12 I made the earth
    and all the people living on it.
  With my own hands I
      stretched out the
      skies,
    and I commanded
      all the armies in
      the sky.
13 I will bring Cyrus to
      do good things,
    and I will make his
      work easy.
  He will rebuild my
      city
    and set my people free
    without any payment or reward.
  The LORD All-powerful says this."

14 The LORD says,
  "The goods made in Egypt and Cush
    and the tall people of Seba
  will come to you
    and will become yours.
  The Sabeans will walk behind you,
    coming along in chains.
  They will bow down before you
    and pray to you, saying,
  'God is with you,
    and there is no other God.'"

15 God and Saviour of Israel,
    you are a God that people cannot
      see.
16 All the people who make idols will be
      put to great shame;

> I am the LORD. There is no other God; I am the only God.
> — Isaiah 45:5

they will go off together in disgrace.
17 But Israel will be saved by the LORD, and that salvation will continue for ever.
Never again will Israel be put to shame.

18 The LORD created the heavens.
He is the God who formed the earth and made it.
He did not want it to be empty, but he wanted life on the earth.
This is what the LORD says:
"I am the LORD. There is no other God.
19 I did not speak in secret or hide my words in some dark place.
I did not tell the family of Jacob to look for me in empty places.
I am the LORD, and I speak the truth;
I say what is right.
20 "You people who have escaped from other nations, gather together and come before me;
come near together.
People who carry idols of wood don't know what they are doing.
They pray to a god who cannot save them.
21 Tell these people to come to me.
Let them talk about these things together.
Who told you long ago that this would happen?
Who told about it long ago?
I, the LORD, said these things.
There is no other God besides me.
I am the only good God. I am the Saviour.
There is no other God.
22 "All people everywhere, follow me and be saved.
I am God. There is no other God.
23 I will make a promise by my own power,
and my promise is true;
what I say will not be changed.
I promise that everyone will bow before me
and will promise to follow me.
24 People will say about me, 'Goodness and power
come only from the LORD.'"
Everyone who has been angry with him
will come to him and be ashamed.
25 But with the LORD's help, the people of Israel
will be found to be good,
and they will praise him.

False Gods are Useless

46 Bel and Nebo bow down.
Their idols are carried by animals.
The statues are only heavy loads that must be carried;
they only make people tired.
2 These gods will all bow down.
They cannot save themselves
but will all be carried away like prisoners.
3 "Family of Jacob, listen to me!
All you people from Israel who are still alive, listen!
I have carried you since you were born;
I have taken care of you from your birth.
4 Even when you are old, I will be the same.
Even when your hair has turned grey, I will take care of you.
I made you and will take care of you.
I will carry you and save you.

5 "Can you compare me to anyone?
No one is equal to me or like me.
6 Some people are rich with gold
and weigh their silver on the scales.

> I made you and will take care of you. I will carry you and save you.
> – Isaiah 46:4

They hire a goldsmith, and he makes
  it into a god.
    Then they bow down and worship it.
7 They put it on their shoulders and
  carry it.
    They set it in its place, and there it
      stands;
    it cannot move from its place.
    People may yell at it, but it cannot
      answer.
    It cannot save them from their
      troubles.

8 "Remember this, and do not forget it!
    Think about these things, you who
      turn against God.
9 Remember what happened long ago.
    Remember that I am God, and
      there is no other God.
    I am God, and there is no one like
      me.
10 From the beginning I told you what
    would happen in the end.
    A long time ago I told you things
      that have not yet happened.
    When I plan something, it happens.
    What I want to do, I will do.
11 I am calling a man from the east to
    carry out my plan;
    he will come like a hawk from a
      country far away.
    I will make what I have said come
      true;
    I will do what I have planned.
12 Listen to me, you stubborn people,
    who are far from what is right.
13 I will soon do the things that are
    right.
    I will bring salvation soon.
    I will save Jerusalem
      and bring glory to Israel."

God will Destroy Babylon

47 The LORD says, "City of Babylon,
      go down and sit in the earth.
    People of Babylon, sit on the ground.
    You are no longer the ruler.
    You will no longer be called
      tender or beautiful.
2   You must use large stones to grind
      grain into flour.
    Remove your veil and your nice
      skirts.
    Uncover your legs and cross the
      rivers.
3 People will see your nakedness;
    they will see your shame.
    I will punish you;
    I will punish every one of you."

4 Our Saviour is named the LORD All-
    powerful;
    he is the Holy One of Israel.

5 "Babylon, sit in darkness and say
    nothing.
    You will no longer be called the
      queen of kingdoms.
6 I was angry with my people,
    so I rejected those who belonged
      to me.
    I gave them to you,
    but you showed them no mercy.
    You even made the old people
      work very hard.
7 You said, 'I will live for ever
    as the queen.'
    But you did not think about these
      things
    or consider what would happen.

8 "Now, listen, you lover of pleasure.
    You think you are safe.
    You tell yourself,
    'I am the only important person.
    I will never be a widow
    or lose my children.'
9 Two things will happen to you
    suddenly, in a single day.
    You will lose your children and
      your husband.
    These things will truly happen to
      you,
    in spite of all your magic,
    in spite of your powerful tricks.
10 You do evil things, but you feel safe
    and say, 'No one sees what I do.'
    Your wisdom and knowledge
      have fooled you.
    You say to yourself,
    'I am God, and no one is equal to
      me.'
11 But troubles will come to you,
    and you will not know how to stop
      them.
    Disaster will fall on you,

and you will not be able to keep it
  away.
You will be destroyed quickly;
  you will not even see it coming.
12 "Keep on using your tricks
  and doing all your magic
  that you have used since you were
    young.
Maybe they will help you;
  maybe you will be able to scare
    someone.
13 You are tired of the advice you have
    received.
So let those who study the sky—
  those who tell the future by looking at
    the stars and the new moons—
  let them save you from what is
    about to happen to you.
14 But they are like straw;
  fire will quickly burn them up.
They cannot save themselves
  from the power of the fire.
They are not like coals that give
    warmth
  nor like a fire that you may sit
    beside.
15 You have worked with these people,
  and they have been with you since
    you were young,
  but they will not be able to help
    you.
Everyone will go his own way,
  and there will be no one left to save
    you."

God Controls the Future

48 The LORD says, "Family of Jacob,
    listen to me.
  You are called Israel,
  and you come from the family of
    Judah.
  You swear by the LORD's name
  and praise the God of Israel,
  but you are not honest or sincere.
2 You call yourselves people of the holy
    city,
  and you depend on the God of
    Israel,
  who is named the LORD All-
    powerful.
3 Long ago I told you what would
    happen.

I said these things and made them
    known;
  suddenly I acted, and these things
    happened.
4 I knew you were stubborn;
  your neck was like an iron
    muscle,
  and your head was like bronze.
5 So a long time ago I told you about
    these things;
  I told you about them before they
    happened
  so you couldn't say, 'My idols did
    this,
  and my wooden and metal statues
    made these things happen.'
6 "You heard and saw everything that
    happened,
  so you should tell this news to
    others.
Now I will tell you about new things,
  hidden things that you don't know
    yet.
7 These things are happening now, not
    long ago;
  you have not heard about them
    before today.
So you cannot say, 'We already knew
    about that.'
8 But you have not heard me; you have
    not understood.
Even long ago you did not listen to
    me.
I knew you would surely turn against
    me;
  you have fought against me since
    you were born.
9 But for my own sake I will be
    patient.
People will praise me for not
    becoming angry
  and destroying you.
10 I have made you pure, but not by fire,
    as silver is made pure.
I have purified you by giving you
    troubles.
11 I do this for myself, for my own
    sake.
I will not let people speak evil
    against me,
  and I will not let some god take my
    glory.

Israel will be Free

12 "People of Jacob, listen to me.
   People of Israel, I have called you
      to be my people.
   I am God;
      I am the beginning and the end.
13 I made the earth with my own hands.
   With my right hand I spread out
      the skies.
   When I call them,
      they come together before me."

14 All of you, come
      together and
      listen.
   None of the gods
      said these things
      would happen.
   The LORD has chosen
      someone
      to attack the
      Babylonians;
   he will carry out
      his wishes
      against Babylon.

15 "I have spoken; I have called him."
   I have brought him, and I will
      make him successful.
16 Come to me and listen to this.
   From the beginning I have spoken
      openly.
   From the time it began, I was
      there."

   Now, the Lord GOD
      has sent me with his Spirit.

17 This is what the LORD, who saves
      you,
   the Holy One of Israel, says:
   "I am the LORD your God,
      who teaches you to do what is
         good,
      who leads you in the way you
         should go.
18 If you had obeyed me,
      you would have had peace like a
         full-flowing river.
   Good things would have flowed to
      you like the waves of the sea.
19 You would have had many children,
      as many as the grains of sand.
   They would never have died out
      nor been destroyed."

20 My people, leave Babylon!
   Run from the Babylonians!
   Tell this news with shouts of joy to
      the people;
   spread it everywhere on earth.
   Say, "The LORD has saved his
      servants, the people of Jacob."
21 They did not become thirsty when he
      led them through the
      deserts.
   He made water
      flow from a rock
      for them.
   He split the rock,
      and water flowed
      out.

22 "There is no peace
      for evil people,"
      says the LORD.

> "There is no peace for evil people," says the LORD.
> — Isaiah 48:22

God Calls His Special Servant

49 All of you people in faraway
      places, listen to me.
   Listen, all you nations far away.
   Before I was born, the LORD called
      me to serve him.
   The LORD named me while I was
      still in my mother's body.
2 He made my tongue like a sharp sword.
   He hid me in the shadow of his
      hand.
   He made me like a sharp arrow.
   He hid me in the holder for his
      arrows.
3 He told me, "Israel, you are my
      servant.
   I will show my glory through you."
4 But I said, "I have worked hard for
      nothing;
   I have used all my power, but I did
      nothing useful.
   But the LORD will decide what my
      work is worth;
   God will decide my reward."
5 The LORD made me in the body of my
      mother

48:15 him This probably refers to Cyrus king of Persia.

to be his servant,
to lead the people of Jacob back to him
so that Israel might be gathered to
him.
The LORD will honour me,
and I will get my strength from my
God.
6 Now he told me,
"You are an important servant to me
to bring back the tribes of Jacob,
to bring back the people of Israel
who are left alive.
But, more importantly, I will make
you a light for all nations
to show people all over the world
the way to be saved."

7 The LORD who saves you
is the Holy One of Israel.
He speaks to the one who is hated by
the people,
to the servant of rulers.
This is what he says: "Kings will see
you and stand to honour you;
great leaders will bow down before
you,
because the LORD can be trusted.
He is the Holy One of Israel, who
has chosen you."

The Day of Salvation

8 This is what the LORD says:
"At the right time I will hear your
prayers.
On the day of salvation I will help
you.
I will protect you,
and you will be the sign of my
agreement with the people.
You will bring back the people to the
land
and give the land that is now
ruined back to its owners.
9 You will tell the prisoners, 'Come out
of your prison.'
You will tell those in darkness,
'Come into the light.'
The people will eat beside the roads,
and they will find food even on
bare hills.
10 They will not be hungry or thirsty.
Neither the hot sun nor the desert
wind will hurt them.

FAITH links

A MOTHER'S LOVE
ISAIAH 49:13-16

Do you ever have to remind your mother or stepmother of your name? Not likely. Even if you come from a family of many children and your mum slips and calls you by your brother's name, you know that your mum knows who you are. She could never forget you.

Isaiah explained that God's love for his people is like a mother's love. To him you are as unforgettable as you are to your mother. God says that even *if* a mother could forget her children (not likely!), he would never forget his people. So, on Mother's Day, give God a thought, too.

Surf on to see how much God loves you:

The Perfect Sacrifice, Leviticus 1—7, p. 135

Your Heavenly Dad, Psalm 103:13, p. 786

What's in a Name? Isaiah 9:6, p. 908

A Hopeful Name, Hosea 1:3–11, p. 1172

Prove It! Matthew 16:1–4, p. 1302

The Doubt Remover, Romans 10:8–10, p. 1533

The God who comforts them will lead
them
and guide them by springs of
water.

11 I will make my mountains into roads,
and the roads will be raised up.
12 Look, people are coming to me from far away,
from the north and from the west,
from Aswan in southern Egypt."

13 Heavens and earth, be happy.
Mountains, shout with joy,
because the LORD comforts his people
and will have pity on those who suffer.

Jerusalem and Her Children

14 But Jerusalem said, "The LORD has left me;
the Lord has forgotten me."

15 The LORD answers, "Can a woman forget the baby she nurses?
Can she feel no kindness for the child to which she gave birth?
Even if she could forget her children, I will not forget you.
16 See, I have written your name on my hand.
Jerusalem, I always think about your walls.
17 Your children will soon return to you,
and the people who defeated you and destroyed you will leave.
18 Look up and look around you.
All your children are gathering to return to you."
The LORD says, "As surely as I live, your children will be like jewels
that a bride wears proudly.

19 "You were destroyed and defeated,
and your land was made useless.
But now you will have more people than the land can hold,
and those people who destroyed you will be far away.
20 Children were born to you while you were sad,
but they will say to you,
'This place is too small for us.
Give us a bigger place to live.'
21 Then you will say to yourself,
'Who gave me all these children?
I was sad and lonely,
defeated and separated from my people.
So who reared these children?
I was left all alone.
Where did all these children come from?'"

22 This is what the Lord GOD says:
"See, I will lift my hand to signal the nations;
I will raise my banner for all the people to see.
Then they will bring your sons back to you in their arms,
and they will carry your daughters on their shoulders.
23 Kings will teach your children,
and daughters of kings will take care of them.
They will bow down before you
and kiss the ground at your feet.
Then you will know I am the LORD.
Anyone who trusts in me will not be disappointed."

24 Can the wealth a soldier wins in war be taken away from him?
Can a prisoner be freed from a powerful soldier?
25 This is what the LORD says:
"The prisoners will be taken from the strong soldiers.
What the soldiers have taken will be saved.
I will fight your enemies,
and I will save your children.
26 I will force those who trouble you to eat their own flesh.
Their own blood will be the wine that makes them drunk.
Then everyone will know
I, the LORD, am the One who saves you;
I am the Powerful One of Jacob who saves you."

Israel was Punished for Its Sin

50 This is what the LORD says:
"People of Israel, you say I divorced your mother.
Then where is the paper that proves it?
Or do you think I sold you

to pay a debt?
Because of the evil things you did, I
    sold you.
Because of the times she turned
    against me, your mother was
    sent away.
2 I came home and found no one
    there;
  I called, but no one answered.
  Do you think I am not able to save
    you?
  Do I not have the power to save
    you?
  Look, I need only to shout and the
    sea becomes dry.
  I change rivers into a desert,
  and their fish rot because there is no
    water;
    they die of thirst.
3 I can make the skies dark;
  I can make them black like clothes
    of sadness."

God's Servant Obeys

4 The Lord GOD gave me the ability to
    teach
  so that I know what to say to make
    the weak strong.
  Every morning he wakes me.
  He teaches me to listen like a
    student.
5 The Lord GOD helps me learn,
  and I have not turned against him
    nor stopped following him.
6 I offered my back to those who beat
    me.
  I offered my cheeks to those who
    pulled my beard.
  I won't hide my face from them
    when they make fun of me and spit
    at me.
7 The Lord GOD helps me,
  so I will not be ashamed.
  I will be determined,
  and I know I will not be disgraced.
8 He shows that I am innocent, and he
    is close to me.
  So who can accuse me?
  If there is someone, let us go to
    court together.
  If someone wants to prove I have
    done wrong,
  he should come and tell me.

9 Look! It is the Lord GOD who helps
    me.
  So who can prove me guilty?
  Look! All those who try will become
    useless like old clothes;
    moths will eat them.
10 Who among you
    fears the
    LORD
    and obeys his
    servant?

50:10 Trust
Find out how to rely on God.

  That person may
    walk in the dark
    and have no light.
  Then let him trust in the LORD
    and depend on his God.
11 But instead, some of you want to light
    your own fires
    and make your own light.
  So, go, walk in the light of your fires,
    and trust your own light to guide
    you.
  But this is what you will receive from
    me:
    you will lie down in a place of pain.

Jerusalem will be Saved

51 The Lord says, "Listen to me,
    those of you who try to live right
    and follow the Lord.
  Look at the rock from which you
    were cut;
    look at the stone quarry from
    which you were dug.
2 Look at Abraham, your ancestor,
    and Sarah, who gave birth to your
    ancestors.
  Abraham had no children when I
    called him,
  but I blessed him and gave him
    many descendants.
3 So the LORD will comfort Jerusalem;
    he will show mercy to those who
    live in her ruins.
  He will change her deserts into a
    garden like Eden;
    he will make her empty lands like
    the garden of the LORD.
  People there will be very happy;
    they will give thanks and sing
    songs.

4 "My people, listen to me;
    my nation, pay attention to me.
  I will give the people my teachings,
    and my decisions will be like a
      light to all people.
5 I will soon show that I do what is
      right.
    I will soon save you.
    I will use my power and judge all
      nations.
  All the faraway places are waiting for
      me;
    they wait for my power to help
      them.
6 Look up to the heavens.
    Look around you at the earth
      below.
  The skies will disappear like clouds of
      smoke.
    The earth will become useless like
      old clothes,
    and its people will die like flies.
  But my salvation will continue for
      ever,
    and my goodness will never end.

7 "You people who know what is right
      should listen to me;
    you people who follow my
      teachings should hear what I
        say.
  Don't be afraid of the evil things
      people say,
    and don't be upset by their insults.
8 Moths will eat those people as if they
      were clothes,
    and worms will eat them as if they
      were wool.
  But my goodness will continue for
      ever,
    and my salvation will continue from
      now on."

9 Wake up, wake up, and use your
      strength,
    powerful LORD.
  Wake up as you did in the old times,
    as you did a long time ago.
  With your own power, you cut Rahab
      into pieces
    and killed that sea monster.
10 You dried up the sea
    and the waters of the deep ocean.
  You made the deepest parts of the
      sea into a road
    for your people to cross over and
      be saved.
11 The people the LORD has freed will
      return
    and enter Jerusalem with joy.
  Their happiness will last for ever.
    They will have joy and gladness,
    and all sadness and sorrow will be
      gone far away.

12 The LORD says, "I am the one who
      comforts you.
    So why should you be afraid of
      people, who die?
    Why should you fear people who
      die like the grass?
13 Have you forgotten the LORD who
      made you,
    who stretched out the skies
      and made the earth?
  Why are you always afraid
    of those angry people who trouble
      you
    and who want to destroy?
  But where are those angry people
      now?

**51:12–13
Fears**
Why should you not fear people?

14 People in prison will soon be set free;
    they will not die in prison,
    and they will have enough food.
15 I am the LORD your God,
    who stirs the sea and makes the
      waves roar.
    My name is the LORD All-powerful.
16 I will give you the words I want you
      to say.
    I will cover you with my hands and
      protect you.
  I made the heavens and the earth,
    and I say to Jerusalem, 'You are my
      people.'"

God Punished Israel

17 Awake! Awake!
    Get up, Jerusalem.
  The LORD was very angry with you;
    your punishment was like wine in a
      cup.

The LORD made you drink that wine;
> you drank the whole cup until you
>> stumbled.
18 Jerusalem had many people,
> but there was not one to lead her.
> Of all the people who grew up there,
>> no one was there to guide her.
19 Troubles came to you two by two,
> but no one will feel sorry for you.
> There was ruin and disaster, great
>> hunger and fighting.
> No one can comfort you.
20 Your people have become weak.
> They fall down and lie on every
>> street corner,
> like animals caught in a net.
> They have felt the full anger of the
>> LORD
> and have heard God's angry shout.

21 So listen to me, poor Jerusalem,
> you who are drunk but not from
>> wine.
22 Your God will defend his people.
> This is what the LORD your God
>> says:
> "The punishment I gave you is like a
>> cup of wine.
> You drank it and could not walk
>> straight.
> But I am taking that cup of my anger
>> away from you,
> and you will never
>> be punished by
>> my anger again.
23 I will now give that
> cup of
> punishment to
> those who gave
> you pain,
> who told you,
> 'Bow down so we
> can walk over
> you.'
> They made your back like dirt for
>> them to walk on;
> you were like a street for them to
>> travel on."

Jerusalem will be Saved

52 Wake up, wake up, Jerusalem!
> Become strong!
> Be beautiful again,
>> holy city of Jerusalem.
> The people who do not worship God
>> and who are not pure
> will not enter you again.
2 Jerusalem, you once were a prisoner.
> Now shake off the dust and stand
>> up.
> Jerusalem, you once were a prisoner.
> Now free yourself from the chains
>> around your neck.
3 This is what the LORD says:
> "You were not sold for a price,
> so you will be saved without cost."
4 This is what the Lord GOD says:
> "First my people went down to Egypt
>> to live.
> Later Assyria made them slaves.

5 "Now see what has happened," says
>> the LORD.
> "Another nation has taken away
>> my people for nothing.
> This nation who rules them makes
>> fun of me," says the LORD.
> "All day long they speak against
>> me.
6 This has happened so my people will
>> know who I am,
> and so, on that future day, they will
>> know
> that I am the one speaking to them.
> It will really be me."

7 How beautiful is the
> person
> who comes over
> the mountains to
> bring good news,
> who announces peace
> and brings good
> news,
> who announces
> salvation
> and says to Jerusalem,
> "Your God is King."
8 Listen! Your guards are shouting.
> They are all shouting for joy!
> They all will see with their own eyes
>> when the LORD returns to
>> Jerusalem.
9 Jerusalem, your buildings are
>> destroyed now,
> but shout and rejoice together,

> How beautiful is the person who comes over the mountains to bring good news.
> – Isaiah 52:7

Isaiah 52:10 966

because the LORD has comforted his
 people.
He has saved Jerusalem.
10 The LORD will show his holy power
 to all the nations.
Then everyone on earth
 will see the salvation of our God.

11 You people, leave, leave; get out of
 Babylon!
Touch nothing that is unclean.
You men who carry the LORD's things
 used in worship,
leave there and make yourselves
 pure.
12 You will not be forced to leave
 Babylon quickly;
you will not be forced to run away,
because the LORD will go before you,
 and the God of Israel will guard
 you from behind.

The Lord's Suffering Servant

13 The LORD says, "See, my servant will
 act wisely.
People will greatly honour and
 respect him.
14 Many people were shocked when
 they saw him.
His appearance was so changed he
 did not look like a man;
his form was changed so much they
 could barely tell he was human.
15 But now he will surprise many
 nations.
Kings will be amazed and shut
 their mouths.
They will see things they had not
 been told about him,
and they will understand things
 they had not heard."

53 Who would have believed what
 we heard?
Who saw the LORD's power in this?
2 He grew up like a small plant before
 the LORD,
like a root growing in a dry land.
He had no special beauty or form to
 make us notice him;
there was nothing in his
 appearance to make us
 desire him.

FAITH links

THE ONE WHO SUFFERED

ISAIAH 53

No one likes to suffer. If you get even the tiniest splinter in your finger, your whole body seems to react to the pain. Now imagine having a splinter in your finger for every person who ever lived. That would hurt a lot more than the one splinter! Isaiah wrote about someone whose whole life would be one of suffering. He would die for the sins of everyone who ever lived. Isaiah was talking about Jesus, who was born hundreds of years after this was written.

God loved us so much that "he gave his one and only Son" (John 3:16) to suffer for us. Now that's amazing love!

The Sign of His Presence, Exodus 40:34–38, p. 130

Approaching God, Numbers 3:10, p. 180

Plans for a Son, 1 Chronicles 22:5–19, p. 548

Believe the Impossible? Ezekiel 37, p. 1131

Clean Inside and Out, Luke 11:39–40, p. 1392

The Gift, John 3:16–18, p. 1427

---

3 He was hated and rejected by people.
He had much pain and suffering.
People would not even look at him.
He was hated, and we didn't even
 notice him.

4 But he took our suffering on him
    and felt our pain for us.
  We saw his suffering
    and thought God was punishing
      him.
5 But he was wounded for the wrong
    we did;
  he was crushed for the evil
    we did.
  The punishment, which made us well,
    was given to him,
  and we are healed because of his
    wounds.
6 We all have wandered away like sheep;
  each of us has gone his own way.

Sin
Does everyone have a sin problem?

  But the LORD has put on him the
    punishment
  for all the evil we have done.
7 He was beaten down and punished,
    but he didn't say a word.
  He was like a lamb being led to be
    killed.
  He was quiet, as a sheep is quiet
    while its wool is being cut;
  he never opened his mouth.
8 Men took him away roughly and
    unfairly.
  He died without children to
    continue his family.
  He was put to death;
  he was punished
    for the sins of
    my people.
9 He was buried with
    wicked men,
  and he died with
    the rich.
  He had done nothing
    wrong,
  and he had never
    lied.
10 But it was the LORD who decided
    to crush him and make him
      suffer.
  The LORD made his life a penalty
    offering,
  but he will still see his descendants
    and live a long life.
  He will complete the things the
    LORD wants him to do.
11 "After his soul suffers many things,
    he will see life and be satisfied.
  My good servant will make many
    people right with God;
  he will carry away their sins.
12 For this reason I will make him a
    great man among people,
  and he will share in all things with
    those who are strong.
  He willingly gave his life
    and was treated like a criminal.
  But he carried away the sins of many
    people
  and asked forgiveness for those
    who sinned."

People will Return to Jerusalem

54 The LORD says, "Sing, Jerusalem.
  You are like a woman who never
    gave birth to children.
  Start singing and shout for joy.
  You never felt the pain of giving
    birth,
  but you will have more children
    than the woman who has a
      husband.
2 Make your tent bigger;
    stretch it out and make it wider.
  Do not hold back.
  Make the ropes longer
    and its stakes stronger,
3 because you will
    spread out to the
    right and to the
    left.
  Your children will
    take over other
    nations,
  and they will again
    live in cities that
    once were
    destroyed.

> My good servant will make many people right with God; he will carry away their sins.
> — Isaiah 53:11

4 "Don't be afraid, because you will not
    be ashamed.
  Don't be embarrassed, because
    you will not be disgraced.
  You will forget the shame you felt
    earlier;
  you will not remember the shame

you felt when you lost your
husband.
5 The God who made you is like your
husband.
His name is the LORD All-powerful.
The Holy One of Israel is the one
who saves you.
He is called the God of all the
earth.
6 You were like a woman whose
husband left her,
and you were very sad.
You were like a wife who married
young
and then her husband left her.
But the LORD called you to be his,"
says your God.
7 God says, "I left you for a short time,
but with great kindness I will bring
you back again.
8 I became very angry
and hid from you for a time,
but I will show you mercy with
kindness for ever,"
says the LORD who saves you.

9 The LORD says, "This day is like the
time of Noah to me.
I promised then that I would never
flood the world again.
In the same way, I promise I will not
be angry with you
or punish you again.
10 The mountains may disappear,
and the hills may come to an end,
but my love will never disappear;
my promise of peace will not come
to an end,"
says the LORD who shows mercy to
you.

11 "You poor city. Storms have hurt you,
and you have not been comforted.
But I will rebuild you with turquoise
stones,
and I will build your foundations
with sapphires.
12 I will use rubies to build your walls
and shining jewels for the gates
and precious jewels for all your
outer walls.
13 All your children will be taught by the
LORD,
and they will have much peace.
14 I will build you using fairness.
You will be safe from those who
would hurt you,
so you will have nothing to fear.
Nothing will come to make you
afraid.
15 I will not send anyone to attack you,
and you will defeat those who do
attack you.
16 "See, I made the blacksmith.
He fans the fire to make it hotter,
and he makes the kind of tool he
wants.
In the same way I have made the
destroyer to destroy.
17 So no weapon that is used against
you will defeat you.
You will show that those who speak
against you are wrong.
These are the good things my
servants receive.
Their victory comes from me,"
says the LORD.

God Gives What is Good

55 The LORD says, "All you who are
thirsty,
come and drink.
Those of you who do not have money,
come, buy and eat!
Come buy wine and milk
without money and without cost.
2 Why spend your money on something
that is not real food?
Why work for something that
doesn't really satisfy you?
Listen closely to me, and you will eat
what is good;
your soul will enjoy the rich food
that satisfies.
3 Come to me and listen;
listen to me so you may live.
I will make an agreement with you
that will last for ever.
I will give you the blessings I
promised to David.
4 I made David a witness of my power
for all nations,
a ruler and commander of many
nations.

5 You will call for nations that you don't
      yet know.
   And these nations that do not know
      you will run to you
   because of the LORD your God,
      because of the Holy One of Israel
         who honours you."

6 So you should look for the LORD
      before it is too late;
   you should call to him while he is
      near.
7 The wicked should stop doing wrong,
   and they should stop their evil
      thoughts.
   They should return to the LORD so he
      may have mercy on them.
   They should come to our God,
      because he will freely forgive
         them.

8 The LORD says, "My thoughts are not
      like your thoughts.
   Your ways are not like my ways.
9 Just as the heavens are higher than
      the earth,
   so are my ways higher than your
      ways
   and my thoughts higher than your
      thoughts.
10 Rain and snow fall from the sky
   and don't return without watering
      the ground.
   They cause the plants to sprout and
      grow,
   making seeds for the farmer
   and bread for the people.
11 The same thing is true of the words I
      speak.
   They will not return to me empty.
   They make the things happen that I
      want to happen,
   and they succeed in doing what I
      send them to do.

12 "So you will go
      out with joy
   and be led
      out in
         peace.
   The mountains
      and hills will burst into song
         before you,

WHAT GOD THINKS
ISAIAH 55:8-9

Do you know what your dad or stepdad is thinking right now? Probably not, because you can't read minds. But sometimes, you *might* know how he will react to something. How is this possible? It's simple: you know how he reacted in the past. Your relationship with him causes you to know a lot about his likes and dislikes. Many times, we think we can figure God out that easily. We think we know what he thinks and how he will react. According to Isaiah, God doesn't think the way that we think. His thoughts and plans are far more superior. Don't try to second-guess God. Rather, trust that God knows what is best for you.

Here are some more links on putting your trust in God:

What He's Really Like, Deuteronomy 4:15–20, p. 233

An Admirable Quality, 1 Kings 10:1–13, p. 451

Plan for Success, 1 Chronicles 14:8–17, p. 538

How God Speaks, Job 33:14–17, p. 696

Future Hope, Joel 3:17–21, p. 1191

The Finished Product, Philippians 1:6, p. 1609

55:12
Joy
A picture of joy.

and all the trees in the fields will
  clap their hands.
13 Large cypress trees will grow where
    thorn-bushes
    were.
  Myrtle trees will
    grow where
    weeds were.
  These things will be a
    reminder of the
    LORD's promise,
    and this reminder
    will never be
    destroyed."

> My Temple will be called a house for prayer for people from all nations.
> – Isaiah 56:7

All Nations will Obey the LORD

56 This is what the LORD says:
  "Give justice to all people,
    and do what is right,
  because my salvation will come to
    you soon.
  Soon everyone will know that I do
    what is right.
2 The person who obeys the law about
    the Sabbath
    will be blessed,
  and the person who does no evil
    will be blessed."

3 Foreigners who have joined the LORD
    should not say,
  "The LORD will not accept me with
    his people."
  The eunuch should not say,
  "Because I cannot have children,
    the LORD will not accept me."
4 This is what the LORD says:
  "The eunuchs should obey the law
    about the Sabbath
    and do what I want
    and keep my agreement.
5 If they do, I will make their names
    remembered
    within my Temple and its walls.
  It will be better for them than
    children.
  I will give them a name that will last
    for ever,
    that will never be forgotten.
6 Foreigners will join the LORD
    to worship him and love him,
    to serve him,
    to obey the law about the Sabbath,
    and to keep my agreement.
7 I will bring these people to my holy
    mountain
    and give them joy
    in my house of
    prayer.
  The offerings and
    sacrifices
    they place on my
    altar will please
    me,
  because my Temple
    will be called
    a house for prayer
    for people from
    all nations."

8 The Lord GOD says—
  he who gathers the Israelites that
    were forced to leave their
    country:
  "I will bring together other people
    to join those who are already
    gathered."

Israel's Leaders are Evil

9 All you animals of the field,
    all you animals of the forest, come
      to eat.
10 The leaders who are to guard the
    people are blind;
  they don't know what they are
    doing.
  All of them are like quiet dogs
    that don't know how to bark.
  They lie down and dream
    and love to sleep.
11 They are like hungry dogs
    that are never satisfied.
  They are like shepherds
    who don't know what they are
      doing.
  They all have gone their own way;
    all they want to do is satisfy
      themselves.
12 They say, "Come, let's drink some
    wine;
    let's drink all the beer we want.
  And tomorrow we will do this
    again,
    or, maybe we will have an even
      better time."

Israel Does Not Follow God

57 Those who are right with God
may die,
but no one pays attention.
Good people are taken away,
but no one understands.
Those who do right are being taken
away from evil
2 and are given peace.
Those who live as God wants
find rest in death.

3 "Come here, you magicians!
Come here, you sons of prostitutes
and those who take part in
adultery!
4 Of whom are you making fun?
Whom are you insulting?
At whom do you stick out your
tongue?
You turn against God,
and you are liars.
5 You have sexual relations under every
green tree
to worship your gods.
You kill children in the ravines
and sacrifice them in the rocky
places.
6 You take the smooth rocks from the
ravines
as your portion.
You pour drink offerings on them to
worship them,
and you give grain offerings to
them.
Do you think this makes me want
to show you mercy?
7 You make your bed on every hill and
mountain,
and there you offer sacrifices.
8 You have hidden your idols
behind your doors and
doorposts.
You have left me, and you have
uncovered yourself.
You have pulled back the covers
and climbed into bed.
You have made an agreement with
those whose beds you love,
and you have looked at their
nakedness.
9 You use your oils and perfumes
to look nice for Molech.
You have sent your messengers to
faraway lands;
you even tried to send them to the
place of the dead.
10 You were tired from doing these
things,
but you never gave up.
You found new strength,
so you did not stop.

11 "Whom were you so afraid of
that you lied to me?
You have not remembered me
or even thought about me.
I have been quiet for a long time.
Is that why you are not afraid of me?
12 I will tell about your 'goodness' and
what you do,
and those things will do you no
good.
13 When you cry out for help,
let the gods you have gathered
help you.
The wind will blow them all away;
just a puff of wind will take them
away.
But the person who depends on me
will receive the land
and own my holy mountain."

The LORD will Save His People

14 Someone will say, "Build a road!
Build a road! Prepare the way!
Make the way clear for my people."
15 And this is the
reason:
God lives
for ever and
is holy.
He is high and
lifted up.
He says, "I live in a high and holy
place,
but I also live with people who are
sad and humble.
I give new life to those who are
humble
and to those whose hearts are
broken.
16 I will not accuse for ever,
nor will I always be angry,
because then human life would grow
weak.

57:15 Humbleness Who does God give new life to?

Human beings, whom I created,
  would die.
17 I was angry because they were
    dishonest in order to make money.
  I punished them and turned away
    from them in anger,
  but they continued to do evil.
18 I have seen what they have done, but
    I will heal them.
  I will guide them and comfort them
    and those who felt sad for them.
  They will all praise me.
19 I will give peace, real peace, to those
    far and near,
  and I will heal them," says the
    LORD.
20 But evil people are like the angry sea,
    which cannot rest,
  whose waves toss up waste and
    mud.
21 "There is no peace for evil people,"
    says my God.

How to Honour God

58 The LORD says, "Shout out loud.
    Don't hold back.
  Shout out loud like a trumpet.
  Tell my people what they have done
    against their God;
    tell the family of Jacob about their
      sins.
2 They still come every day looking for
    me
    and want to learn my ways.
  They act just like a nation that does
    what is right,
    that obeys the commands of its
      God.
  They ask me to judge them fairly.
  They want God to be near them.
3 They say, 'To honour you we had
    special days when we gave up
    eating,
  but you didn't see.
  We humbled ourselves to honour you,
    but you didn't notice.'"

But the LORD says, "You do what
    pleases yourselves on these
    special days,
  and you are unfair to your workers.
4 On these special days when you do
    not eat, you argue and fight

FAITH links

HOW TO WORSHIP GOD
ISAIAH 58

What do you think worshipping God means? Does it just involve going to church every Sunday? Isaiah would say a big "No" to that. True worship means taking care of the poor and homeless. It means giving clothes to those in need, feeding the hungry, and helping friends and relatives. In short it means caring for others. That's the way that God wants to be honoured. If you truly worship God, treat others with kindness.

Want to worship God? Here are some ways to show it:

The MLP, Ruth 1:16–17, p. 345

The Way to Serve God, 1 Kings 9:4, p. 450

Helpful Advice, Job 12:4–5, p. 673

Kindness First, Matthew 9:35–36, p. 1290

The Number One Rule, Mark 12:28–31, p. 1351

The Worst Chore, John 13:3–17, p. 1447

  and hit each other with your fists.
  You cannot do these things as you do
    now
    and believe your prayers are heard
      in heaven.
5 This kind of special day is not what I
    want.
  This is not the way I want people to

be sorry for what they have
done.
I don't want people just to bow their
heads like a plant
and wear rough cloth and lie in
ashes to show their sadness.
This is what you do on your special
days when you do not eat,
but do you
think this is
what the
LORD wants?
6 "I will tell you
the kind of
special day I
want:
free the people you have put in prison
unfairly
and undo their chains.
Free those to whom you are unfair
and stop their hard labour.
7 Share your food with the hungry
and bring poor, homeless people
into your own homes.
When you see someone who has no
clothes, give him yours,
and don't refuse to help your own
relatives.
8 Then your light will shine like the
dawn,
and your wounds will quickly heal.
Your God will walk before you,
and the glory of the LORD will
protect you from behind.
9 Then you will call out, and the LORD
will answer.
You will cry out, and he will say,
'Here I am.'

"If you stop making trouble for
others,
if you stop using cruel words and
pointing your finger at others,
10 if you feed those who are hungry
and take care of the needs of those
who are troubled,
then your light will shine in the
darkness,
and you will be bright like
sunshine at noon.
11 The LORD will always lead you.
He will satisfy your needs in dry
lands

58:5–7
Honouring
God
How is God honoured?

and give strength to your bones.
You will be like a garden that has
much water,
like a spring that never runs dry.
12 Your people will rebuild the old cities
that are now in ruins;
you will rebuild their foundations.
You will be known for repairing the
broken places
and for rebuilding the roads and
houses.

13 "You must obey God's law about the
Sabbath
and not do what pleases yourselves
on that holy day.
You should call the Sabbath a joyful
day
and honour it as the LORD's holy
day.
You should honour it by not doing
whatever you please
nor saying whatever you please on
that day.
14 Then you will find joy in the LORD,
and I will carry you to the high
places above the earth.
I will let you eat the crops of the
land your ancestor Jacob had."
The LORD has said these things.

The Evil That People Do

59 Surely the LORD's power is
enough to save you.
He can hear you when you ask him
for help.
2 It is your evil that has separated
you from your God.
Your sins cause him to turn away
from you,
so he does not hear you.
3 With your hands you have killed
others,
and with your fingers you have
done wrong.
With your lips you have lied,
and with your tongue you say evil
things.
4 People take each other to court unfairly,
and no one tells the truth in
arguing his case.
They accuse each other falsely and
tell lies.

▶ Isaiah 59   974

SIN
Isaiah 59:12–13

Covered with Mud! Ever fallen into mud? It's very hard to get rid of it all. Even after you scrub yourself, you may still find bits of dirt under your fingernails or between your toes. Mud and dirt have a way of messing up everything. Even just a speck of dirt on a clean shirt can make you look pretty bad.

God often talks about sin as being dirty. When you sin, it's as if you went outside and rolled around in mud on purpose. But instead of being dirty on the outside, sin makes you dirty inside. (Look at Isaiah 6.) How can God make you "clean" again?

MORE FAITH links

Red to White, **p. 896**

Dirty Inside, **p. 904**

Real Repentance, **p. 993**

Clean Inside and Out, **p. 1392**

Keeping Clean, **p. 1576**

Do you think a little bit of dirt is OK with God? After all, most of us aren't that bad!

You'd better read some of these other Faithlinks. God hates sin, but he's got the best cleaner in the world for it! Read on!

The Cover-up, Psalm 32:1–2, p. 733
- How long do you think you could hide a bag of smelly rubbish – old food, that sort of thing – in your room? Not very long, right? The smell would give it away. Sin is like that rubbish. How long do you think you can hide a sin from God? What is the only way to get rid of the rubbish of sin?

What God "Hates", Proverbs 6:16–19, p. 835
- Link here to read about things that God hates.

The Sin Habit, Romans 7:15–20, p. 1527
- Ever had a habit you just couldn't break, no matter what you did? Paul had a habit like that – sin. What good things do you find hard to do?
- Connect here to find out how Jesus makes it possible for you to develop a habit of pleasing God.

They cause trouble and create
    more evil.
5 They hatch evil like eggs from
    poisonous snakes.
  If you eat one of those eggs, you
    will die,
    and if you break one open, a
    poisonous snake comes out.
  People tell lies as they would spin a
    spider's web.
6   The webs they make cannot be
    used for clothes;
    you can't cover yourself with those
    webs.
  The things they do are evil,
    and they use their hands to hurt
    others.
7 They eagerly run to do evil,
    and they are always ready to kill
    innocent people.
  They think evil thoughts.
    Everywhere they go they cause
    ruin and destruction.
8 They don't know how to live in
    peace,
    and there is no fairness in their
    lives.
  They are dishonest.
    Anyone who lives as they live will
    never have peace.

Israel's Sin Brings Trouble

9 Fairness has gone far away;
    goodness is nowhere to be
    found.
  We wait for the light, but there is only
    darkness now.
  We hope for a bright light, but all
    we have is darkness.
10 We are like the blind feeling our way
    along a wall.
  We feel our way as if we had no
    eyes.
  In the brightness of day we trip as if it
    were night.
  We are like dead men among the
    strong.
11 All of us growl like the bears.
    We call out sadly like the doves.
  We look for justice, but there isn't
    any.
  We want to be saved, but salvation
    is far away.
12 We have done many wrong things
    against our God;
    our sins show we are wrong.
  We know we have turned against God;
    we know the evil things we have
    done:
13 sinning and
    rejecting
    the LORD,
    turning away
    from our God,
    planning to hurt
    others and to
    disobey God,
  planning and speaking lies.
14 So we have driven away justice,
    and we have kept away from what
    is right.
  Truth is not spoken in the streets;
    what is honest is not allowed to
    enter the city.
15 Truth cannot be found anywhere,
    and people who refuse to do evil
    are attacked.

  The LORD looked and could not find
    any justice,
    and he was displeased.
16 He could not find anyone to help the
    people,
    and he was surprised that there
    was no one to help.
  So he used his own power to save the
    people;
    his own goodness gave him
    strength.
17 He covered himself with goodness
    like armour.
  He put the helmet of salvation on
    his head.
  He put on the clothes of punishment
    and wrapped himself in the coat of
    his strong love.
18 The LORD will pay back his enemies
    for what they have done.
  He will show his anger to those
    who were against him;
    he will punish the people in
    faraway places as they deserve.
19 Then people from the west will fear
    the LORD,
    and people from the east will fear
    his glory.

> **59:12-13 Sin** Read about your sinful state.

The LORD will come quickly like a
    fast-flowing river,
    driven by the breath of the LORD.

20 "Then a Saviour will come to
    Jerusalem
    and to the people of Jacob who
        have turned from sin,"
    says the LORD.

21 The LORD says, "This is my agreement with these people: My Spirit and my words that I give you will never leave you or your children or your grandchildren, now and for ever."

Jerusalem will be Great

60 "Jerusalem, get up and shine,
    because your light has come,
    and the glory of the LORD shines
        on you.
2 Darkness now covers
        the earth;
    deep darkness
        covers her
        people.
    But the LORD shines
        on you,
    and people see his
        glory around you.
3 Nations will come to
        your light;
    kings will come to
        the brightness of your sunrise.

4 "Look around you.
    People are gathering and coming
        to you.
    Your sons are coming from far away,
    and your daughters are coming
        with them.
5 When you see them, you will shine
        with happiness;
    you will be excited and full of joy,
    because the wealth of the nations
        across the seas will be given to
        you;
    the riches of the nations will come
        to you.
6 Herds of camels will cover your land,
    young camels from Midian and
        Ephah.
    People will come from Sheba
        bringing gold and incense,
    and they will sing praises to the
        LORD.
7 All the sheep from Kedar will be
        given to you;
    the rams from Nebaioth will be
        brought to you.
    They will be pleasing sacrifices on my
        altar,
    and I will make my beautiful
        Temple more beautiful.

8 "The people are returning to you like
        clouds,
    like doves flying to their nests.
9 People in faraway lands are waiting
        for me.
    The great trading ships will come
        first,
    bringing your children from faraway
        lands,
    and with them
        silver and gold.
    This will honour the
        LORD your God,
        the Holy One of
        Israel,
        who does
        wonderful things
        for you.

10 "Jerusalem,
        foreigners will
        rebuild your
        walls,
    and their kings will serve you.
    When I was angry, I hurt you,
    but now I want to be kind to you
        and comfort you.
11 Your gates will always be open;
    they will not be closed day or night
    so the nations can bring their wealth
        to you,
    and their kings will be led to you.
12 The nation or kingdom that doesn't
        serve you will be destroyed;
    it will be completely ruined.

13 "The great trees of Lebanon will be
        given to you:
    its pine, fir and cypress trees
        together.
    You will use them to make my
        Temple beautiful,

> Jerusalem, get up and shine, because your light has come, and the glory of the LORD shines on you.
> – Isaiah 60:1

and I will give much honour to this
place where I rest my feet.
14 The people who have hurt you will
bow down to you;
those who hated you will bow
down at your feet.
They will call you The City of the
LORD,
Jerusalem, city of the Holy One of
Israel.

15 "You have been hated and left empty
with no one passing through.
But I will make you great from now
on;
you will be a place of happiness for
ever and ever.
16 You will be given what you need from
the nations,
like a child drinking milk from its
mother.
Then you will know that it is I, the
LORD, who saves you.
You will know that the Powerful
One of Jacob protects you.
17 I will bring you gold in place of
bronze,
silver in place of iron,
bronze in place of wood,
iron in place of rocks.
I will change your punishment into
peace,
and you will be ruled by what is
right.
18 There will be no more violence in
your country;
it will not be ruined or destroyed.
You will name your walls Salvation
and your gates Praise.
19 The sun will no longer be your light
during the day
nor will the brightness from the
moon be your light,
because the LORD will be your light
for ever,
and your God will be your glory.
20 Your sun will never set again,
and your moon will never be dark,
because the LORD will be your light
for ever,
and your time of sadness will end.
21 All of your people will do what is
right.

They will receive the earth for ever.
They are the plant I have planted,
the work of my own hands
to show my greatness.
22 The smallest family will grow to a
thousand.
The least important of you will
become a powerful nation.
I am the LORD,
and when it is time, I will make
these things happen quickly."

The LORD's Message of Freedom

61 The Lord GOD has put his Spirit in
me,
because the LORD has appointed
me to tell the good news to the
poor.
He has sent me to comfort those
whose hearts are broken,
to tell the captives they are free
and to tell the prisoners they are
released.
2 He has sent me to announce the time
when the LORD will show his
kindness
and the time when our God will
punish evil people.
He has sent me to comfort all those
who are sad
3 and to help the sorrowing people
of Jerusalem.
I will give them a crown to replace
their ashes,
and the oil of gladness to replace
their sorrow,
and clothes of praise to replace
their spirit of sadness.
Then they will be called Trees of
Goodness,
trees planted by the LORD to show
his greatness.

4 They will rebuild the old ruins
and restore the places destroyed
long ago.
They will repair the ruined cities
that were destroyed for so long.

5 My people, foreigners will come to
tend your sheep.
People from other countries will
tend your fields and vineyards.

FAITH links

JESUS' MISSION AND YOURS
ISAIAH 61:1-2

When Jesus lived on earth, he stood up in the synagogue one day and read this passage from Isaiah. (See Luke 4:16–20, p. 1374.) He knew that his mission was to spread the good news of God's kingdom. If you're a Christian, that's your mission, too. God doesn't send you out blindly, not knowing how or when to do it. As Isaiah explained, the Holy Spirit is the One who helps you to serve God in the name of the Lord.

A Different Kind of People, Leviticus 11, p. 146

A Picture of the Past, Psalm 105, p. 789

A Bad Reaction, Jeremiah 36, p. 1043

Empty Words, Ezekiel 33:30–33, p. 1127

Love Him? Show It! Amos 2:6–7, p. 1196

People of Faith, Hebrews 11, p. 1679

---

6 You will be called priests of the LORD;
  you will be named the servants of our God.
You will have riches from all the nations on earth,
  and you will take pride in them.
7 Instead of being ashamed, my people will receive twice as much wealth.
Instead of being disgraced, they will be happy because of what they receive.
They will receive a double share of the land,
  so their happiness will continue for ever.
8 "I, the LORD, love justice.
I hate stealing and everything that is wrong.
I will be fair and give my people what they should have,
  and I will make an agreement with them that will continue for ever.
9 Everyone in all nations will know the children of my people,
  and their children will be known among the nations.
Anyone who sees them will know that they are people the LORD has blessed."

10 The LORD makes me very happy;
  all that I am rejoices in my God.

61:10 Joy Reasons to be joyful?

He has covered me with clothes of salvation
  and wrapped me with a coat of goodness,
like a bridegroom dressed for his wedding,
  like a bride dressed in jewels.
11 The earth causes plants to grow,
  and a garden causes the seeds planted in it to grow.
In the same way the Lord GOD will make goodness and praise come from all the nations.

New Jerusalem

62 Because I love Jerusalem, I will continue to speak for her;
  for Jerusalem's sake I will not stop speaking
until her goodness shines like a bright light,
  until her salvation burns bright like a flame.
2 Jerusalem, the nations will see your goodness,

and all kings will see your glory.
Then you will have a new name,
   which the LORD himself will give
   you.
3 You will be like a beautiful crown in
   the LORD's hand,
   like a king's crown in your God's
   hand.
4 You will never again be called the
   People that God Left,
   nor your land the Land that God
   Destroyed.
You will be called the People God
   Loves,
   and your land will be called the
   Bride of God,
because the LORD loves you.
And your land will belong to him as
   a bride belongs to her
   husband.
5 As a young man marries a woman,
   so your
      children
      will marry
      your land.
   As a man
      rejoices over
      his new wife,
   so your God will rejoice over you.
6 Jerusalem, I have put guards on the
   walls to watch.
   They must not be silent day or
   night.
You people who remind the LORD of
   your needs in prayer
   should never be quiet.
7 You should not stop praying to him
   until he builds up Jerusalem
   and makes it a city all people will
   praise.

8 The LORD has made a promise,
   and by his power he will keep his
   promise.
He said, "I will never again give your
   grain
   as food to your enemies.
I will not let your enemies drink the
   new wine
   that you have worked to make.
9 The person who gathers food will eat
   it,
   and he will praise the LORD.

> **62:5 Thankfulness**
> Is God thankful for you?

The person who gathers the grapes
   will drink the wine
   in the courts of my Temple."
10 Go through, go through the gates!
   Make the way ready for the people.
   Build up, build up the road!
   Move all the stones off the road.
   Raise the banner as a sign for the
   people.
11 The LORD is speaking
   to all the faraway lands:
   "Tell the people of Jerusalem,
   'Look, your Saviour is coming.
   He is bringing your reward to you;
   he is bringing his payment with
   him.'"
12 His people will be called the Holy
   People,
   the Saved People of the LORD,
   and Jerusalem will be called the City
   God Wants,
   the City God Has Not Rejected.

The Lord Judges His People

63 Who is this coming from Edom,
   from the city of Bozrah, dressed
   in red?
Who is this dressed in fine clothes
   and marching forwards with his
   great power?
He says, "I, the LORD, speak what is
   right.
I have the power to save you."

2 Someone asks, "Why are your clothes
   bright red
   as if you had walked on the grapes
   to make wine?"

3 The LORD answers, "I have walked in
   the winepress alone,
   and no one among the nations
   helped me.
I was angry and walked on the
   nations
   and crushed them because of my
   anger.
Blood splashed on my clothes,
   and I stained all my clothing.
4 I chose a time to punish people,

and the time has come for me to save.
5 I looked around, but I saw no one to help me.
I was surprised that no one supported me.
So I used my own power to save my people;
my own anger supported me.
6 While I was angry, I walked on the nations.
In my anger I punished them
and poured their blood on the ground."

The Lord's Kindness to His People

7 I will tell about the LORD's kindness
and praise him for everything he has done.
I will praise the LORD for the many good things he has given us

63:7 Kindness What kind of limits are on God's mercy?

and for his goodness to the people of Israel.
He has shown great mercy to us
and has been very kind to us.
8 He said, "These are my people;
my children will not lie to me."
So he saved them.
9 When they suffered, he suffered also.
He sent his own angel to save them.
Because of his love and kindness, he saved them.
Since long ago he has picked them up and carried them.
10 But they turned against him
and made his Holy Spirit very sad.
So he became their enemy,
and he fought against them.
11 But then his people remembered what happened long ago,
in the days of Moses and the Israelites with him.
Where is the LORD who brought the people through the sea,
with the leaders of his people?
Where is the one
who put his Holy Spirit among them,

12 who led Moses by the right hand with his wonderful power,
who divided the water before them
to make his name famous for ever,
13 who led the people through the deep waters?
Like a horse walking through a desert,
the people did not stumble.
14 Like cattle that go down to the valley,
the Spirit of the LORD gave the people a place to rest.
LORD, that is the way you led your people,
and by this you won for yourself wonderful fame.

A Prayer for Help

15 LORD, look down from the heavens and see;
look at us from your wonderful and holy home in heaven.
Where is your strong love and power?
Why are you keeping your love and mercy from us?
16 You are our father.
Abraham doesn't know we are his children,
and Israel doesn't recognise us.
LORD, you are our father.
You are called "the one who has always saved us".
17 LORD, why are you making us wander from your ways?
Why do you make us stubborn so that we don't honour you?
For our sake come back to us,
your servants, who belong to you.
18 Your people had your Temple for a while,
but now our enemies have walked on your holy place and crushed it.
19 We have become like people you never ruled over,
like those who have never worn your name.

64

Tear open the skies and come down to earth
so that the mountains will tremble before you.
2 Like a fire that burns twigs,

Isaiah 65:1   981

like a fire that makes water boil,
let your enemies know who you are.
Then all nations will shake with
fear when they see you.
3 You have done amazing things we did
not expect.
You came down, and the mountains
trembled before you.
4 From long ago no one has ever heard
of a God like you.
No one has ever seen a God
besides you,
who helps the people who trust
you.
5 You help those who enjoy doing good,
who remember how you want them
to live.
But you were angry because we
sinned.
For a long time we disobeyed,
so how can we be saved?
6 All of us are dirty with sin.
All the right things we have done
are like filthy pieces of cloth.
All of us are like
dead leaves,
and our sins,
like the
wind, have
carried us
away.
7 No one worships you
or even asks you to help us.
That is because you have turned
away from us
and have let our sins destroy us.

8 But LORD, you are our father.
We are like clay, and you are the
potter;
your hands made us all.
9 LORD, don't continue to be angry with
us;
don't remember our sins for ever.
Please, look at us,
because we are your people.
10 Your holy cities are empty like the
desert.
Jerusalem is like a desert;
it is destroyed.
11 Our ancestors worshipped you
in our holy and wonderful Temple,
but now it has been burned with fire,
and all our precious things have
been destroyed.
12 When you see these things, will you
hold yourself back from helping
us, LORD?
Will you be silent and punish us
beyond what we can stand?

64:6
Sin
Is anyone free
from sin?

FAITH CHALLENGE

Got another challenge for you. Read 64:8 to find out why you were created in a certain way. Knowing God is the potter, what does this mean to you? How does this affect how you should treat others?

TESTING IT

Isaiah 64:8
But LORD, you are our father. We are like clay, and you are the potter; your hands made us all.

All People will Learn About God

65 The LORD says, "I made myself
known to people who were
not looking for me.
I was found by those who were not
asking me for help.
I said, 'Here I am. Here I am,'

to a nation that was not praying to
    me.
2 All day long I stood ready to accept
    people who turned against me,
  but the way they continue to live is
      not good;
    they do anything they want to do.
3 Right in front of me
    they continue to do things that
      make me angry.
  They offer sacrifices to their gods
      in their gardens,
    and they burn incense on altars of
      brick.
4 They sit among the graves
    and spend their nights waiting to
      get messages from the dead.
  They eat the meat of pigs,
    and their pots are full of soup made
      from meat that is wrong to eat.
5 But they tell others, 'Stay away and
      don't come near me.
    I am too holy for you.'
  These people are like smoke in my
      nose.
    Like a fire that burns all the time,
      they continue to make me
      angry.

6 "Look, it is written here before me.
    I will not be quiet; instead, I will
      repay you in full.
    I will punish you for what you have
      done.
7 I will punish you for your sins and
      your ancestors' sins,"
    says the LORD.
  "They burned incense to gods on the
      mountains
    and shamed me on those hills.
  So I will punish them as they should
      be punished
    for what they did."

8 This is what the LORD says:
  "When there is juice left in the
      grapes,
    people do not destroy them,
      because they know there is good
      left in them.
  So I will do the same thing to my
      servants—
    I will not completely destroy them.

9 I will leave some of the children of
      Jacob,
    and some of the people of Judah
      will receive my mountain.
  I will choose the people who will live
      there;
    my servants will live there.
10 Then the Plain of Sharon will be a
      field for flocks,
    and the Valley of Achor will be a
      place for herds to rest.
  They will be for the people who
      want to follow me.

11 "But as for you who left the LORD,
    who forgot about my holy
      mountain,
  who worship the god Luck,
    who hold religious feasts for the
      god Fate,
12 I decide your fate, and I will punish
      you with my sword.
    You will all be killed,
  because I called you, but you refused
      to answer.
    I spoke to you, but you wouldn't
      listen.
  You did the things I said were evil
    and chose to do things that
      displease me."

13 So this is what the Lord GOD says:
  "My servants will eat,
    but you evil people will be hungry.
  My servants will drink,
    but you evil people will be thirsty.
  My servants will be happy,
    but you evil people will be shamed.
14 My servants will shout for joy
    because of the goodness of their
      hearts,
  but you evil people will cry,
    because you will be sad.
  You will cry loudly, because your
      spirits will be broken.
15 Your names will be like curses to my
      servants,
    and the Lord GOD will put you to
      death.
  But he will call his servants by
      another name.
16 People in the land who ask for
      blessings

will ask for them from the faithful God.
And people in the land who make a promise
will promise in the name of the faithful God,
because the troubles of the past will be forgotten.
I will make those troubles go away.

A New Time is Coming

17 "Look, I will make new heavens and a new earth,
and people will not remember the past
or think about those things.
18 My people will be happy for ever because of the things I will make.
I will make a Jerusalem that is full of joy,
and I will make her people a delight.
19 Then I will rejoice over Jerusalem and be delighted with my people.
There will never again be heard in that city the sounds of crying and sadness.
20 There will never be a baby from that city
who lives only a few days.
And there will never be an older person
who doesn't have a long life.
A person who lives 100 years will be called young,
and a person who dies before he is 100 will be thought of as a sinner.
21 In that city those who build houses will live there.
Those who plant vineyards will get to eat their grapes.
22 No more will one person build a house and someone else live there.
One person will not plant a garden and someone else eat its fruit.
My people will live a long time,

as trees live long.
My chosen people will live there and enjoy the things they make.
23 They will never again work for nothing.
They will never again give birth to children who die young.
All my people will be blessed by the LORD;
they and their children will be blessed.
24 I will provide for their needs before they ask,
and I will help them while they are still asking for help.
25 Wolves and lambs will eat together in peace.
Lions will eat hay like oxen,
and a snake on the ground will not hurt anyone.
They will not hurt or destroy each other
on all my holy mountain,"
says the LORD.

65:17-25 Future Check out what your future holds.

The Lord will Judge All Nations

66 This is what the LORD says: "Heaven is my throne, and the earth is my footstool.
So do you think you can build a house for me?
Do I need a place to rest?
2 My hand made all things.
All things are here because I made them,"
says the LORD.

66:2 Worship How should you respond to God?

"These are the people I am pleased with:
those who are not proud or stubborn
and who fear my word.
3 But those people who kill bulls as a sacrifice to me
are like those who kill people.
Those who kill sheep as a sacrifice
are like those who break the necks of dogs.
Those who give me grain offerings

are like those who offer me the
    blood of pigs."
Those who burn incense
    are like those who worship idols.
These people choose their own ways,
    not mine,
    and they love the terrible things
    they do.
4 So I will choose their punishments,
    and I will punish them with what
    they fear most.
This is because I called to them, but
    they did not listen.
I spoke to them, but they did not
    hear me.
They did things I said were evil;
    they chose to do things I did not
    like."

5 You people who obey the words of the
    LORD,
    listen to what he says:
"Your brothers hated you
    and turned against you because
    you followed me.
Your brothers said, 'Let the LORD be
    honoured
    so we may see you rejoice,'
    but they will be punished.
6 Listen to the loud noise coming from
    the city;
    hear the noise from the Temple.
It is the LORD punishing his enemies,
    giving them the punishment they
    should have.

7 "A woman does not give birth before
    she feels the pain;
    she does not give birth to a son
    before the pain starts.
8 No one has ever heard of that
    happening;
    no one has ever seen that happen.
In the same way no one ever saw a
    country begin in one day;
    no one has ever heard of a new
    nation beginning in one
    moment.
But Jerusalem will give birth to her
    children
    just as soon as she feels the birth
    pains.
9 In the same way I will not cause pain
    without allowing something new to
    be born," says the LORD.
"If I cause you the pain,
    I will not stop you from giving
    birth to your new nation," says
    your God.
10 "Jerusalem, rejoice.
    All you people who love Jerusalem,
    be happy.
Those of you who felt sad for Jerusalem
    should now feel happy with her.
11 You will take comfort from her and be
    satisfied,
    as a child is nursed by its mother.
You will receive her good things
    and enjoy her wealth."

12 This is what the LORD says:

"I will give her peace that will flow to
    her like a river.
The wealth of the nations will come
    to her like a river overflowing its
    banks.
Like babies you will be nursed and
    held in my arms
    and bounced on my knees.
13 I will comfort you
    as a mother comforts her child.
You will be comforted in
    Jerusalem."

14 When you see these things, you will
    be happy
    and you will grow like the grass.
The LORD's servants will see his
    power,
    but his enemies will see his anger.
15 Look, the LORD is coming with fire
    and his armies with clouds of dust.
He will punish those people with his
    anger;
    he will punish them with flames of
    fire.
16 The LORD will judge the people with
    fire
    and he will destroy many people
    with his sword;
    he will kill many people.

66:3 dogs . . . pigs God did not want his people to offer dogs and pigs as sacrifices because they were unclean animals.

17 "These people make themselves holy and pure to go to worship their gods in their gardens. Following each other into their special gardens, they eat the meat of pigs and rats and other hateful things. But they will all be destroyed together," says the Lord.

18 "I know they have evil thoughts and do evil things, so I am coming to punish them. I will gather all nations and all people, and they will come together and see my glory.

19 "I will put a mark on some of the people, and I will send some of these saved people to the nations: to Tarshish, Libya, Lud (the land of archers), Tubal, Greece and all the faraway lands. These people have never heard about what I have done nor seen my glory. So the saved people will tell the nations about my glory. 20 And they will bring all your fellow Israelites from all nations to my holy mountain in Jerusalem. Your fellow Israelites will come on horses, donkeys and camels and in chariots and wagons. They will be like the grain offerings that the people bring in clean containers to the Temple," says the Lord. 21 "And I will choose even some of these people to be priests and Levites," says the Lord.

22 "I will make new heavens and the new earth, which will last for ever," says the Lord. "In the same way, your names and your children will always be with me. 23 All people will come to worship me every Sabbath and every New Moon," says the Lord. 24 "They will go out and see the dead bodies of the people who sinned against me. The worms that eat them will never die, and the fires that burn them will never stop, and everyone will hate to see those bodies."

THE WEEPING PROPHET

Welcome! My name is Jeremiah. It was my sad job to tell God's people that they would soon be conquered by their enemies. I wept when the people refused to be sorry for their sins and turn back to God. In fact, I wept so much that people called me the weeping prophet. All my talk of sin and defeat got me into big trouble. Some people were so angry with me that they threw me down a well and left me to die. You'll have to check out Jeremiah 38:1–13 to find out how I survived.

I wrote this book basically because God told me to write it. I spoke God's words and my friend Baruch wrote them all down. I sent Baruch to the Temple to read the book out loud. I hoped that the people would stop doing bad things and ask God to forgive them. When the king heard God's words, he cut the book into strips and burned it! Baruch and I had to write the book again.

JESUS WATCH

A message of hope is found in Jeremiah 23. The Lord promised to raise up a "good branch" in David's family tree. This "good branch" is Jesus, a descendant of King David. Jesus is a king who rules wisely and always does what is fair and just. Jeremiah gave us another name for Jesus: The Lord Does What Is Right. Jesus brings a new agreement with God. It is not like the old agreement that God made with Moses. In that agreement, God promised to bless his people if they obeyed his law. The people broke the old agreement by worshipping idols. In the new agreement, God promises to forgive our sins when we believe in Jesus. He sends the Holy Spirit to help us be holy and be more like Jesus.

my FAVOURITE links

OTHER CONNECTIONS

Livin' it — How carefully do you watch your words? Do you think that it's important? God does, and the Bible has a lot to say about the way we use our words. Find out why it's best to think first and then speak, when you download Loose Lips? Jeremiah 9:3.

Get the Info — The Israelites were surrounded by people who worshipped false gods. Unfortunately for the Israelites, they quickly forgot about God and chased after these false gods. Check out some of the gods that were worshipped back in Old Testament times at True or False Gods? Jeremiah 48:7, 13.

MORE STUFF...

Object Lessons — God gave Jeremiah these symbols to help him get his message through:
- Pot of boiling water tipping from the north is a symbol of the Babylonians who attacked Israel from the north (Jeremiah 1:13).
- Ruined linen belt represents the people of Israel who refused to listen to God (Jeremiah 13:1–13).
- Potter's clay is an image of God's ability to do whatever he wants with whomever he wants (Jeremiah 18:1–6).

Who's a rotten fig?

You've probably heard of rotten eggs, but a rotten fig? Maybe we should plug into Jeremiah 24 to find out.

did you know?

MORE STUFF ON THE JEREMIAH SURFWATCH
A born-prophet, Jeremiah 1:4–10
Worthless idols, Jeremiah 10:1–5
A ruined belt, Jeremiah 13:1–11
The broken jar, Jeremiah 19
Stolen treasure, Jeremiah 52

FAITHlinks

- Too Young to Serve, Jeremiah 1:4–9
- A Broken Promise, Jeremiah 2:1–8
- All Talk, No Action, Jeremiah 5:1–2
- Bragging Rights, Jeremiah 9:23–24
- A Home Town Hurt, Jeremiah 11:8—12:6
- Stand! Jeremiah 19:14—20:6
- A Hopeful Future, Jeremiah 29:11
- What's Wrong About Rumours, Jeremiah 29:24–32
- A Promise from the Heart, Jeremiah 31:31–33
- Fear God or People? Jeremiah 38:14–21

Jeremiah 1:1

1 These are the words of Jeremiah son of Hilkiah. He belonged to the family of priests who lived in the town of Anathoth in the land of Benjamin. 2 The LORD spoke his word to Jeremiah during the thirteenth year that Josiah son of Amon was king of Judah. 3 The LORD also spoke to Jeremiah while Jehoiakim son of Josiah was king of Judah and during the eleven years that Zedekiah son of Josiah was king of Judah. In the fifth month of his last year, the people of Jerusalem were taken away as captives.

The LORD Calls Jeremiah

4 The LORD spoke his word to me, saying:

5 "Before I made you in your mother's womb, I chose you.
Before you were born, I set you apart for a special work.
I appointed you as a prophet to the nations."

6 Then I said, "But Lord GOD, I don't know how to speak. I am only a boy."

7 But the LORD said to me, "Don't say, 'I am only a boy.' You must go everywhere I send you, and you must say everything I tell you to say. 8 Don't be afraid of anyone, because I am with you to protect you," says the LORD.

9 Then the LORD reached out his hand and touched my mouth. He said to me, "See, I am putting my words in your mouth. 10 Today I have put you in charge of nations and kingdoms. You will pull up and tear down, destroy and overthrow, build up and plant."

Jeremiah Sees Two Visions

11 The LORD spoke his word to me, saying: "Jeremiah, what do you see?"

I answered, "I see a stick of almond wood."

12 The LORD said to me, "You have seen correctly, because I am watching to make sure my words come true."

13 The LORD spoke his word to me again: "What do you see?"

I answered, "I see a pot of boiling water, tipping over from the north."

14 The LORD said to me, "Disaster will come from the north and strike all the people who live in this country. 15 In a short time I will call all of the people in the northern kingdoms," said the LORD.

"Those kings will come and set up their thrones
near the entrance of the gates of Jerusalem.

FAITH links

TOO YOUNG TO SERVE

JEREMIAH 1:4-9

"You're too young!" Have you heard those words recently in connection with something you're not allowed to do? Maybe you're too young to drive a car or vote right now, but there's one thing you're not too young for: serving God. Jeremiah thought that he was too young to speak for God. But God assured Jeremiah that he would help him. God would give him the words to say.

God has a purpose for everyone. God can use anyone to do his will – so let him use you.

Think God can't use you? Link here:

Everyone Can Help, Numbers 4, p. 181

Your Best Work, 1 Kings 6, p. 443

Said It? Do It! Lamentations 2:17, p. 1077

Love Him? Show It! Amos 2:6–7, p. 1196

Just Say Yes! Matthew 9:9–13, p. 1289

My Best Serve, Acts 6:1–6, p. 1473

They will attack all the city walls
around Jerusalem
and all the cities in Judah.
16 And I will announce my judgements
against my people
because of their evil in turning
away from me.
They offered sacrifices to other gods
and worshipped idols they had
made with their own hands.
17 "Jeremiah, get ready. Stand up and tell them everything I command you to say. Don't be afraid of the people, or I will give you good reason to be afraid of them. 18 Today I am going to make you a strong city, an iron pillar, a bronze wall. You will be able to stand against everyone in the land: Judah's kings, officers, priests and the people of the land. 19 They will fight against you, but they will not defeat you, because I am with you to protect you!" says the LORD.

Israel Turns from God

2 The LORD spoke his word to me, saying: 2 "Go and speak to the people of Jerusalem, saying: This is what the LORD says:
'I remember how faithful you were to
me when you were a young
nation.
You loved me like a young bride.
You followed me through the desert,
a land that had never been planted.
3 The people of Israel were holy to the
LORD,
like the first fruits from his
harvest.
Those who tried to hurt Israel were
judged guilty.
Disasters struck them,'" says the
LORD.

4 Hear the word of the LORD, family of
Jacob,
all you family groups of Israel.
5 This is what the LORD says:
"I was fair to your ancestors,
so why did they turn away from
me?
Your ancestors worshipped useless
idols

FAITH links

A BROKEN PROMISE
JEREMIAH 2:1-8

Did someone ever promise you that they would be your friend for ever, but later wound up breaking that promise? God told Jeremiah to tell the Israelites that they had been unfaithful to him. They had promised to be committed to him, but failed. A commitment is a promise to be faithful. Even though the people were unfaithful to God, God remained faithful to them.

When you make a commitment to a friend, that friend expects you to be loyal. If Jesus is your Saviour, you've made a commitment to follow his commands. God wants you to honour your commitment to him.

A Serious Promise, Deuteronomy 23:21–23, p. 257

Loyal to a Friend, 2 Samuel 9, p. 409

The Salt Promise, 2 Chronicles 13:5, p. 576

You Are What You Do, Proverbs 20:11, p. 854

A Christian's Responsibility, Acts 11:26, p. 1484

Hot, Cold or In Between? Revelation 3:15, p. 1735

---

and became useless themselves.
6 Your ancestors didn't say,
'Where is the LORD who brought
us out of Egypt?
He led us through the desert,

through a dry and rocky land,
through a dark and dangerous land.
He led us where no one travels or
lives.'

7 I brought you into a fertile land
so you could eat its fruit and
produce.
But you came and made my land
unclean;
you made it a hateful place.
8 The priests didn't ask,
'Where is the LORD?'
The people who know the teachings
didn't know me.
The leaders turned against me.
The prophets prophesied in the name
of Baal
and worshipped useless idols.

9 "So now I will again tell what I have
against you," says the LORD.
"And I will tell what I have against
your grandchildren.
10 Go across the sea to the island of
Cyprus and see.
Send someone to the land of Kedar
to look closely.
See if there has ever been anything
like this.
11 Has a nation ever exchanged its gods?
(Of course, its gods are not really
gods at all.)
But my people have exchanged their
glorious God
for idols worth nothing.
12 Skies, be shocked at the things that
have happened
and shake with great fear!" says
the LORD.
13 "My people have done two sins:
they have turned away from me,
the spring of living water.
And they have dug their own wells,
which are broken wells that cannot
hold water.
14 Have the people of Israel become
slaves?
Have they become like someone
who was born a slave?
Why were they taken captive?
15 Enemies have roared like lions at
Israel;
they have growled at Israel.

They have destroyed the land of
Israel.
The cities of Israel lie in ruins,
and all the people have left.
16 The men from the cities of Memphis
and Tahpanhes
have disgraced you by shaving the
top of your head.
17 Haven't you brought this on
yourselves
by turning away from the LORD
your God
when he was leading you in the
right way?
18 It did not help to go to Egypt
and drink from the Shihor River.
It did not help to go to Assyria
and drink from the Euphrates
River.
19 Your evil will bring punishment to
you,
and the wrong you have done will
teach you a lesson.
Think about it and understand
that it is a terrible evil to turn away
from the LORD your God.
It is wrong not to fear me,"
says the Lord GOD All-powerful.

20 "Long ago you refused to obey me as
an ox breaks its yoke.
You broke the ropes I used to hold
you
and said, 'I will not serve you!'
In fact, on every high hill
and under every green tree
you lay down as a prostitute.
21 But I planted you as a special vine,
as a very good seed.
How then did you turn
into a wild vine that grows bad
fruit?
22 Although you wash yourself with
cleanser
and use much soap,
I can still see the stain of your
guilt," says the Lord GOD.
23 "How can you say to me, 'I am not
guilty.
I have not worshipped the Baal
idols'?
Look at the things you did in the
valley.

Think about what you have done.
You are like a she-camel in mating
    season
    that runs from place to place.
24 You are like a wild donkey that lives
    in the desert
    and sniffs the wind at mating time.
    At that time who can hold her
        back?
    Any male who chases her will easily
        catch her;
    at mating time, it is easy to find
        her.
25 Don't run until your feet are bare
    or until your throat is dry.
    But you say, 'It's no use!
    I love those other gods
    and I must chase them!'

26 "A thief is ashamed when someone
        catches him stealing.
    In the same way, the family of
        Israel is ashamed—
    they, their kings, their officers,
        their priests and their prophets.
27 They say to things of wood, 'You are
        my father,'
    and to idols of stone, 'You gave
        birth to me.'
    Those people won't look at me;
    they have turned their backs to
        me.
    But when they get into trouble, they
        say,
    'Come and save us!'
28 Where are the idols you made for
        yourselves?
    Let them come and save you
    when you are in trouble!
    People of Judah, you have as many
        idols
    as you have towns!

29 "Why do you complain to me?
    All of you have turned against me,"
        says the LORD.
30 "I punished your people, but it did
        not help.
    They didn't come back when they
        were punished.
    With your swords you killed your
        prophets
    like a hungry lion.

31 "People of Judah, pay attention to
        the word of the LORD:
    have I been like a desert to the
        people of Israel
    or like a dark and dangerous land?
    Why do my people say, 'We are free
        to wander.
    We won't come to you any more'?
32 A young woman does not forget her
        jewellery,
    and a bride does not forget the
        decorations for her dress.
    But my people have forgotten me
    for more days than can be counted.
33 You really know how to chase after
        love.
    Even the worst women can learn
        evil ways from you.
34 Even on your clothes you have the
        blood
    of poor and innocent people,
    but they weren't thieves you
        caught breaking in.
    You do all these things,
35 but you say, 'I am innocent.
    God is not angry with me.'
    But I will judge you guilty of lying,
    because you say, 'I have not
        sinned.'
36 It is so easy for you to change your
        mind.
    Even Egypt will let you down,
    as Assyria let you down.
37 You will eventually leave that place
    with your hands on your head, like
        captives.
    You trusted those countries,
    but you will not be helped by them,
    because the LORD has rejected them.

Judah is Unfaithful

3 "If a man divorces his wife
    and she leaves him and marries
        another man,
    should her first husband come back
        to her again?
    If he went back to her, wouldn't the
        land become completely
        unclean?
    But you have acted like a prostitute
        with many lovers,
    and now you want to come back to
        me?" says the LORD.

2 "Look up to the bare hilltops, Judah.
>   Is there any place where you have not been a prostitute?
> You have sat by the road waiting for lovers
>   like an Arab in the desert.
> You made the land unclean,
>   because you did evil and were like a prostitute.
> 3 So the rain has not come,
>   and there have not been any spring rains.
> But your face still looks like the face of a prostitute.
>   You refuse even to be ashamed of what you did.
> 4 Now you are calling to me,
>   'My father, you have been my friend since I was young.
> 5 Will you always be angry at me?
>   Will your anger last for ever?'
> Judah, you said this,
>   but you did as much evil as you could!"

Judah and Israel are like Sisters

6 When King Josiah was ruling Judah, the LORD said to me, "Did you see what unfaithful Israel did? She was like a prostitute with her idols on every hill and under every green tree. 7 I said to myself, 'Israel will come back to me after she does this evil,' but she didn't come back. And Israel's wicked sister Judah saw what she did. 8 Judah saw that I divorced unfaithful Israel because of her adultery, but that didn't make Israel's wicked sister Judah afraid. She also went out and acted like a prostitute! 9 And she didn't care that she was acting like a prostitute. So she made her country unclean and was guilty of adultery, because she worshipped idols made of stone and wood. 10 Israel's wicked sister didn't even come back to me with her whole heart, but only pretended," says the LORD.

11 The LORD said to me, "Unfaithful Israel had a better excuse than wicked Judah. 12 Go and speak this message towards the north:
> 'Come back, unfaithful people of Israel,' says the LORD.
> 'I will stop being angry with you,
>   because I am full of mercy,' says the LORD.
> 'I will not be angry with you for ever.
> 13 All you have to do is admit your sin—
>   that you turned against the LORD your God
> and worshipped gods under every green tree
>   and didn't obey me,'" says the LORD.

14 "Come back to me, you unfaithful children," says the LORD, "because I am your master. I will take one person from every city and two from every family group, and I will bring you to Jerusalem. 15 Then I will give you new rulers who will be faithful to me, who will lead you with knowledge and understanding. 16 In those days there will be many of you in the land," says the LORD. "At that time people will no longer say, 'I remember the Ark of the Agreement.' They won't think about it any more or remember it or miss it or make another one. 17 At that time people will call Jerusalem The Throne of the LORD, and all nations will come together in Jerusalem to show respect to the LORD. They will not follow their stubborn, evil hearts any more. 18 In those days the family of Judah will join the family of Israel. They will come together from a land in the north to the land I gave their ancestors.

19 "I, the LORD, said,
> 'How happy I would be to treat you as my own children
>   and give you a pleasant land,
>   a land more beautiful than that of any other nation.'
> I thought you would call me 'My Father'

> Then I will give you new rulers who will be faithful to me, who will lead you with knowledge and understanding.
> – Jeremiah 3:15

and not turn away from me.
20 But like a woman who is unfaithful to
her husband,
family of Israel, you have been
unfaithful to me," says the
LORD.

21 You can hear crying on the bare
hilltops.
It is the people of Israel crying and
praying for mercy.
They have become very evil
and have forgotten the LORD their
God.
22 "Come back to me, you unfaithful
children,
and I will forgive you for being
unfaithful."

"Yes, we will come to you,
because you are the LORD our
God.
23 It was foolish to worship idols on the
hills
and on the mountains.
Surely the salvation of Israel
comes from the LORD our God.
24 Since our youth, shameful gods have
eaten up in sacrifice
everything our ancestors worked
for—
their flocks and herds,
their sons and daughters.
25 Let us lie down in our shame,
and let our disgrace cover us like a
blanket.
We have sinned against the LORD our
God,
both we and our ancestors.
From our youth until now,
we have not obeyed the LORD our
God."

4 "If you will return, Israel,
then return to me," says the
LORD.
"If you will throw away your idols
that I hate,
then don't wander away from me.
2 If you say when you make a promise,
'As surely as the LORD lives,'
and you can say it in a truthful,
honest and right way,

then the nations will be blessed by
him
and they will praise him for what
he has done."

FAITH links

REAL REPENTANCE
JEREMIAH 4:1-4

When a person says, "Sorry!" but doesn't look or act sorry, would you believe their apology? Not likely! Their apology would seem unreal if their behaviour remained the same. After Israel had sinned, God told them how to return to him. He wanted to see some real repentance. They had to get rid of their idols and keep the law that Moses had given them.

Repentance is a part of forgiveness. Although God offers forgiveness, he expects us to "turn away" from the things we do or say that displease him. That's real repentance.

Link here to see what God has to say about being really sorry:

Own Up to It, 2 Samuel 12:1–13, p. 412

This Hurts Me More? 2 Chronicles 36:17–22, p. 606

Learning from Mistakes, Psalm 51:12–13, p. 748

Red to White, Isaiah 1:18, p. 896

The Watchman, Ezekiel 3:16–22, p. 1088

The Temptation Fighter, Matthew 4:1–11, p. 1278

3 This is what the LORD says to the people of Judah and to Jerusalem:
"Plough your unploughed fields,
    and don't plant seeds among thorns.
4 Give yourselves to the service of the LORD
    and decide to obey him,
    people of Judah and people of Jerusalem.
If you don't, my anger will spread among you like a fire,
    and no one will be able to put it out,
    because of the evil you have done.

Trouble from the North

5 "Announce this message in Judah and say it in Jerusalem:
    'Blow the trumpet throughout the country!'
Shout out loud and say,
    'Come together!
Let's all escape to the fortified cities!'
6 Raise the signal flag towards Jerusalem!
    Run for your lives and don't wait,
    because I am bringing disaster from the north.
    There will be terrible destruction."

7 A lion has come out of his den;
    a destroyer of nations has begun to march.
He has left his home
    to destroy your land.
Your towns will be destroyed
    with no one left to live in them.
8 So put on rough cloth,
    show how sad you are and cry loudly.
The terrible anger of the LORD
    has not turned away from us.

9 "When this happens," says the LORD,
    "the king and officers will lose their courage.
The priests will be terribly afraid
    and the prophets will be shocked!"
10 Then I said, "Lord GOD, you have tricked the people of Judah and Jerusalem. You said, 'You will have peace,' but now the sword is pointing at our throats!"

11 At that time this message will be given to Judah and Jerusalem: "A hot wind blows from the bare hilltops of the desert towards the LORD's people. It is not a gentle wind to separate grain from chaff. 12 I feel a stronger wind than that. Now even I will announce judgements against the people of Judah."

13 Look! The enemy rises up like a cloud,
    and his chariots come like a windstorm.
His horses are faster than eagles.
    How terrible it will be for us! We are ruined!
14 People of Jerusalem, clean the evil from your hearts so that you can be saved.
    Don't continue making evil plans.
15 A voice from Dan makes an announcement
    and brings bad news from the mountains of Ephraim.
16 "Report this to the nations.
    Spread this news in Jerusalem:
    'Invaders are coming from a faraway country,
    shouting words of war against the cities of Judah.
17 The enemy has surrounded Jerusalem as men guard a field,
    because Judah turned against me,'" says the LORD.
18 "The way you have lived and acted has brought this trouble to you.
This is your punishment.
    How terrible it is!
    The pain stabs your heart!"

Jeremiah's Cry

19 Oh, how I hurt! How I hurt!
    I am bent over in pain.
    Oh, the torture in my heart!
    My heart is pounding inside me.
    I cannot keep quiet,
    because I have heard the sound of the trumpet.
    I have heard the shouts of war.
20 Disaster follows disaster;

the whole country has been
    destroyed.
My tents are destroyed in only a
    moment.
My curtains are torn down quickly.
21 How long must I look at the war flag?
    How long must I listen to the war
        trumpet?

22 The LORD says, "My people are
        foolish.
    They do not know me.
    They are stupid children;
        they don't understand.
    They are skilful at doing evil,
        but they don't know how to do
            good."

Disaster is Coming

23 I looked at the earth
        and it was empty and had no
            shape.
    I looked at the sky
        and its light was gone.
24 I looked at the mountains
        and they were shaking.
    All the hills were trembling.
25 I looked, and there were no people.
    Every bird in the sky had flown
        away.
26 I looked, and the good, rich land had
        become a desert.
    All its towns had been destroyed
        by the LORD and his great anger.

27 This is what the LORD says:
    "All the land will be ruined,
        but I will not completely destroy it.
28 So the people in the land will cry
        loudly
    and the sky will grow dark,
        because I have spoken and will not
            change my mind.
    I have made a decision and I will
        not change it."

29 At the sound of the horsemen and the
        archers,
    all the people in the towns run away.
    They hide in the thick bushes
        and climb up into the rocks.
    All of the cities of Judah are empty;
        no one lives in them.

30 Judah, you destroyed nation, what are
        you doing?
    Why do you put on your finest
        dress
    and decorate yourself with gold
        jewellery?
    Why do you put colour around your
        eyes?
    You make yourself beautiful, but it
        is all useless.
    Your lovers hate you;
        they want to kill you.

31 I hear a cry like a woman having a
        baby,
    distress like a woman having her
        first child.
    It is the sound of Jerusalem gasping
        for breath.
    She lifts her hands in prayer and
        says,
    "Oh! I am about to faint
        before my murderers!"

No One is Right

5 The LORD says, "Walk up and down
    the streets of Jerusalem.
    Look around and discover these
        things.
    Search the public squares of the city.
    If you can find one person who does
        honest things,
    who searches for the truth,
        I will forgive this city.
2 Although the people say, 'As surely as
        the LORD lives!'
    they don't really mean it."

3 LORD, don't you look for truth in
        people?
    You struck the people of Judah,
        but they didn't feel any pain.
    You crushed them,
        but they refused to learn what is
            right.
    They became more stubborn than a
        rock;
    they refused to turn back to God.
4 But I thought,
    "These are only the poor, foolish
        people.
    They have not learned the way of the
        LORD

FAITH links

ALL TALK, NO ACTION
JEREMIAH 5:1-2

The story is told of a Greek philosopher named Diogenes (die-o-juh-knees) who went around Athens in search of an honest man. He claimed not to have found one. God sent Jeremiah in a similar search around Jerusalem. Unlike Diogenes, God already knew that everyone was dishonest. They claimed to worship God, but their actions didn't match their words. They were spiritual phonies – all talk and no action!

God doesn't like spiritual phoniness! He expects his people to be honest. If we tell others that we worship God, but don't really do it, we might fool them – but we never fool God.

Serious About the Sabbath, Exodus 31:15, p. 117

Always Truthful, Numbers 23:19, p. 208

No Middle Ground, Joshua 24:14–15, p. 307

Empty Words, Ezekiel 33:30–33, p. 1127

Perfectly Pleasing? Matthew 5:1–12, p. 1280

One Thing to Do, Romans 4:1–5, p. 1523

---

and what their God wants them to do.

5 So I will go to the leaders of Judah and talk to them.

Surely they understand the way of the LORD
and know what God wants them to do."
But even the leaders had all joined together to break away from the LORD;
they had broken their ties with him.

6 So a lion from the forest will attack them.
A wolf from the desert will kill them.
A leopard is waiting for them near their towns.
It will tear to pieces anyone who comes out of the city,
because the people of Judah have sinned greatly.
They have wandered away from the LORD many times.

7 The LORD said, "Tell me why I should forgive you.
Your children have left me
and have made promises to idols that are not gods at all.
I gave your children everything they needed,
but they still were like an unfaithful wife to me.
They spent much time in houses of prostitutes.
8 They are like well-fed horses filled with sexual desire;
each one wants another man's wife.
9 Shouldn't I punish the people of Judah for doing these things?" says the LORD.
"Shouldn't I give a nation such as this the punishment it deserves?

10 "Go along and cut down Judah's vineyards,
but do not completely destroy them.
Cut off all her people as if they were branches,
because they do not belong to the LORD.
11 The families of Israel and Judah have been completely unfaithful to me," says the LORD.

12 Those people have lied about the Lord
and said, "He will not do anything to us!
Nothing bad will happen to us!
We will never see war or hunger!
13 The prophets are like an empty wind;
the word of God is not in them.
Let the bad things they say happen to them."
14 So this is what the Lord God All-powerful says:
"The people said I would not punish them.
So, the words I give you will be like fire,
and these people will be like wood that it burns up.
15 Listen, family of Israel," says the Lord,
"I will soon bring a nation from far away to attack you.
It is an old nation that has lasted a long time.
The people there speak a language you do not know;
you cannot understand what they say.
16 Their arrows bring death.
All their people are strong warriors.
17 They will eat your crops and your food.
They will eat your sons and daughters.
They will eat your flocks and herds.
They will eat your grapes and figs.
They will destroy with their swords the fortified cities you trust.
18 "Yet even then," says the Lord, "I will not destroy you completely. 19 When the people of Judah ask, 'Why has the Lord our God done all these terrible things to us?' then give them this answer: 'You have left the Lord and served foreign idols in your own land. So now you will serve foreigners in a land that does not belong to you.'

20 "Announce this message to the family of Jacob,
and tell it to the nation of Judah:
21 hear this message, you foolish people who have no sense.
They have eyes, but they don't really see.
They have ears, but they don't really listen.
22 Surely you are afraid of me," says the Lord.
"You should shake with fear in my presence.
I am the one who made the beaches to be a border for the sea,
a border the water can never go past.
The waves may pound the beach, but they can't win over it.
They may roar, but they cannot go beyond it.
23 But the people of Judah are stubborn and have turned against me.
They have turned aside and gone away from me.
24 They do not say to themselves,
'We should fear the Lord our God,
who gives us autumn and spring rains in their seasons,
who makes sure we have the harvest at the right time.'
25 But your evil has kept away both rain and harvest.
Your sins have kept you from enjoying good things.
26 There are wicked men among my people.
Like those who make nets for catching birds,
they set their traps to catch people.
27 Like cages full of birds,
their houses are full of lies.
They have become rich and powerful.
28 They have grown big and fat.
There is no end to the evil things they do.
They won't plead the case of the orphan
or help the poor be judged fairly.
29 Shouldn't I punish the people of Judah for doing these things?" says the Lord.
"Shouldn't I give a nation such as this the punishment it deserves?

30 "A terrible and shocking thing
       has happened in the land of Judah:
31 the prophets speak lies
       and the priests take power into
           their own hands,
       and my people love it this way.
           But what will you do when the end
               comes?

Jerusalem is Surrounded

6 "Run for your lives, people of
       Benjamin!
   Run away from Jerusalem!
   Blow the war trumpet in the town of
       Tekoa!
   Raise the warning flag over the
       town of Beth Hakkerem!
   Disaster is coming from the north;
       terrible destruction is coming to
           you.
2 Jerusalem, I will destroy you,
       you who are fragile and gentle.
3 Shepherds with their flocks will come
       against Jerusalem.
   They will set up their tents all
       around her,
   each shepherd taking care of his
       own section."
4 They say, "Get ready to fight against
       Jerusalem!
   Get up! We will attack at noon!
   But it is already getting late;
       the evening shadows are growing
           long.
5 So get up! We will attack at night.
   We will destroy the strong towers
       of Jerusalem!"
6 This is what the LORD All-powerful
says:
   "Cut down the trees around
       Jerusalem
   and build an attack ramp to the top
       of its walls.
   This city must be punished.
       Inside it is nothing but slavery.
7 Jerusalem pours out her evil
       as a well pours out its water.
   The sounds of violence and
       destruction are heard within her.
   I can see the sickness and hurts of
       Jerusalem.
8 Listen to this warning, Jerusalem,
       or I will turn my back on you
   and make your land an empty desert
       where no one can live."
9 This is what the LORD All-powerful
says:
   "Gather the few people of Israel who
       are left alive,
   as you would gather the last grapes
       on a grapevine.
   Check each vine again,
       like someone who gathers grapes."

10 To whom can I speak? Whom can I
       warn?
   Who will listen to me?
   The people of Israel have closed
       ears,
   so they cannot hear my warnings.
   They don't like the word of the
       LORD;
   they don't want to listen to it!
11 But I am full of the anger of the
       LORD
   and I am tired of holding it in.

   "Pour out my anger on the children
       who play in the street
   and on the young men gathered
       together.
   A husband and his wife will both be
       caught in his anger,
   as will the very old.
12 Their houses will be turned over to
       others,
   along with their fields and wives,
   because I will raise my hand
       and punish the people of Judah,"
           says the LORD.
13 "Everyone, from the least important
       to the greatest,
   is greedy for money.
   Even the prophets and priests
       all tell lies.
14 They tried to heal my people's
       serious injuries
   as if they were small wounds.
   They said, 'It's all right, it's all right.'
       But really, it is not all right.
15 They should be ashamed of the
       terrible way they act,
   but they are not ashamed at all.
   They don't even know how to
       blush about their sins.

So they will fall, along with everyone
    else.
  They will be thrown to the ground
    when I punish them," says the
    Lord.
16 This is what the Lord says:
  "Stand where the roads cross and
    look.
  Ask where the old way is,
  where the good way is, and walk on
    it.
  If you do, you will find rest for
    yourselves.
  But they have said,
    'We will not walk on the good way.'
17 I set watchmen over you
  and told you,
    'Listen for the sound of the war
      trumpet!'
  But they said, 'We will not listen.'
18 So listen, all you nations,
  and pay attention, you witnesses.
  Watch what I will do to the people
    of Judah.
19 Hear this, people of the earth:
  I am going to bring disaster to the
    people of Judah
  because of the evil they plan.
  They have not listened to my
    messages
  and have rejected my teachings.
20 Why do you bring me offerings of
    incense from the land of
    Sheba?
  Why do you bring me sweet-
    smelling cane from a faraway
    land?
  Your burnt offerings will not be
    accepted;
  your sacrifices do not please me."
21 So this is what the Lord says:
  "I will put problems in front of
    Judah.
  Fathers and sons will stumble over
    them together.
  Neighbours and friends will die."
22 This is what the Lord says:
  "Look, an army is coming
  from the land of the north;
  a great nation is coming
  from the far sides of the earth.
23 The soldiers carry bows and spears.
  They are cruel and show no mercy.
  They sound like the roaring ocean
    when they ride their horses.
  That army is coming lined up for
    battle,
  ready to attack you, Jerusalem."

24 We have heard the news about that
    army
  and are helpless from fear.
  We are trapped by our pain,
  like a woman having a baby.
25 Don't go out into the fields
  or walk down the roads,
  because the enemy has swords.
  There is terror on every side.
26 My people, put on rough cloth
  and roll in the ashes to show how
    sad you are.
  Cry loudly for those who are dead,
  as if your only son were dead,
  because the destroyer
  will soon come against us.
27 "Jeremiah, I have made you like a
    worker who tests metal,
  and my people are like the metal.
  You must observe their ways
  and test them.
28 All my people have turned against me
  and are stubborn.
  They go around telling lies about
    others.
  They are like bronze and iron
  that became covered with rust.
  They all act dishonestly.
29 The fire is fanned to make it hotter,
  but the lead does not melt.
  The pure metal does not come out;
  the evil is not removed from my
    people.
30 My people will be called rejected silver,
  because the Lord has rejected
    them."

> Ask where the old way is, where the good way is, and walk on it.
> – Jeremiah 6:16

Jeremiah's Temple Message

7 This is the word that the LORD spoke to Jeremiah: 2 "Stand at the gate of the Temple and preach this message there:

"'Hear the word of the LORD, all you people of the nation of Judah! All you who come through these gates to worship the LORD, listen to this message! 3 This is what the LORD All-powerful, the God of Israel, says: Change your lives and do what is right! Then I will let you live in this place. 4 Don't trust the lies of people who say, "This is the Temple of the LORD. This is the Temple of the LORD. This is the Temple of the LORD!" 5 You must change your lives and do what is right. Be fair to each other. 6 You must not oppress strangers, orphans and widows. Don't kill innocent people in this place! Don't follow other gods, or they will ruin your lives. 7 If you do these things, I will let you live in this land that I gave to your ancestors to keep for ever.

7:5-7 Character Find out how God wants you to treat others.

8 "'But look, you are trusting lies, which is useless. 9 Will you steal and murder and be guilty of adultery? Will you falsely accuse other people? Will you burn incense to the god Baal and follow other gods you have not known? 10 If you do that, do you think you can come before me and stand in this place where I have chosen to be worshipped? Do you think you can say, "We are safe!" when you do all these hateful things? 11 This place where I have chosen to be worshipped is nothing more to you than a hideout for robbers. I have been watching you, says the LORD.

12 "'You people of Judah, go now to the town of Shiloh, where I first made a place to be worshipped. See what I did to it because of the evil things the people of Israel had done. 13 You people of Judah have done all these evil things too, says the LORD. I spoke to you again and again, but you did not listen to me. I called you, but you did not answer. 14 So I will destroy the place where I have chosen to be worshipped in Jerusalem. You trust in that place, which I gave to you and your ancestors, but I will destroy it just as I destroyed Shiloh. 15 I will push you away from me just as I pushed away your relatives, the people of Israel!'

16 "As for you, Jeremiah, don't pray for these people. Don't cry out for them or ask anything for them or beg me to help them, because I will not listen to you. 17 Don't you see what they are doing in the towns of Judah and in the streets of Jerusalem? 18 The children gather wood, and the fathers use the wood to make a fire. The women make the dough for cakes of bread, and they offer them to the Queen Goddess. They pour out drink offerings to other gods to make me angry. 19 But I am not the one the people of Judah are really hurting, says the LORD. They are only hurting themselves and bringing shame upon themselves.

20 "'So this is what the Lord GOD says: I will pour out my anger on this place, on people and animals, on the trees in the field and the crops in the ground. My anger will be like a hot fire that no one can put out.

Obedience is More than Sacrifice

21 "'This is what the LORD All-powerful, the God of Israel, says: Offer burnt offerings along with your other sacrifices, and eat the meat yourselves! 22 When I brought your ancestors out of Egypt, I did not speak to them and give them commands only about burnt offerings and sacrifices. 23 I also gave them this command: obey me, and I will be your God and you will be my people. Do all that I command so that good things will happen to you. 24 But your ancestors did not listen or pay attention to me. They were stubborn and did whatever their evil hearts wanted. They went backwards, not forwards. 25 Since the day your ancestors left Egypt, I have sent my servants, the prophets, again and again to you. 26 But your ancestors did not listen or pay attention to me. They were very stubborn and did more evil than their ancestors.'

27 "Jeremiah, you will tell all these

things to the people of Judah, but they will not listen to you. You will call to them, but they will not answer you. 28 So say to them, 'This is the nation that has not obeyed the LORD its God. These people do nothing when I correct them. They do not tell the truth; it has disappeared from their lips.

The Valley of Killing

29 "'Cut off your hair and throw it away. Go up to the bare hilltop and cry out, because the LORD has rejected these people. He has turned his back on them, and in his anger will punish them. 30 The people of Judah have done what I said was evil, says the LORD. They have set up their hateful idols in the place where I have chosen to be worshipped and have made it unclean. 31 The people of Judah have built places of worship at Topheth in the Valley of Ben Hinnom. There they burned their own sons and daughters as sacrifices, something I never commanded. It never even entered my mind. 32 So, I warn you. The days are coming, says the LORD, when people will not call this place Topheth or the Valley of Ben Hinnom any more. They will call it the Valley of Killing. They will bury the dead in Topheth until there is no room to bury anyone else. 33 Then the bodies of the dead will become food for the birds of the sky and for the wild animals. There will be no one left alive to chase them away. 34 I will end the happy sounds of the bride and bridegroom. There will be no happy sounds in the cities of Judah or in the streets of Jerusalem, because the land will become an empty desert!

8 "The LORD says: At that time they will remove from their tombs the bones of Judah's kings and officers, priests and prophets, and the people of Jerusalem. 2 The bones will be spread on the ground under the sun, moon and stars that the people loved and served and went after and searched for and worshipped. No one will gather up the bones and bury them. So they will be like dung thrown on the ground. 3 I will force the people of Judah to leave their homes and their land. Those of this evil family who are not dead will wish they were, says the LORD All-powerful.'

Sin and Punishment

4 "Say to the people of Judah: 'This is what the LORD says:
When people fall down, don't they get
    up again?
And when someone goes the
    wrong way, doesn't he turn
    back?
5 Why, then, have the people of
    Jerusalem gone the wrong way
    and not turned back?
They believe their own lies
    and refuse to turn around and
    come back.
6 I have listened to them very carefully,
    but they do not say what is right.
They do not feel sorry about their
    wicked ways,
    saying, "What have I done?"
Each person goes his own way,
    like a horse charging into a battle.
7 Even the birds in the sky
    know the right times to do things.
The storks, doves, swifts and
    thrushes
    know when it is time to migrate.
But my people don't know
    what the LORD wants them to do.

8 "'You keep saying, "We are wise,
    because we have the teachings of
    the LORD."
But actually, those who explain the
    Scriptures
    have written lies with their pens.
9 These wise men refused to listen to
    the word of the LORD,
    so they are not really wise at all.
They will be ashamed.
They will be shocked and trapped.
10 So I will give their wives to other men
    and their
    fields to
    new
    owners.
Everyone, from
    the least
    important to
    the greatest,
is greedy for money.

8:10 Greed
Check out God's view of greed.

Even the prophets and priests
  all tell lies.
11 They tried to heal my people's
    serious injuries
  as if they were small wounds.
  They said, "It's all right, it's all right."
  But really, it is not all right.
12 They should be ashamed of the
    terrible way they act,
  but they are not ashamed at all.
  They don't even know how to
    blush about their sins.
  So they will fall, along with everyone
    else.
  They will be thrown to the ground
    when I punish them, says the
    LORD.

13 "I will take away their crops, says
    the LORD.
  There will be no grapes on the
    vine
  and no figs on the fig tree.
  Even the leaves will dry up and
    die.
  I will take away what I gave them.'"

14 "Why are we just sitting here?
  Let's get together!
  We have sinned against the LORD,
    so he has given us poisoned water
    to drink.
  Come, let's run to the fortified
    cities.
  The LORD our God has decided
    that we must die,
  so let's die there.
15 We hoped to have peace,
  but nothing good has come.
  We hoped for a time when he would
    heal us,
  but only terror has come.
16 From the land of Dan,
  the snorting of the enemy's horses
    is heard.
  The ground shakes from the
    neighing of their large horses.
  They have come and destroyed
    the land and everything in it,
  the city and all who live there."

17 "Look! I am sending poisonous
    snakes to attack you.
  These snakes cannot be charmed,
  and they will bite you," says the
    LORD.

Jeremiah's Sadness

18 God, you are my comfort when I am
    very sad
  and when I am afraid.
19 Listen to the sound of my people.
  They cry from a faraway land:
  "Isn't the LORD still in Jerusalem?
  Isn't Jerusalem's king still there?"

  But God says, "Why did the people
    make me angry by worshipping
    idols,
  useless foreign idols?"

20 And the people say, "Harvest time is
    over;
  summer has ended,
  and we have not been saved."

21 Because my people are crushed, I am
    crushed.
  I cry loudly and am afraid for them.
22 Isn't there balm in the land of Gilead?
  Isn't there a doctor there?
  So why aren't the hurts of my people
    healed?

9 I wish my head were like a spring of
    water
  and my eyes like a fountain of
    tears!
  Then I could cry day and night
    for my people who have been
    killed.
2 I wish I had a place in the desert—
  a house where travellers spend the
    night—
  so I could leave my people.
  I could go away from them,
  because they are all unfaithful to God;
  they are all turning against him.

Judah's Failures

3 "They use their
    tongues
  like a bow,
  shooting lies
  from their
  mouths like
  arrows.

9:3
Truth
What's wrong
with lying?

CONTROLLING WHAT I SAY
Jeremiah 9:3

Loose Lips? What do you do when someone tells you a really important secret? Or tells you the latest rumour about that "bad kid" at school? Do you look for the first person you can tell, or do you refuse to pass on gossip? Do you have "loose lips" – telling secrets and spreading juicy stories – or are your lips sealed?

Rumours and gossip can be very harmful to friendships or reputations if they are believed. God is very displeased with rumours and the people who spread them. (Check out Jeremiah 29:24–32.) What can you do when someone passes on a rumour to you? Try to find out the truth, or do the next best thing: ignore it.

MORE FAITH LINKS

A Special Promise, **p. 217**
A Gentle Answer, **p. 847**
What's Wrong About Rumours, **p. 1032**
The Peril of Poisonous Plans, **p. 1221**
The Whole Truth, **p. 1438**
Say What?! **p. 1603**

> If someone says to you, "Did you hear what they're saying about . . ." what do you do?
>
> You'd better check out these links before you do anything!

Just Kidding? Genesis 21:8–10, p. 28
● Has anyone ever said something mean to you, then added, "I'm just kidding"? Have you ever done that to someone? How do you feel when someone teases you? To avoid hurting someone with your words, think how you would feel.

The Problem with Gossip, Proverbs 11:12–13, p. 840
● Gossip doesn't always mean passing on a rumour about someone. Link here to discover what rumours and gossip can lead to.

Trouble with the Tongue, James 3:3–12, p. 1692
● Have you ever said something nice to a friend, then turned around and called your brother or sister a mean name? This Faithlink has a lot to say about what comes out of our mouths!

my FAVOURITE links

Jeremiah 9:4

Lies, not truth,
   have grown strong in the land.
They go from one evil thing to
      another.
   They do not know who I am," says
      the LORD.
4 "Watch out for your friends
      and don't trust your own
         relatives,
   because every relative is a cheat
      and every friend tells lies about
         you.
5 Everyone lies to his friend
      and no one speaks the truth.
   The people of Judah have taught their
      tongues to lie.
   They have become tired from
      sinning.
6 Jeremiah, you live in the middle of
      lies.
   With their lies the people refuse to
      know me," says the LORD.
7 So this is what the LORD All-powerful
says:
   "I will test the people of Judah as a
      person tests metal in a fire.
   I have no other choice,
      because my people have sinned.
8 Their tongues are like sharp arrows.
      Their mouths speak lies.
   Everyone speaks nicely to his
      neighbour,
      but he is secretly planning to attack
         him.
9 Shouldn't I punish the people for
      doing this?" says the LORD.
   "Shouldn't I give a nation like this
      the punishment it deserves?"
10 I, Jeremiah, will cry loudly for the
      mountains
   and sing a funeral song for the
      empty fields.
   They are empty, and no one passes
      through.
   The mooing of cattle cannot be
      heard.
   The birds have flown away,
      and the animals are gone.
11 "I, the LORD, will make the city of
      Jerusalem a heap of ruins,
   a home for wild dogs.

I will destroy the cities of Judah
   so no one can live there."
12 What person is wise enough to understand these things? Is there someone who has been taught by the LORD who can explain them? Why was the land ruined? Why has it been made like an empty desert where no one goes?
13 The LORD answered, "It is because Judah has stopped following my teachings that I gave them. They have not obeyed me or done what I told them to do. 14 Instead, they were stubborn and followed the Baals, as their ancestors taught them to do." 15 So this is what the LORD All-powerful, the God of Israel, says: "I will soon make the people of Judah eat bitter food and drink poisoned water. 16 I will scatter them through other nations that they and their ancestors never knew about. I will chase the people of Judah with the sword until they are all killed."
17 This is what the LORD All-powerful
says:
   "Now, think about these things!
   Call for the women who cry at
      funerals to come.
   Send for those women who are
      good at that job.
18 Let them come quickly
      and cry loudly for us.
   Then our eyes will fill with tears
      and streams of water will flow from
         our eyelids.
19 The sound of loud crying is heard
      from Jerusalem:
   'We are truly ruined!
   We are truly ashamed!
   We must leave our land,
      because our houses are in
         ruins.'"
20 Now, women of Judah, listen to the
      word of the LORD;
   open your ears to hear the words
      of his mouth.
   Teach your daughters how to cry
      loudly.
   Teach one another a funeral
      song.
21 Death has climbed in through our
      windows
   and has entered our strong cities.

FAITH links

BRAGGING RIGHTS
JEREMIAH 9:23-24

What qualities or possessions do you admire? Some people admire those with great personalities, money, cool toys, high scores in video games, or popularity. People with these qualities or possessions might even brag about having them. Bragging about something you have is also known as boasting. Jeremiah told the Israelites about one quality that's worth boasting about: how much a person understands about God and what God wants them to do.

God is kind and fair towards others. Knowing him helps us to be kind and fair, too. That's worth bragging about.

Want to brag about something? Connect here:

From Zero to Hero, Judges 6; 7, p. 319

Plans for a Son, 1 Chronicles 22:5-19, p. 548

More Precious Than Gold, Psalm 19:7-10, p. 723

A Useless Thing, Isaiah 44:9, 18-20, p. 954

God's New Temple, Ezekiel 40—44, p. 1135

The Gift, John 3:16-18, p. 1427

Death has taken away our children
who play in the streets
and the young men who meet in
the city squares.

22 Say, "This is what the LORD says:
'The dead bodies of people will lie
in the open field like dung.
They will lie like grain a farmer has
cut,
but there will be no one to gather
them.'"
23 This is what the LORD says:
"The wise must not boast about their
wisdom.
The strong must not boast about
their strength.
The rich must not boast about their
money.
24 But if someone wants to boast, let
him boast
that he understands and knows me.
Let him boast that I am the LORD,
and that I am kind and fair,
and that I do things that are right
on earth.
This kind of boasting pleases me,"
says the LORD.
25 The LORD says, "The time is coming when I will punish all those who are circumcised only in the flesh: 26 the people of Egypt, Judah, Edom, Ammon and Moab and the desert people who cut their hair short. The men in all those countries are not circumcised. And the whole family of Israel does not give itself to serving me."

The Lord and the Idols

10 Family of Israel, listen to what the LORD says to you. 2 This is what he says:
"Don't live like the people from other
nations,
and don't be afraid of special signs
in the sky,
even though the other nations are
afraid of them.
3 The customs of other people are
worth nothing.
Their idols are just wood cut from
the forest,
shaped by a worker with his chisel.
4 They decorate their idols with silver
and gold.
With hammers and nails they
fasten them down

so they won't fall over.
⁵ Their idols are like scarecrows in melon fields;
they cannot talk.
Since they cannot walk,
they must be carried.
Do not be afraid of those idols,
because they can't hurt you
and they can't help you either."

⁶ LORD, there is no one like you.
You are great,
and your name is great and powerful.
⁷ Everyone should respect you, King of the nations;
you deserve respect.
Of all the wise people among the nations
and in all the kingdoms,
none of them is as wise as you.
⁸ Those wise people are stupid and foolish.
Their teachings come from worthless wooden idols.
⁹ Hammered silver is brought from Tarshish
and gold from Uphaz,
so the idols are made by craftsmen and goldsmiths.
They put blue and purple clothes on the idols.
All these things are made by skilled workers.
¹⁰ But the LORD is the only true God.
He is the only living God, the King for ever.
The earth shakes when he is angry
and the nations cannot stand up to his anger.
¹¹ "Tell them this message: 'These gods did not make heaven and earth; they will be destroyed and disappear from heaven and earth.'"

¹² God made the earth by his power.
He used his wisdom to build the world
and his understanding to stretch out the skies.
¹³ When he thunders, the waters in the skies roar.
He makes clouds rise in the sky all over the earth.
He sends lightning with the rain
and brings out the wind from his storehouses.

¹⁴ People are so stupid and know so little.
Goldsmiths are made ashamed by their idols,
because those statues are only false gods.
They have no breath in them.
¹⁵ They are worth nothing; people make fun of them.
When they are judged, they will be destroyed.
¹⁶ But God, who is Jacob's Portion, is not like the idols.
He made everything
and he chose Israel to be his special people.
The LORD All-powerful is his name.

Destruction is Coming

¹⁷ Get everything you own and prepare to leave,
you people who are trapped by your enemies.
¹⁸ This is what the LORD says:
"At this time I will throw out the people who live in this land.
I will bring trouble to them
so that they may be captured."

¹⁹ How terrible it will be for me because of my injury.
My wound cannot be healed.
Yet I told myself,
"This is my sickness; I must suffer through it."
²⁰ My tent is ruined

> Of all the wise people among the nations and in all the kingdoms, none of them is as wise as you.
> – Jeremiah 10:7

and all its ropes are broken.
My children have gone away and left me.
No one is left to put up my tent again
or to set up a shelter for me.
21 The shepherds are stupid
and don't ask the LORD for advice.
So they do not have success
and all their flocks are scattered and lost.
22 Listen! The news is coming.
A loud noise comes from the north
to make the towns of Judah an empty desert
and a home for wild dogs!

Jeremiah's Prayer

23 LORD, I know that a person's life
doesn't really belong to him.
No one can control his own life.
24 LORD, correct me, but be fair.
Don't punish me in your anger,
or you will destroy me.
25 Pour out your anger on other nations
that do not know you
and do not pray to you.
Those nations have destroyed Jacob's family.
They have eaten him up completely
and destroyed his homeland.

The Agreement is Broken

11 These are the words that the LORD spoke to Jeremiah: 2 "Listen to the words of this agreement and tell them to the people of Judah and those living in Jerusalem. 3 Tell them this is what the LORD, the God of Israel, says: 'Cursed is the person who does not obey the words of this agreement 4 that I made with your ancestors when I brought them out of Egypt. Egypt was like a furnace for melting iron!' I told them, 'Obey me and do everything I command you. Then you will be my people, and I will be your God. 5 Then I will keep the promise I made to your ancestors to give them a fertile land.' And you are living in that country today."

I answered, "Amen, LORD."

6 The LORD said to me, "Announce this message in the towns of Judah and in the streets of Jerusalem: 'Listen to the words of this agreement and obey them. 7 I warned your ancestors to obey me when I brought them out of Egypt. I have warned them again and again to this very day: "Obey me!" 8 But your ancestors did not listen to me. They were stubborn and did what their own evil hearts wanted. So I made all the curses of this agreement come upon them. I commanded them to obey the agreement, but they did not.'"

11:7-8 Obedience
What happens when you disobey?

9 Then the LORD said to me, "I know the people of Judah and those living in Jerusalem have made secret plans. 10 They have gone back to the same sins their ancestors did. Their ancestors refused to listen to my message and followed and worshipped other gods instead. The families of Israel and Judah have broken the agreement I made with their ancestors. 11 So this is what the LORD says: 'I will soon bring a disaster on the people of Judah which they will not be able to escape. They will cry to me for help, but I will not listen to them. 12 The people living in the towns of Judah and the city of Jerusalem will pray to their idols to whom they burn incense. But those idols will not be able to help when disaster comes. 13 Look, people of Judah, you have as many idols as there are towns in Judah. You have built as many altars to burn incense to that shameful god Baal as there are streets in Jerusalem.'

14 "As for you, Jeremiah, don't pray for these people or cry out for them or ask anything for them. I will not listen when they call to me in the time of their trouble.

15 "What is my beloved Judah doing in my Temple
when she makes many evil plans?
Do you think animal sacrifices will stop your punishment?
When you do your evil, then you are happy."

FAITH links

A HOME TOWN HURT
JEREMIAH 11:8—12:6

How would you feel if neighbours plotted to hurt you in some way because of your belief in God? A group of people in Jeremiah's home town plotted to kill him because he spoke for God. They didn't like what he had to say. God wanted Jeremiah to trust him, even if his own family turned against him. God assured Jeremiah that he would take care of him.

If you're the only Christian in your family, you might feel almost as if your family *had* turned against you. Even through this, God wants you to trust in him.

Sometimes it's hard to be a follower of Jesus. Surf here for some encouragement:

The Sacrifice, Genesis 22, p. 29

What Will You Risk? Joshua 2, p. 278

What's Out Becomes In, Judges 11, p. 327

Wronged for What's Right, Ezra 4:4–5, p. 612

The Unpopular Choice, Mark 15:42–43, p. 1360

An Energy Boost, Acts 4:31, p. 1469

---

16 The LORD called you "a leafy olive tree,
  with beautiful fruit and shape."
But with the roar of a strong storm
  he will set that tree on fire,
  and its branches will be burned up.
17 The LORD All-powerful, who planted you, has announced that disaster will come to you. This is because the families of Israel and Judah have done evil and have made him angry by burning incense to Baal.

Evil Plans Against Jeremiah

18 The LORD showed me that men were making plans against me. Because he showed me what they were doing, I knew they were against me. **19** Before this, I was like a gentle lamb waiting to be slaughtered. I did not know they had made plans against me, saying:
  "Let us destroy the tree and its
    fruit.
  Let's kill him so people will forget
    him."
20 But, LORD All-powerful, you are a fair
    judge.
  You know how to test people's
    hearts and minds.
  I have told you what I have against
    them.
  So let me see you give them the
    punishment they deserve.
21 So the LORD speaks about the men from Anathoth who plan to kill Jeremiah and say, "Don't prophesy in the name of the LORD, or we will kill you!" **22** So this is what the LORD All-powerful says: "I will soon punish the men from Anathoth. Their young men will die in war. Their sons and daughters will die from hunger. **23** No one from the city of Anathoth will be left alive, because I will cause a disaster to happen to them that year."

Jeremiah's First Complaint

12 LORD, when I bring my case to
    you,
  you are always right.
  But I want to ask you about the
    justice you give.
  Why are evil people successful?
  Why do dishonest people have
    such easy lives?

2 You have put the evil people here
    like plants with strong roots.
  They grow and produce fruit.
  With their mouths they speak well of
      you,
    but their hearts are really far away
      from you.
3 But you know my heart, LORD.
  You see me and test my thoughts
      about you.
  Drag the evil people away like sheep
      to be slaughtered.
  Set them aside for the day of
      killing.
4 How much longer will the land stay
      dried up
    and the grass in every field be
      dead?
  The animals and birds in the land
      have died,
    because the people are evil.
  Yes, they are even saying,
    "God does not see what happens to
      us."

The LORD's Answer to Jeremiah

5 "If you get tired while racing against
      people,
    how can you race against horses?
  If you stumble in a country that is
      safe,
    what will you do in the thick
      thorn-bushes along the Jordan
      River?
6 Even your own brothers and
      members of your own family
    are making plans against you.
  They are crying out against you.
  Don't trust them,
    even when they say nice things to
      you!

7 "I have left Israel;
    I have left my people.
  I have given the people I love
      over to their enemies.
8 My people have become to me
    like a lion in the forest.
  They roar at me,
    so I hate them.
9 My people have become to me
    like a speckled bird attacked on all
      sides by hawks.
  Go, gather the wild animals.
  Bring them to get something to
      eat.
10 Many shepherds have ruined my
      vineyards
    and trampled the plants in my
      field.
  They have turned my beautiful
      field
    into an empty desert.
11 They have turned my field into a
      desert
    that is wilted and dead.
  The whole country is an empty
      desert,
    because no one who lives there
      cares.
12 Many soldiers have marched over
      those barren hills.
  The LORD is using the armies to
      punish that land
  from one end to the other.
  No one is safe.
13 The people have planted wheat,
    but they have harvested only
      thorns.
  They have worked hard until they
      were very tired,
    but they have nothing for all their
      work.
  They are ashamed of their poor
      harvest,
    because the LORD's terrible anger
      has caused this."

14 This is what the LORD said to me: "Here is what I will do to all my wicked neighbours who take the land I gave my people Israel. I will pull them up and throw them out of their land. And I will pull up the people of Judah from among them. 15 But after I pull them up, I will feel sorry for them again. I will bring each person back to his own property and to his own land. 16 I want them to learn their lessons well. In the past they taught my people to swear by Baal's name. But if they will now learn to swear by my name, saying 'As surely as the LORD lives . . .' I will allow them to rebuild among my people. 17 But if a nation will not listen to my message, I will pull it up completely and destroy it," says the LORD.

Jeremiah's Linen Belt

13 This is what the LORD said to me: "Go and buy a linen belt and put it around your waist. Don't let the belt get wet."

2 So I bought a linen belt, just as the LORD told me, and put it around my waist. 3 Then the LORD spoke his word to me a second time: 4 "Take the belt you bought and are wearing, and go to Perath. Hide the belt there in a crack in the rocks." 5 So I went to Perath and hid the belt there, just as the LORD told me.

6 Many days later the LORD said to me, "Now go to Perath and get the belt I told you to hide there." 7 So I went to Perath and dug up the belt and took it from where I had hidden it. But now it was ruined; it was good for nothing.

8 Then the LORD spoke his word to me. 9 This is what the LORD said: "In the same way I will ruin the pride of the people of Judah and the great pride of Jerusalem. 10 These evil people refuse to listen to my warnings. They stubbornly do only what they want to do, and they follow other gods to serve and worship them. So they will become like this linen belt—good for nothing. 11 As a belt is wrapped tightly around a person's waist, I wrapped the families of Israel and Judah around me," says the LORD. "I did that so they would be my people and bring fame, praise and honour to me. But my people would not listen.

Warnings About Leather Wine Bags

12 "Say to them: 'This is what the LORD, the God of Israel, says: all leather bags for holding wine should be filled with wine.' People will say to you: 'Of course, we know all wine bags should be filled with wine.' 13 Then you will say to them, 'This is what the LORD says: I will make everyone in this land like a drunken person—the kings who sit on David's throne, the priests and the prophets and all the people who live in Jerusalem. 14 I will make them smash against one another, fathers and sons alike, says the LORD. I will not feel sorry or have pity on them or show mercy that would stop me from destroying them.'"

Threat of Slavery

15 Listen and pay attention.
  Don't be too proud,
  because the LORD has spoken to
    you.
16 Give glory to the LORD your God
  before he brings darkness
  and before you slip and fall
    on the dark hills.
  You hope for light,
  but he will turn it into thick
    darkness;
  he will change it into deep gloom.
17 If you don't listen to him,
  I will cry secretly
    because of your pride.
  I will cry painfully,
    and my eyes will overflow with
      tears,
    because the LORD's people will be
      captured.

18 Tell this to the king and the queen
    mother:
  "Come down from your thrones,
  because your beautiful crowns
    have fallen from your heads."
19 The cities of southern Judah are
    locked up
    and no one can open them.
  All Judah will be taken as captives to
    a foreign land;
    they will be carried away
      completely.

20 Jerusalem, look up and see
    the people coming from the north.
  Where is the flock God gave you to
      care for,
    the flock you boasted about?
21 What will you say when they appoint
    as your heads
    those you had thought were your
      friends?
  Won't you have much pain and
      trouble,
    like a woman giving birth to a
      baby?
22 You might ask yourself,
  "Why has this happened to me?"

It happened because of your many
sins.
Because of your sins, your skirt
was torn off
and your body has been treated
badly.
23 Can a person from
Cush change the
colour of his skin?
Can a leopard
change his spots?
In the same way,
Jerusalem, you
cannot change
and do good,
because you are
accustomed to
doing evil.

24 "I will scatter you like chaff that is
blown away by the desert wind.
25 This is what will happen to you;
this is your part in my plans," says
the LORD.
"Because you forgot me
and trusted in false gods,
26 I will pull your skirts up over your
face
so everyone will see your shame.
27 I have seen the terrible things you
have done:
your acts of adultery and your
snorting,
your prostitution,
your hateful acts
on the hills and in the fields.
How terrible it will be for you,
Jerusalem.
How long will you continue being
unclean?"

A Time Without Rain

14 These are the words that the LORD
spoke to Jeremiah about the time
when there was no rain:
2 "The nation of Judah cries as if
someone has died,
and her cities are very sad.
They are distressed over the land.
A cry goes up to God from
Jerusalem.
3 The important men send their
servants to get water.
They go to the wells,
but they find no water.
So they return with empty jars.
They are ashamed and
embarrassed
and cover their
heads in shame.
4 The ground is dry and
cracked open,
because no rain falls
on the land.
The farmers are
upset and sad,
so they cover their
heads in shame.
5 Even the mother deer
in the field
leaves her newborn fawn to die,
because there is no grass.
6 Wild donkeys stand on the bare
hills
and sniff the wind like wild dogs.
But their eyes go blind,
because there is no food."

7 We know that we suffer because of
our sins.
LORD, do something to help us for
the good of your name.
We have left you many times;
we have sinned against you.
8 God, the Hope of Israel,
you have saved Israel in times of
trouble.
Why are you like a stranger in the
land,
or like a traveller who only stays
one night?
9 Why are you like someone who has
been attacked by surprise,
like a warrior who is not able to
save anyone?
But you are among us, LORD,
and we are called by your name
so don't leave us without help!
10 This is what the LORD says about
the people of Judah:
"They really love to wander from
me;
they don't stop themselves from
leaving me.
So now the LORD will not accept
them.

> Can a person from
> Cush change the
> colour of his skin?
> Can a leopard
> change his spots?
> – Jeremiah 13:23

He will now remember the evil
   they do
and will punish them for their
   sins."

11 Then the LORD said, "Don't pray for good things to happen to the people of Judah. **12** Even if they give up eating, I will not listen to their prayers. Even if they offer burnt offerings and grain offerings to me, I will not accept them. Instead, I will destroy the people of Judah with war, hunger and terrible diseases."

13 But I said, "Oh, Lord GOD, the prophets keep telling the people, 'You will not suffer from an enemy's sword or from hunger. I, the LORD, will give you peace in this land.'"

14 Then the LORD said to me, "Those prophets are prophesying lies in my name. I did not send them or appoint them or speak to them. They have been prophesying false visions, idolatries, worthless magic and their own wishful thinking. **15** So this is what I say about the prophets who are prophesying in my name. I did not send them. They say, 'No enemy will attack this country with swords. There will never be hunger in this land.' So those prophets will die from hunger and from an enemy's sword. **16** And the people to whom the prophets speak will be thrown into the streets of Jerusalem. There they will die from hunger and from an enemy's sword. And no one will be there to bury them, or their wives, or their sons or their daughters. I will punish them.

17 "Jeremiah, speak this message to the people of Judah:
'Let my eyes be filled with tears
   night and day, without stopping.
My people have received a terrible
      blow;
   they have been hurt badly.
18 If I go into the country,
   I see people killed by swords.
If I go into the city,
   I see much sickness, because the
people have no food.
Both the priests and the prophets
   have been taken to a foreign
   land.'"

19 LORD, have you completely rejected
      the nation of Judah?
   Do you hate Jerusalem?
Why have you hurt us so badly
   that we cannot be made well
      again?
We hoped for peace,
   but nothing good has come.
We looked for a time of healing,
   but only terror came.
20 LORD, we admit that we are wicked
   and that our ancestors did evil
      things.
   We have sinned against you.
21 For your sake, do not hate us.
   Do not take away the honour from
      your glorious throne.
   Remember your agreement with us,
      and do not break it.
22 Do foreign idols
      have the
      power to bring
      rain?
   Does the sky
      itself have
      the power to
      send down
      showers?
   No, it is you, LORD
      our God.
   You are our only
      hope,
because you are the one who made
   all these things.

15 Then the LORD said to me: "I would not feel sorry for the people of Judah even if Moses and Samuel prayed for them. Send them away from me! Tell them to go! **2** When they ask you, 'Where will we go?' tell them: 'This is what the LORD says:
Those who are meant to die
   will die.
Those who are meant to die in war
   will die in war.
Those who are meant to die from
      hunger
   will die from hunger.

> Do foreign idols have the power to bring rain? Does the sky itself have the power to send down showers?
> – Jeremiah 14:22

Those who are meant to be taken captive
will be taken captive.'
3 "I will send four kinds of destroyers against them," says the LORD. "I will send war to kill, dogs to drag the bodies away, and the birds of the air and wild animals to eat and destroy the bodies. 4 I will make the people of Judah hated by everyone on earth because of what Manasseh did in Jerusalem. (Manasseh son of Hezekiah was king of the nation of Judah.)

5 "Who will feel sorry for you, Jerusalem?
Who will be sad and cry for you?
Who will go out of his way to ask how you are?
6 Jerusalem, you have left me," says the LORD.
"You keep going further and further away,
so I have taken hold of you and destroyed you.
I was tired of holding back my anger.
7 I have separated the people of Judah with my pitchfork
and scattered them at the city gates of the land.
My people haven't changed their ways.
So I have destroyed them and taken away their children.
8 There are more widows than grains of sand in the sea.
I brought a destroyer at noontime against the
mothers of the young men of Judah.
I suddenly brought pain and fear on the people of Judah.
9 When the enemy attacked, a woman with seven sons felt faint because they would all die.
She became weak and unable to breathe.
Her bright day became dark from sadness.
She felt shame and disgrace.
And everyone else left alive in Judah I will hand over to the enemies too!" says the LORD.

Jeremiah's Second Complaint

10 Mother, I am sorry that you gave birth to me
since I must accuse and criticise the whole land.
I have not loaned or borrowed anything,
but everyone curses me.
11 The LORD said,
"I have saved you for a good reason.
I have made your enemies beg you in times of disaster and trouble.
12 No one can smash a piece of iron or bronze
that comes from the north.
13 Your wealth and treasures
I will give to others free of charge, because the people of Judah have sinned
throughout the country.
14 I will make you slaves to your enemies
in a land you have never known.
My anger is like a hot fire,
and it will burn against you."

15 LORD, you understand.
Remember me and take care of me.
Punish for me
those who are hurting me.
Don't destroy me
while you remain patient with them.
Think about the shame I suffer for you.
16 Your words came to me and I listened carefully to them.
Your words made me very happy, because I am called by your name,

> Your words came to me and I listened carefully to them. Your words made me very happy.
> – Jeremiah 15:16

LORD God All-powerful.
17 I never sat with the crowd
    as they laughed and had fun.
  I sat by myself, because you were
    there,
  and you filled me with anger at the
    evil around me.
18 I don't understand why my pain has
    no end.
  I don't understand why my injury
    is not cured or healed.
  Will you be like a brook that goes
    dry?
  Will you be like a spring that stops
    flowing?
19 So this is what the LORD says:
  "If you change your heart and return
    to me, I will take you back.
  Then you may serve me.
  And if you speak things that have
    worth,
    not useless words,
  then you may speak for me.
  Let the people of Judah turn to you,
    but you must not change and be
    like them.
20 I will make you as strong as a wall to
    this people,
    as strong as a wall of bronze.
  They will fight against you,
    but they will not defeat you,
    because I am with you.
  I will rescue you and save you,"
    says the LORD.
21 "I will save you from these wicked
    people
  and rescue you from these cruel
    people."

The Day of Disaster

16 Then the LORD spoke his word to me: 2 "You must not get married or have sons or daughters in this place."

3 The LORD says this about the sons and daughters born in this land and their mothers and fathers: 4 "They will die of terrible diseases, and no one will cry for them or bury them. Their bodies will lie on the ground like dung. They will die in war, or they will starve to death. Their bodies will be food for the birds of the sky and for the wild animals."

5 So this is what the LORD says: "Jeremiah, do not go into a house where there is a funeral meal. Do not go there to cry for the dead or to show your sorrow for them, because I have taken back my blessing, my love and my pity from these people," says the LORD. 6 "Important people and common people will die in the land of Judah. No one will bury them or cry for them or cut himself or shave his head to show sorrow for them. 7 No one will bring food to comfort those who are crying for the dead. No one will offer a drink to comfort someone whose mother or father has died.

8 "Do not go into a house where the people are having a feast to sit down to eat and drink, 9 because this is what the LORD All-powerful, the God of Israel, says: I will soon stop the sounds of joy and gladness and the happy sounds of brides and bridegrooms in this place. This will happen during your lifetime.

10 "When you tell the people of Judah these things, they will ask you, 'Why has the LORD said these terrible things to us? What have we done wrong? What sin have we done against the LORD our God?'

11 "Then say to them: 'This is because your ancestors stopped following me,' says the LORD. 'And they followed other gods and served and worshipped them. Your ancestors left me and stopped obeying my teaching. 12 But you have done even more evil than your ancestors. You are very stubborn and do only what you want to do; you have not obeyed me. 13 So I will throw you out of this country and send you into a land that you and your ancestors never knew. There you can serve other gods day and night, because I will not help you or show you any favours.'

14 "People say, 'As surely as the LORD lives, who brought the people of Israel out of Egypt . . .' But the time is coming," says the LORD, "when people will not say this any more. 15 They will say instead, 'As surely as the LORD lives, who brought the Israelites from the northern land and from all the countries where he had sent them . . .' And I will bring them back to the land I gave to their ancestors.

16 "I will soon send for many fisher-

men to come to this land," says the LORD. "And they will catch the people of Judah. After that, I will send for many hunters to come to this land. And they will hunt the people of Judah on every mountain and hill and in the cracks of the rocks. 17 I see everything they do. They cannot hide from me the things they do; their sin is not hidden from my eyes. 18 I will pay back the people of Judah twice for every one of their sins, because they have made my land unclean. They have filled my country with their hateful idols."

16:17
Sin
Can you hide sin from God?

19 LORD, you are my strength and my protection,
my safe place in times of trouble.
The nations will come to you from all over the world
and say, "Our ancestors had only false gods,
useless idols that didn't help them.
20 Can people make gods for themselves?
They will not really be gods!"

21 The LORD says, "So I will teach those who make idols.
This time I will teach them
about my power and my strength.
Then they will know
that my name is the LORD.

Judah's Guilty Heart

17 "The sin of the people of Judah is written with an iron tool.
Their sins were cut with a hard point into the stone that is their hearts.
Their sins were cut into the corners of their altars.
2 Even their children remember their altars to idols and their Asherah idols
beside the green trees and on the high hills.
3 My mountain in the open country and your wealth and treasures
I will give away to other people.
I will give away the places of worship in your country,
because you sinned by worshipping there.
4 You will lose the land I gave you and it is your own fault.
I will let your enemies take you as their slaves
to a land you have never known.
This is because you have made my anger burn like a hot fire,
and it will burn for ever."

Trusting in Humans or God

5 This is what the LORD says:
"A curse is placed on those who trust other people,
who depend on humans for strength,
who have stopped trusting the LORD.
6 They are like a bush in a desert that grows in a land where no one lives,
a hot and dry land with bad soil.
They don't know about the good things God can give.

7 "But the person who trusts in the LORD will be blessed.
The LORD will show him that he can be trusted.
8 He will be strong, like a tree planted near water
that sends its roots by a stream.
It is not afraid when the days are hot; its leaves are always green.
It does not worry in a year when no rain comes;
it always produces fruit.

9 "More than anything else, a person's mind is evil
and cannot be healed.
No one truly understands it.
10 But I, the LORD, look into a person's heart
and test the mind.
So I can decide what each one deserves;
I can give each one the right payment for what he does."

11 Like a bird hatching an egg it did not lay,
so are the people who get rich by cheating.

> **Jeremiah 17:12**

FAITH links

LIKE A TREE
JEREMIAH 17:5-8

What is the biggest tree you have ever seen? Some redwood trees can grow as tall as 100 metres! Can you imagine being as tall as that? A tree like that needs plenty of sunlight and water in order to grow. According to Jeremiah, trusting God makes you like a well-watered tree with strong, deep roots. Those who trust only in people are like scorched desert bushes – stumpy, dry and crackly. Which would you rather be?

The Cloud Guide, Numbers 9:15-23, p. 188

Listen Up! 1 Kings 19:11-13, p. 467

A Look for the Book, 2 Chronicles 34:14-18, p. 603

How God Speaks, Job 33:14-17, p. 696

What God Thinks, Isaiah 55:8-9, p. 969

Our Heavenly Connection, Matthew 6:9-13, p. 1283

When their lives are half finished,
    they will lose their riches.
At the end of their lives, it will be
    clear they were fools.
12 From the beginning, our Temple has
    been honoured
    as a glorious throne for God.
13 LORD, hope of Israel,
    those who leave you will be
    shamed.
People who stop following the LORD
    will be like a name written in the
    dust,
because they have left the LORD,
    the spring of living water.

Jeremiah's Third Complaint

14 LORD, heal me, and I will truly be
    healed.
Save me, and I will truly be saved.
    You are the one I praise.
15 The people of Judah keep asking me,
    "Where is the word from the
        LORD?
Let's see that message come
    true!"

16 LORD, I didn't run away from being
    the shepherd you wanted.
I didn't want the terrible day to
    come.
You know everything I have said;
    you see all that is happening.
17 Don't be a terror to me.
    I run to you for safety in times of
        trouble.
18 Make those who are hurting me be
    ashamed,
but don't bring shame to me.
Let them be terrified,
    but keep me from terror.
Bring the day of disaster on my
    enemies.
Destroy them, and destroy them
    again.

Keeping the Sabbath Holy

19 This is what the LORD said to me: "Go and stand at the People's Gate of Jerusalem, where the kings of Judah go in and out. And then go to all the other gates of Jerusalem. 20 Say to them there: 'Hear the word of the LORD, kings of Judah, all you people of Judah, and all who live in Jerusalem, who come through these gates into the city. 21 This is what the LORD says: be careful not to carry a load on the Sabbath day or bring it through the gates of Jerusalem. 22 Don't take a load out of your houses on the Sabbath or do any work on that day. But keep the Sabbath as a holy day, as I commanded your ancestors. 23 But your ancestors did

not listen or pay attention to me. They were very stubborn and did not listen. I punished them, but it didn't do any good. 24 But you must be careful to obey me, says the LORD. You must not bring a load through the gates of Jerusalem on the Sabbath, but you must keep the Sabbath as a holy day and not do any work on that day.

25 "'If you obey this command, kings who sit on David's throne will come through the gates of Jerusalem with their officers. They will come riding in chariots and on horses, along with the people of Judah and Jerusalem. And the city of Jerusalem will have people living in it forever. 26 People will come to Jerusalem from the villages around it, from the towns of Judah, from the land of Benjamin, from the western hills, from the mountains and from southern Judah. They will all bring to the Temple of the LORD burnt offerings, sacrifices, grain offerings, incense and offerings to show thanks to God. 27 But you must obey me and keep the Sabbath day as a holy day. You must not carry any loads into Jerusalem on the Sabbath. If you don't obey me, I will start a fire at the gates of Jerusalem, and it will burn until it burns even the strong towers. And it will not be put out.'"

The Potter and the Clay

18 This is the word the LORD spoke to Jeremiah: 2 "Go down to the potter's house, and I will give you my message there." 3 So I went down to the potter's house and saw him working at the potter's wheel. 4 He was using his hands to make a pot from clay, but something went wrong with it. So he used that clay to make another pot the way he wanted it to be.

5 Then the LORD spoke his word to me: 6 "Family of Israel, can't I do the same thing with you?" says the LORD. "You are in my hands like the clay in the potter's hands. 7 There may come a time when I will speak about a nation or a kingdom that I will pull up by its roots or that I will pull down to destroy it. 8 But if the people of that nation stop doing the evil they have done, I will change my mind and not carry out my plans to bring disaster to them. 9 There may come another time when I will speak about a nation that I will build up and plant. 10 But if I see it doing evil by not obeying me, I will change my mind and not carry out my plans to do good for them.

11 "So, say this to the people of Judah and those who live in Jerusalem: 'This is what the LORD says: I am preparing disaster for you and making plans against you. So stop doing evil. Change your ways and do what is right.' 12 But the people of Judah will answer, 'It won't do any good to try! We will continue to do what we want. Each of us will do what his stubborn, evil heart wants!'"

13 So this is what the LORD says:
"Ask the people in other nations this question:
    'Have you ever heard anything like this?'
The people of Israel have done a horrible thing.
14 The snow on the mountains of Lebanon
    never melts from the rocks.
Its cool, flowing streams
    do not dry up.
15 But my people have forgotten me.
    They burn incense to worthless idols
and have stumbled in what they do
    and in the old ways of their ancestors.
They walk along back roads
    and on poor highways.
16 So Judah's country will become an empty desert.
    People will not stop making fun of it.
They will shake their heads as they pass by;
    they will be shocked at how the country was destroyed.
17 Like a strong east wind,
    I will scatter them before their enemies.

18:11 Future What's the future for someone who continues to sin?

At that awful time they will not see
me coming to help them;
they will see me leaving."

Jeremiah's Fourth Complaint

18 Then the people said, "Come, let's make plans against Jeremiah. Surely the teaching of the law by the priest will not be lost. We will still have the advice from the wise men and the words of the prophets. So let's ruin him by telling lies about him. We won't pay attention to anything he says."

19 LORD, listen to me.
Listen to what my accusers are
saying!
20 Good should not be paid back with
evil,
but they have dug a pit in order to
kill me.
Remember that I stood before you
and asked you to do good things
for these people
and to turn your anger away from
them.
21 So now, let their children starve,
and let their enemies kill them with
swords.
Let their wives lose their children and
husbands.
Let the men from Judah be put to
death
and the young men be killed with
swords in battle.
22 Let them cry out in their houses
when you bring an enemy against
them suddenly.
Let all this happen, because my
enemies have dug a pit to
capture me
and have hidden traps for my feet.
23 LORD, you know
about all their plans to kill me.
Don't forgive their crimes
or erase their sins from your mind.
Make them fall from their places;
punish them while you are angry.

Judah is like a Broken Jar

19 This is what the LORD said to me: "Go and buy a clay jar from a potter. 2 Take some of the elders of the people and the priests, and go out to the Valley of Ben Hinnom, near the front of the Potsherd Gate. There speak the words I tell you. 3 Say, 'Kings of Judah and people of Jerusalem, listen to this message from the LORD. This is what the LORD All-powerful, the God of Israel, says: I will soon bring a disaster on this place that will amaze and frighten everyone who hears about it. 4 The people of Judah have stopped following me. They have made this a place for foreign gods. They have burnt sacrifices to other gods that neither they, nor their ancestors, nor the kings of Judah ever knew. They have filled this place with the blood of innocent people. 5 They have built places on hilltops to worship Baal, where they burn their children in the fire to Baal. That is something I did not command or speak about; it never even entered my mind. 6 Now people call this place the Valley of Ben Hinnom or Topheth, but the days are coming, says the LORD, when people will call it the Valley of Killing.

7 "'At this place I will ruin the plans of the people of Judah and Jerusalem. The enemy will chase them, and I will have them killed with swords. I will make their dead bodies food for the birds and wild animals. 8 I will completely destroy this city. People will make fun of it and shake their heads when they pass by. They will be shocked when they see how the city was destroyed. 9 An enemy army will surround the city and will not let anyone go out to get food. I will make the people so hungry that they will eat the bodies of their own sons and daughters, and then they will begin to eat each other.'

10 "While the people with you are watching, break that jar. 11 Then say this: 'The LORD All-powerful says: I will break this nation and this city just as someone breaks a clay jar that cannot be put back together again. The dead people will be buried here in Topheth, because there is no other place for them. 12 This is what I will do to these people and to this place, says the LORD. I will make this city like Topheth. 13 The houses in Jerusalem and the king's palaces will become as unclean as this place, Topheth, because the people

FAITH links

STAND!
JEREMIAH 19:14—20:6

Have you ever been afraid to stand up for something you knew was right? Many people hesitate to take a stand. They think about being made fun of or hurt by others. Jeremiah told the Jewish leaders that God would punish them because of their sin. Because he spoke God's truth, he was arrested. But that didn't stop Jeremiah from speaking the truth!

Taking a stand for the truth can be risky. God can give you the courage to stand for him, just as Jeremiah did.

Here are some more Faithlinks on taking a stand:

Fearful Service? Exodus 4:1–17, p. 80

His OK to Obey, Deuteronomy 2:24–36, p. 230

Give In or Take a Stand? 1 Kings 22:13–14, p. 472

A Memorial for Two Thieves, 1 Chronicles 7:21, p. 530

When Bad Things Happen, Ecclesiastes 3:16–17, p. 876

A Word About Worry, Matthew 6:25–34, p. 1284

---

worshipped gods on the roofs*ⁿ* of their houses. They worshipped the stars and burnt incense to honour them and gave drink offerings to gods.'"

14 When Jeremiah left Topheth where the LORD had sent him to prophesy, he went to the LORD's Temple, stood in the courtyard, and said to all the people: **15** "This is what the LORD All-powerful, the God of Israel, says: 'I will soon bring disaster to Jerusalem and the villages around it, as I said I would. This will happen because the people are very stubborn and do not listen at all to what I say.'"

Pashhur will be Captured

20 Pashhur son of Immer was a priest and the highest officer in the Temple of the LORD. When he heard Jeremiah prophesying in the Temple courtyard, **2** he had Jeremiah the prophet beaten. And he locked Jeremiah's hands and feet between large blocks of wood at the Upper Gate of Benjamin of the LORD's Temple. **3** The next day when Pashhur took Jeremiah out of the blocks of wood, Jeremiah said to him, "The LORD's name for you is not Pashhur. Now his name for you is Terror on Every Side. **4** This is what the LORD says: 'I will soon make you a terror to yourself and to all your friends. You will watch enemies killing your friends with swords. And I will give all the people of Judah to the king of Babylon, who will take them away as captives to Babylon and then will kill them with swords. **5** I will give all the wealth of this city to its enemies—its goods, its valuables and the treasures of the kings of Judah. The enemies will carry all those valuables off to Babylon. **6** And Pashhur, you and everyone in your house will be taken captive. You will be forced to go to Babylon, where you will die and be buried, you and your friends to whom you have prophesied lies.'"

Jeremiah's Fifth Complaint

7 LORD, you tricked me, and I was
    fooled.
        You are stronger than I am, so you
            won.

19:13 roofs In Bible times houses were built with flat roofs. The roof was used for drying things such as flax and fruit. And it was used as an extra room, as a place for worship and as a place to sleep in the summer.

I have become a joke;
  everyone makes fun of me all day
    long.
8 Every time I speak, I shout.
  I am always shouting about
    violence and destruction.
  I tell the people about the message I
    received from the LORD,
  but this only brings me insults.
  The people make fun of me all day
    long.
9 Sometimes I say to myself,
  "I will forget about the LORD.
  I will not speak any more in his
    name."
  But then his message becomes like a
    burning fire inside me,
  deep within my bones.
  I get tired of trying to hold it inside
    me,
  and finally, I cannot hold it in.
10 I hear many people whispering about
    me:
  "Terror on every side!
  Tell on him! Let's tell the rulers
    about him."
  My friends are all just waiting for me
    to make some mistake.
  They are saying,
  "Maybe we can trick him
  so we can defeat him
  and pay him back."

11 But the LORD is with me like a strong
    warrior,
  so those who are chasing me will
    trip and fall;
  they will not defeat me.
  They will be ashamed because they
    have failed,
  and their shame will never be
    forgotten.

12 LORD All-powerful, you test good
    people;
  you look
    deeply into
    the heart
    and mind of
    a person.
  I have told you
    my arguments against these
    people,

20:12
Judgement
Does God know your
thoughts?

so let me see you give them the
  punishment they deserve.
13 Sing to the LORD!
  Praise the LORD!
  He saves the life of the poor
    from the power of the wicked.

Jeremiah's Sixth Complaint

14 Let there be a curse on the day I was
    born;
  let there be no blessing on the day
    when my mother gave birth to
      me.
15 Let there be a curse on the man
    who brought my father the news:
  "You have a son!"
  This made my father very glad.
16 Let that man be like the towns
    the LORD destroyed without pity.
  Let him hear loud crying in the
    morning
  and battle cries at noon,
17 because he did not kill me before I
    was born.
  Then my mother would have been
    my grave;
  she would have stayed pregnant for
    ever.
18 Why did I have to come out of my
    mother's body?
  All I have known is trouble and
    sorrow,
  and my life will end in shame.

God Rejects King Zedekiah's Request

21 This is the word that the LORD spoke to Jeremiah. It came when Zedekiah king of Judah sent Pashhur son of Malkijah and the priest Zephaniah son of Maaseiah to Jeremiah. 2 They said, "Ask the LORD for us what will happen, because Nebuchadnezzar king of Babylon is attacking us. Maybe the LORD will do miracles for us as he did in the past so Nebuchadnezzar will stop attacking us and leave."

3 But Jeremiah answered them, "Tell King Zedekiah this: 4 'Here is what the LORD, the God of Israel, says: you have weapons of war in your hands to defend yourselves against the king of Babylon and

the Babylonians, who are all around the city wall. But I will make those weapons useless. Soon I will bring them into the centre of this city. 5 In my anger, my very great anger, I myself will fight against you with my great power and strength. 6 I will kill everything living in Jerusalem—both people and animals. They will die from terrible diseases. 7 Then, says the LORD, I will hand over Zedekiah king of Judah, his officers and the people in Jerusalem who do not die from the terrible diseases or battle or hunger, to Nebuchadnezzar king of Babylon. I will let those win who want to kill the people of Judah, so the people of Judah and Jerusalem will be killed in war. Nebuchadnezzar will not show any mercy or pity or feel sorry for them!'

8 "Also tell this to the people of Jerusalem: 'This is what the LORD says: I will let you choose to live or die. 9 Anyone who stays in Jerusalem will die in war or from hunger or from a terrible disease. But anyone who goes out of Jerusalem and surrenders to the Babylonians who are attacking you will live. Anyone who leaves the city will save his life as if it were a prize won in war. 10 I have decided to make trouble for this city and not to help it, says the LORD. I will give it to the king of Babylon, and he will burn it with fire.'

11 "Say to Judah's royal family: 'Hear the word of the LORD. 12 Family of David, this is what the LORD says:
You must judge people fairly every
    morning.
Save the person who has been
    robbed
from the power of his attacker.
If you don't, I will become very
    angry.
My anger will be like a fire that no
    one can put out,
because you have done evil
    things.

13 "'Jerusalem, I am against you,
    you who live on top of the
        mountain
    over this valley, says the LORD.
You say, "No one can attack us
    or come into our strong city."

14 But I will give you the punishment
    you deserve, says the LORD.
I will start a fire in your forests
    that will burn up everything
        around you!"'

Judgement Against Evil Kings

22 This is what the LORD says: "Go down to the palace of the king of Judah and prophesy this message there: 2 'Hear the word of the LORD, king of Judah, who rules from David's throne. You and your officers, and your people who come through these gates, listen! 3 This is what the LORD says: do what is fair and right. Save the one who has been robbed from the power of his attacker. Don't mistreat or hurt the foreigners, orphans or widows. Don't kill innocent people here. 4 If you carefully obey these commands, kings who sit on David's throne will come through the gates of this palace with their officers and people, riding in chariots and on horses. 5 But if you don't obey these commands, says the LORD, I swear by my own name that this king's palace will become a ruin.'"

22:3-5
Truth
Learn how to show justice.

6 This is what the LORD says about the palace where the king of Judah lives:
"You are tall like the forests of
    Gilead,
like the mountain tops of Lebanon.
But I will truly make you into a
    desert,
into towns where no one lives.
7 I will send men to destroy the palace,
    each with his weapons.
They will cut up your strong,
    beautiful cedar beams
and throw them into the fire.

8 "People from many nations will pass by this city and ask each other, 'Why has the LORD done such a terrible thing to Jerusalem, this great city?' 9 And the answer will be: 'Because the people of Judah stopped following the agreement with the LORD their God. They worshipped and served other gods.'"

Judgement Against Jehoahaz

10 Don't cry for the dead king or be sad about him.
But cry painfully for the king who is being taken away,
because he will never return or see his homeland again.

11 This is what the LORD says about Jehoahaz son of Josiah who became king of Judah after his father died and who has left this place: "He will never return. 12 He will die where he has been taken captive, and he will not see this land again."

Judgement Against Jehoiakim

13 "How terrible it will be for one who builds his palace by doing evil,
who cheats people so he can build its upper rooms.
He makes his own people work for nothing
and does not pay them.
14 He says, 'I will build a great palace for myself
with large upper rooms.'
So he builds it with large windows
and uses cedar wood for the walls, which he paints red.

15 "Does having a lot of cedar in your house
make you a great king?
Your father was satisfied to have food and drink.
He did what was right and fair,
so everything went well for him.
16 He helped those who were poor and needy,
so everything went well for him.
That is what it means to know God," says the LORD.
17 "But you only look for and think about
what you can get dishonestly.
You are even willing to kill innocent people to get it.
You feel free to hurt people and to steal from them."
18 So this is what the LORD says to Jehoiakim son of Josiah king of Judah:
"The people of Judah will not cry when Jehoiakim dies,
saying: 'Oh, my brother,' or 'Oh, my sister.'
They will not cry for him, saying: 'Oh, master,' or 'Oh, my king.'
19 They will bury him like a donkey,
dragging his body away
and throwing it outside the gates of Jerusalem.

20 "Judah, go up to Lebanon and cry out.
Let your voice be heard in Bashan.
Cry out from Abarim,
because all your friends are destroyed!
21 Judah, when you were successful, I warned you,
but you said, 'I won't listen.'
You have acted like this since you were young;
you have not obeyed me.
22 Like a storm, my punishment will blow all your shepherds away
and send your friends into captivity.
Then you will really be ashamed and disgraced
because of all the wicked things you did.
23 King, you live in your palace,
cosy in your rooms of cedar.
But when your punishment comes,
how you will groan
like a woman giving birth to a baby!

Judgement upon Jehoiachin

24 "As surely as I live," says the LORD, "Jehoiachin son of Jehoiakim king of Judah, even if you were a signet ring on my right hand, I would still pull you off. 25 I will hand you over to Nebuchadnezzar king of Babylon and to the Babylonians—those people you fear because they want to kill you. 26 I will throw you and your mother into another country. Neither of you was born there, but both of you will die there. 27 They will want to come back, but they will never be able to return."

28 Jehoiachin is like a broken pot someone threw away;

he is like something no one wants.
Why will Jehoiachin and his children
    be thrown out
and sent into a foreign land?
29 Land, land, land of Judah,
    hear the word of the Lord!
30 This is what the Lord says:

"Write this down in the record about
    Jehoiachin:
He is a man without children,
    a man who will not be successful in
      his lifetime.
And none of his descendants will be
    successful;
    none will sit on the throne of David
      or rule in Judah."

The Evil Leaders of Judah

23 "How terrible it will be for the leaders of Judah, who are scattering and destroying my people," says the Lord. 2 They are responsible for the people, so the Lord, the God of Israel, says to them: "You have scattered my people and forced them away and not taken care of them. So I will punish you for the evil things you have done," says the Lord. 3 "I sent my people to other countries, but I will gather those who are left alive and bring them back to their own country. Then they will have many children and grow in number. 4 I will place new leaders over my people, who will take care of them. And my people will not be afraid or terrified again, and none of them will be lost," says the Lord.

The Good Branch will Come

5 "The days are coming," says the Lord,
"when I will raise up a good
    branch in David's family.
He will be a king who will rule in a
    wise way;
he will do what is fair and right in
    the land.
6 In his time Judah will be saved
    and Israel will live in safety.
This will be his name:
    The Lord Does What Is Right.
7 "So the days are coming," says the Lord, "when people will not say again: 'As surely as the Lord lives, who brought Israel out of Egypt . . .' 8 but people will say something new: 'As surely as the Lord lives, who brought the descendants of Israel from the land of the north and from all the countries where he had sent them away. . .' then the people of Israel will live in their own land."

FAITH links

YOUR FULL TRUST

JEREMIAH 22:20-22

The Israelites trusted the nations around them for protection. They made agreements with these nations to help each other. Unfortunately, these nations did things that God hated. Israel followed their example. God told Israel that their faith was in the wrong place. Instead of trusting God, they had trusted others.

We may not depend on other nations to help us each day, but we sometimes trust the wrong people. Maybe you've put all of your hope in a friendship that wound up being disappointing. God wants your full trust in him.

Obey? No Way! Exodus 1:15–21, p. 76

When God Says No, 2 Samuel 7, p. 407

Give In or Take a Stand? 1 Kings 22:13–14, p. 472

Two Kinds of People, Psalm 1, p. 710

A Fair-weather Friend, Obadiah 7, p. 1209

The Way to Be Wise, James 1:5, p. 1689

False Prophets will be Punished

9 A message to the prophets:
My heart is broken.
   All my bones shake.
I'm like someone who is drunk,
   like someone who has been
      overcome with wine.
This is because of the LORD
   and his holy words.
10 The land of Judah is full of people
      who are guilty of adultery.
   Because of this, the LORD cursed
      the land.
   It has become a very sad place
      and the pastures have dried up.
   The people are evil
      and use their power in the wrong
         way.
11 "Both the prophets and the priests
      live as if there were no God.
   I have found them doing evil
      things even in my own Temple,"
         says the LORD.
12 "So they will be in danger.
   They will be forced into
      darkness
   where they will be defeated.
   I will bring disaster on them
      in the year I punish them," says
         the LORD.
13 "I saw the prophets of Samaria
      do something wrong.
   Those prophets prophesied by Baal
      and led my people Israel away.
14 And I have seen the prophets of
      Jerusalem
      do terrible things.
   They are guilty of adultery
      and live by lies.
   They encourage evil people to keep
      on doing evil,
      so the people don't stop sinning.
   All of those people are like the city of
      Sodom.
   The people of Jerusalem are like
      the city of Gomorrah to me!"
15 So this is what the LORD All-powerful says about the prophets:
   "I will make those prophets eat bitter
      food
   and drink poisoned water,
because the prophets of Jerusalem
   spread wickedness
      through the whole country."
16 This is what the LORD All-powerful says:
   "Don't pay
      attention to
         what those
            prophets
               are saying
                  to you.
   They are trying
      to fool you.
   They talk about visions their own
      minds made up,
   not about visions from me.
17 They say to those who hate me:
   'The LORD says: you will have
      peace.'
   They say to all those who are
      stubborn and do as they please:
   'Nothing bad will happen to you.'
18 But none of these prophets has stood
      in the meeting of angels
   to see or hear the message of the
      LORD.
   None of them has paid close
      attention to his message.
19 Look, the punishment from the LORD
      will come like a storm.
   His anger will be like a hurricane.
   It will come swirling down on the
      heads of those wicked people.
20 The LORD's anger will not stop
      until he finishes what he plans to
         do.
   When that day is over,
      you will understand this clearly.
21 I did not send those prophets,
      but they ran to tell their message.
   I did not speak to them,
      but they prophesied anyway.
22 But if they had stood in the meeting
      of angels,
   they would have told my message
      to my people.
   They would have turned the people
      from their evil ways
   and from doing evil.

23 "I am a God who is near," says the
      LORD.
   "I am also a God who is far away."

23:16 Hope Does it matter what you hope in?

FAITH CHALLENGE

Try this challenge. Read 23:24 to see what the Lord says about people who try to hide from him. What would make you want to hide from God? What are you hiding from God now? What do you plan to do about it?

TESTING IT

Jeremiah 23:24
"No one can hide where I cannot see him," says the LORD. "I fill all of heaven and earth," says the LORD.

---

24 "No one can hide
 where I cannot see him," says the LORD.
"I fill all of heaven and earth," says the LORD.

25 "I have heard the prophets who prophesy lies in my name. They say, 'I have had a dream! I have had a dream!' 26 How long will this continue in the minds of these lying prophets? They prophesy from their own wishful thinking. 27 They are trying to make the people of Judah forget me by telling each other these dreams. In the same way, their ancestors forgot me and worshipped Baal. 28 Is straw the same thing as wheat?" says the LORD. "If a prophet wants to tell about his dreams, let him! But let the person who hears my message speak it truthfully! 29 Isn't my message like a fire?" says the LORD. "Isn't it like a hammer that smashes a rock?

30 "So I am against the false prophets," says the LORD. "They keep stealing words from each other and say they are from me. 31 I am against the false prophets," says the LORD. "They use their own words and pretend it is a message from me. 32 I am against the prophets who prophesy false dreams," says the LORD. "They mislead my people with their lies and false teachings! I did not send them or command them to do anything for me. They can't help the people of Judah at all," says the LORD.

The Sad Message from the LORD

33 "Suppose the people of Judah, a prophet or a priest asks you: 'Jeremiah, what is the message from the LORD?' You will answer them and say, 'You are a heavy load to the LORD, and I will throw you down, says the LORD.' 34 A prophet or a priest or one of the people might say, 'This is a message from the LORD.' That person has lied, so I will punish him and his whole family. 35 This is what you will say to each other: 'What did the LORD answer?' or 'What did the LORD say?' 36 But you will never again say, 'The message of the LORD', because the only message you speak is your own words. You have changed the words of our God, the living God, the LORD All-powerful. 37 This is how you should speak to the prophets: 'What answer did the LORD give you?' or 'What did the LORD say?' 38 But don't say, 'The message from the LORD'. If you use these words, this is what the LORD says: because you called it a 'message from the LORD', though I told you not to use those words, 39 I will pick you up and throw you away from me, along with Jerusalem, which I gave to your ancestors and to you. 40 And I will make a disgrace of you for ever; your shame will never be forgotten."

The Good and Bad Figs

24 Nebuchadnezzar king of Babylon captured Jehoiachin son of Jehoiakim and king of Judah, his officers and all the craftsmen and metalworkers of Judah. He took them away from Jerusalem and brought them to Babylon. It was then that the LORD showed me two baskets of figs arranged in front of the Temple of the LORD. 2 One of the baskets had very good figs in it, like figs that ripen early in the season. But the other basket had figs too rotten to eat.

3 The LORD said to me, "What do you see, Jeremiah?"

I answered, "I see figs. The good figs are very good, but the rotten figs are too rotten to eat."

4 Then the LORD spoke his word to me: 5 "This is what the LORD, the God of Israel, says: 'I sent the people of Judah out of their country to live in the country of Babylon. I think of those people as good, like these good figs. 6 I will look after them and bring them back to the land of Judah. I will not tear them down, but I will build them up. I will not pull them up, but I will plant them so they can grow. 7 I will make them want to know me, that I am the LORD. They will be my people, and I will be their God, because they will return to me with their whole hearts.

8 "'But the bad figs are too rotten to eat.' So this is what the LORD says: 'Zedekiah king of Judah, his officers and all the people from Jerusalem who are left alive, even those who live in Egypt, will be like those rotten figs. 9 I will make those people hated as an evil people by all the kingdoms of the earth. People will make fun of them and tell jokes about them and point fingers at them and curse them everywhere I scatter them. 10 I will send war, hunger and disease against them. I will attack them until they have all been killed. Then they will no longer be in the land I gave to them and their ancestors.'"

A Summary of Jeremiah's Preaching

25 This is the message that came to Jeremiah concerning all the people of Judah. It came in the fourth year that Jehoiakim son of Josiah was king of Judah and the first year Nebuchadnezzar was king of Babylon. 2 This is the message Jeremiah the prophet spoke to all the people of Judah and Jerusalem:

3 The LORD has spoken his word to me again and again for these past 23 years. I have been a prophet since the thirteenth year of Josiah son of Amon king of Judah. I have spoken messages from the LORD to you from that time until today, but you have not listened.

4 The LORD has sent all his servants the prophets to you over and over again, but you have not listened or paid any attention to them. 5 Those prophets have said, "Stop your evil ways. Stop doing what is wrong so you can stay in the land that the LORD gave to you and your ancestors to live in for ever. 6 Don't follow other gods to serve them or to worship them. Don't make me, the LORD, angry by worshipping idols that are the work of your own hands, or I will punish you."

7 "But you people of Judah did not listen to me," says the LORD. "You made me angry by worshipping idols that were the work of your own hands, so I punished you."

8 So this is what the LORD All-powerful says: "Since you have not listened to my messages, 9 I will send for all the peoples of the north," says the LORD, "along with my servant Nebuchadnezzar king of Babylon. I will bring them all against Judah, those who live there, and all the nations around you, too. I will completely destroy all those countries and leave them in ruins for ever. People will be shocked when they see how badly I have destroyed those countries. 10 I will bring an end to the sounds of joy and happiness, the sounds of brides and bridegrooms, and the sound of people grinding meal. And

> The LORD has sent all his servants the prophets to you . . . but you have not listened or paid any attention to them.
> – Jeremiah 25:4

I will take away the light of the lamp. **11** That whole area will be an empty desert, and these nations will be slaves of the king of Babylon for 70 years.

12 "But when the 70 years have passed, I will punish the king of Babylon and his entire nation for their evil," says the LORD. "I will make that land a desert for ever. **13** I will make happen all the terrible things I said about Babylonia—everything Jeremiah prophesied about all those foreign nations, the warnings written in this book. **14** Even the Babylonians will have to serve many nations and many great kings. I will give them the punishment they deserve for all their own hands have done."

Judgement on the Nations

15 The LORD, the God of Israel, said this to me: "My anger is like the wine in a cup. Take it from my hand and make all the nations, to whom I am sending you, drink all my anger from this cup. **16** They will drink my anger and stumble about and act like madmen because of the war I am going to send among them."

17 So I took the cup from the LORD's hand and went to those nations and made them drink from it. **18** I served this wine to the people of Jerusalem and the towns of Judah, and the kings and officers of Judah, so they would become a ruin. Then people would be shocked and would insult them and speak evil of them. And so it has been to this day. **19** I also made these people drink of the LORD's anger: the king of Egypt, his servants, his officers, all his people **20** and all the foreigners there; all the kings of the land of Uz; all the kings of the Philistines (the kings of the cities of Ashkelon, Gaza, Ekron and the people left at Ashdod); **21** the people of Edom, Moab and Ammon; **22** all the kings of Tyre and Sidon; all the kings of the coastal countries to the west; **23** the people of Dedan and Tema and Buz; all who cut their hair short; **24** all the kings of Arabia; and the kings of the people who live in the desert; **25** all the kings of Zimri, Elam and Media; **26** and all the kings of the north, near and far, one after the other. I made all the kingdoms on earth drink from the cup of the LORD's anger, but the king of Babylon will drink from this cup after all the others.

27 "Then say to them, 'This is what the LORD All-powerful, the God of Israel, says: drink this cup of my anger. Get drunk from it and vomit. Fall down and don't get up because of the war I am sending among you!'

28 "If they refuse to take the cup from your hand and drink, say to them, 'The LORD All-powerful says this: you must drink from this cup. **29** Look! I am already bringing disaster on Jerusalem, the city that is called by my name. Do you think you will not be punished? You will be punished! I am sending war on all the people of the earth, says the LORD All-powerful.'

30 "You, Jeremiah, will prophesy against them with all these words. Say to them:

'The LORD will roar from heaven
   and will shout from his Holy
      Temple.
He will roar loudly against his
      land.
He will shout like people who walk on
      grapes to make wine;
he will shout against all who live on
      the earth.
31 The noise will spread all over the
      earth,
because the LORD will accuse all
      the nations.
He will judge and tell what is wrong
      with all people,
and he will kill the evil people with
      a sword,'" says the LORD.

32 This is what the LORD All-powerful says:

"Disasters will soon spread
   from nation to nation.
They will come like a powerful
   storm
from the faraway places on
   earth."

33 At that time those killed by the LORD will reach from one end of the earth to the other. No one will cry for them or gather up their bodies and bury them. They will be left lying on the ground like dung.

34 Cry, you leaders! Cry out loud!
   Roll around in the dust, leaders of
      the people!
   It is now time for you to be killed.
   You will fall and be scattered,
      like pieces of a broken jar.
35 There will be no place for the leaders
      to hide;
   they will not escape.
36 I hear the sound of the leaders
      shouting.
   I hear the leaders of the people
      crying loudly,
   because the Lord is destroying
      their land.
37 Those peaceful pastures will be like
      an empty desert,
   because the Lord is very angry.
38 Like a lion, he has left his den.
   Their land has been destroyed
   because of the terrible war he
      brought,
   because of his fierce anger.

Jeremiah's Lesson at the Temple

26 This message came from the Lord soon after Jehoiakim son of Josiah became king of Judah. 2 This is what the Lord said: "Jeremiah, stand in the courtyard of the Temple of the Lord. Give this message to all the people of the towns of Judah who are coming to worship at the Temple of the Lord. Tell them everything I tell you to say; don't leave out a word. 3 Perhaps they will listen and stop their evil ways. If they will, I will change my mind about bringing on them the disaster that I am planning because of the evil they have done. 4 Say to them: 'This is what the Lord says: you must obey me and follow my teachings that I gave you. 5 You must listen to what my servants the prophets say to you. I have sent them to you again and again, but you did not listen. 6 If you don't obey me, I will destroy my Temple in Jerusalem as I destroyed my Holy Tent at Shiloh. When I do, people all over the world will curse Jerusalem.'"

7 The priests, the prophets and all the people heard Jeremiah speaking these words in the Temple of the Lord. 8 When Jeremiah finished speaking everything the Lord had commanded him to say, the priests, prophets and all the people grabbed Jeremiah. They said, "You must die! 9 How dare you prophesy in the name of the Lord that this Temple will be destroyed like the one at Shiloh! How dare you say that Jerusalem will become a desert without anyone to live in it!" And all the people crowded around Jeremiah in the Temple of the Lord.

10 Now when the officers of Judah heard about what was happening, they came out of the king's palace and went up to the Temple of the Lord and took their places at the entrance of the New Gate. 11 Then the priests and prophets said to the officers and all the other people, "Jeremiah should be killed. He prophesied against Jerusalem, and you heard him yourselves."

12 Then Jeremiah spoke these words to all the officers of Judah and all the other people: "The Lord sent me to say everything you have heard about this Temple and this city. 13 Now change your lives and start doing good and obey the Lord your God. Then he will change his mind and not bring on you the disaster he has told you about. 14 As for me, I am in your power. Do to me what you think is good and right. 15 But be sure of one thing. If you kill me, you will be guilty of killing an innocent person. You will make this city and everyone who lives in it guilty too! The Lord truly sent me to you to give you this message."

16 Then the officers and all the people said to the priests and the prophets, "Jeremiah must not be killed. What he told us comes from the Lord our God."

17 Then some of the elders of Judah stood up and said to all the people, 18 "Micah, from the city of Moresheth, was a prophet during the time Hezekiah was king of Judah. Micah said to all the people of Judah, 'This is what the Lord All-powerful says:

   Jerusalem will be ploughed like a field.
      It will become a pile of rocks,
   and the hill where the Temple
      stands will be covered with
      bushes.'

19 "Hezekiah king of Judah and the

people of Judah did not kill Micah. You know that Hezekiah feared the LORD and tried to please the LORD. So the LORD changed his mind and did not bring on Judah the disaster he had promised. If we hurt Jeremiah, we will bring a terrible disaster on ourselves!"

20 (Now there was another man who prophesied in the name of the LORD. His name was Uriah son of Shemaiah from the city of Kiriath Jearim. He preached the same things against Jerusalem and the land of Judah that Jeremiah did. 21 When King Jehoiakim, all his army officers and all the leaders of Judah heard Uriah preach, King Jehoiakim wanted to kill Uriah. But Uriah heard about it and was afraid. So he escaped to Egypt. 22 Then King Jehoiakim sent Elnathan son of Acbor and some other men to Egypt, 23 and they brought Uriah back from Egypt. Then they took him to King Jehoiakim, who had Uriah killed with a sword. His body was thrown into the burial place where poor people are buried.)

24 Ahikam son of Shaphan supported Jeremiah. So Ahikam did not hand Jeremiah over to be killed by the people.

26:24 Friendship
Can standing up for a friend make a difference?

Nebuchadnezzar is Made Ruler

27 The LORD spoke his word to Jeremiah soon after Zedekiah son of Josiah was made king of Judah. 2 This is what the LORD said to me: "Make a yoke out of straps and poles, and put it on the back of your neck. 3 Then send messages to the kings of Edom, Moab, Ammon, Tyre and Sidon by their messengers who have come to Jerusalem to see Zedekiah king of Judah. 4 Tell them to give this message to their masters: 'The LORD All-powerful, the God of Israel, says: "Tell your masters: 5 I made the earth, its people and all its animals with my great power and strength. I can give the earth to anyone I want. 6 Now I have given all these lands to Nebuchadnezzar king of Babylon, my servant. I will make even the wild animals obey him. 7 All nations will serve Nebuchadnezzar and his son and grandson. Then the time will come for Babylon to be defeated, and many nations and great kings will make Babylon their servant.

8 "'"But if some nations or kingdoms refuse to serve Nebuchadnezzar king of Babylon and refuse to be under his control, I will punish them with war, hunger and terrible diseases, says the LORD. I will use Nebuchadnezzar to destroy them. 9 So don't listen to your false prophets, those who use magic to tell the future, those who explain dreams, the mediums or magicians. They all tell you, 'You will not be slaves to the king of Babylon.' 10 They are telling you lies that will cause you to be taken far from your homeland. I will force you to leave your homes, and you will die in another land. 11 But the nations who put themselves under the control of the king of Babylon and serve him I will let stay in their own country, says the LORD. The people from those nations will live in their own land and farm it."'"

12 I gave the same message to Zedekiah king of Judah. I said, "Put yourself under the control of the king of Babylon and serve him, and you will live. 13 Why should you and your people die from war, hunger or disease, as the LORD said would happen to those who do not serve the king of Babylon? 14 But the false prophets are saying, 'You will never be slaves to the king of Babylon.' Don't listen to them because they are prophesying lies to you! 15 'I did not send them,' says the LORD. 'They are prophesying lies and saying the message is from me. So I will send you away, Judah. And you and those prophets who prophesy to you will die.'"

16 Then I, Jeremiah, said to the priests

> I made the earth, its people and all its animals with my great power and strength.
> – Jeremiah 27:5

and all the people, "This is what the LORD says: Those false prophets are saying, 'The Babylonians will soon return what they took from the Temple of the LORD.' Don't listen to them! They are prophesying lies to you. 17 Don't listen to those prophets. But serve the king of Babylon, and you will live. There is no reason for you to cause Jerusalem to become a ruin. 18 If they are prophets and have the message from the LORD, let them pray to the LORD All-powerful. Let them ask that the things which are still in the Temple of the LORD and in the king's palace and in Jerusalem not be taken away to Babylon.

19 "This is what the LORD All-powerful says about those things left in Jerusalem, the pillars, the large bronze bowl, which is called the Sea, the stands that can be moved and other things. 20 Nebuchadnezzar king of Babylon did not take these away when he took as captives Jehoiachin son of Jehoiakim king of Judah and all the other important people from Judah and Jerusalem to Babylon. 21 This is what the LORD All-powerful, the God of Israel, says about the things left in the Temple of the LORD and in the king's palace and in Jerusalem: 22 'All of them will also be taken to Babylon. And they will stay there until the day I go to get them,' says the LORD. 'Then I will bring them back and return them to this place.'"

The False Prophet Hananiah

28 It was in that same year, in the fifth month of Zedekiah's fourth year as king of Judah, soon after he began to rule. The prophet Hananiah son of Azzur, from the town of Gibeon, spoke to me in the Temple of the LORD in front of the priests and all the people. He said: 2 "The LORD All-powerful, the God of Israel, says: 'I have broken the yoke the king of Babylon has put on Judah. 3 Before two years are over, I will bring back everything that Nebuchadnezzar king of Babylon took to Babylon from the LORD's Temple. 4 I will also bring back Jehoiachin son of Jehoiakim king of Judah and all the other captives from Judah who went to Babylon,' says the LORD. 'So I will break the yoke the king of Babylon put on Judah.'"

5 Then the prophet Jeremiah spoke to the prophet Hananiah in front of the priests and all the people who were standing in the Temple of the LORD. 6 He said, "Amen! Let the LORD really do that! May the LORD make the message you prophesy come true. May he bring back here everything from the LORD's Temple and all the people who were taken as captives to Babylon.

7 "But listen to what I am going to say to you and all the people. 8 There were prophets long before we became prophets, Hananiah. They prophesied that war, hunger and terrible diseases would come to many countries and great kingdoms. 9 But if a prophet prophesies that we will have peace and that message comes true, he can be recognised as one truly sent by the LORD."

10 Then the prophet Hananiah took the yoke off Jeremiah's neck and broke it. 11 Hananiah said in front of all the people, "This is what the LORD says: 'In the same way I will break the yoke of Nebuchadnezzar king of Babylon. He put that yoke on all the nations of the world, but I will break it before two years are over.'" After Hananiah had said that, Jeremiah left the Temple.

12 The LORD spoke his word to Jeremiah after the prophet Hananiah had broken the yoke off the prophet Jeremiah's neck. 13 The LORD said, "Go and tell Hananiah, 'This is what the LORD says: You have broken a wooden yoke, but I will make a yoke of iron in its place! 14 The LORD All-powerful, the God of Israel, says: I will put a yoke of iron on the necks of all these nations to make them serve Nebuchadnezzar king of Babylon, and they will be slaves to him. I will even give Nebuchadnezzar control over the wild animals.'"

15 Then the prophet Jeremiah said to the prophet Hananiah, "Listen, Hananiah! The LORD did not send you, and you have made the people of Judah trust in lies. 16 So this is what the LORD says: 'Soon I will remove you from the earth. You will die this year, because you

taught the people to turn against the LORD.'"

17 Hananiah died in the seventh month of that same year.

A Letter to the Captives in Babylon

29 This is the letter that Jeremiah the prophet sent from Jerusalem to the elders who were among the captives, the priests and the prophets. He sent it to all the other people Nebuchadnezzar had taken as captives from Jerusalem to Babylon. 2 (This letter was sent after all these people were taken away: Jehoiachin the king and the queen mother; the officers and leaders of Judah and Jerusalem; and the craftsmen and metalworkers from Jerusalem.) 3 Zedekiah king of Judah sent Elasah son of Shaphan and Gemariah son of Hilkiah to Babylon to Nebuchadnezzar king of Babylon. So Jeremiah gave them this letter to carry to Babylon:

4 This is what the LORD All-powerful, the God of Israel, says to all those people I sent away from Jerusalem as captives to Babylon: 5 "Build houses and settle in the land. Plant gardens and eat the food they grow. 6 Get married and have sons and daughters. Find wives for your sons, and let your daughters be married so they also may have sons and daughters. Have many children in Babylon; don't become fewer in number. 7 Also do good things for the city where I sent you as captives. Pray to the LORD for the city where you are living, because if good things happen in the city, good things will happen to you also." 8 The LORD All-powerful, the God of Israel, says: "Don't let the prophets among you and the people who do magic fool you. Don't listen to their dreams. 9 They are prophesying lies to you, saying that their message is from me. But I did not send them," says the LORD.

10 This is what the LORD says: "Babylon will be powerful for 70 years. After that time I will come to you, and I will keep my promise to bring you back to Jerusalem. 11 I say this because I know what I am planning for you," says the LORD. "I have good plans for you, not plans to hurt you. I will give you hope and a good future. 12 Then you will call my name. You will come to me and pray to

29:7 Prayer
Why should you pray for people or places you don't like?

FAITH links

A HOPEFUL FUTURE
JEREMIAH 29:11

What are some of the plans you and your parents have made concerning your future? Maybe your parents have set aside a savings account to help pay for university. Or maybe you've told them about a career that you'd like to try. Whatever the plans are, you know that they were made to make sure that you have a hopeful future. God's plans are like that as well. As Jeremiah explained, God's plans for his people are good, not harmful.

Planning for the future? Connect here first:

Good Advice? Leviticus 20:6, p. 162

The Green Light, 2 Samuel 2:1, p. 401

A Parent's Advice, Proverbs 1:8–9, p. 825

First Place, Haggai 1:7–11, p. 1248

The Choices of a Choice, Luke 5:1–11, p. 1375

Heavenly Treasure, Luke 12:32–34, p. 1394

Jeremiah 29:13 1032

me, and I will listen to you. 13 You will search for me. And when you search for me with all your heart, you will find me! 14 I will let you find me," says the LORD. "And I will bring you back from your captivity. I forced you to leave this place, but I will gather you from all the nations, from the places I have sent you as captives," says the LORD. "And I will bring you back to this place."

15 You might say, "The LORD has given us prophets here in Babylon."

16 But the LORD says this about the king who is sitting on David's throne now and all the other people still in Jerusalem, your relatives who did not go as captives to Babylon with you. 17 The LORD All-powerful says: "I will soon send war, hunger and terrible diseases against those still in Jerusalem. I will make them like bad figs that are too rotten to eat. 18 I will chase them with war, hunger and terrible diseases. I will make them hated by all the kingdoms of the earth. People will curse them and be shocked and will use them as a shameful example wherever I make them go. 19 This is because they have not listened to my message," says the LORD. "I sent my message to them again and again through my servants, the prophets, but they did not listen," says the LORD.

20 You captives, whom I forced to leave Jerusalem and go to Babylon, listen to the message from the LORD. 21 The LORD All-powerful, the God of Israel, says this about Ahab son of Kolaiah and Zedekiah son of Maaseiah: "These two men have been prophesying lies to you, saying that their message is from me. But soon I will hand over those two prophets to Nebuchadnezzar king of Babylon, and he will kill them in front of you. 22 Because of them, all the captives from Judah in Babylon will use this curse: 'May the LORD treat you like Zedekiah and Ahab, whom the king of Babylon burned in the fire.' 23 They have done evil things among the people of Israel. They are guilty of adultery with their neighbours' wives. They have also spoken lies and said those lies were a message from me. I did not tell them to do that. I know what they

FAITH links

WHAT'S WRONG ABOUT RUMOURS
JEREMIAH 29:24-32

Has anyone ever started a rumour about you or one of your friends that wasn't true? Rumours can be very harmful to friendships or reputations if they are believed. God had a message for Shemaiah, a man who spread a rumour about Jeremiah. He told people that Jeremiah was not a true prophet of God. God was very displeased with Shemaiah and promised to punish him.

When a rumour comes your way, you don't have to instantly believe it or pass it on. Instead, try to find out the truth for yourself, or do the next best thing: ignore it.

What do you do when you hear the latest gossip? Link here for some good advice:

The Trouble with Jealousy, Genesis 37, p. 53

The Salt Promise, 2 Chronicles 13:5, p. 576

An Honest Reputation, Nehemiah 13:13, p. 644

Who Do You Prefer? Proverbs 3:32, p. 830

The Verdict Is In? Matthew 7:1–2, p. 1285

The Whole Truth, John 8:31–32, 45, p. 1438

have done; I am a witness to it," says the LORD.

24 Also give a message to Shemaiah from the Nehelamite family. 25 The LORD All-powerful, the God of Israel, says: "Shemaiah, you sent letters in your name to all the people in Jerusalem, to the priest Zephaniah son of Maaseiah, and to all the priests. 26 You said to Zephaniah, 'The LORD has made you priest in place of Jehoiada. You are to be in charge of the Temple of the LORD. You should arrest any madman who acts like a prophet. Lock his hands and feet between wooden blocks, and put iron rings around his neck. 27 Now Jeremiah from Anathoth is acting like a prophet. So why haven't you arrested him? 28 Jeremiah has sent this message to us in Babylon: you will be there for a long time, so build houses and settle down. Plant gardens and eat what they grow.'"

29 Zephaniah the priest read the letter to Jeremiah the prophet. 30 Then the LORD spoke his word to Jeremiah: 31 "Send this message to all the captives in Babylon: 'This is what the LORD says about Shemaiah the Nehelamite: Shemaiah has prophesied to you, but I did not send him. He has made you believe a lie. 32 So the LORD says, I will soon punish Shemaiah the Nehelamite and his family. He will not see the good things I will do for my people, says the LORD. None of his family will be left alive among the people, because he has taught the people to turn against me.'"

Promises of Hope

30 These are the words that the LORD spoke to Jeremiah. 2 The LORD, the God of Israel, said: "Jeremiah, write in a book all the words I have spoken to you. 3 The days will come when I will bring Israel and Judah back from captivity," says the LORD. "I will return them to the land I gave their ancestors, and they will own it!" says the LORD.

4 The LORD spoke this message about the people of Israel and Judah: 5 this is what the LORD said:

"We hear people crying from fear.
They are afraid; there is no peace.
6 Ask this question, and consider it:
a man cannot have a baby.
So why do I see every strong man
holding his stomach in pain like a
woman having a baby?
Why is everyone's face turning
white like a dead man's face?
7 This will be a terrible day!
There will never be another time
like this.
This is a time of great trouble for the
people of Jacob,
but they will be saved from it."

8 The LORD All-powerful says, "At that
time
I will break the yoke from their
necks
and tear off the ropes that hold them.
Foreign people will never again
make my people slaves.
9 They will serve the LORD their God
and David their king,
whom I will send to them.

10 "So people of Jacob, my servants,
don't be afraid.
Israel, don't be frightened," says
the LORD.
"I will soon save you from that
faraway place where you are
captives.
I will save your family from that
land.
The people of Jacob will be safe and
have peace again;
there will be no enemy to frighten
them.
11 I am with you and will save you,"
says the LORD.
"I will completely destroy all those
nations
where I scattered you,
but I will not completely destroy
you.
I will punish you fairly,
but I will still punish you."
12 This is what the LORD says:
"You people have a wound that
cannot be cured;
your injury will not heal.
13 There is no one to argue your case

and no cure for your sores.
So you will not be healed.
14 All those nations who were your
  friends have forgotten you.
  They don't care about you.
  I have hurt you as an enemy would.
  I punished you very hard,
  because your guilt was so great
  and your sins were so many.
15 Why are you crying out about your
  injury?
  There is no cure for your pain.
  I did these things to you because of
  your great guilt,
  because of your many sins.
16 But all those nations that destroyed
  you will now be destroyed.
  All your enemies will become
  captives in other lands.
  Those who stole from you will have
  their own things stolen.
  Those who took things from you in
  war will have their own things
  taken.
17 I will bring back your health
  and heal your injuries," says the
  LORD,
  "because other people forced you
  away.
  They said about you, 'No one cares
  for Jerusalem!'"
18 This is what the LORD says:
  "I will soon make the tents of Jacob's
  people as they used to be,
  and I will have pity on Israel's
  houses.
  The city will be rebuilt on its hill of
  ruins,
  and the king's palace will stand in
  its proper place.
19 People in those places will sing songs
  of praise.
  There will be the sound of laughter.
  I will give them many children
  so their number will not be small.
  I will bring honour to them
  so no one will look down on them.
20 Their descendants will be as they
  were in the old days.
  I will set them up as a strong
  people before me,
  and I will punish the nations who
  have hurt them.
21 One of their own people will lead
  them;
  their ruler will come from among
  them.
  He will come near to me when I
  invite him.
  Who would dare to come to me
  uninvited?" says the LORD.
22 "So you will be my people,
  and I will be your God."
23 Look! It is a storm from the LORD!
  He is angry and has gone out to
  punish the people.
  Punishment will come like a storm
  crashing down on the evil
  people.
24 The LORD will stay angry
  until he finishes punishing the
  people.
  He will stay angry
  until he finishes the punishment he
  planned.
  When that day comes,
  you will understand this.

The New Israel

31 The LORD says, "At that time I will be God of all Israel's family groups, and they will be my people."

2 This is what the LORD says:
  "The people who were not killed by
  the enemy's sword
  found help in the desert.
  I came to give rest to Israel."

3 And from far away the LORD appeared to his people and said,
  "I love you people
  with a love that will last for ever.
  That is why I have continued
  showing you kindness.
4 People of Israel, I will build you up
  again
  and you will be rebuilt.
  You will pick up your tambourines
  again
  and dance with those who are
  joyful.
5 You will plant vineyards again
  on the hills around Samaria.
  The farmers will plant them
  and enjoy their fruit.

Jeremiah 31:13   1035

FAITH links

HIS VALENTINE
JEREMIAH 31:3

You hear a lot about love when Valentine's Day comes around. Many people talk about it as they hand out chocolates and valentine cards. But come February 15, it's like love has ended. The cards stop. The chocolates have gone. But here's some good news. Jeremiah has a valentine from God that you can read any day of the year. God promises to love you for ever. Can anyone else make that claim?

The Rainbow Promise, Genesis 9:1–17, p. 14

A Thanksgiving Reminder, Exodus 12, p. 91

A Holiday Letter, Esther 9:20–23, p. 657

A Love Song, Zephaniah 3:17, p. 1246

How Do I Love You? Malachi 1:1–5, p. 1267

The Gift of Worship, Matthew 2:10–12, p. 1275

---

6 There will be a time when watchmen
   in the mountains of Ephraim
   shout this message:
'Come, let's go up to Jerusalem to
   worship the
   LORD our
   God!'"

31:6 Future — What's the future for believers?

7 This is what the LORD says:
"Be happy and
   sing for the people of Jacob.
Shout for Israel, the greatest of the
   nations.
Sing your praises and shout this:
'LORD, save your people,
   those who are left alive from the
   nation of Israel!'

8 Look, I will soon bring Israel from the
   country in the north,
   and I will gather them from the
   faraway places on earth.
Some of the people are blind and
   crippled.
Some of the women are pregnant,
   and some are ready to give birth.
A great many people will come
   back.
9 They will be crying as they come,
   but they will pray as I bring them
   back.
I will lead those people by streams of
   water
   on an even road where they will
   not stumble.
I am Israel's father,
   and Israel is my firstborn son.

10 "Nations, listen to the message from
   the LORD.
Tell this message in the faraway
   lands by the sea:
'The one who scattered the people of
   Israel will bring them back,
   and he will watch over his people
   like a shepherd.'
11 The LORD will pay for the people of
   Jacob
   and will buy them back from
   people stronger than they were.
12 The people of Israel will come to the
   high points of Jerusalem
   and shout for joy.
Their faces will shine with happiness
   about all the good things from
   the LORD:
   the grain, new wine, oil, young
   sheep and young cows.
They will be like a garden that has
   plenty of water,
   and they will not be troubled any
   more.
13 Then young women of Israel will be
   happy and dance,
   the young men and old men also.

> I will change their sadness into happiness;
> I will give them comfort and joy instead of sadness.
> 14 The priests will have more than enough sacrifices,
> and my people will be filled with the good things I give them!"
> says the LORD.

15 This is what the LORD says:
> "A voice was heard in Ramah
> of painful crying and deep sadness:
> Rachel crying for her children.
> She refused to be comforted,
> because her children are dead!"
> 16 But this is what the LORD says:
> "Stop crying;
> don't let your eyes fill with tears.
> You will be rewarded for your work!"
> says the LORD.
> "The people will return from their enemy's land.
> 17 So there is hope for you in the future," says the LORD.
> "Your children will return to their own land.

18 "I have heard Israel moaning:
> 'LORD, you punished me, and I have learned my lesson.
> I was like a calf that had never been trained.
> Take me back so that I may come back.
> You truly are the LORD my God.
> 19 LORD, after I wandered away from you,
> I changed my heart and life.
> After I understood,
> I beat my breast with sorrow.
> I was ashamed and disgraced,
> because I suffered for the foolish things I did when I was young.'

20 "You know that Israel is my dear son,
> The child I love.
> Yes, I often speak against Israel,
> but I still remember him.
> I love him very much
> and I want to comfort him," says the LORD.

21 "People of Israel, fix the road signs.
> Put up signs to show you the way home.
> Watch the road.
> Pay attention to the road on which you travel.
> People of Israel, come home,
> come back to your towns.
> 22 You are an unfaithful daughter.
> How long will you wander before you come home?
> The LORD has made something new happen in the land:
> a woman will go seeking a man."

23 The LORD All-powerful, the God of Israel, says: "I will again do good things for the people of Judah. At that time the people in the land of Judah and its towns will again use these words: 'May the LORD bless you, home of what is good, holy mountain.' 24 People in all the towns of Judah will live together in peace. Farmers and those who move around with their flocks will live together in peace. 25 I will give rest and strength to those who are weak and tired."

26 After hearing that, I, Jeremiah, woke up and looked around. My sleep had been very pleasant.

27 The LORD says, "The time is coming when I will help the families of Israel and Judah and their children and animals to grow. 28 In the past I watched over Israel and Judah, to pull them up and tear them down, to destroy them and bring them disaster. But now I will watch over them to build them up and make them strong," says the LORD.

29 "At that time people will no longer say:

> 'The parents have eaten sour grapes,
> and that caused the children to grind their teeth from the sour taste.'

30 Instead, each person will die for his own sin; the person who eats sour grapes will grind his own teeth.

The New Agreement

31 "Look, the time is coming," says the LORD,
> "when I will make a new agreement

with the people of Israel
  and the people of Judah.
32 It will not be like the agreement
    I made with their ancestors
  when I took them by the hand
    to bring them out of Egypt.
  I was a husband to them,
    but they broke that agreement,"
  says the LORD.
33 "This is the agreement I will make
    with the people of Israel at that
      time," says the LORD:
  "I will put my teachings in their
      minds
    and write them on their hearts.
  I will be their God,
    and they will be my people.
34 People will no longer have to teach
      their neighbours and relatives
      to know the LORD,
  because all people will know me,
    from the least to the most
      important," says the LORD.
  "I will forgive them for the wicked
      things they did,
    and I will not remember their sins
      any more."

The LORD will Never Leave Israel

35 The LORD makes the sun shine in the
      day
    and the moon and stars to shine at
      night.
  He stirs up the sea so that its waves
      crash on the shore.
    The LORD All-powerful is his
      name.
  This is what the LORD says:
36 "Only if these laws should ever
      fail,"
    says the LORD,
  "will Israel's descendants ever stop
      being a nation before me."
37 This is what the LORD says:
  "Only if people can measure the sky
      above
    and learn the secrets of the earth
      below,
  will I reject all the descendants of
      Israel
    because of what they have done,"
    says the LORD.

Jeremiah 31:37 1037

FAITH links

A PROMISE FROM THE HEART
JEREMIAH 31:31-33

When something is said to be "written in stone" it means it's permanent. When God gave Moses the Ten Commandments, God wrote them on tablets of stone. God used the prophet Jeremiah to make a new promise with the people of Israel. In a future time, God said he would write his teachings on their hearts. That meant he would help them to be obedient. They would want to obey his laws because they loved him.

The heart is the centre of obedience. It is there that we decide whether we will obey God. Believing from the heart is more permanent than stone.

How's your heart condition? Link here to see what God wants your heart to be like:

Lights, Camera, . . . Actions!
Genesis 12:1-3, p. 17

Do What You Want?
Judges 21:25, p. 341

The Wisdom of Obeying God,
1 Kings 11:1-13, p. 453

Like Silver, Psalm 12:6-8,
p. 717

The Power of *If*, Mark 9:14-24,
p. 1344

Out of Your Mind?
1 Corinthians 2:16, p. 1547

The New Jerusalem

38 The LORD says, "The time is coming when Jerusalem will be rebuilt for me—everything from the Tower of Hananel to the Corner Gate. 39 The measuring line will stretch from the Corner Gate straight to the hill of Gareb. Then it will turn to the place named Goah. 40 The whole valley where dead bodies and ashes are thrown, and all the terraces out to the Kidron Valley on the east as far as the corner of the Horse Gate—all that area will be holy to the LORD. The city of Jerusalem will never again be torn down or destroyed."

Jeremiah Buys a Field

32 This is the word the LORD spoke to Jeremiah in the tenth year Zedekiah was king of Judah, which was the eighteenth year of Nebuchadnezzar. 2 At that time the army of the king of Babylon was surrounding Jerusalem. Jeremiah the prophet was under arrest in the courtyard of the guard, which was at the palace of the king of Judah.

3 Zedekiah king of Judah had put Jeremiah in prison there. Zedekiah had asked, "Why have you prophesied the things you have?" (Jeremiah had said, "This is what the LORD says: 'I will soon hand the city of Jerusalem over to the king of Babylon, and he will capture it. 4 Zedekiah king of Judah will not escape from the Babylonian army, but he will surely be handed over to the king of Babylon. And he will speak to the king of Babylon face to face and see him with his own eyes. 5 The king will take Zedekiah to Babylon, where he will stay until I have punished him,' says the LORD. 'If you fight against the Babylonians, you will not succeed.'")

6 While Jeremiah was in prison, he said, "The LORD spoke this word to me: 7 Your cousin Hanamel, son of your uncle Shallum, will come to you soon. Hanamel will say to you, 'Jeremiah, you are my nearest relative, so buy my field near the town of Anathoth. It is your right and your duty to buy that field.'

8 "Then it happened just as the LORD had said. My cousin Hanamel came to me in the courtyard of the guard and said to me, 'Buy for yourself my field near Anathoth in the land of Benjamin. It is your right and duty to buy it and own it.' So I knew this was a message from the LORD.

9 "I bought the field at Anathoth from my cousin Hanamel, weighing out 17 pieces of silver for him. 10 I signed the record and sealed it and had some people witness it. I also weighed out the silver on the scales. 11 Then I took both copies of the record of ownership—the one that was sealed that had the demands and limits of ownership, and the one that was not sealed. 12 And I gave them to Baruch son of Neriah, the son of Mahseiah. My cousin Hanamel, the other witnesses who signed the record of ownership, and many Jews sitting in the courtyard of the guard saw me give the record of ownership to Baruch.

13 "With all the people watching, I told Baruch, 14 'This is what the LORD All-powerful, the God of Israel, says: Take both copies of the record of ownership—the sealed copy and the copy that was not sealed—and put them in a clay jar so they will last a long time. 15 This is what the LORD All-powerful, the God of Israel, says: in the future my people will once again buy houses and fields for grain and vineyards in the land of Israel.'

16 "After I gave the record of ownership to Baruch son of Neriah, I prayed to the LORD, 17 Oh, Lord GOD, you made the skies and the earth with your very great power. There is nothing too hard for you to do. 18 You show love and kindness to thousands of people, but you also bring punishment to children for their parents' sins. Great and powerful God, your name is the LORD All-powerful. 19 You plan and do great things. You see everything that people do, and you reward people for the way they live and for what they do. 20 You did miracles and wonderful things in the land of Egypt. You have continued doing them in Israel and among the other nations even until today. So you have become well known. 21 You brought your people, the Israelites, out of Egypt using signs and miracles and your great power and strength. You brought great terror on everyone. 22 You gave them this land that

you promised to their ancestors long ago, a fertile land. 23 They came into this land and took it for their own, but they did not obey you or follow your teachings. They did not do everything you commanded. So you made all these terrible things happen to them. 24 "Look! The enemy has surrounded the city and has built roads to the top of the walls to capture it. Because of war, hunger and terrible diseases, the city will be handed over to the Babylonians who are attacking it. You said this would happen and now you see it is happening. 25 But now, Lord GOD, you tell me, 'Buy the field with silver and call in witnesses.' You tell me this while the Babylonian army is ready to capture the city."

26 Then the LORD spoke this word to Jeremiah: 27 "I am the LORD, the God of every person on the earth. Nothing is impossible for me. 28 So this is what the LORD says: I will soon hand over the city of Jerusalem to the Babylonian army and to Nebuchadnezzar king of Babylon, who will capture it. 29 The Babylonian army is already attacking the city of Jerusalem. They will soon enter it and start a fire to burn down the city and its houses. The people of Jerusalem offered sacrifices to Baal on the roofs[n] of those same houses and poured out drink offerings to other idols to make me angry. 30 From their youth, the people of Israel and Judah have done only the things I said were wrong. They have made me angry by worshipping idols made with their own hands," says the LORD. 31 "From the day Jerusalem was built until now, this city has made me angry, so angry that I must remove it from my sight. 32 I will destroy it, because of all the evil the people of Israel and Judah have done. The people, their kings and officers, their priests and prophets, all the people of Judah and the people of Jerusalem have made me angry. 33 They turned their backs to me, not their faces. I tried to teach them again and again, but they wouldn't listen or learn. 34 They put their hateful idols in the place where I have chosen to be worshipped, so they made it unclean. 35 In the Valley of Ben Hinnom they built places to worship Baal so they could burn their sons and daughters as sacrifices to Molech. But I never commanded them to do such a hateful thing. It never entered my mind that they would do such a thing and cause Judah to sin.

36 "You are saying, 'Because of war, hunger and terrible diseases, the city will be handed over to the king of Babylon.' But the LORD, the God of Israel, says about Jerusalem: 37 I forced the people of Israel and Judah to leave their land, because I was furious and very angry with them. But soon I will gather them from all the lands where I forced them to go, and I will bring them back to this place, where they may live in safety. 38 The people of Israel and Judah will be my people, and I will be their God. 39 I will make them truly want to be one people with one goal. They will truly want to worship me all their lives, for their own good and for the good of their children after them.

40 "I will make an agreement with them that will last for ever. I will never turn away from them; I will always do good to them. I will make them want to respect me so they will never turn away from me. 41 I will enjoy doing good to them. And with my whole being I will surely plant them in this land and make them grow."

42 This is what the LORD says: "I have brought this great disaster to the people of Israel and Judah. In the same way I will bring the good things that I promise to do for them. 43 You are saying, 'This land is an empty desert, without people or animals. It has been handed over to the Babylonians.' But in the future, people will again buy fields in this land. 44 They will use their money to buy fields. They will sign and seal their agreements and

32:40–41
God's Promises
How long do God's promises last?

32:29 roofs In Bible times houses were built with flat roofs. The roof was used for drying things such as flax and fruit. And it was used as an extra room, as a place for worship and as a place to sleep in the summer.

call in witnesses. They will again buy fields in the land of Benjamin, in the area around Jerusalem, in the towns of Judah and in the mountains, in the western hills and in southern Judah. I will make everything as good for them as it once was," says the LORD.

The Promise of the LORD

33 While Jeremiah was still locked up in the courtyard of the guards, the LORD spoke his word to him a second time: **2** "These are the words of the LORD, who made the earth, shaped it and gave it order, whose name is the LORD: **3** 'Judah, pray to me, and I will answer you. I will tell you important secrets you have never heard before.' **4** This is what the LORD, the God of Israel, says about the houses in Jerusalem and the royal palaces of Judah that have been torn down to be used in defence of the attack by the Babylonian army: **5** 'Some people will come to fight against the Babylonians. They will fill these houses with the bodies of people I killed in my hot anger. I have turned away from this city because of all the evil its people have done.

6 "But then I will bring health and healing to the people there. I will heal them and let them enjoy great peace and safety. **7** I will bring Judah and Israel back from captivity and make them strong countries as in the past. **8** They sinned against me, but I will wash away that sin. They did evil and turned away from me, but I will forgive them. **9** Then 'Jerusalem' will be to me a name that brings joy! And people from all nations of the earth will praise it when they hear about the good things I am doing there. They will be surprised and shocked at all the good things and the peace I will bring to Jerusalem.'

10 "You are saying, 'Our country is an empty desert, without people or animals.' But this is what the LORD says: It is now quiet in the streets of Jerusalem and in the towns of Judah, without people or animals, but it will be noisy there soon! **11** There will be sounds of joy and gladness and the happy sounds of brides and bridegrooms. There will be the sounds of people bringing to the Temple of the LORD their offerings of thanks to the LORD. They will say,

'Praise the LORD All-powerful,
because the LORD is good!
His love continues for ever!'

They will say this because I will again do good things for Judah, as I did in the beginning," says the LORD.

12 This is what the LORD All-powerful says: "This place is empty now, without people or animals. But there will be shepherds in all the towns of Judah and pastures where they let their flocks rest. **13** Shepherds will again count their sheep as the sheep walk in front of them. They will count them in the mountains and in the western hills, in southern Judah and the land of Benjamin, and around Jerusalem and the other towns of Judah!" says the LORD.

The Good Branch

14 The LORD says, "The time is coming when I will do the good thing I promised to the people of Israel and Judah. **15** In those days and at that time,
I will make a good branch sprout
from David's family.
He will do what is fair and right in
the land.
16 At that time Judah will be saved
and the people of Jerusalem will
live in safety.
The branch will be named:
The LORD Does What Is Right."
17 This is what the LORD says: "Someone from David's family will always sit on the throne of the family of Israel. **18** And there will always be priests from the family of Levi. They will always stand before me to offer burnt offerings

> Praise the LORD All-powerful, because the LORD is good! His love continues for ever!
> – Jeremiah 33:11

and grain offerings and sacrifices to me."

19 The LORD spoke his word to Jeremiah, saying: 20 "This is what the LORD says: I have an agreement with day and night that they will always come at the right times. If you could change that agreement, 21 only then could you change my agreement with David and Levi. Only then would my servant David not have a descendant ruling as king on David's throne. And only then would the family of Levi not be priests serving me in the Temple. 22 But I will give many descendants to my servant David and to the family group of Levi who serve me in the Temple. They will be as many as the stars in the sky that no one can count. They will be as many as the grains of sand on the seashore that no one can measure."

23 The LORD spoke his word to Jeremiah, saying: 24 "Jeremiah, have you heard what the people are saying? They say: 'The LORD turned away from the two families of Israel and Judah that he chose.' Now they don't think of my people as a nation any more!"

25 This is what the LORD says: "If I had not made my agreement with day and night, and if I had not made the laws for the sky and earth, 26 only then would I turn away from Jacob's descendants. And only then would I not let the descendants of David my servant rule over the descendants of Abraham, Isaac and Jacob. But I will be kind to them and cause good things to happen to them again."

A Warning to Zedekiah

34 The LORD spoke his word to Jeremiah when Nebuchadnezzar king of Babylon was fighting against Jerusalem and all the towns around it. Nebuchadnezzar had with him all his army and the armies of all the kingdoms and peoples he ruled. 2 This is what the LORD, the God of Israel, said: "Jeremiah, go to Zedekiah king of Judah and tell him:

> I will soon hand the city of Jerusalem over to the king of Babylon, and he will burn it down!
> – Jeremiah 34:2

'This is what the LORD says: I will soon hand the city of Jerusalem over to the king of Babylon, and he will burn it down! 3 You will not escape from the king of Babylon; you will surely be captured and handed over to him. You will see the king of Babylon with your own eyes, and he will talk to you face to face. And you will go to Babylon. 4 But, Zedekiah king of Judah, listen to the promise of the LORD. This is what the LORD says about you: You will not be killed with a sword. 5 You will die in a peaceful way. As people made funeral fires to honour your ancestors, the kings who ruled before you, so people will make a funeral fire to honour you. They will cry for you and sadly say, "Ah, master!" I myself make this promise to you, says the LORD.'"

6 So Jeremiah the prophet gave this message to Zedekiah in Jerusalem. 7 This was while the army of the king of Babylon was fighting against Jerusalem and the cities of Judah that had not yet been taken—Lachish and Azekah. These were the only fortified cities left in the land of Judah.

Slaves are Mistreated

8 The LORD spoke his word to Jeremiah. This was after King Zedekiah had made an agreement with all the people in Jerusalem to free all the Hebrew slaves. 9 Everyone was supposed to free his Hebrew slaves, both male and female. No one was to keep a fellow Jew as a slave. 10 All the officers and all the people accepted this agreement; they agreed to free their male and female slaves and no longer keep them as slaves. So all the slaves were set free. 11 But after that, the people who had slaves changed their minds. So they took back the people they had set free and made them slaves again.

12 Then the LORD spoke his word to Jeremiah: 13 "This is what the LORD, the

God of Israel, says: I brought your ancestors out of Egypt where they were slaves and made an agreement with them. 14 I said to your ancestors: 'At the end of every seven years, each one of you must set his Hebrew slaves free. If a fellow Hebrew has sold himself to you, you must let him go free after he has served you for six years.' But your ancestors did not listen or pay attention to me. 15 A short time ago you changed your hearts and did what I say is right. Each of you gave freedom to his fellow Hebrews who were slaves. And you even made an agreement before me in the place where I have chosen to be worshipped. 16 But now you have changed your minds. You have shown you do not honour me. Each of you has taken back the male and female slaves you had set free, and you have forced them to become your slaves again.

17 "So this is what the LORD says: You have not obeyed me. You have not given freedom to your fellow Hebrews, neither relatives nor friends. But now I will give freedom, says the LORD, to war, to terrible diseases and to hunger. I will make you hated by all the kingdoms of the earth. 18 I will hand over the men who broke my agreement, who have not kept the promises they made before me. They cut a calf into two pieces before me and walked between the pieces." 19 These people made the agreement before me by walking between the pieces of the calf: the leaders of Judah and Jerusalem, the officers of the court, the priests and all the people of the land. 20 So I will hand them over to their enemies and to everyone who wants to kill them. Their bodies will become food for the birds of the air and for the wild animals of the earth. 21 I will hand Zedekiah king of Judah and his officers over to their enemies and to everyone who wants to kill them, and to the army of the king of Babylon, even though they have left Jerusalem. 22 I will give the order, says the LORD, to bring the Babylonian army back to Jerusalem. It will fight against Jerusalem, capture it, set it on fire and burn it down. I will destroy the towns in Judah so that they become ruins where no one lives!"

The Recabite Family Obeys God

35 When Jehoiakim son of Josiah was king of Judah, the LORD spoke his word to Jeremiah, saying: 2 "Go to the family of Recab. Invite them to come to one of the side rooms of the Temple of the LORD, and offer them wine to drink."

3 So I went to get Jaazaniah son of Jeremiah," the son of Habazziniah. And I gathered all of Jaazaniah's brothers and sons and the whole family of the Recabites together. 4 Then I brought them into the Temple of the LORD. We went into the room of the sons of Hanan son of Igdaliah, who was a man of God. The room was next to the one where the officers stay and above the room of Maaseiah son of Shallum, the doorkeeper in the Temple. 5 Then I put some bowls full of wine and some cups before the men of the Recabite family. And I said to them, "Drink some wine."

6 But the Recabite men answered, "We never drink wine. Our ancestor Jonadab son of Recab gave us this command: 'You and your descendants must never drink wine. 7 Also you must never build houses, plant seeds or plant vineyards, or do any of those things. You must live only in tents. Then you will live a long time in the land where you are wanderers.' 8 So we Recabites have obeyed everything Jonadab our ancestor commanded us. Neither we nor our wives, sons or daughters ever drink wine. 9 We never build houses in which to live, or own fields or vineyards, or plant crops. 10 We have lived in tents and have obeyed everything our ancestor Jonadab commanded us. 11 But when Nebuchadnezzar king of Babylon attacked Judah, we said to each other, 'Come, we must enter Jerusalem so we can escape the Babylonian army and the Aramean army.' So we have stayed in Jerusalem."

12 Then the LORD spoke his word to Jeremiah: 13 "This is what the LORD

34:18 They . . . pieces. This showed that the men were willing to be killed, like this animal, if they did not keep their agreement.

35:3 Jeremiah Not the prophet Jeremiah, but a different man with the same name.

All-powerful, the God of Israel, says: Jeremiah, go and tell the men of Judah and the people of Jerusalem: 'You should learn a lesson and obey my message,' says the LORD. 14 'Jonadab son of Recab ordered his descendants not to drink wine, and that command has been obeyed. Until today they have obeyed their ancestor's command; they do not drink wine. But I, the LORD, have given you messages again and again, but you did not obey me. 15 I sent all my servants the prophets to you again and again, saying, "Each of you must stop doing evil. You must change and be good. Do not follow other gods to serve them. If you obey me, you will live in the land I have given to you and your ancestors." But you have not listened to me or paid attention to my message. 16 The descendants of Jonadab son of Recab obeyed the commands their ancestor gave them, but the people of Judah have not obeyed me.'

17 "So the LORD God All-powerful, the God of Israel, says: 'I will soon bring every disaster I said would come to Judah and to everyone living in Jerusalem. I spoke to those people, but they refused to listen. I called out to them, but they did not answer me.'"

18 Then Jeremiah said to the Recabites, "This is what the LORD All-powerful, the God of Israel, says: 'You have obeyed the commands of your ancestor Jonadab and have followed all of his teachings; you have done everything he commanded.' 19 So this is what the LORD All-powerful, the God of Israel, says: 'There will always be a descendant of Jonadab son of Recab to serve me.'"

Jehoiakim Burns Jeremiah's Scroll

36 The LORD spoke this word to Jeremiah during the fourth year that Jehoiakim son of Josiah was king of Judah: 2 "Get a scroll. Write on it all the words I have spoken to you about Israel and Judah and all the nations. Write everything from when I first spoke to you, when Josiah was king, until now. 3 Perhaps the family of Judah will hear what disasters I am planning to bring on them and will stop doing wicked things.

Then I would forgive them for the sins and the evil things they have done."

4 So Jeremiah called for Baruch son of Neriah. Jeremiah spoke the messages the LORD had given him, and Baruch wrote those messages on the scroll. 5 Then Jeremiah commanded Baruch, "I cannot go to the Temple of the LORD. I must stay here. 6 So I want you to go to the Temple of the LORD on a day when the people are

A BAD REACTION
JEREMIAH 36

Have you ever shared your faith with someone, only to have him or her have a bad reaction? Jeremiah dictated the words God gave him to his secretary, Baruch, who wrote them on a scroll. After King Jehoiakim read the scroll, he cut it into pieces and threw it into the fire. He didn't like the truth.

Some people you talk to may not want to hear the truth about God. But don't let that stop you from sharing his truth with others.

Care for the Lost, Deuteronomy 22:1–3, p. 255

On the Wrong Foot, 2 Kings 21:1–2, 16, p. 509

A Picture of the Past, Psalm 105, p. 789

Go! No! Jonah 1, p. 1213

The Greatest Commandment, Matthew 22:36–40, p. 1313

A Friend of Jesus, John 15:9–17, p. 1450

giving up eating. Read from the scroll to all the people of Judah who come into Jerusalem from their towns. Read the messages from the LORD, which are the words you wrote on the scroll as I spoke them to you. 7 Perhaps they will ask the LORD to help them. Perhaps each one will stop doing wicked things, because the LORD has announced that he is very angry with them." 8 So Baruch son of Neriah did everything Jeremiah the prophet told him to do. In the LORD's Temple he read aloud the scroll that had the LORD's messages written on it.

9 In the ninth month of the fifth year that Jehoiakim son of Josiah was king, a special time to give up eating was announced. All the people of Jerusalem and everyone who had come into Jerusalem from the towns of Judah were supposed to give up eating to honour the LORD. 10 At that time Baruch read to all the people there the scroll containing Jeremiah's words. He read the scroll in the Temple of the LORD in the room of Gemariah son of Shaphan, a royal secretary. That room was in the upper courtyard at the entrance of the New Gate of the Temple.

11 Micaiah son of Gemariah, the son of Shaphan, heard all the messages from the LORD that were on the scroll. 12 Micaiah went down to the royal secretary's room in the king's palace where all of the officers were sitting: Elishama the royal secretary; Delaiah son of Shemaiah; Elnathan son of Acbor; Gemariah son of Shaphan; Zedekiah son of Hananiah; and all the other officers. 13 Micaiah told those officers everything he had heard Baruch read to the people from the scroll.

14 Then the officers sent a man named Jehudi son of Nethaniah to Baruch. (Nethaniah was the son of Shelemiah, who was the son of Cushi.) Jehudi said to Baruch, "Bring the scroll that you read to the people and come with me."

So Baruch son of Neriah took the scroll and went with Jehudi to the officers. 15 Then the officers said to Baruch, "Please sit down and read the scroll to us."

So Baruch read the scroll to them. 16 When the officers heard all the words, they became afraid and looked at each other. They said to Baruch, "We must certainly tell the king about these words." 17 Then the officers asked Baruch, "Tell us, please, where did you get all these words you wrote on the scroll? Did you write down what Jeremiah said to you?"

18 "Yes," Baruch answered. "Jeremiah spoke them all to me, and I wrote them down with ink on this scroll."

19 Then the officers said to Baruch, "You and Jeremiah must go and hide, and don't tell anyone where you are."

20 The officers put the scroll in the room of Elishama the royal secretary. Then they went to the king in the courtyard and told him all about the scroll. 21 So King Jehoiakim sent Jehudi to get the scroll. Jehudi brought the scroll from the room of Elishama the royal secretary and read it to the king and to all the officers who stood around the king. 22 It was the ninth month of the year, so King Jehoiakim was sitting in the winter apartment. There was a fire burning in a small firepot in front of him. 23 After Jehudi had read three or four columns, the king cut those columns off of the scroll with a penknife and threw them into the firepot. Finally, the whole scroll was burnt in the fire. 24 King Jehoiakim and his servants heard everything that was said, but they were not frightened! They did not tear their clothes to show their sorrow. 25 Elnathan, Delaiah and Gemariah even tried to talk King Jehoiakim out of burning the scroll, but he would not listen to them. 26 Instead, the king ordered Jerahmeel son of the king, Seraiah son of Azriel and Shelemiah son of Abdeel to arrest Baruch the secretary and Jeremiah the prophet. But the LORD had hidden them.

27 So King Jehoiakim burnt the scroll where Baruch had written all the words Jeremiah had spoken to him. Then the LORD spoke his word to Jeremiah: 28 "Get another scroll. Write all the words on it that were on the first scroll that Jehoiakim king of Judah burnt up. 29 Also say this to Jehoiakim king of Judah: 'This is what the LORD says: you burnt up that scroll and said, "Why, Jeremiah, did you write on it

'the king of Babylon will surely come and destroy this land and the people and animals in it?' 30 So this is what the LORD says about Jehoiakim king of Judah: Jehoiakim's descendants will not sit on David's throne. When Jehoiakim dies, his body will be thrown out on the ground. It will be left out in the heat of the day and in the cold frost of the night. 31 I will punish Jehoiakim and his children and his servants, because they have done evil things. I will bring disasters upon them and upon all the people in Jerusalem and Judah— everything I promised but which they refused to hear."'

32 So Jeremiah took another scroll and gave it to Baruch son of Neriah, his secretary. As Jeremiah spoke, Baruch wrote on the scroll the same words that were on the scroll Jehoiakim king of Judah had burnt in the fire. And many like words were added to the second scroll.

Jeremiah in Prison

37 Nebuchadnezzar king of Babylon had appointed Zedekiah son of Josiah to be king of Judah. Zedekiah took the place of Jehoiachin son of Jehoiakim. 2 But Zedekiah, his servants and the people of Judah did not listen to the words the LORD had spoken through Jeremiah the prophet.

3 Now King Zedekiah sent Jehucal son of Shelemiah and the priest Zephaniah son of Maaseiah with a message to Jeremiah the prophet. This was the message: "Jeremiah, please pray to the LORD our God for us."

4 At that time Jeremiah had not yet been put into prison. So he was free to go anywhere he wanted. 5 The army of the king of Egypt had marched from Egypt towards Judah. Now the Babylonian army had surrounded the city of Jerusalem. When they heard about the Egyptian army marching towards them, the Babylonian army left Jerusalem.

6 The LORD spoke his word to Jeremiah the prophet: 7 "This is what the LORD, the God of Israel, says: Jehucal and Zephaniah, I know Zedekiah king of Judah sent you to seek my help. Tell this to King Zedekiah: 'The army of the king of Egypt came here to help you, but they will go back to Egypt. 8 After that, the Babylonian army will return and attack Jerusalem and capture it and burn it down.'

9 "This is what the LORD says: People of Jerusalem, do not fool yourselves. Don't say, 'The Babylonian army will surely leave us alone.' They will not! 10 Even if you defeated all of the Babylonian army that is attacking you and there were only a few injured men left in their tents, they would come from their tents and burn down Jerusalem!"

11 So the Babylonian army left Jerusalem to fight the army of the king of Egypt. 12 Now Jeremiah tried to travel from Jerusalem to the land of Benjamin to get his share of the property that belonged to his family. 13 When Jeremiah got to the Benjamin Gate of Jerusalem, the captain in charge of the guards arrested him. The captain's name was Irijah son of Shelemiah son of Hananiah. Irijah said, "You are leaving us to join the Babylonians!"

14 But Jeremiah said to Irijah, "That's not true! I am not leaving to join the Babylonians." Irijah refused to listen to Jeremiah, so he arrested Jeremiah and took him to the officers of Jerusalem. 15 Those rulers were very angry with Jeremiah and beat him. Then they put him in jail in the house of Jonathan the royal secretary, which had been made into a prison. 16 So those people put Jeremiah into a cell in a dungeon, and Jeremiah was there for a long time.

17 Then King Zedekiah sent for Jeremiah and had him brought to the palace. Zedekiah asked him in private, "Is there any message from the LORD?"

Jeremiah answered, "Yes, there is. Zedekiah, you will be handed over to the king of Babylon." 18 Then Jeremiah said to King Zedekiah, "What crime have I

> What crime have I done against you or your officers or the people of Jerusalem?
> – Jeremiah 37:18

done against you or your officers or the people of Jerusalem? Why have you thrown me into prison? 19 Where are your prophets that prophesied this message to you: 'The king of Babylon will not attack you or this land of Judah?' 20 But now, my master, king of Judah, please listen to me, and please do what I ask of you. Do not send me back to the house of Jonathan the royal secretary, or I will die there!"

21 So King Zedekiah gave orders for Jeremiah to be put under guard in the courtyard of the guard and to be given bread each day from the street of the bakers until there was no more bread in the city. So he stayed under guard in the courtyard of the guard.

Jeremiah is Thrown into a Well

38 Shephatiah son of Mattan, Gedaliah son of Pashhur, Jehucal son of Shelemiah and Pashhur son of Malkijah heard what Jeremiah was telling all the people. He said: 2 "This is what the LORD says: 'Everyone who stays in Jerusalem will die from war, or hunger or terrible diseases. But everyone who surrenders to the Babylonian army will live; they will escape with their lives and live.' 3 And this is what the LORD says: 'This city of Jerusalem will surely be handed over to the army of the king of Babylon. He will capture this city!'"

4 Then the officers said to the king, "Jeremiah must be put to death! He is discouraging the soldiers who are still in the city, and all the people, by what he is saying to them. He does not want good to happen to us; he wants to ruin us."

5 King Zedekiah said to them, "Jeremiah is in your control. I cannot do anything to stop you."

6 So the officers took Jeremiah and put him into the well of Malkijah, the king's son, which was in the courtyard of the guards. The officers used ropes to lower Jeremiah into the well, which did not have any water in it, only mud. And Jeremiah sank down into the mud.

7 But Ebed-Melech, a Cushite and a servant in the palace, heard that the officers had put Jeremiah into the well. As King Zedekiah was sitting at the Benjamin Gate, 8 Ebed-Melech left the palace and went to the king. Ebed-Melech said to him, 9 "My master and king, these rulers have acted in an evil way. They have treated Jeremiah the prophet badly. They have thrown him into a well and left him there to die! When there is no more bread in the city, he will starve to death."

10 Then King Zedekiah commanded Ebed-Melech the Cushite, "Take 30 men from the palace and lift Jeremiah the prophet out of the well before he dies."

11 So Ebed-Melech took the men with him and went to a room under the storeroom in the palace. He took some old rags and worn-out clothes from that room. Then he let those rags down with some ropes to Jeremiah in the well. 12 Ebed-Melech the Cushite said to Jeremiah, "Put these old rags and worn-out clothes under your arms to be pads for the ropes." So Jeremiah did as Ebed-Melech said. 13 The men pulled Jeremiah up with the ropes and lifted him out of the well. And Jeremiah stayed under guard in the courtyard of the guard.

Zedekiah Questions Jeremiah

14 Then King Zedekiah sent someone to get Jeremiah the prophet and bring him to the third entrance to the Temple of the LORD. The king said to Jeremiah, "I am going to ask you something. Do not hide anything from me, but tell me everything honestly."

15 Jeremiah said to Zedekiah, "If I give you an answer, you will surely kill me. And even if I give you advice, you will not listen to me."

16 But King Zedekiah made a secret promise to Jeremiah, "As surely as the LORD lives who has given us breath and life, I will not kill you. And I promise not to hand you over to the officers who want to kill you."

17 Then Jeremiah said to Zedekiah, "This is what the LORD God All-powerful, the God of Israel, says: 'If you surrender to the officers of the king of Babylon, your life will be saved. Jerusalem will not be burnt down, and you and your family will

FAITH links

FEAR GOD OR PEOPLE?
JEREMIAH 38:14-21

King Zedekiah told Jeremiah that he wanted to know what God had to say to him. When Zedekiah heard that God wanted him to surrender to the Babylonians, he refused to obey. He was more afraid of the people around him than he was of God.

Who do you fear more: God or people? Being obedient to God can be hard when those around you do not believe in God. God wants you to fear him, rather than other people. That means he wants you to be more concerned about what he thinks than about what others might think.

Connect to these Faithlinks on following the right leader:

Following the Crowd, Numbers 13; 14, p. 193

The Heart of the Matter, 1 Samuel 16, p. 375

A Wise Wish, 1 Kings 3:5–9, p. 439

Choosing a Friend, Proverbs 28:7, p. 865

Stand! Jeremiah 19:14—20:6, p. 1019

The Unpopular Choice, Mark 15:42–43, p. 1360

---

live. 18 But if you refuse to surrender to the officers of the king of Babylon, Jerusalem will be handed over to the Babylonian army, and they will burn it down. And you yourself will not escape from them.'"

19 Then King Zedekiah said to Jeremiah, "I'm afraid of some Jews who have already gone over to the side of the Babylonian army. If the Babylonians hand me over to them, they will treat me badly."

20 But Jeremiah answered, "The Babylonians will not hand you over to the Jews. Obey the LORD by doing what I tell you. Then things will go well for you, and your life will be saved. 21 But if you refuse to surrender to the Babylonians, the LORD has shown me what will happen. 22 All the women left in the palace of the king of Judah will be brought out and taken to the important officers of the king of Babylon. Your women will make fun of you with this song:

'Your good friends misled you
    and were stronger than you.
While your feet were stuck in the mud,
    they left you.'

23 "All your wives and children will be brought out and given to the Babylonian army. You yourself will not even escape from them. You will be taken prisoner by the king of Babylon, and Jerusalem will be burned down."

24 Then Zedekiah said to Jeremiah, "Do not tell anyone that I have been talking to you, or you will die. 25 If the officers find out I talked to you, they will come to you and say, 'Tell us what you said to King Zedekiah and what he said to you. Don't keep any secrets from us. If you don't tell us everything, we will kill you.' 26 If they ask you, tell them, 'I was begging the king not to send me back to Jonathan's house to die.'"

27 All the officers did come to question Jeremiah. So he told them everything the king had ordered him to say. Then the officers said no more to Jeremiah, because no one had heard what Jeremiah and the king had discussed.

28 So Jeremiah stayed under guard in the courtyard of the guard until the day Jerusalem was captured.

The Fall of Jerusalem

39 This is how Jerusalem was captured: Nebuchadnezzar king of Babylon marched against Jerusalem with

his whole army and surrounded the city to attack it. This was during the tenth month of the ninth year in which Zedekiah was king of Judah. 2 This lasted until the ninth day of the fourth month in Zedekiah's eleventh year. Then the city wall was broken through. 3 And all these officers of the king of Babylon came into Jerusalem and sat down at the Middle Gate: Nergal-Sharezer of the district of Samgar; Nebo-Sarsekim, a chief officer; Nergal-Sharezer, an important leader; and all the other important officers.

4 When Zedekiah king of Judah and all his soldiers saw them, they ran away. They left Jerusalem at night and went out from the king's garden. They went through the gate that was between the two walls and then headed towards the Jordan Valley. 5 But the Babylonian army chased them and caught up with Zedekiah in the plains of Jericho. They captured him and took him to Nebuchadnezzar king of Babylon, who was at the town of Riblah in the land of Hamath. There Nebuchadnezzar passed his sentence on Zedekiah. 6 At Riblah the king of Babylon killed Zedekiah's sons and all the important officers of Judah as Zedekiah watched. 7 Then he put out Zedekiah's eyes. He put bronze chains on Zedekiah and took him to Babylon.

8 The Babylonians set fire to the palace and to the houses of the people, and they broke down the walls around Jerusalem. 9 Nebuzaradan, commander of the king's special guards, took the people left in Jerusalem, those captives who had surrendered to him earlier and the rest of the people of Jerusalem, and he took them all away to Babylon. 10 But Nebuzaradan, commander of the guard, left some of the poorest people of Judah behind. They owned nothing, but that day he gave them vineyards and fields.

11 Nebuchadnezzar king of Babylon had given these orders about Jeremiah through Nebuzaradan, commander of the guard: 12 "Find Jeremiah and take care of him. Do not hurt him, but do for him whatever he asks you." 13 So Nebuchadnezzar sent these men for Jeremiah: Nebuzaradan, commander of the guards; Nebushazban, a chief officer; Nergal-Sharezer, an important leader; and all the other officers of the king of Babylon. 14 They had Jeremiah taken out of the courtyard of the guard. Then they turned him over to Gedaliah son of Ahikam son of Shaphan, who had orders to take Jeremiah back home. So they took him home and he stayed among the people left in Judah.

> Find Jeremiah and take care of him. Do not hurt him, but do for him whatever he asks you.
> – Jeremiah 39:12

15 While Jeremiah was guarded in the courtyard, the LORD spoke his word to him: 16 "Jeremiah, go and tell Ebed-Melech the Cushite this message: 'This is what the LORD All-powerful, the God of Israel, says: very soon I will make my words about Jerusalem come true through disaster, not through good times. You will see everything come true with your own eyes. 17 But I will save you on that day, Ebed-Melech, says the LORD. You will not be handed over to the people you fear. 18 I will surely save you, Ebed-Melech. You will not die from a sword, but you will escape and live. This will happen because you have trusted in me, says the LORD.'"

Jeremiah is Set Free

40 The LORD spoke his word to Jeremiah after Nebuzaradan, commander of the guards, had set Jeremiah free at the city of Ramah. He had found Jeremiah in Ramah bound in chains with all the captives from Jerusalem and Judah who were being taken away to Babylon. 2 When commander Nebuzaradan found Jeremiah, Nebuzaradan said to him, "The LORD your God announced this disaster would come to this place. 3 And now the LORD has done everything he said he would do. This disaster happened because the people of Judah sinned against the LORD and did not obey him. 4 But today I

am freeing you from the chains on your wrists. If you want to, come with me to Babylon and I will take good care of you. But if you don't want to come, then don't. Look, the whole country is open to you. Go wherever you wish." 5 Before Jeremiah turned to leave, Nebuzaradan said, "Or go back to Gedaliah son of Ahikam, the son of Shaphan. The king of Babylon has chosen him to be governor over the towns of Judah. Go and live with Gedaliah among the people, or go anywhere you want."

Then Nebuzaradan gave Jeremiah some food and a present and let him go. 6 So Jeremiah went to Gedaliah son of Ahikam at Mizpah and stayed with him there. He lived among the people who were left behind in Judah.

The Short Rule of Gedaliah

7 Some officers and their men from the army of Judah were still out in the open country. They heard that the king of Babylon had put Gedaliah son of Ahikam in charge of the people who were left in the land: the men, women and children who were the poorest. They were the ones who were not taken to Babylon as captives. 8 So these soldiers came to Gedaliah at Mizpah: Ishmael son of Nethaniah, Johanan and

SMALL COMFORTS

When one of your friends is going through a bad time, how do you comfort him or her? Here's someone who has a problem in this area. Let's welcome Steve, aged 10, to Connect 2-You.

Steve

Well, my best friend's mum died a few weeks ago, and I'm afraid to talk to him about it. I went to the funeral but I haven't called or seen him since then. I just don't know what to say to him. I'm afraid that if I say the wrong thing, he's going to break down and start crying – and I don't think I could handle that. I know I'm being a terrible friend. What should I do?

The Bible is full of instructions for Christians to encourage one another, support one another and comfort one another. The best thing Steve can do is to be honest with his friend. Tell him exactly how he's feeling. Steve should ask his friend to tell him how he's feeling. The Livin' It page on loving God's way, Mark 12:28-34, p. 1352, has some tips on what the Bible says about comforting others. If this is something you're struggling with, take a look.

Jesus says to love your neighbour as you love yourself. Steve should try putting himself in his friend's position. If it was Steve's mum who had just died, what would he want people to say to him? How would you want your friends to show their love for you?

Jonathan sons of Kareah, Seraiah son of Tanhumeth, the sons of Ephai the Netophathite, Jaazaniah son of the Maacathite and their men.

9 Gedaliah son of Ahikam, the son of Shaphan, made a promise to them, saying, "Do not be afraid to serve the Babylonians. Stay in the land and serve the king of Babylon. Then everything will go well for you. 10 I myself will live in Mizpah and will speak for you before the Babylonians who come to us here. Harvest the wine, the summer fruit and the oil, and put what you harvest in your storage jars. Live in the towns you control."

11 The Jews in Moab, Ammon, Edom and other countries also heard that the king of Babylon had left a few Jews alive in the land. And they heard the king of Babylon had chosen Gedaliah as governor over them. (Gedaliah was the son of Ahikam, the son of Shaphan.) 12 When the people of Judah heard this news, they came back to Judah from all the countries where they had been scattered. They came to Gedaliah at Mizpah and gathered a large harvest of wine and summer fruit.

13 Johanan son of Kareah and all the army officers of Judah still in the open country came to Gedaliah at Mizpah. 14 They said to him, "Don't you know that Baalis king of the Ammonite people wants you dead? He has sent Ishmael son of Nethaniah to kill you." But Gedaliah son of Ahikam did not believe them.

15 Then Johanan son of Kareah spoke to Gedaliah in private at Mizpah. He said, "Let me go and kill Ishmael son of Nethaniah. No one will know anything about it. We should not let Ishmael kill you. Then all the Jews gathered around you would be scattered to different countries again, and the few people of Judah who are left alive would be lost."

16 But Gedaliah son of Ahikam said to Johanan son of Kareah, "Do not kill Ishmael! The things you are saying about Ishmael are not true."

41 In the seventh month Ishmael son of Nethaniah and ten of his men came to Gedaliah son of Ahikam at Mizpah. (Nethaniah was the son of Elishama.) Now Ishmael was a member of the king's family and had been one of the officers of the king of Judah. While they were eating a meal with Gedaliah at Mizpah, 2 Ishmael and his ten men got up and killed Gedaliah son of Ahikam, the son of Shaphan, with a sword. (Gedaliah was the man the king of Babylon had chosen as governor over Judah.) 3 Ishmael also killed all the Jews and the Babylonian soldiers who were there with Gedaliah at Mizpah.

4 The day after Gedaliah was murdered, before anyone knew about it, 5 80 men came to Mizpah bringing grain offerings and incense to the Temple of the LORD. Those men from Shechem, Shiloh and Samaria had shaved off their beards, torn their clothes and cut themselves.[n] 6 Ishmael son of Nethaniah went out from Mizpah to meet them, crying as he walked. When he met them, he said, "Come with me to meet Gedaliah son of Ahikam." 7 So they went into Mizpah. Then Ishmael son of Nethaniah and his men killed 70 of them and threw the bodies into a deep well. 8 But the ten men who were left alive said to Ishmael, "Don't kill us! We have wheat and barley and oil and honey that we have hidden in a field." So Ishmael let them live and did not kill them with the others. 9 Now the well where he had thrown all the bodies had been made by King Asa as a part of his defences against Baasha king of Israel. But Ishmael son of Nethaniah put dead bodies in it until it was full.

10 Ishmael captured all the other people in Mizpah: the king's daughters and all the other people who were left there. They were the ones whom Nebuzaradan, commander of the guard, had chosen Gedaliah son of Ahikam to take care of. So Ishmael son of Nethaniah captured those people, and he started to cross over to the country of the Ammonites.

11 Johanan son of Kareah and all his army officers with him heard about all the evil things Ishmael son of Nethaniah had done. 12 So they took their men and went to fight Ishmael son of Nethaniah and

---

41:5 shaved . . . themselves The men did this to show they were sad about the Temple in Jerusalem being destroyed.

caught him near the big pool of water at Gibeon. 13 When the captives Ishmael had taken saw Johanan and the army officers, they were glad. 14 So all the people Ishmael had taken captive from Mizpah turned around and ran to Johanan son of Kareah. 15 But Ishmael son of Nethaniah and eight of his men escaped from Johanan and ran away to the Ammonites.

16 So Johanan son of Kareah and all his army officers saved the captives that Ishmael son of Nethaniah had taken from Mizpah after he murdered Gedaliah son of Ahikam. Among those left alive were soldiers, women, children and palace officers. And Johanan brought them back from the town of Gibeon.

The Escape to Egypt

17-18 Johanan and the other army officers were afraid of the Babylonians. Since the king of Babylon had chosen Gedaliah son of Ahikam to be governor of Judah and Ishmael son of Nethaniah had murdered him, Johanan was afraid that the Babylonians would be angry. So they decided to run away to Egypt. On the way they stayed at Geruth Kimham, near the town of Bethlehem.

42 While there, Johanan son of Kareah and Jezaniah son of Hoshaiah went to Jeremiah the prophet. All the army officers and all the people, from the least important to the greatest, went along too. 2 They said to him, "Jeremiah, please listen to what we ask. Pray to the LORD your God for all the people left alive from the family of Judah. At one time there were many of us, but you can see that there are few of us now. 3 So pray that the LORD your God will tell us where we should go and what we should do."

4 Then Jeremiah the prophet answered, "I understand what you want me to do. I will pray to the LORD your God as you have asked. I will tell you everything he says and not hide anything from you."

5 Then the people said to Jeremiah, "May the LORD be a true and loyal witness against us if we don't do everything the LORD your God sends you to tell us. 6 It does not matter if we like the message or

42:6 Obedience
Read this to see what happens when you obey.

not. We will obey the LORD our God, to whom we are sending you. We will obey what he says so good things will happen to us."

7 Ten days later the LORD spoke his word to Jeremiah. 8 Then Jeremiah called for Johanan son of Kareah, the army officers with him and all the other people, from the least important to the greatest. 9 Jeremiah said to them, "You sent me to ask the LORD for what you wanted. This is what the God of Israel says: 10 'If you will stay in Judah, I will build you up and not tear you down. I will plant you and not pull you up, because I am sad about the disaster I brought on you. 11 Now you fear the king of Babylon, but don't be afraid of him. Don't be afraid of him,' says the LORD, 'because I am with you. I will save you and rescue you from his power. 12 I will be kind to you, and he will also treat you with mercy and let you stay in your land.'

13 "But if you say, 'We will not stay in Judah,' you will disobey the LORD your God. 14 Or you might say, 'No, we will go and live in Egypt. There we will not see war, or hear the trumpets of war or be hungry.' 15 If you say that, listen to the message of the LORD, you who are left alive from Judah. This is what the LORD All-powerful, the God of Israel, says: 'If you make up your mind to go and live in Egypt, these things will happen: 16 you are afraid of war, but it will find you in the land of Egypt. And you are worried about hunger, but it will follow you into Egypt, and you will die there. 17 Everyone who goes to live in Egypt will die in war or from hunger or terrible disease. No one who goes to Egypt will live; no one will escape the terrible things I will bring to them.'

18 "This is what the LORD All-powerful, the God of Israel, says: 'I showed my anger against the people of Jerusalem. In the same way I will show my anger against you when you go to Egypt. Other nations will speak evil of you. People will be shocked by what will happen to you. You will become a curse

word, and people will insult you. And you will never see Judah again.'

19 "You who are left alive in Judah, the LORD has told you, 'Don't go to Egypt.' Be sure you understand this; I warn you today 20 that you are making a mistake that will cause your deaths. You sent me to the LORD your God, saying, 'Pray to the LORD our God for us. Tell us everything the LORD our God says, and we will do it.' 21 So today I have told you, but you have not obeyed the LORD your God in all that he sent me to tell you. 22 So now be sure you understand this: you want to go to live in Egypt, but you will die there by war, hunger or terrible diseases."

43 So Jeremiah finished telling the people the message from the LORD their God; he told them everything the LORD their God had sent him to tell them.

2 Azariah son of Hoshaiah, Johanan son of Kareah, and some other men were too proud. They said to Jeremiah, "You are lying! The LORD our God did not send you to say, 'You must not go to Egypt to live there.' 3 Baruch son of Neriah is causing you to be against us. He wants you to hand us over to the Babylonians so they can kill us or capture us and take us to Babylon."

4 So Johanan, the army officers and all the people disobeyed the LORD's command to stay in Judah.

5 But Johanan son of Kareah and the army officers led away those who were left alive from Judah. They were the people who had run away from the Babylonians to other countries but then had come back to live in Judah. 6 They led away the men, women and children, and the king's daughters. Nebuzaradan commander of the guard had put Gedaliah son of Ahikam son of Shaphan in charge of those people. Johanan also took Jeremiah the prophet and Baruch son of Neriah. 7 These people did not listen to the LORD. So they all went to Egypt to the city of Tahpanhes.

8 In Tahpanhes the LORD spoke his word to Jeremiah: 9 "Take some large stones. Bury them in the clay in the brick pavement in front of the king of Egypt's palace in Tahpanhes. Do this while the Jews are watching you. 10 Then say to them, 'This is what the LORD All-powerful, the God of Israel, says: I will soon send for my servant, Nebuchadnezzar king of Babylon. I will set his throne over these stones I have buried, and he will spread his covering for shade above them. 11 He will come here and attack Egypt. He will bring death to those who are supposed to die. He will make prisoners of those who are to be taken captive, and he will bring war to those who are to be killed with a sword. 12 Nebuchadnezzar will set fire to the temples of the gods of Egypt and burn them. And he will take the idols away as captives. As a shepherd wraps himself in his clothes, so Nebuchadnezzar will wrap Egypt around him. Then he will safely leave Egypt. 13 He will destroy the stone pillars in the temple of the sun god in Egypt, and he will burn down the temples of the gods of Egypt.'"

Disaster in Egypt

44 Jeremiah received a message from the LORD for all the Jews living in Egypt—in the cities of Migdol, Tahpanhes, Memphis and in southern Egypt. This was the message: 2 "The LORD All-powerful, the God of Israel, says: You saw all the terrible things I brought on Jerusalem and the towns of Judah, which are ruins today with no one living in them. 3 It is because the people who lived there did evil. They made me angry by burning incense and worshipping other gods that neither they nor you nor your ancestors ever knew. 4 I sent all my servants, the prophets, to you again and again. By them I said to you, 'Don't do this terrible thing that I hate.' 5 But they did not listen or pay

> They made me angry by burning incense and worshipping other gods that neither they nor you nor your ancestors ever knew.
> – Jeremiah 44:3

attention. They did not stop doing evil things and burning incense to other gods. 6 So I showed my great anger against them. I poured out my anger in the towns of Judah and the streets of Jerusalem so they are only ruins and piles of stones today.

7 "Now the LORD All-powerful, the God of Israel, says: Why are you doing such great harm to yourselves? You are cutting off the men and women, children and babies from the family of Judah, leaving yourselves without anyone from the family of Judah. 8 Why do you want to make me angry by making idols? Why do you burn incense to the gods of Egypt, where you have come to live? You will destroy yourselves. Other nations will speak evil of you and make fun of you. 9 Have you forgotten about the evil things your ancestors did? And have you forgotten the evil the kings and queens of Judah did? Have you forgotten about the evil you and your wives did? These things were done in the country of Judah and in the streets of Jerusalem. 10 Even to this day the people of Judah are still too proud. They have not learned to respect me or to follow my teachings. They have not obeyed the laws I gave you and your ancestors.

11 "So this is what the LORD All-powerful, the God of Israel, says: I am determined to bring disasters on you. I will destroy the whole family of Judah. 12 The few who were left alive from Judah were determined to go to Egypt and settle there, but they will all die in Egypt. They will be killed in war or die from hunger. From the least important to the greatest, they will be killed in war or die from hunger. Other nations will speak evil about them. People will be shocked by what has happened to them. They will become a curse word, and people will insult them. 13 I will punish those people who have gone to live in Egypt, just as I punished Jerusalem, using swords, hunger and terrible diseases. 14 Of the people of Judah who were left alive and have gone to live in Egypt, none will escape my punishment. They want to return to Judah and live there, but none of them will live to return to Judah, except a few people who will escape."

15 A large group of the people of Judah who lived in southern Egypt were meeting together. Among them were many women of Judah who were burning incense to other gods, and their husbands knew it. All these people said to Jeremiah, 16 "We will not listen to the message from the LORD that you spoke to us. 17 We promised to make sacrifices to the Queen Goddess, and we will certainly do everything we promised. We will burn incense and pour out drink offerings to worship her, just as we, our ancestors, kings and officers did in the past. All of us did these things in the towns of Judah and in the streets of Jerusalem. At that time we had plenty of food and were successful, and nothing bad happened to us. 18 But since we stopped making sacrifices to the Queen Goddess and stopped pouring out drink offerings to her, we have had great problems. Our people have also been killed in war and by hunger."

19 The women said, "Our husbands knew what we were doing. We had their permission to burn incense to the Queen Goddess and to pour out drink offerings to her. Our husbands knew we were making cakes that looked like her and were pouring out drink offerings to her."

20 Then Jeremiah spoke to all the people—men and women—who answered him. 21 He said to them, "The LORD remembered that you and your ancestors, kings and officers, and the people of the land burnt incense in the towns of Judah and in the streets of Jerusalem. He remembered and thought about it. 22 Then he could not be patient with you any longer. He hated the terrible things you did. So he made your country an empty desert, where no one lives. Other people curse that country. And so it is today. 23 All this happened because you burnt incense to other gods. You sinned against the LORD. You did not obey him or follow his teachings or the laws he gave you. You did not keep your part of the agreement with him. So this disaster has happened to you. It is there for you to see."

24 Then Jeremiah said to all those

men and women, "People of Judah who are now in Egypt, hear the word of the LORD: 25 The LORD All-powerful, the God of Israel, says: you and your wives did what you said you would do. You said, 'We will certainly keep the promises we made. We promised to make sacrifices to the Queen Goddess and to pour out drink offerings to her.' So, go ahead. Do the things you promised, and keep your promises. 26 But hear the word of the LORD. Listen, all you Jews living in Egypt. The LORD says, 'I have sworn by my great name: the people of Judah now living in Egypt will never again use my name to make promises. They will never again say in Egypt, "As surely as the Lord GOD lives..." 27 I am watching over them, not to take care of them, but to hurt them. The Jews who live in Egypt will die from swords or hunger until they are all destroyed. 28 A few will escape being killed by the sword and will come back to Judah from Egypt. Then, of the people of Judah who came to live in Egypt, those who are left alive will know if my word or their word came true. 29 I will give you a sign that I will punish you here in Egypt,' says the LORD. 'When you see it happen, you will know that my promises to hurt you will really happen.' 30 This is what the LORD says: 'Hophra king of Egypt has enemies who want to kill him. Soon I will hand him over to his enemies just as I handed Zedekiah king of Judah over to Nebuchadnezzar king of Babylon, who wanted to kill him.'"

A Message to Baruch

45 In the fourth year that Jehoiakim son of Josiah was king of Judah, Jeremiah the prophet told these things to Baruch son of Neriah, and Baruch wrote them on a scroll: 2 "This is what the LORD, the God of Israel, says to you, Baruch: 3 You have said, 'How terrible it is for me! The LORD has given me sorrow along with my pain. I am tired because of my suffering and cannot rest.'"

> The LORD has given me sorrow along with my pain. I am tired because of my suffering and cannot rest.
> – Jeremiah 45:3

4 The LORD said, "Say this to Baruch: 'This is what the LORD says: I will soon tear down what I have built, and I will pull up what I have planted everywhere in Judah. 5 Baruch, you are looking for great things for yourself. Don't look for them, because I will bring disaster on all the people, says the LORD. You will have to go to many places, but I will let you escape alive wherever you go.'"

Messages to the Nations

46 The LORD spoke this word to Jeremiah the prophet about the nations:

2 This message is to Egypt. It is about the army of Neco king of Egypt, which was defeated at the city of Carchemish on the Euphrates River by Nebuchadnezzar king of Babylon. This was in the fourth year that Jehoiakim son of Josiah was king of Judah. This is the LORD's message to Egypt:

3 "Prepare your shields, large and small,
 and march out for battle!
4 Harness the horses
 and get on them!
Go to your places for battle
 and put on your helmets!
Polish your spears.
 Put on your armour!
5 What do I see?
 That army is terrified,
 and the soldiers are running away.
 Their warriors are defeated.
 They run away quickly
 without looking back.
 There is terror on every side!" says the LORD.
6 "The fast runners cannot run away;
 the strong soldiers cannot escape.
 They stumble and fall
 in the north, by the Euphrates River.
7 Who is this, rising up like the Nile River,
 like strong, fast rivers?
8 Egypt rises up like the Nile River,

like strong, fast rivers.
Egypt says, 'I will rise up and cover
the earth.
I will destroy cities and the people
in them!'
9 Horsemen, charge into battle!
Chariot drivers, drive hard!
March on, brave soldiers—
soldiers from the countries of Cush
and Put who carry shields,
soldiers from Lydia who use
bows.

10 "But that day belongs to the Lord
GOD All-powerful.
At that time he will give those
people the punishment they
deserve.
The sword will kill until it is finished,
until it satisfies its thirst for their
blood.
The Lord GOD All-powerful will offer
a sacrifice
in the land of the north, by the
Euphrates River.

11 "Go up to Gilead and get some balm,
people of Egypt!
You have prepared many medicines,
but they will not work;
you will not be healed.
12 The nations have heard of your
shame,
and your cries fill all the earth.
One warrior has run into another;
both of them have fallen down
together!"

13 This is the message the LORD spoke to Jeremiah the prophet about Nebuchadnezzar king of Babylon's coming to attack Egypt:

14 "Announce this message in Egypt,
and preach it in Migdol.
Preach it also in the cities of
Memphis and Tahpanhes:
'Get ready for war,
because the battle is all around
you.'
15 Egypt, why were your warriors
killed?
They could not stand because the
LORD pushed them down.
16 They stumbled again and again

and fell over each other.
They said, 'Get up. Let's go back
to our own people and our
homeland.
We must get away from our
enemy's sword!'
17 In their homelands those soldiers
called out,
'The king of Egypt is only a lot of
noise.
He missed his chance for glory!'"

18 The King's name is the LORD All-
powerful.
He says, "As surely as I live,
a powerful leader will come.
He will be like Mount Tabor
among the mountains,
like Mount Carmel by the sea.
19 People of Egypt, pack your things
to be taken away as captives,
because Memphis will be destroyed.
It will be a ruin, and no one will
live there.

20 "Egypt is like a beautiful young cow,
but a horsefly is coming
from the north to attack her.
21 The hired soldiers in Egypt's army
are like fat calves,
because even they all turn and run
away together;
they do not stand strong against
the attack.
Their time of destruction is coming;
they will soon be punished.
22 Egypt is like a hissing snake that is
trying to escape.
The enemy comes closer and
closer.
They come against Egypt with axes
like men who cut down trees.
23 They will chop down Egypt's army
as if it were a great forest," says
the LORD.
"There are more enemy soldiers than
locusts;
there are too many to count.
24 The people of Egypt will be ashamed.
They will be handed over to the
enemy from the north."

25 The LORD All-powerful, the God of Israel, says: "Very soon I will punish

Amon, the god of the city of Thebes. And I will punish Egypt, her kings, her gods and the people who depend on the king. 26 I will hand those people over to their enemies, who want to kill them. I will give them to Nebuchadnezzar king of Babylon and his officers. But in the future, Egypt will live in peace as it once did," says the LORD.

A Message to Israel

27 "People of Jacob, my servants, don't be afraid;
    don't be frightened, Israel.
I will surely save you from those faraway places
    and your children from the lands where they are captives.
The people of Jacob will have peace and safety again,
    and no one will make them afraid.
28 People of Jacob, my servants, do not be afraid,
    because I am with you," says the LORD.
"I will completely destroy the many different nations
    where I scattered you.
But I will not completely destroy you.
I will punish you fairly,
    but I will not let you escape your punishment."

46:27 Fears Who can save you from your fears?

A Message to the Philistines

47 Before the king of Egypt attacked the city of Gaza, the LORD spoke his word to Jeremiah the prophet. This message is to the Philistine people.
2 This is what the LORD says:
"See, the enemy is gathering in the north like rising waters.
They will become like an overflowing stream
and will cover the whole country like a flood,
    even the towns and the people living in them.
Everyone living in that country will cry for help;
    the people will cry painfully.
3 They will hear the sound of the running horses
    and the noisy chariots
    and the rumbling chariot wheels.
Parents will not help their children to safety,
    because they will be too weak to help.
4 The time has come
    to destroy all the Philistines.
It is time to destroy all who are left alive
    who could help the cities of Tyre and Sidon.
The LORD will soon destroy the Philistines,
    those left alive from the island of Crete.
5 The people from the city of Gaza will be sad and shave their heads.
The people from the city of Ashkelon will be made silent.
Those left alive from the valley,
    how long will you cut yourselves?"

6 "You cry, 'Sword of the LORD,
    how long will you keep fighting?
Return to your holder.
    Stop and be still.'
7 But how can his sword rest
    when the LORD has given it a command?
He has ordered it
    to attack Ashkelon and the seacoast."

A Message to Moab

48 This message is to the country of Moab. This is what the LORD All-powerful, the God of Israel, says:
"How terrible it will be for the city of Nebo,
    because it will be ruined.
The town of Kiriathaim will be disgraced and captured;

47:5 sad and . . . yourselves The people did these things to show their sadness.

Jeremiah 48:8 1057

TRUE OR FALSE GODS?
Jeremiah 48:7, 13

The Israelites were surrounded by people who worshipped false gods. Sometimes the Israelites made the mistake of paying attention to these false gods as if they were real. There was one in particular, Baal, who the Israelites sometimes worshipped. Baal was a god who was supposed to help produce good crops and livestock. (Read Judges 2:10–11, p. 313.)

Each time God's children worshipped these false gods, God himself had to point out their sin and bring them back to reality. Here are a few of the frequently mentioned false gods in the Old Testament.

Ashtoreth	Baal's wife	Judges 2:13, p. 313
Bel	Babylonian god	Isaiah 46:1, p. 957
Chemosh	God of the Moabites and Ammonites	Jeremiah 48:7, 13, p. 1057
Dagon	Philistine god	1 Samuel 5:2–7, p. 360
Molech	Ammonite god	Leviticus 18:21, p. 159
Nebo	Babylonian god of wisdom and the arts	Isaiah 46:1, p. 957
Rimmon	Syrian god of rain	2 Kings 5:18, p. 483

the strong city will be disgraced
and shattered.
2 Moab will not be praised again.
Men in the town of Heshbon plan
Moab's defeat.
They say, 'Come, let us put an end
to that nation!'
Town of Madmen,* you will also be
silenced.
The sword will chase you.
3 Listen to the cries from the town of
Horonaim,
cries of much confusion and
destruction.
4 Moab will be broken up.
Her little children will cry for help.
5 Moab's people go up the path to the
town of Luhith,
crying loudly as they go.

On the road down to Horonaim,
cries of pain and suffering can be
heard.
6 Run! Run for your lives!
Go like a bush being blown
through the desert.
7 You trust in the things you do and in
your wealth,
so you also will be captured.
The god Chemosh will go into
captivity
and his priests and officers with
him.
8 The destroyer will come against every
town;
not one town will escape.

48:2 Madmen This name sounds like the Hebrew word for "be silenced".

The valley will be ruined,
  and the high plain will be destroyed,
  as the LORD has said.
9 Give wings to Moab,
  because she will surely leave her
    land.
  Moab's towns will become empty,
    with no one to live in them.
10 A curse will be on anyone who
    doesn't do what the LORD says,
  and a curse will be on anyone who
    holds back his sword from
    killing.

11 "The people of Moab have never
    known trouble.
  They are like wine left to settle;
  they have never been poured from
    one jar to another.
  They have not been taken into
    captivity.
  So they taste as they did before,
    and their smell has not changed.
12 A time is coming," says the LORD,
  "When I will send people to pour
    you from your jars.
  They will empty Moab's jars
    and smash her jugs.
13 The people of Israel trusted that god
    in the town of Bethel,
  and they were ashamed when
    there was no help.
  In the same way Moab will be
    ashamed of their god Chemosh.

14 "You cannot say, 'We are warriors!
  We are brave men in battle!'
15 The destroyer of Moab and her towns
    has arrived.
  Her best young men will be killed!"
    says the King,
  whose name is the LORD All-
    powerful.
16 "The end of Moab is near,
  and she will soon be destroyed.
17 All you who live around Moab,
  all you who know her, cry for her.
  Say, 'The ruler's power is broken;
  Moab's power and glory are gone.'

18 "You people living in the town of
    Dibon, come down from your
    place of honour
  and sit on the dry ground,
  because the destroyer of Moab has
    come against you.
  And he has destroyed your
    fortified cities.
19 You people living in the town of
    Aroer,
  stand next to the road and watch.
  See the man running away and the
    woman escaping.
  Ask them, 'What happened?'
20 Moab is filled with shame, because
    she is ruined.
  Cry, Moab, cry out!
  Announce at the Arnon River
  that Moab is destroyed.
21 People on the high plain have been
    punished.
  Judgement has come to these
    towns:
  Holon, Jahzah and Mephaath;
22   Dibon, Nebo and Beth Diblathaim;
23   Kiriathaim, Beth Gamul and Beth
    Meon;
24   Kerioth and Bozrah.
  Judgement has come to all the
    towns of Moab, far and near.
25 Moab's strength has been cut off,
  and its arm broken!" says the
    LORD.

26 "The people of Moab thought they
    were greater than the LORD,
  so punish them until they act as if
    they are drunk.
  Moab will fall and roll around in its
    own vomit,
  and people will even make fun of it.
27 Moab, you made fun of Israel.
  Israel was caught in the middle of a
    gang of thieves.
  When you spoke about Israel,
  you shook your head and acted as
    if you were better than it.
28 People in Moab, leave your towns
    empty
  and go and live among the rocks.
  Be like a dove that makes its nest
    at the entrance of a cave.

29 "We have heard that the people of
    Moab are proud,
  very proud.

They are proud, very proud,
  and in their hearts they think they
    are important."
30 The LORD says,
  "I know Moab's great pride, but it
    is useless.
  Moab's boasting accomplishes
    nothing.
31 So I cry sadly for Moab,
    for everyone in Moab.
  I moan for the people from the
    town of Kir Hareseth.
32 I cry with the people of the town of
    Jazer
  for you, the grapevines of the town
    of Sibmah.
  In the past your vines spread all the
    way to the sea,
    as far as the sea of Jazer.
  But the destroyer has taken over
    your fruit and grapes.
33 Joy and happiness are gone
    from the large, rich fields of Moab.
  I have stopped the flow of wine from
    the winepresses.
  No one walks on the grapes with
    shouts of joy.
  There are shouts,
    but not shouts of joy.
34 "Their crying can be heard from
    Moabite towns,
    from Heshbon to Elealeh and Jahaz.
  It can be heard from Zoar as far away
    as Horonaim and Eglath
    Shelishiyah.
  Even the waters of Nimrim are
    dried up.
35 I will stop Moab
    from making burnt offerings at the
    places of worship
  and from burning incense to their
    gods," says the LORD.
36 "My heart cries sadly for Moab like a
    flute playing a funeral song.
  It cries like a flute for the people
    from Kir Hareseth.
  The money they made has all been
    taken away.
37 Every head has been shaved
    and every beard cut off.
  Everyone's hands are cut,
    and everyone wears rough cloth
    around his waist."
38 People are crying on every roof*n* in
    Moab
    and in every public square.
  There is nothing but sadness,

FAITH CHALLENGE

Try this one. Read 48:30 to find out how the Lord feels about people who like to boast about themselves or what they have. How do you feel when you hear people boasting about things they've done? Is there some area in your life where you may be tempted to brag?

TeSTiNG iT

Jeremiah 48:30
The LORD says, "I know Moab's great pride, but it is useless. Moab's boasting accomplishes nothing."

48:37 Every head . . . waist. The people did these things to show their sadness for those who had died.
48:38 roof In Bible times houses were built with flat roofs. The roof was used for drying things such as flax and fruit. And it was used as an extra room, as a place for worship and as a place to sleep in the summer.

because I have broken Moab
like a jar no one wants," says the
LORD.
39 "Moab is shattered! The people are
crying!
Moab turns away in shame!
People all around her make fun of
her.
The things that happened fill them
with great fear."

40 This is what the LORD says:
"Look! Someone is coming, like an
eagle diving down from the sky
and spreading its wings over Moab.
41 The towns of Moab will be captured,
and the fortified cities will be
defeated.
At that time Moab's warriors will be
frightened,
like a woman who is having a baby.
42 The nation of Moab will be
destroyed,
because they thought they were
greater than the LORD.
43 Fear, deep pits and traps wait for you,
people of Moab," says the LORD.
44 "People will run from fear,
but they will fall into the pits.
Anyone who climbs out of the pits
will be caught in the traps.
I will bring the year of punishment to
Moab," says the LORD.

45 "People have run from the powerful
enemy
and have gone to Heshbon for
safety.
But fire started in Heshbon;
a blaze has spread from the home
town of Sihon king of Moab.
It burnt up the leaders of Moab
and destroyed those proud people.
46 How terrible it is for you, Moab!
The people who worship Chemosh
have been destroyed.
Your sons have been taken captive,
and your daughters have been
taken away.

47 "But in days to come,
I will make good things happen
again to Moab," says the LORD.

This ends the judgement on Moab.

A Message to Ammon

49 This message is to the Ammonite people.
This is what the Lord says:
"Do you think that Israel has no
children?
Do you think there is no one to
take the land when the parents
die?
If that were true, why did Molech
take Gad's land
and why did Molech's people settle
in Gad's towns?"
2 The LORD says,
"The time will come when I will
make Rabbah,
the capital city of the Ammonites,
hear the battle cry.
It will become a hill covered with
ruins,
and the towns around it will be
burnt.
Those people forced Israel out of that
land,
but now Israel will force them out!"
says the LORD.
3 "People in the town of Heshbon, cry
sadly because the town of Ai is
destroyed!
Those who live in Rabbah, cry out!
Put on your rough cloth to show your
sadness, and cry loudly.
Run here and there for safety
inside the walls,
because Molech will be taken
captive
and his priests and officers with
him.
4 You boast about your valleys
and about the fruit in your valleys.
You are like an unfaithful child
who believes his treasures will save
him.
You think, 'Who would attack
me?'
5 I will soon bring terror on you
from everyone around you,"
says the Lord GOD All-powerful.
"You will all be forced to run away,
and no one will be able to gather
you.

6 "But the time will come
  when I will make good things
    happen to the Ammonites
    again,"
  says the Lord.

A Message to Edom

7 This message is to Edom. This is what the Lord All-powerful says:
  "Is there no more wisdom in the
    town of Teman?
  Can the wise men of Edom no
    longer give good advice?
  Have they lost their wisdom?
8 You people living in the town of
    Dedan,
  run away and hide in deep caves,
  because I will bring disaster on the
    people of Esau.
  It is time for me to punish them.
9 If workers came and picked the
    grapes from your vines,
  they would leave a few grapes
    behind.
  If robbers came at night,
  they would steal only enough for
    themselves.
10 But I will strip Edom bare.
  I will find all their hiding places,
  so they will not be able to hide
    from me.
  The children, relatives and
    neighbours will die,
  and Edom will be no more.
11 Leave the orphans, and I will take
    care of them.
  Your widows also can trust in me."

12 This is what the Lord says: "Some people did not deserve to be punished, but they had to drink from the cup of suffering anyway. People of Edom, you deserve to be punished, so you will not escape punishment. You must certainly drink from the cup of suffering." 13 The Lord says, "I swear by my own name that the city of Bozrah will become a pile of ruins! People will be shocked by what happened there. They will insult that city and speak evil of it. And all the towns around it will become ruins for ever."

14 I have heard a message from the
    Lord.
  A messenger has been sent among
    the nations, saying,
  "Gather your armies to attack it!
    Get ready for battle!"

15 "Soon I will make you the smallest of
    nations,
  and you will be greatly hated by
    everyone.
16 Edom, you frightened other nations,
  but your pride has fooled you.
  You live in the hollow places of the cliff
    and control the high places of the
      hills.
  Even if you build your home as high
    as an eagle's nest,
  I will bring you down from there,"
    says the Lord.

17 "Edom will be destroyed.
  People who pass by will be shocked
    to see the destroyed cities,
  and they will be amazed at all her
    injuries.
18 Edom will be destroyed like the cities
    of Sodom and Gomorrah
  and the towns around them," says
    the Lord.
  "No one will live there!
  No one will stay in Edom."

19 "Like a lion coming up from the thick
    bushes near the Jordan River
  to attack a strong pen for sheep,
  I will suddenly chase Edom from its
    land.
  Who is the one I have chosen to do
    this?
  There is no one like me,
  no one who can take me to court.
  None of their leaders can stand up
    against me."

20 So listen to what the Lord has
    planned to do against Edom.
  Listen to what he has decided to do
    to the people in the town of
      Teman.
  He will surely drag away the young
    ones of Edom.
  Their home towns will surely be
    shocked at what happens to
      them.

21 At the sound of Edom's fall, the earth will shake.
Their cry will be heard all the way to the Red Sea.
22 The LORD is like an eagle swooping down
and spreading its wings over the city of Bozrah.
At that time Edom's soldiers will become very frightened,
like a woman having a baby.

A Message to Damascus

23 This message is to the city of Damascus:
"The towns of Hamath and Arpad are put to shame,
because they have heard bad news.
They are discouraged.
They are troubled like the tossing sea.
24 The city of Damascus has become weak.
The people want to run away; they are ready to panic.
The people feel pain and suffering, like a woman giving birth to a baby.
25 Damascus was a city of my joy.
Why have the people not left that famous city yet?
26 Surely the young men will die in the city squares,
and all her soldiers will be killed at that time," says the LORD All-powerful.
27 "I will set fire to the walls of Damascus,
and it will completely burn the strong cities of King Ben-Hadad."

A Message to Kedar and Hazor

28 This message is to the tribe of Kedar and the kingdoms of Hazor, which Nebuchadnezzar king of Babylon defeated. This is what the LORD says:
"Go and attack the people of Kedar, and destroy the people of the East.
29 Their tents and flocks will be taken away.
Their belongings will be carried off—
their tents, all their goods and their camels.
Men will shout to them,
'Terror on every side!'
30 "Run away quickly!
People in Hazor, find a good place to hide!" says the LORD.
"Nebuchadnezzar king of Babylon has made plans against you
and wants to defeat you.
31 "Get up! Attack the nation that is comfortable,
that is sure no one will defeat it," says the LORD.
"It does not have gates or fences to protect it.
Its people live alone.
32 The enemy will steal their camels and their large herds of cattle as war prizes.
I will scatter the people who cut their hair short to every part of the earth,
and I will bring disaster on them from everywhere," says the LORD.
33 "The city of Hazor will become a home for wild dogs;
it will be an empty desert for ever.
No one will live there,
and no one will stay in it."

A Message to Elam

34 Soon after Zedekiah became king of Judah, the LORD spoke this word to Jeremiah the prophet. This message is to the nation of Elam.
35 This is what the LORD All-powerful says:
"I will soon break Elam's bow, its greatest strength.
36 I will bring the four winds against Elam
from the four corners of the skies.
I will scatter its people everywhere the four winds blow;
its captives will go to every nation.
37 I will terrify Elam in front of their enemies,
who want to destroy them.
I will bring disaster to Elam

Esther
The Courage to Conquer Fear

Ever feel scared? Maybe you were afraid to try something new. Or, maybe you were afraid that something bad could happen. Did you know that Bible queens like Esther felt scared, too? When you're feeling like the "Cowardly Lion", courage can help you to face your fears. Having courage doesn't mean facing your fears just once. You might have to face them again and again. See how God helped Esther overcome her fears by checking out

Here's the Scoop

on the following page. The numbers match the question numbers on this page. Although God isn't mentioned in the Book of Esther, you can know that he was at work behind the scenes.

1. Would you enter a contest knowing that it could totally change your life? What if winning the contest meant that you would have to leave your family and your neighbourhood and go and live somewhere else?

2. Would you risk your life to save the life of someone else? Would it depend on whether you knew that person? Would you take that risk for someone you didn't know at all? Esther had to make that very choice and decide whether she wanted to risk her life for a lot of people she had never met.

3. Think of the one person in your life that you try to avoid at all costs. Maybe it's an older boy at school who likes to tease you, or the girl next door who is bossy. Would you have the courage to meet that person face-to-face?

4. Everyone probably could face a scary situation – like having an operation – if it was just once. But would you have the courage to go through the same scary situation more than once?

5. If someone started a holiday in honour of you, what would it be for – your football skills, your ability to disappear when there's work to be done, or your courage? What would you like your holiday to honour about you?

Here's the Scoop

1. Entering a contest might not sound scary. But for Esther this was no ordinary contest. Esther's story was like Cinderella's in a way. The king of the land searched for a new wife. So, he set up a "beauty contest". Esther wasn't an important person or someone with high connections. She was a Jewish orphan. Competing in the contest took courage. Out of all of the women, Esther was chosen. (Check out **Esther 2:1–18**, p. 649.)

2. Esther's cousin Mordecai gave Esther some bad news. A man named Haman had an evil plan to kill all of the Jews. Esther knew that the king could stop Haman. When Esther found out about Haman's evil plan, she risked her life to go before the king. Requesting to see the king without permission meant death. So Esther decided to fast and pray. She knew that God could give her the courage to face the king. (Read about it in **Esther 4:1—5:3**, p. 651.)

3. Esther knew all about needing courage to face an enemy. The second part of her plan involved inviting the king and Haman to dinner, not once but twice. Esther didn't blow her cool by screaming at Haman at the first dinner. She knew that she had to wait and plan. God gave her the courage to be patient. Finally, she was able to tell her story to the king. He believed her and took action. (Look up **Esther 5:4–8; 7:1–7**, p. 653.)

4. Trouble wasn't over for Esther and her people. Even though Haman had been caught, the Jewish people were still in danger. The king's law ordering all the Jewish people in the land to be killed was still in effect. Once again Esther had to risk her life and go before the king, suggesting another plan. Thanks to God, the king said yes to Esther's plan. Esther and her people were saved! (See **Esther 8:1–8**, p. 655.)

5. Because of Esther's courage, the Jews were saved from destruction. That's why Purim, a new holiday, was celebrated. Esther wrote a letter telling the Jews about the new holiday. Each year the Jewish people were to gather together and remember the courage of one orphan. (Check out **Esther 9:26–32**, p. 658.) Courage may not earn you a holiday with your name on it. But people will remember the courage God gives you to overcome a fear. Don't believe it? Trust God for courage and see what happens.

Mary Totally Trusting

To trust means to have confidence in someone. The wise person puts his or her trust in someone dependable. God is someone you can always count on. Would you agree? Mary, the mother of Jesus, would. Mary wasn't perfect. She did not have all the answers to the problems she faced throughout her life. At times, she was tempted to doubt. Check out

Here's the Scoop

Look on the next page to find out how Mary's trust in God deepened with each experience. The numbers match the question numbers on this page. Trusting God doesn't make a person perfect. It just means that you know where to go for help!

1 Are you willing to trust God even when he wants you to do something hard? What if it meant that if you obeyed God, people might reject you or think bad things about you? That would be hard to do, wouldn't it? Yet, Mary was asked to do just that. She knew if she said yes to God, it would mean certain rejection and ridicule.

2 If you knew that someone you loved was in danger, would you trust God to keep him or her safe? Would you be able to let God handle your fears and concerns?

3 Being a parent isn't always easy. (You might ask your parents if they would agree!) Ask your parents about what things they trust God for in raising you. Even though Mary was raising God's own son, it wasn't always easy for her, either.

4 Do you believe that God can do impossible things? What are some of the things you trust God to do in your own life? Do you trust that God can do the "impossible" for you?

5 Are you willing to trust God to bring good out of a bad situation? Suppose a grandparent gets ill, or one of your parents has just lost their job. Those are difficult situations for any family. How does trusting God help you and your family through these times?

Here's the Scoop

1. An angel announced that God would give Mary a son – the Son of God! Mary was probably just a teenager at the time. Also she wasn't married – only engaged to be married. If she had a son, others would think bad things about her. But Mary didn't grumble and say, "No way! Not me!" Instead, she said, "I am the servant of the Lord. Let this happen to me as you say!" (**Luke 1:38**). (Read about it in **Luke 1:26-55**, p. 1365.)

2. When Jesus was a young child, a jealous king wanted to kill him. This king was afraid that Jesus would one day take over his throne. But Mary's husband Joseph was warned in a dream to take the family to Egypt. Even though it meant that Mary and Joseph would have to leave their families and live in a foreign land, Mary trusted God to keep her son safe. (Look up **Matthew 2:13-18**, p. 1276.)

3. During a trip home from Jerusalem for the Passover Feast, Mary and Joseph could not find Jesus. Can you imagine how Mary might have felt? Mary and Joseph travelled all the way back to Jerusalem to look for Jesus. There they found him in the Temple, talking with the teachers. Mary didn't always understand her son's actions. As a mother she worried about him. But God taught her that she could trust him to keep Jesus safe. (Check out **Luke 2:41-52**, p. 1370.)

4. At a wedding in Cana, the host ran out of wine. That was embarrassing to the bride and groom. But Mary knew that one of the other wedding guests could help. Who was that guest? Her son Jesus, who was now an adult. She trusted him to do the impossible. And he did! He turned water into wine. Jesus did many more "impossible" things, like making the blind see and forgiving people's sins, to demonstrate God's love and forgiveness. (Read **John 2:1-11**, p. 1424.)

5. One of the worst things that can happen to a parent is to watch their child suffer and be unable to do anything about it. Mary stood near the cross where Jesus was crucified. She couldn't stop him from suffering. She couldn't take his place. She couldn't prevent him from dying. Yet Mary knew that Jesus died to pay the price for the sins of everyone – including her. Mary was willing to trust him – her own son – as her Saviour. Are you willing? (See **John 19:25-26**, p. 1457.)

and show them how angry I am!"
says the LORD.
"I will send a sword
to chase Elam
until I have killed
them all.
38 I will set up my
throne in Elam to
show that I am
king,
and I will destroy
its king and its
officers!" says
the LORD.
39 "But I will make good
things happen to Elam again
in the future," says the LORD.

A Message to Babylon

50 This is the message the LORD spoke to Babylon and the Babylonian people through Jeremiah the prophet.

2 "Announce this to the nations.
Lift up a banner and tell them.
Speak the whole message and say:
'Babylon will be captured.
The god Bel will be put to
shame,
and the god Marduk will be
afraid.
Babylon's gods will be put to
shame,
and her idols will be afraid!'
3 A nation from the north will attack
Babylon
and make it like an empty desert.
No one will live there;
both people and animals will run
away."

4 The LORD says, "At that time
the people of Israel and Judah will
come together.
They will cry and look for the
LORD their God.
5 Those people will ask how to go to
Jerusalem
and will start in that direction.
They will come and join themselves
to the LORD.
They will make an agreement with
him that will last for ever,

an agreement that will never be
forgotten.

6 "My people have been
like lost sheep.
Their leaders have
led them in the
wrong way
and made them
wander around
in the mountains
and hills.
They forgot where
their resting
place was.
7 Whoever saw my people hurt them.
And those enemies said, 'We did
nothing wrong.
Those people sinned against the
LORD, their true resting place,
the God their fathers trusted.'

8 "Run away from Babylon,
and leave the land of the
Babylonians.
Be like the goats that lead the
flock.
9 I will soon bring against Babylon
many great nations from the north.
They will take their places for war
against it,
and it will be captured by people
from the north.
Their arrows are like trained soldiers
who do not return from war with
empty hands.
10 The enemy will take all the wealth
from the Babylonians.
Those enemy soldiers will get all
they want," says the LORD.

11 "Babylon, you are excited and happy,
because you took my land.
You dance around like a young cow in
the grain.
Your laughter is like the neighing
of male horses.
12 Your mother will be very ashamed;
the woman who gave birth to you
will be disgraced.
Soon Babylonia will be the least
important of all the nations.
She will be an empty, dry desert.

> My people have been like lost sheep. Their leaders have led them in the wrong way.
> – Jeremiah 50:6

13 Because of the LORD's anger,
no one will live there.
She will be completely empty.
Everyone who passes by Babylon will
be shocked.
They will shake their heads when
they see all her injuries.

14 "Take your positions for war against
Babylon,
all you soldiers with bows.
Shoot your arrows at Babylon! Do not
save any of them,
because Babylon has sinned
against the LORD.
15 Soldiers around Babylon, shout the
war cry!
Babylon has surrendered, her
towers have fallen,
and her walls have been torn
down.
The LORD is giving her people the
punishment they deserve.
You nations should give her what
she deserves;
do to her what she has done to
others.
16 Don't let the people from Babylon
plant their crops
or gather the harvest.
The soldiers treated their captives
cruelly.
Now, let everyone go back home.
Let everyone run to his own
country.

17 "The people of Israel are like a flock
of sheep that are scattered
from being chased by lions.
The first lion to eat them up
was the king of Assyria.
The last lion to crush their bones
was Nebuchadnezzar king of
Babylon."
18 So this is what the LORD All-powerful, the God of Israel, says:
"I will punish the king of Babylon
and his country
as I punished the king of Assyria.
19 But I will bring the people of Israel
back to their own pasture.
They will eat on Mount Carmel and
in Bashan.
They will eat and be full
on the hills of Ephraim and
Gilead."
20 The LORD says,
"At that time people will try to find
Israel's guilt,
but there will be no guilt.
People will try to find Judah's sins,
but no sins will be found,
because I will leave a few people alive
from Israel and Judah,
and I will forgive their sins.

21 "Attack the land of Merathaim.
Attack the people who live in
Pekod.
Chase them, kill them, and
completely destroy them.
Do everything I commanded you!"
says the LORD.

22 "The noise of battle can be heard all
over the country;
it is the noise of much destruction.
23 Babylon was the hammer of the
whole earth,
but how broken and shattered that
hammer is now.
It is truly the most ruined
of all the nations.
24 Babylon, I set a trap for you,
and you were caught before you
knew it.
You fought against the LORD,
so you were found and taken
prisoner.
25 The LORD has opened up his
storeroom
and brought out the weapons of his
anger,
because the Lord GOD All-powerful
has work to do
in the land of the Babylonians.
26 Come against Babylon from far
away.
Break open her storehouses of
grain.
Pile up her dead bodies like heaps
of grain.
Completely destroy Babylon
and do not leave anyone alive.
27 Kill all the young men in Babylon;
let them be killed like animals.

How terrible it will be for them,
    because the time has come for
    their defeat;
    it is time for them to be
    punished.
28 Listen to the people running to
    escape the country of
    Babylon!
  They are telling Jerusalem
    how the LORD our God is punishing
    Babylon as it deserves
    for destroying his Temple.

29 "Call for the archers
    to come against Babylon.
  Tell them to surround the city,
    and let no one escape.
  Pay her back for what she has
    done;
    do to her what she has done to
    other nations.
  Babylon acted with pride against the
    LORD,
    the Holy One of Israel.
30 So her young men will be killed in
    her streets.
  All her soldiers will die on that
    day," says the LORD.
31 "Babylon, you are too proud, and
    I am against you,"
  says the Lord GOD All-powerful.
  "The time has come
    for you to be punished.
32 Proud Babylon will stumble and
    fall,
    and no one will help her get up.
  I will start a fire in her towns,
    and it will burn up everything
    around her."
33 This is what the LORD All-powerful
  says:
  "The people of Israel
    and Judah are slaves.
  The enemy took them as prisoners
    and won't let them go.
34 But God is strong and will buy them
    back.
  His name is the LORD All-powerful.
  He will surely defend them with
    power
    so he can give rest to their land.
  But he will not give rest to those
    living in Babylon."

35 The LORD says,
  "Let a sword kill the people living in
    Babylon
    and her officers and wise men!
36 Let a sword kill her false prophets,
    and they will become fools.
  Let a sword kill her warriors,
    and they will be full of terror.
37 Let a sword kill her horses and
    chariots
    and all the soldiers hired from
    other countries!
  Then they will be like frightened
    women.
  Let a sword attack her treasures,
    so they will be taken away.
38 Let a sword attack her waters
    so they will be dried up.
  She is a land of idols,
    and the people go insane with fear
    over them.

39 "Desert animals and hyenas will live
    there,
    and owls will live there,
    but no people will ever live there
    again.
  She will never be filled with people
    again.
40 God completely destroyed the cities
    of Sodom and Gomorrah
    and the towns around them," says
    the LORD.
  "In the same way no people will live
    in Babylon,
    and no human being will stay there.

41 "Look! An army is coming from the
    north.
  A powerful nation and many kings
    are coming together from all
    around the world.
42 Their armies have bows and spears.
  The soldiers are cruel and have no
    mercy.
  As the soldiers come riding on their
    horses,
    the sound is loud like the roaring
    sea.
  They stand in their places, ready for
    battle.
  They are ready to attack you, city
    of Babylon.

43 The king of Babylon heard about
   those armies,
   and he became helpless with fear.
Distress has gripped him.
   His pain is like that of a woman
   giving birth to a baby.

44 "Like a lion coming up from the thick
   bushes near the Jordan River
   to attack a strong pen for sheep,
I will suddenly chase the people of
   Babylon from their land.
Who is the one I have chosen to do
   this?
There is no one like me,
   no one who can take me to court.
   None of their leaders can stand up
   against me."

45 So listen to what the LORD has
   planned to do against Babylon.
   Listen to what he has decided to do
   to the people in the city of
   Babylon.
He will surely drag away the young
   ones of Babylon.
   Their home towns will surely be
   shocked at what happens to
   them.

46 At the sound of Babylon's capture,
   the earth will shake.
People in all nations will hear
   Babylon's cry of distress.

51

This is what the LORD says:
"I will soon cause a destroying
   wind to blow
   against Babylon
   and the
   Babylonian
   people.

2 I will send foreign
   people to destroy
   Babylon
   like a wind that
   blows chaff away.
   They will destroy
   the land.
Armies will surround
   the city
   when the day of disaster comes
   upon her.

3 Don't let the Babylonian soldiers
   prepare their bows to shoot.
Don't even let them put on their
   armour.
Don't feel sorry for the young men of
   Babylon,
   but completely destroy her army.

4 They will be killed in the land of the
   Babylonians
   and will die in her streets.

5 The Lord GOD All-powerful
   did not leave Israel and Judah,
   even though they were completely
   guilty
   in the presence of the Holy One of
   Israel.

6 "Run away from Babylon
   and save your lives!
Don't stay and be killed because of
   Babylon's sins.
It is time for the LORD to punish
   Babylon;
   he will give Babylon the
   punishment she deserves.

7 Babylon was like a gold cup in the
   LORD's hand
   that made the whole earth drunk.
The nations drank Babylon's wine,
   and so they went mad.

8 Babylon has suddenly fallen and been
   broken.
Cry for her!
Get balm for her pain,
   and perhaps she can be healed.

9 "Foreigners in Babylon say, 'We tried
   to heal Babylon,
   but she cannot be
   healed.
So let us leave her
   and each go to
   his own country.
Babylon's
   punishment is as
   high as the sky;
   it reaches to the
   clouds.'

10 "The people of Judah
   say, 'The LORD
   has shown us to
   be right.
Come, let us tell in Jerusalem
   what the LORD our God has done.'

> The LORD has shown
> us to be right. Come,
> let us tell in
> Jerusalem what the
> LORD our God has
> done.
> – Jeremiah 51:10

Jeremiah 51:26

11 "Sharpen the arrows!
  Pick up your shields!
 The Lord has stirred up the kings of the Medes,
  because he wants to destroy Babylon.
 The Lord will punish them as they deserve
  for destroying his Temple.
12 Lift up a banner against the walls of Babylon!
  Bring more guards.
 Put the watchmen in their places,
  and get ready for a secret attack!
 The Lord will certainly do what he has planned
  and what he said he would do against the people of Babylon.
13 People of Babylon, you live near much water
  and are rich with many treasures,
 but your end as a nation has come.
  It is time to stop you from robbing other nations.
14 The Lord All-powerful has promised in his own name:
  'Babylon, I will surely fill you with
  so many enemy soldiers they will be like a swarm of locusts.
 They will stand over you and shout their victory.'

15 "The Lord made the earth by his power.
 He used his wisdom to build the world
  and his understanding to stretch out the skies.
16 When he thunders, the waters in the skies roar.
 He makes clouds rise in the sky all over the earth.
 He sends lightning with the rain
  and brings out the wind from his storehouses.

17 "People are so stupid and know so little.
 Goldsmiths are made ashamed by their idols,
 because those statues are only false gods.
 They have no breath in them.
18 They are worth nothing; people make fun of them.
 When they are judged, they will be destroyed.
19 But God, who is Jacob's Portion, is not like the idols.
 He made everything,
  and he chose Israel to be his special people.
 The Lord All-powerful is his name.

20 "You are my war club,
  my battle weapon.
 I use you to smash nations.
 I use you to destroy kingdoms.
21 I use you to smash horses and riders.
 I use you to smash chariots and drivers.
22 I use you to smash men and women.
 I use you to smash old people and young people.
 I use you to smash young men and young women.
23 I use you to smash shepherds and flocks.
 I use you to smash farmers and oxen.
 I use you to smash governors and officers.

24 "But I will pay back Babylon and all the Babylonians for all the evil things they did to Jerusalem in your sight," says the Lord.

25 The Lord says,
 "Babylon, you are a destroying mountain,
  and I am against you.
 You have destroyed the whole land.
 I will put my hand out against you.
 I will roll you off the cliffs,
  and I will make you a burnt out mountain.
26 People will not find any rocks in Babylon big enough for cornerstones.
 People will not take any rocks from Babylon to use for the foundation of a building,
 because your city will be just a pile of ruins for ever," says the Lord.

27 "Lift up a banner in the land!
Blow the trumpet among the nations!
Get the nations ready for battle against Babylon.
Call these kingdoms of Ararat, Minni and Ashkenaz to fight against her.
Choose a commander to lead the army against Babylon.
Send so many horses that they are like a swarm of locusts.
28 Get the nations ready for battle against Babylon—
the kings of the Medes, their governors and all their officers, and all the countries they rule.
29 The land shakes and moves in pain, because the LORD will do what he has planned to Babylon.
He will make Babylon an empty desert,
where no one will live.
30 Babylon's warriors have stopped fighting.
They stay in their protected cities.
Their strength is gone,
and they have become like frightened women.
Babylon's houses are burning.
The bars of her gates are broken.
31 One messenger follows another; messenger follows messenger.
They announce to the king of Babylon
that his whole city has been captured.
32 The river crossings have been captured,
and the swamplands are burning.
All of Babylon's soldiers are terribly afraid."
33 This is what the LORD All-powerful, the God of Israel, says:
"The city of Babylon is like a threshing floor,
where people crush the grain at harvest time.
The time to harvest Babylon is coming soon."
34 "Nebuchadnezzar king of Babylon has defeated and destroyed us.
In the past he took our people away,
and we became like an empty jar.
He was like a giant snake that swallowed us.
He filled his stomach with our best things.
Then he spat us out.
35 Babylon did terrible things to hurt us.
Now let those things happen to Babylon,"
say the people of Jerusalem.
"The people of Babylon killed our people.
Now let them be punished for what they did," says Jerusalem.
36 So this is what the LORD says:
"I will soon defend you, Judah,
and make sure that Babylon is punished.
I will dry up Babylon's sea
and make her springs become dry.
37 Babylon will become a pile of ruins, a home for wild dogs.
People will be shocked by what happened there.
No one will live there any more.
38 Babylon's people roar like young lions;
they growl like baby lions.
39 While they are stirred up,
I will give a feast for them
and make them drunk.
They will shout and laugh.
And they will sleep for ever and never wake up!" says the LORD.
40 "I will take the people of Babylon to be killed.
They will be like lambs,
like rams and goats waiting to be killed.
41 "How Babylon has been defeated!
The pride of the whole earth has been taken captive.
People from other nations are shocked at what happened to Babylon,
and the things they see make them afraid.
42 The sea has risen over Babylon;

its roaring waves cover her.
43 Babylon's towns are ruined and empty.
It has become a dry, desert land,
a land where no one lives.
People do not even travel through Babylon.
44 I will punish the god Bel in Babylon.
I will make him spit out what he has swallowed.
Nations will no longer come to Babylon;
even the wall around the city will fall.

45 "Come out of Babylon, my people!
Run for your lives!
Run from the LORD's great anger.
46 Don't lose courage;
rumours will spread through the land, but don't be afraid.
One rumour comes this year, and another comes the next year.
There will be rumours of terrible fighting in the country,
of rulers fighting against rulers.
47 The time will surely come
when I will punish the idols of Babylon,
and the whole land will be disgraced.
There will be many dead people lying all around.
48 Then heaven and earth and all that is in them
will shout for joy about Babylon.
They will shout because the army comes from the north
to destroy Babylon," says the LORD.

49 "Babylon must fall, because she killed people from Israel.
She killed people from everywhere on earth.
50 You who have escaped being killed with swords,
leave Babylon! Don't wait!
Remember the LORD in the faraway land
and think about Jerusalem."

51 "We people of Judah are disgraced, because we have been insulted.

We have been shamed,
because strangers have gone into the holy places of the LORD's Temple!"

52 So the LORD says, "The time is coming soon
when I will punish the idols of Babylon.
Wounded people will cry with pain all over that land.
53 Even if Babylon grows until she touches the sky,
and even if she makes her highest cities strong,
I will send people to destroy her," says the LORD.

54 "Sounds of people crying are heard in Babylon.
Sounds of people destroying things
are heard in the land of the Babylonians.
55 The LORD is destroying Babylon
and making the loud sounds of the city become silent.
Enemies come roaring in like ocean waves.
The roar of their voices is heard all around.
56 The army has come to destroy Babylon.
Her soldiers have been captured, and their bows are broken,
because the LORD is a God who punishes people for the evil they do.
He gives them the full punishment they deserve.
57 I will make Babylon's rulers and wise men drunk,
and her governors, officers and soldiers too.
Then they will sleep for ever and never wake up," says the King,
whose name is the LORD All-powerful.

58 This is what the LORD All-powerful says:
"Babylon's thick wall will be completely pulled down

and her high gates burnt.
The people will work hard, but it
won't help;
their work will only become fuel
for the flames!"

A Message to Babylon

59 This is the message that Jeremiah the prophet gave to the officer Seraiah son of Neriah, who was the son of Mahseiah. Seraiah went to Babylon with Zedekiah king of Judah in the fourth year of Zedekiah's reign. His duty was to arrange the king's food and housing on the trip. 60 Jeremiah had written on a scroll all the terrible things that would happen to Babylon, all these words about Babylon. 61 Jeremiah said to Seraiah, "As soon as you come to Babylon, be sure to read this message so all the people can hear you. 62 Then say, 'LORD, you have said that you will destroy this place so that no people or animals will live in it. It will be an empty ruin for ever.' 63 After you finish reading this scroll, tie a stone to it and throw it into the Euphrates River. 64 Then say, 'In the same way Babylon will sink and will not rise again because of the terrible things I will make happen here. Her people will fall.'"

The words of Jeremiah end here.

The Fall of Jerusalem

52 Zedekiah was 21 years old when he became king, and he was king in Jerusalem for eleven years. His mother's name was Hamutal daughter of Jeremiah,*n* and she was from Libnah. 2 Zedekiah did what the LORD said was wrong, just as Jehoiakim had done. 3 All this happened in Jerusalem and Judah because the LORD was angry with them. Finally, he threw them out of his presence.

Zedekiah turned against the king of Babylon. 4 Then Nebuchadnezzar king of Babylon marched against Jerusalem with his whole army. They made a camp around the city and built devices all around the city walls to attack it. This happened in Zedekiah's ninth year, tenth month and tenth day as king. 5 And the city was under attack until Zedekiah's eleventh year as king.

6 By the ninth day of the fourth month, the hunger was terrible in the city; there was no food for the people to eat. 7 Then the city wall was broken through, and the whole army of Judah ran away at night. They left the city through the gate between the two walls by the king's garden. Even though the Babylonians were surrounding the city, Zedekiah and his men headed towards the Jordan Valley.

8 But the Babylonian army chased King Zedekiah and caught him in the plains of Jericho. All of his army was scattered from him. 9 So the Babylonians captured Zedekiah and took him to the king of Babylon at the town of Riblah in the land of Hamath. There he passed sentence on Zedekiah. 10 At Riblah the king of Babylon killed Zedekiah's sons as he watched. The king also killed all the officers of Judah. 11 Then he put out Zedekiah's eyes, and put bronze chains on him and took him to Babylon. And the king kept Zedekiah in prison there until the day he died.

12 Nebuzaradan, commander of the king's special guards and servant of the king of Babylon, came to Jerusalem on the tenth day of the fifth month. This was in Nebuchadnezzar's nineteenth year as king of Babylon. 13 Nebuzaradan set fire to the Temple of the LORD, the palace and all the houses of Jerusalem; every important building was burnt. 14 The whole Babylonian army, led by the commander of the king's special guards, broke down all the walls around Jerusalem. 15 Nebuzaradan, the commander of the king's special guards, took captive some of the poorest people, those who were left in Jerusalem, those who had surrendered to the king of Babylon and the skilled craftsmen who were left in Jerusalem. 16 But Nebuzaradan left behind some of the poorest people of the land to take care of the vineyards and fields.

17 The Babylonians broke into pieces the bronze pillars, the bronze stands and the large bronze bowl, called the Sea, which were in the Temple of the LORD.

52:1 Jeremiah This is not the prophet Jeremiah but a different man with the same name.

Then they carried all the bronze pieces to Babylon. 18 They also took the pots, shovels, wick trimmers, bowls, dishes and all the bronze objects used to serve in the Temple. 19 The commander of the king's special guards took away bowls, pans for carrying hot coals, large bowls, pots, lampstands, pans and bowls used for drink offerings. He took everything that was made of pure gold or silver.

20 There was so much bronze that it could not be weighed: two pillars, the large bronze bowl called the Sea with the twelve bronze bulls under it and the movable stands, which King Solomon had made for the Temple of the LORD. 21 Each of the pillars was about 9 metres high, 6 metres around and hollow inside. The wall of each pillar was 8 centimetres thick. 22 The bronze capital on top of the one pillar was about 2.5 metres high. It was decorated with a net design and bronze pomegranates all around it. The other pillar also had pomegranates and was like the first pillar. 23 There were 96 pomegranates on the sides of the pillars. There was a total of 100 pomegranates above the net design.

24 The commander of the king's special guards took as prisoners Seraiah the chief priest, Zephaniah the priest next in rank and the three doorkeepers. 25 He also took from the city the officer in charge of the soldiers, seven people who advised the king, the royal secretary who selected people for the army and 60 other men from Judah who were in the city when it fell. 26 Nebuzaradan, the commander, took these people and brought them to the king of Babylon at the town of Riblah. 27 There at Riblah, in the land of Hamath, the king had them killed.

So the people of Judah were led away from their country as captives. 28 This is the number of the people Nebuchadnezzar took away as captives: in the seventh year, 3,023 Jews; 29 in Nebuchadnezzar's eighteenth year, 832 people from Jerusalem; 30 in Nebuchadnezzar's twenty-third year, Nebuzaradan, commander of the king's special guards, took 745 Jews as captives.

In all 4,600 people were taken captive.

Jehoiachin is Set Free

31 Jehoiachin king of Judah was in prison in Babylon for 37 years. The year Evil-Merodach became king of Babylon he let Jehoiachin king of Judah out of prison. He set Jehoiachin free on the twenty-fifth day of the twelfth month. 32 Evil-Merodach spoke kindly to Jehoiachin and gave him a seat of honour above the seats of the other kings who were with him in Babylon. 33 So Jehoiachin put away his prison clothes, and for the rest of his life, he ate at the king's table. 34 Every day the king of Babylon gave Jehoiachin an allowance. This lasted as long as he lived, until the day Jehoiachin died.

Lamentations

FIVE SAD SONGS

Hi! Jeremiah the prophet, here. Have you ever cried a river of tears? Back when I was carrying God's message to his people, I cried so much I could have filled a river. The city of Jerusalem was in ruins. The walls were broken down, the houses burned, and most of the people were dead or sent away to a foreign land. The few people who remained were starving. Worst of all, the beautiful Temple of the Lord was destroyed and its treasures stolen by our enemies.

I wrote this book to tell people that God himself destroyed Jerusalem and the Temple as punishment for sin. This book is really five laments, or "sad songs", about our suffering. With the Temple destroyed, we had no place to worship. Had God abandoned us? No, his love never ends. Soon the time of punishment would be over and we would be allowed to return to our land. God would restore our nation.

JESUS WATCH

In many ways, Jeremiah reminds us of Jesus. Both men were set apart for special work before they were even born. Jeremiah was chosen to be a prophet. Jesus was chosen to be our saviour and king. Both men suffered rejection by the people around them. For 40 years Jeremiah warned the people that God would punish them for their sins, but people wouldn't listen. They continued to do just as they pleased. Jesus declared that he was the promised Messiah, but only a few people believed him. Some people even picked up rocks to hurl at him. Both wept over Jerusalem. Jeremiah was present when the city was destroyed by the Babylonians and was overcome with sadness. Many years after Jerusalem was rebuilt, Jesus wept because he knew that it would soon be destroyed again. Both men were arrested and left to suffer painful deaths. Jeremiah was thrown into a well where he was meant to sink down into the mud until he suffocated. The king sent soldiers to rescue him. Jesus was nailed to a cross and left to die. On the third day he rose from the dead.

OTHER CONNECTIONS

Livin' it

Stop and really listen – listen to all the different noises around you, to the different voices telling you what to do. Stop to listen and you quickly realise that the world is a pretty noisy place. Now try to hear God's voice above the din. Difficult, isn't it. Connect to Listen Up! Lamentations 3:24–27, for some practical ways you can learn to listen to God's voice.

FAITH links

○ Sow It and Reap, **Lamentations 1:18**

○ Said It? Do It! **Lamentations 2:17**

○ When the Going Gets Tough, **Lamentations 3:22–27**

my FAVOURITE links

_____
_____
_____
_____

When will the Lord's love end?

Do you know the answer to that one? It's never! Check it out in Lamentations 3:22–23.

did YOU know?

SOME OTHER SAD STUFF:
Looking for bread, Lamentations 1:11
God rejects the Temple, Lamentations 2:6–7
Return to the Lord, Lamentations 3:40–42

Jerusalem Cries over Her Loss

1 Jerusalem once was full of people,
   but now the city is empty.
 Jerusalem once was a great city
     among the nations,
   but now she[n] is like a widow.
 She was like a queen of all the other
     cities,
   but now she is a slave.

2 She cries loudly at night,
   and tears are on her cheeks.
 There is no one to comfort her;
   all who loved her are gone.
 All her friends have turned against her
   and are now her enemies.

3 Judah has gone into captivity
   where she suffers and works hard.
 She lives among other nations,
   but she has found no rest.
 Those who chased her caught her
   when she was in trouble.

4 The roads to Jerusalem are sad,
   because no one comes for the
     feasts.
 No one passes through her gates.
   Her priests groan,
 her young women are suffering,
   and Jerusalem suffers terribly.

5 Her foes are now her masters.
   Her enemies enjoy the wealth they
     have taken.
 The LORD is punishing her
   for her many sins.
 Her children have gone away
   as captives of the enemy.

6 The beauty of Jerusalem
   has gone away.
 Her rulers are like deer
   that cannot find food.
 They are weak
   and run from the hunters.

7 Jerusalem is suffering and homeless.
   She remembers all the good things
     from the past.
 But her people were defeated by the
     enemy,
   and there was no one to help her.
 When her enemies saw her,
   they laughed to see her ruined.

8 Jerusalem sinned terribly,
   so she has become unclean.
 Those who honoured her now hate
     her,
   because they have seen her
     nakedness.
 She groans
   and turns away.

9 She made herself dirty by her sins
   and did not think about what would
     happen to her.
 Her defeat was surprising,
   and no one could comfort her.
 She says, "LORD, see how I suffer,
   because the enemy has won."

10 The enemy reached out and took
     all her precious things.
 She even saw foreigners
   enter her Temple.
 The LORD had commanded
     foreigners
   never to enter the meeting place of
     his people.

11 All of Jerusalem's people groan,
     looking for bread.
 They are trading their precious
     things for food
   so they can stay alive.
 The city says, "Look, LORD, and see.
   I am hated."

12 Jerusalem says, "You who pass by on
     the road don't seem to care.
 Come, look at me and see.
   Is there any pain like mine?
     Is there any pain like that he has
       caused me?
 The LORD has punished me
   on the day of his great anger.

13 "He sent fire from above
     that went down into my bones.
 He stretched out a net for my feet
   and turned me back.

1:1 she In this poem the city of Jerusalem is described as a woman.

Lamentations 1:20

He made me so sad and lonely
  that I am weak all day.

14 "He has noticed my sins;
   they are tied together by his hands;
   they hang around my neck.
   He has turned my strength into
     weakness.
   The Lord has handed me over
     to those who are stronger than I.

15 "The Lord has rejected
   all my mighty men inside my
     walls.
   He brought an army against me
     to destroy my young men.
   As if in a winepress, the Lord has
     crushed
     the capital city of Judah.

16 "I cry about these things;
   my eyes overflow with tears.
   There is no one near to comfort me,
     no one who can give me strength
       again.
   My children are left sad and lonely,
     because the enemy has won."

17 Jerusalem reaches out her hands,
   but there is no one to comfort her.
   The LORD commanded the people of
     Jacob
     to be surrounded by their enemies.
   Jerusalem is now unclean
     like those around her.

18 Jerusalem says, "The LORD is right,
   but I refused to obey him.
   Listen, all you people,
     and look at my pain.
   My young women and men
     have gone into captivity.

19 "I called out to my friends,
   but they turned against me.
   My priests and my elders
     have died in the city
     while looking for food
       to stay alive.

20 "Look at me, LORD. I am upset
   and greatly troubled.
   My heart is troubled,

FAITH links

SOW IT AND REAP
LAMENTATIONS 1:18

Ever hear someone say, "You reap what you sow"? Sowing has to do with planting seed. If you plant corn, you expect corn to grow, rather than potatoes. A person's actions are like the seed that is planted. If a person does bad things, bad things will happen to them. The Israelites disobeyed and reaped the consequences of their sin. Captivity in a strange land was the consequence.

When you choose to ignore a rule of your parents or of God, a punishment may result. Being punished is never pleasant. Yet correction can help you know right from wrong. Knowing the difference will help you make right choices in your life.

Need help in making the right decision? Link here:

This Hurts Me More?
2 Chronicles 36:17–22,
p. 606

Mind Guard, Proverbs 4:23,
p. 831

Down on Discipline? Proverbs 29:15, p. 867

A Blueprint for Living, Amos 5:14–15, p. 1200

Faith Workout, Acts 16:4–5,
p. 1493

Cut to the Quick, Hebrews 4:12, p. 1670

because I have been so stubborn.
Out in the streets, the sword kills;
 inside the houses, death destroys.

21 "People have heard my groaning,
 and there is no one to comfort
  me.
All my enemies have heard of my
  trouble,
 and they are happy you have done
  this to me.
Now bring that day you have
  announced
 so that my enemies will be like me.

22 "Look at all their evil.
 Do to them what you have done to
  me
 because of all my sins.
I groan over and over again,
 and I am afraid."

The Lord Destroyed Jerusalem

2 Look how the Lord in his anger
 has brought Jerusalem to shame.
He has thrown down the greatness of
  Israel
 from the sky to the earth;
he did not remember the Temple, his
  footstool,
 on the day of his anger.

2 The Lord swallowed up without
  mercy
 all the houses of the people of
  Jacob;
in his anger he pulled down
 the strong places of Judah.
He threw her kingdom and its rulers
 down to the ground in dishonour.

3 In his anger he has removed
 all the strength of Israel;
he took away his power from Israel
 when the enemy came.
He burnt against the people of Jacob
 like a flaming fire
 that burns up everything around it.

4 Like an enemy, he prepared to shoot
  his bow,
 and his hand was against us.
Like an enemy, he killed

all the good-looking people;
he poured out his anger like fire
 on the tents of Jerusalem.

5 The Lord was like an enemy;
 he swallowed up Israel.
He swallowed up all her palaces
 and destroyed all her strongholds.
He has caused more moaning and
  groaning
 for Judah.

6 He cut down his Temple like a
  garden;
 he destroyed the meeting-place.
The LORD has made Jerusalem
  forget
 the set feasts and Sabbath days.
He has rejected the king and the
  priest
 in his great anger.

7 The Lord has rejected his altar
 and abandoned his Temple.
He has handed over to the enemy
 the walls of Jerusalem's palaces.
Their uproar in the LORD's Temple
 was like that of a feast day.

8 The LORD planned to destroy
 the wall around Jerusalem.
He measured the wall
 and did not stop himself from
  destroying it.
He made the walls and defences sad;
 together they have fallen.

9 Jerusalem's gates have fallen to the
  ground;
 he destroyed and smashed the
  bars of the gates.
Her king and her princes are among
  the nations.
 The teaching of the LORD has
  stopped,
 and the prophets do not have
  visions from the LORD.

10 The elders of Jerusalem
 sit on the ground in silence.
They throw dust on their heads
 and put on rough cloth to show
  their sadness.

The young women of Jerusalem
  bow their heads to the ground in
  sorrow.

11 My eyes have no more tears,
  and I am sick to my stomach.

I feel empty inside,
  because my people have been
    destroyed.
Children and babies are fainting
  in the streets of the city.

12 They ask their mothers,
  "Where is the grain and wine?"
They faint like wounded soldiers
  in the streets of the city
  and die in their mothers' arms.

13 What can I say about you, Jerusalem?
  What can I compare you to?
  What can I say you are like?
  How can I comfort you, Jerusalem?
Your ruin is as deep as the sea.
  No one can heal you.

14 Your prophets saw visions,
  but they were false and worth
    nothing.
They did not point out your sins
  to keep you from being captured.
They preached what was false
  and led you wrongly.

15 All who pass by on the road
  clap their hands at you;
  they make fun of Jerusalem
  and shake their heads.
They ask, "Is this the city that people
    called
  the most beautiful city,
  the happiest place on earth?"

16 All your enemies open their mouths
  to speak against you.
They make fun and grind their teeth
  in anger.
  They say, "We have swallowed you
    up.
  This is the day we were waiting for!
  We have finally seen it happen."

17 The LORD has done what he planned;
  he has kept his word
  that he commanded long ago.
He has destroyed without mercy,
  and he has let your enemies laugh
    at you.
He has strengthened your
  enemies.

FAITH links

SAID IT? DO IT!
LAMENTATIONS 2:17

If your mum or dad says, "Do that one more time and you're for it!" you know they mean what they say. God had told the Israelites that he would punish them if they disobeyed him. God followed through on what he said. Even though the consequence was a hard one for Israel, they learned that God was faithful to his word.

Following words with actions shows that you're a person who keeps your word. You may know someone who is all talk and no action. That person may say he'll do something, but does not follow through. Be a doer, not just a "sayer" of your words.

Ten Ways to Obey, Exodus 20, p. 103

Take My Advice, 1 Kings 2:2–4, p. 436

Mind Guard, Proverbs 4:23, p. 831

Too Young to Serve, Jeremiah 1:4–9, p. 988

Get Ready! Mark 13:26–27, p. 1354

Attention, Please! Luke 8:11–15, p. 1383

18 The people cry out to the Lord.
   Wall of Jerusalem,
 let your tears flow
   like a river day and night.
 Do not stop
   or let your eyes rest.

19 Get up, cry out in the night,
   even as the night begins.
 Pour out your heart like water
   in prayer to the Lord.
 Lift up your hands in prayer to him
   for the life of your children
 who are fainting with hunger
   on every street corner.

20 Jerusalem says: "Look, LORD, and see
   to whom you have done this.
 Women eat their own babies,
   the children they have cared for.
 Priests and prophets are killed
   in the Temple of the Lord.

21 "People young and old
   lie outside on the ground.
 My young women and young men
   have been killed by the sword.
 You killed them on the day of your anger;
   you killed them without mercy.

22 "You invited terrors to come against me
   on every side,
 as if you were inviting them to a feast.
 No one escaped or remained alive
   on the day of the LORD's anger.
 My enemy has killed
   those I cared for and brought up."

The Meaning of Suffering

3 I am a man who has seen the suffering
   that comes from the rod of the LORD's anger.
2 He led me
   into darkness, not light.
3 He turned his hand against me
   again and again, all day long.

4 He wore out my flesh and skin
   and broke my bones.
5 He surrounded me with sadness
   and attacked me with grief.
6 He made me sit in the dark,
   like those who have been dead a long time.

7 He shut me in so I could not get out;
   he put heavy chains on me.
8 I cry out and beg for help,
   but he ignores my prayer.
9 He blocked my way with a stone wall
   and led me in the wrong direction.
10 He is like a bear ready to attack me,
   like a lion in hiding.
11 He led me the wrong way and let me stray
   and left me without help.
12 He prepared to shoot his bow
   and made me the target for his arrows.
13 He shot me in the kidneys
   with the arrows from his bag.
14 I was a joke to all my people,
   who make fun of me with songs all day long.
15 The LORD filled me with misery;
   he made me drunk with suffering.
16 He broke my teeth with gravel
   and trampled me into the ground.
17 I have no more peace.
   I have forgotten what happiness is.
18 I said, "My strength is gone,
   and I have no hope in the LORD."

19 LORD, remember my suffering and
   my misery,
   my sorrow and trouble.
20 Please remember me
   and think about me.
21 But I have hope
   when I think of this:

22 The LORD's love never ends;
   his mercies never stop.
23 They are new every morning;
   LORD, your loyalty is great.
24 I say to myself, "The LORD is mine,
   so I hope in him."

3:21–22
Hope
Can you have hope in bad situations?

Lamentations 3:45

25 The LORD is good to those who hope in him,
   to those who seek him.
26 It is good to wait quietly
   for the LORD to save.
27 It is good for someone to work hard
   while he is young.

28 He should sit alone and be quiet;
   the LORD has given him hard work to do.
29 He should bow down to the ground;
   perhaps there is still hope.
30 He should let anyone slap his cheek;
   he should be filled with shame.

31 The Lord will not reject
   his people for ever.
32 Although he brings sorrow,
   he also has mercy and great love.
33 He does not like to punish people
   or make them sad.

34 He sees if any prisoner of the earth
   is crushed under his feet;
35 he sees if someone is treated unfairly
   before the Most High God;
36 the Lord sees
   if someone is cheated in his case in court.

37 Nobody can speak and have it happen
   unless the Lord commands it.
38 Both bad and good things
   come by the command of the Most High God.
39 No one should complain
   when he is punished for his sins.

40 Let us examine and see what we have done
   and then return to the LORD.
41 Let us lift up our hands and pray from our hearts
   to God in heaven:
42 "We have sinned and turned against you,
   and you have not forgiven us.

43 "You wrapped yourself in anger and chased us;
   you killed us without mercy.
44 You wrapped yourself in a cloud,
   and no prayer could get through.
45 You made us like scum and rubbish
   among the other nations.

FAITH links

WHEN THE GOING GETS TOUGH

LAMENTATIONS 3:22-27

Hard times can make life seem dark and hopeless. Jeremiah witnessed the invasion of Israel and the capture of his people because of God's judgement on their disobedience. Although things looked very bad, Jeremiah knew that God was good. He encouraged the people to put their hope in him. God was faithful. Someday he would help his people.

Whenever things go wrong in your life, you can trust that God is always faithful to his people. He won't forget about you.

Got a big problem? Connect here for some help:

Big Lack Attack, 2 Kings 4:1-7, p. 480

Happiness or Joy? Job 29:18-19, p. 691

Fly Like an Eagle, Isaiah 40:28-31, p. 947

Your Feet on High Places, Habakkuk 3:18-19, p. 1239

Mission Impossible? Mark 5:21-24, 35-43, p. 1337

Keep On Keeping On, Revelation 13:10, p. 1744

Lamentations 3 1080

LISTENING TO GOD
Lamentations 3:24–27

Listen Up! Stop and count all the different people who want you to listen to them. Parents, brothers and sisters, teachers, friends, coaches, club leaders and TV announcers are some of them. And they don't just want you to hear them – they want you to really listen. It's enough to make your ears and brain tired! How do you decide who to listen to and who to ignore?

God wants us to listen to him, too. Ever wonder how God speaks to a person? (Check out Job 33:14–17, p. 696.) God *does* speak to you through the Bible, through the Holy Spirit and through people in your life. Are you quiet enough to hear him and *really* listen?

MORE FAITH links

Learning to Listen, **p. 358**

Listen Up! **p. 467**

How God Speaks, **p. 696**

Hold On! **p. 1639**

Pay Attention! **p. 1668**

Do you like to listen to the radio or your favourite CDs good and loud – so loud you can hardly hear yourself think? (Or maybe you don't need to hear yourself think!)

Well, sometimes we need a bit of quiet, too, so we can hear what God has to say to us. Check it out in these Faithlinks.

An Attention-Getter, Numbers 22, p. 207
- What would you do if your pet suddenly talked to you one morning, instead of barking, squeaking or meowing? It would get your attention, wouldn't it? Link here to find out what God did to get someone's attention.

Prayer Priority, Luke 5:15–16, p. 1376
- What do you take time for each day? Things that are important and you take time for are *priorities*. For Jesus, prayer was a priority – is it for you?

You're a Fake! 2 Peter 2:1, p. 1709
- Two sides of the story? Who do you listen to? This Faithlink helps you answer that question!

That's False! 2 John 7–11, p. 1722
- Everyday your brain is filled with information – from school, from your friends, from the Internet, from TV. Do you know what's true and what's false? How much of the false do you allow in your brain? How do you know if you're listening to what God wants you to hear? If you're not sure, talk to your parents.

my FAVOURITE links

46 "All our enemies
    open their mouths and speak
        against us.
47 We have been frightened and fearful,
    ruined and destroyed."
48 Streams of tears flow from my eyes,
    because my people are destroyed.

49 My tears flow continually,
    without stopping,
50 until the LORD looks down
    and sees from heaven.
51 I am sad when I see
    what has happened to all the
        women of my city.

52 Those who are my enemies for no
        reason
    hunted me like a bird.
53 They tried to kill me in a pit;
    they threw stones at me.
54 Water came up over my head,
    and I said, "I am going to die."
55 I called out to you, LORD,
    from the bottom of the pit.
56 You heard me calling, "Do not close
        your ears
    and ignore my cry and shouts."
57 You came near when I called to you;
    you said, "Don't be afraid."

58 Lord, you have taken my case
    and given me back my life.
59 LORD, you have seen how I have been
        wronged.
    Now judge my case for me.
60 You have seen how my enemies took
        revenge on me
    and made evil plans against me.

61 LORD, you have heard their insults
    and all their evil plans against me.
62 The words and thoughts of my
        enemies
    are against me all the time.
63 Look! In everything they do
    they make fun of me with songs.

64 Pay them back, LORD,
    for what they have done.
65 Make them stubborn,
    and put your curse on them.
66 Chase them in anger, LORD,
    and destroy them from under your
        heavens.

The Attack on Jerusalem

4 See how the gold has lost its shine,
    how the pure gold has lost its shine!
The stones of the Temple are
        scattered
    at every street corner.

2 The precious people of Jerusalem
    were more valuable than gold,
but now they are thought of as clay
        jars
    made by the hands of a potter.

3 Even wild dogs give their milk
    to feed their young,
but my people are cruel
    like ostriches in the desert.

4 The babies are so thirsty
    their tongues stick to the roofs of
        their mouths.
Children beg for bread,
    but no one gives them any.

5 Those who once ate fine foods
    are now starving in the streets.
People who grew up wearing nice
        clothes
    now pick through rubbish piles.

6 My people have been punished
    more than Sodom was.
Sodom was destroyed suddenly,
    and no hands reached out to help
        her.

7 Our princes were purer than snow
    and whiter than milk.
Their bodies were redder than
        rubies;
    they looked like sapphires.

8 But now they are blacker than coal,
    and no one recognises them in the
        streets.
Their skin hangs on their bones;
    it is as dry as wood.

9 Those who were killed in the war
    were better off

than those killed by hunger.
They starve in pain and die,
   because there is no food from the
      field.

10 With their own hands kind women
      cook their own children.
   They became food
      when my people
         were destroyed.

11 The LORD turned
      loose all of his
         anger;
   he poured out his
      strong anger.
   He set fire to
      Jerusalem,
   burning it down to
      the foundations.

12 Kings of the earth and people of the
      world
   could not believe
   that enemies and foes
      could enter the gates of
         Jerusalem.

13 It happened because her prophets
      sinned
   and her priests did evil.
   They killed in the city
      those who did what was right.

14 They wandered in the streets
      as if they were blind.
   They were dirty with blood,
      so no one would touch their
         clothes.

15 "Go away! You are unclean," people
      shouted at them.
   "Get away! Get away! Don't touch
      us!"
   So they ran away and wandered.
      Even the other nations said, "Don't
         stay here."

16 The LORD himself scattered them
      and did not look after them any
         more.
   No one respects the priests
      or honours the elders.

17 Also, our eyes grew tired,
      looking for help that never came.
   We kept watch from our towers
      for a nation to save us.

18 Our enemies hunted us,
      so we could not even walk in the
         streets.
   Our end is near. Our
      time is up.
   Our end has come.

19 Those who chased us
      were faster than
         eagles in the sky.
   They ran us into the
      mountains
   and ambushed us
      in the desert.

20 The LORD's appointed king, who was
      our very breath,
   was caught in their traps.
   We had said about him, "We will be
      protected by him
      among the nations."

21 Be happy and glad, people of Edom,
      you who live in the land of Uz.
   The cup of God's anger will come to
      you;
   then you will get drunk and go
      naked.

22 Your punishment is complete,
      Jerusalem.
   He will not send you into captivity
      again.
   But the LORD will punish the sins of
      Edom;
   he will uncover your evil.

A Prayer to the LORD

5 Remember, LORD, what happened
      to us.
   Look and see our disgrace.
2 Our land has been turned over to
      strangers;
   our houses have been given to
      foreigners.
3 We are like orphans with no father;
   our mothers are like widows.
4 We have to buy the water we drink;

> The LORD turned loose all of his anger; he poured out his strong anger.
> – Lamentations 4:11

Lamentations 5:22

we must pay for the firewood.
5 Those who chase after us want to catch us by the neck.
We are tired and find no rest.
6 We made an agreement with Egypt and with Assyria to get enough food.
7 Our ancestors sinned against you, but they are gone;
now we suffer because of their sins.
8 Slaves have become our rulers, and no one can save us from them.
9 We risk our lives to get our food; we face death in the desert.
10 Our skin is hot like an oven; we burn with starvation.
11 The enemy abused the women of Jerusalem
and the girls in the cities of Judah.
12 Princes were hung by the hands; they did not respect our elders.
13 The young men ground grain at the mill,
and boys stumbled under loads of wood.
14 The elders no longer sit at the city gates;
the young men no longer sing.
15 We have no more joy in our hearts; our dancing has turned to sadness.
16 The crown has fallen from our head.
How terrible it is because we sinned.
17 Because of this we are afraid,
and now our eyes are dim.
18 Mount Zion is empty, and wild dogs wander around it.
19 But you rule for ever, LORD. You will be King from now on.
20 Why have you forgotten us for so long?
Have you left us for ever?
21 Bring us back to you, LORD, and we will return.
Make our days as they were before,
22 or have you completely rejected us? Are you so angry with us?

eMAIL FROM GOD 5:16
Troubles
Find out what causes some hard times.

GLIMPSE OF HEAVEN

Welcome to my WebPage. I'm Ezekiel the prophet. When God called me to be a prophet, he showed me some pretty strange things. Try and imagine this: I saw four living creatures, each with four faces and four wings. Each creature had the face of a human, a lion, an ox and an eagle. The creatures glowed like burning coals and lightning flashed between them. Above the creatures was a dome that sparkled like ice, and above the dome was a throne of sapphire. Check out <u>Ezekiel 1</u> right away to find out who was seated on the throne.

I wrote this book to warn people that God would punish them severely if they did not stop sinning and turn back to him. It was the same message God had given to other prophets, but God often had me act out his messages. Once he told me to lie on my left side for 390 days to symbolise the years that the nation of Israel sinned. Then he told me to lie on my right side for 40 days for the sin of the nation of Judah. Surf over to <u>Ezekiel 4</u> for that story.

JESUS WATCH

In Ezekiel's day, the people were like sheep without a shepherd. Their leaders, who were supposed to be like shepherds, thought only of themselves. They did not lead the people in worshipping the true God, but instead offered sacrifices to false gods. God allowed his people to be conquered and sent to a foreign land as a punishment for their sins. In Ezekiel 34, God promised to send a true shepherd who would care for his sheep. The true shepherd will protect the sheep from harm. He will search for the lost sheep and make the weak sheep strong. God will give them a good place to live, and they will live in peace. Who is the true shepherd? Jesus, of course. Jesus is the good shepherd who leads us to heaven. We can trust him to protect and care for us, because he knows us all by name. Jesus loves us so much that he died for us. He took the punishment we deserve so that we can live for ever in heaven.

my FAVOURITE links

OTHER CONNECTIONS

Here are a few interesting places to stop and surf while reading through the Book of Ezekiel:

- When God told the Israelites to enter the land he had promised them, it wasn't a simple case of just walking in and settling down. The Israelites had to wage a "holy war" to conquer the people already living there. Learn more about the different weapons both the Israelites and their enemies used in battle by logging on to Ancient War and Weapons, Ezekiel 23:24.
- Let's Visit Damascus, Ezekiel 27:18. Find out more about one of the oldest cities still existing in the world, which today is the capital of Syria.
- The Kings of Egypt, Ezekiel 29:1–16. The king of Egypt, also known as Pharaoh, had a lot of power. In fact, during those times, the king owned everything in the land. There were 30 different generations of Pharaohs in Egyptian history. Link here to find out which Bible people had a "Pharaoh encounter".

Did you ever hear of dry bones coming to life?

That sounds pretty odd, doesn't it? Let's download Ezekiel 37 to find out more.

CHECK THESE OUT:
Ezekiel's new hairstyle, Ezekiel 5
Wheels with eyes, Ezekiel 10
The useless vine, Ezekiel 15
A river that gives life, Ezekiel 47:1–12

FAITH links

- Our Awesome God, **Ezekiel 1:26–28**
- The Watchman, **Ezekiel 3:16–22**
- God's Instructions, **Ezekiel 4:1–15**
- Good Enough? **Ezekiel 8**
- The Dead-end of the Occult, **Ezekiel 13:17–23**
- A Model of Forgiveness, **Ezekiel 16:59–63**
- A Hard Place, **Ezekiel 28:25–26**
- Empty Words, **Ezekiel 33:30–33**
- Believe the Impossible? **Ezekiel 37**
- God's New Temple, **Ezekiel 40—44**

Ezekiel's Vision of Living Creatures

1 It was the fifth day of the fourth month of the thirtieth year of our captivity. I was by the Kebar River among the people who had been carried away as captives. The sky opened, and I saw visions of God.

2 It was the fifth day of the month of the fifth year that King Jehoiachin had been a prisoner. 3 The LORD spoke his word to Ezekiel son of Buzi in the land of the Babylonians by the Kebar River. There he felt the power of the LORD.

4 When I looked, I saw a stormy wind coming from the north. There was a great cloud with a bright light around it and fire flashing out of it. Something that looked like glowing metal was in the centre of the fire. 5 Inside the cloud was what looked like four living creatures, who were shaped like humans, 6 but each of them had four faces and four wings. 7 Their legs were straight. Their feet were like a calf's hoofs and sparkled like polished bronze. 8 The living creatures had human hands under their wings on their four sides. All four of them had faces and wings, 9 and their wings touched each other. The living creatures did not turn when they moved, but each went straight ahead.

10 Their faces looked like this: each living creature had a human face and the face of a lion on the right side and the face of an ox on the left side. And each one also had the face of an eagle. 11 That was what their faces looked like. Their wings were spread out above. Each had two wings that touched one of the other living creatures and two wings that covered its body. 12 Each went straight ahead. Wherever the spirit would go, the living creatures would also go, without turning. 13 The living creatures looked like burning coals of fire or like torches. Fire went back and forth among the living creatures. It was bright, and lightning flashed from it. 14 The living creatures ran back and forth like bolts of lightning.

15 Now as I looked at the living creatures, I saw a wheel on the ground by each of the living creatures with its four faces. 16 The wheels and the way they were made were like this: they looked like sparkling chrysolite. All four of them looked the same, like one wheel crossways inside another wheel. 17 When they moved, they went in any one of the four directions, without turning as they went. 18 The rims of the wheels were high and frightening and were full of eyes all around.

19 When the living creatures moved, the wheels moved beside them. When the living creatures were lifted up from the ground, the wheels also were lifted up. 20 Wherever the spirit would go, the living creatures would go. And the wheels were lifted up beside them, because the spirit of the living creatures was in the wheels. 21 When the living creatures moved, the wheels moved. When the living creatures stopped, the wheels stopped. And when the living creatures were lifted from the ground, the wheels were lifted beside them, because the spirit of the living creatures was in the wheels.

22 Now, over the heads of the living creatures was something like a dome that sparkled like ice and was frightening. 23 And under the dome the wings of the living creatures were stretched out straight towards one another. Each living creature also had two wings covering its body. 24 I heard the sound of their wings, like the roaring sound of the sea, as they moved. It was like the voice of God Almighty, a roaring sound like a noisy army. When the living creatures stopped, they lowered their wings.

25 A voice came from above the dome over the heads of the living creatures. When the living creatures stopped, they lowered their wings. 26 Now above the dome there was something that looked like a throne. It looked like a sapphire gem. And on the throne was a shape like a human. 27 Then I noticed that from the waist up the shape looked like glowing metal with fire inside. From the waist down it looked like fire, and a bright light was all around. 28 The surrounding glow looked like the rainbow in the clouds on a rainy day. It seemed to look like the glory of the LORD. So when I saw it, I bowed face

FAITH links

OUR AWESOME GOD
EZEKIEL 1:26-28

You've heard a lot about the love of God and how you can have a relationship with him. Maybe you even think of him as the best friend you've ever had. That's great. But there's one other thing to consider about him: his holiness. The prophet Ezekiel had a vision of the glory of God. When he saw it, he fell face down. Ezekiel was amazed at the presence of God.

God's holiness deserves our respect. How do you show what God's holiness means to you?

A Holiday Every Week, Leviticus 23:1–3, p. 166

A Song of Thanks, 1 Samuel 2, p. 356

Love That Will Last, Psalm 136, p. 813

What God "Hates", Proverbs 6:16–19, p. 835

Your Spiritual Roots, Zechariah 1:1–6, p. 1253

The Gift, John 3:16–18, p. 1427

---

down on the ground and heard a voice speaking.

The LORD Speaks to Ezekiel

2 He said to me, "Human, stand up on your feet so I may speak with you." 2 While he spoke to me, the Spirit entered me and put me on my feet. Then I heard the LORD speaking to me.

3 He said, "Human, I am sending you to the people of Israel. That nation has turned against me and broken away from me. They and their ancestors have sinned against me until this very day. 4 I am sending you to people who are stubborn and who do not obey. You will say to them, 'This is what the Lord GOD says.' 5 They may listen, or they may not, since they are a people who have turned against me. But they will know that a prophet has been among them. 6 You, human, don't be afraid of the people or their words. Even though they may be like thorny branches and thorns all around you, and though you may feel as if you live with poisonous insects, don't be afraid. Don't be afraid of their words or their looks, because they are a people who rebel against me. 7 But speak my words to them. They may listen, or they may not, because they turn against me. 8 But you, human, listen to what I say to you. Don't turn against me as those people do. Open your mouth and eat what I am giving you."

9 Then I looked and saw a hand stretched out to me, and a scroll was in it. 10 He opened the scroll in front of me. Funeral songs, sad writings and words about troubles were written on the front and back.

3 Then the LORD said to me, "Human, eat what you find; eat this scroll. Then go and speak to the people of Israel." 2 So I opened my mouth, and he gave me the scroll to eat.

3 He said to me, "Human, eat this scroll which I am giving you, and fill your stomach with it." Then I ate it, and it was as sweet as honey in my mouth.

4 Then he said to me, "Human, go to the people of Israel, and speak my words to them. 5 You are not being sent to people whose speech you can't understand, whose language is difficult. You are being sent to Israel. 6 You are not being sent to many nations whose speech you can't understand and whose language is difficult and whose words you cannot understand. If I had sent you to them, they would have listened to you. 7 But the people of Israel will not be willing to listen to you, because they are not willing to listen to me. Yes, all the people of Israel are stubborn and will not obey.

Ezekiel 3:8

8 See, I now make you as stubborn and as hard as they are. 9 I am making you as hard as a diamond, harder than stone. Don't be afraid of them or be frightened by them, though they are a people who rebel against me."

10 Also, he said to me, "Human, believe all the words I will speak to you, and listen carefully to them. 11 Then go to the captives, your own people, and say to them, 'The Lord GOD says this.' Tell them this whether they listen or not."

12 Then the Spirit lifted me up, and I heard a loud rumbling sound behind me, saying, "Praise the glory of the LORD in heaven." 13 I heard the wings of the living creatures touching each other and the sound of the wheels by them. It was a loud rumbling sound. 14 So the Spirit lifted me up and took me away. I was unhappy and angry, and I felt the great power of the LORD. 15 I came to the captives from Judah, who lived by the Kebar River at Tel Abib. I sat there seven days where these people lived, feeling shocked.

Israel's Warning

16 After seven days the LORD spoke his word to me again. He said, 17 "Human, I now make you a watchman for Israel. Any time you hear a word from my mouth, warn them for me. 18 When I say to the wicked, 'You will surely die,' you must warn them so they may live. If you don't speak out to warn the wicked to stop their evil ways, they will die in their sin. But I will hold you responsible for their death. 19 If you warn the wicked and they do not turn from their wickedness or their evil ways, they will die because of their sin. But you will have saved your life.

20 "Again, those who do right may turn away from doing good and do evil. If I make something bad happen to them, they will die. Because you have not warned them, they will die because of their sin, and the good they did will not be remembered. But I will hold you responsible for their deaths. 21 But if you have warned those good people not to sin, and they do not sin, they will surely live,

---

FAITH links

THE WATCHMAN
EZEKIEL 3:16-22

The job of the keeper of a lighthouse is to warn ships of upcoming dangers. In the Old Testament, a watchman on a city wall had a similar job with some differences. A watchman had the responsibility of looking out for the approaching enemy. Ezekiel had a similar responsibility. His job was to watch the people of Israel and warn them about God's coming judgement because of their sin. God warned Ezekiel to be faithful.

As Christians, we're to be faithful at telling others about Jesus to help them escape the coming judgement. Jesus' death has already made it possible for anyone to be found "not guilty".

Link here to find out more about sharing your faith:

Can't Live Without It? Genesis 3, p. 7

When Bad Turns to Worse, Exodus 5:6–12, p. 82

You're Out! 2 Kings 17:5–7, p. 501

Red to White, Isaiah 1:18, p. 896

Tell All About Him! Matthew 28:19, p. 1326

Just a Test, Luke 4:1–13, p. 1373

because they believed the warning. And you will have saved your life."

22 Then I felt the power of the LORD there. He said to me, "Get up and go out to the plain. There I will speak to you." 23 So I got up and went out to the plain. I saw the glory of the LORD standing there, like the glory I saw by the Kebar River, and I bowed face down on the ground.

24 Then the Spirit entered me and made me stand on my feet. He spoke to me and said, "Go, shut yourself up in your house. 25 As for you, human, the people will tie you up with ropes so that you will not be able to go out among them. 26 Also, I will make your tongue stick to the roof of your mouth so you will be silent. You will not be able to argue with the people, even though they turn against me. 27 But when I speak to you, I will open your mouth, and you will say to them, 'The Lord GOD says this.' Those who will listen, let them listen. Those who refuse, let them refuse, because they are a people who rebel against me.

The Map of Jerusalem

4 "Now, human, get yourself a brick, put it in front of you, and draw a map of Jerusalem on it. 2 Then surround it with an army. Build battle works against the city and a dirt road to the top of the city walls. Set up camps around it, and put heavy logs in place to break down the walls. 3 Then get yourself an iron plate and set it up like an iron wall between you and the city. Turn your face towards the city as if to attack it and then attack. This is a sign to Israel.

4 "Then lie down on your left side, and take the guilt of Israel on yourself. Their guilt will be on you for the number of days you lie on your left side. 5 I have given you the same number of days as the years of the people's sin. So you will have the guilt of Israel's sin on you for 390 days.

6 "After you have finished these 390 days, lie down for a second time, on your right side. You will then have the guilt of Judah on you. I will give it to you for 40 days, a day for each year of their sin. 7 Then you will look towards Jerusalem, which is being attacked. With your arm bare, you will prophesy against Jerusalem. 8 I will put ropes on you so you cannot turn from one side to the other until you have finished the days of your attack on Jerusalem.

9 "Take wheat, barley, beans, small peas and millet seeds, put them in one bowl, and make them into bread for yourself. You will eat it for the 390 days you lie on your side. 10 You will eat 220

FAITH links

GOD'S INSTRUCTIONS
EZEKIEL 4:1-15

Have you ever been to see a play performed in a theatre? The actors can make a scene come alive. Ezekiel had to act out the coming judgement on Israel. God told him exactly what to do and expected Ezekiel to follow his instructions to the letter.

God wants you to follow his instructions, too. You can find them in the Bible. As you live out these instructions, others will pay attention. Maybe someday, someone will ask you about Jesus.

See the Heart Behind It, Nehemiah 8; 9, p. 636

You're Invited! Psalm 100, p. 784

Jesus' Mission and Yours, Isaiah 61:1–2, p. 978

God's New Temple, Ezekiel 40—44, p. 1135

Pass It On! Joel 1:2–3, p. 1187

Believe It or Not, Luke 1:20, 38, p. 1366

grammes of food every day at set times. 11 You will drink about ½ a litre of water every day at set times. 12 Eat your food as you would eat a barley cake, baking it over human dung where the people can see." 13 Then the LORD said, "In the same way Israel will eat unclean food among the nations where I force them to go."

14 But I said, "No, Lord GOD! I have never been made unclean. From the time I was young until now I've never eaten anything that died by itself or was torn by animals. Unclean meat has never entered my mouth."

15 "Very well," he said. "Then I will give you cow's dung instead of human dung to use for your fire to bake your bread."

16 He also said to me, "Human, I am going to cut off the supply of bread to Jerusalem. They will eat the bread that is measured out to them, and they will worry as they eat. They will drink water that is measured out to them, and they will be in shock as they drink it. 17 This is because bread and water will be hard to find. The people will be shocked at the sight of each other, and they will become weak because of their sin.

Ezekiel Cuts His Hair

5 "Now, human, take a sharp sword, and use it like a barber's razor to shave your head and beard. Then take scales and weigh and divide the hair. 2 Burn a third with fire in the middle of the city when the days of the attack on Jerusalem are over. Then take a third and cut it up with the knife all around the city. And scatter a third to the wind. This is how I will chase them with a sword. 3 Also take a few of these hairs and tie them in the folds of your clothes. 4 Take a few more, throw them into the fire and burn them up. From there a fire will spread to all the people of Israel.

5 "This is what the Lord GOD says: this is Jerusalem. I have put her at the centre

> This is Jerusalem. I have put her at the centre of the nations with countries all around her.
> – Ezekiel 5:5

of the nations with countries all around her. 6 But she has refused to obey my laws and has been more evil than the nations. She has refused to obey my rules, even more than nations around her. The people of Jerusalem have rejected my laws and have not lived by my rules.

7 "So this is what the Lord GOD says: you have caused more trouble than the nations around you. You have not followed my rules or obeyed my laws. You have not even obeyed the laws of the nations around you.

8 "So this is what the Lord GOD says: I myself am against you, and I will punish you as the nations watch. 9 I will do things among you that I have not done before and the like of which I will never do again, because you do the things I hate. 10 So parents among you will eat their children, and children will eat their parents. I will punish you and will scatter to the winds all who are left alive. 11 So the Lord GOD says: you have made my Temple unclean with all your evil idols and the hateful things you do. Because of this, as surely as I live, I will cut you off. I will have no pity, and I will show no mercy. 12 A third of you will die by disease or be destroyed by hunger inside your walls. A third will fall dead by the sword outside your walls. And a third I will scatter in every direction as I chase them with a sword. 13 Then my anger will come to an end. I will use it up against them, and then I will be satisfied. Then they will know that I, the LORD, have spoken. After I have carried out my anger against them, they will know the strength of my feelings.

14 "I will make you a ruin and a shame among the nations around you, to be seen by all who pass by. 15 Then the nations around you will shame you and make fun of you. You will be a warning and a terror to them. This will happen when I punish you in my great anger. I, the LORD, have spoken. 16 I will send a time of hunger to destroy you, and then I will make your hunger get even worse,

and I will cut off your supply of food. 17 I will send a time of hunger and wild animals against you, and they will kill your children. Disease and death will sweep through your people, and I will bring the sword against you to kill you. I, the LORD, have spoken."

Prophecies Against the Mountains

6 Again the LORD spoke his word to me, saying: 2 "Human, look towards the mountains of Israel, and prophesy against them. 3 Say, 'Mountains of Israel, listen to the word of the Lord GOD. The Lord GOD says this to the mountains, the hills, the ravines and the valleys: I will bring a sword against you, and I will destroy your places of idol worship. 4 Your altars will be destroyed and your incense altars broken down. Your people will be killed in front of your idols. 5 I will lay the dead bodies of the Israelites in front of their idols, and I will scatter your bones around your altars. 6 In all the places you live, cities will become empty. The places of idol worship will be ruined; your altars will become lonely ruins. Your idols will be broken and brought to an end. Your incense altars will be cut down, and the things you made will be wiped out. 7 Your people will be killed and fall among you. Then you will know that I am the LORD.

8 "'But I will leave some people alive; some will not be killed by the nations when you are scattered among the foreign lands. 9 Then those who have escaped will remember me, as they live among the nations where they have been taken as captives. They will remember how I was hurt because they were unfaithful to me and turned away from me and desired to worship their idols. They will hate themselves because of the evil things they did that I hate. 10 Then they will know that I am the LORD. I did not bring this terrible thing on them for no reason.'

11 "This is what the Lord GOD says: clap your hands, stamp your feet and groan because of all the hateful, evil things the people of Israel have done.

Ezekiel 7:9 **1091**

They will die by war, hunger and disease. 12 The person who is far away will die by disease. The one who is nearby will die in war. The person who is still alive and has escaped these will die from hunger. So I will carry out my anger on them. 13 Their people will lie dead among their idols around the altars, on every high hill, on all the mountain tops and under every green tree and leafy oak—all the places where they offered sweet-smelling incense to their idols. Then you will know that I am the LORD. 14 I will use my power against them to make the land empty and wasted from the desert to Diblah, wherever they live. Then they will know that I am the LORD.'"

Ezekiel Tells of the End

7 Again the LORD spoke his word to me, saying: 2 "Human, the Lord GOD says this to the land of Israel: an end! The end has come on the four corners of the land. 3 Now the end has come for you, and I will send my anger against you. I will judge you for the way you have lived, and I will make you pay for all your actions that I hate. 4 I will have no pity on you; I will not hold back punishment from you. Instead, I will make you pay for the way you have lived and for your actions that I hate. Then you will know that I am the LORD.

EMAIL FROM GOD
7:3–4
Judgement
Who will judge you?

5 "This is what the Lord GOD says: disaster on top of disaster is coming. 6 The end has come! The end has come! It has stirred itself up against you! Look! It has come! 7 Disaster has come for you who live in the land! The time has come; the day of confusion is near. There will be no happy shouting on the mountains. 8 Soon I will pour out my anger against you; I will carry out my anger against you. I will judge you for the way you have lived and will make you pay for everything you have done that I hate. 9 I will show no pity, and I will not hold back punishment. I will pay you back for the way you have lived and the things you have done that I hate.

Then you will know that I am the LORD who punishes.

10 "Look, the day is here. It has come. Disaster has come, violence has grown and there is more pride than ever. 11 Violence has grown into a weapon for punishing wickedness. None of the people will be left—none of that crowd, none of their wealth and nothing of value. 12 The time has come; the day has arrived. Don't let the buyer be happy or the seller be sad, because my burning anger is against the whole crowd. 13 Sellers will not return to the land they have sold as long as they live, because the vision against all that crowd will not be changed. Because of their sins, they will not save their lives. 14 They have blown the trumpet, and everything is ready. But no one is going to the battle, because my anger is against all that crowd.

15 "The sword is outside, and disease and hunger are inside. Whoever is in the field will die by the sword. Hunger and disease will destroy those in the city. 16 Those who are left alive and who escape will be on the mountains, moaning like doves of the valleys about their own sin. 17 All hands will hang weakly with fear, and all knees will become weak as water. 18 They will put on rough cloth to show how sad they are. They will tremble all over with fear. Their faces will show their shame, and all their heads will be shaved. 19 The people will throw their silver into the streets, and their gold will be like rubbish. Their silver and gold will not save them from the LORD's anger. It will not satisfy their hunger or fill their stomachs, because it caused them to fall into sin. 20 They were proud of their beautiful jewellery and used it to make their idols and their evil statues, which I hate. So I will turn their wealth into rubbish. 21 I will give it to foreigners as treasures from war and to the most evil people in the world as treasure, and they will dishonour it. 22 I will also turn away from the people of Israel, and they will dishonour my treasured place. Then robbers will enter and dishonour it.

23 "Make chains for captives, because the land is full of bloody crimes and the city is full of violence. 24 So I will bring the worst of the nations to take over the people's houses. I will also end the pride of the strong, and their holy places will be dishonoured. 25 When the people are suffering greatly, they will look for peace, but there will be none. 26 Disaster will come on top of disaster, and rumour will be added to rumour. Then they will try to get a vision from a prophet; the teachings of God from the priest and the advice from the older leaders will be lost. 27 The king will cry greatly, the prince will give up hope and the hands of the people who

FAITH CHALLENGE

Here's one for you. Read 7:27 to find out what God thinks about people who judge others. What are some areas in which you tend to judge others (sports, education, where they live, etc.)? How can you work not to judge others?

TESTING IT

Ezekiel 7:27
The way they have judged others is the way I will judge them. Then they will know that I am the LORD.

own land will shake with fear. I will punish them for the way they have lived. The way they have judged others is the way I will judge them. Then they will know that I am the LORD."

Ezekiel's Vision of Jerusalem

8 It was the fifth day of the sixth month of the sixth year of our captivity. I was sitting in my house with the elders of Judah in front of me. There I felt the power of the Lord GOD. 2 I looked and saw something that looked like a human. From the waist down it looked like fire, and from the waist up it looked like bright glowing metal. 3 It stretched out the shape of a hand and caught me by the hair on my head. The Spirit lifted me up between the earth and the sky. He took me in visions of God to Jerusalem, to the entrance to the north gate of the inner courtyard of the Temple. In the courtyard was the idol that caused God to be jealous. 4 I saw the glory of the God of Israel there, as I had seen on the plain.

5 Then he said to me, "Human, now look towards the north." So I looked up towards the north, and in the entrance north of the gate of the altar was the idol that caused God to be jealous.

6 He said to me, "Human, do you see what they are doing? Do you see how many hateful things the people of Israel are doing here that drive me far away from my Temple? But you will see things more hateful than these."

7 Then he brought me to the entry of the courtyard. When I looked, I saw a hole in the wall. 8 He said to me, "Human, dig through the wall." So I dug through the wall and saw an entrance.

9 Then he said to me, "Go in and see the hateful, evil things they are doing here." 10 So I entered and looked, and I saw every kind of crawling thing and hateful beast and all the idols of the people of Israel, carved on the wall all around. 11 Standing in front of these carvings and idols were 70 of the elders of Israel and Jaazaniah son of Shaphan. Each man had his pan for burning incense in his hand, and a sweet-smelling cloud of incense was rising.

FAITH links

GOOD ENOUGH?
EZEKIEL 8

Most of us, if we're honest, think our behaviour is good for the most part. We can easily think that someone else is capable of great evil, but not us! God showed Ezekiel a vision of the things that many leaders in Israel did – things God hated. These leaders thought that God did not notice their sin. But God saw everything. He knew that the people of Israel only pretended to worship him. He wanted them to be faithful to him once more.

God knows our hearts. We were all born with a desire to sin. Only Jesus gives us the freedom to choose to do right.

Here are some more Faithlinks on being faithful to Jesus:

Above the Law, 1 Kings 21, p. 470

A Memorial for Two Thieves, 1 Chronicles 7:21, p. 530

Let's Make a Deal, Daniel 1:8–21, p. 1150

A Fake Apology, Hosea 6:1–7, p. 1177

Perfectly Pleasing? Matthew 5:1–12, p. 1280

A High Price, Romans 6:23, p. 1526

12 Then he said to me, "Human, have you seen what the elders of Israel are doing in the dark? Have you seen each man in the room of his own idol? They say, 'The LORD doesn't see us. The LORD has

left the land.'" 13 He also said to me, "You will see them doing even more hateful things."

14 Then he brought me to the entrance of the north gate of the Temple of the LORD, where I saw women sitting and crying for Tammuz." 15 He said to me, "Do you see, human? You will see things even more hateful than these."

16 Then he brought me into the inner courtyard of the Temple. There I saw about 25 men at the entrance to the Temple of the LORD, between the porch and the altar. With their backs turned to the Temple of the LORD, they faced east and were worshipping the sun in the east.

17 He said to me, "Do you see, human? Is it unimportant that the people of Judah are doing the hateful things they have done here? They have filled the land with violence and made me continually angry. Look, they are insulting me in every way they can. 18 So I will act in anger. I will have no pity, nor will I show mercy. Even if they shout in my ears, I won't listen to them."

Vision of the Angels

9 Then he shouted with a loud voice in my ears, "You who are chosen to punish this city, come near with your weapon in your hand." 2 Then six men came from the direction of the upper gate, which faces north, each with his powerful weapon in his hand. Among them was a man dressed in linen with a writing case at his side. The men went in and stood by the bronze altar.

3 Then the glory of the God of Israel went up from above the creatures with wings, where it had been, to the place in the Temple where the door opened. He called to the man dressed in linen who had the writing case at his side. 4 He said to the man, "Go through Jerusalem and put a mark on the foreheads of the people who groan and cry about all the hateful things being done among them."

5 As I listened, he said to the other men, "Go through the city behind the man dressed in linen and kill. Don't pity anyone, and don't show mercy. 6 Kill and destroy old men, young men and women, little children and older women, but don't touch any who have the mark on them. Start at my Temple." So they started with the elders who were in front of the Temple.

7 Then he said to the men, "Make the Temple unclean, and fill the courtyards with those who have been killed. Go out!" So the men went out and killed the people in the city. 8 While the men were killing the people, I was left alone. I bowed face down on the ground and I cried out, "Oh, Lord GOD! Will you destroy everyone left alive in Israel when you turn loose your anger on Jerusalem?"

> The Temple was filled with the cloud, and the courtyard was full of the brightness from the glory of the LORD.
> – Ezekiel 10:4

9 Then he said to me, "The sin of the people of Israel and Judah is very great. The land is filled with people who murder, and the city is full of people who are not fair. The people say, 'The LORD has left the land, and the LORD does not see.' 10 But I will have no pity, nor will I show mercy. I will bring their evil back on their heads."

11 Then the man dressed in linen with the writing case at his side reported, "I have done just as you commanded me."

The Coals of Fire

10 Then I looked and saw in the dome above the heads of the living creatures something like a sapphire gem which looked like a throne. 2 The LORD said to the man dressed in linen, "Go in between the wheels under the living creatures, fill your hands with coals of fire from between the living creatures, and scatter the coals over the city."

8:14 Tammuz Tammuz was a god in Babylon. Every year people thought this god died when the plants died. After they cried for him, they believed he came back to life and the plants lived again.

As I watched, the man with linen clothes went in. 3 Now the living creatures were standing on the south side of the Temple when the man went in. And a cloud filled the inner courtyard. 4 Then the glory of the LORD went up from the living creatures and stood over the door of the Temple. The Temple was filled with the cloud, and the courtyard was full of the brightness from the glory of the LORD. 5 The sound of the wings of the living creatures was heard all the way to the outer courtyard. It was like the voice of God Almighty when he speaks.

6 When the LORD commanded the man dressed in linen, "Take fire from between the wheels, from between the living creatures," the man went in and stood by a wheel. 7 One living creature put out his hand to the fire that was among them, took some of the fire, and put it in the hands of the man dressed in linen. Then the man took the fire and went out.

The Wheels and the Creatures

8 Something that looked like a human hand could be seen under the wings of the living creatures. 9 I saw the four wheels by the living creatures, one wheel by each living creature. The wheels looked like shining chrysolite. 10 All four wheels looked alike: each looked like a wheel crossways inside another wheel. 11 When the wheels moved, they went in any of the directions that the four living creatures faced. The wheels did not turn about, and the living creatures did not turn their bodies as they went. 12 All their bodies, their backs, their hands, their wings and the wheels were full of eyes all over. Each of the four living creatures had a wheel. 13 I heard the wheels being called "whirling wheels". 14 Each living creature had four faces. The first face was the face of a creature with wings. The second face was a human face, the third was the face of a lion and the fourth was the face of an eagle.

15 Then the living creatures flew up. They were the same living creatures I had seen by the Kebar River. 16 When the living creatures moved, the wheels moved beside them. When the living creatures lifted their wings to fly up from the ground, the wheels did not leave their place beside them. 17 When the living creatures stopped, the wheels stopped. When the creatures went up, the wheels went up also, because the spirit of the living creatures was in the wheels.

18 Then the glory of the LORD left the door of the Temple and stood over the living creatures. 19 As I watched, the living creatures spread their wings and flew up from the ground, with the wheels beside them. They stood where the east gate of the Temple of the LORD opened, and the glory of the God of Israel was over them.

20 These were the living creatures I had seen under the God of Israel by the Kebar River. I knew they were called cherubim. 21 Each one had four faces and four wings, and under their wings were things that looked like human hands. 22 Their faces looked the same as the ones I had seen by the Kebar River. They each went straight ahead.

Prophecies Against Evil Leaders

11 The Spirit lifted me up and brought me to the front gate of the Temple of the LORD, which faces east. I saw 25 men where the gate opens, among them Jaazaniah son of Azzur and Pelatiah son of Benaiah, who were leaders of the people. 2 Then the LORD said to me, "Human, these are the men who plan evil and give wicked advice in this city of Jerusalem. 3 They say, 'It is almost time for us to build houses. This city is like a cooking pot, and we are like the best meat.' 4 So prophesy against them, prophesy, human."

5 Then the Spirit of the LORD entered me and told me to say: "This is what the LORD says: you have said these things, people of Israel, and I know what you are thinking. 6 You have killed many people in this city, filling its streets with their bodies.

7 "So this is what the Lord GOD says: those people you have killed and left in the middle of the city are like the best meat, and this city is like the cooking pot. But I will force you out of the city. 8 You have feared the sword, but I will bring a

sword against you, says the Lord GOD. 9 I will force you out of the city and hand you over to strangers and punish you. 10 You will die by the sword. I will punish you at the border of Israel so you will know that I am the LORD. 11 This city will not be your cooking pot, and you will not be the best meat in the middle of it. I will punish you at the border of Israel. 12 Then you will know that I am the LORD. You did not live by my rules or obey my laws. Instead, you did the same things as the nations around you."

11:12 Decisions
How is peer pressure bad?

13 As I prophesied, Pelatiah son of Benaiah died. Then I bowed face down on the ground and shouted with a loud voice, "Oh no, Lord GOD! Will you completely destroy the Israelites who are left alive?"

Promise to Those Remaining

14 The LORD spoke his word to me, saying, 15 "Human, the people still in Jerusalem have spoken about your own relatives and all the people of Israel who are captives with you, saying, 'They are far from the LORD. This land has been given to us as our property.'

16 "So say, 'This is what the Lord GOD says: I sent the people far away among the nations and scattered them among the countries. But for a little while I have become a Temple to them in the countries where they have gone.'

17 "So say: 'This is what the Lord GOD says: I will gather you from the nations and bring you together from the countries where you have been scattered. Then I will give you back the land of Israel.'

18 "When they come to this land, they will remove all the evil idols and all the hateful images. 19 I will give them a desire to respect me completely, and I will put inside them a new way of thinking. I will take out the stubborn heart of stone from their bodies, and I will give them an obedient heart of flesh. 20 Then

11:19 Following God
Check out how God changes lives.

they will live by my rules and obey my laws and keep them. They will be my people, and I will be their God. 21 But those who want to serve their evil statues and hateful idols, I will pay back for their evil ways, says the Lord GOD."

Ezekiel's Vision Ends

22 Then the living creatures lifted their wings with the wheels beside them, and the glory of the God of Israel was above them. 23 The glory of the LORD went up from inside Jerusalem and stopped on the mountain on the east side of the city. 24 The Spirit lifted me up and brought me to the captives who had been taken from Judah to Babylonia. This happened in a vision given by the Spirit of God, and then the vision I had seen ended. 25 And I told the captives from Judah all the things the LORD had shown me.

Ezekiel Moves Out

12 Again the LORD spoke his word to me, saying: 2 "Human, you are living among a people who refuse to obey. They have eyes to see, but they do not see, and they have ears to hear, but they do not hear, because they are a people who refuse to obey.

3 "So, human, pack your things as if you will be taken away captive, and walk away like a captive in the daytime with the people watching. Move from your place to another with the people watching. Perhaps they will understand, even though they are a people who refuse to obey. 4 During the day when the people are watching, bring out the things you would pack as captive. At evening, with the people watching, leave your place like those who are taken away as captives from their country. 5 Dig a hole through the wall while they watch, and bring your things out through it. 6 Lift them onto your shoulders with the people watching, and carry them out in the dark. Cover your face so you cannot see the ground, because I have made you a sign to the people of Israel."

7 I did these things as I was commanded. In the daytime I brought what I had packed as if I were being taken

away captive. Then in the evening I dug through the wall with my hands. I brought my things out in the dark and carried them on my shoulders as the people watched. 8 Then in the morning the LORD spoke his word to me, saying: 9 "Human, didn't Israel, who refuses to obey, ask you, 'What are you doing?' 10 Say to them, 'This is what the Lord GOD says: this message is about the king in Jerusalem and all the people of Israel who live there.' 11 Say, 'I am a sign to you.'

"The same things I have done will be done to the people in Jerusalem. They will be taken away from their country as captives. 12 The king among them will put his things on his shoulder in the dark and will leave. The people will dig a hole through the wall to bring him out. He will cover his face so he cannot see the ground. 13 But I will spread my net over him, and he will be caught in my trap. Then I will bring him to Babylon in the land of the Babylonians. He will not see that land, but he will die there. 14 All who are around the king—his helpers and all his army—I will scatter in every direction, and I will chase them with a sword. 15 They will know that I am the LORD when I scatter them among the nations and spread them among the countries. 16 But I will save a few of them from the sword and from hunger and disease. Then they can tell of their hateful actions among the nations where they go. Then they will know that I am the LORD."

The Lesson of Ezekiel's Shaking

17 The LORD spoke his word to me, saying: 18 "Human, tremble as you eat your food, and shake with fear as you drink your water. 19 Then say to the people of the land: 'This is what the Lord GOD says about the people who live in Jerusalem in the land of Israel: they will eat their food with fear and drink their water in shock, because their land will be stripped bare because of the violence of the people who live in it. 20 The cities where people live will become ruins, and the land will become empty. Then you will know that I am the LORD.'"

The Visions will Come True

21 The LORD spoke his word to me, saying: 22 "Human, what is this saying you have in the land of Israel: 'The days go by and every vision comes to nothing'? 23 So say to them, 'This is what the Lord GOD says: I will make them stop saying this, and nobody in Israel will use this saying any more.' But tell them, 'The time is near when every vision will come true. 24 There will be no more false visions or pleasing prophecies inside the nation of Israel, 25 but I, the LORD, will speak. What I say will be done, and it will not be delayed. You refuse to obey, but in your time I will say the word and do it, says the Lord GOD.'"

12:17-25
Judgement
God promises judgement for disobedience.

26 The LORD spoke his word to me, saying: 27 "Human, the people of Israel are saying, 'The vision that Ezekiel sees is for a time many years from now. He is prophesying about times far away.' 28 "So say to them: 'The Lord GOD says this: none of my words will be delayed any more. What I have said will be done, says the Lord GOD.'"

Ezekiel Speaks Against False Prophets

13 The LORD spoke his word to me, saying: 2 "Human, prophesy against the prophets of Israel. Say to those who make up their own prophecies: 'Listen to the word of the LORD. 3 This is what the Lord GOD says: how terrible it will be for the foolish prophets who follow their own ideas and have not seen a vision from me! 4 People of Israel, your prophets have been like wild dogs hunting to kill and eat among ruins. 5 Israel is like a house in ruins, but you have not gone up into the broken places or repaired the wall. So how can Israel hold back the enemy in the battle on the LORD's day of judging? 6 Your prophets see false visions and prophesy lies. They say, "This is the

message of the LORD," when the LORD has not sent them. But they still hope their words will come true. 7 You said, "This is the message of the LORD," but that is a false vision. Your prophecies are lies, because I have not spoken.

8 "So this is what the Lord GOD says: because you prophets spoke things that are false and saw visions that do not come true, I am against you, says the Lord GOD. 9 I will punish the prophets who see false visions and prophesy lies. They will have no place among my people. Their names will not be written on the list of the people of Israel, and they will not enter the land of Israel. Then you will know that I am the Lord GOD.

10 "It is because they lead my people the wrong way by saying, "Peace!" when there is no peace. When the people build a weak wall, the prophets cover it with whitewash to make it look strong. 11 So tell those who cover a weak wall with whitewash that it will fall down. Rain will pour down, hailstones will fall and a stormy wind will break the wall down. 12 When the wall has fallen, people will ask you, "Where is the whitewash you used on the wall?"

13 "So this is what the Lord GOD says: I will break the wall with a stormy wind. In my anger rain will pour down, and hailstones will destroy the wall. 14 I will tear down the wall on which you put whitewash. I will level it to the ground so that people will see the wall's foundation. And when the wall falls, you will be destroyed under it. Then you will know that I am the LORD. 15 So I will carry out my anger on the wall and against those who covered it with whitewash. Then I will tell you, "The wall is gone, and those who covered it with whitewash are gone. 16 The prophets of Israel who prophesy to Jerusalem and who see visions of peace for the city, when there is no peace, will be gone, says the Lord GOD."

False Women Prophets

17 "Now, human, look towards the women among your people who make up their own prophecies. Prophesy against

FAITH links

THE DEAD END OF THE OCCULT
EZEKIEL 13:17-23

Ouija boards. Séances. Psychics. They're all just simple party entertainment, right? If you think that, think again. God told Ezekiel to speak out against a group of women who called themselves prophets. They used so-called magic charms and encouraged people to sin. God wanted his people to be free from their lies and to listen only to his truth.

Many people today visit psychics, hoping to catch a glimpse of the future. Others may seek those who claim to practice witchcraft, hoping to gain power. God is against these practices. Instead of being an avenue to truth, they're really a dead end. They allow the enemy of Christians – Satan – to be in control. Don't go there!

Don't get caught in a dead end! Connect here for God's wisdom:

What You Value, Genesis 25:21–34, p. 34

What He's Really Like, Deuteronomy 4:15–20, p. 233

Sitting on the Fence, 1 Kings 18, p. 464

A Hopeful Future, Jeremiah 29:11, p. 1031

Obeying God or Man? Daniel 3:8–30, p. 1154

Long-lasting Hope, Hosea 14, p. 1184

them. 18 Say, 'This is what the Lord GOD says: how terrible it will be for women who sew magic charms on their wrists and make veils of every length to trap people! You ruin the lives of my people but try to save your own lives. 19 For handfuls of barley and pieces of bread, you have dishonoured me among my people. By lying to my people, who listen to lies, you have killed people who should not die, and you have kept alive those who should not live.
20 "'So this is what the Lord GOD says: I am against your magic charms, by which you trap people as if they were birds. I will tear those charms off your arms, and I will free those people you have trapped like birds. 21 I will also tear off your veils and save my people from your hands. They will no longer be trapped by your power. Then you will know that I am the LORD. 22 By your lies you have caused those who did right to be sad, when I did not make them sad. And you have encouraged the wicked not to stop being wicked, and so save their lives. 23 So you will not see false visions or prophesy any more, and I will save my people from your power so you will know that I am the LORD.'"

Stop Worshipping Idols

14 Some of the elders of Israel came to me and sat down in front of me. 2 Then the LORD spoke his word to me, saying: 3 "Human, these men want to worship idols. They put up evil things that cause people to sin. Should I allow them to ask me for help? 4 So speak to them and tell them, 'This is what the Lord GOD says: when any of the people of Israel want to worship idols and put up evil things that cause people to sin and then come to the prophet, I, the LORD, will answer them myself for worshipping idols. 5 Then I will win back my people Israel, who have left me because of all their idols.'

6 "So say to the people of Israel, 'This is what the Lord GOD says: Change your hearts and lives, and stop worshipping idols. Stop doing all the things I hate. 7 Any of the Israelites or foreigners in Israel can separate themselves from me by wanting to worship idols or by putting up the things that cause people to sin. Then if they come to the prophet to ask me questions, I, the LORD, will answer them myself. 8 I will reject them. I will make them a sign and an example, and I will separate them from my people. Then you will know that I am the LORD.

9 "'But if the prophet is tricked into giving a prophecy, it is because I, the LORD, have tricked that prophet to speak. Then I will use my power against him and destroy him from among my people Israel. 10 The prophet will be as guilty as the one who asks him for help; both will be responsible for their guilt. 11 Then the nation of Israel will not leave me any more or make themselves unclean any more with all their sins. They will be my people, and I will be their God, says the Lord GOD.'"

Jerusalem will Not be Spared

12 The LORD spoke his word to me, saying: 13 "Human, if the people of a country sin against me by not being loyal, I will use my power against them. I will cut off their supply of food and send a time of hunger, destroying both people and animals. 14 Even if three great men like Noah, Daniel and Job were in that country, their goodness could save only themselves, says the Lord GOD.

15 "Or I might send wild animals into that land, leaving the land empty and without children. Then no one would pass through it because of the animals. 16 As surely as I live, says the Lord GOD, even if Noah, Daniel and Job were in the land, they could not save their own sons or daughters. They could save only themselves, but that country would become empty.

17 "Or I might bring a war against that

> This is what the Lord GOD says: Change your hearts and lives, and stop worshipping idols. Stop doing all the things I hate.
> – Ezekiel 14:6

country. I might say, 'Let a war be fought in that land,' in this way destroying its people and its animals. 18 As surely as I live, says the Lord GOD, even if those three men were in the land, they could not save their sons or daughters. They could save only themselves.

19 "Or I might cause a disease to spread in that country. I might pour out my anger against it, destroying and killing people and animals. 20 As surely as I live, says the Lord GOD, even if Noah, Daniel and Job were in the land, they could not save their son or daughter. They could save only themselves because they did what was right.

21 "This is what the Lord GOD says: my plans for Jerusalem are much worse! I will send my four terrible punishments against it—war, hunger, wild animals and disease—to destroy its people and animals. 22 But some people will escape; some sons and daughters will be led out. They will come out to you, and you will see what happens to people who live as they did. Then you will be comforted after the disasters I have brought against Jerusalem, after all the things I have brought against it. 23 You will be comforted when you see what happens to them for living as they did, because you will know there was a good reason for what I did to Jerusalem, says the Lord GOD."

Story of the Vine

15 The LORD spoke his word to me, saying: 2 "Human, is the wood of the vine better than the wood of any tree in the forest? 3 Can wood be taken from the vine to make anything? Can you use it to make a peg on which to hang something? 4 If the vine is thrown into the fire for fuel, and the fire burns up both ends and starts to burn the middle, is it useful for anything? 5 When the vine was whole, it couldn't be made into anything. When the fire has burnt it completely, it certainly cannot be made into anything."

6 So this is what the Lord GOD says: "Out of all the trees in the forest, I have given the wood of the vine as fuel for fire. In the same way I have given up the people who live in Jerusalem 7 and will turn against them. Although they came through one fire, fire will still destroy them. When I turn against them, you will know that I am the LORD. 8 So I will make the land empty, because the people have not been loyal, says the Lord GOD."

The LORD's Kindness to Jerusalem

16 The LORD spoke his word to me, saying: 2 "Human, tell Jerusalem about her hateful actions. 3 Say, 'This is what the Lord GOD says to Jerusalem: your beginnings and your ancestors were in the land of the Canaanites. Your father was an Amorite, and your mother was a Hittite. 4 On the day you were born, your cord*n* was not cut. You were not washed with water to clean you. You were not rubbed with salt or wrapped in cloths. 5 No one felt sorry enough for you to do any of these things for you. No, you were thrown out into the open field, because you were hated on the day you were born.

6 "When I passed by and saw you kicking about in your blood, I said to you, "Live!" 7 I made you grow like a plant in the field. You grew up and became tall and became like a beautiful jewel. Your breasts formed, and your hair grew, but you were naked and without clothes.

8 "Later when I passed by you and looked at you, I saw that you were old enough for love. So I spread my robe over you and covered your nakedness. I also made a promise to you and entered into an agreement with you so that you became mine, says the Lord GOD.

9 "Then I bathed you with water, washed all the blood off you, and put oil on you. 10 I put beautiful clothes made with needlework on you and put sandals of fine leather on your feet. I wrapped you in fine linen and covered you with silk. 11 I put jewellery on you: bracelets on your arms, a necklace around your neck, 12 a ring in your nose, earrings in your ears and a beautiful crown on your head. 13 So you wore gold and silver. Your clothes were made of fine linen, silk

---

16:4 cord The umbilical cord that gives the unborn baby food and air from its mother.

and beautiful needlework. You ate fine flour, honey and olive oil. You were very beautiful and became a queen. 14 Then you became famous among the nations, because you were so beautiful. Your beauty was perfect, because of the glory I gave you, says the Lord GOD.

Jerusalem Becomes a Prostitute

15 "But you trusted in your beauty. You became a prostitute, because you were so famous. You had sexual relations with anyone who passed by. 16 You took some of your clothes and made your places of worship colourful. There you carried on your prostitution. These things should not happen; they should never occur. 17 You also took your beautiful jewellery, made from my gold and silver I had given you, and you made for yourselves male idols so you could be a prostitute with them. 18 Then you took your clothes with beautiful needlework and covered the idols. You gave my oil and incense as an offering to them. 19 Also, you took the bread I gave you, the fine flour, oil and honey I gave you to eat, and you offered them before the gods as a pleasing smell. This is what happened, says the Lord GOD.

20 "But your sexual sins were not enough for you. You also took your sons and daughters who were my children, and you sacrificed them to the idols as food. 21 You killed my children and offered them up in fire to the idols. 22 While you did all your hateful acts and sexual sins, you did not remember when you were young, when you were naked and had no clothes and were left in your blood.

23 "How terrible! How terrible it will be for you, says the Lord GOD. After you did all these evil things, 24 you built yourself a place to worship gods. You made for yourself a place of worship in every city square. 25 You built a place of worship at the beginning of every street. You made your beauty hateful, offering your body for sex to anyone who passed by, so your sexual sins became worse and worse. 26 You also had sexual relations with the Egyptians, who were your neighbours and partners in sexual sin. Your sexual sins became even worse, and they caused me to be angry. 27 So then, I used my power against you and took away some of your land. I let you be defeated by those who hate you, the Philistine women, who were ashamed of your evil ways. 28 Also, you had sexual relations with the Assyrians, because you could not be satisfied. Even though you had sexual relations with them, you still were not satisfied. 29 You did many more sexual sins in Babylonia, the land of traders, but even this did not satisfy you.

30 "Truly your will is weak, says the Lord GOD. You do all the things a stubborn prostitute does. 31 You built your place to worship gods at the beginning of every street, and you made places of worship in every city square. But you were not like a prostitute when you refused to accept payment.

32 "You are a wife who is guilty of adultery. You desire strangers instead of your husband. 33 Men pay prostitutes, but you pay all your lovers to come to you. And they come from all around for sexual relations. 34 So you are different from other prostitutes. No man asks you to be a prostitute, and you pay money instead of having money paid to you. Yes, you are different.

The Prostitute is Judged

35 "So, prostitute, hear the word of the LORD. 36 This is what the Lord GOD says: you showed your nakedness to other countries. You uncovered your body in your sexual sins with them as your lovers and with all your hateful idols. You killed your children and offered their blood to your idols. 37 So I will gather all your lovers with whom you found pleasure. Yes, I will gather all those you loved and those you hated. I will gather them against you from all around, and I will strip you naked in front of them so they can see your nakedness. 38 I will punish you as women guilty of adultery or as murderers are punished. I will put you to death because I am angry and jealous. 39 I will also hand you over to your lovers. They will tear down your places of worship and destroy other places where you

worship gods. They will tear off your clothes and take away your jewellery, leaving you naked and bare. 40 They will bring a crowd against you to throw stones at you and cut you into pieces with their swords. 41 They will burn down your houses and will punish you in front of many women. I will put an end to your sexual sins, and you will no longer pay your lovers. 42 Then I will rest from my anger against you, and I will stop being jealous. I will be quiet and not angry any more.

43 "Because you didn't remember when you were young, but have made me angry in all these ways, I will repay you for what you have done, says the Lord GOD. Didn't you add sexual sins to all your other acts which I hate?

44 "Everyone who uses wise sayings will say this about you: 'The daughter is like her mother.' 45 You are like your mother, who hated her husband and children. You are also like your sisters, who hated their husbands and children. Your mother was a Hittite, and your father was an Amorite. 46 Your older sister is Samaria, who lived north of you with her daughters; your younger sister is Sodom, who lived south of you with her daughters. 47 You not only followed their ways and did the hateful things they did, but you were soon worse than they were in all your ways. 48 As surely as I live, says the Lord GOD, this is true. Your sister Sodom and her daughters never did what you and your daughters have done.

49 "This was the sin of your sister Sodom: she and her daughters were proud and had plenty of food and lived in great comfort, but she did not help the poor and needy. 50 So Sodom and her daughters were proud and did things I hate in front of me. So I got rid of them when I saw what they did. 51 Also, Samaria did not do half the sins you do; you have done more hateful things than they did. So you make your sisters look good because of all the hateful things you have done. 52 You will suffer disgrace, because you have provided an excuse for your sisters. They are better than you are. Your sins were even more terrible than theirs. Feel ashamed and suffer disgrace, because you made your sisters look good.

53 "But I will give back to Sodom and her daughters the good things they once had. I will give back to Samaria and her daughters the good things they once had. And with them I will also give back the good things you once had 54 so you may suffer disgrace and feel ashamed for all the things you have done. You even gave comfort to your sisters in their sins. 55 Your sisters, Sodom with her daughters and Samaria with her daughters, will return to what they were before. You and your daughters will also return to what you were before. 56 You humiliated your sister Sodom when you were proud, 57 before your evil was uncovered. And now the Edomite women and their neighbours say bad things about you. Even the Philistine women humiliate you. Those around you hate you. 58 This is your punishment for your terrible sins and for actions that I hate, says the LORD.

God Keeps His Promises

59 "This is what the Lord GOD says: I will do to you what you have done. You hated and broke the agreement you promised to keep. 60 But I will remember my agreement I made with you when you were young, and I will make an agreement that will continue for ever with you. 61 Then you will remember what you have done and feel ashamed when you receive your sisters—both your older and your younger sisters. I will give them to you like daughters, but not because they share in my agreement with you. 62 I will set up my agreement with you, and you will know that I am the LORD. 63 You will remember what you did and feel ashamed. You will not open your mouth again because of your shame, when I forgive you for all the things you have done, says the Lord GOD.'"

The Eagle and the Vine

17 The LORD spoke his word to me, saying: 2 "Human, give a riddle and tell a story to the people of Israel. 3 Say, 'This is what the Lord GOD says: a giant

A MODEL OF FORGIVENESS
EZEKIEL 16:59-63

In order to learn some things, you need a model. If you wanted to draw a bowl of fruit, seeing one in front of you would help. If you wanted to improve your serve in tennis, watching someone else helps. God has always been the model for faithfulness and forgiveness. That's why God told Ezekiel that he would keep his promise to the people of Israel. He would forgive their sins and do even more than he had ever promised them.

Even though we do wrong and sin against God, he is always ready and willing to forgive us. He models forgiveness, so that we can forgive others.

Here are some more Faithlinks on why we need to forgive others:

Dirty Inside, Isaiah 6:1-7, p. 904

The God of Second Chances, Jonah 3, p. 1215

The Temptation Fighter, Matthew 4:1-11, p. 1278

Quick to Forgive? Mark 11:25, p. 1349

Forgive Again? Luke 17:3-4, p. 1402

A Happy Ending, Revelation 22:16-21, p. 1754

---

eagle with big wings and long feathers of many different colours came to Lebanon and took hold of the top of a cedar tree. 4 He pulled off the top branch and brought it to a land of traders, where he planted it in a city of traders.

5 "The eagle took some seed from the land and planted it in a good field near plenty of water. He planted it to grow like a willow tree. 6 It grew and became a low vine that spread over the ground. The branches turned towards the eagle, but the roots were under the eagle. So the seed became a vine, and its branches grew, sending out leaves.

7 "But there was another giant eagle with big wings and many feathers. The vine then bent its roots towards this eagle. It sent out its branches from the area where it was planted towards the eagle so he could water it. 8 It had been planted in a good field by plenty of water so it could grow branches and give fruit. It could have become a fine vine.'

9 "Say to them, 'This is what the Lord GOD says: the vine will not continue to grow. The first eagle will pull up the vine's roots and strip off its fruit. Then the vine and all its new leaves will dry up and die. It will not take a strong arm or many people to pull the vine up by its roots. 10 Even if it is planted again, it will not continue to grow. It will completely dry up and die when the east wind hits it in the area where it grew.'"

Zedekiah Against Nebuchadnezzar

11 Then the LORD spoke his word to me, saying: 12 "Say now to the people who refuse to obey: 'Do you know what these things mean?' Say: 'The king of Babylon came to Jerusalem and took the king and important men of Jerusalem and brought them to Babylon. 13 Then he took a member of the family of the king of Judah and made an agreement with him, forcing him to take an oath. The king also took away the leaders of Judah 14 to make the kingdom weak so it would not be strong again. Then the kingdom of Judah could continue only by keeping its agreement with the king of Babylon. 15 But the

king of Judah turned against the king of Babylon by sending his messengers to Egypt and asking them for horses and many soldiers. Will the king of Judah succeed? Will the one who does such things escape? He cannot break the agreement and escape.

16 "'As surely as I live, says the Lord GOD, he will die in Babylon, in the land of the king who made him king of Judah. The king of Judah hated his promise to the king of Babylon and broke his agreement with him. 17 The king of Egypt with his mighty army and many people will not help the king of Judah in the war. The Babylonians will build devices to attack the cities and to kill many people. 18 The king of Judah showed that he hated the promise by breaking the agreement. He promised to support Babylon, but he did all these things. So he will not escape.

19 "'So this is what the Lord GOD says: as surely as I live, this is true: I will pay back the king of Judah for hating my promise and breaking my agreement. 20 I will spread my net over him, and he will be caught in my trap. Then I will bring him to Babylon, where I will punish him for the unfaithful acts he did against me. 21 All the best of his soldiers who escape will die by the sword, and those who live will be scattered to every wind. Then you will know that I, the LORD, have spoken.

22 "'This is what the Lord GOD says: I myself will also take a young branch from the top of a cedar tree, and I will plant it. I will cut off a small twig from the top of the tree's young branches, and I will plant it on a very high mountain. 23 I will plant it on the high mountain of Israel. Then it will grow branches and give fruit and become a great cedar tree. Birds of every kind will build nests in it and live in the shelter of the tree's branches. 24 Then all the trees in the countryside will know that I am the LORD. I bring down the high tree and make the low tree tall. I dry up the green tree and make the dry tree grow. I am the LORD. I have spoken, and I will do it.'"

God is Fair

18 The LORD spoke his word to me, saying: 2 "What do you mean by using this saying about the land of Israel:

'The parents have eaten sour grapes,
    and that caused the children to
    grind their teeth from the sour
    taste'?

3 "As surely as I live, says the Lord GOD, this is true: you will not use this saying in Israel any more. 4 Every living thing belongs to me. The life of the parent is mine, and the life of the child is mine. The person who sins is the one who will die.

5 "Suppose a person is good and does what is fair and right. 6 He does not eat at the mountain places of worship. He does not look to the idols of Israel for help. He does not have sexual relations with his neighbour's wife or with a woman during her time of monthly bleeding. 7 He does not mistreat anyone but returns what was given as a promise for a loan. He does not rob other people. He gives bread to the hungry and clothes to those who have none. 8 He does not lend money to get too much interest or profit. He keeps his hand from doing wrong. He judges fairly between one person and another. 9 He lives by my rules and obeys my laws faithfully. Whoever does these things is good and will surely live, says the Lord GOD.

10 "But suppose this person has a wild son who murders people and who does any of these other things. 11 (Though the father himself has not done any of these things.) This son eats at the mountain places of worship. He has sexual relations with his neighbour's wife. 12 He mistreats the poor and needy. He steals and refuses to return what was promised for a loan. He looks to idols for help. He does things which I hate. 13 He lends money for too

> As surely as I live, this is true: I will pay back the king of Judah for hating my promise and breaking my agreement.
> – Ezekiel 17:19

much interest and profit. Will this son live? No, he will not live! He has done all these hateful things, so he will surely be put to death. He will be responsible for his own death.

14 "Now suppose this son has a son who has seen all his father's sins, but after seeing them does not do those things. 15 He does not eat at the mountain places of worship. He does not look to the idols of Israel for help. He does not have sexual relations with his neighbour's wife. 16 He does not mistreat anyone or keep something promised for a loan or steal. He gives bread to the hungry and clothes to those who have none. 17 He keeps his hand from doing wrong. He does not take too much interest or profit when he lends money. He obeys my laws and lives by my rules. He will not die for his father's sin; he will surely live. 18 But his father took other people's money unfairly and robbed his brother and did what was wrong among his people. So he will die for his own sin.

19 "But you ask, 'Why is the son not punished for the father's sin?' The son has done what is fair and right. He obeys all my rules, so he will surely live. 20 The person who sins is the one who will die. A child will not be punished for a parent's sin, and a parent will not be punished for a child's sin. Those who do right will enjoy the results of their own goodness; evil people will suffer the results of their own evil.

18:19-20 Family Will children be punished for the family's sin?

21 "But suppose the wicked stop doing all the sins they have done and obey all my rules and do what is fair and right. Then they will surely live; they will not die. 22 Their sins will be forgotten. Because they have done what is right, they will live. 23 I do not really want the wicked to die, says the Lord GOD. I want them to stop their bad ways and live.

24 "But suppose good people stop doing good and do wrong and do the same hateful things the wicked do. Will they live? All their good acts will be forgotten, because they became unfaithful. They have sinned, so they will die because of their sins.

25 "But you say, 'What the Lord does isn't fair.' Listen, people of Israel. I am fair. It is what you do that is not fair! 26 When good people stop doing good and do wrong, they will die because of it. They will die, because they did wrong. 27 When the wicked stop being wicked and do what is fair and right, they will save their lives. 28 Because they thought about it and stopped doing all the sins they had done, they will surely live; they will not die. 29 But the people of Israel still say, 'What the Lord does isn't fair.' People of Israel, I am fair. It is what you do that is not fair.

30 "So I will judge you, people of Israel; I will judge each of you by what you do, says the Lord GOD. Change your hearts and stop all your sinning so sin will not bring your ruin. 31 Get rid of all the sins you have done, and get for yourselves a new heart and a new way of thinking. Why do you want to die, people of Israel? 32 I do not want anyone to die, says the Lord GOD, so change your hearts and lives so you may live.

A Sad Song for Israel

19 "Sing a funeral song for the leaders of Israel. 2 Say:
'Your mother was like a female lion.
She lay down among the young lions.
She had many cubs.
3 When she brought up one of her cubs,
he became a strong lion.
He learned to tear the animals he hunted,
and he ate people.
4 The nations heard about him.
He was trapped in their pit,
and they brought him with hooks to the land of Egypt.

5 "'The mother lion waited and saw that there was no hope for her cub.
So she took another one of her cubs and made him a strong lion.
6 This cub roamed among the lions.
He was now a strong lion.

He learned to tear the animals he
    hunted,
    and he ate people.
7 He tore down their strong places
    and destroyed their cities.
The land and everything in it
    were terrified by the sound of his
        roar.
8 Then the nations came against him
    from areas all around,
    and they spread their net over him.
He was trapped in their pit.
9 Then they put him into a cage with
        chains
    and brought him to the king of
        Babylon.
They put him into prison
    so his roar could not be heard
        again
    on the mountains of Israel.

10 "'Your mother was like a vine in your
        vineyard,
    planted beside the water.
The vine had many branches and
        gave much fruit,
    because there was plenty of
        water.
11 The vine had strong branches,
    good enough for a king's sceptre.
The vine became tall
    among the thick branches.
And it was seen, because it was tall
    with many branches.
12 But it was pulled up by its roots in
        anger
    and thrown down to the ground.
The east wind dried it up.
    Its fruit was torn off.
Its strong branches were broken off
    and burned up.
13 Now the vine is planted in the
        desert,
    in a dry and thirsty land.
14 Fire spread from the vine's main
        branch,
    destroying its fruit.
There is not a strong branch left on it
    that could become a sceptre for a
        king.'

This is a funeral song; it is to be used as a funeral song."

Israel Has Refused God

20 It was the tenth day of the fifth month of the seventh year of our captivity. Some of the elders of Israel came to ask about the LORD and sat down in front of me.

2 The LORD spoke his word to me, saying: 3 "Human, speak to the elders of Israel and say to them: 'This is what the Lord GOD says: did you come to ask me questions? As surely as I live, I will not let you ask me questions.'

4 "Will you judge them? Will you judge them, human? Let them know the hateful things their ancestors did. 5 Say to them: 'This is what the Lord GOD says: When I chose Israel, I made a promise to the descendants of Jacob. I made myself known to them in Egypt, and I promised them, "I am the LORD your God." 6 At that time I promised them I would bring them out of Egypt into a land I had found for them, a fertile land, the best land in the world. 7 I said to them, "Each one of you must throw away the hateful idols you have seen and liked. Don't make yourselves unclean with the idols of Egypt. I am the LORD your God."

8 "'But they turned against me and refused to listen to me. They did not throw away the hateful idols which they saw and liked; they did not give up the idols of Egypt. Then I decided to pour out my anger against them while they were still in Egypt. 9 But I acted for the sake of my name so it would not be dishonoured in full view of the nations where the Israelites lived. I made myself known to the Israelites with a promise to bring them out of Egypt while the nations were watching. 10 So I took them out of Egypt and brought them into the desert. 11 I gave them my rules and told them about my laws, by which people will live if they obey them. 12 I also gave them my Sabbaths to be a sign between us so they would know that I am the LORD who made them holy.

13 "'But in the desert Israel turned against me. They did not follow my rules, and they rejected my laws, by which people will live if they obey them. They dishonoured my Sabbaths. Then I decided to

pour out my anger against them and destroy them in the desert. **14** But I acted for the sake of my name so it would not be dishonoured in full view of the nations who watched as I had brought the Israelites out of Egypt. **15** And in the desert I swore to the Israelites that I would not bring them into the land I had given them. It is a fertile land, the best land in the world. **16** This was because they rejected my laws and did not follow my rules. They dishonoured my Sabbaths and wanted to worship their idols. **17** But I had pity on them. I did not destroy them or put an end to them in the desert. **18** I said to their children in the desert, "Don't live by the rules of your parents, or obey their laws. Don't make yourselves unclean with their idols. **19** I am the LORD your God. Live by my rules, obey my laws and follow them. **20** Keep my Sabbaths holy, and they will be a sign between me and you. Then you will know that I am the LORD your God."

21 "'But the children turned against me. They did not live by my rules, nor were they careful to obey my laws, by which people will live if they obey them. They dishonoured my Sabbaths. So I decided to pour out my anger against them in the desert. **22** But I held back my anger. I acted for the sake of my name so it would not be dishonoured in full view of the nations who watched as I brought the Israelites out. **23** And in the desert I swore to the Israelites that I would scatter them among the nations and spread them among the countries, **24** because they had not obeyed my laws. They had rejected my rules and dishonoured my Sabbaths and worshipped the idols of their parents. **25** I also allowed them to follow rules that were not good and laws by which they could not live. **26** I let the Israelites make themselves unclean by the gifts they brought to their gods when they sacrificed their first children in the fire. I wanted to terrify them so they would know that I am the LORD.'

27 "So, human, speak to the people of Israel. Say to them, 'This is what the Lord GOD says: your ancestors spoke against me by being unfaithful to me in another way. **28** When I had brought them into the land I promised to give them, they saw every high hill and every leafy tree. There they offered their sacrifices to gods. They brought offerings that made me angry and burned their incense and poured out their drink offerings. **29** Then I said to them: what is this high place where you go to worship?'" (It is still called High Place today.)

30 "So say to the people of Israel: 'This is what the Lord GOD says: are you going to make yourselves unclean as your ancestors did? Are you going to be unfaithful and desire their hateful idols? **31** When you offer your children as gifts and sacrifice them in the fire, you are making yourselves unclean with all your idols even today. So, people of Israel, should I let you ask me questions? As surely as I live, says the Lord GOD, I will not accept questions from you.

32 "'What you want will not come true. You say, "We want to be like the other nations, like the people in other lands. We want to worship idols made of wood and stone." **33** As surely as I live, says the Lord GOD, I will use my great power and strength and anger to rule over you. **34** I will bring you out from the foreign nations. With my great power and strength and anger I will gather you from the lands where you are scattered. **35** I will bring you among the nations as I brought your ancestors into the desert with Moses. There I will judge you face to face. **36** I will judge you the same way I judged your ancestors in the desert of the land of Egypt, says the Lord GOD. **37** I will count you like sheep and will bring you into line with my agreement. **38** I will get rid of those who refuse to obey me and who turn against me. I will bring them out of the land where they are now

> I am the LORD your God. Live by my rules, obey my laws and follow them.
> – Ezekiel 20:19

living, but they will never enter the land of Israel. Then you will know that I am the LORD.

39 "This is what the Lord GOD says: people of Israel, go and serve your idols for now. But later you will listen to me; you will not continue to dishonour my holy name with your gifts and gods. 40 On my holy mountain, the high mountain of Israel, all Israel will serve me in the land, says the Lord GOD. There I will accept you. There I will expect your offerings, the first harvest of your offerings, and all your holy gifts. 41 I will accept you like the pleasing smell of sacrifices when I bring you out from the foreign nations and gather you from the lands where you are scattered. Then through you I will show how holy I am so the nations will see. 42 When I bring you into the land of Israel, the land I promised your ancestors, you will know that I am the LORD. 43 There you will remember everything you did that made you unclean, and then you will hate yourselves for all the evil things you have done. 44 I will deal with you for the sake of my name, not because of your evil ways or unclean actions. Then you will know I am the LORD, people of Israel, says the Lord GOD.'"

Babylon, the LORD's Sword

45 Now the LORD spoke his word to me, saying: 46 "Human, look towards the south. Prophesy against the south and against the forest of the southern area. 47 Say to that forest: 'Hear the word of the LORD. This is what the Lord GOD says: I am ready to start a fire in you that will destroy all your green trees and all your dry trees. The flames that burn will not be put out. Every face from south to north will feel their heat. 48 Then all the people will see that I, the LORD, have started the fire. It will not be put out.'"

49 Then I said, "Ah, Lord GOD! The people are saying about me, 'He is only telling stories.'"

21 Then the LORD spoke his word to me, saying: 2 "Human, look towards Jerusalem and speak against the holy place. Prophesy against the land of Israel. 3 Say to Israel: 'This is what the LORD says: I am against you. I will pull my sword out of its holder, and I will cut off from you both the wicked and those who do right. 4 Because I am going to cut off the wicked and those who do right, my sword will come out from its holder and attack all people from south to north. 5 Then all people will know that I, the LORD, have pulled my sword out from its holder. My sword will not go back in again.'

6 "So, human, groan with a breaking heart and great sadness. Groan in front of the people. 7 When they ask you, 'Why are you groaning?' you will say, 'Because of what I have heard is going to happen. When it happens, every heart will melt with fear, and all hands will become weak. Everyone will be afraid; all knees will become weak as water. Look, it is coming, and it will happen, says the Lord GOD.'"

8 The LORD spoke his word to me, saying: 9 "Human, prophesy and say, 'This is what the Lord says:

A sword, a sword,
    made sharp and polished.
10 It is made sharp for the killing.
    It is polished to flash like lightning.

"'You are not happy about this horrible punishment by the sword. But my son Judah, you did not change when you were only beaten with a rod.
11 The sword should be polished.
    It is meant to be held in the hand.
    It is made sharp and polished,
    ready for the hand of a killer.
12 Shout and yell, human,
    because the sword is meant for my
      people,
    for all the rulers of Israel.
They will be killed by the sword,
    along with my people.
So beat your chest in sadness.

13 "'The test will come. And Judah, who is hated by the armies of Babylon, will not last, says the Lord GOD.'

14 "So, human, prophesy
    and clap your hands.
Let the sword strike
    two or three times.
It is a sword meant for killing,
    a sword meant for much killing.

This sword surrounds the people to be killed. 15 Their hearts will melt with fear, and many people will die. I have placed the killing sword at all their city gates. Oh! The sword is made to flash like lightning. It is held, ready for killing. 16 Sword, cut on the right side; then cut on the left side. Cut anywhere your blade is turned. 17 I will also clap my hands and use up my anger. I, the LORD, have spoken."

> Those who are important now will be made unimportant, and those who are unimportant now will be made important.
> – Ezekiel 21:26

Jerusalem to be Destroyed

18 The LORD spoke his word to me, saying: 19 "Human, mark two roads that the king of Babylon and his sword can follow. Both of these roads will start from the same country. And make signs where the road divides and one way goes towards the city. 20 Mark one sign to show the road he can take with his sword to Rabbah in the land of the Ammonites. Mark the other sign to show the road to Judah and Jerusalem, which is protected with strong walls. 21 The king of Babylon has come to where the road divides, and he is using magic. He throws lots with arrows and asks questions of his family idols. He looks at the liver of a sacrificed animal to learn where he should go. 22 The lot in his right hand tells him to go to Jerusalem. It tells him to use logs to break down the city gates, to shout the battle cry and give the order to kill, and to build a dirt road to the top of the walls and devices to attack the walls. 23 The people of Jerusalem have made agreements with other nations to help them fight Babylon. So they will think this prediction is wrong, but it is really proof of their sin, and they will be captured.

24 "So this is what the Lord GOD says: 'You have shown how sinful you are by turning against the LORD. Your sins are seen in all the things you do. Because of this proof against you, you will be taken captive by the enemy.

25 "'You unclean and evil leader of Israel, you will be killed! The time of your final punishment has come. 26 This is what the Lord GOD says: take off the royal turban and remove the crown. Things will change. Those who are important now will be made unimportant, and those who are unimportant now will be made important. 27 A ruin! A ruin! I will make it a ruin! This place will not be rebuilt until the one comes who has a right to be king. Then I will give him that right.'

The Punishment of Ammon

28 "And you, human, prophesy and say: 'This is what the Lord GOD says about the people of Ammon and their insults:
a sword, a sword
    is pulled out of its holder.
It is polished to kill and destroy,
    to flash like lightning!
29 Prophets see false visions about you
    and prophesy lies about you.
The sword will be put on the necks
    of these unclean and evil people.
Their day of judging has come;
    the time of final punishment has come.
30 Put the sword back in its holder.
I will judge you
    in the place where you were created,
    in the land where you were born.
31 I will pour out my anger against you
    and blast you with the fire of my anger.
I will hand you over to cruel men,
    experts in destruction.
32 You will be like fuel for the fire;
    you will die in the land.
You will not be remembered,
    because I, the LORD, have spoken.'"

The Sins of Jerusalem

22 The LORD spoke his word to me, saying: 2 "And you, human, will you judge? Will you judge the city of murderers? Then tell her about all her hateful acts. 3 You are to say: 'This is what the Lord GOD says: you are a city that kills those who come to live there. You make yourself unclean by making idols. 4 You have become guilty of murder and have become unclean by your idols which you have made. So you have brought your time of punishment near; you have come to the end of your years. That is why I have made you a shame to the nations and why all lands laugh at you. 5 Those near and those far away laugh at you with your bad name, you city full of confusion.

6 "'Jerusalem, see how each ruler of Israel in you has been trying to kill people. 7 The people in you hate their fathers and mothers. They mistreat the foreigners in you and wrong the orphans and widows in you. 8 You hate my holy things and dishonour my Sabbaths. 9 The men in you tell lies to cause the death of others. The people in you eat food offered to idols at the mountain places of worship, and they take part in sexual sins. 10 The men in you have sexual relations with their fathers' wives and with women who are unclean, during their time of monthly bleeding. 11 One man in you does a hateful act with his neighbour's wife, while another has shamefully made his daughter-in-law unclean sexually. And another forces his half-sister to have sexual relations with him. 12 The people in you take money to kill others. You take unfair interest and profits and make profits by mistreating your neighbour. And you have forgotten me, says the Lord GOD.

13 "'So, Jerusalem, I will shake my fist at you for stealing money and for murdering people. 14 Will you still be brave and strong when I punish you? I, the LORD, have spoken, and I will act. 15 I will scatter you among the nations and spread you through the countries. That is how I will get rid of your uncleanness. 16 But you, yourself, will be dishonoured in the sight of the nations. Then you will know that I am the LORD.'"

Israel is Worthless

17 The LORD spoke his word to me, saying: 18 "Human, the people of Israel have become useless like scum to me. They are like the copper, tin, iron and lead left in the furnace when silver is purified. 19 So this is what the Lord GOD says: 'Because you have become useless like scum, I am going to put you together inside Jerusalem. 20 People put silver, copper, iron, lead and tin together inside a furnace to melt them down in a blazing fire. In the same way I will gather you in my hot anger and put you together in Jerusalem and melt you down. 21 I will put you together and make you feel the heat of my anger. You will be melted down inside Jerusalem. 22 As silver is melted in a furnace, you will be melted inside the city. Then you will know that I, the LORD, have poured out my anger on you.'"

> I will put you together and make you feel the heat of my anger. You will be melted down inside Jerusalem.
> – Ezekiel 22:21

Sins of the People

23 The LORD spoke his word to me, saying: 24 "Human, say to the land, 'You are a land that has not had rain or showers when God is angry.' 25 Like a roaring lion that tears the animal it has caught, Israel's rulers make evil plans. They have destroyed lives and have taken treasure and valuable things. They have caused many women to become widows. 26 Israel's priests do cruel things to my teachings and do not honour my holy things. They make no difference between holy and unholy things, and they teach there is no difference between clean and unclean things. They do not remember my Sabbaths, so I am dishonoured by them. 27 Like wolves tearing a dead animal, Jerusalem's leaders have killed people for profit. 28 And the prophets try to cover

this up by false visions and by lying messages. They say, 'This is what the Lord GOD says' when the LORD has not spoken. 29 The people cheat others and steal. They hurt people who are poor and needy. They cheat foreigners and do not treat them fairly.

30 "I looked for someone to build up the walls and to stand before me where the walls are broken to defend these people, so I would not have to destroy them. But I could not find anyone. 31 So I let them see my anger. I destroyed them with an anger that was like fire because of all the things they have done, says the Lord GOD."

Samaria and Jerusalem

23 The LORD spoke his word to me, saying: 2 "Human, a woman had two daughters. 3 While they were young, they went to Egypt and became prostitutes. They let men touch and hold their breasts. 4 The older girl was named Oholah, and her sister was named Oholibah. They became my wives and had sons and daughters. Oholah is Samaria, and Oholibah is Jerusalem.*n*

5 "While still my wife, Samaria had sexual relations with other men. She had great sexual desire for her lovers, men from Assyria. The Assyrians were warriors and 6 wore blue uniforms. They were all handsome young captains and commanders riding on horseback. 7 Samaria became a prostitute for all the important men in Assyria and made herself unclean with all the idols of everyone she desired. 8 She continued the prostitution she began in Egypt. When she was young, she had slept with men, and they touched her breasts and had sexual relations with her.

9 "So I handed her over to her lovers, the Assyrians, that she wanted so badly. 10 They stripped her naked and took away her sons and daughters. Then they killed her with a sword. Women everywhere began talking about how she had been punished.

11 "Her sister Jerusalem saw what happened, but she became worse than her sister in her sexual desire and prostitution. 12 She also desired the Assyrians, who were all soldiers in beautiful uniforms—handsome young captains and commanders riding horses. 13 I saw that both girls were alike; both were prostitutes.

14 "But Jerusalem went even further. She saw carvings of Babylonian men on a wall. They wore red 15 and had belts around their waists and turbans on their heads. They all looked like chariot officers born in Babylonia. 16 When she saw them, she wanted to have sexual relations with them and sent messengers to them in Babylonia. 17 So these Babylonian men came and had sexual relations with her and made her unclean. After that, she became sick of them. 18 But she continued her prostitution so openly that everyone knew about it. And I finally became sick of her, as I had her sister. 19 But she remembered how she was a young prostitute in Egypt, so she took part in even more prostitution. 20 She wanted men who behaved like animals in their sexual desire. 21 In the same way you desired to do the sinful things you had done in Egypt. There men touched and held your young breasts.

God's Judgement on Jerusalem

22 "So, Jerusalem, this is what the Lord GOD says: you are tired of your lovers. So now I will make them angry with you and cause them to attack you from all sides. 23 Men from Babylon and all Babylonia and men from Pekod, Shoa and Koa will attack you. All the Assyrians will attack you: handsome young captains and commanders, all of them important men and all riding horses. 24 Those men will attack you with great armies and with their weapons, chariots and wagons. They will surround you with large and small shields and with helmets. And I will give them the right to punish you, and they will give you their own kind of punishment. 25 Then you will see how strong my anger can be when they punish you

---

23:4 Oholah . . . Jerusalem Throughout this chapter Samaria is used in place of Oholah, and Jerusalem is used in place of Oholibah.

ANCIENT WAR AND WEAPONS   Ezekiel 23:24

In Old Testament times, there were a lot of wars over land. The Israelites fought in many of these kinds of wars as they moved into the land that God had promised them. One of the most famous is the war that Joshua led the people in at Jericho. To the Israelites, this was a "holy war" that God called them to fight. In fact, Joshua told the priests and soldiers that the Lord had given them the city of Jericho. (See Joshua 6:16, p. 283.)

The Old Testament weapons used for wars were simple: the bow and arrow, the sling, the sword, the spear or lance, the battleaxe and some protective armour. By the time Solomon became king, armies also used horses for battle, as well as chariots to make their attacks more swift. (Read 1 Kings 10:26, p. 452.)

As the Israelites became a stronger nation and more able to protect themselves, they sometimes trusted more in their own strength than in God's strength. Many of the Old Testament prophets preached to the Israelites about placing their trust in their swords rather than in the Word of God. (Look at Jeremiah 39:18, p. 1048.)

in their anger. They will cut off your noses and ears. They will take away your sons and daughters, and those who are left will be burned. 26 They will take off your clothes and steal your jewellery. 27 I will put a stop to the sinful life you began when you were in Egypt so that you will not desire it or remember Egypt any more.

28 "This is what the Lord GOD says: you became tired of your lovers, but I am going to hand you over to those men you now hate. 29 They will treat you with hate and take away everything you worked for, leaving you empty and naked. Everyone will know about the sinful things you did. Your sexual sins 30 have brought this on you. You have had sexual relations with the nations and made yourselves unclean by worshipping their idols. 31 You did the same things your sister did, so you will get the same punishment, like a bitter cup to drink.

32 "This is what the Lord GOD says: you will drink the same cup your sister did,
and that cup is deep and wide.
Everyone will make fun of you,
because the cup is full.
33 It will make you miserable and drunk.
It is the cup of fear and ruin.
It is the cup of your sister Samaria.
34 You will drink everything in it,
and then you will smash it
and tear at your breasts.
I have spoken, says the Lord GOD.

35 "So this is what the Lord GOD says: you have forgotten me and turned your back on me. So you will be punished for your sexual sins."

Judgement on Samaria and Jerusalem

36 The LORD said to me: "Human, will you judge Samaria and Jerusalem, showing them their hateful acts? 37 They are guilty of adultery and murder. They have taken part in adultery with their idols.

They even offered our children as sacrifices in the fire to be food for these idols. 38 They have also done this to me: they made my Temple unclean and at the same time they dishonoured my Sabbaths. 39 They sacrificed their children to their idols. Then they entered my Temple at that very time to dishonour it. That is what they did inside my Temple!

40 "They even sent for men from far away, who came after a messenger was sent to them. The two sisters bathed themselves for them, painted their eyes and put on jewellery. 41 They sat on a fine bed with a table set before it, on which they put my incense and my oil.

42 "There was the noise of a reckless crowd in the city. Common people gathered, and drunkards were brought from the desert. They put bracelets on the wrists of the two sisters and beautiful crowns on their heads. 43 Then I said about the one who was worn out by her acts of adultery, 'Let them continue their sexual sins with her. She is nothing but a prostitute.' 44 They kept going to her as they would go to a prostitute. So they continued to go to Samaria and Jerusalem, these shameful women. 45 But men who do right will punish them as they punish women who take part in adultery and who murder people, because they are guilty of adultery and murder.

46 "This is what the Lord GOD says: bring together a mob against Samaria and Jerusalem, and hand them over to be frightened and robbed. 47 Let the mob kill them by throwing stones at them, and let them cut them down with their swords. Let them kill their sons and daughters and burn their houses down.

48 "So I will put an end to sexual sins in the land. Then all women will be warned, and they will not do the sexual sins you have done. 49 You will be punished for your sexual sins and the sin of worshipping idols. Then you will know that I am the Lord GOD."

The Pot and the Meat

24 The LORD spoke his word to me on the tenth day of the tenth month of the ninth year of our captivity. He said: 2 "Human, write down today's date, this very date. The king of Babylon has surrounded Jerusalem this very day. 3 And tell a story to the people who refuse to obey me. Say to them: 'This is what the Lord GOD says:

put on the pot; put it on
  and pour water in it.
4 Put in the pieces of meat,
  the best pieces—the legs and the shoulders.
Fill it with the best bones.
5 Take the best of the flock,
  and pile wood under the pot.
Boil the pieces of meat
  until even the bones are cooked.

6 "'This is what the Lord GOD says:
how terrible it will be for the city of murderers!
How terrible it will be for the rusty pot
  whose rust will not come off!
Take the meat out of it, piece by piece.
Don't choose any special piece.

7 "'The blood from her killings is still in the city.
She poured the blood on the bare rock.
She did not pour it on the ground
  where dust would cover it.
8 To stir up my anger and revenge,
I put the blood she spilled on the bare rock
so it will not be covered.

9 "'So this is what the Lord GOD says:
How terrible it will be for the city of murderers!
I myself will pile the wood high for burning.
10 Pile up the wood
  and light the fire.
Finish cooking the meat.
Mix in the spices,
  and let the bones burn.
11 Then set the empty pot on the coals
  so it may become hot and its copper sides glow.
The dirty scum stuck inside it may then melt

and its rust burn away. 12 But efforts to clean the pot have failed. Its heavy rust cannot be removed, even in the fire.

13 "'By your sinful action you have become unclean. I wanted to cleanse you, but you are still unclean. You will never be cleansed from your sin until my anger against you is carried out.

14 "'I, the LORD, have spoken. The time has come for me to act. I will not hold back punishment or feel pity or change my mind. I will judge you by your ways and actions, says the Lord GOD.'"

> I will judge you by your ways and actions, says the Lord GOD.
> – Ezekiel 24:14

The Death of Ezekiel's Wife

15 Then the LORD spoke his word to me, saying: 16 "Human, I am going to take your wife from you, the woman you look at with love. She will die suddenly, but you must not be sad or cry loudly for her or shed any tears. 17 Groan silently; do not cry loudly for the dead. Tie on your turban, and put your sandals on your feet. Do not cover your face, and do not eat the food people eat when they are sad about a death."

18 So I spoke to the people in the morning, and my wife died in the evening. The next morning I did as I had been commanded.

19 Then the people asked me, "Tell us, what do the things you are doing mean for us?"

20 Then I said to them, "The LORD spoke his word to me. He said, 21 'Say to the people of Israel, this is what the Lord GOD says: I am going to dishonour my Temple. You think it gives you strength. You are proud of it, and you look at it with love and tenderness. But your sons and daughters that you left behind in Jerusalem will fall dead by the sword. 22 When that happens, you are to act as I have: you are not to cover your face, and you are not to eat the food people eat when they are sad about a death. 23 Your turbans must stay on your heads, and your sandals on your feet. You must not cry loudly, but you must rot away in your sins and groan to each other. 24 So Ezekiel is to be an example for you. You must do all the same things he did. When all this happens, you will know that I am the Lord GOD.'

25 "And as for you, human, this is how it will be. I will take away the Temple that gives them strength and joy, that makes them proud. They look at it with love, and it makes them happy. And I will take away their sons and daughters also. 26 At that time a person who escapes will come to you with information for you to hear. 27 At that very time your mouth will be opened. You will speak and be silent no more. So you will be a sign for them, and they will know that I am the LORD."

Prophecy Against Ammon

25 The LORD spoke his word to me, saying: 2 "Human, look towards the people of Ammon and prophesy against them. 3 Say to them, 'Hear the word of the Lord GOD. This is what the Lord GOD says: you were glad when my Temple was dishonoured, when the land of Israel was ruined and when the people of Judah were taken away as captives. 4 So I am going to give you to the people of the East to be theirs. They will set up their camps among you and make their homes among you. They will eat your fruit and drink your milk. 5 I will make the city of Rabbah a pasture for camels and the land of Ammon a resting place for sheep. Then you will know that I am the LORD. 6 This is what the Lord GOD says: you have clapped your hands and stamped your feet; you have laughed about all the insults you made against the land of Israel. 7 So I will use my power against you. I will give you to the nations as if you were treasures taken in war. I will wipe you out of the lands so you will no longer

be a nation, and I will destroy you. Then you will know that I am the LORD.'

Prophecy Against Moab and Edom

8 "This is what the Lord GOD says: 'Moab and Edom say, "The people of Judah are like all the other nations." 9 So I am going to take away the cities that protect Moab's borders, the best cities in that land: Beth Jeshimoth, Baal Meon and Kiriathaim. 10 Then I will give Moab, along with the Ammonites, to the people of the East as their possession. Then, along with the Ammonites, Moab will not be a nation any more. 11 So I will punish the people of Moab, and they will know that I am the LORD.'

Prophecy Against Edom

12 "This is what the Lord GOD says: 'Edom took revenge on the people of Judah, and the Edomites became guilty because of it. 13 So this is what the Lord GOD says: I will use my power against Edom, killing every human and animal in it. And I will destroy Edom all the way from Teman to Dedan as they die in battle. 14 I will use my people Israel to take revenge on Edom. So the Israelites will do to Edom what my hot anger demands. Then the Edomites will know what my revenge feels like, says the Lord GOD.'

Prophecy Against Philistia

15 "This is what the Lord GOD says: 'The Philistines have taken revenge with hateful hearts. Because of their strong hatred, they have tried to destroy Judah. 16 So this is what the Lord GOD says: I will use my power against the Philistines. I will kill the Kerethites, and I will destroy those people still alive on the coast of the Mediterranean Sea. 17 I will punish them in my anger and do great acts of revenge to them. They will know that I am the LORD when I take revenge on them.'"

> So I will use my power against you. I will give you to the nations as if you were treasures taken in war.
> – Ezekiel 25:7

Prophecy Against Tyre

26 It was the eleventh year of our captivity, on the first day of the month. The LORD spoke his word to me, saying: 2 "Human, the city of Tyre has spoken against Jerusalem: 'The city that traded with the nations is destroyed. Now we can be the trading centre. Since the city of Jerusalem is ruined, we can make money.' 3 So this is what the Lord GOD says: I am against you, Tyre. I will bring many nations against you, like the sea beating its waves on your island shores. 4 They will destroy the walls of Tyre and pull down her towers. I will also scrape away her ruins and make her a bare rock. 5 Tyre will be an island where fishermen dry their nets. I have spoken, says the Lord GOD. The nations will steal treasures from Tyre. 6 Also, her villages on the shore across from the island will be destroyed by war. Then they will know that I am the LORD.

Nebuchadnezzar to Attack Tyre

7 "This is what the Lord GOD says: I will bring a king from the north against Tyre. He is Nebuchadnezzar king of Babylon, the greatest king, with his horses, chariots, horsemen and a great army. 8 He will fight a battle and destroy your villages on the shore across from the island. He will set up devices to attack you. He will build a road of earth to the top of the walls. He will raise his shields against you. 9 He will bring logs to pound through your city walls, and he will break down your towers with his iron bars. 10 His horses will be so many that they will cover you with their dust. Your walls will shake at the noise of horsemen, wagons and chariots. The king of Babylon will enter your city gates as men enter a city where the walls are broken through. 11 The hoofs of his horses will run over your streets. He will kill your army with the sword, and your strong pillars will fall down to the ground. 12 Also, his men will

take away your riches and will steal the things you sell. They will break down your walls and destroy your nice houses. They will throw your stones, wood and rubbish into the sea. 13 So I will stop your songs; the music of your harps will not be heard any more. 14 I will make you a bare rock, and you will be a place for drying fishing nets. You will not be built again, because I, the LORD, have spoken, says the Lord GOD.

15 "This is what the Lord GOD says to Tyre: the people who live along the sea coast will shake with fear when they hear about your defeat. Those of you who are injured and dying will groan. 16 Then all the leaders of the sea coast will get down from their thrones, take off their beautiful needlework clothes and show how afraid they are. They will sit on the ground and tremble all the time. When they see you, they will be shocked. 17 They will begin singing a funeral song about you and will say to you:

'Tyre, you famous city, you have been destroyed!
You have lost your sea power!
You and your people
had great power on the seas.
You made everyone around you
afraid of you.
18 Now the people who live by the coast tremble,
now that you have fallen.
The islands of the sea
are afraid because you have been defeated.'

19 "This is what the Lord GOD says: I will make you an empty city, like cities that have no people living in them. I will bring the deep ocean waters over you, and the Mediterranean Sea will cover you. 20 At that time I will send you down to the place of the dead to join those who died long ago. I will make you live with the dead below the earth in places that are like old ruins. You will not come back from there or have any place in the world of the living again. 21 Other people will be afraid of what happened to you, and it will be the end of you. People will look for you, but they will never find you again, says the Lord GOD."

A Funeral Song for Tyre

27 The LORD spoke his word to me, saying: 2 "Human, sing a funeral song for the city of Tyre. 3 Speak to Tyre, which has ports for the Mediterranean Sea and is a place for trade for the people of many lands along the sea coast. 'This is what the Lord GOD says:

Tyre, you have said,
"I am like a beautiful ship."
4 You were at home on the high seas.
Your builders made your beauty perfect.
5 They made all your boards
of fir trees from Mount Hermon.
They took a cedar tree from Lebanon
to make a ship's mast for you.
6 They made your oars
from oak trees from Bashan.
They made your deck
from cypress trees from the coast of Cyprus
and set ivory into it.
7 Your sail of linen with designs sewed on it came from Egypt
and became like a flag for you.
Your cloth shades over the deck were blue and purple
and came from the island of Cyprus.
8 Men from Sidon and Arvad used oars to row you.
Tyre, your skilled men were the sailors on your deck.
9 Workers of Byblos were with you,
putting caulk[n] in your ship's seams.
All the ships of the sea and their sailors
came alongside to trade with you.

10 "'Men of Persia, Lydia and Put
were warriors in your army
and hung their shields and helmets on your sides.
They made you look beautiful.
11 Men of Arvad and Cilicia
guarded your city walls all around.
Men of Gammad
were in your watchtowers

27:9 **caulk** Something like tar put between the boards of a ship to make it waterproof.

Ezekiel 27:23 **1117**

LET'S VISIT DAMASCUS   Ezekiel 27:18

Damascus, the current capital of Syria, is one of the oldest cities still existing in the world. A man named Uz (his great granddad was Noah) founded the city of Damascus. Damascus is near a lot of main highways, and so it is called a "trade centre". That means people go there to buy and sell things. Damask, a type of woven cloth, was the most important item sold there in Old Testament times. (See Ezekiel 27:18–19.) That might be where Damascus got its name.

Whenever Damascus is mentioned in the New Testament, it has to do with the apostle Paul. He was on his way to Damascus to persecute Christians. Suddenly, the Lord was revealed to him in a bright flash of light that left him blind. Once he got to Damascus, God used a man named Ananias to heal him of the blindness. Paul became a Christian because of this experience; and instead of tormenting the Christians, he preached to them. (Check out the story in Acts 9:1–24, p. 1478.)

and hung their shields around your walls.
They made your beauty perfect.

12 "People of Tarshish became traders for you because of your great wealth. They traded your goods for silver, iron, tin and lead.

13 "People of Greece, Tubal and Meshech became merchants for you. They traded your goods for slaves and things of bronze.

14 "People of Beth Togarmah traded your goods for work horses, war horses and mules.

15 "People of Rhodes became merchants for you, selling your goods on many coastal lands. They brought back ivory tusks and valuable black wood as your payment.

16 "People of Aram became traders for you, because you had so many good things to sell. They traded your goods for turquoise, purple cloth, cloth with designs sewed on, fine linen, coral and rubies.

17 "People of Judah and Israel became merchants for you. They traded your goods for wheat from Minnith, and for honey, olive oil and balm.

18-19 "People of Damascus became traders for you because you have many good things and great wealth. They traded your goods for wine from Helbon, wool from Zahar and barrels of wine from Izal. They received wrought iron, cassia and sugar cane in payment for your good things.

20 "People of Dedan became merchants for you, trading saddle blankets for riding.

21 "People of Arabia and all the rulers of Kedar became traders for you. They received lambs, rams and goats in payment for you.

22 "The merchants of Sheba and Raamah became merchants for you. They traded your goods for all the best spices, valuable gems and gold.

23 "People of Haran, Canneh and Eden and the traders of Sheba, Asshur

and Kilmad became merchants for you. 24 They were paid with the best clothes, blue cloth, cloth with designs sewed on, carpets of many colours and tightly wound ropes.

25 "Trading ships
  carried the things you sold.
 You were like a ship full of heavy cargo
  in the middle of the sea.
26 The men who rowed you
  brought you out into the high seas,
 but the east wind broke you to pieces
  in the middle of the sea.
27 Your wealth, your trade, your goods,
  your seamen, your sailors, your workers,
 your traders, your warriors
  and everyone else on board
 sank into the sea
  on the day your ship was wrecked.
28 The people on the shore shake with fear
  when your sailors cry out.
29 All the men who row
  leave their ships;
 the seamen and the sailors of other ships
  stand on the shore.
30 They cry loudly about you;
  they cry very much.
 They throw dust on their heads
  and roll in ashes to show they are sad.
31 They shave their heads for you,
  and they put on rough cloth to show they are upset.
 They cry and sob for you;
  they cry loudly.
32 And in their loud crying
  they sing a funeral song for you:
 "No one was ever destroyed like Tyre,
  surrounded by the sea."
33 When the goods you traded went out over the seas,
  you met the needs of many nations.
 With your great wealth and goods,
  you made kings of the earth rich.
34 But now you are broken by the sea
  and have sunk to the bottom.
 Your goods and all the people on board

have gone down with you.
35 All those who live along the shore
  are shocked by what happened to you.
 Their kings are terribly afraid,
  and their faces show their fear.
36 The traders among the nations hiss at you.
 You have come to a terrible end,
  and you are gone for ever.'"

Prophecy Against the King of Tyre

28 The LORD spoke his word to me, saying: 2 "Human, say to the ruler of Tyre: 'This is what the Lord GOD says:
  because you are proud,
   you say, "I am a god.
  I sit on the throne of a god
   in the middle of the seas."
  You think you are as wise as a god,
   but you are a human, not a god.
 3 You think you are wiser than Daniel.
   You think you can find out all secrets.
 4 Through your wisdom and understanding
   you have made yourself rich.
  You have gained gold and silver
   and have saved it in your storerooms.
 5 Through your
   great skill in
   trading,
   you have
   made your
   riches grow.
  You are too proud
   because of your riches.

28:5
Talents
Beware of the talent trap.

6 "'So this is what the Lord GOD says:
 you think you are wise
  like a god,
7 but I will bring foreign people against you,
  the cruellest nation.
 They will pull out their swords
  and destroy all that your wisdom has built,
 and they will dishonour your greatness.
8 They will kill you;
  you will die a terrible death

like those who are killed at sea.
9 While they are killing you,
   you will not be able to say any
      more, "I am a god."
You will be only a human, not a god,
   when your murderers kill you.
10 You will die like an unclean person;
   foreigners will kill you.

I have spoken, says the Lord GOD.'"

11 The LORD spoke his word to me, saying: 12 "Human, sing a funeral song for the king of Tyre. Say to him: 'This is what the Lord GOD says:
   You were an example of what was
      perfect,
      full of wisdom and perfect in
         beauty.
13 You had a wonderful life,
      as if you were in Eden, the garden
         of God.
   Every valuable gem was on you:
      ruby, topaz and emerald,
      yellow quartz, onyx and jasper,
      sapphire, turquoise and chrysolite.
   Your jewellery was made of gold.
   It was prepared on the day you
      were created.
14 I appointed a living creature to guard
      you.
      I put you on the holy mountain of
         God.
      You walked among the gems that
         shone like fire.
15 Your life was right and good
      from the day you were created,
      until evil was found in you.
16 Because you traded with countries far
         away,
      you learned to be cruel, and you
         sinned.
   So I threw you down in disgrace from
      the mountain of God.
   And the living creature who
      guarded you
      forced you out from among the
         gems that shone like fire.
17 You became too proud
      because of your beauty.
   You ruined your wisdom
      because of your greatness.
   I threw you down to the ground.
   Your example taught a lesson to
      other kings.
18 You dishonoured your places of
      worship
      through your many sins and
         dishonest trade.
   So I set on fire the place where you
      lived,
      and the fire burned you up.
   I turned you into ashes on the ground
      for all those watching to see.
19 All the nations who knew you
      are shocked about you.
   Your punishment was so terrible,
      and you are gone for ever.'"

Prophecy Against Sidon

20 The LORD spoke his word to me, saying: 21 "Human, look towards the city of Sidon and prophesy against her. 22 Say: 'This is what the Lord GOD says:
   I am against you, Sidon,
      and I will show my glory among
         you.
   People will know that I am the LORD
      when I have punished Sidon;
      I will show my holiness by
         defeating her.
23 I will send diseases to Sidon,
      and blood will flow in her streets.
   Those who are wounded in Sidon will
      fall dead,
      attacked from all sides.
   Then they will know that I am the
      LORD.

God will Help Israel

24 "'No more will neighbouring nations be like thorny branches or sharp thorns to hurt Israel. Then they will know that I am the Lord GOD.

25 "'This is what the Lord GOD says: I will gather the people of Israel from the nations where they are scattered. I will show my holiness when the nations see what I do for my people. Then they will live in their own land—the land I gave to my servant Jacob. 26 They will live safely in the land and will build houses and plant vineyards. They will live in safety after I have punished all the nations around who hate them. Then they will know that I am the LORD their God.'"

Ezekiel 29:1 1120

| A HARD PLACE |
| EZEKIEL 28:25-26 |

Has your mum or dad ever punished you by grounding you or taking away some other privilege? That's what's known as being in a hard place. Even though you were being punished, perhaps your mum or dad tried to lighten your load by holding out a ray of hope. That's what Ezekiel gave the Israelites. Their sin had earned them a punishment. They were dragged off to a foreign land. But God promised that he would bring them back to their own land someday.

Even when we fail and earn our own punishment, God doesn't leave us in a hard place. He provides hope.

The Perfect Leader? Numbers 20:1–13, p. 203

A Pity Party, Job 10, p. 671

A Swarm of Trouble, Joel 2:25–27, p. 1190

The Sin Habit, Romans 7:15–20, p. 1527

Blessed Are the Weak? 2 Corinthians 12:7–10, p. 1582

You're Correct! Hebrews 12:5–7, p. 1683

Prophecy Against Egypt

29 It was the twelfth day, of the tenth month, in the tenth year of our captivity. The LORD spoke his word to me, saying: 2 "Human, look towards the king of Egypt, and prophesy against him and all Egypt. 3 Say: 'This is what the Lord GOD says:

I am against you, king of Egypt.
You are like a great crocodile that
    lies in the Nile River.
You say, "The Nile is mine;
    I made it for myself."
4 But I will put hooks in your jaws,
    and I will make the fish of the Nile
        stick to your sides.
I will pull you up out of your rivers,
    with all the fish sticking to your
        sides.
5 I will leave you in the desert,
    you and all the fish from your
        rivers.
You will fall onto the ground;
    you will not be picked up or buried.
I have given you to the wild animals
    and to the birds of the sky for food.
6 Then all the people who live in Egypt will know that I am the LORD.

"'Israel tried to lean on you for help, but you were like a crutch made out of a weak stalk of grass. 7 When their hands grabbed you, you splintered and tore open their shoulders. When they leaned on you, you broke and made all their backs twist.

8 "'So this is what the Lord GOD says: I will cause an enemy to attack you and kill your people and animals. 9 Egypt will become an empty desert. Then they will know that I am the LORD.

"'Because you said, "The Nile River is mine, and I have made it," 10 I am against you and your rivers. I will destroy the land of Egypt and make it an empty desert from Migdol in the north to Aswan in the south, all the way to the border of Cush. 11 No person or animal will walk through it, and no one will live in Egypt for 40 years. 12 I will make the land of Egypt the most deserted country of all. Her cities will be the most deserted of all ruined cities for 40 years. I will scatter the Egyptians among the nations, spreading them among the countries.

13 "'This is what the Lord GOD says: after 40 years I will gather Egypt from the nations where they have been scattered. 14 I will bring back the Egyptian captives

THE KINGS OF EGYPT
Ezekiel 29:1–16

Another name for the kings of Egypt was *Pharaoh*. *Pharaoh* really means "great house" and was originally used to describe the king's palace, but as people used it, it came to mean something like "his honour" or "his majesty". The king of Egypt had a lot of power. By the rules of Egyptian government, the king owned everything in the land. The Egyptians believed that the kings would go on to rule the underworld after their deaths. That's part of the reason why the Egyptians took so much trouble to bury kings a certain way. Mummies were often kings who were buried in fancy, beautifully decorated graves along with their belongings.

In all, there were 30 different generations of Pharaohs in Egypt. Many people from the Bible dealt with a king of Egypt. Abraham's wife was called to the king's palace. (See Genesis 12:14–20, p. 18.) Solomon married the daughter of a king of Egypt. (Look at 1 Kings 3:1, p. 438.) Probably the most famous is the king of Egypt who wouldn't let Moses take the Israelites out of Egypt until he and his countrymen had suffered ten plagues. (Check out Exodus 12:29–33, p. 92.)

and make them return to southern Egypt, to the land they came from. They will become a weak kingdom there. **15** It will be the weakest kingdom, and it will never again rule other nations. I will make it so weak it will never again rule over the nations. **16** The Israelites will never again depend on Egypt. Instead, Egypt's punishment will remind the Israelites of their sin in turning to Egypt for help. Then they will know that I am the Lord GOD.'"

Egypt is Given to Babylon

17 It was the first day of the first month of the twenty-seventh year of our captivity. The LORD spoke his word to me, saying: **18** "Human, Nebuchadnezzar king of Babylon made his army fight hard against Tyre. Every soldier's head was rubbed bare and every shoulder was rubbed raw. But Nebuchadnezzar and his army gained nothing from fighting Tyre. **19** So this is what the Lord GOD says: I will give the land of Egypt to Nebuchadnezzar king of Babylon. He will take away Egypt's people and its wealth and its treasures as pay for his army. **20** I am giving Nebuchadnezzar the land of Egypt as a reward for working hard for me, says the Lord GOD.

21 "At that time I will make Israel grow strong again, and I will let you, Ezekiel, speak to them. Then they will know that I am the LORD."

Egypt will be Punished

30 The LORD spoke his word to me, saying: **2** "Human, prophesy and say, 'This is what the Lord GOD says:
Cry and say,
"The terrible day is coming."
3 The day is near;
the LORD's day of judging is near.
It is a cloudy day
and a time when the nations will be judged.
4 An enemy will attack Egypt,
and Cush will tremble with fear.

When the killing begins in Egypt,
  her wealth will be taken away,
  and her foundations will be torn
    down.
5 Cush, Put, Lydia, Arabia, Libya and some of my people who had made an agreement with Egypt will fall dead in war.
6 "This is what the Lord says:
  those who fight on
    Egypt's side will
    fall.
  The power she is
    proud of will be
    lost.
  The people in Egypt
    will fall dead in
    war
  from Migdol in the
    north to Aswan in the south,
  says the Lord God.
7 They will be the most deserted
    lands.
  Egypt's cities will be the worst of
    cities that lie in ruins.
8 Then they will know that I am the
    Lord
  when I set fire to Egypt
  and when all those nations on her
    side are crushed.
9 "At that time I will send messengers in ships to frighten Cush, which now feels safe. The people of Cush will tremble with fear when Egypt is punished. And that time is sure to come.
10 "This is what the Lord God says:
  I will destroy great numbers of
    people in Egypt
  through the power of
    Nebuchadnezzar king of
    Babylon.
11 Nebuchadnezzar and his army,
  the cruellest army of any
    nation,
  will be brought in to destroy the
    land.
  They will pull out their swords
    against Egypt
  and will fill the land with those they
    kill.
12 I will make the streams of the Nile
    River become dry land,
  and then I will sell the land to evil
    people.
  I will destroy the land and everything
    in it
  through the power of foreigners.
  I, the Lord, have spoken.

Egypt's Idols are Destroyed

13 "This is what the Lord God says:
  I will destroy the
    idols
  and take away the
    statues of gods
    from the city of
    Memphis.
  There will no longer
    be a leader in
    Egypt,
  and I will spread fear through the
    land of Egypt.
14 I will make southern Egypt empty
  and start a fire in Zoan
  and punish Thebes.
15 And I will pour out my anger against
    Pelusium,
  the stronghold of Egypt.
  I will destroy great numbers of
    people in Thebes.
16 I will set fire to Egypt.
  Pelusium will be in great pain.
  The walls of Thebes will be broken
    open,
  and Memphis will have troubles
    every day.
17 The young men of Heliopolis and
    Bubastis
  will fall dead in war,
  and the people will be taken away
    as captives.
18 In Tahpanhes the day will be dark
  when I break Egypt's power.
  Then she will no longer be proud
    of her power.
  A cloud will cover Egypt,
  and her villages will be captured
    and taken away.
19 So I will punish Egypt,
  and they will know I am the
    Lord.'"

> This is what the Lord says: those who fight on Egypt's side will fall. The power she is proud of will be lost.
> – Ezekiel 30:6

Egypt Becomes Weak

20 It was in the eleventh year of our captivity, in the first month, on the seventh day of the month. The LORD spoke his word to me, saying: 21 "Human, I have broken the powerful arm of the king of Egypt. It has not been tied up, so it will not get well. It has not been wrapped with a bandage, so it will not be strong enough to hold a sword in war. 22 So this is what the Lord GOD says: I am against the king of Egypt. I will break his arms, both the strong arm and the broken arm, and I will make the sword fall from his hand. 23 I will scatter the Egyptians among the nations, spreading them among the countries. 24 I will make the arms of the king of Babylon strong and put my sword in his hand. But I will break the arms of the king of Egypt. Then when he faces the king of Babylon, he will cry out in pain like a dying person. 25 So I will make the arms of the king of Babylon strong, but the arms of the king of Egypt will fall. Then people will know that I am the LORD when I put my sword into the hand of the king of Babylon and he uses it in war against Egypt. 26 Then I will scatter the Egyptians among the nations, spreading them among the countries. Then they will know that I am the LORD."

A Cedar Tree

31 It was on the first day of the third month of the eleventh year of our captivity. The LORD spoke his word to me, saying: 2 "Human, say to the king of Egypt and his people:
'No one is like you in your greatness.
3 Assyria was once like a cedar tree in
  Lebanon
    with beautiful branches that
      shaded the forest.
It was very tall;
  its top was among the clouds.
4 Much water made the tree grow;
  the deep springs made it tall.
Rivers flowed
  around the bottom of the tree
  and sent their streams
    to all other trees in the
      countryside.
5 So the tree was taller
  than all the other trees in the
    countryside.
Its limbs became long and big
  because of so much water.
6 All the birds of the sky
  made their nests in the tree's limbs.
And all the wild animals
  gave birth under its branches.
All great nations
  lived in the tree's shade.
7 So the tree was great and beautiful,
  with its long branches,
  because its roots reached down to
    much water.
8 The cedar trees in the garden of God
  were not as great as it was.
The pine trees
  did not have such great limbs.
The plane trees
  did not have such branches.
No tree in the garden of God
  was as beautiful as this tree.
9 I made it beautiful
  with many branches,
  and all the trees of Eden in the
    garden of God
    wanted to be like it.

10 "So this is what the Lord GOD says: the tree grew tall. Its top reached the clouds, and it became proud of its height. 11 So I handed it over to a mighty ruler of the nations for him to punish it. Because it was evil, I got rid of it. 12 The cruellest foreign nation cut it down and left it. The tree's branches fell on the mountains and in all the valleys, and its broken limbs were in all the ravines of the land. All the nations of the earth left the shade of that tree. 13 The birds of the sky live on the fallen tree. The wild animals live among the tree's fallen branches. 14 So the trees that grow by the water will not be proud to be tall; they will not put their tops among the clouds. None of the trees that are watered well will grow that tall, because they all are meant to die and go under the ground. They will be with people who have died and have gone down to the place of the dead.

15 "This is what the Lord GOD says: on the day when the tree went down to the

place of the dead, I made the deep springs cry loudly. I covered them and held back their rivers, and the great waters stopped flowing. I dressed Lebanon in black to show her sadness about the great tree, and all the trees in the countryside were sad about it. 16 I made the nations shake with fear at the sound of the tree falling when I brought it down to the place of the dead. It went to join those who have gone down to the grave. Then all the trees of Eden and the best trees of Lebanon, all the well-watered trees, were comforted in the place of the dead below the earth. 17 These trees had also gone down with the great tree to the place of the dead. They joined those who were killed in war and those among the nations who had lived under the great tree's shade.

18 "So no tree in Eden is equal to you, Egypt, in greatness and honour, but you will go down to join the trees of Eden in the place below the earth. You will lie among unclean people, with those who were killed in war.

"'This is about the king of Egypt and all his people, says the Lord GOD.'"

A Funeral Song

32 It was on the first day of the twelfth month of the twelfth year of our captivity. The LORD spoke his word to me, saying: 2 "Human, sing a funeral song about the king of Egypt. Say to him:
'You are like a young lion among the nations.
You are like a crocodile in the seas.
You splash around in your streams and stir up the water with your feet,
making the rivers muddy.

3 "'This is what the Lord GOD says:
I will spread my net over you,
and I will use a large group of people
to pull you up in my net.

4 Then I will throw you on the land
dropping you onto the ground.
I will let the birds of the sky rest on you
and all the animals of the earth eat you until they are full.
5 I will scatter your flesh on the mountains
and fill the valleys with what is left of you.
6 I will drench the land with your flowing blood
as far as the mountains,
and the ravines will be full of your flesh.
7 When I make you disappear,
I will cover the sky and make the stars dark.
I will cover the sun with a cloud,
and the moon will not shine.
8 I will make all the shining lights in the sky
become dark over you;
I will bring darkness over your land,
says the Lord GOD.
9 I will cause many people to be afraid
when I bring you as a captive into other nations,
to lands you have not known.
10 I will cause many people to be shocked about you.
Their kings will tremble with fear because of you
when I swing my sword in front of them.
They will shake every moment on the day you fall;
each king will be afraid for his own life.
11 "'So this is what the Lord GOD says:
the sword of the king of Babylon will attack you.
12 I will cause your people to fall by the swords of mighty soldiers,
the most terrible in the world.

> I will cause many people to be afraid when I bring you as a captive into other nations, to lands you have not known.
> – Ezekiel 32:9

They will destroy the pride of Egypt and all its people. 13 I will also destroy all Egypt's cattle which live alongside much water. The foot of a human will not stir the water, and the hoofs of cattle will not muddy it any more. 14 So I will let the Egyptians' water become clear. I will cause their rivers to run as smoothly as olive oil, says the Lord GOD. 15 When I make the land of Egypt empty and take everything that is in the land, when I destroy all those who live in Egypt, then they will know that I am the LORD.'

16 "This is the funeral song people will sing for Egypt. The women of the nations will sing it; they will sing a funeral song for Egypt and all its people, says the Lord GOD."

Egypt to be Destroyed

17 It was in the twelfth year of our captivity, on the fifteenth day of the month. The LORD spoke his word to me, saying: 18 "Human, cry for the people of Egypt. Bring down Egypt, together with the women of the powerful nations; bring them down to the place of the dead below the earth to join those who go to the place of the dead. 19 Say to them: 'Are you more beautiful than others? Go and lie down in death with those who are unclean.' 20 The Egyptians will fall among those killed in war. The sword is ready; the enemy will drag Egypt and all her people away. 21 From the place of the dead the leaders of the mighty ones will speak about the king of Egypt and the nations which help him: 'The unclean, those killed in war, have come down here and lie dead.'

22 "Assyria and all its army lie dead there. The graves of their soldiers are all around. All were killed in war, 23 and their graves were put in the deepest parts of the place of the dead. Assyria's army lies around its grave. When they lived on earth, they frightened people, but now all of them have been killed in war.

24 "The nation of Elam is there with all its army around its grave. All of them were killed in war. They had frightened people on earth and were unclean, so they went down to the lowest parts of the place of the dead. They must carry their shame with those who have gone down to the place of the dead. 25 A bed has been made for Elam with all those killed in war. The graves of her soldiers are all around her. All Elam's people are unclean, killed in war. They frightened people when they lived on earth, but now they must carry their shame with those who have gone down to the place of the dead. Their graves are with the rest who were killed.

26 "Meshech and Tubal are there with the graves of all their soldiers around them. All of them are unclean and have been killed in war. They also frightened people when they lived on earth. 27 But they are not buried with the other soldiers who were killed in battle long ago, those who went with their weapons of war to the place of the dead. These soldiers had their swords laid under their heads and their shields on their bodies. These mighty soldiers used to frighten people when they lived on earth.

28 "You, king of Egypt, will be broken and lie among those who are unclean, who were killed in war.

29 "Edom is there also, with its kings and all its leaders. They were mighty, but now they lie in death with those killed in war, with those who are unclean, with those who have gone down to the place of the dead.

30 "All the rulers of the north and all the Sidonians are there. Their strength frightened people, but they have gone down in shame with those who were killed. They are unclean, lying with those killed in war. They carry their shame with those who have gone down to the place of the dead.

31 "The king of Egypt and his army will see these who have been killed in war.

Then he will be comforted for all his soldiers killed in war, says the Lord GOD. 32 I made people afraid of the king of Egypt while he lived on earth. But he and all his people will lie among those who are unclean, who were killed in war, says the Lord GOD."

Ezekiel is Watchman for Israel

33 The LORD spoke his word to me, saying: 2 "Human, speak to your people and say to them: 'Suppose I bring a war against a land. The people of the land may choose one of their men and make him their watchman. 3 When he sees the enemy coming to attack the land, he will blow the trumpet and warn the people. 4 If they hear the sound of the trumpet but do nothing, the enemy will come and kill them. They will be responsible for their own deaths. 5 They heard the sound of the trumpet but didn't do anything. So they are to blame for their own deaths. If they had done something, they would have saved their own lives. 6 But if the watchman sees the enemy coming to attack and does not blow the trumpet, the people will not be warned. Then if the enemy comes and kills any of them, they have died because of their own sin. But I will punish the watchman for their deaths.'

7 "You, human, are the one I have made a watchman for Israel. If you hear a word from my mouth, you must warn them for me. 8 Suppose I say to the wicked: 'Wicked people, you will surely die,' but you don't speak to warn the wicked to stop doing evil. Then they will die because they were sinners, but I will punish you for their deaths. 9 But if you warn the wicked to stop doing evil and they do not stop, they will die because they were sinners. But you have saved your life.

10 "So you, human, say to Israel: 'You have said: surely our law-breaking and sins are hurting us. They will kill us. What can we do so we will live?' 11 Say to them: 'The Lord GOD says: as surely as I live, I do not want any who are wicked to die. I want them to stop doing evil and live. Stop! Stop your wicked ways! You don't want to die, do you, people of Israel?'

12 "Human, say to your people: 'The goodness of those who do right will not save them when they sin. The evil of wicked people will not cause them to be punished if they stop doing it. If good people sin, they will not be able to live by the good they did earlier.' 13 If I tell good people, "You will surely live," they might think they have done enough good and then do evil. Then none of the good things they did will be remembered. They will die because of the evil they have done. 14 Or, if I say to the wicked people, "You will surely die," they may stop sinning and do what is right and honest. 15 For example, they may return what somebody gave them as a promise to repay a loan, or pay back what they stole. If they live by the rules that give life and do not sin, then they will surely live, and they will not die. 16 They will not be punished for any of their sins. They now do what is right and fair, so they will surely live.

17 "Your people say: 'The way of the Lord is not fair.' But it is their own ways that are not fair. 18 When the good people stop doing good and do evil, they will die for their evil. 19 But when the wicked stop doing evil and do what is right and fair, they will live. 20 You still say: 'The way of the Lord is not fair.' Israel, I will judge all of you by your own ways."

The Fall of Jerusalem Explained

21 It was on the fifth day of the tenth month of the twelfth year of our captivity. A person who had escaped from Jerusalem came to me and said, "Jerusalem has been captured." 22 Now I had felt the power of the LORD on me the evening before. He had made me able to talk again before this person came to me. I could speak; I was not without speech any more.

23 Then the LORD spoke his word to me, saying: 24 "Human, people who live in the ruins in the land of Israel are saying: 'Abraham was only one person, yet he was given the land as his own.

EMAIL FROM GOD
33:1–6 Responsibility
Are you responsible to help others?

Surely the land has been given to us, who are many, as our very own.' 25 So say to them: 'This is what the Lord GOD says: you eat meat with the blood still in it, you ask your idols for help and you murder people. Should you then have the land as your very own? 26 You depend on your sword and do terrible things which I hate. Each of you has sexual relations with his neighbour's wife. So should you have the land?'

27 "Say to them: 'This is what the Lord GOD says: as surely as I live, those who are among the city ruins in Israel will be killed in war. I will cause those who live in the country to be eaten by wild animals. People hiding in the strongholds and caves will die of disease. 28 I will make the land an empty desert. The people's pride in the land's power will end. The mountains of Israel will become empty so that no one will pass through them. 29 They will know that I am the LORD when I make the land an empty desert because of the things they have done that I hate.'

30 "But as for you, human, your people are talking about you by the walls and in the doorways of houses. They say to each other: 'Come now, and hear the message from the LORD.' 31 So they come to you in crowds as if they were really ready to listen. They sit in front of you as if they were my people and hear your words, but they will not obey them. With their mouths they tell me they love me, but their hearts desire their selfish profits. 32 To your people you are nothing more than a singer who sings love songs and has a beautiful voice and plays a musical instrument well. They hear your words, but they will not obey them.

33 "When this comes true, and it surely will happen, then the people will know that a prophet has been among them."

The Leaders are like Shepherds

34 The LORD spoke his word to me, saying: 2 "Human, prophesy against the leaders of Israel, who are like shepherds. Prophesy and say to them: 'This is what the Lord GOD says: how terrible it will be for the shepherds of Israel who feed only themselves! Why don't the shepherds feed the flock? 3 You eat the milk curds, and you clothe yourselves with the wool. You kill the fat sheep, but you do not feed the flock. 4 You have not made the weak

---

FAITH links

EMPTY WORDS
EZEKIEL 33:30-33

Has anyone ever said they wanted to be your friend, but acted as if they didn't? God told Ezekiel that the Israelites claimed to listen to Ezekiel, but never planned to change the way they acted. Their words were empty. There was nothing behind them.

Actions should always follow words. If you tell God you want to follow his way, your actions should speak louder than your words. Don't just claim it; do it!

Are you a big talker, but don't back up your words with action? Link here:

A Use for Your Abilities, Genesis 41, p. 59

A Different Kind of People, Leviticus 11, p. 146

Your Stats, 1 Kings 15; 16, p. 460

Love Him? Show It! Amos 2:6-7, p. 1196

A Reminder to Do What Is Right and True, Zechariah 7:8-10, p. 1257

Obey or Disobey? Luke 20:20-26, p. 1409

strong. You have not healed the sick or put bandages on those that were hurt. You have not brought back those who strayed away or searched for the lost. But you have ruled the sheep with cruel force. 5 The sheep were scattered, because there was no shepherd, and they became food for every wild animal. 6 My flock wandered over all the mountains and on every high hill. They were scattered all over the face of the earth, and no one searched or looked for them.

7 "'So, you shepherds, hear the word of the LORD. This is what the Lord GOD says: 8 As surely as I live, my flock has been caught and eaten by all the wild animals, because the flock has no shepherd. The shepherds did not search for my flock. No, they fed themselves instead of my flock. 9 So, you shepherds, hear the word of the LORD. 10 This is what the Lord GOD says: I am against the shepherds. I will blame them for what has happened to my sheep and will not let them tend the flock any more. Then the shepherds will stop feeding themselves, and I will take my flock from their mouths so they will no longer be their food.

11 "'This is what the Lord GOD says: I, myself, will search for my sheep and take care of them. 12 As a shepherd takes care of his scattered flock when it is found, I will take care of my sheep. I will save them from all the places where they were scattered on a cloudy and dark day. 13 I will bring them out from the nations and gather them from the countries. I will bring them to their own land and pasture them on the mountains of Israel, in the ravines and in all the places where people live in the land. 14 I will feed them in a good pasture, and they will eat grass on the high mountains of Israel. They will lie down on good ground where they eat grass, and they will eat in rich grassland on the mountains of Israel. 15 I will feed my flock and lead them to rest, says the Lord GOD. 16 I will search for the lost, bring back those that strayed away, put bandages on those that were hurt and make the weak strong. But I will destroy those sheep that are fat and strong. I will tend the sheep with fairness.

17 "'This is what the Lord GOD says: as for you, my flock, I will judge between one sheep and another, between the rams and the male goats. 18 Is it not enough for you to eat grass in the good land? Must you crush the rest of the grass with your feet? Is it not enough for you to drink clear water? Must you make the rest of the water muddy with your feet? 19 Must my flock eat what you crush, and must they drink what you make muddy with your feet?

20 "'So this is what the Lord GOD says to them: I, myself, will judge between the fat sheep and the thin sheep. 21 You push with your side and with your shoulder, and you knock down all the weak sheep with your horns until you have forced them away. 22 So I will save my flock; they will not be hurt any more. I will judge between one sheep and another. 23 Then I will put over them one shepherd, my servant David. He will feed them and tend them and be their shepherd. 24 Then I, the LORD, will be their God, and my servant David will be a ruler among them. I, the LORD, have spoken.

25 "'I will make an agreement of peace with my sheep and will remove harmful animals from the land. Then the sheep will live safely in the desert and sleep in the woods. 26 I will bless them and let them live around my hill. I will cause the rains to come when it is time; there will be showers to bless them. 27 Also the trees in the countryside will give their fruit, and the land will give its harvest. And the sheep will be safe on their land. Then they will know that I am the LORD when I break the bars of their captivity and save them from the power of those who made them slaves. 28 They will not be led captive by the

> As a shepherd takes care of his scattered flock when it is found, I will take care of my sheep.
> – Ezekiel 34:12

nations again. The wild animals will not eat them, but they will live safely, and no one will make them afraid. 29 I will give them a place famous for its good crops, so they will no longer suffer from hunger in the land. They will not suffer the insults of other nations any more. 30 Then they will know that I, the LORD their God, am with them. The nation of Israel will know that they are my people, says the Lord GOD. 31 You, my human sheep, are the sheep I care for, and I am your God, says the Lord GOD.'"

Prophecy Against Edom

35 The LORD spoke his word to me, saying: 2 "Human, look towards Edom and prophesy against it. 3 Say to it: 'This is what the Lord GOD says: I am against you, Edom. I will stretch out my hand against you and make you an empty desert. 4 I will destroy your cities, and you will become empty. Then you will know that I am the LORD.

5 "'You have always been an enemy of Israel. You let them be defeated in war when they were in trouble at the time of their final punishment. 6 So the Lord GOD says, as surely as I live, I will let you be murdered. Murder will chase you. Since you did not hate murdering people, murder will chase you. 7 I will make Edom an empty ruin and destroy everyone who goes in or comes out of it. 8 I will fill its mountains with those who are killed. Those killed in war will fall on your hills, in your valleys and in all your ravines. 9 I will make you a ruin for ever; no one will live in your cities. Then you will know that I am the LORD.

10 "'You said, "These two nations, Israel and Judah, and these two lands will be ours. We will take them for our own." But the LORD was there. 11 So this is what the Lord GOD says: As surely as I live, I will treat you just as you treated them. You were angry and jealous because you hated them. So I will punish

35:11–12
Hate
Will people hate you because you love God?

you and show the Israelites who I am. 12 Then you will know that I, the LORD, have heard all your insults against the mountains of Israel. You said, "They have been ruined. They have been given to us to eat." 13 You have not stopped your proud talk against me. I have heard you. 14 This is what the Lord GOD says: all the earth will be happy when I make you an empty ruin. 15 You were happy when the land of Israel was ruined, but I will do the same thing to you. Mount Seir and all Edom, you will become an empty ruin. Then you will know that I am the LORD.'"

Israel to Come Home

36 "Human, prophesy to the mountains of Israel and say: 'Mountains of Israel, hear the word of the LORD. 2 This is what the Lord GOD says: the enemy has said about you, "Now the old places to worship gods have become ours."' 3 So prophesy and say: 'This is what the Lord GOD says: they have made you an empty ruin and have crushed you from all around. So you became a possession of the other nations. People have talked and whispered against you. 4 So, mountains of Israel, hear the word of the Lord GOD. The Lord GOD speaks to the mountains, hills, ravines and valleys, to the empty ruins and abandoned cities that have been robbed and laughed at by the other nations. 5 This is what the Lord GOD says: I speak in hot anger against the other nations. I speak against the people of Edom, who took my land for themselves with joy and with hate in their hearts. They forced out the people and took their pastureland.' 6 So prophesy about the land of Israel and say to the mountains, hills, ravines and valleys: 'This is what the Lord GOD says: I speak in my jealous anger, because you have suffered the insults of the nations. 7 So this is what the Lord GOD says: I promise that the nations around you will also have to suffer insults.

8 "'But you, mountains of Israel, will grow branches and fruit for my people, who will soon come home. 9 I am concerned about you; I am on your side. You

will be ploughed, and seed will be planted in you. 10 I will increase the number of people who live on you, all the people of Israel. The cities will have people living in them, and the ruins will be rebuilt. 11 I will increase the number of people and animals living on you. They will grow and have many young. You will have people living on you as you did before, and I will make you better off than at the beginning. Then you will know that I am the LORD. 12 I will cause my people Israel to walk on you and own you, and you will belong to them. You will never again take their children away from them.

13 "This is what the Lord GOD says: People say about you, "You eat people and take children from your nation." 14 But you will not eat people any more or take away the children, says the Lord GOD. 15 I will not make you listen to insults from the nations any more; you will not suffer shame from them any more. You will not cause your nation to fall any more, says the Lord GOD.'"

The LORD Acts for Himself

16 The LORD spoke his word to me again, saying: 17 "Human, when the nation of Israel was living in their own land, they made it unclean by their ways and the things they did. Their ways were like a woman's uncleanness in her time of monthly bleeding. 18 So I poured out my anger against them, because they murdered in the land and because they made the land unclean with their idols. 19 I scattered them among the nations, and they were spread through the countries. I punished them for how they lived and what they did. 20 They dishonoured my holy name in the nations where they went. The nations said about them: 'These are the people of the LORD, but they had to leave the land which he gave them.' 21 But I had concern for my holy name, which the nation of Israel had dishonoured among the nations where they went.

22 "So say to the people of Israel, 'This is what the Lord GOD says: Israel, I am going to act, but not for your sake. I will do something to help my holy name, which you have dishonoured among the nations where you went. 23 I will prove the holiness of my great name, which has been dishonoured among the nations. You have dishonoured it among these nations, but the nations will know that I am the LORD when I prove myself holy before their eyes, says the Lord GOD.

24 "'I will take you from the nations and gather you out of all the lands and bring you back into your own land. 25 Then I will sprinkle clean water on you, and you will be clean. I will cleanse you from all your uncleanness and your idols. 26 Also, I will teach you to respect me completely, and I will put a new way of thinking inside you. I will take out the stubborn hearts of stone from your bodies, and I will give you obedient hearts of flesh. 27 I will put my Spirit inside you and help you live by my rules and carefully obey my laws. 28 You will live in the land I gave to your ancestors, and you will be my people, and I will be your God. 29 So I will save you from all your uncleanness. I will command the grain to come and grow; I will not allow a time of hunger to hurt you. 30 I will increase the harvest of the field so you will never again suffer shame among the nations because of hunger. 31 Then you will remember your evil ways and actions that were not good, and you will hate yourselves because of your sins and your terrible acts that I hate. 32 I want you to know that I am not going to do this for your sake, says the Lord GOD. Be ashamed and embarrassed about your ways, Israel.

33 "'This is what the Lord GOD says: this is what will happen on the day I cleanse you from all your sins: I will cause the cities to have people living in them again, and the destroyed places will be rebuilt. 34 The empty land will be ploughed so it will no longer be a ruin for everyone who passes by to see. 35 They will say, "This land was ruined, but now it has become like the garden of Eden. The cities were destroyed, empty and ruined,

> **eMAIL FROM GOD**
> **36:20–21**
> **Following God**
> Does God care about his name?

but now they are protected and have people living in them." 36 Then those nations still around you will know that I, the LORD, have rebuilt what was destroyed and have planted what was empty. I, the LORD, have spoken, and I will do it.'

36:36 Belief
Find out if God means what he says.

37 "This is what the Lord GOD says: I will let myself be asked by the people of Israel to do this for them again: I will make their people grow in number like a flock. 38 They will be as many as the flocks brought to Jerusalem during her holy feasts. Her ruined cities will be filled with flocks of people. Then they will know that I am the LORD."

The Vision of Dry Bones

37 I felt the power of the LORD on me, and he brought me out by the Spirit of the LORD and put me down in the middle of a valley. It was full of bones. 2 He led me around among the bones, and I saw that there were many bones in the valley and that they were very dry. 3 Then he asked me, "Human, can these bones live?"

I answered, "Lord GOD, only you know."

4 He said to me, "Prophesy to these bones and say to them, 'Dry bones, hear the word of the LORD. 5 This is what the Lord GOD says to the bones: I will cause breath to enter you so you will come to life. 6 I will put muscles on you and flesh on you and cover you with skin. Then I will put breath in you so you will come to life. Then you will know that I am the LORD.'"

7 So I prophesied as I was commanded. While I prophesied, there was a noise and a rattling. The bones came together, bone to bone. 8 I looked and saw muscles come on the bones, and flesh grew and skin covered the bones. But there was no breath in them.

9 Then he said to me, "Prophesy to the wind.ⁿ Prophesy, human, and say to the wind, 'This is what the Lord GOD says: wind, come from the four winds, and

FAITH links

BELIEVE THE IMPOSSIBLE?
EZEKIEL 37

In *Through the Looking Glass*, the sequel to *Alice in Wonderland*, the White Queen told Alice that she sometimes believed six impossible things before breakfast. Sounds silly? Yet Ezekiel was called to believe the impossible when he saw a vision of a valley full of bones. These bones represented the people of Israel. In God's eyes, they were spiritually dead. That meant they had no power to do anything for God. Even though they had sinned against God, God promised to give them life once more by forgiving them.

Sin makes a person "lifeless". Thanks to Jesus new life is possible.

The Perfect Sacrifice, Leviticus 1—7, p. 135

Depend on Him! 2 Chronicles 16:1–9, p. 579

Go for the Gold, Job 23:10, p. 685

Dirty Inside, Isaiah 6:1–7, p. 904

Inside the Heart of God, Micah 7:18–20, p. 1228

The Way to Heaven, John 14:1–6, p. 1448

37:9 wind This Hebrew word could also mean "breath" or "spirit".

breathe on these people who were killed so they can come back to life.'" 10 So I prophesied as the LORD commanded me. And the breath came into them, and they came to life and stood on their feet, a very large army.

11 Then he said to me, "Human, these bones are like all the people of Israel. They say, 'Our bones are dried up, and our hope has gone. We are destroyed.' 12 So, prophesy and say to them, 'This is what the Lord GOD says: my people, I will open your graves and cause you to come up out of your graves. Then I will bring you into the land of Israel. 13 My people, you will know that I am the LORD when I open your graves and cause you to come up from them. 14 And I will put my Spirit inside you, and you will come to life. Then I will put you in your own land. And you will know that I, the LORD, have spoken and done it, says the LORD.'"

Judah and Israel Back Together

15 The LORD spoke his word to me, saying, 16 "Human, take a stick and write on it, 'For Judah and all the Israelites with him.' Then take another stick and write on it, 'The stick of Ephraim, for Joseph and all the Israelites with him.' 17 Then join them together into one stick so they will be one in your hand.

18 "When your people say to you, 'Explain to us what you mean by this,' 19 say to them, 'This is what the Lord GOD says: I will take the stick for Joseph and the tribes of Israel with him, which is in the hand of Ephraim, and I will put it with the stick of Judah. I will make them into one stick, and they will be one in my hand.' 20 Hold the sticks on which you wrote these names in your hand so the people can see them. 21 Say to the people, 'This is what the Lord GOD says: I am going to take the people of Israel from among the nations where they have gone. I will gather them from all around and bring them into their own land. 22 I will make them one nation in the land, on the mountains of Israel. One king will rule all of them. They will never again be two nations; they will not be divided into two kingdoms any more. 23 They will not

37:23
Forgiveness
How can you be clean from sin?

continue to make themselves unclean by their idols, their statues of gods which I hate, or by their sins. I will save them from all the ways they sin and turn against me, and I will make them clean. Then they will be my people, and I will be their God.

24 "'My servant David will be their king, and they will all have one shepherd. They will live by my rules and obey my laws. 25 They will live on the land I gave to my servant Jacob, the land in which your ancestors lived. They will all live on the land for ever: they, their children and their grandchildren. David my servant will be their king for ever. 26 I will make an agreement of peace with them, an agreement that continues for ever. I will put them in their land and make them grow in number. Then I will put my Temple among them for ever. 27 The place where I live will be with them. I will be their God, and they will be my people. 28 When my Temple is among them for ever, the nations will know that I, the LORD, make Israel holy.'"

Prophecy Against Gog

38 The LORD spoke his word to me, saying, 2 "Human, look towards Gog of the land of Magog, the chief ruler of the nations of Meshech and Tubal. Prophesy against him 3 and say, 'The Lord GOD says this: I am against you, Gog, chief ruler of Meshech and Tubal. 4 I will turn you around and put hooks in your jaws. And I will bring you out with all your army, horses and horsemen, all of whom will be dressed in beautiful uniforms. They will be a large army with large and small shields and all having swords. 5 Persia, Cush and Put will be with them, all of them having shields and helmets. 6 There will also be Gomer with all its troops and the nation of Togarmah from the far north with all its troops— many nations with you.

7 "'Be prepared. Be prepared, you and all the armies that have come together to make you their commander. 8 After a long

time you will be called for service. After those years you will come into a land that has been rebuilt from war. The people in the land will have been gathered from many nations to the mountains of Israel, which were empty for a long time. These people were brought out from the nations, and they will all be living in safety. 9 You will come like a storm. You, all your troops, and the many nations with you will be like a cloud covering the land.

10 "This is what the Lord GOD says: at that time ideas will come into your mind, and you will think up an evil plan. 11 You will say, "I will march against a land of towns without walls. I will attack those who are at rest and live in safety. All of them live without city walls or gate bars or gates. 12 I will capture treasures and take valuable things. I will turn my power against the rebuilt ruins that now have people living in them. I will attack these people who have been gathered from the nations, who have become rich with farm animals and property, who live at the centre of the world." 13 Sheba, Dedan and the traders of Tarshish, with all its villages, will say to you, "Did you come to capture treasure? Did you bring your troops together to take valuable things? Did you bring them to carry away silver and gold and to take away farm animals and property?"

14 "So prophesy, human, and say to Gog, 'This is what the Lord GOD says: now that my people Israel are living in safety, you will know about it. 15 You will come with many people from your place in the far north. You will have a large group with you, a mighty army, all riding on horses. 16 You will attack my people Israel like a cloud that covers the land. This will happen in the days to come when I bring you against my land. Gog, then the nations will know me when they see me prove how holy I am in what I do through you.

17 "'This is what the Lord GOD says: You are the one about whom I spoke in past days. I spoke through my servants, the prophets of Israel, who prophesied for many years that I would bring you against them. 18 This is what will happen: on the day Gog attacks the land of Israel, I will become very angry, says the Lord GOD. 19 With jealousy and great anger I tell you that at that time there will surely be a great earthquake in Israel. 20 The fish of the sea, the birds of the sky, the wild animals, everything that crawls on the ground and all the people on the earth will shake with fear before me. Also, the mountains will be thrown down, the cliffs will fall and every wall will fall to the ground. 21 Then I will call for a war against Gog on all my mountains, says the Lord GOD. Everyone's sword will attack the soldier next to him. 22 I will punish Gog with disease and death. I will send a heavy rain with hailstones and burning sulphur on Gog, his army and the many nations with him. 23 Then I will show how great I am. I will show my holiness, and I will make myself known to the many nations that watch. Then they will know that I am the LORD.'

eMAIL FROM GOD
38:23 God
Will the world ever see God's greatness?

The Death of Gog and His Army

39 "Human, prophesy against Gog and say, 'This is what the Lord GOD says: I am against you, Gog, chief ruler of Meshech and Tubal. 2 I will turn you around and lead you. I will bring you from the far north and send you to attack the mountains of Israel. 3 I will knock your bow out of your left hand and throw down your arrows from your right hand. 4 You, all your troops and the nations with you will fall dead on the mountains of Israel. I will let you be food for every bird that eats meat and for every wild animal. 5 You will lie fallen on the ground, because I have spoken, says the Lord GOD. 6 I will send fire on Magog and those who live in safety on the coastal lands. Then they will know that I am the LORD.

7 "'I will make myself known among my people Israel, and I will not let myself be dishonoured any more. Then the nations will know that I am the LORD, the Holy One in Israel. 8 It is coming! It will

happen, says the Lord GOD. The time I talked about is coming.

9 "Then those who live in the cities of Israel will come out and make fires with the enemy's weapons. They will burn them, both large and small shields, bows and arrows, war clubs and spears. They will use the weapons to burn in their fires for seven years. 10 They will not need to take wood from the field or chop firewood from the forests, because they will make fires with the weapons. In this way they will take the treasures of those who took their treasures; they will take the valuable things of those who took their valuable things, says the Lord GOD.

11 "At that time I will give Gog a burial place in Israel, in the Valley of the Travellers, east of the Dead Sea. It will block the road for travellers. Gog and all his army will be buried there, so people will call it The Valley of Gog's Army.

12 "The people of Israel will be burying them for seven months to make the land clean again. 13 All the people in the land will bury them, and they will be honoured on the day of my victory, says the Lord GOD.

14 "The people of Israel will choose men to work through the land to make it clean. Along with others, they will bury Gog's soldiers still lying dead on the ground. After the seven months are finished, they will still search. 15 As they go through the land, anyone who sees a human bone is to put a marker by it. The sign will stay there until the gravediggers bury the bone in The Valley of Gog's Army. 16 A city will be there named Hamonah. So they will make the land clean again.'

17 "Human, this is what the Lord GOD says: speak to every kind of bird and wild animal: 'Come together, come! Come together from all around to my sacrifice, a great sacrifice which I will prepare for you on the mountains of Israel. Eat flesh and drink blood! 18 You are to eat the flesh of the mighty and drink the blood of the rulers of the earth as if they were fat animals from Bashan: rams, lambs, goats and bulls. 19 You are to eat and drink from my sacrifice which I have prepared for you, eating fat until you are full and drinking blood until you are drunk. 20 At my table you are to eat until you are full of horses and riders, mighty men and all kinds of soldiers,' says the Lord GOD.

21 "I will show my glory among the nations. All the nations will see my power when I punish them. 22 From that time onwards the people of Israel will know that I am the LORD their God. 23 The nations will know Israel was taken away captive because they turned against me. So I turned away from them and handed them over to their enemies until all of them died in war. 24 Because of their uncleanness and their sins, I punished them and turned away from them.

25 "So this is what the Lord GOD says: Now I will bring the people of Jacob back from captivity, and I will have mercy on the whole nation of Israel. I will not let them dishonour me. 26 The people will forget their shame and how they rejected me when they live again in safety on their own land with no one to make them afraid. 27 I will bring the people back from other lands and gather them from the lands of their enemies. So I will use my people to show many nations that I am holy. 28 Then my people will know that I am the LORD their God, because I sent them into captivity among the nations, but then I brought them back to their own land, leaving no one behind. 29 I will not turn away from them any more, because I will put my Spirit into the people of Israel, says the Lord GOD."

The New Temple

40 It was the twenty-fifth year of our captivity, at the beginning of the year, on the tenth day of the month. It was

> I will show my glory among the nations. All the nations will see my power when I punish them.
> – Ezekiel 39:21

in the fourteenth year after Jerusalem was captured. On that same day I felt the power of the LORD, and he brought me to Jerusalem. **2** In the visions of God he brought me to the land of Israel and put me down on a very high mountain. On the south of the mountain there were some buildings that looked like a city. **3** He took me closer to the buildings, and I saw a man who looked as if he were made of bronze, standing in the gateway. He had a cord made of linen and a stick in his hand, both for measuring. **4** The man said to me, "Human, look with your eyes and hear with your ears. Pay attention to all that I will show you, because that's why you have been brought here. Tell the people of Israel all that you see."

The East Gateway

5 I saw a wall that surrounded the Temple area. The measuring stick in the man's hand was 3 metres long. So the man measured the wall, which was 3 metres thick and 3 metres high.

6 Then the man went to the east gateway. He went up its steps and measured the opening of the gateway. It was 3 metres deep. **7** The rooms for the guards were 3 metres long and 3 metres wide. The walls that came out between the guards' rooms were about 2.5 metres thick. The opening of the gateway next to the porch that faced the Temple was 3 metres deep.

8 Then the man measured the porch of the gateway. **9** It was about 4.5 metres deep, and its side walls were a metre thick. The porch of the gateway faced the Temple.

10 On each side of the east gateway were three rooms, which measured the same on each side. The walls between each room were the same thickness. **11** The man measured the width of the entrance to the gateway, which was 5 metres wide. The width of the gate was about 6.5 metres. **12** And there was a low wall about 50 centimetres high in front of each room. The rooms were 3 metres on each side. **13** The man measured the gateway from the roof of one room to the roof of the opposite room. It was about 12.5 metres from one door to the opposite door. **14** The man also measured the porch, which was about 10 metres wide. The courtyard was around the porch. **15** From the front of the outer side of the

GOD'S NEW TEMPLE
EZEKIEL 40—44

Ezekiel saw a vision of a new Temple of God. The old Temple had been destroyed before the Israelites were taken in captivity to Babylon. But God showed Ezekiel how wonderful he would make the new Temple. More than that, the people of God would truly worship him with their whole hearts.

If you're a Christian, you provide a new temple for God within your own body. That's where the Holy Spirit lives. God wants you to worship him with your whole heart.

Connect to these links on worshipping God:

The Name of the Lord, Exodus 33:19–23; 34:5–8, p. 120

A Life of Thanksgiving, 1 Kings 1:47–48, p. 435

What's in a Name? Isaiah 9:6, p. 908

Your Spiritual Roots, Zechariah 1:1–6, p. 1253

How Do I Love You? Malachi 1:1–5, p. 1267

One Thing to Do, Romans 4:1–5, p. 1523

gateway to the front of the porch of the inner side of the gateway was 25 metres. 16 The rooms and porch had small windows on both sides. The windows were narrower on the side facing the gateway. Carvings of palm trees were on each side wall of the rooms.

The Outer Courtyard

17 Then the man brought me into the outer courtyard where I saw rooms and a pavement of stones all around the court. Thirty rooms were along the edge of the paved walkway. 18 The pavement ran alongside the gates and was as deep as the gates were wide. This was the lower pavement. 19 Then the man measured from the outer wall to the inner wall. The outer court between these two walls was 50 metres on the east and on the north.

The North Gateway

20 The man measured the length and width of the north gateway leading to the outer courtyard. 21 Its three rooms on each side, its inner walls and its porch measured the same as the first gateway. It was 25 metres long and 12.5 metres wide. 22 Its windows, porch and carvings of palm trees measured the same as the east gateway. Seven steps went up to the gateway, and the gateway's porch was at the inner end. 23 The inner courtyard had a gateway across from the northern gateway like the one on the east. The man measured it and found it was 50 metres from inner gateway to outer gateway.

The South Gateway

24 Then the man led me south where I saw a gateway facing south. He measured its inner walls and its porch, and they measured the same as the other gateways. 25 The gateway and its porch had windows all around like the other gateways. It was 25 metres long and 12.5 metres wide. 26 Seven steps went up to this gateway. Its porch was at the inner end, and it had carvings of palm trees on its inner walls. 27 The inner courtyard had a gateway on its south side. The man measured from gate to gate on the south side, which was 50 metres.

The Inner Courtyard

28 Then the man brought me through the south gateway into the inner courtyard. The inner south gateway measured the same as the gateways in the outer wall. 29 The inner south gateway's rooms, inner walls and porch measured the same as the gateways in the outer wall. There were windows all around the gateway and its porch. The gateway was 25 metres long and 12.5 metres wide. 30 Each porch of each inner gateway was about 15 metres long and about 2.5 metres wide. 31 The inner south gateway's porch faced the outer courtyard. Carvings of palm trees were on its side walls, and its stairway had eight steps.

32 The man brought me into the inner courtyard on the east side. He measured the inner east gateway, and it was the same as the other gateways. 33 The inner east gateway's rooms, inside walls and porch measured the same as the other gateways. Windows were all around the gateway and its porch. The inner east gateway was 25 metres long and 12.5 metres wide. 34 Its porch faced the outer courtyard. Carvings of palm trees were on its inner walls on each side, and its stairway had eight steps.

35 Then the man brought me to the inner north gateway. He measured it, and it was the same as the other gateways. 36 Its rooms, inner walls and porch measured the same as the other gateways. There were windows all around the gateway, which was 25 metres long and 12.5 metres wide. 37 Its porch faced the outer courtyard. Carvings of palm trees were on its inner walls on each side, and its stairway had eight steps.

Rooms for Preparing Sacrifices

38 There was a room with a door that opened onto the porch of the inner north

gateway. In this room the priests washed animals for the burnt offerings. 39 There were two tables on each side of the porch, on which animals for burnt offerings, sin offerings and penalty offerings were killed. 40 Outside, by each side wall of the porch, at the entrance to the north gateway, were two more tables. 41 So there were four tables inside the gateway, and four tables outside. In all there were eight tables on which the priests killed animals for sacrifices. 42 There were four tables made of cut stone for the burnt offering. These tables were about 75 centimetres long, 75 centimetres wide and about 50 centimetres high. On these tables the priests put their tools which they used to kill animals for burnt offerings and the other sacrifices. 43 Double shelves 8 centimetres wide were put up on all the walls. The flesh for the offering was put on the tables.

The Priests' Rooms

44 There were two rooms in the inner courtyard. One was beside the north gateway and faced south. The other room was beside the south gateway and faced north. 45 The man said to me, "The room which faces south is for the priests who serve in the Temple area, 46 while the room that faces north is for the priests who serve at the altar. This second group of priests are descendants of Zadok, the only descendants of Levi who can come near the LORD to serve him."

47 The man measured the inner courtyard. It was a square—50 metres long and 50 metres wide. The altar was in front of the Temple.

The Temple Porch

48 The man brought me to the porch of the Temple and measured each side wall of the porch. Each was about 2.5 metres thick. The doorway was 7 metres wide. The side walls of the doorway were each about 1.5 metres wide. 49 The porch was 10 metres long and 6 metres wide, with ten steps leading up to it. Pillars were by the side walls, one on each side of the entrance.

The Holy Place of the Temple

41 The man brought me to the Holy Place and measured its side walls, which were each 3 metres thick. 2 The entrance was 5 metres wide. The walls alongside the entrance were each about 2.5 metres wide. The man measured the Holy Place, which was 25 metres long and 10 metres wide.

3 Then the man went inside and measured the side walls of the next doorway. Each was a metre thick. The doorway was 3 metres wide, and the walls next to it were each more than 3.5 metres thick. 4 Then the man measured the room at the end of the Holy Place. It was 10 metres long and 10 metres wide. The man said to me, "This is the Most Holy Place."

5 Then the man measured the wall of the Temple, which was 3 metres thick. There were side rooms 2 metres wide all around the Temple. 6 The side rooms were on three different storeys, each above the other, with 30 rooms on each storey. All around the Temple walls there were ledges for the side rooms. The upper rooms rested on the ledges but were not attached to the Temple walls. 7 The side rooms around the Temple were wider on each higher storey, so rooms were wider on the top storey. A stairway went up from the lowest storey to the highest through the middle storey.

8 I also saw that the Temple had a raised base all around. Its edge was the foundation for the side rooms, and it was 3 metres thick. 9 The outer wall of the side rooms was about 2.5 metres thick. There was an open area between the side rooms of the Temple 10 and some other rooms. It was 10 metres wide and went all around the Temple. 11 The side rooms had doors which led to the open area around the outside of the Temple. One door faced north, and the other faced south. The open area was about 2.5 metres wide all around.

12 The building facing the private area at the west side was 35 metres wide. The wall around the building was about 2.5 metres thick and 45 metres long.

13 Then the man measured the Temple. It was 50 metres long. The private area, including the building and its walls, was in all 50 metres long. 14 Also the front of the Temple and the private area on its east side were 50 metres wide.

15 The man measured the length of the building facing the private area on the west side, and it was 50 metres from one wall to the other.

The Holy Place, the Most Holy Place and the outer porch 16 had wood panels on the walls. By the doorway, the Temple had wood panels on the walls. The wood covered all the walls from the floor up to the windows, 17 up to the part of the wall above the entrance.

All the walls inside the Most Holy Place and the Holy Place, and on the outside, in the porch, 18 had carvings of creatures with wings and palm trees. A palm tree was between each carved creature, and every creature had two faces. 19 One was a human face looking towards the palm tree on one side. The other was a lion's face looking towards the palm tree on the other side. They were carved all around the Temple walls. 20 From the floor to above the entrance, palm trees and creatures with wings were

CONNECT 2-YOU

ALL IN THE FAMILY

Do you have any friends who are having problems with their families? Here's someone who wants to share some of her problems with us. Let's welcome Lucy, aged 11, to Connect 2-You.

Lucy

My family is driving me mad! Dad works all the time, and even when he's home, you can tell he's still thinking about things at the office. Mum loves to nag me about every little thing I do – the way I eat, the way I dress, the things I watch on TV, you name it. And my brother is completely mad. He painted his whole room black and sits in there all the time listening to weird music. I can't move out for another seven years! How am I going to survive?

God tells us to honour our mother and father, but he doesn't say it will be easy. Living together under one roof takes a lot of patience and a lot of work. If you would like some tips on how to live with your parents and siblings in peace, check out the Livin' It page on living with your family, Exodus 20:12, p. 102.

Maybe the best thing Lucy can do is to ask God to help her find some common ground with each member of her family. She needs to find something they can talk about or do together that won't drive either of them crazy. If she makes the effort to find some common ground, she'll probably find that the things that irritate her about each person don't bother her as much anymore.

carved. The walls of the Holy Place 21 had square doorposts. In front of the Most Holy Place was something that looked like 22 an altar of wood. It was 1.5 metres high and 1 metre wide. Its corners, base and sides were wood. The man said to me, "This is the table that is in the presence of the LORD." 23 Both the Holy Place and the Most Holy Place had double doors. 24 Each of the doors had two pieces that would swing open. 25 Carved on the doors of the Holy Place were palm trees and creatures with wings, like those carved on the walls. And there was a wooden roof over the front Temple porch. 26 There were windows and palm trees on both side walls of the porch. The side rooms of the Temple were also covered by a roof over the stairway.

The Priests' Rooms

42 Then the man led me north out into the outer courtyard and to the rooms across from the private area and the building. 2 These rooms on the north side were 50 metres long and 25 metres wide. 3 There was 10 metres of the inner courtyard between them and the Temple. On the other side, they faced the stone pavement of the outer courtyard. The rooms were built in three storeys like steps and had balconies. 4 There was a path on the north side of the rooms, which was 5 metres wide and 50 metres long. Doors led into the rooms from this path. 5 The top rooms were narrower, because the balconies took more space from them. The rooms on the first and second storeys of the building were wider. 6 The rooms were on three storeys. They did not have pillars like the pillars of the courtyards. So the top rooms were farther back than those on the first and second storeys. 7 There was a wall outside parallel to the rooms and to the outer courtyard. It ran in front of the rooms for 25 metres. 8 The row of rooms along the outer courtyard was 25 metres long, and the rooms that faced the Temple were about 50 metres long. 9 The lower rooms had an entrance on the east side so a person could enter them from the outer courtyard, 10 at the start of the wall beside the courtyard.

There were rooms on the south side, which were across from the private area and the building. 11 These rooms had a path in front of them. They were like the rooms on the north with the same length and width and the same doors. 12 The doors of the south rooms were like the doors of the north rooms. There was an entrance at the open end of a path beside the wall, so a person could enter at the east end.

13 The man said to me, "The north and south rooms across from the private area are holy rooms. There the priests who go near the LORD will eat the most holy offerings. There they will put the most holy offerings—the grain offerings, sin offerings and penalty offerings—because the place is holy. 14 The priests who enter the Holy Place must leave their serving clothes there before they go into the outer courtyard, because these clothes are holy. After they put on other clothes, they may go to the part of the Temple area which is for the people."

Outside the Temple Area

15 When the man finished measuring inside the Temple area, he brought me out through the east gateway. He measured the area all around. 16 The man measured the east side with the measuring stick; it was 250 metres by the measuring stick. 17 He measured the north side; it was 250 metres by the measuring stick. 18 He measured the south side; it was 250 metres by the measuring stick. 19 He went around to the west side; it measured 250 metres by the measuring stick. 20 So he measured the Temple area on all four sides. The Temple area had a wall all around it that was 250 metres long and 250 metres wide. It separated what was holy from that which was not holy.

The LORD Among His People

43 Then the man led me to the outer east gateway, 2 and I saw the glory of the God of Israel coming from the east. It sounded like the roar of rushing water, and its brightness made the earth shine. 3 The vision I saw was like the vision I had seen when the LORD came to destroy the city and also like the vision I had seen by the Kebar River. I bowed face down on the ground. 4 The glory of the LORD came into the Temple area through the east gateway.

5 Then the Spirit picked me up and brought me into the inner courtyard. There I saw the LORD's glory filling the Temple. 6 As the man stood at my side, I heard someone speaking to me from inside the Temple. 7 The voice from the Temple said to me, "Human, this is my throne and the place where my feet rest. I will live here among the Israelites for ever. The people of Israel will not make my holy name unclean again. Neither the people nor their kings will make it unclean with their sexual sins or with the dead bodies of their kings. 8 The kings made my name unclean by putting their doorway next to my doorway, and their doorpost next to my doorpost so only a wall separated me from them. When they did their acts that I hate, they made my holy name unclean, and so I destroyed them in my anger. 9 Now let them stop their sexual sins and take the dead bodies of their kings far away from me. Then I will live among them for ever.

10 "Human, tell the people of Israel about the Temple so they will be ashamed of their sins. Let them think about the plan of the Temple. 11 If they are ashamed of all they have done, let them know the design of the Temple and how it is built. Show them its exits and entrances, all its designs and also all its rules and teachings. Write the rules as they watch so they will obey all the teachings and rules about the Temple. 12 This is the teaching about the Temple: all the area around the top of the mountain is most holy. This is the teaching about the Temple.

> Then the Spirit picked me up and brought me into the inner courtyard. There I saw the LORD's glory filling the Temple.
> – Ezekiel 43:5

The Altar

13 "These are the measurements of the altar, using the measuring stick. The altar's rim is 50 centimetres high and 50 centimetres wide, and its rim is about 25 centimetres around its edge. And the altar is this tall: 14 from the ground up to the lower ledge, it measures 1 metre. It is 50 centimetres wide. It measures 2 metres from the smaller ledge to the larger ledge and is 50 centimetres wide. 15 The place where the sacrifice is burned on the altar is 2 metres high, with its four corners shaped like horns and reaching up above it. 16 It is square, 6 metres long and 6 metres wide. 17 The upper ledge is also square, 7 metres long and 7 metres wide. The rim around the altar is 25 centimetres wide, and its border is 50 centimetres wide all around. Its steps are on the east side."

18 Then the man said to me, "Human, this is what the Lord GOD says: these are the rules for the altar. When it is built, use these rules to offer burnt offerings and to sprinkle blood on it. 19 You must give a young bull as a sin offering to the priests, the Levites who are from the family of Zadok and who come near me to serve me, says the Lord GOD. 20 Take some of the bull's blood and put it on the four corners of the altar, on the four corners of the ledge, and all around the rim. This is how you will make the altar pure and ready for God's service. 21 Then take the bull for the sin offering and burn it in the proper place in the Temple area, outside the Temple building.

22 "On the second day offer a male goat that has nothing wrong with it for a sin offering. The priests will make the altar pure and ready for God's service as they did with the young bull. 23 When you finish making the altar pure and ready, offer a young bull and a ram from the flock, both without defect. 24 You must offer them in the presence of the LORD, and the priests are to throw salt on them

and offer them as a burnt offering to the LORD.

25 "You must prepare a goat every day for seven days as a sin offering. Also, the priests must prepare a young bull and ram from the flock, both without defect. 26 For seven days the priests are to make the altar pure and ready for God's service. Then they will give the altar to God. 27 After these seven days, on the eighth day, the priests must offer your burnt offerings and your fellowship offerings on the altar. Then I will accept you, says the Lord GOD."

The Outer East Gate

44 Then the man brought me back to the outer east gateway of the Temple area, but the gate was shut. 2 The LORD said to me, "This gate will stay shut; it will not be opened. No one may enter through it, because the LORD God of Israel has entered through it. So it must stay shut. 3 Only the ruler himself may sit in the gateway to eat a meal in the presence of the LORD. He must enter through the porch of the gateway and go out the same way."

4 Then the man brought me through the outer north gate to the front of the Temple. As I looked, I saw the glory of the LORD filling the Temple of the LORD, and I bowed face down on the ground.

5 The LORD said to me, "Human, pay attention. Use your eyes to see, and your ears to hear. See and hear everything I tell you about all the rules and teachings of the Temple of the LORD. Pay attention to the entrance to the Temple and to all the exits from the Temple area. 6 Then speak to those who refuse to obey. Say to the people of Israel, 'This is what the Lord GOD says: Stop doing all your acts that I hate, Israel! 7 You brought foreigners into my Holy Place who were not circumcised in the flesh and had not given themselves to serving me. You dishonoured

> See and hear everything I tell you about all the rules and teachings of the Temple of the LORD.
> – Ezekiel 44:5

my Temple when you offered me food, fat and blood. You broke my agreement by all the things you did that I hate. 8 You did not take care of my holy things yourselves but put foreigners in charge of my Temple. 9 This is what the Lord GOD says: foreigners who are not circumcised in the flesh and who do not give themselves to serving me may not enter my Temple. Not even a foreigner living among the people of Israel may enter.

10 "But the Levites who stopped obeying me when Israel left me and who followed their idols must be punished for their sin. 11 These Levites are to be servants in my Holy Place. They may guard the gates of the Temple and serve in the Temple area. They may kill the animals for the burnt offering and the sacrifices for the people. They may stand before the people to serve them. 12 But these Levites helped the people worship their idols and caused the people of Israel to fall, so I make this promise: they will be punished for their sin, says the Lord GOD. 13 They will not come near me to serve as priests, nor will they come near any of my holy things or the most holy offerings. But they will be made ashamed of the things they did that I hate. 14 I will put them in charge of taking care of the Temple area, all the work that must be done in it.

15 "But the priests who are Levites and descendants of Zadok took care of my Holy Place when Israel left me, so they may come near to serve me. They may stand in my presence to offer me the fat and blood of the animals they sacrifice, says the Lord GOD. 16 They are the only ones who may enter my Holy Place. Only they may come near my table to serve me and take care of the things I gave them to do.

17 "When they enter the gates of the inner courtyard, they must wear linen robes. They must not wear wool to serve at the gates of the inner courtyard or in the Temple. 18 They will wear linen

turbans on their heads and linen underclothes. They will not wear anything that makes them perspire. 19 When they go out into the outer courtyard to the people, they must take off their serving clothes before they go. They must leave these clothes in the holy rooms and put on other clothes. Then they will not let their holy clothes hurt the people.

20 "They must not shave their heads or let their hair grow long but must keep the hair of their heads trimmed. 21 None of the priests may drink wine when they enter the inner courtyard. 22 The priests must not marry widows or divorced women. They may marry only virgins from the people of Israel or widows of priests. 23 They must teach my people the difference between what is holy and what is not holy. They must help my people know what is unclean and what is clean.

24 "In court they will act as judges. When they judge, they will follow my teachings. They must obey my laws and my rules at all my special feasts and keep my Sabbaths holy.

25 "They must not go near a dead person, making themselves unclean. But they are allowed to make themselves unclean if the dead person is their father, mother, son, daughter, brother or a sister who has not married. 26 After a priest has been made clean again, he must wait seven days. 27 Then he may go into the inner courtyard to serve in the Temple, but he must offer a sin offering for himself, says the Lord GOD.

28 "These are the rules about the priests and their property: they will have me instead of property. You will not give them any land to own in Israel; I am what they will own. 29 They will eat the grain offerings, sin offerings and penalty offerings. Everything Israel gives to me will be theirs. 30 The best fruits of all the first harvests and all the special gifts offered to me will belong to the priests. You will also give to the priests the first part of your grain that you grind and so bring a blessing on your family. 31 The priests must not eat any bird or animal that died a natural death or one that has been torn by wild animals.

The Land is Divided

45 "When you divide the land for the Israelite tribes by throwing lots, you must give a part of the land to belong to the LORD. It will be about 12 kilometres long and about 10 kilometres wide; all of this land will be holy. 2 From this land, an area 250 metres square will be for the Temple. There will be an open space around the Temple that is 250 metres wide. 3 In the holy area you will measure a part about 12 kilometres long and 5 kilometres wide, and in it will be the Most Holy Place. 4 This holy part of the land will be for the priests who serve in the Temple, who come near to the LORD to serve him. It will be a place for the priests' houses and for the Temple. 5 Another area about 12 kilometres long and more than 5 kilometres wide will be for the Levites, who serve in the Temple area. It will belong to them so they will have cities in which to live.

6 "You must give the city an area that is about 2.5 kilometres wide and about 12 kilometres long, along the side of the holy area. It will belong to all the people of Israel.

7 "The ruler will have land on both sides of the holy area and the city. On the west of the holy area, his land will reach to the Mediterranean Sea. On the east of the holy area, his land will reach to the eastern border. It will be as long as the land given to each tribe. 8 Only this land will be the ruler's property in Israel. So my rulers will not be cruel to my people any more, but they will let each tribe in the nation of Israel have its share of the land.

9 "This is what the Lord GOD says: You have gone far enough, you rulers of Israel!

45:9–11
Honesty
Do what is right.

Stop being cruel and hurting people, and do what is right and fair. Stop forcing my people out of their homes, says the Lord GOD. 10 You must have honest scales, an honest dry measurement and an honest liquid measurement. 11 The dry measure and the liquid measure will be the same: the liquid measure will always be a tenth of a homer,ⁿ and the ephah will always be a tenth of a homer. The measurement they follow will be the homer. 12 The shekelⁿ will be worth 20 gerahs, and a mina will be worth 60 shekels.

Offerings and Holy Days

13 "'This is the gift you should offer: one sixtieth of your harvest of wheat, and one sixtieth of your harvest of barley. 14 The amount of oil you are to offer is one-hundredth of your harvest. (Ten baths make a homer and also make a cor.) 15 You should give one sheep from each flock of 200 from the watering places of Israel. All these are to be offered for the grain offerings, burnt offerings and fellowship offerings to remove sins so you will belong to God, says the Lord GOD. 16 All people in the land will give this special offering to the ruler of Israel. 17 It will be the ruler's responsibility to supply the burnt offerings, grain offerings and drink offerings. These offerings will be given at the feasts, at the New Moons, on the Sabbaths and at all the other feasts of Israel. The ruler will supply the sin offerings, grain offerings and fellowship offerings to pay for the sins of Israel.

18 "'This is what the Lord GOD says: on the first day of the first month take a young bull without defect. Use it to make the Temple pure and ready for God's service. 19 The priest will take some of the blood from this sin offering and put it on the doorposts of the Temple, on the four corners of the ledge of the altar and on the posts of the gate to the inner courtyard. 20 You will do the same thing on the seventh day of the month for anyone who has sinned by accident or without knowing it. This is how you make the Temple pure and ready for God's service.

Passover Feast Offerings

21 "'On the fourteenth day of the first month you will celebrate the Feast of Passover. It will be a feast of seven days when you eat bread made without yeast. 22 On that day the ruler must offer a bull for himself and for all the people of the land as a sin offering. 23 During the seven days of the feast he must offer seven bulls and seven rams that have nothing wrong with them. They will be burnt offerings to the LORD, which the ruler will offer every day of the seven days of the feast. He must also offer a male goat every day as a sin offering. 24 The ruler must give as a grain offering 20 litres for each bull and 20 litres for each ram. He must give 4 litres of olive oil for each 20 litres.

25 "'Beginning on the fifteenth day of the seventh month, when you celebrate the Feast of Shelters, the ruler will supply the same things for seven days: the sin offerings, burnt offerings, grain offerings and the olive oil.

Rules for Worship

46 "'This is what the Lord GOD says: the east gate of the inner courtyard will stay shut on the six working days, but it will be opened on the Sabbath day and on the day of the New Moon. 2 The ruler will enter from outside through the porch of the gateway and stand by the gatepost, while the priests offer the ruler's burnt offering and fellowship offering. The ruler will worship at the entrance of the gateway, and then he will go out. But the gate will not be shut until evening. 3 The people of the land will worship at the entrance of that gateway in the presence of the LORD on the Sabbaths and New Moons. 4 This is the burnt offering the ruler will offer to the LORD on the Sabbath day: six male lambs all without defect and a ram that has nothing wrong with it. 5 He must give a 20 litre grain offering with the ram, but he may give as much grain offering with the lambs as he pleases. He must also give 4 litres of olive oil for each 20 litres of grain.

45:11 homer The Hebrew word means "donkey-load". It measured about 200 litres. So an ephah was about 20 litres, and a bath was about 20 litres.
45:12 shekel In Ezekiel's time a shekel weighed about 11 grammes.

6 On the day of the New Moon he must offer a young bull that has nothing wrong with it. He must also offer six lambs and a ram that have nothing wrong with them. 7 The ruler must give a 20 litre grain offering with the bull and 20 litres with the ram. With the lambs, he may give as much grain as he pleases. But he must give 4 litres of olive oil for each 20 litres of grain. 8 When the ruler enters, he must go in through the porch of the gateway, and he must go out the same way.

9 "When the people of the land come into the LORD's presence at the special feasts, those who enter through the north gate to worship must go out through the south gate. Those who enter through the south gate must go out through the north gate. They must not return the same way they entered; everyone must go out the opposite way. 10 The ruler will go in with the people when they go in and go out with them when they go out.

11 "'At the feasts and regular times of worship 20 litres of grain must be offered with a young bull, and 20 litres of grain must be offered with a ram. But with an offering of lambs, the ruler may give as much grain as he pleases. He should give 4 litres of olive oil for each 20 litres of grain. 12 The ruler may give an offering as a special gift to the LORD; it may be a burnt offering or fellowship offering. When he gives it to the LORD, the inner east gate is to be opened for him. He must offer his burnt offering or his fellowship offering as he does on the Sabbath day. Then he will go out, and the gate will be shut after he has left.

13 "'Every day you will give a year-old lamb that has nothing wrong with it for a burnt offering to the LORD. Do it every morning. 14 Also, you must offer a grain offering with the lamb every morning. For this you will give 3 litres of grain and 1 litre of olive oil, to make the fine flour moist, as a grain offering to the LORD. This is a rule that must be kept from now on. 15 So you must always give the lamb, together with the grain offering and the olive oil, every morning as a burnt offering.

Rules for the Ruler

16 "'This is what the Lord GOD says: if the ruler gives a gift from his land to any of his sons, that land will belong to the son and then to the son's children. It is their property passed down from their family. 17 But if the ruler gives a gift from his land to any of his servants, that land will belong to the servant only until the year of freedom. Then the land will go back to the ruler. Only the ruler's sons may keep a gift of land from the ruler. 18 The ruler must not take any of the people's land, forcing them out of their land. He must give his sons some of his own land so my people will not be scattered out of their own land.'"

The Special Kitchens

19 The man led me through the entrance at the side of the gateway to the priests' holy rooms that face north. There I saw a place at the west end. 20 The man said to me, "This is where the priests will boil the meat of the penalty offering and sin offering and bake the grain offering. Then they will not need to bring these holy offerings into the outer courtyard, because that would hurt the people."

21 Then the man brought me out into the outer courtyard and led me to its four corners. In each corner of the courtyard was a smaller courtyard. 22 Small courtyards were in the four corners of the courtyard. Each small courtyard was the same size, 20 metres long and 15 metres wide. 23 A stone wall was around each of the four small courtyards, and places for cooking were built in each of the stone walls. 24 The man said to me, "These are the kitchens where those who work in the Temple will boil the sacrifices offered by the people."

The River from the Temple

47 The man led me back to the door of the Temple, and I saw water coming out from under the doorway and flowing east. (The Temple faced east.) The water flowed down from the south side wall of the Temple and then south

of the altar. **2** The man brought me out through the outer north gate and led me around outside to the outer east gate. I found the water coming out on the south side of the gate.

3 The man went towards the east with a line in his hand and measured about 500 metres. Then he led me through water that came up to my ankles. **4** The man measured about 500 metres again and led me through water that came up to my knees. Then he measured about 500 metres again and led me through water up to my waist. **5** The man measured about 500 metres again, but it was now a river that I could not cross. The water had risen too high; it was deep enough for swimming; it was a river that no one could cross. **6** The man asked me, "Human, do you see this?"

Then the man led me back to the bank of the river. **7** As I went back, I saw many trees on both sides of the river. **8** The man said to me, "This water will flow towards the eastern areas and go down into the Jordan Valley. When it enters the Dead Sea, it will become fresh. **9** Everywhere the river goes, there will be many fish. Wherever this water goes the Dead Sea will become fresh, and so where the river goes there will be many living things. **10** Fishermen will stand by the Dead Sea. From En Gedi all the way to En Eglaim there will be places to spread fishing nets. There will be many kinds of fish in the Dead Sea, as many as in the Mediterranean Sea. **11** But its swamps and marshes will not become fresh; they will be left for salt. **12** All kinds of fruit trees will grow on both banks of the river, and their leaves will not dry and die. The trees will have fruit every month, because the water for them comes from the Temple. The fruit from the trees will be used for food, and their leaves for medicine."

Borders of the Land

13 This is what the Lord GOD says: "These are the borders of the land to be divided among the twelve tribes of Israel. Joseph will have two parts of land. **14** You will divide the land equally. I promised to give it to your ancestors, so this land will belong to you as family property.

15 "This will be the border line of the land: "On the north side it will start at the Mediterranean Sea. It will go through Hethlon, towards Lebo Hamath and on to the towns of Zedad, **16** Berothah and Sibraim on the border between Damascus and Hamath. Then it will go on to the town of Hazer Hatticon on the border of the country of Hauran. **17** So the border line will go from the Mediterranean Sea east to the town of Hazar Enan, where the land belonging to Damascus and Hamath lies on the north side. This will be the north side of the land.

18 "On the east side the border runs south from a point between Hauran and Damascus. It will go along the Jordan between Gilead and the land of Israel and will continue to the town of Tamar on the Dead Sea. This will be the east side of the land.

19 "On the south side the border line will go east from Tamar all the way to the waters of Meribah Kadesh. Then it will run along the brook of Egypt to the Mediterranean Sea. This will be the south side of the land.

20 "On the west side the Mediterranean Sea will be the border line up to a place across from Lebo Hamath. This will be the west side of your land.

21 "You will divide this land among the tribes of Israel. **22** You will divide it as family property for yourselves and for the foreigners who live and have children among you. You are to treat these foreigners in the same way as people born in Israel; they are to share the land with the tribes of Israel. **23** In whatever tribe the foreigner lives, you will give him some land," says the Lord GOD.

Dividing the Land

48 "These are the areas of the tribes named here: Dan will have

> You are to treat these foreigners in the same way as people born in Israel; they are to share the land with the tribes of Israel.
> – Ezekiel 47:22

one share at the northern border. It will go from the sea through Hethlon to Lebo Hamath, all the way to Hazar Enan, where Damascus lies to the north. It will stop there next to Hamath. This will be Dan's northern border from the east side to the Mediterranean Sea on the west side.

2 "South of Dan's border, Asher will have one share. It will go from the east side to the west side.

3 "South of Asher's border, Naphtali will have one share. It will go from the east side to the west side.

4 "South of Naphtali's border, Manasseh will have one share. It will go from the east side to the west side.

5 "South of Manasseh's border, Ephraim will have one share. It will go from the east side to the west side.

6 "South of Ephraim's border, Reuben will have one share. It will go from the east side to the west side.

7 "South of Reuben's border, Judah will have one share. It will go from the east side to the west side.

8 "South of Judah's border will be the holy area which you are to give. It will be about 12 kilometres wide and as long and wide as one of the tribes' shares. It will run from the east side to the west side. The Temple will be in the middle of this area.

9 "The share which you will give the LORD will be about 12 kilometres long and 10 kilometres wide. 10 The holy area will be divided among these people. The priests will have land about 12 kilometres long on the north and south sides, and 10 kilometres wide on the west and east sides. The Temple of the LORD will be in the middle of it. 11 This land is for the priests who are given the holy duty of serving the LORD. They are the descendants of Zadok who did my work and did not leave me when Israel and the Levites left me. 12 They will have as their share a very holy part of the holy portion of the land. It will be next to the land of the Levites.

13 "Alongside the land for the priests, the Levites will have a share about 12 kilometres long and 5 kilometres wide; its full length will be about 12 kilometres and its full width about 10 kilometres. 14 The Levites are not to sell or trade any of this land. They are not to let anyone else own any of this best part of the land, because it belongs to the LORD.

City Property

15 "The rest of the area will be about 2.5 kilometres wide and 12 kilometres long. It will not be holy but will belong to the city and be used for homes and pastures. The city will be in the middle of it. 16 These are the city's measurements: the north side will be about 2 kilometres, the south side about 2 kilometres, the east side about 2 kilometres and the west side about 2 kilometres. 17 The city's land for pastures will be about 125 metres on the north, 125 metres on the south, 125 metres on the east and 125 metres on the west. 18 Along the long side of the holy area there will be left 5 kilometres on the east and 5 kilometres on the west. It will be used to grow food for the city workers. 19 The city workers from all the tribes of Israel will farm this land. 20 This whole area will be square, 12 kilometres by 12 kilometres. You shall give to the LORD the holy share along with the city property.

21 "Land that is left over on both sides of the holy area and city property will belong to the ruler. That land will extend east of the holy area to the eastern border and west of it to the Mediterranean Sea. Both of these areas run the length of the lands of the tribes, and they belong to the ruler. The holy area with the Holy Place of the Temple will be in the middle. 22 The Levites' land and the city property will be in the middle of the lands belonging to the ruler. Those lands will be between Judah's border and Benjamin's border.

The Other Tribes' Land

23 "Here is what the rest of the tribes will receive: Benjamin will have one share. It will go from the east side to the Mediterranean Sea on the west side.

24 "South of Benjamin's land, Simeon will have one share. It will go from the east side to the west side.

25 "South of Simeon's land, Issachar will have one share. It will go from the east side to the west side.

26 "South of Issachar's land, Zebulun will have one share. It will go from the east side to the west side.

27 "South of Zebulun's land, Gad will have one share. It will go from the east side to the west side.

28 "The southern border of Gad's land will go east from Tamar on the Dead Sea to the waters of Meribah Kadesh. Then it will run along the brook of Egypt to the Mediterranean Sea.

29 "This is the land you will divide among the tribes of Israel to be their shares," says the Lord GOD.

The Gates of the City

30 "These will be the outside borders of the city: the north side will measure more than 2 kilometres. **31** There will be three gates facing north: Reuben's Gate, Judah's Gate and Levi's Gate, named after the tribes of Israel.

32 "The east side will measure more than 2 kilometres. There will be three gates facing east: Joseph's Gate, Benjamin's Gate and Dan's Gate.

33 "The south side will measure more than 2 kilometres. There will be three gates facing south: Simeon's Gate, Issachar's Gate and Zebulun's Gate.

34 "The west side will measure more than 2 kilometres. There will be three gates facing west: Gad's Gate, Asher's Gate and Naphtali's Gate.

35 "The city will measure about 12 kilometres around. From then on the name of the city will be The LORD Is There."

ADVENTURES IN BABYLON

Hi! Daniel here. You have probably heard a few stories about me. I'm the one who survived a night in the lions' den. When I was a young man, my three friends and I were captured by our enemies and taken to live in the king's palace in Babylon. The king wanted us to be his servants, so we learned the language and the customs of Babylon. We were even given Babylonian names. Only one problem: the food. It had been offered to idols! It was against God's law to eat this food, but how could we refuse the food without insulting the king? Plug into Daniel 1 for the answer.

I wrote this book to encourage people to follow God even when times are difficult. One time my three friends had to make a choice: worship a 30-metre high gold statue or be thrown into a blazing furnace. What would you do? Because they refused to worship the statue, they were tied up and thrown into the furnace. Imagine the king's surprise when he saw a fourth person in the fire. Who was it? Surf over to Daniel 3:25–30 to find out.

JESUS WATCH

God gave Daniel the ability to explain dreams. One time, King Nebuchadnezzar had a strange dream and asked Daniel to explain it to him. In his dream the king saw a huge, frightening statue with a head of pure gold. The rest of the body was made of bronze, silver, iron and clay. A rock hit the statue and the statue crumbled. The rock became a large mountain that filled the earth.

Daniel explained that the statue stood for the kingdoms of the world that will come to an end someday. The rock stands for Jesus who will come and establish a kingdom that will never end.

God also gave Daniel dreams and visions about heaven. He saw Jesus coming into heaven on clouds. Jesus came near God's throne and was given the authority, glory and strength of a king. People from every nation will serve him and his kingdom will last for ever.

OTHER CONNECTIONS

Connect to these information bulletin boards about people and places found in the Book of Daniel:

- <u>Let's Visit Babylon, Daniel 2; 7</u>. Find out more about one of the most powerful cities in the world during Bible times and the place where Daniel lived and served under three different kings.
- <u>Who Are the Greeks? Daniel 11:3–35</u>. When Daniel predicted the Greeks would one day be a world power, they were a little known people. Yet Daniel's prediction, given to him in a vision by God, came true. Find out what importance the Greeks and their language were to play in the spread of the gospel throughout the world.

FAITH links

○ Let's Make a Deal, **Daniel 1:8–21**

○ Obeying God or Man? **Daniel 3:8–30**

○ The Writing's on the Wall, **Daniel 5**

○ In the Lions' Den, **Daniel 6**

○ Concern for All, **Daniel 9**

my FAVOURITE links

_____
_____
_____
_____

Why didn't the lions eat Daniel?

Maybe they weren't hungry! We'd better connect to <u>Daniel 6</u> to find out the real story.

OTHER COOL STORIES IN DANIEL:

<u>Eat your veggies! Daniel 1</u>
<u>The heat is on! Daniel 3</u>
<u>A grass-eating king, Daniel 4:28–37</u>
<u>Writing on the wall, Daniel 5:22–31</u>

▶ **Daniel 1:1 1150**

Daniel Taken to Babylon

1 During the third year that Jehoiakim was king of Judah, Nebuchadnezzar king of Babylon came to Jerusalem and surrounded it with his army. 2 The Lord allowed Nebuchadnezzar to capture Jehoiakim king of Judah. Nebuchadnezzar also took some of the things from the Temple of God, which he carried to Babylonia and put in the temple of his gods.

3 Then King Nebuchadnezzar ordered Ashpenaz, his chief officer, to bring some of the Israelite men into his palace. He wanted them to be from important families, including the family of the king of Judah. 4 King Nebuchadnezzar wanted only young Israelite men who had nothing wrong with them. They were to be handsome and well educated, capable of learning and understanding and able to serve in his palace. Ashpenaz was to teach them the language and writings of the Babylonians. 5 The king gave the young men a certain amount of food and wine every day, just like the food he ate. The young men were to be trained for three years, and then they would become servants of the king of Babylon. 6 Among those young men were Daniel, Hananiah, Mishael and Azariah from the people of Judah.

7 Ashpenaz, the chief officer, gave them Babylonian names. Daniel's new name was Belteshazzar, Hananiah's was Shadrach, Mishael's was Meshach and Azariah's was Abednego.

8 Daniel decided not to eat the king's food or drink his wine because that would make him unclean. So he asked Ashpenaz for permission not to make himself unclean in this way.

9 God made Ashpenaz, the chief officer, want to be kind and merciful to Daniel, 10 but Ashpenaz said to Daniel, "I am afraid of my master, the king. He ordered me to give you this food and drink. If you begin to look worse than other young men your age, the king will see this. Then he will cut off my head because of you."

11 Ashpenaz had ordered a guard to watch Daniel, Hananiah, Mishael and Azariah. 12 Daniel said to the guard, "Please give us this test for ten days: don't give us anything but vegetables to eat and

---

FAITH links

LET'S MAKE A DEAL
DANIEL 1:8-21

Suppose your teacher involved your class in an activity that you and your parents agreed was wrong for you. Should you go along with the activity in order to be obedient? Daniel faced a similar situation. He was a servant to the king of Babylon, but he wanted to obey God. The king wanted him to eat the foods all his servants ate. Daniel wanted to eat the healthier food that he thought God would want him to eat. So Daniel suggested a test to see which foods made him healthier.

You may need to bargain with others sometimes. God can give you the wisdom to suggest other choices and to do what is right.

Here are some more Faithlinks on making smart choices:

Take Me to Your Leader, Numbers 27:12–23, p. 214

Who Do You Trust? Joshua 9, p. 287

A Wise Wish, 1 Kings 3:5–9, p. 439

If You Want My Advice . . . Proverbs 13:1, p. 843

That's False! 2 John 7–11, p. 1722

Helpful Hints, 3 John 11, p. 1724

water to drink. 13 After ten days compare how we look with how the other young men look who eat the king's food. See for yourself and then decide how you want to treat us, your servants."

14 So the guard agreed to test them for ten days. 15 After ten days they looked healthier and better fed than all the young men who ate the king's food. 16 So the guard took away the king's special food and wine, feeding them vegetables instead.

17 God gave these four young men wisdom and the ability to learn many things that people had written and studied. Daniel could also understand visions and dreams.

1:17 Talents
Who gives you your talents?

18 At the end of the time set for them by the king, Ashpenaz brought all the young men to King Nebuchadnezzar. 19 The king talked to them and found that none of the young men were as good as Daniel, Hananiah, Mishael and Azariah. So those four young men became the king's servants. 20 Every time the king asked them about something important, they showed much wisdom and understanding. They were ten times better than all the fortune-tellers and magicians in his kingdom! 21 So Daniel continued to be the king's servant until the first year Cyrus was king.

Nebuchadnezzar's Dream

2 During Nebuchadnezzar's second year as king, he had dreams that bothered him and kept him awake at night. 2 So the king called for his fortune-tellers, magicians, wizards and wise men, because he wanted them to tell him what he had dreamed. They came in and stood in front of the king.

3 Then the king said to them, "I have had a dream that bothers me, and I want to know what it means."

4 The wise men answered the king in the Aramaic language, "Our king, live for ever! Please tell us, your servants, your dream. Then we will tell you what it means."

5 King Nebuchadnezzar said to them, "I meant what I said. You must tell me the dream and what it means. If you don't, I will have you torn apart, and I will turn your houses into piles of stones. 6 But if you tell me my dream and its meaning, I will reward you with gifts and great honour. So tell me the dream and what it means."

7 Again the wise men said to the king, "Tell us, your servants, the dream, and we will tell you what it means."

8 King Nebuchadnezzar answered, "I know you are trying to get more time, because you know that I meant what I said. 9 If you don't tell me my dream, you will be punished. You have all agreed to tell me lies and wicked things, hoping things will change. Now, tell me the dream so that I will know you can tell me what it really means!"

10 The wise men answered the king, saying, "No one on earth can do what the king asks! No great and powerful king has ever asked the fortune-tellers, magicians or wise men to do this; 11 the king is asking something that is too hard. Only the gods could tell the king this, but the gods do not live among people."

12 When the king heard their answer, he became very angry. He ordered that all the wise men of Babylon be killed. 13 So King Nebuchadnezzar's order to kill the wise men was announced, and men were sent to look for Daniel and his friends to kill them.

14 Arioch, the commander of the king's guards, was going to kill the wise men of Babylon. But Daniel spoke to him with wisdom and skill, 15 saying, "Why did the king order such a terrible punishment?" Then Arioch explained everything to Daniel. 16 So Daniel went to King Nebuchadnezzar and asked for an appointment so that he could tell the king what his dream meant.

17 Then Daniel went to his house and explained the whole story to his friends Hananiah, Mishael and Azariah. 18 Daniel asked his friends to pray that the God of heaven would show them mercy and help them understand this secret so he and his friends would not

Daniel 2:19 1152

LET'S VISIT BABYLON
Daniel 2; 7

Babylon was the capital of the Babylonian Empire. It was located between two famous rivers: the Tigris and the Euphrates. Babylon was at its richest and finest when King Nebuchadnezzar II was king. Most important cities at that time had walls for protection. Babylon had a *double* wall and eight major gates into the city. The walls were decorated with coloured bricks that had drawings of lions, dragons and bulls. One of the most famous sights in Babylon was King Nebuchadnezzar's Hanging Gardens, one of the seven wonders of the ancient world.

At one time, God's people in Judah were taken as captives to Babylon. The stories that you have heard about Daniel in the lions' den and Daniel's friends in the fiery furnace happened in Babylon. Daniel predicted the destruction of Babylon and today the whole city remains in ruins.

be killed with the other wise men of Babylon.

19 During the night God explained the secret to Daniel in a vision. Then Daniel praised the God of heaven. 20 Daniel said:
"Praise God for ever and ever,
 because he has wisdom and power.
21 He changes the times and seasons of
  the year.
 He takes away the power of kings
  and gives their power to new
  kings.
 He gives wisdom to those who are
  wise
 and knowledge to those who
  understand.
22 He makes known secrets that are
  deep and hidden;
 he knows what is hidden in
  darkness,
 and light is all around him.
23 I thank you and praise you, God of
  my ancestors,
 because you have given me
  wisdom and power.
 You told me what we asked of you;
  you told us about the king's
  dream."

The Meaning of the Dream

24 Then Daniel went to Arioch, the man King Nebuchadnezzar had chosen to kill the wise men of Babylon. Daniel said to him, "Don't put the wise men of Babylon to death. Take me to the king, and I will tell him what his dream means."

25 Very quickly Arioch took Daniel to the king and said, "I have found a man among the captives from Judah who can tell the king what his dream means."

26 The king asked Daniel, who was also called Belteshazzar, "Are you able to tell me what I dreamed and what it means?"

27 Daniel answered, "No wise man, magician or fortune-teller can explain to the king the secret he has asked about. 28 But there is a God in heaven who explains secret things, and he has shown King Nebuchadnezzar what will happen at a later time. This is your dream, the vision you saw while lying on your bed: 29 our king, as you were lying there, you thought about things to come. God, who can tell people about secret things, showed you what is going to happen. 30 God also told this secret to me, not because I have

greater wisdom than any other living person, but so that you may know what it means. In that way you will understand what went through your mind.

31 "Our king, in your dream you saw a huge, shiny and frightening statue in front of you. 32 The head of the statue was made of pure gold. Its chest and arms were made of silver. Its stomach and the upper part of its legs were made of bronze. 33 The lower part of the legs were made of iron, while its feet were made partly of iron and partly of baked clay. 34 While you were looking at the statue, you saw a rock cut free, but no human being touched the rock. It hit the statue on its feet of iron and clay and smashed them. 35 Then the iron, clay, bronze, silver and gold broke to pieces at the same time. They became like chaff on a threshing floor in the summer time; the wind blew them away and there was nothing left. Then the rock that hit the statue became a very large mountain that filled the whole earth.

36 "That was your dream. Now we will tell the king what it means. 37 Our king, you are the greatest king. God of heaven has given you a kingdom, power, strength and glory. 38 Wherever people, wild animals and birds live, God made you ruler over them. King Nebuchadnezzar, you are the head of gold on that statue.

39 "Another kingdom will come after you, but it will not be as great as yours. Next a third kingdom, the bronze part, will rule over the earth. 40 Then there will be a fourth kingdom, strong as iron. In the same way that iron crushes and smashes things to pieces, the fourth kingdom will smash and crush all the other kingdoms.

41 "You saw that the statue's feet and toes were partly baked clay and partly iron. That means the fourth kingdom will be a divided kingdom. It will have some of the strength of iron in it, just as you saw iron was mixed with clay. 42 The toes of the statue were partly iron and partly clay. So the fourth kingdom will be partly strong like iron and partly breakable like clay. 43 You saw the iron mixed with clay, but iron and clay do not hold together. In the same way the people of the fourth kingdom will be a mixture, but they will not be united as one people.

44 "During the time of those kings, the God of heaven will set up another kingdom that will never be destroyed or given to another group of people. This kingdom will crush all the other kingdoms and bring them to an end, but it will continue for ever.

45 "King Nebuchadnezzar, you saw a rock cut from a mountain, but no human being touched it. The rock broke the iron, bronze, clay, silver and gold to pieces. In this way the great God showed you what will happen. The dream is true, and you can trust this explanation."

46 Then King Nebuchadnezzar fell face down on the ground in front of Daniel. The king honoured him and commanded that an offering and incense be presented to him. 47 Then the king said to Daniel, "Truly I know your God is the greatest of all gods, the Lord of all the kings. He tells people about things they cannot know. I know this is true, because you were able to tell these secret things to me."

48 Then the king gave Daniel many gifts plus an important position in his kingdom. Nebuchadnezzar made him ruler over the whole area of Babylon and put him in charge of all the wise men of Babylon. 49 Daniel asked the king to make Shadrach, Meshach and Abednego leaders over the area of Babylon, so the king did as Daniel asked. Daniel himself became one of the people who stayed at the royal court.

The Gold Idol and Blazing Furnace

3 King Nebuchadnezzar made a gold statue 30 metres high and 3 metres wide and set it up on the plain of Dura in the area of Babylon. 2 Then he called for the leaders: the governors, assistant governors, captains of the soldiers, people who advised the king, keepers of the treasury, judges, rulers and all other officers in his kingdom. He wanted them to come to the special service for the statue he had set up. 3 So they all came for the special service and stood in front of the

statue that King Nebuchadnezzar had set up. **4** Then the man who made announcements for the king said in a loud voice, "People, nations and those of every language, this is what you are commanded to do: **5** when you hear the sound of the horns, flutes, lyres, zithers,[n] harps, pipes and all the other musical instruments, you must bow down and worship the gold statue that King Nebuchadnezzar has set up. **6** Anyone who doesn't bow down and worship will immediately be thrown into a blazing furnace."

7 Now people, nations and those who spoke every language were there. When they heard the sound of the horns, flutes, lyres, zithers, pipes and all the other musical instruments they bowed down and worshipped the gold statue King Nebuchadnezzar had set up.

8 Then some Babylonians came up to the king and began speaking against the men of Judah. **9** They said to King Nebuchadnezzar, "Our king, live for ever! **10** Our king, you gave a command that everyone who heard the horns, lyres, zithers, harps, pipes and all the other musical instruments would have to bow down and worship the gold statue. **11** Anyone who wouldn't do this was to be thrown into a blazing furnace. **12** Our king, there are some men of Judah whom you made officers in the area of Babylon that did not pay attention to your order. Their names are Shadrach, Meshach and Abednego. They do not serve your gods and do not worship the gold statue you have set up."

13 Nebuchadnezzar became very angry and called for Shadrach, Meshach and Abednego. When they were brought to the king, **14** Nebuchadnezzar said, "Shadrach, Meshach and Abednego, is it true that you do not serve my gods nor worship the gold statue I have set up? **15** In a moment you will again hear the sound of the horns, flutes, lyres, zithers, harps, pipes and all the other musical instruments. If you bow down and worship the statue I made, that will be good. But if you do not worship it, you will immediately be thrown into the blazing furnace. What god will be able to save you from my power then?"

FAITH links

OBEYING GOD OR MAN?
DANIEL 3:8-30

Imagine being told that you had to bow before a statue of the Member of Parliament for your area. If you didn't bow, you'd be thrown in jail. What would you do? Shadrach, Meshach and Abednego had been told to bow down to a statue of King Nebuchadnezzar. They had to decide if they would obey God or the king.

God wants us to obey the people that are in our government, except when obeying them causes us to disobey God. God honours our obedience to him, even if it means disobeying those in authority.

Who do you obey? Check out these links:

The Sacrifice, Genesis 22, p. 29

Sitting on the Fence, 1 Kings 18, p. 464

A Promise from the Heart, Jeremiah 31:31–33, p. 1037

The Greatest Commandment, Matthew 22:36–40, p. 1313

Believe It or Not, Luke 1:20, 38, p. 1366

A Christian's Responsibility, Acts 11:26, p. 1484

16 Shadrach, Meshach and Abednego answered the king, saying, "Nebuchadnezzar, we do not need to defend our-

---
3:5 zithers Musical instruments with 30 to 40 strings.

selves to you. **17** If you throw us into the blazing furnace, the God we serve is able to save us from the furnace. He will save us from your power, Our king. **18** But even if God does not save us, we want you, Our king, to know this: we will not serve your gods or worship the gold statue you have set up."

19 Then Nebuchadnezzar was furious with Shadrach, Meshach and Abednego, and he changed his mind. He ordered the furnace to be heated seven times hotter than usual. **20** Then he commanded some of the strongest soldiers in his army to tie up Shadrach, Meshach and Abednego and throw them into the blazing furnace.

21 So Shadrach, Meshach and Abednego were tied up and thrown into the blazing furnace while still wearing their robes, trousers, turbans and other clothes. **22** The king's command was very strict, and the furnace was made so hot that the flames killed the strong soldiers who threw Shadrach, Meshach and Abednego into the furnace. **23** Firmly tied, Shadrach, Meshach and Abednego fell into the blazing furnace.

24 Then King Nebuchadnezzar was so surprised that he jumped to his feet. He asked the men who advised him, "Didn't we tie up only three men and throw them into the fire?"

They answered, "Yes, Our king."

25 The king said, "Look! I see four men walking around in the fire. They are not tied up, and they are not burned. The fourth man looks like a son of the gods."

26 Then Nebuchadnezzar went to the opening of the blazing furnace and shouted, "Shadrach, Meshach and Abednego, come out! Servants of the Most High God, come here!"

So Shadrach, Meshach and Abednego came out of the fire. **27** When they came out, the governors, assistant governors, captains of the soldiers and royal advisers crowded around them and saw that the fire had not harmed their bodies. Their hair was not burned, their robes were not burned and they didn't even smell of smoke!

28 Then Nebuchadnezzar said, "Praise the God of Shadrach, Meshach and Abednego. Their God has sent his angel and saved his servants from the fire! These three men trusted their God and refused to obey my command. They were willing to die rather than serve or worship any god other than their own. **29** So I now give this command: anyone from any nation or language who says anything against the God of Shadrach, Meshach and Abednego will be torn apart and have his house turned into a pile of stones. No other god can save his people like this." **30** Then the king promoted Shadrach, Meshach and Abednego in the area of Babylon.

Nebuchadnezzar's Dream of a Tree

4 King Nebuchadnezzar sent this letter to the people, nations and those who speak every language in all the world:

I wish you peace and great wealth!

2 The Most High God has done miracles and wonderful things for me that I am happy to tell you about.

3 His wonderful acts are great,
and his miracles are mighty.
His kingdom goes on for ever,
and his rule continues from now on.

4 I, Nebuchadnezzar, was happy and successful at my palace, **5** but I had a dream that made me afraid. As I was lying on my bed, I saw pictures and visions in my mind that alarmed me. **6** So I ordered all the wise men of Babylon to come to me and tell me what my dream meant. **7** The fortune-tellers, magicians and wise men came, and I told them about the dream. But they could not tell me what it meant.

8 Finally, Daniel came to me. (I called him Belteshazzar to honour my god, because the spirit of the holy gods is in him.) I told my dream to him. **9** I said, "Belteshazzar, you are the most important of all the fortune-tellers. I know that the spirit of the holy gods is in you, so there is no secret that is too hard for you to understand. This was what I dreamed; tell me what it means. 10 These are the visions I saw while I was lying in my bed: I looked, and there in front of me was a tree standing in the middle of the earth. And it was very tall. 11 The tree grew large and strong. The top of the tree touched the sky and could be seen from anywhere on earth. 12 The leaves of the tree were beautiful. It had plenty of good fruit on it, enough food for everyone. The wild animals found shelter under the tree, and the birds lived in its branches. Every animal ate from it.

13 "As I was looking at those things in the vision while lying on my bed, I saw an observer, a holy angel coming down from heaven. 14 He spoke very loudly and said, 'Cut down the tree and cut off its branches. Strip off its leaves and scatter its fruit. Let the animals under the tree run away, and let the birds in its branches fly away. 15 But leave the stump and its roots in the ground with a band of iron and bronze around it; let it stay in the field with the grass around it.

"'Let the man become wet with dew, and let him live among the animals and plants of the earth. 16 Let him not think like a human any longer, but let him have the mind of an animal for seven years.

17 "'The observers gave this command; the holy ones declared the sentence. This is so all people may know that the Most High God rules over every kingdom on earth. God gives those kingdoms to anyone he wants, and he chooses people to rule them who are not proud.'

18 "That is what I, King Nebuchadnezzar, dreamed. Now Belte-

FAITH links

EATING HUMBLE PIE
DANIEL 4

Who is the most powerful person you know? Your dad? Your headmaster? At one time, King Nebuchadnezzar was the most powerful ruler on earth. His palace was one of the wonders of the known world. All of that success went to his head. After Nebuchadnezzar expressed pride in his own "mighty power", God humbled Nebuchadnezzar in an unusual way.

Pride causes a person to think, *Look what I have done.* Humility keeps a person's sight on God. As Nebuchadnezzar learned, "He [God] is able to make proud people humble."

The Trouble with Jealousy, Genesis 37, p. 53

Put Pride Aside, Exodus 2:11–15, p. 78

What I've Got, 2 Kings 20:12–17, p. 508

Just a Test, Luke 4:1–13, p. 1373

Best Seat in the House, Luke 14:7–11, p. 1398

Most Wanted? 2 Corinthians 10:1, p. 1580

shazzar," tell me what the dream means. None of the wise men in my kingdom can explain it to me, but you can, because the spirit of the holy gods is in you."

4:18 **Belteshazzar** Another name for Daniel.

Daniel Explains the Dream

19 Then Daniel, who was called Belteshazzar, was very quiet for a while, because his understanding of the dream frightened him. So the king said, "Belteshazzar, do not let the dream or its meaning make you afraid."

Then Belteshazzar answered, "My master, I wish the dream were about your enemies, and I wish its meaning were for those who are against you! 20 You saw a tree in your dream that grew large and strong. Its top touched the sky, and it could be seen from all over the earth. 21 Its leaves were beautiful, and it had plenty of fruit for everyone to eat. It was a home for the wild animals, and its branches were nesting places for the birds. 22 Our king, you are that tree! You have become great and powerful, like the tall tree that touched the sky. Your power reaches to the far parts of the earth.

23 "Our king, you saw an observer, a holy angel, coming down from heaven who said, 'Cut down the tree and destroy it. But leave the stump and its roots in the ground with a band of iron and bronze around it; leave it in the field with the grass. Let him become wet with dew and live like a wild animal for seven years.'

24 "This is the meaning of the dream, Our king. The Most High God has commanded these things to happen to my master the king: 25 you will be forced away from people to live among the wild animals. People will feed you grass like an ox, and dew from the sky will make you wet. Seven years will pass, and then you will learn this lesson: the Most High God is ruler over every kingdom on earth, and he gives those kingdoms to anyone he chooses.

26 "Since the stump of the tree and its roots were left in the ground, your kingdom will be given back to you when you learn that one in heaven rules your kingdom. 27 So, Our king, please accept my advice. Stop sinning and do what is right. Stop doing wicked things and be kind to the poor. Then you might continue to be successful."

The King's Dream Comes True

28 All these things happened to King Nebuchadnezzar. 29 Twelve months later as he was walking on the roof[n] of his palace in Babylon, 30 he said, "I have built this great Babylon as my royal home. I built it by my power to show my glory and my majesty."

31 The words were still in his mouth when a voice from heaven said, "King Nebuchadnezzar, these things will happen to you: your royal power has been taken away from you. 32 You will be forced away from people. You will live with the wild animals and will be fed grass like an ox. Seven years will pass before you learn this lesson: the Most High God rules over every kingdom on earth and gives those kingdoms to anyone he chooses."

33 Immediately the words came true. Nebuchadnezzar was forced to go away from people, and he began eating grass like an ox. He became wet from dew. His hair grew long like the feathers of an eagle, and his nails grew like the claws of a bird.

34 At the end of that time, I, Nebuchadnezzar, looked up towards heaven, and I could think normally again! Then I gave praise to the Most High God; I gave honour and glory to him who lives for ever.

God's rule is for ever,

4:29 roof In Bible times houses were built with flat roofs. The roof was used for drying things such as flax and fruit. And it was used as an extra room, as a place for worship and as a place to sleep in the summer.

and his kingdom continues for all time. 35 People on earth are not truly important. God does what he wants with the powers of heaven and the people on earth. No one can stop his powerful hand or question what he does.

36 At that time I could think normally again, and God gave back my great honour and power and returned the glory to my kingdom. The people who advised me and the royal family came to me for help again. I became king again and was even greater and more powerful than before. 37 Now I, Nebuchadnezzar, give praise and honour and glory to the King of heaven. Everything he does is right and fair, and he is able to make proud people humble.

The Writing on the Wall

5 King Belshazzar gave a big banquet for 1,000 royal guests and drank wine with them. 2 As Belshazzar was drinking his wine, he gave orders to bring the gold and silver cups that his ancestor Nebuchadnezzar had taken from the Temple in Jerusalem. This was so the king, his royal guests, his wives and his slave women could drink from those cups. 3 So they brought the gold cups that had been taken from the Temple of God in Jerusalem. And the king and his royal guests, his wives and his slave women drank from them. 4 As they were drinking, they praised their gods, which were made from gold, silver, bronze, iron, wood and stone.

5 Suddenly the fingers of a person's hand appeared and began writing on the plaster of the wall, near the lampstand in the royal palace. The king watched the hand as it wrote.

6 King Belshazzar was very frightened. His face turned white, his knees knocked together and he could not stand up because his legs were too weak. 7 The king called for the magicians, wise men and wizards of Babylon and said to them, "Anyone who can read this writing and explain it will receive purple clothes fit for a king and a gold chain around his neck. And I will make that person the third highest ruler in the kingdom."

8 Then all the king's wise men came in, but they could not read the writing or tell the king what it meant. 9 King Belshazzar became even more afraid, and his face became even whiter. His royal guests were confused.

10 Then the king's mother, who had heard the voices of the king and his royal guests, came into the banquet room. She said, "Our king, live for ever! Don't be afraid or let your face be white with fear! 11 There is a man in your kingdom who has the spirit of the holy gods. In the days of your father, this man showed understanding, knowledge and wisdom like the gods. Your father, King Nebuchadnezzar, put this man in charge of all the wise men, fortune-tellers, magicians and wizards. 12 The man I am talking about is named Daniel, whom the king named Belteshazzar. He was very clever and had knowledge and understanding. He could explain dreams and secrets and could answer very hard problems. Call for Daniel. He will tell you what the writing on the wall means."

13 So they brought Daniel to the king, and the king asked, "Is your name Daniel? Are you one of the captives my father the king brought from Judah? 14 I have heard that the spirit of the gods is in you, and that you are very clever and have knowledge and extraordinary understanding. 15 The wise men and magicians were brought to me to read this writing and to explain what it means, but they could not explain it. 16 I have heard that you are able to explain what things mean and can find the answers to hard problems. Read this writing on the wall and explain it to me. If you can, I will give you purple clothes fit for a king and a gold chain to wear around your neck. And you will become the third highest ruler in the kingdom."

17 Then Daniel answered the king, "You may keep your gifts for yourself, or

you may give those rewards to someone else. But I will read the writing on the wall for you and will explain to you what it means.

18 "Our king, the Most High God made your father Nebuchadnezzar a great, important and powerful king. 19 Because God made him important, all the people, nations and those who spoke every language were very frightened of Nebuchadnezzar. If he wanted someone to die, he killed that person. If he wanted someone to live, he let that person live. Those he wanted to promote, he promoted. Those he wanted to be less important, he made less important.

20 "But Nebuchadnezzar became too proud and stubborn, so he was taken off his royal throne. His glory was taken away. 21 He was forced away from people, and his mind became like the mind of an animal. He lived with the wild donkeys and was fed grass like an ox and became wet with dew. These things happened to him until he learned his lesson: the Most High God rules over every kingdom on earth, and he sets anyone he chooses over those kingdoms.

22 "Belshazzar, you already knew these things, because you are a descendant of Nebuchadnezzar. Still you have not been sorry for what you have done. 23 Instead, you have set yourself against the Lord of heaven. You ordered the drinking cups from the Temple of the Lord to be brought to you. Then you and your royal guests, your wives and your slave women drank wine from them. You praised the gods of silver, gold, bronze, iron, wood and stone that are not really gods; they cannot see or hear or understand anything. You did not honour God, who has power over your life and everything you do. 24 So God sent the hand that wrote on the wall.

25 "These are the words that were written on the wall: 'Mene, mene, tekel, parsin'.

26 "This is what the words mean: Mene: God has counted the days until your kingdom will end. 27 Tekel: you have been weighed on the scales and found not good enough. 28 Parsin: your kingdom is being divided and will be given to the Medes and the Persians."

FAITH links

THE WRITING'S ON THE WALL
DANIEL 5

What is the most unusual way you've heard of for a message to be delivered? God delivered a message to Belshazzar in a unique way. He allowed the fingers of a hand to suddenly appear and write a message on a wall!

God has ways of getting his messages across. He doesn't always use a large handwritten note on a wall to get a person's attention. One of the most unique ways he's used was to send his Son to earth to become a human. Unlike the message delivered to Belshazzar, God's Son brought good news. God wants everyone to pay attention to that message. Are you paying attention?

Ten Ways to Obey, Exodus 20, p. 103

An Admirable Quality, 1 Kings 10:1–13, p. 451

More Precious Than Gold, Psalm 19:7–10, p. 723

Going My Way? Hosea 8:1–6, p. 1179

Prove It! Matthew 16:1–4, p. 1302

Want to Know? Ask! Luke 9:45, p. 1386

Daniel 5:29 1160

29 Then Belshazzar gave an order for Daniel to be dressed in purple clothes and to have a gold chain put around his neck. And it was announced that Daniel was the third highest ruler in the kingdom. 30 That very same night Belshazzar, king of the Babylonian people, was killed. 31 So Darius the Mede became the new king when he was 62 years old.

Daniel and the Lions

6 Darius thought it would be a good idea to choose 120 governors who would rule his kingdom. 2 He chose three men as supervisors over those governors, and Daniel was one of the supervisors. The supervisors were to ensure that the governors did not try to cheat the king. 3 Daniel showed that he could do the work better than the other supervisors and governors, so the king planned to put Daniel in charge of the whole kingdom. 4 Because of this, the other supervisors and governors tried to find reasons to accuse Daniel about his work in the government. But they could not find anything wrong with him or any reason to accuse him, because he was trustworthy and not lazy or dishonest.

EMAIL FROM GOD
6:4–5
Character
An example of good character.

5 Finally these men said, "We will never find any reason to accuse Daniel unless it is about the law of his God." 6 So the supervisors and governors went as a group to the king and said: "King Darius, live for ever! 7 The supervisors, assistant governors, governors, the people who advise you and the captains of the soldiers have all agreed that you should make a new law for everyone to obey: for the next 30 days no one should pray to any god or human except to you, Our king. Anyone who doesn't obey will be thrown into the lions' den. 8 Now, Our king, make the law and sign your name to it so that it cannot be changed, because then it will be a law of the Medes and Persians and cannot be cancelled." 9 So King Darius signed the law.

10 Even though Daniel knew that the new law had been written, he went to pray in an upstairs room in his house, which had windows that opened towards Jerusalem. Three times each day Daniel would kneel down to pray and thank God, just as he always had done.

FAITH links

IN THE LIONS' DEN
DANIEL 6

If you've ever been made fun of because you're clever or do all of your homework, you can relate to Daniel's experience. You've probably heard his story many times before. Jealous men came up with a law to trap Daniel. Because of the law, the king had Daniel thrown into the lions' den. But God prevented Daniel from being hurt.

People might try to make trouble for you because of your good work or because you follow God. When that happens, don't think that God has given up on you. He protected Daniel. He'll protect you, too.

Feel like you're up against lions sometimes? Surf on for help:

Moses' Champion, Numbers 12, p. 192

Play Fair or Play Favourites? Deuteronomy 1:16–18, p. 227

Wronged for What's Right, Ezra 4:4–5, p. 612

Go! No! Jonah 1, p. 1213

Keep Up the Good Work! Galatians 6:9–10, p. 1593

The Gentle Way, Titus 3:1–5, p. 1661

11 Then those men went as a group and found Daniel praying and asking God for help. 12 So they went to the king and talked to him about the law he had made. They said, "Didn't you sign a law that says no one may pray to any god or human except you, Our king? Doesn't it say that anyone who disobeys during the next 30 days will be thrown into the lions' den?"

The king answered, "Yes, that is the law, and the laws of the Medes and Persians cannot be cancelled."

13 Then they said to the king, "Daniel, one of the captives from Judah, is not paying attention to you, Our king, or to the law you signed. Daniel still prays to his God three times every day." 14 The king became very upset when he heard this. He wanted to save Daniel, and he worked hard until sunset trying to think of a way to save him.

15 Then those men went as a group to the king. They said, "Remember, Our king, the law of the Medes and Persians says that no law or command given by the king can be changed."

16 So King Darius gave the order, and Daniel was brought in and thrown into the lions' den. The king said to Daniel, "May the God you serve all the time save you!" 17 A big stone was brought and placed over the opening of the lions' den. Then the king used his signet ring and the rings of his royal officers to put special seals on the rock. This showed that no one would move the rock and bring Daniel out. 18 Then King Darius went back to his palace. He did not eat that night, he did not have any entertainment brought to him, and he could not sleep.

19 The next morning King Darius got up at dawn and hurried to the lions' den. 20 As he came near the den, he was worried. He called out to Daniel, "Daniel, servant of the living God! Has your God that you always worship been able to save you from the lions?"

21 Daniel answered, "Our king, live for ever! 22 My God sent his angel to close the lions' mouths. They have not hurt me, because my God knows I am innocent. I never did anything wrong to you, Our king."

23 King Darius was very happy and told his servants to lift Daniel out of the lions' den. So they lifted him out and did not find any injury on him, because Daniel had trusted in his God.

24 Then the king commanded that the men who had accused Daniel be brought to the lions' den. They, their wives and their children were thrown into the den. The lions grabbed them before they hit the floor of the den and crushed their bones.

25 Then King Darius wrote a letter to all people and all nations, to those who spoke every language in the world:

I wish you great peace and wealth.

26 I am making a new law for people in every part of my kingdom. All of you must fear and respect the God of Daniel.
Daniel's God is the living God;
    he lives for ever.
His kingdom will never be
    destroyed,
    and his rule will never end.
27 God rescues and saves people
    and does mighty miracles
    in heaven and on earth.
He is the one who saved Daniel
    from the power of the lions.

28 So Daniel was successful during the time Darius was king and when Cyrus the Persian was king.

Daniel's Dream About Four Animals

7 In Belshazzar's first year as king of Babylon, Daniel had a dream. He saw visions as he was lying on his bed, and he wrote down what he had dreamed.

2 Daniel said: "I saw my vision at night. In the vision the wind was blowing from all four directions, which made the sea very rough. 3 I saw four huge animals come up from the sea, and each animal was different from the others.

4 "The first animal looked like a lion, but had wings like an eagle. I watched this animal until its wings were torn off. It was

lifted from the ground so that it stood up on two feet like a human, and it was given the mind of a human.

5 "Then I saw a second animal before me that looked like a bear. It was raised up on one of its sides and had three ribs in its mouth between its teeth. It was told, 'Get up and eat all the meat you want!'

6 "After that, I looked, and there before me was another animal. This animal looked like a leopard with four wings on its back that looked like a bird's wings. This animal had four heads and was given power to rule.

7 "After that, in my vision at night I saw in front of me a fourth animal that was cruel, terrible and very strong. It had large iron teeth. It crushed and ate what it killed, and then it walked on whatever was left. This fourth animal was different from any animal I had seen before, and it had ten horns.

8 "While I was thinking about the horns, another horn grew up among them. It was a little horn with eyes like a human's eyes. It also had a mouth, and the mouth was boasting. The little horn pulled out three of the other horns.

9 "As I looked,
thrones were put in their places,
and God, who has been alive for ever, sat on his throne.
His clothes were white like snow,
and the hair on his head was white like wool.
His throne was made from fire,
and the wheels of his throne were blazing with fire.
10 A river of fire was flowing
from in front of him.
Many thousands of angels were serving him,
and millions of angels stood before him.
Court was ready to begin,
and the books were opened.

11 "I kept on looking because the little horn was boasting. I kept watching until finally the fourth animal was killed. Its body was destroyed, and it was thrown into the burning fire. 12 (The power and rule of the other animals had been taken from them, but they were permitted to live for a certain period of time.)

13 "In my vision at night I saw in front of me someone who looked like a human being coming on the clouds in the sky. He came near God, who has been alive for ever, and he was led to God. 14 He was given authority, glory and the strength of a king. People of every tribe, nation and language will serve him. His rule will last for ever, and his kingdom will never be destroyed.

> He was given authority, glory and the strength of a king.
> – Daniel 7:14

The Meaning of the Dream

15 "I, Daniel, was worried. The visions that went through my mind frightened me. 16 I came near one of those standing there and asked what all this meant.

"So he told me and explained to me what these things meant: 17 'The four great animals are four kingdoms that will come from the earth. 18 But the holy people who belong to the Most High God will receive the power to rule and will have the power to rule for ever, from now on.'

19 "Then I wanted to know what the fourth animal meant, because it was different from all the others. It was very terrible and had iron teeth and bronze claws. It was the animal that crushed and ate what it killed and then walked on whatever was left. 20 I also wanted to know about the ten horns on its head and about the little horn that grew there. It had pulled out three of the other ten horns and looked greater than the others. It had eyes and a mouth that kept boasting. 21 As I watched, the little horn began making war against God's holy people and was defeating them 22 until God, who has been alive for ever, came. He judged in

favour of the holy people who belong to the Most High God; then the time came for them to receive the power to rule.

23 "And he explained this to me: 'The fourth animal is a fourth kingdom that will come on the earth. It will be different from all the other kingdoms and will destroy people all over the world. It will walk on and crush the whole earth. 24 The ten horns are ten kings who will come from this fourth kingdom. After those ten kings are gone, another king will come. He will be different from the kings who ruled before him, and he will defeat three of the other kings. 25 This king will speak against the Most High God, and he will hurt and kill God's holy people. He will try to change times and laws that have already been set. The holy people that belong to God will be in that king's power for three and a half years.

26 "'But the court will decide what should happen. The power of the king will be taken away, and his kingdom will be completely destroyed. 27 Then the holy people who belong to the Most High God will have the power to rule. They will rule over all the kingdoms under heaven with power and greatness, and their power to rule will last for ever. People from all the other kingdoms will respect and serve them.'

28 "That was the end of the dream. I, Daniel, was very afraid. My face became white from fear, but I kept everything to myself."

Daniel's Vision

8 During the third year of King Belshazzar's rule, I, Daniel, saw another vision, which was like the first one. 2 In this vision I saw myself in the capital city of Susa, in the area of Elam. I was standing by the Ulai Canal 3 when I looked up and saw a ram standing beside the canal. It had two long horns, but one horn was longer and newer than the other. 4 I watched the ram charge to the west, the north and the south. No animal could stand before him, and none could save another animal from his power. He did whatever he wanted and became very powerful.

5 While I was watching this, I saw a male goat come from the west. This goat had one large horn between his eyes that was easy to see. He crossed over the whole earth so fast that his feet hardly touched the ground.

6 In his anger the goat charged the ram with the two horns that I had seen standing by the canal. 7 I watched the angry goat attack the ram and break the sheep's two horns. The ram was not strong enough to stop it. The goat knocked the ram to the ground and then walked all over him. No one was able to save the ram from the goat, 8 so the male goat became very great. But when he was strong, his big horn broke off and four horns grew in place of the one big horn. Those four horns pointed in four different directions and were easy to see.

9 Then a little horn grew from one of those four horns, and it became very big. It grew to the south, the east and towards the beautiful land of Judah. 10 That little horn grew until it reached to the sky. It even threw some of the army of heaven to the ground and walked on them! 11 That little horn set itself up as equal to God, the Commander of heaven's armies. It stopped the daily sacrifices that were offered to him, and the Temple, the place where people worshipped him, was pulled down. 12 Because there was a turning away from God, the people stopped the daily sacrifices. Truth was thrown down to the ground, and the horn was successful in everything it did.

13 Then I heard a holy angel speaking. Another holy angel asked the first one, "How long will the things in this vision last—the daily sacrifices, the turning away from God that brings destruction, the Temple being pulled down and the army of heaven being walked on?"

14 The angel said to me, "This will happen for 2,300 evenings and mornings. Then the holy place will be repaired."

15 I, Daniel, saw this vision and tried to understand what it meant. In it I saw someone who looked like a man standing near me. 16 And I heard a man's voice

calling from the Ulai Canal: "Gabriel, explain the vision to this man."

17 Gabriel came to where I was standing. When he came close to me, I was very afraid and bowed face down on the ground. But Gabriel said to me, "Human being, understand that this vision is about the time of the end."

18 While Gabriel was speaking, I fell into a deep sleep with my face on the ground. Then he touched me and lifted me to my feet. 19 He said, "Now, I will explain to you what will happen in the time of God's anger. Your vision was about the set time of the end.

20 "You saw a ram with two horns, which are the kings of Media and Persia. 21 The male goat is the king of Greece, and the big horn between its eyes is the first king. 22 The four horns that grew in the place of the broken horn are four kingdoms. Those four kingdoms will come from the nation of the first king, but they will not be as strong as the first king.

23 "When the end comes near for those kingdoms, a bold and cruel king who tells lies will come. This will happen when many people have turned against God. 24 This king will be very powerful, but his power will not come from himself. He will cause terrible destruction and will be successful in everything he does. He will destroy powerful people and even God's holy people. 25 This king will succeed by using lies and force. He will think that he is very important. He will destroy many people without warning; he will try to fight even the Prince of princes! But that cruel king will be destroyed, and not by human power.

26 "The vision that has been shown to you about these evenings and mornings is true. But seal up the vision, because those things won't happen for a long time."

27 I, Daniel, became very weak and was sick for several days after that vision.

Then I got up and went back to work for the king, but I was very upset about the vision. I didn't understand what it meant.

Daniel's Prayer

9 These things happened during the first year Darius son of Xerxes was king over Babylon. He was a descendant of the Medes. 2 During Darius' first year as king, I, Daniel, was reading the Scriptures. I saw that the LORD told Jeremiah that Jerusalem would be empty ruins for 70 years.

3 Then I turned to the Lord God and prayed and asked him for help. I did not eat any food. To show my sadness, I put on rough cloth and sat in ashes. 4 I prayed to the LORD my God and told him about all of our sins. I said, "Lord, you are a great God who causes fear and wonder. You keep your agreement of love with all who love you and obey your commands.

9:4–8
Sin
Seek forgiveness for your sins.

5 "But we have sinned and done wrong. We have been wicked and turned against you, your commands and your laws. 6 We did not listen to your servants, the prophets, who spoke for you to our kings, our leaders, our ancestors and all the people of the land.

7 "Lord, you are good and right, but we are full of shame today—the people of Judah and Jerusalem, all the people of Israel, those near and far whom you scattered among many nations because they were not loyal to you. 8 LORD, we are all ashamed. Our kings and leaders and our fathers are ashamed, because we have sinned against you.

9 "But, Lord our God, you show us mercy and forgive us even though we have turned against you. 10 We have not obeyed the LORD our God or the teachings he gave us through his servants, the

> Then I got up and went back to work for the king, but I was very upset about the vision.
> – Daniel 8:27

prophets. 11 All the people of Israel have disobeyed your teachings and have turned away, refusing to obey you. So you brought on us the curses and promises of punishment written in the Teachings of Moses, the servant of God, because we sinned against you.

12 "You said these things would happen to us and our leaders, and you made them happen; you brought on us a great disaster. Nothing has ever been done on earth like what was done to Jerusalem. 13 All this disaster came to us just as it is written in the Teachings of Moses. But we have not pleaded with the LORD our God. We have not stopped sinning. We have not paid attention to your truth. 14 The LORD was ready to bring the disaster on us, and he did it because the LORD our God is right in everything he does. But we still did not obey him.

15 "Lord our God, you used your power and brought us out of Egypt. Because of that, your name is known even today. But we have sinned and have done wrong. 16 Lord, you do what is right, but please do not be angry with Jerusalem, your city on your holy hill. Because of our sins and the evil things done by our ancestors, people all around insult and make fun of Jerusalem and your people.

17 "Now, our God, hear the prayers of your servant. Listen to my prayer for help, and for your sake do good things for your holy place that is in ruins. 18 My God, pay attention and hear me. Open your eyes and see all the terrible things that have happened to us. See how our lives have been ruined and what has happened to the city that is called by your name. We do not ask these things because we are good; instead, we ask because of your mercy. 19 Lord, listen! Lord, forgive! Lord, hear us and do something! For your sake, don't wait, because your city and your people are called by your name."

Gabriel's Explanation

20 While I was saying these things in my prayer to the LORD, my God, confessing my sins and the sins of the people of Israel and praying for God's holy hill,

FAITH links

CONCERN FOR ALL
DANIEL 9

How would you show concern for a large group of people? Would you buy everyone ice cream, if you could? Daniel prayed for a large group of people – the Israelites. He told God that he was sorry for his own sins and for theirs. He also asked God to be merciful.

Praying for others is one way to show your concern for them. You might start a prayer journal, listing the needs of others in one column and the answers you receive in another. As you receive an answer, don't forget to thank God.

Just a Little Respect, 1 Chronicles 11:10–19, p. 534

Seeing the Needs, Nehemiah 1, p. 625

Help for a Friend, Mark 2:1–5, p. 1332

Jesus' Prayer, John 17, p. 1453

An Encouraging Word, 1 Corinthians 1:3–5, p. 1545

The Sacrifice of Service, Philippians 2:17, 25–30, p. 1612

21 Gabriel came to me. (I had seen him in my last vision.) He came flying quickly to me about the time of the evening sacrifice, while I was still praying. 22 He taught me and said to me, "Daniel, I have come to give you wisdom and to help you understand. 23 When you first started praying, an answer was given, and I came to tell

you, because God loves you very much. So think about the message and understand the vision.

24 "God has ordered 490 years for your people and your holy city for these reasons: to stop people from turning against God; to put an end to sin; to take away evil; to bring in goodness that continues for ever; to bring about the vision and prophecy; and to appoint a most holy place.

25 "Learn and understand these things. A command will come to rebuild Jerusalem. The time from this command until the appointed leader comes will be 49 years and 434 years. Jerusalem will be rebuilt with streets and a trench filled with water around it, but it will be built in times of trouble. 26 After the 434 years the appointed leader will be killed; he will have nothing. The people of the leader who is to come will destroy the city and the holy place. The end of the city will come like a flood, and war will continue until the end. God has ordered that place to be completely destroyed. 27 That leader will make firm an agreement with many people for seven years. He will stop the offerings and sacrifices after three and a half years. A destroyer will do terrible things until the ordered end comes to the destroyed city."

Daniel's Vision of a Man

10 During Cyrus' third year as king of Persia, Daniel, whose name was Belteshazzar, received a vision about a great war. It was a true message that Daniel understood.

2 At that time I, Daniel, had been very sad for three weeks. 3 I did not eat any fancy food or meat, or drink any wine or use any perfumed oil for three weeks. 4 On the twenty-fourth day of the first month, I was standing beside the great Tigris River. 5 While standing there, I looked up and saw a man dressed in linen clothes with a belt of fine gold wrapped around his waist. 6 His body was like shiny yellow quartz. His face was bright like lightning, and his eyes were like fire. His arms and legs were shiny like polished bronze, and his voice sounded like the roar of a crowd.

7 I, Daniel, was the only person who saw the vision. The men with me did not see it, because they were so frightened that they ran away and hid. 8 So I was left alone, watching this great vision. I lost my strength, my face turned white like a dead person and I was helpless. 9 Then I heard the man in the vision speaking. As I listened, I fell into a deep sleep with my face on the ground.

10 Then a hand touched me and set me on my hands and knees. I was so afraid that I was shaking. 11 The man in the vision said to me, "Daniel, God loves you very much. Think carefully about the words I will speak to you, and stand up, because I have been sent to you." When he said this, I stood up, but I was still shaking.

12 Then the man said to me, "Daniel, do not be afraid. Some time ago you decided to get understanding and to humble yourself before your God. Since that time God has listened to you, and I have come because of your prayers. 13 But the prince of Persia has been fighting against me for 21 days. Then Michael, one of the most important angels, came to help me, because I had been left there with the king of Persia. 14 Now I have come to explain to you what will happen to your people, because the vision is about a time in the future."

15 While he was speaking to me, I bowed face down and could not speak. 16 Then one who looked like a man touched my lips, so I opened my mouth and started to speak. I said to the one standing in front of me, "Master, I am upset and afraid because of what I saw in the vision. I feel helpless. 17 Master, how can I, your servant, talk with you? My strength is gone, and it is hard for me to breathe."

18 The one who looked like a man touched me again and gave me strength. 19 He said, "Daniel, don't be afraid. God

---

EMAIL FROM GOD
10:5–6
Angels
Meet an amazing angel!

Daniel 11:9 1167

WHO ARE THE GREEKS?   Daniel 11:3–35

The prophet Daniel predicted that Greece would become a great world power. (Read Daniel 11:3–35.) Sure enough, near the end of the Old Testament era, Greece did become a world power under the leadership of Alexander the Great. Alexander's goal was to spread Greek culture and ideas throughout the world. That's why you can still find Greek things almost everywhere, like the columns in some architecture and art.

The other great thing about Greece being a world power was that, during New Testament days, it was much easier to spread the gospel since one government ruled so much of the world. Also, since Greek was the universal language at that time, it was easy for people like the apostle Paul to preach in a lot of different places and still be understood.

---

loves you very much. Peace be with you. Be strong now; be courageous."

When he spoke to me, I became stronger and said, "Master, speak, since you have given me strength."

20 Then he said, "Daniel, do you know why I have come to you? Soon I must go back to fight against the prince of Persia. When I go, the prince of Greece will come, 21 but I must first tell you what is written in the Book of Truth. No one stands with me against these enemies except Michael, the angel ruling over your people.

11 In the first year that Darius the Mede was king, I stood up to support Michael in his fight against the prince of Persia.

Kingdoms of the South and North

2 "Now then, Daniel, I tell you the truth: three more kings will rule in Persia, and then a fourth king will come. He will be much richer than all the kings of Persia before him and will use his riches to get power. He will stir up everyone against the kingdom of Greece. 3 Then a mighty king will come, who will rule with great power and will do anything he wants. 4 After that king has come, his kingdom will be broken up and divided out towards the four parts of the world. His kingdom will not go to his descendants, and it will not have the power that he had, because his kingdom will be pulled up and given to other people.

5 "The king of the South will become strong, but one of his commanders will become even stronger. He will begin to rule his own kingdom with great power. 6 Then after a few years, a new friendship will develop. The daughter of the king of the South will marry the king of the North in order to bring peace. But she will not keep her power, and his family will not last. She, her husband, her child and those who brought her to that country will be killed.

7 "But a person from her family will become king of the South and will attack the armies of the king of the North. He will go into that king's strong, walled city and will fight and win. 8 He will take their gods, their metal idols and their valuable things made of silver and gold back to Egypt. Then he will not bother the king of the North for a few years. 9 Next, the

king of the North will attack the king of the South, but he will be beaten back to his own country.

10 "The sons of the king of the North will prepare for war. They will get a large army together that will move through the land very quickly, like a powerful flood. Later, that army will come back and fight all the way to the strong, walled city of the king of the South. 11 Then the king of the South will become very angry and will march out to fight against the king of the North. The king of the North will have a large army, but he will lose the battle, 12 and the soldiers will be carried away. The king of the South will then be very proud and will kill thousands of soldiers from the northern army, but he will not continue to be successful. 13 The king of the North will gather another army, larger than the first one. After several years he will attack with a large army and many weapons.

14 "In those times many people will be against the king of the South. Some of your own people who love to fight will turn against the king of the South, thinking it is time for God's promises to come true. But they will fail. 15 Then the king of the North will come. He will build roads of earth to the tops of the city walls and will capture a strong, walled city. The southern army will not have the power to fight back; even their best soldiers will not be strong enough to stop the northern army. 16 So the king of the North will do whatever he wants; no one will be able to stand against him. He will gain power and control in the beautiful land of Israel and will have the power to destroy it. 17 The king of the North will decide to use all his power to fight against the king of the South, but he will make a peace agreement with the king of the South. The king of the North will give one of his daughters as a wife to the king of the South so that he can defeat him. But those plans will not succeed or help him. 18 Then the king of the North will turn his attention to cities along the coast of the Mediterranean Sea and will capture them. But a commander will put an end to the pride of the king of the North, turning his pride back on him. 19 After that happens the king of the North will go back to the strong, walled cities of his own country, but he will lose his power. That will be the end of him.

20 "The next king of the North will send out a tax collector so he will have plenty of money. In a few years that ruler will be killed, although he will not die in anger or in a battle.

21 "That ruler will be followed by a very cruel and hated man, who will not have the honour of being from a king's family. He will attack the kingdom when the people feel safe, and he will take power by lying to the people. 22 He will sweep away in defeat large and powerful armies and even a prince who made an agreement. 23 Many nations will make agreements with that cruel and hated ruler, but he will lie to them. He will gain much power, but only a few people will support him. 24 The richest areas will feel safe, but that cruel and hated ruler will attack them. He will succeed where his ancestors did not. He will rob the countries he defeats and will give those things to his followers. He will plan to defeat and destroy strong cities, but he will be successful for only a short time.

25 "That very cruel and hated ruler will have a large army that he will use to stir up his strength and courage. He will attack the king of the South. The king of the South will gather a large and very powerful army and prepare for war. But the people who are against him will make secret plans, and the king of the South will be defeated. 26 People who were supposed to be his good friends will try to destroy him. His army will be swept away in defeat; many of his soldiers will be killed in battle. 27 Those two kings will want to hurt each other. They will sit at the same table and lie to each other, but it will not do either one any good, because God has set a time for their end to come. 28 The king of the North will go back to his own country with much wealth. Then he will decide to go against the holy agreement. He will take action and then return to his own country.

29 "At the right time the king of the

North will attack the king of the South again, but this time he will not be successful as he was before. 30 Ships from the west will come and fight against the king of the North, so he will be afraid. Then he will return and show his anger against the holy agreement. He will be good to those who have stopped obeying the holy agreement.

31 "The king of the North will send his army to make the Temple in Jerusalem unclean. They will stop the people from offering the daily sacrifice, and then they will set up the destroying terror. 32 The king of the North will tell lies and cause those who have not obeyed God to be ruined. But those who know God and obey him will be strong and fight back.

33 "Those who are wise will help the others understand what is happening. But they will be killed with swords or burned, or taken captive or robbed of their homes and possessions. These things will continue for many days. 34 When the wise ones are suffering, they will get a little help, but many who join the wise ones will not help them in their time of need. 35 Some of the wise ones will be killed. But the hard times must come so they can be made stronger and purer and without faults until the time of the end comes. Then, at the right time, the end will come.

The King Who Praises Himself

36 "The king of the North will do whatever he wants. He will boast about himself and praise himself and think he is even better than a god. He will say things against the God of gods that no one has ever heard. And he will be successful until all the bad things have happened. Then what God has planned to happen will happen. 37 The king of the North will not care about the gods his ancestors worshipped or the god that women worship. He won't care about any god. Instead, he will make himself more important than any god. 38 The king of the North will worship power and strength, which his ancestors did not worship. He will honour the god of power with gold and silver, expensive jewels and gifts. 39 That king will attack fortified cities with the help of a foreign god. He will give much honour to the people who join him, making them rulers in charge of many other people. And he will make them pay him for the land they rule.

40 "At the time of the end, the king of the South will fight a battle against the king of the North. The king of the North will attack with chariots, soldiers on horses and many large ships. He will invade many countries and sweep through their lands like a flood. 41 The king of the North will attack the beautiful land of Judah. He will defeat many countries, but Edom, Moab and the leaders of Ammon will be saved from him. 42 The king of the North will show his power in many countries; Egypt will not escape. 43 The king will get treasures of gold and silver and all the riches of Egypt. The Libyan and Nubian people will obey him. 44 But the king of the North will hear news from the east and the north that will make him afraid and angry. He will go to destroy completely many nations. 45 He will set up his royal tents between the sea and the beautiful mountain where the holy Temple is built. But, finally, his end will come, and no one will help him.

The Time of the End

12 "At that time Michael, the great prince who protects your people, will stand up. There will be a time of much trouble, the worst time since nations have been on earth, but your people will be saved. Everyone whose name is written in God's book will be saved. 2 Many people who have already died will live again. Some of them will wake up to have life for ever, but some will wake up to find shame and disgrace for ever. 3 The wise people will shine like the brightness of the sky. Those who teach others to live right will shine like stars for ever and ever.

4 "But you, Daniel, close up the book and seal it. These things will happen at the time of the end. Many people will go here and there to find true knowledge."

5 Then I, Daniel, looked, and saw two other men. One was standing on my side

of the river, and the other was standing on the far side. **6** The man who was dressed in linen was standing over the water in the river. One of the two men spoke to him and asked, "How long will it be before these amazing things come true?"

7 The man dressed in linen, who stood over the water, raised his hands towards heaven. And I heard him swear by the name of God who lives for ever, "It will be for three and a half years. The power of the holy people will finally be broken, and then all these things will come true."

8 I heard the answer, but I did not really understand, so I asked, "Master, what will happen after all these things come true?"

9 He answered, "Go your way, Daniel. The message is closed up and sealed until the time of the end. **10** Many people will be made clean, pure and spotless, but the wicked will continue to be wicked. Those wicked people will not understand these things, but the wise will understand them.

11 "The daily sacrifice will be stopped. Then, 1,290 days later, the destroying terror will be set up. **12** Those who wait for the end of the 1,335 days will be happy.

13 "As for you, Daniel, go your way until the end. You will get your rest, and at the end you will rise to receive your reward."

> As for you, Daniel, go your way until the end. You will get your rest, and at the end you will rise to receive your reward.
> – Daniel 12:13

A CALL TO COME HOME

Hi, there. I'm Hosea, a prophet of God. Have you ever had a really good friend? A friend you cared for deeply? What if that friend promised to go to the pictures with you but at the last minute chose to go to a party with someone else? What if your friend refused to see you or even to talk to you on the phone? You would be sad, but probably not as sad as I was about my wife, Gomer. I loved her with all my heart, but she was not faithful to me. Gomer left me and our children, but one day I brought her home again.

I wrote this book to warn the people of Israel about their unfaithfulness to God. My life with Gomer was a picture of God and the unfaithful nation of Israel. God loved Israel even more than I loved Gomer and wanted Israel to worship him alone. The people of Israel continued to worship false gods, so God allowed them to be conquered by their enemies. But God, like Gomer and me, promised to bring Israel home one day to be his chosen people again.

JESUS WATCH

Gomer, in her unfaithfulness, was eventually held as a slave. Hosea loved her so much that he was willing to pay the price to buy her back. He paid fifteen pieces of silver and 150 kilogrammes of barley to save her from a life of slavery. Before we believe in Jesus, we are slaves, too. Jesus said, "Everyone who lives in sin is a slave to sin" (John 8:34). Jesus loves us so much that he paid the price for our sins. He gave his life as a sacrifice and saved us from a life of sin. Now we are children of God and live to please our Father. God sends us the Holy Spirit who helps us become holy and more like Jesus.

FAITH links

Why did the merchants use dishonest scales?

Sounds like they were a bunch of con men. Let's download Hosea 12:7-8 to find out.

- A Hopeful Name, Hosea 1:3–11
- A Fake Apology, Hosea 6:1–7
- Going My Way? Hosea 8:1–6
- Long-lasting Hope, Hosea 14

Hosea 1:1

1 The LORD spoke his word to Hosea son of Beeri during the time that Uzziah, Jotham, Ahaz and Hezekiah were kings of Judah and Jeroboam son of Jehoash was king of Israel.

Hosea's Wife and Children

2 When the LORD began speaking through Hosea, the LORD said to him, "Go and marry an unfaithful woman and have unfaithful children, because the people in this country have been completely unfaithful to the LORD." 3 So Hosea married Gomer daughter of Diblaim, and she became pregnant and gave birth to Hosea's son.

4 The LORD said to Hosea, "Name him Jezreel,ⁿ because soon I will punish the family of Jehu for the people they killed at Jezreel. In the future I will put an end to the kingdom of Israel 5 and break the power of Israel's army in the Valley of Jezreel."

6 Gomer became pregnant again and gave birth to a daughter. The LORD said to Hosea, "Name her Lo-Ruhamah,ⁿ because I will not pity Israel any more, nor will I forgive them. 7 But I will show pity to the people of Judah. I will save them, but not by using bows or swords, horses or horsemen or weapons of war. I, the LORD their God, will save them."

8 After Gomer had stopped nursing Lo-Ruhamah, she became pregnant again and gave birth to another son. 9 The LORD said, "Name him Lo-Ammi,ⁿ because you are not my people, and I am not your God.

God's Promise to Israel

10 "But the number of the Israelites will become like the grains of sand of the sea, which no one can measure or count. They were called, 'You are not my people', but later they will be called 'children of the living God'. 11 The people of Judah and Israel will join together again and will choose one leader for themselves. They will come up from the land, because the day of Jezreelⁿ will be truly great.

2 "You are to call your brothers, 'my people', and your sisters, 'you have been shown pity'.

FAITH links

A HOPEFUL NAME
HOSEA 1:3-11

Suppose that instead of giving you the name you have, your parents had decided to name you after a characteristic of theirs. For example, "laughs a lot". Ridiculous, you say? Not to the prophet Hosea. The Israelites weren't faithful to God. So God told Hosea to choose names for his children that reflected the people's lack of faithfulness. God later provided hope by giving the people a new name: "children of the living God".

We sometimes choose hopeless names for ourselves when we do wrong things. For example, we might call ourselves "loser" or "hopeless". If you're a Christian, you can claim the name "child of the living God". That is a name to restore hope.

The Rainbow Promise, Genesis 9:1–17, p. 14

The God of Big Things, Joshua 10, p. 289

A Mother's Love, Isaiah 49:13–16, p. 961

Name with a Purpose, Matthew 1:21, p. 1274

Two Birthdays, John 3:1–7, p. 1426

Never Alone, Hebrews 13:5–6, p. 1684

1:4, 11 Jezreel This name in Hebrew means "God plants".
1:6 Lo-Ruhamah This name in Hebrew means "not pitied".
1:9 Lo-Ammi This name in Hebrew means "not my people".

God Speaks About Israel

2 "Plead with your mother.[n]
 Accuse her, because she is no longer my wife,
 and I am no longer her husband.
 Tell her to stop acting like a prostitute,
 to stop behaving like an unfaithful wife.
3 If she refuses, I will strip her naked
 and leave her as bare as on the day she was born.
 I will make her dry like a desert,
 like a land without water,
 and I will kill her with thirst.
4 I will not take pity on her children,
 because they are the children of a prostitute.
5 Their mother has acted like a prostitute;
 the one who became pregnant with them has acted disgracefully.
 She said, 'I will chase after my lovers,[n]
 who give me my food and water,
 wool and flax, wine and olive oil.'
6 So I will block her road with thornbushes;
 I will build a wall around her
 so she cannot find her way.
7 She will run after her lovers,
 but she won't catch them.
 She will look for them,
 but she won't find them.
 Then she will say, 'I will go back to my first husband,[n]
 because life was better then for me than it is now.'
8 But she does not know that I was the one
 who gave her grain, new wine and oil.
 I gave her much silver and gold,
 but she used it for Baal.
9 "So I will come back and take away my grain at harvest time
 and my new wine when it is ready.
 I will take back my wool and linen
 that covered her nakedness.
10 So I will show her nakedness to her lovers,
 and no one will save her from me.
11 I will put an end to all her celebrations:
 her yearly festivals, her New Moon festivals and her Sabbaths.
 I will stop all of her special feasts.
12 I will destroy her vines and fig trees,
 which she said were her pay from her lovers.
 I will turn them into a forest,
 and wild animals will eat them.
13 I will punish her for all the times she burned incense to the Baals.
 She put on her rings and jewellery
 and went chasing after her lovers,
 but she forgot me!"
 says the LORD.

14 "So I am going to attract her;
 I will lead her into the desert
 and speak tenderly to her.
15 There I will give her back her vineyards,
 and I will make the Valley of Trouble a door of hope.
 There she will respond as when she was young,
 as when she came out of Egypt."
16 The LORD says, "In the future she will call me 'my husband';
 no longer will she call me 'my baal.'[n]
17 I will never let her say the names of Baal again;
 people won't use their names any more.
18 At that time I will make an agreement for them
 with the wild animals, the birds and the crawling things.
 I will smash from the land
 the bow and the sword and the weapons of war,
 so my people will live in safety.
19 And I will make you my promised bride for ever.

2:2 mother Refers to the nation of Israel here.
2:5 lovers Refers to the nations surrounding Israel, who led Israel to worship false gods.
2:7 husband Refers to God here.
2:16 baal Another Hebrew word for husband, but it was the same word as the god Baal.

I will be good and fair;
I will show you my love and mercy.
20 I will be true to you as my promised
  bride,
  and you will know the LORD.

21 "At that time I will speak to you,"
  says the LORD.
  "I will speak to the
    skies,
  and they will give
    rain to the earth.
22 The earth will
    produce grain,
    new wine and oil;
  much will grow
    because my
    people are called
    Jezreel."[n]
23 I will plant my people in the land,
  and I will show pity to the one I
    had called 'not shown pity'.
  I will say, 'You are my people'
    to those I had called 'not my
    people'.
  And they will say to me, 'You are
    our God.'"

Hosea Buys a Wife

3 The LORD said to me again, "Go and show your love to a woman loved by someone else, who has been unfaithful to you. In the same way the LORD loves the people of Israel, even though they worship other gods and love to eat the raisin cakes."[n]

2 So I bought her for 15 pieces of silver and 150 kilogrammes of barley. 3 Then I told her, "You must wait for me for many days. You must not be a prostitute, and you must not have sexual relations with any other man. I will act the same way towards you."

4 In the same way Israel will live many days without a king or leader, without sacrifices or holy stone pillars, and without the holy robe or an idol. 5 After this, the people of Israel will return to the LORD their God and follow him and the king from David's family. In the last days they will turn in fear to the LORD, and he will bless them.

The LORD's Word Against Israel

4 People of Israel, listen to the LORD's
  message.
  The LORD has this
    against you who live in the land:
  "The people are not true, not loyal to
    God,
  nor do those who
    live in the land
    even know him.
2 Cursing, lying, killing,
    stealing and
    adultery are
    everywhere.
  One murder
    follows another.
3 Because of this the
    land dries up,
  and all its people
    are dying.
  Even the wild animals and the birds
    of the air
  and the fish of the sea are dying.

God's Case Against the Priests

4 "No one should accuse
    or blame another person.
  Don't blame the people, you priests,
    when they quarrel with you.
5 You will be ruined in the day,
    and your prophets will be ruined
      with you in the night.
  I will also destroy your mother."[n]
6 My people will be destroyed,
    because they have no knowledge.
  You have refused to learn,
    so I will refuse to let you be priests
      to me.
  You have forgotten the teachings of
    your God,
    so I will forget your children.
7 The more priests there are,
    the more they sin against me.
  I will take away their honour
    and give them shame.
8 Since the priests live off the sin

2:22 Jezreel This name in Hebrew means "God plants".
3:1 raisin cakes This food was eaten in the feasts that honoured false gods.
4:5 mother Here "mother" refers to the nation of Israel.

> I will be true to you as my promised bride, and you will know the LORD.
> – Hosea 2:20

offerings of the people,
  they want the people to sin more
    and more.
9 The priests are as wrong as the people,
  and I will punish them both for
    what they have done.
  I will repay them for the wrong
    they have done.

10 "They will eat
    but not have enough;
  they will have sexual relations with
    the prostitutes,
  but they will not have children,
  because they have left the LORD
    to give themselves to
11 prostitution,
  to old and new wine,
  which take away their ability to
    understand.

God's Case Against the People

12 "My people ask wooden idols for
    advice;
  they ask those sticks of wood to
    advise them!
  Like prostitutes, they have chased
    after other gods
  and have left their own God.
13 They make sacrifices on the tops of
    the mountains.
  They burn offerings on the hills,
  under oaks, poplars and other trees,
    because their shade is nice.
  So your daughters become
    prostitutes,
  and your daughters-in-law are
    guilty of adultery.

14 "But I will not punish your daughters
    for becoming prostitutes,
  nor your daughters-in-law
    for their sins of adultery.
  I will not punish them,
  because the men have sexual
    relations with prostitutes
  and offer sacrifices with the temple
    prostitutes.
  A foolish people will be ruined.

15 "Israel, you act like a prostitute,
    but do not be guilty towards the
      LORD.
  Don't go to Gilgal
    or go up to Beth Aven.*
  Don't make promises,
    saying, 'As surely as the LORD
      lives . . .'
16 The people of Israel are stubborn
    like a stubborn young cow.
  Now the LORD will feed them
    like lambs in the open country.
17 The Israelites have chosen to worship
    idols,
    so leave them alone.
18 When they finish their drinking,
    they completely give themselves to
      being prostitutes;
    they love these disgraceful ways.
19 They will be swept away as if by a
    whirlwind,
  and their sacrifices will bring them
    only shame.

God's Word Against the Leaders

5 "Listen, you priests.
  Pay attention, people of Israel.
  Listen, royal family,
    because you will all be judged.
  You have been like a trap at Mizpah
    and like a net spread out at Mount
      Tabor.
2 You have done many evil things,
    so I will punish you all.
3 I know all about the people of Israel;
    what they have done is not hidden
      from me.
  Now that Israel acts like a prostitute,
    it has made itself unclean.

4 "They will not give up their deeds
    and return to their God.
  They are determined to be unfaithful
    to me;
    they do not know the LORD.
5 Israel's pride testifies against them.
  The people of Israel will stumble
    because of their sin,
  and the people of Judah will
    stumble with them.
6 They will come to worship the LORD,
    bringing their flocks and herds,
    but they will not be able to find him,

4:15 Gilgal . . . Beth Aven Cities in Israel where people worshipped false gods.

because he has left them.
7 They have not been true to the LORD;
they are children who do not
belong to him.
So their false worship
will destroy them and their land.

8 "Blow the horn in Gibeah
and the trumpet in Ramah.
Give the warning at Beth Aven,
and be first into battle, people of
Benjamin.
9 Israel will be ruined
on the day of punishment.
To the tribes of Israel
I tell the truth.
10 The leaders of Judah are like those
who steal other people's land.
I will pour my punishment over them
like a flood of water.
11 Israel is crushed by the punishment,
because it decided to follow idols.
12 I am like a moth to Israel,
like a rot to the people of Judah.
13 "When Israel saw its wounds
and Judah saw its wounds,
Israel went to Assyria for help
and sent to the great king of
Assyria.
But he cannot heal you
or cure your
wounds.
14 I will be like a lion to
Israel,
like a young lion to
Judah.
I will attack them
and tear them to
pieces.
I will drag them off,
and no one will be
able to save
them.
15 Then I will go back to my place
until they suffer for their guilt and
turn back to me.
In their trouble they will look for
me."

The People are Not Faithful

6 "Come, let's go back to the LORD.
He has hurt us, but he will heal us.

He has wounded us, but he will
bandage our wounds.
2 In two days he will put new life in us;
on the third day he will raise us up
so that we may live in his presence
3 and know him.
Let's try to learn about the LORD;
He will come to us as surely as the
dawn comes.
He will come to us like rain,
like the spring rain that waters the
ground."

4 The LORD says, "Israel, what should I
do with you?
Judah, what should I do with you?
Your faithfulness is like a morning
mist,
like the dew that goes away early
in the day.
5 I have warned you by my prophets
that I will kill you and destroy you.
My justice comes out like bright
light.
6 I want faithful love
more than I want animal sacrifices.
I want people to know me
more than I want burnt offerings.
7 But they have broken the agreement
as Adam did;
they have been
unfaithful to me.
8 Gilead is a city of
people who do
evil;
their footprints are
bloody.
9 The priests are like
robbers waiting
to attack people;
they murder people
on the road to
Shechem[n]
and do wicked things.
10 I have seen horrible things in Israel.
Look at Israel's prostitution;
Israel has become unclean.

11 "Judah, I have set a harvest time for
you

> In their trouble they
> will look for me.
> – Hosea 5:15

6:9 Shechem A city of safety where people could go for protection.

FAITH links

A FAKE APOLOGY
HOSEA 6:1-7

Have you ever said you were sorry for something you did wrong only because you were caught? God told Hosea to speak out against the repentance of the Israelites. God knew that they weren't genuine when they said that they wanted to learn about him. He also knew that they would soon go back to doing the same sins he caught them doing in the first place.

God is always willing to forgive you when you say you're sorry. But he wants more than just an apology. He wants you to mean what you say. How can you do this? Let your actions show that you're sorry.

Sorry about something you did? Link here on what to do about it:

Facing the Consequences, Deuteronomy 3:21–29, p. 232

A Hidden Sin, Joshua 7, p. 285

Above the Law, 1 Kings 21, p. 470

You Are What You Do, Proverbs 20:11, p. 854

Stand! Jeremiah 19:14—20:6, p. 1019

From Useless to Useful, Philemon 11, p. 1663

---

when I will make the lives of my people good again.
7 When I heal Israel,
Israel's sin will go away,
and so will Samaria's evil.

"They cheat a lot!
Thieves break into houses,
and robbers are in the streets.
2 It never enters their minds
that I remember all their evil deeds.
The bad things they do are all around them;
they are right in front of me.

Israel's Evil Kings

3 "They make the king happy with their wickedness;
their rulers are glad with their lies.
4 But all of them are traitors.
They are like an oven heated by a baker.
While he mixes the dough,
he does not need to stir up the fire.
5 The kings get so drunk they get sick every day.
The rulers become crazy with wine;
they make agreements with those who do not know the true God.
6 They burn like an oven;
their hearts burn inside them.
All night long their anger is low,
but when morning comes, it becomes a roaring fire.
7 All these people are as hot as an oven;
they burn up their rulers.
All their kings fall,
and no one calls on me.

Israel and the Other Nations

8 "Israel mixes with other nations;
he is like a pancake cooked only on one side.
9 Foreign nations have eaten up his strength,
but he doesn't know it.
Israel is weak and feeble, like an old man,
but he doesn't know it.

10 Israel's pride will cause their defeat;
   they will not turn back to the LORD
      their God
   or look to him for help in all this.
11 Israel has become like a pigeon—
      easy to fool and stupid.
   First they call to Egypt for help.
   Then they run to Assyria.
12 When they go, I will catch them in a
      net,
   I will bring them down like birds
      from the sky;
   I will punish them countless times
      for their evil.
13 How terrible for
      them
   because
      they left me!
   They will be
      destroyed,
      because
   they turned against me.
   I want to save them,
   but they have spoken lies against
      me.
14 They do not call to me from their
      hearts.
   They just lie on their beds and cry.
   They come together to ask for grain
      and new wine,
   but they really turn away from me.
15 Though I trained them and gave them
      strength,
   they have made evil plans against
      me.
16 They did not turn to the Most High
      God.
   They are like a loose bow that can't
      shoot.
   Because their leaders boast about
      their strength,
   they will be killed with swords,
   and the people in Egypt
      will laugh at them.

Israel Has Trusted Wrong Things

8 "Put the trumpet to your lips and
      give the warning!
   The enemy swoops down on the
      LORD's people like an eagle.
   The Israelites have broken my
      agreement
   and have turned against my
      teachings.
2 They cry out to me,
   'Our God, we in Israel know you!'
3 But Israel has rejected what is good,
   so the enemy will chase them.
4 They chose their own kings
   without asking my permission.
   They chose their own leaders,
      people I did not know.
   They made their silver and gold into
      idols,
   and for all this they will be
      destroyed.
5 I hate the calf-shaped idol of Israel!
   I am very angry with the people.
   How long will they remain unclean?
6 The idol is something a craftsman
      made;
   it is not God.
   Israel's calf-shaped idol
   will surely be smashed to pieces.

7 "Israel's foolish plans are like
      planting the wind,
   but they will harvest a storm.
   Like a stalk with no head of grain,
      it produces nothing.
   Even if it produced something,
      other nations would eat it.
8 Israel is eaten up;
   the people are mixed among the
      other nations
   and have become useless to me.
9 Israel is like a wild donkey all by
      itself.
   They have run to Assyria;
   They have hired other nations to
      protect them.
10 Although Israel is mixed among the
      nations,
   I will gather them together.
   They will become weaker and
      weaker
   as they suffer under the great king
      of Assyria.

11 "Although Israel built more altars to
      remove sin,
   they have become altars for
      sinning.
12 I have written many teachings for
      them,

Hosea 9:5

FAITH links

GOING MY WAY?
HOSEA 8:1-6

Have you ever made a decision on your own without asking a parent first? Maybe you told a friend you could sleep over at his house before you asked your mum. Some decisions don't require permission, of course. For example, you can choose your own socks. But major decisions need a parent's approval. Hosea told the Israelites that the plans they made were without God's approval. They had rejected God's plans in favour of their own. Because of that, he wouldn't help them when trouble came.

If we claim to be children of God, he wants some say in what we do. When we reject God's plans and follow our own, we can't expect God to help us.

If you want God to help you, then check out these links:

Following the Crowd, Numbers 13; 14, p. 193

Facts About Following, Joshua 6, p. 283

Do What You Want? Judges 21:25, p. 341

A Parent's Advice, Proverbs 1:8–9, p. 825

Faith Workout, Acts 16:4–5, p. 1493

Helpful Hints, 3 John 11, p. 1724

---

but they think the teachings are strange and foreign.
13 The Israelites offer sacrifices to me as gifts
and eat the meat,
but the LORD is not pleased with them.
He remembers the evil they have done,
and he will punish them for their sins.
They will be slaves again as they were in Egypt.
14 Israel has forgotten their Maker and has built palaces;
Judah has built many strong, walled cities.
But I will send fire on their cities
and destroy their strong buildings."

Israel's Punishment

9 Israel, do not rejoice;
don't shout for joy as the other nations do.
You have been like a prostitute against your God.
You love the pay of prostitutes on every threshing floor.
2 But the threshing floor and the winepress will not feed the people,
and there won't be enough new wine.
3 The people will not stay in the LORD's land.
Israel will return to being captives as they were in Egypt,
and in Assyria they will eat food that they are not allowed to eat.
4 The Israelites will not give offerings of wine to the LORD;
they will not give him sacrifices.
Their sacrifices will be like food that is eaten at a funeral;
it is unclean, and everyone who eats it becomes unclean.
Their food will only satisfy their hunger;
they cannot sacrifice it in the Temple.
5 What will you do then on the day of feasts

and on the day of the LORD's
   festival?
6 Even if the people are not destroyed,
   Egypt will capture them;
   Memphis*n* will bury them.
Weeds will grow over their silver
      treasures,
   and thorns will drive them out of
      their tents.
7 The time of punishment has come,
   the time to pay for sins.
Let Israel know this:
you think the prophet
   is a fool,
and you say the
   spiritual person
   is mad.
You have sinned very
   much,
and your hatred is
   great.
8 Is Israel a watchman?
   Are God's people
   prophets?
Everywhere Israel goes, traps are set
   for him.
He is an enemy in God's house.
9 The people of Israel have gone deep
      into sin
   as the people of Gibeah*n* did.
The Lord will remember the evil
      things they have done
   and he will punish their sins.

10 "When I found Israel,
      it was like finding grapes in the
         desert.
   Your ancestors were like
      finding the first figs on the fig tree.
   But when they came to Baal Peor
      they began worshipping an idol,
   and they became as hateful as the
      thing they worshipped.
11 Israel's glory will fly away like a bird;
      there will be no more pregnancy,
         no more births, no more getting
            pregnant.
12 But even if the Israelites bring up
         children,
      I will take them all away.
   How terrible it will be for them
      when I go away from them!
13 I have seen Israel, like Tyre,
   given a pleasant place.
But the people of Israel will soon
      bring out
   their children to be killed."
14 LORD, give them what they should
      have.
What will you give them?
Make their women unable to have
      children;
   give them dried-up breasts that
      cannot feed their babies.

15 "The Israelites were
      very wicked in
      Gilgal,
   so I have hated
      them there.
   Because of the sinful
      things they have
      done,
   I will force them to
      leave my land.
   I will no longer love
      them;
their leaders have turned against
   me.
16 Israel is beaten down;
      its root is dying, and it has no fruit.
   If they have more children,
      I will kill the children they love."

17 God will reject them,
      because they have not obeyed
         him;
   they will wander among the
      nations.

Israel will Pay for Sin

10 Israel is like a large vine
      that produced plenty of fruit.
   As the people became richer,
      they built more altars for idols.
   As their land became better,
      they put up better stone pillars to
         honour gods.
2 Their heart was false,
      and now they must pay for their
         guilt.

9:6 Memphis A city in Egypt famous for its tombs.
9:9 Gibeah The sins of the people of Gibeah caused a civil war. See Judges 19–21.

The LORD will break down their
  altars;
he will destroy their holy stone
  pillars.
3 Then they will say, "We have no king,
  because we didn't honour the
  LORD.
As for the king,
  he couldn't do anything for us."
4 They make many false promises
  and agreements which they don't
  keep.
So people sue each
  other in court;
they are like
  poisonous weeds
  growing in a
  ploughed field.
5 The people from
  Israel are
  worried about
  the calf-shaped idol
  at Beth Aven.
The people will cry about it,
  and the priests will cry about it.
They used to shout for joy about its
  glory,
6 but it will be carried off to Assyria
  as a gift to the great king.
Israel will be disgraced,
  and the people will be ashamed for
  not obeying.
7 Israel will be destroyed;
  its king will be like a chip of wood
  floating on the water.
8 The places of false worship will be
  destroyed,
  the places where Israel sinned.
Thorns and weeds will grow up
  and cover their altars.
Then they will say to the mountains,
  "Cover us!"
  and to the hills, "Fall on us!"
9 "Israel, you have sinned since the
  time of Gibeah,"
  and the people there have
  continued sinning.
But war will surely overwhelm them
  in Gibeah,
  because of the evil they have done
  there.

10 When I am ready,
  I will come to punish them.
Nations will come together against
  them,
  and they will be punished for their
  double sins.
11 Israel is like a well-trained young cow
  that likes to thresh grain.
I will put a yoke on her neck
  and make her work hard in the
  field.
Israel will plough,
  and Judah will
  break up the
  ground.
12 I said, 'Plant
  goodness,
  harvest the fruit of
  loyalty,
  plough the new
  ground of
  knowledge.
Look for the LORD
  until he comes
  and pours goodness on you like
  water.'
13 But you have ploughed evil
  and harvested trouble;
  you have eaten the fruit of your
  lies.
Because you have trusted in your
  own power
  and your many soldiers,
14 your people will hear the noise of
  battle,
  and all your strong, walled cities
  will be destroyed.
It will be like the time King Shalman
  destroyed Beth Arbel in battle,
  when mothers and their children
  were crushed to death.
15 The same will happen to you, people
  of Bethel,
  because you did so much evil.
When the sun comes up,
  the king of Israel will die.

God's Love for Israel

11 "When Israel was a child, I loved
  him,

> Plant goodness,
> harvest the fruit of
> loyalty, plough the
> new ground of
> knowledge.
> – Hosea 10:12

10:9 Gibeah The sins of the people of Gibeah caused a civil war. See Judges 19–21.

and I called
  my son out
  of Egypt."
2 But when I
  called the
  people of
  Israel,
  they went away from me.
They offered sacrifices to the Baals
  and burned incense to the idols.
3 It was I who taught Ephraim to walk,
  and I took them by the arms,
but they did not understand
  that I had healed them.
4 I led them with cords of human
    kindness,
  with ropes of love.
I lifted the yoke from their neck
  and bent down and fed them.

5 "The Israelites will become captives
    again, as they were in Egypt,
  and Assyria will become their king,
    because they refuse to turn back to
    God.
6 War will sweep through their cities
  and will destroy them
and kill them because of their
    wicked plans.
7 My people have made up their minds
  to turn away from me.
The prophets call them to turn to
    me,
  but none of them honours me at
    all.

8 "Israel, how can I
    give you up?
  How can I give you
    away, Israel?
  I don't want to make
    you like Admah
    or treat you like
    Zeboiim."
My heart beats for
    you,
  and my love for you stirs up my
    pity.
9 I won't punish you in my anger,
  and I won't destroy Israel again.
I am God and not a human;
  I am the Holy One, and I am
    among you.

11:1 God Does God love his people?

I will not come against you in
    anger.
10 They will go after the LORD,
  and he will roar like a lion.
When he roars,
  his children will hurry to him from
    the west.
11 They will come swiftly
    like birds from Egypt
  and like doves from Assyria.
I will settle them again in their
    homes,"
  says the LORD.

The LORD is Against Israel

12 Israel has surrounded me with lies;
    the people have made evil plans.
And Judah turns against God,
    the faithful Holy One.

12 What Israel does is as useless as
  chasing the wind;
he chases the east wind all day.
They tell more and more lies
  and do more and more violence.
They make agreements with Assyria,
  and they send a gift of olive oil to
    Egypt.
2 The LORD also has some things
    against Judah.
He will punish Israel for what they
    have done;
  he will give them what they deserve.
3 Their ancestor Jacob held on to his
    brother's heel
  while the two of
    them were being
    born.
When he grew to be
    a man,
  he wrestled with
    God.
4 When Jacob wrestled
    with the angel
    and won,
  he cried and asked
    for his blessing.
Later, God met with him at Bethel
  and spoke with him there.

> You must return to
> your God; love him,
> do what is just, and
> always trust in him
> as your God.
> – Hosea 12:6

11:8 Admah . . . Zeboiim Two other cities destroyed when God destroyed Sodom and Gomorrah.

5 It was the LORD God All-powerful;
   the LORD is his great name.
6 You must return to your God;
   love him, do what is just,
   and always trust in him as your
     God.

7 The merchants use dishonest scales;
   they like to cheat people.
8 Israel said, "I am rich! I am someone
     with power!"
   All their money will do them no
     good
   because of the sins they have
     done.

9 "But I am the LORD your God,
   who brought you out of Egypt.
   I will make you live in tents again
     as you used to do on worship days.
10 I spoke to the prophets
     and gave them many visions;
     through them, I taught my
       lessons to you."
11 The people of Gilead are evil,
     worth nothing.
   Though people sacrifice bulls at
     Gilgal,
     their altars will become like
       piles of stone
   in a ploughed field.
12 Your ancestor Jacob fled to North
     West Mesopotamia
   where he worked to get a wife;
     he tended sheep to pay for her.
13 Later the LORD used a prophet
     to bring Jacob's descendants out of
       Egypt;
   he used a prophet
     to take care of the Israelites.
14 But the Israelites made the Lord
     angry when they killed other
       people,
   and they deserve to die for their
     crimes.
   The Lord will make them pay
     for the disgraceful things they have
       done.

The Final Word Against Israel

13 People used to fear the tribe of
     Ephraim;
   they were important people in
     Israel.
   But they sinned by worshipping Baal,
     so they must die.
2 But they still keep on sinning more
     and more.
   They make idols of their silver,
     idols that are cleverly made,
     the work of a craftsman.
   Yet the people of Israel say to each
     other,
   "Kiss those calf idols and sacrifice
     to them."
3 So those people will be like the
     morning mist;
   they will disappear like the
     morning dew.
   They will be like chaff blown from
     the threshing floor,
   like smoke going out of a
     window.

4 "I, the LORD, have been your God
     since you were in the land of
       Egypt.
   You should have known no other
     God except me.
   I am the only one who saves.
5 I cared for them in the desert
     where it was hot and dry.
6 I gave them food, and they became
     full and satisfied.
   But then they became too proud
     and forgot me.
7 That is why I will be like a lion to them,
     like a leopard waiting by the road.
8 I will attack like a bear robbed of her
     cubs,
   ripping their bodies open.
   I will devour them like a lion
     and tear them apart like a wild
       animal.

9 "Israel, I will destroy you.
   Who will be your helper then?
10 What good is your king?

> You should have known no other God except me. I am the only one who saves.
> — Hosea 13:4

Hosea 13:11 1184

Can he save you in any of your towns?
What good are your leaders?
You said, 'Give us a king and leaders.'
11 So I gave you a king, but only in anger,
and I took him away in my great anger.
12 The sins of Israel are on record, stored away, waiting for punishment.
13 The pain of birth will come for him, but he is like a foolish baby
who won't come out of its mother's womb.
14 Will I save them from the place of the dead?
Will I rescue them from death?
Where is your sickness, death?
Where is your pain, place of death?
I will show them no mercy.
15 Israel is doing well among the nations,
but the LORD will send a wind from the east,
coming from the desert,
that will dry up his springs and wells of water.
It will destroy from their treasure houses everything of value.
16 The nation of Israel will be ruined, because it fought against God.
The people of Israel will die in war; their children will be torn to pieces,
and their pregnant women will be ripped open."

Israel Returns to God

14 Israel, return to the LORD your God,
because your sins have made you fall.
2 Come back to the LORD
and say these words to him:
"Take away all our sin
and kindly receive us,
and we will keep the promises we made to you.
3 Assyria cannot save us,
nor will we trust in our horses.
We will not say again, 'Our gods',

FAITH links

LONG-LASTING HOPE
HOSEA 14

When you were a little kid, you might have counted on your mother's voice, or a dummy or comforter to make everything better when you were upset. What are the things that comfort you now? Hosea warned the Israelites against the false comfort of the idols and heroes that they had chosen. They looked to the wooden gods they made or to other nations to make everything better. But only God could bring them real comfort.

Some things in life will only bring comfort for a short time. Many people trust money, the compliments of others, looks and fame for comfort. When you need long-lasting hope, trust God.

Alone and Forgotten? Genesis 40:23, p. 57

The Wisdom of Obeying God, 1 Kings 11:1–13, p. 453

Like Silver, Psalm 12:6–8, p. 717

The Foundation of Our Hope, Isaiah 31:1–8, p. 934

The Winner's Crown, 1 Corinthians 9:24–27, p. 1555

A Heavenly Sight, Revelation 21:1–4, p. 1753

to the things our hands have made.
You show mercy to orphans."

4 The LORD says,
"I will forgive them for leaving me
and will love them freely,
because I am not angry with them
any more.
5 I will be like the dew to Israel,
and they will blossom like a lily.
Like the cedar trees in Lebanon,
their roots will be firm.
6 They will be like spreading branches,
like the beautiful olive trees
and the sweet-smelling cedars in
Lebanon.
7 The people of Israel will again live
under my protection.
They will grow like the grain,
they will bloom like a vine,
and they will be as famous as the
wine of Lebanon.
8 Israel, have nothing to do with idols.
I, the LORD, am the one who
answers your prayers and
watches over you.
I am like a green pine tree;
your blessings come from me."

9 A wise person will know these
things,
and an understanding person will
take them to heart.
The LORD's ways are right.
Good people live by following
them,
but those who turn against God die
because of them.

HUNGRY LOCUSTS

My name is Joel, which means "the Lord is God". God gave me a message for his people right after swarms of locusts had destroyed all our crops. What's a locust? It's a large grasshopper with a huge appetite. Imagine millions of these insects munching on every plant in sight! The sheep and cattle could find nothing to eat. People were starving. I told the people this terrible destruction was from God. He sent the locusts as a punishment for sin.

I wrote this book to tell the people to turn back to God before it was too late. Another more terrible punishment – worse than locusts – might come if they did not repent and turn away from their sins. God said, "Come back to me with all your heart. Go without food, and cry and be sad" (Joel 2:12). God promises to punish those who sin, but he will richly bless those who follow his laws.

JESUS WATCH

On the night before he died, Jesus promised to send the Holy Spirit, his Helper, to guide us. The Holy Spirit helps us understand God's Word. Joel predicted that one day the Lord would give his Holy Spirit to all kinds of people. On that day, miracles in the sky and on the earth will take place. Then people will know that the Day of the Lord has come. It will be a terrible day of punishment, but anyone who calls on the name of the Lord will be saved. In the Book of Joel, we see Jesus as a judge. He will come on the Day of the Lord and punish those nations who conquered Israel and forced the people to live in foreign lands. Jesus will live on Mount Zion, and Jerusalem will be a holy place.

Have you ever heard of milk flowing from the hills?

Seems strange, doesn't it? Let's surf over to Joel 3:18–21 to find out about it.

FAITH links

- **Pass It On!** Joel 1:2–3
- **A Swarm of Trouble,** Joel 2:25–27
- **Future Hope,** Joel 3:17–21

Locusts Destroy the Crops

1 The LORD spoke his word to Joel son of Pethuel:

2 Elders, listen to this message.
 Listen to me, all you who live in the land.
 Nothing like this has ever happened
  during your lifetime
  or during your ancestors' lifetimes.
3 Tell your children about these things,
  let your children tell their children,
  and let your grandchildren tell their children.
4 What the cutting locusts have left,
  the swarming locusts have eaten;
 what the swarming locusts have left,
  the hopping locusts have eaten,
 and what the hopping locusts have left,
  the destroying locusts[n] have eaten.

5 Drunkards, wake up and cry!
  All you people who drink wine, cry!
 Cry because your wine
  has been taken away from your mouths.
6 A powerful nation has come into my land
  with too many soldiers to count.
 It has teeth like a lion,
  jaws like a female lion.
7 It has made my grapevine a waste
  and made my fig tree a stump.
 It has stripped all the bark off my trees
  and left the branches white.

8 Cry as a young woman cries
  when the man she was going to marry has died.
9 There will be no more grain or drink offerings
  to offer in the Temple of the LORD.
 Because of this, the priests,
  the servants of the LORD, are sad.
10 The fields are ruined;
  the ground is dried up.
 The grain is destroyed,
  the new wine is dried up,
  and the olive oil runs out.
11 Be sad, farmers.
  Cry loudly, you who grow grapes.
 Cry for the wheat and the barley.
  Cry because the harvest of the field is lost.
12 The vines have become dry,
  and the fig trees are dried up.

FAITH links

PASS IT ON!
JOEL 1:2-3

Many people pass on stories of their faith to their kids. They want their kids to love God as much as they do. God told the Israelites to pass on the stories of what God had done for them to their children. That way, their children would learn the importance of knowing God and obeying him. You can pass on stories of faith, too! How? You can tell other people what God has done in your life.

Faith of Our Fathers, Joshua 4:4–9, p. 280

A Picture of the Past, Psalm 105, p. 789

A Bad Reaction, Jeremiah 36, p. 1043

The Watchman, Ezekiel 3:16–22, p. 1088

Love for Free, Romans 5:8, p. 1524

People of Faith, Hebrews 11, p. 1679

1:4 cutting . . . locusts These are different names for an insect like a large grasshopper. The locust can quickly destroy trees, plants and crops, and in this destruction, Joel sees a warning. God will cause this type of destruction when he punishes his people.

The pomegranate trees, the date
    palm trees, the apple trees—
  all the trees in the field have died.
And the happiness of the people has
    died, too.
13 Priests, put on your rough cloth and
    cry to show your sadness.
  Servants of the altar, cry out loud.
Servants of my God,
  keep your rough cloth on all night
    to show your sadness.
Cry because there will be no more
    grain or drink offerings
  to offer in the Temple of your
    God.
14 Call for a day when no one eats food!
  Tell everyone to stop work!
Bring the elders
  and everyone who lives in the land
to the Temple of the LORD your God,
  and cry out to the LORD.
15 What a terrible day it will be!
  The LORD's day of judging is near,
when punishment will come
  like a destroying attack from the
    Almighty.

16 Our food is taken away
    while we watch.
  Joy and happiness are gone
    from the Temple of our God.
17 Though we planted fig seeds,
    they lie dry and dead in the earth.
  The barns are empty and falling
    down.
  The storerooms for grain have
    been broken down,
  because the grain has dried up.
18 The animals are groaning!
  The herds of cattle wander around
    confused,
  because they have no grass to eat;
    even the flocks of sheep suffer.
19 LORD, I am calling to you for help,
    because fire has burned up the
      open pastures,
  and flames have burned all the
    trees in the field.
20 Wild animals also need your help.
  The streams of water have dried
    up,
  and fire has burned up the open
    pastures.

The Coming Day of Judgement

2 Blow the trumpet in Jerusalem;
  shout a warning on my holy
    mountain.
Let all the people who live in the land
    shake with fear,
  because the LORD's day of judging
    is coming;
  it is near.
2 It will be a dark, gloomy day,
    cloudy and black.
  Like the light at sunrise,
    a great and powerful army will
      spread over the mountains.
  There has never been anything like it
    before,
  and there will never be anything
    like it again.

3 In front of them a fire destroys;
    behind them a flame burns.
  The land in front of them is like the
    garden of Eden;
  the land behind them is like an
    empty desert.
  Nothing will escape from them.
4 They look like horses,
    and they run like war horses.
5 It is like the noise of chariots
    rumbling over the tops of the
      mountains,
  like the noise of a roaring fire
    burning dry stalks.
  They are like a powerful army lined
    up for battle.
6 When they see them, nations shake
    with fear,
  and everyone's face becomes
    pale.

7 They charge like soldiers;
    they climb over the wall like
      warriors.
  They all march straight ahead
    and do not move off their path.
8 They do not run into each other,
    because each walks in line.
  They break through all efforts to stop
    them
  and keep coming.
9 They run into the city.
  They run at the wall
    and climb into the houses,

entering through windows like
thieves.
10 Before them, earth and sky shake.
The sun and the moon become dark,
and the stars stop shining.
11 The LORD shouts out orders
to his army.
His army is very large!
Those who obey him are very
strong!
The LORD's day of judging
is an overwhelming and terrible
day.
No one can stand up against it!

Change Your Hearts

12 The LORD says, "Even now, come
back to me with all your heart.
Go without food, and cry and be
sad."

13 Tearing your clothes is not enough to
show you are sad;
let your heart be broken.
Come back to the LORD your God,
because he is kind and shows
mercy.
He doesn't become angry quickly,
and he has great love.
He can change his mind about
doing harm.
14 Who knows? Maybe he will turn back
to you
and leave behind a blessing for
you.
Grain and drink offerings belong to
the LORD your God.

15 Blow the trumpet in Jerusalem;
call for a day when no one eats
food.
Tell everyone to stop work.
16 Bring the people together
and make the meeting holy for the
LORD.
Bring together the elders,
as well as the children,
and even babies that still feed at
their mothers' breasts.
The bridegroom should come from
his room,
the bride from her bedroom.

17 The priests, the LORD's servants,
should cry
between the altar and the entrance
to the Temple.
They should say, "LORD, have mercy
on your people.
Don't let them be put to shame;
don't let other nations make fun of
them.
Don't let people in other nations
ask,
'Where is their God?'"

The LORD Restores the Land

18 Then the LORD became concerned
about his land
and felt sorry for his people.
19 He said to them:
"I will send you grain, new wine
and olive oil,
so that you will have plenty.
No more will I shame you
among the nations.
20 I will force the army from the north
to leave your land
and go into a dry, empty land.
Their soldiers in front will be forced
into the Dead Sea,
and those in the rear into the
Mediterranean Sea.
Their bodies will rot and stink.
The LORD has surely done a
wonderful thing!"

21 Land, don't be afraid;
be happy and full of joy,
because the LORD has done a
wonderful thing.
22 Wild animals, don't be afraid,
because the open pastures have
grown grass.
The trees have given fruit;
the fig trees and the grapevines
have grown much fruit.
23 So be happy, people of Jerusalem;
be joyful in the LORD your God.
Because he does what is right,
he has brought you rain;
he has sent the autumn rain
and the spring rain for you, as
before.
24 And the threshing floors will be full
of grain;

Joel 2:25 1190

FAITH links

A SWARM OF TROUBLE
JOEL 2:25-27

How much can you eat in one day? A swarm of locusts can eat tons of plants in one day. That would destroy a town's food supply! The prophet Joel used locusts as a symbol of destruction when he talked to the people about the punishment for their sins. But God promised to restore all that they had lost when their land was invaded.

Some events may happen that can cause you to feel as if your life is over. But God offers hope, even after something awful has happened.

Here are some more Faithlinks on hope:

Can't Live Without It? Genesis 3, p. 7

When Bad Turns to Worse, Exodus 5:6–12, p. 82

A Hard Place, Ezekiel 28:25–26, p. 1120

Rock Solid, Habakkuk 1:12, p. 1236

That's Much Better! Ephesians 2:4–5, p. 1599

A Happy Ending, Revelation 22:16–21, p. 1754

the barrels will overflow with new
    wine and olive oil.

The LORD Speaks
25 "Though I sent my great army
        against you—
    those swarming locusts and
        hopping locusts,
    the destroying locusts and the
        cutting locusts*n* that ate your
        crops—
    I will pay you back
        for those years of trouble.
26 Then you will have plenty to eat
        and be full.
    You will praise the name of the LORD
        your God,
    who has done miracles for you.
    My people will never again be
        shamed.
27 Then you will know that I am among
        the people of Israel,
    that I am the LORD your God,
        and there is no other God.
    My people will never be shamed
        again.

28 "After this,
    I will pour out my Spirit on all
        kinds of people.
    Your sons and daughters will
        prophesy,
    your old men will dream dreams,
        and your young men will see
        visions.
29 At that time I will pour out my Spirit
    also on male slaves and female
        slaves.
30 I will show miracles
    in the sky and on the earth:
        blood, fire and thick smoke.
31 The sun will become dark,
        the moon red as blood,
    before the overwhelming and
        terrible day of the LORD
        comes.
32 Then anyone who calls on the LORD
        will be saved,
    because on
        Mount Zion
        and in
        Jerusalem
        there will be
        people who
        will be saved,

EMAIL FROM GOD
2:32
Salvation
Who can be saved?

2:25 swarming . . . locusts These are different names for an insect like a large grasshopper. The locust can quickly destroy trees, plants and crops, and in this destruction, Joel sees a warning. God will cause this type of destruction when he punishes his people.

just as the LORD has said.
Those left alive after the day of
    punishment
    are the people whom the LORD
        called.

Punishment for Judah's Enemies

3 "In those days and at that time,
    when I will make things better for
        Judah and Jerusalem,
2 I will gather all the nations together
    and bring them down into the
        Valley Where the LORD Judges.
    There I will judge them,
    because those nations scattered my
        own people Israel
    and forced them to live in other
        nations.
    They divided up my land
3 and threw lots for my people.
    They traded boys for prostitutes,
        and they sold girls to buy wine to
            drink.

4 "Tyre and Sidon and all of you regions of Philistia! What did you have against me? Were you punishing me for something I did, or were you doing something to hurt me? I will very quickly do to you what you have done to me. 5 You took my silver and gold, and you put my precious treasures in your temples. 6 You sold the people of Judah and Jerusalem to the Greeks so that you could send them far from their land.

7 "You sent my people to that faraway place, but I will get them and bring them back, and I will do to you what you have done to them. 8 I will sell your sons and daughters to the people of Judah, and they will sell them to the Sabean people far away." The LORD said this.

God Judges the Nations

9 Announce this among the nations:
        Prepare for war!
    Wake up the soldiers!
        Let all the men of war come near
            and attack.
10 Make swords from your ploughs,
        and make spears from your hooks
            for trimming trees.
    Let even the weak person say,

"I am a soldier."
11 All of you nations, hurry,
        and come together in that place.
    LORD, send your soldiers
        to gather the nations.

12 "Wake up, nations,
        and come to attack in the Valley
            Where the LORD Judges.

FAITH links

FUTURE HOPE

JOEL 3:17-21

Do you ever feel fearful about the future? Maybe you're worried about what will happen when you change year at school. Joel preached a message to the Israelites about hope for the future. Even though they had gone through hard times because of the consequences of their sins, one day God would restore their land.

You don't have to fear what lies ahead. God promised to always be with you. He won't forget his promise.

Worrying got you down? Here are some helpful links:

A Major Problem, Genesis 15:6, p. 20

Who Ya' Gonna Call? Psalm 3:4, p. 711

In Deep Water, Psalm 69, p. 760

A Tight Spot, Jonah 2, p. 1215

A Word About Worry, Matthew 6:25–34, p. 1284

Hope That Doesn't Fail, Acts 26:4–7, p. 1510

Joel 3:13

There I will sit to judge
all the nations on every side.
13 Swing the cutting tool,
because the harvest is ripe.
Come, walk on them as you would
walk on grapes to get their juice,
because the winepress is full
and the barrels are spilling over,
because these people are so evil!"

14 There are huge numbers of people
in the Valley of Decision,[n]
because the LORD's day of judging is
near
in the Valley of Decision.
15 The sun and the moon will become
dark,
and the stars will stop shining.
16 The LORD will roar like a lion from
Jerusalem;
his loud voice will thunder from
that city,
and the sky and the earth will
shake.
But the LORD will be a safe place for
his people,
a strong place of safety for the
people of Israel.

17 "Then you will know that I, the LORD
your God,
live on my holy Mount Zion.
Jerusalem will be a holy place,
and strangers will never even go
through it again.

A New Life Promised for Judah

18 "On that day wine will drip from the
mountains,
milk will flow from the hills,
and water will run through all the
ravines of Judah.
A fountain will flow from the Temple
of the LORD
and give water to the valley of
acacia trees.
19 But Egypt will become empty,
and Edom an empty desert,
because they were cruel to the
people of Judah.
They killed innocent people in that
land.
20 But there will always be people living
in Judah,
and people will live in Jerusalem
from now on.
21 Egypt and Edom killed my people,
so I will definitely punish them."

The LORD lives in Jerusalem!

3:14 Valley of Decision This is like the name "Valley Where the LORD Judges" in 3:2 and 3:12.

A CROOKED NATION

Hi, my name is Amos. I was a shepherd living near Jerusalem when God called me to be a prophet to the nation of Israel.

Do you know what a plumb line is? It is a strong cord with a heavy weight at one end. It's a tool used by builders to see if a wall is really straight. God showed me in a dream that he held a plumb line up to the nation of Israel and found it to be very crooked. The people were not following God's laws.

I wrote this book to tell people to stop sinning and turn back to God. Not only did the people worship idols instead of the true God, but they also did not lead good lives. The nation of Israel was very rich at this time, but the wealthy people did not treat the poor fairly. "They walk on poor people as if they were nothing, and they refuse to be fair to those who are suffering" (Amos 2:7). I warned the people that Israel would be destroyed if they did not turn back to God and stop their evil practices.

JESUS WATCH

The nation of Israel was destroyed because of its sins, but God promised to restore it. Amos described the kingdom of David as a fallen tent that God will set up again. Jesus is the Son of David who will set up a kingdom that will never end. Someday Jesus will come back to judge the nations of the earth. The Day of the Lord will be a terrible day of punishment for people who sinned against God. God is patient and kind, but he will punish all who deserve it. Amos 5:18 says, "Why do you want that day to come? It will bring darkness for you, not light." Christians do not need to fear the Day of the Lord because Jesus promises to reward all who believe in him and follow his commandments.

my FAVOURITE links

OTHER CONNECTIONS

 Stop at <u>Let's Visit Samaria, Amos 3:11–15</u>, to find out about one of the oldest cities founded and built entirely by the Israelites. King Omri built Samaria to be the capital of the Northern Kingdom when Israel was divided into two nations. Check out the different roles Samaria played throughout the Bible.

FAITH links

○ Love Him? Show It!
<u>Amos 2:6–7</u>

○ A Blueprint for Living,
<u>Amos 5:14–15</u>

○ The "Ruler" of Our Lives,
<u>Amos 7:7–9</u>

Who made the stars?

You probably have a good idea, but let's check it out in <u>Amos 5:8</u>.

OTHER STUFF TO SURF:

<u>Justice flowing like a river, Amos 5:24</u>
<u>Go home, Amos, Amos 7:10–17</u>
<u>God's promise, Amos 9:11–15</u>

1 These are the words of Amos, one of the shepherds from the town of Tekoa. He saw this vision about Israel two years before the earthquake. It was at the time Uzziah was king of Judah and Jeroboam son of Jehoash was king of Israel.
2 Amos said,
"The LORD will roar from Jerusalem;
he will send his voice from
Jerusalem.
The pastures of the shepherds will
become dry,
and even the top of Mount Carmel
will dry up."

Israel's Neighbours are Punished

The People of Aram

3 This is what the LORD says:
"For the many crimes of Damascus,
I will punish them.
They drove over the
people of Gilead
with threshing
boards that had
iron teeth.
4 So I will send fire upon
the house of
Hazael
that will destroy the
strong towers of
Ben-Hadad.
5 I will break down the
bar of the gate to Damascus
and destroy the king who is in the
Valley of Aven,
as well as the leader of Beth Eden.
The people of Aram will be taken
captive to the country of Kir,"
says the LORD.

The People of Philistia

6 This is what the LORD says:
"For the many crimes of Gaza,
I will punish them.
They sold all the people of one area
as slaves to Edom.
7 So I will send a fire on the walls of
Gaza
that will destroy the city's strong
buildings.
8 I will destroy the king of the city of
Ashdod,
as well as the leader of Ashkelon.
Then I will turn against the people of
the city of Ekron,
and the last of the Philistines will
die," says the Lord GOD.

The People of Phoenicia

9 This is what the LORD says:
"For the many crimes of Tyre,
I will punish them.
They sold all the people of one area
as slaves to Edom,
and they forgot the agreement
among relatives they had made
with Israel.
10 So I will send fire on the walls of Tyre
that will destroy the city's strong
buildings."

The People of Edom

11 This is what the LORD says:
"For the many crimes
of Edom,
I will punish them.
They hunted down
their relatives,
the Israelites,
with the sword,
showing them no
mercy.
They were angry all
the time
and kept on being
very angry.
12 So I will send fire on the city of Teman
that will even destroy the strong
buildings of Bozrah."[n]

The People of Ammon

13 This is what the LORD says:
"For the many crimes of Ammon,
I will punish them.
They ripped open the pregnant
women in Gilead
so they could take over that land
and make their own country larger.
14 So I will send fire on the city wall of
Rabbah

> The LORD will roar from Jerusalem; he will send his voice from Jerusalem.
> – Amos 1:2

1:12 Teman . . . Bozrah Since Teman was in northern Edom and Bozrah was in southern Edom, this means the whole country will be destroyed.

that will destroy its strong
   buildings.
It will come during a day of battle,
   during a stormy day with strong
   winds.
15 Then their king and leaders will be
   taken captive;
   they will all be taken away
   together," says the LORD.

The People of Moab

2 This is what the LORD says:
"For the many crimes of Moab,
   I will punish them.
   They burned the bones of the king
   of Edom into lime.
2 So I will send fire on Moab
   that will destroy the strong
   buildings of the city of Kerioth.
   The people of Moab will die in a great
   noise,
   in the middle of the sounds of war
   and trumpets.
3 So I will bring an end to the king of
   Moab,
   and I will kill all its leaders with
   him," says the LORD.

The People of Judah

4 This is what the LORD says:
"For the many crimes of Judah,
   I will punish them.
   They rejected the teachings of the
   LORD
   and did not keep his commands;
   they followed the same gods
   as their ancestors had followed.
5 So I will send fire on Judah,
   and it will destroy the strong
   buildings of Jerusalem."

Israel is Punished

6 This is what the LORD says:
"For the many crimes of Israel,
   I will punish them.
   For silver, they sell people who have
   done nothing wrong;
   they sell the poor to buy a pair of
   sandals.
7 They walk on poor people as if they
   were nothing,
   and they refuse to be fair to those
   who are suffering.

FAITH links

LOVE HIM? SHOW IT!
AMOS 2:6-7

Suppose you lost your lunch money at school. What if someone agreed to lend you money, but only if you agreed to pay them back double the amount? How would you feel? The poor Israelites found themselves in a worse situation. Amos warned the rich people that God saw how they cheated the poor people. Although the rich people talked about serving God, they treated others miserably.

God wants us to respond to the needs of those around us, not just give lip service. Helping others is the way to show real love for God.

Want to know how to best serve God? Surf here:

Give What You Can, Numbers 7:1–11, p. 186

Yours, Mine and Ours? 1 Samuel 25, p. 389

Jesus' Mission and Yours, Isaiah 61:1–2, p. 978

Concern for All, Daniel 9, p. 1165

That Thing You Do, Matthew 25:14–30, p. 1319

My Best Serve, Acts 6:1–6, p. 1473

Fathers and sons have sexual
   relations with the same woman,
   and so they ruin my holy name.

8 As they worship at their altars,
   they lie down on clothes taken
      from the poor.
   They fine people,
   and with that money they buy wine
      to drink in the house of their
      god.

9 "But it was I who destroyed the
      Amorites before them,
   who were tall like cedar trees and
      as strong as oaks—
   I destroyed them completely.
10 It was I who brought you from the
      land of Egypt
   and led you for 40 years through
      the desert
   so I could give you the land of the
      Amorites.
11 I made some of your children
      prophets
   and some of your young people
      Nazirites.
   People of Israel, isn't this true?" says
      the LORD.

12 "But you made the Nazirites drink
      wine
   and told the prophets not to
      prophesy.
13 Now I will make you get stuck,
      as a wagon loaded with grain gets
      stuck.
14 No one will escape, not even the
      fastest runner.
   Strong people will not be strong
      enough;
   warriors will not be able to save
      themselves.
15 Soldiers with bows and arrows will
      not stand and fight,
   and even fast runners will not get
      away;
   soldiers on horses will not escape
      alive.
16 At that time even the bravest warriors
      will run away without their
      armour," says the LORD.

Warning to Israel

3 Listen to this word that the LORD has
   spoken against you, people of Israel,
against the whole family he brought out of
Egypt.

2 "I have chosen only you
      out of all the families of the earth,
   so I will punish you
      for all your sins."

3 Two people will not walk together
      unless they have agreed to do so.
4 A lion in the forest does not roar
      unless it has caught an animal;
   it does not growl in its den
      when it has caught nothing.
5 A bird will not fall into a trap
      where there is no bait;
   the trap will not spring shut
      if there is nothing to catch.
6 When a trumpet blows a warning in a
      city,
   the people tremble.
   When trouble comes to a city,
      the LORD has caused it.
7 Before the Lord GOD does anything,
      he tells his plans to his servants
      the prophets.
8 The lion has roared!
      Who wouldn't be afraid?
   The Lord GOD has spoken.
      Who will not prophesy?

9 Announce this to the strong buildings
      of Ashdod
   and to the strong buildings of Egypt:
   "Come to the mountains of Samaria,
      where you will see great confusion
      and people hurting others."

10 "The people don't know how to do
      what is right," says the LORD.
   "Their strong buildings are filled
      with treasures they took by force
      from others."

11 So this is what the Lord GOD says:
   "An enemy will take over the land
      and pull down your strongholds;
   he will take the treasures out of
      your strong buildings."

12 This is what the LORD says:
   "A shepherd might save from a lion's
      mouth
   only two leg bones or a scrap of an
      ear of his sheep.
   In the same way only a few Israelites
      in Samaria will be saved—

▶ **Amos 3:13 1198**

LET'S VISIT SAMARIA
Amos 3:11–15

Back in the Old Testament days Israel was divided into the Northern Kingdom and the Southern Kingdom. King Omri built Samaria to be the capital of the Northern Kingdom.

Samaria is probably best known as the place where Jesus had a conversation with a woman beside a well. (See John 4:5–42, p. 1428.) But Samaria was an important city to Israel even before Jesus' life on earth. There are only two other cities that the Bible mentions more than Samaria. Samaria was one of the few major cities founded and built entirely by the Israelites.

Samaria has been taken over by several different nations: Assyria, Babylonia, Persia, Greece and Rome. When Herod the Great took over Samaria, he named it Sebaste – the Greek term for *Augustus* – in honour of the emperor of Rome.

---

people who now sit on their beds and on their couches."

13 "Listen and be witnesses against the family of Jacob," says the Lord GOD, the God All-powerful.

14 "When I punish Israel for their sins, I will also destroy the altars at Bethel.
The corners of the altar will be cut off, and they will fall to the ground.
15 I will tear down the winter house, together with the summer house.
The houses decorated with ivory will be destroyed,
and the great houses will come to an end," says the LORD.

Israel will Not Return

4 Listen to this message, you cows of Bashan*n* on the Mountain of Samaria.
You take things from the poor and crush people who are in need.
Then you command your husbands, "Bring us something to drink!"
2 The Lord GOD has promised this:
"Just as surely as I am a holy God, the time will come
when you will be taken away by hooks,
and what is left of you with fish-hooks.
3 You will go straight out of the city through holes in the walls,
and you will be thrown on the rubbish dump," says the LORD.

4 "Come to the city of Bethel and sin; come to Gilgal and sin even more.
Offer your sacrifices every morning,
and bring one-tenth of your crops every three days.
5 Offer bread made with yeast as a sacrifice to show your thanks,
and boast about the special offerings you bring,
because this is what you love to do, Israelites," says the Lord GOD.

4:1 Bashan Amos compares the rich, lazy women of Samaria to well-fed cows from Bashan, a place known for its rich animal pastures.

6 "I did not give you any food in your cities,
   and there was not enough to eat in any of your towns,
   but you did not come back to me," says the LORD.
7 "I held back the rain from you three months before harvest time.
   Then I let it rain on one city but not on another.
   Rain fell on one field, but another field got none and dried up.
8 People weak from thirst went from town to town for water,
   but they could not get enough to drink.
   Still you did not come back to me," says the LORD.
9 "I made your crops die from disease and mildew.
   When your gardens and your vineyards got larger,
   locusts ate your fig and olive trees.
   But still you did not come back to me," says the LORD.
10 "I sent disasters against you, as I did to Egypt.
   I killed your young men with swords, and your horses were taken from you.
   I made you smell the stink from all the dead bodies,
   but still you did not come back to me," says the LORD.
11 "I destroyed some of you as I destroyed Sodom and Gomorrah.
   You were like a burning stick pulled from a fire,
   but still you did not come back to me," says the LORD.
12 "So this is what I will do to you, Israel;
   because I will do this to you,

get ready to meet your God, Israel."

13 He is the one who makes the mountains and creates the wind
   and makes his thoughts known to people.
   He changes the dawn into darkness
   and walks over the mountains of the earth.
   His name is the LORD God All-powerful.

> He is the one who makes the mountains and creates the wind and makes his thoughts known to people.
> — Amos 4:13

Israel Needs to Repent

5 Listen to this funeral song that I sing about you, people of Israel.
2 "The young girl Israel has fallen, and she will not rise up again.
   She was left alone in her own land, and there is no one to help her up."

3 This is what the Lord GOD says:
"If 1,000 soldiers leave a city, only 100 will return;
if 100 soldiers leave a city, only ten will return."

4 This is what the LORD says to the nation of Israel:
"Come to me and live.
5 But do not look in Bethel or go to Gilgal,
   and do not go down to Beersheba.
   The people of Gilgal will be taken away as captives,
   and Bethel will become nothing."
6 Come to the LORD and live,
   or he will move like fire against the descendants of Joseph.
   The fire will burn Bethel, and there will be no one to put it out.
7 You turn justice upside down, and you throw on the ground what is right.

Amos 5:8   1200

8 God is the one who made the star
    groups Pleiades and Orion;
  he changes darkness into the
    morning light,
  and the day into dark night.
  He calls for the waters of the sea
    to pour out on the earth.
  The LORD is his name.
9 He destroys the protected city;
    he ruins the strong, walled city.

10 You hate those who speak in court
     against evil,
   and you can't stand those who tell
     the truth.
11 You walk on poor people,
     forcing them to give you grain.
   You have built fancy houses of cut
     stone,
     but you will not live in them.
   You have planted beautiful vineyards,
     but you will not drink the wine
       from them.
12 I know your many crimes,
     your terrible sins.
   You hurt people who do right,
     you take money to do wrong,
   and you keep the poor from getting
     justice in court.
13 In such times the wise person will
     keep quiet,
   because it is a bad time.

14 Try to do good, not evil,
     so that you will live,
   and the LORD God All-powerful will
     be with you
   just as you say he is.
15 Hate evil and love good;
     be fair in the courts.
   Perhaps the LORD God All-powerful
     will be kind
   to the people of Joseph who are left
     alive.

16 This is what the Lord, the LORD
   God All-powerful, says:
   "People will be crying in all the
     streets;
     they will be saying, 'Oh, no!' in the
       public places.
   They will call the farmers to come
     and weep
   and will pay people to cry out loud
     for them.
17 People will be crying in all the
     vineyards,
     because I will pass among you to
       punish you," says the LORD.

The LORD's Day of Judging

18 How terrible it will be for you who
     want
     the LORD's day of judging to come.

FAITH links

A BLUEPRINT FOR LIVING
AMOS 5:14-15

A blueprint is a plan of action for a builder. By following the blueprint, the builder can successfully do his work. Many people say they want to do the right thing, but aren't quite sure how. Amos provides a blueprint for living a life that is pleasing to God. Do good; hate evil. As you follow this blueprint, God offers his help and guarantees you success in completing it.

I'll Never Forget What's-His-Name, Deuteronomy 8, p. 239

What's Out Becomes In, Judges 11, p. 327

A Wise Wish, 1 Kings 3:5–9, p. 439

Mind Guard, Proverbs 4:23, p. 831

Put God First, Acts 5:27–32, p. 1472

What's Good About You? Philemon 4–7, p. 1663

Why do you want that day to come?
   It will bring darkness for you, not
      light.
19 It will be like someone who runs from
      a lion
   and meets a bear,
   or like someone who goes into his
      house
   and puts his hand on the wall,
   and then is bitten by a snake.
20 So the LORD's day of judging will
      bring darkness, not light;
   it will be very dark, not light at all.

21 The LORD says, "I completely hate
      your feasts;
   I cannot stand your religious
      meetings.
22 If you offer me burnt offerings and
      grain offerings,
   I won't accept them.
   You bring your best fellowship
      offerings of fattened cattle,
   but I will ignore them.
23 Take the noise of your songs away
      from me!
   I won't listen to the music of your
      harps.
24 But let justice
      flow like a
      river,
   and let
      goodness
      flow like a
      stream that
      never stops.

**5:24
Character**
Check out what should
never stop!

25 "People of Israel, you did not bring
      me sacrifices and offerings
   while you travelled in the desert
      for 40 years.
26 You have carried with you
   your king, the god Sakkuth
   and Kaiwan your idol,
   and the star gods you have made.
27 So I will send you away as captives
      beyond Damascus,"
   says the LORD, whose name is the
      God All-powerful.

Israel will be Destroyed

6 How terrible it will be for those who
   have an easy life in Jerusalem,
   for those who feel safe living on
      Mount Samaria.
   You think you are the important people
      of the best nation in the world;
   the Israelites come to you for help.
2 Go and look at the city of Calneh,
   and from there go to the great city
      Hamath;
   then go down to Gath of the
      Philistines.
   You are no better than these kingdoms.
   Your land is no larger than theirs.
3 You put off the day of punishment,
   but you bring near the day when
      you can do evil to others.
4 You lie on beds decorated with ivory
   and stretch out on your couches.
   You eat tender lambs
   and fattened calves.
5 You make up songs on your harps,
   and, like David, you compose
      songs on musical instruments.
6 You drink wine by the bowlful
   and use the best perfumed lotions.
   But you are not sad over the ruin
      of Israel,
7 so you will be some of the first ones
      taken as slaves.
   Your feasting and lying around will
      come to an end.

8 The Lord GOD made this promise;
   the LORD God All-powerful says:
   "I hate the pride of the Israelites,
   and I hate their strong buildings,
   so I will let the enemy take the city
      and everything in it."

9 At that time there might be only ten
people left alive in just one house, but they
will also die. 10 When the relatives come
to get the bodies to take them outside, one
of them will call to the other and ask, "Are
there any other dead bodies with you?"
   That person will answer, "No."
   Then the one who asked will say,
"Hush! We must not say the name of the
LORD."

11 The LORD has given the command;
   the large house will be broken into
      pieces,
   and the small house into bits.

12 Horses do not run on rocks,
and people do not plough rocks
with oxen.
But you have changed fairness into
poison;
you have changed what is right
into a bitter taste.
13 You are happy that the town of Lo
Debar was captured,
and you say, "We have taken
Karnaim" by our own strength."

14 The LORD God All-powerful says,
"Israel, I will bring a nation against
you
that will make your people suffer
from Lebo Hamath in the north
to the valley south of the Dead Sea."

The Vision of Locusts

7 This is what the Lord GOD showed me: he was forming a swarm of locusts, after the king had taken his share of the first crop and the second crop had just begun growing. 2 When the locusts ate all the crops in the country, I said, "Lord GOD, forgive us. How could Israel live through this? It is too small already!"

3 So the LORD changed his mind about this. "It will not happen," said the LORD.

The Vision of Fire

4 This is what the Lord GOD showed me: the Lord GOD was calling for fire to come down like rain. It burned up the deep water and was going to burn up the land. 5 Then I cried out, "Lord GOD, stop! How could Israel live through this? It is too small already."

6 So the LORD changed his mind about this too. "It will not happen," said the Lord GOD.

The Vision of the Plumb Line

7 This is what he showed me: the Lord stood by a straight wall, with a plumb line in his hand. 8 The LORD said to me, "Amos, what do you see?"

I said, "A plumb line."

Then the Lord said, "See, I will put a plumb line among my people Israel to show how crooked they are. I will not look the other way any longer.

FAITH links

THE "RULER" OF OUR LIVES
AMOS 7:7-9

Ever try to hang a picture on a wall? You could tell whether the picture was straight by measuring with a ruler. If you didn't use a ruler or tape measure, the picture would hang crookedly. Amos saw a vision of a plumb line. A plumb line was used to measure how straight a wall was. God used the plumb line to measure how "straight" the Israelites were. That meant he wanted to know how willing they were to get rid of their sin.

The Bible is used to measure how "straight" our lives are. It can show us the places where we're "out of line" with God's commands. Where do you need to straighten up?

The Trouble with Sin, Genesis 6—8, p. 11

Try to Remember, Deuteronomy 11:18–21, p. 243

A Look for the Book, 2 Chronicles 34:14–18, p. 603

Our Thirst Quencher, Psalm 42:1–3, p. 741

Life's Rule Book, 2 Timothy 3:15–17, p. 1655

The Sin "Braker", Jude 24–25, p. 1727

6:13 Lo Debar . . . Karnaim These were cities in Israel that the Israelites had captured in war.

9 "The places where Isaac's descendants
    worship will be destroyed,
  Israel's holy places will be turned
    into ruins,
  and I will attack King Jeroboam's
    family with the sword."

Amaziah Speaks Against Amos

10 Amaziah, a priest at Bethel, sent this message to Jeroboam king of Israel: "Amos is making evil plans against you with the people of Israel. He has been speaking so much that this land can't hold all his words. 11 This is what Amos has said:

  'Jeroboam will die by the sword,
    and the people of Israel will be
      taken as captives
    out of their own country.'"

12 Then Amaziah said to Amos, "Seer, go back right now to Judah. Do your prophesying and earn your living there, 13 but don't prophesy any more here at Bethel. This is the king's holy place, and it is the nation's temple."

14 Then Amos answered Amaziah, "I do not make my living as a prophet, nor am I a member of a group of prophets. I make my living as a shepherd, and I take care of sycamore trees. 15 But the LORD took me away from tending the flock and said to me, 'Go and prophesy to my people Israel.' 16 So listen to the LORD's word. You tell me,

  'Don't prophesy against Israel,
    and stop prophesying against the
      descendants of Isaac.'

17 "Because you have said this, the LORD says:

  'Your wife will become a prostitute in
    the city,
  and your sons and daughters will
    be killed with swords.
  Other people will measure your land
    and divide it among
      themselves,
  and you will die in a foreign
    country.
  The people of Israel will definitely be
    taken
  from their own land as captives.'"

The Vision of Ripe Fruit

8 This is what the Lord GOD showed me: a basket of summer fruit. 2 He said to me, "Amos, what do you see?"

I said, "A basket of summer fruit."

Then the LORD said to me, "An end[n] has come for my people Israel, because I will not overlook their sins any more.

3 "On that day the palace songs will become funeral songs," says the Lord GOD. "There will be dead bodies thrown everywhere! Silence!"

4 Listen to me, you who walk on helpless
    people,
  you who are trying to destroy the
    poor people of this country,
      saying,
5 "When will the New Moon festival be
    over
  so we can sell grain?
  When will the Sabbath be over
    so we can bring out wheat to sell?
  We can charge them more
    and give them less,
  and we can change the scales to
    cheat the people.
6 We will buy poor people for silver,
    and needy people for the price of a
      pair of sandals.
  We will even sell the wheat that
    was swept up from the floor."

7 The LORD has sworn by his name, the Pride of Jacob, "I will never forget everything that these people did.
8 The whole land will shake because of it,
    and everyone who lives in the land
      will cry for those who died.
  The whole land will rise like the Nile;
    it will be shaken, and then it will fall
      like the Nile River in Egypt."

9 The Lord GOD says:
  "At that time I will cause the sun to
    go down at noon
    and make the earth dark on a
      bright day.
10 I will change your festivals into days
    of crying for the dead,

8:2 end The Hebrew word for "end" sounds like the Hebrew word for "summer fruit".

and all your songs will become
    songs of sadness.
I will make all of you wear rough
    cloth to show your sadness;
I will make you shave your heads
    as well.
I will make it like a time of crying for
    the death of an only son,
    and its end like the end of an awful
    day."

11 The Lord GOD says:
    "The days are coming
    when I will cause a time of hunger in
        the land.
    The people will not be
        hungry for bread
        or thirsty for water,
    but they will be
        hungry for words
        from the LORD.
12 They will wander from the
        Mediterranean Sea to the Dead
        Sea,
    from the north to the east.
    They will search for the word of the
        LORD,
    but they won't find it.
13 At that time the beautiful young
        women and the young men
    will become weak from thirst.
14 They make promises by the idol in
        Samaria
    and say, 'As surely as the god of
        Dan lives...'
    and, 'As surely as the god of
        Beersheba" lives, we promise...'
    So they will fall
        and never get up again."

Israel will be Destroyed

9 I saw the Lord standing by the altar,
    and he said:
    "Smash the top of the pillars
        so that even the bottom of the
        doors will shake.
    Make the pillars fall on the people's
        heads;
    anyone left alive I will kill with a
        sword.

> The people will not be hungry for bread or thirsty for water, but they will be hungry for words from the LORD.
> – Amos 8:11

Not one person will get away;
    no one will escape.
2 If they dig down as deep as the place of
        the dead,
    I will pull them up from there.
    If they climb up into heaven,
    I will bring them down from there.
3 If they hide at the top of Mount
        Carmel,
    I will find them and take them
        away.
    If they try to hide
        from me at the bottom of the
        sea,
    I will command a snake to bite
        them.
4 If they are captured
        and taken away
        by their enemies,
    I will command the
        sword to kill
        them.
    I will keep watch over them,
        but I will keep watch to give them
        trouble, not to do them good."

5 The Lord GOD All-powerful touches
        the land,
    and the land shakes.
    Then everyone who lives in the
        land cries for the dead.
    The whole land rises like the Nile
        River
    and falls like the river of Egypt.
6 The LORD builds his upper rooms
        above the skies;
    he sets their foundations on the
        earth.
    He calls for the waters of the sea
    and pours them out on the land.
    The LORD is his name.

7 The LORD says,
    "Israel, you are no different to me
        than the people of Cush.
    I brought Israel out of the land of
        Egypt,

8:14 Dan ... Beersheba Dan was the city farthest north in Israel, and Beersheba was the city farthest south. So this means all the people of Israel.

the Philistines from Crete
and the Arameans from Kir.

8 I, the Lord God, am watching the
sinful kingdom Israel.
I will destroy it
from off the earth,
but I will not completely destroy
Jacob's descendants," says the
Lord.
9 "I am giving the command
to scatter the nation of Israel
among all nations.
It will be like someone shaking grain
through a strainer,
but not even a tiny stone falls
through.
10 All the sinners among my people
will die by the sword—
those who say,
'Nothing bad will happen to us.'

The Lord Promises to Restore Israel

11 "The kingdom of David is like a fallen tent,
but in that day I will set it up
again
and mend its broken places.
I will rebuild its ruins
as it was before.
12 Then Israel will take over what is left
of Edom
and the other nations that belong
to me,"
says the Lord,
who will make it happen.

13 The Lord says, "The time is coming
when there will be all kinds of
food.
People will still be harvesting crops
when it's time to plough again.
People will still be taking the juice
from grapes
when it's time to plant again.
Wine will drip from the mountains
and pour from the hills.
14 I will bring my people Israel back
from captivity;
they will build the ruined cities
again,
and they will live in them.

FAITH links

UPROOTED BY CHANGE
AMOS 9:15

If you've ever seen someone move a plant from one place to another, you know how unsettling that can be for the plant. Some plants don't thrive after being uprooted. Some events in life can cause you to feel uprooted. Going to a new school, moving to a new house, or a change in your family situation due to divorce can be pretty scary. The Israelites had been uprooted, their lives completely changed. Amos's book ends with the message of hope for them. There would come a time when they would not have to fear being uprooted again.

Change can be hard, sometimes. When you're feeling uprooted by change, God's presence can bring you stability.

Here are some Faithlinks on how to handle those big changes in your life:

Real Faith or Really Scared? Judges 4, p. 315

Problem Solved, 2 Kings 20:1–11, p. 507

Lower Than Low, Job 19:13–25, p. 680

Future Hope, Joel 3:17–21, p. 1191

A Safe Place, Nahum 1:7, p. 1231

An Energy Boost, Acts 4:31, p. 1469

Amos 9:15

They will plant vineyards and drink
the wine from them;
they will plant gardens and eat
their fruit.
15 I will plant my people on their land,
and they will not be pulled out
again
from the land which I have given
them,"
says the LORD your God.

DESTROY EDOM

It's Obadiah the prophet here. I served God by telling the nation of Edom about God's plan to punish them. Do you remember the story of Jacob and Esau, the twin brothers who started fighting before they were even born? Esau sold his rights as a firstborn son to Jacob for a bowl of soup. Jacob then tricked his father Isaac into giving him the blessing that should have been given to Esau. When he found out that Jacob had stolen his inheritance, Esau was so angry he wanted to kill his brother. (Surf on over to Genesis 25—27, p. 33, for that exciting story.) Esau eventually forgave Jacob; but his descendants, the nation of Edom, were always enemies of Israel.

I wrote this book to tell people that Edom would be destroyed because it was an enemy of God's people. As our relatives, the Edomites should have helped defend Jerusalem from our enemies, but instead they laughed at our trouble. They were happy when Jerusalem was invaded and came to steal our treasures. The Edomites even captured people trying to escape and turned them over to the enemy. God said, "The same evil things you did to other people will happen to you" (Obadiah 15).

JESUS WATCH

The people of Edom were proud of their nation and did not think it could ever be destroyed. Their capital city of Sela was perched on a high cliff and could only be approached through a narrow gorge. How could anyone conquer Sela? Years later Edom was conquered and forced out of its mountain strongholds. The people moved to southern Israel and eventually were completely destroyed by the Romans. Edom was punished for its sins. Obadiah also talks about the day that Jesus will come to judge all the nations. It will be a day of terrible punishment for nations who were enemies of Israel. Jesus will restore the nation of Israel and rule as a king from Mount Zion in Jerusalem.

FAITH links

What will Edom lose?

Everything! Check out Obadiah 6-7.

WHAT ABOUT THIS?
Don't laugh at Israel, Obadiah 12–14
The holy mountain, Obadiah 17

○ Set for Life?
Obadiah 2–4

○ A Fair-weather Friend,
Obadiah 7

The LORD will Punish the Edomites

1 This is the vision of Obadiah.

This is what the Lord GOD says about Edom:[n]
We have heard a message from the LORD.
A messenger has been sent among the nations, saying,
"Attack! Let's go and attack Edom!"

The Lord Speaks to the Edomites

2 "Soon I will make you the smallest of nations.
You will be greatly hated by everyone.
3 Your pride has fooled you,
you who live in the hollow places of the cliff.
Your home is up high,
you who say to yourself,
'No one can bring me down to the ground.'
4 Even if you fly high like the eagle
and make your nest among the stars,
I will bring you down from there,"
says the LORD.
5 "You will really be ruined!
If thieves came to you,
if robbers came by night,
they would steal only enough for themselves.
If workers came and picked the grapes from your vines,
they would leave a few behind.
6 But you, Edom, will really lose everything!
People will find all your hidden treasures!
7 All the people who are your friends
will force you out of the land.
The people who are at peace with you
will trick you and defeat you.
Those who eat your bread with you now
are planning a trap for you,
and you will not notice it."

8 The LORD says, "On that day
I will surely destroy the wise people from Edom,
and those with understanding from the mountains of Edom.
9 Then, city of Teman, your best warriors will be afraid

SET FOR LIFE?
OBADIAH 2-4

Do you think that money, fame, sports achievements or power can make a person secure for life? The Edomites in Obadiah's day believed that their possessions made them secure. They felt proud because their city was like a fortress. No enemies could harm them, or so they thought. But Obadiah warned them that God would humble them.

Many prideful people boast that they "have it all" (money, fame, power) and are secure in themselves. But God can humble anyone.

Think money will solve your problems? Connect here:

Put Pride Aside, Exodus 2:11–15, p. 78

What I've Got, 2 Kings 20:12–17, p. 508

Wisdom About Wealth, Ecclesiastes 5:10–12, p. 878

A Robbery in Progress, Malachi 3:8–10, p. 1270

Your Heart's Desire, Luke 16:13–15, p. 1401

Share and Share Alike? Acts 2:43–47, p. 1466

---

1 Edom The Edomites were the people who came from Esau, Jacob's twin brother. They were enemies of the Israelites.

A FAIR-WEATHER FRIEND
OBADIAH 7

What do you call a friend who is only around some of the time? No, it's not a riddle. Some friends are fair-weather friends. They only hang around when you have something they want. Obadiah warned the Israelites about their "fair-weather allies". These were the nations who claimed to help Israel. But Obadiah warned that one day these same nations would force Israel out of the land.

Fair-weather friends can hurt your feelings by their lack of loyalty. God is a friend who will never be disloyal. You can always depend on God.

Lights, Camera, . . . Actions! Genesis 12:1–3, p. 17

The Gift of Friendship, 1 Samuel 18:1–3; 19, p. 381

Some Friendly Advice, Proverbs 17:9, 14, 17, p. 851

A Hopeful Name, Hosea 1:3–11, p. 1172

The Way to Heaven, John 14:1–6, p. 1448

Thanks for a Friend, 1 Thessalonians 1:1–3, p. 1630

and everyone from the mountains of Edom will be killed.
10 You did violence to your relatives, the Israelites,
so you will be covered with shame and destroyed for ever.
11 You stood aside without helping while strangers carried Israel's treasures away.
When foreigners entered Israel's city gate
and threw lots to decide what part of Jerusalem they would take,
you were like one of them.

Commands That Edom Broke

12 "Edom, do not laugh at your brother Israel in his time of trouble
or be happy about the people of Judah when they are destroyed.
Do not boast when cruel things are done to them.
13 Do not enter the city gate of my people
in their time of trouble
or laugh at their problems
in their time of trouble.
Do not take their treasures
in their time of trouble.
14 Do not stand at the crossroads
to destroy those who are trying to escape.
Do not capture those who escape alive and turn them over to their enemy
in their time of trouble.

The Nations will be Judged

15 "The LORD's day of judging is coming soon
to all the nations.
The same evil things you did to other people
will happen to you;
they will come back upon your own head.

15 Judgement
What happens on the day of judgement?

16 Because you drank in my Temple,
all the nations will drink on and on.
They will drink and drink
until they disappear.
17 But on Mount Zion some will escape the judgement,
and it will be a holy place.

The people of Jacob will take back
their land
from those who took it from them.
18 The people of Jacob will be like a fire
and the people of Joseph[n] like a
flame.
But the people of Esau[n] will be like
dry stalks.
The people of Jacob will set them
on fire and burn them up.
There will be no one left of the people
of Esau."
This will happen because the LORD
has said it.

19 Then God's people will regain
southern Judah from Edom;
they will take back the mountains
of Edom.
They will take back the western hills
from the Philistines.
They will regain the lands of Ephraim
and Samaria,
and Benjamin will take over
Gilead.
20 People from Israel who once were
forced to leave their homes
will take the land of the Canaanites,
all the way to Zarephath.
People from Judah who once were
forced to leave Jerusalem and
live in Sepharad
will take back the cities of southern
Judah.
21 Powerful warriors will go up on
Mount Zion,
where they will rule the people
living on Edom's mountains.
And the kingdom will belong to the
LORD.

---

18 people of Jacob . . . Joseph The people who came from Jacob and Joseph, or the Israelites.
18 people of Esau The people who came from Esau, or the Edomites.

FISH BAIT!

Hi! I'm Jonah. I'll bet you've heard of me. I'm the one who spent three days and three nights inside a fish. When God told me to go and preach to the people of Nineveh, I was shocked. Nineveh was the capital of Assyria, our greatest enemy. Assyrians skinned their enemies while they were still alive and dragged their captives away with giant fish-hooks. I didn't want God to forgive Nineveh; I wanted him to destroy it! Instead of going to Nineveh, I got on a boat sailing in the other direction. So, how did I end up in a fish? You'll have to turn to Jonah 1 for the whole fish tale!

I wrote this book so that people would know that God wants all people to be sorry for their sins and follow his laws. I eventually did go to Nineveh to tell the people that God would destroy their city if they did not stop doing evil things. To my disgust, they listened! The people of Nineveh stopped eating for a while and wore rough clothes to show sadness for their sins. God is kind and merciful to people who are sorry for their sins, even when we aren't.

JESUS WATCH

Jesus worked many miracles, but the teachers of the law asked for a sign that would prove that he was the Son of God. Jesus said that the only sign would be the sign of Jonah. Just as Jonah was in the big fish for three days and nights, Jesus was in his grave for three days and nights. Jonah's experience with the fish reminds us of the death, burial and resurrection of Jesus. When Jesus rose from the dead, he proved that he truly was the Son of God. Jonah's message for the Ninevites shows that God is concerned for all people, not just the people of Israel. God loves the people of the world so much that he sent Jesus to die for their sins. Anyone who believes in Jesus has eternal life. No one is excluded. People from all nations are invited.

my FAVOURITE links

OTHER CONNECTIONS

- Let's Visit Nineveh, Jonah 1—4. Connect here to find out more about the capital of Assyria, one of the most powerful and evil empires during Old Testament times. Today, nothing remains of this ancient capital, fulfilling Bible prophecy.

MORE STUFF...

More Miracles The story of Jonah is filled with miracles that God sent to convince the reluctant prophet Jonah to take his message to the people of Nineveh. Check out what God did to give Jonah a "gentle" push.
- God sent a great storm that threatened the safety of the ship and its crew, including Jonah (Jonah 1:4–5).
- When Jonah was thrown overboard by the crew to save the ship, God provided a great fish to swallow Jonah. Jonah was kept safe inside the fish for three days and three nights (Jonah 1:14–17).
- God caused the fish to throw up Jonah on dry land. This time when God said to go, Jonah obeyed (Jonah 2:10—3:3).

How long did it take to walk around the city of Nineveh?

Too long, probably. Check it out in Jonah 3:3.

CHECK THESE OUT ON THE JONAH SURFWATCH:
A fishy prayer, Jonah 2
Ninevites stop eating, Jonah 3:5–10
The worm turns, Jonah 4

FAITH links

○ Go! No!
Jonah 1

○ A Tight Spot,
Jonah 2

○ The God of Second Chances,
Jonah 3

○ Mercy for an Enemy,
Jonah 4

God Calls and Jonah Runs

1 The LORD spoke his word to Jonah son of Amittai: 2 "Get up and go to the great city of Nineveh and preach against it, because I see the evil things they do."

3 But Jonah got up to run away from the LORD by going to Tarshish. He went to the city of Joppa, where he found a ship that was going to the city of Tarshish. Jonah paid for the trip and went aboard, planning to go to Tarshish to run away from the LORD.

4 But the LORD sent a great wind on the sea, which made the sea so stormy that the ship was in danger of breaking apart. 5 The sailors were afraid, and each man cried to his own god. They began throwing the cargo from the ship into the sea to make the ship lighter.

But Jonah had gone down far inside the ship to lie down, and he fell fast asleep. 6 The captain of the ship came and said, "Why are you sleeping? Get up and pray to your god! Maybe your god will pay attention to us, and we won't die!"

7 Then the men said to each other, "Let's throw lots to see who caused these troubles to happen to us."

When they threw lots, the lot showed that the trouble had happened because of Jonah. 8 Then they said to him, "Tell us, who caused our trouble? What is your job? Where do you come from? What is your country? Who are your people?"

9 Then Jonah said to them, "I am a Hebrew. I fear the LORD, the God of heaven, who made the sea and the land."

10 The men were very afraid, and they asked Jonah, "What terrible thing did you do?" (They knew he was running away from the LORD because he had told them.)

11 Since the wind and the waves of the sea were becoming much stronger, they said to him, "What should we do to you to make the sea calm down for us?"

12 Jonah said to them, "Pick me up and throw me into the sea, and then it will calm down. I know it is my fault that this great storm has come on you."

13 Instead, the men tried to row the ship back to the land, but they could not, because the sea was becoming more stormy.

FAITH links

GO! NO!
JONAH 1

Suppose God told you to go to your worst enemy and tell him God loved him. Would you go? Jonah didn't! The Ninevites were cruel enemies of Israel. So Jonah set off for a city in the opposite direction. But God didn't let Jonah get away with being disobedient.

Sometimes we promise to serve God, but wind up running in the opposite direction when an opportunity to serve comes up that doesn't fit what we had in mind. God doesn't take no for an answer. When he says, "Go," what will you say?

Fearful Service? Exodus 4:1–17, p. 80

Help for the Poor, Leviticus 5:7, p. 138

A Reminder to Be Fair, 2 Chronicles 19:5–11, p. 583

Too Young to Serve, Jeremiah 1:4–9, p. 988

The Most Fun, Acts 20:35, p. 1502

As Strong as Superman? Philippians 4:13, p. 1615

Jonah's Punishment

14 So the men cried to the LORD, "LORD, please don't let us die because of this man's life; please don't think we are guilty of killing an innocent person. LORD, you have caused all this to happen; you wanted it this way." 15 So they picked up

Jonah 1:16 1214

LET'S VISIT NINEVEH Jonah 1—4

Nineveh was founded by Nimrod, a descendant of Noah. (Check out Genesis 10:1–12, p. 14.) For many years Nineveh was the capital city of Assyria, a powerful and evil empire. Whenever most people talk about Nineveh, they think about the prophet Jonah. God asked Jonah to go and preach to the people of Nineveh, but Jonah didn't want to go. Jonah wanted God to punish them for their wickedness! When Jonah finally did preach to them, they repented of their sins . . . at least for a while. (Look at Jonah 3:10.)

About 150 years after Jonah's visit, Nineveh was completely destroyed. The Medes, Babylonians and Scythians attacked the city after a flood that weakened the city wall and dissolved some of the bricks in the buildings. This fulfilled the prophecy of Nahum. (Read Nahum 2:1–6, p. 1232.)

Jonah and threw him into the sea, and the sea became calm. **16** Then they began to fear the LORD very much; they offered a sacrifice to the LORD and made promises to him.

17 The LORD caused a big fish to swallow Jonah, and Jonah was inside the fish for three days and three nights.

2 While Jonah was inside the fish, he prayed to the LORD his God and said,

2 "When I was in danger,
I called to the LORD,
and he answered me.
I was about to die,
so I cried to you
and you heard my voice.
3 You threw me into the sea,
down, down into the deep sea.
The water was all around me,
and your powerful waves flowed over me.
4 I said, 'I was driven out of your presence,
but I hope to see your Holy Temple again.'

2:1 Prayer Can God always hear your prayer?

5 The waters of the sea closed around my throat.
The deep sea was all around me;
seaweed was wrapped around my head.
6 When I went down to where the mountains of the sea start to rise,
I thought I was locked in this prison for ever,
but you saved me from the pit of death,
LORD my God.

7 "When my life had almost gone,
I remembered the LORD.
I prayed to you,
and you heard my prayers in your Holy Temple.

8 "People who worship useless idols
give up their loyalty to you.
9 But I will praise and thank you
while I give sacrifices to you,
and I will keep my promises to you.
Salvation comes from the LORD!"

FAITH links

A TIGHT SPOT
JONAH 2

When you're in a tight spot, what do you do? Jonah was in big trouble. He had disobeyed God and wound up as a fish sandwich – hold the bread – as a result. So, what did he do? He prayed!

When you're in a jam, pray. You can pray wherever you are: outside, in your room, inside a fish. God will always listen to you.

Here are some more Faithlinks on what to do in a jam:

When You're Afraid, Genesis 32:9–12, p. 45

Your Best Defence, 2 Chronicles 20:1–12, p. 584

999, Psalm 28:6, p. 730

Small Beginnings, Zechariah 4:10, p. 1255

The Best Protection Plan, Matthew 2:13–18, p. 1276

Prayer Anywhere, Mark 1:35, p. 1331

FAITH links

THE GOD OF SECOND CHANCES
JONAH 3

Do you do what your parents tell you to do the first time they mention it? Or, do you wait until they ask you again? Jonah didn't obey the first time God told him to go to Nineveh. After a little persuasion (being fish food!), Jonah was ready to listen.

When you blow it, God offers a second chance for obedience. Peter, one of Jesus' followers, also needed a second chance. (You can read about this in John 18 and 21, p. 1454.) Jesus willingly gave it to him. Do you need a second chance? Just ask God. He *is* the God of second chances.

The Perfect Leader? Numbers 20:1–13, p. 203

Two Enemies, Nehemiah 6, p. 631

A Pity Party, Job 10, p. 671

A Model of Forgiveness, Ezekiel 16:59–63, p. 1103

Blessed Are the Weak? 2 Corinthians 12:7–10, p. 1582

A Friendly Welcome, Philemon 18, p. 1664

---

10 Then the LORD spoke to the fish, and the fish threw up Jonah onto the dry land.

God Calls and Jonah Obeys

3 The LORD spoke his word to Jonah again and said, **2** "Get up and go to the great city Nineveh and preach to it what I tell you to say."

3 So Jonah obeyed the LORD and got up and went to Nineveh. It was a very large city; just to walk across it took a person three days. **4** After Jonah had entered the city and walked for one day, he preached to the people, saying, "After 40 days, Nineveh will be destroyed!"

5 The people of Nineveh believed God.

Jonah 3:6

FAITH links

MERCY FOR AN ENEMY
JONAH 4

Ever wonder how God could show love or forgiveness to someone who doesn't deserve it? Jonah did not want God to show love to his enemies, the Ninevites. But that's what God did. The Ninevites told God they were sorry for their sins. Instead of destroying them, he showed compassion by forgiving their sins.

God has mercy on anyone who turns away from their sin. Because he has not treated us the way we deserve, he wants us to show his mercy to our enemies as well.

How do you treat your enemies? Need help? Connect here:

Forgive Instead, Genesis 33, p. 47

Putting an Enemy in Check, 2 Kings 6:8–23, p. 486

Concern for All, Daniel 9, p. 1165

Justice Desserts, Habakkuk 2:4–8, p. 1237

The Number One Rule, Mark 12:28–31, p. 1351

Who Needs Love? Luke 6:27–36, p. 1379

They announced that they would stop eating for a while, and they put on rough cloth to show their sadness. All the people in the city did this, from the most important to the least important.

6 When the king of Nineveh heard this news, he got up from his throne, took off his robe and covered himself with rough cloth and sat in ashes to show how upset he was.

7 He sent this announcement through Nineveh:

> By command of the king and his important men: no person or animal, herd or flock, will be allowed to taste anything. Do not let them eat food or drink water. 8 But every person and animal should be covered with rough cloth, and people should cry loudly to God. Everyone must turn away from evil living and stop doing harm all the time. 9 Who knows? Maybe God will change his mind. Maybe he will stop being angry and then we will not die.

10 When God saw what the people did, that they stopped doing evil, he changed his mind and did not do what he had warned. He did not punish them.

God's Mercy Makes Jonah Angry

4 But this made Jonah very unhappy, and he became angry. 2 He prayed to the LORD, "When I was still in my own country this is what I said would happen, and that is why I quickly ran away to Tarshish. I knew that you are a God who is kind and shows mercy. You don't become angry quickly, and you have great love. I knew you would choose not to cause harm. 3 So now I ask you, LORD, please kill me. It is better for me to die than to live."

4 Then the LORD said, "Do you think it is right for you to be angry?"

5 Jonah went out and sat down east of the city. There he made a shelter for himself and sat in the shade, waiting to see what would happen to the city. 6 The LORD made a plant grow quickly up over Jonah, which gave him shade and helped him to be more comfortable. Jonah was very pleased to have the plant. 7 But the next day when the sun rose, God sent a worm to attack the plant so that it died.

8 As the sun rose higher in the sky, God sent a very hot east wind to blow, and

the sun became so hot on Jonah's head that he became very weak and wished he were dead. He said, "It is better for me to die than to live."

9 But God said to Jonah, "Do you think it is right for you to be angry about the plant?"

Jonah answered, "It is right for me to be angry! I am so angry I could die!"

10 And the LORD said, "You are so concerned for that plant even though you did nothing to make it grow. It appeared one day, and the next day it died. 11 Then shouldn't I show concern for the great city Nineveh, which has more than 120,000 people who do not know right from wrong, and many animals too?"

MAKE GOOD PLANS

Hi, it's Micah here. Welcome to my homepage! I was a prophet of God, who lived about the same time as Isaiah and Hosea. Have you ever made plans to do good things, like play with a friend, plant a garden or work on a school project? The people of Israel made plans, too, but their plans were bad! Rich people cheated the poor out of their property. Judges took money to decide who would win in court. People worshipped false gods instead of the real thing – the true God of Israel. They thought nothing bad would happen to them because they were God's chosen people, but boy, were they wrong! God made some plans, too – to punish them for all their wickedness!

I wrote this book to tell people to stop doing evil things and ask God to forgive them. God told us what he wants: "to do what is right to other people, love being kind to others, and live humbly, obeying your God" (Micah 6:8). God expects us to follow his laws and to be honest in all we do. Why not make some plans today to show kindness to other people?

JESUS WATCH

In Micah 5, we read about God's most important plan. God planned to send a ruler who would take care of his people and bring them peace. The ruler would be born in Bethlehem, but come from very old times. His strength would be from God, and his power would be in the name of the Lord his God. Seven hundred years after Micah wrote these words, God sent Jesus, the long-awaited Messiah, to live among us as a man. Jesus was born in Bethlehem, just as Micah predicted. Jesus is also the Son of God, so he is eternal and comes from very old times. Like a shepherd, Jesus takes care of his people. We have peace with God because Jesus died to take the punishment for our sins. Jesus rules for ever in heaven with the power God gave him. God gave Jesus a name that is above all names. One day everyone will know that Jesus is Lord of all.

my FAVOURITE links

OTHER CONNECTIONS

GET THE INFO

Stop by Let's Visit Bethlehem, Micah 5:2, to find out more about this tiny hamlet nearly five miles south of Jerusalem. Although it probably is best known as the birthplace of Jesus, Bethlehem has played an important role in many Bible events. Check it out!

FAITH links

○ The Peril of Poisonous Plans, **Micah 2:1–3**

○ A Real Crowd-pleaser? **Micah 2:6–11**

○ The Right Ingredients, **Micah 6:8**

○ Inside the Heart of God, **Micah 7:18–20**

Do you think all the people of Israel were doing bad things?

It sounds like it. Better check out Micah 7:1-6. It doesn't sound like you would want to hang out with this crowd!

DON'T MISS THESE GREAT STORIES:

Evil planners, Micah 2:1–2
No more bad news! Micah 2:6–11
A new ruler, Micah 5:2–5
Micah's prayer, Micah 7:14–20

Samaria and Israel to Be Punished

1 During the time that Jotham, Ahaz and Hezekiah were kings of Judah, the word of the LORD came to Micah, who was from Moresheth. He saw these visions about Samaria and Jerusalem.

2 Hear this, all you nations;
    listen, earth and all you who live on it.
The Lord GOD will be a witness against you,
    the Lord from his Holy Temple.
3 See, the LORD is coming out of his place;
    he is coming down to walk on the tops of the mountains.
4 The mountains will melt under him,
    and the valleys will crack open,
like wax near a fire,
    like water running down a hillside.
5 All this is because of Jacob's sin,
    because of the sins of the nation of Israel.
What is the place of Jacob's sin?
    Isn't it Samaria?
What is Judah's place of idol worship?
    Isn't it Jerusalem?

The LORD Speaks

6 "So I will make Samaria a pile of ruins in the open country,
    a place for planting vineyards.
I will pour her stones down into the valley
    and strip her down to her foundations.
7 All her idols will be broken into pieces;
    all the gifts to her idols will be burned with fire.
I will destroy all her idols,
    and because Samaria earned her money by being unfaithful to me,
this money will be carried off by others who are not faithful to me."

Micah's Great Sadness

8 I will moan and cry because of this evil,
    going around barefoot and naked.
I will cry loudly like the wild dogs
    and make sad sounds like the owls do,
9 because Samaria's wound cannot be healed.
    It will spread to Judah;
it will reach the city gate of my people,
    all the way to Jerusalem.
10 Don't tell it in Gath.[n]
    Don't cry in Acco.[n]
    Roll in the dust
    at Beth Ophrah.[n]
11 Pass on your way,
    naked and ashamed,
    you who live in Shaphir.[n]
Those who live in Zaanan[n]
    won't come out.
The people in Beth Ezel[n] will cry,
    but they will not give you any support.
12 Those who live in Maroth[n]
    will be anxious for good news to come,
because trouble will come from the LORD,
    all the way to the gate of Jerusalem.
13 You people living in Lachish,[n]
    harness the fastest horse to the chariot.

> See, the LORD is coming out of his place; he is coming down to walk on the tops of the mountains.
> – Micah 1:3

1:10 Gath This name sounds like the Hebrew word for "tell".
1:10 Acco This name sounds like the Hebrew word for "cry".
1:10 Beth Ophrah This name means "house of dust".
1:11 Shaphir This name means "beautiful".
1:11 Zaanan This name sounds like the Hebrew word for "come out".
1:11 Beth Ezel This name means "house by the side of another", suggesting help or support.
1:12 Maroth This name sounds like the Hebrew word for "sad" or "miserable".
1:13 Lachish This name sounds like the Hebrew word for "horses".

Jerusalem's sins started in you;
yes, Israel's sins were found in you.
14 So you must give farewell gifts
to Moresheth*ⁿ* in Gath.
The houses in Achzib*ⁿ* will be false help
to the kings of Israel.
15 I will bring against you people who will take your land,
you who live in Mareshah.*ⁿ*
The glory of Israel
will go in to Adullam.
16 Cut off your hair to show you are sad
for the children you love.
Make yourself bald like the eagle,
because your children will be taken away to a foreign land.

The Evil Plans of People

2 How terrible it will be for people who plan wickedness,
who lie on their beds and make evil plans.
When the morning light comes, they do what they planned,
because they have the power to do so.
2 They want fields, so they take them;
they want houses, so they take them away.
They cheat people to get their houses;
they rob them even of their property.

3 That is why the LORD says:
"Look, I am planning trouble against such people,
and you won't be able to save yourselves.
You will no longer walk proudly,
because it will be a terrible time.
4 At that time people will make fun of you
and sing this sad song about you:
'We are completely ruined;

1:14 **Moresheth** This may be a play on the word "engaged", referring to a farewell gift to a bride.
1:14 **Achzib** This name means "lie" or "trick".
1:15 **Mareshah** This name sounds like the Hebrew word for a person who captures other cities and lands.

Micah 2:4 **1221**

FAITH links

THE PERIL OF POISONOUS PLANS
MICAH 2:1-3

Micah had a message for the Israelites. The wealthy people cheated the poor out of their homes and land. But God saw what they did. So Micah told them that bad things would happen to those who planned to hurt others.

When you sow evil, you will reap it. Thoughts of getting even with others or plans to cause trouble for someone can sometimes backfire. When "poisonous plans" present themselves to you, put them where they belong – out of your mind.

Check out these Faithlinks on getting even:

More Powerful Than Revenge, Genesis 50:14–21, p. 71

Just a Little Respect, 1 Chronicles 11:10–19, p. 534

A Life-Saving Message, Esther 2:19–22, p. 650

A Gentle Answer, Proverbs 15:1, p. 847

Forgive and Forget, Ephesians 4:32, p. 1604

The Gentle Way, Titus 3:1–5, p. 1661

the LORD has taken away my
    people's land.
Yes, he has taken it away from me
    and divided our fields among our
    enemies!"
5 So you will have no one from the
    LORD's people
to throw lots to divide the land.

Micah is Asked Not to Prophesy

6 The prophets say, "Don't prophesy to
    us!
    Don't prophesy about these things!
    Nothing to make us feel bad will
    happen!"
7 But I must say this, people of Jacob:
    the LORD is becoming angry about
    what you have done.
My words are welcome
    to the person who does what is
    right.
8 But you are fighting against my
    people like an enemy.
You take the coats from people
    who pass by;
you rob them of their safety;
    you plan war.
9 You've forced the women of my
    people
from their nice houses;
you've taken my glory
    from their children for ever.
10 Get up and leave.
    This is not your place of rest any
    more.
You have made this place unclean,
    and it is doomed to destruction.
11 But you people want a false prophet
    who will tell you nothing but lies.
You want one who promises to
    prophesy good things for you
    if you give him wine and beer.
He's just the prophet for you.

The LORD Promises to Rescue His People

12 "Yes, people of Jacob, I will bring all
    of you together;
I will bring together all those left
    alive in Israel.
I will put them together like sheep in
    a pen,
like a flock in its pasture;
the place will be filled with many
    people.
13 Someone will open the way and lead
    the people out.

FAITH links

A REAL CROWD-PLEASER?

MICAH 2:6-11

Have you ever told someone something you thought that person wanted to hear? The Israelites tried to get Micah to say only what they wanted to hear. Micah refused to change the message God had given him just to please the people.

Are you a crowd-pleaser or a God-pleaser? A crowd-pleaser cares more about what others think than about what God thinks. Being a God-pleaser takes courage. God willingly supplies the courage you need to live for him.

Like to please others? Connect to these links:

What Will You Risk? Joshua 2, p. 278

Give In or Take a Stand? 1 Kings 22:13–14, p. 472

Fear God or People? Jeremiah 38:14–21, p. 1047

When the Going Gets Tough, Lamentations 3:22–27, p. 1079

Facing Your Fears, Matthew 8:23–27, p. 1288

The Unpopular Choice, Mark 15:42–43, p. 1360

The people will break through the
gate and leave the city where
they were held captive.
Their king will go out in front of
them,
and the LORD will lead them."

The Leaders of Israel are Guilty of Evil

3 Then I said,
"Listen, leaders of the people of
Jacob;
listen, you rulers of the nation of
Israel.
You should know how to decide cases
fairly,
2 but you hate good and love evil.
You skin my people alive
and tear the flesh off their bones.
3 You eat my people's flesh
and skin them and
break their
bones;
you chop them up like
meat for the pot,
like meat in a
cooking pan.
4 They will cry to the
LORD,
but he won't answer
them.
At that time he will
hide his face from them,
because what they have done is
evil."

5 The LORD says this about the prophets who teach his people the wrong way of living:
"If these prophets are given food to
eat,
they shout, 'Peace!'
But if someone doesn't give them
what they ask for,
they call for a holy war against that
person.
6 So it will become like night for them,
without visions.
It will become dark for them,
without any way to tell the future.
The sun is about to set for the
prophets;
their day will become dark.

7 The seers will be ashamed;
the people who see the future will
be embarrassed.
Yes, all of them will cover their
mouths,
because there will be no answer
from God."

Micah is an Honest Prophet of God

8 But I am filled with power,
with the Spirit of the LORD,
and with justice and strength,
to tell the people of Jacob how they
have turned against God,
and the people of Israel how they
have sinned.
9 Leaders of Jacob and rulers of Israel,
listen to me,
you who hate fairness
and twist what is
right.
10 You build Jerusalem
by murdering
people;
you build it with
evil.
11 Its judges take
money
to decide who wins
in court.
Its priests only teach for pay,
and its prophets only look into the
future when they get paid.
But they lean on the LORD and say,
"The LORD is here with us,
so nothing bad will happen to us."
12 Because of you,
Jerusalem will be ploughed like a
field.
The city will become a pile of rocks,
and the hill on which the Temple
stands will be covered with
bushes.

The Mountain of the LORD

4 In the last days
the mountain on which the LORD's
Temple stands
will become the most important of
all mountains.
It will be raised above the hills,

They will cry to the
LORD, but he won't
answer them.
– Micah 3:4

and people from other nations will
    come streaming to it.
2 Many nations will come and say,
    "Come, let us go up to the
        mountain of the LORD,
    to the Temple of the God of Jacob,
    so that he can teach us his ways
        and we can obey his teachings."
His teachings will go out from
    Jerusalem,
    the word of the LORD from that
        city.
3 The Lord will judge many nations;
    he will make decisions about
        strong nations that are far away.
They will hammer their swords into
    plough blades
    and their spears into hooks for
        trimming trees.
Nations will no longer raise swords
    against other nations;
    they will not train for war any
        more.
4 Everyone will sit under his own vine
    and fig tree,
    and no one will make them afraid,
    because the LORD All-powerful has
        said it.
5 All other nations
    may follow
        their own
        gods,
    but we will
        follow the
        LORD our
    God for ever and ever.

6 The LORD says, "At that time,
I will gather the crippled;
    I will bring together those who
        were sent away,
    those whom I caused to have
        trouble.
7 I will keep alive those who were
    crippled,
    and I will make a strong nation of
        those who were sent away.
The LORD will be their king in Mount
    Zion from now on and for ever.
8 And you, watchtower of the flocks,"
    hill of Jerusalem,
    to you will come the kingdom as in
        the past.

Jerusalem, the right to rule will
    come again to you."

Why the Israelites Must Go to Babylon

9 Now, why do you cry so loudly?
    Is your king gone?
Have you lost your helper,
    so that you are in pain, like a
        woman trying to give birth?
10 People of Jerusalem, strain and be in
    pain.
Be like a woman trying to give birth,
    because now you must leave the city
        and live in the field.
You will go to Babylon,
    but you will be saved from that
        place.
The LORD will go there
    and buy you back from your enemies.

11 But now many nations
    have come to fight against you,
    saying, "Let's destroy Jerusalem.
    We will look at her and be glad we
        have defeated her."
12 But they don't know
    what the LORD is thinking;
    they don't understand his plan.
    He has gathered them like bundles
        of grain to the threshing floor.
13 "Get up and beat them, people of
    Jerusalem.
    I will make you strong as if you
        had horns of iron
    and hoofs of bronze.
    You will beat many nations into
        small pieces
    and give their wealth to the LORD,
        their treasure to the Lord of all the
            earth."

5 So, strong city, gather your soldiers
    together,
    because we are surrounded and
        attacked.
    They will hit the leader of Israel
        in the face with a club.

4:8 watchtower . . . flocks This probably means a part of Jerusalem. The leaders would be like shepherds in a tower watching their sheep.

Email from God 4:4
Fears
Should anyone make you afraid?

Micah 5:8 1225

LET'S VISIT BETHLEHEM   Micah 5:2

Bethlehem is most famous as the home of King David and the place where Jesus was born. It is located five miles south of Jerusalem.

A lot of people visit Bethlehem on holiday. The main attraction is the Church of the Nativity. This church is supposed to be built over the place where Jesus was born, so tourists visit it a *lot* around Christmas. Some other places to sightsee in Bethlehem are the fields of Boaz, where Ruth gathered grain and met her husband (read Ruth, p. 345), and the Shepherds' Field, where the angels announced the birth of Jesus to the shepherds (check out Luke 2:8–18, p. 1368).

The name *Bethlehem* means "House of Bread". This is probably because in the Old Testament Bethlehem was known for producing grain. Later, Jesus called himself the "Bread of Life".

The Ruler to Be Born in Bethlehem

2 "But you, Bethlehem Ephrathah,
    though you are too small to be
        among the army groups from
        Judah,
    from you will come one who will rule
        Israel for me.
    He comes from very old times,
        from days long ago."

3 The LORD will give up his people
    until the one who is having a baby
        gives birth;
    then the rest of his relatives will
        return
    to the people of Israel.

4 At that time the ruler of Israel will
        stand
    and take care of his people
    with the LORD's strength
    and with the power of the name of
        the LORD his God.
    The Israelites will live in safety,
    because his greatness will reach all
        over the earth.

5   He will bring peace.

Rescue and Punishment

Assyria will surely come into our
    country
and walk over our large buildings.
We will set up seven shepherds,
    eight leaders of the people.
6 They will destroy the Assyrians with
        their swords;
    they will conquer the land of
        Assyria with their swords
        drawn.
    They will rescue us from the
        Assyrians when they come into
        our land,
    when they walk over our borders.

7 Then the people of Jacob who are left
        alive
    will be to other people
    like dew from the LORD
    or rain on the grass—
    it does not wait for human beings;
    it does not pause for any person.

8 Those of Jacob's people who are left
        alive
    will be scattered among many
        nations and peoples.

They will be like a lion among the
   animals of the forest,
  like a young lion in a flock of
   sheep:
  as it goes, it jumps on them
   and tears them to pieces,
   and no one can save them.
9 So you will raise your fist in victory
   over your enemies,
  and all your enemies will be
   destroyed.

10 The LORD says, "At that time,
   I will take your horses from you
   and destroy your chariots.
11 I will destroy the cities in your
   country
  and tear down all your defences.
12 I will take away the magic charms
   you use
  so you will have no more fortune-
   tellers.
13 I will destroy your statues of gods
   and the stone pillars you worship
  so that you will no longer worship
   what your hands have made.
14 I will tear down Asherah idols from
   you
  and destroy your cities.
15 In my anger and rage,
   I will pay back the nations that
   have not listened."

The LORD's Case

6 Now hear what the LORD says:
  "Get up; plead your case in front of
   the mountains;
  let the hills hear your story.
2 Mountains, listen to the LORD's legal
   case.
  Foundations of the earth, listen.
  The LORD has a legal case against his
   people,
   and he will accuse Israel."

3 He says, "My people, what did I do to
   you?
  How did I make you tired of me?
   Tell me.
4 I brought you from the land of Egypt
   and freed you from slavery;
  I sent Moses, Aaron and Miriam
   to you.
5 My people, remember
   the evil plans of Balak king of
   Moab
  and what Balaam son of Beor told
   Balak.
  Remember what happened from
   Acacia to Gilgal
  so that you will know the LORD
   does what is right!"

6 You say, "What can I bring with me
   when I come before the LORD,
   when I bow before God on high?
  Should I come before him with burnt
   offerings,
   with year-old calves?
7 Will the LORD be pleased with
   1,000 rams?
  Will he be pleased with
   10,000 rivers of oil?
  Should I give my first child for the
   evil I have done?
  Should I give my very own child
   for my sin?"
8 The LORD has told you, human, what
   is good;
  he has told you what he wants
   from you:
  to do what is right to other people,
   love being kind to others,
   and live humbly, obeying your God.

9 The voice of the LORD calls to the
   city,
  and the wise person honours
   him.
  So pay attention to the rod of
   punishment;
   pay attention to the One who
   threatens to punish.
10 Are there still in the wicked house
   wicked treasures
   and the cursed false measure?
11 Can I forgive people who cheat
   others
  with wrong weights and scales?
12 The rich people of the city
   do cruel things.
  Its people tell lies;
   they do not tell the truth.
13 As for me, I will make you sick.
  I will attack you, ruining you
   because of your sins.

Micah 7:6

THE RIGHT INGREDIENTS
MICAH 6:8

Have you ever used a recipe to cook something? If so, you know that whatever you're making is most likely to turn out nice if you follow the recipe. Micah provides a "recipe" for right living. By following it, your life can be pleasing to God. Doing what is right, showing mercy and being humble are the ingredients of a life that is deliciously pleasing to God.

Show Some Respect, Leviticus 19:32, p. 161

Patience, Please, Psalm 145:8–9, p. 819

Get Hot or Keep Cool? Proverbs 12:16, p. 842

Welcome! Matthew 19:13–15, p. 1307

The Worst Chore, John 13:3–17, p. 1447

Another Lazy Day? 2 Thessalonians 3:6–13, p. 1640

14 You will eat, but you won't become full;
   you will still be hungry and empty.
You will store up, but save nothing,
   and what you store up, the sword will destroy.
15 You will plant,
   but you won't harvest.
You will step on your olives,
   but you won't get any oil from them.
You will crush the grapes,
   but you will not drink the new wine.
16 This is because you obey the laws of King Omri
   and do all the things that Ahab's family does;
   you follow their advice.
So I will let you be destroyed.
   The people in your city will be laughed at,
   and other nations will make fun of you.

The Evil That People Do

7 Poor me! I am like a hungry man,
   and all the summer fruit has been picked—
there are no grapes left to eat,
   none of the early figs I love.
2 All of the faithful people are gone;
   there is not one good person left in this country.
Everyone is waiting to kill someone;
   everyone is trying to trap someone else.
3 With both hands they are doing evil.
   Rulers ask for money,
   and judges' decisions are bought for a price.
Rich people tell what they want,
   and they get it.
4 Even the best of them is like a thorn-bush;
   the most honest of them is worse than a prickly thorn-bush.
The day that your watchmen[n] warned you about has come.
   Now they will be confused.
5 Don't believe your neighbour
   or trust a friend.
Don't say anything,
   even to your wife.
6 A son will not honour his father,
   a daughter will turn against her mother
and a daughter-in-law will be against her mother-in-law;

7:4 watchmen Another name for prophets. The prophets were like guards who stood on a city's wall and watched for trouble coming from far away.

a person's enemies will be
  members of his own family.

The LORD's Kindness

7 Israel says, "I will look to the LORD
    for help.
  I will wait for God to save me;
    my God will hear me.
8 Enemy, don't laugh at me.
  I have fallen, but I will get up again.
  I sit in the shadow of trouble now,
    but the LORD will be a light for
    me.
9 I sinned against the LORD,
    so he was angry with me,
  but he will defend my case in court.
  He will bring about what is right
    for me.
  Then he will bring me out into the
    light,
    and I will see him set things right.
10 Then my enemies will see this,
    and they will be ashamed,
  those who said to me,
    'Where is the LORD your God?'
  I will look down on them.
    They will get walked on, like mud
    in the street."

Israel will Return

11 The time will come when your walls
    will be built again,
  when your country will grow.
12 At that time your people will come
    back to you
  from Assyria and the cities of
    Egypt,
  and from Egypt to the Euphrates
    River,
  and from sea to sea and mountain
    to mountain.
13 The earth will be ruined for the
    people who live in it
  because of their deeds.

A Prayer to God

14 So shepherd your people with your
    stick;
  tend the flock of people who
    belong to you.
  That flock now lives alone in the
    forest
  in the middle of a garden land.
  Let them feed in Bashan and Gilead
    as in days long ago.
15 "As in the days when I brought you
    out of Egypt,
  I will show them miracles."

FAITH links

INSIDE THE HEART OF GOD

MICAH 7:18-20

Ever watch a science programme on TV that showed the inside of something? Maybe the programme featured a look at the heart or eye, using the latest technology. This passage in Micah takes you inside a heart without using technology. Whose heart is it? God's. The descriptions of what God loves to do can help you know what God is like. He is forgiving, merciful, loving, patient and faithful. Is your heart like God's?

Check out these Faithlinks on having a heart like God's:

A Thanksgiving Reminder, Exodus 12, p. 91

How Big Is God? Job 38—41, p. 703

Your Heavenly Dad, Psalm 103:13, p. 786

World News, Isaiah 13—19, p. 913

Remembering Jesus, Matthew 26:26–29, p. 1321

A Family Meal, Mark 14:23–26, p. 1356

16 When the nations see those miracles,
  they will no longer boast about
    their power.
  They will put their hands over their
    mouths,
    refusing to listen.
17 They will crawl in the dust like a
    snake,
  like insects crawling on the ground.
  They will come trembling from their
    holes to the LORD our God
  and will turn in fear before you.
18 There is no God like you.
  You forgive those who are guilty of
    sin;
  you don't look at the sins of your
    people
  who are left alive.
  You will not stay angry for ever,
    because you enjoy being kind.
19 You will have mercy on us again;
  you will conquer our sins.
  You will throw away all our sins
    into the deepest part of the sea.
20 You will be true to the people of
    Jacob,
  and you will be kind to the people
    of Abraham
  as you promised to our ancestors
    long ago.

DOWN WITH NINEVEH!

Hi, there! I'm Nahum the prophet. My message was for the great city of Nineveh, the capital of Assyria. Do you remember Jonah, the prophet who spent three days in the big fish? God sent Jonah to Nineveh to tell the people to stop doing evil things and ask God to forgive them. To Jonah's surprise, the people listened to his message and turned to God. Years passed and the people of Nineveh forgot all about God. They did unspeakably cruel things to their enemies, especially to God's people. The Assyrians conquered Israel and dragged the people away with giant fish-hooks.

I wrote this book to tell everyone that God would destroy the city of Nineveh for its wickedness. Many thought Nineveh was the mightiest city on earth. Its walls were 30 metres high and wide enough for three chariots to ride side by side around the city. Defeat seemed impossible, but God said he would completely destroy Nineveh. Turn to Nahum 2:1–10 to see how the city was attacked. (By the way, can you find Nineveh on any geography map today? What God says, he does!)

JESUS WATCH

Soon after Nahum spoke his prophecy, the River Tigris flooded and destroyed a part of the wall that surrounded Nineveh. The Babylonian army entered Nineveh through the damaged wall and carried off its treasure before setting the city on fire. God used the Babylonians to carry out his judgement. Someday Jesus will return to judge the nations. The Day of the Lord will be a terrible time of punishment for those nations who have not followed God's laws. The Lord will not let the guilty go unpunished. The earth will tremble when he comes to judge people for their sins. But people who believe in Jesus and follow God's laws have no need to fear the Day of the Lord. It will be a great time of joy and celebration! Just like Jesus promised, we will live in heaven with Jesus for ever.

What happens to people who make plans against the Lord?

Trouble, that's what! Connect to Nahum 1:9–10 and find out what God has in store for them.

FAITH links

A Safe Place, Nahum 1:7

DOWNLOAD THESE MESSAGES:
A jealous God, Nahum 1:2–6
Like an army of locusts, Nahum 3:15–17

1 This is the message for the city of Nineveh.[n] This is the book of the vision of Nahum, who was from the town of Elkosh.

The LORD is Angry with Nineveh

2 The LORD is a jealous God who punishes;
 the LORD punishes and is filled with anger.
The LORD punishes those who are against him,
 and he stays angry with his enemies.
3 The LORD does not become angry quickly,
 and his power is great.
The LORD will not let the guilty go unpunished.
Where the LORD goes, there are whirlwinds and storms,
 and the clouds are the dust beneath his feet.
4 He speaks to the sea and makes it dry;
 he dries up all the rivers.
The areas of Bashan and Carmel dry up,
 and the flowers of Lebanon dry up.
5 The mountains shake in front of him,
 and the hills melt.
The earth trembles when he comes;
 the world and all who live in it shake with fear.
6 No one can stay alive when he is angry;
 no one can survive his strong anger.
His anger is poured out like fire;
 the rocks are smashed by him.

7 The LORD is good,
 giving protection in times of trouble.
 He knows who trusts in him.
8 But like a rushing flood,
 he will completely destroy Nineveh;
 he will chase his enemies until he kills them.

9 The LORD will completely destroy anyone making plans against him.
 Trouble will not come a second time.
10 Those people will be like tangled thorns

FAITH links

A SAFE PLACE
NAHUM 1:7

When emergencies strike, everyone looks for a place of protection. If a tornado threatens your home, the best place to go for safety is a basement or a bathroom on the lowest floor of your house. If you get lost when you're out, a police station can be a refuge. According to the prophet Nahum, God is a "place" of protection in times of trouble. God watches over you. Whenever you're afraid, talk to God. No matter what happens in your life, you can turn to God when trouble comes.

Here are some Faithlinks on dealing with those bad days:

When You're Afraid, Genesis 32:9–12, p. 45

Good Times and Bad, 1 Kings 17, p. 462

A Really Bad Day, Job 1:20–22; 2:10, p. 661

When the Going Gets Tough, Lamentations 3:22–27, p. 1079

It's Under Control, Romans 8:28, p. 1529

Hard Times, 2 Corinthians 1:8–10, p. 1570

1:1 Nineveh The capital city of the country of Assyria. Nahum uses Nineveh to stand for all of Assyria.

or like people drunk from their wine;
they will be burned up quickly like dry weeds.
11 Someone has come from Nineveh
who makes evil plans against the LORD
and gives wicked advice.

12 This is what the LORD says:
"Although Assyria is strong and has many people,
it will be defeated and brought to an end.
Although I have made you suffer, Judah,
I will make you suffer no more.
13 Now I will free you from their control
and tear away your chains."

14 The LORD has given you this command, Nineveh:
"You will not have descendants to carry on your name.
I will destroy the idols and metal images
that are in the temple of your gods.
I will make a grave for you, because you are wicked."

15 Look, there on the hills,
someone is bringing good news!
He is announcing peace!
Celebrate your feasts, people of Judah,
and give your promised sacrifices to God.
The wicked will not come to attack you again;
they have been completely destroyed.

Nineveh will be Defeated

2 The destroyer[n] is coming to attack you, Nineveh.
Guard the defences.
Watch the road.
Get ready.
Gather all your strength!

2 Destroyers have destroyed God's people
and ruined their vines,
but the LORD will bring back Jacob's greatness
like Israel's greatness.

3 The shields of his soldiers are red;
the army is dressed in red.
The metal on the chariots flashes like fire
when they are ready to attack;
their horses are excited.
4 The chariots race through the streets
and rush back and forth through the city squares.
They look like torches;
they run like lightning.

5 He[n] calls his officers,
but they stumble on the way.
They hurry to the city wall,
and the shield is put into place.
6 The river gates are thrown open,
and the palace is destroyed.
7 It has been announced that the people of Nineveh
will be captured and carried away.
The slave girls moan like doves
and beat their breasts, because they are sad.
8 Nineveh is like a pool,
and now its water is draining away.
"Stop! Stop!" the people yell,
but no one turns back.
9 Take the silver!
Take the gold!
There is no end to the treasure—
piles of wealth of every kind.
10 Nineveh is robbed, ruined and destroyed.
The people lose their courage, and their knees knock.

> Destroyers have destroyed God's people and ruined their vines.
> – Nahum 2:2

2:1 destroyer The Babylonians, the Scythians and the Medes destroyed Nineveh.
2:5 He This probably means the king of Assyria.

Stomachs ache, and everyone's
  face grows pale.
11 Where is the lions'[n] den
  and the place where they feed their
    young?
  Where did the lion, lioness and cubs
    go
    without being afraid?
12 The lion killed enough for his cubs,
    enough for his mate.
  He filled his cave with the animals he
    caught;
  he filled his den
    with meat he had
    killed.
13 "I am against you,
    Nineveh,"
  says the LORD
    All-powerful.
  "I will burn up your
    chariots in
    smoke,
  and the sword will
    kill your young lions.
  I will stop you from hunting down
    others on the earth,
  and your messengers' voices
    will no longer be heard."

It will be Terrible for Nineveh

3 How terrible it will be for the city that
  has killed so many.
  It is full of lies
  and goods stolen from other
    countries.
  It is always killing somebody.
2 Hear the sound of whips
    and the noise of the wheels.
  Hear horses galloping
    and chariots bouncing along!
3 Horses are charging,
    swords are shining,
    spears are gleaming!
  Many are dead;
    their bodies are piled up—
    too many to count.
  People stumble over the dead
    bodies.
4 The city was like a prostitute;
    she was charming and a lover of
    magic.

She made nations slaves with her
    prostitution
  and her witchcraft.
5 "I am against you, Nineveh," says the
    LORD All-powerful.
  "I will pull your dress up over your
    face
  and show the nations your nakedness
    and the kingdoms your shame.
6 I will throw filthy rubbish on you
    and make a fool of you.
  I will make people stare at you.
7 Everyone who sees
    you will run away
    and say,
    'Nineveh is in ruins.
    Who will cry for
    her?'
  Nineveh, where will I
    find anyone to
    comfort you?"
8 You are no better than
    Thebes,[n]
  who sits by the Nile
    River
  with water all around her.
  The river was her defence;
    the waters were like a wall around
    her.
9 Cush and Egypt gave her endless
    strength;
  Put and Libya supported her.
10 But Thebes was captured
    and went into captivity.
  Her small children were beaten to
    death
    at every street corner.
  Lots were thrown for her important
    men,
  and all of her leaders were put in
    chains.

11 Nineveh, you will be drunk too.
    You will hide;
    you will look for a place safe from
    the enemy.
12 All your defences are like fig trees
    with ripe fruit.

> Everyone who sees
> you will run away
> and say, "Nineveh is
> in ruins. Who will cry
> for her?"
> – Nahum 3:7

2:11 lions' The symbol of Assyria was the lion.
3:8 Thebes A great city in Egypt.

When the tree is shaken, the figs
    fall into the mouth of the eater.
13 Look at your soldiers.
    They are all women!
  The gates of your land
    are wide open for your enemies;
    fire has burned the bars of your
      gates.

14 Get enough water before the long war
      begins.
    Make your defences strong!
    Get mud,
      mix clay,
      make bricks!
15 There the fire will burn you up.
    The sword will kill you;
    like grasshoppers eating crops, the
      battle will completely destroy
      you.
    Grow in number like hopping locusts;
      grow in number like swarming
      locusts!
16 Your traders are more than the stars
      in the sky,
    but like locusts, they strip the land
      and then fly away.
17 Your guards are like locusts.
    Your officers are like swarms of
      locusts
    that hang on the walls on a cold
      day.
    When the sun comes up, they fly
      away,
    and no one knows where they have
      gone.
18 King of Assyria, your rulers are
      asleep;
    your important men lie down to
      rest.
    Your people have been scattered on
      the mountains,
    and there is no one to bring them
      back.
19 Nothing can heal your wound;
    your injury will not heal.
  Everyone who hears about you
      applauds,
    because everyone has felt your
      endless cruelty.

Habakkuk

LOTS OF QUESTIONS

Hi, there! My name is Habakkuk. I'm the prophet who asked God a lot of questions. Have you ever noticed that some kids never get into trouble no matter how many bad things they do? Sometimes, it's the same thing with grown-ups. I asked God why he didn't punish the people of Judah for their many sins. These people were bad! They worshipped idols, the rich cheated the poor, and judges no longer made fair decisions. God replied that he would send the Babylonians to punish the nation of Judah. I was shocked. The Babylonians? Those wicked, cruel people who did not even worship the true God?

I wrote this book to tell people to trust God. God is patient and wants everyone to stop doing evil and turn back to him. He may be slow to become angry, but eventually all those who sin will be punished. God *is* in control. "Those who are right with God will live by trusting in him" (Habakkuk 2:4).

JESUS WATCH

Someday Jesus will come to judge the nations for their sins. The Day of the Lord will be a terrible time of punishment for those people who have not followed God's laws. For people who believe in Jesus, though, the Day of the Lord will be glorious. Habakkuk wrote, "Then, just as water covers the sea, people everywhere will know the LORD's glory" (Habakkuk 2:14). God will make all things new. A new heaven and a new earth will appear. God's presence will be with his people always and the new city of Jerusalem will come down from heaven. The city will not need the sun to shine because God's glory will be its light and Jesus will be its lamp. God's people will live with him for ever in heaven. (Check out what John has to say about this new heaven and earth in Revelation 21 and 22, p. 1752.)

What was Habakkuk waiting for?

He had spoken a complaint against God. We'd better connect to Habakkuk 2 to find out what's going on.

FAITH links

- Rock Solid, **Habakkuk 1:12**
- Justice Desserts, **Habakkuk 2:4–8**
- Your Feet on High Places, **Habakkuk 3:18–19**

Habakkuk 1:1

1 This is the message Habakkuk the prophet received.

Habakkuk Complains

2 LORD, how long must I ask for help
   and you ignore me?
I cry out to you about violence,
   but you do not save us!
3 Why do you make me see wrong things
   and make me look at trouble?
People are destroying things and hurting others in front of me;
   they are arguing and fighting.
4 So the teachings are weak,
   and justice never comes.
Evil people gain while good people lose;
   the judges no longer make fair decisions.

The LORD Answers

5 "Look at the nations!
   Watch them and be amazed and shocked.
I will do something in your lifetime
   that you won't believe even when you are told about it.
6 I will use the Babylonians,
   those cruel and wild people
who march across the earth
   and take lands that don't belong to them.
7 They scare and frighten people.
   They do what they want to do
   and are good only to themselves.
8 Their horses are faster than leopards
   and quicker than wolves at sunset.
Their horse soldiers attack quickly;
   they come from places far away.
They attack quickly, like an eagle swooping down for food.
9 They all come to fight.
Nothing can stop them.
   Their prisoners are as many as the grains of sand.
10 They laugh at kings
   and make fun of rulers.
They laugh at all the fortified cities
   and build mounds of earth to the top of the walls to capture them.
11 Then they leave like the wind and move on.
   They are guilty of worshipping their own strength."

Habakkuk Complains Again

12 LORD, you live for ever,
   my God, my holy God.
   We will not die.
LORD, you have chosen the Babylonians to punish people;

FAITH links

ROCK SOLID
HABAKKUK 1:12

Rock is one of the hardest substances on earth. Rock is pretty solid. Special tools are needed to dig through rock. If you stand on a large rock, you know it won't break under your weight. It also won't shift or slide and cause you to fall. To Habakkuk, God was a rock. He was solid and dependable. That meant he could put his whole trust in God. So can you.

Want to know who to trust? Connect here:

From Hopeless to Hopeful, Exodus 6:9, p. 83

Who Ya' Gonna Call? Psalm 3:4, p. 711

Future Hope, Joel 3:17–21, p. 1191

Mission Impossible? Mark 5:21–24, 35–43, p. 1337

Fully God, Fully Human, John 11:35, p. 1444

Never Alone, Hebrews 13:5–6, p. 1684

our Rock, you picked them to
    punish.
13 Your eyes are too good to look at
        evil;
    you cannot stand to see those who
        do wrong.
    So how can you put up with those evil
        people?
    How can you be quiet when the
        wicked swallow up people who
        are better than they are?
14 You treat people like fish in the sea,
    like sea creatures without a leader.
15 The enemy brings them in with
        hooks.
    He catches them in his net
    and drags them in his nets.
    So he rejoices and sings for joy.
16 The enemy offers sacrifices to his
        net
    and burns incense to worship it,
    because it lets him live like the rich
        and enjoy the best food.
17 Will he keep on taking riches with his
        net?
    Will he go on destroying people
        without showing mercy?

2 I will stand like a guard to watch
    and place myself at the tower.
    I will wait to see what he will say to
        me;
    I will wait to learn how God will
        answer my complaint.

The LORD Answers

2 The LORD answered me:
    "Write down the vision;
    write it clearly on clay tablets
    so whoever reads it can run to tell
        others.
3 It is not yet time for the message to
        come true,
    but that time is coming soon;
    the message will come true.
    It may seem like a long time,
    but be patient and wait for it,
    because it will surely come;
        it will not be delayed.
4 The evil nation is very proud of itself;
    it is not living as it should.
    But those who are right with God
        will live by trusting in him.

5 "Just as wine can fool a person,
    those who are too proud will not
        last,
    because their desire is like a grave's
        desire for death,

FAITH LINKS

JUSTICE DESSERTS
HABAKKUK 2:4-8

"There's no justice in the world!" Have you heard anyone say that? Have *you* ever said that? Some people feel hopeless because of the cruelties of others. Watching people who seem to get away with doing wrong things causes them to wonder if God really cares. Habakkuk told the Israelites about what happens to bullies in the end. They get what their actions deserve. Habakkuk did not spread this message so that the people could gloat over the downfall of their enemies. He said this because of God's faithfulness in caring for those who are wronged by others. When others wrong you, you can trust that justice will be served.

Forgive Instead, Genesis 33, p. 47

Moses' Champion, Numbers 12, p. 192

A Giant Problem, 1 Samuel 17:32–51, p. 377

God's Sure Protection, Psalm 18, p. 721

The Gentle Way, Titus 3:1–5, p. 1661

Keep On Keeping On, Revelation 13:10, p. 1744

and like death they always want more.
They gather other nations for themselves
and collect for themselves all the countries.

6 But all the nations the Babylonians have hurt will laugh at them.
They will make fun of the Babylonians
and say, 'How terrible it will be for the one that steals many things.
How long will that nation get rich by forcing others to pay them?'

7 "One day the people from whom you have taken money will turn against you.
They will realise what is happening and make you shake with fear.
Then they will take everything you have.

8 Because you have stolen from many nations,
those who are left will take much from you.
This is because you have killed many people,
destroying countries and cities and everyone in them.

9 "How terrible it will be for the nation that becomes rich by doing wrong,
thinking they will live in a safe place
and escape harm.

10 Because you have made plans to destroy many people,
you have made your own houses ashamed of you.
Because of it, you will lose your lives.

11 The stones of the walls will cry out against you,
and the boards that support the roof will agree that you are wrong.

12 "How terrible it will be for the nation that kills people to build a city,
that wrongs others just to start a town.

13 The LORD All-powerful will send fire to destroy what those people have built;
all the nations' work will be for nothing.

14 Then, just as water covers the sea, people everywhere will know the LORD's glory.

15 "How terrible for the nation that makes its neighbours drink,
pouring from the jug of wine until they are drunk
so that it can look at their naked bodies.

16 You Babylonians will be filled with disgrace, not respect.
It's your turn to drink and fall to the ground like a drunk person.
The cup of anger from the LORD's right hand is coming around to you.
You will receive disgrace, not respect.

17 You hurt many people in Lebanon, but now you will be hurt.
You killed many animals there, and now you must be afraid
because of what you did
to that land, those cities and the people who lived in them.

The Message About Idols

18 "An idol does no good, because a human made it;
it is only a statue that teaches lies.
The one who made it expects his own work to help him,
but he makes idols that can't even speak!

19 How terrible it will be for the one who says to a wooden statue, 'Come to life!'
How terrible it will be for the one who says to a silent stone, 'Get up!'
It cannot tell you what to do.
It is only a statue covered with gold and silver;
there is no life in it.

20 The LORD is in his Holy Temple;
all the earth should be silent in his presence."

Habakkuk's Prayer

3 This is the prayer of Habakkuk the prophet, on shigionoth.

2 LORD, I have heard the news about you;
  I am amazed at what you have done.
LORD, do great things once again in our time;
  make those things happen again in our own days.
Even when you are angry,
  remember to be kind.

3 God is coming from Teman;
  the Holy One comes from Mount Paran.[n] *Selah*
His glory covers the skies,
  and his praise fills the earth.
4 He is like a bright light.
  Rays of light shine from his hand,
  and there he hides his power.
5 Sickness goes before him,
  and disease follows behind him.
6 He stands and shakes the earth.
  He looks, and the nations shake with fear.
The mountains, which stood for ages, break into pieces;
  the old hills fall down.
God has always done this.

7 I saw that the tents of Cushan were in trouble
  and that the tents of Midian trembled.
8 LORD, were you angry with the rivers,
  or were you angry with the streams?
Were you angry with the sea
  when you rode your horses and chariots of victory?[m]
9 You uncovered your bow
  and commanded many arrows to be brought to you. *Selah*
You split the earth with rivers.
10 The mountains saw you and shook with fear.
The rushing water flowed.
The sea made a loud noise,
  and its waves rose high.
11 The sun and moon stood still in the sky;

Habakkuk 3:11 1239

FAITH links

YOUR FEET ON HIGH PLACES
HABAKKUK 3:18-19

A mountain goat doesn't worry about whether it will fall off a mountain. Its padded, "gripper" hooves give it the confidence it needs to skip nimbly up and down a mountain. Habakkuk assures you that you can have this sort of confidence in God. He gives you the confidence to serve him and the confidence to face whatever "mountains" (good times) or "valleys" (hard times) come your way in life. You can't get this kind of confidence on your own. It only comes from God.

Lacking confidence? Connect here for some help:

Good Plans, Genesis 45:7–8, p. 64

The Weak Link, Judges 16, p. 334

Weak? Great! 2 Chronicles 14:11, p. 577

Too Young to Serve, Jeremiah 1:4–9, p. 988

A Model of Forgiveness, Ezekiel 16:59–63, p. 1103

The Power of *If*, Mark 9:14–24, p. 1344

3:3 Teman . . . Paran God is seen as again coming from the direction of Mount Sinai. He came from Sinai when he rescued his people from Egypt.
3:8 sea . . . victory This is probably talking about the Israelites crossing the Red Sea.

they stopped when they saw the
flash of your flying arrows
and the gleam of your shining
spear.
12 In anger you marched on the earth;
in anger you punished the nations.
13 You came out to save your people,
to save your chosen one.
You crushed the leader of the wicked
ones
and took everything he had, from
head to toe. *Selah*
14 With the enemy's own spear you
stabbed the leader of his army.
His soldiers rushed out like a
storm to scatter us.
They were happy
as they were robbing the poor
people in secret.
15 But you marched through the sea
with your horses,
stirring the great waters.

16 I hear these things, and my body
trembles;
my lips tremble when I hear the
sound.
My bones feel weak,
and my legs shake.

But I will wait patiently for the day of
disaster
that will come to the people who
attack us.
17 Fig trees may not grow figs,
and there may be no grapes on the
vines.
There may be no olives growing
and no food growing in the fields.
There may be no sheep in the pens
and no cattle in the barns.
18 But I will still be glad in the LORD;
I will rejoice in God my Saviour.
19 The Lord GOD is my strength.
He makes me
like a deer
that does
not stumble
so I can walk
on the steep
mountains.

3:17–19
Encouragement
Who helps you be strong?

For the director of music. On my stringed instruments.

OBEY NOW!

Welcome to my homepage! My name is Zephaniah, and I was called by God to be a prophet to King Josiah. Maybe you've heard about Josiah. He was crowned king of Judah when he was only eight years old. Imagine one of your classmates as king or queen! Pretty weird, huh? Even though Josiah was young, he realised what was important. Josiah loved God, so he told people to stop worshipping idols. He sent workmen to repair the Temple of the Lord, so that the people could worship the true God. Was Josiah surprised when the Book of the Teachings was found and read aloud! No one had been following God's laws for years!

I wrote this book to tell people to obey God before it was too late. The Lord's day of judging people and nations was coming soon. The nations who did not follow God would be punished. I told the people, "Do what is right. Learn to be humble. Maybe you will escape on the day the LORD shows his anger" (Zephaniah 2:3). Do you think they listened?

JESUS WATCH

Zephaniah told people to fear the Lord's day of judging. Someday Jesus will come on a cloud from heaven with great power and glory to judge everyone on earth. It will be a terrible time of punishment for those who have not obeyed God, but a day of rejoicing for all who believe in Jesus. Jesus will use a loud trumpet to send his angels all around the earth to gather up his chosen people. He will give his people honour and praise. The people will rejoice with all their hearts, for all sadness will be taken away. Jesus the King will be with them always.

FAITH links

Nobody really knows for sure when the day of the Lord's judging will be, but check out Zephaniah 1:14-18 for some details.

A Love Song, **Zephaniah 3:17**

CHECK THESE OUT:
One last chance, Zephaniah 2:1–3
Total destruction, Zephaniah 3:1–8
A new song! Zephaniah 3:14–17

Zephaniah 1:1

1 This is the word of the LORD that came through Zephaniah while Josiah son of Amon was king of Judah. Zephaniah was the son of Cushi, who was the son of Gedaliah. Gedaliah was the son of Amariah, who was the son of Hezekiah.

The LORD's Judgement

2 "I will sweep away everything
    from the earth," says the LORD.
3 "I will sweep away the people and
    animals;
  I will destroy the birds in the air
    and the fish of the sea.
  I will ruin the evil people,
    and I will remove
      human beings
      from the earth,"
    says the LORD.

The Future of Judah

4 "I will punish Judah
    and all the people
      living in
      Jerusalem.
  I will remove from
    this place
  all signs of Baal,
    the false priests and the other
      priests.
5 I will destroy those who worship
    the stars from the roofs,"
  and those who worship and make
    promises
    by both the LORD and the god
      Molech,
6 and those who turn away from the
    LORD,
    and those who stopped following
      the LORD and praying to him for
      direction.
7 Be silent before the Lord GOD,
    because the LORD's day for judging
      people is coming soon.
  The LORD has prepared a sacrifice;
    he has made holy his invited guests.
8 On the day of the LORD's sacrifice,
    I, the LORD, will punish the princes
      and the king's sons
    and all those who wear foreign
      clothes.
9 On that day I will punish those who
    worship Dagon,

  those who hurt others and tell lies
    in the temples of their gods.
10 "On that day," says the LORD,
    "a cry will be heard at the Fish Gate.
  A wail will come from the new area
    of the city,
  and a loud crash will echo from the
    hills.
11 Cry, you people living in the market
    area,
  because all the merchants will be
    dead;
  all the silver traders will be gone.
12 At that time I, the
    LORD, will search
      Jerusalem with
      lamps.
  I will punish those
    who are satisfied
    with themselves,
    who think, 'The
    LORD won't help
    us or punish us.'
13 Their wealth will be
    stolen
  and their houses
    destroyed.
  They may build houses,
    but they will not live in them.
  They may plant vineyards,
    but they will not drink any wine
      from them.

The LORD's Day of Judging

14 "The LORD's day of judging is coming
    soon;
    it is near and coming fast.
  The cry will be very sad on the day of
    the LORD;
    even soldiers will cry.
15 That day will be a day of anger,
    a day of terror and trouble,
    a day of destruction and ruin,
    a day of darkness and gloom,
    a day of clouds and blackness,
16 a day of alarms and battle cries.

> At that time I, the LORD, will search Jerusalem with lamps. I will punish those who are satisfied with themselves.
> – Zephaniah 1:12

1:5 roof In Bible times houses were built with flat roofs. The roof was used for drying things such as flax and fruit. And it was used as an extra room, as a place for worship and as a place to sleep in the summer.

'Attack the strong, walled cities!
 Attack the corner towers!'
17 I will make life hard for the people;
  they will walk around like the
    blind,
  because they have sinned against
    the LORD.
 Their blood will be poured out like
   dust,
 and their insides will be dumped
   like rubbish.
18 On the day that God will show his
   anger,
  neither their silver nor gold will
    save them.
 The LORD's anger will be like a fire
   that will burn up the whole world;
 suddenly he will bring an end, yes, an
   end
   to everyone on earth."

The LORD Asks People to Change

2 Gather together, gather,
   you unwanted people.
2 Do it before it's too late,
   before you are blown away like
     chaff,
   before the LORD's terrible anger
     reaches you,
   before the day of the LORD's anger
     comes to you.
3 Come to the LORD, all you who are
     not proud,
   who obey his laws.
 Do what is right.
   Learn to be
     humble.
   Maybe you
     will escape
     on the day the
     LORD shows his anger.

2:3 Humbleness Is humility important?

Philistia will be Punished

4 No one will be left in the city of Gaza,
   and the city of Ashkelon will be
     destroyed.
 Ashdod will be empty by noon,
   and the people of Ekron will be
     chased away.
5 How terrible it will be for you who
   live by the Mediterranean Sea,
   you Philistines!

 The word of the LORD is against you,
   Canaan, land of the Philistines.

"I will destroy you
   so that no one will be left."
6 The land by the Mediterranean Sea,
   in which you live,
   will become pastures, fields for
     shepherds and pens for sheep.
7 It will belong to the descendants of
     Judah who are left alive.
   There they will let their sheep eat
     grass.
   At night they will sleep
     in the houses of Ashkelon.
 The LORD their God will pay attention
     to them
   and will make their life good again.

Moab and Ammon will be Punished

8 "I have heard the insults of the
     country of Moab
   and the threats of the people of
     Ammon.
 They have insulted my people
   and have taken their land."
9 So the LORD All-powerful, the God of
     Israel, says,
   "As surely as I live,
 Moab will be destroyed like Sodom,
   and Ammon will be destroyed like
     Gomorrah"
 a heap of weeds, a pit of salt
   and a ruin for ever.
 Those of my people who are left alive
   will take whatever they want
     from them;
 those who are left from my nation
   will take their land."

10 This is what Moab and Ammon get
     for being proud,
   because they insulted and made
     fun of the people of the LORD
     All-powerful.
11 The LORD will frighten them,
   because he will destroy all the
     gods of the earth.

2:9 Sodom . . . Gomorrah Two cities God destroyed because the people were so evil.

Cush and Assyria will be Destroyed

12 "You Cushites also
  will be killed by my sword."
13 Then the LORD will turn against the
    north
  and destroy Assyria.
  He will make Nineveh
  a ruin as dry as a desert.
14 Flocks and herds will lie down there,
  and all wild animals.
  The owls and crows will sit
  on the stone pillars.
  The owl will call through the
    windows,
  rubbish will be in the doorways,
  and the wooden boards of the
  buildings will be gone.
15 This is the happy and safe city
  that thinks there is no one else as
    strong as it is.
  But what a ruin it will be,
  a place where wild animals live.
  All those who pass by will make fun
  and shake their fists.

Jerusalem will be Punished

3 How terrible for the wicked,
  stubborn city of Jerusalem,
  which hurts its own people.
2 It obeys no voice;
  it can't be taught to do right.
  It doesn't trust the LORD;
  it doesn't worship its God.
3 Its officers are like roaring lions.
  Its rulers are like hungry wolves
  that attack in the evening,
  and in the morning nothing is left
  of those they attacked.
4 Its prophets are proud;
  they are people who cannot be
    trusted.
  Its priests don't respect holy things;
  they break God's teachings.
5 But the LORD is good, and he is there
  in that city.
  He does no wrong.
  Every morning he governs the
  people fairly;
  every day he can be trusted.
  But evil people are not ashamed of
  what they do.

6 "I have destroyed nations;
  their towers were ruined.
  I made their streets empty
  so no one goes there any more.
  Their cities are ruined;
  no one lives there at all.
7 I said, 'Surely now Jerusalem will
    respect me
  and will accept my teaching.'
  Then the place where they lived
  would not be destroyed,
  and I would not have to punish
    them.
  But they were still eager
  to do evil in everything they did.
8 Just wait," says the LORD.
  "Some day I will stand up as a
    witness.
  I have decided that I will gather
    nations
  and assemble kingdoms.
  I will pour out my anger on them,
  all my strong anger.
  My anger will be like fire
  that will burn up the whole world.

A New Day for God's People

9 "Then I will give the people of all
    nations pure speech
  so that all of them will speak the
  name of the LORD
  and worship me together.
10 People will come from where the Nile
    River begins;
  my scattered people will come with
  gifts for me.
11 Then Jerusalem will not be
    ashamed
  of the wrongs done against me,
  because I will remove from this city
  those who like to boast;
  there will never be any more proud
    people
  on my holy mountain in
    Jerusalem.
12 But I will leave in the city
  the humble and those who are not
    proud,
  and they will trust in the LORD.

GOD'S LOVE FOR ME
Zephaniah 3:17

God's Love Note Suppose your mum stuck a note in with your lunch or in your backpack that said she loved you and was thinking of you. How would that make you feel? How could it help if you were having a rough day? God loves us and sends us love notes all the time. We can see them in the things around us and read them in the Bible. (Check out Zephaniah 3:17.) Can you imagine God singing with happiness just because of you? But you can believe it because God tells us he does. God's love for you never changes and never ends. That should make you feel like singing, too!

MORE FAITH links

Love That Will Last, **p. 813**
A Mother's Love, **p. 961**
The One Who Suffered, **p. 966**
His Valentine, **p. 1035**
A Love Song, **p. 1246**
The Love Magnet, **p. 1694**

When things just don't go right and you make a real mess of things – like shouting at your brother or fighting with your best friend – it can make life miserable. It can also make you feel downright unlovable.

We all have times when we feel like that. That's the time to read one of God's love notes to you. Read on to find out more about God's amazing love for you!

The Rainbow Promise, Genesis 9:1–17, p. 14
- Link here to find the true meaning of the rainbow and why it is one of God's love notes.

Our Heavenly Shepherd, Psalm 23, p. 726
- Psalm 23 compares God to a shepherd and his people to his sheep. How is God like a good shepherd? How are you like one of his sheep? Why do you need a shepherd? This Faithlink tells you what a wonderful shepherd we have.

Love for Free, Romans 5:8, p. 1524
- If you broke something that belonged to your parents, do you think they would stop loving you? Multiply your parents' love by a thousand and you can begin to understand the kind of love God has for you. You can't earn God's love – it's a gift! That's why God sent his Son, Jesus, to die for us. With whom can you share the good news of God's love?

my FAVOURITE links

Zephaniah 3:13 **1246**

FAITH links

A LOVE SONG
ZEPHANIAH 3:17

Do you ever sing when you're happy? Can you imagine God singing with happiness? Zephaniah explained that in a future time, God would rejoice over his people with songs that showed his gladness because of them.

God sings because of you. That means he's glad to be around you. You can be assured of his love for you. Once you're confident of that love, you might feel like singing, too.

Check out God's love song for you:

A Time to Celebrate, Exodus 15:1–21, p. 95

Gratitude Attitude, Ezra 3, p. 611

Love That Will Last, Psalm 136, p. 813

What's in a Name? Isaiah 9:6, p. 908

Too Busy to Worship? Luke 2:8–20, p. 1368

Always Do This! 1 Thessalonians 5:16–18, p. 1636

---

13 Those who are left alive in Israel
   won't do wrong
   or tell lies;
   they won't trick people with their
      words.
   They will eat and lie down
      with no one to make them afraid."

A Happy Song

14 Sing, Jerusalem.
      Israel, shout for joy!
   Jerusalem, be happy
      and rejoice with all your heart.
15 The LORD has stopped punishing you;
      he has sent your enemies away.
   The King of Israel, the LORD, is with
      you;
      you will never again be afraid of
         being harmed.
16 On that day Jerusalem will be told,
      "Don't be afraid, city of Jerusalem.
      Don't give up.
17 The LORD your God is with you;
      the mighty One will save you.
   He will rejoice over you.
      You will rest in his love;
      he will sing and be joyful about
         you."

18 "I will take away the sadness planned
         for you,
      which would have made you very
         ashamed.
19 At that time I will punish
      all those who harmed you.
   I will save my people who cannot walk
      and gather my people who have
         been thrown out.
   I will give them praise and honour
      in every place where they were
         shamed.
20 At that time I will gather you;
      at that time I will bring you back
         home.
   I will give you honour and praise
      from people everywhere
   when I make things go well again for
         you,
      as you will see with your own
         eyes," says the LORD.

Haggai

GET BUSY!

Hi, there! My name is Haggai, and God sent me with a message to the governor and the high priest of Judah. Have you ever started a project but never taken the time to finish it? In my time, the Temple of the Lord was an unfinished project. God's people returned to their land from a long time of exile in a foreign land. At first, the people began rebuilding the Temple with a lot of enthusiasm and energy. But soon the project came to a screeching halt. Neighbours complained; and all the work on the Temple stopped. People found time to work on their own houses, but never had time to work on the Temple.

I wrote this book to remind people to put God first in their lives. Everyone has lots of things to do, but God's work should always come first. The people listened to my message and work on the Temple started again. God promises to richly bless those who love him and follow his commands. How can you put God first in your life?

JESUS WATCH

God made a promise to Zerubbabel, the governor of Judah, that he would be as important as God's signet ring. A signet ring was pressed into the wax that sealed an important document. It guaranteed that the document was from the owner of the ring. God honoured Zerubbabel for his work on the Temple by making him an ancestor of Jesus. Zerubbabel was a guarantee that God would send the Messiah. God also promised that the new Temple would be greater than the old Temple built by Solomon. Years later Herod the Great spent a fortune improving the Temple. However great the Temple of the Lord was, though, Jesus is greater.

What's wrong with living in a fancy house?

Not sure about that one? Haggai wrote something about it. Let's surf over to Haggai 1:3–11 to see what he says.

FAITH links

○ First Place, Haggai 1:7–11

○ Be Brave! Haggai 2:4

DOWNLOAD THESE VERSES:
A better Temple, Haggai 2:6–9
Before and after, Haggai 2:15–19
Zerubbabel's reward, Haggai 2:20–23

It is Time to Build the Temple

1 The prophet Haggai spoke the word of the LORD to Zerubbabel son of Shealtiel, the governor of Judah, and to Joshua son of Jehozadak, the high priest. This message came in the second year that Darius was king, on the first day of the sixth month:

2 "This is what the LORD All-powerful says: 'The people say the right time has not come to rebuild the Temple of the LORD.'"

3 Then Haggai the prophet spoke the word of the LORD: 4 "Is it right for you to be living in fancy houses while the Temple is still in ruins?"

5 This is what the LORD All-powerful says: "Think about what you have done. 6 You have planted much, but you harvest little. You eat, but you do not become full. You drink, but you are still thirsty. You put on clothes, but you are not warm enough. You earn money, but then you lose it all as if you had put it into a purse full of holes."

7 This is what the LORD All-powerful says: "Think about what you have done. 8 Go up to the mountains, bring back wood and build the Temple. Then I will be pleased with it and be honoured," says the LORD. 9 "You look for much, but you find little. When you bring it home, I destroy it. Why?" asks the LORD All-powerful. "Because you all work hard for your own houses while my house is still in ruins! 10 Because of what you have done, the sky holds back its rain and the ground holds back its crops. 11 I have called for a time without rain on the land, and on the mountains, and on the grain, the new wine, the olive oil, the plants which the earth produces, the people, the farm animals and all the work of your hands."

12 Zerubbabel son of Shealtiel and Joshua son of Jehozadak, the high priest, and all the rest of the people who were left alive obeyed the LORD their God and the message from Haggai the prophet, because the LORD their God had sent him. And the people feared the LORD.

13 Haggai, the LORD's messenger, gave the LORD's message to the people,

---

FAITH links

FIRST PLACE
HAGGAI 1:7-11

Suppose your parents redecorated every room in your home except yours. You'd feel pretty neglected, wouldn't you? The Israelites had returned to their land after being in Babylon for several years. After their return, the prophet Haggai warned them about their neglect in rebuilding God's Temple. They had rebuilt their own homes, but they had forgotten about God's. God wasn't saying that they couldn't fix their houses. He just wanted them to show how important he was to them.

When life gets busy, it's easy to forget about God. We put all other activities first, ahead of doing things for God. But God wants his work to also be important to us. How important is it to you?

Reward for Obedience, Leviticus 26:3–13, p. 171

Plans for a Son, 1 Chronicles 22:5–19, p. 548

A Hopeful Future, Jeremiah 29:11, p. 1031

God's New Temple, Ezekiel 40—44, p. 1135

The Choices of a Choice, Luke 5:1–11, p. 1375

Meeting Together, 1 Corinthians 16:19, p. 1567

saying, "The LORD says, 'I am with you.'" 14 The LORD stirred up Zerubbabel son of Shealtiel, the governor of Judah, and Joshua son of Jehozadak, the high priest, and all the rest of the people who were left alive. So they came and worked on the Temple of their God, the LORD All-powerful. 15 They began on the twenty-fourth day of the sixth month in the second year Darius was king.

The Beauty of the Temple

2 On the twenty-first day of the seventh month, the LORD spoke his word through Haggai the prophet, saying, 2 "Speak to Zerubbabel son of Shealtiel, governor of Judah, and to Joshua son of Jehozadak, the high priest, and to the rest of the people who are left alive. Say, 3 'Do any of you remember how great the Temple was before it was destroyed? What does it look like now? Doesn't it seem like nothing to you?' 4 But the LORD says, 'Zerubbabel, be brave. Also, Joshua son of Jehozadak, the high priest, be brave. And all you people who live in the land, be brave,' says the LORD. 'Work, because I am with you,' says the LORD All-powerful. 5 'I made a promise to you when you came out of Egypt, and my Spirit is still with you. So don't be afraid.'

6 "This is what the LORD All-powerful says: 'In a short time I will once again shake the heavens and the earth, the sea and the dry land. 7 I will shake all the nations, and they will bring their wealth. Then I will fill this Temple with glory,' says the LORD All-powerful. 8 'The silver is mine, and the gold is mine,' says the LORD All-powerful. 9 'The new Temple will be greater than the one before,' says the LORD All-powerful. 'And in this place I will give peace,' says the LORD All-powerful."

10 On the twenty-fourth day of the ninth month in the second year Darius was king, the LORD spoke his word to Haggai the prophet, saying, 11 "This is what the LORD All-powerful says: 'Ask the priests for a teaching. 12 Suppose a person carries in the fold of his clothes some meat made holy for the LORD. If that fold touches bread, cooked food, wine, olive oil or some other food, will that be made holy?'"

The priests answered, "No."

FAITH links

BE BRAVE!
HAGGAI 2:4

God's people had a big job ahead of them when they prepared to rebuild the Temple. God had sent the prophet Haggai to encourage Zerubbabel, the governor of Judah, to begin the work without fear.

What fears, if any, are stopping you from serving God? A fearful situation does not always mean someone is making fun of you for what you believe. The fear of failure and discouragement can also stop you from serving God or doing what is right. God can help you take courage and do whatever he has called you to do.

Link here to find out how you can have courage:

A Message of Courage and Hope, 2 Kings 19:4–10, p. 505

The Big Risk, Esther 4:11—5:2, p. 652

When Bad Things Happen, Ecclesiastes 3:16–17, p. 876

The God of Second Chances, Jonah 3, p. 1215

Blessed Are the Weak? 2 Corinthians 12:7–10, p. 1582

While You Wait, Jude 21, p. 1726

13 Then Haggai said, "A person who touches a dead body will become unclean. If he touches any of these foods, will it become unclean, too?"

The priests answered, "Yes, it would become unclean."

14 Then Haggai answered, "The LORD says, 'This is also true for the people of this nation. They are unclean, and everything they do with their hands is unclean to me. Whatever they offer at the altar is also unclean.

15 "'Think about this from now on! Think about how it was before you started laying stones on top of stones to build the Temple of the LORD. 16 A person used to come to a pile of grain expecting to find 20 basketfuls, but there were only ten. And a person used to come to the wine vat to take out 50 jarfuls, but only 20 were there. 17 I destroyed your work with diseases, mildew and hail, but you still did not come back to me,' says the LORD. 18 'It is the twenty-fourth day of the ninth month, the day in which the people finished working on the foundation of the Temple of the LORD. From now on, think about these things: 19 Do you have seeds for crops still in the barn? Your vines, fig trees, pomegranates and olive trees have not given fruit yet. But from now on I will bless you!'"

The LORD Makes a Promise to Zerubbabel

20 Then the LORD spoke his word a second time to Haggai on the twenty-fourth day of the month. He said, 21 "Tell Zerubbabel, the governor of Judah, 'I am going to shake the heavens and the earth. 22 I will destroy the foreign kingdoms and take away the power of the kingdoms of the nations. I will destroy the chariots and their riders. The horses will fall with their riders, as people kill each other with swords.' 23 The LORD All-powerful says, 'On that day I will take you, Zerubbabel son of Shealtiel, my servant,' says the LORD, 'and I will make you important like my signet ring, because I have chosen you!' says the LORD All-powerful."

UNDER CONSTRUCTION

Hi, it's Zechariah the prophet here. I was part of the first group of people who returned to Jerusalem after spending many years in a foreign country as captives. The big thing going on when I got back to Jerusalem was a major DIY project. Has your family ever redecorated a room in your house? Ripped out the old carpeting, painted the walls, bought new furniture? It's a lot of hard work, but when you've finished the room is beautiful. It was the same with our city. Our enemies had destroyed the city, and now God had plans to bless his people and to make the city of Jerusalem beautiful again.

I wrote this book to encourage God's people to rebuild the Temple of the Lord. Building the Temple was a way to love and honour God. The Temple was the centre of worship for our entire nation, and it was where God himself lived in a special way. God promised to make Jerusalem his chosen city again, if we would obey him and rebuild the Temple. With a new Temple, God said people would come from all over to worship him and Jerusalem would be peaceful and prosperous again.

JESUS WATCH

Many parts of the Book of Zechariah give us snapshots of Jesus. In Zechariah 9, he describes a king coming into Jerusalem on a donkey. In Bible times, a king who rode a horse was ready for war; but a king on a donkey came in peace. A few days before he died, Jesus rode into Jerusalem on a donkey. The people praised him and waved palm branches in his honour. He came to bring people peace with God. Zechariah also described a good shepherd who was rejected and sold for 30 pieces of silver. Jesus called himself the good shepherd. He was betrayed by Judas, one of his own disciples, and handed over to the soldiers for 30 pieces of silver. Another picture of Jesus was a stone with the message "And in one day I will take away the sin of this land" (Zechariah 3:9). On the day he died on the cross, Jesus took away the sin of the whole world. Jesus is the Branch who will build the Temple of the Lord. He will be a priest and a king. As a priest, Jesus asks God to forgive our sins. As a king, he rules for ever from heaven.

OTHER CONNECTIONS

 What do you do when you see the needs of others around you? Ignore them and walk away? Offer to help? God wants us to care for others as he cares for us. Find out more about it by linking to Can I Help You? Zechariah 7:8–9.

- Where Is God's Kingdom? Zechariah 9:9–10. Ever wonder where exactly is the kingdom of God? Are you, like the Israelites, expecting a king with a palace and the whole works? Surf here to check out what the Bible means when it refers to God's kingdom.

FAITH links

○ Your Spiritual Roots, Zechariah 1:1–6

○ Small Beginnings, Zechariah 4:10

○ A Reminder to Do What Is Right and True, Zechariah 7:8–10

○ The Best Advice, Zechariah 10:2

my FAVOURITE links

_____
_____
_____

Why did the high priest need new clothes?

Was it because his old clothes were dirty? Let's find out in Zechariah 3.

MORE ON THE ZECHARIAH SURFWATCH:

A flying scroll, Zechariah 5:1–4
Sins in a basket, Zechariah 5:5–11
Blessings for Jerusalem, Zechariah 8
The king is coming! Zechariah 9:9–17

The Lord Calls His People Back

1 In the eighth month of Darius' second year as king, the Lord spoke his word to the prophet Zechariah son of Berekiah, who was the son of Iddo. The Lord said, 2 "The Lord was very angry with your ancestors. 3 So tell the people: this is what the Lord All-powerful says: 'Return to me, and I will return to you,' says the Lord All-powerful. 4 Don't be like your ancestors. In the past the prophets said to them: this is what the Lord All-powerful says: 'Stop your evil ways and evil actions.' But they wouldn't listen or pay attention to me, says the Lord. 5 Your ancestors are dead, and those prophets didn't live for ever. 6 I commanded my words and laws to my servants the prophets, and they preached to your ancestors, who returned to me. They said, 'The Lord All-powerful did as he said he would. He punished us for the way we lived and for what we did.'"

The Vision of the Horses

7 It was on the twenty-fourth day of the eleventh month, which is the month of Shebat, in Darius' second year as king. The Lord spoke his word to the prophet Zechariah son of Berekiah, who was the son of Iddo.

8 During the night I had a vision. I saw a man riding a red horse. He was standing among some myrtle trees in a ravine, with red, brown and white horses behind him.

9 I asked, "What are these, sir?"

The angel who was talking with me answered, "I'll show you what they are."

10 Then the man standing among the myrtle trees explained, "They are the ones the Lord sent through all the earth."

11 Then they spoke to the Lord's angel, who was standing among the myrtle trees. They said, "We have gone through all the earth, and everything is calm and quiet."

12 Then the Lord's angel asked, "Lord All-powerful, how long will it be before you show mercy to Jerusalem and the cities of Judah? You have been angry with them for 70 years now." 13 So the Lord answered the angel who was talking with me, and his words were comforting and good.

14 Then the angel who was talking to me said to me, "Announce this: this is what the Lord All-powerful says: 'I have a

---

FAITH links

YOUR SPIRITUAL ROOTS

ZECHARIAH 1:1-6

How far back can you trace your roots? The Israelites could trace their roots all the way back to Abraham. Some of their ancestors did not follow God. Through Zechariah, God called his people to stop sinning and return to him. God didn't want them to follow the bad examples of their ancestors, who had turned away from him.

God wants you to follow him, even if you're the first to become a Christian in your family. As a Christian, you're part of the spiritual heritage described in the Bible. (Check out Hebrews 11, p. 1679.)

A Direct Path, Proverbs 3:5–6, p. 829

His Valentine, Jeremiah 31:3, p. 1035

Empty Words, Ezekiel 33:30–33, p. 1127

Inside the Heart of God, Micah 7:18–20, p. 1228

When We Agree, Matthew 18:19–20, p. 1306

One Big, Happy Family, John 1:12, p. 1422

strong love for Jerusalem. 15 And I am very angry with the nations that feel so safe. I was only a little angry at them, but they made things worse.'

16 "So this is what the LORD says: 'I will return to Jerusalem with mercy. My Temple will be rebuilt,' says the LORD All-powerful, 'and the measuring line will be used to rebuild Jerusalem.'

17 "Also announce: this is what the LORD All-powerful says: 'My towns will be rich again. The LORD will comfort Jerusalem again, and I will again choose Jerusalem.'"

The Vision of the Horns

18 Then I looked up and saw four animal horns. 19 I asked the angel who was talking with me, "What are these?"

He said, "These are the horns that scattered the people of Judah, Israel and Jerusalem."

20 Then the LORD showed me four craftsmen. 21 I asked, "What are they coming to do?"

He answered, "They have come to scare and throw down the horns. These horns scattered the people of Judah so that no one could even lift up his head. These horns stand for the nations that attacked the people of Judah and scattered them."

The Vision of the Measuring Line

2 Then I looked up and saw a man holding a line for measuring objects. 2 I asked him, "Where are you going?"

He said to me, "I am going to measure Jerusalem, to see how wide and how long it is."

3 Then the angel who was talking with me left, and another angel came out to meet him. 4 The second angel said to him, "Run and tell that young man, 'Jerusalem will become a city without walls, because there will be so many people and cattle in it. 5 I will be a wall of fire around it,' says the LORD. 'And I will be the glory within it.'

6 "Oh no! Oh no! Run away from Babylon, because I have scattered you like the four winds of heaven," says the LORD.

7 "Oh no, Jerusalem! Escape, you who live right in Babylon." 8 This is what the LORD All-powerful says: "After he has honoured me and sent me against the nations who took your possessions—because whoever touches you hurts what is precious to me— 9 I will shake my hand against them so that their slaves will rob them."

Then you will know that the LORD All-powerful sent me.

10 "Shout and be glad, Jerusalem. I am coming, and I will live among you," says the LORD. 11 "At that time people from many nations will join with the LORD and will become my people.

Then I will live among you, and you will know that the LORD All-powerful has sent me to you. 12 The LORD will take Judah as his own part of the holy land, and Jerusalem will be his chosen city again. 13 Be silent, everyone, in the presence of the LORD. He is coming out of the holy place where he lives."

The Vision of the High Priest

3 Then he showed me Joshua, the high priest, standing in front of the LORD's angel. And Satan was standing by Joshua's right side to accuse him. 2 The LORD said to Satan, "The LORD says "no" to you, Satan! The LORD who has chosen Jerusalem says "no" to you! This man was like a burning stick pulled from the fire."

3 Joshua was wearing dirty clothes and was standing in front of the angel. 4 The angel said to those standing in front of him, "Take off those dirty clothes."

Then the angel said to Joshua, "Look, I have taken away your sin from you, and I am giving you beautiful, fine clothes."

5 Then I said, "Put a clean turban on his head." So they put a clean turban on his head and dressed him while the LORD's angel stood there.

6 Then the LORD's angel said to Joshua, 7 "This is what the LORD All-powerful says: 'If you do as I tell you and serve me, you will be in charge of my Temple and my courtyards. And I will let

you be with these angels who are standing here.

8 "'Listen, Joshua, the high priest, and your friends who are sitting in front of you. They stand for what will happen. I am going to bring my servant called the Branch. 9 Look, I put this stone in front of Joshua, a stone with seven sides. I will carve a message on it,' says the LORD All-powerful. 'And in one day I will take away the sin of this land.'

10 "The LORD All-powerful says, 'In that day, each of you will invite your neighbour to sit under your own grapevine and under your own fig tree.'"

The Vision of the Lampstand

4 Then the angel who was talking with me returned and woke me up as if I had been asleep. 2 He asked me, "What do you see?"

I said, "I see a solid gold lampstand with a bowl at the top. And there are seven lamps and also seven places for wicks. 3 There are two olive trees by it, one on the right of the bowl and the other on the left."

4 I asked the angel who talked with me, "Sir, what are these?"

5 The angel said, "Don't you know what they are?"

"No, sir," I said.

6 Then he told me, "This is the word of the LORD to Zerubbabel: 'You will not succeed by your own strength or power, but by my Spirit,' says the LORD All-powerful.

7 "Who are you, big mountain? In front of Zerubbabel you will become flat land, and he will bring out the topmost stone, shouting, 'It's beautiful! It's beautiful!'"

8 Then the LORD spoke his word to me again, saying, 9 "Zerubbabel has laid the foundation of this Temple, and he will complete it. Then you will know that the LORD All-powerful has sent me to you.

10 "The people should not think that small beginnings are unimportant. They will be happy when they see Zerubbabel with tools, building the Temple.

"(These are the seven eyes of the LORD, which look back and forth across the earth.)"

FAITH links

SMALL BEGINNINGS
ZECHARIAH 4:10

Have you ever felt discouraged over a project that seemed to take for ever? Maybe you've been feeling as if you've hardly made a dent in what you have to do. Or maybe you've witnessed to someone, but that person has barely responded. Although Zerubbabel and the Israelites had laid the foundation of the new Temple, it seemed like a small beginning. They had a long way to go to complete the Temple.

Small beginnings can still bring a rich harvest. Don't allow discouragement over small beginnings to keep you from doing other work for God. When in doubt, remember the story of the mustard seed (plug into Matthew 13:31–32, p. 1297; Mark 4:30–32, p. 1336; or Luke 13:18–19, p. 1395, for that story). That tiny seed was the beginning of a large tree.

Here are some Faithlinks on taking that first, tiny step:

Keep On Praying, 1 Samuel 1, p. 354

Depend on Him! 2 Chronicles 16:1–9, p. 579

999, Psalm 28:6, p. 730

In the Lions' Den, Daniel 6, p. 1160

Your Feet on High Places, Habakkuk 3:18–19, p. 1239

Keep On Keeping On, Revelation 13:10, p. 1744

11 Then I asked the angel, "What are the two olive trees on the right and left of the lampstand?"

12 I also asked him, "What are the two olive branches beside the two gold pipes, from which the olive oil flows to the lamps?"

13 He answered, "Don't you know what they are?"

"No, sir," I said.

14 So he said, "They stand for the two who have been appointed to serve the LORD of all the earth."

The Vision of the Flying Scroll

5 I looked up again and saw a flying scroll.

2 The angel asked me, "What do you see?"

I answered, "I see a flying scroll, 10 metres long and 5 metres wide."

3 And he said to me, "This is the curse that will go all over the land. One side says every thief will be taken away. The other side says everyone who makes false promises will be taken away. 4 The LORD All-powerful says, 'I will send it to the houses of thieves and to those who use my name to make false promises. The scroll will stay in that person's house and destroy it with its wood and stones.'"

The Vision of the Woman

5 Then the angel who was talking with me came forwards and said to me, "Look up and see what is going out."

6 "What is it?" I asked.

He answered, "It is a measuring basket going out." He also said, "It stands for the people's sins in all the land."

7 Then the lid made of lead was raised, and there was a woman sitting inside the basket. 8 The angel said, "The woman stands for wickedness." Then he pushed her back into the basket and put the lid back down.

9 Then I looked up and saw two women going out with the wind in their wings. Their wings were like those of a stork, and they lifted up the basket between earth and the sky.

10 I asked the angel who was talking with me, "Where are they taking the basket?"

11 "They are going to Babylonia to build a temple for it," he answered. "When the temple is ready, they will set the basket there in its place."

The Vision of the Four Chariots

6 I looked up again and saw four chariots going out between two mountains, mountains of bronze. 2 Red horses pulled the first chariot. Black horses pulled the second chariot. 3 White horses pulled the third chariot, and strong, spotted horses pulled the fourth chariot. 4 I asked the angel who was talking with me, "What are these, sir?"

5 He said, "These are the four spirits of heaven. They have just come from the presence of the Lord of the whole world. 6 The chariot pulled by the black horses will go to the land of the north. The white horses will go to the land of the west, and the spotted horses will go to the land of the south."

7 When the powerful horses went out, they were eager to go through all the earth. So he said, "Go through all the earth," and they did.

8 Then he called to me, "Look, the horses that went north have caused my spirit to rest in the land of the north."

A Crown for Joshua

9 The LORD spoke his word to me, saying, 10 "Take silver and gold from Heldai, Tobijah and Jedaiah, who were captives in Babylon. Go that same day to the house of Josiah son of Zephaniah, who came from Babylon. 11 Make the silver and gold into a crown, and put it on the head of Joshua son of Jehozadak, the high priest. 12 Tell him this is what the LORD All-powerful says: 'A man whose name is the Branch will branch out from where he

> A man whose name is the Branch will branch out from where he is, and he will build the Temple of the LORD.
> – Zechariah 6:12

is, and he will build the Temple of the LORD. 13 One man[n] will build the Temple of the LORD, and the other[n] will receive honour. One man will sit on his throne and rule, and the other will be a priest on his throne. And these two men will work together in peace.' 14 The crown will be kept in the Temple of the LORD to remind Heldai, Tobijah, Jedaiah and Josiah son of Zephaniah. 15 People living far away will come and build the Temple of the LORD. Then you will know the LORD All-powerful has sent me to you. This will happen if you completely obey the LORD your God."

The People Should Show Mercy

7 In Darius' fourth year as king, on the fourth day of the ninth month, which is called Kislev, the LORD spoke his word to Zechariah. 2 The city of Bethel sent Sharezer, Regem-Melech and their men to ask the LORD a question. 3 They went to the prophets and priests who were at the Temple of the LORD All-powerful. The men said, "For years in the fifth month of each year we have shown our sadness and gone without food. Should we continue to do this?"

4 The LORD All-powerful spoke his word to me, saying, 5 "Tell the priests and the people in the land: 'For 70 years you went without food and cried in the fifth and seventh months, but that was not really for me. 6 And when you ate and drank, it was really for yourselves. 7 The LORD used the earlier prophets to say the same thing, when Jerusalem and the surrounding towns were at peace and wealthy, and people settled in the southern area and the western hills.'"

8 And the LORD spoke his word to Zechariah again, saying, 9 "This is what the LORD All-powerful says: 'Do what is right and true. Be kind and merciful to each other. 10 Don't hurt widows and orphans, foreigners or the poor; don't even think of doing evil to somebody else.'

11 "But they refused to pay attention;

7:9 Caring
How should you treat others?

FAITH links

A REMINDER TO DO WHAT IS RIGHT AND TRUE
ZECHARIAH 7:8-10

Do you ever complain that your parents are nagging because they say the same things all the time? "Clean your room." "Do your homework." "Don't hit your sister." They say the same things because they want you to remember to do them.

Some messages are the same throughout the Bible. Love God. Love others. Don't seek to harm others. Be fair and honest. Show mercy. This was Zechariah's message to the Israelites. Why these same messages? People often need reminders about how God wants us to live and reminders to *do* what he tells us!

Need a reminder? Connect here:

Yours, Mine and Ours?
1 Samuel 25, p. 389

Take My Advice, 1 Kings 2:2–4, p. 436

See the Heart Behind It, Nehemiah 8; 9, p. 636

A Blueprint for Living, Amos 5:14–15, p. 1200

How to Make God Glad, Ephesians 6:1–2, p. 1605

The True Test, 1 John 3:18, p. 1718

6:13 One man This probably refers to Zerubbabel.
6:13 other This probably refers to Joshua.

▶ **Zechariah 7 1258**

CARING FOR OTHERS
Zechariah 7:8–9

Livin' it

Can I Help You? Have you ever been in a big shop and got lost? Panic starts to set in, and then you hear a sales assistant say, "Can I help you?" Phew! Those words are just what you need! It feels good to be on the receiving end of someone's concern and care, doesn't it? But how do you feel when someone needs your help? What do you do then?

God wants us to respond to the needs of those around us. Helping others is the way to show real love for God. (Read Amos 2:6–7, p. 1196.) How do your words and actions show concern for others?

When three strangers showed up at Abraham's tent, he did everything possible to welcome them. (Check out Genesis 18:1–8, p. 23.) How can you make people feel welcome – anywhere, anytime?

MORE FAITH links

Show You Care, **p. 481**
Seeing the Needs, **p. 625**
Help for the Hurting, **p. 666**
Meaningless Words, **p. 684**
Kindness Counts, **p. 1489**
You're Welcomed! **p. 1494**

> How do you show you care for others?

Makes you stop and think, doesn't it? Let's link to some of the following for some more thoughts on caring.

Care for the Lost, Deuteronomy 22:1–3, p. 255
- Have you ever found a lost dog or cat? What did you do with it?
- God gave Adam the job of caring for the animals. We're still caretakers of the earth. How do you do your part in being a caretaker?

Kindness First, Matthew 9:35–36, p. 1290
- When you approach a crowd of kids, what's the first thing you think of? Are you thinking of someone that you want to avoid? Or why that girl doesn't wear cooler clothes? Jesus' first thought was a kind, caring one. How can you help someone who could do with a kind word or act?

Don't Play Favourites, James 2:1–7, p. 1691
- Link here to see how God wants us to treat all people.

my **FAVOURITE** *links*

they were stubborn and did not want to listen any more. 12 They made their hearts as hard as rock and would not listen to the teachings of the LORD All-powerful. And they would not hear the words he sent by his Spirit through the earlier prophets. So the LORD All-powerful became very angry.

13 "'When I called to them, they would not listen. So when they called to me, I would not listen,' says the LORD All-powerful. 14 'I scattered them like a hurricane to other countries which they did not know. This good land was left so ruined behind them that no one could live there. They had made the desired land a ruin.'"

The LORD will Bless Jerusalem

8 The LORD All-powerful spoke his word, saying, 2 this is what the LORD All-powerful says: "I have a very strong love for Jerusalem. My strong love for her is like a fire burning in me."

3 This is what the LORD says: "I will return to Jerusalem and live in it. Then it will be called the City of Truth, and the mountain of the LORD All-powerful will be called the Holy Mountain."

4 This is what the LORD All-powerful says: "Old men and old women will again sit along Jerusalem's streets, each carrying a cane because of age. 5 And the streets will be filled with boys and girls playing."

6 This is what the LORD All-powerful says: "Those who are left alive then may think it is too difficult to happen, but it is not too difficult for me," says the LORD All-powerful. 7 This is what the LORD All-powerful says: "I will save my people from countries in the east and west. 8 I will bring them back, and they will live in Jerusalem. They will be my people, and I will be their good and loyal God."

9 This is what the LORD All-powerful says: "Work hard, you who are hearing these words today. The prophets spoke these words when the foundation was laid for the house of the LORD All-powerful, for the building of the Temple. 10 Before that time there was no money to hire people or animals. People could not safely come and go because of their enemies; I had turned everyone against his neighbour. 11 But I will not do to these people who are left what I did in the past," says the LORD All-powerful.

12 "They will plant their seeds in peace, their grapevines will have fruit, the ground will give good crops, and the sky will send rain. I will give all this to the people who are left alive. 13 Judah and Israel, your names have been used as curses in other nations. But I will save you, and you will become a blessing. So don't be afraid; work hard."

14 This is what the LORD All-powerful says: "When your ancestors made me angry, I planned to punish you. I did not change my mind," says the LORD All-powerful. 15 "But now I will do something different. I am planning to do good to Jerusalem and Judah. So don't be afraid. 16 These are the things you should do: tell each other the truth. In the courts judge with truth and complete fairness. 17 Do not make plans to hurt your neighbours, and don't love false promises. I hate all these things," says the LORD.

18 The LORD All-powerful spoke his word to me again. 19 This is what the LORD All-powerful says: "The special days when you give up eating in the fourth, fifth, seventh and tenth months will become good, joyful, happy feasts in Judah. But you must love truth and peace."

20 This is what the LORD All-powerful says: "Many people from many cities will still come to Jerusalem. 21 People from one city will go and say to those from another city, 'We are going to pray to the LORD and to ask the LORD All-powerful for help. Come and go with us.' 22 Many people and powerful nations will come to worship the LORD All-powerful in Jerusalem and to pray to the LORD for help."

23 This is what the LORD All-powerful says: "At that time, ten men from different countries will come and take hold of a Judean by his coat. They will say to him, 'Let us go with you, because we have heard that God is with you.'"

Zechariah 9:1 1260

WHERE IS GOD'S KINGDOM?   Zechariah 9:9–10

In Old Testament days, the Israelites looked forward to the coming of the Messiah. They thought the kingdom of God would be like a new king taking over a country. They thought there would be battles, and God would get back at their enemies.

The kingdom of God did begin when Jesus came, but it was not a kingdom of war and conquest. It was a kingdom of God's love, mercy and forgiveness. Jesus brought about God's kingdom by dying for us and forgiving us instead of fighting our enemies for us.

Jesus said, though, that the kingdom of God would be shown in a different way when he comes the next time. Then it will be more like what the Old Testament Israelites had imagined.

Punishment on Israel's Enemies

9 This message is the word of the LORD.

The message is against the land of Hadrach
   and the city of Damascus.
The tribes of Israel and all people
   belong to the LORD.
2 The message is also against the city of Hamath, on the border,
   and against Tyre and Sidon, with their skill.
3 Tyre has built a strong wall for herself.
   She has piled up silver like dust
   and gold like the mud in the streets.
4 But the Lord will take away all she has
   and destroy her power on the sea.
   That city will be destroyed by fire.
5 The city of Ashkelon will see it and be afraid.
   The people of Gaza will shake with fear,
   and the people of Ekron will lose hope.
No king will be left in Gaza,
   and no one will live in Ashkelon any more.
6 Foreigners will live in Ashdod,
   and I will destroy the pride of the Philistines.
7 I will stop them from drinking blood
   and from eating forbidden food.
Those left alive will belong to God.
   They will be leaders in Judah,
   and Ekron will become like the Jebusites.
8 I will protect my Temple
   from armies who would come or go.
No one will hurt my people again,
   because now I am watching them.

The King is Coming

9 Rejoice greatly, people of Jerusalem!
   Shout for joy, people of Jerusalem!
Your king is coming to you.
   He does what is right, and he saves.
   He is gentle and riding on a donkey,
   on the colt of a donkey.
10 I will take away the chariots from Ephraim
   and the horses from Jerusalem.
The bows used in war will be broken.
The king will talk to the nations about peace.

His kingdom will go from sea to
    sea,
and from the Euphrates River to
    the ends of the earth.

11 As for you, because of the blood of
    the agreement with you
I will set your prisoners free from
    the dry pit.
12 You prisoners who have hope,
    return to your place of safety.
Today I am telling you
    that I will give you back twice as
    much as before.
13 I will use Judah like a bow
    and Ephraim like the arrows.
Jerusalem, I will use your men
    to fight the men of Greece.
I will use you like a warrior's
    sword.

14 Then the LORD will appear above
    them,
and his arrows will shoot like
    lightning.
The Lord GOD will blow the trumpet,
    and he will march in the storms of
    the south.
15 The LORD All-powerful will protect
    them;
they will destroy the enemy with
    catapults.
They will drink and shout like
    drunkards.
They will be filled like a bowl
    used for sprinkling blood at the
    corners of the altar.
16 On that day the LORD their God will
    save them
    as if his people were sheep.
They will shine in his land
    like jewels in a crown.
17 They will be so pretty and beautiful.
The young men will grow strong
    on the grain
    and the young women on new
    wine.

The LORD's Promises

10 Ask the LORD for rain during the
    springtime.
The LORD is the one who makes
    the clouds.
He sends the showers
    and gives everyone green fields.
2 Idols tell lies;

FAITH links

THE BEST ADVICE
ZECHARIAH 10:2

What people or places do you consider "in the know" as far as advice is concerned? Newspaper or magazine articles that answer personal questions? The Internet? Horoscopes? Zechariah warned the Israelites against seeking answers through idols or fortune-tellers. Neither provided the truth. Sound familiar? Many people today look for answers from psychics, horoscopes, fortune cookies and other people, places and things. They look everywhere for truth, except to God.

Truth can only be found by listening to God. God provides answers through his word, prayer and the advice of other Christians. Need answers? Seek God's advice.

Who Do You Trust? Joshua 9,
p. 287

Prayer + Action = Success,
Nehemiah 2:4–9, p. 626

The Prayer Habit, Psalm 5:1–3,
p. 712

If You Want My Advice . . .
Proverbs 13:1, p. 843

Believe It or Not, Luke 1:20, 38,
p. 1366

Pay Attention! Hebrews 2:1,
p. 1668

fortune-tellers see false visions
and tell about false dreams.
The comfort they give is worth
nothing.
So the people are like lost sheep.
They are abused, because there is
no shepherd.

3 The LORD says, "I am angry with my
shepherds,
and I will punish the leaders.
I, the LORD All-powerful, care
for my flock, the people of Judah.
I will make them like my proud
war horses.
4 From Judah will come the cornerstone,
and the tent peg,
the battle bow,
and every ruler.
5 Together they will be like soldiers
marching to battle through muddy
streets.
The LORD is with them,
so they will fight and defeat the
horsemen.

6 "I will strengthen the people of Judah
and save the people of Joseph.
I will bring them back,
because I care about them.
It will be as though
I had never left them,
because I am the LORD their God,
and I will answer them.
7 The people of Ephraim will be strong
like soldiers;
they will be as glad as when they
have drunk wine.
Their children will see it and rejoice;
they will be happy in the LORD.
8 I will call my people
and gather them together.
I will save them,
and they will grow in number as
they grew in number before.
9 I have scattered them among the
nations,
but in those faraway places, they
will remember me.
They and their children will live
and return.
10 I will bring them back from the land
of Egypt

and gather them from Assyria.
I will bring them to Gilead and
Lebanon
until there isn't enough room for
them all.
11 They will come through the sea of
trouble.
The waves of the sea will be calm,
and the Nile River will dry up.
I will defeat Assyria's pride
and destroy Egypt's power over
other countries.
12 I will make my people strong,
and they will live as I say," says the
LORD.

11 Lebanon, open your gates
so fire may burn your cedar trees."
2 Cry, pine trees, because the cedar has
fallen,
because the tall trees are ruined.
Cry, oaks in Bashan,
because the mighty forest has been
cut down.
3 Listen to the shepherds crying
because their rich pastures are
destroyed.
Listen to the lions roaring
because the lovely land of the
Jordan River is ruined.

The Two Shepherds

4 This is what the LORD my God says: "Feed the flock that are about to be killed. 5 Their buyers kill them and are not punished. Those who sell them say, 'Praise the LORD, I am rich.' Even the shepherds don't feel sorry for their sheep. 6 I don't feel sorry any more for the people of this country," says the LORD. "I will let everyone be under the power of his neighbour and king. They will bring trouble to the country, and I will not save anyone from them."

7 So I fed the flock about to be killed, particularly the weakest ones. Then I took two sticks; I called one Pleasant and the other Union, and I fed the flock. 8 In one month I got rid of three shepherds. The

---

11:1 trees In this poem, trees, bushes and animals stand for leaders of countries around Judah.

flock did not pay attention to me, and I got impatient with them. 9 I said, "I will no longer take care of you like a shepherd. Let those that are dying die, and let those that are to be destroyed be destroyed. Let those that are left eat each other."
10 Then I broke the stick named Pleasant to break the agreement God made with all the nations. 11 That day it was broken. The weak ones in the flock who were watching me knew this message was from the LORD.
12 Then I said, "If you want to pay me, pay me. If not, then don't." So they paid me 30 pieces of silver.
13 The LORD said to me, "Throw the money to the potter." That is how little they thought I was worth." So I took the 30 pieces of silver and threw them to the potter in the Temple of the LORD.
14 Then I broke the second stick, named Union, to break the brotherhood between Judah and Israel.
15 Then the LORD said to me, "Get the things used by a foolish shepherd again, 16 because I am going to get a new shepherd for the country. He will not care for the dying sheep, or look for the young ones, or heal the injured ones or feed the healthy. But he will eat the best sheep and tear off their hoofs.

17 "How terrible it will
be for the
useless shepherd
who abandoned the
flock.
A sword will strike
his arm and his
right eye.
His arm will lose all
its strength,
and his right eye
will go blind."

Jerusalem will be Saved

12 This message is the word of the LORD to Israel. This is what the LORD says, who stretched out the skies, and laid the foundations of the earth, and put the human spirit within: 2 "I will make Jerusalem like a cup of poison to the nations around her. They will come and attack Jerusalem and Judah. 3 One day all the nations on earth will come together to attack Jerusalem, but I will make it like a heavy rock; anyone who tries to move it will get hurt. 4 At that time I will confuse every horse and cause its rider to go mad," says the LORD. "I will watch over Judah, but I will blind all the horses of the enemies. 5 Then the leaders of Judah will say to themselves, 'The people of Jerusalem are strong, because the LORD All-powerful is their God.'

6 "At that time I will make the leaders of Judah like a fire burning a stack of wood or like a fire burning straw. They will destroy all the people around them left and right. But the people of Jerusalem will remain safe.

7 "The LORD will save the homes of Judah first so that the honour given to David's family and to the people of Jerusalem won't be greater than the honour given to Judah. 8 At that time the LORD will protect the people in Jerusalem. Then even the weakest of them will be strong like David. And the family of David will be like God, like an angel of the LORD in front of them. 9 At that time I will go to destroy all the nations that attack Jerusalem.

Crying for the One They Stabbed

10 "I will pour out on David's family and the people in Jerusalem a spirit of kindness and mercy. They will look at me, the one they have stabbed, and they will cry like someone crying over the death of an only child. They will be as sad as someone who has lost a firstborn son. 11 At that time there will be much crying in Jerusalem, like the crying for Hadad Rimmon in the plain of Megiddo. 12 The land will cry, each family by itself: the

> How terrible it will be for the useless shepherd who abandoned the flock.
> – Zechariah 11:17

11:13 worth This was a small amount. It was about the price paid for a slave.

family of David by itself and their wives by themselves, the family of Nathan by itself and their wives by themselves, 13 the family of Levi by itself and their wives by themselves, the family of Shimei by itself and their wives by themselves, 14 and all the rest of the families by themselves and their wives by themselves.

13 "At that time a fountain will be open for David's descendants and for the people of Jerusalem to cleanse them of their sin and uncleanness."

13:1 Guilt
How can you be made guilt-free?

2 The LORD All-powerful says, "At that time I will get rid of the names of the idols from the land; no one will remember them any more. I will also remove the prophets and unclean spirits from the land. 3 If a person continues to prophesy, his own father and mother, the ones who gave birth to him, will tell him, 'You have told lies using the LORD's name, so you must die.' When he prophesies, his own father and mother who gave birth to him will stab him.

4 "At that time the prophets will be ashamed of their visions and prophecies. They won't try to trick people by wearing the prophet's clothes made of hair. 5 Each of them will say, 'I am not a prophet. I am a farmer and have been a farmer since I was young.' 6 But someone will ask, 'What are the deep cuts on your body?' And each will answer, 'I was hurt at my friend's house.'

The Shepherd is Killed

7 "Sword, hit the shepherd.
   Attack the man who is my friend,"
   says the LORD All-powerful.
"Kill the shepherd,
   and the sheep will scatter,
   and I will punish the little ones."
8 The LORD says, "Two-thirds of the people
   through all the land will die. They will be gone,
   and one-third will be left.
9 The third that is left I will test with fire,

purifying them like silver,
   testing them like gold.
Then they will call on me,
   and I will answer them.
I will say, 'You are my people,'
   and they will say, 'The LORD is our God.'"

The Day of Punishment

14 The LORD's day of judging is coming when the wealth you have taken will be divided among you.

2 I will bring all the nations together to fight Jerusalem. They will capture the city and rob the houses and attack the women. Half the people will be taken away as captives, but the rest of the people won't be taken from the city.

3 Then the LORD will go to war against those nations; he will fight as in a day of battle. 4 On that day he will stand on the Mount of Olives, east of Jerusalem. The Mount of Olives will split in two, forming a deep valley that runs east and west. Half the mountain will move towards the north, and half will move towards the south. 5 You will run through this mountain valley to the other side, just as you ran from the earthquake when Uzziah was king of Judah. Then the LORD my God will come and all the holy ones with him.

6 On that day there will be no light, cold or frost. 7 There will be no other day like it, and the LORD knows when it will come. There will be no day or night; even at evening it will still be light.

8 At that time fresh water will flow from Jerusalem. Half of it will flow east to the Dead Sea, and half will flow west to the Mediterranean Sea. It will flow in summer and winter.

9 Then the LORD will be king over the whole world. At that time there will be only one LORD, and his name will be the only name.

10 All the land south of Jerusalem from Geba to Rimmon will be turned into a plain. Jerusalem will be raised up, but it will stay in the same place. The city will reach from the Benjamin Gate, to the First Gate, to the Corner Gate, and from the Tower of Hananel to the king's wine-

FAITH CHALLENGE

Got another challenge for you. Read 14:9 to find out what kind of government the world can expect in the future. How would the world be different today if the leaders of all countries gave up control to God?

Testing it

Zechariah 14:9
Then the LORD will be king over the whole world. At that time there will be only one LORD, and his name will be the only name.

presses. 11 People will live there, and it will never be destroyed again. Jerusalem will be safe.

12 But the LORD will bring a terrible disease on the nations that fought against Jerusalem. Their flesh will rot away while they are still standing up. Their eyes will rot in their sockets, and their tongues will rot in their mouths. 13 At that time the LORD will cause panic. Everybody will grab his neighbour, and they will attack each other. 14 The people of Judah will fight in Jerusalem. And the wealth of the nations around them will be collected—much gold, silver and clothes. 15 A similar disease will strike the horses, mules, camels, donkeys and all the animals in the camps.

16 All of those left alive of the people who came to fight Jerusalem will come back to Jerusalem year after year to worship the King, the LORD All-powerful, and to celebrate the Feast of Shelters. 17 Anyone from the nations who does not go to Jerusalem to worship the King, the LORD All-powerful, will not have rain fall on his land. 18 If the Egyptians do not go to Jerusalem, they will have no rain. Then the LORD will send them the same terrible disease he sent the other nations that did not celebrate the Feast of Shelters. 19 This will be the punishment for Egypt and any nation which does not go to celebrate the Feast of Shelters.

20 At that time the horses' bells will have written on them: HOLY TO THE LORD. The cooking pots in the Temple of the LORD will be like the holy altar bowls. 21 Every pot in Jerusalem and Judah will be holy to the LORD All-powerful, and everyone who offers sacrifices will be able to take food from them and cook in them. At that time there will not be any buyers or sellers in the Temple of the LORD All-powerful.

Malachi

ONLY THE BEST!

Hi! I'm Malachi, the prophet with a message for God's people. Imagine you are at a big party and you're the guest of honour. A pile of beautifully wrapped presents awaits you. You open the first one and find a beautiful coat with a big rip down the side. You open the second present and find a puzzle with several pieces missing. The next present is a toy car with a broken wheel. You are so hurt. Why would anyone give you presents like this? In my time, these were the kinds of gifts people were offering to God. God's law required that offerings made at the Temple be absolutely perfect, but the priests made offerings that were, at best, second rate. This did not please God at all.

I wrote this book to remind everyone that God deserves the best we can give him – not whatever is left over. Worship God with your whole heart. Obey his commandments with joy. Give generously to God's work. What does God promise for those who honour him? "I will open the windows of heaven for you and pour out all the blessings you need" (Malachi 3:10).

JESUS WATCH

In Malachi 4, God promised to send Elijah the prophet before the terrifying day of the Lord's judging. The "new Elijah" was John the Baptist, who came to prepare people for the Messiah. John told the people to turn away from their sins for the kingdom of heaven was coming soon. People came from all around to hear him preach. When they confessed their sins, John baptised them in the River Jordan. John told the people about the Messiah who was coming, one whose sandals he was not good enough to carry. Who is the Messiah? Jesus, of course! Jesus will return on the day of the Lord's judging to punish those who have refused to obey him. But those who honour and respect God will have their names written in a book to be remembered. Goodness will shine on them like the sun, and they will dance around like well-fed calves. Read about it in Malachi 4!

FAITH links

What was so bad about the things the people were giving to God?

Clue: it has something to do with respect. Why don't we surf over to Malachi 1:6–14 to check it out.

- How Do I Love You? Malachi 1:1–5
- A Half-hearted Offering, Malachi 1:6–14
- A Robbery in Progress, Malachi 3:8–10

1 This message is the word of the LORD given to Israel through Malachi.

God Loves Israel

2 The LORD said, "I have loved you."

But you ask, "How have you loved us?"

The LORD said, "Esau and Jacob were brothers. I loved Jacob, 3 but I hated Esau. I destroyed his mountain country and left his land to the wild dogs of the desert."

4 The people of Edom might say, "We were destroyed, but we will go back and rebuild the ruins."

But the LORD All-powerful says, "If they rebuild them, I will destroy them. People will say, 'Edom is a wicked country. The LORD is always angry with the Edomites.' 5 You will see these things with your own eyes. And you will say, 'The LORD is great, even outside the borders of Israel!'"

The Priests Don't Respect God

6 The LORD All-powerful says, "A child honours his father, and a servant honours his master. I am a father, so why don't you honour me? I am a master, so why don't you respect me? You priests do not respect me.

"But you ask, 'How have we shown you disrespect?'

7 "You have shown it by bringing unclean food to my altar.

"But you ask, 'What makes it unclean?'

"It is unclean because you don't respect the altar of the LORD. 8 When you bring blind animals as sacrifices, that is wrong. When you bring crippled and sick animals, that is wrong. Try giving them to your governor. Would he be pleased with you? He wouldn't accept you," says the LORD All-powerful.

9 "Now ask God to be kind to you, but he won't accept you with such offerings," says the LORD All-powerful.

10 "I wish one of you would close the Temple doors so that you would not light useless fires on my altar! I am not pleased with you and will not accept your gifts," says the LORD All-powerful.

11 "From the east to the west I will be honoured among the nations. Everywhere they will bring incense and clean offerings to me, because I will be honoured among the nations," says the LORD All-powerful.

12 "But you don't honour me. You say about the Lord's altar, 'It is unclean, and the food has no worth.' 13 You say, 'We are tired of doing this,' and you sniff at it in disgust," says the LORD All-powerful.

1:11 Reputation
How great is God's reputation?

FAITH links

HOW DO I LOVE YOU?
MALACHI 1:1-5

What do your parents or guardians do to show their love for you? You could probably come up with a list, couldn't you? The Israelites doubted God's love. So God told Malachi to remind them of his love.

There are times when we doubt God's love for us. Sometimes we need to be reminded of that love. Want a reminder of God's love? Here it is: Jesus.

The Sign of His Presence, Exodus 40:34-38, p. 130

Go for the Gold, Job 23:10, p. 685

Our Heavenly Shepherd, Psalm 23, p. 726

The "Ruler" of Our Lives, Amos 7:7-9, p. 1202

Too Busy to Worship? Luke 2:8-20, p. 1368

MVFM? Galatians 3:26-27, p. 1589

FAITH links

A HALF-HEARTED OFFERING
MALACHI 1:6-14

Suppose you asked a friend for a piece of chewing-gum and he offered you one he had already chewed. What would you think of that offering? More than likely, you would feel that you deserved better. Malachi spoke out against the half-hearted offerings the Israelites gave. In the time of Moses, God had commanded the people to offer perfectly formed animals. Now some of the people half-heartedly offered whatever animals they felt like giving. God hated those offerings. As a king, he deserved better.

Many times, we may half-heartedly offer God our service or our money. He deserves better.

Here are some more links on giving God our best:

Everyone Can Help, Numbers 4, p. 181

Your Best Work, 1 Kings 6, p. 443

Service with a Smile, 1 Chronicles 6:31–49, p. 527

Set for Life? Obadiah 2–4, p. 1208

Your Heart's Desire, Luke 16:13–15, p. 1401

Give Till It Hurts? 2 Corinthians 8:6–9; 9:6–9, p. 1578

"And you bring hurt, crippled and sick animals as gifts. You bring them as gifts, but I won't accept them from you," says the LORD. 14 "The person who cheats will be cursed. He has a male animal in his flock and promises to offer it, but then he offers to the Lord an animal that has something wrong with it. I am a great king," says the LORD All-powerful, "and I am feared by all the nations.

Rules for Priests

2 "Priests, this command is for you. 2 Listen to me. Pay attention to what I say. Honour my name," says the LORD All-powerful. "If you don't, I will send a curse on you and on your blessings. I have already cursed them, because you don't pay attention to what I say.

3 "I will punish your descendants. I will smear your faces with the animal insides left from your feasts, and you will be thrown away with it. 4 Then you will know that I am giving you this command so my agreement with Levi will continue," says the LORD All-powerful. 5 "My agreement for priests was with the tribe of Levi. I promised them life and peace so they would honour me. And they did honour me and fear me. 6 They taught the true teachings and spoke no lies. With peace and honesty they did what I said they should do, and they kept many people from sinning.

7 "A priest should teach what he knows, and people should learn the teachings from him, because he is the messenger of the LORD All-powerful. 8 But you priests have stopped obeying me. With your teachings you have caused many people to do wrong. You have broken the agreement with the tribe of Levi!" says the LORD All-powerful. 9 "You have not been careful to do what I say, but instead you take sides in court cases. So I have caused you to be hated and disgraced in front of everybody."

Judah was Not Loyal to God

10 We all have the same father; the same God made us. So why do people break their promises to each other and show no respect for the agreement our

ancestors made with God? 11 The people of Judah have broken their promises. They have done something God hates in Israel and Jerusalem: the people of Judah did not respect the Temple that the LORD loves, and the men of Judah married women who worship foreign gods. 12 Whoever does this might bring offerings to the LORD All-powerful, but the LORD will still cut that person off from the community of Israel.

13 This is another thing you do. You cover the LORD's altar with your tears. You cry and moan, because he does not accept your offerings and is not pleased with what you bring. 14 You ask, "Why?" It is because the LORD sees how you treated the wife you married when you were young. You broke your promise to her, even though she was your partner and you had an agreement with her. 15 God made husbands and wives to become one body and one spirit for his purpose—so they would have children who are true to God.

So be careful, and do not break your promise to the wife you married when you were young.

16 The LORD God of Israel says, "I hate divorce. And I hate people who do cruel things as easily as they put on clothes," says the LORD All-powerful.

So be careful. And do not break your trust.

The Special Day of Judging

17 You have tired the LORD with your words.

You ask, "How have we tired him?"

You did it by saying, "The LORD thinks anyone who does evil is good, and he is pleased with them." Or you asked, "Where is the God who is fair?"

3 The LORD All-powerful says, "I will send my messenger, who will prepare the way for me. Suddenly, the Lord you are looking for will come to his Temple; the messenger of the agreement, whom you want, will come." 2 No one can live through that time; no one can survive when he comes. He will be like a purifying fire and like laundry soap. 3 Like someone who heats and purifies silver, he will purify the Levites and make them pure like gold and silver. Then they will bring offerings to the LORD in the right way. 4 And the LORD will accept the offerings from Judah and Jerusalem, as it was in the past. 5 The LORD All-powerful says, "Then I will come to you and judge you. I will be quick to testify against those who take part in evil magic, adultery and lying under oath, those who cheat workers of their pay and who cheat widows and orphans, those who are unfair to foreigners, and those who do not respect me.

3:5
Judgement
What is God against?

Stealing from God

6 "I the LORD do not change. So you descendants of Jacob have not been destroyed. 7 Since the time of your ancestors, you have disobeyed my rules and have not kept them. Return to me, and I will return to you," says the LORD All-powerful.

"But you ask, 'How can we return?'

8 "Should a person rob God? But you are robbing me.

"You ask, 'How have we robbed you?'

"You have robbed me in your offerings and the tenth of your crops. 9 So a curse is on you, because the whole nation has robbed me. 10 Bring to the storehouse a full tenth of what you earn so there will be food in my house. Test me in this," says the LORD All-powerful. "I will open the windows of heaven for you and pour out all the blessings you need. 11 I will stop the insects so they won't eat your crops. The grapes won't fall from your vines before they are ready to pick," says the LORD All-powerful. 12 "All the nations will call you blessed, because you will have a pleasant country," says the LORD All-powerful.

The LORD's Promise of Mercy

13 The LORD says, "You have said terrible things about me.

"But you ask, 'What have we said about you?'

14 "You have said, 'It is useless to

FAITH links

A ROBBERY IN PROGRESS
MALACHI 3:8-10

Imagine how you would feel if you heard that someone had robbed your church. Yet a hold-up occurs every Sunday whenever people refuse to give either their time or their money. Malachi delivered a message to the Israelites about giving. God had commanded the people to give a tithe of their harvest to him. A tithe was 10 per cent. When the people forgot to give, God felt "robbed".

Giving to God is not a requirement because God needs what we give. God wants us to give to show the value of sharing what we have with others.

Connect here for more on sharing:

Share What You Have, Exodus 35:5–18, p. 123

Give What You Can, Numbers 7:1–11, p. 186

What's the Use? 2 Kings 12:6–12, p. 495

Wisdom About Wealth, Ecclesiastes 5:10–12, p. 878

My Favourite! Mark 10:17–23, p. 1347

Give from the Heart, Luke 21:1–4, p. 1410

---

serve God. It did no good to obey his laws and to show the LORD All-powerful that we were sorry for what we did. 15 So we say that proud people are happy. Evil people succeed. They challenge God and get away with it.'"

16 Then those who honoured the LORD spoke with each other, and the LORD listened and heard them. The names of those who honoured the LORD and respected him were written in his presence in a book to be remembered.

EMAIL FROM GOD
3:14–18 Following God
Does God care if you follow him?

17 The LORD All-powerful says, "They belong to me; on that day they will be my very own. As a parent shows mercy to his child who serves him, I will show mercy to my people. 18 You will again see the difference between good and evil people, between those who serve God and those who don't.

The Day of the LORD's Judging

4 "There is a day coming that will burn like a hot furnace, and all the proud and evil people will be like straw. On that day they will be completely burned up so that not a root or branch will be left," says the LORD All-powerful. 2 "But for you who honour me, goodness will shine on you like the sun, with healing in its rays. You will jump around, like well-fed calves. 3 Then you will crush the wicked like ashes under your feet on the day I will do this," says the LORD All-powerful.

4 "Remember the teaching of Moses my servant, those laws and rules I gave to him on Mount Sinai for all the Israelites.

5 "But I will send you Elijah the prophet before that great and terrifying day of the LORD's judging. 6 Elijah will help parents love their children and children love their parents. Otherwise, I will come and put a curse on the land."

THE NEW TESTAMENT

A NEW KING

Hi, everyone. You might not know a lot about me. Before I met Jesus, I was a tax collector. If you know anything about tax collectors in my time, you know that we weren't exactly the nicest guys around. Some of us (myself included) often charged people more taxes than we should – and we kept the change. Let's just say I wasn't a very popular man in town. When I began following Jesus, though, things changed! I became one of Jesus' 12 followers and later became a leader in the early church.

I wrote this book because I was a Jew who had become a follower of Jesus, or a Christian, as we were later called. I had a lot of Jewish friends who had become Christians, and I wanted them to understand that Jesus gave new meaning to God's rules. (Take a look at chapters 5—7 of my book, and you'll see me writing about Jesus' new spin on the Old Testament teachings.) I wanted all of my Jewish friends to know that the Messiah had indeed come to save his people. Hallelujah!

JESUS WATCH

Matthew gives us a beautiful picture of the Messiah promised in the Old Testament. To prove that Jesus is the promised Messiah, Matthew reaches back into the Old Testament for some words that help his readers understand who Jesus is. He often calls Jesus the "Son of David" to help his Jewish readers understand Jesus' relationship to their history, belonging to the family tree of King David. This phrase is used nine times in Matthew's book (and that's a lot, considering that same phrase is mentioned only six times in all the other Gospels). He's also called the "Servant of the Lord", connecting him with the God of the Old Testament. Matthew carefully selects stories and quotes from the Old Testament to help his Jewish readers understand just who Jesus is.

my FAVOURITE links

OTHER CONNECTIONS

Livin' it

Want to know how to be the greatest kid ever? Check out what Jesus has to say about serving others by connecting to Being the GREATEST! Matthew 25:14–30.

GET THE INFO

Find out more about some important people and events in Jesus' ministry by downloading these sites:

- Jesus' Sermon Notes, Matthew 5:40. Link here for more information about Jesus' most famous sermon. It's all about how to live your life God's way.
- The Chosen Dozen, Matthew 10:1–29. Who were the men Jesus called to be his first followers? You probably can name a few, but do you know all of them? Find a list of their names by logging on here.

Do you think the religious rulers really hated Jesus?

Connect to Matthew 12 to find out what they said and wanted to do about him.

did YOU know?

CHECK OUT THESE OTHER COOL STORIES:

A get-away trip to Egypt, Matthew 2:13–15
Jesus' first sermon, Matthew 5—7
A faith that grows, Matthew 13:31–35
A deadly plot, Matthew 26:1–5

FAITH links

○ Name with a Purpose, **Matthew 1:21**

○ The Best Protection Plan, **Matthew 2:13–18**

○ Perfectly Pleasing? **Matthew 5:1–12**

○ A Word About Worry, **Matthew 6:25–34**

○ Just Say Yes! **Matthew 9:9–13**

○ Your Choice of Fruit, **Matthew 12:33–35**

○ Prove It! **Matthew 16:1–4**

○ Welcome! **Matthew 19:13–15**

○ The Greatest Commandment, **Matthew 22:36–40**

○ That Thing You Do, **Matthew 25:14–30**

○ Don't Get Mad; Get Even? **Matthew 26:57–63; 27:11–14**

○ Tell All About Him! **Matthew 28:19**

▶ **Matthew 1:1** 1274

The Family History of Jesus

1 This is the family history of Jesus Christ. He came from the family of David, and David came from the family of Abraham.

2 Abraham was the father[n] of Isaac.
Isaac was the father of Jacob.
Jacob was the father of Judah and his brothers.
3 Judah was the father of Perez and Zerah.
(Their mother was Tamar.)
Perez was the father of Hezron.
Hezron was the father of Ram.
4 Ram was the father of Amminadab.
Amminadab was the father of Nahshon.
Nahshon was the father of Salmon.
5 Salmon was the father of Boaz.
(Boaz's mother was Rahab.)
Boaz was the father of Obed.
(Obed's mother was Ruth.)
Obed was the father of Jesse.
6 Jesse was the father of King David.
David was the father of Solomon.
(Solomon's mother had been Uriah's wife.)
7 Solomon was the father of Rehoboam.
Rehoboam was the father of Abijah.
Abijah was the father of Asa.
8 Asa was the father of Jehoshaphat.
Jehoshaphat was the father of Jehoram.
Jehoram was the father of Uzziah.
9 Uzziah was the father of Jotham.
Jotham was the father of Ahaz.
Ahaz was the father of Hezekiah.
10 Hezekiah was the father of Manasseh.
Manasseh was the father of Amon.
Amon was the father of Josiah.
11 Josiah was the grandfather of Jehoiachin and his brothers.
(This was at the time that the people were taken to Babylon.)
12 After they were taken to Babylon:
Jehoiachin was the father of Shealtiel.
Shealtiel was the grandfather of Zerubbabel.
13 Zerubbabel was the father of Abiud.
Abiud was the father of Eliakim.
Eliakim was the father of Azor.

FAITH links

NAME WITH A PURPOSE
MATTHEW 1:21

Do you know what your name means? If you think about it, you might ask your parents to tell you what your name means and why they chose that name for you. Names were very important to people in Bible times. Jesus' name, which means "salvation", points to his purpose for coming to earth: to save people from sin.

If you believe in Jesus, you have a name and a purpose that is shared by millions of other believers. That name is *Christian*, which means "Christ-followers". (See Acts 11:26, p. 1484.) Since you bear the name, you can live up to it by living like Jesus.

Check out these Faithlinks to see what it means to belong to God:

The Perfect Sacrifice, Leviticus 1—7, p. 135

A Different Kind of People, Leviticus 11, p. 146

What's in a Name? Isaiah 9:6, p. 908

A Fake Apology, Hosea 6:1–7, p. 1177

Your Civic Duty, Matthew 17:24–27, p. 1304

It's Free! Ephesians 2:8–9, p. 1600

1:2 father "Father" in Jewish lists of ancestors can sometimes mean grandfather or a more distant relative.

14 Azor was the father of Zadok.
Zadok was the father of Akim.
Akim was the father of Eliud.
15 Eliud was the father of Eleazar.
Eleazar was the father of Matthan.
Matthan was the father of Jacob.
16 Jacob was the father of Joseph. Joseph was the husband of Mary, and Mary was the mother of Jesus. Jesus is called the Christ.

17 So there were fourteen generations from Abraham to David. And there were fourteen generations from David until the people were taken to Babylon. And there were fourteen generations from the time when the people were taken to Babylon until Christ was born.

The Birth of Jesus Christ

18 This is how the birth of Jesus Christ came about. His mother Mary was engaged[n] to marry Joseph, but before they married, she learned she was pregnant by the power of the Holy Spirit. 19 Because Mary's husband, Joseph, was a good man, he did not want to disgrace her in public, so he planned to divorce her secretly.

20 While Joseph thought about these things, an angel of the Lord came to him in a dream. The angel said, "Joseph, descendant of David, don't be afraid to take Mary as your wife, because the baby in her is from the Holy Spirit. 21 She will give birth to a son, and you will name him Jesus,[n] because he will save his people from their sins."

22 All this happened to bring about what the Lord had said through the prophet: 23 "The virgin will be pregnant. She will have a son, and they will name him Immanuel,"[n] which means "God is with us".

24 When Joseph woke up, he did what the Lord's angel had told him to do. Joseph took Mary as his wife, 25 but he did not have sexual relations with her until she gave birth to the son. And Joseph named him Jesus.

Wise Men Come to Visit Jesus

2 Jesus was born in the town of Bethlehem in Judea during the time when

---

FAITH links

THE GIFT OF WORSHIP
MATTHEW 2:10-12

How far do you have to go to worship God? More than likely, the church you attend isn't very far away. The wise men travelled hundreds of miles from their homeland in the east to worship the newborn king, Jesus. They had followed a star in the night sky, which foretold the birth of a great king. They honoured him by giving him gifts worthy of a king.

Like the wise men, we can offer Jesus the gift of worship. This gift can be offered anytime, anywhere. Worship is a gift that is more valuable than gold. What are some ways you worship Jesus?

My Worship Place, Genesis 35:1–14, p. 49

A Thanksgiving Reminder, Exodus 12, p. 91

A Reminder to Be Fair, 2 Chronicles 19:5–11, p. 583

You're Invited! Psalm 100, p. 784

A Friend of Jesus, John 15:9–17, p. 1450

One of the Faithful, Acts 10:1–34, p. 1482

1:18 engaged For the Jewish people an engagement was a lasting agreement, which could only be broken by a divorce. If a bride-to-be was unfaithful, it was considered adultery, and she could be put to death.
1:21 Jesus The name Jesus means "salvation".
1:23 "The virgin . . . Immanuel," Quotation from Isaiah 7:14.

Herod was king. When Jesus was born, some wise men from the east came to Jerusalem. 2 They asked, "Where is the baby who was born to be the king of the Jews? We saw his star in the east and have come to worship him."

3 When King Herod heard this, he was troubled, as well as all the people in Jerusalem. 4 Herod called a meeting of all the leading priests and teachers of the law and asked them where the Christ would be born. 5 They answered, "In the town of Bethlehem in Judea. The prophet wrote about this in the Scriptures:

6 'But you, Bethlehem, in the land of
  Judah,
 are important among the tribes of
  Judah.
 A ruler will come from you
  who will be like a shepherd for my
   people Israel.'"   *Micah 5:2*

7 Then Herod had a secret meeting with the wise men and learned from them the exact time they first saw the star. 8 He sent the wise men to Bethlehem, saying, "Look carefully for the child. When you find him, come and tell me so I can worship him too."

9 After the wise men heard the king, they left. The star that they had seen in the east went before them until it stopped above the place where the child was. 10 When the wise men saw the star, they were filled with joy. 11 They came to the house where the child was and saw him with his mother, Mary, and they bowed down and worshipped him. They opened their gifts and gave him treasures of gold, frankincense and myrrh. 12 But God warned the wise men in a dream not to go back to Herod, so they returned to their own country by a different way.

Jesus' Parents Take Him to Egypt

13 After they left, an angel of the Lord came to Joseph in a dream and said, "Get up! Take the child and his mother and escape to Egypt, because Herod is starting to look for the child so he can kill him. Stay in Egypt until I tell you to return."

14 So Joseph got up and left for Egypt during the night with the child and his mother. 15 And Joseph stayed in Egypt until Herod died. This happened to bring about what the Lord had said through

---

FAITH links

THE BEST PROTECTION PLAN
MATTHEW 2:13-18

Who do you trust for protection when you're scared? A parent or guardian? A big brother or sister? When Jesus was a child, a jealous king wanted to have him killed. This king, Herod, didn't like the fact that the wise men called Jesus the "king of the Jews" (look at Matthew 2:2). Herod wanted that title all to himself! But God wouldn't let anything happen to the One he had sent to save the world. In a series of dreams, God let Joseph know where to take Jesus to keep him safe. That's the kind of protection you can count on.

Surf on over here to find out how God cares for you:

A Major Problem, Genesis 15:6, p. 20

Forgive Instead, Genesis 33, p. 47

God's Pep Talk, Joshua 1:5–9, p. 276

A Hopeful Name, Hosea 1:3–11, p. 1172

Justice Desserts, Habakkuk 2:4–8, p. 1237

Hard Times, 2 Corinthians 1:8–10, p. 1570

the prophet: "I called my son out of Egypt."[n]

Herod Kills the Baby Boys

16 When Herod saw that the wise men had tricked him, he was furious. So he gave an order to kill all the baby boys in Bethlehem and in the surrounding area who were two years old or younger. This was in keeping with the time he learnt from the wise men. 17 So what God had said through the prophet Jeremiah came true:
18 "A voice was heard in Ramah
of painful crying and deep sadness:
Rachel crying for her children.
She refused to be comforted,
because her children are dead."
Jeremiah 31:15

Joseph and Mary Return

19 After Herod died, an angel of the Lord spoke to Joseph in a dream while he was in Egypt. 20 The angel said, "Get up! Take the child and his mother and go to the land of Israel, because the people who were trying to kill the child are now dead."
21 So Joseph took the child and his mother and went to Israel. 22 But he heard that Archelaus was now king in Judea since his father Herod had died. So Joseph was afraid to go there. After being warned in a dream, he went to the area of Galilee, 23 to a town called Nazareth, and lived there. And so what God had said through the prophets came true: "He will be called a Nazarene."[n]

The Work of John the Baptist

3 About that time John the Baptist began preaching in the desert area of Judea. 2 John said, "Change your hearts and lives because the kingdom of heaven is near." 3 John the Baptist is the one Isaiah the prophet was talking about when he said:
"This is a voice of one
who calls out in the desert:
'Prepare the way for the Lord.
Make the road straight for him.'"
Isaiah 40:3
4 John's clothes were made from camel's hair, and he wore a leather belt around his waist. For food, he ate locusts and wild honey. 5 Many people came from

---

FAITH links

A CHANGE OF HEART
MATTHEW 3:1-12

"I'm sorry." Have you said that lately? When we do wrong, many of us are quick to say it, but slow to really mean it.

When John the Baptist told the Israelites to "change your hearts and lives", he meant one thing: repent. To *repent* means more than just saying you're sorry for something you did wrong. It also involves making a decision to avoid doing what you did wrong. That takes action! But you're not in it alone. When you want to make a change, just ask God. He's always glad to help!

Can't Live Without It? Genesis 3, p. 7

Alone and Forgotten? Genesis 40:23, p. 57

The Weak Link, Judges 16, p. 334

A Life-Saving Message, Esther 2:19–22, p. 650

Red to White, Isaiah 1:18, p. 896

The Sin Habit, Romans 7:15–20, p. 1527

2:15 "I called . . . Egypt." Quotation from Hosea 11:1.
2:23 Nazarene A person from the city of Nazareth, a name probably meaning "branch" (see Isaiah 11:1).

Jerusalem and Judea and all the area around the Jordan River to hear John. 6 They confessed their sins, and he baptised them in the Jordan River.

7 Many of the Pharisees and Sadducees came to the place where John was baptising people. When John saw them, he said, "You are all snakes! Who warned you to run away from God's coming punishment? 8 Do the things that show you really have changed your hearts and lives. 9 And don't think you can say to yourselves, 'Abraham is our father.' I tell you that God could make children for Abraham from these rocks. 10 The axe is now ready to cut down the trees, and every tree that does not produce good fruit will be cut down and thrown into the fire."ⁿ

11 "I baptise you with water to show that your hearts and lives have changed. But there is one coming after me who is greater than I am, whose sandals I am not good enough to carry. He will baptise you with the Holy Spirit and fire. 12 He will come ready to clean the grain, separating the good grain from the chaff. He will put the good part of the grain into his barn, but he will burn the chaff with a fire that cannot be put out.'"ⁿ

Jesus is Baptised by John

13 At that time Jesus came from Galilee to the Jordan River and wanted John to baptise him. 14 But John tried to stop him, saying, "Why do you come to me to be baptised? I need to be baptised by you!"

15 Jesus answered, "Let it be this way for now. We should do all things that are God's will." So John agreed to baptise Jesus.

16 As soon as Jesus was baptised, he came up out of the water. Then heaven opened, and he saw God's Spirit coming down on him like a dove. 17 And a voice from heaven said, "This is my Son, whom I love, and I am very pleased with him."

3:10 **The axe ... fire.** This means that God is ready to punish his people who do not obey him.
3:12 **He will ... out.** This means that Jesus will come to separate good people from bad people, saving the good and punishing the bad.

FAITH links

THE TEMPTATION FIGHTER

MATTHEW 4:1-11

How do you handle the temptation to do something wrong? When Jesus was tempted, he used the Scriptures for strength. Every time the devil tried to tempt him, Jesus would say, "It is written." Jesus relied on what God said to help him fight the devil's temptations.

Food helps our bodies grow and stay healthy. But there is another kind of food that can help us when we're tempted. That food is "spiritual food". That's what the Bible provides. It teaches us about God and helps us grow stronger in our faith. So, next time you're facing a tough temptation, remember what's written in the Bible!

Need help resisting that urge to do something wrong? Click here:

The Cloud Guide, Numbers 9:15–23, p. 188

In Deep Water, Psalm 69, p. 760

What God "Hates", Proverbs 6:16–19, p. 835

Eating Humble Pie, Daniel 4, p. 1156

The "Ruler" of Our Lives, Amos 7:7–9, p. 1202

Cut to the Quick, Hebrews 4:12, p. 1670

The Temptation of Jesus

4 Then the Spirit led Jesus into the desert to be tempted by the devil. 2 Jesus ate nothing for 40 days and nights. After this, he was very hungry. 3 The devil came to Jesus to tempt him, saying, "If you are the Son of God, tell these rocks to become bread."

4 Jesus answered, "It is written in the Scriptures, 'A person does not live by eating only bread, but by everything God says.'"*n*

5 Then the devil led Jesus to the holy city of Jerusalem and put him on a high place of the Temple. 6 The devil said, "If you are the Son of God, jump down, because it is written in the Scriptures:
'He has put his angels in charge of you.
They will catch you in their hands so that you will not hit your foot on a rock.'" *Psalm 91:11-12*

7 Jesus answered him, "It also says in the Scriptures, 'Do not test the Lord your God.'"*n*

8 Then the devil led Jesus to the top of a very high mountain and showed him all the kingdoms of the world and all their splendour. 9 The devil said, "If you will bow down and worship me, I will give you all these things."

10 Jesus said to the devil, "Go away from me, Satan! It is written in the Scriptures, 'You must worship the Lord your God and serve only him.'"*n*

4:10 Responsibility
Who is the only One you must serve?

11 So the devil left Jesus, and angels came and took care of him.

Jesus Begins Work in Galilee

12 When Jesus heard that John had been put in prison, he went back to Galilee. 13 He left Nazareth and went to live in Capernaum, a town near Lake Galilee, in the area near Zebulun and Naphtali. 14 Jesus did this to bring about what the prophet Isaiah had said:
15 "Land of Zebulun and land of Naphtali
along the sea,
beyond the Jordan River.

This is Galilee where the non-Jewish people live.
16 These people who live in darkness will see a great light.
They live in a place covered with the shadows of death,
but a light will shine on them."
Isaiah 9:1-2

Jesus Chooses Some Followers

17 From that time Jesus began to preach, saying, "Change your hearts and lives, because the kingdom of heaven is near."

18 As Jesus was walking by Lake Galilee, he saw two brothers, Simon (called Peter) and his brother Andrew. They were throwing a net into the lake because they were fishermen. 19 Jesus said, "Come follow me, and I will make you fish for people." 20 So Simon and Andrew immediately left their nets and followed him.

21 As Jesus continued walking by Lake Galilee, he saw two other brothers, James and John, the sons of Zebedee. They were in a boat with their father Zebedee, mending their nets. Jesus told them to come with him. 22 Immediately they left the boat and their father, and they followed Jesus.

Jesus Teaches and Heals People

23 Jesus went everywhere in Galilee, teaching in the synagogues, preaching the Good News about the kingdom of heaven, and healing all the people's diseases and sicknesses. 24 The news about Jesus spread all over Syria, and people brought all the sick to him. They were suffering from different kinds of diseases. Some were in great pain, some had demons, some were epileptics*n* and some

---

4:4 'A person . . . says.' Quotation from Deuteronomy 8:3.
4:7 'Do . . . God.' Quotation from Deuteronomy 6:16.
4:10 'You . . . him.' Quotation from Deuteronomy 6:13.
4:24 epileptic A person with a disease that causes them sometimes to lose control of their body and perhaps faint, shake strongly or be unable to move.

were paralysed. Jesus healed all of them. 25 Many people from Galilee, the Ten Towns,[n] Jerusalem, Judea and the land across the Jordan River followed him.

Jesus Teaches the People

5 When Jesus saw the crowds, he went up on a hill and sat down. His followers came to him, 2 and he began to teach them, saying:

3 "Those people who know they have great spiritual needs are happy, because the kingdom of heaven belongs to them.

4 Those who are sad now are happy, because God will comfort them.

5 Those who are humble are happy, because the earth will belong to them.

6 Those who want to do right more than anything else are happy, because God will fully satisfy them.

7 Those who show mercy to others are happy, because God will show mercy to them.

8 Those who are pure in their thinking are happy, because they will be with God.

9 Those who work to bring peace are happy, because God will call them his children.

10 Those who are treated badly for doing good are happy, because the kingdom of heaven belongs to them.

11 "People will insult you and hurt you. They will lie and say all kinds of evil things about you because you follow me. But when they do, you will be happy. 12 Rejoice and be glad, because you have a great reward waiting for you in heaven. People did the same evil things to the prophets who lived before you.

You are like Salt and Light

13 "You are the salt of the earth. But if the salt loses its salty taste, it cannot be

---

4:25 **Ten Towns** In Greek, called "Decapolis". It was an area east of Lake Galilee that once had ten main towns.

FAITH links

PERFECTLY PLEASING?
MATTHEW 5:1-12

Parents have their own way of letting kids know what pleases them. Some of these ways are called "rules". Think of the ones you have at home. When the rules are followed, everybody's happy, right? Not always!

Jesus once preached a sermon on a hilltop (see The Sermon on the Mount, p. 1280) to let people know how to please God. The people who are the most happy are those who trust God and want to please him. Pleasing God doesn't mean that life automatically becomes perfect. Also, God isn't expecting everyone to be perfect at pleasing him. He just wants people to be willing.

Link here to find out what else pleases God:

Serious About the Sabbath, Exodus 31:15, p. 117

The Wisdom of Obeying God, 1 Kings 11:1–13, p. 453

Good Enough? Ezekiel 8, p. 1093

A Family Meal, Mark 14:23–26, p. 1356

Helpful Hints, 3 John 11, p. 1724

made salty again. It is good for nothing, except to be thrown out and walked on. 14 "You are the light that gives light to the world. A city that is built on a hill cannot be hidden. 15 And people don't hide a light under a bowl. They put it on a lampstand so the light shines for all the people in the house. 16 In the same way, you should be a light for other people. Live so that they will see the good things you do and will praise your Father in heaven.

The Importance of the Law

17 "Don't think that I have come to destroy the law of Moses or the teaching of the prophets. I have not come to destroy them but to bring about what they said. 18 I tell you the truth, nothing will disappear from the law until heaven and earth are gone. Not even the smallest letter or the smallest part of a letter will be lost until everything has happened. 19 Whoever refuses to obey any command and teaches other people not to obey that command will be the least important in the kingdom of heaven. But whoever obeys the commands and teaches other people to obey them will be great in the kingdom of heaven. 20 I tell you that if you are no more obedient than the teachers of the law and the Pharisees, you will never enter the kingdom of heaven.

Jesus Teaches About Anger

21 "You have heard that it was said to our people long ago, 'You must not murder anyone.'" Anyone who murders another will be judged.' 22 But I tell you, if you are angry with a brother or sister," you will be judged. If you say bad things to a brother or sister, you will be judged by the council. And if you call someone a fool, you will be in danger of the fire of hell.

23 "So when you offer your gift to God at the altar, and you remember that your brother or sister has something against you, 24 leave your gift there at the altar. Go and make peace with that person, and then come and offer your gift.

25 "If your enemy is taking you to court, become friends quickly, before you go to court. Otherwise, your enemy might turn you over to the judge, and the judge might give you to a guard to put you in jail. 26 I tell you the truth, you will not leave there until you have paid everything you owe.

Jesus Teaches About Sexual Sin

27 "You have heard that it was said, 'You must not be guilty of adultery.'" 28 But I tell you that if anyone looks at a woman and wants to sin sexually with her, in his mind he has already done that sin with the woman. 29 If your right eye causes you to sin, take it out and throw it away. It is better to lose one part of your body than to have your whole body thrown into hell. 30 If your right hand causes you to sin, cut it off and throw it away. It is better to lose one part of your body than for your whole body to go into hell.

Jesus Teaches About Divorce

31 "It was also said, 'Anyone who divorces his wife must give her a written divorce paper.'" 32 But I tell you that anyone who divorces his wife forces her to be guilty of adultery. The only reason for a man to divorce his wife is if she has sexual relations with another man. And anyone who marries that divorced woman is guilty of adultery.

Make Promises Carefully

33 "You have heard that it was said to our people long ago, 'Don't break your promises, but keep the promises you make to the Lord.'" 34 But I tell you, never swear an oath. Don't swear an oath using the name of heaven, because heaven is

---

5:21 You . . . anyone. Quotation from Exodus 20:13; Deuteronomy 5:17.
5:22 brother . . . sister Although the Greek text reads "brother" here and throughout this book, Jesus' words were meant for the entire church, including men and women.
5:27 'You . . . adultery.' Quotation from Exodus 20:14; Deuteronomy 5:18.
5:31 'Anyone . . . divorce paper.' Quotation from Deuteronomy 24:1.
5:33 'Don't . . . Lord.' This refers to Leviticus 19:12; Numbers 30:2; Deuteronomy 23:21.

Matthew 5:35 1282

JESUS' SERMON NOTES Matthew 5—7

One of Jesus' most famous sermons is called the "Sermon on the Mount". (Look at Matthew 5—7.) It's called that because Jesus taught from the side of a mountain. The place where this sermon might have been given is marked today by a beautiful little church, called the "Chapel on the Mount of Beatitudes". The sermon is all about how to live life God's way.

Here are some things you might have heard of from this famous sermon:

The beatitudes, or blessings, that come by living God's way (5:1–12)
Jesus' followers are "the salt of the earth" (5:13–16)
Don't fight back (5:38–42)
Jesus' model prayer (6:9–13)
God is more important than money (6:19–24)
The most important rule (7:12)

God's throne. 35 Don't swear an oath using the name of the earth, because the earth belongs to God. Don't swear an oath using the name of Jerusalem, because that is the city of the great King. 36 Don't even swear by your own head, because you cannot make one hair on your head become white or black. 37 Say only yes if you mean yes, and no if you mean no. If you say more than yes or no, it is from the Evil One.

Don't Fight Back

38 "You have heard that it was said, 'An eye for an eye, and a tooth for a tooth.'*n* 39 But I tell you, don't stand up against an evil person. If someone slaps you on the right cheek, turn to him the other cheek as well. 40 If someone wants to sue you in court and take your shirt, let him have your coat as well. 41 If someone forces you to go with him a kilometre, go with him 2 kilometres. 42 If a person asks you for something, give it to him. Don't refuse to give to someone who wants to borrow from you.

Love All People

43 "You have heard that it was said, 'Love your neighbour'*n* and hate your enemies.' 44 But I say to you, love your enemies. Pray for those who hurt you. 45 If you do this, you will be true children of your Father in heaven. He causes the sun to rise on good people and on evil people, and he sends rain to those who do right and to those who do wrong. 46 If you love only the people who love you, you will get no reward. Even the tax collectors do that. 47 And if you are nice only to your friends, you are no better than other people. Even those who don't know God are nice to their friends. 48 So you must be perfect, just as your Father in heaven is perfect.

5:43–44
Love
Love your enemies.

5:38 'An eye . . . tooth.' Quotation from Exodus 21:24; Leviticus 24:20; Deuteronomy 19:21.
5:43 Love your neighbour Quotation from Leviticus 19:18.

Jesus Teaches About Giving

6 "Be careful! When you do good things, don't do them in front of people to be seen by them. If you do that, you will have no reward from your Father in heaven.

2 "When you give to the poor, don't be like the hypocrites. They blow trumpets in the synagogues and on the streets so that people will see them and honour them. I tell you the truth, those hypocrites already have their full reward. 3 So when you give to the poor, don't let anyone know what you are doing. 4 Your giving should be done in secret. Your Father can see what is done in secret, and he will reward you.

Jesus Teaches About Prayer

5 "When you pray, don't be like the hypocrites. They love to stand in the synagogues and on the street corners and pray so people will see them. I tell you the truth, they already have their full reward. 6 When you pray, you should go into your room and close the door and pray to your Father who cannot be seen. Your Father can see what is done in secret, and he will reward you.

7 "And when you pray, don't be like those people who don't know God. They continue saying things that mean nothing, thinking that God will hear them because of their many words. 8 Don't be like them, because your Father knows the things you need before you ask him. 9 So when you pray, you should pray like this:
'Our Father in heaven,
may your name always be kept holy.
10 May your kingdom come
and what you want be done,
here on earth as it is in heaven.
11 Give us the food we need for each day.
12 Forgive us for our sins,
just as we have forgiven those who sinned against us.
13 And do not cause us to be tempted,
but save us from the Evil One.'
14 Yes, if you forgive others for their sins, your Father in heaven will also forgive you for your sins. 15 But if you don't forgive others, your Father in heaven will not forgive your sins.

FAITH links

OUR HEAVENLY CONNECTION

MATTHEW 6:9-13

A baby is not born with a complete understanding of how to speak. As they develop, they learn to make sounds by listening to others. When you were a baby, your parents talked to you to help you learn to communicate with them.

That's how it is with prayer. We can talk to God through prayer. When Jesus preached on the hillside (check out The Sermon on the Mount, p. 1280), he taught his followers how to pray. You can talk to God at any time and tell him whatever is on your mind. When you pray, trust that he cares and will answer.

When You're Afraid, Genesis 32:9–12, p. 45

Help to Understand, 2 Samuel 14, p. 416

A Promise from the Heart, Jeremiah 31:31–33, p. 1037

God's New Temple, Ezekiel 40—44, p. 1135

Prayer Anywhere, Mark 1:35, p. 1331

An Energy Boost, Acts 4:31, p. 1469

Jesus Teaches About Worship

16 "When you give up eating,ⁿ don't put on a sad face like the hypocrites. They make their faces look sad to show people they are giving up eating. I tell you the truth, those hypocrites already have their full reward. 17 So when you give up eating, comb your hair and wash your face. 18 Then people will not know that you are giving up eating, but your Father, whom you cannot see, will see you. Your Father sees what is done in secret, and he will reward you.

God is More Important than Money

19 "Don't store treasures for yourselves here on earth where moths and rust will destroy them and thieves can break in and steal them. 20 But store your treasures in heaven where they cannot be destroyed by moths or rust and where thieves cannot break in and steal them. 21 Your heart will be where your treasure is.

6:19–20 Money
Check out the treasures in heaven.

22 "The eye is a light for the body. If your eyes are good, your whole body will be full of light. 23 But if your eyes are evil, your whole body will be full of darkness. And if the only light you have is really darkness, then you have the worst darkness.

24 "No one can serve two masters. The person will hate one master and love the other, or will follow one master and refuse to follow the other. You cannot serve both God and worldly riches.

Don't Worry

25 "So I tell you, don't worry about the food or drink you need to live, or about the clothes you need for your body. Life is more than food, and the body is more than clothes. 26 Look at the birds in the air. They don't plant or harvest or store

---

6:16 give up eating This is called "fasting". The people would give up eating for a special time of prayer and worship to God. It was also done to show sadness and disappointment.

FAITH links

A WORD ABOUT WORRY
MATTHEW 6:25-34

What do you worry about? Do you spend time thinking about things like who your friends are, who will sit with you at lunch, or whether you'll do well in the maths test? When Jesus preached on the hillside (read about it in The Sermon on the Mount, p. 1280), he talked about worry. God wants us to stop worrying. Why? Because God promises to take care of us each day, that's why. That doesn't mean that bad things will never happen to you. It means that when they do, you will know that God cares about them and that you can talk to him about whatever happens.

Got some major worries? Connect here to find out how to be worry-free:

A Major Problem, Genesis 15:6, p. 20

God's Pep Talk, Joshua 1:5–9, p. 276

Listen Up! 1 Kings 19:11–13, p. 467

Future Hope, Joel 3:17–21, p. 1191

Blessed Are the Weak? 2 Corinthians 12:7–10, p. 1582

A Soldier's Story, 2 Timothy 2:3, p. 1653

food in barns, but your heavenly Father feeds them. And you know that you are worth much more than the birds. 27 You cannot add any time to your life by worrying about it.

28 "And why do you worry about clothes? Look at how the lilies in the field grow. They don't work or make clothes for themselves. 29 But I tell you that even Solomon with his riches was not dressed as beautifully as one of these flowers. 30 God clothes the grass in the field, which is alive today but tomorrow is thrown into the fire. So you can be even more sure that God will clothe you. Don't have so little faith! 31 Don't worry and say, 'What will we eat?' or 'What will we drink?' or 'What will we wear?' 32 The people who don't know God keep trying to get these things, and your Father in heaven knows you need them. 33 The thing you should want most is God's kingdom and doing what God wants. Then all these other things you need will be given to you. 34 So don't worry about tomorrow, because tomorrow will have its own worries. Each day has enough trouble of its own.

Be Careful About Judging Others

7 "Don't judge other people, or you will be judged. 2 You will be judged in the same way that you judge others, and the amount you give to others will be given to you.

3 "Why do you notice the little piece of dust in your friend's eye, but you don't notice the big piece of wood in your own eye? 4 How can you say to your friend, 'Let me take that little piece of dust out of your eye'? Look at yourself! You still have that big piece of wood in your own eye. 5 You hypocrite! First, take the wood out of your own eye. Then you will see clearly to take the dust out of your friend's eye.

**7:3–5
Decisions**
What do you need to do before you criticise others?

6 "Don't give holy things to dogs, and don't throw your pearls before pigs. Pigs will only trample on them, and dogs will turn to attack you.

Ask God for What You Need

7 "Ask, and God will give to you. Search, and you will find. Knock, and the

THE VERDICT IS IN?

MATTHEW 7:1-2

"You're a loser!" Have you ever heard words like that? Have you ever said words like that? Often, we find it easy to make a judgement about someone. We're not always right in our opinions about a person.

Jesus warns us not to judge others. Judging others means seeing something bad in another person. When we judge others, we will be judged. Jesus said that because he knows that we're not God. We don't have God's perfect judgement. So the next time you're tempted to judge someone, keep this word in mind: DON'T.

Download these Faithlinks to find out more about caring for others:

Family Feud, Genesis 27, p. 37

A Special Promise, Numbers 30:1–2, p. 217

Care for the Lost, Deuteronomy 22:1–3, p. 255

A Gentle Answer, Proverbs 15:1, p. 847

You Are What You Do, Proverbs 20:11, p. 854

Ya' Gotta Love It? 1 John 2:15, p. 1715

door will open for you. 8 Yes, everyone who asks will receive. Everyone who searches will find. And everyone who knocks will have the door opened.

9 "If your children ask for bread, which of you would give them a stone? 10 Or if your children ask for a fish, would you give them a snake? 11 Even though you are bad, you know how to give good gifts to your children. How much more will your heavenly Father give good things to those who ask him!

The Most Important Rule

12 "Do to others what you want them to do to you. This is the meaning of the law of Moses and the teaching of the prophets.

The Way to Heaven is Hard

13 "Enter through the narrow gate. The gate is wide and the road is wide that leads to hell, and many people enter through that gate. 14 But the gate is small and the road is narrow that leads to true life. Only a few people find that road.

People Know You by Your Actions

15 "Be careful of false prophets. They come to you looking gentle like sheep, but they are really dangerous like wolves. 16 You will know these people by what they do. Grapes don't come from thornbushes, and figs don't come from thorny weeds. 17 In the same way, every good tree produces good fruit, but a bad tree produces bad fruit. 18 A good tree cannot produce bad fruit, and a bad tree cannot produce good fruit. 19 Every tree that does not produce good fruit is cut down and thrown into the fire. 20 In the same way, you will know these false prophets by what they do.

21 "Not all those who say that I am their Lord will enter the kingdom of heaven. The only people who will enter the kingdom of heaven are those who do what my Father in heaven wants. 22 On the last day many people will say to me, 'Lord, Lord, we spoke for you, and through you we forced out demons and did many miracles.' 23 Then I will tell them clearly, 'Get away from me, you who do evil. I never knew you.'

7:21 Eternal Life — Who will enter heaven?

Two Kinds of People

24 "Everyone who hears my words and obeys them is like a wise man who built his house on rock. 25 It rained hard,

---

FAITH links

ASK, SEARCH, KNOCK
MATTHEW 7:7-10

Have you ever wanted to ask for something, but weren't sure what to ask? Jesus knew that people don't always know what to ask God for. That's why he told his followers to "ask, search and knock". This means to keep on asking for what you need.

Does this mean that God will automatically give us what we ask for if we keep asking him? No. God knows what we need. He answers prayer three ways: "Yes", "No" and "Wait". The final decision is always up to him. He just wants us to keep on asking!

Approaching God, Numbers 3:10, p. 180

Who Do You Trust? Joshua 9, p. 287

Keep On Praying, 1 Samuel 1, p. 354

Plan for Success, 1 Chronicles 14:8–17, p. 538

Think About Him, Isaiah 26:3, p. 926

When We Agree, Matthew 18:19–20, p. 1306

the floods came and the winds blew and hit that house. But it did not fall, because it was built on rock. 26 Everyone who hears my words and does not obey them is like a foolish man who built his house on sand. 27 It rained hard, the floods came and the winds blew and hit that house, and it fell with a big crash."

28 When Jesus finished saying these things, the people were amazed at his teaching, 29 because he did not teach like their teachers of the law. He taught like a person who had authority.

Jesus Heals a Sick Man

8 When Jesus came down from the hill, great crowds followed him. 2 Then a man with a skin disease came to Jesus. The man bowed down before him and said, "Lord, you can heal me if you will." 3 Jesus reached out his hand and touched the man and said, "I will. Be healed!" And immediately the man was healed of his disease. 4 Then Jesus said to him, "Don't tell anyone about this. But go and show yourself to the priest[n] and offer the gift Moses commanded[n] for people who are made well. This will show the people what I have done."

Jesus Heals a Soldier's Servant

5 When Jesus entered the city of Capernaum, an army officer came to him, begging for help. 6 The officer said, "Lord, my servant is at home in bed. He can't move his body and is in much pain."

7 Jesus said to the officer, "I will go and heal him."

8 The officer answered, "Lord, I am not worthy for you to come into my house. You only need to command it, and my servant will be healed. 9 I, too, am a man under the authority of others, and I have soldiers under my command. I tell one soldier, 'Go,' and he goes. I tell another soldier, 'Come,' and he comes. I say to my servant, 'Do this,' and my servant does it."

10 When Jesus heard this, he was amazed. He said to those who were following him, "I tell you the truth, this is the greatest faith I have found, even in Israel. 11 Many people will come from the east and from the west and will sit and eat with Abraham, Isaac and Jacob in the kingdom of heaven. 12 But those people who should be in the kingdom will be thrown outside into the darkness, where people will cry and grind their teeth with pain."

8:12 Hell What will the people in hell be doing?

13 Then Jesus said to the officer, "Go home. Your servant will be healed just as you believed he would." And his servant was healed that same hour.

Jesus Heals Many People

14 When Jesus went to Peter's house, he saw that Peter's mother-in-law was sick in bed with a fever. 15 Jesus touched her hand, and the fever left her. Then she stood up and began to serve Jesus.

16 That evening people brought to Jesus many who had demons. Jesus spoke and the demons left them, and he healed all the sick. 17 He did these things to bring about what Isaiah the prophet had said:

"He took our suffering on him
and carried our diseases." *Isaiah 53:4*

People Want to Follow Jesus

18 When Jesus saw the crowd around him, he told his followers to go to the other side of the lake. 19 Then a teacher of the law came to Jesus and said, "Teacher, I will follow you wherever you go."

20 Jesus said to him, "The foxes have holes to live in, and the birds have nests, but the Son of Man has no place to rest his head."

21 Another man, one of Jesus' followers, said to him, "Lord, first let me go and bury my father."

22 But Jesus told him, "Follow me, and let the people who are dead bury their own dead."

8:4 show . . . priest The law of Moses said a priest must say when a Jewish person with a skin disease was well.

8:4 Moses commanded Read about this in Leviticus 14:1-32.

Jesus Calms a Storm

23 Jesus got into a boat, and his followers went with him. 24 A great storm arose on the lake so that waves covered the boat, but Jesus was sleeping. 25 His followers went to him and woke him, saying, "Lord, save us! We will drown!"

26 Jesus answered, "Why are you afraid? You don't have enough faith." Then Jesus got up and gave a command to the wind and the waves, and it became completely calm.

27 The men were amazed and said, "What kind of man is this? Even the wind and the waves obey him!"

Jesus Heals Two Men with Demons

28 When Jesus arrived at the other side of the lake in the area of the Gadarene[n] people, two men who had demons in them met him. These men lived in the burial caves and were so dangerous that people could not use the road by those caves. 29 They shouted, "What do you want with us, Son of God? Did you come here to torture us before the right time?"

30 Near that place there was a large herd of pigs feeding. 31 The demons begged Jesus, "If you make us leave these men, please send us into that herd of pigs."

32 Jesus said to them, "Go!" So the demons left the men and went into the pigs. Then the whole herd rushed down the hill into the lake and were drowned. 33 The herdsmen ran away and went into the town, where they told about all of this and what had happened to the men who had demons. 34 Then the whole town went out to see Jesus. When they saw him, they begged him to leave their area.

Jesus Heals a Paralysed Man

9 Jesus got into a boat and went back across the lake to his own town. 2 Some people brought to Jesus a man who was paralysed and lying on a mat. When Jesus saw the faith of these people, he said to the paralysed man, "Be encouraged, young man. Your sins are forgiven."

3 Some of the teachers of the law said

8:28 Gadarene From Gadara, an area south east of Lake Galilee.

FACING YOUR FEARS
MATTHEW 8:23-27

Suppose you were in a small boat in the middle of a large lake. Now suppose you faced the worst storm you've ever seen. How would you feel? Jesus' followers were used to fishing on Lake Galilee. But a sudden huge storm terrified them. Where was Jesus when this happened? In the boat, asleep! After his followers expressed their fears, Jesus stopped the storm.

Jesus will help you with any fear that you may have. When you are afraid, don't be afraid to tell him all about it. He can handle any "storm" your life can dish out.

Jesus can chase those fears away! Check it out:

The Rainbow Promise, Genesis 9:1–17, p. 14

Moses' Champion, Numbers 12, p. 192

A Really Bad Day, Job 1:20–22; 2:10, p. 661

Go for the Gold, Job 23:10, p. 685

The Unpopular Choice, Mark 15:42–43, p. 1360

Keep On Keeping On, Revelation 13:10, p. 1744

forgiven,' or to tell him, 'Stand up and walk'? 6 But I will prove to you that the Son of Man has authority on earth to forgive sins." Then Jesus said to the paralysed man, "Stand up, take your mat and go home." 7 And the man stood up and went home. 8 When the people saw this, they were amazed and praised God for giving power like this to human beings.

Jesus Chooses Matthew

9 When Jesus was leaving, he saw a man named Matthew sitting in the tax collector's booth. Jesus said to him, "Follow me," and he stood up and followed Jesus.

10 As Jesus was having dinner at Matthew's house, many tax collectors and "sinners" came and ate with Jesus and his followers. 11 When the Pharisees saw this, they asked Jesus' followers, "Why does your teacher eat with tax collectors and sinners?"

12 When Jesus heard them, he said, "It is not the healthy people who need a doctor, but the sick. 13 Go and learn what this means: 'I want kindness more than I want animal sacrifices.'[n] I did not come to invite good people but to invite sinners."

Jesus' Followers are Criticised

14 Then the followers of John[n] came to Jesus and said, "Why do we and the Pharisees often give up eating for a certain time,[n] but your followers don't?"

15 Jesus answered, "The friends of the bridegroom are not sad while he is with them. But the time will come when the bridegroom will be taken from them, and then they will give up eating.

16 "No one sews a patch of unshrunken cloth over a hole in an old coat. If he does, the patch will shrink and pull away from

---

9:3 blasphemy Saying things against God or not showing respect for God.
9:13 'I want . . . sacrifices.' Quotation from Hosea 6:6.
9:14 John John the Baptist, who preached to people about Christ's coming (Matthew 3, Luke 3).
9:14 give up . . . time This is called "fasting". The people would give up eating for a special time of prayer and worship to God. It was also done to show sadness and disappointment.

FAITH links

JUST SAY YES!
MATTHEW 9:9-13

Imagine Jesus coming up to you in the school playground and asking you to work with him. What would you say? Jesus often did that in the Bible. He approached people where they were working and living and asked them to come and work with him.

Jesus didn't look for those people who were rich or important. He looked for people who would be faithful to him. When you are asked to do something for Jesus, you should always be ready to respond and help. A willing heart that is ready to work for Jesus is very pleasing to him.

The Sacrifice, Genesis 22, p. 29

Play Fair or Play Favourites? Deuteronomy 1:16–18, p. 227

Peace in the Family, Psalm 133, p. 811

Best Seat in the House, Luke 14:7–11, p. 1398

Glad to Help! Romans 15:17–20, p. 1541

Hot, Cold or In Between? Revelation 3:15, p. 1735

---

to themselves, "This man speaks as if he were God. That is blasphemy!"[n]

4 Knowing their thoughts, Jesus said, "Why are you thinking evil thoughts? 5 Which is easier: to say, 'Your sins are

the coat, making the hole worse. 17 Also, people never pour new wine into old leather bags. Otherwise, the bags will break, the wine will spill and the wine bags will be ruined. But people always pour new wine into new wine bags. Then both will continue to be good."

Jesus Gives Life to a Dead Girl and Heals a Sick Woman

18 While Jesus was saying these things, a leader of the synagogue came to him. He bowed down before Jesus and said, "My daughter has just died. But if you come and lay your hand on her, she will live again." 19 So Jesus and his followers stood up and went with the leader.

20 Then a woman who had been bleeding for twelve years came behind Jesus and touched the edge of his coat. 21 She was thinking, "If I can just touch his clothes, I will be healed."

22 Jesus turned and saw the woman and said, "Be encouraged, dear woman. You are made well because you believed." And the woman was healed from that moment on.

23 Jesus continued along with the leader and went into his house. There he saw the funeral musicians and many people crying. 24 Jesus said, "Go away. The girl is not dead, only asleep." But the people laughed at him. 25 After the crowd had been thrown out of the house, Jesus went into the girl's room and took hold of her hand, and she stood up. 26 The news about this spread all around the area.

Jesus Heals More People

27 When Jesus was leaving there, two blind men followed him. They cried out, "Have mercy on us, Son of David!"

28 After Jesus went inside, the blind men went with him. He asked the men, "Do you believe that I can make you see again?"

They answered, "Yes, Lord."

29 Then Jesus touched their eyes and said, "Because you believe I can make you see again, it will happen." 30 Then the men were able to see. But Jesus warned them strongly, saying, "Don't tell anyone about this." 31 But the blind men left and spread the news about Jesus all around that area.

32 When the two men were leaving, some people brought another man to Jesus. This man could not talk because he had a demon in him. 33 After Jesus forced

---

FAITH links

KINDNESS FIRST
MATTHEW 9:35-36

When you approach a crowd of kids at the park or in the corridor at school, what's the first think you think of? Are you thinking about the kid you want to avoid because he made fun of you the other day? Or why that girl doesn't dress better? Jesus' first thought was usually a kind one. He could not move through a crowd without helping someone.

Can you think of someone who could use a kind word or a kind act? Let Jesus' example inspire you to move out in kindness.

Connect to these other links on being the "kind" of kid who pleases God:

Fairness for All, Deuteronomy 24:17, p. 258

Helpful Advice, Job 12:4–5, p. 673

The Problem with Gossip, Proverbs 11:12–13, p. 840

Jesus' Mission and Yours, Isaiah 61:1–2, p. 978

Love Him? Show It! Amos 2:6–7, p. 1196

Welcome! Matthew 19:13–15, p. 1307

THE CHOSEN DOZEN   Matthew 10:1–29

Jesus chose 12 men to work closely with him in his ministry. Some people think he picked 12 because that's how many tribes there were in Israel. Jesus had many more people that helped him in his ministry, but these 12 were his inner circle. Of his 12 followers, 3 were Jesus' closest friends: Peter, James and John.

These 12 men are sometimes called "followers" and sometimes called "apostles". A follower is a person who is learning from someone else. An apostle is someone with a special message or commission. (Check out John 13:16, p. 1447.) These men were both. They followed Jesus and learned from him. Then when he was gone, they carried on his work. The 12 were Simon Peter, Andrew, James the son of Zebedee, John, Philip, Bartholomew, Matthew, Thomas, Simon, James the son of Alphaeus, Thaddaeus and Judas, who betrayed Jesus. (See Matthew 10:1–4.) Matthias was chosen by the apostles to replace Judas after Jesus left earth and went back to heaven. (Read Acts 1:26, p. 1464.)

---

the demon to leave the man, he was able to speak. The crowd was amazed and said, "We have never seen anything like this in Israel."

34 But the Pharisees said, "The prince of demons is the one that gives him power to force demons out."

35 Jesus travelled through all the towns and villages, teaching in their synagogues, preaching the Good News about the kingdom and healing all kinds of diseases and sicknesses. 36 When he saw the crowds, he felt sorry for them because they were hurting and helpless, like sheep without a shepherd. 37 Jesus said to his followers, "There are many people to harvest but only a few workers to help harvest them. 38 Pray to the Lord, who owns the harvest, that he will send more workers to gather his harvest."*n*

Jesus Sends Out His Apostles

10 Jesus called his twelve followers together and gave them authority to drive out evil spirits and to heal every kind of disease and sickness. 2 These are the names of the twelve apostles: Simon (also called Peter) and his brother Andrew; James son of Zebedee, and his brother John; 3 Philip and Bartholomew; Thomas and Matthew, the tax collector; James son of Alphaeus, and Thaddaeus; 4 Simon the Zealot and Judas Iscariot, who turned against Jesus.

5 Jesus sent out these twelve men with the following order: "Don't go to the non-Jewish people or to any town where the Samaritans live. 6 But go to the people of Israel, who are like lost sheep. 7 When you go, preach this: 'The kingdom of heaven is near.' 8 Heal the sick, raise the dead to life again, heal those who have skin diseases and force demons out of people. I give you these powers freely, so help other people freely. 9 Don't carry any money with

---

9:37-38 "There are . . . harvest." As a farmer sends workers to harvest the grain, Jesus sends his followers to bring people to God.

you—gold or silver or copper. 10 Don't carry a bag or extra clothes or sandals or a walking stick. Workers should be given what they need.

11 "When you enter a city or town, find some worthy person there and stay in that home until you leave. 12 When you enter that home, say, 'Peace be with you.' 13 If the people there welcome you, let your peace stay there. But if they don't welcome you, take back the peace you wished for them. 14 And if a home or town refuses to welcome you or listen to you, leave that place and shake its dust off your feet.[n] 15 I tell you the truth, on the Judgement Day it will be better for the towns of Sodom and Gomorrah[n] than for the people of that town.

Jesus Warns His Apostles

16 "Listen, I am sending you out like sheep among wolves. So be as clever as snakes and as innocent as doves. 17 Be careful of people, because they will arrest you and take you to court and whip you in their synagogues. 18 Because of me you will be taken to stand before governors and kings, and you will tell them and the non-Jewish people about me. 19 When you are arrested, don't worry about what to say or how to say it. At that time you will be given the things to say. 20 It will not really be you speaking but the Spirit of your Father speaking through you.

21 "Brothers will give their own brothers to be killed, and fathers will give their own children to be killed. Children will fight against their own parents and have them put to death. 22 All people will hate you because you follow me, but those people who keep their faith until the end will be saved. 23 When you are treated badly in one city, run to another city. I tell you the truth, you will not finish going through all the cities of Israel before the Son of Man comes.

24 "A student is not better than his teacher, and a servant is not better than his master. 25 A student should be satisfied to become like his teacher; a servant should be satisfied to become like his master. If the head of the family is called Beelzebul, then the other members of the family will be called worse names!

Fear God, Not People

26 "So don't be afraid of those people, because everything that is hidden will be shown. Everything that is secret will be made known. 27 I tell you these things in the dark, but I want you to tell them in the light. What you hear whispered in your ear you should shout from the house-tops. 28 Don't be afraid of people, who can kill the body but cannot kill the soul. The only one you should fear is the one who can destroy the soul and the body in hell. 29 Two sparrows cost only a penny, but not even one of them can die without your Father's knowing it. 30 God even knows how many hairs are on your head. 31 So don't be afraid. You are worth much more than many sparrows.

Tell People About Your Faith

32 "All those who stand before others and say they believe in me, I will say before my Father in heaven that they belong to me. 33 But all who stand before others and say they do not believe in me, I will say before my Father in heaven that they do not belong to me.

34 "Don't think that I came to bring peace to the earth. I did not come to bring peace, but a sword. 35 I have come so that

'a son will be against his father,
a daughter will be against her mother,
a daughter-in-law will be against her mother-in-law.

36 A person's enemies will be members of his own family.' *Micah 7:6*

37 "Those who love their father or mother more than they love me are not worthy to be my followers. Those who

10:22 Perseverance
What will you get for keeping on despite rejection?

10:14 shake . . . feet. A warning. It showed that they had rejected these people.
10:15 Sodom and Gomorrah Two cities that God destroyed because the people were so evil.

love their son or daughter more than they love me are not worthy to be my followers. 38 Whoever is not willing to carry the cross and follow me is not worthy of me. 39 Those who try to hold on to their lives will give up true life. Those who give up their lives for me will hold on to true life. 40 Whoever accepts you also accepts me, and whoever accepts me also accepts the One who sent me. 41 Whoever meets a prophet and accepts him will receive the reward of a prophet. And whoever accepts a good person because that person is good will receive the reward of a good person. 42 Those who give one of these little ones a cup of cold water because they are my followers will truly get their reward."

Jesus and John the Baptist

11 After Jesus finished telling these things to his twelve followers, he left there and went to the towns in Galilee to teach and preach.

2 John the Baptist was in prison, but he heard about what Christ was doing. So John sent some of his followers to Jesus. 3 They asked him, "Are you the One who is to come, or should we wait for someone else?"

4 Jesus answered them, "Go and tell John what you hear and see: 5 the blind can see, the crippled can walk and people with skin diseases are healed. The deaf can hear, the dead are raised to life and the Good News is preached to the poor. 6 Those who do not stumble in their faith because of me are blessed."

7 As John's followers were leaving, Jesus began talking to the people about John. Jesus said, "What did you go out into the desert to see? A reed[n] blown by the wind? 8 What did you go out to see? A man dressed in fine clothes? No, those who wear fine clothes live in kings' palaces. 9 So why did you go out? To see a prophet? Yes, and I tell you, John is more than a prophet. 10 This was written about him:
'I will send my messenger ahead of you,
who will prepare the way for you.'
Malachi 3:1
11 I tell you the truth, John the Baptist is greater than any other person ever born, but even the least important person in the kingdom of heaven is greater than John. 12 Since the time John the Baptist came until now, the kingdom of heaven has been going forwards in strength, and people have been trying to take it by force. 13 All the prophets and the law of Moses told about what would happen until the time John came. 14 And if you will believe what they said, you will believe that John is Elijah, whom they said would come. 15 You people who can hear me, listen!

16 "What can I say about the people of this time? What are they like? They are like children sitting in the market place, who call out to each other,

17 'We played music for you, but you did not dance;
we sang a sad song, but you did not cry.'

18 John came and did not eat or drink like other people. So people say, 'He has a demon.' 19 The Son of Man came, eating and drinking, and people say, 'Look at him! He eats too much and drinks too much wine, and he is a friend of tax collectors and sinners.' But wisdom is proved to be right by what it does."

Jesus Warns Unbelievers

20 Then Jesus criticised the cities where he did most of his miracles, because the people did not change their lives and stop sinning. 21 He said, "How terrible for you, Korazin! How terrible for you, Bethsaida![n] If the same miracles I did in you had happened in Tyre and Sidon,[n] those people would have changed their lives a long time ago. They would have worn rough cloth and put ashes on themselves to show they had changed. 22 But I tell you, on the Judgement Day it will be better for Tyre and Sidon than for you. 23 And you, Capernaum,[n] will you be lifted up to

---

11:7 reed This means that John was not ordinary or weak like grass blown by the wind.
11:21 Korazin . . . Bethsaida Towns by Lake Galilee where Jesus preached to the people.
11:21 Tyre and Sidon Towns where wicked people lived.
11:23 Capernaum A town by Lake Galilee where Jesus preached to the people.

heaven? No, you will be thrown down to the depths. If the miracles I did in you had happened in Sodom,* its people would have stopped sinning, and it would still be a city today. 24 But I tell you, on the Judgement Day it will be better for Sodom than for you."

Jesus Offers Rest to People

25 At that time Jesus said, "I praise you, Father, Lord of heaven and earth, because you have hidden these things from the people who are wise and clever. But you have shown them to those who are like little children. 26 Yes, Father, this is what you really wanted.

27 "My Father has given me all things. No one knows the Son, except the Father. And no one knows the Father, except the Son and those whom the Son chooses to tell.

28 "Come to me, all of you who are tired and have heavy loads, and I will give you rest. 29 Accept my teachings and learn from me, because I am gentle and humble in spirit, and you will find rest for your lives. 30 The teaching that I ask you to accept is easy; the load I give you to carry is light."

11:30 Troubles
How can Jesus help with your problems?

Jesus is Lord of the Sabbath

12 At that time Jesus was walking through some fields of grain on a Sabbath day. His followers were hungry, so they began to pick the grain and eat it. 2 When the Pharisees saw this, they said to Jesus, "Look! Your followers are doing what is unlawful to do on the Sabbath day."

3 Jesus answered, "Have you not read what David did when he and the people with him were hungry? 4 He went into God's house, and he and those with him ate the holy bread, which was lawful only for priests to eat. 5 And have you not read in the law of Moses that on every Sabbath day the priests in the Temple break this law about the Sabbath day? But the priests are not wrong for doing that. 6 I tell you that there is something here that is greater than the Temple. 7 The Scripture says, 'I want kindness more than I want animal sacrifices.'* You don't really know what those words mean. If you understood them, you would not judge those who have done nothing wrong.

8 "So the Son of Man is Lord of the Sabbath day."

Jesus Heals a Man's Hand

9 Jesus left there and went into their synagogue, 10 where there was a man with a crippled hand. They were looking for a reason to accuse Jesus, so they asked him, "Is it right to heal on the Sabbath day?"*

11 Jesus answered, "If any of you has a sheep, and it falls into a ditch on the Sabbath day, you will help it out of the ditch. 12 Surely a human being is more important than a sheep. So it is lawful to do good things on the Sabbath day."

13 Then Jesus said to the man with the crippled hand, "Hold out your hand." The man held out his hand, and it became well again, like the other hand. 14 But the Pharisees left and made plans to kill Jesus.

Jesus is God's Chosen Servant

15 Jesus knew what the Pharisees were doing, so he left that place. Many people followed him, and he healed all who were sick. 16 But Jesus warned the people not to tell who he was. 17 He did these things to bring about what Isaiah the prophet had said:

18 "Here is my servant whom I have
    chosen.
  I love him, and I am pleased with
    him.
  I will put my Spirit upon him,
    and he will tell of my justice to all
      people.
19 He will not argue or cry out;
  no one will hear his voice in the
    streets.

11:23 Sodom A city that God destroyed because the people were so evil
12:7 'I . . . sacrifices.' Quotation from Hosea 6:6.
12:10 "Is it right . . . day?" It was against Jewish law to work on the Sabbath day.

20 He will not break a crushed blade of grass
or put out even a weak flame
until he makes justice win the victory.
21 In him will the non-Jewish people find hope." *Isaiah 42:1-4*

Jesus' Power is from God

22 Then some people brought to Jesus a man who was blind and could not talk, because he had a demon. Jesus healed the man so that he could talk and see. 23 All the people were amazed and said, "Perhaps this man is the Son of David!" 24 When the Pharisees heard this, they said, "Jesus uses the power of Beelzebul, the ruler of demons, to force demons out of people."

25 Jesus knew what the Pharisees were thinking, so he said to them, "Every kingdom that is divided against itself will be destroyed. And any city or family that is divided against itself will not continue. 26 And if Satan forces out himself, then Satan is divided against himself, and his kingdom will not continue. 27 You say that I use the power of Beelzebul to force out demons. If that is true, then what power do your people use to force out demons? So they will be your judges. 28 But if I use the power of God's Spirit to force out demons, then the kingdom of God has come to you.

29 "If anyone wants to enter a strong person's house and steal his things, he must first tie up the strong person. Then he can steal the things from the house.

30 "Whoever is not with me is against me. Whoever does not work with me is working against me. 31 So I tell you, people can be forgiven for every sin and everything they say against God. But whoever speaks against the Holy Spirit will not be forgiven. 32 Anyone who speaks against the Son of Man can be forgiven, but anyone who speaks against the Holy Spirit will not be forgiven, now or in the future.

People Know You by Your Words

33 "If you want good fruit, you must make the tree good. If your tree is not good, it will have bad fruit. A tree is known by the kind of fruit it produces. 34 You snakes! You are evil people, so how can you say anything good? The mouth speaks the things that are in the heart. 35 Good people have good things in their hearts, and so they say good things. But evil people have evil in their hearts, so they say evil things. 36 And I tell you that on the Judgement Day people will be responsible

---

FAITH links

YOUR CHOICE OF FRUIT
MATTHEW 12:33-35

Would you expect a fruit tree that has been lovingly cared for to produce rotten fruit? Probably not, right? A good tree produces good fruit. A bad tree . . . well, you get the idea. Jesus used that story to talk about our words. A heart full of love will cause a person to say kind and loving things. A heart full of hate or evil will cause a person to say mean and hateful things. Anyone who hangs around you will know the kind of "tree" you are. So, what kind of fruit are you producing?

Who Do You Prefer? Proverbs 3:32, p. 830

The Right Ingredients, Micah 6:8, p. 1227

How Do I Love You? Malachi 1:1–5, p. 1267

Welcome! Matthew 19:13–15, p. 1307

Who Needs Love? Luke 6:27–36, p. 1379

Full of Faith, 1 Thessalonians 4:1, p. 1633

12:36 Judgement
Will God judge the words you speak?

for every careless thing they have said. 37 The words you have said will be used to judge you. Some of your words will prove you right, but some of your words will prove you guilty."

The People Ask for a Miracle

38 Then some of the Pharisees and teachers of the law answered Jesus, saying, "Teacher, we want to see you work a miracle as a sign."

39 Jesus answered, "Evil and sinful people are the ones who want to see a miracle for a sign. But no sign will be given to them, except the sign of the prophet Jonah. 40 Jonah was in the stomach of the big fish for three days and three nights. In the same way, the Son of Man will be in the grave three days and three nights. 41 On the Judgement Day the people from Nineveh[n] will stand up with you people who live now, and they will show that you are guilty. When Jonah preached to them, they were sorry and changed their lives. And I tell you that someone greater than Jonah is here. 42 On the Judgement Day, the Queen of the South[n] will stand up with you people who live today. She will show that you are guilty, because she came from far away to listen to Solomon's wise teaching. And I tell you that someone greater than Solomon is here.

People Today are Full of Evil

43 "When an evil spirit comes out of a person, it travels through barren places, looking for a place to rest, but it doesn't find it. 44 So the spirit says, 'I will go back to the house I left.' When the spirit comes back, it finds the house still empty, swept clean and made neat. 45 Then the evil spirit goes out and brings seven other spirits even more evil than it is, and they go in and live there. So the person has even more trouble than before. It is the same way with the evil people who live today."

Jesus' True Family

46 While Jesus was talking to the people, his mother and brothers stood outside, trying to find a way to talk to him. 47 Someone told Jesus, "Your mother and brothers are standing outside, and they want to talk to you."

48 He answered, "Who is my mother? Who are my brothers?"

12:50 God's Family
Who are Jesus' true siblings?

49 Then he pointed to his followers and said, "Here are my mother and my brothers. 50 My true brother and sister and mother and father are those who do what my Father in heaven wants."

A Story About Planting Seed

13 That same day Jesus went out of the house and sat by the lake. 2 Large crowds gathered around him, so he got into a boat and sat down, while the people stood on the shore. 3 Then Jesus used stories to teach them many things. He said: "A farmer went out to plant his seed. 4 While he was planting, some seed fell by the road, and the birds came and ate it all up. 5 Some seed fell on rocky ground, where there wasn't much earth. That seed grew very fast, because the ground was not deep. 6 But when the sun rose, the plants dried up, because they did not have deep roots. 7 Some other seed fell among thorny weeds, which grew and choked the good plants. 8 Some other seed fell on good ground where it grew and produced a crop. Some plants made 100 times more, some made 60 times more and some made 30 times more. 9 You people who can hear me, listen."

Why Jesus Used Stories to Teach

10 The followers came to Jesus and asked, "Why do you use stories to teach the people?"

12:41 Nineveh The city where Jonah preached to warn the people. Read Jonah 3.
12:42 Queen of the South The Queen of Sheba. She travelled 1,600 kilometres to learn God's wisdom from Solomon. Read 1 Kings 10:1-13.

11 Jesus answered, "You have been chosen to know the secrets about the kingdom of heaven, but others cannot know these secrets. 12 Those who have understanding will be given more, and they will have all they need. But those who do not have understanding, even what they have will be taken away from them. 13 This is why I use stories to teach the people: they see, but they don't really see. They hear, but they don't really hear or understand. 14 So they show that the things Isaiah said about them are true:

'You will listen and listen, but you will not understand.
You will look and look, but you will not learn.
15 For the minds of these people have become stubborn.
They do not hear with their ears, and they have closed their eyes.
Otherwise they might really understand
what they see with their eyes and hear with their ears.
They might really understand in their minds
and come back to me and be healed.' *Isaiah 6:9-10*

16 But you are blessed, because you see with your eyes and hear with your ears. 17 I tell you the truth, many prophets and good people wanted to see the things that you now see, but they did not see them. And they wanted to hear the things that you now hear, but they did not hear them.

Jesus Explains the Seed Story

18 "So listen to the meaning of that story about the farmer. 19 What is the seed that fell by the road? That seed is like the person who hears the message about the kingdom but does not understand it. The Evil One comes and takes away what was planted in that person's heart. 20 And what is the seed that fell on rocky ground? That seed is like the person who hears the teaching and quickly accepts it with joy. 21 But he does not let the teaching go deep into his life, so he keeps it only a short time. When trouble or persecution comes because of the teaching he accepted, he quickly gives up. 22 And what is the seed that fell among the thorny weeds? That seed is like the person who hears the teaching but lets worries about this life and the temptation of wealth stop that teaching from growing. So the teaching does not produce fruit[n] in that person's life. 23 But what is the seed that fell on the good ground? That seed is like the person who hears the teaching and understands it. That person grows and produces fruit, sometimes 100 times more, sometimes 60 times more and sometimes 30 times more."

13:23 Witnessing Find out how some hear God's Word.

A Story About Wheat and Weeds

24 Then Jesus told them another story: "The kingdom of heaven is like a man who planted good seed in his field. 25 That night, when everyone was asleep, his enemy came and planted weeds among the wheat and then left. 26 Later, the wheat grew and the heads of grain grew, but the weeds also grew. 27 Then the man's servants came to him and said, 'You planted good seed in your field. Where did the weeds come from?' 28 The man answered, 'An enemy planted weeds.' The servants asked, 'Do you want us to pull up the weeds?' 29 The man answered, 'No, because when you pull up the weeds, you might also pull up the wheat. 30 Let the weeds and the wheat grow together until the harvest time. At harvest time I will tell the workers, "First gather the weeds and tie them together to be burnt. Then gather the wheat and bring it to my barn."'"

Stories of Mustard Seed and Yeast

31 Then Jesus told another story: "The kingdom of heaven is like a mustard seed that a man planted in his field. 32 That seed is the smallest of all seeds, but when it grows, it is one of the largest

---

13:22 produce fruit To produce fruit means to have in your life the good things God wants.

garden plants. It becomes big enough for the wild birds to come and build nests in its branches."

33 Then Jesus told another story: "The kingdom of heaven is like yeast that a woman took and hid in a large bowl of flour until it made all the dough rise."

34 Jesus used stories to tell all these things to the people; he always used stories to teach them. 35 This is as the prophet said:

"I will speak using stories;
    I will tell things that have been
        secret since the world was
            made."   *Psalm 78:2*

Jesus Explains About the Weeds

36 Then Jesus left the crowd and went into the house. His followers came to him and said, "Explain to us the meaning of the story about the weeds in the field."

37 Jesus answered, "The man who planted the good seed in the field is the Son of Man. 38 The field is the world, and the good seeds are all of God's children who belong to the kingdom. The weeds are those people who belong to the Evil One. 39 And the enemy who planted the bad seed is the devil. The harvest time is the end of the world, and the workers who gather are God's angels.

40 "Just as the weeds are pulled up and burnt in the fire, so it will be at the end of the world. 41 The Son of Man will send out his angels, and they will gather out of his kingdom all who cause sin and all who do evil. 42 The angels will throw them into the blazing furnace, where the people will cry and grind their teeth with pain. 43 Then the good people will shine like the sun in the kingdom of their Father. You people who can hear me, listen.

Stories of a Treasure and a Pearl

44 "The kingdom of heaven is like a treasure hidden in a field. One day a man found the treasure, and then he hid it in the field again. He was so happy that he went and sold everything he owned to buy that field.

45 "Also, the kingdom of heaven is like a man looking for fine pearls. 46 When he found a very valuable pearl, he went and sold everything he had and bought it.

A Story of a Fishing Net

47 "Also, the kingdom of heaven is like a net that was put into the lake and caught many different kinds of fish. 48 When it was full, the fishermen pulled the net to the shore. They sat down and put all the good fish in baskets and threw away the bad fish. 49 It will be this way at the end of the world. The angels will come and separate the evil people from the good people. 50 The angels will throw the evil people into the blazing furnace, where people will cry and grind their teeth with pain."

51 Jesus asked his followers, "Do you understand all these things?"

They answered, "Yes, we understand."

52 Then Jesus said to them, "So every teacher of the law who has been taught about the kingdom of heaven is like the owner of a house. He brings out both new things and old things he has saved."

Jesus Goes to His Home Town

53 When Jesus finished teaching with these stories, he left there. 54 He went to his home town and taught the people in the synagogue, and they were amazed. They said, "Where did this man get this wisdom and this power to do miracles? 55 He is just the son of a carpenter. His mother is Mary, and his brothers are James, Joseph, Simon and Judas. 56 And all his sisters are here with us. Where then does this man get all these things?" 57 So the people were upset with Jesus.

But Jesus said to them, "A prophet is honoured everywhere except in his home town and in his own home."

58 So he did not do many miracles there because they had no faith.

How John the Baptist Was Killed

14 At that time Herod, the ruler of Galilee, heard the reports about Jesus. 2 So he said to his servants, "Jesus is John the Baptist, who has risen from the dead. That is why he can work these miracles."

3 Some time before this, Herod had arrested John, tied him up, and put him in prison. Herod did this because of Herodias, who had been the wife of Philip, Herod's brother. 4 John had been telling Herod, "It is not lawful for you to be married to Herodias." 5 Herod wanted to kill John, but he was afraid of the people, because they believed John was a prophet.

6 On Herod's birthday, the daughter of Herodias danced for Herod and his guests, and she pleased him. 7 So he promised with an oath to give her anything she wanted. 8 Herodias told her daughter what to ask for, so she said to Herod, "Give me the head of John the Baptist here on a dish." 9 Although King Herod was very sad, he had made a promise, and his dinner guests had heard him. So Herod ordered that what she asked for be done. 10 He sent soldiers to the prison to cut off John's head. 11 And they brought it on a dish and gave it to the girl, and she took it to her mother. 12 John's followers came and got his body and buried it. Then they went and told Jesus.

More than 5,000 Fed

13 When Jesus heard what had happened to John, he left in a boat and went to a lonely place by himself. But the crowds heard about it and followed him on foot from the towns. 14 When he arrived, he saw a great crowd waiting. He felt sorry for them and healed those who were sick.

15 When it was evening, his followers came to him and said, "No one lives in this place, and it is already late. Send the people away so they can go to the towns and buy food for themselves."

16 But Jesus answered, "They don't need to go away. You give them something to eat."

17 They said to him, "But we have only five loaves of bread and two fish."

18 Jesus said, "Bring the bread and the fish to me." 19 Then he told the people to sit down on the grass. He took the five loaves and the two fish and, looking up to heaven, he thanked God for the food. Jesus divided the bread and gave it to his followers, who gave it to the people. 20 All the people ate and were satisfied. Then the followers filled twelve baskets with the leftover pieces of food. 21 There were about 5,000 men there who ate, not counting women and children.

FAITH links

SAD TIMES
MATTHEW 14:13-14

Some things in life are hard. One of the hardest things to deal with is when someone you love dies. When Jesus heard that John the Baptist had been killed, he went off by himself for a while. Still the crowds followed him. Even though he probably wanted to be by himself, he took the time to heal the sick and help those around him.

When you lose someone you love, you're going to feel sad. Just know that you have a Saviour who understands what you're going through. He is always with you.

Jesus does care when you are feeling sad. Check it out:

A Message of Courage and Hope, 2 Kings 19:4–10, p. 505

Problem Solved, 2 Kings 20:1–11, p. 507

Full Circle, Job 42, p. 706

Remembering Jesus, Matthew 26:26–29, p. 1321

Mission Impossible? Mark 5:21–24, 35–43, p. 1337

Who Needs Love? Luke 6:27–36, p. 1379

Jesus Walks on the Water

22 Immediately Jesus told his followers to get into the boat and go ahead of him across the lake. He stayed there to send the people home. 23 After he had sent them away, he went by himself up into the hills to pray. It was late, and Jesus was there alone. 24 By this time, the boat was already far away from land. It was being hit by waves, because the wind was blowing against it.

25 Between three and six o'clock in the morning, Jesus came to them, walking on the water. 26 When his followers saw him walking on the water, they were afraid. They said, "It's a ghost!" and cried out in fear.

27 But Jesus quickly spoke to them, "Have courage! It is I. Do not be afraid."

28 Peter said, "Lord, if it is really you, then command me to come to you on the water."

29 Jesus said, "Come."

And Peter left the boat and walked on the water to Jesus. 30 But when Peter saw the wind and the waves, he became afraid and began to sink. He shouted, "Lord, save me!"

31 Immediately Jesus reached out his hand and caught Peter. Jesus said, "Your faith is small. Why did you doubt?"

32 After they got into the boat, the wind became calm. 33 Then those who were in the boat worshipped Jesus and said, "Truly you are the Son of God!"

34 When they had crossed the lake, they came to shore at Gennesaret. 35 When the people there recognised Jesus, they told people in the area there that Jesus had come, and they brought all their sick to him. 36 They begged Jesus to let them touch just the edge of his coat, and all who touched it were healed.

Obey God's Law

15 Then some Pharisees and teachers of the law came to Jesus from Jerusalem. They asked him, 2 "Why don't your followers obey the unwritten laws which have been handed down to us? They don't wash their hands before they eat."

3 Jesus answered, "And why do you refuse to obey God's command so that you can follow your own teachings? 4 God said, 'Honour your father and your mother,'*n* and 'Anyone who says cruel things to his father or mother must be put to death.'*n* 5 But you say a person can tell his father or mother, 'I have something I could use to help you, but I have given it to God instead.' 6 You teach that person not to honour his father or his mother. You rejected what God said for the sake of your own rules. 7 You are hypocrites! Isaiah was right when he said about you:

8 'These people show honour to me
    with words,
but their hearts are far from me.
9 Their worship of me is worthless.
    The things they teach are nothing
    but human rules.'"   *Isaiah 29:13*

10 After Jesus called the crowd to him, he said, "Listen and understand what I am saying. 11 It is not what people put into their mouths that makes them unclean. It is what comes out of their mouths that makes them unclean."

12 Then his followers came to him and asked, "Do you know that the Pharisees are angry because of what you said?"

13 Jesus answered, "Every plant that my Father in heaven has not planted himself will be pulled up by the roots. 14 Stay away from the Pharisees; they are blind leaders. And if a blind person leads a blind person, both will fall into a ditch."

15 Peter said, "Explain the example to us."

16 Jesus said, "Do you still not understand? 17 Surely you know that all the food that enters the mouth goes into the stomach and then goes out of the body. 18 But what people say with their mouths comes from the way they think; these are the things that make people unclean. 19 Out of the mind come evil thoughts, murder, adultery, sexual sins,

---

15:18 Honesty
Check out what your thoughts and speech should be like.

15:4 'Honour . . . mother.' Quotation from Exodus 20:12; Deuteronomy 5:6.
15:4 'Anyone . . . death.' Quotation from Exodus 21:17.

> **FAITH CHALLENGE**
>
> Here's a challenge for you. Read 15:11 to discover what Jesus has to say about what comes out of our mouths. How do you respond when your friends use bad language or talk about things they shouldn't?
>
> ## TeSTiNG iT
>
> **Matthew 15:11**
> It is not what people put into their mouths that makes them unclean. It is what comes out of their mouths that makes them unclean.

stealing, lying and speaking evil of others. 20 These things make people unclean; eating with unwashed hands does not make them unclean."

Jesus Helps a Non-Jewish Woman

21 Jesus left that place and went to the area of Tyre and Sidon. 22 A Canaanite woman from that area came to Jesus and cried out, "Lord, Son of David, have mercy on me! My daughter has a demon, and she is suffering very much."

23 But Jesus did not answer the woman. So his followers came to Jesus and begged him, "Tell the woman to go away. She is following us and shouting."

24 Jesus answered, "God sent me only to the lost sheep, the people of Israel."

25 Then the woman came to Jesus again and bowed before him and said, "Lord, help me!"

26 Jesus answered, "It is not right to take the children's bread and give it to the dogs."

27 The woman said, "Yes, Lord, but even the dogs eat the crumbs that fall from their masters' table."

28 Then Jesus answered, "Woman, you have great faith! I will do what you asked." And at that moment the woman's daughter was healed.

Jesus Heals Many People

29 After leaving there, Jesus went along the shore of Lake Galilee. He went up on a hill and sat there. 30 Great crowds came to Jesus, bringing with them the lame, the blind, the crippled, those who could not speak and many others. They put them at Jesus' feet, and he healed them. 31 The crowd was amazed when they saw that people who could not speak before were now able to speak. The crippled were made strong. The lame could walk, and the blind could see. And they praised the God of Israel for this.

More than 4,000 Fed

32 Jesus called his followers to him and said, "I feel sorry for these people, because they have already been with me three days, and they have nothing to eat. I don't want to send them away hungry. They might faint while going home."

33 His followers asked him, "How can we get enough bread to feed all these people? We are far away from any town."

34 Jesus asked, "How many loaves of bread do you have?"

They answered, "Seven, and a few small fish."

35 Jesus told the people to sit on the ground. 36 He took the seven loaves of bread and the fish and gave thanks to God. Then he divided the food and gave it

to his followers, and they gave it to the people. 37 All the people ate and were satisfied. Then his followers filled seven baskets with the leftover pieces of food. 38 There were about 4,000 men there who ate, besides women and children. 39 After sending the people home, Jesus got into the boat and went to the area of Magadan.

The Leaders Ask for a Miracle

16 The Pharisees and Sadducees came to Jesus, wanting to trick him. So they asked him to show them a miracle from God.

2 Jesus answered, "At sunset you say we will have good weather, because the sky is red. 3 And in the morning you say that it will be a rainy day, because the sky is dark and red. You see these signs in the sky and know what they mean. In the same way, you see the things that I am doing now, but you don't know their meaning. 4 Evil and sinful people ask for a miracle as a sign, but they will not be given any sign, except the sign of Jonah."*n* Then Jesus left them and went away.

Guard Against Wrong Teachings

5 Jesus' followers went across the lake, but they had forgotten to bring bread. 6 Jesus said to them, "Be careful! Beware of the yeast of the Pharisees and the Sadducees."

7 His followers discussed the meaning of this, saying, "He said this because we forgot to bring bread."

8 Knowing what they were talking about, Jesus asked them, "Why are you talking about not having bread? Your faith is small. 9 Do you still not understand? Remember the five loaves of bread that fed the 5,000? And remember that you filled many baskets with the leftovers? 10 Or the seven loaves of bread that fed the 4,000 and the many baskets you then also filled? 11 I was not talking to you about bread. Why don't you understand that? I am telling you to beware of the yeast of the Pharisees and the Sadducees." 12 Then the followers understood that

---

FAITH links

PROVE IT!
MATTHEW 16:1-4

Are you the kind of person who has to "see it" to believe it? In Jesus' day, the religious leaders – the Pharisees and the Sadducees – wanted proof that Jesus was who he said he was. They wanted a sign from heaven.

The Bible provides proof that Jesus is the Saviour. The Gospels – Matthew, Mark, Luke and John – provide eyewitness proof that Jesus died for your sins, rose from the dead, returned to heaven, and plans to return to earth someday. That's all the proof you need!

When Bad Turns to Worse, Exodus 5:6–12, p. 82

From Zero to Hero, Judges 6; 7, p. 319

Hurry Up and Wait, 2 Samuel 5, p. 405

On the Wrong Foot, 2 Kings 21:1–2, 16, p. 509

Two Ways to Grow, Luke 2:46–52, p. 1370

Life's Rule Book, 2 Timothy 3:15–17, p. 1655

Jesus was not telling them to beware of the yeast used in bread but to beware of the teaching of the Pharisees and the Sadducees.

16:4 sign of Jonah Jonah's three days in the fish are like Jesus' three days in the tomb. The story about Jonah is in the Book of Jonah.

Peter Says Jesus is the Christ

13 When Jesus came to the area of Caesarea Philippi, he asked his followers, "Who do people say the Son of Man is?"

14 They answered, "Some say you are John the Baptist. Others say you are Elijah, and still others say you are Jeremiah or one of the prophets."

15 Then Jesus asked them, "And who do you say I am?"

16 Simon Peter answered, "You are the Christ, the Son of the living God."

17 Jesus answered, "You are blessed, Simon son of Jonah, because no person taught you that. My Father in heaven showed you who I am. 18 So I tell you, you are Peter.ⁿ On this rock I will build my church, and the power of death will not be able to defeat it. 19 I will give you the keys of the kingdom of heaven; the things you don't allow on earth will be the things that God does not allow, and the things you allow on earth will be the things that God allows." 20 Then Jesus warned his followers not to tell anyone he was the Christ.

Jesus Says that He Must Die

21 From that time on Jesus began telling his followers that he must go to Jerusalem, where the older Jewish leaders, the leading priests, and the teachers of the law would make him suffer many things. He told them he must be killed and then be raised from the dead on the third day.

22 Peter took Jesus aside and told him not to talk like that. He said, "God save you from those things, Lord! Those things will never happen to you!"

23 Then Jesus said to Peter, "Go away from me, Satan!ⁿ You are not helping me! You don't care about the things of God, but only about the things people think are important."

24 Then Jesus said to his followers, "If people want to follow me, they must give up the things they want. They must be willing even to give up their lives to follow me.

16:24 Following God
What must you do to follow Jesus?

25 Those who want to save their lives will give up true life, and those who give up their lives for me will have true life. 26 It is worth nothing for them to have the whole world if they lose their souls. They could never pay enough to buy back their souls. 27 The Son of Man will come again with his Father's glory and with his angels. At that time, he will reward them for what they have done. 28 I tell you the truth, some people standing here will see the Son of Man coming with his kingdom before they die."

Jesus Talks with Moses and Elijah

17 Six days later, Jesus took Peter, James and John, the brother of James, up on a high mountain by themselves. 2 While they watched, Jesus' appearance was changed; his face became bright like the sun, and his clothes became white as light. 3 Then Moses and Elijahⁿ appeared to them, talking with Jesus.

4 Peter said to Jesus, "Lord, it is good that we are here. If you want, I will put up three tents here—one for you, one for Moses and one for Elijah."

5 While Peter was talking, a bright cloud covered them. A voice came from the cloud and said, "This is my Son, whom I love, and I am very pleased with him. Listen to him!"

6 When his followers heard the voice, they were so frightened they fell to the ground. 7 But Jesus went to them and touched them and said, "Stand up. Don't be afraid." 8 When they looked up, they saw Jesus was now alone.

9 As they were coming down the mountain, Jesus commanded them not to tell anyone about what they had seen until the Son of Man had risen from the dead.

10 Then his followers asked him,

16:18 Peter The Greek name "Peter", like the Aramaic name "Cephas", means "rock".
16:23 Satan Name for the devil, meaning "the enemy". Jesus means that Peter was talking like Satan.
17:3 Moses and Elijah Two of the most important Jewish leaders in the past. Moses had given them the law, and Elijah was an important prophet.

"Why do the teachers of the law say that Elijah must come first?"

11 Jesus answered, "They are right to say that Elijah is coming and that he will make everything the way it should be. 12 But I tell you that Elijah has already come, and they did not recognise him. They did to him whatever they wanted to do. It will be the same with the Son of Man; those same people will make the Son of Man suffer." 13 Then the followers understood that Jesus was talking about John the Baptist.

Jesus Heals a Sick Boy

14 When Jesus and his followers came back to the crowd, a man came to Jesus and bowed before him. 15 The man said, "Lord, have mercy on my son. He has epilepsy[n] and is suffering very much, because he often falls into the fire or into the water. 16 I brought him to your followers, but they could not cure him."

17 Jesus answered, "You people have no faith, and your lives are all wrong. How long must I put up with you? How long must I continue to be patient with you? Bring the boy here." 18 Jesus gave a strong command to the demon inside the boy. Then the demon came out, and the boy was healed from that time on.

19 The followers came to Jesus when he was alone and asked, "Why couldn't we force the demon out?"

20 Jesus answered, "Because your faith is too small. I tell you the truth, if your faith is as big as a mustard seed, you can say to this mountain, 'Move from here to there,' and it will move. All things will be possible for you." 21[n]

Jesus Talks About His Death

22 While Jesus' followers were gathering in Galilee, he said to them, "The Son of Man will be handed over to people, 23 and they will kill him. But on the third day he will be raised from the dead." And the followers were filled with sadness.

Jesus Talks About Paying Taxes

24 When Jesus and his followers came to Capernaum, the men who collected the Temple tax came to Peter. They

---

FAITH links

YOUR CIVIC DUTY
MATTHEW 17:24-27

Being a Christian makes you an honorary citizen of heaven. But being a Christian doesn't mean you can stop obeying the laws of the land. After all, Jesus willingly paid the required temple tax for himself and for Peter.

This story reminds us to respect and obey our leaders (for example, teachers, headteachers and the police). That way, we can be good citizens of heaven and of earth!

Want the good citizen award? Download these links:

A Use for Your Abilities, Genesis 41, p. 59

A Memorial for Two Thieves, 1 Chronicles 7:21, p. 530

A Reminder to Do What Is Right and True, Zechariah 7:8–10, p. 1257

Too Busy to Worship? Luke 2:8–20, p. 1368

Calling Anyone! Acts 23:12–22, p. 1506

Who's on First? 3 John 9–10, p. 1723

17:15 epilepsy A disease that causes a person sometimes to lose control of their body and perhaps faint, shake strongly or be unable to move.

17:21 Verse 21 Some Greek copies add verse 21: "That kind of spirit comes out only if you use prayer and give up eating."

asked, "Does your teacher pay the Temple tax?"

25 Peter answered, "Yes, Jesus pays the tax."

Peter went into the house, but before he could speak, Jesus said to him, "What do you think? The kings of the earth collect different kinds of taxes. But who pays the taxes—the king's children or others?" 26 Peter answered, "Other people pay the taxes."

Jesus said to Peter, "Then the children of the king don't have to pay taxes. 27 But we don't want to upset these tax collectors. So go to the lake and fish. After you catch the first fish, open its mouth and you will find a coin. Take that coin and give it to the tax collectors for you and me."

Who is the Greatest?

18 At that time the followers came to Jesus and asked, "Who is greatest in the kingdom of heaven?"

2 Jesus called a little child to him and stood the child before his followers. 3 Then he said, "I tell you the truth, you must change and become like little children. Otherwise, you will never enter the kingdom of heaven. 4 The greatest person in the kingdom of heaven is the one who makes himself humble like this child.

5 "Whoever accepts a child in my name accepts me. 6 If one of these little children believes in me, and someone causes that child to sin, it would be better for that person to have a large stone tied around the neck and be drowned in the sea. 7 How terrible for the people of the world because of the things that cause them to sin. Such things will happen, but how terrible for the one who causes them to happen! 8 If your hand or your foot causes you to sin, cut it off and throw it away. It is better for you to lose part of your body and live for ever than to have two hands and two feet and be thrown into the fire that burns for ever. 9 If your eye causes you to sin, take it out and throw it away. It is better for you to have only one eye and live for ever than to have two eyes and be thrown into the fire of hell.

A Lost Sheep

10 "Be careful. Don't think these little children are worth nothing. I tell you that they have angels in heaven who are always with my Father in heaven. 11 *n*

12 "If a man has 100 sheep but one of the sheep gets lost, he will leave the other 99 on the hill and go to look for the lost sheep. 13 I tell you the truth, he is happier about that one sheep than about the 99 that were never lost. 14 In the same way, your Father in heaven does not want any of these little children to be lost.

When a Person Sins Against You

15 "If your fellow believer sins against you, go and tell him in private what he did wrong. If he listens to you, you have helped that person to be your brother or sister again. 16 But if he refuses to listen, go to him again and take one or two other people with you. 'Every case may be proved by two or three witnesses.'*m* 17 If he refuses to listen to them, tell the church. If he refuses to listen to the church, then treat him like a person who does not believe in God or like a tax collector.

18 "I tell you the truth, the things you don't allow on earth will be the things God does not allow. And the things you allow on earth will be the things that God allows.

19 "Also, I tell you that if two of you on earth agree about something and pray for it, it will be done for you by my Father in heaven. 20 This is true because if two or three people come together in my name, I am there with them."

An Unforgiving Servant

21 Then Peter came to Jesus and asked, "Lord, when my fellow believer sins against me, how many times must I

18:11 Verse 11 Some Greek copies add verse 11: "The Son of Man came to save lost people."
18:16 'Every . . . witnesses.' Quotation from Deuteronomy 19:15.

Matthew 18:22

FAITH links

WHEN WE AGREE
MATTHEW 18:19-20

You know that 1 + 1 = 2, right? But did you also know that 1 + 1 = 3? Want to know how? Jesus once said that when two or more believers agree about something in prayer, he promised to be with them.

Need some power behind that prayer? Check out these Faithlinks:

The Name of the Lord, Exodus 33:19–23; 34:5–8, p. 120

Deciding Wisely, 1 Kings 3:16–28, p. 440

Fly Like an Eagle, Isaiah 40:28–31, p. 947

A Useless Thing, Isaiah 44:9, 18–20, p. 954

Pass It On! Joel 1:2–3, p. 1187

You've Got the Power! Acts 1:1–8; 2:1–4, p. 1463

18:21–35 Forgiveness
How many times do you need to forgive?

---

forgive him? Should I forgive him as many as seven times?"

22 Jesus answered, "I tell you, you must forgive him more than seven times. You must forgive him even if he does wrong to you seventy times seven.

23 "The kingdom of heaven is like a king who decided to collect the money his servants owed him. 24 When the king began to collect his money, a servant who owed him several thousand pounds was brought to him. 25 But the servant did not have enough money to pay his master, the king. So the master ordered that everything the servant owned should be sold, even the servant's wife and children. Then the money would be used to pay the king what the servant owed.

26 "But the servant fell on his knees and begged, 'Be patient with me, and I will pay you everything I owe.' 27 The master felt sorry for his servant and told him he did not have to pay it back. Then he let the servant go free.

28 "Later, that same servant found another servant who owed him a few pounds. The servant grabbed him around the neck and said, 'Pay me the money you owe me!'

29 "The other servant fell on his knees and begged him, 'Be patient with me, and I will pay you everything I owe.'

30 "But the first servant refused to be patient. He threw the other servant into prison until he could pay everything he owed. 31 When the other servants saw what had happened, they were very sorry. So they went and told their master all that had happened.

32 "Then the master called his servant in and said, 'You evil servant! Because you begged me to forget what you owed, I told you that you did not have to pay anything. 33 You should have shown mercy to that other servant, just as I showed mercy to you.' 34 The master was very angry and put the servant in prison to be punished until he could pay everything he owed.

35 "This king did what my heavenly Father will do to you if you do not forgive your brother or sister from your heart."

Jesus Teaches About Divorce

19 After Jesus said all these things, he left Galilee and went into the area of Judea on the other side of the Jordan River. 2 Large crowds followed him, and he healed them there.

3 Some Pharisees came to Jesus and tried to trick him. They asked, "Is it right for a man to divorce his wife for any reason he chooses?"

4 Jesus answered, "Surely you have read in the Scriptures: when God made the world, 'he made them male and female'.[n] 5 And God said, 'So a man will leave his father and mother and be united with his wife, and the two will become one body.'[n] 6 So there are not two, but one. God has joined the two together, so no one should separate them."

7 The Pharisees asked, "Why then did Moses give a command for a man to divorce his wife by giving her divorce papers?"

8 Jesus answered, "Moses allowed you to divorce your wives because you refused to accept God's teaching, but divorce was not allowed in the beginning. 9 I tell you that anyone who divorces his wife and marries another woman is guilty of adultery. The only reason for a man to divorce his wife is if his wife has sexual relations with another man."

10 The followers said to him, "If that is the only reason a man can divorce his wife, it is better not to marry."

11 Jesus answered, "Not everyone can accept this teaching, but God has made some able to accept it. 12 There are different reasons why some men cannot marry. Some men were born without the ability to become fathers. Others were made that way later in life by other people. And some men have given up marriage because of the kingdom of heaven. But the person who can marry should accept this teaching about marriage."[n]

Jesus Welcomes Children

13 Then the people brought their little children to Jesus so he could put his hands on them[n] and pray for them. His followers told them to stop, 14 but Jesus said, "Let the little children come to me. Don't stop them, because the kingdom of heaven belongs to people who are like these children." 15 After Jesus put his hands on the children, he left that place.

A Rich Young Man's Question

16 A man came to Jesus and asked, "Teacher, what good thing must I do to have life for ever?"

17 Jesus answered, "Why do you ask

FAITH links

WELCOME!
MATTHEW 19:13-15

Quick! Think of a time when someone made you feel welcome. Jesus took time to make children feel welcome, even though his followers felt that he was "too busy" or important to do so. Jesus even used children to teach a lesson to adults. First, he said that a person needed the faith of a child in order to enter heaven. Then he promised that when a person accepts a child in his name, they accept him as well. So, what will you do this week to welcome others like Jesus?

Roll Out the Welcome Wagon, Genesis 18:2–8, p. 24

Kind or Fair? 1 Samuel 30, p. 395

A Travelling Bible Study, 2 Chronicles 17:9, p. 580

How to Worship God, Isaiah 58, p. 972

A Broken Promise, Jeremiah 2:1–8, p. 989

Get Ready! Mark 13:26–27, p. 1354

19:4 'he made . . . female' Quotation from Genesis 1:27 or 5:2.
19:5 'So . . . body.' Quotation from Genesis 2:24.
19:12 But . . . marriage. This may also mean, "The person who can accept this teaching about not marrying should accept it."
19:13 put his hands on them Showing that Jesus gave special blessings to these children.

me about what is good? Only God is good. But if you want to have life for ever, obey the commands."

18 The man asked, "Which commands?"

Jesus answered, " 'You must not murder anyone; you must not be guilty of adultery; you must not steal; you must not tell lies about your neighbour; 19 honour your father and mother;[n] and love your neighbour as you love yourself.' "[n]

20 The young man said, "I have obeyed all these things. What else do I need to do?"

21 Jesus answered, "If you want to be perfect, then go and sell your possessions and give the money to the poor. If you do this, you will have treasure in heaven. Then come and follow me."

19:21–22 Money
Jesus is more important than your stuff.

22 But when the young man heard this, he left very sad, because he was rich.

23 Then Jesus said to his followers, "I tell you the truth, it will be hard for a rich person to enter the kingdom of heaven. 24 Yes, I tell you that it is easier for a camel to go through the eye of a needle than for a rich person to enter the kingdom of God."

25 When Jesus' followers heard this, they were very surprised and asked, "Then who can be saved?"

26 Jesus looked at them and said, "This is something people cannot do, but God can do all things."

27 Peter said to Jesus, "Look, we have left everything and followed you. So what will we have?"

28 Jesus said to them, "I tell you the truth, when the age to come has arrived, the Son of Man will sit on his great throne. All of you who followed me will also sit on twelve thrones, judging the twelve tribes of Israel. 29 And all those who have left houses, brothers, sisters, father, mother, children or farms to follow me will get much more than they left, and they will have life for ever. 30 Many who have the highest place now will have the lowest place in the future. And many who have the lowest place now will have the highest place in the future.

A Story About Workers

20 "The kingdom of heaven is like a person who owned some land. One morning, he went out very early to hire some people to work in his vineyard. 2 The man agreed to pay the workers a silver coin[n] for working on that day. Then he sent them into the vineyard to work. 3 At about nine o'clock the man went to the market-place and saw some other people standing there, doing nothing. 4 So he said to them, 'If you go and work in my vineyard, I will pay you what your work is worth.' 5 So they went to work in the vineyard. The man went out again at about twelve o'clock and three o'clock and did the same thing. 6 At about five o'clock the man went to the market-place again and saw others standing there. He asked them, 'Why have you stood here all day doing nothing?' 7 They answered, 'No one has given us a job.' The man said to them, 'Then you can go and work in my vineyard.'

8 "At the end of the day, the owner of the vineyard said to the foreman of all the workers, 'Call the workers and pay them. Start with the last people I hired and end with those I hired first.'

9 "When the workers who were hired at five o'clock came to get their pay, each received a silver coin. 10 When the workers who were hired first came to get their pay, they thought they would be paid more than the others. But each one of them also received a silver coin. 11 When they got their coin, they complained to the man who owned the land. 12 They said, 'Those people were hired last and worked only one hour. But you paid them the same as you paid us who worked hard all day in the hot sun.' 13 But the man who owned the vineyard said to one of those

---

19:19 'You . . . mother.' Quotation from Exodus 20:12-16; Deuteronomy 5:16-20.
19:19 'love . . . yourself.' Quotation from Leviticus 19:18.
20:2 coin Roman denarii. A silver coin was the average pay for one day's work.

workers, 'Friend, I am being fair to you. You agreed to work for a silver coin. 14 So take your pay and go. I want to give the man who was hired last the same pay that I gave you. 15 I can do what I want with my own money. Are you jealous because I am good to those people?'

16 "So those who have the last place now will have the first place in the future, and those who have the first place now will have the last place in the future."

Jesus Talks About His Own Death

17 While Jesus was going to Jerusalem, he took his twelve followers aside privately and said to them, 18 "Look, we are going to Jerusalem. The Son of Man will be turned over to the leading priests and the teachers of the law, and they will say that he must die. 19 They will give the Son of Man to the non-Jewish people to laugh at him and beat him with whips and crucify him. But on the third day, he will be raised to life again."

A Mother Asks Jesus a Favour

20 Then the wife of Zebedee came to Jesus with her sons. She bowed before him and asked him to do something for her.

21 Jesus asked, "What do you want?"

She said, "Promise that one of my sons will sit at your right side and the other will sit at your left side in your kingdom."

22 But Jesus said, "You don't understand what you are asking. Can you drink the cup that I am about to drink?"[n]

The sons answered, "Yes, we can."

23 Jesus said to them, "You will drink from my cup. But I cannot choose who will sit at my right or my left; those places belong to those for whom my Father has prepared them."

24 When the other ten followers heard this, they were angry with the two brothers.

25 Jesus called all the followers together and said, "You know that the rulers of the non-Jewish people love to show their power over the people. And their important leaders love to use all their authority. 26 But it should not be that way among you. Whoever wants to become great among you must serve the rest of you like a servant. 27 Whoever wants to become first among you must serve the rest of you

20:25–28
Leadership
Jesus came to serve.

FAITH links

THE WAY TO GREATNESS
MATTHEW 20:20-28

If you wanted others to think you were important, what would you do? The mother of two of Jesus' followers wanted her sons to have important positions in the kingdom of God. Jesus gave his followers some advice about greatness that can be said in two words: "Serve others." You can start by putting others first. That's the way to true greatness.

Download these links for more on true greatness:

Fearful Service? Exodus 4:1–17, p. 80

The Way to Serve God, 1 Kings 9:4, p. 450

Prayer + Action = Success, Nehemiah 2:4–9, p. 626

The Verdict Is In? Matthew 7:1–2, p. 1285

Better Than Some? Luke 18:9–14, p. 1405

A Different Kind of Fruit, Galatians 5:22–23, p. 1592

20:22 drink . . . drink Jesus used the idea of drinking from a cup to ask if they could accept the same terrible things that would happen to him.

like a slave. 28 In the same way, the Son of Man did not come to be served. He came to serve others and to give his life as a ransom for many people."

Jesus Heals Two Blind Men

29 When Jesus and his followers were leaving Jericho, a great many people followed him. 30 Two blind men sitting by the road heard that Jesus was going by, so they shouted, "Lord, Son of David, have mercy on us!"

31 The people warned the blind men to be quiet, but they shouted even more, "Lord, Son of David, have mercy on us!"

32 Jesus stopped and said to the blind men, "What do you want me to do for you?"

33 They answered, "Lord, we want to see."

34 Jesus felt sorry for the blind men and touched their eyes, and at once they could see. Then they followed Jesus.

Jesus Enters Jerusalem as a King

21 As Jesus and his followers were coming closer to Jerusalem, they stopped at Bethphage at the hill called the Mount of Olives. From there Jesus sent two of his followers 2 and said to them, "Go to the town you can see ahead of you. When you enter it, you will quickly find a donkey tied there with its colt. Untie them and bring them to me. 3 If anyone asks you why you are taking the donkeys, say that the Master needs them, and he will send them at once."

4 This was to bring about what the prophet had said:

5 "Tell the people of Jerusalem,
  'Your king is coming to you.
He is gentle and riding on a donkey,
  on the colt of a donkey.'"

Zechariah 9:9

6 The followers went and did what Jesus told them to do. 7 They brought the donkey and the colt to Jesus and laid their coats on them, and Jesus sat on them. 8 Many people spread their coats on the road. Others cut branches from the trees and spread them on the road. 9 The people were walking ahead of Jesus and behind him, shouting,

"Praise*ⁿ* to the Son of David!
God bless the One who comes in the
  name of the Lord!
Praise to God in heaven!" *Psalm 118:26*

10 When Jesus entered Jerusalem, all the city was filled with excitement. The people asked, "Who is this man?"

11 The crowd answered, "This man is Jesus, the prophet from the town of Nazareth in Galilee."

Jesus Goes to the Temple

12 Jesus went into the Temple and threw out all the people who were buying and selling there. He turned over the tables of those who were exchanging different kinds of money, and he upset the benches of those who were selling doves. 13 Jesus said to all the people there, "It is written in the Scriptures, 'My Temple will be called a house for prayer.'*ⁿ* But you are changing it into a 'hideout for robbers'."*ⁿ*

14 The blind and crippled people came to Jesus in the Temple, and he healed them. 15 The leading priests and the teachers of the law saw that Jesus was doing wonderful things and that the children were praising him in the Temple, saying, "Praise*ⁿ* to the Son of David." All these things made the priests and the teachers of the law very angry.

16 They asked Jesus, "Do you hear the things these children are saying?"

Jesus answered, "Yes. Haven't you read in the Scriptures, 'You have taught children and babies to sing praises'?"*ⁿ*

17 Then Jesus left and went out of the city to Bethany, where he spent the night.

The Power of Faith

18 Early the next morning, as Jesus was going back to the city, he became

---

21:9, 15 Praise Literally, "Hosanna", a Hebrew word used at first in praying to God for help. At this time it was probably a shout of joy used in praising God or his Messiah.
21:13 'My Temple . . . prayer.' Quotation from Isaiah 56:7.
21:13 'hideout for robbers' Quotation from Jeremiah 7:11.
21:16 'You . . . praises' Quotation from the Septuagint (Greek) version of Psalm 8:2.

hungry. 19 Seeing a fig tree beside the road, Jesus went to it, but there were no figs on the tree, only leaves. So Jesus said to the tree, "You will never again have fruit." The tree immediately dried up. 20 When his followers saw this, they were amazed. They asked, "How did the fig tree dry up so quickly?" 21 Jesus answered, "I tell you the truth, if you have faith and do not doubt, you will be able to do what I did to this tree and even more. You will be able to say to this mountain, 'Go, fall into the sea.' And if you have faith, it will happen. 22 If you believe, you will get anything you ask for in prayer."

Leaders Doubt Jesus' Authority

23 Jesus went to the Temple, and while he was teaching there, the leading priests and the older leaders of the people came to him. They said, "What authority do you have to do these things? Who gave you this authority?"

24 Jesus answered, "I also will ask you a question. If you answer me, then I will tell you what authority I have to do these things. 25 Tell me: when John baptised people, did that come from God or just from other people?"

They argued about Jesus' question, saying, "If we answer, 'John's baptism was from God', Jesus will say, 'Then why didn't you believe him?' 26 But if we say, 'It was from people', we are afraid of what the crowd will do because they all believe that John was a prophet."

27 So they answered Jesus, "We don't know".

Jesus said to them, "Then I won't tell you what authority I have to do these things.

A Story About Two Sons

28 "Tell me what you think about this: a man had two sons. He went to the first son and said, 'Son, go and work today in my vineyard'. 29 The son answered, 'I will not go'. But later the son changed his mind and went. 30 Then the father went to the other son and said, 'Son, go and work today in my vineyard'. The son answered, 'Yes, sir, I will go and work', but he did not go. 31 Which of the two sons obeyed his father?"

The priests and leaders answered, "The first son".

Jesus said to them, "I tell you the truth, the tax collectors and the prostitutes will enter the kingdom of God before you do. 32 John came to show you the right way to live. You did not believe him, but the tax collectors and prostitutes believed him. Even after seeing this, you still refused to change your ways and believe him.

A Story About God's Son

33 "Listen to this story: there was a man who owned a vineyard. He put a wall around it and dug a hole for a winepress and built a tower. Then he leased the land to some farmers and left for a trip. 34 When it was time for the grapes to be picked, he sent his servants to the farmers to get his share of the grapes. 35 But the farmers grabbed the servants, beat one, killed another and then killed a third servant with stones. 36 So the man sent some other servants to the farmers, even more than he sent the first time. But the farmers did the same thing to the servants that they had done before. 37 So the man decided to send his son to the farmers. He said, 'They will respect my son.' 38 But when the farmers saw the son, they said to each other, 'This son will inherit the vineyard. If we kill him, it will be ours!' 39 Then the farmers grabbed the son, threw him out of the vineyard and killed him. 40 So what will the owner of the vineyard do to these farmers when he comes?"

41 The priests and leaders said, "He will surely kill those evil men. Then he will lease the vineyard to some other farmers who will give him his share of the crop at harvest time."

42 Jesus said to them, "Surely you have read this in the Scriptures:
'The stone that the builders rejected
　became the cornerstone.
The Lord did this,
　and it is wonderful to us.'

Psalm 118:22-23

43 "So I tell you that the kingdom of God will be taken away from you and given to people who do the things God wants in his kingdom. 44 The person who falls on this stone will be broken, and on whomsoever that stone falls, that person will be crushed."ⁿ

45 When the leading priests and the Pharisees heard these stories, they knew Jesus was talking about them. 46 They wanted to arrest him, but they were afraid of the people, because the people believed that Jesus was a prophet.

A Story About a Wedding Feast

22 Jesus again used stories to teach the people. He said, 2 "The kingdom of heaven is like a king who prepared a wedding feast for his son. 3 The king invited some people to the feast. When the feast was ready, the king sent his servants to tell the people, but they refused to come.

4 "Then the king sent other servants, saying, 'Tell those who have been invited that my feast is ready. I have killed my best bulls and calves for the dinner, and everything is ready. Come to the wedding feast.'

5 "But the people refused to listen to the servants and left to do other things. One went to work in his field, and another went to his business. 6 Some of the other people grabbed the servants, beat them and killed them. 7 The king was furious and sent his army to kill the murderers and burn their city.

8 "After that, the king said to his servants, 'The wedding feast is ready. I invited those people, but they were not worthy to come. 9 So go to the street corners and invite everyone you find to come to my feast.' 10 So the servants went into the streets and gathered all the people they could find, both good and bad. And the wedding hall was filled with guests.

11 "When the king came in to see the guests, he saw a man who was not dressed for a wedding. 12 The king said, 'Friend, how were you allowed to come in here? You are not dressed for a wedding.' But the man said nothing. 13 So the king told some servants, 'Tie this man's hands and feet. Throw him out into the darkness, where people will cry and grind their teeth with pain.'

14 "Yes, many people are invited, but only a few are chosen."

Is It Right to Pay Taxes or Not?

15 Then the Pharisees left that place and made plans to trap Jesus into saying something wrong. 16 They sent some of their own followers and some people from the group called Herodians.ⁿ They said, "Teacher, we know that you are an honest man and that you teach the truth about God's way. You are not afraid of what other people think about you, because you pay no attention to who they are. 17 So tell us what you think. Is it right to pay taxes to Caesar or not?"

18 But knowing that these leaders were trying to trick him, Jesus said, "You hypocrites! Why are you trying to trap me? 19 Show me a coin used for paying the tax." So the men showed him a coin.ⁿ 20 Then Jesus asked, "Whose image and name are on the coin?"

21 The men answered, "Caesar's."

22:21
Money
What should you do with your money?

Then Jesus said to them, "Give to Caesar the things that are Caesar's, and give to God the things that are God's."

22 When the men heard what Jesus said, they were amazed and left him and went away.

Some Sadducees Try to Trick Jesus

23 That same day some Sadducees came to Jesus and asked him a question. (Sadducees believed that people would not rise from the dead.) 24 They said, "Teacher, Moses said if a married man

---

21:44 Verse 44 Some copies do not have verse 44.
22:16 Herodians A political group that followed Herod and his family.
22:19 coin Roman denarii. A silver coin was the average pay for one day's work.

dies without having children, his brother must marry the widow and have children for him. 25 Once there were seven brothers among us. The first one married and died. Since he had no children, his brother married the widow. 26 Then the second brother also died. The same thing happened to the third brother and all the other brothers. 27 Finally, the woman died. 28 Since all seven men had married her, when people rise from the dead, whose wife will she be?"

29 Jesus answered, "You don't understand, because you don't know what the Scriptures say, and you don't know about the power of God. 30 When people rise from the dead, they will not marry, nor will they be given to someone to marry. They will be like the angels in heaven. 31 Surely you have read what God said to you about rising from the dead. 32 God said, 'I am the God of Abraham, the God of Isaac and the God of Jacob.'" God is the God of the living, not the dead."

22:30 Angels
Do angels get married?

33 When the people heard this, they were amazed at Jesus' teaching.

The Most Important Command

34 When the Pharisees learned that the Sadducees could not argue with Jesus' answers to them, the Pharisees met together. 35 One Pharisee, who was an expert on the law of Moses, asked Jesus this question to test him: 36 "Teacher, which command in the law is the most important?"

37 Jesus answered, "'Love the Lord your God with all your heart, all your soul and all your mind.'" 38 This is the first and most important command. 39 And the second command is like the first: 'Love your neighbour as you love yourself.'" 40 All the law and the writings of the prophets depend on these two commands."

Jesus Questions the Pharisees

41 While the Pharisees were together, Jesus asked them, 42 "What do you think about the Christ? Whose son is he?"

Matthew 22:42 1313

FAITH links

THE GREATEST COMMANDMENT
MATTHEW 22:36-40

You've read the Ten Commandments, right? (If not, do not pass "Go" until you read Exodus 20:1–17, p. 101.) Of all the commandments, which do you think is the most important? Keep the Sabbath holy? Do not steal? According to Jesus, the most important commandment is to love God with all of your heart, soul and mind. That means loving him with your whole being. The second commandment is to love others as much as you love yourself. Two commandments, one purpose: love. Now, that's not so hard to remember, is it?

Made in His Image, Genesis 1:26–27, p. 4

Help for the Poor, Leviticus 5:7, p. 138

Too Young to Serve, Jeremiah 1:4–9, p. 988

Your Full Trust, Jeremiah 22:20–22, p. 1023

Help for a Friend, Mark 2:1–5, p. 1332

From Useless to Useful, Philemon 11, p. 1663

22:32 'I am . . . Jacob.' Quotation from Exodus 3:6.
22:37 'Love . . . mind.' Quotation from Deuteronomy 6:5.
22:39 'Love . . . yourself.' Quotation from Leviticus 19:18.

They answered, "The Christ is the Son of David."

43 Then Jesus said to them, "Then why did David call him 'Lord'? David, speaking by the power of the Holy Spirit, said,

44 'The LORD said to my Lord:
Sit by me at my right side,
until I put your enemies under
your control.' *Psalm 110:1*

45 David calls the Christ 'Lord', so how can the Christ be his son?"

46 None of the Pharisees could answer Jesus' question, and after that day no one was brave enough to ask him any more questions.

Jesus Accuses Some Leaders

23 Then Jesus said to the crowds and to his followers, 2 "The teachers of the law and the Pharisees have the authority to tell you what the law of Moses says. 3 So you should obey and follow whatever they tell you, but their lives are not good examples for you to follow. They tell you to do things, but they themselves don't do them. 4 They make strict rules and try to force people to obey them, but they are unwilling to help those who struggle under the weight of their rules.

5 "They do good things so that other people will see them. They make the boxes[n] of Scriptures that they wear bigger, and they make their special prayer clothes very long. 6 Those Pharisees and teachers of the law love to have the most important seats at feasts and in the synagogues. 7 They love people to greet them with respect in the market places, and they love to have people call them 'Teacher'.

8 "But you must not be called 'Teacher', because you have only one Teacher, and you are all brothers and sisters together. 9 And don't call any person on earth 'Father', because you have one Father, who is in heaven. 10 And you should not be called 'Master', because you have only one Master, the Christ. 11 Whoever is your servant is the greatest among you. 12 Whoever makes himself great will be made humble. Whoever makes himself humble will be made great.

13 "How terrible for you, teachers of the law and Pharisees! You are hypocrites! You close the door for people to enter the kingdom of heaven. You yourselves don't enter, and you stop others who are trying to enter. 14[n]

15 "How terrible for you, teachers of the law and Pharisees! You are hypocrites! You travel across land and sea to find one person who will change to your ways. When you find that person, you make him more fit for hell than you are.

16 "How terrible for you! You guide the people, but you are blind. You say, 'If people swear by the Temple when they make a promise, that means nothing. But if they swear by the gold that is in the Temple, they must keep that promise.' 17 You are blind fools! Which is greater: the gold or the Temple that makes that gold holy? 18 And you say, 'If people swear by the altar when they make a promise, that means nothing. But if they swear by the gift on the altar, they must keep that promise.' 19 You are blind! Which is greater: the gift or the altar that makes the gift holy? 20 The person who swears by the altar is really using the altar and also everything on the altar. 21 And the person who swears by the Temple is really using the Temple and also everything in the Temple. 22 The person who swears by heaven is also using God's throne and the One who sits on that throne.

23 "How terrible for you, teachers of the law and Pharisees! You are hypocrites! You give to God one-tenth of everything you earn—even your mint, dill and cumin.[n] But you don't obey the really

---

23:5 boxes Small leather boxes containing four important Scriptures. Some Jews tied these to the forehead and left arm, probably to show they were very religious.

23:14 Verse 14 Some Greek copies add verse 14: "How terrible for you, teachers of the law and Pharisees. You are hypocrites. You take away widows' houses, and you say long prayers so that people will notice you. So you will have a worse punishment."

23:23 mint, dill and cumin Herbs grown in gardens and used for spices. Only very religious people would be careful enough to give a tenth of these plants.

important teachings of the law—justice, mercy and being loyal. These are the things you should do, as well as those other things. 24 You guide the people, but you are blind! You are like a person who picks a fly out of a drink and then swallows a camel!ⁿ

25 "How terrible for you, teachers of the law and Pharisees! You are hypocrites! You wash the outside of your cups and dishes, but inside they are full of things you got by cheating others and by pleasing only yourselves. 26 Pharisees, you are blind! First make the inside of the cup clean, and then the outside of the cup can be truly clean.

27 "How terrible for you, teachers of the law and Pharisees! You are hypocrites!

23:27-28
Being Pure
It's what's on the inside that counts.

You are like tombs that are painted white. Outside, those tombs look fine, but inside, they are full of the bones of dead people and all kinds of unclean things. 28 It is the same with you. People look at you and think you are good, but on the inside you are full of hypocrisy and evil.

29 "How terrible for you, teachers of the law and Pharisees! You are hypocrites! You build tombs for the prophets, and you show honour to the graves of those who lived good lives. 30 You say, 'If we had lived during the time of our ancestors, we would not have helped them kill the prophets.' 31 But you give proof that you are children of those who murdered the prophets. 32 And you will complete the sin that your ancestors started.

33 "You are snakes! A family of poisonous snakes! How are you going to escape God's judgement? 34 So I tell you this: I am sending to you prophets and wise men and teachers. Some of them you will kill and crucify. Some of them you will beat in your synagogues and chase from town to town. 35 So you will be guilty for the death of all the good people who have been killed on earth—from the murder of that good man Abel to the murder of Zechariahⁿ son of Berakiah, whom you murdered between the Temple and the altar. 36 I tell you the truth, all of these things will happen to you people who are living now.

Jesus Feels Sorry for Jerusalem

37 "Jerusalem, Jerusalem! You kill the prophets and stone to death those who are sent to you. Many times I wanted to gather your people as a hen gathers her chicks under her wings, but you did not let me. 38 Now your house will be left completely empty. 39 I tell you, you will not see me again until that time when you will say, 'God bless the One who comes in the name of the Lord.'"ⁿ

The Temple will Be Destroyed

24 As Jesus left the Temple and was walking away, his followers came up to him to show him the Temple's buildings. 2 Jesus asked, "Do you see all these buildings? I tell you the truth, not one stone will be left on another. Every stone will be thrown down to the ground."

3 Later, as Jesus was sitting on the Mount of Olives, his followers came to be alone with him. They said, "Tell us, when will these things happen? And what will be the sign that it is time for you to come again and for this age to end?"

4 Jesus answered, "Be careful that no one fools you. 5 Many will come in my name, saying, 'I am the Christ', and they will fool many people. 6 You will hear about wars and stories of wars that are coming, but don't be afraid. These things must happen before the end comes. 7 Nations will fight against other nations; kingdoms will fight against other kingdoms. There will be times when there is no food for people to eat, and there will be earthquakes in different places. 8 These things are like the first pains when something new is about to be born.

9 "Then people will arrest you, hand you over to be hurt and kill you. They will

---

23:24 You . . . camel! Meaning, "You worry about the smallest mistakes but commit the biggest sin."
23:35 Abel . . . Zechariah In the order of the books of the Hebrew Old Testament, the first and last men to be murdered.
23:39 'God . . . Lord.' Quotation from Psalm 118:26.

hate you because you believe in me. 10 At that time, many will lose their faith, and they will turn against each other and hate each other. 11 Many false prophets will come and cause many people to believe lies. 12 There will be more and more evil in the world, so most people will stop showing their love for each other. 13 But those people who keep their faith until the end will be saved. 14 The Good News about God's kingdom will be preached in all the world, to every nation. Then the end will come.

15 "Daniel the prophet spoke about 'the destroying terror'.[n] You will see this standing in the holy place." (You who read this should understand what it means.) 16 "At that time, the people in Judea should run away to the mountains. 17 If people are on the roofs[n] of their houses, they must not go down to get anything out of their houses. 18 If people are in the fields, they must not go back to get their coats. 19 At that time, how terrible it will be for women who are pregnant or have nursing babies! 20 Pray that it will not be winter or a Sabbath day when these things happen and you have to run away, 21 because at that time there will be much trouble. There will be more trouble than there has ever been since the beginning of the world until now, and nothing as bad will ever happen again. 22 God has decided to make that terrible time short. Otherwise, no one would go on living. But God will make that time short to help the people he has chosen. 23 At that time, someone might say to you, 'Look, there is the Christ!' Or another person might say, 'There he is!' But don't believe them. 24 False Christs and false prophets will come and perform great wonders and miracles. They will try to fool even the people God has chosen, if that were possible. 25 Now I have warned you about this before it happens.

26 "If people tell you, 'The Christ is in the desert', don't go there. If they say, 'The Christ is in the inner room', don't believe it. 27 When the Son of Man comes, he will be seen by everyone, like lightning flashing from the east to the west. 28 Wherever the dead body is, there the vultures will gather.

29 "Soon after the trouble of those days,

'the sun will grow dark,
and the moon will not give its light.
The stars will fall from the sky.
And the powers of the heavens will be shaken.' *Isaiah 13:10; 34:4*

30 "At that time, the sign of the Son of Man will appear in the sky. Then all the peoples of the world will cry. They will see the Son of Man coming on clouds in the sky with great power and glory. 31 He will use a loud trumpet to send his angels all around the earth, and they will gather his chosen people from every part of the world.

> But those people who keep their faith until the end will be saved.
> – Matthew 24:13

32 "Learn a lesson from the fig tree: when its branches become green and soft and new leaves appear, you know summer is near. 33 In the same way, when you see all these things happening, you will know that the time is near, ready to come. 34 I tell you the truth, all these things will happen while the people of this time are still living. 35 Earth and sky will be destroyed, but the words I have said will never be destroyed.

When will Jesus Come Again?

36 "No one knows when that day or time will be, not the angels in heaven, not even the Son. Only the Father knows. 37 When the Son of Man comes, it will be like what happened during Noah's time. 38 In those days before the flood, people

---

24:15 'the destroying terror' Mentioned in Daniel 9:27; 12:11 (see also Daniel 11:31).

24:17 roof In Bible times houses were built with flat roofs. The roof was used for drying things such as flax and fruit. And it was used as an extra room, as a place for worship and as a place to sleep in the summer.

were eating and drinking, marrying and giving their children to be married, until the day Noah entered the ark. 39 They knew nothing about what was happening until the flood came and destroyed them. It will be the same when the Son of Man comes. 40 Two men will be in the field. One will be taken, and the other will be left. 41 Two women will be grinding grain with a mill." One will be taken, and the other will be left.

42 "So always be ready, because you don't know the day your Lord will come. 43 Remember this: if the owner of the house knew what time of night a thief was coming, the owner would watch and not let the thief break in. 44 So you also must be ready, because the Son of Man will come at a time you don't expect him.

45 "Who is the wise and loyal servant that the master trusts to give the other servants their food at the right time? 46 When the master comes and finds the servant doing his work, the servant will be blessed. 47 I tell you the truth, the master will choose that servant to take care of everything he owns. 48 But suppose that servant is evil, and thinks to himself, 'My master will not come back soon,' 49 and he begins to beat the other servants and eat and get drunk with others like him? 50 The master will come when that servant is not ready and is not expecting him. 51 Then the master will cut him in pieces and send him away to be with the hypocrites, where people will cry and grind their teeth with pain.

A Story About Ten Bridesmaids

25 "At that time the kingdom of heaven will be like ten bridesmaids who took their lamps and went to wait for the bridegroom. 2 Five of them were foolish and five were wise. 3 The five foolish bridesmaids took their lamps, but they did not take spare oil for the lamps to burn. 4 The wise bridesmaids took their lamps and more oil in jars. 5 Because the bridegroom was late, they became sleepy and went to sleep.

6 "At midnight someone cried out, 'The bridegroom is coming! Come and meet him!' 7 Then all the bridesmaids woke up and got their lamps ready. 8 But the foolish ones said to the wise, 'Give us some of your oil, because our lamps are going out.' 9 The wise bridesmaids answered, 'No, the oil we have might not be enough for all of us. Go to the people who sell oil and buy some for yourselves.'

10 "So while the five foolish bridesmaids went to buy oil, the bridegroom came. The bridesmaids who were ready went in with the bridegroom to the wedding feast. Then the door was closed and locked.

11 "Later the others came back and said, 'Sir, sir, open the door to let us in.' 12 But the bridegroom answered, 'I tell you the truth, I don't want to know you.'

13 "So always be ready, because you don't know the day or the hour the Son of Man will come.

A Story About Three Servants

14 "The kingdom of heaven is like a man who was going to another place for a visit. Before he left, he called for his servants and told them to take care of his things while he was gone. 15 He gave one servant five bags of gold, another servant two bags of gold and a third servant one bag of gold, to each one as much as he could manage. Then he left. 16 The servant who got five bags went quickly to invest the money and earned five more bags. 17 In the same way, the servant who had two bags invested them and earned two more. 18 But the servant who got one bag went out and dug a hole in the ground and hid the master's money.

19 "After a long time the master came home and asked the servants what they had done with his money. 20 The servant who was given five bags of gold brought five more bags to the master and said, 'Master, you trusted me to care for five bags of gold, so I used your five bags to earn five more.' 21 The master answered,

---

24:41 mill Two large, round, flat rocks used for grinding grain to make flour.

EMAIL FROM GOD
25:14–30 Responsibility
How do you earn more responsibility?

▶ Matthew 25 1318

SERVING
Matthew 25:14–30

Being the GREATEST! Would you like to be really great – you know, the person everyone looks up to? How can you get that way? Some people think it's how much money you have or how famous you are. Other people think it's how good someone is at a particular sport or if he or she looks cool.

But Jesus has a different idea of what makes a person great. Jesus said true greatness comes from helping and caring for others. (Check out Matthew 23:11.)

Serving others helps us pay attention to other people and their needs and not just think about ourselves. Jesus himself said that he came to serve others, not to have people serve him. (See Mark 10:45, p. 1348.) Who could be a better example of "greatness" than Jesus? Whose idea of greatness do you plan to follow – Jesus' example or the world's?

MORE FAITH links

The Way to Serve God, **p. 450**

Service with a Smile, **p. 527**

The Worst Chore, **p. 1447**

My Best Serve, **p. 1473**

> It's a bit confusing, isn't it? Jesus says that if we want to be first, we should serve others. How do you think that works?
>
> Better download some of these other links on serving. Maybe we'll get a clue!

Just Say Yes! Matthew 9:9–13, p. 1289
- What do you say when your mum or dad asks you to do something for them?
- How about your brother or sister? What about a friend? What if it's Jesus asking you to do something?

Calling Anyone! Acts 23:12–22, p. 1506
- We all like to feel important. But there are many people who do great things without anyone knowing about it. Find out about one of these people and what he did by linking here!

Help for the Body, Romans 12:3–8, p. 1536
- Everybody is good at doing something. What are you good at doing? Making people smile or singing or helping around the house? How do you use your talents and abilities?

Your Faith Example, 1 Timothy 4:12, p. 1646
- Link here to discover how you can serve God!

my FAVOURITE links

Matthew 25:34

'You did well. You are a good and loyal servant. Because you were loyal with small things, I will let you care for much greater things. Come and share my joy with me.'

22 "Then the servant who had been given two bags of gold came to the master and said, 'Master, you gave me two bags of gold to care for, so I used your two bags to earn two more.' 23 The master answered, 'You did well. You are a good and loyal servant. Because you were loyal with small things, I will let you care for much greater things. Come and share my joy with me.'

24 "Then the servant who had been given one bag of gold came to the master and said, 'Master, I knew that you were a hard man. You harvest things you did not plant. You gather crops where you did not sow any seed. 25 So I was afraid and went and hid your money in the ground. Here is your bag of gold.' 26 The master answered, 'You are a wicked and lazy servant! You say you knew that I harvest things I did not plant and that I gather crops where I did not sow any seed. 27 So you should have put my gold in the bank. Then, when I came home, I would have received my gold back with interest.'

28 "So the master told his other servants, 'Take the bag of gold from that servant and give it to the servant who has ten bags of gold. 29 Those who have much will get more, and they will have much more than they need. But those who do not have much will have everything taken away from them.' 30 Then the master said, 'Throw that useless servant outside, into the darkness where people will cry and grind their teeth with pain.'

The King will Judge All People

31 "The Son of Man will come again in his great glory, with all his angels. He will be King and sit on his great throne. 32 All the nations of the world will be gathered before him, and he will separate them into two groups as a shepherd separates the sheep from the goats. 33 The Son of Man will put the sheep on his right and the goats on his left.

34 "Then the King will say to the

FAITH links

THAT THING YOU DO
MATTHEW 25:14-30

Think about something you do well. Can you draw? Laugh? Tell a joke? Jesus once told a story about a man who gave each of his three servants a different number of bags of gold. He told them to "take care of his things" while he was gone. Two of the servants used the bags of gold to make more gold for their master. The other servant took his one bag of gold and did nothing with it. Jesus told his disciples that the master was pleased with the two servants, but angry with the one who did nothing with what he was given.

God wants each of us to use the gifts he has given us – whether it's a special talent or ability, our money or our time – to serve others. He doesn't give them to us to forget about them or to use for ourselves. When we use our talents and abilities, we sometimes gain more responsibilities, like two of the men did in the story. Just think: when you use your talents to help others, God feels glad. You will, too!

Share What You Have, Exodus 35:5–18, p. 123

Show Some Respect, Leviticus 19:32, p. 161

Take Me to Your Leader, Numbers 27:12–23, p. 214

A Bad Reaction, Jeremiah 36, p. 1043

Too Busy to Worship? Luke 2:8–20, p. 1368

people on his right, 'Come, my Father has given you his blessing. Receive the kingdom God has prepared for you since the world was made. 35 I was hungry, and you gave me food. I was thirsty, and you gave me something to drink. I was alone and away from home, and you invited me into your house. 36 I was without clothes, and you gave me something to wear. I was sick, and you cared for me. I was in prison, and you visited me.'

25:34–40
Sickness
Who should you care for?

37 "Then the good people will answer, 'Lord, when did we see you hungry and give you food, or thirsty and give you something to drink? 38 When did we see you alone and away from home and invite you into our house? When did we see you without clothes and give you something to wear? 39 When did we see you sick or in prison and care for you?'

40 "Then the King will answer, 'I tell you the truth, anything you did for even the least of my people here, you also did for me.'

41 "Then the King will say to those on his left, 'Go away from me. You will be punished. Go into the fire that burns for ever that was prepared for the devil and his angels. 42 I was hungry, and you gave me nothing to eat. I was thirsty, and you gave me nothing to drink. 43 I was alone and away from home, and you did not invite me into your house. I was without clothes, and you gave me nothing to wear. I was sick and in prison, and you did not care for me.'

44 "Then those people will answer, 'Lord, when did we see you hungry or thirsty or alone and away from home or without clothes or sick or in prison? When did we see these things and not help you?'

45 "Then the King will answer, 'I tell you the truth, anything you refused to do for even the least of my people here, you refused to do for me.'

46 "These people will go off to be punished for ever, but the good people will go to live for ever."

The Plan to Kill Jesus

26 After Jesus finished saying all these things, he told his followers, 2 "You know that the day after tomorrow is the day of the Passover Feast. On that day the Son of Man will be given to his enemies to be crucified."

3 Then the leading priests and the Jewish elders had a meeting at the palace of the high priest, named Caiaphas. 4 At the meeting, they planned to set a trap to arrest Jesus and kill him. 5 But they said, "We must not do it during the feast, because the people might cause a riot."

Perfume for Jesus' Burial

6 Jesus was in Bethany at the house of Simon, who had a skin disease. 7 While Jesus was there, a woman approached him with an alabaster jar filled with expensive perfume. She poured this perfume on Jesus' head while he was eating.

8 His followers were upset when they saw the woman do this. They asked, "Why waste that perfume? 9 It could have been sold for a great deal of money and the money given to the poor."

10 Knowing what had happened, Jesus said, "Why are you troubling this woman? She did an excellent thing for me. 11 You will always have the poor with you, but you will not always have me. 12 This woman poured perfume on my body to prepare me for burial. 13 I tell you the truth, wherever the Good News is preached in all the world, what this woman has done will be told, and people will remember her."

Judas Becomes an Enemy of Jesus

14 Then one of the twelve apostles, Judas Iscariot, went to talk to the leading priests. 15 He said, "What will you pay me for giving Jesus to you?" And they gave him 30 silver coins. 16 After that, Judas watched for the best time to turn Jesus over.

Jesus Eats the Passover Meal

17 On the first day of the Feast of Unleavened Bread, the followers came to

Jesus. They said, "Where do you want us to prepare for you to eat the Passover meal?"

18 Jesus answered, "Go into the city to a certain man and tell him, 'The Teacher says: the chosen time is near. I will have the Passover with my followers at your house.'" 19 The followers did what Jesus told them to do, and they prepared the Passover meal.

20 In the evening Jesus was sitting at the table with his twelve followers. 21 As they were eating, Jesus said, "I tell you the truth, one of you will turn against me."

22 This made the followers very sad. Each one began to say to Jesus, "Surely, Lord, I am not the one who will turn against you, am I?"

23 Jesus answered, "The man who has dipped his hand with me into the bowl is the one who will turn against me. 24 The Son of Man will die, just as the Scriptures say. But how terrible it will be for the person who hands the Son of Man over to be killed. It would be better for him if he had never been born."

25 Then Judas, who would give Jesus to his enemies, said to Jesus, "Teacher, surely I am not the one, am I?"

Jesus answered, "Yes, it is you."

The Lord's Supper

26 While they were eating, Jesus took some bread and thanked God for it and broke it. Then he gave it to his followers and said, "Take this bread and eat it; this is my body."

27 Then Jesus took a cup and thanked God for it and gave it to the followers. He said, "Every one of you drink this. 28 This is my blood which is the new agreement that God makes with his people. This blood is poured out for many to forgive their sins. 29 I tell you this: I will not drink of this fruit of the vine" again until that day when I drink it new with you in my Father's kingdom."

30 After singing a hymn, they went out to the Mount of Olives.

Jesus' Followers will Leave Him

31 Jesus told his followers, "Tonight you will all stumble in your faith on

---

FAITH links

REMEMBERING JESUS
MATTHEW 26:26-29

Facing the death of a friend or relative is hard. You can't help remembering how much he or she meant to you. Before Jesus went to the cross, he had one last meal with his 12 followers. During the meal, he gave a piece of bread to each of his followers. The bread represented his body. He passed around a cup, which represented his blood. He did this to teach his followers how to remember him after he was gone.

Today, we call the bread and cup the Lord's Supper or Communion. The Lord's Supper reminds us of how Jesus gave his life for us.

Link here to see what else Jesus does for us:

Reward for Obedience, Leviticus 26:3–13, p. 171

Our Heavenly Shepherd, Psalm 23, p. 726

The Bible: Good for Your Faith, Psalm 119, p. 802

Your Spiritual Roots, Zechariah 1:1–6, p. 1253

Name with a Purpose, Matthew 1:21, p. 1274

Life After Death? 1 Corinthians 15:12–13, p. 1563

26:29 **fruit of the vine** Product of the grapevine; this may also be translated "wine."

account of me, because it is written in the Scriptures:

'I will kill the shepherd,
and the sheep will scatter.'

Zechariah 13:7

32 But after I rise from the dead, I will go ahead of you into Galilee."

33 Peter said, "Everyone else may stumble in their faith because of you, but I will not."

34 Jesus said, "I tell you the truth, tonight before the cockerel crows you will say three times that you don't know me."

35 But Peter said, "I will never say that I don't know you! I will even die with you!" And all the other followers said the same thing.

Jesus Prays Alone

36 Then Jesus went with his followers to a place called Gethsemane. He said to them, "Sit here while I go over there and pray." 37 He took Peter and the two sons of Zebedee with him, and he began to be very sad and troubled. 38 He said to them, "My heart is full of sorrow, to the point of death. Stay here and watch with me."

39 After walking a little farther away from them, Jesus fell to the ground and prayed, "My Father, if it is possible, do not give me this cup*n* of suffering. But do what you want, not what I want." 40 Then Jesus went back to his followers and found them asleep. He said to Peter, "You men, could you not stay awake with me for one hour? 41 Stay awake and pray for strength against temptation. The spirit wants to do what is right, but the body is weak."

42 Then Jesus went away a second time and prayed, "My Father, if it is not possible for this painful thing to be taken from me, and if I must do it, I pray that what you want will be done."

43 Then he went back to his followers, and again he found them asleep, because their eyes were heavy. 44 So Jesus left them and went away and prayed a third time, saying the same thing.

45 Then Jesus went back to his followers and said, "Are you still sleeping and resting? The time has come for the Son of Man to be handed over to sinful people. 46 Get up, we must go. Look, here comes the man who has turned against me."

Jesus is Arrested

47 While Jesus was still speaking, Judas, one of the twelve apostles, came up. With him were many people carrying swords and clubs who had been sent from the leading priests and the Jewish elders of the people. 48 Judas had planned to give them a signal, saying, "The man I kiss is Jesus. Arrest him." 49 At once Judas went to Jesus and said, "Greetings, Teacher!" and kissed him.

50 Jesus answered, "Friend, do what you came to do."

Then the people came and grabbed Jesus and arrested him. 51 When that happened, one of Jesus' followers reached for his sword and pulled it out. He struck the servant of the high priest and cut off his ear.

52 Jesus said to the man, "Put your sword back in its place. All who use swords will be killed with swords. 53 Surely you know I could ask my Father, and he would give me more than twelve armies of angels. 54 But it must happen this way to bring about what the Scriptures say."

55 Then Jesus said to the crowd, "You came to get me with swords and clubs as if I were a criminal. Every day I sat in the Temple teaching, and you did not arrest me there. 56 But all these things have happened so that it will come about as the prophets wrote." Then all of Jesus' followers left him and ran away.

Jesus Before the Leaders

57 Those people who arrested Jesus led him to the house of Caiaphas, the high priest, where the teachers of the law and the Jewish elders were gathered. 58 Peter followed far behind to the courtyard of the high priest's house, and he sat down with the guards to see what would happen to Jesus.

26:39 cup Jesus is talking about the terrible things that will happen to him. Accepting these things will be very hard, like drinking a cup of something bitter.

DON'T GET MAD; GET EVEN?
MATTHEW 26:57-63; 27:11-14

When someone treats you unkindly, what do you do? Do you get mad or think about getting even? (Be honest!) After Jesus was arrested and put on trial, people made fun of him and called him names. He didn't get mad or say mean things. Instead, he remained silent for the most part. He refused to treat them the way they treated him.

When we're mistreated, many of us are tempted to get even. When those times come, think about what Jesus would do. Don't let others cause you to do wrong. Two wrongs never make a right!

Got someone bugging you? Link here for help:

Out of Control? Genesis 4, p. 8

Give Revenge a Rest, Leviticus 19:18, p. 160

The MLP, Ruth 1:16–17, p. 345

Mind Guard, Proverbs 4:23, p. 831

Get Hot or Keep Cool? Proverbs 12:16, p. 842

Forgive Again? Luke 17:3–4, p. 1402

Matthew 26:72 1323

59 The leading priests and the whole Jewish council tried to find something false against Jesus so they could kill him. 60 Many people came and told lies about him, but the council could find no real reason to kill him. Then two people came and said, 61 "This man said, 'I can destroy the Temple of God and build it again in three days.'"

62 Then the high priest stood up and said to Jesus, "Aren't you going to answer? Don't you have something to say about their charges against you?" 63 But Jesus said nothing.

Again the high priest said to Jesus, "I command you by the power of the living God: tell us if you are the Christ, the Son of God."

64 Jesus answered, "Those are your words. But I tell you, in the future you will see the Son of Man sitting at the right hand of God, the Powerful One, and coming on clouds in the sky."

65 When the high priest heard this, he tore his clothes and said, "This man has said things that are against God! We don't need any more witnesses; you all heard him say these things against God. 66 What do you think?"

The people answered, "He should die."

67 Then the people there spat in Jesus' face and beat him with their fists. Others slapped him. 68 They said, "Prove to us that you are a prophet, you Christ! Tell us who hit you!"

Peter Says He Doesn't Know Jesus

69 At that time, as Peter was sitting in the courtyard, a servant girl came to him and said, "You also were with Jesus of Galilee."

70 But Peter said to all the people there that he was never with Jesus. He said, "I don't know what you are talking about."

71 When he left the courtyard and was at the gate, another girl saw him. She said to the people there, "This man was with Jesus of Nazareth."

72 Again, Peter said he was never with him, saying, "I swear I don't know this man Jesus!"

73 A short time later, some people standing there went to Peter and said, "Surely you are one of those who followed Jesus. The way you talk proves it."

74 Then Peter began to place a curse on himself and swear, "I don't know the man." At once, a cockerel crowed. 75 And Peter remembered what Jesus had told him: "Before the cockerel crows, you will say three times that you don't know me." Then Peter went outside and cried bitterly.

Jesus is Taken to Pilate

27 Early the next morning, all the leading priests and elders of the people decided that Jesus should die. 2 They tied him, led him away, and turned him over to Pilate, the governor.

Judas Kills Himself

3 Judas, the one who had given Jesus to his enemies, saw that they had decided to kill Jesus. Then he was very sorry for what he had done. So he took the 30 silver coins[n] back to the priests and the leaders, 4 saying, "I sinned; I handed over to you an innocent man."

The leaders answered, "What is that to us? That's your problem, not ours."

5 So Judas threw the money into the Temple. Then he went off and hanged himself.

6 The leading priests picked up the silver coins in the Temple and said, "Our law does not allow us to keep this money with the Temple money, because it has paid for a man's death." 7 So they decided to use the coins to buy Potter's Field as a place to bury strangers who died in Jerusalem. 8 That is why that field is still called the Field of Blood. 9 So what Jeremiah the prophet had said came true: "They took 30 silver coins. That is how little the Israelites thought he was worth. 10 They used those 30 silver coins to buy the potter's field, as the Lord commanded me."[n]

Pilate Questions Jesus

11 Jesus stood before Pilate the governor, and Pilate asked him, "Are you the king of the Jews?"

Jesus answered, "Those are your words."

12 When the leading priests and the elders accused Jesus, he said nothing.

13 So Pilate said to Jesus, "Don't you hear them accusing you of all these things?"

14 But Jesus said nothing in answer to Pilate, and Pilate was very surprised at this.

Pilate Tries to Free Jesus

15 Every year at the time of Passover the governor would free one prisoner whom the people chose. 16 At that time there was a man in prison, named Barabbas, who was known to be very bad. 17 When the people gathered at Pilate's house, Pilate said, "Whom do you want me to set free: Barabbas or Jesus who is called the Christ?" 18 Pilate knew that the people had turned Jesus over to him because they were jealous.

19 While Pilate was sitting there on the judge's seat, his wife sent this message to him: "Don't have anything to do with that man, because he is innocent. Today I had a dream about him, and it troubled me very much."

20 But the leading priests and elders convinced the crowd to ask for Barabbas to be freed and for Jesus to be killed.

21 Pilate said, "I have Barabbas and Jesus. Which do you want me to set free for you?"

The people answered, "Barabbas."

22 Pilate asked, "So what should I do with Jesus, the one called the Christ?"

They all answered, "Crucify him!"

23 Pilate asked, "Why? What wrong has he done?"

But they shouted louder, "Crucify him!"

24 When Pilate saw that he could do nothing about this and that a riot was starting, he took some water and washed his hands[n] in front of the crowd. Then he

---

27:3 coin Roman dinarii. A silver coin was the average pay for one day's work.
27:10 "They . . . commanded me." See Zechariah 11:12-13 and Jeremiah 32:6-9.
27:24 washed his hands He did this as a sign to show that he wanted no part in what the people did.

said, "I am not guilty of this man's death. You are the ones who are causing it!"

25 All the people answered, "We and our children will be responsible for his death."

26 Then he set Barabbas free. But Jesus was beaten with whips and handed over to the soldiers to be crucified.

27 The governor's soldiers took Jesus into the governor's palace, and they all gathered around him. 28 They took off his clothes and put a red robe on him. 29 Using thorny branches, they made a crown, put it on his head, and put a stick in his right hand. Then the soldiers bowed before Jesus and made fun of him, saying, "Hail, King of the Jews!" 30 They spat on Jesus. Then they took his stick and began to beat him on the head. 31 After they finished, the soldiers took off the robe and put his own clothes on him again. Then they led him away to be crucified.

Jesus is Crucified

32 As the soldiers were going out of the city with Jesus, they forced a man from Cyrene, named Simon, to carry the cross for Jesus. 33 They all came to the place called Golgotha, which means the Place of the Skull. 34 The soldiers gave Jesus wine mixed with gall[n] to drink. He tasted the wine but refused to drink it. 35 When the soldiers had crucified him, they threw lots to decide who would get his clothes. 36 The soldiers sat there and continued watching him. 37 They put a sign above Jesus' head with a charge against him. It said: THIS IS JESUS, THE KING OF THE JEWS. 38 Two robbers were crucified beside Jesus, one on the right and the other on the left. 39 People walked by and insulted Jesus and shook their heads, 40 saying, "You said you could destroy the Temple and build it again in three days. So save yourself! Come down from that cross if you are really the Son of God!"

41 The leading priests, the teachers of the law and the Jewish elders were also making fun of Jesus. 42 They said, "He saved others, but he can't save himself! He says he is the king of Israel! If he is the king, let him come down now from the cross. Then we will believe in him. 43 He trusts in God, so let God save him now, if God really wants him. He himself said, 'I am the Son of God.'" 44 And in the same way, the robbers who were being crucified beside Jesus insulted him.

Jesus Dies

45 At noon the whole country became dark, and the darkness lasted for three hours. 46 At about three o'clock Jesus cried out in a loud voice, "Eli, Eli,[n] lama sabachthani?" This means, "My God, my God, why have you rejected me?"

47 Some of the people standing there who heard this said, "He is calling Elijah."

48 Quickly one of them ran and got a sponge and filled it with vinegar and tied it to a stick and gave it to Jesus to drink. 49 But the others said, "Don't bother him. We want to see if Elijah will come to save him."

50 But Jesus cried out again in a loud voice and died.

51 Then the curtain in the Temple[n] was torn into two pieces, from the top to the bottom. Also, the earth shook and rocks broke apart. 52 The graves opened, and many of God's people who had died were raised from the dead. 53 They came out of the graves after Jesus was raised from the dead and went into the holy city, where they appeared to many people.

54 When the army officer and the soldiers guarding Jesus saw this earthquake and everything else that happened, they were very frightened and said, "He really was the Son of God!"

55 Many women who had followed Jesus from Galilee to help him were standing at a distance from the cross, watching. 56 Mary Magdalene, and Mary the mother of James and Joseph, and the mother of James and John were there.

27:34 gall Probably a drink of wine mixed with drugs to help a person feel less pain.
27:46 Eli, Eli Some bibles translate this as Eloi, Eloi.
27:51 curtain in the Temple A curtain divided the Most Holy Place from the other part of the Temple. That was the special building in Jerusalem where God commanded the Jewish people to worship him.

Jesus is Buried

57 That evening a rich man named Joseph, a follower of Jesus from the town of Arimathea, came to Jerusalem. 58 Joseph went to Pilate and asked to have Jesus' body. So Pilate gave orders for the soldiers to give it to Joseph. 59 Then Joseph took the body and wrapped it in a clean linen cloth. 60 He put Jesus' body in a new tomb that he had cut out of a wall of rock, and he rolled a very large stone to block the entrance of the tomb. Then Joseph went away. 61 Mary Magdalene and the other woman named Mary were sitting near the tomb.

The Tomb of Jesus is Guarded

62 The next day, the day after Preparation Day, the leading priests and the Pharisees went to Pilate. 63 They said, "Sir, we remember that while that liar was still alive he said, 'After three days I will rise from the dead.' 64 So give the order for the tomb to be guarded closely till the third day. Otherwise, his followers might come and steal the body and tell people that he has risen from the dead. That lie would be even worse than the first one."

65 Pilate said, "Take some soldiers and go and guard the tomb the best way you know." 66 So they all went to the tomb and made it safe from thieves by sealing the stone in the entrance and putting soldiers there to guard it.

Jesus Rises from the Dead

28 The day after the Sabbath day was the first day of the week. At dawn on the first day, Mary Magdalene and another woman named Mary went to look at the tomb.

2 At that time there was a strong earthquake. An angel of the Lord came down from heaven, went to the tomb and rolled the stone away from the entrance. Then he sat on the stone. 3 He was shining as bright as lightning, and his clothes were white as snow. 4 The soldiers guarding the tomb shook with fear because of the angel, and they became like dead men.

5 The angel said to the women, "Don't be afraid. I know that you are looking for Jesus, who has been crucified. 6 He is not here. He has risen from the dead as he said he would. Come and see the place where his body was. 7 And then go quickly and tell his followers, 'Jesus has risen from the dead. He is going into

---

FAITH links

TELL ALL ABOUT HIM!

MATTHEW 28:19

Think about someone you admire. If a friend asked you about that person, what would you say about him or her? Before Jesus returned to heaven, his followers were given the job of telling the world about their best friend, Jesus. He was someone *they* admired. If you're a follower of Jesus, that's *your* job, too. Does this mean you have to immediately get on a plane to Australia in order to talk about Jesus? No, unless you and your folks just happen to be going there. It *does* mean, though, being willing to tell people about Jesus wherever you happen to be.

Faith of Our Fathers, Joshua 4:4–9, p. 280

See the Heart Behind It, Nehemiah 8; 9, p. 636

A Picture of the Past, Psalm 105, p. 789

Remember Your Creator, Ecclesiastes 12:1, 13, p. 885

Inside the Heart of God, Micah 7:18–20, p. 1228

The Number One Rule, Mark 12:28–31, p. 1351

Galilee ahead of you, and you will see him there.'" Then the angel said, "Now I have told you."

8 The women left the tomb quickly. They were afraid, but they were also very happy. They ran to tell Jesus' followers what had happened. 9 Suddenly, Jesus met them and said, "Greetings." The women came up to him, took hold of his feet, and worshipped him. 10 Then Jesus said to them, "Don't be afraid. Go and tell my followers to go on to Galilee, and they will see me there."

The Soldiers Report to the Leaders

11 While the women went to tell Jesus' followers, some of the soldiers who had been guarding the tomb went into the city to tell the leading priests everything that had happened. 12 Then the priests met with the Jewish elders and made a plan. They paid the soldiers a large amount of money 13 and said to them, "Tell the people that Jesus' followers came during the night and stole the body while you were asleep. 14 If the governor hears about this, we will satisfy him and save you from trouble." 15 So the soldiers kept the money and did as they were told. And that story is still spread among the Jewish people even today.

Jesus Talks to His Followers

16 The eleven followers went to Galilee to the mountain where Jesus had told them to go. 17 On the mountain they saw Jesus and worshipped him, but some of them did not believe it was really Jesus. 18 Then Jesus came to them and said, "All power in heaven and on earth is given to me. 19 So go and make followers of all people in the world. Baptise them in the name of the Father and the Son and the Holy Spirit. 20 Teach them to obey everything that I have taught you, and I will be with you always, even until the end of this age."

28:19-20 Witnessing
Check out Jesus' final command.

JESUS ON THE MOVE

Hi, there. I'm Mark. I'm glad you're reading my book. I was just a little older than you when I experienced the things in this book. Even though I wasn't one of *the* disciples, I *was* an early follower of Jesus. I spent a lot of time with Jesus, went with Paul on some of his missionary journeys, and I worked with Barnabas (another early missionary) to spread the gospel. In later years, I knew Peter pretty well, and he told me plenty!

So, why did I write this book? I wrote it for a group of non-Jews who formed a church in Rome. I wanted them to know the same Jesus I did. So I wrote this to tell them about him. But I didn't want to give them long, boring stories. I filled my book with a lot of action-packed short stories about Jesus serving everyone he met. A lot of people say this was the first Gospel written. I guess I was in a hurry!

JESUS WATCH

Mark's Gospel gives us snapshots of Jesus' ministry with lots of details. Before the first chapter is over, Mark describes Jesus' baptism, his temptation in the desert, calling the disciples, casting out demons and healing people. Whew! And that's just the first chapter! Jesus' personality in this book can best be described as "immediately". You see Jesus going somewhere "immediately" or doing something "immediately". Jesus was always moving forward to reach his goal.

Mark's way of showing us Jesus in this book is really simple. He offers us a picture of Jesus as the servant-king. Chapters 1–10 portray Jesus on a mission to serve many, in a variety of ways and places. Chapters 11–16 portray Jesus as the perfect servant, giving his life for the sins of the people that he loves.

my FAVOURITE links

OTHER CONNECTIONS

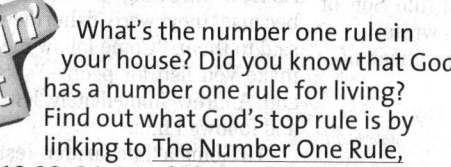

What's the number one rule in your house? Did you know that God has a number one rule for living? Find out what God's top rule is by linking to The Number One Rule, Mark 12:28–34. See if it's one you can live by.

Visit these information bulletin boards to find out more about important places and people you'll find in the Book of Mark:

- A Place to Worship, Mark 6:2. Jesus did not worship in a church like the one you may attend. Instead, Jesus and his family would gather at the local synagogue. Link here for more about this important meeting place.
- Connect to Saints, Sinners or Religious Leaders? Mark 7:1–13, to learn more about the group of men who were most opposed to Jesus and his teachings. Decide for yourself how you would describe these men!
- Jesus – God With Us, Mark 16. Download this map for a look at the key places in Jesus' childhood, his early ministry and his later ministry.

Does Mark's book talk about the end times when Jesus will return?

If you surf through Mark 13 you'll find out that it does, and a lot more. Take a look at these other really cool stories.

The chosen dozen, Mark 1:16–20
A herd of crazy pigs, Mark 5:1–20
The blind see, Mark 10:46–52
Jesus returns to heaven, Mark 16:19–20

FAITH links

- Prayer Anywhere, **Mark 1:35**
- Help for a Friend, **Mark 2:1–5**
- Mission Impossible? **Mark 5:21–24, 35–43**
- The Power of If, **Mark 9:14–24**
- My Favourite! **Mark 10:17–23**
- Quick to Forgive? **Mark 11:25**
- The Number One Rule, **Mark 12:28–31**
- Get Ready! **Mark 13:26–27**
- A Family Meal, **Mark 14:23–26**
- The Unpopular Choice, **Mark 15:42–43**

John Prepares for Jesus

1 This is the beginning of the Good News about Jesus Christ, the Son of God,*ⁿ* 2 as the prophet Isaiah wrote:

> "I will send my messenger ahead of you,
> who will prepare your way."
> *Malachi 3:1*

> 3 "This is a voice of one
> who calls out in the desert:
> 'Prepare the way for the Lord.
> Make the road straight for him.'"
> *Isaiah 40:3*

4 John was baptising people in the desert and preaching a baptism of changed hearts and lives for the forgiveness of sins. 5 All the people from Judea and Jerusalem were going out to him. They confessed their sins and were baptised by him in the Jordan River. 6 John wore clothes made from camel's hair, had a leather belt around his waist and ate locusts and wild honey. 7 This is what John preached to the people: "There is one coming after me who is greater than I; I am not good enough even to kneel down and untie his sandals. 8 I baptise you with water, but he will baptise you with the Holy Spirit."

Jesus is Baptised

9 At that time Jesus came from the town of Nazareth in Galilee and was baptised by John in the Jordan River. 10 Immediately, as Jesus was coming up out of the water, he saw heaven open. The Holy Spirit came down on him like a dove, 11 and a voice came from heaven: "You are my Son, whom I love, and I am very pleased with you."

12 Then the Spirit sent Jesus into the desert. 13 He was in the desert for 40 days and was tempted by Satan. He was with the wild animals, and the angels came and took care of him.

Jesus Chooses Some Followers

14 After John was put in prison, Jesus went into Galilee, preaching the Good News from God. 15 He said, "The right time has come. The kingdom of God is near. Change your hearts and lives and believe the Good News!"

16 When Jesus was walking by Lake Galilee, he saw Simon*ⁿ* and his brother Andrew throwing a net into the lake because they were fishermen. 17 Jesus said to them, "Come follow me, and I will make you fish for people." 18 So Simon and Andrew immediately left their nets and followed him.

19 Going a little farther, Jesus saw two more brothers, James and John, the sons of Zebedee. They were in a boat, mending their nets. 20 Jesus immediately called them, and they left their father in the boat with the hired workers and followed Jesus.

Jesus Forces Out an Evil Spirit

21 Jesus and his followers went to Capernaum. On the Sabbath day he went to the synagogue and began to teach. 22 The people were amazed at his teaching, because he taught like a person who had authority, not like their teachers of the law. 23 Just then, a man was there in the synagogue who had an evil spirit in him. He shouted, 24 "Jesus of Nazareth! What do you want with us? Did you come to destroy us? I know who you are—God's Holy One!"

25 Jesus commanded the evil spirit, "Be quiet! Come out of the man!" 26 The evil spirit shook the man violently, gave a loud cry and then came out of him.

27 The people were so amazed they asked each other, "What is happening here? This man is teaching something new, and with authority. He even gives commands to evil spirits, and they obey him." 28 And the news about Jesus spread quickly everywhere in the area of Galilee.

Jesus Heals Many People

29 As soon as Jesus and his followers left the synagogue, they went with James and John to the home of Simon*ⁿ* and Andrew. 30 Simon's mother-in-law was sick in bed with a fever, and the people

---

1:1 the Son of God Some Greek copies omit these words.
1:16, 29 Simon Simon's other name was Peter.

FAITH LINKS

PRAYER ANYWHERE
MARK 1:35

Suppose someone told you that you could talk to your mum and dad only on Sundays and only while sitting at the dining room table. Sounds pretty silly? Well, God is your heavenly Father. Some people believe that they can only talk to God at certain times and at one certain place – church. What do you believe?

Jesus often woke up early and went off by himself to pray. Prayer can take place anywhere. You can talk to God on your way to school, in the car, or in the playground. God is always ready to listen to you – anytime, anywhere!

Need to talk to God? Connect here:

From Hopeless to Hopeful, Exodus 6:9, p. 83

What Will You Risk? Joshua 2, p. 278

Real Faith or Really Scared? Judges 4, p. 315

No Doubt About It, Job 36:5, p. 699

Hope That Doesn't Fail, Acts 26:4–7, p. 1510

Thoughts on Thoughts, Philippians 4:8–9, p. 1614

---

told Jesus about her. 31 So Jesus went to her bed, took her hand and helped her up. The fever left her, and she began serving them.

32 That evening, after the sun went down, the people brought to Jesus all who were sick and had demons in them. 33 The whole town gathered at the door. 34 Jesus healed many who had different kinds of sicknesses, and he forced many demons to leave people. But he would not allow the demons to speak, because they knew who he was.

35 Early the next morning, while it was still dark, Jesus woke and left the house. He went to a lonely place, where he prayed. 36 Simon and his friends went to look for Jesus. 37 When they found him, they said, "Everyone is looking for you!"

38 Jesus answered, "We should go to other towns around here so I can preach there too. That is the reason I came." 39 So he went everywhere in Galilee, preaching in the synagogues and forcing out demons.

Jesus Heals a Sick Man

40 A man with a skin disease came to Jesus. He fell to his knees and begged Jesus, "You can heal me if you will."

41 Jesus felt sorry for the man, so he reached out his hand and touched him and said, "I will. Be healed!" 42 Immediately the disease left the man, and he was healed.

43 Jesus told the man to go away at once, but he warned him strongly, 44 "Don't tell anyone about this. But go and show yourself to the priest. And offer the gift Moses commanded for people who are made well."[n] This will show the people what I have done." 45 The man left there, but he began to tell everyone that Jesus had healed him, and so he spread the news about Jesus. As a result, Jesus could not enter a town if people saw him. He stayed in remote places [where nobody lived], but people came to him from everywhere.

Jesus Heals a Paralysed Man

2 A few days later, when Jesus came back to Capernaum, the news spread

---

1:44 Moses . . . well Read about this in Leviticus 14:1-32.

Mark 2:2

FAITH links

HELP FOR A FRIEND
MARK 2:1-5

Would you go out of your way to help a friend? Four people wanted to take their paralysed friend to Jesus. Since Jesus was in a crowded house, they made a hole in the roof and lowered him down, bed and all.

Jesus wants you to have the same kind of concern for your friends. You don't have to tear up a roof to help a friend, however. You can tell them about Jesus, pray for them, say kind words to them when they're feeling sad, or just be willing to listen. Your friends will be glad you care!

Here are some more Faithlinks on caring for your friends:

Giving Your Part, Leviticus 27:30, p. 173

An Unsung Hero, Ruth 2:12, 15–16, p. 347

The Heart of the Matter, 1 Samuel 16, p. 375

Lower Than Low, Job 19:13–25, p. 680

God's Instructions, Ezekiel 4:1–15, p. 1089

Kindness First, Matthew 9:35–36, p. 1290

---

that he was at home. 2 Many people gathered together so that there was no room in the house, not even outside the door. And Jesus was teaching them God's message. 3 Four people came, carrying a paralysed man. 4 Since they could not get to Jesus because of the crowd, they dug a hole in the roof right above where he was speaking. When they got through, they lowered the mat with the paralysed man on it. 5 When Jesus saw the faith of these people, he said to the paralysed man, "Young man, your sins are forgiven."

6 Some of the teachers of the law were sitting there, thinking to themselves, 7 "Why does this man say things like that? He is speaking as if he were God. Only God can forgive sins."

8 Jesus knew immediately what these teachers of the law were thinking. So he said to them, "Why are you thinking these things? 9 Which is easier: to tell this paralysed man, 'Your sins are forgiven,' or to tell him, 'Stand up. Take your mat and walk'? 10 But I will prove to you that the Son of Man has authority on earth to forgive sins." So Jesus said to the paralysed man, 11 "I tell you, stand up, take your mat, and go home." 12 Immediately the paralysed man stood up, took his mat and walked out while everyone was watching him.

The people were amazed and praised God. They said, "We have never seen anything like this!"

13 Jesus went to the lake again. The whole crowd followed him there, and he taught them. 14 While he was walking along, he saw a man named Levi*[n]* son of Alphaeus, sitting in the tax collector's booth. Jesus said to him, "Follow me," and he stood up and followed Jesus.

15 Later, as Jesus was having dinner at Levi's house, many tax collectors and "sinners" were eating there with Jesus and his followers. Many people like this followed Jesus. 16 When the teachers of the law who were Pharisees saw Jesus eating with the tax collectors and "sinners", they asked his followers, "Why does he eat with tax collectors and sinners?"

17 Jesus heard this and said to them, "It is not the healthy people who need a doctor, but the sick. I did not come to invite good people but to invite sinners."

2:14 Levi Also known as Matthew.

Jesus' Followers are Criticised

18 Now the followers of John[n] and the Pharisees often gave up eating for a certain time.[n] Some people came to Jesus and said, "Why do John's followers and the followers of the Pharisees often give up eating, but your followers don't?"

19 Jesus answered, "The friends of the bridegroom do not give up eating while the bridegroom is still with them. As long as the bridegroom is with them, they cannot give up eating. 20 But the time will come when the bridegroom will be taken from them, and then they will give up eating.

21 "No one sews a patch of unshrunken cloth over a hole in an old coat. Otherwise, the patch will shrink and pull away—the new patch will pull away from the old coat. Then the hole will be worse. 22 Also, no one ever pours new wine into old leather bags. Otherwise, the new wine will break the bags, and the wine will be ruined along with the bags. But new wine should be put into new leather bags."

Jesus is Lord of the Sabbath

23 One Sabbath day, as Jesus was walking through some fields of grain, his followers began to pick some grain to eat. 24 The Pharisees said to Jesus, "Why are your followers doing what is not lawful on the Sabbath day?"

25 Jesus answered, "Have you never read what David did when he and those with him were hungry and needed food? 26 During the time of Abiathar the high priest, David went into God's house and ate the holy bread, which is lawful only for priests to eat. And David also gave some of the bread to those who were with him."

27 Then Jesus said to the Pharisees, "The Sabbath day was made to help people; they were not made to be ruled by the Sabbath day. 28 So then, the Son of Man is Lord even of the Sabbath day."

Jesus Heals a Man's Hand

3 Another time when Jesus went into a synagogue, a man with a crippled hand was there. 2 Some people watched Jesus closely to see if he would heal the man on the Sabbath day so they could accuse him.

3 Jesus said to the man with the crippled hand, "Stand up here in the middle of everyone."

4 Then Jesus asked the people, "Which is lawful on the Sabbath day: to do good or to do evil, to save a life or to kill?" But they said nothing to answer him.

5 Jesus was angry as he looked at the people, and he felt very sad because they were stubborn. Then he said to the man, "Hold out your hand." The man held out his hand and it was healed. 6 Then the Pharisees left and began making plans with the Herodians[n] about a way to kill Jesus.

Many People Follow Jesus

7 Jesus left with his followers for the lake, and a large crowd from Galilee followed him. 8 Also many people came from Judea, from Jerusalem, from Idumea, from the lands across the Jordan River and from the area of Tyre and Sidon. When they heard what Jesus was doing, many people came to him. 9 When Jesus saw the crowds, he told his followers to get a boat ready for him to keep people from crowding against him. 10 He had healed many people, so all the sick were pushing towards him to touch him. 11 When evil spirits saw Jesus, they fell down before him and shouted, "You are the Son of God!" 12 But Jesus strongly warned them not to tell who he was.

Jesus Chooses His Twelve Apostles

13 Then Jesus went up on a mountain and called to him the men he wanted, and they came to him. 14 Jesus chose twelve men and called them apostles. He wanted

---

2:18 John John the Baptist, who preached to people about Christ's coming (Mark 1:4-8; Luke 1:1-22).

2:18 gave . . . time This is called "fasting". The people would give up eating for a special time of prayer and worship to God. It was also done to show sadness and disappointment.

3:6 Herodians A political group that followed Herod and his family.

Mark 3:15 1334

them to be with him, and he wanted to send them out to preach 15 and to have the authority to force demons out of people. 16 These are the twelve men he chose: Simon (Jesus named him Peter), 17 James and John, the sons of Zebedee (Jesus named them Boanerges, which means "Sons of Thunder"), 18 Andrew, Philip, Bartholomew, Matthew, Thomas, James the son of Alphaeus, Thaddaeus, Simon the Zealot 19 and Judas Iscariot, who later turned against Jesus.

Some People Say Jesus Has a Devil

20 Then Jesus went home, but again a crowd gathered. There were so many people that Jesus and his followers could not eat. 21 When his family heard this, they went to get him because they thought he was out of his mind. 22 But the teachers of the law from Jerusalem were saying, "Beelzebul is living inside him! He uses power from the ruler of demons to force demons out of people."

23 So Jesus called the people together and taught them with stories. He said, "Satan will not force himself out of people. 24 A kingdom that is divided cannot continue, 25 and a family that is divided cannot continue. 26 And if Satan is against himself and fights against his own people, he cannot continue; that is the end of

CONTROL YOURSELF

Ever stop to think about the things you are thankful for? Here is someone who is having some problems in this area. Let's welcome Max, aged 9, to Connect 2-You.

Max

My mum says I spend too much time wishing for things I don't have instead of appreciating what I do have. She says I'm not grateful for the things God has given me. What does that mean? Should I go around saying thank you for every little thing that happens?

Sometimes it's easy to forget how much God does for us. But when you take time to stop and really think about it, you'll be amazed at what comes to mind. If you'd like some tips on how to do this, check out the Livin' It page on being thankful, Colossians 2:6-7, p. 1623. It may help you to develop an attitude of thankfulness!

It also helps if you put yourself in God's position. How would Max feel if he did something really nice for someone and that person never said thank you or even noticed what he'd done? Just as we like to be thanked for things we do, so does God! Remember that next time you find yourself moaning.

Satan. 27 No one can enter a strong person's house and steal his things unless he first ties up the strong person. Then he can steal things from the house. 28 I tell you the truth, all sins that people do and all the things people say against God can be forgiven. 29 But anyone who speaks against the Holy Spirit will never be forgiven; he is guilty of a sin that continues for ever."

30 Jesus said this because the teachers of the law said that he had an evil spirit inside him.

Jesus' True Family

31 Then Jesus' mother and brothers arrived. Standing outside, they sent someone in to tell him to come out. 32 Many people were sitting around Jesus, and they said to him, "Your mother and brothers are waiting for you outside."

33 Jesus asked, "Who are my mother and my brothers?" 34 Then he looked at those sitting around him and said, "Here are my mother and my brothers! 35 My true brother and sister and mother and father are those who do what God wants."

A Story About Planting Seed

4 Again Jesus began teaching by the lake. A great crowd gathered around him, so he sat down in a boat near the shore. All the people stayed on the shore close to the water. 2 Jesus taught them many things, using stories. He said, 3 "Listen! A farmer went out to plant his seed. 4 While he was planting, some seed fell by the road, and the birds came and ate it up. 5 Some seed fell on rocky ground where there wasn't much earth. That seed grew very fast, because the ground was not deep. 6 But when the sun rose, the plants dried up because they did not have deep roots. 7 Some other seed fell among thorny weeds, which grew and choked the good plants. So those plants did not produce a crop. 8 Some other seed fell on good ground and began to grow. It got taller and produced a crop. Some plants made 30 times more, some made 60 times more, and some made 100 times more."

9 Then Jesus said, "You people who can hear me, listen!"

Jesus Tells Why He Used Stories

10 Later, when Jesus was alone, the twelve apostles and others around him asked him about the stories.

11 Jesus said, "You can know the secret about the kingdom of God. But to other people I tell everything by using stories 12 so that:

'They will look and look, but they will
    not learn.
They will listen and listen, but they
    will not understand.
If they did learn and understand,
    they would come back to me and
    be forgiven.'" *Isaiah 6:9-10*

Jesus Explains the Seed Story

13 Then Jesus said to his followers, "Don't you understand this story? If you don't, how will you understand any story? 14 The farmer is like a person who plants God's message in people. 15 Sometimes the teaching falls on the road. This is like the people who hear the teaching of God, but Satan quickly comes and takes away the teaching that was planted in them. 16 Others are like the seed planted on rocky ground. They hear the teaching and quickly accept it with joy. 17 But since they don't allow the teaching to go deep into their lives, they keep it only a short time. When trouble or persecution comes because of the teaching they accepted, they quickly give up. 18 Others are like the seed planted among the thorny weeds. They hear the teaching, 19 but the worries of this life, the temptation of wealth and many other evil desires keep the teaching from growing and producing fruit[n] in their lives. 20 Others are like the seed planted in the good ground. They hear the teaching and accept it. Then they grow and produce fruit—sometimes 30 times more, sometimes 60 times more and sometimes 100 times more."

Use What You Have

21 Then Jesus said to them, "Do you hide a lamp under a bowl or under a bed? No! You put the lamp on a lampstand.

4:19 producing fruit To produce fruit means to have in your life the good things God wants.

22 Everything that is hidden will be made clear and every secret thing will be made known. 23 You people who can hear me, listen!

24 "Think carefully about what you hear. The way you give to others is the way God will give to you, but God will give you even more. 25 Those who have understanding will be given more. But those who do not have understanding, even what they have will be taken away from them."

Jesus Uses a Story About Seed

26 Then Jesus said, "The kingdom of God is like someone who plants seed in the ground. 27 Night and day, whether the person is asleep or awake, the seed still grows, but the person does not know how it grows. 28 By itself the earth produces grain. First the plant grows, then the ear and then all the grain in the ear. 29 When the grain is ready, the farmer cuts it, because the harvest time has come."

A Story About Mustard Seed

30 Then Jesus said, "How can I show you what the kingdom of God is like? What story can I use to explain it? 31 The kingdom of God is like a mustard seed, the smallest seed you plant in the ground. 32 But when planted, this seed grows and becomes the largest of all garden plants. It produces large branches, and the wild birds can make nests in its shade."

33 Jesus used many stories like these to teach the crowd God's message—as much as they could understand. 34 He always used stories to teach them. But when he and his followers were alone, Jesus explained everything to them.

Jesus Calms a Storm

35 That evening, Jesus said to his followers, "Let's go across the lake." 36 Leaving the crowd behind, they took him in the boat just as he was. There were also other boats with them. 37 A very strong wind came up on the lake. The waves came over the sides and into the boat so that it was already full of water. 38 Jesus was at the back of the boat, sleeping with his head on a pillow. His followers woke him and said, "Teacher, don't you care that we are drowning!"

39 Jesus stood up and commanded the wind and said to the waves, "Quiet! Be still!" Then the wind stopped, and it became completely calm.

40 Jesus said to his followers, "Why are you afraid? Do you still have no faith?"

41 The followers were very afraid and asked each other, "Who is this? Even the wind and the waves obey him!"

A Man with Demons Inside Him

5 Jesus and his followers went to the other side of the lake to the area of the Gerasene people. 2 When Jesus got out of the boat, instantly a man with an evil spirit came to him from the burial caves. 3 This man lived in the caves, and no one could tie him up, not even with a chain. 4 Many times people had used chains to tie the man's hands and feet, but he always broke them off. No one was strong enough to control him. 5 Day and night he would wander around the burial caves and on the hills, screaming and cutting himself with stones. 6 While Jesus was still far away, the man saw him, ran to him and fell down before him.

7 The man shouted in a loud voice, "What do you want with me, Jesus, Son of the Most High God? I command you in God's name not to torture me!" 8 He said this because Jesus was saying to him, "You evil spirit, come out of the man."

9 Then Jesus asked him, "What is your name?"

He answered, "My name is Legion," because we are many spirits." 10 He

> The kingdom of God is like a mustard seed, the smallest seed you plant in the ground.
> – Mark 4:31

5:9 Legion Means very many. A legion was about 5,000 men in the Roman army.

Mark 5:26

FAITH links

MISSION IMPOSSIBLE?
MARK 5:21-24, 35-43

Got a hard problem in your life? Maybe you, like Jairus the synagogue leader, are wondering what Jesus can do for you. Jairus didn't have a hard problem. He had an *impossible* problem. His daughter was dying. He knew that only Jesus could help her. By the time Jesus arrived, she had died. But Jesus did the impossible by bringing her back to life.

Hard problems help us learn to trust God. Through them, we learn that Jesus has the power to do anything. When you're faced with the impossible, put your trust in the God of impossibilities.

Good Plans, Genesis 45:7–8, p. 64

A Holiday Letter, Esther 9:20–23, p. 657

Happiness or Joy? Job 29:18–19, p. 691

Prove It! Matthew 16:1–4, p. 1302

Just for the Asking, Romans 3:23–28, p. 1522

Fear-Fighters, 2 Timothy 1:7, p. 1652

Jesus, "Send us into the pigs; let us go into them." 13 So Jesus allowed them to do this. The evil spirits left the man and went into the pigs. Then the herd of pigs—about 2,000 of them—rushed down the hill into the lake and were drowned.

14 The herdsmen ran away and went to the town and to the countryside, telling everyone about this. So people went out to see what had happened. 15 They came to Jesus and saw the man who used to have the many evil spirits, sitting, clothed and in his right mind. And they were frightened. 16 The people who saw this told the others what had happened to the man who had the demons living in him, and they told about the pigs. 17 Then the people began to beg Jesus to leave their area.

18 As Jesus was getting back into the boat, the man who was freed from the demons begged to go with him. 19 But Jesus would not let him. He said, "Go home to your family and tell them how much the Lord has done for you and how he has had mercy on you." 20 So the man left and began to tell the people in the Ten Towns[n] about what Jesus had done for him. And everyone was amazed.

Jesus Gives Life to a Dead Girl and Heals a Sick Woman

21 When Jesus went in the boat back to the other side of the lake, a large crowd gathered around him there. 22 A leader of the synagogue, named Jairus, came there, saw Jesus and fell at his feet. 23 He begged Jesus, saying again and again, "My daughter is dying. Please come and put your hands on her so she will be healed and will live." 24 So Jesus went with him.

A large crowd followed Jesus and pushed very close around him. 25 Among them was a woman who had been bleeding for twelve years. 26 She had suffered very much from many doctors and had

---

begged Jesus again and again not to send them out of that area.

11 A large herd of pigs was feeding on a hill near there. 12 The demons begged

5:20 Ten Towns In Greek, called "Decapolis." It was an area east of Lake Galilee that once had ten main towns.

spent all the money she had, but instead of improving, she was getting worse. 27 When the woman heard about Jesus, she came up behind him in the crowd and touched his coat. 28 She thought, "If I can just touch his clothes, I will be healed." 29 Instantly her bleeding stopped, and she felt in her body that she was healed from her disease.

30 At once Jesus felt power go out from him. So he turned around in the crowd and asked, "Who touched my clothes?"

31 His followers said, "Look at how many people are pushing against you! And you ask, 'Who touched me?'"

32 But Jesus continued looking around to see who had touched him. 33 The woman, knowing that she was healed, came and fell at Jesus' feet. Shaking with fear, she told him the whole truth. 34 Jesus said to her, "Dear woman, you are made well because you believed. Go in peace; be healed of your disease."

35 While Jesus was still speaking, some people came from the house of the synagogue leader. They said, "Your daughter is dead. There is no need to bother the teacher any more."

36 But Jesus paid no attention to what they said. He told the synagogue leader, "Don't be afraid; just believe."

37 Jesus let only Peter, James and John the brother of James go with him. 38 When they came to the house of the synagogue leader, Jesus found many people there making lots of noise and crying loudly. 39 Jesus entered the house and said to them, "Why are you crying and making so much noise? The child is not dead, only asleep." 40 But they laughed at him. So, after throwing them out of the house, Jesus took the child's father and mother and his three followers into the room where the child was. 41 Taking hold of the girl's hand, he said to her, "Talitha, koum!" (This means, "Young girl, I tell you to stand up!") 42 At once the girl stood right up and began walking. (She was twelve years old.) Everyone was completely amazed. 43 Jesus gave them strict orders not to tell people about this. Then he told them to give the girl something to eat.

Jesus Goes to His Home Town

6 Jesus left there and went to his home town, and his followers went with him. 2 On the Sabbath day he taught in the synagogue. Many people heard him and were amazed, saying, "Where did this man get these teachings? What is this wisdom that has been given to him? And where did he get the power to do miracles? 3 He is just the carpenter, the son of Mary and the brother of James, Joseph, Judas and Simon. And his sisters are here with us." So the people were upset with Jesus.

4 Jesus said to them, "A prophet is honoured everywhere except in his home town and with his own people and in his own home." 5 So Jesus was not able to work any miracles there except to heal a few sick people by putting his hands on them. 6 He was amazed at how many people had no faith.

Then Jesus went to other villages in that area and taught. 7 He called his twelve followers together and got ready to send them out two by two and gave them authority over evil spirits. 8 This is what Jesus commanded them: "Take nothing for your trip except a walking stick. Take no bread, no bag and no money in your pockets. 9 Wear sandals, but take only the clothes you are wearing. 10 When you enter a house, stay there until you leave that town. 11 If the people in a certain place refuse to welcome you or listen to you, leave that place. Shake its dust off your feet[n] as a warning to them."

12 So the followers went out and preached that people should change their hearts and lives. 13 They forced many demons out and put olive oil on many sick people and healed them.

How John the Baptist was Killed

14 King Herod heard about Jesus, because he was now well known. Some people said, "He is John the Baptist, who has risen from the dead. That is why he can work these miracles."

6:11 Shake . . . feet A warning. It showed that they were rejecting these people.

Mark 6:26 1339

A PLACE TO WORSHIP
Mark 6:2

The synagogue was a local gathering place where Jews of all ages met to pray and study the teachings of Moses. There were many synagogues in Jerusalem because a new one could be started every time ten or more men committed to studying together. There were no sacrifices offered at the synagogue like there were at the Temple. When people went to the synagogue, they would read from books of the Bible, pray and listen to someone teach. Different men taught at different times. Jesus read the Scriptures in the synagogue in Nazareth (see Luke 4:16–30, p. 1374), and he often taught in synagogues (look up Matthew 4:23, p. 1279).

Synagogue buildings were usually rectangular with a large sitting area, like many church sanctuaries today. The congregation sat on stone benches along the walls or cross-legged on the floor. The main piece of furniture in a synagogue was the place where the sacred scrolls (like our Bible) were kept. The apostle Paul preached at synagogues on his missionary journeys. (Check out Acts 13:5, p. 1486; 14:1, p. 1489.)

15 Others said, "He is Elijah."[n]

Other people said, "Jesus is a prophet, like the prophets who lived long ago."

16 When Herod heard this, he said, "I killed John by cutting off his head. Now he has risen from the dead!"

17 Herod himself had ordered his soldiers to arrest John and put him in prison in order to please his wife, Herodias. She had been the wife of Philip, Herod's brother, but then Herod had married her. **18** John had been telling Herod, "It is not lawful for you to be married to your brother's wife." **19** So Herodias hated John and wanted to kill him. But she couldn't, **20** because Herod was afraid of John and protected him. He knew John was a good and holy man. Also, though John's preaching always bothered him, he enjoyed listening to John.

21 Then the perfect time came for Herodias to cause John's death. On Herod's birthday, he gave a dinner party for the most important government leaders, the commanders of his army and the most important people in Galilee. **22** When the daughter of Herodias came in and danced, she pleased Herod and the people eating with him.

So King Herod said to the girl, "Ask me for anything you want, and I will give it to you." **23** He promised her, "Anything you ask for I will give to you—up to half of my kingdom."

24 The girl went to her mother and asked, "What should I ask for?"

Her mother answered, "Ask for the head of John the Baptist."

25 At once the girl went back to the king and said to him, "I want the head of John the Baptist right now on a dish."

26 Although the king was very sad, he had made a promise, and his dinner guests had heard it. So he did not want to

---

6:15 Elijah A man who spoke for God and who lived hundreds of years before Christ. See 1 Kings 17.

refuse what she asked. 27 Immediately the king sent a soldier to bring John's head. The soldier went and cut off John's head in the prison 28 and brought it back on a dish. He gave it to the girl, and the girl gave it to her mother. 29 When John's followers heard this, they came and got John's body and put it in a tomb.

More than 5,000 Fed

30 The apostles gathered around Jesus and told him about all the things they had done and taught. 31 Crowds of people were coming and going so that Jesus and his followers did not even have time to eat. He said to them, "Come away by yourselves, and we will go to a lonely place to get some rest."

32 So they went in a boat by themselves to a lonely place. 33 But many people saw them leave and recognised them. So from all the towns they ran to the place where Jesus was going, and they got there before him. 34 When he arrived, he saw a great crowd waiting. He felt sorry for them, because they were like sheep without a shepherd. So he began to teach them many things.

35 When it was late in the day, his followers came to him and said, "No one lives in this place, and it is already very late. 36 Send the people away so they can go to the countryside and towns around here to buy themselves something to eat."

37 But Jesus answered, "You give them something to eat."

They said to him, "We would all have to work a month to earn enough money to buy that much bread!"

38 Jesus asked them, "How many loaves of bread do you have? Go and see."

When they found out, they said, "Five loaves and two fish."

39 Then Jesus told his followers to have the people sit in groups on the green grass. 40 So they sat in groups of 50 or 100. 41 Jesus took the five loaves and two fish and, looking up to heaven, he thanked God for the food. He divided the bread and gave it to his followers for them to give to the people. Then he divided the two fish among them all. 42 All the people ate and were satisfied. 43 The followers filled twelve baskets with the leftover pieces of bread and fish. 44 There were 5,000 men who ate.

Jesus Walks on the Water

45 Immediately Jesus told his followers to get into the boat and go ahead of him to Bethsaida across the lake. He stayed behind to send the people home. 46 After sending them away, he went into the hills to pray.

47 That night, the boat was in the middle of the lake, and Jesus was alone on the land. 48 He saw his followers struggling hard to row the boat, because the wind was blowing against them. Between three and six o'clock in the morning, Jesus came to them, walking on the water, and he wanted to walk past the boat. 49 But when they saw him walking on the water, they thought he was a ghost and cried out. 50 They all saw him and were afraid. But immediately Jesus spoke to them and said, "Have courage! It is I. Do not be afraid." 51 Then he got into the boat with them, and the wind became calm. The followers were greatly amazed. 52 They did not understand about the miracle of the five loaves, because their minds were closed.

53 When they had crossed the lake, they came to shore at Gennesaret and tied the boat there. 54 When they got out of the boat, people immediately recognised Jesus. 55 They ran everywhere in that area and began to bring sick people on mats wherever they heard he was. 56 And everywhere he went—into towns, cities or countryside—the people brought the sick to the market-places. They begged him to let them touch just the edge of his coat, and all who touched it were healed.

Obey God's Law

7 When some Pharisees and some teachers of the law came from Jerusalem, they gathered around Jesus. 2 They saw some of Jesus' followers eating food with hands that were not clean, that is, they hadn't washed them. 3 (The Pharisees and all the Jews never eat before

SAINTS, SINNERS OR RELIGIOUS LEADERS?
Mark 7:1–13

The Pharisees and Sadducees were two groups of Jewish religious leaders. Jesus had disagreements with both groups during his life on earth.

The word *Pharisee* means "separated". The Pharisees concentrated on keeping themselves separate from people who did not observe certain religious laws. The Pharisees made up some of these laws. Like if God gave one law, "Keep the Sabbath holy", the Pharisees would interpret that into a lot of rules and regulations about what it meant to keep the Sabbath holy. Jesus didn't ever disagree with God's laws, but he often disagreed with all the rules and regulations that the Pharisees made up and added to God's laws.

The Sadducees were priests, merchants and aristocrats. They stuck to God's original laws, but they did not believe in the resurrection of the dead. You can see how Jesus would disagree with that! (Check out Mark 12:18–27.)

---

washing their hands in a special way according to their unwritten laws. 4 And when they buy something in the market, they never eat it until they have washed themselves in a special way. They also follow many other unwritten laws, such as the washing of cups, pitchers and pots.)

5 The Pharisees and the teachers of the law said to Jesus, "Why don't your followers obey the unwritten laws which have been handed down to us? Why do your followers eat their food with hands that are not clean?"

6 Jesus answered, "Isaiah was right when he spoke about you hypocrites. He wrote,

'These people show honour to me
    with words,
but their hearts are far from me.
7 Their worship of me is worthless.
The things they teach are nothing
    but human rules.' *Isaiah 29:13*

8 You have stopped following the commands of God, and you follow only human teachings."

9 Then Jesus said to them, "You cleverly ignore the commands of God so you can follow your own teachings. 10 Moses said, 'Honour your father and your mother,'ⁿ and 'Anyone who says cruel things to his father or mother must be put to death.'ⁿ 11 But you say a person can tell his father or mother, 'I have something I could use to help you, but it is Corban—a gift to God.' 12 You no longer let that person use that money for his father or his mother. 13 By your own rules, which you teach people, you are rejecting what God said. And you do many things like that."

14 After Jesus called the crowd to him again, he said, "Every person should listen to me and understand what I am saying. 15 There is nothing people put into their bodies that makes them unclean.

7:10 'Honour . . . mother' Quotation from Exodus 20:12; Deuteronomy 5:16.
7:10 'Anyone . . . death.' Quotation from Exodus 21:17.

People are made unclean by the things that come out of them." 16 *n*

17 When Jesus left the people and went into the house, his followers asked him about this story. 18 Jesus said, "Do you still not understand? Surely you know that nothing that enters someone from the outside can make that person unclean. 19 It does not go into the heart, but into the stomach. Then it goes out of the body." (When Jesus said this, he meant that no longer was any food unclean for people to eat.)

20 And Jesus said, "The things that come out of people are the things that make them unclean. 21 All these evil things begin inside people, in the heart: evil thoughts, sexual sins, stealing, murder, adultery, 22 greed, evil actions, lying, doing sinful things, jealousy, speaking evil of others, pride and foolish living. 23 All these evil things come from inside and make people unclean."

Jesus Helps a Non-Jewish Woman

24 Jesus left that place and went to the area around Tyre. When he went into a house, he did not want anyone to know he was there, but he could not stay hidden. 25 A woman whose daughter had an evil spirit in her heard that he was there. So she quickly came to Jesus and fell at his feet. 26 She was Greek, born in Phoenicia, in Syria. She begged Jesus to force the demon out of her daughter.

27 Jesus told the woman, "It is not right to take the children's bread and give it to the dogs. First let the children eat all they want."

28 But she answered, "Yes, Lord, but even the dogs under the table can eat the children's crumbs."

29 Then Jesus said, "Because of your answer, you may go. The demon has left your daughter."

30 The woman went home and found her daughter lying in bed; the demon was gone.

Jesus Heals a Deaf Man

31 Then Jesus left the area around Tyre and went through Sidon to Lake Galilee, to the area of the Ten Towns." 32 While he was there, some people brought a man to him who was deaf and could not talk plainly. The people begged Jesus to put his hand on the man to heal him.

33 Jesus led the man away from the crowd, by himself. He put his fingers in the man's ears and then spat and touched the man's tongue. 34 Looking up to heaven, he sighed and said to the man, "Ephphatha!" (This means, "Be opened.") 35 Instantly the man was able to hear and to use his tongue so that he spoke clearly.

36 Jesus commanded the people not to tell anyone about what happened. But the more he commanded them, the more they told about it. 37 They were completely amazed and said, "Jesus does everything well. He makes the deaf hear! And those who can't talk he makes able to speak."

More than 4,000 People Fed

8 Another time there was a great crowd with Jesus that had nothing to eat. So Jesus called his followers and said, 2 "I feel sorry for these people, because they have already been with me for three days, and they have nothing to eat. 3 If I send them home hungry, they will faint on the way. Some of them live a long way from here."

4 Jesus' followers answered, "How can we get enough bread to feed all these people? We are far away from any town."

5 Jesus asked, "How many loaves of bread do you have?"

They answered, "Seven."

6 Jesus told the people to sit on the ground. Then he took the seven loaves, gave thanks to God, and divided the bread. He gave the pieces to his followers to give to the people, and they did so. 7 The followers also had a few small fish. After Jesus gave thanks for the fish, he told his followers to give them to the

---

7:16 Verse 16 Some Greek copies add verse 16: "You people who can hear me, listen!"

7:31 Ten Towns In Greek, called "Decapolis." It was an area east of Lake Galilee that once had ten main towns.

people as well. 8 All the people ate and were satisfied. Then his followers filled seven baskets with the leftover pieces of food. 9 There were about 4,000 people who ate. After they had eaten, Jesus sent them home. 10 Then right away he got into a boat with his followers and went to the area of Dalmanutha.

The Leaders Ask for a Miracle

11 The Pharisees came to Jesus and began to ask him questions. Hoping to trap him, they asked Jesus for a miracle from God. 12 Jesus sighed deeply and said, "Why do you people ask for a miracle as a sign? I tell you the truth, no sign will be given to you." 13 Then Jesus left the Pharisees and went in the boat to the other side of the lake.

Guard Against Wrong Teachings

14 His followers had only one loaf of bread with them in the boat; they had forgotten to bring more. 15 Jesus warned them, "Be careful! Beware of the yeast of the Pharisees and the yeast of Herod."

16 His followers discussed the meaning of this, saying, "He said this because we have no bread."

17 Knowing what they were talking about, Jesus asked them, "Why are you talking about not having bread? Do you still not see or understand? Are your minds closed? 18 You have eyes, but you don't really see. You have ears, but you don't really listen. Remember when 19 I divided five loaves of bread for the 5,000? How many baskets did you fill with leftover pieces of food?"

They answered, "Twelve."

20 "And when I divided seven loaves of bread for the 4,000, how many baskets did you fill with leftover pieces of food?"

They answered, "Seven."

21 Then Jesus said to them, "Don't you understand yet?"

Jesus Heals a Blind Man

22 Jesus and his followers came to Bethsaida. There some people brought a blind man to Jesus and begged him to touch the man. 23 So Jesus took the blind man's hand and led him out of the village. Then he spat on the man's eyes and put his hands on the man and asked, "Can you see now?"

24 The man looked up and said, "Yes, I see people, but they look like trees walking around."

25 Again Jesus put his hands on the man's eyes. Then the man opened his eyes wide and they were healed, and he was able to see everything clearly. 26 Jesus told him to go home, saying, "Don't go into the town."

Peter Says Jesus is the Christ

27 Jesus and his followers went to the towns around Caesarea Philippi. While they were travelling, Jesus asked them, "Who do people say I am?"

28 They answered, "Some say you are John the Baptist. Others say you are Elijah,[n] and others say you are one of the prophets."

29 Then Jesus asked, "But who do you say I am?"

Peter answered, "You are the Christ."

30 Jesus warned his followers not to tell anyone who he was.

31 Then Jesus began to teach them that the Son of Man must suffer many things and that he would be rejected by the Jewish elders, the leading priests and the teachers of the law. He told them that the Son of Man must be killed and then rise from the dead after three days. 32 Jesus told them plainly what would happen. Then Peter took Jesus aside and began to tell him not to talk like that. 33 But Jesus turned and looked at his followers. Then he told Peter not to talk in that way. He said, "Go away from me, Satan![n] You don't care about the things of God, but only about things people think are important."

34 Then Jesus called the crowd to him, along with his followers. He said, "If people want to follow me, they must give up

---

8:28 Elijah A man who spoke for God and who lived hundreds of years before Christ. See 1 Kings 17.

8:33 Satan Name for the devil meaning "the enemy". Jesus means that Peter was talking like Satan.

the things they want. They must be willing even to give up their lives to follow me. 35 Those who want to save their lives will give up true life. But those who give up their lives for me and for the Good News will have true life. 36 It is worth nothing for them to have the whole world if they lose their souls. 37 They could never pay enough to buy back their souls. 38 The people who live now are living in a sinful and evil time. If people are ashamed of me and my teaching, the Son of Man will be ashamed of them when he comes with his Father's glory and with the holy angels."

9 Then Jesus said to the people, "I tell you the truth, some people standing here will see the kingdom of God come with power before they die."

8:34–36 Money What it means to follow Jesus.

Jesus Talks with Moses and Elijah

2 Six days later, Jesus took Peter, James and John up on a high mountain by themselves. While they watched, Jesus' appearance was changed. 3 His clothes became shining white, whiter than any person could make them. 4 Then Elijah and Moses[n] appeared to them, talking with Jesus.

5 Peter said to Jesus, "Teacher, it is good that we are here. Let us make three tents—one for you, one for Moses and one for Elijah." 6 Peter did not know what to say, because he and the others were so frightened.

7 Then a cloud came and covered them, and a voice came from the cloud, saying, "This is my Son, whom I love. Listen to him!"

8 Suddenly Peter, James and John looked around, but they saw only Jesus there alone with them.

9 As they were coming down the mountain, Jesus commanded them not to tell anyone about what they had seen until the Son of Man had risen from the dead.

10 So the followers obeyed Jesus, but they discussed what he meant about rising from the dead.

FAITH links

THE POWER OF IF
MARK 9:14-24

One of the most powerful words in the English language is the word *if*. That tiny word can mean the difference between belief and unbelief. A father asked Jesus for help for his son. When the father said, "If you can do anything," Jesus knew that he had trouble believing.

Part of learning to trust God is learning to admit when you have a problem believing in him. God is never fooled when we claim to have faith that we really don't have. If you don't have it, admit it! Then, like the father, ask Jesus to help you have faith.

Download these links for more on faith:

Lights, Camera, . . . Actions! Genesis 12:1–3, p. 17

Complaints, Complaints! Exodus 16:1–3, p. 97

A Serious Promise, Deuteronomy 23:21–23, p. 257

Wisdom in Store, Proverbs 2:6–7, p. 828

A Word About Worry, Matthew 6:25–34, p. 1284

Heavenly Treasure, Luke 12:32–34, p. 1394

9:4 Elijah and Moses Two of the most important Jewish leaders in the past. Moses had given them the law, and Elijah was an important prophet.

11 Then they asked Jesus, "Why do the teachers of the law say that Elijah must come first?"

12 Jesus answered, "They are right to say that Elijah must come first and make everything the way it should be. But why does the Scripture say that the Son of Man will suffer much and that people will treat him as if he were nothing? 13 I tell you that Elijah has already come. And people did to him whatever they wanted to do, just as the Scriptures said it would happen."

Jesus Heals a Sick Boy

14 When Jesus, Peter, James and John came back to the other followers, they saw a great crowd around them and the teachers of the law arguing with them. 15 But as soon as the crowd saw Jesus, the people were surprised and ran to welcome him.

16 Jesus asked, "What are you arguing about?"

17 A man answered, "Teacher, I brought my son to you. He has an evil spirit in him that stops him from talking. 18 When the spirit attacks him, it throws him on the ground. Then my son foams at the mouth, grinds his teeth and becomes very stiff. I asked your followers to force the evil spirit out, but they couldn't."

19 Jesus answered, "You people have no faith. How long must I stay with you? How long must I put up with you? Bring the boy to me."

20 So the followers brought him to Jesus. As soon as the evil spirit saw Jesus, it made the boy lose control of himself, and he fell down and rolled on the ground, foaming at the mouth.

21 Jesus asked the boy's father, "How long has this been happening?"

The father answered, "Since he was very young. 22 The spirit often throws him into a fire or into water to kill him. If you can do anything for him, please have pity on us and help us."

23 Jesus said to the father, "You said, 'If you can!' All things are possible for the one who believes."

24 Immediately the father cried out, "I do believe! Help me to believe more!"

25 When Jesus saw that a crowd was quickly gathering, he ordered the evil spirit, saying, "You spirit that makes people unable to hear or speak, I command you to come out of this boy and never enter him again!"

26 The evil spirit screamed and caused the boy to fall on the ground again. Then the spirit came out. The boy looked as if he were dead, and many people said, "He is dead!" 27 But Jesus took hold of the boy's hand and helped him to stand up.

28 When Jesus went into the house, his followers began asking him privately, "Why couldn't we force that evil spirit out?"

29 Jesus answered, "That kind of spirit can only be forced out by prayer."

Jesus Talks About His Death

30 Then Jesus and his followers left that place and went through Galilee. He didn't want anyone to know where he was, 31 because he was teaching his followers. He said to them, "The Son of Man will be handed over to people, and they will kill him. After three days, he will rise from the dead." 32 But the followers did not understand what Jesus meant, and they were afraid to ask him.

Who is the Greatest?

33 Jesus and his followers went to Capernaum. When they went into a house there, he asked them, "What were you arguing about on the road?" 34 But the followers did not answer, because their argument on the road was about which one of them was the greatest.

35 Jesus sat down and called the twelve apostles to him. He said, "Whoever wants to be the most important must be last of all and servant of all."

36 Then Jesus took a small child and had him stand among them. Taking the child in his arms, he said, 37 "Whoever accepts a child like this in my name accepts me. And whoever accepts me accepts the One who sent me."

Anyone Not Against Us is For Us

38 Then John said, "Teacher, we saw someone using your name to force

demons out of a person. We told him to stop, because he does not belong to our group."

39 But Jesus said, "Don't stop him, because anyone who uses my name to do powerful things will not easily say evil things about me. 40 Whoever is not against us is with us. 41 I tell you the truth, whoever gives you a drink of water because you belong to the Christ will truly get his reward.

9:41 Giving
What is your reward for giving to others?

42 "If one of these little children believes in me, and someone causes that child to sin, it would be better for that person to have a large stone tied around his neck and be drowned in the sea. 43 If your hand causes you to sin, cut it off. It is better for you to lose part of your body and live for ever than to have two hands and go to hell, where the fire never goes out. 44 ⁿ 45 If your foot causes you to sin, cut it off. It is better for you to lose part of your body and to live for ever than to have two feet and be thrown into hell. 46 ⁿ 47 If your eye causes you to sin, take it out. It is better for you to enter the kingdom of God with only one eye than to have two eyes and be thrown into hell. 48 In hell the worm does not die; the fire is never put out. 49 Every person will be salted with fire.ⁿ

50 "Salt is good, but if the salt loses its salty taste, you cannot make it salty again. So, be full of salt, and have peace with each other."

Jesus Teaches About Divorce

10 Then Jesus left that place and went into the area of Judea and across the Jordan River. Again, crowds came to him, and he taught them as he usually did.

2 Some Pharisees came to Jesus and tried to trick him. They asked, "Is it right for a man to divorce his wife?"

3 Jesus answered, "What did Moses command you to do?"

4 They said, "Moses allowed a man to write out divorce papers and send her away."ⁿ

5 Jesus said, "Moses wrote that command for you because you were stubborn. 6 But when God made the world, 'he made them male and female'.ⁿ 7 'So a man will leave his father and mother and be united with his wife, 8 and the two will become one body.'ⁿ So there are not two, but one. 9 God has joined the two together, so no one should separate them."

10 Later, in the house, his followers asked Jesus again about the question of divorce. 11 He answered, "Anyone who divorces his wife and marries another woman is guilty of adultery against her. 12 And the woman who divorces her husband and marries another man is also guilty of adultery."

Jesus Accepts Children

13 Some people brought their little children to Jesus so he could touch them, but his followers told them to stop. 14 When Jesus saw this, he was upset and said to them, "Let the little children come to me. Don't stop them, because the kingdom of God belongs to people who are like these children. 15 I tell you the truth, you must accept the kingdom of God as if you were a little child, or you will never enter it." 16 Then Jesus took the children in his arms, put his hands on them and blessed them.

A Rich Young Man's Question

17 As Jesus started to leave, a man ran to him and fell on his knees before Jesus. The man asked, "Good teacher, what must I do to have life for ever?"

18 Jesus answered, "Why do you call me good? Only God is good. 19 You know the commands: 'You must not murder anyone. You must not be guilty of adultery. You must not steal. You must not tell

---

9:44 Verse 44 Some Greek copies of Mark add verse 44, which is the same as verse 48.
9:46 Verse 46 Some Greek copies of Mark add verse 46, which is the same as verse 48.
9:49 Salted with fire Purified by fire as with the action of salt.
10:4 "Moses . . . away." Quotation from Deuteronomy 24:1.
10:6 'he made . . . female' Quotation from Genesis 1:27.
10:8 'So . . . body.' Quotation from Genesis 2:24.

Mark 10:34

FAITH links

MY FAVOURITE!
MARK 10:17-23

Suppose someone were to ask you to give up your most cherished possession to prove your love for God. How willing would you be to give it up?

Jesus once talked to a young man who had a lot of possessions. He knew that the young man loved his possessions more than he loved God. God wants people to love him more than they love things. He's not against your having possessions. He just wants to have first place in your life. So . . . does he?

What You Value, Genesis 25:21-34, p. 34

Obey? No Way! Exodus 1:15-21, p. 76

Care to Be Fair? Joshua 18:1-8, p. 299

A Parent's Advice, Proverbs 1:8-9, p. 825

A Half-hearted Offering, Malachi 1:6-14, p. 1268

A Robbery in Progress, Malachi 3:8-10, p. 1270

---

lies about your neighbour. You must not cheat. Honour your father and mother.'"[n]

20 The man said, "Teacher, I have obeyed all these things since I was a boy."

21 Jesus, looking at the man, loved him and said, "There is one more thing you need to do. Go and sell everything you have, and give the money to the poor and you will have treasure in heaven. Then come and follow me."

22 He was very sad to hear Jesus say this, and he left very sad, because he was rich.

23 Then Jesus looked at his followers and said, "How hard it will be for the rich to enter the kingdom of God!"

24 The followers were amazed at what Jesus said. But he said again, "My children, it is very hard to enter the kingdom of God! 25 It is easier for a camel to go through the eye of a needle than for a rich person to enter the kingdom of God."

26 The followers were even more surprised and said to each other, "Then who can be saved?"

27 Jesus looked at them and said, "This is something people cannot do, but God can. God can do all things."

28 Peter said to Jesus, "Look, we have left everything and followed you."

29 Jesus said, "I tell you the truth, all those who have left houses, brothers, sisters, mother, father, children or farms for me and for the Good News 30 will get more than they left. Here in this world they will have a hundred times more homes, brothers, sisters, mothers, children and fields. And with those things, they will also suffer for their belief. But in the age that is coming they will have life for ever. 31 Many who have the highest place now will have the lowest place in the future. And many who have the lowest place now will have the highest place in the future."

Jesus Talks About His Death

32 As Jesus and the people with him were on the road to Jerusalem, he was leading the way. His followers were amazed, but others in the crowd who followed were afraid. Again Jesus took the twelve apostles aside and began to tell them what was about to happen in Jerusalem. 33 He said, "Look, we are going to Jerusalem. The Son of Man will be turned over to the leading priests and the teachers of the law. They will say that he must die, and they will turn him over to the non-Jewish people, 34 who will laugh

---

10:19 'You . . . mother.' Quotation from Exodus 20:12-16; Deuteronomy 5:16-20.

at him and spit on him. They will beat him with whips and crucify him. But on the third day, he will rise to life again."

Two Followers Ask Jesus a Favour

35 Then James and John, sons of Zebedee, came to Jesus and said, "Teacher, we want to ask you to do something for us."

36 Jesus asked, "What do you want me to do for you?"

37 They answered, "Let one of us sit at your right side and one of us sit at your left side in your glory in your kingdom."

38 Jesus said, "You don't understand what you are asking. Can you drink the cup that I must drink? And can you be baptised with the same kind of baptism that I must go through?"[n]

39 They answered, "Yes, we can."

Jesus said to them, "You will drink the same cup that I will drink, and you will be baptised with the same baptism that I must go through. 40 But I cannot choose who will sit at my right or my left; those places belong to those for whom they have been prepared."

41 When the other ten followers heard this, they began to be angry with James and John.

42 Jesus called them together and said, "The non-Jewish people have rulers. You know that those rulers love to show their power over the people, and their important leaders love to use all their authority. 43 But it should not be that way among you. Whoever wants to become great among you must serve the rest of you like a servant. 44 Whoever wants to become the first among you must serve all of you like a slave. 45 In the same way, the Son of Man did not come to be served. He came to serve others and to give his life as a ransom for many people."

Jesus Heals a Blind Man

46 Then they came to the town of Jericho. As Jesus was leaving there with his followers and a great many people, a blind beggar named Bartimaeus son of Timaeus was sitting by the road. 47 When he heard that Jesus from Nazareth was walking by, he began to shout, "Jesus, Son of David, have mercy on me!"

48 Many people warned the blind man to be quiet, but he shouted even more, "Son of David, have mercy on me!"

49 Jesus stopped and said, "Tell the man to come here."

So they called the blind man, saying, "Cheer up! Get to your feet. Jesus is calling you." 50 The blind man jumped up, left his coat there, and went to Jesus.

51 Jesus asked him, "What do you want me to do for you?"

The blind man answered, "Teacher, I want to see."

52 Jesus said, "Go, you are healed because you believed." At once the man could see, and he followed Jesus on the road.

Jesus Enters Jerusalem as a King

11 As Jesus and his followers were coming closer to Jerusalem, they came to the towns of Bethphage and Bethany near the Mount of Olives. From there Jesus sent two of his followers 2 and said to them, "Go to the town you can see there. When you enter it, you will quickly find a colt tied, which no one has ever ridden. Untie it and bring it here to me. 3 If anyone asks you why you are doing this, tell him its Master needs the colt, and he will send it at once."

4 The followers went into the town, found a colt tied in the street near the door of a house, and untied it. 5 Some people were standing there and asked, "What are you doing? Why are you untying that colt?" 6 The followers answered the way Jesus told them to answer, and the people let them take the colt.

7 They brought the colt to Jesus and put their coats on it, and Jesus sat on it. 8 Many people spread their coats on the road. Others cut branches in the fields and spread them on the road. 9 The people were walking ahead of Jesus and behind him, shouting,

"Praise[n] God!

10:38 Can you . . . through? Jesus was asking if they could suffer the same terrible things that would happen to him.

11:9 Praise Literally, "Hosanna", a Hebrew word used at first in praying to God for help. At this time it was probably a shout of joy used in praising God or his Messiah.

FAITH links

QUICK TO FORGIVE?
MARK 11:25

More than likely, you can easily think of something someone did to make you mad. But how quick are you to forgive the person who hurt you? Are you as fast as a cheetah, quick to forgive? Or, are you a tortoise, slow in forgiving others?

Jesus talked often about forgiveness. God wants you to forgive others for whatever they have done to you. Forgiveness is not something to offer only if you feel like it. It's something God wants you to give, no matter what. When you forgive others, God will forgive you.

Where do you rate on forgiving others? Check it out here:

More Powerful Than Revenge, Genesis 50:14–21, p. 71

What's Out Becomes In, Judges 11, p. 327

Some Friendly Advice, Proverbs 17:9, 14, 17, p. 851

A Model of Forgiveness, Ezekiel 16:59–63, p. 1103

The Choices of a Choice, Luke 5:1–11, p. 1375

The Whole Truth, John 8:31–32, 45, p. 1438

God bless the One who comes in the name of the Lord! *Psalm 118:26*
10 God bless the kingdom of our father David!
That kingdom is coming!
Praise to God in heaven!"

11 Jesus entered Jerusalem and went into the Temple. After he had looked at everything, since it was already late, he went out to Bethany with the twelve apostles.

12 The next day as Jesus was leaving Bethany, he became hungry. 13 Seeing a fig tree in leaf from far away, he went to see if it had any figs on it. But he found no figs, only leaves, because it was not the right season for figs. 14 So Jesus said to the tree, "May no one ever eat fruit from you again." And Jesus' followers heard him say this.

Jesus Goes to the Temple

15 When Jesus returned to Jerusalem, he went into the Temple and began to throw out those who were buying and selling there. He turned over the tables of those who were exchanging different kinds of money, and he upset the benches of those who were selling doves. 16 Jesus refused to allow anyone to carry goods through the Temple courts. 17 Then he taught the people, saying, "It is written in the Scriptures, 'My Temple will be called a house for prayer for people from all nations.'[n] But you are changing God's house into a 'hideout for robbers.'"[n]

18 The leading priests and the teachers of the law heard all this and began trying to find a way to kill Jesus. They were afraid of him, because all the people were amazed at his teaching. 19 That evening, Jesus and his followers left the city.

The Power of Faith

20 The next morning as Jesus was passing by with his followers, they saw the fig tree dry and dead, even to the

---

11:17 'My Temple . . . nations.' Quotation from Isaiah 56:7.
11:17 'hideout for robbers' Quotation from Jeremiah 7:11.

roots. 21 Peter remembered the tree and said to Jesus, "Teacher, look! The fig tree you cursed is dry and dead!"

22 Jesus answered, "Have faith in God. 23 I tell you the truth, you can say to this mountain, 'Go, fall into the sea.' And if you have no doubts in your mind and believe that what you say will happen, God will do it for you. 24 So I tell you to believe that you have received the things you ask for in prayer, and God will give them to you. 25 When you are praying, if you are angry with someone, forgive him so that your Father in heaven will also forgive your sins." 26 *n*

Leaders Doubt Jesus' Authority

27 Jesus and his followers went again to Jerusalem. As Jesus was walking in the Temple, the leading priests, the teachers of the law and the elders came to him. 28 They said to him, "What authority do you have to do these things? Who gave you this authority?"

29 Jesus answered, "I will ask you one question. If you answer me, I will tell you what authority I have to do these things. 30 Tell me: when John baptised people, was that authority from God or just from other people?"

31 They argued about Jesus' question, saying, "If we answer, 'John's baptism was from God,' Jesus will say, 'Then why didn't you believe him?' 32 But if we say, 'It was from other people,' the crowd will be against us." (These leaders were afraid of the people, because all the people believed that John was a prophet.)

33 So they answered Jesus, "We don't know."

Jesus said to them, "Then I won't tell you what authority I have to do these things."

A Story About God's Son

12 Jesus began to use stories to teach the people. He said, "A man planted a vineyard. He put a wall around it and dug a hole for a winepress and built a tower. Then he leased the land to some farmers and left for a trip. 2 When it was time for the grapes to be picked, he sent a servant to the farmers to get his share of the grapes. 3 But the farmers grabbed the servant and beat him and sent him away empty-handed. 4 Then the man sent another servant. They hit him on the head and showed no respect for him. 5 So the man sent another servant, whom they killed. The man sent many other servants; the farmers beat some of them and killed others.

6 "The man had one person left to send, his son whom he loved. He sent him last of all, saying, 'They will respect my son.'

7 "But the farmers said to each other, 'This son will inherit the vineyard. If we kill him, it will be ours.' 8 So they took the son, killed him and threw him out of the vineyard.

9 "So what will the owner of the vineyard do? He will come and kill those farmers and will give the vineyard to other farmers. 10 Surely you have read this Scripture:

'The stone that the builders rejected
became the cornerstone.
11 The Lord did this,
and it is wonderful to us.'"

Psalm 118:22-23

12 The Jewish leaders knew that the story was about them. They wanted to find a way to arrest Jesus, but they were afraid of the people. So the leaders left him and went away.

Is It Right to Pay Taxes or Not?

13 Later, the Jewish leaders sent some Pharisees and Herodians*n* to Jesus to trap him into saying something wrong. 14 They came to him and said, "Teacher, we know that you are an honest man. You are not afraid of what other people think about you, because you pay no attention to who they are. And you teach the truth about God's way. Tell us: is it right to pay taxes to Caesar or not? 15 Should we pay them, or not?"

11:26 Verse 26 Some early Greek copies add verse 26: "But if you don't forgive other people, then your Father in heaven will not forgive your sins."

12:13 Herodians A political group that followed Herod and his family.

But knowing what these men were really trying to do, Jesus said to them, "Why are you trying to trap me? Bring me a coin to look at." 16 They gave Jesus a coin, and he asked, "Whose image and name are on the coin?"

They answered, "Caesar's."

17 Then Jesus said to them, "Give to Caesar the things that are Caesar's, and give to God the things that are God's." The men were amazed at what Jesus said.

Some Sadducees Try to Trick Jesus

18 Then some Sadducees came to Jesus and asked him a question. (Sadducees believed that people would not rise from the dead.) 19 They said, "Teacher, Moses wrote that if a man's brother dies, leaving a wife but no children, then that man must marry the widow and have children for his brother. 20 Once there were seven brothers. The first brother married and died, leaving no children. 21 So the second brother married the widow, but he also died and had no children. The same thing happened with the third brother. 22 All seven brothers married her and died, and none of the brothers had any children. Finally the woman died too. 23 Since all seven brothers had married her, when people rise from the dead, whose wife will she be?"

24 Jesus answered, "Why don't you understand? Don't you know what the Scriptures say, and don't you know about the power of God? 25 When people rise from the dead, they will not marry, nor will they be given to someone to marry. They will be like the angels in heaven. 26 Surely you have read what God said about people rising from the dead. In the book in which Moses wrote about the burning bush," it says that God told Moses, 'I am the God of Abraham, the God of Isaac and the God of Jacob.'" 27 God is the God of the living, not the dead. You Sadducees are wrong!"

The Most Important Command

28 One of the teachers of the law came and heard Jesus arguing with the

FAITH links

THE NUMBER ONE RULE

MARK 12:28-31

Throughout your life, you'll hear a lot of rules. What do you think is the most important rule you can follow? Wash behind your ears? Clean your room? Don't talk with your mouth full? The people of Israel had hundreds of rules to follow to show their obedience to God. The religious leaders made up many of these rules.

A man once asked Jesus to name the most important rule of all. Jesus told him that the most important rule was to love God, and the second was to love others. Love is more important than any sacrifice we can make.

Link here for more on loving your enemies:

Your Worst Enemy, Exodus 7—11, p. 85

No Thanksgiving? 2 Kings 23:21-23, p. 512

Meaningless Words, Job 21:34, p. 684

Two Are Better, Ecclesiastes 4:9-12, p. 877

Obey or Disobey? Luke 20:20-26, p. 1409

Kindness Counts, Acts 14:3, p. 1489

12:26 burning bush Read Exodus 3:1-12 in the Old Testament.
12:26 'I am . . . Jacob.' Quotation from Exodus 3:6.

LOVING GOD'S WAY
Mark 12:28–34

The Number One Rule   Lists, lists and more lists. Everyone loves to look at lists! We have lists of the Top 10 songs, the Top 10 businesses, the Top 10 football teams. On all Top 10 lists, the most important is number one. Do you have a list of rules in your classroom or at home? Is the most important one at the top of the list?

A man once asked Jesus to name the most important rule of all – number one on Jesus' list. Jesus told him that the most important rules were to love God and others. (Look at Mark 12:28–31.) How can you make loving God number one on your Top 10 list of things to do?

MORE FAITH links

- What God Wants, **p. 242**
- Go! No! **p. 1213**
- The Best Choice, **p. 1560**
- Don't Play Favourites, **p. 1691**
- The True Test, **p. 1718**

What's the top rule on your list?

(One that should be pretty near the top is don't surf onto any unsupervised websites. That's a good safety rule.)

But how about downloading these Faithlinks to find out God's number one rule?

Kind or Fair? 1 Samuel 30, p. 395
- Suppose you and a friend did a project together to win a prize, but a third friend chose not to help you. Would it be fair to let the third friend share in the prize? Even though some of his soldiers grumbled, David agreed to share and share alike. When you have to choose between kindness and your idea of fairness, what will you do?

The Worst Chore, John 13:3–17, p. 1447
- What's the worst chore you can think of doing? How would you feel if you had to do it? Link here to see how the disciples felt about Jesus' doing the worst chore anyone could do.

Kindness Counts, Acts 14:3, p. 1489
- What's the one ability you really wish you had? To play a sport or musical instrument better than anyone else? To write a best-seller or paint a masterpiece? What would you do with your ability? How can you use the abilities you *do* have to help others and show love to God?
- Being kind is an ability God gives you. When you're kind to others, they see God's love for them. Remember – kindness counts!

Sadducees. Seeing that Jesus gave good answers to their questions, he asked Jesus, "Which of the commands is most important?"

29 Jesus answered, "The most important command is this: 'Listen, people of Israel! The Lord our God is the only Lord. 30 Love the Lord your God with all your heart, all your soul, all your mind and all your strength.'*ⁿ* 31 The second command is this: 'Love your neighbour as you love yourself.'*ⁿ* There are no commands more important than these."

32 The man answered, "That was a good answer, Teacher. You were right when you said God is the only Lord and there is no other God besides him. 33 One must love God with all his heart, all his mind and all his strength. And one must love his neighbour as he loves himself. These commands are more important than all the animals and sacrifices we offer to God."

34 When Jesus saw that the man answered him wisely, Jesus said to him, "You are close to the kingdom of God." And after that, no one was brave enough to ask Jesus any more questions.

35 As Jesus was teaching in the Temple, he asked, "Why do the teachers of the law say that the Christ is the son of David? 36 David himself, speaking by the Holy Spirit, said:

'The LORD said to my Lord:
   Sit by me at my right side,
   until I put your enemies under
      your control.'   *Psalm 110:1*

37 David himself calls the Christ 'Lord', so how can the Christ be his son?" The large crowd listened to Jesus with pleasure.

38 Jesus continued teaching and said, "Beware of the teachers of the law. They like to walk around wearing fancy clothes, and they love people to greet them with respect in the market-places. 39 They love to have the most important seats in the synagogues and at feasts. 40 But they cheat widows and steal their houses and then try to make themselves look good by saying long prayers. They will receive a greater punishment."

True Giving

41 Jesus sat near the Temple money box and watched the people put in their money. Many rich people gave large sums of money. 42 Then a poor widow came and put in two very small copper coins, which were not even worth a penny.

43 Calling his followers to him, Jesus said, "I tell you the truth, this poor widow gave more than all those rich people. 44 They gave only what they did not need. This woman is very poor, but she gave all she had; she gave all she had to live on."

The Temple will Be Destroyed

13 As Jesus was leaving the Temple, one of his followers said to him, "Look, Teacher! How beautiful the buildings are! How big the stones are!"

2 Jesus said, "Do you see all these great buildings? Not one stone will be left on another. Every stone will be thrown down to the ground."

3 Later, as Jesus was sitting on the Mount of Olives, opposite the Temple, he was alone with Peter, James, John and Andrew. They asked Jesus, 4 "Tell us, when will these things happen? And what will be the sign that they are going to happen?"

5 Jesus began to answer them, "Be careful that no one fools you. 6 Many people will come in my name, saying, 'I am the One,' and they will fool many people. 7 When you hear about wars and stories of wars that are coming, don't be afraid. These things must happen before the end comes. 8 Nations will fight against other nations, and kingdoms against other kingdoms. There will be earthquakes in different places, and there will be times when there is no food for people to eat. These things are like the first pains when something new is about to be born.

12:30 'Listen . . . strength.' Quotation from Deuteronomy 6:4-5.
12:31 'Love . . . yourself.' Quotation from Leviticus 19:18.

---

eMail from God
12:29–30 Love
What is the most important command that God has given you?

Mark 13:9

9 "You must be careful. People will arrest you and take you to court and beat you in their synagogues. You will be forced to stand before kings and governors, to tell them about me. This will happen to you because you follow me. 10 But before these things happen, the Good News must be told to all people. 11 When you are arrested and judged, don't worry ahead of time about what you should say. Say whatever is given to you to say at that time, because it will not really be you speaking; it will be the Holy Spirit.

12 "Brothers will give their own brothers to be killed, and fathers will give their own children to be killed. Children will fight against their own parents and cause them to be put to death. 13 All people will hate you because you follow me, but those people who keep their faith until the end will be saved.

14 "You will see 'the destroying terror'[n] standing where it should not be." (You who read this should understand what it means.) "At that time, the people in Judea should run away to the mountains. 15 If people are on the roofs[n] of their houses, they must not go down or go inside to get anything out of their houses. 16 If people are in the fields, they must not go back to get their coats. 17 At that time, how terrible it will be for women who are pregnant or have nursing babies! 18 Pray that these things will not happen in winter, 19 because those days will be full of trouble. There will be more trouble than there has ever been since the beginning, when God made the world, until now, and nothing as bad will ever happen again. 20 God has decided to make that terrible time short. Otherwise, no one would go on living. But God will make that time short to help the people he has chosen. 21 At that time, someone might say to you, 'Look, there is the Christ!' Or another person might say, 'There he is!' But don't believe them. 22 False Christs and false prophets will come and perform great wonders and miracles. They will try to fool even the people God has chosen, if that were possible. 23 So be careful. I have warned you about all this before it happens.

FAITH links

GET READY!
MARK 13:26-27

You know that a new school year starts every autumn. No one has to convince you that you need to get ready for that event at the end of the summer. You just do what you need to do to get ready, right? (Even if you don't *want* to!)

Jesus told his followers that he would return to earth someday. Although no one knows when that will happen, it *will* happen. We need to be ready for him to return. How do you get ready? Here are some ways: read the Bible, pray and do what God says.

Here are some other links on ways to get ready:

Ten Ways to Obey, Exodus 20, p. 103

The Perfect Sacrifice, Leviticus 1—7, p. 135

The Perfect Leader? Numbers 20:1–13, p. 203

A Tight Spot, Jonah 2, p. 1215

Our Heavenly Connection, Matthew 6:9–13, p. 1283

Prayer Priority, Luke 5:15–16, p. 1376

13:14 'the destroying terror' Mentioned in Daniel 9:27; 12:11 (cf. Daniel 11:31).
13:15 roof In Bible times houses were built with flat roofs. The roof was used for drying things such as flax and fruit. And it was used as an extra room, as a place for worship and as a place to sleep in the summer.

24 "During the days after this trouble comes,
'the sun will grow dark,
and the moon will not give its light.
25 The stars will fall from the sky.
And the powers of the heavens will be shaken.' *Isaiah 13:10; 34:4*
26 "Then people will see the Son of Man coming in clouds with great power and glory. 27 Then he will send his angels all around the earth to gather his chosen people from every part of the earth and from every part of heaven.
28 "Learn a lesson from the fig tree: when its branches become green and soft and new leaves appear, you know summer is near. 29 In the same way, when you see these things happening, you will know that the time is near, ready to come. 30 I tell you the truth, all these things will happen while the people of this time are still living. 31 Earth and sky will be destroyed, but the words I have said will never be destroyed.
32 "No one knows when that day or time will be, not the angels in heaven, not even the Son. Only the Father knows. 33 Be careful! Always be ready, because you don't know when that time will be. 34 It is like a man who goes on a trip. He leaves his house and lets his servants take care of it, giving each one a special job to do. The man tells the servant guarding the door always to be watchful. 35 So always be ready, because you don't know when the owner of the house will come back. It might be in the evening, or at midnight, or in the morning while it is still dark, or when the sun rises. 36 Always be ready. Otherwise he might come back suddenly and find you sleeping. 37 I tell you this, and I say this to everyone: 'Be ready!'"

The Plan to Kill Jesus

14 It was now only two days before the Passover and the Feast of Unleavened Bread. The leading priests and teachers of the law were trying to find a trick to arrest Jesus and kill him. 2 But they said, "We must not do it during the feast, because the people might cause a riot."

A Woman with Perfume for Jesus

3 Jesus was in Bethany at the house of Simon, who had a skin disease. While Jesus was eating there, a woman approached him with an alabaster jar filled with very expensive perfume, made of pure nard. She opened the jar and poured the perfume on Jesus' head.

4 Some who were there became upset and said to each other, "Why waste that perfume? 5 It was worth a full year's work. It could have been sold and the money given to the poor." And they got very angry with the woman.

6 Jesus said, "Leave her alone. Why are you troubling her? She did an excellent thing for me. 7 You will always have the poor with you, and you can help them any time you want. But you will not always have me. 8 This woman did the only thing she could do for me; she poured perfume on my body to prepare me for burial. 9 I tell you the truth, wherever the Good News is preached in all the world, what this woman has done will be told, and people will remember her."

EMAIL FROM GOD
14:6–9 Giving
Check out this example of giving.

Judas Becomes an Enemy of Jesus

10 One of the twelve apostles, Judas Iscariot, went to talk to the leading priests to offer to hand Jesus over to them. 11 These priests were pleased about this and promised to pay Judas money. So he watched for the best time to turn Jesus over.

Jesus Eats the Passover Meal

12 It was now the first day of the Feast of Unleavened Bread when the Passover lamb was sacrificed. Jesus' followers said to him, "Where do you want us to go and prepare for you to eat the Passover meal?"

13 Jesus sent two of his followers and said to them, "Go into the city and a man carrying a jar of water will meet you. Follow him. 14 When he goes into a house, tell the owner of the house, 'The Teacher

says: where is my guest room in which I can eat the Passover meal with my followers?' 15 The owner will show you a large room upstairs that is furnished and ready. Prepare the food for us there."

16 So the followers left and went into the city. Everything happened as Jesus had said, so they prepared the Passover meal.

17 In the evening, Jesus went to that house with the twelve. 18 While they were all eating, Jesus said, "I tell you the truth, one of you will turn against me—one of you eating with me now."

19 The followers were very sad to hear this. Each one began to say to Jesus, "I am not the one, am I?"

20 Jesus answered, "It is one of the twelve—the one who dips his bread into the bowl with me. 21 The Son of Man will die, just as the Scriptures say. But how terrible it will be for the person who hands the Son of Man over to be killed. It would be better for him if he had never been born."

The Lord's Supper

22 While they were eating, Jesus took some bread and thanked God for it and broke it. Then he gave it to his followers and said, "Take it; this is my body."

23 Then Jesus took a cup and thanked God for it and gave it to the followers, and they all drank from the cup.

24 Then Jesus said, "This is my blood which is the new agreement that God makes with his people. This blood is poured out for many. 25 I tell you the truth, I will not drink of this fruit of the vine*n* again until that day when I drink it new in the kingdom of God."

26 After singing a hymn, they went out to the Mount of Olives.

Jesus' Followers Will Leave Him

27 Then Jesus told the followers, "You will all stumble in your faith, because it is written in the Scriptures:

'I will kill the shepherd,
  and the sheep will scatter.'
                              Zechariah 13:7

28 But after I rise from the dead, I will go ahead of you into Galilee."

A FAMILY MEAL
MARK 14:23-26

Mealtimes are times for families to be together. Jesus and his followers were like a family. On the night before Jesus' death, they shared a special meal together. Jesus knew how important it was for them to be together.

As Christians, we're all part of God's family. Although all of us can't fit into one room together, there is a special meal that we can all share no matter where we are in the world. This meal is called the Lord's Supper. The bread and the cup are what we share to remember the most important member of our family – Jesus.

Sitting on the Fence, 1 Kings 18, p. 464

Give In or Take a Stand? 1 Kings 22:13–14, p. 472

Plans for a Son, 1 Chronicles 22:5–19, p. 548

A Fair-Weather Friend, Obadiah 7, p. 1209

Ask, Search, Knock, Matthew 7:7–10, p. 1286

One Big, Happy Family, John 1:12, p. 1422

29 Peter said, "Everyone else may stumble in their faith, but I will not."

30 Jesus answered, "I tell you the

14:25 **fruit of the vine** Product of the grapevine; this may also be translated "wine."

truth, tonight before the cockerel crows twice you will say three times you don't know me."

31 But Peter insisted, "I will never say that I don't know you! I will even die with you!" And all the other followers said the same thing.

Jesus Prays Alone

32 Jesus and his followers went to a place called Gethsemane. He said to them, "Sit here while I pray." 33 Jesus took Peter, James and John with him, and he began to be very sad and troubled. 34 He said to them, "My heart is full of sorrow, to the point of death. Stay here and watch."

35 After walking a little farther away from them, Jesus fell to the ground and prayed that, if possible, he would not have this time of suffering. 36 He prayed, "Abba,ⁿ Father! You can do all things. Take away this cupⁿ of suffering. But do what you want, not what I want."

37 Then Jesus went back to his followers and found them asleep. He said to Peter, "Simon, are you sleeping? Couldn't you stay awake with me for one hour? 38 Stay awake and pray for strength against temptation. The spirit wants to do what is right, but the body is weak."

39 Again Jesus went away and prayed the same thing. 40 Then he went back to his followers, and again he found them asleep, because their eyes were very heavy. And they did not know what to say to him.

41 After Jesus prayed a third time, he went back to his followers and said to them, "Are you still sleeping and resting? That's enough. The time has come for the Son of Man to be handed over to sinful people. 42 Get up, we must go. Look, here comes the man who has turned against me."

Jesus is Arrested

43 At once, while Jesus was still speaking, Judas, one of the twelve apostles, came up. With him were many people carrying swords and clubs who had been sent from the leading priests, the teachers of the law and the Jewish elders.

44 Judas had planned a signal for them, saying, "The man I kiss is Jesus. Arrest him and guard him while you lead him away." 45 So Judas went straight to Jesus and said, "Teacher!" and kissed him. 46 Then the people grabbed Jesus and arrested him. 47 One of his followers standing nearby pulled out his sword and struck the servant of the high priest and cut off his ear.

48 Then Jesus said, "You came to get me with swords and clubs as if I were a criminal. 49 Every day I was with you teaching in the Temple, and you did not arrest me there. But all these things have happened to make the Scriptures come true." 50 Then all of Jesus' followers left him and ran away.

51 A young man, wearing only a linen cloth, was following Jesus, and the people also grabbed him. 52 But the cloth he was wearing came off, and he ran away naked.

Jesus Before the Leaders

53 The people who arrested Jesus led him to the house of the high priest, where all the leading priests, the Jewish elders and the teachers of the law were gathered. 54 Peter followed far behind and entered the courtyard of the high priest's house. There he sat with the guards, warming himself by the fire.

55 The leading priests and the whole Jewish council tried to find something that Jesus had done wrong so they could kill him. But the council could find no proof of anything. 56 Many people came and told false things about him, but all said different things—none of them agreed.

57 Then some people stood up and lied about Jesus, saying, 58 "We heard this man say, 'I will destroy this Temple that people made. And three days later, I will build another Temple not made by

---

14:36 Abba Name that a Jewish child called his father.
14:36 cup Jesus is talking about the terrible things that will happen to him. Accepting these things will be very hard, like drinking a cup of something bitter.

people.'" 59 But even the things these people said did not agree.

60 Then the high priest stood before them and asked Jesus, "Aren't you going to answer? Don't you have something to say about their charges against you?" 61 But Jesus said nothing; he did not answer. The high priest asked Jesus another question: "Are you the Christ, the Son of the blessed God?"

EMAIL FROM GOD
14:61-62 Jesus
Will the Messiah come again?

62 Jesus answered, "I am. And in the future you will see the Son of Man sitting at the right hand of God, the Powerful One, and coming on clouds in the sky."

63 When the high priest heard this, he tore his clothes and said, "We don't need any more witnesses! 64 You all heard him say these things against God. What do you think?"

They all said that Jesus was guilty and should die. 65 Some of the people there began to spit at Jesus. They blindfolded him and beat him with their fists and said, "Prove you are a prophet!" Then the guards led Jesus away and beat him.

Peter Says He Doesn't Know Jesus

66 While Peter was in the courtyard, a servant girl of the high priest came there. 67 She saw Peter warming himself at the fire and looked closely at him.

Then she said, "You also were with Jesus, that man from Nazareth."

68 But Peter said that he was never with Jesus. He said, "I don't know or understand what you are talking about." Then Peter left and went towards the entrance of the courtyard. And the cockerel crowed."

69 The servant girl saw Peter there, and again she said to the people who were standing nearby, "This man is one of those who followed Jesus." 70 Again Peter said that it was not true.

A short time later, some people were standing near Peter saying, "Surely you are one of those who followed Jesus, because you are from Galilee, too."

71 Then Peter began to place a curse on himself and swear, "I don't know this man you're talking about!"

72 At once, the cockerel crowed the second time. Then Peter remembered what Jesus had told him: "Before the cockerel crows twice, you will say three times that you don't know me." Then Peter lost control of himself and began to cry.

Pilate Questions Jesus

15 Very early in the morning, the leading priests, the older leaders, the teachers of the law and all the Jewish council decided what to do with Jesus. They tied him, led him away and turned him over to Pilate, the governor.

2 Pilate asked Jesus, "Are you the king of the Jews?"

Jesus answered, "Those are your words."

3 The leading priests accused Jesus of many things. 4 So Pilate asked Jesus another question, "You can see that they are accusing you of many things. Aren't you going to answer?"

5 But Jesus still said nothing, so Pilate was very surprised.

Pilate Tries to Free Jesus

6 Every year at the time of the Passover the governor would free one prisoner whom the people chose. 7 At that time, there was a man named Barabbas in prison who was a rebel and had committed murder during a riot. 8 The crowd came to Pilate and began to ask him to free a prisoner as he always did.

9 So Pilate asked them, "Do you want me to free the king of the Jews?" 10 Pilate knew that the leading priests had turned Jesus over to him because they were jealous. 11 But the leading priests had persuaded the people to ask Pilate to free Barabbas, not Jesus.

12 Then Pilate asked the crowd again, "So what should I do with this man you call the king of the Jews?"

14:68 And . . . crowed. A few, early Greek copies leave out this phrase.

13 They shouted, "Crucify him!" 14 Pilate asked, "Why? What wrong has he done?"

But they shouted even louder, "Crucify him!" 15 Pilate wanted to please the crowd, so he freed Barabbas for them. After having Jesus beaten with whips, he handed Jesus over to the soldiers to be crucified. 16 The soldiers took Jesus into the governor's palace (called the Praetorium) and called all the other soldiers together. 17 They put a purple robe on Jesus and used thorny branches to make a crown for his head. 18 They began to call out to him, "Hail, King of the Jews!" 19 The soldiers beat Jesus on the head many times with a stick. They spat on him and made fun of him by bowing on their knees and worshipping him. 20 After they finished, the soldiers took off the purple robe and put his own clothes on him again. Then they led him out of the palace to be crucified.

Jesus is Crucified

21 A man named Simon from Cyrene, the father of Alexander and Rufus, was coming from the fields to the city. The soldiers forced Simon to carry the cross for Jesus. 22 They led Jesus to the place called Golgotha, which means the Place of the Skull. 23 The soldiers tried to give Jesus wine mixed with myrrh to drink, but he refused. 24 The soldiers crucified Jesus and divided his clothes among themselves, throwing lots to decide what each soldier would get.

25 It was nine o'clock in the morning when they crucified Jesus. 26 There was a sign with this charge against Jesus written on it: THE KING OF THE JEWS. 27 They also put two robbers on crosses beside Jesus, one on the right, and the other on the left. 28 [n] 29 People walked by and insulted Jesus and shook their heads, saying, "You said you could destroy the Temple and build it again in three days. 30 So save yourself! Come down from that cross!"

31 The leading priests and the teachers of the law were also making fun of Jesus. They said to each other, "He saved other people, but he can't save himself. 32 If he is really the Christ, the king of Israel, let him come down now from the cross. When we see this, we will believe in him." The robbers who were being crucified beside Jesus also insulted him.

Jesus Dies

33 At noon the whole country became dark, and the darkness lasted for three hours. 34 At three o'clock Jesus cried in a loud voice, "Eli, Eli,[n] lama sabachthani." This means, "My God, my God, why have you rejected me?"

35 When some of the people standing there heard this, they said, "Listen! He is calling Elijah."

36 Someone there ran and got a sponge, filled it with vinegar, tied it to a stick, and gave it to Jesus to drink. He said, "We want to see if Elijah will come to take him down from the cross."

37 Then Jesus cried in a loud voice and died.

38 The curtain in the Temple[n] was torn into two pieces, from the top to the bottom. 39 When the army officer who was standing in front of the cross saw what happened when Jesus died, he said, "This man really was the Son of God!"

40 Some women were standing at a distance from the cross, watching; among them were Mary Magdalene, Salome and Mary the mother of James and Joseph. (James was her youngest son.) 41 These women had followed Jesus in Galilee and helped him. Many other women were also there who had come with Jesus to Jerusalem.

Jesus is Buried

42 This was Preparation Day. (That means the day before the Sabbath day.)

15:28 Verse 28 Some Greek copies add verse 28: "And the Scripture came true that says, 'They put him with criminals.'"
15:34 Eli, Eli Some bibles translate this as Eloi, Eloi.
15:38 curtain in the Temple A curtain divided the Most Holy Place from the other part of the Temple. That was the special building in Jerusalem where God commanded the Jewish people to worship him.

▶ **Mark 15:43** 1360

THE UNPOPULAR CHOICE
MARK 15:42-43

How important is popularity to you? Would you be willing to admit you believed in something if doing so made you unpopular? Joseph was an important Jewish leader who believed in Jesus. But Jesus had just been put to death. Many who followed Jesus were afraid they would be treated badly, too. Believing in Jesus as Saviour was not the popular choice! Yet Joseph was brave enough to ask Pontius Pilate, the Roman governor, for Jesus' body in order to bury it.

Serving Jesus takes courage. It involves standing up for what you believe in, even if your beliefs are not the most popular.

Looking to win a popularity contest? Check out these Faithlinks first:

An Example Not to Follow, Leviticus 18:1–3, p. 157

Trailblazers of Faith, 2 Kings 22:1–2, p. 510

Wronged for What's Right, Ezra 4:4–5, p. 612

Go! No! Jonah 1, p. 1213

Be Brave! Haggai 2:4, p. 1249

Faith That Pleases God, Luke 7:1–9, p. 1380

That evening, 43 Joseph from Arimathea was brave enough to go to Pilate and ask for Jesus' body. Joseph, an important member of the Jewish council, was one of the people who was waiting for the kingdom of God to come. 44 Pilate was amazed that Jesus was already dead, so he called the army officer who had guarded Jesus and asked him if Jesus had already died. 45 The officer told Pilate that he was dead, so Pilate told Joseph he could have the body. 46 Joseph bought some linen cloth, took the body down from the cross, and wrapped it in the linen. He put the body in a tomb that was cut out of a wall of rock. Then he rolled a very large stone to block the entrance of the tomb. 47 And Mary Magdalene and Mary the mother of Joseph saw the place where Jesus was laid.

Jesus Rises from the Dead

16 The day after the Sabbath day, Mary Magdalene, Mary the mother of James, and Salome bought some sweet-smelling spices to put on Jesus' body. 2 Very early on that day, the first day of the week, soon after sunrise, the women were on their way to the tomb. 3 They said to each other, "Who will roll away for us the stone that covers the entrance of the tomb?"

4 Then the women looked and saw that the stone had already been rolled away, even though it was very large. 5 The women entered the tomb and saw a young man wearing a white robe and sitting on the right side, and they were afraid.

6 But the man said, "Don't be afraid. You are looking for Jesus from Nazareth, who has been crucified. He has risen from the dead; he is not here. Look, here is the place where they laid him. 7 Now go and tell his followers and Peter, 'Jesus is going into Galilee ahead of you, and you will see him there as he told you before.'"

8 The women were confused and shaking with fear, so they left the tomb and ran away. They did not tell anyone about what happened, because they were afraid.

Mark 16 **1361**

JESUS – GOD WITH US
MARK 16

1. Childhood. Jesus was born in Bethlehem. (Look up Luke 2:1–7, p. 1367.) While he was still a young child, his parents took him to Egypt to escape King Herod's threat to kill all the boy babies in Bethlehem. (Check out Matthew 2:13–15, p. 1276.) Jesus grew up in Nazareth. (Read Matthew 2:19–23, p. 1277.)

2. Beginnings. Jesus' ministry began when his cousin John baptised him in the River Jordan. Jesus then spent 40 days alone in the desert where he was tempted by Satan. (Check out Mark 1:9–13.) Jesus performed his first miracle at a wedding in Cana when he turned water into wine for the guests. (Read John 2:1–12, p. 1424.)

3. Early ministry. Jesus preached his famous Sermon on the Mount. (Check out Matthew 5—7, p. 1280.) He demonstrated his power from God by bringing a young man back to life (read Luke 7:11–17, p. 1380) and getting demons out of a man in Gadara (look at Luke 8:26–39, p. 1383). Jesus' reputation grew, as did opposition from religious leaders to his ministry.

4. Later ministry. Jesus did even more amazing things. He healed ten lepers in Samaria. (See Luke 17:11–19, p. 1402.) He raised his friend Lazarus from the dead in Bethany. (Look up John 11:38–44, p. 1443.) As God planned, Jesus was arrested, crucified and raised from the dead in Jerusalem. (Check out Mark 14—16, p. 1355.)

Mark 16:9

Verses 9-20 are not included in two of the best and oldest Greek copies of Mark.

Some Followers See Jesus

[9 After Jesus rose from the dead early on the first day of the week, he showed himself first to Mary Magdalene. Once in the past, he had forced seven demons out of her. 10 After Mary saw Jesus, she went and told his followers, who were very sad and were crying. 11 But Mary told them that Jesus was alive. She said that she had seen him, but the followers did not believe her.

12 Later, Jesus showed himself to two of his followers while they were walking in the country, but he did not look the same as before. 13 These followers went back to the others and told them what had happened, but again, the followers did not believe them.

Jesus Talks to the Apostles

14 Later Jesus showed himself to the eleven apostles while they were eating, and he criticised them because they had no faith. They were stubborn and refused to believe those who had seen him after he had risen from the dead.

15 Jesus said to his followers, "Go everywhere in the world, and tell the Good News to everyone. 16 Anyone who believes and is baptised will be saved, but anyone who does not believe will be punished. 17 And those who believe will be able to do these things as proof: they will use my name to force out demons. They will speak in new languages." 18 They will pick up snakes and drink poison without being hurt. They will touch the sick, and the sick will be healed."

19 After the Lord Jesus said these things to his followers, he was carried up into heaven, and he sat at the right side of God. 20 The followers went everywhere in the world and told the Good News to people, and the Lord helped them. The Lord proved that the Good News they told was true by giving them power to work miracles.]

16:17 languages This can also be translated "tongues".

THE TRUE HEALER

Hi. Luke here. I'm the only non-Jewish writer in the New Testament, but I was one of the first people to accept that Jesus is God's Son. Most people know that I am a doctor, but did you know that I was also a constant companion of Paul, one of the leaders of the early church? Because I was with Paul, I also ended up in prison with him. (You can check out that story in Colossians 4:14, p. 1627.)

I wrote this book because my friend Theophilus hadn't heard about Jesus and I wanted to tell him everything that I knew. But that's not all. I also wanted to give a very organised and detailed account of what Jesus had done. There were a lot of stories floating around about Jesus. So I wrote this to set the record straight. I made sure that all of my facts were correct, and I double-checked them before I wrote this book.

JESUS WATCH

Luke focuses on two important elements about Jesus in this book – his humanity and his compassion. Luke goes to a lot of trouble to write down a complete history of Jesus' relatives in chapter 3. It traces Jesus' family history all the way back to Adam! This was an important list because it helped the people understand that Jesus was God's Son. Luke also helps us understand Jesus' humanity through a detailed description of the physical things that happened to Jesus at his crucifixion. And he shares a lot about Jesus' compassion for people through telling stories about Jesus healing the sick and caring for hurting people.

More than anything, Luke combines the historical facts about Jesus with the truth of what he did while he walked the earth to paint an amazingly accurate picture of the Messiah.

my FAVOURITE links

OTHER CONNECTIONS

How much is too much stuff? For God's take on that subject click on Such a Lot of Stuff! Luke 12; 13, and see if you may need to downsize your wardrobe a bit!

What's the one thing that you do especially well? Is it easy for you to share that ability or talent with others? Find out how God wants you to use the gifts and abilities he has given you by logging on to Attitude Check, Luke 17:7–10.

Ever mess up big time? Did you feel like running away to the farthest point on the globe? Or like giving up? Before you pack your bags or quit, check out how God views our weaknesses and failures by connecting to Oh No! Not Again! Luke 22:54–62.

You won't want to miss these info bulletin boards:

- A Model Prayer, Luke 11:1. Is it hard sometimes to find the right words when you're praying? Jesus' disciples thought so. In fact, they asked Jesus for advice on how to pray. Link here to find out Jesus' answer.
- Log on to Jesus' Last Week, Luke 22, for an overview of the events that occurred from the time Jesus entered Jerusalem to a cheering crowd, to the darkest hour when he was nailed to a cross.
- One of the key places in Jesus' life and ministry is the small town of Nazareth. Find out more about this town by downloading Let's Visit Nazareth, Luke 24:19.

Do you think Luke actually saw any of the things that he writes about in this book?

The thing is, he probably didn't. But plug into Luke 1:1–4, and see what you think!

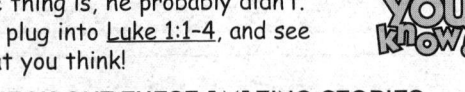

CHECK OUT THESE AMAZING STORIES FROM LUKE'S GOSPEL:

Birth of a king, Luke 2:1–20
Growing up, Luke 2:39–52
A huge lunch, Luke 9:10–17
The risen Lord, Luke 24

FAITH links

- Believe It or Not, **Luke 1:20, 38**
- Exercising Patience, **Luke 2:25–28, 36–37**
- Two Ways to Grow, **Luke 2:46–52**
- The Choices of a Choice, **Luke 5:1–11**
- Who Needs Love? **Luke 6:27–36**
- Faith That Pleases God, **Luke 7:1–9**
- Want to Know? Ask! **Luke 9:45**
- Best Seat in the House, **Luke 14:7–11**
- Your Heart's Desire, **Luke 16:13–15**
- Better Than Some? **Luke 18:9–14**
- Faith God Notices, **Luke 18:35–43**
- Give from the Heart, **Luke 21:1–4**

Luke Writes About Jesus' Life

1 Many have tried to report on the things that happened among us. 2 They have written the same things that we learned from others—the people who saw those things from the beginning and served God by telling people his message. 3 Since I myself have studied everything carefully from the beginning, most excellent[n] Theophilus, it seemed good for me to write it out for you. I arranged it in order 4 to help you know that what you have been taught is true.

Zechariah and Elizabeth

5 During the time Herod ruled Judea, there was a priest named Zechariah who belonged to Abijah's group.[n] Zechariah's wife, Elizabeth, came from the family of Aaron. 6 Zechariah and Elizabeth truly did what God said was good. They did everything the Lord commanded and were without fault in keeping his law. 7 But they had no children, because Elizabeth could not have a baby, and both of them were very old.

8 One day Zechariah was serving as a priest before God, because his group was on duty. 9 According to the custom of the priests, he was chosen by lot to go into the Temple of the Lord and burn incense. 10 There were a great many people outside praying at the time the incense was offered. 11 Then an angel of the Lord appeared to Zechariah, standing on the right side of the incense table. 12 When he saw the angel, Zechariah was startled and frightened. 13 But the angel said to him, "Zechariah, don't be afraid. God has heard your prayer. Your wife, Elizabeth, will give birth to a son, and you will name him John. 14 He will bring you joy and gladness, and many people will be happy because of his birth. 15 John will be a great man for the Lord. He will never drink wine or beer, and even from birth, he will be filled with the Holy Spirit. 16 He will help many people of Israel return to the Lord their God. 17 He will go before the Lord in spirit and power like Elijah. He will make peace between parents and their children and will bring those who are not obeying God back to the right way of thinking, to make a people ready for the coming of the Lord."

18 Zechariah said to the angel, "How can I know that what you say is true? I am an old man, and my wife is old, too."

19 The angel answered him, "I am Gabriel. I stand before God, who sent me to talk to you and to tell you this good news. 20 Now, listen! You will not be able to speak until the day these things happen, because you did not believe what I told you. But they will really happen."

21 Outside, the people were still waiting for Zechariah and were surprised that he was staying so long in the Temple. 22 When Zechariah came outside, he could not speak to them, and they knew he had seen a vision in the Temple. He could only make signs to them and remained unable to speak. 23 When his time of service at the Temple was finished, he went home.

24 Later, Zechariah's wife, Elizabeth, became pregnant and did not go out of her house for five months. Elizabeth said, 25 "Look what the Lord has done for me! My people were ashamed[n] of me, but now the Lord has taken away that shame."

An Angel Appears to Mary

26 During Elizabeth's sixth month of pregnancy, God sent the angel Gabriel to Nazareth, a town in Galilee, 27 to a virgin. She was engaged to marry a man named Joseph from the family of David. Her name was Mary. 28 The angel came to her and said, "Greetings! The Lord has blessed you and is with you."

29 But Mary was very startled by what the angel said and wondered what this greeting might mean.

30 The angel said to her, "Don't be afraid, Mary; God has shown you his grace. 31 Listen! You will become pregnant and give birth to a son, and you will name him Jesus. 32 He will be great and

---

1:3 excellent This word was used to show respect to an important person like a king or ruler.
1:5 Abijah's group The Jewish priests were divided into 24 groups. See 1 Chronicles 24.
1:25 ashamed The Jewish people thought it was a disgrace for women not to have children.

Luke 1:33 1366

FAITH links

BELIEVE IT OR NOT
LUKE 1:20, 38

Did you know that you could choose to believe something if you wanted to believe? An angel brought good news to Zechariah, a priest of Israel, and Mary, the future wife of Joseph the carpenter. Mary chose to believe the angel's news that she would have a son. Zechariah heard similar news – his wife would have a son – but he was doubtful.

God wants us to have faith that he can do the impossible if he chooses to do so. Having faith means choosing to believe, even though you can't see any proof. Choose to believe in God!

What do you believe? Check it out here:

Idol Talk, Exodus 32, p. 118

Our Thorough God, Leviticus 13, p. 149

A Direct Path, Proverbs 3:5–6, p. 829

Believe the Impossible? Ezekiel 37, p. 1131

The Power of If, Mark 9:14–24, p. 1344

Attention, Please! Luke 8:11–15, p. 1383

34 Mary said to the angel, "How will this happen since I am a virgin?"
35 The angel said to Mary, "The Holy Spirit will come upon you, and the power of the Most High will cover you. For this reason the baby will be holy and will be called the Son of God. 36 Now Elizabeth, your relative, is also pregnant with a son though she is very old. Everyone thought she could not have a baby, but she has been pregnant for six months. 37 God can do anything!"
38 Mary said, "I am the servant of the Lord. Let this happen to me as you say!" Then the angel went away.

1:35
Jesus
Check out Jesus' role in the Trinity.

Mary Visits Elizabeth

39 Mary got up and went quickly to a town in the hills of Judea. 40 She came to Zechariah's house and greeted Elizabeth. 41 When Elizabeth heard Mary's greeting, the unborn baby inside her jumped, and Elizabeth was filled with the Holy Spirit. 42 She cried out in a loud voice, "God has blessed you more than any other woman, and he has blessed the baby to whom you will give birth. 43 Why has this good thing happened to me, that the mother of my Lord comes to me? 44 When I heard your voice, the baby inside me jumped with joy. 45 You are blessed because you believed that what the Lord said to you would really happen."

Mary Praises God

46 Then Mary said,
"My soul praises the Lord;
47 my heart rejoices in God my Saviour,
48 because he has shown his concern for his humble servant girl.
From now on, all people will say that I am blessed,
49 because the Powerful One has done great things for me.
His name is holy.
50 God will show his mercy for ever and ever

will be called the Son of the Most High. The Lord God will give him the throne of King David, his ancestor. 33 He will rule over the people of Jacob for ever, and his kingdom will never end."

to those who worship and serve him.

51 He has done mighty deeds by his power.
He has scattered the people who are proud
and think great things about themselves.
52 He has brought down rulers from their thrones
and raised up the humble.
53 He has filled the hungry with good things
and sent the rich away with nothing.
54 He has helped his servant, the people of Israel,
remembering to show them mercy
55 as he promised to our ancestors,
to Abraham and to his children for ever."

56 Mary stayed with Elizabeth for about three months and then returned home.

The Birth of John

57 When it was time for Elizabeth to give birth, she had a boy. 58 Her neighbours and relatives heard how good the Lord was to her, and they rejoiced with her.

59 When the baby was eight days old, they came to circumcise him. They wanted to name him Zechariah because this was his father's name, 60 but his mother said, "No! He will be named John."

61 The people said to Elizabeth, "But no one in your family has this name." 62 Then they made signs to his father to find out what he would like to name him.

63 Zechariah asked for a writing tablet and wrote, "His name is John," and everyone was surprised. 64 Immediately Zechariah could talk again, and he began praising God. 65 All their neighbours became alarmed, and in all the mountains of Judea people continued talking about all these things. 66 The people who heard about them wondered, saying, "What will this child be?" because the Lord was with him.

Zechariah Praises God

67 Then Zechariah, John's father, was filled with the Holy Spirit and prophesied:
68 "Let us praise the Lord, the God of Israel,
because he has come to help his people and has given them freedom.
69 He has given us a powerful Saviour from the family of God's servant David.
70 He said that he would do this through his holy prophets who lived long ago:
71 He promised he would save us from our enemies
and from the power of all those who hate us.
72 He said he would give mercy to our fathers
and that he would remember his holy promise.
73 God promised Abraham, our father,
74 that he would save us from the power of our enemies
so we could serve him without fear,
75 being holy and good before God as long as we live.

76 "Now you, child, will be called a prophet of the Most High God.
You will go before the Lord to prepare his way.
77 You will make his people know that they will be saved
by having their sins forgiven.
78 With the loving mercy of our God, a new day from heaven will dawn upon us.
79 It will shine on those who live in darkness,
in the shadow of death.
It will guide us into the path of peace."

80 And so the child grew up and became strong in spirit. John lived in the desert until the time when he came out to preach to Israel.

The Birth of Jesus

2 At that time, Augustus Caesar sent an order that all people in the countries

under Roman rule must list their names in a register. 2 This was the first registration;[n] it was taken while Quirinius was governor of Syria. 3 And all went to their own towns to be registered.

4 So Joseph left Nazareth, a town in Galilee, and went to the town of Bethlehem in Judea, known as the town of David. Joseph went there because he was from the family of David. 5 Joseph registered with Mary, to whom he was engaged[n] and who was now pregnant. 6 While they were in Bethlehem, the time came for Mary to have the baby, 7 and she gave birth to her first son. Because there were no rooms left in the inn, she wrapped the baby with pieces of cloth and laid him in a box where animals are fed.

Shepherds Hear About Jesus

8 That night, some shepherds were in the fields nearby watching their sheep. 9 Then an angel of the Lord stood before them. The glory of the Lord was shining around them, and they became very frightened. 10 The angel said to them, "Do not be afraid. I am bringing you good news that will be a great joy to all the people. 11 Today your Saviour was born in the town of David. He is Christ, the Lord. 12 This is how you will know him: you will find a baby wrapped in pieces of cloth and lying in a feeding box."

13 Then a very large group of angels from heaven joined the first angel, praising God and saying:
14 "Give glory to God in heaven,
and on earth let there be peace among the people who please God."

15 When the angels left them and went back to heaven, the shepherds said to each other, "Let's go to Bethlehem. Let's see this thing that has happened which the Lord has told us about."

16 So the shepherds went quickly and found Mary and Joseph and the baby, who was lying in a feeding box. 17 When they had seen him, they told what the angels had said about this child. 18 Everyone was amazed at what the shepherds said to them. 19 But Mary treasured these things and continued to think about them.

FAITH links

TOO BUSY TO WORSHIP?
LUKE 2:8-20

Imagine yourself as a busy shepherd, watching a flock of frisky sheep. Suddenly the night sky becomes alive with first one angel, then a very large group of angels. How would you feel? The shepherds who witnessed this event "became very frightened" (Luke 2:9). But when the angels announced the birth of the Saviour, their fear turned to excitement. They left their flocks and went to worship him.

God looks for people who aren't too busy to worship him. He wants you to make worship an important part of your life.

My Worship Place, Genesis 35:1–14, p. 49

A Song of Thanks, 1 Samuel 2, p. 356

Your Heavenly Dad, Psalm 103:13, p. 786

God's Valuable Gift: You, Psalm 127:3–5, p. 809

Faith Workout, Acts 16:4–5, p. 1493

Meeting Together, 1 Corinthians 16:19, p. 1567

2:2 registration Census. A counting of all the people and the things they own.
2:5 engaged For the Jewish people an engagement was a lasting agreement, which could only be broken by a divorce. If a bride-to-be was unfaithful it was considered adultery and she could be put to death.

20 Then the shepherds went back to their sheep, praising God and thanking him for everything they had seen and heard. It had been just as the angel had told them.

21 When the baby was eight days old, he was circumcised and was named Jesus, the name given by the angel before the baby began to grow in Mary's womb.

Jesus is Presented in the Temple

22 When the time came for Mary and Joseph to do what the law of Moses taught about being made pure,[n] they took Jesus to Jerusalem to present him to the Lord. 23 (It is written in the law of the Lord: "Every first-born male shall be given to the Lord.")[n] 24 Mary and Joseph also went to offer a sacrifice, as the law of the Lord says: "You must sacrifice two doves or two young pigeons."[n]

Simeon Sees Jesus

25 In Jerusalem lived a man named Simeon who was a good man and godly. He was waiting for the time when God would take away Israel's sorrow, and the Holy Spirit was in him. 26 Simeon had been told by the Holy Spirit that he would not die before he saw the Christ promised by the Lord. 27 The Spirit led Simeon to the Temple. When Mary and Joseph brought the baby Jesus to the Temple to do what the law said they must do, 28 Simeon took the baby in his arms and thanked God:
29 "Now, Lord, you can let me, your servant,
die in peace as you said.
30 With my own eyes I have seen your salvation,
31 which you prepared before all people.
32 It is a light for the non-Jewish people to see
and an honour for your people, the Israelites."

33 Jesus' father and mother were amazed at what Simeon had said about him. 34 Then Simeon blessed them and said to Mary, "God has chosen this child to cause the fall and rise of many in Israel. He will be a sign from God that many people will not accept 35 so that the

---

FAITH links

EXERCISING PATIENCE
LUKE 2:25-28, 36-37

What is the longest amount of time you've ever waited for something? Simeon and Anna were two people of Israel who waited a long time for God to send the Saviour. God told Simeon that he would not die until he saw the promised Saviour. Anna, too, had grown old waiting.

The birth of the Saviour had been announced over seven hundred years before it actually took place. That's a long time to wait! Sometimes God allows us to wait before he makes things happen. Waiting helps to develop patience within you. Patience doesn't come automatically. It takes... patience to develop.

Need some patience? Download these links:

An Attention-Getter, Numbers 22, p. 207

A Long Wait, Joshua 14:6–15, p. 294

Fly Like an Eagle, Isaiah 40:28–31, p. 947

Stand! Jeremiah 19:14—20:6, p. 1019

Ask, Search, Knock, Matthew 7:7–10, p. 1286

Just a Test, Luke 4:1–13, p. 1373

2:22 pure The law of Moses said that 40 days after a Jewish woman gave birth to a son, she must be cleansed by a ceremony at the Temple. Read Leviticus 12:2-8.
2:23 "Every . . . Lord." Quotation from Exodus 13:2.
2:24 "You . . . pigeons." Quotation from Leviticus 12:8.

thoughts of many will be made known. And the things that will happen will make your heart sad, too."

Anna Sees Jesus

36 There was a prophetess, Anna, from the family of Phanuel in the tribe of Asher. Anna was very old. She had once been married for seven years. 37 Then her husband died, and she was a widow for 84 years. Anna never left the Temple but worshipped God, going without food and praying day and night. 38 Standing there at that time, she thanked God and spoke about Jesus to all who were waiting for God to free Jerusalem.

Joseph and Mary Return Home

39 When Joseph and Mary had done everything the law of the Lord commanded, they went home to Nazareth, their own town in Galilee. 40 The little child grew and became strong. He was filled with wisdom, and God's goodness was upon him.

Jesus as a Boy

41 Every year Jesus' parents went to Jerusalem for the Passover Feast. 42 When he was twelve years old, they went to the feast as they always did. 43 After the feast days were over, they started home. The boy Jesus stayed behind in Jerusalem, but his parents did not know it. 44 Thinking that Jesus was with them in the group, they travelled for a whole day. Then they began to look for him among their family and friends. 45 When they did not find him, they went back to Jerusalem to look for him there. 46 After three days they found Jesus sitting in the Temple with the teachers, listening to them and asking them questions. 47 All who heard him were amazed at his understanding and answers. 48 When Jesus' parents saw him, they were astonished. His mother said to him, "Son, why did you do this to us? Your father and I were very worried about you and have been looking for you."

49 Jesus said to them, "Why were you looking for me? Didn't you know that I must be in my Father's house?" 50 But they did not understand the meaning of what he said.

51 Jesus went with them to Nazareth and was obedient to them. But his mother kept in her mind all that had happened.

FAITH links

TWO WAYS TO GROW
LUKE 2:46-52

Did you know there's more than one way to grow? There's the usual way: eat the right foods, exercise and so on to become strong and healthy. But there's another way to grow – in faith. To grow in faith you also need the right kind of food – "spiritual food". That comes from reading the Bible, going to church, and learning from other Christians about God.

Once, when Jesus was 12, he was found in the Temple, listening to the religious leaders and asking them questions. Asking questions is one way to grow in faith. If you have questions, you can talk to your parents, your Sunday school teacher or your pastor.

A Time to Celebrate, Exodus 15:1–21, p. 95

Our Thirst Quencher, Psalm 42:1–3, p. 741

Jesus' Mission and Yours, Isaiah 61:1–2, p. 978

Said It? Do It! Lamentations 2:17, p. 1077

Pass It On! Joel 1:2–3, p. 1187

The Choices of a Choice, Luke 5:1–11, p. 1375

52 Jesus became wiser and grew physically. People liked him, and he pleased God.

The Preaching of John

3 It was the fifteenth year of the rule of Tiberius Caesar. These men were under Caesar: Pontius Pilate, the ruler of Judea; Herod, the ruler of Galilee; Philip, Herod's brother, the ruler of Iturea and Trachonitis; and Lysanias, the ruler of Abilene. 2 Annas and Caiaphas were the high priests. At this time, the word of God came to John son of Zechariah in the desert. 3 He went all over the area around the Jordan River preaching a baptism of changed hearts and lives for the forgiveness of sins. 4 As it is written in the book of Isaiah the prophet:

This is the voice of one who calls out:
"Prepare in the desert
   the way for the LORD.
Make a straight road in the dry lands
   for our God.
5 Every valley should be raised up,
   and every mountain and hill should
      be made flat.
The rough ground should be made
   level,
   and the rugged ground should be
      made smooth.
6 Then the glory of the LORD will be
   shown,
   and all people together will see it.
The LORD himself said these things."
Isaiah 40:3-5

7 To the crowds of people who came to be baptised by John, he said, "You are all snakes! Who warned you to run away from God's coming punishment? 8 Do the things that show you really have changed your hearts and lives. Don't begin to say to yourselves, 'Abraham is our father.' I tell you that God could make children for Abraham from these rocks. 9 The axe is now ready to cut down the trees, and every tree that does not produce good fruit will be cut down and thrown into the fire.'"[n]

10 The people asked John, "Then what should we do?"

eMAIL FROM GOD
3:7–8 Repentance
What does it mean to repent?

FAITH CHALLENGE

Try this challenge. Read 3:8 to discover how we should act in front of other people. How long would it take for someone who doesn't know you to figure out that you're a Christian?

TeSTiNG iT

Luke 3:8
Do the things that show you really have changed your hearts and lives.

11 John answered, "If you have two shirts, share with the person who does not have one. If you have food, share that also."

12 Even tax collectors came to John to be baptised. They said to him, "Teacher, what should we do?"

13 John said to them, "Don't take more taxes from people than you have been ordered to take."

14 The soldiers asked John, "What about us? What should we do?"

3:9 The axe . . . fire. This means that God is ready to punish his people who do not obey him.

John said to them, "Don't force people to give you money, and don't lie about them. Be satisfied with the pay you get."

15 Since the people were hoping for the Christ to come, they wondered if John might be the one.

16 John answered everyone, "I baptise you with water, but there is one coming who is greater than I am. I am not good enough to untie his sandals. He will baptise you with the Holy Spirit and fire. 17 He will come ready to clean the grain, separating the good grain from the chaff. He will put the good part of the grain into his barn, but he will burn the chaff with a fire that cannot be put out.'" 18 And John continued to preach the Good News, saying many other things to encourage the people.

19 But John spoke against Herod, the governor, because of his sin with Herodias, the wife of Herod's brother, and because of the many other evil things Herod did. 20 So Herod did something even worse: he put John in prison.

Jesus is Baptised by John

21 When all the people were being baptised by John, Jesus also was baptised. While Jesus was praying, heaven opened 22 and the Holy Spirit came down on him in the form of a dove. Then a voice came from heaven, saying, "You are my Son, whom I love, and I am very pleased with you."

The Family History of Jesus

23 When Jesus began his ministry, he was about 30 years old. People thought that Jesus was Joseph's son.
Joseph was the son" of Heli.
24 Heli was the son of Matthat.
Matthat was the son of Levi.
Levi was the son of Melki."
Melki was the son of Jannai.
Jannai was the son of Joseph.
25 Joseph was the son of Mattathias.
Mattathias was the son of Amos.
Amos was the son of Nahum.
Nahum was the son of Esli.
Esli was the son of Naggai.
26 Naggai was the son of Maath.
Maath was the son of Mattathias.
Mattathias was the son of Semein.
Semein was the son of Josech.
Josech was the son of Joda.
27 Joda was the son of Joanan.
Joanan was the son of Rhesa.
Rhesa was the son of Zerubbabel.
Zerubbabel was the grandson of
  Shealtiel.
Shealtiel was the son of Neri.
28 Neri was the son of Melki."
Melki was the son of Addi.
Addi was the son of Cosam.
Cosam was the son of Elmadam.
Elmadam was the son of Er.
29 Er was the son of Joshua.
Joshua was the son of Eliezer.
Eliezer was the son of Jorim.
Jorim was the son of Matthat.
Matthat was the son of Levi.
30 Levi was the son of Simeon.
Simeon was the son of Judah.
Judah was the son of Joseph.
Joseph was the son of Jonam.
Jonam was the son of Eliakim.
31 Eliakim was the son of Melea.
Melea was the son of Menna.
Menna was the son of Mattatha.
Mattatha was the son of Nathan.
Nathan was the son of David.
32 David was the son of Jesse.
Jesse was the son of Obed.
Obed was the son of Boaz.
Boaz was the son of Salmon.
Salmon was the son of Nahshon.
33 Nahshon was the son of Amminadab.
Amminadab was the son of Admin."
Admin was the son of Arni.
Arni was the son of Hezron.
Hezron was the son of Perez.
Perez was the son of Judah.
34 Judah was the son of Jacob.
Jacob was the son of Isaac.
Isaac was the son of Abraham.

3:17 He will . . . out. This means that Jesus will come to separate good people from bad people, saving the good and punishing the bad.
3:23 son "Son" in Jewish lists of ancestors can sometimes mean grandson or more distant relative.
3:24, 28 Melki Some manuscripts spell Melki as Melchi.
3:33 Admin Some manuscripts say, "Amminadab, the son of Ram, the son of Hezron", other manuscripts vary widely.

Abraham was the son of Terah.
Terah was the son of Nahor.
35 Nahor was the son of Serug.
Serug was the son of Reu.
Reu was the son of Peleg.
Peleg was the son of Eber.
Eber was the son of Shelah.
36 Shelah was the son of Cainan.
Cainan was the son of Arphaxad.
Arphaxad was the son of Shem.
Shem was the son of Noah.
Noah was the son of Lamech.
37 Lamech was the son of Methuselah.
Methuselah was the son of Enoch.
Enoch was the son of Jared.
Jared was the son of Mahalalel.
Mahalalel was the son of Kenan.
38 Kenan was the son of Enosh.
Enosh was the son of Seth.
Seth was the son of Adam.
Adam was the son of God.

Jesus is Tempted by the Devil

4 Jesus, filled with the Holy Spirit, returned from the Jordan River. The Spirit led Jesus into the desert 2 where the devil tempted Jesus for 40 days. Jesus ate nothing during that time, and when those days were ended, he was very hungry.

3 The devil said to Jesus, "If you are the Son of God, tell this rock to become bread."

4 Jesus answered, "It is written in the Scriptures: 'A person does not live by eating only bread.'"[n]

5 Then the devil took Jesus and showed him all the kingdoms of the world in an instant. 6 The devil said to Jesus, "I will give you all these kingdoms and all their power and glory. It has all been given to me, and I can give it to anyone I wish. 7 If you worship me, then it will all be yours."

8 Jesus answered, "It is written in the Scriptures: 'You must worship the Lord your God and serve only him.'"[n]

9 Then the devil led Jesus to Jerusalem and put him on a high place of the Temple. He said to Jesus, "If you are the Son of God, jump down. 10 It is written in the Scriptures:

'He has put his angels in charge of you
to watch over you.' *Psalm 91:11*

11 It is also written:

FAITH links

JUST A TEST
LUKE 4:1-13

What tempts you the most? The devil tried to tempt Jesus with food, power and pride. Since Jesus had been in the wilderness for 40 days without food, Satan knew that Jesus would be very hungry. He wanted Jesus to help himself for the wrong reason.

Temptation itself is not a sin. Giving in to temptation is what causes sin. God allows temptation in our lives to help us grow stronger in faith. When temptation comes, think of it as a test that you need to pass. With God on your side, you can pass with flying colours!

Download these links for more help in passing the test!

Facing the Consequences, Deuteronomy 3:21-29, p. 232

Real Repentance, Jeremiah 4:1-4, p. 993

Sow It and Reap, Lamentations 1:18, p. 1075

Forgive Again? Luke 17:3-4, p. 1402

A High Price, Romans 6:23, p. 1526

Lost Love? Revelation 2:4, p. 1733

4:4 'A person . . . bread.' Quotation from Deuteronomy 8:3.
4:8 'You . . . him.' Quotation from Deuteronomy 6:13.

'They will catch you in their hands
so that you will not hit your foot on
a rock.'" *Psalm 91:12*

12 Jesus answered, "But it also says in the Scriptures: 'Do not test the Lord your God.'"[n]

13 After the devil had tempted Jesus in every way, he left him to wait until a better time.

Jesus Teaches the People

14 Jesus returned to Galilee in the power of the Holy Spirit, and stories about him spread throughout all the area. 15 He began to teach in their synagogues, and everyone praised him.

16 Jesus travelled to Nazareth, where he had grown up. On the Sabbath day he went to the synagogue, as he always did, and stood up to read. 17 The book of Isaiah the prophet was given to him. He opened the book and found the place where this is written:

18 "The Lord has put his Spirit in me,
because he appointed me to tell the
Good News to the poor.
He has sent me to tell the captives
they are free
and to tell the blind that they can
see again. *Isaiah 61:1*
God sent me to free those who have
been treated unfairly *Isaiah 58:6*
19 and to announce the time when the
Lord will show his kindness."
Isaiah 61:2

20 Jesus closed the book, gave it back to the assistant and sat down. Everyone in the synagogue was watching Jesus closely. 21 He began to say to them, "While you heard these words just now, they were coming true!"

22 All the people spoke well of Jesus and were amazed at the words of grace he spoke. They asked, "Isn't this Joseph's son?"

23 Jesus said to them, "I know that you will tell me the old saying: 'Doctor, heal yourself.' You want to say, 'We heard about the things you did in Capernaum. Do those things here in your own town!'" 24 Then Jesus said, "I tell you the truth, a prophet is not accepted in his home town. 25 But I tell you the truth, there were many widows in Israel during the time of Elijah. It did not rain in Israel for three and a half years, and there was no food anywhere in the whole country. 26 But Elijah was sent to none of those widows, only to a widow in Zarephath, a town in Sidon. 27 And there were many with skin diseases living in Israel during the time of the prophet Elisha. But none of them were healed, only Naaman, who was from the country of Syria."

28 When all the people in the synagogue heard these things, they became very angry. 29 They got up, forced Jesus out of town, and took him to the edge of the cliff on which the town was built. They planned to throw him off the edge, 30 but Jesus walked through the crowd and went on his way.

Jesus Forces Out an Evil Spirit

31 Jesus went to Capernaum, a city in Galilee, and on the Sabbath day, he taught the people. 32 They were amazed at his teaching, because he spoke with authority. 33 In the synagogue a man who had within him an evil spirit shouted in a loud voice, 34 "Jesus of Nazareth! What do you want with us? Did you come to destroy us? I know who you are—God's Holy One!"

35 Jesus commanded the evil spirit, "Be quiet! Come out of the man!" The evil spirit threw the man down to the ground before all the people and then left the man without hurting him.

36 The people were amazed and said to each other, "What does this mean? With authority and power he commands evil spirits, and they come out." 37 And so the news about Jesus spread to every place in the whole area.

Jesus Heals Many People

38 Jesus left the synagogue and went to the home of Simon.[n] Simon's mother-in-law was sick with a high fever, and they asked Jesus to help her. 39 He came to her side and commanded the fever to leave. It left her, and immediately she got up and began serving them.

4:12 'Do . . . God.' Quotation from Deuteronomy 6:16.
4:38 Simon Simon's other name was Peter.

40 When the sun went down, the people brought those who were sick to Jesus. Putting his hands on each sick person, he healed every one of them. 41 Demons came out of many people, shouting, "You are the Son of God." But Jesus commanded the demons and would not allow them to speak, because they knew Jesus was the Christ.

42 At daybreak, Jesus went to a lonely place, but the people looked for him. When they found him, they tried to keep him from leaving. 43 But Jesus said to them, "I must preach about God's kingdom to other towns, too. This is why I was sent."

44 Then he kept on preaching in the synagogues of Judea.

Jesus' First Followers

5 One day while Jesus was standing beside Lake Galilee, many people were pressing all around him to hear the word of God. 2 Jesus saw two boats at the shore of the lake. The fishermen had left them and were washing their nets. 3 Jesus got into one of the boats, the one that belonged to Simon,* and asked him to push off a little from the land. Then Jesus sat down and continued to teach the people from the boat.

4 When Jesus had finished speaking, he said to Simon, "Take the boat into deep water, and put your nets in the water to catch some fish."

5 Simon answered, "Master, we worked hard all night trying to catch fish, and we caught nothing. But you say to put the nets in the water, so I will." 6 When the fishermen did as Jesus told them, they caught so many fish that the nets began to break. 7 They called to their partners in the other boat to come and help them. They came and filled both boats so full that they were almost sinking.

8 When Simon Peter saw what had happened, he bowed down before Jesus and said, "Go away from me, Lord. I am a sinful man!" 9 He and the other fishermen were amazed at the many fish they

---

5:3 **Simon** Simon's other name was Peter.

THE CHOICES OF A CHOICE
LUKE 5:1-11

You have plans for your life, right? Maybe you've thought about going to university someday and having a fabulous career. Now suppose you met someone who could do amazing things. Would you give up your life plans just to work with that person?

Being a Christian is a choice that leads to other choices. For Jesus' followers, this choice involved giving up their fishing business to be with Jesus full time. Many people say no to Christianity because they think that God wants them to be miserable. But that's not true. A loving God has loving plans for his people. The choice to follow him is up to you.

What's your choice? Connect here to know what choice is best for you:

What You Value, Genesis 25:21–34, p. 34

The Green Light, 2 Samuel 2:1, p. 401

Does Crime Pay? Psalm 37:1–7, p. 736

Choosing a Friend, Proverbs 28:7, p. 865

You've Got the Power! Acts 1:1–8; 2:1–4, p. 1463

Just Say No! Titus 2:11–12, p. 1660

caught, as were 10 James and John, the sons of Zebedee, Simon's partners.

Jesus said to Simon, "Don't be afraid. From now on you will fish for people." 11 When the men brought their boats to the shore, they left everything and followed Jesus.

Jesus Heals a Sick Man

12 When Jesus was in one of the towns, there was a man covered with a skin disease. When he saw Jesus, he bowed before him and begged him, "Lord, you can heal me if you will."

13 Jesus reached out his hand and touched the man and said, "I will. Be healed!" Immediately the disease disappeared. 14 Then Jesus said, "Don't tell anyone about this, but go and show yourself to the priest" and offer a gift for your healing, as Moses commanded." This will show the people what I have done."

15 But the news about Jesus spread even more. Many people came to hear Jesus and to be healed of their sicknesses, 16 but Jesus often slipped away to be alone so he could pray.

Jesus Heals a Paralysed Man

17 One day as Jesus was teaching the people, the Pharisees and teachers of the law from every town in Galilee and Judea and from Jerusalem were there. The power of the Lord was present for him to heal the sick. 18 Just then, some men were carrying on a mat a man who was paralysed. They tried to bring him in and put him down before Jesus. 19 But because there were so many people there, they could not find a way in. So they went up on the roof and lowered the man on his mat through the ceiling into the middle of the crowd right before Jesus. 20 Seeing their faith, Jesus said, "Friend, your sins are forgiven."

21 The Jewish teachers of the law and the Pharisees thought to themselves, "Who is this man who is speaking as if he were God? Only God can forgive sins."

22 But Jesus knew what they were thinking and said, "Why are you thinking these things? 23 Which is easier: to say, 'Your sins are forgiven,' or to say, 'Stand up and walk'? 24 But I will prove to you that the Son of Man has authority on earth to forgive sins." So Jesus said to the

---

FAITH links

PRAYER PRIORITY
LUKE 5:15-16

What do you make time for each day? The things you make time for are called *priorities*. That's another word to describe the things that are important to you.

For Jesus, prayer was a priority each day. He often went to a place where he could be alone to pray. Jesus knew how important it was to talk with his Father, without being interrupted. On your list of priorities, make sure to add prayer. If it was important enough for Jesus, it should be important enough for you!

I'll Never Forget What's-His-Name, Deuteronomy 8, p. 239

Your Heavenly Dad, Psalm 103:13, p. 786

The Writing's on the Wall, Daniel 5, p. 1159

Going My Way? Hosea 8:1–6, p. 1179

Heavenly Treasure, Luke 12:32–34, p. 1394

A Good Habit, Ephesians 6:18, p. 1606

5:14 show . . . priest The law of Moses said a priest must say when a Jewish person with a skin disease was well.
5:14 Moses commanded Read about this in Leviticus 14:1-32.

paralysed man, "I tell you, stand up, take your mat, and go home."

25 At once the man stood up before them, picked up his mat and went home, praising God. 26 All the people were completely amazed and began to praise God. They were filled with much respect and said, "Today we have seen amazing things!"

Levi Follows Jesus

27 After this, Jesus went out and saw a tax collector named Levi[n] sitting in the tax collector's booth. Jesus said to him, "Follow me!" 28 So Levi got up, left everything and followed him.

29 Then Levi gave a big dinner for Jesus at his house. Many tax collectors and other people were eating there, too. 30 But the Pharisees and the men who taught the law for the Pharisees began to complain to Jesus' followers, "Why do you eat and drink with tax collectors and sinners?"

31 Jesus answered them, "It is not the healthy people who need a doctor, but the sick. 32 I have not come to invite good people but sinners to change their hearts and lives."

Jesus Answers a Question

33 They said to Jesus, "John's followers often give up eating[n] for a certain time and pray, just as the Pharisees do. But your followers eat and drink all the time."

34 Jesus said to them, "You cannot make the friends of the bridegroom give up eating while he is still with them. 35 But the time will come when the bridegroom will be taken away from them, and then they will give up eating."

36 Jesus told them this story: "No one takes cloth off a new coat to cover a hole in an old coat. Otherwise, he ruins the new coat, and the cloth from the new coat will not be the same as the old cloth. 37 Also, no one ever pours new wine into old leather bags. Otherwise, the new wine will break the bags, the wine will spill out and the leather bags will be ruined. 38 New wine must be put into new leather bags. 39 No one after drinking old wine wants new wine, because he says, 'The old wine is better.'"

Jesus is Lord over the Sabbath

6 One Sabbath day Jesus was walking through some fields of grain. His followers picked the heads of grain, rubbed them in their hands and ate them. 2 Some Pharisees said, "Why do you do what is not lawful on the Sabbath day?"

3 Jesus answered, "Have you not read what David did when he and those with him were hungry? 4 He went into God's house and took and ate the holy bread, which is lawful only for priests to eat. And he gave some to the people who were with him." 5 Then Jesus said to the Pharisees, "The Son of Man is Lord of the Sabbath day."

Jesus Heals a Man's Hand

6 On another Sabbath day Jesus went into the synagogue and was teaching, and a man with a crippled right hand was there. 7 The teachers of the law and the Pharisees were watching closely to see if Jesus would heal on the Sabbath day so they could accuse him. 8 But he knew what they were thinking, and he said to the man with the crippled hand, "Stand up here in the middle of everyone." The man got up and stood there. 9 Then Jesus said to them, "I ask you, which is lawful on the Sabbath day: to do good or to do evil, to save a life or to destroy it?" 10 Jesus looked around at all of them and said to the man, "Hold out your hand." The man held out his hand, and it was healed.

11 But the Pharisees and the teachers of the law were very angry and discussed with each other what they could do to Jesus.

Jesus Chooses His Apostles

12 At that time Jesus went off to a mountain to pray, and he spent the night praying to God. 13 The next morning, Jesus called his followers to him and chose twelve of them, whom he named apostles: 14 Simon (Jesus named him Peter),

---

5:27 Levi Also known as Matthew.
5:33 give up eating This is called "fasting". The people would give up eating for a special time of prayer and worship to God. It was also done to show sadness and disappointment.

his brother Andrew, James, John, Philip, Bartholomew, 15 Matthew, Thomas, James son of Alphaeus, Simon (called the Zealot), 16 Judas son of James and Judas Iscariot, who later turned Jesus over to his enemies.

Jesus Teaches and Heals

17 Jesus and the apostles came down from the mountain, and he stood on level ground. A large group of his followers were there, as well as many people from all around Judea, Jerusalem, and the sea coast cities of Tyre and Sidon. 18 They all came to hear Jesus teach and to be healed of their sicknesses, and he healed those who were troubled by evil spirits. 19 All the people were trying to touch Jesus, because power was coming from him and healing them all.

20 Jesus looked at his followers and said,
"Happy you people who are poor,
because the kingdom of God
belongs to you.
21 Happy you people who are now hungry,
because you will be satisfied.
Happy you people who are now crying,
because you will laugh with joy.
22 "People will hate you, shut you out, insult you and say you are evil, because you follow the Son of Man. But when they do, you will be happy. 23 Be full of joy at that time, because you have a great reward waiting for you in heaven. Their ancestors did the same things to the prophets.
24 "But how terrible it will be for you who are rich,
because you have had your easy life.
25 How terrible it will be for you who are full now,
because you will be hungry.
How terrible it will be for you who are laughing now,
because you will be sad and cry.
26 "How terrible when everyone says only good things about you, because their ancestors said the same things about the false prophets.

Love Your Enemies

27 "But I say to you who are listening, love your enemies. Do good to those who hate you, 28 bless those who curse you, pray for those who are cruel to you. 29 If anyone slaps you on one cheek, offer him the other cheek, too. If someone takes your coat, do not stop him from taking your shirt. 30 Give to everyone who asks you, and when someone takes something that is yours, don't ask for it back. 31 Do to others what you would want them to do to you. 32 If you love only the people who love you, what praise should you get? Even sinners love the people who love them. 33 If you do good only to those who do good to you, what praise should you get? Even sinners do that! 34 If you lend things to people, always hoping to get something back, what praise should you get? Even sinners lend to other sinners so that they can get back the same amount! 35 But love your enemies, do good to them, and lend to them without hoping to get anything back. Then you will have a great reward and you will be children of the Most High God, because he is kind even to people who are ungrateful and full of sin. 36 Show mercy, just as your Father shows mercy.

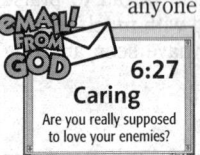

6:27
Caring
Are you really supposed to love your enemies?

Look at Yourselves

37 "Don't judge other people, and you will not be judged. Don't accuse others of being guilty, and you will not be accused of being guilty. Forgive, and you will be forgiven. 38 Give, and you will receive. You will be given much. Pressed down, shaken together and running over, it will spill into your lap. The way you give to others is the way God will give to you."

39 Jesus told them this story: "Can a blind person lead another blind person? No! Both of them will fall into a ditch. 40 A student is not better than the teacher, but the student who has been fully trained will be like the teacher.

41 "Why do you notice the little piece of dust in your friend's eye, but you don't

WHO NEEDS LOVE?
LUKE 6:27-36

Loving friends and family is pretty simple, right? Those who love us and take care of us deserve our love in return.

When Jesus preached his Sermon on the Mount (see the info site on The Sermon on the Mount, p. 1282), he talked about a group that needs love even more. Who are these people? Enemies. In other words, we're to show love to those who treat us badly. This is the kind of love that God has. God's love is given freely. No one has to earn it. Next time you meet an enemy, instead of thinking about getting even, think about praying for him. That's the way to show love.

Here are some more Faithlinks on showing love:

Forgive Instead, Genesis 33, p. 47

More Powerful Than Revenge, Genesis 50:14–21, p. 71

Own Up to It, 2 Samuel 12:1–13, p. 412

Listen Up! 1 Kings 19:11–13, p. 467

Your Choice of Fruit, Matthew 12:33–35, p. 1295

As Strong as Superman? Philippians 4:13, p. 1615

---

notice the big piece of wood in your own eye? 42 How can you say to your friend, 'Friend, let me take that little piece of dust out of your eye' when you cannot see that big piece of wood in your own eye! You hypocrite! First, take the wood out of your own eye. Then you will see clearly to take the dust out of your friend's eye.

Two Kinds of Fruit

43 "A good tree does not produce bad fruit, nor does a bad tree produce good fruit. 44 Each tree is known by its own fruit. People don't gather figs from thornbushes, and they don't get grapes from bushes. 45 Good people bring good things out of the good stored in their hearts. But evil people bring evil things out of the evil stored in their hearts. People speak the things that are in their hearts.

Two Kinds of People

46 "Why do you call me, 'Lord, Lord,' but do not do what I say? 47 I will show you what everyone is like who comes to me and hears my words and obeys. 48 That person is like a man building a house who dug deep and laid the foundation on rock. When the floods came, the water tried to wash the house away, but it could not shake it, because the house was built well. 49 But the one who hears my words and does not obey is like a man who built his house on the ground without a foundation. When the floods came, the house quickly fell and was completely destroyed."

Jesus Heals a Soldier's Servant

7 When Jesus finished saying all these things to the people, he went to Capernaum. 2 There was an army officer who had a servant who was very important to him. The servant was so sick he was nearly dead. 3 When the officer heard about Jesus, he sent some Jewish elders to him to ask Jesus to come and heal his servant. 4 The men went to Jesus and begged him, saying, "This officer is worthy of your help. 5 He loves our people, and he built us a synagogue."

6 So Jesus went with the men. He was getting near the officer's house when the officer sent friends to say, "Lord, don't trouble yourself, because I am not worthy to have you come into my house. 7 That is why I did not come to you myself. But you only need to command it, and my servant will be healed. 8 I, too, am a man under the authority of others, and I have soldiers under my command. I tell one soldier, 'Go,' and he goes. I tell another soldier, 'Come,' and he comes. I say to my servant, 'Do this,' and my servant does it."

9 When Jesus heard this, he was amazed. Turning to the crowd that was following him, he said, "I tell you, this is the greatest faith I have found anywhere, even in Israel."

10 Those who had been sent to Jesus went back to the house where they found the servant in good health.

Jesus Brings a Man Back to Life

11 Soon afterwards Jesus went to a town called Nain, and his followers and a large crowd travelled with him. 12 When he came near the town gate, he saw a funeral. A mother, who was a widow, had lost her only son. A large crowd from the town was with the mother while her son was being carried out. 13 When the Lord saw her, he felt very sorry for her and said, "Don't cry." 14 He went up and touched the coffin, and the people who were carrying it stopped. Jesus said, "Young man, I tell you, get up!" 15 And the son sat up and began to talk. Then Jesus gave him back to his mother.

16 All the people were amazed and began praising God, saying, "A great prophet has come to us! God has come to help his people."

17 This news about Jesus spread through all Judea and into all the places around there.

John Asks a Question

18 John's followers told him about all these things. He called for two of his followers 19 and sent them to the Lord to ask, "Are you the One who is to come, or should we wait for someone else?"

20 When the men came to Jesus, they said, "John the Baptist sent us to you with this question: 'Are you the One who is to

FAITH THAT PLEASES GOD
LUKE 7:1-9

Have you ever been amazed by something someone has said? That's what happened to Jesus. An army officer went to him, hoping that he would heal his servant. But he didn't expect Jesus to come to his house and do it. He knew that Jesus only had to say the word and his servant would be healed. Jesus was "amazed" when he heard that (Luke 7:9).

That's the kind of faith that pleases God. This is not a wishy-washy, gee-I-hope-he-can-do-it kind of faith. This is the kind of faith that moves mountains.

Here are some other links on pleasing God:

Lights, Camera, . . . Actions!
Genesis 12:1–3, p. 17

An Attention-Getter, Numbers 22, p. 207

Sitting on the Fence, 1 Kings 18, p. 464

Remember Your Creator, Ecclesiastes 12:1, 13, p. 885

Heavenly Treasure, Luke 12:32–34, p. 1394

The Doubt Remover, Romans 10:8–10, p. 1533

come, or should we wait for someone else?'"

21 At that time, Jesus healed many people of their sicknesses, diseases and evil spirits, and he gave sight to many blind people. 22 Then Jesus answered John's followers, "Go and tell John what you saw and heard here. The blind can see, the crippled can walk and people with skin diseases are healed. The deaf can hear, the dead are raised to life and the Good News is preached to the poor. 23 Those who do not stumble in their faith because of me are blessed!"

24 When John's followers left, Jesus began talking to the people about John: "What did you go out into the desert to see? A reed*n* blown by the wind? 25 What did you go out to see? A man dressed in fine clothes? No, people who have fine clothes and much wealth live in kings' palaces. 26 But what did you go out to see? A prophet? Yes, and I tell you, John is more than a prophet. 27 This was written about him:

'I will send my messenger ahead of you,
who will prepare the way for you.'
Malachi 3:1

28 I tell you, John is greater than any other person ever born, but even the least important person in the kingdom of God is greater than John."

29 (When the people, including the tax collectors, heard this, they all agreed that God's teaching was good, having been baptised by John. 30 But the Pharisees and experts on the law refused to accept God's plan for themselves; they did not let John baptise them.)

31 Then Jesus said, "What shall I say about the people of this time? What are they like? 32 They are like children sitting in the market place, calling to one another and saying,

'We played music for you, but you did not dance;
we sang a sad song, but you did not cry.'

33 John the Baptist came and did not eat bread or drink wine, and you say, 'He has a demon in him.' 34 The Son of Man came eating and drinking, and you say, 'Look at him! He eats too much and drinks too much wine, and he is a friend of tax collectors and sinners!' 35 But wisdom is proved to be right by what it does."

A Woman Washes Jesus' Feet

36 One of the Pharisees asked Jesus to eat with him, so Jesus went into the Pharisee's house and sat at the table. 37 A sinful woman in the town learnt that Jesus was eating at the Pharisee's house. So she brought an alabaster jar of perfume 38 and stood behind Jesus at his feet, crying. She began to wash his feet with her tears, and she dried them with her hair, kissing them many times and rubbing them with the perfume. 39 When the Pharisee who asked Jesus to come to his house saw this, he thought to himself, "If Jesus were a prophet, he would know that the woman touching him is a sinner!"

40 Jesus said to the Pharisee, "Simon, I have something to say to you."

Simon said, "Teacher, tell me."

41 Jesus said, "Two people owed money to the same banker. One owed 500 silver coins*n* and the other owed 50 silver coins. 42 They had no money to pay what they owed, but the banker told both of them they did not have to pay him. Which person will love the banker more?"

43 Simon, the Pharisee, answered, "I think it would be the one who owed him the most money."

Jesus said to Simon, "You are right." 44 Then Jesus turned towards the woman and said to Simon, "Do you see this woman? When I came into your house, you gave me no water for my feet, but she washed my feet with her tears and dried them with her hair. 45 You gave me no kiss of greeting, but she has been kissing my feet since I came in. 46 You did not put oil on my head, but she poured perfume on my feet. 47 I tell you that her many sins are forgiven, so she showed great love. But the person who is forgiven only a little will love only a little."

7:24 reed It means that John was not ordinary or weak like grass blown by the wind.

7:41 coins Roman denarii. A silver coin was the average pay for one day's work.

48 Then Jesus said to her, "Your sins are forgiven."

49 The people sitting at the table began to say among themselves, "Who is this who even forgives sins?"

50 Jesus said to the woman, "Because you believed, you are saved from your sins. Go in peace."

The Group with Jesus

8 After this, while Jesus was travelling through some cities and small towns, he preached and told the Good News about God's kingdom. The twelve apostles were with him, 2 and also some women who had been healed of sicknesses and evil spirits: Mary, called Magdalene, from whom seven demons had gone out; 3 Joanna, the wife of Chuza (the manager of Herod's house); Susanna; and many others. These women used their own money to help Jesus and his apostles.

A Story About Planting Seed

4 When a great crowd was gathered, and people were coming to Jesus from every town, he told them this story:

5 "A farmer went out to plant his seed. While he was planting, some seed fell by the road. People walked on the seed, and the birds ate it up. 6 Some seed fell on rock, and when it began to grow, it died because it had no water. 7 Some seed fell among thorny weeds, but the weeds grew up with it and choked the good plants. 8 And some seed fell on good ground and grew and made 100 times more."

As Jesus finished the story, he called out, "You people who can hear me, listen!"

9 Jesus' followers asked him what this story meant.

10 Jesus said, "You have been chosen to know the secrets about the kingdom of God. But I use stories to speak to other people so that:

'You will listen and listen, but you will not understand.
You will look and look, but you will not learn.' *Isaiah 6:9*

11 "This is what the story means: the seed is God's message. 12 The seed that fell beside the road is like the people who hear God's teaching, but the devil comes and takes it away from them so they cannot believe it and be saved. 13 The seed that fell on rock is like those who hear God's teaching and accept it gladly, but they don't allow the teaching to go deep into their lives. They believe for a while, but when trouble comes, they give up. 14 The seed that fell among the thorny weeds is like those who hear God's teaching, but they let the worries, riches and pleasures of this life keep them from growing and producing good fruit. 15 And the seed that fell on the good ground is like those who hear God's teaching with good, honest hearts and obey it and patiently produce good fruit.

Use What You Have

16 "No one after lighting a lamp covers it with a bowl or hides it under a bed. Instead, the person puts it on a lampstand so those who come in will see the light. 17 Everything that is hidden will become clear, and every secret thing will be made known. 18 So be careful how you listen. Those who have understanding will be given more. But from those who do not have understanding, even what they think they have will be taken away."

Jesus' True Family

19 Jesus' mother and brothers came to see him, but there was such a crowd they could not get to him. 20 Someone said to Jesus, "Your mother and your brothers are standing outside, wanting to see you."

21 Jesus answered them, "My mother and my brothers are those who listen to God's teaching and obey it!"

Jesus Calms a Storm

22 One day Jesus and his followers got into a boat, and he said to them, "Let's go across the lake." And so they started across. 23 While they were sailing, Jesus fell asleep. A very strong wind blew up on the lake, causing the boat to fill with water, and they were in danger.

FAITH links

ATTENTION, PLEASE!
LUKE 8:11-15

A person's actions tell you how much he or she is paying attention to what is said. For example, if your teacher said to you, "Open your book to page 9," not doing so would show your lack of attention. Jesus once told a story about a person who planted seeds in different types of soil. The story points to the need to pay attention to God's message. The seed represented God's message. The soil represented the way people respond to that news. Often, people hear the news of Jesus, but don't do anything about it. Are you paying attention? What kind of seed are you?

Good Advice? Leviticus 20:6, p. 162

Do What You Want? Judges 21:25, p. 341

This Hurts Me More? 2 Chronicles 36:17–22, p. 606

You Are What You Do, Proverbs 20:11, p. 854

Prayer Priority, Luke 5:15–16, p. 1376

Hold On! 2 Thessalonians 2:15–17, p. 1639

---

24 The followers went to Jesus and woke him, saying, "Master! Master! We will drown!"

Jesus got up and gave a command to the wind and the waves. They stopped, and it became calm. 25 Jesus said to his followers, "Where is your faith?"

The followers were afraid and amazed and said to each other, "Who is this that commands even the wind and the water, and they obey him?"

A Man with Demons Inside Him

26 Jesus and his followers sailed across the lake from Galilee to the area of the Gerasene people. 27 When Jesus got out on the land, a man from the town who had demons inside him came to Jesus. For a long time he had worn no clothes and had lived in the burial caves, not in a house. 28 When he saw Jesus, he cried out and fell down before him. He said with a loud voice, "What do you want with me, Jesus, Son of the Most High God? I beg you, don't torture me!" 29 He said this because Jesus was commanding the evil spirit to come out of the man. Many times it had taken hold of him. Though he had been kept under guard and chained hand and foot, he had broken his chains and had been forced by the demon out into a lonely place.

30 Jesus asked him, "What is your name?"

He answered, "Legion,"ⁿ because many demons were in him. 31 The demons begged Jesus not to send them into eternal darkness.ⁿ 32 A large herd of pigs was feeding on a hill, and the demons begged Jesus to allow them to go into the pigs. So Jesus allowed them to do this. 33 When the demons came out of the man, they went into the pigs, and the herd ran down the hill into the lake and was drowned.

34 When the herdsmen saw what had happened, they ran away and reported this in the town and the countryside. 35 And people went to see what had happened. When they came to Jesus, they found the man sitting at Jesus' feet, clothed and in his right mind, because the demons were gone. But the people were

---

8:30 "Legion" Means very many. A legion was about 5,000 men in the Roman army.
8:31 eternal darkness Literally, "the abyss," something like a pit or a hole that has no end.

frightened. 36 The people who saw this happen told the others how Jesus had made the man well. 37 All the people of the Gerasene country asked Jesus to leave, because they were all very afraid. So Jesus got into the boat and went back to Galilee.

38 The man whom Jesus had healed begged to go with him, but Jesus sent him away, saying, 39 "Go back home and tell people how much God has done for you." So the man went all over town telling how much Jesus had done for him.

Jesus Gives Life to a Dead Girl and Heals a Sick Woman

40 When Jesus got back to Galilee, a crowd welcomed him, because everyone was waiting for him. 41 A man named Jairus, a leader of the synagogue, came to Jesus and fell at his feet, begging him to come to his house. 42 Jairus' only daughter, about twelve years old, was dying.

While Jesus was on his way to Jairus' house, the people were crowding all around him. 43 A woman was in the crowd who had been bleeding for twelve years, but no one was able to heal her. 44 She came up behind Jesus and touched the edge of his coat, and instantly her bleeding stopped. 45 Then Jesus said, "Who touched me?"

When all the people said they had not touched him, Peter said, "Master, the people are all around you and are pushing against you."

46 But Jesus said, "Someone did touch me, because I felt power go out from me." 47 When the woman saw she could not hide, she came forwards, shaking, and fell down before Jesus. While all the people listened, she told why she had touched him and how she had been instantly healed. 48 Jesus said to her, "Dear woman, you are made well because you believed. Go in peace."

49 While Jesus was still speaking, someone came from the house of the synagogue leader and said to him, "Your daughter is dead. Don't bother the teacher any more."

50 When Jesus heard this, he said to Jairus, "Don't be afraid. Just believe, and your daughter will be well."

51 When Jesus went to the house, he let only Peter, John, James and the girl's father and mother go inside with him. 52 All the people were crying and feeling sad because the girl was dead, but Jesus said, "Stop crying. She is not dead, only asleep."

53 The people laughed at Jesus because they knew the girl was dead. 54 But Jesus took hold of her hand and called to her, "My child, stand up!" 55 Her spirit came back into her, and she stood up at once. Then Jesus ordered that she be given something to eat. 56 The girl's parents were amazed, but Jesus told them not to tell anyone what had happened.

Jesus Sends Out the Apostles

9 Jesus called the twelve apostles together and gave them power and authority over all demons and the ability to heal sicknesses. 2 He sent the apostles out to tell about God's kingdom and to heal the sick. 3 He said to them, "Take nothing for your trip, neither a walking stick, bag, bread, money or extra clothes. 4 When you enter a house, stay there until it is time to leave. 5 If people do not welcome you, shake the dust off your feet[n] as you leave the town, as a warning to them."

6 So the apostles went out and travelled through all the towns, preaching the Good News and healing people everywhere.

Herod is Confused About Jesus

7 Herod, the governor, heard about all the things that were happening and was confused, because some people said, "John the Baptist has risen from the dead." 8 Others said, "Elijah has come to us." And still others said, "One of the prophets who lived long ago has risen from the dead." 9 Herod said, "I cut off John's head, so who is this man I hear such things about?" And Herod kept trying to see Jesus.

9:5 shake . . . feet A warning. It showed that they had rejected these people.

More than 5,000 Fed

10 When the apostles returned, they told Jesus everything they had done. Then Jesus took them with him to a town called Bethsaida where they could be alone together. 11 But the people learned where Jesus went and followed him. He welcomed them and talked with them about God's kingdom and healed those who needed to be healed.

12 Late in the afternoon, the twelve apostles came to Jesus and said, "Send the people away. They need to go to the towns and countryside around here and find places to sleep and something to eat, because no one lives in this place."

13 But Jesus said to them, "You give them something to eat."

They said, "We have only five loaves of bread and two fish, unless we go and buy food for all these people." 14 (There were about 5,000 men there.)

Jesus said to his followers, "Tell the people to sit in groups of about 50 people."

15 So the followers did this, and all the people sat down. 16 Then Jesus took the five loaves of bread and two fish, and, looking up to heaven, he thanked God for the food. Then he divided the food and gave it to the followers to give to the people. 17 They all ate and were satisfied, and what was left over was gathered up, filling twelve baskets.

Jesus is the Christ

18 Once when Jesus was praying alone, his followers were with him, and he asked them, "Who do the people say I am?"

19 They answered, "Some say you are John the Baptist. Others say you are Elijah." And others say you are one of the prophets from long ago who has come back to life."

20 Then Jesus asked, "But who do you say I am?"

Peter answered, "You are the Christ from God."

21 Jesus warned them not to tell anyone, saying, 22 "The Son of Man must suffer many things. He will be rejected by the Jewish elders, the leading priests, and the teachers of the law. He will be killed and after three days will be raised from the dead."

23 Jesus said to all of them, "If people want to follow me, they must give up the things they want. They must be willing to give up their lives daily to follow me. 24 Those who want to save their lives will give up their lives. But those who give up their lives for me will have true life. 25 It is worth nothing for them to have the whole world if they themselves are destroyed or lost. 26 If people are ashamed of me and my teaching, then the Son of Man will be ashamed of them when he comes in his glory and with the glory of the Father and the holy angels. 27 I tell you the truth, some people standing here will see the kingdom of God before they die."

9:24 Life Jesus offers true life.

Jesus Talks with Moses and Elijah

28 About eight days after Jesus said these things, he took Peter, John and James and went up on a mountain to pray. 29 While Jesus was praying, the appearance of his face changed, and his clothes became shining white. 30 Then two men, Moses and Elijah," were talking with Jesus. 31 They appeared in heavenly glory, talking about his intended departure which he would soon bring about in Jerusalem. 32 Peter and the others were very sleepy, but when they awoke fully, they saw the glory of Jesus and the two men standing with him. 33 When Moses and Elijah were about to leave, Peter said to Jesus, "Master, it is good that we are here. Let us make three tents—one for you, one for Moses and one for Elijah." (Peter did not know what he was talking about.)

34 While he was saying these things, a cloud came and covered them, and they

---

9:19 Elijah A man who spoke for God and who lived hundreds of years before Christ. See 1 Kings 17.
9:30 Moses and Elijah Two of the most important Jewish leaders in the past. Moses had given them the law, and Elijah was an important prophet.

became afraid as the cloud covered them. 35 A voice came from the cloud, saying, "This is my Son, whom I have chosen. Listen to him!"

36 When the voice finished speaking, only Jesus was there. Peter, John and James said nothing and told no one at that time what they had seen.

Jesus Heals a Sick Boy

37 The next day, when they came down from the mountain, a large crowd met Jesus. 38 A man in the crowd shouted to him, "Teacher, please come and look at my son, because he is my only child. 39 An evil spirit seizes my son, and suddenly he screams. It causes him to lose control of himself and foam at the mouth. The evil spirit keeps on hurting him and almost never leaves him. 40 I begged your followers to force the evil spirit out, but they could not do it."

41 Jesus answered, "You people have no faith, and your lives are all wrong. How long must I stay with you and put up with you? Bring your son here."

42 While the boy was coming, the demon threw him on the ground and made him lose control of himself. But Jesus gave a strong command to the evil spirit and healed the boy and gave him back to his father. 43 All the people were amazed at the great power of God.

Jesus Talks About His Death

While everyone was wondering about all that Jesus did, he said to his followers, 44 "Don't forget what I tell you now: the Son of Man will be handed over to people." 45 But the followers did not understand what this meant; the meaning was hidden from them so they could not understand. But they were afraid to ask Jesus about it.

Who is the Greatest?

46 Jesus' followers began to have an argument about which one of them was the greatest. 47 Jesus knew what they were thinking, so he took a little child and stood the child beside him. 48 Then Jesus said, "Whoever accepts this little child in my name accepts me. And whoever accepts me accepts the One who sent me, because whoever is least among you all is really the greatest."

Anyone Not Against Us is For Us

49 John answered, "Master, we saw someone using your name to force demons

---

FAITH links

WANT TO KNOW? ASK!

LUKE 9:45

When you don't understand something you've heard or studied, what do you do? If you want to be wise, the best thing to do is to ask questions. When Jesus' followers didn't understand what Jesus said, they were afraid to ask him about it. Quite often, people are afraid to ask questions because they're afraid of looking stupid. Whenever you have questions about God, or your Bible, don't be afraid to ask someone to help you. God wants you to know all about him!

Download these links on getting wisdom:

An Example Not to Follow, Leviticus 18:1–3, p. 157

Learning to Listen, 1 Samuel 3, p. 358

Bragging Rights, Jeremiah 9:23–24, p. 1005

The Dead End of the Occult, Ezekiel 13:17–23, p. 1098

The Power of Prayer, Acts 12:5, p. 1485

One Thing to Do, Romans 4:1–5, p. 1523

out of people. We told him to stop, because he does not belong to our group."

50 But Jesus said to him, "Don't stop him, because whoever is not against you is for you."

A Town Rejects Jesus

51 When the time was coming near for Jesus to depart, he was determined to go to Jerusalem. 52 He sent some men ahead of him, who went into a town in Samaria to make everything ready for him. 53 But the people there would not welcome him, because he was set on going to Jerusalem. 54 When James and John, followers of Jesus, saw this, they said, "Lord, do you want us to call fire down from heaven and destroy those people?"[n] 55 But Jesus turned and scolded them. 56 Then[n] they went to another town.

Following Jesus

57 As they were going along the road, someone said to Jesus, "I will follow you anywhere you go."

58 Jesus said to them, "The foxes have holes to live in, and the birds have nests, but the Son of Man has no place to rest his head."

59 Jesus said to another man, "Follow me!"

But he said, "Lord, first let me go and bury my father."

60 But Jesus said to him, "Let the people who are dead bury their own dead. You must go and tell about the kingdom of God."

61 Another man said, "I will follow you, Lord, but first let me go and say goodbye to my family."

62 Jesus said, "Anyone who begins to plough a field but keeps looking back is of no use in the kingdom of God."

Jesus Sends Out the Seventy-two

10 After this, the Lord chose 72[n] others and sent them out in pairs ahead of him into every town and place where he planned to go. 2 He said to them, "There are a great many people to harvest, but there are only a few workers. So pray to God, who owns the harvest, that he will send more workers to help gather his harvest. 3 Go now, but listen! I am sending you out like sheep among wolves. 4 Don't carry a purse, a bag or sandals, and don't waste time talking with people on the road. 5 Before you go into a house, say, 'Peace be with this house.' 6 If peaceful people live there, your blessing of peace will stay with them, but if not, then your blessing will come back to you. 7 Stay in the peaceful house, eating and drinking what the people there give you. A worker should be given his pay. Don't move from house to house. 8 If you go into a town and the people welcome you, eat what they give you. 9 Heal the sick who live there, and tell them, 'The kingdom of God is near you.' 10 But if you go into a town, and the people don't welcome you, then go into the streets and say, 11 'Even the dust from your town that sticks to our feet we wipe off against you.'[n] But remember that the kingdom of God is near.' 12 I tell you, on the Judgement Day it will be better for the people of Sodom than for the people of that town.

Jesus Warns Unbelievers

13 "How terrible for you, Korazin! How terrible for you, Bethsaida! If the miracles I did in you had happened in Tyre and Sidon,[n] those people would have changed their lives long ago. They would have worn rough cloth and put ashes on themselves to show they had changed. 14 But on the Judgement Day it will be better for Tyre and Sidon than for you. 15 And you, Capernaum,[n] will you

---

9:54 Verse 54 Here, some Greek copies add: "... as Elijah did."
9:56 Verses 55-56 Some copies read: "But Jesus turned and scolded them. And Jesus said, 'You don't know what kind of spirit you belong to. 56 The Son of Man did not come to destroy the souls of people but to save them.' Then"
10:1 72 Many Greek copies read 70.
10:11 dust . . . you A warning. It showed that they had rejected these people.
10:13 Tyre and Sidon Towns where wicked people lived.
10:13, 15 Korazin . . . Bethsaida . . . Capernaum Towns by Lake Galilee where Jesus preached to the people.

be lifted up to heaven? No! You will be thrown down to the depths!

16 "Whoever listens to you listens to me, and whoever refuses to accept you refuses to accept me. And whoever refuses to accept me refuses to accept the One who sent me."

Satan Falls

17 When the 72[n] came back, they were very happy and said, "Lord, even the demons obeyed us when we used your name!"

18 Jesus said, "I saw Satan fall like lightning from heaven. 19 Listen, I have given you power to walk on snakes and scorpions, power that is greater than the enemy has. So nothing will hurt you. 20 But you should not be happy because the spirits obey you but because your names are written in heaven."

10:17 Demons Find out who the demons obey.

Jesus Prays to the Father

21 Then Jesus rejoiced in the Holy Spirit and said, "I praise you, Father, Lord of heaven and earth, because you have hidden these things from the people who are wise and clever. But you have shown them to those who are like little children. Yes, Father, this is what you really wanted.

22 "My Father has given me all things. No one knows who the Son is, except the Father. And no one knows who the Father is, except the Son and those whom the Son chooses to tell."

23 Then Jesus turned to his followers and said privately, "You are blessed to see what you now see. 24 I tell you, many prophets and kings wanted to see what you now see, but they did not, and they wanted to hear what you now hear, but they did not."

The Good Samaritan

25 Then an expert on the law stood up to test Jesus, saying, "Teacher, what must I do to get eternal life?"

26 Jesus said, "What is written in the law? What do you read there?"

27 The man answered, "Love the Lord your God with all your heart, all your soul, all your strength and all your mind."[n] Also, "Love your neighbour as you love yourself."[n]

28 Jesus said to him, "Your answer is right. Do this and you will live."

29 But the man, wanting to show the importance of his question, said to Jesus, "And who is my neighbour?"

30 Jesus answered, "As a man was going down from Jerusalem to Jericho, some robbers attacked him. They tore off his clothes, beat him, and left him lying there, almost dead. 31 It happened that a Jewish priest was going down that road. When he saw the man, he walked by on the other side. 32 Next, a Levite[n] came there, and after he went over and looked at the man, he walked by on the other side of the road. 33 Then a Samaritan[n] travelling down the road came to where the hurt man was. When he saw the man, he felt very sorry for him. 34 The Samaritan went to him, poured olive oil and wine[n] on his wounds and bandaged them. Then he put the hurt man on his own donkey and took him to an inn where he cared for him. 35 The next day, the Samaritan brought out two silver coins,[n] gave them to the innkeeper, and said, 'Take care of this man. If you spend more money on him, I will pay it back to you when I come again.'"

36 Then Jesus said, "Which one of these three men do you think was a neighbour to the man who was attacked by the robbers?"

37 The expert on the law answered,

10:17 72 Many Greek copies read 70.
10:27 "Love . . . mind." Quotation from Deuteronomy 6:5.
10:27 "Love . . . yourself." Quotation from Leviticus 19:18.
10:32 Levite Levites were members of the tribe of Levi who helped the Jewish priests with their work in the Temple. Read 1 Chronicles 23:24-32.
10:33 Samaritan Samaritans were people from Samaria. These people were part Jewish, but the Jews did not accept them as true Jews. Samaritans and Jews disliked each other.
10:34 olive oil and wine Oil and wine were used like medicine to soften and clean wounds.
10:35 coins Roman denarii. A silver coin was the average pay for one day's work.

FAITH CHALLENGE

Try this one. Read 10:29 to find out what important question a religious leader wanted Jesus to answer. According to Jesus' definition, who are your neighbours? How do you need to change your definition of a neighbour?

TESTING IT

Luke 10:29
But the man, wanting to show the importance of his question, said to Jesus, "And who is my neighbour?"

"The one who showed him mercy."

Jesus said to him, "Then go and do what he did."

Mary and Martha

38 While Jesus and his followers were travelling, Jesus went into a town. A woman named Martha let Jesus stay at her house. 39 Martha had a sister named Mary, who was sitting at Jesus' feet and listening to him teach. 40 But Martha was busy with all the work to be done. She went in and said, "Lord, don't you care that my sister has left me alone to do all the work? Tell her to help me."

41 But the Lord answered her, "Martha, Martha, you are worried and upset about many things. 42 Only one thing is important. Mary has chosen the better thing, and it will never be taken away from her."

Jesus Teaches About Prayer

11 Once Jesus was praying in a certain place. When he finished, one of his followers said to him, "Lord, teach us to pray as John taught his followers."

2 Jesus said to them, "When you pray, say:

'Father, may your name always be kept holy.
May your kingdom come.
3 Give us the food we need for each day.
4 Forgive us for our sins,
because we forgive everyone who has done wrong to us.
And do not cause us to be tempted.'"

Continue to Ask

5 Then Jesus said to them, "Suppose one of you went to your friend's house at midnight and said to him, 'Friend, loan me three loaves of bread. 6 A friend of mine has come into town to visit me, but I have nothing for him to eat.' 7 Your friend inside the house answers, 'Don't bother me! The door is already locked, and my children and I are in bed. I cannot get up and give you anything.' 8 I tell you, if friendship is not enough to make him get up to give you the bread, your boldness will make him get up and give you whatever you need. 9 So I tell you, ask, and God will give to you. Search, and you will find. Knock, and the door will open for you. 10 Yes, everyone who asks will receive. The one who searches will find. And everyone who knocks will have the door opened. 11 If your children ask for a fish, which of you would give them a snake instead? 12 Or, if your children ask for an egg, would you give them a scorpion? 13 Even though you are bad, you know how to give good things to your children. How much more will your heavenly Father give the Holy Spirit to those who ask him!"

A MODEL PRAYER LUKE 11:1

Jesus said that we should pray with faith and simplicity. He gave us a model prayer to follow. This prayer is sometimes called "The Lord's Prayer". The prayer is in the Bible in the Gospels of Matthew and Luke. In Matthew, the prayer appears in Jesus' famous sermon called "The Sermon on the Mount". (Read Matthew 6:9–13, p. 1283.) In Luke, it appears after the disciples asked Jesus to teach them how to pray. (See Luke 11:1–4.) Here's what the different parts of the prayer mean:

"Our Father in heaven, may your name always be kept holy" (Matthew 6:9).
We can worship and respect God when we pray.
"May your kingdom come and what you want be done, here on earth as it is in heaven" (6:10).
We should want what God wants when we pray.
"Give us the food we need for each day" (6:11).
We can ask God for what we need when we pray.
"Forgive us for our sins, just as we have forgiven those who sinned against us" (6:12).
We can ask God for forgiveness when we pray.
"And do not cause us to be tempted, but save us from the Evil One" (6:13).
We can ask God to protect us from sin and evil when we pray.

Jesus' Power is from God

14 Once Jesus was sending out a demon that could not talk. When the demon came out, the man who had been unable to speak, then spoke. The people were amazed. 15 But some of them said, "Jesus uses the power of Beelzebul, the ruler of demons, to force demons out of people."

16 Other people, wanting to test Jesus, asked him to give them a sign from heaven. 17 But knowing their thoughts, he said to them, "Every kingdom that is divided against itself will be destroyed. And a family that is divided against itself will not continue. 18 So if Satan is divided against himself, his kingdom will not continue. You say that I use the power of Beelzebul to force out demons. 19 But if I use the power of Beelzebul to force out demons, what power do your people use to force demons out? So they will be your judges. 20 But if I use the power of God to force out demons, then the kingdom of God has come to you.

21 "When a strong person with many weapons guards his own house, his possessions are safe. 22 But when someone stronger comes and defeats him, the stronger one will take away the weapons the first man trusted and will give away the possessions.

23 "Anyone who is not with me is against me, and anyone who does not work with me is working against me.

The Empty Person

24 "When an evil spirit comes out of a person, it travels through dry places, looking for a place to rest. But when it

finds no place, it says, 'I will go back to the house I left.' 25 And when it comes back, it finds that house swept clean and made neat. 26 Then the evil spirit goes out and brings seven other spirits more evil than it is, and they go in and live there. So the person has even more trouble than before."

People Who Are Truly Happy

27 As Jesus was saying these things, a woman in the crowd called out to Jesus, "Happy is the mother who gave birth to you and nursed you."

28 But Jesus said, "No, happy are those who hear the teaching of God and obey it."

11:28 Obedience — What will make you really happy?

The People Want a Miracle

29 As the crowd grew larger, Jesus said, "The people who live today are evil. They want to see a miracle for a sign, but no sign will be given them, except the sign of Jonah.[n] 30 As Jonah was a sign for those people who lived in Nineveh, the Son of Man will be a sign for the people of this time. 31 On the Judgement Day the Queen of the South[n] will stand up with the people who live now. She will show they are guilty, because she came from far away to listen to Solomon's wise teaching. And I tell you that someone greater than Solomon is here. 32 On the Judgement Day the people of Nineveh will stand up with the people who live now, and they will show that you are guilty. When Jonah preached to them, they were sorry and changed their lives. And I tell you that someone greater than Jonah is here.

Be a Light for the World

33 "No one lights a lamp and puts it in a secret place or under a bowl, but on a lampstand so the people who come in can see. 34 Your eye is a light for the body. When your eyes are good, your whole body will be full of light. But when your eyes are evil, your whole body will be full of darkness. 35 So be careful not to let the light in you become darkness. 36 If your whole body is full of light, and none of it is dark, then you will shine bright, as when a lamp shines on you."

Jesus Accuses the Pharisees

37 After Jesus had finished speaking, a Pharisee asked Jesus to eat with him. So Jesus went in and sat at the table. 38 But the Pharisee was surprised when he saw that Jesus did not wash his hands[n] before the meal. 39 The Lord said to him, "You Pharisees clean the outside of the cup and the dish, but inside you are full of greed and evil. 40 You foolish people! The same one who made what is outside also made what is inside. 41 So give what is in your dishes to the poor, and then you will be fully clean. 42 How terrible for you Pharisees! You give God one-tenth of even your mint, your rue and every other plant in your garden. But you fail to be fair to others and to love God. These are the things you should do while continuing to do those other things. 43 How terrible for you Pharisees, because you love to have the most important seats in the synagogues, and you love to be greeted with respect in the market places. 44 How terrible for you, because you are like hidden graves, which people walk on without knowing."

Jesus Talks to Experts on the Law

45 One of the experts on the law said to Jesus, "Teacher, when you say these things, you are insulting us, too."

46 Jesus answered, "How terrible for you, you experts on the law! You make strict rules that are very hard for people to obey, but you yourselves don't even try to follow those rules. 47 How terrible for you, because you build tombs for the

---

11:29 sign of Jonah Jonah's three days in the fish are like Jesus' three days in the tomb. See Matthew 12:40.
11:31 Queen of the South The Queen of Sheba. She travelled 1,600 kilometres to learn God's wisdom from Solomon. Read 1 Kings 10:1-3.
11:38 wash his hands This was a Jewish religious custom that the Pharisees thought was very important.

CLEAN INSIDE AND OUT
LUKE 11:39-40

Would you drink out of a cup that was clean on the outside but dirty on the inside? The answer is obvious, wouldn't you say? You'd want the inside to match the outside.

Jesus told the Pharisees that they were clean on the outside, but dirty on the inside. By this he meant they had sinful thoughts and actions, yet they tried to make themselves look good in public. God wants us to be clean outside and in. He doesn't want us to pretend that we have no sin. Being quick to admit that we've done wrong and to ask God to forgive us keeps us clean on the inside.

A Holiday Every Week, Leviticus 23:1–3, p. 166

Does Crime Pay? Psalm 37:1–7, p. 736

Red to White, Isaiah 1:18, p. 896

Real Repentance, Jeremiah 4:1–4, p. 993

The "Ruler" of Our Lives, Amos 7:7–9, p. 1202

Obey or Disobey? Luke 20:20–26, p. 1409

---

prophets whom your ancestors killed! 48 And now you show that you approve of what your ancestors did. They killed the prophets, and you build tombs for them! 49 This is why in his wisdom God said, 'I will send prophets and apostles to them. They will kill some, and they will treat others cruelly.' 50 So you who live now will be punished for the deaths of all the prophets who were killed since the beginning of the world—51 from the killing of Abel to the killing of Zechariah,ⁿ who died between the altar and the Temple. Yes, I tell you that you who are alive now will be punished for them all.

52 "How terrible for you, you experts on the law. You have taken away the key to learning about God. You yourselves would not learn, and you stopped others from learning, too."

53 When Jesus left, the teachers of the law and the Pharisees began to give him trouble, asking him questions about many things and 54 trying to catch him saying something wrong.

Don't Be like the Pharisees

12 So many thousands of people had gathered that they were stepping on each other. Jesus spoke first to his followers, saying, "Beware of the yeast of the Pharisees, because they are hypocrites. 2 Everything that is hidden will be shown, and everything that is secret will be made known. 3 What you have said in the dark will be heard in the light, and what you have whispered in an inner room will be shouted from the housetops.

4 "I tell you, my friends, don't be afraid of people who can kill the body but after that can do nothing more to hurt you. 5 I will show you the one to fear. Fear the one who has the power to kill you and also to throw you into hell. Yes, this is the one you should fear.

6 "Five sparrows are sold for only two pennies, and God does not forget any of them. 7 But God even knows how many hairs you have on your head. Don't be afraid. You are worth much more than many sparrows.

Don't Be Ashamed of Jesus

8 "I tell you, all those who stand before others and say they believe in me, I, the

---

11:51 Abel . . . Zechariah In the Hebrew Old Testament, the first and last men to be murdered.

Son of Man, will say before the angels of God that they belong to me. 9 But all who stand before others and say they do not believe in me, I will say before the angels of God that they do not belong to me.

10 "Anyone who speaks against the Son of Man can be forgiven, but anyone who speaks against the Holy Spirit will not be forgiven.

11 "When you are brought into the synagogues before the leaders and other powerful people, don't worry about how to defend yourselves or what to say. 12 At that time the Holy Spirit will teach you what you must say."

Jesus Warns Against Selfishness

13 Someone in the crowd said to Jesus, "Teacher, tell my brother to divide with me the property our father left us."

14 But Jesus said to him, "Who said I should judge or decide between you?" 15 Then Jesus said to them, "Be careful and guard against all kinds of greed. Life is not measured by how much one owns."

16 Then Jesus told this story: "There was a rich man who had some land, which grew a good crop. 17 He thought to himself, 'What will I do? I have no place to keep all my crops.' 18 Then he said, 'This is what I will do: I will tear down my barns and build bigger ones, and there I will store all my grain and other goods. 19 Then I can say to myself, "I have enough good things stored to last for many years. Rest, eat, drink and enjoy life!"'

20 "But God said to him, 'Foolish man! Tonight your life will be taken from you. So who will get those things you have prepared for yourself?'

21 "This is how it will be for those who store up things for themselves and are not rich towards God."

Don't Worry

22 Jesus said to his followers, "So I tell you, don't worry about the food you need to live, or about the clothes you need in order for your body. 23 Life is more than food, and the body is more than clothes. 24 Look at the birds. They don't plant or harvest, they don't have storerooms or barns, but God feeds them. And you are worth much more than birds. 25 You cannot add any time to your life by worrying about it. 26 If you cannot do even the little things, then why worry about the big things? 27 Consider how the lilies grow; they don't work or make clothes for themselves. But I tell you that even Solomon with his riches was not dressed as beautifully as one of these flowers. 28 God clothes the grass in the field, which is alive today but tomorrow is thrown into the fire. So how much more will God clothe you? Don't have so little faith! 29 Don't always think about what you will eat or what you will drink, and don't keep worrying. 30 All the people in the world are trying to get these things, and your Father knows you need them. 31 But seek God's kingdom, and all the other things you need will be given to you.

Don't Trust in Money

32 "Don't fear, little flock, because your Father wants to give you the kingdom. 33 Sell your possessions and give to the poor. Get for yourselves purses that will not wear out, the treasure in heaven that never runs out, where thieves can't steal and moths can't destroy. 34 Your heart will be where your treasure is.

Always Be Ready

35 "Be dressed, ready for service, and have your lamps shining. 36 Be like servants who are waiting for their master to come home from a wedding party. When he comes and knocks, the servants immediately open the door for him. 37 They will be blessed when their master comes home, because he sees that they were watching for him. I tell you the truth, the master will dress himself to serve and tell the servants to sit at the table, and he will serve them. 38 Those servants will be happy when he comes in and finds them still waiting, even if it is midnight or later.

39 "Remember this: if the owner of the house knew what time a thief was coming, he would not allow the thief to enter his house. 40 So you also must be ready, because the Son of Man will come at a time when you don't expect him!"

> Luke 12:41 1394

FAITH links

HEAVENLY TREASURE
LUKE 12:32-34

Think about what you value most. This might be something you spend most of your time thinking about. This could also be a goal that you have for your life. What you value is what you treasure. Jesus preached a sermon to teach people about God's kingdom. He talked about storing treasure in heaven. If you treasure learning about God and helping others, you'll store up treasure in heaven.

What's important to you? Check out these Faithlinks:

What You Value, Genesis 25:21-34, p. 34

Remembering What He Said, Deuteronomy 6:4-9, p. 236

What God Thinks, Isaiah 55:8-9, p. 969

Empty Words, Ezekiel 33:30-33, p. 1127

The Choices of a Choice, Luke 5:1-11, p. 1375

You're a Fake! 2 Peter 2:1, p. 1709

Who is the Trusted Servant?

41 Peter said, "Lord, did you tell this story to us or to all people?"

42 The Lord said, "Who is the wise and trusted servant that the master trusts to give the other servants their food at the right time? 43 When the master comes and finds the servant doing his work, the servant will be blessed. 44 I tell you the truth, the master will choose that servant to take care of everything he owns. 45 But suppose the servant thinks to himself, 'My master will not come back soon,' and he begins to beat the other servants, men and women, and to eat and drink and get drunk. 46 The master will come when that servant is not ready and is not expecting him. Then the master will cut him in pieces and send him away to be with the others who don't obey.

47 "The servant who knows what his master wants but is not ready, or who does not do what the master wants, will be beaten with many blows! 48 But the servant who does not know what his master wants and does things that should be punished will be beaten with few blows. From everyone who has been given much, much will be demanded. And from the one trusted with much, much more will be expected.

Jesus Causes Division

49 "I came to set fire to the world, and I wish it were already burning! 50 I have a baptism[n] to undergo and I feel very troubled until it is over. 51 Do you think I came to give peace to the earth? No, I tell you, I came to divide it. 52 From now on, a family with five people will be divided, three against two, and two against three. 53 They will be divided: father against son and son against father, mother against daughter and daughter against mother, mother-in-law against daughter-in-law and daughter-in-law against mother-in-law."

> **12:51-53 Family**
> Is there anything that is more important than the family?

Understanding the Times

54 Then Jesus said to the people, "When you see clouds coming up in the west, you say, 'It's going to rain,' and it happens. 55 When you feel the wind begin to blow from the south, you say, 'It will be a hot day,' and it happens. 56 Hypocrites! You know how to under-

---

12:50 I . . . baptism Jesus was talking about the suffering he would soon go through.

stand the appearance of the earth and sky. Why don't you understand what is happening now?

Settle Your Problems

57 "Why can't you decide for yourselves what is right? 58 If your enemy is taking you to court, try hard to settle it on the way. If you don't, your enemy might take you to the judge, and the judge might turn you over to the officer, and the officer might throw you into jail. 59 I tell you, you will not get out of there until you have paid everything you owe."

Change Your Hearts

13 At that time some people were there who told Jesus that Pilate[n] had killed some people from Galilee while they were worshipping. He mixed their blood with the blood of the animals they were sacrificing to God. 2 Jesus answered, "Do you think this happened to them because they were more sinful than all others from Galilee? 3 No, I tell you. But unless you change your hearts and lives, you will be destroyed as they were! 4 What about those eighteen people who died when the tower of Siloam fell on them? Do you think they were more sinful than all the others who live in Jerusalem? 5 No, I tell you. But unless you change your hearts and lives, you will all be destroyed too!"

13:3–5 Repentance
Change your heart – or else!

The Useless Tree

6 Jesus told this story: "A man had a fig tree planted in his vineyard. He came looking for some fruit on the tree, but he found none. 7 So the man said to his gardener, 'I have been looking for fruit on this tree for three years, but I never find any. Cut it down. Why should it waste the ground?' 8 But the servant answered, 'Master, let the tree have one more year to produce fruit. Let me dig up the earth around it and put on some manure. 9 If the tree produces fruit next year, good. But if not, you can cut it down.'"

Jesus Heals on the Sabbath

10 Jesus was teaching in one of the synagogues on the Sabbath day. 11 A woman was there who, for eighteen years, had an evil spirit in her that made her crippled. Her back was always bent; she could not stand up straight. 12 When Jesus saw her, he called her over and said, "Woman, you are free from your sickness." 13 Jesus put his hands on her, and immediately she was able to stand up straight and began praising God.

14 The synagogue leader was angry because Jesus healed on the Sabbath day. He said to the people, "There are six days when one has to work. So come to be healed on one of those days, and not on the Sabbath day."

15 The Lord answered, "You hypocrites! Doesn't each of you untie your work animals and lead them to drink water every day—even on the Sabbath day? 16 This woman that I healed, a daughter of Abraham, has been held by Satan for eighteen years. Surely it is not wrong for her to be freed from her sickness on a Sabbath day!" 17 When Jesus said this, all of those who were criticising him were ashamed, but the entire crowd rejoiced at all the wonderful things Jesus was doing.

Stories of Mustard Seed and Yeast

18 Then Jesus said, "What is God's kingdom like? What can I compare it with? 19 It is like a mustard seed that a man plants in his garden. The seed grows and becomes a tree, and the wild birds build nests in its branches."

20 Jesus said again, "What can I compare God's kingdom with? 21 It is like yeast that a woman took and hid in a large bowl of flour until it made all the dough rise."

The Narrow Door

22 Jesus was teaching in every town and village as he travelled towards Jerusalem. 23 Someone said to Jesus, "Lord, will only a few people be saved?"

13:1 Pilate Pontius Pilate was the Roman governor of Judea from A.D. 26 to A.D. 36.

HANDLING MY STUFF
Luke 12; 13

Livin' it

Such a Lot of Stuff! Do you have to move stuffed toys to get into bed? Are CDs and books overflowing the shelves? Do your clothes get squashed into your wardrobe and dresser drawers? How important is "your stuff" to you? How often do you use what you have? Can you even find it when you want it?

Jesus preached a sermon to help his listeners understand that loving God and loving money or possessions don't mix. (Check <u>Luke 16:13–15</u>.) You can't love God and possessions. Whichever is loved more – God or money – is the heart's desire. What is *your* heart's desire?

MORE FAITH links

Idol Talk, **p. 118**

"Handle" Your Responsibilities, **p. 485**

Wisdom About Wealth, **p. 878**

Set for Life? **p. 1208**

Give Till It Hurts? **p. 1578**

Do you feel like you're being buried by too much stuff?

Have a look at these Faithlinks. They might help you handle all that stuff.

What I've Got, <u>2 Kings 20:12–17, p. 508</u>
- Are you ever tempted to brag about the cool stuff you have? What would you do if you no longer had those things? There's nothing wrong in having nice things. But the stuff you have doesn't make you special. God gives you everything and he makes you special. Now that's something to brag about!

My Favourite! <u>Mark 10:17–23, p. 1347</u>
- Suppose someone asked you to give up your favourite possession to prove you loved God. How willing would you be to give it up? Link here to see how a man reacted to such a suggestion.

Share and Share Alike? <u>Acts 2:43–47, p. 1466</u>
- How willing are you to share what you have with others? Would it make a difference in what you were being asked to share? Early Christians shared everything they had because of their love of God. How can you share some of God's love and some of your possessions with someone today?

my FAVOURITE links

Jesus said, 24 "Try hard to enter through the narrow door, because many people will try to enter there, but they will not be able. 25 When the owner of the house gets up and closes the door, you can stand outside and knock on the door and say, 'Sir, open the door for us.' But he will answer, 'I don't know you or where you come from.' 26 Then you will say, 'We ate and drank with you, and you taught in the streets of our town.' 27 But he will say to you, 'I don't know you or where you come from. Go away from me, all you who do evil!' 28 You will cry and grind your teeth with pain when you see Abraham, Isaac, Jacob and all the prophets in God's kingdom, but you yourselves thrown outside. 29 People will come from the east, west, north and south and will sit down at the table in the kingdom of God. 30 There are those who have the lowest place in life now who will have the highest place in the future. And there are those who have the highest place now who will have the lowest place in the future."

Jesus will Die in Jerusalem

31 At that time some Pharisees came to Jesus and said, "Go away from here! Herod wants to kill you!"

32 Jesus said to them, "Go and tell that fox Herod, 'Today and tomorrow I am forcing demons out and healing people. Then, on the third day, I will reach my goal.' 33 Yet I must be on my way today and tomorrow and the next day. Surely it cannot be right for a prophet to be killed anywhere except in Jerusalem.

34 "Jerusalem, Jerusalem! You kill the prophets and stone to death those who are sent to you. Many times I wanted to gather your people as a hen gathers her chicks under her wings, but you would not let me. 35 Now your house is left completely empty. I tell you, you will not see me until that time when you will say, 'God bless the One who comes in the name of the Lord.'"*n*

Healing on the Sabbath

14 On a Sabbath day, when Jesus went to eat at the home of a leading Pharisee, the people were watching Jesus very closely. 2 And in front of him was a man with dropsy.*n* 3 Jesus said to the Pharisees and experts on the law, "Is it right or wrong to heal on the Sabbath day?" 4 But they would not answer his question. So Jesus took the man, healed him and sent him away. 5 Jesus said to the Pharisees and teachers of the law, "If your child or ox falls into a well on the Sabbath day, will you not pull him out quickly?" 6 And they could not answer him.

Don't Make Yourself Important

7 When Jesus noticed that some of the guests were choosing the best places to sit, he told this story: 8 "When someone invites you to a wedding feast, don't take the most important seat, because someone more important than you may have been invited. 9 The host, who invited both of you, will come to you and say, 'Give this person your seat.' Then you will be embarrassed and will have to move to the last place. 10 So when you are invited, go and sit in a seat that is not important. When the host comes to you, he may say, 'Friend, move up here to a more important place.' Then all the other guests will respect you. 11 All who make themselves great will be made humble, but those who make themselves humble will be made great."

You will Be Rewarded

12 Then Jesus said to the man who had invited him, "When you give a lunch or a dinner, don't invite only your friends, your family, your other relatives and your rich neighbours. At another time they will invite you to eat with them, and you will be repaid. 13 Instead, when you give a feast, invite the poor, the crippled, the lame and the blind. 14 Then you

14:13–14
Caring
Find out the kind of people you should care for.

13:35 'God . . . Lord.' Quotation from Psalm 118:26.
14:2 **dropsy** A sickness that causes the body to swell larger and larger.

Luke 14:15

FAITH links

BEST SEAT IN THE HOUSE
LUKE 14:7-11

Suppose you and a friend were invited to a party to meet someone famous. Now, let's say there was only one seat next to the famous person. Would you take it or would you let your friend have it?

Jesus once told a story about taking the best seats at a party. The people who wanted others to think they were important would take the best seats. Jesus used this story to teach people to be humble. Humble people don't try to make themselves look important. They don't have to. God says he will make the humble great!

Here are some more links on being humble:

Fairness for All, Deuteronomy 24:17, p. 258

The Way to Serve God, 1 Kings 9:4, p. 450

Seeing the Needs, Nehemiah 1, p. 625

Set for Life? Obadiah 2–4, p. 1208

Glad to Help! Romans 15:17–20, p. 1541

Brag on Him! 1 Corinthians 3:18–23, p. 1548

A Story About a Big Banquet

15 One of those at the table with Jesus heard these things and said to him, "Happy are the people who will share in the meal in God's kingdom."

16 Jesus said to him, "A man gave a big banquet and invited many people. 17 When it was time to eat, the man sent his servant to tell the guests, 'Come. Everything is ready.'

18 "But all the guests made excuses. The first one said, 'I have just bought a field, and I must go and look at it. Please excuse me.' 19 Another said, 'I have just bought five pairs of oxen; I must go and try them. Please excuse me.' 20 A third person said, 'I just got married; I can't come.' 21 So the servant returned and told his master what had happened. Then the master became angry and said, 'Go at once into the streets and alleys of the town, and bring in the poor, the crippled, the blind, and the lame.' 22 Later the servant said to him, 'Master, I did what you commanded, but we still have room.' 23 The master said to the servant, 'Go out to the roads and country lanes, and tell the people there to come so my house will be full. 24 I tell you, none of those whom I invited first will eat with me.'"

The Cost of Being Jesus' Follower

25 Large crowds were travelling with Jesus, and he turned and said to them, 26 "If anyone comes to me but loves his father, mother, wife, children, brothers or sisters—or even life—more than me, he cannot be my follower. 27 Whoever is not willing to carry the cross and follow me cannot be my follower. 28 If you want to build a tower, you first sit down and decide how much it will cost, to see if you have enough money to finish the job. 29 If you don't, you might lay the foundation, but you would not be able to finish. Then all who saw it would make fun of you, 30 saying, 'This person began to build but was not able to finish.'

31 "If a king is going to fight another king, first he will sit down and plan. He will decide if he and his 10,000 soldiers can defeat the other king who has 20,000 soldiers. 32 If he can't, then while the

will be blessed, because they have nothing and cannot pay you back. But you will be repaid when the good people rise from the dead."

other king is still far away, he will send some people to speak to him and ask for peace. 33 In the same way, you must give up everything you have to be my follower.

Don't Lose Your Influence

34 "Salt is good, but if it loses its salty taste, you cannot make it salty again. 35 It is no good for the soil or for manure; it is thrown away.

"You people who can hear me, listen."

A Lost Sheep, a Lost Coin

15 The tax collectors and sinners all came to listen to Jesus. 2 But the Pharisees and the teachers of the law began to complain: "Look, this man welcomes sinners and even eats with them."

3 Then Jesus told them this story: 4 "Suppose one of you has 100 sheep but loses one of them. Then he will leave the other 99 sheep in the open field and go out and look for the lost sheep until he finds it. 5 And when he finds it, he happily puts it on his shoulders 6 and goes home. He calls to his friends and neighbours and says, 'Be happy with me because I found my lost sheep.' 7 In the same way, I tell you there is more joy in heaven over one sinner who changes his heart and life, than over 99 good people who don't need to change.

15:7 Repentance *What gives heaven joy?*

8 "Suppose a woman has ten silver coins,ⁿ but loses one. She will light a lamp, sweep the house and look carefully for the coin until she finds it. 9 And when she finds it, she will call her friends and neighbours and say, 'Be happy with me because I have found the coin that I lost.' 10 In the same way, there is joy in the presence of the angels of God when one sinner changes his heart and life."

The Son Who Left Home

11 Then Jesus said, "A man had two sons. 12 The younger son said to his father, 'Give me my share of the property.' So the father divided the property between his two sons. 13 Then the younger son gathered up all that was his and travelled far away to another country. There he wasted his money in foolish living. 14 After he had spent everything, a time came when there was no food anywhere in the country, and the son was poor and hungry. 15 So he got a job with one of the citizens there who sent the son into the fields to feed pigs. 16 The son was so hungry that he wanted to eat the food the pigs were eating, but no one gave him anything. 17 When he realised what he was doing, he thought, 'All my father's servants have plenty of food. But I am here, almost dying with hunger. 18 I will leave and return to my father and say to him, "Father, I have sinned against God and have done wrong to you. 19 I am no longer worthy to be called your son, but let me be like one of your servants."' 20 So the son left and went to his father.

"While the son was still a long way off, his father saw him and felt sorry for his son. So the father ran to him and hugged and kissed him. 21 The son said, 'Father, I have sinned against God and have done wrong to you. I am no longer worthy to be called your son.' 22 But the father said to his servants, 'Hurry! Bring the best clothes and put them on him. Also, put a ring on his finger and sandals on his feet. 23 And get our fat calf and kill it so we can have a feast and celebrate. 24 My son was dead, but now he is alive again! He was lost, but now he is found!' So they began to celebrate.

25 "The older son was in the field, and as he came closer to the house, he heard the sound of music and dancing. 26 So he called to one of the servants and asked what all this meant. 27 The servant said, 'Your brother has come back, and your father killed the fat calf, because your brother came home safely.' 28 The older son was angry and would not go in to the feast. So his father went out and begged him to come in. 29 But the older son said

---

15:8 coins Roman denarii. A silver coin was the average pay for one day's work.

to his father, 'I have served you like a slave for many years and have always obeyed your commands. But you never gave me even a young goat to have at a feast with my friends. 30 But your other son, who wasted all your money on prostitutes, comes home, and you kill the fat calf for him!' 31 The father said to him, 'Son, you are always with me, and all that I have is yours. 32 We had to celebrate and be happy because your brother was dead, but now he is alive. He was lost, but now he is found.'"

15:32 Salvation
Check out a time to celebrate.

True Wealth

16 Jesus also said to his followers, "Once there was a rich man who had a manager to take care of his business. This manager was accused of cheating him. 2 So he called the manager in and said to him, 'What is this I hear about you? Give me an account of what you have done with my money, because you can't be my manager any longer.' 3 The manager thought to himself, 'What will I do since my master is taking my job away from me? I am not strong enough to dig ditches, and I am too proud to beg. 4 I know what I'll do so that when I lose my job people will welcome me into their homes.'

5 "So the manager called in everyone who owed the master any money. He asked the first one, 'How much do you owe?' 6 He answered, '3,000 litres of olive oil.' The manager said to him, 'Take your bill, sit down quickly and write 1,500 litres.' 7 Then the manager asked another one, 'How much do you owe?' He answered, '18 tonnes of wheat.' Then the manager said to him, 'Take your bill and write 14 tonnes.' 8 So, the master praised the dishonest manager for being clever. Yes, worldly people are more clever with their own kind than spiritual people are.

9 "I tell you, make friends for yourselves using worldly riches so that when those riches are gone, you will be welcomed in those homes that continue for ever. 10 Whoever can be trusted with a little can also be trusted with a lot, and whoever is dishonest with a little is dishonest with a lot. 11 If you cannot be trusted with worldly riches, then who will trust you with true riches? 12 And if you cannot be trusted with things that belong to someone else, who will give you things of your own?

13 "No servant can serve two masters. The servant will hate one master and love the other, or will follow one master and refuse to follow the other. You cannot serve both God and worldly riches."

16:13 Money
Can Christians serve both God and money?

God's Law Cannot Be Changed

14 The Pharisees, who loved money, were listening to all these things and made fun of Jesus. 15 He said to them, "You make yourselves look good in front of people, but God knows what is really in your hearts. What is important to people is hateful in God's sight.

16 "The law of Moses and the writings of the prophets were preached until John" came. Since then the Good News about the kingdom of God has been told, and everyone tries to enter it by force. 17 It would be easier for heaven and earth to pass away than for the smallest part of a letter in the law to be changed.

Divorce and Remarriage

18 "If a man divorces his wife and marries another woman, he is guilty of adultery, and the man who marries a divorced woman is also guilty of adultery."

The Rich Man and Lazarus

19 Jesus said, "There was a rich man who always dressed in the finest clothes and lived in luxury every day. 20 And a very poor man named Lazarus, whose body was covered with sores, was laid at the rich man's gate. 21 He wanted to eat only the small pieces of food that fell from

---

16:16 John John the Baptist, who preached to people about Christ's coming (Matthew 3, Luke 3).

FAITH links

YOUR HEART'S DESIRE
LUKE 16:13-15

What do you love? Some people, if they're honest, will say that they love their possessions. Maybe they have some great computer games, or the latest mobile phone. Some just seem to love the money it takes to buy those possessions.

One day Jesus preached a sermon to help his listeners understand how to please God. (Check out The Sermon on the Mount, p. 1280.) He wanted them to know that loving God and loving worldly riches don't mix. You can't love one if you love the other. Loving one or the other means having it as your heart's desire. What is *your* heart's desire?

The Sacrifice, Genesis 22, p. 29

Ten Ways to Obey, Exodus 20, p. 103

When God Says No, 2 Samuel 7, p. 407

A Look for the Book, 2 Chronicles 34:14–18, p. 603

A Robbery in Progress, Malachi 3:8–10, p. 1270

More Money? 1 Timothy 6:10, p. 1649

---

the rich man's table. And the dogs would come and lick his sores. 22 Later, Lazarus died, and the angels carried him to the arms of Abraham. The rich man died, too, and was buried. 23 In the place of the dead, he was in much pain. The rich man saw Abraham far away with Lazarus at his side. 24 He called, 'Father Abraham, have mercy on me! Send Lazarus to dip his finger in water and cool my tongue, because I am suffering in this fire!' 25 But Abraham said, 'Child, remember when you were alive you had the good things in life, but bad things happened to Lazarus. Now he is comforted here, and you are suffering. 26 Besides, there is a big pit between you and us, so no one can cross over to you, and no one can leave there and come here.' 27 The rich man said, 'Father, then please send Lazarus to my father's house. 28 I have five brothers, and Lazarus could warn them so that they will not come to this place of pain.' 29 But Abraham said, 'They have the law of Moses and the writings of the prophets; let them learn from them.' 30 The rich man said, 'No, father Abraham! If someone goes to them from the dead, they would believe and change their hearts and lives.' 31 But Abraham said to him, 'If they will not listen to Moses and the prophets, they will not listen to someone who comes back from the dead.'"

Sin and Forgiveness

17 Jesus said to his followers, "Things that cause people to sin will happen, but how terrible for the person who causes them to happen! 2 It would be better for you to be thrown into the sea with a large stone around your neck than to cause one of these little ones to sin. 3 So be careful!

"If another follower sins, warn him, and if he is sorry and stops sinning, forgive him. 4 If he sins against you seven times in one day and says that he is sorry each time, forgive him."

17:5–6
Faith
Check out how big your faith should be.

How Big is Your Faith?

5 The apostles said to the Lord, "Give us more faith!"

FAITH links

FORGIVE AGAIN?
LUKE 17:3-4

How many times do you think a person should be forgiven for the same offence? Let's say that a friend said something mean to you. Could you forgive her if she said the same thing to you over and over again? Jesus said that we should always be ready to forgive someone, no matter how many times that person asks for forgiveness. Don't worry if you think you can't forgive from the heart. God just wants you to be willing. He's willing to help you when you find it hard to forgive.

Made in His Image, Genesis 1:26–27, p. 4

Yours, Mine and Ours? 1 Samuel 25, p. 389

A Memorial for Two Thieves, 1 Chronicles 7:21, p. 530

Teaching Others, Ezra 7:8–10, p. 617

Help for a Friend, Mark 2:1–5, p. 1332

Give from the Heart, Luke 21:1–4, p. 1410

6 The Lord said, "If your faith were the size of a mustard seed, you could say to this mulberry tree, 'Dig yourself up and plant yourself in the sea,' and it would obey you.

Be Good Servants

7 "Suppose one of you has a servant who has been ploughing the ground or caring for the sheep. When the servant comes in from working in the field, would you say, 'Come in and sit down to eat'? 8 No, you would say to him, 'Prepare something for me to eat. Then get yourself ready and serve me. After I finish eating and drinking, you can eat.' 9 The servant does not get any special thanks for doing what his master commanded. 10 It is the same with you. When you have done everything you are told to do, you should say, 'We are unworthy servants; we have only done the work we should do.'"

Be Thankful

11 While Jesus was on his way to Jerusalem, he was going through the area between Samaria and Galilee. 12 As he came into a small town, ten men who had a skin disease met him there. They did not come close to Jesus 13 but called to him, "Jesus! Master! Have mercy on us!"

14 When Jesus saw the men, he said, "Go and show yourselves to the priests."[n]

As the ten men were going, they were healed. 15 When one of them saw that he was healed, he went back to Jesus, praising God in a loud voice. 16 Then he bowed down at Jesus' feet and thanked him. (And this man was a Samaritan.) 17 Jesus said, "Weren't ten men healed? Where are the other nine? 18 Is this Samaritan the only one who came back to thank God?" 19 Then Jesus said to him, "Stand up and go on your way. You were healed because you believed."

God's Kingdom is Within You

20 Some of the Pharisees asked Jesus, "When will the kingdom of God come?"

Jesus answered, "God's kingdom is coming, but not in a way that you will be able to see with your eyes. 21 People will not say, 'Look, here it is!' or, 'There it is!' because God's kingdom is within[n] you."

22 Then Jesus said to his followers, "The time will come when you will want

---

17:14 show . . . priests The law of Moses said a priest must say when a Jewish person with a skin disease became well.

17:21 within Or "among".

Luke 17 1403

BEING RESPONSIBLE
Luke 17:7–10

Livin' it

Attitude Check Think about something you can do really well. Can you draw? Tell a joke? Sing? Play sports? Listen? Do these talents and abilities help make you popular and everybody's friend?

Of all the things others notice about you, is being *responsible* one of them? Ruth was responsible. She had an attitude of helping others rather than thinking of ways others could help her. (Check Ruth 2:1–7, p. 346.) Do others think of you as a responsible kid?

Jesus once told a story about showing responsibility. In it he shared what God wants us to do with the special gifts, talents and abilities he gives us. (Read about it in Matthew 25:14–30, p. 1317.) How can you use your talents in a way that makes God happy and shows you are responsible?

MORE FAITH Links
- Read My Lips? **p. 260**
- Your Response to Responsibility, **p. 346**
- You Are What You Do, **p. 854**
- That Thing You Do, **p. 1319**

So God wants us to use our talents and abilities in a responsible way – not just waste them.

Hmm! Maybe we need to think about doing a talent check.

If you know what you're good at, how do you think you are getting on with using your talents to help others and to please God?

Promises, Promises, Judges 2:1–3, p. 312
- Have you ever made a promise you didn't keep? What happened?
- Being a responsible person means keeping your promises. How can you do that even when it's hard?

A Christian's Responsibility, Acts 11:26, p. 1484
- As a citizen of a country, you have certain responsibilities. What are some of those responsibilities?
- One of the responsibilities of being a Christian is to grow in faith. How do the people in your church help you to grow?

Say What?! Ephesians 4:22–29, p. 1603
- Do you ever hurt people by what you say? Being responsible for the words that come out of our mouths is important, too!

Trouble with the Tongue, James 3:3–12, p. 1692
- Link here to discover how a small tongue can cause BIG trouble. How can you be responsible for what you say?

My FAVOURITE Links

very much to see one of the days of the Son of Man. But you will not see it. 23 People will say to you, 'Look, there he is!' or, 'Look, here he is!' Stay where you are; don't go away and search.

When Jesus Comes Again

24 "When the Son of Man comes again, he will shine like lightning, which flashes across the sky and lights it up from one side to the other. 25 But first he must suffer many things and be rejected by the people of this time. 26 When the Son of Man comes again, it will be as it was when Noah lived. 27 People were eating, drinking, marrying and giving their children to be married until the day Noah entered the boat. Then the flood came and killed them all. 28 It will be the same as during the time of Lot. People were eating, drinking, buying, selling, planting and building. 29 But the day Lot left Sodom,[n] fire and sulphur rained down from the sky and killed them all. 30 This is how it will be when the Son of Man comes again.

31 "On that day, a person who is on the roof and whose belongings are in the house should not go inside to get them. A person who is in the field should not go back home. 32 Remember Lot's wife.[n] 33 Those who try to keep their lives will lose them. But those who give up their lives will save them. 34 I tell you, on that night two people will be sleeping in one bed; one will be taken and the other will be left. 35 There will be two women grinding grain together; one will be taken, and the other will be left." 36[n]

37 The followers asked Jesus, "Where will this be, Lord?"

Jesus answered, "Where there is a dead body, there the vultures will gather."

God will Answer His People

18 Then Jesus used this story to teach his followers that they should always pray and never lose hope. 2 "In a certain town there was a judge who did not respect God or care about people. 3 In that same town there was a widow who kept coming to this judge, saying, 'Give me my rights against my enemy.' 4 For a while the judge refused to help her. But afterwards, he thought to himself, 'Even though I don't respect God or care about people, 5 I will see that she gets her rights. Otherwise she will continue to bother me until I am worn out.'"

6 The Lord said, "Listen to what the unfair judge said. 7 God will always give what is right to his people who cry to him night and day, and he will not be slow to answer them. 8 I tell you, God will help his people quickly. But when the Son of Man comes again, will he find those on earth who believe in him?"

Being Right with God

9 Jesus told this story to some people who thought they were very good and looked down on everyone else: 10 "A Pharisee and a tax collector both went to the Temple to pray. 11 The Pharisee stood alone and prayed, 'God, I thank you that I am not like other people who steal, cheat or take part in adultery, or even like this tax collector. 12 I give up eating[n] twice a week, and I give one-tenth of everything I earn!'

13 "The tax collector, standing at a distance, would not even look up to heaven. But he beat on his chest because he was so sad. He said, 'God, have mercy on me, a sinner.' 14 I tell you, when this man went home, he was right with God, but the Pharisee was not. All who make themselves great will be made humble, but all who make themselves humble will be made great."

Who will Enter God's Kingdom?

15 Some people brought even their babies to Jesus so he could touch them.

17:29 Sodom A city that God destroyed because the people were so evil.
17:32 Lot's wife A story about what happened to Lot's wife is found in Genesis 19:15-17, 26.
17:36 Verse 36 A few Greek copies add verse 36: "Two people will be in the field. One will be taken, and the other will be left."
18:12 give up eating This is called "fasting". The people would give up eating for a special time of prayer and worship to God. It was also done to show sadness and disappointment.

FAITH links

BETTER THAN SOME?
LUKE 18:9-14

You probably feel pretty good about yourself, right? Most of us, if we're honest, feel that we're pretty good or at least better than some people we might know. Jesus told a story about a Pharisee and a tax collector. The Pharisee thought that he was better than the tax collector. Jesus told the story as a warning about pride. Since God can see what we're *really* like, he's not impressed when we brag about ourselves. So, instead of bragging, remember the tax collector's prayer. The humble way is always the best way.

Check out these links for something to really brag about:

Just Kidding? Genesis 21:8–10, p. 28

Put Pride Aside, Exodus 2:11–15, p. 78

Giving Your Part, Leviticus 27:30, p. 173

Help for the Outsiders, Nehemiah 5:9–10, p. 630

Jesus' Prayer, John 17, p. 1453

The "Eyes" Have It? 1 Corinthians 12, p. 1559

When the followers saw this, they told them to stop. 16 But Jesus called for the children, saying, "Let the little children come to me. Don't stop them, because the kingdom of God belongs to people who are like these children. 17 I tell you the truth, you must accept the kingdom of God as if you were a child, or you will never enter it."

A Rich Man's Question

18 A certain leader asked Jesus, "Good Teacher, what must I do to have life for ever?"

19 Jesus said to him, "Why do you call me good? Only God is good. 20 You know the commands: 'You must not be guilty of adultery. You must not murder anyone. You must not steal. You must not tell lies about your neighbour. Honour your father and mother.'"[n]

21 But the leader said, "I have obeyed all these commands since I was a boy."

22 When Jesus heard this, he said to him, "There is still one more thing you need to do. Sell everything you have and give it to the poor, and you will have treasure in heaven. Then come and follow me." 23 But when the man heard this, he became very sad, because he was very rich.

24 Jesus looked at him and said, "It is very hard for rich people to enter the kingdom of God. 25 It is easier for a camel to go through the eye of a needle than for a rich person to enter the kingdom of God."

Who Can Be Saved?

26 When the people heard this, they asked, "Then who can be saved?"

27 Jesus answered, "God can do things that are not possible for people to do."

28 Peter said, "Look, we have left everything and followed you."

29 Jesus said, "I tell you the truth, all those who have left houses, wives, brothers, parents or children for the kingdom of God 30 will get much more in this life. And in the age that is coming, they will have life for ever."

Jesus will Rise from the Dead

31 Then Jesus took the twelve apostles aside and said to them, "We are going

---

18:20 'You . . . mother.' Quotation from Exodus 20:12-16; Deuteronomy 5:16-20.

Luke 18:32 1406

to Jerusalem. Everything the prophets wrote about the Son of Man will happen. 32 He will be turned over to those who are not Jews. They will laugh at him, insult him, spit on him, 33 beat him with whips and kill him. But on the third day, he will rise to life again." 34 The apostles did not understand this; the meaning was hidden from them, and they did not realise what was said.

Jesus Heals a Blind Man

35 As Jesus came near the city of Jericho, a blind man was sitting beside the road, begging. 36 When he heard the people coming down the road, he asked, "What is happening?"

37 They told him, "Jesus, from Nazareth, is going by."

38 The blind man cried out, "Jesus, Son of David, have mercy on me!"

39 The people leading the group warned the blind man to be quiet. But the blind man shouted even more, "Son of David, have mercy on me!"

40 Jesus stopped and ordered the blind man to be brought to him. When he came near, Jesus asked him, 41 "What do you want me to do for you?"

He said, "Lord, I want to see."

42 Jesus said to him, "Then see. You are healed because you believed."

43 At once the man was able to see, and he followed Jesus, thanking God. All the people who saw this praised God.

Zacchaeus Meets Jesus

19 Jesus was going through the city of Jericho. 2 A man was there named Zacchaeus, who was a very important tax collector, and he was wealthy. 3 He wanted to see who Jesus was, but he was not able because he was too short to see above the crowd. 4 He ran ahead to a place where Jesus would come, and he climbed a sycamore tree so he could see him. 5 When Jesus came to that place, he looked up and said to him, "Zacchaeus, hurry and come down! I must stay at your house today."

6 Zacchaeus came down quickly and welcomed him gladly. 7 All the people saw this and began to complain, "Jesus is staying with a sinner!"

8 But Zacchaeus stood and said to the Lord, "I will give half of my possessions to the poor. And if I have cheated anyone, I will pay back four times more."

9 Jesus said to him, "Salvation has come to this house today, because this man also belongs to the family of Abraham. 10 The Son of Man came to find lost people and save them."

FAITH links

FAITH GOD NOTICES

LUKE 18:35-43

When you need help, how quick are you to ask for it? When you ask for help, how much faith do you have that you'll receive what you ask for? A blind man by the road was quick to yell for help when he heard that Jesus was near. He knew that Jesus could give him sight. The people around him tried to silence him, but he would not be silent. His enthusiastic cry for help showed his faith. Jesus couldn't help but take notice. That's the kind of faith that always pleases God. Do you have that kind of faith?

A Different Kind of People, Leviticus 11, p. 146

Building Tools, Ezra 6:15, p. 615

How God Speaks, Job 33:14–17, p. 696

Hope That Doesn't Fail, Acts 26:4–7, p. 1510

Our Interpreter, Romans 8:26, p. 1528

While You Wait, Jude 21, p. 1726

19:10
Jesus
Why did Jesus come to earth?

A Story About Three Servants

11 As the people were listening to this, Jesus told them a story because he was near Jerusalem and they thought God's kingdom would appear immediately. 12 He said: "A very important man went to a country far away to be made a king and then to return home. 13 So he called ten of his servants and gave a gold coin[n] to each servant. He said, 'Do business with this money until I get back.' 14 But the people in the kingdom hated the man. So they sent a group to follow him and say, 'We don't want this man to be our king.'

15 "But the man became king. When he returned home, he said, 'Call those servants who have my money so I can know how much they earned with it.'

16 "The first servant came and said, 'Sir, I earned ten bags of money with the one you gave me.' 17 The king said to the servant, 'Excellent! You are a good servant. Since I can trust you with small things, I will let you rule over ten of my cities.'

18 "The second servant said, 'Sir, I earned five bags of money with your one.' 19 The king said to this servant, 'You can rule over five cities.'

20 "Then another servant came in and said to the king, 'Sir, here is your bag of money which I wrapped in a piece of cloth and hid. 21 I was afraid of you, because you are a hard man. You even take money that you didn't earn and gather food that you didn't plant.' 22 Then the king said to the servant, 'I will condemn you by your own words, you evil servant. You knew that I am a hard man, taking money that I didn't earn and gathering food that I didn't plant. 23 Why then didn't you put my money in the bank? Then when I came back, my money would have earned some interest.'

24 "The king said to the men who were standing by, 'Take the bag of money away from this servant and give it to the servant who earned ten bags of money.' 25 They said, 'But sir, that servant already has ten bags of money.' 26 The king said, 'Those who have will be given more, but those who do not have anything will have everything taken away from them. 27 Now where are my enemies who didn't want me to be king? Bring them here and kill them before me.'"

Jesus Enters Jerusalem as a King

28 After Jesus said this, he went on towards Jerusalem. 29 As Jesus came near Bethphage and Bethany, towns near the hill called the Mount of Olives, he sent out two of his followers. 30 He said, "Go to the town you can see there. When you enter it, you will find a colt tied there, which no one has ever ridden. Untie it and bring it here to me. 31 If anyone asks you why you are untying it, say that the Master needs it."

32 The two followers went into town and found the colt just as Jesus had told them. 33 As they were untying it, its owners came out and asked the followers, "Why are you untying our colt?"

34 The followers answered, "The Master needs it." 35 So they brought it to Jesus, threw their coats on the colt's back, and put Jesus on it. 36 As Jesus rode towards Jerusalem, others spread their coats on the road before him.

37 As he was coming close to Jerusalem, on the way down the Mount of Olives, the whole crowd of followers began joyfully shouting praise to God for all the miracles they had seen. 38 They said,

"God bless the king who comes in
   the name of the Lord!   *Psalm 118:26*
There is peace in heaven and glory to
   God!"

39 Some of the Pharisees in the crowd said to Jesus, "Teacher, tell your followers not to say these things."

40 But Jesus answered, "I tell you, if my followers didn't say these things, then the stones would cry out."

Jesus Cries for Jerusalem

41 As Jesus came near Jerusalem, he saw the city and cried for it, 42 saying, "I wish you knew today what would bring you peace. But now it is hidden from you. 43 The time is coming when your

---

19:13 coin A Greek "mina". One mina was enough money to pay a person for three months' work.

enemies will build a wall around you and will hold you in on all sides. 44 They will destroy you and all your people, and not one stone will be left on another. All this will happen because you did not recognise the time when God came to save you."

Jesus Goes to the Temple

45 Jesus went into the Temple and began to throw out the people who were selling things there. 46 He said, "It is written in the Scriptures, 'My Temple will be a house for prayer.'ⁿ But you have changed it into a 'hideout for robbers'!"ⁿ

47 Jesus taught in the Temple every day. The leading priests, the experts on the law and some of the leaders of the people wanted to kill Jesus. 48 But they did not know how they could do it, because all the people were listening closely to him.

Jewish Leaders Question Jesus

20 One day Jesus was in the Temple, teaching the people and telling them the Good News. The leading priests, teachers of the law and Jewish elders came up to talk with him, 2 saying, "Tell us what authority you have to do these things? Who gave you this authority?"

3 Jesus answered, "I will also ask you a question. Tell me: 4 when John baptised people, was that authority from God or just from other people?"

5 They argued about this, saying, "If we answer, 'John's baptism was from God,' Jesus will say, 'Then why did you not believe him?' 6 But if we say, 'It was from other people,' all the people will stone us to death, because they believe John was a prophet." 7 So they answered that they didn't know where it came from.

8 Jesus said to them, "Then I won't tell you what authority I have to do these things."

A Story About God's Son

9 Then Jesus told the people this story: "A man planted a vineyard and leased it to some farmers. Then he went away for a long time. 10 When it was time for the grapes to be picked, he sent a servant to the farmers to get some of the grapes. But they beat the servant and sent him away empty-handed. 11 Then he sent another servant. They beat this servant also, and showed no respect for him, and sent him away empty-handed. 12 So the man sent a third servant. The farmers wounded him and threw him out. 13 The owner of the vineyard said, 'What will I do now? I will send my son whom I love. Maybe they will respect him.' 14 But when the farmers saw the son, they said to each other, 'This son will inherit the vineyard. If we kill him, it will be ours.' 15 So the farmers threw the son out of the vineyard and killed him.

"What will the owner of this vineyard do to them? 16 He will come and kill those farmers and will give the vineyard to other farmers."

When the people heard this story, they said, "Let this never happen!"

17 But Jesus looked at them and said, "Then what does this verse mean:

'The stone that the builders rejected
became the cornerstone'?

Psalm 118:22

18 Everyone who falls on that stone will be broken, and the person on whom it falls, that person will be crushed!"

19 The teachers of the law and the leading priests wanted to arrest Jesus at once, because they knew the story was about them. But they were afraid of what the people would do.

Is It Right to Pay Taxes or Not?

20 So they watched Jesus and sent some spies who acted as if they were sincere. They wanted to trap Jesus into saying something wrong so they could hand him over to the authority and power of the governor. 21 So the spies asked Jesus, "Teacher, we know that what you say and teach is true. You pay no attention

---

19:46 'My Temple . . . prayer.' Quotation from Isaiah 56:7.
19:46 'hideout for robbers' Quotation from Jeremiah 7:11.

FAITH links

OBEY OR DISOBEY?
LUKE 20:20-26

Do you think that disobeying a law just because you're a Christian is ever right? Jesus was once asked whether paying taxes to the Romans was the right thing to do. Jesus' answer shows the importance of obeying our leaders. This does not mean doing something that you know is wrong. It does mean showing respect for the leaders in authority.

Download these links on showing respect:

Obey? No Way! Exodus 1:15–21, p. 76

Play Fair or Play Favourites? Deuteronomy 1:16–18, p. 227

Your Best Work, 1 Kings 6, p. 443

Depend on Him! 2 Chronicles 16:1–9, p. 579

Welcome! Matthew 19:13–15, p. 1307

Help for the Body, Romans 12:3–8, p. 1536

---

to who people are, and you always teach the truth about God's way. 22 Tell us, is it right for us to pay taxes to Caesar or not?"

23 But Jesus, knowing they were trying to trick him, said, 24 "Show me a silver coin.ⁿ Whose image and name are on it?"

They said, "Caesar's."

25 Jesus said to them, "Then give to Caesar the things that are Caesar's, and give to God the things that are God's."

26 So they were not able to trap Jesus into anything he said in the presence of the people. And being amazed at his answer, they became silent.

Some Sadducees Try to Trick Jesus

27 Some Sadducees, who believed people would not rise from the dead, came to Jesus. 28 They asked, "Teacher, Moses wrote that if a man's brother dies and leaves a wife but no children, then that man must marry the widow and have children for his brother. 29 Once there were seven brothers. The first brother married and died, but had no children. 30 Then the second brother married the widow, and he died. 31 And the third brother married the widow, and he died. The same thing happened with all seven brothers; they died and had no children. 32 Finally, the woman died also. 33 Since all seven brothers had married her, whose wife will she be when people rise from the dead?"

34 Jesus said to them, "On earth, people marry and are given to someone to marry. 35 But those who will be worthy to be raised from the dead and live again will not marry, nor will they be given to someone to marry. 36 In that life they are like angels and cannot die. They are children of God, because they have been raised from the dead. 37 Even Moses clearly showed that the dead are raised to life. When he wrote about the burning bush,ⁿ he said that the Lord is 'the God of Abraham, the God of Isaac and the God of Jacob.'ⁿ 38 God is the God of the living, not the dead, because all people are alive to him."

eMAIL FROM GOD
20:36 Angels
Can angels die?

39 Some of the teachers of the law said, "Teacher, your answer was good." 40 No one was brave enough to ask him another question.

20:24 coin Roman dinarii. A silver coin was the average pay for one day's work.
20:37 burning bush Read Exodus 3:1-12 in the Old Testament.
20:37 'the God of . . . Jacob' These words are taken from Exodus 3:6.

Is the Christ the Son of David?

41 Then Jesus said, "Why do people say that the Christ is the Son of David? 42 In the book of Psalms, David himself says:

> 'The LORD said to my Lord:
> Sit by me at my right side,
> 43 until I put your enemies under
>   your control.'[n]   *Psalm 110:1*

44 David calls the Christ 'Lord', so how can the Christ be his son?"

Jesus Accuses Some Leaders

45 While all the people were listening, Jesus said to his followers, 46 "Beware of the teachers of the law. They like to walk around wearing fancy clothes, and they love people to greet them with respect in the market places. They love to have the most important seats in the synagogues and at feasts. 47 But they cheat widows and steal their houses and then try to make themselves look good by saying long prayers. They will receive a greater punishment."

True Giving

21 As Jesus looked up, he saw some rich people putting their gifts into the Temple money box." 2 Then he saw a poor widow putting two small copper coins into the box. 3 He said, "I tell you the truth, this poor widow gave more than all those rich people. 4 They gave only what they did not need. This woman is very poor, but she gave all she had to live on."

The Temple will Be Destroyed

5 Some people were talking about the Temple and how it was decorated with beautiful stones and gifts offered to God.

But Jesus said, 6 "As for these things you are looking at, the time will come when not one stone will be left on another. Every stone will be thrown down."

7 They asked Jesus, "Teacher, when will these things happen? What will be the sign that they are about to take place?"

8 Jesus said, "Be careful so you are not fooled. Many people will come in my name, saying, 'I am the One' and, 'The time has come!' But don't follow them. 9 When you hear about wars and riots, don't be afraid, because these things must happen first, but the end will come later."

10 Then he said to them, "Nations will fight against other nations, and kingdoms

---

FAITH links

GIVE FROM THE HEART
LUKE 21:1-4

How much, do you suppose, is enough money to give in an offering at church? Jesus was more impressed with a widow who gave two copper coins in the Temple than he was with a rich man who gave a lot of money. Why? Because the widow was very poor and gave all that she had. God wants all of your heart to be in what you give. So, next time you give, think about giving a gift from the heart.

Help for the Poor, Leviticus 5:7, p. 138

His OK to Obey, Deuteronomy 2:24–36, p. 230

What I've Got, 2 Kings 20:12–17, p. 508

Some Friendly Advice, Proverbs 17:9, 14, 17, p. 851

Your Civic Duty, Matthew 17:24–27, p. 1304

The Most Fun, Acts 20:35, p. 1502

20:43 until . . . control Literally, "until I make your enemies a footstool for your feet".
21:1 money box A special box in the Jewish place of worship where people put their gifts to God.

against other kingdoms. 11 In various places there will be great earthquakes, sicknesses and a lack of food. Fearful events and great signs will come from heaven.

12 "But before all these things happen, people will arrest you and treat you cruelly. They will judge you in their synagogues and put you in jail and force you to stand before kings and governors, because you follow me. 13 But this will give you an opportunity to tell about me. 14 Make up your minds not to worry ahead of time about what you will say. 15 I will give you the wisdom to say things that none of your enemies will be able to stand against or prove wrong. 16 Even your parents, brothers, relatives and friends will turn against you, and they will kill some of you. 17 All people will hate you because you follow me. 18 But none of these things can really harm you. 19 By continuing to have faith you will save your lives.

Jerusalem will Be Destroyed

20 "When you see armies all around Jerusalem, you will know it will soon be destroyed. 21 At that time, the people in Judea should run away to the mountains. The people in Jerusalem must get out, and those who are near the city should not go in. 22 These are the days of punishment to bring about all that is written in the Scriptures. 23 How terrible it will be for women who are pregnant or have nursing babies! Great trouble will come upon this land, and God will be angry with these people. 24 They will be killed by the sword and taken as prisoners to all nations. Jerusalem will be crushed by non-Jewish people until their time is over.

Don't Fear

25 "There will be signs in the sun, moon and stars. On earth, nations will be afraid and confused because of the roar and fury of the sea. 26 People will be so afraid they will faint, wondering what is happening to the world, because the powers of the heavens will be shaken. 27 Then people will see the Son of Man coming in a cloud with power and great glory. 28 When these things begin to happen, look up and hold your heads high, because the time when God will free you is near!"

Jesus' Words will Live for Ever

29 Then Jesus told this story: "Look at the fig tree and all the other trees. 30 When their leaves appear, you know that summer is near. 31 In the same way, when you see these things happening, you will know that God's kingdom is near.

32 "I tell you the truth, all these things will happen while the people of this time are still living. 33 Earth and sky will be destroyed, but the words I have spoken will never be destroyed."

Be Ready All the Time

34 "Be careful not to spend your time feasting, drinking or worrying about worldly things. If you do, that day might come on you suddenly, 35 like a trap on all people on earth. 36 So be ready all the time. Pray that you will be strong enough to escape all these things that will happen and that you will be able to stand before the Son of Man."

37 During the day, Jesus taught the people in the Temple, and at night he went out of the city and stayed on the Mount of Olives. 38 Every morning all the people got up early to go to the Temple to listen to him.

Judas Becomes an Enemy of Jesus

22 It was almost time for the Feast of Unleavened Bread, called the Passover Feast. 2 The leading priests and teachers of the law were trying to find a way to kill Jesus, because they were afraid of the people.

3 Satan entered Judas Iscariot, one of Jesus' twelve apostles. 4 Judas went to the leading priests and some of the soldiers who guarded the Temple and talked to them about a way to hand Jesus over to them. 5 They were pleased and agreed to give Judas money. 6 He agreed and watched for the best time to hand Jesus

▶ Luke 22:7 **1412**

JESUS' LAST WEEK Luke 22

When people talk about Holy Week, they are talking about the last week of Jesus' life before his death and resurrection. The week began when Jesus rode into Jerusalem on a colt to cheering crowds. That is called the "triumphal entry".

Sunday	Jesus enters Jerusalem as a King	Mark 11:1–11, p. 1348
Monday	Jesus kicks merchants out of the Temple	Mark 11:15–19, p. 1349
Tuesday	The leading priests, teachers of the Law, and Jewish elders pick a fight with Jesus	Luke 20:1–8, p. 1408
	Jesus talks about his death and return	Matthew 24; 25, p. 1315
	Judas becomes an enemy of Jesus	Luke 22:3–6, p. 1411
Thursday	Jesus celebrates the Passover	John 13:1–30, p. 1446
	Jesus begins the Lord's Supper tradition	Mark 14:22–26, p. 1356
	Jesus prays for his followers and for us	John 17, p. 1453
Friday	Jesus is arrested	Mark 14:43–50, p. 1357
	Peter says he doesn't know Jesus	John 18:15–27, p. 1455
	Jesus is crucified between two thieves	Mark 15:16–27, p. 1359
Sunday	Jesus is raised from the dead!	Luke 24:1–9, p. 1417

over to them when he was away from the crowd.

Jesus Eats the Passover Meal

7 The Day of Unleavened Bread came when the Passover lambs had to be sacrificed. 8 Jesus said to Peter and John, "Go and prepare the Passover meal for us to eat."

9 They asked, "Where do you want us to prepare it?" 10 Jesus said to them, "After you go into the city, a man carrying a jar of water will meet you. Follow him into the house that he enters, 11 and tell the owner of the house, 'The Teacher asks where is the guest room in which I may eat the Passover meal with my followers?' 12 Then he will show you a large, furnished room upstairs. Prepare the Passover meal there."

13 So Peter and John left and found everything as Jesus had said. And they prepared the Passover meal.

The Lord's Supper

14 When the time came, Jesus and the apostles were sitting at the table. 15 He said to them, "I wanted very much to eat

this Passover meal with you before I suffer. 16 I will not eat another Passover meal until it is given its true meaning in the kingdom of God."

17 Then Jesus took a cup, gave thanks and said, "Take this cup and share it among yourselves. 18 I will not drink again from the fruit of the vine[n] until God's kingdom comes."

19 Then Jesus took some bread, gave thanks, broke it and gave it to the apostles, saying, "This is my body, which I am giving for you. Do this to remember me." 20 In the same way, after supper, Jesus took the cup and said, "This cup is the new agreement that God makes with his people. This new agreement begins with my blood which is poured out for you.

Who will Turn Against Jesus?

21 "But one of you will turn against me, and his hand is with mine on the table. 22 What God has planned for the Son of Man will happen, but how terrible it will be for that one who turns against the Son of Man."

23 Then the apostles asked each other which one of them would do that.

Be like a Servant

24 The apostles also began to argue about which one of them was the most important. 25 But Jesus said to them, "The kings of the non-Jewish people rule over them, and those who have authority over others like to be called 'friends of the people'. 26 But you must not be like that. Instead, the greatest among you should be like the youngest, and the leader should be like the servant. 27 Who is more important: the one sitting at the table or the one serving? You think the one at the table is more important, but I am like a servant among you.

EMAIL FROM GOD
22:27
Pride
Who is the greatest?

28 "You have stayed with me through my struggles. 29 Just as my Father has given me a kingdom, I also give you a kingdom 30 so you may eat and drink at my table in my kingdom. And you will sit on thrones, judging the twelve tribes of Israel.

Don't Lose Your Faith!

31 "Simon, Simon, Satan has asked to test all of you as a farmer tests his wheat. 32 I have prayed that you will not lose your faith! Help your brothers be stronger when you come back to me."

33 But Peter said to Jesus, "Lord, I am ready to go with you to prison and even to die with you!"

34 But Jesus said, "Peter, before the cockerel crows this day, you will say three times that you don't know me."

Be Ready for Trouble

35 Then Jesus said to the apostles, "When I sent you out without a purse, a bag or sandals, did you need anything?"

They said, "No."

36 He said to them, "But now if you have a purse or a bag, carry that with you. If you don't have a sword, sell your coat and buy one. 37 The Scripture says, 'He was treated like a criminal,'[n] and I tell you this scripture must come true. It was written about me, and it is happening now."

38 His followers said, "Look, Lord, here are two swords."

He said to them, "That is enough."

Jesus Prays Alone

39 Jesus left the city and went to the Mount of Olives, as he often did, and his followers went with him. 40 When he reached the place, he said to them, "Pray for strength against temptation."

41 Then Jesus went about a stone's throw away from them. He kneeled down and prayed, 42 "Father, if you are willing, take away this cup[n] of suffering. But do what you want, not what I want." 43 Then an angel from heaven appeared to him to strengthen him. 44 Being full of pain,

---

22:18 fruit of the vine Product of the grapevine; this may also be translated "wine".

22:37 'He . . . criminal' Quotation from Isaiah 53:12.

22:42 cup Jesus is talking about the terrible things that will happen to him. Accepting these things will be hard, like drinking a cup of something bitter.

Luke 22 1414

Failures and Weaknesses
Luke 22:54–62

Oh No! Not Again! Ever had one of those days that no matter how hard you try, everything seems to go wrong? Maybe you've been working on controlling your temper. But then you disagree with the ref's decision during the football match and forget about staying calm. You kick the ball off into the spectators and angry words come pouring out of your mouth! How do you feel when you fail at something? Do you feel it's not worth trying any more because you'll only mess up again?

Timothy had failed in something, and then he was afraid to try something new. Paul had some advice for Timothy. He reminded Timothy that God had given him the gifts of power, love and self-control. These could help him when he was afraid of failure. (Read 2 Timothy 1:7, p. 1650.) How can God help you to deal with failure?

MORE FAITH links

The Perfect Leader? **p. 203**
A Hard Place, **p. 1120**
Blessed Are the Weak? **p. 1582**
You're Correct! **p. 1683**
Toss Those Troubles! **p. 1706**

> We can all probably think of times when we thought we'd made a huge mistake and got things wrong, can't we?
>
> But it's good to know that God is always there for us – even when we make a complete mess of things.

Weak? Great! 2 Chronicles 14:11, p. 577
- Link here to discover what's so great about being weak.

Learning from Mistakes, Psalm 51:12–13, p. 748
- If you saw a friend about to do something you just got grounded for, would you try to stop him? That's what is known as learning from your mistakes. Think of some mistakes you've been corrected for. What did you learn from those mistakes?

The God of Second Chances, Jonah 3, p. 1215
- Do you do what your parents tell you to do the first time they ask? Or, do you wait until they ask again? What happens if they need to ask you several times?
- When you "blow it", God offers a second chance to obey him. What do you need a second (or third) chance for?

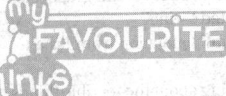

my FAVOURITE links

Jesus prayed even harder. His sweat was like drops of blood falling to the ground. 45 When he finished praying, he went to his followers and found them asleep because of their sadness. 46 Jesus said to them, "Why are you sleeping? Get up and pray for strength against temptation."

Jesus is Arrested

47 While Jesus was speaking, a crowd came up, and Judas, one of the twelve apostles, was leading them. He came close to Jesus so he could kiss him. 48 But Jesus said to him, "Judas, are you using a kiss to give the Son of Man to his enemies?" 49 When those who were standing around him saw what was happening, they said, "Lord, should we strike them with our swords?" 50 And one of them struck the servant of the high priest and cut off his right ear. 51 Jesus said, "Stop! No more of this." Then he touched the servant's ear and healed him. 52 Those who came to arrest Jesus were the leading priests, the soldiers who guarded the Temple and the older Jewish leaders. Jesus said to them, "You came out here with swords and clubs as though I were a criminal. 53 I was with you every day in the Temple, and you didn't arrest me there. But this is your time—the time when darkness rules."

Peter Says He Doesn't Know Jesus

54 They arrested Jesus, and led him away, and brought him into the house of the high priest. Peter followed far behind them. 55 After the soldiers started a fire in the middle of the courtyard and sat together, Peter sat with them. 56 A servant girl saw Peter sitting there in the light, and looking closely at him, she said, "This man was also with him."

57 But Peter said this was not true; he said, "Woman, I don't know him."

58 A short time later, another person saw Peter and said, "You are also one of them."

But Peter said, "Man, I am not!"

59 About an hour later, another man insisted, "Certainly this man was with him, because he is from Galilee, too."

60 But Peter said, "Man, I don't know what you are talking about!"

At once, while Peter was still speaking, a cockerel crowed. 61 Then the Lord turned and looked straight at Peter. And Peter remembered what the Lord had said: "Before the cockerel crows this day, you will say three times that you don't know me." 62 Then Peter went outside and cried bitterly.

The People Make Fun of Jesus

63 The men who were guarding Jesus began making fun of him and beating him. 64 They blindfolded him and said, "Prove that you are a prophet, and tell us who hit you." 65 They said many cruel things to Jesus.

Jesus Before the Leaders

66 When day came, the council of the elders of the people, both the leading priests and the teachers of the law, came together and led Jesus to their highest court. 67 They said, "If you are the Christ, tell us."

Jesus said to them, "If I tell you, you will not believe me. 68 And if I ask you, you will not answer. 69 But from now on, the Son of Man will sit at the right hand of the powerful God."

70 They all said, "Then are you the Son of God?"

Jesus said to them, "You say that I am."

71 They said, "Why do we need witnesses now? We ourselves heard him say this."

Pilate Questions Jesus

23 Then the whole group stood up and led Jesus to Pilate.*n* 2 They began to accuse Jesus, saying, "We caught this man telling things that mislead our people. He says that we should not pay taxes to Caesar, and he calls himself the Christ, a king."

3 Pilate asked Jesus, "Are you the king of the Jews?"

23:1 Pilate Pontius Pilate was the Roman governor of Judea from A.D. 26 to A.D. 36.

Jesus answered, "Those are your words."

4 Pilate said to the leading priests and the people, "I find nothing against this man."

5 They were insisting, saying, "But Jesus makes trouble with the people, teaching all around Judea. He began in Galilee, and now he is here."

Pilate Sends Jesus to Herod

6 Pilate heard this and asked if Jesus was from Galilee. 7 Since Jesus was under Herod's authority, Pilate sent Jesus to Herod, who was in Jerusalem at that time. 8 When Herod saw Jesus, he was very glad, because he had heard about Jesus and had wanted to meet him for a long time. He was hoping to see Jesus work a miracle. 9 Herod asked Jesus many questions, but Jesus said nothing. 10 The leading priests and teachers of the law were standing there, strongly accusing Jesus. 11 After Herod and his soldiers had made fun of Jesus, they dressed him in a kingly robe and sent him back to Pilate. 12 In the past, Pilate and Herod had always been enemies, but on that day they became friends.

Jesus Must Die

13 Pilate called the people together with the leading priests and the Jewish leaders. 14 He said to them, "You brought this man to me, saying he makes trouble among the people. But I have questioned him before you all, and I have not found him guilty of what you say. 15 Also, Herod found nothing wrong with him; he sent him back to us. Look, he has done nothing for which he should die. 16 So, after I punish him, I will let him go free." 17 [n]

18 But the people shouted together, "Take this man away! Let Barabbas go free!" 19 (Barabbas was a man who was in prison for his part in a riot in the city and for murder.)

20 Pilate wanted to let Jesus go free and told this to the crowd. 21 But they shouted again, "Crucify him! Crucify him!"

22 A third time Pilate said to them, "Why? What wrong has he done? I can find no reason to kill him. So I will have him punished and set him free."

23 But they continued to shout, demanding that Jesus be crucified. Their yelling became so loud that 24 Pilate decided to give them what they wanted. 25 He set free the man who was in jail for rioting and murder, and he handed Jesus over to them to do with him as they wished.

Jesus is Crucified

26 As they led Jesus away, Simon, a man from Cyrene, was coming in from the fields. They forced him to carry Jesus' cross and to walk behind him.

27 A large crowd of people was following Jesus, including some women who were sad and crying for him. 28 But Jesus turned and said to them, "Women of Jerusalem, don't cry for me. Cry for yourselves and for your children. 29 The time is coming when people will say, 'Happy are the women who cannot have children and who have no babies to nurse.' 30 Then people will say to the mountains, 'Fall on us!' And they will say to the hills, 'Cover us!' 31 If they act like this now when life is good, what will happen when bad times come?"[n]

32 There were also two criminals led out with Jesus to be put to death. 33 When they came to a place called the Skull, the soldiers crucified Jesus and the criminals—one on his right and the other on his left. 34 Jesus said, "Father, forgive them, because they don't know what they are doing."[n]

The soldiers threw lots to decide who would get his clothes. 35 The people stood there watching. And the leaders made fun of Jesus, saying, "He saved others. Let him save himself if he is God's Chosen One, the Christ."

36 The soldiers also made fun of him, coming to Jesus and offering him some

---

23:17 Verse 17 A few Greek copies add verse 17: "Every year at the Passover Feast, Pilate had to release one prisoner to the people."
23:31 If . . . come? Literally, "If they do these things in the green tree, what will happen in the dry?"
23:34 Verse 34 Some early Greek copies do not have this part of the verse.

vinegar. 37 They said, "If you are the king of the Jews, save yourself!" 38 At the top of the cross these words were written: THIS IS THE KING OF THE JEWS.

39 One of the criminals on a cross began to shout insults at Jesus: "Aren't you the Christ? Then save yourself and us."

40 But the other criminal stopped him and said, "You should fear God! You are getting the same punishment as he is. 41 We are punished justly, getting what we deserve for what we did. But this man has done nothing wrong." 42 Then he said, "Jesus, remember me when you come into your kingdom."

43 Jesus said to him, "I tell you the truth, today you will be with me in paradise."[n]

Jesus Dies

44 It was about noon, and the whole land became dark until three o'clock in the afternoon, 45 because the sun did not shine. The curtain in the Temple[n] was torn in two. 46 Jesus cried out in a loud voice, "Father, I give you my life." After Jesus said this, he died.

47 When the army officer there saw what happened, he praised God, saying, "Surely this was a good man!"

48 When all the people who had gathered there to watch saw what happened, they returned home, beating their chests because they were so sad. 49 But those who were close friends of Jesus, including the women who had followed him from Galilee, stood at a distance and watched.

Joseph Takes Jesus' Body

50 There was a good and religious man named Joseph who was a member of the Jewish council. 51 But he had not agreed to the other leaders' plans and actions against Jesus. He was from the Jewish town of Arimathea and was waiting for the kingdom of God to come. 52 Joseph went to Pilate to ask for the body of Jesus. 53 He took the body down from the cross, wrapped it in cloth, and put it in a tomb that was cut out of a wall of rock. This tomb had never been used before. 54 This was late on Preparation Day, and when the sun went down, the Sabbath day would begin.

55 The women who had come from Galilee with Jesus followed Joseph and saw the tomb and how Jesus' body was laid. 56 Then the women left to prepare spices and perfumes.

On the Sabbath day they rested, as the law of Moses commanded.

Jesus Rises from the Dead

24 Very early on the first day of the week, at dawn, the women came to the tomb, bringing the spices they had prepared. 2 They found the stone rolled away from the entrance of the tomb, 3 but when they went in, they did not find the body of the Lord Jesus. 4 While they were wondering about this, two men in shining clothes suddenly stood beside them. 5 The women were very afraid and bowed their heads to the ground. The men said to them, "Why are you looking for a living person in this place for the dead? 6 He is not here; he has risen from the dead. Do you remember what he told you in Galilee? 7 He said the Son of Man must be handed over to sinful people, be crucified and rise from the dead on the third day." 8 Then the women remembered what Jesus had said.

9 The women left the tomb and told all these things to the eleven apostles and the other followers. 10 It was Mary Magdalene, Joanna, Mary the mother of James, and some other women who told the apostles everything that had happened at the tomb. 11 But they did not

> When the army officer there saw what happened, he praised God, saying, "Surely this was a good man!"
> – Luke 23:47

23:43 paradise A place where people who are obedient to God go when they die.
23:45 curtain in the Temple A curtain divided the Most Holy Place from the other part of the Temple. That was the special building in Jerusalem where God commanded the Jewish people to worship him.

Luke 24:12   1418

LET'S VISIT NAZARETH   Luke 24:19

Nazareth is in southern Galilee about 30 miles from the Mediterranean Sea. It doesn't get really hot or really cold there, making it a great place to live. Nazareth is not mentioned in the Old Testament, but we know that it existed at least 1,500 years before Jesus was born.

It was in Nazareth that the angel appeared to Mary and told her that Jesus would be born. (Read Luke 1:26–38.) After Jesus' family travelled to Egypt, they came back to Nazareth and Jesus grew up there. (Check out Matthew 2:23, p. 1277; Luke 2:39–40.) In fact, Jesus was closely associated with Nazareth. (Check out John 1:45, p. 1423.)

Today Nazareth is called En-Nasira. About 30,000 people live there.

believe the women, because it sounded like nonsense. 12 But Peter got up and ran to the tomb. Bending down and looking in, he saw only the cloth that Jesus' body had been wrapped in. Peter went away to his home, wondering about what had happened.

Jesus on the Road to Emmaus

13 That same day two of Jesus' followers were going to a town named Emmaus, about eleven kilometres from Jerusalem. 14 They were talking about everything that had happened. 15 While they were talking and discussing, Jesus himself came near and began walking with them, 16 but they were kept from recognising him. 17 Then he said, "What are these things you are talking about while you walk?"

The two followers stopped, looking very sad. 18 The one named Cleopas answered, "Are you the only visitor in Jerusalem who does not know what just happened there?"

19 Jesus said to them, "What are you talking about?"

They said, "About Jesus of Nazareth. He was a prophet who said and did many powerful things before God and all the people. 20 Our leaders and the leading priests handed him over to be sentenced to death, and they crucified him. 21 But we were hoping that he would free Israel. Besides this, it is now the third day since this happened. 22 And today some women among us amazed us. Early this morning they went to the tomb, 23 but they did not find his body there. They came and told us that they had seen a vision of angels who said that Jesus was alive! 24 So some of our group went to the tomb, too. They found it just as the women said, but they did not see Jesus."

25 Then Jesus said to them, "You are foolish and slow to believe everything the prophets said. 26 They said that the Christ must suffer these things before he enters his glory." 27 Then starting with what Moses and all the prophets had said about him, Jesus began to explain everything that had been written about himself in the Scriptures.

28 They came near the town of Emmaus, and Jesus acted as if he were going farther. 29 But they begged him, "Stay with us, because it is late; it is almost night." So he went in to stay with them.

30 When Jesus was at the table with them, he took some bread, gave thanks, divided it and gave it to them. 31 And then they were allowed to recognise Jesus. But

when they saw who he was, he disappeared. 32 They said to each other, "It felt like a fire burning in us when Jesus talked to us on the road and explained the Scriptures to us."

33 So the two followers got up at once and went back to Jerusalem. There they found the eleven apostles and others gathered. 34 They were saying, "The Lord really has risen from the dead! He showed himself to Simon."

35 Then the two followers told what had happened on the road and how they recognised Jesus when he divided the bread.

Jesus Appears to His Followers

36 While the two followers were telling this, Jesus himself stood right in the middle of them and said, "Peace be with you." 37 They were fearful and terrified and thought they were seeing a ghost. 38 But Jesus said, "Why are you troubled? Why do you doubt what you see? 39 Look at my hands and my feet. It is I myself! Touch me and see, because a ghost does not have a living body as you see I have."

40 After Jesus said this, he showed them his hands and feet. 41 While they still could not believe it because they were amazed and happy, Jesus said to them, "Do you have any food here?" 42 They gave him a piece of grilled fish. 43 While the followers watched, Jesus took the fish and ate it.

44 He said to them, "Remember when I was with you before? I said that everything written about me must happen—everything in the law of Moses, the books of the prophets and the Psalms."

45 Then Jesus opened their minds so they could understand the Scriptures. 46 He said to them, "It is written that the Christ would suffer and rise from the dead on the third day 47 and that a change of hearts and lives and forgiveness of sins would be preached in his name to all nations, starting at Jerusalem. 48 You are witnesses of these things. 49 I will send you what my Father has promised, but you must stay in Jerusalem until you have received that power from heaven."

24:46–47 Good News
Who is the Good News for?

Jesus Goes Back to Heaven

50 Jesus led his followers as far as Bethany, and he raised his hands and blessed them. 51 While he was blessing them, he was separated from them and carried into heaven. 52 They worshipped him and returned to Jerusalem very happy. 53 They stayed in the Temple all the time, praising God.

GOD WITH US

Hi! I'm John. Want to know more about me? Well, I was a fisherman who left his fishing nets behind to follow Jesus. A lot of people get me confused with John the Baptist, but we're two different people. My brother James and I were part of Jesus' original 12 followers. In fact, I was the one called "the follower Jesus loved". (Check it out in John 13:23.) This isn't the only book I wrote either. I wrote three letters (known as 1, 2 and 3 John) and the Book of Revelation. I lived a very long life, and even served the church in Ephesus for many years before my death. You're probably wondering why I wrote this book. Just read John 20:31 to see why. I wrote this book to let people know that Jesus was truly the Son of God. Since I was both an eyewitness to the things I wrote about and a follower of Jesus, I wanted everyone who read my book to get a clear picture that Jesus was God's own Son.

JESUS WATCH

John's Gospel helps us understand Jesus as God. How does he do this? First, he does this through seven "I Am" statements that Jesus made. Jesus said things like, "I am the bread that gives life" and "I am the way, and the truth, and the life". By presenting these statements, John helps his readers understand Jesus' connection with God. (Remember God's conversation with Moses in Exodus 3, p. 79? God uses the words *I Am* there, too. Take a moment to read that now.) Second, John helps us understand Jesus as a man by allowing us to see Jesus' human side. He lets us see Jesus when he's tired, thirsty, upset, troubled and in anguish.

my FAVOURITE links

OTHER CONNECTIONS

Livin' it

Ever play "Follow the Leader"? The game can be fun. But when it comes down to real life, following the *right* leader is important. Connect to Follow the Right Leader, John 2, to find out how important it is.

Which would you rather be – full of joy, or full of happiness? Do you know the difference? Download what God has to say about it at I Got the Joy, Joy, Joy, Joy, John 16:24.

Here are some interesting facts you'll find in the Book of John:

- Let's Visit Capernaum, John 4:46–54. Stop by this info bulletin board to find out more about this small town where Jesus spent a lot of time during his ministry on earth.
- Jesus referred to himself with many different names. Find out what some of those titles are by logging on to The Names of Jesus, John 6:35.
- Ever wonder why there are four books about Jesus' life and ministry? Stop by Biographies from Every View, John 19, to find out why.
- Let's Visit Lake Galilee, John 21. You may have heard people refer to Lake Galilee as the Sea of Galilee. But if you connect here, you'll find out that this body of fresh water is really a lake.

Hmmm. This could be a bit confusing. How can a man become a word? No, wait a minute. How can a word become a man?

Actually, it's easy if you're God. Read about what Jesus did in John 1:1-14.

WANT TO READ SOME OTHER AMAZING STORIES IN JOHN'S GOSPEL? SURF OVER TO THESE EXCITING STORIES:
John the Baptist, John 1:15–34
Water into wine, John 2:1–10
A prayer for all followers, John 13; 14
The darkest hour, John 19:17–37

- One Big, Happy Family, **John 1:12**
- Two Birthdays, **John 3:1–7**
- The Gift, **John 3:6–18**
- The Whole Truth, **John 8:31–32, 45**
- Our Good Shepherd, **John 10:11–15**
- Fully God, Fully Human, **John 11:35**
- The Worst Chore, **John 13:3–17**
- The Way to Heaven, **John 14:1–6**
- A Friend of Jesus, **John 15:9–17**
- Jesus' Prayer, **John 17**

▶ John 1:1   1422

Christ Comes to the World

1 In the beginning there was the Word.ⁿ The Word was with God, and the Word was God. 2 He was with God in the beginning. 3 All things were made by him, and nothing was made without him. 4 In him there was life, and that life was the light of all people. 5 The Light shines in the darkness, and the darkness has not overpowered it.

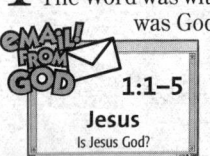

1:1–5 Jesus Is Jesus God?

6 There was a man named Johnⁿ who was sent by God. 7 He came to tell people the truth about the Light so that through him all people could hear about the Light and believe. 8 John was not the Light, but he came to tell people the truth about the Light. 9 The true Light that gives light to all was coming into the world!

10 The Word was in the world, and the world was made by him, but the world did not know him. 11 He came to the world that was his own, but his own people did not accept him. 12 But to all who did accept him and believe in him he gave the right to become children of God. 13 They did not become his children in any human way—by any human parents or human desire. They were born of God.

14 The Word became human and lived among us. We saw his glory—the glory that belongs to the only Son of the Father—and he was full of grace and truth. 15 John tells the truth about him and cries out, saying, "This is the One I told you about: 'The One who comes after me is greater than I am, because he was living before me.'"

16 Because he was full of grace and truth, from him we all received one gift after another. 17 The law was given through Moses, but grace and truth came through Jesus Christ. 18 No one has ever seen God. But God the only Son is very close to the Father,ⁿ and he has shown us what God is like.

John Tells People About Jesus

19 Here is the truth Johnⁿ told when the Jews in Jerusalem sent priests and Levites to ask him, "Who are you?"

FAITH links

ONE BIG, HAPPY FAMILY

JOHN 1:12

Who are some of the people in your family? What's the best thing about being part of your family? If you're a Christian, you also belong to another family – the family of God. Because of Jesus, we "have the right to become children of God". That makes God our heavenly Father! Knowing Jesus is the best thing about being part of this family!

Download these links for more benefits on being part of God's family:

The Name of the Lord, Exodus 33:19–23; 34:5–8, p. 120

A Different Kind of People, Leviticus 11, p. 146

Real Repentance, Jeremiah 4:1–4, p. 993

Name with a Purpose, Matthew 1:21, p. 1274

You've Got the Power! Acts 1:1–8; 2:1–4, p. 1463

Always Do This! 1 Thessalonians 5:16–18, p. 1636

1:1 Word The Greek word is "logos", meaning any kind of communication; it could be translated "message". Here, it means Christ, because Christ was the way God told people about himself.
1:6, 19 John John the Baptist, who preached to people about Christ's coming (Matthew 3, Luke 3).
1:18 But . . . Father This could be translated, "But the only God is very close to the Father." Also, some Greek copies say, "But the only Son is very close to the Father."

20 John spoke freely and did not refuse to answer. He said, "I am not the Christ."

21 So they asked him, "Then who are you? Are you Elijah?"[n]

He answered, "No, I am not."

"Are you the Prophet?"[n] they asked.

He answered, "No."

22 Then they said, "Who are you? Give us an answer to tell those who sent us. What do you say about yourself?"

23 John told them in the words of the prophet Isaiah:

"This is the voice of one who calls out:
'Prepare in the desert
the way for the LORD.'"   Isaiah 40:3

24 Some Pharisees who had been sent asked John: 25 "If you are not the Christ or Elijah or the Prophet, why do you baptise people?"

26 John answered, "I baptise with water, but there is one here with you that you don't know about. 27 He is the One who comes after me. I am not good enough to untie the strings of his sandals."

28 This all happened at Bethany on the other side of the Jordan River, where John was baptising people.

29 The next day John saw Jesus coming towards him. John said, "Look, the Lamb of God,[n] who takes away the sin of the world! 30 This is the One I was talking about when I said, 'A man will come after me, but he is greater than I am, because he was living before me.' 31 Even I did not know who he was, although I came baptising with water so that the people of Israel would know who he is."

32-33 Then John said, "I saw the Spirit come down from heaven in the form of a dove and rest on him. Until then I did not know who the Christ was. But the God who sent me to baptise with water told me, 'You will see the Spirit come down and rest on a man; he is the One who will baptise with the Holy Spirit.' 34 I have seen this happen, and I tell you the truth: this man is the Son of God."

The First Followers of Jesus

35 The next day John[n] was there again with two of his followers. 36 When he saw Jesus walking by, he said, "Look, the Lamb of God!"[n]

37 The two followers heard John say this, so they followed Jesus. 38 When Jesus turned and saw them following him, he asked, "What are you looking for?"

They said, "Rabbi, where are you staying?" ("Rabbi" means "Teacher".)

39 He answered, "Come and see." So the two men went with Jesus and saw where he was staying and stayed there with him that day. It was about four o'clock in the afternoon.

40 One of the two men who followed Jesus after they heard John speak about him was Andrew, Simon Peter's brother. 41 The first thing Andrew did was to find his brother Simon and say to him, "We have found the Messiah." ("Messiah" means "Christ".)

42 Then Andrew took Simon to Jesus. Jesus looked at him and said, "You are Simon son of John. You will be called Cephas." ("Cephas" means "Peter".[n])

43 The next day Jesus decided to go to Galilee. He found Philip and said to him, "Follow me."

44 Philip was from the town of Bethsaida, where Andrew and Peter lived. 45 Philip found Nathanael and told him, "We have found the man that Moses wrote about in the law, and the prophets also wrote about him. He is Jesus, the son of Joseph, from Nazareth."

46 But Nathanael said to Philip, "Can anything good come from Nazareth?"

Philip answered, "Come and see."

47 As Jesus saw Nathanael coming

1:21 Elijah A man who spoke for God. He lived hundreds of years before Christ and was expected to return before Christ (Malachi 4:5-6).

1:21 Prophet They probably meant the prophet that God told Moses he would send (Deuteronomy 18:15-19).

1:29, 36 Lamb of God Name for Jesus. Jesus is like the lambs that were offered for a sacrifice to God.

1:35 John John the Baptist, who preached to people about Christ's coming (Matthew 3, Luke 3).

1:42 Peter The Greek name "Peter", like the Aramaic name "Cephas", means "rock".

towards him, he said, "Here is truly an Israelite. There is nothing false in him."

48 Nathanael asked, "How do you know me?"

Jesus answered, "I saw you when you were under the fig tree, before Philip told you about me."

49 Then Nathanael said to Jesus, "Teacher, you are the Son of God; you are the King of Israel."

50 Jesus said to Nathanael, "Do you believe simply because I told you I saw you under the fig tree? You will see greater things than that." 51 And Jesus said to them, "I tell you the truth, you will all see heaven open and 'angels of God going up and coming down'[n] on the Son of Man."

The Wedding at Cana

2 Two days later there was a wedding in the town of Cana in Galilee. Jesus' mother was there, 2 and Jesus and his followers were also invited to the wedding. 3 When all the wine was gone, Jesus' mother said to him, "They have no more wine."

4 Jesus answered, "Dear woman, why come to me? My time has not yet come."

5 His mother said to the servants, "Do whatever he tells you to do."

6 In that place there were six stone water jars that the Jews used in their washing ceremony.[n] Each jar held about 100 litres.

7 Jesus said to the servants, "Fill the jars with water." So they filled the jars to the top.

8 Then he said to them, "Now take some out and give it to the master of the feast."

So they took the water to the master. 9 When he tasted it, the water had become wine. He did not know where the wine came from, but the servants who had brought the water knew. The master of the wedding called the bridegroom 10 and said to him, "People always serve the best wine first. Later, after the guests have been drinking awhile, they serve the cheaper wine. But you have saved the best wine till now."

11 So in Cana of Galilee Jesus did his first miracle. There he showed his glory, and his followers believed in him.

Jesus in the Temple

12 After this, Jesus went to the town of Capernaum with his mother, brothers and followers. They stayed there for just a few days. 13 When it was almost time for the Jewish Passover Feast, Jesus went to Jerusalem. 14 In the Temple he found people selling cattle, sheep and doves. He saw others sitting at tables, exchanging different kinds of money. 15 Jesus made a whip out of cords and forced all of them, both the sheep and cattle, to leave the Temple. He turned over the tables and scattered the money of those who were exchanging it. 16 Then he said to those who were selling pigeons, "Take these things out of here! Don't make my Father's house a place for buying and selling!"

**2:13–17
Anger**
Do you know what made Jesus angry?

17 When this happened, the followers remembered what was written in the Scriptures: "My strong love for your Temple completely controls me."[n]

18 The Jews said to Jesus, "Show us a miracle to prove you have the right to do these things."

19 Jesus answered them, "Destroy this temple, and I will build it again in three days."

20 The Jews answered, "It took 46 years to build this Temple! Do you really believe you can build it again in three days?"

21 (But the temple Jesus meant was his own body. 22 After Jesus was raised from the dead, his followers remembered that Jesus had said this. Then they believed the Scripture and the words Jesus had said.)

1:51 'angels . . . down' These words are from Genesis 28:12.
2:6 washing ceremony The Jewish people washed themselves in special ways before eating, before worshipping in the Temple and at other special times.
2:17 "My . . . me." Quotation from Psalm 69:9.

FOLLOWING JESUS
John 2

Follow the Right Leader Do you like to play the game "Follow the Leader" or "Simon Says"? What happens in these games if you don't do exactly what the leader does or says? Now think of some situations in real life where it's really important to follow the leader's directions. What could happen if you went your own way?

How do you know you will go to heaven when you die? Jesus answered that question by telling us that the *only* way to heaven is through him. Following Jesus will take you to your heavenly home someday – nothing else will get you there. (Look at John 14:1–6.) How can you follow Jesus?

Before you decide to "follow" anyone, there are a few things you should check out first. Are they a good leader? You don't want to get lost or anything.

Maybe we ought to learn more about what makes a good leader first. Try surfing to these Faithlinks before you follow anyone!

MORE FAITH links

- Your Spiritual Roots, **p. 1253**
- Two Birthdays, **p. 1426**
- The Way to Heaven, **p. 1448**
- The Winner's Crown, **p. 1555**
- An Unselfish Example, **p. 1611**
- The Coming Attraction, **p. 1634**

A Memorial for Two Thieves, 1 Chronicles 7:21, p. 530
- Do you know anything about your family history? Are there any interesting or embarrassing facts about any of your ancestors? If someone wrote about your life, what would your actions say about you? Would it say you followed Jesus – or someone else?

One Big, Happy Family, John 1:12, p. 1422
- What's the best thing about belonging to your family? Link here to find out about another family you belong to.

Hope That Doesn't Fail, Acts 26:4–7, p. 1510
- Imagine being dragged into court and told to defend yourself for being a follower of Jesus. What would you do? What would you say?
- How can following Jesus give you hope? What do you hope for?

23 When Jesus was in Jerusalem for the Passover Feast, many people believed in him because they saw the miracles he did. 24 But Jesus did not trust himself to them because he knew them all. 25 He did not need anyone to tell him about people, because he knew what was in people's minds.

Nicodemus Comes to Jesus

3 There was a man named Nicodemus who was one of the Pharisees and an important Jewish leader. 2 One night Nicodemus came to Jesus and said, "Teacher, we know you are a teacher sent from God, because no one can do the miracles you do unless God is with him."

3 Jesus answered, "I tell you the truth, unless one is born again, he cannot be in God's kingdom."

4 Nicodemus said, "But if a person is already old, how can he be born again? He cannot enter his mother's body again. So how can a person be born a second time?"

5 But Jesus answered, "I tell you the truth, unless one is born from water and the Spirit, he cannot enter God's kingdom. 6 Human life comes from human parents, but spiritual life comes from the Spirit. 7 Don't be surprised when I tell you, 'You must all be born again.' 8 The wind blows where it wants to and you hear the sound of it, but you don't know where the wind comes from or where it is going. It is the same with every person who is born from the Spirit."

9 Nicodemus asked, "How can this happen?"

10 Jesus said, "You are an important teacher in Israel, and you don't understand these things? 11 I tell you the truth, we talk about what we know, and we tell about what we have seen, but you don't accept what we tell you. 12 I have told you about things here on earth, and you do not believe me. So you will not believe me if I tell you about things of heaven. 13 The only one who has ever gone up to heaven is the One who came down from heaven—the Son of Man.

14 "Just as Moses lifted up the snake in the desert,[n] the Son of Man must also be lifted up. 15 So that everyone who believes can have eternal life in him.

16 "God loved the world so much that he gave his one and only Son so that whoever believes in him may not be lost, but have eternal life. 17 God

---

FAITH links

TWO BIRTHDAYS
JOHN 3:1-7

Celebrating a birthday is exciting! Did you know that you could celebrate two birthdays each year? Jesus told a Pharisee named Nicodemus about the second kind of birthday. He called this being "born again". People who accept Jesus become new people, thanks to the Holy Spirit. That's something to celebrate!

The Perfect Sacrifice, Leviticus 1—7, p. 135

The God of Big Things, Joshua 10, p. 289

A Given, 1 Chronicles 5:18–20, p. 526

What's in a Name? Isaiah 9:6, p. 908

A Family Meal, Mark 14:23–26, p. 1356

A Family Resemblance, Galatians 3:6–9, p. 1588

3:15–16 Eternal Life What is needed for eternal life?

3:14 Moses . . . desert When the Israelites were dying from snake bites, God told Moses to put a brass snake on a pole. The people who looked at the snake were healed (Numbers 21:4-9).

did not send his Son into the world to judge the world guilty, but to save the world through him. 18 People who believe in God's Son are not judged guilty. Those who do not believe have already been judged guilty, because they have not believed in God's one and only Son. 19 They are judged by this fact: the Light has come into the world, but they did not want light. They wanted darkness, because they were doing evil things. 20 All who do evil hate the light and will not come to the light, because it will show all the evil things they do. 21 But those who follow the true way come to the light, and it shows that the things they do were done through God."

Jesus and John the Baptist

22 After this, Jesus and his followers went into the area of Judea, where he stayed with his followers and baptised people. 23 John was also baptising in Aenon, near Salim, because there was plenty of water there. People were going there to be baptised. 24 (This was before John was put into prison.)

25 Some of John's followers had an argument with a Jew about religious washing.[n] 26 So they came to John and said, "Teacher, remember the man who was with you on the other side of the Jordan River, the one you spoke about so much? He is baptising, and everyone is going to him."

27 John answered, "A man can get only what God gives him. 28 You yourselves heard me say, 'I am not the Christ, but I am the one sent to prepare the way for him.' 29 The bride belongs only to the bridegroom. But the friend who helps the bridegroom stands by and listens to him. He is thrilled that he gets to hear the bridegroom's voice. In the same way, I am really happy. 30 He must become greater, and I must become less important.

The One Who Comes from Heaven

31 "The One who comes from above is greater than all. The one who is from the earth belongs to the earth and talks about

---

FAITH links

THE GIFT
JOHN 3:16-18

Have you ever given a gift that helped a whole group of people? Maybe you gave a gift to your family that everyone could use. God gave a gift to the whole world. He sent his Son to die for the sins of everyone – including you! How do you receive this gift? All you have to do is to believe that Jesus died for your sins, not just everyone else's. Now you have eternal life. That's quite a gift, isn't it?

Here are some more Faithlinks on God's gift to us:

When Bad Turns to Worse, Exodus 5:6–12, p. 82

Our Heavenly Shepherd, Psalm 23, p. 726

A Direct Path, Proverbs 3:5–6, p. 829

A Love Song, Zephaniah 3:17, p. 1246

A Change of Heart, Matthew 3:1–12, p. 1277

Too Busy to Worship? Luke 2:8–20, p. 1368

---

things on the earth. But the One who comes from heaven is greater than all. 32 He tells what he has seen and heard,

---

3:25 religious washing The Jewish people washed themselves in special ways before eating, before worshipping in the Temple and at other special times.

but no one accepts what he says. 33 Whoever accepts what he says has proven that God is true. 34 The One whom God sent speaks the words of God, because God gives him the Spirit fully. 35 The Father loves the Son and has given him power over everything. 36 Those who believe in the Son have eternal life, but those who do not obey the Son will never have life. God's anger stays on them."

Jesus and a Samaritan Woman

4 The Pharisees heard that Jesus was making and baptising more followers than John, 2 although Jesus himself did not baptise people, but his followers did. 3 Jesus knew that the Pharisees had heard about him, so he left Judea and went back to Galilee. 4 But on the way he had to go through the country of Samaria.

5 In Samaria Jesus came to the town called Sychar, which is near the field Jacob gave to his son Joseph. 6 Jacob's well was there. Jesus was tired from his long trip, so he sat down beside the well. It was about twelve o'clock noon. 7 When a Samaritan woman came to the well to get some water, Jesus said to her, "Please give me a drink." 8 (This happened while Jesus' followers were in town buying some food.)

9 The woman said, "I am surprised that you ask me for a drink, since you are a Jewish man and I am a Samaritan woman." (Jewish people are not friends with Samaritans.*)

10 Jesus said, "If you only knew the free gift of God and who it is that is asking you for water, you would have asked him, and he would have given you living water."

11 The woman said, "Sir, where will you get this living water? The well is very deep, and you have nothing to get water with. 12 Are you greater than Jacob, our father, who gave us this well and drank from it himself along with his sons and flocks?"

13 Jesus answered, "Everyone who drinks this water will be thirsty again, 14 but whoever drinks the water I give will never be thirsty. The water I give will become a spring of water flowing up inside that person, giving eternal life."

15 The woman said to him, "Sir, give me this water so I will never be thirsty again and will not have to come back here to get more water."

16 Jesus told her, "Go and get your husband and come back here."

17 The woman answered, "I have no husband."

Jesus said to her, "You are right to say you have no husband. 18 Really you have had five husbands, and the man you live with now is not your husband. You told the truth."

19 The woman said, "Sir, I can see that you are a prophet. 20 Our ancestors worshipped on this mountain, but you Jews say that Jerusalem is the place where people must worship."

21 Jesus said, "Believe me, woman. The time is coming when neither in Jerusalem nor on this mountain will you actually worship the Father. 22 You Samaritans worship something you don't understand. We understand what we worship, because salvation comes from the Jews. 23 The time is coming when the true worshippers will worship the Father in spirit and truth, and that time is here already. You see, the Father too is actively seeking such people to worship him. 24 God is spirit, and those who worship him must worship in spirit and truth."

eMAIL FROM GOD
4:21-26
Jesus
Jesus is the Messiah.

25 The woman said, "I know that the Messiah is coming." (Messiah is the One called Christ.) "When the Messiah comes, he will explain everything to us."

26 Then Jesus said, "I am he—I, the one talking to you."

27 Just then his followers came back from town and were surprised to see him talking with a woman. But none of them asked, "What do you want?" or "Why are you talking with her?"

28 Then the woman left her water jar and went back to town. She said to the

4:9 Jewish people . . . Samaritans. This can also be translated "Jewish people don't use things that Samaritans have used."

people, 29 "Come and see a man who told me everything I ever did. Do you think he might be the Christ?" 30 So the people left the town and went to see Jesus.

31 Meanwhile, his followers were begging him, "Teacher, eat something."

32 But Jesus answered, "I have food to eat that you know nothing about."

33 So the followers asked themselves, "Has somebody already brought him food?"

34 Jesus said, "My food is to do what the One who sent me wants me to do and to finish his work. 35 You have a saying, 'Four more months till harvest.' But I tell you, open your eyes and look at the fields ready for harvest now. 36 Already, the one who harvests is being paid and is gathering crops for eternal life. So the one who plants and the one who harvests celebrate at the same time. 37 Here the saying is true, 'One person plants, and another harvests.' 38 I sent you to harvest a crop that you did not work for. Others did the work, and you will finish their work."*ⁿ*

> **4:34–38 Witnessing**
> Check out the real harvest.

39 Many of the Samaritans in that town believed in Jesus because of what the woman said: "He told me everything I ever did." 40 When the Samaritans came to Jesus, they begged him to stay with them, so he stayed there two more days. 41 And many more believed because of the things he said.

42 They said to the woman, "First we believed in Jesus because of what you told us, but now we believe because we heard him ourselves. We know that this man really is the Saviour of the world."

Jesus Heals an Officer's Son

43 Two days later, Jesus left and went to Galilee. 44 (Jesus had said before that a prophet is not respected in his own country.) 45 When Jesus arrived in Galilee, the people there welcomed him. They had seen all the things he did at the Passover Feast in Jerusalem, because they had been there, too.

46 Jesus went again to visit Cana in Galilee where he had changed the water into wine. One of the king's important officers lived in the city of Capernaum, and his son was sick. 47 When he heard that Jesus had come from Judea to Galilee, he went to Jesus and begged him to come to Capernaum and heal his son, because his son was almost dead. 48 Jesus said to him, "You people must see signs and miracles before you will believe in me."

49 The officer said, "Sir, come before my child dies."

50 Jesus answered, "Go. Your son will live."

The man believed what Jesus told him and went home. 51 On the way the man's servants came and met him and told him, "Your son is alive."

52 The man asked, "What time did my son begin to get well?"

They answered, "Yesterday at one o'clock the fever left him."

53 The father knew that one o'clock was the exact time that Jesus had said, "Your son will live." So the man and all the people who lived in his house believed in Jesus.

54 That was the second miracle Jesus did after coming from Judea to Galilee.

Jesus Heals a Man at a Pool

5 Later Jesus went to Jerusalem for a special Jewish feast. 2 In Jerusalem there is a pool with five covered porches, which is called Bethesda*ⁿ* in the Jewish language.*ⁿ* This pool is near the Sheep Gate. 3 Many sick people were lying on the porches beside the pool. Some were blind, some were crippled and some were paralysed.*ⁿ* 5 A man was lying there who

---

4:38 But I . . . their work. As a farmer sends workers to harvest grain, Jesus sends his followers out to bring people to God.

5:2 Bethesda Also called Bethsaida or Bethzatha, a pool of water north of the Temple in Jerusalem.

5:2 Jewish language Hebrew or Aramaic, the languages of the Jewish people in the first century.

5:3 Verse 3 Some Greek copies add "and they waited for the water to move". A few later copies add verse 4: "Sometimes an angel of the Lord came down to the pool and stirred up the water. After the angel did this, the first person to go into the pool was healed from any sickness he had."

LET'S VISIT CAPERNAUM — John 4:46-54

Capernaum was a fishing town on the shores of Lake Galilee. The name *Capernaum* means "Village of Nahum". It was probably named for the man who owned the land where the village was built. (This is not the Old Testament prophet, Nahum.)

Jesus spent a lot of time around Capernaum. He healed many people, including an army officer's servant (check out Matthew 8:5-13, p. 1287), a paralysed man (see Mark 2:1-12, p. 1331), and an important officer of the king's son (look at John 4:46-54, p. 1432). It was also near Capernaum, that Jesus called several of his disciples. (Check out Mark 1:16-21, p. 1330; Mark 2:1, 13-14, p. 1331.) Before Jesus died, he cursed this city because of its unbelief (look at Matthew 11:23-24, p. 1293) and predicted its ruin (see Luke 10:15, p. 1387). Today there is nothing left of Capernaum but the ruins.

had been sick for 38 years. 6 When Jesus saw the man and knew that he had been sick for such a long time, Jesus asked him, "Do you want to be well?"

7 The sick man answered, "Sir, there is no one to help me get into the pool when the water starts moving. While I am coming to the water, someone else always gets in before me."

8 Then Jesus said, "Stand up. Pick up your mat and walk." 9 And immediately the man was well; he picked up his mat and began to walk.

The day this happened was a Sabbath day. 10 So the Jews said to the man who had been healed, "Today is the Sabbath. It is against our law for you to carry your mat on the Sabbath day."

11 But he answered, "The man who made me well told me, 'Pick up your mat and walk.'"

12 Then they asked him, "Who is the man who told you to pick up your mat and walk?"

13 But the man who had been healed did not know who it was, because there were many people in that place, and Jesus had left.

14 Later, Jesus found the man at the Temple and said to him, "See, you are well now. Stop sinning so that something worse does not happen to you."

15 Then the man left and told the Jews that Jesus was the one who had made him well.

16 Because Jesus was doing this on the Sabbath day, the Jews began to persecute him. 17 But Jesus said to them, "My Father never stops working, and so I keep working, too."

18 This made the Jews try still harder to kill him. They said, "First Jesus was breaking the law about the Sabbath day. Now he says that God is his own Father, making himself equal with God!"

Jesus Has God's Authority

19 But Jesus said, "I tell you the truth, the Son can do nothing alone. The Son does only what he sees the Father doing, because the Son does whatever the Father does. 20 The Father loves the Son and shows the Son all the things he himself does. But the Father will show the Son even greater things than this so that you can all be amazed. 21 Just as the

Father raises the dead and gives them life, so also the Son gives life to those he wants to. 22 In fact, the Father judges no one, but he has given the Son power to do all the judging 23 so that all people will honour the Son as much as they honour the Father. Anyone who does not honour the Son does not honour the Father who sent him.

24 "I tell you the truth, whoever hears what I say and believes in the One who sent me has eternal life. That person will not be judged guilty but has already left death and entered life. 25 I tell you the truth, the time is coming and is already here when the dead will hear the voice of the Son of God, and those who hear will have life. 26 Life comes from the Father himself, and he has allowed the Son to have life in himself as well. 27 And the Father has given the Son the power to judge, because he is the Son of Man. 28 Don't be surprised at this: a time is coming when all who are dead and in their graves will hear his voice. 29 Then they will come out of their graves. Those who did good will rise and have life for ever, but those who did evil will rise to be judged guilty.

5:24 God's Promises
Check out God's promise to all believers.

5:28–29 Eternal Life
Who will receive eternal punishment?

Jesus is God's Son

30 "I can do nothing alone. I judge only the way I am told, so my judgement is fair. I don't try to please myself, but I try to please the One who sent me.

31 "If only I tell people about myself, what I say does not count. 32 But there is another who tells about me, and I know that the things he says about me are true.

33 "You have sent people to John, and he has told you the truth. 34 It is not that I accept such human telling; I tell you this so you can be saved. 35 John was like a burning and shining lamp, and you were happy to enjoy his light for a while.

36 "But I have a proof about myself that is greater than that of John. The things I do, which are the things my Father gave me to do, prove that the Father sent me. 37 And the Father himself who sent me has given proof about me. You have never heard his voice or seen what he looks like. 38 His teaching does not live in you, because you don't believe in the One the Father sent. 39 You carefully study the Scriptures because you think they give you eternal life. They do in fact tell about me, 40 but you refuse to come to me to have that life.

41 "I don't need praise from people. 42 But I know you—I know that you don't have God's love in you. 43 I have come

FAITH CHALLENGE

Read 5:30 to find out who Jesus cared about pleasing. If you decided to spend a whole day doing things to please God instead of pleasing yourself, where would you go and what would you do?

TeSTiNG iT

John 5:30
I can do nothing alone. I judge only the way I am told, so my judgement is fair. I don't try to please myself, but I try to please the One who sent me.

from my Father and speak for him, but you don't accept me. But when another person comes, speaking only for himself, you will accept him. 44 You try to get praise from each other, but you do not try to get the praise that comes from the only God. So how can you believe? 45 Don't think that I will stand before the Father and say you are wrong. The one who says you are wrong is Moses, the one you hoped would save you. 46 If you really believed Moses, you would believe me, because Moses wrote about me. 47 But if you don't believe what Moses wrote, how can you believe what I say?"

More than 5,000 Fed

6 After this, Jesus went across Lake Galilee (or, Lake Tiberias). 2 Many people followed him because they saw the miracles he did to heal the sick. 3 Jesus went up on a hill and sat down there with his followers. 4 It was almost the time for the Jewish Passover Feast.

5 When Jesus looked up and saw a large crowd coming towards him, he said to Philip, "Where can we buy enough bread for all these people to eat?" 6 (Jesus asked Philip this question to test him, because Jesus already knew what he planned to do.)

7 Philip answered, "We would all have to work a month to buy enough bread for each person to have only a little piece."

8 Another one of his followers, Andrew, Simon Peter's brother, said, 9 "Here is a boy with five loaves of barley bread and two little fish, but that is not enough for so many people."

10 Jesus said, "Tell the people to sit down." This was a very grassy place, and about 5,000 men sat down there. 11 Then Jesus took the loaves of bread, thanked God for them and gave them to the people who were sitting there. He did the same with the fish, giving as much as the people wanted.

12 When they had all had enough to eat, Jesus said to his followers, "Gather the leftover pieces of fish and bread so that nothing is wasted." 13 So they gathered up the pieces and filled twelve baskets with the pieces left from the five barley loaves.

14 When the people saw this miracle that Jesus did, they said, "He must truly be the Prophet[n] who is coming into the world."

15 Jesus knew that the people planned to come and take him by force and make him their king, so he left and went into the hills alone.

Jesus Walks on the Water

16 That evening Jesus' followers went down to Lake Galilee. 17 It was dark now, and Jesus had not yet come to them. The followers got into a boat and started across the lake to Capernaum. 18 By now a strong wind was blowing, and the waves on the lake were getting bigger. 19 When they had rowed the boat about five or six kilometres, they saw Jesus walking on the water, coming towards the boat. The followers were afraid, 20 but Jesus said to them, "It is I. Do not be afraid." 21 Then they were glad to take him into the boat. At once the boat came to land at the place where they wanted to go.

The People Seek Jesus

22 The next day the people who had stayed on the other side of the lake knew that Jesus had not gone in the boat with his followers but that they had left without him. And they knew that only one boat had been there. 23 But then some boats came from Tiberias and landed near the place where the people had eaten the bread after the Lord had given thanks. 24 When the people saw that Jesus and his followers were not there now, they got into boats and went to Capernaum to find Jesus.

Jesus, the Bread of Life

25 When the people found Jesus on the other side of the lake, they asked him, "Teacher, when did you come here?"

26 Jesus answered, "I tell you the truth, you aren't looking for me because

---

6:14 Prophet They probably meant the prophet that God told Moses he would send (Deuteronomy 18:15-19).

GET THE INFO

THE NAMES OF JESUS
John 6:35

The two names Christians use the most for God's Son are *Jesus* and *Christ*. *Jesus* is a form of the Hebrew word for *Joshua*. It means "God is salvation". The name *Christ* came from a Greek term that means "Messiah". Here are some other names for Jesus used in the New Testament.

Alpha and Omega	He is the Beginning and the End	Revelation 21:6, p. 1753
Bread of Life	He is the one essential food	John 6:35, p. 1434
Most Important Stone	He is our sure foundation	Ephesians 2:20, p. 1600
Good Shepherd	He takes care of us	John 10:11, p. 1441
High Priest	He offered the perfect sacrifice for our sins	Hebrews 3:1, p. 1669
Immanuel	This name means "God is with us"	Matthew 1:23, p. 1275
King of Kings	The almighty ruler	Revelation 19:16, p. 1751
Lamb of God	Gave his life as a sacrifice for us	John 1:29, p. 1423
Light of the World	Jesus brings hope in the darkness	John 9:5, p. 1440
Son of Man	Jesus is all human and all God	Matthew 24:30, p. 1316

you saw me do miracles. You are looking for me because you ate the bread and were satisfied. 27 Don't work for the food that spoils. Work for the food that stays good always and gives eternal life. The Son of Man will give you this food, because on him God the Father has put his power."

28 The people asked Jesus, "What are the things God wants us to do?"

29 Jesus answered, "The work God wants you to do is this: believe the One he sent."

30 So the people asked, "What miracle will you do? If we see a miracle, we will believe you. What will you do? 31 Our fathers ate the manna in the desert. This is written in the Scriptures: 'He rained manna down on them to eat.'"[n]

6:31 'He gave . . . eat.' Quotation from Psalm 78:24.

32 Jesus said, "I tell you the truth, it was not Moses who gave you bread from heaven; it is my Father who is giving you the true bread from heaven. 33 God's bread is the One who comes down from heaven and gives life to the world."

34 The people said, "Sir, give us this bread always."

35 Then Jesus said, "I am the bread that gives life. Whoever comes to me will never be hungry, and whoever believes in me will never be thirsty. 36 But as I told you before, you have seen me and still don't believe. 37 The Father gives me my people. Every one of them will come to me, and I will always accept them. 38 I came down from heaven to do what God wants me to do, not what I want to do. 39 Here is what the One who sent me wants me to do: I must not lose even one whom God gave me, but I must raise them all on the last day. 40 Those who see the Son and believe in him have eternal life, and I will raise them on the last day. This is what my Father wants."

41 The Jews began to complain about Jesus because he said, "I am the bread that comes down from heaven." 42 They said, "This is Jesus, the son of Joseph. We know his father and mother. How can he say, 'I came down from heaven'?"

43 But Jesus answered, "Stop complaining to each other. 44 The Father is the One who sent me. No one can come to me unless the Father draws him to me, and I will raise that person up on the last day. 45 It is written in the prophets, 'They will all be taught by God.'ⁿ Everyone who listens to the Father and learns from him comes to me. 46 No one has seen the Father except the One who is from God; only he has seen the Father. 47 I tell you the truth, whoever believes has eternal life. 48 I am the bread that gives life. 49 Your ancestors ate the manna in the desert, but still they died. 50 Here is the bread that comes down from heaven. Anyone who eats this bread will never die. 51 I am the living bread that came down from heaven. Anyone who eats this bread will live for ever. This bread is my flesh, which I will give up so that the world may have life."

52 Then the Jews began to argue among themselves, saying, "How can this man give us his flesh to eat?"

53 Jesus said, "I tell you the truth, you must eat the flesh of the Son of Man and drink his blood. Otherwise, you won't have real life in you. 54 Those who eat my flesh and drink my blood have eternal life, and I will raise them up on the last day. 55 My flesh is true food, and my blood is true drink. 56 Those who eat my flesh and drink my blood live in me, and I live in them. 57 The living Father sent me, and I live because of the Father. So whoever eats me will live because of me. 58 I am not like the bread your ancestors ate. They ate that bread and still died. I am the bread that came down from heaven, and whoever eats this bread will live for ever." 59 Jesus said all these things while he was teaching in the synagogue in Capernaum.

The Words of Eternal Life

60 When the followers of Jesus heard this, many of them said, "This teaching is hard. Who can accept it?"

61 Knowing that his followers were complaining about this, Jesus said, "Does this teaching bother you? 62 Then will it also bother you to see the Son of Man going back to the place where he came from? 63 It is the Spirit that gives life. The flesh doesn't give life. The words I told you are spirit, and they give life. 64 But some of you don't believe." (Jesus knew from the beginning who did not believe and who would turn against him.) 65 Jesus said, "That is the reason I said, 'If the Father does not bring a person to me, that one cannot come.'"

66 After Jesus said this, many of his followers left him and stopped following him.

67 Jesus asked the twelve followers, "Do you want to leave, too?"

6:45 'They . . . God.' Quotation from Isaiah 54:13.

68 Simon Peter answered him, "Lord, where would we go? You have the words that give eternal life. 69 We believe and know that you are the Holy One from God."

70 Then Jesus answered, "I chose all twelve of you, but one of you is a devil." 71 Jesus was talking about Judas, the son of Simon Iscariot. Judas was one of the twelve, but later he was going to turn against Jesus.

Jesus' Brothers Don't Believe

7 After this, Jesus travelled around Galilee. He did not want to travel in Judea, because the Jews there wanted to kill him. 2 It was time for the Jewish Feast of Shelters. 3 So Jesus' brothers said to him, "You should leave here and go to Judea so your followers there can see the miracles you do. 4 Anyone who wants to be well known does not hide what he does. If you are doing these things, show yourself to the world." 5 (Even Jesus' brothers did not believe in him.)

6 Jesus said to his brothers, "The right time for me has not yet come, but any time is right for you. 7 The world cannot hate you, but it hates me, because I tell it the evil things it does. 8 So you go to the feast. I will not go yet to this feast, because the right time for me has not yet come." 9 After saying this, Jesus stayed in Galilee.

10 But after Jesus' brothers had gone to the feast, Jesus went also. But he did not let people see him. 11 At the feast the Jews were looking for him and saying, "Where is that man?"

12 Within the large crowd there, many people were whispering to each other about Jesus. Some said, "He is a good man."

Others said, "No, he fools the people." 13 But no one was brave enough to talk about Jesus openly, because they were afraid of the Jews.

Jesus Teaches at the Feast

14 When the feast was about half over, Jesus went to the Temple and began to teach. 15 The Jews were amazed and said, "This man has never studied. How did he learn so much?"

16 Jesus answered, "The things I teach are not my own, but they come from him who sent me. 17 If people choose to do what God wants, they will know that my teaching comes from God and not from me. 18 Those who teach their own ideas are trying to get honour for themselves. But those who try to bring honour to the one who sent them speak the truth, and there is nothing false in them. 19 Moses gave you the law,* but none of you obeys that law. Why are you trying to kill me?"

20 The people answered, "A demon has come into you. We are not trying to kill you."

21 Jesus said to them, "I did one miracle, and you are all amazed. 22 Moses gave you the law about circumcision. (But really Moses did not give you circumcision; it came from our ancestors.) And yet you circumcise a baby on a Sabbath day. 23 If a baby can be circumcised on a Sabbath day to obey the law of Moses, why are you angry at me for healing a person's whole body on the Sabbath day? 24 Stop judging by the way things look, but judge by what is really right."

> **EMAIL FROM GOD**
> **7:24 Judgement**
> Don't judge by appearances.

Is Jesus the Christ?

25 Then some of the people who lived in Jerusalem said, "This is the man they are trying to kill. 26 But he is teaching where everyone can see and hear him, and no one is trying to stop him. Maybe the leaders have decided he really is the Christ. 27 But we know where this man is from. And when the real Christ comes, no one will know where he comes from."

28 Jesus, teaching in the Temple, cried out, "Yes, you know me, and you know where I am from. But I have not come by my own authority. I was sent by the One who is true, whom you don't know. 29 But

---

7:19 law Moses gave God's people the law that God gave him on Mount Sinai (Exodus 34:29-32).

I know him, because I am from him, and he sent me."

30 When Jesus said this, the people tried to take him. But no one was able to touch him, because it was not yet the right time. 31 But many of the people believed in Jesus. They said, "When the Christ comes, will he do more miracles than this man has done?"

The Leaders Try to Arrest Jesus

32 The Pharisees heard the crowd whispering these things about Jesus. So the leading priests and the Pharisees sent some Temple guards to arrest him. 33 Jesus said, "I will be with you a little while longer. Then I will go back to the One who sent me. 34 You will look for me, but you will not find me. And you cannot come where I am."

35 The Jews said to each other, "Where will this man go so we cannot find him? Will he go to the Greek cities where our people live and teach the Greek people there? 36 What did he mean when he said, 'You will look for me, but you will not find me,' and 'You cannot come where I am'?"

Jesus Talks About the Spirit

37 On the last and most important day of the feast Jesus stood up and said in a loud voice, "Let anyone who is thirsty come to me and drink. 38 If anyone believes in me, rivers of living water will flow out from that person's heart, as the Scripture says." 39 Jesus was talking about the Holy Spirit. The Spirit had not yet been given, because Jesus had not yet been raised to glory. But later, those who believed in Jesus would receive the Spirit.

The People Argue About Jesus

40 When the people heard Jesus' words, some of them said, "This man really is the Prophet."*n*

41 Others said, "He is the Christ."

Still others said, "The Christ will not come from Galilee. 42 The Scripture says that the Christ will come from David's family and from Bethlehem, the town where David lived." 43 So the people did not agree with each other about Jesus.

44 Some of them wanted to arrest him, but no one was able to touch him.

Some Leaders Won't Believe

45 The Temple guards went back to the leading priests and the Pharisees, who asked, "Why didn't you bring Jesus?"

46 The guards answered, "The words he says are greater than the words of any other person who has ever spoken!"

47 The Pharisees answered, "So Jesus has fooled you also! 48 Have any of the leaders or the Pharisees believed in him? No! 49 But these people, who know nothing about the law, are under God's curse."

50 Nicodemus, who had gone to see Jesus before, was in that group.*n* He said, 51 "Our law does not judge a man without hearing him and knowing what he has done."

52 They answered, "Are you from Galilee, too? Study the Scriptures, and you will learn that no prophet comes from Galilee."

Some early Greek manuscripts do not contain 7:53—8:11.

[53 And everyone left and went home.

The Woman Caught in Adultery

8 Jesus went to the Mount of Olives. 2 But early in the morning he went back to the Temple, and all the people came to him, and he sat and taught them. 3 The teachers of the law and the Pharisees brought a woman who had been caught in adultery. They forced her to stand before the people. 4 They said to Jesus, "Teacher, this woman was caught having sexual relations with a man who is not her husband. 5 The law of Moses commands that we stone to death every

---

7:40 Prophet They probably meant the prophet God told Moses he would send (Deuteronomy 18:15-19).
7:50 Nicodemus . . . group. The story about Nicodemus going and talking to Jesus is in John 3:1-21.

woman who does this. What do you say we should do?" 6 They were asking this to trick Jesus so that they could have some charge against him.

But Jesus bent down and started writing on the ground with his finger. 7 When they continued to ask Jesus their question, he rose up and said, "Anyone here who has never sinned can throw the first stone at her." 8 Then Jesus bent over again and wrote on the ground.

9 Those who heard Jesus began to leave one by one, first the older men and then the others. Jesus was left there alone with the woman standing before him. 10 Jesus rose up again and asked her, "Woman, where are they? Has no one judged you guilty?"

11 She answered, "No one, sir."

Then Jesus said, "I also don't judge you guilty. You may go now, but don't sin any more."]

Jesus is the Light of the World

12 Later, Jesus talked to the people again, saying, "I am the light of the world. The person who follows me will never live in darkness but will have the light that gives life."

8:12 Following God
Read to see what you should follow.

13 The Pharisees said to Jesus, "When you talk about yourself, you are the only one to say these things are true. We cannot accept what you say."

14 Jesus answered, "Yes, I am saying these things about myself, but they are true. I know where I came from and where I am going. But you don't know where I came from or where I am going. 15 You judge by human standards. I am not judging anyone. 16 But when I do judge, my judgement is true, because I am not alone. The Father who sent me is with me. 17 Your own law says that when two witnesses say the same thing, you must accept what they say. 18 I am one of the witnesses who speaks about myself, and the Father who sent me is the other witness."

19 They asked, "Where is your father?"

Jesus answered, "You don't know me or my Father. If you knew me, you would know my Father, too." 20 Jesus said these things while he was teaching in the Temple, near where the money is kept. But no one arrested him, because the right time for him had not yet come.

The People Misunderstand Jesus

21 Again, Jesus said to the people, "I will leave you, and you will look for me, but you will die in your sins. You cannot come where I am going."

22 So the Jews asked, "Will Jesus kill himself? Is that why he said, 'You cannot come where I am going'?"

23 Jesus said, "You people are from here below, but I am from above. You belong to this world, but I don't belong to this world. 24 So I told you that you would die in your sins. Yes, you will die in your sins if you don't believe that I am he."

25 They asked, "Then who are you?"

Jesus answered, "I am what I have told you from the beginning. 26 I have many things to say and decide about you. But I tell people only the things I have heard from the One who sent me, and he speaks the truth."

27 The people did not understand that he was talking to them about the Father. 28 So Jesus said to them, "When you lift up the Son of Man, you will know that I am he. You will know that these things I do are not by my own authority but that I say only what the Father has taught me. 29 The One who sent me is with me. I always do what is pleasing to him, so he has not left me alone." 30 While Jesus was saying these things, many people believed in him.

Freedom from Sin

31 So Jesus said to the Jews who believed in him, "If you continue to obey my teaching, you are truly my followers. 32 Then you will know the truth, and the truth will make you free."

33 They answered, "We are Abraham's children, and we have never been anyone's slaves. So why do you say we will be free?"

FAITH links

THE WHOLE TRUTH
JOHN 8:31-32, 45

Has anyone ever lied to you? The next time he or she tells you something, believing that person becomes harder doesn't it? Sometimes people lie because they're afraid that others won't like the truth. Jesus always told the truth, even though doing so often caused trouble for him with the religious leaders of Israel. They didn't like to hear him tell the truth about God or about their sin.

Jesus called himself the truth. Because he *is* the truth, that's what we ought to always tell if we believe in him.

Jesus takes what we say very seriously. So should we! Check it out:

The Best Policy, Genesis 29:16–29, p. 41

Who Do You Prefer? Proverbs 3:32, p. 830

A Broken Promise, Jeremiah 2:1–8, p. 989

The Verdict Is In? Matthew 7:1–2, p. 1285

The Deadliest Lie, Acts 5:1–11, p. 1471

Say What?! Ephesians 4:22–29, p. 1603

34 Jesus answered, "I tell you the truth, everyone who lives in sin is a slave to sin. 35 A slave does not stay with a family for ever, but a son belongs to the family for ever. 36 So if the Son makes you free, you will be truly free. 37 I know you are Abraham's children, but you want to kill me because you don't accept my teaching. 38 I am telling you what my Father has shown me, but you do what your own father has told you."

39 They answered, "Our father is Abraham."

Jesus said, "If you were really Abraham's children, you would do the things Abraham did. 40 I am a man who has told you the truth which I heard from God, but you are trying to kill me. Abraham did nothing like that. 41 So you are doing the things your own father did."

But they said, "We are not like children who never knew who their father was. God is our Father; he is the only Father we have."

42 Jesus said to them, "If God were really your Father, you would love me, because I came from God and now I am here. I did not come by my own authority; God sent me. 43 You don't understand what I say, because you cannot accept my teaching. 44 You belong to your father the devil, and you want to do what he wants. He was a murderer from the beginning and was against the truth,

> **eMAIL FROM GOD 8:44**
> **Satan**
> Is the devil completely evil?

because there is no truth in him. When he tells a lie, he shows what he is really like, because he is a liar and the father of lies. 45 But because I speak the truth, you don't believe me. 46 Can any of you prove that I am guilty of sin? If I am telling the truth, why don't you believe me? 47 The person who belongs to God accepts what God says. But you don't accept what God says, because you don't belong to God."

Jesus is Greater than Abraham

48 The Jews answered, "We say you are a Samaritan and have a demon in you. Are we not right?"

49 Jesus answered, "I have no demon in me. I give honour to my Father, but you dishonour me. 50 I am not trying to get honour for myself. There is One who wants this honour for me, and he is the judge. 51 I tell you the truth, whoever

obeys my teaching will never die."

52 The Jews said to Jesus, "Now we know that you have a demon in you! Even Abraham and the prophets died. But you say, 'Whoever obeys my teaching will never die.' 53 Do you think you are greater than our father Abraham, who died? And the prophets died, too. Who do you think you are?"

54 Jesus answered, "If I give honour to myself, that honour is worth nothing. The One who gives me honour is my Father, and you say he is your God. 55 You don't really know him, but I know him. If I said I did not know him, I would be a liar like you. But I do know him, and I obey what he says. 56 Your father Abraham was very happy that he would see my day. He saw that day and was glad."

57 The Jews said to him, "You have never seen Abraham! You are not even 50 years old."

58 Jesus answered, "I tell you the truth, before Abraham was even born, I am!" 59 When Jesus said this, the people picked up stones to throw at him. But Jesus hid himself, and then he left the Temple.

Jesus Heals a Man Born Blind

9 As Jesus was walking along, he saw a man who had been born blind. 2 His followers asked him, "Teacher, whose sin

DID YOU HEAR ABOUT...?

Do you ever stop and think about gossip? Here's Hannah. She's struggling with this problem. Let's welcome Hannah, aged 11, to Connect 2-You.

Hannah

My friends call me a gossip, and I suppose they're right. I love to talk about what other people are doing. It drives me mad if there are things going on in my friends' lives that I don't know about. And when someone tells me something, I can't wait to tell other people about it. All my friends are the same way. What do you think?

Gossip can be pretty tempting, can't it? But the Bible says we should control our tongues and not let our tongues control us. For some tips on how to get rid of gossip in your life, take a look at the Livin' It page on controlling what you say, Jeremiah 9:3, p. 1003.

When Hannah learns to control her tongue, she may be surprised at what happens with her friends. When people start to realise that she can be trusted not to tell their secrets, she will find that her friendships get deeper and stronger. She should think of it as a reward for obeying God's commands.

caused this man to be born blind—his own sin or his parents' sin?"

3 Jesus answered, "It is not this man's sin or his parents' sin that made him be blind. This man was born blind so that God's power could be shown in him. 4 While it is daytime, we must continue doing the work of the One who sent me. Night is coming, when no one can work. 5 While I am in the world, I am the light of the world."

6 After Jesus said this, he spat on the ground and made some mud with it and put the mud on the man's eyes. 7 Then he told the man, "Go and wash in the Pool of Siloam." (Siloam means Sent.) So the man went, washed and came back seeing.

8 The neighbours and some people who had earlier seen this man begging said, "Isn't this the same man who used to sit and beg?"

9 Some said, "He is the one," but others said, "No, he only looks like him."

The man himself said, "I am the man."

10 They asked, "How did you get your sight?"

11 He answered, "The man named Jesus made some mud and put it on my eyes. Then he told me to go to Siloam and wash. So I went and washed, and then I could see."

12 They asked him, "Where is this man?"

"I don't know," he answered.

Pharisees Question the Healing

13 Then the people took to the Pharisees the man who had been blind. 14 The day Jesus had made mud and healed his eyes was a Sabbath day. 15 So now the Pharisees asked the man, "How did you get your sight?"

He answered, "He put mud on my eyes, I washed, and now I see."

16 So some of the Pharisees were saying, "This man does not keep the Sabbath day, so he is not from God."

But others said, "A man who is a sinner can't do miracles like these." So they could not agree with one another.

17 They asked the man again, "What do you say about him since it was your eyes he opened?"

The man answered, "He is a prophet."

18 The Jews did not believe that he had been blind and could now see again. So they sent for the man's parents 19 and asked them, "Is this your son who you say was born blind? Then how does he now see?"

20 His parents answered, "We know that this is our son and that he was born blind. 21 But we don't know how he can now see. We don't know who opened his eyes. Ask him. He is old enough to speak for himself." 22 His parents said this because they were afraid of the Jews, who had already decided that anyone who said Jesus was the Christ would be put out of the synagogue. 23 That is why his parents said, "He is old enough. Ask him."

24 So for the second time, they called the man who had been blind. They said, "You should give God the glory by telling the truth. We know that this man is a sinner."

25 He answered, "I don't know if he is a sinner. One thing I do know: I was blind, and now I see."

26 They asked, "What did he do to you? How did he make you see again?"

27 He answered, "I have already told you, and you didn't listen. Why do you want to hear it again? Do you want to become his followers, too?"

28 Then they insulted him and said, "You are his follower, but we are followers of Moses. 29 We know that God spoke to Moses, but as for this man we don't even know where he comes from."

30 The man answered, "This is a very strange thing. You don't know where he comes from, and yet he opened my eyes. 31 We all know that God does not listen to sinners, but he listens to anyone who worships and obeys him. 32 Nobody has ever heard of anyone giving sight to a man born blind. 33 If this man were not from God, he could do nothing."

34 They answered, "You were born full of sin! Are you trying to teach us?" And they threw him out.

Spiritual Blindness

35 When Jesus heard that they had thrown him out, Jesus found him and said,

John 10:13 1441

"Do you believe in the Son of Man?"

36 He asked, "Who is the Son of Man, sir, so that I can believe in him?"

37 Jesus said to him, "You have seen him. The Son of Man is the one talking with you."

38 He said, "Lord, I believe!" Then the man worshipped Jesus.

39 Jesus said, "I came into this world so that the world would be judged. I came so that the blind[n] will see and so that those who see will become blind."

40 Some of the Pharisees who were nearby heard Jesus say this and asked, "Are you saying we are blind, too?"

41 Jesus said, "If you were blind, you would not be guilty of sin. But since you keep saying you see, your guilt remains."

The Shepherd and His Sheep

10 Jesus said, "I tell you the truth, the person who does not enter the sheepfold by the door, but climbs in by some other way, is a thief and a robber. 2 The one who enters by the door is the shepherd of the sheep. 3 The one who guards the door opens it for him. And the sheep listen to the voice of the shepherd. He calls his own sheep by name and leads them out. 4 When he brings all his sheep out, he goes ahead of them, and they follow him because they know his voice. 5 But they will never follow a stranger. They will run away from him because they don't know his voice." 6 Jesus told the people this story, but they did not understand what it meant.

Jesus is the Good Shepherd

7 So Jesus said again, "I tell you the truth, I am the door for the sheep. 8 All the people who came before me were thieves and robbers. The sheep did not listen to them. 9 I am the door, and the person who enters through me will be saved and will be able to come in and go out and find pasture. 10 A thief comes to steal and kill and destroy, but I came to give life—life in all its fullness.

11 "I am the good shepherd. The good shepherd gives his life for the sheep. 12 The worker who is paid to keep the sheep is different from the shepherd who owns them. When the worker sees a wolf coming, he runs away and leaves the sheep alone. Then the wolf attacks the sheep and scatters them. 13 The man runs away because he is only a paid

10:10 Life
What did Jesus come to give?

FAITH links

OUR GOOD SHEPHERD
JOHN 10:11-15

If you've ever been around sheep, you know how helpless they are. A shepherd has to help them do just about everything. They also depend on the shepherd for protection.

Guess what? Jesus says that we're like sheep and he is our shepherd. That means he takes care of us. He even gave his life for us. Now that's good news!

God has the best protection plan! Link here for more:

Fearful Service? Exodus 4:1–17, p. 80

What's in a Name? Isaiah 9:6, p. 908

His Valentine, Jeremiah 31:3, p. 1035

A Word About Worry, Matthew 6:25–34, p. 1284

Prove It! Matthew 16:1–4, p. 1302

Most Wanted? 2 Corinthians 10:1, p. 1580

9:39 blind Jesus is talking about people who are spiritually blind, not physically blind.

worker and does not really care about the sheep.

14-15 "I am the good shepherd. I know my sheep, as the Father knows me. And my sheep know me, as I know the Father. I give my life for the sheep. **16** I have other sheep that are not in this flock, and I must bring them also. They will listen to my voice, and there will be one flock and one shepherd. **17** The Father loves me because I give my life so that I can take it back again. **18** No one takes it away from me; I give my own life freely. I have the right to give my life, and I have the right to take it back. This is what my Father commanded me to do."

19 Again the Jews did not agree with each other because of these words of Jesus. **20** Many of them said, "A demon has come into him and made him crazy. Why listen to him?"

21 But others said, "A man who is crazy with a demon does not say things like this. Can a demon open the eyes of the blind?"

Jesus is Rejected

22 The time came for the Feast of Dedication at Jerusalem. It was winter, **23** and Jesus was walking in the Temple in Solomon's Porch. **24** The Jews gathered around him and said, "How long will you make us wonder about you? If you are the Christ, tell us plainly."

25 Jesus answered, "I have already told you, but you did not believe. The miracles I do in my Father's name show who I am. **26** But you don't believe, because you are not my sheep. **27** My sheep listen to my voice; I know them, and they follow me. **28** I give them eternal life, and they will never die, and no one can steal them out of my hand. **29** My Father gave my sheep to me. He is greater than all, and no person can steal my sheep out of my Father's hand. **30** The Father and I are one."

31 Again the Jews picked up stones to kill Jesus. **32** But he said to them, "I have done many good works from the Father. Which of these good works are you killing me for?"

33 The Jews answered, "We are not killing you because of any good work you have done, but because you speak against God. You are only a human, but you say you are the same as God!"

34 Jesus answered, "It is written in your law that God said, 'I said, you are gods.'ᵐ **35** This Scripture called those people gods who received God's message, and Scripture is always true. **36** So why do you say that I speak against God because I said, 'I am God's Son'? I am the one God chose and sent into the world. **37** If I don't do what my Father does, then don't believe me. **38** But if I do what my Father does, even though you don't believe in me, believe what I do. Then you will know and understand that the Father is in me and I am in the Father."

39 They tried to take Jesus again, but he escaped from them.

40 Then he went back across the Jordan River to the place where John had first baptised. Jesus stayed there, **41** and many people came to him and said, "John never did a miracle, but everything John said about this man is true." **42** And in that place many believed in Jesus.

The Death of Lazarus

11 A man named Lazarus was sick. He lived in the town of Bethany, where Mary and her sister Martha lived. **2** Mary was the woman who later put perfume on the Lord and wiped his feet with her hair. Mary's brother was Lazarus, the man who was now sick. **3** So Mary and Martha sent someone to tell Jesus, "Lord, the one you love is sick."

4 When Jesus heard this, he said, "This sickness will not end in death. It is for the glory of God, to bring glory to the Son of God." **5** Jesus loved Martha and her sister and Lazarus. **6** But when he heard that Lazarus was sick, he stayed where he was for two more days. **7** Then Jesus said to his followers, "Let's go back to Judea."

10:25–27
Following God
How can you know Jesus?

10:34 'I . . . gods.' Quotation from Psalm 82:6.

8 The followers said, "But Teacher, the Jews there tried to stone you to death only a short time ago. Now you want to go back there?"

9 Jesus answered, "Are there not twelve hours in the day? If anyone walks in the daylight, he will not stumble, because he can see by this world's light. 10 But if anyone walks at night, he stumbles because there is no light to help him see."

11 After Jesus said this, he added, "Our friend Lazarus has fallen asleep, but I am going there to wake him."

12 The followers said, "But Lord, if he is only asleep, he will be all right."

13 Jesus meant that Lazarus was dead, but his followers thought he meant Lazarus was really sleeping. 14 So then Jesus said plainly, "Lazarus is dead. 15 And I am glad for your sakes I was not there so that you may believe. But let's go to him now."

16 Then Thomas (the one called Didymus) said to the other followers, "Let us also go so that we can die with him."

Jesus in Bethany

17 When Jesus arrived, he learned that Lazarus had already been dead and in the tomb for four days. 18 Bethany was about three kilometres from Jerusalem. 19 Many of the Jews had come there to comfort Martha and Mary about their brother.

20 When Martha heard that Jesus was coming, she went out to meet him, but Mary stayed at home. 21 Martha said to Jesus, "Lord, if you had been here, my brother would not have died. 22 But I know that even now God will give you anything you ask."

23 Jesus said, "Your brother will rise and live again."

24 Martha answered, "I know that he will rise and live again in the resurrection[n] on the last day."

25 Jesus said to her, "I am the resurrection and the life. Those who believe in me will have life even if they die. 26 And everyone who lives and believes in me will never die. Martha, do you believe this?"

27 Martha answered, "Yes, Lord. I believe that you are the Christ, the Son of God, the One who was to come into the world."

Jesus Cries

28 After Martha said this, she went back and talked to her sister Mary alone. Martha said, "The Teacher is here and he is asking for you." 29 When Mary heard this, she got up quickly and went to Jesus. 30 Jesus had not yet come into the town but was still at the place where Martha had met him. 31 The Jews were with Mary in the house, comforting her. When they saw her stand and leave quickly, they followed her, thinking she was going to the tomb to cry there.

32 But Mary went to the place where Jesus was. When she saw him, she fell at his feet and said, "Lord, if you had been here, my brother would not have died."

33 When Jesus saw Mary crying and the Jews who came with her also crying, he was upset and was deeply troubled. 34 He asked, "Where did you bury him?"

"Come and see, Lord," they said.

35 Jesus cried.

36 So the Jews said, "See how much he loved him."

37 But some of them said, "If Jesus opened the eyes of the blind man, why couldn't he keep Lazarus from dying?"

Jesus Raises Lazarus

38 Again feeling very upset, Jesus came to the tomb. It was a cave with a large stone covering the entrance. 39 Jesus said, "Move the stone away."

Martha, the sister of the dead man, said, "But, Lord, it has been four days since he died. There will be a bad smell."

40 Then Jesus said to her, "Didn't I tell you that if you believed you would see the glory of God?"

41 So they moved the stone away from the entrance. Then Jesus looked up and said, "Father, I thank you that you heard me. 42 I know that you always hear me,

11:25 Eternal Life What does Jesus give?

11:24 *resurrection* Being raised from the dead to live again.

FAITH links

FULLY GOD, FULLY HUMAN
JOHN 11:35

When a friend feels sad, you feel sad, too, don't you? Jesus felt exactly the same way. The shortest verse in the Bible tells us that when a friend of his died, Jesus cried. Jesus is God, but he is also human. He has feelings just like you do. That means he can understand when you're feeling sad about something. You can trust that he cares.

Download these links for more about God's care for you:

Your Heavenly Parent, Exodus 2:1–10, p. 77

Depend on Him! 2 Chronicles 16:1–9, p. 579

A Safe Place, Nahum 1:7, p. 1231

It's Under Control, Romans 8:28, p. 1529

Life After Death? 1 Corinthians 15:12–13, p. 1563

Go for It! Hebrews 12:1–4, p. 1682

but I said these things because of the people here around me. I want them to believe that you sent me." 43 After Jesus said this, he cried out in a loud voice, "Lazarus, come out!" 44 The dead man came out, his hands and feet wrapped with pieces of cloth, and a cloth around his face.

Jesus said to them, "Take the cloth off him and let him go."

The Plan to Kill Jesus

45 Many of the Jews, who had come to visit Mary and saw what Jesus did, believed in him. 46 But some of them went to the Pharisees and told them what Jesus had done. 47 Then the leading priests and Pharisees called a meeting of the Jewish council. They asked, "What should we do? This man is doing many miracles. 48 If we let him continue doing these things, everyone will believe in him. Then the Romans will come and take away our Temple and our nation."

49 One of the men there was Caiaphas, the high priest that year. He said, "You people know nothing! 50 You don't realise that it is better for one man to die for the people than for the whole nation to be destroyed."

51 Caiaphas did not think of this himself. As high priest that year, he was really prophesying that Jesus would die for the Jewish nation 52 and for God's scattered children to bring them all together and make them one.

53 That day they started planning to kill Jesus. 54 So Jesus no longer travelled openly among the Jews. He left there and went to a place near the desert, to a town called Ephraim and stayed there with his followers.

55 It was almost time for the Jewish Passover Feast. Many from the country went up to Jerusalem before the Passover to do the special things to make themselves pure. 56 The people looked for Jesus and stood in the Temple asking each other, "Is he coming to the Feast? What do you think?" 57 But the leading priests and the Pharisees had given orders that if anyone knew where Jesus was, he must tell them. Then they could arrest him.

Jesus with Friends in Bethany

12 Six days before the Passover Feast, Jesus went to Bethany, where Lazarus lived, whom Jesus had raised from the dead. 2 There they had a dinner for Jesus. Martha served the food, and Lazarus was one of the people eating with Jesus. 3 Mary brought in half a litre of very expensive perfume made from pure nard. She poured the perfume on

Jesus' feet, and then she wiped his feet with her hair. And the sweet smell from the perfume filled the whole house.

4 Judas Iscariot, one of Jesus' followers, who would later turn against him, was there. Judas said, 5 "This perfume was worth 300 silver coins.*n* Why wasn't it sold and the money given to the poor?" 6 But Judas did not really care about the poor; he said this because he was a thief. He was the one who kept the money bag, and he often stole from it.

7 Jesus answered, "Leave her alone. It was right for her to save this perfume for today, the day for me to be prepared for burial. 8 You will always have the poor with you, but you will not always have me."

The Plot Against Lazarus

9 A large crowd of Jews heard that Jesus was in Bethany. So they went there to see not only Jesus but Lazarus, whom Jesus raised from the dead. 10 So the leading priests made plans to kill Lazarus, too. 11 Because of Lazarus many of the Jews were leaving them and believing in Jesus.

Jesus Enters Jerusalem

12 The next day a great crowd who had come to Jerusalem for the Passover Feast heard that Jesus was coming there. 13 So they took branches of palm trees and went out to meet Jesus, shouting,
 "Praise*n* God!
 God bless the One who comes in the
  name of the Lord!
 God bless the King of Israel!"
Psalm 118:25-26

14 Jesus found a colt and sat on it. This was as the Scripture says,
 15 "Don't be afraid, people of
  Jerusalem!
 Your king is coming,
  sitting on the colt of a donkey."
Zechariah 9:9

16 The followers of Jesus did not understand this at first. But after Jesus was raised to glory, they remembered that this had been written about him and that they had done these things to him.

People Tell About Jesus

17 There had been many people with Jesus when he raised Lazarus from the dead and told him to come out of the tomb. Now they were telling others about what Jesus did. 18 Many people went out to meet Jesus, because they had heard about this miracle. 19 So the Pharisees said to each other, "You can see that nothing is going right for us. Look! The whole world is following him."

Jesus Talks About His Death

20 There were some Greek people, too, who came to Jerusalem to worship at the Passover Feast. 21 They went to Philip, who was from Bethsaida in Galilee, and said, "Sir, we would like to see Jesus." 22 Philip told Andrew, and then Andrew and Philip told Jesus.

23 Jesus said to them, "The time has come for the Son of Man to receive his glory. 24 I tell you the truth, a grain of wheat must fall to the ground and die to make many seeds. But if it never dies, it remains only a single seed. 25 Those who love their lives will lose them, but those who hate their lives in this world will keep true life for ever. 26 Whoever serves me must follow me. Then my servant will be with me everywhere I am. My Father will honour anyone who serves me.

27 "Now I am very troubled. Should I say, 'Father, save me from this time'? No, I came to this time in order to suffer. 28 Father, bring glory to your name!"

Then a voice came from heaven, "I have brought glory to it, and I will do it again."

29 The crowd standing there, who heard the voice, said it was thunder.

But others said, "An angel has spoken to him."

eMAIL FROM GOD
12:26
Following God
How can you know Jesus is near?

12:5 coins A silver Roman denarii coin was the average pay for one day's work.
12:13 Praise Literally, "Hosanna", a Hebrew word used at first in praying to God for help. At this time it was probably a shout of joy used in praising God or his Messiah.

30 Jesus said, "That voice was for your sake, not mine. 31 Now is the time for the world to be judged; now the ruler of this world will be thrown down. 32 If I am lifted up from the earth, I will draw all people towards me." 33 Jesus said this to show how he would die.

34 The crowd said, "We have heard from the law that the Christ will live for ever. So why do you say, 'The Son of Man must be lifted up'? Who is this 'Son of Man'?"

35 Then Jesus said, "The light will be with you for a little longer, so walk while you have the light. Then the darkness will not catch you. If you walk in the darkness, you will not know where you are going. 36 Believe in the light while you still have it so that you will become children of light." When Jesus had said this, he left and hid himself from them.

Some People Won't Believe in Jesus

37 Though Jesus had done many miracles in front of the people, they still did not believe in him. 38 This was to bring about what Isaiah the prophet had said:

"Who would have believed what we heard?
Who saw the Lord's power in this?" *Isaiah 53:1*

39 This is why the people could not believe: Isaiah had also said,
40 "Make the minds of these people dumb.
Shut their ears. Cover their eyes.
Otherwise, they might really understand
what they see with their eyes
and hear with their ears.
They might really understand in their minds
and come back to me and be healed." *Isaiah 6:10*

41 Isaiah said this because he saw Jesus' glory and spoke about him.

42 But many believed in Jesus, even many of the leaders. But because of the Pharisees, they did not say they believed in him for fear they would be put out of the synagogue. 43 They loved praise from people more than praise from God.

44 Then Jesus cried out, "Whoever believes in me is really believing in the One who sent me. 45 Whoever sees me sees the One who sent me. 46 I have come as light into the world so that whoever believes in me would not stay in darkness.

47 "Anyone who hears my words and does not obey them, I do not judge, because I did not come to judge the world, but to save the world. 48 There is a judge for those who refuse to believe in me and do not accept my words. The word I have taught will be their judge on the last day. 49 The things I taught were not from myself. The Father who sent me told me what to say and what to teach. 50 And I know that eternal life comes from what the Father commands. So whatever I say is what the Father told me to say."

Jesus Washes His Followers' Feet

13 It was almost time for the Jewish Passover Feast. Jesus knew that it was time for him to leave this world and go back to the Father. He had always loved those who were his own in the world, and he loved them all the way to the end.

2 Jesus and his followers were at the evening meal. The devil had already persuaded Judas Iscariot, the son of Simon, to turn against Jesus. 3 Jesus knew that the Father had given him power over everything and that he had come from God and was going back to God. 4 So during the meal Jesus stood up and took off his outer clothing. Taking a towel, he wrapped it around his waist. 5 Then he poured water into a bowl and began to wash the followers' feet, drying them with the towel that was wrapped around him.

6 Jesus came to Simon Peter, who said to him, "Lord, are you going to wash my feet?"

7 Jesus answered, "You don't understand now what I am doing, but you will understand later."

8 Peter said, "No, you will never wash my feet."

Jesus answered, "If I don't wash your feet, you are not one of my people."

9 Simon Peter answered, "Lord, then wash not only my feet, but wash my hands and my head, too!"

10 Jesus said, "After a person has had a bath, his whole body is clean. He needs

Jesus Taking the Temptation Test

Those terrible, troublesome temptations! When you least expect it, one will pop into your life – a temptation to eat the last piece of cake; a temptation to cheat on a test; a temptation to disobey your parents. One thing's for sure: everyone faces temptations of some kind. Even Jesus was tempted during his time on earth. But Jesus knew how to handle temptations. Want to find out how Jesus was tempted and what he did? Turn the page to check out

Here's the Scoop

and take a lesson from the Master in how to pass the temptation test! The numbers match the question numbers on this page.

1 Suppose your mum told you not to eat anything before dinner. Now, suppose someone offered you a bar of chocolate, a packet of crisps or a cake. Would you eat it?

2 What are you good at? Skating? Football? Are you ever tempted to show off in front of others? (Be honest!) If someone popular dared you to do something dangerous in order to prove how "good" you really are would you do it? What if you knew, deep down, that it was wrong?

3 What would you do if you were told you could have anything you wanted – even a million pounds? Sounds good so far, doesn't it? But suppose you were told that you had to take a "shortcut", like cheating on a test or obeying someone who does wrong things. Would you do it?

4 If you had the power to get back at someone who hurt you, even if doing it was wrong, would you use that power? Think about a situation where you would be tempted the most to use this power.

5 Suppose you were asked to make a sacrifice that would save someone else, like giving blood or bone marrow. Now suppose you were told that this sacrifice could be really painful. Would you still make the sacrifice?

Here's the Scoop

1. Jesus once fasted for 40 days out of obedience to God the Father. He was really hungry. But when the devil told him to make bread out of stones, Jesus used the Scriptures to tell him "No!" Jesus knew that the devil wanted him to do something selfish to show off his power. He also knew that the Word of God gave a person the power to resist temptation. It will help you to resist temptation, too. (See **Matthew 4:3–4**, p. 1279.)

2. The devil wanted Jesus to throw himself off the Temple to prove that God would help him. This was another way for Jesus to show off in front of others. The devil tried to tempt Jesus by quoting from the Scriptures. Jesus knew that he didn't have to prove who he was. He also didn't have to prove that the Father would take care of him. So he used the Word of God to tell Satan to back off. When was the last time you did that? (Check out **Luke 4:9–12**, p. 1373.)

3. The devil promised to give Jesus the world if Jesus would only worship him. Why was this a temptation? In a way, the devil wanted Jesus to take a "shortcut" by avoiding the cross. Jesus knew that dying on the cross was part of God's plan. Once more Jesus used the Word of God to say no to temptation. He knew that God's plan did not involve a shortcut. When you're tempted to take a shortcut, remember that one word: No! (Read **Luke 4:5–8**, p. 1373.)

4. A crowd of people charged towards Jesus to arrest him in the garden of Gethsemane. Jesus knew that he would be treated badly and would later be put to death. Peter, one of Jesus' disciples, tried to use violence to stop the crowd. But even though Jesus had the power to stop them from taking him, he didn't. Instead, he reminded everyone of what the Word of God said. Guess what he did next. He obeyed it. (Read about it in **John 18:1–11**, p. 1454.)

5. While Jesus was on the cross, people around him made fun of him. They told him that he could save himself if he wanted to. Jesus had the power to save himself or to call angels to rescue him from the cross. But Jesus went to the cross to die for the sins of everyone. If Jesus had given in to the temptation to free himself, we would all be lost! He chose to say no to temptation and yes to obedience. You can, too. (Check out **Mark 15:21–32**, p. 1359.)

Paul — Hope for Hard Times

Everyone goes through bad times at some point in life. What are bad times? Failing a test. Having a pet die. Going through an illness. Being badly treated by others. How do you usually respond when bad times come your way? The way a person acts during hard times shows whether or not they have faith in God. Bad times can strengthen a person's faith, but they can also cause someone weak in faith to turn away from God. Paul experienced bad times as a missionary and apostle for God. Go to

Here's the Scoop

on the following page to find out what happened to his faith. The numbers match the question numbers on this page.

1. If someone spread rumours that weren't true about you to others, how would you feel? What would you do? Would you defend yourself or try to get back at that person by spreading rumours about them? Paul constantly faced situations where people said things about him that weren't true.

2. Suppose you were treated badly, even though you tried to do good. Would you try to get even? Or, would you continue to do good? Paul faced major opposition even as he was trying to do good.

3. How would you respond if you were accused of something that you didn't do? Imagine your teacher walks into the classroom and accuses you of cheating when you didn't. What would you say in your defence?

4. A life-threatening circumstance can be discouraging. Many are tempted to give up or be angry with God. How willing are you to trust God through the difficult times?

5. How do you react when the weather wrecks your plans? Do you cry, "It's not fair!" or do you try to be flexible? Some storms can throw a ship – or a life – off course. How can you stay on course?

Here's the Scoop

1. Paul and another missionary named Barnabas went to a town called Iconium to tell people about Jesus. But some of the Jewish people tried to make trouble for them. They said bad things about Paul and Barnabas. But they refused to stop preaching about Jesus. Instead, Paul and Barnabas trusted God. He gave them hope to make it through the hard times. (Read **Acts 14:1–7**, p. 1489.)

2. Paul and Silas used God's power to help a servant girl. But instead of being thanked for their good deed, they were arrested, beaten and thrown into prison! Amazingly, Paul didn't try to get even and he didn't complain about being treated unfairly. Instead, he sang praise songs with Silas! Later, when God sent an earthquake to shake down the walls of the jail, they stayed to help the jailer! Because of them, the jailer and his family were baptised as believers. (Check out **Acts 16:16–40**, p. 1494.)

3. A group of men accused Paul of making the Jewish Temple unclean. They told the people that what Paul was teaching was against the Law of Moses. The men stirred up the crowd so that they tried to kill him. Roman soldiers finally arrested Paul just to get him safely away from the mob. Even though the men told lies about him, Paul didn't say bad things in return. He continued to tell the Good News of Jesus. (Look up **Acts 21:27–36**, p. 1503.)

4. Over 40 men came up with a plan to kill Paul. Paul's nephew overheard the whole thing and was able to tell the Roman guards about it. During this time while Paul was in jail based on false accusations, Paul didn't get angry with God because he was treated unfairly. He didn't complain and he didn't question what God was doing. Paul continued to pray and trust God to protect him. He chose to keep his eyes on God instead of on his circumstances. (Read **Acts 23:11–22**, p. 1506.)

5. While on his way to stand trial in Rome, Paul's ship was sunk in a storm. How did Paul handle this? Paul prayed. During the storm, God sent an angel to tell Paul that no one's life would be lost. Everyone would make it to shore safely. God took care of Paul. Months later, he sailed on another ship to Rome. So there you have it. Prayer, praise and the power of God helped Paul through the hard times. Are these part of your strategy for getting through bad times? (Check out **Acts 27:13—28:10-11**, p. 1511.)

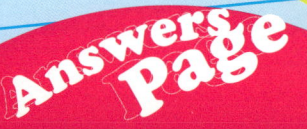

FAITH links

THE WORST CHORE
JOHN 13:3-17

Think of the worst chore that you hope you never have to do. That will give you some idea of how Jesus' followers felt when he began to wash their feet. In Jesus' time, washing a person's feet was considered the worst chore anyone could do. Only servants washed feet. So why did Jesus get up and do it? He wanted to provide an example of service. He wants us to be willing to serve others just as he did. So . . . what will you do?

A Use for Your Abilities, Genesis 41, p. 59

Yours, Mine and Ours? 1 Samuel 25, p. 389

The Way to Serve God, 1 Kings 9:4, p. 450

That Thing You Do, Matthew 25:14–30, p. 1319

You're Welcomed! Acts 16:14–15, p. 1494

The Sacrifice of Service, Philippians 2:17, 25–30, p. 1612

---

only to wash his feet. And you men are clean, but not all of you." 11 Jesus knew who would turn against him, and that is why he said, "Not all of you are clean."

12 When he had finished washing their feet, he put on his clothes and sat down again. He asked, "Do you understand what I have just done for you? 13 You call me 'Teacher' and 'Lord', and you are right, because that is what I am. 14 If I, your Lord and Teacher, have washed your feet, you also should wash each other's feet. 15 I did this as an example so that you should do as I have done for you. 16 I tell you the truth, a servant is not greater than his master. A messenger is not greater than the one who sent him. 17 If you know these things, you will be happy if you do them.

18 "I am not talking about all of you. I know those I have chosen. But this is to bring about what the Scripture said: 'The man who ate at my table has turned against me.'*n* 19 I am telling you this now before it happens so that when it happens, you will believe that I am he. 20 I tell you the truth, whoever accepts anyone I send also accepts me. And whoever accepts me also accepts the One who sent me."

Jesus Talks About His Death

21 After Jesus said this, he was very troubled. He said openly, "I tell you the truth, one of you will turn against me."

22 The followers all looked at each other, because they did not know whom Jesus was talking about. 23 One of the followers sitting*n* next to Jesus was the follower Jesus loved. 24 Simon Peter made signs to him to ask Jesus whom he was talking about.

25 That follower leaned closer to Jesus and asked, "Lord, who is it?"

26 Jesus answered, "I will dip this bread into the dish. The man I give it to is the man who will turn against me." So Jesus took a piece of bread, dipped it, and gave it to Judas Iscariot, the son of Simon. 27 As soon as Judas took the bread, Satan entered him. Jesus said to him, "The thing that you will do—do it quickly." 28 No one at the table understood why Jesus said this to Judas. 29 Since he was the one who kept the money bag, some of the followers thought Jesus was telling him to buy what was needed for the feast or to give something to the poor.

30 Judas took the bread Jesus gave him and immediately went out. It was night.

13:18 'The man . . . me.' Quotation from Psalm 41:9.
13:23 sitting Literally, "lying". The people of that time ate lying down and leaning on one arm.

31 When Judas was gone, Jesus said, "Now the Son of Man receives his glory, and God receives glory through him. 32 If God receives glory through him, then God will give glory to the Son through himself. And God will give him glory quickly."

33 Jesus said, "My children, I will be with you only a little longer. You will look for me, and what I told the Jews, I tell you now: where I am going you cannot come.

34 "I give you a new command: love each other. You must love each other as I have loved you. 35 All people will know that you are my followers if you love each other."

**13:34–35
Love**
You must love each other.

Peter will Say He Doesn't Know Jesus

36 Simon Peter asked Jesus, "Lord, where are you going?"

Jesus answered, "Where I am going you cannot follow now, but you will follow later."

37 Peter asked, "Lord, why can't I follow you now? I am ready to die for you!"

38 Jesus answered, "Are you ready to die for me? I tell you the truth, before the cockerel crows, you will say three times that you don't know me."

Jesus Comforts His Followers

14 Jesus said, "Don't let your hearts be troubled. Trust in God, and trust in me. 2 There are many rooms in my Father's house; I would not tell you this if it were not true. I am going there to prepare a place for you. 3 After I go and prepare a place for you, I will come back and take you to be with me so that you may be where I am. 4 You know the way to the place where I am going."

5 Thomas said to Jesus, "Lord, we don't know where you are going. So how can we know the way?"

6 Jesus answered, "I am the way, and the truth, and the life. The only way to the Father is through me. 7 If you really knew me, you would know my Father, too. But now you do know him, and you have seen him."

8 Philip said to him, "Lord, show us the Father. That is all we need."

9 Jesus answered, "I have been with you a long time now. Do you still not know me, Philip? Whoever has seen me has seen the Father. So why do you say, 'Show us the Father'? 10 Don't you believe that

---

FAITH links

THE WAY TO HEAVEN
JOHN 14:1-6

How do you know you'll go to heaven after you die? Many people often wonder about that question. There's only one sure way to get to heaven: through Jesus. He is the way, the truth and the life. Because Jesus willingly went to the cross for our sins, anyone who trusts him will have a heavenly home someday. That's a promise you can count on!

Here are some more Faithlinks about God's amazing promise to us:

God's New Home, 2 Chronicles 7:11–22, p. 570

How Big Is God? Job 38—41, p. 703

Clean Inside and Out, Luke 11:39–40, p. 1392

Life After Death?
1 Corinthians 15:12–13, p. 1563

The Coming Attraction,
1 Thessalonians 4:13–18, p. 1634

A Heavenly Sight, Revelation 21:1–4, p. 1753

I am in the Father and the Father is in me? The words I say to you don't come from me, but the Father lives in me and does his own work. 11 Believe me when I say that I am in the Father and the Father is in me. Or believe because of the miracles I have done. 12 I tell you the truth, whoever believes in me will do the same things that I do. Those who believe will do even greater things than these, because I am going to the Father. 13 And if you ask for anything in my name, I will do it for you so that the Father's glory will be shown through the Son. 14 If you ask me for anything in my name, I will do it.

The Promise of the Holy Spirit

15 "If you love me, you will obey my commands. 16 I will ask the Father, and he will give you another Helper[n] to be with you for ever— 17 the Spirit of truth. The world cannot accept him, because it does not see him or know him. But you know him, because he lives with you and he will be in you.

18 "I will not leave you all alone like orphans; I will come back to you. 19 In a little while the world will not see me any more, but you will see me. Because I live, you will live, too. 20 On that day you will know that I am in my Father, and that you are in me and I am in you. 21 Those who know my commands and obey them are the ones who love me, and my Father will love those who love me. I will love them and will show myself to them."

22 Then Judas (not Judas Iscariot) said, "But, Lord, why do you plan to show yourself to us and not to the rest of the world?"

23 Jesus answered, "If people love me, they will obey my teaching. My Father will love them, and we will come to them and make our home with them. 24 Those who do not love me do not obey my teaching. This teaching that you hear is not really mine; it is from my Father, who sent me.

25 "I have told you all these things while I am with you. 26 But the Helper will teach you everything and will cause you to remember all that I told you. This Helper is the Holy Spirit whom the Father will send in my name.

27 "I leave you peace; my peace I give you. I do not give it to you as the world does. So don't let your hearts be troubled or afraid. 28 You heard me say to you, 'I am going, but I am coming back to you.' If you loved me, you would be happy that I am going back to the Father, because he is greater than I am. 29 I have told you this now, before it happens, so that when it happens, you will believe. 30 I will not talk with you much longer, because the ruler of this world is coming. He has no power over me, 31 but the world must know that I love the Father, so I do exactly what the Father told me to do.

"Come now, let us go."

Jesus is Like a Vine

15 "I am the true vine; my Father is the gardener. 2 He cuts off every branch of mine that does not produce fruit. And he trims and cleans every branch that produces fruit so that it will produce even more fruit. 3 You are already clean because of the words I have spoken to you. 4 Remain in me, and I will remain in you. A branch cannot produce fruit alone but must remain in the vine. In the same way, you cannot produce fruit alone but must remain in me.

5 "I am the vine, and you are the branches. If any remain in me and I remain in them, they produce much fruit. But without me they can do nothing. 6 If any do not remain in me, they are like a branch that is thrown away and then dies. People pick up dead branches, throw them into the fire and burn them. 7 If you remain in me and follow my teachings, you can ask anything you want, and it will be given to you. 8 You should produce

14:15–23 Obedience
What does it mean to love Jesus?

14:19 Death
Who has power over death?

14:16 Helper "Counsellor" or "Comforter". Jesus is talking about the Holy Spirit.

John 15:9

much fruit and show that you are my followers, which brings glory to my Father. 9 I loved you as the Father loved me. Now remain in my love. 10 I have obeyed my Father's commands, and I remain in his love. In the same way, if you obey my commands, you will remain in my love. 11 I have told you these things so that you can have the same joy I have and so that your joy will be the fullest possible joy.

12 "This is my command: love each other as I have loved you. 13 The greatest love a person can show is to die for his friends. 14 You are my friends if you do what I command you. 15 I no longer call you servants, because a servant does not know what his master is doing. But I call you friends, because I have made known to you everything I heard from my Father. 16 You did not choose me; I chose you. And I gave you this work: to go and produce fruit, fruit that will last. Then the Father will give you anything you ask for in my name. 17 This is my command: love each other.

15:13–15 Friendship
Check out what makes a true friend.

Jesus Warns His Followers

18 "If the world hates you, remember that it hated me first. 19 If you belonged to the world, it would love you as it loves its own. But I have chosen you out of the world, so you don't belong to it. That is why the world hates you. 20 Remember what I told you: a servant is not greater than his master. If people did wrong to me, they will do wrong to you, too. And if they obeyed my teaching, they will obey yours, too. 21 They will do all this to you on account of me, because they do not know the One who sent me. 22 If I had not come and spoken to them, they would not be guilty of sin, but now they have no excuse for their sin. 23 Whoever hates me also hates my Father. 24 I did works among them that no one else has ever done. If I had not done these works, they would not be guilty of sin. But now they have seen what I have done, and yet they have hated both me and my Father. 25 But this happened so that what is written in their law would be true: 'They hated me for no reason.'*n*

26 "I will send you the Helper*n* from the Father; he is the Spirit of truth who comes from the Father. When he comes, he will tell about me, 27 and you also must tell people about me, because you have been with me from the beginning.

FAITH links

A FRIEND OF JESUS
JOHN 15:9-17

Want to know how to be a friend of Jesus? Jesus himself tells you how. First, love others. Second, do what he says. In fact, loving others is one of Jesus' commands. How do you do that? By being willing to serve others. Jesus gave his life for us. More than likely, none of us will be called on to give our lives to help a friend. But we can still do whatever it takes to serve and help others.

Give What You Can, Numbers 7:1–11, p. 186

Care for the Lost, Deuteronomy 22:1–3, p. 255

Loyal to a Friend, 2 Samuel 9, p. 409

Just Say Yes! Matthew 9:9–13, p. 1289

An Encouraging Word, 1 Corinthians 1:3–5, p. 1545

Come On In! 1 Peter 4:9–10, p. 1705

15:25 'They . . . reason.' These words could be from Psalm 35:19 or Psalm 69:4.
15:26 Helper "Counsellor" or "Comforter". Jesus is talking about the Holy Spirit.

John 16:29

16 "I have told you these things to keep you from giving up. 2 People will put you out of their synagogues. Yes, the time is coming when those who kill you will think they are offering service to God. 3 They will do this because they have not known the Father and they have not known me. 4 I have told you these things now so that when the time comes you will remember that I warned you.

The Work of the Holy Spirit

"I did not tell you these things at the beginning, because I was with you then. 5 Now I am going back to the One who sent me. But none of you asks me, 'Where are you going?' 6 Your hearts are filled with sadness because I have told you these things. 7 But I tell you the truth, it is better for you that I go away. When I go away, I will send the Helper[n] to you. If I do not go away, the Helper will not come. 8 When the Helper comes, he will prove to the people of the world the truth about sin, about being right with God and about judgement. 9 He will prove to them that sin is not believing in me. 10 He will prove to them that being right with God comes through my going to the Father and not being seen by you any more. 11 And the Helper will prove to them that judgement happened when the ruler of this world was judged.

12 "I have many more things to say to you, but they are too much for you now. 13 But when the Spirit of truth comes, he will lead you into all truth. He will not speak his own words, but he will speak only what he hears, and he will tell you what is to come. 14 The Spirit of truth will bring glory to me, because he will take what I have to say and tell it to you. 15 All that the Father has is mine. That is why I said that the Spirit will take what I have to say and tell it to you.

Sadness will Become Happiness

16 "After a little while you will not see me, and then after a little while you will see me again."

17 Some of the followers said to each other, "What does Jesus mean when he says, 'After a little while you will not see me, and then after a little while you will see me again'? And what does he mean when he says, 'Because I am going to the Father'?" 18 They also asked, "What does he mean by 'a little while'? We don't understand what he is saying."

19 Jesus saw that the followers wanted to ask him about this, so he said to them, "Are you asking each other what I meant when I said, 'After a little while you will not see me, and then after a little while you will see me again'? 20 I tell you the truth, you will cry and be sad, but the world will be happy. You will be sad, but your sadness will become joy. 21 When a woman gives birth to a baby, she has pain, because her time has come. But when her baby is born, she forgets the pain, because she is so happy that a child has been born into the world. 22 It is the same with you. Now you are sad, but I will see you again and you will be happy, and no one will take away your joy. 23 In that day you will not ask me for anything. I tell you the truth, my Father will give you anything you ask for in my name.

EMAIL FROM GOD
16:23–24 Prayer
In whose name should you pray?

24 Until now you have not asked for anything in my name. Ask and you will receive, so that your joy will be the fullest possible joy.

Victory over the World

25 "I have told you these things, using stories that hide the meaning. But the time will come when I will not use stories like that to tell you things; I will speak to you in plain words about the Father. 26 In that day you will ask the Father for things in my name. I mean, I will not need to ask the Father for you. 27 The Father himself loves you. He loves you because you have loved me and believed that I came from God. 28 I came from the Father into the world. Now I am leaving the world and going back to the Father."

29 Then the followers of Jesus said,

16:7 Helper "Counsellor" or "Comforter". Jesus is talking about the Holy Spirit.

▶ John 16 1452

HAVING JOY
John 16:24

I Got the Joy, Joy, Joy, Joy Did you ever sing the song "I Got the Joy, Joy, Joy, Joy Down in My Heart"? What kind of joy is that? Where does it come from?

God gives you the joy that never goes away no matter what. This is the joy that we have knowing God loves us. (Look at Acts 3:1–16, p. 1466.) Imagine how you'd feel if someone suddenly solved a problem you've had all of your life – like curing a life-threatening disease or helping you become a maths genius overnight. Jesus' death solved the enormous problem of sin in your life by forgiving those sins. Now that's pure joy! How does that make you feel "down in your heart"?

MORE FAITH links

A Life of Thanksgiving, **p. 435**

A Need to Change, **p. 873**

Think About Him, **p. 926**

A Different Kind of Fruit, **p. 1592**

The "Quality" of Life, **p. 1708**

Did you know that you can be joyful even when things are really bad?

Let's see what these Faithlinks have to say about it.

Happiness or Joy? Job 29:18–19, p. 691
- Do you know the difference between happiness and joy? Happiness depends on circumstances. When everything is going great, you feel happy. But happiness doesn't last for ever. Joy comes from God and is always there – in bad times or good times. Which would you rather have: joy or happiness?

Blessed Are the Weak? 2 Corinthians 12:7–10, p. 1582
- No one likes to be thought of as weak – in our bodies or in the way we do things. God helps us when we're weak. Link here to learn where Paul found joy and strength when he was weak.

Always Do This! 1 Thessalonians 5:16–18, p. 1636
- What are some things you always do, besides breathing? Do you laugh a lot? Sing? Complain? Some actions probably depend on what's happening in your life. This Faithlink lists three activities to *always* do. How can you include them in your personal "always do" list?

_____

_____

_____

"You are speaking clearly to us now and are not using stories that are hard to understand. 30 We can see now that you know all things. You can answer a person's question even before it is asked. This makes us believe you came from God."

31 Jesus answered, "So now you believe? 32 Listen to me; a time is coming when you will be scattered, each to his own home. That time is now here. You will leave me alone, but I am never really alone, because the Father is with me. 33 "I told you these things so that you can have peace in me. In this world you will have trouble, but be brave! I have defeated the world."

16:33 Comfort
Having troubles? Take comfort in this.

Jesus Prays for His Followers

17 After Jesus said these things, he looked towards heaven and prayed, "Father, the time has come. Give glory to your Son so that the Son can give glory to you. 2 You gave the Son power over all people so that the Son could give eternal life to all those you gave him. 3 And this is eternal life: that people know you, the only true God, and that they know Jesus Christ, the One you sent. 4 Having finished the work you gave me to do, I brought you glory on earth. 5 And now, Father, give me glory with you; give me the glory I had with you before the world was made.

6 "I showed what you are like to those you gave me from the world. They belonged to you, and you gave them to me, and they have obeyed your teaching. 7 Now they know that everything you gave me comes from you. 8 I gave them the teachings you gave me, and they accepted them. They knew that I truly came from you, and they believed that you sent me. 9 I am praying for them. I am not praying for people in the world but for those you gave me, because they are yours. 10 All I have is yours, and all you have is mine. And my glory is shown through them. 11 I am coming to you; I will not stay in the world any longer. But they are still in the world. Holy Father, keep them safe by the power of your name, the name you gave me, so that they will be one, just as you and I are one.

FAITH links

JESUS' PRAYER
JOHN 17

Suppose you were having the worst day of your life. Would you immediately think about helping someone else? Jesus faced one of the worst days of his life. He knew that he would soon be arrested and put to death. Before he went to the cross, he prayed for his followers. Jesus knew that they would need God's help in all that they did. He also prayed that his followers would get along with each other.

Praying for someone is one way to show concern for that person. Let Jesus' prayer be a reminder to you to pray for the needs of others. Let it remind you, too, of how much Jesus cares for you!

What God Wants, Deuteronomy 10:12–13, p. 242

Just a Little Respect, 1 Chronicles 11:10–19, p. 534

Your Heavenly Dad, Psalm 103:13, p. 786

Concern for All, Daniel 9, p. 1165

Prayer Priority, Luke 5:15–16, p. 1376

Prayer for a Friend, Colossians 1:9–12, p. 1620

12 While I was with them, I kept them safe by the power of your name, the name you gave me. I protected them, and only one of them, the one worthy of destruction, was lost so that the Scripture would come true.

13 "I am coming to you now. But I pray these things while I am still in the world so that these followers can have all my joy in them. **14** I have given them your teaching. And the world has hated them, because they don't belong to the world, just as I don't belong to the world. **15** I am not asking you to take them out of the world but to keep them safe from the Evil One. **16** They don't belong to the world, just as I don't belong to the world. **17** Make them ready for your service through your truth; your teaching is truth. **18** I have sent them into the world, just as you sent me into the world. **19** For their sake, I am making myself ready to serve so that they can be ready for their service of the truth.

17:17
Truth
Is God's Word the truth?

20 "I pray for these followers, but I am also praying for all those who will believe in me because of their teaching. **21** Father, I pray that they can be one. As you are in me and I am in you, I pray that they can also be one in us. Then the world will believe that you sent me. **22** I have given these people the glory that you gave me so that they can be one, just as you and I are one. **23** I will be in them and you will be in me so that they will be completely one. Then the world will know that you sent me and that you loved them just as much as you loved me.

17:23
Salvation
What happens when you are saved?

24 "Father, I want these people that you gave me to be with me where I am. I want them to see my glory, which you gave me because you loved me before the world was made. **25** Father, you are the One who is good. The world does not know you, but I know you, and these people know you sent me. **26** I showed them what you are like, and I will show them again. Then they will have the same love that you have for me, and I will live in them."

Jesus is Arrested

18 When Jesus finished praying, he went with his followers across the Kidron Valley. On the other side there was a garden, and Jesus and his followers went into it.

2 Judas knew where this place was, because Jesus often met his followers there. Judas was the one who turned against Jesus. **3** So Judas came there with a group of soldiers and some guards from the leading priests and the Pharisees. They were carrying torches, lanterns and weapons.

4 Knowing everything that would happen to him, Jesus went out and asked, "Who is it you are looking for?"

5 They answered, "Jesus from Nazareth."

"I am he," Jesus said. (Judas, the one who turned against Jesus, was standing there with them.) **6** When Jesus said, "I am he," they moved back and fell to the ground.

7 Jesus asked them again, "Who is it you are looking for?"

They said, "Jesus of Nazareth."

8 "I told you that I am he," Jesus said. "So if you are looking for me, let the others go." **9** This happened so that the words Jesus said before would come true: "I have not lost any of the ones you gave me."

10 Simon Peter, who had a sword, pulled it out and struck the servant of the high priest, cutting off his right ear. (The servant's name was Malchus.) **11** Jesus said to Peter, "Put your sword back. Shouldn't I drink the cup[n] the Father gave me?"

Jesus is Brought Before Annas

12 Then the soldiers with their commander and the Jewish guards arrested Jesus. They tied him **13** and led him first

---

18:11 cup Jesus is talking about the terrible things that will happen to him. Accepting these things will be very hard, like drinking a cup of something bitter.

to Annas, the father-in-law of Caiaphas, the high priest that year. 14 Caiaphas was the one who had told the Jews that it would be better if one man died for all the people.

Peter Says He Doesn't Know Jesus

15 Simon Peter and another one of Jesus' followers went along after Jesus. This follower knew the high priest, so he went with Jesus into the high priest's courtyard. 16 But Peter waited outside near the door. The follower who knew the high priest came back outside, spoke to the girl at the door, and brought Peter inside. 17 The girl at the door said to Peter, "Aren't you also one of that man's followers?"

Peter answered, "No, I am not!"

18 It was cold, so the servants and guards had built a fire and were standing around it, warming themselves. Peter also was standing with them, warming himself.

The High Priest Questions Jesus

19 The high priest asked Jesus questions about his followers and his teaching. 20 Jesus answered, "I have spoken openly to everyone. I have always taught in synagogues and in the Temple, where all the Jews come together. I never said anything in secret. 21 So why do you question me? Ask the people who heard my teaching. They know what I said."

22 When Jesus said this, one of the guards standing there hit him. The guard said, "Is that the way you answer the high priest?"

23 Jesus answered him, "If I said something wrong, then say what it was. But if what I said is true, why do you hit me?"

24 Then Annas sent Jesus, who was still tied, to Caiaphas the high priest.

Peter Says Again He Doesn't Know Jesus

25 As Simon Peter was standing and warming himself, they said to him, "Aren't you one of that man's followers?"

Peter said it was not true; he said, "No, I am not."

26 One of the servants of the high priest was there. This servant was a relative of the man whose ear Peter had cut off. The servant said, "Didn't I see you with him in the garden?"

27 Again Peter said it wasn't true. At once a cockerel crowed.

Jesus is Brought Before Pilate

28 Early in the morning they led Jesus from Caiaphas' house to the Roman governor's palace. They would not go inside the palace, because they did not want to make themselves unclean;[n] they wanted to eat the Passover meal. 29 So Pilate went outside to them and asked, "What charges do you bring against this man?"

30 They answered, "If he were not a criminal, we wouldn't have brought him to you."

31 Pilate said to them, "Take him yourselves and judge him by your own law."

"But we are not allowed to put anyone to death," the Jews answered. 32 (This happened so that what Jesus said about how he would die would come true.)

33 Then Pilate went back inside the palace and called Jesus to him and asked, "Are you the king of the Jews?"

34 Jesus said, "Is that your own question, or did others tell you about me?"

35 Pilate answered, "I am not Jewish. It was your own people and their leading priests who handed you over to me. What have you done wrong?"

36 Jesus answered, "My kingdom does not belong to this world. If it belonged to this world, my servants would fight so that I would not be given over to the Jews. But my kingdom is from another place."

37 Pilate said, "So you are a king!"

Jesus answered, "You are the one saying I am a king. This is why I was born and came into the world: to tell people the truth. And everyone who belongs to the truth listens to me."

18:28 unclean Going into a non-Jewish place would make them unfit to eat the Passover Feast, according to Jewish law.

▶ John 18:38　1456

BIOGRAPHIES FROM EVERY VIEW　　　John 19

If they all tell about the life of Jesus, why are there four Gospels instead of just one? Maybe because each Gospel writer wrote to a different kind of person and for a different reason, so they explained Jesus' story a different way. Together, the four Gospels give us a better picture of who Jesus was than only one Gospel could have done.

Matthew wrote to the Jews to show them that Jesus was the Messiah promised in the Old Testament. Mark focused on Jesus as a servant who helped people. Luke wrote to Gentiles (non-Jewish people) to give the full story of Jesus' life, from his birth to the birth of the church. John emphasised who Jesus was, rather than what he did. John wanted his readers to understand that Jesus was God himself. (Read John 20:31.)

38 Pilate said, "What is truth?" After he said this, he went out to the Jews again and said to them, "I find nothing against this man. 39 But it is your custom that I free one prisoner to you at Passover time. Do you want me to free the 'king of the Jews'?"

40 They shouted back, "No, not him! Let Barabbas go free!" (Barabbas was a robber.)

19 Then Pilate ordered that Jesus be taken away and whipped. 2 The soldiers made a crown from some thorny branches and put it on Jesus' head and put a purple robe around him. 3 Then they came to him many times and said, "Hail, King of the Jews!" and hit him in the face.

4 Again Pilate came out and said to them, "Look, I am bringing Jesus out to you. I want you to know that I find nothing against him." 5 So Jesus came out, wearing the crown of thorns and the purple robe. Pilate said to them, "Here is the man!"

6 When the leading priests and the guards saw Jesus, they shouted, "Crucify him! Crucify him!"

But Pilate answered, "Crucify him yourselves, because I find nothing against him."

7 The Jews answered, "We have a law that says he should die, because he said he is the Son of God."

8 When Pilate heard this, he was even more afraid. 9 He went back inside the palace and asked Jesus, "Where do you come from?" But Jesus did not answer him. 10 Pilate said, "You refuse to speak to me? Don't you know I have power to set you free and power to have you crucified?"

11 Jesus answered, "The only power you have over me is the power given to you by God. The man who betrayed me to you is guilty of a greater sin."

12 After this, Pilate tried to let Jesus go. But the Jews cried out, "Anyone who makes himself king is against Caesar. If you let this man go, you are no friend of Caesar."

13 When Pilate heard what they were saying, he brought Jesus out and sat down on the judge's seat at the place called The Stone Pavement. (In the Jewish language*n* the name is Gabbatha.) 14 It was about noon on Preparation Day of Passover week. Pilate said to the Jews, "Here is your king!"

19:13 Jewish language Hebrew or Aramaic, the languages of the Jewish people in the first century.

15 They shouted, "Take him away! Take him away! Crucify him!"

Pilate asked them, "Do you want me to crucify your king?"

The leading priests answered, "The only king we have is Caesar."

16 So Pilate handed Jesus over to them to be crucified.

Jesus is Crucified

The soldiers took charge of Jesus. 17 Carrying his own cross, Jesus went out to a place called The Place of the Skull, which in the Jewish language[n] is called Golgotha. 18 There they crucified Jesus. They also crucified two other men, one on each side, with Jesus in the middle. 19 Pilate wrote a sign and put it on the cross. It read: JESUS OF NAZARETH, THE KING OF THE JEWS. 20 The sign was written in the Jewish language, in Latin and in Greek. Many of the Jews read the sign, because the place where Jesus was crucified was near the city. 21 The leading Jewish priests said to Pilate, "Don't write, 'The King of the Jews'. But write, 'This man said, "I am the King of the Jews."'"

22 Pilate answered, "What I have written, I have written."

23 After the soldiers crucified Jesus, they took his clothes and divided them into four parts, with each soldier getting one part. They also took his long shirt, which was all one piece of cloth, woven from top to bottom. 24 So the soldiers said to each other, "We should not tear this into parts. Let's throw lots to see who will get it." This happened so that this Scripture would come true:

"They divided my clothes among them,
and they threw lots for my clothing." *Psalm 22:18*

So the soldiers did this.

25 Standing near his cross were Jesus' mother, his mother's sister, Mary the wife of Clopas, and Mary Magdalene. 26 When Jesus saw his mother and the follower he loved standing nearby, he said to his mother, "Dear woman, here is your son." 27 Then he said to the follower, "Here is your mother." From that time on, the follower took her to live in his home.

Jesus Dies

28 After this, Jesus knew that everything had been done. So that the Scripture would come true, he said, "I am thirsty."[n] 29 There was a jar full of vinegar there, so the soldiers soaked a sponge in it, put the sponge on a branch of a hyssop plant and lifted it to Jesus' mouth. 30 When Jesus tasted the vinegar, he said, "It is finished." Then he bowed his head and died.

31 This day was Preparation Day, and the next day was a special Sabbath day. Since the Jews did not want the bodies to stay on the cross on the Sabbath day, they asked Pilate to order that the legs of the men be broken[n] and the bodies be taken away. 32 So the soldiers came and broke the legs of the first man on the cross beside Jesus. Then they broke the legs of the man on the other cross beside Jesus. 33 But when the soldiers came to Jesus and saw that he was already dead, they did not break his legs. 34 But one of the soldiers stuck his spear into Jesus' side, and at once blood and water came out. 35 (The one who saw this happen is the one who told us this, and whatever he says is true. And he knows that he tells the truth, and he tells it so that you might believe.) 36 These things happened to make the Scripture come true: "Not one of his bones will be broken."[n] 37 And another Scripture says, "They will look at the one they stabbed."[n]

Jesus is Buried

38 Later, Joseph from Arimathea asked Pilate if he could take the body of Jesus. (Joseph was a secret follower of Jesus, because he was afraid of the

---

19:17 Jewish language Hebrew or Aramaic, the languages of the Jewish people in the first century.
19:28 "I am thirsty." Read Psalms 22:15; 69:21.
19:31 broken The breaking of their bones would make them die sooner.
19:36 "Not one . . . broken." Quotation from Psalm 34:20. The idea is from Exodus 12:46; Numbers 9:12.
19:37 "They . . . stabbed." Quotation from Zechariah 12:10.

Jews.) Pilate gave his permission, so Joseph came and took Jesus' body away. 39 Nicodemus, who earlier had come to Jesus at night, went with Joseph. He brought about 30 kilogrammes of myrrh and aloes. 40 These two men took Jesus' body and wrapped it with the spices in pieces of linen cloth, which is how the Jewish people bury the dead. 41 In the place where Jesus was crucified, there was a garden. In the garden was a new tomb that had never been used before. 42 The men laid Jesus in that tomb because it was nearby, and the Jews were preparing to start their Sabbath day.

Jesus' Tomb is Empty

20 Early on the first day of the week, Mary Magdalene went to the tomb while it was still dark. When she saw that the large stone had been moved away from the tomb, 2 she ran to Simon Peter and the follower whom Jesus loved. Mary said, "They have taken the Lord out of the tomb, and we don't know where they have put him."

3 So Peter and the other follower started for the tomb. 4 They were both running, but the other follower ran faster than Peter and reached the tomb first. 5 He bent down and looked in and saw the strips of linen cloth lying there, but he did not go in. 6 Then, following him, Simon Peter arrived and went into the tomb and saw the strips of linen lying there. 7 He also saw the cloth that had been around Jesus' head, which was folded up and laid in a different place from the strips of linen. 8 Then the other follower, who had reached the tomb first, also went in. He saw and believed. 9 (They did not yet understand from the Scriptures that Jesus must rise from the dead.)

Jesus Appears to Mary Magdalene

10 Then the followers went back home. 11 But Mary stood outside the tomb, crying. As she was crying, she bent down and looked inside the tomb. 12 She saw two angels dressed in white, sitting where Jesus' body had been, one at the head and one at the feet.

13 They asked her, "Woman, why are you crying?"

She answered, "They have taken away my Lord, and I don't know where they have put him." 14 When Mary said this, she turned around and saw Jesus standing there, but she did not know it was Jesus.

15 Jesus asked her, "Woman, why are you crying? Whom are you looking for?"

Thinking he was the gardener, she said to him, "Did you take him away, sir? Tell me where you put him, and I will get him."

16 Jesus said to her, "Mary."

Mary turned towards Jesus and said in the Jewish language,* "Rabboni." (This means Teacher.)

17 Jesus said to her, "Don't hold on to me, because I have not yet gone up to the Father. But go to my brothers and tell them, 'I am going back to my Father and your Father, to my God and your God.'"

18 Mary Magdalene went and said to the followers, "I saw the Lord!" And she told them what Jesus had said to her.

Jesus Appears to His Followers

19 When it was evening on the first day of the week, the followers were together. The doors were locked, because they were afraid of the Jews. Then Jesus came and stood right in the middle of them and said, "Peace be with you." 20 After he said this, he showed them his hands and his side. The followers were thrilled when they saw the Lord.

21 Then Jesus said again, "Peace be with you. As the Father sent me, I now send you." 22 After he said this, he breathed on them and said, "Receive the Holy Spirit. 23 If you forgive anyone his sins, they are forgiven. If you don't forgive them, they are not forgiven."

Jesus Appears to Thomas

24 Thomas (called Didymus), who was one of the twelve, was not with them when

---

20:16 Jewish language Hebrew or Aramaic, the languages of the Jewish people in the first century.

Jesus came. 25 The other followers kept telling Thomas, "We saw the Lord."

But Thomas said, "I will not believe it until I see the nail marks in his hands and put my finger where the nails were and put my hand into his side."

26 A week later the followers were in the house again, and Thomas was with them. The doors were locked, but Jesus came in and stood right in the middle of them. He said, "Peace be with you." 27 Then he said to Thomas, "Put your finger here, and look at my hands. Put your hand here in my side. Stop being an unbeliever and believe."

28 Thomas said to him, "My Lord and my God!"

29 Then Jesus told him, "You believe because you see me. Those who believe without seeing me will be truly happy."

Why John Wrote this Book

30 Jesus did many other miracles in the presence of his followers that are not written in this book. 31 But these are written so that you may believe that Jesus is the Christ, the Son of God. Then, by believing, you may have life through his name.

Jesus Appears to Seven Followers

21 Later, Jesus showed himself to his followers again—this time at Lake Galilee.*n* This is how he showed himself: 2 some of the followers were together— Simon Peter, Thomas (called Didymus), Nathanael from Cana in Galilee, the two sons of Zebedee and two other followers. 3 Simon Peter said, "I am going out to fish."

The others said, "We will go with you." So they went out and got into the boat. They fished that night but caught nothing.

4 Early the next morning Jesus stood on the shore, but the followers did not know it was Jesus. 5 Then he said to them, "Friends, did you catch any fish?"

They answered, "No."

6 He said, "Throw your net on the right side of the boat, and you will find some." So they did, and they caught so many fish they could not pull the net back into the boat.

7 The follower whom Jesus loved said to Peter, "It is the Lord!" When Peter heard him say this, he wrapped his coat around himself. (Peter had taken his clothes off.) Then he jumped into the water. 8 The other followers went ashore in the boat, dragging the net full of fish. They were not very far from shore, only about a hundred yards. 9 When the followers stepped out of the boat and onto the shore, they saw a fire of hot coals. There were fish on the fire, and there was bread.

10 Then Jesus said, "Bring some of the fish you have just caught."

11 Simon Peter went into the boat and pulled the net to the shore. It was full of big fish, 153 in all, but even though there were so many, the net did not tear. 12 Jesus said to them, "Come and eat." None of the followers dared ask him, "Who are you?" because they knew it was the Lord. 13 Jesus came and took the bread and gave it to them, along with the fish.

14 This was now the third time Jesus showed himself to his followers after he was raised from the dead.

Jesus Talks to Peter

15 When they finished eating, Jesus said to Simon Peter, "Simon son of John, do you love me more than these?"

He answered, "Yes, Lord, you know that I love you."

Jesus said, "Feed my lambs."

16 Again Jesus said, "Simon son of John, do you love me?"

He answered, "Yes, Lord, you know that I love you."

Jesus said, "Take care of my sheep."

> Those who believe without seeing me will be truly happy.
> – John 20:29

21:1 **Lake Galilee** Literally, "Sea of Tiberias".

LET'S VISIT LAKE GALILEE   John 21

Lake Galilee is almost 13 miles long and about 8 miles wide. The water in it is fresh water, not salt water like in the sea. Because it is so large, sometimes it is referred to as the Sea of Galilee.

Jesus recruited 11 of his disciples from this area. Many of them were fishermen who worked in Lake Galilee. Because of where the lake is located, terrible storms can sweep down from the mountains creating sudden, violent storms. This is probably the type of storm that Jesus miraculously calmed for his disciples. (Check out Matthew 8:27, p. 1288.)

17 A third time he said, "Simon son of John, do you love me?"

Peter was hurt because Jesus asked him the third time, "Do you love me?" Peter said, "Lord, you know everything; you know that I love you!"

He said to him, "Feed my sheep. 18 I tell you the truth, when you were younger, you tied your own belt and went where you wanted. But when you are old, you will put out your hands and someone else will tie you and take you where you don't want to go." 19 (Jesus said this to show how Peter would die to give glory to God.) Then Jesus said to Peter, "Follow me!"

20 Peter turned and saw that the follower Jesus loved was walking behind them. (This was the follower who had leaned against Jesus at the supper and had said, "Lord, who will turn against you?") 21 When Peter saw him behind them, he asked Jesus, "Lord, what about him?"

22 Jesus answered, "If I want him to live until I come back, that is not your business. You follow me."

23 So a story spread among the followers that this one would not die. But Jesus did not say he would not die. He only said, "If I want him to live until I come back, that is not your business."

24 That follower is the one who is telling these things and who has now written them down. We know that what he says is true.

25 There are many other things Jesus did. If every one of them were written down, I suppose the whole world would not be big enough for all the books that would be written.

THE GOOD NEWS SPREADS

Hi, it's Luke again. You remember me, right? I wrote the Gospel of Luke. Here's a little secret that I'll let you in on now. I wrote the Gospel of Luke to tell my friend about what Jesus did. Well, I wrote Acts as part two of the story, to tell people what happened in the lives of Jesus' followers after he returned to heaven. Since I was Paul's travelling companion, I actually saw much of what I wrote about in this book. You'll notice that I use the word *we* when I joined Paul. (Check out Acts 16:10 to see when I joined Paul.)

I wrote this book because I wanted to record the happenings in the lives of Jesus' followers, who became known as Christians. (You can read up on that in Acts 11:19–26.) A lot of people call my book "The Acts of the Holy Spirit" because a lot of what happens in this book is the Holy Spirit working in the lives of Jesus' followers. What's really great about this book is that it's not finished. The acts of his followers are still happening today. Isn't that amazing? This book is still being written!

JESUS WATCH

The living Saviour is the theme of this book. Jesus is alive and well, living in the lives of the early believers, working and struggling with their relationship with him without being able to actually see him. Jesus is presented as both Lord and Saviour through the lives of his followers who do miracles, are persecuted, preach and travel searching for others who haven't heard about Jesus.

my FAVOURITE links

OTHER CONNECTIONS

Livin' it
What do you do with the money you have? For some sound advice on how to use your money, connect to Being Wise About Money, Acts 5:1–5.

Quick! Think of a person in your life who really gets on your nerves. How do you handle that kind of person? Download What *Am* I Going to Do? Acts 15:1–29, for some thoughts on this subject.

Check out these exciting people and places you'll find in the Book of Acts:

- Angels Watching Over Us, Acts 8. Find out about God's special messengers.
- Let's Visit Antioch, Acts 13:1–3. Stop here to find out what made this ancient city important to the early church.
- Let's Visit Athens, Acts 17:15—18:1. Find out more about this famous Greek capital when you link here.
- Let's Visit Philippi, Acts 20. Download the info here about the first European city to have a church.
- Did you know that Paul was a Roman citizen as well as an Israelite? Learn more about A Man of Two Countries, Acts 22.
- Trace the many journeys of Paul when you link to The Life of Paul, Acts 27; 28.

Did you hear about the man who fell asleep during one of Paul's sermons?

It must have been an incredibly long sermon! Did you know that he fell out of the window? Connect to Acts 20:6-12 to get the flash on that story!

did you know?

CHECK OUT THESE OTHER AMAZING THINGS THAT ARE RECORDED IN THIS BOOK:
Fire falls from the sky, Acts 2:1–13
Paul escapes in a basket, Acts 9:19–25
Peter's miraculous jailbreak, Acts 12:3–19
Shipwrecked! Acts 27

FAITH links

○ You've Got the Power!
Acts 1:1–8; 2:1–4

○ Flex Your Faith,
Acts 3:1–16

○ The Deadliest Lie,
Acts 5:1–11

○ Put God First,
Acts 5:27–32

○ My Best Serve,
Acts 6:1–6

○ The Person Most Likely to Give?
Acts 9:36–42

○ The Power of Prayer,
Acts 12:5

○ Kindness Counts,
Acts 14:3

○ You're Welcomed!
Acts 16:14–15

○ Hope That Doesn't Fail,
Acts 26:4–7

Acts 1:13 1463

Luke Writes Another Book

1 To Theophilus.
The first book I wrote was about everything Jesus began to do and teach 2 until the day he was taken up into heaven. Before this, with the help of the Holy Spirit, Jesus told the apostles he had chosen what they should do. 3 After his death, he showed himself to them and proved in many ways that he was alive. The apostles saw Jesus during the 40 days after he was raised from the dead, and he spoke to them about the kingdom of God. 4 Once when he was eating with them, he told them not to leave Jerusalem. He said, "Wait here to receive the promise from the Father which I told you about. 5 John baptised people with water, but in a few days you will be baptised with the Holy Spirit."

Jesus is Taken Up into Heaven

6 When the apostles were all together, they asked Jesus, "Lord, are you now going to give the kingdom back to Israel?"

7 Jesus said to them, "The Father is the only One who has the authority to decide dates and times. These things are not for you to know. 8 But when the Holy Spirit comes to you, you will receive power. You will be my witnesses—in Jerusalem, in all of Judea, in Samaria and in every part of the world."

1:8
Witnessing
Who are you to witness to?

9 After he said this, as they were watching, he was lifted up, and a cloud hid him from their sight. 10 As he was going, they were looking into the sky. Suddenly, two men wearing white clothes stood beside them. 11 They said, "Men of Galilee, why are you standing here looking into the sky? Jesus, whom you saw taken up from you into heaven, will come back in the same way you saw him go."

A New Apostle Is Chosen

12 Then they went back to Jerusalem from the Mount of Olives. (This mountain is about a kilometre from Jerusalem.) 13 When they entered the city, they went to the upstairs room where they were staying. Peter, John, James, Andrew, Philip, Thomas, Bartholomew, Matthew,

---

FAITH links

YOU'VE GOT THE POWER!
ACTS 1:1-8; 2:1-4

Could you lift a bus with your bare hands? Probably not. Yet you could lift one if you were behind the controls of a crane or a large tow truck. That would give you the power to do it.

Jesus told followers to wait in Jerusalem for the Holy Spirit to come. He knew that the Holy Spirit would give them the power to do the work that Jesus did. They couldn't do this work on their own. Neither can we. If you know Jesus, you've got the power – the Holy Spirit. He provides the strength you need to do what God wants you to do.

Download these links for more on the Holy Spirit:

The Sign of His Presence, Exodus 40:34–38, p. 130

Keep On Praying, 1 Samuel 1, p. 354

Empty Words, Ezekiel 33:30–33, p. 1127

Ask, Search, Knock, Matthew 7:7–10, p. 1286

Two Birthdays, John 3:1–7, p. 1426

Our Interpreter, Romans 8:26, p. 1528

James son of Alphaeus, Simon (known as the Zealot) and Judas son of James were there. 14 They all continued praying together with some women, including Mary the mother of Jesus, and Jesus' brothers.

15 During this time there was a meeting of the believers (about 120 of them). Peter stood up and said, 16-17 "Brothers and sisters,ⁿ in the Scriptures the Holy Spirit said through David something that must happen involving Judas. He was one of our own group and served together with us. He led those who arrested Jesus." 18 (Judas bought a field with the money he got for his evil act. But he fell to his death, his body burst open, and all his intestines poured out. 19 Everyone in Jerusalem learned about this so they named this place Akeldama. In their language Akeldama means "Field of Blood".) 20 "In the Book of Psalms," Peter said, "this is written:

'May his place be empty;
    leave no one to live in it.'   *Psalm 69:25*

And it is also written:

'Let another man replace him as
    leader.'   *Psalm 109:8*

21-22 "So now a man must become a witness with us of Jesus' being raised from the dead. He must be one of the men who were part of our group during all the time the Lord Jesus was among us—from the time John was baptising people until the day Jesus was taken up from us to heaven."

23 They put the names of two men before the group. One was Joseph Barsabbas, who was also called Justus. The other was Matthias. 24-25 The apostles prayed, "Lord, you know the thoughts of everyone. Show us which one of these two you have chosen to do this work. Show us who should be an apostle in place of Judas, who turned away and went where he belongs." 26 Then they used lots to choose between them, and the lots showed that Matthias was the one. So he became an apostle with the other eleven.

The Coming of the Holy Spirit

2 When the day of Pentecost came, they were all together in one place. 2 Suddenly a noise like a strong, blowing wind came from heaven and filled the whole house where they were sitting. 3 They saw something like flames of fire that were separated and stood over each person there. 4 They were all filled with the Holy Spirit, and they began to speak different languagesⁿ by the power the Holy Spirit was giving them.

5 There were some religious Jews staying in Jerusalem who were from every country in the world. 6 When they heard this noise, a crowd came together. They were all surprised, because each one heard them speaking in his own language. 7 They were completely amazed at this. They said, "Look! Aren't all these people that we hear speaking from Galilee? 8 Then how is it possible that we each hear them in our own languages? We are from different places: 9 Parthia, Media, Elam, Mesopotamia, Judea, Cappadocia, Pontus, Asia, 10 Phrygia, Pamphylia, Egypt, the areas of Libya near Cyrene, Rome 11 (both Jews and those who had become Jews), Crete and Arabia. But we hear them telling in our own languages about the great things God has done!" 12 They were all amazed and confused, asking each other, "What does this mean?"

13 But others were making fun of them, saying, "They have had too much wine."

Peter Speaks to the People

14 But Peter stood up with the eleven apostles, and in a loud voice he spoke to the crowd: "My fellow Jews, and all of you who are in Jerusalem, listen to me. Pay attention to what I have to say. 15 These people are not drunk, as you think; it is only nine o'clock in the morning! 16 But Joel the prophet wrote about what is happening here today:

17 'God says: In the last days

1:16-17 Brothers and sisters Although the Greek text says "brothers" here and throughout this book, these words of the speakers were meant for the entire church, both men and women.

2:4 languages This can also be translated "tongues."

> I will pour out my Spirit on all kinds of people.
> Your sons and daughters will prophesy.
> Your old men will dream dreams,
> and your young men will see visions.
> 18 At that time I will pour out my Spirit
> also on my male slaves and female slaves.
> 19 I will show miracles in the sky and on the earth:
> blood, fire and thick smoke.
> 20 The sun will become dark,
> the moon red as blood,
> before the overwhelming and terrible day of the LORD comes.
> 21 Then anyone who calls on the LORD will be saved.' *Joel 2:28-32*

22 "People of Israel, listen to these words: Jesus from Nazareth was a very special man. God clearly showed this to you by the miracles, wonders and signs he did through Jesus. You all know this, because it happened right here among you. 23 Jesus was given to you, and with the help of those who don't know the law, you put him to death by nailing him to a cross. But this was God's plan which he had made long ago; he knew all this would happen. 24 God raised Jesus from the dead and set him free from the pain of death, because death could not hold him. 25 For David said this about him:

> 'I keep the LORD before me always.
> Because he is close by my side,
> I will not be hurt.
> 26 So I rejoice and am glad.
> Even my body has hope,
> 27 because you will not leave me in the grave.
> You will not let your holy one rot.
> 28 You will teach me how to live a holy life.
> Being with you will fill me with joy.' *Psalm 16:8-11*

29 "Brothers and sisters, I can tell you truly that David, our ancestor, died and was buried. His grave is still here with us today. 30 He was a prophet and knew God had promised him that he would make a person from David's family a king just as he was.*[n]* 31 Knowing this before it happened, David talked about the Christ rising from the dead. He said:

> 'He was not left in the grave.
> His body did not rot.'

32 So Jesus is the One whom God raised from the dead. And we are all witnesses to this. 33 Jesus was lifted up to heaven and is now at God's right side. The Father has given the Holy Spirit to Jesus as he promised. So Jesus has poured out that Spirit, and this is what you now see and hear. 34 David was not the one who was lifted up to heaven, but he said:

> 'The LORD said to my Lord,
> "Sit by me at my right side,
> 35 until I put your enemies under your control."'*[n]* *Psalm 110:1*

36 "So, all the people of Israel should know this truly: God has made Jesus—the man you nailed to the cross—both Lord and Christ."

37 When the people heard this, they felt guilty and asked Peter and the other apostles, "What shall we do?"

eMAIL FROM GOD
2:37-38
Salvation
What to do when you are saved.

38 Peter said to them, "Change your hearts and lives and be baptised, each one of you, in the name of Jesus Christ for the forgiveness of your sins. And you will receive the gift of the Holy Spirit. 39 This promise is for you, for your children and for all who are far away. It is for everyone the Lord our God calls to himself."

40 Peter warned them with many other words. He begged them, "Save yourselves from the evil of today's people!" 41 Then those people who accepted what Peter said were baptised. About 3,000 people were added to the number of believers that day. 42 They spent their time learning the apostles' teaching,

---

2:30 God . . . was See 2 Samuel 7:13; Psalm 132:11.
2:35 until . . . control Literally, "until I make your enemies a footstool for your feet."

sharing, breaking bread^n and praying together.

The Believers Share

43 The apostles were doing many miracles and signs, and everyone felt great respect for God. 44 All the believers were together and shared everything. 45 They would sell their land and the things they owned and then divide the money and give it to anyone who needed it. 46 The believers met together in the Temple every day. They ate together in their homes, happy to share their food with joyful hearts. 47 They praised God and were liked by all the people. Every day the Lord added those who were being saved to the group of believers.

2:42–45 Money Share what you have with others.

Peter Heals a Crippled Man

3 One day Peter and John went to the Temple at three o'clock, the time set each day for the afternoon prayer service. 2 There, at the Temple gate called Beautiful Gate, was a man who had been crippled all his life. Every day he was carried to this gate to beg for money from the people going into the Temple. 3 The man saw Peter and John going into the Temple and asked them for money. 4 Peter and John looked straight at him and said, "Look at us!" 5 The man looked at them, thinking they were going to give him some money. 6 But Peter said, "I don't have any silver or gold, but I do have something else I can give you. By the power of Jesus Christ from Nazareth, stand up and walk!" 7 Then Peter took the man's right hand and lifted him up. Immediately the man's feet and ankles became strong. 8 He jumped up, stood on his feet and began to walk. He went into the Temple with them, walking and jumping and praising God. 9-10 All the people recognised him as the crippled man who always sat by the Beautiful Gate begging for money. Now they saw this same man walking and praising God, and they were amazed. They wondered how this could happen.

FAITH links

SHARE AND SHARE ALIKE?

ACTS 2:43-47

On a scale of 1 to 10 (10 being very willing), how willing are you to share what you have with others? Would you rank yourself at 8 or 9? Or are you a 3? If we're honest, most of us would say that we have moments when we don't feel like sharing. The first-century Christians believed in sharing everything they had. They shared food, money and other possessions with each other. What made them feel like sharing? God's love. Why not share some of God's love with someone today?

What do you have to give? Link here for more on giving:

Share What You Have, Exodus 35:5–18, p. 123

Give What You Can, Numbers 7:1–11, p. 186

A Small Percent, Deuteronomy 14:22–23, p. 247

Wisdom About Wealth, Ecclesiastes 5:10–12, p. 878

Your Heart's Desire, Luke 16:13–15, p. 1401

Give to Give, 1 Corinthians 16:1–4, p. 1566

2:42 breaking bread This may mean a meal as in verse 46, or the Lord's Supper, the special meal that Jesus told his followers to eat to remember him (Luke 22:14-20).

Peter Speaks to the People

11 While the man was holding on to Peter and John, all the people were amazed and ran to them at Solomon's Porch. 12 When Peter saw this, he said to them, "People of Israel, why are you surprised? You are looking at us as if it were our own power or goodness that made this man walk. 13 The God of Abraham, Isaac and Jacob, the God of our ancestors, gave glory to Jesus, his servant. But you handed him over to be killed. Pilate decided to let him go free, but you told Pilate you did not want Jesus. 14 You did not want the One who is holy and good but asked Pilate to give you a murderer[n] instead. 15 And so you killed the One who gives life, but God raised him from the dead. We are witnesses to this. 16 It was faith in Jesus that made this crippled man well. You can see this man, and you know him. He was made completely well because of trust in Jesus, and you all saw it happen!

17 "Brothers and sisters,[n] I know you did those things to Jesus because neither you nor your leaders understood what you were doing. 18 God said through the prophets that his Christ would suffer and die. And now God has made these things come true in this way. 19 So you must change your hearts and lives! Come back to God, and he will forgive your sins. Then the Lord will give you times of spiritual rest. 20 And he will send Jesus, the One he chose to be the Christ. 21 But Jesus must stay in heaven until the time comes when all things will be made right again. God told about this time long ago when he spoke through his holy prophets. 22 Moses said, 'The Lord your God will give you a prophet like me, who is one of your own people. You must listen to everything he tells you. 23 Anyone who does not listen to that prophet will die, cut off from God's people.'[n] 24 Samuel, and all the other prophets who spoke for God after Samuel, told about this time now. 25 You are descendants of the prophets. You have received the agreement God

Acts 3:25 1467

EMAIL FROM GOD
3:15
Jesus
What does Jesus give?

FAITH links

FLEX YOUR FAITH
ACTS 3:1-16

Imagine how you'd feel if someone suddenly solved a problem you'd had all your life. That's what happened to a lame man who begged for money outside of the Temple gate. Meeting Peter and John, two of Jesus' followers, changed his life. Through the power of the Holy Spirit, the lame man was healed. He had asked for money, but received something better.

Sometimes, God uses problems in our lives to help us grow in faith. Learning about the way God helps others also helps our faith to grow.

Learning to Trust, Psalm 25:4–5, p. 727

The Watchman, Ezekiel 3:16–22, p. 1088

Your Feet on High Places, Habakkuk 3:18–19, p. 1239

Tell All About Him! Matthew 28:19, p. 1326

The Way to Heaven, John 14:1–6, p. 1448

Out of Your Mind? 1 Corinthians 2:16, p. 1547

3:14 murderer Barabbas, the man the crowd asked Pilate to set free instead of Jesus (Luke 23:18). **3:17 Brothers and sisters** Although the Greek text says "brothers" here and throughout this book, Paul's words were meant for the entire church, including men and women. **3:22–23 'The Lord . . . people.'** Quotation from Deuteronomy 18:15,19.

made with your ancestors. He said to your father Abraham, 'Through your descendants all the nations on the earth will be blessed.'* 26 God has raised up his servant Jesus and sent him to you first to bless you by turning each of you away from doing evil."

Peter and John at the Council

4 While Peter and John were speaking to the people, Jewish priests, the captain of the soldiers that guarded the Temple and Sadducees came up to them. 2 They were upset because the two apostles were teaching the people and were preaching that people will rise from the dead through the power of Jesus. 3 The Jewish leaders grabbed Peter and John and put them in jail. Since it was already night, they kept them in jail until the next day. 4 But many of those who had heard Peter and John preach believed the things they said. There were now about 5,000 in the group of believers.

5 The next day the Jewish rulers, the Jewish elders and the teachers of the law met in Jerusalem. 6 Annas the high priest, Caiaphas, John and Alexander were there, as well as everyone from the high priest's family. 7 They made Peter and John stand before them and then asked them, "By what power or authority did you do this?"

8 Then Peter, filled with the Holy Spirit, said to them, "Rulers of the people and you elders, 9 are you questioning us about a good thing that was done to a crippled man? Are you asking us who made him well? 10 We want all of you and all the Jewish people to know that this man was made well by the power of Jesus Christ from Nazareth. You crucified him, but God raised him from the dead. This man was crippled, but he is now well and able to stand here before you because of the power of Jesus. 11 Jesus is

> 'the stone* that you builders rejected,
> which has become the
> cornerstone.' *Psalm 118:22*

12 Jesus is the only One who can save people. His name is the only power in the world that has been given to save people. We must be saved through him."

13 The Jewish leaders saw that Peter and John were not afraid to speak, and they understood that these men had no special training or education. So they were amazed. Then they realised that Peter and John had been with Jesus. 14 Because they saw the healed man standing there beside the two apostles, they could say nothing against them. 15 After the Jewish leaders ordered them to leave the meeting, they began to talk to each other. 16 They said, "What shall we do with these men? Everyone in Jerusalem knows they have done a great miracle, and we cannot say it is not true. 17 But to keep it from spreading among the people, we must warn them not to talk to people any more using that name."

18 So they called Peter and John in again and told them not to speak or to teach at all in the name of Jesus. 19 But Peter and John answered them, "You decide what God would want. Should we obey you or God? 20 We cannot keep quiet. We must speak about what we have seen and heard." 21 The Jewish leaders warned the apostles again and let them go free. They could not find a way to punish them, because all the people were praising God for what had been done. 22 The man who received the miracle of healing was more than 40 years old.

EMAIL FROM GOD
4:19–20
Responsibility
What are you responsible for?

The Believers Pray

23 After Peter and John left the meeting of Jewish leaders, they went to their own group and told them everything the leading priests and the Jewish elders had said to them. 24 When the believers heard this, they prayed to God together, "Lord, you are the One who made the sky, the earth, the sea and everything in them. 25 By the Holy Spirit, through our father David your servant, you said:

> 'Why are the nations so angry?

3:25 'Through . . . blessed.' Quotation from Genesis 22:18; 26:4.
4:11 stone A symbol meaning Jesus.

> Why are the people making
> useless plans?
> 26 The kings of the earth prepare to
> fight,
> and their leaders make plans
> together
> against the LORD
> and his appointed one. *Psalm 2:1-2*

27 These things really happened when Herod, Pontius Pilate, those who are not Jews and the Jewish people all came together against Jesus here in Jerusalem. Jesus is your holy servant, the One you made to be the Christ. 28 These people made your plan happen because of your power and your will. 29 And now, Lord, listen to their threats. Lord, help us, your servants, to speak your word without fear. 30 Help us to be brave by showing us your power to heal. Give proofs and make miracles happen by the power of Jesus, your holy servant."

31 After they had prayed, the place where they were meeting was shaken. They were all filled with the Holy Spirit, and they spoke God's word without fear.

The Believers Share

32 The group of believers were united in their hearts and spirit. All those in the group acted as though their private property belonged to everyone in the group. In fact, they shared everything. 33 With great power the apostles were telling people that the Lord Jesus was truly raised from the dead. And God blessed all the believers very much. 34 No one in the group needed anything. From time to time those who owned fields or houses sold them, brought the money, 35 and gave it to the apostles. Then the money was given to anyone who needed it.

36 One of the believers was named Joseph, a Levite born in Cyprus. The apostles called him Barnabas (which means "one who encourages"). 37 Joseph owned a field, sold it, brought the money and gave it to the apostles.

Ananias and Sapphira Die

5 But a man named Ananias and his wife Sapphira sold some land. 2 He kept back part of the money for himself; his wife knew about this and agreed to it. But he brought the rest of the money and gave it to the apostles. 3 Peter said, "Ananias, why did you let Satan rule your thoughts

---

FAITH links

AN ENERGY BOOST

ACTS 4:31

Some cartoon superheroes have to put on something special (like a costume) in order to gain their super powers. If they didn't have access to those items, they couldn't save the world!

The apostles had access to an amazing power far greater than any made-up superhero's. When the apostles asked God to show his power to them, he made the building shake and filled them with the Holy Spirit. That same power is available to us. God may not cause a building to shake when you pray. But the Holy Spirit can fill you with courage when you're afraid. Now, *that's* power!

Need a power boost? Connect here:

What Will You Risk? Joshua 2, p. 278

Good Times and Bad, 1 Kings 17, p. 462

A Message of Courage and Hope, 2 Kings 19:4–10, p. 505

999, Psalm 28:6, p. 730

Facing Your Fears, Matthew 8:23–27, p. 1288

Prayer Anywhere, Mark 1:35, p. 1331

Acts 5 1470

HANDLING MY MONEY
Acts 5:1–5

Being Wise About Money Imagine entering a contest and winning the grand prize of £1,000. Or maybe you received £100 for your birthday – from a rich relative you didn't know you had! What would you do with that money – spend it right away or save some of it? Would you give some of it away?

Just like everything else you have, your money is a blessing from God. God wants you to use your money wisely and think of it as another way to serve him and other people. (Check Ecclesiastes 5:10–12, p. 878.) Want to be wise about money? Don't make it the centre of your life.

MORE FAITH links
- Giving Your Part, **p. 173**
- Gifts from the Heart, **p. 557**
- Wisdom About Wealth, **p. 878**
- A Robbery in Progress, **p. 1270**
- Give from the Heart, **p. 1410**

If you got quite a bit of money for your birthday, what do you think you'd do with it?

Do you think you might want to buy lots of treats for you and your friends?

Maybe you'd better plan first how to spend your money. Check out these Faithlinks for some help.

Give What You Can, Numbers 7:1–11, p. 186
- Do you give some of your money as a church offering? What are some of the things that the offering money is used for? What if you don't have much money to give? We all have the responsibility to give what we can, whether it's money, time or help.

A Half-hearted Offering, Malachi 1:6–14, p. 1268
- How would you react if you asked your friend for a piece of chewing-gum and he offered you one he had already chewed? Yuck! This Faithlink tells how God feels about half-hearted offerings.

More Money? 1 Timothy 6:10, p. 1649
- What would you do if you won a million pounds? How do you think it would change your life? Can money make a person happy? Paul said that loving money leads to all kinds of evil. He didn't say *money* is sinful – but the love of it can make a person greedy. Money should be used wisely. How will you use your money?

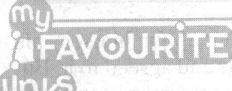

to lie to the Holy Spirit and to keep for yourself part of the money you received for the land? 4 Before you sold the land, it belonged to you. And even after you sold it, you could have used the money in any way you wanted. Why did you think of doing this? You lied to God, not to us!" 5-6 When Ananias heard this, he fell down and died. Some young men came in, wrapped up his body, carried it out and buried it. And everyone who heard about this was filled with fear.

7 About three hours later his wife came in, but she did not know what had happened. 8 Peter said to her, "Tell me, was the money you got for your field this much?"

Sapphira answered, "Yes, that was the price."

9 Peter said to her, "Why did you and your husband agree to test the Spirit of the Lord? Look! The men who buried your husband are at the door, and they will carry you out." 10 At that moment Sapphira fell down by his feet and died. When the young men came in and saw that she was dead, they carried her out and buried her beside her husband. 11 The whole church and all the others who heard about these things were filled with fear.

The Apostles Heal Many

12 The apostles did many signs and miracles among the people. And they would all meet together on Solomon's Porch. 13 None of the others dared to join them, but all the people respected them. 14 More and more men and women believed in the Lord and were added to the group of believers. 15 The people placed their sick on beds and mats in the streets, hoping that when Peter passed by at least his shadow might fall on them. 16 Crowds came from all the towns around Jerusalem, bringing their sick and those who were bothered by evil spirits, and all of them were healed.

Leaders Try to Stop the Apostles

17 The high priest and all his friends (a group called the Sadducees) became very jealous. 18 They took the apostles and put them in jail. 19 But during the night, an angel of the Lord opened the doors of the jail and led the apostles outside. The angel said, 20 "Go and stand in the Temple and tell the people everything about this new life." 21 When the apostles heard this, they obeyed and went into the Temple early in the morning and continued teaching.

When the high priest and his friends arrived, they called a meeting of the Jewish leaders and all the important Jewish elders. They sent some men to the jail to bring the apostles to them. 22 But, upon arriving, the officers could not find

---

FAITH links

THE DEADLIEST LIE
ACTS 5:1-11

One of the scariest stories in the Bible has to be the story of Ananias and Sapphira. Both lied to the apostle Peter about the price of some land that they sold. As the result of that lie, both died on the spot! That scared everyone!

God hates lying. (See Proverbs 6:17, p. 833.) He wants his followers to feel the same way. Do you hate it enough not to do it?

An Honest Reputation, Nehemiah 13:13, p. 644

Who Do You Prefer? Proverbs 3:32, p. 830

What's Wrong About Rumours, Jeremiah 29:24–32, p. 1032

The Whole Truth, John 8:31–32, 45, p. 1438

The Worst Chore, John 13:3–17, p. 1447

With All Your Heart, Colossians 3:23, p. 1626

the apostles. So they went back and reported to the Jewish leaders. 23 They said, "The jail was closed and locked, and the guards were standing at the doors. But when we opened the doors, the jail was empty!" 24 Hearing this, the captain of the Temple guards and the leading priests were confused and wondered what was happening.

25 Then someone came and told them, "Listen! The men you put in jail are standing in the Temple teaching the people." 26 Then the captain and his men went out and brought the apostles back. But the soldiers did not use force, because they were afraid the people would stone them to death.

27 The soldiers brought the apostles to the meeting and made them stand before the Jewish leaders. The high priest questioned them, 28 saying, "We gave you strict orders not to continue teaching in that name. But look, you have filled Jerusalem with your teaching and are trying to make us responsible for this man's death."

29 Peter and the other apostles answered, "We must obey God, not human authority! 30 You killed Jesus by hanging him on a cross. But God, the God of our ancestors, raised Jesus up from the dead! 31 Jesus is the One whom God raised to be on his right side, as Leader and Saviour. Through him, all Jewish people can change their hearts and lives and have their sins forgiven. 32 We saw all these things happen. The Holy Spirit, whom God has given to all who obey him, also proves these things are true."

33 When the Jewish leaders heard this, they became angry and wanted to kill them. 34 But a Pharisee named Gamaliel stood up in the meeting. He was a teacher of the law, and all the people respected him. He ordered the apostles to leave the meeting for a little while. 35 Then he said, "People of Israel, be careful what you are planning to do to these men. 36 Remember when Theudas appeared? He said he was a great man, and about 400 men joined him. But he was killed, and all his followers were scattered; they were able

eMAIL FROM GOD
5:29
Obedience
Check out who you should obey.

FAITH links

PUT GOD FIRST
ACTS 5:27-32

Sometimes you can get into trouble for doing the right thing. Peter and John, two followers of Jesus, were thrown into prison for healing a man at the Temple. The religious leaders demanded to know by whose authority they healed the man. After hearing that Jesus helped them, Peter and John were told not to talk to people in Jesus' name. They chose to obey God, rather than do what the leaders told them to do.

God wants you to obey people in authority. But he wants you to obey him first of all. Put God first!

God wants to be No. 1 in your life. Link here to find out more:

Following the Crowd, Numbers 13; 14, p. 193

I'll Never Forget What's-His-Name, Deuteronomy 8, p. 239

A Hopeful Future, Jeremiah 29:11, p. 1031

A Blueprint for Living, Amos 5:14-15, p. 1200

The Choices of a Choice, Luke 5:1-11, p. 1375

Keeping Clean, 2 Corinthians 7:1, p. 1576

to do nothing. 37 Later, a man named Judas came from Galilee at the time of the registration." He also led a group of followers and was killed, and all his followers were scattered. 38 And so now I tell you: stay away from these men, and leave them alone. If their plan comes from human authority, it will fail. 39 But if it is from God, you will not be able to stop them. You might even be fighting against God himself!"

The Jewish leaders agreed with what Gamaliel said. 40 They called the apostles in, beat them and told them not to speak in the name of Jesus again. Then they let them go free. 41 The apostles left the meeting full of joy because they were given the honour of suffering disgrace for Jesus. 42 Every day in the Temple and in people's homes they continued teaching the people and telling the Good News—that Jesus is the Christ.

Seven Leaders are Chosen

6 The number of followers was growing. But during this same time, the Greek-speaking followers had an argument with the other Jewish followers. The Greek-speaking widows were not getting their share of the food that was given out every day. 2 The twelve apostles called the whole group of followers together and said, "It is not right for us to stop our work of teaching God's word in order to serve tables. 3 So, brothers and sisters, choose seven of your own men who are good, full of the Spirit and full of wisdom. We will put them in charge of this work. 4 Then we can continue to pray and to teach the word of God."

5 The whole group liked the idea, so they chose these seven men: Stephen (a man with great faith and full of the Holy Spirit), Philip," Procorus, Nicanor, Timon, Parmenas and Nicolas (a man from Antioch who had become a Jew). 6 Then they put these men before the apostles, who prayed and laid their hands on" them.

7 The word of God was continuing to spread. The group of followers in Jerusalem increased, and a great number of the Jewish priests believed and obeyed.

FAITH links

MY BEST SERVE
ACTS 6:1-6

Christians in the first century had a problem. The poor weren't being helped. But the apostles had too much work to do. They wanted to be able to preach and teach. So, how did they solve the problem? They chose other believers to help with the work.

God wants his people to work together. One person should not be expected to do everything. Each person in the church is good at something and is important to the church. What are you good at? How can you help out in your church?

Everyone Can Help, **Numbers 4, p. 181**

Your Response to Responsibility, **Ruth 2:1–7, p. 346**

Your Best Work, **1 Kings 6, p. 443**

Operation Co-operation, **Ezra 1:5, p. 609**

The Way to Greatness, **Matthew 20:20–28, p. 1309**

Help for the Body, **Romans 12:3–8, p. 1536**

5:37 registration Census. A counting of all the people and the things they own.
6:5 Philip Not the apostle named Philip.
6:6 laid their hands on The laying on of hands had many purposes, including the giving of a blessing, power or authority.

Stephen is Accused

8 Stephen was richly blessed by God who gave him the power to do great miracles and signs among the people. 9 But some Jewish people were against him. They belonged to the synagogue of Free Men[n] (as it was called), which included Jewish people from Cyrene, Alexandria, Cilicia and Asia. They all came and argued with Stephen.

10 But the Spirit was helping him to speak with wisdom, and his words were so strong that they could not argue with him. 11 So they secretly urged some men to say, "We heard Stephen speak against Moses and against God."

12 This upset the people, the Jewish elders and the teachers of the law. They came and grabbed Stephen and brought him to a meeting of the Jewish leaders. 13 They brought in some people to tell lies about Stephen, saying, "This man is always speaking against this holy place and the law of Moses. 14 We heard him say that Jesus from Nazareth will destroy this place and that Jesus will change the customs Moses gave us." 15 All the people in the meeting were watching Stephen closely and saw that his face looked like the face of an angel.

Stephen's Speech

7 The high priest said to Stephen, "Are these things true?"

2 Stephen answered, "Brothers and fathers, listen to me. Our glorious God appeared to Abraham, our ancestor, in Mesopotamia before he lived in Haran. 3 God said to Abraham, 'Leave your country and your relatives, and go to the land I will show you.'[n] 4 So Abraham left the country of Chaldea and went to live in Haran. After Abraham's father died, God sent him to this place where you now live. 5 God did not give Abraham any of this land, not even a foot of it. But God promised that he would give this land to him and his descendants, even before Abraham had a child. 6 This is what God said to him: 'Your descendants will be strangers in a land they don't own. The people there will make them slaves and will mistreat them for 400 years. 7 But I will punish the nation where they are slaves. Then your descendants will leave that land and will worship me in this place.'[n] 8 God made an agreement with Abraham, the sign of which was circumcision. And so when Abraham had his son, Isaac, Abraham circumcised him when he was eight days old. Isaac also circumcised his son, Jacob, and Jacob did the same for his sons, the twelve ancestors[n] of our people.

9 "Jacob's sons became jealous of Joseph and sold him to be a slave in Egypt. But God was with him 10 and saved him from all his troubles. The king of Egypt liked Joseph and respected him because of the wisdom God gave him. The king made him governor of Egypt and put him in charge of all the people in his palace.

11 "Then all the land of Egypt and Canaan became so dry that nothing would grow, and the people suffered very much. Jacob's sons, our ancestors, could not find anything to eat. 12 But when Jacob heard there was grain in Egypt, he sent his sons there. This was their first trip to Egypt. 13 When they went there a second time, Joseph told his brothers who he was, and the king learned about Joseph's family. 14 Then Joseph sent messengers to invite Jacob, his father, to come to Egypt along with all his relatives (75 persons altogether). 15 So Jacob went down to Egypt, where he and his sons died. 16 Later their bodies were moved to Shechem and put in a grave there. (It was the same grave Abraham had bought for a sum of money from the sons of Hamor in Shechem.)

7:9 Jealousy What can jealousy cause?

6:9 Free Men Jewish people who had been slaves or whose fathers had been slaves, but who were now free.

7:3 'Leave . . . you.' Quotation from Genesis 12:1.

7:7 'Your descendants . . . place.' Quotation from Genesis 15:13-14 and Exodus 3:12.

7:8 twelve ancestors Important ancestors of the Jewish people; the leaders of the twelve Jewish tribes.

Acts 7:43 1475

17 "The promise God made to Abraham was soon to come true, and the number of people in Egypt grew large. 18 Then a new king, who did not know who Joseph was, began to rule Egypt. 19 This king tricked our people and was cruel to our ancestors, forcing them to leave their babies outside to die. 20 At this time Moses was born, and he was very beautiful. For three months Moses was cared for in his father's house. 21 When they put Moses outside, the king's daughter adopted him and raised him as if he were her own son. 22 The Egyptians taught Moses everything they knew, and he was a powerful man in what he said and did.

23 "When Moses was about 40 years old, he thought it would be good to visit his own people, the people of Israel. 24 Moses saw an Egyptian mistreating an Israelite, so he defended the Israelite and punished the Egyptian by killing him. 25 Moses thought his own people would understand that God was using him to save them, but they did not. 26 The next day when Moses saw two men of Israel fighting, he tried to make peace between them. He said, 'Men, you are brothers. Why are you hurting each other?' 27 The man who was hurting the other pushed Moses away and said, 'Who made you our ruler and judge? 28 Are you going to kill me as you killed the Egyptian yesterday?'*ⁿ* 29 When Moses heard him say this, he left Egypt and went to live in the land of Midian where he was a stranger. While Moses lived in Midian, he had two sons.

30 "Forty years later an angel appeared to Moses in the flames of a burning bush as he was in the desert near Mount Sinai. 31 When Moses saw this, he was amazed and went near to look closer. Moses heard the Lord's voice say, 32 'I am the God of your ancestors, the God of Abraham, Isaac and Jacob.'*ⁿ* Moses began to shake with fear and was afraid to look. 33 The Lord said to him, 'Take off your sandals, because you are standing on holy ground. 34 I have seen the troubles my people have suffered in Egypt. I have heard their cries and have come down to save them. And now, Moses, I am sending you back to Egypt.'*ⁿ*

35 "This Moses was the same man the two men of Israel rejected, saying, 'Who made you a ruler and judge?'*ⁿ* Moses is the same man God sent to be a ruler and saviour, with the help of the angel that Moses saw in the burning bush. 36 So Moses led the people out of Egypt. He worked miracles and signs in Egypt, at the Red Sea and then in the desert for 40 years. 37 This is the same Moses that said to the people of Israel, 'God will give you a prophet like me, who is one of your own people.'*ⁿ* 38 This is the Moses who was with the gathering of the Israelites in the desert. He was with the angel that spoke to him at Mount Sinai, and he was with our ancestors. He received commands from God that give life, and he gave those commands to us.

39 "But our ancestors did not want to obey Moses. They rejected him and wanted to go back to Egypt. 40 They said to Aaron, 'Make us gods who will lead us. Moses led us out of Egypt, but we don't know what has happened to him.'*ⁿ* 41 So the people made an idol that looked like a calf. Then they brought sacrifices to it and were proud of what they had made with their own hands. 42 But God turned against them and did not try to stop them from worshipping the sun, moon and stars. This is what is written in the book of the prophets: God says,

'People of Israel, you did not bring
    me sacrifices and offerings
while you travelled in the desert
    for 40 years.
43 You have carried with you
    your king, the god Sakkuth,

7:28 **'Who . . . yesterday?'** Quotation from Exodus 2:14.

7:32 **'I am . . . Jacob.'** Quotation from Exodus 3:6.

7:34 **'Take . . . Egypt.'** Quotation from Exodus 3:5-10.

7:35 **'Who . . . judge?'** Quotation from Exodus 2:14.

7:37 **'God . . . people.'** Quotation from Deuteronomy 18:15.

7:40 **'Make . . . him.'** Quotation from Exodus 32:1.

and Kaiwan your idol
and the star gods you have made.
So I will send you away as captives
    beyond Damascus.'   *Amos 5:25-27*

44 "The Holy Tent where God spoke to our ancestors was with them in the desert. God told Moses how to make this Tent, and he made it like the plan God showed him. 45 Later, Joshua led our ancestors to capture the lands of the other nations. Our people went in, and God forced the other people out. When our people went into this new land, they took with them this same Tent they had received from their ancestors. They kept it until the time of David, 46 who pleased God and asked God to let him build a house for him, the God of Jacob. 47 But Solomon was the one who built the Temple.

48 "But the Most High does not live in houses that people build with their hands. As the prophet says:
49 'Heaven is my throne,
    and the earth is my footstool.
So do you think you can build a
    house for me? says the Lord.
Do I need a place to rest?
50 Remember, my hand made all these
    things!'"   *Isaiah 66:1-2*

51 Stephen continued speaking: "You stubborn people! You have not given your hearts to God, nor will you listen to him! You are always against what the Holy Spirit is trying to tell you, just as your ancestors were. 52 Your ancestors tried to hurt every prophet who ever lived. Those prophets said long ago that the One who is good would come, but your ancestors killed them. And now you have turned against and killed the One who is good. 53 You received the law of Moses, which God gave you through his angels, but you haven't obeyed it."

Stephen is Killed

54 When the leaders heard this, they became furious. They were so cross they were grinding their teeth at Stephen. 55 But Stephen was full of the Holy Spirit. He looked up to heaven and saw the glory of God and Jesus standing at God's right side. 56 He said, "Look! I see heaven open and the Son of Man standing at God's right side."

57 Then they shouted loudly and covered their ears and all ran at Stephen. 58 They took him out of the city and began to throw stones at him to kill him. And those who told lies against Stephen left their coats with a young man named Saul. 59 While they were throwing stones, Stephen prayed, "Lord Jesus, receive my spirit." 60 He fell on his knees and cried in a loud voice, "Lord, do not hold this sin against them." After Stephen said this, he died.

8 Saul agreed that the killing of Stephen was good.

Troubles for the Believers

On that day the church of Jerusalem began to be persecuted, and all the believers, except the apostles, were scattered throughout Judea and Samaria.

2 And some religious people buried Stephen and cried loudly for him. 3 Saul was also trying to destroy the church, going from house to house, dragging out men and women and putting them in jail. 4 And wherever they were scattered, they told people the Good News.

Philip Preaches in Samaria

5 Philip[n] went to the city of Samaria and preached about the Christ. 6 When the people there heard Philip and saw the miracles he was doing, they all listened carefully to what he said. 7 Many of these people had evil spirits in them, but Philip made the evil spirits leave. The spirits made a loud noise when they came out. Philip also healed many weak and crippled people there. 8 So the people in that city were very happy.

9 But there was a man named Simon in that city. Before Philip came there, Simon had practised magic and amazed all the people of Samaria. He boasted and called himself a great man. 10 All the people—the least important to the most important—paid attention to Simon, saying, "This man has the power of God, called 'the Great Power!'" 11 Simon had amazed

---

8:5 Philip Not the apostle named Philip.

Get the Info

ANGELS WATCHING OVER US — Acts 8

In the New Testament, angels are special messengers for God. (See Hebrews 1:14, p. 1668.) An angel named Gabriel brought the news to Mary that she would give birth to Jesus, the Messiah. (Look at Luke 1:26–38, p. 1365.) Besides passing along messages, angels were also used by God to guide and protect his children. On several occasions, angels assisted Jesus during his ministry on earth. For example, angels helped Jesus while he was in the desert (Matthew 4:11, p. 1279) and helped roll away the stone from the tomb (Matthew 28:2–6, p. 1326). Angels still exist today and still do God's work. We don't always see them, but they are there.

Here are some New Testament events that involved angels:

Event	Reference
An angel told Zechariah about the birth of his son	Luke 1:11–20, p. 1365
An angel warned Joseph about Herod's plan to kill Jesus; told Joseph about Herod's death	Matthew 2:13, 19–20, p. 1276
Angels announced Jesus' birth to shepherds	Luke 2:8–15, p. 1368
Angels helped Jesus during his temptation	Matthew 4:11, p. 1279
Angels opened the grave and announced Jesus' resurrection	Matthew 28:2–7, p. 1326
An angel sent Philip into the desert to meet the eunuch	Acts 8:26–27, p. 1478
An angel instructed Cornelius to send for Peter	Acts 10:3–8, p. 1481
An angel released Peter from prison	Acts 12:7, p. 1485
An angel made Herod sick	Acts 12:23, p. 1486
An angel reassured Paul in a storm	Acts 27:23–24, p. 1512

them with his magic so long that the people became his followers. 12 But when Philip told them the Good News about the kingdom of God and the power of Jesus Christ, men and women believed Philip and were baptised. 13 Simon himself believed, and after he was baptised, he stayed very close to Philip. When he saw the miracles and the powerful things Philip did, Simon was amazed.

14 When the apostles who were still in Jerusalem heard that the people of Samaria had accepted the word of God, they sent Peter and John to them. 15 When Peter and John arrived, they prayed that the Samaritan believers might receive the Holy Spirit. 16 These people had been baptised in the name of the Lord Jesus, but the Holy Spirit had not yet come upon any of them. 17 Then, when the two apostles began laying their hands on[n] the people, they received the Holy Spirit.

18 Simon saw that the Spirit was given to people when the apostles laid their hands on them. So he offered the apostles money, 19 saying, "Give me also this power so that anyone on whom I lay my hands will receive the Holy Spirit."

20 Peter said to him, "You and your money should both be destroyed, because you thought you could buy God's gift with money. 21 You cannot share with us in this work since your heart is not right before God. 22 Change your heart! Turn away from this evil thing you have done, and pray to the Lord. Maybe he will forgive you for thinking this. 23 I see that you are full of bitter jealousy and ruled by sin."

24 Simon answered, "Both of you pray for me to the Lord so the things you have said will not happen to me."

25 After Peter and John told the people what they had seen Jesus do and after they had spoken the message of the Lord, they went back to Jerusalem. On the way, they went through many Samaritan towns and preached the Good News to the people.

Philip Teaches an Ethiopian

26 An angel of the Lord said to Philip,[n] "Get ready and go south to the road that leads down to Gaza from Jerusalem—the desert road." 27 So Philip got ready and went. On the road he saw a man from Ethiopia, a eunuch. He was an important officer in the service of Candace, the queen of the Ethiopians; he was responsible for taking care of all her money. He had gone to Jerusalem to worship. 28 Now, as he was on his way home, he was sitting in his chariot reading from the Book of Isaiah, the prophet. 29 The Spirit said to Philip, "Go to that chariot and stay near it."

30 So when Philip ran towards the chariot, he heard the man reading from Isaiah the prophet. Philip asked, "Do you understand what you are reading?"

31 He answered, "How can I understand unless someone explains it to me?" Then he invited Philip to climb in and sit with him. 32 The portion of Scripture he was reading was this:

"He was like a sheep being led to be killed.

He was quiet, as a lamb is quiet while its wool is being cut;
he never opened his mouth.

33   He was shamed and was treated unfairly.

He died without children to continue his family.

His life on earth has ended."

Isaiah 53:7-8

34 The officer said to Philip, "Please tell me, who is the prophet talking about—himself or someone else?" 35 Philip began to speak, and starting with this same Scripture, he told the man the Good News about Jesus.

36 While they were travelling down the road, they came to some water. The officer said, "Look, here is water. Why shouldn't I be baptised?" 37[n] 38 Then the officer commanded the chariot to stop. Both Philip and the officer went down into the water, and Philip baptised him. 39 When they came up out of the water, the Spirit of the Lord took Philip away; the officer never saw him again. And the officer continued on his way home, full of joy. 40 But Philip appeared in a city called Azotus and preached the Good News in all the towns on the way from Azotus to Caesarea.

Saul is Converted

9 In Jerusalem Saul was still threatening the followers of the Lord by saying he would kill them. So he went to the

---

8:17 laying their hands on The laying on of hands had many purposes, including the giving of a blessing, power or authority.

8:26 Philip Not the apostle named Philip.

8:37 Verse 37 Some late copies of Acts add verse 37: "Philip answered, 'If you believe with all your heart, you can.' The officer said, 'I believe that Jesus Christ is the Son of God.'"

high priest 2 and asked him to write letters to the synagogues in the city of Damascus. Then if Saul found any followers of Christ's Way, men or women, he would arrest them and bring them back to Jerusalem.

3 So Saul headed towards Damascus. As he came near the city, a bright light from heaven suddenly flashed around him. 4 Saul fell to the ground and heard a voice saying to him, "Saul, Saul! Why are you persecuting me?"

5 Saul said, "Who are you, Lord?"

The voice answered, "I am Jesus, whom you are persecuting. 6 Get up now and go into the city. Someone there will tell you what you must do."

7 The people travelling with Saul stood there but said nothing. They heard the voice, but they saw no one. 8 Saul got up from the ground and opened his eyes, but he could not see. So those with Saul took his hand and led him into Damascus. 9 For three days Saul could not see and did not eat or drink.

10 There was a follower of Jesus in Damascus named Ananias. The Lord spoke to Ananias in a vision, "Ananias!"

Ananias answered, "Here I am, Lord."

11 The Lord said to him, "Get up and go to Straight Street. Find the house of Judas,*n* and ask for a man named Saul from the city of Tarsus. He is there now, praying. 12 Saul has seen a vision in which a man named Ananias comes to him and lays his hands on him. Then he is able to see again."

13 But Ananias answered, "Lord, many people have told me about this man and the terrible things he did to your holy people in Jerusalem. 14 Now he has come here to Damascus, and the leading priests have given him the power to arrest everyone who worships you."

15 But the Lord said to Ananias, "Go! I have chosen Saul for an important work. He must tell about me to those who are not Jews, to kings and to the people of Israel. 16 I will show him how much he must suffer for my name."

17 So Ananias went to the house of Judas. He laid his hands on*n* Saul and said, "Brother Saul, the Lord Jesus sent me. He is the one you saw on the road on your way here. He sent me so that you can see again and be filled with the Holy Spirit." 18 Immediately, something that looked like fish scales fell from Saul's eyes, and he was able to see again! Then Saul got up and was baptised. 19 After he ate some food, his strength returned.

Saul Preaches in Damascus

Saul stayed with the followers of Jesus in Damascus for a few days. 20 Soon he began to preach about Jesus in the synagogues, saying, "Jesus is the Son of God."

21 All the people who heard him were amazed. They said, "This is the man who was in Jerusalem trying to destroy those who trust in this name! He came here to arrest the followers of Jesus and take them back to the leading priests."

22 But Saul grew more powerful. His proofs that Jesus is the Christ were so strong that the Jewish people in Damascus could not argue with him.

23 After many days, some Jewish people made plans to kill Saul. 24 They were watching the city gates day and night, but Saul learned about their plan. 25 One night some followers of Saul helped him leave the city by lowering him in a basket through an opening in the city wall.

Saul Preaches in Jerusalem

26 When Saul went to Jerusalem, he tried to join the group of followers, but they were all afraid of him. They did not believe he was really a follower. 27 But Barnabas accepted Saul and took him to the apostles. Barnabas explained to them that Saul had seen the Lord on the road and the Lord had spoken to Saul. Then he told them how boldly Saul had preached in the name of Jesus in Damascus.

28 And so Saul stayed with the followers, going everywhere in Jerusalem, preaching boldly in the name of the Lord. 29 He would often talk and argue with the Jewish people who spoke Greek, but they

---

9:11 Judas This is not either of the apostles named Judas.

9:17 laid his hands on The laying on of hands had many purposes, including the giving of a blessing, power or authority.

▶ Acts 9:30 1480

A FRIEND IN NEED
ACTS 9:27

How would you react if the meanest person you know suddenly became nice? Saul, who later became known as the apostle Paul, used to be an enemy of Christians. But, one day, he became a follower of Jesus. He needed a friend to teach him more about Jesus and to show the other believers that he could be trusted. Barnabas was that friend. God looks for people who are willing to befriend those who need Jesus. Are you willing?

Link here to find out more about sharing Jesus with your friends:

The Gift of Friendship,
1 Samuel 18:1–3; 19, p. 381

A Life-Saving Message, Esther 2:19–22, p. 650

Jesus' Mission and Yours, Isaiah 61:1–2, p. 978

Tell All About Him! Matthew 28:19, p. 1326

Quick to Forgive? Mark 11:25, p. 1349

As Strong as Superman? Philippians 4:13, p. 1615

were trying to kill him. 30 When the followers learned about this, they took Saul to Caesarea and from there sent him to Tarsus.

31 The church everywhere in Judea, Galilee and Samaria had a time of peace

9:31
Encouragement
Who is your source of encouragement?

and became stronger. Respecting the Lord by the way they lived, and being encouraged by the Holy Spirit, the group of believers continued to grow.

Peter Heals Aeneas

32 As Peter was travelling through all the area, he visited God's people who lived in Lydda. 33 There he met a man named Aeneas, who was paralysed and had not been able to leave his bed for the past eight years. 34 Peter said to him, "Aeneas, Jesus Christ heals you. Stand up and make your bed." Aeneas stood up immediately. 35 All the people living in Lydda and on the Plain of Sharon saw him and turned to the Lord.

Peter Heals Tabitha

36 In the city of Joppa there was a follower named Tabitha (whose Greek name was Dorcas). She was always doing good deeds and kind acts. 37 While Peter was in Lydda, Tabitha became sick and died. Her body was washed and put in a room upstairs. 38 Since Lydda is near Joppa and the followers in Joppa heard that Peter was in Lydda, they sent two messengers to Peter. They begged him, "Hurry, please come to us!" 39 So Peter got ready and went with them. When he arrived, they took him to the upstairs room where all the widows stood around Peter, crying. They showed him the shirts and coats Tabitha had made when she was still alive. 40 Peter sent everyone out of the room and kneeled and prayed. Then he turned to the body and said, "Tabitha, stand up." She opened her eyes, and when she saw Peter, she sat up. 41 He gave her his hand and helped her up. Then he called the saints and the widows into the room and showed them that Tabitha was alive. 42 People everywhere in Joppa learned about this, and many believed in the Lord. 43 Peter stayed in Joppa for many days with a man named Simon who was a leatherworker.

FAITH links

THE PERSON MOST LIKELY TO GIVE?
ACTS 9:36-42

Who is the kindest, most giving person you know? If the Christians in Joppa were asked this question, they would say Tabitha. Tabitha, also called Dorcas, used her sewing ability to give to others. Because she was so loving to her community, the people in the town made a special request of the apostle Peter. When she died, he brought her back to life through the Holy Spirit!

Tabitha's selfless giving is an example for any Christian. Even if you don't know how to sew on a button, you can still use your abilities to help someone.

Giving Your Part, Leviticus 27:30, p. 173

Show You Care, 2 Kings 4:10, p. 481

Service with a Smile, 1 Chronicles 6:31–49, p. 527

My Favourite! Mark 10:17–23, p. 1347

Share and Share Alike? Acts 2:43–47, p. 1466

Give to Give, 1 Corinthians 16:1–4, p. 1566

Peter Teaches Cornelius

10 At Caesarea there was a man named Cornelius, an officer in the Italian group of the Roman army. 2 Cornelius was a religious man. He and all the other people who lived in his house worshipped the true God. He gave much of his money to the poor and prayed to God often. 3 One afternoon about three o'clock, Cornelius clearly saw a vision. An angel of God came to him and said, "Cornelius!"

4 Cornelius stared at the angel. He became afraid and said, "What do you want, Lord?"

The angel said, "God has heard your prayers. He has seen that you give to the poor, and he remembers you. 5 Send some men now to Joppa to bring back a man named Simon who is also called Peter. 6 He is staying with a man, also named Simon, who is a leatherworker and has a house beside the sea." 7 When the angel who spoke to Cornelius left, Cornelius called two of his servants and a soldier, a religious man who worked for him. 8 Cornelius explained everything to them and sent them to Joppa.

9 About noon the next day as they came near Joppa, Peter was going up to the roof[n] to pray. 10 He was hungry and wanted to eat, but while the food was being prepared, he had a vision. 11 He saw heaven opened and something coming down that looked like a big sheet being lowered to earth by its four corners. 12 In it were all kinds of animals, reptiles and birds. 13 Then a voice said to Peter, "Get up, Peter; kill and eat."

14 But Peter said, "No, Lord! I have never eaten food that is unholy or unclean."

15 But the voice said to him again, "God has made these things clean so don't call them 'unholy'!" 16 This happened three times, and at once the sheet was taken back to heaven.

17 While Peter was wondering what this vision meant, the men Cornelius sent had found Simon's house and were

---

10:9 roof In Bible times houses were built with flat roofs. The roof was used for drying things such as flax and fruit. And it was used as an extra room, as a place for worship and as a place to sleep in the summer.

FAITH links

ONE OF THE FAITHFUL
ACTS 10:1-34

Cornelius was a Roman army officer who served God by his faithfulness in giving generously to the poor and in prayer. Faithfulness is a quality that few may acknowledge. Yet everyone benefits from a faithful giver. God rewarded Cornelius's faithfulness by using him to help Peter understand that God loves *all* people, not just the Jews.

How faithful are you in giving? Connect to these links for help:

Giving Your Part, Leviticus 27:30, p. 173

Give What You Can, Numbers 7:1–11, p. 186

Too Young to Serve, Jeremiah 1:4–9, p. 988

Go! No! Jonah 1, p. 1213

Give from the Heart, Luke 21:1–4, p. 1410

Give Till It Hurts? 2 Corinthians 8:6–9; 9:6–9, p. 1578

---

standing at the gate. 18 They asked, "Is Simon Peter staying here?"

19 While Peter was still thinking about the vision, the Spirit said to him, "Listen, three men are looking for you. 20 Get up and go downstairs. Go with them without doubting, because I have sent them to you."

21 So Peter went down to the men and said, "I am the one you are looking for. Why did you come here?"

22 They said, "A holy angel spoke to Cornelius, an army officer and a good man; he worships God. All the Jewish people respect him. The angel told Cornelius to ask you to come to his house so that he can hear what you have to say." 23 So Peter asked the men to come in and spend the night.

The next day Peter got ready and went with them, and some of the followers from Joppa joined him. 24 On the following day they came to Caesarea. Cornelius was waiting for them and had called together his relatives and close friends. 25 When Peter entered, Cornelius met him, fell at his feet and worshipped him. 26 But Peter helped him up, saying, "Stand up. I too am only a human." 27 As he talked with Cornelius, Peter went inside where he saw many people gathered. 28 He said, "You people understand that it is against our Jewish law for Jewish people to associate with or visit anyone who is not Jewish. But God has shown me that I should not call any person 'unholy' or 'unclean'. 29 That is why I did not argue when I was asked to come here. Now, please tell me why you sent for me."

eMAIL FROM GOD
10:28 Respect
How should you regard others?

30 Cornelius said, "Four days ago, I was praying in my house at this same time—three o'clock in the afternoon. Suddenly, there was a man standing before me wearing shining clothes. 31 He said, 'Cornelius, God has heard your prayer and has seen that you give to the poor and remembers you. 32 So send some men to Joppa and ask Simon Peter to come. Peter is staying in the house of a man, also named Simon, who is a leatherworker and has a house beside the sea.' 33 So I sent for you immediately, and it was very good of you to come. Now we are all here before God to hear everything the Lord has commanded you to tell us."

34 Peter began to speak: "I really understand now that to God every person is the same. 35 In every country God accepts anyone who worships him and does what is right. 36 You know the message

that God has sent to the people of Israel is the Good News that peace has come through Jesus Christ. Jesus is the Lord of all people! 37 You know what has happened all over Judea, beginning in Galilee after John[n] preached to the people about baptism. 38 You know about Jesus from Nazareth, that God gave him the Holy Spirit and power. You know how Jesus went everywhere doing good and healing those who were ruled by the devil, because God was with him. 39 We saw what Jesus did in Judea and in Jerusalem, but the Jews in Jerusalem killed him by hanging him on a cross. 40 Yet, on the third day, God raised Jesus to life and caused him to be seen, 41 not by all the people, but only by the witnesses God had already chosen. And we are those witnesses who ate and drank with him after he was raised from the dead. 42 He told us to preach to the people and to tell them that he is the one whom God chose to be the judge of the living and the dead. 43 All the prophets say it is true that all who believe in Jesus will be forgiven their sins through Jesus' name."

44 While Peter was still saying this, the Holy Spirit came down on all those who were listening. 45 The Jewish believers who came with Peter were amazed that the gift of the Holy Spirit had been given even to those who were not Jews. 46 These Jewish believers heard them speaking in different languages[n] and praising God. Then Peter said, 47 "Can anyone keep these people from being baptised with water? They have received the Holy Spirit just as we did!" 48 So Peter ordered that they be baptised in the name of Jesus Christ. Then they asked Peter to stay with them for a few days.

Peter Returns to Jerusalem

11 The apostles and the believers in Judea heard that some who were not Jewish had accepted God's teaching too. 2 But when Peter came to Jerusalem, some Jewish believers argued with him. 3 They said, "You went into the homes of people who are not circumcised and ate with them!"

4 So Peter explained the whole story to them. 5 He said, "I was in the city of Joppa, and while I was praying, I had a vision. I saw something that looked like a big sheet being lowered from heaven by its four corners. It came very close to me. 6 I looked inside it and saw animals, wild beasts, reptiles and birds. 7 I heard a voice say to me, 'Get up, Peter; kill and eat.' 8 But I said, 'No, Lord! I have never eaten anything that is unholy or unclean.' 9 But the voice from heaven spoke again, 'God has made these things clean, so don't call them unholy.' 10 This happened three times. Then the whole thing was taken back to heaven. 11 Just then three men who were sent to me from Caesarea came to the house where I was staying. 12 The Spirit told me to go with them without doubting. These six believers here also went with me, and we entered the house of Cornelius. 13 He told us about the angel he saw standing in his house. The angel said to him, 'Send some men to Joppa and invite Simon Peter to come. 14 By the words he will say to you, you and all your family will be saved.' 15 When I began my speech, the Holy Spirit came up on them just as he came up on us at the beginning. 16 Then I remembered the words of the Lord. He said, 'John baptised with water, but you will be baptised with the Holy Spirit.' 17 Since God gave them the same gift he gave us who believed in the Lord Jesus Christ, how could I stop the work of God?"

18 When the Jewish believers heard this, they stopped arguing. They praised God and said, "So God is allowing even those who are not Jewish to turn to him and live."

The Good News Comes to Antioch

19 Many of the believers were scattered when they were persecuted after Stephen was killed. Some of them went as

11:2–18 Obedience Read this example of obedience.

10:37 John John the Baptist, who preached to people about Christ's coming (Matthew 3, Luke 3).
10:46 languages This can also be translated "tongues".

Acts 11:20

far as Phoenicia, Cyprus and Antioch telling the message to others, but only to Jews. 20 Some of these believers were people from Cyprus and Cyrene. When they came to Antioch, they spoke also to Greeks, telling them the Good News about the Lord Jesus. 21 The Lord was helping the believers, and a large group of people believed and turned to the Lord.

22 The church in Jerusalem heard about all of this, so they sent Barnabas to Antioch. 23-24 Barnabas was a good man, full of the Holy Spirit and full of faith. When he reached Antioch and saw how God had blessed the people, he was glad. He encouraged all the believers in Antioch always to obey the Lord with all their hearts, and many people became followers of the Lord.

25 Then Barnabas went to the city of Tarsus to look for Saul, 26 and when he found Saul, he brought him to Antioch. For a whole year Saul and Barnabas met with the church and taught many people there. In Antioch the followers were called Christians for the first time.

27 About that time some prophets came from Jerusalem to Antioch. 28 One of them, named Agabus, stood up and spoke with the help of the Holy Spirit. He said, "A very hard time is coming to the whole world. There will be no food to eat." (This happened when Claudius ruled.) 29 The believers all decided to help the followers who lived in Judea, as much as each one could. 30 They gathered the money and gave it to Barnabas and Saul, who brought it to the elders in Judea.

Herod Agrippa Hurts the Church

12 During that same time King Herod began to mistreat some who belonged to the church. 2 He ordered James, the brother of John, to be killed by the sword. 3 Herod saw that the Jewish people liked this, so he decided to arrest Peter, too. (This happened during the time of the Feast of Unleavened Bread.)

4 After Herod arrested Peter, he put him in jail and handed him over to be guarded by sixteen soldiers. Herod

---

FAITH links

A CHRISTIAN'S RESPONSIBILITY

ACTS 11:26

If you were born in Great Britain, you're called a British citizen. As a British citizen, you have certain rights and responsibilities. One of those responsibilities is to obey the laws of the land.

In Antioch during the first century, believers of Jesus were called Christians for the first time. That word means "a follower of Jesus Christ". There are rights and responsibilities attached to being a Christian. One of those responsibilities is to grow in faith. Saul (Paul) and Barnabas helped the believers in Antioch to grow in their faith. How do the people in your church help you to grow?

Download these Faithlinks for some tips on growing in faith:

A Serious Promise, Deuteronomy 23:21–23, p. 257

Promises, Promises, Judges 2:1–3, p. 312

Obeying God or Man? Daniel 3:8–30, p. 1154

Your Civic Duty, Matthew 17:24–27, p. 1304

Faith That Pleases God, Luke 7:1–9, p. 1380

Meeting Together, 1 Corinthians 16:19, p. 1567

planned to bring Peter before the people for trial after the Passover Feast. 5 So Peter was kept in jail, but the church prayed earnestly to God for him.

Peter Leaves the Jail

6 The night before Herod was to bring him to trial, Peter was sleeping between two soldiers, bound with two chains. Other soldiers were guarding the door of the jail. 7 Suddenly, an angel of the Lord stood there, and a light shone in the cell. The angel struck Peter on the side and woke him up. "Hurry! Get up!" the angel said. And the chains fell off Peter's hands. 8 Then the angel told him, "Get dressed and put on your sandals." And Peter did. Then the angel said, "Put on your coat and follow me." 9 So Peter followed him out, but he did not know if what the angel was doing was real; he thought he might be seeing a vision. 10 They went past the first and second guards and came to the iron gate that separated them from the city. The gate opened by itself for them, and they went through it. When they had walked down one street, the angel suddenly left him.

11 Then Peter realised what had happened. He thought, "Now I know that the Lord really sent his angel to me. He rescued me from Herod and from all the things the Jewish people thought would happen."

12 When he considered this, he went to the home of Mary, the mother of John Mark. Many people were gathered there, praying. 13 Peter knocked on the outside door, and a servant girl named Rhoda came to answer it. 14 When she recognised Peter's voice, she was so happy she forgot to open the door. Instead, she ran inside and told the group, "Peter is at the door!"

15 They said to her, "You are mad!" But she kept on saying it was true, so they said, "It must be Peter's angel."

16 Peter continued to knock, and when they opened the door, they saw him and were amazed. 17 Peter made a sign with his hand to tell them to be quiet. He explained how the Lord led him out of the jail, and he said, "Tell James and the other believers what happened." Then he left to go to another place.

18 The next day the soldiers were very upset and wondered what had happened to Peter. 19 Herod looked everywhere for him but could not find him. So he questioned the guards and ordered that they be killed.

FAITH links

THE POWER OF PRAYER
ACTS 12:5

Peter's friends made a big difference in his life while he was in prison. No, they didn't send him a file in a cake. They prayed for him. Because of their faithfulness in prayer, God rescued Peter from prison.

Prayer can be powerful. How powerful? The God who created the universe listens to and answers your prayer. Is that powerful enough for you?

Here are some more Faithlinks on the power of prayer:

Just a Little Respect, 1 Chronicles 11:10–19, p. 534

The Prayer Habit, Psalm 5:1–3, p. 712

When We Agree, Matthew 18:19–20, p. 1306

Prayer Priority, Luke 5:15–16, p. 1376

Jesus' Prayer, John 17, p. 1453

A Good Habit, Ephesians 6:18, p. 1606

LET'S VISIT ANTIOCH Acts 13:1–3

A man named Seleucus started the city of Antioch. He named it after his dad, Antiochus. He built it about 300 miles north of Jerusalem on the bank of a river called Orontes. Antioch was the capital of Syria during New Testament times. It was the third largest city in the whole Roman Empire. Antioch was built on a trade route. That meant many people travelled by on their way to trade and do business. Because of that, Antioch became an important place for sharing the Good News. People could hear the Good News, then go home and tell all their friends. In fact, it was in Antioch that Jesus' followers were first called "Christians". (Check out Acts 11:26.) Antioch also became the birthplace of foreign missions, because Paul used the Antioch church as a base of operations for some of his missionary tours.

The Death of Herod Agrippa

Later Herod moved from Judea and went to the city of Caesarea, where he stayed. 20 Herod was very angry with the people of Tyre and Sidon, but the people of those cities all came in a group to him. After convincing Blastus, the king's personal servant, to be on their side, they asked Herod for peace, because their country got its food from his country.

21 On a chosen day Herod put on his royal robes, sat on his throne and made a speech to the people. 22 They shouted, "This is the voice of a god, not a human!" 23 Because Herod did not give the glory to God, an angel of the Lord immediately caused him to become sick, and he was eaten by worms and died.

24 God's message continued to spread and reach people.

25 After Barnabas and Saul finished their task in Jerusalem, they returned to Antioch, taking John Mark with them.

Barnabas and Saul are Chosen

13 In the church at Antioch there were these prophets and teachers: Barnabas, Simeon (also called Niger), Lucius (from the city of Cyrene), Manaen (who had grown up with Herod, the ruler) and Saul. 2 They were all worshipping the Lord and gave up eating for a certain time." During this time the Holy Spirit said to them, "Set apart for me Barnabas and Saul to do a special work for which I have chosen them."

3 So after they had given up eating and prayed, they laid their hands on" Barnabas and Saul and sent them out.

Barnabas and Saul in Cyprus

4 Barnabas and Saul, sent out by the Holy Spirit, went to the city of Seleucia. From there they sailed to the island of Cyprus. 5 When they came to Salamis, they preached the Good News of God in the Jewish synagogues. John Mark was with them to help.

6 They went across the whole island to Paphos where they met a Jewish magician

---

13:2 gave up . . . time This is called "fasting". The people would give up eating for a special time of prayer and worship to God. It was also done to show sadness and disappointment.

13:3 laid their hands on The laying on of hands had many purposes, including the giving of a blessing, power or authority.

named Bar-Jesus. He was a false prophet 7 who always stayed close to Sergius Paulus, the governor and a clever man. He asked Barnabas and Saul to come to him, because he wanted to hear the message of God. 8 But Elymas, the magician, was against them. (Elymas is the name for Bar-Jesus in the Greek language.) He tried to stop the governor from believing in Jesus. 9 But Saul, who was also called Paul, was filled with the Holy Spirit. He looked straight at Elymas 10 and said, "You son of the devil! You are an enemy of everything that is right! You are full of evil tricks and lies, always trying to change the Lord's truths into lies. 11 Now the Lord will touch you, and you will be blind. For a time you will not be able to see anything—not even the light from the sun."

Then everything became dark for Elymas, and he walked around, trying to find someone to lead him by the hand. 12 When the governor saw this, he believed because he was amazed at the teaching about the Lord.

Paul and Barnabas Leave Cyprus

13 Paul and those with him sailed from Paphos and came to Perga, in Pamphylia. There John Mark left them to return to Jerusalem. 14 They continued their trip from Perga and went to Antioch, a city in Pisidia. On the Sabbath day they went into the synagogue and sat down. 15 After the law of Moses and the writings of the prophets were read, the leaders of the synagogue sent a message to Paul and Barnabas: "Brothers, if you have any message that will encourage the people, please speak."

16 Paul stood up, raised his hand and said, "You Israelites and you who worship God, please listen! 17 The God of the Israelites chose our ancestors. He made the people great during the time they lived in Egypt, and he brought them out of that country with great power. 18 And he was patient with them for 40 years in the desert. 19 God destroyed seven nations in the land of Canaan and gave the land to his people. 20 All this happened in about 450 years.

"After this, God gave them judges until the time of Samuel the prophet. 21 Then the people asked for a king, so God gave them Saul son of Kish. Saul was from the tribe of Benjamin and was king for 40 years. 22 After God took him away, God made David their king. God said about him: 'I have found in David son of Jesse the kind of man I want. He will do all I want him to do.' 23 So God has brought Jesus, one of David's descendants, to Israel to be its Saviour, as he promised. 24 Before Jesus came, John" preached to all the people of Israel about a baptism of changed hearts and lives. 25 When he was finishing his work, he said, 'Who do you think I am? I am not the Christ. He is coming later, and I am not worthy to untie his sandals.'

26 "Brothers, sons of the family of Abraham, and those of you who are not Jews who worship God, listen! The news about this salvation has been sent to us. 27 Those who live in Jerusalem and their leaders did not realise that Jesus was the Saviour. They did not understand the words that the prophets wrote, which are read every Sabbath day. But they made them come true when they said Jesus was guilty. 28 They could not find any real reason for Jesus to be put to death, but they asked Pilate to have him killed. 29 When they had done to him all that the Scriptures had said, they took him down from the cross and laid him in a tomb. 30 But God raised him up from the dead! 31 After this, for many days, those who had gone with Jesus from Galilee to Jerusalem saw him. They are now his witnesses to the people. 32 We tell you the Good News about the promise God made to our ancestors. 33 God has made this promise come true for us, his children, by raising Jesus from the dead. We read about this also in Psalm 2:

'You are my son.

Today I have become your father.'

Psalm 2:7

34 God raised Jesus from the dead, and he will never go back to the grave and become dust. So God said:

13:24 John John the Baptist, who preached to people about Christ's coming (Matthew 3, Luke 3).

▶ **Acts 13:35** 1488

'I will give you the blessings
I promised to David.' *Isaiah 55:3*
35 But in another place God says:
'You will not let your holy one rot.'
Psalm 16:10
36 David did God's will during his lifetime. Then he died and was buried beside his ancestors, and his body did rot in the grave. 37 But the One God raised from the dead did not rot in the grave. 38-39 Brothers, understand what we are telling you: you can have forgiveness of your sins through Jesus. The law of Moses could not free you from your sins. But through Jesus everyone who believes is free from all sins. 40 Be careful! Don't let what the prophets said happen to you:
41 'Look at the nations!
Watch them and be amazed and shocked.
I will do something in your lifetime
that you won't believe even when you are told about it.'" *Habakkuk 1:5*
42 While Paul and Barnabas were leaving the synagogue, the people asked them to tell them more about these things on the next Sabbath. 43 When the meeting was over, many Jews and those who had changed to the Jewish religion and who worshipped God followed Paul and Barnabas from that place. Paul and Barnabas were persuading them to continue trusting in God's grace.
44 On the next Sabbath day, almost everyone in the city came to hear the word of the Lord. 45 Seeing the crowd, the Jewish people became very jealous and said insulting things and argued against what Paul said. 46 But Paul and Barnabas spoke very boldly, saying, "We must speak the message of God to you first. But you refuse to listen. You are judging yourselves not worthy of having eternal life! So we will now go to the people of other nations. 47 This is what the Lord told us to do, saying:
'I have made you a light for the nations;

email FROM GOD
13:38–39
Forgiveness
Who can be forgiven?

FAITH CHALLENGE
Here's one for you. Read 13:47 to find out what the Lord has in mind for his people. How can you be a light to the people around you? In what ways are you already a light?

TeSTiNG iT

Acts 13:47
This is what the Lord told us to do, saying: "I have made you a light for the nations; you will show people all over the world the way to be saved."

you will show people all over the world the way to be saved.'"
Isaiah 49:6
48 When those who were not Jewish heard Paul say this, they were happy and gave honour to the message of the Lord. And the people who were chosen to have life for ever believed the message.
49 So the message of the Lord was spreading through the whole country. 50 But the Jewish people stirred up some of the important religious women and the leaders of the city. They started trouble against Paul and Barnabas and forced them out of their area. 51 So Paul and

Acts 14:15 1489

Barnabas shook the dust off their feet[n] and went to Iconium. 52 But the followers were filled with joy and the Holy Spirit.

Paul and Barnabas in Iconium

14 In Iconium, Paul and Barnabas went as usual to the Jewish synagogue. They spoke so well that a great many Jews and Greeks believed. 2 But some of the Jews who did not believe excited the non-Jewish people and turned them against the believers. 3 Paul and Barnabas stayed in Iconium a long time and spoke bravely for the Lord. He showed that their message about his grace was true by giving them the power to work miracles and signs. 4 But the city was divided. Some of the people agreed with the Jews, and others believed the apostles.

5 Some who were not Jews, some Jews and some of their rulers wanted to mistreat Paul and Barnabas and to stone them to death. 6 When Paul and Barnabas learned about this, they ran away to Lystra and Derbe, cities in Lycaonia, and to the areas around those cities. 7 They announced the Good News there, too.

Paul in Lystra and Derbe

8 In Lystra there sat a man who had been born crippled; he had never walked. 9 As this man was listening to Paul speak, Paul looked straight at him and saw that he believed God could heal him. 10 So he cried out, "Stand up on your feet!" The man jumped up and began walking around. 11 When the crowds saw what Paul did, they shouted in the Lycaonian language, "The gods have become like humans and have come down to us!" 12 Then the people began to call Barnabas "Zeus"[n] and Paul "Hermes",[n] because he was the main speaker. 13 The priest in the temple of Zeus, which was near the city, brought some bulls and flowers to the city gates. He and the people wanted to offer a sacrifice to Paul and Barnabas. 14 But when the apostles, Barnabas and Paul, heard about it, they tore their clothes. They ran in among the people, shouting, 15 "Friends, why are you doing these things? We are only

---

FAITH links

KINDNESS COUNTS
ACTS 14:3

What is the coolest ability you wish you had? To jump over tall buildings at a single bound? To play a sport or musical instrument better than anyone? Paul and Barnabas, two apostles of Jesus, were able to perform miracles. That's pretty cool! They did these not for show but to demonstrate God's kindness.

When you are kind to others, they can see God's love for them. So, remember: kindness counts!

Download these links on how you can make kindness count:

Help for the Poor, Leviticus 5:7, p. 138

Yours, Mine and Ours? 1 Samuel 25, p. 389

Seeing the Needs, Nehemiah 1, p. 625

Your Choice of Fruit, Matthew 12:33–35, p. 1295

The Greatest Commandment, Matthew 22:36–40, p. 1313

Share and Share Alike? Acts 2:43–47, p. 1466

13:51 shook . . . feet A warning. It showed that they had rejected these people.
14:12 "Zeus" The Greeks believed in many gods, of whom Zeus was the most important.
14:12 "Hermes" The Greeks believed he was a messenger for the other gods.

human beings like you. We are bringing you the Good News and are telling you to turn away from these worthless things and turn to the living God. He is the One who made the sky, the earth, the sea and everything in them. 16 In the past, God let all the nations do what they wanted. 17 Yet he proved he is real by showing kindness, by giving you rain from heaven and crops at the right times, by giving you food and filling your hearts with joy." 18 Even with these words, they were barely able to keep the crowd from offering sacrifices to them.

19 Then some Jewish people came from Antioch and Iconium and persuaded the people to turn against Paul. So they threw stones at him and dragged him out of town, thinking they had killed him. 20 But the followers gathered around him, and he got up and went back into the town. The next day he and Barnabas left and went to the city of Derbe.

The Return to Antioch in Syria

21 Paul and Barnabas told the Good News in Derbe, and many became followers. Paul and Barnabas returned to Lystra, Iconium and Antioch, 22 making the followers of Jesus stronger and helping them stay in the faith. They said, "We must suffer many things to enter God's kingdom." 23 They chose elders for each church, by praying and giving up eating for a certain time.[n] These elders had trusted the Lord, so Paul and Barnabas put them in the Lord's care.

24 Then they went through Pisidia and came to Pamphylia. 25 When they had preached the message in Perga, they went down to Attalia. 26 And from there they sailed away to Antioch where the believers had put them into God's care and had sent them out to do this work. Now they had finished.

27 When they arrived in Antioch, Paul and Barnabas gathered the church together. They told the church all about what God had done with them and how God had made it possible for those who were not Jewish to believe. 28 And they stayed there a long time with the followers.

The Meeting at Jerusalem

15 Then some people came to Antioch from Judea and began teaching the non-Jewish believers: "You cannot be saved if you are not circumcised as Moses taught us." 2 Paul and Barnabas were against this teaching and argued with them about it. So the church decided to send Paul, Barnabas and some others to Jerusalem where they could talk more about this with the apostles and elders.

3 The church helped them leave on the trip, and they went through the countries of Phoenicia and Samaria, telling all about how those who were not Jewish had turned to God. This made all the believers very happy. 4 When they arrived in Jerusalem, they were welcomed by the apostles, the elders and the church. Paul, Barnabas and the others told about everything God had done with them. 5 But some of the believers who belonged to the Pharisee group came forwards and said, "The non-Jewish believers must be circumcised. They must be told to obey the law of Moses."

6 The apostles and the elders gathered to consider this problem. 7 After a long debate, Peter stood up and said to them, "Brothers, you know that in the early days God chose me from among you to preach the Good News to those who are not Jewish. They heard the Good News from me, and they believed. 8 God, who knows the thoughts of everyone, accepted them. He showed this to us by giving them the Holy Spirit, just as he did to us. 9 To God, those people are not different from us. When they believed, he made their hearts pure. 10 So now why are you testing God by putting a heavy load around the necks of the non-Jewish believers? It is a load that neither we nor our ancestors were able to carry. 11 But we believe that we and they too will be saved by the grace of the Lord Jesus."

12 Then the whole group became quiet. They listened to Paul and Barnabas

---

14:23 giving up . . . time This is called "fasting". The people would give up eating for a special time of prayer and worship to God. It was also done to show sadness and disappointment.

Acts 15 **1491**

HANDLING CONFLICTS
Act 15:1–29

What *Am* I Going to Do? Is there someone who is always "bugging" you? Maybe someone who always calls you names or makes fun of you? When these things happen, it can make you feel angry, scared or ready to get even. What do you do? Do you ask someone for help? Who?

Jesus tells us how to handle people who cause us problems and sometimes make our life miserable. His way of dealing with those hard-to-love people is very different from what most people would tell you. (Check out Matthew 5:38–48, p. 1282.) Are you willing to be friends with people who act like your enemies? This will not be easy, but with Jesus' help you can do it. You may even turn an "enemy" into a friend!

MORE FAITH links

The Trouble with Jealousy, **p. 53**
Give Revenge a Rest, **p. 160**
Play Fair or Play Favourites? **p. 227**
Wronged for What's Right, **p. 612**
The Peril of Poisonous Plans, **p. 1221**
Winning a Friend, **p. 1654**

What's the fastest way to turn an "enemy" into a friend?

(Hint: it doesn't mean giving them money!)

Log on to these Faithlinks to find out how!

Does Crime Pay? Psalm 37:1–7, p. 736
• This Faithlink tells you to trust God to handle problems and conflicts in your life.

In Deep Water, Psalm 69, p. 760
• Conflicts (problems and troubles) in your life can make you feel like you're in deep water or even mud. Do you think you will never have conflicts in your life? Not likely! What are some conflicts you are dealing with? Link here to learn about David's way of dealing with conflict.

Forgive and Forget, Ephesians 4:32, p. 1604
• When someone is really giving you a hard time, what do you feel like doing? Do you easily forget about that person's bad behaviour towards you? If not, you are holding a grudge.
• What's the opposite of holding a grudge? Forgiving someone. That isn't always easy to do. But since God always forgives us, that's what we ought to do for anyone who hurts us. Know anyone who needs your forgiveness?

tell about all the miracles and signs that God did through them among the non-Jewish people. 13 After they finished speaking, James said, "Brothers, listen to me. 14 Simon has told us how God showed his love for the non-Jewish people. For the first time he is accepting from among them a people to be his own. 15 The words of the prophets agree with this too: 16 'After these things I will return.

> The kingdom of David is like a fallen tent.
> But I will rebuild its ruins,
> and I will set it up.
> 17 Then those people who are left alive
> may ask the Lord for help,
> and the other nations that belong
> to me,
> says the Lord,
> who will make it happen.
> 18 And these things have been known
> for a long time.' *Amos 9:11-12*

19 "So I think we should not bother the non-Jewish people who are turning to God. 20 Instead, we should write a letter to them telling them these things: stay away from food that has been offered to idols (which makes it unclean), any kind of sexual sin, eating animals that have been strangled, and blood. 21 They should do these things, because for a long time in every city the law of Moses has been taught. And it is still read in the synagogue every Sabbath day."

Letter to Non-Jewish Believers

22 The apostles, the elders and the whole church decided to send some of their men with Paul and Barnabas to Antioch. They chose Judas Barsabbas and Silas, who were respected by the believers. 23 They sent the following letter with them:

> From the apostles and elders, your brothers.
> To all the non-Jewish believers in Antioch, Syria and Cilicia:
> Greetings!

24 We have heard that some of our group have come to you and said things that trouble and upset you. But we did not tell them to do this. 25 We have all agreed to choose some messengers and send them to you with our dear friends Barnabas and Paul—26 people who have given their lives to serve our Lord Jesus Christ. 27 So we are sending Judas and Silas, who will tell you the same things. 28 It has pleased the Holy Spirit that you should not have a heavy load to carry, and we agree. You need to do only these things: 29 stay away from any food that has been offered to idols, any animals that have been strangled, blood and any kind of sexual sin. If you stay away from these things, you will do well.

Goodbye.

30 So they left Jerusalem and went to Antioch where they gathered the church and gave them the letter. 31 When they read it, they were very happy because of the encouraging message. 32 Judas and Silas, who were also prophets, said many things to encourage the believers and make them stronger. 33 After some time Judas and Silas were sent off in peace by the believers, and they went back to those who had sent them. 34 *n* 35 But Paul and Barnabas stayed in Antioch and, along with many others, preached the Good News and taught the people the message of the Lord.

Paul and Barnabas Separate

36 After some time, Paul said to Barnabas, "We should go back to all those towns where we preached the message of the Lord. Let's visit the believers and see how they are doing."

37 Barnabas wanted to take John Mark with them, 38 but he had left them at Pamphylia; he did not continue with them in the work. So Paul did not think it was a good idea to take him. 39 Paul and Barnabas had such a serious argument about this that they separated and went different ways. Barnabas took Mark and sailed to Cyprus, 40 but Paul chose Silas

---

15:34 Verse 34 Some Greek copies add verse 34: "... but Silas decided to remain there."

and left. The believers in Antioch put Paul into the Lord's care, 41 and he went through Syria and Cilicia, giving strength to the churches.

Timothy Goes with Paul

16 Paul came to Derbe and Lystra, where a follower named Timothy lived. Timothy's mother was Jewish and a believer, but his father was a Greek. 2 The believers in Lystra and Iconium respected Timothy and said good things about him. 3 Paul wanted Timothy to travel with him, but all the Jews living in that area knew that Timothy's father was Greek. So Paul circumcised Timothy to please the Jews. 4 Paul and those with him travelled from town to town and gave the decisions made by the apostles and elders in Jerusalem for the people to obey. 5 So the churches became stronger in the faith and grew larger every day.

Paul is Called Out of Asia

6 Paul and those with him went through the areas of Phrygia and Galatia since the Holy Spirit did not let them preach the Good News in the country of Asia. 7 When they came near the country of Mysia, they tried to go into Bithynia, but the Spirit of Jesus did not let them. 8 So they passed by Mysia and went to Troas. 9 That night Paul saw in a vision a man from Macedonia. The man stood and begged, "Come over to Macedonia and help us." 10 After Paul had seen the vision, we immediately prepared to leave for Macedonia, understanding that God had called us to tell the Good News to those people.

**16:6–7
God's Will**
Read this to see who will lead you.

Lydia Becomes a Christian

11 We left Troas and sailed straight to the island of Samothrace. The next day we sailed to Neapolis.ⁿ 12 Then we went by land to Philippi, a Roman colonyⁿ and the leading city in that part of Macedonia. We stayed there for several days.

13 On the Sabbath day we went outside the city gate to the river where we

Acts 16:13   1493

FAITH links

FAITH WORKOUT
ACTS 16:4-5

Paul, Silas and Timothy travelled from place to place helping other Christians to grow in faith. When the Christians they met learned about God and his plans for them, their faith grew stronger.

You know what a personal trainer is, right? That's a person who helps someone else get into good physical shape. Other Christians can be like "spiritual personal trainers" in our lives. One of the ways other Christians help us is to explain the Scriptures to us. Think about how your pastor, a parent, or your Sunday school teacher helps you to understand God's Word. When we help each other, we're helped as well.

Try to Remember, Deuteronomy 11:18–21, p. 243

Learning to Listen, 1 Samuel 3, p. 358

Plan for Success, 1 Chronicles 14:8–17, p. 538

Our Thirst Quencher, Psalm 42:1–3, p. 741

Two Ways to Grow, Luke 2:46–52, p. 1370

Out with the Old! Colossians 3:1–14, p. 1625

16:11 Neapolis City in Macedonia. It was the first city Paul visited on the continent of Europe.
16:12 Roman colony A town begun by Romans with Roman laws, customs and privileges.

thought we would find a special place for prayer. Some women had gathered there, so we sat down and talked with them. 14 One of the listeners was a woman named Lydia from the city of Thyatira whose job was selling purple cloth. She worshipped God, and he opened her mind to pay attention to what Paul was saying. 15 She and all the people in her house were baptised. Then she invited us to her home, saying, "If you think I am truly a believer in the Lord, then come and stay in my house." And she persuaded us to stay with her.

Paul and Silas in Jail

16 Once, while we were going to the place for prayer, a servant girl met us. She had a special spirit[n] in her, and she earned a lot of money for her owners by telling fortunes. 17 This girl followed Paul and us, shouting, "These men are servants of the Most High God. They are telling you how you can be saved."

18 She kept this up for many days. This bothered Paul, so he turned and said to the spirit, "By the power of Jesus Christ, I command you to come out of her!" Immediately, the spirit came out.

19 When the owners of the servant girl saw this, they knew that now they could not use her to make money. So they grabbed Paul and Silas and dragged them before the city rulers in the market place. 20 They brought Paul and Silas to the Roman rulers and said, "These men are Jews and are making trouble in our city. 21 They are teaching things that are not right for us as Romans to do."

22 The crowd joined the attack against them. The Roman officers tore the clothes of Paul and Silas and had them beaten with rods. 23 Then Paul and Silas were thrown into jail, and the jailer was ordered to guard them carefully. 24 When he heard this order, he put them far inside the jail and pinned their feet down between large blocks of wood.

FAITH links

YOU'RE WELCOMED!
ACTS 16:14-15

"Hospitality" is another way to say making someone feel welcome. That's what Lydia did for Paul and the other missionaries with whom he travelled. After becoming a believer herself, Lydia invited Paul to stay at her home.

Showing hospitality is one way to care for others. You don't have to own a home or even *be* at home to be hospitable. Hospitality starts with an attitude of welcome. No matter where you are, you can help someone feel welcome.

Know how to make others feel welcomed? Click here to find out:

Care for the Lost, Deuteronomy 22:1–3, p. 255

Show You Care, 2 Kings 4:10, p. 481

Service with a Smile, 1 Chronicles 6:31–49, p. 527

Love Him? Show It! Amos 2:6–7, p. 1196

The Worst Chore, John 13:3–17, p. 1447

Come On In! 1 Peter 4:9–10, p. 1705

---

25 About midnight Paul and Silas were praying and singing songs to God as the other prisoners listened. 26 Suddenly,

16:16 spirit This was a spirit from the devil, which caused her to have special knowledge.

Acts 17:12 1495

there was a strong earthquake that shook the foundation of the jail. Then all the doors of the jail broke open, and all the prisoners were freed from their chains. 27 The jailer woke up and saw that the jail doors were open. Thinking that the prisoners had already escaped, he got his sword and was about to kill himself.*n* 28 But Paul shouted, "Don't hurt yourself! We are all here." 29 The jailer told someone to bring a light. Then he ran inside and, shaking with fear, fell down before Paul and Silas. 30 He brought them outside and said, "Men, what must I do to be saved?" 31 They said to him, "Believe in the Lord Jesus and you will be saved—you and all the people in your house." 32 So Paul and Silas told the message of the Lord to the jailer and all the people in his house. 33 At that hour of the night the jailer took Paul and Silas and washed their wounds. Then he and all his people were baptised immediately. 34 After this the jailer took Paul and Silas home and gave them food. He and his family were very happy because they now believed in God.

35 The next morning, the Roman officers sent the police to tell the jailer, "Let these men go free."

36 The jailer said to Paul, "The officers have sent an order to let you go free. You can leave now. Go in peace."

37 But Paul said to the police, "They beat us in public without a trial, even though we are Roman citizens.*n* And they threw us in jail. Now they want to make us go away quietly. No! Let them come themselves and bring us out."

38 The police told the Roman officers what Paul said. When the officers heard that Paul and Silas were Roman citizens, they were afraid. 39 So they came and told Paul and Silas they were sorry and took them out of jail and asked them to leave the city. 40 So when they came out of the jail, they went to Lydia's house where they saw some of the believers and encouraged them. Then they left.

Paul and Silas in Thessalonica

17 Paul and Silas travelled through Amphipolis and Apollonia and came to Thessalonica where there was a Jewish synagogue. 2 Paul went into the synagogue as he always did, and on each Sabbath day for three weeks, he talked with the Jews about the Scriptures. 3 He explained and proved that the Christ must die and then rise from the dead. He said, "This Jesus I am telling you about is the Christ." 4 Some of the Jews were convinced and joined Paul and Silas, along with many of the Greeks who worshipped God and many of the important women.

5 But the Jews became jealous. So they got some evil men from the market-place, formed a mob and started a riot. They ran to Jason's house, looking for Paul and Silas, wanting to bring them out to the people. 6 But when they did not find them, they dragged Jason and some other believers to the leaders of the city. The people were yelling, "These people have made trouble everywhere in the world, and now they have come here too! 7 Jason is keeping them in his house. All of them do things against the laws of Caesar, saying there is another king, called Jesus."

8 When the people and the leaders of the city heard these things, they became very upset. 9 They made Jason and the others put up a sum of money. Then they let the believers go free.

Paul and Silas Go to Berea

10 That same night the believers sent Paul and Silas to Berea where they went to the Jewish synagogue. 11 These Jews were more willing to listen than the Jews in Thessalonica. The Jews in Berea were eager to hear what Paul and Silas said and studied the Scriptures every day to find out if these things were true. 12 So, many of them believed, as well as many important Greek women

17:11–12 Bible
Find out why reading the Bible is important.

16:27 kill himself He thought the leaders would kill him for letting the prisoners escape.
16:37 Roman citizens Roman law said that Roman citizens must not be beaten before they had a trial.

LET'S VISIT ATHENS   Acts 17:15—18:1

Athens was the capital of a state in Greece called Attica. Athens was the centre of art, architecture, literature and politics during the Golden Age of the Greeks (fifth century B.C.). Some people call it the birthplace of western civilization and culture.

When people visit Athens, one of the most famous sights they go to see is called the Parthenon. The Parthenon is actually the ruins that are left of an ancient Greek building. Another famous spot is Mars' Hill, which was like a courtroom for ancient Greeks.

The apostle Paul visited Athens during his second missionary journey. (Read Acts 17:15—18:1.) He spent some time sightseeing and found a statue built to honour "A GOD WHO IS NOT KNOWN". (See Acts 17:23.) Paul used that statue to teach the people about the one true God.

---

and men. 13 But the Jews in Thessalonica learned that Paul was preaching the word of God in Berea, too. So they came there, upsetting the people and making trouble. 14 The believers quickly sent Paul away to the coast, but Silas and Timothy stayed in Berea. 15 The people leading Paul went with him to Athens. Then they carried a message from Paul back to Silas and Timothy for them to come to him as soon as they could.

Paul Preaches in Athens

16 While Paul was waiting for Silas and Timothy in Athens, he was troubled because he saw that the city was full of idols. 17 In the synagogue, he talked with the Jews and the Greeks who worshipped God. He also talked every day with people in the market-place.

18 Some of the Epicurean and Stoic philosophers[n] argued with him, saying, "This man doesn't know what he is talking about. What is he trying to say?" Others said, "He seems to be telling us about some other gods," because Paul was telling them about Jesus and his rising from the dead. 19 They got Paul and took him to a meeting of the Areopagus,[n] where they said, "Please explain to us this new idea you have been teaching. 20 The things you are saying are new to us, and we want to know what this teaching means." 21 (All the people of Athens and those from other countries who lived there always used their time to talk about the newest ideas.)

22 Then Paul stood before the meeting of the Areopagus and said, "People of Athens, I can see you are very religious in all things. 23 As I was going through your city, I saw the objects you worship. I found an altar that had these words written on it: TO A GOD WHO IS NOT KNOWN. You worship a god that you don't know, and this is the God I am telling you about! 24 The God who made the whole world and everything in it is the Lord of the land and the sky. He does not live in temples built by

---

17:18 Epicurean and Stoic philosophers Philosophers were those who searched for truth. Epicureans believed that pleasures, especially pleasures of the mind, were the goal of life. Stoics believed that life should be without feelings of joy or grief.

17:19 Areopagus A council or group of important leaders in Athens. They were like judges.

human hands. 25 This God is the One who gives life, breath and everything else to people. He does not need any help from them; he has everything he needs. 26 God began by making one person, and from him came all the different people who live everywhere in the world. God decided exactly when and where they must live. 27 God wanted them to look for him and perhaps search all around for him and find him, though he is not far from any of us: 28 'We live in him. We walk in him. We are in him.' Some of your own poets have said: 'For we are his children.' 29 Since we are God's children, you must not think that God is like something that people imagine or make from gold, silver or rock. 30 In the past, people did not understand God, and he ignored this. But now, God tells all people in the world to change their hearts and lives. 31 God has set a day that he will judge all the world with fairness, by the man he chose long ago. And God has proved this to everyone by raising that man from the dead!"

32 When the people heard about Jesus being raised from the dead, some of them laughed. But others said, "We will hear more about this from you later." 33 So Paul went away from them. 34 But some of the people believed Paul and joined him. Among those who believed was Dionysius, a member of the Areopagus, a woman named Damaris and some others.

Paul in Corinth

18 Later Paul left Athens and went to Corinth. 2 Here he met a Jew named Aquila who had been born in the country of Pontus. But Aquila and his wife, Priscilla, had recently moved to Corinth from Italy, because Claudius*ⁿ* commanded that all Jews must leave Rome. Paul went to visit Aquila and Priscilla. 3 Because they were tentmakers, just as he was, he stayed with them and worked with them. 4 Every Sabbath day he talked with the Jews and Greeks in the synagogue, trying to persuade them to believe in Jesus.

5 Silas and Timothy came from Macedonia and joined Paul in Corinth. After this, Paul spent all his time telling people the Good News, showing the Jews that Jesus is the Christ. 6 But they would not accept Paul's teaching and said some evil things. So he shook off the dust from his clothes*ⁿ* and said to them, "If you are not saved, it will be your own fault! I have done all I can do! After this, I will go only to those who are not Jewish." 7 Paul left the synagogue and moved into the home of Titius Justus, next to the synagogue. This man worshipped God. 8 Crispus was the leader of that synagogue, and he and all the people living in his house believed in the Lord. Many others in Corinth also listened to Paul and believed and were baptised.

9 During the night, the Lord told Paul in a vision: "Don't be afraid. Continue talking to people and don't be quiet. 10 I am with you, and no one will hurt you because many of my people are in this city." 11 Paul stayed there for a year and a half, teaching God's word to the people.

18:9 Witnessing
Are you afraid to share your faith?

Paul is Brought Before Gallio

12 When Gallio was the governor of the country of Southern Greece, some of the Jews came together against Paul and took him to the court. 13 They said, "This man is teaching people to worship God in a way that is against our law."

14 Paul was about to say something, but Gallio spoke to the Jews, saying, "I would listen to you Jews if you were complaining about a crime or some wrong. 15 But the things you are saying are only questions about words and names—arguments about your own law. So you must solve this problem yourselves. I don't want to be a judge of these things." 16 And Gallio made them leave the court.

17 Then they all grabbed Sosthenes, the leader of the synagogue, and beat him

---

18:2 Claudius The emperor (ruler) of Rome, A.D. 41-54.

18:6 shook . . . clothes This was a warning to show that Paul would no longer talk to the Jews in that city.

there before the court. But this did not bother Gallio.

Paul Returns to Antioch

18 Paul stayed with the believers for many more days. Then he left and sailed for Syria, with Priscilla and Aquila. At Cenchrea Paul cut off his hair,[n] because he had made a promise to God. 19 Then they went to Ephesus, where Paul left Priscilla and Aquila. While Paul was there, he went into the synagogue and talked with the Jews. 20 When they asked him to stay with them longer, he refused. 21 But as he left, he said, "I will come back to you again if God wants me to." And so he sailed away from Ephesus.

22 When Paul landed at Caesarea, he went and gave greetings to the church in Jerusalem. After that, Paul went to Antioch. 23 He stayed there for a while and then left and went through the regions of Galatia and Phrygia. He travelled from town to town in these regions, giving strength to all the followers.

Apollos in Ephesus and Corinth

24 A Jew named Apollos came to Ephesus. He was born in the city of Alexandria and was a good speaker who knew the Scriptures well. 25 He had been taught about the way of the Lord and was always very excited when he spoke and taught the truth about Jesus. But the only baptism Apollos knew about was the baptism that John[n] taught. 26 Apollos began to speak very boldly in the synagogue, and when Priscilla and Aquila heard him, they took him to their home and helped him better understand the way of God. 27 Now Apollos wanted to go to the country of Southern Greece. So the believers helped him and wrote a letter to the followers there, asking them to accept him. These followers had believed in Jesus because of God's grace, and when Apollos arrived, he helped them very much. 28 He argued very strongly with the Jews before all the people, clearly proving with the Scriptures that Jesus is the Christ.

18:28 Bible What do the Scriptures prove?

Paul in Ephesus

19 While Apollos was in Corinth, Paul was visiting some places on the way to Ephesus. There he found some followers 2 and asked them, "Did you receive the Holy Spirit when you believed?"

They said, "We have never even heard of a Holy Spirit."

3 So he asked, "What kind of baptism did you have?"

They said, "It was the baptism that John[n] taught."

4 Paul said, "John's baptism was a baptism of changed hearts and lives. He told people to believe in the One who would come after him, and that One is Jesus."

5 When they heard this, they were baptised in the name of the Lord Jesus. 6 Then Paul laid his hands on them,[n] and the Holy Spirit came upon them. They began speaking different languages[n] and prophesying. 7 There were about twelve people in this group.

8 Paul went into the synagogue and spoke out boldly for three months. He talked with the Jews and persuaded them to accept the things he said about the kingdom of God. 9 But some of the Jews became stubborn. They refused to believe and said evil things about the Way of Jesus before all the people. So Paul left them, and, taking the followers with him, he went to the school of a man named Tyrannus. There Paul talked with people every day 10 for two years. Because of his work, every Jew and Greek in the country of Asia heard the word of the Lord.

The Sons of Sceva

11 God used Paul to do some very special miracles. 12 Some people took handkerchiefs and clothes that Paul had used

---

18:18 cut . . . hair Jews did this to show that the time of a special promise to God was finished.
18:25, 19:3 John John the Baptist, who preached to people about Christ's coming (Matthew 3, Luke 3).
19:6 laid his hands on them The laying on of hands had many purposes, including the giving of a blessing, power or authority.
19:6 languages This can also be translated "tongues".

and put them on the sick. When they did this, the sick were healed and evil spirits left them.

13 But some Jews also were travelling around and making evil spirits go out of people. They tried to use the name of the Lord Jesus to force the evil spirits out. They would say, "By the same Jesus that Paul talks about, I order you to come out!" 14 Seven sons of Sceva, a leading Jewish priest, were doing this.

15 But on one occasion an evil spirit said to them, "I know Jesus, and I know about Paul, but who are you?"

16 Then the man who had the evil spirit jumped on them. Because he was so much stronger than all of them, they ran away from the house naked and hurt. 17 All the people in Ephesus—Jews and Greeks—learned about this and were filled with fear and gave great honour to the Lord Jesus. 18 Many of the believers began to confess openly and tell all the evil things they had done. 19 Some of them who had used magic brought their magic books and burned them before everyone. Those books were worth about 50,000 silver coins.[n]

20 So in a powerful way the word of the Lord kept spreading and growing.

21 After these things, Paul decided to go to Jerusalem, planning to go through the countries of Macedonia and Southern Greece and then on to Jerusalem. He said, "After I have been to Jerusalem, I must also visit Rome." 22 Paul sent Timothy and Erastus, two of his helpers, ahead to Macedonia, but he himself stayed in Asia for a while.

Trouble in Ephesus

23 And during that time, there was some serious trouble in Ephesus about the Way of Jesus. 24 A man named Demetrius, who worked with silver, made little silver models that looked like the temple of the goddess Artemis.[n] Those who did this work made much money. 25 Demetrius had a meeting with them and some others who did the same kind of work. He told them, "Men, you know that we make a lot of money from our business. 26 But look at what this man Paul is doing. He has convinced and turned away many people in Ephesus and in almost all of Asia! He says the gods made by human hands are not real. 27 There is a danger that our business will lose its good name, but there is also another danger: people will begin to think that the temple of the great goddess Artemis is not important. Her greatness will be destroyed, but Artemis is the goddess that everyone in Asia and the whole world worships."

28 When the others heard this, they became very angry and shouted, "Artemis, the goddess of Ephesus, is great!" 29 The whole city became confused. The people grabbed Gaius and Aristarchus, who were from Macedonia and were travelling with Paul, and ran to the theatre. 30 Paul wanted to go in and talk to the crowd, but the followers did not let him. 31 Also, some leaders of Asia who were friends of Paul sent him a message, begging him not to go into the theatre. 32 Some people were shouting one thing, and some were shouting another. The meeting was completely confused; most of them did not know why they had come together. 33 The Jews put a man named Alexander in front of the people, and some of them told him what to do. Alexander waved his hand so he could explain things to the people. 34 But when they saw that Alexander was a Jew, they all shouted the same thing for two hours: "Great is Artemis of Ephesus!"

35 Then the city clerk made the crowd be quiet. He said, "People of Ephesus, everyone knows that Ephesus is the city that keeps the temple of the great goddess Artemis and her holy stone[n] that fell from heaven. 36 Since no one can say this is not true, you should be quiet. Stop and

---

19:19 50,000 silver coins Probably drachmas. A silver coin was enough to pay a worker for one day's labour.
19:24 Artemis A Greek goddess that the people of Asia Minor worshipped.
19:35 holy stone Probably a meteorite or stone that the people thought looked like Artemis.

19:13-16 Demons
Do evil spirits have power?

think before you do anything. 37 You brought these men here, but they have not said anything evil against our goddess or stolen anything from her temple. 38 If Demetrius and those who work with him have a charge against anyone they should go to the courts and judges where they can argue with each other. 39 If there is something else you want to talk about, it can be decided at the legal town meeting of the people. 40 I say this because some people might see this trouble today and say that we are rioting. We could not explain this, because there is no real reason for this meeting." 41 After the city clerk said these things, he told the people to go home.

Paul in Macedonia and Greece

20 When the trouble stopped, Paul sent for the followers to come to him. After he had encouraged them and said goodbye, he left and went to the country of Macedonia. 2 He said many things to strengthen the followers in the different places on his way through Macedonia. Then he went to Greece, 3 where he stayed for three months. He was ready to sail for Syria, but some Jews were planning something against him. So Paul decided to go back through Macedonia to Syria. 4 The men who went with him were Sopater son of Pyrrhus, from the city of Berea; Aristarchus and Secundus, from the city of Thessalonica; Gaius, from Derbe; Timothy; and Tychicus and Trophimus, two men from the country of Asia. 5 These men went on ahead and waited for us at Troas. 6 We sailed from Philippi after the Feast of Unleavened Bread. Five days later we met them in Troas, where we stayed for seven days.

Paul's Last Visit to Troas

7 On the first day of the week,*ⁿ* we all met together to break bread,*ⁿ* and Paul spoke to the group. Because he was planning to leave the next day, he kept on talking until midnight. 8 We were all together in a room upstairs, and there were many lamps in the room. 9 A young man named Eutychus was sitting in the window. As Paul continued talking, Eutychus was falling into a deep sleep. Finally, he went sound asleep and fell to the ground from the third floor. When they picked him up, he was dead. 10 Paul went down to Eutychus, knelt down and put his arms around him. He said, "Don't worry. He is alive now." 11 Then Paul went upstairs again, broke bread and ate. He spoke to them for a long time, until it was early morning, and then he left. 12 They took the young man home alive and were greatly comforted.

The Trip from Troas to Miletus

13 We went on ahead of Paul and sailed for the city of Assos, where he wanted to join us on the ship. Paul had planned this because he wanted to go to Assos by land. 14 When he met us there, we took him aboard and went to Mitylene. 15 We sailed from Mitylene and the next day came to a place near Chios. The following day we sailed to Samos, and the next day we reached Miletus. 16 Paul had already decided not to stop at Ephesus, because he did not want to stay too long in the country of Asia. He was hurrying to be in Jerusalem on the day of Pentecost, if that were possible.

The Elders from Ephesus

17 Now from Miletus Paul sent to Ephesus and called for the elders of the church. 18 When they came to him, he said, "You know about my life from the first day I came to Asia. You know the way I lived all the time I was with you. 19 The Jews made plans against me, which troubled me very much. But you know I always served the Lord unselfishly, and I often cried. 20 You know I preached to you and did not hold back anything that

---

20:7 first day of the week Sunday, which for the Jews began at sunset on our last day of the week. But if in this part of Asia a different system of time was used, then the meeting was on our Sunday night.
20:7 break bread Probably the Lord's Supper, the special meal that Jesus told his followers to eat to remember him (Luke 22:14-20).

Acts 20:38 **1501**

LET'S VISIT PHILIPPI   Acts 20

Philippi is a European city. At first, Philippi was called Krenides, which means "wells" or "springs". Later, it was renamed after Philip II. (Philip was the father of Alexander the Great, the Greek conqueror.)

From the ruins of the city we know that it had a market. We also know there was a gate. (Read about it in Acts 16:12–13.) There was a seat of judgement (like a courtroom), a library and a jail. This jail might have been the place where Paul and Silas were in prison together. (Look at Acts 16:23–40.) You might remember that they prayed and sang until an earthquake shook the jail during the night. The church at Philippi was the first European church. Paul and Silas founded the church by meeting with a women's prayer group. Lydia, a businesswoman, became the first Christian there. (Read Acts 16:12–15, 40.)

would help you. You know that I taught you in public and in your homes. 21 I warned both Jews and Greeks to change their lives and turn to God and believe in our Lord Jesus. 22 But now I must obey the Holy Spirit and go to Jerusalem. I don't know what will happen to me there. 23 I know only that in every city the Holy Spirit tells me that troubles and even jail wait for me. 24 I don't care about my own life. The most important thing is that I complete my mission, the work that the Lord Jesus gave me—to tell people the Good News about God's grace.

25 "And now, I know that none of you among whom I was preaching the kingdom of God will ever see me again. 26 So today I tell you that if any of you should be lost, I am not responsible, 27 because I have told you everything God wants you to know. 28 Be careful for yourselves and for all the people the Holy Spirit has given to you to care for. You must be like shepherds to the church of God,*n* which he bought with the death of his own Son. 29 I know that after I leave, some people will come like wild wolves and try to destroy the flock. 30 Also, some from your own group will rise up and twist the truth and will lead away followers after them. 31 So be careful! Always remember that for three years, day and night, I never stopped warning each of you, and I often cried over you.

32 "Now I am putting you in the care of God and the message about his grace. It is able to give you strength, and it will give you the blessings God has for all his holy people. 33 When I was with you, I never wanted anyone's money or fine clothes. 34 You know I always worked to take care of my own needs and the needs of those who were with me. 35 I showed you in all things that you should work as I did and help the weak. I taught you to remember the words Jesus said: 'It is more blessed to give than to receive.'"

36 When Paul had said this, he knelt down with all of them and prayed. 37-38 And they all cried because Paul had said they would never see him again. They put their arms around him and kissed him. Then they went with him to the ship.

20:28 of God Some Greek copies say, "of the Lord".

FAITH links

THE MOST FUN
ACTS 20:35

Which do you think is the most fun: giving a gift or receiving a gift? Let's face it – we like to receive. It's fun to get things and to have people serve us. So, receiving is more fun, right? Jesus and the apostle Paul would disagree. Jesus once said, "It is more blessed to give than to receive." Don't believe it? Try it and see!

Download these links to find out the most fun of all:

Share What You Have, Exodus 35:5–18, p. 123

A Small Percent, Deuteronomy 14:22–23, p. 247

Gifts from the Heart, 1 Chronicles 29, p. 557

Happiness or Joy? Job 29:18–19, p. 691

The Person Most Likely to Give? Acts 9:36–42, p. 1481

Give to Give, 1 Corinthians 16:1–4, p. 1566

Paul Goes to Jerusalem

21 After we all said goodbye to them, we sailed straight to the island of Cos. The next day we reached Rhodes, and from there we went to Patara. 2 There we found a ship going to Phoenicia, so we went aboard and sailed away. 3 We sailed near the island of Cyprus, seeing it to the north, but we sailed on to Syria. We stopped at Tyre because the ship needed to unload its cargo there. 4 We found some followers in Tyre and stayed with them for seven days. Through the Holy Spirit they warned Paul not to go to Jerusalem. 5 When we finished our visit, we left and continued our trip. All the followers, even the women and children, came outside the city with us. After we all knelt on the beach and prayed, 6 we said goodbye and got on the ship, and the followers went back home.

7 We continued our trip from Tyre and arrived at Ptolemais, where we greeted the believers and stayed with them for a day. 8 The next day we left Ptolemais and went to the city of Caesarea. There we went into the home of Philip the preacher, one of the seven helpers,*n* and stayed with him. 9 He had four unmarried daughters who had the gift of prophesying. 10 After we had been there for some time, a prophet named Agabus arrived from Judea. 11 He came to us and borrowed Paul's belt and used it to tie his own hands and feet. He said, "The Holy Spirit says, 'This is how the Jews in Jerusalem will tie up the man who wears this belt. Then they will give him to those who are not Jews.'"

12 When we all heard this, we and the people there begged Paul not to go to Jerusalem. 13 But he said, "Why are you crying and making me so sad? I am not only ready to be tied up in Jerusalem, I am ready to die for the Lord Jesus!"

14 We could not persuade him to stay away from Jerusalem. So we stopped begging him and said, "We pray that what the Lord wants will be done."

15 After this, we got ready and started on our way to Jerusalem. 16 Some of the followers from Caesarea went with us and took us to the home of Mnason, where we would stay. He was from Cyprus and was one of the first followers.

Paul Visits James

17 In Jerusalem the believers were glad to see us. 18 The next day Paul went with us to visit James, and all the elders

---

21:8 helpers The seven men chosen for a special work described in Acts 6:1-6.

were there. 19 Paul greeted them and told them everything God had done among the non-Jewish people through him. 20 When they heard this, they praised God. Then they said to Paul, "Brother, you can see that many thousands of Jews have become believers. And they think it is very important to obey the law of Moses. 21 They have heard about your teaching, that you tell the Jews who live among those who are not Jews to leave the law of Moses. They have heard that you tell them not to circumcise their children and not to obey Jewish customs. 22 What should we do? They will learn that you have come. 23 So we will tell you what to do: four of our men have made a promise to God. 24 Take these men with you and share in their cleansing ceremony.*ⁿ* Pay their expenses so they can shave their heads.*ⁿ* Then it will prove to everyone that what they have heard about you is not true and that you follow the law of Moses in your own life. 25 We have already sent a letter to the non-Jewish believers. The letter said: 'Do not eat food that has been offered to idols, or blood or animals that have been strangled. Do not take part in sexual sin.'"

26 The next day Paul took the four men and shared in the cleansing ceremony with them. Then he went to the Temple and announced the time when the days of the cleansing ceremony would be finished. On the last day an offering would be given for each of the men.

27 When the seven days were almost over, some Jews from Asia saw Paul at the Temple. They upset all the people and grabbed Paul. 28 They shouted, "People of Israel, help us! This is the man who goes everywhere teaching against the law of Moses, against our people and against this Temple. Now he has brought some Greeks into the Temple and has made this holy place unclean!" 29 (The Jews said this because they had seen Trophimus, a man from Ephesus, with Paul in Jerusalem. The Jews thought that Paul had brought him into the Temple.)

30 All the people in Jerusalem became upset. Together they ran, took Paul and dragged him out of the Temple. The Temple doors were closed immediately. 31 While they were trying to kill Paul, the commander of the Roman army in Jerusalem learned that there was trouble in the whole city. 32 Immediately he took some officers and soldiers and ran to the place where the crowd was gathered. When the people saw them, they stopped beating Paul. 33 The commander went to Paul and arrested him. He told his soldiers to tie Paul with two chains. Then he asked who he was and what he had done wrong. 34 Some in the crowd were yelling one thing, and some were yelling another. Because of all this confusion and shouting, the commander could not learn what had happened. So he ordered the soldiers to take Paul to the army building. 35 When Paul came to the steps, the soldiers had to carry him because the people were ready to hurt him. 36 The whole mob was following them, shouting, "Kill him!"

37 As the soldiers were about to take Paul into the army building, he spoke to the commander, "May I say something to you?"

The commander said, "Do you speak Greek? 38 I thought you were the Egyptian who started some trouble against the government not long ago and led 4,000 killers out to the desert."

39 Paul said, "No, I am a Jew from Tarsus in the country of Cilicia. I am a citizen of that important city. Please, let me speak to the people."

40 The commander gave permission, so Paul stood on the steps and waved his hand to quiet the people. When there was silence, he spoke to them in the Jewish language.*ⁿ*

Paul Speaks to the People

22 Paul said, "Friends, fellow Jews, listen to my defence to you."

21:24 cleansing ceremony The special things Jews did to end the Nazirite promise.
21:24 shave their heads The Jews did this to show that their promise was finished.
21:40 Jewish language Hebrew or Aramaic, the languages of the Jews in the first century.

A MAN OF TWO COUNTRIES   Acts 22

Paul was a Jewish man, yet he was born in a town that was ruled by Rome. Because of that, he was an Israelite, but he was also a Roman citizen. (Check out Acts 22:28.) A Roman citizen could not be tied up or put into prison without a trial. A Roman citizen also wasn't supposed to be beaten or whipped. Another law said that if a Roman citizen felt he was not receiving a fair trial under local authorities, he could appeal his cause to Rome.

Sometimes being a Roman citizen really helped Paul out. Once he and his partner Silas were bound, beaten and imprisoned by Roman authorities at Philippi. When Paul told the authorities that they were Roman citizens, the authorities let them go immediately. (Read Acts 16:16–40.) Another time in Jerusalem, Paul was taken into custody by Roman soldiers. Because he was a Roman citizen, he was not beaten and was able to get a hearing that eventually led him to Rome. (See Acts 22:24–29.)

2 When the Jews heard him speaking the Jewish language,* they became very quiet. Paul said, 3 "I am a Jew, born in Tarsus in the country of Cilicia, but I grew up in this city. I was a student of Gamaliel,* who carefully taught me everything about the law of our ancestors. I was very serious about serving God, just as are all of you here today. 4 I persecuted the people who followed the Way of Jesus, and some of them were even killed. I arrested men and women and put them in jail. 5 The high priest and the whole council of Jewish elders can tell you this is true. They gave me letters to the Jewish brothers in Damascus. So I was going there to arrest these people and bring them back to Jerusalem to be punished.

6 "At about noon when I came near Damascus, a bright light from heaven suddenly flashed all around me. 7 I fell to the ground and heard a voice saying, 'Saul, Saul, why are you persecuting me?' 8 I asked, 'Who are you, Lord?' The voice said, 'I am Jesus from Nazareth whom you are persecuting.' 9 Those who were with me did not hear the voice, but they saw the light. 10 I said, 'What shall I do, Lord?' The Lord answered, 'Get up and go to Damascus. There you will be told about all the things I have planned for you to do.' 11 I could not see, because the bright light had made me blind. So my companions led me into Damascus.

12 "There a man named Ananias came to me. He was a religious man; he obeyed the law of Moses, and all the Jews who lived there respected him. 13 He stood by me and said, 'Brother Saul, see again!' Immediately I was able to see him. 14 He said, 'The God of our ancestors chose you long ago to know his plan, to see the Righteous One and to hear words from him. 15 You will be his witness to all people, telling them about what you have seen and heard. 16 Now, why wait any longer? Get up, be baptised and wash your sins away, trusting in him to save you.'

17 "Later, when I returned to Jerusa-

22:2 Jewish language Hebrew or Aramaic, the languages of the Jews in the first century.
22:3 Gamaliel A very important teacher of the Pharisees, a Jewish religious group (Acts 5:34).

lem, I was praying in the Temple, and I saw a vision. 18 I saw the Lord saying to me, 'Hurry! Leave Jerusalem now! The people here will not accept the truth about me.' 19 But I said, 'Lord, they know that in every synagogue I put the believers in jail and beat them. 20 They also know I was there when Stephen, your witness, was killed. I stood there agreeing and holding the coats of those who were killing him!' 21 But the Lord said to me, 'Leave now. I will send you far away to the non-Jewish people.'"

22 The crowd listened to Paul until he said this. Then they began shouting, "Kill him! Get him out of the world! He should not be allowed to live!" 23 They shouted, threw off their coats[n] and threw dust into the air.[n]

24 Then the commander ordered the soldiers to take Paul into the army building and beat him. He wanted to make Paul tell why the people were shouting against him like this. 25 But as the soldiers were tying him up, preparing to beat him, Paul said to an officer nearby, "Do you have the right to beat a Roman citizen[n] who has not been proven guilty?"

26 When the officer heard this, he went to the commander and reported it. The officer said, "Do you know what you are doing? This man is a Roman citizen."

27 The commander came to Paul and said, "Tell me, are you really a Roman citizen?"

He answered, "Yes."

28 The commander said, "I paid a lot of money to become a Roman citizen."

But Paul said, "I was born a citizen."

29 The men who were preparing to question Paul moved away from him immediately. The commander was frightened because he had already tied Paul, and Paul was a Roman citizen.

Paul Speaks to Jewish Leaders

30 The next day the commander decided to learn why the Jews were accusing Paul. So he ordered the leading priests and the Jewish council to meet. The commander took Paul's chains off. Then he brought Paul out and stood him before their meeting.

23 Paul looked at the Jewish council and said, "Brothers, I have lived my life with a clear conscience before God up to this day." 2 Ananias,[n] the high priest, heard this and told the men who were standing near Paul to hit him on the mouth. 3 Paul said to Ananias, "God will hit you, too! You are like a wall that has been painted white. You sit there and judge me, using the law of Moses, but you are telling them to hit me, and that is against the law."

4 The men standing near Paul said to him, "You cannot insult God's high priest like that!"

5 Paul said, "Brothers, I did not know this man was the high priest. It is written in the Scriptures, 'You must not curse a leader of your people.'"[n]

6 Some of the men in the meeting were Sadducees, and others were Pharisees. Knowing this, Paul shouted to them, "My brothers, I am a Pharisee, and my father was a Pharisee. I am on trial here because I believe that people will rise from the dead."

7 When Paul said this, there was an argument between the Pharisees and the Sadducees, and the group was divided. 8 (The Sadducees do not believe in angels or spirits or that people will rise from the dead. But the Pharisees believe in them all.) 9 So there was a great uproar. Some of the teachers of the law, who were Pharisees, stood up and argued, "We find nothing wrong with this man. Maybe an angel or a spirit did speak to him."

10 The argument was beginning to turn into such a fight that the commander was afraid the Jews would tear Paul to pieces. So he told the soldiers to go down and take Paul away and put him in the army building.

22:23 threw off their coats This showed that the Jews were very angry with Paul.
22:23 threw dust into the air This showed even greater anger.
22:25 Roman citizen Roman law said that Roman citizens must not be beaten before they had a trial.
23:2 Ananias This is not the man named Ananias in Acts 22:12.
23:5 'You . . . people.' Quotation from Exodus 22:28.

Acts 23:11

11 The next night the Lord came and stood by Paul. He said, "Be brave! You have told people in Jerusalem about me. You must do the same in Rome."

FAITH links

CALLING ANYONE!
ACTS 23:12-22

There are many unsung heroes in life. Paul's nephew learned about an evil plot to kill Paul. He told Paul about the plot and saved his life. Quick! For a chance to be known as the smartest person in the world, what was Paul's nephew's name? Give up? The answer is: no one knows! The Bible doesn't give his name. But we know that what he did for Paul was very important.

Sometimes God causes unknown people to do important things for him. God can use anyone to serve him. You don't have to be brave or have super strength. You just have to be willing.

Check out these links for more on serving God:

A Use for Your Abilities, Genesis 41, p. 59

His OK to Obey, Deuteronomy 2:24–36, p. 230

Your Stats, 1 Kings 15; 16, p. 460

Just Say Yes! Matthew 9:9–13, p. 1289

That Thing You Do, Matthew 25:14–30, p. 1319

The "Eyes" Have It! 1 Corinthians 12, p. 1559

12 In the morning some of the Jews made a plan to kill Paul, and they took an oath not to eat or drink anything until they had killed him. 13 There were more than 40 Jews who made this plan. 14 They went to the leading priests and the Jewish elders and said, "We have taken an oath not to eat or drink until we have killed Paul. 15 So this is what we want you to do: send a message to the commander to bring Paul out to you as though you want to ask him more questions. We will be waiting to kill him while he is on the way here."

16 But Paul's nephew heard about this plan and went to the army building and told Paul. 17 Then Paul called one of the officers and said, "Take this young man to the commander. He has a message for him."

18 So the officer brought Paul's nephew to the commander and said, "The prisoner, Paul, asked me to bring this young man to you. He wants to tell you something."

19 The commander took the young man's hand and led him to a place where they could be alone. He asked, "What do you want to tell me?"

20 The young man said, "The Jews have decided to ask you to bring Paul down to their council meeting tomorrow. They want you to think they are going to ask him more questions. 21 But don't believe them! More than 40 men are hiding and waiting to kill Paul. They have all taken an oath not to eat or drink until they have killed him. Now they are waiting for you to agree."

22 The commander sent the young man away, ordering him, "Don't tell anyone that you have told me about their plan."

Paul is Sent to Caesarea

23 Then the commander called two officers and said, "I need some men to go to Caesarea. Get 200 soldiers, 70 horsemen and 200 men with spears ready to leave at nine o'clock tonight. 24 Get some horses for Paul to ride so he can be taken to Governor Felix safely." 25 And he wrote a letter that said:

26 From Claudius Lysias.
To the Most Excellent Governor Felix:
Greetings.
27 The Jews had taken this man and planned to kill him. But I learned that he is a Roman citizen, so I went with my soldiers and saved him. 28 I wanted to know why they were accusing him, so I brought him before their council meeting. 29 I learned that the Jews said Paul did some things that were wrong by their own laws, but no charge was worthy of jail or death. 30 When I was told that some of the Jews were planning to kill Paul, I sent him to you at once. I also told those Jews to tell you what they have against him."

31 So the soldiers did what they were told and took Paul and brought him to the city of Antipatris that night. 32 The next day the horsemen went with Paul to Caesarea, but the other soldiers went back to the army building in Jerusalem. 33 When the horsemen came to Caesarea and gave the letter to the governor, they turned Paul over to him. 34 The governor read the letter and asked Paul, "What area are you from?" When he learned that Paul was from Cilicia, 35 he said, "I will hear your case when those who are against you come here, too." Then the governor gave orders for Paul to be kept under guard in Herod's palace.

Paul is Accused

24 Five days later Ananias, the high priest, went to the city of Caesarea with some of the Jewish elders and a lawyer named Tertullus. They had come to make charges against Paul before the governor. 2 Paul was called into the meeting, and Tertullus began to accuse him, saying, "Most Excellent Felix! Our people enjoy much peace because of you, and many wrong things in our country are being made right through your wise help. 3 We accept these things always and in every place, and we are thankful for them. 4 But not wanting to take any more of your time, I beg you to be kind and listen to our few words. 5 We have found this man to be a troublemaker, stirring up the Jews everywhere in the world. He is a leader of the Nazarene group. 6 Also, he was trying to make the Temple unclean, but we stopped him." 8 By asking him questions yourself, you can decide if all these things are true." 9 The other Jews agreed and said that all of this was true.

10 When the governor made a sign for Paul to speak, Paul said, "Governor Felix, I know you have been a judge over this nation for a long time. So I am happy to defend myself before you. 11 You can learn for yourself that I went to worship in Jerusalem only twelve days ago. 12 Those who are accusing me did not find me arguing with anyone in the Temple or stirring up the people in the synagogues or in the city. 13 They cannot prove the things they are saying against me now. 14 But I will tell you this: I worship the God of our ancestors as a follower of the Way of Jesus. The Jews say that the Way of Jesus is not the right way. But I believe everything that is taught in the law of Moses and that is written in the books of the Prophets. 15 I have the same hope in God that they have—the hope that all people, good and bad, will surely be raised from the dead. 16 This is why I always try to do what I believe is right before God and people.

17 "After being away from Jerusalem for several years, I went back to bring money to my people and to offer sacrifices. 18 I was doing this when they found me in the Temple. I had finished the cleansing ceremony and had not made any trouble; no people were gathering around me. 19 But there were some Jews from the country of Asia who should be here, standing before you. If I have really done anything wrong, they are the ones who should accuse me. 20 Or ask these Jews here if they found any wrong in me when

---

24:6 Verse 6 Some Greek copies add verses 6b-8a: "And we wanted to judge him by our own law. 7 But the officer Lysias came and used much force to take him from us. 8 And Lysias commanded those who wanted to accuse Paul to come to you."

I stood before the Jewish council in Jerusalem. 21 But I did shout one thing when I stood before them: 'You are judging me today because I believe that people will rise from the dead!'"

22 Felix already understood much about the Way of Jesus. He stopped the trial and said, "When commander Lysias comes here, I will decide your case." 23 Felix told the officer to keep Paul guarded but to give him some freedom and to let his friends bring what he needed.

Paul Speaks to Felix and His Wife

24 After some days Felix came with his wife, Drusilla, who was Jewish, and asked for Paul to be brought to him. He listened to Paul talk about believing in Christ Jesus. 25 But Felix became afraid when Paul spoke about living right, self-control and the time when God will judge the world. He said, "Go away now. When I have more time, I will call for you." 26 At the same time Felix hoped that Paul would give him some money, so he often sent for Paul and talked with him.

27 But after two years, Felix was replaced by Porcius Festus as governor. But Felix had left Paul in prison to please the Jews.

Paul Asks to See Caesar

25 Three days after Festus became governor, he went from Caesarea to Jerusalem. 2 There the leading priests and the important Jewish leaders made charges against Paul before Festus. 3 They asked Festus to do them a favour. They wanted him to send Paul back to Jerusalem, because they had a plan to kill him on the way. 4 But Festus answered that Paul would be kept in Caesarea and that he himself was returning there soon. 5 He said, "Some of your leaders should go with me. They can accuse the man there in Caesarea, if he has really done something wrong."

6 Festus stayed in Jerusalem another eight or ten days and then went back to Caesarea. The next day he told the soldiers to bring Paul before him. Festus was seated on the judge's seat 7 when Paul came into the room. The Jewish people who had come from Jerusalem stood around him, making serious charges against him, which they could not prove. 8 This is what Paul said to defend himself: "I have done nothing wrong against the Jewish law, against the Temple or against Caesar."

9 But Festus wanted to please the Jews. So he asked Paul, "Do you want to go to Jerusalem for me to judge you there on these charges?"

10 Paul said, "I am standing at Caesar's judgement seat now, where I should be judged. I have done nothing wrong to

FAITH CHALLENGE

Read 24:25 to see what one Roman leader said about becoming a Christian. Why do you think some people are afraid to hear about becoming a Christian? What would you tell them about the need to know Jesus?

TeSTiNG iT

Acts 24:25
But Felix became afraid when Paul spoke about living right, self-control and the time when God will judge the world. He said, "Go away now. When I have more time, I will call for you."

the Jews; you know this is true. 11 If I have done something wrong and the law says I must die, I do not ask to be saved from death. But if these charges are not true, then no one can give me to them. I want Caesar to hear my case!"

12 Festus talked about this with his advisors. Then he said, "You have asked to see Caesar, so you will go to Caesar!"

Paul Before King Agrippa

13 A few days later King Agrippa and Bernice came to Caesarea to visit Festus. 14 They stayed there for some time, and Festus told the king about Paul's case. Festus said, "There is a man that Felix left in prison. 15 When I went to Jerusalem, the leading priests and the Jewish elders there made charges against him, asking me to sentence him to death. 16 But I answered, 'When a man is accused of a crime, Romans do not hand him over until he has been allowed to face his accusers and defend himself against their charges.' 17 So when these Jews came here to Caesarea for the trial, I did not waste time. The next day I sat on the judge's seat and commanded that the man be brought in. 18 The Jews stood up and accused him, but not of any serious crime as I thought they would. 19 The things they said were about their own religion and about a man named Jesus who died. But Paul said that he is still alive. 20 Not knowing how to find out about these questions, I asked Paul, 'Do you want to go to Jerusalem and be judged there?' 21 But he asked to be kept in Caesarea. He wants a decision from the emperor." So I ordered that he be held until I could send him to Caesar."

22 Agrippa said to Festus, "I would also like to hear this man myself."

Festus said, "Tomorrow you will hear him."

23 The next day Agrippa and Bernice appeared with great show, acting like very important people. They went into the judgement room with the army leaders and the important men of Caesarea. Then Festus ordered the soldiers to bring Paul in. 24 Festus said, "King Agrippa and all who are gathered here with us, you see this man. All the Jewish people, here and in Jerusalem, have complained to me about him, shouting that he should not live any longer. 25 When I judged him, I found no reason to order his death. But since he asked to be judged by Caesar, I decided to send him. 26 But I have nothing definite to write to the emperor about him. So I have brought him before all of you—especially you, King Agrippa. I hope you can question him and give me something to write. 27 I think it is foolish to send a prisoner to Caesar without telling what charges are against him."

Paul Defends Himself

26 Agrippa said to Paul, "You may now speak to defend yourself."

Then Paul raised his hand and began to speak. 2 He said, "King Agrippa, I am very happy to stand before you and will answer all the charges the Jewish people make against me. 3 You know so much about all the Jewish customs and the things the Jews argue about, so please listen to me patiently.

4 "All the Jewish people know about my whole life, how I lived from the beginning in my own country and later in Jerusalem. 5 They have known me for a long time. If they want to, they can tell you that I was a good Pharisee. And the Pharisees obey the laws of the Jewish religion more carefully than any other group. 6 Now I am on trial because I hope for the promise that God made to our ancestors. 7 This is the promise that the twelve tribes of our people hope to receive as they serve God day and night. My king,

> If I have done something wrong and the law says I must die, I do not ask to be saved from death.
> – Acts 25:11

25:21 emperor The ruler of the Roman Empire, which was almost all the known world.

FAITH links

HOPE THAT DOESN'T FAIL
ACTS 26:4-7

Imagine being dragged into court and told to defend yourself for being a Christian. This was Paul's situation. After being arrested and taken before the Jewish king, Agrippa, Paul stated his defence. His explanation can be summed up in three words: hope in Jesus. This is the kind of hope that won't fail in a crisis. This hope is eternal!

When you believe in Jesus, you have hope because you know that he keeps his promises. He promised to always be with you, no matter what. That's the kind of hope the world needs!

A Message of Courage and Hope, 2 Kings 19:4–10, p. 505

Comfort from the Word, Job 26:3–4, p. 688

A Hopeful Name, Hosea 1:3–11, p. 1172

A Safe Place, Nahum 1:7, p. 1231

Mission Impossible? Mark 5:21–24, 35–43, p. 1337

Our Good Shepherd, John 10:11–15, p. 1441

---

the Jews have accused me because I hope for this same promise! 8 Why do any of you people think it is impossible for God to raise people from the dead?

9 "I, too, thought I ought to do many things against Jesus from Nazareth. 10 And that is what I did in Jerusalem. The leading priests gave me the power to put many of God's people in jail, and when they were being killed, I agreed it was a good thing. 11 In every synagogue, I often punished them and tried to make them speak against Jesus. I was so angry against them I even went to other cities to find them and punish them.

12 "On one occasion the leading priests gave me permission and the power to go to Damascus. 13 On the way there, at noon, I saw a light from heaven. It was brighter than the sun and flashed all around me and those who were travelling with me. 14 We all fell to the ground. Then I heard a voice speaking to me in the Jewish language,[n] saying, 'Saul, Saul, why are you persecuting me? You are only hurting yourself by fighting me.' 15 I said, 'Who are you, Lord?' The Lord said, 'I am Jesus, the one you are persecuting. 16 Stand up! I have chosen you to be my servant and my witness—you will tell people the things that you have seen and the things that I will show you. This is why I have come to you today. 17 I will keep you safe from your own people and also from those who are not Jewish. I am sending you to them 18 to open their eyes so that they may turn away from darkness to the light, away from the power of Satan and to God. Then their sins can be forgiven, and they can have a place with those people who have been made holy by believing in me.'

19 "King Agrippa, after I had this vision from heaven, I obeyed it. 20 I began telling people that they should change their hearts and lives and turn to God and do things to show they really had changed. I told this first to those in Damascus, then in Jerusalem and in every part of Judea, and also to those who are not Jewish. 21 This is why the Jews took me and were trying to kill me in the Temple. 22 But God has helped me, and so I stand here today, telling all people, small and great, what I have seen. But I am saying only what Moses and the prophets said would happen—23 that the Christ would die, and as the first to rise from the dead, he would bring light to the Jewish and non-Jewish people."

26:14 **Jewish language** Hebrew or Aramaic, the languages of the Jews in the first century.

Paul Tries to Persuade Agrippa

24 While Paul was saying these things to defend himself, Festus said loudly, "Paul, you are out of your mind! Too much study has driven you insane!" 25 Paul said, "Most excellent Festus, I am not mad. My words are true and sensible. 26 King Agrippa knows about these things, and I can speak freely to him. I know he has heard about all these things, because they did not happen in a corner. 27 King Agrippa, do you believe what the prophets wrote? I know you believe." 28 King Agrippa said to Paul, "Do you think you can persuade me to become a Christian in such a short time?" 29 Paul said, "Whether it is a short or a long time, I pray to God that not only you but every person listening to me today would be saved and be like me—except for these chains I have."

30 Then King Agrippa, Governor Festus, Bernice and all the people sitting with them stood up 31 and left the room. Talking to each other, they said, "There is no reason why this man should die or be put in jail." 32 And Agrippa said to Festus, "We could let this man go free, but he has asked Caesar to hear his case."

Paul Sails for Rome

27 It was decided that we would sail for Italy. An officer named Julius, who served in the emperor's[n] army, guarded Paul and some other prisoners. 2 We got on a ship that was from the city of Adramyttium and was about to sail to different ports in the country of Asia. Aristarchus, a man from the city of Thessalonica in Macedonia, went with us. 3 The next day we came to Sidon. Julius was very good to Paul and gave him freedom to go and visit his friends, who took care of his needs. 4 We left Sidon and sailed close to the island of Cyprus, because the wind was blowing against us. 5 We went across the sea by Cilicia and Pamphylia and landed at the city of Myra, in Lycia. 6 There the officer found a ship from Alexandria that was going to Italy, so he put us on it.

7 We sailed slowly for many days. We had a hard time reaching Cnidus because the wind was blowing against us, and we could not go any further. So we sailed by the south side of the island of Crete near Salmone. 8 Sailing past it was hard. Then we came to a place called Fair Havens, near the city of Lasea.

9 We had lost much time, and it was now dangerous to sail, because it was already after the Day of Cleansing.[n] So Paul warned them, 10 "Men, I can see there will be a lot of trouble on this trip. The ship, the cargo and even our lives may be lost." 11 But the captain and the owner of the ship did not agree with Paul, and the officer believed what the captain and owner of the ship said. 12 Since that harbour was not a good place for the ship to stay for the winter, most of the men decided that the ship should leave. They hoped we could go to Phoenix and stay there for the winter. Phoenix, a city on the island of Crete, had a harbour which faced south-west and north-west.

The Storm

13 When a good wind began to blow from the south, the men on the ship thought, "This is the wind we wanted, and now we have it." So they pulled up the anchor, and we sailed very close to the island of Crete. 14 But then a very strong wind named the "northeaster" came from the island. 15 The ship was caught in it and could not sail against it. So we stopped trying and let the wind carry us. 16 When we went below a small island named Cauda, we were barely able to bring in the lifeboat. 17 After the men took the lifeboat in, they tied ropes around the ship to hold it together. The men were afraid that the ship would hit the sandbanks of Syrtis,[n] so they lowered the sail and let the wind carry the ship. 18 The next day the storm was blowing us so hard that the men threw out some of the cargo.

27:1 **emperor** The ruler of the Roman Empire, which was almost all the known world.
27:9 **Day of Cleansing** An important Jewish holy day in the autumn of the year. Bad storms arose on the sea at this time of year.
27:17 **Syrtis** Shallow area in the sea near the Libyan coast.

19 A day later with their own hands they threw out the ship's equipment. 20 When we could not see the sun or the stars for many days, and the storm was very bad, we lost all hope of being saved.

21 After the men had gone without food for a long time, Paul stood up before them and said, "Men, you should have listened to me. You should not have sailed from Crete. Then you would not have had all this trouble and loss. 22 But now I tell you to cheer up because none of you will die. Only the ship will be lost. 23 Last night an angel came to me from the God I belong to and worship. 24 The angel said, 'Paul, do not be afraid. You must stand before Caesar. And God has promised you that he will save the lives of everyone sailing with you.' 25 So men, have courage. I trust in God that everything will happen as his angel told me. 26 But we will run aground on an island."

27 On the fourteenth night we were still being carried around in the Adriatic Sea.ⁿ About midnight the sailors thought we were close to land, 28 so they lowered a rope with a weight on the end of it into the water. They found that the water was 20 fathoms deep. They went a little further and lowered the rope again. It was 15 fathoms deep. 29 The sailors were afraid that we would hit the rocks, so they threw four anchors into the water and prayed for daylight to come. 30 Some of the sailors wanted to leave the ship, and they lowered the lifeboat, pretending they were throwing more anchors from the front of the ship. 31 But Paul told the officer and the other soldiers, "If these men do not stay in the ship, your lives cannot be saved." 32 So the soldiers cut the ropes and let the lifeboat fall into the water.

33 Just before dawn Paul began persuading all the people to eat something. He said, "For the past fourteen days you have been waiting and watching and not eating. 34 Now I beg you to eat something. You need it to stay alive. None of you will lose even one hair of your heads." 35 After he said this, Paul took some bread and thanked God for it before all of them. He broke off a piece and began eating. 36 They all felt better and started eating, too. 37 There were 276 people on the ship. 38 When they had eaten all they wanted, they began making the ship lighter by throwing the grain into the sea.

27:35 Thankfulness Check out one way to give thanks.

The Ship is Destroyed

39 When daylight came, the sailors saw land. They did not know what land it was, but they saw a bay with a beach and wanted to sail the ship to the beach if they could. 40 So they cut the ropes to the anchors and left the anchors in the sea. At the same time, they untied the ropes that were holding the rudders. Then they raised the front sail into the wind and sailed towards the beach. 41 But the ship hit a sandbank. The front of the ship stuck there and could not move, but the back of the ship began to break up from the big waves.

42 The soldiers decided to kill the prisoners so none of them could swim away and escape. 43 But Julius, the officer, wanted to let Paul live and did not allow the soldiers to kill the prisoners. Instead he ordered everyone who could swim to jump into the water first and swim to land. 44 The rest were to follow using wooden boards or pieces of the ship. And this is how all the people made it safely to land.

Paul on the Island of Malta

28 When we were safe on land, we learned that the island was called Malta. 2 The people who lived there were very good to us. Because it was raining and very cold, they made a fire and welcomed all of us. 3 Paul gathered a pile of sticks and was putting them on the fire when a poisonous snake came out because of the heat and bit him on the hand. 4 The people living on the island saw the snake hanging from Paul's hand and said to each other,

---

27:27 Adriatic Sea The sea between Greece and Italy, including the central Mediterranean.

THE LIFE OF PAUL

Acts

1. Early life. Saul was born in Tarsus, both a Jew *and* a Roman citizen. (Read Acts 22:3.) He studied with a famous Jewish teacher named Gamaliel and became a well-respected religious leader. Saul hunted down Christians and punished them for their faith. (Look at Acts 8:3.) Later, Saul met Jesus on his way to Damascus and became a leader of Christ-followers, known as Christians. (See Acts 9:1–9.)

2. Preparation. Paul began working at first with the Christians in Damascus (Acts 9:22), Arabia (Galatians 1:17, p. 1587) and Jerusalem. Then he went to Tarsus for about ten years because the Jewish leaders were against him. (Read Acts 9:26–30.)

3. Early missionary work. Paul travelled to Cyprus, Antioch, Iconium, Lystra and Derbe with his good friend Barnabas. They took the message of the gospel to non-Jewish people. (Look at Acts 11:19–26. See also Acts 13 and 14 for more information about their travels.)

4. Later trips. On Paul's second missionary trip, he travelled to Macedonia, Philippi, Thessalonica, Berea, Athens and Corinth. (Look up Acts 16:1—18:23.) On his third missionary trip, he worked with the churches at Ephesus, Troas and Miletus. (Check out Acts 19 and 20.)

5. After he was put in jail for his preaching, Paul appealed his case to Rome. (Read Acts 25.) He travelled by ship to Rome for a trial. (Look up Acts 27.) Even as a prisoner in Rome he continued to preach about Jesus. (See Acts 28:17–31.) It's possible that Paul was executed around A.D. 68.

"This man must be a murderer! He did not die in the sea, but Justice[n] does not want him to live." 5 But Paul shook the snake off into the fire and was not hurt. 6 The people thought that Paul would swell up or fall down dead. They waited and watched him for a long time, but nothing bad happened to him. So they changed their minds and said, "He is a god!"

7 There were some fields around there owned by Publius, an important man on

---

28:4 Justice The people thought there was a god named Justice who would punish bad people.

the island. He welcomed us into his home and was very good to us for three days. 8 Publius' father was sick with a fever and dysentery.ⁿ Paul went to him, prayed and put his hands on the man and healed him. 9 After this, all the other sick people on the island came to Paul, and he healed them, too. 10-11 The people on the island gave us many honours. When we were ready to leave, three months later, they gave us the things we needed.

28:10–11 Giving How can you help God's workers?

Paul Goes to Rome

We got on a ship from Alexandria that had stayed on the island during the winter. On the front of the ship was the sign of the twin gods.ⁿ 12 We stopped at Syracuse for three days. 13 From there we sailed to Rhegium. The next day a wind began to blow from the south, and a day later we came to Puteoli. 14 We found some believers there who asked us to stay with them for a week. Finally, we came to Rome. 15 The believers in Rome heard that we were there and came out as far as the Market of Appiusⁿ and the Three Innsⁿ to meet us. When Paul saw them, he was encouraged and thanked God.

Paul in Rome

16 When we arrived at Rome, Paul was allowed to live alone, with the soldier who guarded him.

17 Three days later Paul sent for the Jewish leaders there. When they came together, he said, "Brothers, I have done nothing against our people or the customs of our ancestors. But I was arrested in Jerusalem and given to the Romans. 18 After they asked me many questions, they could find no reason why I should be killed. They wanted to let me go free, 19 but the Jewish people there argued against that. So I had to ask to come to Rome to have my trial before Caesar. But I have no charge to bring against my own people. 20 That is why I wanted to see you and talk with you. I am bound with this chain because I believe in the hope of Israel."

21 They answered Paul, "We have received no letters from Judea about you. None of our Jewish brothers who have come from there brought news or told us anything bad about you. 22 But we want to hear your ideas, because we know that people everywhere are speaking against this religious group."

23 Paul and the Jewish people chose a day for a meeting and on that day many more of the Jews met with Paul at the place he was staying. He spoke to them all day long. Using the law of Moses and the prophets' writings, he explained the kingdom of God, and he tried to persuade them to believe these things about Jesus. 24 Some believed what Paul said, but others did not. 25 So they argued and began leaving after Paul said one more thing to them: "The Holy Spirit spoke the truth to your ancestors through Isaiah the prophet, saying,

26 'Go and tell this people:
   You will listen and listen, but you will
      not understand.
   You will look and look, but you will
      not learn.
27 Make the minds of these people
      dumb.
   Shut their ears. Cover their
      eyes.
   Otherwise, they might really
      understand
   what they see with their eyes
      and hear with their ears.
   They might really understand in their
      minds
   and come back to me and be
      healed.'   *Isaiah 6:9-10*

28 "I want you to know that God has also sent his salvation to those who are not Jewish, and they will listen!" 29ⁿ

28:8 dysentery A sickness like diarrhoea.
28:10-11 twin gods Statues of Castor and Pollux, gods in old Greek tales.
28:15 Market of Appius A town about 27 miles from Rome.
28:15 Three Inns A town about 30 miles from Rome.
28:29 Verse 29 Some late Greek copies add verse 29: "After Paul said this, the Jews left. They were arguing very much with one another."

30 Paul stayed two full years in his own rented house and welcomed all people who came to visit him. **31** He boldly preached about the kingdom of God and taught about the Lord Jesus Christ, and no one tried to stop him.

BACK TO BASICS

Hi! Paul here. You might have read about me in Luke's book, Acts. I was a Jewish religious leader who had a life-changing encounter with the living Jesus. As a result, instead of killing Jesus' followers, I became a leader in the early church! You can guess I caused quite a stir when I began telling others about Jesus! Some say this book – a letter, written to my friends in Rome – was one of my most important. Read my other books, and you decide!

I wrote this book to help this young church understand the basics about my teachings on Jesus, God, the church, and differences between Jews and non-Jews. The church in Rome was full of all sorts of controversies over what to believe. So, I wrote this letter to them to set the record straight. And in the process I ended up writing what has become a lesson on the Christian faith that is important to all followers at all times.

JESUS WATCH

The significance of Jesus fills this book. What significance? Well, Paul takes time in this book to help believers understand who we are without Jesus and what effect Jesus has on our lives – and ultimately on our eternity.

In Romans, Paul explains that Jesus is the giver of eternal life. It's a gift that's not only free, but also one that frees us from the punishment we would face if we didn't know him. As Paul explains, without Jesus, we would be totally lost. When Jesus died on the cross, he totally defeated death for all those who believe in him. That's a powerful message, and Paul wanted *everyone* to know it and understand it.

my FAVOURITE links

OTHER CONNECTIONS

 What's the first thing you want to do when you get some wonderful news? Do you keep it to yourself or do you rush right out to tell someone else? Connect to Have I Got News for You! Romans 10:14–17, to see what God wants us to do with *his* good news!

Find out what God has to say about keeping the peace in your home, or among your friends, when you download Peace and Quiet? Romans 14:19.

GET THE INFO

Link to Let's Visit Rome, Romans 1:15, to learn more about the largest and most famous city in New Testament times.

Here's a quick question. Does God ever stop loving us?

Check out Romans 8:38–39 to see what Paul has to say about God's love.

THE BOOK OF ROMANS HAS A LOT OF OTHER REALLY FANTASTIC TRUTHS. CHECK OUT THESE:
Everyone needs Jesus! Romans 3:9–20
The father of our faith, Romans 4
God's Spirit rules! Romans 8
Live by God's rules, Romans 12; 13

FAITH links

- Just for the Asking, Romans 3:23–28
- Love for Free, Romans 5:8
- A High Price, Romans 6:23
- The Sin Habit, Romans 7:15–20
- It's Under Control, Romans 8:28
- The Doubt Remover, Romans 10:8–10
- Our Gift to God, Romans 12:1–2
- Glad to Help! Romans 15:17–20

Romans 1:1

1 From Paul, a servant of Christ Jesus. God called me to be an apostle and chose me to tell the Good News.

2 God promised this Good News long ago through his prophets, as it is written in the Holy Scriptures. 3-4 The Good News is about God's Son, Jesus Christ our Lord. As a man, he was born from the family of David. But through the Spirit of holiness he was appointed to be God's Son with great power by rising from the dead. 5 Through Christ, God gave me the special work of an apostle, which was to lead people of all nations to believe and obey. I do this work for him. 6 And you who are in Rome are also called to belong to Jesus Christ.

7 To all of you in Rome whom God loves and has called to be his holy people:

Grace and peace to you from God our Father and the Lord Jesus Christ.

A Prayer of Thanks

8 First I want to say that I thank my God through Jesus Christ for all of you, because people everywhere in the world are talking about your faith. 9 God, whom I serve with my whole heart by telling the Good News about his Son, knows that I always mention you 10 every time I pray. I pray that I will be allowed to come to you, and this will happen if God wants it. 11 I want very much to see you, to give you some spiritual gift to make you strong. 12 I mean that I want us to help each other with the faith we have. Your faith will help me, and my faith will help you. 13 Brothers and sisters,[n] I want you to know that I planned many times to come to you, but this has not been possible. I wanted to come so that I could help you grow spiritually as I have helped the other non-Jewish people.

14 I have a duty to all people—Greeks and those who are not Greeks, the wise and the foolish. 15 That is why I want so much to preach the Good News to you in Rome.

16 I am proud of the Good News, because it is the power God uses to save everyone who believes—to save the Jews first, and also to save those who are not Jews. 17 The Good News shows how God makes people right with himself—that it begins and ends with faith. As the Scripture says, "But those who are right with God will live by trusting in him."[n]

All People Have Done Wrong

18 God's anger is shown from heaven against all the evil and wrong things people do. By their own evil lives they

---

FAITH CHALLENGE

Here's a challenge for you. Read 1:12 to discover how our faith can be strengthened. Who are some people who have helped your faith grow? How can you help your friends' faith to grow?

Testing it

Romans 1:12
I mean that I want us to help each other with the faith we have. Your faith will help me, and my faith will help you.

1:13 Brothers and sisters Although the Greek text says "brothers" here and throughout this book, Paul's words were meant for the entire church, both men and women.
1:17 "But those . . . him." Quotation from Habakkuk 2:4.

LET'S VISIT ROME
Romans 1:15

During New Testament times, Rome was the largest and most famous city of its day. (Have you heard the phrase, "All roads lead to Rome"?) Over a million people lived there. It was the centre of the whole Roman Empire. Sometimes it was called *Urbs Septicollis* ("City of the Seven Hills"), because it was literally built on seven hills.

Some famous sights in Rome are the Forum; the centre of the city with roads in all directions; the Colosseum, where games like the Olympics were held. Rome also had public baths, aqueducts, arches and many temples for worshipping false gods. The apostle Paul was a prisoner in Rome when he wrote letters to churches. These letters are part of the New Testament.

hide the truth. 19 God shows his anger because some knowledge of him has been made clear to them. Yes, God has shown himself to them. 20 There are things about him that people cannot see—his eternal power and all the things that make him God. But since the beginning of the world those things have been easy to understand by what God has made. So people have no excuse for the bad things they do. 21 They knew God, but they did not give glory to God or thank him. Their thinking became useless. Their foolish minds were filled with darkness. 22 They said they were wise, but they became fools. 23 They traded the glory of God who lives for ever for the worship of idols made to look like earthly people, birds, animals and snakes.

24 Because they did these things, God left them and let them go their sinful way, wanting only to do evil. As a result, they became full of sexual sin, using their bodies wrongly with each other. 25 They traded the truth of God for a lie. They worshipped and served what had been created instead of the God who created those things, who should be praised for ever. Amen.

26 Because people did those things, God left them and let them do the shameful things they wanted to do. Women stopped having natural sex and started having sex with other women. 27 In the same way, men stopped having natural sex and began wanting each other. Men did shameful things with other men, and in their bodies they received the punishment for those wrongs.

28 People did not think it was important to have a true knowledge of God. So God left them and allowed them to have their own worthless thinking and to do things they should not do. 29 They are filled with every kind of sin, evil, selfishness and hatred. They are full of jealousy, murder, fighting, lying and thinking the worst about each other. They gossip 30 and say evil things about each other. They hate God. They are rude and conceited and boast about themselves. They invent ways of doing evil. They do not obey their parents. 31 They are foolish, they do not keep their promises, and they show no kindness or mercy to others. 32 They know God's law says that those

1:20 Following God
Has God shown himself to people?

who live like this should die. But they themselves not only continue to do these evil things, they applaud others who do them.

You People Also are Sinful

2 If you think you can judge others, you are wrong. When you judge them, you are really judging yourself guilty, because you do the same things they do. 2 God judges those who do wrong things, and we know that his judging is right. 3 You judge those who do wrong, but you do wrong yourselves. Do you think you will be able to escape the judgement of God? 4 He has been very kind and patient, waiting for you to change, but you think nothing of his kindness. Perhaps you do not understand that God's kindness is meant to lead you to change your hearts and lives. 5 But you are stubborn and refuse to change, so you are making your own punishment even greater on the day he shows his anger. On that day everyone will see God's right judgements. 6 God will reward or punish every person for what that person has done. 7 Some people, by always continuing to do good, live for God's glory, for honour and for life that has no end. God will give them life for ever. 8 But other people are selfish. They refuse to follow truth and, instead, follow evil. God will give them his punishment and anger. 9 He will give trouble and suffering to everyone who does evil—to the Jews first and also to those who are not Jews. 10 But he will give glory, honour and peace to everyone who does good—to the Jews first and also to those who are not Jews. 11 For God judges all people in the same way.

12 People who do not have the law and who are sinners will be lost, although they do not have the law. And, in the same way, those who have the law and are sinners will be judged by the law. 13 Hearing the law does not make people right with God. It is those who obey the law who will be right with him. 14 (Those who are not Jews do not have the law, but when they freely do what the law commands, they are the law for themselves. This is true even though they do not have the law. 15 They show that in their hearts they know what is right and wrong, just as the law commands. And they show this by their thoughts. Sometimes their thoughts tell them they did wrong, and sometimes their thoughts tell them they did right.) 16 All these things will happen on the day when God, through Christ Jesus, will judge people's secret thoughts. The Good News that I preach says this.

2:4
Kindness
God has been kind to you.

The Jews and the Law

17 What about you? You call yourself a Jew. You trust in the law of Moses and boast that you are close to God. 18 You know what he wants you to do and what is important, because you have learned the law. 19 You think you are a guide for the blind and a light for those who are in darkness. 20 You think you can show foolish people what is right and teach those who know nothing. You have the law; so you think you know everything and have all truth. 21 You teach others, so why don't you teach yourself? You tell others not to steal, but you steal. 22 You say that others must not take part in adultery, but you are guilty of that sin. You hate idols, but you steal from temples. 23 You boast about having God's law, but you bring shame to God by breaking his law, 24 just as the Scriptures say: "Those who are not Jews speak against God's name because of you."[n]

25 If you follow the law, your circumcision has meaning. But if you break the law, it is as if you were never circumcised. 26 People who are not Jews are not circumcised, but if they do what the law says, it is as if they were circumcised. 27 You Jews have the written law and circumcision, but you break the law. So those who are not circumcised in their bodies, but still obey the law, will show that you are guilty. 28 They can do this because a person is not a true Jew if he is only a Jew

---

2:24 "Those . . . you." Quotation from Isaiah 52:5; Ezekiel 36:20.

in his physical body; true circumcision is not only on the outside of the body. 29 A person is a Jew only if he is a Jew inside; true circumcision is done in the heart by the Spirit, not by the works of the written law. Such a person gets praise from God rather than from people.

3 So, do Jews have anything that other people do not have? Is there anything special about being circumcised? 2 Yes, of course, there is in every way. The most important thing is this: God trusted the Jews with his teachings. 3 If some Jews were not faithful to him, will that stop God from doing what he promised? 4 No! God will continue to be true even when every person is false. As the Scriptures say:

"So you will be shown to be right
  when you speak,
and you will win your case."
Psalm 51:4

5 When we do wrong, that shows more clearly that God is right. So can we say that God is wrong to punish us? (I am talking as people might talk.) 6 No! If God could not punish us, he could not judge the world.

7 A person might say, "When I lie, it really gives him glory, because my lie shows God's truth. So why am I judged a sinner?" 8 It would be the same to say, "We should do evil so that good will come." Some people find fault with us and say we teach this, but they are wrong and deserve the punishment they will receive.

All People are Guilty

9 So are we Jews better than others? No! We have already said that Jews and those who are not Jews are all guilty of sin. 10 As the Scriptures say:

3:9–12
Guilt
Is everyone guilty of sin?

"There is no one who always does
  what is right,
not even one.

11 There is no one who understands.
  There is no one who looks to God
    for help.

12 All have turned away.
  Together, everyone has become
    useless.
  There is no one who does anything
    good;
  there is not even one." *Psalm 14:1-3*

13 "Their throats are like open graves;
  they use their tongues for telling
    lies." *Psalm 5:9*
"Their words are like snake poison."
Psalm 140:3

14 "Their mouths are full of cursing and
  hate." *Psalm 10:7*

15 "They are always ready to kill
  people.

16 Everywhere they go they cause ruin
  and misery.

17 They don't know how to live in
  peace." *Isaiah 59:7-8*

18 "They have no fear of God." *Psalm 36:1*

19 We know that the law's commands are for those who have the law. This stops all excuses and brings the whole world under God's judgement, 20 because no one can be made right with God by following the law. The law only shows us our sin.

How God Makes People Right

21 But God has a way to make people right with him without the law, and he has now shown us that way which the law and the prophets told us about. 22 God makes people right with himself through their faith in Jesus Christ. This is true for all who believe in Christ, because all people are the same: 23 all have sinned and are not good enough for God's glory, 24 and all need to be made right with God by

3:23
Sin
Can God tolerate sin?

his grace, which is a free gift. They need to be made free from sin through Jesus Christ. 25 God gave him as a way to forgive sin through faith in the blood of Jesus' death. This showed that God always does what is right and fair, as in the past when he was patient and did not punish people for their sins. 26 And God gave Jesus to show today that he does what is right. God did this so he could

Romans 3:27 **1522**

FAITH links

JUST FOR THE ASKING
ROMANS 3:23-28

Got time for some good news and bad news about sin? Let's start with the bad news first. The bad news is that everyone has sinned. *Everyone.* The good news is that we have hope because of Jesus. He's the only One "good enough" to free us from sin. Why? Because he never sinned.

Knowing this helps us to face up to our sin. God knows that we blow it from time to time. He just wants us to own up to it. Because of Jesus, forgiveness is ours for the asking.

Here are some more Faithlinks on forgiveness. Check them out!

The Perfect Sacrifice, Leviticus 1—7, p. 135

The One Who Suffered, Isaiah 53, p. 966

Believe the Impossible? Ezekiel 37, p. 1131

A Change of Heart, Matthew 3:1–12, p. 1277

It's Free! Ephesians 2:8–9, p. 1600

His Best Qualities, 2 Peter 3:9, p. 1711

judge rightly and so he could make right any person who has faith in Jesus.

27 So do we have a reason to boast about ourselves? No! And why not? It is the way of faith that stops all boasting, not the way of trying to obey the law. 28 A person is made right with God through faith, not through obeying the law. 29 Is God only the God of the Jews? Is he not also the God of those who are not Jews? 30 Of course he is, because there is only one God. He will make Jews right with him by their faith, and he will also make those who are not Jews right with him through their faith. 31 So do we destroy the law by following the way of faith? No! Faith causes us to be what the law truly wants.

The Example of Abraham

4 So what can we say that Abraham,[n] the father of our people, learned about faith? 2 If Abraham was made right by the things he did, he had a reason to boast. But this is not God's view, 3 because the Scripture says, "Abraham believed God, and God accepted Abraham's faith, and that faith made him right with God."[n]

4 When people work, their pay is not given as a gift, but as something earned.

4:5 Trust
Trusting in God pays off.

5 But people cannot do any work that will make them right with God. So they must trust in him, who makes even evil people right in his sight. Then God accepts their faith, and that makes them right with him. 6 David said the same thing. He said that people are truly blessed when God, without paying attention to good deeds, makes people right with himself.

7 "Happy are they
   whose sins are forgiven,
   whose wrongs are pardoned.
8 Happy is the person
   whom the Lord does not consider
      guilty."   *Psalm 32:1-2*

9 Is this blessing only for those who are circumcised or also for those who are not circumcised? We have already said that God accepted Abraham's faith and that faith made him right with God. 10 So how did this happen? Did God accept Abraham

---

4:1 Abraham Most respected ancestor of the Jews. Every Jew hoped to see Abraham.
4:3 "Abraham . . . God." Quotation from Genesis 15:6.

FAITH links

ONE THING TO DO
ROMANS 4:1-5

Abraham, one of the founding fathers of the Jewish nation, was a man of faith. He trusted God to save him. He knew that he could not earn God's favour or mercy by something he did.

Often we think we have to do things to earn God's mercy. If that's something you believe, take a lesson from Abraham. Have faith in God. That's all you have to do!

The Wisdom of Obeying God, 1 Kings 11:1–13, p. 453

Remember Your Creator, Ecclesiastes 12:1, 13, p. 885

Let's Make a Deal, Daniel 1:8–21, p. 1150

Perfectly Pleasing? Matthew 5:1–12, p. 1280

The Greatest Commandment, Matthew 22:36–40, p. 1313

Our Gift to God, Romans 12:1–2, p. 1536

---

before or after he was circumcised? It was before his circumcision. 11 Abraham was circumcised to show that he was right with God through faith before he was circumcised. So Abraham is the father of all those who believe but are not circumcised; he is the father of all believers who are accepted as being right with God. 12 And Abraham is also the father of those who have been circumcised and who live following the faith that our father Abraham had before he was circumcised.

God Keeps His Promise

13 Abraham[n] and his descendants received the promise that they would get the whole world. He did not receive that promise through the law, but through being right with God by his faith. 14 If people could receive what God promised by following the law, then faith is worthless. And God's promise to Abraham is worthless, 15 because the law can only bring God's anger. But if there is no law, there is nothing to disobey.

16 So people receive God's promise by having faith. This happens so the promise can be a free gift. Then all of Abraham's children can have that promise. It is not only for those who live under the law of Moses but for anyone who lives with faith like that of Abraham, who is the father of us all. 17 As it is written in the Scriptures: "I am making you a father of many nations."[n] This is true before God, the God Abraham believed, the God who gives life to the dead and who creates something out of nothing.

18 There was no hope that Abraham would have children. But Abraham believed God and continued hoping, and so he became the father of many nations. As God told him, "Your descendants also will be too many to count."[n] 19 Abraham was almost 100 years old, much past the age for having children, and Sarah could not have children. Abraham thought about all this, but his faith in God did not become weak. 20 He never doubted that God would keep his promise, and he never stopped believing. He grew stronger in his faith and gave praise to God. 21 Abraham felt sure that God was able to do what he had promised. 22 So, "God accepted Abraham's faith, and that faith made him right with God."[n] 23 Those words ("God accepted Abraham's faith") were written

---

4:13 Abraham Most respected ancestor of the Jews. Every Jew hoped to see Abraham.
4:17 "I . . . nations." Quotation from Genesis 17:5.
4:18 "Your . . . count." Quotation from Genesis 15:5.
4:22 "God . . . God." Quotation from Genesis 15:6.

not only for Abraham 24 but also for us. God will accept us also because we believe in the One who raised Jesus our Lord from the dead. 25 Jesus was given to die for our sins, and he was raised from the dead to make us right with God.

Right with God

5 Since we have been made right with God by our faith, we have peace with God. This happened through our Lord Jesus Christ, 2 who has brought us into that blessing of God's grace that we now enjoy. And we are happy because of the hope we have of sharing God's glory. 3 We also have joy with our troubles, because we know that these troubles produce patience. 4 And patience produces character, and character produces hope. 5 And this hope will never disappoint us, because God has poured out his love to fill our hearts. He gave us his love through the Holy Spirit, whom God has given to us.

6 When we were unable to help ourselves, at the moment of our need, Christ died for us, although we were living against God. 7 Very few people will die to save the life of someone else although perhaps for a good person someone might possibly die. 8 But God shows his great love for us in this way: Christ died for us while we were still sinners.

9 So through Christ we will surely be saved from God's anger, because we have been made right with God by the blood of Christ's death. 10 While we were God's enemies, he made friends with us through the death of his Son. Surely, now that we are his friends, he will save us through his Son's life. 11 And not only that, now we are also very happy in God through our Lord Jesus Christ. Through him we are now God's friends again.

eMail from God
5:3 Perseverance
What will hard times produce?

FAITH links

LOVE FOR FREE
ROMANS 5:8

If you broke something that belonged to your mum or dad, do you think they would stop loving you? No, right? (Don't break something to try to prove this.) Your mum and dad would love you no matter what. That's the kind of love God has for us. We call this kind of love *unconditional*. That's another way to say love freely given, with no strings attached. You can't earn this love. It's a gift! That's why God sent his Son to die for us. That's what the Good News of the Gospel is all about. Why not share it with someone?

Connect here to find out how to share the Good News with others:

The Sign of His Presence, Exodus 40:34–38, p. 130

A Priest Without Sin, Leviticus 4:3–7, p. 136

God's Sure Protection, Psalm 18, p. 721

One Big, Happy Family, John 1:12, p. 1422

Two Birthdays, John 3:1–7, p. 1426

The Doubt Remover, Romans 10:8–10, p. 1533

Adam and Christ Compared

12 Sin came into the world because of what one man did, and with sin came death. This is why everyone must die— because everyone sinned. 13 Sin was in the world before the law of Moses, but sin is not counted against us as breaking a command when there is no law. 14 But

from the time of Adam to the time of Moses, everyone had to die, even those who had not sinned by breaking a command, as Adam had.

Adam was like the One who was coming in the future. 15 But God's free gift is not like Adam's sin. Many people died because of the sin of that one man. But the grace from God was much greater; many people received God's gift of life by the grace of the one man, Jesus Christ. 16 After Adam sinned once, he was judged guilty. But the gift of God is different. God's free gift came after many sins, and it makes people right with God. 17 One man sinned, and so death ruled all people because of that one man. But now those people who accept God's full grace and the great gift of being made right with him will surely have true life and rule through the one man, Jesus Christ.

18 So as one sin of Adam brought the punishment of death to all people, one good act that Christ did makes all people right with God. And that brings true life for all. 19 One man disobeyed God, and many became sinners. In the same way, one man obeyed God, and many will be made right. 20 The law came to make sin worse. But when sin grew worse, God's grace increased. 21 Sin once used death to rule us, but God gave people more of his grace so that grace could rule by making people right with him. And this brings life for ever through Jesus Christ our Lord.

Dead to Sin but Alive in Christ

6 So do you think we should continue sinning so that God will give us even more grace? 2 No! We died to our old sinful lives, so how can we continue living with sin? 3 Did you forget that all of us became part of Christ when we were baptised? We shared his death in our baptism. 4 When we were baptised, we were buried with Christ and shared his death. So, just as Christ was raised from the dead by the wonderful power of the Father, we also can live a new life.

5 Christ died, and we have been joined with him by dying too. So we will also be joined with him by rising from the dead as he did. 6 We know that our old life died with Christ on the cross so that our sinful selves would have no power over us and we would not be slaves to sin. 7 Anyone who has died is made free from sin's control.

8 If we died with Christ, we know we will also live with him. 9 Christ was raised from the dead, and we know that he cannot die again. Death has no power over him now. 10 Yes, when Christ died, he died to defeat the power of sin just once—enough for all time. He now has a new life, and his new life is with God. 11 In the same way, you should see yourselves as being dead to the power of sin and alive with God through Christ Jesus.

12 So, do not let sin control your life here on earth so that you do what your sinful self wants to do. 13 Do not offer the parts of your body to serve sin, as things to be used in doing evil. Instead, offer yourselves to God as people who have died and now live. Offer the parts of your body to God to be used in doing good. 14 Sin will not be your master, because you are not under law but under God's grace.

Be Slaves of Righteousness

15 So what should we do? Should we sin because we are under grace and not under law? No! 16 Surely you know that when you give yourselves like slaves to obey someone, then you are really slaves of that person. The person you obey is your master. You can follow sin, which brings spiritual death, or you can obey God, which makes you right with him. 17 In the past you were slaves to sin—sin controlled you. But thank God, you fully obeyed the things that you were taught. 18 You were made free from sin, and now you are slaves to goodness. 19 I use this example because this is hard for you to understand. In the past you offered the parts of your body to be slaves to sin and evil; you lived only for evil. In the same way now you must give yourselves to be slaves of goodness. Then you will live only for God.

20 In the past you were slaves to sin, and goodness did not control you. 21 You

did evil things, and now you are ashamed of them. Those things only bring death. 22 But now you are free from sin and have become slaves of God. This brings you a life that is only for God, and this gives you life for ever. 23 When people sin, they earn what sin pays—death. But God gives us a free gift—life for ever in Christ Jesus our Lord.

An Example from Marriage

7 Brothers and sisters, all of you understand the law of Moses. So surely you know that the law rules over people only while they are alive. 2 For example, a woman must stay married to her husband as long as he is alive. But if her husband dies, she is free from the law of marriage. 3 But if she marries another man while her husband is still alive, the law says she is guilty of adultery. But if her husband dies, she is free from the law of marriage. Then if she marries another man, she is not guilty of adultery.

4 In the same way, my brothers and sisters, your old selves died, and you became free from the law through the body of Christ. This happened so that you might belong to someone else—the One who was raised from the dead—and so that we might be used in service to God. 5 In the past, we were ruled by our sinful selves. The law made us want to do sinful things that controlled our bodies, so the things we did were bringing us death. 6 In the past, the law held us like prisoners, but our old selves died and we were made free from the law. So now we serve God in a new way with the Spirit, and not in the old way with written rules.

Our Fight Against Sin

7 You might think I am saying that sin and the law are the same thing. That is not true. But the law was the only way I could learn what sin meant. I would never have known what it means to want to take something belonging to someone else if the law had not said, "You must not want to take your neighbour's things."[a] 8 And sin found a way to use that command and cause me to want all kinds of things I should not want. But without the law, sin has no power. 9 I was alive before I knew the law. But when the law's command

---

FAITH links

A HIGH PRICE
ROMANS 6:23

If you told someone a lie, would you expect the police to suddenly arrest you and a judge to sentence you to death? Chances are you wouldn't, but guess what. According to God's law, any sin we commit earns us the death penalty. That's what Paul means when he says, "When people sin, they earn what sin pays – death." The silver lining in that dark cloud is that Jesus has already paid the price. His sacrifice on the cross makes it possible for you to be pronounced "not guilty" by God – the ultimate judge. God doesn't force you to accept this free gift, however. The choice is yours.

Own Up to It, 2 Samuel 12:1–13, p. 412

Dirty Inside, Isaiah 6:1–7, p. 904

The Watchman, Ezekiel 3:16–22, p. 1088

A Hard Place, Ezekiel 28:25–26, p. 1120

Lost Love? Revelation 2:4, p. 1733

A Happy Ending, Revelation 22:16–21, p. 1754

7:7 "You . . . things." Quotation from Exodus 20:17.

came to me, then sin began to live, 10 and I died. The command was meant to bring life, but for me it brought death. 11 Sin found a way to fool me by using the command to make me die.

12 So the law is holy, and the command is holy and right and good. 13 Does this mean that something that is good brought death to me? No! Sin used something that is good to bring death to me. This happened so that I could see what sin is really like; the command was used to show that sin is very evil.

The War Within Us

14 We know that the law is spiritual, but I am not spiritual since sin rules me as if I were its slave. 15 I do not understand the things I do. I do not do what I want to do, and I do the things I hate. 16 And if I do not want to do the hated things I do, that means I agree that the law is good. 17 But I am not really the one who is doing these hated things; it is sin living in me that does them. 18 Yes, I know that nothing good lives in me—I mean nothing good lives in the part of me that is earthly and sinful. I want to do the things that are good, but I do not do them. 19 I do not do the good things I want to do, but I do the bad things I do not want to do. 20 So if I do things I do not want to do, then I am not the one doing them. It is sin living in me that does those things.

21 So I have learned this rule: when I want to do good, evil is there with me. 22 In my mind, I am happy with God's law. 23 But I see another law working in my body, which makes war against the law that my mind accepts. That other law working in my body is the law of sin, and it makes me its prisoner. 24 What a miserable man I am! Who will save me from this body that brings me death? 25 I thank God for saving me through Jesus Christ our Lord!

So in my mind I am a slave to God's law, but in my sinful self I am a slave to the law of sin.

Be Ruled by the Spirit

8 So now, those who are in Christ Jesus are not judged guilty. 2 Through Christ Jesus the law of the Spirit that brings life made me free from the law that brings sin and death. 3 The law was without power, because the law was made weak by our sinful selves. But God did what the law could not do. He sent his own Son to earth with the same human life that others use for sin. By sending his Son to be an offering to pay for sin, God used a human life to destroy sin. 4 He did this so that we could be the kind of people the law correctly wants us to be. Now we do not live following our sinful selves, but we live following the Spirit.

THE SIN HABIT
ROMANS 7:15-20

Ever had a habit you just couldn't break, no matter what you did? The apostle Paul knew what that was like. In fact, his habit is our habit – sin. As Paul said, "I want to do the things that are good, but I do not do them." But this story has a happy ending. Thanks to Jesus' death on the cross, we can develop a new habit. It's called "pleasing God". As you think about doing that, the sin habit is broken.

The Trouble with Sin, Genesis 6—8, p. 11

Facing the Consequences, Deuteronomy 3:21–29, p. 232

Above the Law, 1 Kings 21, p. 470

A Swarm of Trouble, Joel 2:25–27, p. 1190

Clean Inside and Out, Luke 11:39–40, p. 1392

The Gift, John 3:16–18, p. 1427

5 Those who live following their sinful selves think only about things that their sinful selves want. But those who live following the Spirit are thinking about the things the Spirit wants them to do. 6 If people's thinking is controlled by the sinful self, there is death. But if their thinking is controlled by the Spirit, there is life and peace. 7 When people's thinking is controlled by the sinful self, they are against God, because they refuse to obey God's law and really are not even able to obey God's law. 8 Those people who are ruled by their sinful selves cannot please God.

9 But you are not ruled by your sinful selves. You are ruled by the Spirit, if that Spirit of God really lives in you. But the person who does not have the Spirit of Christ does not belong to Christ. 10 Your body will always be dead because of sin. But if Christ is in you, then the Spirit gives you life, because Christ made you right with God. 11 God raised Jesus from the dead, and if God's Spirit is living in you, he will also give life to your bodies that die. God is the One who raised Christ from the dead, and he will give life through his Spirit that lives in you.

12 So, my brothers and sisters, we must not be ruled by our sinful selves or live the way our sinful selves want. 13 If you use your lives to do the wrong things your sinful selves want, you will die spiritually. But if you use the Spirit's help to stop doing the wrong things you do with your body, you will have true life.

14 The true children of God are those who let God's Spirit lead them. 15 The Spirit we received does not make us slaves again to fear: it makes us children of God. With that Spirit we cry out, "Father." 16 And the Spirit himself joins with our spirits to say we are God's children. 17 If we are God's children, we will receive blessings from God together with Christ. But we must suffer as Christ suffered so that we will have glory as Christ has glory.

8:17–18 Troubles
Here's some hope in bad times.

FAITH links

OUR INTERPRETER
ROMANS 8:26

If you've seen an interpreter work, you know that he or she translates for two parties who can't understand each other. Did you know that we have an interpreter? It's the Holy Spirit. Although God always understands how we feel, often we don't understand how to talk to him or what to ask him for. When we don't know what to pray, the Spirit will speak for us. All we have to do is trust that God knows best!

Connect here to find out how the Holy Spirit helps you pray:

Keep On Praying, 1 Samuel 1, p. 354

Learning to Trust, Psalm 25:4–5, p. 727

When We Agree, Matthew 18:19–20, p. 1306

Flex Your Faith, Acts 3:1–16, p. 1467

An Energy Boost, Acts 4:31, p. 1469

A Good Habit, Ephesians 6:18, p. 1606

Our Future Glory

18 The sufferings we have now are nothing compared to the great glory that will be shown to us. 19 Everything God made is waiting with excitement for God

---

8:15 "Father" Literally, "Abba, Father". Jewish children called their fathers "Abba".

FAITH links

IT'S UNDER CONTROL
ROMANS 8:28

Ever feel that you've blown it so badly that life seems like it's over? At times like that, it's easy to believe that nothing good can ever happen again. That's why it's great to know that God has everything under control. He can make something good happen out of a bad situation. That's what Paul, the writer of the letter to the Romans, wants Christians to know. Why is that important? Knowing this can help us not to worry when things go wrong.

Here are some Faithlinks to help you when you think things are getting out of control:

When Bad Turns to Worse, Exodus 5:6–12, p. 82

Full Circle, Job 42, p. 706

When Bad Things Happen, Ecclesiastes 3:16–17, p. 876

When the Going Gets Tough, Lamentations 3:22–27, p. 1079

Rock Solid, Habakkuk 1:12, p. 1236

Thoughts on Thoughts, Philippians 4:8–9, p. 1614

---

thing God made would be set free from ruin to have the freedom and glory that belong to God's children.

22 We know that everything God made has been waiting until now in pain, like a woman ready to give birth. 23 Not only the world, but we also have been waiting with pain inside us. We have the Spirit as the first part of God's promise. So we are waiting for God to finish making us his own children, which means our bodies will be made free. 24 We were saved, and we have this hope. If we see what we are waiting for, that is not really hope. People do not hope for something they already have. 25 But we are hoping for something we do not have yet, and we are waiting for it patiently.

26 Also, the Spirit helps us with our weakness. We do not know how to pray as we should. But the Spirit himself speaks to God for us, even begs God for us with deep feelings that words cannot explain. 27 God can see what is in people's hearts. And he knows what is in the mind of the Spirit, because the Spirit speaks to God for his people in the way God wants.

28 We know that in everything God works for the good of those who love him. They are the people he called, because that was his plan. 29 God knew them before he made the world, and he decided that they would be like his Son so that Jesus would be the firstborn[n] of many brothers. 30 God planned for them to be like his Son; and those he planned to be like his Son, he also called; and those he called, he also made right with him; and those he made right, he also glorified.

God's Love in Christ Jesus

31 So what should we say about this? If God is with us, no one can defeat us. 32 He did not spare his own Son but gave him for us all. So with Jesus, God will surely give us all things. 33 Who can accuse the people God has chosen? No one, because God is the One who makes

---

to show his children's glory completely. 20 Everything God made was changed to become useless, not by its own wish but because God wanted it and because all along there was this hope: 21 that every-

8:29 firstborn Here this probably means that Christ was the first in God's family to share God's glory.

them right. 34 Who can say God's people are guilty? No one, because Christ Jesus died, but he was also raised from the dead, and now he is on God's right side, begging God for us. 35 Can anything separate us from the love Christ has for us? Can troubles or problems or sufferings or hunger or nakedness or danger or violent death? 36 As it is written in the Scriptures:

"For you we are in danger of death
all the time.
People think we are worth no more
than sheep to be killed."

Psalm 44:22

37 But in all these things we have full victory through God who showed his love for us. 38 Yes, I am sure that neither death, nor life, nor angels, nor ruling spirits, nothing now, nothing in the future, nor powers, 39 nothing above us, nothing below us, nor anything else in the whole world will ever be able to separate us from the love of God that is in Christ Jesus our Lord.

God and the Jewish People

9 I am in Christ, and I am telling you the truth; I do not lie. My feelings are ruled by the Holy Spirit, and they tell me I am not lying. 2 I have great sorrow and always feel much sadness. 3 I wish I could help my Jewish brothers and sisters, my people. I would even wish that I were cursed and cut off from Christ if that would help them. 4 They are the people of Israel, God's chosen children. They have seen the glory of God, and they have the agreements that God made between himself and his people. God gave them the law of Moses and the right way of worship and his promises. 5 They are the descendants of our great ancestors, and they are the earthly family into which Christ was born, who is God over all. Praise him for ever!*n* Amen.

6 It is not that God failed to keep his promise to them. But only some of the people of Israel are truly God's people,*n* 7 and only some of Abraham's*n* descendants are true children of Abraham. But God said to Abraham: "The descendants I promised you will be from Isaac."*n* 8 This means that not all of Abraham's descendants are God's true children. Abraham's true children are those who become God's children because of the promise God made to Abraham. 9 God's promise to Abraham was this: "At the right time I will return, and Sarah will have a son."*n* 10 And that is not all. Rebekah's sons had the same father, our father Isaac. 11-12 But before the two boys were born, God told Rebekah, "The older will serve the younger."*n* This was before the boys had done anything good or bad. God said this so that the one chosen would be chosen because of God's own plan. He was chosen because he was the one God wanted to call, not because of anything he did. 13 As the Scripture says, "I loved Jacob, but I hated Esau."*n*

14 So what should we say about this? Is God unfair? In no way. 15 God said to Moses, "I will show kindness to anyone to whom I want to show kindness, and I will show mercy to anyone to whom I want to show mercy."*n* 16 So God will choose the one to whom he decides to show mercy; his choice does not depend on what people want or try to do. 17 The Scripture says to the king of Egypt: "I made you king for this reason: to show my power in you so that my name will be talked about in all the earth."*n* 18 So God shows mercy where he wants to show mercy, and he makes stubborn the people he wants to make stubborn.

19 So one of you will ask me: "Then why does God blame us for our sins? Who can fight his will?" 20 You are only human, and human beings have no right

---

9:5 born . . . for ever! This can also mean, "born. May God, who rules over all things, be praised for ever!"
9:6 God's people Literally, "Israel", the people God chose to bring his blessings to the world.
9:7 Abraham Most respected ancestor of the Jews. Every Jew hoped to see Abraham.
9:7 "The descendants . . . Isaac." Quotation from Genesis 21:12.
9:9 "At . . . son." Quotation from Genesis 18:10,14.
9:11-12 "The older . . . younger." Quotation from Genesis 25:23.
9:13 "I . . . Esau." Quotation from Malachi 1:2-3.
9:15 "I . . . mercy." Quotation from Exodus 33:19.
9:17 "I . . . earth." Quotation from Exodus 9:16.

to question God. An object should not ask the person who made it, "Why did you make me like this?" 21 The potter can make anything he wants to make. He can use the same clay to make one thing for special use and another thing for daily use.

22 It is the same way with God. He wanted to show his anger and to let people see his power. But he patiently stayed with those people he was angry with—people who were due to be destroyed. 23 He waited with patience so that he could make known his rich glory to the people who receive his mercy. He has prepared these people to have his glory, 24 and we are those people whom God called. He called us not from the Jews only but also from those who are not Jews. 25 As the Scripture says in Hosea:

"I will say, 'You are my people'
   to those I had called 'not my people'.
And I will show my love
   to those people I did not love."
Hosea 2:1, 23

26 "They were called,
   'You are not my people',
but later they will be called
   'children of the living God'."
Hosea 1:10

27 And Isaiah cries out about Israel:
"Israel, your people are many,
   like the grains of sand by the sea.
But only a few of them will be left
   alive to return to the LORD.
28   God has announced that he will
   destroy the land completely and fairly."
Isaiah 10:22

29 It is as Isaiah said:
"The Lord All-powerful
   allowed a few of our people to live.
Otherwise we would have been
   completely destroyed
like the cities of Sodom and
   Gomorrah."[n]
Isaiah 1:9

30 So what does all this mean? Those who are not Jews were not trying to make themselves right with God, but they were made right with God because of their faith. 31 The people of Israel tried to follow a law to make themselves right with God. But they did not succeed, 32 because they tried to make themselves right by the things they did instead of trusting in God to make them right. They stumbled over the stone that causes people to stumble. 33 As it is written in the Scripture:

"I will put in Jerusalem a stone that
   causes people to stumble,
a rock that makes them fall.
Anyone who trusts in it will never be
   disappointed."
Isaiah 8:14; 28:16

10 Brothers and sisters, the thing I want most is for all the Jews to be saved. That is my prayer to God. 2 I can say this about them: they really try to follow God, but they do not know the right way. 3 Because they did not know the way that God makes people right with him, they tried to make themselves right in their own way. So they did not accept God's way of making people right. 4 Christ ended the law so that everyone who believes in him may be right with God.

5 Moses describes how to be made right by following the law. He says, "A person who obeys these things will live because of them."[n] 6 But this is what the Scripture says about being made right through faith: "Don't say to yourself, 'Who will go up into heaven?'" (That means, "Who will go up to heaven and bring Christ down to earth?") 7 "And do not say, 'Who will go down into the world below?'" (That means, "Who will go down and bring Christ up from the dead?") 8 This is what the Scripture says: "The word is near you; it is in your mouth and in your heart."[n] That is the teaching of faith that we are telling. 9 If you use your mouth to say, "Jesus is Lord," and if you believe in your heart that God raised Jesus from the dead, you will be saved. 10 We believe with our hearts, and so we are made right with God. And we use our mouths to say that we believe, and so we

> **EMAIL FROM GOD**
> **10:8–10**
> **Salvation**
> Check out how to be saved.

9:29 Sodom and Gomorrah Two cities that God destroyed because the people were so evil.
10:5 "A person . . . them." Quotation from Leviticus 18:5.
10:8 Verses 6-8 Quotations from Deuteronomy 30:12-14; Psalm 107:26.

SHARING MY FAITH
Romans 10:14–17

Have I Got News for You! Imagine that you just heard some wonderful news – you "aced" a really tough test. Or your mum doesn't have cancer. Or your family's going to Spain for a whole month. What's the first thing you want to do? You probably want to spread the news. Who would you tell? Why would you tell them?

God wants you to spread his Good News – that because Jesus died on the cross and took the punishment for our sins, we can live for ever with him in heaven. That's the best news ever! In fact, did you know that Jesus' final words to his followers instructed them to do just that – to tell everyone about him! (Check out Matthew 28:19, p. 1327.) Do you have family, friends and acquaintances who need to hear about God's great love for them? Make sure you tell them today!

MORE FAITH Links

Learning from Mistakes, **p. 748**

Jesus' Mission and Yours, **p. 978**

Pass It On! **p. 1187**

Tell All About Him! **p. 1326**

Your Faith Story, **p. 1650**

What's Good About You? **p. 1663**

> Do you want to hear some really great news?

> No, you haven't just won a competition – it's much better than that!

> Just surf over to some of these Faithlinks, and you'll find out!

A Life-Saving Message, Esther 2:19–22, p. 650
- Mordecai heard about a plan to kill the king and reported it. The king's life was saved. God has given you an important life-saving message to tell others. Who will you share it with?

A Bad Reaction, Jeremiah 36, p. 1043
- Have you ever shared your faith with someone, only to have him or her have a bad reaction? How did you handle it? What do you do when people don't want to hear about God? How can you keep on sharing your faith?

Attention, Please! Luke 8:11–15, p. 1383
- How much are you paying attention to what God has to say to you? Link here to find out what kind of soil you are for God.

My FAVOURITE Links

FAITH LINKS

THE DOUBT REMOVER
ROMANS 10:8-10

Want to know, really know, without the shadow of a doubt that you're going to heaven? The apostle Paul provides the answer: believe in Jesus and say it! That's all you have to do. Believe that Jesus died for your sins and that God raised Jesus from the dead. Do you believe that Jesus rose from the dead? Do you have faith in God? Have you told someone about what you believe? Then you're going to heaven someday! There's no doubt about it!

Approaching God, Numbers 3:10, p. 180

The God of Big Things, Joshua 10, p. 289

A Picture of the Past, Psalm 105, p. 789

Two Birthdays, John 3:1–7, p. 1426

Flex Your Faith, Acts 3:1–16, p. 1467

People of Faith, Hebrews 11, p. 1679

---

are saved. **11** As the Scripture says, "Anyone who trusts in him will never be disappointed."ⁿ **12** That Scripture says "anyone" because there is no difference between those who are Jews and those who are not. The same Lord is the Lord of all and gives many blessings to all who trust in him, **13** as the Scripture says, "Anyone who calls on the Lord will be saved."ⁿ

14 But before people can ask the Lord for help, they must believe in him; and before they can believe in him, they must hear about him; and for them to hear about the Lord, someone must tell them; **15** and before someone can go and tell them, that person must be sent. It is written, "How beautiful is the person who comes to bring good news."ⁿ

10:14–15 Witnessing
How will people hear the Good News?

16 But not all the Jews accepted the good news. As Isaiah said, "LORD, who believed what we told them?"ⁿ **17** So faith comes from hearing the Good News, and people hear the Good News when someone tells them about Christ.

18 But I ask: Didn't people hear the Good News? Yes, they heard—as the Scripture says:

"Their message went out through all
    the world;
  their words go everywhere on
    earth."   *Psalm 19:4*

19 Again I ask: Didn't the people of Israel understand? Yes, they did understand. First, Moses says:

"So I will use those who are not a
    nation to make them jealous;
  I will use a nation that does not
    understand to make them
    angry."   *Deuteronomy 32:21*

20 Then Isaiah is bold enough to say:

"I was found by those who were not
    asking me for help.
  I said, 'Here I am. Here I am,' to a
    nation that was not praying to
    me."   *Isaiah 65:1*

21 But about Israel God says,

"All day long I stood ready to
    accept
  people who turned against me."
         Isaiah 65:2

10:11 "Anyone . . . disappointed." Quotation from Isaiah 28:16.
10:13 "Anyone . . . saved." Quotation from Joel 2:32.
10:15 "How . . . news." Quotation from Isaiah 52:7.
10:16 "Lord, . . . them?" Quotation from Isaiah 53:1.

God Shows Mercy to All People

11 So I ask: Did God throw out his people? No! I myself am an Israelite from the family of Abraham, from the tribe of Benjamin. 2 God chose the Israelites to be his people before they were born, and he has not thrown his people out. Surely you know what the Scripture says about Elijah, how he prayed to God against the people of Israel. 3 "Lord," he said, "they have killed your prophets, and they have destroyed your altars. I am the only prophet left, and now they are trying to kill me too."[n] 4 But what answer did God give Elijah? He said, "But I have left 7,000 people in Israel who have never bowed down before Baal."[n] 5 It is the same now. There are a few people that God has chosen by his grace. 6 And if he chose them by grace, it is not for the things they have done. If they could be made God's people by what they did, God's gift of grace would not really be a gift.

7 So this is what has happened: although the Israelites tried to be right with God, they did not succeed, but the ones God chose did become right with him. The others were made stubborn and refused to listen to God. 8 As it is written in the Scriptures:

> "God gave the people a dull mind so
>   they could not understand."
>
> *Isaiah 29:10*
>
> "But to this day the LORD has not
>   given you a mind that
>   understands;
> you don't really understand what
>   you see
> with your eyes or hear with your
>   ears."
>
> *Deuteronomy 29:4*

9 And David says:

> "Let their own feasts trap them and
>   cause their ruin;
> let their feasts cause them to
>   stumble and be paid back.
> 10 Let their eyes be closed so they
>   cannot see
> and their backs be for ever weak
>   from troubles."
>
> *Psalm 69:22-23*

11 So I ask: when the Jews fell, did that fall destroy them? No! But their mistake brought salvation to those who are not Jews, in order to make the Jews jealous. 12 The Jews' mistake brought rich blessings for the world, and the Jews' loss brought rich blessings for the non-Jewish people. So surely the world will receive much richer blessings when enough Jews become the kind of people God wants.

13 Now I am speaking to you who are not Jews. I am an apostle to those who are not Jews, and since I have that work, I will make the most of it. 14 I hope I can make my own people jealous and, in that way, help some of them to be saved. 15 When God turned away from the Jews, he became friends with other people in the world. So when God accepts the Jews, surely that will bring them life after death.

16 If the first piece of bread is offered to God, then the whole loaf is made holy. If the roots of a tree are holy, then the tree's branches are holy too.

17 It is as if some of the branches from an olive tree have been broken off. You non-Jewish people are like the branch of a wild olive tree that has been joined to that first tree. You now share the strength and life of the first tree, the Jews. 18 So do not boast about those branches that were broken off. If you boast, remember that you do not support the root, but the root supports you. 19 You will say, "Branches were broken off so that I could be joined to their tree." 20 That is true. But those branches were broken off because they did not believe, and you continue to be part of the tree only because you believe. Do not be proud, but be afraid. 21 If God did not let the natural branches of that tree stay, then he will not let you stay if you don't believe.

22 So you see that God is kind and also very strict. He punishes those who stop following him. But God is kind to you, if you continue following in his kindness. If you do not, you will be cut off

---

11:3 "Lord . . . too." Quotation from 1 Kings 19:10,14.
11:4 "But . . . Baal." Quotation from 1 Kings 19:18.

from the tree. 23 And if the Jews will believe in God again, he will accept them back. God is able to put them back where they were. 24 It is not natural for a wild branch to be part of a good tree. And you who are not Jews are like a branch cut from a wild olive tree and joined to a good olive tree. But since those Jews are like a branch that grew from the good tree, surely they can be joined to their own tree again.

25 I want you to understand this secret, brothers and sisters, so you will understand that you do not know everything: part of Israel has been made stubborn, but that will change when many who are not Jews have come to God. 26 And that is how all Israel will be saved. It is written in the Scriptures:

"Then a Saviour will come to
  Jerusalem
and to the people of Jacob[n] who
  have turned from sin.
27 This is how Israel's guilt will be
  forgiven;
this is how its sins will be taken
  away." *Isaiah 59:20-21; 27:9*

28 The Jews refuse to accept the Good News, so they are God's enemies. This has happened to help you who are not Jews. But the Jews are still God's chosen people, and he loves them very much because of the promises he made to their ancestors. 29 God never changes his mind about the people he calls and the things he gives them. 30 At one time you refused to obey God. But now you have received mercy, because those people refused to obey. 31 And now the Jews refuse to obey, because God showed mercy to you. But this happened so that they also can receive mercy from him. 32 God has given all people over to their stubborn ways so that he can show mercy to all.

Praise to God

33 Yes, God's riches are very great, and his wisdom and knowledge have no end! No one can explain the things God decides or understand his ways. 34 As the Scripture says,

> But God is kind to you, if you continue following in his kindness. If you do not, you will be cut off from the tree.
> – Romans 11:22

"Who has known the
  mind of the
  Lord
or been able to give
  him advice?'
        Isaiah 40:13
35 "No one has ever
  given God
  anything
  that he must
  pay back."
        Job 41:11

36 Yes, God made all things, and everything continues through him and for him. To him be the glory for ever! Amen.

Give Your Lives to God

12 So brothers and sisters, since God has shown us great mercy, I beg you to offer your lives as a living sacrifice to him. Your offering must be only for God and pleasing to him, which is the spiritual way for you to worship. 2 Do not change yourselves to be like the people of this world, but be changed within by a new way of thinking.

12:2 God
Find out what is pleasing to God.

Then you will be able to decide what God wants for you; you will know what is good and pleasing to him and what is perfect. 3 Because God has given me a special gift, I have something to say to everyone among you. Do not think you are better than you are. You must decide what you really are by the amount of faith God has given you. 4 Each one of us has a body with many parts, and these parts all have different uses. 5 In the same way, we are many, but in Christ we are all one body. Each one is a part of that body, and each part belongs to all the other parts. 6 We all have different gifts, each of which came because of the grace God gave us. The person who has the gift of prophecy

---

11:26 Jacob Father of the twelve family groups of Israel, the people God chose to be his own.

▶ Romans 12:7 1536

FAITH links

OUR GIFT TO GOD
ROMANS 12:1-2

If you have a good friend, you know what a gift friendship can be. You offer yourself to your friend wholeheartedly. God offers us a gift through his Son Jesus. The least we can do is offer him a gift in return. Do you know what gift would really please God? You. He wants you to be willing to lay aside your own plans for your life in favour of his plans. He also wants you to be willing to lay aside the desire to do wrong things and do what's right. That's what being "a living sacrifice" is all about.

Connect here to find out more about being a "living sacrifice":

Fearful Service? Exodus 4:1–17, p. 80

Your Best Work, 1 Kings 6, p. 443

Your Stats, 1 Kings 15; 16, p. 460

Too Young to Serve, Jeremiah 1:4–9, p. 988

Your Feet on High Places, Habakkuk 3:18–19, p. 1239

That Thing You Do, Matthew 25:14–30, p. 1319

FAITH links

HELP FOR THE BODY
ROMANS 12:3-8

Your body is made of many parts. Each one is important. A church is made of many people. Each one is important. That's why the church is known as "the body of Christ". God gave each person in the church a gift or ability to do something. Some people have a gift of serving; some have a gift of being generous. What is your gift? Whatever it is, you can use it to help the body!

Check out these links on being responsible:

Everyone Can Help, Numbers 4, p. 181

Your Response to Responsibility, Ruth 2:1–7, p. 346

A Big Responsibility, 2 Kings 11, p. 494

Building Together, Nehemiah 3, p. 627

Love Him? Show It! Amos 2:6–7, p. 1196

A Christian's Responsibility, Acts 11:26, p. 1484

---

should use that gift in agreement with the faith. **7** Anyone who has the gift of serving should serve. Anyone who has the gift of teaching should teach. **8** Whoever has the gift of encouraging others should encourage. Whoever has the gift of giving to others should give freely. Anyone who has the gift of being a leader should try hard when he leads. Whoever has the gift of showing mercy to others should do so with joy.

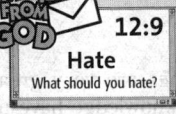

12:9
Hate
What should you hate?

9 Your love must be real. Hate what is evil, and hold on to what is good. 10 Love each other like brothers and sisters. Give each other more honour than you want for yourselves. 11 Do not be lazy but work hard, serving the Lord with all your heart. 12 Be joyful because you have hope. Be patient when trouble comes, and pray at all times. 13 Share with God's people who need help. Bring strangers in need into your homes.

14 Wish good for those who harm you; wish them well and do not curse them. 15 Be happy with those who are happy, and be sad with those who are sad. 16 Live in peace with each other. Do not be proud, but make friends with those who seem unimportant. Do not think how clever you are.

17 If someone does wrong to you, do not pay him back by doing wrong to him. Try to do what everyone thinks is right. 18 Do your best to live in peace with everyone. 19 My friends, do not try to punish others when they wrong you, but wait for God to punish them with his anger. It is written: "I will punish those who do wrong; I will repay them,"[n] says the Lord. 20 But you should do this:

"If your enemy is hungry, feed him.
If he is thirsty, give him a drink.
Doing this will be like pouring burning coals on his head."

Proverbs 25:21-22

21 Do not let evil defeat you, but defeat evil by doing good.

Christians Should Obey the Law

13 All of you must yield to the government rulers. No one rules unless God has given him the power to rule, and no one rules now without that power from God. 2 So those who are against the government are really against what God has commanded. And they will bring punishment on themselves. 3 Those who do right do not have to fear the rulers; only those who do wrong fear them. Do you want to be unafraid of the rulers? Then do what is right, and they will praise you. 4 The ruler is God's servant to help you. But if you do

13:1 Obedience Should Christians obey the government?

FAITH CHALLENGE

Here's another one for you. Read 13:7 to discover what we owe each other and how we are to pay it. What is the best way to show respect and honour to your teacher? Your headteacher? A police officer? Your parents?

TeSTiNG iT

Romans 13:7
Pay everyone, then, what you owe. If you owe any kind of tax, pay it. Show respect and honour to them all.

_____
_____
_____
_____
_____
_____
_____

wrong, then be afraid. He has the power to punish; he is God's servant to punish those who do wrong. 5 So you must yield to the government, not only because you might be punished, but because you know it is right.

6 This is also why you pay taxes. Rulers are working for God and give their time to their work. 7 Pay everyone, then, what you owe. If you owe any kind of tax, pay it. Show respect and honour to them all.

12:19 "I ... them," Quotation from Deuteronomy 32:35.

Loving Others

8 Do not owe people anything, except always owe love to each other, because the person who loves others has obeyed all the law. 9 The law says, "You must not be guilty of adultery. You must not murder anyone. You must not steal. You must not want to take your neighbour's things."[n] All these commands and all others are really only one rule: "Love your neighbour as you love yourself."[n] 10 Love never hurts a neighbour, so loving is obeying all the law.

11 Do this because we live in an important time. It is now time for you to wake up from your sleep, because our salvation is nearer now than when we first believed. 12 The "night"[n] is almost finished, and the "day"[n] is almost here. So we should stop doing things that belong to darkness and take up the weapons used for fighting in the light. 13 Let us live in a right way, like people who belong to the day. We should not have wild parties or get drunk. There should be no sexual sins of any kind, no fighting or jealousy. 14 But clothe yourselves with the Lord Jesus Christ and forget about satisfying your sinful self.

Do Not Criticise Other People

14 Accept into your group someone who is weak in faith, and do not argue about opinions. 2 One person believes it is right to eat all kinds of food.[n] But another, who is weak, believes it is right to eat only vegetables. 3 The one who knows that it is right to eat any kind of food must not reject the one who eats only vegetables. And the person who eats only vegetables must not think that the one who eats all foods is wrong, because God has accepted that person. 4 You cannot judge another person's servant. The master decides if the servant is doing well or not. And the Lord's servant will do well because the Lord helps him do well.

5 Some think that one day is more important than another, and others think that every day is the same. Let all be sure in their own mind. 6 Those who think one day is more important than other days are doing that for the Lord. And those who eat all kinds of food are doing that for the Lord, and they give thanks to God. Others who refuse to eat some foods do that for the Lord, and they give thanks to God. 7 We do not live or die for ourselves. 8 If we live, we are living for the Lord, and if we die, we are dying for the Lord. So living or dying, we belong to the Lord.

9 The reason Christ died and rose from the dead to live again was so he would be Lord over both the dead and the living. 10 So why do you judge your brothers or sisters in Christ? And why do you think you are better than they are? We will all stand before God to be judged, 11 because it is written in the Scriptures:

"'As surely as I live,' says the Lord,
'Everyone will bow before me and will
promise to follow me.'" *Isaiah 45:23*

12 So each of us will have to answer to God.

Do Not Cause Others to Sin

13 For that reason we should stop judging each other. We must make up our minds not to do anything that will make another Christian sin. 14 I am in the Lord Jesus, and I know that there is no food that is wrong to eat. But if a person believes something is wrong, that thing is wrong for him. 15 If you hurt your brother's or sister's faith because of something you eat, you are not really following the way of love. Do not destroy someone's faith by eating food he thinks is wrong, because Christ died for him. 16 Do not allow what you think is good to become what others say is evil. 17 In the kingdom of God, eating and drinking are not important. The important things are living right with God, peace, and joy in the Holy Spirit.

13:9 "You . . . things." Quotation from Exodus 20:13-15, 17.
13:9 "Love . . . yourself." Quotation from Leviticus 19:18.
13:12 "night" This is used as a symbol of the sinful world we live in. This world will soon end.
13:12 "day" This is used as a symbol of the good time that is coming, when we will be with God.
14:2 all . . . food The Jewish law said there were some foods Jews should not eat. When Jews became Christians, some of them did not understand they could now eat all foods.

BEING A PEACEMAKER
Romans 14:19

Peace and Quiet? Is your house always peaceful and quiet? Or are there arguments and disagreements between parents and kids, and amongst the kids themselves? How do you react in these situations? Do you try to be a peacemaker or do you stir things up a bit and become a peacebreaker?

A peacemaker tries to make peace between two people who aren't getting along. A peacebreaker starts trouble wherever he or she goes. God wants his followers to be peacemakers. (Look at James 3:18, p. 1693.) Which would you rather have – the reward of the peacemaker or the trouble of the peacebreaker? How can you be a peacemaker where you are today?

MORE FAITH links
- More Powerful Than Revenge, **p. 71**
- Kind or Fair? **p. 395**
- Some Friendly Advice, **p. 851**
- The Gentle Way, **p. 1661**
- A Peacemaker or a Peacebreaker? **p. 1693**

If your friends fall out with each other, does it make you sad?

What do you think you should do to try and help them sort out their problems and talk to each other?

It could be a bit tricky, couldn't it? Download these Faithlinks and see how you can be a peacemaker in this situation.

Peace in the Family, Psalm 133, p. 811
- Ever wish you and other members of your family could get along all the time? How about you and your friends? What can you do to make this happen?
- God's love makes it possible for people to "live together in peace". Even brothers and sisters!

Winning a Friend, 2 Timothy 2:23–24, p. 1654
- Have you ever argued with someone about something that wasn't really important? Link up here to hear Paul's advice about "foolish and stupid arguments".

The Way to Get Along, 1 Peter 3:8–9, p. 1703
- What was the last thing you argued about with your brother or sister? When you and your brother or sister fight, how do you feel? How does that compare with the way you feel when you get along? This Faithlink gives some great advice for getting along with family and friends. Give it a go!

my **FAVOURITE** links

18 Anyone who serves Christ by living this way is pleasing God and will be accepted by other people.

19 So let us try to do what makes for peace and help one another. 20 Do not let the eating of food destroy the work of God. All foods are all right to eat, but it is wrong to eat food that causes someone else to sin.

14:19 Peace
How can you be a peacemaker?

21 It is better not to eat meat or drink wine or do anything that will cause your brother or sister to sin.

22 Your beliefs about these things should be kept secret between you and God. People are happy if they can do what they think is right without feeling guilty. 23 But those who eat something without being sure it is right are wrong because they did not believe it was right. Anything that is done without believing it is right is a sin.

15 We who are strong in faith should help the weak with their weaknesses, and not please only ourselves. 2 Let each of us please our neighbours for their good, to help them be stronger in faith. 3 Even Christ did not live to please himself. It was as the Scriptures said: "When people insult you, it hurts me."*n*
4 Everything that was written in the past was written to teach us. The Scriptures give us patience and encouragement so that we can have hope. 5 Patience and encouragement come from God. And I pray that God will help you all agree with each other the way Christ Jesus wants. 6 Then you will all be joined together, and you will give glory to God the Father of our Lord Jesus Christ. 7 Christ accepted you, so you should accept each other, which will bring glory to God. 8 I tell you that Christ became a servant of the Jews to show that God's promises to the Jewish ancestors are true. 9 And he also did this so that those who are not Jews could give glory to God for the mercy he gives to them. It is written in the Scriptures:

"So I will praise you, LORD, among the nations.

I will sing praises to your name."

Psalm 18:49

10 The Scripture also says,
"Be happy, you who are not Jews, together with his people."

Deuteronomy 32:43

11 Again the Scripture says,
"All you nations, praise the LORD.
All you people, praise him."

Psalm 117:1

12 And Isaiah says,
"The new king will come from the family of Jesse"
will stand as a banner for all peoples;
the nations will come together around him
and the place where he lives will be filled with glory." *Isaiah 11:10*

13 I pray that the God who gives hope will fill you with much joy and peace while you trust in him. Then your hope will overflow by the power of the Holy Spirit.

Paul Talks About His Work

14 My brothers and sisters, I am sure that you are full of goodness. I know that you have all the knowledge you need and that you are able to teach each other. 15 But I have written to you very openly about some things I wanted you to remember. I did this because God gave me this special gift: 16 to be a minister of Christ Jesus to those who are not Jews. I served God by teaching his Good News, so that the non-Jewish people could be an offering that God would accept—an offering made holy by the Holy Spirit.

15:14 Kindness
What should you be filled with?

17 So I am proud of what I have done for God in Christ Jesus. 18 I will not talk about anything except what Christ has done through me in leading those who are not Jews to obey God. They have obeyed God because of what I have said and done,

---

15:3 "When . . . me." Quotation from Psalm 69:9.
15:12 Jesse Jesse was the father of David, king of Israel. Jesus was from their family.

FAITH links

GLAD TO HELP!
ROMANS 15:17-20

Paul was proud of his work for God because of Jesus. He could be proud because he knew that Jesus helped him in everything that he did. His eagerness to serve showed his worship of God.

There are many ways to serve God. When you're glad, like Paul, to serve God, God is pleased. Pride in doing the work of the Lord through the help of Jesus is the best kind of pride.

Gratitude Attitude, Ezra 3, p. 611

All Talk, No Action, Jeremiah 5:1–2, p. 996

A Half-hearted Offering, Malachi 1:6–14, p. 1268

The Way to Greatness, Matthew 20:20–28, p. 1309

Best Seat in the House, Luke 14:7–11, p. 1398

The "Eyes" Have It?
1 Corinthians 12, p. 1559

---

19 because of the power of miracles and the great things they saw, and because of the power of the Holy Spirit. I preached the Good News from Jerusalem all the way around to Illyricum, and so I have finished that part of my work. 20 I always want to preach the Good News in places where people have never heard of Christ, because I do not want to build on the work someone else has already started. 21 But it is written in the Scriptures:

"Those who were not told about him will see,

and those who have not heard about him will understand."

Isaiah 52:15

Paul's Plan to Visit Rome

22 This is the reason I was stopped many times from coming to you. 23 Now I have finished my work here. Since for many years I have wanted to come to you, 24 I hope to visit you on my way to Spain. After I enjoy being with you for a while, I hope you can help me on my trip. 25 Now I am going to Jerusalem to help God's people. 26 The believers in Macedonia and Southern Greece were happy to give their money to help the poor among God's people at Jerusalem. 27 They were happy to do this, and really they owe it to them. These who are not Jews have shared in the Jews' spiritual blessings, so they should use their material possessions to help the Jews. 28 After I am sure the poor in Jerusalem get the money that has been given for them, I will leave for Spain and visit you on the way. 29 I know that when I come to you I will bring Christ's full blessing.

30 Brothers and sisters, I beg you to help me in my work by praying to God for me. Do this because of our Lord Jesus and the love that the Holy Spirit gives us. 31 Pray that I will be saved from the non-believers in Judea and that this help I bring to Jerusalem will please God's people there. 32 Then, if God wants me to, I will come to you with joy, and together you and I will have a time of rest. 33 The God who gives peace be with you all. Amen.

Greetings to the Christians

16 I recommend to you our sister Phoebe, who is a helper[n] in the church in Cenchrea. 2 I ask you to accept her in the Lord in the way God's people should. Help her with anything she needs, because she has helped me and many other people also.

3 Give my greetings to Priscilla and

16:1 helper Literally, "deaconess". This might mean the same as one of the special women helpers in 1 Timothy 3:11.

Aquila, who work together with me in Christ Jesus 4 and who risked their own lives to save my life. I am thankful to them, and all the non-Jewish churches are thankful as well. 5 Also, greet for me the church that meets at their house.

Greetings to my dear friend Epenetus, who was the first person in the country of Asia to follow Christ. 6 Greetings to Mary, who worked very hard for you. 7 Greetings to Andronicus and Junias, my relatives, who were in prison with me. They are very important apostles. They were believers in Christ before I was. 8 Greetings to Ampliatus, my dear friend in the Lord. 9 Greetings to Urbanus, a worker together with me for Christ. And greetings to my dear friend Stachys. 10 Greetings to Apelles, who was tested and proved that he truly loves Christ. Greetings to all those who are in the family of Aristobulus. 11 Greetings to Herodion, my fellow citizen. Greetings to all those in the family of Narcissus who belong to the Lord. 12 Greetings to Tryphena and Tryphosa, women who work very hard for the Lord. Greetings to my dear friend Persis, who also has worked very hard for the Lord. 13 Greetings to Rufus, who is a special person in the Lord, and to his mother, who has been like a mother to me also. 14 Greetings to Asyncritus, Phlegon, Hermes, Patrobas, Hermas and all the brothers who are with them. 15 Greetings to Philologus and Julia, Nereus and his sister, and Olympas, and to all God's people with them. 16 Greet each other with a holy kiss. All of Christ's churches send greetings to you.

17 Brothers and sisters, I ask you to look out for those who cause people to be against each other and who upset other people's faith. They are against the true teaching you learned, so stay away from them. 18 Such people are not serving our Lord Christ but are only doing what pleases themselves. They use fancy talk and fine words to fool the minds of those who do not know about evil.

16:19 Obedience Does it matter if you obey?

19 All the believers have heard that you obey, so I am very happy because of you. But I want you to be wise in what is good and innocent in what is evil.

20 The God who brings peace will soon defeat Satan and give you power over him.

The grace of our Lord Jesus be with you.

21 Timothy, a worker together with me, sends greetings, as well as Lucius, Jason and Sosipater, my relatives.

22 I am Tertius, and I am writing this letter from Paul. I send greetings to you in the Lord.

23 Gaius is letting me and the whole church here use his home. He also sends greetings to you, as do Erastus, the city treasurer, and our brother Quartus. 24 "

25 Glory to God who can make you strong in faith by the Good News that I tell people and by the message about Jesus Christ. The message about Christ is the secret that was hidden for long ages past but is now made known. 26 It has been made clear through the writings of the prophets. And by the command of the eternal God it is made known to all nations that they might believe and obey.

27 To the only wise God be glory for ever through Jesus Christ! Amen.

16:24 Verse 24 Some Greek copies add verse 24: "The grace of our Lord Jesus Christ be with all of you. Amen."

1 Corinthians

GROWING PAINS

Hi! It's me, Paul. You may know that I was a key figure in spreading the gospel about Jesus, and starting churches. In fact, did you know that I helped start the church in Corinth? I wanted a church in Corinth because it was such a busy city filled with people going from Corinth to all parts of the world. (At the time, Corinth was the second most important city, next to Rome.) Hey, I figured if I could plant a church there, I knew I could reach the whole world!

I wrote this letter because the church in Corinth was having a lot of problems. Since it was a major city, it had people from all over visiting it. These people brought with them all sorts of different beliefs and practices. So, I wrote to the church there to help them answer questions about false gods, marriage, worship, gifts of the Holy Spirit, and other issues . . . you know, the type of stuff normal people in a normal church might struggle with.

JESUS WATCH

You can find Jesus all over this book, because Jesus was the focus of Paul's life. Paul writes about the effect that believing in Jesus has on a follower's life. Paul wanted to tell his Corinthian friends to understand that Jesus and his teachings should be at the very centre of their lives. In other words, he wanted Christians both then and today to know that believing in Jesus impacts every area of life.

Paul says that Jesus "has become for us wisdom from God" (1 Corinthians 1:30). Paul wanted believers to know that Jesus was for everyone. You didn't have to be really smart, or really rich, or really pretty to believe in Jesus. Jesus is someone anyone can approach and have a relationship with.

my FAVOURITE links

OTHER CONNECTIONS

Livin' it What kind of effort do you put into a school project? What about playing your favourite sport? How about dusting your room? Connect to Good, Better, Best, 1 Corinthians 9:24–27, to see what kind of effort God wants from you – no matter what you do.

Everyone on earth will die someday. But as believers in Jesus, Christians don't have to fear death. Link to The Final End? 1 Corinthians 15:50–57, to find out why.

MORE STUFF . . .

Love Notes Jesus' kind of love goes beyond a feeling you have for someone or something. Jesus' love is a choice. In 1 Corinthians 13, Paul gives a list of all the things love is and love is not. Take a look:

- Love is patient, kind and trusting.
- It does not keep track of wrongs that have been done, and it does not get upset with others.
- It is not jealous, rude or selfish.
- Love does not like evil, but is happy with truth.

What was the deal with the Corinthians taking each other to court?

Not sure? Read about it in 1 Corinthians 6:1–8, and let's see what you think.

CHECK OUT THESE OTHER REALLY COOL THINGS IN 1 CORINTHIANS:
The Lord's Supper, 1 Corinthians 10:17–33
Our spiritual gifts, 1 Corinthians 12—14
The book on love, 1 Corinthians 13
Jesus is alive: it's a fact, 1 Corinthians 15

FAITH links

Out of Your Mind?
1 Corinthians 2:16

Brag on Him!
1 Corinthians 3:18–23

I'll Be the Judge!
1 Corinthians 4:4–5

The Winner's Crown,
1 Corinthians 9:24–27

A Family Celebration,
1 Corinthians 11:23–29

The "Eyes" Have It?
1 Corinthians 12

The Best Choice,
1 Corinthians 13

Life After Death?
1 Corinthians 15:12–13

Give to Give,
1 Corinthians 16:1–4

Meeting Together,
1 Corinthians 16:19

1 Corinthians 1:15   **1545**

1 From Paul. God called me to be an apostle of Christ Jesus because that is what God wanted. Also from Sosthenes, our brother in Christ.

2 To the church of God in Corinth, to you who have been made holy in Christ Jesus. You were called to be God's holy people with all people everywhere who pray in the name of the Lord Jesus Christ—their Lord and ours:

3 Grace and peace to you from God our Father and the Lord Jesus Christ.

Paul Gives Thanks to God

4 I always thank my God for you because of the grace God has given you in Christ Jesus. 5 I thank God because in Christ you have been made rich in every way, in all your speaking and in all your knowledge. 6 Just as our witness about Christ has been proved to you, 7 so you have every gift from God while you wait for our Lord Jesus Christ to come again. 8 Jesus will keep you strong until the end so that there will be no wrong in you on the day our Lord Jesus Christ comes again. 9 God, who has called you to share everything with his Son, Jesus Christ our Lord, is faithful.

1:8 Perseverance Who will keep you strong?

Problems in the Church

10 I beg you, brothers and sisters,″ by the name of our Lord Jesus Christ that all of you agree with each other and not be split into groups. I beg that you be completely joined together by having the same kind of thinking and the same purpose. 11 My brothers and sisters, some people from Chloe's family have told me quite plainly that there are quarrels among you. 12 This is what I mean: one of you says, "I follow Paul"; another says, "I follow Apollos"; another says, "I follow Peter"; and another says, "I follow Christ." 13 Christ has been divided up into different groups! Did Paul die on the cross for you? No! Were you baptised in the name of Paul? No! 14 I thank God I did not baptise any of you except Crispus and Gaius 15 so that now no one can say you were baptised

FAITH links

AN ENCOURAGING WORD

1 CORINTHIANS 1:3-5

If you're searching for a good way to help a friend, here is one way: encourage him and pray for him. The apostle Paul was concerned about the church he helped to start in Corinth. So he wrote them a letter. He told them how he thanked God for them. He also encouraged them to rely on God for help.

We may not always know what our friends need. God, however, always knows. So, the next time you have a spare minute, why not pray for a friend? Then, send your friend a note or e-mail to let him know that you care.

Here are some more Faithlinks on being a good friend:

Show Some Respect, Leviticus 19:32, p. 161

Give What You Can, Numbers 7:1–11, p. 186

The MLP, Ruth 1:16–17, p. 345

The Salt Promise, 2 Chronicles 13:5, p. 576

You Are What You Do, Proverbs 20:11, p. 854

Get Ready! Mark 13:26–27, p. 1354

1:10 brothers and sisters Although the Greek text says "brothers" here and throughout this book, Paul's words were meant for the entire church, both men and women.

in my name. 16 (I also baptised the family of Stephanas, but I do not remember that I baptised anyone else.) 17 Christ did not send me to baptise people but to preach the Good News. And he sent me to preach the Good News without using words of human wisdom so that the cross of Christ[n] would not lose its power.

Christ is God's Power and Wisdom

18 The teaching about the cross is foolishness to those who are being lost, but to us who are being saved it is the power of God. 19 It is written in the Scriptures:

"Their wise men will lose their
  wisdom;
 their wise men will not be able to
  understand." *Isaiah 29:14*

20 Where is the wise person? Where is the educated person? Where is the skilled talker of this world? God has made the wisdom of the world foolish. 21 Because of the wisdom of God the world did not know God through its own wisdom. So God chose to use the message that sounds foolish to save those who believe. 22 The Jews ask for miracles, and the Greeks want wisdom. 23 But we preach a crucified Christ. This is a big problem to the Jews, and it is foolishness to those who are not Jews. 24 But Christ is the power of God and the wisdom of God to those people God has called—Jews and Greeks. 25 Even the foolishness of God is wiser than human wisdom, and the weakness of God is stronger than human strength.

26 Brothers and sisters, look at what you were when God called you. Not many of you were wise in the way the world judges wisdom. Not many of you had great influence. Not many of you came from important families. 27 But God chose the foolish things of the world to shame the wise, and he chose the weak things of the world to shame the strong. 28 He chose what the world thinks is unimportant and what the world looks down on and thinks

**1:28
Pride**
What has God chosen?

is nothing in order to destroy what the world thinks is important. 29 God did this so that no one can boast in his presence. 30 Because of God you are in Christ Jesus, who has become for us wisdom from God. In Christ we are put right with God, and have been made holy, and have been set free from sin. 31 So, as the Scripture says, "If someone wants to boast, he should boast only about the Lord."[n]

The Message of Christ's Death

2 Dear brothers and sisters, when I came to you, I did not come preaching God's secret with fancy words or a show of human wisdom. 2 I decided that while I was with you I would forget about everything except Jesus Christ and his death on the cross. 3 So when I came to you, I was weak and fearful and trembling. 4 My teaching and preaching were not with words of human wisdom that persuade people but with proof of the power that the Spirit gives. 5 This was so that your faith would be in God's power and not in human wisdom.

God's Wisdom

6 However, I speak a wisdom to those who are mature. But this wisdom is not from this world or from the rulers of this world, who are losing their power. 7 I speak God's secret wisdom, which he has kept hidden. Before the world began, God planned this wisdom for our glory. 8 None of the rulers of this world understood it. If they had, they would not have crucified the Lord of glory. 9 But as it is written in the Scriptures:

"From long ago no one
  has ever heard of a God like you.

**2:6–8
Wisdom**
Check out the difference between God's wisdom and human wisdom.

1:17 cross of Christ Paul uses the cross as a picture of the gospel, the story of Christ's death and rising from the dead to pay for our sins. The cross, or Christ's death, was God's way to save us.
1:31 "If . . . Lord." Quotation from Jeremiah 9:24.

FAITH links

OUT OF YOUR MIND?
1 CORINTHIANS 2:16

If you could be anyone else in the world, who would you want to be? Why? Do you ever wish you could be the smartest person in the world, or the richest? Many people wish they were someone else, at least for a day. Although you can't really be someone else, there is a way that you can *think* like someone else. The apostle Paul tells us that we have the mind of Christ. That means we can think like Jesus. Thinking like Jesus means letting the Holy Spirit show us how to live. It means wanting what God wants.

Fatherly Advice, Exodus 18, p. 99

A Different Kind of People, Leviticus 11, p. 146

Our Thirst Quencher, Psalm 42:1–3, p. 741

Love Him? Show It! Amos 2:6–7, p. 1196

A Family Meal, Mark 14:23–26, p. 1356

Most Wanted? 2 Corinthians 10:1, p. 1580

No one has ever seen
a God besides you,
who helps the people who trust
you." *Isaiah 64:4*

10 But God has shown us these things through the Spirit. The Spirit searches out all things, even the deep secrets of God. 11 Who knows the thoughts that another person has? Only a person's spirit that lives within him knows his thoughts. It is the same with God. No one knows the thoughts of God except the Spirit of God. 12 Now we did not receive the spirit of the world, but we received the Spirit that is from God so that we can know all that God has given us. 13 And we speak about these things, not with words taught us by human wisdom but with words taught us by the Spirit. And so we explain spiritual truths to spiritual people. 14 A person who does not have the Spirit does not accept the truths that come from the Spirit of God. That person thinks they are foolish and cannot understand them, because they can only be judged to be true by the Spirit. 15 The spiritual person is able to judge all things, but no one can judge him. The Scripture says:

16 "Who has known the mind of the
    LORD
    or been able to give him advice?"
    Isaiah 40:13
But we have the mind of Christ.

Following People is Wrong

3 Brothers and sisters, in the past I could not talk to you as I talk to spiritual people. I had to talk to you as I would to people without the Spirit—babies in Christ. 2 The teaching I gave you was like milk, not solid food, because you were not able to take solid food. And even now you are not ready. 3 You are still not spiritual, because there is jealousy and quarrelling among you, and this shows that you are not spiritual. You are acting like people of the world. 4 One of you says, "I belong to Paul," and another says, "I belong to Apollos." When you say things like this, you are acting like people of the world.

5 Is Apollos important? No! Is Paul important? No! We are only servants of God who helped you believe. Each one of us did the work God gave us to do. 6 I planted the seed, and Apollos watered it. But God is the One who made it grow. 7 So the one who plants is not

**3:5–9
Witnessing**
How can you help others grow in faith?

important, and the one who waters is not important. Only God, who makes things grow, is important. 8 The one who plants and the one who waters have the same purpose, and each will be rewarded for his own work. 9 We are God's workers, working together; you are like God's farm, God's house.

10 Using the gift God gave me, I laid the foundation of that house like an expert builder. Others are building on that foundation, but all people should be careful how they build on it. 11 The foundation that has already been laid is Jesus Christ, and no one can lay down any other foundation. 12 But if people build on that foundation, using gold, silver, jewels, wood, grass or straw, 13 their work will be clearly seen, because the Day of Judgement[n] will make it seen. That Day will appear with fire, and the fire will test everyone's work to show what sort of work it was. 14 If the building that has been put on the foundation still stands, the builder will get a reward. 15 But if the building is burned up, the builder will suffer loss. The builder will be saved, but it will be as one who escaped from a fire.

16 Don't you know that you are God's temple and that God's Spirit lives in you? 17 If anyone destroys God's temple, God will destroy that person, because God's temple is holy and you are that temple.

18 Do not fool yourselves. If you think you are wise in this world, you should become a fool so that you can become truly wise, 19 because the wisdom of this world is foolishness with God. It is written in the Scriptures, "He catches those who are wise in their own clever traps."[n] 20 It is also written in the Scriptures, "The Lord knows what wise people think. He knows their thoughts are just a puff of wind."[n] 21 So you should not boast about human leaders. All things belong to you: 22 Paul, Apollos and Peter; the world, life, death, the present and the future—all these belong to you. 23 And you belong to Christ, and Christ belongs to God.

Apostles are Servants of Christ

4 People should think of us as servants of Christ, the ones God has trusted

---

FAITH links

BRAG ON HIM!
1 CORINTHIANS 3:18-23

Ever brag about who you know? Many people brag to others about famous people they know. That's called "name dropping". For example, "My third cousin is a friend of _____"(fill in the name of someone you admire). They think that knowing these people makes them cool.

Paul wrote to the Christians in Corinth to warn them to stop bragging. They bragged about the leaders they knew. Instead, Paul encouraged them to brag about belonging to Jesus. That's good advice! Knowing him gives us plenty to brag about!

Connect here to find out more about getting rid of pride in your life:

Good Advice? Leviticus 20:6, p. 162

The Weak Link, Judges 16, p. 334

A Right to Get Even? 1 Samuel 24, p. 388

The Problem with Pride, Isaiah 2:11, p. 898

All Talk, No Action, Jeremiah 5:1–2, p. 996

Say What?! Ephesians 4:22–29, p. 1603

3:13 Day of Judgement The day Christ will come to judge all people and take his people to live with him.
3:19 "He . . . traps." Quotation from Job 5:13.
3:20 "The Lord . . . wind." Quotation from Psalm 94:11.

with his secrets. 2 Now in this way those who are trusted with something valuable must show they are worthy of that trust. 3 As for myself, I do not care if I am judged by you or by any human court. I do not even judge myself. 4 I know of no wrong I have done, but this does not make me right before the Lord. The Lord is the One who judges me. 5 So do not judge before the right time; wait until the Lord comes. He will bring to light things that are now hidden in darkness, and will make known the secret purposes of people's hearts. Then God will praise each one of them.

6 Brothers and sisters, I have used Apollos and myself as examples so you could learn through us the meaning of the saying, "Follow only what is written in the Scriptures." Then you will not be more proud of one person than another. 7 Who says you are better than others? What do you have that was not given to you? And if it was given to you, why do you boast as if you did not receive it as a gift?

8 You think you already have everything you need. You think you are rich. You think you have become kings without us. I wish you really were kings so we could be kings together with you. 9 But it seems to me that God has put us apostles in last place, like those sentenced to die. We are like a show for the whole world to see—angels and people. 10 We are fools for Christ's sake, but you are very wise in Christ. We are weak, but you are strong. You receive honour, but we are shamed. 11 Even to this very hour we do not have enough to eat or drink or to wear. We are often beaten, and we have no homes in which to live. 12 We work hard with our own hands for our food. When people curse us, we bless them. When they hurt us, we put up with it. 13 When they tell evil lies about us, we speak nice words about them. Even today, we are treated as though we were the rubbish of the world—the scum of the earth.

14 I am not trying to make you feel ashamed. I am writing this to give you a warning as my own dear children. 15 For though you may have 10,000 teachers in Christ, you do not have many fathers. Through the Good News I became your father in Christ Jesus, 16 so I beg you, please follow my example. 17 That is why I am sending to you Timothy, my son in

FAITH links

I'LL BE THE JUDGE!
1 CORINTHIANS 4:4-5

Has someone ever said something about you that wasn't true? Or made a hurtful comment about something you said or did without knowing why? Being misjudged or misunderstood by someone hurts.

The Christians in Corinth believed something that was untrue about Paul. So he wrote to set the record straight. His warning to them is also a warning to us not to judge other Christians. Only God knows a person's heart. He alone judges perfectly.

Want to know who is the perfect judge? Link here:

Learning to Listen, 1 Samuel 3, p. 358

Help for the Hurting, Job 6:29–30, p. 666

Learning from Mistakes, Psalm 51:12–13, p. 748

Eating Humble Pie, Daniel 4, p. 1156

Better Than Some? Luke 18:9–14, p. 1405

A Family Celebration, 1 Corinthians 11:23–29, p. 1558

the Lord. I love Timothy, and he is faithful. He will help you remember my way of life in Christ Jesus, just as I teach it in all the churches everywhere.

18 Some of you have become proud, thinking that I will not come to you again. 19 But I will come to you very soon if the Lord wishes. Then I will know what the proud ones do, not what they say, 20 because the kingdom of God is present not in talk but in power. 21 Which do you want: that I come to you with punishment or with love and gentleness?

Wickedness in the Church

5 It is actually being said that there is sexual sin among you. And it is a kind that does not happen even among people who do not know God. A man there has his father's wife. 2 And you are proud! You should have been filled with sadness so that the man who did this should be put out of your group. 3 I am not there with you in person, but I am with you in spirit. And I have already judged the man who did that sin as if I were really there. 4 When you meet together in the name of our Lord Jesus, and I meet with you in spirit with the power of our Lord Jesus, 5 then hand this man over to Satan. So his sinful self[n] will be destroyed, and his spirit will be saved on the day of the Lord.

6 Your boasting is not good. You know the saying, "Just a little yeast makes the whole batch of dough rise." 7 Take out all the old yeast so that you will be a new batch of dough without yeast, which you really are. For Christ, our Passover lamb, has been sacrificed. 8 So let us celebrate this feast, but not with the bread that has the old yeast—the yeast of sin and wickedness. Let us celebrate this feast with the bread that has no yeast—the bread of goodness and truth.

9 I wrote to you in my earlier letter not to associate with those who sin sexually. 10 But I did not mean you should not associate with those of this world who sin sexually, or with the greedy, or robbers, or those who worship idols. To get away from them you would have to leave this world. 11 I am writing to tell you that you must not associate with those who call themselves believers in Christ but who sin sexually, or are greedy, or worship idols, or abuse others with words, or get drunk, or cheat people. Do not even eat with people like that.

12-13 It is not my business to judge those who are not part of the church. God will judge them. But you must judge the people who are part of the church. The Scripture says, "You must get rid of the evil person among you."[n]

Judging Problems Among Christians

6 When you have something against another Christian, how can you bring yourself to go before judges who are not right with God? Why do you not let God's people decide who is right? 2 Surely you know that God's people will judge the world. So if you are to judge the world, are you not able to judge small cases as well? 3 You know that in the future we will judge angels, so surely we can judge the ordinary things of this life. 4 If you have ordinary cases that must be judged, are you going to appoint people as judges who mean nothing to the church? 5 I say this to shame you. Surely there is someone among you wise enough to judge a complaint between believers. 6 But now one believer goes to court against another believer—and you do this in front of unbelievers!

> It is not my business to judge those who are not part of the church. God will judge them.
> – 1 Corinthians 5:12–13

6:3 Angels Find out who you will judge someday.

5:5 sinful self Literally, "flesh." This could also mean his body.
5:12-13 "You . . . you." Quotation from Deuteronomy 17:7; 19:19; 22:21, 24; 24:7.

7 The fact that you have lawsuits against each other shows that you are already defeated. Why not let yourselves be wronged? Why not let yourselves be cheated? 8 But you yourselves do wrong and cheat, and you do this to other believers!

9-10 Surely you know that the people who do wrong will not inherit God's kingdom. Do not be fooled. Those who sin sexually, worship idols, take part in adultery, those who are male prostitutes or men who have sexual relations with other men, those who steal, are greedy, get drunk, lie about others or rob—these people will not inherit God's kingdom. 11 In the past, some of you were like that, but you were washed clean. You were made holy, and you were made right with God in the name of the Lord Jesus Christ and in the Spirit of our God.

Use Your Bodies for God's Glory

12 "I am allowed to do all things," but all things are not good for me to do. "I am allowed to do all things," but I will not let anything make me its slave. 13 "Food is for the stomach, and the stomach for food," but God will destroy them both. The body is not for sexual sin but for the Lord, and the Lord is for the body. 14 By his power God has raised the Lord from the dead and will also raise us from the dead. 15 Surely you know that your bodies are parts of Christ himself. So I must never take the parts of Christ and join them to a prostitute! 16 It is written in the Scriptures, "The two will become one body."[n] So you should know that anyone who joins with a prostitute becomes one body with the prostitute. 17 But the one who joins with the Lord is one spirit with the Lord.

18 So run away from sexual sin. Every other sin people do is outside their bodies, but those who sin sexually sin against their own bodies. 19 You should know that your body is a temple for the Holy Spirit who is in you. You have received the Holy Spirit from God. So you do not belong to yourselves, 20 because you were bought by God for a price. So honour God with your bodies.

About Marriage

7 Now I will discuss the things you wrote to me about. It is good for a man not to have sexual relations with a woman. 2 But because sexual sin is a danger, each man should have his own wife, and each woman should have her own husband. 3 The husband should give his wife all that he owes her as his wife. And the wife should give her husband all that she owes him as her husband. 4 The wife does not have full rights over her own body; her husband shares them. And the husband does not have full rights over his own body; his wife shares them. 5 Do not refuse to give your bodies to each other, unless you both agree to stay away from sexual relations for a time so you can give your time to prayer. Then come together again so Satan cannot tempt you because of a lack of self-control. 6 I say this to give you permission to stay away from sexual relations for a time. It is not a command to do so. 7 I wish that everyone were like me, but each person has his own gift from God. One has one gift, another has another gift.

8 Now for those who are not married and for the widows I say this: it is good for them to stay unmarried as I am. 9 But if they cannot control themselves, they should marry. It is better to marry than to burn with sexual desire.

10 Now I give this command for the married people. (The command is not from me; it is from the Lord.) A wife should not leave her husband. 11 But if she does leave, she must not marry again, or she should make up with her husband. Also the husband should not divorce his wife.

12 For all the others I say this (I am saying this, not the Lord): if a Christian man has a wife who is not a believer, and she is happy to live with him, he must not divorce her. 13 And if a Christian woman has a husband who is not a believer, and he is happy to live with her, she must not divorce him. 14 The husband who is not a believer is made holy through his

---

6:16 "The two ... body." Quotation from Genesis 2:24.

believing wife. And the wife who is not a believer is made holy through her believing husband. If this were not true, your children would not be clean, but now your children are holy. 15 But if those who are not believers decide to leave, let them leave. When this happens, the Christian man or woman is free. But God called us to live in peace. 16 Wife, you don't know; maybe you will save your husband. And husband, you don't know; maybe you will save your wife.

Live as God Called You

17 But in any case each one of you should continue to live the way God has given you to live—the way you were when God called you. This is a rule I make in all the churches. 18 If a man was already circumcised when he was called, he should not undo his circumcision. If a man was without circumcision when he was called, he should not be circumcised. 19 It is not important if a man is circumcised or not. The important thing is obeying God's commands. 20 Each one of you should stay the way you were when God called you. 21 If you were a slave when God called you, do not let that bother you. But if you can be free, then make good use of your freedom. 22 Those who were slaves when the Lord called them are free persons who belong to the Lord. In the same way, those who were free when they were called are now Christ's slaves. 23 You all were bought at a great price, so do not become slaves of people. 24 Brothers and sisters, each of you should stay as you were when you were called, and stay there with God.

Questions About Getting Married

25 Now I write about people who are not married. I have no command from the Lord about this; I give my opinion. But I can be trusted, because the Lord has shown me mercy. 26 The present time is a time of trouble, so I think it is good for you to stay the way you are. 27 If you have a wife, do not try to become free from her. If you are not married, do not try to find a wife. 28 But if you decide to marry, you have not sinned. And if a girl who has never married decides to marry, she has not sinned. But those who marry will have trouble in this life, and I want you to be free from trouble.

29 Brothers and sisters, this is what I mean: we do not have much time left. So starting now, those who have wives should live as if they had no wives. 30 Those who are crying should live as if they were not crying. Those who are happy should live as if they were not happy. Those who buy things should live as if they own nothing. 31 Those who use the things of the world should live as if they were not using them, because this world in its present form will soon be gone.

32 I want you to be free from worry. A man who is not married is busy with the Lord's work, trying to please the Lord. 33 But a man who is married is busy with things of the world, trying to please his wife. 34 He must think about two things—pleasing his wife and pleasing the Lord. A woman who is not married or a girl who has never married is busy with the Lord's work. She wants to be holy in body and spirit. But a married woman is busy with things of the world, as to how she can please her husband. 35 I am saying this to help you, not to limit you. But I want you to live in the right way, to give yourselves fully to the Lord without concern for other things.

36 If a man thinks he is not doing the right thing with the girl he is engaged to, if she is almost past the best age to marry and he feels he should marry her, he should do what he wants. They should get married. It is no sin. 37 But if a man is sure in his mind that there is no need for marriage, and has his own desires under control, and has decided not to marry the one to whom he

> You all were bought at a great price, so do not become slaves of people.
> – 1 Corinthians 7:23

is engaged, he is doing the right thing. 38 So the man who marries his girl does right, but the man who does not marry will do better.

39 A woman must stay with her husband as long as he lives. But if her husband dies, she is free to marry any man she wants, but she must marry in the Lord. 40 The woman is happier if she does not marry again. This is my opinion, but I believe I also have God's Spirit.

About Food Offered to Idols

8 Now I will write about meat that is sacrificed to idols. We know that "we all have knowledge". Knowledge puffs you up with pride, but love builds up. 2 If you think you know something, you do not yet know anything as you should. 3 But if any person loves God, that person is known by God.

8:1–3 Wisdom What is true knowledge?

4 So this is what I say about eating meat sacrificed to idols: we know that an idol is really nothing in the world, and we know there is only one God. 5 Even though there are things called gods, in heaven or on earth (and there are many "gods" and "lords"), 6 for us there is only one God—our Father. All things came from him, and we live for him. And there is only one Lord—Jesus Christ. All things were made through him, and we also were made through him.

7 But not all people know this. Some people are still so used to idols that when they eat meat, they still think of it as being sacrificed to an idol. Because their conscience is weak, when they eat it, they feel guilty. 8 But food will not bring us closer to God. Refusing to eat does not make us less pleasing to God, and eating does not make us better in God's sight.

9 But be careful that your freedom does not cause those who are weak in faith to fall into sin. 10 You have "knowledge", so you have freedom to eat in an idol's temple.[n] But someone who is weak in faith might see you eating there and be encouraged to eat meat sacrificed to idols while thinking it is wrong to do so. 11 This weak believer for whom Christ died is ruined because of your "knowledge". 12 When you sin against your brothers and sisters in Christ like this and cause them to do what they feel is wrong, you are also sinning against Christ. 13 So if the food I eat causes them to fall into sin, I will never eat meat again so that I will not cause any of them to sin.

Paul is like the Other Apostles

9 I am a free man. I am an apostle. I have seen Jesus our Lord. You people are all an example of my work in the Lord. 2 If others do not accept me as an apostle, surely you do, because you are proof that I am an apostle in the Lord.

3 This is the answer I give people who want to judge me: 4 do we not have the right to eat and drink? 5 Do we not have the right to bring a believing wife with us when we travel as do the other apostles and the Lord's brothers and Peter? 6 Are Barnabas and I the only ones who must work to earn our living? 7 No soldier ever serves in the army and pays his own salary. No one ever plants a vineyard without eating some of the grapes. No person takes care of a flock without drinking some of the milk.

8 I do not say this by human authority; God's law also says the same thing. 9 It is written in the law of Moses: "When an ox is working in the grain, do not cover its mouth to keep it from eating."[n] When God said this, was he thinking only about oxen? No. 10 He was really talking about us. Yes, that Scripture was written for us, because it goes on to say: "The one who ploughs and the one who works in the grain should hope to get some of the grain for their work." 11 Since we planted spiritual seed among you, is it too much if we should harvest from you some things for this life? 12 If others have the right to get something from you, surely we have this right, too. But we do not use it. No, we put up with everything ourselves so that we

---

8:10 idol's temple Building where a god is worshipped.
9:9 "When an ox ... eating." Quotation from Deuteronomy 25:4.

DOING MY BEST
1 Corinthians 9:24–27

Good, Better, Best Ever go to buy a bike and have three choices: the basic model, the better model, and then the top-of-the-range model? You buy the one that best fits your needs and budget. If you were being rated on how you do things, what rating would you usually get? Would your rating depend on what you were doing? For example, maybe you would do your top-of-the-range work on an important exam, but barely make the grade in room cleaning!

God wants you to do *everything* with your best effort, no matter what you do. (Read Colossians 3:23, p. 1626.) Keeping Jesus in mind as you work will help you give it your all. Try to do your best – whether it's taking out the rubbish or trying to get into the football team!

MORE FAITH links

- A Big Responsibility, **p. 494**
- Building Tools, **p. 615**
- Building Together, **p. 627**
- My Best Serve, **p. 1473**
- With All Your Heart, **p. 1626**

What's your first instinct when you know there are chores to do and you don't want to do them?

Do you keep out of the way, hoping no one will find you, until you think it's safe to come out?

That's not really the best way to handle things. Better surf over to these Faithlinks right now for good advice on doing your best – no matter what the chore is!

An Unsung Hero, Ruth 2:12, 15–16, p. 347
- Have you ever felt unappreciated in what you do to help others? What do you do when you feel that way? Remember, God sees everything. He wants you to do your best even if no one else notices.

Your Best Work, 1 Kings 6, p. 443
- What are the activities you put the most effort into? Only the things you like to do? Everything you do? Link here to see how King Solomon would have answered these questions.

Small Beginnings, Zechariah 4:10, p. 1255
- Read this Faithlink for encouragement about small beginnings.

Another Lazy Day? 2 Thessalonians 3:6–13, p. 1640
- Ever wish there were no chores for you to do or homework or . . . anything else for that matter? We all wish that sometimes. But that's not God's plan – he wants us to be willing to work hard and do our best. How can keeping busy help keep you out of trouble?

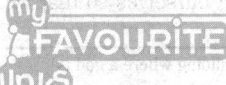

will not keep anyone from believing the Good News of Christ. 13 Surely you know that those who work at the Temple get their food from the Temple, and those who serve at the altar get part of what is offered at the altar. 14 In the same way, the Lord has commanded that those who tell the Good News should get their living from this work.

15 But I have not used any of these rights. And I am not writing this now to get anything from you. I would rather die than have my reason for boasting taken away. 16 Telling the Good News does not give me any reason for boasting. Telling the Good News is my duty—something I must do. And how terrible it will be for me if I do not tell the Good News. 17 If I preach because it is my own choice, I have a reward. But if I preach and it is not my choice to do so, I am only doing the duty that was given to me. 18 So what reward do I get? This is my reward: that when I tell the Good News I can offer it freely. I do not use my full rights in my work of preaching the Good News.

19 I am free and belong to no one. But I make myself a slave to all people to win as many as I can. 20 To the Jews I became like a Jew to win the Jews. I myself am not ruled by the law. But to those who are ruled by the law I became like a person who is ruled by the law. I did this to win those who are ruled by the law. 21 To those who are without the law I became like a person who is without the law. I did this to win those people who are without the law. (But really, I am not without God's law—I am ruled by Christ's law.) 22 To those who are weak, I became weak so I could win the weak. I have become all things to all people so I could save some of them in any way possible. 23 I do all this because of the Good News and so I can share in its blessings.

24 You know that in a race all the runners run, but only one gets the prize. So run to win! 25 All those who compete in the games use self-control so they can win a crown. That crown is an earthly thing that lasts only a short time, but our crown will never be destroyed. 26 So I do not run without a goal. I fight like a boxer who is

FAITH links

THE WINNER'S CROWN
1 CORINTHIANS 9:24-27

Have you ever won a race? Winning can be very exciting, especially if you have something to show for it, like a trophy or a medal.

The apostle Paul compared living the Christian life to running a race. No one easily wins a race. You have to work hard to be good enough to finish a race, let alone win it. Living as a Christian takes work, too. Instead of being handed a trophy that could tarnish or become lost, we have the promise of a crown that "will never be destroyed" (1 Corinthians 9:25). This is the eternal life that God promised.

Download these Faithlinks to find out what it takes to be a true winner:

The Rainbow Promise, Genesis 9:1–17, p. 14

Trailblazers of Faith, 2 Kings 22:1–2, p. 510

Your Best Defence, 2 Chronicles 20:1–12, p. 584

More Precious Than Gold, Psalm 19:7–10, p. 723

The Power of *If*, Mark 9:14–24, p. 1344

Praise Him! Revelation 5:12, p. 1736

hitting something—not just the air. 27 I treat my body hard and make it my slave so that I myself will not be rejected after I have preached to others.

Warnings from Israel's Past

10 Brothers and sisters, I want you to know what happened to our ancestors who followed Moses. They were all under the cloud and all went through the sea. 2 They were all baptised as followers of Moses in the cloud and in the sea. 3 They all ate the same spiritual food, 4 and all drank the same spiritual drink. They drank from that spiritual rock that followed them, and that rock was Christ. 5 But God was not pleased with most of them, so they died in the desert.

6 And these things happened as examples for us, to stop us from wanting evil things as those people did. 7 Do not worship idols, as some of them did. Just as it is written in the Scriptures: "They sat down to eat and drink, and then they got up and sinned sexually."[n] 8 We must not take part in sexual sins, as some of them did. In one day 23,000 of them died because of their sins. 9 We must not test Christ as some of them did; they were killed by snakes. 10 Do not complain as some of them did; they were killed by the angel that destroys.

11 The things that happened to those people are examples. They were written down to teach us, because we live in a time when all these things of the past have reached their goal. 12 If you think you are strong, you should be careful not to fall. 13 The only temptation that has come to you is that which everyone has. But you can trust God, who will not let you be tempted more than you can stand. But when you are tempted, he will also give you a way to escape so that you will be able to stand it.

14 So, my dear friends, run away from the worship of idols. 15 I am speaking to you as to intelligent people; judge for yourselves what I say. 16 We give thanks for the cup of blessing,[n] which is a sharing in the blood of Christ. And the bread that we break is a sharing in the body of Christ. 17 Because there is one loaf of bread, we who are many are one body, because we all share that one loaf.

18 Think about the Israelites: do not those who eat the sacrifices share in the altar? 19 I do not mean that the food sacrificed to an idol is important. I do not mean that an idol is anything at all. 20 But I say that what is sacrificed to idols is offered to demons, not to God. And I do not want you to share anything with demons. 21 You cannot drink the cup of the Lord and the cup of demons also. You cannot share in the Lord's table and the table of demons. 22 Are we trying to make the Lord jealous? We are not stronger than he is, are we?

How to Use Christian Freedom

23 "We are allowed to do all things," but all things are not good for us to do. "We are allowed to do all things," but not all things help others grow stronger. 24 Do not look out only for yourselves. Look out for the good of others also.

25 Eat any meat that is sold in the meat market. Do not ask questions to see if it is meat you think is wrong to eat. 26 You may eat it, "because the earth belongs to the Lord, and everything in it."[n]

27 Those who are not believers may invite you to eat with them. If you want to go, eat anything that is put before you. Do not ask questions to see if you think it might be wrong to eat. 28 But if anyone says to you, "That food was offered to idols," do not eat it. Do not eat it because of that person who told you and because eating it might be thought to be wrong. 29 I don't mean you think it is wrong, but the other person might. But why, you ask, should my freedom be judged by someone else's conscience? 30 If I eat the meal with thankfulness, why am I criticised because of something for which I thank God?

10:7 "They . . . sexually." Quotation from Exodus 32:6.
10:16 cup of blessing The cup of the fruit of the vine that Christians thank God for and drink at the Lord's Supper.
10:26 "because . . . it" Quotation from Psalms 24:1; 50:12; 89:11.

31 The answer is, if you eat or drink, or if you do anything, do it all for the glory of God. 32 Never do anything that might hurt others—Jews, Greeks or God's church— 33 just as I, also, try to please everybody in every way. I am not trying to do what is good for me but what is good for most people so they can be saved.

11 Follow my example, as I follow the example of Christ.

Being Under Authority

2 I praise you because you remember me in everything, and you follow closely the teachings just as I gave them to you. 3 But I want you to understand this: the head of every man is Christ, the head of a woman is the man[n] and the head of Christ is God. 4 Every man who prays or prophesies with his head covered brings shame to his head. 5 But every woman who prays or prophesies with her head uncovered brings shame to her head. She is the same as a woman who has her head shaved. 6 If a woman does not cover her head, she should have her hair cut off. But since it is shameful for a woman to cut off her hair or to shave her head, she should cover her head. 7 But a man should not cover his head, because he is the likeness and glory of God. But woman is man's glory. 8 Man did not come from woman, but woman came from man. 9 And man was not made for woman, but woman was made for man. 10 So that is why a woman should have a symbol of authority on her head, because of the angels. 11 But in the Lord women are not independent of men, and men are not independent of women. 12 This is true because woman came from man, but also man is born from woman. But everything comes from God. 13 Decide this for yourselves: is it right for a woman to pray to God with her head uncovered? 14 Even nature itself teaches you that wearing long hair is shameful for a man. 15 But long hair is a woman's glory. Long hair is given to her as a covering. 16 Some people may still want to argue about this, but I would add that neither we nor the churches of God have any other practice.

The Lord's Supper

17 In the things I tell you now I do not praise you, because when you come together you do more harm than good. 18 First, I hear that when you meet together as a church you are divided, and I believe some of this. 19 (It is necessary to have differences among you so that it may be clear which of you really have God's approval.) 20 When you come together, you are not really eating the Lord's Supper.[n] 21 This is because when you eat, each person eats without waiting for the others. Some people do not get enough to eat, while others have too much to drink. 22 You can eat and drink in your own homes! You seem to think God's church is not important, and you embarrass those who are poor. What should I tell you? Should I praise you? I do not praise you for doing this.

23 The teaching I gave you is the same teaching I received from the Lord: on the night when the Lord Jesus was handed over to be killed, he took bread 24 and gave thanks for it. Then he broke the bread and said, "This is my body; it is for you. Do this to remember me." 25 In the same way, after they ate, Jesus took the cup. He said, "This cup is the new agreement that is sealed with the blood of my death. When you drink this, do it to remember me." 26 Every time you eat

> The answer is, if you eat or drink, or if you do anything, do it all for the glory of God.
> – 1 Corinthians 10:31

11:17–22 Following God
How can you identify followers of God?

11:3 the man This could also mean "her husband".
11:20 Lord's Supper The special meal that Jesus told his followers to eat to remember him (Luke 22:14-20).

FAITH links

A FAMILY CELEBRATION
1 CORINTHIANS 11:23-29

If you've ever been to a family party where two family members weren't getting along, you'll know how uncomfortable that can be. Their disagreement brings a dark cloud to an otherwise joyful celebration.

Paul wrote to the Christians of Corinth about the Lord's Supper. The Lord's Supper is a family celebration in honour of Jesus. Unfortunately, some of the Corinthians weren't getting along. Others had sinful attitudes. Before we participate in the Lord's Supper, we need to make sure our attitudes and actions honour Jesus. That might involve asking for forgiveness from God or from some other person we've hurt. When we do this, the whole "family" will be able to honour Jesus.

What God Wants, Deuteronomy 10:12–13, p. 242

Mourning for an Enemy, 2 Samuel 1, p. 399

God's New Home, 2 Chronicles 7:11–22, p. 570

The Watchman, Ezekiel 3:16–22, p. 1088

The Number One Rule, Mark 12:28–31, p. 1351

Family Time, Hebrews 10:25, p. 1678

---

this bread and drink this cup you are telling others about the Lord's death until he comes.

27 So a person who eats the bread or drinks the cup of the Lord in a way that is not worthy of it will be guilty of sinning against the body and the blood of the Lord. 28 Look into your own hearts before you eat the bread and drink the cup, 29 because all who eat the bread and drink the cup without recognising the body eat and drink judgement against themselves. 30 That is why many in your group are sick and weak, and many have died. 31 But if we judged ourselves in the right way, God would not judge us. 32 But when the Lord judges us, he punishes us so that we will not be destroyed along with the world.

33 So my brothers and sisters, when you come together to eat, wait for each other. 34 Anyone who is too hungry should eat at home so that in meeting together you will not bring God's judgement on yourselves. I will tell you what to do about the other things when I come.

Gifts from the Holy Spirit

12 Now, brothers and sisters, I want you to understand about spiritual gifts. 2 You know the way you lived before you were believers. You let yourselves be influenced and led away to worship idols—things that could not speak. 3 So I want you to understand that no one who is speaking with the help of God's Spirit says, "Jesus be cursed." And no one can say, "Jesus is Lord," without the help of the Holy Spirit.

4 There are different kinds of gifts, but they are all from the same Spirit. 5 There are different ways to serve but the same Lord to serve. 6 And there are different ways that God works through people but the same God. God works in all of us in everything we do. 7 Something from the Spirit can be seen in each person, for the common good. 8 The Spirit gives one person the ability to speak with wisdom, and the same Spirit gives another the ability to speak with knowledge. 9 The same Spirit gives faith to one person. And, to another, that one Spirit gives gifts of

healing. **10** The Spirit gives to another person the power to do miracles, to another the ability to prophesy. And he gives to another the ability to know the difference between good and evil spirits. The Spirit gives one person the ability to speak in different kinds of languages*[n]* and to another the ability to interpret those languages. **11** One Spirit, the same Spirit, does all these things, and the Spirit decides what to give each person.

The Body of Christ Works Together

12 A person's body is only one thing, but it has many parts. Though there are many parts to a body, all those parts make only one body. Christ is like that also. **13** Some of us are Jews, and some are Greeks. Some of us are slaves, and some are free. But we were all baptised into one body through one Spirit. And we were all made to share in the one Spirit.

14 The human body has many parts. **15** The foot might say, "Because I am not a hand, I am not part of the body." But saying this would not stop the foot from being a part of the body. **16** The ear might say, "Because I am not an eye, I am not part of the body." But saying this would not stop the ear from being a part of the body. **17** If the whole body were an eye, it would not be able to hear. If the whole body were an ear, it would not be able to smell. **18-19** If each part of the body were the same part, there would be no body. But truly God put all the parts, each one of them, in the body as he wanted them. **20** So then there are many parts, but only one body.

21 The eye cannot say to the hand, "I don't need you!" And the head cannot say to the foot, "I don't need you!" **22** No! Those parts of the body that seem to be the weaker are really necessary. **23** And the parts of the body we think are less are the parts to which we give the most honour. We give special respect to the parts we want to hide. **24** The more beautiful parts of our body need no special care. But God put the body together and gave more honour to the parts that need it **25** so our body would not be divided.

FAITH links

THE "EYES" HAVE IT?
1 CORINTHIANS 12

Suppose your whole body was made up of only one eye. What would happen? Well, for one thing, you'd have trouble walking, breathing and eating.

In a physical body, every part is important. That's the way the church – Jesus' "body" – is, too! The Spirit has given each member a special ability. Some teach, some encourage others, and others preach. Sometimes, however, we start to wish we had someone else's ability. Or, we might think our ability is better than someone else's. When that happens, we stop working together. God wants us to be thankful for the gifts he has given us and to respect the gifts of others.

Want to know how to use your gifts? Connect here:

Serious About the Sabbath, Exodus 31:15, p. 117

Loyal to a Friend, 2 Samuel 9, p. 409

The Problem with Pride, Isaiah 2:11, p. 898

The Right Ingredients, Micah 6:8, p. 1227

Jesus' Prayer, John 17, p. 1453

The Sacrifice of Service, Philippians 2:17, 25–30, p. 1612

12:10 languages This can also be translated "tongues".

God wanted the different parts to care the same for each other. 26 If one part of the body suffers, all the other parts suffer with it. Or if one part of our body is honoured, all the other parts share its honour.

27 Together you are the body of Christ, and each one of you is a part of that body. 28 In the church God has given a place first to apostles, second to prophets and third to teachers. Then God has given a place to those who do miracles, those who have gifts of healing, those who can help others, those who are able to govern, and those who can speak in different languages." 29 Not all are apostles. Not all are prophets. Not all are teachers. Not all do miracles. 30 Not all have gifts of healing. Not all speak in different languages. Not all interpret those languages. 31 But you should truly want to have the greater gifts.

Love is the Greatest Gift

And now I will show you the best way of all.

13 I may speak in different languages" of people or even angels. But if I do not have love, I am only a noisy bell or a crashing cymbal. 2 I may have the gift of prophecy. I may understand all the secret things of God and have all knowledge, and I may have faith so great I can move mountains. But even with all these things, if I do not have love, then I am nothing. 3 I may give away everything I have, and I may even give my body as an offering to be burnt." But I gain nothing if I do not have love.

4 Love is patient and kind. Love is not jealous, it does not boast, and it is not proud. 5 Love is not rude, is not selfish, and does not get upset with others. Love does not count up wrongs that have been done. 6 Love is not happy with evil but is happy with the truth. 7 Love patiently accepts all things. It always trusts, always hopes, and always remains strong.

8 Love never ends. There are gifts of

13:4–8
Love
What is true love?

FAITH links

THE BEST CHOICE
1 CORINTHIANS 13

Who or what do you love? Many people think they know what love is, but their actions prove otherwise! This chapter in 1 Corinthians is sometimes called the "love chapter". It explains what love is and what it is not. Love is not a feeling. It is an act of the will, or a choice you make. You can choose to love someone by not being rude to him or her, or by letting him or her go first. In fact, God commands us to love others, including our enemies. Love is the greatest gift we can have or offer. Choose love today!

Click here to find out more about loving others God's way:

Roll Out the Welcome Wagon, Genesis 18:2–8, p. 24

Anger: Quick or Slow? Psalm 86:15, p. 776

Who Do You Prefer? Proverbs 3:32, p. 830

Sow It and Reap, Lamentations 1:18, p. 1075

Just Say Yes! Matthew 9:9–13, p. 1289

The True Test, 1 John 3:18, p. 1718

12:28; 13:1 languages This can also be translated "tongues".
13:3 Verse 3 Other Greek copies read: "hand over my body in order that I may boast."

prophecy, but they will be ended. There are gifts of speaking in different languages, but those gifts will stop. There is the gift of knowledge, but it will come to an end. 9 The reason is that our knowledge and our ability to prophesy are not perfect. 10 But when perfection comes, the things that are not perfect will end. 11 When I was a child, I talked like a child, I thought like a child, I reasoned like a child. When I became a man, I stopped those childish ways. 12 It is the same with us. Now we see a dim reflection, as if we were looking into a mirror, but then we shall see clearly. Now I know only a part, but then I will know fully, as God has known me. 13 So these three things continue for ever: faith, hope and love. And the greatest of these is love.

Desire Spiritual Gifts

14 You should seek after love, and you should truly want to have the spiritual gifts, especially the gift of prophecy. 2 I will explain why. Those who have the gift of speaking in different languages[n] are not speaking to people; they are speaking to God. No one understands them; they are speaking secret things through the Spirit. 3 But those who prophesy are speaking to people to give them strength, encouragement and comfort. 4 The ones who speak in different languages are helping only themselves, but those who prophesy are helping the whole church. 5 I wish all of you had the gift of speaking in different kinds of languages, but more, I wish you would prophesy. Those who prophesy are greater than those who can only speak in different languages—unless someone is there who can explain what is said so that the whole church can be helped.

6 Brothers and sisters, will it help you if I come to you speaking in different languages? No! It will help you only if I bring you a new truth or some new knowledge, or prophecy, or teaching. 7 It is the same as with lifeless things that make sounds—like a flute or a harp. If they do not make clear musical notes, you will not know what is being played. 8 And in a war, if the trumpet does not give a clear sound, who will prepare for battle? 9 It is the same with you. Unless you speak clearly with your tongue, no one can understand what you are saying. You will be talking into the air! 10 It may be true that there are all kinds of sounds in the world, and none is without meaning. 11 But unless I understand the meaning of what someone says to me, I will be a foreigner to him, and he will be a foreigner to me. 12 It is the same with you. Since you want spiritual gifts very much, seek most of all to have the gifts that help the church grow stronger.

13 The one who has the gift of speaking in a different language should pray for the gift to interpret what is spoken. 14 If I pray in a different language, my spirit is praying, but my mind does nothing. 15 So what should I do? I will pray with my spirit, but I will also pray with my mind. I will sing with my spirit, but I will also sing with my mind. 16 If you praise God with your spirit, those persons there without understanding cannot say amen[n] to your prayer of thanks, because they do not know what you are saying. 17 You may be thanking God in a good way, but the other person is not helped.

18 I thank God that I speak in different kinds of languages more than all of you. 19 But in the church meetings I would rather speak five words I understand in order to teach others than thousands of words in a different language.

20 Brothers and sisters, do not think like children. In evil things be like babies, but in your thinking you should be like adults. 21 It is written in the Scriptures:

"With people who use strange words
    and foreign languages
The LORD will speak to these
    people.
But people would not listen to
    me,"   *Isaiah 28:11-12*

says the Lord.

22 So the gift of speaking in different kinds of languages is a proof for those who do not believe, not for those who

---

14:2 languages This can also be translated "tongues".
14:16 amen To say amen means to agree with the things that were said.

do believe. And prophecy is for people who believe, not for those who do not believe. 23 Suppose the whole church meets together and everyone speaks in different languages. If some people come in who do not understand or do not believe, they will say you are mad. 24 But suppose everyone is prophesying and some people come in who do not believe or do not understand. If everyone is prophesying, their sin will be shown to them, and they will be judged by all that they hear. 25 The secret things in their hearts will be made known. So they will bow down and worship God saying, "Truly, God is with you."

Meetings Should Help the Church

26 So, brothers and sisters, what should you do? When you meet together, one person has a song, and another has a teaching. Another has a new truth from God. Another speaks in a different language,[n] and another person interprets that language. The purpose of all these things should be to help the church grow strong. 27 When you meet together, if anyone speaks in a different language, it should be only two, or not more than three, who speak. They should speak one after the other, and someone else should interpret. 28 But if there is no interpreter, then those who speak in a different language should be quiet in the church meeting. They should speak only to themselves and to God.

29 Only two or three prophets should speak, and the others should judge what they say. 30 If a message from God comes to another person who is sitting, the first speaker should stop. 31 You can all prophesy one after the other. In this way all the people can be taught and encouraged. 32 The spirits of prophets are under the control of the prophets themselves. 33 God is not a God of confusion but a God of peace.

As is true in all the churches of God's people, 34 women should keep quiet in the church meetings. They are not allowed to speak, but they must yield to this rule as the law says. 35 If they want to learn something, they should ask their own husbands at home. It is shameful for a woman to speak in the church meeting. 36 Did God's teaching come from you? Or are you the only ones to whom it has come?

37 Those who think they are prophets or spiritual persons should understand that what I am writing to you is the Lord's command. 38 Those who ignore this will be ignored by God.

39 So my brothers and sisters, you should truly want to prophesy. But do not stop people from using the gift of speaking in different kinds of languages. 40 But let everything be done in a right and orderly way.

The Good News About Christ

15 Now, brothers and sisters, I want you to remember the Good News I brought to you. You received this Good News and continue strong in it. 2 And you are being saved by it if you continue believing what I told you. If you do not, then you believed for nothing.

3 I passed on to you what I received, of which this was most important: that Christ died for our sins, as the Scriptures say; 4 that he was buried and was raised to life on the third day as the Scriptures say; 5 and that he was seen by Peter and then by the twelve apostles. 6 After that, Jesus was seen by more than 500 of the believers at the same time. Most of them are still living today, but some have died. 7 Then he was seen by James and later by all the apostles. 8 Last of all he was seen by me—as by a person not born at the normal time. 9 All the other apostles are greater than I am. I

> God is not a God of confusion but a God of peace.
> – 1 Corinthians 14:33

14:26 language This can also be translated "tongue".

am not even good enough to be called an apostle, because I persecuted the church of God. 10 But God's grace has made me what I am, and his grace to me was not wasted. I worked harder than all the other apostles. (But it was not I really; it was God's grace that was with me.) 11 So if I preached to you or the other apostles preached to you, we all preach the same thing, and this is what you believed.

We will be Raised from the Dead

12 Now since we preached that Christ was raised from the dead, why do some of you say that people will not be raised from the dead? 13 If no one is ever raised from the dead, then Christ has not been raised. 14 And if Christ has not been raised, then our preaching is worth nothing, and your faith is worth nothing. 15 And also, we are guilty of lying about God, because we testified of him that he raised Christ from the dead. But if people are not raised from the dead, then God never raised Christ. 16 If the dead are not raised, Christ has not been raised either. 17 And if Christ has not been raised, then your faith has nothing to it; you are still guilty of your sins. 18 And those in Christ who have already died are lost. 19 If our hope in Christ is for this life only, we should be pitied more than anyone else in the world.

20 But Christ has truly been raised from the dead—the first one, and proof that those who sleep in death will also be raised. 21 Death has come because of what one man did, but the rising from death also comes because of one man. 22 In Adam all of us die. In the same way, in Christ all of us will be made alive again. 23 But everyone will be raised to life in the right order. Christ was first to be raised. When Christ comes again, those who belong to him will be raised to life, 24 and then the end will come. At that time Christ will destroy all rulers, authorities and powers, and he will hand over the kingdom to God the Father. 25 Christ

EMAIL FROM GOD
15:12–21
Resurrection
The bottom line of Christian faith.

FAITH links

LIFE AFTER DEATH?
1 CORINTHIANS 15:12-13

Ever hear someone talk about life after death? Some people believe that after a person dies, nothing happens. He or she just doesn't exist anymore. So, what do you believe will happen after you die? Is the thought too scary to think about?

If you're a Christian, you don't have to be too scared to think about death. You know that your life will go on, even after you die! That's what Paul wanted the Christians in Corinth to know and believe. A Christian's hope is in Jesus. Since he was raised from the dead, you will be, too, someday. There is life after death: eternal life!

Link here to find out more about why Christians shouldn't fear death:

A Friend in Deed, Job 2:13, p. 662

Who Ya' Gonna Call? Psalm 3:4, p. 711

Love That Will Last, Psalm 136, p. 813

Sad Times, Matthew 14:13–14, p. 1299

The Coming Attraction, 1 Thessalonians 4:13–18, p. 1634

Never Alone, Hebrews 13:5–6, p. 1684

▶ 1 Corinthians 15 1564

DEATH
1 Corinthians 15:50–57

The Final End? If someone close to you has died, you probably felt an overwhelming sadness and may have spent a lot of time crying. If you have ever been to a funeral, you know that is how people react to the loss of a loved one. People feel sad because they know they will miss seeing that person and talking to him or her. But Christians, even in their sadness, can feel happiness because they know that they *will* see the person again someday – in heaven. How can knowing that comfort you and help you comfort others?

Some people believe that after someone dies, that's the end – he or she just doesn't exist anymore. Paul wanted Christians not to fear death, but to know the truth. (Read 1 Corinthians 15:12–13.) If you're a Christian, you know that there is life after death: eternal life through Jesus.

MORE FAITH LINKS

Sad Times, p. 1299
Remembering Jesus, p. 1321
Mission Impossible? p. 1337
Life After Death? p. 1563
The Coming Attraction, p. 1634

> Do you ever think about death? It can be such a scary topic that some people don't like to think about it.
>
> Although it can be scary to think about, if you connect to these links you'll find out that believers in Jesus have another way of thinking about death.

Love That Will Last, Psalm 136, p. 813
- Is there anything you know that lasts for ever? Some bad things may seem to last for ever but eventually they go away. How about people, do they last for ever? Christians don't live on earth for ever, but where *do* they last for ever? This Faithlink tells about another thing that you can count on to last for ever.

Fully God, Fully Human, John 11:35, p. 1444
- When a friend feels sad, you feel sad, too, don't you? And when someone you love dies, you feel very sad. Link here to find out how Jesus felt about a sad situation.

A Heavenly Sight, Revelation 21:1–4, p. 1753
- What is the most beautiful place you have ever seen? What did you like best about that place?
- What do you think heaven will be like? If you fear what the future may hold, think about this description of heaven, and be glad!

must rule until he puts all enemies under his control. 26 The last enemy to be destroyed will be death. 27 The Scripture says that God put all things under his control.*ⁿ* When it says "all things" are under him, it is clear this does not include God himself. God is the One who put everything under his control. 28 After everything has been put under the Son, then he will put himself under God, who had put all things under him. Then God will be the complete ruler over everything.

29 If the dead are never raised, what will people do who are being baptised for the dead? If the dead are not raised at all, why are people being baptised for them? 30 And what about us? Why do we put ourselves in danger every hour? 31 I die every day. That is true, brothers and sisters, just as it is true that I boast about you in Christ Jesus our Lord. 32 If I fought wild animals in Ephesus only with human hopes, I have gained nothing. If the dead are not raised, "Let us eat and drink, because tomorrow we will die."*ⁿ*

33 Do not be fooled: "Bad friends will ruin good habits." 34 Come back to your right way of thinking and stop sinning. Some of you do not know God—I say this to shame you.

What Kind of Body will We Have?

35 But someone may ask, "How are the dead raised? What kind of body will they have?" 36 Foolish person! When you sow a seed, it must die in the ground before it can live and grow. 37 And when you sow it, it does not have the same "body" it will have later. What you sow is only a bare seed, maybe wheat or something else. 38 But God gives it a body that he has planned for it, and God gives each kind of seed its own body. 39 All things made of flesh are not the same: people have one kind of flesh, animals have another, birds have another and fish have another. 40 Also there are heavenly bodies and earthly bodies. But the beauty of the heavenly bodies is one kind, and the beauty of the earthly bodies is another. 41 The sun has one kind of beauty, the moon has another beauty and the stars have another. And each star is different in its beauty.

42 It is the same with the dead who are raised to life. The body that is "planted" will ruin and decay, but it is raised to a life that cannot be destroyed. 43 When the body is "planted", it is without honour, but it is raised in glory. When the body is "planted", it is weak, but when it is raised, it is powerful. 44 The body that is "planted" is a physical body. When it is raised, it is a spiritual body.

There is a physical body, and there is also a spiritual body. 45 It is written in the Scriptures: "The first man, Adam, became a living person."*ⁿ* But the last Adam became a spirit that gives life. 46 The spiritual did not come first, but the physical and then the spiritual. 47 The first man came from the dust of the earth. The second man came from heaven. 48 People who belong to the earth are like the first man of earth. But those people who belong to heaven are like the man of heaven. 49 Just as we were made like the man of earth, so we will also be made like the man of heaven.

50 I tell you this, brothers and sisters: flesh and blood cannot have a part in the kingdom of God. Something that will ruin cannot have a part in something that never ruins. 51 But look! I tell you this secret: we will not all sleep in death, but we will all be changed. 52 It will take only a second—as quickly as an eye blinks—when the last trumpet sounds. The trumpet will sound, and those who have died will be raised to live for ever, and we will all be changed. 53 This body that can be destroyed must clothe itself with something that can never be destroyed. And this body that dies must clothe itself with something that can never die. 54 So this body that can be destroyed will clothe itself with that which can never be destroyed, and this body that dies will

15:27 God put . . . control. From Psalm 8:6.
15:32 "Let us . . . die." Quotation from Isaiah 22:13; 56:12.
15:45 "The first . . . person." Quotation from Genesis 2:7.

clothe itself with that which can never die. When this happens, this Scripture will be made true:

"Death is destroyed for ever."
Isaiah 25:8
55 "Death, where is your victory?

Where is your pain, place of death?" *Hosea 13:14*
56 Death's power to hurt is sin, and the power of sin is the law. 57 But we thank God! He gives us the victory through our Lord Jesus Christ.

58 So my dear brothers and sisters, stand strong. Do not let anything change you. Always give yourselves fully to the work of the Lord, because you know that your work in the Lord is never wasted.

The Gift for Other Believers

16 Now I will write about the collection of money for God's people. Do the same thing I told the Galatian churches to do: 2 on the first day of every week, each one of you should put aside money as you have been blessed. Save it up so you will not have to collect money after I come. 3 When I arrive, I will send whomever you approve to take your gift to Jerusalem. I will send them with letters of introduction, 4 and if it seems good for me to go also, they will go along with me.

Paul's Plans

5 I plan to go through Macedonia, so I will come to you after I go through there. 6 Perhaps I will stay with you for a time or even all winter. Then you can help me on my trip, wherever I go. 7 I do not want to see you now just in passing. I hope to stay a longer time with you if the Lord allows it. 8 But I will stay at Ephesus until Pentecost, 9 because a good opportunity for a great and growing work has been given to me now. And there are many people working against me.

10 If Timothy comes to you, see to it that he has nothing to fear with you, because he is working for the Lord just as I am. 11 So none of you should treat Timothy as unimportant, but help him on his way in peace so that he can come back to me. I am expecting him to come with the brothers.

12 Now about our brother Apollos: I strongly encouraged him to visit you with the other brothers. He did not at all want to come now; he will come when he has the opportunity.

GIVE TO GIVE
1 CORINTHIANS 16:1-4

Paul wrote to remind the Corinthian Christians to give money to help poor Christians in Jerusalem. Giving is something we do to help one another. Most churches use the offerings received each week to pay the salaries of church workers, to help people in need and to support missionaries. When members of a church family give what they can, that allows the church to do what it does best – help people learn about Jesus.

Here are some more Faithlinks on giving your best to God:

Giving Your Part,
Leviticus 27:30, p. 173

Give What You Can,
Numbers 7:1–11, p. 186

The Way to Serve God,
1 Kings 9:4, p. 450

Love Him? Show It!
Amos 2:6–7, p. 1196

Give Till It Hurts?
2 Corinthians 8:6–9; 9:6–9, p. 1578

Hot, Cold or In Between?
Revelation 3:15, p. 1735

Paul Ends His Letter

13 Be careful. Continue strong in the faith. Have courage, and be strong. 14 Do everything in love.

16:13 Courage
What should you do when you're afraid?

15 You know that the family of Stephanas were the first believers in Southern Greece and that they have given themselves to the service of God's people. I ask you, brothers and sisters, 16 to follow the leading of people like these and anyone else who works and serves with them.

17 I am happy that Stephanas, Fortunatus and Achaicus have come. You are not here, but they have filled your place. 18 They have refreshed my spirit and yours. You should recognise the value of people like these.

19 The churches in the country of Asia send greetings to you. Aquila and Priscilla greet you in the Lord, as does the church that meets in their house. 20 All the brothers and sisters here send greetings. Give each other a holy kiss when you meet.

21 I, Paul, am writing this greeting with my own hand.

22 If anyone does not love the Lord, let him be separated from God—lost for ever! Come, O Lord!

23 The grace of the Lord Jesus be with you.

24 My love be with all of you in Christ Jesus.

FAITH links

MEETING TOGETHER
1 CORINTHIANS 16:19

Do you remember the finger-play game, "This is the church, this is the steeple; open the door, and there are the people"? In that game, the fingers represent the people in the church. It shows that the church is not a building, but a living "body" of people who meet together regularly.

The apostle Paul ended his letter with a greeting from a married couple named Aquila and Priscilla. They were part of a church group that met in their home. Whether Christians meet in homes, schools or other types of buildings, God is pleased when his people meet together to worship him. Is attending church regularly part of your weekly routine?

A Thanksgiving Reminder,
Exodus 12, p. 91

Serious About the Sabbath,
Exodus 31:15, p. 117

Facts About Following,
Joshua 6, p. 283

Inside the Heart of God,
Micah 7:18–20, p. 1228

Heavenly Treasure,
Luke 12:32–34, p. 1394

Two Birthdays, John 3:1–7,
p. 1426

2 Corinthians

A CASE FOR THE DEFENCE

It's me again – Paul. This is my second letter to my friends in Corinth. And, in case you're wondering, this book *is* different from 1 Corinthians. That first book was all about the problems that the church in Corinth was having. But this one is entirely different. I'm not complaining here, but serving God can be really hard. It's not always fun being poor and hungry and tired and in constant danger. It wasn't always fun, but I wanted my friends to understand that I would go through *anything* to tell people about Jesus!

I wrote this letter to set the record straight. You see, a lot of the Jewish leaders didn't like my message or me. So they started telling lies about me. (They even accused me of being a false teacher!) I wanted my friends to understand that the Christian life is not all about success, power and fame, like they were saying. It's about following and obeying Jesus – even if it means suffering and being misunderstood!

JESUS WATCH

Paul's ministry was all about telling people about Jesus, and this letter is no exception. In this letter, Paul focuses on helping us understand Jesus as our comforter in the bad times. And Paul promises that for all followers, bad times happen. Throughout the book, Paul talks about Jesus as our comforter (1:5), our victory (2:14), our Lord (4:5), our light (4:6) and our gift (9:15). Paul faced many tough times, but he was able to continue in spite of his difficulties because he knew the truth – Jesus is always with us. We can be encouraged by that same truth today!

my FAVOURITE links

OTHER CONNECTIONS

 Do you mind sharing your stuff with other kids? Or do you worry about your stuff getting lost, or ruined? What's more important – your stuff or your friends? Find out what the Bible has to say about the things we own by linking to Sharing Your Stuff, 2 Corinthians 8:1–9.

GET THE INFO

- Let's Visit Corinth, 2 Corinthians 6. Connect here to find out why Corinth was such a perfect place for Paul to preach about the Good News.

Does Paul really talk about giving to the church in this letter?

Let's find out by reading what Paul writes about in 2 Corinthians 8:7–15.

OTHER COOL STUFF IN THIS BOOK:

Victory! 2 Corinthians 2:14–17
Becoming God's friend, 2 Corinthians 5:11–21
Paul's defence, 2 Corinthians 10

FAITH links

○ Hard Times, **2 Corinthians 1:8–10**

○ Keeping Clean, **2 Corinthians 7:1**

○ Give Till It Hurts? **2 Corinthians 8:6–9; 9:6–9**

○ Most Wanted? **2 Corinthians 10:1**

○ Blessed Are the Weak? **2 Corinthians 12:7–10**

2 Corinthians 1:1

1 From Paul, an apostle of Christ Jesus. I am an apostle because that is what God wanted. Also from Timothy our brother in Christ.

To the church of God in Corinth, and to all of God's people everywhere in Southern Greece:

2 Grace and peace to you from God our Father and the Lord Jesus Christ.

Paul Gives Thanks to God

3 Praise be to the God and Father of our Lord Jesus Christ. God is the Father who is full of mercy and all comfort. 4 He comforts us every time we have trouble, so when others have trouble, we can comfort them with the same comfort God gives us. 5 We share in the many sufferings of Christ. In the same way, much comfort comes to us through Christ. 6 If we have troubles, it is for your comfort and salvation, and if we have comfort, you also have comfort. This helps you to accept patiently the same sufferings we have. 7 Our hope for you is strong, knowing that you share in our sufferings and also in the comfort we receive.

8 Brothers and sisters,* we want you to know about the trouble we suffered in Asia. We had great burdens there that were beyond our own strength. We even gave up hope of living. 9 Truly, in our own hearts we believed we would die. But this happened so we would not trust in ourselves but in God, who raises people from the dead. 10 God saved us from these great dangers of death, and he will continue to save us. We have put our hope in him, and he will save us again. 11 And you can help us with your prayers. Then many people will give thanks for us—that God blessed us because of their many prayers.

EMAIL FROM GOD
1:3–11 Comfort
Are sad people important to God?

1:8 Brothers and sisters Although the Greek text says "brothers" here and throughout this book, Paul's words were meant for the entire church, both men and women.

FAITH links

HARD TIMES
2 CORINTHIANS 1:8-10

What is your first reaction when hard times come? Many people tend to panic or get angry with God. They think, *Why is this happening to me? Why did God allow this to happen? Does God still care about me?*

The apostle Paul faced many tough situations as a missionary. At times, he even thought he would die! But the hard times helped him to trust God for help.

God never promised that we would not go through hard times. As Jesus once said, "In this world you will have trouble" (John 16:33). Like Paul, we can trust that God will help us.

Connect to these links for more on trusting God:

A Major Problem, Genesis 15:6, p. 20

Moses' Champion, Numbers 12, p. 192

A Pity Party, Job 10, p. 671

Dirty Inside, Isaiah 6:1–7, p. 904

Facing Your Fears, Matthew 8:23–27, p. 1288

Keep On Keeping On, Revelation 13:10, p. 1744

The Change in Paul's Plans

12 This is what we are proud of, and I can say it with a clear heart: in everything we have done in the world, and especially with you, we have had an honest and sincere heart from God. We did this by God's grace, not by the kind of wisdom the world has. 13-14 We write to you only what you can read and understand. And I hope that as you have understood some things about us, you may come to know everything about us. Then you can be proud of us, as we will be proud of you on the day our Lord Jesus Christ comes again.

15 I was so sure of all this that I made plans to visit you first so you could be blessed twice. 16 I planned to visit you on my way to Macedonia and again on my way back. I wanted to get help from you for my trip to Judea. 17 Do you think that I made these plans without really meaning it? Or maybe you think I make plans as the world does, so that I say "yes, yes" and at the same time "no, no."

18 But if you can believe God, you can believe that what we tell you is never both "yes" and "no". 19 The Son of God, Jesus Christ, that Silas and Timothy and I preached to you, was not "yes" and "no". In Christ it has always been "yes". 20 The "yes" to all of God's promises is in Christ, and through Christ we say "yes" to the glory of God. 21 Remember, God is the One who makes you and us strong in Christ. God made us his chosen people. 22 He put his mark on us to show that we are his, and he put his Spirit in our hearts to be a guarantee for all he has promised.

23 I tell you this, and I ask God to be my witness that this is true: the reason I did not come back to Corinth was to keep you from being punished or hurt. 24 We are not trying to control your faith. You are strong in faith. But we are workers with you for your own joy.

2 So I decided that my next visit to you would not be another one to make you sad. 2 If I make you sad, who will make me glad? Only you can make me glad—particularly the person whom I made sad. 3 I wrote you a letter for this reason: that when I came to you I would not be made sad by the people who should make me happy. I felt sure of all of you, that you would share my joy. 4 When I wrote to you before, I was very troubled and unhappy in my heart, and I wrote with many tears. I did not write to make you sad, but to let you know how much I love you.

Forgive the Sinner

5 Someone there among you has caused sadness, not to me, but to all of you. I mean he caused sadness to all in some way. (I do not want to make it sound worse than it really is.) 6 The punishment that most of you gave him is enough for him. 7 But now you should forgive him and comfort him to keep him from having too much sadness and giving up completely. 8 So I beg you to show that you love him. 9 I wrote to you to test you and to see if you obey in everything. 10 If you forgive someone, I also forgive him. And what I have forgiven—if I had anything to forgive—I forgave it for you, as if Christ were with me. 11 I did this so that Satan would not win anything from us, because we know very well what Satan's plans are.

Paul's Concern in Troas

12 When I came to Troas to preach the Good News of Christ, the Lord gave me a good opportunity there. 13 But I had no peace, because I did not find my brother Titus. So I said goodbye to them at Troas and went to Macedonia.

Victory Through Christ

14 But thanks be to God, who always leads us in victory through Christ. God uses us to spread his knowledge everywhere like a sweet-smelling perfume. 15 Our offering to God is this: we are the sweet smell of Christ among those who are being saved and among those who are being lost. 16 To those who are lost, we are the smell of death that brings death, but to those who are being saved, we are the smell of life that brings life. So who is able to do this work? 17 We do not sell the word of God for a profit as many other people do. But in Christ we

speak the truth before God, as messengers of God.

Servants of the New Agreement

3 Are we starting to boast about ourselves again? Do we need letters of introduction to you or from you, like some other people? 2 You yourselves are our letter, written on our hearts, known and read by everyone. 3 You show that you are a letter from Christ sent through us. This letter is not written with ink but with the Spirit of the living God. It is not written on stone tablets" but on human hearts.

4 We can say this, because through Christ we feel certain before God. 5 We are not saying that we can do this work ourselves. It is God who makes us able to do all that we do. 6 He made us able to be servants of a new agreement from himself to his people. This new agreement is not a written law, but it is of the Spirit. The written law brings death, but the Spirit gives life.

7 The law that brought death was written in words on stone. It came with God's glory, which made Moses' face so bright that the Israelites could not continue to look at it. But that glory later disappeared. 8 So surely the new way that brings the Spirit has even more glory. 9 If the law that judged people guilty of sin had glory, surely the new way that makes people right with God has much greater glory. 10 That old law had glory, but it really loses its glory when it is compared to the much greater glory of this new way. 11 If that law which disappeared came with glory, then this new way which continues for ever has much greater glory.

12 We have this hope, so we are very bold. 13 We are not like Moses, who put a covering over his face so the Israelites would not see it. The glory was disappearing, and Moses did not want them to see it fade. 14 But their minds were closed, and even today that same covering hides the meaning when they read the old agreement. That covering is taken away only through Christ. 15 Even today, when they read the law of Moses, there is a covering over their minds. 16 But when a person changes and follows the Lord, that covering is taken away. 17 The Lord is the Spirit, and where the Spirit of the Lord is, there is freedom. 18 Our faces, then, are not covered. We all show the Lord's glory, and we are being changed to be like him. This change in us brings ever greater glory, which comes from the Lord, who is the Spirit.

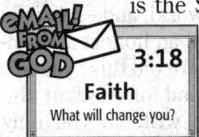

3:18 Faith What will change you?

Preaching the Good News

4 God, with his mercy, gave us this work to do, so we don't give up. 2 But we have turned away from secret and shameful ways. We use no trickery, and we do not change the teaching of God. We teach the truth plainly, showing everyone who we are. Then they can know in their hearts what kind of people we are in God's sight. 3 If the Good News that we preach is hidden, it is hidden only to those who are lost. 4 The devil who rules this world has blinded the minds of those who do not believe. They cannot see the light of the Good News—the Good News about the glory of Christ, who is exactly like God. 5 We do not preach about ourselves, but we preach that Jesus Christ is Lord and that we are your servants for Jesus. 6 God once said, "Let the light shine out of the darkness!" This is the same God who made his light shine in our hearts by letting us know the glory of God that is in the face of Christ.

Spiritual Treasure in Clay Jars

7 We have this treasure from God, but we are like clay jars that hold the treasure. This shows that the great power is from God, not from us. 8 We have troubles all around us, but we are not defeated. We do not know what to do, but we do not give up the hope of living. 9 We are persecuted, but God does not leave us. We are hurt sometimes, but we are not destroyed.

3:3 stone tablets Meaning the law of Moses that was written on stone tablets (Exodus 24:12; 25:16).

FAITH CHALLENGE

Here's a challenge for you. Read 4:1 to discover how Paul encouraged his Christian friends. How does knowing that God gave us work to do encourage you? What would you say to someone who told you that being a Christian is too much work?

Testing it

2 Corinthians 4:1
God, with his mercy, gave us this work to do, so we don't give up.

10 We carry the death of Jesus in our own bodies so that the life of Jesus can also be seen in our bodies. 11 We are alive, but for Jesus we are always in danger of death so that the life of Jesus can be seen in our bodies that die. 12 So death is working in us, but life is working in you.

4:8–12 Worry
Does God care about your worries?

13 It is written in the Scriptures, "I believed, so I spoke."[n] Our faith is like this too. We believe, and so we speak. 14 God raised the Lord Jesus from the dead, and we know that God will also raise us with Jesus. God will bring us together with you, and we will stand before him. 15 All these things are for you. And so the grace of God that is being given to more and more people will bring increasing thanks to God for his glory.

Living by Faith

16 So we do not give up. Our physical body is becoming older and weaker, but our spirit inside us is made new every day. 17 We have small troubles for a while now, but they are helping us gain an eternal glory that is much greater than the troubles. 18 We set our eyes not on what we see but on what we cannot see. What we see will last only a short time, but what we cannot see will last for ever.

5 We know that our body—the tent we live in here on earth—will be destroyed. But when that happens, God will have a house for us. It will not be a house made by human hands; instead, it will be a home in heaven that will last for ever. 2 But now we groan in this tent. We want God to give us our heavenly home, 3 because it will clothe us so we will not be naked. 4 While we live in this body, we have burdens, and we groan. We do not want to be naked, but we want to be clothed with our heavenly home. Then this body that dies will be fully covered with life. 5 This is what God made us for, and he has given us the Spirit to be a guarantee for this new life.

6 So we always have courage. We know that while we live in this body, we are away from the Lord.

5:6–7 Death
Find out what your ultimate destination is.

7 We live by what we believe, not by what we can see. 8 So I say that we have courage. We really want to be away from this body and be at home with the Lord. 9 Our only goal is to please God whether we live here or there, 10 because we must all stand before Christ to be judged. Each of us will receive what we

---

4:13 "I . . . spoke." Quotation from Psalm 116:10.

should get—good or bad—for the things we did in the earthly body.

Becoming Friends with God

11 Since we know what it means to fear the Lord, we try to help people accept the truth about us. God knows what we really are, and I hope that in your hearts you know too. 12 We are not trying to prove ourselves to you again, but we are telling you about ourselves so you will be proud of us. Then you will have an answer for those who are proud about things that can be seen rather than what is in the heart. 13 If we are out of our minds, it is for God. If we have our right minds, it is for you. 14 The love of Christ controls us, because we know that One died for all, so all have died. 15 Christ died for all so that those who live would not continue to live for themselves. He died for them and was raised from the dead so that they would live for him.

16 From this time on we do not think of anyone as the world does. In the past we thought of Christ as the world thinks, but we no longer think of him in that way. 17 If anyone belongs to Christ, there begins a new creation. The old things have gone: everything is made new! 18 All this is from God. Through Christ, God made peace between us and himself, and God gave us the work of telling everyone about the peace we can have with him.

**5:18–21
Witnessing**
What does God want you to share?

19 God was in Christ, making peace between the world and himself. In Christ, God did not hold the world guilty of its sins. And he gave us this message of peace. 20 So we have been sent to speak for Christ. It is as if God is calling to you through us. We speak for Christ when we beg you to be at peace with God. 21 Christ had no sin, but God made him become sin so that in Christ we could become right with God.

6 We are workers together with God, so we beg you: do not let the grace that you received from God be for nothing. 2 God says,

"At the right time I will hear your
  prayers.
On the day of salvation I will help
  you."   *Isaiah 49:8*

I tell you that the "right time" is now, and the "day of salvation" is now.

3 We do not want anyone to find fault with our work, so nothing we do will be a problem for anyone. 4 But in every way we show we are servants of God: in accepting many hard things, in troubles, in difficulties and in great problems. 5 We are beaten and thrown into prison. We meet those who become upset with us and start riots. We work hard, and sometimes we get no sleep or food. 6 We show we are servants of God by our pure lives, our understanding, patience and kindness, by the Holy Spirit, by true love, 7 by speaking the truth and by God's power. We use our right living to defend ourselves against everything. 8 Some people honour us, but others blame us. Some people say evil things about us, but others say good things. Some people say we are liars, but we speak the truth. 9 We are not known, yet we are well known. We seem to be dying, but we continue to live. We are punished, but we are not killed. 10 We have much sadness, but we are always rejoicing. We are poor, but we are making many people rich in faith. We have nothing, but really we have everything.

11 We have spoken freely to you in Corinth and have opened our hearts to you. 12 Our feelings of love for you have not stopped, but you have stopped your feelings of love for us. 13 I speak to you as if you were my children. Do to us as we have done—open your hearts to us.

Warning About Those Who Do Not Believe

14 You are not the same as those who do not believe. So do not join yourselves to them. Good and bad do not belong together. Light and darkness cannot share together. 15 How can Christ and Belial, the devil, have any agreement? What can a believer have together with a non-believer? 16 The temple of God cannot have any agreement with idols, and we are the temple of the living God. As God said:

2 Corinthians 7:10 **1575**

LET'S VISIT CORINTH — 2 Corinthians 6

Today Corinth is a small town, but when the apostle Paul was alive, it was a busy city full of industry and sales. It was on a narrow strip of land in Greece with water on both sides, making it a convenient port for ships. That was one reason why it was a good place for Paul to preach. He knew that his listeners would go from there to many other places, and then they could share the Good News.

Corinth also had many temples to false gods. When people in Corinth became Christians, they had to learn a lot about living holy lives. Paul wrote two letters to the church there, which we know as 1 and 2 Corinthians. Both of those books contain instructions on living for Christ in an evil environment.

"I will live with them and walk with them.
And I will be their God, and they will be my people."[n]

17 "You people, leave, leave,
 get out of Babylon!
 Touch nothing that is unclean."
 Isaiah 52:11; Ezekiel 20:34,41

18 "I will be your father,
 and you will be my sons and
  daughters,
 says the Lord Almighty."
 2 Samuel 7:14; 7:8

7 Dear friends, we have these promises from God, so we should make ourselves pure—free from anything that makes body or soul unclean. We should try to become holy in the way we live, because we respect God.

Paul's Joy

2 Open your hearts to us. We have not done wrong to anyone, we have not ruined the faith of anyone, and we have not cheated anyone. 3 I do not say this to blame you. I told you before that we love you so much we would live or die with you. 4 I feel very sure of you and am very proud of you. You give me much comfort, and in all of our troubles I have great joy.

5 When we came into Macedonia, we had no rest. We found trouble all around us. We had fighting on the outside and fear on the inside. 6 But God, who comforts those who are troubled, comforted us when Titus came. 7 We were comforted, not only by his coming but also by the comfort you gave him. Titus told us about your wish to see me and that you are very sorry for what you did. He also told me about your great care for me, and when I heard this, I was much happier.

8 Even if my letter made you sad, I am not sorry I wrote it. At first I was sorry, because it made you sad, but you were sad only for a short time. 9 Now I am happy, not because you were made sad, but because your sorrow made you change your lives. You became sad in the way God wanted you to, so you were not hurt by us in any way. 10 The kind of sorrow God wants makes people change their hearts and lives. This leads to salvation, and you cannot be sorry for that. But the kind

---

6:16 "I . . . people." Quotation from Leviticus 26:11-12; Jeremiah 32:38; Ezekiel 37:27.

2 Corinthians 7:11 1576

FAITH links

KEEPING CLEAN
2 CORINTHIANS 7:1

Let's say you've just put on some new clothes, clothes you really like. Would you immediately go outside and jump into the nearest puddle? You probably wouldn't. You'd want to keep as clean as possible to avoid messing up your new clothes. God wants his people to be as clean as possible on the inside. Keeping clean and pure means avoiding people or things that could harm you spiritually. These include television programmes or films that your parents don't want you to watch, kids who try to influence you to do things you know are wrong, and so on. Keeping clean honours God.

Download these Faithlinks for ways to keep clean for God:

Can't Live Without It,
Genesis 3, p. 7

A Choice to Make,
Deuteronomy 30:15–20, p. 265

In Your Best Interests,
Ruth 3, p. 349

Down on the Ant Farm,
Proverbs 6:6–11, p. 833

Prayer for a Friend,
Colossians 1:9–12, p. 1620

The Way to Be Wise,
James 1:5, p. 1689

---

of sorrow the world has brings death. 11 See what this sorrow—the sorrow God wanted you to have—has done to you: it has made you very serious. It made you want to prove you were not wrong. It made you angry and afraid. It made you want to see me. It made you care. It made you want the right thing to be done. You proved you were innocent in the problem. 12 I wrote that letter, not because of the one who did the wrong or because of the person who was hurt. I wrote the letter so you could see, before God, the great care you have for us. 13 That is why we were comforted.

Not only were we very comforted, we were even happier to see that Titus was so happy. All of you made him feel much better. 14 I boasted to Titus about you, and you showed that I was right. Everything we said to you was true, and you have proved that what we boasted about to Titus is true. 15 And his love for you is stronger when he remembers that you were all ready to obey. You welcomed him with respect and fear. 16 I am very happy that I can trust you fully.

Christian Giving

8 And now, brothers and sisters, we want you to know about the grace God gave the churches in Macedonia. 2 They have been tested by great troubles, and they are very poor. But they gave much because of their great joy. 3 I can tell you that they gave as much as they were able and even more than they could afford. No one told them to do it. 4 But they begged and pleaded with us to let them share in this service for God's people. 5 And they gave in a way we did not expect: they first gave themselves to the Lord and to us. This is what God wants. 6 So we asked Titus to help you finish this special work of grace since he is the one who started it. 7 You are rich in everything—in faith, in speaking, in knowledge, in truly wanting to help, and in the love you learned from us. In the same way, be strong also in the grace of giving.

8 I am not commanding you to give. But I want to see if your love is true by comparing you with others that really want to help. 9 You know the grace of our Lord Jesus Christ. You know that Christ

SHARING
2 Corinthians 8:1–9

Livin' it

Sharing Your Stuff Sharing your stuff with someone can be hard. Maybe it'll get ruined, or lost, or never returned. And how about sharing your money? The money you get for gifts, for pocket money, or for doing jobs should be yours to use any way you want, right? Maybe you feel like you *have* to give some of your money to church or Sunday school but you'd really like that new computer game instead. Paul talked a lot about giving and sharing – and it doesn't always involve things or money. (Look at 2 Corinthians 8:6–9; 9:6–9.)

Jesus doesn't say you have to share or give away everything. What he does want, though, is for you to give willingly and cheerfully. (Check out Luke 21:1–4, p. 1410.) How do you share what you have – because you want to, or because you *have* to?

MORE FAITH links

Give What You Can, **p. 186**
Yours, Mine and Ours? **p. 389**
Kind or Fair? **p. 395**
Share and Share Alike? **p. 1466**
The Person Most Likely to Give? **p. 1481**
Give Till It Hurts? **p. 1578**

How do you feel about sharing your crisps or chocolate with friends? Are you happy to do it – even if you're really hungry?

You'd better check out what God has to say about sharing!

Share What You Have, Exodus 35:5–18, p. 123
- God wants us to share what we have with others. How do you share your money, time and talents to do the work of God?

Care to Be Fair? Joshua 18:1–8, p. 299
- When you need to share with someone, what do you do to be fair?
- God wants us to care about being fair. What is one way you've come up with to share what God gives you?

What's the Use? 2 Kings 12:6–12, p. 495
- Do you know what your church's offering money is used for? If you're not sure, ask someone who knows (like your pastor).

my FAVOURITE links

_____
_____
_____
_____

FAITH links

GIVE TILL IT HURTS?
2 CORINTHIANS 8:6-9; 9:6-9

Many people give out of obligation. They feel they have to give, especially to the church. In his letter to the Corinthian Christians, Paul talked a lot about giving. He wanted them to know that they were not forced to give. In fact, God wants people to be "glad givers". As Paul said, a person should give what his or her heart tells them to give. Giving doesn't always involve money. You can "give" your time to help someone. You can also donate clothes or toys to people in need. You'll be glad you did!

Fairness for All, Deuteronomy 24:17, p. 258

A Reminder to Be Fair, 2 Chronicles 19:5–11, p. 583

Set for Life? Obadiah 2–4, p. 1208

Go! No! Jonah 1, p. 1213

The Gift of Worship, Matthew 2:10–12, p. 1275

The Way to Greatness, Matthew 20:20–28, p. 1309

was rich, but for you he became poor so that by his becoming poor you might become rich. 10 This is what I think you should do: last year you were the first to want to give, and you were the first who gave. 11 So now finish the work you started. Then your "doing" will be equal to your "wanting to do". Give from what you have. 12 If you want to give, your gift will be accepted. It will be judged by what you have, not by what you do not have. 13 We do not want you to have troubles while other people are at ease, but we want everything to be equal. 14 At this time you have plenty. What you have can help others who are in need. Then later, when they have plenty, they can help you when you are in need, and all will be equal. 15 As it is written in the Scriptures, "The person who gathered more did not have too much, nor did the person who gathered less have too little."[n]

Titus and His Companions Help

16 I thank God because he gave Titus the same love for you that I have. 17 Titus accepted what we asked him to do. He wanted very much to go to you, and this was his own idea. 18 We are sending with him the brother who is praised by all the churches because of his service in preaching the Good News. 19 Also, this brother was chosen by the churches to go with us when we deliver this gift of money. We are doing this service to bring glory to the Lord and to show that we really want to help.

20 We are being careful so that no one will criticise us for the way we are handling this large gift. 21 We are trying hard to do what the Lord accepts as right and also what people think is right.

22 Also, we are sending with them our brother, who is always ready to help. He has proved this to us in many ways, and he wants to help even more now, because he has much faith in you.

23 Now about Titus—he is my partner who is working with me to help you. And about the other brothers—they are sent from the churches, and they bring glory to Christ. 24 So show these men the proof of your love and the reason we are proud of you. Then all the churches can see it.

Help for Fellow Christians

9 I really do not need to write to you about this help for God's people. 2 I know you want to help. I have been

---

8:15 "The person . . . little." Quotation from Exodus 16:18.

boasting about this to the people in Macedonia, telling them that you in Southern Greece have been ready to give since last year. And your desire to give has made most of them ready to give also. 3 But I am sending the brothers to you so that our boasting about you in this will not be empty words. I want you to be ready, as I said you would be. 4 If any of the people from Macedonia come with me and find that you are not ready, we will be ashamed that we were so sure of you. (And you will be ashamed too!) 5 So I thought I should ask these brothers to go to you before we do. They will finish getting in order the generous gift you promised so it will be ready when we come. And it will be a generous gift—not one that you did not want to give.

6 Remember this: the person who plants a little will have a small harvest, but the person who plants a lot will have a big harvest. 7 Each one should give as he has decided in his heart to give. You should not be sad when you give, and you should not give because you feel forced to give. God loves the person who gives happily. 8 And God can give you more blessings than you need. Then you will always have plenty of everything—enough to give to every good work. 9 It is written in the Scriptures:

"He gives freely to the poor.
The things he does are right and will continue for ever." *Psalm 112:9*

10 God is the One who gives seed to the farmer and bread for food. He will give you all the seed you need and make it grow so there will be a great harvest from your goodness. 11 He will make you rich in every way so that you can always give freely. And your giving through us will cause many to give thanks to God. 12 This service you do not only helps the needs of God's people, it also brings much more thanks to God. 13 It is a proof of your faith. Many people will praise God because you obey the Good News of Christ—the gospel you say you believe—

9:6–8 Giving
What kind of giver does God love?

and because you freely share with them and with all others. 14 And when they pray, they will wish they could be with you because of the great grace that God has given you. 15 Thanks be to God for his gift that is too wonderful for words.

Paul Defends His Ministry

10 I, Paul, am begging you with the gentleness and the kindness of Christ. Some people say that I am easy on you when I am with you and bold when I am away. 2 They think we live in a worldly way, and I plan to be very bold with them when I come. I beg you that when I come I will not need to use that same boldness with you. 3 We do live in the world, but we do not fight in the same way the world fights. 4 We fight with weapons that are different from those the world uses. Our weapons have power from God that can destroy the enemy's strong places. We destroy people's arguments 5 and every proud thing that raises itself against the knowledge of God. We capture every thought and make it give up and obey Christ. 6 We are ready to punish anyone there who does not obey, but first we want you to obey fully.

7 You must look at the facts before you. If you feel sure that you belong to Christ, you must remember that we belong to Christ just as you do. 8 It is true that we boast freely about the authority the Lord gave us. But this authority is to build you up, not to tear you down. So I will not be ashamed. 9 I do not want you to think I am trying to scare you with my letters. 10 Some people say, "Paul's letters are powerful and sound important, but when he is with us, he is weak. And his speaking is nothing." 11 They should know this: we are not there with you now, so we say these things in letters. But when we are there with you, we will show the same authority that we show in our letters. 12 We do not dare to compare ourselves with those who think they are very important. They

10:12–13 Pride
Check out how to measure your value.

FAITH links

MOST WANTED?
2 CORINTHIANS 10:1

What are the qualities that you admire most in a person? Some admire people with strong personalities. Others like people who have a sense of humour. Humbleness and gentleness are not usually in the top five "most admired" qualities! The apostle Paul appealed to the Corinthian believers "with the gentleness and the kindness of Christ". These qualities require that we lay aside our pride as they develop. Sounds hard? It is. That's why the Holy Spirit has to do the work for us!

Connect here to find out about the qualities God admires:

The Cloud Guide, Numbers 9:15–23, p. 188

A Friend in Deed, Job 2:13, p. 662

Mind Guard, Proverbs 4:23, p. 831

What God "Hates", Proverbs 6:16–19, p. 835

Believe It or Not, Luke 1:20, 38, p. 1366

Don't Play Favourites, James 2:1–7, p. 1691

use themselves to measure themselves, and they judge themselves by what they themselves are. This shows that they know nothing. 13 But we will not boast about things outside the work that was given us to do. We will limit our boasting to the work that God gave us, and this includes our work with you. 14 We are not boasting too much, as we would be if we had not already come to you. But we have come to you with the Good News of Christ. 15 We limit our boasting to the work that is ours, not what others have done. We hope that as your faith continues to grow, you will help our work to grow much larger. 16 We want to tell the Good News in the areas beyond your city. We do not want to boast about work that has already been done in another person's area. 17 But, "If someone wants to boast, he should boast only about the Lord."[n] 18 It is not those who say they are good who are accepted but those who the Lord thinks are good.

Paul and the False Apostles

11 I wish you would be patient with me even when I am a little foolish, but you are already doing that. 2 I am jealous over you with a jealousy that comes from God. I promised to give you to Christ, as your only husband. I want to give you as his pure bride. 3 But I am afraid that your minds will be led away from your true and pure following of Christ just as Eve was tricked by the snake with his evil ways. 4 You are very patient with anyone who comes to you and preaches a different Jesus from the one we preached. You are very willing to accept a spirit or good news that is different from the Spirit and Good News you received from us.

5 I do not think that those "great apostles" are any better than I am. 6 I may not be a trained speaker, but I do have knowledge. We have shown this to you clearly in every way.

7 I preached God's Good News to you without pay. I made myself unimportant to make you important. Do you think that was wrong? 8 I accepted pay from other churches, taking their money so I could serve you. 9 If I needed something when I was with you, I did not trouble any of you. The brothers who came from Macedonia

---

10:17 "If . . . Lord." Quotation from Jeremiah 9:24.

gave me all that I needed. I did not allow myself to depend on you in any way, and I will never depend on you. 10 No one in Southern Greece will stop me from boasting about that. I say this with the truth of Christ in me. 11 And why do I not depend on you? Do you think it is because I do not love you? God knows that I love you.

12 And I will continue doing what I am doing now, because I want to stop those people from having a reason to boast. They would like to say that the work they boast about is the same as ours. 13 Such men are not true apostles but are workers who lie. They change themselves to look like apostles of Christ. 14 This does not surprise us. Even Satan changes himself to look like an angel of light.[n] 15 So it does not surprise us if Satan's servants also make themselves look like servants who work for what is right. But in the end they will be punished for what they do.

11:14 Satan Satan disguises himself.

Paul Tells About His Sufferings

16 I tell you again: no one should think I am a fool. But if you think so, accept me as you would accept a fool. Then I can boast a little, too. 17 When I boast because I feel sure of myself, I am not talking as the Lord would talk but as a fool. 18 Many people are boasting about their lives in the world. So I will boast too. 19 You are wise, so you will gladly be patient with fools! 20 You are even patient with those who order you around, or use you, or trick you, or think they are better than you, or hit you in the face. 21 It is shameful to me to say this, but we were too "weak" to do those things to you!

But if anyone else is brave enough to boast, then I also will be brave and boast. (I am talking as a fool.) 22 Are they Hebrews?[n] So am I. Are they Israelites? So am I. Are they from Abraham's family? So am I. 23 Are they serving Christ? I am serving him more. (I am mad to talk like this.) I have worked much harder than they. I have been in prison more often. I have been hurt more in beatings. I have been near death many times. 24 Five times the Jews have given me their punishment of 39 lashes with a whip. 25 Three different times I was beaten with rods. One time I was almost stoned to death. Three times I was in ships that were wrecked, and one of those times I spent a night and a day in the sea. 26 I have gone on many travels and have been in danger from rivers, thieves, my own people, the Jews and those who are not Jews. I have been in danger in cities, in places where no one lives and on the sea. And I have been in danger with false Christians. 27 I have done hard and tiring work, and many times I did not sleep. I have been hungry and thirsty, and many times I have been without food. I have been cold and without clothes. 28 Besides all this, there is on me every day the load of my concern for all the churches. 29 I feel weak every time someone is weak, and I feel upset every time someone is led into sin.

30 If I must boast, I will boast about the things that show I am weak. 31 God knows I am not lying. He is the God and Father of the Lord Jesus Christ, and he is to be praised for ever. 32 When I was in Damascus, the governor under King Aretas wanted to arrest me, so he put guards around the city. 33 But my friends lowered me in a basket through a hole in the city wall. So I escaped from the governor.

A Special Blessing in Paul's Life

12 I must continue to boast. It will do no good, but I will talk now about visions and revelations[n] from the Lord. 2 I know a man in Christ who was taken up to the third heaven fourteen years ago. I do not know whether the man was in his body or out of his body, but God knows. 3-4 And I know that this man was

11:14 angel of light Messenger from God. The devil fools people so that they think he is from God.
11:22 Hebrews A name for the Jews that some Jews were very proud of.
12:1 revelations Revelation is making known a truth that has been hidden.

taken up to paradise.ⁿ I don't know if he was in his body or away from his body, but God knows. He heard things he is not able to explain, things that no human is allowed to tell. 5 I will boast about a man like that, but I will not boast about myself, except about my weaknesses. 6 But if I wanted to boast about myself, I would not be a fool, because I would be telling the truth. But I will not boast about myself. I do not want people to think more of me than what they see me do or hear me say.

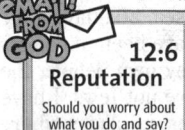

12:6 Reputation
Should you worry about what you do and say?

7 So that I would not become too proud of the wonderful things that were shown to me, a painful problemⁿ was given to me. This problem was a messenger from Satan, sent to beat me and keep me from being too proud. 8 I begged the Lord three times to take this problem away from me. 9 But he said to me, "My grace is enough for you. When you are weak, my power is made perfect in you." So I am very happy to boast about my weaknesses. Then Christ's power can live in me. 10 For this reason I am happy when I have weaknesses, insults, hard times, sufferings and all kinds of troubles for Christ. Because when I am weak, then I am truly strong.

Paul's Love for the Christians

11 I have been talking like a fool, but you made me do it. You are the ones who should say good things about me. I am worth nothing, but those "great apostles" are not worth any more than I am!
12 When I was with you, I patiently did the things that prove I am an apostle—signs, wonders and miracles. 13 So you received everything that the other churches have received. Only one thing was different: I was not a burden to you. Forgive me for this!
14 I am now ready to visit you the third time, and I will not be a burden to you. I

BLESSED ARE THE WEAK?
2 CORINTHIANS 12:7-10

No one likes to be thought of as weak. The old saying "survival of the fittest" shows how society views weakness. Yet everyone has a weakness of some sort. Paul wrote about a physical weakness that he asked God to remove. But God said no. Instead, he told Paul that he was strong when Paul was weak.

God helps us when we're weak. What is a weakness? Fear is, for one thing. Our weaknesses remind us to rely on God. When we're weak, he's strong. Next time you're feeling weak, ask God to lend you some of his strength. He'll be glad to do it.

Want to be strong? Better be weak first! Check it out:

When You're Afraid,
Genesis 32:9–12, p. 45

The Perfect Leader?
Numbers 20:1–13, p. 203

The God of Big Things,
Joshua 10, p. 289

What God Thinks,
Isaiah 55:8–9, p. 969

Facing Your Fears, Matthew 8:23–27, p. 1288

Thoughts on Thoughts,
Philippians 4:8–9, p. 1614

12:3-4 paradise A place where good people go when they die.
12:7 painful problem Literally, "thorn in the flesh."

want nothing from you, except you. Children should not have to save up to give to their parents. Parents should save to give to their children. 15 So I am happy to give everything I have for you, even myself. If I love you more, will you love me less?

16 It is clear I was not a burden to you, but you think I was sly and lied to catch you. 17 Did I cheat you by using any of the messengers I sent to you? No, you know I did not. 18 I asked Titus to go to you, and I sent our brother with him. Titus did not cheat you, did he? No, you know that Titus and I did the same thing and with the same spirit.

19 Do you think we have been defending ourselves to you all this time? We have been speaking in Christ and before God. You are our dear friends, and everything we do is to make you stronger. 20 I am afraid that when I come, you will not be what I want you to be, and I will not be what you want me to be. I am afraid that among you there may be arguing, jealousy, anger, selfish fighting, evil talk, gossip, pride and confusion. 21 I am afraid that when I come to you again, my God will make me ashamed before you. I may be saddened by many of those who have sinned because they have not changed their hearts or turned from their sexual sins and the shameful things they have done.

Final Warnings and Greetings

13 I will come to you for the third time. "Every case must be proved by two or three witnesses."ⁿ 2 When I was with you the second time, I gave a warning to those who had sinned. Now I am away from you, and I give a warning to all the others. When I come to you again, I will not be easy with them. 3 You want proof that Christ is speaking through me. My proof is that he is not weak among you, but he is powerful. 4 It is true that he was weak when he was killed on the cross, but he lives now by God's power. It is true that we are weak in Christ, but for you we will be alive in Christ by God's power.

> It is true that we are weak in Christ, but for you we will be alive in Christ by God's power.
> – 2 Corinthians 13:4

5 Look closely at yourselves. Test yourselves to see if you are living in the faith. You know that Jesus Christ is in you—unless you fail the test. 6 But I hope you will see that we ourselves have not failed the test. 7 We pray to God that you will not do anything wrong. It is not important to see that we have passed the test, but it is important that you do what is right, even if it seems we have failed. 8 We cannot do anything against the truth, but only for the truth. 9 We are happy to be weak, if you are strong, and we pray that you will become complete. 10 I am writing this while I am away from you so that when I come I will not have to be harsh in my use of authority. The Lord gave me this authority to build you up, not to tear you down.

11 Now, brothers and sisters, I say goodbye. Try to be perfect. Do what I have asked you to do. Agree with each other, and live in peace. Then the God of love and peace will be with you.

12 Greet each other with a holy kiss. 13 All of God's holy people send greetings to you.

14 The grace of the Lord Jesus Christ, the love of God, and the fellowship of the Holy Spirit be with you all.

13:1 "Every . . . witnesses." Quotation from Deuteronomy 19:15.

REAL FREEDOM

Hi, people! It's me, Paul. You probably remember me from a few other books I've written. I was a really good Pharisee – a well-known and popular religious leader, who hated those followers of a man called Jesus. But then I met Jesus on a dusty road while on my way to kill even more Christians. That wonderful moment changed the direction of my life for ever; and since then I have spent hours and hours telling everyone about what Jesus has done in my life.

I wrote this letter to the church in a place called Galatia because my friends there were hearing two different messages about what Jesus had done for them. One message was true: that Jesus died for them . . . and that was all they needed. The other message was wrong: that Jesus died for them, but that they also needed to keep a bunch of ancient rules. So, to clear things up, I wrote this letter to them to remind them about who Jesus was and what he had done.

JESUS WATCH

In this book, Jesus is portrayed as someone who frees people who are slaves to obeying every single rule in the law. These people believed that by obeying *all* the rules, they could be saved from their sin. Paul tells his readers that Jesus' death on the cross is all a person needs to be saved and freed from sin. This message was true for believers then, and it's true for believers now. The really cool thing is that all God wants from us is our complete faith in the work done by his Son – nothing more, nothing less.

my FAVOURITE links

OTHER CONNECTIONS

What are some "good" things that you do? Ever consider why you do good things? Link to That (Good) Thing You Do, Galatians 6:9–10, to discover why God wants us to do good things.

MORE STUFF . . .
Good Fruit, Bad Fruit   In Galatians 5:16–26, Paul outlined two types of behaviour: behaving according to our human nature and behaving according to our spirit nature. Check out the differences in the type of "fruit", or our actions, each produce:

- Human nature: worshipping gods; making trouble; hating; being jealous; being angry; being selfish; making people angry with each other; feeling envy.
- Spirit nature: love; joy; peace; patience; kindness; goodness; faithfulness; gentleness; self-control.

What kind of fruit do you produce?

Do you think we're really supposed to serve other people?

Well, we are. And we're supposed to do it with love. Check out Galatians 5:13 to see what it says.

MORE COOL STUFF TO SURF:
Peter is wrong! Galatians 2:11–21
Real faith, Galatians 3:6–9
Fruit for the soul, Galatians 5:22–26
A good harvest, Galatians 6:7–10

FAITH links

○ A Family Resemblance, **Galatians 3:6–9**

○ MVFM? **Galatians 3:26–27**

○ At the Right Time, **Galatians 4:4**

○ A Different Kind of Fruit, **Galatians 5:22–23**

○ Keep Up the Good Work! **Galatians 6:9–10**

1 From Paul, an apostle. I was not chosen to be an apostle by human beings, nor was I sent from human beings. I was made an apostle through Jesus Christ and God the Father who raised Jesus from the dead. 2 This letter is also from all those of God's family[n] who are with me.

To the churches in Galatia:[n]

3 Grace and peace to you from God our Father and the Lord Jesus Christ. 4 Jesus gave himself for our sins to free us from this evil world we live in, as God the Father planned. 5 The glory belongs to God for ever and ever. Amen.

The Only Good News

6 God, by his grace through Christ, called you to become his people. So I am amazed that you are turning away so quickly and believing something different from the Good News. 7 Really, there is no other Good News. But some people are confusing you; they want to change the Good News of Christ. 8 We preached to you the Good News. So if we ourselves, or even an angel from heaven, should preach to you something different, we should be judged guilty! 9 I said this before, and now I say it again: you have already accepted the Good News. If anyone is preaching something different to you, he should be judged guilty!

10 Do you think I am trying to make people accept me? No, God is the One I am trying to please. Am I trying to please people? If I still wanted to please people, I would not be a servant of Christ.

Paul's Authority is from God

11 Brothers and sisters,[n] I want you to know that the Good News I preached to you was not made up by human beings. 12 I did not get it from humans, nor did anyone teach it to me, but Jesus Christ showed it to me.

13 You have heard about my past life in the Jewish religion. I attacked the church of God and tried to destroy it. 14 I was becoming a leader in the Jewish religion, doing better than most other Jews of my age. I tried harder than anyone else to follow the teachings handed down by our ancestors.

FAITH CHALLENGE

Got another challenge for you. Read 1:10 to discover what Paul said to those who accused him of trying to please people. What's wrong with trying to please other people? How would you describe yourself – as a people-pleaser or a God-pleaser? What do you need to change?

TeSTiNG iT

Galatians 1:10
Do you think I am trying to make people accept me? No, God is the One I am trying to please. Am I trying to please people? If I still wanted to please people, I would not be a servant of Christ.

15 But God had special plans for me and set me apart for his work even before I was born. He called me through his grace 16 and showed his Son to me so that I might tell the Good News about him

---

1:2 those . . . family The Greek text says "brothers".
1:2 Galatia Probably the same country where Paul preached and began churches on his first missionary trip. Read the Book of Acts, chapters 13 and 14.
1:11 Brothers and sisters Although the Greek text says "Brothers" here and throughout this book, Paul's words were meant for the entire church, both men and women.

to those who are not Jewish. When God called me, I did not get advice or help from any person. 17 I did not go to Jerusalem to see those who were apostles before I was. But, without waiting, I went away to Arabia and later went back to Damascus.

18 After three years I went to Jerusalem to meet Peter and stayed with him for fifteen days. 19 I met no other apostles, except James, the brother of the Lord. 20 God knows that these things I write are not lies. 21 Later, I went to the areas of Syria and Cilicia.

22 In Judea the churches in Christ had never met me. 23 They had only heard it said, "This man who was attacking us is now preaching the same faith that he once tried to destroy." 24 And these believers praised God because of me.

Other Apostles Accepted Paul

2 After fourteen years I went to Jerusalem again, this time with Barnabas. I also took Titus with me. 2 I went because God showed me I should go. I met with the believers there, and in private I told their leaders the Good News that I preach to the non-Jewish people. I did not want my past work and the work I am now doing to be wasted. 3 Titus was with me, but he was not forced to be circumcised, even though he was a Greek. 4 We talked about this problem because some false believers had come into our group secretly. They came in like spies to overturn the freedom we have in Christ Jesus. They wanted to make us slaves. 5 But we did not give in to those false believers for a minute. We wanted the truth of the Good News to continue for you.

6 Those leaders who seemed to be important did not change the Good News that I preach. (It doesn't matter to me if they were "important" or not. To God everyone is the same.) 7 But these leaders saw that I had been given the work of telling the Good News to those who are not Jewish, just as Peter had the work of telling the Jews. 8 God

2:6
Jealousy
Should you envy other Christians?

gave Peter the power to work as an apostle for the Jewish people. But he also gave me the power to work as an apostle for those who are not Jews. 9 James, Peter and John, who seemed to be the leaders, understood that God had given me this special grace, so they accepted Barnabas and me. They agreed that they would go to the Jewish people and that we should go to those who are not Jewish. 10 The only thing they asked us was to remember to help the poor—something I really wanted to do.

Paul Shows that Peter was Wrong

11 When Peter came to Antioch, I challenged him to his face, because he was wrong. 12 Peter ate with the non-Jewish people until some Jewish people sent from James came to Antioch. When they arrived, Peter stopped eating with those who weren't Jewish, and he separated himself from them. He was afraid of the Jews. 13 So Peter was a hypocrite, as were the other Jewish believers who joined with him. Even Barnabas was influenced by what these Jewish believers did. 14 When I saw they were not following the truth of the Good News, I spoke to Peter in front of them all. I said, "Peter, you are a Jew, but you are not living like a Jew. You are living like those who are not Jewish. So why do you now try to force those who are not Jewish to live like Jews?"

15 We were not born as non-Jewish "sinners", but as Jews. 16 Yet we know that a person is made right with God not by following the law, but by trusting in Jesus Christ. So we, too, have put our faith in Christ Jesus, that we might be made right with God because we trusted in Christ. It is not because we followed the law, because no one can be made right with God by following the law.

17 We Jews came to Christ, trying to be made right with God, and it became clear that we are sinners too. Does this mean that Christ encourages sin? No! 18 But I would really be wrong to begin teaching again those things that I gave up. 19 It was the law that put me to death, and

Galatians 2:20 1588

I died to the law so that I can now live for God. 20 I was put to death on the cross with Christ, and I do not live any more— it is Christ who lives in me. I still live in my body, but I live by faith in the Son of God who loved me and gave himself to save me. 21 By saying these things I am not going against God's grace. Just the opposite, if the law could make us right with God, then Christ's death would be useless.

Blessing Comes Through Faith

3 You people in Galatia were told very clearly about the death of Jesus Christ on the cross. But you were foolish; you let someone trick you. 2 Tell me this one thing: how did you receive the Holy Spirit? Did you receive the Spirit by following the law? No, you received the Spirit because you heard the Good News and believed it. 3 You began your life in Christ by the Spirit. Now are you trying to make it complete by your own power? That is foolish. 4 Were all your experiences wasted? I hope not! 5 Does God give you the Spirit and work miracles among you because you follow the law? No, he does these things because you heard the Good News and believed it.

6 The Scriptures say the same thing about Abraham: "Abraham believed God, and God accepted Abraham's faith, and that faith made him right with God."ⁿ 7 So you should know that the true children of Abraham are those who have faith. 8 The Scriptures, telling what would happen in the future, said that God would make the non-Jewish people right through their faith. This Good News was told to Abraham beforehand, as the Scripture says: "All nations will be blessed through you."ⁿ 9 So all who believe as Abraham believed are blessed just as Abraham was. 10 But those who depend on following the law to make them right are under a curse, because the Scriptures say, "Anyone will be cursed who does not always obey what is written in the Book of the Law."ⁿ 11 Now it is clear that no one can be made right with God by the law, because the Scriptures say, "Those who are right with God will live by trusting in him."ⁿ 12 The

FAITH links

A FAMILY RESEMBLANCE
GALATIANS 3:6-9

Has anyone ever told you that you look like your mum or dad? You can't help but share a family resemblance. If you're a Christian, you also look like Abraham, one of Israel's founding fathers. You don't have to run to a mirror to check. The resemblance is not physical. As Christians, we share the same faith as Abraham. He believed that God would save him, and so do we. Because of this faith, we are Abraham's children and we will be blessed like Abraham was.

Download these Faithlinks to find out more about being part of God's family:

On the Wrong Foot, 2 Kings 21:1–2, 16, p. 509

Trailblazers of Faith, 2 Kings 22:1–2, p. 510

Jesus' Mission and Yours, Isaiah 61:1–2, p. 978

Name with a Purpose, Matthew 1:21, p. 1274

Remembering Jesus, Matthew 26:26–29, p. 1321

A Christian's Responsibility, Acts 11:26, p. 1484

3:6 "Abraham . . . God." Quotation from Genesis 15:6.
3:8 "All . . . you." Quotation from Genesis 12:3; 18:18.
3:10 "Anyone . . . Law." Quotation from Deuteronomy 27:26.
3:11 "Those . . . him." Quotation from Habakkuk 2:4.

law is not based on faith. It says, "A person who obeys these things will live because of them."[n] 13 Christ took away the curse the law put on us. He changed places with us and put himself under that curse. It is written in the Scriptures, "Anyone whose body is displayed on a tree[n] is cursed." 14 Christ did this so that God's blessing promised to Abraham might come through Jesus Christ to those who are not Jews. Jesus died so that by our believing we could receive the Spirit that God promised.

The Law and the Promise

15 Brothers and sisters,[n] let us think in human terms: even an agreement made between two persons is firm. After that agreement is accepted by both people, no one can stop it or add anything to it. 16 God made promises both to Abraham and to his descendant. God did not say, "and to your descendants". That would mean many people. But God said, "and to your descendant". That means only one person; that person is Christ. 17 This is what I mean: God had an agreement with Abraham and promised to keep it. The law, which came 430 years later, cannot change that agreement and so destroy God's promise to Abraham. 18 If the law could give us Abraham's blessing, then the promise would not be necessary. But that is not possible, because God freely gave his blessings to Abraham through the promise he had made.

19 So what was the law for? It was given to show that the wrong things people do are against God's will. And it continued until the special descendant, who had been promised, came. The law was given through angels who used Moses for a mediator[n] to give the law to people. 20 But a mediator is not needed when there is only one side, and God is only one.

The Purpose of the Law of Moses

21 Does this mean that the law is against God's promises? Never! That would be true only if the law could make us right. But God did not give a law that

---

FAITH links

MVFM?
GALATIANS 3:26-27

A birth certificate lets the world know whose child you are. Your last name is also an indication of where you belong. You're a valuable member of your family. As a Christian, you also belong to God because of your faith in Jesus. You're a valuable member of that family, too! Consider yourself an MVFM: Most Valuable Family Member!

Find out more about how valuable you are to God:

The Rainbow Promise, Genesis 9:1–17, p. 14

Approaching God, Numbers 3:10, p. 180

How Big Is God? Job 38—41, p. 703

Perfectly Pleasing? Matthew 5:1–12, p. 1280

A Family Celebration, 1 Corinthians 11:23–29, p. 1558

The Finished Product, Philippians 1:6, p. 1609

3:12 "A person . . . them." Quotation from Leviticus 18:5.
3:13 displayed on a tree Deuteronomy 21:22-23 says that when a person was killed for doing wrong, the body was hung on a tree to show shame. Paul means that the cross of Jesus was like that.
3:15 brothers and sisters Although the Greek text says "brothers" here and throughout this book, the words of Paul were meant for the entire church, both men and women.
3:19 mediator A person who helps one person talk to or give something to another person.

can bring life. 22 Instead, the Scriptures showed that the whole world is bound by sin. This was so the promise would be given through faith to people who believe in Jesus Christ.

23 Before this faith came, we were all held prisoners by the law. We had no freedom until God showed us the way of faith that was coming. 24 In other words, the law was our guardian leading us to Christ so that we could be made right with God through faith. 25 Now the way of faith has come, and we no longer live under a guardian.

26-27 You were all baptised into Christ, and so you were all clothed with Christ. This means that you are all children of God through faith in Christ Jesus. 28 In Christ, there is no difference between Jew and Greek, slave and free person, male and female. You are all the same in Christ Jesus. 29 You belong to Christ, so you are Abraham's descendants. You will inherit all of God's blessings because of the promise God made to Abraham.

email FROM GOD
3:28-29 Respect
Are some people better than others?

4 I want to tell you this: while those who will inherit their fathers' property are still children, they are no different from slaves. It does not matter that the children own everything. 2 While they are children, they must obey those who are chosen to care for them. But when the children reach the age set by their fathers, they are free. 3 It is the same for us. We were once like children, slaves to the useless rules of this world. 4 But when the right time came, God sent his Son who was born of a woman and lived under the law. 5 God did this so he could buy freedom for those who were under the law and so we could become his children.

6 Since you are God's children, God sent the Spirit of his Son into your hearts, and the Spirit cries out, "Father".*
7 So now you are not a slave; you are God's child, and God will give you the blessing he promised, because you are his child.

FAITH links

AT THE RIGHT TIME
GALATIANS 4:4

Ever wish that time would speed up or slow down? Maybe you waited for something wonderful to happen. Or, maybe you waited for something that you dreaded. Sometimes we wish that time would speed up when we're waiting for God to answer our prayers. God wants us to trust his timing. He knows just when to make things happen. He waited for the perfect time to send his Son to earth. Since God is perfect, his timing is also perfect. He's always on time!

If you have trouble waiting, check out these links:

Can't Live Without It? Genesis 3, p. 7

From Hopeless to Hopeful, Exodus 6:9, p. 83

Learning to Trust, Psalm 25:4-5, p. 727

999, Psalm 28:6, p. 730

Exercising Patience, Luke 2:25-28, 36-37, p. 1369

His Best Qualities, 2 Peter 3:9, p. 1711

Paul's Love for the Christians

8 In the past you did not know God. You were slaves to gods that were not real. 9 But now you know the true God. Really, it is God who knows you. So why

---

4:6 "Father" Literally, "Abba, Father". Jewish children called their fathers "Abba".

do you turn back to those weak and useless rules you followed before? Do you want to be slaves to those things again? 10 You still follow teachings about special days, months, seasons and years. 11 I am afraid for you, that my work for you has been wasted.

12 Brothers and sisters, I became like you, so I beg you to become like me. You were very good to me before. 13 You remember that it was because of sickness that I came to you the first time, preaching the Good News. 14 Though my sickness was a trouble for you, you did not hate me or make me leave. But you welcomed me as an angel from God, as if I were Jesus Christ himself! 15 You were very happy then, but where is that joy now? I am ready to testify that you would have taken out your eyes and given them to me if that were possible. 16 Now am I your enemy because I tell you the truth?

17 Those people*[n]* are working hard to persuade you, but this is not good for you. They want to persuade you to turn against us and follow only them. 18 It is good for people to show interest in you, but only if their purpose is good. This is always true, not just when I am with you. 19 My little children, again I feel the pain of childbirth for you until you truly become like Christ. 20 I wish I could be with you now and could change the way I am talking to you, because I do not know what to think about you.

The Example of Hagar and Sarah

21 Some of you still want to be under the law. Tell me, do you know what the law says? 22 The Scriptures say that Abraham had two sons. The mother of one son was a slave woman, and the mother of the other son was a free woman. 23 Abraham's son from the slave woman was born in the normal human way. But the son from the free woman was born because of the promise God made to Abraham.

24 This story teaches something else: the two women are like the two agreements between God and his people. One agreement is the law that God made on Mount Sinai,*[n]* and the people who are under this agreement are like slaves. The mother named Hagar is like that agreement. 25 She is like Mount Sinai in Arabia and is a picture of the earthly Jewish city of Jerusalem. This city and its people, the Jews, are slaves to the law. 26 But the heavenly Jerusalem, which is above, is like the free woman. She is our mother. 27 It is written in the Scriptures:

"Be happy, Jerusalem.
 You are like a woman who never
  gave birth to children.
 Start singing and shout for joy.
 You never felt the pain of giving
  birth,
 but you will have more children
  than the woman who has a
  husband." *Isaiah 54:1*

28 My brothers and sisters, you are God's children because of his promise, as Isaac was then. 29 The son who was born in the normal way treated the other son badly. It is the same today. 30 But what does the Scripture say? "Throw out the slave woman and her son. The son of the slave woman should not inherit anything. The son of the free woman should receive it all."*[n]* 31 So, my brothers and sisters, we are not children of the slave woman, but of the free woman.

Keep Your Freedom

5 We have freedom now, because Christ made us free. So stand strong. Do not change and go back into the slavery of the law. 2 Listen, I, Paul, tell you that if you go back to the law by being circumcised, Christ does you no good. 3 Again, I warn every man: if you allow yourselves to be circumcised, you must follow all the law. 4 If you try to be made right with God through the law, your life with Christ is over—you have left God's grace. 5 But we have the true hope that comes from being made right with God, and by the

---

4:17 Those people They are the false teachers who were bothering the believers in Galatia (Galatians 1:7).
4:24 Mount Sinai Mountain in Arabia where God gave his laws to Moses (Exodus 19 and 20).
4:30 "Throw . . . all." Quotation from Genesis 21:10.

Spirit we wait eagerly for this hope. 6 When we are in Christ Jesus, it is not important if we are circumcised or not. The important thing is faith—the kind of faith that works through love.

7 You were running a good race. Who stopped you from following the true way? 8 This change did not come from the One who chose you. 9 Be careful! "Just a little yeast makes the whole batch of dough rise." 10 But I trust in the Lord that you will not believe those different ideas. Whoever is confusing you with such ideas will be punished.

11 My brothers and sisters, I do not teach that a man must be circumcised. If I teach circumcision, why am I still being attacked? If I still taught circumcision, my preaching about the cross would not be a problem. 12 I wish the people who are bothering you would castrate*n* themselves!

13 My brothers and sisters, God called you to be free, but do not use your freedom as an excuse to do what pleases your sinful self. Serve each other with love. 14 The whole law is made complete in this one command: "Love your neighbour as you love yourself."*n* 15 If you go on hurting each other and tearing each other apart, be careful, or you will completely destroy each other.

The Spirit and Human Nature

16 So I tell you: live by following the Spirit. Then you will not do what your sinful selves want. 17 Our sinful selves want what is against the Spirit, and the Spirit wants what is against our sinful selves. The two are against each other, so you cannot do just what you please. 18 But if the Spirit is leading you, you are not under the law.

19 The wrong things the sinful self does are clear: being sexually unfaithful, not being pure, taking part in sexual sins, 20 worshipping gods, doing witchcraft, hating, making trouble, being jealous, being angry, being selfish, making people angry with each other, causing divisions among people, 21 feeling envy, being drunk, having wild and wasteful parties, and doing other things like these. I warn

---

FAITH links

A DIFFERENT KIND OF FRUIT
GALATIANS 5:22-23

What's your favourite fruit? Did you know that the Spirit has some fruit that are his favourites? They're not the kind you might be thinking about. He prefers fruit like love, joy, peace, patience, kindness, goodness, faithfulness, gentleness and self-control. In fact, this "fruit" is called the fruit of the Spirit. Why is it called that? Because it helps us grow in faith. As we trust God, love, joy, peace, and so on, are the fruit that the Holy Spirit develops within us. What "fruit" do you need more of in your life?

I Want It *Now!* Judges 14:1–3, p. 332

Fair All the Time? 2 Samuel 8:15, p. 408

The Way to Serve God, 1 Kings 9:4, p. 450

One Big, Happy Family, John 1:12, p. 1422

Always Do This! 1 Thessalonians 5:16–18, p. 1636

The "Quality" of Life, 2 Peter 1:5–8, p. 1708

5:12 castrate To cut off part of the male sex organ. Paul wanted to show that he is very upset with the false teachers.
5:14 "Love . . . yourself." Quotation from Leviticus 19:18.

Galatians 6:12

you now as I warned you before: those who do these things will not inherit God's kingdom. 22 But the Spirit produces the fruit of love, joy, peace, patience, kindness, goodness, faithfulness, 23 gentleness, self-control. There is no law that says these things are wrong. 24 Those who belong to Christ Jesus have crucified their own sinful selves. They have given up their old selfish feelings and the evil things they wanted to do. 25 We get our new life from the Spirit, so we should follow the Spirit. 26 We must not be proud or make trouble with each other or be jealous of each other.

Help Each Other

6 Brothers and sisters, if someone in your group does something wrong, you who are spiritual should go to that person and gently help make him right again. But be careful, because you might be tempted to sin too. 2 By helping each other with your troubles, you truly obey the law of Christ. 3 If anyone thinks he is important when he really is not, he is only fooling himself. 4 Each person should judge his own actions and not compare himself with others. Then he can be proud for what he himself has done. 5 Each person must be responsible for himself.

6 Anyone who is learning the teaching of God should share all the good things he has with his teacher.

Life is like Planting a Field

7 Do not be fooled: you cannot cheat God. People harvest only what they plant. 8 If they plant to satisfy their sinful selves, their sinful selves will bring them ruin. But if they plant to please the Spirit, they will receive eternal life from the Spirit. 9 We must not become tired of doing good. We will receive our harvest of eternal life at the right time if we do not give up. 10 When we have the opportunity to help anyone, we should do it. But we should give special attention to those who are in the family of believers.

Paul Ends His Letter

11 See what large letters I use to write this myself. 12 Some people are trying to

FAITH links

KEEP UP THE GOOD WORK!
GALATIANS 6:9-10

Who has the most fun in movies or on TV: the good guy or the villain? The good guy, you say? Nope! Usually, the bad guy looks like he's having fun destroying everything. The good guy has a hard time saving the world and is rarely thanked by anyone.

Movies and TV show what the world values. What's bad is sometimes seen as good. God still wants his people to do good things. Unfortunately, we can easily become discouraged. That's why the apostle Paul said to not give up doing good works. The good things we can do include saying kind things to each other, telling people about Jesus and praying for one another. Don't miss out on an opportunity to do something good today!

Here are some more Faithlinks on being a good guy:

Lights, Camera, . . . Actions! Genesis 12:1–3, p. 17

Roll Out the Welcome Wagon, Genesis 18:2–8, p. 24

The Green Light, 2 Samuel 2:1, p. 401

Small Beginnings, Zechariah 4:10, p. 1255

You're Welcomed! Acts 16:14–15, p. 1494

Your Faith Example, 1 Timothy 4:12, p. 1646

DOING GOOD
Galatians 6:9–10

That (Good) Thing You Do Some people do "random acts of kindness". That means that they do something good for someone because that person needs help. Sometimes the person receiving the help doesn't even know who has helped him or her. Why do *you* do good things? Do you expect to receive something from doing good? What?

God wants his people to do good things. Sometimes we can become discouraged when we see others doing anything they please, without giving a thought to anyone else. Paul said never to give up doing good. (Read Galatians 6:9–10.) What good thing can you do for someone today?

MORE FAITH links

The Right Thing to Do, **p. 391**

On the Wrong Foot, **p. 509**

The Right Ingredients, **p. 1227**

Keep Up the Good Work! **p. 1593**

Helpful Hints, **p. 1724**

> If you do a good deed, do you expect something in return? Or do you hope that everyone will know that it was you who did it?
>
> It's good to do good things, but maybe you ought to surf over to these links to see why God wants us to do good things.

A Blueprint for Living, Amos 5:14–15, p. 1200
- A blueprint is a plan of action for a builder. Link here to find out about God's blueprint for your life. Following it carefully can lead to success in your life!

A Reminder to Do What Is Right and True, Zechariah 7:8–10, p. 1257
- Do you ever complain that your parents are nagging because they say the same things all the time? Why do they need to say the same things? What might happen if they never reminded you of what you are to do? Some messages are repeated over and over in the Bible. Can you think of some of those messages? Why do they need to be repeated?

The True Test, 1 John 3:18, p. 1718
- If someone said they loved you but never said anything nice about you or did nice things for you, would you believe them? Love is more than just words; it's showing that love in the good things we do. What good thing can you do for someone today to show that you love him or her?

my FAVOURITE links

force you to be circumcised so the Jews will accept them. They are afraid they will be attacked if they follow only the cross of Christ.ⁿ 13 Those who are circumcised do not obey the law themselves, but they want you to be circumcised so they can boast about what they forced you to do. 14 I hope I will never boast about things like that. The cross of our Lord Jesus Christ is my only reason for boasting. Through the cross of Jesus my world was crucified, and I died to the world. 15 It is not important if a man is circumcised or uncircumcised. The important thing is being the new people God has made. 16 Peace and mercy to those who follow this rule—and to all of God's people.

17 So do not give me any more trouble. I have scars on my body that showⁿ I belong to Christ Jesus.

18 My brothers and sisters, the grace of our Lord Jesus Christ be with your spirit. Amen.

6:12 cross of Christ Paul uses the cross as a picture of the gospel, the story of Christ's death and rising from the dead to pay for our sins. The cross, or Christ's death, was God's way to save us.
6:17 that show Many times Paul was beaten and whipped by people who were against him because he was teaching about Christ. The scars were from these beatings.

NOTHING BUT CHRISTIAN

Welcome, newbie! I'm glad you're reading this letter. I'm Paul and I hope you remember who I am. I was a well-known Jewish leader who spent a lot of time arresting and hassling followers of Jesus, known as Christians. After I met Jesus, though, I became the champion of the church – teaching new believers and telling others about Jesus. (You can check out that incredible story by downloading Acts 9, p. 1478.) I wrote this letter from jail. I spent a lot of time in jail because the Jewish leaders and others did not like my message. (Kind of like how I was before I met Jesus!)

My friends at the church in Ephesus were facing a critical issue. Those who had been Jews before they met Jesus claimed that if you wanted to become a Christian, you had to become a Jew first and obey all the laws of Moses. Ridiculous! So, I wrote this letter to tell my friends at Ephesus that there's no such thing as a Jewish Christian or a non-Jewish Christian. We're all just Christians!

JESUS WATCH

Through his writings, Paul became known for the phrase "in Christ". That phrase appears several times in this book. In fact, Paul covers just about every important issue for believers in this book and answers with the assurance that we are "in Jesus". For example, Paul says that we were adopted through Christ (Ephesians 1:5). We are made alive together through Jesus (Ephesians 2:5). And, as followers, we share in the promise that God made in Jesus (Ephesians 3:6). Paul takes great care to help the believers in Ephesus, and even us, understand that Jesus is our key for everyday living, as well as for eternal living. Without Jesus, we'd be lost!

my FAVOURITE links

OTHER CONNECTIONS

- Let's Visit Ephesus, Ephesians 3. Today there's nothing left but ruins of this ancient Greek city, but during New Testament times Ephesus was a thriving, important centre. Download the info here to find out more.

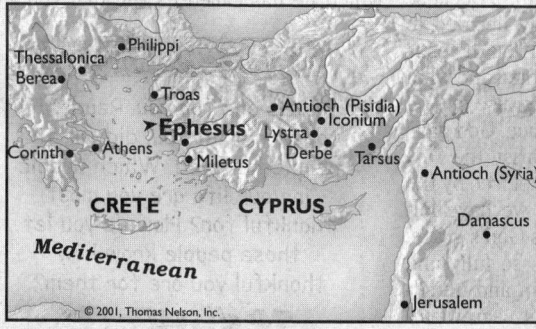

FAITH links

- That's Much Better!
  Ephesians 2:4–5

- It's Free!
  Ephesians 2:8–9

- Say What?!
  Ephesians 4:22–29

- Forgive and Forget,
  Ephesians 4:32

- How to Make God Glad,
  Ephesians 6:1–2

- A Good Habit,
  Ephesians 6:18

What's the deal about children obeying their parents?

Paul had a lot to say about that! Let's connect to Ephesians 6:1–4 and find out.

did YOU know?

DON'T MISS THESE GREAT STORIES:
Paul's special prayer, Ephesians 1:15–23
Don't be a baby! Ephesians 4:11–16
Living in light, Ephesians 5:1–14
Get ready for battle! Ephesians 6:10–18

1

1 From Paul, an apostle of Christ Jesus. I am an apostle because that is what God wanted.

To God's holy people living in Ephesus, believers in Christ Jesus:

2 Grace and peace to you from God our Father and the Lord Jesus Christ.

Spiritual Blessings in Christ

3 Praise be to the God and Father of our Lord Jesus Christ. In Christ, God has given us every spiritual blessing in the heavenly world. **4** That is, in Christ, he chose us before the world was made so that we would be his holy people—people without blame before him. **5** Because of his love, God had already decided to make us his own children through Jesus Christ. That was what he wanted and what pleased him, **6** and it brings praise to God because of his wonderful grace. God gave that grace to us freely, in Christ, the One he loves. **7** In Christ we are set free by the blood of his death, and so we have forgiveness of sins. How rich is God's grace, **8** which he has given to us so fully and freely. God, with full wisdom and understanding, **9** let us know his secret purpose. This was what God wanted, and he planned to do it through Christ. **10** His goal was to carry out his plan, when the right time came, that all things in heaven and on earth would be joined together in Christ as the head.

11 In Christ we were chosen to be God's people, because from the very beginning God had decided this in keeping with his plan. And he is the One who makes everything agree with what he decides and wants. **12** We are the first people who hoped in Christ, and we were chosen so that we would bring praise to God's glory. **13** So it is with you. When you heard the true teaching—the Good News about your salvation—you believed in Christ. And in Christ, God put his special mark of ownership on you by giving you the Holy Spirit that he had promised. **14** That Holy Spirit is the guarantee that we will receive what God promised for his people until God gives full freedom to those who are his—to bring praise to God's glory.

Paul's Prayer

15 That is why since I heard about your faith in the Lord Jesus and your love for all God's people, **16** I have not stopped giving thanks to God for you. I always remember you in my prayers, **17** asking the God of our Lord Jesus Christ, the glorious Father, to give you a spirit of wisdom and revelation so that you will know him better. **18** I pray also that you will have greater understanding in your heart so you will know the hope to which he has called us and that you will

1:15–16 Thankfulness
Should you ever stop giving thanks?

FAITH CHALLENGE

Here's one for you. Read 1:16 to learn what Paul did for the people he loved. Which people in your life are you most thankful for? How do you let those people know how thankful you are for them?

TESTING IT

Ephesians 1:16
I have not stopped giving thanks to God for you. I always remember you in my prayers.

know how rich and glorious are the blessings God has promised his holy people. 19 And you will know that God's power is very great for us who believe. That power is the same as the great strength 20 God used to raise Christ from the dead and put him at his right side in the heavenly world. 21 God has put Christ over all rulers, authorities, powers and kings, not only in this world but also in the next. 22 God put everything under his power and made him the head over everything for the church, 23 which is Christ's body. The church is filled with Christ, and Christ fills everything in every way.

We Now Have Life

2 In the past you were spiritually dead because of your sins and the things you did against God. 2 Yes, in the past you lived the way the world lives, following the ruler of the evil powers that are above the earth. That same spirit is now working in those who refuse to obey God. 3 In the past all of us lived like them, trying to please our sinful selves and doing all the things our bodies and minds wanted. We should have suffered God's anger because of the way we were. We were the same as all other people.

4 But God's mercy is great, and he loved us very much. 5 Though we were spiritually dead because of the things we did against God, he gave us new life with Christ. You have been saved by God's grace. 6 And he raised us up with Christ and gave us a seat with him in the heavens. He did this for those in Christ Jesus 7 so that for all future time he could show the very great riches of his grace by being kind to us in Christ Jesus. 8 I mean that you have been saved by grace through believing. You did not save yourselves: it was a gift from God. 9 It was not the result of your own work, so you cannot boast about it. 10 God has made us what we are. In Christ Jesus, God made us to do good works, which God planned in advance for us to live our lives doing.

One in Christ

11 You were not born Jewish. You are the people the Jews call "uncircumcised". Those who call you "uncircumcised" call themselves "circumcised". (Their circumcision is only something they themselves do on their bodies.) 12 Remember that in

---

FAITH links

THAT'S MUCH BETTER!
EPHESIANS 2:4-5

Let's suppose you did something wrong, like telling a lie. After admitting that you told a lie, suppose you were given a hug instead of being punished. How would you feel? That's what mercy is all about. *Mercy means not giving someone the punishment that he deserves.* As sinners, we deserve punishment. God treats us much better than we deserve. Since he's merciful to us, shouldn't we treat other people much better than they deserve, too?

Download these links for more on how to treat others:

The Trouble with Jealousy, Genesis 37, p. 53

World News, Isaiah 13—19, p. 913

A Model of Forgiveness, Ezekiel 16:59–63, p. 1103

Inside the Heart of God, Micah 7:18–20, p. 1228

Forgive and Forget, Ephesians 4:32, p. 1604

It's Guaranteed! 1 John 1:9–10, p. 1714

FAITH links

IT'S FREE!
EPHESIANS 2:8-9

What did you do to earn your family's love this week? Did you do everything right? Did you get along with everyone? What's that you say? You did absolutely nothing to earn their love? Not one teensy, weensy little thing? The fact is, you can't earn their love. God's grace is the same way. We can't earn it – it's a gift. You could no more earn it than you could fly to the moon under your own power. God sent his Son to die for us. Because of that, we are saved from the punishment for our sins. That's a free gift!

Made in His Image, Genesis 1:26–27, p. 4

Big Lack Attack, 2 Kings 4:1–7, p. 480

Dirty Inside, Isaiah 6:1–7, p. 904

A Hard Place, Ezekiel 28:25–26, p. 1120

A Family Celebration, 1 Corinthians 11:23–29, p. 1558

From Useless to Useful, Philemon 11, p. 1663

---

the past you were without Christ. You were not citizens of Israel, and you had no part in the agreements[n] with the promise that God made to his people. You had no hope, and you did not know God. **13** But now in Christ Jesus, you who were far away from God are brought near through the blood of Christ's death. **14** Christ himself is our peace. He made both Jewish people and those who are not Jews one people. They were separated as if there were a wall between them, but Christ broke down that wall of hate by giving his own body. **15** The Jewish law had many commands and rules, but Christ ended that law. His purpose was to make the two groups of people become one new people in him and in this way make peace. **16** It was also Christ's purpose to end the hatred between the two groups, to make them into one body, and to bring them back to God. Christ did all this with his death on the cross. **17** Christ came and preached peace to you who were far away from God, and to those who were near to God. **18** Yes, it is through Christ we all have the right to come to the Father in one Spirit.

19 Now you who are not Jewish are not foreigners or strangers any longer, but are citizens together with God's holy people. You belong to God's family. **20** You are like a building that was built on the foundation of the apostles and prophets. Christ Jesus himself is the most important stone[n] in that building, **21** and that whole building is joined together in Christ. He makes it grow and become a holy temple in the Lord. **22** And in Christ you, too, are being built together with the Jews into a place where God lives through the Spirit.

2:14 Peace
Who is your peace?

Paul's Work in Telling the Good News

3 So I, Paul, am a prisoner of Christ Jesus for you who are not Jews. **2** Surely you have heard that God gave me this work through his grace to help you.

2:12 agreements The agreements that God gave to his people in the Old Testament.
2:20 most important stone Literally, "cornerstone". The first and most important stone in a building.

Ephesians 3:19 **1601**

LET'S VISIT EPHESUS   Ephesians 3

Today the city of Ephesus is in ruins, but in New Testament days, it was an important city with a huge auditorium that held 25,000 people. It had gymnasiums and impressive public buildings. One of the Seven Wonders of the Ancient World, the temple of Diana, can be found in Ephesus.

The church at Ephesus may have been started by Priscilla and Aquila. (Check out Acts 18:18–21, p. 1498.) The church was about two years old when Paul came to town. Later, the apostle John (one of Jesus' disciples) settled at Ephesus and ministered there after Paul. John was exiled on the Isle of Patmos just off the coast. While he was there, God used him to write the Book of Revelation. In it, he wrote to seven churches, and one of them was the church at Ephesus. (See Revelation 1:11; 2:1–7, p. 1732.)

3 He let me know his secret by showing it to me. I have already written a little about this. 4 If you read what I wrote then, you can see that I truly understand the secret about the Christ. 5 People who lived in other times were not told that secret. But now, through the Spirit, God has shown that secret to his holy apostles and prophets. 6 This is that secret: that through the Good News those who are not Jews will share with the Jews in God's blessing. They belong to the same body, and they share together in the promise that God made in Christ Jesus.

7 By God's special gift of grace given to me through his power, I became a servant to tell that Good News. 8 I am the least important of all God's people, but God gave me this gift—to tell those who are not Jews the Good News about the riches of Christ, which are too great to understand fully. 9 And God gave me the work of telling all people about the plan for his secret, which has been hidden in him since the beginning of time. He is the One who created everything. 10 His purpose was that through the church all the rulers and powers in the heavenly world will now know God's wisdom, which has so many forms. 11 This agrees with the purpose God had since the beginning of time, and he carried out his plan through Christ Jesus our Lord. 12 In Christ we can come before God with freedom and without fear. We can do this through faith in Christ. 13 So I ask you not to become discouraged because of the sufferings I am having for you. My sufferings are for your glory.

The Love of Christ

14 So I bow in prayer before the Father 15 from whom every family in heaven and on earth gets its true name. 16 I ask the Father in his great glory to give you the power to be strong inwardly through his Spirit. 17 I pray that Christ will live in your hearts by faith and that your lives will be strong in love and be built on love. 18 And I pray that you and all God's holy people will have the power to understand the greatness of Christ's love—how wide and how long and how high and how deep that love is. 19 Christ's love is greater than anyone can ever know, but I pray that you will be able to know that love. Then you can be filled with the fullness of God.

20 With God's power working in us, God can do much, much more than anything we can ask or imagine. 21 To him be glory in the church and in Christ Jesus for all time, for ever and ever. Amen.

The Unity of the Body

4 I am in prison because I belong to the Lord. God chose you to be his people, so I tell you now to live the life to which God called you. 2 Always be humble, gentle and patient, accepting each other in love. 3 You are joined together with peace through the Spirit, so do all you can to continue together in this way. 4 There is one body and one Spirit, and God called you to have one hope. 5 There is one Lord, one faith and one baptism. 6 There is one God and Father of everything. He rules everything and is everywhere and is in everything.

7 Christ gave each one of us the special gift of grace, showing how generous he is. 8 That is why it says in the Scriptures,

"When he went up to the heights,
he led a parade of captives,
and he gave gifts to all peoples."

Psalm 68:18

9 When it says, "He went up," what does it mean? It means that he first came down to the earth. 10 So Jesus came down, and he is the same One who went up above all the sky. Christ did that to fill everything with his presence. 11 And Christ gave gifts to people—he made some to be apostles, some to be prophets, some to go and tell the Good News, and some to have the work of caring for and teaching God's people. 12 Christ gave those gifts to prepare God's holy people for the work of serving, to make the body of Christ stronger. 13 This work must continue until we are all joined together in the same faith and in the same knowledge of the Son of God. We must become like a mature person, growing until we become like Christ and have his perfection.

14 Then we will no longer be babies. We will not be tossed about like a ship that the waves carry one way and then another. We will not be influenced by every new teaching we hear from people who are trying to fool us. They make plans and try any kind of trick to fool people into following the wrong path. 15 No! Speaking the truth with love, we will grow up in every way into Christ, who is the head. 16 The whole body depends on Christ, and all the parts of the body are joined and held together. Each part does its own work to make the whole body grow and be strong with love.

4:2 Love — How can you love other people?

4:13–14 Learning — When should you stop learning about God?

The Way You Should Live

17 In the Lord's name, I tell you this. Do not continue living like those who do not believe. Their thoughts are worth nothing. 18 They do not understand, and they know nothing, because they refuse to listen. So they cannot have the life that God gives. 19 They have lost all feeling of shame, and they use their lives for doing evil. They continually want to do all kinds of evil. 20 But what you learned in Christ was not like this. 21 I know that you heard about him, and you are in him, so you were taught the truth that is in Jesus. 22 You were taught to leave your old self—to stop living the evil way you lived before. That old self becomes worse, because people are fooled by the evil things they want to do. 23 But you were taught to be made new in your hearts, 24 to become a new person. That new person is made to be like God—made to be truly good and holy.

25 So you must stop telling lies. "Tell each other the truth,"*n* because we all belong to each other in the same body. 26 When you are angry, do not sin, and be sure to stop being angry

4:26–27 Anger — Check out this good advice on anger.

4:25 "Tell . . . truth," Quotation from Zechariah 8:16.

FAITH links

SAY WHAT?!
EPHESIANS 4:22-29

Words can hurt. Think about the last time someone said something mean to you. Those words hurt, didn't they? Name-calling, telling lies, gossip and bad language are ways we use words to hurt others and ourselves. Paul, the writer of Ephesians, warned the Ephesian Christians to watch their words. Instead of putting others down, they were told to build others up with their words. Kind words are the way to "help others become stronger". Be a builder, not a destroyer, with your words!

Here are some more links on choosing your words carefully:

Just Kidding? Genesis 21:8–10, p. 28

The Best Policy, Genesis 29:16–29, p. 41

A Special Promise, Numbers 30:1–2, p. 217

Peace in the Family, Psalm 133, p. 811

I'll Be the Judge! 1 Corinthians 4:4–5, p. 1549

The Gentle Way, Titus 3:1–5, p. 1661

---

29 When you talk, do not say harmful things, but say what people need—words that will help others become stronger. Then what you say will do good to those who listen to you. 30 And do not make the Holy Spirit sad. The Spirit is God's proof that you belong to him. God gave you the Spirit to show that God will make you free when the final day comes. 31 Do not be bitter or angry or cross. Never shout angrily or say things to hurt others. Never do anything evil. 32 Be kind and loving to each other, and forgive each other just as God forgave you in Christ.

Living in the Light

5 You are God's children whom he loves, so try to be like him. 2 Live a life of love just as Christ loved us and gave himself for us as a sweet-smelling offering and sacrifice to God.

3 But there must be no sexual sin among you, or any kind of evil or greed. Those things are not right for God's holy people. 4 Also, there must be no evil talk among you, and you must not speak foolishly or tell evil jokes. These things are not right for you. Instead, you should be giving thanks to God. 5 You can be sure of this: no one will have a place in the kingdom of Christ and of God who sins sexually, or does evil things, or is greedy. Anyone who is greedy is serving a false god.

6 Do not let anyone fool you by telling you things that are not true, because these things will bring God's anger on those who do not obey him. 7 So have nothing to do with them. 8 In the past you were full of darkness, but now you are full of light in the Lord. So live like children who belong to the light. 9 Light brings every kind of goodness, right living and truth. 10 Try to learn what pleases the Lord. 11 Have nothing to do with the things done in darkness, which are not worth anything. But show that they are wrong. 12 It is shameful even to talk about what those people do in secret. 13 But the light makes all things easy to see, 14 and everything that is made easy to see can become light. This is why it is said:

"Wake up, sleeper!

---

before the end of the day. 27 Do not give the devil a way to defeat you. 28 Those who are stealing must stop stealing and start working. They should earn an honest living for themselves. Then they will have something to share with those who are poor.

Ephesians 5:15 1604

FAITH links

FORGIVE AND FORGET
EPHESIANS 4:32

What's the opposite of holding a grudge? Forgiving someone. Although that question was easy to answer, the answer itself is not always easy to do. Or so we think. The apostle Paul encouraged the Christians in the city of Ephesus to forgive others. Since God always forgives us, that's what we ought to do for anyone who hurts us.

Here is more on what God has to say about forgiveness:

More Powerful Than Revenge, Genesis 50:14–21, p. 71

Putting an Enemy in Check, 2 Kings 6:8–23, p. 486

Does Crime Pay? Psalm 37:1–7, p. 736

Mercy for an Enemy, Jonah 4, p. 1216

The Best Protection Plan, Matthew 2:13–18, p. 1276

Who Needs Love? Luke 6:27–36, p. 1379

Rise from death,
and Christ will shine on you."

15 So be very careful how you live. Do not live like those who are not wise, but live wisely. 16 Use every chance you have for doing good, because these are evil times. 17 So do not be foolish but learn what the Lord wants you to do. 18 Do not be drunk with wine, which will ruin you, but be filled with the Spirit. 19 Speak to each other with psalms, hymns and spiritual songs, singing and making music in your hearts to the Lord. 20 Always give thanks to God the Father for everything, in the name of our Lord Jesus Christ.

5:20 Thankfulness How much do you have to be thankful for?

Wives and Husbands

21 Yield to obey each other because you respect Christ.

22 Wives, yield to your husbands, as you do to the Lord, 23 because the husband is the head of the wife, as Christ is the head of the church. And he is the Saviour of the body, which is the church. 24 As the church yields to Christ, so you wives should yield to your husbands in everything.

25 Husbands, love your wives as Christ loved the church and gave himself for it 26 to make it belong to God. Christ used the word to make the church clean by washing it with water. 27 He died so that he could give the church to himself like a bride in all her beauty. He died so that the church could be pure and without fault, with no evil or sin or any other wrong thing in it. 28 In the same way, husbands should love their wives as they love their own bodies. The man who loves his wife loves himself. 29 No one ever hates his own body, but feeds and takes care of it. And that is what Christ does for the church, 30 because we are parts of his body. 31 The Scripture says, "So a man will leave his father and mother and be united with his wife, and the two will become one body."ⁿ 32 That secret is very important—I am talking about Christ and the church. 33 But each one of you must love his wife as he loves himself, and a wife must respect her husband.

Children and Parents

6 Children, obey your parents as the Lord wants, because this is the right thing to do. 2 The command says, "Honour

---

5:31 "So . . . body." Quotation from Genesis 2:24.

Ephesians 6:18

FAITH links

HOW TO MAKE GOD GLAD
EPHESIANS 6:1-2

Want to make God glad? Do you really want to please him? Then read the three words at the end of this sentence carefully: *obey your parents*. Before you roll your eyes, think about it for a minute. Your parents love you and want what's best for you. If you really want to show respect for your parents (see verse 2), then listen to what they say, and do it!

Want advice on handling your parents? Connect here:

Fatherly Advice, Exodus 18, p. 99

Care for the Lost, Deuteronomy 22:1–3, p. 255

In Your Best Interests, Ruth 3, p. 349

When I Need Advice, 1 Kings 12:1–17, p. 455

If You Want My Advice... Proverbs 13:1, p. 843

Your Civic Duty, Matthew 17:24–27, p. 1304

Slaves and Masters

5 Slaves, obey your masters here on earth with fear and respect and from a sincere heart, just as you obey Christ. 6 You must do this not only while they are watching you, to please them. With all your heart you must do what God wants as people who are obeying Christ. 7 Do your work with enthusiasm. Work as if you were serving the Lord, not as if you were serving only men and women. 8 Remember that the Lord will give a reward to everyone, slave or free, for doing good.

9 Masters, in the same way, be good to your slaves. Do not threaten them. Remember that the One who is your Master and their Master is in heaven, and he treats everyone alike.

Wear the Full Armour of God

10 Finally, be strong in the Lord and in his great power. 11 Put on the full armour of God so that you can fight against the devil's evil tricks. 12 Our fight is not against people on earth but against the rulers and authorities and the powers of this world's darkness, against the spiritual powers of evil in the heavenly world. 13 That is why you need to put on God's full armour. Then on the day of evil you will be able to stand strong. And when you have finished the whole fight, you will still be standing. 14 So stand strong, with the belt of truth tied around your waist and the protection of right living on your chest. 15 On your feet wear the Good News of peace to help you stand strong. 16 And also use the shield of faith with which you can stop all the burning arrows of the Evil One. 17 Accept God's salvation as your helmet, and take the sword of the Spirit, which is the word of God. 18 Pray in the Spirit at all times with all kinds of prayers, asking for everything you need. To do this you must

6:13 Perseverance
What do you need to keep standing?

your father and mother."[n] This is the first command that has a promise with it—

6:1–3 Obedience
What commandment comes with a promise?

3 "Then everything will be well with you, and you will have a long life on the earth."[n]

4 Fathers, do not make your children angry, but raise them with the training and teaching of the Lord.

6:2 "Honour . . . mother." Quotation from Exodus 20:12; Deuteronomy 5:16.
6:3 "Then . . . earth." Quotation from Exodus 20:12; Deuteronomy 5:16.

> Ephesians 6:19 **1606**

A GOOD HABIT
EPHESIANS 6:18

What are some of your habits? Some habits are good; some are bad. It is said that a habit takes 21 days to develop. So, for the next 21 days, why not make daily prayer a habit? You'll find that once you start, this is one habit you won't want to break. God tells us to never stop praying for each other. Does this mean you have to mutter a prayer for 24 hours straight? No. It just means be prepared to pray.

Link here for more about good habits for a healthy faith:

When God Says No, 2 Samuel 7, p. 407

Building Together, Nehemiah 3, p. 627

The Bible: Good for Your Faith, Psalm 119, p. 802

Wisdom in Store, Proverbs 2:6–7, p. 828

Tell All About Him! Matthew 28:19, p. 1326

Faith Workout, Acts 16:4–5, p. 1493

always be ready and never give up. Always pray for all God's people.

19 Also pray for me that when I speak, God will give me words so that I can tell the secret of the Good News without fear. 20 I have been sent to preach this Good News, and I am doing that now, here in prison. Pray that when I preach the Good News I will speak without fear, as I should.

Final Greetings

21 I am sending to you Tychicus, our brother whom we love and a faithful servant of the Lord's work. He will tell you everything that is happening with me. Then you will know how I am and what I am doing. 22 I am sending him to you for this reason—so that you will know how we are, and he can encourage you.

23 Peace and love with faith to you from God the Father and the Lord Jesus Christ. 24 Grace to all of you who love our Lord Jesus Christ with love that never ends.

NUMBER ONE!

OK, you know who this is, right? It's me, Paul. Remember who I was before I met Jesus? I was a powerful Jewish leader, who arrested and killed Jesus' followers. I was convinced that Jesus was nothing more than a rebellious troublemaker. Until Jesus met me on the road to Damascus, that is. After he changed my life, Jesus became the most important person in my life. My mission became telling others about Jesus and serving them. It was important to me that believers should work together and help each other. My friends at Philippi often helped me. (Check out Philippians 4:14–16.) In fact, the church at Philippi was one of my favourite churches. Which is why I wrote this letter.

The church in Philippi was having trouble and I wanted to help them. Some people were telling them that they had to follow Jesus' teaching *and* Moses' teaching in order to be a true Christian. But that wasn't the truth – they only needed to follow Jesus' teachings. I wanted my friends in Philippi to understand that Jesus should be the most important person in their lives. A lot of us know people who are very important to us – our friends, our parents, our teachers. But for Christians, Jesus needs to be Number One!

JESUS WATCH

Paul gives us several snapshots of Jesus in this letter. Paul calls Jesus his life (Philippians 1:21); he is the picture of true unselfishness (Philippians 2:5); and Jesus is Paul's power source (Philippians 4:13). Paul talks a lot about Jesus in this book. He helps us understand that a life lived for Jesus isn't always easy, but it *is* one that is exciting and always changing. Paul shows us how his belief in Jesus has affected his life. Then he encourages his friends (and us!) to give their lives to Jesus – the only way they'll ever be really happy.

my FAVORITE links

OTHER CONNECTIONS

livin' it — Each school year you "grow" in the amount of knowledge you have. Each year, you grow physically. But how do you "grow" in faith? Find out by downloading How Are You Growing? Philippians 1:1–11.

How do you feel when your best friend gets a better bike than you? How about when the kid down the street beats you into the football team? Link to The Perfect Life! Philippians 4:10–13, to learn how to be content with whatever you have.

MORE STUFF...

Joy Philippians is sometimes called the "joy letter". The word "joy" is mentioned more than 15 times. But did you know that Paul wrote this letter while he was in jail? Not a very joyful place, yet Paul found plenty of reasons to be joyful. Here are a few things he said about joy:

- Pray with joy (Philippians 1:4).
- Join each other in joy (Philippians 2:17–18).
- Welcome those who work for Jesus with joy (Philippians 2:25–30).
- Enjoy your faith in the Lord (Philippians 3:1).
- Enjoy being with other Christians (Philippians 4:1).
- Always be joyful (Philippians 4:4).

You know, the secret of true happiness doesn't involve getting lots of cool stuff.

Plug into Philippians 4:10-13 to find out what the secret really is.

did YOU know?

MORE ON THE PHILIPPIANS SURFWATCH:

No grumbling allowed, Philippians 2:14–18
Getting first prize, Philippians 3:12–14
What, me worry? Philippians 4:5–9

FAITH links

○ The Finished Product, **Philippians 1:6**

○ An Unselfish Example, **Philippians 2:5–8**

○ The Sacrifice of Service, **Philippians 2:17, 25–30**

○ Thoughts on Thoughts, **Philippians 4:8–9**

○ As Strong as Superman? **Philippians 4:13**

○ But I Want It? **Philippians 4:19**

1 From Paul and Timothy, servants of Christ Jesus.

To all of God's holy people in Christ Jesus who live in Philippi, including your elders and deacons:

2 Grace and peace to you from God our Father and the Lord Jesus Christ.

Paul's Prayer

3 I thank my God every time I remember you, 4 always praying with joy for all of you. 5 I thank God for the help you gave me while I preached the Good News—help you gave from the first day you believed until now. 6 God began doing a good work in you, and I am sure he will continue it until it is finished when Jesus Christ comes again.

7 And I know that I am right to think like this about all of you, because I have you in my heart. All of you share in God's grace with me while I am in prison and while I am defending and proving the truth of the Good News. 8 God knows that I want to see you very much, because I love all of you with the love of Christ Jesus.

9 This is my prayer for you: that your love will grow more and more; that you will have knowledge and understanding with your love; 10 that you will see the difference between good and bad and will choose the good; that you will be pure and without wrong for the coming of Christ; 11 that you will do many good things with the help of Christ to bring glory and praise to God.

Paul's Troubles Help the Work

12 I want you brothers and sisters[n] to know that what has happened to me has helped to spread the Good News. 13 All the palace guards and everyone else knows that I am in prison because I am a believer in Christ. 14 Because I am in prison, most of the believers have become more bold in Christ and are not afraid to speak the word of God.

15 It is true that some preach about Christ because they are jealous and ambitious, but others preach about Christ because they want to help. 16 They preach because they have love, and they know that God gave me the work of defending the Good News. 17 But the others preach about Christ for selfish and wrong reasons, wanting to make trouble for me in prison.

18 But it doesn't matter. The important thing is that in every way, whether for

---

FAITH links

THE FINISHED PRODUCT
PHILIPPIANS 1:6

When you start a project, you like to see it through, don't you? Just think: you are a project for God. First, God helped you trust Jesus as your Saviour. Because of that, God will keep working in you throughout your life to help you grow in faith. He won't give up on you. You can count on God to finish the "job"!

Here are some Faithlinks to encourage you to keep on going:

Good Plans, Genesis 45:7–8, p. 64

Always Truthful, Numbers 23:19, p. 208

The Prayer Habit, Psalm 5:1–3, p. 712

Your Full Trust, Jeremiah 22:20–22, p. 1023

Empty Words, Ezekiel 33:30–33, p. 1127

A Friend of Jesus, John 15:9–17, p. 1450

1:12 brothers and sisters Although the Greek text says "brothers" here and throughout this book, Paul's words were meant for the entire church, both men and women.

Philippians 1 1610

GROWING IN FAITH
Philippians 1:1–11

How Are You Growing? You've probably heard from someone (like a grandma or an aunt), "Look how tall you are! You're growing like a weed!" There are other ways to grow, too, besides physically. You can grow in the amount of knowledge you learn at school. You can grow socially in learning how to get along with others. You can also grow in faith. Growing in faith means learning more about God and what's important to him, as you read the Bible, attend Sunday school and trust God more.

Most of your physical growth takes place before you're an adult. But growing in faith should never stop, even if you live to be 100. (Check out <u>Philippians 1:6</u>.) God will keep working in you to help you grow in faith. He never gives up – count on him to finish the "job"! How is your faith growing?

MORE FAITH links
- Trailblazers of Faith, **p. 510**
- Two Ways to Grow, **p. 1370**
- Faith Workout, **p. 1493**
- Full of Faith, **p. 1633**
- How Do You Grow? **p. 1659**

Everybody can tell how much you've grown month-by-month – it's obvious by how much taller you are (and by how much shorter your trousers are!).

But did you know that you can grow spiritually, too? Download these Faithlinks to find out how!

The "Ruler" of Our Lives, Amos 7:7–9, p. 1202
- Ever try to hang a picture? Did it hang straight? You can tell if it's straight by using a ruler. The Bible is used to measure how "straight" our lives are. It can show us where we are crooked or "out of line" with how God wants us to live. Where do you need to straighten up?

Inside the Heart of God, Micah 7:18–20, p. 1228
- This Faithlink helps you to know what God is like.

Prove It! Matthew 16:1–4, p. 1302
- Are you the kind of person who doesn't believe something unless you can see it? Do you think "seeing is believing"? Many people in Jesus' day and today want proof that Jesus is the Saviour. Where can you find that proof? Why can you believe every bit of it?

A Different Kind of Fruit, Galatians 5:22–23, p. 1592
- What's your favourite fruit? The Holy Spirit has some fruits that are his favourites, too. They're not the kind you might be thinking about, though. Link here to discover the kind of "fruits" that help you grow in faith.

my FAVOURITE links

right or wrong reasons, they are preaching about Christ. So I am happy, and I will continue to be happy. 19 Because you are praying for me and the Spirit of Jesus Christ is helping me, I know this trouble will bring my freedom. 20 I expect and hope that I will not fail Christ in anything but that I will have the courage now, as always, to show the greatness of Christ in my life here on earth, whether I live or die. 21 To me the only important thing about living is Christ, and dying would be profit for me. 22 If I continue living in my body, I will be able to work for the Lord. I do not know what to choose—living or dying. 23 It is hard to choose between the two. I want to leave this life and be with Christ, which is much better, 24 but you need me here in my body. 25 Since I am sure of this, I know I will stay with you to help you grow and have joy in your faith. 26 You will be very happy in Christ Jesus when I am with you again.

27 Only one thing concerns me: be sure that you live in a way that brings honour to the Good News of Christ. Then whether I come and visit you or am away from you, I will hear that you are standing strong with one purpose, that you work together as one for the faith of the Good News, 28 and that you are not afraid of those who are against you. All of this is proof that your enemies will be destroyed but that you will be saved by God. 29 God gave you the honour not only of believing in Christ but also of suffering for him, both of which bring glory to Christ. 30 When I was with you, you saw the struggles I had, and you hear about the struggles I am having now. You yourselves are having the same kind of struggles.

2 Does your life in Christ give you strength? Does his love comfort you? Do we share together in the Spirit? Do you have mercy and kindness? 2 If so, make me very happy by having the same thoughts, sharing the same love, and having one mind and purpose. 3 When you do things, do not let selfishness or pride be

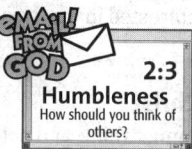

2:3 Humbleness
How should you think of others?

your guide. Instead, be humble and give more honour to others than to yourselves. 4 Do not be interested only in

AN UNSELFISH EXAMPLE
PHILIPPIANS 2:5-8

Have you ever seen a mould that's used to make copies of something? For example, a mould, or model, is used to make plastic statues and other things. In much the same way, Jesus is our mould. He is the model for unselfishness. First, he left heaven to become a human on earth. He willingly gave his life so that we could have God's forgiveness for our sins.

The Holy Spirit uses the "mould" of Jesus to shape your life as a Christian. This does not mean that you lose everything that is uniquely you. It just means that you become more and more like Jesus.

The Perfect Leader? Numbers 20:1–13, p. 203

Help to Understand, 2 Samuel 14, p. 416

Help for the Outsiders, Nehemiah 5:9–10, p. 630

Mind Guard, Proverbs 4:23, p. 831

Just Say Yes! Matthew 9:9–13, p. 1289

A Different Kind of Fruit, Galatians 5:22–23, p. 1592

your own life, but be interested in the lives of others.

Be Unselfish like Christ

5 In your lives you must think and act like Christ Jesus.
6 Christ himself was like God in everything.
But he did not think that being equal with God was something to be used for his own benefit.
7 But he gave up his place with God and made himself nothing.
He was born to be a man and became like a servant.
8 And when he was living as a man, he humbled himself and was fully obedient to God,
even when that caused his death— death on a cross.
9 So God raised him to the highest place.
God made his name greater than every other name
10 so that every knee will bow to the name of Jesus—
everyone in heaven, on earth and under the earth.
11 And everyone will confess that Jesus Christ is Lord
and bring glory to God the Father.

Be the People God Wants You to Be

12 My dear friends, you have always obeyed God when I was with you. It is even more important that you obey now while I am away from you. Keep on working to complete your salvation with fear and trembling, 13 because God is working in you to help you want to do and be able to do what pleases him.

14 Do everything without complaining or arguing. 15 Then you will be innocent and without any wrong. You will be God's children without fault. But you are living with crooked and evil people all around you, among whom you shine like stars in the dark world. 16 You offer the teaching that gives life. So when Christ comes again, I can be happy because my work was not wasted. I ran the race and won.

FAITH links

THE SACRIFICE OF SERVICE

PHILIPPIANS 2:17, 25-30

If you've read some of the Old Testament books, you know about the animal sacrifices the people of Israel gave to God. Sacrifices were the only way that people could be forgiven for their sins. When Jesus died on the cross, he was the once-and-for-all sacrifice for sins. Animal sacrifices were no longer required. Instead, we give service as a sacrifice to God. Think about the missionaries you've read about or the ones your church sponsors. Many missionaries have given their lives to serve God. That's the ultimate sacrifice. What will you do to serve God?

Download these Faithlinks on serving others:

Made in His Image, Genesis 1:26–27, p. 4

What God Wants, Deuteronomy 10:12–13, p. 242

From Zero to Hero, Judges 6; 7, p. 319

You Are What You Do, Proverbs 20:11, p. 854

Obey or Disobey? Luke 20:20–26, p. 1409

The Worst Chore, John 13:3–17, p. 1447

17 Your faith makes you offer your lives as a sacrifice in serving God. If I have to offer my own blood with your sacrifice, I will be happy and full of joy with all of you. 18 You also should be happy and full of joy with me.

Timothy and Epaphroditus

19 I hope in the Lord Jesus to send Timothy to you soon. I will be happy to learn how you are. 20 I have no one else like Timothy, who truly cares for you. 21 Other people are interested only in their own lives, not in the work of Jesus Christ. 22 You know the kind of person Timothy is. You know he has served with me in telling the Good News, as a son serves his father. 23 I plan to send him to you quickly when I know what will happen to me. 24 I am sure that the Lord will help me to come to you soon.

25 Epaphroditus, my brother in Christ, works and serves with me in the army of Christ. When I needed help, you sent him to me. I think now that I must send him back to you, 26 because he wants very much to see all of you. He is worried because you heard that he was sick. 27 Yes, he was sick, and nearly died, but God had mercy on him and me too so that I would not have more sadness. 28 I want very much to send him to you so that when you see him you can be happy, and I can stop worrying about you. 29 Welcome him in the Lord with much joy. Give honour to people like him, 30 because he almost died for the work of Christ. He risked his life to give me the help you could not give in your service to me.

The Importance of Christ

3 My brothers and sisters, be full of joy in the Lord. It is no trouble for me to write the same things to you again, and it will help you to be more ready. 2 Watch out for those who do evil, who are like dogs, who insist on cutting[n] the body. 3 We are the ones who are truly circumcised. We worship God through his Spirit, and our pride is in Christ Jesus. We do not put trust in ourselves or anything we can do, 4 although I might be able to put trust in myself. If anyone thinks he has a reason to trust in himself, he should know that I have greater reason for trusting in myself. 5 I was circumcised eight days after my birth. I am from the people of Israel and the tribe of Benjamin. I am a Hebrew,[n] and my parents were Hebrews. I had a strict view of the law, which is why I became a Pharisee. 6 I was so enthusiastic I tried to hurt the church. No one could find fault with the way I obeyed the law of Moses. 7 Those things were important to me, but now I think they are worth nothing because of Christ. 8 Not only those things, but I think that all things are worth nothing compared with the greatness of knowing Christ Jesus my Lord. Because of him, I have lost all those things, and now I know they are worthless rubbish. This allows me to have Christ 9 and to belong to him. Now I am right with God, not because I followed the law, but because I believed in Christ. God uses my faith to make me right with him. 10 I want to know Christ and the power that raised him from the dead. I want to share in his sufferings and become like him in his death. 11 Then I have hope that I myself will be raised from the dead.

Continuing Towards Our Goal

12 I do not mean that I am already as God wants me to be. I have not yet reached that goal, but I continue trying to reach it and to make it mine. Christ wants me to do that, which is the reason he made me his. 13 Brothers and sisters, I know that I have not yet reached that goal, but there is one thing I always do. Forgetting the past and straining towards what is ahead, 14 I keep trying to reach the goal and get the prize for which God called me through Christ to the life above.

15 All of us who are spiritually mature should think this way too. And if there are things you do not agree with, God will

email FROM GOD
3:12–14
Faith
What is your ultimate goal?

3:2 cutting The word in Greek is like the word "circumcise," but it means "to cut completely off".
3:5 Hebrew A name for the Jews that some Jews were very proud of.

make them clear to you. 16 But we should continue following the truth we already have.

17 Brothers and sisters, all of you should try to follow my example and to copy those who live the way we showed you. 18 Many people live like enemies of the cross of Christ. I have often told you about them, and it makes me cry to tell you about them now. 19 In the end, they will be destroyed. They do whatever their bodies want, they are proud of their shameful acts, and they think only about earthly things. 20 But our homeland is in heaven, and we are waiting for our Saviour, the Lord Jesus Christ, to come from heaven. 21 By his power to rule all things, he will change our simple bodies and make them like his own glorious body.

What the Christians are to Do

4 My dear brothers and sisters, I love you and want to see you. You bring me joy and make me proud of you, so stand strong in the Lord as I have told you.

2 I ask Euodia and Syntyche to agree in the Lord. 3 And I ask you, my faithful friend, to help these women. They served with me in telling the Good News, together with Clement and others who worked with me, whose names are written in the book of life."

4 Be full of joy in the Lord always. I will say again, be full of joy.

5 Let everyone see that you are gentle and kind. The Lord is coming soon. 6 Do not worry about anything, but pray and ask God for everything you need, always giving thanks. 7 And God's peace, which is so great we cannot understand it, will keep your hearts and minds in Christ Jesus.

8 Brothers and sisters, think about the things that are good and worthy of praise. Think about the things that are true and honourable and right and pure and beautiful and respected. 9 Do

4:8–9
Life
What should you be thinking about?

4:3 **book of life** God's book that has the names of all God's chosen people (Revelation 3:5; 21:27).

FAITH links

THOUGHTS ON THOUGHTS

PHILIPPIANS 4:8-9

Which is easier: to think good thoughts or bad thoughts? Sadly, thinking bad thoughts is easier. What are bad thoughts? Some include worrying over a problem, thoughts of revenge and other angry thoughts, and the ever-popular "what-ifs?" What-if thoughts are usually fears over what might be. For example, *What if I fail my maths test? What if no one likes me?* Thoughts like those can make you miserable. That's why the apostle Paul suggested that we think of what's true, honourable, right, pure, beautiful and respected. Thoughts like those can bring you peace.

Need help in controlling those thoughts? Connect here:

When You're Afraid, Genesis 32:9–12, p. 45

What's Out Becomes In, Judges 11, p. 327

Who Ya' Gonna Call? Psalm 3:4, p. 711

When Bad Things Happen, Ecclesiastes 3:16–17, p. 876

Who Needs Love? Luke 6:27–36, p. 1379

Keep On Keeping On, Revelation 13:10, p. 1744

FAITH links

AS STRONG AS SUPERMAN?
PHILIPPIANS 4:13

If you've ever worried about what you can't do, here is some good news. You have the strength to do anything! How is that possible? If you trust Jesus as your Saviour, you can "do all things". Although this does not mean you'll be able to lift a train, it does mean you can do things you didn't think were possible. What kinds of things? Well, you can forgive someone who hurt you. You can overcome your fears. You can even show love to an enemy. With Jesus, you can do it!

Want to do the impossible? Anything is possible with God. Check it out!

Alone and Forgotten? Genesis 40:23, p. 57

Moses' Champion, Numbers 12, p. 192

Get Hot or Keep Cool? Proverbs 12:16, p. 842

Don't Get Mad; Get Even? Matthew 26:57–63; 27:11–14, p. 1323

Mission Impossible? Mark 5:21–24, 35–43, p. 1337

A Friendly Welcome, Philemon 18, p. 1664

FAITH links

BUT I WANT IT?
PHILIPPIANS 4:19

Want to stop worrying about what you have or don't have? Then read what Paul says in this verse. God will give you everything you need. Before you head to the nearest shopping centre to buy, buy, buy, consider this: God will give you what you need, but those needs may not include your *wants*. Needs include food, clothing, shelter and so on. As for wants, well, you know what those are. You can trust that God will provide what you need.

Connect here to find out how God takes care of your needs:

Your Heavenly Parent, Exodus 2:1–10, p. 77

Listen Up! 1 Kings 19:11–13, p. 467

Lower Than Low, Job 19:13–25, p. 680

999, Psalm 28:6, p. 730

A Tight Spot, Jonah 2, p. 1215

Love for Free, Romans 5:8, p. 1524

Paul Thanks the Christians

10 I am very happy in the Lord that you have shown your care for me again. You continued to care about me, but there was no way for you to show it. 11 I am not telling you this because I need anything. I have learned to be satisfied with the things I have and with everything that happens. 12 I know how to live when I am

what you learned and received from me, what I told you, and what you saw me do. And the God who gives peace will be with you.

Philippians 4 **1616**

BEING CONTENT
Philippians 4:10–13

The Perfect Life! What would make your life perfect? Would it be having more things? Would it be living somewhere else or maybe having your brother or sister live somewhere else for a while? What keeps you from feeling satisfied (being content) with what you have?

Paul tells you how to be content with what you *do* have. You can do this by trusting God to give you everything you need. (Look at Philippians 4:19.) What is the difference between what you *want* and what you *need*?

MORE FAITH links

Complaints, Complaints!
p. 97

A Life of Thanksgiving,
p. 435

Wisdom About Wealth,
p. 878

Think About Him,
p. 926

More Money?
p. 1649

> Do you ever find yourself thinking, "If only I had a million pounds – then I could have whatever I wanted! And I could buy stuff for all my friends."
>
> Maybe you'd better surf over to these Faithlinks to find out the difference between wanting more and being happy with what you have.

When the Green-eyed Monster Strikes, 1 Samuel 18:6–9, p. 379
- Has someone ever compared you with someone else? Did the comparison make you feel good or bother you? Why?
- Jealousy is called the "green-eyed monster" because it can make us act like one. Have you ever been jealous? What did you do about it? You can always tell God how you feel, and he can help you be content.

A Need to Change, Ecclesiastes 1:1–11, p. 873
- What makes you bored and not content with your life? How do you act when you are bored? The next time you find life "Boooorrring!" think of how you can change the situation. What can you do to be more content?

Mission Impossible? Mark 5:21–24, 35–43, p. 1337
- Link here to discover how God handles hard problems and brings contentment.

poor, and I know how to live when I have plenty. I have learned the secret of being happy at any time in everything that happens, when I have enough to eat and when I go hungry, when I have more than I need and when I do not have enough. 13 I can do all things through Christ, because he gives me strength.

14 But it was good that you helped me when I needed it. 15 You Philippians remember when I first preached the Good News there. When I left Macedonia, you were the only church that gave me help. 16 Several times you sent me things I needed when I was in Thessalonica. 17 Really, it is not that I want to receive gifts from you, but I want you to have the good that comes from giving. 18 And now I have everything, and more. I have all I need, because Epaphroditus brought your gift to me. It is like a sweet-smelling sacrifice offered to God, who accepts that sacrifice and is pleased with it. 19 My God will use his wonderful riches in Christ Jesus to give you everything you need. 20 Glory to our God and Father for ever and ever! Amen.

21 Greet each of God's people in Christ. Those who are with me send greetings to you. 22 All of God's people greet you, particularly those from the palace of Caesar.

23 The grace of the Lord Jesus Christ be with you all.

Colossians

ONLY JESUS

Let's take a test to see if you know who I am. I was a well-known religious leader who hated Christians. One day, I met Jesus. After that, I became *the* spokesman for Jesus. Because of my message, I made a lot of people mad and spent a lot of time in jail. You got it! It's me, Paul. In fact, I wrote this letter from jail. (My friend Timothy helped me. Check out Colossians 1:1.) I never visited the church at Colosse, but I worked in Ephesus, about 100 miles away. Most likely, a young man named Epaphras heard the truth about Jesus and told others in Colosse. That's how news spread in those days.

The church in Colosse was having problems that were similar to those many other young churches were having – false teachings. In fact, the city was full of people teaching wrong things. Some taught that the human body was evil. Others were teaching that Christians should worship angels! So, I wrote this letter to my fellow believers to help them understand that the body isn't an evil thing and that we're supposed to worship only Jesus.

JESUS WATCH

In this book, Paul portrays Jesus as the ruler who is "over all rulers and powers". Paul presents Jesus as a "cosmic Christ" (in other words, he explains how Jesus is in charge of everything in the universe). How does he do this? He explains that Jesus existed before anything else (Colossians 1:17); he is the head of the church (Colossians 1:18); he is the risen Lord (Colossians 3:1). Paul's portrayal of Jesus as an all-powerful leader isn't so people would fear Jesus. Instead, Paul was out to prove to people that Jesus was everything they ever dreamed that he could be. We can trust Jesus because he was everything he said he was!

my FAVOURITE links

OTHER CONNECTIONS

Livin' it — What are the things you are most thankful for? Do you have a hard time remembering to say thank you? Connect to Thanks a Million! Colossians 2:6–7, to learn what the Bible has to say about having a gratitude attitude.

If you were to make a list of the top qualities you would like to develop, what would those be? Being smarter or more athletic? Being strong or being kind? When you become a Christian, God begins to work from the inside out to change you into the person he wants you to become. Check it out by linking to Out with the Old! Colossians 3:1–14.

MORE STUFF...

The New You Ever heard the expression "get a life"? In one sense that's what happens when you believe in Jesus – you get a *new* life and become a new person in Jesus. That means you need to get rid of the old way of doing things and do things that God wants you to do. Here are a few examples from Colossians 3:1–14:

- Get rid of being greedy and doing evil things.
- Get rid of bad tempers, doing or saying things to hurt others, and using bad language when you speak.
- Do be kind, gentle, humble and patient with others. Love each other!

Do you know who was in prison with Paul?

No? Check out the prisoner list in Colossians 4:10–14 to find out.

DOWNLOAD THESE AMAZING STORIES:

God's enemies, Colossians 1:21–23
By Jesus' rules, Colossians 2:16–23
A new life, Colossians 3:1–11

FAITH links

○ Prayer for a Friend, Colossians 1:9–12

○ Just Like a Tree, Colossians 1:23

○ Out with the Old! Colossians 3:1–14

○ With All Your Heart, Colossians 3:23

did you know?

Colossians 1:1

1 From Paul, an apostle of Christ Jesus. I am an apostle because that is what God wanted. Also from Timothy, our brother.

2 To the holy and faithful brothers and sisters[n] in Christ that live in Colosse:

Grace and peace to you from God our Father.

3 In our prayers for you we always thank God, the Father of our Lord Jesus Christ, 4 because we have heard about the faith you have in Christ Jesus and the love you have for all of God's people. 5 You have this faith and love because of your hope, and what you hope for is kept safe for you in heaven. You learned about this hope when you heard the message about the truth, the Good News 6 that was told to you. Everywhere in the world that Good News is bringing blessings and is growing. This has happened with you too, since you heard the Good News and understood the truth about the grace of God. 7 You learned about God's grace from Epaphras, whom we love. He works together with us and is a faithful servant of Christ for us. 8 He also told us about the love you have from the Holy Spirit.

9 Because of this, since the day we heard about you, we have continued praying for you, asking God that you will know fully what he wants. We pray that you will also have great wisdom and understanding in spiritual things 10 so that you will live the kind of life that honours and pleases the Lord in every way. You will produce fruit in every good work and grow in the knowledge of God. 11 God will strengthen you with his own great power so that you will not give up when troubles come, but you will be patient. 12 And you will joyfully give thanks to the Father who has made you able to have a share in all that he has prepared for his people in the kingdom of light. 13 God has freed us from the power of darkness and brought us into the kingdom of his dear Son. 14 The Son paid for our sins, and in him we have forgiveness.

1:2 brothers and sisters Although the Greek text says "brothers" here and throughout this book, Paul's words were meant for the entire church, both men and women.

FAITH links

PRAYER FOR A FRIEND
COLOSSIANS 1:9-12

If you were to pray for a friend, what would you ask God for? In his letter to the Christians in the city of Colosse, Paul prayed that they would have God's best. What was God's best? He prayed that they would have wisdom and understanding. He also prayed that they would know what God wanted them to do for him.

Paul was glad to pray for the Colossian Christians since he could not be with them. He knew that God would always take care of them. The best thing you can do for a friend is to pray for them and ask for God's wisdom and strength for them.

God really wants to help your friends. Connect here to find out more:

What He's Really Like, Deuteronomy 4:15–20, p. 233

A Long Wait, Joshua 14:6–15, p. 294

Learning from Mistakes, Psalm 51:12–13, p. 748

You've Got the Power! Acts 1:1–8; 2:1–4, p. 1463

The Finished Product, Philippians 1:6, p. 1609

Pay Attention! Hebrews 2:1, p. 1668

Colossians 1:27 **1621**

The Importance of Christ

15 No one can see God, but Jesus Christ is exactly like him. He ranks higher than everything that has been made. 16 Through his power all things were made—things in heaven and on earth, things seen and unseen, all powers, authorities, lords and rulers. All things were made through Christ and for Christ. 17 He was there before anything was made, and all things continue because of him. 18 He is the head of the body, which is the church. Everything comes from him. He is the first one who was raised from the dead. So in all things Jesus has first place. 19 God was pleased for all of himself to live in Christ. 20 And through Christ, God has brought all things back to himself again—things on earth and things in heaven. God made peace through the blood of Christ's death on the cross.

**1:15–16
Jesus**
Did Jesus create the world?

21 At one time you were separated from God. You were his enemies in your minds, and the evil things you did were against God. 22 But now God has made you his friends again. He did this through Christ's death in the body so that he might bring you into God's presence as people who are holy, with no wrong, and with nothing of which God can judge you guilty. 23 This will happen if you continue strong and sure in your faith. You must not be moved away from the hope brought to you by the Good News that you heard. That same Good News has been told to everyone in the world, and I, Paul, help in preaching that Good News.

Paul's Work for the Church

24 I am happy in my sufferings for you. There are things that Christ must still suffer through his body, the church. I am accepting, in my body, my part of these things that must be suffered. 25 I became a servant of the church because God gave me a special work to do that helps you, and that work is to tell fully the message of God. 26 This message is the secret that was hidden from everyone since the beginning of time, but now it is made known to God's holy people. 27 God decided to let his people know this rich

---

FAITH links

JUST LIKE A TREE

COLOSSIANS 1:23

A seed or plant needs to be placed deeply enough in the ground to allow it to take root and grow. Shallow soil won't let the roots grow deeply enough, resulting in a weak plant. A tree with strong, healthy roots is hard to move.

Paul wanted the Christians in the city of Colosse to have strong, deeply rooted faith. How can you have that kind of faith? Reading the Bible, praying and learning from other Christians can help. As you grow older, your faith will be stronger. Pray that God will continue to grow your faith deep and strong.

Here are more Faithlinks on growing faith as strong as a tree:

A Life of Thanksgiving, 1 Kings 1:47–48, p. 435

An Admirable Quality, 1 Kings 10:1–13, p. 451

Bragging Rights, Jeremiah 9:23–24, p. 1005

The Best Advice, Zechariah 10:2, p. 1261

Best Seat in the House, Luke 14:7–11, p. 1398

How Do You Grow? Titus 1:1, p. 1659

and glorious secret which he has for all people. This secret is Christ himself, who is in you. He is our only hope for glory. 28 So we continue to preach Christ to each person, using all wisdom to warn and to teach everyone, in order to bring each one into God's presence as a mature person in Christ. 29 To do this, I work and struggle, using Christ's great strength that works so powerfully in me.

2 I want you to know how hard I work for you, those in Laodicea, and others who have never seen me. 2 I want them to be strengthened and joined together with love so that they may be rich in their understanding. This leads to their knowing fully God's secret, that is, Christ himself. 3 In him all the treasures of wisdom and knowledge are safely kept.

4 I say this so that no one can fool you by arguments that seem good, but are false. 5 Though I am absent from you in my body, my heart is with you, and I am happy to see your good lives and your strong faith in Christ.

Continue to Live in Christ

6 As you received Christ Jesus the Lord, so continue to live in him. 7 Keep your roots deep in him and have your lives built on him. Be strong in the faith, just as you were taught, and always be thankful.

2:7 Perseverance — How should you live?

8 Be sure that no one leads you away with false and empty teaching that is only human, which comes from the ruling spirits of this world, and not from Christ. 9 All of God lives in Christ fully (even when Christ was on earth), 10 and you have a full and true life in Christ, who is ruler over all rulers and powers.

11 Also in Christ you had a different kind of circumcision, a circumcision not done by hands. It was through Christ's circumcision, that is, his death, that you were made free from the power of your sinful self. 12 When you were baptised, you were buried with Christ, and you were raised up with him through your faith in God's power that was shown when he raised Christ from the dead. 13 When you were spiritually dead because of your sins and because you were not free from the power of your sinful self, God made you alive with Christ, and he forgave all our sins. 14 He cancelled the debt, which listed all the rules we failed to follow. He took away that record with its rules and nailed it to the cross. 15 God stripped the spiritual rulers and powers of their authority. With the cross, he won the victory and showed the world that they were powerless.

Don't Follow People's Rules

16 So do not let anyone make rules for you about eating and drinking or about a religious feast, a New Moon Festival or a Sabbath day. 17 These things were like a shadow of what was to come. But what is true and real has come and is found in Christ. 18 Do not let anyone disqualify you by making you humiliate yourself and worship angels. Such people enter into visions, which fill them with foolish pride because of their human way of thinking. 19 They do not hold tightly to Christ, the head. It is from him that all the parts of the body are cared for and held together. So it grows in the way God wants it to grow.

20 Since you died with Christ and were made free from the ruling spirits of the world, why do you act as if you still belong to this world by following rules like these: 21 "Don't eat this", "Don't taste that", "Don't even touch that thing"? 22 These rules refer to earthly things that are gone as soon as they are used. They are only man-made commands and teachings. 23 They seem to be wise, but they are only part of a man-made religion. They make people pretend not to be proud and make them punish their bodies, but they do not really control the evil desires of the sinful self.

Your New Life in Christ

3 Since you were raised from the dead with Christ, aim at what is in heaven, where Christ is sitting at the right hand of God. 2 Think only about the things in heaven, not the things on earth. 3 Your

BEING THANKFUL
Colossians 2:6–7

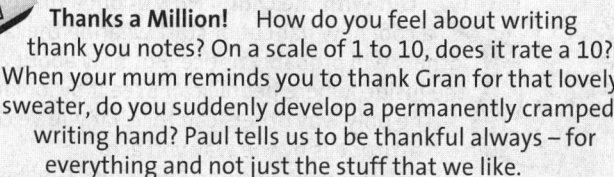

Thanks a Million! How do you feel about writing thank you notes? On a scale of 1 to 10, does it rate a 10? When your mum reminds you to thank Gran for that lovely sweater, do you suddenly develop a permanently cramped writing hand? Paul tells us to be thankful always – for everything and not just the stuff that we like.

Things aren't the only items we should be thankful for. God also wants us to be thankful for the people in our lives who love and help us. (Read 1 Thessalonians 1:1–3, p. 1630.) Who are the people in your life you are thankful for? Why are you thankful for them? Tell them how you feel – how about saying, "Thanks a million!"

MORE FAITH links

A Thanksgiving Reminder, **p. 91**

A Life of Thanksgiving, **p. 435**

Gratitude Attitude, **p. 611**

A Holiday Letter, **p. 657**

Thanks for a Friend, **p. 1630**

Who are you most thankful for?

Are you thankful for all your friends and family, and all the nice things you have?

Those are all good things to be thankful for. Here are some other thoughts on things to be thankful for. Check them out!

A Song of Thanks, 1 Samuel 2, p. 356
- When you're feeling thankful, how do you show it? What are you thankful to God for? Link here to join Hannah in a song of thanks.

No Thanksgiving? 2 Kings 23:21–23, p. 512
- Can you imagine what it would be like if everyone waited until the end of the year to say thanks for things that they'd been given? Pretty strange, huh? But you don't need to wait for a special day to be thankful. What are some ways you show thankfulness to God every day – 365 days a year?

Ten Things I Like About You, 2 Thessalonians 1:3–4, p. 1638
- Have you ever bragged to someone else about what a friend could do? What did you tell them about your friend? Why did you do it?
- How has God helped someone you know? How will you thank God for his help? How will you let that person know that you're proud of them?

my FAVOURITE links

Colossians 3 1624

GENTLENESS
Colossians 3:1–14

Livin' it

Out with the Old! How about a makeover? If you get a cool new haircut or start wearing the latest styles, others will probably notice. But how about a makeover on the inside, where people can't see it by looking at you? The only way others can tell that you've changed your attitude is by the way you act.

When we become Christians, God begins to change us, starting from the inside out. We need to get rid of stuff like anger, jealousy and bad attitudes. God helps make us over with better stuff – like patience, kindness and gentleness. (Check out Colossians 3:1–14.) What kind of an inside makeover do you need? What new attitudes and actions will take the place of the old ones?

MORE FAITH links
- Just Kidding? **p. 28**
- Help for the Hurting, **p. 666**
- A Gentle Answer, **p. 847**
- The Right Ingredients, **p. 1227**
- Kindness First, **p. 1290**
- I'll Be the Judge! **p. 1549**

It's not much good wearing great clothes and looking really fab if the way we talk about people is horrid!

Being thoughtful to others – that's what really counts. Check it out in these Faithlinks.

Who Needs Love? Luke 6:27–36, p. 1379
- Who needs your love, kindness and gentleness the most? Link here to find out how Jesus answers that question.

Most Wanted? 2 Corinthians 10:1, p. 1580
- What are the Top 10 qualities you admire most in a person? What makes you really like someone? Is it someone who is a leader or someone who is always funny? Link here to discover which qualities made Paul's Top 10 list. You may be surprised!

The Gentle Way, Titus 3:1–5, p. 1661
- What's the first thing you think of doing when your brother or sister says something mean to you? Do you ever think of being kind and gentle? Showing kindness instead of getting back at someone isn't always easy. How can you do this the next time someone annoys you?

my FAVOURITE links

old sinful self has died, and your new life is kept with Christ in God. 4 Christ is our life, and when he comes again, you will share in his glory.

5 So put all evil things out of your life: sexual sinning, doing evil, letting evil thoughts control you, wanting things that are evil and greed. This is really serving a false god. 6 These things make God angry." 7 In your past, evil life you also did these things.

8 But now also put these things out of your life: anger, bad temper, doing or saying things to hurt others and using evil words when you talk. 9 Do not lie to each other. You have left your old sinful life and the things you did before. 10 You have begun to live the new life, in which you are being made new and are becoming like the One who made you. This new life brings you the true knowledge of God. 11 In the new life there is no difference between Greeks and Jews, those who are circumcised and those who are not circumcised, or people who are foreigners, or Scythians." There is no difference between slaves and free people. But Christ is in all believers, and Christ is all that is important.

12 God has chosen you and made you his holy people. He loves you. So always do these things: show mercy to others, be kind, humble, gentle and patient. 13 Get along with each other, and forgive each other. If someone does wrong to you, forgive that person because the Lord forgave you. 14 Do all these things; but most important, love each other. Love is what holds you all together in perfect unity. 15 Let the peace that Christ gives control your thinking, because you were all called together in one body" to have peace. Always be thankful. 16 Let the teaching of Christ live in you richly. Use all wisdom to teach and instruct each other by singing psalms, hymns and spiritual songs with thankfulness in your hearts to God.

3:8–9 Life Check out some things you shouldn't do.

3:16 Music Why should you make music?

FAITH links

OUT WITH THE OLD!
COLOSSIANS 3:1-14

When we become Christians, God begins to change us, starting from the inside out. There are certain things we have to get rid of – like anger and jealousy and bad attitudes. When we get rid of those things, God can begin to make us new and help us do the right things – like being patient and kind with others; getting along and, above all else, loving others as Jesus loves us.

What attitudes do you need to get rid of? Connect here:

A Shortcut, 1 Samuel 13:1–14, p. 369

Give In or Take a Stand? 1 Kings 22:13–14, p. 472

A Memorial for Two Thieves, 1 Chronicles 7:21, p. 530

Patience, Please, Psalm 145:8–9, p. 819

A Direct Path, Proverbs 3:5–6, p. 829

Kindness First, Matthew 9:35–36, p. 1290

17 Everything you do or say should be done to obey Jesus your Lord. And in all you do, give thanks to God the Father through Jesus.

3:6 These . . . angry Some Greek copies add: "against the people who do not obey God".
3:11 Scythians The Scythians were known as very wild and cruel people.
3:15 body The spiritual body of Christ, meaning the church or his people.

FAITH links

WITH ALL YOUR HEART
COLOSSIANS 3:23

What are some tasks that you find hardest to do? Homework? Chores? When you're faced with a task you don't particularly like, what do you do? Some of us tend to work half-heartedly, just trying to get the chore done. Sometimes we even complain about having to do the work in the first place. Are you ever tempted to do that?

God wants you to do everything with your best effort, no matter what you do. Keeping Jesus in mind as you work will help you put your whole heart into what you do. That was Paul's advice to the Colossian Christians — and for you.

Need an attitude adjustment on doing your best?
Link here:

Everyone Can Help, Numbers 4, p. 181

Operation Co-operation, Ezra 1:5, p. 609

Down on the Ant Farm, Proverbs 6:6–11, p. 833

Love for a Lifetime, Song of Solomon 6:8–9, p. 891

The Gift of Worship, Matthew 2:10–12, p. 1275

Better Than Some? Luke 18:9–14, p. 1405

Your New Life with Other People

18 Wives, yield to the authority of your husbands, because this is the right thing to do in the Lord.

19 Husbands, love your wives and be gentle with them.

20 Children, obey your parents in all things, because this pleases the Lord.

21 Fathers, do not nag your children. If you are too hard to please, they may want to stop trying.

22 Slaves, obey your masters in all things. Do not obey just when they are watching you, to gain their favour, but serve them honestly, because you respect the Lord. 23 In all the work you are doing, work the best you can. Work as if you were doing it for the Lord, not for people. 24 Remember that you will receive your reward from the Lord, which he promised to his people. You are serving the Lord Christ. 25 But remember that anyone who does wrong will be punished for that wrong, and the Lord treats everyone the same.

4 Masters, give what is good and fair to your slaves. Remember that you have a Master in heaven.

What the Christians are to Do

2 Continue praying, keeping alert and always thanking God. 3 Also pray for us that God will give us an opportunity to tell people his message. Pray that we can preach the secret that God has made known about Christ. This is why I am in prison. 4 Pray that I can speak in a way that will make it clear, as I should.

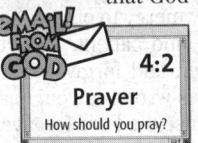
4:2 Prayer
How should you pray?

5 Be wise in the way you act with people who are not believers, making the most of every opportunity. 6 When you talk, you should always be kind and pleasant so you will be able to answer everyone in the way you should.

4:6 Witnessing
What should your words reflect?

News About the People with Paul

7 Tychicus is my dear brother in Christ and a faithful minister and servant with me in the Lord. He will tell you all the things that are happening to me. 8 This is why I am sending him: so you may know how we are and he may encourage you. 9 I send him with Onesimus, a faithful and dear brother in Christ, and one of your group. They will tell you all that has happened here.

10 Aristarchus, a prisoner with me, and Mark, the cousin of Barnabas, greet you. (I have already told you what to do about Mark. If he comes, welcome him.) 11 Jesus, who is called Justus, also greets you. These are the only Jewish believers who work with me for the kingdom of God, and they have been a comfort to me.

12 Epaphras, a servant of Jesus Christ, from your group, also greets you. He always prays for you that you will grow to be spiritually mature and have everything God wants for you. 13 I know he has worked hard for you and the people in Laodicea and in Hierapolis. 14 Demas and our dear friend Luke, the doctor, greet you.

15 Greet the brothers in Laodicea. And greet Nympha and the church that meets in her house. 16 After this letter is read to you, be sure it is also read to the church in Laodicea. And you read the letter that I wrote to Laodicea. 17 Tell Archippus, "Be sure to finish the work the Lord gave you."

18 I, Paul, greet you and write this with my own hand. Remember me in prison. Grace be with you.

1 Thessalonians

JESUS WILL RETURN!

Hi, it's Paul again. You're about to read one of the first letters I wrote after I became a follower of Jesus. I actually began the church in Thessalonica (a city in Greece). I spent three Sabbath days preaching in the Jewish place of worship, called a synagogue. (For more on synagogues, connect to Mark 6, p. 1338.) When the Jewish people wouldn't believe what I was saying, I went to the non-Jewish people and preached to them. I did this a lot. I told everybody I could about the change that Jesus had made in my life.

Thessalonica was a seaport city with nearly 200,000 people in it. That is a big city! You can imagine all of the different types of beliefs that were circulating through that city. I wrote this letter to help believers there understand one key truth – the promised return of Jesus. You see, some people were spreading rumours that Jesus had *already* returned. So I wrote to them to give them all of the facts that I could about Jesus' return. Jesus *is* coming, but he hasn't come yet!

JESUS WATCH

Guess what. You can count on Jesus returning. He promised it. The Old Testament even promised it. Much of the portrayal of Jesus in this book focuses on the fact that Jesus is coming back. He's presented as the believer's hope and our deliverer (1 Thessalonians 1:10). Paul spends most of his time in this book helping the Thessalonians understand that Jesus *is* returning. And when Jesus comes back, all who believe in him will experience the most incredible homecoming ever! We *will* see Jesus again!

my FAVORITE links

OTHER CONNECTIONS

Livin' it — How good are you at waiting for things? Can you sit quietly or do you get fidgety? Download Let Me Do It! 1 Thessalonians 5, to find out how good you are at waiting for things — and what it takes to be good at the waiting game.

Get the Info

- Let's Visit Thessalonica, 1 Thessalonians 3. Do you know who the city of Thessalonica was named after? Connect here to find out the answer and more about this ancient Greek city that still exists today.

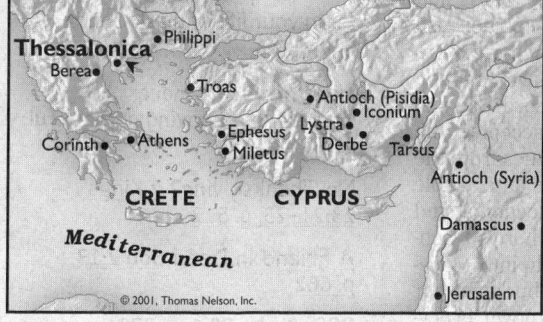

FAITH links

○ Thanks for a Friend, **1 Thessalonians 1:1–3**

○ Full of Faith, **1 Thessalonians 4:1**

○ The Coming Attraction, **1 Thessalonians 4:13–18**

○ Always Do This! **1 Thessalonians 5:16–18**

Do you think we'll know when Jesus comes back?

Download 1 Thessalonians 4:13–18 to see what will happen.

did you know?

MORE COOL SITES TO CHECK OUT:
Paul's pride and joy, 1 Thessalonians 2:17–20
A life that pleases God, 1 Thessalonians 4:1–12
Get ready for Jesus, 1 Thessalonians 5:1–11

1 From Paul, Silas and Timothy.
To the church in Thessalonica, the church in God the Father and the Lord Jesus Christ:
Grace and peace to you.

The Faith of the Thessalonians

2 We always thank God for all of you and mention you when we pray. 3 We continually recall before God our Father the things you have done because of your faith and the work you have done because of your love. And we thank him that you continue to be strong because of your hope in our Lord Jesus Christ.

4 Brothers and sisters,[n] God loves you, and we know he has chosen you, 5 because the Good News we brought to you came not only with words, but with power, with the Holy Spirit and with sure knowledge that it is true. Also you know how we lived when we were with you in order to help you. 6 And you became like us and like the Lord. You suffered much, but still you accepted the teaching with the joy that comes from the Holy Spirit. 7 So you became an example to all the believers in Macedonia and Southern Greece. 8 And the Lord's teaching spread from you not only into Macedonia and Southern Greece, but now your faith in God has become known everywhere. So we do not need to say anything about it. 9 People everywhere are telling about the way you accepted us when we were there with you. They tell how you stopped worshipping idols and began serving the living and true God. 10 And you wait for God's Son, whom God raised from the dead, to come from heaven. He is Jesus, who saves us from God's angry judgement that is sure to come.

1:4–5 Good News Does believing in the Good News help you?

Paul's Work in Thessalonica

2 Brothers and sisters, you know our visit to you was not a failure. 2 Before we came to you, we suffered in Philippi. People there insulted us, as you know, and many people were against us. But our God helped us to be brave and to tell you

---

FAITH links

THANKS FOR A FRIEND
1 THESSALONIANS 1:1-3

For whom are you thankful? Each time Paul wrote a letter to a group of Christians, he mentioned how thankful he was for them. In this letter to Christians in Thessalonica, Paul spoke for Silas and Timothy, two missionaries who travelled with him. Not only were they thankful, they also prayed for the Thessalonian Christians.

It's great to be thankful to God for the people in our lives. Think of the people you are thankful for in your life and ask God to help them.

Here are some more Faithlinks on having a thankful attitude:

No Thanksgiving? 2 Kings 23:21–23, p. 512

A Friend in Deed, Job 2:13, p. 662

999, Psalm 28:6, p. 730

A Fair-weather Friend, Obadiah 7, p. 1209

An Encouraging Word, 1 Corinthians 1:3–5, p. 1545

Always Do This! 1 Thessalonians 5:16–18, p. 1636

1:4 Brothers and sisters Although the Greek text says "Brothers" here and throughout this book, Paul's words were meant for the entire church, both men and women.

1 Thessalonians 2:19

> **FAITH CHALLENGE**
>
> Try this challenge. Read 2:2 to find out what happened to Paul in Philippi. What would you do if you saw kids making fun of one of your Christian friends at school?
>
> ## Testing it
>
> **1 Thessalonians 2:2**
> Before we came to you, we suffered in Philippi. People there insulted us, as you know, and many people were against us. But our God helped us to be brave and to tell you his Good News.

his Good News. 3 Our appeal does not come from lies or wrong reasons, nor were we trying to trick you. 4 But we speak the Good News because God tested us and trusted us to do it. When we speak, we are not trying to please people, but God, who tests our hearts. 5 You know that we never tried to influence you by saying nice things about you. We were not trying to get your money; we had no selfishness to hide from you. God knows that this is true. 6 We were not looking for human praise, from you or anyone else, 7 even though as apostles of Christ we could have used our authority over you.

But we were very gentle with you, like a mother caring for her little children. 8 Because we loved you, we were happy to share not only God's Good News with you, but even our own lives. You had become so dear to us! 9 Brothers and sisters, I know you remember our hard work and difficulties. We worked night and day so we would not burden any of you while we preached God's Good News to you.

10 When we were with you, we lived in a holy and honest way, without fault. You know this is true, and so does God. 11 You know that we treated each of you as a father treats his own children. 12 We encouraged you, we told you and we insisted that you live good lives for God, who calls you to his glorious kingdom.

13 Also, we always thank God because when you heard his message from us, you accepted it as the word of God, not the words of humans. And it really is God's message which works in you who believe. 14 Brothers and sisters, your experiences have been like those of God's churches in Christ that are in Judea.*n* You suffered from the people of your own country, as they suffered from the Jews, 15 who killed both the Lord Jesus and the prophets and forced us to leave that country. They do not please God and are against all people. 16 They try to stop us from teaching those who are not Jews so they may be saved. By doing this, they are increasing their sins to the limit. The anger of God has come to them at last.

2:13 Belief
How is God able to work through you?

Paul Wants to Visit Them Again

17 Brothers and sisters, though we were separated from you for a short time, our thoughts were still with you. We wanted very much to see you and tried hard to do so. 18 We wanted to come to you. I, Paul, tried to come more than once, but Satan stopped us. 19 You are our hope, our joy and the crown we will take

---

2:14 Judea The Jewish land where Jesus lived and taught and where the church first began.

1 Thessalonians 2:20 1632

LET'S VISIT THESSALONICA   1 Thessalonians 3

Thessalonica was founded by the Macedonian king Cassander in 315 B.C. He named the city after his wife (she was the sister of the Greek military conqueror, Alexander the Great). The apostle Paul worked for several months in Thessalonica and later wrote two letters, which we now call 1 and 2 Thessalonians, to the church there. Paul visited Thessalonica during his second missionary journey through Macedonia. (Check out Acts 17:1–9, p. 1495.) He loved the Thessalonian church. (See 1 Thessalonians 2:1–12, p. 1630.)

An important road in Thessalonica was called the Egnatian Way. It was a Roman military highway. Today Thessalonica is called Salonika. The Egnatian Way is still one of the main roads.

---

pride in when our Lord Jesus Christ comes. 20 Truly you are our glory and our joy.

3 When we could not wait any longer, we decided it was best to stay in Athens alone 2 and send Timothy to you. Timothy, our brother, works with us for God and helps us tell people the Good News about Christ. We sent him to strengthen and encourage you in your faith 3 so none of you would be upset by these troubles. You yourselves know that we must face these troubles. 4 Even when we were with you, we told you we all would have to suffer, and you know it has happened. 5 Because of this, when I could wait no longer, I sent Timothy to you so I could learn about your faith. I was afraid the devil had tempted you, and then our hard work would have been wasted.

6 But Timothy now has come back to us from you and has brought us good news about your faith and love. He told us that you always remember us in a good way and that you want to see us just as much as we want to see you. 7 So, brothers and sisters, while we have much trouble and suffering, we are encouraged about you because of your faith. 8 Our life is really full if you stand strong in the Lord. 9 We have so much joy before our God because of you. We cannot thank him enough for all the joy we feel. 10 Night and day we continue praying with all our heart that we can see you again and give you all the things you need to make your faith strong.

11 Now may our God and Father himself and our Lord Jesus prepare the way for us to come to you. 12 May the Lord make your love grow more and multiply for each other and for all people so that you will love others as we love you. 13 May your hearts be made strong so that you will be holy and without fault before our God and Father when our Lord Jesus comes with all his holy ones.

A Life that Pleases God

4 Brothers and sisters, we taught you how to live in a way that will please God, and you are living that way. Now we ask and encourage you in the Lord Jesus to live that way even more. 2 You know what we told you to do by the authority of the Lord Jesus. 3 God wants you to be

FAITH links

FULL OF FAITH
1 THESSALONIANS 4:1

Who is your favourite teacher? Many people have said that their favourite teacher happened to be the one who was the strictest. Why? Because that teacher knew what her student could do. She wanted the best for that student and made sure he lived up to his potential.

Paul had taught the Christians in Thessalonica about God and how to please him. He knew that they were capable of doing great things for God. He wanted them to live up to that potential. That's what the people at your church want for you. Your pastor or your Sunday school teacher wants you to grow in faith and reach your full faith potential.

Help for the Poor, Leviticus 5:7, p. 138

Plans for a Son, 1 Chronicles 22:5–19, p. 548

How Big Is God? Job 38—41, p. 703

What's in a Name? Isaiah 9:6, p. 908

Help for a Friend, Mark 2:1–5, p. 1332

You're Correct! Hebrews 12:5–7, p. 1683

---

holy and to stay away from sexual sins. 4 He wants each of you to learn to control your own body*n* in a way that is holy and honourable. 5 Don't use your body for sexual sin like the people who do not know God. 6 Also, do not wrong or cheat another Christian in this way. The Lord will punish people who do those things as we have already told you and warned you. 7 God called us to be holy and does not want us to live in sin. 8 So the person who refuses to obey this teaching is disobeying God, not simply a human teaching. And God is the One who gives us his Holy Spirit.

9 We do not need to write to you about having love for your Christian family, because God has already taught you to love each other. 10 And truly you do love the Christians in all of Macedonia. Brothers and sisters, now we encourage you to love them even more.

11 Do all you can to live a peaceful life. Take care of your own business, and do your own work as we have already told you. 12 If you do, then people who are not believers will respect you, and you will not have to depend on others for what you need.

EMAIL FROM GOD
4:11 Life
What should you take care of?

The Lord's Coming

13 Brothers and sisters, we want you to know about those Christians who have died so you will not be sad, as others who have no hope. 14 We believe that Jesus died and that he rose again. So, because of him, God will raise with Jesus those who have died. 15 What we tell you now is the Lord's own message. We who are living when the Lord comes again will not go before those who have already died. 16 The Lord himself will come down from heaven with a loud command, with the voice of the archangel*n* and with the trumpet call of God. And those who have died believing in Christ will rise first. 17 After that, we who are still alive will be gathered up with them in the clouds to meet the Lord in the air. And we will be

---

4:4 learn . . . body This might also mean "learn to live with your own wife."
4:16 archangel The leader among God's angels or messengers.

FAITH links

THE COMING ATTRACTION
1 THESSALONIANS 4:13-18

You've seen film trailers, right? They're those mini-movies that are shown right before the main feature. They pump up your excitement about a film that "is coming to a theatre near you soon!" This passage is like a "trailer" for Jesus' return to earth. Before he left, Jesus promised that he would come back someday. Paul wanted to remind the Christians in Thessalonica of the wonderful future in store for Christians. When the Lord returns, all believers, even those who have died, will be with Jesus. That was encouraging news then and now.

Download these Faithlinks on your wonderful future:

His Valentine, Jeremiah 31:3, p. 1035

God's New Temple, Ezekiel 40—44, p. 1135

A Hopeful Name, Hosea 1:3–11, p. 1172

A Word About Worry, Matthew 6:25–34, p. 1284

Fully God, Fully Human, John 11:35, p. 1444

Hope That Doesn't Fail, Acts 26:4–7, p. 1510

---

with the Lord for ever. 18 So encourage each other with these words.

Be Ready for the Lord's Coming

5 Now, brothers and sisters, we do not need to write to you about times and dates. 2 You know very well that the day the Lord comes again will be a surprise, like a thief that comes in the night. 3 While people are saying, "We have peace and we are safe," they will be destroyed quickly. It is like pains that come quickly to a woman having a baby. Those people will not escape. 4 But you, brothers and sisters, are not living in darkness, and so that day will not surprise you like a thief. 5 You are all people who belong to the light and to the day. We do not belong to the night or to darkness. 6 So we should not be like other people who are sleeping, but we should be awake and have self-control. 7 Those who sleep, sleep at night. Those who get drunk, get drunk at night. 8 But we belong to the day, so we should control ourselves. We should wear faith and love to protect us, and the hope of salvation should be our helmet. 9 God did not choose us to suffer his anger but to have salvation through our Lord Jesus Christ. 10 Jesus died for us so that we can live together with him, whether we are alive or dead when he comes. 11 So encourage each other and give each other strength, just as you are doing now.

Final Instructions and Greetings

12 Now, brothers and sisters, we ask you to appreciate those who work hard among you, who lead you in the Lord and teach you. 13 Respect them with a very special love because of the work they do.

Live in peace with each other. 14 We ask you, brothers and sisters, to warn those who do not work. Encourage the people who are afraid. Help those who are weak. Be patient with

---

EMAIL FROM GOD

4:13–18 Pain
Check out how to treat each other in times of pain.

EMAIL FROM GOD

5:12–14 Laziness
Who should you encourage to work?

PATIENCE
1 Thessalonians 5

Let Me Do It! Suppose you're baking a cake for your mum, and your six-year-old sister is helping. She takes *for ever* to measure out things, and she stirs in slow motion. How patient would you be? Would you wait or take over? What things or people make you the most impatient? When are you the most patient?

Fortunately for us, God is very patient. Even when we make the same mistakes over and over, God patiently loves us and forgives us. He wants us to be patient, too. Sometimes that means waiting a long, long time. (Look at Luke 2:25–28, 36–37, p. 1369.) How do you feel about waiting for something? Does it drive you nuts? Waiting helps to develop patience within you – and that doesn't just happen overnight.

MORE FAITH links

I Want It *Now!* p. 332

A Shortcut, p. 369

Exercising Patience, p. 1369

At the Right Time, p. 1590

His Best Qualities, p. 1711

While You Wait, p. 1726

> Sometimes we can get so excited waiting for something that we can hardly sit still. We get all jittery and have butterflies in our stomachs.
>
> This is when a bit of patience is called for. You could always surf over to these Faithlinks while you're waiting! It may just help.

A Long Wait, Joshua 14:6–15, p. 294
- How do you feel when you have to wait 40 minutes for something? How about 40 days? Or 40 weeks? Now imagine having to wait 40 years to get something you were promised? Would you wait or give up? Link here to find out that God always keeps his promises – even though you may have to wait.

Hurry Up and Wait, 2 Samuel 5, p. 405
- How would you rate yourself on the patience scale (1=not at all patient; 10= very patient)? One way to become more patient is to try not to predict when something is going to happen. How can trusting in God's timing help you?

A Happy Ending, Revelation 22:16–21, p. 1754
- Do you like stories with happy endings? Want to know a real-life story that has a guaranteed happy ending? It's your story if you trust Jesus as your Saviour. Christians wait patiently for the day when their life story will have a happy ending as they live with Jesus in heaven. Do you look forward to Jesus' return?

my FAVOURITE links

everyone. 15 Be sure that no one pays back wrong for wrong, but always try to do what is good for each other and for all people.

16 Always be joyful. 17 Pray continually, 18 and give thanks whatever happens. That is what God wants for you in Christ Jesus.

19 Do not hold back the work of the Holy Spirit. 20 Do not treat prophecy as if it were unimportant. 21 But test everything. Keep what is good, 22 and stay away from everything that is evil.

23 Now may God himself, the God of peace, make you pure, belonging only to him. May your whole self—spirit, soul and body—be kept safe and without fault when our Lord Jesus Christ comes. 24 You can trust the One who calls you to do that for you.

25 Brothers and sisters, pray for us.

26 Give each other a holy kiss when you meet. 27 I tell you by the authority of the Lord to read this letter to all the believers.

28 The grace of our Lord Jesus Christ be with you.

FAITH links

ALWAYS DO THIS!
1 THESSALONIANS 5:16-18

What are some things you always do, besides breathing? Do you laugh a lot? Sing? Complain? Some actions probably depend on what's happening in your life. If you're feeling sick, you may not feel like laughing.

Paul gave the Christians in Thessalonica three activities to always do: be joyful, pray, give thanks. That's good advice for us, too. Does this mean you have to be joyful or thank God if someone steals your bike? No. It means having an attitude of thanks. It means being joyful that God is with you always. That's something to always be thankful for!

Check out all you have to be thankful for:

A Thanksgiving Reminder, Exodus 12, p. 91

A Life of Thanksgiving, 1 Kings 1:47–48, p. 435

A Wise Wish, 1 Kings 3:5–9, p. 439

Love That Will Last, Psalm 136, p. 813

Our Gift to God, Romans 12:1–2, p. 1536

A Different Kind of Fruit, Galatians 5:22–23, p. 1592

2 Thessalonians

JESUS' RETURN – PART TWO

It's Paul here. This is my second letter to my friends at Thessalonica (a city that's located in Greece), written about six months after the first letter. I loved the church at Thessalonica. I started this church as part of my desire to tell everyone about who I used to be – a Jewish religious leader who hated Christians. (To find out how the church got started, surf over to 1 Thessalonians, p. 1628.) After Jesus had changed my life, I wanted everyone to know that he could do the same for them.

My pals in Thessalonica were *still* having trouble understanding when Jesus would return. In my first letter to them (check it out if you haven't read it yet), I tried to help them understand that Jesus had *not* returned yet ('cos they were being told that he *had* returned). Well, now they were believing that Jesus would return soon, and they didn't have to do anything . . . just sit around and wait! Imagine, believers in the city weren't going to work or anything. Not a cool scene! So, I wrote this letter to help them understand (again) when Jesus would return.

JESUS WATCH

Seeing Jesus in this letter is a lot like seeing Jesus in Paul's first letter to the Thessalonians. Jesus' return is portrayed as something that believers can trust in and look forward to. But Paul also helps his readers understand the other side of Jesus' return. Those who haven't received Jesus as Saviour have an entirely different event awaiting them. People who don't know Jesus can expect terrifying things to happen to them. (Check out 2 Thessalonians 1:6–10 and 2:8–12 for the details on this.)

Jesus is presented as someone believers can trust. Unbelievers must surrender to him or prepare for an unpleasant awakening at his return. But Paul's aim isn't to strike depression in the lives of unbelievers. He does all of this, hoping that those who haven't trusted Jesus yet will give their lives to him.

FAITH links

Guess what Paul said to do about people who refused to listen to him?

(You can find the answer in 2 Thessalonians 3:14–15.)

○ **Ten Things I Like About You,**
2 Thessalonians 1:3–4

○ **Hold On!**
2 Thessalonians 2:15–17

○ **Another Lazy Day?**
2 Thessalonians 3:6–13

▶ **2 Thessalonians 1:1** 1638

1 From Paul, Silas and Timothy.
To the church in Thessalonica in God our Father and the Lord Jesus Christ:
2 Grace and peace to you from God the Father and the Lord Jesus Christ.

Paul Talks About God's Judgement

3 We must always thank God for you, brothers and sisters.*n* This is only right, because your faith is growing more and more, and the love that every one of you has for each other is increasing. 4 So we boast about you to the other churches of God. We tell them about the way you continue to be strong and have faith even though you are being treated badly and are suffering many troubles.

5 This is proof that God is right in his judgement. He wants you to be counted worthy of his kingdom for which you are suffering. 6 God will do what is right. He will give trouble to those who trouble you. 7 And he will give rest to you who are troubled and to us also when the Lord Jesus appears with burning fire from heaven with his powerful angels. 8 Then he will punish those who do not know God and who do not obey the Good News about our Lord Jesus Christ. 9 Those people will be punished with a destruction that continues for ever. They will be kept away from the Lord and from his great power. 10 This will happen on the day when the Lord Jesus comes to receive glory because of his holy people. And all the people who have believed will be amazed at Jesus. You will be in that group, because you believed what we told you.

11 That is why we always pray for you, asking our God to help you live the kind of life he called you to live. We pray that with his power God will help you do the good things you want and perform the works that come from your faith. 12 We pray all this so that the name of our Lord Jesus Christ will have glory in you, and you will have glory in him. That glory comes from the grace of our God and the Lord Jesus Christ.

Evil Things will Happen

2 Brothers and sisters, we have something to say about the coming of our

---

FAITH links

TEN THINGS I LIKE ABOUT YOU

2 THESSALONIANS 1:3-4

Have you ever bragged to someone else about what a friend could do? Maybe you were happy when a friend learned to ski or got an A on a test. That's news worth sharing.

Paul was thankful for the way God helped the Christians in Thessalonica. He was proud of how their faith had grown. He told Christians in other cities about the Thessalonian Christians. How has God helped someone you know? How will you let that person know that you're proud of him or her?

Here are some more Faithlinks on learning to be thankful:

Time to Celebrate, Exodus 15:1–21, p. 95

A Holiday Every Week, Leviticus 23:1–3, p. 166

Uniquely You, Psalm 139:13–14, p. 815

Think About Him, Isaiah 26:3, p. 926

Perfectly Pleasing? Matthew 5:1–12, p. 1280

The Power of *If*, Mark 9:14–24, p. 1344

1:3 brothers and sisters Although the Greek text says "brothers" here and throughout this book, Paul's words were meant for the entire church, both men and women.

Lord Jesus Christ and the time when we will meet together with him. 2 Do not become easily upset in your thinking or afraid if you hear that the day of the Lord has already come. Someone may say this in a prophecy or in a message or in a letter as if it came from us. 3 Do not let anyone fool you in any way. That day of the Lord will not come until the turning away[n] from God happens and the Man of Evil, who is on his way to hell, appears. 4 He will be against and put himself above anything called God or anything that people worship. And that Man of Evil will even go into God's Temple and sit there and say that he is God.

5 I told you when I was with you that all this would happen. Do you not remember? 6 And now you know what is stopping that Man of Evil so he will appear at the right time. 7 The secret power of evil is already working in the world, but there is one who is stopping that power. And he will continue to stop it until he is taken out of the way. 8 Then that Man of Evil will appear, and the Lord Jesus will kill him with the breath that comes from his mouth and will destroy him with the glory of his coming. 9 The Man of Evil will come by the power of Satan. He will have great power, and he will do many different false miracles, signs and wonders. 10 He will use every kind of evil to trick those who are lost. They will die, because they refused to love the truth. (If they loved the truth, they would be saved.) 11 For this reason God sends them something powerful that leads them away from the truth so they will believe a lie. 12 So all those will be judged guilty who did not believe the truth, but enjoyed doing evil.

You are Chosen for Salvation

13 Brothers and sisters, whom the Lord loves, God chose you from the beginning to be saved. So we must always thank God for you. You are saved by the Spirit that makes you holy and by your faith in the truth. 14 God used the Good News that we preached to call you to be saved so you can share in the glory of our Lord Jesus Christ. 15 So, brothers and sisters, stand strong and continue to believe the teachings we gave you in our speaking and in our letter.

2:3 **turning away** Or "the rebellion".

FAITH links

HOLD ON!
2 THESSALONIANS 2:15-17

What information do you find yourself holding on to? Maybe a commercial jingle is going around in your head right now. Or maybe you know exactly how many nose hairs a rhinoceros has, if any.

Paul wrote two letters to the Christians in Thessalonica. In this second letter, he told them to hold on to what they had been taught about Jesus. That information was worth holding on to.

What have you been taught about God? Listening to your pastor, thinking about Scriptures and praying are three ways to help you to hold on to what you know about God.

Alone and Forgotten? Genesis 40:23, p. 57

Good Times and Bad, 1 Kings 17, p. 462

What God "Hates", Proverbs 6:16–19, p. 835

A Bad Reaction, Jeremiah 36, p. 1043

Faith Workout, Acts 16:4–5, p. 1493

One Thing to Do, Romans 4:1–5, p. 1523

16-17 May our Lord Jesus Christ himself and God our Father encourage you and strengthen you in every good thing you do and say. God loved us, and through his grace he gave us a good hope and encouragement that continues for ever.

Pray for Us

3 And now, brothers and sisters, pray for us that the Lord's teaching will continue to spread quickly and that people will give honour to that teaching, just as you did. 2 And pray that we will be protected from stubborn and evil people, because not all people believe.

3 But the Lord is faithful and will give you strength and will protect you from the Evil One. 4 The Lord makes us feel sure that you are doing and will continue to do the things we told you. 5 May the Lord lead your hearts into God's love and Christ's patience.

The Duty to Work

6 Brothers and sisters, by the authority of our Lord Jesus Christ we command you to stay away from any believer who refuses to work and does not follow the teaching we gave you. 7 You yourselves know that you should live as we live. We were not lazy when we were with you. 8 And when we ate another person's food, we always paid for it. We worked very hard night and day so we would not be an expense to any of you. 9 We had the right to ask you to help us, but we worked to take care of ourselves so we would be an example for you to follow. 10 When we were with you, we gave you this rule: "Anyone who refuses to work should not eat."

11 We hear that some people in your group refuse to work. They do nothing but busy themselves in other people's lives. 12 We command those people and beg them in the Lord Jesus Christ to work quietly and earn their own food. 13 But you, brothers and sisters, never become tired of doing good.

14 If some people do not obey what we tell you in this letter, then take note of them. Have nothing to do with them so they will feel ashamed. 15 But do not treat them as enemies. Warn them as fellow believers.

FAITH links

ANOTHER LAZY DAY?
2 THESSALONICA 3:6-13

Ever wish there were no chores for you to do, or homework, or ... anything else for that matter? If so, you're not the only one to wish that. Some of the Christians in Thessalonica didn't want to work. But Paul had a warning for them. Those who didn't work shouldn't eat. He didn't want the Christians to be lazy.

God wants us to be willing to work hard. When we spend a lot of time doing nothing, it can lead us to do the wrong thing. Some people begin to gossip about others or cause trouble in other ways. Keeping busy helps us to keep out of trouble.

Don't like to work too hard? Think again and download these links:

A Use for Your Abilities, Genesis 41, p. 59

Fearful Service? Exodus 4:1–17, p. 80

Your Response to Responsibility, Ruth 2:1–7, p. 346

Meaningless Words, Job 21:34, p. 684

Exercising Patience, Luke 2:25–28, 36–37, p. 1369

Trouble with the Tongue, James 3:3–12, p. 1692

Final Words

16 Now may the Lord of peace give you peace at all times and in every way. The Lord be with all of you.

17 I, Paul, end this letter now in my own handwriting. All my letters have this to show they are from me. This is the way I write.

18 The grace of our Lord Jesus Christ be with you all.

1 & 2 Timothy

GOOD ADVICE

It's Paul again. I hope you remember who I am! On top of all that happened to me (like persecuting believers, being persecuted when Jesus changed my life, and travelling all over to train believers), I also had a select group of people that I spent extra time with to help them with the ministry that God had given them. These are really my last letters to Timothy. I wrote this letter while in prison in Rome, awaiting execution for my faith.

Timothy was a young pastor who was a good friend. I loved him like a son. A while back, I spent a lot of time with Timothy. I wrote this letter as a sort of review – to remind him of the things I taught him. But that's not all. Timothy was also dealing with a lot of false teachings. So I wanted to give him advice about how to deal with that. I also wanted to advise him on how he ought to live his life – pastors should be role models for their congregations! Both 1 and 2 Timothy are about how church leaders should act and what it takes to be a leader in the church. I hope you learn as much from these letters as Timothy did!

JESUS WATCH

Jesus is presented in both 1 and 2 Timothy as someone who stands in the gap between humans and God, to help make us right before our holy Father. In 1 Timothy, Jesus is presented as the "one way humans can reach God" (1 Timothy 2:5) and the source of our spiritual strength, faith and love (1 Timothy 1:12–14). Paul also helps us understand that Jesus came to give himself as a "payment to free all people" (1 Timothy 2:6). Paul wants us to know that Jesus came for us. And when he did, whatever barrier existed between God and us was torn down.

In 2 Timothy, Paul gives us snapshots of Jesus' ability to conquer death and offer eternal life to everyone who believes in Jesus. For example, Paul says that Jesus offers us a salvation that comes with a glory that doesn't end (2 Timothy 2:10). Those who believe in Jesus will also get a crown for waiting "with love for him to come again" (2 Timothy 4:8).

My FAVOURITE links

OTHER CONNECTIONS

 If things don't go your way, what do you usually do? Throw a fit? Walk away? Go up to your room and slam the door? Take a few tips from the Bible on learning how to increase your self-control by logging on to In Control, 2 Timothy 1:7.

GET THE INFO

- Powerful Women of Faith, 2 Timothy 4. Connect here to discover where you can find some of the most powerful women in the New Testament – women like Jesus' mother Mary, Elizabeth, Priscilla and others.

MORE STUFF...
Good Workers It takes a lot of work and self-control to be a faithful follower of Jesus. Paul uses several examples in telling us how to "keep the faith". Check it out:
- Be a good servant and use our faith (1 Timothy 4:6–10).
- Be a good soldier who wants to please Jesus (2 Timothy 2:3–4).
- Be an athlete who trains hard and follows all the rules (2 Timothy 2:5).

Did you know that Paul explains in one of his letters to Timothy how to get rich quick?!

Check out 1 Timothy 6:6-10 to see what Paul is really talking about.

MORE ON THE TIMOTHY SURFWATCH:
The secret to worship, 1 Timothy 2; 3
The good fight, 1 Timothy 6:12–16
A loyal soldier, 2 Timothy 2:1–13
Key to wisdom, 2 Timothy 3:14–17

FAITH links

○ The Leaders in Your Life, **1 Timothy 2:1–4**

○ Your Faith Example, **1 Timothy 4:12**

○ More Money? **1 Timothy 6:10**

○ Your Faith Story, **2 Timothy 1:5**

○ Fear-Fighters, **2 Timothy 1:7**

○ A Soldier's Story, **2 Timothy 2:3**

○ Winning a Friend, **2 Timothy 2:23–24**

○ Life's Rule Book, **2 Timothy 3:15–17**

1 Timothy 1:1

1 From Paul, an apostle of Christ Jesus, by the command of God our Saviour and Christ Jesus our hope.

2 To Timothy, a true child to me because you believe:

Grace, mercy and peace from God the Father and Christ Jesus our Lord.

1:2 Jesus
Is Jesus merciful?

Warning Against False Teaching

3 I asked you to stay longer in Ephesus when I went into Macedonia so you could command some people there to stop teaching false things. 4 Tell them not to spend their time on stories that are not true and on long lists of names in family histories. These things only bring arguments; they do not help God's work, which is done in faith. 5 The purpose of this command is for people to have love, a love that comes from a pure heart and a good conscience and a true faith. 6 Some people have missed these things and turned to useless talk. 7 They want to be teachers of the law, but they do not understand either what they are talking about or what they are sure about.

8 But we know that the law is good if someone uses it correctly. 9 We also know that the law is not made for good people but for those who are against the law and for those who refuse to follow it. It is for people who are against God and are sinful, who are not holy and have no religion, who kill their fathers and mothers, who murder, 10 who take part in sexual sins, who have sexual relations with people of the same sex, who sell slaves, who tell lies, who speak falsely and who do anything against the true teaching of God. 11 That teaching is part of the Good News of the blessed God that he gave me to tell.

Thanks for God's Mercy

12 I thank Christ Jesus our Lord, who gave me strength, because he trusted me and gave me this work of serving him. 13 In the past I spoke against Christ and persecuted him and did all kinds of things to hurt him. But God showed me mercy, because I did not know what I was doing. I did not believe. 14 But the grace of our Lord was fully given to me, and with that grace came the faith and love that are in Christ Jesus.

15 What I say is true, and you should fully accept it: Christ Jesus came into the world to save sinners, of whom I am the worst. 16 But I was given mercy so that in me, the worst of all sinners, Christ Jesus could show that he has patience without limit. His patience with me made me an example for those who would believe in him and have life for ever. 17 To the King that rules for ever, who will never die, who cannot be seen, the only God, be honour and glory for ever and ever. Amen.

18 Timothy, my child, I am giving you a command that agrees with the prophecies that were given about you in the past. I tell you this so you can follow them and fight the good fight. 19 Continue to have faith and do what you know is right. Some people have rejected this, and their faith has been shipwrecked. 20 Hymenaeus and Alexander have done that, and I have given them to Satan so they will learn not to speak against God.

1:18–19 Following God
How can you live a godly life?

Some Rules for Men and Women

2 First, I tell you to pray for all people, asking God for what they need and being thankful to him. 2 Pray for rulers and for all who have authority so that we can have quiet and peaceful lives full of worship and respect for God. 3 This is good, and it pleases God our Saviour, 4 who wants all people to be saved and to know the truth. 5 There is one God and one way human beings can reach God. That way is through Christ Jesus, who is himself human. 6 He gave himself as a payment to free all people. He is proof that came at the right time. 7 That is why I was chosen to tell the Good News and to be an apostle. (I am telling the truth; I am not lying.) I was chosen to teach those who are not Jews to believe and to know the truth.

FAITH links

THE LEADERS IN YOUR LIFE
1 TIMOTHY 2:1-4

Who are the leaders in your life? These may include teachers, police officers, the headteacher of your school, the Prime Minister. When Paul wrote a letter to Timothy, a young pastor, he told Timothy to pray for the people in authority. God wants us to pray for our leaders. If we do, God tells us that we will have a "quiet and peaceful" life. What could you pray for? You can pray that these leaders will make wise and fair decisions. You can also ask God to protect each leader from harm.

Check out these Faithlinks on how to show respect to others:

Fatherly Advice, Exodus 18, p. 99

Big Lack Attack, 2 Kings 4:1–7, p. 480

Prayer + Action = Success, Nehemiah 2:4–9, p. 626

Like Silver, Psalm 12:6–8, p. 717

Our Heavenly Connection, Matthew 6:9–13, p. 1283

I'll Be the Judge! 1 Corinthians 4:4–5, p. 1549

---

8 So, I want men everywhere to pray, lifting up their hands in a holy manner, without anger and arguments.

9 Also, women should wear proper clothes that show respect and self-control, not using plaited hair or gold or pearls or expensive clothes. 10 Instead, they should do good deeds, which is right for women who say they worship God.

11 Let a woman learn by listening quietly and being ready to co-operate in everything. 12 But I do not allow a woman to teach or to have authority over a man, but to listen quietly, 13 because Adam was formed first and then Eve. 14 And Adam was not tricked, but the woman was tricked and became a sinner. 15 But she will be saved through having children if they continue in faith, love and holiness, with self-control.

Elders in the Church

3 What I say is true: anyone wanting to become an elder desires a good work. 2 An elder must not give people a reason to criticise him, and he must have only one wife. He must be self-controlled, wise, respected by others, ready to welcome guests and able to teach. 3 He must not drink too much wine or like to fight, but rather be gentle and peaceful, not loving money. 4 He must be a good family leader, having children who co-operate with full respect. 5 (If someone does not know how to lead the family, how can that person take care of God's church?) 6 But an elder must not be a new believer, or he might be too proud of himself and be judged guilty just as the devil was. 7 An elder must also have the respect of people who are not in the church so he will not be criticised by others and caught in the devil's trap.

Deacons in the Church

8 In the same way, deacons must be respected by others, not saying things they do not mean. They must not drink too much wine or try to get rich by cheating others. 9 With a clear conscience they must follow the secret of the faith that God made known to us. 10 Test them first. Then let them serve as deacons if

you find nothing wrong in them. 11 In the same way, women*ⁿ* must be respected by others. They must not speak evil of others. They must be self-controlled and trustworthy in everything. 12 Deacons must have only one wife and be good leaders of their children and their own families. 13 Those who serve well as deacons are making an honourable place for themselves, and they will be very bold in their faith in Christ Jesus.

The Secret of Our Life

14 Although I hope I can come to you soon, I am writing these things to you now. 15 Then, even if I am delayed, you will know how to live in the family of God. That family is the church of the living God, the support and foundation of the truth. 16 Without doubt, the secret of our life of worship is great:

He was shown to us in a human body,
 proved right in spirit,
 and seen by angels.
He was preached to those who are
 not Jews,
 believed in by the world,
 and taken up in glory.

3:16 Jesus
Why you worship Jesus.

A Warning About False Teachers

4 Now the Holy Spirit clearly says that in the later times some people will stop believing the faith. They will follow spirits that lie and teachings of demons. 2 Such teachings come from the false words of liars whose understanding is destroyed as if by a hot iron. 3 They forbid people to marry and tell them not to eat certain foods which God created to be eaten with thanks by people who believe and know the truth. 4 Everything God made is good, and nothing should be refused if it is

4:1 Satan
Who are on Satan's team?

3:11 women This might mean the wives of the deacons, or it might mean women who serve in the same way as deacons.

FAITH links

YOUR FAITH EXAMPLE
1 TIMOTHY 4:12

In Paul's letter to his friend Timothy, Paul gave Timothy some good advice. Timothy was the pastor of a church. Paul told Timothy not to let others put him down because he was young. He also reminded Timothy that he could set an example for the people in his church family.

Did you ever think that you could be an example for others? You can! The same God who helped Timothy will help you, too. You can start by getting involved at church. Ask your parents, pastor or Sunday school teacher what you can do to help out. You are never too young to serve God!

Download these Faithlinks to find out how you can be a good example:

Share What You Have, Exodus 35:5–18, p. 123

The Heart of the Matter, 1 Samuel 16, p. 375

Learning from Mistakes, Psalm 51:12–13, p. 748

Your Spiritual Roots, Zechariah 1:1–6, p. 1253

Exercising Patience, Luke 2:25–28, 36–37, p. 1369

Your Faith Story, 2 Timothy 1:5, p. 1650

accepted with thanks, 5 because it is made holy by what God has said and by prayer.

Be a Good Servant of Christ

6 By telling these things to the brothers and sisters,[n] you will be a good servant of Christ Jesus. You will be made strong by the words of the faith and the good teaching which you have been following. 7 But do not follow foolish stories that disagree with God's truth, but train yourself to serve God. 8 Training your body helps you in some ways, but serving God helps you in every way by bringing you blessings in this life and in the future life too. 9 What I say is true, and you should fully accept it. 10 This is why we work and struggle: we hope in the living God who is the Saviour of all people, especially of those who believe.

11 Command and teach these things. 12 Do not let anyone treat you as if you are unimportant because you are young. Instead, be an example to the believers with your words, your actions, your love, your faith, and your pure life. 13 Until I come, continue to read the Scriptures to the people, strengthen them, and teach them. 14 Use the gift you have, which was given to you through prophecy when the group of elders laid their hands on[n] you. 15 Continue to do those things; give your life to doing them so your progress may be seen by everyone. 16 Be careful in your life and in your teaching. If you continue to live and teach rightly, you will save both yourself and those who listen to you.

Rules for Living with Others

5 Do not speak angrily to an older man, but plead with him as if he were your father. Treat younger men like brothers, 2 older women like mothers and younger women like sisters. Always treat them in a pure way.

3 Take care of widows who are truly widows. 4 But if a widow has children or grandchildren, let them first learn to do their duty to their own family and to repay their parents or grandparents. That pleases God. 5 The true widow, who is all alone, puts her hope in God and continues to pray night and day for God's help. 6 But the widow who uses her life to please herself is really dead while she is alive. 7 Tell the believers to do these things so that no one can criticise them. 8 Whoever does not care for his own relatives, especially his own family members, has turned against the faith and is

FAITH CHALLENGE

Read 5:4 to learn what God expects from children. How do you typically react when your parents ask you to do things around the house? What can you do about your attitude at home?

TeSTiNG iT

1 Timothy 5:4
But if a widow has children or grandchildren, let them first learn to do their duty to their own family and to repay their parents or grandparents. That pleases God.

4:6 brothers and sisters Although the Greek text says "brothers" here and throughout this book, Paul's words were meant for the entire church, both men and women.
4:14 laid their hands on The laying on of hands had many purposes, including the giving of a blessing, power or authority.

worse than someone who does not believe in God.

9 To be on the list of widows, a woman must be at least 60 years old. She must have been faithful to her husband. 10 She must be known for her good works—works such as raising her children, accepting strangers, washing the feet of God's people, helping those in trouble and giving her life to do all kinds of good deeds.

11 But do not put younger widows on that list. After they give themselves to Christ, they may be pulled away from him by their physical needs, and then they will want to marry again. 12 They will be judged for not doing what they first promised to do. 13 Besides that, they would learn to waste their time, going from house to house. And they not only waste their time but also may begin to gossip and busy themselves with other people's lives, saying things they should not say. 14 So I want the younger widows to marry, have children and take care of their homes. Then no enemy will have any reason to criticise them. 15 But some have already turned away to follow Satan.

16 If any woman who is a believer has widows in her family, she should care for them herself. The church should not have to care for them. Then it will be able to take care of those who are truly widows.

17 The elders who lead the church well should receive double honour, especially those who work hard by speaking and teaching, 18 because the Scripture says: "When an ox is working in the grain, do not cover its mouth to keep it from eating,"[n] and "A worker should be given his pay."[n]

19 Do not listen to someone who accuses an elder, without two or three witnesses. 20 Tell those who continue sinning that they are wrong. Do this in front of the whole church so that the others will have a warning.

21 Before God and Christ Jesus and the chosen angels, I command you to do these things without showing favour of any kind to anyone.

22 Think carefully before you lay your hands on[n] anyone, and don't share in the sins of others. Keep yourself pure.

23 Stop drinking only water, but drink a little wine to help your stomach and your frequent sicknesses.

24 The sins of some people are easy to see even before they are judged, but the sins of others are seen only later. 25 So also good deeds are easy to see, but even those that are not easily seen cannot stay hidden.

6 All who are slaves under a yoke should show full respect to their masters so no one will speak against God's name and our teaching. 2 The slaves whose masters are believers should not show their masters any less respect because they are believers. They should serve their masters even better, because they are helping believers they love.

You must teach and preach these things.

False Teaching and True Riches

3 Anyone who has a different teaching does not agree with the true teaching of our Lord Jesus Christ and the teaching that shows the true way to serve God. 4 This person is full of pride and understands nothing, but is sick with a love for arguing and fighting about words. This brings jealousy, fighting, speaking against others, evil mistrust 5 and constant quarrels from those who have evil minds and have lost the truth. They think that serving God is a way to get rich.

6 Serving God does make us very rich, if we are satisfied with what we have. 7 We brought nothing into the world, so we can take nothing out. 8 But, if we have food and clothes, we will be satisfied with that. 9 Those who want to become rich bring temptation to themselves and are caught in a trap. They want many foolish and harmful things that ruin and destroy

---

5:18 "When . . . eating," Quotation from Deuteronomy 25:4.
5:18 "A worker . . . pay." Quoted in Luke 10:7.
5:22 lay your hands on The laying on of hands had many purposes, including the giving of a blessing, power or authority.

1 Timothy 6:21 1649

FAITH links

MORE MONEY?
1 TIMOTHY 6:10

Can money make a person happy? Some people would say yes. The apostle Paul would say no. In his first letter to his friend Timothy, Paul told him that loving money leads to "all kinds of evil". Paul did not say that *money* is sinful. What he meant was that the desire for riches makes a person greedy. It also leads to other problems.

Money is one of the resources available to us. Like any resource, money should be used wisely. How will you use your money?

Here are some links on being content with what you have:

A Small Percent, Deuteronomy 14:22–23, p. 247

Take My Advice, 1 Kings 2:2–4, p. 436

Uniquely You, Psalm 139:13–14, p. 815

First Place, Haggai 1:7–11, p. 1248

Give to Give, 1 Corinthians 16:1–4, p. 1566

The "Quality" of Life, 2 Peter 1:5–8, p. 1708

---

people. 10 The love of money causes all kinds of evil. Some people have left the faith, because they wanted to get more money, but they have caused themselves much sorrow.

Some Things to Remember

11 But you, man of God, run away from all those things. Instead, live in the right way, serve God, have faith, love, patience and gentleness. 12 Fight the good fight of faith, grabbing hold of the life that continues for ever. You were called to have that life when you confessed the good confession before many witnesses. 13 In the sight of God, who gives life to everything, and of Christ Jesus, I give you a command. Christ Jesus made the good confession when he stood before Pontius Pilate. 14 Do what you were commanded to do without wrong or blame until our Lord Jesus Christ comes again. 15 God will make that happen at the right time. He is the blessed and only Ruler, the King of all kings and the Lord of all lords. 16 He is the only One who never dies. He lives in light so bright no one can go near it. No one has ever seen God, or can see him. May honour and power belong to God for ever. Amen.

6:11–12 Following God
Check out how to live the right way.

17 Command those who are rich with things of this world not to be proud. Tell them to hope in God, not in their uncertain riches. God richly gives us everything to enjoy. 18 Tell the rich people to do good, to be rich in doing good deeds, to be generous and ready to share. 19 By doing that, they will be saving a treasure for themselves as a strong foundation for the future. Then they will be able to have the life that is true life.

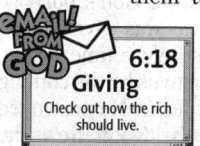
6:18 Giving
Check out how the rich should live.

20 Timothy, guard what God has trusted to you. Stay away from foolish, useless talk and from the arguments of what is falsely called "knowledge". 21 By saying they have that "knowledge", some have missed the true faith.

Grace be with you.

2 Timothy 1:1

1 From Paul, an apostle of Christ Jesus by the will of God. God sent me to tell about the promise of life that is in Christ Jesus.

2 To Timothy, a dear child to me:

Grace, mercy and peace to you from God the Father and Christ Jesus our Lord.

Encouragement for Timothy

3 I thank God as I always mention you in my prayers, day and night. I serve him, doing what I know is right as my ancestors did. 4 Remembering that you cried for me, I want very much to see you so I can be filled with joy. 5 I remember your true faith. That faith first lived in your grandmother Lois and in your mother Eunice, and I know you now have that same faith. 6 This is why I remind you to keep using the gift God gave you when I laid my hands on*[n]* you. Now let it grow, as a small flame grows into a fire. 7 God did not give us a spirit that makes us afraid but a spirit of power and love and self-control.

8 So do not be ashamed to tell people about our Lord Jesus, and do not be ashamed of me, in prison for the Lord. But suffer with me for the Good News. God, who gives us the strength to do that, 9 saved us and made us his holy people. That was not because of anything we did ourselves but because of God's purpose and grace. That grace was given to us through Christ Jesus before time began, 10 but it is now shown to us by the coming of our Saviour Christ Jesus. He destroyed death, and through the Good News he showed us the way to have life that cannot be destroyed. 11 I was chosen to tell that Good News and to be an apostle and a teacher. 12 I am suffering now because I tell the Good News, but I am not ashamed, because I know Jesus, the One in

1:12 God's Promises Find out what Jesus promises to those who trust him.

1:6 laid my hands on The laying on of hands had many purposes, including the giving of a blessing, power or authority.

FAITH links

YOUR FAITH STORY
2 TIMOTHY 1:5

Think about something you've learned from a parent or grandparent. Maybe your mum taught you a recipe that was passed down from generation to generation. Maybe your grandpa taught you how to whistle.

In Paul's letter to his friend Timothy, Paul reminded Timothy about what he learned from his mother and grandmother. They taught Timothy about God. Parents and grandparents today can "pass down" their faith by telling their children about God and how they lived their lives as Christians. What have your parents or grandparents taught you about God? Pass it on!

Download these Faithlinks about sharing your faith:

A Use for Your Abilities, Genesis 41, p. 59

On the Wrong Foot, 2 Kings 21:1–2, 16, p. 509

Love for a Lifetime, Song of Solomon 6:8–9, p. 891

Two Ways to Grow, Luke 2:46–52, p. 1370

The Finished Product, Philippians 1:6, p. 1609

What's Good About You? Philemon 4–7, p. 1663

SELF-CONTROL
2 Timothy 1:7

In Control When small children don't get their way, they sometimes scream and stamp their feet. They may even throw themselves on the floor and yell. They haven't learned to control their emotions and actions. How about you? Have you developed self-control, or do you still do a bit of foot-stamping, screaming and door-slamming?

Which is easier – to think good thoughts or bad thoughts? To be calm and controlled or to lose it? Paul has some suggestions for gaining self-control. (Look at Philippians 4:8–9, p. 1614.) How can good thoughts help you be more in control of your life?

MORE FAITH links
- A Gentle Answer, p. 847
- The Right Ingredients, p. 1227
- Fear-Fighters, p. 1652
- Just Say No! p. 1660
- The "Quality" of Life, p. 1708

Have you ever been asked to do something all over again – like re-doing an essay for homework because you handed in a messy piece of paper?

Although it may seem unfair at the time, learning some discipline is good for us – it helps us develop self-control. Check it out!

I Want It *Now!* Judges 14:1–3, p. 332
- Do you find it hard to wait for something you really want? How do you react when you can't have something immediately? Do you pout? Whine? Beg? Do those methods usually work?
- Part of self-control means learning to control your need to have something *right now!* A person with self-control takes time to make wise choices about his or her wants. Can't stand to wait? God can help – just ask him.

Get Hot or Keep Cool? Proverbs 12:16, p. 842
- If someone called you a name, what would you do? Get mad and call the person the same name – or worse? Sulk about it? Keep your cool and ignore it? Link here to see what God has to say about it.

Down on Discipline? Proverbs 29:15, p. 867
- Wish your parents would never nag you about things you do wrong? Why do parents and others who care about you correct you? How does their correction make you feel? This Faithlink gives some very good reasons for discipline. How can discipline help *you* develop self-control?

my FAVOURITE links

FAITH links

FEAR-FIGHTERS
2 TIMOTHY 1:7

Have you ever been afraid that you couldn't do something? Maybe a recent failure has caused you to be afraid to try something new. Paul's friend Timothy felt that way. In his letter to Timothy, Paul had some advice. He told Timothy that God gave him gifts to help him. What were these gifts? Power, love and self-control. If you're a Christian, you have these gifts, too. Whenever you fear that you can't do something, think about what you can do: trust God to help you.

Next time you're afraid, think about these Faithlinks:

Your Heavenly Parent, Exodus 2:1–10, p. 77

Always Truthful, Numbers 23:19, p. 208

Stand! Jeremiah 19:14—20:6, p. 1019

In the Lions' Den, Daniel 6, p. 1160

A Different Kind of Fruit, Galatians 5:22–23, p. 1592

The "Quality" of Life, 2 Peter 1:5–8, p. 1708

---

whom I have believed. And I am sure he is able to protect what he has trusted me with until that day." 13 Follow the pattern of true teachings that you heard from me in faith and love, which are in Christ Jesus. 14 Protect the truth that you were given; protect it with the help of the Holy Spirit who lives in us.

15 You know that everyone in the country of Asia has left me, even Phygelus and Hermogenes. 16 May the Lord show mercy to the family of Onesiphorus, who has often helped me and was not ashamed that I was in prison. 17 When he came to Rome, he looked eagerly for me until he found me. 18 May the Lord allow him to find mercy from the Lord on that day. You know how many ways he helped me in Ephesus.

A Loyal Soldier of Christ Jesus

2 You then, Timothy, my child, be strong in the grace we have in Christ Jesus. 2 You should teach people whom you can trust the things you and many others have heard me say. Then they will be able to teach others. 3 Share in the troubles we have like a good soldier of Christ Jesus. 4 A soldier wants to please the enlisting officer, so no one serving in the army wastes time with everyday matters. 5 Also an athlete who takes part in a contest must obey all the rules in order to win. 6 The farmer who works hard should be the first person to get some of the food that was grown. 7 Think about what I am saying, because the Lord will give you the ability to understand everything.

8 Remember Jesus Christ, who was raised from the dead, who is from the family of David. This is the Good News I preach, 9 and I am suffering because of it to the point of being bound with chains like a criminal. But God's teaching is not in chains. 10 So I patiently accept all these troubles so that those whom God has chosen can have the salvation that is in Christ Jesus. With that salvation comes glory that never ends.

11 This teaching is true:
If we died with him, we will also live with him.
12 If we accept suffering, we will also rule with him.

1:12 day The day Christ will come to judge all people and take his people to live with him.

2 Timothy 2:26   1653

A Worker Pleasing to God

14 Continue teaching these things, warning people in God's presence not to argue about words. It does not help anyone, and it ruins those who listen. 15 Do the best you can to give yourself to God as the kind of person he will accept. Be a worker who is not ashamed and who uses the true teaching in the right way. 16 Stay away from foolish, useless talk, because that will lead people further away from God. 17 Their evil teaching will spread like a sickness inside the body. Hymenaeus and Philetus are like that. 18 They have left the true teaching, saying that the rising from the dead has already taken place, and so they are destroying the faith of some people. 19 But God's strong foundation continues to stand. These words are written on the seal: "The Lord knows those who belong to him,"[n] and "Everyone who wants to belong to the Lord must stop doing wrong."

20 In a large house there are not only things made of gold and silver, but also things made of wood and clay. Some things are used for special purposes, and others are made for ordinary jobs. 21 All who make themselves clean from evil will be used for special purposes. They will be made holy, useful to the Master, ready to do any good work.

22 But run away from the evil young people like to do. Try hard to live right and to have faith, love and peace, together with those who trust in the Lord from pure hearts. 23 Stay away from foolish and stupid arguments, because you know they grow into quarrels. 24 And a servant of the Lord must not quarrel but must be kind to everyone, a good teacher and patient. 25 The Lord's servant must gently teach those who disagree. Then maybe God will let them change their minds so they can accept the truth. 26 And they may wake up and

2:22 Temptation Here's what to do when faced with temptation.

2:19 "The Lord . . . him" Quotation from Numbers 16:5.

FAITH links

A SOLDIER'S STORY
2 TIMOTHY 2:3

Think a soldier's life is easy? No way. A soldier has to perform hard duties, obey commanding officers and march, march, march. A soldier's life is one of endurance. They are trained to do their job without complaining.

Paul encouraged Timothy to endure suffering like a soldier would. How can you do that? Persevere (which is another way of saying, don't give up!). Instead of looking for the easy way out, keep on going.

Need some encouragement? Download here:

When You're Afraid, Genesis 32:9–12, p. 45

Two Enemies, Nehemiah 6, p. 631

A Really Bad Day, Job 1:20–22; 2:10, p. 661

Future Hope, Joel 3:17–21, p. 1191

The Power of Prayer, Acts 12:5, p. 1485

Keep Going! James 1:2–3, p. 1688

If we refuse to accept him, he will refuse to accept us.
13 If we are not faithful, he will still be faithful,
because he cannot be false to himself.

2 Timothy 3:1 **1654**

FAITH links

WINNING A FRIEND
2 TIMOTHY 2:23-24

Have you ever argued with someone about something that was not really important? Paul had advice for his friend Timothy about "foolish and stupid arguments". What was his advice? Avoid them! Instead, be kind to everyone.

Next time you find yourself in an argument ask yourself these questions: Is this worth arguing about? Is it important for me to be right or to win this argument? If you find that it is not important, you can stop the argument by giving in to your friend. Let him know that your friendship is more important than the argument. You will win him over with your kindness!

Family Feud, Genesis 27, p. 37

Care to Be Fair? Joshua 18:1–8, p. 299

A Friend in Deed, Job 2:13, p. 662

Some Friendly Advice, Proverbs 17:9, 14, 17, p. 851

Welcome! Matthew 19:13–15, p. 1307

Trouble with the Tongue, James 3:3–12, p. 1692

---

ple will love themselves, love money, boast and be proud. They will say evil things against others and will not obey their parents or be thankful or be the kind of people God wants. 3 They will not love others, will refuse to forgive, will gossip and will not control themselves. They will be cruel, will hate what is good, 4 will turn against their friends and will do foolish things without thinking. They will be conceited, will love pleasure instead of God, 5 and will act as if they serve God but will not have his power. Stay away from those people. 6 Some of them go into homes and get control of weak women who are full of sin and are led by many evil desires. 7 These women are always learning new teachings, but they are never able to understand the truth fully. 8 Just as Jannes and Jambres were against Moses, these people are against the truth. Their thinking has been ruined, and they have failed in trying to follow the faith. 9 But they will not be successful in what they do, because as with Jannes and Jambres, everyone will see that they are foolish.

Obey the Teachings

10 But you have followed what I teach, the way I live, my goal, faith, patience and love. You know I never give up. 11 You know how I have been hurt and have suffered, as in Antioch, Iconium and Lystra. I have suffered, but the Lord saved me from all those troubles. 12 Everyone who wants to live as God desires, in Christ Jesus, will be hurt. 13 But people who are evil and cheat others will go from bad to worse. They will fool others, but they will also be fooling themselves.

14 But you should continue following the teachings you learned. You know they are true, because you trust those who taught you. 15 Since you were a child you have known the Holy Scriptures which are able to make you wise. And that wisdom leads to salvation through faith in Christ Jesus. 16 All Scripture is given

escape from the trap of the devil, who catches them to do what he wants.

The Last Days

3 Remember this! In the last days there will be many troubles, 2 because peo-

3:16 Bible
Check out who really wrote the Bible.

FAITH links

LIFE'S RULE BOOK
2 TIMOTHY 3:15-17

Have you ever tried to learn a new sport? What did you do to learn it? Many people try to watch videos or read books about the sport. The videos and books explain the rules and provide tips on how to improve. If a person didn't know the rules of the sport they would not be able to play the game well.

In his second letter to Timothy, Paul encouraged Timothy to study the Bible. The Bible is our "rule book" for life. It teaches us about God and helps us to grow stronger in our faith. It's all we need to know about how to live in a way that honours God.

Here are some more Faithlinks about playing by the rules:

What He's Really Like, Deuteronomy 4:15–20, p. 233

Read My Lips? Deuteronomy 26:16–19, p. 260

The Problem with Gossip, Proverbs 11:12–13, p. 840

The Foundation of Our Hope, Isaiah 31:1–8, p. 934

Our Heavenly Connection, Matthew 6:9–13, p. 1283

How Do You Grow? Titus 1:1, p. 1659

---

by God and is useful for teaching, for showing people what is wrong in their lives, for correcting faults and for teaching how to live right. 17 Using the Scriptures, the person who serves God will be capable, having all that is needed to do every good work.

4 I give you a command in the presence of God and Christ Jesus, the One who will judge the living and the dead, and by his coming and his kingdom: 2 preach the Good News. Be ready at all times, and tell people what they need to do. Tell them when they are wrong. Encourage them with great patience and careful teaching, 3 because

4:1–2 Witnessing When should you witness?

the time will come when people will not listen to the true teaching but will find many more teachers who please them by saying the things they want to hear. 4 They will stop listening to the truth and will begin to follow false stories. 5 But you should control yourself at all times, accept troubles, do the work of telling the Good News and complete all the duties of a servant of God.

6 My life is being given as an offering to God, and the time has come for me to leave this life. 7 I have fought the good fight, I have finished the race, I have kept the faith. 8 Now, a crown is being held for me—a crown for being right with God. The Lord, the judge who judges rightly, will give the crown to me on that day*—not only to me but to all those who have waited with love for him to come again.

Personal Words

9 Do your best to come to me as soon as you can, 10 because Demas, who loved this world, left me and went to Thessalonica. Crescens went to Galatia, and Titus went to Dalmatia. 11 Luke is the only one still with me. Get Mark and bring him with you when you come, because he can help me in my work here. 12 I sent Tychicus to Ephesus. 13 When I was in

---

4:8 day The day Christ will come to judge all people and take his people to live with him.

2 Timothy 4 1656

POWERFUL WOMEN OF FAITH   2 Timothy 4

Mary, the mother of Jesus, is perhaps the most famous woman of the New Testament. Think about it . . . she was the very first person to believe in Jesus. She is an example of faith, humility and service. (Read Luke 1:26–56, p. 1365.)

Other important women in the New Testament include:

Anna	Recognised baby Jesus as the Messiah	Luke 2:36–38, p. 1370
Elizabeth	Mother of John the Baptist	Luke 1:5, 13, p. 1365
Eunice	Timothy's mother, who passed on her faith to him	2 Timothy 1:5, p. 1650
Lois	Timothy's grandma, who passed on her faith to him	2 Timothy 1:5, p. 1650
Lydia	Was converted by Paul during his ministry in Philippi	Acts 16:14, p. 1494
Martha and Mary	Sisters of Lazarus and friends of Jesus	Luke 10:38–42, p. 1389
Mary Magdalene	Jesus cast demons out of this woman; a follower of Jesus	Matthew 27:56–61, p. 1325; Mark 16:9, p. 1362
Priscilla	Worked with Paul at Corinth and Ephesus	Acts 18:2, 18, 19, p. 1497
Salome	Mother of Jesus' disciples, James and John	Matthew 20:20–24, p. 1309; Matthew 27:56, p. 1325; Mark 15:40, p. 1359
Tabitha (Dorcas)	Peter raised her from the dead	Acts 9:36–41, p. 1480

Troas, I left my coat there with Carpus. So when you come, bring it to me, along with my books, particularly the ones written on parchment."

14 Alexander the metalworker did many harmful things against me. The Lord will punish him for what he did. 15 You also should be careful that he does not hurt you, because he fought strongly against our teaching.

16 The first time I defended myself, no one helped me; everyone left me. May they be forgiven. 17 But the Lord stayed with me and gave me strength so I could fully tell the Good News to all those who are not Jews. So I was saved from the lion's mouth. 18 The Lord will save me when anyone tries to hurt me, and he will bring me safely to his heavenly kingdom. Glory for ever and ever be the Lord's. Amen.

Final Greetings

19 Greet Priscilla and Aquila and the family of Onesiphorus. 20 Erastus stayed in Corinth, and I left Trophimus sick in Miletus. 21 Try as hard as you can to come to me before winter.

Eubulus sends greetings to you. Also Pudens, Linus, Claudia and all the brothers and sisters in Christ greet you.

22 The Lord be with your spirit. Grace be with you.

4:13 parchment A writing paper made from the skins of sheep.

ADVICE FOR A PASTOR

Hi! It's me again, Paul. You remember me, right? Well, in case you've forgotten, let me fill you in on my background. I used to persecute Christians. Then, one day, I met Jesus and he changed my life. After that moment, I spent my life encouraging believers in the faith and telling others about the change Jesus made in my life.

I wrote this letter to my friend Titus – a non-Jew (sometimes called a Gentile) who was a Christian and had become a pastor. My friend really needed some advice about the inner workings of the church. I advised him about how he could create order in the church so it would run smoothly. I also gave him some advice about how to elect elders and other church officials. That's not all. I also instructed Titus to teach the truth and gave him advice about how believers in the church should treat each other. I think this letter is still helping pastors and ministers today!

JESUS WATCH

While Paul spends much of his time writing about the basics of church management, he also takes time to paint a rich portrait of Jesus. In just a few words, Paul presents Jesus as both God and our Saviour, who paid the price for our sins. Paul urges Titus to wait for "our great hope and the coming of the glory of our great God and Saviour Jesus Christ" (Titus 2:13). Paul wants believers to be patient and wait for Jesus, the promise and hope of their salvation. Paul's other purpose in writing this letter is to help people who are called to serve in the church to know they're not alone. Serving Jesus won't always be easy, but Jesus promises that he'll be present with us to comfort us and help us when things get out of control. God will never give us more than we can handle. Amazing!

Do you know what the people of Crete were like? (And, no, before you say it, they weren't like Crete-tures . . .) If you really want to know about them, connect to Titus 1:10-16 for Paul's description.

FAITH links

- How Do You Grow?
  Titus 1:1
- Just Say No!
  Titus 2:11–12
- The Gentle Way,
  Titus 3:1–5

1 From Paul, a servant of God and an apostle of Jesus Christ. I was sent to help the faith of God's chosen people and to help them know the truth that shows people how to serve God. 2 That faith and that knowledge come from the hope of life for ever, which God promised to us before time began. And God cannot lie. 3 At the right time God let the world know about that life through preaching. He trusted me with that work, and I preached by the command of God our Saviour.

4 To Titus, my true child in the faith which we share:

Grace and peace from God the Father and Christ Jesus our Saviour.

Titus' Work in Crete

5 I left you in Crete so you could finish doing the things that still needed to be done and so you could appoint elders in every town, as I directed you. 6 An elder must not be guilty of doing wrong, must have only one wife, and must have believing children. They must not be known as children who are wild and do not obey. 7 As a manager of God's work, an elder must not be guilty of doing wrong, being selfish or becoming angry quickly. He must not drink too much wine, like to fight or try to get rich by cheating others. 8 An elder must be ready to welcome guests, love what is good, be wise, live right and be holy and self-controlled. 9 By holding on to the trustworthy word just as we teach it, an elder can help people by using true teaching, and he can show those who are against the true teaching that they are wrong.

10 There are many people who refuse to obey, who talk about worthless things and lead others into the wrong way—mainly those who say all who are not Jews must be circumcised. 11 These people must be stopped, because they are upsetting whole families by teaching things they should not teach, which they do to get rich by cheating people. 12 Even one of their own prophets said, "Cretan people are always liars, evil animals and lazy people who do nothing but eat." 13 The words that prophet said are true. So firmly tell those people they are wrong so they may become strong in the faith, 14 not accepting Jewish false stories and

FAITH links

HOW DO YOU GROW?
TITUS 1:1

If you've heard the nursery rhyme "Mary, Mary, quite contrary", you know how her garden grows. Gardens aren't the only things capable of growth. Paul described his purpose for writing a letter to a church leader named Titus. He wanted to help Titus grow in faith. He also described how that faith would grow.

Your faith can grow, too. How does your faith grow? It grows as you read the Bible, pray and talk to other Christians about God. When you learn more about God, your faith in him becomes stronger.

Here are some more Faithlinks on giving your faith a workout:

A Given, 1 Chronicles 5:18–20, p. 526

Peace in the Family, Psalm 133, p. 811

Like a Tree, Jeremiah 17:5–8, p. 1016

God's Instructions, Ezekiel 4:1–15, p. 1089

The Temptation Fighter, Matthew 4:1–11, p. 1278

Faith God Notices, Luke 18:35–43, p. 1406

the commands of people who reject the truth. 15 To those who are pure, all things are pure, but to those who are full of sin and do not believe, nothing is pure. Both their minds and their thinking have been ruined. 16 They say they know God, but their actions show they do not accept him. They are hateful people, they refuse to obey and they are useless for doing anything good.

Following the True Teaching

2 But you must tell everyone what to do to follow the true teaching. 2 Teach older men to be self-controlled, serious, wise, strong in faith, in love and in patience.

3 In the same way, teach older women to be holy in their behaviour, not speaking against others or having the habit of too much wine, but teaching what is good. 4 Then they can teach the young women to love their husbands, to love their children, 5 to be wise and pure, to be good workers at home, to be kind and to yield to their husbands. Then no one will be able to criticise the teaching God gave us.

6 In the same way, encourage young men to be wise. 7 In every way be an example of doing good deeds. When you teach, do it with honesty and seriousness. 8 Speak the truth so that you cannot be criticised. Then those who are against you will be ashamed because there is nothing bad to say about us.

9 Slaves should yield to their own masters at all times, trying to please them and not arguing with them. 10 They should not steal from them but should show their masters they can be fully trusted so that in everything they do they will make the teaching of God our Saviour attractive.

11 That is the way we should live, because God's grace that can save everyone has come. 12 It teaches us not to live against God nor to do the evil things the world wants to do. Instead, that grace teaches us to live now in a wise and right way and in a way that shows we serve God. 13 We should live like that while we wait for our great hope and the coming of the glory of our great God and Saviour Jesus Christ. 14 He gave himself for us so he might pay the price to free us from all evil and to make us pure people who belong only to him—people who are always wanting to do good deeds.

FAITH links

JUST SAY NO!
TITUS 2:11-12

What's a two-letter word that begins with *N* and is the opposite of yes? *No*. Yet when it comes to not giving in to temptation, we sometimes forget that simple little word.

Paul wrote to Titus with advice on how to live. He told Titus to say no to doing wrong things and say yes to what's right. Each day you'll be faced with making similar choices. Think about some of the choices you're faced with right now. When you're tempted to do something that you know is wrong, remember that simple little word, and just say no!

Download these links on saying *NO* to temptations:

Complaints, Complaints! Exodus 16:1–3, p. 97

I Want It *Now*! Judges 14:1–3, p. 332

The Prayer Habit, Psalm 5:1–3, p. 712

What's Wrong About Rumours, Jeremiah 29:24–32, p. 1032

The Right Ingredients, Micah 6:8, p. 1227

A Friend of Jesus, John 15:9–17, p. 1450

15 Say these things and encourage the people and tell them what is wrong in their lives, with all authority. Do not let anyone treat you as if you were unimportant.

The Right Way to Live

3 Remind the believers to yield to the authority of rulers and government leaders, to obey them, to be ready to do good, 2 to speak no evil about anyone, to live in peace and to be gentle and polite to all people.

3 In the past we also were foolish. We did not obey, we were wrong, and we were slaves to many things our bodies wanted and enjoyed. We spent our lives doing evil and being jealous. People hated us, and we hated each other. 4 But when the kindness and love of God our Saviour was shown, 5 he saved us because of his mercy. It was not because of good deeds we did to be right with him. He saved us through the washing that made us new people through the Holy Spirit. 6 God poured out richly upon us that Holy Spirit through Jesus Christ our Saviour. 7 Being made right with God by his grace, we could have the hope of receiving the life that never ends.

3:7 Eternal Life — What is your hope?

8 This teaching is true, and I want you to be sure the people understand these things. Then those who believe in God will be careful to use their lives for doing good. These things are good and will help everyone.

9 But stay away from those who have foolish arguments and talk about useless family histories and argue and quarrel about the law. Those things are worth nothing and will not help anyone. 10 After a first and second warning, avoid someone who causes arguments. 11 You can know that such people are evil and sinful; their own sins prove them wrong.

Some Things to Remember

12 When I send Artemas or Tychicus to you, try hard to come to me at Nicopolis, because I have decided to stay there this winter. 13 Do all you can to help Zenas the lawyer and Apollos on their journey so that they have everything they need. 14 Our people must learn to use their lives for doing good deeds to provide what is necessary so that their lives will not be useless.

15 All who are with me greet you. Greet those who love us in the faith.

Grace be with you all.

FAITH links

THE GENTLE WAY
TITUS 3:1-5

What's the first thing you think about doing when a brother or sister says something mean to you? Did you ever think about being kind and gentle? That was Paul's advice to Titus. Paul knew that Titus would have to teach other Christians. That was one of his duties as a church leader. So Paul told Titus to remind Christians how to live. Paul's advice to Titus is for you today. Showing kindness instead of getting back at someone is not always easy. But since God is kind to us, we can be kind towards others – even those who treat us unkindly.

Family Feud, Genesis 27, p. 37

Give Revenge a Rest, Leviticus 19:18, p. 160

Patience, Please, Psalm 145:8–9, p. 819

A Gentle Answer, Proverbs 15:1, p. 847

Quick to Forgive? Mark 11:25, p. 1349

That's Much Better! Ephesians 2:4–5, p. 1599

FREE AT LAST!

Hello, everybody. It's me again, Paul. This very short letter is one of the last letters written by me in the Bible. It's also one of my most personal letters. While many of my other letters were written to churches, this one is written to my good friend Philemon, who was a Christian living in Colosse. I was in prison in Rome when I wrote this letter. While in prison, I met Onesimus, Philemon's slave who had run away. He came to Rome looking for his freedom from physical slavery, but he received much more when he found and became a follower of Jesus.

I wrote this letter to Philemon on Onesimus's behalf. I wanted Philemon (and the others who were members of Philemon's house church) to understand that Onesimus was now a brother in Christ and to accept him as a fellow believer. So, I asked Philemon to release Onesimus from slavery. It was a bold request, but do you know what happened? Philemon did set Onesimus free, and it's possible that Onesimus became a leader in the church. Praise God!

JESUS WATCH

Sin and forgiveness are painted in an incredible picture through the retelling of the story of Onesimus – the runaway slave. Paul feels compelled to encourage Philemon to forgive Onesimus and then agrees to take on whatever debt Onesimus owes Philemon. In a very practical way, Paul's efforts demonstrate what Jesus does for us.

Many people have a lot of stuff to say about our sins. Some people want us to believe that we'll never get rid of our sin. Others want us to believe that Jesus forgives our sins, but he never forgets them. But Paul's letter to Philemon completely blows those ideas out of the water. Through Jesus' saving work on the cross, our debt of sin is forgiven and we can enter into a relationship with God.

FAITH links

Does Paul really say that he'll repay Onesimus's debt?

You can read about it in Philemon 18–19.

- What's Good About You? Philemon 4–7
- From Useless to Useful, Philemon 11
- A Friendly Welcome, Philemon 18

Philemon 7

1 From Paul, a prisoner of Christ Jesus, and from Timothy, our brother.

To Philemon, our dear friend and worker with us; 2 to Apphia, our sister; to Archippus, a worker with us; and to the church that meets in your home:

3 Grace and peace to you from God our Father and the Lord Jesus Christ.

Philemon's Love and Faith

4 I always thank my God when I mention you in my prayers, 5 because I hear about the love you have for all God's holy people and the faith you have in the Lord Jesus. 6 I pray that the faith you share may make you understand every blessing we have in Christ. 7 I have great joy and

---

FAITH links

WHAT'S GOOD ABOUT YOU?
PHILEMON 4-7

Think of a time when someone said something nice about you. Maybe he or she told you about a quality you have that they liked. Paul complimented his friend Philemon on how he shared his faith with others. The work Philemon did for the Lord made Paul feel glad. Would you like someone to think that of you? There's one way you can be sure that someone does: tell someone about Jesus.

Want to help out a friend? Tell them about Jesus!

From Zero to Hero, Judges 6; 7, p. 319

Operation Co-operation, Ezra 1:5, p. 609

Jesus' Mission and Yours, Isaiah 61:1–2, p. 978

Stand! Jeremiah 19:14—20:6, p. 1019

Help for a Friend, Mark 2:1–5, p. 1332

Calling Anyone! Acts 23:12–22, p. 1506

FAITH links

FROM USELESS TO USEFUL
PHILEMON 11

Have you ever messed up so badly that you felt useless? Onesimus's story can help you take heart. Although the name *Onesimus* meant "useful", he made himself useless by stealing from his master Philemon. He then ran away to avoid being punished. Yet, something happened when Onesimus met Paul. He became a Christian and was very helpful to Paul.

Feeling useless? God is always willing to give you a second chance. When you accept his forgiveness, you're on your way to becoming useful once more.

Facing the Consequences, Deuteronomy 3:21–29, p. 232

You're Out! 2 Kings 17:5–7, p. 501

Justice Served, Isaiah 35:3–4, p. 940

A Change of Heart, Matthew 3:1–12, p. 1277

Your Choice of Fruit, Matthew 12:33–35, p. 1295

Your Faith Example, 1 Timothy 4:12, p. 1646

comfort, my brother, because the love you have shown to God's people has refreshed them.

Accept Onesimus as a Brother

8 So, in Christ, I could be bold and order you to do what is right. 9 But because I love you, I am pleading with you instead. I, Paul, an old man now and also a prisoner for Christ Jesus, 10 am pleading with you for my child Onesimus, who became my child while I was in prison. 11 In the past he was useless to you, but now he has become useful for both you and me.

12 I am sending him back to you, and with him I am sending my own heart. 13 I wanted to keep him with me so that in your place he might help me while I am in prison for the Good News. 14 But I did not want to do anything without asking you first so that any good you do for me will be because you want to do it, not because I forced you. 15 Maybe Onesimus was separated from you for a short time so you could have him back for ever— 16 no longer as a slave, but better than a slave, as a loved brother. I love him very much, but you will love him even more, both as a person and as a believer in the Lord.

17 So if you consider me your partner, welcome Onesimus as you would welcome me. 18 If he has done anything wrong to you or if he owes you anything, charge that to me. 19 I, Paul, am writing this with my own hand. I will pay it back, and I will say nothing about what you owe me for your own life. 20 So, my brother, I ask that you do this for me in the Lord: refresh my heart in Christ. 21 I write this letter, knowing that you will do what I ask you and even more.

22 One more thing—prepare a room for me in which to stay, because I hope God will answer your prayers and I will be able to come to you.

Final Greetings

23 Epaphras, a prisoner with me for Christ Jesus, sends greetings to you. 24 And also Mark, Aristarchus, Demas and Luke, workers together with me, send greetings.

25 The grace of our Lord Jesus Christ be with your spirit.

FAITH links

A FRIENDLY WELCOME
PHILEMON 18

Paul wanted Philemon to forgive his runaway slave Onesimus. Not only that, Paul wanted Philemon to treat Onesimus like a Christian brother. Legally, Philemon had the right to have Onesimus punished or put to death. After all, Onesimus had stolen from his master and had run away. Running away was enough to earn Onesimus a severe punishment. Paul wanted Philemon to treat Onesimus the way Jesus once treated Philemon.

Jesus always welcomes us back no matter what we do. Since he's willing to do that, he wants us to be willing to forgive those who wrong us. Has someone hurt you recently? Ask God to help you forgive that person.

Is there someone you need to forgive? God can help. Connect here to find out more:

The Perfect Leader? Numbers 20:1–13, p. 203

Count on His Mercy, Judges 2:16–17; 3, p. 313

A Mother's Love, Isaiah 49:13–16, p. 961

Name with a Purpose, Matthew 1:21, p. 1274

Forgive Again? Luke 17:3–4, p. 1402

The Finished Product, Philippians 1:6, p. 1609

NEVER GO BACK!

Hi, everyone. No one really knows who wrote this letter, but I (Paul again!) will tell you about it. Some people think I wrote it anyway because the way it was written looks a lot like the other stuff I've written. Others think that it was written by Apollos, (check out Acts 18:24 and 19:1, p. 1498), or another one of my travelling companions. It doesn't really matter who wrote Hebrews because the most important thing is it's full of unbelievable truth.

The letter was written to a church that met in a home in the Jewish section of Rome. The church was experiencing a lot of problems. The writer wanted to tell the people two things: first, they needed to pay attention to the things that God was saying; second, they needed to *do* what God was telling them. You see, these people were tempted to go back to the old way of doing things and follow the old Jewish traditions. But the message in Hebrews is clear for those people struggling in their faith and for you, too: "Never, never, never go back." Life in Christ, and eventually eternal life, is far, far better than anything else around. It's worth the struggle and worth the wait.

JESUS WATCH

The writer of Hebrews makes one of the strongest cases in the New Testament for Jesus' divine (or godly) nature. The writer describes Jesus as our divine, yet human, prophet, priest and king. Whew! That's a tall order! But not for Jesus – he's God! The writer of Hebrews takes on Jesus' humanity and his deity and describes, explains and praises both aspects. In fact, the writer of this book uses over 20 different words to describe Jesus' attributes and accomplishments. The bottom-line conclusion that Hebrews makes is that Jesus is the best! There is no better than Jesus. He's all-powerful. He's the highest king. He's the perfect Saviour. And he lived just like we did. Now that's an awesome God!

my FAVOURITE links

OTHER CONNECTIONS

Livin' it

When you hear the word "faithful", what do you think of? A dog? Your best friend? How about God? What about you? Learn what it means to be faithful from the wonderful examples of faith you'll find by connecting to True Blue, Hebrews 11.

Get the Info

- Death on a Cross, Hebrews 6:6. Almost everyone knows that Jesus died on a cross, but did you know that crucifixion – to be killed on a cross – was the worst form of punishment the Romans used? Find out more by linking here.

MORE STUFF...

It Takes Faith What does it mean to have faith? The writer of Hebrews defines faith in Hebrews 11 by saying it is being sure of what God will do even if you can't touch it, see it, or even feel it. Check out the list of people who pleased God because of their faith and have made it into the Hall of Faith: Abel, Enoch, Noah, Abraham, Isaac, Jacob, Moses, Rahab and others.

Did you ever wonder what faith is all about?

Sometimes it can be hard to understand exactly what people mean by faith. But if you download Hebrews 11, you'll learn a lot.

MORE ON THE HEBREWS SURFWATCH:
Better than angels, Hebrews 1
The greatest of all, Hebrews 3
Grow up! Hebrews 6:1–12

FAITH links

- Touched by an Angel?
  Hebrews 1:3–4

- Pay Attention!
  Hebrews 2:1

- Cut to the Quick,
  Hebrews 4:12

- Family Time,
  Hebrews 10:25

- People of Faith,
  Hebrews 11

- Go for It!
  Hebrews 12:1–4

- You're Correct!
  Hebrews 12:5–7

- Never Alone,
  Hebrews 13:5–6

God Spoke Through His Son

1 In the past God spoke to our ancestors through the prophets many times and in many different ways. 2 But now in these last days God has spoken to us through his Son. God has chosen his Son to own all things, and through him he made the world. 3 The Son reflects the glory of God and shows exactly what God is like. He holds everything together with his powerful word. When the Son made people clean from their sins, he sat down at the right side of God, the Great One in heaven. 4 The Son became much greater than the angels, and God gave him a name that is much greater than theirs.

5 This is because God never said to any of the angels,

"You are my Son.
Today I have become your Father."
Psalm 2:7

Nor did God say of any angel,

"I will be his father,
and he will be my son." *2 Samuel 7:14*

6 And when God brings his firstborn Son into the world, he says,

"All the gods should worship him."[n]
Psalm 97:7

7 This is what God said about the angels:

"God makes his angels become like winds.
He makes his servants become like flames of fire." *Psalm 104:4*

8 But God said this about his Son:

"God, your throne will last for ever and ever.
You will rule your kingdom with fairness.

9 You love right and hate evil,
so God has chosen you from among your friends;
he has set you apart with much joy." *Psalm 45:6-7*

10 God also says,

"In the beginning you made the earth,
and your hands made the skies.

1:6 "All . . . him." These words are found in Deuteronomy 32:43 in the Septuagint, the Greek version of the Old Testament, and in a Hebrew copy among the Dead Sea Scrolls.

FAITH links

TOUCHED BY AN ANGEL?
HEBREWS 1:3-4

Have you ever wondered about angels? Maybe you've seen television programmes or read books about angels. They're powerful messengers God created to serve him. Some spend all their time praising him. Although angels are important and powerful, there is someone who is greater than they are. Who is that? Jesus. That's what the writer of Hebrews wanted Christians to know. Some first-century Christians believed that angels were to be worshipped. The Bible tells us that Jesus has been given authority over everyone – including angels. That means only he deserves to be worshipped.

Download these links for more reasons to praise God:

The Name of the Lord, Exodus 33:19–23; 34:5–8, p. 120

You're Invited! Psalm 100, p. 784

Concern for All, Daniel 9, p. 1165

A Family Meal, Mark 14:23–26, p. 1356

An Unselfish Example, Philippians 2:5–8, p. 1611

Fear-Fighters, 2 Timothy 1:7, p. 1652

Hebrews 1:11

11 They will be destroyed, but you will
remain.
They will all wear out like clothes.
12 And, like clothes, you will change
them and throw them away.
But you never change,
and your life will never end."
Psalm 102:25-27
13 And God never said this to an angel:
"Sit by me at my right side
until I put your enemies under your
control."[n] *Psalm 110:1*
14 All the angels are spirits who serve God and are sent to help those who will receive salvation.

1:14 Help How do angels help Christians?

Our Salvation is Great

2 So we must be more careful to follow what we were taught. Then we will not stray away from the truth. 2 The teaching God spoke through angels was shown to be true, and anyone who did not follow it or obey it received the punishment that was earned. 3 So surely we also will be punished if we ignore this great salvation. The Lord himself first told about this salvation, and it was proven true to us by those who heard him. 4 God also proved it by using wonders, great signs, many kinds of miracles and by giving people gifts through the Holy Spirit, just as he wanted.

Christ Became like Humans

5 God did not choose angels to be the rulers of the new world that was coming, which is what we have been talking about. 6 It is written in the Scriptures,

"But why are people important to
you?
Why do you take care of human
beings?
7 You made them a little lower than the
angels
and crowned them with glory and
honour. You put them in charge
of everything you made.
8 You put all things under their
control." *Psalm 8:4-6*

When God put everything under their control, there was nothing left that they

---

FAITH links

PAY ATTENTION!
HEBREWS 2:1

What are the things you pay attention to easily? Your favourite TV programmes or DVDs? A computer game? We usually pay attention to whatever we're interested in.

The writer of Hebrews wanted to remind Christians to pay attention to God's Word. Why was that important? There were many teachers who claimed to know about God, but did not tell the truth about him. Knowing the truth of God's Word would keep the Christians from believing lies. That was true then and now. So, how can you pay attention to God's Word? The best way is to read it and do what it says.

Here are some more Faithlinks on knowing God's Word:

Ten Ways to Obey, Exodus 20, p. 103

Learning to Listen, 1 Samuel 3, p. 358

Wronged for What's Right, Ezra 4:4–5, p. 612

A Promise from the Heart, Jeremiah 31:31–33, p. 1037

The Way to Be Wise, James 1:5, p. 1689

You're a Fake! 2 Peter 2:1, p. 1709

1:13 until . . . control Literally, "until I make your enemies a footstool for your feet."

did not rule. Still, we do not yet see them ruling over everything. 9 But we see Jesus, who for a short time was made lower than the angels. And now he is wearing a crown of glory and honour because he suffered and died. And by God's grace, he died for everyone.

10 God is the One who made all things, and all things are for his glory. He wanted to have many children share his glory, so he made the One who leads people to salvation perfect through suffering.

11 Jesus, who makes people holy, and those who are made holy are from the same family. So he is not ashamed to call them his brothers and sisters.ⁿ 12 He says,

"Then, I will tell my fellow Israelites about you;
I will praise you in the public meeting." *Psalm 22:22*

13 He also says,

"I will trust in God." *Isaiah 8:17*

And he also says,

"I am here, and with me are the children God has given me." *Isaiah 8:18*

14 Since these children are people with physical bodies, Jesus himself became like them. He did this so that, by dying, he could destroy the one who has the power of death—the devil— 15 and free those who were like slaves all their lives because of their fear of death. 16 Clearly, it is not angels that Jesus helps, but the people who are from Abraham.ⁿ 17 For this reason Jesus had to be made like his brothers in every way so he could be their merciful and faithful high priest in service to God. Then Jesus could bring forgiveness for their sins. 18 And now he can help those who are tempted, because he himself suffered and was tempted.

Jesus is Greater than Moses

3 So all of you holy brothers and sisters, who were called by God, think about Jesus, who was sent to us and is the high priest of our faith. 2 Jesus was faithful to God as Moses was in God's family. 3 Jesus has more honour than Moses, just as the builder of a house has more honour than the house itself. 4 Every house is built by someone, but the builder of everything is God himself. 5 Moses was faithful in God's family as a servant, and he told what God would say in the future. 6 But Christ is faithful as a Son over God's house. And we are God's house if we keep on being very sure about our great hope.

> Every house is built by someone, but the builder of everything is God himself.
> – Hebrews 3:4

We Must Continue to Follow God

7 So it is as the Holy Spirit says:

"Today listen to what he says.
8 Do not be stubborn as in the past
when you turned against God,
when you tested God in the desert.
9 There your ancestors tried me and tested me
and saw the things I did for 40 years.
10 I was angry with them.
I said, 'They are not loyal to me
and have not understood my ways.'
11 I was angry and made a promise,
'They will never enter my rest.'"ⁿ
Psalm 95:7-11

12 So brothers and sisters, be careful that none of you has an evil, unbelieving heart that will turn you away from the living God. 13 But encourage each other every day while it is "today".ⁿ Help each other so none of you will become hardened because sin has tricked you. 14 We

---

2:11 brothers and sisters Although the Greek text says "brothers" here and throughout this book, the writer's words refer to the entire church, both men and women.

2:16 Abraham Most respected ancestor of the Jews. Every Jew hoped to see Abraham.

3:11 rest A place in which to rest God promised to give his people.

3:13 "today" This word is taken from verse 7. It means that it is important to do these things now.

all share in Christ if we keep till the end the sure faith we had in the beginning. 15 This is what the Scripture says:

"Today listen to what he says.
Do not be stubborn as in the past when you turned against God."

Psalm 95:7-8

16 Who heard God's voice and was against him? It was all those people Moses led out of Egypt. 17 And with whom was God angry for 40 years? He was angry with those who sinned, who died in the desert. 18 And to whom was God talking when he promised that they would never enter his rest? He was talking to those who did not obey him. 19 So we see they were not allowed to enter and have God's rest, because they did not believe.

4 Now, since God has left us the promise that we may enter his rest, let us be very careful so none of you will fail to enter. 2 The Good News was preached to us just as it was to them. But the teaching they heard did not help them, because they heard it but did not accept it with faith. 3 We who have believed are able to enter and have God's rest. As God has said,

"I was angry and made a promise, 'They will never enter my rest.'"

Psalm 95:11

But God's work was finished from the time he made the world. 4 In the Scriptures he talked about the seventh day of the week: "And on the seventh day God rested from all his works."[n] 5 And again in the Scripture God said, "They will never enter my rest."

6 It is still true that some people will enter God's rest, but those who first heard the way to be saved did not enter, because they did not obey. 7 So God planned another day, called "today". He spoke about that day through David a long time later in the same Scripture used before:

"Today listen to what he says.
Do not be stubborn." *Psalm 95:7-8*

8 We know that Joshua[n] did not lead the people into that rest,[n] because God spoke later about another day. 9 This shows that the rest for God's people is still coming. 10 Anyone who enters God's rest will rest from his work as God did. 11 Let us try as

FAITH links

CUT TO THE QUICK
HEBREWS 4:12

If you've ever seen a sword or seen someone use one on TV, you know that a sword is sharp enough to cut through a lot of things. The writer of Hebrews compared God's Word – the Bible – to a double-edged sword. Why? When you hear it, it acts as a sword on your heart. That means it reveals your hidden attitudes and causes you to want to do better. The truth can hurt sometimes. When we follow the truth, however, we feel better. Let God's Word cut out the bad attitudes and thoughts in your life.

The Trouble with Sin, Genesis 6—8, p. 11

A Holiday Every Week, Leviticus 23:1–3, p. 166

Your Stats, 1 Kings 15; 16, p. 460

How Do I Love You? Malachi 1:1–5, p. 1267

Too Busy to Worship? Luke 2:8–20, p. 1368

Hold On! 2 Thessalonians 2:15–17, p. 1639

4:4 "And . . . works." Quotation from Genesis 2:2.
4:8 Joshua After Moses died, Joshua became leader of the Jewish people and led them into the land that God promised to give them.
4:8 rest Literally, "sabbath rest," meaning a sharing in the rest that God began after he created the world.

hard as we can to enter God's rest so that no one will fail by following the example of those who refused to obey.

12 God's word is alive and working and is sharper than a double-edged sword. It cuts all the way into us, where the soul and the spirit are joined, to the centre of our joints and bones. And it judges the thoughts and feelings in our hearts. 13 Nothing in all the world can be hidden from God. Everything is clear and lies open before him, and to him we must explain the way we have lived.

> Even though Jesus was the Son of God, he learned obedience by what he suffered.
> – Hebrews 5:8

Jesus is Our High Priest

14 Since we have a great high priest, Jesus the Son of God, who has gone into heaven, let us hold on to the faith we have. 15 For our high priest is able to understand our weaknesses. When he lived on earth, he was tempted in every way that we are, but he did not sin. 16 Let us, then, feel very sure that we can come before God's throne where there is grace. There we can receive mercy and grace to help us when we need it.

eMail from God
4:16
Courage
Where can you find help when you need it?

5 Every high priest is chosen from among other people. He is given the work of going before God for them to offer gifts and sacrifices for sins. 2 Since he himself is weak, he is able to be gentle with those who do not understand and who are doing wrong things. 3 Because he is weak, the high priest must offer sacrifices for his own sins and also for the sins of the people.

4 To be a high priest is an honour, but no one chooses himself for this work. He must be called by God as Aaron[n] was. 5 So also Christ did not choose himself to have the honour of being a high priest, but God chose him. God said to him,

"You are my Son.
Today I have become your Father."
Psalm 2:7

6 And in another Scripture God says,
"You are a priest for ever,
a priest like Melchizedek."[n]
Psalm 110:4

7 While Jesus lived on earth, he prayed to God and asked God for help. He prayed with loud cries and tears to the One who could save him from death, and his prayer was heard because he trusted God. 8 Even though Jesus was the Son of God, he learned obedience by what he suffered. 9 And because his obedience was perfect, he was able to give eternal salvation to all who obey him. 10 In this way God made Jesus a high priest, a priest like Melchizedek.

Warning Against Falling Away

11 We have much to say about this, but it is hard to explain because you are so slow to understand. 12 By now you should be teachers, but you need someone to teach you again the first lessons of God's message. You still need the teaching that is like milk. You are not ready for solid food. 13 Anyone who lives on milk is still a baby and knows nothing about right teaching. 14 But solid food is for those who are grown up. They have practised in order to know the difference between good and evil.

6 So let us go on to grown-up teaching. Let us not go back over the beginning lessons we learned about Christ. We should not again start teaching about faith in God and about turning away from those acts that lead to death. 2 We should not return to the teaching about baptisms,[n] about laying on of hands,[n] about the

---

5:4 Aaron Aaron was Moses' brother and the first Jewish high priest.
5:6 Melchizedek A priest and king who lived in the time of Abraham. (Read Genesis 14:17-24.)
6:2 baptisms The word here may refer to Christian baptism, or it may refer to the Jewish ceremonial washings.
6:2 laying on of hands The laying on of hands had many purposes, including the giving of a blessing, power or authority.

DEATH ON A CROSS
Hebrews 6:6

The Romans used crucifixion – to be killed on a cross – as their worst form of the death penalty. It was used only for criminals and slaves. Sometimes when a person was killed on a cross, their wrists were tied to a crossbeam of wood. Other times their wrists were actually nailed to the wood. Then the crossbeam would be attached to a tall stake. Their feet might also be nailed to the tall stake.

When people were hung on a cross like this, they had a hard time holding themselves up so they could breathe. Eventually, they died because they got too tired to hold themselves up. It was a horrible way to die. In fact, it was so horrible that the Israelites wouldn't even talk about it in everyday conversation. Some people wondered how Jesus could be the Messiah and yet die such a shameful death. Paul said, though, that Jesus' death on a cross was the power of God for all of us. (Check out 1 Corinthians 1:23–24, p. 1546.)

raising of the dead and eternal judgement. **3** And we will go on to grown-up teaching if God allows.

4 Some people cannot be brought back again to a changed life. They were once in God's light, and enjoyed heaven's gift, and shared in the Holy Spirit. **5** They found out how good God's word is, and they received the powers of his new world. **6** But they fell away from Christ. It is impossible to bring them back to a changed life again, because they are nailing the Son of God to a cross again and are shaming him in front of others.

7 Some people are like land that gets plenty of rain. The land produces a good crop for those who work it, and it receives God's blessings. **8** Other people are like land that grows thorns and weeds and is worthless. It is in danger of being cursed by God and will be destroyed by fire.

9 Dear friends, we are saying this to you, but we really expect better things from you that will lead to your salvation. **10** God is fair; he will not forget the work you did and the love you showed for him by helping his people. And he will remember that you are still helping them. **11** We want each of you to go on with the same hard work all your lives so you will surely get what you hope for. **12** We do not want you to become lazy. Be like those who through faith and patience will receive what God has promised.

13 God made a promise to Abraham.ⁿ And as there is no one greater than God, he used himself when he swore to Abraham, **14** saying, "I will surely bless you and give you many descendants."ⁿ **15** Abraham waited patiently for this to happen, and he received what God promised.

16 People always use the name of someone greater than themselves when they swear. The oath proves that what they say is true, and this ends all arguing. **17** God wanted to prove that his promise was true to those who would get what he

---

6:13 Abraham Most respected ancestor of the Jews. Every Jew hoped to see Abraham.
6:14 "I . . . descendants." Quotation from Genesis 22:17.

promised. And he wanted them to understand clearly that his purposes never change, so he made an oath. 18 These two things cannot change: God cannot lie when he makes a promise, and he cannot lie when he makes an oath. These things encourage us who came to God for safety. They give us strength to hold on to the hope we have been given. 19 We have this hope as an anchor for the soul, sure and strong. It enters behind the curtain in the Most Holy Place in heaven, 20 where Jesus has gone ahead of us and for us. He has become the high priest for ever, a priest like Melchizedek.[n]

6:18 Truth Can God lie?

The Priest Melchizedek

7 Melchizedek[n] was the king of Salem and a priest for God Most High. He met Abraham when Abraham was coming back after defeating the kings. When they met, Melchizedek blessed Abraham, 2 and Abraham gave him a tenth of everything he had brought back from the battle. First, Melchizedek's name means "king of goodness", and he is king of Salem, which means "king of peace". 3 No one knows who Melchizedek's father or mother was,[n] where he came from, when he was born, or when he died. Melchizedek is like the Son of God; he continues being a priest for ever.

4 You can see how great Melchizedek was. Abraham, the great father, gave him a tenth of everything that he won in battle. 5 Now the law says that those in the tribe of Levi who become priests must collect a tenth from the people—their own people—even though the priests and the people are from the family of Abraham. 6 Melchizedek was not from the tribe of Levi, but he collected a tenth from Abraham. And he blessed Abraham, the man who had God's promises. 7 Now everyone knows that the more important person blesses the less important person. 8 Priests receive a tenth, even though they are only men who live and then die. But Melchizedek, who received a tenth from Abraham, continues living, as the Scripture says. 9 We might even say that Levi, who receives a tenth, also paid it when Abraham paid Melchizedek a tenth. 10 Levi was not yet born, but he was in the body of his ancestor when Melchizedek met Abraham.

11 The people were given the law[n] based on a system of priests from the tribe

FAITH CHALLENGE

Here's a challenge for you. Read 6:12 to find out what kind of people we should look up to. What person has had the biggest impact on your life? What areas of your life are you most tempted to be "lazy" in? School work? Chores at home? Bible study?

Testing it

Hebrews 6:12
We do not want you to become lazy. Be like those who through faith and patience will receive what God has promised.

6:20; 7:1 Melchizedek A priest and king who lived in the time of Abraham. (Read Genesis 14:17-24.)

7:3 No one . . . was Literally, "Melchizedek was without father, without mother, without genealogy."

7:11 The . . . law This refers to the people of Israel who were given the law of Moses.

> Hebrews 7:12   1674

of Levi, but they could not be made perfect through that system. So there was a need for another priest to come, a priest like Melchizedek, not Aaron. 12 And when a different kind of priest comes, the law must be changed, too. 13 We are saying these things about Christ, who belonged to a different tribe. No one from that tribe ever served as a priest at the altar. 14 It is clear that our Lord came from the tribe of Judah, and Moses said nothing about priests belonging to that tribe.

Jesus is like Melchizedek

15 And this becomes even more clear when we see that another priest comes who is like Melchizedek. 16 He was not made a priest by human rules and laws but through the power of his life, which continues for ever. 17 It is said about him,

"You are a priest for ever,
a priest like Melchizedek."

Psalm 110:4

18 The old rule is now set aside, because it was weak and useless. 19 The law of Moses could not make anything perfect. But now a better hope has been given to us, and with this hope we can come near to God. 20 It is important that God did this with an oath. Others became priests without an oath, 21 but Christ

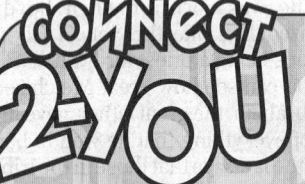

DOING YOUR BEST

How important is it to you to do your best? Do you do it only sometimes or all the time? Let's meet someone who's having some problems in this area. Welcome Richard, aged 9, to Connect 2-You.

Richard

My problem is school. I must be thick or something because I have to work twice as hard as everyone else just to get a C. It's not fair. My teacher says she wishes she had a whole class of students just like me, but I think she's just saying that. Is it really worth it to work so hard just to be average?

Good question. The Bible has some interesting things to say about this topic. You won't find any verses that tell us to get As or to be the best at something. What the Bible does tell us is to run the race that is set before us. That means to do our best in every situation. That's all God asks from us – our best, whether our best earns us an A or a C. If you would like some tips in this area, check out the Livin' It page on doing your best, 1 Corinthians 9:24-27, p. 1554.

God doesn't judge us based on how well we do compared to other people. He judges us based on what we do with the talents and abilities he has given us. If Richard keeps doing his best, he won't find it a waste of time.

became a priest with God's oath. God said:

"The Lord has made a promise
and will not change his mind.
'You are a priest for ever.'"

Psalm 110:4

22 This means that Jesus is the guarantee of a better agreement[n] from God to his people.

23 When one of the other priests died, he could not continue being a priest. So there were many priests. 24 But because Jesus lives for ever, he will never stop serving as priest. 25 So he is able always to save those who come to God through him because he always lives, asking God to help them.

26 Jesus is the kind of high priest we need. He is holy, sinless, pure, not influenced by sinners and he is raised above the heavens. 27 He is not like the other priests who had to offer sacrifices every day, first for their own sins, and then for the sins of the people. Christ offered his sacrifice only once and for all time when he offered himself. 28 The law chooses high priests who are people with weaknesses, but the word of God's oath came later than the law. It made God's Son to be the high priest, and that Son has been made perfect for ever.

Jesus is Our High Priest

8 Here is the point of what we are saying: we have a high priest who sits on the right side of God's throne in heaven. 2 Our high priest serves in the Most Holy Place, the true place of worship that was made by God, not by humans.

3 Every high priest has the work of offering gifts and sacrifices to God. So our high priest must also offer something to God. 4 If our high priest were now living on earth, he would not be a priest, because there are already priests here who follow the law by offering gifts to God. 5 The work they do as priests is only a copy and a shadow of what is in heaven. This is why God warned Moses when he was ready to build the Holy Tent: "Be very careful to make everything by the plan I showed you on the mountain."[n] 6 But the priestly work that has been given to Jesus is much greater than the work that was given to the other priests. In the same way, the new agreement that Jesus brought from God to his people is much greater than the old one. And the new agreement is based on promises of better things.

8:6 Jesus What does Jesus do for you?

7 If there had been nothing wrong with the first agreement,[n] there would have been no need for a second agreement. 8 But God found something wrong with his people. He says:

"Look, the time is coming, says the
  L ORD ,
when I will make a new agreement
  with the people of Israel
  and the people of Judah.
9 It will not be like the agreement
  I made with their ancestors
when I took them by the hand
  to bring them out of Egypt.
But they broke that agreement,
  and I turned away from them, says
  the L ORD .
10 This is the agreement I will make
  with the people of Israel at that
  time, says the L ORD .
I will put my Teachings in their
  minds
and write them on their hearts.
I will be their God,
  and they will be my people.
11 People will no longer have to teach
  their neighbours and relatives
  to know the L ORD ,
because all people will know me,
  from the least to the most
  important.
12 I will forgive them for the wicked
  things they did,

7:22 agreement God gives a contract or agreement to his people. For the Jews, this agreement was the law of Moses. But now God has given a better agreement to his people through Christ.

8:5 "Be . . . mountain." Quotation from Exodus 25:40.

8:7 first agreement The contract God gave the Jewish people when he gave them the law of Moses.

and I will not remember their sins any more." *Jeremiah 31:31-34*

13 God called this a new agreement, and so he has made the first agreement old. And anything that is old and worn out is ready to disappear.

The Old Agreement

9 The first agreement[n] had rules for worship and a man-made place for worship. 2 The Holy Tent was set up for this. The first area in the Tent was called the Holy Place. In it were the lamp and the table with the bread that was made holy for God. 3 Behind the second curtain was a room called the Most Holy Place. 4 In it was a golden altar for burning incense and the Ark covered with gold that held the old agreement. Inside this Ark was a golden jar of manna, Aaron's rod that once grew leaves, and the stone tablets[n] of the old agreement. 5 Above the Ark were the creatures that showed God's glory, whose wings reached over the lid. But we cannot tell everything about these things now.

6 When everything in the Tent was made ready in this way, the priests went into the first room every day to worship. 7 But only the high priest could go into the second room, and he did that only once a year. He could never enter the inner room without taking blood with him, which he offered to God for himself and for sins the people did without knowing they did them. 8 The Holy Spirit uses this to show that the way into the Most Holy Place was not open while the system of the old Holy Tent was still being used. 9 This is an example for the present time. It shows that the gifts and sacrifices offered cannot make the conscience of the worshipper perfect. 10 These gifts and sacrifices were only about food and drink and special washings. They were rules for the body, to be followed until the time of God's new way.

The New Agreement

11 But when Christ came as the high priest of the good things we now have, he entered the greater and more perfect tent. It is not made by humans and does not belong to this world. 12 Christ entered the Most Holy Place only once—and for all time. He did not take with him the blood of goats and calves. His sacrifice was his own blood, and by it he set us free from sin for ever. 13 The blood of goats and bulls and the ashes of a cow are sprinkled on the people who are unclean, and this makes their bodies clean again. 14 How much more is done by the blood of Christ! He offered himself through the eternal Spirit[n] as a perfect sacrifice to God. His blood will make our consciences pure from useless acts so we may serve the living God.

15 For this reason Christ brings a new agreement from God to his people. Those who are called by God can now receive the blessings he has promised, blessings that will last for ever. They can have those things because Christ died so that the people who lived under the first agreement could be set free from sin.

16 When there is a will,[n] it must be proven that the one who wrote that will is dead. 17 A will means nothing while the person is alive; it can be used only after the person dies. 18 This is why even the first agreement could not begin without blood to show death. 19 First, Moses told all the people every command in the law. Next he took the blood of calves and mixed it with water. Then he used red wool and a branch of the hyssop plant to sprinkle it on the Book of the law and on all the people. 20 He said, "This is the blood that begins the Agreement that God commanded you to obey."[n] 21 In the same way, Moses sprinkled the blood on the Holy Tent and over all the things used in worship. 22 The law says that almost

---

9:1 first agreement The contract God gave the Jewish people when he gave them the law of Moses.
9:4 stone tablets They were the two stone tablets on which God wrote the Ten Commandments.
9:14 Spirit This refers to the Holy Spirit, to Christ's own spirit, or to the spiritual and eternal nature of his sacrifice.
9:16 will A legal document that shows how a person's money and property are to be distributed at the time of death. This is the same word in Greek as "agreement" in verse 15.
9:20 "This . . . obey." Quotation from Exodus 24:8.

everything must be made clean by blood, and sins cannot be forgiven without blood to show death.

Christ's Death Takes Away Sins

23 So the copies of the real things in heaven had to be made clean by animal sacrifices. But the real things in heaven need much better sacrifices. 24 Christ did not go into the Most Holy Place made by humans, which is only a copy of the real one. He went into heaven itself and is there now before God to help us. 25 The high priest enters the Most Holy Place once every year with blood that is not his own. But Christ did not offer himself many times. 26 Then he would have had to suffer many times since the world was made. But Christ came only once and for all time at just the right time to take away all sin by sacrificing himself. 27 Just as everyone must die once and be judged, 28 so Christ was offered as a sacrifice once to take away the sins of many people. And he will come a second time, not to offer himself for sin, but to bring salvation to those who are waiting for him.

9:27–28 Salvation What Jesus will bring at his second coming.

10 The law is only an unclear picture of the good things coming in the future; it is not the real thing. The people under the law offer the same sacrifices every year, but these sacrifices can never make perfect those who come near to worship God. 2 If the law could make them perfect, the sacrifices would have already stopped. The worshippers would be made clean, and they would no longer have a sense of sin. 3 But these sacrifices remind them of their sins every year, 4 because it is impossible for the blood of bulls and goats to take away sins.

5 So when Christ came into the world, he said:
  "You do not want sacrifices and offerings,
    but you have prepared a body for me.
6 You do not ask for burnt offerings and sacrifices to take away sins.
7 Then I said, 'Look, I have come.
    It is written about me in the book.
  My God, I want to do what you want.'" *Psalm 40:6-8*

8 In this Scripture he first said, "You do not want sacrifices and offerings. You do not ask for burnt offerings and offerings to take away sins." (These are all sacrifices that the law commands.) 9 Then he said, "Look, I have come to do what you want." God ends the first system of sacrifices so he can set up the new system. 10 And because of this, we are made holy through the sacrifice Christ made in his body once and for all time.

11 Every day the priests stand and do their religious service, often offering the same sacrifices. Those sacrifices can never take away sins. 12 But after Christ offered one sacrifice for sins, for ever, he sat down at the right side of God. 13 And now Christ waits there for his enemies to be put under his power. 14 With one sacrifice he made perfect for ever those who are being made holy.

15 The Holy Spirit also tells us about this. First he says:
16 "This is the agreement*n* I will make
    with them at that time, says the LORD.
  I will put my teachings in their minds
    and write them on their hearts." *Jeremiah 31:33*
17 Then he says:
  "Their sins and the evil things they do—
    I will not remember any more." *Jeremiah 31:34*

18 Now when these have been forgiven, there is no more need for a sacrifice for sins.

Continue to Trust God

19 So, brothers and sisters, we are completely free to enter the Most Holy Place without fear because of the blood of Jesus' death. 20 We can enter through a new and living way that Jesus opened for

---
10:16 agreement God gives a contract or agreement to his people. For the Jews, this agreement was the law of Moses. But now God has given a better agreement to his people through Christ.

us. It leads us through the curtain—Christ's body. 21 And since we have a great priest over God's house, 22 let us come near to God with a sincere heart and a sure faith, because we have been made free from a guilty conscience, and our bodies have been washed with pure water. 23 Let us hold firmly to the hope that we have confessed, because we can trust God to do what he promised.

24 Let us think about each other and help each other to show love and do good deeds. 25 You should not stay away from the church meetings, as some are doing, but you should meet together and encourage each other. Do this even more as you see the day[n] coming.

26 If we decide to go on sinning after we have learnt the truth, there is no longer any sacrifice for sins. 27 There is nothing but fear in waiting for the judgement and the terrible fire that will destroy all those who live against God. 28 Anyone who refused to obey the law of Moses was found guilty from the proof given by two or three witnesses. He was put to death without mercy. 29 So what do you think should be done to those who do not respect the Son of God, who look at the blood of the agreement that made them holy as no different from others' blood, who insult the Spirit of God's grace? Surely they should have a much worse punishment. 30 We know that God said, "I will punish those who do wrong; I will repay them."[n] And he also said, "The Lord will judge his people."[n] 31 It is a terrible thing to fall into the hands of the living God.

32 Remember those days in the past when you first learnt the truth. You had a hard struggle with many sufferings, but you continued strong. 33 Sometimes you were hurt and attacked before crowds of people, and sometimes you shared with those who were being treated that way. 34 You helped the prisoners. You even had joy when all that you owned was taken from you, because you knew you had something better and more lasting.

35 So do not lose the courage you had in the past, which has a great reward. 36 You must hold on, so you can do what

FAITH links

FAMILY TIME
HEBREWS 10:25

Think about how life would change if you and your family only met together once every two or three months. You would hardly know each other, would you? Even though they may bug you at times, you've got to admit that your family is pretty cool. (C'mon, admit it.)

God wants his family to be close. That's why the writer of Hebrews encouraged Christians to meet together often. That's why church involvement is important. When we're together as a church family, we can encourage each other. We can show love to one another. Who can you encourage today in your family? How about in your church family?

Family Feud, Genesis 27, p. 37

Approaching God, Numbers 3:10, p. 180

The MLP, Ruth 1:16–17, p. 345

Peace in the Family, Psalm 133, p. 811

Faith Workout, Acts 16:4–5, p. 1493

MVFM? Galatians 3:26–27, p. 1589

10:25 day The day Christ will come to judge all people and take his people to live with him.
10:30 "I . . . them." Quotation from Deuteronomy 32:35.
10:30 "The Lord . . . people." Quotation from Deuteronomy 32:36; Psalm 135:14.

God wants and receive what he has promised. 37 For in a very short time,

"The One who is coming will come
and will not be delayed.
38 The person who is right with me
will live by trusting in me.
But if he turns back with fear,
I will not be pleased with him."

Habakkuk 2:3-4

39 But we are not those who turn back and are lost. We are people who have faith and are saved.

What is Faith?

11 Faith means being sure of the things we hope for and knowing that something is real even if we do not see it. 2 Faith is the reason we remember great people who lived in the past.

11:1 Faith How do you define faith?

3 It is by faith we understand that the whole world was made by God's command so what we see was made by something that cannot be seen.

4 It was by faith that Abel offered God a better sacrifice than Cain did. God said he was pleased with the gifts Abel offered and called Abel a good man because of his faith. Abel died, but through his faith he is still speaking.

5 It was by faith that Enoch was taken to heaven so he would not die. He could not be found, because God had taken him away. Before he was taken, the Scripture says that he was a man who truly pleased God. 6 Without faith no one can please God. Anyone who comes to God must believe that he is real and that he rewards those who truly want to find him.

7 It was by faith that Noah heard God's warnings about things he could not yet see. He obeyed God and built a large boat to save his family. By his faith, Noah showed that the world was wrong, and he became one of those who are made right with God through faith.

8 It was by faith Abraham obeyed God's call to go to another place God promised to give him. He left his own country, not knowing where he was to go.

FAITH links

PEOPLE OF FAITH
HEBREWS 11

Who is one of your heroes? Maybe this is a person you've read about in a story. Chapter 11 of Hebrews describes some real-life heroes. They're "heroes of the faith". Why are their lives so special? They had great faith. That's why this chapter is called the "faith" chapter of the Bible. You've probably heard some of these stories in Sunday school. Abraham and Sarah, Jacob, Joseph, Moses and others show us what having faith in God is like.

You can be a hero of faith to someone. How? You can start by sharing your faith with someone. Let that person know what God has done in your life. You'll be a true hero!

Download these Faithlinks on telling others what God has done for you:

A Bad Reaction, Jeremiah 36, p. 1043

How Do I Love You? Malachi 1:1–5, p. 1267

Just Say Yes! Matthew 9:9–13, p. 1289

The Unpopular Choice, Mark 15:42–43, p. 1360

Prayer Priority, Luke 5:15–16, p. 1376

The Gift, John 3:16–18, p. 1427

Hebrews 11 **1680**

Being Faithful
Hebrews 11

Livin' it

True Blue Have you ever heard someone say, "He's a true-blue friend"? What do you think that means – a friend who fell into a bath of blue paint? Or someone who went out in mid-winter with no coat? 'Fraid not. It's describing someone who is loyal and sticks with you, no matter what. Do you have a friend like that? Are you that kind of friend?

The writer of Hebrews tells about some people who were "heroes of the faith". They were loyal and faithful to God. They showed this great faith in their lives. (Look at Hebrews 11.) How can you be a hero of faith? You can start by letting others know what God has done in your life! Then you can be "true blue" to God!

MORE FAITH links
- An Unsung Hero, **p. 347**
- Loyal to a Friend, **p. 409**
- The Salt Promise, **p. 576**
- Love for a Lifetime, **p. 891**
- A Broken Promise, **p. 989**
- One of the Faithful, **p. 1482**

Who are some of your heroes?

Let's guess – they probably wear skin-tight suits and have amazing powers that help them save the world from destruction every week, right?

Those guys are cool, but check out some real heroes when you download these links.

Lights, Camera, . . . Actions! Genesis 12:1–3, p. 17
- Imagine being asked to pack your things and move to a foreign country – one you know nothing about. Would you go? Check out this link to see what Abraham did.
- Being faithful to God involves actions, not just words. What do your actions tell about you?

Read My Lips? Deuteronomy 26:16–19, p. 260
- Suppose you told your mother you would take out the rubbish, but didn't do it. Would she believe that you really meant what you said? God wants us to do what we say. Do you mean what you say? Then act like it!

Believe It or Not, Luke 1:20, 38, p. 1366
- Did you know that you could choose to believe something if you wanted to believe? Link here to learn about faithful people who believed God could do the impossible.

my FAVOURITE links

9 It was by faith that he lived like a foreigner in the country God promised to give him. He lived in tents with Isaac and Jacob, who had received that same promise from God. **10** Abraham was waiting for the city*ⁿ* that has real foundations—the city planned and built by God.
11 He was too old to have children, and Sarah could not have children. It was by faith that Abraham was made able to become a father, because he trusted God to do what he had promised. **12** This man was so old he was almost dead, but from him came as many descendants as there are stars in the sky. Like the sand on the seashore, they could not be counted.
13 All these great people died in faith. They did not get the things that God promised his people, but they saw them coming far in the future and were glad. They said they were like visitors and strangers on earth. **14** When people say such things, they show they are looking for a country that will be their own. **15** If they had been thinking about the country they had left, they could have gone back. **16** But they were waiting for a better country—a heavenly country. So God is not ashamed to be called their God, because he has prepared a city for them.
17 It was by faith that Abraham, when God tested him, offered his son Isaac as a sacrifice. God made the promises to Abraham, but Abraham was ready to offer his own son as a sacrifice. **18** God had said, "The descendants I promised you will be from Isaac."*ⁿ* **19** Abraham believed that God could raise the dead, and really, it was as if Abraham got Isaac back from death.
20 It was by faith that Isaac blessed the future of Jacob and Esau. **21** It was by faith that Jacob, as he was dying, blessed each one of Joseph's sons. Then he worshipped as he leaned on the top of his walking stick.
22 It was by faith that Joseph, while he was dying, spoke about the Israelites leaving Egypt and told about what to do with his body.
23 It was by faith that Moses' parents hid him for three months after he was born. They saw that Moses was a beautiful baby, and they were not afraid to disobey the king's order.
24 It was by faith that Moses, when he grew up, refused to be called the son of the king of Egypt's daughter. **25** He chose to suffer with God's people instead of enjoying sin for a short time. **26** He thought it was better to suffer for the Christ than to have all the treasures of Egypt, because he was looking for God's reward. **27** It was by faith that Moses left Egypt and was not afraid of the king's anger. Moses continued strong as if he could see the God that no one can see. **28** It was by faith that Moses prepared the Passover and spread the blood on the doors so the one who brings death would not kill the first-born sons of Israel.
29 It was by faith that the people crossed the Red Sea as if it were dry land. But when the Egyptians tried it, they were drowned.
30 It was by faith that the walls of Jericho fell after the people had marched around them for seven days.
31 It was by faith that Rahab, the prostitute, welcomed the spies and was not killed with those who refused to obey God.
32 Do I need to give more examples? I do not have time to tell you about Gideon, Barak, Samson, Jephthah, David, Samuel and the prophets. **33** Through their faith they defeated kingdoms. They did what was right, received God's promises and shut the mouths of lions. **34** They stopped great fires and were saved from being killed with swords. They were weak, and yet were made strong. They were powerful in battle and defeated other armies. **35** Women received their dead relatives raised back to life. Others were tortured and refused to accept their freedom so they could be raised from the dead to a better life. **36** Some were laughed at and beaten. Others were put in chains and thrown into prison. **37** They were stoned

---

11:10 city The spiritual "city" where God's people live with him. Also called "the heavenly Jerusalem". (See Hebrews 12:22.)
11:18 "The descendants . . . Isaac." Quotation from Genesis 21:12.

to death, they were cut in half and they were killed with swords. Some wore the skins of sheep and goats. They were poor, abused and treated badly. 38 The world was not good enough for them! They wandered in deserts and mountains, living in caves and holes in the earth.

39 All these people are known for their faith, but none of them received what God had promised. 40 God planned to give us something better so that they would be made perfect, along with us.

Follow Jesus' Example

12 We have around us many people whose lives tell us what faith means. So let us run the race that is before us and never give up. We should remove from our lives anything that would get in the way and the sin that so easily holds us back. 2 Let us look only to Jesus, the One who began our faith and who makes it perfect. He suffered death on the cross. But he accepted the shame as if it were nothing because of the joy that God put before him. And now he is sitting at the right side of God's throne. 3 Think about Jesus' example. He held on while wicked people were doing evil things to him. So do not get tired and stop trying.

God is Like a Father

4 You are struggling against sin, but your struggles have not yet caused you to be killed. 5 You have forgotten the encouraging words that call you his children:

"My child, don't think the Lord's
    discipline is worth nothing,
and don't get angry when he
    corrects you.
6 The Lord corrects those he loves,
    and he punishes everyone he
    accepts as his child." *Proverbs 3:11-12*

7 So hold on through your sufferings, because they are like a father's discipline. God is treating you as children. All children are disciplined by their fathers. 8 If you are never disciplined (and every child must be disciplined), you are not true children. 9 We have all had fathers here on earth who disciplined us, and we respected them. So it is even

---

FAITH links

GO FOR IT!
HEBREWS 12:1-4

Have you ever seen a marathon runner competing in a race? Running a marathon takes endurance. You can't stop at the first mile and still call yourself a marathon runner. You have to run all 26 miles to cross the finish line.

The writer of Hebrews compared the Christian life to a race. Being a Christian requires endurance, just like being a marathon runner does. You have to endure hard times, disappointments and other struggles. But God promises his presence and his help. He's with you all the way, cheering you on!

Link here to find out about your biggest cheerleader:

From Hopeless to Hopeful, Exodus 6:9, p. 83

Your Worst Enemy, Exodus 7—11, p. 85

Faith of Our Fathers, Joshua 4:4–9, p. 280

A Given, 1 Chronicles 5:18–20, p. 526

Attention, Please! Luke 8:11–15, p. 1383

The Sacrifice of Service, Philippians 2:17, 25–30, p. 1612

---

eMAIL FROM GOD
12:7–11
Correction
Why is discipline good?

Hebrews 12:23

FAITH links

YOU'RE CORRECT!
HEBREWS 12:5-7

Not many of us like to be disciplined, even when we do wrong. What does discipline mean? It means to correct someone. Why do parents discipline their children? They do it because they love them and want the best for their children.

The writer of Hebrews wrote advice for Christians about discipline. Like any parent, God disciplines his children when they do wrong. God's discipline shows his love for us.

From Hopeless to Hopeful, Exodus 6:9, p. 83

The Weak Link, Judges 16, p. 334

A Shortcut, 1 Samuel 13:1–14, p. 369

A Model of Forgiveness, Ezekiel 16:59–63, p. 1103

Believe It or Not, Luke 1:20, 38, p. 1366

Don't Play Favourites, James 2:1–7, p. 1691

---

more important that we accept discipline from the Father of our spirits so we will have life. 10 Our fathers on earth disciplined us for a short time in the way they thought was best. But God disciplines us to help us, so we can become holy as he is. 11 We do not enjoy being disciplined. It is painful, but later, after we have learned from it, we have peace, because we start living in the right way.

Be Careful How You Live

12 You have become weak, so make yourselves strong again. 13 Live in the right way so that you will be saved and your weakness will not cause you to be lost.

14 Try to live in peace with all people, and try to live free from sin. Anyone whose life is not holy will never see the Lord. 15 Be careful that no one fails to receive God's grace and begins to cause trouble among you. A person like that can ruin many of you. 16 Be careful that no one takes part in sexual sin or is like Esau and never thinks about God. As the elder son, Esau would have received everything from his father, but he sold all that for a single meal. 17 You remember that after Esau did this, he wanted to get his father's blessing, but his father refused. Esau could find no way to change what he had done, even though he wanted the blessing so much that he cried.

18 You have not come to a mountain that can be touched and that is burning with fire. You have not come to darkness, sadness and storms. 19 You have not come to the noise of a trumpet or to the sound of a voice like the one the people of Israel heard and begged not to hear another word. 20 They did not want to hear the command: "If anything, even an animal, touches the mountain, it must be put to death with stones."[n] 21 What they saw was so terrible that Moses said, "I am shaking with fear."[n]

22 But you have come to Mount Zion, to the city of the living God, the heavenly Jerusalem. You have come to thousands of angels gathered together with joy. 23 You have come to the meeting of God's first-born[n] children whose names are written in heaven. You have come

---

12:20 "If . . . stones." Quotation from Exodus 19:12-13.
12:21 "I . . . fear." Quotation from Deuteronomy 9:19.
12:23 first-born The first son born in a Jewish family was given the most important place in the family and received special blessings. All of God's children are like that.

to God, the judge of all people, and to the spirits of good people who have been made perfect. 24 You have come to Jesus, the One who brought the new agreement from God to his people, and you have come to the sprinkled blood*ⁿ* that has a better message than the blood of Abel.*ⁿ*

25 So be careful and do not refuse to listen when God speaks. Others refused to listen to him when he warned them on earth, and they did not escape. So it will be worse for us if we refuse to listen to God who warns us from heaven. 26 When he spoke before, his voice shook the earth, but now he has promised, "Once again I will shake not only the earth but also the heavens."*ⁿ* 27 The words "once again" clearly show us that everything that was made—things that can be shaken—will be destroyed. Only the things that cannot be shaken will remain.

28 So let us be thankful, because we have a kingdom that cannot be shaken. We should worship God in a way that pleases him with respect and fear, 29 because our God is like a fire that burns things up.

13 Keep on loving each other as brothers and sisters. 2 Remember to welcome strangers, because some who have done this have welcomed angels without knowing it. 3 Remember those who are in prison as if you were in prison with them. Remember those who are suffering as if you were suffering with them.

4 Marriage should be honoured by everyone, and husband and wife should keep their marriage pure. God will judge as guilty those who take part in sexual sins. 5 Keep your lives free from the love of money, and be satisfied with what you have. God has said,

"I will never leave you;
   I will never forget you."

Deuteronomy 31:4

6 So we can be sure when we say,
"I will not be afraid, because the Lord
      is my helper.
   People can't do anything to me."

Psalm 118:6

7 Remember your leaders who taught

FAITH links

NEVER ALONE
HEBREWS 13:5-6

Quick! Name someone who is always with you – not just some of the time, but always. Can't think of anyone? God is with you 24/7. Know what else? He will never forget about you. N-E-V-E-R. Can anyone else make that claim?

That's why the writer of Hebrews quoted God's promise from the Book of Deuteronomy. God promised his people in Old Testament times that he wouldn't leave them or forget about them. That promise is for you, too. He also promises to help you. You don't have to be afraid of anything. Isn't that good news?

Connect here for more good news:

Good Plans, Genesis 45:7–8, p. 64

The Perfect Sacrifice, Leviticus 1—7, p. 135

Real Faith or Really Scared? Judges 4 , p. 315

Long-lasting Hope, Hosea 14, p. 1184

Mission Impossible? Mark 5:21–24, 35–43, p. 1337

Hard Times, 2 Corinthians 1:8–10, p. 1570

12:24 sprinkled blood The blood of Jesus' death.
12:24 Abel The son of Adam and Eve, who was killed by his brother Cain (Genesis 4:8).
12:26 "Once . . . heavens." Quotation from Haggai 2:6, 21.

God's message to you. Remember how they lived and died, and copy their faith. 8 Jesus Christ is the same yesterday, today and for ever.

9 Do not let all kinds of strange teachings lead you into the wrong way. Your hearts should be strengthened by God's grace, not by obeying rules about foods, which do not help those who obey them.

10 We have a sacrifice, but the priests who serve in the Holy Tent cannot eat from it. 11 The high priest carries the blood of animals into the Most Holy Place where he offers this blood for sins. But the bodies of the animals are burnt outside the camp. 12 So Jesus also suffered outside the city to make his people holy with his own blood. 13 So let us go to Jesus outside the camp, holding on as he did when he bore our disgrace.

14 Here on earth we do not have a city that lasts for ever, but we are looking for the city that we will have in the future. 15 So through Jesus let us always offer to God our sacrifice of praise, coming from lips that speak his name. 16 Do not forget to do good to others, and share with them, because such sacrifices please God.

> **eMAIL FROM GOD**
> **13:15**
> **Thankfulness**
> What can you offer God?

17 Obey your leaders and act under their authority. They are watching over you, because they are responsible for your souls. Obey them so that they will do this work with joy, not sadness. It will not help you to make their work hard.

18 Pray for us. We are sure that we have a clear conscience, because we always want to do the right thing. 19 I especially beg you to pray so that God will send me back to you soon.

20-21 I pray that the God of peace will give you every good thing you need so you can do what he wants. God raised from the dead our Lord Jesus, the Great Shepherd of the sheep, because of the blood of his death. His blood began the eternal agreement that God made with his people. I pray that God will do in us what pleases him, through Jesus Christ, and to him be glory for ever and ever. Amen.

22 My brothers and sisters, I beg you to listen patiently to this message I have written to encourage you, because it is not very long. 23 I want you to know that our brother Timothy has been let out of prison. If he arrives soon, we will both come to see you.

24 Greet all your leaders and all of God's people. Those from Italy send greetings to you.

25 Grace be with you all.

FAITH IN ACTION

Hi! I'm James, and I'm glad you're reading this book. You're probably wondering who I am. I was the half-brother of Jesus. And I was also the leader of the church in Jerusalem. If you connect to Acts 15:12–21, p. 1490, you'll see that I was really the head of the whole church. I often worked together with Paul. Even though we didn't always agree on everything, we made major decisions for the church.

I wrote this book to Christians who were having trouble living out their faith. You know, believing in Jesus is much more than just knowing about him. To be a true follower of Jesus it's important that we not only say that we are Christians, but we also have to show it by doing good things. We've got to behave like Jesus is with us all of the time. And, we've got to treat other people the same. That's a lot. But Jesus helps us do it!

JESUS WATCH

The Book of James doesn't say much about Jesus. James doesn't talk specifically about the life of Jesus, and he doesn't speak about the return of Jesus. But, throughout his book, James describes the life of someone who's been invaded by Jesus. He talks about people who have turned their lives over to Jesus and how that should affect their lives. His book also describes many of the teachings of Jesus and makes many references to the Sermon on the Mount (check out Matthew 5:10–12, p. 1280, and Matthew 6:19, p. 1284).

James wants to give us a picture of Jesus as the role model for our own lives. We can't just know a lot about Jesus and his teachings. We've got to take what we know and apply it to our lives. It's called "walking the walk *and* talking the talk". You can do it!

my FAVOURITE links

OTHER CONNECTIONS

Livin' it — Does it take a lot to make you angry? Or does the smallest thing set you off? Find out what God has to say about anger and some advice on how to handle your fuse – whether it's short or long – by downloading You Make Me Sooo Mad! James 1:19–21.

MORE STUFF...

Growing Close to God James gives five keys to growing closer to God. Take a look at these five ways from James 4:7–10:
- Be willing to follow God no matter what (v. 7).
- Don't give in to the devil's temptations to do things you know are wrong (v. 7).
- Stop doing those things that displease God; focus instead on things that please God (v. 8).
- When you do something wrong, don't be *sorry*; be *sorrowful* over how you have disappointed God (v. 9).
- Remember who God is – he is the One who gives you your worth and value (v. 10). Depend on him!

FAITH links

○ Keep Going!
  James 1:2–3

○ The Way to Be Wise,
  James 1:5

○ Don't Play Favourites,
  James 2:1–7

○ Trouble with the Tongue,
  James 3:3–12

○ A Peacemaker or a Peacebreaker?
  James 3:18

○ The Love Magnet,
  James 4:7–8

Do you know what James describes as having the most deadly poison?

You're thinking it must be some kind of snake, right?

Nope, you're wrong. Better check out James 3:7–10 to find out. You're in for a surprise!

did YOU know?

DON'T MISS WHAT JAMES HAS TO SAY ABOUT...
Bad times, James 1:1–8
Faith that's dead, James 2:14–26
Real wisdom, James 3:13–18
The power of prayer, James 5:13–18

James 1:1

1 From James, a servant of God and of the Lord Jesus Christ.

To all of God's people who are scattered everywhere in the world:

Greetings.

Faith and Wisdom

2 My brothers and sisters,* when you have many kinds of troubles, you should be full of joy, 3 because you know that these troubles test your faith, and this will give you patience. 4 Let your patience show itself perfectly in what you do. Then you will be perfect and complete and will have everything you need. 5 But if any of you needs wisdom, you should ask God for it. He is generous and enjoys giving to all people, so he will give you wisdom. 6 But when you ask God, you must believe and not doubt. Anyone who doubts is like a wave in the sea, blown up and down by the wind. 7-8 Such who doubt are thinking two different things at the same time, and they cannot decide about anything they do. They should not think they will receive anything from the Lord.

True Riches

9 Believers who are poor should be proud, because God has made them spiritually rich. 10 Those who are rich should be proud, because God has helped them to see that they are spiritually poor. The rich will die like a wild flower in the grass. 11 The sun rises with burning heat and dries up the plants. The flower falls off, and its beauty is gone. In the same way the rich will die while they are still taking care of business.

Temptation is Not from God

12 When people are tempted and still continue strong, they should be happy. After they have proved their faith, God will reward them with life for ever. God promised this to all those who love him. 13 When people are tempted, they should not say, "God is tempting me." Evil cannot tempt God, and God himself does not tempt anyone. 14 But people are tempted

KEEP GOING!
JAMES 1:2–3

Your mum or dad gets sick. A bigger kid picks on you at school. Sometimes bad things happen. How do you respond to hard times? Some people are tempted to give up. Others become angry with God. They may say, "If God loved me, this wouldn't happen."

When hard times come, James says, "Don't give up. Instead, keep going!" Hard times help to produce patience in your life. Patience helps you not to give up. Having faith in hard times is difficult. But when the hard times are over, your faith will be stronger!

Here is some more hope for hard times:

Meaningless Words, Job 21:34, p. 684

When the Going Gets Tough, Lamentations 3:22–27, p. 1079

The God of Second Chances, Jonah 3, p. 1215

Ask, Search, Knock, Matthew 7:7–10, p. 1286

Just a Test, Luke 4:1–13, p. 1373

Hard Times, 2 Corinthians 1:8–10, p. 1570

1:2 brothers and sisters Although the Greek text says "brothers" here and throughout this book, James' words were meant for the entire church, both men and women.

James 1:27 1689

FAITH links

THE WAY TO BE WISE
JAMES 1:5

Psst. Come closer. Closer. That's close enough. Want to know the secret to being wise? Two words: *ask God*. That's James's advice for wisdom seekers. God is the source of wisdom. Having wisdom does not mean you become a know-it-all. It means you're willing to learn to do what's right.

What do you need wisdom for? For those hard situations where you have to make a choice between doing what's right and doing what's wrong. Wisdom helps you know when to ask for help. The best thing about having wisdom is this: God helps you to use it.

Check out these Faithlinks on wising up:

The Cloud Guide, Numbers 9:15–23, p. 188

Plan for Success, 1 Chronicles 14:8–17, p. 538

Seeing the Needs, Nehemiah 1, p. 625

Wisdom in Store, Proverbs 2:6–7, p. 828

Prayer Priority, Luke 5:15–16, p. 1376

Keeping Clean, 2 Corinthians 7:1, p. 1576

---

when their own evil desire leads them away and traps them. 15 This desire leads to sin, and then the sin grows and brings death.

16 My dear brothers and sisters, do not be fooled about this. 17 Every good action and every perfect gift is from God. These good gifts come down from the Creator of the sun, moon and stars, who does not change like their shifting shadows. 18 God decided to give us life through the word of truth so we might be the most important of all the things he made.

Listening and Obeying

19 My dear brothers and sisters, always be willing to listen and slow to speak. Do not become angry easily, 20 because anger will not help you live the right kind of life God wants. 21 So put out of your life every evil thing and every kind of wrong. Then in gentleness accept God's teaching that is planted in your hearts, which can save you.

22 Do what God's teaching says; when you only listen and do nothing, you are fooling yourselves. 23 Those who hear God's teaching and do nothing are like people who look at themselves in a mirror. 24 They see their faces and then go away and quickly forget what they looked like. 25 But the truly happy people are those who carefully study God's perfect law that makes people free, and they continue to study it.

E-MAIL FROM GOD
1:25 Blessings
What brings you real happiness?

They do not forget what they heard, but they obey what God's teaching says. Those who do this will be made happy.

The True Way to Worship God

26 People who think they are religious but say things they should not say are just fooling themselves. Their "religion" is worth nothing. 27 Religion that God accepts as pure and without fault is this: caring for orphans or widows who need help, and keeping yourself free from the world's evil influence.

James 1 1690

ANGER
James 1:19–21

You Make Me Sooo Mad! What things or people drive you up the wall and make you so angry that you just want to scream? Is it your little brother getting into your things? Or a big kid always picking on you? Or maybe a computer that crashes when you're winning a game? How do you handle your anger?

Instead of spouting off and really letting someone have it when you're angry with them, God has a better idea. Be willing to forgive others for the mean things they do. (Read Luke 17:3–4, p. 1401.) How do you think forgiving someone might make you less angry?

Is it ever OK to be angry? Yes, when you are angry about disobedience to God and his Word. Jesus became angry when he saw what was happening in the Temple. (Look at Matthew 21:12–13, p. 1310.) Do you ever become angry at situations where God is being ignored? How do you handle a situation like that?

MORE FAITH links

Patience, Please, **p. 819**

What God "Hates", **p. 835**

Justice Served, **p. 940**

Don't Get Mad; Get Even? **p. 1323**

Out with the Old! **p. 1625**

What makes you maddest of all? Is it when your computer gets all jammed up and crashes! Does is make you so angry you can hardly see straight?

If that's the case, it sounds like you have a problem with your temper. Why don't you count to 10 and then download these Faithlinks. They'll help you cool down!

Out of Control? Genesis 4, p. 8
- Link here to see how terrible anger can become when it is out of control.

Anger: Quick or Slow? Psalm 86:15, p. 776
- Which are you quick to do – get angry with someone or show kindness to people? When someone really bugs you, what's the easiest thing to do? Get angry, right? Which do you think God does the quickest: become angry or show kindness to you? What do you need to do to be more like that?

A Gentle Answer, Proverbs 15:1, p. 847
- Have you ever noticed that when someone makes you mad and you say something mean back to that person, you both feel angrier? What usually happens if you are sarcastic or start shouting? Does anything get settled? Link here to find a better way to handle that situation.

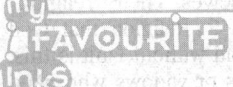

Love All People

2 My dear brothers and sisters, as believers in our glorious Lord Jesus Christ, never think some people are more important than others. 2 Suppose someone comes into your church meeting wearing nice clothes and a gold ring. At the same time a poor person comes in wearing old, dirty clothes. 3 You show special attention to the one wearing nice clothes and say, "Please, sit here in this good seat." But you say to the poor person, "Stand over there," or, "Sit on the floor by my feet." 4 What are you doing? You are making some people more important than others, and with evil thoughts you are deciding that one person is better.

5 Listen, my dear brothers and sisters! God chose the poor in the world to be rich with faith and to receive the kingdom God promised to those who love him. 6 But you show no respect to the poor. The rich are always trying to control your lives. They are the ones who take you to court. 7 And they are the ones who speak against Jesus, who owns you.

8 This royal law is found in the Scriptures: "Love your neighbour as you love yourself."*n* If you obey this law, you are doing right. 9 But if you treat one person as being more important than another, you are sinning. You are guilty of breaking God's law. 10 A person who follows all of God's law but fails to obey even one command is guilty of breaking all the commands in that law. 11 The same God who said, "You must not be guilty of adultery,"*n* also said, "You must not murder anyone."*n* So if you do not take part in adultery but you murder someone, you are guilty of breaking all of God's law. 12 In everything you say and do, remember that you will be judged by the law that makes people free. 13 So you must show mercy to others, or God will not show mercy to you when he judges you. But the person who shows mercy can stand without fear at the judgement.

Faith and Good Works

14 My brothers and sisters, if people say they have faith, but do nothing, their faith is worth nothing. Can faith like that

---

FAITH links

DON'T PLAY FAVOURITES
JAMES 2:1-7

How would you feel if your teacher only gave good marks to students who could buy her nice things? You'd probably feel terrible if you weren't one of the students who could do that. Besides, your teacher wouldn't be a very good teacher if she did that! That's why God does not want us to play favourites. Playing favourites means only being nice to certain people. In James's day, some Christians were nice to the rich but ignored the poor. That's not the way God wants us to be! We're to treat all people the same – with kindness.

Just Kidding? Genesis 21:8–10, p. 28

A Small Percent, Deuteronomy 14:22–23, p. 247

Your Best Work, 1 Kings 6, p. 443

The Problem with Pride, Isaiah 2:11, p. 898

The Way to Greatness, Matthew 20:20–28, p. 1309

Who's on First? 3 John 9–10, p. 1723

2:8 "Love . . . yourself." Quotation from Leviticus 19:18.
2:11 "You . . . adultery," Quotation from Exodus 20:14; Deuteronomy 5:18.
2:11 "You . . . anyone." Quotation from Exodus 20:13; Deuteronomy 5:17.

save them? 15 A brother or sister in Christ might need clothes or food. 16 If you say to that person, "God be with you! I hope you stay warm and get plenty to eat," but you do not give what that person needs, your words are worth nothing. 17 In the same way, faith that is alone—that does nothing—is dead.

18 Someone might say, "You have faith, but I have deeds." Show me your faith without doing anything, and I will show you my faith by what I do. 19 You believe there is one God. Good! But the demons believe that too, and they tremble with fear.

20 You foolish person! Must you be shown that faith that does nothing is worth nothing? 21 Abraham, our ancestor, was made right with God by what he did when he offered his son Isaac on the altar. 22 So you see that Abraham's faith and the things he did worked together. His faith was made perfect by what he did. 23 This shows the full meaning of the Scripture that says: "Abraham believed God, and God accepted Abraham's faith, and that faith made him right with God."[n] And Abraham was called God's friend.[n] 24 So you see that people are made right with God by what they do, not by faith only.

25 Another example is Rahab, a prostitute, who was made right with God by something she did. She welcomed the spies into her home and helped them escape by a different road.

26 Just as a person's body that does not have a spirit is dead, so faith that does nothing is dead!

Controlling the Things We Say

3 My brothers and sisters, not many of you should become teachers, because you know that we who teach will be judged more strictly. 2 We all make many mistakes. If people never said anything wrong, they would be perfect and able to control their entire selves too. 3 When we put bits into the mouths of horses to make them obey us, we can control their whole bodies. 4 Also a ship is very big, and it is pushed by strong winds. But a very small rudder controls that big ship,

---

FAITH links

TROUBLE WITH THE TONGUE
JAMES 3:3-12

Have you ever said something nice to someone? Think about how that person felt. Have you ever said something that you wished you hadn't said? Maybe it was something that hurt someone. How do you think *that* person felt? How did you feel after saying it? Just think – both statements came out of the same mouth. James tells us to watch what we say. The same mouth should not be used for good *and* for evil. God wants us to use our words for good!

Need help controlling your words? Connect here:

More Powerful Than Revenge, Genesis 50:14–21, p. 71

A Right to Get Even? 1 Samuel 24, p. 388

The Peril of Poisonous Plans, Micah 2:1–3, p. 1221

Kindness First, Matthew 9:35–36, p. 1290

The Whole Truth, John 8:31–32, 45, p. 1438

Another Lazy Day? 2 Thessalonians 3:6–13, p. 1640

2:23 "Abraham . . . God." Quotation from Genesis 15:6.
2:23 God's friend These words about Abraham are found in 2 Chronicles 20:7 and Isaiah 41:8.

James 4:2 1693

FAITH links

A PEACEMAKER OR A PEACEBREAKER?

JAMES 3:18

Are you a peacemaker or a peacebreaker? A peacemaker tries their best to make peace between two people who aren't getting along. A peacemaker also tries to get along with others. A peacebreaker starts trouble wherever he or she goes. Maybe he doesn't like the game the other kids are playing and demands that another be played. Maybe she tries to start a rumour about another girl.

James reminds us that peacemakers will be rewarded. Peacebreakers don't receive anything but trouble. Which would you rather have?

Download these links on keeping the peace:

Forgive Instead, Genesis 33, p. 47

Kind or Fair? 1 Samuel 30, p. 395

Peace in the Family, Psalm 133, p. 811

The Verdict Is In? Matthew 7:1–2, p. 1285

I'll Be the Judge! 1 Corinthians 4:4–5, p. 1549

The Way to Get Along, 1 Peter 3:8–9, p. 1703

---

making it go wherever the person wants. 5 It is the same with the tongue. It is a small part of the body, but it boasts about great things.

A big forest fire can be started with only a little flame. 6 And the tongue is like a fire. It is a whole world of evil among the parts of our bodies. The tongue spreads its evil through the whole body. The tongue is set on fire by hell, and it starts a fire that influences all of life. 7 People can tame every kind of wild animal, bird, reptile and fish, and they have tamed them, 8 but no one can tame the tongue. It is wild and evil and full of deadly poison. 9 We use our tongues to praise our Lord and Father, but then we curse people, whom God made like himself. 10 Praises and curses come from the same mouth! My brothers and sisters, this should not happen. 11 Do good and bad water flow from the same spring? 12 My brothers and sisters, can a fig tree make olives, or can a grapevine make figs? No! And a well full of salty water cannot give good water.

True Wisdom

13 Are there those among you who are truly wise and understanding? Then they should show it by living right and doing good things with a gentleness that comes from wisdom. 14 But if you are selfish and have bitter jealousy in your hearts, do not boast. Your boasting is a lie that hides the truth. 15 That kind of "wisdom" does not come from God but from the world. It is not spiritual; it is from the devil. 16 Where jealousy and selfishness are, there will be confusion and every kind of evil. 17 But the wisdom that comes from God is first of all pure, then peaceful, gentle and easy to please. This wisdom is always ready to help those who are troubled and to do good for others. It is always fair and honest. 18 People who work for peace in a peaceful way plant a good crop of good living.

Give Yourselves to God

4 Do you know where your fights and arguments come from? They come from the selfish desires that war within you. 2 You want things, but you do not have them. So you are ready to kill and are jealous of other people, but you still cannot get what you want. So you argue and fight. You do not get what you want,

because you do not ask God. 3 Or when you ask, you do not receive because the reason you ask is wrong. You want things so you can use them for your own pleasures.

4 So, you are not loyal to God! You should know that loving the world is the same as hating God. Anyone who wants to be a friend of the world becomes God's enemy. 5 Do you think the Scripture means nothing that says, "The Spirit that God made to live in us wants us for himself alone."[n] 6 But God gives us even more grace, as the Scripture says,

"God is against the proud,
but he gives grace to the humble."

Proverbs 3:34

7 So give yourselves completely to God. Stand against the devil, and the devil will run from you. 8 Come near to God, and God will come near to you. You sinners, clean sin out of your lives. You who are trying to follow God and the world at the same time, make your thinking pure. 9 Be sad, cry and weep! Change your laughter into crying and your joy into sadness. 10 Don't be too proud in the Lord's presence, and he will make you great.

4:8 Worship
How can God come closer to you?

You Are Not the Judge

11 Brothers and sisters, do not tell evil lies about each other. If you speak against your fellow believers or judge them, you are judging and speaking against the law they follow. And when you are judging the law, you are no longer a follower of the law. You have become a judge. 12 God is the only Lawmaker and Judge. He is the only One who can save and destroy. So it is not right for you to judge your neighbour.

Let God Plan Your Life

13 Some of you say, "Today or tomorrow we will go to some city. We will stay there a year, do business and make money." 14 But you do not know what will happen tomorrow! Your life is like a mist. You can see it for a short time, but then it goes away. 15 So you should say, "If the Lord wants, we will live and do this or that." 16 But now you are proud and you boast. All of this boasting is wrong. 17 Anyone who knows the right thing to do, but does not do it, is sinning.

FAITH links

THE LOVE MAGNET
JAMES 4:7-8

Think of a magnet, one of those horseshoe-shaped ones. Now think of a piece of metal. How long would it take for the metal to be pulled close to the magnet? No time at all, right? Now think of God as the magnet and yourself as the piece of metal. Unlike the magnet, God doesn't snatch you to him. He waits for you to come. That's why James tells us to come near to God. As we come near to God, he comes near to us. God's love is what attracts us to him. It's more powerful than any magnet!

Time to Celebrate, Exodus 15:1–21, p. 95

Your Total Trust, Deuteronomy 1:32, p. 229

Happiness or Joy? Job 29:18–19, p. 691

A Direct Path, Proverbs 3:5–6, p. 829

The Best Protection Plan, Matthew 2:13–18, p. 1276

Faith That Pleases God, Luke 7:1–9, p. 1380

4:5 "The Spirit . . . alone." These words may be from Exodus 20:5.

A Warning to the Rich

5 You rich people, listen! Cry and be very sad because of the troubles that are coming to you. 2 Your riches have rotted, and your clothes have been eaten by moths. 3 Your gold and silver have rusted, and that rust will be a proof that you were wrong. It will eat your bodies like fire. You saved your treasure for the last days. 4 The pay you did not give the workers who harvested your fields cries out against you, and the cries of the workers have been heard by the Lord All-powerful. 5 Your life on earth was full of rich living and pleasing yourselves with everything you wanted. You made yourselves fat, like an animal ready to be killed. 6 You have judged guilty and then murdered innocent people, who were not against you.

Be Patient

7 Brothers and sisters, be patient until the Lord comes again. A farmer patiently waits for his valuable crop to grow from the earth and for it to receive the autumn and spring rains. 8 You, too, must be patient. Do not give up hope, because the Lord is coming soon. 9 Brothers and sisters, do not complain against each other or you will be judged guilty. And the Judge is ready to come! 10 Brothers and sisters, follow the example of the prophets who spoke for the Lord. They suffered many hard things, but they were patient. 11 We say they are happy because they did not give up. You have heard about Job's patience, and you know the Lord's purpose for him in the end. You know the Lord is full of mercy and is kind.

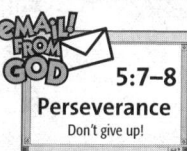

5:7–8 Perseverance Don't give up!

Be Careful What You Say

12 My brothers and sisters, above all, do not use an oath when you make a promise. Don't use the name of heaven, earth or anything else to prove what you say. When you mean yes, say only "yes", and when you mean no, say only "no" so you will not be judged guilty.

The Power of Prayer

13 Anyone who is having troubles should pray. Anyone who is happy should sing praises. 14 Anyone who is sick should call the church's elders. They should pray for and pour oil on the person[n] in the name of the Lord. 15 And the prayer that is said with faith will make the sick person well; the Lord will heal that

---

5:14 pour oil on the person Oil was used in the name of the Lord as a sign that the person was now set apart for God's special attention and care.

FAITH CHALLENGE

Got another one for you. Read 5:13 for some important instructions. If you prayed more often, what effect do you think it would have on your life? What are some things in your life for which you can "sing praises"?

TESTING IT

James 5:13
Anyone who is having troubles should pray. Anyone who is happy should sing praises.

person. And if the person has sinned, the sins will be forgiven. 16 Confess your sins to each other and pray for each other so God can heal you. When a believing person prays, great things happen. 17 Elijah was a human being just like us. He prayed that it would not rain, and it did not rain on the land for three and a half years! 18 Then Elijah prayed again, and the rain came down from the sky, and the land produced crops again.

5:16 Courage
Find out why prayer is important.

Saving a Soul

19 My brothers and sisters, if one of you wanders away from the truth, and someone helps that person come back, 20 remember this: anyone who brings a sinner back from the wrong way will save that sinner's soul from death and will cause many sins to be forgiven.

1 & 2 Peter

ADVICE TO LIVE ON

Hello! I'm Peter, and I hope that you like these two books. I certainly knew a lot about being a follower of Jesus. I was one of the first twelve disciples and one of Jesus' three closest friends. Before I was a disciple, I was a fisherman. I followed Jesus during all of his ministry. And I was with him just before he was killed. I wasn't always the best follower, though. I made a *lot* of mistakes. In fact, when Jesus was facing his greatest trial, I told people I didn't even know him. It was one of the worst moments of my life. But the good news for me – and for you – is that Jesus forgives and loves us.

I wrote these two letters to give believers advice on how to live their lives for Jesus. So, I give advice to husbands and wives, teachers and church leaders. I also warn believers about false teachers and some untrue things they were saying. And, a lot was also being said about the return of Jesus, so I try to clear up some of the things believers were hearing.

JESUS WATCH

The world we live in can be cruel and unforgiving. It's not easy to live out the beliefs that Jesus calls us to. But, 1 Peter addresses this by presenting Jesus as the example we're to follow when we're facing rejection, troubles or suffering because of what we believe. Jesus is our hope! And he's the source of our strength and unbelievable joy – even when we're going through some bad times.

2 Peter takes a similar approach, but applies it in a new way. In 1 Peter, Jesus is our strength when we're suffering. In 2 Peter, Jesus is our source of knowledge and power. In other words, if we're ever going to grow up in our faith, we've got to rely on Jesus to help us grow.

my FAVOURITE links

OTHER CONNECTIONS

Livin' it — Ever have one of those days when everything seemed to go wrong? God not only offers to help carry the load for you when things go bad, but God also can guide you through the tough times. Check it out by logging on to Help! 1 Peter 4:12–19.

- A Fisher of People, 1 Peter 1. If you think you've had times when you disappointed God, you'll be glad to meet Peter. Peter went through some low points in his walk with Jesus before becoming a bold leader in the early church. Find out more about Peter's life by linking here.

MORE STUFF . . .

Service, Please! How do you describe Christian service? Peter describes different ways you can serve others. You can read more about it in 1 Peter 4:7–11:

- Love each other deeply.
- Forgive each other's sins.
- Welcome guests into your home.

What do you think will happen to people who teach false things?

One thing's for sure – they'll be in big trouble. Surf over to 2 Peter 2, and see what you think.

LOOK AT THESE OTHER COOL STORIES:
  The "living stone", 1 Peter 2:4–10
  Passing the test, 1 Peter 4:12–19
  Like a thief, 2 Peter 3:8–13

FAITH links

- The Way to Get Along, 1 Peter 3:8–9
- Come On In! 1 Peter 4:9–10
- Toss Those Troubles! 1 Peter 5:7
- The "Quality" of Life, 2 Peter 1:5–8
- You're a Fake! 2 Peter 2:1
- His Best Qualities, 2 Peter 3:9

1 Peter 1:2 **1699**

Get the Info

A FISHER OF PEOPLE

1 Peter 1

1. Simon Peter was born at Bethsaida. He was a fisherman until Jesus called him to "fish for people". (Check out Luke 5:1–11, p. 1375.)

2. In Caesarea Philippi, Jesus changed Simon's name to Peter, which means "rock", after Peter recognised Jesus as the Son of the living God. (Read Matthew 16:13–16, p. 1303.)

3. Peter, along with James and John, went with Jesus to a high mountain. They watched as Jesus' appearance changed and Jesus' face became as bright as the sun. (See Matthew 17:1–9, p. 1303.)

4. Peter hit his lowest point the night before Jesus was crucified when he said three times that he didn't even know Jesus. (See Matthew 26:69–75, p. 1323.) After Jesus was raised from the dead, he appeared to Peter and the other disciples in Jerusalem. (Look at Luke 24:33–49, p. 1419.)

5. Peter became a bold leader in the early church at Jerusalem. (Check out Acts 2:14–41, p. 1464.) He also preached to non-Jewish people after God gave him a vision in Joppa. (Read Acts 10:9–23, p. 1481.)

---

1 From Peter, an apostle of Jesus Christ. To God's chosen people who are away from their homes and are scattered all around the countries of Pontus, Galatia, Cappadocia, Asia and Bithynia. 2 God

1:2
Obedience
What does God want you to do?

planned long ago to choose you by making you his holy people, which is the Spirit's work. God wanted you to obey him and to be made clean by the blood of the death of Jesus Christ.

Grace and peace be yours more and more.

We Have a Living Hope

3 Praise be to the God and Father of our Lord Jesus Christ. In God's great mercy he has caused us to be born again into a living hope, because Jesus Christ rose from the dead. 4 Now we hope for the blessings God has for his children. These blessings, which cannot be destroyed or be spoiled or lose their beauty, are kept in heaven for you. 5 God's power protects you through your faith until salvation is shown to you at the end of time. 6 This makes you very happy, even though now for a short time different kinds of troubles may make you sad. 7 These troubles come to prove that your faith is pure. This purity of faith is worth more than gold, which can be proved to be pure by fire but will ruin. But the purity of your faith will bring you praise and glory and honour when Jesus Christ is shown to you. 8 You have not seen Christ, but still you love him. You cannot see him now, but you believe in him. So you are filled with a joy that cannot be explained, a joy full of glory. 9 And you are receiving the goal of your faith—the salvation of your souls.

10 The prophets searched carefully and tried to learn about this salvation. They prophesied about the grace that was coming to you. 11 The Spirit of Christ was in the prophets, telling in advance about the sufferings of Christ and about the glory that would follow those sufferings. The prophets tried to learn about what the Spirit was showing them, when those things would happen, and what the world would be like at that time. 12 It was shown them that their service was not for themselves but for you, when they told about the truths you have now heard. Those who preached the Good News to you told you those things with the help of the Holy Spirit who was sent from heaven—things into which angels desire to look.

A Call to Holy Living

13 So prepare your minds for service and have self-control. All your hope should be for the gift of grace that will be yours when Jesus Christ is shown to you. 14 Now that you are obedient children of God do not live as you did in the past. You did not understand, so you did the evil things you wanted. 15 But be holy in all you do, just as God, the One who called you, is holy. 16 It is written in the Scriptures: "You must be holy, because I am holy."ⁿ

17 You pray to God and call him Father, and he judges each person's work equally. So while you are here on earth, you should live with respect for God. 18 You know that in the past you were living in a worthless way, a way passed down from the people who lived before you. But you were saved from that useless life. You were bought, not with something that ruins like gold or silver, 19 but with the precious blood of Christ, who was like a pure and perfect lamb. 20 Christ was chosen before the world was made, but he was shown to the world in these last times for your sake. 21 Through Christ you believe in God, who raised Christ from the dead and gave him glory. So your faith and your hope are in God.

1:18–19 Salvation How was your salvation bought?

22 Now that you have made your souls pure by obeying the truth, you can have true love for your Christian brothers and sisters.ⁿ So love each other deeply with all your heart. 23 You have been born again, and this new life did not come from something that dies, but from something that cannot die. You were born again through God's living message that continues for ever. 24 The Scripture says,

"All people are like the grass,

1:16 "You must be . . . holy." Quotation from Leviticus 11:45; 19:2; 20:7.
1:22 brothers and sisters Although the Greek text says "brothers" here and throughout this book, Peter's words refer to the entire church, both men and women.

and all their glory is like the
flowers of the field.
The grass dies and the flowers fall,
25 but the word of the Lord will live
for ever."
Isaiah 40:6-8

And this is the word that was preached to you.

Jesus is the Living Stone

2 So then, rid yourselves of all evil, all lying, hypocrisy, jealousy and evil speech. 2 As newborn babies want milk, you should want the pure and simple teaching. By it you can grow up and be saved, 3 because you have already examined and seen how good the Lord is.

4 Come to the Lord Jesus, the "stone"[n] that lives. The people of the world did not want this stone, but he was the stone God chose, and he was precious. 5 You also are like living stones, so let yourselves be used to build a spiritual temple—to be holy priests who offer spiritual sacrifices to God. He will accept those sacrifices through Jesus Christ. 6 The Scripture says:

"I will put a stone in the ground in
   Jerusalem.
Everything will be built on this
   important and precious rock.
Anyone who trusts in him
   will never be disappointed."
Isaiah 28:16

7 This stone is worth much to you who believe. But to the people who do not believe,

"the stone that the builders rejected
   has become the cornerstone."
Psalm 118:22

8 Also, he is

"a stone that causes people to
   stumble,
a rock that makes them fall."
Isaiah 8:14

They stumble because they do not obey what God says, which is what God planned to happen to them.

9 But you are a chosen people, royal priests, a holy nation, a people for God's own possession. You were chosen to tell about the wonderful acts of God, who called you out of darkness into his wonderful light. 10 At one time you were not a people, but now you are God's people. In the past you had never received mercy, but now you have received God's mercy.

Live for God

11 Dear friends, you are like foreigners and strangers in this world. I beg you to avoid the evil things your bodies want to do that fight against your soul. 12 People who do not believe are living all around you and might say that you are doing wrong. Live such good lives that they will see the good things you do and will give glory to God on the day when Christ comes again.

Yield to Every Human Authority

13 For the Lord's sake, yield to the people who have authority in this world: the king, who is the highest authority, 14 and the leaders who are sent by him to punish those who do wrong and to praise those who do right. 15 It is God's desire that by doing good you should stop foolish people from saying stupid things about you. 16 Live as free people, but do not use your freedom as an excuse to do evil. Live as servants of God. 17 Show respect for all people: love the brothers and sisters of God's family, respect God, honour the king.

2:15 Respect Why should you do good things?

Follow Christ's Example

18 Slaves, yield to the authority of your masters with all respect, not only those who are good and kind, but also those who are dishonest. 19 A person might have to suffer even when it is unfair, but if he thinks of God and stands the pain, God is pleased. 20 If you are beaten for doing wrong, there is no reason to praise you for being patient in your punishment. But if you suffer for doing good, and you are patient, then God is pleased. 21 This is what you were called to do, because Christ suffered for you and gave you an

---

2:4 "**stone**" The most important stone in God's spiritual temple or house (his people).

> 1 Peter 2:22   1702

FAITH CHALLENGE

Here's another challenge for you. Read 2:19 to find out what to do when people are unfair to you. What is the most unfair thing that's ever happened to you? How did you handle it? How does knowing this verse help you?

TeSTiNG iT

1 Peter 2:19
A person might have to suffer even when it is unfair, but if he thinks of God and stands the pain, God is pleased.

example to follow. So you should do as he did. 22 "He had never sinned,
  and he had never lied." *Isaiah 53:9*

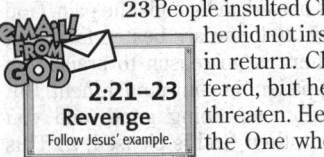

**2:21–23
Revenge**
Follow Jesus' example.

23 People insulted Christ, but he did not insult them in return. Christ suffered, but he did not threaten. He let God, the One who judges rightly, take care of him. 24 Christ carried our sins in his body on the cross so we would stop living for sin and start living for what is right. And you are healed because of his wounds. 25 You were like sheep that wandered away, but now you have come back to the Shepherd and Protector of your souls.

Wives and Husbands

3 In the same way, you wives should yield to your husbands. Then, if some husbands do not obey God's teaching, they will be persuaded to believe without anyone saying a word to them. They will be persuaded by the way their wives live. 2 Your husbands will see the pure lives you live with your respect for God. 3 It is not fancy hair, gold jewellery or fine clothes that should make you beautiful. 4 No, your beauty should come from within you—the beauty of a gentle and quiet spirit that will never be destroyed and is very precious to God. 5 In this same way the holy women who lived long ago and followed God made themselves beautiful, yielding to their own husbands. 6 Sarah obeyed Abraham, her husband, and called him her master. And you women are true children of Sarah if you always do what is right and are not afraid.

7 In the same way, you husbands should live with your wives in an understanding way, since being answered they are weaker than you. But show them respect, because God gives them the same blessing he gives to you—the grace that gives true life. Do this so that nothing will stop your prayer.

Suffering for Doing Right

8 Finally, all of you should be in agreement, understanding each other, loving each other as family, being kind and humble. 9 Do not do wrong to repay a wrong, and do not insult to repay an insult. But repay with a blessing, because you yourselves were called to do this so that you might receive a blessing. 10 The Scripture says,

**3:9
Enemies**
Check out how to repay an insult.

"You must do these things
  to enjoy life and have many happy
    days.
You must not say evil things,
  and you must not tell lies.

FAITH links

THE WAY TO GET ALONG
1 PETER 3:8-9

What was the last thing you argued about with your brother or sister? Sometimes people argue because they don't understand something about another person. When you and your brother or sister fight, how do you feel? Compare that feeling to the way you feel when you do get along.

Peter, one of Jesus' twelve followers, wrote a letter to help Christians learn about God. He gave advice to help them get along with each other. He told them to try to understand each other, love each other and be kind. That's the way to get along. Try it sometime with a family member or a friend and see what happens.

Here are some more Faithlinks about getting along with others:

Family Feud, Genesis 27, p. 37

Give Revenge a Rest, Leviticus 19:18, p. 160

A Parent's Advice, Proverbs 1:8–9, p. 825

Justice Desserts, Habakkuk 2:4–8, p. 1237

Best Seat in the House, Luke 14:7–11, p. 1398

Winning a Friend, 2 Timothy 2:23–24, p. 1654

---

11 Stop doing evil and do good.
  Look for peace and work for it.
12 The Lord sees the good people
  and listens to their prayers.
  But the Lord is against
    those who do evil." *Psalm 34:12-16*

13 If you are trying hard to do good, no one can really hurt you. 14 But even if you suffer for doing right, you are blessed.

"Don't be afraid of what they fear;
  do not dread those things."
Isaiah 8:12-13

15 But respect Christ as the holy Lord in your hearts. Always be ready to answer everyone who asks you to explain about the hope you have, 16 but answer in a gentle way and with respect. Keep a clear conscience so that those who speak evil of your good life in Christ will be made ashamed. 17 It is better to suffer for doing good than for doing wrong if that is what God wants. 18 Christ himself suffered for sins once. He was not guilty, but he suffered for those who are guilty to bring you to God. His body was killed, but he was made alive in the spirit. 19 And in the spirit he went and preached to the spirits in prison 20 who refused to obey God long ago in the time of Noah. God was waiting patiently for them while Noah was building the boat. Only a few people—eight in all—were saved by water. 21 And that water is like baptism that now saves you—not the washing of dirt from the body, but the promise made to God from a good conscience. And this is because Jesus Christ was raised from the dead. 22 Now Jesus has gone into heaven and is at God's right side ruling over angels, authorities and powers.

Change Your Lives

4 Since Christ suffered while he was in his body, strengthen yourselves with the same way of thinking Christ had. The person who has suffered in the body is finished with sin. 2 Strengthen yourselves so that you will live here on earth doing what God wants, not the evil things people want. 3 In the past you wasted too much time doing what non-believers enjoy. You were guilty of sexual sins, evil desires,

HANDLING BAD TIMES
1 Peter 4:12–19

Help! Do you lug a backpack full of books and papers to school each day? Does it ever get heavy? Imagine carrying twice the heaviest load you've ever carried all day, everywhere you go. Pretty soon you would feel bent over and dragging along. What if someone offered to take the heavy load from you? How would you feel then?

The things you worry about and the bad times you have can cause you to feel loaded down. But God offers to take that heavy load from you. (Read 1 Peter 5:7.) God takes on your load because he loves you. So, go ahead. Give God those troubles!

MORE FAITH Links

- When Bad Turns to Worse, **p. 82**
- Good Times and Bad, **p. 462**
- A Really Bad Day, **p. 661**
- When the Going Gets Tough, **p. 1079**
- A Soldier's Story, **p. 1653**

Has someone who is close to you – a friend, your mum or dad, or your gran – ever been ill? How did it make you feel? You probably worried a lot.

When something bad happens to someone you care about, that can get you down. But there is someone who can help! Connect to these Faithlinks to learn more.

A Giant Problem, 1 Samuel 17:32–51, p. 377
- Do you ever feel small and worthless – like an ant meeting up with the bottom of a giant shoe? Sometimes problems can make us feel that way. What are some giant problems in your life? Talk to God about them. He can cut those problems down to size.

Lower Than Low, Job 19:13–25, p. 680
- Job had terrible problems and he felt miserable. Link here to discover what Job did when he hit "rock bottom".

Sad Times, Matthew 14:13–14, p. 1299
- Have you ever had someone you loved die? How did you feel? What was the hardest part? One of Jesus' friends died and he felt sad about it. He went off by himself for a while. When you feel sad about someone dying, remember that Jesus understands and is with you. How can that help you?

Hard Times, 2 Corinthians 1:8–10, p. 1570
- What is your first reaction when hard times come? Do you panic or get angry with God? Paul went through lots of hard times – he even thought he would die. Link here to see how Paul reacted to these bad times.

my FAVOURITE links

getting drunk, wild and drunken parties, and hateful idol worship. 4 Non-believers think it is strange that you do not do the many wild and wasteful things they do, so they insult you. 5 But they will have to explain this to God, who is ready to judge the living and the dead. 6 For this reason the Good News was preached to those who are now dead. Even though they were judged like all people, the Good News was preached to them so they could live in the spirit as God lives.

Use God's Gifts Wisely

7 The time is near when all things will end. So think clearly and control yourselves so that you will be able to pray. 8 Most importantly, love each other deeply, because love will cause many sins to be forgiven. 9 Open your homes to each other, without complaining. 10 Each of you has received a gift to use to serve others. Be good servants of God's various gifts of grace. 11 Anyone who speaks should speak words from God. Anyone who serves should serve with the strength God gives so that in everything God will be praised through Jesus Christ. Power and glory belong to him for ever and ever. Amen.

Suffering as a Christian

12 My friends, do not be surprised at the terrible trouble which now comes to test you. Do not think that something strange is happening to you. 13 But be happy that you are sharing in Christ's sufferings so that you will be happy and full of joy when Christ comes again in glory. 14 When people insult you because you follow Christ, you are blessed, because the glorious Spirit, the Spirit of God, is with you. 15 Do not suffer for murder, theft or any other crime, nor because you trouble other people. 16 But if you suffer because you are a Christian, do not be ashamed. Praise God because you wear that name. 17 It is time for judgement to begin with God's family. And if that judging begins with us, what will happen to those people who do not obey the Good News of God?

18 "If it is very hard for a good person to be saved,

FAITH links

COME ON IN!

1 PETER 4:9-10

Who do you like to invite to your house? Your best friend? Any friend? Only certain ones? In his first letter, Peter encouraged the Christians to be hospitable to *any* believers who showed up at their house. Being hospitable means being kind to the people who visit you. In Bible times, there were no hotels and motels like the ones we enjoy today. Travellers generally depended on the kindness of others.

You can be hospitable to anyone, anywhere you are. Being hospitable doesn't mean being choosy about whom you welcome. It means welcoming anyone who comes.

Care for the Lost, Deuteronomy 22:1–3, p. 255

The MLP, Ruth 1:16–17, p. 345

Kind or Fair? 1 Samuel 30, p. 395

Jesus' Mission and Yours, Isaiah 61:1–2, p. 978

The Right Ingredients, Micah 6:8, p. 1227

The Worst Chore, John 13:3–17, p. 1447

---

eMAIL FROM GOD
4:12–19
Troubles
Find the joy in your troubles.

the wicked person and the sinner
will surely be lost!"[n]

19 So those who suffer as God wants should trust their souls to the faithful Creator as they continue to do what is right.

The Flock of God

5 Now I have something to say to the elders in your group. I also am an elder. I have seen Christ's sufferings, and I will share in the glory that will be shown to us. I beg you to 2 shepherd God's flock, for whom you are responsible. Watch over them because you want to, not because you are forced. That is how God wants it. Do it because you are happy to serve, not because you want money. 3 Do not be like a ruler over people you are responsible for, but be good examples to them. 4 Then when Christ, the Chief Shepherd, comes, you will get a glorious crown that will never lose its beauty.

5 In the same way, younger people should be willing to be under older people. And all of you should be very humble with each other.

"God is against the proud,
but he gives grace to the humble."
Proverbs 3:34

6 Be humble under God's powerful hand so he will lift you up when the right time comes. 7 Give all your worries to him, because he cares about you.

8 Control yourselves and be careful! The devil, your enemy, goes around like a roaring lion looking for someone to eat. 9 Refuse to give in to him, by standing strong in your faith. You know that your Christian family all over the world is having the same kinds of suffering.

10 And after you suffer for a short time, God, who gives all grace, will make everything right. He will make you strong and support you and keep you from falling. He called you to share in his glory in Christ, a glory that will continue for ever. 11 All power is his for ever and ever. Amen.

5:8
Satan
Who is the devil's enemy?

FAITH links

TOSS THOSE TROUBLES!

1 PETER 5:7

What is the heaviest load you have ever carried? Imagine carrying twice that load all day, everywhere you went. (If you have trouble imagining that, grab about five or six heavy books and lug them around.) Now imagine someone offering to take that heavy load from you. Imagine how much lighter you would feel! That's what Peter says God does for you. The things that worry you can cause you to feel loaded down. God promises you can toss your load of worries onto him. Why? Because he loves you. So, go ahead. Toss those troubles. He can handle 'em!

Don't worry! Connect here to see how God can take care of those fears:

The Trouble with Sin, Genesis 6—8, p. 11

Your Worst Enemy, Exodus 7—11, p. 85

A Pity Party, Job 10, p. 671

999, Psalm 28:6, p. 730

Future Hope, Joel 3:17–21, p. 1191

The God of Second Chances, Jonah 3, p. 1215

4:18 "If . . . lost!" Quotation from Proverbs 11:31 in the Septuagint, the Greek version of the Old Testament.

Final Greetings

12 I wrote this short letter with the help of Silas, who I know is a faithful brother in Christ. I wrote to encourage you and to tell you that this is the true grace of God. Stand strong in that grace.

13 The church in Babylon, chosen like you, sends you greetings. Mark, my son in Christ, also greets you. 14 Give each other a kiss of Christian love when you meet.

Peace to all of you who are in Christ.

2 Peter 1:1 1708

1 From Simon Peter, a servant and apostle of Jesus Christ.

To you who have received a faith as valuable as ours, because our God and Saviour Jesus Christ does what is right.

2 Grace and peace be given to you more and more, because you truly know God and Jesus our Lord.

God Has Given Us Blessings

3 Jesus has the power of God, by which he has given us everything we need to live and to serve God. We have these things because we know him. Jesus called us by his glory and goodness. 4 Through these he gave us the very great and precious promises. With these gifts you can share in being like God, and the world will not ruin you with its evil desires.

5 Because you have these blessings, do your best to add these things to your lives: to your faith, add goodness; and to your goodness, add knowledge; 6 and to your knowledge, add self-control; and to your self-control, add patience; and to your patience, add service for God; 7 and to your service for God, add kindness for your brothers and sisters" in Christ; and to this kindness, add love. 8 If all these things are in you and are growing, they will help you to be useful and productive in your knowledge of our Lord Jesus Christ. 9 But anyone who does not have these things cannot see clearly. He is blind and has forgotten that he was made clean from his past sins.

10 My brothers and sisters, try hard to be certain that you really are called and chosen by God. If you do all these things, you will never fall. 11 And you will be given a very great welcome into the eternal kingdom of our Lord and Saviour Jesus Christ.

12 You know these things, and you are

1:5–8 Perseverance
Check out how to grow in faith.

1:7 brothers and sisters Although the Greek text says "brothers" here and throughout this book, Peter's words were meant for the entire church, both men and women.

FAITH links

THE "QUALITY" OF LIFE
2 PETER 1:5-8

Ever hear people talk about what they need to make life better? Some might feel they need more money to improve their quality of life. Others might feel they need something meaningful to do.

Peter, one of Jesus' followers, has some advice for making life better. In the second letter that he wrote, he talked about some spiritual qualities Christians could add to their lives to make life better *for others*. What are these qualities? Goodness, knowledge, self-control, patience, service, kindness and love. These are also the fruits of the Spirit. (See Galatians 5:22–23, p. 1592.) Don't leave home without 'em!

Check out what qualities you should be taking along each day:

Learning to Listen, 1 Samuel 3, p. 358

The Green Light, 2 Samuel 2:1, p. 401

Our Thirst Quencher, Psalm 42:1–3, p. 741

Down on the Ant Farm, Proverbs 6:6–11, p. 833

Want to Know? Ask! Luke 9:45, p. 1386

A Different Kind of Fruit, Galatians 5:22–23, p. 1592

very strong in the truth, but I will always help you remember them. 13 I think it is right for me to help you remember as long as I am in this body. 14 I know I must soon leave this body, as our Lord Jesus Christ has shown me. 15 I will try my best so that you may be able to remember these things even after I am gone.

We Saw Christ's Glory

16 When we told you about the powerful coming of our Lord Jesus Christ, we were not telling just clever stories that someone invented. But we saw the greatness of Jesus with our own eyes. 17 Jesus heard the voice of God, the Greatest Glory, when he received honour and glory from God the Father. The voice said, "This is my Son, whom I love, and I am very pleased with him." 18 We heard that voice from heaven while we were with Jesus on the holy mountain.

19 This makes us more sure about the message the prophets gave. It is good for you to follow closely what they said as you would follow a light shining in a dark place, until the day begins and the morning star rises in your hearts. 20 Most of all, you must understand this: no prophecy in the Scriptures ever comes from the prophet's own interpretation. 21 No prophecy ever comes from what a person wanted to say, but people led by the Holy Spirit spoke words from God.

False Teachers

2 There used to be false prophets among God's people, just as you will have some false teachers in your group. They will secretly teach things that are wrong—teachings that will cause people to be lost. They will even refuse to accept the Master, Jesus, who bought their freedom. So they will bring quick ruin on themselves. 2 Many will follow their evil ways and say evil things about the way of truth. 3 Those false teachers only want your money, so they will use you by telling you lies. Their judgement spoken against them long ago is still coming, and their ruin is certain.

FAITH links

YOU'RE A FAKE!
2 PETER 2:1

Imagine how you'd feel if someone suddenly walked into your classroom at school and announced that your teacher was a fake and taught you stuff that was wrong. You'd be pretty amazed, wouldn't you? Peter made a similar announcement when he talked about a group of teachers in the area. He called them false teachers. These teachers did not tell the truth about God. Peter warned the Christians about them so that they would continue believing what was true.

When people talk to you about God, you might wonder how you can know what's true and what's false. The Bible can help. It will always tell you what's true!

Download these Faithlinks to get the real truth:

Good Advice? Leviticus 20:6, p. 162

Remembering What He Said, Deuteronomy 6:4–9, p. 236

The Prayer Habit, Psalm 5:1–3, p. 712

Long-lasting Hope, Hosea 14, p. 1184

Hope That Doesn't Fail, Acts 26:4–7, p. 1510

That's False! 2 John 7–11, p. 1722

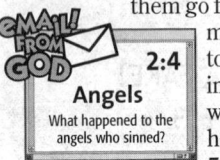

2:4 Angels
What happened to the angels who sinned?

4 When angels sinned, God did not let them go free without punishment. He sent them to hell and put them in caves of darkness where they are being held for judgement. 5 And God punished the world long ago when he brought a flood to the world that was full of people who were against him. But God saved Noah, who preached about being right with God, and seven other people with him. 6 And God also destroyed the evil cities of Sodom and Gomorrah[n] by burning them until they were ashes. He made those cities an example of what will happen to those who are against God. 7 But he saved Lot from those cities. Lot, a good man, was troubled because of the dirty lives of evil people. 8 (Lot was a good man, but because he lived with evil people every day, his good heart was hurt by the evil things he saw and heard.) 9 So the Lord knows how to save those who serve him when troubles come. He will hold evil people and punish them, while waiting for the Judgement Day. 10 That punishment is especially for those who live by doing the evil things their sinful selves want and who hate authority.

These false teachers are bold and do anything they want. They are not afraid to speak against the angels. 11 But even the angels, who are much stronger and more powerful than false teachers, do not accuse them with insults before the Lord. 12 But these people speak against things they do not understand. They are like animals that act without thinking, animals born to be caught and killed. And, like animals, these false teachers will be destroyed. 13 They have caused many people to suffer, so they themselves will suffer. That is their pay for what they have done. They take pleasure in openly doing evil, so they are like dirty spots and stains among you. They delight in trickery while eating meals with you. 14 Every time they look at a woman they want her, and their desire for sin is never satisfied. They lead weak people into the trap of sin, and they have taught their hearts to be greedy. God will punish them! 15 These false teachers left the right road and lost their way, following the way Balaam went. Balaam was the son of Beor, who loved being paid for doing wrong. 16 But a donkey, which cannot talk, told Balaam he was sinning. It spoke with a man's voice and stopped the prophet's mad thinking.

17 Those false teachers are like springs without water and clouds blown by a storm. A place in the blackest darkness has been kept for them. 18 They boast with words that mean nothing. By their evil desires they lead people into the trap of sin—people who are just beginning to escape from others who live in error. 19 They promise them freedom, but they themselves are not free. They are slaves of things that will be destroyed. For people are slaves of anything that controls them. 20 They were made free from the evil in the world by knowing our Lord and Saviour Jesus Christ. But if they return to evil things and those things control them, then it is worse for them than it was before. 21 Yes, it would be better for them to have never known the right way than to know it and to turn away from the holy teaching that was given to them. 22 What they did is like this true saying: "A dog goes back to what it has thrown up,"[n] and, "After a pig is washed, it goes back and rolls in the mud."

Jesus will Come Again

3 My friends, this is the second letter I have written you to help your honest minds remember. 2 I want you to think about the words the holy prophets spoke in the past, and remember the command our Lord and Saviour gave us through your apostles. 3 It is most important for you to understand what will happen in the last days. People will laugh at you. They will live doing the evil things they want to do. 4 They will say, "Jesus promised to come again. Where is he? Our fathers have died, but the world continues the

---

2:6 Sodom and Gomorrah Two cities God destroyed because the people were so evil.
2:22 "A dog . . . up" Quotation from Proverbs 26:11.

FAITH links

HIS BEST QUALITIES
2 PETER 3:9

What do you think is your best quality? Your winning personality? Your smile? Your kindness? All of God's qualities are his best ones. But Peter talked about two in particular: his faithfulness and patience. Some of the Christians in Peter's day wondered what was taking Jesus so long to return. Peter wanted them to know that God was faithful in keeping his promises. He patiently allows everyone the opportunity to ask for his forgiveness. If you haven't done that yet, what are you waiting for?

The Perfect Sacrifice, Leviticus 1—7, p. 135

A Shortcut, 1 Samuel 13:1–14, p. 369

Hurry Up and Wait, 2 Samuel 5, p. 405

A Hard Place, Ezekiel 28:25–26, p. 1120

A High Price, Romans 6:23, p. 1526

It's Guaranteed! 1 John 1:9–10, p. 1714

---

way it has been since it was made." 5 But they do not want to remember what happened long ago. By the word of God heaven was made, and the earth was made from water and with water. 6 Then the world was flooded and destroyed with water. 7 And that same word of God is keeping heaven and earth that we now have in order to be destroyed by fire. They are being kept for the Judgement Day and the destruction of all who are against God.

8 But do not forget this one thing, dear friends: to the Lord one day is as a thousand years, and a thousand years is as one day. 9 The Lord is not slow in doing what he promised—the way some people understand slowness. But God is being patient with you. He does not want anyone to be lost, but he wants all people to change their hearts and lives.

10 But the day of the Lord will come like a thief. The skies will disappear with a loud noise. Everything in them will be destroyed by fire, and the earth and everything in it will be burnt up.*n* 11 In that way everything will be destroyed. So what kind of people should you be? You should live holy lives and serve God, 12 as you wait for and look forward to the coming of the day of God. When that day comes, the skies will be destroyed with fire, and everything in them will melt with heat. 13 But God made a promise to us, and we are waiting for a new heaven and a new earth where goodness lives.

14 Dear friends, since you are waiting for this to happen, do your best to be without sin and without fault. Try to be at peace with God. 15 Remember that we are saved because our Lord is patient. Our dear brother Paul told you the same thing when he wrote to you with the wisdom that God gave him. 16 He writes about this in all his letters. Some things in Paul's letters are hard to understand, and people who are ignorant and weak in faith explain these things falsely. They also falsely explain the other Scriptures, but they are destroying themselves by doing this.

17 Dear friends, since you already know about this, be careful. Do not let those evil people lead you away by the wrong they do. Be careful so you will not fall from your strong faith. 18 But grow in the grace and knowledge of our Lord and Saviour Jesus Christ. Glory be to him now and for ever! Amen.

3:10 will be burnt up Many Greek copies say, "will be found". One copy says, "will disappear".

1, 2, & 3 John

REAL JESUS

Hi, guys! It's me again, John. I'm glad you're reading my short letters. You may remember that I wrote another book about Jesus to let people know that he truly was the Son of God. Just in case you *don't* remember all of that stuff about me, let me fill you in. I was Jesus' favourite disciple. In fact, I was an eyewitness to everything that Jesus did. In other words, I was with Jesus all of the time. Imagine, being that close to God – every day! It was incredible!

I wrote these letters to believers about three different topics. So you won't get confused, let me give you one quick idea about each letter. I wrote 1 John because there were some people who were saying that Jesus looked like a human but really wasn't. Well, I lived and ate and walked with Jesus. I *knew* this wasn't true. I wrote 2 John to remind Christians to stay away from people who say that Jesus wasn't really human. And I wrote 3 John to my good friend Gaius to encourage him to continue to seek the truth and help those who were teaching the truth. Remember what the truth is? (Hint: download John 14:6, p. 1448.)

JESUS WATCH

John's three letters remind believers that Jesus is a real person – and he's really God. John's portrayal through these three letters is built on a firm foundation that Jesus walked with believers as fully God and completely human (a really tough thing to understand!). These three books help both John's first readers and us to realise that Jesus isn't someone who doesn't understand our daily lives and needs. He loves us, and he loves being with us – even today!

my FAVOURITE links

OTHER CONNECTIONS

 What would you consider the hardest thing about being a kid? Is close to the top of your list trying to obey all the rules that you are given – rules at home, rules at school, rules at Sunday school? What about obeying God's rules? Download <u>Loving to Obey, 1 John 2:3–6</u>, to learn how important it is to follow God's rules.

MORE STUFF . . .
Good and Bad Teachers How can you tell the difference between a good teacher and a false teacher? In his letters, John gives some important differences. Check it out below:
- Good teachers believe that Jesus came to earth as a human (1 John 4:2).
- False teachers refuse to admit that Jesus came to earth (1 John 4:3).
- Those who don't believe in God listen to false teachers; God's people listen to good teachers (1 John 4:5–6).
- False teachers don't follow only Jesus' teachings, but add other teachings (2 John 9–11).
- False teachers do evil things; good teachers obey God (3 John 11).

Do you know who John calls a liar?

Think you know the answer to that one? Let's surf over to <u>1 John 2:22–23</u> to make sure.

CHECK OUT SOME OTHER COOL STUFF IN JOHN'S BOOKS:
<u>Source of love, 1 John 4:7–21</u>
<u>Ask anything! 1 John 5:13–15</u>
<u>False teachers not wanted, 2 John 7–11</u>
<u>The greatest joy, 3 John 4</u>

FAITH links

○ It's Guaranteed!
  1 John 1:9–10

○ Ya' Gotta Love It?
  1 John 2:15

○ The True Test,
  1 John 3:18

○ Love and Obey,
  2 John 6

○ That's False!
  2 John 7–11

○ What Any Parent Wants,
  3 John 3–4

○ Who's on First?
  3 John 9–10

○ Helpful Hints,
  3 John 11

1 We write to you now about what has always existed, which we have heard, we have seen with our own eyes, we have looked at, and we have touched with our hands. We write to you about the Word[n] that gives life. 2 He who gives life was shown to us. We saw him and can give proof about it. And now we announce to you that he has life that continues for ever. He was with God the Father and was shown to us. 3 We announce to you what we have seen and heard, because we want you also to have fellowship with us. Our fellowship is with God the Father and with his Son, Jesus Christ. 4 We write this to you so you can be full of joy with us.

God Forgives our Sins

5 Here is the message we have heard from Christ and now announce to you: God is light,[n] and in him there is no darkness at all. 6 So if we say we have fellowship with God, but we continue living in darkness, we are liars and do not follow the truth. 7 But if we live in the light, as God is in the light, we can share fellowship with each other. Then the blood of Jesus, God's Son, cleanses us from every sin.

8 If we say we have no sin, we are fooling ourselves, and the truth is not in us. 9 But if we confess our sins, he will forgive our sins, because we can trust God to do what is right. He will cleanse us from all the wrongs we have done. 10 If we say we have not sinned, we make God a liar, and we do not accept God's teaching.

Jesus is our Helper

2 My dear children, I write this letter to you so you will not sin. But if anyone does sin, we have a helper in the presence of the Father—Jesus Christ, the One who does what is right. 2 He is the way our sins are taken away, and not only our sins but the sins of all people.

3 We can be sure that we know God if

IT'S GUARANTEED!
1 JOHN 1:9-10

Some items you buy may come with a money-back guarantee. A guarantee is a promise. If you're not completely satisfied with what you bought, you can return it to the manufacturer and receive a full refund. It's great to have a guarantee, especially one with no strings attached. But having one is no good unless the manufacturer honours that guarantee.

In his first letter, John, one of Jesus' 12 followers, wrote about a guarantee that God will honour. If you do something wrong and confess what you've done, God promises to forgive you. Why? Because he's faithful. You have his word on it.

Download these links to find out how God deals with your sin:

A Priest Without Sin, **Leviticus 4:3–7, p. 136**

A Hidden Sin, **Joshua 7, p. 285**

A Pity Party, **Job 10, p. 671**

Believe the Impossible? **Ezekiel 37, p. 1131**

One Big, Happy Family, **John 1:12, p. 1422**

It's Free! **Ephesians 2:8–9, p. 1600**

2:3 Obedience
What is a sign that you know God?

1:1 Word The Greek word is "logos," meaning any kind of communication. Here, it means Christ, who was the way God told people about himself.
1:5 light Here, this word is used as a symbol of God's goodness or truth.

1 John 2:16 1715

how we can be sure we are living in God: 6 whoever says that he lives in God must live as Jesus lived.

The Command to Love Others

7 My dear friends, I am not writing a new command to you but an old command you have had from the beginning. It is the teaching you have already heard. 8 But also I am writing a new command to you, and you can see its truth in Jesus and in you, because the darkness is passing away, and the true light is already shining. 9 Anyone who says, "I am in the light,"[n] but hates a brother or sister,[n] is still in the darkness. 10 Whoever loves a brother or sister lives in the light and will not cause anyone to stumble in their faith. 11 But whoever hates a brother or sister is in darkness, lives in darkness and does not know where to go, because the darkness has made that person blind.

12 I write to you, dear children,
    because your sins are forgiven
      through Christ.
13 I write to you, parents,
    because you know the One who
      existed from the beginning.
I write to you, young people,
    because you have defeated the Evil
      One.
14 I write to you, children,
    because you know the Father.
I write to you, parents,
    because you know the One who
      existed from the beginning.
I write to you, young people,
    because you are strong;
    the teaching of God lives in you,
    and you have defeated the Evil
      One.

15 Do not love the world or the things in the world. If you love the world, the love of the Father is not in you. 16 These are the ways of the world: wanting to please our sinful selves, wanting the sinful things we

---

FAITH links

YA' GOTTA LOVE IT?
1 JOHN 2:15

You probably get lots of advice from your mum and dad, right? Your parents want to make sure you know what's right and what's wrong. The apostle John wrote a letter to Christians to help them know what was right and what was wrong. That's why he warned them to avoid loving the things of the world. What is the world? It includes the people and ideas that are opposed to God. Loving the things of the world means wanting or doing the wrong things, like being greedy or selfish. These attitudes make us unable to love people the way that God loves.

An Example Not to Follow, Leviticus 18:1–3, p. 157

Fairness for All, Deuteronomy 24:17, p. 258

Comfort from the Word, Job 26:3–4, p. 688

The Verdict Is In? Matthew 7:1–2, p. 1285

Best Seat in the House, Luke 14:7–11, p. 1398

You've Got the Power! Acts 1:1–8; 2:1–4, p. 1463

---

we obey his commands. 4 Anyone who says, "I know God," but does not obey God's commands is a liar, and the truth is not in that person. 5 But if someone obeys God's teaching, then in that person God's love has truly reached its goal. This is

---

2:9 light Here, this word is used as a symbol of God's goodness or truth.

2:9 brother or sister Although the Greek text says "brother" here and throughout this book, John's words were meant for the entire church, both men and women.

1 John 2 1716

OBEYING GOD
1 John 2:3–6

Loving to Obey Blah, blah, blah – same old warning over and over again? Why do things need repeating a zillion times? Maybe it's because lots of people do what *they* think is right, rather than what God says. God wants us to be obedient to him and not follow what *we* think is right and wrong. (Check out Judges 21:25, p. 342.)

God gives us advice about right and wrong. He tells us to stay away from people and ideas that go against God. If we love the things of the world, it means we can't love God. You can't love the world *and* God at the same time. (Look up 1 John 2:15.) Which will you choose – loving the world, or loving God?

MORE FAITH links

Obeying God or Man? **p. 1154**

A Reminder to Do What Is Right and True, **p. 1257**

The Number One Rule, **p. 1351**

Your Heart's Desire, **p. 1401**

Obey or Disobey? **p. 1409**

Love and Obey, **p. 1721**

You know, obeying God is one of the most important things you can do.

Just download some of these Faithlinks to see what else God has to say about obeying him.

Ten Ways to Obey, Exodus 20, p. 103
- Who makes the rules at home or at school? How do you feel about rules?
- God gave us a set of rules called the Ten Commandments. Which one of the commandments is the hardest for you to obey?

I Insist! 1 Samuel 8; 9, p. 363
- Have you ever begged your parents for something that you later wished you hadn't?
- How about insisting on having your own way? What happens if your way isn't God's way? Are you still going to do it?

The Greatest Commandment, Matthew 22:36–40, p. 1313
- What do you think is the No. 1 rule to obey? Link here to find out what Jesus has to say about it.

Put God First, Acts 5:27–32, p. 1472
- Did you ever get into trouble for doing the right thing? What happened?
- What if someone in authority asked you to do something that God says is wrong? What would you do?

see and being too proud of what we have. None of these come from the Father, but all of them come from the world. 17 The world and everything that people want in it are passing away, but the person who does what God wants lives for ever.

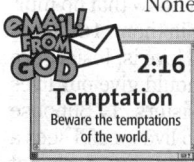

2:16 Temptation
Beware the temptations of the world.

Reject the Enemies of Christ

18 My dear children, these are the last days. You have heard that the enemy of Christ is coming, and now many enemies of Christ are already here. This is how we know that these are the last days. 19 These enemies of Christ were in our fellowship, but they left us. They never really belonged to us; if they had been a part of us, they would have stayed with us. But they left, and this shows that none of them really belonged to us.

20 You have the gift[n] that the Holy One gave you, so you all know the truth. 21 I do not write to you because you do not know the truth but because you do know the truth. And you know that no lie comes from the truth.

22 Who is the liar? It is the person who does not accept Jesus as the Christ. This is the enemy of Christ: the person who does not accept the Father and his Son. 23 Whoever does not accept the Son does not have the Father. But whoever confesses the Son has the Father, too.

24 Be sure you continue to follow the teaching you heard from the beginning. If you continue to follow what you heard from the beginning, you will stay in the Son and in the Father. 25 And this is what the Son promised to us—life for ever.

26 I am writing this letter about those people who are trying to lead you the wrong way. 27 Christ gave you a special gift that is still in you, so you do not need any other teacher. His gift teaches you about everything, and it is true, not false. So continue to live in Christ, as his gift taught you.

28 Yes, my dear children, live in him so that when Christ comes back, we can be without fear and not be ashamed in his presence. 29 If you know that Christ is all that is right, you know that all who do right are God's children.

We are God's Children

3 The Father has loved us so much that we are called children of God. And we really are his children. The reason the people in the world do not know us is that they have not known him. 2 Dear friends, now we are children of God, and we have not yet been shown what we will be in the future. But we know that when Christ comes again, we will be like him, because we will see him as he really is. 3 Christ is pure, and all who have this hope in Christ keep themselves pure like Christ.

4 The person who sins breaks God's law. Yes, sin is living against God's law. 5 You know that Christ came to take away sins and that there is no sin in Christ. 6 So anyone who lives in Christ does not go on sinning. Anyone who goes on sinning has never really understood Christ and has never known him.

7 Dear children, do not let anyone lead you the wrong way. Christ is all that is right. So to be like Christ a person must do what is right. 8 The devil has been sinning since the beginning, so anyone who continues to sin belongs to the devil. The Son of God came for this purpose: to destroy the devil's work.

3:7–8 Satan
Who destroys the devil's work?

9 Those who are God's children do not continue sinning, because the new life from God remains in them. They are not able to go on sinning, because they have become children of God. 10 So we can see who God's children are and who the devil's children are: those who do not do what is right are not God's children, and those who do not love their brothers and sisters are not God's children.

We Must Love Each Other

11 This is the teaching you have heard from the beginning: we must love each

---

2:20 gift This might mean the Holy Spirit, or it might mean teaching or truth as in verse 24.

FAITH links

THE TRUE TEST
1 JOHN 3:18

If someone said that they loved you, but acted as if they didn't want to be around you, would you believe that they loved you? You wouldn't, would you? You'd want to see some proof of that love. John, one of Jesus' 12 followers, had a lot to say about love in his letter. Love is more than just words. Love involves action. Don't just say you love someone, John says. Show it!

Here's some help on how to pass the "love" test:

Show Some Respect, Leviticus 19:32, p. 161

Choosing Sides, 1 Samuel 20, p. 382

Building Together, Nehemiah 3, p. 627

A Friend of Jesus, John 15:9–17, p. 1450

The Best Choice, 1 Corinthians 13, p. 1560

Who's on First? 3 John 9–10, p. 1723

other. 12 Do not be like Cain who belonged to the Evil One and killed his brother. And why did he kill him? Because the things Cain did were evil, and the things his brother did were good.

13 Brothers and sisters, do not be surprised when the people of the world hate you. 14 We know we have left death and have come into life because we love each other. Whoever does not love is still dead. 15 Everyone who hates a brother or sister is a murderer," and you know that no murderers have eternal life in them. 16 This is how we know what real love is: Jesus gave his life for us. So we should give our lives for our brothers and sisters. 17 Suppose someone has enough to live on and sees a brother or sister in need, but does not help. Then God's love is not living in that person. 18 My children, we should love people not only with words and talk, but by our actions and true caring.

19-20 This is the way we know that we belong to the way of truth. When our hearts make us feel guilty, we can still have peace before God. God is greater than our hearts, and he knows everything. 21 My dear friends, if our hearts do not make us feel guilty, we can come without fear into God's presence. 22 And God gives us what we ask for because we obey God's commands and do what pleases him. 23 This is what God commands: that we believe in his Son, Jesus Christ, and that we love each other, just as he commanded. 24 The people who obey God's commands live in God, and God lives in them. We know that God lives in us because of the Spirit God gave us.

Warning Against False Teachers

4 My dear friends, many false prophets have gone out into the world. So do not believe every spirit, but test the spirits to see if they are from God. 2 This is how you can know God's Spirit: every spirit who confesses that Jesus Christ came to earth as a human is from God. 3 And every spirit who refuses to say this about Jesus is not from God. It is the spirit of the enemy of Christ, which you have heard is coming, and now he is already in the world.

4 My dear children, you belong to God and have defeated them, because God's Spirit, who is in you, is greater than the

---

3:15 Everyone ... murderer If one person hates a brother or sister, then in the heart that person has killed that brother or sister. Jesus taught about this sin to his followers (Matthew 5:21-26).

1 John 5:2

FAITH CHALLENGE

Try this one. Read 4:18 to find out why we don't have to be afraid of anything. What kinds of things scare you? How does knowing this verse help you?

TESTING IT

1 John 4:18
Where God's love is, there is no fear, because God's perfect love drives out fear. It is punishment that makes a person fear, so love is not made perfect in the person who fears.

---

us: he sent his one and only Son into the world so that we could have life through him. 10 This is what real love is: it is not our love for God; it is God's love for us in sending his Son to be the way to take away our sins.

11 Dear friends, if God loved us that much we also should love each other. 12 No one has ever seen God, but if we love each other, God lives in us, and his love is made perfect in us.

13 We know that we live in God and he lives in us, because he gave us his Spirit. 14 We have seen and can testify that the Father sent his Son to be the Saviour of the world. 15 Whoever confesses that Jesus is the Son of God has God living inside, and that person lives in God. 16 And so we know the love that God has for us, and we trust that love.

God is love. Those who live in love live in God, and God lives in them. 17 This is how love is made perfect in us: that we can be without fear on the day God judges us, because in this world we are like him. 18 Where God's love is, there is no fear, because God's perfect love drives out fear. It is punishment that makes a person fear, so love is not made perfect in the person who fears.

4:18 Fears
What can drive away your fears?

19 We love because God first loved us. 20 If people say, "I love God," but hate their brothers or sisters, they are liars. Those who do not love their brothers and sisters, whom they have seen, cannot love God, whom they have never seen. 21 And God gave us this command: those who love God must also love their brothers and sisters.

devil, who is in the world. 5 And they belong to the world, so what they say is from the world, and the world listens to them. 6 But we belong to God, and those who know God listen to us. But those who are not from God do not listen to us. That is how we know the Spirit that is true and the spirit that is false.

Love Comes from God

7 Dear friends, we should love each other, because love comes from God. Everyone who loves has become God's child and knows God. 8 Whoever does not love does not know God, because God is love. 9 This is how God showed his love to

Faith in the Son of God

5 Everyone who believes that Jesus is the Christ is God's child, and whoever loves the Father also loves the Father's children. 2 This is how we know we love God's children: when we love God and obey his commands.

5:1–3 Obedience
How can you show love for others?

3 Loving God means obeying his commands. And God's commands are not too hard for us, 4 because everyone who is a child of God conquers the world. And this is the victory that conquers the world—our faith. 5 So the one who wins against the world is the person who believes that Jesus is the Son of God.

6 Jesus Christ is the One who came by water[n] and blood.[n] He did not come by water only, but by water and blood. And the Spirit says that this is true, because the Spirit is the truth. 7 So there are three witnesses that tell us about Jesus: 8 the Spirit, the water and the blood; and these three witnesses agree. 9 We believe people when they say something is true. But what God says is more important, and he has told us the truth about his own Son. 10 Anyone who believes in the Son of God has the truth that God told us. Anyone who does not believe makes God a liar, because that person does not believe what God told us about his Son. 11 This is what God told us: God has given us eternal life, and this life is in his Son. 12 Whoever has the Son has life, but whoever does not have the Son of God does not have life.

We Have Eternal Life Now

13 I write this letter to you who believe in the Son of God so you will know you have eternal life. 14 And this is the boldness we have in God's presence: that if we ask God for anything that agrees with

5:13–15 Prayer
How do you know God hears your prayers?

what he wants, he hears us. 15 If we know he hears us every time we ask him, we know we have what we ask from him.

16 If anyone sees a brother or sister sinning (sin that does not lead to eternal death), that person should pray, and God will give the sinner life. I am talking about people whose sin does not lead to eternal death. There is sin that leads to death. I do not mean that a person should pray about that sin. 17 Doing wrong is always sin, but there is sin that does not lead to eternal death.

18 We know that those who are God's children do not continue to sin. The Son of God keeps them safe, and the Evil One cannot touch them. 19 We know that we belong to God, but the Evil One controls the whole world. 20 We also know that the Son of God has come and has given us understanding so that we can know the True One. And our lives are in the True One and in his Son, Jesus Christ. He is the true God and the eternal life.

21 So, dear children, keep yourselves away from gods.

5:6 water This probably means the water of Jesus' baptism.
5:6 blood This probably means the blood of Jesus' death.

From the Elder.[n]
To the chosen lady[n] and her children: I love all of you in the truth,[n] and all those who know the truth love you. 2 We love you because of the truth that lives in us and will be with us for ever.

3 Grace, mercy and peace from God the Father and his Son, Jesus Christ, will be with us in truth and love.

4 I was very happy to learn that some of your children are following the way of truth, as the Father commanded us. 5 And now, dear lady, this is not a new command but is the same command we have had from the beginning. I ask you that we all love each other. 6 And love means living the way God commanded us to live. As you have heard from the beginning, his command is this: live a life of love.

7 Many false teachers are in the world now who do not confess that Jesus Christ came to earth as a human. Anyone who does not confess this is a false teacher and an enemy of Christ. 8 Be careful yourselves that you do not lose everything you have worked for, but that you receive your full reward.

9 Anyone who goes beyond Christ's teaching and does not continue to follow only his teaching does not have God. But whoever continues to follow the teaching of Christ has both the Father and the Son. 10 If someone comes to you and does not bring this teaching, do not welcome or accept that person into your house. 11 If you welcome such a person, you share in the evil work.

12 I have many things to write to you, but I do not want to use paper and ink. Instead, I hope to come to you and talk face to face so we can be full of joy.

13 The children of your chosen sister[n] greet you.

5
Love
What should Christians be known for?

FAITH links

LOVE AND OBEY
2 JOHN 6

What's the connection between love and obedience? One goes with the other. If you love your parents, you do what they tell you to do. If you love God, you do what he tells you to do.

That's what John, one of Jesus' followers, wrote about in his second letter. Jesus once told his followers that those who loved him obeyed his commands. (See John 15:14, p. 1450. John wrote that book, too!) Know what one of his commands is? Love others. So . . . how will you obey that command this week?

Give Revenge a Rest, Leviticus 19:18, p. 160

The Gift of Friendship, 1 Samuel 18:1–3; 19, p. 381

Help for the Outsiders, Nehemiah 5:9–10, p. 630

A Friend in Deed, Job 2:13, p. 662

Your Choice of Fruit, Matthew 12:33–35, p. 1295

Forgive Again? Luke 17:3–4, p. 1402

---

1 Elder "Elder" means an older person. It can also mean a special leader in the church (as in Titus 1:5).
1 lady This might mean a woman, or in this letter it might mean a church. If it is a church, then "her children" would be the people of the church.
1 truth The truth or "Good News" about Jesus Christ that joins all believers together.
13 sister Sister of the "lady" in verse 1. This might be another woman or another church.

2 John 1722

THAT'S FALSE!
2 JOHN 7-11

Has anyone ever tried to make you believe something that was not true? The apostle John warned Christians about false teachers in the area. These teachers did not believe that Jesus was God. John told the Christians not to even allow these teachers to enter their homes.

You may not have people coming to your door with false information. But you receive a lot of information each day at school, in your neighbourhood, on the Internet and on TV. Do you know what's true and what's false? How much of what's false do you allow into your brain? If you're not sure about what you're hearing or reading, talk to your parents or your pastor.

Here are some more Faithlinks on knowing what to believe:

The Sacrifice, Genesis 22, p. 29

Take Me to Your Leader, Numbers 27:12–23, p. 214

A Look for the Book, 2 Chronicles 34:14–18, p. 603

The One Who Suffered, Isaiah 53, p. 966

Faith Workout, Acts 16:4–5, p. 1493

The Way to Be Wise, James 1:5, p. 1689

FAITH links

WHAT ANY PARENT WANTS
3 JOHN 3-4

What do you think your parents want for your life? Most parents or guardians want their children to grow up to be respected members of society – fully mature and wise. John was like a father to the Christians he wrote letters to. He had hopes and dreams for them, just like any parent. One dream was for them to live in a way that would please God. He wanted them to keep believing what was true about God. Guess what? That's what *your* parents want for you, too.

Check out God's plans and hopes for you:

Forgive Instead, Genesis 33, p. 47

Obey? No Way! Exodus 1:15–21, p. 76

More Precious Than Gold, Psalm 19:7–10, p. 723

Pass It On! Joel 1:2–3, p. 1187

Quick to Forgive? Mark 11:25, p. 1349

How to Make God Glad, Ephesians 6:1–2, p. 1605

FAITH links

WHO'S ON FIRST?
3 JOHN 9-10

Is there a Diotrephes in your life? No, that's not a new kind of video game. Diotrephes was a church leader who made trouble for visiting church leaders sent by John. Instead of welcoming them, Diotrephes ignored them and tried to stop anyone else in the church from helping them. He wanted to be seen as the most important person in his church community.

All Christians are part of a team. There are no MVPs (Most Valuable Players). Part of the team's duty includes respecting church leaders and welcoming those who visit. That duty takes humility and a willingness to serve others. Are you willing?

Play Fair or Play Favourites? Deuteronomy 1:16–18, p. 227

Your Response to Responsibility, Ruth 2:1–7, p. 346

Building Together, Nehemiah 3, p. 627

Best Seat in the House, Luke 14:7–11, p. 1398

An Unselfish Example, Philippians 2:5–8, p. 1611

The True Test, 1 John 3:18, p. 1718

From the Elder.[n]
To my dear friend Gaius, whom I love in the truth:[n]

2 My dear friend, I know your soul is doing fine, and I pray that you are doing well in every way and that your health is good. 3 I was very happy when some

---

1 Elder "Elder" means an older person. It can also mean a special leader in the church (as in Titus 1:5).

1 truth The truth or "Good News" about Jesus Christ that joins all believers together.

3 John 4 1724

brothers and sisters[n] came and told me about the truth in your life and how you are following the way of truth. 4 Nothing gives me greater joy than to hear that my children are following the way of truth.

5 My dear friend, it is good that you help the brothers and sisters, even those you do not know. 6 They told the church about your love. Please help them to continue their trip in a way worthy of God. 7 They started out in service to Christ, and they have been accepting nothing from non-believers. 8 So we should help such people; when we do, we share in their work for the truth.

9 I wrote something to the church, but Diotrephes, who loves to be their leader, will not listen to us. 10 So if I come, I will talk about what Diotrephes is doing, about how he lies and says evil things about us. But more than that, he refuses to accept the other brothers and sisters; he even stops those who do want to accept them and puts them out of the church.

11 My dear friend, do not follow what is bad; follow what is good. The one who does good belongs to God. But the one who does evil has never known God.

EMAIL FROM GOD
11
Life
Read about following what is good.

12 Everyone says good things about Demetrius, and the truth agrees with what they say. We also speak well of him, and you know what we say is true.

13 I have many things I want to write you, but I do not want to use pen and ink. 14 I hope to see you soon and talk face to face.

15 Peace to you. The friends here greet you. Please greet each friend there by name.

---

3 brothers and sisters Although the Greek text says "brothers" here and throughout this book, John's words were meant for the entire church, both men and women.

FAITH links

HELPFUL HINTS
3 JOHN 11

Did your mother ever say, "If so-and-so jumped off a bridge, would you do the same?" That's an answer many parents give in response to their children's desire to do something everyone else does. Usually, that "something" is an activity the parent isn't crazy about.

In his letter, the apostle John didn't mention any bridges. Instead, he told the Christians not to follow a bad example. Instead, they should do what was right. Want to do what's right? You'll need a model for right behaviour. The Bible mentions the perfect role model: Jesus. Follow him, and you can't go wrong!

Connect here to find out more about the perfect role model:

What's Out Becomes In, Judges 11, p. 327

I Insist! 1 Samuel 8; 9, p. 363

Mind Guard, Proverbs 4:23, p. 831

Small Beginnings, Zechariah 4:10, p. 1255

Two Ways to Grow, Luke 2:46–52, p. 1370

Out with the Old! Colossians 3:1–14, p. 1625

FIGHT FOR THE FAITH!

Hi, I'm Jude. You probably don't know who I am – I'm the older brother of James (he wrote James and was the leader of the church in Jerusalem) and Jesus' half-brother. It's hard to imagine, but I didn't actually believe in Jesus until *after* he rose from the dead. I had a lot to learn about Jesus when I finally believed. The Bible doesn't talk a lot about me, but I probably served in the Jerusalem church with James and was certainly around very important biblical people.

I wrote this book to let the first believers know that it was important to understand what they believed. A lot of Christians were running around saying they were believers, but they weren't really thinking about what that meant; and a lot of the teachings floating around about Jesus were really wrong. There were also many rebellious people in the church – and I wanted these people to stop being rebellious.

JESUS WATCH

Jude gives us two very distinct pictures of Jesus. On the one hand, believers are told to fight for their faith they know is true and to keep themselves in the love of God. Jude calls them (and us) to look for God's mercy and seek eternal life, because those who don't will be punished. At the same time, Jude reminds us that Jesus protects us and keeps us from stumbling in our walk with him.

If we'll "keep ourselves in Jesus" and trust in God's ability to guard every step we take, Jude promises that we'll enter into a type of friendship with God that is wonderful. Knowing God can feel impossible, and following what God commands can be unbelievably difficult. But Jude reassures us that God is strong and able to keep us from falling.

FAITH links

Do you know what God did to those angels who rebelled against him?

Try connecting to Jude 6, and see what you can find out.

○ While You Wait, **Jude 21**

○ The Sin "Braker", **Jude 24–25**

Jude 1

1 From Jude, a servant of Jesus Christ and a brother of James.

To all who have been called by God. God the Father loves you, and you have been kept safe in Jesus Christ:

2 Mercy, peace and love be yours richly.

God will Punish Sinners

3 Dear friends, I wanted very much to write to you about the salvation we all share. But I felt the need to write to you about something else: I want to encourage you to fight hard for the faith that was given the holy people of God once and for all time. 4 Some people have secretly entered your group. Long ago the prophets wrote about these people who will be judged guilty. They are against God and have changed the grace of our God into a reason for sexual sin. They also refuse to accept Jesus Christ, our only Master and Lord.

5 I want to remind you of some things you already know: remember that the Lord saved his people by bringing them out of the land of Egypt. But later he destroyed all those who did not believe. 6 And remember the angels who did not keep their place of power but left their proper home. The Lord has kept these angels in darkness, bound with everlasting chains, to be judged on the great day. 7 Also remember the cities of Sodom and Gomorrah*ⁿ* and the other towns around them. In the same way they were full of sexual sin and people who desired sexual relations that God does not allow. They suffer the punishment of eternal fire, as an example for all to see.

8 It is the same with these people who have entered your group. They are guided by dreams and make themselves dirty with sin. They reject God's authority and speak against the angels. 9 Not even the

EMAIL FROM GOD 6
Hell
What happened to angels who rebelled?

---

7 **Sodom and Gomorrah** Two cities God destroyed because they were so evil.

FAITH links

WHILE YOU WAIT
JUDE 21

What events do you find the hardest to wait for? Your birthday? Christmas? Many Christians have a hard time waiting for Jesus' return to earth. Jude, the half-brother of Jesus, wrote a letter to encourage Christians to stay in God's love while they waited for Jesus to return. Staying in God's love means living for him and obeying what he says.

Jude knew that false teachers would try to lure the Christians that he wrote to away from God. That's why he told them to stick with God. We should, too. How do you stick with God? You can pray, read your Bible and get involved at church.

Check out these Faithlinks on the best way to stick with God:

Our Thorough God, Leviticus 13, p. 149

Patience, Please, Psalm 145:8–9, p. 819

The Gift of Worship, Matthew 2:10–12, p. 1275

Faith God Notices, Luke 18:35–43, p. 1406

Keeping Clean, 2 Corinthians 7:1, p. 1576

A Heavenly Sight, Revelation 21:1–4, p. 1753

FAITH LINKS

THE SIN "BRAKER"
JUDE 24-25

If you've ever been on inline skates, you know what falling is like. As you learn to skate better, you learn how to brake and keep your knees bent to avoid falling.

Jude, the half-brother of Jesus, wrote about another type of falling. To "fall" means to sin. Trusting in God's strength helps to keep you from giving in to the temptation to sin. These verses are a prayer that many churches use at the end of a service. Next time you're out skating, think about how God puts the brakes on sin in your life.

The Trouble with Jealousy, Genesis 37, p. 53

A Long Wait, Joshua 14:6–15, p. 294

World News, Isaiah 13—19, p. 913

Facing Your Fears, Matthew 8:23–27, p. 1288

The Way to Be Wise, James 1:5, p. 1689

A Happy Ending, Revelation 22:16–21, p. 1754

---

archangel[n] Michael, when he argued with the devil about who would have the body of Moses, dared to judge the devil guilty. Instead, he said, "The Lord punish you." 10 But these people speak against things they do not understand. And what they do know, by feeling, as dumb animals know things, are the very things that destroy them. 11 It will be terrible for them. They have followed the way of Cain, and for money they have given themselves to doing the wrong that Balaam did. They have fought against God as Korah did, and like Korah, they surely will be destroyed. 12 They are like dirty spots in your special Christian meals you share. They eat with you and have no fear, caring only for themselves. They are clouds without rain, which the wind blows around. They are autumn trees without fruit that are pulled out of the ground. So they are twice dead. 13 They are like wild waves of the sea, tossing up their own shameful actions like foam. They are like stars that wander in the sky. A place in the blackest darkness has been kept for them for ever.

14 Enoch, the seventh descendant from Adam, said about these people: "Look, the Lord is coming with many thousands of his holy angels to 15 judge every person. He is coming to punish all who are against God for all the evil they have done against him. And he will punish the sinners who are against God for all the evil they have said against him."

16 These people complain and blame others, doing the evil things they want to do. They boast about themselves, and they flatter others to get what they want.

A Warning and Things to Do

17 Dear friends, remember what the apostles of our Lord Jesus Christ said before. 18 They said to you, "In the last times there will be people who laugh about God, following their own evil desires which are against God." 19 These are the people who divide you, people whose thoughts are only of this world, who do not have the Spirit. 20 But dear friends, use your most holy

EMAIL FROM GOD
20 Prayer
What's the best way to build faith?

---

9 archangel The leader among God's angels or messengers.

Jude 21   1728

faith to build yourselves up, praying in the Holy Spirit. 21 Keep yourselves in God's love as you wait for the Lord Jesus Christ with his mercy to give you life for ever.

22 Show mercy to people who have doubts. 23 Take others out of the fire, and save them. Show mercy mixed with fear to others, hating even their clothes which are dirty from sin.

Praise God

24 God is strong and can keep you from falling. He can bring you before his glory without any wrong in you and can give you great joy. 25 He is the only God, the One who saves us. To him be glory, greatness, power and authority through Jesus Christ our Lord for all time past, now and for ever. Amen.

A NEW BEGINNING

Hi, everyone! It's John here. Do you remember which other books I wrote? That's right. I wrote the Gospel of John and three letters (1, 2 and 3 John). I was known as the disciple Jesus loved the most. But being a disciple of Jesus wasn't always easy. Because I was a leader of a church, the Roman emperor Domitian sent me away to the island of Patmos, which was really like a prison. (Do you know that the enemies of the faith wanted to do me harm? Praise God that he protected me!) I wrote this letter (my last one) while I was there.

Why did I write this book? I wanted to give my friends and fellow believers hope by letting them know that Jesus was in control of *everything* – even when they were facing some pretty tough times. But I didn't want the Roman officials to understand what I was saying. (I'm sure they would try to get rid of more Christians.) So I used a lot of symbols in my book that only believers would understand. Kind of like writing to your friends in a secret code! Pretty sneaky, eh?

JESUS WATCH

John's book gives a dramatic and powerful glimpse – or revelation – into what will happen when Jesus returns to earth. John portrays Jesus as the conquering king, the judge over all the earth and the loving redeemer. The book begins with a picture of Jesus' breathtaking glory and shows his power over the entire church. Want some quick snapshots of Jesus in Revelation? Jesus is: ruler of the kings of the earth (Revelation 1:5); the First and the Last (Revelation 1:17); the One who sits on the throne (Revelation 5:13); the Word of God (Revelation 19:13); the King of Kings and Lord of Lords (Revelation 19:16); the Alpha and the Omega (Revelation 22:13). We worship an awesome God!

Through these pictures, believers are offered hope. God's message throughout this book, and through the life of Jesus, is clear – trusting Jesus for eternal life is essential. We could live apart from Jesus – but we'd lack so much. Power, wisdom, blessings. The list is long. Choosing to live for Jesus might not offer us an easy life, but it does mean that we get to spend eternity with the conquering, loving and redeeming Lamb of God. What will you choose to do?

OTHER CONNECTIONS

Get the Info

- **The Follower Jesus Loved, Revelation 1.** Along with Peter and his brother James, John was one of the followers closest to Jesus. In fact, John refers to himself as "the follower Jesus loved". Find out more about John's life and ministry by connecting here.
- **What Do You Call the Devil? Revelation 12:9.** Some people think of the devil as that cute character in the red suit with the horns and pitchfork. But the Bible tells us that the devil is the very enemy of God. Download this info bulletin board to find out the various names used for Satan in the Scriptures.

Faith Links

- Lost Love? **Revelation 2:4**
- Hot, Cold or In Between? **Revelation 3:15**
- Praise Him! **Revelation 5:12**
- Keep On Keeping On, **Revelation 13:10**
- A Heavenly Sight, **Revelation 21:1–4**
- A Happy Ending, **Revelation 22:16–21**

My Favourite Links

_____
_____
_____
_____

Did You Know?

Did you read the part about there being a "new Jerusalem"?

That's not all! John tells us about a new heaven and a new earth! You'd better surf over to Revelation 21 right now. This sounds too good to miss!

CHECK OUT THESE OTHER COOL STORIES:

A heavenly sight, Revelation 4
Bowls of anger, Revelation 15; 16
Satan's last stand, Revelation 20:1–15
The river of life, Revelation 22:1–2
Final words, Revelation 22:18–21

Revelation 1:5   1731

THE FOLLOWER JESUS LOVED   Revelation 1

1. John was a fisherman along Lake Galilee with his brother James, when Jesus called them to be his followers. (Look up Matthew 4:21–22, p. 1279.) He and his brother were nicknamed "Sons of Thunder".

2. Along with Peter and James, John was one of the followers closest to Jesus throughout his ministry. He also went with Jesus to a high mountain, where he saw Jesus' appearance change. (Read Matthew 17:1–9, p. 1303.)

3. John stayed close to Jesus during his final week. He was there at the Lord's Supper, Jesus' prayer time in Gethsemane, Jesus' trial, and even his death on the cross. (Look up John 19:25–27, p. 1457.)

4. John worked with Peter as leader of the early church in Jerusalem. (See Acts 3 and 4, p. 1466.)

5. John was sent to live alone on the island called Patmos as punishment for preaching the Word of God. That's probably where he wrote his message about Jesus and his letters that are a part of the New Testament. That's also where he wrote the Book of Revelation, the last book in the New Testament. (Check out Revelation 1:1–11, p. 1731.)

John Tells About this Book

1 This is the revelation[n] of Jesus Christ, which God gave to him, to show his servants what must soon happen. And Jesus sent his angel to show it to his servant John, 2 who has told everything he has seen. It is the word of God; it is the message from Jesus Christ. 3 Happy is the one who reads the words of God's message, and happy are the people who hear this message and do what is written in it. The time is near when all of this will happen.

Jesus' Message to the Churches

4 From John.

To the seven churches in the country of Asia:

Grace and peace to you from the One who is and was and is coming, and from the seven spirits before his throne, 5 and from Jesus Christ. Jesus is the faithful witness, the first among those raised from

---

1:1 revelation A making known of truth that has been hidden.

the dead. He is the ruler of the kings of the earth.

He is the One who loves us, who made us free from our sins with the blood of his death. 6 He made us to be a kingdom of priests who serve God his Father. To Jesus Christ be glory and power for ever and ever! Amen.

7 Look, Jesus is coming with the clouds, and everyone will see him, even those who stabbed him. And all peoples of the earth will cry loudly because of him. Yes, this will happen! Amen.

8 The Lord God says, "I am the Alpha and the Omega."[n] I am the One who is and was and is coming. I am the Almighty."

9 I, John, am your brother. All of us share with Christ in suffering, in the kingdom and in patience to continue. I was on the island of Patmos,[n] because I had preached the word of God and the message about Jesus. 10 On the Lord's day I was in the Spirit, and I heard a loud voice behind me that sounded like a trumpet. 11 The voice said, "Write what you see in a book and send it to the seven churches: to Ephesus, Smyrna, Pergamum, Thyatira, Sardis, Philadelphia and Laodicea."

12 I turned to see who was talking to me. When I turned, I saw seven golden lampstands 13 and someone among the lampstands who was "like a Son of Man".[n] He was dressed in a long robe and had a gold band around his chest. 14 His head and hair were white like wool, as white as snow, and his eyes were like flames of fire. 15 His feet were like bronze that glows hot in a furnace, and his voice was like the noise of flooding water. 16 He held seven stars in his right hand, and a sharp two-edged sword came out of his mouth. He looked like the sun shining at its brightest time.

17 When I saw him, I fell down at his feet like a dead man. He put his right hand on me and said, "Do not be afraid. I am the First and the Last. 18 I am the One who lives; I was dead, but look, I am alive for ever and ever! And I hold the keys to death and to the place of the dead. 19 So write the things you see, what is now and what will happen later. 20 Here is the secret of the seven stars that you saw in my right hand and the seven golden lampstands: the seven lampstands are the seven churches, and the seven stars are the angels of the seven churches.

To the Church in Ephesus

2 "Write this to the angel of the church in Ephesus:

"The One who holds the seven stars in his right hand and walks among the seven golden lampstands says this: 2 I know what you do, how you work hard and never give up. I know you do not put up with the false teachings of evil people. You have tested those who say they are apostles but really are not, and you found they are liars. 3 You have patience and have suffered troubles for my name and have not given up.

4 "But I have this against you: you have left the love you had in the beginning. 5 So remember where you were before you fell. Change your hearts and do what you did at first. If you do not change, I will come to you and will take away your lampstand from its place. 6 But there is something you do that is right: you hate what the Nicolaitans[n] do, as much as I.

7 "Every person who has ears should listen to what the Spirit says to the churches. To those who win the victory I will give the right to eat the fruit from the tree of life, which is in the garden of God.

To the Church in Smyrna

8 "Write this to the angel of the church in Smyrna:

"The One who is the First and the Last, who died and came to life again, says this: 9 I know your troubles and that you are poor, but really you are rich! I know the bad things some people say about you. They

---

1:8 Alpha and the Omega The first and last letters of the Greek alphabet. This means "the beginning and the end."
1:9 Patmos A small island in the Aegean Sea, near the coast of Asia Minor (modern Turkey).
1:13 "like . . . Man" "Son of Man" is a name Jesus called himself.
2:6 Nicolaitans This is the name of a religious group that followed false beliefs and ideas.

Revelation 2:19 1733

put some of you in prison to test you, and you will suffer for ten days. But be faithful, even if you have to die, and I will give you the crown of life.

11 "Everyone who has ears should listen to what the Spirit says to the churches. Those who win the victory will not be hurt by the second death.

To the Church in Pergamum

12 "Write this to the angel of the church in Pergamum:

"The One who has the sharp, two-edged sword says this: 13 I know where you live. It is where Satan has his throne. But you are true to me. You did not refuse to tell about your faith in me even during the time of Antipas, my faithful witness who was killed in your city, where Satan lives.

14 "But I have a few things against you: you have some there who follow the teaching of Balaam. He taught Balak how to cause the people of Israel to sin by eating food offered to idols and by taking part in sexual sins. 15 You also have some who follow the teaching of the Nicolaitans.ⁿ 16 So change your hearts and lives. If you do not, I will come to you quickly and fight against them with the sword that comes out of my mouth.

17 "Everyone who has ears should listen to what the Spirit says to the churches.

"I will give some of the hidden manna to everyone who wins the victory. I will also give to each one who wins the victory a white stone with a new name written on it. No one knows this new name except the one who receives it.

To the Church in Thyatira

18 "Write this to the angel of the church in Thyatira:

"The Son of God, who has eyes that blaze like fire and feet like shining bronze, says this: 19 I know what you do. I know about your love, your faith, your service and your patience. I know that you are doing more now than you did at first.

2:15 Nicolaitans This is the name of a religious group that followed false beliefs and ideas.

FAITH links

LOST LOVE?
REVELATION 2:4

Have you ever stopped being friends with someone? Maybe this was a friend you used to play with all the time, but don't any longer. Some relationships change over time. That's because our feelings sometimes change. But there are some relationships we have that we hope will never change.

In Ephesians 1:15, Paul complimented the Ephesians on how much love they had for Jesus. Here, Jesus told them that they didn't have as much love as they used to have. They had lost the enthusiasm they had had for Jesus. Jesus wanted them to confess any sins in their lives and ask for his forgiveness. Is that what you need to do? Don't wait!

Count on His Mercy, Judges 2:16–17; 3, p. 313

A Memorial for Two Thieves, 1 Chronicles 7:21, p. 530

Anger: Quick or Slow? Psalm 86:15, p. 776

Concern for All, Daniel 9, p. 1165

Remembering Jesus, Matthew 26:26–29, p. 1321

A Christian's Responsibility, Acts 11:26, p. 1484

---

say they are Jews, but they are not true Jews. They are a synagogue that belongs to Satan. 10 Do not be afraid of what you are about to suffer. I tell you, the devil will

20 "But I have this against you: you let that woman Jezebel spread false teachings. She says she is a prophetess, but by her teaching she leads my people to take part in sexual sins and to eat food that is offered to idols. 21 I have given her time to change her heart and turn away from her sin, but she does not want to change. 22 So I will throw her on a bed of suffering. And all those who take part in adultery with her will suffer greatly if they do not turn away from the wrongs she does. 23 I will also kill her followers. Then all the churches will know I am the One who searches hearts and minds, and I will repay each of you for what you have done.

24 "But others of you in Thyatira have not followed her teaching and have not learned what some call Satan's deep secrets. I say to you that I will not put any other load on you. 25 Only continue in your loyalty until I come.

26 "I will give power over the nations to everyone who wins the victory and continues to be obedient to me until the end. 27 'You will rule over them with an iron rod,
as when pottery is broken into pieces.' *Psalm 2:9*
28 This is the same power I received from my Father. I will also give him the morning star. 29 Everyone who has ears should listen to what the Spirit says to the churches.

To the Church in Sardis

3 "Write this to the angel of the church in Sardis:

"The One who has the seven spirits and the seven stars says this: I know what you do. People say that you are alive, but really you are dead. 2 Wake up! Make yourselves stronger before what you have left dies completely. I have found that what you are doing is less than what my God wants. 3 So do not forget what you have received and heard. Obey it, and change your hearts and lives. So you must wake up, or I will come like a thief, and you will not know when I will come to you. 4 But you have a few there in Sardis who have kept their clothes clean, so they will walk with me and will wear white clothes, because they are worthy. 5 Those who win the victory will be dressed in white clothes like them. And I will not erase their names from the book of life, but I will say they belong to me before my Father and before his angels. 6 Everyone who has ears should listen to what the Spirit says to the churches.

To the Church in Philadelphia

7 "Write this to the angel of the church in Philadelphia:

"This is what the One who is holy and true, who holds the key of David, says. When he opens a door, no one can close it. And when he closes it, no one can open it. 8 I know what you do. I have put an open door before you, which no one can close. I know you have a little strength, but you have obeyed my teaching and were not afraid to speak my name. 9 Those in the synagogue that belongs to Satan say they are Jews, but they are not true Jews; they are liars. I will make them come before you and bow at your feet, and they will know that I have loved you. 10 You have obeyed my teaching about not giving up your faith. So I will keep you from the time of trouble that will come to the whole world to test those who live on earth.

11 "I am coming soon. Continue strong in your faith so no one will take away your crown. 12 I will make those who win the victory to become pillars in the temple of my God, and they will never have to leave it. I will write on them the name of my God and the name of the city of my God, the new Jerusalem,ⁿ that comes down out of heaven from my God. I will also write on them my new name. 13 Everyone who has ears should listen to what the Spirit says to the churches.

To the Church in Laodicea

14 "Write this to the angel of the church in Laodicea:

3:12 Jerusalem This name is used to mean the spiritual city God built for his people. See Revelation 21-22.

FAITH links

HOT, COLD OR IN BETWEEN?
REVELATION 3:15

Cold, hot and lukewarm are three different temperatures. We like cocoa to be hot and soft drinks to be cold. Not many people like anything lukewarm. Jesus feels the same way.

One day, the apostle John saw a vision of the risen Jesus. Jesus had a message for Christians in the city of Laodicea. He didn't like the fact that they were lukewarm. That meant they were half-hearted about God. When you have faith in God and do what he says, you're "on fire" for God. If you don't believe in God, that means you're cold. Jesus wants you to be hot or cold, not in between! Go for hot!

Check out these Faithlinks on having a faith that is "hot":

Always Truthful, Numbers 23:19, p. 208

A Reminder to Be Fair, 2 Chronicles 19:5–11, p. 583

A Picture of the Past, Psalm 105, p. 789

Dirty Inside, Isaiah 6:1–7, p. 904

Tell All About Him! Matthew 28:19, p. 1326

Attention, Please! Luke 8:11–15, p. 1383

Revelation 4:4 1735

"The Amen," the faithful and true witness, the beginning of all God has made, says this: 15 I know what you do, that you are neither hot nor cold. I wish that you were either hot or cold! 16 But because you are warm—neither hot, nor cold—I am ready to spit you out of my mouth. 17 You say, 'I am rich, and I have become wealthy and do not need anything.' But you do not know that you are really miserable, pitiful, poor, blind and naked. 18 I advise you to buy

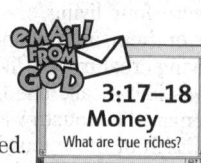

3:17–18 Money
What are true riches?

from me gold made pure in fire so you can be truly rich. Buy from me white clothes so you can be clothed and so you can cover your shameful nakedness. Buy from me medicine to put on your eyes so you can truly see.

19 "I correct and punish those whom I love. So be eager to do right, and change your hearts and lives. 20 Here I am! I stand at the door and knock. If you hear my voice and open the door, I will come in and eat with you, and you will eat with me.

21 "Those who win the victory will sit with me on my throne in the same way that I won the victory and sat down with my Father on his throne. 22 Everyone who has ears should listen to what the Spirit says to the churches."

John Sees Heaven

4 After the vision of these things I looked, and there before me was an open door in heaven. And the same voice that spoke to me before, that sounded like a trumpet, said, "Come up here, and I will show you what must happen after this." 2 Immediately I was in the Spirit, and before me was a throne in heaven, and someone was sitting on it. 3 The One who sat on the throne looked like precious stones, like jasper and carnelian. All around the throne was a rainbow the colour of an emerald. 4 Around the throne there were 24 other thrones with 24 elders sitting on them. They were dressed in white and had

---

3:14 Amen Used here as a name for Jesus; it means to agree fully that something is true.

golden crowns on their heads. 5 Lightning flashes and noises and thundering came from the throne. Before the throne seven lamps were burning, which are the seven spirits of God. 6 Also before the throne there was something that looked like a sea of glass, clear like crystal.

In the centre and around the throne were four living creatures with eyes all over them, in front and behind. 7 The first living creature was like a lion. The second was like a calf. The third had a face like a man. The fourth was like a flying eagle. 8 Each of these four living creatures had six wings and was covered all over with eyes, inside and out. Day and night they never stop saying: "Holy, holy, holy is the Lord God Almighty. He was, he is, and he is coming."

4:8 Heaven
What will you see in heaven?

9 These living creatures give glory, honour and thanks to the One who sits on the throne, who lives for ever and ever. 10 Then the 24 elders bow down before the One who sits on the throne, and they worship him who lives for ever and ever. They put their crowns down before the throne and say:
11 "You are worthy, our Lord and God,
to receive glory and honour and power,
because you made all things.
Everything existed and was made,
because you wanted it."

5 Then I saw a scroll in the right hand of the One sitting on the throne. The scroll had writing on both sides and was kept closed with seven seals. 2 And I saw a powerful angel calling in a loud voice, "Who is worthy to break the seals and open the scroll?" 3 But there was no one in heaven or on earth or under the earth who could open the scroll or look inside it. 4 I cried hard because there was no one who was worthy to open the scroll or look inside. 5 But one of the elders said to me, "Do not cry! The Lion[n] from the tribe of Judah, David's descendant, has won the victory so that he is able to open the scroll and its seven seals."

FAITH links

PRAISE HIM!
REVELATION 5:12

Do you like to sing in church? What songs do you like to sing? Songs about Jesus help us praise him and express our love for him. Have you ever seen a large group of people singing the chorus to Handel's *Messiah*? Imagine seeing not people, but *angels* singing praises to God — more angels than you ever thought you would see and hear. In a vision of heaven, the apostle John saw and heard thousands and thousands of angels praising Jesus. Since God is so awesome, they couldn't help *but* praise him. Do you feel the same way? If so, give him some praise!

Want to tell God you love him? Connect here:

Idol Talk, Exodus 32, p. 118

Do What You Want? Judges 21:25, p. 341

How Big Is God? Job 38—41, p. 703

Our Awesome God, Ezekiel 1:26–28, p. 1087

Two Birthdays, John 3:1–7, p. 1426

The Sin Habit, Romans 7:15–20, p. 1527

6 Then I saw a Lamb standing in the centre of the throne and in the middle of

---
5:5 Lion Here refers to Christ.

the four living creatures and the elders. The Lamb looked as if he had been killed. He had seven horns and seven eyes, which are the seven spirits of God that were sent into all the world. 7 The Lamb came and took the scroll from the right hand of the One sitting on the throne. 8 When he took the scroll, the four living creatures and the 24 elders bowed down before the Lamb. Each one of them had a harp and golden bowls full of incense, which are the prayers of God's holy people. 9 And they all sang a new song to the Lamb:
"You are worthy to take the scroll
and to open its seals,
because you were killed,
and with the blood of your death
you bought people for God
from every tribe, language, people
and nation.
10 You made them to be a kingdom of
priests for our God,
and they will rule on the earth."

11 Then I looked, and I heard the voices of many angels around the throne, and the four living creatures, and the elders. There were thousands and thousands of angels, 12 saying in a loud voice: "The Lamb who was killed is worthy
to receive power, wealth, wisdom and
strength,
honour, glory and praise!"
13 Then I heard all creatures in heaven and on earth and under the earth and in the sea saying:
"To the One who sits
on the throne
and to the Lamb
be praise and honour
and glory and
power
for ever and ever."
14 The four living creatures said, "Amen," and the elders bowed down and worshipped.

6 Then I watched while the Lamb opened the first of the seven seals. I heard one of the four living creatures say with a voice like thunder, "Come!" 2 I looked, and there before me was a white horse. The rider on the horse held a bow, and he was given a crown, and he rode out, determined to win the victory.

3 When the Lamb opened the second seal, I heard the second living creature say, "Come!" 4 Then another horse came out, a red one. Its rider was given power to take away peace from the earth and to make people kill each other, and he was given a big sword.

5 When the Lamb opened the third seal, I heard the third living creature say, "Come!" I looked, and there before me was a black horse, and its rider held a pair of scales in his hand. 6 Then I heard something that sounded like a voice coming from the middle of the four living creatures. The voice said, "A litre of wheat for a day's pay, and 3 litres of barley for a day's pay, and do not damage the olive oil and wine!"

7 When the Lamb opened the fourth seal, I heard the voice of the fourth living creature say, "Come!" 8 I looked, and there before me was a pale horse. Its rider was named death, and Hades*n* was following close behind him. They were given power over a quarter of the earth to kill people by war, by starvation, by disease and by the wild animals of the earth.

9 When the Lamb opened the fifth seal, I saw under the altar the souls of those who had been killed because they were faithful to the word of God and to the message they had received. 10 These souls shouted in a loud voice, "Holy and true Lord, how long until you judge the people of the earth and punish them for killing us?" 11 Then each one of them was given a white robe and was told to wait a short time longer. There were still some of their fellow servants and brothers and sisters*n* in the service

> Holy and true Lord, how long until you judge the people of the earth and punish them for killing us?
> – Revelation 6:10

6:8 Hades The unseen world of the dead.
6:11 brothers and sisters Although the Greek text says "brothers" here and throughout this book, John's words refer to the entire church, both men and women.

of Christ who must be killed as they were. They had to wait until all of this was finished.

12 Then I watched while the Lamb opened the sixth seal, and there was a great earthquake. The sun became black like rough black cloth, and the whole moon became red like blood. 13 And the stars in the sky fell to the earth like figs falling from a fig tree when the wind blows. 14 The sky disappeared as a scroll when it is rolled up, and every mountain and island was moved from its place.

15 Then the kings of the earth, the rulers, the generals, the rich people, the powerful people, the slaves and the free people hid themselves in caves and in the rocks on the mountains. 16 They called to the mountains and the rocks, "Fall on us. Hide us from the face of the One who sits on the throne and from the anger of the Lamb! 17 The great day for their anger has come, and who can stand against it?"

The 144,000 People of Israel

7 After the vision of these things I saw four angels standing at the four corners of the earth. The angels were holding the four winds of the earth to keep them from blowing on the land or on the sea or on any tree. 2 Then I saw another angel coming up from the east who had the seal of the living God. And he called out in a loud voice to the four angels to whom God had given power to harm the earth and the sea. 3 He said to them, "Do not harm the land or the sea or the trees until we mark with a sign the foreheads of the people who serve our God." 4 Then I heard how many people were marked with the sign. There were 144,000 from every tribe of the people of Israel.

5 From the tribe of Judah 12,000 were marked with the sign,
from the tribe of Reuben 12,000,
from the tribe of Gad 12,000,
6 from the tribe of Asher 12,000,
from the tribe of Naphtali 12,000,
from the tribe of Manasseh 12,000,
7 from the tribe of Simeon 12,000,
from the tribe of Levi 12,000,
from the tribe of Issachar 12,000,
8 from the tribe of Zebulun 12,000,
from the tribe of Joseph 12,000,
and from the tribe of Benjamin 12,000 were marked with the sign.

The Great Crowd Worships God

9 After the vision of these things I looked, and there was a great number of people, so many that no one could count them. They were from every nation, tribe, people and language of the earth. They were all standing before the throne and before the Lamb, wearing white robes and holding palm branches in their hands. 10 They were shouting in a loud voice, "Salvation belongs to our God, who sits on the throne, and to the Lamb." 11 All the angels were standing around the throne and the elders and the four living creatures. They all bowed down on their faces before the throne and worshipped God, 12 saying, "Amen! Praise, glory, wisdom, thanks, honour, power and strength belong to our God for ever and ever. Amen!"

13 Then one of the elders asked me, "Who are these people dressed in white robes? Where did they come from?"

14 I answered, "You know who they are, sir."

And the elder said to me, "These are the people who have come out of the great distress. They have washed their robes and made them white in the blood of the Lamb.ⁿ 15 Because of this, they are before the throne of God. They worship him day and night in his temple. And the One who sits on the throne will be present with them. 16 Those people will never be hungry again, and they will never be thirsty again. The sun will not hurt them, and no heat will burn them,

---

7:14 washed . . . Lamb This means they believed in Jesus so that their sins could be forgiven through Christ's blood.

17 because the Lamb at the centre of the throne will be their shepherd. He will lead them to springs of water that give life. And God will wipe away every tear from their eyes."

7:17 Heaven Check out who will be at the centre of heaven.

The Seventh Seal

8 When the Lamb opened the seventh seal, there was silence in heaven for about half an hour. 2 And I saw the seven angels who stand before God and to whom were given seven trumpets.

3 Another angel came and stood at the altar, holding a golden pan for incense. He was given much incense to offer with the prayers of all God's holy people. The angel put this offering on the golden altar before the throne. 4 The smoke from the incense went up from the angel's hand to God with the prayers of God's people. 5 Then the angel filled the incense pan with fire from the altar and threw it on the earth, and there were flashes of lightning, thunder and loud noises, and an earthquake.

The Seven Angels and Trumpets

6 Then the seven angels who had the seven trumpets prepared to blow them.

7 The first angel blew his trumpet, and hail and fire mixed with blood were poured down on the earth. And a third of the earth, and all the green grass, and a third of the trees were burnt up.

8 Then the second angel blew his trumpet, and something that looked like a big mountain, burning with fire, was thrown into the sea. And a third of the sea became blood, 9 a third of the living things in the sea died, and a third of the ships were destroyed.

10 Then the third angel blew his trumpet, and a large star, burning like a torch, fell from the sky. It fell on a third of the rivers and on the springs of water. 11 The name of the star is Wormwood.ⁿ And a third of all the water became bitter,

and many people died from drinking the water that was bitter.

12 Then the fourth angel blew his trumpet, and a third of the sun, and a third of the moon, and a third of the stars were struck. So a third of them became dark, and a third of the day was without light, and also the night.

13 While I watched, I heard an eagle that was flying high in the air cry out in a loud voice, "Trouble! Trouble! Trouble for those who live on the earth because of the remaining sounds of the trumpets that the other three angels are about to blow!"

9 Then the fifth angel blew his trumpet, and I saw a star fall from the sky to the earth. The star was given the key to the deep hole that leads to the bottomless pit. 2 Then it opened up the hole that leads to the bottomless pit, and smoke came up from the hole like smoke from a big furnace. Then the sun and sky became dark because of the smoke from the hole. 3 Then locusts came down to the earth out of the smoke, and they were given the power to sting like scorpions.ⁿ 4 They were told not to harm the grass on the earth or any plant or tree. They could harm only the people who did not have the sign of God on their foreheads. 5 These locusts were not given the power to kill anyone, but to cause pain to the people for five months. And the pain they felt was like the pain a scorpion gives when it stings someone. 6 During those days people will look for a way to die, but they will not find it. They will want to die, but death will run away from them.

7 The locusts looked like horses prepared for battle. On their heads they wore what looked like crowns of gold, and their faces looked like human faces. 8 Their hair was like women's hair, and their teeth ere like lions' teeth. 9 Their chests looked like iron breastplates, and the sound of their wings was like the noise of many

8:11 Wormwood Name of a very bitter plant; used here to give the idea of bitter sorrow.
9:3 scorpions A scorpion is an insect-like creature with a poisonous sting.

Revelation 9:10 1740

horses and chariots hurrying into battle. 10 The locusts had tails with stingers like scorpions, and in their tails was their power to hurt people for five months. 11 The locusts had a king who was the angel of the bottomless pit. His name in the Hebrew language is Abaddon and in the Greek language is Apollyon."

12 The first trouble is past; there are still two other troubles that will come.

13 Then the sixth angel blew his trumpet, and I heard a voice coming from the horns on the golden altar that is before God. 14 The voice said to the sixth angel who had the trumpet, "Free the four angels who are tied at the great river Euphrates." 15 And they let loose the four angels who had been kept ready for this hour and day and month and year so they could kill a third of all people on the earth. 16 I heard how many troops on horses were in their army—200,000,000.

17 The horses and their riders I saw in the vision looked like this: they had breastplates that were fiery red, dark blue and yellow like sulphur. The heads of the

9:11 Abaddon, Apollyon Both names mean "Destroyer".

FORGIVE ME

Is there someone in your life that you need to forgive or that you need forgiveness from? Here's a friend who's struggling in this area. Please welcome James, aged 10, to Connect 2-You.

James

A few weeks ago, my little sister destroyed my football programme collection. She was mad at me, so she went into my room and started ripping up the programmes. Some of them were even pretty valuable! She said she was sorry, and my mum made me say I forgive her. But I really don't want to forgive her. I'm still so mad at her! What would you do?

Can you understand how James is feeling? It is hard to forgive someone when they do something mean to us. But think of it in this way: God forgives us for everything we do – no matter how bad it is – if we ask him to. And he wants us to do the same for people who ask us for forgiveness. If you would like some tips on how to accept apologies, check out the Livin' It page on forgiveness, Genesis 50:14-21, p.72.

James is mad at his sister. But it's important for him to forgive her. It's pretty tough to ask God to forgive us if we're not willing to forgive others.

horses looked like heads of lions, with fire, smoke and sulphur coming out of their mouths. 18 A third of all the people on earth were killed by these three terrible disasters coming out of the horses' mouths: the fire, the smoke and the sulphur. 19 The horses' power was in their mouths and in their tails; their tails were like snakes with heads, and with them they hurt people.

20 The other people who were not killed by these terrible disasters still did not change their hearts and turn away from what they had made with their own hands. They did not stop worshipping demons and idols made of gold, silver, bronze, stone and wood—things that cannot see or hear or walk. 21 These people did not change their hearts and turn away from murder or evil magic, from their sexual sins or stealing.

The Angel and the Small Scroll

10 Then I saw another powerful angel coming down from heaven dressed in a cloud with a rainbow over his head. His face was like the sun, and his legs were like pillars of fire. 2 The angel was holding a small scroll open in his hand. He put his right foot on the sea and his left foot on the land. 3 Then he shouted loudly like the roaring of a lion. And when he shouted, the voices of seven thunders spoke. 4 When the seven thunders spoke, I started to write. But I heard a voice from heaven say, "Keep hidden what the seven thunders said, and do not write them down."

5 Then the angel I saw standing on the sea and on the land raised his right hand to heaven, 6 and he made a promise by the power of the One who lives for ever and ever. He is the One who made the skies and all that is in them, the earth and all that is in it, and the sea and all that is in it. The angel promised, "There will be no more waiting! 7 In the days when the seventh angel is ready to blow his trumpet, God's secret will be finished. This secret is the Good News God told to his servants, the prophets."

8 Then I heard the same voice from heaven again, saying to me: "Go and take the open scroll that is in the hand of the angel that is standing on the sea and on the land."

9 So I went to the angel and told him to give me the small scroll. And he said to me, "Take the scroll and eat it. It will be sour in your stomach, but in your mouth it will be sweet as honey." 10 So I took the small scroll from the angel's hand and ate it. In my mouth it tasted sweet as honey, but after I ate it, it was sour in my stomach. 11 Then I was told, "You must prophesy again about many peoples, nations, languages and kings."

The Two Witnesses

11 I was given a measuring stick like a rod, and I was told, "Go and measure the temple of God and the altar, and count the people worshipping there. 2 But do not measure the yard outside the temple. Leave it alone, because it has been given to those who are not God's people. And they will trample on the holy city for 42 months. 3 And I will give power to my two witnesses to prophesy for 1,260 days, and they will be dressed in rough cloth to show their sadness."

4 These two witnesses are the two olive trees and the two lampstands that stand before the Lord of the earth. 5 And if anyone tries to hurt them, fire comes from their mouths and kills their enemies. And if anyone tries to hurt them in whatever way, in that same way that person will die. 6 These witnesses have the power to stop the sky from raining during the time they are prophesying. And they have power to make the waters become blood, and they have power to send every kind of trouble to the earth as many times as they want.

7 When the two witnesses have

> He is the One who made the skies and all that is in them, the earth and all that is in it.
> – Revelation 10:6

finished telling their message, the beast that comes up from the bottomless pit will fight a war against them. He will defeat them and kill them. 8 The bodies of the two witnesses will lie in the street of the great city where the Lord was killed. This city is named Sodom[n] and Egypt, which has a spiritual meaning. 9 Those from every race of people, tribe, language and nation will look at the bodies of the two witnesses for three and a half days, and they will refuse to bury them. 10 People who live on the earth will rejoice and be happy because these two are dead. They will send each other gifts, because these two prophets brought much suffering to those who live on the earth.

11 But after three and a half days, God put the breath of life into the two prophets again. They stood on their feet, and everyone who saw them became very afraid. 12 Then the two prophets heard a loud voice from heaven saying, "Come up here!" And they went up into heaven in a cloud as their enemies watched.

13 In the same hour there was a great earthquake, and a tenth of the city was destroyed. 7,000 people were killed in the earthquake, and those who did not die were very afraid and gave glory to the God of heaven.

14 The second trouble is finished. Pay attention: the third trouble is coming soon.

The Seventh Trumpet

15 Then the seventh angel blew his trumpet. And there were loud voices in heaven, saying:

"The power to rule the world
now belongs to our Lord and his Christ,
and he will rule for ever and ever."

16 Then the 24 elders, who sit on their thrones before God, bowed down on their faces and worshipped God. 17 They said:

"We give thanks to you, Lord God Almighty,
who is and who was,
because you have used your great power
and have begun to rule!
18 The people of the world were angry,
but your anger has come.
The time has come to judge the dead
and to reward your servants the prophets
and your holy people,
all who respect you, great and small.
The time has come to destroy those who destroy the earth!"

19 Then God's temple in heaven was opened. The Ark that holds the agreement God gave to his people could be seen in his temple. Then there were flashes of lightning, noises, thunder, an earthquake and a great hailstorm.

The Woman and the Dragon

12 And then a great wonder appeared in heaven: a woman was clothed with the sun, and the moon was under her feet, and a crown of twelve stars was on her head. 2 She was pregnant and cried out with pain, because she was about to give birth. 3 Then another wonder appeared in heaven: there was a giant red dragon with seven heads and seven crowns on each head. He also had ten horns. 4 His tail swept a third of the stars out of the sky and threw them down to the earth. He stood in front of the woman who was ready to give birth so he could eat her baby as soon as it was born. 5 Then the woman gave birth to a son who will rule all the nations with an iron rod. And her child was taken up to God and to his throne. 6 The woman ran away into the desert to a place God

> Then the seventh angel blew his trumpet.
> – Revelation 11:15

11:8 Sodom City that God destroyed because the people were so evil.

Revelation 12:12 **1743**

WHAT DO YOU CALL THE DEVIL? Revelation 12:9

Satan is the enemy of God, his people and all that is good. He is evil. He is a liar. He constantly tempts people to sin. (Read 1 Thessalonians 3:5, p. 1632.) He fell from God's service and talked other angels into following him. (See Revelation 12:9.) When Jesus returns, Satan will be completely defeated and thrown into the lake of burning sulphur. (Look at Revelation 20:1–10.)

Here are some of the names for Satan used in the New Testament:

Beelzebul, ruler of demons	Matthew 12:24, p. 1295
The enemy	Matthew 13:39, p. 1298
A liar; the father of lies	John 8:44, p. 1438
Ruler of darkness	Ephesians 6:12, p. 1605
A roaring lion	1 Peter 5:8, p. 1706
Angel of the bottomless pit	Revelation 9:11, p. 1740
The dragon	Revelation 12:7, p. 1743
Old snake	Revelation 20:2, p. 1752

prepared for her where she would be taken care of for 1,260 days.

7 Then there was a war in heaven. Michael[n] and his angels fought against the dragon, and the dragon and his angels fought back. **8** But the dragon was not strong enough, and he and his angels lost their place in heaven. **9** The giant dragon was thrown down out of heaven. (He is that old snake called the devil or Satan, who tricks the whole world.) The dragon with his angels was thrown down to the earth.

10 Then I heard a loud voice in heaven saying:

"The salvation and the power and the
    kingdom of our God
and the authority of his Christ have
    now come.
The accuser of our brothers and
    sisters,
who accused them day and night
    before our God,
has been thrown down.
11 And our brothers and sisters defeated him
by the blood of the Lamb's death
and by the message they
    preached.
They did not love their lives so much
    that they were afraid of death.
12 So rejoice, you heavens
    and all who live there!
But it will be terrible for the earth
    and the sea,

12:7 Michael The archangel—leader among God's angels or messengers (Jude 9).

because the devil has come down
to you!
He is filled with anger,
because he knows he does not
have much time."

13 When the dragon saw he had been thrown down to the earth, he hunted for the woman who had given birth to the son. 14 But the woman was given the two wings of a great eagle so she could fly to the place prepared for her in the desert. There she would be taken care of for three and a half years, away from the snake. 15 Then the snake poured water out of its mouth like a river towards the woman so the flood would carry her away. 16 But the earth helped the woman by opening its mouth and swallowing the river that came from the mouth of the dragon. 17 Then the dragon was very angry at the woman, and he went off to make war against all her other children—those who obey God's commands and who have the message Jesus taught.

18 And the dragon stood on the seashore.

The Two Beasts

13 Then I saw a beast coming up out of the sea. It had ten horns and seven heads, and there was a crown on each horn. A name against God was written on each head. 2 This beast looked like a leopard, with feet like a bear's feet and a mouth like a lion's mouth. And the dragon gave the beast all of his power and his throne and great authority. 3 One of the heads of the beast looked as if it had been killed by a wound, but this death wound was healed. Then the whole world was amazed and followed the beast. 4 People worshipped the dragon because he had given his power to the beast. And they also worshipped the beast, asking, "Who is like the beast? Who can make war against it?"

5 The beast was allowed to say proud words and words against God, and it was allowed to use its power for 42 months. 6 It used its mouth to speak against God, against God's name, against the place where God lives, and against all those who live in heaven. 7 It was given power to make war against God's holy people and to defeat them. It was given power over every tribe, people, language and nation. 8 And all who live on earth will worship the beast—all the people since the beginning of the world whose names are not

---

FAITH links

KEEP ON KEEPING ON

REVELATION 13:10

The apostle John had a vision of the future. He saw God's people going through a difficult time. They weren't going through hard times because they had done wrong. They were going through hard times because they were faithful to Jesus.

No one escapes hard times in this life. Hard times help develop perseverance. That's a long word meaning the determination to keep on going, no matter what. Those who endure to the end are rewarded. So, keep on being faithful to Jesus.

Here are some links to help you when the going gets tough:

Alone and Forgotten? Genesis 40:23, p. 57

Who Ya' Gonna Call? Psalm 3:4, p. 711

Be Brave! Haggai 2:4, p. 1249

Our Good Shepherd, John 10:11–15, p. 1441

The Winner's Crown, 1 Corinthians 9:24–27, p. 1555

Keep Going! James 1:2–3, p. 1688

written in the Lamb's book of life. The Lamb is the One who was killed.

9 Anyone who has ears should listen:
10 If you are to be a prisoner,
then you will be a prisoner.
If you are to be killed with the sword,
then you will be killed with the sword.

This means that God's holy people must have patience and faith.

11 Then I saw another beast coming up out of the earth. It had two horns like a lamb, but it spoke like a dragon. 12 This beast stands before the first beast and uses the same power the first beast has. By this power it makes everyone living on earth worship the first beast, who had the death wound that was healed. 13 And the second beast does great miracles so that it even makes fire come down from heaven to earth while people are watching. 14 It fools those who live on earth by the miracles it has been given the power to do. It does these miracles to serve the first beast. The second beast orders people to make an idol to honour the first beast, the one that was wounded by the deadly sword but sprang to life again. 15 The second beast was given power to give life to the idol of the first one so that the idol could speak. And the second beast was given power to command all who will not worship the image of the beast to be killed. 16 The second beast also forced all people, small and great, rich and poor, free and slave, to have a mark on their right hand or on their forehead. 17 No one could buy or sell without this mark, which is the name of the beast or the number of its name. 18 This takes wisdom. Let the one who has understanding find the meaning of the number, which is the number of a person. Its number is 666.

The Song of the Saved

14 Then I looked, and there before me was the Lamb standing on Mount Zion.*n* With him were 144,000 people who had his name and his Father's name written on their foreheads. 2 And I heard a sound from heaven like the noise of flooding water and like the sound of loud thunder. The sound I heard was like people playing harps. 3 And they sang a new song before the throne and before the four living creatures and the elders. No one could learn the new song except the 144,000 who had been bought from the earth. 4 These are the ones who did not do sinful things with women, because they kept themselves pure. They follow the Lamb everywhere he goes. These

FAITH CHALLENGE

Here's a challenge! Read 14:6–7 to get an idea of what God's judgement will be like. How do you feel when you hear that God will one day judge all people?

TESTING IT

Revelation 14:6–7
Then I saw another angel flying high in the air. He had the eternal Good News to preach to those who live on earth . . . "Fear God and give him praise, because the time has come for God to judge all people. So worship God who made the heavens, and the earth, and the sea, and the springs of water."

14:1 Mount Zion Another name for Jerusalem; here meaning the spiritual city of God's people.

144,000 were bought from among the people of the earth as people to be offered to God and the Lamb. 5 They were not guilty of telling lies; they are without fault.

The Three Angels

6 Then I saw another angel flying high in the air. He had the eternal Good News to preach to those who live on earth—to every nation, tribe, language and people. 7 He preached in a loud voice, "Fear God and give him praise, because the time has come for God to judge all people. So worship God who made the heavens, and the earth, and the sea, and the springs of water."

8 Then the second angel followed the first angel and said, "Ruined, ruined is the great city of Babylon! She made all the nations drink the wine of the anger of her adultery."

9 Then a third angel followed the first two angels, saying in a loud voice: "If anyone worships the beast and his idol and gets the beast's mark on the forehead or on the hand, 10 that one also will drink the wine of God's anger, which is prepared with all its strength in the cup of his anger. And that person will be put in pain with burning sulphur before the holy angels and the Lamb. 11 And the smoke from their burning pain will rise for ever and ever. There will be no rest, day or night, for those who worship the beast and his idol or who get the mark of his name." 12 This means God's holy people must be patient. They must obey God's commands and keep their faith in Jesus.

13 Then I heard a voice from heaven saying, "Write this: happy are the dead who die from now on in the Lord."

The Spirit says, "Yes, they will rest from their hard work, and the reward of all they have done stays with them."

The Earth is Harvested

14 Then I looked, and there before me was a white cloud, and sitting on the white cloud was One who looked like a Son of Man.ⁿ He had a gold crown on his head and a sharp sickleⁿ in his hand. 15 Then another angel came out of the temple and called out in a loud voice to the One who was sitting on the cloud, "Take your sickle and harvest the earth, because the time to harvest has come, and the fruit of the earth is ripe." 16 So the One who was sitting on the cloud swung his sickle over the earth, and the earth was harvested.

17 Then another angel came out of the temple in heaven, and he also had a sharp sickle. 18 And then another angel, who has power over the fire, came from the altar. This angel called to the angel with the sharp sickle, saying, "Take your sharp sickle and gather the bunches of grapes from the earth's vine, because its grapes are ripe." 19 Then the angel swung his sickle over the earth. He gathered the earth's grapes and threw them into the great winepress of God's anger. 20 They were trampled in the winepress outside the city, and blood flowed out of the winepress as high as horses' bridles for a distance of about 300 kilometres.

The Last Troubles

15 Then I saw another wonder in heaven that was great and amazing. There were seven angels bringing seven disasters. These are the last disasters, because after them, God's anger is finished.

2 I saw what looked like a sea of glass mixed with fire. All of those who had won the victory over the beast and his idol and over the number of his name were standing by the sea of glass.

They had harps that God had given them. 3 They sang the song of Moses, the servant of God, and the song of the Lamb:

"You do great and wonderful things,

Lord God Almighty.

Psalm 111:2
Amos 3:13

EMAIL FROM GOD
15:3-4
Worship
Will everyone worship God someday?

14:14 Son of Man "Son of Man" is a name Jesus called himself.

14:14 sickle A farming tool with a curved blade. It was used to harvest grain.

Everything the LORD does is right
and true, *Psalm 145:17*
King of the nations.
4 Everyone will respect you, Lord,
Jeremiah 10:7
and will honour you.
Only you are holy.
All the nations will come
and worship you, *Psalm 86:9-10*
because the right things you have
done
are now made known." *Deuteronomy 32:4*
5 After this I saw that the temple (the Tent of the Agreement) in heaven was opened. 6 And the seven angels bringing the seven disasters came out of the temple. They were dressed in clean, shining linen and wore golden bands tied around their chests. 7 Then one of the four living creatures gave to the seven angels seven golden bowls filled with the anger of God, who lives for ever and ever. 8 The temple was filled with smoke from the glory and the power of God, and no one could enter the temple until the seven disasters of the seven angels were finished.

The Bowls of God's Anger

16 Then I heard a loud voice from the temple saying to the seven angels, "Go and pour out the seven bowls of God's anger on the earth."

2 The first angel left and poured out his bowl on the land. Then ugly and painful sores came upon all those who had the mark of the beast and who worshipped his idol.

3 The second angel poured out his bowl on the sea, and it became blood like that of a dead man, and every living thing in the sea died.

4 The third angel poured out his bowl on the rivers and the springs of water, and they became blood. 5 Then I heard the angel of the waters saying:

"Holy One, you are the One who is and who was.
You are right to decide to punish these evil people.

6 They have poured out the blood of your holy people and your prophets.
So now you have given them blood to drink as they deserve."

7 And I heard a voice coming from the altar saying:
"Yes, Lord God Almighty,
the way you punish evil people is right and fair."

8 The fourth angel poured out his bowl on the sun, and he was given power to burn the people with fire. 9 They were burned by the great heat, and they cursed the name of God, who had control over these disasters. But the people refused to change their hearts and lives and give glory to God.

10 The fifth angel poured out his bowl on the throne of the beast, and darkness covered its kingdom. People bit their tongues because of the pain. 11 They also cursed the God of heaven because of their pain and the sores they had, but they refused to change their hearts and turn away from the evil things they did.

12 The sixth angel poured out his bowl on the great river Euphrates so that the water in the river was dried up to prepare the way for the kings from the east to come. 13 Then I saw three evil spirits that looked like frogs coming out of the mouth of the dragon, out of the mouth of the beast and out of the mouth of the false prophet. 14 These evil spirits are the spirits of demons, which have power to do miracles. They go out to the kings of the whole world to gather them together for the battle on the great day of God Almighty.

15 "Listen! I will come as a thief comes! Happy are those who stay awake and keep their clothes on so that they will not walk around naked and have people see their shame."

16 Then the evil spirits gathered the kings together to the place that is called Armageddon in the Hebrew language.

> "Holy One, you are the One who is and who was. You are right to decide to punish these evil people."
> – Revelation 16:5

Revelation 16:17

17 The seventh angel poured out his bowl into the air. Then a loud voice came out of the temple from the throne, saying, "It is finished!" 18 Then there were flashes of lightning, noises, thunder, and a big earthquake—the worst earthquake that has ever happened since people have been on earth. 19 The great city split into three parts, and the cities of the nations were destroyed. And God remembered the sins of Babylon the Great, so he gave that city the cup filled with the wine of his terrible anger. 20 Then every island ran away, and mountains disappeared. 21 Giant hailstones, each weighing up to 50 kilogrammes, fell from the sky upon people. People cursed God for the disaster of the hail, because this disaster was so terrible.

The Woman on the Animal

17 Then one of the seven angels who had the seven bowls came and spoke to me. He said, "Come, and I will show you the punishment that will be given to the great prostitute, the one sitting over many waters. 2 The kings of the earth sinned sexually with her, and the people of the earth became drunk from the wine of her sexual sin."

3 Then the angel carried me away by the Spirit to the desert. There I saw a woman sitting on a red beast. It was covered with names insulting to God written on it, and it had seven heads and ten horns. 4 The woman was dressed in purple and red and was shining with the gold, precious jewels and pearls she was wearing. She had a golden cup in her hand, a cup filled with evil things and the uncleanness of her sexual sin. 5 On her forehead a title was written that was secret. This is what was written:

THE GREAT BABYLON
MOTHER OF PROSTITUTES
AND OF THE EVIL THINGS OF THE EARTH

6 Then I saw that the woman was drunk with the blood of God's holy people and with the blood of those who were killed because of their faith in Jesus.

When I saw the woman, I was very amazed. 7 Then the angel said to me, "Why are you amazed? I will tell you the secret of this woman and the beast she rides—the one with seven heads and ten horns. 8 The beast you saw was once alive but is not alive now. But soon it will come up out of the bottomless pit and go away to be destroyed. There are people who live on earth whose names have not been written in the book of life since the beginning of the world. They will be amazed when they see the beast, because he was once alive, is not alive now, but will come again.

9 "You need a wise mind to understand this. The seven heads on the beast are seven mountains where the woman sits. 10 And they are seven kings. Five of the kings have already been destroyed, one of the kings lives now, and another has not yet come. When he comes, he must stay a short time. 11 The beast that was once alive, but is not alive now, is also an eighth king. He belongs to the first seven kings, and he will go away to be destroyed.

12 "The ten horns you saw are ten kings who have not yet begun to rule, but they will receive power to rule with the beast for one hour. 13 All ten of these kings have the same purpose, and they will give their power and authority to the beast. 14 They will make war against the Lamb, but the Lamb will defeat them, because he is Lord of lords and King of kings. He will defeat them with his called, chosen and faithful followers."

> He will defeat them with his called, chosen and faithful followers.
> – Revelation 17:14

15 Then the angel said to me, "The waters that you saw, where the prostitute sits, are peoples, races, nations and languages. 16 The ten horns and the beast you saw will hate the prostitute. They will take everything she has and leave her naked. They will eat her body and burn her with fire. 17 God made the ten horns want to carry out his

purpose by agreeing to give the beast their power to rule, until what God has said comes about. 18 The woman you saw is the great city that rules over the kings of the earth."

Babylon is Destroyed

18 After the vision of these things, I saw another angel coming down from heaven. This angel had great power, and his glory made the earth bright. 2 He shouted in a powerful voice:

"Ruined, ruined is the great city of Babylon!
    She has become a home for demons
and a prison for every evil spirit,
    and a prison for every unclean bird
        and unclean beast.
3 She has been ruined, because all the peoples of the earth
    have drunk the wine of the desire of her sexual sin.
She has been ruined also because the kings of the earth
    have sinned sexually with her,
and the merchants of the earth
    have grown rich from the great wealth of her luxury."

4 Then I heard another voice from heaven saying:
    "Come out of that city, my people,

WISE WORDS

Do you sometimes have a problem with listening to what other people say. Here's someone who does have a problem in this area. Let's let him tell you about it. Please welcome Dan, aged 10, to Connect 2-You.

Dan

Well, I hate to call him a problem because I love him, but it's my grandfather. He's always trying to give me advice about what I should and shouldn't do. He always says it in a nice way, but it's still hard to listen to him. I mean, what does he know? He was a kid 60 years ago.

We can all understand how Dan's feeling. It can be frustrating to have people always telling you what's best for you. But the Bible says Dan's grandfather's words are a valuable treasure. Dan shouldn't let them go to waste.

It's called wisdom, and it means knowing the right thing to do. Because Dan's grandfather has been around for so long and has seen so much, he knows things that Dan may never learn – unless he listens to him. God has put him in Dan's life for a reason. For more tips in this area, check out the Livin' It page on wisdom, Proverbs 2, p. 827.

so that you will not share in her sins,
so that you will not receive the disasters that will come to her.

5 Her sins have piled up as high as the sky,
and God has not forgotten the wrongs she has done.
6 Give that city the same as she gave to others.
Pay her back twice as much as she did.
Prepare wine for her that is twice as strong
as the wine she prepared for others.
7 She gave herself much glory and rich living.
Give her the same amount of suffering and sadness.
She says to herself, 'I am a queen sitting on my throne.
I am not a widow; I will never be sad.'
8 So these disasters will come to her in one day:
death, and crying, and great hunger,
and she will be destroyed by fire,
because the Lord God who judges her is powerful."

9 The kings of the earth who sinned sexually with her and shared her wealth will see the smoke from her burning. Then they will cry and be sad because of her death. 10 They will be afraid of her suffering and stand far away and say:
"Terrible! How terrible for you, great city,
powerful city of Babylon,
because your punishment has come in one hour!"

11 And the merchants of the earth will cry and be sad about her, because now there is no one to buy their cargoes— 12 cargoes of gold, silver, jewels, pearls; fine linen, purple cloth, silk, red cloth; all kinds of citron wood and all kinds of things made from ivory, expensive wood, bronze, iron and marble; 13 cinnamon, spice, incense, myrrh, frankincense; wine, olive oil, fine flour, wheat; cattle, sheep, horses, carriages; slaves and human lives.

14 The merchants will say,
"Babylon, the good things you wanted are gone from you.
All your rich and fancy things have disappeared.
You will never have them again."
15 The merchants who became rich from selling to her will be afraid of her suffering and will stand far away. They will cry and be sad 16 and say:
"Terrible! How terrible for the great city!
She was dressed in fine linen, purple and red cloth,
and she was shining with gold, precious jewels and pearls!
17 All these riches have been destroyed in one hour!"

Every sea captain, all those who travel, the sailors, and all those who earn their living from the sea stood far away from Babylon. 18 As they saw the smoke from her burning, they cried out loudly, "There was never a city like this great city!" 19 And they threw dirt on their heads and cried, weeping and were sad. They said:
"Terrible! How terrible for the great city!
All the people who had ships on the sea
became rich because of her wealth!
But she has been destroyed in one hour!
20 Be happy because of this, heaven!
Be happy, God's holy people and apostles and prophets!
God has punished her because of what she did to you."

21 Then a powerful angel picked up a large stone, like one used for grinding grain, and threw it into the sea. He said:
"In the same way, the great city of Babylon will be thrown down,
and it will never be found again.
22 The music of people playing harps and other instruments, flutes and trumpets,
will never be heard in you again.
No workman doing any job
will ever be found in you again.

The sound of grinding grain
    will never be heard in you again.
23 The light of a lamp
    will never shine in you again,
    and the voices of a bridegroom and
        bride
    will never be heard in you again.
Your merchants were the world's
        great people,
    and all the nations were tricked by
        your magic.
24 You are guilty of the death of the
        prophets and God's holy
        people
    and all who have been killed on
        earth."

People in Heaven Praise God

19 After this vision and announcement I heard what sounded like a great many people in heaven saying:
"Hallelujah!*ⁿ*
Salvation, glory and power belong to
    our God,
2 because his judgements are true
    and right.
He has punished the prostitute
    who made the earth evil with her
        sexual sin.
He has paid her back for the death of
    his servants."
3 Again they said:
"Hallelujah!
She is burning, and her smoke will
    rise for ever and ever."
4 Then the 24 elders and the four living creatures bowed down and worshipped God, who sits on the throne. They said: "Amen, Hallelujah!"
5 Then a voice came from the throne, saying: "Praise our God, all
    you who serve
        him
and all you who
    honour him, both small and
        great!"
6 Then I heard what sounded like a great many people, like the noise of flooding water and like the noise of loud thunder. The people were saying:

"Hallelujah!
    Our Lord God, the Almighty, rules.
7 Let us rejoice and be happy
    and give God glory,
because the wedding of the Lamb has
        come,
    and the Lamb's bride has made
        herself ready.
8 Fine linen, bright and clean, was
    given to her to wear."
(The fine linen means the good things done by God's holy people.)
9 And the angel said to me, "Write this: happy are those who have been invited to the wedding meal of the Lamb!" And the angel said, "These are the true words of God."
10 Then I bowed down at the angel's feet to worship him, but he said to me, "Do not worship me! I am a servant like you and your brothers and sisters who have the message of Jesus. Worship God, because the message about Jesus is the spirit that gives all prophecy."

The Rider on the White Horse

11 Then I saw heaven opened, and there before me was a white horse. The rider on the horse is called Faithful and True, and he is right when he judges and makes war. 12 His eyes are like burning fire, and on his head are many crowns. He has a name written on him, which no one but himself knows. 13 He is dressed in a robe dipped in blood, and his name is the Word of God. 14 The armies of heaven, dressed in fine linen, white and clean, were following him on white horses. 15 Out of the rider's mouth comes a sharp sword that he will use to defeat the nations, and he will rule them with a rod of iron. He will crush out the wine in the winepress of the terrible anger of God the Almighty. 16 On his robe and on his upper leg was written this name: KING OF KINGS AND LORD OF LORDS.

> On his robe and on his upper leg was written this name:
> KING OF KINGS AND LORD OF LORDS.
> – Revelation 19:16

19:1 **Hallelujah** This means "praise God!"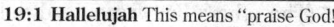

Revelation 19:17

17 Then I saw an angel standing in the sun, and he called with a loud voice to all the birds flying in the sky: "Come and gather together for the great feast of God **18** so that you can eat the bodies of kings, generals, mighty people, horses and their riders, and the bodies of all people—free, slave, small and great."

19 Then I saw the beast and the kings of the earth. Their armies were gathered together to make war against the rider on the horse and his army. **20** But the beast was captured and with him the false prophet who did the miracles for the beast. The false prophet had used these miracles to trick those who had the mark of the beast and worshipped his idol. The false prophet and the beast were thrown alive into the lake of fire that burns with sulphur. **21** And their armies were killed with the sword that came out of the mouth of the rider on the horse, and all the birds ate the bodies until they were full.

The 1,000 Years

20 I saw an angel coming down from heaven. He had the key to the bottomless pit and a large chain in his hand. **2** The angel grabbed the dragon, that old snake who is the devil and Satan, and tied him up for 1,000 years. **3** Then he threw him into the bottomless pit, closed it and locked it over him. The angel did this so he could not trick the people of the earth any more until the 1,000 years were ended. After 1,000 years he must be set free for a short time.

4 Then I saw some thrones and people sitting on them who had been given the power to judge. And I saw the souls of those who had been killed because they were faithful to the message of Jesus and the message from God. They had not worshipped the beast or his idol, and they had not received the mark of the beast on their foreheads or on their hands. They came back to life and ruled with Christ for 1,000 years. **5** (The others that were dead did not live again until the 1,000 years were ended.) This is the first raising of the dead. **6** Happy and holy are those who share in this first raising of the dead. The second death has no power over them. They will be priests for God and for Christ and will rule with him for 1,000 years.

7 When the 1,000 years are over, Satan will be set free from his prison. **8** Then he will go out to trick the nations in all the earth—Gog and Magog—to gather them for battle. There are so many people they will be like sand on the seashore. **9** And Satan's army marched across the earth and gathered around the camp of God's people and the city God loves. But fire came down from heaven and burnt them up. **10** And Satan, who tricked them, was thrown into the lake of burning sulphur with the beast and the false prophet. There they will be punished day and night for ever and ever.

> Happy and holy are those who share in this first raising of the dead. The second death has no power over them.
> – Revelation 20:6

People of the World are Judged

11 Then I saw a great white throne and the One who was sitting on it. Earth and sky ran away from him and disappeared. **12** And I saw the dead, great and small, standing before the throne. Then books were opened, and the book of life was opened. The dead were judged by what they had done, which was written in the books. **13** The sea gave up the dead who were in it, and Death and Hades" gave up the dead who were in them. Each person was judged by what he had done. **14** And Death and Hades were thrown into the lake of fire. The lake of fire is the second death. **15** And anyone whose name was not found written in the book of life was thrown into the lake of fire.

The New Jerusalem

21 Then I saw a new heaven and a new earth. The first heaven and the first

---

20:13 Hades The unseen world of the dead.

earth had disappeared, and there was no sea any more. 2 And I saw the holy city, the new Jerusalem,[n] coming down out of heaven from God. It was prepared like a bride dressed for her husband. 3 And I heard a loud voice from the throne, saying, "Now God's presence is with people, and he will live with them, and they will be his people. God himself will be with them and will be their God. 4 He will wipe away every tear from their eyes, and there will be no more death, sadness, crying or pain, because all the old ways are gone."

21:4 Heaven
Will you be sad in heaven?

5 The One who was sitting on the throne said, "Look! I am making everything new!" Then he said, "Write this, because these words are true and can be trusted."

6 The One on the throne said to me, "It is finished. I am the Alpha and the Omega,[n] the Beginning and the End. I will give free water from the spring of the water of life to anyone who is thirsty. 7 Those who win the victory will receive this, and I will be their God, and they will be my children. 8 But cowards, those who refuse to believe, who do evil things, who kill, who sin sexually, who do evil magic, who worship idols and who tell lies— all these will have a place in the lake of burning sulphur. This is the second death."

9 Then one of the seven angels who had the seven bowls full of the seven last troubles came to me, saying, "Come with me, and I will show you the bride, the wife of the Lamb." 10 And the angel carried me away by the Spirit to a very large and high mountain. He showed me the holy city, Jerusalem, coming down out of heaven from God. 11 It was shining with the glory of God and was bright like a very expensive jewel, like a jasper, clear as crystal. 12 The city had a great high wall with twelve gates with twelve angels at the gates, and on each gate was written the name of one of the twelve tribes of Israel. 13 There were three gates on the east, three on the north, three on the south and three on the west. 14 The walls of the city were built on twelve foundation stones, and on the stones were written the names of the twelve apostles of the Lamb.

15 The angel who talked with me had a measuring rod made of gold to measure

---

FAITH links

A HEAVENLY SIGHT
REVELATION 21:1-4

What is the most beautiful city you have ever seen? What did you like best about it? The apostle John saw a vision of heaven. What an amazing place! God had created a new heaven and a new earth. No one would be sad or lonely or filled with hate ever again. This was a hopeful sight for John.

If you fear what the future may hold, think about John's vision of heaven. We have a bright future ahead!

Fearful Service? Exodus 4:1–17, p. 80

Approaching God, Numbers 3:10, p. 180

All Talk, No Action, Jeremiah 5:1–2, p. 996

Uprooted by Change, Amos 9:15, p. 1205

Just a Test, Luke 4:1–13, p. 1373

The Way to Heaven, John 14:1–6, p. 1448

21:2 new Jerusalem The spiritual city where God's people live with him.
21:6 Alpha and the Omega The first and last letters of the Greek alphabet. This means "the beginning and the end."

the city, its gates and its wall. **16** The city was built in a square, and its length was equal to its width. The angel measured the city with the rod. The city was 2,200 kilometres long, 2,200 kilometres wide and 2,200 kilometres high. **17** The angel also measured the wall. It was 80 metres high, by human measurements, which the angel was using. **18** The wall was made of jasper, and the city was made of pure gold, as pure as glass. **19** The foundation stones of the city walls were decorated with every kind of jewel. The first foundation was jasper, the second was sapphire, the third was chalcedony, the fourth was emerald, **20** the fifth was onyx, the sixth was carnelian, the seventh was chrysolite, the eighth was beryl, the ninth was topaz, the tenth was chrysoprase, the eleventh was jacinth, and the twelfth was amethyst. **21** The twelve gates were twelve pearls, each gate having been made from a single pearl. And the street of the city was made of pure gold as clear as glass.

22 I did not see a temple in the city, because the Lord God Almighty and the Lamb are the city's temple. **23** The city does not need the sun or the moon to shine on it, because the glory of God is its light, and the Lamb is the city's lamp. **24** By its light the people of the world will walk, and the kings of the earth will bring their glory into it. **25** The city's gates will never be shut on any day, because there is no night there. **26** The glory and the honour of the nations will be brought into it. **27** Nothing unclean and no one who does shameful things or tells lies will ever go into it. Only those whose names are written in the Lamb's book of life will enter the city.

22 Then the angel showed me the river of the water of life. It was shining like crystal and was flowing from the throne of God and of the Lamb **2** down the middle of the street of the city. The tree of life was on each side of the river. It produces fruit twelve times a year, once each month. The leaves of the tree are for the healing of all the nations. **3** Nothing that God judges guilty will be in that city. The throne of God and of the Lamb will be

---

FAITH links

A HAPPY ENDING
REVELATION 22:16-21

What's your favourite story? Most people like a story with a happy ending. Want to know a real-life story that has a guaranteed happy ending? Your story. If you trust Jesus as your Saviour, you have that hope of Jesus' return. He's already made it possible for you to be forgiven of sin. Now he's preparing a place for you to live in heaven with him for ever.

In this passage, the apostle John looked forward to the second coming of Jesus. John was tired of hard times and the evil that never seemed to go away. The thought of Jesus' return gave him comfort. Do you look forward to Jesus' return? Then, join John and Christians throughout the ages in saying, "Amen. Come, Lord Jesus!"

Worried about the future? Download these links:

A Holiday Every Week, Leviticus 23:1–3, p. 166

The One Who Suffered, Isaiah 53, p. 966

A Fair-weather Friend, Obadiah 7, p. 1209

Rock Solid, Habakkuk 1:12, p. 1236

Prove It! Matthew 16:1–4, p. 1302

Just for the Asking, Romans 3:23–28, p. 1522

there, and God's servants will worship him. 4 They will see his face, and his name will be written on their foreheads. 5 There will never be night again. They will not need the light of a lamp or the light of the sun, because the Lord God will give them light. And they will rule as kings for ever and ever.

6 The angel said to me, "These words can be trusted and are true." The Lord, the God of the spirits of the prophets, sent his angel to show his servants the things that must happen soon.

7 "Listen! I am coming soon! Happy is the one who obeys the words of prophecy in this book."

8 I, John, am the one who heard and saw these things. When I heard and saw them, I bowed down to worship at the feet of the angel who showed these things to me. 9 But the angel said to me, "Do not worship me! I am a servant like you, your brothers the prophets and all those who obey the words in this book. Worship God!"

22:8–9 Heaven Who had a vision of heaven?

10 Then the angel told me, "Do not keep secret the words of prophecy in this book, because the time is near for all this to happen. 11 Let whoever is doing evil continue to do evil. Let whoever is unclean continue to be unclean. Let whoever is doing right continue to do right. Let whoever is holy continue to be holy."

12 "Listen! I am coming soon! I will bring my reward with me, and I will repay each one of you for what you have done. 13 I am the Alpha and the Omega,*ⁿ* the First and the Last, the Beginning and the End.

14 "Happy are those who wash their robes*ⁿ* so that they will receive the right to eat the fruit from the tree of life and may go through the gates into the city. 15 Outside the city are the evil people, those who do evil magic, who sin sexually, who murder, who worship idols, and who love lies and tell lies.

16 "I, Jesus, have sent my angel to tell you these things for the churches. I am the descendant from the family of David, and I am the bright morning star."

17 The Spirit and the bride say, "Come!" Let the one who hears this say, "Come!" Let whoever is thirsty come; whoever wishes may have the water of life as a free gift.

18 I warn everyone who hears the words of the prophecy of this book: if anyone adds anything to these words, God will add to that person the disasters written about in this book. 19 And if anyone takes away from the words of this book of prophecy, God will take away that one's share of the tree of life and of the holy city, which are written about in this book.

20 Jesus, the One who says these things are true, says, "Yes, I am coming soon."

Amen. Come, Lord Jesus!

21 The grace of the Lord Jesus be with all. Amen.

22:13 Alpha and the Omega The first and last letters of the Greek alphabet. This means "the beginning and the end."

22:14 wash their robes This means they believed in Jesus so that their sins could be forgiven through Christ's blood.

SEARCH ENGINE

ACTIONS

Lights, Camera,...Actions!
Genesis 12:1–3, p. 17

What You Value
Genesis 25:21–34, p. 34

A Use for Your Abilities
Genesis 41, p. 59

Serious About the Sabbath
Exodus 31:15, p. 117

A Different Kind of People
Leviticus 11, p. 146

An Example Not to Follow
Leviticus 18:1–3, p. 157

A Special Promise
Numbers 30:1–2, p. 217

Facing the Consequences
Deuteronomy 3:21–29, p. 232

I'll Never Forget What's-His-Name
Deuteronomy 8, p. 239

Read My Lips?
Deuteronomy 26:16–19, p. 260

Promises, Promises
Judges 2:1–3, p. 312

A Right to Get Even?
1 Samuel 24, p. 388

A Memorial for Two Thieves
1 Chronicles 7:21, p. 530

Prayer + Action = Success
Nehemiah 2:4–9, p. 626

Standing for What's Right
Esther 3:2–4, p. 651

Get Hot or Keep Cool?
Proverbs 12:16, p. 842

You Are What You Do
Proverbs 20:11, p. 854

FAITH CHALLENGE
Proverbs 22:6, p. 857

Sow It and Reap
Lamentations 1:18, p. 1075

Said It? Do It!
Lamentations 2:17, p. 1077

Empty Words
Ezekiel 33:30–33, p. 1127

Let's Make a Deal
Daniel 1:8–21, p. 1150

Going My Way?
Hosea 8:1–6, p. 1179

A Blueprint for Living
Amos 5:14–15, p. 1200

Attention, Please!
Luke 8:11–15, p. 1383

Clean Inside and Out
Luke 11:39–40, p. 1392

Calling Anyone!
Acts 23:12–22, p. 1506

A Family Celebration
1 Corinthians 11:23–29, p. 1558

LIVIN' IT: That (Good) Thing You Do
Galatians 6:9–10, p. 1594

Always Do This!
1 Thessalonians 5:16–18, p. 1636

Hold On!
2 Thessalonians 2:15–17, p. 1639

Your Faith Example
1 Timothy 4:12, p. 1646

Don't Play Favourites
James 2:1–7, p. 1691

FAITH CHALLENGE
James 5:13, p. 1695

Hot, Cold or in Between?
Revelation 3:15, p. 1735

ADVICE

CONNECT 2-YOU: The Truth Hurts
p. 54

Fatherly Advice
Exodus 18, p. 99

Good Advice?
Leviticus 20:6, p. 162

In Your Best Interests
Ruth 3, p. 349

Search Engine

Take My Advice
- **1 Kings 2:2–4, p. 436**

When I Need Advice
- **1 Kings 12:1–7, p. 455**

Advice from a Kid
- **2 Kings 5, p. 484**

A Friend in Deed
- **Job 2:13, p. 662**

Helpful Advice
- **Job 12:4–5, p. 673**

If You Want My Advice . . .
- **Proverbs 13:1, p. 843**

The Best Advice
- **Zechariah 10:2, p. 1261**

Always Do This!
- **1 Thessalonians 5:16–18, p. 1636**

Your Faith Example
- **1 Timothy 4:12, p. 1646**

Winning a Friend
- **2 Timothy 2:23–24, p. 1654**

ANGELS

Roll Out the Welcome Wagon
- **Genesis 18:2–8, p. 24**

God to the Rescue!
- **1 Samuel 23, p. 386**

A Special Angel
- **1 Chronicles 21:6–22, p. 547**

Too Busy to Worship?
- **Luke 2:8–20, p. 1368**

Angels Watching Over Us
- **Acts 8, p. 1477**

Touched by an Angel?
- **Hebrews 1:3–4, p. 1667**

Praise Him!
- **Revelation 5:12, p. 1736**

ANGER

Out of Control?
- **Genesis 4, p. 8**

Give Revenge a Rest
- **Leviticus 19:18, p. 160**

The Perfect Leader?
- **Numbers 20:1–13, p. 203**

CONNECT 2-YOU: Temper, Temper
- **p. 742**

Anger: Quick or Slow?
- **Psalm 86:15, p. 776**

A Gentle Answer
- **Proverbs 15:1, p. 847**

Don't Get Mad; Get Even?
- **Matthew 26:57–63; 27:11–14, p. 1323**

LIVIN' IT: You Make Me Sooo Mad!
- **James 1:19–21, p. 1690**

ANSWERS TO PRAYERS

Prayer + Action = Success
- **Nehemiah 2:4–9, p. 626**

Ask, Search, Knock
- **Matthew 7:7–10, p. 1286**

ARGUING

Winning a Friend
- **2 Timothy 2:23–24, p. 1654**

The Way to Get Along
- **1 Peter 3:8–9, p. 1703**

AUTHORITY

The Leaders in Your Life
- **1 Timothy 2:1–4, p. 1645**

BAD TIMES

When Bad Turns to Worse
- **Exodus 5:6–12, p. 82**

Wronged for What's Right
- **Ezra 4:4–5, p. 612**

A Really Bad Day
- **Job 1:20–22; 2:10, p. 661**

Full Circle
- **Job 42, p. 706**

FAITH CHALLENGE
- **Psalm 118:18, p. 799**

When the Going Gets Tough
- **Lamentations 3:22–27, p. 1079**

Mission Impossible?
- **Mark 5:21–24, 35–43, p. 1337**

▶ **Search Engine 1758**

- It's Under Control
  Romans 8:28, p. 1529
- Hard Times
  2 Corinthians 1:8–10, p. 1570
- Go for It!
  Hebrews 12:1–4, p. 1682
- Keep Going!
  James 1:2–3, p. 1688
- LIVIN' IT: Help!
  1 Peter 4:12–19, p. 1704
- Keep On Keeping On
  Revelation 13:10, p. 1744

BEHAVIOUR

- Just Kidding?
  Genesis 21:8–10, p. 28
- What You Value
  Genesis 25:21–34, p. 34
- Complaints, Complaints!
  Exodus 16:1–3, p. 97
- Idol Talk
  Exodus 32, p. 118
- Share What You Have
  Exodus 35:5–18, p. 123
- A Different Kind of People
  Leviticus 11, p. 146
- An Example Not to Follow
  Leviticus 18:1–3, p. 157
- LIVIN' IT: Totally "Uncool"?
  Leviticus 18:1–5, p. 158
- The Perfect Leader?
  Numbers 20:1–13, p. 203
- Facing the Consequences
  Deuteronomy 3:21–29, p. 232
- Read My Lips?
  Deuteronomy 26:16–19, p. 260
- Promises, Promises
  Judges 2:1–3, p. 312
- FAITH CHALLENGE
  Psalm 81:8–9, p. 772
- Said It? Do It!
  Lamentations 2:17, p. 1077
- Good Enough?
  Ezekiel 8, p. 1093
- A Change of Heart
  Matthew 3:1–12, p. 1277
- Your Choice of Fruit
  Matthew 12:33–35, p. 1295

- FAITH CHALLENGE
  Luke 3:8, p. 1371
- Calling Anyone!
  Acts 23:12–22, p. 1506
- Out with the Old!
  Colossian 3:1–14, p. 1625
- Another Lazy Day?
  2 Thessalonians 3:6–13, p. 1640
- Don't Play Favourites
  James 2:1–7, p. 1691
- Helpful Hints
  3 John 11, p. 1724
- Hot, Cold or in Between?
  Revelation 3:15, p. 1735

BELIEVING

- A Major Problem
  Genesis 15:6, p. 20
- A Home Town Hurt
  Jeremiah 11:8—12:6, p. 1008
- Get Ready!
  Mark 13:26–27, p. 1354
- Believe It or Not
  Luke 1:20, 38, p. 1366
- Out with the Old!
  Colossians 3:1–14, p. 1625
- Hot, Cold or in Between?
  Revelation 3:15, p. 1735

BIBLE STUDY

- A Travelling Bible Study
  2 Chronicles 17:9, p. 580
- A Look for the Book
  2 Chronicles 34:14–18, p. 603
- The Bible: Good for Your Faith
  Psalm 119, p. 802
- CONNECT 2-YOU: The B-I-B-L-E
  p. 901
- What's in a Name?
  Isaiah 9:6, p. 908

BLESSINGS

- Uniquely You
  Psalm 139:13–14, p. 815

BRAVERY

- God's Pep Talk
  Joshua 1:5–9, p. 276
- What Will You Risk?
  Joshua 2, p. 278
- Claiming the Promised Land
  Joshua 11, p. 291
- From Zero to Hero
  Judges 6:7, p. 319
- A Giant Problem
  1 Samuel 17:32–51, p. 377

CARING FOR ANIMALS

- FAITH CHALLENGE
  Genesis 24:17–19, p. 31
- CONNECT 2-YOU: The Truth Hurts
  p. 54
- FAITH CHALLENGE
  Genesis 48:1, p. 68
- Care for the Lost
  Deuteronomy 22:1–3, p. 255

CARING FOR OTHERS

- CONNECT 2-YOU: The Truth Hurts
  p. 54
- FAITH CHALLENGE
  Genesis 48:1, p. 68
- Help for the Poor
  Leviticus 5:7, p. 138
- FAITH CHALLENGE
  Deuteronomy 15:6, p. 248
- Care for the Lost
  Deuteronomy 22:1–3, p. 255
- Fairness for All
  Deuteronomy 24:17, p. 258
- What's Out Becomes In
  Judges 11, p. 327
- Your Response to Responsibility
  Ruth 2:1–7, p. 346
- Yours, Mine and Ours?
  1 Samuel 25, p. 389
- Big Lack Attack
  2 Kings 4:1–7, p. 480

Search Engine **1759**

- Show You Care
  2 Kings 4:10, p. 481
- FAITH CHALLENGE
  Ezra 8:36, p. 619
- Seeing the Needs
  Nehemiah 1, p. 625
- Help for the Outsiders
  Nehemiah 5:9–10, p. 630
- Meaningless Words
  Job 21:34, p. 684
- FAITH CHALLENGE
  Proverbs 14:21, p. 846
- Two Are Better
  Ecclesiastes 4:9–12, p. 877
- Love Him? Show It!
  Amos 2:6–7, p. 1196
- LIVIN' IT: Can I Help You?
  Zechariah 7:8–9, p. 1258
- Help for a Friend
  Mark 2:1–5, p. 1332
- Jesus' Prayer
  John 17, p. 1453

CELEBRATING

- Can't Live Without It
  Genesis 3, p. 7
- Time to Celebrate
  Exodus 15:1–21, p. 95
- A Feast for Remembering
  Deuteronomy 16:1–8, p. 249
- A Cause for Celebration
  1 Kings 8:62–66, p. 449
- FAITH CHALLENGE
  Nehemiah 12:27, p. 642
- A Holiday Letter
  Esther 9:20–23, p. 657

CHANGE

- A Need to Change
  Ecclesiastes 1:1–11, p. 873
- Uprooted by Change
  Amos 9:15, p. 1205
- Out with the Old!
  Colossians 3:1–14, p. 1625

Search Engine 1760

CHOICES

- Can't Live Without It?
  Genesis 3, p. 7
- What You Value
  Genesis 25:21–34, p. 34
- An Example Not to Follow
  Leviticus 18:1–3, p. 157
- LIVIN' IT: Totally "Uncool"?
  Leviticus 18:1–5, p. 158
- One Potato, Two Potato . . .
  Numbers 26:55–56, p. 212
- A Choice to Make
  Deuteronomy 30:15–20, p. 265
- LIVIN' IT: This or That?
  Deuteronomy 30:15–20, p. 267
- CONNECT 2-YOU: A Chance to Be Popular
  p. 296
- No Middle Ground
  Joshua 24:14–15, p. 307
- I Want It *Now*!
  Judges 14:1–3, p. 332
- The Heart of the Matter
  1 Samuel 16, p. 375
- Choosing Sides
  1 Samuel 20, p. 382
- The Right Thing to Do
  1 Samuel 26, p. 391
- FAITH CHALLENGE
  1 Samuel 28:7, p. 393
- Deciding Wisely
  1 Kings 3:16–28, p. 440
- Sitting on the Fence
  1 Kings 18, p. 464
- CONNECT 2-YOU:
  TV or Not TV: That Is the Question
  p. 490
- On the Wrong Foot
  2 Kings 21:1–2, 16, p. 509
- Two Kinds of People
  Psalm 1, p. 710
- The Unpopular Choice
  Mark 15:42–43, p. 1360
- The Choices of a Choice
  Luke 5:1–11, p. 1375
- Attention, Please!
  Luke 8:11–15, p. 1383
- LIVIN' IT: Such a Lot of Stuff!
  Luke 12; 13, p. 1396

- A Good Habit
  Ephesians 6:18, p. 1606
- Pay Attention!
  Hebrews 2:1, p. 1668
- FAITH CHALLENGE
  Hebrews 6:12, p. 1673
- Helpful Hints
  3 John 11, p. 1724

CHRISTIAN(S)

- God's New Home
  2 Chronicles 7:11–22, p. 570
- Jesus' Mission and Yours
  Isaiah 61:1–2, p. 978
- Jesus' Sermon Notes
  Matthew 5—7, p. 1282
- Two Ways to Grow
  Luke 2:46–52, p. 1370
- The Choices of a Choice
  Luke 5:1–11, p. 1375
- A Christian's Responsibility
  Acts 11:26, p. 1484
- Meeting Together
  1 Corinthians 16:19, p. 1567
- A Family Resemblance
  Galatians 3:6–9, p. 1588
- MVFM?
  Galatians 3:26–27, p. 1589
- Your Faith Story
  2 Timothy 1:5, p. 1650
- While You Wait
  Jude 21, p. 1726

CHURCH ATTENDANCE

- Serious About the Sabbath
  Exodus 31:15, p. 117
- A Holiday Every Week
  Leviticus 23:1–3, p. 166
- Too Busy to Worship?
  Luke 2:8–20, p. 1368

CHURCH

- Giving Your Part
  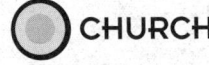
  Leviticus 27:30, p. 173

- Everyone Can Help
  Numbers 4, p. 181
- CONNECT 2-YOU: For Better or Worship
  p. 522
- Meeting Together
  1 Corinthians 16:19, p. 1567
- Family Time
  Hebrews 10:25, p. 1678

COMFORTING OTHERS

- Help for the Poor
  Leviticus 5:7, p. 138
- Comfort from the Word
  Job 26:3–4, p. 688
- Full Circle
  Job 42, p. 706
- CONNECT 2-YOU: Small Comforts
  p. 1049

COMPASSION

- Help for the Hurting
  Job 6:29–30, p. 666
- No Doubt About It
  Job 36:5, p. 699
- Full Circle
  Job 42, p. 706
- Your Heavenly Dad
  Psalm 103:13, p. 786

CONFESSING MY SINS

- Idol Talk
  Exodus 32, p. 118
- A Priest Without Sin
  Leviticus 4:3–7, p. 136
- See the Heart Behind It
  Nehemiah 8; 9, p. 636
- Lost Love?
  Revelation 2:4, p. 1733

CONFLICTS

- In Deep Water
  Psalm 69, p. 760

Search Engine **1761**

- LIVIN' IT: What *Am* I Going to Do?
  Acts 15:1–29, p. 1491

CONTENTMENT

- LIVIN' IT: The Perfect Life!
  Philippians 4:10–13, p. 1616

CONTROLLING WHAT I SAY

- Just Kidding?
  Genesis 21:8–10, p. 28
- Complaints, Complaints!
  Exodus 16:1–3, p. 97
- Show Some Respect
  Leviticus 19:32, p. 161
- Moses' Champion
  Numbers 12, p. 192
- LIVIN' IT: Loose Lips?
  Jeremiah 9:3, p. 1003
- Trouble with the Tongue
  James 3:3–12, p. 1692

COURAGE

- Following the Crowd
  Numbers 13; 14, p. 193
- God's Pep Talk
  Joshua 1:5–9, p. 276
- LIVIN' IT: Captain Courageous?
  Joshua 1:6–9, p. 277
- What Will You Risk?
  Joshua 2, p. 278
- From Zero to Hero
  Judges 6; 7, p. 319
- A Giant Problem
  1 Samuel 17:32–51, p. 377
- A Message of Courage and Hope
  2 Kings 19:4–10, p. 505
- A Life-saving Message
  Esther 2:19–22, p. 650
- The Big Risk
  Esther 4:11—5:2, p. 652
- Stand!
  Jeremiah 19:14—20:6, p. 1019
- Your Feet on High Places
  Habakkuk 3:18–19, p. 1239

▶ **Search Engine** 1762

○ Be Brave!
Haggai 2:4, p. 1249

⬤ CREATION

○ Made in His Image
Genesis 1:26–27, p. 4
○ Garden of Delight
Genesis 2:8–10, p. 5

⬤ DEATH

○ CONNECT 2-YOU: Life After Life
p. 550
○ The Big Risk
Esther 4:11—5:2, p. 652
○ Remembering Jesus
Matthew 26:26–29, p. 1321
○ The Deadliest Lie
Acts 5:1–11, p. 1471
○ A High Price
Romans 6:23, p. 1526
○ Life After Death?
1 Corinthians 15:12–13, p. 1563
○ LIVIN' IT: The Final End?
1 Corinthians 15:50–57, p. 1564
○ Death on a Cross
Hebrews 6:6, p. 1672

⬤ DEPENDABILITY

○ Depend on Him!
2 Chronicles 16:1–9, p. 579
○ An Unsung Hero
Ruth 2:12, 15–16, p. 347
○ A Broken Promise
Jeremiah 2:1–8, p. 989
○ All Talk, No Action
Jeremiah 5:1–2, p. 996

⬤ DETERMINATION

○ From Hopeless to Hopeful
Exodus 6:9, p. 83
○ Building Tools
Ezra 6:15, p. 615

⬤ DISAPPOINTMENTS

○ Alone and Forgotten?
Genesis 40:23, p. 57
○ Keep On Praying
1 Samuel 1, p. 354

⬤ DISCIPLINE

○ A Shortcut
1 Samuel 13:1–14, p. 369
○ LIVIN' IT: Eyes on the Prize
2 Chronicles 1:7–12, p. 562
○ This Hurts Me More?
2 Chronicles 36:17–22, p. 606
○ Down on the Ant Farm
Proverbs 6:6–11, p. 833
○ FAITH CHALLENGE
Proverbs 22:6, p. 857
○ Down on Discipline?
Proverbs 29:15, p. 867
○ A Hard Place
Ezekiel 28:25–26, p. 1120
○ The Right Ingredients
Micah 6:8, p. 1227
○ A Reminder to Do What Is Right and True
Zechariah 7:8–10, p. 1257
○ You're Correct!
Hebrews 12:5–7, p. 1683

⬤ DISCOURAGEMENT

○ When Bad Turns to Worse
Exodus 5:6–12, p. 82
○ Good Times and Bad
1 Kings 17, p. 462
○ Lower Than Low
Job 19:13–25, p. 680
○ When Bad Things Happen
Ecclesiastes 3:16–17, p. 876
○ Small Beginnings
Zechariah 4:10, p. 1255

⬤ DOING MY BEST

○ Try to Remember
Deuteronomy 11:18–21, p. 243

Search Engine

- A Choice to Make
  Deuteronomy 30:15–20, p. 265
- Your Best Work
  1 Kings 6, p. 443
- An Honest Reputation
  Nehemiah 13:13, p. 644
- Let's Make a Deal
  Daniel 1:8–21, p. 1150
- FAITH CHALLENGE
  John 5:30, p. 1431
- The Most Fun
  Acts 20:35, p. 1502
- Our Gift to God
  Romans 12:1–2, p. 1536
- LIVIN' IT: Good, Better, Best
  1 Corinthians 9:24–27, p. 1554
- Prayer for a Friend
  Colossians 1:9–12, p. 1620
- With All Your Heart
  Colossians 3:23, p. 1626
- CONNECT 2-YOU: Doing Your Best
  p. 1674

DUTIES

- A Serious Promise
  Deuteronomy 23:21–23, p. 257
- Read My Lips?
  Deuteronomy 26:16–19, p. 260
- A Big Responsibility
  2 Kings 11, p. 494
- FAITH CHALLENGE
  Romans 13:7, p. 1537

ENCOURAGEMENT

- CONNECT 2-YOU: I Can't Do It!
  p. 420
- Good Times and Bad
  1 Kings 17, p. 462
- Listen Up!
  1 Kings 19:11–13, p. 467
- Two Enemies
  Nehemiah 6, p. 631
- FAITH CHALLENGE
  Psalm 146:8, p. 820
- Fly Like an Eagle
  Isaiah 40:28–31, p. 947
- A Swarm of Trouble
  Joel 2:25–27, p. 1190
- Your Feet on High Places
  Habakkuk 3:18–19, p. 1239
- Hope That Doesn't Fail
  Acts 26:4–7, p. 1510
- Keep Up the Good Work!
  Galatians 6:9–10, p. 1593
- Toss Those Troubles!
  1 Peter 5:7, p. 1706
- While You Wait
  Jude 21, p. 1726

ENCOURAGING OTHERS

- FAITH CHALLENGE
  Romans 1:12, p. 1518
- An Encouraging Word
  1 Corinthians 1:3–5, p. 1545

ENDURANCE

- Building Tools
  Ezra 6:15, p. 615
- Faith God Notices
  Luke 18:35–43, p. 1406
- As Strong as Superman?
  Philippians 4:13, p. 1615
- Go for It!
  Hebrews 12:1–4, p. 1682

ENEMIES

- Your Worst Enemy
  Exodus 7—11, p. 85
- Mourning for an Enemy
  2 Samuel 1, p. 399
- Putting an Enemy in Check
  2 Kings 6:8–23, p. 486
- Two Enemies
  Nehemiah 6, p. 631
- Who Ya' Gonna Call?
  Psalm 3:4, p. 711
- Does Crime Pay?
  Psalm 37:1–7, p. 736
- LIVIN' IT: Now You're Asking for It!
  Proverbs 25:21–22, p. 862

Search Engine 1764

- Who Needs Love?
  Luke 6:27–36, p. 1379
- Hope That Doesn't Fail
  Acts 26:4–7, p. 1510

ENVY

- The Trouble with Jealousy
  Genesis 37, p. 53

ETERNAL LIFE

- The Gift
  John 3:16–18, p. 1427
- The Way to Heaven
  John 14:1–6, p. 1448
- The Doubt Remover
  Romans 10:8–10, p. 1533
- The Winner's Crown
  1 Corinthians 9:24–27, p. 1555
- A Happy Ending
  Revelation 22:16–21, p. 1754

FAILURES

- CONNECT 2-YOU: My Fault
  p. 587
- LIVIN' IT: Oh No! Not Again!
  Luke 22:54–62, p. 1414

FAIRNESS

- Lights, Camera, . . . Actions!
  Genesis 12:1–3, p. 17
- A Major Problem
  Genesis 15:6, p. 20
- Play Fair or Play Favourites?
  Deuteronomy 1:16–18, p. 227
- Fairness for All
  Deuteronomy 24:17, p. 258
- Care to Be Fair?
  Joshua 18:1–8, p. 299
- Kind or Fair?
  1 Samuel 30, p. 395
- Fair All the Time?
  2 Samuel 8:15, p. 408
- A Reminder to Be Fair
  2 Chronicles 19:5–11, p. 583
- FAITH CHALLENGE
  Psalm 106:3, p. 790

FAITH

- Lights, Camera, . . . Actions!
  Genesis 12:1–3, p. 17
- A Major Problem
  Genesis 15:6, p. 20
- Good Plans
  Genesis 45:7–8, p. 64
- Your Heavenly Parent
  Exodus 2:1–10, p. 77
- What Will You Risk?
  Joshua 2, p. 278
- Faith of Our Fathers
  Joshua 4:4–9, p. 280
- Real Faith or Really Scared?
  Judges 4, p. 315
- An Unsung Hero
  Ruth 2:12, 15–16, p. 347
- Women Who Made a Difference
  Ruth 4, p. 350
- A Giant Problem
  1 Samuel 17:32–51, p. 377
- Trailblazers of Faith
  2 Kings 22:1–2, p. 510
- Plan for Success
  1 Chronicles 14:8–17, p. 538
- Ask, Search, Knock
  Matthew 7:7–10, p. 1286
- Just Say Yes!
  Matthew 9:9–13, p. 1289
- Prove It!
  Matthew 16:1–4, p. 1302
- The Power of *If*
  Mark 9:14–24, p. 1344
- Faith That Pleases God
  Luke 7:1–9, p. 1380
- One of the Faithful
  Acts 10:1–34, p. 1482
- FAITH CHALLENGE
  Romans 1:12, p. 1518
- One Thing to Do
  Romans 4:1–5, p. 1523
- LIVIN' IT: How Are You Growing?
  Philippians 1:1–11, p. 1610
- Just Like a Tree
  Colossians 1:23, p. 1621

Search Engine 1765

- Full of Faith
  1 Thessalonians 4:1, p. 1633
- Powerful Women of Faith
  2 Timothy 4, p. 1656
- How Do You Grow?
  Titus 1:1, p. 1659
- People of Faith
  Hebrews 11, p. 1679
- LIVIN' IT: True Blue
  Hebrews 11, p. 1680
- Keep Going!
  James 1:2–3, p. 1688

FAMILY

- More Powerful Than Revenge
  Genesis 50:14–21, p. 71
- LIVIN' IT: Give Me Space!
  Exodus 20:12, p. 102
- Moses' Champion
  Numbers 12, p. 192
- What's Out Becomes In
  Judges 11, p. 327
- CONNECT 2-YOU: Me and My Parents
  p. 330
- Peace in the Family
  Psalm 133, p. 811
- Love for a Lifetime
  Song of Solomon 6:8–9, p. 891
- CONNECT 2-YOU: All in the Family
  p. 1138
- One Big, Happy Family
  John 1:12, p. 1422
- MVFM?
  Galatians 3:26–27, p. 1589
- Family Time
  Hebrews 10:25, p. 1678

FEARS

- When You're Afraid
  Genesis 32:9–12, p. 45
- Fearful Service?
  Exodus 4:1–17, p. 80
- What God Wants
  Deuteronomy 10:12–13, p. 242
- God's Pep Talk
  Joshua 1:5–9, p. 276
- Real Faith or Really Scared?
  Judges 4, p. 315
- A Message of Courage and Hope
  2 Kings 19:4–10, p. 505
- Your Best Defence
  2 Chronicles 20:1–12, p. 584
- CONNECT 2-YOU: No Fear
  p. 676
- Who Ya' Gonna Call?
  Psalm 3:4, p. 711
- LIVIN' IT: Scared to Death!
  Isaiah 43:1–2, p. 951
- Future Hope
  Joel 3:17–21, p. 1191
- Be Brave!
  Haggai 2:4, p. 1249
- Facing Your Fears
  Matthew 8:23–27, p. 1288
- Blessed Are the Weak?
  2 Corinthians 12:7–10, p. 1582
- Fear-Fighters
  2 Timothy 1:7, p. 1652
- FAITH CHALLENGE
  1 John 4:18, p. 1719

FIGHTING

- The Perfect Sacrifice
  Leviticus 1—7, p. 135
- CONNECT 2-YOU: Cheek to Cheek
  p. 141
- Some Bad Guys
  1 Samuel 31:1–4, p. 396
- Peace in the Family
  Psalm 133, p. 811
- Ancient War and Weapons
  Ezekiel 23:24, p. 1112
- The Way to Get Along
  1 Peter 3:8–9, p. 1703

FOLLOWING JESUS

- More Powerful Than Revenge
  Genesis 50:14–21, p. 71
- The Perfect Sacrifice
  Leviticus 1—7, p. 135
- A Priest Without Sin
  Leviticus 4:3–7, p. 136

Search Engine 1766

- Wronged for What's Right
  Ezra 4:4–5, p. 612
- Good Enough?
  Ezekiel 8, p. 1093
- Name With a Purpose
  Matthew 1:21, p. 1274
- Jesus' Sermon Notes
  Matthew 5—7, p. 1282
- The Chosen Dozen
  Matthew 10:1–29, p. 1291
- When We Agree
  Matthew 18:19–20, p. 1306
- Don't Get Mad; Get Even?
  Matthew 26:57–63; 27:11–14, p. 1323
- My Favourite!
  Mark 10:17–23, p. 1347
- The Unpopular Choice
  Mark 15:42–43, p. 1360
- A Model Prayer
  Luke 11:1, p. 1390
- Your Heart's Desire
  Luke 16:13–15, p. 1401
- LIVIN' IT: Follow the Right Leader
  John 2, p. 1425
- The Way to Heaven
  John 14:1–6, p. 1448
- Out of Your Mind?
  1 Corinthians 2:16, p. 1547
- An Unselfish Example
  Philippians 2:5–8, p. 1611
- The Coming Attraction
  1 Thessalonians 4:13–18, p. 1634
- A Happy Ending
  Revelation 22:16–21, p. 1754

FORGIVENESS

- Forgive Instead
  Genesis 33, p. 47
- CONNECT 2-YOU: The Truth Hurts
  p. 54
- More Powerful Than Revenge
  Genesis 50:14–21, p. 71
- LIVIN' IT: You Want Me to Do What?
  Genesis 50:15–21, p. 72
- CONNECT 2-YOU: Cheek to Cheek
  p. 141
- Learning from Mistakes
  Psalm 51:12–13, p. 748
- Red to White
  Isaiah 1:18, p. 896
- Real Repentance
  Jeremiah 4:1–4, p. 993
- It's Guaranteed!
  1 John 1:9–10, p. 1714

FORGIVING OTHERS

- A Model of Forgiveness
  Ezekiel 16:59–63, p. 1103
- Quick to Forgive?
  Mark 11:25, p. 1349
- Forgive Again?
  Luke 17:3–4, p. 1402
- Forgive and Forget
  Ephesians 4:32, p. 1604
- From Useless to Useful
  Philemon 11, p. 1663
- A Friendly Welcome
  Philemon 18, p. 1664
- CONNECT 2-YOU: Forgive Me
  p. 1740

FRIENDSHIPS

- CONNECT 2-YOU: You're Not Alone
  p. 126
- An Example Not to Follow
  Leviticus 18:1–3, p. 157
- LIVIN' IT: Totally "Uncool"?
  Leviticus 18:1–5, p. 158
- Following the Crowd
  Numbers 13; 14, p. 193
- CONNECT 2-YOU: A Chance to Be Popular
  p. 296
- The Heart of the Matter
  1 Samuel 16, p. 375
- LIVIN' IT: The Perfect Friend
  1 Samuel 18:1, p. 378
- The Gift of Friendship
  1 Samuel 18:1–3; 19, p. 381
- Choosing Sides
  1 Samuel 20, p. 382
- Choosing a Friend
  Proverbs 28:7, p. 865
- Some Friendly Advice
  Proverbs 17:9, 14, 17, p. 851

- Help For a Friend
  Mark 2:1–5, p. 1332
- CONNECT 2-YOU: Did You Hear About. . .?
  p. 1439
- A Friend of Jesus
  John 15:9–17, p. 1450
- A Friend in Need
  Acts 9:27, p. 1480
- Thanks For a Friend
  1 Thessalonians 1:1–3, p. 1630
- Winning a Friend
  2 Timothy 2:23–24, p. 1654

GENTLENESS

- LIVIN' IT: Out with the Old!
  Colossians 3:1–14, p. 1624
- The Gentle Way
  Titus 3:1–5, p. 1661

GIFTS FROM GOD

- A Use for Your Abilities
  Genesis 41, p. 59
- Time for Breakfast
  Numbers 11:4–9, p. 191
- A Wise Wish
  1 Kings 3:5–9, p. 439
- An Admirable Quality
  1 Kings 10:1–13, p. 451
- CONNECT 2-YOU: The Haves and Have Nots
  p. 566
- God's Valuable Gift: You
  Psalm 127:3–5, p. 809
- That Thing You Do
  Matthew 25:14–30, p. 1319
- The Gift
  John 3:16–18, p. 1427
- Love for Free
  Romans 5:8, p. 1524
- The Winner's Crown
  1 Corinthians 9:24–27, p. 1555
- The "Eyes" Have It?
  1 Corinthians 12, p. 1559
- Fear-Fighters
  2 Timothy 1:7, p. 1652

Search Engine 1767

GIVING

- Give What You Can
  Numbers 7:1–11, p. 186
- Gifts from the Heart
  1 Chronicles 29, p. 557
- Give from the Heart
  Luke 21:1–4, p. 1410
- The Person Most Likely to Give?
  Acts 9:36–42, p. 1481
- The Most Fun
  Acts 20:35, p. 1502
- Give to Give
  1 Corinthians 16:1–4, p. 1566
- Give Till It Hurts?
  2 Corinthians 8:6–9; 9:6–9, p. 1578

GOALS

- LIVIN' IT: Eyes on the Prize
  2 Chronicles 1:7–12, p. 562

GOD

- Made in His Image
  Genesis 1:26–27, p. 4
- Alone and Forgotten?
  Genesis 40:23, p. 57
- Your Heavenly Parent
  Exodus 2:1–10, p. 77
- The Name of the Lord
  Exodus 33:19–23; 34:5–8, p. 120
- The Sign of His Presence
  Exodus 40:34–38, p. 130
- Our Thorough God
  Leviticus 13, p. 149
- God's Presence with the Israelites
  Leviticus 16:1–15, p. 155
- Approaching God
  Numbers 3:10, p. 180
- The Cloud Guide
  Numbers 9:15–23, p. 188
- What He's Really Like
  Deuteronomy 4:15–20, p. 233
- The God of Big Things
  Joshua 10, p. 289
- God's New Home
  2 Chronicles 7:11–22, p. 570

▶ **Search Engine 1768**

- How God Speaks
  Job 33:14–17, p. 696
- FAITH CHALLENGE
  Job 37:14, p. 701
- How Big Is God?
  Job 38—41, p. 703
- Our Thirst Quencher
  Psalm 42:1–3, p. 741
- A Picture of the Past
  Psalm 105, p. 789
- What God "Hates"
  Proverbs 6:16–19, p. 835
- Remember Your Creator
  Ecclesiastes 12:1, 13, p. 885
- Dirty Inside
  Isaiah 6:1–7, p. 904
- World News
  Isaiah 13—19, p. 913
- What God Thinks
  Isaiah 55:8–9, p. 969
- FAITH CHALLENGE
  Isaiah 64:8, p. 981
- FAITH CHALLENGE
  Jeremiah 23:24, p. 1025
- Our Awesome God
  Ezekiel 1:26–28, p. 1087
- Long-lasting Hope
  Hosea 14, p. 1184
- Inside the Heart of God
  Micah 7:18–20, p. 1228
- FAITH CHALLENGE
  Zechariah 14:9, p. 1265

● **GOOD DEEDS**

- The Person Most Likely to Give?
  Acts 9:36–42, p. 1481
- The Most Fun
  Acts 20:35, p. 1502

● **GOSSIP**

- The Problem with Gossip
  Proverbs 11:12–13, p. 840
- FAITH CHALLENGE
  Ecclesiastes 10:20, p. 883
- What's Wrong About Rumours
  Jeremiah 29:24–32, p. 1032

- CONNECT 2-YOU: Did You Hear About. . .?
  p. 1439

● **GRACE**

- A Holiday Letter
  Esther 9:20–23, p. 657
- It's Free!
  Ephesians 2:8–9, p. 1600

● **GREED**

- Do What You Want?
  Judges 21:25, p. 341
- Your Heart's Desire
  Luke 16:13–15, p. 1401

● **GUILTY**

- FAITH CHALLENGE
  Psalm 7:4, p. 714

● **HAPPINESS**

- Happiness or Joy?
  Job 29:18–19, p. 691

● **HEAVEN**

- Our Awesome God
  Ezekiel 1:26–28, p. 1087
- God's New Temple
  Ezekiel 40—44, p. 1135
- A Heavenly Sight
  Revelation 21:1–4, p. 1753

● **HOLY SPIRIT**

- The Sign of His Presence
  Exodus 40:34–38, p. 130
- Jesus' Mission and Yours
  Isaiah 61:1–2, p. 978
- Two Birthdays
  John 3:1–7, p. 1426
- You've Got the Power!
  Acts 1:1–8; 2:1–4, p. 1463
- Flex Your Faith
  Acts 3:1–16, p. 1467

Search Engine

- An Energy Boost
  Acts 4:31, p. 1469
- Our Interpreter
  Romans 8:26, p. 1528
- Out of Your Mind?
  1 Corinthians 2:16, p. 1547
- A Different Kind of Fruit
  Galatians 5:22–23, p. 1592
- An Unselfish Example
  Philippians 2:5–8, p. 1611
- The "Quality" of Life
  2 Peter 1:5–8, p. 1708

HONESTY

- Family Feud
  Genesis 27, p. 37
- The Best Policy
  Genesis 29:16–29, p. 41
- CONNECT 2-YOU: The Truth Hurts
  p. 54
- FAITH CHALLENGE
  Genesis 48:1, p. 68
- Own Up to It
  2 Samuel 12:1–13, p. 412
- An Honest Reputation
  Nehemiah 13:13, p. 644
- LIVIN' IT: Friends with God
  Psalm 15, p. 719
- Who Do You Prefer?
  Proverbs 3:32, p. 830
- All Talk, No Action
  Jeremiah 5:1–2, p. 996
- Empty Words
  Ezekiel 33:30–33, p. 1127
- A Fake Apology
  Hosea 6:1–7, p. 1177
- Better Than Some?
  Luke 18:9–14, p. 1405
- You're a Fake!
  2 Peter 2:1, p. 1709
- That's False!
  2 John 7–11, p. 1722

HONOURING PARENT(S)

- Family Feud
  Genesis 27, p. 37

- FAITH CHALLENGE
  Genesis 48:1, p. 68
- How to Make God Glad
  Ephesians 6:1–2, p. 1605
- FAITH CHALLENGE
  1 Timothy 5:4, p. 1647
- What Any Parent Wants
  3 John 3–4, p. 1723
- Who's on First?
  3 John 9–10, p. 1723
- CONNECT 2-YOU: Wise Words
  p. 1749

HOPE

- From Hopeless to Hopeful
  Exodus 6:9, p. 83
- A Message of Courage and Hope
  2 Kings 19:4–10, p. 505
- The Foundation of Our Hope
  Isaiah 31:1–8, p. 934
- A Hopeful Future
  Jeremiah 29:11, p. 1031
- A Hopeful Name
  Hosea 1:3–11, p. 1172
- It's Under Control
  Romans 8:28, p. 1529

HOSPITALITY

- Roll Out the Welcome Wagon
  Genesis 18:2–8, p. 24
- Welcome!
  Matthew 19:13–15, p. 1307
- You're Welcomed!
  Acts 16:14–15, p. 1494
- Come On In!
  1 Peter 4:9–10, p. 1705
- Who's on First?
  3 John 9–10, p. 1723

HUMBLENESS

- Tower of Pride
  Genesis 11:3–9, p. 16
- Eating Humble Pie
  Daniel 4, p. 1156

▶ **Search Engine 1770**

- The Way to Greatness
  Matthew 20:20–28, p. 1309
- Best Seat in the House
  Luke 14:7–11, p. 1398

JEALOUSY

- The Trouble with Jealousy
  Genesis 37, p. 53
- CONNECT 2-YOU: Look at Me!
  p. 367
- When the Green-eyed Monster Strikes
  1 Samuel 18:6–9, p. 379
- CONNECT 2-YOU: The Haves and Have Nots
  p. 566

JOY

- Happiness or Joy?
  Job 29:18–19, p. 691
- LIVIN' IT: I Got the Joy, Joy, Joy, Joy
  John 16:24, p. 1452

JUDGEMENT

- Ten Curses
  Exodus 9, p. 87
- You're Out!
  2 Kings 17:5–7, p. 501
- Help for the Hurting
  Job 6:29–30, p. 666
- Justice Served
  Isaiah 35:3–4, p. 940
- God's Instructions
  Ezekiel 4:1–15, p. 1089
- FAITH CHALLENGE
  Ezekiel 7:27, p. 1092
- The Writing's on the Wall
  Daniel 5, p. 1159
- A Swarm of Trouble
  Joel 2:25–27, p. 1190
- Justice Desserts
  Habakkuk 2:4–8, p. 1237
- The Verdict Is In?
  Matthew 7:1–2, p. 1285
- FAITH CHALLENGE
  Acts 24:25, p. 1508
- I'll Be the Judge!
  1 Corinthians 4:4–5, p. 1549

- FAITH CHALLENGE
  Revelation 14:6–7, p. 1745

KINDNESS

- Help for the Poor
  Leviticus 5:7, p. 138
- Help for the Outsiders
  Nehemiah 5:9–10, p. 630
- FAITH CHALLENGE
  Proverbs 14:21, p. 846
- Kindness First
  Matthew 9:35–36, p. 1290
- Kindness Counts
  Acts 14:3, p. 1489
- Don't Play Favourites
  James 2:1–7, p. 1691

LEADERS

- Take Me to Your Leader
  Numbers 27:12–23, p. 214
- The Deliverer
  Deuteronomy 34, p. 272
- God's Pep Talk
  Joshua 1:5–9, p. 276
- Count on His Mercy
  Judges 2:16–17; 3, p. 313
- Real Faith or Really Scared?
  Judges 4, p. 315
- From Zero to Hero
  Judges 6; 7, p. 319
- The Judges
  Judges 9, p. 324
- Just a Little Respect
  1 Chronicles 11:10–19, p. 534
- Your Civic Duty
  Matthew 17:24–27, p. 1304
- Saints, Sinners or Religious Leaders?
  Mark 7:1–13, p. 1341
- The Leaders in Your Life
  1 Timothy 2:1–4, p. 1645

LISTENING TO GOD

- The Sacrifice
  Genesis 22, p. 29

- When Bad Turns to Worse
  Exodus 5:6–12, p. 82
- Fatherly Advice
  Exodus 18, p. 99
- CONNECT 2-YOU: You're Not Alone
  p. 126
- FAITH CHALLENGE
  Leviticus 10:3, p. 145
- An Attention-Getter
  Numbers 22, p. 207
- Facts About Following
  Joshua 6, p. 283
- Learning to Listen
  1 Samuel 3, p. 358
- Listen Up!
  1 Kings 19:11–13, p. 467
- Too Young to Serve
  Jeremiah 1:4–9, p. 988
- LIVIN' IT: Listen Up!
  Lamentations 3:24–27, p. 1080
- Your Spiritual Roots
  Zechariah 1:1–6, p. 1253

LISTENING TO OTHERS

- Help to Understand
  2 Samuel 14, p. 416
- Advice from a Kid
  2 Kings 5, p. 484
- On the Wrong Foot
  2 Kings 21:1–2, 16, p. 509
- Want to Know? Ask!
  Luke 9:45, p. 1386
- Your Faith Story
  2 Timothy 1:5, p. 1650

LONELINESS

- CONNECT 2-YOU: You're Not Alone
  p. 126

LOVE

- Made in His Image
  Genesis 1:26–27, p. 4
- FAITH CHALLENGE
  Psalm 48:9, p. 746
- Love That Will Last
  Psalm 136, p. 813
- Love Him? Show It!
  Amos 2:6–7, p. 1196
- How Do I Love You?
  Malachi 1:1–5, p. 1267
- The Greatest Commandment
  Matthew 22:36–40, p. 1313
- The Number One Rule
  Mark 12:28–31, p. 1351
- The Best Choice
  1 Corinthians 13, p. 1560
- The Love Magnet
  James 4:7–8, p. 1694
- The True Test
  1 John 3:18, p. 1718
- Love and Obey
  2 John 6, p. 1721

LOVING LIKE GOD LOVES

- Count on His Mercy
  Judges 2:16–17; 3, p. 313
- Go for the Gold
  Job 23:10, p. 685
- A Mother's Love
  Isaiah 49:13–16, p. 961
- The One Who Suffered
  Isaiah 53, p. 966
- His Valentine
  Jeremiah 31:3, p. 1035
- LIVIN' IT: God's Love Note
  Zephaniah 3:17, p. 1245
- A Love Song
  Zephaniah 3:17, p. 1246
- LIVIN' IT: The Number One Rule
  Mark 12:28–34, p. 1352
- One of the Faithful
  Acts 10:1–34, p. 1482
- Love for Free
  Romans 5:8, p. 1524
- The Finished Product
  Philippians 1:6, p. 1609
- Ya' Gotta Love It?
  1 John 2:15, p. 1715

▶ Search Engine | 1772

FAITH CHALLENGE
1 John 4:18, p. 1719

● LOYALTY

- Family Feud
  Genesis 27, p. 37
- The MLP
  Ruth 1:16–17, p. 345
- The Gift of Friendship
  1 Samuel 18:1–3; 19, p. 381
- Choosing Sides
  1 Samuel 20, p. 382
- Loyal to a Friend
  2 Samuel 9, p. 409
- The Salt Promise
  2 Chronicles 13:5, p. 576
- FAITH CHALLENGE
  Jeremiah 23:24, p. 1025
- A Fair-weather Friend
  Obadiah 7, p. 1209

● LYING

- Family Feud
  Genesis 27, p. 37
- Who Do You Trust?
  Joshua 9, p. 287
- Promises, Promises
  Judges 2:1–3, p. 312
- Own Up to It
  2 Samuel 12:1–13, p. 412
- The Deadliest Lie
  Acts 5:1–11, p. 1471

● MARRIAGE

- More Powerful Than Revenge
  Genesis 50:14–21, p. 71

● MERCY

- The Boat That Saved the World
  Genesis 7, p. 12
- Just Kidding?
  Genesis 21:8–10, p. 28
- More Powerful Than Revenge
  Genesis 50:14–21, p. 71
- Count on His Mercy
  Judges 2:16–17; 3, p. 313
- FAITH CHALLENGE
  Psalm 123:3–4, p. 808
- Mercy for an Enemy
  Jonah 4, p. 1216
- The Right Ingredients
  Micah 6:8, p. 1227
- That's Much Better!
  Ephesians 2:4–5, p. 1599

● MISTAKES

- CONNECT 2-YOU: My Fault
  p. 587

● MOCKING OTHERS

- Just Kidding?
  Genesis 21:8–10, p. 28
- Help for the Outsiders
  Nehemiah 5:9–10, p. 630
- FAITH CHALLENGE
  Psalm 123:3–4, p. 808
- FAITH CHALLENGE
  Ecclesiastes 10:20, p. 883
- FAITH CHALLENGE
  1 Thessalonians 2:2, p. 1631

● MONEY

- The Trouble with Sin
  Genesis 6—8, p. 11
- Share What You Have
  Exodus 35:5–18, p. 123
- Giving Your Part
  Leviticus 27:30, p. 173
- Give What You Can
  Numbers 7:1–11, p. 186
- A Small Percent
  Deuteronomy 14:22–23, p. 247
- What's the Use?
  2 Kings 12:6–12, p. 495
- Gifts from the Heart
  1 Chronicles 29, p. 557

Search Engine

- Wisdom About Wealth
  Ecclesiastes 5:10–12, p. 878
- LIVIN' IT: Such a Lot of Stuff!
  Luke 12; 13, p. 1396
- Give from the Heart
  Luke 21:1–4, p. 1410
- LIVIN' IT: Being Wise About Money
  Acts 5:1–5, p. 1470
- Give to Give
  1 Corinthians 16:1–4, p. 1566
- More Money?
  1 Timothy 6:10, p. 1649

NEED(S)

- Lights, Camera,... Actions!
  Genesis 12:1–3, p. 17
- Weak? Great!
  2 Chronicles 14:11, p. 577
- But I Want It?
  Philippians 4:19, p. 1615

OBEYING GOD

- The Trouble with Sin
  Genesis 6—8, p. 11
- Lights, Camera,... Actions!
  Genesis 12:1–3, p. 17
- The Sacrifice
  Genesis 22, p. 29
- FAITH CHALLENGE
  Genesis 24:17–19, p. 31
- Obey? No Way!
  Exodus 1:15–21, p. 76
- Fearful Service?
  Exodus 4:1–17, p. 80
- A Thanksgiving Reminder
  Exodus 12, p. 91
- Ten Ways to Obey
  Exodus 20, p. 103
- Idol Talk
  Exodus 32, p. 118
- Reward for Obedience
  Leviticus 26:3–13, p. 171
- His OK to Obey
  Deuteronomy 2:24–36, p. 230
- Remembering What He Said
  Deuteronomy 6:4–6, p. 236
- What God Wants
  Deuteronomy 10:12–13, p. 242
- Facts About Following
  Joshua 6, p. 283
- FAITH CHALLENGE
  Joshua 22:18, p. 304
- FAITH CHALLENGE
  Judges 8:23, p. 323
- A Shortcut
  1 Samuel 13:1–14, p. 369
- The Wisdom of Obeying God
  1 Kings 11:1–13, p. 453
- Your Stats
  1 Kings 15; 16, p. 460
- FAITH CHALLENGE
  1 Chronicles 21:8, p. 545
- Plans for a Son
  1 Chronicles 22:5–19, p. 548
- Standing for What's Right
  Esther 3:2–4, p. 651
- Too Young to Serve
  Jeremiah 1:4–9, p. 988
- A Promise from the Heart
  Jeremiah 31:31–33, p. 1037
- Obeying God or Man?
  Daniel 3:8–30, p. 1154
- Go! No!
  Jonah 1, p. 1213
- The God of Second Chances
  Jonah 3, p. 1215
- Perfectly Pleasing?
  Matthew 5:1–12, p. 1280
- Just Say Yes!
  Matthew 9:9–13, p. 1289
- FAITH CHALLENGE
  John 5:30, p. 1431
- Put God First
  Acts 5:27–32, p. 1472
- A Soldier's Story
  2 Timothy 2:3, p. 1653
- LIVIN' IT: Loving to Obey
  1 John 2:3–6, p. 1716

OBEYING OTHERS

- FAITH CHALLENGE
  Genesis 24:17–19, p. 31
- Give Revenge a Rest
  Leviticus 19:18, p. 160

▶ **Search Engine 1774**

- See the Heart Behind It
  Nehemiah 8; 9, p. 636
- Your Civic Duty
  Matthew 17:24–27, p. 1304
- Love and Obey
  2 John 6, p. 1721

OBEYING THE LAW

- Put Pride Aside
  Exodus 2:11–15, p. 78
- Above the Law
  1 Kings 21, p. 470
- A Promise from the Heart
  Jeremiah 31:31–33, p. 1037
- Your Civic Duty
  Matthew 17:24–27, p. 1304
- Obey or Disobey?
  Luke 20:20–26, p. 1409
- FAITH CHALLENGE
  Romans 13:7, p. 1537

OBLIGATIONS

- FAITH CHALLENGE
  2 Chronicles 25:2, p. 590

PARENT(S)

- CONNECT 2-YOU: Me and My Parents
  p. 330
- The MLP
  Ruth 1:16–17, p. 345
- Plans for a Son
  1 Chronicles 22:5–19, p. 548
- A Parent's Advice
  Proverbs 1:8–9, p. 825
- LIVIN' IT: How to Be a Real Wise Guy!
  Proverbs 6:20–23, p. 834
- A Word to the Wise
  Proverbs 10:1, p. 838

PATIENCE

- Alone and Forgotten?
  Genesis 40:23, p. 57
- The Green Light
  2 Samuel 2:1, p. 401
- Hurry Up and Wait
  2 Samuel 5, p. 405
- 999
  Psalm 28:6, p. 730
- Patience, Please
  Psalm 145:8–9, p. 819
- Exercising Patience
  Luke 2:25–28, 36–37, p. 1369
- LIVIN' IT: Let Me Do It!
  1 Thessalonians 5, p. 1635

PEACE

- Think About Him
  Isaiah 26:3, p. 926
- A Hopeful Future
  Jeremiah 29:11, p. 1031

PEACEMAKING

- LIVIN' IT: Give Me Space!
  Exodus 20:12, p. 102
- Peace in the Family
  Psalm 133, p. 811
- Get Hot or Keep Cool?
  Proverbs 12:16, p. 842
- LIVIN' IT: Peace and Quiet?
  Romans 14:19, p. 1539
- A Peacemaker or a Peacebreaker?
  James 3:18, p. 1693

PEER PRESSURE

- LIVIN' IT: Totally "Uncool"?
  Leviticus 18:1–5, p. 158
- Give In or Take a Stand?
  1 Kings 22:13–14, p. 472
- Fear God or Fear People?
  Jeremiah 38:14–21, p. 1047
- A Real Crowd-pleaser?
  Micah 2:6–11, p. 1222

PERSEVERANCE (KEEP GOING)

- My Worship Place
  Genesis 35:1–14, p. 49

Search Engine **1775**

- Your Worst Enemy
  Exodus 7—11, p. 85
- CONNECT 2-YOU: Cheek to Cheek
  p. 141
- Keep On Praying
  1 Samuel 1, p. 354
- CONNECT 2-YOU: I Can't Do It!
  p. 420
- Building Tools
  Ezra 6:15, p. 615
- Two Enemies
  Nehemiah 6, p. 631
- LIVIN' IT: Hang in There!
  Job 17:9, p. 679
- Faith God Notices
  Luke 18:35–43, p. 1406
- The Power of Prayer
  Acts 12:5, p. 1485
- FAITH CHALLENGE
  2 Corinthians 4:1, p. 1573
- A Soldier's Story
  2 Timothy 2:3, p. 1653
- Keep Going!
  James 1:2–3, p. 1688
- Keep On Keeping On
  Revelation 13:10, p. 1744

POPULARITY

- CONNECT 2-YOU: A Chance to Be Popular
  p. 296

PRAISING GOD

- My Worship Place
  Genesis 35:1–14, p. 49
- A Thanksgiving Reminder
  Exodus 12, p. 91
- No Thanksgiving?
  2 Kings 23:21–23, p. 512
- A Holiday Letter
  Esther 9:20–23, p. 657
- You're Invited!
  Psalm 100, p. 784
- Praise Him!
  Revelation 5:12, p. 1736
- FAITH CHALLENGE
  Revelation 14:6–7, p. 1745

PRAYING

- Tower of Pride
  Genesis 11:3–9, p. 16
- Put Pride Aside
  Exodus 2:11–15, p. 78
- Approaching God
  Numbers 3:10, p. 180
- Keep On Praying
  1 Samuel 1, p. 354
- Problem Solved
  2 Kings 20:1–11, p. 507
- Prayer + Action = Success
  Nehemiah 2:4–9, p. 626
- The Prayer Habit
  Psalm 5:1–3, p. 712
- CONNECT 2-YOU: Ask and You Shall Receive
  p. 767
- LIVIN' IT: No Answering Machine
  Psalm 86:1–7, p. 775
- Concern for All
  Daniel 9, p. 1165
- Our Heavenly Connection
  Matthew 6:9–13, p. 1283
- When We Agree
  Matthew 18:19–20, p. 1306
- Prayer Anywhere
  Mark 1:35, p. 1331
- Prayer Priority
  Luke 5:15–16, p. 1376
- A Model Prayer
  Luke 11:1, p. 1390
- The Power of Prayer
  Acts 12:5, p. 1485
- A Good Habit
  Ephesians 6:18, p. 1606
- Prayer for a Friend
  Colossians 1:9–12, p. 1620
- FAITH CHALLENGE
  James 5:13, p. 1695

PRIDE

- Tower of Pride
  Genesis 11:3–9, p. 16
- LIVIN' IT: Struttin' Our Stuff
  Deuteronomy 8:11–18, p. 238
- CONNECT 2-YOU: Look at Me!
  p. 367

▶ Search Engine 1776

- What I've Got
  2 Kings 20:12–17, p. 508
- The Problem with Pride
  Isaiah 2:11, p. 898
- FAITH CHALLENGE
  Jeremiah 48:30, p. 1059
- Set for Life?
  Obadiah 2–4, p. 1208
- Best Seat in the House
  Luke 14:7–11, p. 1398
- Better Than Some?
  Luke 18:9–14, p. 1405
- Glad to Help!
  Romans 15:17–20, p. 1541
- Brag on Him!
  1 Corinthians 3:18–23, p. 1548
- Most Wanted?
  2 Corinthians 10:1, p. 1580
- Ten Things I Like About You
  2 Thessalonians 1:3–4, p. 1638
- Who's on First?
  3 John 9–10, p. 1723

● PRIORITIES

- Remembering What He Said
  Deuteronomy 6:4–9, p. 236
- Try to Remember
  Deuteronomy 11:18–21, p. 243
- CONNECT 2-YOU:
  TV or Not TV: That Is the Question
  p. 490
- Down on the Ant Farm
  Proverbs 6:6–11, p. 833
- First Place
  Haggai 1:7–11, p. 1248
- Prayer Priority
  Luke 5:15–16, p. 1376
- FAITH CHALLENGE
  Luke 10:29, p. 1389
- Pay Attention!
  Hebrews 2:1, p. 1668

● PROBLEMS

- When Bad Turns to Worse
  Exodus 5:6–12, p. 82
- Good Times and Bad
  1 Kings 17, p. 462
- Problem Solved
  2 Kings 20:1–11, p. 507
- Depend on Him!
  2 Chronicles 16:1–9, p. 579
- Does Crime Pay?
  Psalm 37:1–7, p. 736
- Sow It and Reap
  Lamentations 1:18, p. 1075
- Mission Impossible?
  Mark 5:21–24, 35–43, p. 1337
- Flex Your Faith
  Acts 3:1–16, p. 1467

● PROMISES

- The Rainbow Promise
  Genesis 9:1–17, p. 14
- Always Truthful
  Numbers 23:19, p. 208
- A Special Promise
  Numbers 30:1–2, p. 217
- What God Wants
  Deuteronomy 10:12–13, p. 242
- A Serious Promise
  Deuteronomy 23:21–23, p. 257
- A Long Wait
  Joshua 14:6–15, p. 294
- Promises, Promises
  Judges 2:1–3, p. 312
- FAITH CHALLENGE
  2 Samuel 21:7, p. 426
- A Broken Promise
  Jeremiah 2:1–8, p. 989
- Heavenly Treasure
  Luke 12:32–34, p. 1394
- Never Alone
  Hebrews 13:5–6, p. 1684
- His Best Qualities
  2 Peter 3:9, p. 1711

● PROTECTION

- The Perfect Sacrifice
  Leviticus 1—7, p. 135
- Our Thorough God
  Leviticus 13, p. 149
- The Cloud Guide
  Numbers 9:15–23, p. 188

Search Engine 1777

- Time for Breakfast
  Numbers 11:4–9, p. 191
- Moses' Champion
  Numbers 12, p. 192
- An Attention-Getter
  Numbers 22, p. 207
- His OK to Obey
  Deuteronomy 2:24–36, p. 230
- A Feast for Remembering
  Deuteronomy 16:1–8, p. 249
- God's Sure Protection
  Psalm 18, p. 721
- Our Heavenly Shepherd
  Psalm 23, p. 726
- Your Heavenly Dad
  Psalm 103:13, p. 786
- A Direct Path
  Proverbs 3:5–6, p. 829
- In the Lions' Den
  Daniel 6, p. 1160
- A Safe Place
  Nahum 1:7, p. 1231
- The Best Protection Plan
  Matthew 2:13–18, p. 1276
- Our Good Shepherd
  John 10:11–15, p. 1441

QUITTING

- What You Value
  Genesis 25:21–34, p. 34
- From Hopeless to Hopeful
  Exodus 6:9, p. 83

REPENTANCE

- The Perfect Sacrifice
  Leviticus 1—7, p. 135
- FAITH CHALLENGE
  Psalm 118:18, p. 799
- Real Repentance
  Jeremiah 4:1–4, p. 993
- Concern for All
  Daniel 9, p. 1165
- A Change of Heart
  Matthew 3:1–12, p. 1277
- From Useless to Useful
  Philemon 11, p. 1663

REPUTATION

- What You Value
  Genesis 25:21–34, p. 34
- Family Feud
  Genesis 27, p. 37
- The MLP
  Ruth 1:16–17, p. 345
- An Admirable Quality
  1 Kings 10:1–13, p. 451
- Your Stats
  1 Kings 15; 16, p. 460
- A Memorial for Two Thieves
  1 Chronicles 7:21, p. 530
- FAITH CHALLENGE
  1 Chronicles 28:6–7, p. 556
- An Honest Reputation
  Nehemiah 13:13, p. 644

RESPECTING MY ELDERS

- Just Kidding?
  Genesis 21:8–10, p. 28
- FAITH CHALLENGE
  Genesis 24:17–19, p. 31
- Family Feud
  Genesis 27, p. 37
- Fatherly Advice
  Exodus 18, p. 99
- Show Some Respect
  Leviticus 19:32, p. 161

RESPECTING OTHERS

- Just Kidding?
  Genesis 21:8–10, p. 28
- Ten Ways to Obey
  Exodus 20, p. 103
- FAITH CHALLENGE
  Exodus 22:28, p. 106
- A Right to Get Even?
  1 Samuel 24, p. 388
- The Right Thing to Do
  1 Samuel 26, p. 391
- Mourning for an Enemy
  2 Samuel 1, p. 399

Search Engine 1778

- Fair All the Time?
  2 Samuel 8:15, p. 408
- Just a Little Respect
  1 Chronicles 11:10–19, p. 534
- Help for the Outsiders
  Nehemiah 5:9–10, p. 630
- LIVIN' IT: Just a Little Respect
  Job 31:13–14, p. 694
- The "Eyes" Have It?
  1 Corinthians 12, p. 1559

RESPONSIBILITY

- A Use for Your Abilities
  Genesis 41, p. 59
- Remembering What He Said
  Deuteronomy 6:4–9, p. 236
- A Serious Promise
  Deuteronomy 23:21–23, p. 257
- Read My Lips?
  Deuteronomy 26:16–19, p. 260
- What's Out Becomes In
  Judges 11, p. 327
- Your Response to Responsibility
  Ruth 2:1–7, p. 346
- An Unsung Hero
  Ruth 2:12, 15–16, p. 347
- Loyal to a Friend
  2 Samuel 9, p. 409
- "Handle" Your Responsibilities
  2 Kings 6:5–7, p. 485
- A Big Responsibility
  2 Kings 11, p. 494
- The Watchman
  Ezekiel 3:16–22, p. 1088
- LIVIN' IT: Attitude Check
  Luke 17:7–10, p. 1403
- A Christian's Responsibility
  Acts 11:26, p. 1484

RESURRECTION

- The Doubt Remover
  Romans 10:8–10, p. 1533
- Life After Death?
  1 Corinthians 15:12–13, p. 1563

REVENGE

- More Powerful Than Revenge
  Genesis 50:14–21, p. 71
- Your Worst Enemy
  Exodus 7—11, p. 85
- Give Revenge a Rest
  Leviticus 19:18, p. 160
- Justice Served
  Isaiah 35:3–4, p. 940

RULES

- Out of Control?
  Genesis 4, p. 8
- Ten Ways to Obey
  Exodus 20, p. 103
- A Different Kind of People
  Leviticus 11, p. 146
- Our Thorough God
  Leviticus 13, p. 149
- FAITH CHALLENGE
  Judges 8:23, p. 323
- CONNECT 2-YOU: Me and My Parents
  p. 330
- This Hurts Me More?
  2 Chronicles 36:17–22, p. 606
- The "Ruler" of Our Lives
  Amos 7:7–9, p. 1202
- The Right Ingredients
  Micah 6:8, p. 1227
- A Reminder to Do What Is Right and True
  Zechariah 7:8–10, p. 1257
- Life's Rule Book
  2 Timothy 3:15–17, p. 1655

RUMOURS

- What's Wrong About Rumours
  Jeremiah 29:24–32, p. 1032

SADNESS

- A Pity Party
  Job 10, p. 671
- Sad Times
  Matthew 14:13–14, p. 1299

Fully God, Fully Human
John 11:35, p. 1444

SALVATION

Just Kidding?
Genesis 21:8–10, p. 28

Believe the Impossible?
Ezekiel 37, p. 1131

Prove It!
Matthew 16:1–4, p. 1302

Remembering Jesus
Matthew 26:26–29, p. 1321

A Family Meal
Mark 14:23–26, p. 1356

Heavenly Treasure
Luke 12:32–34, p. 1394

FAITH CHALLENGE
Acts 13:47, p. 1488

Just for the Asking
Romans 3:23–28, p. 1522

The Doubt Remover
Romans 10:8–10, p. 1533

SELF-CONTROL

Out of Control?
Genesis 4, p. 8

Idol Talk
Exodus 32, p. 118

I Want It *Now*!
Judges 14:1–3, p. 332

Do What You Want?
Judges 21:25, p. 341

A Shortcut
1 Samuel 13:1–14, p. 369

A Right to Get Even?
1 Samuel 24, p. 388

The Green Light
2 Samuel 2:1, p. 401

CONNECT 2-YOU: My Fault
p. 587

CONNECT 2-YOU: Control Yourself
p. 1334

FAITH CHALLENGE
Acts 24:25, p. 1508

Our Gift to God
Romans 12:1–2, p. 1536

LIVIN' IT: In Control
2 Timothy 1:7, p. 1651

SELF-ESTEEM

Made in His Image
Genesis 1:26–27, p. 4

CONNECT 2-YOU: My Fault
p. 587

Flex Your Faith
Acts 3:1–16, p. 1467

An Energy Boost
Acts 4:31, p. 1469

FAITH CHALLENGE
1 Thessalonians 2:2, p. 1631

SELFISHNESS

FAITH CHALLENGE
Genesis 24:17–19, p. 31

Play Fair or Play Favourites?
Deuteronomy 1:16–18, p. 227

I Insist!
1 Samuel 8; 9, p. 363

Yours, Mine and Ours?
1 Samuel 25, p. 389

SERVING

FAITH CHALLENGE
Genesis 24:17–19, p. 31

Everyone Can Help
Numbers 4, p. 181

The Way to Serve God
1 Kings 9:4, p. 450

Good Times and Bad
1 Kings 17, p. 462

Service with a Smile
1 Chronicles 6:31–49, p. 527

Operation Co-operation
Ezra 1:5, p. 609

FAITH CHALLENGE
Ezra 8:36, p. 619

Building Together
Nehemiah 3, p. 627

How to Worship God
Isaiah 58, p. 972

Search Engine **1779**

▶ **Search Engine 1780**

○ The Way to Greatness
Matthew 20:20–28, p. 1309

○ LIVIN' IT: Being the GREATEST!
Matthew 25:14–30, p. 1318

○ The Worst Chore
John 13:3–17, p. 1447

○ FAITH CHALLENGE
Galatians 1:10, p. 1586

○ The Sacrifice of Service
Philippians 2:17, 25–30, p. 1612

◯ SHARING

○ Fatherly Advice
Exodus 18, p. 99

○ Share What You Have
Exodus 35:5–18, p. 123

○ Care to Be Fair?
Joshua 18:1–8, p. 299

○ Kind or Fair?
1 Samuel 30, p. 395

○ Share and Share Alike?
Acts 2:43–47, p. 1466

○ My Best Serve
Acts 6:1–6, p. 1473

○ LIVIN' IT: Sharing Your Stuff
2 Corinthians 8:1–9, p. 1577

◯ SHARING MY FAITH

○ CONNECT 2-YOU: Sharing with a Friend
p. 199

○ A Life-saving Message
Esther 2:19–22, p. 650

○ You're Invited!
Psalm 100, p. 784

○ Bragging Rights
Jeremiah 9:23–24, p. 1005

○ A Bad Reaction
Jeremiah 36, p. 1043

○ The Watchman
Ezekiel 3:16–22, p. 1088

○ Pass It On!
Joel 1:2–3, p. 1187

○ Tell All About Him!
Matthew 28:19, p. 1326

○ LIVIN' IT: Have I Got News for You!
Romans 10:14–17, p. 1532

○ Brag on Him!
1 Corinthians 3:18–23, p. 1548

○ What's Good About You?
Philemon 4–7, p. 1663

◯ SINS

○ The Trouble with Sin
Genesis 6—8, p. 11

○ A Priest Without Sin
Leviticus 4:3–7, p. 136

○ The Perfect Leader?
Numbers 20:1–13, p. 203

○ Facing the Consequences
Deuteronomy 3:21–29, p. 232

○ A Hidden Sin
Joshua 7, p. 285

○ You're Out!
2 Kings 17:5–7, p. 501

○ The Cover-up
Psalm 32:1–2, p. 733

○ What God "Hates"
Proverbs 6:16–19, p. 835

○ Red to White
Isaiah 1:18, p. 896

○ Dirty Inside
Isaiah 6:1–7, p. 904

○ LIVIN' IT: Covered with Mud!
Isaiah 59:12–13, p. 974

○ A Fake Apology
Hosea 6:1–7, p. 1177

○ Clean Inside and Out
Luke 11:39–40, p. 1392

○ Just for the Asking
Romans 3:23–28, p. 1522

○ The Sin Habit
Romans 7:15–20, p. 1527

○ Keeping Clean
2 Corinthians 7:1, p. 1576

○ From Useless to Useful
Philemon 11, p. 1663

○ The Sin "Braker"
Jude 24–25, p. 1727

◯ STEWARDSHIP

○ Giving Your Part
Leviticus 27:30, p. 173

Search Engine

- Give What You Can
  Numbers 7:1–11, p. 186
- FAITH CHALLENGE
  Numbers 18:25–26, p. 201
- What's the Use?
  2 Kings 12:6–12, p. 495
- A Half-hearted Offering
  Malachi 1:6–14, p. 1268
- A Robbery in Progress
  Malachi 3:8–10, p. 1270
- Give to Give
  1 Corinthians 16:1–4, p. 1566

SUFFERING

- CONNECT 2-YOU: A Good Kind of Suffering
  p. 923
- The One Who Suffered
  Isaiah 53, p. 966
- FAITH CHALLENGE
  1 Peter 2:19, p. 1702

SUNDAY SCHOOL

- Serious About the Sabbath
  Exodus 31:15, p. 117
- A Holiday Every Week
  Leviticus 23:1–3, p. 166
- CONNECT 2-YOU: For Better or Worship
  p. 522
- Teaching Others
  Ezra 7:8–10, p. 617
- Two Ways to Grow
  Luke 2:46–52, p. 1370
- Faith Workout
  Acts 16:4–5, p. 1493

SUPERSTITION

- Idol Talk
  Exodus 32, p. 118
- Good Advice?
  Leviticus 20:6, p. 162
- FAITH CHALLENGE
  1 Samuel 28:7, p. 393
- Sitting on the Fence
  1 Kings 18, p. 464
- FAITH CHALLENGE
  Psalm 81:8–9, p. 772

- A Useless Thing
  Isaiah 44:9, 18–20, p. 954
- True or False Gods?
  Jeremiah 48:7, 13, p. 1057
- The Dead End of the Occult
  Ezekiel 13:17–23, p. 1098
- Obeying God or Man?
  Daniel 3:8–30, p. 1154
- Long-lasting Hope
  Hosea 14, p. 1184
- The Best Advice
  Zechariah 10:2, p. 1261

TALENTS

- Can't Live Without It
  Genesis 3, p. 7
- Building Together
  Nehemiah 3, p. 627
- That Thing You Do
  Matthew 25:14–30, p. 1319
- My Best Serve
  Acts 6:1–6, p. 1473
- Help for the Body
  Romans 12:3–8, p. 1536
- Give Till It Hurts?
  2 Corinthians 8:6–9; 9:6–9, p. 1578

TEACHERS

- Remembering What He Said
  Deuteronomy 6:4–9, p. 236
- Teaching Others
  Ezra 7:8–10, p. 617
- A Christian's Responsibility
  Acts 11:26, p. 1484
- Faith Workout
  Acts 16:4–5, p. 1493
- Full of Faith
  1 Thessalonians 4:1, p. 1633
- You're a Fake!
  2 Peter 2:1, p. 1709

TEMPTATION

- Can't Live Without It?
  Genesis 3, p. 7

Search Engine 1782

- CONNECT 2-YOU: A Chance to Be Popular
  p. 296
- LIVIN' IT: Go Ahead; Try It
  Isaiah 33:15–16, p. 936
- The Temptation Fighter
  Matthew 4:1–11, p. 1278
- Just a Test
  Luke 4:1–13, p. 1373
- Keeping Clean
  2 Corinthians 7:1, p. 1576
- Another Lazy Day?
  2 Thessalonians 3:6–13, p. 1640
- Just Say No!
  Titus 2:11–12, p. 1660
- The Sin "Braker"
  Jude 24–25, p. 1727

THANKFULNESS

- A Thanksgiving Reminder
  Exodus 12, p. 91
- A Song of Thanks
  1 Samuel 2, p. 356
- A Life of Thanksgiving
  1 Kings 1:47–48, p. 435
- No Thanksgiving?
  2 Kings 23:21–23, p. 512
- Gratitude Attitude
  Ezra 3, p. 611
- FAITH CHALLENGE
  Nehemiah 12:27, p. 642
- A Picture of the Past
  Psalm 105, p. 789
- FAITH CHALLENGE
  Ephesians 1:16, p. 1598
- LIVIN' IT: Thanks a Million!
  Colossians 2:6–7, p. 1623
- Thanks for a Friend
  1 Thessalonians 1:1–3, p. 1630

THOUGHTS

- From Hopeless to Hopeful
  Exodus 6:9, p. 83
- Mind Guard
  Proverbs 4:23, p. 831
- The Peril of Poisonous Plans
  Micah 2:1–3, p. 1221
- Clean Inside and Out
  Luke 11:39–40, p. 1392
- A Family Celebration
  1 Corinthians 11:23–29, p. 1558
- Thoughts on Thoughts
  Philippians 4:8–9, p. 1614

TREASURES IN HEAVEN

- Reward for Obedience
  Leviticus 26:3–13, p. 171
- Heavenly Treasure
  Luke 12:32–34, p. 1394

TROUBLES

- When You're Afraid
  Genesis 32:9–12, p. 45
- Your Best Defence
  2 Chronicles 20:1–12, p. 584
- Wronged for What's Right
  Ezra 4:4–5, p. 612
- A Tight Spot
  Jonah 2, p. 1215
- Hard Times
  2 Corinthians 1:8–10, p. 1570

TRUSTING IN GOD

- When You're Afraid
  Genesis 32:9–12, p. 45
- Good Plans
  Genesis 45:7–8, p. 64
- Your Heavenly Parent
  Exodus 2:1–10, p. 77
- Time for Breakfast
  Numbers 11:4–9, p. 191
- Following the Crowd
  Numbers 13; 14, p. 193
- Your Total Trust
  Deuteronomy 1:32, p. 229
- His OK to Obey
  Deuteronomy 2:24–36, p. 230
- Who Do You Trust?
  Joshua 9, p. 287
- When God Says No
  2 Samuel 7, p. 407

Search Engine   1783

- Putting an Enemy in Check
  2 Kings 6:8–23, p. 486
- A Given
  1 Chronicles 5:18–20, p. 526
- Depend on Him!
  2 Chronicles 16:1–9, p. 579
- Go for the Gold
  Job 23:10, p. 685
- Learning to Trust
  Psalm 25:4–5, p. 727
- LIVIN' IT: Trustometer
  Psalm 56, p. 752
- A Home Town Hurt
  Jeremiah 11:8—12:6, p. 1008
- Like a Tree
  Jeremiah 17:5–8, p. 1016
- In the Lions' Den
  Daniel 6, p. 1160
- Rock Solid
  Habakkuk 1:12, p. 1236
- One Thing to Do
  Romans 4:1–5, p. 1523
- A Family Resemblance
  Galatians 3:6–9, p. 1588
- At the Right Time
  Galatians 4:4, p. 1590
- Toss Those Troubles!
  1 Peter 5:7, p. 1706

TRUSTING IN OTHERS

- Depend on Him!
  2 Chronicles 16:1–9, p. 579
- A Direct Path
  Proverbs 3:5–6, p. 829
- Your Full Trust
  Jeremiah 22:20–22, p. 1023

TRUTHFULNESS

- The Whole Truth
  John 8:31–32, 45, p. 1438
- Pay Attention!
  Hebrews 2:1, p. 1668
- You're a Fake!
  2 Peter 2:1, p. 1709
- That's False!
  2 John 7–11, p. 1722

WEAKNESSES

- Good Advice?
  Leviticus 20:6, p. 162
- The Weak Link
  Judges 16, p. 334
- Weak? Great!
  2 Chronicles 14:11, p. 577
- LIVIN' IT: Oh No! Not Again!
  Luke 22:54–62, p. 1414
- Blessed Are the Weak?
  2 Corinthians 12:7–10, p. 1582

WISDOM

- CONNECT 2-YOU: The Truth Hurts
  p. 54
- Who Do You Trust?
  Joshua 9, p. 287
- In Your Best Interests
  Ruth 3, p. 349
- A Wise Wish
  1 Kings 3:5–9, p. 439
- Deciding Wisely
  1 Kings 3:16–28, p. 440
- The Wisdom of Obeying God
  1 Kings 11:1–13, p. 453
- LIVIN' IT: Wise or Wise Guy?
  Proverbs 2, p. 827
- Wisdom in Store
  Proverbs 2:6–7, p. 828
- Want to Know? Ask!
  Luke 9:45, p. 1386
- As Strong as Superman?
  Philippians 4:13, p. 1615
- Prayer for a Friend
  Colossians 1:9–12, p. 1620
- The Way to Be Wise
  James 1:5, p. 1689
- CONNECT 2-YOU: Wise Words
  p. 1749

Search Engine 1784

● WORDS

● FAITH CHALLENGE
  Matthew 15:11, p. 1301
● Say What?!
  Ephesians 4:22–29, p. 1603
● CONNECT 2-YOU: Wise Words
  p. 1749

● WORD OF GOD

● Ten Ways to Obey
  Exodus 20, p. 103
● Moses' Champion
  Numbers 12, p. 192
● Try to Remember
  Deuteronomy 11:18–21, p. 243
● Like Silver
  Psalm 12:6–8, p. 717
● More Precious Than Gold
  Psalm 19:7–10, p. 723
● LIVIN' IT: A Burning Lamp
  Psalm 119:12–18, p. 801
● Stand!
  Jeremiah 19:14—20:6, p. 1019
● The Temptation Fighter
  Matthew 4:1–11, p. 1278
● Cut to the Quick
  Hebrews 4:12, p. 1670

● WORRYING

● 999
  Psalm 28:6, p. 730
● A Word About Worry
  Matthew 6:25–34, p. 1284
● But I Want It?
  Philippians 4:19, p. 1615

● WORSHIPPING GOD

● My Worship Place
  Genesis 35:1–14, p. 49
● Church on the Road
  Exodus 27:9–19, p. 111
● Serious About the Sabbath
  Exodus 31:15, p. 117
● A Holiday Every Week
  Leviticus 23:1–3, p. 166
● I'll Never Forget What's-His-Name
  Deuteronomy 8, p. 239
● CONNECT 2-YOU: For Better or Worship
  p. 522
● LIVIN' IT: An Awesome God
  Nehemiah 8:6, p. 634
● How to Worship God
  Isaiah 58, p. 972
● The Gift of Worship
  Matthew 2:10–12, p. 1275

KIDSBIBLE.COM
TOP 50 BIBLE SITES

Want to know where to quickly find the Top 50 most visited sites in the Bible?

It's easy! Just stop here and you'll find where to go to read all the well-known stories, like David and Goliath, or Noah and the flood, or when Jesus came into Jerusalem, or when Jesus fed all those hungry people with just two fish and five loaves of bread. When you've finished reading each story, come back here, tick it off the list, and go on to the next site.

This is an easy and quick way to read through the highlights in the Bible – all you have to do is choose where you want to start!

Tick box after visiting each site ☑

A
- Abraham and Isaac
  Genesis 11:27—25:11, p. 17 ❏
- Adam and Eve
  Genesis 2:4—3:24, p. 5 ❏

B
- Beatitudes
  Matthew 5:1–12, p. 1280 ❏
  Luke 6:20–23, p. 1378 ❏

C
- Cain and Abel
  Genesis 4:1–24, p. 8 ❏
- Creation
  Genesis 1:1—2:3, p. 1 ❏
  Genesis 2:4–25, p. 5 ❏

D
- Daniel
  Daniel 1—6, p. 1150 ❏
- Daniel and His Friends
  Daniel 3, p. 1153 ❏
- David, the King
  1 Samuel 16—30, p. 374 ❏
  2 Samuel 1—24, p. 399 ❏
  1 Chronicles 11—22; 28; 29, p. 534 ❏
- David and Goliath
  1 Samuel 17, p. 375 ❏

E
- Elijah the Prophet
  1 Kings 17—19; 21, p. 462 ❏

F
- Fruit of the Spirit
  Galatians 5:22–23, p. 1593 ❏

▶ **Top 50 Sites** **1786**

G

○ Golden Rule
   Matthew 7:12, p. 1286 ❏
○ Good Samaritan
   Luke 10:25–37, p. 1388 ❏
○ Great Commandment
   Matthew 22:34–40, p. 1313 ❏
   Mark 12:28–34, p. 1351 ❏
   Luke 10:25–28, p. 1388 ❏
○ Great Commission
   Matthew 28:18–20, p. 1327 ❏

J

○ Jacob
   Genesis 25:19—33:20; 35, p. 34 ❏
○ Jesus' Birth and Boyhood
   Matthew 1:18—2:23, p. 1275 ❏
   Luke 2, p. 1367 ❏
○ Jesus' Baptism
   Matthew 3:13–17, p. 1278 ❏
   Mark 1:9–11, p. 1330 ❏
   Luke 3:21–22, p. 1372 ❏
○ Jesus' Temptation
   Matthew 4:1–11, p. 1279 ❏
   Mark 1:12–13, p. 1330 ❏
   Luke 4:1–13, p. 1373 ❏
○ Jesus' Glory Revealed (Transfiguration)
   Matthew 17:1–13, p. 1303 ❏
   Mark 9:2–13, p. 1344 ❏
   Luke 9:28–36, p. 1385 ❏
○ Jesus Entering Jerusalem
   Matthew 21:1–11, p. 1310 ❏
   Mark 11:1–11, p. 1348 ❏
   Luke 19:28–40, p. 1407 ❏
   John 12:12–19, p. 1445 ❏
○ Jesus' Last Supper (the Lord's Supper)
   Matthew 26:26–30, p. 1321 ❏
   Mark 14:22–26, p. 1356 ❏
   Luke 22:14–38, p. 1412 ❏
   1 Corinthians 11:23–25, p. 1557 ❏
○ Jesus' Arrest
   Matthew 26:47–56, p. 1322 ❏
   Mark 14:43–50, p. 1357 ❏
   Luke 22:47–53, p. 1415 ❏

   John 18:3–14, p. 1454 ❏
○ Jesus' Crucifixion (death)
   Matthew 27:32–66, p. 1325 ❏
   Mark 15:21–47, p. 1359 ❏
   Luke 23:26–56, p. 1416 ❏
○ Jesus' Resurrection
   Matthew 28:1–15, p. 1326 ❏
   Mark 16:1–13, p. 1360 ❏
   Luke 24:1–12, p. 1417 ❏
   John 20:1–18, p. 1458 ❏
○ Jesus' Ascension (going to heaven)
   Mark 16:19–20, p. 1362 ❏
   Luke 24:50–53, p. 1419 ❏
   JESUS' MIRACLES (SELECTED)
○ Calming the Storm
   Matthew 8:23–27, p. 1288 ❏
   Mark 4:35–41, p. 1336 ❏
   Luke 8:22–25, p. 1382 ❏
○ Feeding the Crowds
   Matthew 14:13–21, p. 1299 ❏
   Matthew 15:32–39, p. 1301 ❏
   Mark 6:30–44, p. 1340 ❏
   Mark 8:1–10, p. 1342 ❏
   Luke 9:10–17, p. 1385 ❏
   John 6:5–15, p. 1432 ❏
○ Raising Lazarus from the Dead
   John 11:1–44, p. 1442 ❏
○ John the Baptist
   Matthew 3:1–12, p. 1277 ❏
   Mark 1:1–8, p. 1330 ❏
   Luke 3:1–20, p. 1371 ❏
   John 1:19–28, p. 1422 ❏
○ Jonah
   Jonah 1—4, p. 1213 ❏
○ Joseph, the Boy Sold by His Brothers
   Genesis 37; 39—50, p. 51 ❏
○ Joshua
   Joshua 1—12; 23; 24, p. 276 ❏

L

○ Lord's Prayer
   Matthew 6:9–13, p. 1283 ❏
   Luke 11:1–4, p. 1389 ❏
○ Love Chapter
   1 Corinthians 13, p. 1560 ❏

Top 50 Sites 1787 ◀

M

○ Moses
  Exodus 2—19; 32—34, p. 77 ❏

N

○ New Birth
  John 3, p. 1426 ❏
○ Noah and the Flood
  Genesis 6:9—8:22, p. 10 ❏

P

○ Passover
  Exodus 12:1–30, p. 90 ❏
○ Paul
  Acts 9—28, p. 1478 ❏
○ Pentecost
  Acts 2:1–42, p. 1464 ❏
○ Prodigal Son
  Luke 15:11–32, p. 1399 ❏

R

○ Ruth
  Ruth 1—4, p. 345 ❏

S

○ Samson
  Judges 13—16, p. 330 ❏
○ Samuel
  1 Samuel 1—3; 7—16, p. 354 ❏
○ Saul, King of Israel
  1 Samuel 8—11; 13; 15; 28; 31, p. 362 ❏
○ Sermon on the Mount
  Matthew 5—7, p. 1280 ❏
  Luke 6:20–49, p. 1378 ❏
○ Shepherd Psalm
  Psalm 23, p. 726 ❏
○ Sower and the Seeds
  Matthew 13:1–23, p. 1296 ❏
  Mark 4:1–20, p. 1335 ❏
  Luke 8:4–15, p. 1382 ❏

T

○ Ten Commandments
  Exodus 20:1–17, p. 101 ❏
  Deuteronomy 5:1–21, p. 235 ❏

Z

○ Zacchaeus
  Luke 19:1–10, p. 1406 ❏

HOW TO READ YOUR
KIDSBIBLE.COM

Everybody knows that it's a good thing to read your Bible. But it's such a big book! How are you supposed to get started?

It's a good question. And believe it or not, there are a lot of different ways to read through your Bible. When you think about it, the Bible is really a mini-library because it's one book that contains 66 different books.

But there are several different ways you can read KidsBible.com that break the Bible into easy-to-manage pieces. Take a look below at the different ways you can get started on this exciting, life-changing journey!

"ROAD MAP" TO KIDSBIBLE.COM

 ### 30 DAYS WITH JESUS

On this *KidsBible.com* journey, you will spend 30 days retracing the path Jesus took while he was here on earth. You'll read about his much-awaited birth, his boyhood, the beginning of his ministry, his key teachings, and about the ultimate sacrifice Jesus made so we can live with him in heaven for all eternity. You won't want to miss a day!

 ### 50 DAYS IN THE NEW TESTAMENT

These next 50 days will focus on what happened *after* Jesus returned to heaven. You'll meet many of the leaders of the early church — Peter, James, Stephen, John, and of course, Paul. You will follow Paul's adventures and struggles as he spreads the Good News of Jesus to the world, and you'll hear many of his key teachings to those early Christian communities.

You will read letters from James (Jesus' half-brother), Peter and John with teaching that is as important to us today as it was to those early believers. You'll complete your trek by reading about the final, yet-to-happen event – when Jesus will return and establish a new world and a new kingdom!

50 DAYS IN THE OLD TESTAMENT

In the beginning . . . those words are probably familiar to you, and you have probably heard many of the stories from the Old Testament. But have you ever followed the stories from the beginning to see where they fit into the history of Israel? Here's an opportunity to spend 50 days in the Old Testament, hitting the highlights of some familiar Bible heroes, like Abraham, Moses, David, Daniel, and others. You will discover that the Old Testament is really one story about God's love for his people and his ultimate plan to send a Saviour for people then and today – his Son, Jesus Christ.

TIPS ON STUDYING KIDSBIBLE.COM

So, you've got your KidsBible.com; you've got your "road map" for reading the Bible; you're all set to go!

But, before you start, you'll probably benefit from knowing something about how to study the Bible.

Now, don't panic! That doesn't mean to say that there's going to be a test or anything like that.

Remember, the Bible is God's Word. It's filled with lots of good instructions on how to live, how to handle those difficult situations in your life, and how to be a follower of Jesus. If you're just reading the stories and not really thinking about what these stories mean to you, then you'll probably miss out on a lot of what God has to say to you!

Reading Plans 1790

> So... what do you have to do?

> Well, it's simple. There are many different ways to study the Bible but here's one that uses just four questions. When you read a Bible passage or story, you can ask:

○ **Who are the people in the story?** This helps you identify who's involved in the Bible passage or story. Take the story of David and Goliath, for example, <u>1 Samuel 17, p. 375</u>. The main characters involved in this familiar story are the Israelites led by King Saul; their archenemies, the Philistines; the Philistines' champion fighter, Goliath; and a young shepherd boy named David.

In a Bible passage, the people may not be as easy to identify. But remember, the people can be the ones hearing the story or teaching and/or the person telling the story or teaching.

○ **What's the problem or the teaching in this story or passage?** This question is asking you to tell in your own words what is going on in the story or what the person is teaching about in a Bible passage. There are many different problems going on in the story of David and Goliath, but the ***big*** problem is the 3-metre tall giant, Goliath, who is taunting the Israelites.

○ **What is the lesson being taught or the moral of the story?** This question helps you identify what is the main point of the story or the main teaching in a Bible passage. To discover the point, you can ask two questions: "What is this story/passage teaching you about God?" or "What is this story/passage teaching you about how people should live?" In this story, you learn that God can help you defeat the big problems in your life and that God wants his people to trust and depend on him.

○ **What does God want me to do?** This is where God speaks to you! Maybe you decide that God wants you to face the "giants" in your life – whether it's tomorrow's maths test or the boy down the street who calls you names. Or maybe God wants you to trust him to help you through the battles in your life.

One more thing: when you read your Bible, you might want to write down your answers to these four questions, or to any others that you may have about the passage. You don't have to write a lot, just jot down a sentence or two. There are a few blank lines with each Bible reading entry so you can write down what you have learned in your KidsBible.com.

> OK, so now you're ready. Let the journey begin!

30 DAYS WITH JESUS

1. John 1:1–51 ☐
   What I learned . . .

2. Luke 2:1–52 ☐
   What I learned . . .

3. Mark 1:1–11 ☐
   What I learned . . .

4. Luke 4:1–44 ☐
   What I learned . . .

5. John 3:1–36 ☐
   What I learned . . .

6. Luke 5:1–39 ☐
   What I learned . . .

7. John 4:1–54 ☐
   What I learned . . .

8. Luke 6:1–49 ☐
   What I learned . . .

9. Luke 7:1–50 ☐
   What I learned . . .

10. Luke 8:1–56 ☐
    What I learned . . .

11. Mark 8:1–38 ☐
    What I learned . . .

12. Luke 10:1–52 ☐
    What I learned . . .

13. Matthew 5:1–48 ☐
    What I learned . . .

14. Matthew 6:1–34 ☐
    What I learned . . .

15. Matthew 7:1–29 ☐
    What I learned . . .

16. Luke 14:1–35 ☐
    What I learned . . .

Reading Plans 1792

17. Luke 15:1–32 ☐
    What I learned . . .
    _____
    _____
    _____

18. Luke 16:1–31 ☐
    What I learned . . .
    _____
    _____
    _____

19. John 8:1–59 ☐
    What I learned . . .
    _____
    _____
    _____

20. Luke 17:1–37 ☐
    What I learned . . .
    _____
    _____
    _____

21. Luke 18:1–43 ☐
    What I learned . . .
    _____
    _____
    _____

22. John 9:1–41 ☐
    What I learned . . .
    _____
    _____
    _____

23. Luke 19:1–48 ☐
    What I learned . . .
    _____
    _____
    _____

24. Luke 20:1–47 ☐
    What I learned . . .
    _____
    _____
    _____

25. John 10:1–42 ☐
    What I learned . . .
    _____
    _____
    _____

26. John 11:1–57 ☐
    What I learned . . .
    _____
    _____
    _____

27. Mark 13:1–37 ☐
    What I learned . . .
    _____
    _____
    _____

28. Luke 22:1–71 ☐
    What I learned . . .
    _____
    _____
    _____

29. Matthew 27:1–66 ☐
    What I learned . . .
    _____
    _____
    _____

30. Luke 24:1–53 ☐
    What I learned . . .
    _____
    _____
    _____

… Reading Plans **1793**

50 DAYS IN THE NEW TESTAMENT

1. Acts 1:1–11 ☐
   What I learned . . .

2. Acts 2:1–47 ☐
   What I learned . . .

3. Acts 8:26–40 ☐
   What I learned . . .

4. Acts 9:1–31 ☐
   What I learned . . .

5. Acts 11:1–18 ☐
   What I learned . . .

6. Acts 16:11–40 ☐
   What I learned . . .

7. Acts 17:16–33 ☐
   What I learned . . .

8. Acts 21:1–16, 27–40 ☐
   What I learned . . .

9. Acts 26:1–32 ☐
   What I learned . . .

10. Acts 27:13–44 ☐
    What I learned . . .

11. Acts 28:16–31 ☐
    What I learned . . .

12. Romans 3:1–31 ☐
    What I learned . . .

13. Romans 8:1–39 ☐
    What I learned . . .

14. Romans 12:1–21 ☐
    What I learned . . .

15. 1 Corinthians 13:1–13 ☐
    What I learned . . .

16. 1 Corinthians 15:1–58 ☐
    What I learned . . .

▶ **Reading Plans   1794**

17. 2 Corinthians 1:15–2:11 ❑
    What I learned . . .
    _____
    _____
    _____

18. 2 Corinthians 4:1–18 ❑
    What I learned . . .
    _____
    _____
    _____

19. 2 Corinthians 8:1–15 ❑
    What I learned . . .
    _____
    _____
    _____

20. Galatians 2:11–21 ❑
    What I learned . . .
    _____
    _____
    _____

21. Galatians 5:1–26 ❑
    What I learned . . .
    _____
    _____
    _____

22. Galatians 6:1–10 ❑
    What I learned . . .
    _____
    _____
    _____

23. Ephesians 2:1–22 ❑
    What I learned . . .
    _____
    _____
    _____

24. Ephesians 5:1–21 ❑
    What I learned . . .
    _____
    _____
    _____

25. Ephesians 5:22—6:9 ❑
    What I learned . . .
    _____
    _____
    _____

26. Ephesians 6:10–20 ❑
    What I learned . . .
    _____
    _____
    _____

27. Philippians 1:3–26 ❑
    What I learned . . .
    _____
    _____
    _____

28. Philippians 2:5–18 ❑
    What I learned . . .
    _____
    _____
    _____

29. Philippians 3:1–16 ❑
    What I learned . . .
    _____
    _____
    _____

30. Philippians 4:1–13 ❑
    What I learned . . .
    _____
    _____
    _____

31. Colossians 1:15–29 ❑
    What I learned . . .
    _____
    _____
    _____

32. Colossians 3:1—4:1 ❑
    What I learned . . .
    _____
    _____
    _____

33. 1 Thessalonians 4:1–18 ❑
    What I learned . . .
    _____
    _____
    _____

34. 1 Thessalonians 5:1–11 ❑
    What I learned . . .
    _____
    _____
    _____

Reading Plans 1795

35. 2 Thessalonians 2:1–12 ❏
    What I learned . . .

36. 1 Timothy 6:1–19 ❏
    What I learned . . .

37. 2 Timothy 2:1–26 ❏
    What I learned . . .

38. Titus 3:1–11 ❏
    What I learned . . .

39. Philemon 8–20 ❏
    What I learned . . .

40. Hebrews 11:1–40 ❏
    What I learned . . .

41. Hebrews 12:1–11 ❏
    What I learned . . .

42. James 1:1–27 ❏
    What I learned . . .

43. James 2:1–19 ❏
    What I learned . . .

44. James 3:1–18 ❏
    What I learned . . .

45. James 5:1–18 ❏
    What I learned . . .

46. 1 Peter 1:3–25 ❏
    What I learned . . .

47. 2 Peter 1:3–21 ❏
    What I learned . . .

48. 1 John 1:1—2:17 ❏
    What I learned . . .

49. Revelation 4:1–11 ❏
    What I learned . . .

50. Revelation 21:1—22:21 ❏
    What I learned . . .

▶ **Reading Plans** 1796

50 DAYS IN THE OLD TESTAMENT

1. Genesis 1:1—2:3 ❏
   What I learned . . .
   _____
   _____
   _____

2. Genesis 3:1–24 ❏
   What I learned . . .
   _____
   _____
   _____

3. Genesis 6:9—7:24 ❏
   What I learned . . .
   _____
   _____
   _____

4. Genesis 8:1—9:17 ❏
   What I learned . . .
   _____
   _____
   _____

5. Genesis 17:1–22 ❏
   What I learned . . .
   _____
   _____
   _____

6. Genesis 22:1–19 ❏
   What I learned . . .
   _____
   _____
   _____

7. Genesis 25:19–34 ❏
   What I learned . . .
   _____
   _____
   _____

8. Genesis 27:1—28:9 ❏
   What I learned . . .
   _____
   _____
   _____

9. Genesis 37:1–36 ❏
   What I learned . . .
   _____
   _____
   _____

10. Genesis 41:1–57 ❏
    What I learned . . .
    _____
    _____
    _____

11. Genesis 45:1–28 ❏
    What I learned . . .
    _____
    _____
    _____

12. Exodus 1:8—2:15 ❏
    What I learned . . .
    _____
    _____
    _____

13. Exodus 3:1—4:17 ❏
    What I learned . . .
    _____
    _____
    _____

14. Exodus 5:1—6:13 ❏
    What I learned . . .
    _____
    _____
    _____

15. Exodus 12:1–42 ❏
    What I learned . . .
    _____
    _____
    _____

16. Exodus 13:17—14:31 ❏
    What I learned . . .
    _____
    _____
    _____

Reading Plans 1797

17. Exodus 20:1–21 ☐
    What I learned . . .

18. Numbers 13:1–33 ☐
    What I learned . . .

19. Joshua 2:1–24 ☐
    What I learned . . .

20. Joshua 6:1–27 ☐
    What I learned . . .

21. Judges 16:4–31 ☐
    What I learned . . .

22. 1 Samuel 1:1–28 ☐
    What I learned . . .

23. 1 Samuel 3:1–21 ☐
    What I learned . . .

24. 1 Samuel 10:1–27 ☐
    What I learned . . .

25. 1 Samuel 16:1–13 ☐
    What I learned . . .

26. 1 Samuel 17:1–58 ☐
    What I learned . . .

27. 1 Samuel 24:1–22 ☐
    What I learned . . .

28. 2 Samuel 11:1—12:25 ☐
    What I learned . . .

29. 1 Kings 3:1–28 ☐
    What I learned . . .

30. 1 Kings 17:8–24 ☐
    What I learned . . .

31. 1 Kings 18:1–46 ☐
    What I learned . . .

32. 2 Kings 2:1–18 ☐
    What I learned . . .

33. 2 Kings 4:8–37 ☐
    What I learned . . .

34. 2 Chronicles 35:20—36:23 ☐
    What I learned . . .

Reading Plans 1798

35. Esther 2:1–23 ☐
    What I learned . . .

36. Esther 6:1—8:8 ☐
    What I learned . . .

37. Job 1:1—2:13 ☐
    What I learned . . .

38. Job 42:1–17 ☐
    What I learned . . .

39. Psalm 23 ☐
    What I learned . . .

40. Psalm 51 ☐
    What I learned . . .

41. Psalm 100 ☐
    What I learned . . .

42. Psalm 121 ☐
    What I learned . . .

43. Psalm 145 ☐
    What I learned . . .

44. Proverbs 4:1–27 ☐
    What I learned . . .

45. Ecclesiastes 11:9—12:14 ☐
    What I learned . . .

46. Isaiah 53:1–12 ☐
    What I learned . . .

47. Daniel 1:1–21 ☐
    What I learned . . .

48. Daniel 3:1–30 ☐
    What I learned . . .

49. Daniel 6:1–28 ☐
    What I learned . . .

50. Jonah 1:1—4:11 ☐
    What I learned . . .